CHAMBERS
CROSSWORD COMPLETER

CHAMBERS CROSSWORD COMPLETER

an alternate letter word list

New edition

compiled by
Peter Schwarz

with Foreword by
Don Manley

CHAMBERS

CHAMBERS
An imprint of Chambers Harrap Publishers Ltd
7 Hopetoun Crescent
Edinburgh EH7 4AY

This edition first published by Chambers 1995
Previous edition by W & R Chambers Ltd, 1987
Reprinted 1995, 1996, 1997, 1998

We have made every effort to mark as such all words which we believe to be trademark. We should also like to make it clear that the presence of a word in the book, whether marked or unmarked, in no way effects it legal status as a trademark.

A CIP catalogue record for this book is available from the British Library

ISBN 0-550-19051-1

Managing editor Catherine Schwarz

Typeset by Hewer Text Composition Services, Edinburgh
Printed and bound in Great Britain by
Cox & Wyman Ltd, Reading, Berkshire

Foreword

Most cryptic crosswords have answers with alternate letters 'checked' by crossing answers. The other letters are 'unchecked'. This means that you may find yourself with a diagram entry like this:

a_a_e_

where the answer could be azalea

or like this:

_a_a_e

where the answer could be parade

This unique 'alternate letter dictionary' helps the crossword solver to explore the different alternatives - or indeed the setter to complete filling up the grid with words. *Chambers Crossword Completer* is based on all the words in the latest edition of *The Chambers Dictionary*, including some words only found in phrases but considered meaningful in their own right, such as 'Alzheimer's' and 'Dresden', and abbreviations that are commonly used instead of the full form, eg 'AWOL' and 'EPOS'. Phrases, and most plural forms and verb endings, are *not* included, but irregular plurals, and irregular verb and adjectival forms, *are* listed. Plurals, even when regular, are listed if they are mentioned in definitions in the dictionary, often as having different meanings, eg 'briefs'.

Where the dictionary indicates that the word can be spelt with or without an initial capital letter, often with different meanings, this is shown by the symbol △. Accents have been retained since they often point to separate meanings (eg 'pate' and 'pâté') or to the foreign origin of the word.

Entries, ranging from 4-letter words to 15-letter ones, are arranged by length and then alphabetically according to the alternate letters. These letters are shown in bold for the first word in the group of words for which they are relevant.

For quick and easy reference, the *Crossword Completer* is divided into two sections. The first lists the words according to the alphabetical order of the *odd* letter (eg **a**b**a**c ... **a**b**b**a and so on to **z**o**o**p**h**y**s**i**o**l**o**g**i**s**t** and

zoophytological); the second lists them according to the *even* letters (eg **baba** ... **barb** and so on to **systematization** and **Czechoslovakian**).

You may have to solve a few clues of course, but there is no harm in having your inspiration prompted from time to time!

Don Manley
Oxford 1995

Words arranged according to ODD LETTERS

4 b□s□

ab**a**c
Adam
Adar
adaw
afar
agar
ajar
Ajax
alae
alap
△alar
alas
alay
amah
anal
anan
anas
ana's
apay
Arab
arak
Aran
arar
åsar
atap
aval
away
ayah
azan
ab**b**a
abbé
albe
ambo
arba
an**c**e
arch
arco
asci
AC/**D**C
aide
AIDS
awdl
ab**e**d
abet
acer
Ades
aged
agee
agen
ages
ahem
ajee
akee
alee
alew
△amen
Amex
anew
apes
△apex
area
ared
areg
Ares
aret
arew
aver
Aves
awed
axel
axes
ayes
af**f**y
alfa
anfo
al**g**a
Argo
ac**h**e
achy
agha
ashy
Ab**i**b
abid
acid
adit
agin
agio
akin
alit
amid
amie
amir
amis
anil
anis
aria
arid
aril
aris
avid
axil
axis
al**k**y
ankh
ab**l**e
ably
alls
ally
amla
arle
aula
auld
axle
ac**m**e
agma
alma
alme
alms
ammo
arms
△army
ac**n**e
aîné
ain't
Ainu
anna
anno
arna
aune
△aunt
awny
Ab**o**s
ados
aeon
agog
agon
ahoy
alod
△aloe
alow
amok
anoa
anon
anow
apod
arow
a-row
atoc
atok
atom
atop
avow
AWOL
axon
Al**p**s
ac**r**e
adry
aero
aery
△afro
airn
airs
airt
airy
'Arry
aura
awry
ayre
ae**s**c
also
apse
arse
ac**t**a
aitu
alto
anta
ante
anti
ants
△arts
arty
Asti
auto
ab**u**t
ague
alum
anus
aqua
arum
ar**v**o
ab**y**e
acyl
amyl
aryl
azym
ad**z**e
Ba**a**l
baas
bead
beak
beam
bean
bear
beat
beau
bias
blab
blad
blae
blag
blah
blat
blay
boak
boar
boat
brad
brae
brag
bran
bras
brat
braw
△bray
buat
ba**b**a
babe
Babi
babu
baby
boba
bobs
buba
△bubo
△**b**a**c**h
back
beck
bice
bock
buck
ba**d**e
bede
Bedu
bide
bode
body
budo
ba**e**l
Beeb
beef
been
beep
beer
bees
beet
bhel
bien
bier
bleb
bled
blee
blet
blew
bley
Boer
bred
bree
△bren
brer
brew
byes
ba**f**f
baft
biff
boff
buff
bufo
ba**g**s
bego
biga
bigg
bogy
ba**h**t
buhl
ba**i**l
bait
bein
blin
blip
boil
Brie
brig
brim
brio
△brit
Brix
buik
ba**j**u
ba**k**e
bike
boke
boko
buke
byke
ba**l**d
bale
balk
ball
balm
Balt
balu
bell
belt
bile
bilk
△bill
bold
bole
boll
bolo
bolt
bulb
bulk
△bull
be**m**a
boma
bomb
bumf
bump
ba**n**c
△band
bane
bang
bani
bank
bant
bend
bene
beni
benj
bent
bind
bine
bing
bink
bint
bona
bond
bone
bong
bonk
bony
buna
△bund
bung
bunk
bunt
bi**o**g
bios
blob
bloc
blot
blow
boob
booh
△book
bool
boom
boon
boor
boot
brod
brog
broo
brow
buoy
ba**p**u
ba**r**b
△bard
bare
barf
bark
barm
barn
barp
bars
bere
berg
berk
berm
bird
birk
birl
Biro®
birr
bora
bord
bore
born
bort
brrr
burd
burg
burk
burl
burn
burp
burr
bury
byre
ba**s**e
bash
bask
bass
bast
best
bise
bish
bisk
bosh
bosk
bo's'n
bos'n
boss
bush
busk
buss

Words marked △ may be spelled also with a capital letter

4 b□t□

bust
busy
ba**t**e
△bath
bats
batt
△beta
bete
bête
beth
bite
bito
bits
bitt
both
bots
bott
△bute
buts
butt
byte
ba**u**d
bauk
baur
blub
blue
blur
Blut
bouk
boun
bout
Brum
brut
be**v**y
ba**w**d
bawl
bawn
bawr
bowl
bowr
bows
Bi**x**a
boxy
ba**y**e
bays
bayt
boyg
boyo
boys
bo**z**o
buzz
ce**a**s
△chad
chai
chal
cham
chap
char
chat
chaw
chay
ciao
clad
clag
clam
clan
clap
clat
claw
clay
coal
coat
coax
co-ax
△crab
crag
cram
cran
crap
craw
cyan
czar
ca**b**a
cobb
cube
ce**c**a
coca
cock
coco
ca**d**e
cadi
cede
cedi
coda
code
ch**e**f
cher
chew
chez
ciel
clef
cleg
clem
clew
coed
cred
△cree
crew
cued
ca**f**e
café
caff
coff
coft
cuff
ca**g**e
cagy
co**h**o
△**c**a**i**n
ceil
chic
chid
chik
chin
chip
chit
chiv
chiz
Clio
clip
coif
coil
coin
coir
coit
crib
crim
crit
cuif
cuit
ca**k**e
caky
△coke
coky
ca**l**f
calk
call
calm
calp
calx
cell
△celt
cill
△cola
cold
cole
coll
Colt®
colt
cull
△culm
cult
Ca**m**a
came
camp
coma
comb
come
comp
coms
cyma
cyme
ca**n**e
cang
cann
cans
cant
can't
cany
cens
cent
cine
ciné
cond
cone
conk
conn
cons
cony
cunt
ce**ò**l
choc
chon
chop
chou
△chow
cion
clod
clog
clop
clot
clou
clow
cloy
coof
cook
cool
coom
coon
coop
co-op
coot
croc
crop
crow
ca**p**a
△cape
capi
capo
caps
cope
Copt
copy
cups
ca**r**b
card
care
cark
carl
carp
carr
cart
cere
cert
ciré
cirl
cord
core
corf
cork
corm
corn
cory
curb
curd
cure
curé
curl
curn
curr
curt
ca**s**a
case
cash
cask
cast
cess
cist
cose
cosh
coss
△cost
cosy
cush
cusk
cusp
cuss
cyst
ca**t**e
cats
cete
cite
cito
cits
△city
cote
coth
cott
cute
ca**u**f
cauk
caul
caum
caup
chub
chug
chum
chut
club
clue
coup
cour
crud
crux
ca**v**e
cavy
cive
cove
ca**w**k
cowl
cowp
cows
co**x**a
Cox's
coxy
co**z**e
cozy
D-d**a**y
dead
deaf
deal
△dean
dear
deaw
dhak
dhal
dial
Dian
doab
doat
drab
drad
drag
DRAM
dram
drap
drat
draw
dray
duad
dual
duan
duar
dwam
dyad
Dyak
Da**b**s
debt
dibs
dubs
da**c**e
deck
△deco
dice
dich
△dick
dict
dock
duce
duck
duct
Da**d**a
dado
dido
dodo
dods
dude
duds
de**e**d
deek
deem
deen
△deep
deer
deev
dieb
died
dies
△diet
Dieu
doek
doen
doer
does
dree
dreg
drek
drew
drey
duel
dues
duet
dyed
dyer
da**f**f
daft
deft
defy
doff
duff
da**g**o
digs
doge
dogs
dogy
da**h**l
dohs
dzho
Dá**i**l
dais
deid
deil
doit
drib
drip
do**j**o
di**k**a
dike
△duke
dyke
da**l**e
dali
dalt
dele
delf
deli
dell
delt
dill
dole
doll
dolt
dule
dull
duly
da**m**e
damn

Words marked △ may be spelled also with a capital letter

4 f□u□

damp
dams
deme
demo
demy
dime
dome
domy
duma
dumb
dump
Dane
dang
dank
dant
dene
dent
deny
dine
ding
dink
dint
Doña
dona
done
dong
don't
dune
dung
dunk
dunt
dyne
dhow
doob
dook
dool
doom
door
drop
drow
duos
dopa
dope
dopy
dupe
Dard
dare
darg
dari
dark
darn
dart
dere
derm
dern
derv
dire
dirk
dirl
dirt
Dora
dork
dorm
dorp
dorr
dort
dory
dura
dure
durn
duro
dash
desk
disa
disc
dish
disk
diss
dose
dosh
doss
dost
dush
dusk
dust
data
date
dita
dite
ditt
dote
doth
doty
duty
daub
daud
daur
daut
deus
douc
doup
dour
dout
drub
drug
drum
Druz
Davy
deva
Devi
diva
dive
divi
dove
dawd
dawk
dawn
dawt
dewy
dowd
dowf
dowl
down
dowp
dows
dowt
dixi
dixy
doxy
days
daze
doze
dozy
ecad
Edam
egad
egal
élan
eoan
état
exam
eyas
each
ecce
ecco
eech
etch
Edda
eddo
eddy
ends
Eden
eger
emeu
enew
épée
eten
even
ever
evet
ewer
exes
eyed
eyes
edge
edgy
eggs
eggy
ergo
ergs
euge
eugh
eche
echo
echt
epha
ethe
edit
Efik
E-fit®
egis
emir
emit
epic
eric
evil
△exit
ekka
Esky®
esky
eale
eely
eild
egma
elmy
emma
Emmy
eine
EPNS
erne
esne
etna
eyne
ebon
ecod
enow
EPOS
epos
Eros
Eton
euoi
evoe
exon
eyot
espy
expo
eard
△earl
earn
ears
ecru
eery
eorl
euro
eyra
eyre
eyry
ease
△east
easy
else
Erse
erst
esse
eath
eats
Esth
Elul
étui
exul
eevn
eev'n
envy
emys
feal
fear
feat
fiar
fiat
flab
flag
flak
flam
flan
flap
flat
flaw
flax
flay
foal
foam
frab
frae
frag
frap
△frau
fray
face
fact
feck
fico
foci
fuci
fuck
fade
fado
fady
Fido
feed
fee'd
feel
feer
feet
fief
flea
fled
flee
fleg
flew
flex
fley
foen
foes
free
fret
fuel
faff
fife
fuff
fegs
figo
fogy
△fehm
föhn
faik
fail
fain
fair
faix
feis
flic
flip
flit
flix
foid
foil
foin
frig
fris
frit
friz
fake
fike
fiky
fyke
fa-la
fall
falx
fell
felt
file
fill
film
filo
fils
fold
folk
full
fyle
fame
feme
fume
fumy
fand
fane
fang
fank
fend
feni
fent
find
fine
fini
fink
Finn
fino
fond
fone
font
fund
fung
funk
feod
floe
flog
flop
flor
flow
flox
food
fool
foot
△frog
from
frow
fard
fare
farl
farm
faro
fart
fere
ferm
fern
fire
firk
firm
firn
fora
forb
ford
fore
fork
form
fort
furl
furr
△fury
fyrd
fash
fast
fess
fest
fisc
fish
fisk
fist
foss
fusc
fuse
fuss
fust
fate
feta
fête
fett
fits
fitt
faun
faux
feud
flub
flue
flux
foud
foul
four

Words marked △ may be spelled also with a capital letter

4 f□v□

fave
five
fawn
fowl
foxy
faze
fizz
fozy
fuze
fuzz
geal
gean
gear
geat
ghat
glad
glam
G-man
gnar
gnat
gnaw
goad
goaf
goal
Goan
△goat
grab
grad
Graf
gram
gran
grat
gray
guan
guar
gyal
gaby
gibe
gobo
goby
go-by
gybe
geck
guck
gade
gadi
gods
gude
Gaea
gaed
Gael
geek
geep
Geëz
ghee
gied
gien
gled
glee
gleg
glei
glen
gley
goel
goer
goes
goey
gree
gren
grew
grey
gaff
gift
goff
guff
gaga
gage
giga
gogo
go-go
guga
Gaia
gaid
gain
gair
gait
geit
glia
glib
glid
glim
Glis
glit
grid
grig
grim
grin
grip
gris
grit
guid
gajo
gala
gale
gall
geld
gelt
gila
gild
gill
gilt
gold
gole
golf
golp
gula
gule
△gulf
gull
gulp
guly
gamb
game
gamp
gamy
gimp
gump
gymp
gane
gang
gant
gena
gene
gêne
gens
gent
genu
ging
gink
ginn
gone
gong
Gonk®
gonk
gunk
guns
Günz
gyny
gaol
geos
gios
glob
glom
glop
glow
△good
goof
gook
gool
goon
goop
goor
grog
grot
grow
gape
gapó
garb
gare
gart
gere
germ
gird
girl
girn
△giro
girr
girt
gore
gorm
gorp
gory
gurl
gurn
guru
gyre
gyro
gash
gasp
gast
gest
gism
gist
gosh
Goss
gush
gust
gate
gath
geta
gite
gîte
Goth
guts
gyte
gaud
Gaul
gaum
gaun
gaup
gaur
△geum
glue
glug
glum
glut
gnus
gouk
gout
goût
△grub
grue
grum
gave
give
gyve
gawd
gawk
gawp
gowd
gowf
gowk
gowl
gown
goys
guys
gaze
gazy
gizz
haaf
haar
head
heal
heap
hear
heat
hoar
hoas
hoax
△**hebe**
hobo
hack
hech
heck
hick
△hock
huck
hade
hadj
hide
haem
haet
heed
heel
hied
hoed
hoer
hued
huer
hyen
haff
haft
heft
hi-fi
huff
hagg
high
hogg
hogh
huge
hugy
ha-ha
he-he
hohs
haik
hail
hain
hair
ha'it
heid
heil
heir
hoik
huia
huis
haji
hajj
haka
hake
hike
hoke
hoki
hyke
hale
half
hall
halm
halo
halt
held
hele
△hell
he'll
helm
help
hila
hild
hili
hill
hilt
hold
hole
Holi
holm
holp
hols
holt
holy
hula
hule
hulk
hull
hyle
hame
heme
hemp
home
△homo
homy
huma
humf
hump
hymn
hand
hang
hank
ha'n't
hend
hent
hind
hing
hint
hond
hone
hong
honk
hung
hunk
hunt
hood
hoof
hook
hoon
hoop
hoot
Huon
hept
hipt
hope
hops
hype
hypo
hard
hare
hark
harl
harm
harn
haro
harp
hart
herb
herd
here
herl
herm
hern
△hero
Herr
hers
hery
hire
hore
horn
hors
hurl
hurt
hash
hask
hasp
hass
hast
hesp
hest
hish
hisn
his'n
hiss
hist
hose
hoss
△host
hush
husk
huso
huss
hate
hath
hete
hote
hots
haud
haul
haut
houf
hour
hout

Words marked △ may be spelled also with a capital letter

4 l□o□

have
hive
Hova
hove
hawk
hawm
hewn
howe
howf
howk
howl
hiya
hoya
hwyl
haze
hazy
hizz
igad
ikat
△imam
Igbo
inby
Inca
inch
itch
ibex
iced
icer
idea
idée
idem
△ides
ilea
ilex
item
iffy
info
ingo
ibis
ilia
inia
irid
iris
iwis
ixia
icky
ilka
inky
idle
idly
illy
inly
isle
it'll
iamb
isn't
lynx
Ibos
icon
idol
ikon

△iron
impi
I-spy
inro
iure
inst
inti
into
iota
idyl
ivy'd
jean
jeat
jiao
Joan
jibe
jobe
jobs
juba
jube
△jack
△jock
joco
jade
judo
△judy
jeel
Jeep
jeer
Jeez
joes
△joey
J-pen
jeff
jiff
juga
Jehu
△john
jail
Jain
join
juju
ju-ju
jake
joke
joky
juke
jell
jill
jilt
jole
joll
jolt
July
jamb
jimp
jomo
jump
△jane
jann
Jena

jink
jinn
jinx
June
junk
Juno
△jynx
jook
jape
jark
jarl
jerk
jird
△jura
jure
jury
jasp
jass
jasy
jess
jest
Jesu
jism
josh
joss
just
jato
jeté
jota
△jute
jaup
jeux
jouk
jour
Java
jive
Jove
juve
Jawi
jaws
jowl
jazy
jazz
jizz
△khan
khat
knag
knap
knar
koan
krab
ksar
kyat
kibe
keck
kick
kade
kadi
kudu
keek
keel

keen
keep
kier
knee
knew
koff
kago
kohl
kaid
kaie
kaif
kail
kaim
kain
keir
knit
kris
kaka
kaki
kike
kuku
kale
△kali
kell
kelp
△kelt
kild
kill
kiln
kilo
kilp
kilt
kola
kolo
kyle
△kama
kame
kami
kemb
kemp
kana
kang
kans
kant
keno
kent
kina
kind
kine
△king
kink
kino
kond
konk
kynd
kyne
kaon
khor
knob
knop
knot

know
kook
Kroo
kepi
kept
kipe
△kipp
koph
kara
kart
kerb
kerf
kern
△kirk
kirn
kora
kore
Kurd
kuri
kuru
kesh
kest
kish
kiss
kist
koss
kata
kati
keta
kite
kith
koto
kyte
khud
knub
knur
knut
kava
kiva
kiwi
kayo
△keys
kazi
lead
leaf
leak
△leal
leam
lean
leap
lear
leat
liar
Lias
load
loaf
loam
loan
luau
lyam
lobe

lobi
lobo
lace
lack
lacy
lech
lice
lich
lick
loch
loci
lock
loco
luce
luck
lade
△lady
Lide
lido
lode
ludo
laer
leek
leep
leer
lees
leet
lied
lief
lien
lier
lieu
lues
△left
life
lift
lo-fi
loft
luff
lags
Lego®
loge
logo
logy
luge
lehr
laic
laid
laik
lain
lair
leir
loid
loin
loir
luit
lake
lakh
laky
leke
like

loke
Loki
luke
la-la
lill
Lilo®
lilo
lilt
lily
loll
lull
lulu
△lama
△lamb
lame
lamé
lamp
leme
lima
limb
lime
limn
limo
limp
limy
loma
lome
lump
lyme
lana
△land
△lane
lang
lank
lant
lanx
lend
leng
leno
△lens
△lent
lind
△line
ling
link
linn
lino
lint
liny
lone
long
luna
lune
lung
lunt
lyne
lynx
△lion
loof
look
loom

Words marked △ may be spelled also with a capital letter

4 l□p□

loon
loop
loor
loos
loot
Lyon
Lapp
lips
lope
lard
lare
lark
larn
lere
lerp
lira
lire
lirk
△lord
lore
lorn
lory
lure
lurk
Lyra
lyre
lase
lash
lass
last
lese
less
'less
lest
lisk
△lisp
list
'list
lose
losh
loss
löss
lost
lush
lusk
lust
lyse
late
lath
Lett
lite
lith
lota
lote
loth
loto
lots
lute
lutz
lyte
laud

lauf
loud
loun
loup
lour
lout
lava
lave
leva
leve
levy
live
love
lawk
lawn
lewd
lowe
lown
lowt
luxe
laze
lazo
lazy
leze
lezz
ma'am
maar
mead
meal
mean
meat
moan
moat
M-way
myal
Mace®
mace
Mach
mack
mica
mice
mick
mico
moch
mock
much
△muck
made
Mede
△midi
mode
modi
△mods
meed
meek
meer
meet
mien
mzee
miff
muff

mage
magg
magi
mags
mega
Moho
mohr
Mohs
maid
maik
mail
maim
△main
mair
mein
moil
moit
muid
muil
muir
mojo
make
mako
mike
moke
moki
moko
male
mali
mall
malm
malt
mela
meld
mell
melt
mild
mile
milk
mill
milo
milt
mola
mold
mole
moll
molt
moly
mule
mull
mama
memo
mime
mome
mumm
mump
mana
mand
mane
mang
mani

mano
Manx
many
mend
mene
meng
ment
menu
mina
mind
mine
△ming
mini
mink
mino
mint
minx
miny
mona
mong
'mong
monk
mono
mony
mung
munt
myna
meow
mhos
mood
Moog®
mooi
mook
mool
△moon
moop
△moor
moot
muon
mope
Mopp
mopy
mara
marc
mard
mare
marg
mark
marl
marm
Mars
mart
△mary
merc
mere
meri
merk
merl
Mira
mire
miri

mirk
mirs
MIRV
mirv
miry
mora
more
morn
Moro
mort
mure
murk
murl
masa
mase
mash
mask
△mass
mast
masu
mesa
mese
mesh
△mess
mise
miso
△miss
mist
mose
moss
most
Musa
△muse
mush
musk
muso
muss
must
mate
maté
math
matt
maty
mete
mite
mitt
mity
MOT'd
mote
moth
mott
△motu
mute
muti
mutt
myth
maud
maul
maun
moue
moup

meve
move
mawk
mawr
mewl
mews
mowa
mown
maxi
mixt
mixy
moxa
△maya
moya
moyl
maze
mazy
meze
mézé
mizz
moze
mozz
naam
naan
neal
neap
near
neat
nyas
nabk
nabs
nibs
nach
neck
nice
△nick
nock
nada
nide
nidi
node
nodi
nude
need
neem
neep
ne'er
nief
Noel
Noël
noes
naff
nife
niff
nuff
naga
nigh
nogg
no-go
Naia
naif

naïf
naik
nail
nain
Nair
neif
noil
Naja
Nike
nuke
nala
nill
n'ill
nole
noll
null
△name
nemn
nimb
noma
nome
numb
nana
NAND
nene
△nine
none
nong
no-no
non-U
naos
neon
nook
noon
noop
napa
nape
△nipa
nope
Nupe
narc
nard
nare
nark
nary
nerd
nerk
nirl
nori
nork
norm
Norn
nurd
nurl
nurr
nesh
ness
nest
nisi
nose
nosh

Words marked △ may be spelled also with a capital letter

nosy
Nato
nete
nets
nett
nite
note
n'ote
no'te
not-l
nott
nuts
neuk
neum
noul
noun
noup
nous
nout
nave
△navy
névé
nevi
nova
news
newt
nowl
nown
nowt
nowy
next
nixy
naze
Nazi
odal
ofay
ogam
okay
opah
opal
oral
oval
ombu
ombú
orby
once
orca
ouch
odds
olds
oldy
obey
odea
ogee
Ogen
OKed
Olea
oleo
omen
omer
oner

△open
oven
over
owed
ower
oxen
oxer
oyer
oyes
oyez
oafs
orfe
orgy
oche
obia
obit
odic
Odin
olid
olio
omit
otic
Oaks
oaky
ogle
oils
oily
olla
only
orle
ould
oulk
owly
oink
oint
oons
oont
oboe
obol
obos
odor
ohos
Ogpu
olpe
oops
oppo
ouph
oary
ogre
okra
orra
ourn
ours
owre
oast
odso
onst
oose
oosy
ossa
oust

oath
oats
octa
okta
onto
orts
otto
outs
onus
opus
ovum
odyl
onyx
oryx
ooze
oozy
ouzo
peag
peak
peal
pean
pear
peas
peat
plan
plap
plat
play
prad
pram
prat
prau
pray
pyat
peba
paca
△pace
pack
paco
pact
pacy
pech
peck
pecs
△pica
pice
pick
pics
Pict
pock
poco
puce
△puck
pads
pudu
peek
peel
peen
peep
peer
phew

pied
pier
piet
plea
pleb
pled
poem
poet
pree
prep
prex
prey
puer
pyet
puff
page
pegh
pogo
pugh
paid
paik
pail
△pain
pair
pais
pein
phiz
plié
plim
prig
prim
Prix
puir
puja
Paki
peke
pika
pike
poke
poky
puke
puku
△pale
Pali
pall
palm
palp
paly
pela
△pele
pelf
pell
pelt
pila
pile
pili
pill
Pils
△pole
polk
△poll

polo
polt
poly
pula
pule
pulk
pull
pulp
pulu
puly
pimp
pome
pomp
puma
pump
pumy
pand
pane
pang
pant
pend
pene
peni
penk
pent
piña
pine
ping
pink
pins
pint
piny
△pond
pone
pong
ponk
pons
pont
pony
puna
punk
punt
puny
pyne
peon
phoh
phon
phos
phot
pion
pioy
plod
plop
plot
△plow
ploy
pood
poof
pooh
pook
pool

poon
poop
poor
poot
proa
prob
△prod
△prof
prog
PROM
prom
proo
prop
pros
prow
pyot
papa
pape
pepo
pipa
pipe
pipi
pips
pipy
△pope
pops
pupa
Pará
para
pard
pare
△park
parp
parr
part
père
peri
perk
perm
pern
pert
Peru
perv
pirl
pirn
pore
pork
porn
port
pory
pure
puri
purl
purr
pyre
pyro
pash
pass
past
peso
pest

pisé
pish
piss
pose
posé
posh
poss
post
posy
psst
push
puss
pate
pâté
path
pita
pith
pits
pity
pote
pots
pott
putt
putz
paua
paul
phut
pium
plug
plum
plus
pouf
pouk
pour
pout
pruh
pave
pavé
Pavo
pawa
pawk
pawl
pawn
pown
pixy
poxy
PAYE
pays
Pnyx
prys
pize
pozz
△quad
quag
quat
quay
qadi
quep
quey
quid
quim

Words marked △ may be spelled also with a capital letter

quin
quip
quit
quiz
qu**o**d
quop
qo**p**h
re**a**d
reak
real
ream
rean
reap
rear
rial
road
roam
roan
roar
ryal
ra**b**i
robe
'robe
rube
ruby
ra**c**a
race
rach
rack
racy
reck
rice
rich
rick
ricy
roch
△rock
ruck
ra**d**e
redd
rede
redo
reds
ride
rode
rudd
rude
re**e**d
reef
reek
reel
reen
△rhea
riel
riem
roed
rued
ra**f**f
raft
reft
rife
riff
rift
ruff
ryfe
ra**g**a
rag'd
rage
ragg
ragi
rags
rego
rigg
Ra**h**u
ra**i**d
raik
rail
rain
rait
reif
reik
rein
reis
roil
roin
ruin
ra**j**a
roji
ra**k**e
raki
raku
reke
roke
roky
rukh
ryke
ra**l**e
râle
rely
rile
rill
role
rôle
roll
rule
ruly
Ra**m**a
rami
ramp
rams
rima
rime
rimu
rimy
roma
Rome
romp
rume
△rump
△**r**a**n**a
△rand
rang
rani
rank
rant
rend
rent
reny
rind
rine
ring
rink
rone
rong
ront
rund
rune
rung
runs
runt
rynd
rh**o**s
riot
△rood
roof
rook
room
roon
roop
root
ryot
ra**p**e
rapt
repo
repp
reps
ripe
ripp
ript
rope
ropy
rype
ra-**r**a
rare
rore
ro-ro
rort
rory
rurp
ruru
ra**s**e
rash
rasp
rast
rest
rise
risk
risp
Riss
Rosa
rose
rosé
rost
rosy
rusa
ruse
rusé
rush
rusk
Russ
rust
ra**t**a
rate
rath
rats
ratu
rete
rite
ritt
△ritz
△rota
rote
roti
rotl
Ruta
ruth
ra**u**n
rhus
roué
roul
roum
roup
rout
roux
ra**v**e
riva
rive
rivo
rove
ra**w**n
rowt
ra**z**e
razz
riza
Sa**a**m
scab
scad
scag
scam
scan
scar
scat
scaw
seal
seam
sean
sear
seas
seat
shad
shag
shah
sham
△shan
shat
shaw
shay
sial
skag
skat
skaw
slab
slae
slag
slam
slap
slat
Slav
slaw
slay
snab
snag
snap
snar
soak
soap
soar
Soay
spae
spag
Spam®
span
spar
spat
spaw
spay
stab
stag
stap
star
staw
stay
swab
swad
swag
swam
swan
swap
swat
sway
Sa**b**a
sibb
sybo
sa**c**k
sech
seco
sect
sice
sich
sick
soca
sock
such
suck
syce
sa**d**e
sida
side
soda
sods
sudd
suds
se**e**d
seek
seel
seem
seen
seep
seer
shea
shed
she'd
shes
she's
shet
shew
sien
skeg
skeo
skep
sker
skew
sled
slee
slew
sley
smee
smew
sneb
sned
snee
spec
sped
spek
△spet
spew
sted
stem
△sten
step
stet
stew
stey
sued
suer
suet
swee
swey
syen
sa**f**e
sift
sofa
Sofi
soft
Sufi
sa**g**a
sage
sago
sagy
sego
sigh
sign
so**h**o
so-ho
sa**i**c
said
sail
saim
sain
sair
seif
seik
seil
seir
Shia
shim
shin
ship
shir
shit
shiv
skid
ski'd
skim
skin
skio
skip
skis
skit
slid
'slid
△slim
slip
slit
smir
smit
snib
snig
snip
soil
spic
spie
spik
spin
spit
spiv
stie
stir
suid
suit
swig
swim
swiz
Se**j**m
sijo
soja
sa**k**e

Words marked △ may be spelled also with a capital letter

saké
saki
△sekt
sika
sike
Sikh
soke
sukh
syke
sa**l**e
Salk
salp
salt
seld
sele
self
sell
sild
sile
silk
sill
silo
silt
sola
sold
sole
soli
solo
sols
sulk
△sulu
sa**m**a
same
Sami
samp
semé
semi
shmo
sima
simi
simp
△soma
some
sumo
sump
sa**n**d
sane
sang
sank
sans
△sant
sena
send
sens
sent
sind
sine
sing
sinh
sink
sone

song
△sung
sunk
sunn
sync
synd
syne
sc**o**g
scop
scot
scow
shod
shoe
shog
shoo
△shop
shot
show
skol
slob
sloe
slog
slop
slot
slow
smog
snob
snod
snog
snot
snow
sook
soom
soon
soop
soot
spot
stoa
stob
STOL
stop
stot
stow
swob
swop
swot
se**p**s
sept
sipe
soph
supe
sype
△**s**a**r**d
sari
sark
scry
sera
Serb
sere
serf
serk

serr
Shri
sire
siri
skry
sora
△sorb
sord
sore
sori
sorn
sort
spry
sura
surd
sure
surf
sa**s**h
sass
sese
sess
siss
sist
so-so
soss
suss
Susu
sa**t**e
sati
seta
sett
site
sith
sa**u**l
saut
△scud
scug
scul
scum
scup
scur
scut
shul
shun
'shun
shut
Sium
skua
skug
slub
slue
slug
slum
slur
slut
smug
smur
smut
snub
snug
souk

soul
soum
soup
sour
sous
sout
spud
spue
spun
spur
stub
stud
stum
stun
swum
sa**v**e
Siva
sa**w**n
sewn
shwa
sowf
sowl
sowm
sown
sowp
Sa**x**e
sext
sexy
sa**y**s
scye
Skye
skyr
snye
soya
stye
si**z**e
sizy
Ta**a**l
T-bar
tea'd
teak
teal
team
Tean
tear
teat
thae
Thai
than
thar
that
thaw
tiar
toad
trad
tram
trap
trat
tray
tsar
tuan

twae
twal
'twas
twat
tway
tzar
ta**b**i
tabs
tabu
to-be
△toby
tuba
△tube
ta**c**e
tach
tack
taco
tact
tech
tice
△tich
tick
Tico
tock
toco
tuck
te**d**y
tide
tidy
to-do
tody
tyde
ta**e**l
ta'en
teed
tee'd
teel
teem
teen
teer
Thea
thee
them
then
thew
they
tied
tier
toea
toed
toes
toey
tree
tref
trek
très
tret
trew
trey
trez
twee

te**f**f
tiff
tift
toff
toft
tofu
tufa
tuff
tuft
ta**g**s
tegg
tegu
tige
toga
toge
togs
ta**h**a
tahr
tehr
toho
Tshi
Ta**i**g
tail
tait
teil
thig
thin
thir
this
toil
trie
trig
trim
trin
trio
trip
twig
twin
twit
ta**k**a
take
taki
taky
tika
tike
tiki
toke
toko
tyke
ta**l**a
talc
tale
tali
talk
tall
tela
teld
tell
telt
tile
till

tilt
tola
told
tole
toll
tolt
△tolu
tule
ta**m**e
tamp
teme
temp
tems
△time
tomb
tome
tump
tymp
ta**n**a
tane
ta'ne
△tang
T'ang
tanh
tank
tend
tene
tent
tind
tine
ting
tink
tint
tiny
tone
tong
tonk
tons
△tony
tuna
tund
tune
tuny
tynd
tyn'd
tyne
th**o**n
Thor
thou
took
tool
toom
toon
toot
trod
trog
tron
△trot
trow
troy
ta**p**a

Words marked △ may be spelled also with a capital letter

4 t□r□

tape
taps
tapu
tipi
tipt
tope
topi
tops
Tupi
Tupí
type
typo
tara
tare
tarn
taro
tarp
tart
terf
term
tern
thro
thro'
thru
tire
tirl
tiro
tirr
torc
tore
tori
torn
torr
tort
Tory
turd
turf
△turk
turm
turn
tyre
tyro
tash
task
tass
test
tosa
tose
tosh
toss
tost
tush
tusk
ta-ta
tate
tath
tatt
tatu
tête
tite
titi

tits
tote
tuts
tutu
tyte
taut
thud
thug
thus
touk
toun
tour
tout
true
trug
tava
tawa
taws
tawt
town
towt
towy
taxa
taxi
text
trye
tryp
tizz
toze
tuzz
udal
unau
upas
Ural
urao
utas
umbo
unbe
upby
unce
unci
unco
unde
undé
undo
urdé
Urdu
urdy
ulex
urea
used
user
uses
Utes
uvea
upgo
urge
Unio
unit
uric
Urim

utis
Uzis
ugli®
ugly
ulna
udos
ufos
upon
umph
upsy
Ursa
unto
urus
ulva
urva
V-day
veal
vial
voar
vibs
△**vice**
vade
Veda
vide
veep
veer
vied
vier
△view
vlei
vagi
△vega
△**vehm**
vail
vain
vair
veil
vein
void
vril
vale
vali
△vela
veld
vele
vell
vild
vile
vill
vola
vole
volk
volt
vuln
vamp
vane
vang
vant
vena
vend
Venn

vent
vina
vine
vino
vint
viny
viol
vrow
VTOL
vara
vare
vary
Vera
verb
vers
vert
△very
vire
virl
vasa
vase
vast
vest
visa
vise
visé
vatu
veto
Vita®
vita
vite
vote
vaut
viva
vive
vivo
vext
vizy
Waac
Waaf
weak
weal
wean
wear
wham
whap
what
woad
wrap
wack
wice
wich
wick
wock
wych
wadd
wade
wadi
wadt
wady
wide

weed
week
weel
weem
ween
weep
weet
whee
when
whe'r
whet
whew
whey
wiel
woes
△wren
Wafd
waff
waft
weft
wife
wage
waid
waif
wail
△wain
wait
weid
weil
weir
whid
△whig
whim
whin
whip
whir
△whit
whiz
writ
waka
wake
△wakf
weka
woke
wald
wale
wali
walk
△wall
waly
weld
welk
well
we'll
△welt
△wild
wile
wili
will
wilt
wily

wold
wolf
wull
wame
wemb
wimp
womb
wand
wan'd
wane
wang
wank
want
wany
△wend
went
wind
wine
wing
wink
winn
wino
win't
winy
wont
won't
wynd
wynn
whoa
who'd
whom
whop
who's
whot
whow
wood
woof
wool
woon
woot
woo't
wept
wipe
△**waqf**
ward
ware
wark
warm
warn
warp
wart
wary
were
we're
wert
wire
wiry
△word
wore
work
worm

worn
wort
Würm
wase
wash
wasm
wasp
wast
△west
wise
wish
wisp
wist
wost
wuss
wate
wats
watt
weta
wite
with
wits
wots
wyte
wauk
waul
waur
wave
wavy
we've
wive
wove
wawe
wawl
wowf
waxy
wexe
ways
Xian
Xmas
X-ray
Xema
Xosa
xyst
yead
yeah
yean
year
yuan
yack
yech
yock
yuca
yuck
yede
yode
ybet
yeed
ylem
yaff
yuft

Words marked △ may be spelled also with a capital letter

△**yag**i
yegg
yoga
yogh
yogi
yuga
yo-**h**o
ywi**s**
yike
ylke
yoke
yuke
yuko
yuky
yal**d**
Yale®
yale
y'all
yeld
yelk
yell
yelm
yelp
yelt
yill
yold
yolk
△yule
Yama
yomp
yump
△**y**a**ng**
△yank
yond
yoni
yont
yunx
ygoe
yoof
yoop
yapp
yips
ympe
ympt
△**yar**d
yare
yarn
yarr
yerd
yerk
yird
yirk
yore
york
yurt
yesk
yes's
yest
yate
yeti
yett
yite
yaud
yaup
yeuk
you'd
youk
your
yeve
yawl
yawn
yawp
yaws
yawy
yowe
yowl
yo-**y**o
zeal
zebu
zobo
zobu
zack
zoe**a**
ziff
zein
zoic
zila
△zulu
zimb
zyme
zany
Zend
zinc
zing
zona
zone
zonk
Zuni
Zuñi
Zion
zoom
zoon
zop**p**
zupa
zarf
zero
zurf
zest
zati
zeta
zite
ziti
'**zbu**d
Zeus
zouk
zeze
zizz

Words marked △ may be spelled also with a capital letter

5 a□a□a

abaca
abaya
afara
Agama
alapa
anana
araba
asana
aband
afald
aland
apaid
apayd
award
abase
abate
adage
agape
agate
a'gate
agave
agaze
alate
amate
amaze
apace
apage
arame
avale
awake
aware
awave
alang
abash
awash
abaci
acari
agami
Amati
aback
abask
alack
avail
alarm
again
amain
awarn
alaap
Adam's
adays
amass
AWACS
aways
abaft
adapt
agast
apart
avant
avast
await
alary
Araby
ataxy
albee
amble
album
Alban
amban
amber
△arbor
ambos
abbot
ambit
abbey
ambry
aecia
arced
abcee
ancle
ASCII
ancon
arcus
ascus
ascot
accoy
aldea
Ardea
ardeb
Asdic
aided
addle
ardri
ard-ri
add-on
addio
add-to
audio
adder
aider
alder
ardor
aedes
aidos
Ardas
audit
addax
Akela
ameba
areca
arena
Avena
acerb
ahead
amend
an-end
aread
aredd
abele
agene
akene
aleye
amene
anele
arede
arere
arête
aleph
Adeni
Azeri
apeak
apeek
a-week
areal
aweel
abeam
adeem
aweto
aheap
ayelp
abear
afear
ameer
anear
arear
avens
adept
agent
ahent
aleft
alert
ament
anent
apert
aren't
arett
avert
aiery
apery
arefy
awful
affix
algid
△**algae**
△angle
Argie
argue
aygre
aggri
algal
Algol
angel
argal
argil
argol
algum
algin
argan
argon
aggro
Anglo
agger
anger
Apgar
auger
augur
aegis
△argus
avgas
△**angst**
argot
aught
aggry
angry
aphid
ashen
abhor
aphis
△ashes
ashet
agila
aliya
anima
Arita
ahind
abide
afire
agile
Alice
alike
aline
A-line
alive
amice
amide
amine
anile
anime
animé
anise
arise
aside
A-side
avine
avise
avize
axile
azide
azine
aging
a-wing
ahigh
Amish
anigh
apish
arish
acini
alibi
amici
apiol
△ariel
axial
apism
axiom
alien
align
anion
apian
Arian
Asian
avian
avion
amigo
amino
aviso
abies
adiós
agios
alias
amiss
Aries
agist
ahint
ariot
atilt
adieu
amity
atimy
alkyd
ackee
alkie
ankle
alkyl
anker
asker
akkas
ankus
askew
ad-lib
△**aulic**
abled
allod
aglee
all-be
allée
Allah
auloi
aflaj
allel
allyl
Allen
all-in
all-to
all-up
abler
allis
arles
△atlas
aulos
ablet
aglet
allot
ablow
aglow
allow
agley
allay
alley
alloy
armed
almug
almah
almeh
armil
aumil
adman
ad-man
admin
amman
△ammon
atman
axman
armor
admit
armet
admix
awmry
amnia
apnea
awned
aînée
annal
annul
awner
Alnus
annat
arnut
annex
annoy
aunty
agora
aloha
Anona
aroba
aroma
A-bomb
azoic
abord
acold
agood
ahold
aloed
aloud
A-road
aroid
avoid
axoid
abode
abore
above
adobe
adore
afore
agoge
agone
alone
alowe
amove
anode
apode
arose
atoke
atone
awoke
azote
aloof
along
among
azoth
aioli
aïoli
acock
awork
aboil
afoul
atoll
acorn
adorn
adown
apoop
amour
aloes
abort
about
adopt
afoot
aloft
amort
aport
ayont
a'body
agony
anomy
atomy
atony
atopy
alpha
aspic
ample
apple
appui
ampul
appal
appel
aspen
appro
asper
Ampex®
amply
appay
apply
appuy
aorta
atria
Afric
auric
acred
acrid

Words marked △ may be spelled also with a capital letter

5 b□o□e

adrad
adred
aerie
agree
aurae
ayrie
arrah
aurei
April
aural
abram
abrim
abrin
agrin
apron
atrip
airer
Abrus
acres
après
arras
arris
auras
afrit
amrit
arrêt
arrow
abray
array
aisle
assai
adsum
arson
aesir
apsis
arses
arsis
asses
absit
asset
assot
absey
assay
antra
antic
artic
△attic
Aztec
antae
antre
aitch
artal
artel
actin
acton
astun
attap
actor
after
altar
alter

antar
aster
astir
attar
altos
autos
aptly
artsy
abuna
alula
Anura
adunc
agued
abune
abuse
acute
alure
amuse
azure
aduki
aguti
amuck
ahull
azurn
adult
adust
azury
abuzz
anvil
△arval
arvos
advew
aswim
ajwan
alway
asway
auxin
adyta
avyze
△azyme
abysm
Aryan
abyss
as-yet
azygy
Anzac
aizle
brava
bwana
beard
bland
blaud
board
braid
brand
beare
blade
blame
blare
blasé
blate

blaze
brace
brake
brame
brave
braze
buaze
bhang
beach
beath
blash
brach
brash
bravi
bwazi
△**black**
blank
brack
brank
be-all
brail
brawl
blain
brain
brawn
beano
bravo
beads
blaes
brass
braws
△**beast**
beaut
blast
blatt
boart
boast
bract
brast
beaux
beady
beaky
beamy
braky
braxy
bobac
Babee
△bible
bobak
△**babel**
babul
bubal
baboo
bebop
Bibby
bobby
bubby
bacca
bocca
becke
boche

bacon
bacco
bucko
Backs
buchu
bucku
baccy
biccy
bedad
bided
badge
bedye
bodge
bodle
budge
bodhi
bedel
bedim
bidon
budos
bidet
bedew
baddy
badly
biddy
buddy
bield
bleed
blend
bread
breed
by-end
brede
breme
brere
breve
beech
bleak
break
bream
breem
bleep
blear
breer
beefs
bless
bleat
blent
blest
brent
beefy
beery
buffa
bifid
buffe
befog
buffi
buffo
buffs
befit
baffy

bigha
begad
bigae
bogie
bogle
bugle
bagel
begem
begum
began
begin
begun
bogan
begar
bogus
begat
beget
begot
bight
bigot
baggy
biggy
bogey
boggy
buggy
bohea
Bahai
Baha'i
bahut
blind
build
baize
beige
blite
blive
bribe
bride
brine
brisé
brize
B-side
brief
ba'ing
△being
boing
bring
blini
blink
boink
brick
brink
brisk
brill
bairn
△**blimp**
briar
brier
bliss
blist
bui'lt
buist

blimy
briny
blitz
bajra
bajri
△**bajan**
Bajau
bijou
baked
bikie
bekah
baken
△**baker**
biker
bokos
balsa
belga
△bulla
balk'd
belee
belie
belle
bilge
bulge
bulse
belah
belch
baloo
bilbo
baler
balas
balks
balls
bells
bolas
bolos
bolts
bolus
below
bylaw
bolix
baldy
balky
bally
balmy
belay
belly
bilgy
billy
bulgy
bulky
bully
bemad
bemud
bombe
bombé
bumph
bimbo
bombo
bumbo
bumps

bumpy
banda
△bania
Binca®
bonza
bunia
bunya
boned
Bände
benne
binge
bonce
bonie
bonne
bonze
bunce
bunje
bench
bunch
benni
banal
banco
banjo
bingo
bongo
bunco
bunko
boner
bands
bangs
banns
bends
bonds
bones
bonus
Banat
benet
△**bantu**
bundu
bandy
bendy
benny
benty
bingy
bonny
Bundy®
bungy
bunjy
bunny
bunty
biota
blond
blood
boord
broad
brond
brood
biome
bloke
blore
boose

Words marked △ may be spelled also with a capital letter

5 b□o□g

booze
broke
brose
boong
booth
broch
brogh
broth
block
brock
brook
broil
brool
bloom
broom
blown
brown
bloop
blows
boobs
books
boots
biont
bloat
boost
Bronx
blowy
booby
boody
booky
booty
boozy
biped
bipod
bepat
buppy
barca
burka
burqa
bursa
berob
baric
boric
barbe
barge
barre
barré
barye
birle
birse
borde
boree
borne
borné
burke
burse
berth
birch
birth
burgh
borak

beryl
borel
baron
boron
buran
burin
bardo
borgo
buroo
burro
bar-b-**q**
borer
barbs
bards
Bart's
birds
Biros
beret
buret
burnt
burst
borax
bardy
barky
barmy
beray
berry
birsy
burly
burry
basta
△**basic**
based
basse
baste
besee
bassi
basal
basil
besom
bosom
basan
basin
bason
bison
boson
bosun
bo'sun
basho
basso
basto
bases
basis
buses
beset
besit
besot
bussu
bassy
bosky
bossy

busby
bushy
busky
busty
batta
Butea
bated
betid
bathe
bitte
botte
butte
batch
bitch
botch
butch
batik
betel
botel
butyl
baton
béton
biter
baths
batts
bitos
bitts
botts
batty
betty
bitsy
bitty
bothy
botty
butty
blurb
bluid
bound
bourd
blude
bouge
boule
bouse
brûlé
brume
brute
bluff
bourg
blush
bough
brush
baulk
blunk
bourn
Bruin
△**blues**
blunt
blurt
boult
bruit
brunt

brust
bludy
bluey
bousy
bovid
bevue
bevel
bavin
Bevin
bever
bevvy
bivvy
bowed
bowie
bowne
bowse
bewig
bowel
bower
bowes
bowls
bewet
bowat
bowet
bawdy
byway
buxom
boxen
△**boxer**
bayle
buy-in
boyar
buyer
bayou
boyau
bezel
bazar
buzzy
Caaba
chara
chaya
coarb
chard
cease
ceaze
chace
chafe
chape
chare
chase
chave
clade
clame
Clare
clave
coate
crake
crame
crane
crape
crare

crate
crave
craze
chaff
clang
craig
clash
coach
crash
coati
chack
△chalk
chank
chark
clack
clank
crack
crank
crawl
charm
chasm
claim
chain
chaco
claro
champ
clamp
clasp
cramp
chair
charr
chaos
chaps
chars
ciaos
claes
class
coals
craps
crass
chaft
chant
chart
clart
claut
coact
coapt
△coast
craft
chary
clary
coaly
crapy
crazy
cobia
cobra
cobza
cabob
cubeb
caboc
cubic

cable
cabré
coble
cabal
cibol
Cobol
cabin
Cuban
caber
cabas
Cebus
cubit
cabby
cobby
cubby
cocoa
cycad
cache
cycle
cacti
cocci
cecal
cecum
cacao
cocco
cyclo
cocos
cocky
cadee
cadge
cadie
cadre
codon
cedar
cider
cyder
cedis
cadet
codex
caddy
cadgy
cuddy
caeca
△cheka
chela
crena
△**creed**
caese
chère
clepe
cleve
creme
crème
crême
crepe
crêpe
crewe
ctene
Czech
check
cheek

cleck
cleek
clerk
creak
△creek
creel
cream
clean
△**credo**
cheap
cheep
cleep
creep
cheer
clear
chess
cress
cheat
chert
chest
cleat
cleft
crept
crest
chevy
chewy
crepy
crêpy
Cufic
cuffo
caged
cogie
cogue
cigar
cagot
ci-gît
cagey
ciggy
cohab
cohoe
cohog
cohos
chica
△china
cnida
chimb
climb
caird
child
cried
chide
△chile
chime
chine
chiné
chive
clime
cline
clipe
crime
crine

Words marked △ may be spelled also with a capital letter

crise
chief
cliff
cling
cuing
chich
crith
cuish
ceili
chili
chick
△chink
chirk
click
clink
crick
chiel
chill
chirl
chirm
cairn
Chian
coign
chiao
chico
chimo
chino
chimp
chirp
crimp
crisp
chirr
crier
chips
cries
chirt
clift
clint
clipt
chivy
chizz
△**cajun**
cakes
cokes
cakey
calla
calpa
cella
cilia
colza
celeb
colic
calid
calve
calif
culch
celom
colin
colon
cello
'cello

△**calor**
color
calfs
calms
culet
calix
calyx
culex
cylix
calmy
coley
colly
cully
comma
comic
cumec
comae
combe
camel
comal
caman
cumin
cameo
campo
combo
commo
compo
cimar
△comer
cymar
camas
camis
camus
combs
comms
△comus
comet
compt
cimex
campy
comby
comfy
commy
Cymry
canna
conga
conia
conic
△cynic
canid
contd
canoe
cense
congé
conne
Conté
conte
conté
caneh
cinch
conch

canal
canon
cañon
conin
canto
cento
condo
congo
conto
convo
Canis
canst
cinct
Candu
candy
canny
canty
coney
conky
cundy
chota
clomb
coomb
cromb
chord
cloud
cooed
crowd
chode
choke
chore
chose
cloke
clone
△close
clote
clove
cloze
cooee
crome
crone
crore
croze
choof
cloff
cloth
choli
chock
chook
cloak
clock
clonk
croak
crock
cronk
crook
ceorl
△**choom**
cloam
clown
croon

△crown
choco
choko
chomp
clomp
cloop
croup
choir
clour
chops
△cross
chott
chout
cloot
clout
coopt
co-opt
coost
Croat
croft
crout
choux
choky
cooey
cooky
cooly
coomy
crony
copra
cuppa
△**cupid**
caple
copse
Capri
cippi
capul
copal
cupel
capon
caper
coper
capos
capot
caput
coppy
copsy
capiz
carta
ceria
circa
curia
Carib
carob
ceric
cored
carse
carte
carve
cerge
cerne
corbe

corse
curie
curse
curve
curch
cardi
carpi
cerci
cirri
corgi
corni
cursi
carol
△coral
carom
CD-ROM
coram
cargo
corno
corso
curio
carap
carer
corer
curer
cards
Ceres
circs
cords
corps
carat
caret
curat
curst
cornu
carex
carby
cardy
Carey
carny
carry
carvy
certy
corey
corky
corny
curdy
curly
curny
curry
curvy
costa
cosec
cusec
caste
cesse
coste
casco
cisco
costs
coset

cissy
cushy
cotta
cutie
catch
cutch
cetyl
cital
cutin
cut-in
cyton
cutto
cut-up
cater
citer
cates
cutis
catty
cutey
cutty
causa
chufa
Chubb®
courb
crumb
cauld
could
courd
cause
'cause
chuse
chute
coudé
coupe
coupé
coure
crude
cruse
cruve
chuff
clung
couch
cough
couth
crush
caulk
chuck
chunk
cluck
clunk
cruck
churl
cruel
churn
chump
clump
crump
churr
cruor
clubs
count

court
cruet
crust
crusy
civic
coved
cavie
cuvée
cavel
cavil
civil
coven
covin
caver
cover
civet
covet
civvy
covey
cowed
crwth
cowal
cowan
cower
cowry
coxed
coxae
coxal
caxon
Coxes
chynd
chyle
chyme
clype
crypt
coypu
coyly
cozen
Diana
drama
deare
deave
drake
drape
drave
dwale
draff
dwarf
dwang
death
D-mark
drank
do-all
drail
drawl
dwalm
dwaum
dearn
drain
drawn
diazo

Words marked △ may be spelled also with a capital letter

5 d□a□s

Draco
drabs
dealt
diact
draft
drant
deary
deawy
diary
Debye
debag
debug
debel
Dobro®
debar
debus
dibbs
debit
debut
début
debby
dobby
dacha
Decca®
dicta
decad
diced
decal
ducal
decko
decor
décor
dicer
decks
docks
ducks
dicht
dicot
docht
ducat
decay
decoy
decry
dicey
dicky
dicty
duchy
ducky
dodge
dedal
dados
didos
dodos
didst
daddy
diddy
doddy
dodgy
duddy
dweeb
dread
deere
deeve
diene
drere
doeth
dreck
dwell
dream
drear
dregs
dress
duets
doest
drent
drest
duett
dwelt
deedy
defer
defat
daffy
dagga
dogma
dogie
degum
Dagon
doggo
dagos
degas
dight
digit
daggy
doggy
dohyo
dried
daine
de-ice
drive
dwile
dwine
doing
D-ring
dying
drink
drill
deism
deign
djinn
drier
dribs
dries
daint
deist
doilt
drift
daily
dairy
daisy
deify
△deity
doily
drily
dojos
dekko
daker
diker
dikey
dykey
delta
dolia
dolma
dulia
dalle
delve
dolce
dulse
delph
dilli
Dalek
dildo
dolor
delfs
delft
dally
delay
dilly
Dolby®
dolly
dully
dumka
demob
demic
domed
damme
domal
daman
deman
demon
dumbo
damar
demur
dimer
demos
dumps
demit
dempt
dampy
dimly
dumky
dummy
dumpy
donga
Donna
Deneb
dinic
dance
dense
dinge
donee
donne
donné
dunce
donah
dunch
dunsh
denim
danio
dingo
dunno
dinar
diner
donor
don'ts
Donat
Donet
donut
dandy
denay
dingy
dinky
dungy
dunny
diota
doona
dhole
diode
doole
drôle
drome
drone
drove
droog
dhobi
dhoti
duomi
drook
drouk
dholl
droil
droll
drool
doorn
drown
dsobo
dsomo
duomo
droop
dooms
drops
dross
droit
doomy
drony
duple
depth
dipso
doper
duper
depot
dippy
dopey
duply
duppy
darga
derma
dorsa
durra
daric
Doric
dared
dorad
darre
dirge
dirke
doree
dorse
daraf
derig
derth
darzi
dural
durum
dares
darts
Doras
Doris
dorts
duros
durst
Darby
darcy
darky
deray
△derby
derry
dirty
dorky
dormy
dorty
durgy
duroy
desse
disme
doseh
disco
desex
dishy
dusky
dusty
dated
doted
ditch
△dutch
Datuk
datal
Datel®
dital
dotal
datum
Datin
ditto
dater
deter
doter
detox
ditsy
ditty
ditzy
dotty
douma
doura
△**druid**
daube
deuce
douce
douse
drupe
△druse
Druze
dough
drunk
douar
drugs
dault
daunt
doubt
dauby
Douay
drusy
druxy
David
dived
dovie
devel
△devil
daven
Devon
divan
diver
dover
Dives
davit
dévot
divot
duvet
divvy
downa
dowed
dowie
dowle
dowse
dowel
dewan
diwan
dewar
dowar
dower
△**downs**
Dewey
dowdy
downy
dowry
dixie
dryad
Dayak
doyen
dryer
daynt
doyly
dryly
dazed
dozed
dizen
dozen
dazer
dozer
dizzy
eland
elate
enate
erase
étage
étape
evade
e-la-mi
△**e-mail**
enarm
Erato
Elaps
enact
epact
exact
exalt
erbia
embed
embog
embar
ember
embus
elbow
embow
embox
embay
emcee
elchi
excel
escot
Eddic
ended
endue
eldin
end-on
eider
elder
ex-div
endew
endow
edema
enema
emend
exeme
elemi
Eyeti
exeem
emeer
evens

Words marked △ may be spelled also with a capital letter

egest
eject
elect
erect
event
evert
ewest
exeat
exert
elegy
emery
enemy
every
elfin
enfix
edged
eagle
eagre
eigne
Elgin
ergon
eager
edger
eggar
egger
eight
ergot
ethic
ephod
evhoe
ephah
ethal
△ethyl
ephor
ether
ethos
ewhow
erica
eniac
eliad
edile
elide
elite
élite
esile
evite
△exile
exine
eying
erick
Elian
exies
exits
edict
evict
exist
edify
enjoy
eikon
eskar
esker
Eolic
Eblis
éclat
elmen
emmer
Emmys
emmet
emmew
enmew
Ernie
ennui
éloge
elope
emote
emove
epode
erode
erose
evohe
evoke
exode
emong
epoch
enoki
enorm
eloin
△**elops**
Etons
E-boat
epopt
ebony
elogy
epoxy
eupad
elpee
expel
expos
expat
empty
eared
erred
eerie
eyrie
△**earth**
enrol
EPROM
eprom
error
épris
euros
Eurus
earst
egret
early
easle
ensue
easel
eisel
eusol
Epsom
Elsan®
elsin
eosin
esses
ensew
Essex
ensky
essay
entia
extra
estoc
eathe
ettle
Eytie
extol
eaten
ettin
estro
estop
eater
enter
ester
entry
Eruca
exurb
equid
educe
elude
elute
emule
emure
enure
étude
exude
equal
equip
Equus
educt
eruct
erupt
exult
envoi
eeven
elvan
erven
elver
eaves
elves
envoy
etwee
etyma
Egypt
Enzed
franc
fa'ard
fraud
feare
flake
flame
flare
frame
frate
flaff
flash
frati
flack
flank
flask
frack
△frank
flail
frail
flamm
fraim
flawn
flair
fiars
flats
frass
feast
fract
flaky
flamy
flary
flawy
flaxy
foamy
fable
fibre
fibro
fiber
fubby
fubsy
facia
faced
fiche
fecal
focal
facer
feces
ficos
ficus
focus
fucus
facet
fecht
fecit
fichu
fadge
fidge
fudge
fader
fados
faddy
frena
field
fiend
freed
fremd
feese
feeze
fiere
fleme
frère
flesh
fresh
fleck
freak
fleam
foehn
Freon®
freon
fuero
fleer
freer
flews
fient
△fleet
freet
freit
faery
fiery
△**fifth**
fifer
fifty
fuffy
fogle
fugie
fugle
fugue
fugal
Fagin
Fagus
figos
fagot
fight
fogey
foggy
fuggy
△**fehme**
fried
faine
flite
frize
fling
faith
frith
flick
flisk
frisk
frill
feign
flimp
flier
friar
frier
fains
flies
fries
faint
feint
flint
flirt
flitt
foist
frist
fairy
fritz
frizz
faker
fakir
fakes
fella
folia
folic
felid
filed
false
fille
folie
F-clef
filch
filth
falaj
felon
folio
filar
filer
Felis
films
folks
filet
felly
felty
filly
filmy
folly
fully
famed
femme
femal
femur
fomes
fumes
fumet
fonda
fence
finch
Fanti
fundi
fungi
fanal
final
fanon
fango
finer
fenks
fines
finis
finks
finos
fonds
funds
fancy
fanny
fendy
fenny
finny
fonly
fundy
funky
funny
flora
flota
fiord
fjord
△flood
frond
F-word
f-hole
flote
frore
froze
feoff
flong
flosh
froth
flock
frock
flown
frorn
frown
floor
flour
floss
foots
float
flout
front
frost
flory
foody
footy
frory
frowy
farad
fired
farce
farle
farse
△force
forge
forme
forte
furze
firth
forth
furth
farci
Farsi
fermi
feral
forel
fural
furol
forum

5 f□r□n

furan
fordo
forgo
firer
furor
first
forex
farcy
ferly
ferny
ferry
firry
foray
forby
forky
△forty
furry
furzy
festa
△fossa
fesse
fosse
fusee
fasci
fasti
fusil
Fusus
fishy
fisty
fussy
fusty
fatwa
fetta
fetwa
fated
fetid
fitte
fytte
fetch
fitch
fatal
fetal
futon
fatso
fit-up
f-stop
fetor
Fates
fetus
fatly
fatty
fitly
fauna
faurd
fluid
found
Fauve
fluke
flume
flute
foulé
fluff
flung
faugh
flush
fouth
frush
flunk
Fluon®
flump
frump
feuar
fluor
flurr
fours
fault
fouat
fouet
fount
fruit
frust
fluey
fluky
fluty
fovea
favel
favor
fever
fiver
favus
fives
fowth
fowls
fixed
foxed
fixer
fayne
fayre
flype
flyte
foyle
foyne
Flymo®
fry-up
flyer
foyer
fryer
fly-by
fazed
fuzee
fezes
fizzy
fuzzy
grama
guana
guava
gland
grand
guard
geare
glacé
glade
glare
glaze
△grace
grade
grame
grape
grate
grave
graze
graff
gnash
graph
ghazi
glaik
gnarl
graal
△grail
glaum
gnawn
grain
guaco
guano
graip
grasp
glair
glaur
gnarr
glans
glass
goals
goats
grabs
grass
ghast
ghaut
giant
graft
grant
Glaux
glady
glary
glazy
goary
goaty
grapy
gravy
gable
gobbi
gibel
gobbo
gebur
giber
gobar
gibus
gobos
gabby
△gecko
gucky
gadge
gadje
gadso
godso
Gadus
godet
giddy
godly
gleed
greed
gyeld
geese
glebe
glede
grebe
grece
grège
grese
greve
Guelf
gleek
Greek
gleam
glean
△green
grein
grego
grees
Greys
guess
ghest
gleet
glent
great
greet
guest
Gueux
geeky
gleby
goety
gaffe
gofer
gigue
gigot
grind
guild
glide
glike
grice
gride
grike
grime
gripe
grise
grize
△guide
guile
guise
gliff
grief
griff
going
grith
glisk
glial
grill
guiro
guimp
gains
grips
grits
gaitt
geist
glift
glint
grift
griot
grist
guilt
gaily
grimy
grisy
glitz
gajos
galea
gelid
golpe
G-clef
gulag
galah
gulch
gulph
Galam
golem
galop
gular
gilts
gules
△galut
gilet
gally
gelly
gilly
gilpy
goldy
golly
gulfy
gully
gamba
gamma
gemma
gompa
gumma
gamic
gamme
gimme
gemel
gamin
gambo
gombo
△gumbo
△games
gamut
gemot
gamay
gamey
gammy
gemmy
gimpy
gummy
ganja
△genoa
gonia
gonna
genic
gonad
genie
genre
gunge
gynae
gynie
ganch
genii
genal
genom
Genro
gonzo
genip
goner
gents
gents'
genus
gonys
Gantt
genet
gandy
genty
ginny
gundy
gungy
gunny
gynny
groma
geoid
goold
geode
globe
glode
glove
gloze
gnome
goose
grone
grope
△grove
go-off
groof
grouf
glogg
ghoul
growl
gloom
groom
groan
groin
grown
good-o
gloop
group
gloss
goods
gross
ghost
gloat
glout
groat
grout
globy
glory
goody
gooey
goofy
gooly
goopy
goosy
grody
gopak
gippo
gyppo
gaper
gapes
gapós
gappy
gippy
gipsy
guppy
gyppy
gypsy
garda
garbe
garre
gerbe
gerle
gerne
gorge
gorse
gurge
garth
gerah
girth
garni
goral
gyral
garum
giron
gyron
garbo
giros
gyrus
Gerry
girly
gormy
gorsy
gurly
gurry
gusla
gesse

Words marked △ may be spelled also with a capital letter

geste
gosse
gusle
gusli
gesso
gismo
gusto
gases
gosht
gaspy
gassy
gushy
gussy
gusty
gotta
gutta
gated
get-up
getas
gutsy
gutty
Gouda
△goura
glued
gourd
gauge
gauje
gauze
glume
gouge
grufe
grume
gruff
gruel
gluon
grump
gluer
gauss
△**gault**
gaunt
giust
grunt
g-suit
gaucy
gaudy
gaumy
gauzy
gluey
gouty
gavel
given
giver
gowan
gawcy
gawky
gawsy
gryce
gryde
gryke
grype
guyle
guyse
glyph
gayal
ghyll
goyim
geyan
gayer
grypt
guyot
gazal
gazon
gazoo
gizmo
gazer
heald
heard
hoard
heame
heare
heave
heath
heads
heaps
Hyads
heart
heast
hiant
hoast
heady
heapy
heavy
hoary
hable
heben
hobos
habit
hobby
hubby
haček
hocus
Hecat
hecht
hodja
△hydra
hedge
Hodge
hadji
hadal
hydro
hider
Hades
hadn't
hadst
hedgy
hyena
heeze
H-beam
hiems
heedy
hefte
hefty
huffy
hogan
hogen
hight
ho-hum
hi-hat
hoise
hying
Haikh
haith
heigh
haick
hoick
heist
hoist
haiku
haily
hairy
hejra
hijra
hejab
hijab
hajji
hakam
hakim
hokum
hiker
hokku
hokey
halfa
halma
halva
holla
hylic
halo'd
halse
halve
helve
hyleg
hilch
halal
hilum
halon
hallo
hello
hillo
hollo
hullo
haler
hilar
halfs
halls
halos
hilts
hilus
hulks
helot
△**helix**
hilly
holey
holly
hulky
hully
hamza
hemic
humic
humid
homme
humph
hamal
hemal
he-man
hemin
human
△hymen
homer
humor
homos
humus
hammy
hempy
homey
humpy
Hansa
henna
hance
Hanse
hence
henge
hinge
hynde
hanch
hunch
Hindi
hongi
hanap
honer
honor
hands
hunks
Hindu
handy
hanky
henny
△henry
hinny
honey
honky
hunky
△**haoma**
hoo-ha
hooka
H-bomb
hoord
hyoid
hoove
hooch
hoosh
hoo-oo
hoofs
hooey
hooky
hooly
hypha
hippo
hepar
hoper
hyper
hypos
haply
happy
hippy
hoppy
herma
hurra
hired
heroe
herse
herye
horde
horme
horse
harsh
horal
haram
harem
harim
heron
hirer
hards
harns
haros
herms
horns
Horus
hurds
horst
hurst
△**hyrax**
hardy
harpy
harry
herby
herry
horny
horsy
hurly
hurry
hertz
hasta
hosta
Hasid
hosed
haste
hosen
hyson
hoses
husks
husos
hasn't
hashy
hasty
hushy
husky
hussy
hatha
hutia
hi-tec
hithe
hythe
hatch
hitch
hotch
hutch
hotel
hoten
hater
hotly
Hausa
hauld
hound
hause
haute
△house
houff
haugh
heuch
heugh
hough
houri
haulm
hours
hault
haunt
△**hevea**
havoc
hovel
haven
hoven
haver
hiver
hover
haves
hives
Hovas
hewed
hawse
howbe
howre
howff
hewgh
howso
how-to
hewer
hawks
howdy
hexad
hayle
huzza
hazel
△**hizen**
hazer
huzzy
Itala
izard
image
inane
irade
irate
△**imari**
Iraqi
imaum
inarm
igapó
imago
inapt
imbed
imbue
inbye
imbar
incle
Incan
in-car
incur
incus
incut
itchy
Indra
Indic
iodic
indie
indue
indri
indol
indew
index
ileac
Iceni
ideal
I-beam
ileum
inerm
ileus
inept
inert
infra
infer
infix
ingle
ingan
ingot
ichor
△**iliac**
Iliad
ivied
imide
imine
icing
Irish
idiom
△ilium
Ilian
inion
lai-do
idiot

Words marked △ may be spelled also with a capital letter

5 i□i□y

Idist	jnana	jinks	**knarl**	**kylie**	**kopje**	loads
icily	**jeans**	jinns	kraal	kyloe	**kapok**	**leant**
Injun	**jebel**	**janty**	**krans**	**kalif**	**kaput**	leapt
inkle	**jiber**	△jenny	kvass	**kulak**	**karma**	least
icker	**jabot**	jonty	**kraft**	**kelim**	korma	liart
inker	**Jacob**	junky	krait	kilim	kurta	loast
illth	**jocko**	**japan**	△kraut	**kulan**	**kerne**	lyart
Islam	**jacks**	jupon	**kranz**	kylin	kerve	**leady**
igloo	**Jacky**	**japer**	**kabab**	**kilos**	kurre	leafy
idler	**jaded**	**jarta**	kabob	kolos	Kyrie	leaky
Iblis	**judge**	jirga	kebab	**kylix**	**karri**	leany
inlet	**jodel**	**jerid**	kebob	**kelly**	kirri	leary
islet	△**judas**	**jarul**	**koban**	kelpy	**Karen**	leavy
in-law	**Jeeze**	jural	**kacha**	kelty	Koran	loamy
inlay	**jeely**	**joram**	**kecks**	kiley	**Karoo**	**labda**
iambi	**Jaffa**	jorum	kicks	kilty	**karat**	labia
immit	**jiffy**	**juror**	**kedge**	**kamme**	karst	labra
immew	**jugal**	**jerks**	kidge	**kamik**	**karsy**	△libra
immix	**jugum**	**jurat**	**Kodak®**	**kembo**	karzy	lubra
△**ionic**	**jäger**	**jerky**	**kidel**	kimbo	**kasha**	**lobed**
I-and-I	jagir	△jerry	**kid-on**	**Khmer**	**kisan**	**label**
inner	**jigot**	**jaspe**	**kiddo**	**kamis**	**kesar**	libel
inorb	**jaggy**	jaspé	**kudos**	kemps	**kithe**	**labor**
in-off	**jehad**	Jesse	**kydst**	**kempt**	kythe	liber
iroko	jihad	**Jesus**	**kudzu**	**kombu**	**ketch**	Libor
irons	**Jaina**	jésus	**kedgy**	**kanga**	kutch	lobar
irony	**juice**	**jasey**	kiddy	kinda	**katti**	**labis**
ivory	**joint**	**jeton**	**kheda**	**kente**	**kotos**	lobus
impel	joist	jotun	kwela	kynde	Kotys	**lobby**
ippon	**juicy**	**jatos**	**knead**	**kenaf**	**kotow**	**Lycra®**
impis	**jokol**	**jetty**	kneed	**kaneh**	**kitty**	**laced**
impot	**joker**	jutty	knee'd	**kanji**	**kaugh**	lucid
input	**jakes**	**jeune**	**keeve**	**Kanak**	**kauri**	**lucre**
imply	**jokey**	joule	kieve	**kinin**	**knurl**	lycée
ihram	**jelab**	**joual**	**kreng**	**kendo**	**knurr**	**lichi**
issue	**jello**	**jougs**	**keech**	ken-no	**klutz**	**local**
imshi	**jalap**	**jaunt**	**kneel**	**Kings**	**kevel**	**locum**
issei	julep	joust	knell	kinos	**keyed**	**Lucan**
inset	**jelly**	△**javel**	**keeps**	**kanzu**	**kayle**	**licks**
imshy	jolly	**Javan**	**knelt**	**kandy**	**kayak**	locks
intra	jolty	**jiver**	**kofta**	kindy	**kayos**	locos
ictic	**jambe**	**jawed**	**Kufic**	kinky	**Kazak**	locus
istle	**jambo**	**jewel**	**Kafir**	**khoja**	**kazoo**	luces
ixtle	jumbo	**jawan**	kefir	krona	**liana**	**lacet**
ictal	**jumar**	**jowar**	**kagos**	króna	llama	licht
Intal®	**james**	**Jewry**	**kight**	**knowe**	**liard**	licit
intil	jumps	jowly	**kahal**	krone	**leare**	**lacey**
intro	**jambu**	**joyed**	**knife**	**kloof**	lease	△lucky
inter	**jammy**	**jazzy**	knive	**koori**	leave	**ludic**
ictus	jemmy	**Kaaba**	△koine	**kiosk**	leaze	**laded**
inula	△jimmy	kaama	**KOing**	knock	liane	**ladle**
inure	jimpy	khaya	**knish**	**knoll**	loave	ledge
inurn	jumby	koala	**kaiak**	**known**	**liang**	lodge
Inuit	jumpy	**knave**	**krill**	**knosp**	**leach**	**ledum**
inust	**junta**	**kiang**	**kails**	**kaons**	leash	**laden**
Invar®	**Jonah**	klang	**kokra**	**knout**	loach	Ladin
inwit	**jinni**	krang	**kikoi**	**Kuo-yü**	loath	loden
idyll	△**jingo**	kyang	kukri	**kooky**	**learn**	**lidos**
Iyyar	junco	**khadi**	**kokum**	**kappa**	**llano**	ludos
izzat	junto	khaki	**koker**	kippa	**leads**	**ledgy**
jhala	**Janus**	**knack**	**kalpa**	koppa	leaps	**leese**

Words marked △ may be spelled also with a capital letter

5 m□m□y

leeze
liege
lieve
leech
lie-in
leear
loess
leery
luffa
lefte
lifer
lefty
lofty
logia
logic
legge
ligge
ligne
logie
legal
lagan
ligan
logan
lager
leger
liger
Luger®
luger
Lagos
△logos
legit
light
leggy
lahar
laika
laird
loipe
Luing
lying
laigh
laith
leish
loins
lairy
△laity
lakin
liken
likin
laker
liker
lilac
lolog
laldy
lolly
lamia
lemma
Lemna
limma
lumme
lymph
Limbi

lemel
leman
lemon
limen
lumen
△**limbo**
lemur
limes
limos
limit
limax
lammy
limey
lummy
lumpy
linga
longa
linac
lined
lance
lande
longe
lunge
lanch
linch
lunch
lynch
lenti
lungi
linen
linin
lento
lingo
liner
loner
lunar
lenes
lenis
lenos
lines
links
linos
longs
lanky
liney
lingy
linny
linty
L-dopa
loofa
loord
leone
loose
Lions
loofs
looks
loons
looby
loony
loopy
lepra

lepta
lepid
lipid
lapje
lapse
lapel
lupin
leper
loper
lapis
△lupus
lippy
larva
Lerna
loric
lyric
lurid
large
Lerne
larch
lurch
△**lurgi**
loral
lorel
larum
loran
largo
lares
Larus
liras
Lords
loris
Lurex®
lardy
larky
lordy
lorry
lurgy
lurry
Lassa
lyssa
lisle
los'te
lassi
losel
lysol
losen
lysin
lasso
lesbo
laser
loser
lists
lysis
lassu
lossy
lushy
lusty
lytta
lotic
lated

lathe
latke
Lethe
lithe
litre
lythe
latch
letch
lotah
lathi
laten
Latin
litho
lotto
let-up
later
liter
luter
laths
lotos
△lotus
latex
lathy
laura
laund
lound
loupe
loure
louse
lauch
laugh
leuch
leugh
lough
lauds
louis
loury
lousy
lavra
lived
livid
levee
livre
level
levin
liven
laver
lever
liver
livor
lover
lavas
Levis®
levis
lives
lovat
lovey
lownd
lowne
lowse
lawin

lowan
△**lower**
lawks
△lewis
lawny
lowly
lexis
luxes
laxly
loyal
lay-up
layer
lay-by
lazzi
lozen
lazzo
lazar
lezzy
meal'd
mear'd
meane
meare
mease
meath
miaul
myall
miasm
means
meant
miaow
mealy
meany
meaty
moble
mebos
mobby
Mecca
micra
△mocha
mucic
mucid
macle
miche
Mâcon
macon
mucin
macho
macro
micro
mucro
macer
mucor
micas
micos
mocks
mucus
macaw
McCoy
micky
mochy
mucky

media
mudra
△**medic**
Médoc
madid
madge
medle
midge
mudge
modii
medal
modal
model
△**madam**
modem
mid-on
moder
mudir
Midas
modus
midst
'midst
Medau
madly
middy
muddy
Moera
mieve
mneme
△**mafia**
mafic
△**mufti**
miffy
mifty
magma
magic
Magog
△**mogul**
maggs
△magus
magot
might
moggy
muggy
mahua
mahwa
mahoe
Mahdi
Mehdi
mohel
mohur
mbira
Moira
maile
maire
maise
maize
moire
moiré
meith
Meiji

maiko
mains
meint
moist
muist
meiny
mujik
△**major**
mojos
mikra
makar
△maker
makos
mokos
Malta
malva
△melba
Melia
molla
mulga
malic
melic
mêlée
mille
mulse
milch
mulch
mulsh
malik
melik
molal
melon
milko
molto
malar
miler
milor
molar
milos
molas
mulct
malax
Malay
malty
milky
molly
muley
miltz
mamba
mamma
momma
mimic
mamee
mambo
mimer
memos
Mimus
Momus
mumps
mammy
mimsy

Words marked △ may be spelled also with a capital letter

5 m□n□a

mommy
mummy
mumsy
manga
mania
manna
△manta
Mensa
Munda
manic
maned
monad
mange
manse
menge
mense
minae
mince
minge
Minié
minke
monte
maneh
mensh
month
munch
mynah
manul
monal
Monel®
minim
mango
manto
mento
mondo
mungo
Munro
manor
minar
miner
△minor
moner
manes
Manis
manos
manus
mends
minas
minds
minos
minus
△monas
monos
manet
muntu
mangy
manky
manly
manty
mingy
minty

money
Muntz
moola
myoma
myoid
moose
moove
myope
M-roof
moong
mooch
Maori
mooli
mhorr
mools
myops
moody
mooly
moony
moory
moped
△**maple**
mop-up
moper
mopes
mopus
mopey
moppy
mopsy
maqui
maria
Mirza
moria
morra
murra
murva
marid
mered
marae
marge
marle
merge
merle
merse
morne
morné
△morse
murre
marah
△march
marsh
mirth
morph
myrrh
merel
meril
moral
morel
mural
maron
mirin

moron
morro
maror
marks
marls
mores
Moros
Morus
merit
morat
mpret
murex
mardy
marly
marry
mercy
merry
mirky
mirly
moray
murky
murly
murry
massa
misca'
△missa
Musca
musha
mesic
music
mused
massé
mesne
musse
musth
Masai
Musci
Musak
mesal
mesel
Mosel
mason
meson
mesto
misdo
misgo
maser
miser
muser
misos
Moses
musos
muset
musit
mashy
massy
masty
meshy
messy
missy
misty

mosey
mossy
mushy
musky
mussy
musty
matza
motza
metic
meted
moted
muted
matte
metre
mitre
motte
△**metif**
motif
match
mitch
mutch
metal
metol
motel
matin
moten
muton
matlo
matzo
me-too
△metro
△métro
motto
mater
meter
miter
motor
maths
meths
Metis
△métis
moths
△motus
motet
matey
Mitty
motey
mothy
motty
maund
mould
mound
mauve
meuse
mouse
mvule
mouch
mouth
Mouli®
mourn
mouls

moult
△mount
moust
mousy
moved
movie
maven
mavin
mover
mavis
mowra
mowed
mower
mawky
mixed
moxie
△**maxim**
mixen
mix-in
mix-up
mixer
maybe
moyle
Mayan
△**mayor**
mayst
meynt
mezze
Muzak®
mizen
mezzo
mazer
mazut
muzzy
ngana
nyala
neafe
nyaff
neath
'neath
Naafi
ngaio
nabla
nubia
nabob
noble
nebek
nebel
Nobel
nobby
nobly
nubby
nucha
nicad
nache
nacre
niche
△**nicol**
Nicam
nacho
nudge

nudie
nidal
nodal
nadir
nidor
nidus
nodus
△**neddy**
noddy
neemb
neeld
naeve
neele
neese
neeze
niece
nieve
naevi
needs
needy
niffy
nifty
nugae
△**negro**
nagor
niger
△**negus**
night
naggy
△**nahal**
nihil
nohow
naira
naiad
naive
naïve
neive
noise
nying
neigh
Naias
noils
neist
noint
'noint
noisy
naked
naker
nikau
nalla
nulla
nylon
nelis
Nilot
nelly
nomic
named
nomad
nymph
nimbi
nomoi

no-man
nomen
numen
namer
names
nomos
nempt
Nimby
nanna
△ninja
△**nance**
nonce
ninth
Nandi
ninon
△**nones**
no-nos
no-no's
nonet
nandu
△**nancy**
nanny
ninny
nonny
Nantz
Niobe
no-one
noose
Ngoni
nooky
nappa
nappe
nopal
napoo
neper
Nupes
nepit
nappy
△nippy
nerka
noria
△norma
Norna
narre
nerve
Norse
nurse
△**north**
narco
naras
narcs
nares
narky
nerdy
nervy
nirly
nyssa
nosed
nisse
Neski
nisei

Words marked △ may be spelled also with a capital letter

5 p□i□s

Nasik
nasal
Nisan
noser
nisus
nasty
nosey
nitid
noted
nitre
natch
notch
natal
notal
notum
niton
niter
noter
nates
Notus
natty
netty
nitry
nitty
nutty
nould
n'ould
neume
noule
Nguni
nouns
naunt
nouny
novae
naval
navel
nevel
nival
novel
novum
never
nevus
novas
navew
navvy
nawab
nowed
ngwee
newel
△nowel
no-win
newly
newsy
noway
nixie
noxal
nexus
nixes
n-type
Nayar
noyes
noyau
△**nizam**
nazir
omasa
orate
Osage
ovate
obang
orang
orach
okapi
okays
orant
oracy
otary
ovary
orbed
ombre
ombré
ombus
ombús
oobit
orbit
oubit
ox-bot
ox-bow
owche
occam
orcin
Oscan
occur
oncer
Oscar
oncus
oucht
oidia
oldie
olden
older
order
on-dit
oddly
omega
opera
opéra
oleic
ogee'd
oread
obese
opepe
ox-eye
obeah
obeli
ozeki
odeum
oleum
ocean
odeon
olein
one-er
oleos
olent
overt
onely
offal
Oxfam
offer
orgia
orgic
orgue
oggin
organ
ought
oshac
ochre
ogham
ocher
other
ochry
Oliva
Oriya
Ouija®
ouija
ogive
ojime
olive
opine
ovine
oxide
oxime
OD'ing
O-ring
owing
oribi
oriel
odism
odium
opium
onion
Orion
osier
olios
obiit
odist
ovist
on-job
objet
oakum
oaken
oaker
△ocker
onkus
oiled
oflag
omlah
Orlon®
orlop
oxlip
ogler
oiler
owler
owlet
ollav
ogmic
ohmic
osmic
oomph
ormer
ounce
owner
ornis
oundy
ovoid
ohone
ozone
on-off
oboli
ovoli
ovolo
odour
ology
ouphe
orpin
oppos
ocrea
oared
oorie
ourie
owrie
omrah
orris
o'erby
ossia
Ossie
ousel
owsen
oases
△oasis
odsos
onset
ostia
Optic®
optic
octad
outed
outré
octal
oaten
often
ortho
outdo
outgo
oater
opter
ottar
otter
outer
oxter
oaths
octet
outby
ovule
oculi
orval
oaves
Oryza
odyle
ouzel
ouzos
playa
plaza
poaka
prana
plaid
peace
peare
pease
peaze
phage
phare
phase
△place
plage
plane
'plane
plate
poake
prase
prate
phang
prang
peach
plash
poach
plack
plank
prank
pearl
plasm
praam
psalm
plain
prawn
piano
peart
plait
plant
plast
pratt
prahu
peaky
peaty
peavy
platy
praty
pzazz
pubic
pubes
pubis
△**pacha**
Picea
picra
pucka
paced
pecke
picul
pecan
pacer
paces
pacos
Picus
Pecht
picot
pacey
piccy
picky
pocky
padma
podia
pudic
padle
padre
podge
pudge
pi-dog
pedal
podal
pedro
pudor
podex
△**paddy**
poddy
podgy
puddy
pudgy
pudsy
pietà
presa
piel'd
piend
plead
pseud
peece
peepe
peeve
phene
phese
piece
pièce
prese
preve
preif
plesh
△**paean**
paeon
pheon
pleon
preen
piezo
pheer
plebs
△press
P-Celt
piert
P-Kelt
pleat
prent
prest
peeoy
peery
piety
poesy
predy
premy
prexy
puffy
pagod
pagle
pogge
pagri
pugil
pygal
pagan
pager
pages
Peght
pight
peggy
piggy
pigmy
puggy
pygmy
pshaw
paisa
plica
prima
plied
poind
pried
paire
paise
peise
peize
poise
price
pride
prime
prise
prize
prief
pling
plink
prick
prink
phial
prial
prill
prism
prion
psion
primo
primp
plier
prier
prior
paiks

Words marked △ may be spelled also with a capital letter

5 p□i□t

pains
pairs
plies
pries
paint
point
print
poilu
pricy
primy
△privy
pi-jaw
pakka
pukka
piked
poked
pekoe
pikul
pokal
pekan
Pekin
piker
poker
puker
pokes
pokey
palea
palla
pelma
pelta
pilea
polka
pulka
pulse
pilch
palki
palpi
pilei
pilum
pylon
polio
pulmo
polyp
piler
polar
poler
puler
palas
piles
pills
pilus
poles
polls
polos
polys
palet
pilot
pilau
pilaw
pilow
△**phlox**

Pulex
palay
pally
palmy
palsy
poley
△polly
pulpy
pampa
pombe
pumie
Pomak
pumas
pommy
panda
panga
penna
△pinna
pinta
ponga
punga
punka
panic
Punic
paned
pance
panne
pence
penie
penne
ponce
punce
pinch
△punch
panel
penal
panim
piñon
panto
pingo
pinko
pinto
pongo
punto
pin-up
pants
penes
penis
△**pinot**
panax
pandy
pansy
panty
penny
piney
pinky
pinny
poncy
poney
pongy
ponty

punty
△**phoca**
pooja
pooka
psora
proud
pyoid
phone
'phone
pioye
poove
probe
proke
prole
prone
prore
prose
prove
proof
plong
prong
pooch
paoli
poori
plonk
plook
plouk
pronk
proll
proul
prowl
pro-am
proem
proin
proyn
paolo
photo
promo
proso
Proto®
△proto
Provo
pions
pious
pools
Proms
props
psoas
ploat
poort
peony
phony
piony
poofy
poovy
prosy
proxy
poppa
piped
pupae
△**papal**

pipal
pipul
pupal
pupil
pop-up
paper
△piper
pepos
pipes
pupas
pipit
papaw
pappy
peppy
pippy
poppy
popsy
puppy
pique
piqué
Parca
parka
Parma
Perca
porta
parge
parle
parse
perce
perse
perve
porge
Porte
puree
purée
purge
△purse
parch
perch
porch
pardi
parki
Parsi
parti
perai
pirai
parol
peril
poral
pyral
purim
purin
pareo
Parvo
porno
parer
porer
Paris
parts
Pyrus
perst

pareu
perdu
Purex
Pyrex®
pardy
parky
parly
parry
party
perdy
perky
perry
porgy
porky
porty
purpy
pursy
purty
△**pasha**
pasta
passé
paste
piste
posse
pusle
Pasch
Pesah
pashm
paseo
pesto
poser
pesos
posit
paspy
pasty
pesky
pisky
posey
pushy
pussy
Patna
△pitta
pated
putid
patte
patté
petre
patch
pitch
potch
△**petri**
putti
petal
paten
patin
piton
potin
put-in
put-on
patio
potoo

potto
putto
put-up
pater
petar
peter
paths
petit
patly
patsy
patty
△petty
pithy
potty
putty
plumb
pound
pause
plume
pouke
poule
poupe
Pruce
prude
prune
pluff
plush
pouch
pluck
plunk
Pluto
plump
poulp
poult
poupt
prunt
plumy
pouty
paved
pavid
pavan
paven
pavin
paver
pavis
pivot
pownd
powre
powan
powin
power
pewit
pawaw
pawky
powny
pixie
pixel
pyxis
phyla
payed
paysd

payee
peyse
phyle
poyse
pryse
p-type
psych
psyop
payer
pryer
poynt
pizza
puzel
pozzy
quayd
quake
quale
quare
quaff
quash
quasi
quack
quark
quail
qualm
quair
quant
quart
quaky
qibla
quena
queme
queue
quell
quean
△queen
quern
queyn
queer
Q-Celt
Q-Kelt
quest
query
Q-ship
quina
quine
quire
quite
quiff
quich
qui-hi
quick
quirk
quill
quipo
quids
quits
quiet
quilt
quint
quirt

Words marked △ may be spelled also with a capital letter

5 s□a□e

quist
quipu
Qajar
qanat
quota
quoad
quote
quoif
quoth
quonk
quoll
quoin
Quorn®
Q-boat
Q-sort
quoit
Qoran
Quran
Qur'an
quyte
reata
riata
ruana
reame
reate
reave
roate
reach
roach
realm
rearm
realo
reaks
reams
rears
roads
react
reast
riant
roast
ready
reamy
roary
Rubia
rabic
rebec
rabid
rebid
△rebbe
roble
ruble
△rabbi
△rubai
rebel
robin
rubin
re-bar
rebus
Ribes
robes
Rubus

rabat
rebut
robot
rybat
ribby
recta
rache
recce
ruche
recti
recal
racon
ricin
recco
recto
recap
racer
recur
ricer
races
rocks
récit
richt
reccy
ricey
rocky
redia
redid
radge
ridge
rudie
radii
radon
redan
radio
rodeo
redip
radar
rider
rudas
radix
redox
reddy
redly
ridgy
ruddy
reede
reeve
rieve
reech
△rheum
reels
reest
reedy
reeky
rifle
rifte
ruffe
refel
reffo
refer

refit
rifty
regma
raged
rigid
ragde
ragee
régie
rogue
regal
Rigel
Rigil
rigol
reggo
rager
regar
regur
rigor
△roger
△right
raggy
roguy
△rugby
ruggy
rehab
raita
raird
reird
raile
raine
raise
reive
rhime
△rhine
ruing
Reich
reign
rhino
rails
rains
reins
ruins
reist
roist
rainy
reify
roily
rejig
re-jig
rajah
rejón
rakee
raker
roker
relic
relie
rille
rolag
Ralph
ruler
Rolls

△rules
relet
relax
rally
relay
△riley
rumba
Romic
rimed
ramee
ramie
rimae
rymme
ramal
romal
rumal
ramen
ramin
reman
remen
△roman
Ruman
rumen
Romeo
rumbo
rimer
rumor
ramus
romas
remit
remex
remix
Rumex
rammy
rumly
rummy
rumpy
renga
runic
runed
rance
ranee
range
ranke
renne
rente
rinse
ronde
ronne
ronte
renig
ranch
runch
renal
renin
run-in
run-on
rondo
Roneo®
roneo
run-up

rands
ranks
renew
randy
rangy
renay
reney
rindy
runny
runty
Rioja
roosa
rhomb
rhone
roose
roofs
rooms
roots
roost
rhody
roofy
rooky
roomy
roopy
rooty
repla
rupia
rapid
roped
raphe
raphé
rupee
repel
ripen
repro
raper
riper
roper
ryper
repos
ropes
repot
repay
reply
ropey
roque
roric
rorid
rorie
roral
rural
rerun
ro-ros
rorty
△rasta
rusma
rased
rosed
rasae
rasse
rishi

resin
risen
rosin
riser
risus
△roses
resat
reset
resit
roset
rosit
raspy
resay
resty
risky
rushy
rusty
rated
rathe
retie
ratch
retch
rotch
ratel
rotal
ratan
rutin
ratio
ratoo
△retro
rater
rotor
rates
rites
rotis
rotls
ratty
retry
ritzy
rutty
rhumb
round
reuse
rouge
roule
rouse
route
rough
routh
roust
roupy
rived
revie
revue
ravel
revel
rival
rivel
raven
ravin
riven

raver
river
rover
rivos
revet
rivet
rownd
rowme
rewth
rowth
rowel
rowan
rowen
rower
rawly
rowdy
rhyta
rayed
rayle
rayne
rhyme
rhyne
royne
rayah
riyal
royal
rayon
royst
razed
razee
razoo
razor
rozet
rozit
scala
scapa
shama
shaya
scald
scand
scaud
shand
shard
shar'd
skald
slaid
spald
spard
spayd
staid
stal'd
stand
sward
Saame
△scale
scape
'scape
scare
seame
seare
sease

5 s□a□f

seaze
shade
shake
shale
shame
shape
share
shave
skate
slade
slake
slane
slate
slave
snake
snare
soare
Soave
space
spade
spake
spale
spane
spare
spate
stade
stage
stake
stale
stane
stare
state
stave
suave
swage
swale
sware
scaff
scarf
staff
swarf
Shang
slang
spang
staig
stang
swang
scath
shash
slash
smash
snash
snath
staph
stash
swash
swath
scapi
spahi
△swami
Swazi

shack
shank
shark
skank
slack
smack
smaik
snack
snark
spank
spark
stack
stalk
stank
stark
swack
swank
scail
scall
shall
shawl
skail
small
snail
snarl
spall
spaul
spawl
stall
swayl
shalm
shawm
smalm
smarm
spasm
swarm
sdayn
sharn
slain
spain
spawn
stain
starn
swain
shako
spado
scalp
scamp
scarp
scaup
sharp
stamp
swamp
scaur
spaer
stair
starr
scads
shaps
snaps
stars

stays
swats
scant
scart
scatt
shaft
shakt
shalt
sha'n't
shan't
skart
skatt
slant
smalt
smart
spalt
spart
start
swapt
swart
snafu
scaly
scary
seamy
shady
shaky
shaly
slaty
snaky
snary
soapy
spacy
stagy
swaly
sabra
sable
Sabme
sabre
sybbe
syboe
subah
Sabmi
Sabal
△sibyl
△sybil
sebum
sabin
saber
sober
suber
sabot
Sebat
sybow
subby
sacra
socle
sucre
sycee
shchi
succi
Sicel

Sican
secco
sicko
socko
socks
sucks
sadza
sidha
Sudra
sodic
sided
sadhe
sedge
sidle
sedum
Sodom
sedan
Seder
sider
sudor
sedes
sides
sadhu
sadly
sedgy
soddy
sudsy
scena
Sheba
Shema
sheva
stela
scend
'scend
seeld
shend
sherd
sield
snead
speed
speld
spend
stead
stedd
steed
stend
scene
shere
siege
sieve
skene
stede
stele
steme
stere
suede
suède
△swede
sheaf
shelf
skelf

swerf
skegg
sieth
sheik
sleek
smeek
sneak
sneck
speak
speck
spelk
steak
steek
sheal
sheel
shell
she'll
△sheol
△she'ol
skell
smell
snell
speal
speel
spell
steal
steel
steil
stell
sweal
sweel
swell
skelm
sperm
steam
steem
sdein
sheen
shewn
skean
skein
spean
stean
steen
stein
stern
sheep
skelp
sleep
sneap
steep
sweep
shear
sheer
skear
skeer
smear
sneer
spear
speer
speir

stear
steer
swear
sweer
sweir
skeos
specs
speos
steps
stews
sceat
scent
sheet
shent
sient
skeet
sleet
slept
smelt
speat
spelt
spent
stent
stept
sweat
sweet
swelt
swept
seedy
seely
seepy
spewy
stewy
suety
softa
Sufic
sofar
softs
Sufis
softy
sigla
sigma
segue
segol
sigil
sagum
segno
segar
Seger
soger
sugar
segos
signs
sight
saggy
soggy
schwa
△**sahib**
schmo
saiga
Saiva

Shiva
spica
spina
stipa
stilb
shied
skied
spied
stied
saice
saine
seine
seise
seize
shine
shire
shite
shive
skite
skive
slice
slide
'slife
slime
slipe
slive
smile
smite
snide
snipe
spice
spide
spike
spile
spine
spire
spite
stile
stime
stipe
stire
stive
suite
swine
swipe
swire
swive
skiff
sniff
spiff
stiff
sling
sting
suing
△swing
saith
Shiah
slish
smith
stich
swish

Words marked △ may be spelled also with a capital letter

swith
sci-fi
saick
shirk
skink
slick
slink
smirk
snick
spick
spink
stick
stink
stirk
swink
shiel
shill
skill
skirl
spial
spiel
spill
still
swill
swirl
seism
scion
skimp
stirp
shier
shirr
skier
skirr
slier
smirr
shies
shits
skids
skies
skios
slips
snips
spies
sties
suits
Swiss
swits
△**saint**
saist
shift
shirt
skint
skirt
slipt
snift
snirt
spilt
spirt
stilt
stint
suint

swift
seity
shily
shiny
skiey
skivy
slily
slimy
snipy
soily
spicy
spiky
spiny
spiry
stimy
stivy
spitz
sujee
sajou
sakia
Sakta
sokah
Sakai
Sakti
Sikel
soken
saker
syker
sekos
salpa
salsa
sella
selva
silva
sol-fa
sulfa
sylva
△**salic**
salad
silo'd
solid
salle
salse
salue
salve
selle
solde
solve
selah
solah
sylph
salmi
soldi
sulci
salal
sclim
sklim
solum
△**salon**
silen
solan

Solon
Salmo
salto
salvo
soldo
salep
salop
shlep
siler
solar
soler
sales
salts
selfs
sells
silos
soles
solos
solus
sulks
salet
splat
split
Sclav
salix
silex
sally
salty
silky
silly
silty
splay
sulky
sully
samba
summa
sumac
semée
semie
shmoe
sumph
sampi
shmek
samel
simul
saman
samen
semen
soman
sambo
simar
symar
semis
somas
sumos
Samit
samfu
samey
Sammy
sansa
Santa

senna
sensa
senza
Sunna
Sinic
sonic
△**synod**
sense
since
singe
sonce
sonde
sonne
sonse
synch
synth
Sindi
Sunni
sanko
sunup
Señor
△sonar
sands
sinus
sinew
△**sandy**
senvy
sinky
sonny
sonsy
sunny
scopa
shola
Shona
stoma
△**stoic**
scold
shoed
sloid
sloyd
snood
stond
stood
sword
scone
scope
score
shone
shope
shore
shote
shove
slope
slove
△smoke
smore
smote
snoke
snore
soole
soote

△spode
spoke
spore
stoae
stoke
stole
stone
stope
store
stove
swone
swore
scoff
skoff
spoof
scoog
scoug
stong
slosh
sloth
sooth
sposh
shogi
shoji
stoai
Suomi
shock
shook
smock
snoek
snook
snowk
spook
stock
stonk
stook
stork
scowl
shoal
shool
skoal
snool
spoil
spool
stool
sloom
spoom
storm
scorn
shoon
shorn
shown
sloan
spoon
stoln
stonn
stoun
stown
swoln
swoon
sworn

swoun
slo-mo
smoko
scoop
scoup
scowp
sloop
snoop
stoep
stomp
stoop
stoup
swoop
scour
shoer
smoor
spoor
stoor
stour
Scops
Scots
shoes
slops
spots
stoas
stoss
scoot
△scout
'sfoot
shoat
shoot
short
shott
shout
sloot
smolt
smoot
smout
smowt
snoot
snort
snout
spoot
sport
spout
stoat
stoit
stout
swopt
shoyu
Sioux
showy
slopy
smoky
snowy
sooty
stogy
stony
story
sepia
septa

sopra
sapid
sepad
Sophi
sepal
sapan
sapor
sopor
super
sappy
sepoy
Sophy
soppy
serra
sorda
sorra
stria
surra
Surya
scrab
scrub
shrub
serac
sérac
△seric
siroc
sared
sarod
scrod
shred
sprad
spred
sprod
strad
saree
sarge
scrae
scree
serge
serre
serve
soree
spree
sprue
strae
surge
serif
scrag
scrog
shrug
sprag
sprig
sprog
sprug
strig
sirih
surah
△syrah
serai
skrik
seral

Words marked △ may be spelled also with a capital letter

5 s□r□m

soral
sorel
sural
Sarum
scram
scrim
scrum
serum
strum
Saran®
sarin
scran
serin
seron
△siren
skran
syren
sargo
servo
sorbo
sordo
sorgo
scrap
scrip
sirup
strap
strep
strip
strop
syrup
saros
sarus
serfs
Serps
sorts
sorus
scrat
sprat
sprit
strut
surat
scraw
screw
scrow
serow
shrew
shrow
sprew
straw
strew
strow
sorex
sarky
scray
serry
sorry
spray
stray
stroy
surfy
surgy
surly
sessa
sasse
sushi
sisal
sasin
sysop
sassy
sesey
sissy
Sitka
Sitta
sutra
sated
setae
sithe
sythe
shtum
Satan
satin
seton
sit-in
set-to
Sotho
set-up
shtup
satyr
sitar
sutor
situs
satay
sauba
sauna
scuba
scuta
shura
sputa
stupa
slubb
slurb
squab
squib
slued
sound
squad
squid
sauce
sauté
scuse
’scuse
scute
shule
shute
sluse
souce
souse
spule
spume
stupe
sture
scuff
scurf
snuff
stuff
slung
squeg
stung
swung
sauch
saugh
shush
slush
snush
sough
△south
scudi
sculk
shuck
skulk
skunk
slunk
snuck
spunk
stuck
stunk
scull
skull
stull
stulm
stumm
shuln
spurn
scudo
sculp
slump
slurp
stump
scuds
shuls
spurs
stubs
sault
saunt
scuft
shunt
sluit
souct
spurt
squat
squit
stunt
sturt
squaw
saucy
saury
soupy
spumy
study
scuzz
squiz
saved
savin
seven
Sivan
saver
savor
sever
siver
syver
savey
△savoy
savvy
sawed
sewed
sowed
sownd
sowce
sowle
sowne
sowse
sowff
sawah
sowth
sewel
sewen
sewin
sawer
sewer
sowar
sower
Sawny
sexed
sixte
sixth
Saxon
sexer
sixer
sixes
sixty
sayid
styed
sayne
skyre
skyte
slype
soyle
spyre
style
styme
styre
styte
styli
spyal
sayon
seyen
say-so
stylo
swy-up
sayer
shyer
skyer
slyer
styes
sayst
shyly
skyey
slyly
Soyuz
sized
sizel
sizar
sizer
thana
tiara
tra-la
teaed
teade
tease
teaze
thane
toaze
trace
trade
trape
trave
twang
teach
trash
tuath
thagi
tragi
thack
thank
track
traik
twank
trail
T-rail
trawl
thaim
train
twain
tramp
teals
tears
traps
trass
T-cart
toast
tract
trait
trant
tratt
tuart
teary
thawy
toady
tabla
tibia
tabid
tubed
table
tubae
tubal
△**tabun**
taboo
tabor
tubar
△tuber
tabes
tabus
tubas
tubes
Tebet
Tibet
Tobit
tabby
tubby
ticca
tache
Tyche
tical
△**tacan**
tacho
tacos
ticks
Ticos
tocos
tacet
tacit
tacky
techy
tichy
ticky
todde
tidal
Tudor
to-dos
△**teddy**
tiddy
today
toddy
theca
thema
theta
trefa
trema
theic
teend
they’d
tread
trend
tweed
teene
theme
there
these
thete
’twere
thelf
treif
teeth
theek
treck
tweak
T-cell
tweel
therm
thegn
tie-in
toe-in
treen
’tween
tie-up
twerp
their
tweer
teens
thews
tress
trews
theft
treat
trest
tweet
theow
teeny
thewy
tafia
tuffe
△**taffy**
toffy
tufty
tagma
tugra
toga’d
toged
togue
tigon
tiger
tight
taggy
te-hee
tohos
taiga
taira
teind
third
△triad
tried
trild
thine
toile
toise
tribe
trice
tride
trike
trine
tripe
trite
twice
twine
twire
twite
thief

Words marked △ may be spelled also with a capital letter

triff
thing
toing
tying
taish
thigh
thick
thilk
think
trick
twink
thill
thiol
thirl
△trial
trill
twill
'twill
twirl
tuism
Teian
Taino
twirp
trier
trior
twier
tails
toils
Trias
tries
trios
Twins
taint
'taint
trist
twilt
twist
'twixt
tripy
twiny
Tajik
tikka
takhi
Tokaj
taken
takin
token
taker
tokos
△**tokay**
talea
talma
△talpa
telia
Tilia
telic
tell'd
tiled
telae
tilde
tulle

tilth
talak
taluk
talon
tulip
talaq
talar
taler
tiler
tyler
tales
talks
talus
telos
tiles
telex
talcy
talky
tally
telly
tilly
temed
timed
timid
tumid
Tempe
temse
tempi
tamal
Tamil
tamin
△timon
toman
tempo
timbó
tamer
timer
tumor
tamis
△times
timps
tempt
'tempt
tammy
△tommy
tummy
tumpy
tanga
△tanka
tanna
tenia
△tinea
tonga
tonic
tunic
tined
toned
tuned
tyned
tenné
tense

tenue
tinge
tonne
tynde
tench
tenth
tangi
tanti
tondi
tonal
tenon
tango
tanto
tenno
tondo
ton-up
tenor
toner
tuner
tongs
tonus
Tonys
tunas
tenet
tinct
Tunku
tangy
tanky
tansy
tenny
tenty
tinny
tinty
toney
tunny
trona
Troic
tronc
thou'd
troad
T-bone
thole
those
trode
troke
trone
trope
thong
Thoth
tooth
troth
tholi
trock
thowl
troll
thorn
thorp
tromp
troop
two-up
twoer

thous
tools
toots
trots
thoft
troat
trout
tappa
Typha
topic
typic
tepid
tepee
topee
tophi
topoi
topek
tupek
tupik
tepal
typal
tapen
tap-in
typto
tip-up
top-up
taper
tapir
toper
tapas
tapis
topos
typos
tapet
tippy
tipsy
Topsy
topaz
toque
tuque
targa
terga
terra
throb
taroc
toric
thrid
tired
tyred
targe
tarre
terce
terfe
terne
terse
thrae
three
throe
torse
torte
turme

Torah
torch
tarsi
terai
torii
torsi
Turki
tarok
△terek
torsk
thrum
toran
tyran
torso
turbo
Turco
taros
teras
teres
terms
terts
△tiros
torus
turfs
turps
tyros
tarot
thraw
threw
throw
tardy
tarry
tarty
terry
turfy
tesla
testa
tasse
taste
teste
Tisri
tasar
Taser®
taser
'tisn't
tasty
testy
toshy
tossy
tushy
tusky
tetra
tatie
tithe
title
titre
tutee
tythe
△**titch**
Tutsi
tutti

total
totem
△**tatin**
△titan
titup
Tatar
tater
titer
tutor
Tatts
tatou
tatty
titty
totty
tutty
thuja
thuya
tsuba
Tsuga
thumb
tauld
taube
taupe
Thule
touse
touze
truce
teuch
teugh
touch
tough
truth
truck
trunk
trull
thump
trump
truss
taunt
trust
tousy
touzy
truly
tavah
taver
Tevet
tawie
tawse
towse
towze
tewel
towel
tawer
tower
tewit
tawny
towny
towsy
towzy
toxic
taxed

△**taxol**
Texel
taxon
Texan
toxin
taxer
taxor
taxes
taxis
Taxus
△texas
texts
tayra
thyme
thymi
try-on
toyer
tryer
twyer
tryst
thymy
tazza
tazze
tozie
tizzy
ukase
urate
usage
urali
urari
unarm
Urals
unapt
umbra
unbed
unbid
umbre
upbye
unbag
Uzbeg
Uzbek
umbel
urban
umber
unbar
umbos
up-bow
unbox
△**uncle**
uncap
ulcer
uncos
uncus
uncut
undid
undee
undée
undue
urdee
urdée
undug

5 u□d□m

undam
udder
under
ulema
urena
ureic
U-bend
upend
up-end
uneth
uteri
ureal
uveal
uredo
urent
usen't
unfed
unfit
unfix
ugged
ungod
ungag
ungum
urger
unget
ungot
uh-huh
unhip
usher
unhat
unite
urine
urite
utile
umiak
urial
△**union**
Uniat
unify
unity
upjet
unked
unkid
unket
unled
unlid
upled
uhlan
unlet
unlit
unlaw
unlay
uplay
ulmin
unman
urman
Ulmus
unmet
unmew
usnea
urned

ulnae
urnal
ulnar
U-boat
U-bolt
upped
unpeg
unpen
unpin
upper
umpty
unpay
Ugric
unred
unrid
unrig
uprun
unrip
U-trap
unsod
upsee
urson
Ursus
unset
upset
unsew
unsex
unsay
upsey
ultra
untie
uptie
uptak
until
untin
utter
untax
uvula
usure
U-tube
usual
U-turn
usurp
uhuru
urubu
usury
unwed
unwon
unwet
unwit
ulyie
ulzie
unzip
vraic
viand
veale
Vlach
vealy
vibes
vibex
vacua

vocab
vocal
△**vicar**
voces
△**vichy**
Vedda
vodka
Vedic
video
Vedas
veena
V-neck
veery
viewy
vifda
vigia
vague
vegie
vogie
vogue
vagal
vigil
△**vegan**
vigor
vagus
vuggy
△**vehme**
voilà
vairé
voice
voile
vying
V-sign
vails
vairy
veily
veiny
vakil
villa
volta
volva
vulva
valid
valse
value
valve
vilde
volae
volte
volve
villi
velum
vulgo
valor
velar
volar
vales
valet
veldt
volet
vomer

vomit
vinca
vaned
venae
venge
venue
venal
vinal
vinyl
venom
venin
viner
△**venus**
vinos
vinew
veney
viola
viold
vroom
vrouw
vapid
vapor
viper
varna
virga
varec
virid
varve
verge
verse
verve
virge
viral
varan
verso
vireo
Virgo
varus
vires
virus
verst
vertu
virtu
varix
vardy
verry
vespa
vesta
vista
visie
visne
vasal
vison
visto
visor
visit
vasty
vitta
vatic
vetch
vital

voter
vitas
Vitis
vitex
vaute
vouge
vouch
vault
vaunt
voulu
vivda
vivid
viver
vives
vivat
vowed
vawte
vowel
vower
vexed
vixen
vexer
vozhd
vezir
vizir
vizor
weamb
△**weald**
weave
△whale
whare
wrate
wharf
whang
wrath
whack
wrack
wrawl
whaup
whaur
wraps
wrapt
wrast
weary
weber
webby
△**wicca**
wacke
wacko
wecht
wacky
wicky
wedge
wodge
width
widen
Wodan
Woden
wader
△**widow**
waddy

wedgy
widdy
wield
weeke
weete
where
whelk
wreak
wreck
wheal
wheel
whelm
wheen
whelp
whear
weeds
weeks
wheat
wheft
wrest
waefu'
weedy
weeny
weepy
wefte
wifie
woful
wafer
△**wagon**
wigan
wager
wages
wight
wahoo
weird
waide
waite
waive
weise
weize
while
whine
△white
write
whiff
wring
weigh
which
whish
whilk
whisk
wrick
whirl
whirr
wrier
waifs
waits
whiss
waift
waist
whift

whipt
whist
wrist
whiny
△whity
whizz
waked
waken
woken
waker
wakes
walla
wilga
wilja
welke
wolve
Wolof
△**welch**
△welsh
wilco
waler
wales
walks
walls
wilds
wiles
wills
welkt
△**wally**
walty
welly
willy
wolly
waltz
wamed
△**woman**
women
wamus
Wimpy®
wimpy
womby
wanna
winna
wonga
waned
wanle
wanze
wince
winge
winze
wench
winch
wongi
wants
winds
wings
winks
winos
waney
wanky
wanly

wanty
wenny
windy
winey
wingy
wonky
wooed
woold
whole
whore
whose
who've
wroke
wrote
wrong
woosh
wroth
who'll
whorl
whoso
whoop
wooer
woods
whoot
whort
wroot
woody
woofy
woozy
wootz
wiper
wired
△world
warre
worse
wersh
worth
wirer
wares
wires
words
works
worms
warst
worst
wurst
warby
warty
wordy
wormy
worry
waste
△**wushu**
washy
waspy
wispy
withe
watch
witch
witan
Wotan
watap
water
wetly
withy
witty
would
wound
wauff
wrung
waugh
waulk
waved
woven
waver
waves
wives
wavey
wowee
waxed
waxen
woxen
waxer
wryer
wryly
wizen
wazir
xoana
X-rays
xebec
xylic
xylol
xylyl
xylem
xenia
xenon
Xhosa
X-body
xeric
Xeres
Xyris
Xerox®
xysti
yeard
ysame
yealm
yearn
years
yeast
yrapt
ya-boo
yobbo
yabby
yacca
yucca
yacht
yucky
yodle
yodel
yield
yfere
yrent
yogic
yogin
yager
Yahve
Yahwe
△**yahoo**
yrivd
ylike
yoick
yojan
yakka
yokel
yokul
yikes
Yakut
yakow
yukky
yclad
ycled
yulan
yolky
yamen
yummy
yenta
yince
yrneh
yonks
ycond
ybore
Y-moth
ymolt
ytost
yapok
Yupik
yapon
yupon
yappy
yippy
yuppy
yarfa
yarta
yerba
ydrad
ydred
yarto
Yorks
yeses
yesty
yauld
you're
you've
young
youth
you'll
yourn
yours
yourt
yeven
yowie
yewen
yawey
yawny
Yezdi
zabra
zebra
zebub
zebec
zibet
zocco
Z-bend
zoeae
zoeal
zoeas
zygal
zigan
zygon
Zohar
zaire
zoism
zoist
zakat
zilch
zamia
zymic
zimbi
△zombi
zaman
zambo
zanja
zonda
zineb
Zenic
zoned
△**zante**
zanze
zinke
zonae
zonal
zinco
Zener
Zeno's
zincy
zingy
zinky
zooea
zooid
zhomo
zooks
zoons
zloty
zip-in
zip-on
zupan
zippo
zoppo
zappy
zippy
zerda
zoril
zorro
zeros
zesty
△**zowie**
zizel

Words marked △ may be spelled also with a capital letter

6 a□a□a

Agadah
agapae
anabas
ananas
atabal
ataman
avatar
anarch
awatch
abased
abated
acater
acates
agazed
alated
anadem
Aranea
atabeg
atabek
awaked
awaken
awayes
azalea
△apache
apathy
abatis
acacia
acarid
adagio
Adamic
Agadic
agamic
agamid
agaric
alalia
△arabic
arabin
arabis
aralia
ataxia
ataxic
Azania
ananke
afawld
anally
arable
availe
avails
alarms
avaunt
abator
acajou
amadou
amatol
△amazon
analog
araise
arayse
abattu
acanth

anatta
anatto
avanti
abacus
acarus
alarum
asarum
abbacy
albedo
aubade
ambler
albugo
ambage
albeit
albums
Albany
albino
Albion
albert
ambery
anbury
auburn
abbess
ambush
albata
albite
arbute
arbour
abbeys
arctan
ascian
aucuba
accede
arcade
Arcady
accrew
arched
archer
△arches
arcked
accoil
Alcaic
Archie
archil
arcsin
△arctic
ancile
archly
ancome
accend
accent
Ancona
arcana
arcane
arcing
ascend
ascent
accloy
anchor
arccos

archon
accept
auceps
accord
ancora
Access®
access
accost
accuse
accite
accrue
aecium
alcove
am-dram
Andean
abdabs
abduce
abduct
addict
adduce
adduct
addeem
addled
Andrew
aldrin
aedile
audile
addend
add-ons
aidant
aiding
Aldine
Andine
ardent
addios
addoom
audios
aldern
aldose
aidful
ardour
acetal
akedah
alegar
apeman
axeman
agency
alerce
amerce
aperçu
areach
agenda
amende
amends
aneses
apexes
abeigh
alegge
avenge
aweigh

abelia
acedia
acetic
alevin
alexia
alexic
alexin
amebic
amelia
anemia
anemic
anesis
anetic
avenir
age-old
anerly
areola
areole
ageing
apedom
awetos
afeard
aweary
ageism
ageist
apepsy
a-per-se
averse
Alecto
amenta
aneath
aseity
Avesta
△avenue
acetyl
aye-aye
affear
affrap
affray
affect
affyde
affeer
affied
affret
affair
aefald
affine
affirm
afford
afflux
△afghan
arghan
Augean
angico
aiglet
angled
angler
arguer
argufy
algoid

Anguis
△angola
argala
argali
arguli
argyle
Argyll
angina
argand
argent
Anglos
Aegypt
angary
△angora
Asgard
augury
argosy
△august
algate
argute
augite
Argive
achkan
ash-can
ashlar
ash-pan
ashram
aphids
ash-key
ashler
awheel
achage
Alhagi
aphtha
ash-bin
ash-pit
ashake
awhile
ashame
at-home
achene
aching
aphony
ashine
Athena
Athene
a'thing
athrob
awhape
adhere
ashery
ashore
Ashura
a'where
aghast
alidad
aliyah
animal
apical
Ativan®

avital
akimbo
apiece
abided
aliped
apices
arisen
axises
alight
anight
aright
acidic
adipic
avidin
acidly
afield
aridly
arilli
avidly
axilla
alisma
azione
Amidol®
amigos
avisos
apiary
aviary
ahimsa
amidst
ariosi
arioso
arista
aristo
aviate
acinus
adieus
adieux
anicut
animus
abject
adjoin
abjure
adjure
adjust
ack-ack
aikido
acknew
ankled
anklet
auklet
alkali
Ankole
aikona
alkane
alkene
alkyne
askant
acknow
ackers
askari

Words marked △ may be spelled also with a capital letter

6 a□u□n

arkose
arkite
afloat
agleam
all-day
allice
anlace
allude
allied
allies
all-red
asleep
allege
anlage
Aglaia
all-hid
aslake
allele
aflame
aplomb
ablins
adland
ailing
allons
aslant
abloom
aslope
allure
ablest
ablush
ablate
aplite
atlatl
ablaut
allium
all-out
alleys
ablaze
asmear
almuce
armada
armlet
△almain
armpit
aumail
awmrie
aemule
Almany
almond
admire
almery
armory
armure
aumbry
Aymara
admass
ad-mass
almost
acmite
almous

armful
armour
awmous
anneal
annual
Aonian
arnica
apnoea
aunter
alnage
Aeneid
agnail
△auntie
annals
annuli
auntly
agname
Annona
awning
amnion
agnise
adnate
agnate
adnoun
Arnaut
annexe
agnize
aboral
Adonai
ajowan
amoral
anodal
anorak
apodal
atokal
atonal
avowal
azonal
amoeba
amorce
avouch
adorer
amoret
apogee
apozem
atoner
avocet
avoset
avowed
avower
avoyer
awoken
anough
Adonia
Adonic
Adonis
Aeolic
agogic
agonic
alogia

anodic
anomic
anomie
anoxia
anoxic
aporia
atocia
atomic
atonic
atopic
azonic
azotic
abolla
△apollo
arolla
azolla
aborne
abound
agoing
a-going
amount
anoint
aroint
around
aroynt
agorot
aboard
adoors
amours
Anoura
avoure
avowry
ahorse
arouse
abouts
agouta
agouti
agouty
Acorus
amomum
amoove
anonym
appeal
appear
alpaca
aspect
aspick
alpeen
apples
appaid
appair
ampule
△alpine
Alpini
Alpino
append
arpent
aspine
ampere
ampère

apport
aspire
asport
appose
aspout
appayd
asquat
acquit
abroad
adread
aerial
air-car
airgap
air-gas
airman
air-sac
airway
aortal
arrear
atrial
aerobe
arroba
arrack
arrect
awrack
abrade
arride
afreet
agreed
air-bed
air-sea
'Arriet
Azrael
adrift
aurify
abrégé
agrégé
Auriga
abraid
adroit
afraid
aortic
airily
Abroma
afront
airing
arrant
awrong
abrupt
Atropa
air-arm
air-dry
△aurora
across
afresh
agrise
aorist
arrest
arrish
at-risk

aurist
aerate
amrita
aurate
Air-bus®
air-bus
air-gun
atrium
aureus
aurous
arrive
acrawl
arrows
arrowy
arroyo
abrazo
agrize
agryze
aisled
answer
Auster
assign
abseil
arshin
assail
assoil
Aussie
adsuki
alsike
assume
awsome
absent
arsine
assent
alsoon
absorb
absurd
adsorb
assart
assert
assort
assure
assess
assist
ansate
assets
assott
assize
actual
amtman
Amtrak
antiar
astral
astray
attrap
antick
antics
attach
attack
aether

althea
anthem
anther
antler
Astrex
Altaic
Altair
△antlia
attain
attrit
astely
asthma
autumn
acting
anting
astone
astony
attend
attent
attone
attune
action
astoop
author
acture
afters
altern
antara
artery
astare
astart
astern
astert
attire
attorn
artist
attask
attest
autism
aptote
astute
antrum
artful
astrut
auteur
active
alteza
aoudad
abuser
acumen
aludel
amulet
amused
amuser
abulia
Anubis
anuria
Aquila
alumna
alumni

6 a□u□s

aburst
aguise
aguish
avulse
acuity
aguize
advice
abvolt
advene
△advent
alvine
adverb
advert
advise
atweel
atween
atwain
aswing
aswoon
adward
aswarm
aswirl
ayword
atwixt
always
Amytal®
amytal
anyway
anyone
anyhow
azygos
adytum
amylum
asylum
adzuki
Aizoon
bhajan
bharal
Bharat
biaxal
blanch
blanco
branch
boards
braide
brandy
beaded
beaked
beaker
beamer
bearer
beaten
beater
beaver
bhagee
bhajee
biased
bladed
blades
blamed
blazed
blazer
blazes
boatel
boater
bracer
braces
brayer
brazen
beachy
blashy
brashy
Baalim
beanie
boatie
△brazil
blacks
blanky
branks
branky
beadle
beagle
bragly
brails
branle
brawly
Brahma
Brahmi
baaing
Beaune
brains
brainy
branny
brawny
beacon
beanos
blazon
bravos
braird
blaise
braise
brassy
beauty
bhakti
bratty
beat-up
blague
blaize
braize
bablah
bobcat
babaco
bibber
bobbed
buboes
bobbin
bobwig
babble
babbly
bobble
bobbly
bob-fly
bubble
bubbly
bebung
baboon
by-blow
Babism
Babist
bibful
buccal
backed
backer
backet
becket
bicker
bucker
bucket
bocage
buckie
becall
becalm
buckle
became
become
beckon
biceps
backra
becurl
bicarb
bicorn
buckra
back-up
badman
△bedlam
bedpan
bedral
bodrag
bedeck
beduck
bodach
bodice
bedide
bedyde
△badger
bedded
bedder
bed-key
bedyed
bidden
bidder
bodger
bodied
bodies
budded
budger
△budget
bodega
△buddha
baddie
bedrid
bed-sit
△beduin
bodgie
bodkin
budgie
bedell
boddle
bodily
buddle
bedung
bident
biding
boding
bedrop
badass
bedash
bedust
bedaub
bedbug
bedaze
beegah
beenah
bye-law
bleach
blench
breach
breech
bieldy
blende
beeper
beeves
brevet
brewer
brewis
bleaky
breeks
bee-fly
△beetle
bregma
blenny
brenne
△brehon
△breton
bleary
breare
breast
breese
breath
beer-up
brew-up
baetyl
bye-bye
breeze
breezy
befoam
buffer
buffet
biffin
boffin
baffle
befall
befeld
befell
bifold
befana
befool
before
biform
Bofors
by-form
beflum
befoul
bagman
beggar
begnaw
bogoak
buggan
bagged
bag-net
begged
bigger
bogies
bugged
△bugger
bugler
buglet
begift
baggit
bagnio
baguio
bagwig
beguin
béguin
biggie
biggin
bigwig
buggin
begild
boggle
bigamy
begone
begunk
bogong
bugong
bvgone
begird
begirt
bog-ore
bagful
big-bud
bug-out
bogeys
behead
bahada
behalf
beheld
behold
behind
bohunk
behoof
Bihari
behest
behote
behave
behove
behowl
Bairam
bridal
bhindi
bailee
bailer
△bailey
baiter
beigel
blimey
boiled
boiler
briber
briefs
bridge
blight
blithe
bright
bailie
bainin
blinis
bridie
blinks
bricky
brisky
bailli
bridle
briony
bailor
Briton
Briard
briery
bhisti
blintz
brigue
bajada
bejade
bajree
bejant
bijoux
Bokmål
bukshi
baking
biking
bikini
bakery
bekiss
Balaam
ballad
ballan
ballat
balsam
beldam
Belial

Words marked △ may be spelled also with a capital letter

bilian
bulbar
Bulgar
bullae
Baluch
belace
bolide
baleen
balker
balled
ballet
belied
belief
belier
belled
belted
belter
bilges
bilker
billed
billet
bolden
bolled
bollen
bolter
bulbed
bulbel
bulger
bulker
buller
bullet
beluga
bolshy
Baltic
Belgic
billie
bollix
bulbil
belike
baldly
boldly
belamy
bulimy
Belone
belong
by-lane
byline
balboa
ballon
ballot
ballow
bellow
bilbos
billon
billow
bolt-on
belfry
bolero
ballsy
balata

belate
boleti
ballup
belaud
bulbul
bulgur
belive
belove
bylive
billy-o
bemean
bemoan
bombax
bumbag
bemock
bammer
△bembex
bomber
bum-bee
bummed
bummel
bummer
bumper
△bembix
bemoil
bumkin
bumalo
△bumble
bummle
Bimana
bamboo
bampot
bimbos
bombos
bumbos
bemire
bemuse
bemete
bemaul
Bombyx
bandar
banian
banjax
Bannat
bantam
banyan
banzai
Bengal
benzal
bin-bag
binman
bonsai
buntal
banded
banged
banger
banker
banket
banner
banter

bended
bendee
bender
bennet
binder
binger
binned
bonded
bonder
bonnet
bonzer
bungee
bungey
bunjee
bunker
△bunsen
bunted
△bunter
benign
△binghi
bunchy
bandit
ben-oil
benzil
bonnie
bonxie
bungie
bunjie
bunnia
bunyip
bangle
bingle
bundle
bungle
bename
benumb
byname
by-name
banana
boning
bandog
banjos
benzol
bingos
bonbon
bongos
buncos
bunion
bunkos
binary
banish
Benesh
bonism
bonist
Banate
binate
bonito
bang-up
ben-nut
bonduc

bunkum
benzyl
baobab
biogas
brogan
blotch
broach
bronco
brooch
blonde
blonde®
bloody
boorde
broody
biogen
blowed
blower
boomer
booted
bootee
Boötes
boozed
boozer
boozey
broken
broker
brolga
brough
broché
bionic
biopic
biotic
biotin
blowie
B-movie
boodie
boogie
bookie
bromic
blocks
blocky
boorka
boodle
brolly
bloomy
broomy
browny
booboo
boo-hoo
biopsy
blouse
blowse
blowsy
booksy
broose
browse
browst
browsy
blotto
blotty

blow-up
brogue
blowze
blowzy
bronze
bronzy
brouze
by-play
bo-peep
bopper
bepuff
bepelt
by-plot
bypass
by-past
bepity
bypath
barkan
barman
barrat
Berean
bordar
△boreal
Boreas
bureau
burial
burlap
Burman
bursae
bursal
bursar
byrlaw
byroad
barock
borsch
Bursch
boride
barbed
barbel
barber
barbet
barded
bargee
barken
barker
barley
barney
barred
barrel
barren
barret
barter
Berber
berley
berret
birder
birken
birler
bordel
△border

boreen
borrel
burden
burgee
burger
burhel
buried
burler
burley
burned
burner
burnet
burrel
bereft
barege
barège
borage
△bertha
berthe
△barbie
bardic
barrio
berlin
birdie
birkie
burdie
byrnie
barely
barfly
birsle
burble
burgle
bireme
barong
barony
borane
boring
barrow
barton
baryon
borgos
borrow
borzoi
burbot
burgoo
burros
burrow
△burton
byroom
barish
barite
baryta
berate
borate
buriti
barful
barium
barque
burn-up
baraza

6 b□s□a

bashaw
bespat
bestad
bestar
bismar
bus-bar
busman
byssal
basics
bisect
beside
basher
basket
basnet
basset
baster
beseem
beseen
besped
bested
bister
bosker
bosket
bossed
bushed
bushel
busied
busked
busker
busket
busses
busted
bustee
buster
besigh
△bosche
besoin
bespit
bestir
buskin
basalt
basely
bastle
busily
bustle
bosoms
bosomy
basing
besing
besung
busing
bassos
bastos
bespot
bestow
bishop
bisson
bosbok
boston
busboy
besort
bistre
bistro
Basuto
Basutu
boshta
△basque
besmut
bestud
bisque
bust-up
byssus
bateau
batman
betray
bitmap
bothan
betide
bather
batler
batlet
batted
battel
batten
batter
beteem
bethel
betted
better
bitted
bitten
bitter
bother
butler
butter
bitchy
botchy
betoil
betrim
bittie
bothie
betake
battle
Betula
botfly
bottle
buttle
betime
by-time
bating
betony
biting
△botany
botoné
butane
but-end
butene
bathos
batoon
betook
betrod
bettor
bittor
bottom
button
bêtise
betoss
batata
battue
bittur
Beulah
brumal
brutal
brumby
bounce
bouncy
brunch
bluidy
bounds
bouget
boules
brunet
bruter
bouffe
bludge
bluggy
blunge
bouche
bouché
bought
brushy
bludie
bougie
Brücke
bauble
bluely
bouclé
boulle
bluing
bourne
bouton
bauera
beurre
beurré
bluesy
bluish
△bourse
bruise
bounty
Brutus
bovver
Bovril®
bovine
bovate
bivium
bewray
bowman
bow-oar
bow-saw
bawbee
bawler
bawley
beweep
bowget
bowled
bow-leg
bowler
△bowser
bowyer
bewail
bowfin
bawble
bowels
bowing
bow-boy
bowpot
bowwow
bewept
bawdry
beware
△bowery
byword
by-work
boxcar
box-day
baxter
box-bed
boxing
boxful
△beyond
bryony
buying
△bayard
boyish
boyaux
buy-out
bazaar
bezoar
buzzer
bezzle
bezant
bizone
byzant
bazazz
bezazz
bizazz
chadar
chagan
chalan
charas
cravat
crabby
crambo
chance
chancy
clatch
cranch
cratch
chafer
chalet
chapel
chared
charet
chaser
claret
claver
claves
clawed
clayed
clayey
coaler
coatee
coater
coaxer
crases
crater
craven
craver
crayer
crazed
chaufe
chauff
change
'change
charge
chargé
claggy
craggy
cha-cha
coachy
Chadic
Charis
Chasid
clavie
clavis
crania
crasis
cyanic
cyanin
chalky
chapka
charka
cranky
czapka
cradle
craple
crawly
chacma
chammy
charms
chasmy
clammy
chaîné
chains
chaunt
cranny
chador
Charon
chaton
clamor
claros
craton
crayon
chappy
cramps
crampy
crappy
chakra
charry
chaise
chasse
chassé
classy
clause
coarse
chaeta
chafts
chanty
charta
charts
chaste
chatta
chatti
chatty
clarts
clarty
clasts
coaita
crafty
crants
claque
cratur
cabman
cabobs
cubica
cablet
cobber
cobweb
cubbed
cubage
cabbie
cabrie
cabrit
cobric
cuboid
cybrid
cabala
cobalt
cobble
Cybele
cabana
Cabiri
coburg
cyborg
cubism
cubist
cobnut
coccal
cicada
cachet

cocked
△cocker
cocket
cycler
coccid
Cochin
cyclic
cackle
cecils
cicala
cicely
cockle
cachou
cacoon
coccos
cocoon
cuckoo
cyclos
△cicero
cocksy
cecity
cicuta
cactus
coccus
cock-up
cyclus
coccyx
cadeau
caduac
cadger
codded
codder
codger
cudden
cudgel
codify
caddie
caddis
codlin
cuddie
cuddin
cedula
coddle
cuddle
cuddly
cadent
coding
cedarn
cidery
codist
caecal
△caesar
Ceefax®
chelae
chenar
chetah
coeval
credal
Cretan
clench

cleuch
coerce
creach
chenet
cheven
chevet
chewer
chewet
clever
crenel
crepey
crewel
cyeses
cierge
clergy
cleugh
creagh
cleché
△crèche
chemic
chenix
chesil
chevin
chewie
cleric
clevis
credit
△cretic
cretin
cyesis
checky
cheeky
creaky
creeky
△creole
chemmy
creamy
creant
cueing
coelom
credos
cremor
crepon
cresol
cheapo
cheapy
creepy
cheers
cheery
cherry
chèvre
cheese
cheesy
crease
creasy
creese
creesh
cueist
cherty
chesty

create
cuesta
caecum
cheque
chequy
cherub
cherup
cleave
cleeve
caftan
coffed
coffee
coffer
coffin
cuffin
cafila
coffle
cuffle
cafard
Caffre
Cognac
cogged
cogger
cygnet
ciggie
coggie
cagily
coggle
coggly
caging
cogent
cagoul
cahier
cohoes
coheir
cohune
cohere
cohorn
cohort
co-host
caimac
caiman
chinar
chiral
chital
climax
cnidae
coital
crinal
chiack
chinch
clinch
childe
ceiled
chided
chider
chimer
chimes
△chinee
chisel

coiner
crikey
crimen
cripes
crises
cuiter
cliffy
clingy
cringe
chicha
chichi
chi-chi
△chi-rho
cliché
chitin
clinic
clitic
clivia
crisis
critic
chinks
△chinky
cricky
caille
chicle
chicly
chield
chilli
chilly
criblé
client
coigne
criant
chibol
chicon
chigoe
chikor
chinos
Chiron
chiton
clip-on
chippy
chirpy
crimpy
crisps
crispy
chigre
chirre
chiasm
crissa
cuisse
chintz
chitty
clifty
clints
crista
caique
caïque
chiaus
clique

cliquy
coitus
crinum
chivvy
cojoin
cajole
caking
calcar
callan
calpac
celiac
cellae
cellar
collar
Colmar
colobi
calico
cilice
cultch
calced
calces
calker
caller
callet
calmed
calver
calves
calxes
celled
collet
colter
Culdee
culler
cullet
culmen
culter
culver
calefy
caligo
colugo
caltha
calcic
calkin
callid
Celtic
collie
cullis
cultic
calmly
coldly
calami
calima
column
colons
colony
callow
cellos
collop
caliph
△calory

celery
colors
colure
calash
call-up
callus
calque
cilium
coleus
colour
cultus
combat
comsat
cymbal
comice
comedo
comedy
comodo
camber
camlet
camper
cimier
combed
comber
commer
compel
comper
cumber
cummer
camsho
cambia
comfit
commie
commis
commit
commix
cummin
cymoid
Cymric
cample
camply
comble
comely
comply
cumuli
cement
coming
cameos
camion
campos
combos
come-on
common
commos
commot
compos
compot
camera
cembra
comarb

Words marked △ may be spelled also with a capital letter

6 c□m□s

comart
camash
camass
camese
camise
comose
cymose
camote
comate
comity
campus
comous
cymous
cancan
cannae
Cantal
cantar
canvas
cental
confab
cuneal
Canuck
conics
cañada
cancel
△cancer
canker
canned
cannel
canner
canted
canter
censer
center
cinder
conder
confer
congee
conger
conjee
conker
conned
conner
convex
convey
cunner
canthi
concha
conche
conchs
conchy
candid
candie
condie
confit
confix
conoid
candle
cangle
cantle

canula
cinema
conima
canine
caning
conine
candor
cannon
cannot
canton
cantor
cantos
canyon
censor
centos
cineol
condom
condor
congou
con-rod
contos
convoy
canapé
canopy
canard
canary
cendré
centra
centre
centry
contra
conure
cenote
canful
cangue
cantus
census
centum
cinque
concur
consul
choral
clonal
crotal
coombe
choccy
choice
cloaca
crotch
crouch
chorda
cloddy
cloudy
choked
choker
chokey
choler
chorea
choree
chosen

closed
closer
closet
cloven
clover
cloves
cloyed
cooker
cooler
cooper
cooser
cronet
crowed
chough
cloggy
clough
chocho
cloche
clothe
Clotho
cloths
croche
cholic
chopin
choria
choric
clonic
cookie
coolie
cootie
chocko
croaky
clodly
coolly
choana
cooing
croton
choppy
croppy
croupe
croupy
chokra
chokri
chowri
chowry
choose
choosy
chouse
crosse
crouse
Cloots
clotty
coolth
coonty
croûte
chorus
clonus
cloqué
crocus
croove

capias
captan
cupman
copeck
caplet
capped
capper
cipher
copied
copier
copped
copper
copter
cupped
cupper
cypher
caplin
capric
caprid
Capris
capsid
coppin
Coptic
cupric
cup-tie
cyprid
cypris
copple
copula
cupola
cupule
coping
captor
capers
capita
capote
copita
capful
cippus
cop-out
cupful
cyprus
coquet
carfax
carman
carnal
carpal
carrat
cercal
cereal
circar
corban
Corfam®
corral
corsac
cursal
curtal
caribe
carack
caract

Carica
curacy
corody
carder
careen
career
caries
carnet
carney
carpel
carper
carpet
carrel
carsey
cartel
carter
carved
carvel
carven
carver
cermet
certes
corbel
corded
corked
corker
cormel
cornea
corned
cornel
corner
cornet
corset
Cortes
cortex
corvée
corves
corvet
curfew
curiet
curled
curler
curlew
curney
curpel
cursed
curser
curved
curves
curvet
carafe
cerris
certie
cervid
cervix
corbie
corkir
corrie
corvid
currie

caroli
cerule
circle
corals
curdle
curtly
curule
△carême
chroma
chrome
chromo
corymb
Caranx
△carina
caring
corona
carbon
carboy
carfox
carlot
carron
carrot
carton
ceroon
cordon
corsos
curios
cursor
Carapa
ceriph
curara
curare
curari
caress
cerise
ceruse
chrism
Christ
corpse
curtsy
cerate
cerite
curate
carpus
cercus
cereus
cerium
cerous
circus
cirque
cirrus
corium
cormus
cornua
corpus
△corvus
curium
cursus
corozo
coryza

Words marked △ may be spelled also with a capital letter

6 d□d□i

casbah
cashaw
△casual
costae
costal
co-star
cushat
cushaw
cosech
cashew
casket
casted
caster
cesser
cisted
cosher
cosier
cosmea
cosset
costed
coster
cusped
cussed
cusser
casein
△cassia
cassis
cessio
cistic
cosmic
cossie
cuspid
cystic
cystid
castle
cosily
costly
casing
casino
cosine
cascos
Caslon
△castor
cestos
ciscos
cosmos
custom
custos
casern
cesura
cesure
casque
cesium
cestui
cestus
cissus
cistus
costus
cuscus
Cathar

cat-lap
catnap
coteau
cottar
cotwal
cytode
catnep
cither
cotted
cotter
cutler
cutlet
cutter
citify
cityfy
cut-off
catcht
catchy
cutcha
catkin
catnip
citric
citrin
cottid
cytoid
catalo
cattle
citole
cotyle
cutely
cuttle
catena
cetane
cation
citron
cotton
cuttoe
citess
cotise
cutesy
cytase
cytisi
catgut
catsup
△citrus
cottus
cut-out
caudad
caudal
causal
chukar
coucal
cougar
crural
chubby
clubby
crumbs
crumby
△church
clunch

clutch
crunch
crutch
chuddy
cruddy
caudex
cauker
caules
causen
causer
causey
cautel
cauter
cauves
C-cubed
Clupea
coulée
couped
coupee
couper
couter
cruces
crumen
cruset
cruxes
chuffy
caught
couché
couthy
caulis
clusia
coulis
cousin
coutil
crusie
chucks
chukka
chunky
clucky
caudle
couple
cruels
chummy
crummy
chukor
cou-cou
coupon
clumps
clumpy
crumpy
clumsy
course
cruise
county
crusta
crusty
caucus
cruive
caveat
caviar

civics
cave-in
caving
covent
coving
covyne
cavern
cavort
covary
covers
covert
cavass
civism
cavity
cowman
cowpat
cawker
cowled
cowpea
cowage
cowrie
cawing
cowboy
cowpox
coward
cowish
Caxton
cayman
chyack
chylde
crying
Ceylon
chypre
cayuse
coyote
crypto
cozier
drabby
diarch
deaden
deader
deafen
dealer
deaner
diadem
dialed
diaper
doater
dragée
drakes
draped
draper
drapes
drapet
drawee
drawer
drazel
draffy
dwarfs
draggy

deathy
drachm
dearie
deasil
deawie
diacid
diapir
dualin
dyadic
deadly
deafly
dearly
diable
doable
drably
dually
dyable
dharma
dharna
draunt
deacon
dead-on
dialog
diatom
diaxon
diazos
△dragon
Dralon®
drappy
dearth
drafts
drafty
diamyl
dabbed
dabber
debted
debtee
dibbed
dibber
dobbed
dobber
dubbed
debris
débris
dobbie
dobbin
dubbin
dabble
debile
dibble
debunk
debtor
debark
debase
debosh
deboss
debate
de-blur
dybbuk
decoct

decade
decide
decode
dacker
decked
decker
decree
decrew
dectet
dicker
dickey
docken
docker
docket
ducker
decaff
dacoit
△deccie
deceit
dickie
decoke
deckle
docile
decamp
décime
decane
decani
decant
decent
dicing
docent
Dacron®
deckos
doctor
decarb
decare
decern
Dectra®
decury
dicast
dacite
dickty
Docete
dictum
dactyl
dodman
deduce
deduct
dadoes
didder
didoes
dodded
dodder
Dodgem®
dodger
dodoes
dudder
dudeen
dodkin
duddie

6 d□d□l

daddle
diddle
doddle
dedans
dudish
dudism
daedal
deejay
dee-jay
dreich
drench
duende
deemed
deepen
diesel
dieses
dieter
djebel
dzeren
dredge
dreggy
deepie
diesis
drecky
deeply
duello
dreamt
dreamy
duenna
dyeing
daemon
dièdre
dreare
dreary
dressy
duetti
duetto
duetts
dueful
daftar
defeat
defray
deface
defect
defied
defier
defies
deflex
differ
doffer
duffel
duffer
daftie
daftly
deffly
defile
deftly
duffle
defame
defend
define
deform
defast
defus'd
defuse
defoul
defuze
degras
dog-ear
dagaba
dagoba
dagger
dagoes
degree
digged
digger
dog-bee
dogged
△dogger
dog-hep
dog-leg
dégagé
doggie
dog-hip
daggle
digamy
dog-end
dugong
diglot
dogfox
dog-ape
degust
digest
dogate
dégoût
dugout
dahlia
dehorn
dehort
daiker
daimen
de-icer
doiled
doited
drivel
driven
driver
duikep
duiker
doings
daimio
deific
deixis
doitit
daidle
djinni
daikon
daimon
drippy
driest
dainty
drifty
deject
diktat
dakoit
dik-dik
dekkos
dikkop
dukery
dikast
Delian
dollar
dolman
dolmas
delice
delict
delude
dalles
delver
delves
dolmen
dulcet
deluge
delphs
Dalila
dolent
dolina
doline
dallop
dalton
dildoe
dildos
dollop
delope
delate
delete
dilate
dilute
dolium
dolour
dammar
demean
démodé
dammed
dammer
damned
dampen
damper
damsel
demies
dimmed
dimmer
dumper
damage
dammit
demain
dimwit
domain
damply
dimble
dimple
dimply
dumbly
dumple
demand
dement
demons
domino
damson
demark
demure
damask
demise
demiss
demist
dumose
demote
dimity
domett
dim-out
dumdum
dumous
denial
dental
donnat
denude
dynode
dancer
dander
danger
Daniel
denied
denier
dennet
dentel
dentex
dinged
dinger
dinges
dingey
dinned
dinner
donder
donkey
donned
donnée
donnés
donzel
dunder
△dunker
dunned
dinghy
Dandie
dentil
dentin
donsie
dunlin
dandle
dangle
dangly
dindle
dingle
dinnle
dongle
denims
dynamo
doning
danios
danton
donjon
donnot
dun-cow
Dunlop
denary
donary
Danish
Danisk
dynast
Danite
denote
donate
dunite
dengue
dinful
dingus
dinkum
deodar
dioxan
doodad
doodah
droich
dooket
doomed
droger
drover
drongo
dioxin
doolie
dromic
drop-in
drosky
dhooly
doodle
drolly
droome
Diodon
doocot
doo-wop
dromoi
dromon
dromos
duomos
droopy
dropsy
drossy
drowse
drowsy
dhooti
drouth
drogue
dipsas
depict
dipody
dapper
diplex
dip-net
dipped
△dipper
△dopper
duplet
duplex
depths
doppie
dapple
dipole
daphne
depend
depone
dopant
doping
deploy
diploe
diplon
Dipnoi
dipsos
dupion
depart
deport
dupery
depose
depute
deputy
Dardan
derham
dermal
dirdam
dirham
Dorcas
Dorian
dorsal
durbar
durgan
Durham
durian
direct
deride
dirndl
△dorado
darken
darkey
darned
darnel
darner
darred
darter
dirhem
dormer
dorsel
dorser
dorter

Words marked △ may be spelled also with a capital letter

dirige
Dardic
darkie
derail
dermic
dermis
derris
dormie
durrie
dargle
darkle
darkly
dartle
dernly
dor-fly
daring
durant
during
durion
dartre
dorise
Dorism
duress
derate
dirdum
dor-bug
dorsum
durdum
derive
darcys
dorize
desman
disbar
discal
△dismal
disman
dismay
distal
dossal
dosi-do
dasher
dished
dispel
dossel
dosser
dusken
duster
design
dosage
dassie
desmid
distil
dossil
desalt
disple
duskly
desine
desyne
despot
discos
descry
desert
desire
desorb
disarm
dysury
desist
disuse
disbud
△discus
diseur
dust-up
disown
dittay
detach
detect
dither
ditted
dotted
dutied
dotage
detail
detain
dittit
dottle
dating
detent
détenu
detune
ditone
dotant
doting
dittos
datary
datura
detort
dotard
detest
dotish
detour
dative
dauber
dauner
deuced
doucet
douser
douter
drupel
drudge
druggy
douche
dought
doughy
dautie
double
doubly
drumly
douane
deuton
dhurra
device
divide
devvel
devoid
devoir
devall
Divali
divine
diving
divers
divert
devest
devise
divest
dovish
devote
dévote
duvets
devour
devout
dyvour
dewlap
dowlas
dawner
downed
downer
dowser
dowset
dawtie
Downie®
dawdle
Dewali
dewily
Diwali
dewani
dowlne
dew-bow
dawbry
dawish
dewitt
dexter
dryads
day-bed
doyley
duyker
day-fly
dayglo
Day-Glo
day-old
dry-fly
drying
day-boy
dry-rot
dryish
dizain
dazzle
dozens
dozing
elance
enarch
eparch
exarch
elanet
elater
E-layer
enamel
erased
eraser
evader
examen
eyalet
Elaeis
egally
enable
epaule
enamor
etalon
elapse
écarté
Elanus
embace
embody
emblem
embail
emblic
emboil
ecbole
embale
emball
embalm
emboly
embank
embark
embers
embase
emboss
embost
embusy
embrue
erbium
embryo
eschar
encode
escudo
excide
Eccles
elchee
eschew
etcher
exceed
encage
eucain
encalm
encamp
excamb
Eocene
escroc
escrol
escrow
escape
except
encore
escarp
escort
euchre
encase
encash
encyst
excess
excise
excuse
excite
encave
endear
eddied
eddoes
Eddaic
eidola
end-all
eident
elding
ending
endart
endure
eadish
eddish
eldest
endoss
endite
endive
enemas
evejar
egence
egency
elench
éperdu
eleven
evener
eyelet
emerge
energy
Edenic
Egeria
elegit
emesis
emetic
emetin
eremic
eyelid
eye-pit
Eyetie
evenly
eterne
exeunt
eyeing
elevon
erenow
exempt
epeira
exedra
egesta
ejecta
émeute
Erebus
exequy
eye-cup
eyeful
enerve
effray
efface
effect
enface
enfree
ewftes
effigy
effeir
enfold
effing
enfant
effere
effort
enfire
enform
effuse
elfish
effete
efflux
engram
engobe
eaglet
eggler
erg-ten
eughen
ewghen
engage
engagé
engild
engulf
edging
engine
egg-box
eggnog
engaol
eggery
engird
engirt
engore
eighth
eights
eighty
ergate
eggcup
englut
ephebe
ephebi
ethics
echoed
echoer
echoes
echoic

Words marked △ may be spelled also with a capital letter

6 e□h□l

ethnic
enhalo
exhale
exhume
ethane
ethene
ethyne
Ethiop
exhort
epical
Evipan®
eriach
evince
epimer
exited
eringo
elicit
elixir
exilic
edible
enisle
evilly
△enigma
editor
epigon
epilog
epizoa
émigré
Erinys
enjoin
enjamb
Eskimo
Eolian
eyliad
enlace
enlock
eel-set
eulogy
éclair
esloin
enlink
ellops
enlard
eclose
enlist
eolith
enlevé
Emmies
ermine
emmesh
enmesh
enmity
emmove
enmove
ennead
Etnean
esnecy
eunuch
ennage
eonism
ennuyé
enodal
euouae
evovae
Elodea
eloper
enoses
epopee
eposes
eroded
evoker
Exocet®
exogen
eloign
enough
epocha
Elohim
enosis
epodic
erotic
exodic
exomis
exonic
exotic
étoile
exopod
egoism
egoist
egoity
econut
évolué
△exodus
evolve
eponym
exonym
espial
expect
espada
espied
espies
expugn
esprit
empale
expand
expend
employ
euphon
empare
emparl
empart
empery
△empire
expert
expire
expiry
export
△empusa
empuse
expose
exposé
ear-cap
earlap
earwax
enrobe
eirack
enrace
enrich
earner
étrier
enrage
enragé
earthy
earwig
eureka
eerily
enroll
Euro-MP
earing
enrank
enring
errand
errant
erring
earbob
earcon
enroot
enrapt
egress
éprise
errata
earful
enseal
enseam
ensear
exsect
eassel
△easter
ensued
ensign
eassil
elshin
essoin
easily
eisell
ensile
Essene
ensure
exsert
ensate
ersatz
ensoul
essive
entrap
estral
estray
entice
either
entrée
entrez
eothen
esteem
eatage
eatche
eltchi
entail
entoil
eathly
extold
entame
entomb
eating
extant
extend
extent
extine
Eftpos
ectopy
ectype
eatery
entera
entire
extern
extirp
extort
eftest
extasy
entêté
entity
estate
estrum
estrus
eutaxy
eluder
emulge
emunge
écurie
epulis
erucic
ekuele
eluant
eluent
equant
equine
elutor
équipe
épuisé
evulse
eluate
equate
equity
envied
envier
elvish
enwrap
enwall
enwomb
enwind
emydes
eryngo
etymic
etypic
etymon
elytra
enzian
Eozoic
eczema
enzyme
enzone
evzone
Eozoon
fracas
flabby
flambé
fiancé
fiasco
flanch
franco
fratch
feared
flakes
flamed
flamen
flares
flaser
flawed
flaxen
flayed
flayer
framer
frater
flaggy
flange
flashy
flavin
frazil
featly
flatly
fiaunt
flaune
flaunt
fraena
flacon
flagon
flavor
fragor
flappy
frappé
fiacre
fratry
fraise
fealty
feague
flatus
franzy
Fabian
fabled
fabler
fibbed
fibber
fibred
fabric
fibril
fibrin
fibula
fibros
facial
fecial
facade
façade
facies
fucked
fucker
factis
fucoid
facile
facula
feckly
fecula
fickle
fo'c'sle
facing
fecund
factor
fictor
facete
factum
fuck-up
fidget
fodder
fade-in
faddle
fiddle
fiddly
fuddle
fading
fedora
fade-up
fadeur
faecal
foeman
foetal
fierce
fleece
fleech
fleecy
flench
fletch
△french
fresco
faeces
feeder
feeler
flewed
foemen
fledge
fledgy
flèche
fleshy
faerie
féerie

Words marked △ may be spelled also with a capital letter

feerin
flemit
foetid
fremit
freaky
feeble
feebly
freely
feeing
frenne
flexor
foetor
fueros
fleury
flense
freest
fiesta
freety
freity
fretty
foetus
frenum
freez'd
freeze
frenzy
Fifers
Fifish
fogman
fogram
fagged
figged
fogged
fogger
fogies
fag-end
faggot
fog-bow
fog-dog
fegary
figure
fogash
fugato
fogeys
Führer
△fehmic
Friday
flinch
flitch
faikes
failed
foiled
frisée
fridge
fringe
fringy
flight
fricht
fright
frigid
flicks

flisky
friska
frisky
faible
faille
fainly
fairly
foible
frills
frilly
friand
friend
faitor
feijoa
foison
frigot
frijol
fripon
frivol
friary
flimsy
faints
fainty
feints
feisty
flinty
flirty
frieze
frizzy
fakery
fikery
fikish
fallal
fellah
filial
foliar
fulham
fullam
fullan
fulmar
falces
fallen
faller
falser
falter
feller
felter
filler
fillet
filter
folder
fuller
filthy
fall-in
falsie
felsic
fill-in
fillip
filmic
folkie

fulfil
fulgid
fulvid
feline
felony
filing
falcon
fallow
felloe
△fellow
filfot
folios
follow
fulgor
fylfot
filtre
fulcra
filose
folksy
folate
folium
fumado
fumage
family
female
fimble
fumble
famine
foment
femora
femurs
famish
fumets
famous
fumous
fantad
fan-tan
Fenian
fenman
fingan
finial
finjan
finnac
finnan
fin-ray
fontal
fungal
fanded
fanged
fan-jet
fanned
fannel
fanner
Fantee
fenced
fencer
fences
fender
fennec
fennel

finder
fineer
finger
finned
finner
fonded
funded
funder
funnel
Finnic
fundie
funkia
finsko
fangle
fankle
finale
finals
finely
fondle
fondly
fining
fandom
fangos
fanion
fantod
fantom
fynbos
finery
finish
funest
finite
fondue
fundus
fungus
feodal
florae
floral
floras
flocci
Fronde
floret
flotel
flowed
flower
footed
footer
froren
frozen
△froggy
frothy
fiorin
florid
florin
foodie
footie
frolic
frowie
flocks
footle
foozle

froing
frorne
flow-on
floppy
floury
footra
floosy
flossy
flouse
floush
froise
frowst
frowsy
floaty
frosty
floozy
frowzy
fipple
faquir
ferial
firman
forbad
forçat
forgat
formal
format
forrad
forray
forsay
furcal
foreby
fardel
farden
farfet
farmer
farren
ferrel
ferret
firmer
forced
forcer
△forces
forfex
forger
forget
forked
forker
formed
former
forpet
forren
fortes
furder
furred
far-off
forage
forego
forthy
forwhy
furphy

farcin
farm-in
ferric
fervid
firkin
forbid
fordid
formic
fornix
forpit
forrit
fortis
△ferula
ferule
firmly
furole
forums
farand
farina
ferine
firing
forane
forint
furane
farrow
firlot
forgot
forhoo
forhow
formol
furrow
furore
forest
ferity
far-out
fureur
furfur
forbye
festal
fiscal
fossae
fasces
fasten
faster
fester
fisher
fishes
fossed
foster
fusser
fustet
fascia
fascio
fisgig
fistic
fossil
fusain
fustic
fastly
fissle

Words marked △ may be spelled also with a capital letter

6 f□s□o

fusile
fossor
fusion
fustoc
fescue
fat-cat
fatwa'd
fatwah
fetial
fetich
fat-hen
△father
fatted
fatten
fatter
fetter
fitted
fitter
fother
fitché
fitchy
fatsia
fettle
futile
fathom
fatsos
future
fetish
fitful
fit-out
faucal
faunae
faunal
faunas
feudal
frugal
fruict
fauces
faucet
flugel
flügel
flukey
fluted
fluter
fouter
frutex
fluffy
flushy
fought
flunky
foully
fluent
fautor
frumpy
feutre
flurry
foutra
foutre
foussa
faulty

fluate
fourth
fousty
fruits
fruity
frusta
foul-up
foveae
foveal
favela
△favell
favism
favose
favour
favous
fawner
fewmet
fewter
fowler
fox-bat
fixing
foxing
fixure
fixate
fixity
fixive
fly-man
flyway
△flysch
flying
frying
fezzed
fezzes
fizzed
fizzen
fizzer
fizgig
fizzle
fuzzle
ghazal
Graeae
graham
Graiae
glance
glands
grande
△guards
geared
ghazel
glazed
glazen
glazer
gnawed
gnawer
goatee
graben
graced
△graces
grader
grades

grapes
grapey
grated
grater
graved
gravel
graven
graver
△graves
grazer
grange
guango
glacis
goalie
gradin
Gräfin
gratin
gratis
gravid
glaiks
gladly
gnarly
graile
grakle
graple
grayle
gnamma
gramma
gramme
Grammy
goanna
graine
grains
grainy
granny
geason
glamor
guacos
guanos
grappa
gharri
gharry
glairy
glaury
glassy
grassy
graith
Granth
graste
giaour
gradus
glaive
gib-cat
gubbah
gabbed
gabber
gabled
gablet
gibbed
gibber

gibbet
giblet
gobbet
goblet
goboes
gobiid
goblin
gabble
gobble
gobang
gobony
gabion
gibbon
gabbro
geckos
go-cart
giddap
goddam
gadded
gadder
gadget
Gadhel
gidgee
gidjee
godded
godden
god-den
gadgie
gadoid
geddit
godwit
gadfly
guddle
gadsos
Gideon
godson
giddup
godown
go-down
geegaw
gherao
greece
greedy
gee-gee
geezer
Gheber
gleyed
Gueber
gledge
greige
Gaelic
goetic
greyly
gleamy
greens
greeny
gregos
guenon
Guelph
Ghebre

Guebre
ghesse
gneiss
grease
greasy
greese
ghetto
gleety
Greats
greete
Gnetum
gleave
greave
guffaw
gaffer
gifted
goffer
guffie
gagman
gigman
gagged
gagger
gigged
giglet
goglet
gag-bit
giggit
gagaku
gaggle
giggle
giggly
gigolo
goggle
goggly
guggle
giglot
guitar
glitch
griece
gainer
gaiter
glider
Glires
Goidel
goiter
gricer
grices
griper
gripes
grivet
△guider
guiled
guiler
guinea
guiser
guizer
griffe
gringo
geisha
gaijin

gainly
glibly
grille
grimly
griple
grisly
glioma
grison
guidon
guiros
grippe
grippy
goitre
grigri
'gainst
griesy
grilse
gaiety
gritty
guilty
Griqua
grieve
glitzy
go-kart
gilgai
golias
gollan
gollar
Gullah
gelada
gallet
galley
gelded
gelder
gelled
gilded
gilden
gilder
gillet
gilpey
golden
golfer
goller
gulden
guller
gullet
gulley
gulper
gylden
galage
galago
△gallic
Gallio
gilgie
gillie
galant
galena
galiot
gallon
gallop

Words marked △ may be spelled also with a capital letter

gallow
galoot
gollop
galère
galore
galosh
gelosy
golosh
galuth
gelati
gelato
gallus
gilcup
△galaxy
gemmae
gemman
gimbal
gimmal
gymbal
gymmal
gambet
Gamgee®
gamgee
gammer
gemmed
gemmen
gimlet
gimmer
gimmes
gummed
gambir
gambit
gymnic
gomoku
gamble
gamely
gamine
gaming
△gemini
geminy
gemony
gambol
gammon
gimmor
gumbos
Gemara
gamash
gamesy
gamete
gomuti
gomuto
gumnut
genial
gingal
gunman
gunyah
gander
ganger
gannet
gansey
gender
gennel
gennet
gentes
ginger
ginned
ginnel
ginner
gunnel
gunner
gunsel
gunter
gynney
ginkgo
gung-ho
gun-shy
ganoid
ganoin
gingko
gangly
gentle
gently
gingle
genome
△gentoo
gonion
gantry
genera
gentry
Ganesa
gunite
gangue
genius
geneva
global
gnomae
globby
grouch
goonda
gaoler
globed
gloved
glover
gloves
glower
gnomes
gnoses
goober
gooley
gooney
gooses
goosey
grocer
gromet
groper
groser
groset
grovel
grovet
grower
George
groggy
grough
geodic
globin
gloria
gnomic
gnosis
goolie
goodly
google
googly
grooly
growly
gloomy
ground
groyne
gnomon
good-oh
googol
gooroo
grog-on
gloopy
groupy
gloire
glossa
glossy
grouse
ghosty
groats
grotto
grotty
grouty
growth
grog-up
groove
groovy
Geomys
gipsen
gopher
gypped
gyppie
gaping
gippos
gyppos
gopura
gypsum
gardai
garial
garjan
garran
△german
gurrah
△garuda
garden
garget
garner
garnet
garred
garret
△garter
germen
girded
girder
girnel
girner
gorged
gorget
gurlet
gurnet
gurney
garage
Gurkha
garlic
garvie
gerbil
germin
girkin
girlie
girnie
gorgia
gorgio
garble
gargle
girdle
gorily
gurgle
goramy
gurami
gerent
gerund
goring
gyrant
garbos
garçon
garron
garrot
△gorgon
garish
gyrose
gyrate
gurjun
gyrous
garrya
gasbag
gasman
gas-tar
gossan
guslar
gasket
gasper
gassed
gasser
gaster
Goshen
goslet
gospel
gusher
gusset
gasify
gaskin
gaslit
gestic
gossib
gossip
gussie
gustie
gashly
△gascon
gismos
go-slow
gateau
gâteau
guttae
gather
getter
gotten
gutsed
gutser
gutted
gutter
gutzer
△gothic
guttle
gating
gitana
gitano
gutrot
get-out
gutful
ghubar
grubby
gaunch
grutch
gourde
gourds
gourdy
gaufer
gauger
gauper
glutei
gluten
grudge
grunge
grungy
gauche
gaucho
gaucie
glumly
grumly
gluing
glumps
glumpy
grumph
grumps
grumpy
gaufre
gru-gru
gluish
giusto
gousty
goutte
gaupus
gavial
gavage
giving
govern
gewgaw
gowlan
gowf-ba'
gawker
gawper
gowfer
gowned
gowpen
gowany
gawpus
geyser
guyler
glycin
grysie
gay-you
glycol
gryfon
gayest
goyish
gryesy
gozzan
gazebo
gizzen
guzzle
gazump
gazoon
gizmos
headed
header
healer
hearer
heated
heater
heaved
△heaven
heaver
heaves
hoaxer
Hyades
heathy
hearie
heaume
hyaena
head-on
hearse
hearsy
hoarse
health
hearth
hearts
hearty
heaste
head-up

6 h□b□a

hiatus
hobday
hub-cap
Hebrew
hoboes
Hebrid
hobbit
hubris
hybrid
hybris
habile
hobble
hebona
haboob
hobjob
hobnob
hubbub
hackee
hacker
hickey
hocker
hockey
hachis
hectic
hackle
hackly
heckle
huckle
hector
Hecate
hiccup
hodman
hadden
hedger
hidden
hidder
hodden
hudden
hidage
haddie
hydria
hydric
heddle
hoddle
huddle
hiding
hydyne
hadron
hydros
Hedera
Hadith
huddup
haemal
heehaw
Hielan'
hiemal
hyetal
heeled
heeler
haemic

haemin
heezie
hieing
hoeing
haffet
haffit
hog-rat
hagden
hagged
haglet
△higher
hogged
hogger
hogget
hog-pen
hugged
haggis
hoggin
hogtie
haggle
higgle
highly
hugely
hagdon
hegira
highth
hagbut
high-up
haikai
hainch
hairdo
hailer
hained
haired
heifer
hoiden
hoised
height
hoicks
hairst
haiduk
haique
hijrah
hijack
hejira
Hyksos
hallal
hallan
halvah
heliac
halide
halfen
haloed
haloes
halsed
halser
halter
halver
halves
heller

helmed
helmet
helped
helper
hilled
holden
holder
holies
holler
holpen
haloid
holmia
holmic
holily
holing
halloa
halloo
hallos
hallow
hellos
holloa
hollos
hollow
hullos
Hilary
holism
holist
hylism
hylist
halite
hallux
helium
hold-up
hammal
hammam
hamzah
Humean
Humian
hymnal
humect
hamlet
hammer
hamper
hemmed
hempen
hummed
hummel
hummer
humped
△humpen
humper
hymned
humefy
humify
homage
humlie
hymnic
hamble
hamuli
homely

homily
humble
humbly
hummle
hemina
homing
hominy
humane
hombre
humeri
hamose
Humism
Humist
humusy
hamate
Hamite
humite
humpty
hamous
humbug
humhum
hummum
hummus
humour
humous
hangar
hanjar
handed
hander
hanged
hanger
hanker
hansel
henner
hen-pen
hinder
hinged
honied
honker
hunger
hunker
hunter
honcho
hand-in
hankie
hen-bit
hennin
honkie
Hunnic
handle
hantle
hansom
Hindoo
hungry
honest
hang-up
hen-run
honour
henrys
hoo-hah

hookah
hoorah
hooray
hootch
hooded
hoofed
hoofer
hooked
hooker
hookey
hooley
hooper
hooter
hooven
Hoover®
hoover
hooves
hoodie
hoop-la
hoodoo
hoopoe
hooroo
hook-up
hep-cat
heptad
huppah
hyphae
hyphal
happed
happen
hapten
hipped
hopped
hopper
hyphen
hop-off
haptic
hippic
hippie
hypnic
hypoid
hop-fly
hopple
hip-hop
hippos
hopdog
Hypnos
hypate
hippus
hypnum
harman
hartal
herbal
herbar
hereat
hermae
hurrah
hurray
hereby
harden

hareem
harken
harper
harten
herden
Hermes
heroes
herpes
Herren
hersed
hirsel
horkey
horned
horner
hornet
horses
horsey
hurden
hurler
hurley
hurter
hirage
harmin
herdic
herein
hermit
hernia
heroic
heroin
hormic
Hornie
horrid
hardly
hareld
herald
hirple
hirsle
hurdle
hurtle
hiring
harbor
hard-on
harlot
harrow
hereof
hereon
heriot
heroon
horror
horson
Herero
horary
harass
harish
heresy
hereto
hard-up
hassar
Hesvan
hussar

Words marked △ may be spelled also with a capital letter

6 i□z□r

haslet
hasten
Hesper
hosier
hostel
hushed
husher
husked
husker
Hassid
hispid
histie
hussif
hassle
hustle
hyssop
hostry
hetman
hit-man
hatpeg
hatred
hatted
hatter
hether
hither
Hitler
hitter
hotbed
hotted
hotter
hutted
hitchy
hatpin
hot-air
hottie
hatbox
hot-dog
hotpot
hetero
hatful
houdah
houdan
haunch
hounds
hauler
housel
houses
haught
hourly
haüyne
haulst
houmus
Havana
haven't
having
have-on
havers
haw-haw
howdah
howzat

hawked
hawker
hawkey
hawser
howe'er
howker
howled
howler
howlet
hawkie
hawkit
howdie
hewing
hexact
hexane
hexene
hexing
hexose
heyday
haysel
hoyden
haying
haybox
haymow
huzza'd
hazily
hazing
huzoor
hazard
inarch
imaret
isabel
isatin
Isatis
△italic
imagos
imbibe
imbody
imbrex
inbred
inbent
in-bond
imbark
inborn
imbase
imbosk
imboss
imbrue
incubi
incede
inched
inches
incage
inclip
ischia
in-calf
incult
income
incony
incept

incase
incest
incise
incuse
incite
incave
incavi
incavo
Indian
indaba
indict
induce
induct
iodide
indeed
Indies
indign
indigo
indris
indole
indult
indene
indent
induna
iodine
indoor
indart
iodise
iodism
indite
iodate
indium
iodous
iodize
icecap
ipecac
ibexes
ilexes
iberis
irenic
icebox
ideate
ireful
iterum
in-foal
infect
infeft
infall
infelt
infill
infold
infula
infame
infamy
infant
inflow
infare
infere
infirm
inform

infest
infuse
influx
ingram
ingoes
ingulf
ingénu
ingine
ingest
ingate
ingrum
Ishtar
inhale
inhume
inhoop
inhere
inhaul
iridal
idiocy
ibices
ibidem
ilices
irides
irised
irises
imidic
iridic
iritic
iritis
icicle
inisle
inject
in-joke
injera
injure
injury
ink-bag
ink-cap
ink-sac
inkpot
illiad
inlace
inlock
illude
inlier
ill-off
inlaid
illume
inland
in-line
island
ill-got
illipe
illupi
ill-use
illite
iolite
in-laws
iambic
immane

immune
immure
immask
immesh
inmesh
inmost
inmate
iambus
Ionian
Innuit
ignomy
inning
ionone
ignaro
ignore
△ionise
Ionism
Ionist
ignite
innate
ionium
△ionize
isobar
ironer
isohel
isomer
iconic
ironic
irokos
isogon
isopod
Idoist
idolum
impact
impede
impies
implex
impugn
impair
impala
impale
impend
impone
improv
impark
imparl
impart
import
impure
impish
impose
impost
impute
impave
impawn
inroad
irrupt
inrush
inseam
inspan

instal
instar
insect
inside
inseem
instep
issuer
Iastic
inship
instil
insole
insula
insult
itself
insane
insert
insure
insist
in-situ
insoul
in-tray
intact
intoed
in-toed
intuit
intake
intima
intime
intomb
intend
intent
intine
intone
intron
intros
intern
intire
intuse
intown
inulin
iguana
invade
invoke
invent
invert
invest
invis'd
invite
inwrap
inwick
inwall
inwind
inward
in-word
inwork
inworn
inwith
inwove
inyala
izzard

Words marked △ may be spelled also with a capital letter

6 j□a□e

Jeames
joanna
jibbah
jubbah
jabber
jibbed
jibber
jobbed
jobber
jobbie
jabble
job-lot
jabers
jabiru
jubate
jackal
jacket
jockey
jacana
jaçana
jacent
jocund
jockos
jacksy
jocose
jack-up
Jacque
Judean
Judica
judder
Judges
judogi
Judaic
judoka
jadery
jadish
Jaeger®
jaeger
jeerer
jeelie
jaguar
jigsaw
jagged
jagger
jigged
jigger
jogged
jogger
jugged
juglet
jaghir
jigjig
jig-jig
jiggle
jiggly
joggle
juggle
jig-jog
jugate
jugful
jug-jug
Jahveh
△johnny
jailer
joiner
juiced
juicer
jailor
jojoba
jujube
jejune
Julian
jillet
jolley
jolter
juliet
jilgie
jellos
jalopy
jamjar
jampan
jimjam
jumbal
jambee
jamber
jammed
jammer
jumper
jumbie
jimply
jumble
jumbly
jymold
jemima
jiminy
jambok
jambos
jampot
jumbos
jumart
jambul
jump-up
jandal®
jingal
janker
jantee
jennet
jinker
jinnee
jinxed
△junker
junket
junkie
jansky
jangle
jangly
jingle
jingly
jungle
jungli
jungly
juncos
△junior
juntos
juncus
japing
jupati
jarrah
△jordan
jarred
jarvey
jereed
jerker
△jersey
jarvie
jerbil
jerkin
jirble
jurant
jargon
jarool
jerboa
jurist
jarful
jerque
Jashar
Jasher
jasper
jessed
jestee
jester
josher
josser
jaspis
△jessie
Jesuit
joskin
jostle
justle
justly
jissom
△joseph
jet-lag
jetsam
jetted
jitney
jitter
jotted
jotter
jutted
jataka
jet-ski
jötunn
jetsom
jetson
jetton
jaunce
jounce
journo
jaunse
jaunty
J-curve
△jovial
Jovian
jowled
jowler
jawing
jawbox
jawari
jowari
△jewess
Jewish
joying
joy-pop
joyful
joyous
jazzer
jezail
keasar
khalat
knawel
kraken
krater
khanga
kiaugh
knaggy
kwacha
keavie
khalif
kharif
Khalka
knacky
△klaxon
kia-ora
Khalsa
krantz
khanum
kwanza
keblah
kiblah
kababs
kabobs
kebabs
kebobs
kebbie
kabuki
kabala
kabele
Kabyle
kebele
kibble
kobold
kobang
kibosh
kybosh
kibitz
kabaya
kicker
Kuchen
kaccha
keckle
kecksy
kick-up
keddah
kidnap
Kodiak
kedger
kidded
kidder
kidlet
kidney
kidgie
kiddle
kid-fox
kvetch
keeker
keeled
keeler
keener
keeper
klepht
keelie
kie-kie
kierie
keenly
Kneipe
kreese
kaftan
△kaffer
keffel
△kaffir
kafila
k'thibh
kaikai
khilat
knitch
kaiser
knives
krises
keight
knight
khilim
knicks
kakapo
Ku-Klux
keksye
△kikuyu
kalian
kalpak
killas
△kelper
kelter
killer
kilted
kilter
kalmia
kalpis
keloid
kelpie
Keltic
keltie
△kelvin
kiltie
kalong
kelson
kilerg
kalium
killut
Kultur
kamees
kameez
kemper
kimmer
kümmel
kimchi
kamsin
kamala
kamela
kamila
kemple
kimono
kumara
kumari
kumiss
kantar
kunkar
Kanuck
kanten
kenned
kennel
kenner
kennet
kinder
kinred
kynded
kangha
kantha
kanjis
△kentia
△kanaka
kindle
kindly
kingle
kingly
kinkle
kinema
kinone
kincob
kinase
kunkur
konfyt
koolah
knobby
klooch
knower
kronen
kroner
kyogen
kaolin
kookie

Words marked △ may be spelled also with a capital letter

khodja
kgotla
koodoo
kronor
Kronos
knotty
krónur
kopeck
kipper
kephir
keppit
koppie
kaputt
Kirman
kirpan
Korean
kurgan
kirsch
karsey
karter
kermes
kernel
kersey
kirbeh
kurvey
karait
karmic
kermis
△kerria
kirkin'
korkir
karaka
kirtle
koruna
Karroo
karyon
korero
korora
kaross
karate
karite
kasbah
Kisleu
Kislev
kismet
kissel
kisser
kosher
kishke
kiss-me
kosmos
kathak
kit-bag
kit-car
Kit-Cat
kit-cat
kotwal
kitsch
kitten
kutcha
kettle
kittle
kittly
katana
ketone
kiting
kation
katipo
ketose
kittul
koulan
knubby
Keuper
kludge
knurly
kouros
khurta
Kevlar®
kavass
kowhai
kewpie
kowtow
keypad
key-way
kayoed
kayoes
Kazakh
laager
leaded
leaden
leader
leafed
leaker
leaned
leaped
leaper
leaser
leaved
leaven
leaver
leaves
loaded
loaden
loader
loafer
loaves
leachy
loathe
loathy
lead-in
lea-rig
leally
leanly
liable
learnt
leasow
llanos
liaise
lealty
lean-to
league
labial
lablab
Lib-Lab
Libyan
libido
labret
lebbek
libber
libken
lobbed
lubber
labrid
lubric
labile
lobule
lobuli
libant
lobing
libero
lobose
libate
lobate
labium
△labour
labrum
Labrus
labrys
lochan
laches
lacker
lackey
lecher
lichee
lichen
licker
locker
locket
locoed
locoes
lucken
lychee
lactic
lectin
lochia
luckie
locale
locule
loculi
locums
lucuma
lucumo
lacing
lacuna
lucent
Lucina
lector
lictor
lucern
locust
Lycosa
locate
Lucite®
lacmus
lock-up
△lyceum
lechwe
lac-dye
Lydian
la-di-da
ladder
ladies
ladies'
ledden
ledger
lidded
lidger
lodger
ladify
ladyfy
laddie
lading
Ladino
leeway
lienal
lieder
liefer
lieger
liever
laesie
Leerie
Liebig
luetic
leetle
lierne
lifter
lofted
lofter
leftie
lifull
lyfull
leglan
leg-man
loggat
log-jam
log-man
log-saw
legacy
lagged
laggen
lagger
legged
legger
leglen
leglet
liggen
ligger
logged
logger
lugged
lugger
laggin
leglin
lignin
loggia
loggie
luggie
ligula
ligule
legume
lagena
lag-end
lagune
legend
ligand
luging
lagoon
△legion
logion
loglog
ligure
legist
ligase
legate
legato
ligate
lights
lignum
log-hut
laical
laiker
leiger
loipen
loiter
luiten
laidly
leipoa
laisse
likely
liking
lakish
Lakota
lallan
lilied
loller
loligo
laldie
lalang
lollop
L-plate
Lilium
lolium
Lammas
lampad
lampas
lemmas
lumbar
lum-hat
lambda
△**lambeg**
lamber
lammer
limbec
limbed
limber
limmer
limner
limpet
lumber
lumpen
lumper
lambie
lammie
limail
limbic
limpid
lamely
limply
lament
lamina
lemans
lemony
liming
loment
lumens
lumina
lumine
△**limbos**
lummox
lemurs
lamish
limits
Limbus
limous
landau
lineal
linear
lingam
linhay
longan
lunacy
lancer
lances
lancet
landed
Länder
lander
lanner
lender
lenger
lenses
△lenten
linden
lingel
linger
linker
linnet
linney
linsey
lintel

Words marked △ may be spelled also with a capital letter

6 l□n□f

linter
longer
lunged
lunker
lynxes
lenify
lanugo
linage
lynage
lentic
lentil
lintie
lungie
lunyie
lankly
lingle
lonely
longly
lunula
lunule
lining
lentor
lentos
lenvoy
lingot
lunary
lanose
lanate
length
lenity
lunate
langue
langur
line-up
lingua
link-up
loofah
lionel
lionet
looker
looped
looper
loosen
looten
looter
looves
Leonid
look-in
loonie
lionly
lipide
lapped
lappel
lapper
lappet
lapsed
lepped
lipped
lippen
lopped

lopper
luppen
lappie
lipoid
lippie
lipoma
loping
lupine
lapdog
laptop
lepton
lipase
Lapith
Laputa
lapful
lapsus
loquat
liquid
liquor
lariat
larnax
larvae
larval
lurdan
lorica
lyrics
larder
largen
larker
lurden
lurker
lorcha
laroid
lordly
larine
larynx
loring
lardon
largos
loriot
lyrism
lyrist
lorate
lyrate
larrup
lascar
Lusiad
lasher
lasket
laster
lessee
lessen
lesser
lisper
lisses
listed
listel
listen
lister
lusher

luster
lassie
lesbic
lastly
lushly
lasing
losing
lysine
lassos
lesbos
lesion
lesson
lessor
Lisbon
lissom
lustra
lustre
lash-up
lasque
Latian
lethal
luteal
let-a-be
lateen
lathee
lathen
lather
latten
latter
lethee
letted
letter
lither
litten
litter
lotted
lutten
let-off
litchi
latria
Lettic
lithia
lithic
lutein
lately
little
latent
Latina
Latino
litany
luting
latron
lithos
lotion
lottos
lettre
latest
latish
lutist
let-out

litmus
lituus
launce
launch
lauder
laurel
louden
loupen
louses
louver
lounge
laughy
louche
lauric
leucin
loupit
loudly
louvre
Laurus
lauryl
lavabo
laveer
levied
lavage
lovage
live-in
love-in
lavolt
lively
lovely
△levant
living
loving
livery
lavish
△levite
levity
law-day
lawman
law-man
low-cal
low-fat
low-tar
lawyer
low-key
Lowrie
lowsit
lewdly
lawing
lowing
lowboy
lowery
lowest
lawful
low-cut
lexeme
luxury
laxism
laxist
laxity

luxate
lay-day
layman
lay-off
laying
layout
lay-bye
lay-bys
lazily
lozell
Luzula
△lizard
luzern
meatal
meat-ax
mealer
meawes
meazel
moaner
moated
mganga
meathe
mealie
meanie
mia-mia
meanly
measle
measly
miasma
miasms
meadow
meagre
meatus
mob-cap
mob-law
mobbed
mobled
mobbie
mobble
mobile
machan
Micmac
macaco
mocock
mocuck
macled
micher
△mickey
mocker
muchel
△mucker
mochie
mucoid
mackle
macula
macule
mickle
muchly
muckle
machos

macron
macros
micron
micros
mucros
mucosa
micate
mucate
mock-up
muck-up
mucluc
mucous
macoya
madcap
madman
madras
mediae
medial
△median
medlar
midday
midway
mudcat
medick
medico
madden
madder
medley
midden
midget
mid-leg
mid-sea
mudder
mudger
madefy
mid-off
modify
mid-age
midair
midrib
medaka
mid-sky
meddle
medfly
△middle
module
moduli
modulo
muddle
△madame
madams
medina
modena
△modern
Medise
Medism
△medusa
modest
modish
modist

Words marked △ may be spelled also with a capital letter

medium
medius
mid-gut
modius
Medize
maenad
Moerae
meeken
meered
maelid
meemie
mnemic
myelin
meekly
meetly
muesli
mnemon
myelon
Muftat
miffed
△maffia
muffin
Muftis
muffle
muflon
magian
magmas
△magyar
moggan
Mughal
maglev
magnes
magnet
maguey
muggee
mugger
megohm
magpie
megrim
moggie
magilp
megilp
moguls
mygale
maggot
magnon
Magnox®
magnox
mignon
magism
megass
mighty
magnum
mugful
mug-ewe
mahmal
mihrab
Mohock
mahsir
mohair

mahzor
Mahoun
mahout
△mohawk
maidan
Moirai
△maiden
mailed
mailer
maimed
meiney
moider
moiler
moiser
meishi
meinie
mainly
maikos
mainor
maigre
moiety
mojoes
△majlis
Mejlis
majors
make-do
mikado
making
mikron
make-up
mukluk
Malian
mallam
malmag
mellay
mollah
mullah
Malibu
malice
Milice
Molech
△moloch
malady
melody
miladi
milady
mallee
mallet
malted
melder
melted
milden
mildew
milieu
milken
milker
milled
miller
millet
milsey

milter
molten
mulled
muller
mullet
mulley
Malaga
malign
milage
maltha
maleic
malkin
mollie
mildly
melano
moline
mallow
mellow
melton
malgre
malgré
milord
malism
malist
molest
mulish
malate
Milvus
mulmul
multum
mammae
mammal
mimbar
mammee
mammer
mammet
mamzer
member
mimsey
mommet
momzer
mummed
mummer
mumper
memoir
mummia
mumble
moment
mambos
△mammon
Memnon
memory
mimosa
man-day
mangal
maniac
manoao
manual
menial
mensal

mental
minbar
Minoan
minyan
Monday
monial
menace
mensch
monact
Munich
monody
mangel
manger
mangey
manned
manner
manred
mantel
mender
meneer
menged
menses
mentee
minced
mincer
minded
Mindel
minder
minged
minter
minuet
monger
monied
monies
monkey
montem
minify
munify
manage
manège
menage
ménage
manche
Manchu
months
munshi
mandir
mantic
mantid
mantis
menhir
menyie
mingin
minnie
mundic
muntin
manuka
mangle
△manila
mantle

mingle
minima
mañana
manent
meninx
mining
mandom
manioc
mantos
mentor
mentos
minion
minnow
△mongol
mungos
Munros
mantra
manure
minors
monera
montre
minish
'mongst
monism
monist
monosy
manati
manito
minute
moneth
munite
mancus
manful
manqué
mantua
Mensur
mentum
minium
monaul
moneys
moolah
miombo
mooned
mooner
mooter
myogen
Maoris
miosis
miotic
Moonie
muonic
myopia
myopic
myosin
myosis
myotic
moo-cow
Maoism
Maoist
moorva

mapped
mapper
mopped
mopper
moppet
map-pin
mopoke
mopane
mopani
mopish
△maquis
Marcan
margay
Marian
marram
mercat
merman
Morgan
morgay
mornay
morsal
mortal
mortar
murlan
murram
murray
myriad
maraca
Myrica
△marcel
marked
marker
market
marled
marmem
marred
martel
marten
marvel
marver
mercer
merger
Mersey
moreen
morgen
morned
morsel
murder
murren
murrey
mirage
murage
marshy
morpho
murphy
murrha
margin
marlin
martin
merkin

6 m□r□k

merlin
morbid
morkin
morris
murlin
murrin
markka
marble
marbly
merell
merels
merely
merils
morale
morall
morals
morula
myrtle
merome
marina
marine
merino
murena
murine
marmot
maroon
marrow
merlon
Merlot
mirror
morion
Mormon
morros
morrow
Merops
marish
Marist
merism
morass
morish
Morisk
morose
merits
miriti
maraud
mark-up
marque
marrum
morbus
morgue
murmur
Myrtus
martyr
mescal
mesial
mesian
messan
mishap
mislay
missal
missay
moshav
Mossad
muscae
muscat
masher
masked
masker
masses
masted
△master
mestee
misfed
misken
miskey
misled
missee
missel
misses
misset
△mister
Moslem
musher
musked
muskeg
musket
mussel
mustee
muster
mashie
masjid
maslin
massif
mastic
mesail
misaim
misdid
misfit
mishit
missis
△mosaic
mossie
muscid
Muslim
muslin
mystic
mascle
masula
mistle
mostly
muscle
muscly
muskle
myself
mishmi
Mishna
musang
musing
mascon
mascot
musmon
musrol
Masora
misère
misery
misuse
misust
meseta
mashua
masque
mess-up
miscue
missus
mosque
museum
musive
matzah
matzas
mitral
mutual
matico
motuca
mutuca
matjes
matted
matter
métier
metred
mither
mitten
mothed
mother
motley
motser
mutter
metage
matric
matrix
mattie
metric
mythic
matoke
matily
metals
mettle
motile
mottle
mutely
mutule
△matins
mutant
mutine
mutiny
matlos
matlow
matron
matzoh
matzos
matzot
meteor
method
métros
motion
motmot
motto'd
mutton
mythos
metope
mature
Mithra
motory
mutism
metate
motett
mutate
mutuum
mythus
motive
Motown®
methyl
moutan
△maundy
moulds
mouldy
maumet
Mauser
mouser
mousey
mouter
maungy
mzungu
mought
mouths
mouthy
mauvin
moujik
moulin
mousie
mousle
mousmé
maunna
mouton
maugre
mousse
Mounty
miurus
muu-muu
maulvi
movies
moving
movers
mawmet
mewses
mawkin
mowing
mawpus
maxima
myxoma
maxixe
mayday
mayhap
May-dew
mayhem
mayfly
maying
mayest
moyity
mizvah
mazhbi
mizzen
mezail
mozzie
muzhik
muzaky
mazily
mizzle
mizzly
mozzle
muzzle
mazuma
mezzos
mazard
mazout
mezuza
nyalas
near-by
nuance
nhandu
neaped
nearer
neaten
neaffe
neanic
niacin
Nyanja
nearly
neatly
ngaios
nyanza
nebeck
nobody
nabbed
nabber
nebbed
neb-neb
nibbed
nebris
nubbin
nebula
nebule
nebulé
nebuly
nibble
no-ball
nobble
nubble
nubbly
nubile
nybble
nebish
nebbuk
nobbut
nectar
nickar
nuchae
nuchal
nacket
nacred
necked
niched
nicher
nickel
nicker
nochel
nocket
nuclei
nocake
nicely
nucule
Nicene
nocent
nachos
nicish
nicety
nickum
△noctua
nidget
nodded
nodder
nudger
nidify
nudnik
noddle
nodule
nudely
Na-Dene
niding
nid-nod
nodose
nudism
nudist
nudity
nodous
need-be
naeves
needer
noesis
noetic
needle
needly
nielli
niello
naevus
niffer
nuffin
naffly
nefast
nuggar
nagged
nagger

Words marked △ may be spelled also with a capital letter

6 o□h□e

nigger	non-net	narcos	native	orally	overdo
nogged	no-noes	nardoo	nitryl	ovally	obeyer
nugget	nonage	narrow	neural	ozaena	O-level
noggin	non-ego	Norroy	nougat	orator	omelet
nogaku	nankin	Nernst	nounal	ovator	omened
niggle	nuncio	Nerita	nautch	Onagra	oneyer
niggly	nuncle	nerite	noulde	omasum	opener
nighly	nonane	norite	nausea	opaque	ox-eyed
nagana	nandoo	Nerium	neuter	ox-bird	one-off
nigh-on	nincom	nosean	naught	orbita	overgo
nig-nog	non-com	no-side	nought	orbity	obeche
no-good	non-con	nester	nautic	orchat	olefin
nagari	nonary	Nissen	Ngunis	opcode	orexis
negate	nanism	nisses	nousle	orchel	ocelli
nights	ninety	nosher	neuron	orcein	openly
nighty	nincum	Naskhi	Novial	orchid	overly
no-hope	nooner	Neskhi	novice	orchil	odeums
naiads	niobic	nastic	Navaho	△orchis	one-one
nailed	nookie	nestle	navaid	occult	Oberon
nailer	noodle	nosily	Navajo	oscula	ocelot
noises	Nuphar	nosing	novels	oscule	operon
naiant	napped	nasion	novena	occamy	oneyre
Nikkei	napper	Nesiot	Nivôse	oncome	obeism
nekton	nephew	Nestor	novity	orcine	oleate
nallah	nipped	no-show	new-sad	oscine	omenta
nilgai	nipper	nostoc	New-Age	occupy	omerta
nilgau	nipter	nostos	new-age	oecist	omertà
nullah	napkin	nasard	Newfie	oncost	owelty
nelies	Nippie	nasute	newell	oocyte	obelus
nilled	napalm	nosh-up	new-old	odd-man	Olenus
nellie	Nepali	no-tech	Nowell	ogdoad	one-two
nelson	nipple	notice	newton	old-hat	off-day
Nilote	napron	natter	newish	old-man	office
Nilots	Nippon	nether	nowise	ordeal	olfact
Nemean	napery	netted	noways	oodles	off-key
numbat	nepeta	nutlet	nix-nie	old-age	offset
numdah	narial	nutmeg	nextly	ordain	off-air
numnah	narras	nutted	nay-say	oedema	onfall
nomade	nerval	nutter	noyade	ondine	offend
nomady	norlan'	notify	Naypic	onding	offing
nimbed	normal	notchy	noyous	odd-job	off-job
nimmed	△norman	nitric	nozzer	odds-on	onflow
nimmer	Norway	nitwit	nuzzer	Old-Boy	△oxford
numbed	nurhag	nutria	Nazify	old-boy	oafish
number	narked	nettle	nozzle	obdure	offish
nympho	nerved	nettly	nuzzle	orders	offcut
nim-oil	nerver	natant	Nazism	ordure	offput
namely	nerves	nutant	omasal	oddish	orgeat
nimble	nirled	nation	okayed	oldest	orgies
nimbly	norsel	natron	onager	oldish	ouglie
numbly	nurser	notion	opaled	oddity	oughly
naming	△nereid	natura	△orange	on-dits	oogamy
nomina	nirlie	△nature	otalgy	oidium	oogeny
numina	nirlit	nitery	orache	one-day	organa
Nimrod	Nordic	notary	ogamic	one-man	orgone
nomism	neroli	notate	okapis	one-way	oxgang
numpty	nurdle	nutate	oxalic	overby	orgasm
nimbus	nursle	netful	oxalis	owerby	oxgate
ninjas	narine	notour	Ozalid®	oreads	oxhead
non-fat	nerine	not-out	△oracle	oreide	ochrea

6 o□h□n

ochrey
ochone
ochery
others
Ophism
△ophite
obi-man
obital
ogival
ooidal
origan
ovisac
obiter
△oliver
olivet
orifex
oniric
opioid
origin
Osiris
otitis
oriole
oniony
△orient
orison
ovibos
osiery
obiism
otiose
opiate
odious
Ojibwa
object
objure
oikist
oak-nut
oilcan
oil-gas
oilman
oil-pan
owl-car
o'clock
oillet
oblige
oology
oilily
ollamh
oblong
ogling
on-lend
on-line
oolong
oulong
oxland
oilers
oilery
owlery
oblast
owlish
oblate

△oolite
oil-cup
oilnut
oomiac
oomiak
oompah
ohmage
ormolu
osmund
osmose
osmate
osmium
osmous
Ormazd
Ormuzd
omnify
ornery
ornate
omnium
oroide
orogen
oboist
obolus
orphan
osprey
oppugn
Orphic
orpine
oppose
oar-lap
ocreae
o'erlay
oorial
ourebi
O-grade
oarage
ourali
orrery
ourari
ogress
ogrish
onrush
Ossian
onside
ouster
oyster
ossify
obsign
ossein
oxslip
obsess
on-site
osteal
Ostiak
ostial
Ostyak
outbar
outeat
outgas
outlaw

outlay
outman
obtect
optics
ostler
Ostmen
Ostrea
outher
outjet
outler
outlet
outred
outset
outage
obtain
outbid
outfit
outhit
outlie
outsit
outvie
outwin
outwit
oxtail
outfly
optima
optime
obtend
obtund
octane
Octans
octant
optant
ostent
outing
octroi
octuor
option
orthos
outbox
outfox
outtop
outcry
obtest
obtuse
out-ask
octett
opt-out
ostium
outgun
outjut
output
outrun
outsum
octave
octavo
ottava
outbye
ocular
ovular

opuses
oeuvre
oculus
opulus
obvert
ouvert
onward
oxygen
oxymel
onycha
oozily
plagal
planar
platan
pearce
plaice
planch
prance
pranck
pea-hen
peaked
peavey
phased
phases
placed
placer
placet
planer
planet
plated
platen
plater
plates
played
player
prater
prayed
prayer
piaffe
pa'anga
peachy
plashy
poachy
phaeic
phasic
phasis
phatic
placid
placit
pratie
praxis
pranky
pearly
phalli
prawle
Phasma
plasma
Psalms
△plains
plaint

peacod
peapod
peason
pharos
pianos
pearst
praise
planta
plaste
peanut
plague
plaguy
plaque
piazza
public
pebble
pebbly
pachak
pochay
po'chay
packer
packet
pecker
pecten
picked
picker
picket
pocked
pocket
pucker
pacify
pectic
pectin
picnic
picric
pycnic
pickle
puckle
picene
picine
pycnon
Pecora
picoté
pactum
pick-up
pad-nag
padsaw
Paduan
pedlar
podial
padded
padder
pedder
podded
podley
pudden
pudder
pudsey
pidgin
paddle

pedalo
peddle
piddle
puddle
puddly
padang
pedant
Podunk
pudent
podsol
podzol
Podura
pedate
podite
padauk
padouk
podium
pieman
Pleiad
prefab
prepay
pre-tax
pre-war
plebby
pierce
pleach
pleuch
preace
preach
pseudo
peeled
peeler
peeper
peeved
peever
peewee
piecen
piecer
pieces
prefer
pre-let
premed
preses
preset
preife
peenge
pledge
pleugh
peerie
peewit
phenic
pierid
Pieris
poetic
précis
prefix
prelim
premia
premie
premix

Words marked △ may be spelled also with a capital letter

6 p□o□e

pteria
pterin
Pteris
pyemia
pyemic
paella
△pueblo
pneuma
preamp
paeony
pieing
pyeing
phenol
phenom
pie-dog
plexor
pretor
pye-dog
preppy
pheere
pleura
poetry
pheese
pierst
please
prease
plenty
presto
pretty
peepul
plenum
plexus
pre-buy
precut
prevue
preeve
phenyl
prewyn
pheeze
puffed
puffer
puffin
piffle
poffle
pig-man
pig-rat
pagoda
pegged
peg-leg
pig-bed
pigged
piglet
pigpen
piggie
piggin
puggie
puggle
paging
pigsny
peg-box

peg-top
pigeon
pogrom
pug-dog
pygarg
pigsty
pignut
Pahari
plicae
plical
primal
ptisan
paiock
peinct
prince
pained
paired
Philem
poised
poiser
priced
pricer
pricey
primer
priser
privet
prized
prizer
priefe
plight
painim
paidle
paigle
primly
prisms
prismy
pliant
puisne
puisny
phizog
poison
primos
prison
pliers
priory
plissé
priest
prissy
painty
plinth
pointe
points
pointy
paid-up
Primus®
primus
prieve
pajock
pyjama
pokies

pakeha
pyknic
pukeko
poking
pakora
Pakhto
Pakhtu
pokeys
paleae
pallae
pallah
Pallas
Palmae
palmar
palpal
△pelham
pillar
pillau
pole-ax
pollan
pulsar
pultan
pulwar
palace
Polack
police
policy
palkee
palled
pallet
palmed
palmer
palter
pellet
pelmet
pelter
pelves
phloem
pilfer
polder
polled
pollen
poller
pollex
puller
pullet
pulley
pulper
pulsed
pulver
pilaff
palagi
pelage
phlegm
pulkha
pallia
pallid
palmie
peloid
pelvic

pelvis
pull-in
pulpit
pulvil
palely
palolo
pilula
pilule
palama
paling
piling
Poland
poling
polony
puling
pylons
pallor
pillow
polios
pull-on
pulton
polype
polypi
polyps
paltry
pelory
peltry
palish
pilose
△polish
palate
pelite
pelota
polite
polity
palpus
Phleum
pileum
pile-up
pileus
pilous
Pollux
pull-up
pulque
pultun
poleyn
pampas
Pamyat
pomace
pumice
pomade
pamper
pommel
△pompey
pummel
pumped
pumper
pimple
pimply
pomelo

pumelo
piment
Pomona
pompom
pompon
pomroy
pomato
pandar
penial
penman
pennae
pennal
pen-pal
pentad
pineal
pin-man
pinnae
pontal
punkah
panick
Punica
panada
pander
Pangea
pangen
panned
panter
panzer
pencel
penned
penner
pensée
pensel
Pentel®
pentel
pincer
pinder
Pinger®
pinger
pinked
pin-leg
pinned
pinner
pinnet
poncey
ponder
pongee
pontes
punier
punned
punner
punnet
puntee
punter
pang-fu'
poncho
punchy
pandit
pencil
pen-nib

pensil
pinkie
pinnie
pinxit
Pinyin
pongid
△pontic
pontie
pontil
pundit
penile
penult
pingle
pinole
pintle
punily
△panama
ponent
panton
pantos
pennon
pingos
pinion
pinkos
pintos
pondok
pongos
ponton
puntos
panary
pantry
penury
pinery
panisc
panisk
punish
piñata
pineta
pinite
puncta
puncto
panful
pannus
pantun
penful
pen-gun
pensum
pent-up
phocae
phocas
△pholas
phonal
poojah
poonac
△phoebe
poonce
ploidy
phoner
phoney
phooey

Words marked △ may be spelled also with a capital letter

6 p□o□f

piolet
pioned
pioner
pioney
pioted
plover
pooped
△pooter
prober
proker
proleg
proler
propel
proper
proser
protea
proved
proven
prover
ptoses
pyoner
proofs
plongd
plonge
△plough
proign
phobia
phobic
phonic
photic
pionic
pookit
probit
profit
prolix
prosit
psocid
psoric
ptosis
plonky
people
poodle
poorly
Progne
proine
proing
proyne
phonon
photon
photos
poo-poo
promos
proton
Provos
prompt
phossy
plotty
pronto
poogye
propyl

protyl
Papuan
Popian
poplar
papacy
pepper
pipped
popper
poppet
pupped
puppet
pipage
papain
pepsin
peptic
pipkin
pippin
poplin
poppit
poprin
papula
papule
popple
popply
pepino
piping
peplos
popjoy
papers
papery
papyri
popery
papish
papism
papist
popish
pupate
pappus
pepful
peplum
peplus
pop-gun
papaya
pop-eye
piquet
Parcae
pardal
pariah
parial
Parian
parlay
parral
partan
perfay
phreak
portal
portas
purdah
piracy
parade

parody
parcel
parded
parget
parkee
parker
parley
parpen
parrel
parsec
Parsee
parser
parted
parter
percen
perfet
porker
porter
Purdey®
purger
purler
purser
pursew
purvey
purify
parage
pardie
parkie
parkin
partim
parvis
perdie
pereia
perkin
permit
Persic
pirnie
pirnit
porgie
purlin
purpie
peruke
parkly
parole
partly
pertly
portly
purely
purfle
purfly
purple
purply
Pyrola
paramo
Paraná
parang
parent
paring
perone
piraña

Purana
purine
pyrene
pardon
parlor
parrot
parson
parton
period
Pernod®
perron
person
paraph
pyrope
parure
parish
perish
peruse
phrase
phrasy
porism
porose
purism
purist
parity
periti
pirate
purity
pyrite
perdue
persue
porous
pursue
piraya
pascal
pasear
postal
Pesach
pesade
posada
passed
passée
passer
pastel
paster
pester
Pisces
pissed
posnet
posser
posset
poster
pushed
pusher
pussel
pusser
pashim
passim
pastil
pastis

pistil
possie
postie
postil
pestle
poshly
pesant
posing
pastor
pistol
piston
pastry
Pashto
Pashtu
peseta
Pushto
Pushtu
passus
piss-up
poseur
Possum®
possum
'possum
push-up
pesewa
peshwa
Pathan
pet-day
pe-tsai
pitman
pit-pat
pit-saw
potman
puteal
pataca
putsch
patted
pattée
patten
patter
patzer
pether
petrel
petted
petter
pitied
pitier
pitted
pitten
pitter
poteen
pother
potted
potter
putted
puttee
putten
putter
putzes
put-off

potage
patchy
pitchy
potche
pathic
pat-lid
patois
pet-sit
pot-lid
putois
putrid
puttie
Pythia
Pythic
Pitaka
pattle
pettle
pottle
puteli
patent
patina
patine
potent
pathos
patios
patrol
patron
petrol
pithos
potboy
potion
pottos
putlog
△python
patera
petara
petard
petary
pitara
pituri
puture
potash
pot-ash
potass
petite
potato
potful
potgun
put-put
pausal
plural
paunce
paunch
pounce
pounds
pauper
pauser
plumed
plused
pluses

Words marked △ may be spelled also with a capital letter

6 r□f□g

pouder
poufed
pourer
pouter
pruner
prunes
pluffy
pouffe
plunge
plushy
pouchy
piupiu
plug-in
poukit
pourie
△prusik
pyuria
plucky
plummy
pruina
pruine
pluton
plumpy
poulpe
poudre
pousse
prunus
pavage
pavane
paving
pavone
pavior
pavise
pawpaw
powwaw
pawnce
△pawnee
pawner
pewter
powder
powney
powter
pownie
powwow
powers
paxwax
pay-day
psywar
pay-off
△psyche
psycho
paynim
physic
physio
ptyxis
payola
phyllo
psylla
paying
plying

prying
pay-box
phyton
poyson
peyote
pay-out
phylum
puzzel
pizzle
puzzle
pezant
pazazz
Peziza
pizazz
Quapaw
quasar
quaich
quatch
△quaker
quaver
quagga
quaggy
quaigh
quango
qualia
quar'le
qualmy
quaint
quahog
quaere
quarry
quanta
quarte
quarto
quartz
queach
quelch
quench
quetch
Q-fever
quelea
queued
quethe
queeny
queint
queasy
queest
qwerty
queazy
qigong
quidam
quince
quitch
quited
quiver
quiche
quight
quinic
quinie
quirky

quinoa
quinol
quipos
quinsy
quinta
quinte
qui-hye
quinze
qintar
quotas
quoter
quotes
quotha
quokka
quooke
quoist
quoits
quorum
quotum
Q-train
qasida
qiviut
riancy
reader
reamer
reaper
rearer
reaver
roamer
roarer
rhaphe
read-in
realia
roadie
roarie
really
re-ally
rearly
realos
reason
realty
reasty
Rialto
ribibe
reback
rebeck
rabbet
rabies
ribbed
riblet
robbed
robber
rubbed
rubber
rubbet
rubied
rubies
rebuff
rubefy
rubify

rabbin
rabbis
rabbit
reboil
rubbit
rubric
rebuke
rabble
ribald
robalo
rubble
rubbly
rebind
riband
robing
rubine
ribbon
rebore
reborn
rebury
ribose
robust
rabato
rebate
rebato
rebite
rubati
rubato
ribaud
rubout
racial
reckan
rectal
ric-rac
rictal
rococo
recede
re-cede
recode
racked
racker
racket
recced
recces
recked
richen
riches
ricked
ricker
rochet
△rocker
rocket
rachis
rechie
recoil
recoin
Riccia
racily
recall
recule

richly
rickle
rickly
ruckle
rucola
raceme
racing
recant
△recent
racoon
reccos
reckon
rector
rectos
recept
recipe
record
recure
racism
racist
recast
recess
recuse
recite
recoup
rectum
rectus
rictus
ruckus
radial
radian
redcap
redeal
red-hat
rediae
redial
red-mad
red-man
redraw
rodman
redact
reduce
redden
redder
redeem
redleg
ridded
ridden
ridder
ridged
ridgel
ridger
rodded
rudded
rudder
reduit
ridgil
raddle
radula
reddle

riddle
ruddle
rudely
radome
redone
rident
△riding
rodent
roding
radios
red-box
red-dog
red-hot
redtop
rodeos
rudery
radish
rudish
redate
radium
radius
redbud
red-gum
red-wud
redowa
red-eye
reeded
reeden
reeder
reefer
reeler
reeved
riever
roemer
re-echo
reechy
Raetia
re-edit
reekie
rhexis
ruelle
rheums
rheumy
rueing
reebok
rhetor
reesty
△rhesus
rueful
reflag
reface
refect
rafter
reffed
reflet
reflex
refuel
rifler
ruffed
refuge

6 r□f□i

raffia
ruffin
rafale
raffle
refill
rifely
riffle
ruffle
refine
refund
re-fund
reffos
reflow
refoot
reform
re-form
refuse
refute
reflux
rufous
ragbag
raglan
ragman
ragtag
reggae
regnal
ragged
raggee
reglet
regret
rigged
rigger
rugged
rugger
regain
riglin
raggle
raguly
regale
regula
Regulo®
regulo
rigoll
regime
régime
raging
ragini
regent
△regina
ragtop
region
regard
regest
rugose
righto
rights
rugate
ragout
rag-out
regius

rigour
rig-out
rugous
regive
rehear
reheat
reheel
rehang
rehung
rehash
raiyat
rhinal
raider
railer
raiser
raited
reiter
reiver
ruined
ruiner
raisin
rhizic
railly
rhinos
reject
rejoin
Rajput
raking
rakery
rakish
reload
relics
relict
reluct
relide
relied
relief
relier
rillet
△rolfer
rolled
△roller
relaid
relume
relent
reline
Roland
ruling
roll-on
relish
relate
Rallus
roll-up
relive
rallye
ramcat
rameal
Ramean
remead
remade

remede
remedy
remuda
ramjet
rammed
rammer
ramper
rimmed
romper
rummer
Rumper
ramify
romage
ram-air
remain
remeid
Romaic
rumkin
remake
ramble
ramuli
remble
rumble
rumbly
rumple
remand
remind
remint
Romani
Romany
rumina
ramrod
ramson
Romeos
rumbos
remark
re-mark
remora
Ramism
Ramist
ramose
remise
remiss
rimose
Romish
ramate
remote
ramous
remoud
rimous
rum-bud
rumour
rumpus
remove
randan
rental
runway
rancel
randem
△ranger

ranked
ranker
ransel
ranter
ranzel
render
renied
rennet
renter
rentes
rinded
ringed
ringer
rinser
rondel
runlet
runnel
runner
runnet
runted
run-off
renege
rancho
rancid
randie
rennin
runrig
rankle
rankly
ranula
rundle
runkle
rename
ranine
rancor
random
randon
ransom
renvoi
renvoy
rondos
Roneos
ronyon
renown
ryokan
rhombi
reopen
Rhodes
rioter
roofed
roofer
roomed
roomer
rooted
rooter
rhodic
rhodie
rhotic
rookie
roomie

roopit
rootle
riotry
rootsy
△repeal
repeat
replan
replay
riprap
rip-rap
rip-saw
rupiah
repack
ripeck
rypeck
rapids
rapier
rapped
rappee
rappel
rapper
repped
ripped
ripper
rip-off
repugn
△raphia
raphis
repaid
repair
raptly
repulp
ripely
ripple
ripply
ropily
rapine
raping
repand
repent
repine
repone
roping
raptor
repros
Rippon
report
repure
ropery
rapist
repass
repast
repose
repost
repute
replum
roquet
requit
reread
rorter

rarefy
rerail
rarely
raring
re-roof
rarity
rascal
reseal
reseat
réseau
roseal
resect
rosace
Reseda
réséda
reside
rasher
rasper
raster
reskew
restem
rester
risker
rosier
rosser
roster
rushee
rushen
rusher
rushes
russel
russet
rusted
resign
re-sign
resaid
reship
roscid
△russia
rustic
Russki
Russky
rashly
resale
resell
resile
resold
resole
result
rosily
rosula
rustle
resume
résumé
resent
rising
rosiny
rusine
rasure
resorb

Words marked △ may be spelled also with a capital letter

resort
rosary
rosery
rostra
rustre
resist
re-site
rosety
rescue
reskue
risque
risqué
ruscus
ratbag
rattan
rat-tat
retial
retral
ritual
rottan
rather
ratted
ratten
ratter
retree
retted
ritter
rother
rotted
rotten
rotter
rutted
rutter
ratify
rotche
ratlin
rat-pit
retail
retain
retrim
retake
rattle
rattly
retell
retile
retold
rotolo
rotula
rutile
retama
retime
ratine
ratiné
rating
retene
retina
retund
retune
rotund
ration
ratios
ratoon
ratton
retook
retool
retrod
retros
re-type
retard
retire
retort
returf
return
re-turn
△rotary
retuse
ratite
rotate
rat-run
retour
rotgut
Rouman
rhumba
raunch
rounce
rouncy
rounds
rouser
routed
router
raunge
reurge
raught
rought
roughy
raucid
roupit
raucle
rouble
roucou
reveal
revied
review
re-view
revved
ravage
rivage
rivlin
revoke
revels
revile
revolt
revamp
ravin'd
ravine
raving
roving
reverb
revere
revers
revert
revery
rivery
ravish
revest
revise
rave-up
rêveur
revive
rewrap
rawing
rewind
rowing
row-dow
reward
rewire
reword
rework
rawish
raylet
rhymed
rhymer
rhythm
△**royals**
rhyton
rizzar
rizzer
rozzer
razzia
razzle
rezone
rizzor
razure
rizard
scalae
scalar
scarab
seaman
Seanad
searat
seaway
shaman
spayad
stalag
statal
swaraj
scabby
shabby
shamba
slabby
swabby
scarce
scatch
sealch
séance
searce
search
slatch
smatch
snatch
stance
stanch
stanck
starch
swatch
shandy
stadda
swaddy
swardy
Saanen
scaled
scaler
△scales
scamel
scared
scarer
scarey
seabed
Seabee
sealed
sealer
seamer
seared
seated
seater
shaded
shades
shaked
shaken
shaker
shamed
shamer
shaped
shapen
shaper
shared
sharer
shares
shaved
shaven
shaver
skater
skates
slated
slater
slaver
slavey
slayed
slayer
snarer
soaked
soaken
soaker
soaper
soarer
spaced
spacer
spacey
spader
spades
spahee
sparer
staged
stager
stagey
stakes
stamen
stapes
starer
stated
stater
△states
staved
staves
stawed
stayed
stayer
swayed
swayer
scarfs
staffs
sealgh
shaggy
slaggy
slangs
slangy
snaggy
sparge
Svarga
Swarga
scathe
snathe
spathe
swashy
swathe
swathy
sea-pig
△sharia
sharif
shavie
sialic
Slavic
soapie
spadix
sparid
spavie
spavin
stadia
stasis
static
statim
shacko
shaikh
slacks
sparke
sparks
sparky
stalko
stalky
swanky
shalli
smalls
'snails
snaily
snarly
spalle
spauld
stable
stably
stalls
staple
suable
suably
shammy
smalmy
smarmy
spammy
sdaine
shanny
sharny
spaing
spawny
stayne
swanny
scazon
seahog
season
shadow
shakos
shalom
shalot
shamoy
△sharon
sialon
slalom
spados
stator
stay-on
Syalon®
scampi
scarpa
scarph
sharps
snappy
swampy
scarr'd
scarre
scarry
scaury
shairn
slairg
sparre
sparry
stairs
starry
stayre
sparse
scaith
scanty
scarth

6 s□a□u

scatty
Shakta
Shakti
shanty
skaith
skarth
smalti
smalto
smarty
snaste
Sparta
sparth
stacte
staith
starts
swarth
swarty
scapus
Scarus
shaduf
shamus
slap-up
statua
statue
status
Shaiva
starve
swarve
snazzy
stanza
stanze
stanzo
sabbat
Sabean
Sabian
subman
subway
subact
sables
sobbed
subbed
subdew
subfeu
sublet
subsea
subset
syboes
sabkha
sobeit
subbie
submit
subtil
sobole
subtle
subtly
Sabine
suborn
suburb
sebate
subito
subdue
subgum
sybows
sacral
siccan
siccar
social
socman
succah
secede
sachem
sachet
sacker
sacred
seckel
secret
sicken
sicker
soccer
socket
succès
sucked
sucken
sucker
sucket
socage
sickie
suck-in
seckle
sickle
sickly
suckle
secant
second
secund
saccos
seccos
sector
succor
secern
secure
secesh
sacque
sacrum
succus
seduce
sadden
sadder
sedged
sodden
sodger
sudden
sudder
sudser
saddhu
siddha
siddhi
sodaic
sodain
saddle
sedile
sodomy
sedent
siding
side-on
sudary
sadism
sadist
sedate
sudate
siddur
sodium
seesaw
Shebat
she-oak
stelae
stelar
snebbe
sheuch
sketch
sleech
smeech
speccy
speech
spence
spetch
stench
speedo
speedy
steady
stedde
steddy
steedy
saeter
seeded
seeder
△seeker
seemer
shekel
shewed
shewel
sieger
skewed
skewer
sleded
slewed
soever
spewer
stereo
steven
stewed
stewer
sweven
Szekel
sheafy
shelfy
sdeign
sheugh
skeigh
sledge
sleigh
Swerga
seethe
scenic
△sheria
sherif
specie
step-in
steric
sheikh
sleeky
sneaky
specks
specky
seemly
sheila
shelly
skeely
skelly
smelly
snelly
steale
stealt
steeld
steels
steely
smegma
steamy
stemma
stemme
scerne
seeing
△sheeny
sienna
steane
sweeny
sterol
sheepo
sheepy
△sherpa
sleepy
steepy
steppe
sweepy
shears
'sheart
sheers
sherry
sierra
skeary
skeery
skerry
smeary
sneery
speary
sperre
steard
steare
steery
sweard
sweert
sweirt
she-ass
smeuse
sneesh
speiss
sperse
sperst
sceatt
'sdeath
sheath
sheets
sheety
Shelta
shelty
siesta
sleety
sleuth
smeath
smeeth
sneath
svelte
sweaty
sweets
sweety
skelum
step-up
sheave
shelve
shelvy
sleave
sleeve
steeve
sterve
swerve
sleaze
sleazy
sleezy
sneeze
sneezy
sifter
soften
suffer
soffit
softie
suffix
sifaka
safely
siffle
softly
safari
Sofism
Sufism
safety
saggar
seggar
signal
sagged
sagger
segued
sigher
signer
signet
sogged
sagoin
saguin
sagely
sagene
seghol
segnos
△signor
sugary
sphear
sahiba
schlep
sphaer
schtik
schuit
schelm
schema
scheme
sphene
△sphinx
school
schorl
sphere
sphery
schism
schist
schuss
schout
schuyt
schizo
shibah
shikar
Shiraz
shivah
smilax
spicae
spicas
spinal
spinar
spiral
spital
Suidae
smirch
snitch
stitch
switch
shindy
smiddy
saikei
sailed
sailer
seiner
seised
seiten
seizer
shined
shiner

Words marked △ may be spelled also with a capital letter

6 s□n□h

Shires
shited
shiver
shives
skiver
slicer
slided
slider
slimes
slived
sliven
sliver
smiler
smilet
smiter
sniper
snivel
soiled
soirée
spiced
spicer
spider
spiked
spikes
spined
spinel
spinet
spirea
spired
stilet
stipel
stipes
stived
stiver
suited
suivez
swiper
swipes
swipey
swivel
swivet
sniffy
spiffy
stingo
stingy
swinge
swingy
saithe
seiche
slight
'slight
smight
smithy
spight
stithy
swishy
seisin
seizin
skivie
spiric
△spirit
stimie
slinky
smirky
sticks
sticky
stinko
stinks
swink't
scilla
shield
skills
skilly
slimly
stifle
stilly
swirly
shimmy
stigma
stigme
swimmy
scient
shinne
shinny
skiing
skinny
soigné
spinny
sailor
sciroc
shivoo
skibob
skidoo
Ski-doo®
slip-on
spigot
suitor
shippo
skimpy
skippy
slippy
snippy
stirps
sbirri
sbirro
shirra
smirry
stirra
stirre
saidst
shiest
Shiism
shiksa
shikse
sliest
slimsy
shifty
Shiite
Shinto
shinty
shirty
shitty
snifty
spilth
stilty
stinty
saique
slip-up
skivvy
spivvy
stieve
sejant
sukkah
sakieh
sakkos
Sukkot
salaam
Salian
sallad
sallal
salpae
salpas
selvas
silvae
silvan
silvas
soldan
sol-fa'd
sollar
sulcal
sultan
sylvae
sylvan
sylvas
sell-by
select
shlock
silica
solace
splice
salade
solidi
sallee
sallet
salted
salter
salue'd
salve'd
salver
seller
selves
silken
siller
siloed
silver
solder
solgel
sol-gel
soller
solver
spleen
sullen
salify
sclaff
scliff
skliff
spliff
silage
sulpha
sylphy
salmis
salvia
selkie
silkie
solein
sylvia
saluki
saltly
solely
salami
solemn
salina
saline
silane
silene
△sileni
silent
sklent
solano
so-long
spline
splint
sallow
salmon
saloon
saloop
saltos
salvor
salvos
'sblood
seldom
solion
salary
sclera
sclere
solera
splore
sultry
Salish
splash
splosh
salute
sclate
sklate
solito
solute
splits
saltus
Seljuk
soleus
sulcus
sulfur
saliva
sclave
solive
salewd
samaan
sambal
sambar
Samian
sampan
simial
simian
simpai
summae
summar
summat
shmock
shmuck
sumach
samiel
samlet
Samoed
seméed
semper
semsem
Semtex®
shmoes
simmer
simnel
simper
somber
summed
summer
samshu
semeia
semmit
simkin
summit
sumpit
samekh
samely
sample
semble
semple
simile
simple
simply
sememe
simony
sambos
samfoo
Samiot
samlor
Samson
'simmon
simoom
simoon
summon
symbol
samara
sempre
simorg
simurg
sombre
samosa
samite
samiti
Semite
somata
somite
sambur
sancai
sandal
sangar
sanjak
sanpan
santal
sendal
sontag
sundae
Sunday
sungar
sunhat
Sunnah
sunray
suntan
syngas
syntan
syntax
Seneca
sonics
sanded
sander
sanies
sansei
sended
sender
sennet
sensed
senses
singed
singer
sinker
sinned
sinner
sinnet
sinter
sonnet
sunbed
sunder
sundew
sunken
sunket
sunned
sunset
syndet
sanify
senega
sancho

Words marked △ may be spelled also with a capital letter

6 s□n□i

sandhi	smouch	**shonky**	**shogun**	Syriac	shreik
Sindhi	**shoddy**	snooks	slow-up	Syrian	sordid
sannie	swords	spooky	**snooze**	**scribe**	sortie
santir	**scolex**	stocks	snoozy	scrobe	spraid
sennit	scorer	stocky	**sappan**	Scrubs	sprain
sonsie	scoter	**shoaly**	sepmag	strobe	spruik
sunkie	shoder	shoole	septal	**sprack**	spruit
sunlit	shorer	should	**sapped**	spruce	straik
syndic	shovel	skolly	sapper	strich	strain
sanely	shover	slowly	sephen	strict	strait
senile	showed	smoile	sepses	struck	surfie
single	shower	smoyle	septet	**scryde**	syrtis
singly	sloken	spoils	sipped	spredd	**scrike**
sonant	sloven	spoilt	sipper	stride	shrike
sankos	smoked	stools	sippet	strode	strake
santon	smoker	**sloomy**	sopped	**sardel**	strike
Senhor	snorer	stormy	supped	sarney	stroke
senior	soogee	**Sloane**	supper	sarsen	**scroll**
sensor	soojey	spoony	sypher	screed	shrill
sindon	sooner	stonne	**sapego**	screen	sorell
sunbow	spoken	stound	**Sappho**	scried	sorely
sundog	stogey	stownd	**sepsis**	scryer	spryly
sun-god	stoker	swound	septic	series	stroll
Syncom	stokes	swoune	**sapele**	server	surely
synroc	stoled	swownd	sapple	shreek	**scramb**
senary	stolen	swowne	sipple	shriek	scrimp
Señora	stoned	**sholom**	supple	sirred	scrump
sentry	stonen	smokos	supply	sirree	serums
soneri	stoner	spot-on	**supine**	skreen	shrimp
sundra	storer	stolon	**siphon**	skryer	skrimp
sundri	stores	**shoppy**	syphon	sorbet	skrump
sundry	storey	sloppy	**superb**	sorner	stramp
Senusi	stover	snoopy	**sapota**	sorrel	stroma
sanity	stower	stoope	sopite	sorter	stromb
senate	**spoffy**	**stoury**	**sapful**	sortes	struma
sonata	**shough**	stowre	Sapium	spryer	**saring**
sannup	slough	**scorse**	sepium	streek	sarong
santur	smoggy	△scouse	septum	streel	scrine
send-up	sponge	skoosh	**supawn**	△street	scrunt
sensum	spongy	sloosh	**sequel**	surbed	scryne
sinful	stodge	smouse	**sequin**	surbet	serang
sinewy	stodgy	spouse	**screak**	surfer	△serene
Scogan	stooge	stoush	scream	surrey	serine
scopae	stop-go	swoosh	serdab	survew	shrank
scopas	storge	**Scotty**	serial	survey	shrine
shofar	**sloshy**	scouth	serrae	syrtes	shrink
shoran	soothe	scowth	serran	**scruff**	shrunk
Siouan	sposhy	shorts	serras	shrift	sprang
slogan	**scolia**	shorty	serval	shroff	sprent
Slovak	scoria	shotte	sircar	strafe	△spring
Sno-cat®	△scotia	smooth	sirdar	straff	sprint
stomal	Scotic	snooty	Sirian	strife	sprong
storax	shojis	snorty	sirkar	strift	sprung
slobby	shoo-in	snotty	sirrah	**sorage**	strand
snobby	skolia	snouty	spread	Strega®	strene
sconce	soogie	sports	streak	striga	Strine
scorch	stobie	sporty	stream	**sorgho**	string
△scotch	stogie	spotty	striae	**sarnie**	strond
slouch	stolid	spouty	stroam	serail	strong
smooch	Suomic	stouth	surtax	serein	strung

Words marked △ may be spelled also with a capital letter

strunt
syrinx
sargos
sartor
scroop
sermon
seroon
sorgos
sorrow
strook
sarape
scrape
script
serape
seraph
seriph
stripe
stripy
syrupy
serosa
sprush
strass
stress
Syrism
scruto
sprite
strata
strath
Sûreté
surety
sargus
serous
△shroud
Sirius
sorbus
sprout
stroud
stroup
strout
scrive
shrive
△shrove
strive
strove
scrawl
scrawm
screwy
scrowl
scrows
shrewd
shrowd
sprawl
strawn
strawy
strewn
strown
scraye
strays
syrlye
scruze

sashay
sestet
sister
sussed
△system
siskin
suslik
seseli
sesame
sasine
seston
sissoo
sistra
Sathan
satnav
satrap
sittar
shtick
shtuck
sateen
settee
setter
sithen
sithes
sitrep
sitter
sotted
sutler
suttee
sythes
set-off
shtchi
Sothic
settle
setule
situla
sutile
suttle
suttly
shtumm
satang
satiny
set-tos
set-to's
shtook
shtoom
sitcom
satara
satire
satori
Saturn
satyra
suture
setose
shtetl
set-out
sative
scutal
soutar
squeak

squeal
slubby
snubbe
snubby
stubby
scutch
sluice
sluicy
smutch
source
stucco
sounds
spuddy
squids
sturdy
saucer
sauger
saurel
sautés
souled
souper
soused
souses
souter
squier
stumer
scurfy
snuffy
squiff
stuffy
saulge
scunge
scungy
sludge
sludgy
smudge
smudgy
snudge
spunge
spurge
stuggy
slushy
sought
saulie
shut-in
squail
studio
stupid
shucks
spunky
sculle
sculls
smugly
snugly
souple
sourly
squall
squill
scummy
slummy

squama
squame
spurne
squint
squiny
stupor
sculpt
slumpy
stumps
stumpy
scurry
skurry
slurry
smurry
souari
spurry
△square
squire
squirm
squirr
squirt
sourse
squash
squish
stuns'l
shufti
shufty
smutty
scutum
sputum
scurvy
squawk
spulye
scuzzy
sovran
savvey
Sèvres
△soviet
savage
savant
savine
saving
sevens
savory
severe
severy
savate
savour
sawder
△sawney
sawyer
sowder
sowter
sewage
sawpit
saw-fly
sawing
sewing
sowans
sowens

sowing
△siwash
sowsse
sextan
sexual
six-day
sextet
sexfid
sixain
△saxony
sexpot
sexton
sexism
sexist
saxaul
six-gun
△skylab
skyman
skyway
stylar
styrax
stylet
scyphi
scythe
sayyid
stymie
Scylla
saying
shying
skying
spying
stying
stylos
sayest
shyest
shyish
skyish
slyest
slyish
stylus
sazhen
syzygy
sizzle
sozzle
sozzly
sizing
sizism
sizist
thanah
tiara'd
trapan
tsamba
thatch
trance
teamed
teamer
tearer
teasel
teaser
teated

teazel
thaler
thawer
tracer
traces
traded
trader
trades
trapes
travel
Tuareg
twangy
trashy
Thalia
tragic
travis
thanks
tracks
Tuanku
teagle
teazle
thalli
trauma
teaing
thanna
tranny
trayne
teapot
teapoy
trappy
thairm
transe
toasty
twaite
teacup
Teague
tragus
tebbad
Tib-cat
tibiae
tibial
tibias
tabbed
tabled
tables
tablet
tabret
tabued
tubber
tabefy
tubage
tabula
tubule
tubing
taboos
tabard
taberd
Tibert
Tyburn
Tebeth

6 t□b□u

tubate
tabour
tubful
tic-tac
tacked
tacker
tacket
teckel
ticked
ticken
ticker
ticket
tickey
tocher
tucker
tucket
tactic
tocsin
tuck-in
tackle
tickle
tickly
techno
tachos
tycoon
tectum
tuchun
tedded
tedder
tidied
taddie
Tadjik
teddie
tidbit
tiddle
tiddly
tidily
toddle
tedium
Theban
thecae
thecal
thenar
tietac
toecap
toerag
trepan
thence
thetch
tierce
tiercé
trench
trendy
tweeds
tweedy
tee-hee
teemed
teemer
teepee
tee-tee

teeter
Thebes
themed
theses
thewed
thewes
tiered
tmeses
tee-off
teethe
taenia
Themis
Theria
thesis
thetic
tiepin
tie-wig
tmesis
tremie
trémie
trepid
trevis
Thecla
they'll
treble
trebly
tweely
therms
teeing
theine
toeing
tweeny
tierod
toetoe
trek-ox
tremor
theirs
theory
they're
teensy
theism
theist
tressy
tsetse
tzetse
teenty
treaty
twenty
theave
they've
△twelve
tweeze
toffee
tuffet
tufted
tufter
taffia
tiffin
to-fall
Teflon®

tofore
tifosi
tifoso
tagrag
taguan
tagged
taggee
tagger
tegmen
tigged
togaed
togged
tugged
tugger
tugrik
tegula
toggle
tag-end
tiglon
tigery
tughra
tights
togate
tchick
tahsil
tahina
tahini
T-shirt
taipan
thiram
tribal
tricar
trinal
trilby
taisch
triact
twitch
triode
tailed
taiver
△thibet
thivel
toiled
toiler
toilet
tri-jet
trimer
tripey
trivet
twicer
twined
twiner
things
thingy
triage
twiggy
twinge
taiaha
twight
trifid

trivia
twilit
thicko
thicky
tricks
tricky
taigle
taille
thible
thinly
trials
trifle
trigly
trillo
trimly
triple
triply
tuille
twilly
twirly
triune
tailor
Tainos
toison
toitoi
tricot
trigon
tripod
tripos
△triton
thirst
thirty
triste
twisty
thin'un
trisul
thieve
tailye
tajine
takahe
take-in
taking
token'd
tykish
take-up
taleae
tallat
tele-ad
telial
tellar
tulban
tulwar
teledu
Toledo
talced
talker
tallet
talweg
telfer
tellen

teller
tiller
tilted
tilter
toller
tolsel
tolsey
Toltec
tolter
tolzey
telega
Telegu
Telugu
talkie
talk-in
tellin
til-oil
toluic
talcky
taluka
talant
talent
tiling
toling
talbot
talion
tallot
tallow
telson
tol-lol
toluol
Tulipa
telary
tilery
telesm
T-cloth
T-plate
tylote
talcum
△talmud
telium
△tellus
tambac
tammar
tam-tam
timbal
tombac
tombak
tomcat
tomial
tymbal
tympan
tamber
tamper
tempeh
temper
timber
tumefy
tumphy
tombic

tomtit
tamale
tamely
△temple
timely
tumble
tumuli
tumult
tamanu
tamine
taming
timing
tampon
tempos
timbós
tomboc
tomboy
tompon
tom-tom
tamara
tamari
timbre
tamise
timist
tomato
Tammuz
timous
tomium
tumour
tum-tum
tankas
tannah
tan-vat
teniae
tincal
tindal
tineal
tinman
tonnag
Tanach
tenace
tan-bed
tandem
tanged
tanked
tanker
tanned
tanner
tanrec
tended
tender
tenner
tenrec
tented
tenter
tenues
tinded
tinder
tinier
tinies

Words marked △ may be spelled also with a capital letter

tinker
tinned
tinner
tinsel
tinsey
tinted
tinter
Tonies
tonker
tonlet
Tunker
△tunnel
tangie
tankia
tannic
tannin
tan-pit
tenail
tennis
tenpin
tentie
tenuis
tineid
tinnie
tonsil
tinaja
Tengku
tangle
tangly
tingle
tingly
tinily
tinkle
tinkly
to-name
toneme
tenant
tonant
toning
tuning
tangos
Tannoy®
tannoy
tendon
tenson
tensor
tenzon
tinpot
tondos
tonsor
△tantra
tendre
tenure
tundra
tanist
tonish
tenuto
tonite
tangun
tenour

tinful
tongue
tundun
Tungus
Thorah
thorax
trocar
Trojan
Troyan
two-way
troade
thowel
tooler
tooter
trover
trowel
though
troggs
trough
toothy
troche
trophi
trophy
thoria
toorie
tropic
two-bit
troika
tootle
troely
trolly
troule
two-ply
'twould
thorny
tholoi
tholos
thoron
too-too
trogon
thorpe
trompe
troops
troppo
troupe
tooart
Taoism
Taoist
tootsy
trouse
tsotsi
trouts
trouty
tholus
trotyl
tipcat
top-hat
topman
Tupian
tapped

tapper
tappet
tipped
tipper
tippet
Tippex
Tipp-Ex®
Tophet
topped
topper
tupped
tepefy
tip-off
typify
tappit
Tupaia
tipple
tipula
topple
tupelo
typing
tiptoe
tiptop
△typhon
tephra
tapist
typist
tapeta
tapeti
tophus
typhus
Tarmac®
tarmac
tarnal
tarpan
tarras
tarsal
Tartan®
tartan
△tartar
Tarzan
tergal
ternal
terrae
Terran
terras
thread
threap
threat
throat
turban
Tyrian
thrice
turaco
teredo
tirade
tarcel
target
tarred
tarsel

tercel
tercet
termer
Termes
terret
three-D
threep
throes
tiroes
torret
torsel
torten
tortes
tureen
turfed
turfen
turkey
turned
turner
turret
turves
tyroes
tariff
terefa
thrift
Torify
Toryfy
tarsia
terbic
tercio
territ
tertia
tirrit
toroid
torpid
torrid
turbid
turbit
turgid
Turkic
turkis
turn-in
turnip
tartly
termly
thrall
thrill
torula
toruli
turtle
tarand
taring
thrang
threne
throne
throng
tiring
torana
to-rend
to-rent

tyrant
tar-box
tarboy
tarpon
tarrow
termor
△terror
torpor
torsos
turbos
turbot
Turcos
turgor
turion
turn-on
teraph
thrips
torero
T-cross
thrash
thresh
thrist
thrush
thrust
torose
tarots
terata
terete
Targum
tarsus
tergum
T-group
torous
torque
Turdus
turn-up
thrave
thrive
throve
thrawn
thraws
throwe
thrown
tiswas
Tuscan
tuskar
tussah
tussal
tisick
tasker
taslet
tassel
tasset
tasted
taster
testee
tester
testes
tosher
tossed

tossen
tosser
tusked
tusker
tusseh
tusser
tusche
tassie
testis
tushie
tussis
tystie
tussle
tisane
teston
Tishri
tissue
toss-up
tetrad
△titian
to-tear
T-strap
tutman
tutsan
tatler
tatter
tether
tetter
titfer
tithed
tither
titled
titler
titles
ti-tree
titter
tother
t'other
totted
totter
tutted
tetchy
titchy
tattie
tettix
titbit
tottie
tutrix
titoki
tattle
titely
tittle
titule
tatami
tetany
tattoo
tattow
titupy
Tatary
totara

Words marked △ may be spelled also with a capital letter

6 t□t□u

tittup
tut-tut
Tethys
tetryl
toucan
thumby
tauten
toupee
toupet
tourer
touser
touter
thuggo
trudge
taught
touché
touchy
truthy
taupie
tauric
tautit
thulia
tourie
toutie
tsuris
trunks
tautly
tousle
touzle
truant
tautog
Teuton
trumps
truism
trusty
Taurus
tavern
tavers
tavert
towbar
tow-rag
thwack
tawney
towhee
townee
tow-net
△towser
towage
tawpie
tawtie
tewhit
townie
townly
tawing
towing
Tswana
towmon
tu-whoo
tawdry
tawery
tewart
thwart
toward
towery
taxman
tuxedo
taxied
taxies
Tex-Mex
toxoid
taxing
toyman
thymic
thyine
toying
trying
thymol
Trygon
tuyère
twyere
thyrse
thyrsi
toyish
thymus
try-out
tazzas
tizwas
ujamaa
usance
unawed
usager
usages
uracil
Uralic
Urania
uranic
uranin
unable
usable
usably
uraeus
Uranus
uranyl
umbrae
umbral
umbras
unbear
unbias
upbear
upbeat
up-beat
upbray
umbles
umbrel
unbred
umbril
upboil
unbelt
unbolt
unbend
unbent
unbind
unbone
upbind
urbane
unboot
upblow
umbery
unbare
unbark
unborn
unbury
unbusy
unbitt
uncial
unclad
uncock
unclew
uncage
uncoil
upcoil
urchin
uncolt
upcome
uncini
unclog
uncool
uncape
uncope
uncart
uncord
uncork
uncurl
upcurl
uncase
upcast
uncate
uncowl
undead
undeaf
undear
undraw
updrag
updraw
undeck
undock
undies
undoer
undyed
unduly
undine
undone
undern
undate
update
ureide
uneven
uneyed
ureter
unedge
uredia
uremia
uremic
uresis
uretic
usedn't
unease
uneasy
uberty
uneath
used-up
useful
uterus
uveous
unfact
unfeed
unfree
unfair
unfelt
unfold
upfill
unfine
unfool
upflow
unfirm
unform
unfurl
upfurl
ungear
unglad
ungual
ungues
upgrew
ungain
unguis
ungild
ungilt
ungula
upgang
urgent
urging
upgrow
ungird
ungirt
ungord
Utgard
upgush
unglue
ungyve
ungown
upgaze
unhead
unheal
upheap
unhair
unhele
unhelm
unholy
upheld
uphild
uphill
uphold
unhand
unhang
unhung
uphand
uphang
unhood
unhook
unhoop
uphroe
unhurt
uphurl
unhasp
unhusk
uphaud
unhive
unhewn
unital
urinal
uniped
unisex
united
uniter
ulitis
unific
ukiyo-e
ulicon
ulikon
unipod
unison
ubiety
Uniate
ubique
unique
unjust
upkeep
unknit
upknit
unkent
unkind
unking
unknot
unkept
uakari
uckers
unkiss
unlead
unleal
unload
uplead
uplean
upleap
unlace
unlich
unlock
uplock
unlade
uglify
uplift
ullage
unlaid
unlike
uglily
unlime
ulling
unline
unlink
upland
up-line
uplink
uplook
unlord
unlash
unlast
unless
unlost
umlaut
unlive
unlove
unmade
unmeek
unmeet
unmake
upmake
unmoor
unmard
unmiry
unmask
upmost
utmost
unmown
unnail
urning
ulnare
unnest
urnful
unowed
up-over
ulosis
urosis
△utopia
uropod
unpray
unpack
unpick
unpaid
unpent
upping
unprop
unpope
umpire
uppers
uppish
uppity
unplug
Ugrian
unread
unreal
uprear

Words marked △ may be spelled also with a capital letter

6 v□s□u

uproar
unrobe
unredy
unrude
unreel
unrein
unrake
unroll
unrule
unruly
uproll
unrent
unroof
unroot
uproot
unripe
unrope
unrest
uprest
uprise
uprist
uprose
uprush
upryst
uprate
unseal
unseam
unseat
unsnap
unspar
upstay
upsway
upside
ulster
unseel
unseen
unshed
unsped
unstep
unsafe
unsoft
unsaid
unship
unspi'd
unsuit
unself
unsold
ugsome
unsent
unsung
upsend
ursine
unshod
unshoe
unshot
unstop
unstow
upshot
unsure
unshut

unsoul
unspun
unsewn
unsown
unteam
unthaw
uptear
untack
untuck
urtica
untidy
untied
untrim
uptake
untile
untold
up-till
uptilt
ultima
ultimo
untame
untomb
untent
untune
ultion
untrod
ustion
untorn
unturf
unturn
uptorn
upturn
untrue
uptown
urtext
uvulae
uvular
uvulas
unused
uruses
usurer
unvail
unveil
unweal
unwrap
upwrap
upwaft
unwell
unwill
upwell
unwind
unwont
upwind
up-wind
unwept
unware
unwary
unwire
unwork
unworn

upward
usward
unwise
unwish
unwist
unwive
unyoke
Veadar
viands
vealer
viable
viator
Vibram®
vibrio
vibist
vacked
victim
vocals
vocule
vacant
vicuña
vector
victor
vicary
vacate
vacuum
vidual
vidame
videos
vadose
Vedism
Vedist
veduta
vedute
viewer
vielle
viewly
vegies
voguer
voguey
veggie
vagile
vagina
vagrom
vagary
vigoro
vegete
vigour
△**vehmic**
vahine
V-shape
vihara
veiled
veined
voiced
voicer
voided
voidee
voider
vainly

Vaisya
vakeel
△**viking**
vakass
vallar
valval
valvar
villan
villar
△vulcan
vulgar
vulval
vulvar
veloce
valley
valued
valuer
values
valved
vellet
velvet
volley
vulned
Vulpes
vilify
volage
vildly
vilely
volume
valine
Volans
volant
volens
vellon
volvox
Velcro®
velure
volary
volery
valise
volost
valeta
valete
valuta
velate
veleta
volute
valgus
Valium®
vallum
valour
vellum
velour
villus
vulgus
vomica
vamper
Vimule®
vimana
vamose

vomito
△**vandal**
venial
Venice
vanned
vanner
vendee
vender
veneer
venger
vennel
vented
venter
vendis
ventil
venule
vendor
ven'son
venery
venire
ventre
vinery
vintry
vanish
venose
vanity
venite
vendue
venous
vinous
venewe
violer
violet
violin
voodoo
vapour
varsal
verbal
vermal
vernal
versal
vorpal
varech
varied
varier
varlet
varved
varvel
verdet
verger
verier
△vermes
verrel
verrey
versed
verser
verset
vertex
'vervel
verven

vervet
virger
vortex
verify
virago
vorago
verbid
verdin
verdit
Verein
verlig
vermil
vermin
vermis
versin
△virgin
viroid
verily
virile
Varuna
virent
virino
vorant
△**varroa**
verdoy
versos
vireos
virion
verism
verist
virose
verity
versus
vertue
virous
virtue
vassal
△vestal
vestas
vista'd
vistal
visual
vesica
△**vesper**
vessel
vested
visaed
viséed
visier
visage
viscid
viscin
vastly
visile
Vishnu
vision
vistos
vestry
visite
△**viscum**

Words marked △ may be spelled also with a capital letter

6 V□S□V

viscus
visive
△vatman
vittae
vatted
vatter
vetoes
vetted
voteen
vetchy
vitric
vitals
vittle
votary
vatful
votive
vaunce
voulge
vaudoo
voudou
vaulty
vaunty
vivace
vivres
vivify
vively
vivary
vivers
vowels
vaward
vowess
vexing
voyage
voyeur
vizier
vizzie
vizsla
vizard
weaken
weanel
weaner
wearer
weasel
weaved
weaver
weazen
whaler
whaten
woaded
wharfs
wrathy
wealk'd
whacko
whacky
weakly
whally
wraxle
whammo
whammy
whatna
weapon
whatso
wrasse
wealth
wraith
wharve
webbed
wabain
wabbit
wabble
wobble
wobbly
waboom
wiccan
wacker
wicked
wicken
wicker
wicket
wadmal
wadded
wadset
wedded
wedder
wedged
widget
waddie
wedgie
widgie
waddle
△wedeln
widdle
widely
wading
wadmol
waders
widish
whenas
wheech
whence
wrench
wretch
wieldy
weeded
weeder
weeper
weeten
weever
wee-wee
wheyey
Wiener
wheugh
wrethe
weepie
weevil
wienie
whelk'd
whelky
weekly
wheels
wheely
wheare
wherry
wheesh
wreath
waeful
woeful
wheeze
wheezy
wafted
wafter
waffle
waffly
wifely
wafery
wigwag
wigwam
wagged
wigged
waggle
waggly
wiggle
wiggly
woggle
waggon
wigeon
wah-wah
Wahabi
wahine
whidah
weirdo
Weirds
wailer
waiter
waiver
whiles
whiner
whited
whiten
whites
△whitey
writer
whiffy
whinge
weight
whisht
wright
writhe
whisky
whilly
whirly
whimmy
whinny
wait-on
whilom
whippy
whirry
whilst
whimsy
wriest
wristy
wakiki
wakane
waking
wake-up
Walian
wallah
△walker
walled
waller
wallet
welder
welter
wilder
willed
willer
willet
willey
wolfer
wolver
wolves
walk-in
wallie
welkin
wellie
willie
wiltja
wildly
wilily
walk-on
wallop
wallow
weldor
willow
Wilton
walise
walk-up
walnut
walrus
wilful
wombat
wampee
wombed
wamble
wambly
wimble
wimple
woman'd
womera
Wemyss
wammus
wampum
wampus
wangan
windac
windas
wander
wanker
wanned
wannel
wanted
wanter
wended
wincer
wincey
winded
winder
winged
winger
winker
winner
winsey
winter
wonder
wonned
wonted
wunner
Wendic
wandle
wangle
wankle
windle
winkle
winnle
wintle
waning
woning
wandoo
wanion
wanton
△window
winnow
winery
wintry
wangun
wind-up
wooded
wooden
woofed
woofer
woolen
woosel
wroken
woodie
wholly
woolly
wooing
whoops
whoosh
woodsy
wroath
woobut
wapped
wapper
wippen
wopped
wiping
wapiti
warman
warran
warray
worral
warded
warden
warder
warmed
warmer
warner
warped
warper
warred
warren
warrey
warted
worded
worked
worker
wormed
wormer
worrel
worsen
worser
wurley
worthy
work-in
worrit
warble
warily
warmly
warsle
wirily
wortle
wiring
wardog
warmth
warm-up
washed
washen
washer
wasted
wastel
waster
wastes
wester
wisher
wishes
wisket
wash-in
waspie
Westie
wisely
wistly
wesand
wisent
△wisdom
wastry
wisard
wash-up
witgat
withal

Words marked △ may be spelled also with a capital letter

6 z□u□v

wether
wetted
wither
witted
witter
wotted
wuther
witchy
within
with-it
wattle
wet-fly
wittol
waters
watery
woundy
wauker
waured
waucht
waught
woubit
wou-wou
waurst
wavily
waving
wavery
wivern
wyvern
wowser
wow-wow
wax-red
waxily
waxing
waylay
whydah
why-not
weyard
wryest

way-out
wizier
wuzzle
wezand
wizard
X-rated
xoanon
xyloid
xyloma
xylene
xylose
xenial
xenium
Xhosan
X-craft
xeroma
xyster
xystoi
xystos
xystus
ynambu
yearly
yeasty
yabber
yabbie
yobbos
yacker
yicker
yucker
yodler
Y-level
yaffle
yagger
yogini
yogurt
yogism
Yahveh
Yahweh

yo-ho-ho
yshend
yah-boo
ypight
yoicks
yojana
yakker
yikker
yoking
yukata
yakuza
yelper
yolked
yblent
Y-alloy
yellow
yclept
yplast
yammer
△yumpie
Yemeni
yum-yum
Yankee
yanker
yonder
yonker
yankie
yanqui
yeoman
yeomen
ybound
yoo-hoo
yaourt
yapock
yapper
yippee
yipper
yopper

yappie
△yuppie
yaqona
Yoruba
Y-track
yorker
yarpha
Yardie
△yorkie
ywroke
yarely
ybrent
yarrow
yes-man
yesses
yester
yes-but
yatter
yttria
yttric
youths
youthy
you-all
yaupon
yawper
yowley
Yezidi
△zealot
Zabian
zebeck
zabeta
zoccos
zodiac
zaddik
zoetic
zaffer
zufoli
zufolo

zaffre
zigzag
zagged
zigged
zygoma
zygose
zygote
zillah
zelant
zeloso
Zimmer®
zimmer
zombie
zymoid
zymome
zamang
zambos
zymase
zymite
△zambuk
Zunian
Zuñian
zander
zinced
zingel
zinger
zinked
zonked
zendik
zinnia
zonoid
zincky
zonula
zonule
zenana
zoning
zincos
zonary

zonure
Zenist
zenith
zonate
zooeal
zoonal
zoonic
zoozoo
zlotys
zapper
zipped
zipper
zip-off
ziptop
zapata
△zephyr
Zyrian
zareba
zariba
zereba
zeriba
zarnec
zeroed
zorino
zircon
zorros
zarape
zeroth
zester
zoster
zither
zythum
zounds
zeugma
Zouave

Words marked △ may be spelled also with a capital letter

7 a□a□a

apadana
atalaya
Aramaic
anatase
apanage
atamans
adamant
agaçant
amarant
ataraxy
anarchy
acaudal
Abaddon
abandon
alameda
araneid
academe
Araceae
Araneae
acaleph
amateur
anapest
academy
amalgam
abashed
ataghan
arachis
Acarida
Acarina
amanita
arabica
acarine
Adamite
alanine
amabile
amative
apatite
arabise
arabize
avarice
amazing
awaking
abaxial
adaxial
anaxial
Arabism
atavism
Acadian
acarian
amation
Arabian
Azanian
acacias
adagios
Ananias
Arabist
anaemia
anaemic
alarmed
acapnia
alannah

against
araroba
acaroid
agamoid
abalone
alamode
anagoge
apagoge
acatour
agamous
alamort
amatory
anagogy
analogy
anatomy
anagram
atabrin
acantha
atactic
adapted
abactor
adapter
adaptor
abattis
anattos
abature
alarums
analyse
analyze
analyst
ambs-ace
arblast
albedos
ambient
albugos
ambages
ambling
aiblins
albumen
albumin
albinic
albinos
ambones
ambroid
ambered
auberge
Alberti
albergo
arboret
Abbasid
ambassy
albitic
ambatch
arbiter
arbutus
ambitty
archaic
arcuate
acclaim
arc-lamp
accoast

accablé
aecidia
ascidia
arcaded
accidie
acceder
Alcides
alchera
accrete
ancress
△archeus
ancient
alchemy
archery
arch-foe
alcohol
accoied
arctiid
alcaide
archive
ascribe
arcking
auction
Alcaics
alcalde
archlet
accompt
accinge
asconce
arcanum
accents
ancones
arctoid
anchovy
alcorza
ascarid
accurse
Alcoran
ascaris
accurst
accused
accusal
accuser
ascesis
ascetic
ascitic
ascites
accrual
account
accourt
ascaunt
archway
accoyed
accoyld
alcayde
alchymy
alcázar
audible
audibly
adducer
address

aidless
addrest
audient
andvile
ardrigh
ard-righ
abdomen
addenda
aidance
andante
ardency
android
arduous
andiron
auditor
acerate
acetate
amenage
ames-ace
anelace
average
abeyant
agelast
apetaly
acerbic
alembic
amender
axe-head
ageless
aweless
alength
avenger
aheight
ape-shit
Amerind
adenine
alepine
alewife
alerion
atelier
acetify
amenity
areolae
Ameslan
areolar
adermin
Avernus
adenoma
adenoid
aneroid
apehood
acerose
acetone
acetose
ale-pole
anemone
awesome
ale-hoof
agelong
acerous
acetous

alecost
averred
aleuron
aneurin
atebrin
amearst
apepsia
asepses
asepsis
amentia
aseptic
Avestic
abetted
averted
aventre
abettal
amental
amentum
Avertin®
Avestan
abetter
abettor
adeptly
alertly
ale-bush
asexual
areaway
affeard
affear'd
affeare
aufgabe
affable
affably
affiche
A-effect
affaire
affying
affairs
afflict
alfalfa
awfully
affined
affoord
affront
alfaquí
alforja
afforce
alférez
aefauld
aggrace
aggrade
aggrate
algebra
angicos
aggress
augment
△**anglice**
anguine
angling
anguish
Anglian

Words marked △ may be spelled also with a capital letter

7 a□o□o

anglist
anglify
angrily
angekok
angelic
Angolan
angular
angelus
argulus
alginic
anginal
angioma
argyria
augural
augurer
angerly
algesia
auguste
algesis
arguses
augitic
algates
Angevin
ashrama
athwart
adhibit
aphides
athleta
achieve
athlete
Achaean
ash-heap
awheels
aphagia
aphthae
atheise
atheize
athrill
atheism
Achaian
atheist
aphelia
aphylly
ashamed
aphonia
aphonic
athanor
ash-hole
atheous
acharya
adharma
Amharic
acharné
Acheron
adherer
athirst
ash-tray
aphasia
aphasic
aphesis
aphetic

aphotic
△**achates**
ashiver
agitate
alidade
animate
alizari
abigail
agitato
Arimasp
alicant
amiable
amiably
abidden
amildar
aniseed
aliment
agilely
atingle
atishoo
a-tishoo
a-rights
apishly
aniline
asinine
axinite
abiding
animism
△**apician**
Azilian
asinico
animist
ability
acidify
acidity
agility
anility
aridity
avidity
axillae
axillar
arillus
axially
anionic
Asianic
avionic
aliened
alienee
aliunde
aginner
alienor
acinose
adipose
aciform
aliform
aviform
acinous
alimony
aripple
abiosis
aliases

ariosos
arietta
abiotic
Asiatic
ariette
aviette
agister
agistor
aviator
aristos
Avicula
azimuth
aliquot
apiezon
adjudge
abjoint
adjoint
adjunct
abjurer
adjourn
awkward
asklent
alkalis
ack-emma
askance
alkanet
anklong
acknown
Alkoran
askaris
askesis
anklung
aulnage
all-hail
axle-box
alledge
allseed
allheal
all-seer
allness
ailment
alleged
allegge
allegro
alleger
awlbird
all-time
all-wing
allying
aclinic
allonge
allonym
ailanto
aplanat
aplenty
all-good
all-work
aileron
allurer
allergy
aplasia

atlases
ailette
ablator
all-star
ally-tor
ally-taw
alluvia
all-over
allowed
alleyed
allayer
armband
Asmoday
aimless
armless
arm-rest
alms-fee
armiger
Almaine
armoire
Acmeism
Acmeist
armilla
alms-man
ammonia
almanac
ammonal
almoner
almonry
armhole
armlock
Armoric
almirah
admiral
ammiral
Aymaran
admirer
Aymaras
ammeter
armfuls
armoury
annicut
awnless
alnager
annuity
annelid
annular
annulus
annulet
agnamed
agnomen
aeneous
Arnaout
agnosia
amnesia
amnesic
amnesty
annatta
agnatic
annatto
arnotto

annates
annoyed
annoyer
abomasa
avocado
amorant
anomaly
apogamy
amoebic
amoebae
amoebas
acouchi
acouchy
apogeal
apogean
alonely
anorexy
aloofly
abought
alongst
amongst
apothem
another
aconite
adonise
adonize
agonise
agonize
amosite
anodise
anodize
atomise
atomize
azotise
azotize
abolish
amorini
alodial
asocial
alodium
amorism
Anobium
atomism
△**aeolian**
aeonian
amorino
agogics
agonist
amorist
atomist
aboulia
apollos
apoplex
anosmia
acorned
amorosa
apocope
axolotl
amoroso
amorous
apodous

Words marked △ may be spelled also with a capital letter

7 a□o□o

atokous
azotous
apology
arousal
arouser
anoeses
anoesis
aloetic
anoetic
adopted
△**apostle**
apostil
adopter
avoutry
anonyma
acolyte
anodyne
acolyth
applaud
appease
appeach
asprawl
asphalt
aspidia
aspread
adpress
appress
applied
appuied
apprise
apprize
applier
appoint
amplify
ampulla
appulse
appalti
appalto
amphora
approve
approof
alphorn
asprout
asperge
asperse
apparel
apperil
aspirin
apports
apparat
Aspasia
apposer
ampassy
amputee
ampoule
appuyed
asphyxy
acquest
acquire
acquite
acquist
asquint
air-raid
airward
acreage
airbase
air-lane
airwave
arriage
aureate
abroach
air-bath
airmail
air-rail
arrears
abreact
abreast
already
aerobic
aerobus
acrobat
auricle
African
aurochs
apricot
abridge
acridin
airhead
arreede
arriéré
air-bell
air-cell
arriero
airless
agraffe
acrogen
alright
airship
airline
airside
airtime
'Arryish
airsick
arraign
air-miss
airlift
aureity
aurelia
acrylic
Acrilan®
airflow
aurally
acromia
Ahriman
Aaronic
arrange
adrenal
acronym
aureola
abrooke
airhole
aureole
airlock
air-lock
air-cool
airfoil
airport
agrapha
atropia
atropin
apropos
Atropos
atrophy
aurorae
auroral
air-drop
air-trap
auroras
air-crew
atresia
agrised
arrased
agraste
aerosol
aurated
airstop
acroter
aerator
aground
air-pump
atriums
agravic
arrival
apraxia
△**abraxas**
arrayal
arrayer
arroyos
abrazos
assuage
asswage
abstain
apsidal
apsides
assiege
Auslese
austere
arsheen
abscess
assagai
assegai
assigns
Aeschna
abscind
abscise
arshine
auspice
aisling
absciss
absolve
assumed
arsenic
absence
absinth
arsenal
abscond
alsoone
asshole
Austric
assured
△**austral**
also-ran
assurer
apsaras
Alsatia
ansated
assault
assever
assayer
assizer
assizes
althaea
astrand
abthane
actuate
amtrack
attract
actuary
actable
astable
autobus
attaboy
antacid
anticke
article
attaché
autocue
autocar
Actaeon
Aetnean
antbear
actress
aptness
artless
antient
attuent
antefix
antigen
ant-eggs
antigay
aitches
antbird
antliae
astride
attrite
attuite
Althing
ant-hill
asteism
antlion
astrict
attaint
attrist
astelic
astilbe
antilog
astylar
artsman
attempt
automat
autumny
actinia
antenna
actinic
attonce
actinal
antonym
autonym
actinon
attones
anthoid
astroid
asthore
art-song
artwork
althorn
aftmost
Anthony
autopsy
antique
apteria
asteria
altered
asterid
alterne
Astarte
apteral
Antares
anthrax
apteryx
autarky
altesse
artiste
artisan
attaskt
aptotic
astatic
astatki
astound
autovac
antiwar
altezza
abusage
adulate
ajutage
asudden
asunder
azurean
azulejo
aculeus
acutely
aquafer
aquifer
ague-fit
ahungry

Words marked △ may be spelled also with a capital letter

7 b□e□k

acushla
alumina
abusive
alunite
amusive
azurine
azurite
amusing
alumish
alumium
abusion
△**aquilon**
alumnae
alumnus
anurous
aqueous
aquaria
aquatic
abutted
abuttal
abutter
arugula
aquiver
aquavit
alveary
advices
advance
alveole
alveoli
adverse
advised
adviser
advisor
akvavit
anxiety
anxious
auxesis
auxetic
amylase
anyways
amygdal
amylene
anywhen
anytime
anywise
azymite
acyclic
abysmal
amyloid
anyroad
azygous
azymous
anybody
abyssal
alyssum
asylums
anziani
Bharati
bradawl
bravado
Bravais

blatant
blabbed
brabble
bramble
beanbag
blaubok
blabber
brambly
braccia
braccio
bear-cat
branchy
bearded
braided
branded
beardie
bladder
boarder
brander
blandly
by-and-by
brasero
braless
beanery
beavery
bravely
bravery
beaufin
beaufet
boat-fly
bhangra
bragged
brangle
blagger
beached
blather
brachet
Baalite
beading
beaming
bearing
beating
biasing
boating
bracing
beamish
bearish
beauish
boarish
biaxial
Baalism
brasier
brazier
beamily
beatify
blacken
bracken
blanket
bracket
blackly
blankly

Braille
beagler
brawler
beamlet
beadman
boatman
Brahman
△brahmin
brained
brawned
braunch
beatnik
bran-new
blarney
bravoes
blawort
bran-pie
biassed
bransle
brassie
brasset
bran-tub
blasted
blatted
boasted
beastie
brantle
brattle
blaster
blatter
boaster
beastly
bravura
bobtail
babiche
babuche
Bobadil
babudom
bebeeru
bobbery
Babygro®
bobbing
babyish
bobbish
Babiism
babuism
△**babbitt**
biblist
bubukle
bobsled
Babylon
babbler
bobbles
bubalis
Bubalus
bibelot
bubinga
bubonic
baboosh
bibcock
Babesia

baby-sit
babassu
baccara
baclava
baccare
baccate
backare
becharm
bicycle
back-end
buck-eye
buckeen
Becher's
△**bacchic**
Bacchae
backhoe
bacchii
Bacchus
buccina
backing
bucking
buckish
biccies
bycoket
bucolic
backlog
bacilli
baculum
buckler
backlot
baconer
becloud
bichord
buckoes
backpay
bicorne
buckram
back-row
bécasse
bucksom
backset
backsaw
bucksaw
backsey
bycatch
because
bedward
bedwarf
badmash
bed-bath
budmash
bedfast
body-bag
bidie-in
budgero
badness
budless
bed-rest
bodeful
bedight
bed-rite

bedside
bedtime
bedding
bidding
bodying
budding
baddish
bedtick
baddies
bodikin
bedeman
bedsore
bedrock
bed-work
bed-roll
bedroom
budworm
badious
bedpost
bedropt
bidarka
bederal
bodhrán
△**bedouin**
bedevil
Bedawin
bedazed
bedizen
beerage
brewage
beefalo
blewart
blesbok
breccia
blended
breaded
breadth
bleeder
blender
breeder
breveté
brewers'
brewery
beet-fly
beef-ham
brecham
beechen
blether
beehive
bee-kite
beeline
brewing
blemish
brevier
blewits
brevity
break-in
bee-skep
break-up
breaker
bleakly

7 b□e□l

bee-glue
beer-mat
beesome
bee-moth
brewpub
bleeper
bleared
△**blessed**
bheesty
beef-tea
bletted
breathe
bleater
breathy
beeswax
bye-byes
beffana
buffalo
bifocal
buffing
baffler
bifilar
buffoon
beghard
big-band
boggard
bogland
baggage
bugbane
buggane
bagwash
boggart
beggary
bugaboo
big-head
bogbean
bugbear
bigness
biggest
buggery
bagpipe
begrime
beguile
beguine
béguine
big-time
bagging
begging
bugging
by-going
biggish
bogyism
baggies
bagnios
baguios
baggily
boggler
bogy-man
begonia
beginne
bigener

bygones
bug-word
big-note
begloom
bighorn
bog-moss
bugloss
bigfoot
bugwort
begorra
begored
bagarre
bog-iron
bagasse
bigoted
bigotry
bagfuls
bug-eyed
Bahadur
behight
Bahaite
Bahaism
Bahaist
behoove
behaved
brigand
brigade
Baisaki
brioche
blinded
brinded
builded
brindle
build-up
blinder
builder
blindly
buirdly
Brinell
boilery
bribery
brimful
briefly
bringer
blither
blighty
bainite
bailiff
baiting
boiling
briming
brinish
British
brinjal
beinked
blinked
brickie
brickle
bricken
brisken
blinker

brisket
briskly
bridled
baillie
bridler
brimmed
brimmer
beignet
bairnly
bricole
bridoon
bail-out
briared
briered
britska
bhistee
blintze
bristle
brittle
Bristol
built-in
built-up
blister
bristly
brittly
brisure
briquet
britzka
bejewel
baklava
beknave
bukshee
beknown
bikeway
belgard
bollard
ballade
beldame
Beltane
bullace
bullate
bulwark
ballant
ballast
balsamy
biliary
bullary
bilobed
belabor
bilobar
bullbar
bullbat
ball-boy
bell-boy
Baluchi
△**bulldog**
baladin
believe
balneal
baleful
Bologna

bolshie
bellhop
belcher
bulghur
bellied
bullied
bulgine
balding
balking
balling
belting
belying
billing
bolting
bulging
bulling
baldish
bullish
ballium
Belgian
billion
bullion
billies
balmily
bulkily
bell-jar
bulimia
bulimic
bilimbi
bellman
beltman
billman
bulimus
△**balance**
balancé
Balanus
baloney
boloney
Bellona
biltong
bollock
bullock
balloon
bellows
bilboes
bilious
bulbous
balcony
billowy
bull-pen
bull-pup
baldric
boleros
balista
Belisha
balls-up
boluses
belated
bolster
△**boletus**
bulrush

beloved
bolivar
Baldwin
beltway
belayed
billy-oh
bombard
bumbaze
bummalo
bombast
bemedal
bimodal
bumming
bumping
bambini
bambino
bumpily
bumpkin
bumbler
bomblet
bimanal
bombora
bummock
bum-boat
bemired
bemused
bemouth
bemazed
bandana
Band-aid®
band-aid
bandage
bondage
beneath
bone-ash
Bengali
bunraku
bone-bed
band-box
binocle
bone-dry
benzene
banteng
bonkers
bandeau
bindery
benefic
baneful
benefit
benight
benthic
bunched
banshee
bencher
benthos
bunches
bandied
benzine
bonfire
banding
banging

7 b□s□l

banking
banting
bending
binding
binning
bonding
bunting
bandits
bonnily
bangled
bungler
bendlet
Benelux
banally
bonamia
benamed
bondman
benempt
bynempt
bonanza
bananas
bandora
benzoic
bandore
benzole
bandook
bannock
bundook
benzoyl
bone-oil
benzoin
bonjour
bonsoir
banjoes
bandrol
banksia
benison
bonasus
boneset
band-saw
bonitos
bandura
banquet
Banbury
Bunbury
biodata
brocard
brocade
brocage
brokage
bromate
buoyage
biomass
buoyant
bloubok
boom-box
bronchi
broncho
broncos
blotchy
blooded
brodded
broaden
broider
brooder
blow-dry
broadly
book-end
Boolean
booze-up
biogeny
brokery
bookful
blowfly
brogged
blowgun
brought
brothel
brochan
biophor
brother
boodied
boogied
biocide
biotite
bromide
bromine
blowing
booking
booming
boozing
broking
bookish
boorish
bromism
bionics
boonies
boozily
blowjob
blocked
brocked
Brocken
brodkin
blocker
brocket
brockit
bootleg
broiler
booklet
boomlet
bookman
bloomer
brommer
Brownie®
△brownie
boo-word
blow-off
boobook
blow-out
biology
blooper
blowsed
bloosme
booksie
blossom
blouson
browser
biontic
bloated
blotted
bloater
blotter
booster
biotype
blowzed
bronzed
bronzen
bronzer
Buphaga
biplane
byplace
bepearl
bipedal
baptise
baptize
baptism
△**baptist**
bepaint
bipolar
beprose
bequest
bergama
barmaid
barbate
barrace
barrage
bereave
burgage
bardash
berdash
burdash
biryani
barrack
bargain
bureaus
burlaps
bureaux
Barbary
Barnaby
bursary
byrlady
bark-bed
boracic
baracan
barocco
borscht
bird-dog
boredom
Bursera
bur-reed
burweed
bergère
Burmese
berserk
bar-bell
borrell
burrell
burgeon
Barrens
Borders
burdens
burgess
bargest
berceau
burghal
burghul
burrhel
barchan
barkhan
birchen
burthen
△**burgher**
berried
Berbice
berline
bornite
barking
barring
birding
birling
burning
burying
burnish
birlinn
barrico
burrito
barrier
barrios
barmkin
barilla
burbler
burglar
birdman
byreman
boronia
Byronic
baronne
borings
baronet
barbola
barwood
burdock
bar-room
Barbour®
burnous
burn-out
baroque
bar-iron
bortsch
biretta
barytic
bursted
Barotse
burette
borstal
baryton
bursten
burst-up
burster
barytes
Bermuda
barbule
bordure
borough
bergylt
borazon
bastard
bustard
beshame
beslave
bespake
bespate
boscage
boskage
bus-fare
basmati
bestain
bass-bar
basoche
bush-cat
basidia
besides
bespeed
bestead
beseeke
besiege
beseech
bespeak
besmear
bashful
bush-fly
bastide
beshine
bespice
byssine
bashing
basting
bushing
busking
bussing
busting
busying
bestick
ba'spiel
bestial
bestill
busgirl
bastion
bushido
bustier
bassist
besaint
bossily
bashlik
basilar

Words marked △ may be spelled also with a capital letter

7 b□s□l

bustler
bas-bleu
besomed
bosomed
baseman
△bushman
basenji
basinet
byssoid
beshone
bespoke
bestorm
bassoon
besport
bespout
bistort
bestrid
bistred
bistros
beshrew
bestrew
bostryx
boshter
Basutos
bush-tit
basqued
bascule
bismuth
bestuck
biscuit
bosquet
bit-rate
bit-part
bateaux
batable
betided
bottega
betread
butt-end
beteeme
between
bittern
battero
bathers
battels
betters
bitless
bitters
butment
battery
butlery
buttery
betight
botcher
butcher
betaine
bottine
batting
batwing
betting
bitting
by-thing
batfish
bethink
battill
betwixt
betaken
betoken
bottled
bottle-o
battler
bottler
bathmic
bitumed
batsman
bitumen
betimes
botanic
bitonal
butanol
bothole
betroth
bittock
buttock
bittour
bottoms
buttons
bottony
buttony
butyric
botargo
batiste
bathtub
betitle
battuta
bethumb
bethump
bathyal
bruhaha
boutade
Bauhaus
blubbed
△bourbon
blubber
bluecap
bouncer
bounded
bounden
△bourdon
blunder
boulder
bounder
bourder
blue-eye
bluffer
bluffly
bludger
blunger
bruchid
brushed
bauchle
bouchée
brush-up
blucher
blusher
brusher
blushet
bauxite
brucine
brucite
blueing
bousing
bruting
brutish
bruxism
brutify
bourkha
bruckle
blunker
bouilli
bourlaw
Brummie
brummer
bausond
boudoir
brumous
brusque
baudric
blurred
bourrée
blue-rot
bruiser
blue-sky
bluette
bluster
boulter
bluntly
bouquet
brulyie
brulzie
Bovidae
bevvied
bivalve
bivious
buvette
bivouac
bow-hand
bow-wave
bowyang
bowlder
bowhead
bawbees
bowbent
bowlful
bowshot
bow-tied
bowline
bow-side
bawling
bowling
bawdily
bawdkin
bywoner
bowknot
bewhore
bawcock
bewitch
box-calf
box-haul
box-seat
box-kite
boxwood
boxroom
box-coat
box-tree
box-iron
boxfuls
buy-back
buyable
Brython
bay-line
bay-tine
boy-girl
bayonet
boyhood
boycott
Bryozoa
buzzard
bazzazz
bezzazz
bizzazz
bez-tine
buzzing
bizonal
bazooka
bezique
bizarre
buzz-saw
bazouki
buzz-wig
chalaza
chamade
charade
clavate
cranage
cyanate
chapati
clarain
clamant
coal-bed
crabbed
chambré
chamber
clabber
clamber
crabber
coal-box
chalcid
chancre
chancel
chancer
chances
claucht
chancey
Chaldee
czardom
chaddar
chaddor
chalder
cladder
csárdás
czardas
chapess
co-agent
chapeau
château
cramesy
chaffer
chamfer
chaufer
charged
clagged
cragged
changer
charger
clanger
clangor
changes
charges
claught
coachee
clachan
clasher
coacher
cyathus
czarina
chalice
chamise
coalise
Coalite®
coalize
cyanide
cyanine
cyanise
cyanite
cyanize
ceasing
charing
chasing
coaming
coating
craving
clayish
clarini
coaxial
cranial
charism
cladism
cranium
czarism
clarion
chamiso
clarino
clavier
crazies

chariot
cladist
czarist
charily
charity
clarify
clarity
crazily
charkha
clarkia
cracked
crackle
crankle
clacker
cracker
crackly
challie
△charlie
challah
challan
crawler
Chablis
challis
chamlet
chaplet
△**charley**
chasmic
charmed
chasmed
clammed
crammed
chasmal
chapman
coalman
charmer
chaumer
claimer
crammer
chained
chaunce
chaunge
crannog
craunch
△**channel**
charnel
channer
clapnet
chalone
chayote
cladode
chabouk
crab-oil
clamour
chamois
claroes
chanoyu
champac
chapped
clapped
cramped
chappie

charpie
champak
chappal
claypan
crampon
clamper
clapper
clasper
clay-pit
crampet
crampit
charpoy
charqui
charred
chagrin
classic
Chassid
classed
clausal
chanson
coarsen
chassis
classis
crassly
chaotic
clastic
chatted
chaetae
chantie
chattel
coastal
chasten
chanter
chantor
chapter
charter
chatter
clatter
coaltar
coal-tar
△coaster
chantey
chantry
chalutz
chauvin
cabbala
cabbage
cab-rank
cabbagy
cubicle
cubical
Cebidae
cubless
cob-pipe
cabling
cubbing
cubbish
Cabeiri
cobbler
△**cabinet**
cubhood

caboose
cobloaf
cab-tout
ciboria
Cabiric
cabaret
cubital
cubitus
cob-swan
cockade
co-chair
cacodyl
cockeye
cachexy
cacoepy
Cocagne
cocaine
coctile
cucking
cycling
coction
cyclist
cockily
cochlea
cichlid
cockled
cackler
cockles
cacolet
coconut
△**cockney**
coccoid
cuckold
cycloid
cyclone
△**cyclops**
cocopan
cockpit
cacique
cockshy
cocotte
cecitis
cedrate
cadrans
cadeaux
caducei
codicil
codices
Cedrela
cudweed
Cadmean
cudbear
cudgels
caddice
cedrine
codeine
codding
codling
caddish
codfish
cadmium

cedilla
codilla
cadelle
codille
cadenza
cadence
cadency
cedared
△**cidaris**
codetta
cadaver
caddyss
chelate
cremate
crenate
creedal
Cheddar
crewels
clement
credent
chéchia
Czechic
Chechen
coeliac
chemise
crevice
cieling
cherish
chewink
cnemial
caesium
chemism
cretism
credits
chekist
chemist
Cheviot
coexist
clerisy
cleeked
check-in
check-up
checker
cleekit
clerkly
creamer
cleanse
creance
chetnik
clean-up
cleaner
chesnut
cleanly
△**cremona**
cheloid
ctenoid
chelone
coehorn
cheroot
cheapie
creepie

cheapen
cheeper
creeper
cheaply
chevron
cheerio
cheerer
clearer
cheerly
clearly
Chelsea
cheesed
chessel
creosol
cremsin
creaser
chesses
cresset
creeshy
creatic
chested
crested
cheetah
creatin
creston
cheater
△creator
caestus
caesura
caerule
cleruch
coequal
chequer
cherubs
cleaved
chervil
Chesvan
cleaver
caffein
caffila
coffret
cognate
cage-cup
cognise
cognize
cogging
cogence
cogener
cogency
cagoule
cohabit
cohibit
cahoots
coherer
chicana
chikara
chicane
climate
coinage
crinate
Chicago

Words marked △ may be spelled also with a capital letter

7 c□i□a

△chicano
cuirass
climbed
cribbed
cribble
climber
childed
chidden
childer
△**chindit**
childly
chimera
Cairene
chimere
△chinese
Chilean
clivers
crivens
cliffed
clip-fed
chiffon
chiefer
chiefly
chiefry
cringle
chigger
clinger
cringer
cliché'd
chikhor
crimina
chiliad
Cainite
caitive
crimine
crinite
cuisine
caitiff
ceiling
chiding
coining
ceilidh
crimini
Chilian
coition
△**chinkie**
crinkle
chicken
clicker
clinker
clicket
cricket
crickey
crinkly
chilled
chillum
criollo
chiller
chillis
Chislev
chimley
crimmer
cairned
Chianti
chignon
chimney
cricoid
crinoid
crinose
chibouk
△chinook
clip-ons
chicory
chipped
clipped
chippie
clippie
crimple
cripple
crispin
chipper
chirper
clipper
crimper
crisper
crisply
chirrup
chiasma
chiasmi
crissum
caisson
crimson
cuisser
chiasms
clifted
cristae
cuittle
chitter
clitter
critter
crittur
chintzy
cliquey
chinwag
cajoler
cojones
cajeput
cajuput
Ciliata
collard
ciliate
collage
collate
calpack
callant
calmant
△**calvary**
ciliary
colobid
calibre
colibri
Caliban
caliber
colobus
call-box
call-boy
culicid
caliche
calicle
calycle
calices
calicos
calyces
culices
cylices
colicky
celadon
caldera
college
Caltech
colleen
collect
culvert
cologne
colugos
culchie
cullied
calcine
calcite
collide
calling
colling
culling
coldish
coltish
cultish
calcium
cultism
cullion
collier
Celsius
Collins
cellist
'cellist
cultist
calcify
calumba
Columba
celomic
calomel
columel
△**calamus**
chlamys
calumet
calumny
colonic
△**colonel**
calando
Calanus
calends
colones
Cellnet®
colloid
calzone
cellose
calzoni
callous
collops
call-out
calipee
calypso
caliper
caloric
chloric
△**calorie**
chloral
caldron
chlorin
caltrap
caltrop
culprit
celesta
celeste
colossi
calotte
calathi
colitis
coletit
calluna
cellule
collude
culture
calculi
Calmuck
colours
coloury
caliver
calyxes
caloyer
campana
command
compage
compare
comrade
Campari
cembali
cembalo
cymbalo
compass
compact
compart
compast
company
camp-bed
comical
Comecon
cimices
comedic
comedos
commend
commère
compère
compete
compear
compeer
comment
cumbent
camogie
camphor
cumshaw
combine
compile
comping
cambial
cambism
cambium
Comtism
campion
Comtian
cambist
Comtist
camaïeu
cimelia
camelid
△**complin**
cumulus
camelot
complot
complex
camelry
camwood
camboge
commode
commote
commove
componé
compose
compote
come-off
commodo
△**commons**
comb-out
comfort
comport
compost
compony
comique
△**camorra**
cambric
camerae
cambrel
cameral
camaron
cumarin
cameras
comfrey
comitia
cometic
comital
cami-top
compter
commune
commute
compute
combust

7 c□p□i

cumquat
cantala
cantata
cantate
centage
centare
concave
connate
cuneate
cannach
canbank
contain
centavo
Cinzano®
centaur
canvass
cineast
contact
cenobia
cenacle
conacre
conical
cynical
conidia
Canidae
cantdog
candela
contend
concede
convene
conteck
conceal
congeal
conseil
canteen
concern
condemn
contemn
concedo
confess
conkers
candent
conceit
concent
concept
concert
confect
confest
congest
conject
connect
consent
content
contest
context
convent
convert
cankery
cannery
cindery
conifer
conchae
conchie
conchal
canthus
conches
candida
cantina
candied
centime
concise
confide
confine
coniine
connive
convive
canning
canting
conning
cunning
confirm
cantion
condign
consign
cantico
centimo
candies
congius
consist
convict
cannily
Canajan
canakin
canikin
canella
canulae
canulas
cantlet
conflux
canonic
centner
△**canonry**
canzona
concord
canzone
cineole
condole
condone
connote
console
convoke
canzoni
candock
conform
conjoin
candour
contour
cannons
consols
concoct
consort
contort
Canopic
Canopus
cinerea
conaria
centric
cantred
centred
congree
congrue
cantref
central
control
centrum
cinerin
cantrip
contrat
concrew
canasta
cunette
conster
conatus
cannula
contund
censure
conduce
confuse
confute
conjure
consume
contuse
censual
conquer
canfuls
concuss
conduct
conduit
consult
century
concupy
conjury
condyle
crotala
chorale
cromack
coolant
crombie
choc-bar
clobber
clotbur
crowbar
cloacae
cloacal
cooncan
clodded
clouded
crowded
chondre
chordae
chordee
croodle
crowdie
coondog
chondri
chordal
chobdar
chowder
clowder
crowder
cholera
choreic
close-in
crocein
close-up
crop-ear
choreus
cholent
closely
clovery
cookery
coopery
cropful
clogged
clogger
clothed
clothes
crochet
choc-ice
choline
chopine
chorine
closing
cloying
coolish
chorial
chorism
chorion
chorizo
crosier
crozier
chorist
clocked
crocked
crooked
chookie
chocker
clocker
croaker
crocket
crowned
choanae
crooner
crowner
choanas
crownet
choenix
choroid
cookout
chopped
cropped
croupon
chopper
cropper
crouper
crossed
cloison
chooser
Croesus
crosses
choosey
crossly
clotted
clouted
chortle
△clootie
coontie
crottle
crow-toe
croûton
clotter
clouter
crofter
△**choctaw**
choltry
closure
cloture
croquis
croquet
Chogyal
cap-case
caprate
cupcake
cupgall
△**captain**
capable
capuche
copycat
capuera
cypsela
Cepheid
cuphead
Cepheus
cypress
coppery
copshop
copaiba
copaiva
cup-tied
caprice
caprine
capsize
captive
coppice
cuprite
cyprine
capping
copying
c-spring
cupping
copyism
Capsian
caption
△cyprian
copyist

Words marked △ may be spelled also with a capital letter

7 c□p□i

Cypriot
caprify
Capella
cupeled
cupola'd
capelin
cipolin
copular
cupolar
cupular
capelet
copilot
co-pilot
caproic
copious
cuprous
copepod
cap-a-pie
cap-à-pie
caporal
caperer
capital
Capitol
capitan
capstan
capsule
capture
capouch
cupfuls
coquina
coquito
cariama
Circaea
curtana
carcake
carcase
carfare
carnage
cartage
cirrate
cordage
cordate
corkage
cornage
corrade
corsage
curtate
curvate
car-wash
currach
curragh
carpark
carrack
cure-all
curtail
certain
curtain
corsair
carcass
corcass
carract

currant
cerebra
carabid
curable
carabin
Cariban
carabao
Carabus
caribou
curaçoa
caroche
coracle
caracal
caracol
caracul
curaçao
carices
Corydon
cariere
cortège
carrell
corbeil
corneal
Circean
carve-up
carneys
carrect
Corbett
cornett
correct
current
cardecu
corbeau
carvery
curtesy
corn-fed
careful
cornfly
corrida
cardiac
carried
curried
carbide
carbine
carline
carmine
cervine
cordite
cornice
corsive
cortile
corvine
cursive
carking
carling
carping
carving
cording
corking
curling
cursing

curving
carlish
Cornish
currish
cortili
carrick
car-sick
cerrial
cordial
Carlism
carrion
carrier
currier
curlies
Carlist
Corfiot
cornist
carnify
certify
curvity
coralla
corella
corolla
circled
circlip
circler
carolus
circles
corylus
circlet
corslet
caramba
ceramic
chromic
caramel
caromel
ceramal
chromel
cerumen
chromos
caranna
chronic
corsned
coronae
Corinth
coronal
chronon
coranto
coroner
coronas
coronis
coronet
△**carioca**
córdoba
corpora
curiosa
carload
cirsoid
cariole
carnose
cirrose

corrode
carlock
cardoon
cartoon
cargoes
carious
cereous
cirrous
corious
cormous
curious
car-coat
carport
carroty
corrody
cursory
Corypha
coryphe
cornrow
chrisom
cerasin
ceresin
△**christy**
curtsey
cerotic
carotid
cerated
curette
carotin
curator
caritas
carauna
curcuma
carouse
cornute
cornual
cornuto
carduus
circuit
corrupt
circusy
caravel
corival
caravan
caraway
cartway
carry-on
corozos
cascara
cassata
cassava
costard
custard
cascade
costate
cuspate
Cossack
casuals
cash-box
cistern
costean

coshery
Castile
costive
Cushite
cystine
casting
cosmism
cession
cushion
cassino
cashier
casuist
cosmist
castled
case-law
caseman
casinos
cestoid
cissoid
cystoid
cassone
cestode
cast-off
cassock
castock
custock
caseous
ciscoes
customs
castory
custody
cesspit
caserne
castral
cesural
costrel
custrel
cistron
cesuras
cesures
costume
cithara
cotland
citrate
cottage
cut-rate
Cathari
cat-walk
cutback
catcall
cattalo
Cathars
cutlass
cattabu
coteaux
citable
Cetacea
cuticle
catechu
citadel
cotidal

Words marked △ may be spelled also with a capital letter

cathead
cat's-eye
cithern
cittern
cat's-ear
cattery
cutlery
catched
catchen
catchup
catcher
catbird
catlike
citrine
cottise
cutline
catling
cutting
catfish
cattish
Cataian
cottier
catmint
cattily
catskin
cutikin
catalpa
cotylae
catalog
catelog
Catalan
cat-flap
catalos
cotyles
cotinga
catenae
catenas
cathood
cottoid
cathode
cathole
cot-folk
cutwork
catworm
cutworm
cottown
citrous
cuttoes
catboat
cottony
catapan
cat's-paw
coterie
catarrh
cateran
caterer
catasta
cytisus
cothurn
catsuit
cut-over
catawba
cutaway
cat-eyed
Catayan
citizen
caudate
courage
couvade
crusade
chupati
crusado
cruzado
courant
clubbed
crumble
clubber
clumber
crumbly
council
churchy
crunchy
cruddle
chuddah
clued-up
chuddar
chunder
clupeid
crubeen
couvert
cautery
crudely
chuffed
cludgie
crushed
couchee
couchée
couthie
cougher
crusher
Cluniac
cauline
crucial
Couéism
caution
crucian
crusian
courier
chutist
Couéist
crucify
crudity
chuckie
chuckle
crunkle
caulker
chukker
courlan
coupler
cruller
cruells
couplet
club-law
chumley
cruelly
cruelty
clubman
△**chunnel**
chunner
chutney
coulomb
caulome
couloir
crumple
chuppah
clumper
crupper
crumpet
caudron
churrus
cruores
cruisie
counsel
courser
cruiser
courses
caustic
counted
crustae
crustal
chunter
cluster
clutter
coulter
counter
country
courtly
coupure
couture
couguar
caviare
ceviche
civvies
cavalla
covelet
cavally
cavalry
civilly
caveman
covered
cover-up
coveted
cuvette
cavetti
cavetto
cowhand
cowbane
cowhage
cow-calf
cowherb
cowherd
cow-weed
cowbell
cowheel
cowshed
cowbird
cowhide
co-write
cowling
cowfish
cowlick
cowgirl
cowslip
cowpoke
cowtree
cowitch
cow-dung
coxcomb
caymans
crybaby
clypeal
clypeus
coyness
cryogen
chylify
chymify
cryonic
cayenne
chymous
cryptic
cryptal
crystal
crypton
clyster
coyotes
cozener
cazique
deaf-aid
diabase
diapase
drayage
drabble
drabber
drag-bar
drawbar
drabbet
draw-boy
dead-cat
diarchy
duarchy
dyarchy
dvandva
diandry
dead-end
dead-eye
drawers
dialect
deanery
drapery
dwarfed
dragged
draggle
draught
drachma
deathly
diarise
diarize
dealing
dialing
doating
drawing
deasiul
diarial
dualism
diarian
drapier
dialist
diarist
dualist
duality
dialled
dialler
drabler
drawler
dead-men
drag-man
drayman
drainer
dragnet
draw-net
dearnly
diamond
Diasone®
Dracone®
dracone
deasoil
dragoon
diabolo
diazoes
drappie
deadpan
dead-pay
diagrid
diadrom
diagram
dead-set
drastic
dratted
draftee
draw-top
diaster
drafter
draft-ox
dwarves
dialyse
dialyze
dobhash
debacle
débâcle
Debrett
dubiety
débride
debrief
dabbing
dibbing

Words marked △ may be spelled also with a capital letter

7 d□b□i

dobbing
dubbing
dabbity
dabbler
dibbler
dubious
dibasic
debased
debaser
dibutyl
dabster
debater
debitor
debauch
debouch
decease
deciare
declare
dictate
dockage
ducdame
declaim
declass
duck-ant
docible
decibel
dice-box
duck-coy
decidua
decided
decadal
decider
decoder
decreed
dickens
duchess
decreet
decagon
decried
deceive
decline
dockise
dockize
ductile
decking
docking
ducking
decrial
diction
decrier
dacoity
deckled
decolor
ducally
decimal
decuman
decanal
decency
d'accord
dichord
decrown
doctors
decapod
decuple
decuria
decurve
decorum
Docetic
Docetae
docquet
decayed
decrypt
doddard
didicoi
didicoy
dudgeon
dudheen
Dodgems®
dodgems
doddery
dodgery
duddery
dodging
Dadaism
Dadaist
didakai
didakei
dedalic
diddler
dedimus
daddock
die-hard
dieback
die-cast
dietary
dyeable
dreaded
Dresden
dreader
duendes
dreadly
deedful
deep-fet
deep-fry
dredger
diethyl
dietine
dyeline
drevill
dietist
deedily
doe-skin
duelled
dwelled
dueller
dweller
duellos
deerlet
dreamed
dreamer
dye-wood
die-work
dye-work
diedral
deep-sea
dressed
dresser
deep-set
duetted
dyester
duettos
die-away
doe-eyed
defraud
deflate
defiant
defacer
deficit
deflect
daffing
defying
duffing
defiler
defence
defense
definer
defunct
defrock
difform
defrost
deforce
defaste
diffuse
default
degrade
dogbane
dogeate
dogvane
digraph
dogdays
dogcart
dog-head
dog's-ear
daggers
digress
doggess
dog-belt
doggery
dogship
digging
dogging
dogfish
doggish
dog-sick
dog-tick
dignify
dignity
dogskin
dogsled
digamma
Digynia
digonal
dagwood
dogwood
doggone
doghole
daglock
dogtown
dogbolt
dog-crab
doggrel
dogtrot
digital
Dogstar
degauss
diglyph
dehisce
dribble
djibbah
dribber
dribbly
dwindle
drip-dry
deiseal
drive-in
dyingly
daisied
deified
deicide
driving
deifier
dailies
daimios
doitkin
drinker
driller
driblet
deiform
dripped
deictic
deistic
drip-tip
drifter
drizzle
drizzly
dejecta
dejeune
dukedom
dakoiti
dika-oil
deltaic
dullard
deleble
delible
deluded
dolldom
deluder
dulness
diluent
doleful
delight
△**delphic**
delphin
△dolphin
dollied
delaine
dulcite
dilling
dollish
doltish
dullish
dulcian
dallier
dollier
dulcify
Dalilah
Delilah
dilemma
delimit
delenda
deltoid
dulcose
dildoes
delapse
deliria
dulosis
dulotic
dilated
dilutee
delator
dilater
dilator
diluter
dilutor
delouse
deliver
delayed
delayer
demeane
dum-palm
dumpbin
domical
domicil
demoded
dimness
demigod
damages
demaine
damming
damning
damping
dimming
dampish
dimmish
dumpish
dumaist
damnify
dimpled
demonic
dominee
dominie
démenti
dominos
demonry
damfool

Words marked △ may be spelled also with a capital letter

dimeric
dambrod
demerge
demerse
dimorph
demirep
demerit
demesne
damosel
domatia
demotic
dimeter
demount
demayne
damozel
donnard
dentate
dunnage
donnart
dunnart
dentary
dingbat
donnerd
Daniell
Dantean
dungeon
danseur
donkeys
données
donnert
densely
duncery
dung-fly
donship
dun-bird
Dunciad
dentine
dunnite
dancing
denying
dinning
donning
dunning
dankish
donnish
dun-fish
dunnish
Dunkirk
donnism
dinkies
dunlins
Dantist
dentist
dandify
dandily
densify
density
Dansker
dandler
dangler
△**danelaw**

dynamic
dynamos
dentoid
dunnock
dingoes
△**dinmont**
denarii
dendron
dynasty
dinette
donator
denture
dinky-di
denizen
Dionaea
diorama
deodand
deodate
dioxane
Dioecia
droichy
do-or-die
drosera
duodena
diocese
doomful
dropfly
drongos
drought
drogher
droshky
diorite
dioxide
D-notice
dooming
droving
dronish
diorism
drookit
droukit
doodler
droplet
doormat
dvornik
drowner
drop-net
dromond
duotone
drop-out
duopoly
dropped
dropple
dropper
deontic
dioptre
diopter
drostdy
drouthy
droguet
doorway
deplane

deprave
dupable
dépêche
△**diptera**
deplete
depress
deprive
depside
dip-pipe
dipping
dopping
depaint
dappled
dipolar
Doppler
Daphnia
daphnid
diploma
diploid
dapsone
deplore
diphone
Diplock
dipnoan
diplont
dip-trap
deposal
deposer
deposit
dopatta
dupatta
deplume
diptych
daquiri
dorlach
dorhawk
darrain
darrayn
dormant
durmast
dirt-bed
durable
durably
derider
dorados
dareful
dernful
direful
dureful
darshan
dirtied
dormice
darling
darning
darting
Dorking
darkish
△dervish
derrick
dornick
deraign

dernier
darbies
darcies
dirtily
duramen
dirempt
derange
durance
dermoid
dariole
dortour
dirt-pie
dart-sac
duresse
daresay
dastard
disband
discard
dismayd
descale
discage
discase
disease
disfame
dispace
disrate
distaff
disbark
dismask
dispark
disrank
dismayl
disdain
distain
despair
△**dismals**
descant
discant
dismast
dispart
distant
disable
dustbin
disobey
disedge
dysodil
dos-à-dos
dosi-dos
descend
dispend
distend
disleaf
dasheki
disleal
dishelm
dasheen
discern
discerp
descent
dessert
discept

disgest
disject
disnest
disseat
dissect
dissent
dissert
distent
dishful
dislimb
desmine
despise
despite
destine
discide
dislike
dashing
dishing
distich
duskish
dashiki
dislink
deskill
distill
dislimn
dossier
dismiss
destiny
duskily
dustily
disally
display
dustman
dyspnea
desmoid
despond
discoed
discoid
discord
disload
dishome
dispone
dispose
disrobe
disyoke
despoil
disform
disgown
dishorn
disjoin
discoer
disport
dispost
disroot
distort
dyslogy
dasypod
dust-pan
Dasypus
dash-pot
dysuria

7 d□s□r

dysuric
disprad
dispred
deserve
dish-rag
desirer
destroy
disused
desktop
disturb
dasyure
discure
diseuse
disjune
dispute
distune
discuss
disgust
disrupt
disavow
distyle
detrain
detract
dittany
datable
databus
Dyticus
dithery
dutiful
ditcher
dotting
dottled
détente
détenue
detinue
dittoed
duteous
dataria
deterge
dottrel
detrude
datival
drubbed
drumble
druidic
daunder
douleia
douceur
doucets
daubery
doucely
drugged
druggie
drudger
drugger
drugget
dauphin
doughty
doucine
dourine
daubing

Drusian
drucken
drunken
drumlin
doubler
doubles
doublet
double-u
drummed
drummer
diurnal
dhurrie
doubted
daunton
daunter
doubter
duumvir
Deutzia
deviate
deviant
dovecot
davidia
divider
divvied
devoice
devling
doveish
devoirs
dovekie
deviled
devalue
devolve
divulge
develop
devilet
dovelet
devilry
diviner
devious
diverge
diverse
divorce
divorcé
devisee
devisal
divisim
deviser
devisor
divisor
devoted
devotee
duvetyn
dyvoury
dew-fall
downa-do
dewlapt
down-bed
dowable
downbow
dowcets
dowager

dawning
dowdily
dawdler
dew-claw
dawn-man
dewanny
dowlney
dew-pond
dawcock
dew-worm
dew-drop
dewater
dewfull
dextral
dextran
dextrin
daytale
dry-wash
daymark
dry-salt
dry-iced
dryades
dry-cell
day-peep
dryness
drybeat
dry-shod
daytime
day-girl
dry-fist
day-lily
daysman
doyenne
daylong
day-book
day-work
dry-dock
day-coal
day-boat
dry-foot
daystar
dry-cure
dry-eyed
dizzard
dazedly
dizzied
dizzily
dazzler
dozenth
emanate
étalage
exarate
emanant
épatant
ébauche
eparchy
exarchy
étagère
evangel
edaphic
erathem

elative
evasive
examine
evanish
epaxial
etacism
elation
enation
erasion
evasion
edacity
egality
enabler
epaulet
enarmed
epagoge
enamour
example
epacrid
etaerio
epacris
elastic
exalted
elastin
enactor
exacter
exactor
exactly
erasure
evacuee
embraid
emblaze
embrace
embrave
emblema
embread
embrewe
ebbless
embogue
ebbtide
ecbolic
embolic
embolus
embroil
embloom
embrown
embargo
embased
embaste
embosom
embassy
embathe
embound
embrute
embowed
embowel
embower
embayld
embryon
embryos
enchafe

enchase
enclave
escuage
euclase
exclave
encharm
exclaim
enchain
enclasp
enchant
etchant
encraty
escudos
excudit
excreta
excrete
encheer
escheat
excheat
eccrine
escribe
eucaine
eucrite
etching
escalop
escolar
encomia
encloud
enclose
escroll
escapee
escaper
euchred
excurse
excerpt
excusal
excuser
excited
exciton
exciter
excitor
exclude
encrust
each-way
encrypt
endgame
endlang
endways
endless
endogen
endship
endwise
eddying
eidolon
endemic
endlong
endmost
endorse
endarch
enderon
endiron

Words marked △ may be spelled also with a capital letter

endurer
elderly
end-user
ecdysis
eidetic
endowed
endower
endozoa
enemata
ewe-lamb
emerald
elevate
eye-bath
eyelash
eye-wash
eyeball
elegant
elenchi
éperdue
exegete
ewe-neck
eye-beam
elevens
eyeless
element
Everest
energic
energid
epergne
exergue
Erewhon
eye-shot
elegiac
eyeliad
elegise
elegize
emetine
eremite
evening
emeriti
ewe-milk
eye-wink
E-region
etesian
elegist
eye-flap
△**eternal**
even-odd
eye-hole
eyesore
erelong
eyehook
emerods
eyebolt
exempla
exemple
eye-spot
epeirid
exedrae
eye-drop
eyebrow

emersed
erepsin
Eleatic
erected
edental
electro
ejector
△elector
erecter
erector
eventer
evertor
erectly
execute
elfland
enflame
enframe
effable
effects
Enfield
enflesh
elf-shot
enfiled
effulge
enfelon
effendi
elfhood
enfeoff
elf-bolt
efforce
enforce
enguard
egg-case
engrace
engrave
engraff
eggwash
engrail
engrain
engrasp
eggmass
engraft
ergodic
Euglena
egghead
egg-cell
engaged
△**engager**
egg-bird
erg-nine
English
engulph
egg-plum
egg-flip
eugenia
eugenic
eugenol
enginer
englobe
engloom
engross

egg-cosy
engorge
eagerly
eightvo
ergates
ephebic
ephebes
ephebos
ephebus
exhibit
ethical
echidna
ephedra
exhedra
echoise
echoize
echoing
echoism
echoist
echelon
ephelis
exhumer
enhance
ethanol
echinus
ethmoid
ethiops
échappé
etheric
exhaust
emicate
emirate
epilate
evirate
evitate
epitaph
epicarp
emicant
epitaxy
epicede
epicene
epigene
epigeal
epigean
eminent
evident
exigent
epithem
epithet
edified
edifice
erinite
elitism
élitism
epicism
edition
elision
exilian
edifier
épicier
elitist

élitist
epicist
exility
etiolin
epizoic
ericoid
epidote
epigone
episode
episome
epitome
epitope
△**epigoni**
epizoan
epizoon
epigons
epigram
ekistic
eristic
emitted
△**epistle**
edictal
emitter
evictor
epicure
Erinyes
epigyny
enjoyer
Eskimos
elkhorn
ellwand
eelfare
eulogia
ellagic
eclogue
enlight
eilding
erl-king
eelworm
eelpout
eclipse
ellipse
enlarge
enliven
esloyne
ermelin
ermined
elmwood
ennoble
ennuied
eanling
ennuyed
evocate
exocarp
exogamy
écorché
exordia
erotema
eroteme
exoderm
erodent

esotery
emonges
emongst
epochal
erotica
exotica
ebonise
ebonite
ebonize
ecocide
egotise
egotize
emotive
epoxide
erosive
egotism
elogium
erodium
erotism
emotion
erosion
Etonian
exomion
ebonist
egotist
elogist
Elohist
exodist
enounce
eloiner
ecology
economy
enomoty
étourdi
ego-trip
elocute
evolute
evolver
ecotype
emplace
emplane
enplane
expiate
empeach
explain
explant
empyema
ekpwele
empress
express
empight
emptied
empaire
emprise
espying
emption
emptier
empties
enprint
emptily
expulse

Words marked △ may be spelled also with a capital letter

7 e□p□n

expanse
expense
expunge
empanel
expunct
explode
explore
exploit
euphony
euphory
eupepsy
emporia
empiric
expired
emperce
euphroe
expurge
esparto
emperor
exports
exposed
exposal
exposer
empathy
expound
emplume
espouse
empower
empayre
enquire
esquire
enquiry
ebriate
earbash
earmark
errable
earache
earldom
enrheum
earless
earnest
ebriety
enraged
earthen
earshot
earthly
errhine
earning
earring
earpick
earlier
earlies
earplug
earflap
eirenic
enrange
étrenne
errands
Euronet
ear-bone
ear-hole

earlobe
ebriose
earlock
euripus
Etruria
eardrum
eardrop
erratic
erratum
Euratom
enround
enrough
enriven
enslave
ensnare
ensnarl
enstamp
△**ecstasy**
eustacy
eustasy
enshell
eastern
ensteep
ensweep
easeful
exscind
easting
ensuing
eastlin
epsilon
essence
easy-osy
ensurer
essayed
enstyle
essoyne
eustyle
essayer
estrade
entrail
entrall
entrain
entrant
extract
extrait
estuary
eatable
enticer
esthete
estrepe
extreme
entreat
estreat
extreat
entwine
estoile
estrich
entrism
entrist
entwist
entomic

entente
extense
extinct
entroid
estrous
entropy
eutropy
ectopia
ectopic
entopic
ectypal
enteric
Euterpe
externe
enteral
enthral
enteron
enterer
ectases
ectasis
entasis
entotic
extatic
entêtée
entitle
enthuse
extrude
entrust
estival
estover
eutexia
ecthyma
entayle
ectozoa
entozoa
educate
emulate
epurate
exudate
epulary
exurbia
equable
exurban
equably
Equidae
elusive
erudite
exuviae
eluvial
exuvial
eluvium
elusion
elution
écuelle
equally
equinia
equinal
equinox
emulous
elusory
equerry

épuisée
emulsin
emulsor
eductor
equator
eevning
envying
envelop
envenom
envious
environ
envault
enwheel
eryngos
Elysium
Elysian
etymons
elytral
elytrum
elytron
enzymic
Elzevir
flatbed
frabbit
flaccid
fiancée
flat-cap
fiascos
fratchy
flag-day
flare-up
frame-up
flâneur
fratery
fearful
flaffer
flamfew
flagged
flanged
fragged
flaught
fraught
feather
flasher
flavine
fragile
flaming
flaring
flaying
foaming
framing
fraying
Flavian
franion
foamily
flacker
flanker
flacket
flasket
frankly
flatlet

frailly
frailty
flaunch
flannel
fraenum
flannen
flaunty
flavone
flavour
featous
flapped
frapped
frappée
frampal
flapper
frantic
flatted
fracted
fractal
flatten
feaster
flatter
Fraktur
feature
frazzle
fibbery
fubbery
febrile
fabling
fibbing
fabliau
fabular
fibular
fibroma
fibroid
fibrose
fibroin
fibrous
fibered
Fabergé
fibster
factice
factive
fictile
fictive
fucking
faction
fiction
faculae
facular
faculty
focally
faceman
façonné
factoid
face-off
factory
fuchsia
focused
fucused
focuses

Words marked △ may be spelled also with a capital letter

fucuses
faceted
fechter
facture
factual
fadable
fidibus
fadedly
fidgets
fidgety
fadaise
faddish
faddism
fideism
faddist
fideist
fuddled
fiddler
fuddler
fiddley
fade-out
fedarie
federal
fedayee
fee-farm
free-arm
freebee
freebie
flea-bag
fleeced
fleecer
frescos
Frenchy
fielded
fiefdom
freedom
fielder
fretful
fledged
freight
fleshed
freshen
flesher
fresher
freshet
fleshly
freshly
flexile
feeding
feeling
feering
fleeing
Fleming
freeing
△**flemish**
flexion
fierily
flecked
freckle
flecker
freckly

fuelled
fueller
feedlot
freeman
freemen
△**fresnel**
fleapit
fleuron
fleerer
Fuehrer
fleuret
freesia
fretsaw
fretted
fletton
fleetly
frenula
flexure
freeway
freezer
fifteen
fifthly
fifties
foggage
fog-bank
fog-lamp
fogydom
fig-leaf
fog-bell
fogless
figment
faggery
figgery
fig-bird
fagging
figging
fogyish
fogyism
fuguist
foggily
fugally
foghorn
figwort
figured
fig-tree
figural
fagotti
fagotto
fighter
fugatos
fahlerz
fahlore
frigate
friable
fribble
Frisbee®
flip-dog
flinder
fair-day
friseur
fritfly

frigged
fringed
flinger
frigger
flighty
failing
fairing
foiling
fairish
Frisian
fairily
flicker
frisker
frisket
feigned
faience
faïence
friande
Friends
frijole
faitour
flipper
fripper
friarly
Friesic
frisson
fainted
flitted
fritted
flip-top
flitter
foister
fritter
faintly
failure
frisure
friture
flivver
fairway
friezed
frizzed
frizzle
frizzly
fajitas
falbala
falcade
falcate
faldage
fellate
filiate
foliage
foliate
fullage
fellahs
fallacy
Félibre
filabeg
filibeg
felicia
felucca
folacin

filacer
Filices
Felidae
filmdom
filberd
fulness
filbert
fulgent
fullest
falsely
full-fed
falafel
felafel
Filofax®
fall-guy
filcher
full-hot
felsite
fulmine
falling
felting
filling
folding
falsish
filmish
fullish
fulfill
falsism
falsies
falsify
falsity
filemot
Falange
Felinae
filings
felonry
folioed
foliole
foliose
fulsome
fulgour
fulvous
fallout
fall-out
felwort
fold-out
full-out
felspar
△**filaria**
fulcrum
Falasha
filasse
filmset
felt-tip
falcula
folkway
filazer
fumados
fumbler
famulus
feminal

fimbria
Fumaria
fumaric
femoral
fumette
fumetti
fumetto
femiter
fomites
fenland
fanfare
finback
finnack
fantail
fantasm
funfair
fantads
fantast
fondant
fantasy
finable
funèbre
funicle
finical
finicky
fanteeg
fannell
finders
fingers
finless
finagle
finched
fancied
fan-wise
fanzine
fen-fire
fanning
fencing
finding
funding
funning
fennish
fineish
Finnish
fancier
funnies
funnily
finikin
fangled
fondler
fontlet
finally
finance
finings
fanfold
fin-toed
fungoid
finnock
fantods
fungous
funeral

Words marked △ may be spelled also with a capital letter

7 f□n□r

findram
finesse
finnsko
fanatic
fenitar
funster
froward
flotage
flowage
footage
flokati
flotant
feodary
Froebel
footbar
frogbit
footboy
floccus
flooded
fronded
Floréal
flowers
floreat
flowery
foolery
feoffee
foodful
feoffer
feoffor
flogged
frogged
froughy
flowing
fooling
footing
foolish
foodism
florist
foot-jaw
frocked
foozler
froglet
footman
footmen
frogman
flounce
frounce
flouncy
footpad
floored
floorer
footrot
floosie
△footsie
flotsam
frowsty
fronted
frosted
floatel
frontal
foot-ton

fronton
floater
floruit
footway
floozie
foppery
fopling
foppish
fermata
Ferrara
forlana
furlana
farrand
forward
fardage
fermate
ferrate
forbade
forgave
formate
forsake
furcate
furnace
forzati
firearm
forearm
forwarn
farrago
forzato
forfair
furfair
farrant
formant
firebug
fire-bar
firebox
forecar
faradic
firedog
faraday
fore-day
fore-end
forfend
forlend
forlese
fur-seal
farceur
forbear
farness
forceps
ferment
fervent
forfeit
forhent
forlent
fornent
forwent
farmery
fernery
ferrety
forgery

furmety
forkful
firefly
forager
foregut
farthel
farther
further
Formica®
farcied
ferried
ferrite
fertile
forgive
forpine
furtive
farcing
farding
farming
ferning
firring
forging
forming
furring
furbish
furnish
fermium
fermion
foreign
farrier
furrier
△forties
farcify
fortify
furmity
forelie
forsloe
foreleg
fartlek
fortlet
forslow
forelay
fireman
foramen
foreman
foremen
fire-new
fir-wood
fir-cone
forbode
forbore
fordone
forgone
forlore
furlong
forsook
fern-owl
forlorn
forworn
furioso
fervour

ferrous
furious
farmost
furrowy
firepan
firepot
forepaw
fir-tree
foreran
forerun
Fortran
foresee
foresaw
foresay
foretop
firstly
farruca
formula
furcula
ferrule
fortune
ferrugo
forever
faraway
forayer
fusible
fusidic
fast-day
fish-day
fisheye
Fastens
Fastext
fashery
fishery
fish-fag
fishful
fistful
fish-god
fishgig
fascine
festive
fissile
fissive
fasting
fishing
fastish
fossick
fascial
△fascism
fashion
fission
fushion
fustian
△fascist
fishify
fussily
fustily
fusilli
fist-law
fish-net
fish-oil

festoon
fuscous
fuss-pot
fusarol
fistula
fossula
fissure
fish-way
fat-face
futhark
fetiche
fat-head
fathers
fatness
fetters
fitness
fattest
fitment
fittest
fateful
fatigue
fitchée
futchel
fitchet
fitchew
fatling
fatting
fitting
fattish
fitlier
fatuity
fettler
fatally
Fatimid
futhorc
fetlock
futhork
futtock
fathoms
fatsoes
fatuous
futures
fat-lute
foulard
fougade
four-ale
foumart
feudary
flubbed
f-number
fluidic
fluidal
foulder
founder
foundry
fourgon
flushed
fauchon
flusher
foughty
flutina

Words marked △ may be spelled also with a capital letter

fluxive
feuding
fluting
faucial
fluvial
Fauvism
fluxion
Fourier
faunist
Fauvist
feudist
flutist
frutify
flunkey
flummox
fluence
fluency
four-oar
frumple
fluoric
foudrie
fourses
Flustra
fructed
fruited
fouetté
frustum
fluster
flutter
fruiter
foveate
five-bar
five-day
favrile
foveola
foveole
fivepin
favored
fevered
favorer
favours
fewmets
fewness
fawning
fowling
fox-mark
fox-tail
fixable
fixedly
foxship
fixings
foxhole
fox-trap
foxtrot
fox-trot
fixture
fox-hunt
fox-evil
flybane
fly-half
fly-past

flyable
flyleaf
flybelt
flyting
fly-fish
fly-kick
fly-flap
flyblow
fly-slow
fayence
flybook
flyboat
flytrap
flyover
flyaway
fizzgig
fizzing
fuzzily
fazenda
guaraná
gradate
gramash
Guaraní
guarani
guanaco
gramary
Granary®
granary
grabbed
grabble
grab-bag
grabber
gearbox
Glaucus
Giardia
grandma
grandpa
gladded
grandad
guarded
gladdie
grandee
guardee
grandam
gladden
gladdon
graddan
glandes
grandly
glacéed
go-ahead
goateed
Goanese
glareal
gradely
grapery
gravely
goat-fig
gladful
granfer
grayfly

goat-god
granger
guangos
gnathic
graphic
gnathal
gnasher
Graphis
granita
gracile
gradine
granite
gratiné
guanine
gearing
glaring
glazing
grating
graving
grazing
goatish
guarish
gradini
gharial
glacial
gradino
glacier
glazier
grazier
gladius
gratify
gravity
grackle
glaiket
glaikit
gnarled
Grallae
gravlax
grammar
grained
grannie
graunch
grapnel
grannam
grainer
granola
glamour
gealous
grapple
graupel
grasper
grampus
gnarred
glairin
grassum
glassen
grasser
glasses
granted
grantee
Granthi

grafter
granter
grantor
ghastly
giantly
giantry
granule
gravure
guayule
gradual
glaived
gabbard
gabnash
gabbart
giblets
gabfest
gabbing
gibbing
gubbins
gabelle
Gobelin
gabbler
gobbler
gobioid
gibbose
gibbous
goburra
gabbros
geckoes
godward
gadwall
goddamn
Gadidae
△**godhead**
godsend
gudgeon
△**goddess**
godless
godship
godlike
gadding
gadling
god-king
godling
giddily
godlily
gadsman
gudeman
godhood
gadroon
godroon
△**godetia**
go-devil
giddy-up
gregale
grenade
gheraos
Gaeldom
guerdon
guelder
guereza

Guelfic
gleeful
geechee
greyhen
△**grecise**
△grecize
guérite
greying
greyish
gremial
Grecism
△**grecian**
gherkin
grey-lag
gremlin
gleeman
greenie
greenth
gleaner
greener
greenly
glenoid
glebous
grey-out
Gregory
grecque
ghessed
greisen
greaser
guesser
greisly
greeted
greaten
guesten
greater
greeter
ghettos
greatly
geebung
greaves
Gaekwar
gaffing
gag-rein
gagging
gigging
goggled
giggler
goggler
gigolos
goggles
G-agents
gagster
gahnite
Gehenna
guisard
grimace
guidage
gribble
grieced
grinded
griddle

Words marked △ may be spelled also with a capital letter

7 g□i□d

gliadin
glidder
gridder
grinder
guilder
guildry
gaiters
grisely
gainful
griffin
griffon
ghilgai
gringos
geishas
guichet
gwiniad
gliding
gricing
griping
△guiding
guising
grimily
griskin
grilled
grisled
ghillie
glimmer
gliomas
grinned
△**guignol**
grinner
gripped
glimpse
gripple
gripper
goitred
grigris
griesie
gliosis
gainsay
griesly
gristle
glisten
glister
glitter
grifter
gritter
gristly
guipure
griever
Gaikwar
grizzle
grizzly
goliard
golland
galeate
gallate
△**goliath**
goldarn
gallant
galabea
galabia
gold-bug
galoche
giltcup
gelidly
goldeye
galleon
gulleys
gilbert
gallery
gullery
gallfly
galagos
Galahad
gullied
△**gallice**
gallise
gallize
galling
gelding
gelling
gilding
golfing
goldish
gullish
gallium
gillion
Gallios
gullies
galliot
galilee
galumph
galanga
Galenic
gallnut
galloon
gallows
galopin
galipot
galatea
galette
gelatin
gummata
gemmate
gambado
gimbals
gymnast
gemsbok
gombeen
gemmery
gumshoe
gummite
gemming
gumming
gampish
gemfish
gimmick
gambier
gambist
gamelan
gambler
Geminid
Geminis
gamboge
gammock
gumboil
gummous
gumboot
gambrel
gomeral
gomeril
gumdrop
gametic
gametal
gomutos
gemmule
gunnage
gunwale
gingall
gang-bye
gonidia
gonadic
gonidic
gonadal
gunnera
Genoese
ginseng
genteel
gunless
gingery
ginnery
gunnery
gingham
ginshop
gunship
gunshot
ganoine
△gentile
genuine
gunfire
ganging
ginning
gunning
gingili
gentian
Günzian
ganglia
gantlet
gunplay
genomic
gondola
genlock
gunlock
gunroom
gunboat
gunport
genappe
genipap
generic
gangrel
△general
Ganesha
genista
geneses
△genesis
genuses
genetic
genette
genital
genitor
Genevan
gangway
genizah
globate
geofact
geomant
good-bye
grow-bag
gnocchi
grouchy
Geordie
geoidal
good-den
good-day
good-e'en
gooleys
gropers
grosert
geodesy
geogeny
goosery
grocery
georgic
gloried
gloving
glowing
glozing
growing
gnomish
goodish
Grobian
Grotian
grodier
Grolier
goodies
goolies
gnomist
glorify
goofily
Goorkha
grockle
growler
glommed
△**goodman**
grommet
groined
grown-up
groaner
grounds
good-now
globoid
globose
glonoin
giocoso
globous
geogony
geology
groupie
grouper
grogram
Glossic
glossal
good-son
glosser
grouser
grossly
glottic
△gnostic
glottal
gloater
grouter
glottis
grottos
ghostly
globule
groover
gypping
guppies
gopuram
garland
gormand
gurnard
garbage
germane
germain
Germans
gardant
gertcha
gyrocar
gurudom
△**gerbera**
△**gorsedd**
△**gardens**
garners
garters
garment
gargety
giraffe
garigue
garpike
girding
garfish
garnish
girlish
guruism
Gordian
Gordius
gorgios
gorilla
garbled
girdled
garbler
girdler
gyrally

Words marked △ may be spelled also with a capital letter

gironic
gyronic
gerenuk
gyronny
girlond
garrote
garvock
gorcock
garboil
gorsoon
gorcrow
girasol
girosol
garotte
Gore-Tex®
garbure
gestate
goshawk
△**gestapo**
△**gestalt**
gestant
Gospels
gashful
gustful
Gasthof
gasahol
gasohol
gas-lime
gasping
gassing
gosling
gushing
gaskins
gaseity
gossipy
Gosplan
gas-coke
gas-coal
gossoon
gaseous
gessoes
gastric
gisarme
gastrin
gesture
gas-buoy
guttate
gytrash
gateaus
gâteaux
gittern
gathers
gutless
gutters
gutsful
gutcher
göthite
gatling
getting
G-string
gutsing
gutting
Gothick
guttier
gateleg
gateman
gitanos
gateway
getaway
goulash
glutaei
gourami
grubbed
grubble
grumble
grubber
grumbly
gouache
gougère
Gruyère
gluteal
gluteus
gaudery
gauffer
goutfly
gruffly
glugged
gaudgie
gauchos
glucina
gauging
Gaulish
grunion
gaudily
gourmet
grummet
glucose
grumose
goujons
grumous
glue-pot
glutted
grufted
gruntle
glutton
grutten
gaulter
grunter
gauntly
gauntry
gavotte
gowland
gownboy
gowpens
gownman
gowaned
grysbok
gayness
grysely
glyphic
gryphon
gwyniad
glycine
gaysome
glycose
guy-rope
goyisch
gryesly
glyptic
glyptal
gizzard
gazebos
gazeful
gazelle
guzzler
gazania
gazooka
△**gazette**
headage
heal-all
huanaco
hoarder
heave-ho
heavens
heathen
heather
hyacine
hyaline
hyalite
heading
healing
heaping
hearing
heating
heaving
heavier
heavies
headily
heavily
hoarily
hearken
headman
haaf-net
hyaloid
headrig
hoarsen
headset
hearsay
hearted
hearten
healthy
heartly
headway
hoatzin
Hebraic
hobnail
habdabs
hibachi
hobodom
hobbish
Hobbism
hoboism
Hobbian
Hobbist
hobbler
hob-a-nob
hebenon
Hobson's
habited
habitué
habitus
habitat
hectare
hackbut
Hock-day
hackery
hacking
hack-log
hackler
heckler
hackles
hacklet
hackney
hickory
hocused
hack-saw
hicatee
hachure
hiccupy
hydrate
hydrant
hydride
hedging
hidling
hidlins
hidalga
huddled
hidalgo
hedonic
hydroid
hadrome
haddock
hideous
hydrous
hideout
hydroxy
hederal
hydatid
Hieland
hoe-cake
Hielant
hueless
heedful
heeling
hoedown
haemony
heel-tap
huff-cap
huffish
hafnium
heftily
huffily
huffkin
hafflin
Haggada
haggard
hogward
hog-mane
hogwash
hogback
highboy
hag-seed
hag-weed
hogweed
hygiene
hog-deer
highest
hoggery
high-fed
high-hat
hag-ride
hog-line
hogging
hugging
hagfish
haggish
highish
hog-fish
hoggish
Hygeian
hog-skin
high-key
hog-plum
haggler
higgler
high-low
highman
highmen
hoghood
hog-nose
hagdown
hugeous
hagbolt
high-set
high-top
highway
hahnium
huitain
haircut
heirdom
hairdos
hair-eel
heiress
heigh-ho
haining
Haitian
hairnet
heinous
hairpin
heister
hoister
Heimweh
hijinks
halyard
holland

Words marked △ may be spelled also with a capital letter

7 h□l□a

half-ape
holy-ale
hallali
hold-all
holla-ho
helibus
halibut
holibut
hell-box
Halacha
helical
helicon
half-cap
helices
half-cut
hell-cat
Helodea
halidom
holydam
half-day
holiday
halberd
Hellene
Hulsean
halvers
halbert
helpful
halogen
halling
halting
helping
hilding
holding
hulking
hylding
hellish
holmium
hallian
hallion
hellion
hellier
hyloist
Halakah
halflin
heliman
hillmen
halimot
hellova
helcoid
half-one
hillock
holm-oak
holloes
helipad
half-pay
holesom
hilltop
holster
halitus
helotry
helluva
halavah
halfwit
halfway
hallway
helixes
halcyon
hallyon
hummaum
hymnary
humidor
humidly
himself
humogen
homager
hem-line
hemming
humming
hymning
hymnist
hammily
homolog
homelyn
hamular
hamulus
humbles
hominid
hymenal
homonym
humanly
hemiola
hemione
hammock
hemlock
hommock
hummock
hymnody
Homeric
Homerid
humeral
humoral
humdrum
humerus
Hamitic
hematic
hematin
hamster
Hamburg
Homburg
humbuzz
Hansard
hennaed
henbane
Hungary
handbag
handcar
hangdog
henpeck
hunkers
hennery
handful
handgun
hind-gut
hen-wife
hanging
hinging
honking
hunting
Hunnish
handier
henries
handily
handjar
handled
hindleg
handler
hangman
hanuman
hen-toed
hand-off
hen-coop
handout
hand-out
hangout
hanaper
hundred
handsel
hands-on
hunt's-up
handset
handsaw
honesty
henotic
Honiton
honours
honeyed
hoop-ash
hoosgow
hoodlum
hoodman
hoolock
hook-pin
hoofrot
hop-yard
heptane
hip-bath
hopsack
hop-sack
hop-oast
hyped-up
hop-head
hapless
hipness
hip-belt
hopeful
hypogea
hip-shot
hopbind
hopbine
hoplite
hop-vine
happing
hipping
hopping
hippish
haptics
happily
hop-flea
hopples
hip-knob
ha'pence
hyponym
ha'penny
haploid
hypnoid
hip-bone
hop-pole
hypnone
hip-roof
hip-lock
hip-gout
hop-tree
hap'orth
hypural
heparin
hyperon
hepatic
hepster
hipster
hypoxia
hypoxic
harmala
herbage
hireage
hersall
harmans
herbary
hirable
hornbug
hurlbat
herdboy
hyraces
haricot
hirudin
herself
Hordeum
hordein
harness
herdess
hurleys
harvest
horrent
hartely
harmful
hornful
hurtful
hard-got
harshen
hership
hard-hit
harshly
harried
hurried
harmine
heroine
heroise
heroize
hircine
harling
herling
herring
hirling
horning
horsing
hurling
hardish
hornish
hernial
heroism
hornito
harrier
heroics
hurdies
harpist
herbist
hornist
hardily
horrify
Harijan
hare-lip
hurdler
hurdles
harslet
herblet
hornlet
horn-mad
herdman
horn-nut
heronry
hardoke
herbose
hormone
hordock
harpoon
harbour
herbous
horrors
harmost
harmony
hard-pan
harn-pan
hard-run
Hereros
hérissé
hard-set
haroset
heretic
hirstie
hardtop
heritor
hirsute
hard-won
hyraxes
horizon
husband

Words marked △ may be spelled also with a capital letter

hastate
hostage
hushaby
Hasidic
Hasidim
has-been
hostess
hosiery
hospice
hostile
Hussite
huswife
hissing
hosting
husking
hashish
△**hessian**
hastily
huskily
hostler
hustler
hoseman
hosanna
hose-net
histoid
histone
hassock
history
histrio
Heshvan
hatband
hatrack
hetmans
hatable
hetaera
hothead
hatless
hotness
hot-melt
hottest
hutment
hateful
hatchel
hatcher
hitcher
hatches
hatchet
hotshot
hetaira
Hittite
hotline
hatting
hitting
hotting
hutting
hottish
hattock
hotfoot
hutzpah
Hotspur
hot-trod
heteros
hatfuls
haulage
hautboy
heureka
hauberk
hauteur
haughty
housing
houting
heurism
haulier
hoummos
haunted
haunter
have-a-go
hive-bee
hoveled
havened
havings
have-not
hive-off
haveour
haviour
haverel
hawkbit
howbeit
hawking
howling
hawkish
hawbuck
however
howdy-do
hexadic
hexagon
hexapla
hexapod
hexarch
hayband
hayward
hey-pass
hayseed
hayride
haywire
hayrick
hay-bote
haycock
hayfork
hayloft
heyduck
huzzaed
hazelly
igarapé
imamate
in-and-in
imagery
inanely
irately
imagine
isatine
imaging
△**imagism**
itacism
Iranian
Italian
italics
imagist
Italiot
inanity
isagoge
imagoes
inaptly
iracund
inboard
imbrast
imbiber
inbreed
inbreak
inbeing
inbring
in-built
imbrown
imburse
inburst
imbosom
imbathe
inbound
imbrute
imbower
inchase
inclasp
incubus
incudes
incline
ischial
ischium
incomer
incense
inconie
inconnu
inclose
incross
inchpin
incipit
incurve
incised
incisor
inciter
include
incrust
incivil
indrawn
indraft
indicia
Indocid®
indican
inducer
indices
indwell
indwelt
indigos
indulge
indulin
indoors
in-depth
indorse
ioduret
indusia
inditer
indexal
indoxyl
indexer
indexes
ikebana
Iceland
iterate
icepack
iceball
inexact
iterant
iceberg
ice-belt
itemise
itemize
Iberian
irenics
ice-blue
ideally
ice-cold
iceboat
ice-foot
ice-free
inearth
Isegrim
ileuses
inertia
identic
ileitis
ineptly
inertly
inflame
inflate
infract
infidel
infield
inflect
inflict
infulae
infimae
infimum
infanta
infante
infancy
inforce
△**inferno**
infarct
infuser
infaust
ingrate
ingrain
ingraft
ingress
ingoing
ingulph
ingénue
ingener
inglobe
ingrown
ingroup
ingross
ingesta
Ishmael
ichabod
inhabit
inhibit
ichthic
ichthys
ichnite
inhaler
inhuman
inhumer
inherce
inherit
in-house
inhaust
imitate
irisate
imitant
iliacus
Irideae
irideal
iciness
iridise
iridize
initial
iridial
iridium
iridian
idiotic
idiotcy
injoint
injelly
injunct
injurer
ilkaday
ink-feed
in-kneed
inkwell
inkling
ink-fish
ink-blot
irksome
inkhorn
inkspot
Inkatha
illicit
illness
illogic
illegal
inlying
ill-will
Islamic
isleman
illapse

Words marked △ may be spelled also with a capital letter

7 i□l□r

ill-bred
ill-used
idlesse
inlayer
Ismaili
iambics
iambist
immense
immerge
immerse
immoral
ismatic
innyard
ignoble
ignobly
ionomer
innings
igneous
innerve
ignorer
ignaros
innards
ioniser
igniter
ionizer
isobare
isobase
isolate
isobath
isogamy
isomere
isogeny
isochor
ivoried
iconise
iconize
idolise
idolize
ironise
ironize
isoline
ironing
idolism
Ivorian
ivories
idolist
ironist
ivorist
iconify
ipomoea
isodoma
Isopoda
isotone
isotope
isodont
isokont
isonomy
isotopy
iron-pan
isospin
isogram

isotron
isoetes
isotype
isohyet
implate
inphase
impeach
impearl
implant
impresa
implead
implete
imprese
impregn
impress
imprest
impiety
implied
impaint
imprint
impulse
impalas
impinge
impanel
implode
implore
improve
impious
imperia
imperil
imports
impasse
impaste
impasto
imposer
imputer
impetus
impound
impavid
inquere
inquest
inquire
inquiet
inquiry
inqilab
inroads
Israeli
ivresse
inscape
insnare
instate
install
instant
issuant
Insecta
insider
insides
instead
inshell
inspect
insofar

insigne
insight
inspire
inswing
instill
insulse
insulin
insular
insanie
insinew
inshore
in-store
insooth
insipid
insured
insurer
insculp
intrada
intrant
intreat
integer
ijtihad
intwine
in-thing
intwist
intimae
isthmus
intense
intoner
introld
introit
icteric
icterid
interne
inthral
△**interim**
icterus
ictuses
intrude
intrust
inulase
iguanid
invader
invoice
inveigh
invalid
involve
invenit
invious
inverse
invitee
inviter
invexed
inweave
inwards
inwoven
idyllic
ivy-bush
joannes
jealous
jib-sail

jobless
jobbery
jibbing
jobbing
Jobclub
jubilee
jib-boom
jib-door
jackass
△**jacobin**
jacobus
jackdaw
△**jackeen**
jacchus
jocular
jackman
jacamar
jacinth
jaconet
jackpot
jacksie
Jacuzzi®
jacuzzi
Jeddart
jadedly
Judaean
Judaica
jadeite
Judaise
Judaize
Judaism
Judaist
judoist
jodhpur
j'adoube
jeepers
jeering
jeepney
jug-ears
Juglans
jughead
joggers
jaggery
jaghire
jagging
jigging
jogging
jugging
jiggish
juggins
jigajig
jig-a-jig
jigajog
joggled
juggler
jugular
jogtrot
jugfuls
Jahvism
Johnian
Jahvist

△**johnnie**
Jehovah
joinder
joinery
joining
Jainism
Jainist
jointed
jointer
jointly
jejunum
ju-jitsu
juke-box
jukskei
jellaba
jellied
jillion
△**jollies**
jellify
jollify
jollily
jollity
jalapic
jalapin
jaloppy
jalouse
jollyer
jamdani
jampani
jimjams
jump-cut
jamadar
jemadar
jemidar
jambeau
jambeux
Jamaica
jambiya
jemmied
jamming
jambier
jumpily
jump-jet
jumelle
jumbler
jambone
jump-off
jambool
jim-crow
jumbuck
juncate
January
jankers
Janeite
jinjili
Jungian
Jenkins
janskys
jangler
jingler
jinglet

Words marked △ may be spelled also with a capital letter

junkman
jannock
jingoes
juncoes
juniper
Joneses
janitor
jonquil
janizar
jeopard
jeofail
jookery
jipyapa
Jap-silk
Japonic
Jupiter
jury-box
Jericho
juridic
jarring
jerking
Jersian
jurally
jarkman
juryman
jurymen
jargoon
jerquer
jarfuls
jessant
jessamy
jaspery
jestful
jasmine
jussive
justice
jesting
justify
Jethart
jitters
jittery
jettied
jetting
jotting
jutting
jetfoil
joukery
journal
journos
journey
jauntee
jauntie
jouster
jive-ass
Javelle
javelin
juvenal
jawfall
Jew's-ear
jewfish
jewelry
jawbone
jawhole
jaw-foot
jaywalk
Joycean
joyless
joy-ride
joyance
Jezebel
jazzily
jazzman
jazz-pop
khanate
knaidel
khaddar
knavery
khalifa
kyanise
kyanite
kyanize
knavish
klavier
khanjar
knacker
knapped
knapple
knapper
knarred
khamsin
kabbala
kabaddi
kebbock
kibitka
kebbuck
kibbutz
kachcha
kuchcha
kacheri
kachina
kick-off
kidding
kidling
Kaddish
kiddier
kiddies
kidskin
kiddush
keelage
kneecap
knee-cap
kneader
knevell
khediva
khedive
keeling
keening
keeping
kneeled
△kremlin
kneeler
keelman
keepnet
Kleenex®
knee-pad
knee-pan
keelson
knees-up
Knesset
Kaffers
koftgar
Kaffirs
kufiyah
kagoule
Kuh-horn
kahawai
klipdas
Krishna
kainite
knifing
Krilium®
klinker
knicker
keitloa
krimmer
kail-pat
kail-pot
knitted
knittle
keister
knitter
kajawah
kakodyl
kikumon
kokanee
kakapos
kellaut
kilobar
kilobit
kylices
killcow
killdee
kiln-dry
kolkhoz
Kallima
killing
killick
killjoy
kalends
killock
kiloton
Kalmuck
kamichi
kamseen
Kommers
kemping
kimonos
kimboed
kampong
kamerad
komatik
kumquat
Kannada
kingcup
kingdom
kantela
kantele
kennels
kinless
kinchin
kinship
king-hit
kunzite
kenning
Kentish
Kennick
Kantism
Kantian
Kantist
kindler
kinglet
kinsman
kinfolk
king-pin
kindred
king-rod
kenosis
kinesis
kenotic
kinetic
know-all
knobbed
knobble
khotbah
khotbeh
knobber
knobbly
Kroo-boy
knowhow
know-how
kaoline
knowing
knock-on
knock-up
knocker
Kroo-man
knotted
klootch
knotter
kippage
kip-skin
kurbash
kursaal
Kurhaus
Kartell
kirmess
kerygma
kerogen
Karaite
kernite
Karling
karting
kerning
kirking
kernish
Kurdish
karaism
△karakul
kirtled
keramic
kirimon
Koranic
Karenni
karaoke
karstic
keratin
kirkton
Kushite
kishkes
△kashmir
kiss-off
kestrel
△kashrus
△kashrut
kithara
Ketubah
kitschy
katydid
kittens
kitteny
kitchen
ketchup
kitling
kitenge
kathode
kit-boat
katorga
ketosis
Kotytto
knubble
khutbah
knubbly
koumiss
knuckle
knuckly
knurled
kruller
kouprey
key-desk
keyless
key-seat
keyline
kayoing
key-ring
key-cold
keyword
keyhole
keynote
krytron
krypsis
krypton
leafage
leakage
leafbud
llanero

7 l□a□e

leafery
loathed
leather
loather
loathly
leading
leafing
leaning
leaping
leasing
leaving
loading
loafing
loaning
leaflet
learned
learner
lianoid
leasowe
lead-out
Liassic
liaison
lean-tos
leasure
△**leaguer**
libbard
lubbard
labiate
librate
library
libidos
lubfish
Librium®
labella
lobelia
libelee
libeler
lobular
lobulus
lobelet
labroid
labrose
lobworm
lobiped
△**liberal**
labarum
liberos
liberty
lobster
lobbyer
lac-lake
lactase
lactate
lockage
lack-all
lucidly
Lycaena
lacteal
lectern
lackeys
lechery

lockful
△**lucifer**
lucigen
lacking
licking
lochial
lection
Lockian
Locrian
Lockist
luckily
lockjaw
locular
locules
loculus
locally
lace-man
lockman
locoman
lucumos
lacinia
△**laconic**
Lychnic
lacunae
licence
license
lacunal
lacunar
lychnis
lock-nut
lucency
lactone
lactose
lich-owl
lockout
lycopod
Lacerta
lucarne
lucerne
lockram
△**locusta**
lichtly
licitly
Lactuca
lecture
lecturn
lacquer
lace-ups
lyceums
lacquey
lichway
ladybug
ladycow
lidless
laddery
ladyfly
ludship
Luddite
lyddite
lodging
ladyish

ladyism
Luddism
ladykin
ladanum
Ladinos
ladrone
leeward
laetare
lee-gage
lee-lane
lie-abed
Laender
liefest
lievest
leechee
leering
lie-down
lift-boy
lifeful
luffing
leftish
leftism
leftist
loftily
lift-man
left-off
lift-off
laggard
lignage
luggage
lugsail
loggats
legible
legibly
logical
log-head
log-reel
legwear
legless
leg-rest
log-chip
leg-show
leg-side
lignite
logline
lagging
Lagting
legging
ligging
logging
løgting
lugeing
lugging
leggism
loggias
lignify
ligular
legally
legumin
logania
logwood

lignose
lughole
legwork
logbook
log-roll
legroom
lugworm
leghorn
ligroin
leg-spin
leg-iron
lighted
legatee
legitim
lighten
Loghtan
Loghtyn
legator
lighter
legatos
lightly
leg-pull
leg-over
lairage
lying-in
leidger
lyingly
laithfu'
laicise
laicize
lairise
lairize
laicity
leisler
leister
leisure
likable
Lakshmi
lokshen
lekking
lakelet
Lollard
Lallans
lullaby
lulibub
lalling
Lalique
lambada
lemmata
Limnaea
Lymnaea
Lombard
lamb-ale
limbate
limeade
lumbang
lumbago
lambast
limacel
limaçon
limaces

lum-head
limbeck
lampern
lampers
limbers
lambent
lambert
lamp-fly
lamiger
lymphad
lempira
lamming
lamping
lemming
limning
limping
lumping
lompish
lumpish
Lamaism
lampion
Lemnian
Lamaist
lumpily
lambkin
limpkin
lumpkin
lamella
△**limulus**
limelit
lomenta
laminae
liminal
lumenal
luminal
laminar
lampoon
lamboys
limbous
limepit
Lemuria
lemures
lamprey
limosis
limited
lameter
lamiter
limiter
lymiter
limites
lampuka
lampuki
langaha
lantana
laniard
lanyard
lindane
lineage
lineate
linkage
linsang

long-ago
laniary
longbow
linkboy
linocut
long-day
linseed
lantern
Linnean
lyncean
lancers
linters
lengest
lenient
longest
lungful
lanugos
luncher
linchet
lynchet
landing
lending
longing
lunging
longish
lentisk
lentigo
lankily
long-leg
lanolin
ländler
lunular
land-law
landman
lensman
lineman
linkman
linings
lentoid
long-oil
lentous
lingoes
line-out
Londony
langrel
land-rat
lunatic
lunated
lunette
Landtag
lengths
linctus
land-tax
lengthy
△**lingula**
langued
languid
lingual
languor
languet
laneway
leopard
leotard
lion-cub
lioncel
Lyomeri
lioness
loosely
looful
lyophil
△**leonine**
lionise
lionize
looning
looping
looting
lionism
lookism
Laotian
loobily
lookout
look-see
lapsang
lapheld
lip-read
lip-deep
lipless
liplike
lapping
lapwing
lipping
lopping
Lappish
lapilli
lupulin
leprose
leptome
lapwork
leprous
leptons
leprosy
Laputan
Lapiths
lip-sync
liquate
liqueur
liquefy
larvate
lurdane
loricae
lyrical
lyricon
Laridae
luridly
lorrell
lernean
largess
larceny
largely
larchen
lurcher
lording
lurking
largish
larkish
larmier
lordkin
Lorelei
lorimer
lorgnon
loriner
lardoon
lyrated
lorette
lyra-way
lastage
Lusiads
losable
listeth
listful
lustful
lasagna
lasagne
lashing
lasting
lisping
listing
luskish
lustick
△**lesbian**
lustily
lashkar
lassoed
lissome
lassock
lassoes
lustral
lustrum
lustres
lispund
lithate
latrant
latices
lethean
lettern
luthern
letters
lathery
lithely
littery
lottery
latchet
lethied
latrine
lattice
lithite
lathing
letting
lotting
Lettish
lithium
Latvian
luthier
Latakia
littlin
latence
Latiner
latency
lithoid
let-down
luteous
lateral
literal
Lythrum
Lateran
liturgy
litotes
latitat
lettuce
latexes
launder
lounder
laundry
laurels
loutery
lounger
leuchen
leughen
laugher
lauwine
leucine
leucite
louring
loudish
loutish
lousily
leucoma
leukoma
louvred
livable
lovable
lavabos
live-box
lived-in
lividly
love-day
levying
lavolta
livelod
livener
live-oak
lovered
leveret
loverly
levitic
levator
lawland
lowland
low-paid
law-calf
△**lowveld**
low-tech
low-bell
low-gear
lawless
lowness
low-life
low-rise
law-list
lowlily
law-book
low-born
low-down
low-cost
low-bred
low-brow
lewisia
lewdsby
lawsuit
lexical
lexicon
laxness
loxygen
laxator
layback
laytime
loyally
loyalty
laylock
lay-down
layered
layette
layaway
lazy-bed
lozenge
lozengy
lazaret
meat-axe
meal-ark
meander
moanful
meat-fly
myalgia
myalgic
Moabite
meaning
myalism
mealies
meatily
maatjes
measled
measles
miasmic
miasmal
meal-man
meat-man
miasmas
meacock
meadowy
meat-tea
meat-tub
measure
mobbing
mobbish
mobsman

Words marked △ may be spelled also with a capital letter

7 m□b□t

mobster
mace-ale
macramé
mockage
macrami
Meccano®
mockado
machair
macabre
macacos
macadam
machete
mochell
muchell
mockers
mockery
mucigen
macchie
machine
miching
mocking
miction
micella
mycelia
maculae
micelle
Mechlin
macular
meconic
meconin
microbe
microns
macaque
machree
mucosae
mycosis
mycotic
△**mycetes**
Macrura
machzor
madrasa
Midgard
△midland
mediate
Midrash
mudbath
mudlark
mudpack
mediant
mediacy
medacca
medical
modicum
medicos
mudscow
△**mid-week**
midterm
mid-year
madness
maddest
middest

mid-Lent
Midwest
midship
Madeira
muddied
mid-life
midsize
midwife
midwive
midriff
madding
madling
mudfish
muddily
mudéjar
medulla
medaled
modeled
modelli
modello
mudflap
meddler
modeler
modular
muddler
modulus
medalet
mudflat
modally
Madonna
madroña
Modiola
madrone
mud-cone
mudhole
Maddock
mudhook
madzoon
midnoon
madroño
mid-hour
madwort
midmost
mud-boat
mudwort
madoqua
mudiria
mad-bred
midiron
medusae
modiste
medusan
medusas
modesty
mud-lump
mediums
meercat
mueddin
meeting
meemies
meerkat

moellon
myeloma
myeloid
maestri
maestro
muezzin
muffish
maffick
Muftiat
miffily
maffled
muffled
mafflin
muffler
△**mafiosi**
△**mafioso**
mofette
magmata
mug-lamb
magnate
migrate
migrant
megabar
megabit
magical
Mogadon®
Megaera
magneto
megafog
mugshot
mugging
muggish
megrims
muggins
magnify
moguled
magalog
magsman
magenta
mugwort
maggoty
Maghreb
Maghrib
megarad
megaron
megasse
megaton
mightst
mugwump
magnums
mugfuls
Mahican
Mohican
mahseer
Mohegan
Mahdism
Mahdist
mahonia
mah-jong
mahatma
Mahound

mridang
mailbag
mailbox
mail-car
moineau
mail-gig
moither
mailing
maiming
maidish
maidism
maillot
mailman
moidore
mainour
Meissen
meioses
meiosis
myiasis
meiotic
moisten
maintop
maister
maistry
moistly
mailvan
majorat
majesty
makable
mikados
makings
mikrons
mukhtar
mallard
maleate
maltase
mileage
miliary
milk-bar
malacia
malicho
milk-cow
melodic
milldam
mylodon
△**maltese**
mill-eye
mullein
malleus
milieus
milreis
milieux
mildewy
malefic
malaise
mellite
millime
milvine
malling
malting
melting

milking
milling
meltith
Millian
million
mullion
milkily
mollify
milk-leg
melilot
maltman
milkman
molimen
malonic
melanic
melange
mélange
melanin
Malines
melanos
molinet
maltose
mullock
milfoil
Miltown®
mellowy
milk-pan
malaria
milk-run
millrun
molerat
malarky
melisma
Molasse
molossi
malison
milk-sop
malmsey
militia
mulatta
mulcted
mulatto
militar
mollusc
multure
mollusk
mulmull
Malayam
Malayan
mammate
mammary
mimical
mimicry
mamzers
momzers
mummery
mummied
mumming
mumpish
mimmick
memoirs

Words marked △ may be spelled also with a capital letter

7 m□r□n

mummify
mamilla
mamelon
mumbler
mimulus
momenta
memento
mim-mou'd
mammoth
mammock
mummock
membral
mu-meson
mimesis
mimetic
mancala
mandala
manyata
mansard
△**mandate**
man-made
miniate
mintage
montage
montane
mundane
manjack
man-jack
manpack
mondain
man-days
manoaos
minyans
montant
minibus
minicab
monacid
manacle
monocle
minicam
menacer
mini-car
monocot
monadic
monodic
Monodon
minuend
man-week
manteel
montero
man-year
minceur
mynheer
manners
monkeys
manrent
manteau
mongery
monkery
mindful
monofil

manager
manihoc
menthol
Manchoo
muncher
manchet
Manihot
monthly
mandira
mandioc
mankind
man-like
mannite
man-size
manning
mending
mincing
minding
munting
mannish
monkish
minnick
mondial
mansion
mention
munnion
mundify
muntjac
muntjak
manakin
manikin
minikin
moniker
△**manilla**
monilia
manille
mangler
mingler
mantlet
manumea
minimal
minimum
Manxman
mint-man
monomer
minimus
manumit
minimax
mint-new
mandola
mandora
mineola
mangold
manhood
manhole
mannose
menfolk
minnock
monsoon
man-hour
mangoes

mantoes
Mantoux
man-body
monopod
maniple
Minerva
Minorca
monarda
△**menorah**
monarch
mandrel
mandril
mineral
mongrel
mantram
moneron
mantrap
manurer
minaret
mini-sub
menisci
mono-ski
monosis
mindset
minutia
manatee
minette
Minitel
minster
monitor
monster
munster
minutes
manitou
monture
mensual
Mantuan
manhunt
minever
miniver
minivet
man-o'-war
men-o'-war
monaxon
moneyed
moneyer
moorage
miombos
moon-bow
Miocene
mooneye
Mooress
Moorery
moon-god
moorhen
moocher
mooring
mooting
moonish
△moorish
moorill

muonium
△**moonies**
moodily
moorlog
moonlet
moonlit
moorman
mootman
maormor
Mjölnir
myosote
myology
moor-pan
myogram
moonset
mooktar
myotube
Mao-suit
mophead
mappery
mapwise
mapping
mopping
mappist
Marsala
mermaid
mirbane
muriate
myrbane
murlain
murrain
marcato
Marrano
mormaor
mordant
marybud
mirable
marabou
miracle
moriche
morocco
maracas
murices
Muridae
mirador
△**muraena**
murgeon
marrels
margent
martext
mordent
morceau
mercery
mirific
morphia
morrhua
morphic
myrrhic
marshal
myrrhol
Märchen

marcher
markhor
murther
marches
morphos
merchet
morphew
married
marline
Marmite®
marmite
moraine
morrice
mortice
mortise
murrine
marking
marling
marring
merling
morling
morning
moreish
murkish
Martini
Martini®
martini
martial
Marxism
Martian
Marxian
mersion
morrion
murrion
marrier
Marxist
mercify
merrily
mortify
murkily
markkaa
markkas
marbled
morello
marbler
morular
marbles
merells
marplot
martlet
morally
Morglay
maremma
marimba
markman
Maranta
Moringa
myringa
moronic
meronym
morendo

Words marked △ may be spelled also with a capital letter

7 m□r□n

mariner
marines
merinos
margosa
marmose
morwong
Marconi®
marconi
merfolk
Mormops
marrowy
marl-pit
Moresco
△morisco
morassy
Maratha
Marathi
marital
marquee
morsure
marquis
△**mercury**
murexes
martyry
mascara
mastaba
mislaid
missaid
mustard
massage
message
misdate
misease
misfare
misgave
mismade
mismake
mismate
misname
misrate
mistake
mustang
miscall
misfall
mista'en
miscast
mishapt
musk-bag
musk-cod
musical
musk-cat
Mustela
misdeed
misfeed
mislead
misread
missend
miswend
misdeal
misfell
mistell
misdeem
misseem
misterm
misween
masseur
mishear
missent
miswent
mostest
mastery
mistery
mystery
mast-fed
mastful
mistful
museful
moss-hag
mestiza
massive
misfile
misfire
misgive
mislike
mislive
missile
missive
mistime
mastiff
mashing
meshing
missing
misting
moshing
mastich
△messiah
missish
misdial
Mosaism
mission
mestizo
mistico
△**messias**
misdiet
messily
mistily
mushily
muskily
mustily
mystify
mascled
meseled
muscled
Moselle
mashlam
mashlim
mashlum
mesclum
mashlin
mesclun
Musales
mesally
misally
misplay
mishmee
mashman
musimon
masonic
mesonic
Mishnic
Mishnah
mist-net
misknow
masonry
Massora
mastoid
mistold
misword
muscoid
misdone
misgone
misyoke
muscone
muscose
muskone
mistook
misform
Mas-John
Mes-John
misborn
misjoin
misdoer
miscopy
△muscovy
musk-pod
Masorah
mesarch
mistral
muskrat
misdraw
miserly
musk-sac
misuser
mash-tub
musette
mash-tun
mess-tin
misstep
meshuga
misrule
mistune
misluck
mesquin
masquer
museums
mesquit
missuit
masculy
moshvei
mash-vat
Mesozoa
methane
matrass
matzahs
metcast
mutable
mutably
metical
maticos
matador
matweed
mittens
moth-eat
mattery
mothery
mitogen
mutagen
matched
matcher
matrice
mythise
mythize
matting
methink
mythism
mattins
metrics
metrist
mythist
Matilda
metaled
mettled
mottled
Mytilus
matelot
metally
metamer
mutanda
Metonic
matinee
matinée
matinal
metonym
mattoid
mottoed
matooke
matzoth
mattock
matzoon
me-tooer
matlows
matross
motions
mottoes
muttons
Methody
muttony
metopic
metopon
Mithras
△**métisse**
mitoses
mitosis
mitotic
matsuri
motivic
mitsvah
mitzvah
métayer
△**metazoa**
mousaka
moulage
mauvais
maunder
moulder
mauvein
maulers
mousery
maulgre
mauther
moucher
mouther
mauvine
mousing
Maurist
mouillé
maudlin
mouflon
mousmee
mourner
mounted
Mountie
moulten
mounter
movable
movably
Mevlevi
Moviola®
Mawlawi
mawseed
mawther
mawkish
maw-worm
mowburn
mixable
Mexican
mixed-up
mixedly
maxwell
mixtion
maxilla
maximal
maximum
maximin
mixture
May-game
Mayfair
May-lady
mayweed
may-bird
Maytime
may-lily
May-lord
maypole
May-morn

mayoral
mayster
may-duke
mazzard
mizmaze
Mazdean
mazeful
muzzily
muzzler
mazurka
Mozarab
Mazarin
mozetta
mezuzah
nuanced
nearest
Noachic
Nyanjas
naartje
nabbing
nibbing
nebbich
nebbish
niblick
nobbily
nebulae
nebular
nibbler
nobbler
nebulas
nictate
nectary
nucleic
nucleal
Nicaean
nuclein
nucleon
nuclear
nucleus
nacrite
nuclide
necking
niceish
nacelle
nucelli
necklet
necrose
nacrous
nocuous
nacarat
necktie
noctuid
noctule
nocturn
nodical
nodding
noduled
nodular
nodally
nodated
△**ne'erday**

needful
Noetian
needily
needler
needles
niellos
naevoid
naebody
naffing
niftily
no-fines
no-fault
niggard
nagmaal
△**negress**
neglect
niggery
nuggety
negligé
négligé
nagging
nogging
Negrito
nigrify
nigella
niggler
△**negroid**
Negroes
nagapie
nighted
nightie
nightly
Nahuatl
nihonga
no-hoper
nail-bed
naiades
naïveté
naiveté
nailery
naively
naïvely
naivety
naïvety
neither
nailing
naivist
noisily
noisome
nail-rod
nainsel'
nakedly
niks-nie
nilgais
nilgaus
nylghau
nulling
nullify
nullity
nelumbo
Nilotic

Nilotes
nummary
namable
nomadic
name-day
△**numbers**
nimiety
nymphic
nymphae
nymphal
nymphos
nymphet
nymphly
numbing
nombles
numbles
nimonic
nominee
nominal
nimious
numeric
nomarch
nemoral
nombril
numeral
nemesia
namaste
name-son
Nemeses
△nemesis
nematic
non-term
nankeen
non-hero
nunnery
nonaged
nonagon
nunship
ninthly
nannied
nandine
nundine
nunnish
Nancies
nannies
nuncios
non-skid
non-flam
non-slip
nonplus
nunhood
non-come
nonuple
ninepin
Nynorsk
non-iron
non-drip
non-user
nonette
nonetti
nunatak

nonetto
non-stop
nonsuch
nonsuit
nun-buoy
Neogaea
neonate
niobate
neo-Nazi
noonday
Neogene
Niobean
neoteny
niobite
nooning
neolith
niobium
Neozoic
niobous
neology
noology
napless
nippers
napping
nipping
nuptial
nappies
nippily
Nepalis
nephric
nephron
naphtha
nepotic
Neptune
△**nirvana**
norland
norward
nor'ward
narrate
nervate
Normans
nurhags
nor'-east
norteña
narceen
norteño
nor'-west
nursery
Nurofen®
nuraghe
nuraghi
narwhal
norther
△**narthex**
nargile
nervine
nursing
nereids
nargily
nervily
nartjie

norimon
Neronic
Norfolk
narrows
nervous
neritic
nervule
nervure
nurture
nosebag
nascent
noshery
nestful
nashgab
nosegay
nesting
nastily
nose-led
Nasalis
nasally
no-score
nose-rag
nostril
nostrum
nitrate
nutcase
netball
nutgall
notable
notably
notedly
nutmeal
notaeum
nathemo
nattery
nuttery
notched
notchel
notcher
nitride
nitrile
nitrite
nutlike
netting
nithing
nothing
nutting
net-fish
nit-pick
natrium
Nitrian
nattily
nitrify
nuttily
notelet
net-play
notanda
Nitinol
nutwood
network
nut-hook

Words marked △ may be spelled also with a capital letter

7 n□t□o

nitroso
nations
nitrous
notions
note-pad
natured
niterie
nut-tree
natural
notitia
netsuke
no-trump
noumena
nousell
nouveau
noughts
naughty
neurine
neurite
nourice
nourish
nautili
neurism
nautics
nauplii
neuroma
neurone
neutral
neutron
noursle
neuston
Navahos
navvied
Navajos
novalia
novella
novelle
novelty
niveous
navarch
navarin
navarho
navette
new-laid
Newgate
new-made
New-Wave
new-wave
newsboy
nowhere
newness
nowness
newsman
newcome
newborn
new-mown
noxious
nayward
noyance
nayword
noysome
Naziism
oxalate
ouakari
ouabain
otalgia
orangey
ocarina
opaline
otarine
oxazine
okaying
odalisk
onanism
oralism
orarium
orarian
orarion
oration
ovarian
ovation
otaries
onanist
opacity
orality
odaller
opacous
△**oratory**
oratrix
onboard
on-board
oxblood
orbital
orbiter
orchard
oscheal
oncogen
osculum
oscular
obconic
orcinol
Oscines
occiput
oncosts
occlude
oddball
oddness
oldness
oddment
odd-like
old-time
on-drive
oodlins
oddsman
ordinee
ordinal
ordinar
Oedipal
Oedipus
orderer
orderly
ondatra
oldster
odd-even
operand
operate
overage
over-age
overawe
overall
over-all
overarm
oregano
open-air
operant
overact
overbid
overbuy
overdue
overdye
oreades
open-end
oreweed
overeye
oneself
oneness
overeat
overfed
overfar
overfly
overget
one-shot
overhit
obelise
obelize
olefine
one-time
Owenite
opening
obelisk
Owenism
obelion
Owenian
Owenist
obesity
overjoy
overlie
overlap
ocellar
ocellus
overlay
overman
oceanic
△**oceanid**
overnet
oceloid
onefold
operose
onerous
overpay
overply
olearia
oneiric
overred
overran
overren
overrun
over-rev
oversea
oversee
overset
oversew
oversow
orectic
omental
omentum
one-step
one-stop
open-top
overtop
oven-tit
overtax
overtly
overuse
one-eyed
offhand
off-ward
offtake
offscum
officer
offices
offpeak
off-peak
off-beam
offbeat
off-line
offside
off-site
ooftish
off-plan
offence
offense
ox-fence
offload
off-road
off-come
off-fore
off-spin
offered
od-force
offeree
offerer
offeror
off-duty
orgiast
ongoing
on-going
oogonia
organza
organic
organum
organon
Ophidia
ochreae
oghamic
ochroid
ochrous
△**ophitic**
ophiura
origane
oxidase
oxidate
origami
oxidant
olivary
Oniscus
olivine
orifice
ovicide
oxidise
oxidize
Odinism
opinion
Osirian
Ovidian
Odinist
oligist
oriency
oviform
okimono
ominous
olitory
osiered
omicron
omitted
opiated
omitter
obitual
oviduct
Ojibwas
oak-gall
oak-mast
oakleaf
oak-fern
oakling
oak-wood
oak-tree
oak-lump
oil-cake
oil-bath
oil-palm
orleans
oil-seed
oil-belt
onliest
obligee
obligor
oil-bird
owl-like
oil-rich
oil-silk
oil-mill
oilskin
oolakan
oulakan

Words marked △ may be spelled also with a capital letter

7 p□a□m

owl-moth
oblique
obloquy
oil-tree
oil-drum
oolitic
owl-eyed
osmiate
oomiack
osmunda
Osmanli
osmious
osmosis
ommatea
osmotic
omniana
omnibus
omniety
omnific
omneity
oenomel
Odonata
obovate
odorate
odorant
obolary
ovoidal
oropesa
orogeny
oporice
ozonise
ozonize
otolith
oxonium
Oxonian
obovoid
oloroso
odorous
orology
otology
odoured
opossum
odontic
orotund
otocyst
oppidan
Orphean
oppress
Orpheus
Orphism
orphrey
opposer
oophyte
ocreate
o'ergang
oarweed
ourself
oarless
ogreish
owre'lay
oarsman

o'erword
o'ercome
oar-lock
oersted
on-stage
ossuary
ossicle
onstead
obscene
ossific
od's-life
oustiti
osselet
opsonic
opsonin
onshore
on-shore
oospore
od's-bobs
osseous
obsequy
observe
oestral
oestrum
oestrus
osseter
obscure
ostraca
ostraka
outland
outward
oatcake
ostiate
outdare
outdate
outface
outgate
outname
outpace
outrace
outrage
outrate
outtake
out-take
out-half
outlash
outwash
Ostmark
outback
outrank
outtalk
outwalk
outfall
outhaul
outsail
out-wall
outcast
outlast
outpart
ostiary
October

optical
octadic
outedge
outweed
oatmeal
outsell
outtell
outwell
outleap
outpeep
outweep
outpeer
outwear
outness
outjest
outwent
octofid
octagon
outshot
outwind
outgive
outhire
outline
outlive
outride
outside
outsize
outwing
ostrich
outwith
outwick
orthian
outlier
ortolan
outflow
outplay
optimal
optimum
△**ottoman**
osteoma
osteoid
ostiole
outcome
outgone
outmode
outmove
outrope
outsole
outvote
outlook
outwork
outworn
outroop
outdoor
outgoer
outpour
outroar
outsoar
options
outgoes
outfoot

outmost
outport
outpost
outroot
octapla
octopod
octuple
outspan
octopus
outbred
outbrag
outcrop
orthros
outgrow
outpray
out-tray
octette
outstep
outstay
obtrude
outdure
outgush
outrush
outburn
outturn
outjump
octaval
out-over
octavos
out-owre
outswim
outhyre
oculate
ovulate
opuscle
opulent
oculist
oeuvres
opuntia
obviate
ouvrage
Orvieto
ouvrier
obvious
obverse
ouverte
onwards
oxy-salt
oxy-acid
onychia
odylism
Ogygian
oxytone
olycook
olykoek
onymous
Olympia
Olympic
Olympus
△**odyssey**
odzooks

placard
placate
platane
Pharaoh
peasant
play-act
phalanx
peatary
peat-bed
prabble
peat-bog
playbus®
play-box
playboy
peascod
. **prancke**
prancer
placcat
plaided
plaudit
play-day
placebo
prayers
plateau
peatery
playful
piaffer
peat-hag
peacher
poacher
plashet
placita
platina
praline
peaking
placing
plating
playing
prating
praying
planish
phaeism
pianism
plagium
pianino
pianist
piarist
pravity
prankle
placket
phallic
pearled
pearlin
phallin
prawlin
pearler
△**phallus**
playlet
pyaemia
plasmic
ptarmic

Words marked △ may be spelled also with a capital letter

7 p□a□m

pyaemic
phasmid
plasmid
peatman
plasmin
planned
praunce
planner
plainly
Pianola®
phacoid
placoid
plafond
play-off
peacock
peafowl
platoon
pea-soup
pea-coat
playpen
pea-crab
prairie
pea-iron
Prakrit
praiser
praeses
praises
plastic
practic
plaited
plastid
platted
piastre
prattle
phantom
phaeton
Plantin
plaiter
plantar
planter
plaster
platter
praetor
△psalter
peartly
planula
peanuts
plaguey
planury
play-way
planxty
pharynx
pébrine
publish
pebbled
pabulum
pabular
pibroch
puberal
puberty
pubises
pochard
pockard
package
pickaxe
picrate
peccavi
peccant
peccary
pacable
picador
pace-egg
pickeer
pschent
pickery
puckery
△**pacific**
pectise
pectize
picrite
pycnite
packing
pecking
picking
peckish
Pictish
puckish
pachisi
paction
piccies
pickled
△**pucelle**
pickler
pickles
packman
picamar
pickmaw
pectose
puccoon
piccolo
pochoir
piceous
pockpit
pack-rat
picotee
picture
picquet
packway
pedrail
pedlary
pedicab
pedicle
pedicel
pidgeon
padrero
pedrero
podagra
padding
podding
pudding
padella
podalic
pedaled
paddler
peddler
piddler
puddler
pedalos
pudenda
pudency
padrone
padroni
paddock
padlock
piddock
puddock
pad-tree
podestà
pedesis
pedetic
precava
piebald
prefard
prepaid
pyebald
peerage
phenate
pierage
Pléiade
predate
preface
prefade
prelate
prepare
presage
pre-wash
prepack
prevail
prewarm
predawn
prewarn
peekabo
Pleiads
precast
plenary
prelacy
prelaty
pierced
pre-echo
piercer
preachy
pleaded
pleader
preverb
prebend
prehend
pretend
precede
prevene
pre-sell
preterm
plebean
pre-teen
peeress
peevers
poetess
precess
precept
prefect
preheat
prelect
present
pretest
pretext
prevent
preyful
pledgee
pledger
pledgor
pledget
pie-shop
poe-bird
Peelite
poetise
poetize
precise
premise
preside
previse
puerile
peeling
peevish
piedish
plenish
prejink
predial
pietism
premium
Pierian
pterion
plenipo
premier
poetics
prelims
premiss
pietist
plenist
predict
preview
plebify
phellem
pueblos
preemie
pre-empt
paeonic
pfennig
pleroma
pteroic
plerome
premove
prepone
prepose
precook
precool
predoom
preform
preborn
pleopod
prepped
pleurae
pleural
preoral
pleuron
△**pierrot**
pleased
pressed
preasse
pressie
press-up
pleaser
plessor
presser
pressor
plectra
P-Celtic
P-Keltic
pleated
peep-toe
plectre
Prestel®
pre-stun
pleater
prestos
paenula
plexure
prelude
prepuce
presume
preludi
prequel
prerupt
pteryla
pie-eyed
prenzie
prezzie
pretzel
pheazar
puff-box
po-faced
piffero
puffery
puffing
puffily
piffler
pigwash
Pugwash
pigtail
pageant
page-boy
pigfeed
pig-herd
pig-lead
pigweed
pigmean
pygmean

7 p□n□i

pig-deer
pigmeat
pigment
piggery
puggery
pegging
pigging
pigling
pogoing
pugging
pig-fish
piggish
puggish
pug-mill
piggies
pig-lily
pigskin
puggled
pigsnie
paginal
pigsney
pigmoid
pygmoid
pug-nose
pug-moth
peg-tops
pigboat
pagurid
puggree
pig-iron
△pegasus
pightle
pig-jump
pig-eyed
Pahlavi
Pehlevi
plicate
primage
primate
prisade
prisage
private
paisano
poinado
prisado
privado
primacy
△primary
privacy
pliable
pribble
pliably
paiocke
princox
poinder
primero
primeur
primely
pailful
painful
prigged
prigger
peishwa
prithee
primine
pairing
priming
pairial
pridian
pricier
privily
privity
pliskie
prickle
pricker
pricket
prickly
paillon
paisley
primmed
primmer
psionic
pliancy
pair-oar
△priapic
Priapus
poitrel
primsie
poisson
painted
pointed
philtre
pointel
painter
philter
pointer
printer
primula
pajocke
pyjama'd
pajamas
pyjamas
pokeful
pak-choi
pukekos
pikelet
pikeman
pakfong
paktong
pakapoo
Pakhtun
pollard
palmate
palpate
peltate
pileate
pillage
pole-axe
poll-axe
pulsate
pellach
pellack
pollack
peltast
polyact
palmary
palabra
pill-bug
pill-box
polacca
polacre
pelican
pile-cap
palm-cat
polecat
paludic
paludal
paladin
pulleys
pollent
pilfery
palmful
pelagic
polygam
polygon
phlegmy
pilcher
palsied
palling
pelting
pilling
polling
pulvini
pallial
pallium
pillion
palmiet
palmist
poloist
pollicy
pulpify
pulpily
Palilia
pilular
palolos
polemic
palamae
pollman
Pullman
polymer
△phlomis
polenta
Polonia
polynia
polynya
polonie
Pilsner
pili-nut
palooka
polyoma
pallone
pellock
pillock
pollock
palm-oil
pilcorn
pultoon
pileous
pulpous
pull-out
pillory
pillowy
Pelopid
polypod
polypes
polypus
peloria
peloric
pyloric
pilgrim
polaron
puldron
pelorus
Polaris
pylorus
pilcrow
palfrey
pelisse
pull-tab
pelitic
politic
palette
palatal
palmtop
pilotis
paletot
poll-tax
pollute
pulture
palaver
phloxes
palmyra
Polyzoa
palazzi
palazzo
pompano
pemican
pommelé
pampean
pampero
pompelo
pimping
pompion
pumpion
pompier
pumpkin
pimpled
pomelos
pimento
pompoon
pompous
△pomfret
pomeroy
pi-meson
pomatum
Pangaea
poniard
pancake
pannage
pen-case
pennate
pentane
pincase
pinnace
pinnate
pondage
pontage
Panjabi
pindari
Punjabi
pinball
pintail
pintado
pendant
pennant
pentact
pangamy
panacea
panocha
panache
panicle
penuche
pinocle
penuchi
Panicum
panicky
Panadol®
pinhead
pangene
pentene
pink-eye
Pandean
pincers
pandect
pendent
pungent
puniest
ponceau
Panagia
punt-gun
penthia
pinched
punch-up
panther
pincher
puncher
ponchos
panchax
pansied
pennied
pensiv'd
pantile
pantine
pennine
pensile

Words marked △ may be spelled also with a capital letter

7 p□n□i

pensive
pentice
pentise
pin-fire
pontile
pontiff
panging
panning
panting
pending
penning
pinking
pinning
punning
pinfish
pinkish
pannick
pennill
Pandion
Peneian
pension
pannier
panties
pennies
paneity
pontify
punalua
pantler
pingler
Pan-Slav
penally
penalty
penance
△**pandora**
penfold
pinfold
pinnoed
pandore
pannose
pentode
pentose
pinhole
pinnock
pantoum
pindown
pontoon
pandoor
pandour
pingoes
pinkoes
pongoes
pint-pot
panoply
Pan-Arab
pangram
penises
pinetum
punctum
Pinxter
punster
penates

punctos
pandura
pinnula
pinguid
pinnule
penguin
pinguin
panfuls
pin-dust
pin-eyed
prosaic
proband
provand
peonage
phonate
probate
proface
profane
prolate
pronate
propage
propale
propane
prorate
probang
pronaoi
proball
pronaos
provant
Pooh-Bah
Phoebus
poor-box
plodded
prodded
plodder
proudly
proverb
proceed
propend
proteid
protend
provend
phoneme
propene
protégé
phone-in
△protean
protein
pioneer
proneur
process
profess
proteus
prowess
project
protect
protest
plovery
poovery
progeny
pronely

plotful
proffer
pronged
prothyl
prophet
phocine
plosive
profile
pro-life
proline
promise
propine
provide
provine
pioning
prosing
proving
poorish
peonism
phobism
photism
protium
plosion
proviso
proximo
phonics
photics
pionies
profits
phobist
protist
probity
prodigy
prosify
prosily
prop-jet
plookie
ploukie
plonker
problem
proller
prouler
prowler
poor-law
prommer
phoenix
pronota
promote
propone
propose
protore
provoke
prolong
poon-oil
pronoun
poor-oot
provost
prosody
plopped
propped
prosper

program
piously
prootic
plotted
plottie
pooftah
proctal
plotter
plouter
plowter
poofter
proctor
procure
produce
profuse
product
propyla
poogyee
protyle
Procyon
papable
popadum
popedom
pop-weed
pipless
poppers
pap-meat
peppery
pipeful
pop-shop
paprika
poppied
pepsine
peptide
peptise
peptize
pipping
popping
pupping
poppish
pupfish
Paphian
peptics
pipe-key
papilla
papulae
△**papilio**
papular
popular
pupilar
papules
papally
pupunha
papoose
pappose
peptone
popcorn
pappous
pap-boat
puparia
piperic

poperin
paperer
papyrus
pipette
Papaver
popover
pop-eyed
piquant
pargana
pardale
parpane
partake
percale
percase
pertake
pervade
portage
portate
pertain
perhaps
parfait
periapt
persant
parable
paracme
pericon
parodic
parador
parados
peridot
paradox
parpend
perpend
Perseid
portend
Purbeck
peraeon
Perseus
porpess
portess
parpent
percept
perfect
perpent
pervert
porrect
portent
parvenu
parafle
porifer
piragua
perigee
pirogue
peregal
paragon
perigon
pyrogen
△**pyrrhic**
parched
perched
percher

Words marked △ may be spelled also with a capital letter

7 p□u□d

porthos
pareira
partita
pereira
parried
pardine
partite
parvise
percine
perlite
porcine
purline
parking
parsing
parting
purging
purling
purring
parkish
perjink
partial
Parsism
Persism
pereion
Permian
Persian
portion
persico
porrigo
portico
Perrier®
perrier
porkies
△**persist**
purlieu
purview
perfidy
perkily
peruked
parella
purfled
pyralid
parelle
parolee
parulis
purples
△pyralis
△**partlet**
perplex
parsley
pyramid
portman
paramos
pyramis
piranha
phrenic
Puranic
paranym
paronym
parsnep
parsnip
pardner
partner
phrensy
pergola
persona
percoid
purpose
pyrrole
part-off
parrock
partook
Porlock
parboil
perform
purloin
parlour
parlous
periods
perlous
persons
portous
percoct
periost
purport
parroty
pork-pie
pyropus
parapet
Perspex®
perique
parerga
para-red
portray
parasol
perusal
phrasal
parison
peruser
phraser
paresis
poroses
porosis
pyrosis
paratha
paretic
parotic
piratic
pyretic
pyritic
parotid
△**puritan**
paritor
parotis
peritus
pyrites
phratry
△**purpura**
perturb
parture
perdure
perfume
perfuse
perjure
permute
pertuse
purpure
pursual
pursuer
percuss
parquet
pursuit
perfumy
perjury
pyruvic
periwig
parkway
pyrexia
pyrexic
△**parazoa**
passade
passage
postage
passado
passant
pessary
piscary
postbag
postbus
postbox
post-doc
pastern
posteen
postern
paste-up
possess
pestful
pushful
postfix
paschal
pessima
piscina
passive
pastime
piscine
pismire
passing
pasting
posting
pushing
△**passion**
Peshito
pasties
peskily
passkey
passman
postman
pesante
pistole
push-off
pissoir
passout
push-out
push-pin
piss-pot
pushrod
posited
push-tug
Pashtun
positon
Pushtun
Pushtoo
pasture
posaune
poseuse
posture
pustule
pascual
Pasquil
Pasquin
pesaunt
postwar
pesewas
pottage
potlach
patball
pitfall
petrary
patible
potable
potiche
pithead
pot-head
pattern
potheen
patrero
patness
patient
pothery
pottery
putrefy
pithful
pitiful
patagia
potager
patched
pitched
putchuk
patch-up
potshop
patcher
pitcher
potcher
putcher
pituita
puttied
Petrine
△pittite
pituite
patting
petting
pitting
pitying
potting
putting
pettish
patrick
pit-mirk
pot-sick
patrial
Pittism
pythium
Pythian
patrico
puttier
patriot
petrify
pettily
pithily
△**patella**
patulin
potamic
putamen
patamar
△**petunia**
patined
patonce
potence
potencé
patency
potency
petiole
pothole
petcock
pothook
putlock
puttock
pit-coal
patroon
put-down
petrous
piteous
pit-pony
pitapat
paterae
pitarah
Patarin
potoroo
pitprop
potassa
petasus
potfuls
pathway
poulard
plumage
plumate
plusage
plumbic
plumbum
plumber
pounced
plumcot
pouncet
paunchy
pouldre

Words marked △ may be spelled also with a capital letter

7 p□u□d

poundal
plunder
poulder
pounder
pluteal
pluteus
prudent
plumery
prudery
pouffed
plugged
plugger
plunger
pouched
pouther
plushes
plug-hat
paughty
Pauline
pausing
plusing
pouring
pouting
pruning
prudish
pluvial
Paulian
prurigo
plumist
paucity
plucked
plucker
plunker
plummet
plumose
plumous
pour-out
plumpie
plumpen
plumper
plumply
prussic
plussed
poursue
poussin
plusses
poursew
prunted
pouftah
poufter
poulter
poultry
plumula
plumule
△**pavlova**
paviour
poverty
pivoted
pivotal
pivoter
pew-rent

powdery
pawkily
powered
pyxidia
pyxides
pixy-led
paxiuba
paysage
payback
poynant
payable
pay-desk
payment
psychic
prythee
pr'ythee
psych-up
psychos
poy-bird
pay-bill
physics
physios
pay-dirt
pay-list
psyllid
ptyalin
payslip
pay-load
plywood
payfone
payroll
pay-roll
pazzazz
pizzazz
puzzler
quayage
quahaug
quamash
Quapaws
quavery
quaffer
quangos
△**quashee**
△quashie
quaking
qualify
quality
quackle
quacker
quannet
quadric
quarrel
quadrat
quassia
quantic
quartic
quantal
quantum
quartan
quarter
quartos

quartet
quartzy
qabalah
Qaddish
Quercus
queachy
queechy
Quechua
queried
queuing
querist
queller
queenie
queynie
queenly
queerly
quetsch
Q-Celtic
Q-Keltic
quester
questor
quetzal
quinate
quidams
quinary
quibble
quinche
quiddle
quiddit
quivery
Quichua
quinine
quiting
quickie
quicken
quickly
quilled
quillai
quiblin
quillon
quillet
quinnat
quinoid
quinone
quiesce
quintic
quilted
quitted
quintal
quittal
quieten
quintan
quieter
quilter
quitter
quittor
quietus
quintet
quietly
quizzed
quizzer

quizzes
quorate
quondam
quodlin
Quonset
quoiter
reawake
readapt
rhatany
road-bed
rhabdom
rear-dos
rhabdus
reamend
road-end
reagent
realgar
reached
road-hog
reacher
rhachis
rhaphis
realise
realize
rearise
reading
reaming
roading
roaming
roaring
△**realism**
realign
readier
readies
realist
readily
reality
reallie
reallot
roadman
road-map
Réaumur
readmit
Rhamnus
reannex
readopt
read-out
reapply
Rhaetia
Rhaetic
realtie
reactor
re-alter
Realtor®
realtor
roaster
roadway
ribband
rebrace
ribcage
reboant

ribible
Rebecca
△**rubicon**
rabidly
ribless
rubbers
robbery
rubbery
rebuild
riblike
ribbing
robbing
rubbing
rubying
rubbish
rabbins
rabbits
rabbity
rebuker
rubella
rabbler
robalos
rabanna
△robinia
rubeola
rib-bone
rabboni
ribwork
rebloom
rubdown
ribbons
rubious
ribwort
ribbony
ruby-red
rebirth
robusta
rebuses
robotic
rabatte
ribston
rebater
rubatos
rebound
rybauld
rechate
réclame
reclaim
rechart
rock-cod
recycle
race-cup
rococos
recceed
recheck
rock-elm
rackets
rickets
rackett
recheat
rackety

Words marked △ may be spelled also with a capital letter

rickety
rockery
reclimb
reccied
receive
recline
recuile
racking
rocking
ruching
rachial
rection
ruction
rockier
Rockies
receipt
rectify
rockily
rocklay
racemic
racemed
recense
Ricinus
recency
reclose
rock-oil
raccoon
racloir
recross
rectory
recipes
recurve
rectrix
ricksha
ricotta
recatch
recital
reciter
Richter
rock-tar
recluse
recoure
rectums
racquet
recount
re-count
recruit
rocquet
recover
re-cover
recower
raceway
recoyle
△**radiata**
radiale
radiate
red-tape
redback
radiant
redraft
ridable
reduced
radicle
△**radical**
radicel
reducer
radices
redhead
redneck
redsear
redness
redress
re-dress
rodless
reddest
redbird
ruddied
red-line
redrive
rodlike
redding
redwing
ridding
ridging
rodding
reddish
redfish
ruddier
ruddily
redskin
raddled
radulae
radular
riddler
rodsman
redwood
red-wood
red-book
ruddock
red-cowl
redpoll
redcoat
redroot
ridered
ruderal
rudesby
ridotto
rodster
redound
redoubt
rodeway
re-enact
reedbed
re-endow
ryepeck
roe-deer
re-elect
re-erect
reechie
reeding
reefing
reeking
reeling
Rhemish
Rhenish
rhenium
Raetian
re-exist
Rhemist
re-edify
ruellia
rheumed
reelman
rye-roll
riempie
re-enter
re-entry
roebuck
re-equip
reflate
reframe
refrain
refract
refocus
refresh
reflect
refugia
refugee
reffing
rifling
raffish
ruffian
ruffled
raffler
riffler
ruffler
raftman
refined
refiner
refloat
referee
refusal
refuser
refutal
refuter
refound
rufiyaa
regmata
riggald
regrade
regrate
rag-fair
regnant
regrant
rag-baby
Rigsdag
rigidly
Rigveda
raghead
ragweed
regrede
regress
ragment
regreet
raggedy
raggery
roguery
rageful
regrind
ragtime
ragging
rigging
rigling
roguing
rugging
riggish
roguish
regalia
raguled
regulae
regular
△**regulus**
regally
regimen
regence
reginal
regency
rag-book
ragwork
rag-doll
rag-wool
ragworm
rug-gown
regroup
ragbolt
ragwort
regorge
regards
regatta
right-oh
righten
right-on
righter
rightos
rightly
rag-bush
rag-dust
rehouse
ruinate
rein-arm
railbed
railbus
rainbow
rail-car
raiment
rhizine
railing
raising
raiting
ruining
roinish
railman
rhizoid
rhizome
ruinous
reissue
reinter
roister
railway
rejudge
rejoice
rejoneo
rejones
Rajpoot
rejourn
rokkaku
Riksdag
rakshas
rokelay
Riksmål
rake-off
rikishi
release
reliant
rulable
roll-bar
relâche
relieve
rilievi
relievo
rilievo
relight
rallied
ralline
relying
△rolfing
rolling
rellish
rollick
rullion
rallier
rollmop
rollock
rullock
rollout
relapse
relique
rulesse
related
roll-top
relater
relator
reliver
relaxin
relayed
ram-raid
rampage
remuage
rummage
rampant
rampart
remnant
Rommany
remodel
Ramadan

Words marked △ may be spelled also with a capital letter

7 r□m□e

romneya
rump-end
remueur
rimless
rompers
rumness
rump-fed
remiges
rum-shop
rim-shot
romaika
rampike
rampire
ramming
ramping
rimming
rammish
rompish
rummish
rampick
rampion
remains
rummily
ramakin
ramekin
Ramilie
remblai
rambler
ramular
rumbler
ramulus
ramenta
Romanic
remanié
△romance
Romansh
Romanes
remanet
rim-lock
rameous
ramsons
remerge
remorse
remarry
remercy
rematch
ramstam
remould
remount
romaunt
removed
removal
remover
rundale
ransack
runback
ringbit
Ranidae
rent-day
Rangers
ringent

rondeau
renague
renegue
röntgen
reneger
ringgit
ranched
rancher
ranchos
Rankine
run-time
ranking
ranting
renning
renying
ringing
rinsing
ronning
running
runtish
runnion
rondino
rentier
rundled
ringlet
rundlet
runflat
ringman
rangoli
rundown
run-down
rancour
ring-taw
rondure
renewal
renewer
ringway
runaway
renayed
rootage
rhombic
rhomboi
rhombos
rhombus
rhonchi
root-cap
reorder
rookery
roomful
riotise
riotize
rioting
roofing
rooting
rookish
rhodium
Rhodian
roomily
raoulia
rootlet
rooinek

rhodora
rhodous
riotous
rooftop
rooster
replace
rupiahs
replant
reptant
ropable
rapidly
replete
ripieni
ripieno
repress
re-press
replevy
replica
replied
raphide
Rappite
reprime
reprise
reprive
reprize
reptile
riptide
rapping
repping
ripping
replier
rippier
Rappist
repaint
repoint
reprint
repulse
rippler
ripples
ripplet
repoman
repiner
repunit
rip-cord
reprove
reproof
raploch
rapport
repaper
repique
roper-in
reposed
riposte
reposal
reposit
reputed
ripstop
rapture
rupture
ropeway
repryve

requere
request
require
requite
requiem
requote
rarebit
reredos
rurally
reroute
rorqual
rescale
re-scale
reshape
restage
restate
roseate
restaff
réseaus
resiant
△restart
réseaux
rosebud
risible
rose-bug
rosebay
rosacea
rose-cut
residua
residue
resider
rest-day
rosiere
respeak
respell
respect
russety
restful
riskful
raschel
rosehip
rescind
reseize
respire
respite
restive
restiff
rasping
resting
rusting
Rissian
Roscian
Russian
Roscius
riskily
Russify
rustily
rosaker
rosalia
rosella
rusalka

resolve
roselle
rosolio
rustler
rosined
resiner
roseola
respond
rescore
restore
rissole
restock
rose-red
rustred
reserve
resurge
rostral
rastrum
rostrum
Rasores
respray
Rosetta
rosette
risotto
rosetty
rescued
resound
rescuer
restyle
retrace
retrate
ratpack
rat-tail
retrain
retract
retrait
retiary
ratable
retable
ratably
reticle
rate-cap
retread
Ruthene
ratteen
rathest
retreat
re-treat
rattery
rettery
ratafia
ruthful
rotifer
rotchie
ratchet
retsina
retried
ratline
rut-time
ratling
ratting

Words marked △ may be spelled also with a capital letter

retting
rotting
rutting
rattish
ruttish
ratfink
rethink
retrial
retaken
retaker
rat-flea
rattlin
rattler
rotolos
rotunda
retinae
retinue
retinal
retinol
ratings
retinas
rat-hole
rations
retired
retiree
retiral
rat-trap
retirer
returns
Ratitae
retitle
rotator
rat-a-tat
retouch
rhubarb
roulade
rousant
raunchy
rounded
roundle
roundel
round-up
rounder
roundly
rouleau
roughie
routhie
roughen
rougher
roughly
reunite
routine
rouming
rousing
routing
reunion
reunify
rouille
raucous
routous
reutter

rouster
riviera
rivière
ravager
revving
revying
rivlins
revalue
revolve
ravelin
reviler
rivulet
revelry
rivalry
ravined
revenge
revenue
ravener
ravioli
rivered
reverie
reverse
reversi
reverso
reverer
riveret
revisal
reviser
revisor
revisit
riveted
riveter
rêveuse
revival
reviver
revivor
rowable
rawhead
rawness
rawhide
rewrite
reweigh
rowdily
rawbone
rewrote
rowlock
rowboat
row-port
rewound
△**reynard**
Ray-Bans®
rayless
rhytina
rhyming
roynish
rhymist
royalet
royally
royalty
Reynold
royster

rizzart
rozelle
seamaid
seaward
smaragd
scalade
scavage
seakale
seaware
soakage
siamang
sladang
seabank
seahawk
seamark
scalado
shamans
sealant
statant
scabbed
slabbed
stabbed
swabbed
scabble
scamble
shabble
shamble
snabble
sjambok
slabber
stabber
swabber
soapbox
shambly
spancel
snatchy
starchy
sraddha
scaldic
Scandic
skaldic
sharded
swarded
staddle
standee
swaddle
scandal
Slavdom
stardom
standen
stand-in
so-and-so
stand-to
stand-up
scalder
slander
stander
△**spandex**
shandry
staidly
stand-by

seaweed
scalene
△siamese
siameze
scaleni
shake-up
shape-up
△**shakers**
stamens
starers
starets
sea-beat
sealery
shapely
slavery
sparely
stagery
stalely
stately
suavely
staretz
scarfed
scaffie
snaffle
staffer
shagged
slagged
snagged
swagged
spangle
swaggie
slanger
spadger
sparger
stagger
swagger
spangly
spathic
slashed
smashed
spathed
stashie
smash-up
slasher
slather
smasher
swasher
stachys
stamina
stasima
seabird
sea-fire
sea-like
sealine
seaside
seawife
stabile
statice
stative
suasive
scaling

sealing
searing
seating
shading
shaking
shaping
sharing
shaving
skating
slating
snaring
soaking
soaring
spacing
sparing
staging
staring
staying
swaling
swaying
slavish
snakish
Spanish
Swahili
seasick
spacial
spaniel
spatial
stadial
staniel
Slavism
stadium
statism
Shavian
station
suasion
scabies
statics
sea-girt
△shariat
statist
scarify
shadily
shakily
Slavify
snakily
soapily
stagily
suavity
shanked
stacked
stalked
shackle
sparkie
sparkle
swankie
slacken
starken
sharker
slacker
smacker

Words marked △ may be spelled also with a capital letter

7 s□a□k

spanker
stacker
stalker
swanker
stacket
slackly
sparkly
starkly
swankey
scaglia
scalled
snarled
stalled
star-led
sea-blue
shawlie
shallon
scallop
shallop
snarl-up
snarler
stabler
stapler
stables
scarlet
shallot
starlet
starlit
swallet
shallow
swallow
shawley
spasmic
shammed
slammed
stammel
spaeman
swagman
shammer
slammer
stammer
swarmer
shammes
stannic
scanned
spanned
stained
Shawnee
slàinte
starnie
staunch
stamnoi
stannel
scanner
spanner
spawner
stainer
stamnos
seafood
sialoid
sparoid
scatole
skatole
sea-wolf
shadoof
seacock
seafolk
seafowl
seaworm
sea-born
sea-worn
scazons
shakoes
spadoes
seaport
shadowy
suasory
scarped
slapped
snapped
swapped
scapple
sharpie
stapple
Shar-Pei
scalpel
sharpen
shampoo
scalper
scamper
scarper
scauper
sharper
slapper
snapper
stamper
swamper
swapper
sharply
scabrid
scarred
sparred
staired
starred
spairge
sparrer
sparrow
S-matrix
seamset
shastra
spastic
scatted
shafted
slanted
slatted
spalted
swatted
scantle
smartie
sparthe
spattee
staithe
startle
△**shaitan**
smarten
△spartan
start-up
scatter
shafter
shaster
shatter
slatter
smatter
spatter
starter
swatter
smaltos
scantly
shantey
slantly
smartly
startly
swarthy
scapula
spatula
statued
seasure
spatule
stature
statute
seagull
shakudo
Shavuot
starved
scarves
shalwar
sealwax
stanyel
swazzle
stanzos
subbase
sublate
Sabbath
subtack
sebacic
subacid
subadar
subedar
subedit
subhead
subtend
subsere
Sabaean
subdean
subteen
subzero
sabreur
subject
subtext
subvert
sebific
sabkhah
Sabahan
sibship
sabkhat
sublime
subside
subtile
sibling
sobbing
subbing
subring
Sabaism
submiss
subsist
subsidy
sabella
sibylic
soboles
subplot
subunit
sebundy
subzone
subsong
Sabaoth
subcool
subgoal
subsoil
subjoin
subaqua
sub-aqua
saburra
subarea
suberic
subarid
suberin
suburbs
soberly
sybotic
subatom
sabaton
subfusc
subdued
subduce
subsume
subfusk
subdual
subduer
subduct
subtype
saccade
saccate
sackage
soccage
sociate
succade
sucrase
sectary
sickbed
sackbut
seceder
secreta
succeed
secrete
sockeye
sacless
secrets
success
secrecy
society
sackful
socager
saclike
sectile
siclike
succise
sacking
sacring
socking
sucking
sickish
section
suction
sucrier
sacrist
sacrify
siccity
sacella
sickled
seculum
secular
suckler
seconde
secondi
Seconal®
secondo
seconds
succose
suck'ole
sucrose
Succoth
succour
succous
sick-out
succory
securer
sycosis
sacaton
succuba
succumb
saccule
seclude
sacculi
succubi
succuss
sidearm
sidebar
side-bar
seducer
sidecar
sadness
saddest
Siddhis
sodaine
sodding

Words marked △ may be spelled also with a capital letter

saddish
sedilia
saddler
sideman
sidemen
sudamen
Sudanic
sideral
sudoral
sadiron
sad-eyed
steward
seepage
shebang
scenary
seedbed
seeable
sueable
stembok
sherbet
seedbox
stencil
stew-can
spencer
step-cut
sketchy
sleechy
stenchy
sledded
sleided
speeded
steaded
smeddum
speldin
speed-up
shedder
skelder
slender
speeder
spelder
spender
speedos
Sienese
stelene
shereef
shebeen
spelean
she-bear
seeress
shekels
siemens
stereos
sievert
scenery
Szekely
skepful
sdeigne
stengah
skegger
sledger
sleight
seethed
seether
shehita
Shemite
sterile
syenite
sheriff
seeding
seeling
seeming
seewing
stewing
Swedish
special
sferics
species
△**sheriat**
seedily
specify
sheikha
sneaked
speckle
sleeken
sneak-up
sleeker
sneaker
speaker
sleekit
steekit
sleekly
seed-lac
shellac
shelled
smelled
spelled
stealed
steeled
stelled
swelled
skellie
stealth
skellum
seedlip
sheller
smeller
speeler
speller
stealer
stellar
sweller
Szekler
stemlet
sterlet
spermic
steamed
stemmed
steamie
steamer
stemmer
sternal
sternum
stepney
sternly
sweeney
steroid
seed-oil
skepped
stepped
steeple
stemple
stempel
steepen
stewpan
steep-to
sleeper
steeper
stepper
sweeper
sheepos
Sherpas
skew-put
stewpot
sleepry
steeply
stearic
sheared
speared
sweered
sierran
stearin
shearer
sneerer
steerer
swearer
sherris
sheerly
spersed
stemson
stepson
Stetson
scepsis
skepsis
speoses
spectra
△**sceptic**
skeptic
smectic
scented
sheeted
stetted
sweated
swelted
sceptre
sheathe
sheltie
spectre
sperthe
△sweetie
sweeten
scepter
shelter
skeeter
skelter
slenter
smelter
specter
spelter
stentor
sweater
swelter
sheaths
sceptry
sheathy
sweetly
sweltry
specula
scedule
sheaved
sleaved
sleeved
sleever
swerver
sheaves
shelves
sneezer
suffete
suffect
suffice
sifting
softish
saffian
safrole
Suffolk
saffron
soft-top
suffuse
saggard
sigmate
signage
saguaro
signary
signeur
segment
suggest
sighful
sagging
sighing
signing
sogging
sugging
Signior
signify
soggily
sagaman
△**signora**
sigmoid
△**signore**
signori
signors
signory
sugared
△**sagitta**
sighted
sighter
sagathy
sightly
sagouin
spheare
schnaps
sahibah
sphaere
schmeck
schnell
schlepp
schmelz
schlich
schtick
scholia
scholar
schemer
sphenic
sthenic
schanse
schanze
schoole
schlock
schmock
schnook
schtook
schtoom
schnorr
schloss
schmoes
schools
schmooz
schappe
spheric
sphered
scherzi
spheral
Saharan
scherzo
schisma
schmuck
schtuck
schizos
spiraea
soilage
spicate
spinate
spinach
shikari
shimaal
spirant
skiable
stibble
switchy
skidded
spindle
stiddie
swindge
swindle
shindig
slidden

Words marked △ may be spelled also with a capital letter

7 s□i□d

swidden
shidder
skidder
slidder
spindly
spin-dry
stipend
spireme
shiness
saidest
shivery
snidely
spicery
spidery
spikery
swinery
skiffle
sniffle
shipful
skilful
skinful
stiffen
sniffer
stiffly
stir-fry
stinged
swigged
shingle
sniggle
swingle
smidgen
smidgin
slinger
snigger
stinger
swigger
swinger
stingos
shingly
swing-by
stichic
stishie
stichoi
slither
swisher
swither
stichos
shit-hot
Saivite
spilite
stibine
suicide
sailing
seining
seizing
shining
shiting
skiving
slicing
sliding
smiling
sniping
soiling
spiling
suiting
swinish
saimiri
stibial
Saivism
stibium
suidian
spirits
slimily
spicily
spikily
spirity
shicksa
sticked
swinked
stickle
slicken
stick-up
shicker
shirker
skinker
slicker
slinker
smicker
snicker
sticker
stinker
smicket
snicket
stickit
slickly
smickly
skilled
spilled
stifled
sciolto
shiplap
spieler
spiller
stifler
stiller
swiller
skillet
skimmia
seismic
skimmed
slimmed
seismal
shipman
shipmen
shimmer
skimmer
slimmer
swimmer
stigmas
shimmey
skinned
△**science**
soignée
spignel
skinner
spinner
spinnet
spinney
spiroid
spinode
spinose
spin-off
spinous
spinout
shipped
skipped
slipped
snipped
stipple
swipple
shippen
shippon
skidpan
skin-pop
shipper
skipper
slipper
snipper
Scirpus
stirpes
shilpit
skippet
snippet
sciarid
shirred
stirred
stirrah
stirrup
stirrer
Sciurus
skirret
scissel
scissil
scissor
Swisses
sciatic
Shiitic
sainted
shifted
shitted
skirted
spitted
stilted
stinted
skittle
smittle
snirtle
spirtle
spittle
shittah
shittim
smitten
spitten
Stilton
shifter
skirter
skitter
slinter
slitter
snifter
spitter
stilter
stinter
swifter
shiatsu
shiatzu
saintly
swiftly
spicula
seizure
soilure
spicule
spinule
stipule
stimuli
ski-jump
shipway
slipway
swizzle
Switzer
sejeant
sojourn
saksaul
Saktism
Sikhism
sokeman
Sukkoth
sakeret
sakiyeh
sultana
salband
sol-faed
saltate
salvage
selvage
solvate
sulcate
sulfate
sullage
syllabi
saltato
soldado
salaams
saltant
salable
soluble
saltbox
salably
silicic
silicle
salicin
silicon
splicer
salices
salicet
saltcat
solicit
splodge
solidum
solidus
solidly
splodgy
self-end
salvete
solfège
salfern
saltern
silvern
salient
solvent
Sillery
silvery
spleeny
self-fed
salt-fat
saligot
silphia
sylphid
sulphur
salchow
sallied
sullied
saltire
sulfide
sulfite
sylvine
sylvite
salting
salving
selfing
saltish
selfish
selfism
salpian
Sylvian
saltier
soldier
selfist
soloist
salpinx
salsify
saltily
silkily
sillily
sulkily
salamon
silk-man
Solomon
salamis
selenic
splenic
silence
solanum
silenus
solanos

Words marked △ may be spelled also with a capital letter

Salsola
saltoed
sulfone
sell-off
sillock
salmons
salvoes
sell-out
sallowy
soliped
siliqua
Salique
silique
silurid
splurge
scleral
Silurus
splurgy
silesia
self-sow
splashy
solatia
splatch
splotch
soliton
saluter
Solpuga
salival
seltzer
samsara
summand
summate
summary
samadhi
someday
sumless
summery
samshoo
somehow
Samnite
sampire
summing
somnial
semeion
summist
simpkin
semi-log
sampler
similar
similor
simpler
simular
similes
simplex
shmaltz
seminal
seminar
Samiote
shmoose
shmooze
someone

symbole
simious
summons
semiped
simarre
simurgh
samurai
samisen
samosas
sumatra
sematic
Semitic
somatic
somitic
somital
symptom
semitar
simitar
sumpter
symitar
sambuca
samovar
someway
somewhy
Samoyed
Sinhala
sunward
sensate
sinkage
sinuate
sondage
sunbake
sunbath
sundari
syntagm
sunlamp
syncarp
suntans
sunfast
syngamy
sandbag
sandbox
sandboy
sanicle
sinical
Senecan
senecio
synodic
synodal
sincere
sondeli
sundeck
sunbeam
Sinaean
sanders
sinless
sonless
sunkets
sunless
sunbeat
△sunbelt

sintery
songful
sandfly
Sankhya
sand-hog
synthon
synchro
sonship
sanchos
sunbird
sensile
sunlike
Sunnite
sunrise
sunwise
sanding
sending
sensing
singing
sinking
sinning
sunning
sunfish
sundial
sensism
Sunnism
sonties
sensist
sunnily
sun-clad
singles
singlet
sunglow
sandman
songman
sonance
synonym
sonancy
sangoma
Senhora
sinuose
syncope
send-off
sunroof
sundown
santour
sanious
sinuous
sensory
syntony
sinopia
synapse
synapte
sinopis
sandpit
sunspot
sangria
senarii
suntrap
synergy
Senussi

sinuses
synesis
sanctum
senator
Sanctus
△senatus
sensual
synfuel
sunburn
singult
sunsuit
synovia
sinewed
synaxis
sinsyne
stomata
scopate
storage
stowage
stomach
saouari
shofars
Scomber
slobber
swobber
showbox
shop-boy
showbiz
△**stoical**
snowcap
slot-car
Scotchy
slouchy
snodded
snooded
spondee
spondyl
stooden
scolder
scowder
smolder
sworder
snoddit
Slovene
shoneen
stonern
smoke-ho
storeys
soonest
showery
snow-fed
shopful
scoffer
spoofer
shoofly
shogged
slogged
shoggle
shoogie
shoogle
showghe

Scoggin
shotgun
spongin
stopgap
slogger
sponger
stodger
shoggly
shoogly
sloughy
sloshed
shophar
smother
soother
shochet
soothly
scoriac
stonied
storied
scoriae
Scotice
snow-ice
scoring
shoeing
shoring
showing
sloping
slowing
smoking
snoring
sooping
stoning
stoping
stoving
stowing
slowish
snowish
Suomish
Scotism
spodium
scolion
Scotian
skolion
stories
stovies
Scotist
scorify
Scotify
showily
smokily
snowily
sootily
stonily
shocked
snorkel
slocken
shocker
snooker
stocker
stonker
stooker

Words marked △ may be spelled also with a capital letter

7 s□o□l

spoiled
skollie
stoolie
stollen
swollen
scollop
spoiler
spooler
shopman
showman
snowman
swooned
scorner
swounds
'swounds
spooney
scotoma
show-off
stopoff
stop-off
scotomy
scooped
shopped
slopped
stooped
stopped
swopped
stopple
Scorpio
scooper
scorper
shopper
snooper
stomper
stooper
stopper
swopper
shotput
scourge
scourie
scourse
scowrie
sporran
scourer
scowrer
spoorer
sponsal
spousal
sponson
scorser
scouser
smouser
sponsor
shotted
slotted
snouted
spotted
swotted
Scottie
shortie
shottle

snottie
shorten
shotten
stouten
scooter
scouter
shooter
shouter
slotter
snorter
snotter
sporter
spotter
spouter
stoiter
stotter
swotter
shortly
stoutly
scopula
sporule
snoozle
swozzle
snoozer
septate
soprani
suppawn
sapsago
soprano
saphena
saphead
supreme
suprême
supremo
sapless
sapient
△**sapphic**
septime
sapling
sapping
sipping
sopping
supping
sophism
sophist
soppily
sapajou
sapples
saponin
sapwood
saprobe
suppose
sepiost
support
Septrin®
Siporex®
septuor
seppuku
sequela
sequent
sequoia

sardana
serfage
seriate
serrate
sirname
sorbate
spreaze
striate
surbase
surbate
surface
surname
sirgang
spreagh
serkali
sarcasm
Syriasm
surpass
servant
screaky
streaky
streamy
strobic
scribal
soroban
scriber
scrubby
shrubby
soroche
Saracen
sericin
sericon
sirocco
soredia
spredde
strodle
strudel
serfdom
sarsden
stridor
strides
shreddy
seriema
screeve
scriene
scrieve
seruewe
servewe
shrieve
spreeze
survewe
screech
scriech
shriech
skriech
skriegh
surreal
surgeon
streets
sarment
△serpent

sorbent
spryest
surfeit
surgent
servery
sorcery
streety
surgery
sarafan
serafin
scruffy
strigae
strigil
Striges
shright
spright
scraggy
scroggy
spriggy
syrphid
sorghum
sorehon
sorghos
Syrphus
serried
sardine
service
servile
Servite
sorbite
surmise
survive
sarking
scrying
serving
sirring
sorning
sorting
surfing
surging
scraich
scraigh
screich
screigh
serfish
skreigh
Sorbish
sordini
Sercial
Serbian
Servian
Sorbian
serpigo
sordino
sorrier
sardius
straits
spraint
straint
surview
sorrily

surdity
surlily
stroken
striker
stroker
surplus
shrilly
strumae
suramin
surfman
scrimpy
scrummy
scrumpy
shrimpy
seringa
Sirenia
△syringa
saronic
sirenic
springe
strange
surance
syringe
scranch
scrunch
sarangi
shrinal
Surinam
strings
strunts
sarsnet
scranny
scrunty
springy
stringy
sarcoma
sarcoid
sarcode
△scrooge
strooke
sirloin
surloin
sarcous
serious
surcoat
surtout
Sarapic
Serapic
striped
scrapie
scruple
strophe
scraper
Sarapis
seraphs
Serapis
seropus
stripes
scrappy
strappy
stripey

Words marked △ may be spelled also with a capital letter

stroppy
sororal
serosae
serosas
sorosis
stretta
soritic
strette
△**scratch**
scritch
shritch
stretch
stretti
scrotal
scrotum
stratum
scrutin
stretto
scrutos
sorites
stratus
serpula
scrouge
scrauch
scraugh
shrouds
shroudy
shrived
strived
shrivel
shriven
striven
shriver
striver
screwed
strawed
strewed
strowed
scrowle
strewth
strawen
screw-up
screwer
strewer
strower
scrawly
scrawny
sprawly
sprayed
strayed
scroyle
spray-on
sprayer
strayer
sprayey
sustain
sassaby
suspend
suspens
sestett
suspect
sestina
sessile
sestine
Sistine
suspire
sossing
sashimi
session
systole
sistrum
systyle
satiate
setuale
situate
setback
setwall
sitfast
satrapy
Sotadic
setness
sithens
satiety
sutlery
satchel
setline
sittine
setting
sitting
sotting
sottish
settled
situlae
settler
settlor
△**satanic**
Satanas
satinet
set-down
sit-down
sit-upon
satiric
satyric
satyrid
sutured
satyral
sutural
satisfy
shtetel
shtetls
△**satsuma**
sausage
scutage
scutate
soutane
sfumato
squeaky
slubbed
snubbed
stubbed
scumble
stubble
stumble
scumbag
scumber
slubber
slumber
snubber
slumbry
squabby
stubbly
stumbly
stucco'd
soupçon
squacco
stuccos
scudded
studded
scuddle
squidge
studdle
souldan
studden
scudder
shudder
sounder
soundly
spun-dry
squaddy
squidgy
sautéed
shut-eye
squeeze
student
stupent
squeezy
stupefy
stuffed
scuffle
shuffle
snuffle
souffle
soufflé
soulful
snuffer
stuffer
snuffly
squiffy
snugged
smuggle
snuggle
slugger
smudger
stushie
scuchin
souther
studied
soubise
spuriae
souming
souring
sousing
sourish
saurian
saucier
studier
squails
studies
studios
saucily
spunkie
stuck-up
shucker
skulker
squilla
squalid
squelch
souslik
scudler
sculler
skudler
squalor
squills
squally
scummed
stummed
squamae
stummel
scummer
skummer
slummer
△sturmer
shunned
stunned
squinch
sputnik
scunner
shunner
spurner
stunner
sturnus
squinny
sauroid
shut-off
sourock
sautoir
soukous
spumous
shut-out
spun-out
sculpin
skulpin
scupper
slurper
stumper
slurred
spurred
squared
scurril
spurrer
squarer
spurrey
squirmy
soursop
squashy
squishy
smutted
stunted
scuttle
shuttle
skuttle
spurtle
squitch
saunter
scutter
shunter
shutter
sputter
stutter
squatty
spurway
squawky
spulyie
snuzzle
spulzie
save-all
savable
Sivaite
Sivaism
saveloy
savanna
seventh
savings
seventy
△**saviour**
several
savarin
sevruga
savoury
sowback
saw-edge
sawfish
sawbill
sawmill
sow-skin
sawn-off
saw-wort
sowarry
sawbuck
sawdust
six-pack
△**sextans**
△**sextant**
sexed-up
sixteen
sexless
sexpert
sextett
sixthly
sextile
sixaine
sixties
Saxonic
sixfold
sexfoil

7 S□X□O

saxhorn
six-foot
sextuor
scybala
skyward
scytale
stylate
skyjack
skylark
skysail
sayable
styrene
shyness
slyness
scythed
scyther
scyphus
stymied
skyline
stylise
stylite
stylize
sky-high
stylish
Stygian
stylist
skyclad
sky-blue
styloid
spyhole
shy-cock
Shylock
skyhook
skyborn
sky-bred
smytrie
stypsis
styptic
shyster
seysure
sizable
sizeism
sizeist
sozzled
sizzler
sazerac®
tuatara
tiaraed
twafald
thanage
thalami
travail
traybit
tranced
tranche
tramcar
thatcht
trap-cut
twaddle
tsaddik
tzaddik
tsardom
tsaddiq
tzaddiq
twaddly
trapeze
trade-in
travels
traject
tranect
tracery
tragedy
traffic
tearful
trayful
trangle
twangle
trangam
tear-gas
trachea
teachie
teach-in
teacher
tsarina
toadied
teatime
teaming
tearing
teasing
thawing
tracing
trading
tsarism
thalian
Tsabian
tsarist
tracked
thankee
trankum
thanker
tracker
traikit
twankay
thallic
trailer
trawler
thallus
trammed
trammel
traumas
Thammuz
trained
trainee
trannie
thannah
trainer
twasome
travois
trapped
traipse
trample
tramper
trapper
trampet
transom
transit
toasted
toastie
twattle
toaster
tractor
traitor
tranter
tractus
traduce
tragule
thalweg
tramway
to-brake
tubfast
tobacco
tabrere
to-break
tableau
tubeful
tubifex
tabbied
tabbing
tabling
tabuing
tubbing
tubbish
tubfish
tablier
△**toby-jug**
tabulae
tubulin
tabular
tubular
tabanid
Tabanus
tabinet
tabloid
tabooed
taborin
taborer
tabaret
taboret
Tabasco®
tabetic
Tibetan
to-brusd
tubfuls
toccata
tackety
tactful
tactile
tacking
ticking
tachism
tactism
tychism
taction
tactics
tachist
tackily
techily
tackled
tackler
tickler
technic
tuck-out
tectrix
tacitly
tactual
tachyon
Tadzhik
tedding
tidying
tiddled
tiddler
toddler
tiddley
tidings
tadpole
tedious
tide-rip
tedesca
tedesco
tideway
themata
trehala
Thebaic
Thebaid
teenage
thecate
trepang
tieback
tietack
toenail
trenail
therapy
tremble
treybit
trembly
tierced
treacle
tiercel
tiercet
treacly
treadle
treddle
tweedle
treader
Tuesday
tee-heed
thereof
tie-neck
therein
thereon
thereto
tieless
toeless
thereat
thereby
△**twelfth**
teemful
treague
thether
theriac
taeniae
trenise
teeming
taedium
therian
taenias
treviss
trekked
trekker
treille
toeclip
trellis
thermic
thermae
thermal
Thermos®
Thermit®
theroid
toehold
trefoil
tremolo
toe-loop
theoric
theorem
theorbo
theurgy
tressed
tressel
treason
theatre
trestle
trental
treetop
theater
treater
tweeter
teentsy
toe-jump
twelves
△**tiffany**
taffeta
taffety
tiffing
tufting
toffish
tagmata
tag-tail
tagmeme
taggers
tigress
toggery
tegmina
tigrine
tagging
tigging

Words marked △ may be spelled also with a capital letter

togging
tugging
tigrish
tegulae
Tagalog
Tagálog
tegular
tigroid
tugboat
tughrik
tigerly
togated
tighten
tagetes
tightly
tohunga
T-shaped
toheroa
tailard
tribade
tsigane
tridarn
tribady
trigamy
trinary
tzigany
thimble
triable
tribble
trilbys
triacid
twiscar
twitchy
triadic
trindle
twiddle
thirdly
twiddly
tail-end
Trilene®
trireme
triseme
toisech
taivers
triceps
taivert
trident
trisect
tripery
tritely
triffic
triffid
toilful
tail-fly
tringle
twiggen
thigger
trigger
twigger
thiggit
Tlingit

thither
trishaw
tritide
tailing
T'ai-p'ing
toiling
twining
trilith
trivial
twibill
tritium
trivium
tuition
△**trinity**
trickle
twinkle
trinkum
thicken
thick'un
think-in
thinker
tricker
thickos
thicket
trinket
thickly
trickly
tricksy
trilled
twilled
taillie
thiller
trifler
twirler
tailles
triblet
triglot
triolet
triplet
Triplex®
triplex
trimmed
triumph
thiamin
trimmer
trismus
tzimmes
thinned
twinned
trionym
thinner
triones
Tritoma
twifold
trilobe
trisome
tritone
trizone
tripoli
triform
tricorn

Tritons
trifoly
trilogy
tripody
trisomy
tripped
tripple
tripper
trippet
triarch
trigram
thiasus
tripsis
twinset
thirsty
trimtab
twin-tub
triatic
tainted
twisted
twitted
thistle
twitten
twinter
twister
twistor
twitter
thistly
trisula
tribune
tribute
triduum
triduan
thieves
triaxon
tuilyie
tailzie
tuilzie
twizzle
takable
tektite
tokamak
takings
take-off
takeout
tallage
tillage
tollage
toluate
tallboy
telecom
Toledos
til-seed
toluene
tallent
taleful
telefax
Telugus
tulchan
telpher
tile-hat

Tellima
tallied
tillite
talcing
talking
telling
tilling
tilting
tolling
tallish
tallith
Tullian
tallier
talkies
tallies
talcked
telamon
tollman
taloned
talooka
talcose
tall-oil
talcous
teleost
tallowy
tilapia
taliped
tylopod
talipes
talipat
talipot
talaria
tile-red
telergy
telesis
tyloses
tylosis
Telstar
teletex
talaunt
tilbury
tally-ho
talayot
tympana
timbale
timpani
tympani
timpano
tympano
Tammany
tympany
tamable
timidly
tumidly
tempera
Tempean
timbers
tempest
tumshie
tamping
tampion

tompion
Tampico
Tamilic
Tamulic
templed
temblor
△templar
tumbler
tumular
tumulus
templet
temenos
tamandu
tombola
tempore
tomfool
tombolo
tambour
timeous
timbrel
tumbrel
tumbril
tamarin
tamarao
Tom-trot
tamarau
timarau
Tamarix
tamasha
tumesce
△**tempter**
timothy
tambura
tempura
tantara
tankard
tanyard
Tynwald
tankage
tannage
tannate
teniate
tentage
tinware
tonnage
tunnage
tanbark
tintack
tone-arm
tent-bed
tenable
tunable
tunably
tunicle
tunicin
tank-car
tanadar
tonnell
tangelo
tangent
tiniest

Words marked △ may be spelled also with a capital letter

7 t□n□e

tonneau
tannery
tensely
tindery
tendenz
tankful
tentful
tuneful
tent-fly
△**tanagra**
tanager
tonight
tent-guy
tinchel
tanghin
tenthly
tan-ride
tensile
tensive
tontine
tanking
tanling
tanning
tenting
tinging
tinning
tinting
tunning
tonnish
tun-dish
tondini
tension
tentigo
tondino
tenpins
tantivy
tensity
tenuity
tangled
tangler
tingler
tinkler
tonally
tonemic
tinamou
tenoner
tenancy
tangoed
tenfold
tenioid
tan-ooze
tinfoil
tung-oil
tinhorn
tandoor
tenuous
ten-foot
tantony
tonepad
△**tantric**
tenured

tendril
tangram
tantrum
tendron
tonetic
tenutos
tongued
tonsure
tinfuls
tongues
taniwha
tintype
two-hand
two-pair
two-part
trouble
toolbag
toolbar
toolbox
twoccer
trodden
thonder
twoness
thonged
trogged
thought
trophic
toothed
trochee
trochal
thother
△**trochus**
thorite
two-line
two-time
tooling
Thomism
thorium
tropism
tromino
tropics
Thomist
tropist
trocken
toolkit
troelie
troolie
trollop
troller
trolley
trommel
toolman
thorned
trounce
two-inch
twofold
twosome
two-tone
two-down
two-four
two-foot

trooper
trouper
tsouris
tootsie
trouser
trouses
trotted
two-step
trotter
trouter
two-eyed
taplash
topsail
tip-cart
topmast
topiary
type-bar
topical
typical
tepidly
topless
tap-shoe
tappice
topline
topside
tapping
tipping
topping
tupping
tap-kick
tipsify
tipsily
tippler
tupelos
tapsman
topsman
to-pinch
toponym
topknot
tapioca
tiptoed
typhoid
top-hole
topsoil
taproom
top-down
typhoon
typhous
tap-bolt
taproot
top-boot
topcoat
topmost
topspin
tapered
toparch
taperer
typeset
tapetal
tapetum
tapster

tipster
tapstry
topfull
T-square
tequila
tartana
tar-sand
turband
tartane
△tartare
ternate
terrace
terrane
threave
tornade
torsade
terrain
tornado
threads
turbant
Tartary
ternary
thready
throaty
turbary
△**terebra**
turacin
turacos
turndun
teredos
tiredly
tarweed
terpene
terrene
turpeth
tar-heel
tar-seal
terreen
torpedo
Turkess
torment
torrent
turgent
tersely
torpefy
torrefy
turnery
terefah
thrifty
torchon
torcher
tormina
tarried
tardive
tartine
tergite
termite
terrine
torsive
tortile
tortive

turbine
turdine
turfite
tarring
turfing
turning
tarnish
tartish
Toryish
turbith
Turkish
termini
tertial
terbium
Toryism
ternion
tersion
tertian
tordion
torsion
turdion
tarrier
tarsier
terrier
Tarsius
tercios
tertius
torpids
turkies
tardily
terrify
Turkify
turnkey
torulae
torulin
turtler
torulus
tartlet
thrilly
thrimsa
thrymsa
thrombi
turfman
Turkman
Turkmen
thrummy
throned
tyranne
threnos
tyrones
tyranny
turbond
turdoid
turnoff
turn-off
torgoch
tortoni
tarrock
turmoil
△**terrors**
turnout

Words marked △ may be spelled also with a capital letter

tar-spot
toreros
tortrix
tirasse
thristy
thrutch
thretty
torqued
Tartufe
torture
tarbush
through
Targums
thrived
thriven
thriver
throw-in
thrower
thruway
tostada
testate
toshach
testacy
test-bed
test-ban
tessera
tassell
testern
tushery
test-fly
tussive
tasking
tasting
testing
tossing
tusking
tastily
testify
testily
tossily
tushkar
tushker
tussore
tussock
testoon
tosspot
Tasered
testril
△**testudo**
titrate
titlark
tetract
tatters
tutress
totient
tattery
tottery
titmice
tatting
tithing
titling

totting
tutting
tittish
Titoism
Titoist
tattily
tattler
titular
tutelar
totally
totemic
Titania
tutania
tetanic
△titanic
tutenag
tetanal
tetanus
△titanis
totanus
tetrode
titmose
tutwork
tituped
Tataric
to-torne
tatouay
tittupy
trucage
tsunami
touraco
thumbed
truncal
thudded
trundle
thunder
△**taurean**
trumeau
truffle
thuggee
trudgen
trudger
thuggos
touched
toughie
toughen
toucher
teuchat
toughly
taurine
thulite
touring
tousing
trucial
thulium
tourism
tourist
thurify
trunked
truckie
truckle

trucker
Trullan
Thummim
trueman
tourney
truancy
thumper
trumpet
trussed
trusser
trusses
toustie
trustee
taunter
truster
taverna
towpath
towable
tow-head
town-end
thwaite
towline
townish
toweled
Tswanas
towmond
towrope
towboat
towmont
towered
to-worne
tow-iron
towards
taxable
taxably
taxicab
toxical
tuxedos
taxless
textile
taxiing
taxying
toxemia
toxemic
taximan
text-man
tax-free
texture
textual
taxiway
trysail
thyself
toyless
toyshop
thymine
toylike
thyroid
twyfold
thylose
toysome
toylsom

trypsin
thyrses
thyrsus
tryptic
tryster
unaware
unaided
urachus
unalike
unalive
uralite
uranide
uranite
unaking
uranism
uranium
Uralian
△uranian
unalist
unasked
udaller
uraemia
uraemic
unaimed
unarmed
up-along
uranous
unaired
uva-ursi
unacted
unaptly
upbraid
umbrage
unbrace
upbrast
umbrere
upbreak
unbless
unblent
unblest
unbegun
unbeget
unbegot
unblind
unbuild
upbuild
unbeing
upbring
Umbrian
unbuilt
unbaked
umbonal
umbones
umbrose
unbroke
unblock
unblown
upblown
umbrous
umbered
unburnt

upburst
unbosom
unbated
unbound
upbound
unbowed
uncrate
uncharm
unchain
unclasp
upcoast
unchary
uncheck
unclean
unclear
upcheer
upclimb
unchild
unction
unclipt
uncinus
uncanny
uncloud
unclose
upclose
uncloak
uncrown
uncross
ulcered
uncured
uncurse
uncited
upcatch
uncouth
upchuck
uncivil
uncover
updrawn
undealt
undress
undight
undried
undoing
undying
undeify
uddered
underdo
undergo
undated
undrunk
ukelele
useless
urethra
urethan
uredine
uterine
uredium
uberous
uneared
unearth
utensil

Words marked △ may be spelled also with a capital letter

7 u□e□t

uveitic
uneaten
uveitis
unequal
unfaded
unfreed
unflesh
unfaith
unfiled
unfilde
unfamed
unfumed
unfunny
unfrock
upfront
up-front
unfired
unfitly
unfeued
unfound
upflung
unflush
unfixed
unfazed
unguard
upgrade
ungodly
unguent
upgoing
unguled
ungulae
urgence
urgency
unglove
ungrown
upgrown
ungored
ungorg'd
ungirth
unglued
ungyved
ungazed
unheard
unhoard
uphoard
upheave
unheart
unhable
unheedy
uphoist
unhuman
unhinge
unhandy
uphoord
unhoped
U-shaped
unhappy
unhired
unhorse
unherst
unhardy
unhasty
unhitch
unhouse
unitard
uricase
urinate
urinant
unitary
urinary
unidea'd
unideal
ulichon
unified
unitise
unitive
unitize
uridine
utilise
utilize
uniting
unition
unifier
unities
unicity
utility
urinose
uniform
△**unicorn**
urinous
unjaded
unjoint
unkempt
unknown
unleash
unlearn
unlucky
unladen
uillean
uplying
unlimed
unlined
unloose
unlaste
unlatch
unloved
unmeant
upmaker
unmanly
unmoral
unmarry
unmated
unmeted
unmould
unmount
unmoved
unmixed
unneath
unnoble
unnamed
ulnaria
unnerve
unnoted
urnfuls
unorder
Urodela
urodele
uromere
urolith
uxorial
utopism
△**utopian**
utopist
unoiled
unowned
urosome
ufology
urology
unoften
unplace
unplait
unpaced
umpteen
unpaged
unpaint
uppiled
unpanel
unpinkt
unpaper
unpared
unpurse
unperch
unposed
unplumb
unplume
unpaved
unqueen
unquiet
unquote
unreave
unready
unraced
utricle
unreeve
unruffe
unright
upright
upraise
unraked
unruled
unrimed
unroost
uprisal
unrisen
uprisen
unrated
unround
uprouse
unrough
unravel
unriven
upriver
unrivet
unroyal
unskan'd
unstaid
unswai'd
upstand
unscale
unshale
unshape
unstate
upscale
upspake
upstage
upstare
upstate
unstack
unsnarl
upswarm
unslain
upstair
unsmart
upstart
unscary
upsides
unsneck
unspeak
upspeak
unshell
unspell
unsteel
upswell
unshewn
upsweep
unswear
upspear
unshent
unspent
unsweet
unswept
upswept
unsight
unspied
unspide
unsling
upswing
unstick
unsaint
unspilt
unsolid
upsilon
unsense
unsinew
unsonsy
unsunny
upstood
unsmote
unsoote
unspoke
upspoke
unstock
unshorn
unshown
unsworn
unshoot
unshout
upshoot
unsured
upsurge
unstrap
unstrip
unscrew
unsated
unsound
unslung
unstuck
unstuft
unsaved
unsewed
unsexed
unsized
untrace
unteach
uptrain
up-train
untread
uptrend
uptight
untried
untride
untwine
untying
unthink
untwist
untaken
untiled
untamed
up-tempo
untoned
untuned
untenty
untired
utterer
upthrow
utterly
untruth
untruss
untrust
untruly
untaxed
ululate
ululant
usucapt
ukulele
usuress
unurged
usuring
usually
usurous
usurped
usurper
unusual
unvocal
unvaile

Words marked △ may be spelled also with a capital letter

7 v□t□a

unvoice
upvalue
unvisor
unvital
unvexed
unweave
unweary
unwaged
umwhile
unwrite
upwhirl
unwhipt
unwaked
unweldy
unwoman
unwooed
unwiped
unwarie
unworth
unwares
upwards
unwitch
unwater
unwitty
unwound
upwound
unwrung
unwived
unwoven
unwayed
unyoked
unzoned
vialful
viatica
vialled
viaduct
vibrate
vibrato
vibrant
vibices
vibrios
vacuate
viciate
vocable
vocoder
vaccine
vacking
Vectian
vacuist
vacuity
vocalic
vocular
vocally
vicomte
vacance
vicinal
vacancy
vacuole
vacuous
vicious
△victory

victrix
viceroy
vacatur
victual
vacuums
viduage
Vidicon®
viduity
vedalia
vidimus
Vedanta
videnda
Veddoid
videoed
viduous
vedette
vidette
veering
viewing
V-necked
Vietnam
vagrant
vaguely
voguing
voguish
veggies
veganic
vaginae
vaginal
V-agents
vaginas
vegetal
vagitus
vehicle
vihuela
V-shaped
vyingly
Vaishya
veiling
veining
voicing
voiding
veinlet
vaivode
voivode
veinous
voiture
voltaic
valuate
valvate
village
voltage
volvate
△vulgate
vulvate
villain
viliaco
viliago
volcano
valiant
vallary

villany
volable
voluble
volubil
volubly
validly
villein
valleys
volleys
velvety
veliger
vulpine
volpino
volumed
velamen
volumes
valonea
△valonia
valance
valence
volante
valency
villose
valgous
villous
Volapük
velaria
valeric
velaric
△völuspa
volatic
velated
voluted
volutin
valvula
valvule
velouté
vulture
vulturn
velours
vilayet
vampire
vamping
vampish
vamoose
vomited
vomitus
ventana
vanward
vantage
vendace
vendage
ventage
vintage
ventail
vanadic
Vendean
venefic
vinegar
ventige
vanning

venting
vendiss
vanilla
Vinalia
venally
venomed
vintner
Ventôse
ventose
vent-peg
vine-rod
ventral
venerer
vanessa
vinasse
venison
venatic
vingt-un
venator
vanitas
vincula
venture
△venturi
vinewed
△vandyke
violate
violent
violist
violone
vapidly
vapours
vapoury
vaquero
variate
virgate
vervain
verbals
variant
verdant
vernant
versant
varices
verbena
vermeil
vermell
varment
veriest
variety
viragos
verdite
versine
varying
versing
varnish
vermian
version
vertigo
vernier
varmint
verdict
varsity

verbify
vermily
verminy
versify
verglas
virelay
viremia
viremic
veranda
viranda
Veronal®
veronal
virando
Varanus
variola
variole
verbose
Virgoan
various
verismo
virosis
viretot
verruca
verruga
vareuse
verdure
versute
virgule
virtual
vistaed
vassail
vessail
visuals
visible
visibly
vesicae
vesicle
vesical
viscera
Vosgean
△vespers
visaged
vespine
vestige
vesting
Vosgian
vastity
vespoid
viscose
viscous
visnomy
visored
vestral
visitee
visiter
visitor
vascula
vesture
vis-à-vis
vitiate
vitrage

Words marked △ may be spelled also with a capital letter

7 v□t□a

vittate
vitrail
vitrain
vitraux
vatable
Vatican
vitreum
votress
Vitrina
vitrine
vatting
vetting
vitriol
vitrics
vitrify
vitelli
vitular
vittles
vitally
vitamin
vetkoek
veteran
vettura
vatfuls
vetiver
vouchee
voucher
vaurien
Vaudois
vaudoux
vaulted
vaunted
vaulter
vaunter
vividly
vivific
vivency
vivaria
△viverra
vowelly
vexedly
vexilla
vixenly
voyager
Viyella®
vizored
weasand
weazand
Wealden
whate'er
whalery
whangee
wrangle
whangam
weather
wearied
wearing
weaving
whaling
wearish
wearily
whacked
wracked
whacker
whackos
whammed
whatnot
whapped
wrapped
whample
wrapper
whaisle
whatsis
whatsit
whatten
wealthy
wharves
whaizle
webbing
wabbler
wobbler
web-toed
webworm
webfoot
wabster
webster
wych-elm
wickiup
wadmaal
widgeon
wadsett
wide-gab
wadding
wedding
wedging
waddler
widener
wedlock
wadmoll
widower
wheedle
wielder
weekday
weekend
wee-weed
whereof
wherein
whereon
whereso
whereto
whene'er
where'er
waeness
whereas
whereat
weedery
whereby
whether
weeding
weeping
weeting
wheyish
weevily
whelked
wreaked
wreaker
wrecker
wheeled
wheelie
wheeler
whemmle
wheenge
waesome
woesome
woe-worn
wheeple
wherret
Wheeson
wheesht
whetted
wreathe
wrestle
wheaten
whetter
wrester
wreaths
wreathy
wheezle
waftage
weftage
wafting
waffler
wofully
wafture
wagtail
wigless
waggery
wiggery
wiglike
wagging
wigging
waggish
wiggler
wagoner
wagerer
wightly
Wahabee
wainage
whipcat
whidded
weirdie
whidder
weirdos
weirdly
weigela
whilere
write-in
write-up
whitely
whiffle
wailful
whiffer
whiffet
whigged
wringed
wriggle
whinger
wringer
wriggly
weighed
weigh-in
writhen
weigher
whither
weights
weighty
wailing
waiting
whining
whiting
△writing
whitish
wrinkle
whicker
whisker
whisket
whiskey
wrinkly
wrizled
whirler
whitlow
whimmed
waivode
waiwode
woiwode
whipped
whimple
whimper
whipper
whisper
whippet
whirred
whirret
whitret
Whitsun
whipsaw
whimsey
waisted
whirtle
whistle
whittle
written
whip-top
waister
whitter
whittaw
whizzed
whizzer
wakeful
wakeman
wakened
wakener
wallaba
welfare
wallaby
wildcat
wolf-dog
wall-eye
willest
well-fed
wileful
willful
welcher
welsher
walking
walling
welding
welling
wilding
willing
wolfing
wolving
wildish
wolfish
wolvish
Wolfian
wallies
wellies
willies
wolfkin
Walkman®
welcome
well-off
Walloon
walk-out
willowy
wolfram
well-set
well-won
walkway
welaway
waltzer
wameful
wampish
wimpish
womanly
wimbrel
wannabe
wantage
windage
windbag
wanness
winkers
winters
Wonders
wintery
wanigan
windgun
wencher
wongied
wanting
wincing
winding
winking
winning

Words marked △ may be spelled also with a capital letter

wonning
wannish
Wendish
wennish
wannion
wendigo
windigo
Windies
windily
wing-led
wangler
winkler
winglet
wanhope
windore
winsome
Wenlock
windock
winnock
windows
wondred
windrow
wine-sap
Windsor
want-wit
woorara
woorali
whoobub
whomble
woodcut
woolded
woolder
woomera
woosell
woolfat
wronger
wrought
wrongly
whorish
wholism
wholist
woozily
whorled
woolled
woollen
whommle
woodman
woolman
whopped
whoopee
whooper
whopper
woodsia
woolsey
woofter
whoever
woodwax
wappend
wapping
wopping
wipeout

warrand
warfare
wordage
warpath
warrant
workbag
workbox
worlded
workday
worldly
warhead
wurleys
wormery
workful
warthog
warship
△worship
wergild
worried
warlike
wartime
warding
warling
warming
warning
warping
warring
wording
working
warmish
wordish
Wardian
Wormian
Würmian
warrior
worrier
wurlies
wordily
warbler
wireman
workman
warlord
warwolf
werwolf
warlock
war-worn
work-out
worn-out
wardrop
warison
workshy
worsted
waratah
wiretap
worktop
wireway
wastage
wassail
washday
△**western**
washers

washery
wastery
wishful
wistful
wosbird
washing
wasting
westing
wishing
waspish
wistiti
westlin
washout
wash-out
washpot
washrag
wastrel
washtub
wysiwyg
wetland
wattage
wetware
wetback
witwall
wotteth
wetness
withers
witless
witness
wottest
Watteau
wet-shod
witchen
watcher
wotcher
watches
watchet
wetting
witling
witting
wotting
wettish
wittily
wattled
wattles
witloof
wet-look
without
watered
waterer
wourali
would-be
wounder
wouldst
wauling
wauring
waulker
whummle
wavelet
waverer
waveson

wawling
waxwing
waxbill
waxwork
waylaid
wayward
weyward
wayfare
waymark
wryneck
wayless
wryness
wayment
wrythen
wayside
waybill
wrybill
waygone
waywode
wayworn
waypost
whyever
waza-ari
wizened
X-factor
x-height
xylogen
xylomas
xylonic
xylenol
Xylopia
xylitol
xanthic
xantham
xanthan
xanthin
Xenopus
Xenurus
Xiphias
xiphoid
xerafin
xeromas
xerarch
xerasia
xerosis
xerotic
xerotes
yealdon
year-end
yearner
yobbery
yobbish
yobbism
yibbles
yobboes
yachtie
yachter
Yiddish
yielder
yeggman
yoghurt

Yahvist
Yahwist
yakhdan
ycleap'd
ycleepe
yplight
yelling
yelping
yslaked
yelloch
yellows
yellowy
ycleped
yolk-sac
yamulka
yanking
ymolten
yuppify
yapster
yardage
yardang
yard-arm
Yoruban
Yorkish
Yorkist
yardman
Y-fronts
yestern
yeshiva
ypsilon
yashmak
yu-stone
yatagan
yttrium
youngth
younger
youngly
youthly
younker
yawning
yowling
Yezidee
zealant
zealful
zoarium
zealous
zebrass
zebrina
zebrine
zabtieh
zebroid
zebrula
zebrule
zoccolo
zedoary
Zadkiel
zaddiks
zoeform
ziffius
zuffoli
zuffolo

Words marked △ may be spelled also with a capital letter

7 z□g□e

Zygaena
zagging
zigging
zygomas
ziganka
zygosis
zygotic
Zairean
Zoilean
zoisite
Zoilism
Zoilist
zakuska
zakuski
Zolaism
zillion
zelator
zimocca
zymogen
Zambian
zombify
zampone
zamponi
zamarra
zamarro
zymurgy
zymosis
zemstva
zymotic
zemstvo
zamouse
zambuck
Zincala
Zingana
Zingara
Zingane
Zingare
Zincali
Zingani
Zingari
Zincalo
Zingano
Zingaro
zanjero
zincite
zincing
zinking
zanyism
Zantiot
Zennist
zincify
zinkify
zincked
zanella
zonular
zonulet
zincoid
zincode
zincous
Zonurus
zonated
zoogamy
zootaxy
zooecia
zooidal
zoogeny
zoopery
zeolite
zoolite
zoonite
zoolith
Zionism
Zionist
zoogony
zoology
zoonomy
zootomy
zootype
zip-neck
zipping
zaptiah
zaptieh
Ziphius
ziplock
zareeba
zorgite
zeroing
zarnich
zorille
zorillo
zorinos
zero-sum
Zostera
zestful
zithern
zetetic
zeuxite
Zeuxian
Zezidee
zizania

Words marked △ may be spelled also with a capital letter

agar-agar
amadavat
Aramaean
avadavat
anasarca
apanaged
anabasis
anabatic
ataraxia
ataraxic
abatable
arapaima
anapaest
Aramaism
agaçante
amaranth
Atalanta
amaracus
anarchal
anarchic
analcime
analcite
amandine
acaudate
Araldite®
Araneida
Acalepha
acalephe
academia
academic
agacerie
apatetic
amazedly
analemma
amaretto
analecta
analects
araceous
araneous
arachnid
anathema
anaphora
anaphase
acaridan
Adamical
Agamidae
Adamitic
Aganippe
abat-jour
agalloch
acauline
availing
anableps
anaglyph
acaulose
availful
alaiment
alarming
alarmism
alarmist
anaconda
araponga
anabolic
anagogic
analogic
anatomic
apagogic
analogon
analogue
abampere
acarpous
anaerobe
anatropy
alacrity
abattoir
acanthin
alastrim
awanting
adaption
acanthus
adaptive
abacuses
arapunga
abat-voix
analyser
analyses
analyzer
analysis
analytic
akaryote
ambiance
albacore
albicore
ambience
aubretia
aubrieta
ambulant
arbalest
arbalist
ambulate
Albanian
albiness
albinism
ambrosia
arboreal
alberghi
amberoid
arborist
amberite
arboreta
alburnum
amberous
arborous
Abbaside
asbestic
asbestos
abbatial
arbitral
ambition
albitise
albitize
arboured
ambivert
Archaean
arcuated
archaise
archaism
archaist
△archaeus
archaize
Accadian
Arcadian
ascidian
archduke
accident
arcading
aecidium
ascidium
accredit
alchemic
ancients
alcahest
archival
archives
arc-light
atchieve
accolade
archlute
arch-mock
ascender
arcanely
accentor
arcanist
archness
anchoret
accepted
accepter
arch-poet
acceptor
accuracy
accorder
accursed
accorage
ascorbic
accurate
accusing
accustom
ancestor
ancestry
alcatras
accouter
accoutre
accounts
Arcturus
archwise
addebted
abductee
addicted
abdicant
abducent
adducent
abductor
adductor
abdicate
audacity
audience
aldehyde
ardently
addendum
androgen
Abderian
alderman
addorsed
aldermen
Alderney
alder-fly
Anderson
Abderite
andesine
andesite
addition
audition
auditory
additive
auditive
abeyance
abeyancy
averages
Arenaria
amenable
amenably
Alemaine
ageratum
areca-nut
acerbate
acerbity
ayenbite
acescent
amelcorn
Aberdeen
anecdote
alebench
ale-berry
avenging
anechoic
amethyst
American
alewives
adenitis
aperitif
apéritif
aperient
areolate
abetment
averment
agedness
adenomas
adenoids
ameiosis
ale-house
adespota
awearied
aberrant
aleurone
averring
aneurism
aneurysm
aberrate
aseismic
aversely
aversion
abessive
adessive
aversive
agential
a-weather
aventail
ale-stake
abetting
axe-stone
aleatory
aperture
aventure
aseptate
anestrum
anestrus
agentive
adequacy
adequate
acervate
affiance
afflated
affrayed
afflatus
affected
affecter
alfresco
affeered
affright
affinity
affronté
affirmer
afferent
afforest
affusion
affluent
aggraced
alguacil
alguazil
arguable
arguably
algicide
algidity
aigrette
argufier
Anglican
anguiped
aiguille
Anguilla
aggrieve
angekkok
△angelica
algology
Angeleno
angklung

8 a□g□l

angulate
argemone
argument
Algonkin
arginine
alginate
△argonaut
aegrotat
angiomas
aeglogue
Algerian
algaroba
auger-bit
aegirine
△algerine
algorism
aegirite
argyrite
Augustan
Argestes
augustly
argutely
Ångström
angstrom
aphicide
anhedral
aphidian
ash-leach
achiever
athletic
ashy-grey
aphthous
an-heires
aphelian
achillea
ash-blond
ash-plant
atheling
aphelion
ashaming
Alhambra
achenial
Athenian
achingly
an-hungry
athanasy
aphanite
achenium
aphonous
achromat
Achernar
△abhorrer
atheroma
adherent
Atherina
atherine
aphorise
aphorism
aphorist
aphorize
aphasiac

adhesion
adhesive
athetoid
ash-stand
aphetise
athetise
aphetize
athetize
abidance
agitated
animated
animater
alizarin
animalic
animatic
amicable
amicably
animally
apically
avifauna
agitator
animator
aligarta
akinesia
akinesis
anisette
acid-head
alighted
arillode
axiology
arilloid
arillary
axillary
arillate
axiality
amidmost
avionics
alienage
acidness
alienism
alienist
Arianise
Arianism
aridness
avidness
alienate
Adiantum
amiantus
Arianize
acidosis
amitosis
amitotic
aniconic
△agitprop
agit-prop
apiarian
acierage
apiarist
aviarist
acierate
aliasing

amissing
agiotage
aviatrix
aviation
aristate
acicular
aliquant
abjectly
adjacent
adjuring
adjuster
adjustor
adjutage
adjutant
adjuvant
Akkadian
ark-shell
alkahest
alkalies
alkalify
alkaloid
alkaline
alkalise
ankylose
alkalize
acknowne
ankerite
alliance
aulnager
ad-libber
allocate
allodial
allodium
allogamy
allegros
allegory
alligate
all-thing
all-fired
all-fives
all-giver
allnight
all-right
all-risks
all-clear
alleluia
aglimmer
Atlantes
Atlantic
Atlantis
ailantos
all-round
all-fours
allsorts
allspice
allopath
aularian
allergen
allergic
alluring
allerion

aplastic
allusion
aplustre
allosaur
allusive
aflutter
aglitter
allotted
allottee
axle-tree
ablation
ablution
ablative
allative
alluvial
alluvion
alluvium
alleycat
alley-taw
alleyway
allaying
alley-tor
armgaunt
alms-deed
alms-dish
Asmodeus
alms-folk
Armagnac
armigero
Almagest
△almighty
armchair
atmology
atmolyse
Armalite
atmolyze
armament
ammoniac
Armenian
Arminian
ammonoid
Armenoid
arm-in-arm
admonish
ammonite
ammonium
armorial
armorist
admitted
armature
armoured
armourer
armozeen
armozine
annealer
annually
abnegate
Annelida
annulled
annalise
annalist

annulose
Annulata
annulate
annalize
amniotic
abnormal
amnesiac
agnostic
adnation
agnation
annattos
annotate
announce
annexion
annexure
annoying
abomasal
amorance
apogaeic
apogamic
aromatic
adorable
adorably
avowable
avocados
abomasum
abomasus
amoeboid
aboideau
alopecia
anoretic
anorexia
anorexic
avowedly
amoretti
amoretto
apophyge
apothegm
alogical
atomical
aborigen
agonised
agonized
atomiser
atomizer
aborigin
aconitic
apomixis
apositia
apositic
aconitum
Apolline
Apollyon
Anoplura
axoplasm
apoplexy
acosmism
acosmist
acoemeti
Anointed
anointer

Words marked △ may be spelled also with a capital letter

aborning
acorn-cup
apodosis
apologia
amorosos
apologue
apospory
apocrine
apograph
anourous
acoustic
avoision
aboiteau
avoutrer
anorthic
abortion
adoption
amortise
apostasy
apostate
abortive
adoptive
amortize
azoturia
Apocynum
alphabet
appearer
appeaser
applause
appraise
aspidium
apple-pie
aspheric
amplexus
arpeggio
appriser
apprizer
Amphibia
amphipod
appliqué
ampullae
appalled
appanage
appendix
alpinism
alpinist
amphorae
approval
approach
approver
asphodel
amphoric
asperger
asperges
amperage
aspartic
apperill
apparent
aspirant
aspiring
asperate
asperity
aspirate
asperous
appestat
apposite
appetent
appetise
amputate
appetite
appetize
asphyxia
applying
appuying
acquaint
arquebus
acquiral
acquired
acquight
airwards
aerially
Aerobics®
aerobics
aerobomb
abricock
apricock
airscrew
auricled
△**auricula**
apricate
atrocity
abridger
Airedale
abradant
acridine
aerodyne
aerodart
acridity
air-bends
agreeing
arrieros
aerofoil
acre-foot
aeriform
auriform
aerogram
arrogant
abrogate
arrogate
airshaft
Ayrshire
airliner
airtight
aortitis
adroitly
airfield
Afro-jazz
Aprilian
aurelian
aerology
agrology
acrolein
airplane
air-plant
Aprilish
acrolith
aerolite
aerolith
Abram-man
acromial
atremble
acrimony
agrémens
agrément
agrimony
atrament
acromion
apron-man
arranger
arrantly
aeronomy
agronomy
airiness
aeronaut
apronful
airwoman
air-force
air-cover
air-power
aureoled
air-to-air
airborne
air-house
airspace
airspeed
agraphia
agraphic
abruptly
atropine
agraphon
atropism
atropous
agrarian
aurorean
Afro-rock
air-brick
aircraft
air-drain
air-brake
airdrome
airframe
airgraph
air-brush
airdrawn
aerostat
agrestal
arrestee
arrester
acrostic
agrestic
aoristic
apres-ski
après-ski
acrosome
arrasene
abrasion
arrestor
abrasive
airstrip
aeration
acrotism
arraught
air-built
airburst
aardvark
aardwolf
atrazine
answerer
absterge
assiento
Ansafone®
assegaai
assignat
assignee
assignor
arsehole
aesthete
aestival
assailer
auspices
abscisin
abscissa
abscisse
absolver
△**absolute**
assemble
assemblé
assembly
assuming
Ausonian
arsenide
absentee
assenter
absinthe
absently
absonant
assonant
assentor
arsonist
arsenate
arsenite
arsonite
assonate
aasvogel
Assyrian
Austrian
abstract
abstrict
absorbed
absorber
asserter
assorted
assorter
absurdly
anserine
assertor
adscript
abstruse
assisted
assassin
assessor
Alsatian
assotted
aesculin
Aesculus
assaying
astragal
anteater
actually
actuator
antibody
△**autobahn**
Antabuse®
autocrat
antecede
autocade
anticked
articled
articles
attached
attacker
anti-chip
autacoid
autocarp
Atticise
Atticism
astucity
anticous
anticize
Atticize
auto-da-fé
autodyne
antedate
antidote
antlered
ants'-eggs
anthelia
anthelix
anthemia
anthesis
asthenia
asthenic
artefact
artifact
artifice
anti-fade
antefixa
astigmia
autogamy
autogeny
autogiro
autogyro
anti-hero
autoharp
altrices

Words marked △ may be spelled also with a capital letter

8 a□t□i

- **astringe**
- **antliate**
- **anti-lock**
- **antilogy**
- autology
- **antelope**
- Antilope
- **autolyse**
- **autolyze**
- **autumnal**
- **attemper**
- **antimony**
- **antimask**
- **automata**
- automate
- **astomous**
- **actiniae**
- actinian
- actinias
- antennae
- antennal
- antennas
- attentat
- **actinide**
- antinode
- **astonied**
- attendee
- attender
- **actinoid**
- **antinomy**
- antonymy
- autonomy
- **actinism**
- artiness
- astonish
- **antenati**
- autunite
- **actinium**
- **although**
- **Anthozoa**
- **antrorse**
- art-house
- **antipode**
- **autopsia**
- autoptic
- **antipole**
- **antiphon**
- **antipope**
- **antepast**
- ante-post
- **after-tax**
- alternat
- arterial
- Asterias
- **attorney**
- **altarage**
- **autarchy**
- **asteroid**
- autarkic
- **anti-roll**
- **alterant**
- attiring
- **anterior**
- anteroom
- antiriot
- attercop
- **antirust**
- apterism
- asterisk
- asterism
- **alterity**
- **apterium**
- apterous
- **aftereye**
- **antistat**
- △artesian
- **attested**
- attester
- **antiship**
- antiskid
- artistic
- autistic
- **autosome**
- **attestor**
- **antisera**
- artistry
- **altitude**
- aptitude
- attitude
- **antithet**
- **astutely**
- **autotomy**
- **antitank**
- astatine
- **antitype**
- autotype
- **artfully**
- **altruism**
- altruist
- **actively**
- **antevert**
- **activism**
- activist
- **activate**
- activity
- **adularia**
- **amusable**
- **adulator**
- **aquacade**
- **ague-cake**
- **aduncate**
- aduncity
- aguacate
- **aduncous**
- **aqueduct**
- **abundant**
- **amuletic**
- **amusedly**
- **azulejos**
- **aculeate**
- amusette
- **abutilon**
- **aluminum**
- **aqualung**
- aquiline
- **abutment**
- **aquanaut**
- **aquarian**
- **alum-root**
- **aquarist**
- **aquarium**
- Aquarius
- **aguishly**
- **avulsion**
- **aquatics**
- **abuttals**
- **abutting**
- aquatint
- **adultery**
- **Ayurveda**
- **alveated**
- **advocaat**
- **advocacy**
- **Arvicola**
- arvicole
- △**advocate**
- **advanced**
- **alveolar**
- **alveolus**
- **advising**
- **advisory**
- **advoutry**
- **advowson**
- **atwitter**
- **auxiliar**
- **adynamia**
- adynamic
- **amygdala**
- amygdale
- amygdule
- **asynergy**
- **apyretic**
- apyrexia
- **anything**
- **anywhere**
- **atypical**
- **Aryanise**
- **Aryanize**
- **asystole**
- **bearable**
- bearably
- beatable
- blamable
- blamably
- **bravados**
- **blah-blah**
- **boatbill**
- **bearbine**
- blabbing
- **Bradbury**
- **branched**
- brancher
- bratchet
- **branchia**
- **brancard**
- **braccate**
- **boat-deck**
- **brandade**
- **brandied**
- brand-new
- **boarding**
- braiding
- **bladdery**
- **blandish**
- Braidism
- brandise
- brandish
- **brakeman**
- brake-van
- **beam-ends**
- **beavered**
- blazered
- bracelet
- **brazenly**
- **braseros**
- **brazenry**
- **blameful**
- **beauffet**
- **Beaufort**
- **boarfish**
- **bragging**
- **braggart**
- **brachial**
- **biathlon**
- boat-hook
- **blathers**
- **Baathism**
- Ba'athism
- Baathist
- Ba'athist
- **brachium**
- **bearings**
- **beatific**
- brazilin
- **beak-iron**
- **blackcap**
- black-cat
- **blackleg**
- **bean-king**
- blacking
- blanking
- **blackboy**
- black-fox
- blacktop
- **blackish**
- brackish
- **blankety**
- **blackout**
- **bear-lead**
- boat-load
- **brailler**
- **beagling**
- bratling
- brawling
- **beamless**
- **bran-mash**
- **biannual**
- brainpan
- **brainbox**
- **brainish**
- **braunite**
- **blazoner**
- **blazonry**
- **bratpack**
- **beanpole**
- **beau-pere**
- **blanquet**
- △**boatrace**
- **bead-roll**
- **baasskap**
- beadsman
- bear's-ear
- Bradshaw
- **brassica**
- **bearskin**
- **brassily**
- **biassing**
- boat-song
- **brassard**
- brassart
- **bracteal**
- **brattice**
- **beauties**
- bractlet
- **beautify**
- blast-off
- **blastoid**
- boattail
- **beastily**
- blastula
- **blastema**
- **blasting**
- blattant
- blatting
- boasting
- **brattish**
- **boastful**
- **blagueur**
- **bearward**
- **beauxite**
- **baby-doll**
- **Babeeism**
- **babyfood**
- **Babygros**
- **bobwheel**
- **babyhood**
- **bob-white**
- **biblical**
- **bobbinet**
- **Babbitry**
- **babbling**
- bobolink
- bubaline
- **babeldom**
- **babelish**

Words marked △ may be spelled also with a capital letter

babelism
bibulous
bob-apple
babirusa
babushka
baby-talk
bibation
bobstays
babouche
bobby-pin
baccarat
bechance
bechamel
béchamel
backache
buckaroo
buckayro
backbeat
buckbean
backband
backbond
backbone
backbite
backchat
back-comb
back-door
backdrop
back-date
backdown
bacteria
bacteric
bachelor
buckeroo
backfall
backfile
backfill
back-foot
backfire
bacchiac
Bacchian
back-heel
back-hair
bacchant
backhand
buckhorn
bacchius
beck-iron
bick-iron
Buccinum
bacillar
back-load
bucellas
becalmed
backlift
back-lill
back-lilt
backland
baculine
buckling
backlash
backlist

baculite
△bacillus
Buckley's
becoming
backmost
Baconian
biconvex
backpack
Bactrian
by-corner
buckrake
backroom
back-rope
back-seat
backside
buckshee
backspin
bicuspid
buckskin
backstop
buckshot
backveld
backward
backword
backwork
backwash
buck-wash
backyard
badlands
bedwards
bedeafen
bedmaker
beddable
bed-table
biddable
bedabble
bud-scale
bedrench
budgeree
budgeted
badgerly
budgeros
budgerow
bedeguar
bedaggle
bed-sheet
Buddhism
Buddhist
bed-linen
bedright
buddleia
bodyline
body-line
bodiless
bed-plate
bedimmed
bodement
bidental
badinage
bedcover
bedsocks

badmouth
bedarken
bedesman
badassed
bodysuit
bedstead
bedstraw
bed-staff
Bedouins
bodywork
badly-off
beddy-bye
bedazzle
bee-eater
bien-aimé
beefalos
bleuâtre
bleacher
breeched
breeches
beefcake
bleeding
blending
breeding
breadnut
Baedeker
breveted
bien-être
bretesse
△brethren
Blenheim
beerhall
blethers
breviary
breviate
break-jaw
breakage
breaking
break-vow
break-out
beetling
bdellium
bregmata
biennial
Biennale
Blennius
Brezonek
bee-house
breloque
beer-pump
bee-bread
beetroot
breasted
brewster
bheestie
breaskit
blessing
Boeotian
brettice
breathed
breather

beesting
beestung
bleating
bletting
beeswing
beef-wood
breezily
bifacial
buff-coat
bifocals
befuddle
buffered
befringe
befriend
befallen
baffling
befinned
beflower
befitted
bog-Latin
beggarly
baguette
bagpiper
bagpipes
beguiler
bigamist
bigamous
beginner
bignonia
bughouse
bigmouth
begorrah
bigarade
begirded
begetter
begotten
begrudge
bogey-man
bogeyism
beheadal
beholden
beholder
Bahamian
Bohemian
behemoth
behappen
behatted
behovely
behavior
bailable
brigalow
bail-ball
bailbond
blimbing
britches
bail-dock
brindled
blindage
blinding
building
blinders

brindisi
blind-gut
brideman
brine-pan
bride-bed
brine-pit
bride-ale
brief-bag
brim-full
briefing
baitfish
bridging
bringing
blighted
blighter
brighten
blithely
brightly
brickbat
brinkman
brick-red
brick-tea
blinking
bricking
brick-nog
blinkard
blinkers
briskish
buik-lear
brisling
brimless
bailment
brimming
beinness
blimpish
Briarean
bailsman
blissful
bristled
brittley
bristols
blistery
briguing
britzska
blizzard
bejabers
Bajocian
bijwoner
bejesuit
Bakelite®
bakemeat
Bakewell
bakeware
balladin
balsamic
Bulgaric
balladry
bilabial
bull-beef
buln-buln
bellbind

Words marked △ may be spelled also with a capital letter

8 b□l□b

bell-buoy
billbook
bell-bird
bilobate
belabour
ballclay
ballcock
bull-calf
bald-coot
bellcote
bale-dock
baladine
bulldust
bulldoze
believer
belleter
billeted
balletic
bulletin
balneary
bilberry
balled-up
bold-face
billfold
bullfrog
bale-fire
bill-fish
ball-game
bullgine
ball-girl
ball-gown
bald-head
billhead
bolthead
bulkhead
bullhead
bolthole
billhook
bull-hoof
bull-horn
billiard
ballista
balkline
balanced
balancer
belonger
bilander
bylander
baldness
Balinese
boldness
bullnose
balmoral
balconet
ballonet
balloted
ballotee
bellower
billowed
ballocks
bollocks
bullocky
bell-pull
ballpark
bellpush
baldpate
baldrick
belfried
bull-ring
ballroom
bell-rope
bolt-rope
baluster
bullshit
bull's-eye
belittle
bell-tent
bulrushy
beloving
bullwhip
bellwort
boll-worm
ballyrag
billy-can
bullyrag
bully-off
bellying
bullying
ballyhoo
belly-god
billyboy
bully-boy
bullyism
bellyful
bemoaner
bummaree
bimbashi
bemuddle
bimbette
bemuffle
bambinos
bum-clock
bumbling
bumaloti
bimanual
bimanous
bombsite
by-motive
bombycid
bondager
bone-ache
△benjamin
bankable
binnacle
bandanna
bungalow
bank-bill
bonibell
bank-book
band-call
bone-cave
Benedick
△benedict
bunodont
bone-dust
bandelet
bannered
banneret
banterer
bonneted
bunkered
bankerly
bonsella
banderol
bannerol
bontebok
bandeaux
benefact
benefice
boniface
banoffee
band-fish
benignly
benthoal
bonehead
bank-high
bunghole
Banthine®
bunching
bin-liner
bun-fight
bone-idle
banditry
banditti
banlieue
bindi-eye
bone-lace
bantling
bundling
bungling
buntline
banalise
boneless
banality
banalize
binomial
bone-meal
benumbed
bondmaid
bone-mill
bonamani
bonamano
boniness
bank-note
buncombe
bonhomie
banjoist
benzoate
bonspiel
band-pass
bona-roba
bongrace
bankroll
banxring
bankrupt
bank-rate
bandsman
banksman
bondsman
bandster
bangster
banister
beniseed
bonassus
bénitier
bang-tail
binaural
banausic
bung-vent
bindweed
bentwood
bendwise
bandyman
bandying
boneyard
bunny-hug
buoyance
buoyancy
brocaded
brocatel
bookable
browbeat
blow-back
blowball
browband
bloncket
blotched
broacher
bronchia
broccoli
bronchos
bioscope
bookcase
bronchus
blood-tax
broadway
brood-sac
book-debt
bloodied
blood-red
blood-wit
bloodily
brodding
blood-hot
broidery
broadish
blowdown
biogenic
brodekin
broken-in
bromelia
bromelin
brokenly
biometry
blokeish
booked-up
blowfish
brougham
brogging
brouhaha
blowhole
book-hand
boot-hook
biophore
blowhard
brochure
brothers
boothose
biocidal
bootikin
bromidic
boom-iron
boot-jack
brockram
blockade
brooklet
blockage
brockage
block-tin
blocking
blockish
brookite
book-lear
booklice
bootlace
bootlick
blowlamp
bookland
booklore
bioblast
bioplasm
bioplast
bookless
bootlast
bootless
browless
blooming
bloomers
bloomery
bookmark
book-mate
brown-bag
Brownian
browning
brownish
Brownism
Brownist
brownout
bionomic
biomorph
book-oath
blowpipe
book-post
biograph
bookrest

Words marked △ may be spelled also with a capital letter

bioassay
blossomy
browsing
bookshop
boob-tube
boortree
boot-tree
bloating
blotting
brow-tine
broguish
bookwork
bookworm
biolysis
boodying
boobyish
boobyism
bronzify
bronzing
bronzite
biphasic
bepraise
B-Special
buplever
biphenyl
bepommel
Baphomet
bepepper
biparous
bepester
beplumed
bepowder
bequeath
barracan
barbasco
barranca
barranco
barbated
bereaved
bereaven
burganet
berdache
barbaric
△borealis
byrlakin
barracks
barnacle
Barbados
barrator
bergamot
barratry
bareboat
bareback
bird-bolt
barebone
beriberi
birdbath
Burschen
birdcage
borachio
birdcall
borecole
baroccos
boracite
Buridan's
barn-door
bargeman
barterer
bird-eyed
bordered
borderer
berberis
bergenia
bargello
bordello
barberry
Burberry
bargeese
berceuse
barbette
barrette
burletta
barbecue
barbeque
berceaux
Bordeaux
bergfall
barefoot
barogram
baregine
berghaan
birthday
berthage
borehole
barchane
birthing
birthdom
bar-chart
barghest
barbican
barbital
bartisan
bartizan
barbicel
bursitis
barricos
burritos
barriers
bird-lice
bird-life
beryllia
birdlike
Bartlemy
bird-lime
bardling
burbling
burglary
barkless
bergmehl
barometz
biramous
baronial
baronage
boringly
bareness
baroness
burinist
Byronism
bar-coded
borrowed
borrower
burgonet
bargoose
burnouse
bar-graph
burgrave
barostat
Burnsian
burnside
birdseed
bardship
birdsong
birdshot
baresark
Burnsite
birds-eye
bird'seye
burnt-ear
barathea
borstall
baritone
barytone
Bermudan
Bermudas
△burgundy
barrulet
barouche
birdwing
berrying
biriyani
barnyard
Biscayan
bastardy
bestadde
beslaver
bostangi
biscacha
bistable
beshadow
bush-baby
bush-buck
busybody
baseball
best-ball
baseband
base-born
bisector
basicity
basidial
basidium
by-speech
besieger
Bessemer
boss-eyed
beseemly
basketry
bushfire
besognio
boschbok
besmirch
bassinet
besuited
buskined
△bastille
bestiary
base-load
Basilian
basilica
basaltic
base-line
baselard
baseless
bashless
basilisk
basement
besoming
besonian
baseness
business
busyness
basanite
basinful
bestowal
bespoken
bestower
bistoury
basophil
bespread
bestreak
biserial
bestride
bestrode
bescreen
by-street
besprent
bush-rope
bescrawl
bestrewn
bestrown
besetter
besotted
besmutch
besouled
besought
basquine
biscuity
bushveld
bushwalk
basswood
bisexual
betrayal
betrayer
battalia
bittacle
bathcube
betacism
△bethesda
batteler
battered
bettered
bathetic
batterie
bitterly
bitchily
batching
botching
butching
bitchery
botchery
butcher's
butchery
battle-ax
bit-slice
batology
butylene
bottle-oh
bateless
botulism
bateleur
betel-nut
batement
bathmism
botanise
botanist
botanize
batwoman
bottomed
bottomry
bathorse
bottom-up
bathrobe
bethrall
bathroom
botargos
buttress
butyrate
betatron
Batavian
bethwack
batswing
bothyman
buttyman
botryoid
Botrytis
botryose
brutally
Brumaire
blueback
bluebuck
bluebell
blubbing
bluebird
bluecoat
blue-chip
bouncily

Words marked △ may be spelled also with a capital letter

8 b□u□c

bouncing
bounding
boundary
blue-eyed
baudekin
bouderie
Brunella
brunette
bouffant
bluefish
blue-grey
bludgeon
bourgeon
bluegown
boughten
brush-off
blushing
brushing
boughpot
blushful
bauhinia
bauxitic
boutique
bruilzie
baubling
bouillon
blueness
△bluenose
bouzouki
boutonné
baudrick
△**baudrons**
blurring
boursier
△**brussels**
bruising
bountree
bourtree
blurting
boulting
blustery
bluntish
blueweed
bluewing
bevelled
beveller
bivalent
bovinely
beverage
bevatron
bowyangs
bawd-born
bi-weekly
bewigged
bewailed
bewilder
bowelled
bowsprit
bewetted
box-wagon
Bixaceae

box-pleat
box-cloth
boxiness
box-lobby
box-frame
bi-yearly
bayadère
bayberry
bryology
bayonets
boyishly
bizcacha
bozzetti
bozzetto
bezonian
buzzword
chalazae
chalazas
clamancy
clavated
charango
characid
characin
chapatti
chambray
clawback
cramboes
clambake
coalball
crabbily
clay-bank
chapbook
chambers
charcoal
cratches
clay-cold
△**chancery**
coat-card
Chaldean
Claudian
chandler
Chaldaic
cladding
chaldron
chawdron
clapdish
clarence
co-agency
coalesce
clavecin
cranefly
cravenly
czarevna
chamelot
chaperon
chapelry
chapeaux
châteaux
coalface
chauffer
cram-full

chaffing
chaffron
chamfron
claw-foot
chaffery
coalfish
cragfast
crawfish
crayfish
clagging
clanging
clangbox
clangour
coachman
crash-mat
crashpad
clashing
coaching
crashing
coachdog
chamisal
chaliced
chamises
chapiter
Charites
clarinet
claviger
caatinga
coamings
Chasidic
clavicle
charisma
craniums
chamisos
clarinos
czaritsa
Craniata
crackjaw
cracknel
chalkpit
crankily
clanking
cracking
clackbox
crackpot
crackers
charlock
charlady
chaology
chaplain
crablike
chatline
chat-line
cradling
crawling
chapless
clawless
coatless
clammily
charming
claimant

clamming
coalmine
cramming
clay-marl
claymore
charmful
chainman
chainsaw
charneco
chainlet
chaunter
crannied
channels
chauntry
clannish
crab-nuts
charoset
cyanogen
cyanosed
chalonic
cyanosis
cyanotic
chaconne
cramoisy
clapping
clasping
cramping
champion
clay-pipe
champart
champers
clappers
claspers
Coalport
chappess
chairman
coatrack
chair-bed
charring
chayroot
clansman
classman
cragsman
clarsach
classics
chausses
classify
clanship
clap-sill
clausula
coarsely
claustra
classism
classist
coarsish
chasseur
claptrap
chaptrel
chattles
chantage
chastely

chattels
craftily
chatting
coasting
coaction
co-author
clatters
clattery
△**chartism**
△chartist
chastise
chastity
coactive
Chanukah
cyanuret
chasuble
claqueur
coagulum
crab-wood
crabwise
crab-yaws
caboceer
caboched
cabochon
cable-car
cableway
cobwebby
cabretta
cubiform
cuboidal
cabriole
caballed
caballer
cobaltic
cobbling
cobblers
cobblery
cabalism
cabalist
cabin-boy
caboodle
Cabirian
cabernet
ciborium
caboshed
cubistic
cabotage
cab-stand
cibation
cubature
cocoa-fat
cyclamen
Cockayne
cachalot
ciclaton
cockatoo
cocoanut
cockboat
cockbird
Coca-Cola®
cock-crow

Words marked △ may be spelled also with a capital letter

8 c□l□a

cacodoxy
cycleway
cockerel
cockeyed
cachexia
cachepot
cacafogo
Coccidae
cyclical
△**coccidia**
Cocaigne
cochleae
cochlear
cockloft
cacology
cichloid
cucumber
cacomixl
cocknify
cicinnus
△**cyclopes**
cycloses
cecropia
cyclonic
cyclopic
cyclosis
cacholot
coco-palm
cocoplum
cucurbit
cicerone
ciceroni
cicisbei
cicisbeo
cockshot
cocksure
cockshut
cockspur
coco-tree
cicatrix
cocktail
cactuses
cachucha
Cocculus
coco-wood
coccyges
codebook
caducean
caducity
caduceus
caducous
codified
codifier
codpiece
co-driver
cadenced
code-name
ciderkin
cider-and
cedar-nut
cider-cup
cadastre
ci-devant
crepance
chevalet
crenated
clematis
chewable
chelator
cremator
crevasse
chee-chee
△**crescent**
coercion
coercive
crescive
cleidoic
creodont
cheddite
clemency
credence
credenda
cheverel
cheveril
creperie
cleverly
crenelle
Cheyenne
cheveron
cleveite
crevette
cheverye
credenza
Cheshvan
chechako
Cheshire
chemical
clerical
cheliped
clerihew
caecitis
chenille
cheville
credible
credibly
creditor
caesious
crepitus
check-key
check-off
cheekily
creakily
clecking
clerkdom
checkers
Cherkess
clerkess
clerkish
checkout
check-out
Chellean
creolian
creolist
creamery
cream-bun
cream-nut
cleanser
cleaning
cleaners
clean-cut
Cherokee
Chelonia
coelomic
coenobia
cremosin
cremorne
cretonne
chenopod
creeping
clearway
clearage
cheerily
chevrony
clearing
cheerios
cheerful
clear-cut
clear-out
chessman
creasote
creosote
creutzer
creatrix
cheating
coextend
creatine
△**creation**
C-section
cheaters
cheatery
creature
chestful
chestnut
creative
caesurae
caesural
caesuras
chemurgy
cleruchy
cherubic
cherubim
cherubin
chequers
coenurus
cleavage
cleaving
cleavers
cheewink
cresylic
coenzyme
cofactor
coffered
caffeine
caffeism
cagebird
cogwheel
cageling
cogently
caginess
cagyness
cognosce
cognomen
cognovit
cogitate
cagework
cohobate
coherent
cohesion
cohesive
caimacam
chicanas
Chinaman
climatal
chicaner
chivaree
clinamen
crinated
climatic
Cnidaria
chicanos
chinampa
△**chimaera**
chiragra
chivalry
cribbled
cribbage
climbing
cribbing
chitchat
coincide
clincher
chin-chin
clip-clop
chiccory
childbed
children
childing
childish
chimeric
cricetid
criteria
clitella
cribella
Cricetus
crimeful
chiffons
chiefdom
chiefery
coiffure
chiefess
chiefest
coiffeur
cringing
clithral
clichéed
coinhere
clinical
criminal
critical
cuitikin
chiliasm
chiliast
clinique
critique
chickpea
chickens
clicking
clinking
chinkara
caillach
chillada
chillies
chillily
chilling
criollos
chinless
chipmuck
chipmunk
cliental
clitoral
clitoris
chilopod
crippled
crispies
chirpily
chipping
chirping
clipping
crispate
chirrupy
cribrose
cribrate
cribrous
chiasmas
chiastic
chip-shop
chiasmus
coistrel
coistril
ceinture
cristate
cliquish
cliquism
crivvens
cribwork
cajolery
cokernut
cakewalk
calcanea
calcanei
cellarer
cellaret
collagen
collared
calcaria

Words marked △ may be spelled also with a capital letter

8 c□l□a

caldaria
calvaria
colza-oil
culpable
culpably
chloasma
Calvados
collator
collapse
celibacy
calibred
colubrid
coloboma
call-bird
calabash
celibate
calicoes
calycled
calycoid
calycule
calycine
culicine
calidity
caladium
cul-de-sac
calvered
colleger
collegia
culverin
calceate
cell-free
Califont®
coliform
call-girl
colchica
calthrop
cultivar
calliper
collider
cultigen
calcific
△**calliope**
colliery
calfless
calf-love
Columban
columnal
columnar
columned
columbic
calamine
calamint
calamari
calamary
calamite
calamity
Columbus
calendar
colonial
calender
colander

Colonies
cylinder
calanthe
calendry
culinary
calmness
coldness
colonise
colonist
call-note
colonize
calzones
collogue
colloque
colloquy
caliphal
Calippic
calypsos
colophon
calipers
calyptra
calipash
celeriac
chlordan
chloride
chlorine
colorant
caltrops
calorist
calcrete
celerity
chlorate
chlorite
cultrate
chlorous
calcspar
coleslaw
colossal
coleseed
calfskin
coliseum
colossus
calisaya
calathea
culottes
calc-tufa
calc-tuff
calf-time
colotomy
calutron
calotype
calathus
calcular
cellular
cultural
coleuses
colluder
△coloured
colourer
cultured
calculus

cold-weld
cold-work
colewort
Calixtin
collyria
cullying
cullyism
commando
combated
compages
campaign
campagna
cembalos
cimbalom
cymbalos
compadre
cum-savvy
comeback
comedian
comeddle
comedown
commence
commerce
compesce
cumbered
cumberer
commerge
campfire
camshoch
cam-wheel
camshaft
camphane
camphene
camphine
camphire
compital
combined
compiler
combings
cymbidia
cambiums
camaïeux
compleat
complect
complice
cameleer
complied
complier
camellia
cameloid
complain
cameline
compline
cameleon
camelish
combless
complish
cumulose
cimolite
complete
cumulate

camomile
cementer
campness
ciminite
cementum
camporee
commoner
commoney
composed
composer
commonly
compound
Comsomol
comforts
Cambrian
comprint
compress
comprise
cumbrous
camisade
camisado
camisole
camp-shot
Camisard
campsite
comether
camstane
camstone
cemetery
cemitare
cometary
comatose
cymatium
communal
campuses
commuter
computer
compulse
combwise
cinnabar
contango
cannabic
cannabin
cannabis
cinnamic
cuneatic
centavos
cinnamon
centaury
concause
cineaste
cinéaste
cunabula
cenobite
cenobium
Canicula
cynicism
cenocyte
Canadian
conidial
conodont

conidium
conveyal
cankered
centeses
conceder
conferee
congener
convener
convexed
conveyer
converge
centesis
congenic
cancelli
convexly
canoeing
convenor
conveyor
cunjevoi
contempt
canoeist
condense
contessa
converse
conceity
concepti
concerti
concerto
concetti
concetto
confetti
contents
conceive
conferva
conserve
coniform
conchoid
cinching
cinchona
canthook
canthari
conchate
candidal
cannibal
conoidal
convince
centinel
confider
confined
confiner
confines
conniver
consider
cannikin
conoidic
canaille
candidly
canfield
canticle
canticos
canticoy

Words marked △ may be spelled also with a capital letter

8 c□r□a

canaigre
centiare
congiary
canticum
continua
continue
continuo
conglobe
conflict
conclude
contline
canalise
conflate
conclave
canalize
cane-mill
cynanche
canoness
canonise
canonist
caninity
canonize
cantonal
canzonas
confocal
cantoned
canzonet
centones
consoler
cantoris
canoodle
consommé
confound
conjoint
contorno
concolor
cannonry
concours
centoist
Congoese
convolve
canopied
cineplex
canephor
conspire
cinereal
conarial
conurban
contract
centrode
canaries
congreet
cancroid
cant-rail
centroid
contrail
contrair
conurbia
contrôlé
centrums
Cinerama®
cancrine
centring
confront
cinerary
confrère
contrary
Canarese
centrism
centrist
△congress
contrast
contrist
concrete
congrats
contrate
contrite
canorous
conarium
controul
Congreve
contrive
canaster
canister
cynosure
cane-toad
canstick
canities
constant
conation
cenotaph
cincture
constate
construe
conative
cannulae
cannular
cannulas
conjugal
consular
conjunct
confused
conjurer
consumer
cinquain
centuple
conjuror
consumpt
△**conquest**
convulse
conducti
consulta
cingulum
cony-wool
condylar
Cenozoic
coolabah
choragic
chorally
clonally
cookable
coolamon
choragus
crotalum
Crotalus
crow-bill
cookbook
crotched
crotchet
choicely
choo-choo
chop-chop
chow-chow
clop-clop
chondral
cloudlet
cloudage
chondrin
cloudily
chording
clodding
clouding
cloddish
Chordata
chordate
△**chondrus**
closeted
clovered
cholemia
cholemic
choleric
choregic
croceate
choregus
clotebur
croceous
cropfull
cropfuls
crowfoot
cloth-cap
clothier
clothing
clochard
chokidar
coolibah
coolibar
chorioid
chorisis
cootikin
choliamb
choriamb
C-horizon
croakily
clocking
croaking
crockery
cromlech
cropland
choultry
cloyless
cookmaid
cloyment
chounter
crownlet
cooingly
clowning
crooning
crowning
clownery
clownish
coolness
cromorna
cromorne
crocoite
croupade
croupier
clodpole
clodpoll
chopping
cropping
choppers
clodpate
croupous
choirman
choirboy
choy-root
cookroom
crossbar
crossway
cloister
crosslet
coonskin
cross-rib
crosstie
cross-ply
crousely
cloysome
coon-song
crossing
crossbow
cross-row
crossish
crosscut
cross-eye
Croatian
clotting
crofting
co-option
co-optive
chorused
crocuses
cookware
cronyism
cephalad
coplanar
cap-paper
Capparis
cephalic
cephalin
copybook
capybara
△**capuchin**
capacity
cupidity
copperas
copy-edit
capoeira
cupreous
copyhold
Capridae
Caprinae
capsizal
capricci
cyprides
caprifig
cyprinid
capriole
Cypriote
capsicum
captious
capellet
cupelled
cupolaed
capeline
cupeling
copulate
cupulate
copemate
caponier
caponise
caponize
coprosma
cupboard
caproate
Copepoda
copyread
caper-tea
capeskin
capitula
capitani
capitano
capstone
capitate
capitayn
capsular
capturer
capework
caprylic
coquetry
coquette
coquilla
coquille
coquitos
carraway
Circaean
carnauba
carcanet
curvated
carbamic
caryatic
caryatid
cercaria
carnally
curbable
curtains

8 c□r□a

carcajou
cardamom
cardamon
cariacou
carjacou
cornacre
curranty
cardamum
carbaryl
cerebral
corn-baby
corn-beef
cerebric
cornball
carabine
corybant
cerebrum
carucage
coracoid
corn-cake
caracole
caracara
corn-cure
corocore
corocoro
card-case
carucate
carceral
cervelat
cornetcy
currency
carpeted
corbeled
cornered
corselet
corseted
cortexes
curveted
cursedly
corsetry
cargeese
cornetti
cornetto
corvette
cardecue
carneous
Cerberus
corneous
cornflag
carefree
coraggio
card-game
coregent
carl-hemp
cornhusk
cardigan
△cardinal
carnival
cervical
corrival
cortical

Corvidae
Corvinae
curvital
carritch
carnifex
cervices
cervixes
circiter
cirriped
cordiner
corniced
cortices
carriage
corniche
cardioid
carditis
cornific
carriole
cornicle
curricle
corridor
cortisol
cursitor
Corfiote
curlicue
corn-kist
Carolean
cartload
cerulean
carolled
caroller
cornloft
cerulein
Cyrillic
Carolina
Caroline
circling
cornland
carillon
careless
cordless
coreless
curbless
cureless
corallum
ceramics
cornmill
cerement
ceremony
chromene
coramine
ceramist
chromate
chromite
cornmoth
chromium
coranach
coronach
carangid
coronoid
Cyrenaic

caruncle
corantos
coronary
curtness
carinate
coronate
coronium
corundum
Caryocar
cordovan
corporal
corporas
cartouch
carbolic
carbonic
Coriolis
cargoose
carbonyl
carboxyl
carapace
coryphee
carap-oil
cornpipe
carap-nut
cartroad
cornrent
curarine
curarise
curarize
chrismal
curbside
cerastes
christen
Chrissie
Christie
Christly
cork-sole
ceresine
christom
curassow
cerusite
corktree
ceratoid
curatrix
caretake
carotene
cerotype
curatory
curative
carousal
circular
carburet
carousel
carouser
cornuted
curculio
curcumin
corduroy
cornutos
circussy
circuity

cernuous
card-vote
cordwain
corkwing
cordwood
corkwood
careworn
cornworm
carryall
carry-all
carrying
carry-ons
currying
carrycot
carry-out
castaway
cascabel
Castanea
castanet
costated
casually
casualty
casebook
cash-book
cosecant
cosherer
cosseted
cosmesis
cosmetic
cisterna
cysteine
cassette
cost-free
caschrom
cosmical
cuspidal
Cushitic
cystitis
cushions
cushiony
cassinos
cast-iron
cuspidor
case-load
ciselure
cashless
ciseleur
casement
cashmere
casimere
costmary
casemate
cosiness
Casanova
custodes
customed
customer
cesspool
cost-plus
Cesarean
castrate

castrati
castrato
case-shot
cislunar
cistuses
costumed
costumer
cistvaen
casework
case-worm
cussword
Cathaian
Cathayan
cottaged
cottager
cottagey
cut-water
citrange
citeable
cattalos
cottabus
Cuthbert
cetacean
catacomb
catechol
catheter
cathexes
cathexis
cutie-pie
cathedra
cathetus
citreous
citified
cityfied
cat's-foot
category
catch-pit
catch-all
catchfly
catching
cutchery
Cottidae
cathisma
cytokine
cetology
cytology
cotyloid
Catiline
coteline
cotillon
catalase
catalyse
catalyst
cutglass
cattleya
catalyze
cat's-meat
catamite
Catonian
catenane
cotenant

Words marked △ may be spelled also with a capital letter

8 d□b□r

catenary
cuteness
cutinise
catenate
cutinize
cathodal
cathodic
△catholic
chthonic
catworks
cathouse
cot-house
catapult
cataract
ceterach
cut-price
catering
cateress
cytosome
cytisine
cytosine
cat-stick
cat's-tail
citation
citatory
cotquean
cothurni
cothurns
cutpurse
cetywall
Cotswold
caudated
crusader
coumaric
coumarin
causally
clubable
crusados
cruzados
chupatti
courante
clubbing
clubbish
clubbism
clubbist
clutches
crutched
churchly
couscous
cauldron
causeway
crumenal
caudexes
causerie
clupeoid
cruzeiro
club-face
club-foot
chugging
club-head
couchant
couching
coughing
crushing
crumhorn
club-haul
caudices
crucifer
crudités
churinga
crucifix
caudicle
caudillo
caulicle
cousinly
coutille
crucible
cousinry
△**coulisse**
cruciate
cautious
chuckies
caulking
chunking
clubland
club-line
coupling
churlish
clueless
crummack
crummock
chummage
churning
churn-owl
crumpled
chumping
clumping
clubroom
clubroot
clubrush
clumsily
coursing
court-day
courtier
courtlet
crustily
courting
countrol
clustery
countess
courtesy
crustate
count-out
chutzpah
cave-bear
cavicorn
civilian
△**cavalier**
cavilled
caviller
covalent
civilise
civilist
civility
civilize
covenant
Coventry
covinous
caverned
coverlet
coverage
coverlid
coverall
covertly
covering
cavesson
cavitied
cavatina
coveting
covetise
cavitate
covetous
cow-leech
cowberry
cowheard
cow-wheat
cow-pilot
cow-plant
cowslip'd
cowhouse
co-worker
cowardly
cowardry
cowgrass
coxalgia
coxiness
coxswain
cly-faker
clypeate
cryogeny
cryolite
cryonics
cayenned
cryostat
coystrel
coystril
cryotron
chyluria
cozenage
diabasic
dramatic
drawable
Dracaena
diapason
diapause
diamanté
dead-beat
drawback
drabbler
Drambuie®
dead-bolt
dead-born
drabbish
dealbate
diarchal
diarchic
diascope
dead-cart
dead-deal
Diandria
draw-down
diazepam
deadener
diabetes
diademed
diameter
diabetic
diapente
drabette
dead-fall
dead-fire
dealfish
draffish
dwarfish
dwarfism
draw-gear
dragging
draughts
draughty
deadhead
dead-head
dead-heat
death-cap
death-ray
drachmae
drachmai
drachmas
death-bed
dead-hand
diaphone
drag-hunt
death-cup
deathful
dealings
drawings
diapiric
draw-leaf
deadlock
dead-lock
dead-lift
diallage
deadline
dearling
dialling
dragline
diaglyph
diablery
dead-meat
drammach
drammock
deaf-mute
drainage
deadness
deafness
dearness
diagnose
drabness
dearnful
diaconal
diagonal
dianodal
dragoman
diamonds
dragonet
diadochi
diabolic
dialogic
diatomic
diatonic
△draconic
dragonné
deaconry
dialogue
dead-pull
△**diaspora**
diaspore
diatribe
diarrhea
dead-rope
diagraph
dragsman
dragster
deanship
draisene
draisine
dead-shot
drag-shot
dram-shop
draft-bar
draw-tube
diastole
diastyle
diastema
diactine
diastase
dianthus
dead-wall
draw-well
dead-wind
dead-wood
dead-work
dialyser
dialyses
dialyzer
dialysis
dialytic
dobber-in
dabchick
dobchick
debelled
dabbling
debility
debonair
Doberman
debarred

Words marked △ may be spelled also with a capital letter

8 d□b□s

debussed
debasing
débutant
dubitate
débouché
deceased
declared
declarer
dichasia
dictator
déclassé
duckbill
dice-coal
dicyclic
dicacity
deciduae
decidual
deciduas
dock-dues
decadent
decedent
△decretal
docketed
decrepit
Duchenne
decrease
duchesse
decagram
decigram
deck-game
dickhead
deck-hand
duck-hawk
declinal
deceiver
deck-load
dockland
duckling
ductless
docility
decolour
dochmiac
December
decemvir
duckmole
document
docimasy
decimate
dochmius
decanter
decently
dicentra
doctoral
dicrotic
doctorly
dice-play
Decapoda
decipher
duck-pond
decurved
dichroic
doctrine
decurion
doctress
decorate
decorous
dockside
dicastic
decision
duck-shot
decisory
decisive
duck-tail
ducatoon
Docetism
Docetist
declutch
decouple
duckweed
dactylar
dactylic
Dactylis
decrying
dockyard
didrachm
didactic
dedicant
dedicate
didactyl
doddered
dodderer
diddicoy
△dedalian
didymium
didymous
Dodonian
didapper
daedalic
drencher
deep-dyed
dieldrin
dreadful
diereses
diegesis
dieresis
dietetic
deepfelt
deer-hair
deerhorn
deer-horn
djellaba
deer-lick
deep-laid
duelling
dwelling
deedless
duellist
dreamily
dreaming
dreamery
deepmost
dreamful
deer-neck
deepness
daemonic
dye-works
dye-house
deer-park
deep-read
drearily
drearing
deemster
dressage
deerskin
dress-tie
duelsome
dressing
die-stock
dyestuff
duetting
duettino
duettist
diestrus
d'oeuvres
△dielytra
defrayal
defiance
deflater
defrayed
defrayer
deflator
defector
defecate
deflexed
defreeze
defilade
defaming
defenced
defended
defender
daftness
deftness
definite
deflower
daffodil
deferral
diffract
deferred
deferrer
deformed
deformer
deferent
deforest
defatted
diffused
diffuser
defluent
dog-watch
degraded
dog-eared
dog-faced
dog-Latin
dogmatic
diggable
dog-daisy
dogsbody
dog's-body
dog-leech
doggerel
doggedly
△dogberry
dog-weary
degrease
dog-cheap
dog-wheat
dog-whelk
dog-tired
daggings
diggings
dogfight
dogsleep
dog's-meat
digamist
digamous
digynian
degender
dog's-nose
digynous
doggoned
do-gooder
dog-house
dog-louse
dogtooth
dog-trick
dog-grass
digester
dogeship
digitise
digitate
digitize
doggy-bag
dahabieh
dihybrid
dihedral
dihydric
dihedron
dehorner
dehorter
drivable
dribbler
dribblet
driveway
drip-feed
deisheal
drisheen
deicidal
deifical
dricksie
drinking
daidling
drilling
daimonic
dripping
drift-way
drift-ice
drift-net
driftage
driftpin
daintily
daiquiri
dairyman
dairying
deifying
dejected
déjeuner
dekalogy
dukeling
Dukhobor
Dukeries
dukeship
dollared
dolmades
dalmatic
dalmahoy
delibate
delubrum
delicacy
△dolichos
delicate
dull-eyed
delegacy
diligent
delegate
Delphian
dollhood
dulcimer
Dulcinea
dulciana
dulcitol
dolomite
dullness
doldrums
doloroso
dolerite
delirium
dolorous
dalesman
dolesome
delusion
delusory
delusive
dule-tree
dilatant
delation
deletion
dilation
dilution
deletory
dilatory
deletive
dilative
diluvial
diluvian
diluvion
delivery

Words marked △ may be spelled also with a capital letter

diluvium
dilly-bag
dallying
delaying
dolly-mop
dolly-tub
damnable
damnably
demeanor
demobbed
dumb-bell
△democrat
Damocles
domicile
dumb-cane
dummerer
demagogy
domainal
damoisel
demijohn
demi-jour
demology
demi-lune
dumpling
demolish
demoniac
demonian
domanial
demander
demanned
demented
domineer
dominoes
dementia
dominant
dominion
dampness
demoness
demonise
demonism
demonist
diminish
dumbness
dominate
demonize
dumfound
damboard
demersal
demurral
demerger
demersed
demurred
demurrer
démarche
demurely
demerara
dimerise
dimerism
dimerous
dimerize
demister

dempster
damaskin
damassin
demyship
domestic
demissly
dumb-show
dumosity
dimetric
demotion
demotist
domatium
dimethyl
demiurge
demi-volt
demi-wolf
dentated
dungaree
dentalia
dentaria
dunnakin
deniable
deniably
Denebola
dingbats
dung-cart
ding-dong
denudate
donnered
dentelle
duncedom
danseuse
dancette
dancetté
dancetty
dung-fork
danegeld
danegelt
dung-heap
dane-hole
dene-hole
dung-hill
dun-diver
denticle
don't-know
Danelagh
dangling
dynamics
dungmere
dynamise
dynamism
dynamist
dynamite
dynamize
dankness
doneness
dandriff
dandruff
dinarchy
dendroid
Dinornis

dendrite
denarius
diner-out
dynastic
dinosaur
donation
dynatron
denature
donatary
donatory
donatism
Donatist
denotate
donative
denounce
do-naught
do-nought
dandy-hen
dinky-die
dandyish
dandyism
denazify
dioramic
doolally
doorbell
Dioscuri
dioecism
door-case
drop-dead
diocesan
duodenal
Diogenic
duodenum
drop-goal
drongoes
droogish
droughty
drophead
dromical
dioritic
drop-kick
drooking
drouking
doorknob
drop-leaf
droplock
drolling
drollery
drollish
drownded
doornail
drowning
duologue
doom-palm
droopily
dropping
doorpost
drop-ripe
doomsday
doomsman
doorsman

doors-man
diopside
doomster
doorstep
dropsied
door-sill
drowsily
doorstop
drop-shot
deontics
dioptric
dioptase
drop-wort
dropwise
Dionysia
door-yard
depraved
△dipsades
Dipsacus
depicter
depictor
dipteral
dipteran
duplexer
diplegia
dapperly
dipteros
diphenyl
dipchick
deprival
depeinct
deprived
dip-slope
depilate
dopamine
dupondii
deponent
dopiness
diplomat
diploidy
diplogen
diplopia
diplozoa
dipnoous
departed
departer
deportee
depurant
depurate
dipstick
deputise
deputize
dormancy
darraign
dermatic
dorsally
darraine
durables
directly
déraciné
director

Doricism
doridoid
dirigent
dirigism
derogate
derailer
dormient
derrière
durukuli
derelict
darkling
darkmans
diriment
dart-moth
daring-do
deranged
daringly
darkness
der-doing
dormouse
dirt-poor
dirt-road
darkroom
dartrous
darksome
derision
derisory
derisive
derating
deration
duration
derivate
dirtying
Darbyite
despatch
dispatch
distance
dastardy
discandy
diseased
disgavel
dispathy
dyspathy
desyatin
dishabit
dishable
dismally
distally
disfavor
distaste
disvalue
disabled
dust-ball
disabuse
dust-bath
dust-bowl
dust-coat
dustcart
dysodile
dysodyle
disadorn

8 d□s□e

disbench
dispeace
dispence
dishevel
dissever
Disneyfy
disherit
dysgenic
dyslexia
dyslexic
dysmelia
dysmelic
dispense
disperse
disseise
dyspepsy
diskette
disleave
disserve
disseize
designer
disagree
dysphagy
dust-hole
disthene
deschool
dyschroa
despisal
discinct
distinct
despiser
disliken
despight
dissight
distichs
dispirit
disciple
deselect
displace
displode
desilver
dosology
disclaim
displume
displant
disallow
disclose
disclost
disflesh
diskless
dustless
desolate
dyspneal
disannex
disinter
dyspnoea
dyspneic
desinent
disendow
disenrol
disunion
disinure
duskness
disunite
disunity
disannul
despotat
disloyal
disposal
disvouch
disbowel
discover
dismoded
disponee
disponer
disposed
disposer
disgorge
dislodge
disloign
disponge
despotic
dystocia
dystonia
dystonic
dystopia
discoing
discount
disjoint
dismount
disbosom
discolor
dishonor
discoure
dishorse
dishouse
dissolve
disapply
disarray
dispread
describe
destruct
disfrock
disgrace
distract
district
disgrade
descried
deserter
deserved
deserver
destrier
disarmer
discreet
disorbed
disorder
distrail
distrain
distrait
disproof
distress
distrust
discrete
desirous
descrive
disprove
discrown
disprize
disaster
disusage
dust-shot
disjunct
dissuade
disputer
disquiet
dispunge
disburse
disguise
dispurse
Dasyurus
disowner
desk-work
dateable
dutiable
détraqué
databank
database
detached
detector
dithecal
ditherer
dotterel
ditheism
ditheist
duty-free
Dutchman
Dutchmen
ditch-dog
detrital
detailed
detainee
detainer
detritus
ditokous
dataller
date-line
dateless
datolite
dotingly
detonate
dittoing
duty-paid
date-palm
Datapost®
date-plum
deterred
daturine
dethrone
dytiscid
Dytiscus
date-tree
dotation
detoxify
ditty-bag
ditty-box
drumbeat
drubbing
deuddarn
△druidess
druidism
deuce-ace
douzeper
drupelet
diuresis
diuretic
deucedly
deuteron
drumfire
drumfish
drugging
drudgery
drudgism
druggist
drumhead
daughter
dauphine
dough-boy
druthers
doughnut
drunkard
doubling
doubloon
drummock
drumming
douanier
dourness
doum-palm
doubting
doubtful
duumviri
duumvirs
deviance
deviancy
deviator
dive-bomb
dove-cote
dividual
dividant
dividend
dividing
dividers
dividivi
dove-eyed
divagate
devilled
devilkin
dovelike
Davy-lamp
deviling
divalent
devildom
develope
deviltry
deviless
devilish
devilism
Devonian
divan-bed
divinify
divinely
divinise
divinity
divinize
divorcee
divorcée
divorcer
diversly
division
divisive
dovetail
duvetine
duvetyne
devotion
devourer
devoutly
divvying
downbeat
down-come
downcast
dewy-eyed
dew-berry
downfall
downflow
downhill
downhole
down-home
down-haul
download
dowel-pin
downland
down-line
dowel-rod
downmost
dewiness
dowfness
Dow-Jones
dewpoint
downplay
downpipe
downpour
downrush
downside
downsize
downtime
down-trod
downturn
down-town
downwind
downward
dowdyish
dowdyism
duxelles
doxology
dextrine
dextrose

Words marked △ may be spelled also with a capital letter

dextrous
daytaler
day-level
day-shift
daylight
day-sight
dry-bible
dry-clean
dry-plate
day-to-day
day-woman
dey-woman
dry-goods
dry-point
drymouth
daybreak
daydream
dayes-man
dry-stane
dry-stone
dry-stove
dry-nurse
dazzling
doziness
dizzying
erasable
evadable
exarchal
enarched
ecaudate
evanesce
elaterin
elatedly
evangely
elaphine
examinee
examiner
evasible
étatisme
emaciate
eradiate
étatiste
edacious
enallage
enabling
enaunter
epagogic
epanodos
examplar
etaerios
Erastian
exanthem
enacting
exacting
enaction
exaction
enacture
elastase
enactive
evacuant
evacuate

evaluate
embraced
embracer
embraces
emblazon
embrasor
embodied
embalmer
embolden
embolism
embanker
embarked
embarred
emborder
embossed
embosser
embussed
embusqué
embitter
embattle
embryoid
embryons
embezzle
enchased
encharge
exchange
eucharis
encradle
eschalot
excubant
encyclic
eucyclic
eschewal
excretal
eschewer
excreter
ecclesia
encaenia
encierro
encrease
encrinal
eccrisis
eccritic
enclisis
enclitic
encrinic
eucritic
enceinte
escalade
escalado
escalier
excelled
esculent
escallop
escalope
eucalypt
encolure
escalate
encolour
encumber
encomion

encomium
encroach
encloser
enclothe
enchoric
escapade
escapado
encipher
exceptor
escapism
escapist
encircle
escarole
escargot
eucaryon
eucaryot
excerpta
encarpus
excursus
encysted
excuse-me
excision
excusive
excitant
exciting
etcetera
excluded
excludee
excluder
excavate
endeared
end-paper
endeavor
endocarp
endodyne
endoderm
Erdgeist
endogamy
endogeny
eldritch
endeixis
endemial
endamage
eudemony
endemism
endanger
Eldorado
endorsed
endorsee
endorser
endermic
enduring
elder-gun
endosarc
endozoic
endozoon
elegance
elegancy
emeraude
elevated
eye-water

elevator
eye-salve
elenctic
exercise
elenchus
emendals
emendate
even-down
ebenezer
eye-level
exegesis
exegetic
elements
eleventh
evenfall
exergual
emergent
emerging
energise
energize
eyeshade
erewhile
eye-rhyme
elephant
erethism
emetical
eremital
eye-piece
eyeliner
evenings
eyesight
eremitic
elegiast
ébéniste
emeritus
eye-black
eyeglass
evermore
eternise
evenness
eternity
eternize
eye-tooth
exemplar
exemplum
execrate
eyebrows
evensong
emersion
eversion
eventual
eventide
electret
electric
erectile
eyestalk
eventing
egestion
ejection
election
electron

electros
erection
evection
exertion
Edentata
edentate
electrum
eventful
egestive
ejective
elective
erective
exertive
exequial
executer
exequies
executor
executry
enervate
emery-bag
everyday
△everyman
everyway
everyone
effraide
efficacy
effecter
effector
effierce
enfierce
enfeeble
enfreeze
effigies
elf-child
elf-shoot
enfilade
effulged
enflower
enfrosen
elflocks
enforcer
efferent
elf-arrow
enforest
enfested
effusion
effusive
enfetter
effetely
effluvia
effluent
egg-dance
engraved
engraven
engraver
engramma
edgebone
Eugubine
eagle-ray
eagle-owl
ergogram

8 e□g□g

engaging
eggshell
egg-whisk
egg-timer
engrieve
egg-slice
egg-plant
edgeless
egg-glass
eugenics
engender
engineer
enginery
edginess
eugenism
eugenist
egg-bound
egg-tooth
engroove
egg-apple
egg-spoon
engorged
egg-fruit
engirdle
eight-day
eight-oar
eighteen
eighties
ergatoid
eighthly
eightvos
ergotise
ergotism
ergative
ergotize
engouled
egg-purse
edgewise
edgeways
ethnarch
enhearse
ethicise
ethicism
ethicist
ethicize
exhedrae
enhydros
echogram
ethnical
ethology
ethylene
exhalant
echoless
ethylate
ephemera
exhumate
enhancer
enhunger
echinoid
Echinops
echinate

Ethiopic
Eohippus
ethercap
ethereal
etherial
exhorter
etherify
etherion
etherise
etherism
etherist
etherize
Ephesian
epigaeal
epigaean
exitance
epitases
epigamic
epitasis
epically
evitable
epilator
epinasty
epicalyx
episcope
episcopy
evincive
evil-doer
eminence
eminency
evidence
exigence
exigency
epicedes
evil-eyed
epicedia
epidemic
epimeric
exigeant
episemon
erigeron
epilepsy
epigeous
epithema
epithems
Epiphany
epiphyte
eligible
eligibly
exigible
elicitor
eximious
Ewigkeit
etiology
epiploic
epiploon
epiblast
etiolate
ebionise
ebionism
evilness

Ebionite
erionite
ebionize
epifocal
episodal
epigones
epidotic
epilogic
epinosic
epipolic
episodic
epitomic
epitonic
epilogue
epicotyl
episperm
epispore
emigrant
epigraph
editress
emigrate
epitrite
emissile
emission
emissary
emissive
ekistics
epistler
epistyle
emitting
existent
emiction
eviction
emictory
epidural
exiguity
exiguous
epicycle
edifying
enjoiner
enkindle
elkhound
enkernel
eukaryon
eukaryot
ex-libris
eulachan
eclectic
eulachon
éolienne
eulogies
eulogise
eulogist
eclogite
eklogite
eulogium
eulogize
enlumine
eclampsy
eel-spear
ellipses

ecliptic
ellipsis
elliptic
eolipile
eelwrack
enlarged
enlargen
enlarger
eelgrass
eclosion
eolithic
eglatere
Emmental
Emmanuel
emmarble
eumerism
enmossed
enneadic
enneagon
ennuying
eco-label
egomania
exogamic
evocable
exorable
evocator
exorcise
exorcism
exorcist
exorcize
exordial
exordium
erogenic
erotesis
erotetic
esoteric
exoteric
eloigner
emongest
elongate
esophagi
exophagy
erotical
erodible
exoplasm
exosmose
enormity
enormous
ecologic
economic
ecotoxic
epopoeia
exotoxic
exotoxin
exospore
ecofreak
étourdie
exoergic
exocrine
egoistic
ecostate

eloquent
evolvent
eponymic
euonymin
euonymus
emphases
emphasis
emphatic
expiable
expiator
especial
empacket
expected
expecter
expedite
empierce
empleach
ekpweles
empyemic
empyesis
espiègle
empressé
espresso
expresso
explicit
empoison
empolder
espalier
expelled
expellee
espumoso
expander
expender
expenses
expunger
exponent
expandor
employed
employee
employer
exploded
exploder
△explorer
emplonge
euphobia
euphonia
euphonic
euphoria
euphoric
empeople
eupepsia
eupeptic
empyreal
empyrean
exporter
empurple
expertly
expirant
expiring
espartos
emperise

Words marked △ may be spelled also with a capital letter

emperish
euphrasy
emporium
emperize
exposure
empathic
eupatrid
empatron
espousal
espouser
euphuise
△euphuism
euphuist
euphuize
emptysis
emptying
Esquimau
enquirer
esquisse
ebriated
Eurobond
Eurocrat
enridged
earth-bag
earthman
earthwax
earth-fed
earth-pea
ear-shell
earphone
earth-hog
earth-nut
earpiece
earnings
earwiggy
earliest
enrolled
enroller
Euromart
étranger
étrennes
errantly
erringly
errantry
eeriness
European
europium
Etrurian
eardrops
errorist
Etruscan
Eurasian
Euroseat
écraseur
△**eurythmy**
earmuffs
enraunge
enravish
enslaved
enslaver
enswathe
ecstasis
ecstatic
eustatic
Eusebian
easy-care
easterly
ensheath
ensiform
ensigncy
easy-goer
ensphere
essoiner
enshield
ensilage
eastland
eastling
eastlins
easeless
ensample
ensemble
easement
eastmost
epsomite
Essencia
easiness
Essenism
essonite
ensconce
exserted
enshrine
enshroud
eastward
elsewise
essaying
essayish
essayist
entrance
estrange
entrails
extrados
enthalpy
entr'acte
eatables
estacade
eutectic
enticing
ectoderm
entoderm
entrench
entremes
esteemed
extremer
extremes
enthetic
esthesia
esthetic
Eutheria
entrepot
entrepôt
entresol
entreaty
ectogeny
entailer
estridge
extolled
extoller
entellus
estimate
Estonian
entender
extended
extender
estancia
entangle
extensor
estrogen
eutrophy
ectropic
eutropic
eftsoons
extrorse
estopped
estoppel
entoptic
ettercap
external
externat
esterify
enthrall
entirely
entering
enthrone
exterior
enterate
entirety
ectosarc
extruder
estivate
eutaxite
entryism
entryist
ectozoan
entozoal
ectozoic
entozoic
ectozoon
entozoon
educated
educable
educator
emulator
ecumenic
enuresis
enuretic
emulgent
evulgate
educible
eludible
esurient
exuviate
equalled
equalise
equality
equalize
eburnean
equinity
epulotic
equipped
equipage
erumpent
emulsify
emulsoid
emulsion
evulsion
emulsive
equities
equitant
exultant
eduction
equation
eruption
eructate
eruptive
equivoke
enviable
enviably
enveigle
envelope
elvanite
environs
envassal
envisage
envision
enwallow
euxenite
eryngoes
eryngium
erythema
etypical
Erysimum
epyllion
Epyornis
Egyptian
Enzedder
enzootic
Fragaria
flambeau
flatboat
flatback
flambéed
flabbily
flax-bush
fiascoes
flanched
flax-comb
francium
fraudful
frame-saw
flamenco
flamelet
flânerie
flagella
feateous
flare-out
flat-foot
foalfoot
flatfish
flagging
fragging
△**flathead**
flashily
flashing
feathery
flashgun
flamingo
feasible
feasibly
flatiron
Fraxinus
flapjack
frabjous
frank-fee
franklin
fracking
Frankish
frailtee
△**fräulein**
flax-lily
flatling
flatlong
fearless
flawless
foamless
frailish
flammule
flax-mill
fragment
flatmate
flaunter
flannels
flatness
frampler
flagpole
frampold
flapping
frappant
frapping
flagrant
fragrant
flax-seed
flagship
fearsome
feast-day
frautage
feasting
flatting
feast-won
fraction
flattery
fracture
flattish
flautist
feastful
features

Words marked △ may be spelled also with a capital letter

flatuses
featuous
flatuous
flag-worm
flatware
flatworm
flatwise
flatways
fob-watch
feblesse
febrific
fibrilla
fabliaux
fabulise
fabulist
fabulous
fabulize
fibromas
fibrosis
fibrotic
faburden
February
face-ache
facially
face-card
fucoidal
factious
face-lift
facilely
feculent
faceless
feckless
focalise
facility
focalize
face-mask
factotum
focussed
focusing
fuchsine
fuchsite
facetiae
fade-away
fiducial
fade-down
fidgeted
fodderer
fiddious
fedelini
fiddling
fuddling
fadeless
fidelity
federacy
federary
federate
fedayeen
foedarie
fredaine
feedback
flea-bane
freeborn
freebase
flea-bite
frescade
fletcher
frescoed
frescoer
frescoes
fiercely
fuel-cell
free-cost
free-city
freedman
Freudian
field-dew
freedmen
fielding
fiendish
frenetic
free-fall
Freefone®
feelgood
feel-good
feed-head
freshman
fresh-new
flesh-fly
freehold
freehand
freshish
fresh-run
feelings
flexible
flexibly
fremitus
freckled
freakish
freakful
freak-out
freeload
feed-line
fuelling
feeblish
feetless
freeness
feed-pump
feed-pipe
free-port
Freepost®
fee-grief
free-reed
fleering
free-soil
fleasome
free-shot
Flextime®
fleeting
fretting
flection
flexural
frequent
flexuose
flexuous
frenulum
free-will
fleawort
fretwork
frenzied
freezing
freeze-up
fiftieth
fiftyish
Fagaceae
fugacity
fugleman
fughetta
figuline
fog-smoke
fogbound
figurant
figurine
figurist
figurate
fagoting
fighting
fugitive
fogeydom
fogeyish
fogeyism
fahlband
fricadel
Frimaire
fribbler
flincher
fail-dike
flinders
fainéant
frisette
flim-flam
flip-flap
flip-flop
flinging
frigging
flichter
flighted
frighten
△faithful
fainites
frigidly
friskily
frisking
friskful
fair-lead
frillies
frilling
friended
friendly
feigning
fainness
fairness
frijoles
flippant
flipping
frippery
Friesian
flip-side
fail-safe
flimsily
Friesish
flintify
flintily
fainting
flirting
flitting
fritting
friction
flittern
flitters
faintish
flirtish
flix-weed
fairydom
fairyism
fakement
fakirism
foldaway
falcated
foliaged
foliated
full-aged
fellahin
fellatio
fellable
filially
filmable
foldable
faltboat
foldboat
fall-back
fullback
full-bore
full-cock
filicide
felicity
falderal
fulgency
filleted
full-eyed
folderol
faldetta
falsetto
full-face
folk-free
filiform
file-fish
feldgrau
filagree
filigree
filmgoer
filthily
filching
falchion
fillibeg
filliped
fillings
felsitic
fulminic
fallible
fallibly
follicle
filmland
folkland
folklore
filament
folkmoot
filander
filename
fellness
fullness
felinity
felonous
falconer
falconet
follower
fellowly
folioing
follow-on
falconry
filioque
follow-up
full-page
full-pelt
Filipina
Filipino
filarial
fulcrums
filtrate
fulcrate
feldspar
feldsher
full-sail
folk-song
fall-trap
folk-tale
full-tilt
full-time
felstone
folk-tune
filatory
filature
fulgural
fumadoes
fumigant
fumigate
familial
familiar
fameless
△familism
Familist
femality
fomenter
feminine
feminise
feminism

Words marked △ may be spelled also with a capital letter

feminist
feminity
feminize
femerall
fumarole
fumerole
fumosity
femetary
fumatory
fumitory
famously
fontanel
fandango
fontange
fantasia
fundable
fanfaron
funebral
finochio
fine-draw
fingered
finnesko
fen-berry
Fanagalo
fin-whale
funkhole
fannings
findings
fanlight
fencible
fanciful
fantigue
fondling
fangless
finalise
finalism
finalist
fineless
fundless
finality
finalize
finances
fineness
fondness
fantoosh
funereal
Fanariot
funerary
finesser
finished
finisher
fenestra
fine-spun
finitude
finitely
fine-tune
function
funguses
Funtumia
fancying
frowards

florally
football
fool-born
foot-bath
floccule
flocculi
floscule
food-card
floccose
floodway
frondage
floodlit
flooding
frondent
frondose
frondeur
△**florence**
flowered
flowerer
floweret
fromenty
footfall
frou-frou
food-fish
frog-fish
footgear
flogging
frogging
froggery
foothill
foothold
froth-fly
frothily
frothery
florigen
floridly
flotilla
flock-bed
frocking
footling
foozling
frogling
foodless
footless
footmuff
footmark
flounder
frowning
footnote
footpace
footpage
floppily
foot-pump
footpost
footpath
foot-race
footrule
flooring
foot-rope
flourish
footrest

foolscap
footstep
frowster
frog-spit
flossing
footslog
footsore
frontman
frontier
frontlet
floatage
frontage
frottage
frostily
floatant
floating
front-end
frosting
frontoon
front-row
frotteur
footwear
footwell
footwork
footworn
fippence
fermatas
forwards
forrader
forsaken
furcated
formalin
fern-ally
fordable
forfault
forhaile
formable
formally
firearms
forfairn
forwaste
firebrat
forebear
fire-back
forebode
fore-body
fireball
fire-bomb
furibund
fernbird
fire-bird
fire-bote
forebitt
fire-clay
forecast
feracity
ferocity
furacity
foredeck
firedamp
foredoom

faradise
faradism
foredate
faradize
forgeman
fervency
ferreted
ferreter
fire-eyed
force-fed
fire-edge
fore-edge
forcedly
forkedly
formerly
farnesol
furbelow
forweary
farceuse
fornenst
forfeits
furmenty
ferreous
forceful
fire-flag
forefeel
forefeet
forefelt
forkfuls
forefoot
foregoer
foregone
forehead
forkhead
farm-hand
farthing
forehand
forehent
forthink
fire-hook
farthest
furthest
farcical
fornical
forcipes
forgiven
ferriage
ferritic
ferritin
fervidly
forcible
forcibly
Fervidor
farriery
furriery
formiate
fortieth
foreking
foreknow
firelock
forelock

forslack
forelift
fork-lift
forelimb
far-flung
foreland
forelend
forelent
fireless
firmless
formless
foremean
fireman's
foramina
firemark
foremast
foremost
Faringee
forinsec
Feringhi
forensic
furuncle
forename
forenoon
farinose
firmness
fire-opal
furlough
forhooie
forborne
fordoing
forgoing
furiosos
far-forth
forsooth
forepeak
foreplan
foreplay
forspeak
far-spent
forspend
forspent
fire-plow
forepart
forepast
fire-plug
foreread
Furcraea
fore-rank
fire-risk
fortress
fernshaw
forestal
forestay
fireside
foreside
fern-seed
fire-step
foreseen
foreshew
forested

Words marked △ may be spelled also with a capital letter

8 f□r□s

△forester
fireship
foresaid
foresail
foreship
foreskin
foreshow
foreslow
forestry
fire-trap
first-day
fire-tube
first-aid
forktail
foretell
foretold
foretime
feretory
farm-toun
formulae
formular
formulas
furcular
furfural
furfuran
fortuned
forjudge
farouche
furfurol
fortuity
forswear
fireweed
farewell
fire-walk
forewent
forewind
forewing
forswink
forswunk
firewood
firework
fireworm
firmware
foreward
forewarn
foreword
formwork
forswore
forsworn
forswatt
ferryman
ferrying
farmyard
fortyish
farcy-bud
festally
fiscally
fishable
fastback
fastball
fishball
fuss-ball
fish-bone
fish-dive
fastener
fosterer
fossette
fish-farm
fusiform
fish-guts
fish-glue
Fasching
fish-hook
fish-hawk
festival
fistical
fissiped
fascicle
fasciola
fasciole
△**fascismo**
fashions
fistiana
fasciate
△fascista
Fascisti
Fascists
fashious
fusileer
fusilier
fuselage
fusel-oil
fish-meal
fistmele
fastness
fisnomie
fish-pond
fusarole
fostress
fish-stew
fishskin
fish-tail
fast-talk
fistulae
fistular
fistulas
fissured
fastuous
fishwife
fish-weir
fess-wise
fat-faced
feticide
Fête-Dieu
fattener
fatherly
fatigued
fatigues
fatigate
fetching
fittings
fitliest
futilely
fettling
fatalism
fatalist
fatality
futility
fattrels
futurism
futurist
futurity
fatstock
fitfully
feudally
Foucault
frugally
fougasse
four-ball
flubbing
faulchin
flue-cure
fluidics
fluidify
founding
fluidise
fluidity
fluidize
four-eyes
fauteuil
fauvette
frumenty
fourfold
four-foot
foul-fish
foughten
flushing
fauchion
flush-box
frutices
fluxions
four-leaf
fluellin
flummery
foulmart
faux-naïf
fluently
foulness
faubourg
four-pack
four-part
frumpish
fluoride
flurried
fluorine
fluorite
foursome
△**faustian**
fruit-bat
fourteen
fruitlet
fructify
fruitage
fountain
faultily
fourthly
fruit-fly
frustule
frustums
fructans
fruiting
fruition
flustery
fruitery
fructose
faultful
fountful
fruit-bud
fruitful
fructive
fruitive
fluework
fivefold
five-line
Favonian
fivepins
feverfew
feverish
favorite
feverous
favoured
favourer
fowl-pest
fewtrils
fox-earth
foxberry
foxshark
foxglove
foxiness
foxhound
fox-grape
fox-brush
fixation
fixature
fixative
flymaker
flypaper
fly-sheet
flywheel
flypitch
fayalite
fly-blown
fly-under
fly-tower
fly-spray
fly-speck
fly-drive
fly-tying
fuzz-ball
foziness
Ghanaian
gravamen
gradatim
guaranis
gradable
gram-atom
guanacos
guaranty
△**guaiacum**
gramarye
grabbler
goalball
grabbing
giambeux
glaucoma
glancing
gear-case
Graecise
Graecism
glaucous
Graecize
granddad
guardian
guardage
glandule
gladding
guardant
grandson
glanders
grandeur
grave-wax
gramercy
glabella
gravelly
glacéing
glareous
graceful
grateful
Graafian
goatfish
graffiti
graffito
graphics
grapheme
glad-hand
gnashers
goatherd
guacharo
gnathite
graphite
graphium
gravitas
glacises
gratinée
granitic
gladiole
gladioli
gradient
graviton
gracioso
grazioso
glaciate
gladiate
gracious
gralloch

Words marked △ may be spelled also with a capital letter

8 g□n□r

gnatling
goatling
grayling
gearless
goalless
goat-moth
grainage
graining
gladness
glasnost
gramoche
go-around
gealousy
grasping
goalpost
glam-rock
glabrate
glabrous
glassman
goadsman
goadster
glassify
goatskin
grass-oil
glassily
gladsome
glassine
grassing
Glassite
glassful
goat's-rue
grattoir
graithly
grafting
giantess
giantism
ghastful
granular
graduand
graduate
gratuity
goatweed
Gobiidae
gabeller
gabbling
Gobelins
gibingly
gabioned
gabbroic
gabbroid
gibbsite
Geckones
godwards
gadabout
gude-dame
Gadhelic
gadgetry
gado-gado
godchild
God-given
god-smith
gadzooks
△godspeed
Gadarene
gudesire
gudewife
god-awful
Gnetales
gregatim
grey-coat
greedily
grey-eyed
greffier
grey-fish
greegree
goethite
guerilla
guéridon
△greeking
Greekdom
Greekish
gleaming
green-bag
greenies
greenlet
△guernsey
greenfly
gleaning
greening
greenery
greenish
greyness
greasies
gneissic
greasily
gleesome
greesing
gressing
guessing
ghettoes
greeting
gift-book
giftedly
gefuffle
giff-gaff
go-faster
giftshop
gift-wrap
gig-lamps
gaggling
giggling
goggling
gigantic
gag-tooth
go-getter
gigawatt
guidance
gainable
guidable
glibbery
guimbard
gliadine
grinding
gliddery
grindery
Griselda
Goidelic
gridelin
grisette
griseous
guileful
gliffing
griefful
gairfowl
grisgris
gris-gris
goings-on
gainings
gridiron
gridlock
grillade
grillage
grilling
gaillard
gainless
glimmery
gliomata
grinning
glibness
grimness
Guicowar
grimoire
gripping
goitrous
gripsack
glissade
gainsaid
gainsays
guiltily
griptape
glittery
grittest
grievous
glitzier
grizzled
grizzler
glitzily
Gujarati
Gujerati
goliardy
galeated
gallabea
gallabia
galvanic
gullable
gillaroo
galbanum
galabeah
galabiah
galabieh
galabiya
Galician
galactic
gelidity
gold-ends
galleted
galleria
goldenly
galleass
goldfish
gilt-head
Gallican
gallivat
gullible
golfiana
gallipot
golliwog
galliard
galliass
Galilean
gall-less
goldless
galangal
galenoid
Galenism
Galenist
galenite
Galloway
Golconda
galloper
Golgotha
galtonia
galapago
gelastic
gulosity
goldsize
gilt-tail
gelatine
gelation
galluses
gallumph
galowses
gulfweed
gull-wing
giltwood
gold-wasp
gillyvor
gollywog
gammadia
gymnasia
gymnasic
gambados
gemma-cup
gamecock
gambeson
gambetta
gemmeous
gymkhana
gumphion
gemshorn
gimmicky
gemology
gambling
Geminian
gameness
gaminess
gamyness
geminate
geminous
gammoner
gambogic
gummosis
gimcrack
gambroon
gamester
gamesome
gematria
gemstone
gumption
gunlayer
gunmaker
genially
gendarme
gonfalon
gonfanon
gang-bang
genocide
gonocyte
gynecium
gonadial
gonidial
gonidium
gondelay
gunmetal
gingelly
gingerly
gannetry
ginkgoes
Gandhian
Gandhism
Gandhist
gingival
Ganoidei
gunfight
gentilic
gingkoes
gangliar
ginglymi
gangland
gangling
gantline
gunflint
ganglion
gantlope
Ganymede
gunsmith
gynandry
goneness
gunpoint
ginhouse
gunhouse
gentrice
gentrify
generale
gangrene

8 g□n□r

generant
gang-rape
generate
generous
gangsman
Genesiac
gangster
ganister
gongster
genetics
gunstick
gunstock
genetrix
genitrix
genitals
gunstone
genotype
geniture
genitive
geniuses
Genevese
Genovese
Gondwana
gynny-hen
geomancy
globated
geotaxis
globally
growable
geocarpy
geolatry
grosbeak
goofball
gaol-bird
groschen
good-dame
goose-cap
geometer
groveled
groveler
goose-egg
geodesic
geodetic
goosegob
goosegog
geometry
Georgian
Georgics
groo-groo
groggery
geophagy
geophone
geophyte
△**gloxinia**
gloriole
gloriosa
grodiest
glorious
good-lack
goodlier
glowlamp
growling
growlery
ghoulish
gloomily
gloaming
glomming
glooming
gloomful
grounded
grounden
grounder
groaning
groining
geognost
geognosy
goodness
groanful
geologer
geogonic
geologic
geoponic
gnomonic
grouplet
groupage
grouping
groupers
groupist
glossily
glosseme
glossina
grog-shop
glossary
goodsire
grossart
gross-out
grottoes
goodtime
ghosting
grouting
globular
globulet
globulin
goodwife
goodwill
gromwell
glow-worm
goodyear
glory-pea
geomyoid
glorying
gypseous
gapingly
gapeseed
gapeworm
gypsydom
gypsyism
garlands
garganey
Germanic
germaine
garbanzo
gyrodyne
gardener
garreted
△**gardenia**
gorgerin
gor-belly
gorgeous
giraffid
garefowl
garaging
garagist
Gurkhali
girlhood
△**germinal**
gyroidal
garcinia
garlicky
gerbille
garrison
garrigue
gorblimy
garbling
girtline
gormless
gyrolite
Garamond
gerontic
Girondin
Geronimo
geraniol
goriness
geranium
Gorgonia
gargoyle
gurgoyle
garboard
garrotte
geropiga
gyrostat
guruship
garishly
girasole
garotted
garotter
gyration
gyratory
Gurmukhi
gurdwara
gardyloo
gas-water
gossamer
gustable
gestapos
△**gesneria**
gasifier
gastfull
gasiform
gasogene
Gasthaus
gas-fired
gossiped
gaslight
gas-tight
gasfield
gossipry
gas-globe
gust-lock
gasalier
gaselier
gasolier
gasolene
gasoline
gas-plant
gastness
gospodar
gas-works
gas-motor
gastraea
gastrula
gestural
gossypol
guttated
gettable
gatherer
gatefold
gate-fine
guttiest
gateless
gatepost
guttural
gate-vein
glutaeal
glutamic
glucagon
glutaeus
grumbler
grubbing
glutelin
glumella
goujeers
gruffish
glugging
grudging
glucinum
grueling
Gaullism
Gaullist
gaumless
gourmand
glumness
grumness
glucosic
grumphie
grumpily
glumpish
△**gaussian**
gruesome
gauntlet
gauntree
gruntled
glutting
gluttony
grunting
goutweed
△**glühwein**
goutwort
gaudy-day
giveaway
give-away
gavelman
gavelock
governor
gownsman
glyceria
glyceric
glycerin
glycerol
glyceryl
glycogen
glycolic
glyconic
glycosyl
glyptics
gazpacho
gazeboes
gazogene
gazement
gazunder
gazetted
headache
headachy
healable
huanacos
headband
head-boom
head-butt
headcase
hoarding
heavenly
headfast
headgear
hoarhead
heath-hen
headhunt
heathens
heathery
heaviest
hyacinth
headlock
headlamp
headland
headline
headlong
headless
headmark
headmost
headnote
headrace
headrail
headring
headroom
headrope
headrest

Words marked △ may be spelled also with a capital letter

headsman
headship
hoarsely
healsome
headshot
heatspot
hoastman
hearties
heartlet
heartpea
hoactzin
heartily
heart-rot
head-tire
hiatuses
huaquero
headword
headwork
Hyblaean
hobdayed
Hebraise
Hebraism
Hebraist
Hebraize
hibachis
hobbitry
hobbling
habanera
hebdomad
hobnobby
hibernal
hub-brake
△hibiscus
habitual
habitude
hebetude
habitans
habitant
hebetant
hebetate
hubbuboo
hobbyism
hobbyist
hiccatee
hackbolt
hock-cart
Hock-days
hacienda
hackette
hectical
heckling
hectorer
hiccough
hectorly
hocussed
huckster
hocusing
Hock-tide
hecatomb
hiccuped
hickwall
hack-work
hide-away
hydranth
hedgepig
hydremia
hiddenly
hedgehog
hedge-hop
hedgerow
hidy-hole
hidlings
Hodgkin's
hidalgas
hidalgos
hedonics
hedonism
hedonist
hydrogen
hydromel
hadronic
hidrosis
hidrotic
hydropic
hydroski
△hydrozoa
hydropsy
Hydromys
hydroxyl
hydatoid
had-I-wist
hielaman
hierarch
haematic
haematin
hieratic
heel-ball
haeremai
heedless
hierurgy
Haggadah
Hogmanay
hag-taper
hog-maned
Haggadic
huggable
hog's-back
high-bred
highball
highbrow
high-born
hog-score
hoggerel
hygienic
Huguenot
hagberry
higher-up
hog-reeve
high-five
high-gear
hogshead
highjack
Hegelian
higgling
△highland
high-lone
hegemony
highmost
△highness
hugeness
highroad
hog-frame
high-rise
high-risk
high-tech
hightail
high-test
hair-ball
hairbell
hair-band
hairgrip
heighten
heich-how
hairlike
hairline
heirloom
hairless
heirless
huissier
heirship
hailshot
hoistman
hoistway
hair-tail
hoisting
hair-work
hair-worm
hair-wave
hijacker
hoky-poky
heliacal
Hollands
Helladic
helpable
hallaloo
holla-hoa
half-beak
holdback
half-bred
hell-bred
half-ball
hell-bent
half-boot
hell-born
half-butt
hylobate
half-blue
Halachah
half-cock
Halachic
helicoid
half-calf
Holocene
halicore
hylicism
hylicist
half-dead
helideck
holydame
half-done
half-door
hall-door
hull-down
holidays
halteres
halve-net
helmeted
Hellenic
Helvetic
half-face
hillfolk
hellfire
hell-fire
hill-fort
holdfast
hologram
hell-gate
hell-hole
hula-hula
hula-hoop
half-hose
half-hour
hellicat
hollidam
holdings
halliard
helminth
hell-kite
half-loaf
halalled
half-life
halfling
halflins
helpline
helmless
helpless
helpmeet
half-moon
hall-moot
hallmark
half-mast
halimote
helpmate
haleness
△holiness
half-note
helenium
hallowed
holdover
△haliotis
heliosis
hillocky
hollowly
halloumi
heliodor
Heliozoa
halfpace
holoptic
half-pike
half-pint
heliport
holy-rood
hilarity
helmsman
hillside
half-step
Holostei
holistic
half-sole
holesome
helistop
half-size
half-tide
helotage
Holstein
half-time
half-tint
half-tone
halation
holotype
half-term
helotism
halitous
half-text
halluces
hellward
half-year
holly-oak
holozoic
hummable
humpback
hump-back
home-bred
home-brew
hymn-book
home-born
homicide
hemocyte
humidify
homodont
homodyne
humidity
hammerer
homefelt
home-farm
home-fire
homogamy
homogeny
home-life
homology
homaloid
homelike
homelily
homeland
humbling

8 h□m□l

homeless
homilist
hamulate
humility
Himalaya
home-made
hymeneal
hymenean
hymenial
hominoid
humanoid
homuncle
humanely
homonymy
humanise
humanism
humanist
humanity
hymenium
humanize
hemiolia
hemiolic
hemiopia
hemiopic
homeosis
homeotic
hummocky
homeobox
hemionus
hemp-palm
hamartia
humoresk
humorist
humorous
hemostat
homesick
hampster
hemp-seed
homespun
hematoid
hematoma
homotony
himation
homotype
homotypy
hematite
humstrum
home-town
humoured
Hamburgh
homeward
homework
hamewith
hangable
hen-padle
hen-party
hung-beef
hand-ball
handbell
handbill
handbook
hangbird
handclap
handcuff
handcart
hinderer
hungerly
hanger-on
handfuls
hindfoot
hangfire
handfast
handgrip
henchman
hindhead
henchmen
hand-held
handhold
hand-horn
handicap
hangings
handiest
Hanukkah
hand-knit
hindlegs
handling
hand-loom
handless
handlist
hen-flesh
handmade
handmaid
hand-mill
hindmost
hangnail
hangnest
handover
hangover
hen-court
hen-house
hen-roost
handplay
hand-pick
hanepoot
hand-post
henequen
henequin
heniquin
hundreds
handrail
hungrily
honorand
honorary
huntress
huntsman
hony-seed
hands-off
honestly
handsome
hand-sewn
honoured
honourer
hen-hussy
Hinduise
Hinduism
Hinduize
hindwing
handwork
hindward
honewort
handyman
honey-bag
honey-sac
honey-bee
honeydew
honey-dew
Hinayana
honey-ant
honeying
honeypot
honeybun
hoofbeat
hyoscine
hoosegow
hoolican
hooligan
hoodless
hoofless
hoof-mark
hoodooed
hoot-toot
hoodwink
hook-worm
heptarch
hipparch
heptagon
hypobole
hypocist
hypoderm
hyphened
hyphenic
hapteron
hopped-up
hypogeal
hypogean
hypogaea
hypogene
hypogyny
hypogeum
hypalgia
hip-flask
hopeless
hopingly
hyponymy
haploidy
hypnotee
hypnosis
hypnotic
hip-joint
Hyperion
hypernym
Hepatica
hypothec
hipsters
hepatise
hepatite
hepatize
hippuric
Hippuris
hippydom
haqueton
hereaway
hard-a-lee
herbaged
harmalin
herbaria
hireable
hardbeam
hornbeak
hornbeam
hardback
hark-back
hartbees
herb-beer
hardbake
hardball
harebell
hornbill
herd-book
hornbook
Heraclid
hyracoid
hard-copy
hard-core
heredity
Harleian
horsecar
horseman
horseway
hardened
hardener
herbelet
hermetic
herpetic
horsefly
horse-boy
hardface
hornfels
hare-foot
herefrom
hard-fern
Hereford
harigals
horngeld
hiragana
hardhead
hardhack
hurcheon
harridan
heroical
harpings
horrific
heroicly
horrible
horribly
horridly
hirrient
hornitos
hara-kiri
hari-kari
hard-luck
horologe
horology
heraldic
hardline
hireling
hurdling
heraldry
harmless
herbless
hornless
hurtless
harambee
Huronian
heronsew
hardness
hereness
harangue
hormonal
harborer
harmonic
hormonic
harlotry
harmosty
hornpipe
horn-pout
hard-rock
Hereroes
horn-rims
hare's-ear
harp-seal
herdsman
hernshaw
harassed
harasser
haruspex
hardship
heroship
herisson
haroseth
Horatian
hardtack
heritage
heritrix
horntail
hereupon
harrumph
hereunto
herdwick
hardwood
harewood
hardware
hornwork
hornworm
hornwort

herewith
harrying
hurrying
Hertzian
hastated
Hispanic
hush-boat
Hasidism
Hasidist
hastener
hosteler
hesperid
Hesperis
hysteria
hysteric
has-beens
hostelry
hasheesh
Hesperus
hush-hush
hospital
hastings
hustings
Hassidic
histioid
hospitia
hustling
hashmark
hospodar
histogen
historic
hassocky
hosepipe
hose-reel
histrion
histrios
hesitant
hesitate
hot-hatch
hateable
hetaerae
Hatteria
hitherto
hotted-up
hatchway
hitchily
hatching
hotchpot
hatchery
hot-short
hatchety
hetairai
hetairas
hetairia
hotelier
hat-plant
hateless
hothouse
hot-brain
haterent
hatbrush

hot-press
hatstand
hatguard
hautbois
houseman
house-tax
heuretic
house-sit
housefly
houseboy
house-dog
housetop
houseful
hausfrau
housings
hauriant
haurient
hourlong
housling
haunting
hout-tout
havocked
havildar
havelock
hovelled
hoveller
hivelike
hiveless
hive-nest
have-nots
hover-car
hover-bed
hover-fly
hover-bus
hiveward
hawkbell
hawk-eyed
hawthorn
Hawaiian
hawfinch
hawklike
hawk-moth
howitzer
hawkweed
how-d'ye-do
hexafoil
hexagram
hexaglot
hexylene
hexaplar
Hexapoda
hexapody
haymaker
hay-de-guy
hey-de-guy
hayfield
hey-go-mad
haystack
huzzaing
hazelnut
haziness

hazardry
inarable
isabella
imaginal
imaginer
imagines
Italiote
inasmuch
isagogic
inaurate
inaction
inactive
imbecile
imbrices
imborder
imbitter
incubate
incubous
incident
ischemia
ischemic
increase
increate
inclined
inchmeal
incoming
itch-mite
incenser
incensor
incentre
inconnue
incloser
inchoate
inceptor
incurred
incurved
incorpse
incision
incisory
incisure
incisive
incitant
inch-tape
included
ischuria
incivism
itchweed
inch-worm
Indiaman
indebted
indicial
induciae
indictee
inductee
indocile
indecent
indicant
inductor
indicate
indicium
indrench

iodoform
indigoes
indigene
indigent
indigest
indagate
indulger
indolent
induline
indamine
indented
indenter
indirect
indurate
iodyrite
indusial
industry
indusium
induviae
induvial
indexing
iterance
ice-ledge
ideogram
Isengrim
irenical
inedited
icefield
inedible
irenicon
ice-skate
ideology
iceblink
idealise
idealism
idealist
ideality
idealize
inermous
icebound
inexpert
ice-cream
inerrant
inessive
inertial
identify
icestone
ideation
identity
ideative
irefully
inequity
inflamed
inflamer
inflated
infrared
inflator
inflatus
infecund
infector
inficete

inflexed
infefted
infringe
in-flight
infamise
infamous
infamize
infantry
iffiness
infinite
infinity
inferiae
infernal
informal
inferred
informed
informer
infirmly
inferior
infernos
infusion
infusory
infusive
influent
inguinal
ingenium
ingrowth
ingroove
ingather
inhearse
ichthyic
inholder
inhalant
inhumane
inhumate
inherent
ichorous
inhesion
inhauler
imitancy
imitable
imitator
iriscope
Irishman
Irishism
inimical
initiate
idiolect
idiotish
idiotism
△iniquity
injector
inkberry
inkiness
inkstand
inkstone
ill-faced
ill-fated
ill-faurd
ill-faste
ill-being

Words marked △ may be spelled also with a capital letter

8 i□l□h

idlehood
ill-timed
illumine
Islamise
Islamism
Islamite
Islamize
inlander
islander
idleness
illinium
ill-spent
illiquid
ill-treat
Illyrian
islesman
ill-usage
illision
illusion
illusory
illusive
illation
illative
illuvial
illuvium
inlaying
immobile
immodest
immolate
immoment
Immanuel
immanely
immingle
immanent
imminent
immunise
ilmenite
immanity
imminute
immunity
immunize
immortal
immersed
immitted
immature
iambuses
innocent
Ionicise
Ionicize
innuendo
ianthine
ignominy
ignaroes
ignorant
ionising
Ignatian
innately
ignition
ignitron
innative
innovate

ionizing
idolater
isobaric
isogamic
isolable
isolator
idolatry
ironbark
iron-clad
iron-clay
isomeric
isometry
iron-gray
iron-grey
isocheim
isochime
isochore
isothere
isotherm
isochasm
ironical
idoliser
idolizer
inositol
isodicon
isocline
isogloss
isopleth
iron-mine
inornate
isogonal
isopodan
isogonic
isonomic
isotonic
isotopic
isodomon
isomorph
isodomum
isologue
isospory
isocracy
isocryme
isobront
isoprene
isotropy
idocrase
iron-sick
Ironside
iron-sand
Isoptera
isostasy
inoculum
ironwood
ironware
ironwork
ivory-nut
impocket
impudent
impleach
impledge

impresse
impugner
impaired
impairer
implicit
imprimis
imprison
impolicy
impelled
impeller
impolder
impolite
impannel
iopanoic
imponent
impanate
impunity
implorer
improper
improver
imperial
imparter
importer
impurely
impurple
imparity
impurity
imperium
impasted
imposter
impishly
imposing
impasto'd
impastos
impostor
inputter
impetigo
impotent
implunge
impluvia
implying
inquirer
irrigate
irrision
irrisory
irritant
irritate
instance
instancy
issuance
inswathe
instable
issuable
issuably
insucken
insecure
insignia
insphere
instinct
inspired
inspirer

inspirit
inscient
insulter
insolent
insolate
insulate
insomuch
insomnia
Ibsenian
insanely
Ibsenism
Ibsenite
insanity
insconce
inscribe
instruct
inserted
inserter
inscroll
inshrine
insurant
instress
insculpt
intrados
intubate
intrench
intrepid
intifada
integral
intaglio
intrince
intuited
intrigue
Intelsat
isthmian
intimacy
intimism
intimist
intimate
intimity
intonaco
intended
intender
intently
intoning
intonate
intromit
introrse
interlay
internal
interval
interwar
interact
internee
internet
interred
interrex
intersex
intorted
intarsia
intermit

intermix
intertie
inthrall
icterine
intercom
interior
Interpol
interess
interest
intercut
intitule
intruder
inurbane
inundant
inundate
inustion
inveagle
inviable
invecked
invected
inveigle
involute
inventor
inverted
inverter
invertin
invertor
izvestia
invasion
investor
invasive
inviting
inwardly
idyllian
idyllist
jeanette
jealouse
jealousy
jabberer
jib-sheet
jobshare
jibbings
jubilant
△**jubilate**
jib-crane
Jebusite
jobation
jackaroo
jickajog
jack-bean
Jacobean
Jacobian
jackboot
Jacobite
jacketed
jackeroo
jockette
Jack-fool
jack-high
jaculate
jocundly

Words marked △ may be spelled also with a capital letter

jack-pine
jocosely
jocosity
jack-tree
△**jacquard**
judicial
Judaical
Judaiser
Judaizer
judgment
jodhpurs
jigsawed
jogpants
jiggered
jaggedly
joggling
juggling
jugglery
jugulate
Jugoslav
Jugo-Slav
johannes
Jehovist
jail-bait
jail-bird
joined-up
join-hand
joint-fir
joint-oil
jointure
jejunely
jejunity
jokingly
jokesome
jillaroo
jolleyer
julienne
jolthead
jalapeño
jelutong
jalousie
jelly-pan
jollying
jim-dandy
jampanee
jumpable
jump-ball
jambeaux
jumped-up
Jamaican
jambiyah
jimpness
jambolan
jamboree
jumboise
jumboize
jimcrack
jump-rope
Jamesian
jump-seat
jump-shot
jemmying
joncanoe
junkanoo
jingbang
junketed
Janiform
Januform
jangling
jongleur
Junonian
jingoish
jingoism
jingoist
junk-ring
junk-shop
Jonathan
janitrix
junction
juncture
junk-yard
janizary
jeopardy
Japhetic
japonica
japanned
japanner
Japanese
Japanesy
Japanise
Japanize
jeroboam
jordeloo
jerrican
jirkinet
jeremiad
Jeremiah
jurymast
jararaca
jararaka
Jurassic
juristic
jarosite
juratory
jerquing
jerrycan
jestbook
justicer
Jesuitic
Jesuitry
jostling
justness
jetliner
jettison
jet-skier
jet-black
jetplane
jet-plane
jaundice
jiu-jitsu
journeys
jauntily
jaunting
jovially
juvenile
Javanese
Jews'-harp
Jew's-harp
jewelled
jeweller
jowing-in
jaw-tooth
Jewishly
joy-wheel
joy-rider
joy-stick
joyfully
joyously
jazz-funk
jazz-rock
jazerant
krameria
khalifah
khalifat
Kwakiutl
knackers
knackery
knackish
knapping
Klansman
knapscal
knapsack
khansama
knapweed
kabbalah
kabeljou
kibitzer
kickable
kachahri
kickback
kickball
kickdown
keckling
kickshaw
kedgeree
kidology
kid-glove
keelboat
kvetcher
knee-deep
knee-high
klephtic
kneehole
keeshond
keelhaul
khedival
knee-jerk
kreplach
keenness
keepsake
keepsaky
knee-stop
kreasote
kreosote
kreutzer
kreatine
kefuffle
koftgari
kaffiyeh
keffiyeh
koftwork
kohlrabi
kaimakam
khilafat
knife-man
kaiserin
knife-box
knife-boy
knightly
knickers
kail-runt
knittles
knitting
knitwear
△**kailyard**
kakiemon
kakemono
kala-azar
killadar
kilobyte
killcrop
killdeer
kilogram
kilogray
kiln-hole
keloidal
kalamdan
kalumpit
kalendar
kolinsky
kalinite
killogie
kyllosis
kalyptra
Kolarian
kill-time
kalotype
Kalevala
kilovolt
kilowatt
Kaliyuga
kamacite
Kamadeva
kymogram
kamikaze
Komsomol
komissar
komitaji
kangaroo
kinkajou
king-bolt
king-bird
king-crab
king-crow
kinsfolk
kingfish
kinghood
kink-host
kantikoy
kingklip
kinakina
king-like
kindlily
kindling
kingling
kindless
kingless
kindness
kenspeck
kingpost
Kanarese
king's-man
kinesics
kingship
king-size
kinetics
kingwood
knowable
△**klondike**
△klondyke
kromesky
knot-hole
kaoliang
knocking
Khoikhoi
knockers
knockout
knotless
knotting
knotweed
knotwork
kephalic
kephalin
kipperer
kyphosis
kyphotic
kirn-baby
korfball
kernelly
kyrielle
kurveyor
kermesse
kerchief
kirn-milk
karyotin
kurtosis
kerbside
Kuroshio
kerosene
kerosine
karstify
keratoid
karateka
keratose
kirkward

Words marked △ may be spelled also with a capital letter

8 k□r□y

kirkyard
kissable
kiss-curl
Kushitic
Kashmiri
△**kashruth**
kistvaen
kottabos
katakana
ketamine
Kitemark
kite-mark
kourbash
krumhorn
kauri-gum
khuskhus
kouskous
knurling
key-plate
keyboard
key-fruit
keystone
klystron
keypunch
keybugle
kazatzka
leasable
loanable
loanback
lean-burn
leaf-base
loaf-cake
leaf-curl
leadenly
lease-rod
llaneros
lead-free
leaf-fall
leap-frog
Loaghtan
leaching
loathing
leathern
leathers
leathery
leachate
leachour
leachtub
loathful
leavings.
leaflike
leadline
leadless
leafless
learning
leanness
leaf-roll
leaprous
leadsman
leaf-scar
loadstar

leaf-soil
Labiatae
labially
Labrador
libraire
labdanum
libeccio
lubberly
libretti
libretto
lobe-foot
Labridae
lubrical
labelled
libelled
libellee
libeller
libelant
libeling
lobeline
lability
lobulate
labellum
libelous
Lebanese
loblolly
liberate
laburnum
lobotomy
libation
lobation
libatory
laboured
labourer
lobbying
lobbyist
lackaday
lockaway
lockable
lichanos
lace-boot
lacebark
lucidity
lichened
Lachesis
lichenin
licker-in
lacteous
△**locofoco**
lockfast
lichgate
lychgate
lacrimal
lactific
lace-leaf
Lucullan
Lucullic
lackland
luculent
localise
localism

localist
luckless
locality
loculate
lack-love
localize
locomote
laciniae
Laconian
licensed
licensee
licenser
licensor
lacunars
lacunary
lecanora
laconism
lacunose
lacunate
lacrosse
lockpick
licorice
lacerant
lectress
lacerate
locksman
locustae
lockstep
lecithin
Lecythis
location
locution
locutory
lecythus
locative
lecturer
lacqueys
locoweed
lichwake
lacewing
lacrymal
lucky-bag
lucky-dip
ladybird
lodicula
lodicule
laddered
ladleful
ladified
ladyfied
lady-fern
lady-help
ladyhood
lodgings
ladylike
lady-love
lodgment
Ladinity
lodesman
lodestar
ladyship

lee-gauge
liegeman
liegedom
leechdom
lee-board
lientery
liftable
lifeboat
liftback
lifebelt
left-bank
lifebuoy
lift-girl
lifehold
left-hand
lifelike
lifeline
lifelong
lifeless
leftover
lift-pump
life-raft
life-rent
lifespan
lifesome
life-size
lifetime
left-wing
leftward
life-work
luggable
log-canoe
lagnappe
logician
logicise
logicism
logicist
logicize
ligneous
logogram
lug-chair
Lagthing
leggings
lignitic
liguloid
Legoland
legalese
legalise
legalism
legalist
log-glass
legality
ligulate
log-slate
legalize
ligament
legendry
lagoonal
leg-woman
legioned
logboard

log-house
legering
legerity
logistic
legatine
lighting
legation
ligation
light-box
logotype
legatary
ligature
lightish
lightful
logjuice
leg-guard
lah-di-dah
laitance
laid-back
loiterer
Laingian
lyings-in
leisured
likeable
△**lakeland**
likeness
lakeside
lekythos
likewake
lykewake
likewalk
lykewalk
lukewarm
likewise
Lollardy
l'allegro
lollipop
Lilliput
lolloped
lallygag
lollygag
limnaeid
lumbagos
lampasse
lambaste
Limaceae
limacine
lambdoid
lambency
lumberer
limnetic
lumberly
lumpenly
lumpfish
lymphoid
lamphole
lymphoma
lamp-hour
lammiger
limpidly
limekiln

Words marked △ may be spelled also with a capital letter

lamellae
lamellar
lamb-like
lambling
limbless
limbmeal
lemon-dab
lemonade
lamented
lamantin
luminant
laminary
luminary
lameness
laminose
liminess
limpness
luminist
laminate
limonite
lomentum
luminous
lamppost
lemurian
limerick
lemuroid
lemurine
lamp-room
lampreys
lambskin
lamasery
lime-tree
lime-twig
limiting
limation
limitary
Limousin
lima-wood
lime-wood
limewash
lumpy-jaw
Linnaean
lentando
lineated
lineally
linearly
linkable
land-army
longboat
lung-book
land-crab
lonicera
longcase
Lonsdale
landdros
lancegay
longeval
lenience
leniency
lancelet
lanceted
lanneret
lingerer
lynx-eyed
lingerie
lungeing
longeron
longeurs
landfall
landfill
landform
long-firm
land-fish
line-fish
lung-fish
land-girl
long-head
lunkhead
lynch-law
linchpin
long-hair
lynchpin
longhand
luncheon
land-herd
lanthorn
longhorn
land-haul
long-haul
lenticel
lenticle
landlady
long-life
long-legs
linoleic
lent-lily
land-line
lanoline
long-line
linalool
landlord
landless
lunulate
langlauf
linoleum
land-laws
land-mine
liniment
landmark
landmass
long-nine
lankness
Leninism
Leninist
loneness
longness
Leninite
lunanaut
Londoner
land-poor
lunarian
landrace
langrage
landrail
land-roll
lunarist
Landsmål
landsman
Langshan
linesman
long-stay
landside
Landseer
langspel
lingster
linkster
lintseed
land-ship
landskip
landslip
lantskip
longship
lonesome
longsome
long-spun
linstock
lengthen
long-togs
long-tail
long-time
lenition
lunation
Linotype®
lincture
long-term
lenitive
lingular
language
linguine
linguini
languish
linguist
longueur
Landwehr
longwall
landwind
landward
lindworm
linkwork
lungwort
longwise
long-wave
longways
loo-table
loosener
looker-in
looker-on
loose-cut
lyophobe
loophole
lyophile
lionlike
loop-line
lop-eared
lapsable
lip-salve
lapidify
lapidary
lapidate
lepidote
lappeted
lipogram
lopsided
lapelled
lupuline
lip-gloss
lipomata
leptonic
lap-joint
lap-board
Lupercal
leporine
lopgrass
liparite
liposome
Lapithae
Laputian
lipstick
lapstone
lip-synch
liquable
liquesce
liquidly
liquidus
loquitur
liquored
lernaean
larnakes
larvated
lyre-bird
lyricism
lyricist
loricate
larcener
larderer
largesse
lyriform
larrigan
lordings
larrikin
lorikeet
lordling
lordless
laryngal
larynges
larynxes
lordosis
lordotic
larboard
liripoop
liripipe
lordship
larkspur
lyra-viol
lyra-wise
lorry-hop
listener
listeria
last-gasp
lashings
luscious
lustique
lasslorn
listless
lustless
losingly
lushness
lissomly
lassoing
lispound
lysergic
lustrums
lustrine
lustring
lustrate
lustrous
lysosome
Lusation
lysozyme
Letraset®
lethargy
litharge
Lothario
lethally
lettable
lutecium
Lutheran
lettered
letterer
littered
latterly
litherly
lothfull
litigant
litigate
latchkey
letching
lathlike
let-alone
Lettland
littling
latently
lateness
Latinise
Latinism
Latinist
lutanist
lutenist
Latinate
Latinity
Latinize
littoral
luteolin
literacy
liturgic

Words marked △ may be spelled also with a capital letter

8 l□t□r

literary
literose
laterite
literate
literati
literato
Lutetian
latitude
latitant
lutetium
latewake
lathyrus
Laurasia
laudable
laudably
laudanum
launcher
louvered
leukemia
leukemic
laureate
lounging
laughter
louchely
laughing
laughful
leucitic
loudness
Leucojum
louis-d'or
leviable
liveable
live-axle
loveable
lavaboes
live-bait
live-born
lovebird
lovebite
lividity
love-drug
love-feat
lavaform
levigate
love-hate
love-knot
Lovelace
lovelock
levelled
△leveller
livelily
lovelily
livelong
livelood
lovelorn
levulose
loveless
lava-lava
lavement
lavender
△levanter
lovingly
love-nest
laverock
liveried
leverage
live-rail
liver-rot
liverish
levirate
love-seat
lovesick
love-suit
lavishly
lovesome
love-song
lavation
lavatera
lavatory
levitate
live-well
liveware
Lowlands
law-maker
low-level
lawyerly
law-giver
low-lived
lowlight
low-slung
lewdness
law-court
low-noise
lowering
Lewisian
lewdster
lewisson
lewisite
lawfully
luxmeter
lexigram
luxurist
luxation
laxative
lixivial
lixivium
layabout
lay-shaft
△loyalist
laywoman
layering
laystall
lazy-jack
lazulite
lozenged
laziness
Lazarist
lazurite
mbaqanga
meatball
mean-born
meanders
meathead
meatless
miasmata
miasmous
meanness
meal-poke
meagrely
meal-tide
meal-tree
mealtime
meantime
mean-tone
measured
measurer
measures
meatuses
mealworm
mobocrat
mobilise
mobility
mobilize
mechanic
moccasin
mockable
mocuddum
mackerel
Macleaya
muckheap
macahuba
mackinaw
machismo
micellar
mycelial
muckluck
mucilage
mycology
muculent
maculose
maculate
macallum
mycelium
Macanese
muchness
meconate
meconium
microbar
microcar
mucrones
microbic
macropod
microdot
microbus
muck-rake
macaroni
macaroon
macarise
macarism
macerate
macarize
macassar
mocassin
mucosity
mycetoma
macrural
micrurgy
muck-worm
madrasah
△midlands
medially
mediator
madrassa
Medibank
Medicean
midi-coat
mid-ocean
△medicaid
modicums
medicine
△medicare
medicate
medieval
modified
modifier
midships
madrigal
med'cinal
mid-wifed
mid-wived
midwives
midnight
Medjidie
midfield
medullae
medullar
medullas
mudslide
medalled
modelled
modeller
medallic
medaling
meddling
middling
modeling
modellos
mud-clerk
medalist
modalism
modalist
modality
modulate
madwoman
modiolar
mid-point
madroños
mediocre
madhouse
△modiolus
mad-apple
mudirieh
madbrain
midbrain
modernly
maderise
moderate
moderato
maderize
medusoid
modestly
modishly
mudstone
meditate
mudpuppy
mudguard
modiwort
muddying
maenadic
Maecenas
myelitis
Maeonian
meekness
meetness
mnemonic
muenster
maestros
maestoso
maffling
mofussil
△magdalen
magmatic
migraine
migrator
megabuck
megabyte
magician
magicked
megacity
megadyne
megadose
magnesia
magnetic
magneton
magnetos
McGuffin
mug-sheep
magnific
megillah
megalith
magnolia
mignonne
mug-house
megapode
magister
mageship
magot-pie
mightily
mightest
mightful
megavolt
megawatt
magazine
Mahratta
Mahadeva

Words marked △ may be spelled also with a capital letter

8 m□n□l

mahogany
Mahdiism
Mahdiist
mahi-mahi
mah-jongg
mahzorim
Moharram
Muharram
Muharrem
maharaja
maharani
Mahayana
mridanga
mailable
mail-boat
mainboom
muirburn
mail-clad
mail-cart
mail-drag
main-deck
maindoor
maidenly
mailgram
maidhood
maiolica
mainland
mainline
maidless
mainmast
meionite
maid-pale
muir-poot
muir-pout
mailroom
mainstay
mailsack
mainsail
mailshot
moistify
maintain
moisture
maieutic
mainyard
majolica
majority
majestic
makeable
makebate
mokaddam
makeless
mako-mako
makimono
makeover
malvasia
miliaria
mullarky
molybdic
Milicien
molecule
molecast
maledict
melodica
melodics
mule-deer
mylodont
melodeon
melodion
malt-dust
melodise
melodist
malodour
meltdown
melodize
milleped
mole-eyed
mallecho
malvesie
moltenly
△mulberry
malleate
multeity
malefice
male-fern
milkfish
maligner
malignly
mill-girl
Malagash
Malagasy
mill-head
molehill
mill-hand
molehunt
milch-cow
millibar
mulligan
milliner
milliped
millirem
Mulciber
multiped
mellitic
multifid
multifil
multiple
multiply
multi-ply
millième
millions
milliard
milliare
milliary
multigym
malt-kiln
milk-loaf
milklike
milkless
melilite
molality
milkmaid
malt-mill
melamine
malamute
malemute
malander
malinger
melanoma
melanism
mildness
Molinism
Molinist
malonate
melanite
melinite
mylonite
melanous
mulloway
miltonia
Miltonic
mellowly
millpond
malapert
mile-post
malarial
malarian
maltreat
millrace
malgrado
malarkey
millrind
molarity
melismas
Milesian
maltster
molasses
molester
moleskin
mulishly
molossus
malstick
milk-tree
muleteer
milltail
△militant
mulattos
military
militate
Mollusca
multurer
milk-weed
milk-walk
milkwood
maltworm
milk-warm
milkwort
mill-work
moldwarp
malaxage
malaxate
Mammalia
mem-sahib
mimicked
mimicker
membered
mamzerim
momzerim
mamselle
mammetry
Memphian
Memphite
mammifer
mammilla
mamillae
mamillar
mameluco
Mameluke
mumbling
momently
mementos
momentum
memorial
membrane
memorise
memorize
mimester
mimetite
mummying
Mandaean
maniacal
mancando
man-eater
mangabey
manna-dew
menhaden
△mandarin
manganic
Manganin®
minyanim
monoacid
montaria
manually
mentally
mondaine
mandator
manna-ash
manyatta
montanto
mandamus
mind-body
manubria
minibike
monachal
monocrat
Manichee
monicker
monocled
menacing
manicure
mind-cure
mongcorn
monocarp
mungcorn
minacity
monocyte
Monachus
monodont
minidisk
monadism
monodist
mannered
mantelet
many-eyed
Ménière's
mince-pie
Monoecia
man-weeks
mannerly
manzello
minneola
monteros
man-years
monteith
manteaus
manteaux
menseful
man-of-war
men-of-war
mindfuck
manifold
manyfold
maniform
manifest
monkfish
monogram
monogamy
managing
monogeny
monogony
monogyny
monoglot
Mon-Khmer
munchies
manshift
munchkin
minshuku
man-child
monohull
monkhood
mandioca
manrider
man-sized
Mandingo
mannikin
manciple
mandible
mantilla
monticle
Montilla
mansions
mannitol
mantissa
△monsieur
menology
monology

8 m□n□l

mantling
mingling
maneless
mindless
monolith
monomial
monomode
△**menomini**
miniment
moniment
monument
muniment
mint-mark
monomark
minimise
minimism
minimist
Minamata
minimize
meninges
monandry
mangonel
manpower
mandolin
Mongolic
menfolks
mandorla
man-hours
mansonry
mongoose
mungoose
monopode
minipill
monopole
△monopoly
menopome
manorial
manurial
menarche
Monarcho
monarchy
monorail
mandrake
mandrill
manuring
many-root
Minoress
Minorite
minority
mangrove
monk-seal
minister
mini-skis
monastic
monistic
ministry
meniscus
minutiae
minstrel
minutely
monotint
monotone
monotony
monition
munition
△**monotype**
minatory
monetary
monitory
monstera
monetise
manitous
menstrua
Minotaur
monitive
monetize
mensural
monaural
mancuses
maneuver
Mensuren
manfully
mansuete
Menevian
menswear
mansworn
monaxial
monoxide
money-bag
moneyman
money-box
monazite
myomancy
mootable
moonbeam
moon-ball
moor-band
moorcock
mooncalf
moon-eyed
myogenic
moonface
moon-fish
moorfowl
moon-gate
moot-hall
moot-hill
moorings
myositis
Maoridom
Mjöllnir
moorland
moonless
myoblast
myosotis
myotonia
myotonic
moor-poot
moor-pout
moonrock
moonroof
myograph
moonrise
moonseed
moonshee
moonsail
moonshot
moo-juice
moonwalk
moonwort
moody-mad
mopehawk
mephitic
mephitis
Mephisto
mopingly
mopboard
mopishly
mapstick
mopstick
muqaddam
maquette
moquette
mordancy
muriated
mariachi
margaric
margarin
muriatic
mortally
Marranos
martagon
Mercator
myriapod
myriadth
mersalyl
mortbell
moribund
marabout
Moraceae
miracles
marocain
moroccos
mericarp
merycism
muricate
meridian
mire-drum
mark-down
mergence
marketed
marketer
murderee
murderer
murrelet
marcella
markedly
martello
morceaux
muriform
marigram
mortgage
marigold
maraging
merogony
marchman
marsh-gas
marsh-man
morphean
mort-head
murphies
merchild
morpheme
merchant
morphine
morphing
murrhine
myrrhine
marchesa
marchese
mirthful
Morpheus
marginal
marzipan
morainal
margined
Marsilea
martinet
morticer
mortiser
markings
marriage
mornings
Marsilia
morainic
morbific
mortific
morbidly
morbilli
mirliton
△myrmidon
merciful
moraller
marbling
mortling
morellos
moralise
moralism
moralist
muralist
morality
Merulius
moralize
mortmain
merimake
Maronian
marinade
meronymy
marinera
Marinism
Marinist
miriness
marinate
Maronite
merengue
meringue
marjoram
marmoset
marooner
mirrored
moreover
myriopod
mirepoix
marsport
morepork
mariposa
maroquin
margrave
marksman
meresman
meristem
mort-safe
marasmic
meristic
myristic
morosely
merosome
mirksome
murksome
Moriscos
morosity
marasmus
Moresque
maritage
Marattia
maritime
△**marathon**
moratory
marauder
murmurer
mercuric
mortuary
marquess
marquise
Moravian
maravedi
merryman
martyria
marrying
mismatch
Mesdames
messages
mismated
mistaken
muscadel
Muscadet
muscatel
mustache
mescalin
moshavim
muscadin
mesially
missable
misfalne
mascaron

Words marked △ may be spelled also with a capital letter

massacre
miscarry
mismarry
misfaith
mossback
mass-bell
musk-ball
mass-book
Musaceae
musician
musicker
musicale
moss-crop
mesocarp
musk-cavy
mesoderm
misteach
masseter
miscegen
miskeyed
musterer
misfeign
mesmeric
misleeke
masterly
misdealt
misbegot
misletoe
misdempt
mismetre
musketry
masseuse
moss-flow
misogamy
misogyny
masthead
mischief
moss-hagg
misthink
misshood
misshape
mestizas
Muscidae
mystical
misgiven
misliker
missives
mistimed
muslined
muslinet
moslings
misdight
mislight
mastitis
miscible
misfield
mistitle
massicot
masticot
Messidor
mestizos
misticos
missilry
misbirth
mystique
Mass-John
Mess-John
misplead
Musulman
mashloch
misplace
misalign
misology
mossland
muscling
misallot
mastless
mesolite
mishmash
messmate
Mishnaic
musingly
misandry
misentry
masoolah
Massorah
misdoubt
misnomer
massoola
miscount
misdoing
misdonne
mispoint
mastodon
miscolor
misroute
misspeak
misapply
misspell
misspelt
misspend
misspent
musk-plum
misarray
misdread
mistreat
mistrial
miscreed
misorder
misgraff
misgraft
mesaraic
misprint
mess-room
mushroom
△**miserere**
mesprise
misprise
△mistress
mistrust
mistryst
moss-rose
Masorete
Masoreth
miswrite
masurium
misproud
mesprize
misprize
misusage
mesotron
misstate
muscular
misguide
meshugga
meshugge
messuage
misjudge
mesquine
musquash
mesquite
misquote
mosquito
mostwhat
mesh-work
Mesozoic
methanal
mutually
methadon
methanol
Metabola
mothball
miticide
matachin
muticous
matadora
matadore
mittened
mutterer
mathesis
motherly
matfelon
mitigant
mitigate
mutchkin
mote-hill
matching
matchbox
metrical
mythical
matrices
matrixes
métairie
metritis
methinks
mittimus
metalled
motelier
metallic
mytiloid
metaling
mottling
mateless
metalist
matelote
motility
mutilate
metalize
metamere
matamata
mutineer
mutinied
metanoia
metonymy
matiness
muteness
mutandum
mutinous
matronal
motional
meteoric
methodic
matronly
me-tooism
metaphor
metaplot
metopism
metopryl
material
maternal
motor-car
motorial
motorman
motorway
matériel
Mithraea
motor-jet
Mithraic
motorail
maturely
matgrass
mattress
motorise
motorist
maturate
maturity
motor-bus
motorium
motorize
mateship
matutine
mutation
mutatory
mutative
Mathurin
mitzvahs
mitzvoth
motivate
motivity
metewand
métayage
methylic
methysis
meteyard
metazoan
metazoic
metazoon
mauvaise
moulding
mouse-ear
mouterer
mousekin
mauveine
maumetry
mouse-dun
moufflon
mouchoir
mouchard
mouthful
moulinet
meunière
mourning
mournful
mounseer
moussaka
△**mountain**
moulting
mountant
mounting
moveable
moveably
movables
Mevlevis
moveless
movement
movingly
△**maverick**
Mawlawis
mawmetry
mawbound
mowburnt
myxedema
maxillae
maximise
maximist
myxomata
Maxim-gun
mixy-maxy
maximize
Mayology
mayoress
Mazdaism
Mazdaist
Mazdeism
mozzetta
mizzling
mazeltov
mazement
maziness
mazarine
mezereon
mezereum
mezuzahs
mezuzoth
Nearctic

Words marked △ may be spelled also with a capital letter

8 n□a□g

near-gaun
Noachian
near-hand
neat-herd
nearness
neatness
nearside
near-silk
nubecula
nobleman
noblemen
noblesse
nubiform
nebbishe
nibbling
Nibelung
nebulise
nobility
nubility
nebulium
nebulous
nobelium
nubilous
nebulize
neckatee
nectared
no-claims
neckbeef
neckband
neck-bone
nucleide
nickeled
nickelic
nucleole
nucleoli
nuclease
nucleate
nacreous
neckgear
noctilio
nucellar
necklace
neckline
nucellus
nick-nack
nocently
nickname
niceness
necrosis
necrotic
necropsy
Nichrome®
nicotian
niceties
nicotine
nocturne
noctuary
neckwear
neckweed
nicky-tam
nudicaul
nodalise
nodulose
nodality
nodulous
nodalize
nudeness
nidering
nidorous
nodosity
nudities
nidation
nodation
nudation
nieveful
needfire
naething
nielloed
needless
niellist
needment
Niflheim
no-frills
niffnaff
naffness
nigh-hand
negligee
negligée
Negrillo
Negritos
niggling
nighness
nigrosin
negroism
nightcap
night-hag
nightjar
night-man
night-fly
negation
negatron
night-dog
night-foe
night-ape
negatory
nugatory
negative
night-owl
△nihilism
nihilist
nihility
nohowish
nuisance
nail-bomb
noisette
noiseful
nail-file
nail-head
nail-hole
neighbor
nailless
nainsell
naissant
nainsook
nylghaus
nelumbos
nullness
nolition
naloxone
nameable
name-drop
nomadise
nomadism
nomadize
numberer
nomogram
nomogeny
nymphean
Nymphaea
nymphish
numskull
nomology
nameless
numbness
nominate
numinous
name-part
numeracy
Nemertea
nomarchy
numerals
numerary
numerate
nemorous
numerous
namaskar
nomistic
namesake
Nematoda
nematode
nematoid
nametape
Nembutal®
nummular
nimbused
nimbuses
nimbyism
non-dairy
non-party
non-metal
Nintendo®
nine-eyes
nankeens
nonsense
ninefold
nine-foot
nanogram
nunchaku
nine-hole
non-thing
nuncheon
non-white
nennigai
nundinal
nine-inch
non-rigid
ninjitsu
non-elect
non-claim
nine-mile
nonanoic
non-union
non-entry
non-moral
nonpolar
non-voter
non-ionic
non-toxic
△nenuphar
nonuplet
ninepins
nonesuch
non-stick
nineteen
nineties
nunataks
nonettos
△nonjuror
ninjutsu
non-quota
non-event
nannygai
nannying
△nancy-boy
nannyish
Neogaean
neonatal
neopagan
Neo-Latin
neotenic
neoteric
noometry
neophobe
neophile
neophyte
neoblast
neoplasm
neologic
neotoxin
neoprene
noontide
noontime
neomycin
napiform
nuptials
△napoleon
Nepalese
nepenthe
nepionic
Naperian
nephroid
nephrite
naphthol
nepotism
nepotist
normalcy
normally
narrator
naricorn
Norseman
norteñas
Norweyan
nervelet
narceine
norteños
nuraghic
Northman
narghile
narghily
northing
northern
nargileh
nereides
nargilly
narcissi
nursling
niramiai
Neronian
narcoses
narcosis
narcotic
narrowly
Neritina
nervular
nurtural
nurturer
narquois
nastalik
nasta'liq
nystatin
noseband
nose-cone
nosedive
nascence
nascency
nisberry
nose-herb
nescient
nose-leaf
nosology
nestlike
nestling
nasalise
noseless
nasality
noselite
nasalize
neshness
nosiness
nose-ring
nuthatch
not-pated
notables
notebook
notecase

Words marked △ may be spelled also with a capital letter

nattered
natterer
nutmeggy
not-being
notified
notifier
natiform
Notogaea
nutshell
notching
nothings
Nethinim
nutrient
nathless
noteless
natality
notandum
△national
notional
nitrogen
nuthouse
nitrosyl
nitroxyl
notarial
nutarian
notornis
naturing
naturism
naturist
nit-grass
notarise
nut-grass
nut-brown
notarize
natation
notation
nutation
natatory
no-trumps
natively
nativism
nativist
△nativity
naumachy
neurally
noumenal
nouvelle
nauseant
noumenon
nauseate
nauseous
nautical
neuritic
neuritis
nautilus
nauplius
neuromas
neuronal
neuroses
neuronic
neuropil
neurosis
neurotic
neutrino
ngultrum
navicula
navicert
navigate
novellae
novellas
noveldom
navalism
novelese
novelise
novelish
novelism
novelist
novelize
November
novenary
never-was
novercal
navarchy
noverint
Novatian
novation
navvying
newscast
nowadays
nowhence
newsgirl
nowt-herd
newshawk
new-risen
newelled
newsless
new-blown
newcomer
new-model
Newtonic
new-found
△newspeak
newsreel
newsroom
newishly
newswire
newly-wed
next-door
nextness
naythles
Nazarean
Nazarene
Nazarite
Nazirite
on-and-off
orangery
Orangism
omadhaun
opalised
opalized
ovaritis
ovariole
odalique
oragious
ovarious
Ozacling®
oratorio
oratress
oracular
opaquely
ombrella
Oxbridge
Orbilius
Orcadian
△occident
oncidium
orchesis
orchella
oncogene
orchitic
orchitis
orchilla
occulted
oecology
oncology
occultly
osculant
osculate
oncoming
Occamism
Occamist
oscinine
once-over
occupied
occupier
occupant
occupate
occurred
occasion
oncotomy
oscitant
oscitate
occlusal
occluder
occlusor
ordnance
oddments
old-timer
ordainer
ordalian
ordalium
ordinand
ordinant
ordinary
ordinate
Old-World
old-world
Oedipean
oldsquaw
obduracy
ordering
obdurate
ordurous
opera-hat
overarch
operatic
openable
operable
overalls
operator
oreganos
overbear
overbeat
overboil
overbrim
overbold
overbulk
overblow
overbook
overbrow
oven-bird
overburn
overbusy
overbite
Oleaceae
overclad
overcoat
overcraw
one-acter
opercula
overcall
overcome
overcloy
overcook
over-cool
overcrop
overcrow
open-cast
overcast
over-club
one-idea'd
overdraw
overdoer
okey-doke
overdone
open-door
overdose
overdust
open-eyed
omelette
operetta
overfeed
overfree
overfall
overfill
overfold
overfull
overfine
overfond
overfund
overflow
overfish
overgall
overgang
overgrow
overgive
overhead
overhear
overheat
overhair
overhale
overhold
overhand
overhang
overhent
overhung
overhype
obeahism
overhaul
one-piece
one-liner
one-sided
one-night
obedient
olefiant
overjump
overkeep
overknee
overkill
overkind
overking
overkest
overleaf
overleap
overload
overlock
overlade
overlier
oreology
overlaid
overlain
overland
overlend
overlent
overlong
overlook
overlard
△overlord
ocellate
overloud
owerloup
overlive
overmuch
overmast
Oceanian
overneat
overnice
oceanids
oleander
overname
one-on-one
openness
oceanaut
one-to-one
one-horse

8 o□e□p

open-plan
overplay
overpeer
overpage
overpart
overpass
overpast
overpost
overplus
overread
one-track
overrack
override
overrode
one-armed
overruff
overrake
overrule
overrank
overripe
overrash
overrate
orecrowe
overseas
oversman
overstay
oversway
overside
oleaster
overseen
overseer
overstep
oversail
overskip
overslip
overspin
overswim
oversell
oversold
obeisant
overshoe
over-shoe
overshot
oversoul
oversize
overteem
overtoil
overtrip
overtake
overtalk
overtime
overtone
ore-stare
overtire
overture
overturn
overtask
overview
overveil
overwear
overween
overwent
overwind
overwing
ovenwood
openwork
ovenware
overword
overwore
overwork
overworn
overwash
overwise
overyear
off-wards
off-sales
official
off-shake
off-shakt
offshoot
offshore
off-white
offsider
off-piste
offended
offender
off-and-on
off-comer
off-board
off-sorts
off-break
offering
offprint
off-drive
off-stage
ongoings
orgulous
oogamous
oogonial
organdie
organise
organism
organist
organity
oogonium
organize
orgasmic
orgastic
ophidian
ochidore
ochreate
ochreous
ocherous
Ochotona
Ophitism
ophiuran
ophiurid
oligarch
opinable
olibanum
origanum
oniscoid
Olivetan
oximeter
oligemia
olive-oil
orichalc
oliphant
original
opificer
oxidiser
oxidizer
opinicus
oeillade
orielled
orillion
opiumism
△oriental
oriented
obi-woman
oviposit
osier-bed
omission
otiosity
omissive
omitting
ouistiti
oviducal
oliguria
odiously
obituary
objector
oak-egger
Oak-apple
△ockerism
oil-paper
oil-gauge
oulachon
obligant
obliging
oologist
obligate
obligati
obligato
oil-fired
owl-light
oilfield
oil-gland
Owl-glass
oilcloth
oiliness
onlooker
obliquid
owl-train
oil-press
oilstone
oblation
oblatory
oblivion
ohmmeter
ommateum
own-label
osnaburg
omniform
oenology
ointment
ornament
oenophil
own-brand
ornithic
ornately
omnivore
omnivory
opopanax
otoscope
odometer
orogenic
odometry
omophagy
ozoniser
ozonizer
ocotillo
omoplate
oloroso
odograph
odontoid
odontoma
odontist
omohyoid
omphalic
omphalos
ox-pecker
Orpheans
oppugner
oppilate
orpiment
opponent
oophoron
opposing
opposite
owrecome
△oerlikon
ourology
owreword
Ossianic
obstacle
obsidian
ossified
oosphere
orseille
orsellic
obsolete
opsimath
opsonium
od's-nouns
obsequie
on-stream
obstruct
observer
oystrige
oestrous
ossarium
onsetter
obscurer
outdance
outmarch
outmatch
outrance
outwatch
outlands
outwards
outdated
outtaken
oathable
ostracod
ostracon
ostrakon
outlawry
outcaste
outvalue
optician
oiticica
obtected
outscold
outscorn
outreach
ostreger
outremer
outreign
outweigh
on-the-job
out-Herod
outvenom
outlearn
outweary
ontogeny
outshine
outthink
outshoot
outrival
obtainer
ofttimes
outrider
outsider
outsides
outsized
outfight
outnight
outright
outsight
osteitis
outfield
orthicon
outskirt
outsleep
ontology
optology
outflank
outfling
outglare
outclass
outflash
outflush
obtemper
outsmart

Words marked △ may be spelled also with a capital letter

8 p□d□c

optimise
optimism
optimist
optimate
Ottamite
Ottomite
optimize
octantal
octonary
ostinato
ox-tongue
optional
outvoice
orthoses
osteogen
outmoded
outpower
outroper
outvoter
orthosis
orthotic
outworks
outbound
outgoing
outpoint
△orthodox
orthopod
orthoepy
outboard
outdoors
outhouse
outworth
outspeak
octapody
Octopoda
octuplet
outspend
outspent
outsport
octopush
outbreak
outprice
outbreed
outdrink
octaroon
octoroon
oat-grass
outcross
outwrest
obturate
outbrave
outdrive
outfrown
outprize
obtusely
obtusity
outstrip
outstand
outstare
optative
obtruder

outguard
outburst
ottavino
outswear
outdwell
outswell
outswing
outlying
oculated
ocularly
opuscula
opuscule
opulence
Orvietan
ouvrière
obvolute
onwardly
ox-warble
onychite
onychium
oxytocic
oxytocin
oxymoron
△olympiad
Olympian
△olympics
Odyssean
ooziness
phalange
placable
placably
playable
platanna
peasanty
Platanus
playback
playbill
peat-bank
platband
playbook
planched
planchet
prancing
placcate
praecava
plaidman
praedial
prandial
play-debt
plaiding
pear-drop
plaudite
plaudits
placeman
plateman
placemen
platelet
peacenik
△phacelia
planetic
peasecod

placebos
peaberry
plateasm
pianette
placenta
peaceful
plateaus
plateaux
plateful
poaceous
praefect
pratfall
platform
play-goer
plangent
playgirl
pea-chick
peat-hagg
peat-hole
plashing
poaching
pea-viner
Pharisee
platinic
pea-rifle
placidly
pianinos
plagiary
pianiste
placitum
platinum
pratique
plank-bed
planking
pranking
plankton
prankish
prankful
peak-load
pearlies
phalloid
pea-plant
pearling
pearlins
peat-land
pearl-ash
phallism
planless
play-list
pearlite
pearl-eye
pharmacy
psalmody
pearmain
peat-moor
play-mare
peat-moss
△psalmist
playmate
psammite
plainant

plaining
planning
plainish
plainful
△platonic
peacocky
pea-soupy
pear-push
Prairial
pea-green
peat-reek
prairied
playroom
piassaba
plaister
peatship
playsuit
playsome
praising
Praesepe
piassava
plausive
pea-straw
plastral
plastics
practice
practick
practics
praktics
pear-tree
plantlet
prattler
plantage
Plantago
plantain
plantule
phantomy
playtime
pea-stone
plaiting
planting
platting
Phaethon
plant-pot
plastron
plastery
△psaltery
phantasm
phantasy
practise
practive
piacular
planulae
planular
planuria
plaguily
platysma
platypus
piazzian
publican
publicly

pebbling
pabulous
pubertal
pub-crawl
pabouche
peccancy
packaged
packager
pachalic
peccavis
piccanin
peccable
po'chaise
pickback
pickerel
picketed
picketer
pocketed
pochette
picker-up
pacifier
packfong
pacifism
pacifist
puckfist
pectinal
pectines
pickings
Puccinia
pachinko
picnicky
pack-load
△peculiar
picklock
pucelage
peculate
peculium
pack-mule
pockmark
pick-me-up
pick-'n'-mix
pecan-nut
pectoral
pycnosis
piccolos
Picariae
picarian
picaroon
pacation
picotite
pictural
pictures
pichurim
picayune
paduasoy
podiatry
pudibund
pedicled
pediculi
pedicure
podocarp

Words marked △ may be spelled also with a capital letter

8 p□d□c

pudicity
podagral
pedigree
pedagogy
podagric
Podogona
puddings
puddingy
pedalier
pedalled
pedaller
pedaloes
pedology
podology
paddling
pedaling
peddling
piddling
puddling
paddlers
pad-cloth
pediment
pudendal
pedantic
peduncle
pedantry
pudendum
podsolic
pad-horse
pedipalp
paderero
pederero
pederast
podargus
padishah
pedestal
pedately
Paddyism
prenasal
prenatal
Pleiades
prepared
preparer
presager
poematic
prelatic
peekaboo
predator
plenarty
presbyte
preacher
piercing
prescind
pleading
pseudery
pseudish
plebeian
presence
pretence
piecener
phenetic
precepit
premedic
preterit
predella
pre-teens
preceese
prepense
pretense
presents
preserve
pyengadu
pledgeor
preggers
phengite
pier-head
peep-hole
plethora
psephism
psephite
Pieridae
poetical
precinct
Pierides
précised
premised
premises
presidia
presidio
pyelitic
pyelitis
premiums
plenipos
premiere
première
precious
previous
pre-elect
preclude
phelloid
pie-plant
peerless
psellism
preamble
piedmont
plein-air
pfenning
pregnant
piedness
pleonasm
pleonast
prehnite
phenogam
premolar
phenolic
pteropod
premorse
preppily
prepping
poetries
preorder
pre-print
piecrust
pleurisy
pressfat
pressman
poetship
pheasant
pleasant
pleasing
pressing
peep-show
pression
pleasure
pressure
pleaseth
pressful
prentice
'prentice
plectres
pretties
prettify
prestige
prettily
plectron
plectrum
prehuman
plexuses
presumer
prejudge
preludio
precurse
peesweep
peetweet
pre-exist
pterylae
phenylic
pterygia
puffball
puffbird
pifferos
piffling
puff-puff
pigmaean
pygmaean
pig-faced
pug-faced
puggaree
pygidial
pygidium
pagehood
pugilism
pugilist
paganise
paganish
paganism
paginate
paganize
pig-woman
pug-nosed
pegboard
pigeonry
pagurian
Pegasean
pigswill
pig's-wash
pahoehoe
primatal
philabeg
plicated
Primates
privates
primatic
primally
prizable
paisanos
philamot
privados
pair-bond
princock
princely
Pliocene
princess
prie-dieu
poinding
primeval
prizeman
prideful
prigging
priggery
priggish
priggism
peishwah
plighted
plighter
philibeg
priciest
pricking
phialled
painless
prismoid
primming
phinnock
psionics
poignado
peignoir
pliantly
phisnomy
poignant
primness
Philomel
poisoner
prisoner
phimosis
psilocin
psilosis
psilotic
ptilosis
philomot
Psilotum
Priapean
priapism
paitrick
primrose
primrosy
prioress
priorate
priority
plimsole
△plimsoll
priestly
puissant
pliosaur
painting
pointing
printing
pristane
pristine
paint-box
painture
pointers
print-out
pairwise
pyjamaed
pejorate
pike-head
Pekinese
pokerish
Pakhtuns
Pakhtoon
pokeweed
polyarch
palmated
pileated
pillager
palladic
pelmatic
polyacid
pulza-oil
palpable
palpably
polka-dot
polyaxon
pulsator
pellagra
palabras
Polabian
palebuck
pull-back
pulicide
policies
pale-dead
paludine
paludism
paludose
paludous
Piltdown
pull-down
pale-eyed
palleted
palterer
pilferer
△pilsener
pulsejet
Palmerin

Words marked △ may be spelled also with a capital letter

palmette
palmetto
paleface
poltfoot
paliform
piliform
△pelagian
polygala
polygamy
polygene
polygeny
polygony
polygyny
phlegmon
polyglot
pillhead
pilchard
pollical
poloidal
pulvinar
palmiped
pelvises
pollices
pulpited
pulpiter
pulsidge
palmitic
palmitin
pollicie
pollinia
pollinic
polliwig
pulsific
pulvilio
pallidly
pellicle
pulville
pulvilli
polliwog
palliard
pulpitry
palliate
pulpitum
pulvinus
pelology
polemics
Polymnia
pall-mall
pell-mell
pulpmill
palamino
palimony
palomino
polymery
polemise
polemist
palamate
polymath
polemize
Polonian
palinode

palinody
Polander
pulingly
paleness
polonise
polonism
polonium
polonize
pillowed
pullover
pulmones
pulsojet
pulmonic
Pulmotor®
pilhorse
polyonym
palm-play
polypide
polypody
polypoid
Pilipino
polypine
polyphon
polypary
polypite
polypous
Polaroid®
paltrily
pelerine
poltroon
pelorism
polarise
polarity
polarize
palisade
palisado
pilaster
polished
polisher
pollster
Pelasgic
polyseme
polysemy
polysome
polysomy
palestra
pilosity
palatial
pilotman
politick
politico
politics
palm-tree
palstaff
pilotage
politely
△palatine
polytene
palstave
polluted
polluter

pellucid
polyuria
palm-wine
pulpwood
pilework
pile-worm
pilewort
pillworm
pillwort
palewise
pollywig
pollywog
polyzoan
polyzoic
polyzoon
pomwater
pompanos
pumicate
Pompeian
pamperer
pamperos
pompelos
pimiento
pommetty
pump-head
pamphlet
pumphood
pemmican
pomology
pemoline
pomander
pimentos
pembroke
pump-room
pomatoes
pump-well
pentarch
pindaree
pin-maker
pinnated
Punjabee
pangamic
Panhagia
pentadic
Pindaric
pantable
pentacle
pinnacle
pintable
pantalon
△pentagon
pintados
Pandanus
panacean
panicked
panicled
pinscher
pinacoid
penuchle
pinochle
panic-buy

ponderal
pendency
penneech
penneeck
pungence
pungency
pince-nez
pink-eyed
ponderer
pandemia
pandemic
Pentelic
panderly
Pandects
ponceaux
pang-full
pinafore
panegyry
punch-bag
pin-wheel
pinch-hit
penchant
pinching
pancheon
panchion
Pantheon
puncheon
pinchers
pinchgut
pannikel
Pan-pipes
pantiled
pen-wiper
pinniped
pontifex
penlight
panmixia
panmixis
pannikin
pontific
pannicle
pendicle
punditry
pinakoid
punaluan
panelled
pond-life
penology
pingling
pangless
penalise
penalize
penumbra
penoncel
penknife
pinkness
puniness
pentosan
penwoman
pandowdy
pennoned

pin-money
pansophy
pangolin
Panionic
pentomic
pantofle
pinpoint
pundonor
penn'orth
panoptic
punt-pole
Ping-Pong®
ping-pong
pancreas
pin-prick
pencraft
panorama
pentroof
pinkroot
panislam
puntsman
pinaster
Pinkster
punisher
ponyskin
pint-size
punctual
penstock
ponytail
punctule
penitent
punition
puncture
punitory
punctate
punitive
pendular
pinguefy
pendulum
pondweed
pinewood
pine-wool
penny-fee
penny-pig
penny-dog
penny-bun
pholades
profaner
protases
psoralen
prolamin
protasis
protatic
probable
probably
provable
provably
Phocaena
procaine
ptomaine
pronator

Words marked △ may be spelled also with a capital letter

8 p□o□a

propanol
prolapse
prosaism
prosaist
Phoebean
plodding
prodding
proudish
proudful
prometal
proseman
prose-man
Proverbs
proceeds
protégée
phonemic
phoner-in
phonetic
progeria
pyogenic
properly
provedor
propense
protease
protense
proteose
property
proofing
plougher
phosgene
proggins
prong-hoe
prophecy
prophage
prochain
prochein
prophyll
prophase
prophesy
Phocidae
prodigal
proviral
proximal
procinct
province
profiler
profiter
pro-lifer
promisee
promiser
provided
provider
pyonings
△photinia
prohibit
prolific
prolixly
proviant
proditor
promisor
providor

provisor
provisos
Protista
provirus
poor-John
plonking
proclaim
prowling
plotless
proclive
proemial
phorminx
△phormium
poorness
prodnose
pronotal
proposal
photogen
promoter
proposer
provoker
prolonge
Photofit®
photofit
photopia
photopic
propolis
prosodic
protonic
proforma
pro-forma
profound
propound
promotor
prosopon
protocol
△protozoa
proto-ore
photopsy
prologue
pronotum
prorogue
△prospect
prompter
Prospekt
promptly
plopping
proppant
propping
△phosphor
piou-piou
pooh-pooh
protract
prograde
protrude
prodrome
prodromi
prop-root
progress
poolside
poor's-box

prostyle
plotting
poontang
poortith
prostate
procurer
producer
profuser
promulge
poorwill
poon-wood
propylic
propylon
pappadom
poppadum
pipeclay
pipe-case
pupa-case
pepperer
puppetry
pipefuls
pipefish
popehood
poplitic
pop-visit
Popsicle®
papillae
papillar
pupillar
populace
pupilage
pipelike
pipeline
popeling
papilios
papillon
pupilary
papalise
papalism
papalist
papulose
pipeless
populism
populist
populate
pupilate
papulous
populous
papalize
popinjay
pappoose
puppodum
pap-spoon
paper-day
puparial
pipe-rack
papering
peperino
peperoni
piperine
paper-boy

puparium
Pepysian
papisher
pipe-stem
papistic
popeship
popishly
papistry
pipe-tree
pupation
pipe-wine
pipework
pipewort
puppy-fat
poppy-oil
puppy-dog
puppydom
puppyish
puppyism
piquancy
parlance
pernancy
portance
parlando
partaken
partaker
purdahed
pardalis
perradii
phreatic
portable
persaunt
Portaloo®
perianth
periagua
portague
periblem
pure-bred
parabola
parabole
periboli
parabema
parochin
pork-chop
pericope
pericarp
peracute
peridial
parodied
paradigm
pyridine
paradrop
periderm
△paradise
parodist
peridote
peridium
paradoxy
parietal
Parmesan
perdendo

parcener
pargeted
pargeter
purse-net
parhelia
parhelic
paroemia
porterly
perceant
purveyor
parterre
permease
perverse
porpesse
portesse
perfecta
perfecti
perfecto
permeate
perseity
porteous
purseful
perceive
purified
purifier
paraffin
parafoil
paraffle
Porifera
port-fire
pyriform
paragram
Paraguay
perigeal
perigean
Phrygian
paragoge
porogamy
perigone
perigyny
Parthian
porthole
perching
perchery
Porphyra
porphyry
porthors
parchesi
purchase
perthite
pyrrhous
partisan
partizan
Percidae
parritch
porridge
perlitic
partible
particle
persicot
porrigos

Words marked △ may be spelled also with a capital letter

porticos
portière
Parsiism
perviate
Partitur
pervious
pirlicue
portigue
purlicue
purlieus
parakeet
parallax
parallel
perilled
paralogy
purslain
parklike
parkland
perilune
porkling
△portland
purblind
purfling
purslane
purulent
paralyse
parclose
portlast
purplish
pyrolyse
perilous
paralyze
pyrolyze
pyramids
parament
paramese
paramour
parental
perineal
peroneal
Pyrenean
paranoea
paranoia
paranoic
paranoid
pyrenoid
paronymy
partners
Peronism
Peronist
pertness
phrenism
poriness
pureness
paranete
perineum
peroneus
Pareoean
personae
personal
personas

pornomag
portolan
perforce
pardoner
parroted
parroter
purposed
purposes
parsonic
percolin
periodic
periotic
parpoint
parrotry
porpoise
portoise
perspire
piri-piri
peripety
periplus
paraquat®
paroquet
parbreak
pirarucu
portrait
purtraid
parergon
portress
perorate
purtrayd
Parisian
pyrostat
parishen
perished
perisher
poristic
puristic
piroshki
Pyrosoma
pyrosome
parasang
part-song
phrasing
perisarc
parasite
porosity
part-time
pyritise
pyritous
pyritize
portulan
persuade
perfumed
perfumer
perjured
perjurer
pertused
Portugee
parousia
purpuric
purpurin

pursuant
pursuing
perruque
Peruvian
paravail
paravane
paravant
pyruvate
perswade
port-wine
port-winy
parkward
partwork
pyrexial
peroxide
pyroxyle
pyroxene
paroxysm
parrying
partyism
parazoan
pirozhki
parazoon
pastance
piss-a-bed
pashalik
passable
passably
poseable
postally
passados
piscator
paspalum
pass-back
push-bike
push-ball
pass-book
postcode
postcard
push-cart
postcava
postdate
passer-by
Passeres
paste-eel
pesterer
post-echo
postface
post-free
pisiform
pisshead
pasch-egg
pessimal
piscinae
piscinas
pasticci
pastiche
postiche
passible
passibly
pastille

possible
possibly
Poseidon
Peshitta
Peshitto
pessimum
postlude
posology
passless
pisolite
pashmina
passment
postmark
puss-moth
posingly
poshness
postnati
pastoral
postoral
Passover
pistolet
push-over
post-obit
pastorly
pishogue
post-paid
push-pull
postpone
passport
postpose
pastrami
poshteen
Pashtuns
positing
Pushtuns
position
positron
positive
pastural
postural
pustular
posturer
password
pussy-cat
Puseyism
Puseyite
pittance
potlatch
phthalic
phthalin
pitiable
pitiably
pithball
petechia
poticary
patience
pattened
patterer
potterer
pathetic
pettedly

pot-belly
putter-on
pita-flax
patagial
patagium
pitchman
putchock
patchily
pita-hemp
patching
pitching
patch-box
putcheon
patchery
petchary
potshard
potshare
potsherd
petrific
phthisic
phthisis
putridly
pettifog
patriate
patellae
patellar
patellas
petalody
petalled
petaloid
pithlike
petaline
petulant
pathless
petalism
pithless
pitiless
patulous
petalous
putamina
patentee
patently
potently
patentor
petuntse
pétanque
petuntze
patronal
petiolar
petrosal
pathogen
petioled
petronel
potholer
petrolic
pythonic
patronne
pot-bound
pothouse
pot-roast
paternal

8 p□t□r

peterman
peter-man
pityroid
Patarine
Peterloo
paterero
pot-ashes
potassic
pith-tree
potatoes
pot-still
potstone
petition
potation
petitory
potatory
putative
pot-au-feu
patty-pan
pitty-pat
puttying
plumaged
plurally
pourable
poulaine
△**plumbago**
plumbing
plumbery
plumbism
plumbate
plumbite
plumbous
plum-cake
plum-duff
poundage
pauldron
pouldron
prudence
plumelet
△**prunella**
prunelle
prunello
pauseful
plugging
plunging
pouchful
plumiped
prusiked
plurisie
pruritic
prurient
prurigos
Pluviôse
pluviose
pluvious
pruritus
pluckily
pruinose
△**plutonic**
plumpish
Paul's-man
Prussian
Prussify
plussage
poursuit
plussing
pourtray
poultice
plum-tree
plus-twos
plumulae
plumular
plug-ugly
pavilion
pavement
pavonian
pavonine
pivot-man
pivoting
pewterer
powdered
pew-chair
powsowdy
power-amp
powerful
pawnshop
pyxidium
poxvirus
pax-board
pax-brede
pixy-ring
phylarch
prytanea
physalia
physalis
physeter
phyletic
psychics
pay-sheet
psychoid
pay-phone
psychism
psychist
physical
physicky
paynimry
physique
phyllode
phyllody
phylloid
phyllome
phyllary
ptyalise
ptyalism
phyllite
ptyalize
pryingly
phytosis
Plymouth
peyotism
peyotist
pizzeria
puzzling
pezizoid
quandang
quandong
quandary
quaverer
Quakerly
quackery
Quaalude®
quailing
qualming
quagmire
quagmiry
qualmish
quaintly
quatorze
quarried
quarrier
quadriga
quatrain
quadrans
quadrant
quadroon
quadrate
quayside
quaestor
quartier
quantify
quartile
quantong
quart-pot
quartern
quarters
quantise
quantity
quartett
quantize
quencher
Quebecer
quenelle
queueing
Quechuan
queenlet
queening
queendom
queenite
queerdom
queerish
queerity
queasily
questant
questing
question
querying
qaimaqam
quibbler
quincunx
quiddler
quiddany
quiddity
quivered
quinella
Quichuan
Quirinal
Quirites
Quirinus
quickset
quick-fix
quirkily
quirkish
quillman
quill-pen
Quillaia
quill-nib
Quillaja
quilling
quisling
quidnunc
quixotic
quixotry
quippish
quit-rent
quinsied
quipster
quietude
quintain
quintile
quieting
quilting
quitting
quietism
quietist
quintett
quietive
quizzify
quizzing
quizzery
qalamdan
quotable
quotably
quotient
rear-arch
reawaken
rhagades
readable
readably
road-book
reascend
reascent
reaedify
rhabdoid
reagency
reaffirm
rhaphide
reaching
realiser
realizer
readiest
readjust
rear-lamp
roadless
rearmice
rearmost
realness
reasoned
reasoner
read-only
rearouse
reappear
rear-rank
rearrest
roadsman
rhapsode
rhapsody
roadside
reanswer
roadster
reassign
reassume
roadshow
reabsorb
reassert
reassure
reassess
Rhaetian
reattach
reattain
realtime
reactant
roasting
reaction
road-test
reactive
road-user
rear-view
readvise
rearward
ready-mix
rubicund
rabidity
rubidium
rabbeted
△**rubaiyat**
rubrical
rabbiter
rubbishy
△**rabbinic**
rabbitry
rubellan
rebelled
rebeller
rabbling
rebeldom
rebellow
ribaldry
ribbonry
rib-roast
reburial
roborant
reborrow
rib-grass
roburite
robustly

Words marked △ may be spelled also with a capital letter

ribosome
rebuttal
robotics
rabatoes
rebatoes
rebutted
rebutter
ruby-tail
rabatine
ribstone
rubstone
rebutton
robotise
robotize
ribaudry
ribozyme
rockaway
recharge
racially
rectally
rock-alum
rice-beer
race-ball
rice-bird
rock-bird
ricochet
rock-cook
racecard
rock-cork
receding
racketed
racketer
rocketer
Roccella
Rochelle
recceing
recreant
racketry
rocketry
richesse
raclette
recreate
ricketty
rock-fall
rockfish
racegoer
rice-glue
racahout
rock-hewn
receival
rachides
rachises
received
receiver
reclined
recliner
recoiler
rachitic
rachitis
rectitic
rectitis

rachilla
rocaille
ructions
récollet
rich-left
reckling
rockling
rock-lark
reckless
recommit
racemise
racemism
racemose
racemate
racemize
recanter
reconvey
recently
recentre
raciness
richness
rectoral
reckoner
reclothe
recaptor
receptor
racepath
ricercar
rick-rack
△recorder
recurred
recurved
rack-rail
rack-rent
rectress
rickshaw
ruckseat
rucksack
recessed
recesses
recusant
recision
rice-soup
recourse
Racovian
recovery
rockweed
rock-wood
rackwork
rockwork
reccying
rickyard
radiance
radiancy
riddance
radiated
red-faced
redwater
radialia
radially
rideable

radiator
radwaste
radicule
ridicule
radicant
reducing
redactor
radicate
ridgeway
reddenda
reddendo
△redeemer
redbelly
redefine
redshank
redshare
redshire
redshort
red-light
ruddiest
redolent
riddling
ridgling
redeless
radulate
rudiment
Rodentia
rudeness
raddocke
redeploy
redbrick
redirect
radar-gun
redargue
redesign
redistil
ridottos
redstart
radiuses
redouble
redivide
reduviid
ruddying
rhematic
re-embody
reed-band
reed-bird
re-embark
rheocord
re-emerge
re-engage
reef-knot
rheology
reedling
Riesling
re-enlist
ryeflour
reedmace
rhetoric
re-expand
reed-pipe

re-export
ryebread
reed-rand
reed-rond
rheostat
reedstop
rye-straw
△roentgen
rheotome
roestone
ruefully
reed-wren
Rh-factor
rifleman
raftered
reflexed
rifle-pit
reflexly
refreeze
refigure
refugium
refringe
refelled
ruffling
riftless
refunder
refining
refinery
rifeness
reflower
raft-port
referral
reformat
referred
△reformed
re-formed
△reformer
riff-raff
referent
raft-rope
reforest
raftsman
refusnik
refusion
refluent
rag-paper
regrater
Ragnarök
regrator
regicide
rigidify
rigadoon
rigidise
rigidity
rigidize
raggedly
ruggedly
regreets
ragwheel
ragtimer
regainer

regalian
rugelach
reguline
regalism
regalist
regulise
rugulose
regality
regelate
regolith
regulate
regulize
regiment
ragingly
rag-woman
regional
rag-money
regrowth
Rogerian
regarder
rogering
rigorism
rigorist
rigorous
register
rugosely
registry
rugosity
regather
ragstone
rigatoni
righting
△rogation
rogatory
rightish
rightist
rightful
reheater
rehearse
rehoboam
rehandle
raisable
ruinable
rainband
rain-bird
rainbowy
raincoat
railcard
reindeer
raindrop
raindate
reinette
rainfall
reinfund
reinform
reinfuse
railhead
△reichian
rein-hand
railings
rhinitis

8 r□i□l

reillume
raillery
railless
rainless
reinless
re-ignite
rhizobia
raisonné
Rhinodon
rhizopod
rhizopus
reimport
reimpose
railroad
reinsman
reinsert
reinsure
rain-tree
roisting
re-invent
reinvest
rainwear
rain-wash
rejecter
rejector
rejigger
rejoicer
rajaship
rakehell
rakshasa
rekindle
rakishly
reliance
releasee
releaser
reliable
reliably
rollable
releasor
roll-call
relucent
relocate
reliever
relievos
religion
relegate
Rallidae
ruleless
relumine
rillmark
roll-neck
roll-over
role-play
relapsed
relapser
roly-poly
relation
relative
relaunch
relevant
relaxant
relaxing
rallying
rallyist
rampancy
rummager
rampauge
rump-bone
Ramadhan
remedial
remediat
remedied
remodify
rumbelow
ramified
ramiform
remigial
remigate
ram's-horn
rum-shrub
rampired
rum-ti-tum
Ramilies
Ramillie
rambling
rumbling
ramulose
rumpless
ramulous
remember
Romanian
Rumanian
Romansch
Rumansch
Rumonsch
reminder
romancer
△**romantic**
remanent
ruminant
Romanise
Romanish
Romanism
Romanist
ruminate
ramentum
Romanize
rump-post
ramequin
remarked
remarker
rim-brake
remarque
remurmur
rumorous
rampsman
remaster
remissly
Rome-scot
remittal
remitted
remittee
remitter
remotely
remittor
remotion
rambutan
rum-punch
rumourer
Romeward
Ramayana
rondavel
rondache
rentable
rinsable
runnable
rent-a-mob
roncador
ring-bolt
ringbone
ring-bark
runabout
ring-dial
ring-dyke
ring-dove
renderer
renverse
renverst
rondeaux
runner-up
rent-free
raniform
reniform
renegade
renegado
reneguer
ronggeng
renegate
runagate
ranchman
ringhals
rinkhals
ranching
ranchero
△**renminbi**
rinsings
rinsible
runcible
rondinos
rindless
ringless
renumber
ring-mark
rankness
renforce
ransomer
randomly
renforst
re'nforst
ring-pull
ranarian
ranarium
ringside
ringster
ringtail
ring-tail
ring-time
renitent
renounce
renovate
renowned
renowner
ring-walk
ring-wall
renewing
ringwork
ringworm
ringwise
renaying
rendzina
rhodanic
rhopalic
rood-beam
rhomboid
root-ball
rhonchal
reoccupy
rhonchus
reordain
reopener
Rhodesia
rootedly
roomette
roomfuls
reoffend
root-fast
root-hair
roothold
Rhodites
reorient
root-knot
rood-loft
rooflike
rootlike
roofless
rootless
room-mate
roof-rack
roomsome
rood-tree
rooftree
ryotwari
rapparee
△repealer
repeated
repeater
replacer
raphania
ropeable
Raphanus
republic
rapacity
rapidity
replevin
ripienos
repreeve
reprisal
raphides
repairer
repriefe
Reptilia
replicon
reprieve
repelled
repeller
rippling
repenter
repining
ripeness
ropiness
reproval
reproach
Raptores
reprover
repeople
riparial
riparian
repartee
reporter
repurify
rope-ripe
reperuse
rephrase
rapeseed
reposall
reposure
repetend
reputing
raptured
repoussé
rope-walk
ropework
repaying
replying
rope-yarn
roquette
requital
required
requirer
requited
requiter
requight
requoyle
rere-arch
rarefied
ruralise
ruralism
ruralist
rurality
ruralize
reremice
rareness
rare-ripe
rerevise
rereward

Words marked △ may be spelled also with a capital letter

Rastaman
research
re-search
resiance
rascally
rascasse
resubmit
rust-belt
rosebush
rosebowl
Rosaceae
rose-comb
rest-cure
residual
resident
rose-drop
rosy-drop
residuum
respects
rispetti
rispetto
rosefish
resigned
resigner
rosoglio
rose-hued
rest-home
rustical
raspings
rispings
rose-knot
resalgar
risaldar
rose-leaf
reselect
resolved
resolver
roselike
rushlike
resplend
Roseland
rustling
restless
roseless
rustless
resalute
resolute
risoluto
rosulate
resemble
rosemary
Russniak
resenter
resinify
resinoid
rosin-oil
resonant
rashness
resinise
rosiness
resinata
resinate
resonate
rosinate
resinous
resinize
restorer
Responsa
response
resupine
rose-pink
rasorial
rosarian
restrict
reserved
reserves
resorter
resurvey
resorcin
restrain
restring
rush-ring
rose-root
rescript
rose-rash
rostrate
rosarium
resistor
resetter
rose-tree
rosetted
resettle
risottos
resource
rescuing
rosewood
retraict
rateable
rateably
retrally
ritually
retraite
retraitt
rutabaga
ratsbane
Rutaceae
reticule
reticent
retrench
ruthenic
rottenly
ratified
ratifier
retiform
Rotifera
rat-rhyme
retailer
retainer
retrieve
retaking
reteller
rattline
rattling
rutilant
riteless
ruthless
retinoid
retinula
rotundly
rotenone
retinite
ritenuto
rational
retroact
ratooner
retrofit
retrorse
rataplan
Rotarian
retiracy
rat-arsed
retarded
retarder
retorted
retorter
returnee
returner
ritornel
roturier
returnik
retiring
ratproof
rathripe
rotgrass
rat's-tail
rot-stone
rotation
rotatory
rotative
rat-guard
rotavate
rotovate
retrying
rhubarby
reusable
rout-cake
roundlet
rounding
round-top
round-arm
rounders
roundure
roundish
routeman
routeing
roulette
rouleaus
rouleaux
rough-hew
roughage
rough-dry
roughish
rough-out
rout-seat
revealer
revieval
reviewer
revved-up
reveille
ravelled
revelled
reveller
revolted
revolter
revolver
rivalled
rivelled
reviling
rivaless
rivalise
revolute
rivality
rivalize
revenger
revenges
revenued
revanche
ravingly
rovingly
ravening
revenant
ravenous
rove-over
reversal
riverman
river-rat
riverway
reversed
reverser
reverted
river-bed
reversis
riverain
△**reverend**
reverent
riverine
reversos
river-god
river-hog
reverist
ravisher
revision
revestry
revisory
revetted
rivetted
riveting
revivify
reviving
row-barge
rowndell
rowdedow
rowelled
rawboned
rewarder
rewarewa
rowdydow
rowdyish
rowdyism
rhythmal
rhythmed
rhythmic
rhythmus
Rhytisma
royalise
royalism
△royalist
rhyolite
royalize
roysting
razmataz
razor-cut
scalawag
soakaway
soaraway
stayaway
seawards
scarabee
scavager
seafarer
seawater
staragen
Scalaria
shamanic
sparaxis
scalable
seamanly
shakable
shamable
shapable
sparable
statable
scalados
swayback
sway-back
scambler
shambles
snap-brim
shabbily
soap-ball
slam-bang
slap-bang
stabbing
swabbing
shadblow
scabbard
shag-bark
slabbery
soapbark
swabbers
shadbush
searcher
snatcher
stanchel
stancher

Words marked △ may be spelled also with a capital letter

8 s□a□c

starched
starcher
scarcely
shauchle
shauchly
stanchly
seascape
scarcity
staccato
Scandian
Shandean
shaddock
spandrel
swaddler
standoff
stand-off
spandril
scalding
scaldini
scaldino
scandent
standing
standard
slap-dash
standish
stardust
scandium
shake-bag
shake-rag
shareman
spaceman
spademan
slaverer
stamened
stapedes
scavenge
space-age
Swadeshi
snake-oil
snake-pit
spageric
spanemia
spanemic
stapelia
statedly
scalenus
shake-out
shameful
share-out
spadeful
stake-out
staffage
scarf-pin
scaffold
spatfall
scarfing
scarfish
starfish
shanghai
spanghew
spangled

spangler
spanglet
shaggily
slangily
shagging
slagging
slanging
snagging
swagging
staggard
staggers
slangish
star-gaze
scaphoid
shashlik
seashell
scathing
slashing
smashing
swashing
stanhope
seashore
swanherd
spathose
spar-hawk
Scaridae
Sparidae
statical
shamisen
spadices
spavined
sea-fight
spagiric
spadille
spadillo
suasible
stadiums
shamiana
stasimon
Spaniard
Scabiosa
Shafiite
scabious
scarious
spacious
slapjack
snack-bar
shackles
sparkler
sparklet
stalkoes
sharking
skanking
smacking
spanking
stacking
stalking
swanking
swankpot
starkers
sparkish

smallsat
Stahlian
stallman
stall-fed
smallage
stallage
starlike
swanlike
seaplane
shawling
snap-link
snarling
soapland
spalling
span-long
sparling
stabling
stalling
starling
swayling
scallion
shalloon
smallpox
stallion
small-arm
snailery
scarless
seamless
seatless
smallish
soapless
spanless
△spätlese
stablish
Stahlism
starless
stayless
seablite
shallows
scarmoge
smalmily
smarmily
scammony
shamming
slamming
swarming
swan-mark
shammash
swan-neck
scanning
spanning
spawning
stagnant
staining
swaining
swanning
△stannary
swannery
searness
swainish
stagnate

stannate
stannite
stannous
seasonal
seawoman
seasoned
seasoner
shadower
spadones
Slavonia
Slavonic
seaborne
sea-going
seahound
seamount
seaboard
seacoast
seahorse
starosta
starosty
△seaspeak
stampede
stampedo
sharp-set
spalpeen
shagpile
snappily
scalping
scalpins
scamping
scarping
sharping
slapping
snapping
stamping
swapping
shampoo'd
shampoos
seal-pipe
scampish
sharpish
snappish
scalprum
sharp-cut
star-pav'd
stairway
star-read
shabrack
shamrock
sea-green
shagreen
seacraft
starrily
seadrome
scarring
seafront
sparring
starring
shagroon
soaproot
spadroon

sea-grape
scabrous
swagsman
soapsuds
seamster
slaister
sealskin
staysail
swanskin
swan-skin
spansule
sparsely
swan-song
scansion
slapshot
snapshot
starspot
swagshop
swan-shot
swap-shop
sparsity
scanties
startled
startler
svastika
swastika
scantily
scatting
shafting
shantung
slanting
starting
swatting
swaption
scattery
shattery
slattern
slattery
starters
Shaktism
smartass
smartish
startish
scantity
scawtite
smaltite
startful
scapulae
scapular
scapulas
spatular
shamuses
statured
statuses
seaquake
seacunny
statuary
Shabuoth
Shavuoth
starving
Shaivism

Words marked △ may be spelled also with a capital letter

Shaivite
spaewife
spaw-well
soapwort
stalwart
starwort
△sealyham
scaly-leg
spagyric
stanzoes
stanzaic
subbasal
sabbatic
Sobranje
subcaste
Sobranye
subabbot
subacrid
subucula
subacute
subadult
submerge
subgenre
sublease
submerse
subtense
subverse
subverst
sabre-cut
subgenus
subserve
subagent
subahdar
subchief
subchord
subshrub
subsizar
subtidal
subviral
sublimed
subfield
subtilly
subtitle
sobriety
subtilty
sibyllic
subclaim
sabuline
sibilant
subfloor
sabulose
subclass
sibilate
subtlety
subulate
sabulous
sibilous
subimago
subpolar
subsolar
subtotal
subvocal
subzonal
subsonic
subtonic
subtopia
subpoena
subcosta
subequal
saburral
suburban
subtribe
suberect
subtract
subgrade
subtrude
subbreed
suborder
suborner
suburbia
subframe
sobering
subprior
soberise
subcrust
suberise
suberose
subtrist
suberate
△sybarite
suberous
subgroup
soberize
suberize
sebesten
sabotier
sabotage
substage
substyle
subitise
sybotism
substate
saboteur
subitize
subaural
subdural
subhuman
sublunar
Subbuteo®
subaudio
subhumid
subduple
subovate
suboxide
saccadic
sacraria
Socratic
sociable
sociably
socially
sectator
secodont
societal
sickener
socketed
suckener
suckered
sachemic
secretin
sacredly
secretly
sickerly
sockette
sackfuls
suck-hole
succinct
succinic
sacristy
succinyl
Sicilian
Siculian
sicklied
so-called
suchlike
sicklily
suckling
Siceliot
sucklers
sackless
sacellum
sycamine
sycamore
sycomore
Sicanian
Socinian
secondee
seconder
secantly
secondly
sickness
suchness
secundum
syconium
sectoral
Suctoria
sucurujú
securely
sickroom
security
secesher
saccular
succubae
succubas
saccules
secluded
sacculus
succubus
suchwise
sad-faced
sidearms
sideband
seducing
seductor
suddenly
suddenty
sidekick
sidelock
sidalcea
soda-lake
sideline
sideling
sidelong
saddlery
sedulity
sodalite
sodality
sedulous
sodamide
sediment
sudamina
sodomise
△sodomite
sodomize
Sudanese
sidenote
sidepath
sidereal
sideroad
sederunt
siderate
siderite
sudarium
sudorous
sidesman
sidestep
sadistic
sideslip
sideshow
sedately
sedation
sedition
sudation
sudatory
sedative
Sadducee
siddurim
sidewalk
sidewall
sideward
sidewise
sideways
spelaean
seecatch
scenario
Sheraton
skewback
stembuck
skewbald
spekboom
seed-coat
skeechan
sketcher
swelchie
seedcake
seed-corn
seedcase
speedway
shelduck
steadied
steadier
speldrin
speedily
spendall
steadily
stepdame
sheading
shedding
sledding
speeding
spelding
spending
steading
speed-cop
speedful
step-down
scelerat
sceneman
skeletal
skene-dhu
she-devil
stereome
skeleton
suedette
siege-gun
seed-fish
stedfast
shelf-ful
sleigher
Spergula
Svengali
sledging
seething
stephane
△shepherd
shechita
scenical
shehitah
Shekinah
specimen
specific
syenitic
sterigma
speciate
specious
sneaksby
speckled
sneakily
sleeking
sneaking
speaking
sheikdom
sneakish
sneak-cup
speakout
seed-leaf

Words marked △ may be spelled also with a capital letter

8 s□e□l

steelman
seed-lobe
shell-ice
△sherlock
skelloch
stenlock
seemlier
steelmen
stellify
stealthy
seedlike
seedling
shealing
sheeling
sheiling
shelling
△shetland
smelling
spelling
sperling
stealing
steeling
△sterling
swealing
swelling
steelbow
stellion
swelldom
swell-mob
seedless
seemless
stemless
swellish
stellate
shellful
spellful
steamily
steaming
stemming
spermary
stemmata
spermous
sternway
sternage
skean-dhu
steaning
steening
steining
steenbok
sternson
seedness
Siennese
skewness
shea-nuts
sternite
stenosed
stenoses
stenosis
stenotic
stegodon
sweep-saw

sheep-pen
steepled
sweep-net
sheep-dip
steapsin
sleepily
skelping
skepping
sleeping
sneaping
stepping
stewpond
sweeping
seed-plot
sheepdog
sheep-pox
sheep-rot
sleepery
sheepish
steepish
sheep-run
sleep-out
shearman
smear-dab
spearman
skerrick
shearleg
sheerleg
stearage
steerage
smearily
shearing
sneering
stearine
steering
swearing
shear-hog
stearate
seedsman
sneeshan
△spetsnaz
speisade
sneeshin
sceattas
sceptral
spectral
sweet-bay
sceptred
sheathed
shea-tree
sweetpea
sheet-tin
sweet-oil
seed-time
steatoma
scenting
sheeting
smelting
stetting
sweating
sweeting

sweetsop
sheltery
smeltery
sweetish
smectite
spectate
steatite
scentful
spectrum
stentour
specular
Shevuoth
saeculum
speculum
sleeveen
steevely
shelving
sleeving
steeving
swerving
sherwani
stepwise
seedy-toe
△**spetznaz**
sleazily
sneezing
safranin
softback
soft-boil
softball
soft-core
softener
sufferer
softhead
suffixal
sufficer
siftings
soffioni
softling
sufflate
siffleur
safeness
softness
safronal
suffrage
saffrony
safarist
soft-soap
Sufistic
soft-sell
soft-shoe
soft-slow
softwood
software
signaled
signaler
sigmatic
signally
saguaros
sagacity
signeted

segreant
segueing
signieur
signless
segolate
sagamore
sageness
sagenite
saginate
signoria
sago-palm
signpost
sugaring
sigisbei
sigisbeo
sagittal
sightsee
sighting
schläger
schnapps
schmaltz
schedule
schiedam
schnecke
schleppy
sphygmic
sphagnum
sphygmus
Sahelian
schiller
scholion
schellum
scholium
schimmel
scheming
schemata
sphinges
sphinxes
sphenoid
sphingid
schantze
schooled
schooner
schlocky
schmooze
schapska
spherics
spheroid
spherule
scherzos
Schizaea
schizoid
schizont
shikaree
shiralee
shivaree
spicated
spirated
sailable
seizable
spiracle

spirally
suitable
suitably
Shivaism
Shivaite
suivante
sail-boat
stibbler
shinbone
stilbene
stilbite
sticcado
snitcher
spitcher
stitched
stitcher
stitches
switchel
scincoid
slipcase
suitcase
spiccato
sticcato
slip-dock
skin-deep
swindler
skidding
sliddery
shireman
shiverer
spikelet
sciaenid
Spigelia
shigella
snivelly
swine-pox
seicento
spinette
stiletto
swine-sty
smileful
spiteful
stived-up
sniffler
sniffles
sainfoin
sniffily
sniffing
spiffing
skinfood
slipform
△spitfire
sailfish
stiffish
skiagram
sting-ray
shingled
shingler
shingles
sniggler
stingily

stinging
swigging
swinging
smidgeon
swingism
shithead
skinhead
shithole
slightly
swishing
slithery
smithers
smithery
scimitar
suicidal
scilicet
spinifex
spirited
stipites
suitings
spilikin
spilitic
spirilla
spiritus
skipjack
stickjaw
spicknel
stickler
stickily
skinking
slicking
sticking
stinking
slipknot
stinkard
stickful
shipload
spillway
shielder
spillage
stillage
saibling
shieling
shilling
skilling
skirling
slimline
spilling
spirling
stifling
stilling
suilline
swilling
skillion
stillion
saikless
sailless
sciolism
sciolist
shipless
skilless
skinless
soilless
stirless
Seidlitz
sciolous
skillful
swill-tub
shipment
skimming
slimming
swimming
shimmery
seismism
skirmish
slimmest
slimmish
shipmate
stigmata
scienced
sciences
scienter
spinnies
skinning
spinning
seignior
seignory
spinnery
slimness
stibnite
seigneur
spinneys
scirocco
slip-over
slivovic
sailorly
smilodon
stippled
stippler
slippage
skimpily
shipping
skimping
skipping
slipping
snipping
slippery
snippety
sciuroid
sliprail
sciurine
shirring
stirring
sailroom
suitress
scirrhus
snip-snap
spinster
swimsuit
scissile
swissing
scission
slipshod
slip-shoe
slipslop
scissors
scissure
Swiftian
sciatica
skittles
swiftlet
shiitake
shiftily
shirtily
shifting
shirting
shitting
skirting
slitting
spitting
stilting
stinting
saintdom
skiatron
spittoon
stiction
ship-tire
snifters
saintess
saintish
saintism
skittish
stiltish
spintext
spin-text
spicular
stipular
stipuled
spiculum
stimulus
stievely
spivvery
swimwear
shipworm
slipware
sail-yard
shipyard
Sikelian
Sikeliot
△sikorsky
sukiyaki
silladar
saltando
selvagee
sulcated
△sylvaner
silvatic
sultanic
syllabic
sylvatic
saleable
saleably
salvable
sellable
solvable
syllable
sol-faing
soldados
sol-faism
sol-faist
sillabub
syllabub
syllabus
self-born
saltbush
selictar
silicide
selected
selectee
silicify
silicula
silicule
salicine
silicone
selector
solecise
solecism
solecist
salacity
saliceta
salt-cote
silicate
solicity
silicium
solecize
solidify
solidago
salading
seladang
solidare
solidary
solidish
solidism
solidist
solidate
solidity
salience
saliency
solvency
solderer
solleret
selvedge
solfeggi
silverly
sullenly
salified
salt-foot
saltfish
silaging
selfheal
sulphide
sylphide
self-help
sulphone
selfhood
sulphury
sylphish
self-hate
sulphate
sulphite
△silphium
salvific
Salvinia
sylviine
salpicon
saltiers
soldiery
sulfinyl
salt-junk
self-left
self-life
self-like
saltless
selfless
self-lost
self-love
self-made
shlemiel
solemnis
solemnly
salt-mine
selenian
Solonian
splenial
selenide
silenced
silencer
solander
splinter
solenoid
splendid
silently
solanine
splendor
saltness
selfness
soleness
salinity
selenate
selenite
solonets
solonetz
selenium
selenous
splenium
splenius
salmonet
salmonid
selcouth
△salopian
shlepper
self-pity
salariat
Silurian
salaried

8 s□l□r

sclereid
scleroid
siluroid
self-rule
sultrily
sclerema
scleroma
salering
saleroom
sclerose
△silurist
solarise
solarism
solarist
sclerite
sclerous
solarium
solarize
Salesian
salesman
Salishan
seldseen
splasher
Silastic®
silastic
self-same
self-sown
solstice
solitude
splatter
split-new
splitted
splitter
splutter
split-off
splotchy
silktail
solation
solution
salutary
solitary
solatium
solutive
saltuses
Seleucid
solpugid
sulfuric
salivary
salivate
silkweed
self-will
saltwort
silkworm
sally-man
sallying
sullying
silly-how
saleyard
sympathy
semi-arid
semi-axis
somebody
semibold
semibull
semicoma
somedeal
somedele
semi-dome
simperer
summerly
symmetry
somegate
symphile
symphily
Symphyla
symphony
samphire
sumphish
summital
sumpitan
samnitis
somnific
symbiont
summitry
somniate
semplice
symploce
simplify
sampling
semblant
semilune
semolina
simpling
simulant
Sémillon
samplery
similise
simplism
simplist
symplast
simulate
simulium
shmaltzy
similize
semi-mute
simoniac
semi-nude
semantic
semuncia
Seminole
semantra
seminary
sameness
simonist
seminate
semi-opal
summoner
semiotic
symbolic
sympodia
symposia
Sumerian
simaruba
somerset
sombrely
semi-ring
sombrero
samarium
sombrous
semester
sempster
semi-soft
Semitics
sometime
semitone
sumotori
symitare
Semitise
Semitism
Semitist
somatism
somatist
semitaur
Semitize
Samaveda
Sama-Veda
somewhat
somewhen
somewise
someways
samizdat
△**simazine**
sandarac
sunwards
sangaree
sin-eater
sinuated
sunbaked
sunbathe
santalin
syngamic
singable
syntagma
syntagms
syncarpy
Santalum
sandbank
songbook
sonobuoy
songbird
Sanscrit
synechia
synectic
senecios
sinecure
sand-cast
sinicise
Sinicism
sinicize
synedria
sand-dune
sanidine
sand-dart
sentence
sundered
sunderer
sanserif
syndesis
syndetic
syntexis
sunbeamy
singeing
sunberry
senseful
sand-flag
songfest
sonogram
sandheap
sunshade
sandhill
sinkhole
sunshine
sunshiny
syndical
sandiver
sentinel
sindings
syndings
sennight
se'nnight
sunlight
Sinaitic
sinuitis
sensible
sensibly
sensilla
sentient
sinciput
Sanskrit
sunblock
sanglier
Sinology
songlike
senilely
sandling
singling
sunblind
sun-blind
sun-blink
syncline
sand-lark
songless
sunglass
senility
Senonian
son-in-law
synanthy
synonymy
saneness
syncopal
santonin
sensoria
sinfonia
syncopic
syntonic
syntonin
sand-peep
synaphea
synapses
synopses
Sinophil
synapsis
synaptic
synopsis
synoptic
sandpump
sinapism
sinopite
Sangraal
Sangreal
Sangrado
sengreen
sun-dried
sundries
sentry-go
synarchy
Sangrail
synergic
synergid
syndrome
sonorant
sunproof
sundrops
syngraph
sundress
Señorita
sonority
senarius
sonorous
sand-star
sinister
songster
Senussis
sinusoid
sing-sing
singsong
sandshoe
synastry
sanctify
sonatina
sunstone
sanction
sanatory
sanitary
sanitise
sanctity
sanitate
sanative
sanitize
singular
sun-cured
sanguify
sinfully
sanguine
sunburnt

Words marked △ may be spelled also with a capital letter

Senoussi
sunburst
sensuous
synovial
sandwich
sandworm
sandwort
syncytia
sannyasi
stomatal
stowaway
stomachy
sporadic
stomatic
smokable
storable
stovaine
showboat
slowback
scombrid
shoebill
snowball
stopbank
smørbrød
snowboot
slobbery
slow-burn
snobbery
snowbird
slobbish
sloebush
snobbish
snobbism
snowbush
slop-bowl
stopcock
stoccado
scorched
scorcher
sloucher
shot-clog
snow-capt
showcase
stoicism
stoccata
sword-law
swordman
spondaic
shoddily
scolding
snowdrop
sword-arm
scordato
sword-cut
showdown
slow-down
stowdown
shoreman
stone-mad
stonerag
stoneraw

storeman
scoleces
shoveler
sloe-eyed
snow-eyes
storeyed
Stone-Age
stone-age
△scolecid
scopelid
slovenly
stonefly
smoke-box
slovenry
smoke-dry
Scopelus
scofflaw
scot-free
shot-free
snowfall
scoffing
spoofery
scomfish
spoffish
sloughed
spongoid
spongily
stodgily
shogging
slogging
shop-girl
showgirl
soothsay
shothole
snow-hole
Shoshone
Shoshoni
sloshing
soothing
shoehorn
smothery
slothful
soothful
Scotican
skokiaan
scolices
sporidia
stotinka
stotinki
stolidly
scolioma
spoliate
scorious
stocious
stotious
stockman
stockade
spookily
stockily
shocking
smocking

stocking
stonking
stockpot
spookery
spookish
stockist
shoelace
shoulder
smoulder
spoilage
snowlike
Scotland
scowling
shoaling
shouldn't
slobland
snobling
snowline
stowlins
smouldry
shoeless
shouldst
snowless
sootless
spotless
stopless
stop-loss
spoilful
stormily
spooming
storming
stormful
spoonfed
spoon-fed
spoonily
scorning
swooning
scoinson
slowness
scornful
spoonful
Scolopax
scotomas
stopover
Scopolia
scotomia
scotopia
scotopic
slogorne
Sporozoa
scoop-net
stoppage
slop-pail
slowpoke
sloppily
scooping
shopping
slopping
stooping
stopping
swopping

△scorpion
Scorpios
scoopful
Scorpius
scourger
scouring
showroom
shofroth
Scotsman
spousage
snowslip
stooshie
spousals
sponsing
slop-shop
snowshoe
sponsion
short-day
Scottice
scouther
scowther
shoetree
shouther
sloetree
smoothen
smoother
Scottify
shortage
short-oil
smoothie
smoothly
snootily
snottily
sportily
spottily
scouting
shooting
shotting
shouting
slotting
snorting
sporting
spotting
spouting
Storting
swotting
scontion
spontoon
shortarm
snottery
Scottish
shootist
shortish
stoutish
shoot-out
short-cut
snootful
sportful
sportive
shogunal
sporular

spot-weld
shopworn
slopwork
slowworm
scolytid
storying
showyard
Scolytus
sforzati
sforzato
smorzato
Sephardi
septaria
sapsagos
sopranos
sapucaia
sapidity
sapience
suppeago
sapremia
sapremic
sopheric
sopherim
supremos
septette
sept-foil
sapphics
sapphire
△sapphism
sapphist
septimal
syphilis
supplial
sepalody
supplied
supplier
supplies
sepaloid
supplely
sepaline
supplant
sepalous
septleva
sepiment
saponify
supinely
saponite
supinate
Sapindus
siphonal
supposal
sapropel
siphonet
supposed
supposer
supposes
siphonic
superman
supernal
supertax
superadd

8 s□p□r

sap-green
superjet
superego
superbly
superior
superloo
superspy
soporose
suppress
separate
superate
saporous
soporous
supergun
sapi-utan
septuple
sequelae
sequence
sequined
surbahar
sarpanch
sortance
Syriarch
screamer
serrated
spreader
streaked
streaker
streamer
striated
surbased
surbated
surfaced
surfacer
spreathe
Sarmatia
Sarmatic
sarrasin
sarrazin
seriatim
serranid
siriasis
sorbaria
serially
sortable
sargasso
servants
Serranus
serratus
striatum
scrabbed
scrubbed
scrubber
Scrabble®
scrabble
scribble
scribbly
strobila
strobile
strobili
saraband
scribing
surfbird
scribism
strabism
surucucu
sprocket
stricken
soricoid
sprackle
sprucely
strickle
strictly
soricine
siroccos
sericite
suricate
soredial
shredded
shredder
spredden
stridden
shraddha
shred-pie
straddle
striddle
stroddle
strident
stradiot
soredium
shrieval
surveyal
sarcenet
sarsenet
screeder
screener
screever
shrieker
shrieved
sorcerer
streeted
screechy
spreethe
sardelle
sergeant
serjeant
sur-reyn'd
surveyor
surcease
sarmenta
sirvente
surgeful
surrebut
scrofula
serafile
sure-fire
surffish
scragged
spragged
sprigged
scroggie
seraglio
scraggly
scriggle
scriggly
straggle
straggly
struggle
scrag-end
strigine
Strigops
strigose
strigate
sorehead
serfhood
surgical
surmisal
survival
△services
spruiker
strained
strainer
straiten
surmiser
straicht
straight
streight
sorbitic
sordidly
straitly
surtitle
servient
streigne
servitor
sorbitol
survivor
sorriest
spraints
striking
stroking
surplice
scrolled
stroller
serology
serflike
strelitz
scramjet
scrammed
scrimped
scrummed
shrimper
strammel
Strimmer®
strummed
strummel
strumpet
scramble
scrimply
sortment
scrumpox
scrimure
stramash
strumose
stromata
strombus
strumous
sirenian
springal
serenade
scrannel
shrinker
shrunken
springed
springer
sprinter
stranded
stranger
stringed
stringer
stronger
syringes
syrinxes
scrunchy
strontia
serenely
sprangle
springle
sprinkle
strangle
strinkle
strongly
sirenise
soreness
spryness
sureness
serenata
serenate
serenity
strength
strongyl
sirenize
sarcomas
surroyal
Sarcodes
sermoner
sermonet
sorrowed
sorrower
strooken
sarcodic
sardonic
sermonic
Sorbonne
surmount
surround
sardonyx
scrap-man
Strepyan
scrapped
scripted
scrupler
scruples
shrapnel
strapped
strapper
stripped
stripper
stropped
seraphic
seraphim
seraphin
strap-oil
strophic
scrapple
scraping
strepent
striping
Strephon
Serapeum
Sartrian
sororial
sororise
surprise
sororate
sorority
sororize
stressed
serfship
stressor
serosity
spritzer
strutted
strutter
stratify
Saratoga
strategy
scratchy
stretchy
spritzig
struthio
scrattle
sprattle
spritely
scrutiny
serotine
sorption
serotype
stratose
stratous
serpulae
stroupan
sprauncy
surquedy
scrouger
shrouded
sorbuses
sprouted
scrounge
straunge
straucht
straught
surculus
stravaig
Serevent®
shriving

Words marked △ may be spelled also with a capital letter

striving
straw-hat
scrawler
sprawler
scrowdge
strewage
shrewdie
shrewdly
screwing
strewing
strowing
screwtop
shrewish
straying
sorryish
Sassanid
sesterce
suspence
systemed
systemic
sisterly
suspense
sestette
sestetto
syssitia
sessions
sesamoid
sassolin
systolic
sesspool
sastruga
sastrugi
sasarara
siserary
susurrus
Sathanas
satrapal
situated
satiable
sitz-bath
setscrew
Sotadean
sithence
sitter-in
setter-on
setter-up
setiform
set-piece
satelles
sitology
settling
sateless
setulose
setulous
se-tenant
satanism
Satanist
satanity
shtupped
Saturday
soterial
sutorial
sutorian
Saturnia
saturnic
saturant
satirise
satirist
satyress
satyrisk
saturate
satirize
set-aside
slug-a-bed
squeaker
squealer
soutache
sfumatos
stubbled
stumbler
squabble
slubbing
snubbing
stubbing
studbook
slumbery
stubborn
snubbish
squabash
scutcher
sous-chef
stuccoed
stuccoer
sour-cold
sourcing
squaccos
soundman
souldier
sturdied
squaddie
sturdily
scudding
sounding
sourdine
spudding
studding
squadron
shuddery
Stundism
Stundist
shutdown
saucepan
sour-eyed
squeegee
squeezer
souvenir
scutella
souterly
sautéing
Sauterne
saucebox
souped-up
scuffler
shuffler
snuffler
snuffles
squiffer
stuffily
snuffing
stuffing
snuffbox
snuffers
studfarm
scumfish
slugfest
smuggled
smuggler
squegger
smudgily
spur-gall
squiggle
squiggly
snugging
sturgeon
saufgard
sluggard
snuggery
sluggish
southpaw
southsay
souchong
southing
scuchion
△southron
slughorn
△southern
scutiger
squailer
stupidly
sauciest
saucisse
spurious
studious
shucking
skulking
stunkard
skullcap
squaller
squilgee
squelchy
spuilzie
squaloid
souvlaki
sculling
spurling
squalene
scullion
scullery
slumlord
shunless
soulless
spurless
slummock
squamula
squamule
scumming
slumming
stumming
squamose
Squamata
squamate
squamous
squander
squinter
stub-nail
sturnoid
shunning
spurning
stunning
sturnine
smugness
snugness
sourness
sauropod
stumpage
sculpsit
stumpily
sculptor
scuppers
sourpuss
scuppaug
spur-rial
spur-ryal
squarial
scurrier
spurrier
squireen
squirrel
squirter
squirage
scurrile
squarely
squirely
slurring
spurring
squaring
squarson
squarish
squiress
stuprate
soul-scat
soul-sick
squasher
stunsail
soul-scot
soul-shot
stuntman
scuttler
squatted
squatter
stultify
smuttily
squattle
shunting
shutting
sluttery
sputtery
sluttish
Saururae
scurvily
squawman
squawker
studwork
studying
spunyarn
sovranly
sovranty
sovietic
savagely
savagery
savegard
savagism
savannah
seven-day
savingly
suversed
severely
severity
savorous
savoured
savourly
△savoyard
saw-edged
sawed-off
sawshark
sawblade
sewellel
sawbones
saw-tones
sawhorse
sawtooth
sewer-gas
sewer-rat
sowbread
sowarree
sewerage
saw-frame
sewering
sow-drunk
sawdusty
sexually
sixscore
sixpence
sixpenny
sextette
sixtieth
sexology
Saxonian
Saxondom
Saxonise
Saxonism
Saxonist
sexiness
saxonite
Saxonize

8 S□X□O

sextolet
saxatile
sextuple
skywards
scybalum
skyscape
Scythian
say-piece
skydiver
skylight
spyplane
spyglass
sayonara
spy-money
slyboots
styluses
sizeable
syzygial
syzygies
sizzling
siziness
suzerain
tearaway
thanadar
thataway
thalamic
tearable
tradable
thalamus
trap-ball
thatched
thatcher
tranchet
trauchle
twaddler
T-bandage
trapdoor
teaseled
teaseler
traveled
traveler
trade-off
trapezia
tsarevna
thanedom
travelog
teaberry
traverse
trabeate
travesty
tradeful
toadflax
trap-fall
trayfuls
toadfish
twanging
tracheae
tracheal
trashcan
trashman
tracheid

trashily
trachoma
teaching
trashery
trachyte
tragical
traditor
trahison
tsaritsa
trackman
trackway
trackage
thanking
tracking
thankyou
thankful
trail-net
trawl-net
thalloid
traplike
thalline
trailing
tramline
trawling
tearless
thawless
thallium
thallous
Teasmade®
trammels
tramming
team-mate
traumata
train-oil
training
trainers
thatness
tragopan
teaboard
trappean
trampler
tramping
trapping
teaspoon
trampish
Trappist
tranquil
tramroad
traprock
toadrush
transact
transect
transude
teamster
transfer
transmew
toad-spit
transfix
tranship
transmit
transume

tram-stop
transept
transire
twattler
tractrix
tray-trip
tractile
tjanting
toasting
traction
tractors
tractate
tractive
traducer
trapunto
teamwork
teamwise
toadying
toadyish
toadyism
tzatziki
tubicole
tobaccos
table-mat
tabletop
tableaux
table-cut
tableful
tubefuls
tubiform
taboggan
toboggan
toboggin
Tubigrip®
tub-thump
tabbinet
tubelike
Tebilise
tubeless
tabulate
tubulate
tubulous
Tebilize®
tubenose
tabloidy
to-broken
tabooing
taberdar
tubercle
tuberose
Taborite
tuberous
tabashir
tabouret
tabourin
to-bruise
tube-well
tabbying
tuckahoe
tic-tac-to
ticketed

tacked-on
tacahout
tactical
tachinid
tachisme
tachiste
tocology
tackling
tickling
tactless
ticklish
tuck-mill
technics
taconite
tick-over
tectonic
Tychonic
tacksman
tick-shop
tick-tack
tick-tick
tick-tock
tucotuco
tucutuco
taciturn
tac-au-tac
tack-weld
tadvance
tide-gate
tide-lock
tideland
toddling
tideless
tidemill
tidemark
tidiness
tidesman
tedesche
tedeschi
tedisome
tidivate
tidewave
toddy-cat
toe-dance
teenaged
teenager
thematic
trematic
trevally
thebaine
thesauri
trembler
trembles
therblig
Theaceae
theocrat
treacher
trencher
△trenches
tree-calf
theodicy

treadler
tweedler
trendily
treading
Tremella
therefor
trecento
thereout
theogony
teething
trephine
thetical
theriaca
toe-piece
taenioid
tredille
taeniate
trekking
tweaking
theology
teemless
thewless
treeless
thermion
thermite
treenail
theonomy
tweeness
teetotal
theropod
toe-to-toe
tremolos
teetotum
△**thespian**
trespass
tie-break
thearchy
theurgic
theorbos
theorise
theorist
theorize
trewsman
tsessebe
theistic
treeship
themself
theosoph
treasure
△treasury
tressure
theatral
twenties
theatric
Theatine
treating
trey-tine
treatise
twelvemo
tweezers
taffetas

Words marked △ may be spelled also with a capital letter

tafferel
tefillah
tefillin
taffrail
taghairm
tagmemic
teguexin
tegmenta
tug-of-war
taglioni
Togolese
tegument
tigerish
tigerism
tiger-eye
tightwad
together
tightish
Tahitian
trimaran
thio-acid
tribadic
tribasic
twin-axis
tribally
△tridacna
trivalve
tailback
trilbies
tail-boom
twin-born
tail-coat
twitcher
twiddier
thirding
Triodion
triadist
tripedal
tripeman
toiseach
tail-ends
toileted
trimeter
trimeric
trisemic
trilemma
taileron
toiletry
toilette
trifecta
triffidy
thingamy
thigging
tailgate
trichoid
twichild
trichome
trichina
triphone
trip-hook
trichord

trichite
tritical
toilinet
tailings
twilight
twi-night
tritiate
Triticum
thickoes
thickset
tricklet
twinkler
trickily
triskele
thinking
tricking
trickery
thickish
trickish
thickety
trial-day
trialled
trilloes
thirlage
triploid
tail-like
tail-lamp
trifling
trilling
triplane
tripling
twinling
trillion
triglyph
tailless
toilless
trialism
trialist
triality
tailleur
trillium
triumvir
thiamine
trimming
triangle
thinning
twinning
thinners
thinness
thinnest
thinnish
thisness
trigness
trimness
triunity
trifocal
trigonal
tripodal
trizonal
tailored
trilobed

triforia
trigonic
trisomic
tritonia
Trizonia
tricorne
tricolor
triapsal
thiophen
trippler
thiophil
trippant
tripping
tailpipe
trippery
tailrace
tribrach
triarchy
tail-rope
trigraph
thirster
tailskid
tailspin
Triassic
twinship
thio-salt
toilsome
twigsome
thin-spun
thin-sown
tric-trac
triptych
tristich
thirteen
thirties
triptane
twisting
twitting
tainture
twittery
triptote
tristful
triethyl
tribunal
thiourea
tributer
Trimurti
thieving
thievery
thievish
toil-worn
tripwire
triaxial
trioxide
Trigynia
tricycle
thiazide
thiazine
takeaway
takeable
take-down

take-home
tokology
takamaka
takingly
tokenism
takeover
talkable
tellable
tillable
tiltable
tollable
tilt-boat
talkback
toll-bait
telechir
telecoms
telecine
telecast
tolldish
talk-down
Toltecan
telferic
toll-free
telefilm
talkfest
tilefish
telegram
telegony
toll-gate
tile-hung
talliate
talukdar
talcking
telemark
telomere
talented
tallness
talionic
tolbooth
teleplay
Tylopoda
talapoin
thlipsis
tulipant
teleport
telepath
telergic
tolerant
tolerate
talesman
talisman
telestic
telesale
teleseme
talkshow
telltale
tell-tale
telethon
teletron
Teletype®
teletext

tellural
Talmudic
telluric
teleview
televise
toleware
tallyman
tallying
tally-ho'd
tally-hos
tilt-yard
tympanal
tympanic
tameable
tympanum
time-ball
time-bill
timecard
timidity
tumidity
tamperer
tempered
temperer
timbered
tumefied
tomogram
tomahawk
Tamilian
tomalley
temulent
tumbling
tump-line
temblors
tumulary
tameless
timeless
tombless
template
timoneer
tamanoir
tameness
Timonise
Timonism
Timonist
tamandua
tomentum
Timonize
temporal
Tom-noddy
tombolos
tamboura
△tamworth
tamarack
timbrel'd
tamarind
timariot
tomorrow
tamarisk
temerity
temerous
timorous

8 t□m□t

tumorous
tomatoes
tomatoey
tempting
tamburin
timously
time-worn
tommy-rot
tommy-gun
time-zone
tendance
△**tantalic**
teniasis
tan-balls
tannable
tentacle
tuneable
tantalum
△tantalus
△**tenebrae**
△**tenebrio**
tunicked
tenacula
ten-score
tenacity
tonicity
Tunicata
tunicate
tone-deaf
tangency
tendence
tendency
tenpence
tenderer
tinkerer
tinseled
tunneled
tunneler
tenderly
tinselly
tunbelly
tenpenny
tingeing
tangelos
tinselry
tonneaus
tonneaux
tankfuls
tuna-fish
Tineidae
tonsilar
tontiner
tangible
tangibly
tenaille
tensible
tondinos
tanaiste
tenuious
tinnitus
tangling
tingling
tinkling
tentless
tinglish
tintless
toneless
tuneless
Tanalith®
tinplate
tonalite
tonality
tenement
tinsmith
tinsnips
tenantry
tininess
tenendum
tangoing
ten-pound
tandoori
tangoist
tenurial
tenoroon
Tantrism
Tantrist
tenorist
tenorite
tongster
tungsten
tungstic
tonishly
tanistry
tenesmus
tank-trap
tung-tree
tenotomy
tinstone
tint-tool
tincture
tong-test
tonsured
Tunguses
Tungusic
tonguing
tent-work
tentwise
thoracal
thoraces
thoraxes
two-faced
thoracic
troparia
teocalli
troubled
troubler
trombone
twoccing
two-score
trot-cozy
two-edged
twopence
twopenny
trogging
thoughts
trochlea
trophied
trochaic
trochoid
toothily
trochisk
trophesy
trochite
toothful
trothful
tropical
two-piece
two-sided
two-timer
two-digit
trominos
teosinte
trollies
trolling
trotline
toodle-oo
trollopy
thowless
troilism
troilist
troilite
trollius
trolleys
thornset
trouncer
two-power
△**thorough**
two-horse
troopial
troupial
two-speed
tool-room
tool-shed
Taoistic
thousand
trossers
trousers
trowsers
troutlet
trottoir
trotting
trouting
trout-rod
two-start
troutful
trouvère
trouveur
tap-dance
topmaker
tapeable
tappable
tippable
type-body
tapacolo
tapaculo
typecast
tapadera
tapadero
tepidity
tuppence
top-level
tuppenny
top-heavy
type-face
typified
typifier
type-high
top-shelf
top-shell
topliner
topsides
toppings
topology
typology
tapelike
tapeline
tape-loop
tape-lure
tapeless
tapenade
toponymy
Typhoean
top-notch
△typhonic
tap-house
toplofty
Typhoeus
toparchy
tapiroid
tapering
top-dress
tephrite
top-proud
tapestry
tape-tied
tipstaff
top-stone
topotype
tapeworm
tipsy-key
topazine
tequilla
toquilla
tarlatan
Tyrtaean
tar-paper
tartaned
tar-water
terraced
terraces
threaden
threader
threaten
throated
turbaned
△**tartaric**
Tartarie
terrapin
terraria
threapit
tornadic
tarnally
△tartarly
tarragon
toreador
tornados
tartanry
Tartarus
terrazzo
terebrae
terebras
turnback
turn-back
throbbed
terebene
turf-clad
turncoat
turncock
thridace
torn-down
turn-down
Tarpeian
three-man
three-way
targeted
tercelet
turreted
threepit
turmeric
terrella
three-ply
torpedos
terzetta
terzetti
terzetto
tarted-up
teraflop
tara-fern
torchier
tarwhine
torching
Tyrrhene
torchère
terminal
torminal
toroidal
turbinal
tarsiped
Tarsipes
terminer
tirrivee
turbined
turbines
turnings
tarsioid

Words marked △ may be spelled also with a capital letter

8 u□b□a

terrific
tirrivie
terrible
terribly
torpidly
torridly
tortilla
turbidly
turgidly
△**tertiary**
△**terminus**
tortious
tarakihi
terakihi
Tyrolean
thriller
Terylene®
tireling
turtling
thraldom
termless
tireless
torulose
tyreless
Tyrolese
thrum-cap
thrummed
thrummer
thrombin
tyramine
tiramisu
thrombus
tarantas
Tironian
Turanian
threnode
threnody
thronged
tyrannic
tyrannis
tartness
turbocar
turbofan
Turcoman
Turkoman
turbojet
turnover
turlough
tarboosh
tarboush
tortoise
thripses
teraphim
turnpike
thrapple
thropple
tar-brush
tartrate
thrasher
threshel
thresher

thrissel
thruster
turnskin
turnspit
thristle
throstle
turnsole
tiresome
tyrosine
teratoid
throttle
teratoma
term-time
teru-tero
teratism
torcular
tortured
torturer
Tartuffe
Targumic
toreutic
torquate
tortuous
thriving
throwing
thraward
thrawart
throw-out
teriyaki
tarrying
tastable
testable
testator
testamur
testatum
tesserae
tesseral
tasseled
tastevin
tasselly
tessella
tasteful
testicle
tuskless
tussocky
testrill
test-tube
testudos
tasswage
task-work
tetrarch
tetracid
tetradic
tetrapla
tithable
tetragon
tetrapod
tetraxon
titubant
titubate
tattered

titterer
tottered
totterer
tithe-pig
tetchily
totalled
tutelage
tattling
titulary
tutelary
totalise
totality
totalize
totemism
totemist
Titanian
tetanoid
tetanise
△titaness
△titanism
titanate
titanite
titanium
titanous
tetanize
tetronal
tattooed
tattooer
titmouse
titupped
tituping
Tatarian
tutorial
tutorage
tott'ring
tutoring
tutoress
tutorise
tutorism
tityre-tu
tutorize
totitive
tittuped
titivate
toucanet
touracos
true-bred
thumbpot
true-born
thumbnut
thumbs-up
true-blue
truncate
trundler
thudding
thundery
trumeaux
truffled
trudging
trudgeon
thuggery

thuggism
truchman
teuchter
truchmen
touchily
touching
touch-box
toughish
truthful
thurifer
thurible
touristy
truckman
truckler
truckage
trucking
trunking
trunkful
true-love
trunnion
tournure
truantry
tautness
thusness
trueness
tautomer
Teutonic
tautonym
thumping
trumping
trumpery
Teucrian
Thursday
truistic
tsutsumu
trussing
trustier
trustily
taunting
trusting
trustful
truquage
truqueur
thuswise
tovarich
taverner
tovarish
thwacker
towelled
toweling
townland
townling
tow-plane
townless
thwarted
thwarter
tawdrily
thwartly
towardly
towering
townsman

township
townskip
town-talk
taxiarch
tax-payer
textbook
Taxaceae
toxicant
toxocara
toxicity
tuxedoes
Taxodium
toxaemia
toxaemic
text-hand
textless
taxonomy
taxation
taxative
textural
textured
textuary
thyreoid
tayberry
tryingly
toywoman
thyloses
thylosis
thyroxin
try-house
thyrsoid
toyishly
unabated
unamazed
unawares
upadaisy
unanchor
up-anchor
unaneled
unargued
unaching
Upanisad
unarisen
uralitic
uranitic
unallied
unadored
unatoned
unavowed
unafraid
upas-tree
unartful
unactive
unamused
uranylic
umbrated
unbeaten
unbiased
unblamed
unbraced
umbratic

Words marked △ may be spelled also with a capital letter

8 u□b□a

unbraste
unbacked
unbuckle
unbedded
unbidden
unbodied
unbudded
unboding
unbreech
umble-pie
umbrella
umbrello
umbrette
unbegged
unbaited
unbridle
umbriere
umbellar
unbelief
unbelted
unbolted
unbanded
unbanked
unbended
unbonnet
unbenign
unbundle
urbanely
urbanise
umbonate
urbanite
urbanity
urbanize
unbloody
unblowed
unbooked
unbroken
unbarbed
unbarked
unbarred
unburden
unburied
unburned
unbereft
unburrow
unbeseem
unbishop
unbathed
unbitted
unbutton
unbrused
unbought
unchancy
uncoated
uncharge
unclassy
unchaste
unclench
unchewed
upcheard
uncreate

unciform
uncoined
uncalled
unculled
uncombed
uncomely
upcoming
uncommon
uncandid
uncinate
uncloudy
unchosen
unclosed
uncloven
uncooked
unclothe
urceolus
uncipher
uncurbed
uncurled
uncurved
upcurved
uncaring
ulcerate
ulcerous
uncashed
uncostly
unchurch
unclutch
uncaused
uncaught
upcaught
uncouple
unctuous
uncowled
uncoyned
undraped
undubbed
undecked
undocked
undecent
undeeded
undreamt
undefide
undefied
undriven
undulled
undulant
undulose
undulate
undulous
undammed
undamned
undamped
undimmed
undinted
undinism
undoomed
undrossy
undipped
under-jaw

underlap
underlay
underman
underpay
undersay
underway
underact
underfed
underlet
undersea
underset
under-age
underbid
underdid
underlie
underlip
underpin
underwit
undersky
under-boy
underdog
undertow
underarm
underuse
udderful
underbuy
undercut
underfur
underrun
undashed
undesert
undouble
undivine
undevout
undazzle
unelated
unending
ureteral
ureteric
unevenly
urethrae
urethral
urethras
urethane
unedited
uredines
uredinia
uteritis
unespied
unearned
unerring
uneasily
uneathes
usefully
unenvied
unfeared
unflawed
unframed
unfabled
unfading
unfreeze

unfairly
unfriend
unfilial
unfallen
unfelled
unfilled
unfilmed
unfolded
unfolder
upfollow
unfanned
unfenced
unfunded
unfooted
unfrozen
unformal
unforced
unforged
unformed
unfurred
unforbid
unforgot
unfasten
unfished
unfetter
unfitted
unfeudal
unfought
unfaulty
unfixity
ungeared
unglazed
ungraced
ungraded
ungrazed
upgrader
ungifted
unguided
ungainly
unguilty
ungalled
ungilded
Ungulata
ungulate
ungummed
ungenial
ungentle
ungently
urgently
ungloved
unground
upgrowth
ungirded
ungorged
ungotten
upgather
ungauged
ungiving
ungowned
upheaval
unhealed

unheated
unhearse
unhealth
unhacked
unhedged
unhidden
unheeded
unhailed
unhaired
unhalsed
unhelmed
unhelped
unholpen
upholder
unholily
unhallow
unhomely
unhanged
unhinged
unhunted
unhonest
unhooded
unheppen
unharmed
unheroic
ushering
usheress
unhatted
unhatch'd
unhoused
urinator
univalve
unimbued
unitedly
universe
unifilar
utiliser
utilizer
unionise
△unionism
△unionist
unionize
unilobar
unipolar
unisonal
univocal
unilobed
unironed
unicolor
uninured
uniquely
ubiquity
uniaxial
unicycle
unifying
unjustly
unjoyful
unjoyous
unknight
unkenned
unkennel

Words marked △ may be spelled also with a capital letter

unkindly
unkingly
unkissed
unleaded
unleased
unloaded
unloader
unlearnt
unlicked
unlocked
uplocked
unlidded
unlading
uilleann
uplifted
uplifter
unlikely
unlimber
unlineal
unlinked
uplander
ugliness
unlooked
unloosen
unlopped
unlorded
unlordly
unlisted
unlively
unlovely
unliving
unloving
unlawful
unmoaned
Ulmaceae
unmodish
unmade-up
unmeetly
unmuffle
unmailed
unmaimed
unmaking
upmaking
unmelted
unmilked
unmilled
unmanned
unminded
unmonied
unmantle
unmarked
unmarred
up-market
unmasked
unmasker
unmissed
un-Mosaic
unmoving
unmuzzle
uintaite
unneeded
urnfield
unnaneld
unnerved
unnethes
unnetted
unnative
uroscopy
urodelan
udometer
unobeyed
unopened
Ulothrix
urochord
utopiast
uxorious
urologic
urostege
urostyle
urostomy
unplaced
unplayed
unpraise
unpacked
unpacker
unpicked
unpreach
unpeeled
unpeered
unpoetic
unpretty
unpained
unpaired
unpoised
unpriced
unprimed
unprized
unpliant
unpoison
unprison
unpriest
umptieth
unpolled
unpulled
unpolish
unpolite
unpanged
unpannel
unpenned
unpinked
unpinned
unproper
unproved
unproven
unpeople
unpurged
umpirage
unperson
uppercut
unposted
uppishly
unpathed
unpitied
unpruned
umquhile
unquoted
unreaped
upreared
unreally
unreason
unribbed
unrubbed
unracked
unrecked
utriculi
unridden
unriddle
unrifled
unruffle
unrigged
unraised
unreined
upraised
unringed
uprootal
unroofed
unrooted
uprooter
unripped
unrepaid
unrepair
uprising
unrotted
unrotten
unrouged
unroused
unrhymed
unstarch
unscaled
unsealed
unseamed
unseated
unshaded
unshaked
unshaken
unshamed
unshaped
unshapen
unshared
unshaved
unshaven
unslaked
unsoaped
unspared
unstated
unstayed
unswayed
unswathe
unstable
unseason
unshadow
upstairs
unsubtle
unsocial
unsecret
unsicker
unsocket
unsucked
unsodden
unsaddle
unsteady
ulstered
unseeded
unseemly
unseeing
unsued-to
unsifted
unsafely
unsafety
unsigned
unsphere
unstitch
unsailed
unsained
unseized
unsliced
unsoiled
unsuited
unsalted
unsolder
unsolved
unsolemn
Ursuline
unseldom
unsummed
unsensed
unsunned
unspoken
unspoilt
unsmooth
unsapped
unsupple
upstream
unshrubd
unstruck
unsorted
upstroke
unsprung
unstring
unstrung
upsprang
upspring
upsprung
unshroud
unsashed
upsetter
unsettle
unsating
unsluice
unsouled
unsoured
unstuffy
unsought
unsexual
unsexist
unthatch
ultrared
unthawed
untraced
untraded
ultraism
ultraist
untucked
untackle
urticant
urticate
untidily
up-to-date
untailed
untilled
uptilted
Ustilago
ultimacy
untemper
untombed
untimely
ultimata
ultimate
Ultonian
untanned
untended
untender
untented
untinged
untinned
untangle
untenant
untapped
unthread
untarred
unturned
upturned
unthrift
unturbid
unthrone
untiring
uttering
ulterior
upthrust
utterest
untasted
untested
untether
untitled
untaught
untruism
untrusty
uptowner
untoward
unusable
unusably
uvularly
unuseful
uvulitis
usurious

8 u□u□p

usurping
usufruct
unviable
unviewed
unveiled
unveiler
unvoiced
unvulgar
unvalued
unvented
unvaried
unversed
unvirtue
unvetted
unvizard
unweaned
unweapon
unwebbed
unwedded
unwieldy
unweeded
unweened
unwifely
unwigged
unwalled
unwilled
unwilful
unwanted
unwinged
unwonted
unwooded
unwarded
unwarmed
unwarned
unwarped
unworded
unworked
unwormed
unworthy
unwarely
unwarily
upwardly
unwashed
unwashen
unwasted
unwished
unwisely
unwisdom
unwetted
unwatery
unyeaned
vraicker
viameter
viaticum
vibrancy
vibrator
vibratos
vibrissa
vibronic
viburnum
vice-dean

vacherin
vaccinal
vaccinia
vice-king
vocalion
viceless
vocalese
vocalise
vocalism
vocalist
vocality
vocalize
vicinage
vacantly
vicenary
vicinity
vacuolar
△**victoria**
vicarial
vicarage
vicaress
victress
vicarate
vacation
vocation
vocative
victuals
Vichyite
Vodafone®
Vedantic
videndum
videotex
videofit
videoing
viewable
Vietcong
viewdata
viewless
Viennese
vee-joint
vagrancy
vagabond
vogueing
vigneron
vignette
vigilant
vagility
Vegemite®
vaginula
vaginule
vaginant
△**veganism**
vaginate
vagaries
vagarish
vigorish
vigorous
vegetant
vegetate
vegetive
△**vehmique**

vehement
voidance
voidable
voice-box
vainesse
voiceful
voidings
veilless
vainness
voidness
valiance
valiancy
villager
villagio
villatic
volcanic
△vulcanic
Valhalla
valuable
valuably
vulgarly
villainy
valuator
viliacos
viliagos
villadom
voltaism
Volscian
velocity
validate
validity
valvelet
velveret
velveted
volleyed
volleyer
vulsella
velleity
vilified
vilifier
villiago
vulvitis
volpinos
velskoen
volplane
velamina
volumist
valanced
vildness
vileness
vallonia
Vellozia
vilipend
valerian
valorise
velarise
valorous
velarium
valorize
velarize
volutoid

volatile
valeting
volitant
volition
volution
velatura
volitate
volitive
valvulae
valvular
Volsungs
volvulus
Valkyrie
vampiric
vamplate
vambrace
vomerine
vomiting
vomitory
vomitive
vintager
vendange
Vandalic
venially
ventaile
ventayle
vindaloo
vine-clad
vanadate
vanadium
vanadous
venidium
veneerer
vendeuse
vendetta
vengeful
vine-gall
vinegary
vent-hole
vendible
vendibly
venville
vincible
vine-leaf
vinology
vanillin
vinolent
vaneless
venality
Vinylite
venomous
vine-prop
vent-pipe
vent-plug
venereal
venerean
ventring
venerate
ventrous
vent'rous
Venusian

vanisher
venosity
vinosity
Venetian
Venutian
venation
Vanitory®
vanitory
venturer
vanguard
vanquish
vinculum
vandyked
vineyard
violater
violable
violably
violator
violence
vapidity
vapulate
viperine
vaporise
viperish
vaporous
viperous
vaporize
vapoured
vapourer
vaqueros
variance
verdancy
vartabed
verbatim
variable
variably
verbally
vernally
viricide
virucide
verecund
varactor
varicose
veracity
voracity
viridian
Varidase®
viridite
viridity
varietal
verse-man
vergence
vergency
verderer
verselet
vertexes
vortexes
verdelho
viraemia
viraemic
variedly

Words marked △ may be spelled also with a capital letter

8 w□i□t

verderor
varletry
vertebra
varletto
verified
verifier
variform
viragoes
voragoes
virogene
vertical
virginal
vortical
verditer
vermined
vertices
vortices
verbiage
verticil
Virginia
vernicle
versicle
virginly
vertigos
verligte
virology
virulent
verbless
virilism
virility
virement
veranda'd
verandah
veronica
virandos
variolar
verboten
vermouth
variorum
verkramp
veristic
varistor
verities
veratrin
veratrum
verrucae
verrucas
verrugas
verjuice
verdured
vargueño
verquere
verquire
virtuosa
virtuose
virtuosi
virtuoso
vertuous
virtuous
viscacha
visually
vassalry
visibles
vesicula
vesicant
vesicate
vesperal
visceral
vasiform
visagist
Visigoth
Vespidae
vestigia
vespiary
vestiary
Vaseline®
vestment
vastness
visional
visioned
visioner
visnomie
△**viscount**
△**visitant**
visiting
vascular
vestural
vestured
vesturer
vasculum
△**vesuvian**
vitiable
vitiator
Vitaceae
vaticide
viticide
vitreous
vitiligo
vitellin
vituline
vitalise
vitalism
vitalist
voteless
vitality
vitellus
vitalize
vitamine
votaress
votarist
vitative
vauncing
voutsafe
voussoir
vaultage
vauntage
vaulting
vaunting
vauntery
vauntful
vivacity
vividity
vivifier
vivipary
vivarium
vivisect
vavasory
vavasour
vowelled
vowelise
vowelize
vexillum
vexingly
vixenish
vexation
vexatory
voyageur
vizcacha
vizament
vizirial
vizarded
vizirate
wearable
whaleman
weakener
weak-eyed
weaseler
weazened
whatever
weaselly
wharfage
wharfing
weakfish
wrangler
wrathily
wrathful
weariful
whackoes
whacking
wrackful
what-like
weakling
weanling
wraxling
whamming
weakness
whatness
weaponed
wrapover
weaponry
wrappage
whapping
wrapping
wealsman
wearying
wobegone
webwheel
wabbling
wobbling
wickered
wickedly
wide-area
widebody
wide-eyed
waddling
wideness
Wodenism
wide-open
widowman
Wedgwood®
wretched
wheedler
whenever
wherever
wye-level
wherefor
whereout
whey-face
weel-far'd
weel-far't
weephole
weeviled
weevilly
wreckage
wrecking
wreakful
wreckful
wheelman
wheeling
weedless
weetless
wheel-cut
wherries
wheatear
wreathed
wreathen
wreather
wrestler
whetting
waesucks
woefully
wheezily
wheezing
wifehood
wifelike
waffling
wifeless
wig-maker
wageless
wagonage
wagon-lit
wagonful
△**waggoner**
wagmoire
wage-push
Wahabism
Wahabite
Wahiguru
wait-a-bit
writable
whimbrel
whizbang
whipbird
whinchat
whipcord
whidding
whitecap
white-leg
whitener
write-off
white-tie
whitefly
writerly
Whiteboy
white-hot
whitepot
while-ere
white-out
white-eye
whiffled
whiffler
whiffing
wriggler
whigging
wringing
Whiggery
Whiggish
Whiggism
writhled
weighage
weighing
writhing
weigh-out
△**writings**
whiniard
whinid'st
whipjack
wrinkled
whisking
whiskers
whiskery
whirlbat
whiplike
whirling
whitling
Whieldon
wait-list
whiplash
whimming
whinnied
whipping
whispers
whispery
whirring
waitress
whipster
whitster
Whigship
whimsily
wainscot
whistled
whistler
whittler
whittret
wristlet

8 w□i□t

whiptail
whim-wham
whipworm
whinyard
whizzing
wakeless
wakening
wakerife
walk-away
welladay
wellaway
Walhalla
walkable
weldable
willable
wallaroo
well-bred
well-born
wild-born
wild-duck
well-doer
well-done
wall-eyed
wildered
wild-eyed
walker-on
Wolffian
wildfire
wallfish
wolf-fish
wildfowl
wellhead
Welshman
well-hung
waldhorn
williwaw
well-knit
well-kept
wildlife
wildland
wolfling
wall-less
weldless
will-less
well-made
walkmill
walk-mill
Walkmans
weldment
Weldmesh®
weldmesh
well-nigh
wellness
wildness
wiliness
walk-over
walloper
wallowed
wallower
welcomer
willowed
well-read
waldrapp
Wellsian
well-seen
wolfskin
wallsend
well-to-do
wilfully
wildwood
wallwort
well-worn
well-wish
Walkyrie
willyard
willyart
waltzing
womblike
wambling
womanise
womanish
womanize
wannabee
winnable
wingbeat
windblow
windburn
wingding
wandered
△wanderer
wintered
wondered
wonderer
wingedly
winterly
wanderoo
windfall
windgall
winchman
wanthill
winnings
wangling
windlass
windless
wingless
wontless
windmill
wanwordy
windowed
winnowed
winnower
wantonly
wanworth
windpipe
wind-rode
windring
windrose
wondrous
wingspan
windsock
windsail
windship
wineskin
wing-shot
windsurf
windward
woodbind
△woodbine
wood-born
woodchat
woodcock
woodchip
wool-dyed
woolding
whomever
whosever
wood-evil
woodenly
whole-hog
whoredom
whoreson
woolfell
wrongful
wrongous
whoa-ho-ho
woodhole
whorlbat
woodlice
woollies
woodland
woodlark
woodless
woodmeal
wooingly
woodness
woodnote
woolpack
whoopsie
woodpile
whooping
whopping
woodruff
woodroof
woodrush
woodsman
△**woolsack**
woodshed
woolshed
woodskin
who-dun-it
woodwale
woodwind
wood-wool
woodward
woodwork
woodworm
woolward
woolwork
woodwose
woodyard
warragal
workaday
warfarer
war-gamer
warfarin
warhable
warragle
workable
warranty
warragul
workboat
warm-boot
wordbook
workbook
wardcorn
wormcast
wiredraw
word-deaf
world-old
warrener
wardenry
war-weary
warmed-up
workfolk
workfare
weregild
wordgame
workgirl
wire-heel
worthies
wire-hair
wormhole
worthily
worthful
warrigal
workings
warrison
wirricow
worricow
workload
wartlike
warbling
warplane
wordlore
wareless
wartless
wireless
wordless
workless
wariment
wardmote
workmate
wariness
warmness
wiriness
work-over
warhorse
wordplay
wardrobe
wardroom
war-proof
workroom
wardress
wormseed
wardship
worksome
workshop
wire-sewn
workwear
wartweed
workweek
werewolf
wormwood
wartwort
wirework
wireworm
wirewove
worky-day
worrying
worrycow
wurtzite
wash-away
wistaria
washable
wastable
wiseacre
washball
wishbone
washbowl
wash-dirt
Wesleyan
wisteria
westerly
wastelot
washed-up
wasteful
wastfull
washings
wise-like
washland
westlins
wiseling
westmost
waspnest
wastness
wiseness
wastrife
washroom
washwipe
westward
wish-wash
wetlands
withdraw
withdrew
withered
wet-lease
watchman
withheld
withhold
watching
witching
watchbox
watchdog
witchery
watchful

Words marked △ may be spelled also with a capital letter

watch-out
watt-hour
wattling
witeless
witblits
wittolly
water-gas
waterman
waterway
waterhen
water-jet
waterage
water-ski
watering
waterlog
Waterloo
waterpox
waterish
wet-nurse
withwind
woundily
wounding
waukmill
waukrife
waveband
waveform
wivehood
wavelike
waveless
waviness
wavering
waverous
waxberry
waxcloth
waxiness
waxworks
wayfarer
waylayer
way-maker
wayleave
waywiser
way-going
wayboard
waygoose
waybread
wizardly

wizardry
xylocarp
xyloidin
xylology
xylomata
Xylonite®
xylonite
xenogamy
Xanthian
xanthein
xanthoma
xanthene
xanthine
Xanthura
xanthate
Xanthium
xanthous
Xantippe
xenolith
xenophya
xenurine
xenotime
xeromata
xeransis
xerantic
xeraphim
yea-sayer
yearbook
yeanling
yearling
yearlong
yearning
yachting
Ygdrasil
yodeller
yielding
yoghourt
Yugoslav
Yugo-slav
yokelish
yakimona
yoke-mate
yoke-toed
yakitori
yokozuna
yeldrock

yeldring
yoldring
△**yuletide**
yglaunst
yonderly
Yenglish
Yinglish
yongthly
yeomanly
yeomanry
ybounden
yarraman
yardbird
yersinia
yardland
yarmulka
yarmulke
yardwand
yeshivah
yeshivas
yeshivot
ypsiloid
yestreen
yataghan
yttrious
ytterbia
youngest
youngish
youthful
yourself
zealless
zealotry
Zoanthus
zabaione
zebrinny
zibeline
zuchetta
zuchetto
zecchine
zecchini
zecchino
zucchini
zoccolos
zodiacal
zaddikim
zoetrope

zigzaggy
zygodont
zygaenid
zygomata
ziggurat
Zigeuner
zugzwang
Zwieback
zoiatria
zikkurat
Zelanian
zylonite
Zalophus
zelatrix
zombiism
zymology
zamindar
zemindar
zambomba
zampogna
zomboruk
zamarras
zamarros
zemstvos
zanjeros
zingiber
Zantippe
Zentippe
Zantiote
zinckify
zincking
zoneless
zaniness
zenithal
zonation
zoomancy
zoolater
zoopathy
zoolatry
zooscopy
zooecium
zooperal
zoogenic
zoometry
Zoophaga
zoophagy

zoophile
zoophily
zoothome
zoochore
zoochory
Zoophyta
zoophyte
zeolitic
zoolitic
zoonitic
zoogloea
zooblast
zoonoses
zoonomia
zoonomic
zoonosis
zoonotic
zootomic
zootoxin
zoomorph
zoosperm
zoospore
zoograft
zootrope
Zionward
zoocytia
zootypic
zippered
zeppelin
zopilote
zip-front
zircaloy
zero-base
zorillos
zerumbet
zirconia
zirconic
Zircoloy®
zero-rate
zaratite
zarzuela
zero-zero
zastruga
zastrugi
zizyphus

Words marked △ may be spelled also with a capital letter

9 a□a□a

avalanche
alabamine
atacamite
alalagmos
agalactia
ataractic
amarantin
alabaster
Amarantus
adamantly
anarchise
anarchize
anarchial
anarchism
anarchist
avascular
araucaria
abandoned
abandonee
anandrous
agateware
Araneidae
awareness
abasement
abatement
amazement
Acalephae
acalephan
asafetida
awakening
academism
academics
academist
Agamemnon
Agapemone
arabesque
analectic
analeptic
amarettos
analgesia
analgesic
abashedly
abashless
abashment
Arachnida
anathemas
arachnoid
anaphoric
anacharis
apathetic
apathaton
acaridean
amazingly
acaricide
Adamitism
acaridian
arabinose
acariasis
anabiosis
anabiotic
atavistic
alack-a-day
available
availably
Anaglypta®
anaplasty
alarmedly
alarm-bell
anamneses
anamnesis
amazon-ant
amazonite
anabolite
analogise
analogize
anatomise
anatomize
aragonite
amatorial
anabolism
amatorian
△amazonian
Anatolian
analogist
anatomist
△**ayatollah**
analogous
acarology
anaerobic
anabranch
amaurosis
anacruses
anacrusis
amaurotic
amassable
amassment
Adansonia
adaptable
apartheid
apartness
apartment
acanthine
abactinal
acanthoid
acanthous
ananthous
avant-goût
anastasis
anastatic
anaptyxis
ayahuasco
analysand
amaryllid
amaryllis
arblaster
ambiguity
ambagious
ambiguous
albricias
aubrietia
ambulacra
ambulance
ambulator
album-leaf
albinoism
albinotic
ambrosial
△**ambrosian**
ambrotype
amberjack
albertite
aubergine
amber-fish
albarelli
albarello
alburnous
arboreous
ambergris
arboretum
ambassage
ambuscade
ambuscado
albescent
albespine
asbestine
Ambystoma
asbestous
albespyne
arbitrage
arbitrate
arbitrary
arbitress
abbotship
arbitrium
albatross
ambitious
amblyopia
archangel
arcuation
archaiser
archaizer
archducal
archduchy
accedence
accidence
arch-druid
archeress
arch-enemy
asclepiad
accretive
alchemise
alchemize
accretion
asclepias
Asclepios
Asclepius
alchemist
arcsecond
anciently
ancientry
archetype
arch-fiend
arch-felon
alcoholic
Archibald
acclimate
archimage
Arctiidae
architect
archivist
acclivity
archilowe
acclivous
archivolt
architype
ancillary
accompany
accumbent
ascendant
ascendent
ascensive
ascending
arc-en-ciel
accension
△ascension
accentual
Arctogaea
anchorage
anchoveta
anchoress
arctophil
anchor-ice
anchorite
auctorial
Alcyonium
anchor-man
archology
archontic
acceptant
acceptive
ancipital
accipiter
alcarraza
ascorbate
ascertain
accordant
Ascaridae
ascarides
according
accordion
accessary
accusable
accession
arch-stone
ascospore
accessory
ancestral
ascetical
ascitical
accourage
accoutred
anchylose
Aldebaran
abdicable
adducible
addictive
adductive
abduction
addiction
adduction
audacious
abdicator
audiencia
addlement
addressed
addressee
addresser
addressor
addresses
abdominal
andantino
audiotape
△**andromeda**
audiophil
andrology
audiology
audiogram
arduously
androgyne
androgyny
audiphone
adderwort
andesitic
auditress
auditoria
Aceraceae
alewashed
acetamide
Amerasian
arenation
Alemannic
amenaunce
Ametabola
apetalous
asepalous
agelastic
acetabula
alembroth
acescence
acescency
amendable
amendment
anecdotal
avengeful
Americana
Amerindic
aperiodic
aperitive
americium
Aretinian
amenities
acellular
areolated
areometer
Abernethy

Words marked △ may be spelled also with a capital letter

adenomata
adenoidal
awesomely
adenosine
ale-conner
anemology
anemogram
Areopagus
ademption
aneuploid
Averroism
Averroist
aberrance
aberrancy
ale-draper
Aleurites
area-sneak
areostyle
avertable
avertible
avertedly
adeptness
alertness
apertness
aventaile
awestrike
azeotrope
anestrous
aleatoric
awestruck
alectryon
asexually
acetylene
affianced
afflation
affective
affecting
affection
affidavit
affrended
affricate
afflicted
affiliate
awfulness
affronted
affrontee
affrontée
affirmant
affluxion
affluence
aggravate
algebraic
argy-bargy
aggregate
anglesite
anglewise
angleworm
aigre-doux
aggressor
augmented
Augmentin®

augmenter
augmentor
anguipede
angriness
anguished
anglicise
anglicize
anglicism
anglicist
anguiform
aggrieved
angel-cake
angelical
argillite
angel-fish
Angelenos
angel-food
angelhood
angulated
△**argentine**
argentite
Algonkian
Argentino
Algonquin
angiomata
△**anglophil**
angiogram
angophora
angerless
augurship
algarroba
auger-hole
auger-worm
algarrobo
algorithm
Augustine
Angostura
Argus-eyed
ashramite
ashlaring
Ashtaroth
anhydrase
anhydride
anhydrite
anhedonia
anhedonic
anhydrous
aphidious
ashlering
achaenium
athletics
atheistic
Achillean
ash-blonde
aphyllous
ashamedly
achimenes
athematic
Athenaeum
anhungred
ashen-grey

Ashtoreth
atheology
athrocyte
abhorrent
abhorring
adherence
aphoriser
apheresis
aphorizer
adhesions
arhythmia
arhythmic
athetosic
athetesis
athetosis
athetotic
Acheulean
Acheulian
ash-bucket
avisandum
avizandum
agitative
alizarine
animalise
animalize
animating
animalism
animatism
agitation
animation
animalist
animality
adiabatic
aliveness
alinement
avisement
alimental
avizefull
acidfreak
apishness
aliphatic
abidingly
acidified
acidifier
asininity
aciniform
animistic
arillated
axiomatic
alienable
alignment
amianthus
alienator
adipocere
aniconism
aniconist
adiposity
animosity
apivorous
adiaphora
Adi-Granth

amissible
amidships
Aristides
aviatress
agistment
Aristarch
aciculate
acidulate
apiculate
acidulent
azimuthal
acidulous
alicyclic
adjective
abjection
adjacency
adjoining
adjunctly
adjutancy
adjuvancy
awkwardly
ankle-jack
ankle-boot
ankylosed
alkalosis
ankylosis
All-father
ad-libbing
allocable
allicholy
allocarpy
all-seeing
axle-guard
allograph
allegiant
allograft
allegedly
alligarta
allegoric
alligator
alleluiah
allemande
allomorph
allometry
Atlantean
ailanthus
all-ending
allantoic
allantoid
allantois
allenarly
aplanatic
allcomers
alloplasm
arle-penny
allophone
allopathy
allergist
allostery
Aylesbury
allotment

allottery
allotting
allotrope
ablutions
allotropy
ablatival
aflatoxin
all-ruling
alleviate
allowable
allowably
allowedly
allowance
auld-warld
allayment
admeasure
alms-drink
armadillo
aimlessly
armigeral
alms-house
armillary
atmolysis
atmometer
adminicle
almandine
almond-oil
admonitor
Axminster
admirable
admirably
Armorican
Admiralty
admirance
admissive
△armistice
admission
admitting
asmoulder
alms-woman
admixture
annualise
annualize
annealing
annectent
abnegator
annuitant
annulment
annulling
annulated
adnominal
agnominal
amniotomy
abnormity
abnormous
adnascent
agnatical
annotator
announcer
annexment
annoyance

Words marked △ may be spelled also with a capital letter

9 a□o□a

Anonaceae
aromatise
aromatize
amoralism
atonalism
adoration
avocation
amoralist
atonalist
atonality
anomalous
apogamous
Avogadro's
amoebaean
avoidable
abondance
avoidance
aforehand
aforesaid
aloneness
abodement
△atonement
aforetime
alopecoid
anorectic
anorectal
aloofness
alongside
apothecia
anopheles
apophasis
apophyses
apophysis
apophatic
abominate
Anobiidae
adoringly
atoningly
△**aborigine**
aconitine
aeolipile
agonising
agonizing
abolition
atomicity
atonicity
agonistic
apodictic
apomictic
atomistic
agonistes
aeolipyle
acock-bill
adornment
abounding
amornings
apoenzyme
apocopate
apologise
apologize
apologist
amorosity
amorously
amorphism
amorphous
△**apocrypha**
amourette
acoustics
aloes-wood
anoestrum
anoestrus
about-face
abortuary
about-ship
anorthite
△**apostolic**
apostille
adoptious
avouterer
apostatic
about-turn
acoluthic
akoluthos
anonymise
anonymize
anonymity
anonymous
applauder
appealing
alphasort
appraisal
appraiser
asphaltic
asphaltum
asphalter
aspectual
aspidioid
apple-jack
apple-cart
apple-tart
apprehend
ampleness
apple-wife
asplenium
apple-John
apple-tree
adpressed
arpeggios
applicate
applicant
appliable
amplified
apprising
apprizing
amphibian
amplifier
appliance
Amphipoda
amphibole
amphiboly
amphigory
appointed
appointee
appointor
amplitude
amphioxus
appellate
appellant
arpillera
appalling
Appaloosa
appendage
appendant
appanaged
aspen-like
alpenhorn
approbate
Aepyornis
amplosome
ampholyte
alpargata
ampersand
amperzand
aspartame
appertain
asparagus
aspersive
aspergill
apportion
aspersion
apparency
aspersoir
aspersory
apparitor
aspirator
apparatus
appetible
appetence
appetency
appetiser
amputator
appetizer
asphyxial
acquiesce
acquitted
acquittal
arrearage
Afro-Asian
aerialist
aeriality
air-cavity
air-jacket
aerobiont
acrobatic
arracacha
auricular
Africaner
atrocious
aerodrome
agreeable
agreeably
agreement
airy-fairy
aerograph
acrogenic
arrogance
abrogator
air-piracy
air-minded
arraigner
Afrikaans
Afrikaner
April-fish
aerolitic
agréments
aeromancy
aerometer
aeromotor
aerometry
air-intake
Aaronical
acronical
acronycal
air-engine
Adrenalin®
adrenalin
acronymic
agronomic
apriorism
apriorist
apriority
air-pocket
air-cooled
agriology
airworthy
aeroplane
atrophied
abruption
air-splint
acropolis
aerophobe
aerophone
acrophony
acropetal
aerophyte
air-bridge
aurorally
aerospace
aeroshell
acrospire
arrestive
agrestial
auriscope
après-goût
aerotrain
airstream
air-strike
acroteria
aerotaxis
air-bubble
arrivance
arrivancy
arrivisme
arriviste
arrow-head
arrow-shot
arrowwood
arrowroot
arrayment
Ausländer
assuasive
assuaging
abstainer
associate
assiduity
apsidiole
assiduous
austerely
austenite
austerity
abscessed
assientos
assuetude
aesthesia
aesthesis
aesthetic
Anschluss
aestivate
auspicate
assailant
abstinent
abseiling
abscissae
abscissin
abscissas
abscisses
assoilzie
Ausgleich
assumable
assumably
assumedly
assembler
assumpsit
arseniate
arsenical
assentive
assonance
arsenious
absconder
absorbate
adsorbate
assurable
assuredly
absorbent
adsorbent
assurgent
assertive
absorbing
absurdism
assertion
absurdist
absurdity
australes
assurance
assertory

Words marked △ may be spelled also with a capital letter

9 b□a□e

apsarases
assistant
assaulter
arsy-versy
assayable
astragals
astraddle
attrahens
attrahent
astrakhan
actualise
actualize
actuarial
actuation
actualist
actuality
astrantia
attractor
autoclave
autocracy
autocycle
anticline
autocrime
anticking
antichlor
articular
artichoke
antechoir
astichous
astucious
autocross
anticivic
antidotal
anthelion
anthemion
artlessly
authentic
autoflare
anti-flash
△artificer
autofocus
arty-farty
antefixal
antefixes
autograph
autograft
autoguide
autogamic
antigenic
autogenic
autogiros
autogyros
antihelix
aitchbone
attainder
astringer
attuitive
altricial
attrition
attuition
attribute
antiknock
antelucan
Autolycus
attollens
attollent
artillery
autolysed
autolysis
autolytic
autolatry
autolyzed
antimonic
artemisia
asthmatic
automatic
automaton
altimeter
attempter
altimetry
attenuate
attendant
attenuant
antennary
antinodal
antinoise
attentive
attention
actinally
antinomic
antonymic
autonomic
antenatal
antennule
anti-novel
Actinozoa
astrolabe
anthocarp
astronaut
astrofell
authoress
astrophel
authorise
authorize
authoring
authorish
authorial
authorism
actionist
authority
astrodome
aetiology
anthology
astrology
astronomy
Astroturf®
astrocyte
anthocyan
Altiplano
autophagy
antipodal
△antipodes
autopoint
autopilot
antiphony
autophoby
autophony
antipapal
autopista
antipasto
antipathy
antiquate
antiquark
antiquary
antiquely
antiquity
afterward
aftercare
aftergame
altercate
alternate
aftermath
after-damp
alternant
alterable
anthracic
afterdeck
attorneys
afterheat
autarchic
after-life
aftertime
altarwise
autarkist
after-clap
afterglow
afterings
altar-tomb
afterword
arteriole
afternoon
aftermost
anthropic
arthropod
after-crop
arthrosis
Antarctic
arthritic
arteritis
arthritis
autoroute
apteryxes
autos-da-fé
antispast
antiscian
altissimo
autosomal
artisanal
autoscopy
antiserum
antitrade
antitragi
altitudes
antitheft
autotelic
autotimer
autotroph
antitypic
antitypal
antitrust
antitoxic
antitoxin
autotoxin
astounded
anthurium
Arthurian
antivenin
antiviral
antivirus
activator
Antrycide®
adulation
adulatory
aquaboard
adumbrate
aquabatic
avuncular
aduncated
abundance
abundancy
aquadrome
acuteness
amusement
aculeated
ahungered
acuminate
aluminate
abusively
amusingly
aluminise
aluminize
aluminium
acuminous
aluminous
anucleate
aquilegia
acupoints
aquaplane
aquaphobe
ague-proof
aquarobic
aquariist
aquarelle
aquariums
alum-shale
alum-slate
alum-stone
aquatinta
adulthood
adulterer
△ayurvedic
adviceful
advection
advocator
advantage
adventive
Adventist
adventure
alveolate
adversary
advertent
adversely
advertise
advertize
adverbial
adversity
advisable
advisably
advisedly
advoutrer
auxiliary
auxometer
anxiously
aryballos
amygdalin
Amygdalus
asyndetic
asyndeton
asynergia
arytenoid
acyclovir
abysmally
asymmetry
amyloidal
amylopsin
asymptote
Aizoaceae
bravadoes
blatantly
brambling
Bradburys
Bradbury's
bear-berry
blaeberry
branchery
branchiae
branching
branchial
branchlet
board-game
brand-name
boardwalk
brandreth
beardless
blandness
brandling
boardroom
board-foot
bladdered
brandered
brand-iron
brake-fade
blameable
blameably
blameless

9 b□a□e

brakeless
brazeless
Boanerges
brake-shoe
brakes-man
blade-bone
bladework
beanfeast
brangling
brachiate
beach-ball
beachhead
biathlete
blatherer
Brachyura
boar-hound
bead-house
boathouse
beau-ideal
brazilein
beaminess
beamingly
bearishly
Brazilian
beatitude
blackband
blackface
blackgame
blackwash
blackjack
blackball
blackmail
blackhead
blacklead
blackness
blankness
Blackfeet
blackbird
blackfish
blacklist
blackwood
blackcock
Blackfoot
blackbuck
beadledom
Braillist
Brahmanic
Brahminic
Brahminee
braincase
brain-wave
brainwash
brain-dead
brainless
△**béarnaise**
brainsick
blaspheme
blasphemy
bead-proof
beanstalk
boatswain

brassiere
brassière
boar-spear
bear's-foot
brasserie
bracteate
boat-train
boastless
bractless
blastment
beautiful
beastlike
blast-pipe
brattling
blastular
beastings
beasthood
blast-hole
bracteole
beauteous
bratwurst
bobtailed
babacoote
bibacious
bebeerine
bob-cherry
biblicism
biblicist
bobbin-net
Babbittry
bubble-car
bubble-gum
bobsleigh
baboonery
baboonish
babirussa
baby-tooth
bobbysock
bacharach
beccaccia
buccaneer
beccafico
buccanier
buckayros
back-board
buckboard
backboned
back-bench
back-block
backbiter
back-crawl
back-chain
bicyclist
back-cloth
back-cross
backcourt
bucketful
bacterise
bacterize
bucketing
bacterial

bacterium
bacterian
bacteroid
backfield
backfisch
bacchante
bacchanal
bacchants
buckhound
buckishly
bacciform
bacillary
bucolical
back-light
Baculites
bicameral
biconcave
Bucentaur
back-plate
back-pedal
backpiece
bicipital
backspace
backstage
back-slang
back-spaul
backstall
backstays
backspeer
backspeir
backsight
backslide
backswing
backshish
buckshish
buckskins
back-shift
backsword
buck's-horn
backtrack
bucktooth
buckthorn
becquerel
buckwheat
buck-wagon
backwoods
backwards
backwater
buckyball
bedraggle
bedlamite
bedlamism
bed-jacket
body-check
body-curer
budgetary
badger-dog
budgeting
bedfellow
bed-settee
bodyguard

bodeguero
bedridden
badminton
bed-sitter
bedelship
bed-closet
bedimming
bidentate
bedropped
bed-bottle
bed-worthy
bedspread
bodyshell
beddy-byes
bedazzled
bedizened
bretasche
beefaloes
bee-master
bleachers
bleachery
bleaching
breeching
breed-bate
breadhead
breadline
breadroom
bread-corn
breadroot
breveting
boerewors
beekeeper
brevetted
beefeater
beech-mast
beech-fern
Brechtian
beech-wood
bletherer
beer-house
brew-house
beeriness
breakback
breakfast
breakable
breakneck
bleakness
break-wind
breaktime
breakdown
break-even
breakaway
bee-flower
beer-money
bregmatic
bee-orchis
bleareyed
blessedly
beefsteak
breast-fed
breastpin

breathful
breathing
breathily
beestings
biestings
Bretwalda
Beelzebub
breezeway
buffaloes
buffeting
bifoliate
bafflegab
befalling
bifurcate
bifarious
befortune
buff-stick
befitting
buff-wheel
beggardom
biguanide
beggar-man
beglamour
big-screen
bugle-band
bugger-all
bugle-call
beglerbeg
bigheaded
bugle-weed
bugle-horn
béguinage
bagginess
bogginess
beggingly
bagpiping
big-ticket
beginning
Big-endian
bigeneric
bog-cotton
begetting
bagatelle
bog-butter
bug-hunter
bog-myrtle
beheading
beholding
buhrstone
behoveful
bahuvrihi
behaviour
brigandry
brigadier
Britannia
Britannic
bricabrac
bric-à-brac
blindless
blindness
blind-side

Words marked △ may be spelled also with a capital letter

blindfish
blindfold
blind-coal
blindworm
bridemaid
bridecake
baisemain
bridewell
bridesman
bride's-man
brief-case
briefless
briefness
bridgable
beingless
beingness
blighting
brininess
Britisher
Briticise
Briticize
bailiwick
Briticism
brinjarry
brickyard
brickwall
briskness
brick-kiln
brickclay
brickwork
blinkered
brick-dust
bailliage
brilliant
bain-marie
bairn-team
baignoire
bairnlike
bairn-time
Britoness
brier-wood
brier-root
blissless
britschka
brimstone
brimstony
brittlely
bristling
Brittonic
briquette
blizzardy
bijection
bakeapple
bakeboard
baksheesh
bakehouse
bakhshish
bakestone
balmacaan
Balaam-box
balladeer
baldachin
Balsamina
Balaamite
△balkanise
△balkanize
ballabile
balladine
balzarine
Bulgarise
Bulgarize
ballabili
Bulgarian
balladist
balsawood
billabong
Bellatrix
ballasted
baldaquin
beleaguer
△**bilharzia**
billboard
bull-board
bilabiate
bull-beans
bilobular
△**balaclava**
balection
bolection
bilocular
bile-ducts
ball-dress
bull-dance
bulldozer
belle-mère
belvedere
bilge-keel
bald-eagle
ballerina
ballerine
believing
billeting
bolletrie
bulletrie
bilge-pump
bald-faced
bold-faced
bullfight
balefully
bullfinch
bell-glass
△**bolognese**
△**balthasar**
△**bolshevik**
△**balthazar**
balkiness
balminess
bulginess
bulkiness
balkingly
bulgingly
bullishly
billionth
Baltimore
bellibone
bellicose
baldicoot
billiards
ballistic
balalaika
belemnite
bilimbing
baldmoney
belomancy
bell-metal
bolometer
bolometry
belamoure
Belonidae
bull-nosed
balanitis
bilingual
ballot-box
balconied
balloting
billowing
bulbosity
Baltoslav
biliously
bulbously
ballpoint
bell-punch
ball-proof
baldpated
bilirubin
ballsed-up
belatedly
bull-trout
bolstered
bilateral
biliteral
boletuses
bell-tower
boliviano
bullwhack
belly-band
belly-ache
bully-beef
belly-flop
billycock
bully-rook
billy-goat
bully-tree
bombardon
bombasine
bombazine
bemoaning
bum-baylie
bummaloti
bombastic
bomb-happy
bombilate
bombinate
bumpiness
bomb-ketch
bumble-bee
Bumbledom
bimonthly
bemonster
bumpology
bamboozle
bomb-proof
bump-start
bombshell
bomb-sight
bomb-squad
bumptious
bumsucker
Bengalese
bank-agent
bengaline
bungaloid
bandalore
bandbrake
bone-black
baneberry
binocular
benedight
bannerall
benne-seed
bantering
bandelier
banderole
bone-earth
Bundesrat
Bundestag
beneficed
banefully
benefited
bent-grass
benignant
benignity
benighted
benighten
benighter
benchmark
benthonic
bench-hole
bunkhouse
benni-seed
bonnibell
bonniness
bendingly
benzidine
bandicoot
bannister
bonilasse
binominal
boning-rod
bandobast
bandoleon
bandoneon
bandolero
bandoleer
bandoline
bentonite
benzoline
bandonion
bandolier
bonhommie
bonhomous
bundobust
bank-paper
binervate
bandstand
bond-slave
banisters
bangsring
band-stone
bondstone
bank-stock
banjulele
banausian
binturong
banqueted
banquette
Bantustan
banqueter
bone-weary
bandwidth
band-wheel
bandwagon
bondwoman
bandy-ball
△**bunny-girl**
biohazard
buonamani
buonamano
bioparent
bootblack
brow-bound
blotching
bronchial
broadband
blond-lace
blood-bath
broadtail
blood-rain
broadways
broadcast
boondocks
blood-feud
broad-leaf
bloodless
broadness
bloodheat
bloodshed
bloodshot
blood-bird
blood-fine
blood-line
blood-wite
broadside
broadwise
bloodying

Words marked △ may be spelled also with a capital letter

9 b□o□d

broadbill
by-ordinar
bloodwood
blood-worm
broadloom
bloodroot
broad-brim
brondyron
broiderer
blood-dust
bloodlust
brokerage
boomerang
bromelain
bromeliad
biogenous
booked-out
biometric
boot-faced
brotherly
brochette
booziness
boorishly
biomining
boogieing
brominism
boodie-rat
blockhead
brookweed
block-ship
brooklime
blockhole
block-book
blockwork
block-coal
booklouse
broomrape
broomball
bloomless
bookmaker
bootmaker
broom-corn
brownness
brown-nose
bionomics
biologist
bromoform
bookplate
biosphere
biography
bookstand
boomslang
bookstall
bookshelf
bookstore
bootstrap
biostable
bioethics
book-token
blowtorch
brogueish
blow-valve
booby-trap
beplaster
buprestid
Buprestis
baptismal
baptistry
bipinnate
by-product
bipartite
bipyramid
by-passage
bepatched
bird-alane
burd-alane
burrawang
△bergamask
born-again
barbascos
barrancos
bargander
berg-adder
bergander
barbarise
barbarize
Barnabite
bursarial
barbarism
Barbadian
barbarian
barbarity
barracker
barnacled
barnacles
byrlaw-man
bargainer
bar-magnet
barcarole
bird-alone
barracoon
Barbadoes
barbarous
barbastel
barracuda
barmbrack
bark-bound
bard-craft
berg-cedar
borachios
bark-cloth
barm-cloth
barrelage
barret-cap
bartender
bordereau
barrelful
Barmecide
berberine
berkelium
berserker
berserkly
barrelled
bargellos
bordellos
bargepole
burdenous
barkeeper
burlesque
barperson
Barberton
barretter
barrefull
barefaced
barograph
baragouin
birth-rate
birthmark
barghaist
birthwort
borghetto
bird-house
barricade
barricado
barminess
burliness
burningly
burnisher
birlieman
barbitone
bursiform
barricoes
barrister
△barmizvah
Burakumin
beryllium
Bartlemew
bark-louse
bird-louse
bird-lover
barometer
barometry
baronetcy
bergomask
barrow-boy
barbotine
borrowing
bird's-nest
barasinga
baroscope
burrstone
barnstorm
bird's-foot
bird-table
burnt-cork
barathrum
Bermudian
byrewoman
bystander
bastardly
bespangle
bashawism
bescatter
bespatter
baseboard
bushcraft
bisection
basically
base-court
besteaded
basketful
beseeched
beseecher
bas-relief
beseeming
besieging
bespeckle
busheller
bushelman
basifugal
bashfully
bush-fruit
basifixed
besognios
boschveld
bush-house
bastinade
bastinado
boskiness
bossiness
bushiness
bismillah
bastioned
besainted
△basmizvah
bisulcate
basilical
basilican
basilicon
baseliner
base-level
besom-head
bush-metal
basin-wide
basinfuls
beslobber
bishopdom
bishopess
bishopric
bespotted
baseplate
basipetal
biserrate
bus-driver
bestrewed
besetment
besetting
besitting
besotting
beslubber
besmutted
bushwhack
bushwoman
△batrachia
battalion
bethankit
bit-mapped
bath-brick
butadiene
butlerage
butterbur
butter-box
buttercup
battement
butter-fat
butterfly
butterine
battening
bettering
bitterish
butternut
bitter-pit
butter-pat
butcherly
bathhouse
bath-house
△batmizvah
battle-axe
battle-cry
Betelgeuz
bottleful
bottle-gas
bottle-imp
betumbled
botanical
betrodden
bethought
betrothed
betrothal
batholite
batholith
Bathonian
battology
botargoes
butt-shaft
bath-sheet
bath-salts
bath-towel
bethumbed
bytownite
batswoman
bathwater
butty-gang
bathylite
bathylith
bathybius
brutalise
brutalize
brutalism
brutalist
brutality
bourasque
△bluebeard
blue-black
blubbered

Words marked △ may be spelled also with a capital letter

blueberry
boundless
blunderer
boulevard
bruteness
brutelike
bluffness
bluegrass
blue-green
bourgeois
Bruchidae
blushless
brush-fire
brushwood
blush-rose
brushwork
brutishly
brutified
△**brummagem**
Brunonian
boutonnée
blueprint
brusquely
baudricke
blue-rinse
bluestone
bluntness
△**bountiful**
bountyhed
blustrous
bounteous
blusterer
blutwurst
bevel-gear
bevelment
bevelling
bivalence
bivalency
bavardage
bivariate
bivariant
bow-backed
bow-legged
bowler-hat
bow-window
bawdiness
bewailing
bowelling
bower-bird
bowstring
bowstrung
box-camera
boxwallah
boxkeeper
box-office
box-girder
buxomness
box-spring
Brythonic
bay-antler
bayoneted
boycotter
Bryophyta
bryophyte
boyfriend
bezoardic
buzzingly
Byzantine
bez-antler
charabanç
char-à-banc
Characeae
chabazite
cyanamide
chalazion
clavation
crab-apple
chaparral
coadapted
character
clamantly
clapboard
coal-black
coal-brass
chawbacon
clabby-doo
crabbedly
clapbread
chambered
chamberer
cranberry
coarctate
chanceful
chancroid
chancrous
Chaldaean
Chandler's
coat-dress
chandlery
chaldaism
chandelle
châtelain
claret-cup
clarendon
chavender
chameleon
ceaseless
chapeless
cease-fire
czarevich
chaperone
craterous
chaseport
chamfrain
crab-faced
coalfield
chauffeur
chaffinch
chamfered
coal-fired
chafferer
charge-cap
changeful
chargeful
charge-man
crashland
clathrate
cha-cha-cha
crash-test
coachwhip
coach-hire
coachline
coachload
coachwood
coachwork
coach-horn
coalhouse
charivari
chariness
craziness
coaxingly
clarified
cyaniding
Chasidism
coalition
clarifier
charities
coaxially
clarionet
claviform
clavicorn
cladistic
clavicula
coadjutor
chalkface
crankcase
crackhead
cracknels
crankness
crackling
clackdish
cracksman
crackdown
challenge
chapleted
charlotte
charlatan
crab-louse
claimable
crammable
charmless
coalminer
charmeuse
chain-gear
chainless
chainshot
channeler
chainwork
Charolais
chatoyant
charoseth
ceanothus
chamomile
clamorous
cladogram
clamourer
cyanotype
crampbark
clappy-doo
champlevé
champagne
cramp-ring
cramp-fish
champaign
cramp-bone
clampdown
cramp-iron
champerty
chairlift
cuadrilla
chagrined
chaprassi
chaprassy
cranreuch
coatstand
classmate
clay-slate
classable
classible
classical
Chassidic
clamshell
classless
crassness
classific
chapstick
crabstick
clausulae
clausular
class-book
classroom
chassepot
claustral
claustrum
crab's-eyes
coastward
chaetodon
chantress
chartless
craftless
coastline
coastwise
Chantilly
craftsman
claytonia
chastened
chastener
craftwork
chart-room
chaetopod
chartered
charterer
chatterer
clatterer
chanteuse
clavulate
coadunate
coagulase
coagulate
coagulant
crapulent
chalumeau
Chanukkah
crapulous
charwoman
Charybdis
chalybean
chalybite
cabbalism
cabbalist
cubically
cebadilla
cable-laid
Cobdenite
Cobdenism
cablegram
cabriolet
cobriform
caballero
caballine
cobaltite
caballing
cobalamin
cabaletta
cabalette
cybernate
cyberpunk
cab-driver
cab-runner
cubby-hole
cyclamate
Cactaceae
cockateel
Cockaigne
cockatiel
cachaemia
cachaemic
cocoa-wood
ciclatoun
cock-a-hoop
cock-broth
cacodylic
cacodemon
coco-de-mer
cache-sexe
cacoëthes
cachectic
cacafuego
cacafogos
cockfight
cockhorse
cochineal
cockiness
cocainise
cocainize

Words marked △ may be spelled also with a capital letter

9 c□c□i

cyclizine
cocainism
coccidium
cyclicism
cocainist
cyclicity
cactiform
cochleate
cucullate
cocklebur
Cichlidae
cocklaird
cockleman
coculture
cacuminal
cockmatch
cockneyfy
cyclorama
cycloidal
cuckoldom
cuckoldry
cyclopean
cocoonery
coccolite
cyclonite
cocooning
coccolith
cyclolith
cyclopian
cacholong
cyclotron
△**cyclopses**
cock-padle
cacophony
caciquism
cockroach
cock-robin
Ciceronic
cicerones
cockswain
cockscomb
cock's-comb
cocuswood
cocksfoot
cicatrice
cicatrise
cicatrize
cacotopia
coccygeal
coccygian
cuddeehih
cudgelled
cudgeller
codifying
caddis-fly
cod-fisher
cadential
code-named
cedar-bird
cedarwood
cadastral

cadetship
cadaveric
Caesarean
chelaship
cheralite
Caesarism
Caesarian
chelation
cremation
crenation
chevalier
Caesarist
crematory
cremaster
crenature
cheechako
coercible
coercibly
cherchef't
crescendo
crenelate
credendum
cleverish
crewelist
crenelled
coeternal
clerecole
clemently
chevelure
clergyman
chechaqua
chechaquo
clericate
crepitate
clericals
crepitant
chelicera
crepiness
cherished
Ctesiphon
cretinise
cretinize
cretinism
caecilian
clericity
chemicked
cherimoya
cretinoid
cheliform
cteniform
cretinous
chemistry
chemitype
chemitypy
checkmate
checkrail
checkrein
clerkship
check-till
checklist
cheekbone

checkbook
checkroom
checkered
clew-lines
creolised
cheilitis
creolized
creamlaid
cream-cake
creamware
creamwove
cleanness
cleansing
cleanskin
cheongsam
chernozem
Coelomata
coenosarc
coelomate
cremocarp
cheloidal
coenobite
crepoline
coenobium
Chekovian
chelonian
Caenozoic
coenourus
chemostat
coelostat
coenocyte
cheap-jack
cheapness
cee-spring
coemption
cheapener
creep-hole
creepered
cherry-bob
cheerless
clearness
clearwing
clearskin
chevroned
clearance
clearcole
cherry-pie
cherry-pit
chevrette
clear-eyed
clepsydra
caen-stone
cheesevat
creatress
crestless
chest-note
cleithral
creatural
crenulate
crepuscle
caerulean

chemurgic
cleruchia
cherubims
credulity
coequally
credulous
chequered
cleavable
cofferdam
coffinite
cafeteria
cuffuffle
cognation
cognisant
cognizant
cognitive
cognition
cognomens
cognomina
cigarillo
cigarette
cogitable
cageyness
cohabitee
cohabitor
coheiress
cohyponym
coherence
coherency
coheritor
cohesible
△**chinaware**
chicanery
climatise
climatize
chicaning
cnidarian
chirality
Chinatown
chinaroot
chiragric
chivalric
chimaerid
climactic
climature
chipboard
clipboard
chilblain
climbable
climb-down
chip-based
chiacking
chincapin
chincough
childless
childness
childlike
child-wife
childhood
crimeless
chimerism

criterion
chiselled
clitellum
cribellum
chiseller
clitellar
cribellar
cliff-face
cliffhang
chieftain
chiefless
chiefship
chiefling
coiffeuse
clingfilm
criminate
ceilinged
chiliagon
criticise
criticize
criticism
clinician
cuisinier
chirimoya
chitinoid
chitinous
criminous
chiliarch
chickadee
chickweed
chickling
chinkapin
chickaree
cricketer
cailleach
cailliach
chillness
chidlings
chitlings
clientage
clientele
clientèle
clianthus
cairngorm
chipolata
chiyogami
Crinoidea
crinoidal
chipochia
crinoline
chinovnik
Chilopoda
Cainozoic
chirology
chironomy
chiropody
chibouque
clinoaxis
Crimplene®
crispness
crippling

Words marked △ may be spelled also with a capital letter

clinquant
chiarezza
chiasmata
chinstrap
Cointreau®
chihuahua
cellarage
calcaneal
calcaneum
calcanean
calcaneus
calcarine
calmative
collative
caldarium
collation
cellarist
collagist
cellarman
colcannon
caliatour
cellarous
culpatory
collapsar
calibrate
celebrate
celebrant
calabrese
colubrine
celebrity
coldblood
calaboose
calibered
colobuses
calf-bound
Culicidae
calyculus
colocynth
calycinal
cilicious
colectomy
Colocasia
cold-drawn
calfdozer
cullender
called-for
colleague
collegial
collegium
collegian
culver-key
cul-de-four
calcedony
calceated
collected
collector
colchicum
colligate
collimate
culminate
cultivate
culminant
collinear
callipers
calcimine
Calvinism
Celticism
collision
calvities
Calvinist
Celticist
callidity
cullionly
calcicole
Callippic
calligram
calcifuge
celsitude
columbate
columbary
chlamydia
chlamydes
△columbine
columbite
columbium
Columbian
columnist
columella
calamanco
call-money
calembour
chlamyses
celomatic
colonnade
celandine
colonelcy
calandria
calendric
cylindric
calendrer
colonitis
calendula
calenture
ciliolate
collocate
colloidal
colcothar
collodion
callosity
caliology
callously
colloquia
collotype
caliphate
calyptera
cellphone
colophony
chlordane
chloracne
calorific
colorific
chlorella
chlorosis
chloritic
chlorotic
cultrated
colosseum
△celestine
celestite
celestial
calmstone
calf's-foot
cold-short
coltsfoot
colostomy
colostric
colostrum
calculate
cellulase
colourant
calculary
coloureds
colourful
cellulite
collusive
colourise
colourize
colouring
collusion
colluvies
colourist
culturist
colour-mag
colourman
△celluloid®
calculose
cellulose
calculous
colour-sup
colourway
calavance
Calixtine
collyrium
combatant
come-and-go
commander
compander
compandor
commandos
campanero
comradely
companied
campanile
combative
combating
companing
campanili
companion
campanist
cembalist
cymbalist
cymbaloes
compasses
compacted
compactor
compactly
campanula
camp-chair
Cimicidae
comically
campeachy
compendia
commendam
campeador
competent
Commelina
cambering
Cimmerian
campesino
compelled
compeller
commensal
commenter
commentor
camp-fever
cymagraph
cymograph
camphoric
camsheugh
combinate
comminate
commingle
combining
cymbidium
cambiform
cymbiform
commissar
committed
committee
committal
cambistry
comfiture
comminute
camelback
compliant
Camelidae
complying
complaint
completed
cumulated
completer
complexus
complexly
Camembert
camanachd
Comintern
cementite
Cominform
commonage
cameo-part
commorant
camcorder
campodeid
component
△composite
commoning
come-o'-will
Cambodian
commotion
compotier
commodity
common-law
cameo-rôle
commodore
△comforter
composter
composure
cymophane
Cambridge
comprador
Camorrism
Camorrist
camarilla
cameraman
cumbrance
comprisal
camera-shy
camerated
combretum
camisades
camisados
camp-stool
camass-rat
camsteary
comptable
comptible
comitadji
camstairy
comatulid
comptroll
comitatus
△communard
commutate
computant
communise
communize
communing
△communism
△communion
△communist
computist
△community
camouflet
combustor
commutual
cantabank
Cingalese
concavely
contangos
contadina
cantabile
contadine
contadini
contagium
connation

Words marked △ may be spelled also with a capital letter

9 c□n□a

contagion
contadino
concavity
container
cantaloup
centaurea
Centaurus
canvasser
contactor
cant-board
canebrake
cenobitic
cane-chair
conscient
conscribe
conscript
canicular
conically
cynically
conscious
cony-catch
cancerate
centenary
contender
conger-eel
canceleer
centering
congenial
Cancerian
connexion
centesimo
cancelier
centenier
congeries
convexity
cancelled
concealer
concerned
condemned
contemned
contemner
contemnor
cancerous
cankerous
contemper
conferred
conferrer
confessed
condenser
confessor
consensus
contessas
conceited
concerted
congested
connected
contented
contested
concentre
concenter
connecter
connector
contester
convector
converter
convertor
concentus
conceptus
concertos
confestly
cannelure
confervae
conserver
confervas
Coniferae
canefruit
cynegetic
cinchonic
cantharid
cantharis
cantharus
conchitis
candidate
confidant
candidacy
condiddle
cantilena
centipede
centinell
confiseur
△confiteor
canniness
cantiness
condiment
confident
connivent
conticent
△continent
concisely
cunningly
confiding
confining
convivial
condition
conciliar
△**canticles**
confirmed
confirmee
confirmer
confirmor
consigned
consignee
consigner
consignor
cincinnus
condignly
cuneiform
concierge
centigram
continued
configure
confiture
continual
continuum
continuer
continuos
canal-rays
concluded
canal-cell
confluent
canellini
Candlemas
candlenut
canal-boat
cinematic
canonical
conundrum
cannonade
centonate
connotate
convocate
consonant
concordat
Cantonese
Congolese
cannoneer
condolent
cantonise
cantonize
connotive
cantoning
cantorial
censorial
censorian
cannonier
consocies
centonist
conformal
conformer
conjoined
contornos
consonous
contoured
concourse
consortia
consorted
contorted
concocter
concoctor
consorter
consolute
convolute
canopying
can-opener
canephora
canephore
conspirer
concreate
centrical
congruent
centreing
congruity
contrôlée
contralti
contralto
centrally
cineramic
confronté
centriole
cinereous
congruous
cineraria
confrérie
contrasty
cinerator
contrived
contriver
canescent
cane-sugar
cane-trash
constrain
constable
constrict
constancy
cinctured
cunctator
construer
construct
cannulate
conjugate
consulage
consulate
conjugant
contumacy
contumely
concubine
conducive
contusive
conjuring
consuming
centurial
connubial
centurion
Confucian
confusion
contusion
△**conqueror**
consultee
conductor
consulter
consultor
conductus
centumvir
concyclic
condyloma
condyloid
candytuft
crotaline
crotalism
choralist
cholaemia
cholaemic
Cro-Magnon
crowberry
cropbound
crotchety
choiceful
cook-chill
cloacalin
cloacinal
cloudland
cloud-capt
cloudless
chondrite
chondrify
clogdance
coordinal
co-ordinal
chondroid
chondrule
choleraic
cooperage
cooperate
co-operate
chokedamp
co-operant
closehead
choke-pear
closeness
closeting
coopering
cholelith
clovepink
close-knit
chokebore
chokecoil
closedown
crop-eared
clove-tree
choke-full
cholecyst
crowfoots
cloth-yard
cloth-hall
crocheted
coonhound
chophouse
chop-house
cookhouse
coolhouse
clonicity
chorionic
chorizont
crosiered
chorister
crookback
chowkidar
crookedly
clockwise
clock-golf
clockwork
cloakroom
chock-full
choplogic
crop-marks

Words marked △ may be spelled also with a capital letter

crown-bark
crown-head
crownless
crownwork
crown-post
chocolate
chocolaty
crocodile
crocosmia
chorology
clodpated
crow-quill
choir-girl
crossband
cross-fade
croustade
crossjack
cross-talk
crosswalk
crossfall
croissant
crosshead
crossbeam
crossness
crow-steps
crow's-nest
crosswind
crossbite
crossfire
crosswise
crossfish
chopstick
cross-kick
crossbill
cross-sill
crow's-bill
cloisonné
crossroad
crossword
crosstown
crow's-foot
crossbred
crosstree
cloistral
crossette
cross-ruff
crossbuck
crossover
cross-eyed
clout-nail
clout-shoe
chorusing
croquante
croquette
cephalate
capsaicin
captaincy
captainry
cephalous
capocchia
capacious

cepaceous
copacetic
capacitor
copresent
ciphering
coppering
copperish
copsewood
cupbearer
Cupressus
captivate
capriccio
coppicing
captivity
cyprinoid
caprifole
caprifoil
capriform
Capricorn
capillary
capelline
cupelling
cipollino
copolymer
co-polymer
cupolated
caponiere
coping-saw
coprolite
coprolith
coprozoic
coprology
copiously
copyright
co-portion
copartner
caparison
caper-bush
copes-mate
copestone
copataine
copatriot
capitella
capitulum
capitular
capitally
capitanos
capotasto
capsulate
capsulary
capsulise
capsulize
caprylate
coquetted
coquilles
carbamate
curtalaxe
coriander
Cornaceae
carrageen
carbachol

carbamide
cardamine
carnalise
carnalize
cercariae
curvative
carnalism
curialism
carbanion
carnation
cercarian
circadian
corrasion
curtation
curvation
caryatids
carnalist
curialist
carnality
corralled
certainly
certainty
carbazole
currajong
currawong
carvacrol
Cordaites
carnahuba
curvature
cardboard
corkboard
cerebrate
cornbrake
cornbrash
Carabidae
cornbread
Caribbean
cerebella
carabiner
corybants
corkborer
cornborer
cerebrums
corncrake
cerecloth
ceraceous
corocoros
corydalis
careenage
correlate
cursenary
carpet-bed
carpetbag
carpet-bag
corner-boy
cerberean
△carmelite
cartelise
cartelize
carpeting
corbeling

corseting
curveting
careerism
cartelism
carnelian
Cartesian
cerberian
cornelian
Cordelier
corsetier
careerist
cartelist
cornetist
corbelled
corbeille
corner-man
curvesome
carpet-rod
curvetted
carpenter
corrector
carpentry
correctly
currently
cornemuse
cornflake
cornfield
carefully
cornflour
cerograph
coraggios
Coregonus
cirrhopod
cart-horse
Corchorus
cirrhosis
cirrhotic
cart-house
corfhouse
cartilage
circinate
corticate
curtilage
cardiacal
card-index
cirripede
carbineer
corkiness
curdiness
curliness
corrigent
cursively
carpingly
currishly
certified
cormidium
carbinier
certifier
cardialgy
cordially
carcinoma

Carnivora
corticoid
carnivore
cortisone
cirriform
cordiform
corniform
curviform
corridors
cursitory
corbicula
curricula
certitude
corollary
coral-reef
△coralline
corallite
corolline
carolling
coral-fish
Corallian
coralloid
coral-rock
ceruleous
coralroot
coralwort
caroluses
corsleted
chromidia
chromogen
chromakey
ceromancy
carambola
carambole
corymbose
chromatic
chromatid
chromatin
chronicle
chronical
carangoid
corantoes
coronated
coroneted
chronaxie
carbonade
carbonate
carronade
cartonage
corporate
Carbonari
carbonado
cormorant
corposant
cursorary
cartouche
corporeal
cornopean
corrodent
carbonise
carbonize

9 c□r□o

carnotite
corrosive
cursorial
corrosion
carnosity
corporify
curiosity
cursorily
carpology
cartology
cordotomy
cartogram
carrousel
caryopses
caryopsis
coreopsis
curiously
coryphaei
coryphene
cardpunch
carap-wood
cardphone
curlpaper
cartridge
coruscate
cornstalk
cart's-tail
card-sharp
coruscant
caressive
cerussite
caressing
cerastium
Christian
chrysalid
corn-salad
chrysalis
Christmas
chrysanth
cornstone
curbstone
corkscrew
curettage
cart-track
card-table
ceratodus
curstness
caretaker
ceratitis
carburate
circulate
corrugate
cartulary
carbuncle
corpuscle
corpulent
carfuffle
curfuffle
carburise
carburize
co-routine
curcumine
curculios
corduroys
corrupter
circuitry
corruptly
corivalry
caravaned
caravance
caravaner
cartwheel
carrytale
carry-back
Carlylese
curry-leaf
Carlylean
cordyline
Carlylism
currycomb
cispadane
Cassandra
Cistaceae
cassareep
castanets
costalgia
casuarina
cassaripe
casualise
casualize
c'est-à-dire
casualism
caseation
cassation
Castalian
cessation
co-starred
cascadura
case-bound
caste-mark
casteless
coshering
cosseting
cosmetics
castellum
castellan
cisternae
casserole
cosphered
castigate
cuspidate
cassimere
cystidean
costively
cassingle
Castilian
coseismic
coseismal
cushioned
cushionet
cespitose
cuspidore
cystiform
cashierer
casuistic
casuistry
case-knife
cisalpine
cisplatin
casemaker
casemated
cosmorama
cassonade
cystocarp
cosmonaut
cassowary
customary
Cystoidea
cystocele
castoreum
cosmogeny
customise
customize
cystolith
custodial
custodian
custodier
cassocked
cassoulet
castor-oil
cosmogony
cosmology
cystotomy
cosmotron
cosmocrat
cosponsor
castrated
cesarevna
cast-steel
case-study
custumary
costumier
catharise
catharize
cottaging
Catharism
Catharist
citharist
cat-hammed
cattaloes
catharses
catharsis
cathartic
catabolic
catabasis
cataclasm
catechise
catechize
catechism
catechist
coticular
cuticular
cetaceous
cataclysm
Cytherean
cotter-pin
cathedral
cathectic
cut-leaved
catafalco
citigrade
categoric
catchable
catchweed
catchment
catchword
catchpole
catchpoll
cut-throat
catch-crop
cutcherry
cattiness
cat-rigged
cattishly
cat-witted
cat-silver
cytokinin
cotyledon
catalogue
cataloger
cotillion
cattleman
catalepsy
catalyser
catalysis
cytolysis
catalytic
côtelette
catalexis
catalyzer
catamenia
catamaran
cytometer
cytometry
catamount
cat-and-dog
cotangent
co-tenancy
cutaneous
cottonade
cotton-gin
chthonian
cataplasm
cytoplasm
cataplexy
cytopenia
catoptric
cataphyll
caterwaul
catarrhal
catarhine
cityscape
catatonia
catatonic
cytotoxic
cytotoxin
cothurnus
cutty-sark
citizenry
causative
Caucasian
causation
causality
Caucasoid
cruzadoes
clubbable
crumblies
chubb-lock
courbaril
crumb-tray
courbette
church-ale
churching
churchism
councilor
churchman
churchway
cauldrife
cauterant
Clupeidae
causeless
crudeness
cauterise
cauterize
cauterism
cautelous
cruzeiros
courgette
crushable
cauchemar
couchette
clubhouse
cousinage
churidars
caulinary
crucified
crucifier
caudillos
cautioner
cautionry
cauliform
cruciform
coulisses
chuckling
chuckhole
chuck-full
coupledom
cruelness
churnmilk
crumpling
churr-worm
chuprassy
counselor
caumstone
cruiseway

Words marked △ may be spelled also with a capital letter

court-card
courtyard
countable
Crustacea
countless
crustless
court-leet
countship
courtship
countline
courtlike
courtling
Courtelle®
court-roll
courtroom
count-down
courteous
clustered
courtesan
crustated
courtezan
couturier
clubwoman
civically
cevadilla
cave-earth
cavalcade
covellite
cavilling
covalency
civilised
civiliser
civilized
civilizer
cavendish
covin-tree
cevapcici
covariant
coverslip
coveralls
cavernous
coverture
covetable
cevitamic
cowfeeder
cowdie-gum
cowardice
cowardree
cowl-staff
△coxsackie
coxcombic
coxcombry
ceylanite
cly-faking
Clydeside
cryogenic
chymistry
cryometer
Ceylonese
ceylonite
cryoprobe

cryoscope
cryoscopy
cryptical
cryptadia
cryptogam
coyotillo
cryptonym
dead-alive
Dramamine®
dramatise
dramatize
dramatics
dramatist
diamagnet
dramaturg
drabbling
drag-chain
dratchell
dead-doing
diandrous
draperied
deadening
deafening
diapering
dianetics®
draperies
diametric
diametral
dialectic
dialectal
diazeuxis
draughter
draught-ox
deathward
death-rate
death-mask
diaphragm
death-damp
death-bell
death-cell
deathless
death-fire
deathlike
diachylum
diachylon
death-blow
deathsman
death-song
death-roll
dray-horse
death-trap
diathermy
diaphysis
diathesis
diathetic
draghound
deadhouse
death-duty
diapirism
Dravidian
dualistic

diallagic
diablerie
dead-level
dharmsala
dead-march
drainable
drainpipe
drain-tile
drain-trap
diagnoses
diagnosis
diaconate
dragomans
diamonded
deaconess
dragoness
dragonfly
diabolise
diabolize
dialogise
dialogite
dialogize
diatomite
dragonise
dragonize
dragonish
diabolism
diacodium
diazonium
△draconism
dragonism
diacodion
△draconian
diabolist
dialogist
diatomist
diabology
dianoetic
△dracontic
dial-plate
draw-plate
drag-queen
diarrheic
diarrheal
diarrhoea
diatropic
diaereses
diaeresis
diacritic
diatretum
draw-sheet
deadstock
draw-table
diastolic
draftsman
diactinic
diactinal
diastasic
diastasis
diastatic
dead-water

diapyesis
diapyetic
debagging
debelling
debenture
dubiosity
dubiously
Dobermann
debarrass
debarment
debarring
debussing
debatable
dubitable
dubitably
debateful
débutante
dib-stones
dubitancy
debauched
debauchee
debaucher
de-blurred
debruised
declarant
dichasial
dichasium
dictation
declaimer
dictatory
dictatrix
déclassée
dictature
duck-board
decubitus
deckchair
dock-cress
decoctive
decoction
decachord
dicacious
deck-cargo
decocture
docudrama
deciduate
decidable
decidedly
decadence
decadency
deciduous
△decretals
decrement
decretive
decreeing
docketing
decretist
déchéance
decretory
Decagynia
decagonal
decoherer

deckhouse
dacoitage
declinate
declinant
deceitful
diclinism
declivity
ductility
declivous
diclinous
decollate
décolleté
decalogue
decillion
decalcify
decalitre
decilitre
deciliter
decumbent
decemviri
decemvirs
decomplex
decimally
decompose
Decameron
decametre
decimetre
decimator
decimeter
decantate
decennary
decongest
decennial
decennium
decencies
Decandria
decontrol
doctorand
doctorate
dichogamy
doctoress
doctorial
dicrotism
dicrotous
dichotomy
decapodal
decapodan
deceptive
deception
deceptory
decurrent
decursive
dichroite
dichroism
decursion
dichromic
dichromat
doctrinal
decorated
decorator
decussate

9 d□c□s

decastere
decistere
duck's-meat
dicastery
decastich
decession
Dicksonia
duckshove
duck's-foot
dachshund
decastyle
Dicotylae
decathlon
Docetists
decaudate
decoupage
découpage
dictyogen
dicky-bird
dactylist
decoy-duck
didrachma
deducible
dodecagon
deductive
deduction
didactics
dedicated
dedicatee
dedicator
doddering
doddipoll
Dadaistic
Didelphia
didelphic
didelphid
Didelphis
Didelphys
Dodonaean
Didynamia
doddypoll
drepanium
△daedalian
dietarian
diet-bread
deerberry
deep-drawn
dreadless
diet-drink
dieselise
dieselize
dietetics
dae-nettle
deer-fence
dredge-box
deer-hound
drerihead
dietician
dietitian
die-sinker
djellabah
dream-land
dreamless
dreamtime
dreamhole
dreamboat
deer-mouse
dressmake
dyer's-weed
dyer's-weld
dress-coat
dress-suit
deep-toned
duettinos
defrauder
defraying
defeatism
deflation
defeatist
defiantly
defeature
deficient
defective
defection
defecator
defaecate
dufferdom
different
dufferism
deflexion
deflected
deflector
deflexure
diffident
duffing-up
difficile
difficult
defalcate
defoliate
defoliant
diffluent
defendant
definable
definably
Defenders
definiens
defensive
deflorate
defroster
deferable
deferment
deferring
deformity
deference
defatting
diffusely
diffusive
defluxion
diffusion
defaulter
dog-paddle
dog-eat-dog
dogmatise
dogmatize
degrading
dogmatism
dogmatics
dogmatist
dog-salmon
dogmatory
degree-day
dog-legged
doggerman
dog-kennel
dog-letter
dogshores
dignitary
dogginess
doggishly
dignified
dog-violet
do-goodery
do-gooding
do-goodism
dog-collar
degarnish
dogaressa
degustate
digestive
digestion
digastric
digitalin
digitalis
dog's-tooth
digitiser
digitated
digitizer
dahabeeah
dahabiyah
dahabiyeh
dehydrate
dehiscent
deiparous
driveable
drivelled
driveller
dyingness
dziggetai
drink-hail
drinkable
drillship
drill-hole
deinosaur
Deinornis
drip-stone
drift-land
drift-sail
deistical
drift-weed
driftless
driftwood
drift-bolt
deid-thraw
dairymaid
dairy-farm
dejection
dejectory
dika-bread
Dekabrist
Dukhobors
dulcamara
delta-wing
Dalmatian
Dalradian
dulocracy
delicious
deludable
dolefully
delegable
diligence
delighted
delphinia
Delphinus
dolphinet
doll-house
dolliness
doltishly
dalliance
Dulcitone®
dulcitude
dolomitic
delineate
delundung
△daltonism
Daltonian
delapsion
deliquium
deliriant
dolorific
delirious
doleritic
deliriums
delusions
Delftware
dilatable
dilutable
dilatancy
dilatator
deliverer
deliverly
dill-water
dolly-shop
Domdaniel
damnation
dimyarian
demeanour
damnatory
demobbing
△democracy
democraty
Damoclean
domiciled
dumb-cluck
dimidiate
demi-deify
demi-devil
damselfly
dumbfound
demagogic
demagogue
demi-gorge
dumminess
dumpiness
dumpishly
demulcent
demulsify
demi-lance
demi-monde
dementate
demandant
dominical
Dominican
demanding
demanning
dimension
dominance
dominancy
dominions
dominator
dumb-piano
damp-proof
demipique
demarcate
demurrage
dimorphic
demurring
demersion
demisable
△damascene
damaskeen
demissive
demission
domestics
demystify
dimissory
damasquin
demitasse
demiurgic
demiurgus
demi-volte
dungarees
dentalium
dentation
dune-buggy
Dinoceras
dance-band
dance-hall
danceable
denseness
dandelion
donkey-man
dungeoner
dangerous
Dantesque
dannebrog

Words marked △ may be spelled also with a capital letter

dancettee
dance-tune
denigrate
dandiacal
dinginess
denyingly
dandified
dentition
densifier
dentiform
dandiprat
dentistry
dynamical
dynamiter
dynamotor
dining-car
Dinantian
Dundonian
Dundreary
dendritic
denitrate
denotable
Dunstable
dinothere
do-nothing
denitrify
denouncer
dandy-cart
dandy-cock
dandy-roll
dandyprat
dandyfunk
door-cheek
dioecious
Dioscorea
drop-drill
dromedare
dromedary
duodenary
drone-pipe
duodecimo
drove-road
drop-forge
diosgenin
deoxidate
droningly
dronishly
deoxidise
deoxidize
dioristic
doorknock
doodlebug
drollness
doorn-boom
deodorant
deodorise
deodorize
door-plate
drop-press
droppings
dropsical
door-stead
drop-scene
drowsihed
doorstone
drop-scone
dropstone
dioestrus
doomsayer
dioptrate
dioptrics
doomwatch
Dionysiac
Dionysian
depravity
depictive
depiction
depicture
Dipodidae
deprecate
depredate
deprehend
depletive
depletion
dipterist
dipterous
depletory
depressed
depressor
dip-sector
dope-fiend
depthless
depth-bomb
duplicand
duplicate
dip-circle
duplicity
dapple-bay
depilator
dependant
dependent
depending
dupondius
diplomate
diplomacy
diplozoon
deprogram
dipeptide
departing
depurator
departure
deposable
depositor
depasture
diphthong
dip-switch
△**diphysite**
darraigne
Dardanian
dermatoid
dermatome
dartboard
dirt-cheap
directive
direction
△**directory**
directrix
Dorididae
dare-devil
dor-beetle
darkfield
direfully
dirigible
dirigisme
dirigiste
dark-house
dirtiness
derring-do
derringer
dartingly
dormitive
Darwinism
Darwinian
dormition
Darwinist
dorsiflex
dormitory
Duralumin®
duralumin
darklings
doronicum
Dormobile®
derisible
dirt-track
derivable
derivably
disparage
disparate
discalced
discandie
dastardly
dismayful
dismaying
dissaving
d'escalier
dismality
disparity
disjaskit
dishallow
disdained
disfavour
dispauper
dismantle
distantly
dashboard
dust-brand
disoblige
deskbound
desk-bound
dust-brush
desecrate
desiccate
desiccant
disaccord
dish-cloth
dish-clout
dish-cover
dust-devil
disregard
desperate
desperado
disrepair
dissemble
dismember
dissembly
descended
descender
disbelief
disrelish
dysgenics
dispelled
discerner
dispeople
destemper
distemper
dyspepsia
dispensed
dispersal
disseisin
dispenser
disperser
disseisor
dyslectic
dyspeptic
dystectic
dissected
dissector
△dissenter
desuetude
disrepute
désoeuvré
disseizin
disseizor
dish-faced
disaffect
disaffirm
designate
designful
designing
dysphagia
dysphagic
dysthymia
dysthymic
dysphonia
dysphonic
dyschroia
disthrone
dysphoria
dysphoric
discharge
dischurch
dysphasia
dysthesia
dysthetic
dosshouse
disshiver
destinate
dissipate
duskiness
dustiness
dissident
distingué
dashingly
distichal
duskishly
dissimile
distilled
distiller
dismissal
destitute
disfigure
displease
disfluent
desulphur
desalting
desultory
dysplasia
desolater
desolator
disillude
displayed
displayer
disembark
disemploy
disembody
dose-meter
dosimeter
dosimetry
disimmure
disengage
disentail
disenable
dyspnoeic
dyspnoeal
disinfect
disinfest
disinvest
dysentery
disanchor
disanoint
desinence
disentomb
disinhume
despotate
dislocate
dissonant
disgodded
dispondee
discoidal
discovert
disforest
dishonest
discovery
discomfit
disbodied

Words marked △ may be spelled also with a capital letter

9 d□s□o

disposing
dissocial
desmodium
despotism
dystopian
despoiler
discommon
desmosome
discolour
dishonour
dosiology
discourse
distorted
disposure
dissolute
disappear
desipient
dustproof
desirable
describer
desirably
disgracer
discredit
disorient
disprofit
dispraise
distraite
descrying
deserving
disarming
desertion
distraint
disbranch
disproove
dystrophy
dyscrasia
disprison
disproved
disproval
disproven
dyspraxia
destroyed
destroyer
disesteem
dustsheet
dust-storm
disattire
disattune
dishtowel
despumate
disputant
disturbed
discumber
disturber
disburden
dissuader
dissunder
dishumour
disguised
disbursal
disguiser

discursus
disgusted
dislustre
disrupter
disruptor
dispurvey
disavouch
disavowal
dash-wheel
dishwater
dusty-foot
dittander
dot-matrix
detractor
détraquée
duty-bound
detective
detection
datacomms
△**dithelete**
△**dithelism**
dithecous
dutifully
dottiness
detriment
detrition
dithionic
dottipoll
datum-line
detention
detonator
ditrochee
dittology
duteously
detergent
determent
deterrent
determine
detersive
deterring
detersion
detorsion
detortion
dethroner
date-stamp
date-shell
date-sugar
detrusion
dithyramb
drum-belly
druidical
deuterate
doucepere
douceness
douzepers
deuteride
deuterium
drug-fiend
dough-ball
Doukhobor
doughtily

drunkenly
double-axe
double-bar
doubleton
double-you
drum-major
diurnally
drumstick
drug-store
doubtable
dauntless
doubtless
diuturnal
duumviral
deviation
deviatory
deviceful
dove-drawn
dividable
dividedly
dividuous
dove-house
devaluate
divulgate
devil's-bit
devilment
divellent
devilship
divulsive
devilling
devil-fish
divulsion
divalency
developed
developer
devil-crab
davenport
devonport
divinator
deviously
divergent
diversely
divertive
divorcive
diverging
diverting
diversion
diversify
diversity
devastate
devisable
divisible
divisibly
dove's-foot
divesture
devotedly
devitrify
devotions
devouring
dewlapped
downburst

downforce
downgrade
down-going
down-gyved
dowdiness
downiness
dowelling
down-lying
down-quilt
dowerless
downright
downstage
downstair
downswing
downspout
down-train
downtrend
dowitcher
down-throw
downwards
Dexedrine®
Dixieland
dexterity
dexterous
dextrally
dextrorse
day-sailor
dry-waller
day-labour
drysalter
day-school
day-length
day-nettle
day-return
dayr'house
dry-fisted
dayspring
Dryasdust
dizygotic
dizziness
emanative
emanation
evagation
exaration
emanatist
Elaeagnus
emanatory
eparchate
exarchate
exarchist
Ecardines
égarement
erasement
elaterite
elaterium
enamelled
enameller
evangelic
eradicate
evaginate
examinate

exanimate
examinant
evasively
examining
evanition
emaciated
epaulette
état-major
epaenetic
epainetic
elaborate
evaporate
enamorado
elaeolite
evaporite
enamoured
exactable
exaltedly
exanthema
exactness
exactress
exanthems
enactment
exactment
elastomer
elastance
ejaculate
evacuator
embraceor
embracery
embrangle
embracive
embracing
embrasure
embrazure
embedment
embedding
embodying
emblemata
emblemise
emblemize
embreathe
embrittle
emballing
embalming
embellish
embrocate
embroider
embroglio
emblossom
embarrass
Ember-days
Ember-week
embarking
embarring
embargoed
embargoes
emboscata
embassade
embassage
embussing

Words marked △ may be spelled also with a capital letter

9 e□i□e

embattled
elbow-room
embayment
embryonic
embryonal
embryo-sac
embryotic
embezzler
esclandre
exchanger
Encratite
Encratism
Eucharist
enchanted
enchanter
excrement
excretive
exceeding
ecclesial
excretion
excretory
encierros
encheason
escheator
△**exchequer**
enchilada
escribano
Euclidean
encrinite
encrimson
exculpate
Excalibur
excellent
excelling
encolpium
encolpion
△**excelsior**
eucalypti
euchloric
escalator
encompass
encomiast
excambium
excambion
encomiums
encanthis
eccentric
excentric
enchorial
euchology
enclosure
exclosure
exceptant
escapable
excipient
exceptive
excepting
exception
escopette
escortage
excarnate
excoriate
encurtain
excurrent
excursive
excursion
eucaryote
excerptum
excerptor
excisable
excusable
excusably
excessive
exciseman
excitable
excitedly
excitancy
encourage
excaudate
exclusive
exclusion
exclusory
encaustic
encounter
excavator
eachwhere
encrypted
endearing
endeavour
eudialyte
endoblast
endecagon
endocrine
end-reader
eudaemony
endlessly
eidograph
endogamic
endogenic
endeictic
endolymph
endemical
endamoeba
eudemonia
eudemonic
endomorph
endomixis
endungeon
endenizen
endoplasm
endophagy
endophyte
endurable
endurably
endorphin
eldership
endurance
eiderdown
eider-duck
ecdysiast
endosteal
endosperm
endosteum
endoscope
endosmose
endospore
endoscopy
endowment
Ebenaceae
epedaphic
elevation
edematose
edematous
elevatory
elegantly
exerciser
exercises
emendable
emendator
eyeleteer
événement
exegetics
exegetist
ewe-necked
elevenses
elemental
△**everglade**
evergreen
energumen
exergonic
emergence
emergency
energetic
eyeshadow
ewe-cheese
erethitic
elegiacal
eremitism
eye-glance
epeolatry
eternally
esemplasy
exemplary
eye-splice
exemption
exemplify
eye-opener
execrable
execrably
Epeiridae
eyebright
eversible
eventrate
eventuate
eyestrain
electuary
electable
eleutheri
electress
erectness
ejectment
electrise
electrize
eye-string
electrify
electrode
electoral
executant
executive
execution
executory
executrix
exequatur
edelweiss
everywhen
everybody
efficient
effective
effectual
enfreedom
exfoliate
effulgent
effulging
effortful
efference
effluvial
effluvium
effluxion
effluence
Englander
engravery
engraving
engrained
engrainer
engrenage
eagle-hawk
eaglewood
egg-beater
eagle-eyed
ergograph
Englisher
Englishry
Englified
ergomania
ergometer
ergonomic
engine-man
eigentone
engendure
egg-powder
engrossed
engrosser
engarland
eagerness
engiscope
engyscope
eightieth
eightsman
ergataner
eightfold
eightsome
eightfoil
eight-hour
eightfoot
eight-foot
engoûment
englutted
ethnarchy
enhearten
ephialtes
exhibiter
exhibitor
ethically
echidnine
enhydrite
ephedrine
enhydrous
ethnicism
ethnicity
exhalable
ephelides
ethologic
echolalia
ephemerid
ephemerae
ephemeral
ephemeron
ephemeras
ephemeris
enhancive
echinated
ethmoidal
ethnocide
Ethiopian
ethnology
etherical
ephoralty
ethereous
exhausted
exhauster
echeveria
Ericaceae
epitaphic
epitapher
epitaxial
emication
epilation
evitation
epigaeous
epinastic
evincible
evincibly
episcopal
exilement
epicedial
epicedium
epicedian
epidermic
epidermal
epidermis
exigeante
eviternal
epineural
epileptic
epicentre

Words marked △ may be spelled also with a capital letter

9 e□i□e

epicenter
eminently
evidently
exigently
epizeuxis
epiphragm
epiphanic
epiphyses
epiphysis
epithesis
epiphytic
epithetic
epiphytal
epitheton
eliminate
eliminant
edificial
epinician
epinicion
epinikian
epinikion
edibility
epicleses
epiclesis
etiolated
enigmatic
eriometer
ebionitic
epidosite
epilogise
epilogize
epitomise
epitomize
editorial
episodial
epilobium
epipolism
epilogist
epitomist
epizootic
epirrhema
epigraphy
epicritic
eristical
epistolic
epistoler
epistolet
edictally
epistemic
existence
epistases
epistasis
epistatic
epistaxis
△**epicurean**
epicurise
epicurize
epicurism
etiquette
epicyclic
epigynous
enjoyable
enjoyably
enjoyment
enkindled
eukaryote
eel-basket
ex-librism
ex-librist
eclectics
enlighten
eulogiums
eclampsia
eclamptic
eglantine
ealdorman
ellipsoid
enlivener
Eumycetes
eumelanin
Eumenides
Emmenthal
emmetrope
ennobling
eunuchise
eunuchize
eunuchism
eunuchoid
egomaniac
evocative
evocation
exoration
exogamous
evocatory
exorciser
exorcizer
exordiums
exonerate
elopement
esoterica
esoterism
exodermal
exodermis
erogenous
exogenous
elongated
ecophobia
esophagus
egotheism
eroticise
eroticize
emotivism
eroticism
exoticism
eroticist
emotional
egotistic
Elohistic
emolliate
emollient
exosmosis
exosmotic
eloinment
exoenzyme
economise
economize
exopodite
economism
economics
ecologist
economist
ecosphere
exosphere
exosporal
écossaise
erostrate
exostoses
exostosis
emolument
evolutive
elocution
evolution
eloquence
elocutory
evolvable
eponymous
ecosystem
esplanade
emphasise
emphasize
expiation
explainer
expiatory
Euphausia
euphausid
emplastic
emplaster
expectant
expecting
expedient
expediter
expeditor
euphemise
euphemize
expletive
euphemism
euphenics
expletory
espressos
expressly
empaestic
emplectum
emplecton
espagnole
explicate
emptiness
emptional
expellant
expellent
expulsive
expelling
expulsion
emphlyses
emphlysis
espumosos
empennage
exponible
expansile
expansive
expensive
expansion
empanoply
espionage
euphorbia
euphonise
euphonize
explosive
exploring
euphonism
euphonium
explosion
exploiter
expurgate
expirable
empirical
expertise
expertize
esperance
Esperanto
ekphrasis
empyreuma
emporiums
episcate
exposable
expositor
exposture
expatiate
empathise
empathize
espousals
expounder
emphysema
Esquimaux
esquiress
exquisite
Eurocracy
enrheumed
earnestly
egregious
earthward
earth-bath
earthfall
earthfast
earthling
earthflax
earth-tone
earthwolf
earthwork
earthworm
earthborn
earth-bred
earth-star
eard-house
earliness
ébrillade
enrolment
enrolling
errand-boy
eirenicon
étrangère
enranckle
erroneous
ebriosity
ear-cockle
Europhile
enrapture
Euraquilo
Eurospeak
egression
erratical
eurytherm
écritoire
△**eurhythmy**
ecstasied
ecstasise
ecstasize
enstatite
Euskarian
eastbound
exsiccate
easy-chair
exsiccant
exsection
exsuccous
East-ender
easterner
ensheathe
enshelter
easy-going
eastlings
essential
ensorcell
exsertile
ex-service
exsertion
elsewhere
erstwhile
eastwards
essayette
estrapade
euthanasy
extravert
eutrapely
estranged
estranger
extraught
estuarine
extradite
estradiol
estuarial
estuarian
entralles
entrammel
extrapose
entrapper

Words marked △ may be spelled also with a capital letter

extractor
ectoblast
entoblast
establish
ectocrine
Eutychian
eutectoid
entremets
extremest
extremely
entrechat
extremism
eutherian
euthenics
euthenist
extremist
extremity
entrecôte
estafette
ectogenic
extricate
estrildid
extrinsic
entelechy
extolment
extolling
estimable
estimably
entamoeba
estaminet
extempore
ectomorph
estimator
extenuate
extendant
extensile
extensive
extension
extensity
extincted
extrovert
eutrophic
ectropium
entropium
ectropion
entropion
Esthonian
eutropous
extrorsal
estoppage
ectoplasm
estopping
entoptics
ectophyte
entophyte
entertake
extirpate
entertain
externals
enterable
Euterpean
extermine
extorsive
extortive
extortion
exteriors
enteritis
ectotherm
entourage
En-Tout-Cas®
extrusive
extrusion
extrusory
eutaxitic
enthymeme
educative
emulative
exudative
education
emulation
epulation
epuration
épuration
exudation
educatory
enunciate
emunction
emunctory
enumerate
exuberate
exuberant
educement
enurement
ecumenism
ecumenics
emulgence
elucidate
elusively
eruditely
erudition
esurience
esuriency
eruciform
eduskunta
enucleate
equalness
ebullient
equalling
equaliser
equalizer
eburneous
emulously
equipment
equipoise
equipping
elutriate
equisetic
equisetum
equitable
equitably
exultance
exultancy
equivocal
equivalve
equivoque
ervalenta
enveloped
envenomed
enviously
envermeil
eavesdrip
eavesdrop
envoyship
enwreathe
Edwardian
erythrina
erythrite
erythrism
erythemal
etymology
enzymatic
flambeaus
flambeaux
flaccidly
fraîcheur
fratchety
franchise
flanching
fratching
francolin
fraudsman
fraudster
flare-path
flamencos
flame-leaf
flameless
flabellum
flagellum
flageolet
fraternal
framework
flap-eared
flame-tree
flay-flint
fearfully
Franglais
frangible
flaughter
flashback
feathered
flashbulb
flashcube
flash-over
flagitate
flakiness
foaminess
fragilely
flamingos
flamingly
flaringly
foamingly
fragility
frankness
Frankenia
frailness
flatlings
flammable
flaunting
flannelly
flavoring
flavorous
flappable
flagrance
fragrance
flagrancy
fragrancy
flagstaff
flagstick
flagstone
flaptrack
franticly
feast-rite
fractious
flatterer
flatulent
featurely
flax-wench
flag-waver
Fabianism
Fabianist
fabaceous
fibreless
fabricate
fabricant
febricity
febrility
fibrillae
fibrillin
fibrillar
fibriform
fibrinous
febricula
febricule
febrifuge
Fibonacci
fibromata
fibroline
fibrolite
fibrocyte
fiberless
face-cream
face-cloth
face-guard
facsimile
factitive
facticity
factional
fictional
feculence
feculency
focimeter
fecundate
facundity
fecundity
factorage
factorise
factorize
factoring
factorial
factotums
face-plate
focussing
face-saver
facetious
fiduciary
fadedness
fidgeting
foddering
faddiness
fideistic
fiddle-bow
fuddle-cap
federarie
fee-faw-fum
free-board
free-bench
freebooty
fleeching
frescoing
frescoist
Frenchify
Frenchman
Frenchmen
fieldward
fieldfare
fiend-like
fieldsman
fieldvole
fieldwork
free-diver
foederati
fretfully
fledgling
freighter
fleshless
freshness
flesh-meat
fleshment
fleshling
flesh-tint
freshener
fleshings
fleshhood
flesh-hook
fleshworm
flechette
fléchette
fieriness
feelingly
flexitime
foeticide
fleckless
freckling
freelance
free-liver

9 f□e□m

△free-lover
△freemason
freephone
free-rider
free-range
fleurette
free-space
freesheet
freestone
feedstock
feedstuff
freestyle
fleetness
fleet-foot
frequence
frequency
freewheel
freewoman
freewomen
feed-water
freezable
frenzical
freeze-dry
freeze-out
fifteenth
fifteener
fife-major
fogramite
fogramity
fagaceous
fugacious
fig-pecker
fogginess
fog-signal
faggoting
figurable
figurante
fightback
fightable
fagottist
fricative
frigatoon
fricassee
fribbling
fribblish
foilborne
flip-chart
flinching
friedcake
feiseanna
fainéance
faineancy
fair-faced
faithless
frightful
frithgild
flightily
frithborh
faithcure
foiningly
frigidity
frikkadel
feignedly
friending
frivolity
frivolous
flippancy
fripperer
friarbird
faintness
flirt-gill
flintlock
fritterer
fairyland
fairytale
fairylike
fairy-ring
fairyhood
frizzante
fellaheen
fallalery
falcation
fellation
filiation
foliation
fellatios
foliature
full-blast
Félibrige
full-blood
full-blown
full-bound
full-cream
felicific
Filicales
filaceous
feliciter
full-dress
folk-dance
false-card
filter-bed
fullerene
falseness
faltering
filleting
Folketing
falsehood
falsework
filter-tip
falsettos
fulgently
full-faced
full-front
filigrane
filigrain
filigreed
full-grown
fill-horse
fulminate
fulminant
fillipeen
filminess
falsified
filliping
falsifier
fulfilled
fulfiller
falciform
fulminous
fillister
folkloric
filanders
△**falangism**
△**falangist**
felonious
foliolate
full-orbed
fulsomely
falconine
following
Fallopian
fellow-man
foliolose
fulgorous
filopodia
Filipinos
filoplume
filtrable
folk-right
Falernian
full-scale
feldspath
full-speed
filoselle
full-split
faldstool
film-strip
full-timer
falculate
fulgurate
fulgurant
fulgurite
fulgurous
folk-weave
fumigator
Fomalhaut
femineity
fimbriate
fumarolic
fumatoria
fanfarade
Finlander
fundament
fandangle
fandangos
fantasied
fantasise
fantasize
Fenianism
fantasist
fantailed
fanfarona
fantasque
fantastic
fantastry
funebrial
finickety
finocchio
finicking
funicular
funiculus
finically
fine-drawn
finger-end
fenceless
fingering
funnelled
funnel-net
fingertip
funnel-web
find-fault
fenugreek
fan-shaped
fanciable
fanciless
funkiness
funniness
fungicide
fungibles
fungiform
financial
financier
fining-pot
fungoidal
finnochio
fungosity
fin-footed
finessing
finishing
font-stone
fenestral
fanatical
fine-tooth
fen-sucked
fancy-sick
fancywork
fancy-free
frowardly
flotation
footboard
flowchart
floccular
floscular
flocculus
footcloth
floodgate
floodmark
floodwall
floodtide
flowerage
flower-bed
flower-bud
flowering
flowerpot
floreated
frog-eater
feoffment
footfault
frothless
foothills
froth-fomy
fool-happy
foolhardy
flophouse
Florideae
floridean
flowingly
foolishly
floridity
frolicked
floriform
floristic
floriated
floristry
fioritura
fioriture
frockless
frock-coat
footlight
footloose
frogmarch
flowmeter
frogmouth
flouncing
footplate
footprint
foolproof
foot-pound
floorhead
flourishy
footstalk
foot-stall
footsteps
footstool
foodstuff
frontward
front-page
front-rank
frost-nail
frontways
floatable
frontiers
frontless
frostless
frontager
front-line
frontwise
frostbite
frostlike
frostwork
foppishly
fire-alarm
forwander
forwarder
forwardly

Words marked △ may be spelled also with a capital letter

firmament
foreanent
forgather
formalise
formalize
formative
fortalice
forsaking
formalism
formation
furcation
formalist
formality
forjaskit
farragoes
fire-arrow
formatted
forfaiter
formatter
firebrand
fore-brace
forebrain
fire-blast
foreboder
fire-break
firebrick
forecabin
fore-caddy
firecrest
foreclose
forecloth
feracious
ferocious
furacious
fore-cited
fork-chuck
forecourt
fire-drake
force-land
forgeable
fardel-bag
force-feed
farmeress
forceless
forcemeat
forgetful
forgetive
far-seeing
ferreting
forjeskit
forcepses
fermented
fire-eater
forfeiter
forgetter
fervently
force-pump
firefloat
forefront
fireguard
fire-grate
forage-cap
foregleam
foregoing
forthwith
forthcome
fore-horse
furtherer
farmhouse
firehouse
forcipate
forficate
formicate
fornicate
fortilage
formicant
formicary
forbiddal
forbidden
forbidder
forkiness
furriness
furniment
fertilely
furtively
furnished
furbisher
furnisher
fortified
fertilise
fertilize
forgiving
fortifier
fertility
fervidity
foreigner
fire-irons
Forficula
fortitude
furniture
forejudge
foreknown
firelight
feralised
feralized
foraminal
forenight
fortnight
Feringhee
farandine
forensics
forenamed
farandole
far-sought
furiosity
forlornly
fervorous
ferrogram
furiously
forgotten
ferrotype
farm-place
fireplace
forepoint
fireproof
fire-power
forereach
fire-robed
forestage
foreslack
forestall
forestair
farmstead
forespend
forespeak
foresteal
foreshewn
forespent
forest-fly
foresight
forestine
fire-stick
foreskirt
firestone
foreshore
foreshock
forest-oak
fire-storm
foreshown
forasmuch
first-hand
first-rate
foreteach
fernticle
foreteeth
first-time
firstling
forethink
foretoken
foretooth
firethorn
first-born
first-foot
foretaste
formulaic
formulate
fortunate
formulary
formulise
formulize
fortunize
formulism
formulist
furfurole
furfurous
fore-wheel
foreweigh
firewoman
forewoman
forewomen
forswonck
fireworks
fire-water
forky-tail
forsythia
△forty-five
ferry-boat
fish-creel
fosterage
Fasten-e'en
fesse-wise
fastening
fostering
fisherman
foster-son
fish-guano
fish-garth
fascinate
festinate
fustigate
fissipede
fishiness
fussiness
fustiness
festively
fossilise
fossilize
fastigium
festivity
fissility
fossicker
fascicled
fashioner
festivous
festilogy
fascistic
fasciated
fascicule
fisticuff
fasciculi
fustilugs
fish-joint
fish-knife
fusillade
fish-louse
fossorial
fusionism
fusionist
festology
fish-plate
fish-spear
fish-slice
fish-scrap
fast-track
fossulate
fistulose
fistulous
fish-woman
fishyback
fat-tailed
feticidal
fetichise
fetichize
fetichism
fetichist
fatidical
fetidness
fat-headed
fattening
fatefully
fatigable
fatiguing
fattiness
fittingly
fatuitous
fat-witted
fetlocked
fatiscent
fetishise
fetishize
fetishism
fetishist
fetoscopy
fettucine
fettucini
feudalise
feudalize
feudalism
feudalist
frugalist
feudality
frugality
Foucault's
feudatory
foul-brood
four-by-two
faulchion
Fourcroya
flue-cured
fluidness
foundress
foundling
flûte-à-bec
flute-bird
flugelman
fluke-worm
four-flush
flushness
four-horse
four-hours
fluxional
fruticose
faunistic
fluviatic
feuilleté
fourpence
fourpenny
flurrying
fluorspar
fluoresce
fluorosis
fourscore
fluctuate
Fluothane®
flustrate

9 f□u□t

fructuate
fruit-cage
fruitcake
frustrate
fluctuant
fructuary
Fructidor
faultless
fruitless
fruitwood
fructuous
fruit-tree
fruiterer
four-wheel
five-a-side
faveolate
fivepence
fivepenny
favorable
favorably
favorless
fever-heat
fever-tree
favourite
fawningly
fixedness
fixed-wing
fox-hunter
flyweight
fly-fisher
fly-bitten
frying-pan
fly-by-wire
fuzziness
gravamina
gradation
guaranies
gravadlax
guacamole
guanazolo
gradatory
guarantee
guarantor
grandmama
grandpapa
guardrail
guardable
grandaddy
guardedly
grandness
guardless
guardship
guard-ship
grandsire
glandular
guardsman
grandiose
guard-book
guardroom
glandered
grand-aunt
graveyard
grapeseed
graceless
grapeless
graveless
graveness
grapeshot
grapevine
gravelled
glabellae
glabellar
gravel-pit
grapetree
Gradgrind
graphical
graphicly
graphemic
gnathonic
guacharos
graphitic
gratinate
gravitate
Gramineae
glaringly
gratingly
gratified
granitise
granitite
granitize
gratifier
gracility
gravidity
gladioles
gladiolus
granitoid
granivore
graciosos
gladiator
graticule
gratitude
gear-lever
grammatic
goalmouth
grauncher
glamorise
glamorize
glamorous
graspable
graspless
glaireous
grassland
glassware
glass-gall
goat's-hair
glasslike
gear-stick
gearshift
grass-plot
Gladstone
glass-rope
glasswork
grasshook
glasswort
glass-crab
glassfuls
grantable
ghastness
giantship
gianthood
ghastfull
granulate
gratulate
gratulant
granulary
granulite
gradually
granuloma
granulose
granulous
graduated
graduator
graywacke
gearwheel
gravy-soup
gobbeline
gibberish
gubbinses
gabionade
gabionage
Gibeonite
Gibbonian
gibbosity
gibbously
gabardine
gaberdine
go-between
godparent
godfather
goddamned
gadgeteer
godlessly
giddiness
godliness
God-gifted
God-a-mercy
godmother
gadrooned
godrooned
Gnetaceae
Gregarina
gregarine
grenadine
gregarian
grenadier
greybeard
gier-eagle
greegrees
glengarry
grewhound
greyhound
gaelicise
gaelicize
gmelinite
gaelicism
Greekless
Greekling
Glenlivet®
greenhand
△greensand
greengage
greenwash
greenback
greenmail
greenweed
greenness
Greenwich
greenwood
green-bone
greenroom
greenhorn
green-eyed
gremolata
glenoidal
Gregorian
guerrilla
guessable
gneissoid
gneissose
greystone
guesswork
Gaeltacht
greatness
ghettoise
ghettoize
guestwise
gee-string
guest-room
greatcoat
great-aunt
greywacke
goffering
gigmanity
gigahertz
goggle-box
gigantean
gigantism
go-getting
gris-amber
guitarist
grimalkin
grisaille
guildhall
guildsman
guideless
guileless
guideship
Ghibeline
guideline
guidebook
guidepost
guinea-pig
griefless
grief-shot
gainfully
goings-out
going-over
going-away
griminess
glidingly
gripingly
guilloche
guillemot
grillwork
gaillarde
glissandi
glissando
gritstone
gainsayer
guiltless
grist-mill
grievance
glitziest
Gujarathi
Gujerathi
galravage
gilravage
goliardic
gallabeah
gallabiya
galvanise
galvanize
gallabiah
gallabieh
galvanism
galvanist
gallantly
gallantry
gold-brick
galabiyah
galabiyeh
goldcrest
galactose
gold-cloth
gala-dress
gelidness
golden-eye
gilt-edged
galleried
gelsemine
galleting
gelsemium
Galwegian
goldenrod
goldfield
gillflirt
goldfinch
goldfinny
gold-fever
gelignite
gill-house
gallinazo
galliwasp
gallivant
gallingly

Words marked △ may be spelled also with a capital letter

△gallicise
△gallicize
gallisise
gallisize
△gallicism
gallinule
gold-laced
galumpher
golomynka
goldminer
galengale
galingale
Galenical
galantine
gallonage
gallopade
gallopers
galiongee
Gallophil
gilsonite
galloping
gallooned
gallowses
gold-plate
galapagos
galdragon
goldsmith
goldspink
goldstick
goldsinny
gallstone
goldstone
goloshoes
gully-hole
gally-crow
gemmative
gymnasial
gymnasium
gammadion
gammation
gemmation
gymnasien
gimmalled
gambadoes
gummatous
gymnastic
Gammexane®
gumshield
gomphoses
gomphosis
gumminess
gum-digger
gimmickry
gemel-ring
gaminerie
gammoning
gambogian
gummosity
gambolled
gymnosoph
gemmology

gemütlich
gumptious
genialise
genialize
goniatite
geniality
gendarmes
genealogy
gangboard
gynocracy
gonococci
genocidal
gingerade
gynaeceum
gynney-hen
ganderism
gynaecium
gynoecium
genteelly
gynaecoid
gingerous
genuflect
Gandhi-ism
genuinely
gentilise
gentilize
gentilish
gentilism
gentility
gannister
gangliate
gentleman
gentlemen
ginglymus
ganglions
gunpowder
Gongorism
gondolier
Gongorist
guncotton
gangplank
gang-punch
gonophore
gynophore
generable
generical
gonorrhea
generalia
generally
ginormous
generator
gong-stick
Genesitic
genetical
genitalia
genitalic
genotypic
genitival
gunrunner
geomancer
goosander

globalise
globalize
globalism
geocarpic
geomantic
geotactic
gaol-break
good-cheap
grouchily
glomerate
gooseherd
goose-neck
goose-wing
groveling
goose-fish
goose-girl
geodetics
groceries
geodesist
goose-skin
goose-club
grovelled
groveller
gloves-off
goosefoot
grotesque
geometric
geometrid
globe-trot
goose-step
glomerule
glomeruli
gronefull
goodfaced
gaol-fever
grosgrain
georgette
geophilic
geophones
geophytic
goodiness
goofiness
glowingly
gropingly
glorified
goodliest
groomsman
groundage
ground-ash
goodnight
groundhog
grounding
ground-ivy
groundman
groundnut
groundsel
geognosis
geologise
geologize
geologian
geoponics

gnomonics
geologist
globosity
groupable
geosphere
geotropic
geography
good-speed
grossness
grossular
glossator
glossitis
good-sized
gnostical
glottides
ghostlike
growthist
glottises
geostatic
globulite
globulous
good-willy
goodyears
Geomyidae
gypsywort
gerfalcon
gyrfalcon
germander
garlandry
germanely
gargarise
gargarize
Germanice
Germanise
Germanize
Germanish
gargarism
Germanism
germanium
Germanist
geriatric
garbanzos
garibaldi
gore-blood
garreteer
gardening
garderobe
garmented
giraffine
giraffoid
garagiste
girthline
germinate
germinant
garnishee
garnisher
garnishry
girlishly
germicide
garniture
gorilline

gorillian
gorblimey
gorilloid
gyromancy
gerundive
gerundial
Girondism
Girondist
girandola
girandole
gorgoneia
gorgonise
gorgonize
gorgonian
garbology
garrotted
garrotter
gyroplane
gyroscope
garotting
garrulity
garrulous
gyrovague
garryowen
gas-carbon
gossamery
gessamine
gestative
goslarite
gustative
gestation
gustation
gestatory
gustatory
gaspereau
gospelise
gospelize
gospeller
gas-retort
gaspiness
gassiness
gustiness
gaspingly
gushingly
gossiping
gas-filled
gas-fitter
gas-liquor
gasometer
gasometry
gastnesse
gasconade
gasholder
gasconism
gas-cooled
gismology
gas-bottle
gastraeum
gastropod
gastritis
gas-burner

Words marked △ may be spelled also with a capital letter

9 g□s□y

gossypine
Gossypium
Gothamite
guttation
Gothamist
gatecrash
gathering
gettering
guttering
gutter-man
gatehouse
gutsiness
gothicise
gothicize
Gothicism
Gothicist
gate-money
get-at-able
gate-tower
gutbucket
glutamate
glutamine
grumbling
Grundyism
gourd-worm
gaugeable
gaudeamus
glutenous
gauze-tree
gauleiter
gruffness
grudgeful
gaucherie
gauchesco
gaudiness
gauziness
goutiness
glucinium
glutinous
gruelling
glucoside
gruppetti
gruppetto
grubstake
gauntness
goustrous
glueyness
gavelkind
givenness
governall
governess
governing
gowpenful
gawkiness
gawkihood
gowdspink
geyserite
glyceride
glycerine
glycoside
glycollic
glycocoll
Glyptodon
gazpachos
gaze-hound
gizmology
gazetteer
gazetting
headboard
head-crash
headchair
headcloth
headdress
haanepoot
headframe
hoar-frost
heathbird
heathenry
heathcock
heath-fowl
hoarhound
headiness
heaviness
hoariness
healingly
hyalinise
hyalinize
hearkener
headlease
headlight
headliner
headlines
Hyaenidae
hyalonema
headpeace
headpiece
headphone
headreach
head-rhyme
headshake
headscarf
headstall
heapstead
headstick
headstone
hoar-stone
headstock
heartland
heartache
heartseed
heart-dear
heartless
heartbeat
heartfelt
healthful
heartling
heart-sick
healthily
heartikin
heart-bond
heartwood
heartsome
heart-sore
heart-free
hearth-rug
hearth-tax
heartburn
head-woman
head-water
heavy-duty
Hebraical
hobnailed
Hebraiser
Hebraizer
Hebrewess
Hebrewism
Hobbesian
Hebridean
hybridise
hybridize
hybridism
Hebridian
hybridity
hybridoma
Hobbinoll
hybridous
hubristic
hibakusha
habilable
hob-and-nob
hobjobber
hobgoblin
hibernate
habergeon
haberdine
hibernise
hibernize
Hibernian
habituate
habitable
habitably
hobbyless
huckaback
hackamore
hackberry
hecogenin
hackneyed
hectoring
hectorism
hectogram
huckstery
hocussing
hiccuping
hacqueton
hodmandod
hydrangea
hydrazine
hydration
hydraulic
hydraemia
hydrazoic
hide-bound
hiddenite
hedgebill
hodiernal
hedge-bote
hedge-born
hodograph
hydriodic
heddle-eye
hodometer
hodometry
hydrovane
hadrosaur
hydronaut
hydrocele
hydroxide
hideosity
hydrosoma
hydrosome
hydrofoil
hydrozoan
hydrozoon
hydrology
hideously
hydroptic
hydrostat
hydropult
hydrolyse
hydrolyte
hydrolyze
hedyphane
hederated
hodoscope
hydathode
hidey-hole
hierarchy
hieratica
haematite
hieracium
haematoma
haematoid
haecceity
heedfully
heediness
haemocoel
hierology
hyetology
hierogram
hierocrat
haemostat
hierodule
haemocyte
heel-piece
heftiness
huffiness
huffishly
hagiarchy
haggardly
Haggadist
high-blest
high-blown
highchair
high-class
high-dried
hygienics
hygienist
△high-flier
high-flown
△high-flyer
high-grade
high-grown
hag-ridden
hog-ringer
haggishly
hoggishly
hygristor
highlight
Highlands
high-level
hegemonic
hygrodeik
hygrophil
hagiology
hygrology
hugeously
hygrostat
high-place
high-proof
high-speed
high-toned
high-taper
high-viced
heir-at-law
hair-brush
haircloth
hairdrier
hairdryer
hair-grass
hairiness
heinously
hairpiece
hailstone
hail-storm
hairst-rig
hairspray
hairstyle
hair-waver
half-adder
Hollander
hallalled
hell-black
half-breed
half-baked
hill-billy
half-blood
hell-broth
halobiont
heliborne
Hylobates
half-bound
Helicidae
half-cheek
helictite
holocrine

Words marked △ may be spelled also with a capital letter

helically
half-close
half-crown
half-caste
holy-cruel
△**holocaust**
helidrome
half-dozen
holderbat
△**hellenise**
△hellenize
Hellenism
helvetium
Helvetian
Holmesian
Hellenist
hellebore
halieutic
half-frame
half-faced
holograph
half-hardy
hell-hated
half-hitch
hellhound
hilliness
haltingly
hellishly
half-light
halalling
halflings
half-miler
holing-axe
holloware
Hallowe'en
Hallowmas
heliozoic
heliozoan
heliology
heliostat
heliotype
heliotypy
half-plate
half-price
halophile
halophily
helipilot
halfpence
halfpenny
halophobe
holophote
half-pound
halophyte
holophyte
hylophyte
Haloragis
hilarious
Holarctic
half-round
half-royal
hallstand

Hallstatt
half-shell
heli-skier
half-shift
half-sword
holystone
heliscoop
halothane
half-track
half-timer
holotypic
holstered
halitosis
halitotic
half-title
half-truth
hellwards
holly-fern
Hollywood
hollyhock
hylozoism
hylozoist
ham-handed
hemialgia
Himyarite
hamfatter
homebound
homebuyer
humectate
homecraft
humectant
hemicycle
homicidal
humective
home-comer
hemoconia
home-croft
humidness
hamadryad
homoeobox
hammering
hammerkop
hummeller
hammerman
homoeosis
homoeotic
hammer-toe
home-guard
homograph
homograft
homogamic
home-grown
hemihedry
humdinger
ham-fisted
humiliate
humiliant
humble-bee
homologue
humble-pie
humblesse

hemolysis
hemolytic
homiletic
Himalayan
homemaker
△**hamamelis**
homomorph
hymeneals
Hominidae
hymenaeal
hymenaean
humanness
humankind
humanlike
homonymic
humongous
humungous
homuncule
homunculi
homeopath
homeomery
hymnodist
hummocked
homeowner
hymnology
hemiopsia
homoplasy
Hemiptera
Homoptera
homophile
homopolar
homophobe
homophone
homophony
homophyly
Homeridae
humorless
home-ruler
humorally
hemispace
homestall
homestead
hemistich
hamstring
hematinic
homotonic
hemitrope
homotypic
homotypal
hematuria
hematosis
hem-stitch
hamstrung
home-truth
homotaxic
homotaxis
humbugged
hamburger
humbugger
homousian
homewards

hen-paddle
hen-paidle
Hungarian
handbrake
hindbrain
hindberry
handclasp
handcraft
handcuffs
hinder-end
hungerful
hankering
Hunterian
henpecked
hanselled
Hanseatic
hand-glass
hang-glide
handgrips
hunchback
hendiadys
handiness
hintingly
handiwork
hen-witted
handlebar
hand-press
hand-paper
hundredth
hundreder
hundredor
honorific
hindrance
honoraria
hen-driver
handstand
handshake
handstaff
hindsight
handspike
hone-stone
hands-free
hand-screw
handsturn
handtowel
hind-wheel
honey-cart
honey-seed
honey-bear
honeyless
honey-bird
honey-blob
honeycomb
handywork
honky-tonk
honeymoon
honeypots
hunky-dory
honey-trap
hoolachan
hoof-bound

hooped-pot
hood-mould
hootnanny
hook-nosed
hoodooing
hoofprint
hoop-snake
haphazard
heptarchy
hop-garden
Hipparion
heptaglot
heptapody
hypoblast
hope-chest
hypocrite
hypocrisy
hopscotch
hypocotyl
hypocaust
hypoderma
hyphenate
hyphenise
hyphenize
happening
hyphenism
haplessly
hopefully
hypogaeal
hypogaeum
hypogaean
hypogeous
hip-girdle
hippiedom
happiness
hop-picker
hippiatry
hypallage
hypomania
hypomanic
hypinosis
hyponasty
hippodame
hypnoidal
hypnogeny
hypnotise
hypnotize
hypnotism
hypnotist
hip-pocket
hop-pocket
hypnotoid
haplology
hippology
hoplology
hypnology
hippocras
hypermart
hypergamy
Hypericum
hypertext

9 h□p□r

hyperfine
hyperlink
hyperemia
hyperemic
hyperbola
hyperbole
hyperopia
hypercube
hypernymy
hypostyle
Hepaticae
hepatical
hypotonia
hypotonic
hepatitis
hypotaxis
hippurite
hypoxemia
hypoxemic
hermandad
harmaline
hortative
herbalism
herbarium
herbarian
hortation
herbalist
hereabout
hortatory
harmattan
hereafter
hardboard
Heraclean
hard-cured
hard-drawn
harmdoing
Hirudinea
horseback
horsetail
horsehair
horseless
horsemeat
horseshoe
horsewhip
horsehide
hardening
hermetics
horsemint
hordeolum
horseplay
herpetoid
horsepond
horse-foot
harvester
Herpestes
harlequin
harmfully
hurtfully
herb-grace
hardgrass
harigalds
herd-groom
harshness
horehound
hermitage
△hurricane
hurricano
hurriedly
hardihead
hardiness
hermitess
horniness
horsiness
hardiment
herriment
harbinger
herringer
horrified
herbicide
herbivora
hardihood
herbivore
herbivory
herniated
horologic
horologer
hardliner
hartlesse
horn-maker
hard-metal
horometry
heronshaw
hirundine
hardnosed
harangued
haranguer
harborage
hariolate
hercogamy
herkogamy
harmonica
harmonise
Harmonite
harmonize
herborise
herborize
harrowing
harmonium
Harrovian
harmonics
△harmonist
herborist
hircosity
harpooner
harmotome
harbourer
hardparts
herb-Paris
hard-paste
herb-Peter
hard-ruled
hare-stane
hardshell
harp-shell
harassing
haruspicy
hornstone
horoscope
hartshorn
hare's-foot
horoscopy
heritable
heritably
heretical
heritress
harquebus
hereunder
△herculean
hirsutism
hornwrack
hard-wired
hornyhead
herryment
hercynite
Hercynian
husbandly
husbandry
histamine
Hesychasm
Hesychast
Hesperian
hysterics
hosteller
hesternal
hysteroid
hospitage
hospitale
hastiness
huskiness
hostilely
hissingly
histidine
Hassidism
hospitium
hispidity
hostility
hostlesse
hyson-skin
histogeny
hessonite
historism
historian
historify
histology
histogram
hesitance
hesitancy
hesitator
hetmanate
hit-parade
hotheaded
Hitlerite
hetaerism
Hitlerism
hetaerist
Hitlerist
△hottentot
hatefully
hatchback
hatchment
hitch-hike
hatchling
hut-circle
hetairism
hetairist
hôtel-Dieu
hot-and-hot
hit-and-run
hot-dogger
Huttonian
heterodox
hit-or-miss
heteronym
heteropod
heterosis
heterotic
hour-angle
hound-fish
housemaid
hause-bane
house-mate
house-carl
house-leek
houseless
house-line
housewife
houselled
household
house-bote
hause-lock
housework
houseroom
houseboat
housecoat
houseful s
house-hunt
house-duty
hour-glass
Houyhnhnm
haughtily
heuristic
hourplate
haustella
haustoria
have-at-him
havocking
hive-honey
hovel-post
haversack
haversine
haverings
hoverport
hivewards
hawsepipe
hawsehole
hawkishly
hawk-nosed
howtowdie
howsoever
hawksbill
hexachord
Hexagynia
hexagonal
hexahedra
hexameter
Hexandria
hexaploid
hexastich
hexastyle
Hexateuch
haymakers
haymaking
hoydenish
hoydenism
hey-presto
Hizbollah
hazardize
hazardous
Hizbullah
irascible
irascibly
inaidable
inaudible
inaudibly
imageable
imageless
inaneness
inaugural
inanimate
imaginary
italicise
italicize
imagining
Italicism
inanition
imaginist
inability
imagistic
isallobar
inamorata
inamorato
isagogics
inaptness
imbrangle
imbecilic
inbreathe
imbricate
imbalance
inbrought
imbroglio
inburning
in-between
ischaemia
ischaemic
incubuses

Words marked △ may be spelled also with a capital letter

incubator
incidence
incremate
inclement
increment
incretion
increaser
incognito
ischiadic
itchiness
inclining
ischiatic
inculcate
inculpate
incumbent
incommode
incunable
incentive
incondite
incensory
inclosure
incapable
incapably
incipient
inceptive
inception
incarnate
incurvate
incertain
incurable
incurably
incorrect
incurrent
incursive
incurring
incursion
incurvity
incurious
incorrupt
incessant
inclusive
including
incaution
inclusion
indraught
Indianise
Indianize
Indianist
indubious
indocible
inducible
inductile
inductive
indiction
induction
indecency
indecorum
△**indicator**
indweller
indignant
indignify
indignity
indigence
indigency
indigotin
indagator
indelible
indelibly
indulgent
indolence
indolency
indemnify
indemnity
indumenta
indention
indenture
iodophile
indirubin
indurated
indusiate
indispose
iddy-umpty
induviate
indexical
indexless
index-link
Icelandic
Icelander
iterative
iteration
inelastic
inexactly
ice-action
inelegant
isenergic
ineffable
ineffably
ideograph
irenicism
ice-skater
idealless
ideologic
idealogue
ideologue
idealiser
idealizer
ideomotor
irenology
ideophone
inebriate
inebriant
inerrable
inerrably
inebriety
inerrancy
inebrious
ileostomy
identical
ineptness
inertness
identikit
Identi-Kit
inequable
inerudite
inflative
inflation
infracted
infractor
infective
infection
infielder
inflexion
inflexure
inflicter
inflictor
infilling
infantile
infantine
inflowing
infuriate
informant
infirmary
inferable
infertile
inferring
infirmity
inference
infortune
infuscate
infusible
△**infusoria**
infatuate
influxion
influenza
influence
ingrately
ingrained
ingleneuk
ingle-side
inglenook
ingenuity
ingenious
ingenuous
ingrowing
ingestive
ingestion
ingluvial
ingluvies
inhabiter
inhibiter
inhibitor
ichneumon
ichthyoid
inhalator
inhumanly
ichnolite
ichnology
inherence
inherency
inharmony
inheritor
Iridaceae
imitative
imitation
irisation
imidazole
idioblast
itinerate
itinerant
itineracy
itinerary
idiograph
isinglass
Irishness
initialed
initially
initiator
idiomatic
Isidorian
iridology
iridotomy
idioplasm
idiophone
idiotical
idioticon
injection
injurious
injustice
ink-jerker
inkholder
irksomely
ink-bottle
ink-eraser
ill-manned
ill-haired
illiberal
illicitly
ill-headed
ill-hedded
ill-deedly
ill-versed
illegible
illegibly
illogical
illegally
ill-wisher
ill-omened
illuminer
Islamitic
illimited
ill-boding
ill-gotten
ill-judged
ill-humour
immediate
immediacy
immodesty
immigrate
immigrant
Ismailism
Ismailian
Immelmann
immolator
immanacle
immensely
immunogen
immensity
immanence
imminence
immanency
imminency
△**immortals**
immersion
immorally
immission
immutable
immutably
ismatical
immitting
immovable
immovably
immixture
innocuity
innocence
innocency
innocuous
innuendos
innkeeper
ionophore
ionopause
innervate
ignorable
innerwear
ignoramus
ignorance
innermost
ignescent
ignitable
ignitible
innovator
innoxious
isogamete
isobathic
isolative
isolation
isogamous
isotactic
iron-bound
iso-octane
isosceles
iron-cased
isomerase
isomerise
isomerize
isomerism
isogenous
isomerous
isometric
inorganic
isochimal
isochrone
isochoric
isotheral
inopinate
ixodiasis

Words marked △ may be spelled also with a capital letter

9 i□o□i

isoniazid
isoclinic
isoclinal
iron-miner
isopolity
inodorous
isodomous
isologous
isonomous
isopodous
iconology
Isokontae
isodontal
isokontan
iconostas
isocrymal
inotropic
isotropic
isopropyl
isocratic
iron-sided
Ironsides
ironsmith
ironstone
isosteric
isostatic
inoculate
Iroquoian
ironworks
ivory-palm
isocyclic
ivory-tree
isohyetal
impeacher
impeccant
impacable
impactite
impactive
impaction
impedance
impudence
imprecate
impresari
impleader
implement
imprecise
impletion
implexion
implicate
impliedly
impairing
impellent
impulsive
impelling
impulsion
impolitic
impennate
impendent
impingent
impending
impinging
impundulu
implodent
implosive
improvise
impsonite
improving
implosion
improbity
impromptu
impiously
important
imperfect
impartial
imperious
imperator
importune
imposable
impassive
impassion
impastoed
impostume
imposture
impetrate
imputable
imputably
impeticos
impatiens
impatient
in-patient
impetigos
inputting
impotence
impotency
impetuous
impetuses
impounder
imprudent
inpouring
impluvium
impavidly
inpayment
inquinate
inquiline
inquiring
inquietly
inquorate
irreality
irradiate
irradiant
Israelite
irrigable
irregular
irriguous
irrigator
irrelated
iprindole
irruptive
irruption
inrushing
irritable
irritably
irritancy
irritator
installed
inshallah
inspanned
instantly
itsy-bitsy
insectary
insectile
insection
inside-car
insidious
issueless
insheathe
inshelter
inspector
insphear'd
instigate
inswinger
instilled
inscience
institute
insultant
insoluble
insolubly
inselberg
insolvent
insulting
insulsity
insolence
insularly
insulator
insomniac
insensate
insinuate
insincere
insipidly
insipient
insurable
inscriber
insurgent
in-service
insertion
insurance
insistent
insatiate
insatiety
integrand
integrate
integrant
intaglios
integrity
intricate
intrigant
intricacy
intuitive
intuition
intrinsic
intriguer
intellect
intimiste
intumesce
intensate
intendant
intenable
intenible
intensely
intensive
intentive
intension
intention
intensify
intensity
intonator
introject
introvert
iatrogeny
introitus
introduce
interlard
interface
interlace
interpage
intervale
interdash
interbank
internals
icterical
Icteridae
intercede
interfere
intervene
interleaf
interdeal
intervein
intercept
interject
interment
intersect
intersert
interwind
interdine
interline
interring
interlink
intorsion
intortion
interdict
internist
interview
intercity
interflow
interplay
interknit
interfold
interlope
internode
interpone
interpose
interzone
interlock
interwork
interjoin
interbred
intercrop
inter-arts
interpret
intergrow
interesse
interests
interfuse
interlude
intermure
interrupt
intestate
intestacy
intestine
intrusive
intrusion
inumbrate
inunction
inurement
inusitate
inutility
Iguanidae
iguanodon
ibuprofen
Inuktitut
invective
invidious
inveigler
involucre
involucel
invalidly
involuted
inventive
Irvingite
Irvingism
invention
inventory
inviolate
invertase
invariant
Inverness
inversely
inversive
inversion
invisible
invisibly
izvestiya
inwreathe
inwrought
inworking
ivy-leaved
jealously
job-master
jabbering
△**jobcentre**
jubilance
jubilancy
jaborandi
jobernowl
Jebusitic

Words marked △ may be spelled also with a capital letter

9 l□a□e

jobsworth
Jack-a-Lent
jactation
jackalled
Jacobinic
jack-block
Jacobitic
jockeyism
jack-fruit
jackknife
jocularly
jaculator
joculator
jocundity
jack-plane
jacaranda
Jack-slave
jack-staff
jack-stays
jackshaft
jack-snipe
jacksmith
jockstrap
△**jack-straw**
Jack-sauce
jockteleg
Jacquerie
judiciary
judicable
judicious
judicator
judge-made
judgement
judgeship
Judaistic
Judas-kiss
Judas-hole
Judas-tree
jeeringly
jaghirdar
jigamaree
Jagannath
Jugannath
jiggumbob
John-apple
Johannean
Johannine
Johnny-raw
jail-break
jaileress
juiceless
jail-fever
jailhouse
juiciness
joint-heir
jointless
jointness
jointress
jointworm
joint-worm
juke-joint

jokesmith
jolleying
jillflirt
jolliness
jolliment
joltingly
jelliform
jalousied
jollyhead
jellybean
jellyfish
jollyboat
jambalaya
jam-packed
jemminess
jumpiness
jambolana
jump-start
Juncaceae
juneating
Juneberry
Junkerdom
junketeer
jenneting
junketing
Jansenism
Junkerism
Jansenist
Junoesque
junkiness
jingo-ring
Jonsonian
juniority
Juniperus
janissary
janitress
Jenny-wren
jeoparder
japanning
Japaneses
jequirity
jerfalcon
Jordanian
juridical
jerkiness
jarringly
jargoneer
jargonise
jargonize
jargonist
Jerusalem
jurywoman
jurywomen
jerkwater
jerry-shop
jessamine
joss-block
jesserant
jasperise
jasperize
jasperous

joss-house
jaspidean
jestingly
justified
Jesuitism
justiciar
justifier
joss-stick
jet-lagged
jettatura
jitterbug
jet-setter
jut-window
jettiness
juttingly
jet-driven
jetstream
jet-stream
jaundiced
journeyed
journeyer
jouisance
joviality
juvenilia
jawbation
jaw-fallen
jewel-case
jewel-weed
jewellery
jewelling
jewelfish
jawboning
Jew's-pitch
Jew's-stone
△**jews'-trump**
juxtapose
jaywalker
joylessly
joy-riding
jazziness
knaidloch
knaveship
khalifate
knavishly
knackered
khansamah
knapscull
knapskull
kabeljouw
kibbutzim
kickstand
kickshaws
kick-start
kidnapped
kidnapper
kidney-ore
kidstakes
kiddywink
knee-cords
kneidlach
knee-drill

klendusic
kieserite
klephtism
knee-holly
khedivate
keelivine
khedivial
knee-joint
knee-swell
keelyvine
Kshatriya
knife-edge
kaiserdom
knifeless
knife-rest
kaiserism
knightage
kniphofia
knickered
Kainozoic
klinostat
kailyaird
kok-saghyz
kakemonos
kilocycle
killdeers
kiln-dried
kilderkin
kilohertz
killifish
Kelticism
kallitype
kilojoule
kalamkari
kilometre
Kalamazoo®
kalanchoe
kalsomine®
kymograph
Komintern
Kominform
Kamasutra
△**kangaroos**
king-apple
kent-bugle
kingcraft
king-cobra
kink-cough
kingdomed
kennelled
kennel-man
kinsfolks
kentledge
kintledge
kingmaker
kinematic
konimeter
koniology
king's-hood
kinescope
koniscope

king's-evil
king-sized
kinetical
Kunstlied
kinswoman
kloochman
kloochmen
klondiker
klondyker
knotgrass
knowingly
kaolinise
kaolinite
kaolinize
knock-back
knock-knee
knock-down
knocker-up
knowledge
knob-stick
Keplerian
kopasetic
kurrajong
karabiner
kermesite
Kirbigrip®
kirbigrip
karyogamy
karyosome
karyology
karyotype
kerbstone
karateist
keratoses
keratosis
keratitis
kerfuffle
Kerguelen
kirkyaird
kirby-grip
kissagram
kissogram
kathakali
katharsis
katabolic
katabasis
katabatic
kitschily
kittenish
kite-flyer
kitchener
kittiwake
kettleful
kauri-pine
krummhorn
Keynesian
kryometer
keystroke
loaf-bread
lease-band
leaseback

Words marked △ may be spelled also with a capital letter

9 l□a□e

lease-lend
leavening
loaferish
leasehold
leaperous
leavenous
lean-faced
leaf-green
loathsome
lyam-hound
leafiness
leakiness
loaminess
Leavisite
liability
leafleted
leaf-metal
leaf-mould
learnable
learnedly
leaf-nosed
leaporous
lead-paint
leaf-stalk
loadstone
leaf-trace
leastways
leastwise
labialise
labialize
labdacism
labialism
librarian
libration
libratory
librairie
libecchio
libeccios
lobectomy
lobscouse
libidinal
librettos
lubricate
lubricant
lubricity
lubricous
libellant
labelling
libelling
labelloid
libellous
lobulated
libertine
liberties
liberally
labyrinth
laborious
liberator
Labourite
labourism
labourist
Lubavitch
lucrative
lactarian
lactation
luctation
lack-beard
lucubrate
lack-brain
lock-chain
lucidness
lickerish
lichenism
lichenist
lichenoid
lichenose
lecherous
lichenous
lace-frame
locofocos
luciferin
lockhouse
lacrimals
lacrimary
luckie-dad
luckiness
lacrimose
lacrimoso
locellate
Lucullean
Lucullian
lack-linen
localiser
lack-Latin
localizer
lucumones
locomotor
laciniate
laconical
lacunaria
licensure
lectorate
laccolite
laccolith
locoplant
locuplete
lickpenny
luck-penny
lace-paper
lacerable
lacertine
lacertian
lachrymal
lacerated
Lycosidae
locksmith
locatable
lacquerer
lacrymary
lacrymose
lidocaine
lodiculae
ludically
ludicrous
lodge-gate
lodgement
lodgepole
ladlefuls
lady's-maid
lodestone
lady-smock
liegeless
liege-lord
laevigate
leeringly
lienteric
laevulose
life-blood
life-cycle
left-field
life-force
lifeguard
loftiness
leftovers
life-saver
lifestyle
life-sized
life-table
life-weary
Luftwaffe
leftwards
lignaloes
lign-aloes
logically
logograph
logogriph
legginess
laggingly
lignified
ligniform
lagrimoso
lagniappe
logomachy
lagomorph
legendary
legendist
legionary
logaoedic
Liguorian
log-roller
logopedic
logophile
logorrhea
leger-line
logarithm
legislate
logistics
light-ball
light-fast
logothete
light-year
lightless
lightness
lightship
lightning
light-mill
lightsome
light-foot
light-dues
leg-puller
△lehrjahre
loincloth
lairdship
loitering
Leicester
leitmotif
leitmotiv
leisurely
lake-basin
Lollardry
Liliaceae
lallation
lollingly
lollipops
lilangeni
lolloping
loll-shrob
lily-white
lampadary
Lombardic
Lemnaceae
lemmatise
lemmatize
lampadist
lamp-black
lampbrush
limaceous
Lambegger
lumbering
lumberman
lumber-pie
lambently
lamp-glass
lyme-grass
lime-green
lymphatic
lime-hound
lyme-hound
lumpiness
limpingly
lumpishly
lambitive
limpidity
lamaistic
lamellate
lamplight
limelight
lamelloid
lamellose
laminable
lemon-weed
luminaire
lamenting
lemonfish
luminance
lemon-sole
Laminaria
luminesce
limonitic
laminated
lamington
laminator
laminitis
lampooner
limnology
lumbrical
lumbricus
lampshade
lamp-shell
lump-sugar
Lymeswold®
△limestone
lamb's-wool
lamaserai
limitable
limitedly
limitless
Limburger
limousine
limewater
land-agent
lineament
lineation
lineality
linearity
landaulet
landamman
longaeval
long-chain
long-coats
longcloth
landdamne
landdrost
long-dated
lance-jack
lingering
longevity
lintelled
lanterloo
lanceolar
lance-wood
longevous
long-eared
leniently
long-faced
line-fence
land-flood
landforce
landgrave
line-grove
lung-grown
lunch-time
lanthanum
lunch-hour
longhouse

9 m□b□l

lancinate
lankiness
longingly
lanciform
lentiform
longicorn
longitude
lend-lease
linolenic
landloper
land-loper
lunulated
long-lived
linen-fold
Langobard
Longobard
lineolate
Londonese
Londonise
Londonize
Londonish
Londonism
Londonian
landowner
langouste
land-plane
land-pilot
lunarnaut
langridge
land-reeve
long-range
lincrusta
Land-Rover®
landscape
land-shark
Landsmaal
landslide
Landsting
langspiel
lunisolar
longshore
lintstock
line-storm
landscrip
Landsturm
long-sixes
long-track
lunitidal
lengthful
lengthily
linctuses
lingulate
languidly
languaged
lingually
languette
land-value
lintwhite
landwards
land-yacht
look-alike
lioncelle
loosehead
loose-leaf
looseness
lyomerous
lookers-on
lion-heart
lyophobic
lyophilic
Laodicean
looniness
loop-light
△lyonnaise
loon-pants
look-round
lion-tamer
Laplander
lipectomy
lapidific
lapideous
lip-reader
lippening
Lippizana
lippitude
lupulinic
leptotene
leprosery
leprosity
lap-roller
leptosome
lophodont
liposomal
lapstrake
lapstreak
liquation
loquacity
liquefied
liquefier
laquearia
liquidate
liquidise
liquidize
liquidity
liquorice
liquorish
lardalite
Largactil®
lyrically
luridness
largeness
larcenist
larcenous
larghetto
larkiness
larvicide
larvikite
largition
larviform
larum-bell
laryngeal
lorgnette
lark's-heel
lardy-cake
lorazepam
last-ditch
Listerise
Listerize
Listerism
Listerian
lustfully
lysigenic
lush-house
lustihead
lustiness
lastingly
lispingly
lustihood
lassitude
lossmaker
lysimeter
lissomely
lessoning
Lusophile
laser-beam
lysergide
laserwort
lethargic
latration
Lotharios
lethality
laticlave
late-comer
litter-bug
letterbox
latter-day
litheness
letter-gae
lettering
Lutherism
Lutherist
lithesome
lothefull
latter-wit
latifondi
litigable
litigious
luteinise
luteinize
latticini
latticino
lithiasis
lithistid
littleane
lithoidal
latrociny
lithopone
lithotome
luteolous
lithology
lithotomy
lithocyst
Lotophagi
liturgics
liturgist
laterally
literally
lateritic
literatim
literator
literatus
Lotus-land
latescent
lutescent
latitancy
lathyrism
Lauraceae
laudative
laudation
Laurasian
leucaemia
leukaemia
leucaemic
laudatory
laundress
launderer
laurelled
louse-wort
lounge-bar
laughable
laughably
laughsome
Leuciscus
lousiness
louringly
loutishly
loudmouth
leuco-base
leuko-base
leucotome
leukotome
leucotomy
leukotomy
leucocyte
leukocyte
△leviathan
love-apple
love-arrow
livraison
love-charm
love-child
lividness
love-feast
levigable
love-juice
lavaliere
lovelight
levelling
level-coil
lovemaker
love-match
loving-cup
△levantine
loverless
leveraged
liver-wing
liveryman
liverwort
love-shaft
livestock
love-story
levitical
Leviticus
love-token
△lowlander
low-necked
lawlessly
low-minded
lowlihead
lowliness
lowlights
law-giving
Lowrie-tod
lawnmower
low-loader
lawmonger
low-downer
lawn-party
lower-case
lower-deck
lowermost
law-writer
lexically
loxodrome
loxodromy
luxuriate
luxuriant
luxurious
lixiviate
lixivious
layperson
lay-figure
layer-cake
lazzarone
lazzaroni
lazy-bones
lazar-like
lazaretto
lazy-tongs
meandrian
meandrous
meandered
meat-eater
moanfully
mealiness
meatiness
meaningly
miasmatic
meadow-rue
means-test
measuring
meanwhile
mob-handed
mobocracy
mobiliser

9 m□b□l

mobilizer
Maccabean
Maccabees
mechanise
mechanize
mechanism
mactation
mechanics
mechanist
mockadoes
micaceous
macédoine
macadamia
muckender
mockernut
machinate
mochiness
muckiness
machinery
mockingly
machinist
mycologic
machmeter
Mycenaean
macintosh
microcard
microwave
mucronate
micromesh
microchip
microlite
microwire
microlith
micro-mini
microbial
microfilm
macrobian
microbian
macrocode
macrodome
microcode
micropore
microsome
microtome
microtone
macrocosm
microcosm
microform
macrocopy
macrology
microcopy
micrology
microtomy
microgram
micro-brew
micropsia
micropump
macro-axis
macrocyte
microcyte
micropyle

mycophagy
Mecoptera
mycorhiza
muck-raker
Mucorales
macaronic
macaronis
macerator
mica-slate
mucksweat
mycotoxin
Mycetozoa
micturate
MacGuffin
macrurous
macaw-palm
macaw-tree
machzorim
mediately
Midrashim
mediatise
mediative
mediatize
mediation
mediatory
mediatrix
madrassah
mediaeval
medicable
medically
medicinal
mediciner
medicated
medaewart
maddening
madrepore
medresseh
mid-season
mid-heaven
modifying
muddiness
midwifery
maddingly
midwifing
midwiving
mid-wicket
mydriasis
mydriatic
mid-winter
△mudéjares
medullate
middle-age
medullary
madeleine
medalling
modelling
medallion
modillion
medallist
middleman
middlings

modulator
midinette
mudlogger
mad-doctor
modernise
modernize
△modernism
△modernist
modernity
madarosis
moderator
midi-skirt
midstream
meditated
midsummer
Maeonides
mnemonics
mnemonist
Mnemosyne
△maelstrom
muffettee
muffin-cap
muffineer
miffiness
mafficker
muffin-pan
△magdalene
Magyarise
Magyarize
mugearite
magianism
magnalium
Magyarism
migration
migratory
megabucks
megacycle
magicking
magically
megacurie
megadeath
magnesite
magnetise
magnetite
magnetize
magnesium
magnetism
magnesian
magnetics
magnetist
magnetron
megaflora
megafarad
megafauna
megagauss
megahertz
mugginess
magnified
magnifico
magnifier
magnitude

megajoule
megillahs
megilloth
maggot-pie
megaphone
magistery
megascope
megaspore
megastore
magistral
mag-stripe
mug-hunter
Mahometan
maharajah
maharanee
maharishi
mahlstick
mridamgam
mridangam
mainbrace
mail-coach
maid-child
maidenish
mainframe
meiofauna
mainliner
mailmerge
mail-order
mail-plane
mainprise
mainsheet
mail-train
moistness
maistring
maieutics
mujahedin
mujahidin
majorship
major-domo
majorette
majuscule
mako-makos
makimonos
mekometer
make-peace
make-ready
makeshift
mallander
Malvaceae
Meliaceae
maltalent
millboard
molybdate
Meliboean
Malebolge
molybdous
Miliciens
malachite
molochise
molochize
molecular

malicious
melocoton
melodrama
melodrame
melodious
maladroit
millenary
malleable
mallender
millepede
mallee-hen
millerite
Millerian
malleolar
malleolus
millennia
millepore
mallemuck
milken-way
maleffect
malt-floor
milk-float
milk-fever
milk-gland
△malignant
malagueña
malignity
mylohyoid
malt-horse
mill-horse
malt-house
milk-house
multipara
multi-wall
millipede
multipede
milkiness
millinery
meltingly
Malpighia
mollified
mollifier
mollities
multiplet
multiplex
mullioned
millionth
millimole
multimode
multifoil
multiform
multiuser
multitude
multihull
milk-molar
melomania
melomanic
melampode
milometer
melon-pear
malanders

Words marked △ may be spelled also with a capital letter

malingery
malengine
melanemia
melanomas
melanuria
melanuric
melanosis
melanotic
mylonitic
meliorate
Melpomene
meliorism
Miltonism
Miltonian
meliorist
meliority
malformed
mill-owner
millocrat
malvoisie
milk-punch
melaphyre
malarious
melismata
milk-shake
millscale
mole-spade
molestful
milk-sugar
Molossian
moleskins
Melastoma
malmstone
milestone
millstone
Malathion®
melatonin
militancy
milk-tooth
mill-tooth
mulattoes
militaria
molluscan
molluskan
milk-vetch
mill-wheel
milk-white
melt-water
malaxator
mollymawk
Malaysian
Malayalam
mammalian
mammalogy
mimicking
mamselles
mumchance
Memphitic
mumpishly
mummified
memoirism

memoirist
mammillae
mammiform
mummiform
mamillate
mamillary
mamelucos
momentany
momentary
mementoes
momentous
mammonite
mammonish
mammonism
Memnonian
mammonist
mammogram
memorials
memorable
memorably
memoranda
memoriter
mumpsimus
mimetical
mum-budget
mummy-case
manganate
mandatary
manhandle
manganese
mundanely
manzanita
mandarine
manganite
monoamine
Mondayish
mentalism
Montanism
mentation
miniation
mentalist
Montanist
mendacity
mentality
mundanity
manganous
mandatory
Manhattan
miniature
minibreak
manubrial
manubrium
monobasic
monocracy
Manichean
monactine
monocline
monachism
Munichism
monachist
monocular

manically
monochord
minacious
monecious
municipal
monocoque
mind-curer
monoceros
monodrama
monadical
monodical
mini-dress
menadione
monadnock
Minnesang
monkey-bag
menseless
mincemeat
mongering
monkeyish
△**mannerism**
Mendelism
monkeyism
monoecism
Mendelian
Mindelian
△**mannerist**
monkey-jar
manzellos
monkey-nut
mangetout
monkey-pot
monkey-run
mannequin
manoeuvre
minefield
manifolds
mindfully
manifesto
monograph
monogamic
Monogynia
monogenic
menagerie
McNaghten
monthling
Menshevik
mancipate
mendicant
mandiocca
man-minded
manginess
manliness
minginess
Mandingos
mincingly
menticide
manriding
mandilion
menuisier
mendicity

Monsignor
manticora
manticore
monticule
mint-julep
monologic
monologue
monolater
monolatry
man-slayer
mine-layer
monolayer
monomachy
monomania
△**menominee**
muniments
monomeric
manometer
monometer
manometry
man-and-dog
meningeal
Monandria
mandoline
Mennonite
Mongolise
Mongolize
monzonite
mentoring
mentorial
△**mongolism**
Monroeism
Mongolian
Monroeist
monsoonal
mine-owner
△**mongoloid**
mangouste
mongooses
mangostan
monophase
monoplane
monophagy
Menippean
maniplies
manyplies
moniplies
monyplies
monopulse
manipular
monoptote
monophony
monopsony
monopitch
menopause
manor-seat
minirugby
menorrhea
monarchic
man-orchid
monorchid

monarchal
minorship
monorhine
monergism
mongrelly
manurance
monorhyme
many-sided
monk's-seam
mane-sheet
monastery
monostich
mono-skier
miniskirt
meniscoid
monkshood
minestone
Minkstone
Monastral
miniscule
mint-sauce
minuscule
monostyle
Minitrack®
monotreme
monitress
minute-gun
monatomic
△**minuteman**
monotonic
Monotropa
minutiose
monotroch
monstrous
munitions
monotypic
man-at-arms
menstrual
menstruum
manducate
mundungus
Mancunian
Manxwoman
monoxylon
monaxonic
moneybags
moneyless
money-bill
△**mandylion**
moneywort
Mao-jacket
myomantic
moonblind
moot-court
mooseyard
moon-faced
moon-glade
moot-house
Maoriland
moodiness
myofibril

9 m□o□k

moon-knife
myoglobin
moonlight
moon-loved
myologist
moonphase
moonquake
moonraker
myography
moonscape
moonshine
moonshiny
moonstone
mepacrine
mop-headed
mappemond
mephitism
maquisard
marmalade
mermaiden
Myrtaceae
mariachis
margarita
marcasite
margarine
margarite
marialite
marmarise
marmarize
morganite
mortalise
mortalize
mordacity
mortality
murrained
Myriapoda
merganser
mercaptan
mordantly
mirabilia
mirabelle
myrobalan
△**mirabilis**
mortcloth
moraceous
muricated
mercenary
market-day
△**marketeer**
murderess
marmelise
marmelize
mercerise
mercerize
marketing
marcelled
martelled
marvelled
martellos
market-man
myrmecoid

murderous
merpeople
mirifical
marigraph
mortgagee
mortgager
mortgagor
marihuana
marshland
marchpane
mirthless
march-dike
marshalcy
morphemic
marshwort
murtherer
morphosis
morphetic
morphotic
march-dyke
marginate
marxisant
merciable
merciless
merriness
murkiness
merriment
mortified
mercifide
mortician
mortifier
morbidity
martially
Martinmas
mirligoes
meroistic
marijuana
Martlemas
moraliser
myrtle-wax
moralizer
marinière
maranatha
myriorama
marmoreal
marrowfat
Mormonite
marooning
mirroring
marrowish
Mormonism
marrow-men
Mariology
Maryology
marrowsky
Meropidae
meropidan
mare's-tail
mare's-nest
mareschal
marischal

Myristica
mire-snipe
Marasmius
marlstone
merestone
mort-stone
Morescoes
Moriscoes
maritally
moratoria
mercurate
mercurise
mercurize
marauding
murmuring
marsupial
△mercurial
marsupium
mercurous
murmurous
marquetry
mark-white
merry-make
martyrdom
mercy-seat
martyrise
martyrize
martyrium
merozoite
mismanage
mishandle
mistaught
mustachio
muscadine
muscarine
messaging
misfaring
missaying
mistaking
mescalism
massagist
mashallah
misfallen
mystagogy
mishappen
mishanter
mesoblast
Mössbauer
music-rack
misoclere
music-demy
musicking
masochism
masochist
musically
musaceous
misadvise
misregard
masterate
misbehave
misrelate

mishegaas
masterdom
misleader
miscegene
misbeseem
misdemean
musketeer
misdesert
masterful
messenger
mesmerise
mesmerize
miscegine
musteline
misbelief
mastering
mesmerism
Moslemism
mysteries
mesmerist
misreckon
master-key
musselled
misdeemed
misbecome
musketoon
misreport
mistemper
misleared
misfeasor
misbestow
musefully
mesogloea
moss-grown
mischance
mischancy
misshaped
misshapen
mischarge
moschatel
masthouse
masticate
mussitate
massiness
messiness
mistiness
mossiness
mushiness
muskiness
mussiness
mustiness
misdirect
massively
missilery
missingly
mystified
misgiving
misliking
mosaicism
Muslimism
mysticism

mystifier
mosaicist
mispickel
△**messianic**
missioner
mislippen
mistigris
△**messieurs**
misplease
misallege
misallied
muscleman
mistletoe
misemploy
mesomorph
mushmouth
misintend
mesentery
masonried
misoneism
misoneist
misinform
muscovado
mastoidal
Massorete
misgovern
moskonfyt
△**muscovite**
Muscovian
miscolour
muscology
museology
misgotten
mossplant
musk-plant
musk-pouch
mesophyte
mesophyll
miscreate
miscreant
miserable
miserably
miscredit
mispraise
misprised
Masoretic
misgrowth
misesteem
musk-sheep
misassign
musk-shrew
meshugaas
misguided
misguider
misguggle
masculine
Mussulman
Mussulmen
musculous
misaunter
mosquitos

Words marked △ may be spelled also with a capital letter

9 n□l□i

misavised
massymore
mutualise
mutualize
mutualism
mutuality
mitraille
mattamore
methadone
metabolic
metabasis
metabatic
miticidal
matachina
matachini
motocross
matterful
△**mothering**
muttering
mother-lye
metheglin
mitre-wort
moth-eaten
mitigable
mitogenic
mutagenic
mitigator
matchable
Matthaean
matchless
match-play
match-cord
matchwood
matchlock
metricate
matricide
metricise
metricize
mythicise
mythicize
mythicism
metrician
metrifier
metricist
mythicist
matriliny
mitriform
matrimony
matriarch
matricula
Mytilidae
metalline
metallise
metallize
metalling
metallist
metalloid
metalwork
matelasse
matelassé
mutilated

mutilator
metameric
mutinying
metonymic
matronage
mythomane
methought
mutton-ham
matronise
matronize
meteorite
methodise
methodize
meteorism
Methodism
meteorist
△methodist
motionist
metroplex
motion-man
meteoroid
metronome
meteorous
mythopoet
metrology
mythology
metaphase
metaplasm
metapelet
mothproof
motorcade
materials
maturable
motorable
Mithraeum
motor-ship
motor-bike
Mithraism
Mithraist
maternity
motor-boat
motoscafi
motoscafo
metestick
mutoscope
motettist
matutinal
Mathurine
motivator
methylate
methylene
mateyness
methystic
mould-made
mouldwarp
mouldable
mound-bird
mould-loft
maunderer
mouse-tail
mouse-deer

mouse-hole
mouse-trap
mouse-hunt
moufflons
mouth-made
mouthwash
mouth-harp
mouthable
mouthfeel
mouthless
mouthfuls
moudiwart
Mauritius
moudiwort
mournings
mournival
mausoleum
mausolean
maulstick
moustache
moveables
movieland
moviegoer
mowdiwart
mawkishly
mowdiwort
mixedness
myxedemic
myxoedema
maxillary
maxillula
maximally
myxovirus
Moygashel®
moygashel
mayflower
mayorship
mayoralty
mezzanine
muzziness
muzzle-bag
mizzonite
mezzotint
Mozarabic
Mozartean
Mozartian
no-account
neat-house
neat-stall
neat's-foot
niaiserie
near-white
nubeculae
nobleness
nobbiness
nebbisher
nobiliary
nobilesse
nebuliser
nebulizer
Nabataean

nectareal
nectarean
nectarine
nectarial
nictation
nectarous
nyctalops
neckcloth
nickeline
nickelise
nickelize
nickeling
nickelled
nucleolar
nucleolus
nickelous
nucleated
nucleator
nictitate
Nickie-ben
noctiluca
nicompoop
nick-nacky
necrophil
necrotise
necrotize
niccolite
necrology
necrotomy
nocuously
neckpiece
nickpoint
necessary
nickstick
necessity
nicotiana
nachtmaal
nicotinic
nicotined
Noctuidae
nocturnal
neckverse
niddering
noddingly
nodulated
niderling
neesberry
needfully
neediness
needleful
needle-gun
nielloing
niellated
needle-tin
needy-hood
niftiness
niff-naffy
nefandous
nefarious
niggardly
négociant

niggerdom
niggerish
niggerism
neglecter
nigricant
negligent
Nigritian
Negrillos
negritude
négritude
nigritude
negroidal
negrohead
negrophil
nigrosine
negro-corn
nightward
negotiate
nightmare
nighthawk
night-walk
nightfall
night-rail
negotiant
night-cart
nightmary
night-bell
nightgear
nightwear
nightless
night-rest
nightbird
nightfire
nightlife
night-line
night-side
night-tide
night-time
nightclub
night-robe
nightlong
night-work
night-fowl
night-soil
nightgown
nightspot
night-crow
night-rule
nuisancer
nail-biter
nail-brush
naiveness
naïveness
noiseless
neighbour
noisiness
noisomely
nakedness
nullipara
nullified
nullifier

9 n□l□i

nullipore
nelumbium
Nilometer
no-meaning
nomocracy
name-child
nomograph
nymphical
nymphaeum
nymphlike
nymphalid
numbingly
numble-pie
nimblesse
nominable
nominally
nominator
name-plate
nemophila
numerable
numerably
numerical
nemertean
nemertine
numeraire
numéraire
nemertian
numerally
numerator
numbskull
nomothete
nummulary
nummuline
nummulite
nonpareil
non-racial
nunnation
nonparous
non-access
non-verbal
non-member
non-reader
non-lethal
nunneries
non-sexist
non-person
nun's-flesh
nonagonal
nineholes
non-linear
nonillion
nonplused
non-smoker
nanometre
nine-metre
nonentity
non-voting
ninepence
ninepenny
non-driver
non-usager

ninescore
ninetieth
nunataker
nuncupate
nonjuring
nannyghai
nanny-goat
neo-Nazism
neoterise
neoterize
neoterism
neoterist
neoteinia
neotenous
neophobia
neophobic
neophilia
neophytic
Neolithic
neopilina
noodledom
Neo-Gothic
neologise
neologize
neologism
Neocomian
neologian
neonomian
neologist
noosphere
neodymium
nephalism
nephalist
nepheline
nephelite
Napierian
nipperkin
nipcheese
nappiness
nippiness
nippingly
Nepenthes
Nipponese
nephology
nephogram
nephralgy
nephrosis
nephritic
nephrotic
nephritis
naphthene
neptunium
Neptunian
Neptunist
narrative
normalise
normalize
Normanise
Normanize
normative
Normanism

narration
nervation
normality
narratory
nor'-easter
nervature
nursemaid
nurse-tend
nerveless
nurselike
nurseling
Norwegian
norseller
Norueyses
nor'wester
nor'-wester
northland
northward
north-east
north-west
narghilly
northmost
northerly
nerviness
narcissus
narcotine
narcotise
narcotize
narrowing
narcotism
narcotist
nervously
Neritidae
nurturant
nostalgia
nostalgic
nystagmic
nystagmus
nosebleed
naseberry
nose-flute
nastiness
nescience
Nestorian
nostology
nose-piece
no-strings
Nostratic
nose-wheel
nitratine
nitration
notabilia
notochord
notedness
Notodonta
Notre-Dame
not-headed
natheless
netheless
nutmegged
nutpecker

net-veined
nathemore
nut-weevil
notifying
Notogaeic
Notogaean
notchback
nattiness
nuttiness
nutriment
net-winged
nitrified
nutritive
nitriding
nutrition
nit-picker
nitwitted
net-player
Notonecta
nutjobber
natrolite
nitro-silk
notionist
networker
notaphily
notepaper
notoriety
nature-god
naturally
nut-wrench
notorious
Nithsdale
Nototrema
natatoria
no-trumper
nutbutter
neuralgia
neuralgic
naumachia
neuration
naughtily
nourisher
neurility
nouriture
nauplioid
neuromata
neuropath
neurochip
neuroglia
neurology
neurotomy
neurogram
neutrally
neutrinos
neutretto
noviciate
Novocaine®
navicular
novodamus
navigable
navigably

navigator
novelties
navelwort
noveliser
novelette
novelizer
novennial
nevermore
Navaratra
Navaratri
novitiate
newsagent
newmarket
new-fallen
newsflash
newshound
newsiness
nowhither
Newtonian
newsprint
newspaper
new-create
news-stand
news-sheet
newstrade
news-value
newswoman
noxiously
Nazaritic
ovalbumin
orangeade
opal-glass
Orangeism
Orangeman
orang-utan
orange-tip
odalisque
onanistic
oratorial
△**oratorian**
oratorios
oraculous
orbicular
△**ombudsman**
Ombudsmen
obbligati
obbligato
oubliette
ombrophil
orchestra
orchestic
oncogenic
Orchideae
orchidist
oscillate
occulting
occultism
occultist
oncolysis
oncolytic
oecumenic

Words marked △ may be spelled also with a capital letter

oncometer
oncomouse
obconical
occupying
occupance
occupancy
occipital
obcordate
occurrent
occurring
oncostman
occasions
oscitancy
occludent
occlusive
occlusion
Oddfellow
ordinaire
ordinance
Oudenarde
odd-jobber
odd-jobman
odd-lotter
orderless
order-book
one-handed
one-parent
ore-raught
operative
operating
operation
overalled
open-armed
overboard
overbuild
overblown
overbound
open-chain
overcheck
operculum
opercular
overcloud
overcrowd
oleaceous
overcarry
overcatch
overcount
overcover
overdraft
overdress
overdight
overdrive
okey-dokey
overdated
over-exact
open-ended
obeseness
over-exert
one-legged
Olenellus
orepearch

ore-rested
open-field
o're-office
overflown
overflush
overglaze
overgraze
oleograph
overgrain
overgrass
overgreen
overgreat
overgoing
overgloom
overgrown
overgorge
overheads
open-heart
overhaile
overhappy
overhaste
overhasty
obeliscal
overinked
obedience
overissue
overjoyed
overladen
overlying
overlusty
ocellated
overmerry
overmatch
overmount
oceanides
overnight
operosely
operosity
onerously
overplast
overpedal
overpress
overpoise
overprice
overprize
overpaint
overprint
overproud
overproof
overperch
overpitch
overpower
overreach
overreact
overroast
oven-ready
overrider
overruler
olecranal
olecranon
overripen

oleo-resin
overstand
overshade
overstare
overstate
overstaff
overstain
overspend
open-steek
overswell
oversleep
oversteer
overswear
overspent
oversight
overshine
Odelsting
overstink
overspill
overshirt
overskirt
obeisance
overscore
overstock
over-shoes
overshoot
overstrew
overstuff
overstunk
overstudy
oversexed
over-sexed
oversized
over-trade
overtrain
overtrick
overtaken
overtimer
orestunck
overtones
overtures
overthrow
overtrump
overtrust
overtower
overvalue
open-weave
overweary
overwhelm
overwrest
overwrite
overweigh
overwatch
overwound
offhanded
offsaddle
officiate
officiant
office-boy
olfactive
olfaction

officinal
officious
olfactory
offseason
off-centre
off-chance
off-the-peg
off-limits
offensive
offending
off-colour
offspring
offerable
Oxfordian
offerings
offertory
obfuscate
off-stream
off-street
off-cutter
off-putter
orgiastic
orgillous
organical
organ-bird
organ-pipe
organzine
organelle
organised
organiser
oogenesis
oogenetic
organized
organizer
oughtness
ophiolite
ophiology
ochlocrat
otherness
otherwise
Ophiuchus
ophiuroid
oricalche
oligarchy
oxidation
oviparity
oligaemia
oviparous
olive-yard
olive-back
olivenite
Origenism
Oliverian
Origenist
oviferous
ovigerous
originate
originals
orificial
opinioned
Oriolidae

oriflamme
orientate
orienteer
onion-skin
onion-eyed
Oligocene
ovibovine
oligopoly
onirology
ominously
omissible
omittance
oviductal
objective
objection
objectify
objurgate
Ockhamism
Ockhamist
oakenshaw
Orleanism
Orleanist
oil-tanker
owl-parrot
on-licence
oil-beetle
Owle-glass
obligatos
oil-filled
oil-engine
onlooking
oil-colour
obliquely
obliquity
oil-burner
oblivious
osmometer
osmometry
ommatidia
osmeteria
omnibuses
oenomania
ornaments
oenomancy
oenometer
oenanthic
oenophile
oenophily
ownerless
ownership
Oenothera
ornithoid
obnoxious
Orobanche
obovately
ozonation
odonatist
opobalsam
onomastic
opodeldoc
ozocerite

9 o□o□e

ozokerite
ovotestes
ovotestis
omophagia
omophagic
ocotillos
orologist
otologist
odorously
ororotund
odourless
otorrhoea
orography
odontalgy
odontomas
orphanage
omphacite
orphanism
orpharion
omphaloid
oppressor
oppugnant
opponency
Orpington
opportune
opposable
ouroboros
ourselves
oar-footed
obreption
orris-root
ouroscopy
oarswoman
onslaught
obsecrate
ossicular
oyster-bed
obscenely
obscenity
obstetric
ossifraga
ossifrage
ossifying
obsignate
obstinate
obstinacy
obsolesce
opsomania
opsimathy
oesophagi
obsequent
obsequial
obsequies
△observant
obstruent
oestrogen
observing
obsessive
obsession
onsetting
obscurant
obscurely
obscurity
outlander
outwardly
ostracean
outraigne
ostracise
ostracize
out-parish
ostracism
Ostracion
outbacker
outhauler
outlaunce
outlaunch
Ostracoda
outmantle
Octobrist
optically
octachord
outredden
ostleress
ottrelite
outrelief
on-the-spot
out-sentry
out-of-date
out-of-work
out-of-door
out-of-body
Octogynia
ontogenic
octagonal
octahedra
outlinear
outsiders
outrigger
outgiving
outwitted
outfitter
outskirts
ontologic
octillion
optimally
octameter
optometer
optimates
optometry
oftenness
obtundent
ostensive
octennial
obtention
out-and-out
ostensory
ortanique
Octandria
octonarii
ostinatos
ostiolate
osteopath
osteoderm
orthopedy
osteogeny
outtongue
optronics
orthotics
orthotist
outworker
outjockey
outbounds
outgoings
orthotone
osteotome
Ostrogoth
orthodoxy
osteology
osteotomy
orthoepic
outrooper
outpourer
outdoorsy
orthoptic
out-porter
orthoaxes
orthoaxis
octapodic
octopodes
outspread
outspring
outspoken
octaploid
octoploid
optophone
octopuses
outerwear
outcrafty
outermost
obturator
outtravel
outgrowth
octastich
octastyle
octostyle
outstrain
outstrike
outnumber
obtrusive
obtruding
obtrusion
outrunner
outlustre
ottavinos
ovulation
ocularist
obumbrate
opusculum
opulently
obviation
obvolvent
obvoluted
obvention
obviously
obversely
obversion
Orwellian
oxy-halide
oxygenate
oxygenise
oxygenize
oxygenous
onychitis
oxy-iodide
ouzel-cock
pranayama
praeamble
phalangid
phalangal
phalanger
phalanges
placation
planarian
planation
Phanariot
pea-jacket
pharaonic
phalarope
placatory
play-actor
peasantry
phalanxes
praecoces
peat-creel
plaid-neuk
platemark
planetary
peaceable
peaceably
phagedena
pease-meal
peaseweep
peaceless
phaseless
placeless
placement
prayerful
plate-ship
peace-pipe
peacetime
plate-like
phaseolin
planetoid
piacevole
plate-room
pease-soup
played-out
plane-tree
placentae
placental
placentas
playfully
play-going
plangency
playgroup
peach-palm
peach-blow
peach-wood
peach-tree
playhouse
pharisaic
pratingly
prayingly
planisher
platinise
platinize
placidity
platinoid
platinous
placitory
pianistic
platitude
plackless
pranksome
prankster
pearl-sago
praeludia
pearl-edge
pearlings
pearlwort
pearl-spar
pearl-gray
pearl-grey
pearlised
phalluses
pearlitic
pearl-eyed
pearlized
plasmodia
psalmodic
Phasmidae
ptarmigan
psalm-book
plasmatic
pragmatic
psammitic
psalm-tune
plain-Jane
plain-darn
plainness
plaintful
phaenogam
plaintive
plaintiff
plainsman
plainsmen
praenomen
plainsong
plain-cook
plainwork
Planorbis
phacoidal
placoderm
phacolite
piano-wire

Words marked △ may be spelled also with a capital letter

9 p□e□r

Platonise
Platonize
phacolith
Platonism
△**platonics**
pianolist
Platonist
pea-souper
phagocyte
Prakritic
peat-spade
praiseach
peat-stack
plausible
plausibly
praesidia
play-spell
praiseful
phansigar
peat-smoke
plaustral
plantable
practical
practicum
plantless
psaltress
plant-lice
plant-like
plantling
plaything
practolol
plantsman
plant-lore
plastique
practique
psalteria
plastered
plasterer
phantasma
practised
phantosme
plastisol
phantasim
practiser
phantasms
planuloid
plague-pit
plaquette
play-world
pharyngal
pharynges
pharynxes
publisher
publicise
publicize
publicist
publicity
public-key
pebble-bed
pubescent
pickaback

pickapack
piccadell
pickadell
packaging
piccadill
pickadill
pictarnie
peccantly
pack-cinch
pack-cloth
picocurie
pack-drill
pocketful
picketing
pocketing
pickeerer
pacifical
Puck-hairy
pack-horse
pectinate
pectineal
pycnidium
picnicked
picnicker
pactional
peculator
pacemaker
pockmanky
pecuniary
pecunious
pecan-tree
pectolite
pictorial
pictogram
pick-purse
packstaff
packsheet
pick-thank
pack-train
pack-twine
pick-tooth
pachyderm
pad-saddle
pedicular
△**pediculus**
puddening
pedigreed
pedagogic
pedagogue
podagrous
podginess
pudginess
paddle-box
pedalling
pedal-bone
pademelon
padymelon
pedometer
pedantise
pedantize
pedantism

pudendous
Pedipalpi
pedereros
pederasty
pedatifid
paddy-bird
pre-cancel
prelatess
prevalent
phenacite
phenakite
precative
predative
prelatise
prelatize
prelatish
prefacial
prelatial
phenakism
prelatism
predation
prelation
prelatist
plenarily
predacity
prepacked
prehallux
precatory
predatory
prefatory
poetaster
poetastry
prelature
premature
presbyope
presbyopy
presbytic
presbyter
prescient
prescribe
preaching
prescript
preachify
preachily
preocular
preschool
pre-echoes
prescious
prescutum
preoccupy
pleadable
pre-adamic
pseudonym
pleadings
pseudopod
pseudaxis
piece-rate
paederast
preverbal
pretended
prebendal

△**pretender**
piecemeal
pieceless
precedent
preselect
predefine
pre-senile
preterite
preceding
predesign
phenetics
preterist
pretermit
pre-vernal
prerecord
predevote
piece-work
preferred
preferrer
prehensor
paedeutic
presentee
precentor
preceptor
prelector
presenter
preventer
presently
preserver
preserves
pier-glass
phengites
pre-shrink
plethoric
psephitic
△**peel-house**
predicate
predicant
predikant
precincts
predigest
predilect
president
precisely
peevishly
pieridine
poeticise
poeticize
precipice
precisive
précising
presidial
poeticism
presidium
Pteridium
puerilism
Phenician
precisian
precision
prefixion
prevision

presidios
puerility
plexiform
plenipoes
pietistic
prebiotic
predicter
predictor
paediatry
plenilune
plenitude
poeticule
précieuse
prefigure
phellogen
preflight
pre-employ
pneumonia
pneumonic
pre-embryo
pneumatic
pre-emptor
pre-engage
pregnable
pregnance
pregnancy
pleonaste
pleonexia
premosaic
phenolate
pterosaur
△**piepowder**
phenomena
Pleiocene
prepotent
pleiomery
preconise
preconize
premonish
precocial
phelonion
premotion
prenotion
prerosion
precocity
prenotify
prepollex
Pteropoda
pheromone
paedology
phenology
poenology
pyelogram
precoital
prepostor
phenotype
preoption
puerperal
preordain
poetresse
pleuritic

Words marked △ may be spelled also with a capital letter

9 p□e□r

pierrette
pleuritis
press-gang
pressmark
peep-sight
pleaseman
pleasance
pheasants
presswork
pressroom
pleasurer
pressures
pier-table
plentiful
prettyish
prettyism
plectrons
plenteous
plectrums
△**peel-tower**
prejudice
prejudize
prelusive
prenubile
presuming
preludial
preputial
prelusory
precurrer
precursor
pre-exilic
pterygial
pterygium
pterygoid
puff-adder
puftaloon
pifferari
pifferaro
puffiness
puffingly
pegmatite
pugnacity
pageantry
pigsconce
pogo-dance
pignerate
pigheaded
pigmented
pigmental
piggishly
pug-engine
pignorate
pigeon-pea
page-proof
pygostyle
page-three
piggyback
piggy-bank
△**philander**
privateer
philately
plicately
privately
privatise
privative
privatize
primatial
plication
privation
primality
primarily
poinadoes
privadoes
peirastic
plicature
primaeval
poinciana
princedom
princekin
princelet
principia
principle
principal
princesse
priceless
prideless
primeness
prime-time
paideutic
painfully
plightful
pair-horse
philhorse
primipara
privilege
priciness
primitiae
△primitive
primitial
primitias
△**philippic**
Philister
prickling
prickwood
prick-song
phillabeg
phillibeg
phialling
Phillyrea
paillasse
paillette
prismatic
poignancy
philomath
Philomela
philopena
Philomene
poison-gas
poison-ivy
poison-nut
poison-oak
poisonous
prisonous
philology
philogyny
priorship
primrosed
pair-royal
priestess
puissance
priest-rid
puissaunt
point-lace
△**paintball**
paintable
printable
Psittacus
pointedly
printhead
paintress
pointless
printless
pointillé
pointsman
painterly
point-duty
primuline
pokeberry
Pekingese
pyknosome
pike-perch
poker-work
pikestaff
Pakistani
Pakhtoons
pillar-box
polyarchy
polyandry
palmately
polianite
polyamide
pulsatile
pulsative
polyaxial
△**palladium**
△pelmanism
Palladian
palmarian
palmation
palpation
pulsation
pillarist
palladous
pulsatory
pellagrin
pulpboard
polybasic
phlebitis
palace-car
Pulicidae
phlyctena
pole-clipt
policeman
polyconic
palm-court
palm-civet
Paludrine®
paludinal
pilferage
pulse-rate
pulse-wave
pulseless
palletise
palletize
pelletise
pelletize
polverine
pulverine
pulverise
pulverize
pilfering
pelletify
pulverous
palpebral
pollen-sac
palaestra
polyester
palmettos
palafitte
palsgrave
polygraph
Polygamia
polygamic
Polygynia
polygenic
polygonal
polygonum
polyglott
polyhedra
palm-honey
palmhouse
△pele-house
palmitate
palpitate
pollinate
pulvinate
palpitant
palmipede
pulpiteer
pulpiness
peltingly
pollinium
pallidity
pulvilled
pulvillio
pulvillar
pulvillus
pillicock
pelviform
pellitory
palliasse
palmistry
pulvinule
palilalia
polylemma
palillogy
polemical
palominos
poll-money
palampore
palempore
polymeric
polemarch
polymorph
polymasty
polymathy
palankeen
polonaise
palanquin
paleogaea
Pulmonata
pulmonate
pulmonary
pillow-cup
Paleocene
Paleogene
pilloried
pillorise
pillorize
paleolith
polyomino
Paleozoic
paleotype
polyonymy
polyphase
polyphagy
polypidom
polyploid
polyphone
polyphony
Polyporus
polyposis
polyptych
pilgrimer
pelorised
polarised
polariser
palfreyed
pelorized
polarized
polarizer
palm-sugar
Pelasgian
pulpstone
palestric
palestral
palustral
polystyle
pilot-jack
palatable
palatably
political
politicos
politicly
polythene

pilotless
pilot-fish
pilot-flag
polytonal
pilot-boat
polytypic
politique
politesse
Politburo
△**pele-tower**
pullulate
pollutant
pollutive
pollusion
pollution
polyvinyl
palaverer
pole-vault
polywater
△**pollyanna**
polyzoary
polyzonal
polyzooid
pompadour
pomace-fly
pomaceous
pumiceous
pomoerium
pommelled
pummelled
pimpernel
pimientos
pemphigus
pompholyx
pomposity
pompously
pome-water
pump-water
pantagamy
Punjaubee
pentarchy
panhandle
pantaleon
pantalets
pentamery
pinnately
pentangle
Pindarise
Pindarize
pin-making
pennalism
Pindarism
pandation
Pindarist
pinnacled
pintailed
pantables
△**pantaloon**
pentalogy
pentapody
pentalpha
pineapple
pentagram
pennatula
panachaea
panicking
piña-cloth
panic-bolt
ponderate
panderess
panderism
pandemian
pannelled
Pan-German
panderous
ponderous
Pentecost
△**pinkerton**
pendently
pungently
pansexual
pine-finch
pinafored
panegoism
panegyric
punch-card
punch-ball
pinchbeck
pantheism
pantheist
pinchfist
panthenol
pinchcock
punch-bowl
punch-prop
penthouse
pine-house
panchayat
pinnipede
pannikell
penniless
pinkiness
punkiness
pensively
pantingly
punningly
penninite
pontifice
pantiling
pensility
pencilled
penciller
pendicler
pontianac
pontianak
pensioner
pantihose
pencil-ore
penniform
panniered
panmictic
panoistic
penultima
panelling
penillion
panellist
Pan-Slavic
pontlevis
penumbral
pen-and-ink
peninsula
pentosane
pennoncel
penholder
pontoneer
pantoffle
pantoufle
pansophic
Pentothal®
pantomime
pentoxide
panlogism
pontonier
pondokkie
pinhooker
pancosmic
pontooner
peneplane
peneplain
panoplied
panspermy
Pan-Arabic
pen-friend
pendragon
panoramic
pantryman
penurious
pancratic
pen-driver
punishing
penistone
pint-stoup
pint-sized
penetrate
punctuate
penetrant
pin-stripe
panatella
punctilio
penstemon
penitence
penitency
panettone
panettoni
punctured
puncturer
punctated
punctator
pandurate
pendulate
pinnulate
pen-pusher
penduline
penguinry
pendulous
pendulums
pennyland
penny-bank
pentylene
penny-rent
penny-wise
penny-post
penny-wort
propagate
prosaical
protandry
prosateur
profanely
prolately
promachos
probative
prolamine
prolative
protamine
phonation
probation
prolation
pronation
proration
procacity
profanity
protanope
phonatory
probatory
prolapsus
prolactin
propagule
procaryon
prokaryon
procaryot
prokaryot
proactive
proscribe
proscript
proudness
proud-pied
Ptolemaic
phonecard
promenade
proletary
probeable
proveable
proveably
proseucha
proseuche
Provençal
properdin
proceeder
provender
proneness
phonetise
phonetize
phonetism
Pooterism
prooemium
prooemion
phonemics
phonetics
phonetist
procerity
propelled
propeller
proteinic
provedore
processed
professed
prowessed
processor
professor
prolepses
prolepsis
proteuses
proleptic
protected
progestin
projector
prorector
prosector
△protector
protester
protestor
procedure
prosecute
proselyte
proof-mark
proofread
proofless
proffered
profferer
ploughboy
ploughing
ploughman
ploughmen
pronghorn
prongbuck
pro-choice
prothalli
prothorax
prothesis
prophetic
prothetic
poorhouse
proximate
provinces
profiteer
phoniness
prosiness
procident
prominent
provident
prolicide
profiting
promising
providing
prosimian

9 p□o□i

provision
profilist
prolixity
proximity
provisoes
proditory
provisory
promissor
psoriasis
protistic
psoriatic
poodle-dog
profluent
proclisis
proclitic
proembryo
phonmeter
poor-mouth
prognoses
prognosis
proenzyme
prorogate
provocant
proboscis
protonema
photogene
photocell
propodeum
propodeon
proponent
photogeny
prolonger
photophil
phonolite
prologise
prologize
promotive
protogine
protoxide
provoking
prosodial
promotion
prosodian
photonics
prosodist
pronounce
protozoic
phonopore
protozoal
protozoan
protozoon
phonology
photocopy
phonogram
photogram
photopsia
proconsul
protostar
Photostat®
provostry
protoavis

phonotype
photolyse
phototype
prototype
phonotypy
phototypy
protogyny
phosphate
prompt-box
phosphene
phosphide
phosphine
phosphite
prompting
plot-proof
prompture
procreate
procreant
propriety
prodromic
programme
prodromal
prodromus
pyorrhoea
proustite
Proustian
poor's-roll
pro-estrus
prostrate
Prontosil®
proptosis
prostatic
proctitis
procuracy
pronuncio
promuscis
procureur
procuress
profusely
profusion
prolusion
pronuclei
prolusory
propulsor
propylaea
propylene
propylite
prozymite
pepper-box
puppeteer
peppering
poppering
Popperian
pepperoni
pepper-pot
pepsinate
peptidase
popliteal
pepticity
papillate
pupillage

pupillate
papillary
pupillary
pipe-light
pupilship
papilloma
papillose
papillote
papillous
popularly
papillule
pipe-layer
peptonise
peptonize
pipsqueak
paper-case
paperware
paperback
paper-reed
paperless
paper-file
paper-girl
paper-mill
paper-clip
peperomia
piperonal
paperwork
paper-coal
paper-pulp
paparazzi
paparazzo
pipestone
pipe-track
papeterie
poppy-head
puppyhood
poppycock
piquantly
parrakeet
permanent
pargasite
percaline
pervasive
portatile
portative
purgative
partaking
perradial
pervasion
purgation
perradius
permalloy
purgatory
Parnassus
periaktos
parabrake
periblast
parabolic
periboloi
parabolas
peribolos

peribolus
pure-blood
parabasis
periclase
pyroclast
pericrany
pericycle
△**paraclete**
Periclean
parochine
pericline
parochial
pyracanth
pericones
parecious
paracusis
parachute
parodical
parodying
peridinia
peridrome
paradores
paradisic
paradisal
peridotic
paradoxal
pyridoxin
paradoxer
porterage
porcelain
parcenary
perceable
permeable
permeably
persevere
porteress
porbeagle
porrenger
paroemiac
perseline
pargeting
paroemial
Parseeism
parhelion
parcelled
permeance
parge-work
peraeopod
Pernettya
percental
perfecter
perfector
perverter
perfectos
perfectly
persecute
perpetual
perfervid
parleyvoo
perceiver
perfervor

paraffine
purifying
paraffiny
portfolio
poriferal
poriferan
paragraph
paragogic
paragogue
peregrine
porogamic
pyrogenic
paregoric
parchedly
Parcheesi®
parchment
Pyrrhonic
perchance
Parthenon
porphyria
percheron
porphyrin
porphyrio
parrhesia
purchaser
perthitic
porthouse
pervicacy
perkiness
pursiness
pertinent
porwiggle
porringer
purringly
parricide
partitive
Persicise
Persicize
partition
perdition
partially
persimmon
portioned
persienne
portioner
porticoed
perciform
paroicous
porticoes
parcimony
parsimony
pereiopod
permitted
permitter
partitura
perikarya
parfleche
Pyralidae
paralogia
paralegal
perilling

Words marked △ may be spelled also with a capital letter

paralalia
perilymph
purulence
parklands
purulency
paralyser
paralysis
pyrolysis
paralytic
pyrolytic
pyrolater
pyrolatry
paralexia
paralyzer
paramecia
paramedic
pyramidic
pyramidal
pyramidon
pyramides
pyromania
pyromancy
poromeric
paramorph
perimorph
pyramises
paramatta
parameter
perimeter
pyrometer
perimetry
pyrometry
paramount
parentage
perennate
Pyreneans
paranoeic
perinaeal
perinaeum
Pyrenaean
paranoiac
pyreneite
parenting
phrentick
perennial
perennity
paranymph
Peronista
Peronismo
parenesis
phrenesis
phrenetic
phrenitic
perinatal
phrenitis
parsonage
percolate
perforate
periodate
personage
personate
porporate
portolani
portolano
perforans
perforant
parlor-car
parrot-cry
purposely
personise
personize
purposive
pardoning
parsonish
purdonium
personify
parrot-jaw
performer
personnel
part-owner
purloiner
parroquet
periplast
parapodia
periphery
periptery
pyrophone
periproct
porcpisce
peripetia
parapeted
△**peripatus**
paraquito
partridge
portreeve
pararhyme
portrayal
portrayer
parasceve
perisperm
parischan
perishing
periscian
phraseman
periscope
peristome
poroscope
pyroscope
poroscopy
parasitic
peristyle
piratical
pyritical
peritrich
part-timer
paratonic
puritanic
△**pyrethrum**
pyrethrin
parotitis
perttaunt
parataxis
portulaca
perfusate
permutate
pertusate
perturbed
pursuable
perturber
persuader
purpureal
perfumery
perfusive
porcupine
perfusion
pertusion
parbuckle
pursuance
pergunnah
perjurous
percussed
pertussal
percussor
pertussis
parqueted
pirouette
parquetry
Portuguee
perovskia
paravaunt
parkwards
pyroxylic
pyroxylin
pyroxenic
parhypate
party-call
party-size
party-jury
pistareen
passament
pistachio
passadoes
piscatory
piscatrix
push-chair
push-cycle
pass-check
passement
passenger
passepied
passerine
posterior
posterity
paste-down
pesterous
possessed
possessor
passers-by
post-entry
pushfully
posigrade
posthorse
posthaste
pesthouse
posthouse
passivate
pasticcio
pastiness
pushiness
pestilent
passively
pushingly
pesticide
passivism
pessimism
postilion
passivist
pessimist
passivity
postiller
possibles
passioned
passional
pisciform
posticous
pisolitic
postnasal
postnatal
pastorale
pastorate
pistoleer
pistolled
pestology
postponer
postrider
push-start
poss-stick
post-synch
piss-taker
pasturage
postulate
pustulate
postulant
pustulant
posturist
pasquiler
pustulous
post-viral
postwoman
pussyfoot
phthalate
phthalein
pot-hanger
pot-waller
pit-sawyer
petechiae
petechial
putschist
pothecary
putrefied
pottering
pathetics
pithecoid
putter-out
patiently
pitifully
pitch-dark
patchable
patchocke
pitchpine
pitchpipe
pitch-pole
patchwork
pitchfork
pitch-poll
pitch-tree
patchouli
patchouly
pituitary
pettiness
pithiness
pottiness
pottingar
pottinger
pityingly
pettishly
petrified
patricide
pethidine
Petrinism
△**patrician**
patriliny
putridity
patricoes
pettitoes
petticoat
patrimony
patriarch
pituitrin
patriotic
patristic
pet-sitter
patellate
pétillant
petulance
petulancy
pottle-pot
potometer
potentate
potentise
potentize
potential
patinated
patronage
petiolate
petrolage
petroleum
pétroleur
patroness
△pythoness
pathogeny
patronise
patronize
potholing
patrolled

Words marked △ may be spelled also with a capital letter

9 p□t□o

petrolled
patroller
pot-boiler
patrolman
pathology
patrology
petrology
potpourri
petrogram
piteously
petiolule
petersham
paternity
patercove
peter-boat
patereros
potassium
petaurine
petaurist
put-putted
pot-hunter
pluralise
pluralize
pluralism
Poujadism
pluralist
Poujadist
plurality
plumbless
plumbagos
pourboire
plumbeous
pounce-box
pounching
plumdamas
plunderer
pauperess
pauseless
plumeless
plume-bird
pauperise
pauperize
pauperism
prunellos
plume-moth
prudently
plus-fours
prud'homme
pouchfuls
pluripara
pausingly
poutingly
prudishly
prusiking
Paulinism
Paulician
Paulinian
Paulinist
prurience
pruriency
pousowdie
Plutonism
plutonium
Plutonian
Plutonist
paulownia
plutology
plutonomy
plutocrat
plumpness
pourpoint
prussiate
poursuitt
plum-stone
poussette
pourtrayd
poultfoot
poulterer
plumulate
plumulose
pavonazzo
Pavlovian
pivotally
pew-fellow
pawkiness
powellise
△powellite
powellize
Powellism
pew-holder
pew-opener
powerless
power-dive
powerplay
powerboat
pixilated
pixy-stool
phylarchy
prytaneum
paysagist
pay-packet
paymaster
pay-office
psychical
psychogas
psychoses
psychosis
psychotic
physicism
physician
physicist
physicked
Psyllidae
phyllopod
phylogeny
phytogeny
phycology
phytology
phytotomy
phytotron
phycocyan
pay-gravel
pizzaiola
pizzicato
puzzledom
puzzle-peg
pozzolana
puzzolana
Quakerdom
quarenden
quarender
Quakeress
quavering
Quakerish
Quakerism
quakiness
quakingly
qualified
qualitied
qualifier
qualities
Quasimodo
quail-call
quail-pipe
qualmless
quadrifid
quadrigae
quarrying
quadrella
quadrille
quadruman
quarryman
quadruped
quadruple
quadruply
quarry-sap
quadratic
quaeritur
quadratus
quaesitum
quantical
quartzite
quartzose
quartered
quarterly
quartette
quartetti
quartetto
quenching
quercetum
quercetin
Quebecker
Québecois
queue-jump
querimony
queen-cake
queen's-arm
queenless
queenship
queen-like
queen-size
queen-fish
queenhood
queen-post
quebracho
queerness
questrist
querulous
quetzales
quibbling
quitclaim
quiverful
quivering
quiverish
quinidine
quirister
quicksand
quickbeam
quickness
quick-fire
quicklime
quickener
quick-born
quickstep
quick-eyed
quillwort
quinoidal
quinoline
quixotism
quinonoid
quinolone
quinquina
quiescent
quietness
quittance
quietsome
quintroon
quintuple
quintette
quintetti
quintetto
quizzical
qinghaosu
quotative
quotation
quotidian
quotition
quodlibet
road-agent
Reaganite
Reaganism
roadblock
road-borne
roadcraft
readdress
reaedifye
rear-dorse
rearguard
reachable
rhachides
rhaphides
reachless
rearhorse
rhachises
rhachitis
roadhouse
reanimate
readiness
roaringly
realising
realizing
realistic
rear-light
realmless
road-maker
road-metal
rearmouse
reasoning
rearousal
rhapontic
reappoint
rhamphoid
reapparel
reacquire
rearrange
rhapsodic
roadstead
road-sense
reassurer
reactuate
road-train
roast-beef
roast-meat
reattempt
reactance
readvance
read-write
roadworks
ready-made
ready-wash
Rubiaceae
reboation
rubicelle
rabidness
robber-fly
rubberise
rubberize
rabbeting
rebbetzin
rabbinate
rubricate
rubbishly
rabbinite
rabbinism
rubrician
rabbinist
rebukable
rebukeful
rebel-like
rubellite
rebelling
rebellion
rib-plough
robe-maker
rubineous

Words marked △ may be spelled also with a capital letter

Ribbonism
Ribbon-man
reblossom
rebaptise
rebaptize
rebaptism
rubescent
ribosomal
rabatment
rebutment
rabatting
rebutting
ribattuta
ribaudred
rybaudrye
Richardia
réchauffé
rectangle
Rechabite
racialism
raciation
ructation
racialist
reclaimer
raccahout
recharter
rock-brake
rock-borer
rock-basin
rock-bound
rockcress
recyclist
recherché
racketeer
rocketeer
recrement
racketing
ricketily
recreance
recreancy
rice-field
rock-flour
ricegrain
rock-guano
rice-grass
recognise
recognize
racegoing
racehorse
reclinate
recoinage
rockiness
rectified
receiving
reclining
rachidial
rachidian
rectifier
rectitude
recalment
recollect
re-collect
recalesce
rechlesse
recompact
recommend
recumbent
recombine
recompose
rocambole
recomfort
reconvene
raconteur
reconnect
reconvert
reconcile
recondite
reconfirm
recension
Ricinulei
rock-'n'-roll
reconquer
rectorate
rectoress
reckoning
rectorial
recipient
receptive
recaption
reception
rack-punch
rock-pipit
rock-perch
recapture
ricercata
ricercare
rectrices
recurrent
recursive
recording
recurring
recursion
Ricardian
recordist
rickstand
rock-shaft
rock-socks
recessive
rickstick
recession
rock-solid
recusance
recusancy
racetrack
reclusely
reclusive
reclusion
reclusory
recountal
recruital
recruiter
recoveree
recoverer
recoveror
rice-water
rockwater
redhanded
radiately
radialise
radialize
radiative
red-tapism
radiation
red-tapist
radiality
radiatory
red-carpet
radial-ply
red-haired
red-rattle
radiantly
reductase
redecraft
reductant
reducible
radicchio
reductive
redaction
reduction
radicular
ridiculer
radically
radicated
ridgeback
red-headed
reddendum
reddendos
red-legged
ridge-tile
redeeming
rudbeckia
red-heeled
ridge-bone
ridge-pole
ridge-rope
rodgersia
redresser
red-letter
ruddiness
redding-up
rodfisher
red-lining
red-figure
red-plague
raddleman
reddleman
ruddleman
redolence
riddlings
redolency
redeliver
rudiments
redundant
redingote
riding-rod
radiothon
radionics
red-looked
red-polled
radiology
radiogram
redbreast
riderless
redescend
redstreak
redoubted
redevelop
redivivus
re-examine
rheochord
re-endorse
re-elevate
rue-leaved
re-enforce
reed-grass
reediness
reelingly
re-edifier
reed-knife
rheologic
rheumatic
rheometer
rheumatiz
reed-organ
rhetorise
rhetorize
re-entrant
rheotrope
rheotaxis
re-educate
reflagged
reflation
refracted
refractor
ruff-a-duff
refection
refectory
refreshen
refresher
rifle-shot
rifle-bird
reflexive
raftering
reflexion
reflected
reflecter
reflector
raffinate
raffishly
ruffianly
raffinose
refulgent
refelling
Rafflesia
refinedly
reflowing
reformade
reformado
referable
referring
refurbish
refurnish
reformism
reformist
refortify
referenda
reference
refusable
rufescent
refashion
refusenik
refutable
refutably
refitment
refitting
refounder
refluence
regrating
rigmarole
regicidal
rigidness
ruggelach
rug-headed
reguerdon
regretful
rogueship
ruggedise
ruggedize
regretted
rigwiddie
roguishly
rag-picker
regularly
regulator
regiminal
regionary
rigwoodie
regardant
rag-trader
regardful
regarding
régisseur
registrar
right-hand
rightward
right-bank
rightable
rightless
rightness
right-wing
right-down
righteous
rehearing
rehearsal
rehearser

9 r□h□d

rehydrate
rehousing
ruination
rail-borne
reimburse
rain-bound
rainbowed
raincheck
rain-cloud
reindeers
reiterate
reiterant
raiseable
Rhineodon
rail-fence
reinforce
rain-gauge
reinhabit
Reichsrat
Reichstag
rhipidate
raininess
railingly
rhipidium
rhipidion
rainmaker
rail-motor
rhizocaul
rhizocarp
rhizoidal
rhinolith
△rhizobium
Rhizopoda
rhinology
ruinously
reimplant
rain-print
rainproof
reinstate
reinstall
reinspect
reinspire
rain-stone
rainstorm
reinsurer
reistafel
raintight
roisterer
reinvolve
railwoman
rainwater
rejective
rejection
rajahship
rejoinder
rejoicing
rijstafel
rakehelly
rakeshame
roll-about
reluctate
reluctant
relieving
rillettes
relegable
religieux
religiose
religioso
religious
relenting
relapsing
reliquary
reliquiae
rulership
relations
relatival
relevance
relevancy
relay-race
ram-raider
rampaging
rampantly
remeasure
remediate
remedying
ramfeezle
ramifying
remigrate
remainder
rumminess
rompingly
rompishly
rampicked
Ramillies
remontant
remindful
romancing
remanence
remanency
reminisce
Romaniser
ruminator
Romanizer
Rome-penny
remercied
remarqued
remissive
remission
remissory
remitment
remittent
remitting
remoulade
rémoulade
rum-runner
rum-butter
removable
removably
Romewards
rangatira
ransacker
rentaller
runecraft
ring-canal
ring-cross
ring-dance
rangeland
rinseable
rennet-bag
rendering
ranterism
run-resist
ranzelman
renversed
runners-up
ring-fence
renegados
ring-gauge
ranshakle
rancheria
rancherie
rancheros
runcinate
ranginess
rantingly
ringingly
runningly
rendition
rancidity
rantipole
renfierst
ringleted
ring-money
ranunculi
randomise
randomize
rancorous
rencontre
rank-rider
runaround
ringstand
ring-shake
ring-snake
rune-stave
ring-small
ringsider
renascent
renitency
renouncer
renovator
renewable
rinky-dink
rhodanate
rhodamine
rhodanise
rhodanize
rhoeadine
rhotacise
rhotacize
rhopalism
rhotacism
roof-board
rhombuses
root-bound
rhonchial
Rhodesian
root-eater
roof-guard
root-house
roominess
rooming-in
rhodolite
rhodonite
rhodopsin
riotously
roof-plate
root-prune
roofscape
rootstock
rood-tower
repeating
reptation
Ripuarian
republish
repackage
repechage
rapacious
repudiate
rapidness
rapid-fire
rope-dance
reprehend
represent
re-present
replenish
repletion
ripienist
rappelled
repressed
repressor
repugnant
rope-house
reprimand
replicate
rippingly
reptilian
repairman
reptiloid
reprieval
repellant
repellent
repulsive
repelling
repulsion
rope-maker
repentant
reprobate
reprobacy
reprocess
reproving
raptorial
reprogram
reproduce
reportage
reparable
reparably
reporting
repertory
reperusal
repercuss
repassage
reposedly
repossess
reposeful
rope-soled
repositor
repasture
reputable
reputably
reputedly
repotting
rope-trick
rapturise
rapturize
rapturist
rapturous
ropeworks
repayable
repayment
Roquefort
requester
requisite
requiring
requicken
requitted
rerebrace
Rorschach
reradiate
reredorse
reredosse
raree-show
rare-earth
rarefying
ruralness
reremouse
Ruritania
△rastafari
rascaldom
ressaldar
rosmarine
rascalism
rascality
rascaille
raspatory
rose-apple
resnatron
restarter
raspberry
resection
rosaceous
rose-cross
residuary
residence
residency
residuous

rose-elder
rostering
russeting
rostellum
rostellar
respecter
restfully
rosefinch
rush-grown
rasp-house
rest-house
rusticate
riskiness
rushiness
rustiness
restively
raspingly
rusticise
rusticize
rusticial
rusticism
Rosminian
rusticity
restiform
restitute
resultant
resoluble
resilient
resolvent
resultful
rushlight
resulting
resumable
resembler
risk-money
rosin-weed
resentful
resentive
resonance
Rosinante
resinosis
resonator
responder
Russophil
Raskolnik
responsum
responser
responsor
rust-proof
resorbent
resurgent
resurrect
reserpine
reservist
restraint
restringe
reservoir
rostrated
resistant
resistent
resistive
rosa-solis
rose-topaz
rescuable
resources
reshuffle
rosewater
rusty-back
ritualise
ritualize
ritualism
retiarius
ritualist
rat-tailed
retracted
retractor
reticella
△reticulum
reticular
reticence
reticency
rutaceous
retreaded
ratherest
ratheripe
rattening
ratherish
ruthenium
Ruthenian
ratifying
ruthfully
rotiferal
rotograph
retchless
retaining
retribute
retrieval
retriever
retaliate
rattlebag
rutilated
Rotameter®
rotundate
retentive
retention
rotundity
retinulae
retinular
retinitis
ritenutos
rationale
rationals
retrodden
retrocede
retroject
retrovert
retroflex
retroussé
rat-poison
rotaplane
ratepayer
retardate
retardant
retiredly
ritornell
retortive
retorsion
retortion
rotatable
retoucher
rotavirus
Rotavator®
Rotovator®
rotovator
retexture
Roumanian
Roumansch
rhumb-line
raunchily
rounceval
roundhand
Roundhead
roundness
round-fish
roundelay
roundsman
roundworm
round-down
roundarch
round-trip
round-eyed
rousement
route-step
roughcast
roughneck
rough-hewn
roughness
roughshod
rough-draw
routineer
routinely
rousingly
routinise
routinize
routinism
routinist
Rauwolfia
raucously
routously
roussette
revealing
revocable
revocably
revictual
revokable
rivalless
ravelment
rivalship
revulsive
ravelling
revelling
revolting
revolving
rivalling
revulsion
revalenta
revel-rout
revelator
revengive
revenging
raven-bone
raven-duck
river-sand
riverbank
river-jack
river-wall
reverable
river-head
riverweed
riverless
reversely
revertive
riverlike
riverside
river-tide
reversing
reversion
river-flat
reverence
river-boat
revisable
ravishing
rivet-head
revetment
revetting
rivetting
rivet-hole
revivable
revivably
rowdiness
rewritten
rowel-head
rowelling
rowel-spur
rowan-tree
row-dow-dow
rewardful
rewarding
rix-dollar
Roxburghe
Rhynchota
rhymeless
rhyme-word
rhymester
rhythmise
rhythmize
rhythmics
rhythmist
rhyolitic
roysterer
ray-fungus
Rozinante
razor-back
razorable
razor-edge
razor-fish
razor-bill
razor-clam
scarabaei
seawardly
shamateur
shanachie
sea-bather
star-anise
seafaring
△shamanism
swarajism
shamanist
swarajist
sea-walled
spanaemia
spanaemic
scaraboid
star-apple
spadassin
stalactic
starboard
scambling
shambling
shambolic
swag-belly
slabberer
shadberry
soapberry
searching
stanching
stanchion
snatchily
starchily
star-crost
staccatos
standgale
scaldhead
staidness
scaldship
skaldship
standpipe
scaldfish
stardrift
stag-dance
scaldings
slanderer
standards
scald-crow
stander-by
shareware
stage-name
stalemate
skatepark
space-walk
shamefast
spare-part
shakeable
shameable
shapeable

9 s□a□e

scare-head
snakeweed
scaleless
scapeless
shadeless
shameless
shapeless
slakeless
spaceless
spareless
spareness
staleness
stateless
scapement
statement
scavenger
spaceship
snakebird
scalelike
scare-line
snakebite
snakelike
snakewise
space-time
spadelike
spare-time
△stateside
statewide
shaveling
slavering
spadefish
stapedial
Shakerism
stapedius
spagerist
statelily
snakeskin
sharesman
spadesman
statesman
snakewood
statehood
scalework
slave-fork
spadework
stateroom
shakedown
scapegoat
snakeroot
shag-eared
snare-drum
sharecrop
scarecrow
slate-gray
slate-grey
sea-beaten
spadefuls
slave-hunt
spacesuit
scaff-raff
scarfwise

scarf-ring
scarfskin
staffroom
staff-tree
shanghai'd
shaggy-dog
Shangri-la
spangling
slangular
swan-goose
staggered
staggerer
swaggerer
slaughter
stargazer
stargazey
scatheful
shashlick
snaphance
swashwork
scaphopod
slap-happy
smasheroo
spaghetti
staghound
stabilate
staminate
scaliness
seaminess
shadiness
shakiness
slatiness
snakiness
soapiness
staginess
suasively
soakingly
soaringly
sparingly
staringly
sea-fisher
slavishly
scarified
stabilise
stabilize
Stagirite
Stalinism
stasidion
scarifier
spagirist
Stalinist
stability
suability
spadillio
spatially
shamianah
stational
stationer
staminoid
staminode
staminody

statistic
stackyard
slack-bake
slackness
sparkless
stalkless
starkness
sparkling
sparklies
sharkskin
shankbone
stackroom
stalk-eyed
small-hand
stableboy
stall-feed
Stahlhelm
shawlless
smallness
starlight
small-time
snail-like
snail-fish
spauld-ill
snail-slow
stableman
scablands
scagliola
small-bore
small-coal
small-town
scalloped
small-arms
scallawag
scallywag
swallower
shallowly
△**spasmodic**
swarm-cell
slammakin
staymaker
stammerer
shammosim
spasmatic
seannachy
stainless
stauncher
staunchly
stagnancy
stannator
Slavophil
scapolite
Slavonise
Slavonize
sea-roving
seasoning
shadowing
sialolith
statolith
Slavonian
sea-rocket

scatology
sialogram
slavocrat
scazontic
seabottle
scazontes
seaworthy
statocyst
swampland
scalpless
sharpness
sharp-shod
sealpoint
sharpener
scarpines
shampooed
star-proof
scamp-work
shampooer
scarpetti
scarpetto
sharp-eyed
staircase
stairhead
stairwell
stairwise
stairlift
stairwork
stairfoot
sea-island
slab-sided
sparsedly
slaistery
starshine
seat-stick
slapstick
slabstone
soapstone
starstone
swansdown
swans-down
swart-back
slantways
smartweed
scantness
shaftless
smartness
swartness
slantwise
sparteine
scantling
startling
startlish
smart-alec
shantyman
scattered
shattered
scart-free
smartarse
sparterie
scatterer

smatterer
slant-eyed
spatulate
scapulary
statutory
statuette
stalworth
soap-works
scaly-bark
Stagyrite
spagyrist
subcaudal
subwarden
subjacent
sabbatine
sabbatise
sabbatize
submarine
sabbatism
Sabianism
sublation
subcavity
subfamily
subsample
subsacral
submatrix
subvassal
subcantor
suboctave
subacidly
subschema
subscribe
subaction
subscript
subocular
sebaceous
sabadilla
subeditor
subtenant
subdeacon
subgenera
submerged
sublethal
subsecive
sabre-wing
subaerial
subregion
subseries
subsellia
subcellar
subdermal
subhedral
subneural
submersed
sublessee
subversal
sublessor
subjected
submental
submentum
subletter

Words marked △ may be spelled also with a capital letter

subverter
subtenure
suboffice
subagency
subahdary
subahship
subphylum
sublimate
subniveal
subnivean
sublinear
sublimely
subtilely
subtilety
sobbingly
subdivide
sublimise
sublimize
subsidise
subsidize
subtilise
subtilize
subliming
sublimity
subtility
subtitles
submicron
submissly
submitted
submitter
sobriquet
subaltern
△**sibylline**
subalpine
Sabellian
Sibyllist
subclimax
sibilance
sibilancy
sibilator
subclause
subimagos
subentire
subincise
subrogate
subpotent
subtopian
subsoiler
subnormal
subpoena'd
subdolous
subtorrid
subdorsal
subcostal
subcortex
subapical
se-baptist
soberness
subursine
subbranch
subereous

subtropic
subarctic
△sybaritic
subastral
substrata
substrate
substract
substylar
subatomic
substance
substruct
subjugate
sublunate
sublunary
subduable
subduedly
subbureau
submucosa
submucous
subsultus
subsystem
sacrament
sacralgia
sacralise
sacralize
siccative
socialise
socialite
socialize
sociative
Socratise
Socratize
sectarial
sacrarium
△socialism
sectarian
sociation
△**socialist**
sociality
sackcloth
secretage
secretary
sachemdom
succeeder
secretive
sickening
socketing
secretion
Socceroos
secretory
successor
succentor
suck-holer
saccharic
△**saccharum**
saccharin
succinate
sacrilege
sickishly
sacrifice
sacrifide

succinite
sectility
sectional
sacciform
sacristan
siciliana
siciliane
siciliano
sicklemia
sickleman
secularly
△**secondary**
secundine
sicknurse
sociopath
succotash
sociolect
sectorise
sectorize
sectorial
suctorial
suctorian
sociology
sociogram
succourer
sycophant
securable
secernent
securance
securitan
△**secession**
sick-tired
secateurs
sacculate
succulent
seclusive
succubine
seclusion
succubous
succursal
sideboard
sidebones
sideburns
seductive
seduction
side-dress
sedgeland
saddlebag
saddlebow
sidelight
saddle-lap
sidelined
sidelines
sudaminal
sodomitic
sedentary
sudorific
siderosis
sideritic
sideswipe
sideshoot

sidetrack
seditious
Sadducean
Sadducism
sodbuster
side-wheel
sidewards
skedaddle
stewardry
scenarise
scenarize
steradian
scenarios
scenarist
stewartry
shewbread
stepbairn
spec-built
speechful
stepchild
sketchily
speechify
sterculia
stenciled
seed-coral
stercoral
sheldrake
speedball
steadfast
spendable
steadicam®
speedwell
speedless
steadiest
speldring
steadying
seed-drill
speedboat
slenderly
speedster
sheldduck
scelerate
shebeener
stevedore
shelf-mark
seed-field
shelf-life
shelflike
shelfroom
shelf-fuls
sleighing
Shechinah
shechitah
sterilant
seediness
spewiness
seemingly
specified
sterilise
sterilize
sherifian

sterility
specially
specialty
sneak-raid
speakeasy
speakable
sheikhdom
sleekness
speckless
shell-sand
steelyard
shellback
shellbark
shell-marl
spellable
spellican
shell-less
smell-less
seemliest
seemlihed
seemlyhed
spellbind
shellfire
shell-like
shell-lime
shellfish
shell-pink
steel-clad
steel-blue
stellular
shell-hole
shellwork
steelwork
spelldown
stellerid
smell-trap
steel-gray
steel-grey
stellated
shellduck
steam-haul
steamship
steamboat
spermaria
spermatia
spermatic
spermatid
sternward
sternfast
sternebra
sternness
steenkirk
steinkirk
steinbock
sternmost
sternport
sternpost
steenbras
stegnosis
stegnotic
sternitic

9 s□e□o

stenopaic
stegosaur
stegodont
Stenotype®
stenotypy
shemozzle
sheep-wash
sheepwalk
sweepback
seed-pearl
seed-plant
sheep's-bit
sleepless
steepness
sheep-lice
sheepskin
sweepings
sheepfold
sheepcote
sheep-hook
sleepsuit
steerable
spearhead
sheerlegs
sweirness
shearling
steerling
spearfish
spearmint
stearsman
steersman
speerings
speirings
swear-word
spearwort
shear-hulk
sheer-hulk
seed-stalk
skeesicks
sneeshing
sweet-gale
sweet-talk
sweptback
skew-table
spectacle
sceptical
skeptical
sheet-feed
sheet-lead
sweetmeal
scentless
sweetness
sweetmeat
sheathing
sweptwing
sheatfish
sweetfish
sweet-flag
sweetener
sweetwood
sweetcorn
sweet-wort
sceptered
sheltered
sweltered
sheet-iron
shelterer
steatosis
steatitic
spectator
sweatsuit
speculate
spelunker
skew-whiff
sherwanis
sleazebag
safranine
softcover
softening
suffering
safeguard
soft-grass
soft-goods
siftingly
sufficing
suffixion
siffleuse
safflower
soft-nosed
suffocate
soft-pedal
softpaste
suffragan
saffroned
soft-shell
safetyman
suffusive
suffusion
signalise
signalize
signaling
sigmatism
sigmation
signalled
signaller
signalman
signatory
sigmatron
signature
signboard
sagebrush
sagacious
segregate
signeurie
segmented
segmental
suggester
sage-green
sogginess
sighingly
signified
signifier
significs
sigillate
sigillary
sagenitic
segholate
sigmoidal
△**signorina**
signorine
signorini
signorial
△**signorino**
sagapenum
sugarcane
sugarless
sugarplum
sugarally
sugarloaf
sugar-free
sugar-cube
sugar-lump
sagittate
sagittary
sightable
sight-read
sightseer
sightless
sightline
sight-sing
sightsman
sight-hole
schiavone
schnapper
schmaltzy
schnauzer
schechita
sphacelus
scheduled
scheduler
scheelite
sphaerite
schlemiel
schlemihl
schnecken
schlepped
schlepper
sphygmoid
sphagnous
schlieren
schnitzel
scholiast
schilling
scholarch
scholarly
schematic
△**sphenodon**
sphendone
sphincter
school-age
schoolbag
schoolboy
schoolday
schoolery
schooling
schnorkel
schlocker
schoolman
schnorrer
schnozzle
spherical
spherular
schistose
schistous
schmutter
schizopod
spinacene
spiralism
spiration
spiralist
spirality
stirabout
spiraster
spiracula
sailboard
shipboard
slip-board
soil-bound
slip-coach
stir-crazy
sticcados
snitchers
stitchery
stitching
switching
switchman
sailcloth
spiccatos
sticcatos
spin-dried
spindling
swindling
spin-drier
spindrift
skin-diver
spin-dryer
spikenard
slimeball
spike-nail
swineherd
swivel-eye
shineless
smileless
snideness
spineless
spireless
swivel-gun
spirewise
shivering
snipefish
spikefish
swine-fish
Spigelian
snivelled
swivelled
sniveller
spiderman
sciaenoid
swinehood
shire-moot
stilettos
spicebush
spike-rush
stiffware
stiffness
skinflick
skinflint
skilfully
stiffener
skiagraph
slingback
swing-back
swingtail
stingless
slingshot
shingling
sniggling
swingeing
swingling
swing-wing
stingfish
swing-door
swingboat
stingaree
swingtree
sniggerer
stingbull
stichidia
slighting
slightish
sticheron
stipitate
soi-disant
spicilege
shininess
sliminess
soiliness
spiciness
spikiness
spininess
spiritful
shiningly
slidingly
smilingly
swinishly
ski-kiting
spiriting
spiritism
spiritist
spirillum
spirillar
spiniform
spiritoso
spiritous
spiritual

Words marked △ may be spelled also with a capital letter

spirituel
slinkweed
slickness
stink-bird
slinkskin
stinkwood
stickwork
stinkhorn
shickered
slickered
shield-arm
shillaber
still-head
skill-less
stillness
still-life
shielding
ski-flying
spillikin
shillalah
shield-may
stillroom
stillborn
shielduck
still-hunt
spillover
swimmable
seismical
sciamachy
skiamachy
sail-maker
swimmeret
stigmatic
skinny-dip
scientise
scientize
sciential
scientism
scientist
spinnaker
seigniory
skinny-rib
seignoral
spinneret
sgian-dubh
sciroccos
slivovica
spilosite
sailoring
skijoring
Spinozism
Spinozist
spinosity
slivovitz
slivowitz
sailor-man
ship-owner
spirogram
spirogyra
shimozzle
sailplane
stippling
skidproof
slippered
shippound
Sciaridae
Sciuridae
shirralee
scirrhoid
scirrhous
shipshape
skiascopy
sciosophy
scissorer
shirtband
sciatical
stiltedly
stintedly
shiftless
shirtless
skirtless
stintless
swiftness
skin-tight
saintship
stiltbird
saintlike
saintling
Shintoism
Shintoist
scintilla
skirtings
sainthood
skip-tooth
saintfoin
swift-foot
spiculate
spinulate
stimulate
stipulate
stimulant
stipulary
shibuichi
spinulose
spinulous
ski-jumper
shipwreck
sojourner
sokemanry
solfatara
self-aware
sulfatase
sultanate
syllabary
sultaness
sulcalise
sulcalize
syllabise
syllabize
sylvanite
syllabism
saltation
△salvation
siltation
solvation
sulcation
sulfation
syllabics
syllabify
syllabled
saliaunce
saltatory
salvatory
salvarsan
self-abuse
self-begot
self-build
self-built
salubrity
selective
selachian
selection
salicylic
select-man
salacious
siliceous
silicious
solacious
silicosis
silicotic
salicetum
solicitor
saltchuck
solidness
self-drive
splodgily
self-doubt
spleenful
solfeggio
silverise
silverize
silvering
soldering
spleenish
solferino
sallee-man
syllepses
syllepsis
Salientia
sylleptic
saliently
self-faced
Solifugae
salifying
salt-glaze
silk-grass
silageing
sylph-like
sulphonic
sulphinyl
sulphuric
salt-horse
sulphuret
sulphatic
silphiums
self-image
Sylviidae
saltiness
silkiness
silliness
sulkiness
saltishly
selfishly
sylvinite
Sylviinae
salpiform
soldierly
soliloquy
solemness
solemnise
solemnize
solemnify
solemnity
Salomonic
Solomonic
salt-money
salimeter
shlimazel
salangane
solenodon
splendent
splintery
solonchak
splendour
selenious
selenitic
splenetic
solenette
splenitis
Sellotape®
sellotape
sulfonate
syllogise
syllogize
sallowish
sulfonium
syllogism
salmonoid
soleplate
self-pride
solipsism
solipsist
self-pious
saltpetre
saltpeter
siliquose
Siluridae
sclereide
salaryman
scleromas
sclerosed
sclerosal
scleroses
sclerosis
sclerotia
sclerotic
sclerotal
sclerotin
saleratus
scleritis
self-rowld
self-slain
splashing
splashily
siltstone
salesroom
seldshown
self-study
Solutrean
spluttery
solitaire
splatting
splitting
Solutrian
self-trust
sulfurate
sclaunder
spleuchan
Seljukian
self-wrong
self-worth
saltworks
saltwater
sallyport
splay-foot
semiangle
sympathin
summarise
summarize
summative
semi-Arian
summation
simpatico
summarist
summarily
sympatric
semibreve
semi-bajan
semicolon
simpering
summering
sommelier
symmetric
symmetral
summerset
Simmental
semifinal
semifluid
semi-grand
symphonic
symphysis
symphytic
Symphytum
summiteer
summing-up

Words marked △ may be spelled also with a capital letter

9 s□m□i

symbiosis
semeiotic
symbiotic
simulcast
semblable
semblably
simulacra
simulacre
simplices
semblance
semilunar
similarly
simplesse
simpliste
simulated
simpleton
simulator
semi-metal
semanteme
semantide
semuncial
semantics
seminally
simonious
semantron
simon-pure
somnolent
symposiac
Samsonite®
Simeonite
symbolise
symbolize
sympodial
symposial
△**symbolism**
sympodium
symposium
semiotics
symbolics
symbolist
symbolled
semiology
symbology
summonses
someplace
semaphore
semiplume
semi-rigid
sombreros
Samaritan
simarouba
semisolid
sumpsimus
somascope
semestral
Semi-Saxon
sumptuary
something
sometimes
semitonic
sumptuous

sumotoris
symptosis
symptotic
semi-truck
semivowel
somewhere
somewhile
Samoyedic
sink-a-pace
sandarach
Sinhalese
sinuately
sennachie
sunbather
sin-eating
sensation
sinuation
sandalled
suntanned
singalong
syngamous
sans-appel
syntactic
syndactyl
synkaryon
sandblast
sand-blind
songcraft
sunscreen
synectics
synodical
synedrial
synedrium
synedrion
synodsman
sand-devil
sonnetary
sentencer
syngeneic
synoecete
synoekete
sonneteer
senseless
sincerely
sonnetise
sonnetize
synoecise
synoecize
sundering
synoecism
sanbenito
sincerity
sunbeamed
Sanhedrim
Sanhedrin
sinlessly
syntectic
sunbeaten
songfully
sangfroid
sonograph

sandglass
synagogue
synagogal
synchrony
synchysis
syntheses
synthesis
synthetic
syndicate
sandiness
sunniness
sentiment
sinningia
singingly
sincipita
sensitise
sensitive
sensitize
sunrising
sensillum
sons-in-law
sentience
sentiency
synoicous
sinciputs
single-end
Sinologue
synclinal
single-sex
singleton
sunflower
synanthic
synangium
synonymic
syncopate
santolina
santonica
Senhorita
Sanforise
Sanforize
syntonise
syntonize
sensorial
sensorium
seniority
sensorily
sinuosity
sundowner
syntonous
sinuously
syncoptic
synaptase
synapheia
Sinophile
synopsise
synopsize
synoptist
Sinophily
sandpaper
sandpiper
sunbright

synergise
synergize
synergism
synergist
syndromic
syneresis
syncretic
sand-snake
senescent
seneschal
songsmith
singspiel
△**sandstone**
sandstorm
sandspout
sinistral
sand-screw
sinusitis
sanctuary
sunstroke
sanatoria
sanitaria
sunstruck
sensually
sunburned
singultus
synovitic
synovitis
sinewless
sand-yacht
syncytial
syncytium
sannyasin
synizesis
stoma-care
sloganeer
sporangia
stomachic
stomached
stomachal
stomacher
sloganise
sloganize
Slovakian
shopboard
snowboard
shoeblack
showbread
snow-blind
snowblink
slop-built
scombroid
snow-broth
snowberry
slop-basin
scorbutic
snowbound
showbizzy
slowcoach
stoccados
spot-check

sconcheon
slop-chest
scorching
slouching
stoically
Scotchman
stoccatas
sword-hand
sword-cane
sword-rack
sword-tail
sword-bean
swordless
sword-belt
swordlike
swordfish
sword-bill
snowdrift
spondulix
swordplay
swordsman
sword-knot
scorecard
shoreward
stonehand
stone-hard
stoneware
smoke-jack
smoke-ball
smoke-sail
stonewall
stonecast
shoreweed
stone-dead
stone-deaf
shoreless
smokeless
stoneless
shovelful
showerful
stonechat
stoneshot
shorebird
scolecite
scoreline
shoreline
shore-side
slopewise
spokewise
stone-pine
stovepipe
showering
stonefish
Slovenian
stone-lily
sooterkin
shovelled
shoveller
shoresman
spokesman
spokesmen

Words marked △ may be spelled also with a capital letter

smoke-bomb
scolecoid
scopeloid
smokehood
stokehold
stone-cold
stokehole
stonework
smoke-room
storeroom
stoneboat
stonewort
smoketree
stonecrop
smokebush
snowflake
sootflake
stop-frame
snowfield
snowfleck
snowflick
shop-floor
shopfront
shotfirer
spongebag
spongiose
spongeous
spongious
sloggorne
soothfast
soothlich
shophroth
smothered
sloghorne
smotherer
shochetim
slow-hound
sporidesm
showiness
smokiness
snowiness
sootiness
stoniness
slopingly
△**scotified**
sporidial
Scoticism
sporidium
scorifier
'sbodikins
stolidity
scoliosis
scoliotic
Scotistic
storiated
storiette
spoliator
stockyard
smock-race
stocktake
shockable

shock-head
stockless
stockpile
stockfish
stocklist
snorkeler
stockings
stockinet
stockwork
stockroom
stockhorn
stoolball
shoalness
shouldest
spotlight
stoplight
shoalwise
spoilfive
spoilsman
stormless
stormbird
shoemaker
shotmaker
showmanly
storm-cock
slow-march
spoonways
spoonbait
spoon-feed
spoonwise
spoonbill
stownlins
stornelli
stornello
spoonhook
scoundrel
spoonfuls
scotomata
sporocarp
sporogeny
sporophyl
scorodite
sporozoan
spodogram
sporocyst
showplace
slow-paced
Scorpaena
showpiece
stop-press
scorpioid
shotproof
slop-pouch
scoopfuls
scorrendo
scourings
snowscape
soopstake
sponsible
shoeshine
sponsalia

snowstorm
shorthand
shortcake
short-wave
shortfall
short-haul
shootable
sportable
short-head
short-term
shortness
sportless
spoutless
stoutness
scouthery
short-life
short-time
shoutline
smoothing
Storthing
smoothish
short-list
sportsman
shoot-'em-up
sportance
shortener
short-cord
shorthold
spout-hole
shortgown
shorthorn
sloethorn
short-coat
stouthrie
shortstop
scopulate
shogunate
sporulate
spodumene
snow-white
stopwatch
snow-water
storyline
scolytoid
storybook
storyette
sforzandi
sforzando
smorzando
sforzatos
Sephardic
Sephardim
sopranini
septarium
septarian
septation
sopranino
sopranist
sapraemia
sapraemic
sapidless

sapidness
sapodilla
septenary
supremacy
September
sapheaded
supremely
septemfid
supremity
septennia
saphenous
sapiently
septemvir
sapogenin
sapphired
sappiness
soppiness
syphilise
syphilize
septicity
syphiloma
syphiloid
septimole
septiform
sophistic
sophister
sophistry
suppliant
supplicat
sepulchre
sepulcher
supplying
sepulture
sapanwood
saponaria
supinator
siphonage
siphonate
saprolite
sepiolite
supposing
saprozoic
sophomore
sapi-outan
supporter
supersafe
superfast
supermart
supersalt
separable
superable
separably
superably
supergene
supersede
supervene
supersell
superhero
superheat
soporific
superthin

superfine
superhive
supervise
superrich
supermini
superbity
superglue
superplus
superflux
supernova
superbold
supercold
superpose
supercoil
supercool
supersoft
superbrat
superette
separatum
separator
superstar
separates
superfuse
suppurate
siphuncle
sapsucker
septuplet
sequacity
sequencer
sequestra
sequester
sequinned
sarbacane
seriately
serialise
serialize
stream-ice
screaming
spreading
streaking
streaming
surfacing
serialism
Syriacism
Syrianism
Sarmatian
seriation
serration
sortation
striation
serialist
seriality
streakily
streamlet
serranoid
sorb-apple
sargassum
sargassos
sarcastic
stream-tin
surmaster

9 s□r□a

servantry
serrature
striature
scrubland
surfboard
scribable
shrubless
shrubbery
shrublike
scrabbing
scrubbing
strobilae
scrabbler
scribbler
strobilus
sarabande
Soricidae
sprechery
strictish
spreckled
strychnia
Saracenic
strychnic
sericeous
sericitic
stricture
structure
sorediate
shredless
shredding
stridling
scroddled
stridence
stridency
streetage
streetboy
streetcar
surrender
surrendry
sorceress
surgeless
streetful
screecher
serrefile
screeding
screening
screeving
shrieking
surveying
surveille
surreined
sergeancy
serjeancy
serjeanty
surgeoncy
shriek-owl
surrejoin
sorcerous
surfeited
sarmentum
surfeiter
serpentry
shroffage
strifeful
sgraffiti
sgraffito
serigraph
scragging
shrugging
spragging
sprigging
strigging
seraglios
scraggily
straggler
struggler
sprightly
scrog-bush
scrog-buss
Syrphidae
surcharge
sortilege
sorriness
surliness
servilely
sortilegy
surcingle
sorbitise
sorbitize
straining
surmising
surviving
surficial
servilism
Sardinian
sortition
servility
spraickle
serricorn
serpigoes
serviette
servitude
strikeout
surpliced
scrolling
shrilling
strolling
strelitzi
scrimmage
scrummage
skrimmage
stramaçon
scrimshaw
scramming
scrumming
shrimping
strumming
scrimpily
scrambler
scrumdown
stromatic
strumatic
strumitis
stramazon
springald
shrinkage
strongarm
string-bag
△springbok
strongbox
serenader
syringeal
stringent
strongest
strangely
shrinking
springing
sprinting
stringing
strongish
strontium
strontian
springily
strenuity
stringily
sprinkler
strangler
strangles
springlet
strongman
strenuous
Stringops
serinette
strangury
strongyle
sarcomata
Sarvodaya
surrogate
sarcocarp
surrogacy
sarcomere
sermoneer
sorrowful
Sarcodina
sermonise
sermonize
sermoning
sorrowing
sartorial
sardonian
sartorian
Serbonian
sartorius
Sorbonist
sarcology
seriously
sarcoptic
Sarcoptes
scrapyard
scrippage
strap-game
strap-hang
strappado
strip-leaf
scrapheap
strapless
scrapegut
seraphine
strapline
scrapping
strapping
stripling
stripping
stropping
seraphims
seraphins
scrappily
scrapbook
strapwort
scriptory
surfperch
△scripture
surprised
surprisal
surpriser
strossers
stressful
seraskier
spritsail
scrutable
soritical
spriteful
strategic
stratagem
stretched
scratcher
stretcher
scratches
scrutoire
strutting
stratonic
serotinal
serotonin
scrutator
serrulate
stroupach
surquedry
scrounger
sprauchle
serpulite
shrouding
sprouting
strouding
surmullet
surculose
shriveled
scrivener
screwball
strewment
screw-pile
shrewmice
strawlike
scrawling
sprawling
screw-worm
strawworm
screw-down
straw-stem
strayling
sassarara
sussarara
Sassanian
sustained
sustainer
saskatoon
sassafras
systaltic
Sassenach
sisserary
suspended
suspender
systemise
systemize
sistering
suspenser
suspensor
sestertia
suspected
susceptor
sestettos
sostenuto
suscitate
sustinent
sissified
suspicion
sessional
sisal-hemp
sassolite
Sisyphean
susurrate
susurrant
sasquatch
satiation
situation
setaceous
satedness
sutteeism
setter-off
setter-out
sottishly
sottisier
sitzkrieg
settle-bed
satellite
suttletie
satanical
satinwood
satinetta
satinette
sitiology
shtupping
saturable
satirical
satyrical
saturniid

Words marked △ may be spelled also with a capital letter

saturnine
saturnism
Saturnian
saturnist
suturally
Satyrinae
saturated
saturator
satisfied
satisfice
satisfier
shtetlach
sitatunga
situtunga
Soudanese
squeakery
squeaking
squealing
squeamish
squeakily
scumbling
squibbing
squabbish
squabbler
slumbrous
slumberer
scuncheon
scutcheon
scutching
sour-crout
soul-curer
soundless
soundness
soundbite
sound-bite
scuddaler
soundings
squadrone
sourdough
spulebane
souteneur
saucerful
stupefied
sautéeing
squeezing
stupefier
scutellum
scutellar
Sauternes
spulebone
sou'-wester
studentry
smug-faced
shuffling
snuffling
snuff-dish
soulfully
soul-force
snuff-mull
sluggabed
slung-shot
smuggling
squegging
sour-gourd
southland
southward
south-east
south-west
Southdown
Southroun
southmost
slughorne
southerly
studiedly
sauciness
sourishly
squailing
stupidity
△sauvignon
scutiform
saucisson
skunkbird
squalidly
squelcher
squalling
souvlakia
squamella
scummings
squamosal
shunnable
Sturnidae
squint-eye
squinting
squinancy
snub-nosed
Sauropoda
stuporous
sculpture
squireage
square-cut
squiredom
squirrely
squirting
squiralty
souari-nut
squarrose
scurriour
squirarch
soubrette
spur-royal
squashily
soupspoon
squatness
squitters
squatting
shuttered
saunterer
sputterer
stutterer
shubunkin
spur-whang
squawking
scuzzball
sovietise
sovietize
sovietism
savagedom
Sivaistic
seventeen
seventhly
seventies
sovenance
sevenfold
severable
sovereign
severally
severalty
severance
savourily
sexvalent
sexualise
sexualize
sexualism
sexualist
sexuality
sextantal
sixteenth
sixteenmo
sixteener
Saxifraga
saxifrage
sex-change
sex-linked
sexennial
sextoness
six-footer
saxophone
saxitoxin
sextuplet
skyjacker
skylarker
scybalous
say-master
spymaster
styleless
stylebook
scytheman
Scyphozoa
stylishly
sky-diving
styliform
stylistic
stylobate
stylolite
skyrocket
Styrofoam®
styrofoam
styptical
sizarship
thanatism
thanatist
travailed
thanatoid
thalassic
tea-taster
tway-blade
trancedly
thatching
tray-cloth
twaddling
tsaddikim
tzaddikim
tsaddiqim
tzaddiqim
tradename
tragelaph
trademark
trade-last
traceable
tradeable
traceably
traceless
tradeless
thaneship
traceried
teaseling
trapesing
traveling
tsarevich
trapezial
trapezium
tragedian
trapezius
teaselled
travelled
tea-dealer
teaseller
traveller
tradesman
thanehood
trapezoid
traversed
traversal
traverser
trabeated
travertin
toad-eater
trabecula
tearfully
toadgrass
twangling
Thargelia
Tracheata
tracheate
tracheary
teachable
teachless
tracheide
trachinus
trashtrie
teacherly
trachytic
trachitis
twalhours
teasingly
traditive
△tradition
traditors
trackball
trackable
thankless
trackless
thankings
trackroad
track-boat
trailable
trail-less
trawl-line
trawl-fish
tramlined
tramlines
thalluses
traumatic
thaumatin
trainband
trainable
trainless
twa-lofted
traipsing
trampling
trampolin
trappings
twalpenny
trampette
transfard
translate
trap-stair
transcend
tearsheet
transfect
transient
transvest
transship
trans-ship
transpire
trap-stick
transumpt
transenna
transonic
toadstone
transmove
transpose
toadstool
transform
transport
tear-strip
transfuse
transhume
transmute
transeunt
transaxle
tractable
tractably
traitress
twattling

9 t□a□t

trattoria
trattorie
traitorly
tractator
teacupful
traguline
traducing
Traducian
tablature
tubicolar
tobaccoes
tubectomy
tableland
table-maid
tableware
table-talk
table-leaf
table-beer
tablewise
table-book
table-work
tubbiness
tabellion
Tubularia
tabularly
tubulated
tabulator
Tabanidae
tabbouleh
tubercled
tubercule
tabasheer
tabescent
tabbyhood
tacmahack
toccatina
Tocharish
Tocharian
tuckerbag
tuckerbox
ticketing
tactfully
tackiness
techiness
tactician
tactilist
tacticity
tactility
tectiform
tacamahac
technical
technique
tycoonate
tycoonery
tectorial
tectonics
tachogram
tectrices
tucotucos
tucutucos
tacitness

tactually
tachylite
tachypnea
tachylyte
tide-gauge
tediosity
Tod-lowrie
tediously
tidewater
toddy-palm
Theravada
toeragger
theralite
therapist
tee-marker
trepanned
trepanner
Trematoda
trematoid
trematode
thenabout
thesaurus
therapsid
tremblant
trembling
Theobroma
trenchand
trenchard
trenchant
theocracy
theocrasy
treachery
tiercelet
treachour
theaceous
tierceron
treadling
treadmill
trendyism
themeless
thereness
Thelemite
tee-heeing
therewith
thereinto
thereunto
therefore
tregetour
thereupon
therefrom
thereaway
twelfthly
theogonic
trephiner
tree-house
trepidant
theriacal
theglther
taeniasis
treillage
theologic

theologue
theologer
tree-lined
trellised
thermical
theomachy
△**thermidor**
thermally
theomania
theomancy
thermotic
treenware
tie-and-dye
'tween-deck
teeing-off
theandric
tremolant
treponema
treponeme
tremolite
trefoiled
Theropoda
thecodont
therology
teetotums
theophagy
theophany
theopathy
tee-square
thearchic
theorbist
theurgist
tredrille
theorique
theoriser
theoretic
theorizer
tree-snake
theosophy
tressured
treasurer
Thersitic
tree-stump
treatable
twentieth
treatment
twentyish
theatrics
theotokos
theft-bote
theftuous
theftboot
twenty-two
tree-trunk
tremulate
tremulant
trebuchet
tremulous
twelvemos
Teeswater
tie-dyeing

thelytoky
tufaceous
tagmemics
tegmental
tegmentum
tug-of-love
tuggingly
tigrishly
tegularly
tegulated
tiger's-eye
tiger-wood
tight-lace
tight-head
tightness
tightener
tight-knit
tightrope
tahsildar
trivalent
trifacial
triradial
tribadism
tribalism
trisagion
tribalist
trigamist
trigamous
tridactyl
trivalved
tailboard
thin-belly
twin-birth
triactine
twitching
triecious
third-hand
third-rate
Third-Ager
twiddling
thirdsman
twice-laid
tail-ender
tribeless
triteness
trimethyl
tripe-shop
thio-ether
tripe-wife
tricerion
tri-weekly
tribesman
twice-told
twice-born
trimerous
trimetric
trihedral
trihedron
toilet-set
tridented
tridental

trimester
trisector
thin-faced
thief-like
thingness
thingummy
thinghood
tailgater
tritheism
tritheist
trichinae
trichinas
trichroic
thighbone
trichrome
trichosis
trichitic
△**tripitaka**
triticale
trilinear
twiningly
trilithic
trilithon
triticism
trivially
tuitional
trinitrin
think-tank
thinkable
thickhead
thickness
trickless
trickling
twinkling
thick-lips
thickskin
triskelia
thick-knee
thickener
tricksome
thick-sown
thicketed
trickster
trinketer
trinketry
thick-eyed
trialogue
tail-light
trial-fire
trialling
triallist
triploidy
triclinic
trillions
tuillette
triumphal
triumpher
triumviri
triumvirs
triumviry
trimmings

triennial
triangled
triangles
trionymal
Triandria
trilobate
trifocals
tailoress
Trilobita
trilobite
tailoring
trinomial
trifolium
triforium
twiforked
triformed
twiformed
tricolour
trigonous
tribology
tailplane
twin-plane
tailpiece
thiophene
trierarch
tricrotic
tail-rhyme
thirstful
thirstily
tailstock
twin-screw
twin-track
twistable
tristichs
thirtieth
taintless
thirtyish
triathlon
triatomic
taint-worm
triptyque
trieteric
twitterer
tristesse
tribunate
triturate
tributary
Tribunite
tripudium
tricuspid
triquetra
tailwheel
tridymite
trigynian
tricyclic
tricycler
trigynous
trihydric
trihybrid
Tokharish
Tokharian
take-leave
tokoloshe
taking-off
teknonymy
Tiliaceae
talkathon
talkative
tollbooth
tylectomy
telferage
taligrade
telegraph
talegalla
telegenic
telegonic
telpheric
tollhouse
talliable
talking-to
tellingly
toluidine
tellinoid
telamones
telematic
telemeter
telemetry
teleosaur
tallow-dip
tallowish
tol-lolish
teleology
teleonomy
Teleostei
talbotype
telophase
telepheme
telepoint
tulipwood
telephone
telephoto
tulip-root
telephony
tulip-tree
telepathy
tolerable
tolerably
tularemia
tularemic
tolerance
tolerator
talismans
telestich
telescope
tile-stone
telescopy
tellurate
telluride
tellurise
tellurite
tellurize
tellurium
tellurian
tellurion
Talmudist
tellurous
televiser
televisor
tallyshop
tally-hoed
timpanist
tympanist
timocracy
timidness
tumidness
temperate
tampering
tempering
timbering
timber-man
timeframe
tumefying
tomograph
tim-whisky
tumble-bug
tumble-car
tumble-dry
temulence
temulency
time-lapse
temblores
timenoguy
tomentose
tomentous
tamponade
tamponage
temporary
temporise
temporize
tomboyish
tambourin
timeously
timepiece
tamarillo
timorsome
timescale
time-share
tumescent
tombstone
temptable
timetable
temptress
tomatillo
Timbuctoo
tamoxifen
tommy-shop
△temazepam
tantarara
tantalate
Tantalean
tonga-bean
tonka-bean
tantalise
tantalite
tantalize
tentative
ting-a-ling
tantalism
Tantalian
tentation
tentacled
tantalous
tanka-boat
tentacula
tenebrism
tenebrios
tenebrist
tenebrity
tenebrose
tint-block
tenebrous
tenaculum
tent-cloth
tenacious
tunicated
tinderbox
tenseless
tenseness
△tangerine
tenderise
tenderize
tendering
tinkering
tinseling
tunneling
tinselled
tunnelled
tunneller
tunnel-net
tunefully
tanagrine
tenth-rate
tanghinin
tintiness
tonnishly
tensility
tan-pickle
tenaillon
tonsillar
tensional
tendinous
tan-liquor
tanalised
tanalized
tent-maker
tonometer
tonometry
tuning-key
tuning-peg
tuning-pin
tentorial
tonsorial
tentorium
tenuously
tin-opener
tenurable
tungstate
tunesmith
tinguaite
Tungusian
tonguelet
tongue-tie
tank-wagon
tunny-fish
two-handed
two-hander
troparion
two-masted
two-parted
two-master
troubling
troublous
trot-cosey
two-headed
two-leafed
two-legged
two-decker
trowelled
troweller
twoseater
two-leaved
thoughted
thoughten
toothwash
toothache
Trochidae
trochlear
toothless
trothless
toothlike
troth-ring
toothpick
trochilic
trochilus
toothcomb
toothsome
toothwort
toolhouse
two-timing
trominoes
two-lipped
Thomistic
tropistic
two-fisted
trollopee
toodle-pip
toolmaker
thornback
thornless
trouncing
thornbill
thorntree
thornbush
tholobate
two-forked

Words marked △ may be spelled also with a capital letter

9 t□o□o

two-roomed
tropology
two-footed
two-bottle
thorow-wax
troop-ship
taoiseach
trousseau
thousands
trousered
trout-farm
troutless
troutling
twostroke
two-storey
two-by-four
tap-dancer
Typhaceae
topmaking
topiarian
topiarist
top-hamper
top-sawyer
tapacolos
tapaculos
topically
typically
topectomy
tepidness
tapaderas
tapaderos
tappet-rod
typifying
type-genus
tip-cheese
Tupaiidae
tap-cinder
tipsiness
topping-up
toppingly
tappit-hen
tephillah
tephillin
topminnow
tephigram
tip-tilted
Tipulidae
topologic
top-flight
typhlitic
typhlitis
typomania
type-metal
toponymic
toponymal
tip-and-run
typhoidal
tiptoeing
tuptowing
△typhonian
taphonomy
top-booted
taperness
taperwise
tephroite
tephritic
top-drawer
tipstaffs
tipstaves
typewrite
terramara
terramare
turnagain
termagant
Tartarean
tervalent
ternately
threatful
threadfin
tarsalgia
tartarise
tartarize
torbanite
terracing
terrarium
tarnation
Tartarian
throatily
tarmacked
tarpaulin
Tarragona
terraform
tornadoes
turnabout
tirra-lyra
terrazzos
terebrate
terebrant
throbless
throbbing
terebinth
turf-drain
tiredness
teredines
three-card
three-pair
three-part
three-deck
targeteer
terseness
threeness
terrenely
turret-gun
turkey-hen
torrefied
three-line
three-pile
targeting
Turnerian
terpenoid
threefold
threesome
three-four
torpedoer
torpedoes
three-foot
tormented
tormentil
tormentum
three-star
tormenter
tormentor
terzettos
turgently
thriftier
thriftily
toruffled
torch-race
torchière
torch-lily
torchwood
torch-song
terminate
turbinate
turribant
termitary
terpineol
tardiness
tarriness
tartiness
turfiness
turnip-fly
tarnished
tarnisher
terrified
turbidite
Turkicise
Turkicize
terminism
terrifier
terminist
torpidity
torridity
tortility
turbidity
turgidity
tarriance
torsional
terricole
torminous
△territory
turnip-top
torpitude
turpitude
thrillant
thralldom
thrilling
torulosis
thrumming
thrombose
thrum-eyed
tarantara
tarantass
threnodic
tyranness
throngful
tyrannise
tyrannize
thronging
tarantism
Terentian
tyrannous
threnetic
△tarantula
Turkomans
terrorful
tarboggin
Turcophil
terrorise
terrorize
threonine
terrorism
terrorist
turcopole
turboprop
turn-penny
tortricid
tortrices
turnround
turf-spade
thrust-hoe
turnstile
thrashing
threshing
thrusting
thrasonic
threshold
turnstone
turn-screw
turntable
teratogen
throttler
teru-teros
turbulent
throughly
turquoise
torturing
Tartufish
Tartufism
Tartufian
toreutics
Targumist
torturous
torquated
throwback
tire-woman
throw-down
throwster
throwaway
taraxacum
△testament
Tasmanian
testation
testatrix
test-drive
tesseract
tasteless
tasseling
tasselled
tessellae
tessellar
task-force
task-group
tastiness
testiness
testified
testifier
testimony
tessitura
tasimeter
Tisiphone
tusk-shell
tetrarchy
tête-à-tête
tetradite
titration
tetralogy
tetrapody
△tetragram
tête-bêche
titubancy
titleless
tittering
tottering
tetterous
tithe-free
tittivate
tattiness
totting-up
titillate
tittlebat
totalling
titularly
totaliser
totalizer
tetroxide
tutiorism
tattooist
tutiorist
tutworker
tit-for-tat
titupping
totaquine
tutorship
tittuping
tittupped
thumb-mark
thumbtack
thumbnail
thumbless
thumblike
thumbling
thumb-ring
thumbkins
thumb-hole

Words marked △ may be spelled also with a capital letter

9 u□d□r

truncheon
T-junction
truncated
thundrous
thunderer
truceless
Trubenise
Trubenize®
truffling
touchback
touchmark
truchmans
touchable
touchless
toughness
truthless
touchline
truthlike
toughener
touchwood
touch-hole
Touchtone®
touchtone
touchdown
touch-type
tauriform
touristic
trunk-call
trunk-mail
truck-farm
truck-shop
trunk-line
truckling
trunkfish
truck-load
trunk-road
trunk-hose
trunk-work
trunkfuls
tournedos
tourneyer
Teutonise
Teutonize
Teutonism
Teutonist
tautology
trump-card
trumped-up
truepenny
trumpeted
trumpeter
truss-beam
trustless
trustiest
truculent
tovarisch
thwacking
tow-headed
townhouse
tawniness
towel-rack
towel-rail
towelling
towing-net
towerless
thwarting
townscape
townsfolk
tax-paying
tax-farmer
toxically
taxaceous
taxidermy
taxameter
taximeter
taxonomic
taxonomer
textorial
toxaphene
toxophily
textphone
texturise
texturize
textually
tax-exempt
thylacine
thyratron
Thysanura
toylesome
thymidine
thyristor
thyroxine
twyforked
twyformed
thymocyte
try-square
Thyestean
Thyestian
tayassuid
unabashed
unadapted
unaccused
unaidable
up-and-down
up-and-over
unamerced
unamended
unavenged
unashamed
unamiable
uraniscus
Upanishad
uralitise
uralitize
uraninite
unanimity
usability
unaligned
unanimous
unallayed
unalloyed
unadmired
unavoided
uvarovite
unadorned
uranology
unadopted
unapplied
unapparel
unassumed
unassured
unassayed
unactable
unaptness
upaithric
unaltered
unattired
unamusing
unadvised
unanxious
unbearded
unbraided
upbraider
umbratile
unbearing
unbiassed
unblended
umbrella'd
umbrellos
unblessed
unbaffled
unbeguile
unblinded
unbridged
un-British
unbridled
unbuilt-on
unbrizzed
unbeknown
umbellate
umbilical
umbilicus
unbelieve
unbalance
umbellule
unbeloved
unbending
unbinding
unblooded
upbrought
unbookish
unblotted
unbaptise
unbaptize
unberufen
unburthen
umber-bird
upburning
unbespeak
unbashful
unbosomer
unbespoke
unbounded
upbounden
unbrushed
unbruised
unblunted
unchanged
uncharged
unceasing
uncharity
uncharmed
unclaimed
unchained
uncharnel
up-Channel
unclassed
uncharted
uncleship
unchecked
uncleaned
uncleanly
uncheered
uncleared
upcheered
unclearly
uncreated
unclipped
uncombine
uncongeal
unconcern
unconfine
uncannily
uncanonic
unconform
uncandour
uncinated
urceolate
unclouded
uncrowded
unclogged
unclothed
uncrowned
uncropped
uncrossed
uncapable
uncertain
uncurtain
uncurable
uncurrent
up-current
uncareful
uncurling
uncordial
uncurdled
uncurious
unchrisom
uncorrupt
uncessant
uncrudded
uncouthly
uncoupled
uncrumple
uncounted
uncourtly
up-country
uncivilly
uncovered
up-draught
undrained
undebased
undecided
undeceive
undecimal
undecayed
undreaded
undreamed
undressed
undefaced
undefiled
undefined
undignify
undyingly
undrilled
undeluded
undelight
undulancy
undiluted
undulated
undelayed
undamaged
undrowned
undercard
underhand
underlaid
underpaid
underrate
undersaye
undertake
undertane
underlain
underta'en
underpass
undercart
undercast
underpart
underfeed
underself
underdeck
underseal
undersell
underkeep
underpeep
underbear
underwear
udderless
underfelt
undervest
undershot
undergird
underbite
underfire
under-five
underline
undermine

9 u□d□r

under-ripe
underside
undertime
underking
underling
under-ring
underwing
underfish
undersign
undertint
underclub
underclad
underplot
underflow
underclay
underplay
underwood
underdone
undernote
undertone
under-roof
underfong
undersong
undercook
undertook
underwork
undercool
undersoil
undergown
underdoer
undercoat
underfoot
undermost
underbred
undergrad
underprop
underdraw
underfund
underhung
underbush
undesired
undeserve
undutiful
unduteous
undaunted
undoubted
undivided
undawning
undazzled
unexalted
unexcited
unendowed
uselessly
unelected
uneffaced
unengaged
un-English
unethical
Uredineae
uredinial
uredinium
uredinous
uterotomy
unemptied
unexpired
unexposed
unearthed
unearthly
unessence
unessayed
uneatable
unextreme
unextinct
unentered
unequable
unequally
unenvying
unenvious
unfearful
unfraught
unfearing
unfranked
unfocused
unfadable
unfledged
unfleshed
unfleshly
unfeeling
unfuelled
unfreeman
unfretted
unfigured
unfailing
unfeigned
unfolding
upfilling
unfrocked
unfloored
unfurnish
unfortune
unfitness
unfitting
unfounded
unguarded
ungravely
ungrassed
ungodlike
ungodlily
unguessed
ungainful
unguiform
ungallant
ungenteel
ungenuine
upgrowing
ungroomed
unglossed
unghostly
ungermane
ungirthed
ungarbled
upgushing
ungrudged
ungazed-at
unheard-of
upheaping
unhearsed
unhealthy
unheedful
unheeding
unheedily
unhelpful
upholding
upholster
Up-Helly-Aa
unhumbled
unhandily
unhandled
unhopeful
unhappily
unharness
unharmful
unhurtful
ushership
unhurried
unharming
unharbour
usherette
unhasting
unhatched
unhatting
unhaunted
univalent
urinative
△unitarian
urination
uniparous
uniramous
unincited
unindexed
uniserial
universal
unisexual
unifiable
unitively
utilities
uliginose
uliginous
uninjured
unillumed
uniplanar
Unionidae
unionised
unionized
unisonant
Uriconian
uniformed
uniformly
unicolour
unisonous
urinology
unimpeded
unimposed
uninsured
uninvited
unjealous
unjointed
unknelled
unkindled
unknowing
unloading
unlearned
unluckily
unlocated
uplifting
unlogical
unlighted
uplighted
uplighter
unlikable
unlimited
uplinking
uplandish
unlosable
unlivable
unlovable
unlived-in
unmeaning
ulmaceous
unmakable
unmanacle
unmindful
unmanaged
upmanship
unmanlike
unmingled
unmanured
unmoneyed
unmarried
unmerited
unmusical
unmasking
unmatched
unmatured
unmotived
unmoulded
unmourned
unmounted
unmovable
unmovably
unmovedly
unmixedly
unmuzzled
uintahite
unneedful
urn-shaped
unnamable
unnerving
unnoticed
unnatural
urolagnia
uroscopic
unordered
unorderly
urodelous
urogenous
udometric
unoffered
urochrome
Urochorda
urokinase
urolithic
uxoricide
uxorially
ufologist
urologist
unopposed
ulotrichy
urography
unobvious
uropygial
uropygium
unplanked
unplained
unplanned
unpraised
unplaited
unplanted
unplagued
unpacking
unprepare
unpierced
unpledged
unprecise
unpredict
umpteenth
unpleased
unpressed
unpleated
unpliable
unpliably
unpainful
up-pricked
unpainted
unpointed
unprinted
unpoliced
unpalsied
unpolitic
unpiloted
unpennied
unprovide
unpeopled
unprovoke
unpropped
unpopular
unpapered
upper-case
unperfect
unpervert
up-perched
unpartial
unperplex
uppermost
unpursued

unpotable
unpitiful
unpitying
up-putting
unplumbed
unplugged
unplucked
unpayable
unqualify
unquelled
unqueened
unqueenly
unquietly
unreached
unrealise
unrealize
unrealism
unreadily
unreality
unrebuked
unrebated
utricular
utriculus
unridable
unreduced
unredrest
unriddler
unruffled
unrefined
unrefuted
uprightly
Ukrainian
unrelated
unrelaxed
unrumpled
unremoved
unrenewed
uprooting
unripping
unripened
Utraquism
Utraquist
unrestful
unresting
unrosined
unreserve
unrounded
unrevoked
unrevised
unroyally
unrazored
unswaddle
unshapely
unscathed
unsparing
unstaying
upstaring
unshackle
unscanned
unstained
unstamped
unscarred
unsubject
unsubdued
unsuccess
unsickled
unsecular
unsecured
unseduced
ups-a-daisy
upsy-daisy
unsaddled
unseeable
unsued-for
unsterile
unseeming
Ulsterman
unscented
unsheathe
unslept-in
unsighing
unsighted
unsightly
unskilful
unsmiling
unsuiting
unskilled
unspilled
unstifled
unstilled
unskimmed
unskinned
unstirred
unstinted
unsmitten
unsaintly
unsalable
unsolaced
unsolidly
unsullied
unselfish
unsaluted
unsinewed
unshocked
unstocked
unspoiled
unstopped
unstopper
unscoured
unspotted
unserious
unstriped
unshrived
unshriven
unsuspect
unsisting
unsatiate
unsatable
upsetting
upsitting
unsettled
unsourced
unsounded
unsoundly
unsnuffed
unstuffed
unstudied
unshunned
unsquared
unshutter
unsevered
unsavoury
unsayable
unscythed
unsizable
uitlander
ultra-high
unthanked
untracked
untrained
urticaria
untressed
untreated
untoiling
uptrilled
untrimmed
untainted
untwisted
untamable
untamably
untumbled
untimeous
untempted
ultimatum
untenable
untunable
untunably
untuneful
untangled
untrodden
untypable
untypical
untirable
utterable
utterless
utterness
unthrifty
unturning
upturning
utterance
uttermost
untutored
upthunder
untouched
untrussed
untrusser
ululation
usucapion
unushered
usualness
usurpedly
unuttered
unusually
unveiling
unvoicing
unvarying
unvisited
unwearied
unweeting
unwreaked
unwreathe
unweighed
unwriting
unwrinkle
unwhipped
unwritten
unwakened
unwilling
upwelling
unwelcome
unwomanly
unwinding
unwinking
unwrought
upwrought
unworldly
unworried
unwarlike
unworking
unwishful
unwasting
unwishing
unwatched
unwitting
unwittily
unwatered
unwounded
unzealous
vraicking
viaticals
viability
viaticums
viatorial
vibraharp
vibratile
vibrative
vibration
vibratory
vibrantly
vibracula
vibrissae
vibriosis
vacuation
vocabular
vice-chair
vaccinate
victimise
victimize
vaccinial
vaccinium
vacillate
vacillant
vocalness
vocaliser
vocalizer
vicennial
vacuolate
victoress
vectorise
vectorize
victorine
vectoring
vectorial
Victorian
viciosity
vacuously
viciously
vice-queen
vicariate
vice-regal
vicarship
vicereine
Victrola®
victrola
vicarious
vicesimal
videlicet
vade-mecum
videotape
videotext
videodisc
videogram
Vodaphone
vedutista
vedutisti
viewiness
veeringly
viewpoint
viewphone
vee-gutter
vagueness
vignetter
vigilance
vigilante
vaginulae
vaginally
vaginated
vaginitis
vagarious
vigesimal
vegetable
vegetably
vegetated
vehicular
vehemence
vehemency
voice-mail
voiceless
voice-over
vainglory
Vaishnava
voisinage
veilleuse
veinstone
veinstuff

9 v□i□u

voiturier
vikingism
villanage
villagery
volcanise
volcanize
vulcanise
vulcanite
vulcanize
vulgarise
vulgarize
△**volcanism**
△vulcanism
vulgarism
valuation
volcanian
△vulcanian
vulgarian
villagios
△**volcanist**
△vulcanist
vulgarity
valuables
viliacoes
viliagoes
villanous
volcanoes
villagree
valvassor
valiantly
volucrine
validness
velodrome
vellenage
villenage
volte-face
vulnerate
vulnerary
velveteen
valueless
valveless
velveting
vulsellae
vulsellum
Valdenses
vallecula
vilifying
volageous
vellicate
voltigeur
villiagos
vulpicide
vulpinite
voltinism
vulpinism
villiform
vulviform
voluminal
voltmeter
volumeter
voluntary
volunteer
△**valentine**
villosity
velarised
velarized
△**volksraad**
Volkslied
veldskoen
volitient
vol-au-vent
veloutine
vulturine
vulturish
vulturism
vulturous
Valkyriur
Valkyries
vampirise
vampirize
vampirism
vimineous
vambraced
vandalise
vandalize
vintaging
vandalism
veniality
vantbrace
vant-brass
vinaceous
vengeable
vengeably
vengement
veneering
vindemial
vengeance
venefical
ventilate
vindicate
ventifact
vendition
ventiduct
ventosity
venerable
venerably
ventricle
ventrally
venireman
venereous
venerator
vanishing
vine-stock
venatical
vingt-et-un
venturing
venturous
Violaceae
violative
violation
violently
violin-bow
violinist
voodooism
voodooist
vapidness
vaporware
vaporable
Viperidae
vaporific
vaporiser
vaporetti
vaporetto
vaporizer
vapouring
vapourish
Verbascum
variative
verbalise
verbalize
vernalise
vernalize
versatile
verbalism
variation
verbarian
vernation
verbalist
verbality
vernality
verballed
verdantly
viricidal
virucidal
varicella
veracious
voracious
veridical
variegate
verberate
varletess
varieties
varvelled
vervelled
vermeille
vertebrae
vertebral
verifying
viragoish
verminate
virginals
varnisher
versified
verbicide
vermicide
virginium
vorticism
Vergilian
vermilion
Virgilian
Virginian
versifier
vorticist
verticity
virginity
vorticity
versional
versioner
vorticose
vermiform
versiform
verminous
vertigoes
vertiport
verdigris
vermicule
vermifuge
virulence
virulency
virilised
virilized
Varanidae
Varangian
véronique
variolate
verbosely
variolite
verbosity
varioloid
variolous
variously
virescent
variscite
veritable
veritably
veratrine
Varityper®
virgulate
verjuiced
virtually
vargueños
verrucose
verdurous
verrucous
virtuosic
virtuosos
vassalage
vassaless
vistaless
visualise
visualize
visualist
visuality
vesiculae
vesicular
vasectomy
viscerate
visagiste
vestiment
vestigial
vestigium
vastidity
viscidity
vastitude
vestibule
vestiture
vasomotor
Vishnuite
Vishnuism
visionary
visioning
visionist
viscosity
viscounty
visor-mask
vestryman
visitable
visitress
visitator
vasculums
vitiation
vaticinal
viticetum
Vitreosil®
vetchling
vitrified
vitriolic
vitriform
vitellary
vitelline
vitaliser
vitalizer
Vitrolite®
vitiosity
vitascope
vetturini
Vitruvian
vetturino
vouchsafe
vivianite
vivacious
vividness
vivifying
vivamente
vivandier
viverrine
vivariums
vow-fellow
vowelless
vexedness
vexillary
vexatious
voyeurism
vizierate
vizierial
vizirship
wyandotte
whaleback
whale-head
weaseller
whalebone
whaleboat
wrangling
wrathless
weathered

Words marked △ may be spelled also with a capital letter

weatherly
weariless
weariness
wearingly
wearisome
weak-kneed
wrappings
wrapround
whatsoe'er
wealthily
wobbegong
webfooted
wych-alder
wych-hazel
wackiness
Wyclifite
wideawake
wide-angle
Wednesday
wedgewise
wadsetter
widthways
widthwise
widowhood
wrenching
whencever
wieldable
wieldless
wheedling
weekender
whereness
wherewith
whereinto
whereunto
wherefore
woebegone
whereupon
wherefrom
whey-faced
weel-faird
weel-faur'd
weel-faurt
weed-grown
weediness
weepingly
weetingly
weedicide
weevilled
wreakless
wreckfish
wheelbase
wheelwork
weeknight
wherryman
whet-slate
whensoe'er
whetstone
wheatmeal
wrestling
wheatworm
wofulness

waghalter
Wagnerite
Wagnerism
Wagnerian
Wagnerist
waggishly
wagon-lits
wagons-lit
wagonload
wagenboom
wagonette
Wahabiite
Wahabiism
Wehrmacht
writative
whimberry
whinberry
whipcordy
weirdness
waiterage
white-face
whiteware
whitewash
write-back
Whitehall
whitewall
whitebass
whitebait
whitehead
whitebeam
white-seam
whiteness
writeress
white-shoe
waitering
whitening
whitewing
whitewood
write-down
whitecoat
whifflery
whiffling
whip-graft
whingeing
wriggling
weigh-bauk
weighable
weighting
weightily
whichever
whininess
wailingly
waitingly
whiningly
wrinklies
whiskered
whirligig
whirlwind
whirlpool
whillywha
whinnying

whipper-in
whimperer
whisperer
whip-round
whipstaff
whipstall
whimsical
whinstone
whipstock
waistband
wristband
waist-deep
waistbelt
waistline
whistling
whittling
waist-high
waistboat
waistcoat
whittawer
Whitworth
whizz-bang
wakefully
wake-robin
wellanear
walkathon
welfarism
Wallabies
welfarist
well-aimed
walkabout
wallboard
wellbeing
well-built
well-borer
wolfberry
Walachian
well-doing
Willesden
wolverene
willemite
wolverine
wulfenite
weltering
wildering
wyliecoat
Waldenses
well-famed
well-found
waldflute
well-faurt
waldgrave
wildgrave
Weltgeist
wild-goose
well-given
wolfhound
wellhouse
willingly
wolfishly
wolvishly

well-known
well-lined
well-meant
walloping
wallowing
welcoming
willowish
Waltonian
well-oiled
wallpaper
willpower
wolfsbane
Weltstadt
well-spent
well-set-up
well-tried
well-timed
Walpurgis
Welsummer
well-woman
welly-boot
wallydrag
wambenger
wimpishly
womanless
womankind
womenkind
womanlike
womanhood
womenfolk
woman-born
woman-body
womaniser
womanizer
wink-a-peep
windbreak
windblown
windborne
wineberry
windbound
wind-chill
wonderful
winterise
winterize
wandering
wondering
wonderous
wineglass
wanchancy
windhover
windiness
windingly
winkingly
winningly
winsomely
wantonise
wantonize
wincopipe
windowing
winnowing
winepress

windproof
wind-shak'd
windshake
windswept
wind-swift
wine-stone
windstorm
windtight
windthrow
windwards
woodblock
wood-borer
woodcraft
woodchuck
wholesale
woomerang
wholemeal
wholeness
whole-life
wholefood
wholesome
whole-body
woodentop
wrongness
wrongdoer
wrong-foot
wrought-up
whoa-ho-hoa
woodhorse
woodhouse
woodiness
wooziness
whorishly
wholistic
woodlouse
woodmouse
whosoever
woodreeve
woodspite
woodstone
woodscrew
whodunnit
woodwaxen
wipe-clean
wapper-jaw
wapentake
wapenshaw
wapinshaw
warfaring
warranted
war-wasted
warrantee
warranter
warrantor
wordbreak
word-blind
workbench
△warmblood
waribashi
wart-biter
wordbound

Words marked △ may be spelled also with a capital letter

9 w□r□d

wiredrawn
worldwide
worldling
world-view
worseness
wernerite
Wernerian
workerist
worm-eaten
worcester
workfolks
workforce
worthless
wormholed
workhorse
warehouse
workhouse
worriedly
wordiness
worriment
warningly
worrisome
workmanly
warmonger
warlockry
workplace
workpiece
wirephoto
wardrober
worksheet
wordsmith
worst-case
worktable
workwoman
worrywart
worryguts
wassailer
wassailry
west-about
washboard
washbasin
westbound
wisecrack
washcloth
wasteland
wasteness
wasterful
wasterife
westering
washerman
wasserman
△**westerner**
washed-out
wishfully
wistfully
wasegoose
washhouse

washiness
washing-up
waspishly
west-north
washstand
wasp-stung
westwards
witwanton
withdrawn
witherite
withering
wuthering
witnesser
witlessly
watchcase
watchable
witchmeal
witchlike
witch-wife
witchknot
watchword
witchetty
withhault
wittiness
wittingly
witticism
wattmeter
wet-and-dry
wit-monger
withouten
Watergate
water-wave
watermark
waterfall
waterweed
waterless
watershed
water-shot
waterline
waterside
waterlily
water-ski'd
water-core
waterwork
water-cool
waterfowl
water-worn
withstand
withstood
withywind
woundable
woundless
woundwort
waulkmill
whunstane
wavefront
waveguide

wavellite.
wavemeter
waveshape
waxworker
waywardly
wayfaring
waylaying
wry-necked
wayzgoose
X-particle
xylograph
xyloidine
xylometer
Xylophaga
xylophage
xylophone
xylorimba
xenocryst
xenograft
xanthomas
Xanthippe
Xanthoura
xanthoxyl
xenomania
xenomenia
xenophile
xenophobe
xenophoby
Xenarthra
Xiphiidae
xiphoidal
Xiphosura
xerochasy
Xyridales
xeroderma
xeromorph
xerophagy
xerophily
xerophyte
xerostoma
yravished
year-round
yeastlike
yobbishly
yacht-club
yachtsman
Yiddisher
yieldable
Yggdrasil
yo-heave-ho
yohimbine
Yajurveda
yoke-devil
yakety-yak
yakity-yak
yellow-boy
yellowish

yolk-stalk
yammering
Yankeedom
Yankeeism
yuppiedom
yird-house
yersiniae
yersinias
Yorkshire
yardstick
yesterday
yestereve
yeshivahs
yeshivoth
yattering
ytterbium
youngness
youngthly
youngling
youngster
young-eyed
youthhead
youthhood
youthsome
yawningly
zealotism
zealously
Zwanziger
zebra-wood
zibelline
zuchettas
zuchettos
zecchinos
zucchinis
zucchetto
Zechstein
zoechrome
zoetropic
zigzagged
zygaenine
zygaenoid
zygomatic
zygantrum
zygophyte
zygosperm
zygospore
Zwinglian
△**zeitgeist**
zoiatrics
zillionth
zelatrice
zelotypia
zymogenic
zymologic
zymolysis
zymolytic
zymometer

zamindari
zemindari
zamindary
zemindary
zamboorak
zumbooruk
△**zinfandel**
zinc-bloom
zinkenite
zante-wood
zanthoxyl
Zanzibari
Zonuridae
zoogamete
zoogamous
zoolatria
zoomantic
zooscopic
zootechny
zooperist
zoogenous
zoo-keeper
zoometric
zoophobia
zoothecia
zoophagan
zootheism
zoophilia
zoophoric
zoophorus
zoophytic
zoolithic
zoobiotic
zoogloeic
zooplasty
zoologist
zoonomist
zootomist
zoogonous
zoomorphy
zoosporic
zoography
zootrophy
zoocytium
Zapodidae
Ziphiidae
zapateado
zapotilla
Zernebock
zirconium
zero-rated
zestfully
Zeuglodon
zeugmatic

Words marked △ may be spelled also with a capital letter

asarabacca
alabandine
alabandite
anacardium
acatalepsy
acanaceous
anapaestic
adamantean
adamantine
amarantine
anabaptise
anabaptism
△anabaptist
agapanthus
Amaranthus
anabaptize
anarchical
academical
amazedness
arabesqued
amateurish
amateurism
alang-alang
amalgamate
arachnidan
anaphylaxy
anachronic
Araliaceae
Adamitical
avaricious
availingly
anaglyphic
anaglyptic
alablaster
anaclastic
anaplastic
alarm-radio
alarm-clock
alarmingly
anamnestic
araeometer
araeometry
acarophily
anagogical
analogical
anatomical
apagogical
anabolitic
amatorious
Amazon-like
anamorphic
anacoustic
asafoetida
araeostyle
anacolutha
analphabet
acarpelous
anadromous
anatropous
anacrustic
avant-garde
anaptyctic
apartments
anastigmat
adactylous
anastomose
anastrophe
avanturine
anarthrous
adaptation
adaptative
adaptively
amanuenses
amanuensis
ayahuascos
analysable
analyzable
analytical
anadyomene
amboceptor
ambidexter
abbreviate
Albigenses
ambagitory
ambulacral
ambulacrum
arbalester
arbalister
ambulation
ambulatory
albuminoid
albumenise
albuminise
albuminate
albuminous
albumenize
albuminize
albinistic
Ambarvalia
aubergiste
albarellos
ambassador
ambuscados
albescence
ambushment
Ambisonics®
ambisonics
asbestosis
ambisexual
arbitrager
arbitrable
arbitrator
ambivalent
abbey-laird
abbey-piece
Amblyopsis
Amblystoma
archaicism
archaistic
arcubalist
archbishop
accubation
arch-chimic
archdeacon
accidental
accidented
accrescent
arc-welding
archerfish
alchemical
accredited
alcheringa
archeology
archegonia
ance-errand
archetypal
arch-flamen
alcoholise
alcoholism
alcoholize
ascribable
Archimedes
alcaicería
auctioneer
auctionary
architrave
ascription
Alcelaphus
accelerant
accelerate
accultural
ascomycete
accumbency
accomplice
accomplish
accumulate
accomptant
ascendance
ascendancy
ascendable
ascendence
ascendency
ascendible
arcaneness
accentuate
Arctogaean
Alcyonaria
Arctogaeic
anchoretic
anchor-hold
arctophile
arctophily
anchoritic
anchorless
aeciospore
anchor-ring
archonship
archontate
acceptance
acceptancy
acceptable
acceptably
acceptedly
arch-priest
arch-pirate
ancipitous
accordance
accordancy
ascariasis
accordable
accursedly
accurately
accostable
accessible
accessibly
accusement
accusingly
accustomed
ancestress
accusation
accusatory
accusative
asceticism
accoutered
accoucheur
accoutring
accountant
accounting
anchylosed
anchylosis
audibility
abdication
aide-de-camp
addle-pated
aldohexose
Andalusian
aedileship
andalusite
abdominous
andantinos
androecial
androecium
audiometer
androgenic
audiophile
androphore
audiograph
aldermanic
aldermanly
aldermanry
adderstone
adder's-wort
additament
additional
auditorium
alexanders
aceraceous
arenaceous
avenaceous
ametabolic
adelantado
arefaction
acetabular
acetabulum
amerceable
amerciable
amercement
Aberdonian
anecdotage
amendatory
anecdotist
aberdevine
ateleiosis
adenectomy
Aberglaube
areography
avengement
avengeress
acephalous
Amerindian
ameliorate
areolation
anemometer
anemometry
anemophily
adenovirus
amenorrhea
anemograph
Areopagite
axe-breaker
age-bracket
Averrhoism
Averrhoist
aneurismal
aneurysmal
aberration
averseness
asepticise
asepticism
asepticize
anesthesia
avertiment
azeotropic
aventurine
agentivity
acesulfame
asexuality
adequately
adequative
acervately
acervation
acetylenic
affability
affectedly
affectless
affeerment
affricated
affrighted
affrighten
afflicting
affliction
afflictive
affiliable
Aufklärung
affinitive

Words marked △ may be spelled also with a capital letter

10 a□f□o

affronting
affrontive
affirmance
affirmable
affordable
affettuoso
affluently
aggravated
aggrandise
aggrandize
angwantibo
algebraist
angleberry
aigre-douce
angledozer
aggression
aggressive
anguifauna
Anguillula
anglistics
angel-water
algolagnia
algologist
angelology
avgolemono
angularity
angulation
argumentum
Algonquian
argonautic
△anglomania
Anglo-Saxon
△anglophobe
△anglophile
△anglophone
angiosperm
Anglo-Irish
algophobia
argyrodite
auger-shell
Angaraland
algarrobos
augustness
arguteness
agglutinin
ashlar-work
adhibition
aphidicide
Ashkenazim
achievable
aphaeresis
anhelation
anhungered
Athanasian
achromatic
achromatin
aphrodisia
athermancy
abhorrence
abhorrency
Acherontic
anharmonic
aphoristic
adhesively
Achitophel
animalcula
animalcule
agitatedly
animatedly
acinaceous
Arimaspian
animadvert
amiability
alineation
alimentary
abiogenist
arithmetic
Ahithophel
acidimeter
acidimetry
aficionado
acidifying
axiologist
Alismaceae
axiomatics
alienation
axinomancy
anisotropy
amido-group
amino-group
adiaphoron
acieration
aristocrat
Asiaticism
aristology
Aristippus
aciculated
Avicularia
Aviculidae
abiturient
apiculture
aviculture
adjectival
adjacently
abjectness
adjudicate
adjudgment
abjunction
adjunction
adjunctive
abjuration
adjuration
adjuratory
adjustable
adjustably
adjustment
awkwardish
ankle-chain
ankle-biter
alkalinise
alkalinity
alkalinize
ankylosaur
alliaceous
allhallond
allhallown
All-Hallows
able-bodied
all-obeying
allochiria
aplacental
allycholly
allocation
allocution
all-telling
all-weather
allegeance
allegiance
allegretto
allogamous
allegorise
allegorist
allegorize
allegation
alligation
all-firedly
allnighter
all-play-all
allometric
allonymous
aplanatism
allhollown
all-rounder
allophonic
allopathic
allopatric
allargando
all-dreaded
allergenic
allurement
alluringly
allosteric
arles-penny
Allosaurus
allusively
allotheism
ablutomane
allotropic
alliterate
all-purpose
alleviator
all-overish
allowances
almacantar
almucantar
armadillos
Armageddon
armigerous
armillaria
atmologist
arms-length
ammoniacal
ammoniated
ammoniacum
almond-eyed
administer
almond-tree
admonition
ammunition
admonitory
admonitive
armipotent
admiringly
admiration
admirative
admiraunce
atmosphere
admissible
admittance
admittable
admittedly
armour-clad
armourless
abnegation
annihilate
annularity
annalistic
annulation
annunciate
annuntiate
abnormally
annotation
annexation
annoyingly
anonaceous
apocarpous
apolaustic
△apocalypse
amoebiasis
amoebiform
avouchable
avouchment
above-named
aposematic
apodeictic
adolescent
above-board
apopemptic
azobenzene
alongshore
apothecial
apothecary
apothecium
apophthegm
anopheline
apochromat
apotheoses
apotheosis
abominable
abominably
abominator
agonisedly
agonizedly
△aboriginal
apolitical
agonistics
a-cockhorse
apoplectic
Apollonian
acorn-shell
abonnement
anointment
apologetic
apomorphia
aeolotropy
acolouthic
acolouthos
akolouthos
aposporous
apocryphal
apotropaic
apocryphon
apotropous
ahorseback
acoustical
anoestrous
aborticide
apostolise
apostolate
apostolize
abortional
apostrophe
apostatise
apostatize
abortively
acotyledon
appearance
appealable
appeasable
applauding
alphabetic
alphameric
alphametic
applausive
appraisive
aspectable
Ampicillin®
aspidistra
appreciate
apple-woman
apprentice
arpeggione
arpeggiate
amphimacer
applicable
applicably
applicator
amphiscian
Amphineura
amphimixis
amphibious
amphibolic
amphibrach
Amphitryon
amphictyon

Words marked △ may be spelled also with a capital letter

ampliation
ampliative
appointive
amplifying
ampelopses
ampelopsis
appendices
appendixes
alpenstock
approvance
approvable
approaches
amphoteric
approximal
Alphonsine
apperceive
asparagine
aspergilla
apparelled
apparently
aspiringly
asperities
apparition
aspiration
aspiratory
appositely
apposition
appositive
ampussy-and
appetising
amputation
appetition
appetitive
appetizing
asphyxiant
asphyxiate
acquainted
acquirable
acquitment
acquitting
acroamatic
air-marshal
air-passage
airmanship
abreaction
abreactive
△**adriamycin**®
aerobiosis
aerobiotic
acrobatics
aerobatics
acrobatism
auriculate
Africander
Africanoid
Africanise
Africanism
Africanist
Africanize
atracurium
aprication
abridgable
abridgment
arrière-ban
aero-engine
acriflavin
air-officer
auriferous
aerography
aerogramme
aérogramme
arrogantly
arragonite
acrogenous
aeruginous
abrogation
agrégation
arrogation
abrogative
Abraham-man
arraigning
adroitness
Afrikander
air-bladder
aerologist
agrologist
acrylamide
acre-length
acrolithic
acromegaly
atramental
aerometric
acronychal
abranchial
aerenchyma
adrenaline
agronomial
agronomics
aeronomist
agronomist
acronymous
adrenergic
apron-stage
aeronautic
air-cooling
air-hostess
Aureomycin®
abruptness
acrophobia
acrophonic
aerophobia
aerophobic
air-traffic
afrormosia
air-brushed
air-grating
aerostatic
arrestable
arrestment
aerotactic
aerotropic
acroterial
acroterion
acroterium
amritattva
air-cushion
arrow-grass
arrhythmia
arrhythmic
assibilate
associable
answerable
answerably
abstergent
austenitic
abstemious
answerless
arsmetrick
abstersion
abstersive
abstention
assafetida
assignable
assignment
aesthetics
Anschauung
assailable
Aussiedler
abstinence
abstinency
auspicious
assailment
assoilment
abscission
arse-licker
absolvitor
absolutely
absolution
absolutory
absolutism
absolutist
assemblage
assimilate
assumingly
△**assumption**
assumptive
assentator
absinthism
assentient
assonantal
absorbable
adsorbable
assertable
abstracted
abstracter
abstractly
abstractor
absorbency
assurgency
absorbedly
Australian
Australorp
australite
assortment
austringer
absurdness
abstrusely
absorption
adsorption
absorptive
assistance
assessable
assessment
assythment
auscultate
asseverate
assay-piece
△**astragalus**
actualités
antiaditis
attractant
attracting
attraction
attractive
actability
ante-bellum
antibiosis
antibiotic
antechapel
autocratic
attachable
attackable
arty-crafty
antecedent
anticlimax
anticlinal
articulacy
astacology
autecology
Articulata
articulate
altocumuli
attachment
anticipant
anticipate
Antichrist
artocarpus
antecessor
Antichthon
autochthon
anticivism
autodidact
antidromic
anthelices
antheridia
antler-moth
autoerotic
anthersmut
anthemwise
artificial
antifreeze
autography
astigmatic
autogamous
autogenics
antagonise
antagonism
antagonist
autogenous
antagonize
altogether
anti-heroic
attainable
astringent
attainment
auto-immune
Aethiopian
astriction
attainture
astrictive
antilogous
autologous
antilopine
autumnally
automobile
attempered
antimonial
antimonide
antimonate
antimonite
ante-mortem
antimasque
antimatter
automatons
automation
automatism
automatist
astomatous
automotive
attendance
attendancy
attenuated
attenuator
ante-Nicene
attentions
actinolite
antinomian
autonomics
attendment
attunement
autonomist
antonymous
autonomous
astonished
anthomania
actionable
actionably
astrolatry
astrometry
Antiochian
Antiochene
anthophore
Authorized
authorless
astrologer

Words marked △ may be spelled also with a capital letter

10 a□t□o

astronomer
astrologic
astronomic
Anthonomus
authorship
autophagia
autoplasty
△antipodean
autoptical
antepenult
antiphonal
antiphoner
antiphonic
autophobia
antiproton
antipathic
antiquated
alternance
afterwards
aftersales
asteriated
alternatim
altar-rails
afterpains
alternator
aftertaste
anthracoid
anthracene
anti-racism
anti-racist
anthracite
asteridian
apterygial
Apterygota
aftershock
aftershaft
autarchist
aftershave
asteroidal
autarkical
afterpiece
altarpiece
Asteroidea
after-light
afterbirth
arthralgia
arthralgic
altar-cloth
after-image
attirement
attornment
arthromere
afterworld
anteriorly
astarboard
Arthropoda
anthropoid
aftergrass
asterisked
altar-stone
alteration
alterative
after-guard
afterswarm
antistatic
attestable
antisocial
artistical
anti-Semite
altisonant
autoscopic
antisepsis
antiseptic
autostrada
antiserums
altostrati
antisyzygy
antitragus
antitheses
antithesis
antithetic
antitheism
antitheist
autotheism
autotheist
autoteller
altitonant
astuteness
astounding
Arthuriana
artfulness
altruistic
antivenene
activeness
activities
activation
altazimuth
aquabatics
abundantly
aquafortis
acuminated
anucleated
Adullamite
aquamanale
aquamanile
aquamarine
aquaplaner
aquaphobia
aquaphobic
aquarobics
adulterant
adulterine
adulteress
adulterise
adulterate
adulterous
adulterize
advice-boat
arvicoline
advocation
advocatory
avvogadore
adventurer
alveolitis
adversaria
advertence
advertency
advertiser
advisement
advisorate
advisatory
anxiolytic
amylaceous
aryballoid
arytaenoid
asynartete
asynchrony
amygdaloid
anywhither
asymmetric
Asymmetron
asymptotic
Abyssinian
asyntactic
asystolism
amyotrophy
Alzheimer's
bragadisme
Bramah-lock
blancmange
branchiate
branch-line
branchless
branch-work
board-wages
brandy-ball
brand-image
beard-grass
bladder-nut
brandy-snap
brazen-face
beam-engine
brake-wheel
brake-block
brazenness
beaver-tree
blamefully
beaver-wood
braggingly
braggartly
beach-la-mar
brachyaxis
brachydome
brachylogy
brachiopod
beachfront
brachyural
beatifical
braaivleis
beatitudes
brazil-wood
Beaujolais
blackfaced
blackwater
blackberry
blackheart
Blackshirt
blackthorn
blackamoor
blacksmith
blackboard
blanketing
black-bully
blackguard
beadlehood
beadleship
Brahmanism
Brahminism
biannually
boat-necked
brainchild
braininess
brawniness
brainpower
brainstorm
blasphemer
blanquette
boat-racing
brass-faced
brassiness
beadswoman
beautician
blastocoel
bratticing
blastocyst
blastoderm
beautifier
Blastoidea
blastomere
brant-goose
blastopore
boastfully
bradyseism
biblically
bobbin-lace
bibliology
bibliomane
bibliopegy
bibliophil
bibliopole
bibliopoly
Babbittism
baby-jumper
bubbly-jock
babblement
Babylonian
Babylonish
babelesque
babblative
bibulously
baby-minder
bubonocele
baby-ribbon
babiroussa
babesiasis
babesiosis
baby-sitter
baby-walker
bobbysoxer
beccaficos
back-blocks
buck-basket
backbiting
béche-de-mer
bacteremia
bucketfuls
bacterioid
back-friend
backgammon
background
bacchantes
back-handed
back-hander
bacchanals
buccinator
buck-jumper
bacillemia
baculiform
bicultural
becomingly
Buchmanism
Buchmanite
backmarker
back-number
back-office
Bucephalus
backpacker
buck-rabbit
bichromate
backspacer
back-spauld
backstairs
backsheesh
backstitch
backslider
back-street
back-stroke
bacitracin
back-to-back
backvelder
backworker
backwardly
bedraggled
body-cavity
budgerigar
badderlock
bed-wetting
bodegueros
bedchamber
Buddhistic
Bedlington
by-drinking
bedellship
bedclothes
bidentated

Words marked △ may be spelled also with a capital letter

bidonville
body-popper
bedpresser
bedevilled
bed-swerver
body-warmer
buddy-buddy
beef-brewis
beefburger
beer-barrel
beer-bottle
brecciated
breechless
breadberry
breadboard
breadfruit
breadcrumb
bread-stick
breadstuff
beer-engine
beekeeping
brevetting
by-election
beer-garden
blethering
beech-drops
blepharism
breakdance
breakwater
breakables
bierkeller
breakpoint
break-front
beetle-eyed
beetlehead
beetmaster
beetmister
brewmaster
biennially
beer-parlor
bleary-eyed
bleariness
bienséance
breastbone
breast-deep
breast-feed
breast-high
breast-knot
bressummer
breast-pump
breastrail
breastwork
breathable
breathless
brent-goose
breath-test
beeswinged
beef-witted
breezeless
breeziness
buffalo-nut

befriender
buff-jerkin
bufflehead
bafflement
bafflingly
buffoonery
bifurcated
beforehand
beforetime
bufotenine
baggage-car
big-bellied
big-hearted
bigamously
bigmouthed
bogtrotter
bagassosis
behind-door
behindhand
behavioral
brigandage
brigandine
brigantine
blind-alley
blind-drunk
baisemains
bride's-cake
bridesmaid
bride's-maid
bride-price
bridegroom
bridgeable
bridgehead
bridgeless
Bridgerama
bridge-work
bright-eyed
blitheness
brightness
blithering
blithesome
brightsome
bright-work
Britishism
bailieship
bricklayer
brickmaker
brick-earth
brickfield
brickworks
brilliance
brilliancy
bridle-hand
bridle-path
bridle-road
bridle-rein
bridle-wise
bairn's-part
blissfully
blister-fly
blistering

boisterous
blitzkrieg
blizzardly
bijouterie
bejewelled
baking-soda
Bollandist
ballabiles
bellarmine
belladonna
bellamoure
bull-beeves
bull-beggar
balibuntal
bill-broker
ball-barrow
ball-buster
bel-accoyle
bilocation
bilge-water
believable
balderdash
billet-doux
ballet-girl
billet-head
bullet-head
ballerinas
balneology
beliefless
belletrist
bullet-tree
balneation
ball-flower
bell-flower
bald-headed
bull-headed
bellhanger
bolshevise
bolshevism
bolshevist
bolshevize
△belshazzar
bullionist
ballistics
ballistite
bolometric
bull-necked
belongings
bilinguist
balconette
bollocking
ballooning
balloonist
ball-player
billposter
bull-roarer
Balbriggan
bell-ringer
Belgravian
bell-shaped
balustered

bell-siller
ballsiness
balustrade
belittling
bell-turret
bolstering
balbutient
bolivianos
biliverdin
boll-weevil
bell-wether
belly-dance
belly-laugh
ballyhooed
bombardier
bumbailiff
bimodality
bumpkinish
bimillenia
bumble-foot
bimanually
bumfreezer
bimestrial
bimetallic
bumsucking
bomb-vessel
Bombycidae
bunya-bunya
bank-cheque
binoculars
band-clutch
△benedicite
Benedictus
Bundesbank
banderilla
banker-mark
Benzedrine®
Bundesrath
Bundeswehr
beneficial
beneficent
benefactor
benefitted
benefiting
benignancy
benighting
bone-headed
bond-holder
Benthamism
Benthamite
bunchiness
bunch-grass
bonnilasse
bantingism
bannisters
bunglingly
bonamiasis
benumbment
bandmaster
Bananaland
benzocaine

bandoleros
benzpyrene
bankruptcy
boneshaker
banishment
bondswoman
band-string
bonesetter
bond-timber
binaurally
banqueteer
banqueting
benevolent
brocatelle
brow-antler
browbeater
blow-by-blow
bookbinder
bioscience
bronchitic
bronchitis
bronchiole
bioecology
broad-based
broad-gauge
blood-wagon
bloody-eyed
Brobdignag
boondoggle
broadsheet
broadpiece
blood-sized
blonde-lace
blood-plate
broadcloth
broodingly
bloodiness
broodiness
blood-royal
brood-pouch
blood-money
bloodhound
blood-horse
broidering
broad-arrow
broadbrush
blood-group
bloodstock
bloodstain
bloodstone
blood-guilt
broadsword
broken-down
biogenesis
biogenetic
biomedical
brokenness
biometrics
brome-grass
book-holder
biochemist

Words marked △ may be spelled also with a capital letter

10 b□o□h

brother-man
biophysics
biorhythms
biotically
bookkeeper
block-chain
blockboard
blockhouse
bootlicker
bootlegger
bioplasmic
bootlessly
bookmobile
Bloomsbury
bookmaking
bootmaking
bookmarker
book-muslin
broomstick
broomstaff
Brownshirt
brownfield
brown-noser
brownstone
biopoiesis
biological
biomorphic
biospheric
biographee
biographer
biographic
bookseller
blossoming
bootstraps
blottesque
brontosaur
biodynamic
booby-prize
bronze-wing
bipedalism
baptistery
bipolarity
bipinnaria
baphometic
bipartisan
bipetalous
bequeathal
biquintile
bureaucrat
Bernardine
barracking
bar-parlour
barcarolle
barracoota
barracouta
barratrous
bursarship
barramunda
barramundi
burramundi
barebacked

bark-beetle
beribboned
bird-cherry
barley-bree
barrel-bulk
barley-broo
△barleycorn
Berkeleian
barrelfuls
Barmecidal
borderland
borderline
borderless
barbellate
barrenness
barge-board
burdensome
barbershop
barber-shop
barkentine
burnettise
burnettize
barbed-wire
barrenwort
barefooted
bareheaded
birthnight
birthright
birthplace
Bartholmew
barehanded
bird-hipped
bur-thistle
birthstone
borghettos
bartizaned
barricados
barring-out
burnishing
△barmitsvah
barbituric
△barmitzvah
barelegged
burglarise
burglarize
barometric
baronetage
baronetess
bardolatry
burrow-duck
barrow-tram
bird-pepper
bordraging
bird-scarer
barysphere
bird-spider
bird-skiing
Bergsonian
barasingha
Bergsonism
birostrate

burr-walnut
bird-witted
bastard-bar
bastardise
bastardism
bastardize
byssaceous
bashawship
best-before
baseballer
base-burner
basketball
basket-case
basketfuls
basket-hilt
beseeching
bespeckled
Boswellian
bushelling
Boswellise
Boswellism
Boswellize
bissextile
basketwork
bush-harrow
bastinaded
bestialise
bestialism
bestiality
bestialize
byssinosis
△basmitsvah
△basmitzvah
bisulphide
bisulphate
bush-lawyer
besom-rider
base-minded
bushmaster
bastnäsite
bishop-bird
bestowment
bassoonist
bishopweed
basophilic
bescribble
bestridden
bestraddle
baserunner
bushranger
besprinkle
bestraught
bestseller
bush-shrike
besottedly
bushwalker
bisexually
bossyboots
batrachian
battailous
bit-mapping

butter-bean
butter-boat
butter-bake
better-ball
butter-ball
butter-bump
Battenberg
Battenburg
butter-bird
butterdock
butter-dish
butter-fish
butterhead
bitter-king
batteilant
bitterling
butter-milk
betterment
bettermost
betterness
bitterness
betweenity
bitter-root
bitter-spar
butlership
bothersome
butter-tree
butter-wife
bitterwood
butterwort
buttery-bar
bitchiness
butchering
bathing-box
bathing-hut
△batmitsvah
△batmitzvah
Betulaceae
battledoor
battledore
Betelgeuse
bottle-feed
bottlefuls
bottle-fish
batologist
bottle-head
battlement
bottle-neck
bottle-nose
battleship
bottle-tree
bituminise
bituminate
bituminous
bituminize
△bathmizvah
bitonality
button-back
button-ball
Battonberg
button-bush

bathometer
buttoned-up
bottom-fish
buttonhold
buttonhole
button-hook
batholitic
batfowling
bottom-land
bottomless
bottommost
bottomness
button-wood
bathyscape
bathymeter
bathymetry
botryoidal
bathylitic
bluebreast
blue-bonnet
Bourbonism
Bourbonist
bluebottle
blue-cheese
blue-collar
bounciness
blundering
bourgeoise
brushwheel
blushingly
bousingken
Bourignian
brutifying
bluejacket
bouillotte
blue-pencil
brusquerie
blue-rocket
blue-rinsed
blue-tongue
bluethroat
blustering
blusterous
bluey-green
bivalvular
bivouacked
beweltered
bewildered
bowdlerise
bowdlerism
bowdlerize
bow-fronted
bowerwoman
bewitching
bewitchery
bawdy-house
box-pleated
box-spanner
bryologist
boyishness
bizarrerie

charabancs
char-à-bancs
chaparajos
clarabella
chaparejos
Characidae
chamaeleon
coat-armour
Charadrius
charactery
chambranle
crabbiness
Chambertin
chambering
chamberpot
chamber-lye
chalcocite
Chalcidian
chalcedony
chancellor
chanceless
Chaucerian
Chaucerism
coal-cutter
chandlerly
chaud-mellé
chandelier
chardonnay
chaudfroid
châtelaine
cranesbill
crane's-bill
coalescent
Clarenceux
crakeberry
czarevitch
cravenness
Charentais
coacervate
chauffeuse
chapfallen
chaffingly
changeable
changeably
chargeable
chargeably
charge-card
charge-hand
craigfluke
changeling
changeless
chargeless
cragginess
changeover
clangorous
coach-horse
crash-proof
coachbuilt
charitable
charitably
clarichord
clavichord
craniology
coati-mondi
cladistics
charioteer
craniotomy
clavicular
coati-mundi
clarifying
charity-boy
coadjacent
clamjamfry
coadjutrix
coadjutant
crankshaft
chank-shell
crank-sided
cracklings
crackajack
chalkiness
crankiness
chalkboard
crackbrain
chalkstone
chaplaincy
chaplainry
challenged
challenger
cradlesong
charleston
chaulmugra
chasmogamy
charmingly
clamminess
coalmaster
claymation
chainwheel
channelled
channelise
channelize
chain-smoke
chainbrake
chauntress
clannishly
chatoyance
chatoyancy
clapometer
cyanometer
Charophyta
cyanophyte
Charollais
clapped-out
champignon
coal-porter
clappering
clapperboy
chairwoman
claircolle
chairborne
chairbound
chair-organ
chasse-café
classicise
classicism
classicist
classicize
Chassidism
classified
classifier
classiness
coarseness
clanswoman
crab-stones
crassitude
chaussures
coastwards
△chartreuse
chartulary
chaptalise
chaptalize
Clactonian
chasteness
chattiness
craftiness
charthouse
Chaetopoda
chattering
chatterbox
coaptation
coastguard
△chautauqua
coactivity
coagulable
coagulator
crapulence
chalumeaux
craquelure
chauvinism
chauvinist
Charybdian
chalybeate
cabbage-fly
cibachrome
cobwebbery
cobalt-blue
caballeros
cabalistic
cabalettas
cybernated
cybernetic
cyberspace
cub-hunting
cocoa-beans
cactaceous
cock-a-bondy
cockalorum
cockatrice
cockabully
cockchafer
cacodaemon
cicadellid
Cecidomyia
cockernony
cacafuegos
cacography
cacogenics
cack-handed
cyclically
coccineous
cachinnate
cacciatora
cacciatore
cochleated
cucullated
cucumiform
cacomistle
coconut-shy
coconut-oil
cockneydom
cockneyish
cockneyism
cycloramic
cycloidian
cuckoldise
cuckoldize
cyclopedia
cyclopedic
cyclothyme
cyclograph
cyclo-cross
cuckoo-spit
cyclostyle
cyclostome
cock-paddle
cacophonic
cucurbital
Ciceronian
cocksucker
cicisbeism
cocksiness
cockteaser
cecutiency
cicatrices
cicatrixes
cocktailed
cicatricle
cacotrophy
cacotopian
cockyleeky
codicology
cudgelling
caddis-case
cod-fishing
cod-fishery
caddis-worm
cuddlesome
code-number
cider-press
cadaverous
codswallop
cod's-wallop
coelacanth
coetaneous
△cretaceous
Caesarship
cheechalko
cheechakos
crescented
crescentic
crescendos
coercively
coercivity
chevesaile
crewellery
crenellate
cleverness
coeternity
crêpe-soled
crève-coeur
credential
△clementine
clerestory
crewelwork
clergiable
clergyable
clew-garnet
Chekhovian
chevisance
chemically
creditable
creditably
chelicerae
chemisette
chewing-gum
chemicking
cherimoyer
chemiatric
coexistent
checklaton
cheekpiece
checkclerk
cheekiness
cheekpouch
checkpoint
cheektooth
Cherkesses
cream-slice
creaminess
cleansable
crew-necked
chemotaxis
coelomatic
chemonasty
Ctenophora
ctenophore
coenobitic
coenosteum
Caerphilly
cheapskate
creepingly
creepmouse
caespitose
cherry-coal
cheirology

10 c□e□r

cheironomy
cheeriness
chevrotain
clearstory
cheerfully
cheesecake
cheese-head
chessylite
cheesemite
cheesiness
chersonese
chessboard
cheesewood
cheesewire
creatinine
creational
creaturely
creatively
creativity
crenulated
cheque-book
crepuscule
cherubical
cherubimic
coequality
coffer-fish
caffeinism
cognisance
cognizance
cognisable
cognisably
cognizable
cognizably
cognominal
cigarillos
cogitation
cogitative
cohabitant
cohibition
cohibitive
coherently
cohesively
chinachina
climatical
chitarrone
Chinagraph®
chivalrous
cuirassier
crib-biting
coincident
△chinchilla
childbirth
Childermas
childproof
childishly
child-study
Cuisenaire
chimerical
chiselling
chief-baron
chiffchaff
chiffonier
ca'ing-whale
cringeling
cringingly
clinginess
clingstone
crithidial
clish-clash
clinically
criminally
critically
chiliarchy
chiliastic
click-clack
chickenpox
clinkstone
cricketing
chilliness
chionodoxa
clientship
chimneypot
chiromancy
ceilometer
clinometer
clinometry
crinolette
crinolined
cnidoblast
chirognomy
chilopodan
chironomer
chironomic
chironomid
Chironomus
chirograph
Chiroptera
chimpanzee
chirpiness
crispbread
crispation
chinquapin
cribriform
cribration
crio-sphinx
criss-cross
cristiform
clistogamy
chittagong
chittaroni
chittering
chirurgeon
chirurgery
cliquiness
cajolement
collatable
cellar-book
collateral
collagenic
collarette
calcareous
cellar-flap
collar-work
celebrated
calibrator
celebrator
Colubridae
calico-bush
calyciform
culiciform
calyculate
calico-tree
calico-wood
Caledonian
cul-de-lampe
Collembola
calves'-foot
calceiform
colleagued
collegiums
collegiate
culver-keys
calceolate
calcedonio
culvertage
Colbertine
collecting
collection
collective
calefactor
caligraphy
Caligulism
caliginous
calf-ground
colchicums
colchicine
calcinable
cultivable
collimator
cultivator
Callicarpa
calciferol
calcitonin
calliature
colliquant
colliquate
colliculus
columnated
columbaria
chlamydial
chlamydate
calumniate
calumnious
columellae
calamander
calamancos
colemanite
calamitous
calendarer
colonnaded
colonially
calendries
cylindroid
cylindrite
Celtomania
colposcope
colposcopy
cellophane®
Ciliophora
coleorhiza
cellobiose
colportage
coleoptile
Coleoptera
colporteur
colloquial
calmodulin
collocutor
colloquise
colloquist
colloquium
colloquize
collotypic
calyptrate
colorectal
caloricity
chlorodyne
chloridise
chloridate
chloridize
calorifier
chloroform
cultriform
cold-rolled
chloralism
chloralose
chlorinise
chlorinate
chlorinity
chlorinize
chlorophyl
chloroquin
coloration
coloratura
calescence
calc-sinter
colostrous
colossuses
calotypist
colatitude
calculated
cellulated
calculable
calculably
colourable
colourably
culturable
culturally
calculator
colour-code
colourfast
cellulitis
colourless
cellulosic
colour-supp
calculuses
colourwash
collyriums
combatable
come-at-able
comparable
comparably
comparator
commandeer
commandant
commanding
commandery
campaneros
campaigner
campaniles
compatible
compatibly
comparison
compatriot
compassing
compassion
compactify
compaction
campanular
companying
comicality
comedienne
comédienne
comedietta
cummerbund
commercial
compendium
competence
competency
campesinos
competitor
compelling
cumberless
cumberment
compearant
cumbersome
commeasure
compensate
campestral
commentary
commentate
Camberwell
campground
camphorate
come-hither
combinable
compilator
commingled
Commiphora
cymbidiums
commitment
commission
commissary
commissure
committing

Words marked △ may be spelled also with a capital letter

commixtion
commixture
comminuted
compliance
compliancy
compliable
complicacy
complected
complacent
complicant
complicate
complicity
cumuliform
complainer
complement
compliment
comeliness
complanate
camel-corps
camelopard
complotted
completely
completion
cumulation
completory
completive
cumulative
compluvium
complexify
complexion
complexity
comanchero
commonable
compotator
commonalty
componency
composedly
cameo-shell
commonhold
Compositae
compositor
commodious
compounder
commonness
composture
commonweal
compradore
camerlengo
comprehend
camerlingo
Camorrista
compromise
Cameronian
compressed
compressor
cameration
cumbrously
camerawork
comestible
comstocker
cimetidine

camsteerie
cymotrichy
cometology
Camptonite
comitative
communally
commutable
computable
commutator
computator
comburgess
communique
communiqué
camouflage
camoufleur
compulsion
compursion
compulsory
compulsive
combustion
combustive
cinnabaric
canvasback
convalesce
contadinas
cannabinol
contagious
cinnamonic
cantaloupe
centaurian
cantatrice
contactual
confabular
connatural
canvas-work
cony-burrow
cenobitism
conscience
conacreism
convenance
conveyance
convenable
conveyable
candelabra
△**canterbury**
cannel-coal
candescent
condescend
contendent
contending
confederal
△**conference**
conférence
congeneric
congenetic
cankeredly
Cinderella
convexedly
convergent
converging
centesimal

congenital
candelilla
convenient
cancelling
cannellini
cannelloni
cancellate
cancellous
conferment
centennial
concerning
contemning
convexness
conferring
consecrate
consensual
conversely
confessant
conversant
concession
confession
consension
conversion
condensery
condensate
concessive
conceptual
contextual
△conventual
concentred
concentric
concertina
concertino
contestant
contesting
convertend
△**conception**
confection
congestion
connection
contention
convection
convention
conjecture
consectary
contexture
concettism
concettist
convertite
conceitful
conceptive
congestive
connective
convective
consequent
confervoid
conservant
cankerworm
coniferous
conchiform
conchiglie

conchoidal
conchology
cynghanedd
cinchonine
cinchonise
cinchonism
cinchonize
conchiolin
connivance
cannibally
confinable
confidante
convincing
confiscate
confidence
confidency
connivence
connivency
continence
continency
cantilever
centimeter
considered
confiserie
centimetre
contingent
conoidical
consimilar
centiliter
concipient
conditions
consilient
centilitre
conciliary
conciliate
centillion
cantillate
confirmand
confirming
consignify
cancionero
candidness
cincinnate
concinnity
concinnous
centigrade
consistent
conniption
conviction
consistory
convictism
convictive
continuums
continuant
contiguity
continuate
continuity
contiguous
continuous
conglobate
candle-coal

canaliculi
concluding
candle-doup
confluence
candlefish
conclusion
conclusory
conclusive
candle-tree
conflation
conclavist
candlewick
candlewood
cinema-goer
canonicals
canonicate
canonicity
cenenchyma
canonistic
consonance
consonancy
condonable
consolable
cannonball
concordial
concordant
condolence
canzonetta
canzonette
cannon-game
consociate
censorious
cantonment
conformist
conformity
confounded
conjointly
censorship
cannon-shot
concoction
contortion
consortism
consortium
concoctive
contortive
convoluted
conspectus
canophilia
cynophilia
canophobia
cynophobia
canephorus
conspiracy
conspirant
centre-back
contraband
canary-bird
contrabass
contribute
contracted
contractor

10 c□n□r

centricity
contrecoup
contradict
congruence
congruency
centrifuge
centrefold
contraflow
cancriform
centre-fire
congregant
congregate
centre-half
contrahent
centroidal
contre-jour
controlled
controller
centreline
contraltos
centralise
centralism
centralist
centrality
centralize
centromere
contraplex
contraprop
centre-rail
contrarily
cinerarium
canary-seed
centrosome
concretely
contritely
cineration
concretion
contrition
concretise
concretism
concretist
concretive
concretize
canorously
contravene
controvert
canary-wood
cancrizans
canescence
constraint
constringe
constantan
Constantia
constantly
constipate
cunctation
cunctatory
constitute
constative
cunctative
Conjugatae
conjugated
censurable
censurably
confusable
confutable
conjugally
consumable
conjurator
conjunctly
confusedly
consumedly
cinquefoil
conducible
confusible
consummate
cinquepace
concurrent
concurring
conquering
conqueress
consulship
convulsant
concussion
convulsion
consubsist
concussive
convulsive
consuetude
consultant
consulting
conduction
consultory
conductive
consultive
centumviri
condylomas
crotalaria
clonazepam
Crotalidae
chocaholic
cholagogic
cholagogue
coomceiled
cloacaline
choiceness
crouch-ware
cloudscape
cloudberry
chondritic
chondritis
cloudiness
co-ordinate
chondromas
cropduster
chordotomy
cloud-built
cloudburst
co-operator
closed-door
chokeberry
clove-hitch
cloverleaf
choregraph
close-stool
chopfallen
crow-flower
clogginess
Coolgardie
cloth-eared
coolheaded
clodhopper
clothes-peg
clothes-pin
crocheting
cooling-off
clomiphene
choliambic
choriambic
choriambus
clofibrate
clockmaker
clock-radio
chock-tight
chockstone
choanocyte
crown-wheel
clownishly
chocolatey
Crocodilia
Crocodilus
chocoholic
crocoisite
croupiness
cross-match
crosspatch
cross-party
crossbench
cloistered
cloisterer
cross-refer
crosscheck
crosspiece
crosslight
chopsticks
crossfield
crossclaim
crossandra
crossroads
crossbones
crossbower
cross-armed
crossbreed
cloistress
cross-staff
cross-stone
caoutchouc
clostridia
clottiness
co-optation
co-optative
cephalagra
cephalitis
cephalopod
capability
capacitate
cupidinous
capodastro
copresence
co-presence
copperhead
capreolate
copperwork
copperworm
copyholder
captivance
capsizable
capriccios
cypripedia
Cyprinidae
capricious
captiously
capillaire
cipollinos
copulation
copulatory
copulative
cup-and-ball
cup-and-ring
capnomancy
coprolalia
coprophagy
coprolitic
caper-sauce
Capernaite
Cyperaceae
coparcener
Copernican
copartnery
capernoity
copesettic
capitolian
capitoline
capitulant
capitulary
capitalise
capitalism
capitalist
capitulate
capitellum
capitalize
copy-typing
capotastos
capitation
cappuccino
copywriter
coppy-stool
coquelicot
coquetting
coquettish
coquimbite
Cortaderia
coriaceous
cornaceous
curvaceous
carragheen
caryatidal
caryatides
caryatidic
curvacious
corralling
carnallite
carmagnole
carnassial
△circassian
currant-bun
cardboardy
cornbrandy
cerebritis
cerebellar
cerebellic
curability
cerebellum
carabineer
carabinier
corybantes
corybantic
care-crazed
Caricaceae
corncockle
cardcastle
cork-cutter
corn-cutter
caricature
corn-dealer
coradicate
co-radicate
corn-dollie
corydaline
curselarie
cornerback
curfew-bell
corselette
corregidor
Cordeliers
corsetière
corbelling
carpellary
carpellate
carpet-moth
cursedness
correspond
circensial
circensian
cordectomy
cornettino
curvetting
correction
correption
correctory
cornettist
corrective
cornerwise
cornerways
cornflakes

Words marked △ may be spelled also with a capital letter

corn-factor
cornflower
ceriferous
cerography
coregonine
cork-heeled
card-holder
carphology
carthamine
cirrhipede
Cirrhopoda
Carthusian
cornhusker
cardiganed
corticated
cardinally
corrivalry
corrigenda
Cirripedia
cardiogram
cervicitis
corrigible
cardiology
cardialgia
cordillera
cordialise
cordiality
cordialize
carcinomas
carcinogen
carcinosis
cirrigrade
certiorari
cordierite
corbiculae
curricular
corniculum
curriculum
certifying
Carolinian
corylopsis
carelessly
corelation
corelative
ceramicist
chromidium
chromogram
corn-maiden
corn-miller
caramelise
caramelize
chromomere
ceremonial
ceremonies
△coromandel
ceruminous
chromophil
curbmarket
chromosome
chromatics
chromatype
chromotype
chrematist
chronicler
Chronicles
chronicity
chronogram
Cerinthian
Corinthian
Carangidae
chronology
chronotron
coronation
caruncular
cartomancy
corporally
carbonados
corporator
carbon-copy
cariogenic
corporeity
cartophile
cartophily
carpophore
cormophyte
corrodible
corrosible
carbonnade
cartonnage
cartoonish
cartoonist
corroboree
carboxylic
coryphaeus
carapacial
cornstarch
corpse-gate
Christhood
corn-spirit
chrysalids
Christlike
Christless
chrysolite
Christmasy
chrysophan
chrysotile
curbtrader
carotenoid
carotinoid
cork-tipped
ceratopsid
curatorial
curateship
corrugated
circulable
circularly
circulator
corrugator
carbuncled
corpuscule
circumcise
circumduce
circumduct
corpulence
corpulency
carbureter
carburetor
circumflex
circumfuse
curmudgeon
circummure
cornucopia
circumpose
curmurring
circuiteer
corruption
circuitous
corruptive
circumvent
caravaneer
caravanned
caravanner
caravaning
curbvendor
cordwainer
cartwright
careworker
carrying-on
cistaceous
cascarilla
casualness
co-starring
case-bottle
cash-credit
Cistercian
cosmetical
costean-pit
costeaning
cussedness
cashew-nuts
Cassegrain
cystectomy
case-harden
cuspidated
cosmically
castigator
cassia-bark
cysticerci
casting-net
cessionary
cystinosis
Cassiopeia
cashiering
cystinuria
cash-keeper
costliness
casemented
casinghead
cosentient
cosmoramic
customable
cosmolatry
cystoscope
cystoscopy
cestoidean
cosmogenic
cassolette
customised
customized
custom-made
cosmogonic
cosmodrome
cystostomy
cismontane
cispontine
Cestracion
castration
cesarevich
costus-root
cassumunar
caseworker
cat's-brains
catabolism
cat's-cradle
catechesis
catechetic
catechiser
catechizer
catacumbal
cytochrome
catechumen
catafalque
categorial
categories
categorise
categorist
categorize
catch-basin
catchpenny
catch-drain
cote-hardie
cottierism
cuttle-bone
catalectic
cotyliform
cuttlefish
cataloguer
cytologist
catalogize
cataleptic
catamenial
cytometric
Cotingidae
catenarian
catenation
cotton-boll
cathode-ray
citronella
△catholicon
Catholicos
cotton-mill
cottonseed
cottontail
cottonweed
cottonwood
cotton-worm
catapultic
cataphonic
cataphract
catoptrics
cat-cracker
catarrhine
catarrhous
catastasis
cat-burglar
citrulline
cutty-stool
citizeness
citizenise
citizenize
courageous
coumarilic
chubbiness
churchgoer
councilman
councillor
churchless
church-rate
churchward
churchyard
chunderous
causewayed
caulescent
chuff-chuff
chuffiness
club-footed
club-headed
crushingly
Cruciferae
cousinhood
cauliflory
cautionary
cousinship
cautiously
cauliculus
crucifying
chucker-out
couplement
churlishly
clubmaster
churn-drill
churn-staff
coulometer
coulometry
clumpiness
counselled
counsellor
clumsiness
cruisewear
coursework
court-baron
crustacean
causticity
courtierly
crustiness

10 c□u□t

courthouse
counteract
courtcraft
counterbid
clustering
counterspy
cluster-cup
countersue
courtesied
cruet-stand
crustation
countryman
couturière
Cavicornia
cavalierly
civilities
cavalryman
covenanted
covenantee
covenanter
covenantor
covariance
covetingly
cavitation
covetously
cowcatcher
cow-parsley
cow-chervil
cowdie-pine
cowrie-pine
cowl-necked
coweringly
cowardship
cowpuncher
coxcomical
chylaceous
cryoconite
Clydesdale
clypeiform
Clydesider
cryogenics
cryometric
cryophilic
cryophorus
cryoscopic
cryptogram
cryptogamy
cryptology
dramatical
diacaustic
diamantine
dramaturge
dramaturgy
drawbridge
drabbiness
dealbation
dearbought
Drawcansir
dead-centre
diazeuctic
diagenesis
diagenetic
diapedesis
diapedetic
diabetical
Diadelphia
dealership
dialectics
drakestone
dead-finish
dwarfishly
dead-ground
draught-bar
draughtman
draught-net
deathwatch
deathwards
death-adder
death-agony
death's-head
death-throe
death-knell
diaphanous
death-token
diachronic
death-wound
diathermal
diathermic
drawing-pen
drawing-pin
diaskeuast
diallagoid
dead-lights
drawlingly
deadliness
dead-letter
dharmshala
deaf-mutism
drainpipes
diagnostic
dead-nettle
diagonally
diagometer
dragon-fish
dragonhead
deaconhood
diabolical
draconites
diaconicon
dragonlike
dragonnade
dragon-root
deaconship
diacoustic
dragon-tree
Dracontium
dray-plough
deaspirate
diatribist
drag-racing
diarrhoeal
diarrhoeic
diagraphic
diatropism
deadstroke
drawstring
draw-string
diastaltic
diastemata
draftiness
draft-horse
deactivate
dead-weight
dialysable
dialyzable
Dibranchia
debriefing
dabblingly
debilitate
debonnaire
debonairly
debentured
debasement
debasingly
debateable
debatement
debatingly
dubitation
dubitative
debauchery
debouchure
de-blurring
declarable
declarator
declaredly
Dictaphone®
declaimant
declaiming
dictatress
declassify
decrassify
deck-bridge
duck-billed
docibility
decoctible
dickcissel
decadently
decreeable
decrescent
Dickensian
declension
duck-footed
decagramme
decigramme
decagynian
decagynous
decahedral
decahedron
deceivable
deceivably
declinable
declinator
dictionary
decollated
decollator
deckle-edge
duck-legged
decalogist
decolonise
decolonize
decolorant
dichlorvos
decolorise
decelerate
decolorate
decolorize
dochmiacal
decumbence
decumbency
Decemberly
decemviral
docimology
decimalise
decimalism
decimalist
decimalize
decampment
documental
decomposer
decompound
Decembrist
decompress
decamerous
dock-master
docimastic
decimation
dicynodont
decennoval
decandrian
decinormal
decandrous
doctor-fish
dichotomic
Dictograph®
doctorship
dice-player
decapodous
decipherer
deceptible
deceptious
decapitate
deck-quoits
decurrency
dichroitic
dichromism
dichromate
decoration
decorative
decorously
decussated
duckshover
decisively
decathlete
deck-tennis
Docetistic
decoupling
decivilise
decivilize
decryption
didactical
deductible
deducement
dedication
dedicatory
dedicative
didgeridoo
didelphian
didelphine
didelphous
didynamian
didynamous
Didunculus
didascalic
die-casting
deep-browed
dreadlocks
dreadfully
dietetical
dielectric
deep-freeze
deer-forest
dregginess
die-sinking
dreikanter
dreamwhile
dreamingly
dreaminess
dream-world
drearihead
drearihood
veariment
dreariness
deep-rooted
drearisome
deep-seated
dressmaker
dress-shirt
deep-sinker
dress-goods
dyer's-broom
dressguard
defeasance
defrayable
defeasible
defrayment
deflagrate
deficience
deficiency
defectible
defacement
defacingly
defecation
difference
differency
deflection

Words marked △ may be spelled also with a capital letter

10 d□p□o

deflective
diffidence
difficulty
defoliated
defalcator
defoliator
defilement
defamation
defamatory
defendable
defenceman
defenseman
definienda
defensible
defensibly
definement
definitude
definitely
definition
defunction
definitive
defunctive
deflowerer
daffodilly
difformity
deferrable
deformable
deformedly
deforciant
diffusedly
diffusible
degradable
dog-fancier
dog-handler
dogmatical
dogmatiser
dogmatizer
digladiate
dog-parsley
doggedness
daguerrean
degreasant
degression
digression
degressive
digressive
digger-wasp
dog's-fennel
dog-biscuit
dignifying
daggle-tail
degeneracy
degenerate
degenerous
digoneutic
dog-soldier
digestedly
digestible
digitiform
digitalise
digitalize
dog's-tongue
digitorium
digitately
digitation
dehydrater
dehydrator
dehumidify
dehumanise
dehumanize
dehiscence
drivelling
driverless
driving-box
drinking-up
drink-money
drink-drive
drill-press
Deinoceras
deinothere
daintiness
daisy-wheel
daisy-chain
dejectedly
dejections
dijudicate
dika-butter
dukkeripen
dike-louper
dollarless
dollarship
dull-browed
deliberate
delibation
delectable
delectably
dilucidate
Dolichotis
dilacerate
delicately
dolichurus
dolcemente
diligently
delegation
deligation
delightful
delphinoid
dolphin-fly
delphinium
deltiology
dulciloquy
dilemmatic
delaminate
dolomitise
delimitate
dolomitize
delineavit
delineable
delineator
delinquent
dildo-glass
dilapidate
deliquesce
deliration
dolorously
dolesomely
delusional
doll's-house
delustrant
delusively
dilettante
dilettanti
diluteness
dilatorily
dilatation
dull-witted
dilly-dally
delayingly
demeasnure
demobilise
demobilize
democratic
demi-cannon
damp-course
demodulate
demi-ditone
damselfish
demography
damageable
demagogism
damagingly
Demogorgon
demoiselle
damping-off
dumbledore
dimplement
demolisher
demolition
demoniacal
demandable
diminuendo
dementedly
demonology
dominantly
diminished
diminution
domination
demonetise
diminutive
dominative
demonetize
dumfounder
demurrable
dimorphism
dimorphous
demoralise
demoralize
demureness
demirepdom
damasceene
dame-school
domestical
dumbstruck
demoticist
demotivate
dumb-waiter
dumpy-level
dentaliums
dung-beetle
denudation
dense-media
dunderfunk
dinner-gown
dunderhead
dinnerless
dinner-pail
donkey-pump
dunderpate
dinner-time
dance-music
donkey-work
denigrator
denegation
dung-hunter
densimeter
densimetry
dentifrice
dynamicist
dynamogeny
denominate
dynamistic
dynamitard
△dinanderie
dining-hall
denunciate
dining-room
denervated
dendrobium
dendriform
dendrogram
dendroidal
dendrology
dendrophis
dynastical
Dinosauria
dinosauric
denotement
denaturant
denaturise
denaturize
donatistic
denotation
denotative
denouement
dénouement
duniwassal
dandy-fever
dandy-horse
△donnybrook
dandy-brush
denization
duodecimal
duodenitis
duodecimos
△diothelism
△dyothelism
△diothelete
△dyothelete
△dyothelite
drop-hammer
△diophysite
△dyophysite
deoxidiser
deoxidizer
door-keeper
drop-letter
drosometer
drosophila
deodoriser
deodorizer
deoppilate
droopingly
droopiness
drowsihead
drossiness
drowsiness
doomsaying
door-to-door
dioptrical
deontology
diorthosis
diorthotic
depravedly
dupability
depletable
deprecable
deprecator
depredator
depreciate
dapperling
dapperness
depressant
depressing
depression
depressive
deprivable
duplicator
dapple-grey
depolarise
dopplerite
depolarize
depilation
depilatory
dependance
dependacie
dependable
dependably
dependence
dependency
diplomatic
dipsomania
deplorable
deplorably
deployment
diprotodon

10 d□p□o

diplodocus
depopulate
department
deportment
depuration
depuratory
depurative
deposition
depositary
depository
depositive
diphtheria
diphtheric
dipetalous
deputation
diphyodont
diphyletic
dermatitis
dermatogen
dermatoses
dermatosis
Dermaptera
durability
directness
deracinate
Directoire
directress
deridingly
dirt-eating
deregulate
dark-ground
deregister
derogately
derogation
derogatory
derogative
dorsifixed
dérailleur
derailment
dorsigrade
diremption
Dermoptera
dirt-rotten
derestrict
derisively
durational
derivation
derivative
disparager
disparates
despatches
dispatcher
dispatches
diseaseful
dissatisfy
déshabillé
dishabille
disbarment
disharmony
disgarnish
dismalness

discarnate
disdainful
despairing
despairful
dispassion
dismantler
disnatured
disability
desecrater
desecrator
desiccator
diseconomy
disadvance
desiderata
desiderate
desiderium
desperados
dissembler
disselboom
descendant
descendent
descending
dissevered
disbenefit
Disneyfied
disherison
disheritor
disbelieve
dispelling
dispermous
discerning
disrespect
dishearten
dispersoid
distensile
dispersant
descension
dispersion
dissension
distension
dispensary
dispersive
distensive
dissecting
dissenting
disgestion
disjection
dissection
distention
disfeature
dissertate
dissective
disservice
disc-floret
disc-flower
designable
designator
designedly
designless
designment
dissheathe

dischuffed
dysthymiac
dysphemism
deschooler
discharger
dissipated
despicable
despicably
despisable
dislikable
dissipable
distinctly
dissidence
dyskinesia
despiteful
despiteous
dislikeful
dispiteous
distinguée
distichous
dissimilar
dispirited
dissilient
discipline
distilland
distilling
distillery
distillate
distilment
discission
dismission
dismissory
dismissive
dessiatine
displeased
disyllabic
disyllable
disfluency
disulphide
disulphate
disulfiram
disclaimer
desalinise
displenish
desalinate
desalinize
disglorify
dysplastic
displosion
disclosure
desolately
desolation
desolatory
disimagine
disamenity
disembowel
disembosom
disembogue
disembroil
disimprove
disengaged

disinherit
dysenteric
disenvelop
disenthral
disinthral
disenchain
disenchant
disinhibit
disentitle
disenviron
disanalogy
disincline
disenclose
disinclose
disenslave
disanimate
disendowed
disennoble
disinvolve
disentrail
disentrain
disentwine
dissonance
dissonancy
disloyally
disposable
disloyalty
disconcert
dispondaic
despondent
desponding
discordant
discordful
discoverer
disposedly
dishonesty
discomfort
discophile
Discophora
despotical
desmodiums
dispositor
dissociate
discommode
discommend
disconnect
discounsel
discounter
disjointed
disjoining
desmosomal
dishonorer
discobolus
discompose
discoursal
discourser
discourage
disworship
disconsent
dispossess
discontent

distortion
distortive
dissoluble
dissolvent
dissolving
disapparel
desipience
disepalous
disappoint
disapprove
disarrange
disorganic
distribute
distracted
destructor
dispredden
disordered
deservedly
discreetly
disorderly
désorienté
disprofess
dysarthria
dispraiser
distrainee
distrainer
distrainor
desertless
desireless
descramble
distringas
disprinced
disgruntle
dysgraphia
dysgraphic
dystrophia
dystrophic
dystrophin
discrepant
descriptor
distressed
distresser
distruster
dyscrasite
dysprosium
discretely
desorption
discretion
discretive
distraught
desirously
distrouble
disprovide
destroying
desistance
desistence
disespouse
disastrous
disutility
disputable
disputably

Words marked △ may be spelled also with a capital letter

disturbant
disturbing
disjunctor
disquieten
disquietly
Dasyuridae
discutient
disqualify
desquamate
disfurnish
disculpate
disguising
discursion
discussion
dissuasion
discursory
dissuasory
discursist
discursive
discussive
dissuasive
disburthen
disgusting
△**disruption**
disgustful
disruptive
disavaunce
disownment
dishwasher
dessyatine
detracting
detraction
detractory
detractive
detachable
detectable
date-coding
detachedly
detectible
detachment
△**ditheletic**
ditheistic
ditch-water
Dutchwoman
Dutchwomen
detainable
ditriglyph
detainment
dithionate
datum-level
datum-plane
datamation
detonation
ditrochean
detergence
detergency
deterrence
determined
determiner
dethroning
detestable
detestably
detruncate
detoxicant
detoxicate
drug-addict
drupaceous
drumbledor
drudgingly
dough-baked
doughfaced
Doukhobors
daughterly
dauphiness
doughiness
double-bank
double-bass
double-dyed
double-eyed
double-flat
double-gild
double-hung
double-knit
doubleness
double-page
double-park
doubletree
double-take
double-talk
diurnalist
deutoplasm
doulocracy
douloureux
drug-pusher
drug-runner
doubtingly
doubtfully
diuturnity
duumvirate
dive-bomber
devocalise
dove-colour
devocalize
dive-dapper
divagation
divulgence
developing
devalorise
devalorize
devilishly
devolution
diving-bell
△**devanagari**
divineness
divineress
diving-suit
divination
divinatory
divaricate
divergence
divergency
divertible
devastavit
devastator
divestible
divestment
divisional
divisively
devitalise
devitalize
devotement
devotional
devourment
devoutness
down-and-out
down-at-heel
down-easter
dew-retting
downfallen
dawdlingly
downlooked
dowel-joint
down-market
△**dewar-flask**
dower-house
downstairs
downstream
downstroke
downturned
dewatering
downwardly
dexterwise
doxography
dextrogyre
dextrality
dextrously
day-patient
drysaltery
day-scholar
day-release
day-wearied
day-neutral
day-boarder
daydreamer
day-tripper
dry-cupping
day-nursery
dazzlement
dazzlingly
dizzyingly
emalangeni
epanaphora
emasculate
emancipist
emancipate
ecardinate
exacerbate
evanescent
enamelling
enamellist
elatedness
evangeliar
evangelise
evangelism
△evangelist
evangelize
emarginate
exaggerate
edaphology
eradicated
eradicable
examinable
eradicator
examinator
emaciation
eradiation
edaciously
epaulement
eyas-musket
evaporable
elaborator
enamorados
evaporator
epagomenal
enamouring
exasperate
enarration
elasticise
elasticate
elasticity
elasticize
exactingly
enantiomer
enantiosis
exactitude
exaltation
evacuation
evaluation
evacuative
evaluative
emblazoner
emblazonry
eubacteria
embodiment
emblematic
emblements
emboldener
embalmment
embolismal
embolismic
embankment
embonpoint
embroidery
embroglios
embrowning
embarkment
embargoing
ember-goose
embassador
embasement
embossment
embittered
embitterer
embouchure
embruement
elbow-chair
embowelled
embryogeny
embryology
embryulcia
embryonate
embryotomy
escharotic
enchanting
encyclical
escadrille
excrescent
excrementa
ecclesiast
escheatage
excogitate
escribanos
encrinital
encrinitic
encoignure
escritoire
exculpable
escaladoes
excellence
△excellency
escalloped
escallonia
Esculapian
eucalyptol
eucalyptus
euchlorine
escalation
escalatory
encomienda
encampment
escamotage
encincture
encroacher
encloister
encephalic
encephalin
encephalon
escapadoes
exceptious
escapology
escapeless
exceptless
escapement
eccoprotic
excursions
encircling
escarpment
eucaryotic
excerpting
excerption
excursuses
encasement
encashment
encystment
excusatory

Words marked △ may be spelled also with a capital letter

10 e□c□t

ex-cathedra
escutcheon
excitement
excitingly
excitation
excitatory
excitative
encourager
excludable
excruciate
excavation
ecchymosed
ecchymosis
ecchymotic
encryption
endearment
endocrinal
endocrinic
endocritic
endodermal
endodermic
endodermis
eudaemonia
eudaemonic
endogamous
endogenous
endemicity
endamoebae
eudemonics
eudemonism
endomorphy
endangerer
eudiometer
endopodite
endopleura
endophytic
endermatic
endorsable
end-product
elderberry
endermical
endorhizal
enduringly
endoscopic
endosmosis
endosmotic
endothelia
end-stopped
eye-catcher
emerald-cut
elecampane
emendation
emendatory
epexegeses
epexegesis
epexegetic
eyelet-hole
exegetical
eye-legible
eleven-plus
eleventhly
elementary
eye-service
eye-servant
Everglades
emergently
energetics
Erewhonian
even-handed
erethismic
erethistic
emetically
eremitical
eye-witness
ever-living
even-minded
eternalise
eternalist
eternalize
eye-spotted
epeirogeny
execration
execratory
execrative
Eleusinian
eventually
epentheses
epenthesis
epenthetic
electrical
erectility
edentulous
electrogen
electromer
electronic
electorial
electoress
electorate
exenterate
electively
electivity
executancy
executable
executress
enervating
enervation
enervative
emery-paper
emery-wheel
everything
everywhere
everyplace
emery-cloth
emery-board
effaceable
efficacity
efficience
efficiency
effectible
effectless
effacement
enfacement
effectuate
effleurage
effigurate
exfoliator
effulgence
enfoldment
effeminacy
effeminise
effeminate
effeminize
effloresce
effrontery
effervesce
enforcedly
effortless
enfestered
effusively
effeteness
egg-capsule
ergodicity
Euglenales
eagle-stone
engagement
engagingly
egg-binding
Englishman
Englishism
engulfment
ergomaniac
eigenvalue
eugenecist
eugenicist
egg-and-dart
engenderer
ergonomics
ergonomist
engine-room
engendrure
engrossing
ergophobia
engarrison
ergosterol
eightscore
eightpence
eighteenmo
eightpenny
eighteenth
ergatogyne
ergativity
engouement
englutting
exhibition
exhibitory
exhibitive
ethicality
enhydritic
ethnically
ethologist
ethylamine
exhilarant
exhilarate
exhalation
ephemerist
euhemerise
Euhemerism
euhemerist
ephemerous
euhemerize
exhumation
ethambutol
echinoderm
Echinoidea
Etheostoma
echopraxia
echopraxis
ethereally
exheredate
enharmonic
euharmonic
exhaustion
exhaustive
ericaceous
epitaphian
epitaphist
epicanthic
epigastric
epicanthus
evincement
Emi-Scanner®
episcopacy
episcopant
episcopise
episcopate
episcopize
eviscerate
Eriocaulon
episematic
epideictic
epidendrum
epigenesis
epigenetic
epimeletic
epidemical
epidermoid
eviternity
eminential
epicentral
evidential
epithelial
epithelium
epithemata
epiphonema
epithermal
epiphytism
eliminable
eliminator
epilimnion
epidiorite
episiotomy
eximiously
epididymis
edibleness
epiblastic
epiplastra
epiglottic
epiglottis
etiolation
evil-minded
enigmatise
enigmatist
enigmatize
ebionitism
epicondyle
episodical
epitomical
epidotised
epidotized
epitomiser
epitomizer
editorship
epizootics
epiloguise
epiloguize
eriophorum
epispastic
epigrapher
epigraphic
emigration
emigratory
emissivity
ekistician
epistolary
epistolise
epistolist
epistolize
epistemics
epistrophe
episternal
episternum
epicuticle
exiguously
evil-worker
epicycloid
edifyingly
enjoinment
enjambment
enkephalin
eukaryotic
enlacement
eulogistic
eglandular
elliptical
enlargedly
enlistment
enlevement
enlèvement
Emmentaler
emmenology
emmetropia
emmetropic
Enneandria
enneagonal
enneastyle

Words marked △ may be spelled also with a capital letter

exorbitant
exorbitate
exonerator
exogenetic
exoterical
egocentric
eloignment
elongation
esophageal
exophagous
exothermal
exothermic
exotically
exobiology
exoticness
éboulement
emollition
enormously
erotomania
erotogenic
ecological
economical
economiser
economizer
exopoditic
eco-tourism
ecospecies
exospheric
exosporous
étourderie
ego-tripper
egoistical
emoluments
evolutions
eloquently
evolvement
eponychium
exocytosis
emphatical
euphausiid
emplastron
emplastrum
expectance
expectancy
especially
expectable
expectably
expectedly
expedience
expediency
espadrille
expeditely
expedition
expeditate
expeditive
expressman
expressway
expressage
expression
expressure
expressive
expugnable
explicable
explicator
Empfindung
explicitly
empoisoned
empalement
expandable
expendable
expansible
expansibly
empanelled
expunction
employable
euphorbium
ecphoneses
ecphonesis
euphonical
explosible
euphoriant
euphonious
employment
exprobrate
exploitage
exploitive
exportable
expurgator
ecphractic
emphractic
empiricism
empiricist
emparadise
experience
experiment
expertness
Euphrosyne
expiration
expiratory
exposition
expository
expositive
expatiator
empathetic
expatriate
euphuistic
empoverish
emphysemic
Eurocratic
ebracteate
Eurocheque
enrichment
Euroclydon
Eurafrican
enragement
enregiment
enregister
earthwards
earth-table
earth-shine
earth-light
earth-plate
earth-smoke
eard-hunger
eard-hungry
earthiness
earthwoman
earthmover
earthbound
earth-board
earth-house
earthquake
ear-witness
earlierise
earlierize
ear-kissing
enrollment
Euromarket
errand-girl
eurypterid
Eurypterus
enraptured
ear-trumpet
Eurotunnel
éprouvette
ear-bussing
Eurovision
eurhythmic
Eustachian
exsiccator
△eisteddfod
easselgate
easterling
eastermost
Eastertide
Eastertime
easselward
exsufflate
ensignship
ease-giving
enschedule
eosinophil
ensanguine
exsanguine
ensoulment
essayistic
euthanasia
entrancing
eutrapelia
extraneity
extraneous
estrangelo
entrapment
extradotal
extra-solar
extractant
extraction
extractive
extramural
enticeable
enticement
enticingly
ectodermal
ectodermic
entremesse
entreasure
entreating
entreative
ectoenzyme
ectogenous
extricable
entailment
entoilment
ecthlipses
ecthlipsis
entamoebae
entomology
entombment
extemporal
ectomorphy
estimation
estimative
extendable
extenuator
extendedly
extendible
extensible
estanciero
extinction
extincture
extinctive
extinguish
Eatanswill
estrogenic
estipulate
entophytal
ectophytic
entophytic
externally
extirpable
extirpator
enterocele
enterdeale
enthralled
enthraldom
enterolith
enthronise
entireness
enthronize
exteriorly
enterprise
enterotomy
estatesman
entitative
extrusible
enthusiasm
enthusiast
estivation
Euthyneura
Entryphone®
emulatress
equability
exurbanite
enunciable
enunciator
edulcorant
edulcorate
exulcerate
exuberance
exuberancy
enumerator
erubescent
erubescite
ecumenical
enuredness
egurgitate
elucidator
esuriently
exuviation
ebullience
ebulliency
ebullition
equanimity
equanimous
eburnation
equiparate
equipotent
elutriator
emulsifier
equestrian
exultantly
exultingly
eruptional
equatorial
equitation
eructation
exultation
eruptivity
equivocate
equivalent
environics
enwrapment
enwrapping
Edwardiana
erythritic
erysipelas
elytriform
Egyptology
enzymology
eczematous
framboesia
flabbiness
flag-basket
flamboyant
flaccidity
fianchetti
fianchetto
franchisee
franchiser
flanconade
Francophil
Franciscan
flap-dragon
fraudulent
flapdoodle

Words marked △ may be spelled also with a capital letter

10 f□a□d

fraudfully
frame-maker
Fratercula
flavescent
flake-white
flagellant
flabellate
Flagellata
flagellate
fraternise
fraternity
fraternize
frame-house
flame-grill
feateously
flat-footed
flagginess
frangipane
frangipani
fraughtage
flashlight
flashiness
flash-point
flash-board
flash-house
featherbed
feathering
fraxinella
flamingoes
Flamingant
flaminical
flagitious
frabjously
fearlessly
fragmental
fragmented
flaunching
flannelled
fearnought
flavorless
flavouring
flavorsome
flapperish
fratricide
flagrantly
fragrantly
fearsomely
frantic-mad
fractality
fractional
flattering
flatterous
flatulence
flatulency
flag-waving
fibrescope
fibreglass
fibreboard
fabricator
fibrillary
fibrillose
fibrillate
fibrillous
fibrinogen
febrifugal
fabulosity
fabulously
fibrositis
fibroblast
fiberscope
fiberglass
fiberboard
face-fungus
face-harden
facsimiled
facsimiles
factitious
fictitious
factionary
factionist
fictionist
factiously
facileness
fickleness
fecklessly
facilities
facilitate
facinorous
factorable
factorship
face-powder
face-saving
face-to-face
factuality
faceworker
fiducially
fiddleback
fiddle-back
fiddlehead
fadelessly
fiddlewood
federalise
federalism
federalist
federalize
federation
federative
fuddy-duddy
flea-beetle
freebooter
flea-bitten
fleeceless
fleechment
fierceness
fleece-wool
fieldwards
fieldpiece
freedwoman
freedwomen
fieldworks
fieldmouse
fieldboots
fiendishly
fieldstone
free-diving
foederatus
fremescent
frenetical
free-fooder
free-footed
free-for-all
free-fisher
fledgeling
freight-car
freightage
feed-heater
flesh-eater
freshwater
freeholder
fresh-blown
free-handed
fleshiness
fresherdom
flesh-brush
flesh-broth
foeticidal
foetidness
flexi-cover
flexihours
freakiness
freakishly
freeloader
free-labour
freelancer
feebleness
free-minded
free-market
freemartin
foetoscopy
fleur-de-lis
fleur-de-lys
fleeringly
free-school
free-soiler
free-select
free-spoken
freestyler
free-trader
fleetingly
frequenter
frequently
free-verser
fifty-pence
fifty-penny
fifty-fifty
figurehead
figuration
figurative
figurework
fugitation
fugitively
Fahrenheit
fricandeau
fricasseed
fair-boding
friability
flindersia
fringillid
fringeless
fairground
fair-headed
flight-deck
frightened
fair-haired
flightless
frithsoken
frightsome
frithstool
faithfully
fritillary
frigidness
flick-knife
friskingly
friskiness
fair-leader
fair-minded
friendlies
friendlily
friendless
friendship
frigorific
foisonless
flippantly
flimsiness
fair-spoken
faint-heart
flint-heart
flirtingly
feistiness
flintiness
frictional
flirtation
fairy-beads
fairy-money
fairy-stone
fairy-cycle
foliaceous
fallacious
full-bodied
filibuster
full-bottom
full-cocked
Filicineae
filicinean
full-circle
file-cutter
felicitate
felicitous
false-faced
filterable
fuliginous
full-handed
filchingly
filthiness
fulmineous
falling-off
falsidical
fulfilling
fulfilment
faldistory
follicular
falsifying
file-leader
full-length
folklorist
folk-memory
fellmonger
full-manned
fallow-chat
falcon-eyed
fellow-heir
fallowness
fellowship
filopodium
felspathic
filariasis
full-rigged
fellrunner
filtration
folk-speech
full-sailed
full-summed
folk-singer
folksiness
felt-tipped
full-voiced
fell-walker
full-winged
fimicolous
fumigation
fumigatory
familiarly
fumblingly
femaleness
familistic
feminality
feminility
femininely
femininism
femininity
feministic
fimbriated
famishment
fumatorium
famousness
fontanelle
fantastico
finicality
funiculate
fingerbowl
fingerhold
fingerhole
fingerling
fingerless
fingermark

Words marked △ may be spelled also with a capital letter

10 f□x□d

fingernail
fingerpost
finger's-end
fund-holder
fontinalis
fungicidal
fancifully
fonticulus
fantoccini
Finno-Ugric
fan-cricket
fen-cricket
△fenestella
fine-spoken
fenestrate
fanaticise
fanaticism
fanaticize
fine-tuning
finiteness
functional
fungus-gall
foolbegged
footbridge
Froebelian
footballer
Froebelism
flocculent
flocculate
flosculous
foot-candle
floodwater
floodlight
flood-plain
flower-bell
florescent
flower-girl
flower-head
flowerless
flower-show
△florentine
footguards
frothiness
frog-hopper
florilegia
florideous
frolicking
floridness
frolicsome
floristics
floribunda
flock-paper
foot-licker
footlights
frowningly
floppiness
foot-patrol
foot-racing
floorcloth
floorboard
flourished

frog's-march
frog's-mouth
frontwards
front-bench
front-wheel
frost-smoke
floatingly
floutingly
frostiness
frostbound
float-board
float-stone
floatation
foot-warmer
fore-and-aft
farrandine
ferrandine
forwarding
forsakenly
formaliter
forfaiting
formatting
fore-advise
foreboding
fire-blight
fire-basket
forebitter
forechosen
forecasted
forecaster
forecastle
forecourse
fore-damned
fer-de-lance
far-fetched
forfeuchen
fervescent
fortepiano
forcedness
forkedness
forbearant
forbearing
forgetting
forfeiture
forgettery
fermentive
forcefully
forefinger
forefather
foreground
foregather
forthright
fore-hammer
forehanded
forthgoing
forcipated
formicaria
farcically
forgivable
formidable
formidably

fornicator
forbidding
forcing-pit
far-sighted
fertiliser
fertilizer
ferniticle
fervidness
foreignism
fortissimo
forkit-tail
fortifying
formlessly
foraminous
fire-master
forinsecal
firing-step
fore-notice
furuncular
foreordain
fire-office
forfoughen
ferronière
ferro-alloy
farborough
ferrograms
ferro-print
furrow-weed
fire-policy
fire-plough
fore-quoted
fire-raiser
forerunner
foreshadow
forest-bred
forest-born
foreshewed
foreseeing
fire-shovel
foreshowed
firescreen
forest-tree
fernticled
ferntickle
first-aider
fork-tailed
foreteller
first-floor
first-class
first-fruit
foretaught
fortuitism
fortuitist
fortuitous
fire-walker
fire-warden
forty-niner
fernyticle
ferry-house
fustanella
fuss-budget

fusibility
fishburger
fish-carver
foster-home
fosterling
Fescennine
fesse-point
Fastens-eve
fish-finger
fish-farmer
fish-gutter
fast-handed
fascinator
fishing-rod
fastigiate
fastidious
fossicking
fashionist
fustianise
fustianist
fustianize
fasciation
fascicular
fisticuffs
fasciculus
fish-kettle
fish-ladder
fishmonger
fish-manure
fusionless
festoonery
fish-trowel
fatherhood
fetterlock
fatherlike
fatherland
fatherless
fetterless
fathership
fatiguable
fitting-out
fat-kidney'd
fatalistic
fathomable
fathometer
fathom-line
fathomless
fatbrained
futurology
futureless
futuristic
futurition
fatiscence
fettuccine
fitfulness
four-by-four
fourchette
four-colour
founderous
foundation
flugelhorn

flügelhorn
flutemouth
four-figure
fluffiness
four-footed
four-handed
four-inched
four-in-hand
fluvialist
fluxionary
fluxionist
Fourierism
fluviatile
flunkeydom
flunkeyish
flunkeyism
four-leafed
four-leaved
feuilleton
four-legged
four-letter
fluentness
four-o'clock
four-parted
four-poster
fluoridise
fluoridate
fluoridize
fluorinate
fluorotype
foudroyant
four-seater
foul-spoken
fourscorth
four-stroke
four-square
frustrated
fourteener
fourteenth
fruit-knife
faultiness
fruitarian
fruiteress
fourth-rate
fruitfully
five-eighth
fivefinger
five-finger
five-o'clock
five-parted
feverishly
favoritism
five-stones
five-square
favourable
favourably
favourless
fowling-net
fowl-plague
fixed-wheel
fixed-price

Words marked △ may be spelled also with a capital letter

10 f□x□e

fox-terrier
foxtrotted
fox-hunting
flycatcher
flypitcher
fly-fishing
fly-tipping
fly-flapper
faying-face
flyposting
fly-fronted
fly-dumping
fly-by-night
fizzenless
fazendeiro
fuzzy-wuzzy
granadilla
guaranteed
glauberite
gearchange
gear-change
glance-coal
glancingly
glauconite
granddaddy
giardiasis
grandmamma
glandiform
grandchild
grand-niece
glandulous
grand-uncle
guardhouse
glanderous
grandstand
grand-ducal
grave-maker
gravelling
graveolent
grape-louse
grapefruit
Gravettian
grapestone
gravestone
gracefully
gratefully
gravel-walk
graffitist
grangerise
Grangerism
grangerize
graphicacy
graphology
gnaphalium
graphemics
glad-hander
gnashingly
graphitoid
graphitise
graphitize
gravimeter

gravimetry
gramineous
gramicidin
glaciology
glacialist
gratillity
gradienter
graciosity
glaciation
gladiatory
graciously
gravity-fed
gratifying
goalkicker
goalkeeper
graplement
grammarian
grammatist
glasnostic
△gramophone
gramophony
granophyre
Glagolitic
graspingly
glass-faced
goatsucker
goat's-beard
goat's-thorn
goat-sallow
glass-cloth
gladsomely
glassiness
grassiness
glass-coach
glassworks
glasshouse
grass-roots
grasswrack
grass-green
grass-grown
graptolite
goal-tender
grant-in-aid
ghastfully
granulated
granulater
granularly
granulator
granulitic
gradualism
gradualist
graduality
granulomas
graduation
gratuitous
Glaswegian
goat-willow
Gibberella
gabblement
gobsmacked
gubernator

gabbroitic
gobstopper
God-fearing
gadolinite
gadolinium
gadrooning
godrooning
giddy-paced
grenadilla
gregarious
grey-coated
greediness
glendoveer
glebe-house
grey-headed
grey-haired
gleemaiden
Greenpeace
greenheart
greenshank
greenfinch
greenfield
greencloth
greenhouse
greenspeak
green-drake
greenstick
greenstuff
greenstone
greensward
Greco-Roman
greaseball
greaseband
gneissitic
guessingly
greasiness
greisenise
greisenize
gressorial
greasewood
great-niece
guest-night
great-uncle
guest-house
grey-wether
giftedness
gaff-rigged
goggle-eyed
gigglesome
gag-toothed
grindingly
grindstone
gripe-water
Ghibelline
guilefully
griffinish
griffinism
gaingiving
grith-stool
gridlocked
grisliness

grimlooked
grillsteak
guillotine
grille-work
glimmering
gliomatous
glissandos
gainstrive
gainsaying
guilty-like
grittiness
guiltiness
glistering
glitterand
glittering
glitterati
grievingly
grievously
glitziness
gilravager
goliardery
goliathise
goliathize
gallabiyah
galravitch
gilravitch
gallabiyeh
galvaniser
galvanizer
gold-beater
gold-digger
gold-end-man
gelder-rose
Gilbertian
Gilbertine
galley-worm
galley-west
galleryite
gallinazos
galliambic
goldilocks
galimatias
Gallomania
Gallophobe
Gallophile
galloglass
gallows-lee
goloptious
goluptious
gillravage
gelatinoid
gelatinise
gelatinate
gelatinous
gelatinize
gold-washer
gully-raker
gemmaceous
gymnasiums
gymnasiast
gymnastics

game-dealer
gimlet-eyed
gombeen-man
gambit-pawn
gamekeeper
gemologist
gaminesque
gemination
gambolling
gymnosophy
gymnosperm
gametangia
gamotropic
gem-cutting
genialness
genealogic
gangbuster
gynocratic
gonococcal
gonococcic
gonococcus
geniculate
gensdarmes
genderless
genteelise
genteelish
genteelism
genteelize
gander-moon
gingersnap
Ginkgoales
gentilesse
gunfighter
gingivitis
gangliated
gentlefolk
gangliform
gentlehood
ginglimoid
gunslinger
gentleness
ganglionic
gynandrism
gynandrous
gyniolatry
goniometer
goniometry
genophobia
gynophobia
gynophobic
gentrifier
gonorrheal
gonorrhoea
gonorrheic
generalled
generalise
generalist
generalate
generality
generalize
gangrenous

Words marked △ may be spelled also with a capital letter

generosity
generatrix
generation
generative
generously
Genesiacal
geneticist
genethliac
genitalial
genitively
gunrunning
genevrette
Genevanism
geoscience
gooneybird
groceteria
gooseberry
geotechnic
geodesical
geodetical
geomedical
glove-fight
gnoseology
grovelling
gooseflesh
glove-money
goosefoots
geometrise
geometrist
goose-grass
geometrize
geocentric
glomerular
goose-quill
glomerulus
goodfellow
good-father
grogginess
geophagism
geophagist
geophagous
geophilous
geochemist
good-humour
geothermal
geothermic
geophysics
Geodimeter®
growing-bag
gnosiology
Grobianism
gloriously
glorifying
goodlihead
goodlyhead
good-liking
growlingly
goodliness
good-looker
ghoulishly
gloominess
good-morrow
good-mother
groundbait
ground-bass
ground-dove
groundedly
ground-hold
groundling
groundless
groundmass
groundplot
groundprox
groundsman
geognostic
groundsell
groundsill
good-nature
groundwork
geological
geoponical
gnomonical
gnotobiote
googolplex
geographer
geographic
geotropism
glossology
glossiness
glossarial
glossarist
good-sister
Gnosticise
Gnosticism
Gnosticize
glottidean
glottology
gloatingly
ghost-write
geostatics
grotto-work
globularly
geodynamic
goody-goody
gypsophila
gap-toothed
garlandage
gormandise
gormandism
gormandize
garbageman
geriatrics
geriatrist
△gargantuan
gyrocopter
gor-bellied
garnet-rock
garmenture
gorgeously
girlfriend
germinable
garnishing
germicidal
garnierite
gerundival
gorgoneion
gargoylism
garrotting
Gorgonzola
gyrostatic
garishness
gyroscopic
gyrational
Gorbymania
gestaltism
Gestaltist
gospellise
gospellize
gasteropod
gashliness
gasometric
Gesundheit
gasconader
gas-bracket
gastrology
gastralgia
gastronome
gastronomy
Gastropoda
gastrosoph
gastrotomy
gas-furnace
gas-guzzler
gut-scraper
Guttiferae
gate-keeper
gate-legged
get-up-and-go
gutturally
glumaceous
glutaminic
gourdiness
gauffering
grudgingly
gauging-rod
glucosuria
glucosuric
grumpiness
gruesomely
Grubstreet
gauntleted
gaultheria
gruntingly
gluttonise
gluttonish
gluttonous
gluttonize
gaudy-night
gaudy-green
governance
governable
governante
governessy
△government
gay-bashing
glycogenic
glycosidic
glycosuria
glycosuric
glycolysis
glycolytic
glyptodont
glyoxaline
head-bummer
head-banger
headcheese
head-centre
heaven-bred
heaven-born
heaven-sent
heavenward
hoar-headed
head-hugger
headhunter
heathendom
heathenise
heathenish
heathenism
heathenize
heath-poult
hearing-aid
head-lugged
headmaster
hyalomelan
hyalophane
hyaloplasm
headphones
headsheets
hearse-like
hoarseness
head-stream
heatstroke
headstrong
headsquare
heartwater
healthcare
heartsease
heart's-ease
head-to-head
heart-whole
heart-throb
heart-block
heart-blood
healthless
heartiness
heart-spoon
heartbreak
heart-grief
healthsome
heart-quake
headworker
heavy-laden
heavy-armed
Hebraicism
Hebraistic
hybridiser
hybridizer
Hobbianism
hobble-bush
habiliment
hobblingly
habilatory
habilitate
hebdomadal
hebdomadar
hebdomader
hobjobbing
hobnobbing
hibernacle
habit-maker
habitually
habit-cloth
habitation
hebetation
habitaunce
hobby-horse
hackbuteer
hectically
huckle-bone
hackmatack
hackneyman
hectometre
hectolitre
hectograph
hectorship
hectostere
hocus-pocus
huckstress
hydrazides
hydraulics
hydragogue
hodden-grey
hiddenmost
hiddenness
hodgepodge
hydrically
hidalgoish
hidalgoism
hedonistic
hydromancy
hydropathy
hydromania
hydrotaxis
hydroscope
hydrometer
hydrometry
hydrotheca
hydrophily
hydrophane
hydrophone
hydrochore
hydrophyte
hydroplane
hydrosomal
hydropower

10 h□d□o

hydrosomes
hydrologic
hydroponic
hydropolyp
hydrospace
hydrograph
hydrolysis
hydrolytic
hoddy-doddy
hierarchal
hierarchic
haematinic
hiera-picra
haematosis
hye-battel'd
Haemanthus
haematuria
heedlessly
hieromancy
hierolatry
hieroscopy
hyetometer
hierophant
hieroglyph
haemoconia
hierologic
hierocracy
hierograph
hyetograph
haemolysis
haemolytic
Hieronymic
highbinder
high-energy
hug-me-tight
highermost
high-flying
high-heeled
hog-cholera
high-handed
highjacker
high-kilted
highlights
△**highlander**
hegemonial
high-minded
hegemonism
hegemonist
high-necked
hogen-mogen
hagiolater
hagiolatry
hagioscope
hygroscope
hygrometer
hygrometry
hygrophobe
hygrochasy
hygrophyte
hagiologic
hagiocracy

hygrograph
high-octane
high-placed
high-priced
high-reared
high-raised
high-roller
high-ranker
high-street
high-strung
high-souled
high-tasted
high-vacuum
highwayman
higry-pigry
hail-fellow
hair-pencil
hair-powder
hair-raiser
hairstreak
hairspring
hair-waving
hoity-toity
Hakenkreuz
hokey-pokey
heliacally
hullabaloo
Hollandish
hallalling
half-a-dozen
half-a-crown
Helianthus
hellbender
halobiotic
half-cocked
helicoidal
Heliconian
helicopter
halocarbon
hill-digger
half-dollar
half-duplex
holodiscus
halberdier
halfe-horsy
halieutics
halleluiah
hallelujah
holoenzyme
holography
halogenate
halogenous
holohedral
holohedron
half-hunter
half-hourly
helminthic
half-kirtle
half-length
helplessly
holing-pick

heliolater
heliotaxis
heliolatry
helioscope
heliometer
hollow-eyed
heliophyte
Haliotidae
hollowness
heliograph
heliotrope
heliotropy
halloysite
hollow-ware
heliotypic
holophotal
holophrase
halophytic
holophytic
holosteric
heli-skiing
holus-bolus
half-sister
hylotheism
hylotheist
hylotomous
half-volley
hillwalker
halfwitted
half-yearly
hylozoical
Himyaritic
hemianopia
homoblasty
hump-backed
home-brewed
hemicrania
hemocyanin
hemicyclic
homocyclic
home-coming
Hemichorda
homocercal
homochromy
humidifier
humidistat
hamadryads
hammer-fish
hammerhead
hammerlock
hammerless
homoeomery
homoerotic
hammer-pond
homoeopath
homogamous
homogenise
homogenate
homogenous
homogenize
hemoglobin

hamshackle
hemihedral
hemihedron
humming-top
humiliator
homologise
homologate
homologous
homologize
homaloidal
humblingly
homeliness
humbleness
homiletics
hemangioma
homonymity
homonymous
humaneness
humanistic
humanities
hemp-nettle
homuncular
homunculus
homeopathy
homeomeric
homeomorph
homoousian
homoplasmy
hemipteral
hemipteran
hemiplegia
hemiplegic
hemophilia
homophobia
homophobic
homophonic
hemoptysis
humgruffin
hemorrhage
hemorrhoid
Homorelaps
humoralism
humoralist
humoristic
humoresque
humorously
hemostasis
hemostatic
hamesucken
home-signal
hemisphere
homosexual
homothally
hematocrit
hematocele
hematology
homotonous
hemitropal
hemitropic
home-thrust
homotaxial

Homburg-hat
hamburgher
humbugging
humdudgeon
humbuggery
humourless
humoursome
homeworker
homozygote
hemizygous
homozygous
hansardise
hansardize
hen-harrier
hand-barrow
hand-basket
hinderance
hendecagon
henpeckery
hanselling
hinderland
hinderlans
hinderlins
hinterland
hindermost
handedness
hinge-bound
hinge-joint
henceforth
hen-hearted
hang-glider
hand-gallop
henchwoman
henchwomen
hunting-cap
hunting-cat
hunting-box
hunting-cog
huntiegowk
hand-in-hand
handicraft
handicuffs
hand-lotion
hand-me-down
handmaiden
honorarium
honor-guard
handstaves
handstaffs
hony-suckle
handselled
handsomely
hand-screen
handspring
hand-sewing
henotheism
henotheist
hand-to-hand
△**honourable**
honourably
honourless

Words marked △ may be spelled also with a capital letter

honours-man
Hindustani
Hanoverian
hand-weeded
handworked
handy-dandy
honey-eater
hanky-panky
honey-wagon
honey-chile
honey-mouse
honeymonth
honey-crock
honey-stalk
honey-stone
honeybunch
honey-guide
honey-sweet
hootananny
Hyoscyamus
hootenanny
hookedness
hoodie-crow
hyoplastra
hootnannie
hoots-toots
heortology
heptarchic
Heptandria
Heptateuch
heptameter
Heptameron
heptachlor
heptathlon
heptachord
hop-sacking
heptagonal
heptapodic
heptatonic
hypnagogic
Heptagynia
hypabyssal
hypocritic
hypocentre
hypocorism
hypodermal
hypodorian
hypodermic
hypodermis
hyphenated
hypaethral
hypaethron
hippety-hop
hypogaeous
hypogynous
hopping-mad
hupaithric
hippiatric
hop-bitters
hypolydian
hypalgesia
hypalgesic
hopelessly
hypanthium
hippomanes
hippocampi
hypnoidise
hypnoidize
hypsometer
hypnogenic
hypsometry
hippophobe
hypsophobe
hippophagy
hippophile
hypsophyll
hypnotiser
hypnotizer
hypnogogic
hippogriff
hippodrome
Hippocrene
hippogryph
hypoplasia
hypophyses
hypophysis
hyperbaric
hyperbatic
hypermania
hypermanic
hyperbaton
hyperacute
hyperaemia
hyperaemic
hop-trefoil
hyperbolas
hyperfocal
hyperbolic
hypergolic
hypersonic
hypertonic
hyperspace
hyperdulia
hypostases
hypostasis
hypostatic
hypostress
hypotactic
hypotheses
hypothesis
hypothetic
hepatology
hypotenuse
hip-huggers
hippuritic
hypoxaemia
hypoxaemic
harman-beck
herbaceous
herbariums
hereabouts
Herbartian
hardbacked
hornblende
hard-boiled
hard-billed
herb-bennet
hurlbarrow
hard-bitten
Heracleian
Heraclidan
△hyracoidea
hirudinean
hirudinoid
hirudinous
hereditary
hereditist
horse-faced
horse-tamer
horselaugh
horrendous
horse-leech
hartebeest
horseshoer
horse-thief
hermetical
horse-rider
horseflesh
horse-cloth
horse-gowan
horse-woman
horse-coper
horsepower
horned-pout
horse-bread
hard-earned
harvestman
harvest-fly
harvest-bug
Herrenvolk
horn-footed
hard-fisted
hard-fought
horography
herb-garden
hard-gotten
hard-headed
hard-handed
heroically
hermit-crab
hartie-hale
herbicidal
hermitical
heroicness
horridness
heroi-comic
herniotomy
horrifying
herald-duck
horologist
△horologium
hare-lipped
hurdle-race
heraldship
harmlessly
hurtlessly
Herrnhuter
haranguing
heriotable
harmonical
harmoniser
harmonizer
harmonicon
harmonious
harpooneer
harpoon-gun
harbour-bar
harbourage
hard-pushed
herb-Robert
hard-riding
horn-rimmed
heresiarch
harassedly
heresy-hunt
haruspical
haruspices
harassment
horoscopic
hereticate
heretofore
heritrices
heritrixes
harquebuse
harquebuss
harpy-eagle
hirdy-girdy
hurryingly
hurdy-gurdy
hurly-burly
horizontal
husbandman
husbandage
hysteresis
hysteretic
hysterical
Hesperides
hysteritis
hystericky
hostelling
hospitaler
hospitable
hospitably
histiocyte
husking-bee
histiology
histogenic
historical
histoblast
histologic
histolysis
histolytic
histrionic
hesitantly
hesitation
hesitatory
hesitative
hetmanship
hithermost
hitherside
hetherward
hitherward
hitch-hiker
hotchpotch
hot-livered
hot-blooded
hate-monger
hit-and-miss
hot-dogging
hot-cockles
hot-working
hot-mouthed
Hitopadesa
heterocont
Heterocera
heterodont
heterodyne
heterodoxy
heterogamy
heterogeny
heterogony
hot-brained
heterokont
heterology
heteronomy
Heteropoda
heterotaxy
hateworthy
hitty-missy
heulandite
hour-circle
hounds-foot
house-party
houselling
housebound
housecraft
house-proud
heuristics
houts-touts
haustellum
hauntingly
haustorium
hoveringly
hover-mower
hovercraft
hovertrain
hawk-beaked
hawk-billed
hawser-laid
Howleglass
howsomever
how-do-you-do
hawksbeard
hexactinal
hexaëmeron

10 h□x□g

hexagynian
hexagynous
hexahedral
hexahedron
hexamerous
hexametric
hexandrian
hexandrous
hexaplaric
hoydenhood
hay-de-guyes
hey-de-guyes
hay-de-guise
hey-de-guise
hazardable
inadaptive
inaccuracy
inaccurate
isabelline
inadequacy
inadequate
ilang-ilang
inaugurate
imaginable
imaginably
imaginings
Italianise
Italianism
Italianist
Italianate
Italianize
inamoratas
inamoratos
inapposite
inappetent
inartistic
inaptitude
inactively
inactivate
inactivity
iracundity
imbibition
imbecility
inbreeding
inbringing
imbroccata
imbroglios
imbruement
incrassate
incubation
incubatory
incubative
incidental
incedingly
increscent
inclemency
incredible
incredibly
increasing
incognitos
incogitant
incoherent
inclinable
inculpable
inculpably
inculcator
incompared
incumbency
incomplete
incomposed
incantator
incunables
incunabula
incandesce
incendiary
incinerate
inconstant
inchoately
inchoation
inchoative
incapacity
incipience
incipiency
Incaparina
incurvated
incurrable
incurrence
incoronate
incorporal
incessancy
incisiform
incasement
incisorial
incestuous
incisively
incitement
incitingly
incitation
incitative
includable
ischuretic
includible
incautious
incivility
inductance
indictable
indicolite
indocility
indictment
inducement
indecently
indecorous
indecision
indecisive
indication
indicatory
indicative
indwelling
indefinite
indignance
Indigofera
indigolite
indigently
indigenise
indigenous
indigenize
indigested
indagation
indagatory
indagative
indelicacy
indelicate
indulgence
indulgency
indolently
indumentum
iodometric
Indonesian
indentures
indapamide
indirectly
induration
indurative
indistinct
indisposed
industrial
indiscreet
indiscrete
inditement
individual
individuum
indexation
inerasable
inerasably
Iceland-dog
inerasible
inerasibly
inesculent
inelegance
inelegancy
inefficacy
ideography
inevitable
inevitably
irenically
ineligible
ineligibly
inexistant
inexistent
ice-skating
ideologist
idealistic
inexorable
inexorably
ineloquent
inexpiable
inexpiably
inexplicit
idempotent
icebreaker
identified
identifier
inextended
ideational
isentropic
ineptitude
ineducable
inequality
irefulness
inequation
inflatable
infeasible
infraposed
infrasonic
infrasound
infragrant
infraction
infrahuman
infibulate
infectious
infidelity
inflexible
inflexibly
inflection
inflective
infrequent
infeftment
infighting
in-fighting
infliction
inflictive
infelicity
infallible
infallibly
infiltrate
infamonise
infamonize
infamously
infanthood
infinitude
infinitely
infinitant
infinitary
infinitate
infinitive
infirmarer
infernally
inferrable
informally
inferrible
infirmness
inferiorly
infarction
infusorial
infusorian
infatuated
influenzal
ingrateful
ingratiate
ingle-cheek
ingredient
ingression
ingressive
ingeminate
ingenerate
inglorious
ingestible
Ishmaelite
inhabitant
inhibition
inhibitory
inhibitive
ichthyosis
ichthyotic
inhalation
inhumanely
inhumanity
inhumation
inherently
inharmonic
inheritrix
iridaceous
itinerancy
iridescent
iridectomy
Irishwoman
inimically
inimitable
inimitably
initialled
initialing
initialise
initialize
initiation
initiatory
initiative
idiolectal
idiolectic
iridosmine
iridosmium
idiopathic
imipramine
idiot-proof
iniquitous
injectable
injudicial
injunction
injunctive
ink-slinger
ink-stained
ill-matched
ill-natured
Illecebrum
illocution
ill-advised
ill-behaved
ill-defined
illegalise
illegality
illegalize
Islamicise
Islamicist
Islamicize
illuminant
illuminism

Words marked △ may be spelled also with a capital letter

10 i□t□m

illuminist
illuminate
△illuminati
ill-looking
ill-founded
illaqueate
illustrate
illusively
illiteracy
ill-starred
illiterate
illatively
illaudable
illaudably
immeasured
immobilise
immobilism
immobility
immobilize
immaculacy
△**immaculate**
immoderacy
immoderate
immodestly
iambically
Ismailitic
immolation
immemorial
immunoblot
immunology
immanental
imminently
immanation
imminution
immortally
immortelle
inmarriage
immoralism
immoralist
immorality
immurement
immeritous
immiscible
immiserise
immiserize
immaterial
immaturely
immaturity
immoveable
immovables
ignobility
innocently
innuendoes
innominate
innumeracy
ignimbrite
innumerate
innumerous
ignipotent
ignorantly
ignoration
ionosphere
ionisation
innutrient
innateness
innovation
innovatory
innovative
ionization
Icosandria
isogametic
icosahedra
idolatress
idolatrise
idolatrous
idolatrize
inosculate
inordinacy
inordinate
inoperable
inoperably
isoleucine
isogenetic
inobedient
isometrics
isoseismal
isoseismic
iron-fisted
iron-glance
isocheimal
isocheimic
iron-handed
isochronal
isothermal
isochasmic
iconically
ironically
isokinetic
isoniazide
iron-liquor
isoglossal
isoglottal
isoglottic
ironmonger
isoaminile
iron-mining
ironmaster
isoantigen
iconolater
iconomachy
iconomatic
iconolatry
iconoscope
iconometer
iconometry
iconoclasm
iconoclast
idoloclast
isomorphic
isosporous
isotropism
isotropous
Isoetaceae
isopterous
inoculable
inoculator
iron-willed
iron-worded
iron-witted
isodynamic
ivory-black
isocyanide
implacable
implacably
impeccancy
impeccable
impeccably
impictured
impudicity
impediment
impudently
impeditive
impresario
impregnant
impregnate
impression
impressure
impressive
implexuous
impugnable
impugnment
impugation
imprimatur
implicitly
impairment
impuissant
imprinting
impalpable
impalpably
impaludism
impalement
impolitely
impendence
impendency
impenitent
impanation
improbable
improbably
improvable
improvably
implorator
improperly
improviser
imparlance
importance
importancy
impartable
imperially
importable
imparadise
impartible
impartibly
impervious
imperilled
impartment
impureness
impersonal
imperative
importuner
impassable
impassably
imposthume
impassible
impassibly
impossible
imposingly
impishness
imposition
impostumed
impatience
impotently
imputation
imputative
impoundage
imprudence
impoverish
inquirendo
inquilinic
inquisitor
inquietude
irradiance
irradiancy
irradicate
Israelitic
irrigation
irrigative
irreligion
irrelation
irrelative
irrelevant
irremeable
irremeably
irrenowned
irresolute
irrational
irritation
irritative
irreverent
installant
installing
instalment
inspanning
instantial
insobriety
insociable
insecurely
insecurity
inspection
inspective
insufflate
insightful
inspirable
inspirator
instigator
instilling
instilment
inspissate
instituter
institutes
institutor
insolvable
insolvably
insultable
insolidity
insolvency
inselberge
insultment
insolently
insulinase
insularism
insularity
insolation
insulation
insalutary
insalivate
insomnious
inseminate
insinuator
insensible
insensibly
insentient
insaneness
insanitary
insensuous
insipidity
insipience
inseparate
insertable
instructor
insurgence
insurgency
instrument
insurancer
insistence
insistency
insatiable
insatiably
insouciant
insoulment
intradoses
intramural
intubation
intactness
intrepidly
integrable
integrally
integrator
integument
intrigante
intriguant
intriguing
intolerant
intimidate
intemerate
intimately

Words marked △ may be spelled also with a capital letter

10 i□t□m

intimation
intendance
intendancy
intendedly
intangible
intangibly
intentions
intendment
intoningly
intentness
intenerate
intinction
intonation
iatrogenic
introspect
introrsely
introducer
intercalar
interramal
interlaced
internally
intermarry
interfaith
interregal
interceder
interferer
interreges
intervener
interregna
interferon
intervenor
interleave
interweave
intermezzi
intermezzo
interchain
interphone
interphase
intertidal
intervital
interplead
interclude
interplant
internment
interunion
intermodal
internodal
interpolar
interposal
interzonal
interloper
interposer
interiorly
interwound
intervolve
interspace
interurban
intergrade
interbreed
intertrigo
interbrain
intercross
intergrown
interested
internship
interstice
interstate
interlunar
intertwine
intertwist
intestinal
intestines
intoxicant
intoxicate
inurbanely
inurbanity
inundation
inuredness
invocation
invocatory
invigilate
invaginate
invigorant
invigorate
invaluable
invaluably
involucral
involucrum
invaliding
invalidism
invalidate
invalidity
involution
inventable
invendible
inventible
invincible
invincibly
inventress
inviolated
inviolable
inviolably
invariance
invariable
invariably
inveracity
invertedly
invisibles
investment
invitement
invitingly
inveteracy
inveterate
invitation
invitatory
inwardness
ivy-mantled
jabberwock
jubilantly
jubilation
job-hopping
Jack-a-dandy
jackanapes
Jacobinise
Jacobinism
Jacobinize
jackbooted
Jacobethan
Jacobitism
jockeyship
jackhammer
jocularity
jaculation
jaculatory
jocundness
Jack-priest
jack-rabbit
jack-rafter
jocoseness
jack-straws
Jacky-Jacky
judicially
judication
judicatory
judicature
judicative
Judaically
judgmental
Judenhetze
jaguarondi
jaguarundi
jigger-mast
jaggedness
△**juggernaut**
jiggety-jog
jugglingly
Jugendstil
Johnny-cake
Johnsonian
Johnsonese
Johnsonism
Jehovistic
jeistiecor
jointuress
joint-stock
joint-stool
jejuneness
jolterhead
July-flower
jellygraph
jamahiriya
jumping-off
jump-jockey
jumblingly
jumhouriya
jimson-weed
Jamesonite
juncaceous
junk-bottle
junk-dealer
junketings
jinrikisha
jinricksha
jingoistic
Janus-faced
janitorial
janizarian
jeopardise
jeopardous
jeopardize
jippi-jappa
japan-earth
Japanesery
Japanesque
jerked-meat
jerkinhead
jardinière
jargonelle
jury-rudder
jury-rigged
juristical
jerry-built
jasperware
jaspideous
Jesuitical
justiciary
just-in-time
justifying
jostlement
jet-setting
journal-box
journalese
journalise
journalism
journalist
journalize
journeyman
journeying
jouysaunce
jauntiness
jovialness
javelin-man
Juvenalian
juvenilely
juvenility
jovysaunce
Jew-baiting
jewel-house
Jew's-myrtle
jaw-breaker
jaw-crusher
Jewishness
jaw-twister
jaywalking
joyfulness
joyousness
knap-bottle
knave-bairn
klangfarbe
knagginess
knackiness
knackwurst
kibbutznik
kack-handed
kicksorter
kidnapping
kidney-bean
kiddiewink
kidologist
klendusity
kieselguhr
keeperless
keepership
khediviate
knee-length
klebsiella
knee-timber
Kafkaesque
kaffir-boom
knife-money
knife-point
knife-board
kaisership
kriegspiel
Krishnaism
knighthood
knightless
knick-knack
knickpoint
khidmutgar
khitmutgar
Kilmarnock
kilogramme
Keltomania
kimberlite
kempery-man
kymography
king-at-arms
king-archon
kennel-coal
kennelling
kennel-maid
kingfisher
kinchin-lay
Kensington
Kentish-man
Kentish-rag
Kantianism
kinglihood
kindliness
kingliness
kinematics
king-of-arms
kenspeckle
kenophobia
king's-chair
kind-spoken
king's-spear
kinesipath
kenoticist
kookaburra
knobbiness
kaolinitic
kaolinosis
Kuomintang

Words marked △ may be spelled also with a capital letter

knockabout
knock-kneed
knobkerrie
knockwurst
klootchman
knottiness
Karmathian
kersantite
kirn-dollie
kerseymere
kerygmatic
kerchiefed
kerb-market
karyoplasm
karyolysis
karyotypic
karyolymph
kerb-trader
keratinise
keratinous
keratinize
keratotomy
kerb-vendor
katabolism
kitten-moth
kite-flying
kitchen-fee
kitchendom
kettledrum
kettle-pins
kittle-pins
kite-marked
△krugerrand
knuckle-bow
keyboarder
lead-arming
leaf-bridge
leaf-cutter
leaderette
leadenness
leadership
loan-holder
loathingly
leaf-hopper
leathering
leaf-insect
leafleteer
leafletted
leafleting
loadmaster
leaf-mosaic
loan-office
lead-pencil
leaf-sheath
leaf-spring
leastaways
lean-witted
libecchios
libidinist
libidinous
librettist
lobe-footed
lubricator
lubricious
lobulation
Lebensraum
liberalise
liberalism
liberalist
liberality
liberalize
liberation
laboratory
liberatory
liberty-man
lobotomise
lobotomize
lobster-pot
laboursome
lackadaisy
lucubrator
lactescent
Lycaenidae
lucifugous
Luciferian
luciferase
luciferous
lacrimator
locking-nut
lectionary
lock-keeper
loculament
luculently
lackluster
lucklessly
lacklustre
locomobile
locomotion
locomotory
locomotive
laciniated
licensable
laconicism
licentiate
licentious
Lychnapsia
lactoscope
lactometer
lactogenic
laccolitic
lectorship
△lycopodium
lace-pillow
Lacertilia
lachrymals
lachrymary
lachrymose
laceration
lacerative
Locustidae
lockstitch
lacustrine
locateable
lacquering
lacrymator
lucky-piece
ladder-back
ledger-bait
ledger-line
ladieswear
lady-killer
lederhosen
lady's-smock
leechcraft
lieutenant
laeotropic
lherzolite
life-estate
left-footed
left-footer
life-giving
left-handed
left-hander
luffing-jib
life-jacket
lifelessly
life-mortar
life-rocket
life-renter
life-saving
life-tenant
left-winger
leftwardly
luggage-van
lugubrious
legibility
logicality
laggen-gird
loggerhead
logography
lignifying
legalistic
ligamental
leguminous
loganberry
lageniform
logan-stone
lignocaine
log-rolling
logopedics
logopaedic
logorrhoea
logarithms
legislator
logistical
light-faced
light-table
light-tight
light-o'-love
legitimacy
legitimise
legitimism
legitimist
legitimate
legitimize
lightening
lighting-up
light-tower
lighthouse
lighterman
light-organ
light-armed
lighterage
light-proof
legateship
leg-pulling
leishmania
Leibnizian
leiotrichy
leisurable
leisurably
likelihood
likeliness
lake-lawyer
like-minded
lukewarmly
lukewarmth
Lollardism
liliaceous
loll-shraub
lumbang-oil
Limnaeidae
Lammas-tide
lamp-burner
lime-burner
limaciform
limacology
limicolous
lambdacism
lambdoidal
lumber-camp
lumberjack
lumber-mill
limber-neck
lumber-room
lumbersome
lumpectomy
lumber-yard
limb-girdle
lymphocyte
lymphogram
lymphokine
lampholder
lemniscate
limpidness
lamellated
lamentable
lamentably
laminarian
laminarise
lemon-grass
luminarism
luminarist
laminarize
luminosity
lamination
lumination
luminously
lampoonery
lampoonist
lumbricoid
Lemuroidea
Lamarckian
Lamarckism
lambrequin
lamb's-tails
lumpsucker
limitrophe
limitarian
limitation
limitative
limburgite
lentamente
Lancashire
landammann
longaevous
linebacker
land-breeze
land-bridge
lenocinium
linseed-oil
Langerhans
lanceolate
lanternist
laniferous
line-fisher
lanuginose
lanuginous
lanigerous
long-headed
lunch-table
long-haired
landholder
land-hunger
landing-net
lentigines
lentivirus
lentissimo
lenticular
land-jobber
lanzknecht
land-lubber
land-locked
long-legged
loneliness
land-louper
land-mining
link-motion
land-owning
lincomycin
longprimer
land-pirate
lansquenet
long-staple
Landsthing

Words marked △ may be spelled also with a capital letter

10 l□n□s

lonesomely
land-spring
line-squall
long-termer
lengthsman
lengthwise
lengthways
Lingulella
linguiform
languorous
languished
languisher
linguister
linguistic
linguistry
land-values
land-waiter
long-winded
Lyon-at-arms
leopard-cat
leopardess
lyophilise
lyophilize
lion-hunter
looking-for
leontiasis
Laplandish
lipochrome
lapidified
lepidolite
lapidarian
lapidarist
lapidation
lip-reading
lappet-head
leprechaun
leprechawn
lapper-milk
lip-service
lipography
Lippizaner
Lippizzana
lipomatous
leproserie
lophophore
lap-jointed
leptosomic
Leptospira
Lupercalia
laparotomy
Lipizzaner
loquacious
liquescent
liquefying
liquidator
liquidiser
liquidizer
liquidness
lardaceous
lorication
large-scale
lark-heeled
larghettos
larvicidal
lordliness
laryngitic
laryngitis
lordolatry
lust-dieted
listenable
listener-in
lysigenous
lascivious
lesbianism
lusciously
loss-leader
listlessly
last-minute
Lysenkoism
lissomness
lustreless
lustration
lustrously
lustreware
Lusitanian
lethargied
lethargise
lethargize
letter-bomb
letter-book
latter-born
letter-clip
letter-card
letter-file
letterhead
letterless
litter-lout
latter-mint
lattermost
lattermath
littermate
letter-wood
latifundia
litigation
latticinio
Lithistida
little-ease
littleness
litany-desk
lithomancy
lithomarge
litholatry
lithophane
lithophysa
lithophyse
lithophyte
lithoglyph
lithoclast
lithologic
lithotomic
Lithodomus
lithoprint
lithograph
lithotrite
lithotrity
Lythraceae
liturgical
literalise
literalism
literalist
laterality
literality
literalize
literarily
literosity
literation
literature
lotus-eater
latescence
lutestring
latitation
Lithuanian
lauraceous
launcegaye
laundrette
laurdalite
Laundromat®
loundering
laundry-man
louver-door
leukemogen
Laurentian
laureation
loungingly
leuchaemia
loudhailer
laughingly
louping-ill
loud-lunged
leucopenia
leukopenia
leucoderma
leukoderma
leucoblast
leucoplast
leukoblast
leukoplast
leucocytic
leukocytic
louvre-door
Louis-Seize
laurustine
loud-voiced
laurvikite
livability
love-broker
love-favour
levigation
livelihead
lovelihead
livelihood
lavallière
liveliness
loveliness
love-letter
lovemaking
love-monger
lovingness
living-room
love-potion
lever-watch
lover's-knot
laverbread
liver-grown
leviration
liverwurst
lavishment
lavishness
lavatorial
lovat-green
levitation
loveworthy
lovey-dovey
law-abiding
lawrencium
low-tension
Lawrentian
law-officer
low-pitched
low-country
law-breaker
low-profile
lower-class
loweringly
lawfulness
law-burrows
lexicology
loxodromic
lexigraphy
luxuriance
luxuriancy
ley-farming
lazarettos
meandering
meaningful
measliness
meal-monger
miasmatous
miarolitic
meagreness
meatscreen
myasthenia
myasthenic
measurable
measurably
measuredly
mobocratic
Mabinogion
Maccabaean
mechanical
Michaelmas
mace-bearer
macadamise
macadamize
mucedinous
muciferous
mock-heroic
machinator
machineman
machinegun
mackintosh
mycologist
maculation
maculature
muck-midden
mock-modest
maconochie
meconopses
meconopsis
microfarad
mucronated
mock-orange
△macrozamia
macrofauna
microfauna
macrocarpa
microscale
microscope
microscopy
micrometer
micrometre
micrometry
microseism
macrophage
microphone
microphyte
microfiche
microlight
microlitic
macrobiota
macrobiote
microbiota
microskirt
microcline
macroflora
microflora
microsomal
microtonal
micrococci
micrologic
micropolis
microtomic
macrospore
microspore
microprobe
microcrack
microprint
micrograph
macroprism
microprism
microburst
micropylar
macrocycle
mycoplasma
mock-privet

Words marked △ may be spelled also with a capital letter

10 m□n□g

mycorrhiza
mycorhizal
muck-raking
Mucorineae
macaronics
macaronies
maceration
mica-schist
muckspread
mycetology
mycetozoan
mediagenic
mediatress
mediastina
medicalise
medicalize
medicament
medicaster
medication
medicative
medievally
midden-cock
madder-lake
madreporic
Midwestern
modifiable
midshipman
midnightly
midfielder
medullated
middle-aged
middlebrow
muddlehead
middlemost
Madelenian
mudslinger
modularity
modalistic
meddlesome
modulation
madonnaish
mudlogging
mid-morning
mediocrity
madbrained
moderniser
modernizer
modernness
moderatrix
moderately
moderation
moderatism
medusiform
modishness
midi-system
meditation
meditative
medium-term
mnemonical
myeloblast
meerschaum

muffin-bell
mafficking
mefloquine
migraineur
migrainous
magnetical
magnetiser
magnetizer
magnifical
Magnificat
magnifying
△magellanic
megalosaur
megalithic
magi-marker
meganewton
mignonette
megaphonic
megaparsec
megascopic
magistracy
magistrand
magistrate
mightiness
mugwumpery
Muhammadan
Mahommedan
Mohammedan
Muhammedan
Mahayanist
maidenhead
maidenhair
maidenhood
maidenlike
maiden-meek
maimedness
maidenweed
meiofaunal
mainlander
mainlining
maisonette
mainpernor
mainstream
mainspring
maintained
maintainer
moisturise
moisturize
mujaheddin
majestical
majuscular
make-belief
makunouchi
make-weight
mallanders
malvaceous
meliaceous
molybdenum
molybdosis
Malabar-rat
malacology

melaconite
melic-grass
mile-castle
melicotton
melocotoon
maledicent
maladapted
maladdress
malodorous
mallee-bird
mallenders
malleiform
mallee-fowl
millesimal
millefiori
millennial
millennium
muliebrity
millet-seed
malfeasant
malleation
maleficial
maleficent
malefactor
malignance
malignancy
malaguetta
malignment
molehunter
Malthusian
multifaced
multimedia
millimetre
melting-pot
Malpighian
multiphase
millilitre
mollitious
multivious
multiplied
multiplier
multiplane
millionary
multipolar
multivocal
multilobed
multiloquy
mulligrubs
multi-track
multigrade
multi-stage
multistory
multicycle
mollifying
malo-lactic
melomaniac
moliminous
melanocyte
malentendu
malingerer
melanaemia

melancholy
molendinar
melanomata
Melanesian
melanistic
mylonitise
mylonitize
meliorator
mileometer
Mallophaga
mellophone
mellowness
millocracy
malcontent
multocular
malapropos
malapertly
melismatic
mulishness
mild-spoken
mill-stream
militiaman
militantly
militarily
militarise
militarism
militarist
mulattress
militarize
molluscoid
molluscous
malevolent
millwright
malaxation
Malayalaam
membership
mammectomy
mimography
mumping-day
mummifying
mamillated
mumblement
mumblingly
mumble-news
mammogenic
mammograph
mimeograph
Mumbo-Jumbo
mumbo-jumbo
membranous
memorandum
memorative
Mimosaceae
mammy-wagon
mummy-wheat
mummy-cloth
manna-larch
maniacally
mangabeira
man-machine
manzanilla

mendacious
Montagnard
manna-grass
manna-croup
mandamuses
minibudget
mini-budget
montbretia
mini-buffet
mind-bender
Manichaean
monochasia
monocratic
monocyclic
Manicheism
monactinal
monoclinal
monoclinic
monoculous
menacingly
monoclonal
monocarpic
monochroic
monochrome
monochromy
manicurist
monocerous
monadiform
menu-driven
monadology
monkey-boat
monkey-gaff
montelimar
monoecious
montero-cap
monkey-pump
monkey-rail
monkey-rope
monkey-suit
manteltree
monkey-tail
Montezuma's
manoeuvrer
manoeuvres
man-servant
munificent
munifience
manifolder
many-folded
manifoldly
mini-floppy
manifestly
manifestos
monography
manageable
manageably
management
monogamist
monogamous
monogynian
monogenism

10 m□n□g

monogenist
monogenous
monogynous
managerial
manageress
Monegasque
many-headed
mind-healer
monohybrid
monohydric
manchineel
mine-hunter
Manchurian
Manchester
Munchausen
mendicancy
Mandingoes
mansionary
Monsignore
Monsignori
Monsignors
mandibular
monticulus
moniliasis
moniliform
monologise
monologist
monologize
minglement
minglingly
mindlessly
monolithic
monomachia
minimalism
minimalist
monomaniac
monumental
Menominees
mint-master
minimising
manumitted
manometric
minimizing
man-entered
meningitis
meningioma
monandrous
monzonitic
mentorship
mangosteen
monophasic
monopodial
monopodium
monopteral
monoplegia
monopteron
monopteros
monopolise
monopolist
manipulate
monopolize

monophobia
monophobic
monophonic
menopausal
mind-reader
mandragora
monarchial
Monarchian
menorrhoea
monarchise
monarchism
monarchist
monorchism
monarchize
monorhinal
mineralogy
mineralise
mineralist
mongrelise
mongrelism
mineralize
mongrelize
manor-house
monorhymed
ministeria
monastical
monistical
miniseries
minestrone
ministrant
manuscript
ministress
minuscular
meniscuses
monostylar
monstrance
man-stealer
minute-bell
minute-book
monotocous
minute-drop
monotheical
minstrelsy
monotheism
monotheist
minute-hand
minute-jack
minuteness
monotonous
monitorial
monetarism
monetarist
menstruums
menstruate
menstruous
monstruous
manducable
mensurable
minauderie
man-queller
manfulness

mansuetude
minivolley
monovalent
mine-worker
monoxylous
Monaxonida
money-maker
money-taker
money-bound
money-order
myocardial
myocardium
moon-flower
Maoritanga
myoblastic
myological
moon-raised
moonraking
myographic
moonshiner
moonstruck
moonstrike
map-reading
mephitical
map-mounter
meperidine
mopishness
maquillage
morganatic
myrtaceous
myriadfold
margaritic
mordacious
marmarosis
mercaptide
mercantile
marcantant
Myricaceae
miracidium
miraculous
meridional
marketable
market-bell
marker-bomb
marcescent
marker-flag
market-hall
Muraenidae
merceriser
mercerizer
marvelling
martellato
marvellous
martensite
market-town
Marcgravia
morigerate
morigerous
marchlands
marsh-fever
morphogeny

marshalled
marshaller
Marshalsea
morphology
morphemics
marchantia
merchantry
marshiness
morphinism
marsh-robin
marshlocks
march-stone
mirthfully
marginated
marginalia
marginally
morbidezza
martingale
marking-ink
marking-nut
martialism
martialist
morbillous
Marcionist
Marxianism
morbidness
Marcionite
morris-pike
Morris-tube
mercifully
mortifying
moralistic
myringitis
Mariolater
Maryolater
Mariolatry
Maryolatry
marrow-bone
myrioscope
marionette
marrowless
mirrorwise
marprelate
margravine
margravate
mare's-tails
maraschino
Morisonian
moroseness
markswoman
meritocrat
marathoner
moratorium
marguerite
marquisate
merrymaker
merry-night
mistakable
miswandred
mustard-oil
muscardine

mistakenly
message-boy
mustachios
muscarinic
mismanners
maskalonge
maskanonge
mystagogic
mystagogue
mystagogus
mascarpone
miscanthus
musk-beetle
misobserve
mossbunker
musicianer
musicianly
music-shell
musicology
musicality
music-house
misocapnic
misadvised
misbehaved
muster-book
missel-bird
master-card
misleading
misreading
muster-file
master-hand
masterhood
mesmerical
Mustelidae
Mustelinae
mesmeriser
mesmerizer
mysterious
misbelieve
miscellany
masterless
mastermind
misdeeming
misseeming
misdeemful
mussel-plum
muster-roll
musket-rest
mastership
musket-shot
mismeasure
missel-tree
mastectomy
misfeature
misventure
masterwork
masterwort
mystery-man
mist-flower
mishguggle
misogamist

Words marked △ may be spelled also with a capital letter

misogynist
misogynous
mischmetal
mischanter
mesohippus
misthought
masticable
mosaically
mystically
masticator
mashing-tub
muslin-kale
missionary
Messianism
Messianist
missionise
missionize
maskinonge
maskirovka
mystifying
misologist
moss-litter
Mesolithic
misallying
musk-mallow
mass-market
mesomorphy
mesomerism
misimprove
mesenteric
mesenteron
mesenchyme
misentreat
misandrist
misandrous
Mishnayoth
muscovados
misconceit
misconduct
miswording
Massoretic
Muscovitic
miscounsel
misjoinder
miscompute
miscorrect
misconster
misworship
miscontent
misfortune
mastodynia
masspriest
misspelled
mysophobia
mesophytic
miscreance
miscreancy
miscreated
misarrange
miscreator
misericord

mushroomer
mistrysted
mistressly
misprision
misdrawing
mistrayned
mesoscaphe
mesosphere
Mosasauros
mesothorax
muscularly
masturbate
Mussulmans
masquerade
mosquitoes
musquetoon
metabolise
metabolism
metabolite
mutability
metabolize
meticulous
metacentre
metacarpal
metacarpus
mathematic
mitten-crab
mother-cell
mother-city
mitre-wheel
mitre-shell
motherhood
motherland
matterless
motherless
mitre-joint
Methedrine®
mother-spot
mother-to-be
motherwort
moth-flower
metagalaxy
mutagenise
mutagenize
mitigation
mitigatory
mitigative
matchmaker
match-maker
moth-hunter
match-joint
matchboard
matchstick
metrically
mythically
matricidal
mythiciser
mythicizer
methinketh
matricliny
methionine

matrifocal
matrilocal
matriarchy
matricular
matellasse
mytiliform
metalepsis
metaleptic
mettlesome
mutilation
metallurgy
metempiric
metamerism
mutinously
methomania
metromania
mythomania
mutton-chop
mutton-fist
muttonhead
matronhood
meteorital
methodical
meteoritic
matron-like
matrocliny
motionless
mythologer
metrologic
metronomic
metropolis
mythologic
mythopoeia
mythopoeic
mutton-suet
matronship
metrostyle
matronymic
metronymic
metaplasia
metaplasis
metaphoric
metaphrase
metaphrast
metaphysic
materially
maternally
mithridate
matureness
motor-coach
motor-lorry
motormouth
maturation
motor-cycle
metastases
metastasis
metastatic
mutessarif
metastable
metatheses
Metatheria

metathesis
metathetic
metathorax
mutational
metatarsal
metatarsus
Methuselah
motiveless
motivation
methylated
methyldopa
matryoshka
mouldiness
mouldboard
maundering
Mauretania
mouvementé
mousepiece
mouse-sight
mouthparts
mouthpiece
mouth-organ
moucharaby
Moulinette®
moudiewart
moudiewort
maudlinism
mourningly
mournfully
mousseline
mountebank
moustached
moustaches
mountained
Mousterian
movability
movie-maker
movelessly
moving-coil
mavourneen
mowdiewart
mowdiewort
mixed-media
myxoedemic
△mixolydian
maxilliped
maxillulae
myxomycete
maximalist
myxomatous
maxi-single
mixty-maxty
Mayologist
mayonnaise
May-morning
mozzarella
mizzen-mast
mizzen-sail
mezzo-piano
mezzotinto
mezzo-forte

mazarinade
near-begaun
neat-cattle
△neandertal
neat-handed
near-legged
△neapolitan
noblewoman
noblewomen
nubiferous
nubigenous
Nibelungen
nibblingly
nebulosity
nobilitate
nebulously
Nabathaean
nectareous
nyctalopes
nyctalopia
nyctalopic
nickelling
nucleolate
nucleonics
nuclearise
nuclearize
nucleoside
nucleosome
nucleotide
nucleation
nuciferous
nyctinasty
noctilucae
necklacing
nick-nacket
necromancy
necrolater
necrolatry
nectocalyx
necroscopy
necrophobe
necrophile
necrophily
nicrosilal
necrologic
necropolis
nécessaire
Nachschlag
nicotinism
nickumpoop
nucivorous
nudibranch
nidicolous
nidderling
nudge-nudge
nidificate
nidifugous
nidulation
nodulation
nidamental
nidamentum

10 n□e□a

noematical
ne'er-do-weel
ne'er-do-well
Noetianism
needle-book
needle-bath
needlecord
needle-case
needlefish
needlessly
needlework
niffy-naffy
niggardise
niggardize
nigrescent
niggerhead
niggerling
neglection
neglectful
neglective
negligence
negligible
negligibly
nigglingly
nigromancy
negrophobe
negrophile
night-latch
night-watch
night-raven
night-taper
negotiable
negotiator
night-palsy
night-heron
nightshade
night-chair
night-churr
nightshirt
nightpiece
nightrider
night-light
night-night
night-sight
night-blind
nightclass
night-glass
night-cloud
night-house
night-spell
nightdress
nightstick
night-steed
nightstand
night-stool
negatively
negativism
negativist
negativity
nihilistic
nail-biting
Naiadaceae
noisemaker
nail-headed
neighborly
nulla-nulla
nullifying
nelumbiums
numberless
nomography
nympholept
numskulled
nomologist
nimbleness
namelessly
no-man's-land
nominalise
nominalism
nominalist
nominalize
nominately
nomination
nominative
Nemertinea
numerology
numerosity
numeration
numerously
numismatic
nematocyst
nomothetes
nomothetic
Nematoidea
nematology
nummulated
nummulitic
nameworthy
namby-pamby
non-payment
non-natural
non-ability
non-ferrous
nun's-fiddle
nonchalant
non-violent
non-vintage
non-fiction
nunciature
non-aligned
nonplussed
nonplusing
non-playing
non-smoking
no-nonsense
non-society
non-joinder
nincompoop
non-content
non-soluble
non-arrival
non-gremial
non-drinker
nanosecond
nanisation
nineteenth
non-utility
non-starter
non-current
non-swimmer
nanization
Neofascism
Neofascist
Neo-Kantian
neogenesis
neogenetic
noogenesis
neoterical
neorealism
neorealist
neophiliac
neoclassic
neoplastic
neological
nootropics
nuptiality
napkin-ring
Napoleonic
nipplewort
nepenthean
nephoscope
nephologic
nephograph
nephridium
nephrology
nephralgia
nephropexy
nephrotomy
naphthalic
naphthenic
nepotistic
narratable
nero-antico
nurse-child
nursehound
Norbertine
nurseryman
northwards
northbound
northerner
nursing-bra
narcissism
narcissist
Ndrangheta
'Ndrangheta
narrow-boat
narrowcast
narcolepsy
narrowness
nurturable
nystagmoid
nosocomial
nosography
nesting-box
nosologist
nostopathy
nostomania
nostologic
nosophobia
△nasturtium
nitrazepam
notability
noticeable
noticeably
notodontid
nathelesse
nutmegging
natterjack
nethermore
nethermost
netherward
notifiable
notch-board
nothingism
net-fishing
net-fishery
nutritious
nit-picking
nitwittery
nitrifying
nettle-cell
nettle-fish
nettlelike
nettle-rash
nettlesome
natalitial
nettle-tree
notonectal
nationally
notionally
Nothofagus
nitrometer
nationhood
networking
nationless
nitro-group
nationwide
notaphilic
notarially
Notoryctes
nutcracker
nature-cure
naturalise
naturalism
naturalist
naturalize
nature-myth
naturopath
naturistic
notaryship
note-shaver
notational
nutational
natatorial
natatorium
native-born
nativeness
nativistic
noteworthy
naumachiae
naumachias
naumachies
neuraminic
noumenally
neurectomy
nauseating
nauseative
nauseously
nautically
nourice-fee
neurilemma
nourishing
nautiluses
neuropathy
neurogenic
neurolemma
neuroblast
neuroplasm
neurotoxic
neurotoxin
△neuroptera
neurolysis
neutralise
neutralism
neutralist
neutrality
neutralize
neutrophil
neutrettos
nourriture
novicehood
novaculite
noviceship
navigation
novelistic
Never-Never
never-never
newfangled
new-married
nowcasting
newscaster
newsdealer
new-fledged
newsletter
newsmonger
newsreader
newishness
news-vendor
news-writer
newsworthy
Nazaritism
opalescent
orange-lily
orange-peel
orange-root
orange-tree

Words marked △ may be spelled also with a capital letter

orange-wife
orange-wood
ovariotomy
oratorical
Onagraceae
ox-antelope
oracularly
opaqueness
obbligatos
ombrometer
ombrophobe
ombrophile
orchardman
orcharding
orchardist
△**occidental**
once-errand
orchestral
orchestics
orchestric
once-for-all
orchideous
oscillator
oncologist
occultness
osculation
osculatory
oecumenism
occupation
occupative
occurrence
occasional
occasioner
oscitantly
oscitation
old-maidish
old-maidism
ordainable
ordainment
oedematose
oedematous
ordonnance
ordinarily
ordinately
ordination
odd-looking
old-fogyish
obdurately
obduration
Ordovician
olde-worlde
oleraceous
opera-cloak
opera-glass
overabound
overbidder
overbridge
overboldly
overburden
overbought
overcharge
operculate
overcolour
overcanopy
overcaught
overdaring
overdosage
overexcite
overexpose
operettist
overfreely
overflight
overfondly
overflowed
oleiferous
overglance
oleography
oreography
overgreedy
oleaginous
overground
overgrowth
open-hearth
open-handed
overhanded
obeliscoid
one-sidedly
overinform
one-nighter
obediently
overinsure
overleaven
overlabour
overlocker
oreologist
overlander
overlooker
ocellation
overlaunch
overlaying
open-minded
overmantel
overmaster
overmatter
ocean-basin
overnicely
oceanology
ocean-going
oceanarium
overoffice
one-worlder
overplaced
overpraise
overpriced
oleophilic
overpeople
overreckon
overridden
overriding
over-refine
oneirology
overruling
overrunner
overrashly
ore-wrought
overraught
overstayer
overslaugh
overshadow
oversubtle
oversleeve
Odelsthing
open-stitch
overshower
oversupply
overspread
overstruck
overstride
overstrain
overstrike
overstrong
overstrung
overstress
over-the-top
overtimely
overturner
overthrust
overthwart
overweight
overwinter
overworked
overwisely
officially
officiator
officialty
office-book
office-girl
olfactible
offsetable
off-licence
offendedly
offenceful
offendress
off-spinner
obfuscated
off-putting
organicism
organicist
organogram
organogeny
organ-point
organismal
organismic
oughtlings
ochraceous
ophicleide
ophthalmia
ophthalmic
ophiolater
ophiolatry
ophiolitic
ophiologic
ophiomorph
ochlocracy
othergates
otherwhile
otherwhere
otherworld
otherguess
Ophiuridae
oligarchal
oligarchic
olivaceous
olive-shell
originally
oxidisable
oxidizable
originator
opinionist
opium-eater
orientated
orientally
orientator
oniromancy
oniroscopy
opisometer
ovipositor
oligoclase
oligopsony
onirodynia
otioseness
odiousness
obituarist
object-ball
objectless
object-soul
objuration
oak-leather
obligement
obligingly
obligation
obligatory
Oblomovism
Owlspiegle
owlishness
oblateness
oblational
obliterate
osmidrosis
osmiridium
ommatidium
osmeterium
obnubilate
omniferous
omnigenous
oenologist
ornamental
ornamenter
omniparity
omniparous
omnipotent
omniscient
ornateness
ornithosis
ornithopod
omnivorous
onomastics
orogenesis
orogenetic
onocentaur
omophagous
oropharynx
omophorion
opotherapy
odorimetry
orological
orographic
odontocete
odontogeny
odontology
odontalgia
odontalgic
odontolite
odontomata
orotundity
orphanhood
orpheoreon
oppression
oppressive
oppugnancy
oppilation
oppilative
oophoritis
opprobrium
opposeless
oppositely
opposition
oppositive
Oireachtas
o'er-drowsed
obsidional
oyster-bank
oyster-farm
oyster-park
obstetrics
oyster-wife
ossiferous
obsoletely
obsoletion
obsoletism
opsomaniac
opsiometer
oesophagus
obsequious
observance
observancy
observable
observably
observator
obstructer
obstructor
oestradiol
ossivorous
outbalance
outlandish

Words marked △ may be spelled also with a capital letter

10 o□t□a

ostraceous
outrageous
outbargain
out-patient
outdacious
ostracodan
outgassing
outpassion
octodecimo
outgeneral
outperform
out-pension
outmeasure
outjetting
outsetting
out-of-doors
octogenary
octogynous
octahedral
octahedron
octohedron
obtainable
outside-car
ostrich-egg
ostrichism
outfielder
outvillain
obtainment
outfitting
outwitting
ontologist
optologist
outbluster
outclassed
outflowing
optimalise
optimalize
octamerous
optimistic
oftentimes
ostensible
ostensibly
octandrian
octonarian
octandrous
octonarius
octangular
orthopaedy
osteopathy
optionally
orthocaine
Orthoceras
orthogenic
orthopedia
orthopedic
osteogenic
Osteolepis
outlodging
orthophyre
osteophyte
Ostpolitik
orthoclase
osteoblast
osteoclast
orthopnoea
orthogonal
orthoboric
orthotonic
orthotopic
osteocolla
orthoepist
outcompete
orthodromy
outpouring
orthograph
orthotropy
orthoprism
orthopraxy
orthoptics
△**orthoptera**
orthoptist
outspeckle
octopodous
octaploidy
octoploidy
octopusher
outbreath'd
outbreathe
otter-shrew
otter-hound
otter-board
otter-trawl
obturation
outwrought
obtuseness
outstretch
outstation
optatively
obtruncate
outjutting
outsweeten
out-dweller
outswinger
oculomotor
ouvirandra
oxygenator
onyx-marble
oxymoronic
oxy-bromide
oryctology
phalangeal
phalangist
play-acting
praecocial
planchette
prancingly
peat-caster
plauditory
peacemaker
plate-layer
planetaria
plane-table
phagedaena
peace-party
phagedenic
placer-gold
planetical
plate-fleet
plate-glass
prayerless
phanerogam
plate-proof
pease-brose
pease-straw
peacefully
playfellow
plangently
playground
peach-water
peach-bloom
poachiness
peashooter
peacherino
peach-stone
pharisaism
pratincole
planimeter
planimetry
placidness
planigraph
plagiarise
plagiarism
plagiarist
plagiarize
pianissimo
prankingly
planktonic
playleader
phallocrat
phallicism
praeludium
pearl-shell
pearl-white
pearl-diver
phalloidin
phaelonion
pearliness
pearl-stone
pharmacist
plasmodial
plasmodesm
psalmodise
psalmodist
plasmodium
psalmodize
plasmogamy
plasmolyse
plasmolyze
pearmonger
praemunire
psammophil
plasmosoma
plasmosome
pragmatics
pragmatise
pragmatism
pragmatist
pragmatize
plainchant
phaenology
plaintless
praenomens
praenomina
phaenotype
planometer
Platonical
peacockery
peacock-ore
peacockish
planoblast
pianoforte
piano-organ
piano-stool
phagocytic
praepostor
peat-reeker
pea-trainer
pear-shaped
praesidium
playschool
pear-switch
praiseless
praisingly
practician
practicals
Plasticine®
plasticise
plasticity
plasticize
plastidule
prattlebox
plastogamy
plastilina
platteland
phantomish
plant-house
plant-louse
practiques
praetorial
praetorian
psalterian
plastering
praetorium
psalterium
phantasmal
phantasmic
phantastic
phantasime
practisant
practising
phantastry
plantation
plaguesome
plague-spot
plague-sore
play-writer
playwright
pharyngeal
platypuses
publicness
pebbledash
pebble-ware
puberulent
puberulous
pubescence
pack-animal
peccadillo
piccadillo
piccadilly
piccalilli
piccaninny
pickaninny
pace-bowler
pick-cheese
packet-boat
pocket-book
pocket-comb
picket-duty
pocketfuls
pace-egging
pocket-hole
picket-line
pocketless
pickedness
packet-note
packet-ship
peckerwood
pacifiable
pacificism
pacificist
pacificate
pectinated
packing-box
pichiciago
picnicking
peculiarly
poculiform
peculation
pockmantie
pockmarked
pectorally
pycnometer
pictorical
picrotoxin
pycnogonid
pycnospore
pictograph
pycnostyle
pick-pocket
pockpitted
picaresque
picosecond
pack-saddle
pace-setter
pack-thread

Words marked △ may be spelled also with a capital letter

10 p□i□r

picture-hat
picture-rod
pachymeter
picayunish
pediatrics
podiatrist
pediculate
Pediculati
pediculous
pedicurist
pedagogics
pedagogism
podagrical
pudding-bag
padding-ken
pudding-pie
paddle-boat
pedologist
podologist
pedal-point
pedal-board
pedal-organ
paddle-wood
pedimental
pedimented
pedantical
peduncular
pedipalpus
pedereroes
pederastic
Podostemon
pedestrian
paddymelon
paddy-whack
paddy-field
prepayable
preparator
peel-and-eat
prevalence
prevalency
phenacetin
preparedly
pied-à-terre
predaceous
presageful
prelatical
premarital
premaxilla
precarious
predacious
prevailing
prepayment
paedagogic
pteranodon
paedagogue
precaution
poetastery
presbyopia
presbyopic
presbytery
presbytism
pierceable
prescience
prescriber
preachment
piercingly
pleochroic
pseudoacid
pseudobulb
pseudocode
pseudocarp
pseudology
pseudimago
pre-Adamite
pleadingly
preadapted
prevenancy
preferable
preferably
paederasty
pretendant
pretendent
prebendary
precedence
precedency
preference
predevelop
predecease
prerelease
premedical
prevenient
preferment
piece-goods
preferring
prehensile
prepensely
precession
prehension
presension
pretension
pre-tension
prehensory
prehensive
prepensive
preceptial
present-day
presential
paedeutics
precentrix
predestine
predestiny
presetting
prelection
prevention
preceptory
prefecture
predentate
preceptive
presentive
preventive
pledgeable
peelgarlic
psephology
poetically
predicable
plebiscite
presidency
pleximeter
pleximetry
prelingual
plenishing
precipiced
precipitin
presidiums
presidiary
△**plexiglass**
presignify
predispose
preciosity
plesiosaur
paediatric
prediction
prefixture
prehistory
predictive
plenilunar
preciously
previously
pre-glacial
phelloderm
peerlessly
preclusion
psellismus
preclusive
pre-eminent
pleomorphy
pre-embryos
pneumatics
pre-emption
pre-emptive
pleonectic
pregnantly
pleonastic
prednisone
Phenogamae
phenogamic
pleromatic
preconceit
preconcert
precordial
precondemn
Piepowders
phenomenal
prepotence
prepotency
piezometer
phenomenon
paedophile
plerophory
premonitor
prepositor
precocious
prepollent
pie-counter
precognize
precompose
paedotribe
phenocryst
preconsume
prepossess
Plecoptera
Piemontese
phenotypic
preppiness
preappoint
puerperium
prearrange
pleurodont
prefrontal
pleurotomy
pleasantly
pleasingly
pressingly
pheasantry
pleasantry
presswoman
pressurise
pressurize
prettiness
presternum
plentitude
prestation
presumable
presumably
prepuberty
prefulgent
prejudiced
preludious
pre-qualify
presurmise
presuppose
precursory
precursive
prenuptial
pre-exilian
pterylosis
Pterygotus
pegmatitic
pugnacious
peg-tankard
pagoda-tree
pigmentary
pugilistic
pogonotomy
pagination
pigeonhole
pigeon-pair
pigeon-post
pigeon-toed
pigeon-wing
pig-sticker
page-turner
pohutukawa
philatelic
primatical
privatiser
privatizer
pliability
princified
princehood
princelike
princeling
principial
principled
principles
principate
principium
princessly
primevally
prizefight
prizewoman
paideutics
pridefully
priggishly
Pliohippus
primiparae
primiparas
privileged
poikilitic
Philippian
philippina
philippine
Philippise
Philippize
Philistean
Philistian
△**philistine**
prick-eared
pain-killer
prick-louse
phialiform
phillumeny
painlessly
prismoidal
poignadoes
poignantly
pliantness
philomathy
poisonable
primordial
primordium
philoxenia
primogenit
poison-fang
prisonment
philologer
philosophe
philosophy
philologic
philopoena
philologue
psilocybin
priorities
prioritise
prioritize

Words marked △ may be spelled also with a capital letter

10 p□i□s

painstaker
priesthood
priest-king
priest-like
priestling
puissantly
puir's-hoose
puir's-house
priestship
poinsettia
puissaunce
psittacine
point-blank
paintiness
paintworks
printworks
paint-brush
pejoration
pejorative
poke-bonnet
pike-keeper
pyknometer
poker-faced
pokerishly
pulsatance
Palearctic
Polyandria
paleaceous
palmaceous
pultaceous
palmatifid
Pulsatilla
palladious
pilgarlick
polyatomic
polyaxonic
Pelmatozoa
pillar-root
pellagrous
Polianthes
polyactine
polyanthus
palm-branch
pall-bearer
phlebolite
palm-butter
phlebotomy
phlyctaena
Polychaeta
polychaete
polycyclic
phlyctenae
polyclinic
polycrotic
Pelecypoda
pilocarpin
polycarpic
polychroic
polychrome
polychromy
polychrest
Pilocarpus
policy-shop
polycotton
pulp-cavity
polydactyl
poll-degree
pile-driver
paludament
paludinous
polydipsia
pulverable
Palaeocene
pallescent
palaeogaea
Palaeogene
pulp-engine
palletiser
palletizer
pulveriser
pulverizer
palaeolith
pollenosis
palaestral
pollen-tube
palmettoes
palaestric
palaeotype
palmer-worm
Palaeozoic
polt-footed
piliferous
polygraphy
phlegmasia
phlegmatic
palm-grease
polygamist
polygamous
polygynian
polygenism
polygenist
palagonite
polygenous
polygynous
phlegmonic
phlogopite
phlogistic
phlogiston
polyhybrid
polyhedral
polyhedric
polyhydric
polyhedron
polyhalite
Polyhymnia
polyhistor
pulvinated
pollinator
pelvimeter
pulsimeter
pelvimetry
pulvilised
pulvilized
pilliwinks
pulvilling
pulvillios
palliament
pallidness
pillionist
palliation
palliatory
palliative
pellicular
palm-kernel
polemicist
peltmonger
polemonium
polymeride
polymerase
polymerise
polymerism
polymerous
polymerize
polymastia
polymastic
palimpsest
polymathic
palynology
polynomial
palindrome
Polynesian
Pulmonaria
pillow-beer
pillow-bere
pillowcase
pulsometer
pileorhiza
polyominos
pillow-lace
pillow-lava
pillowslip
paleotypic
polyonymic
pillorying
polyphagia
polyphasic
Polypodium
Polyphemic
Polyphemus
Polypterus
polyploidy
polyphonic
pill-popper
poll-parrot
pilgrimage
pilgrimise
pilgrimize
palfrenier
paltriness
pelargonic
pultrusion
polyrhythm
polishable
palisadoes
pilastered
polishings
polishment
polysemant
palisander
palustrian
palustrine
polystylar
politician
politicker
politicoes
politicise
polytocous
politicize
polytheism
polytheist
pilot-whale
pilot-plant
palatalise
palatalize
polytunnel
politeness
palatinate
pilot-house
pollutedly
pellucidly
polyvalent
palsy-walsy
pump-action
pome-citron
pummelling
pompelmous
pumie-stone
pomiferous
pemphigoid
pemphigous
pump-handle
Pimpinella
pomologist
pumple-nose
Pomeranian
panhandler
Pentandria
panjandrum
Pentateuch
pentameter
Pentameron
pentahedra
pennaceous
pentathlon
pentachord
pentathlum
pinnatiped
pinnatifid
pentaploid
pentagonal
pentapodic
pentapolis
pentatomic
pentatonic
pantaloons
pantagraph
pentagraph
pentaprism
penmanship
pentastich
pentastyle
pennatulae
pennatulas
Pentagynia
pine-beauty
pine-beetle
pine-barren
pine-chafer
Punicaceae
pinacoidal
penicillin
paniculate
pine-carpet
panic-grass
ponderance
ponderancy
ponderable
pince-nezed
pangenesis
pangenetic
penteteric
Pontederia
Pentelican
ponderment
pandermite
△**pandemonic**
Pontefract
pen-feather
pin-feather
pandectist
pendentive
Pan-African
panegyrise
panegyrist
panegyrize
punch-ladle
pinchpenny
pinchingly
pinchpoint
pantherine
punch-drunk
pantheress
pantherish
penthouses
pencil-case
Pinnipedia
ponticello
pentimenti
pentimento
Pennisetum
pontifical
pontifices
pencil-lead
pencilling
pensionnat

Words marked △ may be spelled also with a capital letter

pensionary
pundigrion
pensieroso
panniculus
pinakoidal
pinakothek
penologist
penelopise
penelopize
Panglossic
Pan-Slavism
Pan-Slavist
Panamanian
penumbrous
pond-master
penoncelle
penannular
△peninsular
pantoscope
pantophagy
pansophism
pansophist
pantomimic
pancosmism
pontonnier
pundonores
pantograph
panton-shoe
panoptical
panopticon
panophobia
panspermia
panspermic
pancreatic
pancreatin
Pan-Arabism
ponerology
pantrymaid
pancratian
pancratist
panaritium
pancratium
panislamic
punishable
pentstemon
punishment
penetrance
penetrancy
penetralia
penetrable
penetrably
punctually
penetrator
punctuator
pin-striped
punctilios
punctulate
penitently
punctation
pandurated
pinnulated
Pinguicula
pinguidity
pin-cushion
penguinery
pin-buttock
pinguitude
panty-waist
penny-piece
penny-pinch
penny-plain
penny-a-line
pennyroyal
pennyworth
pennycress
penny-stane
penny-stone
△propaganda
propagable
proratable
propagator
prosaicism
procacious
protanopia
protanopic
propagulum
procaryote
prokaryote
proscriber
proscenium
prosciutti
prosciutto
proud-flesh
ploddingly
Ptolemaean
provenance
promenader
phonematic
Ptolemaist
proverbial
proseuchae
Proteaceae
Provençale
proceeding
propendent
pyogenesis
proteiform
Promethean
pronephric
pronephros
prometheum
promethium
phonetical
progenitor
proveditor
propellant
propellent
propelling
proteolyse
propelment
phoneyness
properness
proteinous
processual
propensely
professing
procession
profession
propension
protension
propensity
protensity
propensive
protensive
propertied
protectrix
projectile
projecting
protecting
△protestant
projection
protection
provection
projecture
protectory
pro-oestrus
projective
protective
procedural
prosecutor
protervity
proof-sheet
proof-house
proffering
ploughable
ploughgate
plough-iron
ploughland
ploughman's
plough-team
plough-tree
plough-tail
ploughwise
prothallia
prothallic
prothallus
prophesied
prophesier
prophetess
prophetism
provitamin
phonically
prodigally
profitable
profitably
providable
proximally
provincial
procidence
prominence
prominency
△providence
proairesis
promiseful
prolicidal
prolifical
prohibiter
proficient
prosilient
provisions
prohibitor
propitiate
prodigious
prolixious
propitious
profitless
prolixness
propionate
pholidosis
promissory
promissive
profluence
profligacy
profligate
proclaimer
problemist
prowlingly
proglottis
proclivity
phorminges
proembryos
Phoenician
prognostic
prognathic
phoenixism
protopathy
phototaxis
promotable
proposable
provocable
provokable
provocator
photonasty
protonemal
phonometer
photometer
phocomelia
photogenic
photometry
prolongate
photophobe
photophily
photophone
photophony
phonophore
photophore
Protophyta
protophyte
pronominal
prosodical
photodiode
phonolitic
photoflood
photoglyph
protoplasm
protoplast
procoelous
pronounced
pronouncer
propounder
profoundly
protocolic
protozoans
phonograph
photograph
phototrope
phototropy
protostele
proportion
promontory
Psocoptera
protohuman
prolocutor
prologuise
prologuize
prototypal
protoxylem
phonotypic
photolysis
photolytic
phototypic
phosphatic
prompt-book
prospector
prompt-copy
prospectus
promptness
prompt-note
phosphoret
phosphoric
phosphorus
prosperity
prosperous
phosphuret
promptuary
procreator
protracted
proproctor
protractor
protrudent
propraetor
proprietor
poor-relief
programmed
programmer
pyorrhoeal
pyorrhoeic
procrypsis
procryptic
protreptic
protrusile
protrusion
protrusive
poor's-house
prostheses

Words marked △ may be spelled also with a capital letter

10 p□o□t

prosthesis
prosthetic
proctology
proctalgia
prostomial
prostomium
plottingly
proctorial
proctorage
proctorise
proctorize
prostatism
prostitute
procurable
procurator
procumbent
pronuncios
profundity
profulgent
promulgate
producible
pronuclear
pronucleus
propulsion
propulsory
propulsive
productile
production
productive
propylaeum
Papiamento
pepper-cake
peppercorn
peppermill
peppermint
puppet-play
puppet-show
pepperwort
pupigerous
poplinette
pepsinogen
papillated
papillitis
pipelining
popularise
popularity
popularize
papulation
population
populously
pipe-laying
pipe-opener
pupiparous
paper-faced
paper-maker
paper-gauge
paper-mâché
Piperaceae
piperidine
paper-chase
paper-cigar

paper-birch
papyrology
paper-cloth
paper-knife
paperbound
paperboard
paper-ruler
piperazine
papistical
papaverine
papaverous
pipe-wrench
popsy-wopsy
Portakabin®
parramatta
permanence
permanency
pyro-acetic
portamenti
portamento
porraceous
parmacitie
permafrost
Parnassian
periastron
parablepsy
paraboloid
parabolise
parabolist
parabolize
parabemata
parabiosis
parabiotic
port-crayon
pericyclic
periclinal
portcullis
periculous
pyracantha
paradoctor
paradiddle
peridinian
△**peridinium**
peridermal
paradisean
paradisiac
paradisial
paradisian
paradisaic
parodistic
peridotite
pyridoxine
paradoxure
paradoxist
purtenance
purveyance
parcel-bawd
perdendosi
paraenesis
paraenetic
periegesis

purse-seine
parcel-gilt
permethrin
paroecious
Purbeckian
parcelling
Parnellism
Parnellite
purse-pride
perpetrate
purse-proud
pursership
perversely
perversion
perversity
perversive
perceptual
percentage
percentile
pargetting
porpentine
perception
perfection
permeation
porrection
portentous
perceptive
perfective
permeative
persecutor
perpetuate
perpetuity
perceiving
perfervour
parpen-wall
parcelwise
paraffinic
portfolios
poriferous
pyrography
paraglider
pyrogallic
pyrogallol
perigonial
paragonite
perigonium
perigynous
pyrogenous
paragnosis
paraglossa
pyrrhicist
parchmenty
perihelion
Pyrrhonian
Pyrrhonism
Pyrrhonist
perchloric
porphyrios
porphyrite
porphyrous
pyrrhotine

pyrrhotite
persicaria
pertinence
pertinency
parting-cup
parricidal
participle
percipient
perficient
perfidious
pernicious
perjinkety
perjinkity
pernickety
persiflage
partialise
partialism
partialist
partiality
persifleur
partialize
△**parliament**
persiennes
Persianise
portionist
Persianize
Parkinson's
permission
permissive
permitting
persistent
persistive
particular
perviously
park-keeper
perikaryon
parakiting
parkleaves
purple-born
Pyrolaceae
paralleled
parallelly
paralogise
paralogism
paralogize
purple-hued
paralympic
purblindly
purulently
portliness
paralipses
paralipsis
pyrolusite
perilously
perplexing
perplexity
△**paramecium**
paramedico
pyrimidine
pyramidion
pyramidist

paramnesia
pyromaniac
pyromantic
portmantle
portmantua
pyromeride
perimysium
parametral
perimetral
pari-mutuel
parametric
perimetric
pyrometric
peremptory
paramouncy
parentally
△**paronychia**
pyrenocarp
parenteral
Pyrenaeans
parenchyma
parenthood
paranoidal
phrensical
phrenology
parentless
paronomasy
paronymous
paranormal
phrenesiac
perineural
perforated
personated
personalia
pardonable
pardonably
perforable
personable
personally
percolator
perforator
personator
portolanos
personalty
perforatus
parrot-beak
parrot-bill
parson-bird
parrot-coal
purposeful
parrot-fish
personhood
parsonical
periodical
perfoliate
parvovirus
porlocking
pardonless
performing
pornotopia
parlour-car

Words marked △ may be spelled also with a capital letter

pornocracy
periosteal
pernoctate
periosteum
paraphasia
paraphasic
parapodial
parapodium
peripheral
peripteral
paraplegia
paraplegic
peripheric
paraphilia
parapineal
paraphonia
paraphonic
periphonic
pyrophobia
pyrophobic
pyrophoric
△**pyrophorus**
paraphrase
paraphrast
periphrase
perspirate
peripetian
peripeteia
paraphyses
paraphysis
periphyton
paraquitos
parbreaked
partridges
pararthria
peroration
parastatal
porismatic
pyrostatic
perishable
perishably
parascenia
Parisienne
parischane
poristical
puristical
parastichy
paraselene
phraseless
peristomal
periscopic
poroscopic
parasitoid
parasitise
parasitism
parasitize
peristylar
paratactic
peritectic
pyrotechny
parathesis
perithecia
perstringe
peritricha
pyretology
peritoneal
puritanise
puritanism
peritoneum
puritanize
paratroops
pyrethroid
perdurance
perdurable
perdurably
permutable
Portugaise
perturbant
perturbate
parturient
percutient
perjurious
pursuantly
pursuingly
porousness
percurrent
percussant
percussion
persuasion
percursory
persuasory
perquisite
percussive
persuasive
parquetted
pirouetter
perruquier
Portuguese
pursuivant
perovskite
periwigged
parawalker
periwinkle
peroxidase
peroxidise
peroxidize
pyroxyline
pyroxenite
paroxysmal
paroxytone
passageway
passamezzo
pistachios
post-bellum
push-button
post-chaise
postcoital
post-echoes
post-exilic
posteriors
pastellist
pesterment
pasteboard
Pasteurian
paste-grain
pasteurise
pasteurism
pasteurize
possession
possessory
possessive
pasigraphy
puschkinia
posthumous
piscifauna
pestilence
passimeter
pasticheur
pesticidal
pistillode
postillion
passiflora
pistillary
pistillate
postillate
passionary
Passionist
passionate
postliminy
post-modern
post-mortem
pastmaster
postmaster
post-Nicene
pastorally
post-office
pistolling
pastorship
postocular
pistol-whip
postperson
postpartum
post-partum
pastrycook
push-stroke
PostScript®
postscript
piss-taking
positional
positioned
positively
positivism
positivist
positivity
postulancy
postulates
pasturable
postulator
postulatum
pasquilant
pasquinade
pasty-faced
Puseyistic
pot-wabbler
Petrarchal
Petrarchan
pot-valiant
Pythagoras
patibulary
putrescent
putrescine
pathetical
pot-bellied
pettedness
patter-song
putrefying
pathfinder
Patagonian
pitch-wheel
pitch-black
pitchiness
pitchwoman
put-through
patchcocke
patchboard
pitcherful
pitchstone
pettichaps
patricidal
phthisical
phthisicky
patriciate
pit-village
patricliny
patrialise
patrialism
patriality
patrialize
putridness
patrifocal
patrilocal
patriarchy
petrissage
patristics
patriation
patriotism
pittie-ward
petrifying
pottle-deep
petulantly
pitilessly
potamology
patentable
potentilla
potentiary
potentiate
put-and-take
patination
petiolated
petrolatum
pot-wobbler
pathogenic
pythogenic
petronella
pétroleuse
petroleous
patroniser
patronizer
patrocliny
patrolling
petrolling
pot-boiling
petroglyph
patronless
pathognomy
petromoney
pathologic
petrodrome
patronymic
pit-a-patted
pityriasis
paternally
Peter-see-me
patereroes
patisserie
pâtisserie
△**petitioner**
pot-hunting
put-putting
Patavinity
putty-faced
potty-chair
petty-chaps
putty-knife
plumassier
plum-colour
pouncet-box
plunderage
plunderous
pluperfect
plume-grass
prudential
pausefully
pruning-saw
pruriently
Paulianist
pluckiness
plutolatry
plutocracy
pourparler
pousse-café
pourtraict
pourtrahed
poultroone
Plumularia
pawnbroker
pewter-mill
powerhouse
powertrain
powerfully
pawnticket
pixillated
pixilation
phylactery
psychiater

Words marked △ may be spelled also with a capital letter

10 p□y□h

psychiatry
psychicism
psychicist
psychogram
psychogony
psychology
psychopomp
psychopath
physically
physiocrat
physicking
physiology
Phyllopoda
phyllotaxy
phylloxera
Phytolacca
phytogenic
phytotoxic
phytotoxin
pay-station
pizzicatos
puzzle-head
puzzlement
puzzlingly
pozzolanic
pozzuolana
quarantine
Quaker-bird
quaternion
△**quaternary**
quaternate
quaternity
quagginess
qualifying
qualmishly
quaintness
quatorzain
quarriable
quadricone
quadriceps
quatrefoil
quadriform
quadriller
quarrelled
quarreller
quadrumvir
Quadrumana
quadrumane
quadrantal
quadrantes
quarrender
quadrennia
quadrangle
quadruplet
quadruplex
quadripole
quadrireme
quadrisect
quadratics
quadratrix
quadratura
quadrature
quadrivial
quadrivium
quaestuary
quantifier
quartzitic
quartz-mill
quarter-day
quarter-saw
quartz-rock
quarterage
quarter-ill
quartering
quarter-boy
quarteroon
quartation
quantitive
quesadilla
quenchable
quenchless
quercitron
Queensland
queencraft
quernstone
quebrachos
queasiness
quersprung
questingly
questionee
questioner
queryingly
quinacrine
quinaquina
Quirinalia
quick-match
quick-sandy
quick-water
quick-hedge
quickthorn
quick-firer
quickening
quirkiness
quink-goose
quicktrick
quick-stick
quick-lunch
quizmaster
quiescence
quiescency
quinsy-wort
quietening
quintuplet
quietistic
quizziness
quotatious
rear-boiled
road-bridge
reaccustom
rhabdolith
rear-dorter
readership
real-estate
reafforest
roadheader
realisable
realizable
reaming-bit
reading-boy
reallocate
road-making
rearmament
road-mender
Rhamnaceae
reasonable
reasonably
reasonless
readoption
reappraise
reacquaint
road-roller
roadrunner
rhapsodise
rhapsodist
rhapsodize
reap-silver
reassemble
reassembly
reassuring
reastiness
reactional
reactively
reactivate
reactivity
roadworthy
ready-mixed
ready-to-eat
ready-money
ready-to-sew
rubiaceous
Rebeccaism
Rebeccaite
rub-a-dub-dub
robber-crab
rubberneck
rubber-room
rubberwear
riboflavin
rubiginose
rubiginous
rubrically
rubricator
rabbitfish
rabbit-hole
rubbishing
rabbinical
rib-tickler
rebukingly
rebellious
rabblement
rubble-work
robing-room
ribbonfish
ribbon-seal
rib-roaster
ribbon-weed
ribbon-worm
rebirthing
roberdsman
robertsman
roborating
robustious
robustness
rebuttable
rebatement
ruby-throat
rectangled
rockabilly
reclaimant
rackabones
reclassify
rock-badger
rickburner
rick-barton
rock-butter
recyclable
ricocheted
racecourse
recidivism
recidivist
recreantly
racket-tail
rickettsia
recreation
recreative
recogniser
recognizer
rock-hopper
receivable
reclinable
recoilless
rectifying
recallable
rick-lifter
recallment
recolonise
recolonize
recklessly
rock-lizard
recommence
recompence
recumbence
recumbency
recompense
Rachmanism
Rachmanite
recompress
racemation
raconteuse
recondense
reconciler
reconsider
recontinue
ricinoleic
recentness
reconquest
raccoon-dog
rectorship
receptacle
recipience
recipiency
receptible
reciprocal
recuperate
recapturer
recordable
rock-ribbed
rock-rabbit
rectricial
recurrence
recurrency
recureless
rack-renter
rechristen
rocksteady
rock-steady
rock-salmon
recusation
rock-temple
rock-turbot
recitation
recitative
recitativi
recitativo
recrudesce
recoupment
recruiting
rock-violet
race-walker
ride-and-tie
red-lattice
ridability
radiciform
radicalise
Radicalism
radiculose
radicality
ridiculous
radicalize
redecorate
radication
rededicate
redeemable
redeemably
rudder-fish
ridge-piece
redeemless
rudderless
redressive
redshifted
rodfishing
red-figured
raduliform
riddle-like
redolently

Words marked △ may be spelled also with a capital letter

riddlingly
red-blooded
redelivery
rudimental
redemption
redemptory
redemptive
redundance
redundancy
riding-boot
riding-coat
riding-crop
riding-hood
rodent-like
riding-robe
riding-suit
riding-whip
radiopager
Radiolaria
radiopaque
radioscope
radioscopy
radiometer
radiogenic
radiophone
radiophony
radiosonde
radiologic
radiotoxic
radiograph
radiolysis
radiolytic
radarscope
rediscover
rediscount
redissolve
redescribe
redisburse
redounding
redruthite
red-murrain
redcurrant
redivision
rue-bargain
Riemannian
riebeckite
re-election
re-erection
re-eligible
rheologist
re-enlister
rheumatics
rheumatoid
rheumatise
rheumatism
rheumatize
Rheinberry
rhetorical
re-entrance
re-entrancy
rheotropic
reel-to-reel
re-entering
reed-thrush
ruefulness
reflagging
refracting
refraction
refractary
refractory
refracture
refractive
raft-bridge
refuelable
rafter-bird
refreshing
refreshful
reflexible
rifle-corps
rifle-green
reflecting
reflection
reflective
refringent
ruffianish
ruffianism
refulgence
refulgency
refundable
refinement
refundment
referrable
reformable
reformados
referrible
referendum
refutation
ragmatical
rigidified
ragged-lady
raggedness
ruggedness
regression
regressive
regretting
regainable
regainment
regalement
regularise
regularity
regularize
regelation
regulation
regulatory
regulative
△ragamuffin
regimental
regent-bird
regeneracy
regenerate
regentship
regionally
rag-rolling
regardable
regardless
rigorously
registered
registrant
registrary
rightwards
right-of-way
right-lined
right-drawn
rightfully
rehearsing
rehandling
raiyatwari
reincrease
rain-doctor
reiterance
reiterated
Rhineberry
Rhinegrave
△rhinestone
rainforest
Reichsbank
Reichsland
reichsmark
Reichsrath
raising-bee
Rhipiptera
reim-kennar
reillumine
rainmaking
rhinolalia
rhinoscope
rhinoscopy
rhizogenic
rhinoceros
rhinocerot
rhinotheca
rhinophyma
Rhizophora
rhizophore
rhinovirus
rhizoplane
raisonneur
rhizomorph
rain-plover
railroader
reissuable
rain-shadow
reinspirit
roistering
roisterous
railwayman
reioyndure
rejectable
rejectible
rejoindure
rejoiceful
rejoicings
rejoneador
rajpramukh
rijsttafel
rejuvenise
rejuvenate
rejuvenize
rakishness
releasable
reluctance
reluctancy
rollcollar
relocation
relievable
reliefless
religieuse
religioner
relegation
rolling-pin
rollicking
relentless
relentment
relinquish
rollocking
reliquaire
relishable
Rolls-Royce®
relational
relatively
relativise
relativism
relativist
△relativity
relativize
relevantly
relaxation
relaxative
rallyingly
rally-cross
ram-raiding
rampageous
rampacious
rampallian
remediable
remediably
remedially
remediless
romper-suit
remigation
ramshackle
Ramphastos
rumple-bane
ramblingly
rumblingly
rum-blossom
rememberer
romancical
romantical
Ruminantia
ruminantly
remunerate
Romanistic
Romanesque
rumination
remonetise
ruminative
remonetize
remarkable
remarkably
remorseful
remortgage
remarriage
remoralise
remoralize
Rome-runner
remissible
remissness
remittance
remoteness
rumbullion
rum-running
rumfustian
rumpy-pumpy
rent-an-army
rent-a-crowd
rent-charge
rangelands
renderable
runner-bean
rannel-balk
Ranzellaar
Ringelmann
rinderpest
rangership
rendezvous
ring-finger
röntgenise
röntgenize
renegation
Rh-negative
ranshackle
run-through
rancidness
ringleader
randle-balk
rannle-balk
rantle-balk
randle-tree
ringmaster
ring-necked
Ranunculus
ransomable
rondoletto
randomiser
randomizer
ransomless
rencounter
randomwise
ring-porous
rank-riding
△renascence
rune-singer
ring-tailed
ranivorous

Words marked △ may be spelled also with a capital letter

10 r□n□v

renovation
renewables
Rhoeadales
rhomboidal
rhomboides
rhoicissus
rootedness
root-fallen
room-fellow
reorganise
reorganize
rhodophane
root-rubber
room-ridden
rootsiness
rood-screen
Rhodymenia
repealable
repeatable
repeatedly
△republican
rupicoline
rupicolous
repudiable
repudiator
ripidolite
rope-dancer
rappelling
repression
repressive
repugnance
repugnancy
repaginate
repairable
replicator
ripping-saw
reptilious
repair-shop
repainting
repellance
repellancy
rope-ladder
repellence
repellency
ripple-mark
ripplingly
rope-making
repentance
roping-down
repinement
repiningly
ripsnorter
reprobance
reprobater
reprobator
reproacher
rip-roaring
rapportage
rapporteur
reproducer
repopulate
reportable
reportedly
repurchase
repertoire
reparation
reparatory
reparative
rupestrian
reposition
re-position
repository
Rh-positive
repatriate
reputeless
repetition
reputation
répétiteur
repetitive
reputative
repoussage
repoussoir
rope-walker
roquelaure
requirable
requitable
requiteful
requisitor
requiescat
reredorter
rarefiable
reregulate
reregister
rere-supper
Ruritanian
resealable
researcher
rascal-like
rascallion
restaurant
rust-bucket
rose-beetle
risibility
rose-chafer
rose-colour
rose-combed
rush-candle
rest-centre
△resedaceae
residenter
russel-cord
rose-engine
rostellate
Russellite
respectant
respecting
respectful
respective
rosy-footed
resignedly
resignment
rose-garden
reschedule
rush-holder
rest-harrow
rusticated
respirable
rustically
respirator
rusticator
reshipment
Russianise
Russianism
Russianist
Russianize
rescission
rescissory
restitutor
rustic-ware
rustic-work
resolvable
resilience
resiliency
resolvedly
resultless
rustlingly
rose-lipped
restlessly
resolutely
resolution
re-solution
resolutive
rose-laurel
resemblant
resembling
resumption
resumptive
resentence
rosaniline
rosin-plant
resentment
resonantly
resinously
restorable
respondent
Russophobe
Russophile
responsory
responsive
resupinate
reservable
restricted
resorbence
resurgence
reservedly
restrained
restrainer
resorcinol
resorption
resorptive
△resistance
resistible
resistibly
resistless
rose-tinted
resounding
rose-window
rat-catcher
retransfer
retransmit
retractile
retraction
retractive
ratability
reticulary
reticulate
rutherford
ruthenious
rottenness
retreatant
rotiferous
retainable
retailment
retainment
retributor
retrieving
retaliator
rattle-head
rattle-pate
ruthlessly
rattle-trap
ritt-master
retinacula
retinalite
rationally
ration-book
ration-card
retrochoir
retrovirus
retrospect
retrograde
retrogress
retrorsely
ritardando
returnable
ritornelle
ritornelli
ritornello
returnless
retardment
retirement
retiringly
rotorcraft
rotisserie
rôtisserie
rotational
rat-hunting
△rottweiler
rhubarbing
round-eared
round-faced
round-table
roundabout
round-nosed
roundhouse
round-mouth
route-march
rouseabout
rough-hewer
rough-rider
rough-hound
rough-house
rough-draft
rough-grind
rough-stuff
reunionism
reunionist
roustabout
revealable
revealment
rove-beetle
revocation
revocatory
reviewable
revokement
revalidate
revolvency
revilement
revilingly
revalorise
revalorize
△revelation
revolution
revelatory
revelative
raven's-bone
raven's-duck
revengeful
revanchism
revanchist
ravenously
river-water
riverscape
reversedly
reversible
revertible
reverencer
reverently
river-horse
river-mouth
rivercraft
river-drift
riverfront
revestiary
ravishment
revisional
revisitant
revitalise
revitalize
revivified
revivalism
revivalist
revivement
revivingly
rowing-boat

Words marked △ may be spelled also with a capital letter

10 s□b□l

rowan-berry
rewardable
rewardless
rowdy-dowdy
rhyme-royal
rhythmical
rhythmless
Rhyniaceae
roysterous
razzmatazz
razor-shell
razor-blade
razor-strop
scarabaean
sharawadgi
sharawaggi
scarabaeid
scarabaeus
smaragdine
smaragdite
spatangoid
stay-at-home
sea-bathing
seamanlike
Sparagmite
stalagmite
Scaramouch
sialagogic
sialagogue
sparagrass
seamanship
stalactite
star-bright
stabbingly
scabbiness
shabbiness
slabbiness
searchable
stanchable
swatchbook
spatchcock
starchedly
spancelled
searchless
stanchless
scarcement
scarceness
stanchness
snapdragon
scaldberry
shandygaff
scandalled
stand-alone
scandalise
scandalous
scandalize
shard-borne
standpoint
standers-by
slanderous
standstill
shandrydan
shamefaced
stavesacre
sealed-beam
scavenging
scavengery
snake's-head
scape-wheel
Swadeshism
spagerical
shale-miner
state-aided
spaceplane
suaveolent
searedness
spacewoman
stagecoach
spaceborne
skateboard
snake-house
sea-keeping
scapegrace
spacecraft
stagecraft
statecraft
shame-proof
shave-grass
snakestone
shamefully
scaredy-cat
snaffle-bit
scaffolder
scaffolage
scarf-joint
seal-fisher
shanghaied
shanghaier
slang-whang
slangingly
shagginess
slanginess
sparganium
staggering
swaggering
slaughtery
stargazing
stag-headed
shag-haired
stadholder
staphyloma
staphyline
scatheless
spathulate
scathingly
Scaphopoda
snaphaunce
snaphaunch
shamiyanah
statically
spadiceous
sealing-wax
sea-fishing
spagirical
stabiliser
stabilizer
spaniolise
spaniolate
spatiality
spaniolize
stationary
stationery
statistics
spaciously
scarifying
stark-naked
spankingly
slackening
sparkishly
snail-paced
spauld-bone
snail-shell
small-pipes
stablemate
stallenger
stallinger
snarlingly
stableness
small-tooth
scarlatina
spallation
shallowing
spasmodist
swan-maiden
starmonger
smalminess
smarminess
swarm-spore
slammerkin
stammering
swan-mussel
shammashim
seannachie
staunching
stagnantly
Stannaries
stagnation
stannotype
seasonable
seasonably
seasonally
statoscope
shadowcast
Slavophobe
scatophagy
Slavophile
seasonless
shadowless
sialogogic
sialogogue
slavocracy
sharp-edged
stamp-hinge
snappingly
swampiness
sharp-nosed
scampishly
snappishly
shabracque
scabridity
shagreened
starry-eyed
staurolite
starriness
scabrously
star-shaped
sparseness
scansorial
seamstress
start-naked
Spartacist
spasticity
scaithless
skaithless
slantingly
startingly
scantiness
scattiness
shaft-horse
slatternly
scattering
smattering
scatter-gun
shantytown
scapulated
shakuhachi
statutable
statutably
scaturient
swan-upping
seaquarium
statuesque
starveling
starvation
stalwartly
spagyrical
sub-Saharan
submanager
subnascent
subtangent
Sabbath-day
sabbatical
subcabinet
subcaliber
submariner
subcalibre
subvariety
subcarrier
subnatural
suboceanic
subacidity
subscribed
subscriber
subacutely
subacetate
suboctuple
subdecanal
subtenancy
sabretache
subheading
subgeneric
subterfuge
submediant
subceiling
subsellium
subdeanery
sabre-tooth
subterrain
subterrane
subterrene
subsessile
submersion
subversion
subversive
subcentral
subjectify
subfertile
subletting
subception
subjection
subreption
subsection
subvention
subjective
subreptive
subgenuses
subsequent
subofficer
sebiferous
subphrenic
subchelate
subchanter
subchapter
subcharter
subshrubby
sublimated
sublimable
subcircuit
subsidence
subsidency
sublingual
subkingdom
subliminal
subdivider
subsidiary
subdialect
subtilness
submission
submissive
submitting
subsistent
subglobose
subglacial
sibilantly
subtleness

10 s□b□l

sibilation
sibilatory
subclavian
subintrant
subangular
subcordate
subsoiling
subjoinder
subpoenaed
subcompact
submontane
subroutine
subspecies
subspinous
subaquatic
subaqueous
subtracter
subtractor
subprefect
subprogram
seborrhoea
subtrahend
suborbital
subordinal
sobersides
subarticle
subcranial
soberingly
subtropics
subcrustal
△sybaritish
△sybaritism
subarcuate
substratal
substratum
substellar
subatomics
substernal
substation
substitute
subsumable
subjugator
subfuscous
subsurface
subaudible
subnuclear
subduement
submucosae
submucosal
subduction
subculture
subsultory
subsultive
subaverage
sucralfate
socialness
succedanea
societally
secretaire
succeeding
sacredness
secretness
sickerness
sachemship
succession
successful
successive
sick-fallen
saccharide
saccharify
saccharoid
saccharine
saccharase
saccharise
saccharose
saccharate
saccharize
succinctly
sucking-pig
sacrificer
sectionise
sectionize
sicilianos
sicklebill
sickle-cell
sicilienne
sickliness
secularise
secularism
secularist
secularity
secularize
sick-listed
sick-making
second-best
second-hand
secundines
secondment
second-rate
sacrosanct
socdolager
sociopathy
sociometry
socdoliger
sacroiliac
socdologer
sociologic
sycophancy
sack-posset
securiform
secernment
securement
secureness
sacerdotal
securities
securitise
Securitate
securitize
sacculated
succulence
succulency
secludedly
succussion
succussive
succubuses
sideboards
seducement
seducingly
seductress
soddenness
suddenness
sad-hearted
saddleback
saddlebill
saddle-fast
saddleless
saddle-nose
saddleroom
saddle-sore
saddletree
sedulously
siderolite
siderostat
sideration
sidesaddle
sideswiper
soda-siphon
sidestream
sidestreet
sidestroke
sedateness
sudatorium
Sadducaean
sidewinder
seecatchie
skedaddler
sherardise
stewardess
sherardize
shenanigan
steganopod
sueability
shea-butter
sketchable
sketchbook
stencilled
stenciller
stenciling
speechless
Spencerian
skew-corbel
stercorary
stercorate
speech-song
stepdancer
speediness
steadiness
slenderise
slenderize
speedfully
stereobate
skene-occle
stereocard
seemelesse
shereefian
stereogram
speleology
shebeening
siegeworks
stereopsis
siegecraft
speleothem
stereotomy
stereotype
stereotypy
stepfather
sdeignfull
stephanite
see-through
scenically
speciocide
sheriffdom
specifical
steriliser
sterilizer
specialise
specialism
specialist
speciality
specialize
sterigmata
speciesism
speciesist
speciosity
speciation
speciously
specifying
shecklaton
sneak-thief
sneakingly
speakingly
sneakiness
steakhouse
speakerine
sneakishly
sleekstone
shellycoat
shellacked
stepladder
skelly-eyed
smell-feast
stellified
stelliform
seemlihead
shellshock
spellcheck
stealthily
stealthing
stellulate
Shetlander
Shetlandic
spellingly
stealingly
swellingly
seemliness
shelliness
smelliness
steeliness
shell-money
steelworks
shellbound
spellbound
shelldrake
shellproof
stellately
spermicide
spermaceti
spermaduct
spermiduct
spermogone
sperm-whale
steamtight
steaminess
spermarium
stepmother
spermatium
stemmatous
sternwards
sternsheet
stern-chase
sternalgia
sternalgic
sternworks
sternboard
stenopaeic
stenotopic
skeuomorph
stenograph
seed-oyster
sheep-faced
sheep's-eyes
sweep-seine
sheep's-foot
sheep's-head
sleepy-head
sheepshank
sheep-biter
sheep-plant
sweepingly
sleepiness
steepiness
sheep-louse
step-parent
sheepishly
sweepstake
seed-potato
shearwater
spear-shaft
sperrylite
stearsmate
steersmate
sneeringly
smeariness
spear-point
shear-steel

seersucker
Spenserian
step-sister
sweetwater
sweet-water
spectrally
sweatpants
sheathbill
sweath-band
spectacled
spectacles
steatocele
scepticism
skepticism
sheet-metal
sweetie-pie
sweetheart
sheathfish
sweatshirt
sweat-shirt
sheathless
sheet-glass
sweetening
sleetiness
sweatiness
stentorian
sweetbread
sweet-briar
sweet-brier
sheltering
sweltering
stertorous
sweet-stuff
spectatrix
speculator
spelunking
sleevehand
sleeveless
swerveless
seed-vessel
stemwinder
sleazeball
sleaziness
sneezeweed
sneezewood
sneezewort
soft-bodied
soft-boiled
soft-billed
safe-blower
sufferance
sufferable
sufferably
soft-finned
soft-footed
soft-headed
suffigance
suffisance
sufficient
sufflation
suffragism
suffragist
soft-spoken
signalling
segregable
suggestion
segmentary
segmentate
suggestive
seguidilla
signifying
Sigillaria
sigillarid
sign-manual
sagination
sogdolager
sogdoliger
sogdologer
sugar-candy
sugar-baker
sugarallie
sugariness
sugarhouse
Sagittaria
sagittally
sightlines
sign-writer
schwarzlot
sphacelate
sphaeridia
schlepping
schefflera
schlimazel
sphalerite
scholastic
schalstein
schematise
schematism
schematist
schematize
schemozzle
sphenogram
sphenoidal
Sphingidae
sphinxlike
school-bred
schooldays
schoolgirl
school-ma'am
schoolmaid
school-marm
school-mate
schoolroom
schooltide
schooltime
schoolward
schoolwork
schipperke
scherzandi
scherzando
sphericity
spherocyte
spheroidal
spherelike
sphereless
spherulite
schorl-rock
schismatic
schizocarp
schizogony
schizoidal
Schizopoda
spinaceous
Shivaistic
spiracular
spiraculum
shibboleth
shipbroker
shin-barker
spin-bowler
switchback
spitchcock
sticcadoes
switchgear
stiacciato
switch-over
sticcatoes
stitchwork
stitchwort
spin-doctor
skin-diving
spinescent
spiceberry
shire-reeve
swivel-hook
Sciaenidae
spiderlike
snivelling
swivelling
stipellate
swine-drunk
stilettoed
swinestone
spitefully
spiderwork
spiderwort
sniffingly
stiffening
sniffiness
sail-flying
swingle-bar
swing-wheel
swing-shelf
stingingly
swingingly
stinginess
sniggering
swing-stock
slingstone
swing-music
swing-swang
stichidium
ship-holder
stichology
slightness
smithereen
smithcraft
sticharion
suicidally
spirit-blue
spiritedly
spiritless
stibialism
spinigrade
spirituous
skikjöring
stickybeak
skip-kennel
smirkingly
stinkingly
stickiness
smickering
snick-a-snee
slickstone
stinkstone
stillicide
spiflicate
smifligate
shield-hand
still-video
stillbirth
spillikins
shillelagh
shieldlike
shieldling
shieldless
shield-maid
Scillonian
stiflingly
stillhouse
shieldrake
sciolistic
still-stand
stillatory
skillfully
shieldwall
seismicity
seismogram
seismology
skimmingly
swimmingly
stigmarian
shimmering
shipmaster
skirmisher
stigmatise
stigmatism
stigmatist
stigmatose
stigmatize
scientific
skinniness
seignorage
spinnerule
seigneurie
skibobbing
spirometer
spirometry
spirophore
sailorlike
sailorless
ski-touring
spirograph
stimpmeter
skimpingly
skippingly
slippiness
slipperily
skippering
ship-rigged
stirringly
spinsterly
slipsloppy
slipstream
scissor-leg
slip-string
spinstress
spissitude
shirtwaist
spittlebug
scintigram
skin-tights
stintingly
shiftiness
shirtiness
shittiness
stiltiness
scintiscan
skittishly
stimulancy
stimulable
stimulator
stipulator
ski-jumping
shipwright
sojourning
△salmanazar
solfataras
△salmanaser
solfataric
saltarelli
saltarello
syllabical
sultanship
self-acting
self-action
salmagundi
salmagundy
self-abuser
syllabuses
self-breath
salubrious
solubilise
salability
solubility

Words marked △ may be spelled also with a capital letter

10 s□l□b

solubilize
self-binder
salt-butter
self-bounty
Salicaceae
self-cocker
silicified
saltcellar
salicylism
siliculose
salicylate
self-colour
solacement
selectness
salicional
salicornia
solecistic
solicitude
salicetums
solicitant
soliciting
solicitous
self-deceit
solidified
self-driven
self-denial
self-danger
solidarism
solidarist
solidarity
solid-state
silverback
silverbill
silver-bath
sallenders
salverform
silverfish
silver-gilt
solfeggios
self-exiled
solferinos
silverling
spleenless
sullenness
silverside
silverskin
salientian
self-esteem
silvertail
silverweed
spleenwort
salifiable
solifidian
self-feeder
self-filler
saliferous
self-glazed
selegiline
silkgrower
self-giving
sylphidine
sulfhydryl
sulphonate
sulphonium
sulphurise
sulphurate
sulphurous
sulphurize
self-hatred
sulphation
sulphatase
salpingian
salvifical
self-inject
saltigrade
soldiering
self-killed
self-killer
self-loving
solemniser
solemnizer
Solomonian
salamander
solemnness
self-murder
self-mettle
self-motion
self-moving
shlemozzle
Solanaceae
selenodont
splanchnic
solenoidal
splendidly
silentiary
selenology
silentness
splendrous
solonetzic
splenative
splintwood
salmonella
silhouette
Salmonidae
syllogiser
syllogizer
Selbornian
sallowness
seldomness
salmon-pink
self-praise
solipedous
self-poised
self-profit
self-parody
salopettes
scleriasis
scleroderm
self-regard
self-raised
self-rolled
self-ruling
scleromata
sultriness
self-repose
self-rising
sclerotial
sclerotomy
sclerotise
sclerotium
sclerotize
self-slayer
splash-back
splashdown
self-seeder
self-seeker
salesclerk
saleswoman
silkscreen
self-severe
self-styled
split-level
splutterer
splotchily
split-image
solutional
solitarian
split-brain
salutarily
solitarily
solstitial
salutation
salutatory
self-taught
self-unable
salbutamol
Seleucidae
Seleucidan
solivagant
Sclavonian
salivation
self-willed
silly-billy
seltzogene
somnambule
sympathies
sympathise
sympathize
semi-annual
somebodies
semichorus
semicircle
semicirque
semi-double
semi-divine
semi-drying
Sympetalae
simnel-cake
summerlike
symmetrian
symmetrise
symmetrize
Simmenthal
summertide
summertime
summerwood
symphilism
symphilous
symphylous
symphonion
symphonist
symphyseal
symphysial
semeiology
summitless
somniloquy
semeiotics
somniatory
somniative
semilucent
simplicity
simulacrum
simplified
simplifier
Simuliidae
simillimum
simpleness
semilunate
semi-liquid
similarity
simplistic
similitude
simulation
simulatory
semblative
similative
simulative
simoniacal
seminality
seminarial
seminarian
seminarist
semination
summonable
semi-opaque
somnolence
somnolency
symbolical
symboliser
symbolizer
symposiast
semipostal
semiquaver
somersault
samariform
samarskite
sombreness
sombrerite
semestrial
sempstress
somatology
semiterete
somatotype
semi-uncial
somewhence
semi-weekly
somewhiles
sunbathing
syntagmata
syncarpous
syndactyly
sandalwood
sandbagged
sandbagger
sand-binder
synecology
synecdoche
sinecurism
sinecurist
sandcastle
sunderance
synaeresis
synderesis
Syngenesia
syngenesis
syngenetic
synteresis
syndetical
sinsemilla
sanbenitos
synoecious
sanderling
sunderment
syntenoses
syntenosis
sinke-a-pace
Sanhedrist
sentential
sunsetting
sonography
sandgroper
Singhalese
synchronal
synchronic
synthronus
sand-hopper
synthesise
synthesist
synthesize
synthetise
synthetist
synthetize
syndicator
syneidesis
singing-man
sincipital
sensitised
sensitiser
sensitized
sensitizer
sensibilia
Sandinismo
Sandinista
santioneer
Sanskritic

Words marked △ may be spelled also with a capital letter

single-eyed
synaloepha
single-foot
Sinologist
singlehood
singleness
single-step
sunglasses
synclastic
singletree
synanthous
synonymise
synonymist
synonymity
synonymous
synonymize
synandrium
synandrous
syncopated
syncopator
sensoriums
sunlounger
synoptical
Sangradoes
synergetic
△sinarchism
sinarchist
syncretise
syncretism
syncretist
syncretize
sonorously
△sinarquism
sinarquist
sandsucker
senescence
sinisterly
sinusoidal
synostoses
synostosis
songstress
sinistrous
sanctified
△sanctifier
sanctimony
sanitarian
senatorial
sanitarily
sanitarist
sanatorium
sanitarium
sanctitude
sanctities
sanitation
singularly
sensualise
sensualism
sensualist
sensuality
sensualize
sanguinely
sanguinary
sinfulness
sanguinity
sensuously
songwriter
synaxarion
sporangial
sporangium
stomachful
stomachous
sporadical
stomatitis
saouari-nut
shopaholic
stomatopod
showboater
slop-bucket
Scombresox
Scombridae
snowblower
spot-barred
snobbishly
Scotchness
snow-capped
sword-dance
spondaical
sword-blade
spondylous
scoldingly
shoddiness
swordcraft
scowdering
swordproof
sword-grass
sword-stick
scordatura
sword-guard
shorewards
stone-eater
stonemason
stone's-cast
shovelfuls
shovelhead
scoresheet
spokeshave
Scopelidae
smoketight
smoke-black
slovenlike
shovelling
stone-blind
showerless
shovelnose
stoneborer
shore-going
scoreboard
smokeboard
smokehouse
stonehorse
storehouse
shove-groat
stonebreak
smoke-dried
stone-broke
storefront
smokeproof
stonebrash
stone-crazy
smokestack
stone-still
stolenwise
scoffingly
slow-footed
spongeable
spongebags
sponge-down
spongiform
slow-gaited
spongology
sponginess
stodginess
showground
spongewood
spongeware
soothsayer
soothingly
smother-fly
smothering
stochastic
slothfully
storiology
stolidness
shop-in-shop
spoliation
spoliatory
spoliative
Scotifying
showjumper
smock-faced
stork'sbill
shopkeeper
stockinged
stockinger
shockingly
spookiness
stockiness
stockhorse
smock-frock
shock-proof
shockstall
stock-still
shouldered
shop-lifter
spoylefull
scowlingly
spoilsport
spotlessly
snowmobile
shoemaking
shotmaking
storminess
stormbound
stormproof
slow-motion
stormfully
slow-moving
swooningly
spoondrift
spoonerism
scornfully
spodomancy
scotometer
Scotophobe
Scotophile
sporophyll
sporophore
sporophyte
scotodinia
sporogonia
sporozoite
snobocracy
scooped-out
scorpaenid
sloop-of-war
stoopingly
sloppiness
snowplough
scorpionic
smørrebrød
shopsoiled
slop-seller
spouseless
Scotswoman
sponsional
sponsorial
shoestring
short-dated
short-range
smooth-bore
Scotticise
Scotticism
Scotticize
stoutherie
Scottified
short-lived
shoutingly
snortingly
sportingly
shortening
smoothness
snootiness
snottiness
sportiness
spottiness
smoothpate
shortbread
short-track
short-order
stouthrief
scoutcraft
smooth-shod
sportfully
sportively
sportswear
shortsword
snow-wreath
spot-welder
Scolytidae
storyboard
stony-broke
sforzandos
scorzonera
suprarenal
sopraninos
supralunar
suprapubic
sappanwood
suppedanea
supperless
sapperment
septennial
septennate
septennium
sapiential
suppertime
septemviri
septemvirs
sapphirine
septically
septicemia
septicidal
syphilitic
septillion
suppliance
supplicant
supplicate
sepulchral
supplejack
supplement
supplyment
supplanter
suppleness
supply-side
suppletion
suppletory
suppletive
sepultural
saponified
supineness
supination
sipunculid
supposable
supposably
saprogenic
sapropelic
supposedly
saprophyte
Sophoclean
siphonogam
sophomoric
supporting
supporture
supportive
supersaver

10 s□p□r

supercargo
supernally
superacute
superseder
superdense
superfecta
superheavy
supersharp
supervisal
supervisee
supertitle
supergiant
supervisor
superaltar
superclean
superfluid
superalloy
superclass
superbness
supernovae
supernovas
super-royal
superwoman
superposed
superpower
supersonic
supertonic
superiorly
supersound
superspeed
superorder
superbrain
supergrass
supergroup
suppressed
suppressor
separatrix
separately
separation
superation
separatory
superstore
separatism
separatist
superstate
separative
superhuman
superlunar
super-duper
supersweet
superoxide
superexalt
Sapotaceae
Septuagint
sequacious
sequencing
sequential
sequestrum
serrasalmo
surfaceman
streamered

sarracenia
serradella
sordamente
stream-gold
spreaghery
Serranidae
serradilla
serrations
streamline
streamling
streamless
spread-over
surpassing
servant-man
surfactant
scrobicule
strobiloid
scribbling
strobiline
strobilate
strabismal
strabismic
strabismus
surf-bather
strabotomy
soricident
sericteria
shriche-owl
stracchini
stracchino
sdrucciola
strychnine
Saracenism
spruceness
strictness
strychnism
surfcaster
structural
strictured
structured
stridelegs
stridulant
stridulate
stridulous
stridently
Stradivari
strideways
surveyance
shrievalty
street-cred
streetfuls
screech-owl
shriech-owl
screenings
streetlamp
surrealism
surrealist
serjeantry
sure-enough
screenplay
streetroom

serpentine
surfeiting
surjection
sarmentose
serpentise
sarmentous
serpentize
streetward
streetwise
strifeless
scrofulous
surefooted
strife-torn
serigraphy
strigiform
scrag-whale
scraggling
straggling
struggling
stroganoff
scrog-apple
sprightful
soreheaded
surcharged
surcharger
survivance
surgically
surmisable
survivable
serviceman
sortileger
straitened
strainedly
serving-man
straighten
straightly
serpigines
sordidness
straitness
servitress
strikingly
Struldbrug
serologist
shrillness
surplusage
strelitzes
strelitzia
scrollwork
scrollwise
scrimmager
scrummager
scrimshank
skrimshank
scrambling
scrimpness
stramonium
stromatous
shrinkable
springbuck
spring-cart
stringency

stringendo
strandflat
springhaas
springhead
springhalt
stringhalt
stronghold
springhase
syringitis
strong-knit
shrinelike
springlike
sprinkling
strinkling
springless
stringless
sereneness
shrinkpack
strongroom
springtide
strengthen
springtail
springtime
shrink-wrap
strandwolf
springwood
springwort
surrogatum
sarcolemma
sermonette
Sarcophaga
sarcophagi
sardonical
sermonical
Sorbonical
surnominal
sermoniser
sermonizer
sarcoplasm
sorrowless
surmounted
surmounter
Sorbonnist
seriocomic
sarcocolla
servomotor
Serbo-Croat
strappados
striptease
scrapegood
seraphical
strippings
strophiole
stripeless
scrupulous
strapontin
stripiness
strip-poker
scriptoria
streperous
strepitant

strepitoso
strepitous
scriptural
sororially
sororicide
surf-riding
surprising
stressless
stratocrat
stratified
stratiform
strategics
strategist
scratch-wig
scratchily
scratching
scritch-owl
shritch-owl
struthioid
struthious
scrutineer
scrutinise
scrutinous
serotinous
scrutinize
serotyping
strathspey
suretyship
serrulated
Sertularia
scrounging
shroud-laid
shroudless
stravaiger
shrivelled
shriveling
strivingly
scrivening
Shrovetide
strawberry
shrewdness
strawboard
shrewmouse
shrewishly
spray-paint
spray-dried
sustaining
sustenance
systematic
suspenders
sisterhood
sisterlike
sisterless
systemless
suspensoid
suspension
suspensory
suspensive
sustention
sustentate
sestertium

Words marked △ may be spelled also with a capital letter

suspectful
susceptive
sustentive
suscipient
suspicious
suspirious
sisal-grass
satyagraha
setterwort
setiferous
setigerous
satchelled
settleable
satellites
satellitic
settlement
satanology
sitophobia
△**saturnalia**
satyriasis
satyresque
saturation
suturation
satisfying
set-stitch'd
sousaphone
stubble-fed
stumblebum
snubbingly
stubbiness
stubbornly
slubbering
slumbering
slumberful
slumberous
squabasher
sourcebook
sluicegate
sculduddry
'sbuddikins
sourdeline
spudding-in
soundingly
sturdiness
squadronal
squadroned
soundtrack
shuddering
soundproof
squeezable
spumescent
stupendous
saucer-eyed
squeeze-box
saucerfuls
spuleblade
sauce-alone
scutellate
souterrain
stupefying
snuff-paper
snuff-taker
shuffle-cap
scurfiness
snuffiness
stuffiness
snuff-brown
smudginess
sluggishly
southwards
spur-heeled
south-polar
southbound
△**southerner**
southernly
southering
Saurischia
stupidness
spuriosity
spuriously
studiously
skulkingly
spunkiness
squalidity
squelching
soullessly
squamiform
squamulose
squamosity
squamation
squandered
squanderer
squint-eyed
squint-eyes
stunningly
Sauropsida
stumpiness
sculptress
sculptural
sculptured
squirearch
squirrelly
square-face
squarehead
squirehood
squirelike
squireling
scurrility
squirality
scurrilous
squareness
soubriquet
squirarchy
sauerkraut
square-sail
squireship
square-toed
square-toes
stupration
squarewise
squashable
saussurite
Skupshtina
squeteague
soup-ticket
scuttleful
stultified
stultifier
smuttiness
shunt-wound
sauntering
shuttering
sputtering
stuttering
shutterbug
sluttishly
scurviness
spur-winged
savageness
seven-score
sevenpence
sevenpenny
△**seventh-day**
seventieth
savingness
seven-a-side
severeness
savourless
sewage-farm
saw-toothed
sexpartite
saxicoline
saxicolous
saxicavous
sixteenmos
sexagenary
Sexagesima
six-shooter
sex-limited
sextillion
sexologist
sextonship
sexlocular
sex-starved
sexivalent
skyjacking
skylarking
skyscraper
scyphiform
scyphozoan
stylistics
stylometry
stylopised
stylopized
stylolitic
stylograph
sky-writing
stypticity
sky-surfing
sky-jumping
sizzlingly
suzerainty
tragacanth
thanatosis
thalassian
tea-tasting
thatchless
trade-falne
travelator
tradesfolk
tsarevitch
trapeziums
teaselling
travelling
trace-horse
travelogue
tradecraft
thale-cress
travel-sick
traversing
toad-eating
travertine
trabeation
trajection
trajectory
trabeculae
trabecular
trafficked
trafficker
twangingly
tracheated
Trachearia
tracheitis
trachelate
trashiness
trachytoid
tragically
traditores
tragicomic
thalictrum
tear-jerker
tracklayer
track-scout
thankfully
trap-ladder
thalliform
tea-planter
Thailander
trailingly
trawlerman
traymobile
trammelled
trammeller
trammel-net
thaumasite
traumatise
traumatism
traumatize
travolator
tramontana
tramontane
trampoline
trappiness
tranquilly
tea-drinker
translator
transvalue
transactor
transudate
transience
transiency
transferee
transgenic
transferor
transverse
trans-shape
transplant
transonics
transposal
transposer
trans-sonic
transposon
transeptal
transcribe
transcript
transgress
transistor
transition
transitory
transitive
translunar
transducer
transfuser
transmuter
transputer
translucid
tractrices
tractility
tractional
△**tractarian**
trattorias
traitorism
traitorous
teacupfuls
traducible
traduction
traductive
tablanette
tubicolous
table-d'hôte
tablecloth
table-cover
tablespoon
table-sport
table-music
tobogganed
tobogganer
Tobagonian
tub-thumper
tubularian
tabularise
tubularity
tabularize
tabulation
tubulation

Words marked △ may be spelled also with a capital letter

10 t□b□l

tabulatory
tubulature
tibiotarsi
tuboplasty
tabernacle
Tuberaceae
tuberiform
tuberosity
Tyburn-tree
tubercular
tuberculin
tuberculum
tabescence
tibouchina
toccatella
tocher-good
tocherless
ticker-tape
tickety-boo
tactically
ticking-off
tactlessly
ticklishly
technician
technocrat
technicise
technicism
technicist
technicize
technofear
technology
technopole
technetium
tachometer
tachometry
tachograph
tocopherol
tectricial
taciturnly
tactuality
tachymeter
tachymetry
tachylitic
tachypnoea
tachygraph
tachylytic
tiddlywink
tediousome
Tudoresque
tidivation
tide-waiter
toddy-ladle
toddy-stick
Theravadin
tsesarevna
trepanning
thenabouts
trey-antler
tree-burial
trenchancy
theocratic
trench-coat
treacherer
trench-feet
trench-foot
theodicean
△tweedledee
Tweedledum
tread-wheel
theodolite
trendiness
tweediness
thereabout
tremendous
thereafter
thereamong
thereunder
thereanent
trecentist
Twelfth-day
theogonist
trephining
thetically
taeniacide
taeniafuge
treillaged
theologian
theologise
theologist
theologate
theologize
trebleness
thermoform
thermogram
thermology
thermalise
Thermalite®
thermalize
theomaniac
theomantic
thermionic
thermophil
thermopile
thermostat
thermistor
thermotics
'tweendecks
theonomous
tremolandi
tremolando
teetotally
treponemas
treponemes
tremolitic
tremorless
theophanic
theopneust
theophobia
theophoric
trespasser
tie-breaker
theurgical
theoretics
trekschuit
theistical
themselves
treasonous
theosopher
theosophic
theotechny
twentyfold
twenty-four
twenty-five
theatrical
tweet-tweet
twelvefold
twelve-note
twelve-tone
teeny-weeny
tuffaceous
tuftaffeta
tuftaffety
toffee-nose
tuft-hunter
tagliarini
toggleiron
tegumental
tigerishly
tight-laced
tight-lacer
tightishly
tchoukball
tricameral
trilateral
trivalence
trivalency
triradiate
trifarious
tritanopia
tritanopic
△trinacrian
tripartism
tripartite
twi-natured
thimblerig
thimbleful
thiocyanic
triactinal
triaconter
third-party
third-class
trigeminal
trioecious
triternate
thimerosal
tripe-woman
tripehound
toiletries
trisectrix
Tridentine
trisection
tridentate
thief-taker
triffidian
twinflower
thingumbob
thinginess
triggerman
trichiasis
trichogyne
triphthong
trichology
trichinise
trichinose
trichinous
trichinize
trichromat
trichromic
trithionic
trichroism
teichopsia
Triphysite
trichotomy
Trichiurus
tritically
triniscope
triliteral
toilinette
trilineate
triticeous
trilingual
twilighted
twi-nighter
trivialise
trivialism
triviality
trivialize
tuitionary
tripinnate
trinitrate
tritiation
thick-skull
triskelion
thinkingly
thickening
trickiness
trick-track
thick-grown
trickishly
trinketing
triplicate
triplicity
triflingly
tripleness
triclinium
thill-horse
trillionth
triglyphic
triumphant
triumphing
triumphery
triumviral
trimmingly
triandrian
triandrous
triangular
trilobated
tailor-bird
teinoscope
tribometer
tricoteuse
trilobitic
trifoliate
tailor-made
tailormake
trimorphic
thixotrope
thixotropy
trimonthly
tricostate
trilocular
triapsidal
thiopental
trippingly
tripperish
tribrachic
trigrammic
trierarchy
tricrotism
tricrotous
thirstless
toilsomely
twin-sister
tristichic
thirteenth
thirtyfold
triathlete
twittingly
Thirty-nine
twittering
tripterous
thiouracil
triturator
trifurcate
trisulcate
tripudiary
tripudiate
triquetral
triquetrum
thievishly
thin-walled
tricycling
tricyclist
takingness
tokenistic
tillandsia
tiliaceous
talebearer
telebridge
tollbridge
telechiric
telecamera
telecasted
telecaster
tillerless

Words marked △ may be spelled also with a capital letter

10 t□r□e

tiller-rope
tellership
telegraphy
telegonous
telegnosis
tilt-hammer
telpherman
telpherway
telpherage
telling-off
telematics
telemetric
talentless
talent-spot
tallow-face
teleologic
teleonomic
teliospore
teleostean
teleostome
Teleostomi
tulip-eared
telophasic
telephoner
telephonic
telepathic
telerecord
tularaemia
tularaemic
tolerantly
toleration
talismanic
telesmatic
telescopic
telescreen
tale-teller
Talmudical
televiewer
televérité
televisual
television
telewriter
teleworker
talky-talky
tilly-fally
tilly-vally
tallywoman
tally-hoing
tally-trade
tympanites
tympanitic
tympanitis
Tammanyism
Tammanyite
tamability
time-barred
timocratic
temperance
temperable
timber-head
timberland
timberline
timber-mare
timber-toes
timber-tree
tempestive
timberyard
tomography
tim-whiskey
timekeeper
time-killer
tumble-cart
tumble-dung
tumbledown
temulently
timeliness
tumblerful
timelessly
tumultuary
tumultuate
tumultuous
tumbleweed
temporally
temporalty
temporiser
temporizer
tomfoolery
tambourine
tumorgenic
timbrology
temerously
timorously
time-sharer
tumescence
time-served
time-server
time-saving
tomatillos
temptingly
time-thrust
temptation
tantaliser
tantalizer
tantamount
tanka-boats
tennantite
tentacular
tentaculum
tenebrific
tenebrious
tenability
tankbuster
tenderfeet
tenderfoot
tenterhook
tenderiser
tenderizer
tunbellied
tenderloin
tinder-like
tenderling
tinselling
tunnelling
tenderness
tangential
tendential
Tinseltown
tandemwise
tank-farmer
tennis-ball
tensimeter
tendinitis
tonsilitic
tonsilitis
tonsillary
tennis-shoe
tanglefoot
tanglement
tanglingly
tinklingly
tonelessly
tanglesome
tonalitive
tangleweed
tenemental
tenantable
tuning-fork
tenantless
tenantship
Tintometer®
tendonitis
ten-pointer
ten-pounder
tenurially
tendrillar
tendrilled
tonishness
tenotomist
tinctorial
tonguelike
tongueless
tonguester
tongue-tied
tongue-work
tropaeolin
tropaeolum
troubadour
troubledly
trombonist
trou-de-loup
trowelling
two-year-old
thoughtful
toothpaste
two-wheeled
two-wheeler
toothshell
trochoidal
trophology
Trophonian
trochanter
toothiness
toothbrush
trophesial
trochiscus
trochotron
tropically
troglodyte
Trollopean
Trollopian
trolloping
trollopish
trolley-car
trolley-man
trolleybus
trou-madame
toolmaking
thornhedge
thorniness
tropopause
tromometer
thoroughly
tropophyte
Trogonidae
tropologic
troop-horse
toolpusher
trousseaus
trousseaux
thousandth
trouser-leg
trousering
Trotskyism
Trotskyist
Trotskyite
troctolite
trout-spoon
troutstone
trouvaille
tap-dancing
tophaceous
typhaceous
topgallant
topicality
typicality
type-cutter
tepidarium
tappet-loom
tappet-ring
Tupperware®
topography
typography
type-holder
topping-out
topologist
typologist
typhlology
toponymics
topknotted
top-notcher
topsoiling
taphonomic
toploftily
topophilia
tape-record
taperingly
tapestried
tapescript
typescript
typesetter
tapotement
typewriter
topi-wallah
topsy-turvy
topazolite
tarmacadam
termagancy
tartanalia
throat-band
threadbare
thread-cell
tersanctus
threatened
threatener
terracette
tartareous
throat-full
terrariums
tirra-lirra
tarmacking
thread-lace
tarpauling
throat-lash
turnaround
terra-rossa
terracotta
threadworm
throatwort
Terramycin®
turnbuckle
turnbroach
tirocinium
taradiddle
targetable
three-parts
turkey-cock
torpescent
turgescent
threescore
threepence
threepenny
three-phase
three-piece
three-piled
three-sided
three-cleft
terreplein
tortellini
torbernite
torpedo-net
three-point
three-pound
torpedoist
three-speed
turret-ship

10 t□r□e

torrential
tormenting
turpentine
turpentiny
torrent-bow
turkey-trot
torrefying
tortfeasor
thriftiest
tariffless
thriftless
torch-dance
torchlight
Tyrrhenian
torch-staff
turbinated
Terminalia
terminable
terminably
terminally
terminator
Turritella
turning-saw
tirling-pin
tirailleur
torpidness
torridness
turbidness
turgidness
Tardigrada
tardigrade
terminuses
tortiously
tarsia-work
terrifying
turtleback
turtledove
Tyrolienne
turtleneck
tirelessly
turtle-soup
Turkmenian
thromboses
thrombosis
thrombotic
tyrant-bird
threnodial
threnodist
tarantella
tyrannical
Tyrannidae
throneless
throne-room
tiring-room
Turko-Tatar
Turcophobe
Turcophile
terroriser
terrorizer
torporific
terrorless
thruppence
thruppenny
tartrazine
tiresomely
tyrosinase
teratogeny
teratology
throttling
teratomata
turbulator
turbulence
turbulency
torturedly
Tartuffian
Tartuffish
Tartuffism
throughway
throughout
throughput
Targumical
tortuosity
tortuously
thriveless
thrivingly
thrown-silk
throw-stick
testaceous
tassel-gent
tasselling
tessellate
tusser-silk
tastefully
teschenite
tossicated
tosticated
testicular
testifying
test-market
taskmaster
tasimetric
taseometer
testudinal
testudines
tetrabasic
tetrarchic
Tetrandria
tetrameral
tête-à-têtes
tetrameter
tetrasemic
tetrahedra
tetrathlon
tetrachord
tetraploid
tetragonal
tetrapodic
tetrapolis
tetratomic
Tetramorph
tetraspore
tetrastich
tetrastyle
tetractine
tetraptote
tetraethyl
Tetragynia
titubation
tête-de-pont
Tattersall
tetchiness
tattie-claw
tithingman
tattie-shaw
titillator
tattlingly
titularity
tattle-tale
totemistic
Titanesque
tutworkman
tetrotoxin
totipotent
tutorially
tittupping
tut-tutting
tatpurusha
titivation
thumbscrew
thumbs-down
thumbpiece
thumbikins
tourbillon
thumb-index
thunbergia
thumbprint
thumbstall
truncately
truncation
trundle-bed
thuddingly
thunder-egg
thundering
thunderbox
thunder-god
thunderous
truffle-pig
truffle-dog
touch-paper
truth-value
touch-me-not
touch-piece
touch-plate
touch-and-go
touchingly
toughening
touchiness
touchstone
touch-judge
truthfully
trunk-maker
truckle-bed
tourmaline
tournament
trunnioned
tourniquet
truantship
tauromachy
tautomeric
tautophony
tautologic
thumpingly
trumpeting
tauntingly
trustingly
trustiness
trust-house
trustfully
truculence
truculency
towel-gourd
towel-horse
towing-path
thwartedly
tower-shell
tawdry-lace
toweringly
tawdriness
towardness
thwartship
thwartwise
thwartways
town's-bairn
townswoman
taxability
toxicology
toxication
taxi-driver
taxidermal
taxidermic
text-editor
taxonomist
toxiphobia
texturally
textualism
textualist
thysanuran
twy-natured
thymectomy
thyrsoidal
toyishness
tryptophan
tuzzi-muzzy
tuzzy-muzzy
unawakened
unacademic
unavailing
Ural-Altaic
unanalysed
unanalyzed
unanalytic
uranalysis
unaccented
unascended
unanchored
up-and-under
unamenable
un-American
unaffected
unarguable
unarguably
unanimated
unadjusted
usableness
unallotted
unadmiring
unadmitted
unarmoured
unannealed
unatonable
unavowedly
uranometry
unappeased
unapprised
unappalled
unapproved
unapparent
unaspiring
unacquaint
unabridged
unarranged
unassuaged
unanswered
unassigned
unassailed
unabsolved
unassuming
unassisted
unactuated
unattached
unattended
unaltering
unattested
unartistic
unartfully
unamusable
unbearable
unbearably
unbeatable
unblamable
unblamably
unbranched
upbraiding
unbeavered
unbiasedly
umbrageous
umbratical
unboastful
umbraculum
unbiblical
unbecoming
unbudgeted
unbedimmed
unbedinned
unbleached

Words marked △ may be spelled also with a capital letter

unblenched
unbreached
unbreeched
umbrellaed
umbrelloes
unbreathed
unbeguiled
unbegotten
unbeholden
unbailable
unbribable
upbuilding
upbringing
unblinking
unblissful
umbellated
umbilicate
unbelieved
unbeliever
umbellifer
unbalanced
unbendable
unbonneted
unbenignly
urbanology
unbundling
urbaneness
urbanistic
urbanities
umbonation
upbuoyance
unbloodied
unbrokenly
unbaptised
unbaptized
unbarbered
unburdened
unbirthday
unborrowed
upbursting
unbespoken
unbestowed
unbesought
unbetrayed
unbattered
unbettered
unbuttered
unbottomed
unbuttoned
unblushing
unbewailed
unchanging
uncharming
unchastely
unchastity
unclerical
uncredible
uncleansed
uncheerful
uncreating
uncoffined
uncritical
uncoloured
uncultured
uncumbered
uncommonly
uncommuted
unconfined
uncandidly
uncanonise
uncanonize
uncensored
unconsoled
unconstant
unconjugal
uncensured
unconfused
unconsumed
uncloister
uncurbable
uncerebral
uncared-for
uncarpeted
uncorseted
unchristen
ulceration
ulcerative
ulcerously
uncustomed
unclubable
unctuosity
unctuously
undramatic
undebarred
undeclared
undeceived
undecimole
undoctored
undecisive
undreading
undreaming
undressing
undefeated
undefended
undigested
undulately
undulating
undulation
undulatory
undelaying
undomestic
undeniable
undeniably
undrooping
undepraved
undeprived
undeplored
underjawed
underlayer
undernamed
undertaken
undertaker
underwater
underearth
underpants
undervalue
undirected
underactor
underscore
underscrub
undersexed
underbelly
underlease
undersense
underneath
underagent
underwhelm
undershoot
undershirt
undershrub
underminde
underlinen
underminer
undersized
undertimed
underwired
underskirt
undercliff
underplant
underslung
underfloor
under-clerk
underclass
underglaze
undervoice
undercover
undernoted
under-power
undertoned
underbough
underworld
underborne
undergoing
under-board
underspend
under-trick
under-craft
undercroft
underdrain
underproof
underbrush
undercrest
underdress
underprise
underwrite
underdrive
undergrove
undergrown
underprize
understock
understudy
understeer
underntime
understand
understood
understory
understate
under-tunic
underbuild
underburnt
underquote
underlying
undismayed
undesigned
undisposed
undescried
undeserved
undeserver
undesiring
undesirous
undisputed
undetected
undeterred
undoubting
undoubtful
undivulged
undiverted
undivorced
undivested
unerasable
unexamined
unexampled
unexacting
unembodied
unexcelled
unenclosed
unescorted
unexciting
unexcluded
unendeared
unendingly
ureteritis
unevenness
uterectomy
uneventful
unexecuted
uneffected
unenforced
urethritic
urethritis
Uredinales
unedifying
uneclipsed
Übermensch
uneconomic
uredosorus
uredospore
uredo-stage
unexpiated
unemphatic
unexpected
unexpanded
unemployed
unexplored
unenriched
unerringly
unenslaved
uneasiness
unentailed
unextended
unentitled
uneducated
uneducable
unequalled
usefulness
unenviable
unenviably
unflagging
upflashing
unfeasible
unfeatured
unfocussed
unfadingly
unfrequent
unfrighted
unfaithful
unfriended
unfriendly
unfeigning
unfairness
unfilially
unfillable
unfilleted
unfiltered
unfallible
unfellowed
unfamiliar
unfeminine
unfinished
unforsaken
unfordable
unforcedly
unforgiven
unforcible
unfurrowed
unforeseen
unforested
unforetold
unfortuned
unfastened
unfostered
unfathered
unfettered
unfatherly
unfathomed
unfoughten
unfruitful
upgradable
ungraceful
ungrateful
ungracious
unguentary
ungainsaid
ungenerous
ungrounded

10 u□g□r

ungarnered
ungartered
ungathered
ungrudging
ungoverned
unhealable
unheededly
unhygienic
unhelpable
unhelmeted
unholiness
unhallowed
upholstery
uphillward
unhampered
unhomelike
unhumanise
unhumanize
unhindered
unhandsome
unhonoured
unhoped-for
unhardened
unheroical
unheralded
unhurrying
unhistoric
unhouseled
unhouzzled
unhazarded
unicameral
unilateral
univalence
univalency
unimagined
univariant
unilabiate
univariate
unipartite
urinalysis
uninclosed
unindeared
uniseriate
Unigenitus
unidealism
unitedness
university
unicentral
uninflamed
uninflated
uninfected
uninforced
uninformed
unitholder
utilisable
utilizable
uniliteral
unilingual
uniflorous
unimmortal
unisonance
unisonally
univocally
urinoscopy
urinometer
unifoliate
uniformity
univoltine
unicostate
unilobular
unilocular
unimpaired
unimplored
unimproved
unimparted
unimposing
uninspired
unintended
uninuclear
ubiquinone
uniqueness
ubiquarian
ubiquitary
ubiquitous
uninvolved
uninvested
uninviting
uniaxially
unjustness
unknighted
unknightly
unkinglike
unkindness
unknowable
unleavened
unlabelled
unlaboured
unlockable
unlicensed
unladylike
unlifelike
unleisured
unlikeable
unlikeness
unlamented
unliquored
unlistened
unlessoned
unlettable
unlettered
unliterary
unliveable
unloveable
unlovingly
unlawfully
unmeasured
unmechanic
unmodified
unmeetness
unmailable
unmaidenly
unmellowed
unmolested
unmilitary
unmanacled
unmannered
unmannerly
unmanfully
unmortised
unmerciful
unmorality
unmeriting
unmastered
unmotherly
unmetrical
unmetalled
unmaterial
unmaternal
unmoveable
unmoveably
unmuzzling
uintathere
unnameable
unnumbered
unnurtured
unnoticing
unoccupied
uroscopist
unordained
unordinary
unovercome
urogenital
unobedient
unofficial
unoffended
urochordal
unoriginal
uxoricidal
unoxidised
unoxidized
utopianise
utopianism
utopianize
uxorilocal
uxoriously
uropoiesis
urological
urographic
unossified
unobserved
unobscured
urosthenic
urostegite
unobtained
unorthodox
Uto-Aztecan
unplayable
unpeaceful
unplausive
unpickable
unpuckered
unpacified
unprepared
unpeerable
unpoetical
unpregnant
unpleasant
unpleasing
unprizable
unprincely
unpoisoned
unprisoned
unpriestly
unpillared
unpolicied
unpillowed
unpolished
unpolitely
unpolluted
unpampered
unpanelled
unpunished
unpunctual
unprofaned
unprovable
unphonetic
unproperly
unploughed
unprofited
unpromised
unprovided
unprolific
unproposed
unprovoked
unprompted
unproduced
unpeppered
unpopulous
unpurvaide
unparadise
unpurveyed
unpurified
unparallel
upper-class
unperilous
unparental
unparented
unpardoned
unpurposed
upperworks
upper-crust
unperished
umpireship
unperfumed
unperjured
unpassable
unpossible
uppishness
unpastoral
unpastured
unpathetic
unpatented
unpowdered
unqualited
unquarried
usquebaugh
unquenched
unquotable
unreadable
unrealised
unrealized
uproarious
unreasoned
unreactive
unreceived
unrecalled
unreckoned
unrecorded
unrecuring
unrideable
unredeemed
unruffable
Ugro-Finnic
unreformed
unregarded
upright-man
unrightful
unrejoiced
unreliable
unrelieved
unruliment
unrelentor
unruliness
unrelished
unrelative
unremedied
unromantic
unremarked
unremitted
unrendered
unransomed
unrenowned
unrepealed
unrepeated
unrepaired
unrepelled
unrepented
unrepining
unripeness
unreproved
unreported
unreposing
unrequired
unrequited
unrespited
unresolved
unresented
unrestored
unreserved
unresisted
unratified
unretarded
unreturned
unrevealed
unravelled

Words marked △ may be spelled also with a capital letter

unraveller
unrivalled
unrevenged
unreversed
unreverted
unreverend
unreverent
unravished
unrewarded
unscalable
unshakable
unshakably
unswayable
unscabbard
unsearched
unstanched
unstarched
upstanding
unshakenly
unshackled
unseasoned
unshadowed
unsublimed
unsociable
unsociably
unsocially
unseconded
upside-down
upsideowne
unsteadily
ulsterette
unspecific
unspeaking
unsleeping
unswearing
unsceptred
unsheathed
unswerving
unsoftened
unsafeness
unschooled
unseizable
unsuitable
unsuitably
unsmirched
unsmiled-on
unshingled
unspirited
unshielded
unslipping
unshifting
unstinting
unsaleable
unsellable
unsolvable
unsolidity
unsalaried
unsympathy
unsummered
unsymmetry
unseminar'd
ugsomeness
unsummoned
unsinkable
unsensible
unsensibly
unsinnowed
unsanctify
unsanitary
unscorched
unshowered
unstooping
unsmoothed
unsporting
unsupplied
unstreamed
unstriated
unsurfaced
unshrubbed
upsurgence
unscreened
unsurveyed
unstrained
unsurmised
unscramble
unstringed
unscripted
unscrupled
unstrapped
unstripped
unstressed
unsistered
unsisterly
unsatiated
unsatiable
unsettling
unsizeable
ultrabasic
ultra-rapid
untearable
unthatched
ultrashort
ultrafiche
unthankful
ultrasonic
ultrasound
untrampled
untranquil
Urticaceae
untochered
untuckered
urticarial
urtication
untidiness
untrenched
untreasure
unthinking
untainting
untwisting
untellable
untillable
untalked-of
untalented
ustulation
untameable
untameably
untempered
untimbered
ultimately
untuneable
untendered
untenderly
untangible
untenanted
untroubled
ultroneous
unthorough
unthreaded
unturnable
untyreable
untiringly
ulteriorly
untortured
untasteful
untethered
untruthful
untrueness
untrussing
untrustful
untowardly
usucapient
usucaption
unusefully
unutilised
unutilized
usuriously
unuplifted
usurpingly
usurpation
usurpatory
usurpature
usurpative
unvaluable
unvendible
unviolated
unvariable
unveracity
unverified
unvirtuous
unvitiated
unwearable
unweakened
unweaponed
unwearying
unwedgable
unwieldily
unwifelike
unweighing
unwrinkled
unwellness
unwelcomed
unwontedly
unwinnowed
unworkable
unworthily
unwareness
unwariness
upwardness
unwiseness
unwithered
unwithheld
unwatchful
unwavering
unyielding
vibraphone
vibrations
vibraculum
vibrometer
vibrograph
vocabulary
vocabulist
vice-consul
vice-county
vociferant
vociferate
vociferous
vicegerent
vaccinator
victimiser
victimizer
victimless
vicomtesse
vacantness
vacuolated
△**victoriana**
victorious
vectograph
viceregent
vocational
vacationer
victualled
victualler
vichyssois
videophone
viewership
viewfinder
voetganger
view-halloo
viewlessly
Vietnamese
voetstoots
vegeburger
vignettist
vigilantly
vaginismus
vigorously
vegetarian
vegetating
vegetation
vegetative
vehemently
voiceprint
Vulcanalia
voltameter
villanelle
villagioes
volcanised
volcanized
villainage
villainess
villainous
Villanovan
Voltairean
Voltairian
Voltairism
volubility
velocipede
validation
vulnerable
volleyball
velvet-crab
velvet-duck
value-added
velvet-leaf
villeinage
velvet-pile
valleculae
vallecular
villiagoes
voluminous
volumetric
Volapükist
voluptuary
voluptuous
valerianic
valorously
veldschoen
volatilise
volatility
volatilize
velutinous
volitional
volitorial
velitation
volitation
volutation
valvulitis
vampire-bat
vomitorium
vine-branch
vanadinite
vindemiate
veneer-moth
Vincentian
vengefully
veneficous
venography
vinegar-eel
vinegar-fly
vinegarish
ventilable
vindicable
ventilator
vindicator
vindictive

Words marked △ may be spelled also with a capital letter

10 v□n□l

vinylidene
vinologist
vine-mildew
venomously
ventricule
ventriculi
ventricose
ventricous
veneration
Venus-shell
vanishment
Venetianed
venational
venatorial
vanquisher
violaceous
vapulation
vaporiform
viperiform
vaporosity
vaporettos
vaporously
viperously
vapour-bath
verballing
vernacular
varicocele
varicellar
varicosity
varicotomy
veridicous
variegated
verse-maker
verbena-oil
varietally
variegator
verse-smith
verge-board
Vertebrata
vertebrate
vergership
verifiable
viraginian
viraginous
voraginous
vertically
virginally
vortically
virgin-born
vermicelli
vorticella
varnishing
virginhood
vermicidal
vertigines
versionist
vernissage
vermicular
vermifugal
versicular
vorticular
versifying
virologist
Verulamian
virulently
virilising
virilizing
verandahed
variolator
Vertoscope®
variometer
Vireonidae
variolitic
verkrampte
virescence
varitypist
virtualism
virtualist
virtueless
virtuality
virtuosity
virtuously
viscachera
visualiser
visualizer
visibility
vesiculose
vesiculate
vesication
vesicatory
vesper-bell
vespertine
Visigothic
vestibular
vestibulum
vestmental
vestmented
visionally
viscometer
visiogenic
viscometry
visiophone
visionless
viscountcy
vest-pocket
vestry-room
visitorial
△visitation
visitative
vascularly
vitrailled
viticolous
Vaticanism
Vaticanist
vaticinate
vitrescent
vitreosity
vitiferous
vitriolise
vitriolate
vitriolize
vitellicle
vitalistic
vitalising
vitalities
vitalizing
vitaminise
vitaminize
vituperate
veterinary
vaudeville
vouchsafed
vauntingly
vivandière
viviparism
viviparity
viviparous
Viverridae
△viverrinae
vivisector
vowel-rhyme
vexingness
voyageable
viziership
vizard-mask
wraparound
whatabouts
wharfinger
weak-headed
weak-handed
weak-hinged
wrathiness
weatherman
weathering
weatherise
weatherize
wrathfully
whaling-gun
wearifully
weakliness
weak-minded
weaponless
weapon-shaw
wrap-rascal
whatsoever
weak-willed
wearyingly
wabbliness
wobbliness
wickedness
wickerwork
Wycliffite
wide-bodied
widershins
widespread
widescreen
wretchedly
weeldlesse
wieldiness
whereabout
weekending
whereafter
whewellite
whereunder
whereuntil
wheresoe'er
woe-wearied
weedkiller
wheelchair
wheel-clamp
wheelhorse
wheelhouse
whensoever
wheatsheaf
wheatfield
wreathless
Wheatstone
woefulness
wheeziness
wifeliness
wage-earner
wag-at-the-wa'
Weimaraner
wait-a-while
white-faced
white-water
whitebeard
white-heart
waiterhood
whitethorn
white-slave
whitesmith
writership
whiggamore
Whiggarchy
Whiggishly
weigh-bauks
weightless
writhingly
weighboard
weigh-house
writing-pad
writing-ink
whiskified
whirlybird
whirl-about
whirlblast
whillywhaw
whippiness
whimpering
whispering
waitperson
whippeting
whip-stitch
Whitsunday
whimsiness
wainscoted
wristwatch
whiptailed
waistcloth
whitterick
wainwright
whity-brown
whizzingly
Wykehamist
Wallachian
walk-around
well-boring
well-beseen
well-chosen
wildcatter
wildebeest
wilderment
Wilhelmine
wilderness
well-earned
Waldensian
wall-facing
wallflower
well-formed
wildfowler
well-graced
well-gotten
well-heeled
Welshwoman
wellie-boot
wellington
Williamite
Wolfianism
well-judged
well-liking
will-lessly
well-minded
well-marked
willowherb
well-placed
well-padded
wall-rocket
wolframite
well-sinker
well-spoken
wellspring
well-thewed
well-to-live
well-turned
wall-to-wall
wilfulness
walnutwood
well-willer
wall-washer
well-wished
well-wisher
walky-talky
willy-nilly
willy-willy
wamblingly
wambliness
woman-hater
woman-child
woman-tired
womenfolks
woman-grown
womanishly
woman-built
womanfully

10 z□u□l

womenswear
wampumpeag
wonga-wonga
wine-bibber
wind-broken
wine-cooler
winter-clad
winceyette
Wanderjahr
winterkill
wunderkind
wonderland
wanderlust
wonderment
wontedness
wintertide
wintertime
wanrestful
wonderwork
windfallen
windflower
wing-footed
wine-grower
wanthriven
wanchancie
Winchester
Winchester®
windjammer
wentletrap
window-bole
windowless
wantonness
windowpane
windowsill
window-shop
wintriness
wondrously
wind-shaken
wind-sucker
windshield
wingspread
windscreen
windsurfer
wine-taster
wing-walker
wood-boring
wool-comber
woodcarver
wool-carder
wood-cutter
wool-driver
wholesaler
wholewheat
woodenhead
whole-plate
woodenness
whorehouse
wholegrain
wrong-timed
wool-grower
wrongdoing
woodgrouse
wrongfully
wrongously
whoa-hoa-hoa
woollyback
woollybutt
woodlander
woodpecker
wool-packer
wool-picker
woodpigeon
whomsoever
woolsorter
woodshrike
woodthrush
whodunitry
wool-winder
woodworker
wapper-eyed
wappenshaw
wapenschaw
wapinschaw
warrandice
workaholic
warranting
warrantise
workbasket
wiredrawer
worldscale
world-weary
world-class
wire-dancer
warmed-over
war-wearied
wardenship
worm-eating
workfellow
word-finder
worthwhile
wire-haired
worthiness
worshipped
worshipper
worshipful
Wertherian
work-harden
Wertherism
warming-pan
working-day
warrioress
warblingly
workmaster
werwolfish
wire-puller
workpeople
work-to-rule
werewolves
wire-walker
wireworker
worryingly
washateria
wassailing
West-Banker
wash-bottle
wastepaper
washeteria
westernise
westernism
westernize
wastefully
washing-day
wishing-cap
wasp-tongu'd
wasp-tongue
westwardly
wishy-washy
witgatboom
withdrawal
withdrawer
Watteauish
watchmaker
witch-hazel
watch-night
withholden
withholder
watchglass
witchingly
watchtower
witchcraft
watchstrap
watchfully
watchguard
wattlebark
wattlebird
wattlework
wit-snapper
wit-cracker
watermelon
watertight
water-skied
water-skier
waterflood
waterglass
watersmeet
wateriness
waterworks
waterborne
water-borne
water-bound
watercolor
waterspout
watercraft
water-brain
waterfront
waterproof
watercress
waterdrive
waterquake
woundingly
wavelength
waveringly
wax-proofed
wry-mouthed
wizen-faced
xylochrome
xylography
xylogenous
xylophagan
xylophonic
xylotomous
xenobiotic
xenogenous
xanthomata
xanthopsia
xenophobia
xenarthral
xiphopagic
xiphopagus
xiphosuran
Xyridaceae
xerodermia
xerodermic
xerography
xerophytic
xerostomia
ylang-ylang
yearningly
year-on-year
yeastiness
yackety-yak
yacht-built
Yiddishism
yieldingly
yaffingale
Yggdrasill
Yugoslavic
ythundered
yoke-fellow
yellowback
yellowbird
yellowcake
yellow-girl
yellowhead
yellowness
yellow-root
yellow-weed
yellow-wood
yellow-wort
yellow-yite
Yankeefied
yerd-hunger
yird-hunger
yerd-hungry
yird-hungry
yard-master
Yarborough
yesterdays
yestereven
yestermorn
yesteryear
ypsiliform
youngberry
youthfully
you-know-who
yourselves
Zoantharia
Zoanthidae
zoanthropy
zabaglione
zucchettos
zidovudine
zigzagging
zigzaggery
zygobranch
zygocactus
zygodactyl
Zygaenidae
zygomycete
zygomorphy
zygosphene
zwitterion
zelophobia
zelophobic
Zollverein
Zimbabwean
zymologist
zumbooruck
Zend-Avesta
zinc-blende
zincograph
zincolysis
zone-ticket
zinc-worker
zoolatrous
zoophobous
zoothecial
zoothecium
zoophagous
zoophilism
zoophilist
zoophilous
zoothapses
zoothapsis
zootherapy
zoochorous
zoophytoid
zoogloeoid
zooplastic
zoological
zootomical
zoogonidia
zoomorphic
zoosporous
zoographer
zoographic
zootrophic
zootsuiter
zooculture
Zaporogian
zapateados
zero-coupon
zero-rating
zero-valent
zeuglodont

11 a□a□a

acatalectic
acataleptic
alabastrine
amaranthine
anarchistic
abandonedly
abandonment
academicals
academicism
academician
amateurship
anaphylaxis
arachnoidal
anachronism
anachronous
arachnology
anaphorical
apathetical
arabisation
arabization
araliaceous
amativeness
anadiplosis
anaplerosis
anaplerotic
acaulescent
anagnorisis
Apatosaurus
araeometric
amatorially
acarologist
analogously
anamorphous
amazon-stone
anacoluthia
anacoluthon
analphabete
acarpellous
anaerobiont
Anacreontic
anaesthesia
anaesthesis
anaesthetic
Acanthaceae
apartmental
anastomoses
anastomosis
anastomotic
abactinally
avant-propos
analyticity
abbreviator
Albigensian
albugineous
ambiguously
Amboina-wood
ambilateral
albuminuria
ambrosially
arboraceous
arborescent

ambuscadoes
asbestiform
arbitrageur
arbitrament
arbitration
arbitrarily
arbitratrix
arbitrement
ambitiously
ambivalence
ambivalency
ambiversion
Amboyna-wood
abbey-lubber
acclamation
acclamatory
archaically
archangelic
archaeology
Arcadianism
archduchess
archdukedom
accidentals
archdiocese
accrescence
Asclepiadic
archeometry
archegonial
archegonium
ancientness
archenteron
arch-heretic
acclimatise
acclimatize
acclimation
△archipelago
Archimedean
acclivitous
architraved
accelerando
accelerator
acculturate
accompanier
accompanist
Ascomycetes
accumulator
accommodate
accomptable
ascensional
accentually
alcyonarian
arctophilia
anchor-stock
anchovy-pear
acceptation
arch-prelate
acceptivity
accipitrine
accordantly
accordingly
accustomary

accessorise
accessorize
accessorial
ancestorial
accessorily
ancestrally
accusatival
arch-traitor
ascetically
ascititious
accoutering
accoucheuse
accountable
accountably
accountancy
account-book
arch-villain
audibleness
audaciously
addle-headed
addressable
aide-mémoire
abdominally
androgenous
audiometric
audiovisual
audiologist
arduousness
audiotyping
audiotypist
androgynous
aldopentose
aldermanity
alder-leaved
AIDS-related
aides-de-camp
auditorship
auditoriums
addititious
Amelanchier
△alexandrine
alexandrite
Alexandrian
amenability
ametabolism
ametabolous
adelantados
alembicated
Azerbaijani
amerciament
anencephaly
anecdotical
anecdotally
abecedarian
awelessness
atelectasis
atelectatic
areographic
aleggeaunce
amethystine
Americanise

Americanize
Americanism
Americanist
arenicolous
adenomatous
awesomeness
anemometric
anemophobia
axerophthol
amenorrhoea
anemography
Areopagitic
averruncate
areosystile
amentaceous
awe-stricken
affranchise
anfractuous
affectation
affectively
affectingly
affectivity
affectioned
affectional
afficionado
affricative
affrication
affrightful
affiliation
affirmative
affirmation
affirmatory
afforcement
affirmingly
aggravating
aggradation
aggravation
angwantibos
algebraical
aggregately
argie-bargie
argle-bargle
aggregative
aggregation
augmentable
Anglicanism
aiguillette
angelically
algological
angelolatry
angelophany
Argentinian
△anglomaniac
agglomerate
△anglophobia
△anglophobic
△anglophilia
△anglophilic
△anglophonic
angioplasty
Anglo-Indian

Words marked △ may be spelled also with a capital letter

Anglo-Romani
Anglo-Norman
Anglo-French
angiography
algorithmic
Augustinian
Argathelian
△**angst-ridden**
agglutinate
agglutinant
achievement
athleticism
achaenocarp
atheistical
ashamedness
abhominable
Aphaniptera
achromatise
achromatize
achromatism
achromatous
aphrodisiac
Aphrodisian
Atharvaveda
athermanous
abhorrently
Atherinidae
animalcular
animalcules
animatingly
amicability
acinaciform
animatronic
acidanthera
amiableness
abiogenesis
abiogenetic
acidifiable
aficionados
axiological
alismaceous
axiomatical
amino-acetic
anisocercal
anisomerous
anisotropic
aminobutene
adiaphorism
adiaphorist
adiaphorous
aristocracy
adiathermic
ahistorical
adjectively
adjudicator
adjudgement
adjournment
awkwardness
alkalimeter
alkalimetry
alkalescent

acknowledge
allhallowen
ablactation
allocheiria
allocatable
auld-farrant
allegrettos
allegorical
allegoriser
allegorizer
all-cheering
all-electric
allelomorph
allelopathy
all-American
allineation
ailanthuses
Atlanticism
Atlanticist
aplanospore
all-powerful
alloplastic
allopurinol
allopathist
ailurophile
ailurophobe
ablutionary
allotropism
allotropous
ablatitious
all-building
alleviative
alleviation
alleviatory
allez-vous-en
aimlessness
arm-chancing
Arminianism
adminicular
ammophilous
admiralship
atmospheric
armoured-car
armour-plate
annabergite
annihilator
annunciator
Aeneolithic
abnormalism
abnormality
agnosticism
agnatically
anniversary
agoraphobia
agoraphobic
anomalistic
apogamously
apocalyptic
adolescence
aponeuroses
aponeurosis

aponeurotic
above-ground
apophyllite
apotheosise
apotheosize
abomination
atomisation
atomization
abolishable
abolishment
agonisingly
agonizingly
apoliticism
abolitional
aposiopesis
aposiopetic
agonistical
apodictical
apomictical
apollonicon
Apollinaris
apocopation
Azotobacter
apologetics
axonometric
agonothetes
apomorphine
azo-compound
aeolotropic
amorousness
acolouthite
amorphously
apotropaism
amour-propre
avoirdupois
atom-smasher
acoustician
△**adoptianism**
adoptianist
apostleship
amontillado
apostolical
about-sledge
apostrophic
apostrophus
anorthosite
△**adoptionism**
abortionist
adoptionist
apostatical
Apocynaceae
apodyterium
anonymously
appearances
appeasement
alphabetise
alphabetize
appeachment
appealingly
appeasingly
appraisable

amphetamine
aspheterise
aspheterize
aspheterism
amplexicaul
appreciable
appreciably
appleringie
appreciator
apple-blight
apple-squire
appressoria
amphipathic
applicative
application
applicatory
△**amphisbaena**
amphimictic
amphibolite
amphibolous
amphipodous
amphibology
amphiprotic
appointment
amphictyony
appellative
appellation
appallingly
ampullosity
approbative
approbation
approbatory
approximate
approvingly
appropinque
appropriate
aspergation
asportation
appurtenant
appartement
appertinent
△**aspergillum**
Aspergillus
apparelment
apparelling
aspersorium
apparatchik
aspirations
apparatuses
asphyxiated
asphyxiator
arquebusade
arquebusier
acquirement
acquisitive
acquisition
acquiescent
acquittance
aerobraking
aerobically
acre-breadth

Words marked △ may be spelled also with a capital letter

11 a□r□b

atrabilious
aerobiology
agrobiology
abracadabra
auricularly
auriculated
agriculture
acrocentric
Afrocentric
Afro-centric
atrociously
abridgeable
abridgement
aerodynamic
aeroelastic
air-mechanic
arrhenotoky
airlessness
acriflavine
Aurignacian
air-sickness
arraignment
aerological
agrological
acromegalic
acrimonious
atramentous
air-umbrella
arrangement
abranchiate
agranulosis
agronomical
acronymania
apron-string
aeronautics
air-corridor
agriproduct
acropetally
agrarianism
aircraftman
aerostation
arrestation
aerostatics
agrostology
aerotropism
arrivederci
arrow-headed
arrow-poison
assuagement
assubjugate
associative
association
assiduities
assiduously
austereness
answerphone
abstentious
assafoetida
assignation
aesthetical
aestivation

abstinently
arse-licking
assimilable
assemblyman
assemblance
assentation
absenteeism
assentingly
abscondence
assortative
abstractive
abstraction
abstriction
assuredness
assertively
absorbingly
Assyriology
adscription
assassinate
assessorial
Aesculapian
auscultator
assay-master
astraphobia
actuarially
attractable
antibilious
Antiburgher
antechamber
autochanger
anticyclone
antecedence
antecedents
attaché-case
articulable
autecologic
articulated
articulator
altocumulus
astuciously
autocephaly
anticipator
anticathode
autochthons
autochthony
antheridium
autoerotism
antherozoid
artlessness
authentical
Anthesteria
artefactual
anti-federal
anti-feedant
antifouling
autographic
astigmatism
autogravure
autogenesis
antihelices
anti-heroine

astringency
attuitively
attritional
attuitional
attainments
attaintment
attributive
attribution
△**antijacobin**
△anti-Jacobin
antijamming
autokinesis
autokinetic
artillerist
automobilia
antemundane
antimoniate
antimonious
automorphic
attemptable
asthmatical
automatical
antimutagen
attenuation
actinically
attendement
attentively
attentional
antenniform
antinomical
autonomical
Actinomyces
antonomasia
actinometer
antenuptial
astonishing
antineutron
anthomaniac
artiodactyl
anteorbital
authorcraft
anthochlore
antioxidant
anthologise
anthologize
astronomise
astronomize
anthologist
anthocyanin
astrocytoma
autophagous
autophanous
autoplastic
antependium
antiphonary
antiphrasis
antipyretic
antipathist
antiquarian
antiquation
antiqueness

antiquities
alternately
altercative
alternative
arterialise
arterialize
alternating
altercation
alternation
anthracnose
anthracosis
anthracitic
arthrodesis
attorneydom
attorneyism
after-effect
altoruffled
anterograde
autarchical
antirrhinum
after-dinner
alto-relievo
alto-rilievo
anteriority
arteriotomy
anthropical
arthropodal
arthropathy
aftergrowth
arthrospore
arthroscopy
afterburner
aftersupper
auto-reverse
attestative
attestation
antispastic
anti-Semitic
antistrophe
altostratus
antithalian
altitudinal
attitudinal
autotrophic
antitypical
antitussive
astoundment
anteversion
antivitamin
adumbrative
adumbration
aquaculture
aquiculture
aquafortist
acumination
abusiveness
amusiveness
aquanautics
aquaplaning
aguardiente
aquarellist

Words marked △ may be spelled also with a capital letter

acupressure
adulterator
acupuncture
advancement
adventuress
adventurism
adventurist
adventurous
adversative
adversarial
adverseness
advertently
advertising
adverbially
advertorial
advisedness
advisership
auxiliaries
auxanometer
anxiousness
asynartetic
amyloidosis
alycompaine
amyotrophic
Bramah-press
brabblement
bramble-bush
boat-builder
bear-baiting
branchiopod
branch-pilot
bias-drawing
boardsailor
board-school
brandy-glass
bladder-worm
bladderwort
△beaverboard
blamelessly
brazen-faced
brace-and-bit
blameworthy
branfulness
△braggadocio
braggartism
brachiation
beach-master
beachcomber
Brachiopoda
brachyprism
brachyurous
bearishness
black-market
blackmailer
blackheaded
black-fellow
black-beetle
blackbirder
black-fisher
black-figure
Black-and-Tan

black-and-tan
black-boding
black-coated
brankursine
black-browed
blanketweed
black-a-vised
beaumontage
Brahmanical
Brahminical
brain-teaser
brainlessly
brainsickly
blarney-land
blasphemous
bear's-breech
brass-rubber
blastocoele
beautifully
blastogenic
beastliness
bracteolate
beauteously
brattishing
beastly-head
bradycardia
bradypeptic
baby-bouncer
baby-farming
bibliolater
bibliolatry
bibliomania
bibliomancy
bibliopegic
bibliophile
bibliophily
bibliopolic
bibliotheca
bubble-shell
baby-sitting
beblubbered
backbreaker
backbencher
back-blocker
back-country
back-draught
bacteraemia
bactericide
bacteriosis
bachelordom
bachelorism
bucket-wheel
backfitting
back-ganging
bacchanalia
buccinatory
bacciferous
backing-down
baccivorous
Bacillaceae
back-loading

bacillaemia
bucolically
bacillicide
bacilliform
baculovirus
Baconianism
bicentenary
backpacking
buck-passing
bicarbonate
bicorporate
backscatter
bicuspidate
backsliding
backscratch
buck-washing
body-builder
baddeleyite
bad-tempered
Bodhisattva
badging-hook
body-popping
bedevilment
bedevilling
bedizenment
beef-brained
bleach-field
bread-basket
breadthways
breadthwise
breadwinner
breadcrumbs
Biedermeier
beech-marten
blepharitis
blemishment
breakdancer
beetlebrain
beer-parlour
bienséances
blessedness
breastplate
breathalyse
breathalyze
breathiness
buffalo-bird
buffalo-robe
buff-leather
baffle-board
bifoliolate
baffle-plate
bifurcation
bifariously
befittingly
beguilement
bagging-hook
begging-bowl
beguilingly
Begoniaceae
bogtrotting
bog-asphodel

△bohemianism
behaviorism
behaviorist
behavioural
blind-felled
blind-storey
bridemaiden
bridewealth
brine-shrimp
boiler-maker
brise-soleil
bribery-oath
brimfulness
bridgeboard
bridge-drive
bridge-house
bright-field
blightingly
Britishness
bricklaying
brickmaking
brickshaped
brilliantly
baillieship
brissel-cock
bristle-tail
bristle-fern
brittleness
bristlecone
bristle-worm
brittle-star
bristliness
Bristol-milk
ball-and-claw
ball-bearing
bold-beating
ball-breaker
bull-baiting
ball-busting
bill-chamber
balm-cricket
belle-de-nuit
believingly
balderlocks
balletomane
bullet-proof
billets-doux
bellettrist
bullfighter
balefulness
bull-fronted
bell-founder
bell-foundry
bell-heather
bell-housing
belligerent
bulbiferous
bullishness
billionaire
bellicosely
bellicosity

Words marked △ may be spelled also with a capital letter

11 b□l□i

billiard-cue
bull-mastiff
bilingually
△balmorality
Baltoslavic
balloon-back
balloon-vine
ballot-paper
biliousness
bulbousness
bellows-fish
bell-ringing
Belorussian
balls-aching
billsticker
bullshitter
belatedness
bull-terrier
bilaterally
belowstairs
belly-dancer
belly-timber
ballyhooing
belly-button
Bombacaceae
bombardment
bumbershoot
bombilation
bombination
bimolecular
bimillenary
bumble-puppy
bumpsadaisy
bimetallism
bimetallist
bumptiously
bankability
bone-breccia
binocularly
Benedictine
benedictive
benediction
benedictory
banteringly
bonne-bouche
bonnet-piece
bandeirante
bonnet-rouge
beneficiate
beneficiary
benefaction
beneficence
benefactory
banefulness
benefitting
benignantly
benightment
bunch-backed
bank-holiday
benchership
benthoscope
bank-manager
bondmanship
bandoleered
bandoliered
bonbonnière
beneplacito
Bonapartean
Bonapartism
Bonapartist
bondservant
bond-service
benevolence
bond-washing
bandy-legged
benzylidine
biocatalyst
book-account
biomaterial
buoyantness
browbeating
bookbindery
bookbinding
blotchiness
broach-spire
boot-catcher
broadcasted
broadcaster
bloody-bones
bloodletter
broad-leaved
bloody-faced
broad-church
broadminded
blood-flower
Brobdingnag
blood-bought
bloodsprent
blood-spavin
Broederbond
blood-frozen
bloody-sweat
bloodstream
bloodsucker
blood-guilty
blood-typing
biofeedback
biomedicine
biochemical
brotherlike
brotherhood
biophysical
bromination
booking-hall
bookishness
boorishness
bromidrosis
bookkeeping
blockbuster
block-system
book-learned
bootlicking
bootlegging
bioengineer
biocoenoses
biocoenosis
biocoenotic
bookselling
Brotstudien
bloatedness
blotting-pad
boot-topping
biodynamics
Buprestidae
baptismally
bipartition
biquadratic
bureaucracy
bereavement
barrage-fire
barbaresque
bur-marigold
barrack-room
bersaglieri
barbarously
burial-place
barbastelle
bird-brained
Burschenism
barycentric
bird-catcher
Burseraceae
bargemaster
barley-brake
barley-break
barley-broth
barrel-house
barrel-organ
barley-sugar
barge-stones
barefacedly
bird-fancier
birth-weight
Bartholomew
Berthon-boat
barricadoes
burling-iron
burnishment
bar-sinister
barbiturate
bursiculate
bare-knuckle
berylliosis
burglarious
Barclaycard
Byronically
bird-nesting
baronetical
burgomaster
burrowstown
borborygmic
borborygmus
bergschrund
barnstormer
burn-the-wind
burnt-sienna
barquentine
birdwatcher
Bessarabian
bastard-wing
bespattered
bisociative
bisociation
basket-chair
besiegement
basset-hound
bastel-house
beseemingly
besiegingly
△basket-maker
Baskerville
basketweave
bushelwoman
bashfulness
bastinading
bastinadoed
Bashi-Bazouk
bastinadoes
bastle-house
bushmanship
bastnaesite
businessman
bespreading
bestridable
bestselling
biscuit-root
bushwhacker
bushwalking
bisexuality
bushy-tailed
beta-blocker
botheration
bitter-apple
bitter-cress
butter-cloth
bitter-earth
butterflies
butteriness
butter-knife
between-maid
betweenness
betweentime
butter-plate
butter-print
butter-paper
bittersweet
butter-woman
butcher-bird
bathing-suit
bottle-blond
bottle-brush
bottle-chart
battledress
betel-pepper

battlefield
bottle-glass
batological
bottle-green
bottle-gourd
bottle-nosed
battleplane
battle-piece
bottle-party
batsmanship
△bathmitsvah
△bathmitzvah
botanically
baton-charge
biting-louse
botanomancy
bottom-glade
bottom-grass
bottom-heavy
bathophobia
betrothment
buttonholer
batholithic
buttock-mail
button-mould
butyraceous
bathyscaphe
bathymetric
bathylithic
bathysphere
Butazolidin®
blue-blooded
boulder-clay
blunderbuss
brucellosis
bourguignon
bourgeoisie
blushlessly
brutishness
bauson-faced
boutonnière
brusqueness
bourtree-gun
bountifully
blunt-witted
bounteously
bouquetière
bevel-wheels
bivouacking
bow-windowed
bewhiskered
bewildering
bowdleriser
bowdlerizer
bower-anchor
bewitchment
bowstringed
boxing-glove
boysenberry
bay-windowed
bryological
by-your-leave
Byzantinism
Byzantinist
claw-and-ball
crag-and-tail
characinoid
chalazogamy
chamaephyte
clay-brained
cramboclink
crabbedness
chambermaid
chamberlain
coarctation
chance-comer
chalcedonic
chalcedonyx
chancellery
chancellory
chancroidal
clam-chowder
charcuterie
chandlering
clandestine
crapehanger
Clarencieux
coalescence
crane-necked
chameleonic
ceaselessly
clavecinist
crateriform
chaperonage
chapeau-bras
chaff-engine
chaff-cutter
craggedness
changefully
change-house
charge-house
chargenurse
chargesheet
crash-helmet
craniectomy
clavigerous
chafing-gear
chafing-dish
craniognomy
coalitional
coalitioner
charismatic
craniometer
craniometry
Clavicornia
cranioscopy
charity-girl
coadjacency
clanjamfray
coadjutress
crankhandle
crackleware
crackerjack
challenging
chaulmoogra
charlatanic
charlatanry
charmlessly
chasmogamic
claim-jumper
channelling
chainplates
chain-smoker
chaenomeles
chain-driven
chainstitch
caaing-whale
clamorously
championess
clapperclaw
champertous
crappit-head
crappit-heid
clairschach
chairperson
clairvoyant
chars-à-bancs
classically
class-leader
class-fellow
classifying
chansonnier
chansonette
chanticleer
chaotically
chartaceous
chaetognath
chastenment
chantarelle
chanterelle
chastisable
chart-buster
Chautauquan
craftswoman
coadunative
coagulative
coadunation
coagulation
coagulatory
crapulosity
cabbage-palm
cabbage-rose
cabbage-moth
cabbage-worm
cabbagetown
cabbage-root
cabbage-tree
cabbalistic
cubicalness
cable-length
cablevision
cable-stitch
cobblestone
cabinetwork
cybernation
cybernetics
cyberphobia
cock-and-bull
cockaleekie
cock-a-leekie
cocoa-butter
cycadaceous
cachectical
cacographic
cacographer
cacogastric
cyclicality
Cochin-China
coccidiosis
cockleshell
coconscious
coconut-palm
coconut-milk
cyclopaedia
cyclopaedic
cyclohexane
cycloserine
cyclothymia
cyclothymic
cycloplegia
cyclosporin
cacophonous
cock-sparrow
cicatricula
code-breaker
codicillary
caddishness
co-dependant
co-dependent
cheval-glass
crémaillère
crematorial
crematorium
clenbuterol
cheechakoes
clench-built
crescograph
coercimeter
crescentade
coercionist
crepehanger
cleverality
coenenchyma
crenellated
coeternally
credentials
coefficient
clergywoman
crepitative
clericalism
crepitation
clericalist
chelicerate
cheliferous

Words marked △ may be spelled also with a capital letter

11 c□e□i

cherishment
credibility
coexistence
check-string
cream-cheese
clean-shaven
clean-limbed
cleanliness
clean-living
chemotactic
ctenophoran
coenobitism
chemosphere
chemotropic
coevolution
creophagous
clear-headed
cheerleader
cheirognomy
cheiromancy
cheironomic
cheironomer
Cheiroptera
cherry-stone
cheeseboard
cheesecloth
coessential
cleistogamy
cheesepress
cheeseparer
cheesewring
creatianism
crestfallen
coextensive
coextension
creationism
creationist
creatorship
coeducation
crepuscular
chemurgical
coelurosaur
credulously
chequerwise
chequerwork
café-concert
coffee-maker
caffeinated
coffee-table
cognateness
cognitively
cognitivity
cognitional
cognoscible
cognoscente
cognoscenti
cognominate
cigar-shaped
cigar-holder
cohortative
climatology

chiragrical
Chimaeridae
climactical
climacteric
cuir-bouilli
cuir-bouilly
coincidence
coincidency
childminder
clindamycin
cliffhanger
chieftaincy
chieftainry
chiffonnier
crithomancy
coinherence
coinheritor
criminalese
criminalise
criminalize
criminative
crimination
criminalist
criminality
criticality
criminatory
criticaster
crinigerous
criminology
chick-a-biddy
chicken-feed
Chillingham
cliometrics
chimney-nook
chimney-nuik
chiromantic
clinometric
clinochlore
Chilognatha
chiropodial
chirologist
chiropodist
chirography
chinoiserie
chiropteran
Chippendale
chiaroscuro
chiastolite
coinsurance
chitty-faced
chitterling
chirurgical
collagenase
collagenous
culpability
calcariform
call-at-large
collaborate
collapsable
collapsible
chloanthite

calibration
celebration
celebratory
colubriform
cold-blooded
Calabar-bean
call-barring
calycanthus
cold-casting
calf-country
collembolan
collenchyma
colleaguing
culverineer
collegianer
calceolaria
collectable
collectible
collectedly
collectanea
collections
calefacient
calefactive
calefaction
calefactory
cold-forging
californium
cologarithm
cold-hearted
colligative
calcination
colligation
collimation
culmination
cultivation
calciferous
celliferous
culmiferous
calling-crab
Calvinistic
calcicolous
Callitriche
calligramme
calligraphy
Callistemon
colliquable
calcifugous
callipygean
callipygous
columbarium
columnarity
chlamydeous
columniated
calumniator
calamancoes
calendarise
calendarize
colonialism
calendarist
colonialist
calendering

colonelship
colonelling
calendrical
cylindrical
colonoscope
colonoscopy
collocation
callousness
coleopteral
coleopteran
coleopteron
collocutory
colloquiums
calypsonian
calyptrogen
calorimeter
chlorimeter
chlorometer
colorimeter
calorimetry
chlorimetry
chlorometry
colorimetry
chlorinator
chloroplast
chloroprene
chlorophyll
chloroquine
calisthenic
celestially
calculative
calculating
calculation
colouration
colour-blind
cultureless
collusively
cold-welding
comparative
commandment
comradeship
compaginate
companioned
campaniform
campanology
compassable
compactedly
compactness
compartment
campanulate
Campbellite
comicalness
comedogenic
commendable
commendably
compendious
commendator
compendiums
competently
competitive
competition

Words marked △ may be spelled also with a capital letter

11 c□n□i

compellable
commemorate
compearance
commensally
compensator
campestrian
commentator
camphorated
combinative
comminative
combination
commination
compilation
combinatory
comminatory
compilatory
commiserate
compilement
commissural
comminution
camel-backed
compliantly
complacence
complacency
complicated
complainant
complaisant
complaining
compliments
cameleopard
Camaldolese
Camaldolite
completable
complotting
complexness
camp-meeting
cementation
cementatory
comancheros
cement-stone
cement-water
compotation
commonality
compotatory
Campodeidae
componental
compositive
composition
commodities
commotional
compositous
commonplace
compossible
commonsense
common-shore
comfortable
comfortably
comfortless
comportment
cymophanous
camaraderie

camerlengos
camerlingos
comprimario
camera-ready
comprisable
compressive
compression
compressure
comestibles
comstockery
comstockism
comet-finder
Comptometer®
comptroller
communalise
communalize
commutative
computative
communalism
commutation
computation
communalist
compunction
computerate
computerese
computerise
computerize
compurgator
communicate
communicant
communistic
comeuppance
compulsitor
combustible
combustious
cinnabarine
concatenate
contango-day
consanguine
contaminate
contaminant
cinnarizine
cannabinoid
Convallaria
containable
containment
confarreate
contactable
confabulate
cine-biology
ciné-biology
cenobitical
cynicalness
consciously
cony-catcher
conveyancer
convenances
canceration
centenarian
congelation
candelabrum

candelabras
canterburys
candescence
△**confederate**
△**confederacy**
contenement
congenerous
convergence
convergency
congenially
convenience
conveniency
concealable
congealable
concealment
congealment
cancellated
conterminal
condemnable
contemnible
concernedly
concernment
concernancy
contemplate
contemplant
conferrable
consecrator
concessible
condensable
conversable
conversably
confessedly
conversance
conversancy
concentrate
congestible
connectable
connectible
contestable
convertible
convertibly
conceptacle
conventicle
conceitedly
connectedly
contentedly
conceitless
contentless
consentient
contentment
concentring
concertante
concertinos
concert-goer
conceptious
connections
contentious
concentered
conjectural
conjecturer
conceptuses

consecutive
consecution
consequence
conceivable
conservable
conceivably
conservancy
conservator
cenogenesis
cinchoninic
cantharidic
cantharidal
cantharides
cannibalise
cannibalize
cannibalism
candidature
confiscable
convincible
condisciple
confiscator
considerate
conciseness
confineless
confinement
considering
centimetric
continental
confidently
continently
cunningness
contingence
contingency
canting-coin
conciliable
cunnilingus
confidingly
consimility
convicinity
convivially
conditioned
consilience
conditional
conditioner
concipiency
candidiasis
conciliator
confirmable
confirmator
consignable
condignness
consignment
cancioneros
centimorgan
centigramme
consistence
consistency
convictions
configurate
continuable
continuedly

Words marked △ may be spelled also with a capital letter

11 c□n□i

continually
continuance
continuator
Canellaceae
candleberry
conflictive
conflicting
confliction
canalicular
canaliculus
confluently
conflagrate
conflagrant
candlelight
candle-power
candlestick
conclusions
cinema-organ
CinemaScope®
canonically
connotative
condonation
connotation
consolation
convocation
condolatory
consolatory
consolatrix
consonantal
consonantly
concordance
condolences
condolement
consolement
consolidate
concomitant
condominium
consociated
conformable
conformably
cannon-metal
contorniate
concolorate
concolorous
cannon-proof
connoisseur
condottiere
condottieri
consortiums
convolution
convolvulus
conspecific
conspicuity
conspicuous
canophilist
cynophilist
conspirator
conurbation
centreboard
centrobaric
contrabasso
contributor
contractile
contractive
contraction
centrically
contracture
contractual
contradance
contredance
centrifugal
canary-grass
congregated
controlment
controlling
congruously
centrepiece
contraption
centripetal
contrariety
contrarious
concrescent
contrastive
Congressman
conirostral
contretemps
contra-tenor
cineritious
contrivable
contrivance
controverse
controversy
contrayerva
canisterise
canisterize
cenospecies
cenesthesia
cenesthesis
constrained
constricted
constrictor
constellate
constuprate
constipated
consternate
constituent
cunctatious
constitutor
construable
constructer
constructor
confutative
conjugative
conjugating
confutation
conjugation
conjuration
conjugality
contumacity
conjunctiva
conjunctive
conjunction
cinquecento
conjuncture
connumerate
conducement
confutement
consumerism
consumerist
contubernal
concubinage
concubitant
concubinary
conducingly
connubially
centuriator
consummator
consumptive
consumption
conquerable
concurrence
concurrency
convulsible
convulsions
conductible
conductress
conductance
consultancy
condylomata
cloxacillin
clog-almanac
choice-drawn
crotcheteer
cloudlessly
co-ordinator
co-ordinates
cloud-topped
Chondrostei
chordophone
crop-dusting
crowd-puller
close-banded
close-handed
co-operative
co-operating
co-operation
close-hauled
close-barred
close-reefed
choreograph
clovergrass
chokecherry
close-lipped
close-fisted
close-bodied
choregraphy
cholesteric
cholesterol
cholesterin
cholestasis
cookery-book
cook-general
clodhopping
clothes-line
clothes-pole
clothes-prop
chorisation
chorization
cholinergic
crocidolite
cookie-shine
crookbacked
chock-a-block
crookedness
chocolatier
choroiditis
crocodilian
chorologist
chorography
choirmaster
choirscreen
choirstalls
crossbanded
cross-dating
cross-garnet
crossbarred
cross-legged
crossbearer
cross-leaved
cross-tining
cloisonnage
cross-infect
crossbowman
cross-or-pile
cross-stitch
clostridial
clostridium
cool-tankard
Cromwellian
cephalalgia
cephalalgic
coplanarity
Cephalaspis
Cappah-brown
captainship
cephalocele
Cephalopoda
cephalotomy
capableness
capaciously
capacitance
capodastros
copper-beech
copper-faced
copy-editing
cappernoity
copperplate
coppersmith
copperworks
captivating
captivaunce
capriccioso
cypripedium
cupriferous

11 C□S□O

Cyprinodont
cupellation
capillarity
copple-crown
Cupuliferae
capillitium
copple-stone
coping-stone
coprolaliac
caprolactam
coprophagic
coprophagan
coprophilia
cupro-nickel
Cypro-Minoan
copiousness
coprosterol
copyreading
Capernaitic
cyperaceous
coparcenary
coparcenery
capernoited
capernoitie
caper-spurge
caparisoned
capitularly
cappuccinos
carrageenan
carrageenin
caryatidean
carnationed
curialistic
curtailment
curtail-step
curtain-fire
currant-cake
currant-wine
currant-loaf
carnaptious
curnaptious
cerebralism
cerebration
cerebralist
curableness
cerebriform
cerebellous
cerebellums
carabiniere
carabinieri
corybantism
cerebroside
corn-cracker
curb-crawler
coraciiform
caricatural
correlative
correlation
carvel-built
curlew-berry
carpet-snake
cornerstone
correctable
correctible
correctness
currentness
current-cost
carpentaria
carefulness
cerographic
Cirrhipedia
cornhusking
cardinalate
carminative
cornice-rail
corrigendum
cornice-pole
cornice-hook
corniferous
cornigerous
cardiograph
curling-pond
carriageway
currishness
certificate
certifiable
certifiably
curvilineal
curvilinear
carnificial
car-sickness
cordialness
cardiomotor
carrion-crow
carcinomata
carnivorous
corticolous
carcinology
corbie-steps
corbiculate
corniculate
curriculums
coralliform
corolliform
Carolingian
coralloidal
carillonist
circle-rider
chrominance
ceremonious
chromoplast
chromophore
chromosomal
chromoscope
chronically
chronograph
coronagraph
coronograph
chronologic
chronologer
chronometer
chronometry
chronoscope
caruncuIate
carunculous
corporately
carbonalite
corporative
Carbonarism
corporatism
carbonation
corporation
corporatist
corporality
carbonadoes
corporeally
Corrodentia
cardophagus
cartophilic
cormophytic
cursoriness
corrosively
corroborate
corroborant
carpogonium
carpospores
cartography
caryopsides
curiousness
caryopteris
Carborundum®
carbonylate
carbocyclic
ceroplastic
cerargyrite
coruscating
coruscation
chrismatory
card-sharper
chrysoberyl
chrysocracy
chrysocolla
Christ-cross
Christendom
christening
christingle
caressingly
△christiania
Christianly
chrysalides
chrysalises
chrisom-robe
Christmassy
Christology
Christogram
chrysoprase
chrysarobin
curettement
ceratopsian
curatorship
circularise
circularize
circulative
circulating
carburation
circulation
corrugation
circularity
circulatory
carbuncular
corpuscular
circumciser
carburetion
carburetted
carburetter
carburettor
corpulently
circumflect
circumfused
carousingly
circumlunar
cornucopian
circumpolar
circumspect
circumsolar
corruptible
corruptibly
corruptness
circumvolve
corivalship
caravansary
caravanning
caravanette
cordwainery
curly-headed
Carlylesque
carryings-on
curly-greens
cash-account
cost-account
cost-benefit
cosmeticise
cosmeticize
cosmeticism
cosmetician
castellated
cosmetology
cosignatory
castigation
castigatory
cysticercus
costiveness
cassiterite
casting-vote
cushion-tire
cushion-tyre
cassiopeium
cashierment
casuistical
castle-guard
customarily
custom-built
cosmotheism
cosmothetic

Words marked △ may be spelled also with a capital letter

11 c□s□o

cosmopolite
cosmogonist
cosmologist
cosmosphere
cosmography
cosmocratic
cash-railway
cesarevitch
cesarewitch
citharistic
cathartical
cataclasmic
cataclastic
catechetics
catechising
catechizing
catechismal
catechistic
catachresis
catacaustic
cataclysmic
catadromous
catheterism
cathedratic
catafalcoes
cytogenesis
cytogenetic
categorical
catch-phrase
catch-the-ten
cattishness
catallactic
cytological
cataloguise
cataloguize
catalytical
cotoneaster
cat-and-mouse
citronellal
△**catholicise**
△catholicize
△**catholicism**
catholicity
cottonmouth
cytoplasmic
cataplectic
catapultier
cataphonics
cat-cracking
Caterpillar®
caterpillar
coterminous
catercorner
cater-cousin
catastrophe
cat's-whisker
citizenship
causatively
clubability
churchgoing
crunchiness
churchwoman
churchwards
causelessly
cauterising
cauterizing
cruciverbal
cauligenous
cruciferous
crucifixion
cauliflower
caulicolous
cauliculate
chuckle-head
coupling-box
clubmanship
coulometric
Coulommiers
counselling
causticness
caustically
crustaceous
courtierism
courtliness
countrified
countenance
courteously
countermand
counterbase
counterpace
counterpane
countermark
countervail
counterpart
counterseal
cluster-bean
counterfect
counterfeit
countermine
counter-time
countersink
countersign
counter-view
counterplea
counter-plot
counterblow
counter-glow
counterbond
counterbore
countermove
counter-vote
counterwork
counter-work
counterfoil
counter-roll
counterfort
counterdraw
countermure
counterbuff
countersunk
counter-turn
courtesying
country-seat
countryfied
countryside
countrywide
country-folk
country-rock
cave-dweller
civilianise
civilianize
cavillation
cavalierish
cavalierism
civilisable
civilizable
cavo-rilievo
cavernously
cavernulous
coxcombical
cryobiology
chyliferous
chymiferous
chylomicron
cryophysics
cryosurgery
cryptically
cryotherapy
cryptograph
Cryptogamia
cryptogamic
cryptogenic
crystalline
crystallise
crystallite
crystallize
crystalloid
cryptomeria
cryptorchid
clyster-pipe
deaf-and-dumb
dramaticism
diamagnetic
dramaturgic
dual-control
dead-clothes
diascordium
drap-de-Berry
dram-drinker
dual-density
diadelphous
diametrical
diametrally
diatessaron
dialectical
dialectally
dead-freight
draggle-tail
draughtsman
death-marked
diaphragmal
death-rattle
deathliness
diaphaneity
diachronism
diachronous
diathermacy
diathermous
diaphoresis
diaphoretic
death-stroke
death-duties
drawing-room
drawn-thread
diagnosable
diagnostics
diamond-back
diamond-dust
diapophyses
diapophysis
diapositive
dialogistic
dragonnades
dragoon-bird
diabolology
diamorphine
dragon's-head
diacoustics
dual-purpose
diacritical
drastically
diastematic
draft-dodger
diastrophic
diarthrosis
△**dracunculus**
débridement
dubiousness
debarcation
debarkation
debasedness
debauchedly
debauchment
debouchment
declarative
declamation
declaration
declamatory
declaratory
doch-an-doris
dictatorial
docibleness
decrescendo
decrepitate
decrepitude
declination
dockisation
dockization
declinatory
declinature
ductileness
deceitfully
ducking-pond
declivitous

Words marked △ may be spelled also with a capital letter

decollation
décolletage
deckle-edged
decillionth
decelerator
decolourise
decolourize
Decemberish
decumbently
decemvirate
decumbiture
documentary
decomposite
decameronic
decantation
deconstruct
dichogamous
dichotomise
dichotomize
dichotomist
dichotomous
dicephalous
deceptively
deck-passage
decurvation
decerebrate
decerebrise
decerebrize
decurrently
decorticate
decursively
dichromatic
doctrinaire
doctrinally
decarbonate
decurionate
decarbonise
decarbonize
dichroscope
decorations
decarburise
decarburize
decussately
decussation
dicotyledon
dock-warrant
dactylology
dactylogram
dedramatise
dedramatize
Dodecagynia
deductively
didacticism
Dodecandria
dodecaphony
dodecastyle
didactylous
Didelphidae
dreadnaught
deep-drawing
dreadlessly

dreadnought
dredging-box
dreikanters
dreamlessly
deep-mouthed
de-emphasise
de-emphasize
dressmaking
deerstalker
dress-length
dress-reform
dress-shield
dress-circle
dyer's-rocket
defeasanced
defraudment
deflagrable
deflagrator
defiantness
defibrinate
defibrinise
defibrinize
deficiently
defectively
differentia
differently
deflexional
diffidently
duffing-over
difficultly
defalcation
defiliation
defoliation
defensative
definiendum
defenceless
Defenderism
definientia
defensively
defloration
deformation
diffractive
diffraction
deforcement
deferential
defeudalise
defeudalize
diffuseness
diffusively
diffusivity
degradation
digladiator
dogmatology
daggerboard
Dogberrydom
Dogberryism
dégringoler
doggishness
dog's-mercury
degustation
degustatory

digestively
digitigrade
deglutinate
deglutitive
deglutition
deglutitory
doggy-paddle
dehydration
dehypnotise
dehypnotize
dehortative
dehortation
dehortatory
drivability
dwindlement
deification
driving-band
driving-gear
drink-driver
drill-barrow
drill-harrow
drill-master
drill-plough
dripping-pan
deictically
deistically
drift-mining
drift-anchor
daisy-cutter
Dukhobortsy
Della-Robbia
dull-brained
dolabriform
deliberator
delectation
deliciously
dolefulness
delightedly
delightless
delightsome
delphically
Delphinidae
dolphin-fish
dolphinaria
delphiniums
dollishness
doltishness
dulcifluous
delineative
delineation
delinquency
dilapidated
dilapidator
deliriously
délassement
dull-sighted
delusionist
dilutionary
deleterious
delitescent
diluvialism

diluvialist
deliverable
delivery-man
deliverance
delivery-van
damnability
demi-bastion
democratise
democratize
democratist
domiciliate
domiciliary
dimidiation
demodulator
demyelinate
dumbfounder
demographic
demographer
demigration
demigoddess
demagnetise
demagnetize
demagogical
demagoguery
demagoguism
damping-down
dampishness
dumpishness
demulsifier
demoniacism
demonianism
demonocracy
diminuendos
domineering
dimensioned
dimensional
demonologic
demonolater
demonolatry
demonomania
diminishing
demonstrate
dominations
demi-pension
demarcation
demarkation
damascening
Demosthenic
domesticate
domesticise
domesticize
domesticity
dame's-violet
dámask-steel
demiurgical
demiurgeous
demountable
deniability
duniewassal
dinner-dance
dangerously

Words marked △ may be spelled also with a capital letter

11 d□n□e

dinner-wagon
denigration
dentigerous
densimetric
dancing-girl
denticulate
dynamically
dynamograph
dynamometer
dynamometry
denominable
denominator
denumerable
denumerably
denunciator
dining-table
dendrachate
dendroglyph
dendrolatry
dendrometer
dendritical
denitration
dinotherium
dandy-rigged
denizenship
drop-curtain
Droseraceae
duodecimals
drop-forging
△**diotheletic**
△dyotheletic
△dyothelitic
Diophantine
deoxidation
dronishness
dioristical
doorknocker
dromophobia
doorstepped
doorstepper
deobstruent
drouthiness
doomwatcher
deoxygenate
deoxygenise
deoxygenize
deoxyribose
Dipsacaceae
depravation
depravement
depravingly
deprecative
deprecating
deprecation
depredation
deprecatory
depredatory
depreciator
dipterocarp
depressible
depth-charge

deprivative
duplicative
deprivation
duplication
duplicature
deprivement
duplicitous
dephlegmate
dependingly
diplomatese
dipsomaniac
diplomatise
diplomatize
deploration
diplomatics
diplomatist
deploringly
diplococcus
diprotodont
deprogramme
depopulator
Depo-Provera®
deportation
département
diphtheroid
diphthongic
diphthongal
deplumation
depauperate
depauperise
depauperize
diphycercal
△**diphysitism**
dermatology
durableness
deracialise
deracialize
direct-grant
derecognise
derecognize
directivity
directional
△**directorate**
directorial
directrices
dare-devilry
direfulness
Durchlaucht
dorsiferous
dereliction
dark-lantern
derangement
daring-hardy
dermography
dorsolumbar
derivatives
disparately
discalceate
dispatchful
dastardness
disbandment

discardment
dyspareunia
dismayfully
Distalgesic®
dyspathetic
destabilise
destabilize
de-Stalinise
de-Stalinize
disharmonic
dysharmonic
disfavourer
disgarrison
distantness
dismastment
distasteful
disobedient
disablement
disobliging
desacralise
desacralize
desiccative
desecration
desiccation
disaccustom
desideratum
desperately
desperation
desperadoes
dissembling
dismembered
descendable
descendible
disremember
dishevelled
Disneyesque
Disneyfying
disseminate
dissepiment
disseminule
disbeliever
discernible
discernibly
discernment
discerpible
discerptive
discerption
distempered
dispensable
distensible
dispensably
dispersedly
dispensator
dissectible
dyspeptical
dissentient
dissentious
disceptator
dissertator
disaffected
disafforest

designative
designation
designatory
desegregate
désagrément
designingly
disthronize
deschooling
dysrhythmia
dissipative
destination
dissipation
distinctive
distinction
distincture
dislikeable
dislikeness
distinguish
duskishness
dissimilate
dispiriting
dissilience
distillable
disciplinal
discipliner
dessignment
dismissible
dissimulate
destitution
displeasant
displeasing
disyllabism
disyllabify
displeasure
deselection
desilverise
desilverize
disulphuric
disulphuret
desalinator
desultorily
disillusive
disillusion
disembitter
disemployed
disembodied
disimprison
disemburden
disentangle
disinterest
disinterred
disinfector
disenthrall
disenshroud
disenthrone
desensitise
desensitize
disinclined
desinential
disunionist
disentrance

Words marked △ may be spelled also with a capital letter

disentrayle
disencumber
disannuller
dislocation
dissonantly
despondence
discordance
despondency
discordancy
disbowelled
dishonestly
discomfited
dislodgment
discotheque
discothèque
discophoran
dissociable
dissociably
disposingly
dispositive
disposition
dyslogistic
despoilment
dishonorary
discoloured
dishonourer
discourtesy
discoursive
desmodromic
discography
disportment
discontinue
dissolutely
dissolutive
dissolution
dissolvable
discomycete
Dasipodidae
disapproval
disarmament
disorganise
disorganize
describable
distribuend
distributee
distributer
distributor
disgraceful
destructive
distractive
distracting
destruction
distraction
disgracious
disordinate
deservingly
deserpidine
disgruntled
descriptive
description
discrepance
discrepancy
disproperty
distressful
distrustful
distressing
disprovable
destroyable
disassemble
disassembly
disputative
despumation
dismutation
disputation
disturbance
disjunctive
disjunction
dysfunction
disjuncture
disquietful
disquietive
disquieting
disquietous
disquietude
discussable
discussible
disguisable
disguisedly
disgustedly
disaventure
desexualise
desexualize
dusty-miller
dissyllable
dissymmetry
detrainment
detractress
detectivist
△**ditheletism**
△**dithelitism**
dutifulness
detribalise
detribalize
detrimental
doting-piece
dittography
duteousness
determinate
determinant
determinacy
determinism
determinist
deteriorate
deteriorism
deteriority
detestation
dithyrambic
deuteration
deuteranope
deuterogamy
Deuteronomy
doughtiness
druckenness
drunkenness
double-agent
double-blind
double-check
double-cross
double-digit
double-Dutch
double-ender
double-edged
double-eagle
double-entry
double-faced
double-fault
double-lived
double-quick
double-shade
double-space
double-sharp
double-speak
double-stout
doublethink
douroucouli
drug-running
Deutschmark
dauntlessly
doubtlessly
dive-bombing
doveishness
devaluation
divulgation
devolvement
divulgement
divellicate
devil-dodger
developable
development
diving-board
diving-dress
deviousness
divorceable
divergement
divorcement
divergently
divergingly
divertingly
diversified
diverticula
devastative
devastating
devastation
divestiture
divisionary
△**divisionism**
divisionist
devotedness
dovetailing
devotionist
devouringly
down-draught
down-hearted
downlighter
down-setting
down-sitting
down-the-line
down-to-earth
down-trodden
dexterously
doxographer
dexiotropic
day-labourer
dry-transfer
epanalepses
epanalepsis
emanational
emasculator
emancipator
evanescence
evangeliary
evangelical
exaggerated
exaggerator
eradicative
egalitarian
eradication
evagination
examination
exanimation
evasiveness
evanishment
elaborately
elaborative
evaporative
elaboration
evaporation
elaboratory
exasperator
Erastianism
elasticness
elastically
elasticated
exaltedness
exanthemata
elastomeric
Elastoplast®
Eoanthropus
enarthrosis
ejaculative
ejaculation
ejaculatory
embracement
embracingly
ecblastesis
eubacterium
emblematise
emblematize
emblematist
emboîtement
embellisher
embrocation
embroiderer
embroilment

Words marked △ may be spelled also with a capital letter

11 e□b□r

embarcation
embarkation
embarrassed
embittering
embowelment
embowelling
elbow-grease
embowerment
embryologic
embryonated
exclamative
exclamation
exclamatory
Eucharistic
enchainment
eschatology
enchantress
enchantment
excrescence
excrescency
excremental
excrementum
exceedingly
Escherichia
ecclesiarch
escheatable
escheatment
excogitator
enchiridion
escritorial
eccrinology
encrimsoned
exculpation
exculpatory
excellently
eccaleobion
eucalyptole
encomiastic
encomendero
encumbrance
excommunion
eccentrical
enchondroma
euchologion
encephaline
encephaloid
encephalous
exceptional
encapsulate
encarnalise
encarnalize
excarnation
excoriation
excorticate
excursively
escarmouche
excerptible
encystation
excessively
excitedness
encouraging
exclusively
exclusivism
exclusivist
exclusivity
encrustment
endearingly
endocardiac
endocardial
endocardium
endochylous
eudaemonism
eudaemonics
eudaemonist
endlessness
endemically
endemiology
endomorphic
endometrial
endometrium
endomitosis
endoplasmic
endophagous
endoplastic
ex-directory
endorsement
elderliness
elder-flower
endospermic
eidetically
endothelial
endothelium
endothermic
endotrophic
eremacausis
eye-catching
exercisable
elementally
energetical
elephantine
elephantoid
elegiacally
evening-star
△everlasting
emetophobia
exemplarily
exemplarity
esemplastic
exemplified
exemplifier
epeirogenic
eyebrowless
eventualise
eventualize
eventration
eventuality
eleutherian
electrified
electrician
electricity
ejectamenta
electioneer
electrolier
electronics
electrotint
electrology
electrocute
electrolyse
electrolyte
electrolyze
electrotype
electrotypy
ejector-seat
electorship
executively
executioner
executorial
executrices
executrixes
everywhence
emery-powder
enfranchise
efficacious
efficiently
effectively
effectually
exfoliative
exfoliation
effulgently
enfeoffment
enforceable
enforcement
enfouldered
engrailment
engrammatic
Enghalskrug
engraftment
eagle-winged
eugenically
engineering
egg-and-spoon
engrossment
engorgement
ergatocracy
eighteenmos
ergatomorph
eight-square
ethicalness
ethological
exhilarator
Ephemeridae
ephemerides
Echinoderma
enhancement
ethnobotany
ethnologist
ethnography
etherealise
etherealize
exhortative
exhortation
ethereality
exhortatory
etheromania
echo-sounder
exhaustible
exhaustless
Elizabethan
epitaxially
epigastrium
episcopally
eviscerator
Eriodendron
epipetalous
episepalous
epidendrone
epigenetics
epigenesist
epinephrine
epidemicity
eviternally
evidentiary
epileptical
epicheirema
epithalamia
epithalamic
epithelioma
epiphyllous
epithymetic
epiphytical
eliminative
edification
elicitation
elimination
edificatory
eliminatory
eligibility
epidiascope
epiplastral
epiplastron
enigmatical
editorially
epilogistic
eriophorous
epitrochoid
epigraphist
evil-starred
epistolical
epistilbite
existential
enjambement
enkephaline
eclecticism
eglandulose
ellipticity
ellipsoidal
enlargement
enlivenment
emmenagogic
emmenagogue
Emmenthaler
enneandrian
enneandrous
enneahedral

Words marked △ may be spelled also with a capital letter

11 e□u□v

enneahedron
ennoblement
einsteinium
Einsteinian
egomaniacal
evocatively
exorability
exorbitance
exorbitancy
exonerative
exoneration
esotericism
exotericism
esotericist
epoch-making
emotionable
emotionless
emotionally
egotistical
exoskeletal
exoskeleton
erotomaniac
erotogenous
econometric
erotophobia
ecofriendly
emolumental
evolutional
explanative
explanation
explanatory
emplacement
explainable
expectative
expectation
expectantly
expectingly
expectorate
expectorant
expediently
expeditious
empiecement
euphemistic
espièglerie
expressible
expressness
expugnation
explicative
explication
explicatory
expansively
expensively
expansivity
expansional
expenditure
empanelment
empanelling
exponential
explorative
exploration
exploratory
explosively
expromissor
expropriate
exploitable
eupepticity
exportation
expurgation
emparlaunce
expurgatory
empirically
empiricutic
experienced
Esperantist
emperorship
empyreumata
expiscation
expiscatory
exposedness
empassioned
expositress
expostulate
expatiative
expatiation
expatiatory
empowerment
empty-handed
empty-headed
emphyteusis
emphyteutic
empty-nester
enquiration
exquisitely
Eurocentric
Euro-dollars
earnestness
egregiously
Earthshaker
earthliness
earth-pillar
earth-closet
earthenware
earthmoving
earth-tremor
earth-hunger
earthquaked
ear-piercing
erroneously
europeanise
europeanize
Europeanism
Europeanist
Eurypharynx
Eurypterida
eurypteroid
Euro-sceptic
Etruscology
erratically
eurythermic
eurythermal
eurhythmics
eurhythmist
enslavement
east-by-north
east-by-south
exsiccative
exsiccation
eisteddfods
Epstein-Barr
easternmost
exstipulate
essentially
ensanguined
exsanguined
ensepulchre
elsewhither
extravagate
extravasate
extravagant
estramazone
estranghelo
extra-virgin
extradition
extrafloral
entrainment
extrapolate
extractable
extractible
ectoblastic
entablature
entablement
established
establisher
extremeness
estrepement
esthesiogen
entreatable
entreatment
ectogenesis
ectogenetic
extrication
Estrildidae
extrinsical
extemporary
extemporise
extemporize
entomophagy
entomophily
ectomorphic
extenuative
extenuating
extenuation
extenuatory
eating-apple
eating-house
extensively
extensional
estancieros
ectoplasmic
ectoplastic
entophytous
externalise
externalize
extirpative
externalism
extirpation
externalist
externality
entertainer
extirpatory
enterectomy
exterminate
extorsively
extortioner
enthralment
enthralling
exteriorise
exteriorize
exteriority
enterpriser
enterostomy
enterotoxin
enterovirus
entitlement
ectothermic
ectotrophic
entrustment
equiangular
educability
educational
equableness
equibalance
enunciative
enunciation
enunciatory
edulcorator
equidistant
enumerative
enumeration
exuberantly
erubescence
erubescency
ecumenicism
elucidative
elucidation
elucidatory
enucleation
equilibrate
equilibrium
equilibrist
equilibrity
ebulliently
equilateral
equinoctial
elusoriness
emulousness
equipollent
elutriation
emulsionise
emulsionize
Equisetales
Equisetinae
equivocally
equivocator

11 e□u□v

equivalence
equivalency
envelopment
enviousness
environment
erythematic
erythrocyte
etymologise
etymologize
etymologist
flabbergast
flamboyance
flamboyante
flamboyancy
flaccidness
franc-tireur
fiançailles
Francomania
flag-captain
Francophile
Francophobe
△francophone
flax-dresser
fraudulence
fraudulency
frater-house
flagellated
flagellator
fraternally
fraterniser
fraternizer
flat-earther
fearfulness
feather-pate
feather-edge
feather-head
feather-star
flagitation
fragileness
feasibility
franklinite
frank-pledge
frankfurter
flammulated
fragmentary
flap-mouthed
flauntingly
flannelette
flag-officer
flavourless
flavoursome
flapperhood
fratricidal
franticness
frantically
fractionate
fractionary
fractionise
fractionize
fractionlet
fractiously
featureless
flatulently
flag-wagging
fabricative
fabrication
fibrillated
fibrocement
fibrocement®
face-flannel
fact-finding
facsimilist
facultative
facilitator
fecundation
facinerious
factory-gate
factory-ship
facetiously
factualness
fidgetiness
faddishness
fiddle-de-dee
fiddlestick
free-and-easy
freebootery
freebooting
Frenchiness
Frenchwoman
Frenchwomen
fieldworker
field-cornet
fremescence
fretfulness
free-falling
flesh-market
free-hearted
fleshliness
fleshmonger
flesh-colour
fee-fi-faw-fum
feelingless
flexibility
freeloading
freemasonic
△**freemasonry**
flexography
fleurs-de-lis
fleurs-de-lys
freethinker
free-tongued
free-thought
freeze-frame
fifteenthly
figure-dance
Fehmgericht
fricandeaux
friableness
flinchingly
fair-dealing
fainéantise
fringilline
frighteners
frightening
faith-healer
faithlessly
frightfully
flightiness
faithworthy
frigidarium
flickertail
feignedness
fairniticle
fairnyticle
frigorifico
friponnerie
frivolously
fair-seeming
flirtatious
fair-weather
fairy-butter
fallalishly
full-acorned
full-blooded
full-charged
false-bedded
falteringly
filter-paper
fuller's-herb
full-fraught
full-fledged
full-frontal
full-hearted
fulminating
fulmination
fulminatory
fulling-mill
falsifiable
fallibilism
fallibilist
fallibility
folliculose
folliculous
fell-lurking
filamentary
filamentous
full-mouthed
feloniously
follow-board
fulsomeness
fallow-finch
filmography
felspathoid
fell-running
feldspathic
filmsetting
Falstaffian
fulguration
fell-walking
fume-chamber
familiarise
familiarize
familiarity
fomentation
Fumariaceae
fimbriation
fumatoriums
Fontarabian
fundamental
fanfaronade
fantastical
finicalness
fingerboard
fingerguard
fingerglass
finger-grass
fence-lizard
fingerplate
finger-paint
fingerprint
fingerstall
fender-stool
finch-backed
funambulate
funambulist
financially
Finno-Ugrian
funerreally
fund-raising
fenestrated
fanatically
functionate
functionary
fine-toothed
frowardness
footbreadth
footballing
footballist
flocculence
frondescent
florescence
flower-clock
floweriness
flower-stalk
froth-blower
froth-hopper
foolhardise
foolhardize
florilegium
floriferous
flowingness
foolishness
flock-master
foot-lambert
floorwalker
flourishing
frowstiness
foot-soldier
footslogger
footstooled
front-ranker
frontlessly
frostbitten
frontolysis

Words marked △ may be spelled also with a capital letter

front-loaded
front-loader
foot-tapping
front-runner
foppishness
fipple-flute
forwardness
forwandered
firmamental
formational
farraginous
formalistic
fire-balloon
fire-bombing
firecracker
fire-crested
fire-control
ferociously
foreclosure
fardel-bound
far-reaching
forgetfully
forget-me-not
forbearance
fermentable
forfeitable
forgettable
fire-flaught
fire-fighter
farthingale
forthcoming
furthcoming
furtherance
farthermore
furthermore
furthersome
farthermost
furthermost
formicarium
forcipation
formication
fornication
farcicality
forbiddance
forbiddenly
forgiveness
furtiveness
ferriferous
furciferous
forcing-pump
furnishment
furnishings
fortifiable
forcibility
fernitickle
foreignness
forficulate
foreknowing
ferulaceous
firelighter
foraminifer

foraminated
fire-marshal
foremastman
farinaceous
fortnightly
furunculous
farm-offices
forfoughten
ferro-chrome
ferro-nickel
ferronnière
forlornness
ferrography
furiousness
forepayment
forequarter
forereading
fore-recited
fire-raising
forestation
forestaller
foreseeable
foresignify
foresighted
foreshorten
fore-spurrer
ferntickled
first-person
forethinker
forethought
first-footer
foretopmast
first-fruits
first-attack
first-strike
fortunately
formularise
formularize
formulation
fortune-tell
fortuneless
ferruginous
forevermore
forevouched
fire-walking
fire-worship
forewarning
fire-watcher
farawayness
fernytickle
fast-breeder
fish-bellied
foster-child
Fastern's-e'en
foster-nurse
fast-forward
fish-farming
fish-gutting
festinately
fascinating
fissiparism

fascination
festination
fustigation
fustilarian
fissiparity
fissiparous
fascia-board
fossil-fired
fishing-line
fishing-frog
fustilirian
festivities
fastigiated
fashionable
fissionable
fashionably
fushionless
fasciculate
fusillation
fusing-point
fish-packing
festschrift
fast-talking
fish-torpedo
fetichistic
fatidically
fothergilla
father-in-law
fatefulness
fatigue-duty
fatiguingly
fetch-candle
fitting-shop
fatuousness
fetishistic
feudalistic
fauxbourdon
foundations
four-flusher
frugiferous
frugivorous
foul-mouthed
four-pounder
fluorimeter
fluorometer
fluorescein
fluorescent
fluoroscope
fluoroscopy
fluctuating
frustrating
fluctuation
flustration
fructuation
frustration
faultlessly
fruitlessly
fault-finder
fountain-pen
flusterment
four-wheeled

four-wheeler
fivefingers
favoredness
favouritism
fawningness
foxtrotting
fly-dressing
fazendeiros
fuzzy-haired
gradationed
gradational
glauconitic
Graeco-Roman
glaucescent
gnatcatcher
grandparent
grandfather
grandmaster
guardedness
grandeeship
grand-nephew
glandularly
grandiosely
grandmother
grandiosity
gravel-blind
gracelessly
grave-digger
gladfulness
graphicness
graphically
graphologic
graphomania
gnathonical
gravitative
gravitation
graniteware
guaniferous
gravimetric
glaringness
goatishness
granitiform
gladioluses
gradiometer
granivorous
gravity-feed
goalkicking
glaikitness
Grallatores
grammalogue
grammatical
glasnostian
gramophonic
granophyric
granolithic
glamorously
glamourpuss
glass-gazing
glass-blower
Gladstonian
glassworker

11 g□a□s

grasshopper
grass-rooter
glass-cutter
grass-cutter
geanticline
ghastliness
giant-killer
graptolitic
goal-tending
granulative
granulation
gratulation
granularity
gratulatory
granuliform
granulomata
granulocyte
gibberellic
gibberellin
gobe-mouches
gibbousness
gubernation
gaberlunzie
goddaughter
godlessness
goddess-ship
God-almighty
△god-forsaken
giddy-headed
Gregarinida
greenockite
green-wellie
green-keeper
greenbottle
greengrocer
guerrillero
grease-heels
guesstimate
greaseproof
gressorious
great-nephew
Grenzgänger
gaff-topsail
gegenschein
gigantesque
giganticide
gigantology
griddle-cake
guildswoman
guilelessly
gainfulness
glimmer-gowk
gliomatosis
geitonogamy
guiltlessly
gristliness
gallantness
gold-beating
Goldbergian
gull-catcher
gold-digging
goldenberry
galley-foist
gelseminine
gallimaufry
Gallicanism
gullibility
gelliflowre
galliambics
galliardise
Gallowegian
gallowglass
Gallovidian
gallowsness
gallows-bird
gallows-ripe
gallows-foot
gallows-free
gallows-tree
gillravitch
goldsmithry
gelatiniser
gelatinizer
gally-bagger
gally-beggar
gillyflower
gully-hunter
gymnasiarch
gymnastical
game-chicken
gammerstang
gamogenesis
gemmiparous
gemmiferous
gummiferous
gambit-piece
gemological
gaming-house
gaming-table
gymnorhinal
gemmologist
gimcrackery
gametangium
gamotropism
gametophyte
gemmulation
goniatitoid
gendarmerie
genealogise
genealogize
gonfalonier
genealogist
gangbusting
gonococcoid
geniculated
△gingerbread
genteelness
gander-month
gynaecomast
gynaecology
genuflexion
genuineness
gentilhomme
gentilitial
gentilitian
gentianella
gentlemanly
gentlenesse
gentlewoman
gentlewomen
gonimoblast
goniometric
Gongoristic
generically
gonorrhoeic
gonorrhoeal
generalship
generalling
generations
gangsterdom
gangsterism
gynostemium
genetically
genitivally
genouillère
geomagnetic
geotactical
good-brother
grog-blossom
grouchiness
glomeration
good-evening
glove-shield
geotechnics
goose-winged
Globerigina
geomedicine
globeflower
goose-flower
grotesquely
grotesquery
geometrical
Geometridae
geotectonic
glomerulate
geochemical
geophysical
globigerina
good-looking
gloom-monger
good-morning
groundburst
ground-robin
groundspeed
groundswell
groundsheet
ground-sloth
ground-to-air
good-natured
geopolitics
gnotobiosis
gnotobiotic
gnomonology
groupuscule
glossectomy
glossodynia
grossièreté
glossolalia
geostrategy
gnostically
glottogonic
ghostliness
geostrophic
ghost-writer
groatsworth
globularity
geodynamics
geosyncline
gypsiferous
garlandless
gormandiser
gormandizer
germaneness
Germanesque
Germanistic
Germanophil
Gargantuism
Gargantuist
gyrocompass
gyre-carline
garden-glass
garden-house
garnet-paper
garter-snake
garmentless
germinative
germination
gurgitation
girlishness
garnishment
girdlestead
Geraniaceae
gerontophil
gerontology
garbologist
gyrostatics
garrulously
gerrymander
gestational
gestatorial
Gasteropoda
gas-fittings
gesticulate
gaseousness
gastrectomy
gastrologer
gastromancy
gastronomic
gastronomer
gastroscope
gastrostomy
gastrosophy
gas-guzzling
gutta-percha

Words marked △ may be spelled also with a capital letter

gatecrasher
gutterblood
guttersnipe
guttiferous
go-to-meeting
get-together
gutturalise
gutturalize
glutaminase
grumblingly
gauze-winged
gouvernante
glumiferous
Glumiflorae
glutinously
gourmandise
gourmandism
grummet-hole
glue-sniffer
glyphograph
glycosylate
glyptotheca
gazing-stock
head-banging
headborough
heavenwards
haaf-fishing
headhunting
heathenesse
hyacinthine
hyalomelane
head-station
headscarves
hearse-cloth
heart-easing
heart's-blood
hearth-brush
heartlessly
healthfully
heart-shaped
healthiness
hearth-money
hearth-penny
heart-urchin
heartbroken
hearth-stone
heart-strike
heart-string
heart-strook
heart-struck
heavy-handed
heavy-headed
heavyweight
Hebraically
Hobbistical
hobbledehoy
habiliments
habilitator
hebdomadary
hobgoblinry
hebephrenia
hebephrenic
haberdasher
hibernation
hibernacula
△hibernicise
△hibernicize
Hibernicism
habituation
habitudinal
heckelphone
hacking-coat
huckleberry
hectogramme
hucksterage
hucksteress
hide-and-seek
hydra-headed
hydrargyral
hydrargyrum
Hudibrastic
hedge-parson
hedge-school
hedge-priest
hedge-writer
hedge-hyssop
hedging-bill
hiding-place
hydrocarbon
hydropathic
Hydnocarpus
hydromantic
hydrotactic
hydrogenate
hydrometeor
hydrogenise
hydrogenize
hydrogenous
hydrometric
hydromedusa
hydrophobia
hydrophobic
Hydrophidae
hydrophilic
hydrochoric
Hydrocharis
hydrothorax
hydrophytic
hydrophyton
hydrosomata
hydroponics
hydrologist
hydrosphere
hydrobromic
hydrotropic
hydrography
hideousness
hydrostatic
hydrolysate
hydrocyanic
hierarchism
haemangioma
haematocele
haematology
haematocrit
heedfulness
hierophobia
hierophobic
haemophilia
haemoglobin
hierologist
haemorrhage
haemorrhoid
hierography
hyetography
hierocratic
haemoptysis
haemostasis
haemostatic
Hieronymite
Hieronymian
haemocyanin
hierurgical
huffishness
haggardness
Haggadistic
high-alumina
highblooded
highbrowism
high-battled
high-density
high-feeding
highfalutin
high-hearted
hog-shouther
hoggishness
Hegelianism
highlighted
highlighter
Highlandman
highly-sexed
hegemonical
high-mettled
hogen-mogens
hagioscopic
hygroscopic
hygrometric
hygrophytic
hagiologist
Hagiographa
hagiography
hugeousness
high-profile
high-pitched
high-powered
high-rolling
high-ranking
high-stepper
high-sighted
high-tension
high-voltage
highwrought
hair-brained
hairbreadth
hairdresser
heinousness
hair-raising
hairstylist
hair-trigger
half-and-half
hollandaise
holoblastic
hall-bedroom
holobenthic
half-binding
half-blooded
half-brother
halobiontic
half-baptise
half-baptize
half-checked
helicograph
half-century
△helichrysum
holocaustic
holocaustal
helve-hammer
halfendeale
Hellenistic
hälleflinta
helleborine
helmet-shell
Heldentenor
helpfulness
holographic
hellgramite
hylogenesis
half-hearted
holohedrism
half-holiday
hellishness
half-integer
helminthoid
helminthous
half-leather
half-landing
half-measure
hylomorphic
helioscopic
heliometric
heliophobic
heliochrome
heliochromy
heliotropic
heliotropin
heliography
hylophagous
halophilous
halfpennies
hill-pasture
hylopathism
hylopathist
half-pounder
holophytism

Words marked △ may be spelled also with a capital letter

11 h□l□r

hilariously
Halbstarker
half-starved
helispheric
holothurian
hallucinate
hillwalking
hylozoistic
home-and-home
home-and-away
hemianopsia
hemianoptic
homoblastic
humectation
homocentric
home-crofter
home-defence
hamadryades
hammer-brace
hammercloth
homoeomeric
homoeomorph
homoerotism
homoeopathy
homogeneity
homogeneous
homogeniser
homogenesis
homogenetic
homogenizer
hemihedrism
humming-bird
homoiousian
home-keeping
humiliative
humiliating
humiliation
humiliatory
homological
Hamiltonian
homiletical
hemimorphic
homomorphic
Hymenoptera
homeopathic
homeomerous
hymnologist
homeomorphy
hymnography
homeostasis
homeostatic
homoplastic
hemipterous
homopterous
hemophiliac
homopolymer
homophonous
humgruffian
hemorrhagic
hemeralopia
homesteader

hemispheric
hemistichal
homosporous
home-stretch
homothallic
hematoblast
homothermic
homothermal
hamstringed
hematolysis
hematemesis
hemitropous
hematoxylin
Hematoxylon
humbuggable
homeworking
homozygosis
homozygotic
hangability
hand-breadth
handbagging
hunt-counter
hinderingly
hinderlands
hinderlings
hunter's-moon
hand-feeding
handfasting
hang-gliding
hunchbacked
henchperson
handicapped
handicapper
hunting-mass
hunting-seat
hunting-whip
hunting-tide
hunting-song
hunting-horn
Huntington's
hunting-crop
handkercher
hand-painted
hand-promise
hundredfold
honorifical
hand-running
honorariums
handshaking
handselling
honest-to-God
hunt-the-gowk
hand-to-mouth
honour-bound
honour-point
handwriting
handwritten
handwrought
honey-waggon
honey-badger
honeycombed

honeymooner
honey-locust
honeysuckle
honey-suckle
honey-sucker
hootanannie
hyoscyamine
hook-climber
hootenannie
hooliganism
hyoplastral
hyoplastron
haphazardly
heptarchist
heptandrous
heptamerous
hypoaeolian
heptagynous
hypoblastic
hypocycloid
hypocorisma
hyphenation
haplessness
hippeastrum
hopefulness
hypoglossal
hypogastric
hippiatrics
hippiatrist
hypallactic
hypolimnion
Hepplewhite
hop-o'-my-thumb
hyponitrite
hyponitrous
hypnopaedia
hippodamist
hippodamous
hippocampal
hippocampus
hypnogenous
hypsometric
hypsophobia
hypnotistic
hippopotami
hippologist
hoplologist
hypnopompic
hippodromic
haptotropic
haplography
hypsography
Hippocratic
hypoplastic
hypophyseal
hypophysial
hypermarket
hypergamous
hyperdactyl
hyperactive
hyperacusis

hyperphagia
hypercharge
hyperplasia
hyperemesis
hyperemetic
hyperinosis
hyperinotic
hyperborean
hyperbolise
hyperbolize
hyperbolism
hyperdorian
hypersonics
hypersomnia
hyperboloid
hypertrophy
hypercritic
hypersthene
hyperstress
hyperlydian
hypostasise
hypostasize
hypostatise
hypostatize
hypostrophe
hepatectomy
hypothecate
hypothecary
hypothesise
hypothesize
hypothetise
hypothetize
hypothermia
hypothermal
hypothenuse
hypotensive
hypotension
hypotyposis
hepatoscopy
hypothyroid
hard-and-fast
hortatively
hortatorily
hare-brained
hornblendic
Heracleidan
Heraclitean
hereditable
horse-racing
horseradish
horse-dealer
hermeneutic
hurley-house
horse-riding
hermeticity
horse-litter
horse-collar
herpetology
horse-couper
horse-doctor
horse-drench

harness-cask
harness-room
harvest-mite
harvest-tick
harvest-home
harmfulness
hurtfulness
horographer
hard-grained
hard-hearted
hard-hitting
hurricanoes
hereinafter
hurriedness
herring-pond
herring-bone
herring-gull
herring-buss
horripilate
horripilant
horrisonant
herbivorous
horrisonous
hurtleberry
horological
hurdle-racer
harum-scarum
horn-madness
hardmouthed
hariolation
hercogamous
hircocervus
herb-of-grace
harrowingly
harmoniphon
harmonistic
harmonogram
harbourless
harbour-dues
hard-pressed
harpsichord
haruspicate
harassingly
hart's-tongue
hornswoggle
horoscopist
heresiology
heretically
herb-trinity
hirsuteness
hard-visaged
hard-wearing
hero-worship
hardworking
hardwareman
horny-handed
hurly-hacket
hurry-scurry
hurry-skurry
husbandland
husbandless
husbandlike
histaminase
△hispanicise
△hispanicize
hispanicism
Hesychastic
hysteresial
Hesperiidae
hesperidium
hysteroidal
hysterogeny
hysterotomy
hostess-ship
hospitalise
hospitalize
hospitality
hospitaller
histiocytic
hostilities
historicise
historicize
historicism
historicist
historicity
historiated
historiette
histologist
histrionism
histrionics
hasty-witted
hetaerismic
hot-tempered
hatlessness
hitherwards
hatefulness
hatchettite
hatti-sherif
hetairismic
hotel-keeper
hot-spirited
heteroclite
heterocercy
heteroecism
heterograft
Heteroptera
heteroscian
heterospory
heterostyly
heterotroph
heterotopia
heterotopic
heterotypic
heterotaxis
△heterousian
hounds-berry
hound's-tooth
houseparent
house-father
house-factor
housemaster
housekeeper
housewifely
housewifery
householder
house-mother
house-broken
house-hunter
haughtiness
haustellate
hover-barrow
hawkishness
howsomdever
hexadecimal
hexagonally
hexahedrons
hexametrise
hexametrize
hexametrist
hexaplarian
hexastichal
hexateuchal
hazardously
inadaptable
inaugurator
inanimately
imaginative
imagination
inanimation
inalienable
inalienably
isapostolic
itacolumite
inappetence
inappetency
inauthentic
inattentive
inattention
inalterable
inalterably
inadvertent
inadvisable
imbricately
imbrication
incrassated
incremation
incoercible
incremental
inclemently
increasable
increaseful
incredulity
incredulous
incognisant
incognizant
incogitable
incogitancy
incoherence
incoherency
inclination
inclinatory
incriminate
inculcative
inculcation
inculpation
inculcatory
inculpatory
incalescent
incompetent
incumbently
incompliant
incomposite
incommodity
incantation
incensation
incantatory
incunabulum
incunabular
inconscient
inconscious
incensement
incense-boat
incontinent
incentivise
incentivize
incendivity
inconsonant
incongruent
incongruity
incongruous
incinerator
inconstancy
incrossbred
incapacious
incipiently
incapsulate
incarnadine
△incarnation
incurvation
incertainty
incurvature
incarcerate
incorrectly
incardinate
incarvillea
incertitude
incoronated
incorporate
incorporall
incorporeal
incuriosity
incuriously
incorruptly
incessantly
inclusively
itchy-palmed
india-rubber
indubitable
indubitably
indeciduate
indeciduous
Indo-Chinese
inductively
inductility

11 i□d□c

inductivity
inductional
indifferent
indefinable
indefinably
indignation
indignantly
indigestive
indigestion
indehiscent
Indo-Iranian
indulgently
indemnified
indumentums
indomitable
Indomitably
indentation
induplicate
△independent
indirection
indesignate
industrials
industrious
individuate
individable
indivisible
indivisibly
indexterity
index-finger
index-linked
iteratively
inelaborate
inenarrable
inexactness
ipecacuanha
inescapable
inexcusable
inexcusably
inexcitable
inelegantly
inexecrable
inexecution
inefficient
ineffective
ineffectual
ideographic
inexhausted
inedibility
inexistence
ideological
ineloquence
ideopraxist
inexpectant
inexpedient
inexpensive
idempotency
icebreaking
inebriation
inessential
inertia-reel
identically

identifying
inestimable
inestimably
inextension
ineluctable
inequitable
inequitably
infrangible
infrangibly
inflatingly
inflammable
inflammably
infracostal
infecundity
inflexional
infrequence
infrequency
infiltrator
infomercial
infanticide
infantilism
infundibula
infantryman
infantrymen
infangthief
infinitival
informative
infuriating
infirmarian
information
infuriation
informatics
infernality
informality
informatory
infertility
inferential
inferiority
infestation
infatuation
infeudation
influential
infructuous
ingratitude
ingeniously
ingenuously
ingurgitate
ingathering
inhabitable
inhabitress
inhabitance
inhabitancy
ichthyosaur
ichthyoidal
ichthyolite
ichthyornis
ichthyology
ichnography
ithyphallic
△ithyphallus
inheritable

inheritress
inheritance
imitatively
imitability
idioblastic
itinerantly
iridescence
idiographic
idioglossia
iridisation
iridization
inimicality
initialling
idiomorphic
iridologist
idiotically
injudicious
injuriously
inking-table
irksomeness
ink-horn-mate
ill-mannered
ill-favoured
illiberally
illicitness
ill-tempered
ill-affected
illogically
ill-disposed
illuminable
illuminance
illuminator
illimitable
illimitably
ill-informed
illiquation
illaqueable
illiquidity
ill-wresting
illusionism
illusionist
ill-assorted
illustrious
illustrated
illustrator
ill-humoured
illuviation
immediately
immediatism
immedicable
immigration
immomentous
immunoassay
immenseness
immunogenic
immanentism
immanentist
immunotoxic
immunotoxin
immortalise
immortalize

immortality
immarginate
immitigable
immitigably
immoveables
ignobleness
innocuously
innominable
ignominious
innumerable
innumerably
innervation
ignoramuses
Ignorantine
ionospheric
innutrition
innavigable
innavigably
ion-exchange
innoxiously
icosandrian
icosandrous
icosahedral
icosahedron
isolability
isomagnetic
inoperative
isolecithal
inobedience
isometrical
isogeotherm
inofficious
inoffensive
iron-founder
iron-foundry
inorganised
inorganized
iron-hearted
isothenuria
isochronise
isochronize
isochronism
isochronous
isorhythmic
isodiaphere
isoelectric
ironmongery
isoantibody
isotonicity
iconologist
inodorously
isomorphism
isomorphous
iconography
iconostasis
inopportune
isoxsuprine
inobservant
inobtrusive
inoculative
inoculation

Words marked △ may be spelled also with a capital letter

11 i□t□r

inoculatory
idoxuridine
implacental
impeachable
impeachment
implausible
implausibly
impractical
impecunious
impedimenta
imprecation
impresarios
imprecatory
implemental
imprecisely
imprecision
impregnable
impregnably
impressible
impressment
impignorate
implicative
implication
impuissance
impulsively
impolitical
impoliticly
impingement
imponderous
impenetrate
impenitence
impenitency
imploration
improbation
imploratory
improvement
improvisate
improvident
imploringly
improvingly
impropriate
impropriety
impermanent
imperialise
imperialize
imperialism
imparkation
impartation
importation
imperialist
imperiality
importantly
imperceable
impermeable
impermeably
imperfectly
imperviable
impertinent
impartially
imperilment
imperforate
impersonate
imperiously
importunate
importunacy
importunely
importuning
importunity
impastation
imposthumed
impassively
impassivity
impassioned
impostumate
impetrative
impetration
impetratory
impatiently
impetigines
impetuosity
impetuously
input-output
impoundable
impoundment
imprudently
inquination
inquiration
inquirendos
inquiringly
inquisitive
inquilinism
△inquisition
inquilinity
inquilinous
irreceptive
irrecusable
irrecusably
irradiative
irradiation
irreducible
irreducibly
irreduction
△irredentism
△irredentist
Israelitish
irreflexion
irrefutable
irrefutably
irregularly
irreligious
irrelevance
irrelevancy
irremissive
irremission
irremovable
irremovably
irruptively
irreparable
irreparably
irresoluble
irresolubly
irretentive
irretention
ipratropium
irrevocable
irrevocably
irreverence
instatement
instability
installment
instaurator
instantiate
insectarium
insecticide
Insectivora
insectivore
insectiform
insectifuge
insectology
insidiously
insufflator
inspirative
instigative
inspiration
instigation
inspiratory
instinctive
instinctual
inspiringly
inspiriting
institorial
inspissated
inspissator
institutive
institution
institutist
insalubrity
insultingly
ipselateral
ipsilateral
inseminator
insensately
insinuative
insinuating
insinuation
insinuatory
insincerely
insincerity
insensitive
insentience
insentiency
insipidness
insipiently
inseparable
insuperable
inseparably
insuperably
instreaming
inscribable
instructive
instruction
insertional
inscriptive
inscription
inscrutable
inscrutably
insistently
insessorial
insatiately
insouciance
insculpture
inseverable
intradermal
intravenous
intrasexual
intrathecal
intractable
intractably
intrenchant
intrepidity
intreatfull
integrative
integration
integrality
intagliated
intricately
intuitively
intuitivism
intuitional
intrinsical
intriguante
intellected
intelligent
intolerable
intolerably
intolerance
intemperate
intemperant
intumescent
intensative
intenseness
intensively
intensified
intensitive
intensifier
intentioned
intensional
intentional
Istiophorus
intromitted
intromitter
intercalate
intercalary
interjacent
intertangle
internalise
internalize
interfacing
interfacial
interracial
interradial
interradius
internality
intervallic

11 i□t□r

intervallum
intertarsal
interactant
interactive
interscribe
interaction
interocular
interbedded
intermeddle
interdepend
intercedent
internecine
internecive
intervening
intermedial
intermedium
interleukin
interdealer
interregnum
interneural
intercensal
intercessor
interdental
interseptal
intersertal
intercepter
interceptor
interjector
interventor
intersexual
interleaves
intermezzos
interchange
interminate
inturbidate
interlinear
△**interlingua**
intermingle
interlining
interviewee
interviewer
interfluent
interallied
interfluous
Interglossa
interpolate
interrogate
interrogant
internodial
interiority
intercooled
intercooler
intercourse
intercostal
interspinal
intersperse
intertribal
intertrigos
intercrural
interpreter
intergrowth
interosseal
interesting
interatomic
icteritious
interlunary
internuncio
interludial
interfusion
interrupted
interrupter
interruptor
intrusively
Intoximeter®
intoximeter
inusitation
inutterable
inviability
invidiously
invigilator
invigorator
involucrate
invalidness
invalidhood
involvement
involuntary
inventively
inventorial
inviolately
investigate
investitive
investiture
investments
idyllically
jealousness
jealoushood
jabberingly
joblessness
jabberwocky
Jacobinical
Jacobitical
jactitation
Jack-pudding
jocoserious
Jacqueminot
judiciously
judgemental
Judaisation
Judaization
judgment-day
△**judas-window**
jagging-iron
John-a-dreams
Johnsoniana
joint-tenant
jumping-hare
jumping-jack
jumping-bean
jumping-deer
jimpson-weed
Janian-faced
jinrickshaw
jungle-green
janitorship
Japanophile
juridically
jury-process
jerrymander
justiceship
justiciable
justifiable
justifiably
josephinite
journey-work
jaunting-car
juvenescent
jawbreaking
joylessness
kwashiorkor
knavishness
kibble-chain
kidney-stone
kneecapping
knee-capping
keelhauling
keeping-room
kleptocracy
knee-tribute
kleptomania
kaisar-i-Hind
knife-switch
kriegsspiel
knick-knacky
kilocalorie
killikinick
kalashnikov
Kulturkreis
Kulturkampf
Kommersbuch
kymographic
kamelaukion
Kimeridgian
Kendal-green
kangaroo-hop
kangaroo-rat
kingdomless
kinderspiel
kind-hearted
kinchin-cove
kinchin-mort
kinnikinick
kinematical
kindredness
kindredship
kinesiatric
king's-yellow
kinesthesia
kinesthesis
kinesthetic
kinesiology
kinesipathy
kinetochore
kinetograph
kinetoscope
king-vulture
knowingness
knock-rating
knocked-down
know-nothing
klootchmans
kerb-crawler
kernicterus
keratometer
keratophyre
kiss-and-tell
kiss-me-quick
kite-balloon
katabothron
katadromous
kitchen-maid
kitchenware
kitchen-sink
kitchenette
katavothron
knuckle-head
knuckle-bone
keystroking
load-bearing
leaf-climber
leaf-cushion
leaf-cutting
leave-taking
leader-cable
leaseholder
leap-frogged
loathedness
loathliness
loathsomely
leather-back
leather-head
leather-neck
leather-coat
leatherette®
leach-trough
leaving-shop
leaping-time
liabilities
leafletting
learnedness
loan-society
loadsamoney
leaguer-lass
leaguer-lady
librational
labradorite
labefaction
lubricative
lubrication
lubritorium
Lobeliaceae
libellously
labiodental
loblolly-bay
loblolly-boy

Words marked △ may be spelled also with a capital letter

libertarian
libertinage
liberticide
libertinism
liberalness
labyrinthic
labyrinthal
laboriously
liberty-boat
Lubavitcher
lobby-member
Lochaber-axe
lucratively
lucubration
luckenbooth
lactescence
luckengowan
lickerishly
lichenology
lecherously
lock-forward
lacrimatory
lactiferous
lactifluous
lacrimosely
loculicidal
laciniation
laconically
lycanthrope
lycanthropy
lychnoscope
laccolithic
lactoflavin
lick-platter
Lycopodinae
lacertilian
lachrymator
locorestive
lickspittle
locust-years
locutionary
lectureship
lacquer-tree
lacrymatory
lacrymosely
ludicrously
lodge-keeper
lady's-mantle
lady-trifles
leesome-lane
lieutenancy
luffer-board
life-history
left-luggage
lifemanship
life-rentrix
life-support
loggan-stone
legibleness
logicalness
logodaedaly
loggerheads
leglessness
leg-of-mutton
logographic
logographer
lignivorous
logomachist
ligamentary
ligamentous
Leguminosae
lagomorphic
Loganiaceae
legionnaire
logopaedics
legerdemain
logarithmic
legislative
legislation
legislature
logistician
light-handed
light-headed
light-legged
lightweight
light-heeled
light-minded
light-winged
light-footed
legatissimo
leg-business
lignum-swamp
lignum-scrub
loiteringly
leishmaniae
leishmanias
laicisation
laicization
Leibnitzian
lake-dweller
lukewarmish
△lilliputian
lily-livered
lalapalooza
lumbaginous
lamp-chimney
lammergeier
lammergeyer
lymphangial
lumpishness
limelighted
lamplighter
lamelliform
lamellicorn
lamentation
lemon-yellow
lamentingly
luminescent
limnologist
Lumbricidae
lumbricalis
lamprophyre
limitedness
limited-over
limitlessly
limitations
limp-wristed
longanimity
longanimous
landaulette
Lancastrian
long-clothes
linseed-cake
linseed-meal
lingeringly
lanceolated
lance-knecht
lance-knight
landfilling
line-fishing
landgravate
land-grabber
landgravine
landholding
lanthanides
luncheon-bar
lancinating
lancination
landing-beam
landing-gear
landing-ship
lentiginose
lentiginous
longinquity
land-jobbing
lonely-heart
landlordism
land-measure
long-measure
linen-scroll
linen-draper
langoustine
long-playing
line-printer
long-purples
landscaping
landscapist
land-steward
long-sighted
landsknecht
line-shooter
lengthiness
long-tongued
languidness
languescent
languishing
linguistics
long-visaged
longwearing
long-waisted
leopard-wood
leopard-moth
loose-limbed
loose-bodied
loosestrife
lion-hearted
lapidifying
Lepidoptera
Lepidosteus
lapidescent
Lepidosiren
Lippizzaner
lapilliform
lip-smacking
lipomatosis
leprosarium
leptodactyl
leptocercal
lip-rounding
leptorrhine
lophobranch
lipoprotein
laparoscope
laparoscopy
liposuction
liquescence
liquescency
liquefiable
Liquidambar
liquidation
large-handed
large-minded
larcenously
larviparous
larrikinism
laryngismus
laryngology
laryngotomy
listeners-in
listening-in
listeriosis
lustfulness
lysigenetic
lastingness
luskishness
lese-majesté
lese-majesty
lissomeness
Laserpicium
Laserpitium
lethargical
littérateur
Lutheranism
letter-board
letterboxed
letterpress
letter-stamp
latifundium
litigiously
latch-string
lattice-leaf
lattice-work
lethiferous
littleworth

11 l□t□n

litany-stool
litholapaxy
lithogenous
lithochromy
lithophysae
lithophytic
latrocinium
lithologist
lithotomist
lithodomous
lithotomous
lithosphere
lithography
lithotripsy
lithotritic
lithotritor
lythraceous
laterigrade
literalness
literaliser
literalizer
literaryism
latirostral
lateritious
literatured
Lotus-eaters
lotus-eating
latiseptate
latitudinal
laudability
leucaemogen
launderette
laundry-maid
louver-board
laurel-water
laughing-gas
laughworthy
loutishness
loudmouthed
leucodermia
leukodermia
leucodermic
leukodermic
leucodermal
leukodermal
leucoplakia
leukoplakia
leucorrhoea
leukorrhoea
leucocratic
leukocratic
louvre-board
loudspeaker
Louis-Treize
Louis-Quinze
loup-the-dyke
laurustinus
liveability
love-in-a-mist
level-headed
level-pegged
Livingstone
liver-colour
leviratical
levitically
law-merchant
lawlessness
low-spirited
low-pressure
loxodromics
lexigraphic
luxulianite
luxulyanite
luxuriation
luxuriantly
luxuriously
lixiviation
leze-liberty
leze-majesty
meaningless
meadow-brown
meadow-grass
meadowsweet
measureless
measurement
mechanicals
mechanician
mechanistic
MacFarlane's
Machaerodus
Machairodus
mechatronic
mycodomatia
mock-heroics
machination
machine-made
machine-shop
machine-work
mockingbird
machicolate
mycological
mock-modesty
macrogamete
microgamete
macrodactyl
macroscopic
microscopic
microneedle
microcephal
Micronesian
micrometric
microphonic
microphytic
microlithic
microfiches
microfiling
macrobiotic
microfloppy
microampere
microinject
micrococcal
micrococcus
micrologist
microtomist
macrocosmic
microcosmic
microporous
macrofossil
microfossil
microgroove
micrography
microwriter
microtubule
microswitch
macrocyclic
mycophagist
mycoplasmas
McCarthyite
McCarthyism
mycorrhizal
maceranduba
mycotrophic
Michurinism
micturition
Micawberish
Micawberism
mediateness
mediatorial
mediatrices
mediastinal
mediastinum
mediaevally
medico-legal
medicinable
medicinally
medievalism
medievalist
maddeningly
madreporite
middenstead
madefaction
midshipmate
madrigalian
madrigalist
midlittoral
middle-class
middle-earth
mudslinging
modularised
modularized
middle-sized
middle-world
madonnawise
Madonna-lily
modernistic
moderations
mid-Atlantic
medium-dated
mediumistic
muddy-headed
Moeso-gothic
muffin-fight
muffin-worry
Magdalenian
magnanimity
magnanimous
magnetician
Maglemosian
magnesstone
magnifiable
magnificent
magnificoes
megaloblast
megalomania
megalopolis
maggotorium
magisterial
magisterium
magistratic
Megatherium
megatonnage
megavitamin
magazine-gun
Mahabharata
Mohammedism
Mohorovicic
mail-carrier
mail-catcher
maisonnette
maidservant
maintenance
maintopsail
maintopmast
maisterdome
moisturiser
moisturizer
majoritaire
majoretting
make-believe
Mekhitarist
make-or-break
multangular
multanimous
molybdenite
Malacca-cane
mole-cricket
molecularly
maliciously
malacophily
molecatcher
maledictive
malediction
maledictory
melodiously
maladroitly
maladaptive
maladjusted
millenarism
millenarian
millet-grass
millefleurs
millenniums
mulberry-fig
malfeasance

11 m□r□e

malt-extract
malefaction
malefically
maleficence
malefactory
malignantly
multivalent
multiracial
multiparity
multiparous
multiscreen
multi-access
multiserial
Mulciberian
millisecond
melliferous
meltingness
milking-time
multilineal
multilinear
multifidous
mellifluent
multiplying
mellifluous
multiplexer
multiplexor
milliampere
millionaire
millionfold
multilobate
multisonant
multipotent
multinomial
multicolour
mellivorous
multispiral
multistrike
multiethnic
multistorey
multijugate
multi-author
multijugous
multicuspid
milk-kinship
malakatoone
milk-livered
melanochroi
melanterite
melancholia
melancholic
molendinary
melanophore
meliorative
melioration
malposition
melioristic
meliphagous
milk-pudding
malapropism
malpractice
malariology
molestation
milk-thistle
malfunction
△milquetoast
malevolence
mollycoddle
mammalogist
mimographer
mammiferous
mumpishness
mammillaria
mamillation
mamilliform
momentarily
momentously
mammoth-tree
mammonistic
mammoplasty
mammography
mumbo-jumbos
memorialise
memorialize
memorialist
memorabilia
membraneous
memorandums
mimosaceous
mimetically
man-watching
mansard-roof
mandarinate
manna-lichen
Montanistic
manna-groats
mangalsutra
miniaturise
miniaturize
miniaturist
monoblepsis
mind-bending
mind-blowing
monochasial
Manichaeism
monochasium
minicabbing
monoclinous
monoculture
mine-captain
municipally
monocardian
monochromic
monochromat
monocarpous
Monocotylae
monocrystal
Monadelphia
Monodelphia
monodelphic
mont-de-piété
monkey-board
monkey-bread
monkey-block
mendelevium
Montenegrin
monkey-gland
monkey-grass
Monseigneur
Minnesinger
manneristic
mantelpiece
mantelshelf
monkey-shine
men-servants
monkey-wheel
munificence
manufactory
manufacture
mindfulness
manifestoes
monographic
monographer
montgolfier
monogenesis
monogenetic
managership
mind-healing
Munchhausen
men-children
mentholated
monchiquite
mancipation
mancipatory
manniferous
mannishness
man-milliner
mentionable
monticolous
mandibulate
monticulate
monticulous
monological
monologuise
monologuize
monologuist
monolingual
monolatrous
monomyarian
monomorphic
manumission
manumitting
mononuclear
Minenwerfer
mind-numbing
meningocele
Munro-bagger
Mennonitism
mentonnière
monophagous
manipulable
monopoliser
manipulator
monopolizer
monopsonist
monophthong
△monophysite
mind-reading
monarchical
menorrhagia
mineraliser
mineralizer
minoritaire
ministering
ministerial
monasterial
ministerium
menispermum
minesweeper
monasticism
Monotremata
△monothelete
△monothelite
△monothelism
monothecous
minute-glass
many-tongued
munitioneer
monstrosity
monstrously
monitorship
mine-thrower
minute-while
minute-watch
mensurative
manducation
mensuration
manducatory
mantua-maker
monovalence
monovalency
money-making
money-market
moneylender
money-spider
money-broker
money's-worth
monozygotic
myocarditis
moorbuzzard
moon-goddess
mooring-mast
myoelectric
moonlighter
moon-madness
myographist
map-measurer
meprobamate
maquiladora
mortarboard
meroblastic
moribundity
mariculture
mercenarism
mercenarily

11 m□r□e

marcescible
Marie-Jeanne
market-house
merveilleux
myrmecology
murderously
market-place
market-price
morgenstern
martensitic
market-value
market-woman
mirifically
merogenesis
merogenetic
marshlander
marshmallow
marsh-mallow
mirthlessly
morphologic
marshalship
marshalling
merchandise
merchandize
merchanting
merchantman
merchantmen
marchioness
morphotropy
marginalise
marginalize
marginalism
marginalist
marginality
martinetism
mortice-lock
mortise-lock
morbiferous
mortiferous
mercilessly
morning-land
marriage-bed
morning-tide
morning-gift
morning-room
morning-gown
morsing-horn
martialness
myrmidonian
merdivorous
marlinspike
marble-edged
marble-paper
Marantaceae
Moringaceae
myringotomy
marrow-bones
marionberry
mirror-glass
mirror-image
marconigram
Mariologist
Maryologist
margraviate
maraschinos
meritocracy
Marathonian
meritorious
moratoriums
mercuration
murmuration
murmuringly
Marsupialia
mercurially
murmurously
marquessate
marquisette
marqueterie
Moravianism
Merovingian
marivaudage
merrymaking
merry-andrew
martyrology
mustard-tree
Mesoamerica
message-girl
mustachioed
maskallonge
mishallowed
muscatorium
miscarriage
mismarriage
mesoblastic
mossbluiter
music-seller
moss-cheeper
masochistic
musicalness
music-holder
mesocephaly
misidentify
misrelation
master-class
misdescribe
misperceive
master-clock
miscegenate
misremember
miscegenist
misdemeanor
masterfully
misbeliever
master-joint
miscellanea
muskellunge
master-mason
misbecoming
misdevotion
misbegotten
masterpiece
musket-proof
mistempered
mispersuade
mussel-scalp
mussel-scaup
mussel-shell
misfeasance
misfeatured
misbestowal
master-wheel
missheathed
mischievous
Muschelkalk
mastication
mussitation
masticatory
massiveness
misdiagnose
missishness
Messiahship
miscibility
mispleading
muscle-bound
mésalliance
misalliance
misclassify
mesomorphic
mush-mouthed
mesenterial
misanthrope
misanthropy
misoneistic
misinformer
misinstruct
misdoubtful
misconceive
mastoiditis
misgovernor
museologist
mastodontic
misconstrue
misfortuned
misspelling
mass-produce
miscreative
mistreading
miscreation
miscreaunce
misericorde
miserliness
mistrustful
misestimate
mesothelial
mesothelium
musk-thistle
moss-trooper
musculation
muscularity
musculature
masturbator
misguidedly
misguidance
misjudgment
meshuggenah
meshuggeneh
masculinely
masculinise
masculinize
masculinist
masculinity
mesquinerie
masquerader
Mussulwoman
mitrailleur
mutableness
metacentric
metachrosis
mathematise
mathematize
mutteration
mathematics
motherboard
mothercraft
mutteringly
mother-in-law
mother-naked
mother-right
mother's-mark
mother-water
metafiction
metagenesis
mutagenesis
metagenetic
mitogenetic
matchmaking
matchlessly
metrication
matrilineal
matrilinear
matriclinic
matrimonial
matriarchal
matriculate
metaldehyde
mottle-faced
metalliding
metalloidal
metallogeny
metalworker
metallurgic
metempirics
metamorphic
metonymical
mythomaniac
meteoritics
Methodistic
matroclinic
meteorolite
mythologise
mythologize
mythologian
metrologist
mythologist

mythopoeist
meteorology
methodology
meteorogram
mythopoetic
mythography
metaplastic
metaphorist
metaphrasis
metoposcopy
metapsychic
metaphysics
motor-bandit
materialise
materialize
materialism
materialist
materiality
motor-launch
△mithradatic
△mithridatic
Mithraicism
motor-driven
metastasise
metastasize
metasilicic
metasomatic
metasequoia
mitotically
metathesise
metathesize
mutationist
methylamine
methylation
mould-candle
mould-facing
Mauretanian
mouse-colour
mouth-honour
mouth-friend
moustachial
mountaineer
mountainous
mountain-top
mountenance
moveability
movableness
mawkishness
moxibustion
maxillipede
Myxomycetes
maxim-monger
maximaphily
myxomatosis
Myxophyceae
mixotrophic
May-December
May-meetings
maysterdome
Mezzogiorno
mezzotintos
△neanderthal
near-sighted
noble-minded
nubbing-cove
nectar-guide
nyctanthous
nociceptive
nickel-bloom
neckerchief
nucleolated
nickelodeon
nickel-ochre
nucleoplasm
nuclear-free
nickel-steel
neck-herring
noctivagant
nictitating
nictitation
noctivagous
nyctinastic
nyctitropic
noctilucent
noctilucous
nick-nackery
necromancer
necromantic
necroscopic
necrophobia
nyctophobia
necrophobic
necrophilia
necrophilic
necrobiosis
necrobiotic
necropoleis
necrologist
nocuousness
necessarian
necessaries
necessarily
necessitate
necessitied
necessitous
nocturnally
nudicaudate
nudicaulous
needcessity
needfulness
needlecraft
needle-furze
needlepoint
needlestick
needlewoman
Niersteiner
Nietzschean
nefariously
nigrescence
neglectable
negligeable
negligently
negrophobia
nightfaring
night-waking
nightmarish
negotiation
night-walker
negotiatrix
night-cellar
night-season
night-shriek
night-flying
night-flower
nightingale
negationist
night-worker
night-porter
night-attire
night-hunter
noiselessly
neighboring
neighbourly
noisomeness
nikethamide
nulliparity
nulliparous
nullifidian
name-calling
nomadically
name-dropper
nomographic
nomographer
Nymphalidae
nympholepsy
nymphomania
nomological
nomenclator
nominatival
nimbostrati
numerically
numismatics
numismatist
nematoblast
nematodirus
nematophore
nummulation
non-harmonic
non-marrying
non-partisan
non-naturals
non-abrasive
non-academic
non-metallic
nondescript
non-resident
non-delivery
non-believer
nonsensical
non-feasance
non-sequence
nonagesimal
nonchalance
nunnishness
non-dividing
non-violence
non-elective
non-election
non-electric
non-allergic
nonillionth
non-clinical
nonplussing
non-invasive
non-unionist
non-volatile
non-specific
non-priority
non-provided
none-sparing
non-issuable
nonetheless
non-standard
nuncupative
nuncupation
nuncupatory
nun's-veiling
non-existent
ninny-hammer
Nancy-pretty
neopaganise
neopaganize
neopaganism
Neo-Catholic
neonatology
neovitalism
neovitalist
Neoplatonic
neologistic
Neotropical
nook-shotten
nephelinite
napoleonite
Napoleonism
Napoleonist
nephologist
nephrectomy
nephrolepis
nephropathy
nephritical
naphthalene
naphthalise
naphthalize
Nornamesque
narratively
normatively
nurse-tender
nervelessly
nurserymaid
northwardly
north-easter
north-wester
northernise
northernize

11 n□r□h

northernism
northermost
narcissuses
narcoleptic
narrow-gauge
nervousness
nervuration
nasofrontal
nosographic
nosographer
nasogastric
nosological
nose-nippers
nasopharynx
nostradamic
Nostradamus
nitraniline
notableness
notice-board
notochordal
netherlings
netherstock
netherworld
netherwards
nutrimental
nothingness
nothing-gift
nutritively
nutritional
nettle-cloth
notungulate
nationalise
nationalize
nitrosamine
nationalism
nitrosation
nationalist
notionalist
nationality
nitrogenase
nitrogenise
nitrogenize
nitrogenous
nitrometric
nitrocotton
notaphilism
notaphilist
net-practice
naturalness
natural-born
notoriously
naturopathy
Nototherium
natatoriums
nitty-gritty
nautch-girls
naughtiness
nourishable
nourishment
naupliiform
neuropathic
neuroleptic
neuroticism
neurofibril
neurologist
neurotomist
neurotropic
neurotrophy
neuropteran
neutraliser
neutralizer
navel-gazing
navel-orange
navel-string
novelettish
novelettist
never-fading
never-ending
Novatianism
Novatianist
newscasting
news-theatre
noxiousness
ob-and-soller
opalescence
orange-grass
orange-stick
orange-tawny
orang-outang
Oxalidaceae
onagraceous
oracularity
oraculously
orbiculares
orbicularis
orbicularly
orchestrate
orchestrina
orchestrion
oncogenesis
Orchidaceae
orchiectomy
orchid-house
orchidology
oscillative
oscillating
occultation
oscillation
oscillatory
oscillogram
oecumenical
occipitally
old-maidhood
old-womanish
old-fogeyish
orderliness
opera-dancer
open-and-shut
overachieve
operatively
operational
over-anxiety
over-anxious
overbearing
overblanket
overbidding
over-breathe
overbrimmed
overbalance
overburthen
overcoating
operculated
overcrowded
overcorrect
overcareful
overcasting
overdraught
over-drowsed
opeidoscope
overdevelop
overearnest
overfraught
overfreedom
overfreight
overfulness
overflowing
overforward
oreographic
overgrazing
overgrainer
overgarment
overheating
open-hearted
overhandled
overhastily
overindulge
obediential
overleather
overlocking
oreological
overmeasure
open-mouthed
overnighter
ocean-stream
operoseness
one-worldism
onerousness
overpicture
overprepare
over-precise
overproduce
overpitched
overpayment
overreached
oneirodynia
oneiromancy
overrunning
oneiroscopy
overstrooke
overstretch
overstuffed
over-trading
overtedious
overthrower
overviolent
overweather
overweening
overwrestle
overwrought
over-zealous
offhandedly
officialdom
officialese
officialism
officiality
office-block
olfactology
officiously
offscouring
offset-litho
off-the-shelf
offenceless
offensively
off-coloured
off-Broadway
obfuscation
obfuscatory
organ-screen
organically
organisable
organistrum
organizable
ophicalcite
ophidiarium
ophthalmist
ochlophobia
ochlophobic
ophiologist
ochlocratic
otherwhiles
Ophiuroidea
oviparously
oeil-de-boeuf
Origenistic
originative
origination
originality
olivine-rock
opinionated
opinionator
oriel-window
opium-smoker
orientalise
orientalize
Orientalism
orientation
Orientalist
orientality
oligomerous
Oligochaeta
oligochaete
oligochrome
oviposition
onirocritic

11 p□a□n

ominousness
object-glass
objectivate
objectively
objectivise
objectivize
objectivism
objectivist
objectivity
objurgative
objurgation
objurgatory
olla-podrida
obliquation
obliqueness
obliquitous
obliterated
obliterator
obliviously
Osmundaceae
osmotically
ommatophore
obmutescent
omniformity
omnifarious
oenological
ornamentist
omnipresent
oenophilist
omnipatient
omnipotence
omnipotency
owner-driver
omniscience
Ornithogaea
ornithosaur
Ornithopoda
ornithology
ornithopter
obnoxiously
odonatology
onomasticon
ozonisation
ozonization
odoriferous
ozoniferous
ozonosphere
odorousness
odontoblast
odontograph
odontogenic
odontologic
odontophore
oppignerate
oppignorate
opprobrious
opportunely
opportunism
opportunist
opportunity
oarsmanship

Ossianesque
obsecration
obsidionary
obsceneness
oyster-field
oyster-knife
oyster-plant
oyster-patty
obstetrical
oyster-shell
oyster-tongs
oyster-woman
oyster-wench
obsignation
obsignatory
obstinately
obstipation
od's-pitikins
obsolescent
od's-bodikins
oesophageal
observative
observation
observatory
observantly
obstructive
obstriction
obstruction
oestrogenic
observingly
obsessional
obscuration
obscureness
obscurement
out-paramour
outwardness
ostracoderm
ostracodous
outmarriage
octachordal
octodecimos
ostreaceous
ostreophage
ostreophagy
out-of-the-way
out-of-pocket
octagonally
ontogenesis
ontogenetic
octahedrite
octahedrons
ostrich-farm
ostrich-like
outdistance
ontological
octillionth
obtemperate
optometrist
ostentation
octonocular
octingenary

ostensively
octennially
out-and-outer
orthopaedic
osteopathic
orthoscopic
orthogenics
orthopedics
orthopedist
osteodermic
osteodermal
osteogenous
orthocentre
orthophyric
osteophytic
osteoclasis
osteoplasty
orthoborate
Ostrogothic
osteologist
orthodontia
orthodontic
orthoepical
orthodromic
orthotropic
orthography
osteography
orthopraxis
orthostichy
orthopteran
orthopteron
orthostatic
octuplicate
outbreeding
outcrossing
obtestation
octastichon
outstanding
obtrusively
outbuilding
outquarters
octave-flute
obumbration
ovuliferous
obviousness
oxygenation
onychomancy
oxyrhynchus
oxy-chloride
onychophagy
Onychophora
oxy-fluoride
oxy-compound
oxy-hydrogen
Platanaceae
placability
phalanstery
play-actress
plaice-mouth
praecordial
peat-casting

peacemaking
planetarium
plate-basket
plate-warmer
phagedaenic
peace-parted
peace-keeper
plateresque
prayerfully
place-kicker
planetoidal
plate-powder
peace-monger
place-monger
Phanerozoic
planetology
player-piano
plate-armour
Placentalia
place-hunter
playfulness
platforming
peacherinos
peach-brandy
pharisaical
plagioclase
Praxitelean
phariseeism
planimetric
playing-card
△**platinotype**
planisphere
psaligraphy
plagiostome
Plagiostomi
placket-hole
pearl-barley
pearl-fisher
pearl-millet
pearl-powder
pearl-mussel
pearl-button
pearl-oyster
psalmodical
plasmolysis
plasmolytic
plasminogen
psammophile
psammophyte
plasmatical
pragmatical
Phasmatodea
Phasmatidae
pragmatiser
pragmatizer
phaenogamic
Phaenogamae
plaintively
phaenomenon
plain-spoken
plainstanes

11 p□a□o

plainstones
planogamete
piano-school
phagophobia
Platonicism
peacock-like
peacock-fish
peacock-blue
piano-player
pianofortes
plano-convex
phagocytism
phagocytose
plantocracy
practicable
practicably
practically
plasticiser
plasticizer
prattlement
plantigrade
phantomatic
Phaethontic
praetorship
plasterwork
phantasmata
phantasiast
plantswoman
piacularity
planuliform
pharyngitic
pharyngitis
platyrrhine
publication
publishable
publishment
pebble-stone
pick-and-pick
peccability
peccadillos
pace-bowling
pococurante
picket-fence
picket-guard
pocket-glass
pickelhaube
pocket-piece
pocketphone
pocket-sized
pacifically
pacificator
pectinately
pectination
pectisation
pectization
packing-case
peckishness
pichiciagos
peculiarise
peculiarize
peculiarity
pecuniarily
pictorially
Pycnogonida
pycnogonoid
pictography
pock-pudding
picture-card
picture-rail
picture-wire
picture-play
picture-cord
picture-book
picture-goer
picturesque
Pickwickian
pachydactyl
pachydermia
pachydermic
pachydermal
pick-your-own
pudibundity
pedicellate
Pedicularis
pediculosis
pediculated
pedder-coffe
pedagogical
pedagoguery
pedagoguish
pedagoguism
pudding-pipe
pudding-time
Pedaliaceae
paddle-board
pedal-action
pedological
pad-elephant
paddle-staff
paddle-shaft
paddle-wheel
pedanticise
pedanticize
pedanticism
pedantocrat
Podsnappery
pedunculate
Pedipalpida
Podophyllum
podophyllin
pedestalled
pedetentous
preparative
preparation
preparatory
Pre-Cambrian
presanctify
presagement
prelateship
prevalently
prevaricate
premaxillae
prevailment
prefatorial
predatorily
prefatorily
prêt-à-porter
precautions
precautious
prematurely
prematurity
presbycusis
plea-bargain
presbyteral
presciently
preachiness
prescindent
preschooler
pleochroism
prescission
preoccupate
preoccupant
preoccupied
preacquaint
pseudocubic
pseudograph
pseudologia
pseudologue
pre-adamical
pseudomonad
pseudomonas
pseudomorph
pre-adamitic
preadmonish
pseudopodia
preadaptive
pseudoscope
plebeianise
plebeianize
plebeianism
paederastic
pretendedly
predeceased
predecessor
precedented
preselector
precedently
preterhuman
premedicate
premeditate
preteritive
preterition
prevenience
prerecorded
preferrable
Pherecratic
prehensible
presentable
preventable
preventible
presentably
precentress
preceptress
presentness
presentient
presentment
prefectship
pretentious
prefectural
preservable
pre-ignition
plethorical
predicament
predicative
predication
prelibation
predicatory
preciseness
pleximetric
predilected
peevishness
Pterichthys
precipitate
precipitant
preliminary
previsional
precipitous
plenipotent
pteridology
premiership
predictable
predictably
pietistical
paediatrics
paediatrist
prehistoric
prefigurate
peelie-wally
pre-election
preclinical
pre-emphasis
piedmontite
pre-eminence
pneumonitis
pleomorphic
pre-emptible
pneumatical
pneumathode
preambulate
preambulary
plein-airist
preannounce
prerogative
phenogamous
Pterosauria
pterodactyl
preconceive
premovement
phenomenise
phenomenize
phenomenism
phenomenist
pleiomerous
paedophilia

11 p□n□a

paedophilic
plerophoria
predominate
prenominate
predominant
premonitive
prepositive
premonition
preposition
pre-position
premonitory
prepollence
prepollency
precognosce
precolonial
paedologist
phenologist
poenologist
paedodontic
pre-conquest
pleiotropic
paedotrophy
pyelography
precontract
puerperally
pleurodynia
pleuritical
precritical
plessimeter
plessimetry
Pleistocene
pleasurable
pleasurably
pleasureful
pieds-à-terre
press-button
pre-stressed
plentifully
prestigious
plenteously
Plectoptera
peep-through
prestissimo
prepunctual
prepubertal
prejudgment
prejudicate
prejudicant
prelusively
presumingly
prejudicial
pre-judicial
preaudience
prelusorily
presumptive
presumption
pre-existent
pigheadedly
pig-ignorant
piggishness
pignoration

pigeon-berry
pigeon-chest
pigeon-flier
pigeon-flyer
pigeonholer
pigeonholes
pigeon-house
pig-sticking
philanderer
privateness
primateship
philatelist
primariness
privatively
primatology
primaevally
pliableness
pair-bonding
Priscianist
principally
pricelessly
price-fixing
prize-winner
painfulness
philhellene
primiparity
primiparous
primigenial
pairing-time
priming-wire
priming-iron
primitively
primitivism
primitivist
poikilocyte
prickle-back
prickliness
prickly-pear
phillipsite
prismatical
Psilotaceae
philomathic
psilomelane
primogenial
poison-gland
Psilophyton
philosophic
philosopher
philologian
philologist
poisonously
poison-sumac
philogynist
philogynous
painstaking
priestcraft
psittacosis
pointedness
point-device
point-devise
print-seller

pointlessly
point-of-sale
pointillism
pointillist
printing-ink
point-source
paint-bridge
Primulaceae
poking-stick
polyandrous
palmatisect
palpability
pilgarlicky
pillar-saint
polyactinal
palebiology
phlyctaenae
palm-cabbage
police-court
police-judge
polyculture
pelican-fish
polycentric
polycrotism
pilocarpine
polychroism
polychromic
polycarpous
policewoman
polycrystal
polydactyly
pulveration
pallescence
pollen-grain
poltergeist
pilferingly
Palaearctic
pullet-sperm
palaeotypic
pulverulent
polygraphic
palsgravine
Pelagianism
polygonally
polygenesis
polygenetic
polygonatum
phlegmonoid
phlegmonous
polyglottic
polyglottal
pale-hearted
polyhedrons
polyhydroxy
pulchritude
polyhistory
palpitation
pollination
pillion-seat
pilniewinks
polemically

polymorphic
polymastism
palingenesy
palindromic
pillow-block
poliorcetic
pillow-fight
Paleolithic
paleobotany
pulmobranch
paleography
Pelton-wheel
polyonymous
polyphagous
Polyphemian
polyphonist
polypeptide
pilgrimager
polarimeter
polarimetry
poltroonery
pelargonium
polariscope
Polystichum
Palestinian
palestrical
polystyrene
pilot-jacket
politicking
politically
polytechnic
pelotherapy
Polytrichum
pull-through
Politbureau
pullulation
pellucidity
pale-visaged
pole-vaulter
palmyra-wood
palmyra-nuts
pollyannish
polyzoarial
polyzoarium
pomiculture
Pompeian-red
pampelmoose
pompelmoose
pampelmouse
pompelmouse
pomegranate
pamphleteer
pomological
pompousness
pump-priming
Pandanaceae
pentavalent
pan-galactic
pentadactyl
pentandrian
pentandrous

11 p□n□a

panjandarum
pentamerism
pentamerous
pentahedral
pentahedron
pantaletted
pantalettes
pentangular
pentathlete
pinnatisect
pentamidine
pentaploidy
pentazocine
pantalooned
Pentacrinus
pentastichs
pentactinal
pendant-post
pentagynian
pentacyclic
pentagynous
punicaceous
penicillate
Penicillium
paniculated
panic-monger
pinacotheca
pinocytosis
panic-struck
panic-buying
ponderation
Pinteresque
ponderingly
△**panhellenic**
△**pandemoniac**
△**pandemonium**
△**pandemonian**
ponderosity
ponderously
Pentecostal
penteconter
punt-fishing
panegyrical
panegyricon
pantheistic
pinch-hitter
penthemimer
punching-bag
Punchinello
pantheology
pencil-cedar
pensileness
pensiveness
ponticellos
pinking-iron
pinkishness
pontificate
pontificals
pensionable
pantisocrat
pencil-stone

penological
penultimate
pentlandite
Panglossian
Pan-Slavonic
Pont-l'Évêque
panomphaean
Pan-American
panentheism
panentheist
Pan-Anglican
peninsulate
pennoncelle
pantoscopic
pantophobia
pansophical
pantothenic
pantomimist
pantography
Pantocrator
panspermism
panspermist
penuriously
pancratiast
panislamism
panislamist
panpsychism
panpsychist
panesthesia
punishingly
penetrative
punctuative
penetrating
penetralian
penetration
punctuation
punctualist
punctuality
Panathenaea
Panathenaic
punctilious
punctulated
penitential
panduriform
pan-European
pendulosity
pendulously
pennyweight
penny-wisdom
pennywinkle
pinnywinkle
penny-a-liner
propagative
profanation
propagation
profanatory
prosaicness
prosaically
protandrous
profaneness
prolateness

probabilism
probabilist
probability
probational
probationer
protanomaly
protagonist
prosauropod
procaryotic
prokaryotic
prosciuttos
proud-minded
proterandry
proletarian
proletariat
proteaceous
prosenchyma
proceedings
procerebral
procerebrum
proper-false
procephalic
phonemicise
phonemicize
phoneticise
phoneticize
phoneticism
phonetician
phonemicist
phoneticist
provenience
proveditore
progenitrix
progeniture
Procellaria
proteolysis
proteolytic
prolegomena
Proterozoic
proterogyny
prose-writer
professedly
proleptical
protectress
projectment
progestogen
protectoral
prosecution
prosecutrix
proselytise
proselytize
proselytism
proofreader
proof-charge
proof-puller
prong-horned
ploughshare
plough-staff
plough-stilt
ptochocracy
prothallial

prothallium
prothalamia
prothalloid
prophylaxis
prothrombin
prochronism
prothoracic
prothoraces
prothoraxes
prophesying
prophetical
prophetship
prophethood
proximately
prodigalise
prodigalize
proximation
prodigality
promiscuity
promiscuous
proliferate
promiseless
profiterole
proliferous
prominently
providently
prolificacy
propitiable
promisingly
prohibitive
△**prohibition**
prolificity
proficience
△**provisional**
proficiency
prosiliency
prohibitory
propitiator
provisorily
propinquity
profit-taker
poodle-faker
proclaimant
problematic
prognathism
prognathous
protogalaxy
provocateur
protopathic
provocative
prorogation
provocation
provocatory
photonastic
phototactic
protomartyr
Proboscidea
proboscides
photoactive
proboscises
protonemata

Words marked △ may be spelled also with a capital letter

provokement
photoperiod
photo-relief
photoresist
photometric
prolongable
photo-ageing
phonophobia
photophobia
photophobic
photophilic
photophonic
photochromy
Prototheria
protophytic
phonofiddle
provokingly
protolithic
photo-finish
proposition
promotional
photoglyphy
pronouncing
protonotary
protococcal
Protococcus
prosopopeia
protocolise
protocolize
photocopier
phonologist
protocolist
protocolled
photosphere
phototropic
phonography
photography
proconsular
provostship
proportions
prolocution
prolocutrix
phonotypist
protogynous
phosphatide
phosphatise
phosphatize
prospective
prospecting
prospection
promptitude
phosphorate
phosphorise
phosphorite
phosphorize
phosphonium
phosphorism
phosphorous
procreative
procreation
protractile
protractive
protraction
protrudable
proprietary
proprietrix
programming
△**propranolol**
protrusible
Procrustean
△**progressive**
progressism
progression
progressist
prostration
proctodaeal
proctodaeum
prosthetics
prosthetist
proctorship
proctoscope
proctoscopy
prostitutor
prostatitis
procuration
procuratory
protuberate
protuberant
profuseness
procurement
producement
promulgator
propylamine
proxy-wedded
promycelium
propylitise
propylitize
Procyonidae
pop-lacrosse
pop-fastener
pipe-cleaner
pipe-dreamer
peppercorny
pepper-grass
pepperiness
papier-mâché
poppet-valve
puppet-valve
peptisation
peptization
pupillarity
pipe-lighter
papilliform
populariser
popularizer
papillulate
paper-hanger
paper-making
paper-sailor
papyraceous
piperaceous
paper-feeder
paper-weight
paper-office
paper-enamel
paper-folder
paper-credit
paper-muslin
paper-cutter
pipe-stapple
pipe-stopple
pipistrelle
papovavirus
puppy-walker
puppy-headed
park-and-ride
permanently
permanganic
pervasively
purgatively
parvanimity
portability
purgatorial
purgatorian
parablepsis
parableptic
parabolical
parabolanus
pyroballogy
parabematic
pure-blooded
parabaptism
pork-butcher
pericranial
pericranium
pyroclastic
periclitate
parochially
Paracelsian
pericentric
pericentral
paracrostic
pericardiac
pericardial
pericarpial
pericardium
pericardian
paracetamol
parachutist
perichylous
peridiniums
peridesmium
paradoxical
Paradoxides
purse-taking
perseverate
perseverant
persevering
purse-seiner
purse-bearer
porterhouse
porter-house
parheliacal
permeameter
perpetrable
perpetrator
porte-crayon
parpen-stone
perceptible
perfectible
pervertible
perceptibly
perfectness
perpetuable
persecutive
persecution
perpetually
perpetuance
persecutory
perpetuator
perceivable
perceivably
purificator
paraffinoid
paraffin-oil
paraffin-wax
paragraphia
paragraphic
paragrapher
periglacial
pyrogravure
paragogical
peregrinate
paragliding
peregrinity
paragenesia
paragenesis
perigenesis
paragenetic
pyrogenetic
paraglossae
paraglossal
pyrognostic
Perigordian
perigastric
parchedness
perchlorate
perihepatic
porphyritic
purchasable
pertinacity
pervicacity
pertinently
participate
participant
partitively
participial
partibility
percipience
partitioner
percipiency
porriginous
portionless
parti-coated

Words marked △ may be spelled also with a capital letter

11 p□r□i

permissible
permissibly
permittance
persistence
persistency
particulate
pyrokinesis
parallactic
parallelise
parallelize
paralleling
parallelism
parallelist
paraldehyde
paraleipses
paraleipsis
paralympics
Portlandian
perplexedly
parsley-pert
paramedical
pyramidical
paramedicos
pyramidally
paramaecium
paramoecium
portmanteau
paramorphic
perimorphic
paramastoid
perambulate
paramountcy
paramountly
perennation
parent-craft
paronychial
paranthelia
parentheses
parenthesis
parenthetic
perennially
phrenologic
paronomasia
paranephric
perinephric
paranephros
partnership
phrenetical
perineurium
perforative
personalise
personalize
personative
personating
personalism
percolation
perforation
personation
personalist
personality
purposeless
purpose-like
park-officer
personified
pyrrolidine
personifier
periodicity
performable
performance
pornotopian
periodontia
periodontal
personpower
parlour-maid
pornography
purportedly
purportless
periostitic
periostitis
perlocution
perspective
perspicuity
perspicuous
paraphiliac
paripinnate
parapenting
pyrophorous
perspirable
paraphrenia
paraphraser
paraparesis
periphrases
periphrasis
paraparetic
paraphraxia
paraphraxis
peripeteian
peripatetic
part-payment
parapsychic
portraitist
portraiture
purpresture
pyrargyrite
peristalith
perishables
peristalsis
peristaltic
parascender
peristerite
parascenium
perispermic
perispermal
paresthesia
perishingly
parasuicide
parasailing
parascience
parishioner
paraselenae
phrasemaker
part-singing
peristomial
perissology
phraseology
phraseogram
perestroika
parasitical
parasitemia
parasitosis
piratically
pyrotechnic
parotiditis
perithecial
perithecium
pyritohedra
puritanical
peritonaeal
peritonaeum
peritonitic
peritonitis
paratrooper
paratyphoid
parathyroid
perduration
permutation
perturbable
perturbedly
perturbance
perturbator
perfunctory
persuadable
perfumeless
parturition
perduellion
persulphate
persuasible
perquisitor
perlustrate
periwigging
part-writing
party-pooper
party-coated
passacaglia
passage-boat
passamezzos
piscatorial
pissasphalt
push-bicycle
pesteringly
post-exilian
posteriorly
△**pasteurella**
pasteuriser
pasteurizer
possessable
pushfulness
pasigraphic
post-glacial
paschal-lamb
passiveness
pestiferous
pestilently
passing-bell
passing-note
possibilism
possibilist
passibility
possibility
pessimistic
postillator
passionless
Passiontide
Poseidonian
piscicolous
piscivorous
posological
post-lingual
post-nuptial
pastoralism
pastoralist
pestologist
pastourelle
post-primary
postponence
postscenium
post-tension
positronium
postulation
pustulation
postulatory
pasture-land
pastureless
pasquinader
post-vocalic
post-vintage
pussy-willow
pussyfooter
Petrarchise
Petrarchize
Petrarchism
Petrarchian
Petrarchist
pot-walloner
pot-walloper
Pythagorean
Pythagorism
pot-valorous
putrescible
putrescence
putrefiable
potteringly
pattern-shop
pitifulness
pitchperson
pitchblende
pitch-roofed
patch-pocket
pettishness
patrilineal
patrilinear
patricianly
phthiriasis
patriclinic

Words marked △ may be spelled also with a capital letter

pettifogger
patrimonial
petticoated
patriarchal
patristical
patelliform
petalomania
potamogeton
potentially
potentiated
patent-right
patent-rolls
poting-stick
pathogenous
Pythonesque
pathophobia
patronising
patronizing
patroclinic
petroglyphy
patroonship
pathologist
petrologist
petropounds
pittosporum
Petrodromus
pathography
petrography
piteousness
patrol-wagon
patrolwoman
pit-a-patting
pataphysics
'pataphysics
paternalism
△**paternoster**
pâte-sur-pâte
potato-bogle
petitionary
petitioning
petitionist
pit-dwelling
putty-powder
pluralistic
plum-blossom
plumber-work
pound-master
pound-keeper
pauselessly
plume-pluckt
prudentials
pluriserial
plumigerous
pruning-bill
pruning-hook
prudishness
pruriginous
Paulinistic
pluviometer
plutologist
plutonomist
plutocratic
plum-pudding
pourparlers
Prussianise
Prussianize
Prussianism
poultry-farm
plumularian
paving-stone
pawnbroking
powerlessly
power-diving
power-driven
pixillation
phylacteric
psychiatric
psychically
psychodrama
psychedelia
psychodelia
psychedelic
psychodelic
psychograph
psychagogue
psychogenic
psychologic
psychometer
psychomotor
psychometry
psychonomic
psychophily
psychopathy
psychotoxic
physicalism
physicalist
physicality
physiocracy
physiognomy
physitheism
physicianer
physiciancy
physiologic
physiologus
physiolater
physiolatry
phylloclade
ptyalagogic
ptyalagogue
phyllomania
phyllotaxis
phycophaein
phytophagic
phytochrome
phytoalexin
phycologist
phytologist
phytotomist
phytography
Plymouthite
Plymouthism
Plymouthist
phytosterol
phycomycete
phycocyanin
quandong-nut
quaveringly
quaternion'd
quaternions
qualitative
qualifiable
qualifiedly
quacksalver
quadriennia
quarrel-pane
quarrelling
quadrillion
quarrelsome
quarrellous
quadrennial
quadrennium
quarrington
quadrupedal
quadraphony
quadrophony
quadratical
quarry-water
quaestorial
Quantometer®
quantometer
quarterback
quarter-jack
quarter-rail
quarter-sawn
quarterdeck
quarter-seal
quarter-wind
quarter-road
quarter-note
quarter-tone
quarter-bred
quarter-evil
queene-apple
Queensberry
queen-regent
queenliness
queen-stitch
queer-basher
questionary
questioning
questionist
querulously
queez-maddam
quibblingly
quincuncial
quiveringly
quick-change
quick-firing
quick-witted
quicksilver
quicken-tree
quick-freeze
quick-frozen
quick-sticks
quill-driver
quinquereme
quinquennia
quinsy-berry
quiescently
quintillion
quilting-bee
quizzically
quotability
quoteworthy
quodlibetic
reawakening
readability
rhagadiform
Reaganomics
reascension
rhabdomancy
rhabdomyoma
Rhabdophora
reamendment
reach-me-down
road-hoggish
roadholding
realisation
realization
reanimation
reading-lamp
reading-desk
reading-book
reaping-hook
reading-room
realignment
reallotment
road-mending
readmission
rhamnaceous
reappraisal
reappraiser
Rhamphastos
realpolitik
reapportion
rear-roasted
rhapsodical
reassertion
reassurance
road-scraper
reattribute
reactionary
reactionist
readvertise
ready-witted
ready-to-wear
ready-monied
rib-vaulting
rubicundity
rubber-cored
rabbet-joint
rubber-stamp
rubefacient
rubefaction

Words marked △ may be spelled also with a capital letter

11 r□b□i

rubrication
rubbing-post
rubbish-heap
rib-tickling
rebukefully
Rabelaisian
rabble-rouse
rubble-stone
ribonucleic
rebroadcast
ribbon-grass
rib-roasting
rebarbative
Ribesiaceae
rabattement
reclamation
rock-and-roll
rectangular
Rechabitism
racialistic
reclaimable
reclaimably
rock-breaker
rice-biscuit
ricocheting
ricochetted
rock-climber
racket-court
recremental
ricketiness
racket-press
rickettsiae
rickettsial
rickettsias
rock-forming
recognitive
recognition
recognitory
reclination
rectipetaly
rectiserial
rocking-tool
recriminate
rectifiable
rectilineal
rectilinear
rock-leather
recollected
recalescent
recalculate
recommender
recumbently
recombinant
recommittal
recantation
recondition
reconnoitre
reconnoiter
reconstruct
receptacula
receptivity

reciprocate
reciprocant
reciprocity
recuperable
recuperator
recordation
recurrently
rack-railway
recirculate
rock-sparrow
recessively
recessional
recitativos
recluseness
recountment
recruitment
recoverable
race-walking
reductively
radicalness
radicellose
redactorial
Rediffusion®
redding-kame
redding-comb
reddishness
riddle-me-ree
redeliverer
rodomontade
rudimentary
redemptible
redundantly
riding-cloak
riding-glove
riding-habit
riding-horse
rodenticide
riding-light
riding-rhyme
riding-skirt
radiocarbon
radiopaging
radiolarian
radioactive
radiometric
radiophonic
radiologist
radiography
reduplicate
redirection
Rudesheimer
Rüdesheimer
rediscovery
redetermine
redoubtable
re-enactment
reef-builder
re-encourage
reed-drawing
re-endowment
re-elevation

re-emergence
re-existence
rheological
rheumatical
rheumaticky
rheumateese
rhetorician
re-emphasise
re-emphasize
re-expansion
reed-sparrow
re-establish
rheotropism
re-education
refrangible
refractable
refectioner
refocillate
rifacimenti
rifacimento
refectorian
△refreshment
refreshener
reflexively
reflexivity
refuellable
reflexology
reflectance
refrigerate
refrigerant
refringency
raffishness
ruffian-like
refinedness
refinancing
reflowering
reformative
△reformation
re-formation
reformadoes
reformatory
referendary
referential
referendums
reformulate
rigidifying
regretfully
regredience
ragged-Robin
regrettable
regrettably
rigging-loft
rigging-tree
roguishness
regimentals
regenerable
regenerator
regionalise
regionalize
regionalism
regionalist

regardfully
regurgitate
regurgitant
registrable
right-handed
right-hander
right-of-ways
right-minded
right-winger
right-angled
right-to-life
righteously
rights-of-way
rehydration
rhizanthous
rain-chamber
reincarnate
reiterative
reiteration
reinflation
reification
rhizomatous
rhizocarpic
rhinoscopic
rhinocerote
rhizogenous
rhinoplasty
rhinologist
rhizosphere
rhinorrhoea
ruinousness
reinstation
reinsertion
reinsurance
reintegrate
reintroduce
reinterment
reinterpret
re-invention
rejoicement
rejoicingly
rejoneadora
rejuvenesce
rejuvenator
releasement
reliability
reluctation
reluctantly
relic-monger
Rollerblade®
rollerblade
roller-skate
rallentando
roller-towel
religionary
religionise
religionize
religionism
religionist
religiosity
religiously

Words marked △ may be spelled also with a capital letter

rolling-mill
rule-of-thumb
role-playing
relatedness
relationism
relationist
rallying-cry
remediation
remigration
rumti-iddity
rompishness
remembrance
romanticise
romanticize
romanticism
romanticist
remunerable
remunerator
reminiscent
remonstrate
△remonstrant
remorseless
remittently
rumgumption
ramgunshoch
rumbustical
rumbustious
removedness
rentability
ring-carrier
rangefinder
rannell-balk
ring-fencing
renegotiate
rinthereout
running-hand
running-gear
△renaissance
randle-perch
Runyonesque
rondolettos
rancorously
rinforzando
renormalise
renormalize
ring-stopper
ring-straked
renewedness
ring-winding
Rhopalocera
rhombohedra
root-climber
room-divider
rhodium-wood
reorientate
rhododaphne
riotousness
root-pruning
rood-steeple
replaceable
replacement

raptatorial
republisher
rapscallion
rapaciously
repudiative
repudiation
reprehender
repleteness
representee
representer
representor
repleviable
replenished
replenisher
repressible
repressibly
reprivatise
reprivatize
replication
reptilianly
repellantly
repellently
repulsively
repellingly
rope-machine
repentantly
repentingly
ripsnorting
reprobative
reprobation
reprobatory
reproachful
reprovingly
reprogramme
reprography
reportingly
repartition
reportorial
reparations
reposedness
repossessor
reposefully
repatriator
repetitious
raptureless
rupturewort
rapturously
requiteless
requirement
requitement
requisition
requisitory
reradiation
ruridecanal
rarefactive
rarefaction
△rastafarian
researchful
restatement
rascalliest
rush-bearing

rosy-bosomed
rose-cheeked
rosy-cheeked
rose-campion
Rosicrucian
rose-diamond
residential
respectable
respectably
respectless
restfulness
resignation
respiration
rustication
respiratory
restiveness
Russianness
restitutive
restitution
restitutory
resultative
reselection
resiliently
resplendent
resemblance
resentfully
resentingly
restorative
△restoration
respondence
respondency
Russophobia
Russophobic
responsible
responsibly
responsions
resipiscent
reservation
reservatory
restrictive
restriction
restructure
resurrector
restraining
restringent
resuscitate
resuscitant
resistively
resistingly
resistivity
resourceful
rescue-grass
rosewood-oil
rat-catching
retraceable
rat-kangaroo
rateability
ritualistic
retranslate
retractable
reticularly

reticulated
rate-capping
rate-cutting
rother-beast
rottenstone
rotogravure
retributive
retribution
retributory
retrievable
retrievably
retaliative
retaliation
retaliatory
rattle-brain
rattle-pated
rattlesnake
retinaculum
retinacular
retentively
retentivity
retinispora
retinospora
retinoscope
retinoscopy
rationalise
rationalize
rationalism
rationalist
rationality
retroactive
retroaction
retrocedent
retrolental
retrophilia
ratiocinate
retrofitted
retroflexed
ration-money
retro-rocket
retroussage
retrobulbar
ritardandos
retardative
Rotarianism
retardation
retardatory
retiredness
ritornellos
ratatouille
ritournelle
rhumb-course
raunchiness
round-backed
roundedness
round-headed
round-leaved
round-winged
roundarched
rouge-et-noir
rough-handle

11 r□u□h

rough-legged
reupholster
rough-coated
rough-footed
rough-spoken
rough-string
rouping-wife
raucousness
revaccinate
rival-hating
revaluation
revoltingly
Revelations
revengeless
revengement
revendicate
revindicate
revengingly
reverberate
reverberant
reverseless
reversional
reversioner
reverential
river-bottom
riverworthy
river-dragon
river-driver
river-mussel
ravishingly
revisionary
revisionism
revisionist
rivet-hearth
revivifying
revivescent
reviviscent
rhynchocoel
rhynchodont
rhyme-scheme
rhyme-letter
rhythmicity
razzamatazz
scarabaeist
scarabaeoid
svarabhakti
scalariform
shamanistic
sparagmatic
stalagmitic
△**scaramouche**
stalactical
stalactitic
stalactited
stalactital
scabbedness
scamblingly
shad-bellied
swag-bellied
starch-grain
starchiness

searchingly
snatchingly
stanchioned
searchlight
star-crossed
snatch-purse
snatch-thief
span-counter
standpatter
standoffish
scandaliser
scandalizer
standardise
standardize
stage-manage
spacefaring
sharefarmer
shamelessly
statemented
stave-church
shapeliness
stateliness
slaveringly
sharemilker
snake-hipped
stage-player
statesmanly
shareholder
slaveholder
scaremonger
shameworthy
slave-trader
scale-armour
slate-writer
slave-driver
stage-struck
share-pusher
scaberulous
stateswoman
stagflation
snaffle-rein
scaffoldage
scaffolding
seal-fishing
staff-system
shanghaiing
shaggedness
shagge-eared
spang-cockle
swagger-cane
slaughterer
spathaceous
staphylitis
swan-hopping
suasiveness
scapigerous
sparingness
skating-rink
shaving-soap
searing-iron
slavishness

snakishness
stabilisers
stabilizers
seasickness
sea-milkwort
spaniel-like
staminodium
stasimorphy
statistical
slack-handed
shackle-bone
shackle-bolt
sparklessly
sparklingly
sharksucker
Stahlianism
stallmaster
small-screen
Stahlhelmer
small-minded
stalling-ken
smallholder
scarlet-bean
swallow-tail
shallowness
swallow-dive
swallow-wort
spasmodical
spasmatical
shawnee-wood
stainlessly
staunchable
staunchless
staunchness
spawning-bed
seasonality
shadowgraph
shadowiness
Slavonicise
Slavonicize
sialorrhoea
sialography
scalpriform
sharp-witted
sharp-ground
staircasing
staurolitic
stauroscope
sparrow-hawk
sparrow-bill
snapshooter
seamstressy
star-studded
smarty-boots
spastically
scant-o'-grace
swarthiness
startlingly
smart-ticket
stactometer
staktometer

stadtholder
smartypants
shatter-pate
spatterdash
scatterable
scatteredly
scattershot
scatterling
scattergood
spatterdock
spatterwork
statutorily
△**sabbatarian**
subpanation
subparallel
subcardinal
subbasement
subcategory
sublanguage
submarginal
Sabbathless
subtacksman
subharmonic
subcapsular
subacidness
subschemata
subscribing
subeconomic
subscapular
sabre-rattle
subdeaconry
submergible
submergence
subterhuman
subdelirium
subaerially
subregional
subcellular
subterminal
submersible
subsensible
subvertical
subjectless
subjectship
subsequence
subservient
subaffluent
subchloride
sublimation
subdiaconal
sublimeness
subtileness
subdivisive
subdivision
subvitreous
submissible
submissness
subdistrict
subsistence
sublittoral
subglobular

Words marked △ may be spelled also with a capital letter

suballiance
subclinical
subimaginal
subimagines
subumbrella
subindicate
subincision
Subungulata
subungulate
subindustry
subrogation
submolecule
subdominant
subcontract
subcontrary
subcortical
subspecific
suburbanise
suburbanite
suburbanize
suburbanism
saburration
subarration
subornation
suburbanity
subtreasury
subtractive
subtraction
subfreezing
seborrhoeic
subirrigate
subordinate
subordinary
sober-minded
subarboreal
subprioress
subtropical
subcritical
△sybaritical
sober-suited
subassemble
subassembly
substrative
substractor
substandard
substantive
substantial
subitaneous
substituent
substituted
subjugation
subluxation
subjunctive
subjunction
subduedness
subaudition
subsumptive
subsumption
submultiple
subcultural
subaxillary

such-and-such
sacramental
sociability
socialistic
sockdolager
sockdoliger
sockdologer
succedaneum
secretarial
secretariat
secretively
sickeningly
secretional
sucker-punch
successless
Sachertorte
saccharated
succinctory
sacrilegist
sucking-fish
sickishness
sacrificial
sectionally
Socinianism
secondarily
second-class
second-floor
second-guess
sicknursing
second-rater
sociopathic
sociometric
sociologese
sociologism
sociologist
sacrocostal
succourable
succourless
sycophantic
sycophantry
secessional
sacculation
succulently
sacculiform
seductively
Sydneysider
sedigitated
saddlecloth
saddleg-irth
saddle-nosed
sedimentary
sodomitical
sedentarily
siderophile
sideropenia
seditionary
seditiously
Sadduceeism
side-wheeler
stewardship
shenanigans

spelaeothem
spelaeology
steganogram
stepbrother
speechcraft
speech-crier
sketchiness
speechifier
stencilling
speechmaker
steadfastly
steady-going
spendthrift
speedometer
stepdancing
slenderness
steady-state
stereoblind
stereobatic
stereograph
stevengraph
stereometer
stereometry
skeletonise
skeletonize
stereoptics
stereophony
stereosonic
stereoscope
stereoscopy
stereotypic
stereotyped
stereotyper
stereotaxia
stereotaxic
stereotaxis
shelftalker
sledge-chair
Spenglerian
sdeignfully
Spergularia
stephanotis
shepherdess
stethoscope
stethoscopy
sheriffship
sheriffalty
seemingness
specificate
specifiable
specificity
specialogue
specialiser
specializer
sleek-headed
speakership
shell-jacket
shellacking
steel-headed
swell-headed
stellifying

spellbinder
steel-plated
stellionate
steelworker
stelleridan
shell-crater
stellarator
spermicidal
spermogonia
steam-roller
spermophile
spermaphyte
spermophyte
steam-driven
spermatical
spermatheca
spermatozoa
Steinberger
sternsheets
stern-chaser
sternotribe
sternutator
stenocardia
△stegosaurus
sceuophylax
stenochrome
stenochromy
stenotropic
scenography
stenography
stenotypist
sweep-washer
sleepwalker
sheep-farmer
sheep-master
steeplejack
sleeplessly
steeplebush
sheep-biting
sheep-silver
sweepstakes
sherris-sack
spessartine
spessartite
spectrality
stentmaster
spectacular
sceptically
skeptically
sheet-feeder
sceptreless
sweetie-wife
sleuth-hound
sheet-anchor
spectrology
sheet-copper
spectrogram
steatopygia
scepterless
shelterless
steatorrhea

Words marked △ may be spelled also with a capital letter

11 s□e□t

sweater-girl
spectatress
sheet-rubber
speculative
speculation
speculatist
speculatory
speculatrix
safe-breaker
safe-blowing
safe-cracker
soft-centred
safe-conduct
safe-deposit
soft-hearted
suffixation
sufficience
sufficiency
safe-keeping
suffocative
suffocating
suffocation
suffragette
soft-shelled
safety-catch
suffumigate
sagaciously
segregative
segregation
suggestible
segmentally
significate
significant
signifiable
sigillarian
sigillation
sigmoidally
sign-painter
sugar-coated
sagittarian
Sagittarius
sight-reader
sightseeing
sightlessly
sightliness
sight-singer
sagittiform
sight-player
sightworthy
sign-writing
sphragistic
schwärmerei
sphacelated
schecklaton
schreech-owl
sphaeridium
schrecklich
sphagnology
sphygmology
sphygmogram
scholiastic
schillerise
schillerize
scholarship
scholar-like
schematical
sphingosine
sphincteric
sphincteral
schoolcraft
schoolchild
schoolgoing
schoolhouse
schoolwards
scherzandos
spherically
spheroidise
spheroidize
spherulitic
spherometer
schorlomite
schismatise
schismatize
schistosity
Schistosoma
schistosome
schottische
schizogenic
schizanthus
schizopodal
Schizophyta
schizophyte
spinach-beet
Scitamineae
suitability
spiraliform
spiraculate
sailboarder
swim-bladder
ship-breaker
shipbuilder
stilbestrol
spin-bowling
switchboard
switchblade
stitchcraft
scincoidian
switch-plant
spindle-legs
spine-basher
swivelblock
swivel-chair
spinescence
stipendiate
stipendiary
spinelessly
shiveringly
shigellosis
stilettoing
stiff-necked
spifflicate
skilfulness
swing-handle
swingle-hand
swingletree
swingeingly
swing-plough
swingometer
swing-bridge
slightingly
stichometry
smithsonite
Smithsonian
smithereens
spiniferous
spinigerous
shiningness
smilingness
sliding-rule
swinishness
spiritistic
spirillosis
suicidology
spirituelle
spiritually
spiritualty
stickleback
stickleader
slickenside
snickersnee
skillcentre
skilligalee
skilligolee
stifle-joint
spill-stream
still-hunter
slimmed-down
seismograph
seismologic
seismometer
seismometry
seismonasty
skimmington
shimmy-shake
skirmishing
seismoscope
stigmatical
scientistic
seigniorage
seigniorial
Scientology®
spinnerette
seigneurial
spirometric
Spirochaeta
spirochaete
Spinozistic
spirography
shinplaster
skin-popping
slipperwort
spinsterdom
spinsterish
spinsterial
spinsterian
shit-stirrer
scissortail
scissorwise
scissor-bill
stilt-walker
saintpaulia
stiltedness
stintedness
skittle-ball
shiftlessly
saintliness
swift-winged
shirtlifter
scintillate
scintillant
shirt-sleeve
stilt-plover
swift-footed
shinty-stick
stimulative
stimulating
stimulation
stipulation
stipulatory
sojournment
syllabarium
salvageable
saltarellos
soldatesque
self-affairs
syllabicate
saleability
salvability
solvability
syllabicity
sulfadoxine
saltatorial
self-assumed
self-assured
salableness
self-blinded
self-basting
self-charity
self-cocking
salicaceous
self-created
selectively
selectivity
self-culture
self-command
self-concern
self-conceit
self-concept
self-content
self-centred
self-control
self-closing
selectorial
salaciously

Words marked △ may be spelled also with a capital letter

self-covered
solidifying
self-defence
splodginess
self-delight
self-damning
self-denying
solid-hoofed
self-despair
self-devoted
self-example
self-excited
self-elected
silver-grain
silveriness
self-evident
self-evolved
self-express
silver-point
sallee-rover
silversides
silversmith
silver-stick
spleenstone
sylleptical
silvestrian
sylvestrian
silver-white
self-feeding
self-feeling
self-figured
self-fertile
solifluxion
salt-glazing
selaginella
self-healing
self-harming
sulphureous
sulphureted
sulphurator
sulphhydryl
sillimanite
solmisation
solmization
saltimbocca
saltimbanco
self-induced
saltirewise
salpingitic
salpingitis
saltishness
selfishness
self-imposed
soldiership
saltierwise
soldierlike
self-invited
self-knowing
self-loading
self-locking
self-limited
soliloquise
soliloquize
soliloquist
self-mockery
self-mastery
self-misused
solanaceous
splenectomy
selenograph
self-neglect
splendidous
salinometer
splendorous
splenetical
sulfonamide
sulfonation
salmonberry
self-opening
salmonellae
salmonellas
self-offence
self-opinion
syllogistic
seldom-times
sallow-thorn
self-planted
solipsistic
self-pruning
self-powered
sclerocauly
scleroderma
self-raising
self-reliant
self-relying
sclerometer
solarimeter
self-reproof
sclerophyll
self-respect
sclerotioid
sclerotitis
self-sealing
self-starter
splashboard
self-subdued
self-sterile
self-seeking
salesperson
splashproof
self-support
self-service
self-serving
self-trained
split-screen
spluttering
split-second
self-tempted
solutionist
self-tapping
self-torment
self-torture
silk-thrower
sclate-stane
salsuginous
self-winding
silkworm-gut
self-worship
splay-footed
somnambulic
somnambular
sympathique
sympathiser
sympathetic
sympathizer
summariness
summational
semi-annular
semi-aquatic
semicircled
semi-diurnal
symmetalism
symmetallic
sympetalous
simnel-bread
summerhouse
simperingly
semi-ellipse
symmetrical
summersault
sempervivum
symphonious
sempiternal
sempiternum
somniferous
summit-level
semi-jubilee
simpliciter
simulacrums
simplifying
sampler-work
semi-monthly
semanticist
somnolently
semiotician
sympodially
symposiarch
symbolistic
semiologist
symbolology
semipalmate
sempstering
semi-skilled
semasiology
semi-trailer
semi-tubular
somatically
somatogenic
somatologic
symptomatic
sumptuosity
sumptuously
somatoplasm
somatotonia
somatotonic
somewhither
Santalaceae
sensational
syntagmatic
syntactical
synecologic
sansculotte
synecdochic
sand-casting
sang-de-boeuf
synodically
Sandemanian
sincereness
senselessly
sansevieria
synoeciosis
syndesmoses
syndesmosis
syndesmotic
synoecology
sinlessness
sunlessness
sanderswood
syntectical
sententious
sonofabitch
sin-offering
songfulness
sonographer
synagogical
synchromesh
synchronise
synchronize
synchronism
synchronous
synchrotron
sancho-pedro
synchoresis
synthesiser
synthesizer
synthetical
synthetiser
synthetizer
syndicalism
syndication
syndicalist
sentinelled
sentimental
singing-bird
sensitively
sensibility
sensitivity
Sanskritist
single-cross
single-digit
single-entry
Sinological
synclinoria
single-phase

11 s□n□l

singlestick
single-soled
synanthesis
synanthetic
synonymical
synonymicon
synonymatic
syngnathous
syncopation
sinfonietta
sindonology
sinuousness
Sinophilism
synoptistic
sinupallial
synergistic
sundrenched
sinisterity
sand-skipper
sinistrally
sinistrorse
sanctuarise
sanctuarize
sanctifying
senate-house
senatorship
sanatoriums
sanitariums
sand-thrower
singularise
singularize
singularism
singularist
singularity
sensualness
sanguineous
sanguinaria
Sensurround®
Sanguisorba
syndyasmian
sporangiola
sporangiole
stomachache
stomachical
stomachless
stomachfuls
sloganising
sloganizing
Stomatopoda
stomatology
snobbocracy
shopbreaker
scorchingly
Scotch-Irish
stoicalness
Scotchwoman
sword-bearer
sword-shaped
spondulicks
spondylosis
spondylitic
spondylitis
swordplayer
sword-dollar
snow-dropper
stonewashed
stonewaller
shovelboard
smokescreen
storekeeper
smokelessly
showeriness
scoleciform
stone-colour
showerproof
stoneground
stone's-throw
stonecutter
spokeswoman
spokeswomen
snow-goggles
smörgåsbord
soothsaying
soothfastly
scoriaceous
scoring-card
showjumping
stocktaking
stock-farmer
shock-headed
shopkeeping
stockpiling
snorkelling
stockinette
stockjobber
stockholder
shock-horror
stockbroker
shouldering
smouldering
shop-lifting
Scotlandite
storm-beaten
showmanship
storm-tossed
stormtroops
storm-stayed
scoundrelly
scopolamine
scotomatous
spodomantic
scolopendra
sporogenous
scopophobia
Scotophobia
Scotophobic
scopophilia
Scotophilia
scopophilic
sporophoric
sporophytic
sporogonium
snobography
sporocystic
scorpaenoid
stopping-out
Scorpionida
slow-release
saourari-nut
slow-sighted
show-stopper
sponsorship
snowsurfing
short-handed
scoutmaster
sportcaster
smooth-bored
spottedness
scouthering
short-termer
smooth-faced
Scottifying
short-change
short-winded
spontaneity
spontaneous
snotty-nosed
shortcoming
smooth-paced
short-spoken
short-priced
short-staple
sportswoman
sporulation
storyteller
supracostal
sapucaia-nut
suppedaneum
supremacism
△suprematism
septenarius
supremacist
△suprematist
Septembrist
supremeness
saplessness
septentrial
septentrion
septicaemia
septiferous
syphilology
septifragal
sophistical
suppliantly
supplicavit
sepulchrous
supply-sider
saponaceous
saponifying
sipunculoid
sapropelite
saprolegnia
saprogenous
saprophytic
suppositive
supposition
suppository
saprobiotic
siphonogamy
supportable
supportably
supportless
supportress
supportment
sepiostaire
supportance
supernatant
superjacent
supersafety
superlative
superfamily
supertanker
supermarket
superdainty
superfatted
supernature
superabound
superoctave
superscreen
superactive
superscribe
superscript
superfetate
supersedere
supersedeas
superrefine
superweapon
superheater
supersedure
superphylum
supercharge
supercherie
superficial
supervision
superficies
supervisory
superfluity
superfluous
supersleuth
superimpose
superintend
superinfect
superinduce
superioress
supersonics
superiority
supercoiled
supernormal
supervolute
superbright
superpraise
suppressant
suppressive
suppression

Words marked △ may be spelled also with a capital letter

superstring
superstruct
superlunary
superfusion
supersubtle
sapotaceous
suppurative
suppuration
sequestrate
sequestrant
sequestered
serrasalmos
surtarbrand
surbasement
spread-eagle
streakiness
streaminess
screamingly
spreadingly
streamingly
streamlined
surpassable
spreadsheet
servant-maid
servant-lass
servantless
servantship
servant-girl
serratulate
scrobicular
scribacious
shrubberied
shrubbiness
strabometer
stroboscope
surf-bathing
sericterium
sericulture
Saracenical
seroconvert
surfcasting
suraddition
stridulator
screencraft
sarcenchyme
surrenderee
surrenderer
surrenderor
screech-hawk
shriekingly
surveillant
streetlight
street-level
surgeonship
surgeonfish
streetscape
streetsmart
sarsen-stone
serpentlike
serpentinic
serpent-star

surrebuttal
surrebutter
screen-wiper
streetwards
series-wound
scruffiness
serigraphic
serigrapher
scragginess
sprightless
survivalism
survivalist
serviceable
serviceably
serviceless
straight-arm
straight-cut
straightish
straight-out
straightway
serpiginous
strait-laced
servitorial
surmistress
strikebound
serological
scrimshoner
scrimshandy
scrimpiness
stramineous
scrumptious
springboard
stringboard
spring-clean
strangeness
stringently
springhouse
springiness
stringiness
shrinkingly
serendipity
strenuosity
syringotomy
strenuously
strongpoint
shrink-proof
strengthful
strangulate
springwater
stringy-bark
strongyloid
surrogation
sarcomatous
sarcoidosis
sorrowfully
sarcophagal
sarcophagus
sartorially
Sorbonnical
surmounting
surrounding

seriousness
sarcocystis
strap-hanger
strap-shaped
scrappiness
Soroptimist
scriptorial
scriptorium
scripophile
scripophily
scrapepenny
scripturism
scripturist
surprisedly
stressed-out
stratocracy
serotherapy
stratifying
strategical
scratchback
scratchless
stretchless
scratch-work
scratch-coat
struttingly
Struthiones
scrutiniser
scrutinizer
stratopause
serrulation
sertularian
surturbrand
scriveboard
shrivelling
scrawlingly
strawflower
straw-colour
screw-wrench
screwdriver
syssarcoses
syssarcosis
sustainable
sustainedly
sustainment
systematise
systematize
systematism
systematics
systematist
system-built
sister-in-law
system-maker
suspensible
suspenseful
susceptible
suspectable
susceptibly
suspectedly
suspectless
susceptance
sustentator

suscitation
suspiration
sessile-eyed
sessionally
susurration
sesquialter
sesquioxide
sesquipedal
satiability
situational
setter-forth
sitting-room
sottishness
settledness
satellitise
satellitize
satanically
satanophany
sitiophobia
saturnalian
satirically
soteriology
satisfiable
satisficing
squeakiness
squeakingly
squeamishly
shunamitism
stumblingly
slumbrously
slumberland
slumberless
slumbersome
spud-bashing
sculduddery
skulduddery
slum-dweller
soundlessly
sculduggery
skulduggery
shuddersome
spumescence
sauce-crayon
studentship
snuff-taking
soul-fearing
shufflingly
snuff-dipper
soulfulness
snuff-colour
sluggardise
sluggardize
southlander
southwardly
south-easter
south-wester
southernise
southernize
southernism
southermost
saurischian

11 s□u□i

studiedness
soul-killing
squalidness
squandering
squintingly
sauropodous
sauropsidan
scuppernong
sculpturing
squirearchy
square-built
square-dance
squarsonage
squirarchal
sauerbraten
soul-sleeper
squashiness
saussuritic
stuntedness
shuttlewise
shuttlecock
scuttlebutt
stultifying
squattiness
savableness
savoir-faire
savoir-vivre
seven-league
seventeenth
sovereignly
sovereignty
severalfold
Sivatherium
savouriness
sewage-works
sex-reversal
sixteenthly
sexlessness
sexagesimal
sexological
sexennially
sextodecimo
saxophonist
Styracaceae
scyphistoma
scythe-stone
stylisation
stylization
styliferous
stylishness
stylopodium
sky-coloured
stylography
sky-aspiring
travail-pang
travail-pain
thanatology
thanatopsis
thalassemia
thalassemic
tracasserie
tharborough
thatch-board
Thatcherite
Thatcherism
Tragelaphus
trade-fallen
tracelessly
tragedienne
tragédienne
trapeziform
trapezoidal
traversable
trabeculate
tradeswoman
trafficless
trafficking
trafficator
tearfulness
tear-falling
twanglingly
trachearian
Trachinidae
tracheotomy
teacherless
teachership
traditional
traditioner
tragicomedy
thalidomide
tear-jerking
tracklaying
track-walker
tracklement
thanklessly
tracklessly
thanksgiver
thankworthy
trackerball
trailbaston
trail-blazer
Thallophyta
thallophyte
trammelling
thaumatrope
thaumaturge
thaumaturgy
traineeship
train-bearer
trampoliner
twalpennies
teaspoonful
Trappistine
tranquilize
tranquility
transpadane
transmanche
transcalent
transparent
translative
transmarine
translation
tear-stained
translatory
transvaluer
transaction
transection
transferase
transferred
transferral
transferrin
transferrer
transversal
transvestic
transiently
transsexual
trans-sexual
transceiver
transfinite
transfixion
transhipper
transpierce
transmitted
toad-spittle
transmittal
transmitter
transfigure
transilient
transalpine
transandean
transandine
translocate
transponder
transposing
trans-sonics
transformed
transformer
toad-spotted
transported
transportal
transporter
trapshooter
transeptate
transcriber
transuranic
transitable
transit-duty
transhumant
translunary
translucent
transfusive
transfusion
transductor
tea-strainer
toastmaster
traitorship
traitorhood
traducement
traducingly
tobacco-pipe
tobacconist
tables-d'hôte
tabletopped
tabefaction
tubiflorous
tobogganing
tobogganist
tub-thumping
tibiotarsus
taboparesis
tabernacled
tuberaceous
tuberculate
tuberculise
tuberculize
tuberculoma
tuberculose
tuberculous
tacheometer
tacheometry
tschernosem
ticket-punch
tickettyboo
tactfulness
tucking-mill
tectibranch
tickle-brain
technocracy
Technicolor®
technically
technomania
technomusic
technophile
technopolis
technophobe
tachometric
tichorrhine
tick-tack-toe
tick-tack-too
taciturnity
tack-welding
tachycardia
tachymetric
tachyphasia
tachygraphy
toddlerhood
tiddlywinks
tediousness
Tudorbethan
trepanation
tsesarevich
tsesarewich
therapeutic
Therapeutae
thesauruses
tremblement
tremblingly
theobromine
trenchantly
trencher-fed
trencherman
treachetour
treacherous
treecreeper

Words marked △ may be spelled also with a capital letter

thenceforth
Theocritean
treacliness
trench-knife
theocentric
trendle-tail
trendsetter
theodolitic
teeter-board
thereabouts
therebeside
therewithal
therewithin
theretofore
Twelfth-cake
Twelfth-tide
theogonical
trepidation
trepidatory
theriolatry
theriomorph
treble-dated
theological
theologiser
theologizer
trellis-work
thermocline
theomachist
thermically
thermoduric
thermograph
thermogenic
thermolysis
thermolytic
thermometer
thermometry
thermonasty
thermionics
thermophile
theomorphic
thermoscope
thermotical
thesmothete
thermotaxic
thermotaxis
theanthropy
tremolandos
teetotalism
teetotaller
treponemata
Theromorpha
theophagous
theopneusty
theophobiac
theophobist
theorematic
theoretical
treasonable
treasonably
theosophise
theosophize
theosophism
theosophist
Thersitical
theotechnic
trestlework
theatre-goer
theatricals
theatricise
theatricize
theatricism
theftuously
tremulously
twelvemonth
twelve-penny
tree-worship
thelytokous
teeny-bopper
tweezer-case
toffee-apple
toffee-nosed
tuft-hunting
toffishness
tufftaffeta
tufftaffety
tigrishness
tagliatelle
tegumentary
tiger-flower
tiger-footed
tight-lacing
tight-lipped
tight-fisted
tightly-knit
tiggywinkle
thio-alcohol
tribalistic
tritagonist
trivalvular
thimble-case
thimbleweed
thimblefuls
twin-brother
thiocyanate
trindle-tail
third-stream
triceratops
tripetalous
toilet-cloth
toilet-cover
toilet-glass
tripe-visag'd
trimetrical
Trimetrogon
tripersonal
toilet-table
trimestrial
tribeswoman
tail-feather
thingliness
thingamybob
thingumabob
thingamyjig
thingumajig
triggerfish
trigger-fish
triphibious
tritheistic
triphyllous
trichomonad
Trichomonas
trichinella
trichinosis
trichinotic
trithionate
trichronous
Trichoptera
thitherward
Trinidadian
Trinitarian
trivialness
thick-headed
trickle-down
thick-ribbed
tricksiness
thick-lipped
thick-witted
thinking-cap
thick-coming
triumvirate
thigmotaxis
triennially
triangulate
tridominium
tribologist
tricoloured
trimorphism
trimorphous
thixotropic
thiopentone
trierarchal
thirstiness
thin-skinned
tristichous
thistledown
taintlessly
twitter-bone
thirty-twomo
tribulation
trituration
tributarily
trifurcated
tribuneship
tribunicial
tribunitial
tribunician
tribunitian
trisulphide
triquetrous
trisyllabic
trisyllable
teknonymous
telearchics
talkatively
talkability
Taliacotian
talebearing
telecommand
telecommute
telocentric
telecontrol
telecasting
telecottage
tiller-chain
téléférique
telegraphic
telegrapher
telegrammic
telegnostic
telpherline
telekinesis
telekinetic
Telemessage®
Teleosaurus
tallow-catch
tallow-faced
teleologism
teleologist
teleprinter
tulipomania
telephonist
tulip-poplar
telepathise
telepathize
telepathist
telesthesia
telesthetic
telescience
teleselling
Telescopium
telescopist
tolbutamide
telluretted
Talmudistic
teleworking
talk-you-down
tally-system
tameability
tympaniform
tamableness
time-bargain
temperament
temperately
temperative
temperature
timber-hitch
tamper-proof
time-expired
tempestuous
tempest-tost
tumefacient
tumefaction
tomographic
time-killing

11 t□m□l

tumble-drier
tumbling-box
tumblerfuls
Tom-and-Jerry
tempolabile
temporaries
temporality
temporarily
tomboyishly
temporising
temporizing
time-pleaser
tumorigenic
time-release
timbromania
timbrophily
temerarious
time-sharing
time-service
time-serving
tomatilloes
temptatious
tummy-button
tentatively
tantalising
tantalizing
tentaculate
Tantalus-cup
tentaculite
tentaculoid
tenableness
tunableness
tenebrosity
tankbusting
tenaciously
tendencious
tender-dying
tenderfoots
tenterhooks
tangentally
tendentious
tunefulness
tank-farming
tennis-court
tonnishness
tangibility
tensibility
tentiginous
tonsillitic
tonsillitis
tennis-match
tensiometer
tensiometry
tensionless
tensionally
tenementary
tan-coloured
tenuousness
tent-pegging
tenorrhaphy
tendrillous
tonetically
tin-streamer
tonquin-bean
thoracotomy
trombiculid
troublesome
trouble-town
troublefree
troublously
two-penn'orth
trough-fault
trough-shell
thought-wave
thoughtcast
thoughtless
thought-sick
trophoblast
tooth-picker
Trochilidae
troth-plight
trochometer
toothsomely
trophoplasm
trochophore
tooth-drawer
trophotaxis
trophozoite
Thomistical
troglodytic
Troglodytes
troll-my-dame
thornproofs
twofoldness
tromometric
thorough-pin
thoroughwax
tropophytic
troposphere
tropomyosin
trous-de-loup
trouser-clip
trouserings
trout-basket
two-storeyed
trout-stream
typicalness
taphephobia
toplessness
tepefaction
type-founder
type-foundry
typographia
topographic
typographic
topographer
typographer
topological
typological
toponymical
taphophobia
taphonomist
toploftical
tephromancy
top-priority
tap-dressing
top-dressing
type-species
typesetting
typewriting
typewritten
termagantly
threatening
tarradiddle
threadiness
throatiness
throat-latch
threadmaker
targa-topped
thread-paper
throat-strap
terraqueous
terebration
terebratula
throbbingly
three-handed
three-masted
three-parted
three-master
torpescence
turgescence
turgescency
turret-clock
three-leafed
three-legged
three-decker
Turneresque
three-leaved
torpedinous
Turbellaria
terremotive
three-nooked
three-colour
three-bottle
three-volume
three-square
turkey-shoot
tormentedly
terrestrial
torrentuous
three-suited
thriftiness
tyroglyphid
Tyroglyphus
torchbearer
torch-singer
torch-staves
terminative
termitarium
termination
terminatory
terrigenous
turbine-pump
torsiograph
turfing-iron
tarnishable
terribility
torsibility
territoried
territorial
Torridonian
torticollis
terricolous
terminology
turriculate
thrillingly
turtle-shell
turtle-stone
thrummingly
thrombocyte
tiring-glass
tiring-house
tyrannicide
Tironensian
Tyronensian
tyrannosaur
tyrannously
threnetical
tiring-woman
turbo-ram-jet
Turcophobia
terroristic
turcopolier
turnpike-man
Tortricidae
Terpsichore
thrasonical
teratogenic
teratologic
taratantara
torturesome
turbulently
throughfare
throughgaun
through-bolt
torturingly
Targumistic
torque-meter
tire-valiant
tardy-gaited
tarry-breeks
tessaraglot
testamental
testamentar
tussac-grass
tastelessly
tassell-gent
tessellated
tostication
testificate
testimonial
testiculate
tussock-moth
testudinary

Words marked △ may be spelled also with a capital letter

tetravalent
tetradactyl
tetrarchate
tetrandrian
tetrandrous
tetramerism
tetramerous
Titianesque
tetrahedral
tetrahedron
tetratheism
tetraplegia
tetraplegic
tetraploidy
tetragonous
tetrapodous
tetrasporic
tetradrachm
tetractinal
tetrapteran
tetradymite
tetragynian
tetracyclic
tetragynous
tithe-paying
totteringly
title-holder
Tattersall's
tittivation
tattie-bogle
tutti-frutti
titillative
titillating
titillation
totalisator
totalizator
tetanically
△titanically
Titanomachy
totipalmate
totipotency
têtes-à-têtes
thumb-marked
tourbillion
truncheoned
truncheoner
trundle-tail
thunder-dart
thunderhead
thunder-peal
thunderless
thunderbird
thunder-like
thunderclap
thunderbolt
true-devoted
true-hearted
touch-screen
truth-teller
tough-minded
touch-in-goal

touch-typist
thuriferous
truck-farmer
trunksleeve
tous-les-mois
tautomerism
tautometric
tautophonic
tautochrone
Teutonicism
tautologise
tautologize
taurobolium
tautologism
tautologist
tautologous
tautonymous
trumpet-call
trumpet-fish
trumpet-wood
trumpet-tone
trumpet-tree
true-seeming
trusteeship
trustworthy
trustbuster
truculently
town-dweller
town-meeting
towing-bitts
tow-coloured
town-planner
thwartingly
thwartships
townscaping
townspeople
tax-gatherer
textbookish
toxicogenic
toxicologic
toxicomania
taxidermise
taxidermize
taxidermist
taxonomical
toxoplasmic
toxiphagous
toxophilite
toxiphobiac
textureless
trypanocide
Trypanosoma
trypanosome
thysanurous
thyroiditis
thyrotropin
Thyrostraca
T-lymphocyte
trysting-day
tryptophane
unawareness

unawakening
unavailable
unavailably
unadaptable
unambiguous
unambitious
unaccusable
unaccusably
unaddressed
up-and-coming
unamendable
unavertable
unavertible
unaffecting
unaugmented
unashamedly
unalienable
unalienably
unanimously
unallowable
unannotated
unannounced
Uranoscopus
unavoidable
unavoidably
unabolished
uranoplasty
uranography
unapostolic
unappealing
unappointed
unapproving
unaspirated
unagreeable
unabrogated
unassertive
unassisting
unauthentic
unattainted
unattempted
unattentive
unattending
unalterable
unalterably
unamusingly
unadvisable
unadvisably
unadvisedly
unblameable
unblameably
umbratilous
unbiassedly
unbeautiful
umbraculate
unblenching
unblemished
unbreakable
umbrella-ant
umbrella-fir
unbreathing
unbefitting

unbeginning
unblindfold
umbriferous
unbeknownst
umbellately
unballasted
unbelieving
unbeneficed
unbenefited
unbenignant
unbenighted
unbendingly
unbrotherly
unburthened
unbarricade
unburnished
unbeseeming
unboundedly
unceasingly
unclassical
unchastened
unchartered
unchastised
unchastized
uncuckolded
uncheckable
uncleanness
unclearness
unchildlike
urchin-shows
uncalled-for
uncollected
uncompanied
uncompacted
uncommended
uncompelled
uncommitted
uncompliant
uncomplying
uncompleted
uncomforted
uncomatable
unconscious
uncongenial
unconcealed
unconcerned
uncontemned
unconfessed
unconcerted
unconnected
uncontested
unconverted
unconceived
unconvinced
uncanniness
unconniving
unconfirmed
unconvicted
uncanonical
uncanonised
uncanonized

11 u□c□n

unconcocted
uncontrived
unconquered
uncurtailed
uncurtained
uncertainly
uncertainty
uncorrected
uncertified
unchristian
uncorrupted
upcast-shaft
unclubbable
uncrushable
uncouthness
uncountable
uncourteous
uncluttered
uncivilised
uncivilized
undrainable
undiagnosed
undebauched
undecidable
undecidedly
undeclining
undefinable
undignified
undriveable
undyingness
undrinkable
undelegated
undelighted
undelivered
undemanding
undepressed
undepending
underhanded
undertaking
undermanned
underdamper
undermasted
undervaluer
under-sawyer
underaction
under-school
undertenant
underweight
underseller
underkeeper
underbearer
underletter
undershapen
undercharge
undershorts
underthirst
underthrust
underbidder
undermining
underwiring
undersigned
underbitten
underviewer
undersleeve
underclothe
undercovert
underhonest
underlooker
underworker
under-bonnet
underbreath
underpriced
underbridge
underpraise
underwriter
underground
under-driven
undergrowth
under-espial
understrata
understorey
understated
underfulfil
underbudget
undersupply
underexpose
undescended
undiscerned
undispensed
undesigning
undistilled
undisclosed
undespoiled
undistorted
undissolved
undescribed
undesirable
undesirably
undeserving
undestroyed
undisturbed
undiscussed
undisguised
undutifully
undauntable
undoubtable
undauntedly
undoubtedly
undeviating
undividable
undividedly
undeveloped
undiverting
unelaborate
unenchanted
unescapable
unexcitable
unexclusive
unexcavated
unendurable
unendurably
unexercised
uselessness
un-English
unexhausted
unevidenced
urediospore
unenjoyable
unemotioned
unemotional
unexplained
unexpectant
unexpressed
unexpensive
unexploited
unexperient
unenquiring
unessential
unequitable
unequivocal
unfearfully
unfeathered
unflavoured
unflappable
unflappably
unfeelingly
unflinching
unfailingly
unfeignedly
unfaltering
unfulfilled
unfiltrable
unfinishing
unformatted
unfermented
unforfeited
unforbidden
unfurnished
unfortified
unforgiving
unforeknown
unforgotten
unfortunate
unfashioned
unfittingly
unfeudalise
unfeudalize
unfoundedly
unfructuous
unflustered
unfixedness
upgradation
unguardedly
upgradeable
ungratified
ungrammatic
ungodliness
unguerdoned
unguiculate
ungallantly
unguligrade
ungenteelly
ungentility
ungenitured
ungarmented
ungarnished
ungetatable
unget-at-able
ungazed-upon
unhealthful
unhealthily
unhabitable
unhackneyed
unhidebound
unheedfully
unheedingly
upholstress
upholsterer
unhingement
unhandiness
unhandseled
unhopefully
unhappiness
unharnessed
unharvested
unharmfully
unhurtfully
unhurriedly
unharboured
unhusbanded
unhazardous
univalvular
uninchanted
uniserially
unigeniture
unicellular
universally
unipersonal
unisexually
uninflected
uninforming
uninhabited
uninhibited
unification
unitisation
unitization
utilisation
utilitarian
utilization
uriniparous
uriniferous
uninitiated
unidiomatic
unillumined
unipolarity
uniformness
unicorn-moth
unicolorate
unicolorous
unicoloured
unimpeached
unimpededly
unimpressed
unit-pricing

Words marked △ may be spelled also with a capital letter

unimportant
uninquiring
uninspiring
uninscribed
uninucleate
uninvidious
uninventive
unjustified
unjaundiced
unknowingly
unknownness
unlearnedly
unlaborious
unlabouring
unluckiness
upliftingly
unlightened
unlightsome
unleisurely
unlimitedly
unlooked-for
unliquefied
unlistening
unloverlike
unluxuriant
unluxurious
unmeaningly
unmechanise
unmechanize
unmodulated
unmeditated
unmoistened
unmalicious
unmelodious
unmalleable
unmemorable
unmindfully
unmanliness
unmercenary
unmortgaged
unmarriable
unmortified
unmoralised
unmoralized
unmeritable
unmeritedly
unmurmuring
unmusically
unmasculine
unmitigable
unmitigably
unmitigated
unmatchable
unmutilated
unmotivated
unnecessary
unneedfully
unnaturally
unnourished
unnavigable
unnavigated
unoperative
unofficious
unofficered
unoffensive
unoffending
unorganised
unorganized
Urochordata
urochordate
unoriginate
utopianiser
utopianizer
unobnoxious
ulotrichous
unobservant
unobserving
unorthodoxy
unobtrusive
unpeaceable
unplausible
unplausibly
unpractical
unplastered
unpractised
unpublished
unpedigreed
unpreaching
unpreferred
unprevented
unpresuming
unpaintable
unprintable
unpolarised
unpolarized
unpalatable
unpalatably
unpolitical
upping-block
unpensioned
upping-stone
upping-stock
unprocessed
unprofessed
unprojected
unprotected
unprotested
unprophetic
unprovident
unprofiting
unpromising
unprovoking
unpopularly
unpopulated
unperverted
unperfectly
unperceived
unparagoned
unpurchased
unportioned
unperplexed
unpardoning
unperformed
unperishing
unperturbed
unpersuaded
unpossessed
unpassioned
unpatterned
unpitifully
unpityingly
unpatriotic
unpathwayed
unqualified
unqualitied
unquantised
unquantized
unqueenlike
unquickened
unquietness
unreachable
unreadiness
unrealistic
unreasoning
unreclaimed
unrectified
unreceipted
unrecalling
utricularia
unreceptive
unrecounted
unrecovered
unreducible
unredressed
unrefracted
unrefreshed
unreflected
unregulated
unregarding
uprightness
unrighteous
unrehearsed
unrejoicing
unreluctant
unreligious
unrelenting
unremaining
unromanised
unromanized
unremittent
unremitting
unremovable
unrepugnant
unreprieved
unrepentant
unrepenting
unreproving
unreposeful
unrequisite
unrespected
unrescinded
unrestingly
unresentful
unresenting
unrestraint
unresisting
unretentive
unreturning
unretouched
unrevealing
unravelment
unravelling
unrewarding
unstaidness
unshakeable
unshakeably
unsparingly
unswallowed
unstainable
unstaunched
unseaworthy
unsharpened
unsubmerged
unsubjected
unsubduable
unsocialism
unsectarian
unsociality
unsucceeded
unsuccoured
unsteadfast
unspecified
unspeakable
unspeakably
unsweetened
unsheltered
Ulsterwoman
unsoftening
unsighed-for
unsegmented
unscheduled
unscholarly
unskilfully
unsmilingly
unspiritual
unscissored
unsyllabled
unsolicited
unselfishly
unsoldierly
unsandalled
unsentenced
unsensitive
unshockable
unstoppable
unstoppably
unsupported
unseparable
unseparated
unsurpassed
unshrinking
unsprinkled
unsurprised
unscratched

11 u□s□s

unsustained
unsuspended
unsuspected
unsuspicion
unsatiating
unsettledly
unsatirical
unsaturated
unsatisfied
unslumbrous
unsoundable
unsoundness
unshunnable
unsavourily
ultramarine
untraceable
untravelled
untraversed
unteachable
ultraviolet
ultrafilter
ultra-modern
ultrasonics
untractable
urticaceous
untechnical
urticarious
untrembling
untreatable
untremulous
unthinkable
unthickened
untaintedly
untamedness
untempering
untimeously
untunefully
untinctured
unthought-of
untormented
unthriftily
untarnished
unterrified
untouchable
usucaptible
unutterable
unutterably
unusualness
unvocalised
unvocalized
unvulgarise
unvulgarize
upvaluation
unvenerable
unveracious
unvarnished
unvisitable
unvitrified
unweathered
unweariable
unweariably
unweariedly
unwedgeable
unweetingly
unwillingly
unwelcomely
unwandering
unwinkingly
unwholesome
unwarranted
unwished-for
unwithering
unwitnessed
unwittingly
unwithstood
unwoundable
vibratility
vibrational
vice-admiral
vociferance
vociferator
vicegerency
vaccination
vaccinatory
victimology
vacillating
vacillation
vacillatory
vice-marshal
vacuolation
vectorially
vacuousness
viciousness
vectorscope
victoryless
vicar-choral
vicar-forane
vicariously
viceroyship
viceroyalty
vicissitude
vacationist
vacuum-clean
victuallage
victualless
victualling
vichyssoise
vedette-boat
vagabondage
vagabondise
vagabondize
vagabondish
vagabondism
vigilantism
Vehmgericht
vaivodeship
voivodeship
volcanicity
vulcanicity
valuational
volcanology
vulcanology
villanously
volt-amperes
volubleness
velocimeter
velocimetry
velocipeder
valediction
valedictory
vulneration
velvetiness
velvet-paper
valleculate
vellication
villication
Vallisneria
volumometer
Valoniaceae
voluntative
voluntarism
voluntarist
voluntarily
Valentinian
Volkskammer
Volkslieder
volitionary
vomeronasal
vantageless
viniculture
vine-dresser
vine-disease
Vendémiaire
venefically
veneficious
vinificator
vine-fretter
venographic
ventilative
vindicative
venditation
ventilation
vindication
vindicatory
vendibility
vincibility
vinaigrette
vinblastine
ventricular
ventriculus
ventriloquy
venereology
vincristine
venesection
venisection
vanishingly
venatically
venturesome
venturingly
venturously
vanguardism
violinistic
violoncello
voodooistic
△voortrekker
vaporimeter
vaporisable
vaporizable
vapouringly
versatilely
variability
versability
versatility
variational
verd-antique
varicelloid
varicellous
veraciously
voraciously
veridically
viridescent
Verbenaceae
verse-making
variegation
verberation
verde-antico
verse-monger
vertebrally
vertebrated
vermination
verticality
verbigerate
vorticellae
varnish-tree
vertiginous
vortiginous
vermivorous
vermiculate
vermiculite
vermiculous
verslibrist
virological
virilescent
verumontana
variolation
verboseness
varsovienne
variousness
verisimilar
verdureless
verruciform
virtue-proof
visibleness
vesiculated
vasodilator
vespertinal
vestimental
viscometric
viscountess
viscousness
vasopressin
vasopressor
vestry-clerk
visiting-day

Words marked △ may be spelled also with a capital letter

vascularise
vascularize
vascularity
vasculature
vasculiform
vesuvianite
vitraillist
viticulture
vaticinator
vitrescible
vitrescence
vitrifiable
vituperable
vituperator
vouchsafing
vivaciously
vivacissimo
vivisective
vivisection
vexillation
vexillology
vexatiously
voyeuristic
weasand-pipe
wearability
weasel-faced
whale-fisher
wranglesome
weak-hearted
weatherable
weather-fend
weather-wise
weathercock
weather-worn
weathermost
wearilessly
whaling-port
wearisomely
weak-kneedly
weapon-schaw
weak-sighted
whatsomever
wealthiness
web-fingered
widechapped
wedge-tailed
wedge-heeled
wedge-shaped
widdershins
wide-ranging
widowerhood
wide-watered
whenceforth
wheedlesome
whereabouts
wherewithal
wheresoever
Wienerwurst
weeping-ripe
weeding-fork
weeding-hook
wheyishness
wreckmaster
wheelbarrow
wheelwright
wheel-cutter
weeny-bopper
wag-'n-bietjie
Wagneresque
wage-earning
waggishness
wagonwright
white-handed
whitewasher
white-tailed
white-haired
white-headed
whitethroat
Whitechapel
white-winged
white-billed
white-listed
△**whiteboyism**
white-collar
white-rumped
whiffletree
weightiness
whichsoever
whitherward
weighbridge
weight-train
waiting-maid
writing-case
writing-desk
whiting-time
waiting-list
writing-book
waiting-room
whitishness
whisky-liver
whiskerando
whiskeyfied
whitleather
whitlow-wort
whigmaleery
Weismannism
waivodeship
whippletree
whipping-boy
whipping-top
waitressing
whimsically
Whitsuntide
wainscoting
wainscotted
whistleable
whistle-stop
whistlingly
waistcloths
whist-player
wakefulness
weldability
welfaristic
well-advised
well-behaved
well-beloved
wallclimber
well-covered
well-dressed
well-defined
well-derived
well-desired
well-endowed
well-entered
well-founded
wildfowling
waldgravine
well-groomed
walking-cane
walking-beam
willingness
walking-song
wellingtons
Welwitschia
well-judging
well-looking
well-meaning
well-ordered
welcomeness
welcomingly
Weltpolitik
well-rounded
well-stacked
△**waldsterben**
Weltschmerz
well-sinking
well-trodden
well-thumbed
will-worship
well-wishing
wimpishness
womb-leasing
woman-vested
womanliness
wing-and-wing
winnability
wine-bibbing
Windbreaker®
windbaggery
windcheater
want-catcher
winter-bloom
winterberry
wonderfully
wintergreen
wanderingly
wonderingly
Wanderjahre
winter-sweet
wine-growing
winningness
winning-post
windlestrae
windlestraw
Wensleydale
window-barne
winsomeness
wind-sucking
windsurfing
wine-tasting
wing-walking
wool-bearing
wool-combing
woodcarving
wool-carding
woodcutting
whoremaster
whole-length
wholesomely
whole-hoofed
whole-hogger
whoremonger
whole-souled
whole-footed
whosesoever
wholestitch
wood-fretter
wrong-headed
wrong-minded
wool-growing
wrought-iron
whorishness
wholly-owned
wool-stapler
wood-sanicle
whodunnitry
woody-tongue
wapper-jawed
wappenschaw
workability
workaholism
warrantable
warrantably
warm-blooded
wiredrawing
world-famous
world-beater
worldliness
wire-dancing
worldly-wise
warm-hearted
worthlessly
worshipable
worshipless
worshipping
warehousing
warlikeness
working-beam
working-over
wordishness
workmanship
workmanlike
word-of-mouth
word-painter

Words marked △ may be spelled also with a capital letter

11 w□r□p

wire-pulling
word-perfect
word-puzzler
work-sharing
worsted-work
werewolfery
werewolfish
werewolfism
wireworking
workwatcher
wash-and-wear
west-by-north
west-by-south
Wesleyanism
wasterfully
westernmost
washerwoman
wishfulness
wistfulness
wash-gilding
wise-hearted
wishing-well
washing-line
washing-blue
washing-soda
wishing-bone
wishing-tree
waspishness
wash-leather
Westminster
Westphalian
wishtonwish
wasp-waisted
witheringly
witlessness
withershins
wither-wrung
watchmaking
witch-ridden
witch-finder
watchspring
witenagemot
without-door
watered-down
Water-bearer
water-heater
water-finder
water-skiing
watering-can
watering-cap
watering-pot
waterlogged
water-cooled
water-cooler
watercolour
watercourse
withstander
wauking-song
wax-chandler
waywardness
X-chromosome
xylocarpous
xylographic
xylographer
xylophagous
xylophilous
xylophonist
xenodochium
xenogenesis
xenogenetic
xenoglossia
Xanthochroi
xanthophyll
Xanthoxylum
xenomorphic
xenoplastic
xiphopagous
xyridaceous
xerographic
xeromorphic
xeranthemum
xerophilous
xerotripsis
yeard-hunger
yeard-hungry
yackety-yack
yachtswoman
Yugoslavian
Y-chromosome
yellow-ammer
yellow-belly
yince-errand
yersiniosis
yesternight
yatteringly
yttriferous
yttro-cerite
you-know-what
zealousness
zoantharian
zoanthropic
zygocardiac
Zygomycetes
zygomorphic
zygopleural
Zygophyllum
zwischenzug
zymological
zymosimeter
zymotically
zymotechnic
Zanthoxylum
zinciferous
zinkiferous
zincography
Zonotrichia
zoomagnetic
zoodendrium
zootechnics
zoocephalic
zootheistic
zoochemical
zoophytical
zeolitiform
zooplankton
zoogonidium
zoomorphism
zoospermium
zoografting
zoographist
zip-fastener
Zoroastrian
zero-grazing
zestfulness

Words marked △ may be spelled also with a capital letter

anacatharsis
anacathartic
anapaestical
Amarantaceae
anabaptistic
anarchically
academically
amateurishly
amalgamation
amalgamative
agathodaimon
anaphylactic
anathematise
anathematize
arachnophobe
azathioprine
avariciously
acaridomatia
availability
agalmatolite
agamogenesis
anagogically
analogically
anatomically
apagogically
acarodomatia
anamorphoses
anamorphosis
araeosystyle
analphabetic
anaerobiosis
anaerobiotic
anagrammatic
anaesthetics
anaesthetise
anaesthetist
anaesthetize
avant-gardism
avant-gardist
acanthaceous
adaptability
anastigmatic
avant-courier
anarthrously
adaptiveness
analytically
ambidextrous
abbreviation
abbreviatory
abbreviature
ambulanceman
arborescence
arborisation
arborization
ambassadress
ambitionless
abbey-counter
acciaccatura
archaeometry
archdeaconry
accidentally
aecidiospore
Asclepiadean
archegoniate
archetypical
acclimatiser
acclimatizer
archipelagic
archipelagos
architecture
Archilochian
acceleration
acceleratory
accelerative
accompanyist
accomplished
accomplisher
accumulation
accumulative
accommodable
accommodator
aichmophobia
Ascension-day
accentuality
accentuation
anchoretical
arctophilist
anchoritical
accursedness
accordionist
accurateness
accustrement
accusatorial
accusatively
accouterment
accouchement
accoutrement
addictedness
addle-brained
androcentric
audiological
androsterone
aldermanlike
aldermanship
alder-liefest
adder's-tongue
additionally
andouillette
acetaldehyde
amenableness
alembication
Azerbaijanis
anencephalia
anencephalic
anecdotalist
aye-remaining
aperiodicity
alexipharmic
amelioration
ameliorative
awe-inspiring
anemophilous
anemographic
averruncator
aberrational
agent-general
amentiferous
adequateness
affectedness
affectionate
afficionados
arfvedsonite
affrightened
affrightedly
affrightment
apfelstrudel
affrontingly
afforestable
affluentness
aggressively
augmentation
augmentative
anguilliform
argillaceous
angelica-tree
angiosarcoma
angiocarpous
agglomerated
angiogenesis
Anglocentric
△anglophobiac
Angiospermae
angiospermal
angiostomous
agglutinable
agglutinogen
achlamydeous
athletically
Alhambresque
atheological
athrocytoses
athrocytosis
atheromatous
adhesiveness
animalculism
animalculist
avitaminosis
amicableness
animatronics
animadverter
alimentation
alimentative
arithmetical
arithmomania
arithmometer
alienability
amitotically
amissibility
aristocratic
aristolochia
Aristophanic
Aristotelean
Aristotelian
Aristotelism
apiculturist
adjectivally
adjudication
adjudicative
adjunctively
alkalescence
alkalescency
Ankylosauria
Ankylosaurus
all-important
aplanogamete
all-inclusive
all-roundness
all-or-nothing
ailurophilia
ailurophilic
ailurophobia
ailurophobic
allusiveness
alliteration
alliterative
ailourophobe
ailourophile
allowability
armamentaria
adminiculate
admonishment
administrant
administrate
atmospherics
armour-bearer
armour-plated
annihilation
annihilative
△annunciation
annunciative
announcement
aromatherapy
adorableness
avowableness
apodeictical
above-the-line
aforethought
apogeotropic
apothegmatic
apochromatic
anotherguess
aboriginally
apolitically
abolitionary
abolitionism
abolitionist
apoplectical
Apollinarian
apologetical
acoustically
amontillados
apostolicism
apostolicity
apostrophise

12 a□o□t

apostrophize
amortisement
amortisation
abortiveness
amortizement
amortization
apocynaceous
applaudingly
alphabetical
alphamerical
alpha-blocker
appraisement
applausively
appraisively
alphanumeric
apprehension
apprehensive
appreciation
appreciatory
appreciative
apple-blossom
appressorium
arpeggiation
appoggiatura
amphigastria
amphisbaenic
amphitheatre
amphibrachic
amphitropous
appointments
amphistomous
amphictyonic
ampelography
appendectomy
appendicitis
approachable
approach-shot
appropriator
appertaining
appurtenance
apperception
apperceptive
asparaginase
appercipient
aspergillums
apparentness
aspiringness
apparatchiki
apparatchiks
apparitional
aspirational
appositeness
appositional
appetisement
appetisingly
appetizingly
asphyxiation
acquaintance
acquiescence
acroamatical
Afro-American

agribusiness
agrobusiness
agrochemical
agricultural
Afrocentrism
aerodynamics
aeroembolism
agreeability
arrière-garde
agroforestry
acrogenously
agroindustry
Afrikanerdom
air-ambulance
acronychally
apron-strings
aeronautical
aeroneurosis
air-condition
air-commodore
aeroplankton
acrophonetic
air-breathing
aircraftsman
aerostatical
aerosiderite
acrostically
assibilation
associations
assuefaction
abstemiously
arsphenamine
aesthesiogen
aesthetician
aestheticise
aestheticism
aestheticist
aestheticize
adscititious
auspiciously
absoluteness
assimilation
assimilative
assemblaunce
assentaneous
absinthiated
absent-minded
abstractedly
abstractness
alstroemeria
assortedness
Australasian
Austronesian
abstruseness
absorptivity
assassinator
assessorship
absquatulate
auscultation
auscultatory
asseverating

asseveration
anti-abortion
anti-aircraft
autoantibody
attractingly
attractively
antibacchius
antibarbarus
anticyclonic
antecedently
anticlerical
autocritique
astacologist
articulately
articulation
articulatory
anticipation
anticipatory
anticipative
autocatalyse
autocatalyze
antichthones
autochthones
anticatholic
autodidactic
antediluvial
antediluvian
autodestruct
antidiuretic
anthelmintic
antherozooid
autoexposure
authenticate
authenticity
artificially
antifriction
anti-Gallican
antagonistic
antigropelos
antihalation
autohypnosis
astringently
auto-immunity
attributable
artilleryman
△antilegomena
altaltissimo
automobilism
automobilist
antimacassar
antimnemonic
antimalarial
antemeridian
automorphism
antimetabole
automaticity
altimetrical
antoninianus
astonishment
anti-national
antineutrino

anthocarpous
astronautics
anthoxanthin
Artiodactyla
astrogeology
anthophilous
astrophysics
authorisable
authorizable
aetiological
astrological
astronomical
action-taking
astrocytomas
anteprandial
anti-predator
autoptically
antiphonally
antiphonical
antiparticle
antiparallel
antiperiodic
antiphrastic
antipathetic
antipetalous
antipruritic
alterability
antirachitic
autorickshaw
attorneyship
antarthritic
afterthought
aethrioscope
arthroplasty
anthropogeny
anthropogony
anthropoidal
anthropology
anthropotomy
afterburning
antisocially
antasthmatic
artistically
autistically
anti-Semitism
antisepalous
antistrophic
antistrophon
attitudinise
altitudinous
attitudinize
antithetical
antitheistic
antithrombin
astoundingly
ayuntamiento
adulteration
adulterously
advantageous
adventitious
adverbialise

Words marked △ may be spelled also with a capital letter

12 b□o□s

adverbialize
advisability
asynchronism
asynchronous
amygdaloidal
asymmetrical
asymptomatic
asymptotical
bearableness
blamableness
bramble-berry
bramble-finch
blabbermouth
blanc-de-Chine
Branchiopoda
boardsailing
brandy-bottle
board-measure
branding-iron
boarding-pike
brandy-pawnee
bladderwrack
blandishment
blamefulness
△braggadocios
brachycephal
brachydactyl
brachygraphy
beachcombing
blatherskite
beatifically
blackballing
black-hearted
black-visaged
blackbirding
black-fishing
blacklisting
black-figured
black-and-blue
brackishness
bracket-creep
black-pudding
black-quarter
blackguardly
blackcurrant
beaumontague
brainwashing
brass-bounder
brassfounder
brass-rubbing
blastulation
blastosphere
blast-furnace
boastfulness
baby-batterer
Bible-thumper
Bible-pounder
bibliography
bibliologist
bibliomaniac
bibliopegist
bibliopolist
bibliophobia
bibble-babble
bubble-headed
bibulousness
babingtonite
baby-snatcher
bobby-dazzler
baccalaurean
buccaneering
buccaneerish
backbreaking
backboneless
bactericidal
bacteriology
bacteriostat
bachelor-girl
bachelorhood
bachelorship
bacchanalian
buckle-beggar
back-lighting
becomingness
bicameralism
bicameralist
back-mutation
bicentennial
back-slapping
backstarting
backswordman
backtracking
back-to-nature
backwoodsman
backwardness
back-wounding
body-building
body-checking
bodice-ripper
badger-legged
body-snatcher
bedazzlement
breeches-buoy
breech-loader
bread-chipper
bletherskate
bletheration
brevipennate
breakdancing
breakfast-set
breakthrough
break-promise
beetle-browed
beetleheaded
blennorrhoea
Byelorussian
breastplough
breastsummer
breaststroke
breathalyser
breathalyzer
breathlessly
breathtaking
buffalo-berry
buffalo-grass
buffing-wheel
baggage-train
beggarliness
Bignoniaceae
behaviorally
behaviourism
behaviourist
brigade-major
blind-stamped
bride-chamber
brimfullness
blithesomely
boiling-point
brinkmanship
brickfielder
brick-nogging
brilliantine
brilliant-cut
blimpishness
blissfulness
bristle-grass
Bristol-brick
blister-steel
boisterously
baking-powder
Balaam-basket
Balaamitical
balladmonger
ballanwrasse
bilharziasis
bilharziosis
ball-bearings
ball-breaking
bell-bottomed
ballet-dancer
bullet-headed
balletically
balneologist
ballet-master
balletomania
belletristic
bullfighting
belligerence
belligerency
billingsgate
bolting-hutch
billiard-ball
balance-sheet
balance-wheel
bilingualism
bollock-naked
bull-of-the-bog
bullshitting
belittlement
bilateralism
below-the-line
belly-landing
bombacaceous
bomb-disposal
bimilleniums
bimillennium
benzaldehyde
benjamin-tree
bantamweight
banderillero
bonnet-monkey
bandersnatch
beneficially
beneficently
benefactress
benightening
bench-warrant
banalisation
banalization
benumbedness
banana-bender
Bananalander
bunko-steerer
bend-sinister
benevolently
bonny-clabber
biosatellite
bronco-buster
bioscientist
bronchoscope
bronchoscopy
broadcasting
bloodletting
bloodthirsty
bloody-minded
blood-brother
bloodstained
blood-pudding
bloodsucking
broken-backed
broker-dealer
biogeography
biomechanics
Bromeliaceae
biometrician
broken-winded
bromhidrosis
biochemistry
brother-in-law
biophysicist
biorhythmics
biodiversity
booking-clerk
boogie-woogie
blockbusting
book-learning
bootlessness
bioflavonoid
blow-moulding
biologically
biocoenology
boomps-a-daisy
biographical
book-scorpion

brontosaurus
bioavailable
biosynthesis
biosynthetic
bipropellant
bequeathable
bequeathment
bureaucratic
burial-ground
barratrously
bare-breached
bird-catching
barodynamics
burseraceous
barber-monger
barge-couples
birefringent
Berufsverbot
Boraginaceae
birthday-book
birthday-suit
Bertholletia
birding-piece
burying-place
burning-glass
burning-point
burning-house
bertillonage
barristerial
bare-knuckled
barometrical
baron-officer
bardolatrous
burrowing-owl
baroreceptor
bird's-nesting
borosilicate
barnstorming
borough-reeve
bird-watching
barmy-brained
basidiospore
beseechingly
basket-making
basket-stitch
bespectacled
Besserwisser
bastinadoing
baselessness
base-levelled
businesslike
bus-conductor
basso-relievo
basso-rilievo
base-spirited
besottedness
bushwhacking
bate-breeding
beta-carotene
butter-cooler
butterfly-bow
butterfly-nut
battering-ram
butter-muslin
between-decks
betweentimes
butterscotch
buttery-hatch
bathing-dress
bottle-blonde
battleground
bottle-holder
battlemented
bottle-opener
bottle-slider
bottle-washer
battological
bottom-sawyer
buttress-root
bathypelagic
butty-collier
bougainvilia
bound-bailiff
blunderingly
boulevardier
bourgeoisify
bluestocking
blusteringly
bowling-alley
bowling-green
bewilderment
bow-compasses
bewitchingly
boy-meets-girl
buzzard-clock
chalazogamic
Charadriidae
characterise
characterism
characterful
characterize
coadaptation
crambo-jingle
chalcography
Chalcolithic
chance-medley
chalcanthite
chalcopyrite
claudication
crapehanging
clare-obscure
coacervation
clangorously
crash-landing
crash-matting
coachbuilder
clavicembalo
clarinettist
coalitionism
coalitionist
craniologist
chalicothere
clamjamphrie
crackbrained
chaplainship
Chaplinesque
cradle-scythe
charlatanism
chain-gearing
chain-breaker
clannishness
cladogenesis
cyanogenesis
cladosporium
championship
clapperboard
chairmanship
clair-obscure
clairvoyance
clairvoyancy
clairaudient
classicalism
classicalist
classicality
chassé-croisé
classifiable
Crassulaceae
crassulacean
chaise-longue
crassamentum
claustration
coat-trailing
claptrappery
craftmanship
chaetiferous
chartography
coast-to-coast
craftspeople
craftsperson
charterparty
charter-chest
clatteringly
chapterhouse
Charterhouse
chastisement
chart-busting
chauvinistic
cabbage-white
cable-railway
cable's-length
cable-tramway
cabalistical
cabinetmaker
cubistically
cyclandelate
cockfighting
coccidiostat
cockieleekie
cachinnation
cachinnatory
Cicindelidae
cichoraceous
cyclographic
cyclopropane
Cyclostomata
cyclostomous
cacophonical
cacophonious
cicatrichule
code-breaking
cedrelaceous
codification
co-dependency
coelacanthic
cremationist
coerciveness
crepehanging
clever-clever
crêpe-de-chine
crenellation
coenesthesia
Coelenterata
coelenterate
Czechoslovak
credibleness
creditworthy
checkweigher
checking-room
checkerberry
checkerboard
creolisation
creolization
caenogenesis
chemotherapy
coenobitical
coenospecies
chemotropism
creepy-crawly
clear-obscure
cheirography
clear-sighted
cheirologist
cherry-laurel
cheiromantic
cheiropteran
cherry-pepper
cheerishness
cheerfulness
cheeseburger
cheesecutter
cheesehopper
cheesemonger
cleistogamic
cheeseparing
cheese-rennet
cheesetaster
chesterfield
creatureship
creativeness
crepusculous
cherubically
cheluviation
café-chantant
cohabitation

Words marked △ may be spelled also with a capital letter

12 c□n□e

cohesibility
cohesiveness
chivalrously
coincidental
coincidently
clincher-work
Cain-coloured
childbearing
child-bearing
childcrowing
childishness
chimerically
cliffhanging
chieftainess
cringe-making
cliché-ridden
criticalness
chiliahedron
criticisable
criticizable
criminogenic
chick-a-diddle
clinker-built
chimney-sweep
Chimonanthus
coin-operated
Chironomidae
chiropractic
chiropractor
chirographer
chiropterous
crimping-iron
chiaroscuros
cuisse-madame
cristobalite
chitterlings
chiquichiqui
chirurgeonly
cliquishness
collaterally
culpableness
collaborator
celibatarian
Calyciflorae
calico-flower
calycoideous
calycanthemy
collegialism
collegiality
calceamentum
culvertailed
collectorate
collectively
collectivise
collectivism
collectivist
collectivity
collectivize
caliginosity
cultivatable
collinearity
calligrapher
calligraphic
callisthenic
colliquation
colliquative
calumniation
columniation
calumniatory
calumniously
calamitously
cold-moulding
calendar-line
cylindricity
cylindriform
colonisation
colonization
coleopterist
coleopterous
colloquially
coloquintida
chloroformer
chlorimetric
chlorometric
chlorambucil
chlorination
calisthenics
cold-shoulder
colossus-wise
coletitmouse
colluctation
collywobbles
Commandments
commandingly
companionway
companionate
compatriotic
Campanularia
come-by-chance
camp-drafting
commercially
commencement
commendation
commendatory
compellation
compellative
commemorable
commemorator
commensalism
commensality
commensurate
compensation
compensatory
compensative
commentation
camp-follower
combinations
commiserable
commiserator
commissioned
commissioner
commissarial
commissariat
committeeman
camiknickers
complacently
cumulocirrus
complication
complicative
complaisance
complemental
complimental
complimenter
cumulonimbus
complanation
completeness
cumulatively
complexional
complexioned
cement-copper
cementitious
Cominformist
campodeiform
composedness
componential
commorientes
commodiously
common-riding
△commonwealth
camp-preacher
comprimarios
compressible
Combretaceae
cumbrousness
camp-shedding
camp-sheeting
cometography
cymotrichous
compunctious
compurgation
compurgatory
communicable
communicably
communicator
communitaire
communion-cup
compulsorily
compulsatory
compulsative
compulsively
contabescent
convalescent
contaminable
contagionist
contagiously
cantankerous
containerise
containerize
connaturally
confabulator
cane-bottomed
conscription
conscionable
conscionably
conidiophore
conidiospore
conveyancing
canterburies
conférencier
conferencing
congenerical
cankeredness
concelebrant
concelebrate
conferential
centesimally
congenitally
congeniality
conveniently
cancellarial
cancellarian
cancellation
conterminant
conterminate
conterminous
condemnation
condemnatory
conveyor-belt
contemplable
contemplator
contemptible
contemptibly
cancerphobia
contemporary
contemporise
contemporize
contemptuous
consecration
consecratory
consecrative
consensually
confessional
confessoress
condensation
conversation
conversative
contextually
concentrator
conventicler
consentience
concentrical
concertinaed
consentingly
contestingly
convectional
conventional
confectioner
conventioner
concentering
contentation
contestation
connectively
connectivity
consequences

12 c□n□e

consequently
conservatrix
conservation
conservatory
△conservatism
△conservative
conchiferous
conchologist
cantharidian
cantharidine
convincement
convincingly
confiscation
confiscatory
considerance
considerable
considerably
cantilevered
confidential
canting-wheel
contingently
conning-tower
cunnilinctus
convivialist
conviviality
conditioning
conditionate
conciliation
conciliatory
conciliative
centillionth
cantillation
cantillatory
confirmation
confirmatory
confirmative
consignation
contignation
consignatory
consistently
consistorial
consistorian
continuation
continuative
contiguously
continuously
conglobulate
conglobation
canaliculate
candle-holder
conglomerate
conclamation
candle-paring
canalisation
conclusively
conglutinant
conglutinate
candle-waster
canalization
cinematheque
cinemathèque
canonisation
canonization
concordantly
cannon-fodder
concomitance
concomitancy
consolidated
consolidator
consociation
censoriously
conformation
confoundedly
concorporate
contortional
conspectuity
conspiringly
contrabbasso
contribution
contributary
contributory
contributive
contractable
contractedly
centroclinal
contractible
contractural
contradictor
congregation
controllable
concremation
confrontment
contranatant
contrapuntal
contrapposto
contrariness
contrariwise
concrescence
centrosphere
congratulant
congratulate
concreteness
contriteness
contriturate
canorousness
contrivement
constabulary
constringent
constriction
constrictive
constipation
constituency
constatation
constitution
constitutive
construction
constructive
contumacious
conjunctival
contumelious
contubernyal
confusedness
concubitancy
concupiscent
connubiality
Confucianism
Confucianist
centuriation
centuplicate
conduplicate
consummately
consummation
consummatory
consummative
concurrently
conqueringly
conquistador
convulsional
convulsively
consultation
consultatory
consultative
conductivity
centumvirate
cloud-seeding
chondriosome
cloud-kissing
co-ordinately
co-ordination
co-ordinative
chondroblast
chondrostian
chordophonic
cloddishness
cloven-footed
choreography
cloven-hoofed
cholerically
close-fitting
close-tongued
close-mouthed
close-grained
close-cropped
clothes-sense
clothes-horse
clothes-brush
clothes-press
Choripetalae
cooking-range
cooking-apple
chorizontist
cookie-pusher
clock-watcher
clownishness
chocolate-box
chorological
chorographer
chorographic
crossbanding
cross-lateral
crossbencher
cross-selling
cross-section
cross-lighted
cross-linking
cross-and-pile
cross-country
cross-grained
cross-purpose
cross-current
cross-buttock
crosscutting
cross-examine
Cappagh-brown
cuprammonium
cephalometry
capabilities
capacitation
copper-bottom
copper-fasten
cupping-glass
capriciously
Capricornian
captiousness
capillaceous
cupuliferous
co-polymerise
co-polymerize
coprophagist
coprophagous
coprophilous
cupboard-love
capercaillie
capercailzie
capitalistic
capitulation
capitulatory
coquettishly
carragheenin
carnal-minded
circassienne
Cordaitaceae
currant-jelly
currant-bread
cerebrotonia
cerebrotonic
corn-chandler
curb-crawling
card-carrying
caricaturist
correlatable
carpetbagger
curietherapy
Cartesianism
carpet-knight
carte-blanche
carpetmonger
correctional
correctioner
carpenter-bee
carpenter-ant
correctitude
cerographist
cardinal-bird

curvicaudate
cardinalship
corrivalship
corrie-fisted
cardiography
carriageable
carriage-free
carving-knife
carriage-paid
curling-stone
certificated
carriwitchet
cardiologist
carcinogenic
curvifoliate
curvirostral
curvicostate
curliewurlie
corallaceous
corollaceous
carillonneur
circle-riding
carelessness
ceramography
ceremonially
chromophilic
chromophonic
corn-merchant
curb-merchant
chromosphere
chromaticism
chromaticity
chromatogram
chromatopsia
chrematistic
chronography
chronologise
chronologist
chronologize
chronometric
carbonaceous
corporalship
corporealise
corporealism
corporealist
corporeality
corporealize
carpophagous
cartophilist
Carlovingian
corroborable
corroborator
cartological
carton-pierre
cartographer
cartographic
cirro-stratus
cirro-cumulus
carbohydrate
ceroplastics
christianise
Christianism
Christianity
christianize
Christliness
chrisom-cloth
chrestomathy
Christolatry
corespondent
christophany
Christ's-thorn
corn-shucking
Ceratosaurus
circumcentre
circumcision
circumfusile
circumfusion
circumfluent
circumfluous
curmudgeonly
circumgyrate
circumjacent
circumlocute
circumnutate
circumstance
circumscribe
circuitously
caravansarai
caravanserai
cash-and-carry
cashew-apples
cosmetically
costermonger
cushion-plant
coscinomancy
cosmonautics
cosmoplastic
cosmogonical
cosmological
cosmopolitan
cosmopolitic
cosmographer
cosmographic
customs-house
cash-register
catechetical
catachrestic
catacoustics
catadioptric
cathetometer
citification
cityfication
cytogenetics
categorially
catallactics
cotyledonary
cotyledonous
cattle-lifter
catilinarian
cattle-plague
catamountain
cutinisation
cut-and-thrust
cutinization
cottonocracy
cathodograph
cataphoresis
cataphractic
cataphysical
cataphyllary
caterwauling
cytoskeletal
cytoskeleton
catastrophic
cytotoxicity
courageously
causationism
causationist
clubbability
Churchillian
churchianity
churchpeople
church-parade
churchwarden
cousin-german
cautiousness
chuckie-stane
chuckie-stone
caulking-iron
churlishness
coulombmeter
counsellable
court-martial
courtierlike
countenancer
counting-room
county-people
countermarch
counter-paled
counter-gauge
counterscarp
counter-weigh
counter-tenor
counterpeise
counter-sense
counteroffer
counter-agent
countercheck
counter-wheel
countershaft
countercharm
counterlight
counterplead
counterbluff
counter-claim
counter-flory
counterblast
counter-force
counterpoint
counterpoise
counterbrace
counter-drain
counterproof
counter-punch
counter-guard
countrywoman
country-house
civilisation
civilization
covetousness
covetiveness
cowardliness
cryoglobulin
crymotherapy
chymotrypsin
cryptography
cryptogamian
cryptogamist
cryptogamous
crystal-gazer
cryptologist
crystallitis
crystal-clear
cryptomnesia
cryptomnesic
cryptanalyst
cryptonymous
dead-and-alive
dramatically
dramatisable
dramatizable
diamagnetism
dramaturgist
deambulatory
de-alcoholise
de-alcoholize
dialectician
dialecticism
dialectology
diageotropic
dwarfishness
draughtiness
draught-hooks
draughtboard
draught-horse
draught-house
draught-proof
death-warrant
death-dealing
diaphanously
diathermancy
drawing-paper
drawing-table
doating-piece
drawing-knife
drawing-frame
drawlingness
drainage-tube
diatomaceous
diamond-wheel
diamond-hitch
diamond-field
diamond-drill
diapophysial

12 d□a□o

diabolically
diatonically
dragon's-blood
dracontiasis
deaspiration
diagrammatic
dearticulate
draft-dodging
diastrophism
deactivation
Dibranchiata
dibranchiate
debilitating
debilitation
debilitative
debonairness
dubitatively
doch-an-dorach
dictatorship
decrescendos
decrepitness
decreasingly
declensional
decaffeinate
ducking-stool
declinometer
dock-labourer
decalcomania
deceleration
decoloration
decalescence
decommission
decomposable
decompressor
deconsecrate
decongestant
decongestion
decongestive
decentralise
decentralize
decipherable
decipherment
decapitalise
decapitalize
decapitation
dicarpellary
dichromatism
doctrinarian
dichrooscope
dichroscopic
decoratively
decorousness
decasyllabic
decasyllable
decisiveness
decitizenise
decitizenize
decrustation
dactylically
dactyliology
dactyloscopy
deducibility
dodecagynian
dodecagynous
dodecahedral
dodecahedron
didactically
dodecandrous
dodecaphonic
dedicational
dedicatorial
Didelphyidae
diencephalon
dreadfulness
dietetically
diethylamine
deerstalking
dressing-case
dressing-down
dressing-gown
dressing-room
dressing-sack
deepwaterman
deepwatermen
defraudation
deflationary
deflationist
deflagration
defectionist
differentiae
differential
deflectional
difficulties
defamatorily
definability
definiteness
definitional
definitively
deformedness
deforciation
diffrangible
diffusedness
diffusionism
diffusionist
dogmatically
digladiation
digressional
digressively
dégringolade
degenerately
degenerating
degeneration
degenerative
dogtooth-spar
digitisation
digitization
dehumidifier
driveability
driving-wheel
driving-shaft
drinking-bout
drinking-horn
drink-driving
deinotherium
do-it-yourself
dejectedness
dijudication
dollarocracy
Della-Cruscan
deliberately
deliberation
deliberative
dilucidation
dilaceration
delicateness
delicatessen
delightfully
dolphinarium
deltiologist
delamination
delimitation
delimitative
delinquently
dilapidation
deliquescent
doloriferous
dolorousness
delusiveness
dilettantish
dilettantism
dilatability
dilatoriness
delitescence
delivery-pipe
delivery-tube
dolly-mixture
damnableness
democratical
demi-culverin
demodulation
demi-distance
demagnetiser
demagnetizer
demilitarise
demilitarize
demi-mondaine
demoniacally
diminuendoes
dementedness
demonologist
demineralise
demineralize
diminishable
diminishment
demonstrable
demonstrably
demonstrator
diminutively
dumortierite
demoralising
demoralizing
dimerisation
dimerization
Domesday-book
domesticated
domesticable
domestically
domesticator
denuclearize
donkey-engine
dunderheaded
Donnerwetter
dentilingual
densitometer
densitometry
dentirostral
denticulated
dunniewassal
dingle-dangle
dynamometric
denomination
denominative
denunciation
denunciatory
Dantophilist
dendrologist
dendrologous
dynastically
do-nothingism
denaturalise
denaturalize
donatistical
denotatively
denouncement
droseraceous
duodecennial
duodenectomy
drongo-cuckoo
drongo-shrike
droughtiness
△**dyotheletism**
doom-merchant
dropped-scone
deoppilation
deoppilative
dropping-well
Doomsday-book
doorstepping
deontologist
doomwatching
depravedness
depredations
doppelganger
doppelgänger
depreciation
depreciatory
depreciative
depressingly
depressurise
depressurize
diprionidian
dephlegmator
depolymerise
depolymerize

Words marked △ may be spelled also with a capital letter

depoliticise
depoliticize
diplomatical
diplogenesis
depopulation
departmental
depositional
deposítation
diphtheritic
diphtheritis
diphthongise
diphthongize
dermatophyte
dermabrasion
deracination
directorship
dormer-window
deregulation
derogatorily
derogatively
dorsiventral
Darlingtonia
dorsiflexion
dormitory-car
duraluminium
derisiveness
derivational
derivatively
dispatch-boat
distanceless
discandering
diseasedness
dismayedness
dissatisfied
destabiliser
destabilizer
disharmonise
disharmonize
disdainfully
dispauperise
dispauperize
despairingly
disobedience
disaccharide
disaccordant
disadvantage
disadventure
desideration
desiderative
disregardful
dissemblance
disseverance
dysteleology
dishevelling
dishevelment
disseverment
disseminated
disseminator
disrelishing
dysmenorrhea
discerptible
distemperate
disheartened
descensional
dispensation
dispensatory
dispensative
dysaesthesia
dysaesthetic
dissentingly
dessertspoon
dissenterish
dissenterism
disceptation
dissertation
dissertative
disreputable
disreputably
disaffection
disaffiliate
disagreeable
disagreeably
disagreement
disaggregate
dysphemistic
dissipatedly
distinctness
despisedness
despitefully
dispiteously
dissimilarly
dispiritedly
dispiritment
disciplinant
disciplinary
discipleship
distillation
distillatory
dissimulator
displeasance
displeasedly
displaceable
displacement
desulphurise
desulphurate
desulphurize
disclamation
desalination
disallowance
disallowable
desolateness
disembarrass
disembellish
disambiguate
disembrangle
disinherison
disinterment
disinterring
disintegrate
disinfectant
disinfection
disincentive
disingenuity
disingenuous
disenchanter
desensitiser
desensitizer
disanalogous
disinflation
disendowment
disintricate
disannulling
disannulment
dislocatedly
despondently
despondingly
discordantly
discoverable
disbowelling
discoverture
Discomedusae
discomedusan
discomfiting
discomfiture
disgorgement
dislodgement
discophorous
despotically
dissocialise
dissociality
dissocialize
despoliation
dissociation
dissociative
discommodity
discommunity
discountable
disconnected
disjointedly
disconnexion
dishonorable
dishonorably
despotocracy
discorporate
discomposure
discourteise
discourteous
discouraging
discographer
disconsolate
dispossessed
dispossessor
discontented
Discomycetes
disappointed
disoperation
dasyphyllous
disorganised
disorganized
desirability
distribution
distributary
distributive
distractedly
destructible
distractible
disgradation
deservedness
discreetness
disorientate
disgregation
distrainable
distrainment
discriminant
discriminate
disfranchise
dispropriate
distrustless
discreteness
discretional
discretively
desirousness
disprivacied
disprivilege
disestablish
disassembler
disassociate
disastrously
desaturation
disputatious
disturbative
disquietness
disauthorise
disauthorize
disqualified
disqualifier
desquamation
desquamatory
desquamative
disguiseless
disbursement
disguisement
disquisition
disquisitory
disquisitive
discursively
dissuasively
disgustingly
disgustfully
disruptively
disaventrous
dissymmetric
detractingly
detractively
detachedness
detectophone
△**ditheletical**
ditheistical
ditriglyphic
detumescence
determinable
determinably
determinedly
dethronement

detruncation
detoxication
dithyrambist
deuteranopia
deuteranopic
deuteroscopy
deuteroplasm
Deuteronomic
daughterling
dough-kneaded
deuch-an-doris
doughnutting
double-acting
double-bubble
double-banked
double-biting
double-bottom
double-charge
double-dealer
double-decked
double-decker
double-dagger
double-dotted
double-figure
double-formed
double-glazed
double-headed
double-header
double-handed
double-locked
double-manned
double-minded
double-storey
double-tongue
deutoplasmic
doubtfulness
deviationism
deviationist
devil-may-care
devil-in-a-bush
devil-worship
divinatorial
divarication
divertimenti
divertimento
diversionary
diversionist
diverticular
diverticulum
diversifying
divisibility
divisiveness
devotionally
down-and-outer
downwardness
dextrocardia
dextrogyrate
dextrousness
day-blindness
Elaeagnaceae
exalbuminous
emasculation
emasculatory
emancipation
emancipatory
exacerbation
evanescently
evangelicism
evangelistic
emargination
exaggeration
exaggeratory
exaggerative
examinership
edaciousness
elasmobranch
evaporimeter
evaporometer
evaporograph
epanorthoses
epanorthosis
exasperating
exasperation
exasperative
Epacridaceae
exanthematic
enantiopathy
enantiomeric
enantiomorph
enantiotropy
enantiostyly
enarthrodial
embranchment
emblazonment
emblematical
embarquement
embitterment
embattlement
embourgeoise
embryologist
embezzlement
exchangeable
exchangeably
eschatologic
enchantingly
encyclopedia
encyclopedic
ecclesiology
Ecclesiastes
ecclesiastic
encheiridion
excogitation
excogitative
enclitically
eucalyptuses
encumberment
encomenderos
encumbrancer
eccentricity
encroachment
enchondromas
encephalitic
encephalitis
escapologist
excursionise
excursionist
excursionize
encirclement
eschscholzia
excitability
escutcheoned
exclusionary
exclusionism
exclusionist
excruciating
excruciation
encrustation
endocarditis
endamagement
endometritis
endonuclease
endangerment
endoparasite
endophyllous
endoskeletal
endoskeleton
endosymbiont
endosmometer
epencephalic
epencephalon
exercise-book
exercitation
epexegetical
exegetically
eleventh-hour
elementalism
elephant's-ear
etepimeletic
evening-dress
eleemosynary
eternisation
eternization
exemplifying
execratively
electability
eleutherarch
electrically
electrifying
even-tempered
electroscope
electrometer
electrogenic
electromeric
electrometry
electroshock
electrophile
electroplate
electropolar
electrosonde
electrotonic
electromotor
electrotonus
electro-optic
electrograph
electron-volt
electrotyper
electrolysis
electrolytic
electrotypic
exenteration
executorship
everydayness
everywhither
effectuality
effectuation
enfeeblement
effiguration
effeminately
efflorescent
effervescent
effusiometer
effusiveness
engraftation
eagle-sighted
Euglenoidina
engagingness
Englishwoman
egg-and-anchor
engine-driver
engenderment
engine-fitter
egg-and-tongue
engine-turned
egg-apparatus
eighteen-hole
eighteenthly
ephebophilia
exhibitioner
exhibitively
exhilarating
exhilaration
exhilaratory
exhilarative
ephemeridian
ephemerality
euhemeristic
Echinocactus
echinococcus
echinodermal
ethnoscience
ethnocentric
ethnological
ethnographer
ethnographic
etheostomine
enhypostasia
enhypostatic
exheredation
etheromaniac
enharmonical
etherisation
etherization
echo-sounding
exhaustively

12 f□a□e

episcopalian
episcopalism
evisceration
epideictical
epidemically
epidemiology
evidentially
evil-favoured
epithalamion
epithalamium
epitheliomas
epiphenomena
epididymides
evil-mindedly
episodically
editorialise
editorialize
epirrhematic
epigrammatic
emigrational
evil-speaking
epistolarian
epistolatory
evil-tempered
epistemology
Epicureanism
epicuticular
exiguousness
epicycloidal
eclectically
eulogistical
elliptically
ellipsograph
enlargedness
eunuchoidism
eco-labelling
exorbitantly
esoterically
exoterically
epoch-marking
exophthalmia
exophthalmic
exophthalmos
exophthalmus
exothermally
exobiologist
emotionalism
emotionality
emollescence
enormousness
econometrics
econometrist
ecologically
economically
exospherical
egoistically
emolumentary
elocutionary
evolutionary
elocutionist
evolutionism
evolutionist
emphatically
Euphausiacea
Euphausiidae
explantation
expectations
expectorator
expediential
expeditation
empressement
expressional
expressively
expressivity
espagnolette
explicitness
empoisonment
expansionary
expansionism
expansionist
expromission
euphoniously
expropriable
expropriator
exprobration
exprobratory
exprobrative
exploitation
exploitative
experiential
experimental
experimented
experimenter
empyreumatic
empassionate
expositional
expositively
expostulator
expatriation
Euro-American
ebracteolate
Eurocentrism
Eurocurrency
earnest-penny
earnest-money
earthshaking
earth-created
earthquaking
ear-splitting
Euro-passport
Eurosterling
eurythermous
euroterminal
early-warning
eurhythmical
early-closing
enswathement
ecstatically
eisteddfodau
eisteddfodic
exsufflicate
exsufflation
East-Indiaman
essentialism
essentialist
essentiality
eosinophilia
eosinophilic
exsanguinate
exsanguinity
exsanguinous
enstructured
ex-serviceman
enshrinement
extravagance
extravagancy
extravaganza
extramarital
euthanasiast
entrancement
extraversion
extrasensory
extraversive
extra-regular
extraneously
estrangement
extraditable
extralimital
entraînement
extrapolator
extra-special
extra-uterine
extramundane
extranuclear
entrenchment
entrepreneur
entreatingly
entomologise
entomologist
entomologize
Entomostraca
extensimeter
extensionist
entanglement
extensometer
extinguisher
extroversion
extroversive
entoplastral
entoplastron
ectypography
ectoparasite
entertaining
exteroceptor
enterchaunge
exterminable
exterminator
extortionary
extortionist
extortionate
entertissued
enthrallment
Enteromorpha
enthronement
enteropneust
enteroptosis
enterprising
enthusiastic
educationist
edulcoration
exulceration
edulcorative
equidistance
ecumenically
equilibrator
ebullioscope
ebullioscopy
equalisation
equalitarian
equalization
equimultiple
equanimously
equipollence
equipollency
equiprobable
equiparation
equestrienne
Equisetaceae
equisetiform
equatorially
eruptiveness
elucubration
equivocality
equivocation
equivocatory
equivalently
enviableness
envisagement
eavesdropped
eavesdropper
Edwardianism
erythematous
erythropenia
erythroblast
erythromycin
etymological
etymologicon
etymologicum
elytrigerous
Egyptologist
enzymologist
flamboyantly
Franco-German
△francophobia
fraudulently
Frauendienst
flame-thrower
flabelliform
flagelliform
flabellation
flagellation
flagellatory
frame-breaker
flame-grilled

frangibility
flashforward
featheriness
feather-brain
feather-grass
flagitiously
feasibleness
frankalmoign
frankincense
Frankenstein
fearlessness
flammability
flammiferous
flammulation
flannelboard
flannelgraph
fragrantness
fractography
fractionally
fractionator
flatteringly
flatterously
febrifacient
fibrillation
fibrinolysin
fabulousness
Febronianism
fibroblastic
facsimileing
factitiously
fictitiously
factionalism
factionalist
fictionalise
fictionalize
factiousness
fecklessness
focalisation
facilitation
facilitative
focalization
fiddle-faddle
fiddlesticks
fiddle-string
French-polish
field-spaniel
fiendishness
frenetically
Freightliner®
freightliner
freight-train
freshmanship
flesh-pottery
fuel-injected
flexibleness
freakishness
feeble-minded
feeing-market
free-standing
free-swimming
free-selector
free-thinking
frequentness
freewheeling
freeze-drying
freezing-down
fugie-warrant
figurability
figure-caster
figuratively
fugitiveness
Fehmgerichte
fricasseeing
Fringillidae
faith-healing
faithfulness
flickeringly
friendliness
fairnitickle
fairnytickle
frigorificos
flippantness
faint-hearted
flint-hearted
flint-knapper
frictionless
flitter-mouse
faintishness
fallaciously
filibusterer
full-bottomed
felicitation
felicitously
false-hearted
filter-passer
fuliginosity
fuliginously
folliculated
falcon-gentil
falcon-gentle
fellow-member
filtrability
feldspathoid
full-throated
fully-fledged
fume-cupboard
feminineness
feminisation
feminization
fantasticoes
fantasticism
fantasticate
finger-and-toe
fence-mending
fennel-flower
fingerlickin'
fancifulness
fent-merchant
funambulator
financialist
fenestration
functionally
functionless
foot-and-mouth
flocculation
foot-dragging
frondiferous
floodlighted
frondescence
flower-delice
flower-de-luce
flower-deluce
flower-garden
foolish-witty
frolicsomely
floriculture
footplateman
footplatemen
footslogging
front-bencher
frontiersman
front-of-house
front-loading
frontispiece
fore-and-after
formaldehyde
forsakenness
fore-admonish
forebodement
forebodingly
foreclosable
forecarriage
faradisation
faradization
force-feeding
fortepianist
forbearingly
forset-seller
forgettingly
fermentation
fermentative
forcefulness
fire-fighting
foregoneness
forthrightly
farthingland
farthingless
forth-putting
fornicatress
forbiddingly
forcing-house
forcibleness
foreign-built
ferricyanide
forejudgment
foreknowable
farm-labourer
formlessness
Foraminifera
forensically
furunculosis
ferrocyanide
fireproofing
forequarters
forestalling
forestalment
foreseeingly
foresightful
first-nighter
foretokening
furfuraceous
ferrugineous
fortuitously
forswornness
fire-watching
fast-and-loose
foster-father
foster-mother
foster-parent
fosset-seller
foster-sister
fish-hatchery
fissilingual
fastidiously
fustillirian
fissirostral
fissicostate
fasciculated
fashiousness
fish-salesman
fish-strainer
father-figure
fatherliness
father-lasher
fathers-in-law
fatigue-party
fatigue-dress
futilitarian
futtock-plate
futurologist
fluidisation
foundational
foundationer
fluidization
frumentation
fourfoldness
Fourieristic
fluorochrome
fluorocarbon
fluoridation
fluorimetric
fluorometric
fluorination
fluorescence
fluoroscopic
fruit-machine
fourteenthly
fructiferous
fault-finding
fountain-head
fountainless
fruitfulness
fructivorous
feverishness

favouredness
fowling-piece
fixed-penalty
fly-on-the-wall
guaranteeing
goat-antelope
glaucomatous
glaucescence
guardianship
glandiferous
glandulously
Grandisonian
grapeseed-oil
grave-clothes
gracefulness
gratefulness
gravel-voiced
Gradgrindery
graphologist
graphophobia
graminaceous
glaciologist
gravitometer
gladiatorial
gladiatorian
graciousness
gratifyingly
grallatorial
gram-molecule
grammaticise
grammaticism
grammaticize
grammatology
Gram-negative
gramophonist
granodiorite
grapple-plant
graspingness
Gram-positive
glassyheaded
grass-widower
glass-blowing
gladsomeness
glass-cutting
geanticlinal
giant-killing
giant's-kettle
granulations
gradualistic
granulocytic
graduateship
gratuitously
Gibraltarian
gobbledegook
gobbledygook
gibble-gabble
gubernacular
gubernaculum
god-forgotten
gregarianism
gregariously

greengrocery
greenishness
guerrilleros
great-bellied
great-hearted
guest-chamber
gigantically
gigantomachy
glioblastoma
guild-brother
griseofulvin
Geiger-Müller
guilefulness
gainlessness
glimmeringly
glisteringly
glitteringly
grievousness
galvanically
galvanoscope
galvanometer
galvanometry
galactagogue
galactometer
galactosemia
gallinaceous
galligaskins
gallows-maker
gallsickness
gall-sickness
goldsmithery
gelatination
Gemeinschaft
gambling-hell
gem-engraving
gymnosophist
gemmological
gamopetalous
gamophyllous
gamesmanship
gamesomeness
gamosepalous
genealogical
geniculately
geniculation
gynodioecism
gonadotropic
gonadotropin
gander-mooner
gynaecomasty
gynaecologic
gynaecocracy
genuflection
gingivectomy
gentilitious
Gentianaceae
generatrices
generousness
gangsterland
gang-there-out
genethliacal

genethliacon
genotypicity
Gondwanaland
geomagnetism
geomagnetist
good-breeding
gaol-delivery
geotechnical
geodetically
goose-pimples
grotesquerie
geometrician
globetrotter
geocentrical
geotectonics
geochemistry
good-humoured
geophysicist
globigerinae
growing-pains
growing-point
Grolieresque
gloriousness
glockenspiel
ghoulishness
ground-beetle
ground-cuckoo
ground-feeder
groundlessly
ground-pigeon
geognostical
geologically
gnomonically
geopolitical
gnotobiology
gnotobiotics
group-captain
geographical
glossography
glossologist
grossularite
glossarially
geostrategic
good-tempered
geodynamical
geosynclinal
gormandising
gormandizing
Germanically
Germanophobe
Germanophile
geriatrician
garret-master
garter-stitch
gorgeousness
gyromagnetic
gerontophobe
gerontophile
gerontocracy
Gastarbeiter
Gesneriaceae

gas-permeable
gasification
gas-discharge
gossip-monger
gesticulator
gossip-writer
Gesellschaft
gasometrical
gas-condenser
Gastrocnemii
gastrulation
gastronomist
gastropodous
gastrosopher
gathering-cry
get-rich-quick
glucoprotein
glue-sniffing
gruesomeness
gluttonously
governmental
governorship
glyphography
glycogenesis
glycogenetic
glycoprotein
glyptography
gazetteerish
heat-apoplexy
heaven-fallen
heaven-gifted
heavenliness
heater-shield
heathenishly
heather-bleat
headmistress
headquarters
headshrinker
heart-failure
heartwarming
heart-rending
heart-service
heart-to-heart
heartbreaker
heart-strings
heartburning
heavy-hearted
Hebraistical
Hobbesianism
hybridisable
hybridizable
hubble-bubble
habilitation
hebdomadally
Hobson-Jobson
hobgoblinism
hebephreniac
haberdashery
hibernaculum
Hibernically
Hibernianism

12 h□b□t

habitualness
habitability
hebetudinous
habit-forming
habitational
huckle-backed
hectographic
hydrargyrism
hydraulicked
Hudibrastics
hedge-warbler
hedge-parsley
hedge-sparrow
hedge-creeper
hodge-pudding
hedge-mustard
hydropathist
hydrogenated
hydrogeology
Hydromedusae
hydromedusan
hydrophobous
hydrophilite
hydrophilous
hydrophanous
hydrochloric
hydrothermal
hydrotherapy
hydrophytous
hydrozincite
hydrokinetic
hydrobiology
hydrofluoric
hydroelastic
hydrological
hydrographer
hydrographic
hydrotropism
hydrostatics
hydroquinone
hydrodynamic
hydatidiform
hierarchical
haematemesis
haematoblast
haematolysis
haematoxylin
Haematoxylon
heedlessness
haemophiliac
hierophantic
hieroglyphic
hierological
haemorrhagic
hierogrammat
haemorrhoids
hierographer
hierographic
hyetographic
heeby-jeebies
high-coloured
hygienically
hugger-mugger
high-fidelity
highfaluting
high-five-sign
higgle-haggle
highly-strung
hygrophilous
hygrochastic
hagiological
hagiographer
hagiographic
hygrographic
hog-constable
high-pressure
high-priestly
high-reaching
high-seasoned
high-stepping
high-spirited
high-sounding
highty-tighty
high-velocity
heir-apparent
heir-by-custom
hairdressing
hairlessness
hair-splitter
hair's-breadth
hallan-shaker
Helianthemum
holidaymaker
halter-necked
Hildebrandic
Heldentenöre
Heldentenors
hellgrammite
half-integral
helplessness
half-measures
hylomorphism
half-marathon
half-mourning
heliolatrous
heliocentric
hollow-ground
heliophilous
heliochromic
heliotherapy
heliographer
heliographic
heliotropism
heliogravure
holoplankton
holophrastic
half-seas-over
holistically
half-timbered
hallucinogen
hallucinosis
Hollywoodise
Hollywoodize
hemp-agrimony
Hemichordata
home-crofting
homochromous
hemodialysis
hammer-headed
homoeomorphy
homoeomerous
homoeopathic
homoeostasis
homoeostatic
humification
homoiomerous
homologumena
homologation
homelessness
hemimorphism
homomorphism
hemimorphite
homomorphous
homonymously
hymenopteran
humanisation
humanitarian
humanization
homeopathist
homeothermal
homeothermic
homeomorphic
hymnographer
homopolarity
home-produced
hemiparasite
Hemerocallis
hemorrhoidal
hamarthritis
hamartiology
humorousness
homesickness
homesteading
hemispheroid
home-straight
homothallism
Humpty-dumpty
homothermous
hematogenous
hematologist
hendecagonal
hunger-bitten
hunter-killer
henceforward
hunger-strike
hindforemost
hunting-field
hunting-knife
hunting-lodge
hunting-sword
handkerchief
Hindoostanee
hindquarters
hundred-gated
huntsmanship
handsomeness
henotheistic
honeycombing
honey-tongued
honey-mouthed
honey-buzzard
hoodman-blind
hood-moulding
heortologist
hypocritical
hypochlorite
hypochlorous
hypochondria
hypocoristic
happenstance
hypoeutectic
hypognathism
hypognathous
hypogastrium
hypoglycemia
hypoglycemic
hip-hip-hooray
hip-hip-hurrah
hopelessness
hypnogenesis
hypnogenetic
hippocentaur
hippophagist
hippophagous
hypnotherapy
hypnotically
hypnotisable
hypnotizable
hippopotamic
hippopotamus
hippocrepian
haptotropism
Hippocratise
Hippocratism
Hippocratize
hypoplastron
hypophrygian
hypersarcoma
hyperdactyly
Hypericaceae
hyperacidity
hyperidrosis
hypersensual
hypertension
hypertensive
hyperthermal
hyperthermia
hyperalgesia
hyperalgesic
hyperplastic
hyperbolical
hypercorrect
hypertrophic
hypersthenia

Words marked △ may be spelled also with a capital letter

12 i□d□e

hypersthenic
hyperpyretic
hyperpyrexia
hypostatical
hyposulphate
hyposulphite
hypothalamic
hypothalamus
hepaticology
hypothecator
hypothetical
hephthemimer
hepatologist
hepatomegaly
hypotrochoid
hepatisation
hepatization
happy-go-lucky
Heracleitean
hereditament
hereditarian
hereditarily
horsemanship
horrendously
horse-dealing
hermeneutics
hermeneutist
horseshoeing
hermetically
horse-knacker
herpetofauna
herpetologic
horse-courser
horse-breaker
horse-trading
horse-trainer
harness-maker
harvest-feast
harvest-field
harvest-goose
harvest-louse
harlequinade
hard-featured
hard-favoured
heroicalness
hereinbefore
horrifically
horribleness
heroi-comical
horticulture
horrifyingly
heraldically
hurdle-racing
harmlessness
hurtlessness
horometrical
harmonically
harmoniphone
harmonichord
harmoniumist
harmoniously
harmonometer
harmonograph
harbour-light
horror-struck
hire-purchase
hard-standing
hard-sectored
heresy-hunter
heritability
horizontally
Hispanically
hispaniolise
hispaniolize
hysterectomy
hysterically
hysteromania
hysterogenic
hospital-ship
Histiophorus
histogenesis
histogenetic
histochemist
historically
historiology
histological
histrionical
hesitatingly
hatchet-faced
hatelessness
heteroblasty
heterocyclic
heteroclitic
Heterocontae
heterocercal
heterochrony
heterodactyl
heteroecious
heterogamous
heterogonous
heterokontan
heterologous
heteromorphy
heteromerous
heteronomous
△**heteroousian**
heteroplasia
heteroplasty
heterophylly
Heterosomata
heterosexual
heterosexism
heterosexist
heterostyled
heterothally
heterotactic
heterotrophy
heterauxesis
heterozygote
heterozygous
hound's-tongue
house-warming
housekeeping
housey-housey
house-sitting
house-to-house
house-breaker
house-trained
house-steward
house-husband
house-hunting
haussmannise
haussmannize
hexachloride
hexadactylic
hexafluoride
hexametrical
inadaptation
irascibility
inaccurately
inaccessible
inaccessibly
inaudibility
image-worship
inadequately
inauguration
inauguratory
inadmissible
inadmissibly
inappeasable
inapplicable
inapplicably
inappellable
inappositely
inabstinence
inauspicious
inarticulacy
inarticulate
inartificial
inactivation
iracundulous
inadvertence
inadvertency
imbibitional
incharitable
incrassation
incrassative
incoagulable
incidentally
increasingly
incognisance
incognizance
incognisable
incognizable
incogitative
incoherently
inclinometer
incalescence
incalculable
incalculably
incomparable
incomparably
incompatible
incompatibly
incompetence
incompetency
incompliance
incompletely
incompletion
incomunicado
incommodious
incommutable
incommutably
incomputable
incunabulist
incandescent
inconvenient
inconversant
inconsequent
incontinence
incontinency
inconcinnity
inconcinnous
incendiarism
inconsistent
incontiguous
inconclusion
inconclusive
inconsonance
inconsolable
inconsolably
incineration
inconstantly
inconsumable
inconsumably
inco-ordinate
incrossbreed
incapability
incapacitate
incurability
incorrigible
incorrigibly
incoronation
incorporated
incorporator
incorporeity
incorrodible
incorrosible
incorruption
incorruptive
incestuously
incisiveness
incatenation
incautiously
incrustation
incivilities
indebtedness
indeclinable
indeclinably
indoctrinate
indecorously
indecisively
indicatively
Indo-European

indefeasible
indefeasibly
indefectible
indifference
indifferency
indefensible
indefensibly
indefinitely
indigenously
Indo-Germanic
indigestible
indigestibly
indehiscence
indoleacetic
indelibility
indelicately
indemnifying
indomethacin
induplicated
△**independence**
△independency
indirectness
indistinctly
indiscipline
indissoluble
indissolubly
industrially
indiscreetly
indiscretely
indiscretion
indisputable
indisputably
indetectable
indetectible
indetermined
individually
indivertible
index-linking
ineradicable
ineradicably
inelasticity
inexactitude
inescutcheon
inexecutable
ineffability
ineffaceable
ineffaceably
inefficiency
inexhaustive
idealisation
idealization
ineloquently
inexpectancy
inexpedience
inexpediency
inexpressive
inexpugnable
inexpugnably
inexplicable
inexplicably
inexpansible
inexpungible
inexperience
inexpertness
identifiable
identifiably
inextricable
inextricably
inextensible
ideationally
inextirpable
inequipotent
inflationary
inflationism
inflationist
inflammation
inflammatory
infraorbital
infibulation
infectiously
inflectional
infrequently
infringement
infelicitous
infiltration
infiltrative
infanticidal
infundibular
infundibulum
infiniteness
infinitively
informidable
infusibility
infotainment
ingravescent
ingratiating
ingratiation
ingemination
ingloriously
Ishmaelitish
inhabitation
ichthyolatry
ichthyophagy
ichthyolitic
ichthyocolla
ichnographic
inharmonical
inharmonious
inhospitable
inhospitably
imitableness
iridescently
inimicalness
inimicitious
idiorhythmic
idiosyncrasy
idiothermous
iniquitously
injudicially
injunctively
inking-roller
ill-naturedly
illiberalise
illiberality
illiberalize
ill-beseeming
illegibility
illogicality
illegitimacy
illegitimate
illuminating
illumination
illuminative
Islamisation
illimitation
Islamization
illaqueation
ill-treatment
illustration
illustratory
illustrative
illusiveness
illiterately
immeasurable
immeasurably
immaculately
immoderately
immoderation
immemorially
immunologist
immunisation
immensurable
immunization
immersionism
immersionist
immiseration
immutability
immethodical
immaterially
immatureness
immovability
innominables
ionophoresis
ignitability
ignitibility
innutritious
isolationism
isolationist
idolatrously
inosculation
inoccupation
inordinately
inordination
inoperculate
isoperimeter
isoperimetry
inobediently
isocheimenal
isochromatic
isochronally
isothermally
isobilateral
ironing-board
isodiametric
isodimorphic
iconomachist
iconophilism
iconophilist
iconoclastic
isoprenaline
isotretinoin
inobservance
inobservable
isostemonous
ivory-towered
implantation
impedimental
impierceable
impregnation
impressively
implicitness
imprisonable
imprisonment
impoliteness
imponderable
impenetrable
impenetrably
impenitently
improvisator
improvidence
impropriator
impermanence
impermanency
imperfection
imperceptive
imperfective
impertinence
impertinency
impercipient
impartiality
impersistent
imperviously
imperforated
imperforable
impersonally
impersonator
imperishable
imperishably
imperatorial
imperatively
imposthumate
impassionate
imposingness
imputability
impetiginous
imputatively
inquisitress
irrealisable
irrealizable
irrebuttable
irreconciled
irreciprocal
irredeemable
irredeemably

Words marked △ may be spelled also with a capital letter

irrefragable
irrefragably
irreflection
irreflective
irreformable
irreformably
irregularity
irrigational
irrelatively
irrelevantly
irremediable
irremediably
irremissible
irrepealable
irrepealably
irrepairable
irreprovable
irreprovably
irrespective
irrespirable
irresolvable
irresolvably
irresolutely
irresolution
irresponsive
irresistance
irresistible
irresistibly
irritability
irrationally
irreversible
irreversibly
irreverently
installation
instauration
insubjection
inspectingly
inspectional
inspectorial
inspectorate
insufferable
insufferably
insufficient
insufflation
instillation
inspissation
insalubrious
insolubilise
insolubility
insolubilize
insalivation
insemination
insomnolence
insanitation
inseparables
insurability
instructible
instructions
instructress
insurrection
instrumental
instrumented
insusceptive
insouciantly
intracardiac
intracranial
intrapreneur
intransigent
intransitive
intrauterine
intramundane
intrenchment
intuitionism
intuitionist
intrinsicate
intriguingly
intellectual
intellection
intellective
intelligence
intelligible
intelligibly
intolerantly
intoleration
intimidation
intimidatory
intemperance
intempestive
intemerately
intumescence
intensifying
inteneration
introversion
introversive
introjection
introvertive
iatrochemist
intromission
intromissive
intromittent
intromitting
introducible
introduction
introductory
introductive
intercalated
interjacency
interlaminar
internalised
internalized
intermaxilla
interoceanic
inter-science
interoceptor
intermeddler
interbedding
interference
intermediacy
intervenient
intermediary
intermediate
interpellant
interpellate
interregnums
interfemoral
intercession
intercessory
interfertile
internetting
interception
interjection
intersection
intervention
intertexture
interceptive
interservice
interchanger
interchapter
interminable
interminably
interkinesis
interlingual
interdigital
intercipient
intertissued
intermission
intermissive
intermittent
interdiction
interdictory
intermixture
interdictive
interpleader
interglacial
interfluence
interclusion
interpleural
interpolater
interrogatee
intervocalic
interpolable
interrogable
interpolator
interrogator
interfoliate
intercolline
intercommune
interconnect
intermontane
interlobular
interlocutor
interconvert
interspinous
interspersal
interspatial
interwreathe
intertraffic
interorbital
interfrontal
intercropped
interfretted
interpretess
interpretate
interpretive
interwrought
interestedly
interosseous
interstadial
interstellar
interstitial
internuncial
internuncios
intermundane
intercurrent
interruption
interruptive
intertwining
intussuscept
intrusionist
intoxicating
intoxication
invigilation
invagination
invigoration
inveiglement
invalidation
invulnerable
invulnerably
involutional
invultuation
Invertebrata
invertebrate
invisibility
investigable
investigator
invitingness
inveterately
Jack-a-lantern
△**jack-in-office**
△**jack-in-the-box**
Jack-o'-lantern
Jacquard-loom
judgement-day
judgment-debt
judgment-hall
judgment-seat
Jeffersonian
Juglandaceae
jail-delivery
joint-tenancy
jointing-rule
jointer-plane
jumping-mouse
Jimmy-o'Goblin
jimmy-o'goblin
jingle-jangle
Jenny-spinner
jeopardously
japonaiserie
juristically
jurisdiction
jurisdictive
jurisconsult
jurisprudent

Words marked △ may be spelled also with a capital letter

12 j□r□y

jerry-builder
jesting-stock
Jesuitically
justificator
△justicialism
jet-propelled
journalistic
journey-bated
juvenileness
juvenilities
juvenescence
kicking-strap
kickie-wickie
kicksy-wicksy
kidney-potato
kiddiewinkie
knee-breeches
knee-crooking
keeking-glass
Kremlinology
kleptocratic
knee-trembler
kleptomaniac
knife-and-fork
knife-grinder
knight-errant
knightliness
knick-knacket
klipspringer
kakistocracy
kill-courtesy
kaleidoscope
kaleidophone
kilfud-yoking
Kimmeridgian
kindergarten
kinaesthesia
kinaesthesis
kinaesthetic
kinesiatrics
kinesipathic
king's-cushion
knowableness
knocking-shop
knowledgable
knowledgably
kerb-crawling
kirschwasser
kurchatovium
kerb-merchant
karyokinesis
keratogenous
keratoplasty
keraunograph
kissing-crust
katharevousa
katharometer
katzenjammer
kitchen-range
kitchen-wench
kitchen-knave
kitchen-stuff
kettle-holder
kettlestitch
knuckle-bones
knuckle-joint
Keynesianism
leap-frogging
leather-cloth
leather-knife
leathergoods
loathfulness
leasing-maker
leaping-house
learnability
loan-sharking
libidinosity
libidinously
labanotation
loblolly-tree
liberticidal
liberalistic
labyrinthian
labyrinthine
labour-saving
lickety-split
lucifer-match
lock-hospital
lucklessness
localisation
localization
locomobility
locum-tenency
locomotivity
lycanthropic
licentiously
lactoprotein
Lycopodiales
Lycopodineae
lachrymosely
lachrymosity
lachrymation
lachrymatory
lick-trencher
ledger-tackle
lady's-thistle
lady's-slipper
lady's-cushion
lieutenantry
life-and-death
left-handedly
life-interest
lifelessness
left-of-centre
lugubriously
legacy-hunter
logodaedalic
logodaedalus
loggerheaded
ligniperdous
logging-stone
Liguliflorae
liguliflora
legalisation
legalization
lagomorphous
Legionnaire's
Legionnaires'
legislatress
light-hearted
lightning-rod
lightning-bug
legitimately
legitimation
laisser-faire
laisser-aller
laissez-faire
laissez-aller
leiotrichous
lake-dwelling
lukewarmness
lallapalooza
lollapalooza
Lillibullero
Lilliburlero
lampadedromy
lampadomancy
limacologist
lumber-jacket
lymphography
lymphangitis
lomentaceous
Lamentations
luminiferous
Lymantriidae
luminescence
luminousness
limnophilous
limnological
lumbriciform
lamprophyric
lamp-standard
lamb's-lettuce
Lancasterian
long-breathed
long-drawn-out
long-distance
line-engraver
lanceolately
lantern-jawed
lantern-wheel
land-grabbing
landgraviate
luncheonette
luncheon-meat
longicaudate
lenticellate
longipennate
landing-field
landing-place
landing-speed
landing-craft
landing-stage
landing-strip
lenticularly
longitudinal
land-lubberly
long-standing
lonesomeness
longshoreman
land-surveyor
Languedocian
languageless
languorously
linguistical
languishment
land-yachting
leopard's-bane
loose-jointed
Laodiceanism
looking-glass
lapidicolous
lepidomelane
lapidescence
lappered-milk
leptosomatic
loquaciously
liquefacient
liquefaction
liqueur-glass
large-hearted
lurking-place
larking-glass
laryngectomy
laryngoscope
laryngoscopy
laryngophony
laryngospasm
liriodendron
lord-superior
lorry-hopping
lost-and-found
lust-breathed
listenership
lese-humanity
lasciviously
lusciousness
listlessness
laticiferous
letter-writer
letter-weight
Little-endian
litholatrous
lithophagous
lithophilous
lithological
lithotomical
lithospheric
lithospermum
lithographer
lithotripter
lithographic
lithotriptic
lithotriptor

12 m□n□d

lithotritise
lithotritist
lithotritize
liturgically
liturgiology
literalistic
literariness
latirostrate
laterisation
laterization
lath-splitter
latitudinous
laudableness
launching-pad
laundry-woman
leukemogenic
laureateship
louver-window
lounge-lizard
leucoplastid
leukoplastid
leucopoiesis
leukopoiesis
leucocytosis
leukocytosis
louvre-window
live-feathers
level-pegging
levelling-rod
lovelornness
levorotatory
Liverpudlian
low-watermark
Low-Churchman
Low-Churchism
low-thoughted
lower-bracket
law-stationer
lexicography
lexicologist
loxodromical
luxullianite
laxativeness
lizard-hipped
meat-offering
mean-spirited
meat-salesman
measuring-rod
mealy-mouthed
mobilisation
mobilization
mechanically
machairodont
mechatronics
macaberesque
mycodomatium
mickey-taking
mock-heroical
machinations
machine-ruler
Mechitharist
Macmillanite
machicolated
mucilaginous
microbalance
microwavable
microhabitat
microcapsule
macrodactyly
microscopist
macrocephaly
microcephaly
microseismic
microphysics
microfilaria
microcircuit
micropipette
microbiology
macrobiotics
microclimate
microanatomy
Macropodidae
micrological
microtomical
microcopying
microprinted
microgranite
micrographer
micrographic
microgravity
micro-brewery
macropterous
micropterous
microsurgeon
microsurgery
microtubular
mycoplasmata
mucopurulent
muckspreader
Machtpolitik
mediatorship
mediaevalism
mediaevalist
medicamental
madreporitic
Midwesterner
modification
modificatory
modificative
mid-Victorian
modulability
muddleheaded
middle-income
middleweight
△**mademoiselle**
maderisation
moderateness
maderization
meditatively
muddy-mettled
meeting-house
mnemotechnic
migrationist
magnetically
magnetisable
magnetizable
magnetometer
magnetometry
magnetograph
magnifically
magnificence
magniloquent
megalomaniac
megalosaurus
Muggletonian
Magnoliaceae
magistrature
mail-carriage
maidenliness
maintainable
moistureless
majolicaware
major-general
majestically
majesticness
make-and-break
milk-and-water
molybdenosis
malacologist
molecularity
Malacostraca
melodramatic
malleability
millefeuille
millesimally
miller's-thumb
malversation
mulligatawny
multilateral
multivalence
multivalency
multifaceted
multivariate
multifarious
multivarious
multitasking
multicauline
multipartite
multiscience
multiseriate
multiversity
multicentral
multicentric
multidentate
multiseptate
melting-point
milking-stool
multichannel
multivitamin
multilingual
multicipital
millisievert
multipliable
multiplicand
multiplicate
multiplicity
mellifluence
multiflorous
multinominal
multifoliate
multiformity
multivoltine
multicostate
multilobular
multilocular
multiloquent
multiloquous
multipresent
multigravida
multisulcate
multinuclear
multipurpose
mill-mountain
melanochroic
melancholiac
melanotropin
mallophagous
malformation
malcontented
milk-porridge
malapertness
maltreatment
mill-sixpence
militaristic
molluscicide
Molluscoidea
multungulate
malnutrition
malevolently
mammalogical
mammee-sapota
mammillarias
momentaneous
miminy-piminy
memorability
memorisation
memorization
mendaciously
mind-altering
mind-boggling
man-about-town
Manicheanism
monocultural
many-coloured
mono-compound
minicomputer
municipalise
municipalism
municipality
municipalize
monochromasy
monochromist
monochromate
monodramatic

12 m□n□d

monodelphian
monadelphous
monodelphous
mine-detector
monkey-engine
monkey-flower
monkey-hammer
monkey-jacket
mannerliness
monkey-puzzle
Montessorian
monkey-tricks
manoeuvrable
monkey-wrench
mangel-wurzel
man-of-war's-man
munificently
minification
manufactural
manufacturer
monofilament
manifoldness
manifestable
manifestible
manifestness
monographist
monogenistic
monticellite
mansion-house
mandibulated
mini-lacrosse
mingle-mangle
monolinguist
mindlessness
manslaughter
monomaniacal
monumentally
monomorphous
minimisation
manometrical
monometallic
mini-motorway
minimization
Munro-bagging
monopodially
monopolistic
manipulation
manipulatory
manipulative
monopetalous
monophyodont
monophyletic
△monophysitic
monarchistic
mineralogise
mineralogist
mineralogize
monts-de-piété
meniscectomy
monastically
monostichous
monosyllabic
monosyllable
monosepalous
monostrophic
ministration
ministrative
monothalamic
△monotheletic
monotheistic
monotonously
munitionette
monitorially
monetisation
monstruosity
menstruation
monetization
moneylending
money-changer
money-spinner
money-grubber
moonlighting
myographical
moon-stricken
maquiladoras
marcatissimo
mordaciously
mercantilism
mercantilist
miraculously
meridionally
marker-beacon
market-garden
Marseillaise
merveilleuse
marvellously
market-making
Myrmecophaga
myrmecophile
myrmecophily
myrmecologic
morigeration
marsh-harrier
morphography
morphallaxis
morphologist
merchantable
merchandiser
merchandizer
merchantlike
march-treason
morphotropic
mirthfulness
marginal-unit
morris-dancer
Marsileaceae
marline-spike
marriageable
marriage-bone
morning-after
morning-glory
marriage-ring
Martini-Henry
morbilliform
Marcionitism
mercifulness
marble-cutter
marbled-white
moralisation
morality-play
moralization
marimbaphone
myringoscope
Mariolatrous
Maryolatrous
marconigraph
Marcobrunner
marrow-squash
mirror-writer
marksmanship
meristematic
meritocratic
Marattiaceae
meretricious
mercurialise
mercurialism
mercurialist
mercurialize
merrythought
merry-go-round
massaranduba
miscalculate
mismatchment
△mesoamerican
mistakenness
message-stick
mystagogical
musicianship
musicologist
mesocephalic
miseducation
misadventure
misadvisedly
master-at-arms
masseranduba
misbehaviour
misleadingly
miscegenator
misdemeanant
misdemeanour
Messeigneurs
mysteriously
misbelieving
misreckoning
masterliness
miscellanist
muster-master
misrepresent
master-switch
mastersinger
masterstroke
misfeaturing
missel-thrush
misventurous
misogynistic
moschiferous
mischallenge
mischanceful
mysticalness
misdirection
misdiagnosis
missionarise
missionarize
Mastigophora
misplacement
misallotment
mistle-thrush
mesomorphous
misinterpret
misanthropic
misanthropos
misinformant
misknowledge
mosbolletjie
misformation
misconstruct
miscontented
mass-produced
misapprehend
mistreatment
mistranslate
mispronounce
mistressless
mistrustless
mistress-ship
mesothelioma
mesothoracic
moss-trooping
misstatement
masturbation
masturbatory
mispunctuate
misjudgement
missummation
misquotation
mitrailleuse
methanometer
methaqualone
meticulously
mitochondria
metachronism
mathematical
mathematised
mathematized
Mitteleuropa
Mittel-Europa
motherfucker
motherliness
mother-liquor
motley-minded
matter-of-fact
mothers-in-law
metagnathous
metagalactic

Words marked △ may be spelled also with a capital letter

mutagenicity
matriclinous
matriarchate
matriculator
metallically
metalanguage
metallogenic
metallophone
metalworking
metaleptical
metallurgist
metempirical
metamorphism
metamorphist
metamorphose
mutinousness
mutton-cutlet
mythogenesis
mutton-headed
meteorically
methodically
meteoritical
matroclinous
metrological
metropolitan
mythological
metropolises
mythologiser
mythologizer
meteorologic
meteorograph
metrorrhagia
mythographer
methotrexate
metaphorical
metaphrastic
metoposcopic
metapsychics
metaphysical
materialness
motor-scooter
mithridatise
mithridatism
mithridatize
motor-bicycle
motor-tractor
motorisation
maturational
motorcycling
motorcyclist
motorization
mutessarifat
metasilicate
metasomatism
metathetical
metathoracic
mutationally
motivational
mound-builder
mouse-milking
mouse-buttock
mouth-filling
mouth-to-mouth
mouth-breeder
mourning-band
mourning-dove
mourning-ring
mournfulness
mousquetaire
moustache-cup
mountain-high
mountainside
mountenaunce
moveableness
movelessness
mixobarbaric
mixed-ability
myxedematous
mixter-maxter
mixtie-maxtie
May-September
mizzen-course
muzzle-loader
mezzo-relievo
mezzo-rilievo
mezzo-soprano
△neandertaler
nubbing-cheat
nebulisation
nobilitation
nebulousness
nebulization
noctambulism
noctambulist
nucleophilic
nickel-silver
nyctitropism
noctilucence
neck-moulding
nectocalyces
necrophagous
necrophiliac
necrophilism
necrophilous
necrophorous
necrological
necropolises
necrographer
nychthemeral
nychthemeron
nicotinamide
nidification
niddle-noddle
noematically
needlessness
neglectingly
neglectfully
negrophilism
negrophilist
negotiatress
night-fishery
nightclubber
nightclothes
nugatoriness
night-brawler
night-crawler
negativeness
negativistic
nail-head-spar
neighborhood
neighborless
neighbouring
nail-scissors
name-dropping
nomadisation
nomadization
numberlessly
Nymphaeaceae
nympholeptic
nymphomaniac
nimble-footed
namelessness
nimble-witted
nominalistic
nomenclature
nomenklatura
nomenclative
niminy-piminy
nominatively
numinousness
nimbostratus
numerability
numerologist
numerousness
nematocystic
nomothetical
nematologist
Nematomorpha
namby-pambies
non-objective
non-absorbent
non-scheduled
non-admission
non-addictive
Nintendoitis
non-technical
non-residence
non-resistant
non-resisting
non-effective
non-efficient
nonagenarian
non-Christian
nonchalantly
non-fictional
non-alignment
non-flammable
non-alcoholic
non-flowering
non-intrusion
non-combatant
non-conductor
non-communion
non-committal
non-complying
non-poisonous
nanoplankton
non-breakable
non-essential
none-so-pretty
nineteenthly
non-attention
non-nucleated
non-Euclidean
non-automatic
non-custodial
non-executive
non-existence
Neo-Darwinian
Neo-Darwinism
Neo-Darwinist
Neoceratodus
neoterically
Neohellenism
neorealistic
Neo-Christian
neoclassical
Neoplatonism
Neoplatonist
neologically
neonomianism
nephelometer
nephelometry
Naples-yellow
nipple-shield
Nepenthaceae
nephological
nephrologist
nephroptosis
noradrenalin
nerve-racking
nurse-tending
north-eastern
north-seeking
north-western
Northumbrian
north-country
northernmost
nursing-chair
narcissistic
narco-therapy
narcotically
narrow-minded
nosebleeding
nesting-place
nasolacrymal
nasalisation
nasalization
Nestorianism
nostological
nose-painting
Notodontidae
Netherlander
Netherlandic

Words marked △ may be spelled also with a capital letter

12 n□t□f

notification
nothingarian
nutritionist
nutritiously
Notonectidae
nitromethane
nitrobenzene
nitrophilous
nitro-aniline
nitroso-group
nitrotoluene
naturalistic
naturopathic
notoungulate
noteworthily
neurasthenia
neurasthenic
nauseatingly
nauseousness
nourishingly
neuropathist
neuroscience
neurogenesis
neuropeptide
neurotically
neurobiology
neurofibroma
neuroanatomy
neurological
neurohormone
neurotrophic
neuropterans
neuropterist
neuropterous
neurosurgeon
neurosurgery
neutralistic
neurypnology
navigability
navigational
novelisation
novelization
never-failing
nevertheless
neverthemore
newfangledly
new-fashioned
newsmagazine
Newfoundland
newspaperman
newspaperdom
newspaperism
Nazification
orange-flower
ovariotomist
oratorically
oracularness
ombrophobous
ombrophilous
once-accented
orchard-house
orchard-grass
occidentally
orchestrator
orchidaceous
orchidectomy
orchilla-weed
orchidomania
oscilloscope
oscillograph
oecumenicism
obcompressed
occupational
oncornavirus
Oncorhynchus
occasionally
old-fashioned
ordinariness
odd-come-short
obdurateness
over-and-under
operatically
opera-glasses
over-cannoped
overcanopied
overcrowding
overcapacity
overexertion
overexposure
overestimate
overfullness
overfineness
overfondness
overfinished
overflourish
overinclined
one-sidedness
obedientiary
overkindness
overlordship
overmultiply
overniceness
oceanography
oceanologist
one-and-thirty
one-upmanship
overprepared
overpressure
overpopulate
overpersuade
Oreopithecus
overpowering
overreaction
oneirocritic
oneiromancer
overripeness
overrashness
oversubtlety
overschutcht
oversimplify
overstrained
overscutched
overwhelming
over-weighted
office-bearer
office-holder
office-hunter
olfactometry
olfactronics
office-seeker
offscourings
off-reckoning
off-the-record
oughly-headed
organ-gallery
organography
organoleptic
organ-grinder
organiser-bag
organisation
organ-builder
organizer-bag
organization
ophthalmitis
ophiolatrous
ochroleucous
ochlophobiac
ophiophagous
ophiophilist
Ophioglossum
ophiological
ophiomorphic
otherworldly
oligarchical
orichalceous
opinionately
opinionative
orienteering
oniroscopist
oligotrophic
oeils-de-boeuf
omissiveness
opisthotonic
opisthodomos
opisthotonos
opisthograph
object-finder
object-lesson
obligingness
obligational
obligatorily
oblanceolate
obliteration
obliterative
obliviscence
obmutescence
obnubilation
ornamentally
omnipresence
omnipotently
omnisciently
Ornithischia
ornithomancy
ornithogalum
ornithoscopy
ornithophily
ornithomorph
onomatopoeia
onomatopoeic
otosclerosis
ororotundity
orographical
odontography
odontologist
odontomatous
odontophoral
odontophoran
odontophobia
Odontophorus
orphan-asylum
omphalomancy
oppressively
oophorectomy
opposability
oppositeness
oppositional
ourang-outang
obreptitious
obstetrician
ossification
obsolescence
obsoleteness
oesophagitis
obsequiously
Observantine
obstropalous
obstropulous
obstreperate
obstreperous
obsessionist
obscurantism
obscurantist
outward-bound
outlandishly
outrageously
outfangthief
optoacoustic
outmanoeuvre
oath-breaking
out-pensioner
out-of-the-body
octogenarian
outplacement
optimisation
optometrical
optimization
ostentatious
osteomalacia
osteosarcoma
orthopaedics
orthopaedist
osteopathist
orthogenesis
orthogenetic

Words marked △ may be spelled also with a capital letter

osteogenesis
osteogenetic
orthopedical
osteodermous
orthorhombic
orthosilicic
osteoplastic
orthognathic
orthoboracic
orthogonally
orthotonesis
osteological
osteoporosis
orthocousins
orthodontics
orthodontist
orthodromics
orthographer
orthographic
orthotropism
orthotropous
orthopteroid
orthopterist
orthopterous
outspreading
octopetalous
otter-hunting
obtuse-angled
octastichous
octostichous
octosyllabic
octosyllable
octosepalous
octastrophic
outstretched
oxy-acetylene
platanaceous
placableness
Phalaenopsis
pease-bannock
peace-warrant
praseodymium
planetesimal
peace-keeping
plate-leather
peace-officer
prayerlessly
pease-blossom
prayer-monger
Phanerogamae
Phanerogamia
phanerogamic
phanerophyte
peace-breaker
planet-struck
placentiform
placentology
placentation
pease-pudding
peacefulness
peach-yellows
peach-blossom
playing-field
praxinoscope
planispheric
plagiotropic
pearl-tapioca
phallocratic
pearl-sheller
pearl-fishing
pearl-fishery
Pralltriller
pearl-essence
pharmacology
pharmaceutic
psammophytic
plasmosomata
plain-dealing
plain-hearted
phaenogamous
plainclothes
phaeomelanin
Phaeophyceae
platonically
peacock-stone
plano-concave
plano-conical
phagocytical
phagocytosis
plausibility
praiseworthy
practicalism
practicalist
practicality
Platt-Deutsch
plasteriness
plasterboard
plasterstone
phantasmally
phantasmical
practitioner
pharyngology
pharyngotomy
public-domain
public-school
pebble-powder
peccadilloes
piccadilloes
pickerel-weed
pocket-pistol
pacification
pacificatory
pectinaceous
packing-paper
packing-sheet
packing-press
picrocarmine
pictorically
pectoriloquy
pictographic
picornavirus
Pecksniffian
Picturephone®
picture-house
picture-frame
pachycarpous
Pachydermata
pachydermous
pedicellaria
pediculation
podoconiosis
pudding-faced
pudding-plate
pudding-stone
pedal-clavier
pedal-pushers
pedantically
pedantocracy
pedunculated
paddock-stool
pre-cancerous
preparedness
prelatically
prevaricator
premaxillary
precariously
prevailingly
prefabricate
prelapsarian
precautional
poetastering
presbyacusis
presbycousis
presbyterial
△presbyterian
presbyterate
pre-eclampsia
preachership
prescription
prescriptive
piercingness
preoccupancy
pseudocyesis
pseudography
pseudo-Gothic
pseudomonads
pseudomartyr
pseudonymity
pseudonymous
pseudopodium
pseudorandom
pretenceless
pretendingly
predetermine
precedential
preferential
preselection
premeditated
preheminence
predesignate
pretermitted
prenegotiate
prehensility
precessional
pre-tensioned
prehensorial
premenstrual
presentially
presentiment
predestinate
preceptorial
prefectorial
presentation
presentative
preventative
preventively
prerequisite
preservation
preservatory
preservative
phengophobia
prechristian
pre-Christian
psephologist
plebiscitary
presidential
predigestion
predilection
presidentess
precipitance
precipitancy
precipitator
precisianism
precisianist
precisionist
pteridomania
plenipotence
plenipotency
Pteridophyta
pteridophyte
pteridosperm
predisposing
Plesiosaurus
prehistorian
predictively
preciousness
previousness
prefloration
preclassical
peerlessness
preclusively
pneumococcus
preamplifier
pre-eminently
pleomorphism
pleomorphous
pre-embryonic
pneumaticity
pneumatology
pneumothorax
pleonastical
prerogatived
pterosaurian
pterodactyle

Words marked △ may be spelled also with a capital letter

12 p□e□o

paedobaptism
paedobaptist
preponderant
preponderate
precondition
phenomenally
paedogenesis
paedogenetic
paedophiliac
pleiochasium
predominance
predominancy
prefoliation
precociously
preformation
preformative
precognition
precognitive
precognizant
paedological
phenological
poenological
paedomorphic
paedodontics
pleiotropism
preconscious
preconstruct
Premonstrant
prepossessed
plecopterous
preposterous
pre-Columbian
phenotypical
preoperative
preordinance
Pleuronectes
pleurisy-root
Pre-Dravidian
pre-establish
plessimetric
pleasantness
pleasingness
pleasantries
pheasant's-eye
pressure-cook
pleasureless
pleasure-pain
preassurance
prenticeship
'prenticeship
Plectognathi
prestigiator
prestriction
pretty-pretty
prestissimos
pretty-spoken
prepubescent
prejudgement
presumptuous
pregustation
pre-existence
phenylalanin
puftaloonies
pufftaloonas
pugnaciously
pigmentation
pugilistical
pigeon-flying
pigeon's-blood
privat-docent
privat-dozent
△philadelphus
privateering
philanthrope
philanthropy
psilanthropy
prince-bishop
princeliness
△principality
prizefighter
pridefulness
price-cutting
priggishness
philhellenic
philharmonic
poikilotherm
primigravida
Philistinise
△philistinism
Philistinize
phillumenist
painlessness
primordially
△philodendron
primogenital
primogenitor
philosophess
philosophise
philosophism
philosophist
philosophize
philological
poison-sumach
priestliness
priest-ridden
print-through
pointillisme
pointilliste
printing-head
point-to-point
primulaceous
pejoratively
Polyadelphia
Palladianism
palpableness
polyanthuses
phlebotomise
phlebotomist
phlebotomize
policy-holder
police-manure
pelican's-foot
polycythemia
paludicolous
pile-dwelling
polydemonism
paludamentum
pollen-basket
palaeobotany
polyembryony
palaeography
polyethylene
pulverisable
pulverizable
palaebiology
Palaeolithic
palaestrical
pulverulence
palification
phlegmatical
phlegmagogic
phlegmagogue
Polygalaceae
polygamously
Polygonaceae
polyglottous
polyhistoric
polling-booth
pulvilliform
pillion-rider
polyisoprene
polymyositis
polymorphism
polymorphous
palingeneses
palingenesia
palingenesis
palynologist
palindromist
Polonisation
polyneuritis
Polonization
paleoecology
poliorcetics
paleobiology
paleoclimate
paleobotanic
paleozoology
paleographer
paleographic
paleocrystic
paleontology
polypharmacy
polypetalous
polyphyodont
polyphyletic
polyphyllous
polarography
polarimetric
polarisation
polyrhythmic
polarization
polysyllabic
polysyllable
polysiloxane
polysyndeton
polysepalous
pilot-balloon
palatability
politicaster
palette-knife
polytheistic
polytonality
polyurethane
pollutedness
pellucidness
pollyannaish
pollyannaism
pamperedness
pumpernickel
pompholygous
pandanaceous
pentadactyle
pentadactyly
pentateuchal
pentahedrons
pinealectomy
△pandaemonium
pentagonally
pentapolitan
pantaloonery
pentacrinoid
paniculately
pantechnicon
panhellenion
Panhellenism
Panhellenist
panhellenium
Pan-Germanism
Pentecostals
pen-feathered
pin-feathered
panaesthesia
pansexualism
pansexualist
panification
Punchinellos
panchromatic
pinchcommons
panpharmacon
Panchatantra
pontifically
pantisocracy
pencil-sketch
pinniewinkle
penalisation
penalization
Penang-lawyer
pantophagist
pantophagous
pantomimical
pantographer
pantographic
panspermatic

Words marked △ may be spelled also with a capital letter

12 p□r□e

pancreatitis
panarthritis
Panathenaean
pony-trekking
punctulation
penitentials
penitentiary
puncturation
penny-wedding
penny-whistle
propagandise
propagandism
propagandist
propagandize
propaedeutic
procathedral
probationary
pro-marketeer
protagonists
phonasthenia
protactinium
proscription
proscriptive
proud-hearted
proletariate
proverbially
Provence-rose
pro-celebrity
proteoglycan
promethazine
phonemically
phonetically
progenitress
procellarian
prolegomenon
propenseness
processional
professional
processioner
professorial
professoress
professorate
protectingly
protestingly
projectional
prosectorial
protectorial
progesterone
△**protectorate**
protestation
protectively
projectivity
prosecutable
procès-verbal
proselytiser
proselytizer
proofreading
proof-correct
plough-jogger
ploughwright
prophylactic
prothalamion
prothalamium
prothonotary
propheticism
provincially
profiteering
providential
prolifically
proficiently
provisionary
prolificness
prodigiosity
propitiation
propitiatory
propitiative
prodigiously
propitiously
profitlessly
proditorious
promissorily
profit-taking
protistology
profligately
problematics
proclamation
proclamatory
proglottides
pro-and-conned
phonocamptic
phonotactics
proboscidean
proboscidian
protonematal
photogeology
photorealism
photosetting
prolongation
photophilous
photochemist
photochromic
prototherian
phototherapy
pronominally
prosodically
photokinesis
photobiology
photofission
proto-history
photoglyphic
protoplasmal
photoelastic
protoplasmic
protoplastic
probouleutic
pronouncedly
profoundness
prosopopeial
phonological
protozoology
protocolling
prosopopoeia
protomorphic
photomontage
photovoltaic
photocopying
photospheric
photo-process
phonographer
photographer
phonographic
photographic
prototrophic
phototropism
photogravure
proconsulate
photo-etching
proportional
proportioned
Photostatted
phonotypical
prototypical
phosphaturia
prospectuses
phosphoresce
phospholipid
prosperously
protractedly
protractible
progradation
proprietress
programmatic
programmable
protreptical
protrusively
poor-spirited
prostacyclin
proctologist
prostanthera
proctorially
prostitution
promuscidate
protuberance
promulgation
propugnation
productional
productively
productivity
prosyllogism
progymnasium
pepper-caster
pepper-castor
pupilability
papuliferous
Papilionidae
populousness
Papanicolaou
paper-marbler
paper-washing
papyrologist
paper-stainer
papistically
Papaveraceae
pergameneous
permanganate
phreatophyte
permaculture
paraboloidal
paracyanogen
perichaetial
pyroclastics
perichaetium
pyrochemical
paroccipital
parochialise
parochialism
parochiality
parochialize
para-compound
paracentesis
pericynthion
perichoresis
pericarditis
parachronism
peradventure
paradigmatic
parade-ground
paradisiacal
paradise-fish
paradisaical
Paradiseidae
paradoxidian
paradoxology
paradoxurine
porcelainise
porcelainous
porcelainize
permeability
part-exchange
perseverance
perseverator
paraenetical
pyro-electric
purse-sharing
paroemiology
porcellanise
porcellanite
porcellanous
porcellanize
porte-cochère
porte-bonheur
porte-monnaie
perpetration
perverseness
paraesthesia
purse-strings
perceptional
perfectation
portentously
perfectively
perceptivity
perpetualism
perpetualist
perpetuality

Words marked △ may be spelled also with a capital letter

12 p□r□e

perpetuation
perfervidity
△**purification**
purificatory
purificative
paragnathism
paragraphist
paragnathous
peregrinator
paraglossate
pyrognostics
parchmentise
parchmentize
pertinacious
pervicacious
partisanship
parking-place
participable
participator
partitionist
perfidiously
perniciously
parsimonious
Parkinsonism
permissively
persistently
persistingly
permittivity
particularly
perviousness
parallelwise
pyroligneous
purblindness
paralanguage
paralipomena
perilousness
perplexingly
parsley-piert
pyramidology
paramagnetic
paramilitary
pyromaniacal
portmanteaus
portmanteaux
paramorphism
pyromorphite
perimorphous
parametrical
perimetrical
pyrometrical
peremptorily
perambulator
parenterally
Pirandellian
paranthelion
paranthropus
parenthesise
parenthesize
perenniality
phrontistery
phrenologise
phrenologist
phrenologize
paronomastic
perinephrium
perineuritis
purpose-built
purposefully
periodically
perfoliation
personifying
performative
periodontics
periodontist
pornographer
pornographic
periostracum
pernoctation
parrot-wrasse
perionychium
perspicacity
perspectival
peripherical
paraphimosis
parapophyses
parapophysis
paraphrastic
periphrastic
perspiration
perspiratory
parapsychism
pyrophyllite
paraquadrate
portrait-bust
porismatical
parascending
peristeronic
parasphenoid
puristically
parisyllabic
pyrosulphate
periselenium
phrasemonger
parasyntheta
peristomatic
perispomenon
phraseologic
phraseograph
peristrephic
parasiticide
parasitaemia
parasitology
paratactical
pyrotechnics
pyrotechnist
pyritiferous
pyritohedral
pyritohedron
peritrichous
pyrithiamine
pyrotartaric
pyrotartrate
percutaneous
perturbation
perturbatory
perturbative
perfusionist
persulphuric
percussional
perquisition
percussively
persuasively
periwig-pated
peroxidation
party-capital
party-verdict
passage-money
passableness
Pestalozzian
post-doctoral
post-diluvial
post-diluvian
passe-partout
passemeasure
posteriority
Pasteurellae
Pasteurellas
possessional
possessioned
possessively
postgraduate
posthumously
post-hypnotic
pestilential
posliminious
passibleness
postillation
passionately
Passion-music
pisciculture
postliminary
postliminous
postmeridian
postmistress
pestological
postprandial
postponement
postposition
postpositive
post-synching
Post-Tertiary
positiveness
positivistic
posture-maker
pasque-flower
passy-measure
Puseyistical
pitiableness
pot-walloping
potichomania
putrefacient
putrefaction
putrefactive
patience-dock
pathetically
pattern-maker
pattern-wheel
pitter-patter
pitch-and-toss
pitcher-plant
Patripassian
petrifaction
petrifactive
putting-cleek
putting-green
putting-stone
patrilineage
patriclinous
pettifogging
pettifoggery
patriarchism
patriarchate
patristicism
pottle-bodied
patellectomy
petaliferous
pitilessness
potamologist
potentiality
potentiation
pathogenesis
pathogenetic
petrogenesis
petrogenetic
petrophysics
patroclinous
petroglyphic
pathological
petrological
petrodollars
pythonomorph
petrographer
petrographic
pityrosporum
plumbiferous
plumbaginous
plumber-block
pound-foolish
prudentially
pluriseriate
pruning-knife
pluriliteral
pluviometric
plurilocular
pauciloquent
plummer-block
plum-porridge
Prussianiser
Prussianizer
plumulaceous
pavilion-roof
powdering-tub
powder-skiing
power-sharing

powerlifting
power-dressed
powerfulness
psychiatrist
psychoactive
psychobabble
psychography
psychologise
psychologism
psychologist
psychologize
psychometric
psychonomics
psychrometer
psychrometry
psychopathic
psychosocial
psychosexual
psychoticism
psychotropic
physiocratic
physiography
physiognomic
physiologist
phyllotactic
phytonadione
phycoxanthin
phylogenesis
phylogenetic
phytogenesis
phytogenetic
phytobenthos
phytophagous
phycological
phytological
phytohormone
phytographer
phytographic
Phycomycetes
pay-as-you-earn
puzzle-headed
puzzle-monkey
Quaker-colour
quaking-grass
qualificator
quasi-stellar
quacksalving
qualmishness
quadriennial
quadriennium
Quadragesima
quadrumanous
quarrymaster
quadrinomial
quadrangular
quadraplegia
quadraplegic
quadriplegia
quadriplegic
quadraphonic
quadrophonic
quadrivalent
quaestionary
quaestorship
quantifiable
quartz-iodine
quattrocento
quarter-sawed
quarter-final
quarter-miler
quarterlight
quartern-loaf
quarter-blood
quarter-plate
quarter-bound
quarter-pound
quarter-round
quarter-horse
quarterstaff
quarter-guard
quartz-schist
quantisation
quantitative
quantitively
quantivalent
quantization
quaquaversal
quenchlessly
queue-jumping
querimonious
queen-meadows
queen-regnant
Queenslander
queen-dowager
queen-consort
queer-bashing
questionable
questionably
questionless
question-mark
quidditative
quick-scented
quick-selling
quick-sighted
quicksilvery
quill-feather
quill-driving
quixotically
quinquenniad
quinquennial
quinquennium
quintessence
quizzicality
quotableness
readableness
readaptation
rhabdosphere
reach-me-downs
readjustment
reallocation
readmittance
reannexation
reappearance
rhamphotheca
reassignment
reassemblage
reassumption
road-surveyor
reassuringly
reabsorption
reassessment
reattachment
roasting-jack
re-alteration
reactiveness
reactivation
ready-moneyed
ruby-coloured
rabbeting-saw
rubbing-stone
rabbinically
rabbit-sucker
rabbit-warren
rebelliously
ribble-rabble
rabble-rouser
ribonuclease
robustiously
ruby-throated
ricochetting
rock-climbing
racketeering
racket-ground
Rochelle-salt
racket-tailed
recreational
recognisance
recognizance
recognisable
recognisably
recognizable
recognizably
rachischisis
receivership
rocking-chair
rocking-horse
rocking-stone
recriminator
receiving-set
rectirostral
recollection
recollective
recalcitrant
recalcitrate
recalescence
recklessness
recommitment
recommission
recomforture
racemisation
racemization
reconveyance
raconteuring
reconsecrate
reconversion
reconcilable
reconcilably
reconnoitrer
reconstitute
raccoon-berry
receptacular
receptaculum
receptionist
reciprocally
reciprocator
recuperation
recuperatory
recuperative
recapitalise
recapitulate
recapitalize
recordership
record-player
record-sleeve
rock-scorpion
reciting-note
recrudescent
reducibility
radicicolous
reductionism
reductionist
ridiculously
redecoration
radicivorous
radiesthesia
redefinition
rodomontader
redemptioner
Redemptorist
redintegrate
riding-master
riding-school
radiophonics
radiophonist
radio-therapy
radio-thorium
radiomimetic
radiobiology
radioelement
radiological
radiographer
radiographic
radio-isotope
radionuclide
redeployment
rediscoverer
redistribute
redoublement
re-embodiment
reefer-jacket
re-engagement
re-enlistment
rheometrical
rheumatology

12 r□e□m

rheumatismal
rhetorically
reed-pheasant
roebuck-berry
reflationary
refractorily
refractivity
rifleman-bird
refreshments
refreshingly
refreshfully
rifle-grenade
reflectogram
reflectingly
reflectively
reflectivity
refrigerator
raffle-ticket
refoundation
regressively
regressivity
raggle-taggle
regeneration
regeneratory
regenerative
regardlessly
rigorousness
registration
right-and-left
right-to-lifer
rags-to-riches
rightfulness
rehabilitate
reimbursable
reimbattell'd
reiteratedly
Rhinegravine
Rhipidoptera
rhizocarpous
rhizogenetic
Rhizocephala
rhinocerical
rhinoceroses
rhinocerotes
rhinocerotic
rhizophagous
rhizophilous
rhinoplastic
rhinological
rhinorrhagia
rhinorrhoeal
reimpression
reimposition
reinstalment
reinspection
rail-splitter
reinvigorate
reinvestment
rejectamenta
rejectionist
rejoneadores
rejuvenation
reliableness
rollerblader
roller-hockey
roller-skater
rallentandos
religionless
rolling-stock
relentlessly
relationally
relationless
relationship
relativeness
relativistic
relativities
relativitist
remedilessly
ramification
remainder-man
rumble-tumble
rememberable
rememberably
remembrancer
remembrances
romantically
remineralise
remineralize
remuneration
remuneratory
remunerative
reminiscence
Romanisation
remonstrance
remonstrator
ruminatingly
ruminatively
Romanization
Ramapithecus
remorsefully
Rembrandtish
Rembrandtism
rumpti-iddity
rambunctious
removability
ring-armature
ring-compound
ring-dropping
ring-dotterel
rangefinding
ringed-plover
renversement
rendezvoused
rendezvouses
run-of-the-mill
röntgenogram
röntgenology
renegotiable
running-board
renunciation
renunciatory
renunciative
ranunculuses
ring-streaked
renounceable
renouncement
rhopaloceral
rhombohedral
rhombohedron
reoccupation
reordination
rooming-house
rooflessness
rhododendron
Rhodophyceae
rhodomontade
replantation
rope-drilling
reprehension
reprehensory
reprehensive
representant
replevisable
repressively
repagination
ripple-marked
reproachable
reproachless
reprocessing
reprographer
reprographic
reproducible
reproduction
reproductive
reparability
repercussion
repercussive
repossession
repatriation
repetitional
repetitively
reputatively
reregulation
ruralisation
ruralization
restauration
restaurateur
rush-bottomed
rose-coloured
rosy-coloured
rust-coloured
residentiary
residentship
respectfully
respectively
rosy-fingered
resignedness
rescheduling
resting-place
resting-spore
resting-stage
Rosminianism
respirometer
resolvedness
resplendence
resplendency
restlessness
resoluteness
△resolutioner
resumptively
resiniferous
resonance-box
respondentia
Russocentric
Russophobist
Russophilism
Russophilist
responseless
responsorial
responsively
resupination
resipiscence
resipiscency
restrictedly
reservedness
△resurrection
resurrective
restrainable
restrainedly
△risorgimento
resuscitable
resuscitator
resistlessly
resettlement
resourceless
resoundingly
rushy-fringed
retractility
retractation
retractively
reticulately
reticulation
retrenchment
ratification
ratchet-wheel
retainership
retrievement
rattle-headed
ruthlessness
retentionist
retrocession
retroversion
retrocessive
retrojection
retrophiliac
retromingent
retrofitting
retroflected
retroflexion
retropulsion
retropulsive
retiringness
rotor-station
rhumb-sailing

Words marked △ may be spelled also with a capital letter

roundaboutly
round-mouthed
rough-perfect
rough-grained
rough-wrought
reunionistic
revocability
revictualled
revalidation
revulsionary
revelational
revolutional
revolutioner
revengefully
ravenousness
reverberator
river-terrace
reversionary
revisitation
revivability
revivalistic
revivescence
revivescency
reviviscence
reviviscency
Rhynchonella
Rhynchophora
rhythmically
rhythmometer
rhythmopoeia
rhytidectomy
razzle-dazzle
Scarabaeidae
scarabaeuses
shamateurism
stalactiform
scabbardless
starchedness
standpattism
scandalously
standing-room
Scandinavian
△standardbred
standardiser
standardizer
slanderously
stage-manager
shamefacedly
share-capital
scapegallows
scare-heading
stapedectomy
space-heating
statementing
scavengering
snake-charmer
shareholding
slaveholding
skateboarder
scapegoating
statesperson
sharecropper
slate-writing
shamefulness
snaffling-lay
span-farthing
snap-fastener
snaggleteeth
snaggletooth
slang-whanger
staggeringly
swaggeringly
swagger-stick
slaughterman
slaughterous
slash-and-burn
smash-and-grab
stakhanovism
stakhanovite
swashbuckler
shaving-brush
shaving-stick
scarificator
stabilisator
stabilizator
Stanislavski
statistician
spaciousness
sparking-plug
snack-counter
Stahlhelmist
small-clothes
snarling-iron
snarling-tool
smallholding
stablishment
stammeringly
stanniferous
scanning-disc
swainishness
shadow-boxing
scatophagous
seasoning-tub
scatological
sharpshooter
sharp-sighted
scalping-tuft
sharp-tongued
sharp-looking
sharp-pointed
sharp-toothed
scampishness
snappishness
stauroscopic
scabrousness
sparrow-grass
△star-spangled
snapshooting
slantingways
scatteringly
smatteringly
scattermouch
scatterbrain
shatter-brain
shatterproof
scapulimancy
scapulomancy
statuesquely
stalwartness
submaxillary
△sublapsarian
subfactorial
subhastation
subabdominal
subscribable
suboccipital
subscription
subscriptive
subeditorial
subfeudation
subfeudatory
subreference
subcelestial
submergement
subdelirious
subterjacent
sabre-toothed
subtemperate
subterranean
subvertebral
subfertility
subjectively
subjectivise
subjectivism
subjectivist
subjectivity
subjectivize
subsequently
subservience
subserviency
subaggregate
subthreshold
subdiaconate
sublineation
subliminally
subcivilised
subcivilized
subdivisible
subsidiarily
subsidiarity
subminiature
sublibrarian
submissively
subglacially
subalternant
subalternate
subalternity
soboliferous
Sabellianism
subumbrellar
subantarctic
subinfeudate
subinspector
subintroduce
subnormality
subcommunity
subcommittee
subconscious
subcontinent
subopercular
suboperculum
subapostolic
subtreasurer
subarachnoid
subarrhation
subordinancy
subprincipal
suberisation
subarcuation
suberization
substraction
substantival
substantiate
substitution
substitutive
substruction
substructure
subcutaneous
subauricular
subduplicate
subsultorily
sacramentary
saccadically
Socratically
sectarianise
sectarianism
sectarianize
sociableness
sick-building
sack-doudling
succedaneous
secretariate
successantly
successional
successfully
successively
saccharoidal
saccharinity
succinctness
sacrilegious
sectionalise
sectionalism
sectionalist
sectionalize
sickle-celled
secularistic
sickle-shaped
second-strike
second-to-none
sociometrist
sociobiology
sacroiliitis
sociological
sycophantise

12 s□c□p

sycophantish
sycophantize
sacerdotally
secessionism
secessionist
seclusionist
succussation
sodden-witted
saddlebacked
saddle-shaped
sedulousness
sudoriferous
siderophilic
sudoriparous
Steganopodes
steganograph
speechlessly
speechmaking
stercoranism
stercoranist
speedballing
speedskating
speedboating
Speedwriting®
stepdaughter
scene-painter
stereoacuity
stereochrome
stereochromy
scene-of-crime
stereography
scene-shifter
stereoisomer
speleologist
stereometric
stereopticon
stereophonic
stereoscopic
stereotactic
stereotropic
stereotyping
sledgehammer
shepherdling
shepherdless
stethoscopic
specifically
specialistic
speciousness
speckledness
specksioneer
specktioneer
speaking-tube
speakerphone
sneck-drawing
sneakishness
stelliferous
shellshocked
stealthiness
shealing-hill
sheeling-hill
sheiling-hill

Stellenbosch
steelworking
swell-mobsman
spermogonium
spermaphytic
spermophytic
spermatocele
spermatocyte
spermathecal
spermatogeny
spermatozoal
spermatozoan
spermatozoic
spermatozoid
spermatozoon
stern-wheeler
sternutation
sternutatory
sternutative
stegocarpous
stegosaurian
stegophilist
skeuomorphic
stenographer
scenographic
stenographic
sleepwalking
sheep-scoring
steeplechase
steeple-crown
sheepshearer
sweepingness
sleeping-suit
sheepishness
sheep-stealer
spear-thrower
spear-running
sneeshin-mull
sweet-scented
steatomatous
sweet-and-sour
spectroscope
spectroscopy
spectrometer
spectrometry
spectrograph
sweet-toothed
steatopygous
steatorrhoea
stertorously
sweetishness
spectatorial
sheath-winged
safe-breaking
safe-cracking
sufficiently
softly-softly
suffruticose
soft-sectored
segmentation
suggestively

significance
significancy
significator
sugar-refiner
sight-reading
sight-singing
sight-playing
sage-thrasher
sphragistics
sphacelation
Schneiderian
sphygmoscope
sphygmometer
sphygmophone
sphygmograph
sphairistike
scholastical
sphincterial
schindylesis
schindyletic
schoolboyish
school-divine
school-friend
schoolfellow
school-leaver
schoolmaster
school-taught
schorlaceous
sphericality
schismatical
schizocarpic
Schizaeaceae
schizogonous
schizomycete
schizopodous
schizophrene
schizophytic
schizothymia
schizothymic
scitamineous
suitableness
soixante-neuf
sailboarding
stilboestrol
shipbuilding
slip-carriage
swindle-sheet
spine-bashing
swine-keeping
spine-chiller
spider-legged
spire-steeple
spitefulness
stiff-hearted
spiegeleisen
swinging-boom
swinging-post
sniggeringly
stichometric
stichomythia
stichomythic

spiritedness
spiritlessly
spiritualise
spiritualism
△spiritualist
spirituality
spiritualize
spirituosity
stickability
stickler-like
slickensided
snicker-snack
shield-bearer
spiflication
still-peering
shield-maiden
shieling-hill
shilling-hill
shillingless
shield-shaped
shilly-shally
skillfulness
seismography
seismologist
seismometric
swimming-bell
swimming-bath
swimmingness
swimming-pond
swimming-pool
seismonastic
seismoscopic
skinny-dipper
scientifical
spinning-mill
seigniorality
seigniorship
skipping-rope
slipperiness
snippetiness
spinsterhood
spinstership
scissiparity
scissor-tooth
skirt-dancing
shirtwaister
skittle-alley
spittle-house
scintigraphy
scintillator
shirtsleeves
snifter-valve
skittishness
stipulaceous
spinulescent
swizzle-stick
self-analysis
salvage-corps
self-affected
self-adhesive
syllabically

Words marked △ may be spelled also with a capital letter

saltationism
saltationist
Salvationism
Salvationist
sulfadiazine
saleableness
saltatorious
self-anointed
self-applause
self-approval
self-assembly
self-absorbed
self-activity
self-advocacy
self-begotten
salubriously
self-betrayal
silicicolous
self-cleaning
self-creation
siliciferous
self-critical
salicylamide
self-coloured
self-contempt
self-consumed
solecistical
self-catering
solicitation
solicitously
self-deceived
self-deceiver
solidifiable
self-delusion
self-directed
self-director
self-disliked
self-destruct
self-distrust
self-devotion
silver-beater
self-exciting
self-endeared
self-electing
self-election
self-exertion
self-elective
self-effacing
silver-glance
self-evidence
self-existent
silver-plated
self-employed
salver-shaped
self-educated
silver-voiced
self-flattery
self-focusing
salification
solifluction
self-gracious

self-glorious
sulphonamide
sulphonation
self-hypnosis
sulphuretted
sulphureting
sulphuration
saltimbancos
self-identity
selling-price
salvifically
Salviniaceae
salpiglossis
self-interest
silviculture
sylviculture
self-involved
self-judgment
self-lighting
self-luminous
soliloquiser
soliloquizer
selflessness
salamandrian
salamandroid
salamandrine
self-murderer
selenography
solenoidally
splendidious
splendidness
selenologist
splenomegaly
solonisation
splenisation
solonization
splenization
salsolaceous
salmon-colour
self-occupied
self-ordained
salmon-fisher
saloon-keeper
self-prepared
self-pleasing
self-produced
self-portrait
saltpetreman
scleroderma
sclerodermic
self-rigorous
self-righting
self-reliance
sclerometric
sclerenchyma
solar-powered
self-reproach
sclerophylly
solarisation
self-reverent
solarization

self-standing
salesmanship
self-schooled
self-sameness
solitudinous
salutiferous
splotchiness
self-thinking
salutariness
solitariness
solstitially
salutational
salutatorian
salutatorily
self-violence
splay-mouthed
somnambulant
somnambulary
somnambulism
somnambulist
somnambulate
semi-Arianism
semi-annually
semi-attached
semicylinder
semicomatose
semicircular
semi-diameter
semideponent
semi-detached
symmetallism
Simmenthaler
summer-weight
semifinalist
semi-finished
semiglobular
sumphishness
somnifacient
semi-imbecile
sempiternity
somniloquise
somniloquism
somniloquist
somniloquize
semeiotician
simultaneity
simultaneous
simple-minded
semiliterate
simoniacally
seminiferous
semantically
somnolescent
semi-official
symbolically
symbololatry
semiological
semi-precious
semipalmated
Semi-Pelagian
semipellucid

semiparasite
Simarubaceae
Samaritanism
symptomatise
symptomatize
semi-tropical
somatopleure
somatostatin
Semitisation
somatotensic
somatotropic
somatotropin
Semitization
semi-water-gas
santalaceous
sensationism
sensationist
singableness
syntagmatite
syndactylism
syndactylous
sandblasting
synectically
synecologist
sansculottic
synecdochism
synadelphite
syngenesious
syndetically
sententially
synaesthesia
synaesthetic
synchroscope
synchronical
synchroniser
synchronizer
synchroflash
syntheticism
sentinelling
singing-hinny
sensibleness
sensitometer
single-acting
single-action
single-decker
single-figure
single-handed
single-minded
synclinorium
single-parent
single-seater
single-wicket
Sinanthropus
synantherous
synonymously
sun-and-planet
Syngnathidae
sensorimotor
sindonophany
synoptically
sinupalliate

12 s□n□r

synarthroses
synarthrosis
syncretistic
sonorousness
sinisterwise
sinusoidally
sinistrality
sinistrorsal
sinistrously
sanctifiable
sanctifiedly
senatorially
sanitisation
sanitization
sanguiferous
sensualistic
sanguinolent
sanguineness
sanguinarily
sensuousness
sanguivorous
sun-expelling
sand-yachting
sloganeering
sporangiolum
sporadically
stomatodaeum
snowboarding
shot-blasting
shopbreaking
slobbishness
snobbishness
slouch-hatted
stoechiology
stoichiology
slop-clothing
sword-bayonet
spondoolicks
sword-breaker
stonewalling
stonemasonry
storekeeping
slovenliness
spokespeople
spokesperson
stone-breaker
stonecutting
spongicolous
spongologist
snow-gatherer
smotheringly
smotheriness
slothfulness
scoring-board
storiologist
snow-in-summer
shockability
stocking-feet
stocking-foot
stockingless
shockingness
stock-in-trade
stocking-sole
slockdolager
stockjobbing
stockjobbery
stockbreeder
stockbroking
shoulder-high
spotlessness
stormfulness
scornfulness
scolopaceous
Scolopacidae
scolopendrid
sporogenesis
scopophiliac
sporophorous
snobographer
Scorpaenidae
snooperscope
sportability
smooth-browed
smooth-coated
sportscaster
short-termism
short-termist
stout-hearted
short-changer
short-circuit
short-sighted
smooth-leaved
scoptophilia
scoptophobia
sportsperson
Scottishness
smooth-spoken
short-staffed
sportfulness
sportiveness
sportswriter
storytelling
stony-hearted
supraciliary
supraorbital
supracrustal
supramundane
Septembriser
Septembrizer
Septemberish
septennially
sapientially
septentrions
septemvirate
sapphire-wing
septilateral
sophisticate
supplicating
supplication
supplicatory
supplemental
supplementer
sapindaceous
saponifiable
Sipunculacea
Siphonaptera
saprophagous
saprophytism
supposititious
Siphonophora
siphonophore
sophomorical
siphonostele
supercargoes
superpatriot
supermassive
supernacular
supernatural
supernaculum
separability
supersedence
superrefined
supervenient
superrealism
superrealist
superheroine
supersensual
supersession
supersensory
supervention
soporiferous
supercharger
superhighway
superficials
superciliary
supercilious
superglacial
supercluster
superplastic
supereminent
superimposed
superannuate
superposable
superconduct
superiorship
superpolymer
superspecies
superorganic
supererogant
supererogate
superordinal
superfrontal
supergravity
suppressedly
suppressible
superstratum
separateness
superstardom
superstition
superhumanly
supermundane
superhumeral
superluminal
supersubtile
superevident
superovulate
Septuagintal
septuagenary
Septuagesima
sequentially
sequestrable
sequestrator
sarsaparilla
surface-to-air
surface-craft
surpassingly
surfboarding
scrobiculate
strobiliform
scribblement
scribblingly
strobilation
strabismical
stroboscopic
sprachgefühl
sprechgesang
strychninism
sprechstimme
structurally
stridelegged
stridulantly
stridulation
stridulatory
Stradivarius
sorbefacient
sir-reverence
scrieveboard
streetkeeper
surveillance
surrealistic
sergeant-fish
sergeantship
serjeantship
surrejoinder
surveyorship
street-raking
serpent-eater
serpentiform
serpentinely
serpentining
serpentinise
serpentinite
serpentinous
serpentinize
serpent-stone
screenwriter
streetwalker
surefootedly
scraggedness
Strigiformes
stragglingly
strugglingly
sprightfully
serviceberry

servicewoman
straightaway
straightener
straightedge
straightness
straightways
straitjacket
servitorship
survivorship
strikingness
shrill-gorged
shrill-voiced
scrimshander
skrimshanker
scramblingly
stromatolite
spring-bladed
seronegative
spring-heeled
strontianite
springkeeper
spring-loaded
stranglehold
stranglement
strangle-weed
strong-minded
strengthener
strengthless
strangulated
strongylosis
sarcomatosis
sarcophagous
sardonically
sarcoplasmic
surmountable
surroundings
seriocomical
servocontrol
strophanthin
strophanthus
seraphically
strophiolate
Strepsiptera
scrupulosity
scrupulously
streptococci
streptosolen
streptomycin
seropurulent
scraperboard
seropositive
strepitation
scrophularia
scripturally
scriptwriter
surprisingly
seraskierate
stratocratic
straticulate
sprat-weather
stratigraphy
scratchingly
scratchiness
scratchbuild
scratchbuilt
scrutinising
scrutinously
scrutinizing
stratosphere
stratotanker
serotaxonomy
sarrusophone
shriving-time
straw-breadth
shrewishness
systematical
systematiser
systematizer
sisterliness
system-monger
sisters-in-law
suspensorial
suspensorium
suspensively
sustentation
sustentative
susceptivity
suspiciously
session-clerk
session-house
sesquialtera
sesquitertia
Sittlichkeit
satanophobia
satisfaction
satisfactory
site-specific
satisfyingly
squeaky-clean
slubberingly
slumberingly
stubbornness
slumberously
sound-carrier
studdingsail
studding-sail
shudderingly
saucepan-fish
stupefacient
stupefaction
stupefactive
stupendously
scutellation
shuffle-board
snuff-dipping
spurge-laurel
sluggishness
south-eastern
south-seeking
south-western
soughing-tile
Southcottian
southernmost
southernwood
spuriousness
studiousness
scullery-maid
soullessness
skullduggery
slumpflation
sculpturally
squirearchal
squirrel-cage
squirrel-tail
scurrilously
square-rigged
square-rigger
soul-stirring
spurtle-blade
shunt-winding
squattocracy
skutterudite
saunteringly
sputteringly
stutteringly
sluttishness
seventy-eight
Sivapithecus
sexcentenary
sexagenarian
sextodecimos
styracaceous
scyphistomae
scyphistomas
sky-tinctured
stylographic
tralaticious
tralatitious
thalassaemia
thalassaemic
tragelaphine
traceability
tradescantia
trapezohedra
tradespeople
travel-soiled
trabeculated
teachability
trachomatous
tracheoscopy
tracheophyte
tracheostomy
trachypterus
tragicalness
traditionary
traditionist
tragicomical
△thanksgiving
thank-you-ma'am
thankfulness
trail-blazing
thallophytic
thaumatogeny
thaumatology
traumatology
thaumaturgic
thaumaturgus
trainability
training-ship
train-spotter
trampolinist
teaspoonfuls
tranquilizer
tranquillise
tranquillity
tranquillize
tranquilness
translatable
transcalency
transparence
transparency
transpacific
transoceanic
transactions
transudation
transudatory
transferable
transcendent
transference
transgenesis
transferring
transversely
transversion
transleithan
transfection
transvestism
transvestist
transvestite
transshipper
transpirable
transhipment
transhipping
transmigrant
transmigrate
transmission
transmissive
transmitting
transpicuous
transiliency
transplanter
transaminase
transumption
transumptive
transposable
transforming
transformism
transformist
transmogrify
transmontane
transpontine
transporting
trapshooting
transportive
transuranian

12 t□a□s

transuranium
transgressor
transitional
transit-trade
transitorily
transitively
transitivity
transhumance
transfusable
transmutable
transmutably
transmundane
translucence
translucency
transfusible
transduction
tractibility
toasting-fork
toasting-iron
tractoration
traitorously
Traducianism
Traducianist
tobacco-heart
tobacco-pouch
table-rapping
table-turning
Tubuliflorae
tubulifloral
tabernacular
tuberiferous
Tyburn-ticket
Tyburn-tippet
tuberculated
tuberculosed
tuberculosis
ticket-holder
tacheometric
ticket-office
ticket-porter
ticket-writer
tactlessness
ticklishness
technobabble
technocratic
technicality
technicolour
technography
technologist
technomaniac
technophobia
technophobic
technostress
tectonically
tachyphrasia
tachygrapher
tachygraphic
tiddledywink
tsesarevitch
tsesarewitch
therapeutics

therapeutist
thematically
theocratical
trench-plough
trendsetting
tremendously
thereagainst
therethrough
thereinafter
teeter-totter
Twelfth-night
Theriodontia
Theriomorpha
theologaster
treelessness
thermocouple
Thermidorian
thermography
thermolabile
thermometric
thermophilic
Thesmophoria
theomorphism
thermostatic
thermostable
thermosphere
thermoscopic
thermosiphon
thermotactic
thermotropic
teeing-ground
theanthropic
theopneustic
Theopaschite
theopathetic
theophylline
theorematist
theoretician
theosophical
treasure-city
teensy-weensy
trestle-table
twenty-fourmo
theatrically
theatromania
theatrophone
twenty-twenty
Tagliacotian
tigerishness
togetherness
trilaterally
trinacriform
tridactylous
tripartition
thiobacillus
thiodiglycol
triadelphous
Third-Worlder
thirdborough
trimethylene
tricephalous

tribespeople
tricentenary
thief-catcher
thingummyjig
thingummybob
trigger-happy
triphthongal
trichologist
trichiniasis
trichinellae
trichinellas
trichromatic
trichophyton
thitherwards
triphosphate
trichotomise
trichotomous
trichotomize
Trichiuridae
triticalness
thick-sighted
thick-skulled
thick-skinned
thick-and-thin
trickishness
trickstering
triglyceride
triplication
triple-headed
triflingness
triple-tongue
triple-turned
Trismegistus
triumphalism
triumphalist
triumphantly
thigmotactic
thigmotropic
triangularly
trinomialism
trinomialist
trigonometer
trigonometry
tricorporate
trigrammatic
thiosulphate
toilsomeness
thirteenthly
twitteringly
twitter-boned
thirty-second
thirty-twomos
trifurcation
trituberculy
tribute-money
tripudiation
tricuspidate
thievishness
telecommuter
telaesthesia
telaesthetic

talkee-talkee
tilley-valley
telegraphese
telegraphist
toll-gatherer
talking-point
teleosaurian
tallow-candle
teleological
teleostomous
téléphérique
teleprompter
tolerability
telergically
talismanical
telesmatical
telesoftware
telescopical
teleservices
tellurometer
teleutospore
Telautograph®
televisually
televisional
tameableness
time-bewasted
timocratical
timed-release
temperalitie
time-exposure
time-honoured
timely-parted
tumbler-drier
tamelessness
timelessness
tumultuation
tumultuously
temporaneous
temporalness
tambourinist
Tamaricaceae
timbrologist
timbromaniac
timorousness
temptability
temptingness
tone-deafness
tender-hefted
tangentially
tonsilectomy
tangibleness
tonsillotomy
tintinnabula
tenuirostral
tennis-player
tennis-racket
tangle-netter
tangle-picker
tonelessness
tenant-at-will
tuning-hammer

tin-streaming
tongue-tacked
thoracoscope
thoracostomy
troublemaker
troubleshoot
trouble-mirth
trouble-world
trouble-house
trouble-state
thoughtfully
trocheameter
trophobiosis
trophobiotic
trophallaxis
trochanteric
tooth-drawing
trochosphere
trophotactic
trophotropic
two-sidedness
troglodytism
trolling-bait
troll-my-dames
trolley-table
trolley-wheel
troposcatter
△thoroughbred
thorough-bass
thoroughfare
thoroughness
tropophilous
tropological
tropospheric
troop-carrier
thousandfold
thousand-legs
thousand-year
tootsy-wootsy
tapsalteerie
type-cylinder
tappet-motion
typification
type-founding
typographist
topside-turvy
tapsieteerie
taphonomical
toploftiness
topsy-turvily
Threadneedle
terraforming
terebratulae
terebratulas
terebinthine
turacoverdin
threeha'porth
torrefaction
three-centred
tercel-gentle
three-wheeler

Torpedinidae
tercel-jerkin
turbellarian
three-pounder
Tardenoisian
three-monthly
three-pricker
torrentially
tormentingly
tercentenary
three-quarter
thriftlessly
torch-thistle
turbinacious
Torricellian
tergiversate
turning-lathe
turning-point
terrifically
turbidimeter
terribleness
turriculated
tirlie-wirlie
terrifyingly
turtle-necked
tirelessness
thrombolytic
taramasalata
tyrannically
tyrannicidal
Turcophilism
turbocharged
turbocharger
terror-struck
turnpike-road
terephthalic
throstle-cock
tiresomeness
teratologist
throttle-pipe
teratomatous
through-going
through-other
through-stane
through-stone
tortuousness
thrivingness
testamentary
tassel-gentle
tessellation
tastefulness
testificator
testiculated
taskmistress
tussock-grass
testosterone
testudineous
tissue-typing
tetradactyly
tetrarchical
tetrahedrons

tetrahedrite
tetrachordal
tetrachotomy
tetragonally
tetrapolitan
tetramorphic
tetrasporous
tetrastichal
tetrastichic
tetrapterous
Tetradynamia
tetracycline
tithe-proctor
totalisation
totalitarian
tittle-tattle
totalization
titaniferous
tetanisation
Titanosaurus
tetanization
tetrodotoxin
Thurberesque
thunder-sheet
thunder-plump
thunderflash
thundercloud
thunderingly
thunder-drive
thunder-stone
thunderstorm
thunderously
truce-breaker
truth-telling
touchingness
truthfulness
truck-farming
tauromachian
Teutonically
tautological
trumpet-major
trumpet-shell
trustfulness
town-planning
towardliness
toxicologist
toxicophobia
toxocariasis
tax-sheltered
taxing-master
tax-collector
toxophilitic
trypaflavine
trypanocidal
Thysanoptera
thyrotrophin
trysting-tree
unanalysable
unanalyzable
unanalytical
unaccredited

unascendable
unascendible
unacceptance
unacceptable
unaccustomed
unaffectedly
unaffiliated
unachievable
unamiability
unadmonished
unapologetic
uranographer
uranographic
unappealable
unappeasable
unapplausive
unapplicable
unapproached
unapparelled
unaspiringly
unappetising
unappetizing
unacquainted
unassociated
unanswerable
unanswerably
unassignable
unassailable
unauspicious
unassumingly
unassistedly
unattractive
unarticulate
unartificial
unattainable
unattainably
unauthorised
unauthorized
unartistlike
unadulterate
unadventrous
unadvertised
unbiasedness
umbrageously
unbecomingly
unbreachable
umbrella-bird
umbrella-tree
unbreathable
unbreathed-on
unbefriended
unblinkingly
umbilication
unbelievable
unbelievably
Umbelliferae
unbeneficial
urbanologist
urbanisation
urbanization
unbrokenness

12 u□b□t

unbetterable
unblushingly
unchaperoned
unchangeable
unchangeably
unchangingly
uncharitable
uncharitably
unchallenged
unclassified
unchasteness
uncreditable
uncheerfully
unchivalrous
uncritically
uncelebrated
uncultivated
uncultivable
uncalculated
uncomeatable
uncommercial
uncomeliness
uncomposable
uncompounded
uncommonness
unconcealing
unconcerning
unconsecrate
unconversant
unconsenting
unconfinable
unconvincing
unconsidered
unconfinedly
uncandidness
unconclusive
uncensorious
unconforming
unconformity
uncontrolled
unconstraint
unconfusedly
uncloistered
uncapsizable
uncoquettish
unchronicled
unchristened
ulcerousness
uncatalogued
uncounselled
unctuousness
uncovenanted
undeceivable
undocumented
undecomposed
undeliberate
undelectable
undelightful
undulatingly
undemocratic
undiminished
undependable
undiplomatic
undertakable
under-hangman
undergarment
underpayment
underpassion
underachieve
undertenancy
underdevelop
underperform
undersealing
undermeaning
underpeopled
underbearing
underletting
undersheriff
under-sheriff
underkingdom
underpinning
underskinker
underblanket
underclothed
underclothes
under-and-over
underpowered
under-workman
under-produce
underdressed
underwriting
underwrought
underdrawing
understratum
understaffed
underutilise
underutilize
understanded
understander
underfunding
undersurface
underbuilder
under-turnkey
underrunning
undercurrent
undispatched
undespairing
undismantled
undissembled
undiscerning
undesignedly
undischarged
undiscipline
undiscordant
undiscording
undiscovered
undissolving
undistracted
undisordered
undeservedly
undisturbing
undisputedly
undetectable
undetermined
undoubtingly
undivestedly
unelaborated
unembittered
unencumbered
unendangered
unendingness
uneventfully
user-friendly
urethroscope
urethroscopy
uneconomical
unexpectedly
unexpressive
unexpugnable
unemployable
unemployment
unexpurgated
unerringness
unextenuated
unenthralled
unfranchised
unflaggingly
unflattering
unfadingness
unfrequented
unfrequently
unfrightened
unfaithfully
unfriendlily
unfriendship
unfilterable
unfamiliarly
unformalised
unformalized
unforeboding
unforgivable
unformidable
unfertilised
unfertilized
unforeseeing
unformulated
unforewarned
unfossilised
unfossilized
unfastidious
unfittedness
unfathomable
unfathomably
unfruitfully
unfavourable
unfavourably
ungracefully
ungratefully
ungraciously
unguentarium
ungainliness
unguiculated
ungentleness
ungenerously
ungroundedly
ungrudgingly
ungovernable
ungovernably
unhabituated
unhandsomely
unhyphenated
unheroically
unharmonious
unhospitable
unhistorical
unhesitating
unilaterally
unimaginable
unimaginably
△**unitarianism**
unincumbered
uniseriately
unidealistic
universalise
Universalism
Universalist
universality
universalize
unidentified
unisexuality
uninfluenced
unionisation
unionization
urinogenital
unimolecular
unifoliolate
unicorn-shell
unicorn-whale
unimpressive
unimpugnable
unimprisoned
unimportance
unimportuned
uninstructed
unintegrated
unintroduced
uninterested
ubiquitarian
ubiquitously
unkindliness
unlibidinous
uglification
unlikelihood
unlikeliness
unliquidated
unlistened-to
unliveliness
unloveliness
unlovingness
unlawfulness
unmeasurable
unmeasurably
unmechanical
unmechanised

Words marked △ may be spelled also with a capital letter

12 u□w□r

unmechanized
unmodifiable
unmodernised
unmodernized
unmaintained
unmanageable
unmanageably
unmunitioned
unmiraculous
unmarketable
unmercifully
unmoralising
unmoralizing
unmistakable
unmistakably
unmethodical
unmethodised
unmethodized
Uintatherium
unnoticeable
unnaturalise
unnaturalize
unnourishing
unoverthrown
unofficially
urolithiasis
unoriginated
uxoriousness
unornamental
unornamented
unoppressive
Ulotrichales
unobservance
unobservable
unobstructed
unobservedly
unobtainable
unorthodoxly
unpeacefully
unpreparedly
unprelatical
unprevailing
unprescribed
unpretending
unpoetically
unpleasantly
unpleasingly
unpleasantry
unprettiness
unprejudiced
unprincipled
unprivileged
unpolishable
unpoliteness
unpunishable
unpunishably
unpunctuated
unpropertied
unprotesting
unprocedural
unprofitable
unprofitably
unprovidedly
unprohibited
unpropitious
unproclaimed
unprovokedly
unpronounced
unprosperous
unprocurable
unproductive
unpopularity
unperfection
unperceptive
unpersecuted
unparalleled
unperforated
unpardonable
unpardonably
unperforming
upper-bracket
unperishable
unpersuasive
unpossessing
unpassionate
unpatronised
unpatronized
unpavilioned
unquantified
unquenchable
unquenchably
unquestioned
uproariously
unreasonable
unreasonably
unrecognised
unrecognized
unrecallable
unreconciled
unreckonable
unredeemable
unriddleable
unrefreshing
unreflecting
unreflective
unreformable
unregimented
unregeneracy
unregenerate
unregistered
unrightfully
unrelievable
unrelievedly
unremembered
unromantical
unremarkable
unremorseful
unremittedly
unrepealable
unrepeatable
unrepairable
unrepulsable
unrepentance
unrepiningly
unreprovable
unreproached
unreportable
unrequitedly
unrespective
unresolvable
unresponsive
unrestricted
unreservedly
unrestrained
unresistible
unreturnable
unrevealable
unrevengeful
unrewardedly
unrhythmical
unsearchable
unsearchably
unstanchable
unstableness
unseasonable
unseasonably
unshadowable
unstatutable
unstatutably
unsubscribed
unsublimated
unsubsidised
unsubsidized
unsubmissive
unsubmitting
unsocialised
unsocialized
unsuccessful
unsuccessive
unsteadiness
unsterilised
unsterilized
unseemliness
unspectacled
unswervingly
unsufferable
unsufficient
unsegregated
unscientific
unsailorlike
unstimulated
unsalability
unsolicitous
unseminaried
unsensitised
unsensitized
unsanctified
unsanctioned
unsensualise
unsensualize
unstockinged
unscottified
unsepulchred
unsuppleness
unsupposable
unsupervised
unsuppressed
unstructured
unshrinkable
unscrupulous
unscriptural
unstratified
unsustaining
unsystematic
unsuspecting
unsuspicious
unsettlement
unsaturation
unsatisfying
unslumbering
unsculptured
ultrasensual
unthankfully
untrammelled
ultramontane
untranslated
untransmuted
ultramundane
untremendous
unthinkingly
Ustilagineae
ustilaginous
untimeliness
untumultuous
untenability
untenantable
untroubledly
ultroneously
unthoughtful
unthreatened
unthriftyhed
unterminated
unterrifying
untruthfully
untrustiness
untowardness
unusefulness
usuriousness
usufructuary
unutterables
unvaccinated
unvulnerable
unventilated
unvanquished
unvariegated
unverifiable
unvirtuously
unvoyageable
unwearyingly
unwieldiness
unwontedness
unworthiness
unworshipped
unworshipful

unwithholden
unwatchfully
unwaveringly
unyieldingly
vibraphonist
vibratiuncle
vibracularia
vocabularian
vocabularied
vice-chairman
vocicultural
vociferosity
vociferation
vociferously
vice-governor
Vacciniaceae
vocalisation
vocalization
Victorianism
victoriously
vicar-general
vocationally
vacationless
vacuum-packed
veggie-burger
vaginicoline
vaginicolous
vigorousness
vegetatively
Vehmgerichte
voicefulness
vainglorious
voiding-lobby
Volga-Baltaic
volcanically
vulcanisable
vulcanizable
valuableness
villainously
velocipedean
velocipedian
velocipedist
velvet-guards
velvet-scoter
vilification
voluminosity
voluminously
volumetrical
voluntaryism
voluntaryist
Valenciennes
Velloziaceae
vulvo-uterine
voluptuosity
voluptuously
valorisation
velarisation
valorization
velarization
valetudinary
volatileness
volitionally
volitionless
volitational
vomiturition
vinicultural
vengefulness
vinification
veneficously
vinegarrette
vinegar-plant
vindicatress
vendibleness
vindictively
venom'd-mouth'd
venomousness
venepuncture
venipuncture
ventriloqual
ventripotent
vanquishable
vanquishment
violin-string
violoncellos
vaporisation
vaporousness
vaporization
variationist
variableness
vernacularly
varicoloured
veridicality
viridescence
verbenaceous
vertebration
verification
verificatory
verticalness
versificator
verticillate
verticillium
vermin-killer
virgin's-bower
vermiculated
vermiculture
verslibriste
virilescence
virilisation
virilization
verumontanum
verisimility
verisimilous
virtuosoship
virtuousness
visibilities
vesiculation
vasodilatory
viscerotonia
viscerotonic
vestimentary
vestibulitis
viscosimeter
viscosimetry
viscoelastic
viscountship
vase-painting
visiting-book
visiting-card
visitational
visitatorial
vaticination
vitreousness
vitrifaction
vitrifacture
vitriolation
vitalisation
vitilitigate
vitalization
vitro-di-trina
vituperation
vituperatory
vituperative
veterinarian
vitativeness
vaudevillean
vaudevillian
vaudevillist
vaunt-courier
vivification
viviparously
weal-balanced
whale-fishing
whale-fishery
wranglership
weathercloth
weather-bound
weatherboard
weatherproof
wrathfulness
weak-mindedly
what's-her-name
weak-spirited
what's-his-name
what's-its-name
wicket-keeper
wide-spectrum
wretchedness
whencesoever
whereagainst
wherethrough
weeding-tongs
weeping-cross
wife-swapping
Wagnerianism
wagger-pagger
wiggle-waggle
wag-at-the-wall
wag-by-the-wall
whip-and-derry
white-bellied
white-bearded
white-livered
white-knuckle
white-fronted
white-crested
write-protect
white-crowned
whip-grafting
Whiggishness
weight-lifter
whitherwards
writing-paper
writing-table
waiting-woman
whisky-frisky
whiskerandos
whigmaleerie
whipping-post
whippoorwill
whimperingly
whisperingly
whisperously
whimsicality
wainscotting
whistle-drunk
waistcoateer
waistcoating
well-affected
wollastonite
well-becoming
well-breathed
well-balanced
wallcovering
well-dressing
well-directed
well-disposed
well-deserved
well-educated
welterweight
well-favoured
well-grounded
well-informed
△**wellingtonia**
walking-frame
walking-stick
walking-staff
walkie-talkie
williewaught
will-lessness
well-mannered
will-o'-the-wisp
well-pleasing
well-plighted
Wall-Streeter
well-tempered
well-timbered
wallydraigle
womanishness
woman-queller
wind-changing
wine-coloured
winter-beaten
winterbourne
winter-ground

Words marked △ may be spelled also with a capital letter

wunderkinder
wondermonger
wonder-struck
winter-weight
wonder-worker
wineglassful
winding-sheet
winnowing-fan
wondrousness
wing-shooting
woodburytype
whole-hearted
wood-engraver
woodenheaded
whole-skinned
wrongfulness
woolly-headed
woolly-haired
woolly-minded
woodlessness
wood-offering
woodshedding
whortleberry
workableness
word-building
word-deafness
world-wearied
world-beating
world-shaking
worshipfully
warehouseman
working-class
workmistress
warmongering
word-painting
wire-stitched
wordsmithery
wire-stringed
word-wrapping
wisecracking
wastefulness
△washingtonia
washing-board
washing-house
wishing-stone
withdrawment
witheredness
withholdment
watchfulness
Water-carrier
watermanship
water-parting
water-gilding
water-diviner
water-flowing
watering-call
watering-hole
water-cooling
water-soluble
water-spaniel
water-drinker
watercresses
waterishness
water-strider
waulking-song
waveringness
xylobalsamum
xanthochroia
xanthochroic
xanthochroid
xanthomatous
xanthopterin
xiphisternum
xerodermatic
xeromorphous
yieldingness
yellowhammer
yellow-rocket
yellow-rattle
yellow-yowley
Yankee-Doodle
youthfulness
zygodactylic
zygomycetous
zygomorphism
zygomorphous
zygapophyses
zygapophysis
Zwinglianism
Zwinglianist
Zeitvertreib
zalambdodont
zymotechnics
zantedeschia
zincographer
zincographic
zoopathology
zoomagnetism
zoogeography
zoochemistry
zoophytology
zoologically
zootomically
zoospermatic
zoographical
zero-dividend
Zarathustric
Zeuglodontia

13 a□a□a

acatamathesia
Anacardiaceae
Amaranthaceae
amarantaceous
academicalism
anaphylactoid
anathematical
arachnoiditis
arachnophobia
anaphrodisiac
anachronistic
arachnologist
anachronously
anaphorically
apathetically
acaridomatium
availableness
araeometrical
acarodomatium
analogousness
anaerobically
anagrammatise
anagrammatize
anagrammatism
anagrammatist
avant-gardiste
adaptableness
anastigmatism
avant-couriers
ambidexterity
ambidexterous
ambiguousness
arboriculture
ambassadorial
arbitrariness
ambitiousness
archaeometric
archaeologist
archaeopteryx
archbishopric
accidentalism
accidentality
accident-prone
accreditation
Archegoniatae
alcoholometer
alcoholometry
acclimatation
archimandrite
archipelagoes
architectonic
architectural
archidiaconal
accelerometer
acculturation
accompaniment
accommodative
accommodating
accommodation
Ascensiontide
acceptability
acceptilation
ascertainable
ascertainment
accessibility
accouterments
accoutrements
accoustrement
audaciousness
Addressograph®
androdioecism
audiovisually
audio-engineer
audio-location
acetification
adenoidectomy
anemometrical
averruncation
agents-general
acetylcholine
anfractuosity
affreightment
affenpinscher
affirmatively
affordability
afforestation
aggravatingly
algebraically
anglicisation
anglicization
algologically
argumentative
argumentation
argentiferous
Anglo-Catholic
Anglo-Saxondom
agglomerative
agglomeration
Anglo-American
aggiornamento
angiospermous
agglutinative
agglutinating
agglutination
atheistically
apheliotropic
athematically
aphanipterous
achromaticity
achromatopsia
animalisation
animalization
animadversion
animal-worship
adiabatically
arithmetician
arithmophobia
acidification
axiomatically
anisophyllous
adiaphoristic
amitryptyline
aristocratism
adiathermancy
Aviculariidae
All-hallowmass
All-hallowtide
allochthonous
allegorically
alligator-pear
allelomorphic
Atlantosaurus
ailourophobia
ailourophobic
ailourophilia
ailourophilic
allowableness
admeasurement
armamentarium
almond-blossom
administrable
administrator
admirableness
atmospherical
admissibility
armoured-train
amniocentesis
annexationist
apocatastasis
anomalistical
apocalyptical
apogeotropism
alongshoreman
apophlegmatic
apothegmatise
apothegmatize
apothegmatist
apochromatism
aboriginalism
△aboriginality
apoliticality
agonistically
apodictically
apomictically
atomistically
acorn-barnacle
amorphousness
abortifacient
apostolically
acotyledonous
alphabetarian
alphabetiform
appealingness
apprehensible
applicability
amphigastrium
amphitheatric
amphitheatral
amplification
appellatively
appellational
appendiculate
approximately
approximative
approximation
appropinquate
appropinquity
appropriately
appropriative
appropriation
appertainment
appertainance
aspergillosis
apportionment
appeteezement
acquirability
acquisitively
acquiescently
acquiescingly
aerobiologist
agrobiologist
acrobatically
agriculturist
atrociousness
Afro-Caribbean
aerodynamical
agreeableness
arrière-pensée
aerogenerator
acrylonitrile
aerolithology
acrimoniously
air-compressor
airworthiness
aircraftwoman
agrostologist
associateship
associability
associativity
assiduousness
answerability
abstentionism
abstentionist
aesthetically
assemblywoman
Assumptionist
assentiveness
arsenopyrites
absorbability
adsorbability
Austroasiatic
abstractively
abstractional
assertiveness
Australianism
Assyriologist
assistantship
assassination
asset-stripper
actualisation
actualization
astrapophobia
antiasthmatic
antiarthritic

Words marked △ may be spelled also with a capital letter

13 b□r□e

antibacterial
antiballistic
autobiography
anticoagulant
anticlimactic
anticlinorium
astacological
autecological
anticlockwise
autocephalous
anticorrosive
antichristian
autocatalysis
autocatalytic
autochthonism
autochthonous
auto-digestion
antidesiccant
anthelminthic
autoeroticism
asthenosphere
authentically
authenticator
artificialise
artificialize
artificiality
antigenically
antigropeloes
antihistamine
attainability
attributively
antilogarithm
antimicrobial
anti-modernist
anti-marketeer
asthmatically
automatically
actinobacilli
attentiveness
antenniferous
antinomianism
actinomycosis
actinomorphic
antinephritic
astonishingly
actinotherapy
Antiochianism
anthophyllite
astrophysical
authoritative
authorisation
authoritarian
authorization
astrodynamics
astrocytomata
anti-personnel
antipsychotic
antiquitarian
alternatively
arteriography
anthropogenic
anthropolatry
anthropomorph
anthropometry
anthropophagi
anthropophagy
anthropopathy
anthropophyte
anthroposophy
antispasmodic
antisubmarine
antisocialism
antisocialist
antisociality
autoschediaze
autoschediasm
antiscorbutic
antisepticise
antisepticize
antisepticism
attitudiniser
attitudinizer
antiterrorist
adumbratively
arundinaceous
Aquifoliaceae
aluminiferous
ayuntamientos
acupuncturist
advantageable
advanced-level
adventuresome
adventuristic
adventurously
advertisement
advertizement
advisableness
amygdalaceous
anythingarian
abyssopelagic
blanchisseuse
branch-officer
boarding-house
bladder-cherry
blandishments
blameableness
brachycephaly
brachydactyly
△brachiosaurus
brachypterous
beatification
blackberrying
black-and-white
blankety-blank
blackguardism
brainlessness
brainchildren
brainsickness
brainstorming
blasphemously
boatswain-bird
brassfounding
brattice-cloth
blastogenesis
beauteousness
baby-battering
Bible-thumping
Bible-pounding
bibliographic
bibliographer
bibliological
bibliolatrist
bibliolatrous
bibliophagist
bibliophilism
bibliophilist
bibliopolical
bibliothecary
bubble-chamber
baby-snatching
△baccalaureate
back-calculate
bacteriolysin
bacteriolysis
bacteriolytic
bacteriophage
back-formation
biculturalism
back-pedalling
backscratcher
backwardation
badger-baiting
badger-drawing
bidding-prayer
bidirectional
breech-loading
blepharospasm
breakfast-room
breakableness
breaking-point
beetlebrained
beetle-crusher
breast-feeding
breathing-time
breathing-hole
baggage-animal
begging-letter
beginningless
bignoniaceous
behaviourally
blindman's-buff
building-board
building-block
bridge-builder
brinksmanship
brilliantness
blister-beetle
belt-and-braces
Balsaminaceae
△balkanisation
△balkanization
balsamiferous
ballast-heaver
beleaguerment
ball-cartridge
ballet-dancing
belles-lettres
balneotherapy
belligerently
billiard-cloth
billiard-table
Balanoglossus
bullock's-heart
Baltoslavonic
ballot-rigging
bulbourethral
Bildungsroman
bombastically
bamboozlement
bumptiousness
benedictional
banderilleros
bonheur-du-jour
beneficiation
beneficential
benthopelagic
bone-turquoise
bioscientific
book-canvasser
bronchoscopic
bronchography
blood-relative
blood-relation
bloodlessness
Brobdignagian
broadmindedly
blood-boltered
broad-spectrum
bloodcurdling
biogeographer
broken-hearted
biotechnology
bromeliaceous
biodegradable
biochemically
brother-german
brotherliness
brothers-in-law
booking-office
Bloomsburyite
bioenergetics
bioconversion
biopsychology
blotting-paper
biosystematic
bureaucratise
bureaucratize
bureaucratist
barbarisation
barbarization
barnacle-goose
bargain-hunter
barbarousness
barrel-chested

Words marked △ may be spelled also with a capital letter

13 b□r□e

Berkeleianism
Berberidaceae
barber-surgeon
barrel-vaulted
barefacedness
birefringence
boraginaceous
Birminghamise
Birminghamize
burying-beetle
burning-mirror
burying-ground
bernicle-goose
barristership
burglariously
barnsbreaking
burnt-offering
borough-monger
basset-hornist
beseemingness
businesswoman
bespottedness
bestsellerdom
butter-and-eggs
butter-biscuit
butter-fingers
butterfly-weed
butterfly-fish
betweenwhiles
butcher's-broom
bottle-coaster
battle-cruiser
battle-scarred
baton-sinister
button-through
bathymetrical
brutalisation
brutalization
bougainvillea
boundlessness
boundary-layer
boundary-rider
bourguignonne
bouillabaisse
bountifulness
boulting-hutch
boustrophedon
bounteousness
bowling-crease
bewilderingly
bowstring-hemp
characterless
chalcographic
chalcographer
clandestinely
clandestinity
chameleon-like
△**chateaubriand**
changeability
charge-capping
charge-coupled
changefulness
change-ringing
coachwhip-bird
coachbuilding
clavicembalos
clarification
craniological
clay-ironstone
cranioscopist
charity-school
coadjutorship
cracker-barrel
challengeable
challengingly
charlatanical
cyanoacrylate
clamorousness
clapperclawer
clapperboards
clairaudience
classicalness
coarse-grained
crassulaceous
claustrophobe
craftsmanship
coagulability
cabbalistical
cable-moulding
cobelligerent
cobaltiferous
cabinetmaking
cyberneticist
Cyclanthaceae
cacographical
cocainisation
cocainization
cochleariform
coconut-butter
cyclodialysis
cyclospermous
cuckoo-spittle
cock-of-the-rock
Cucurbitaceae
Ciceronianism
cicatrisation
cicatrization
codeclination
codicological
cheval-de-frise
△**caesaropapism**
coenaesthesis
cream-coloured
clean-timbered
chemoreceptor
cheerlessness
cheirographer
cheiropterous
Cheirotherium
cleistogamous
coeducational
credulousness
cleavableness
coffee-housing
cognomination
climatologist
climatography
climactically
climacterical
cribbage-board
climbing-frame
clincher-built
chieftainship
clishmaclaver
coinheritance
criminologist
criminousness
coin-in-the-slot
crinicultural
chicken-hazard
chicken-and-egg
chinkerinchee
clickety-clack
clickety-click
client-centred
chimney-corner
chimneybreast
chiromantical
clinopinacoid
clinopinakoid
clinodiagonal
chirographist
criss-cross-row
calcariferous
collaborative
collaboration
caliature-wood
cold-bloodedly
colleagueship
collectedness
collecting-box
collectorship
calefactories
cold-heartedly
calcification
Calvinistical
calligraphist
collieshangie
callisthenics
chlamydomonas
chlamydospore
cylindrically
cylindraceous
colposcopical
colloquialism
colloquialist
chlorobromide
chlorocruorin
chloroformist
Chloromycetin
chloroplastal
Chlorophyceae
chlorargyrite
calculational
colourisation
colourization
celluliferous
comparatively
comparability
commandership
compagination
combativeness
compatibility
companionable
companionably
companionless
companionship
companionhood
campanologist
compatriotism
compassionate
compactedness
Campanulaceae
commercialese
commercialise
commercialize
commercialism
commercialist
commerciality
compendiously
Commelinaceae
commemorative
commemoration
commemoratory
commeasurable
commensurable
commensurably
camphoraceous
combinability
combinatorial
combinatorics
commiserative
commiseration
cummingtonite
committeeship
complications
complaisantly
complainingly
complementary
complimentary
cumulostratus
complexedness
compositeness
compositional
comprehensive
comprehension
compressional
comprovincial
camp-sheathing
Compsognathus
commutatively
commutability
computational
communautaire

Words marked △ may be spelled also with a capital letter

computer-aided
communicative
communication
communitarian
communicatory
compulsionist
campylobacter
canvas-climber
concatenation
contabescence
convalescence
convalescency
consanguinity
contaminative
contamination
concavo-convex
confarreation
confabulation
confabulatory
conscientious
consciousness
condescending
condescension
confederative
confederation
consenescence
consenescency
cancellariate
concernedness
cancerophobia
convexo-convex
contemplative
contemplation
contemplatist
Contemptibles
concessionary
confessionary
concessionist
confessorship
conversazione
conversazioni
concentrative
conceptualise
conceptualize
contextualise
contextualize
conceptualism
concentration
conceptualist
concertmaster
conceitedness
contentedness
concentricity
concertinaing
consentaneity
consentaneous
connecting-rod
confectionary
conventionary
conventioneer
confectionery
connectionism
Conceptionist
conventionist
contentiously
convertiplane
conjecturable
conjecturally
consecutively
consequential
conservatoire
conchological
cinchonaceous
canthaxanthin
candidateship
cannibalistic
considerately
considerative
consideration
consideringly
consimilarity
confidingness
consimilitude
conditionally
configuration
continuedness
canaliculated
candle-dipping
conflagration
candle-lighter
conglomeratic
candle-snuffer
conglutinator
cinematograph
convocational
consolidative
cantonisation
cantonization
consolidation
concomitantly
confoundingly
contortionate
contortionism
contortionist
conspicuously
conspurcation
contrabandism
contrabandist
contrabassoon
contributable
canary-creeper
contractility
contractional
centricalness
contraceptive
contraception
contradictive
contradiction
contradictory
centrifugally
centrifugence
contrafagotto
centre-forward
contralateral
confrontation
congruousness
contrapuntist
contrappostos
contrariously
contristation
congressional
Congresswoman
congratulable
congratulator
concretionary
contraterrene
confraternity
Congreve-match
contravention
controversial
controvertist
constrainable
constrainedly
constableship
constablewick
constringency
constellation
constellatory
Constantinian
constupration
consternation
constructable
constructible
conjugational
conjunctively
conjunctional
connumeration
concupiscible
concupiscence
consumptively
consumptivity
conquistadors
convulsionary
convulsionist
cinque-spotted
conductorship
concyclically
condylomatous
choreographic
choreographer
chorepiscopal
cholecystitis
clothes-basket
cook-housemaid
clock-watching
cloak-and-sword
crown-of-thorns
chopping-board
chopping-block
chopping-knife
cross-hatching
cross-matching
cross-vaulting
cross-magnetic
cross-gartered
cloister-garth
cross-division
cross-springer
crossbreeding
cross-dressing
cross-crosslet
cross-purposes
cross-quarters
cross-question
cross-cultural
Capparidaceae
cephalisation
cephalization
cephalothorax
cephalosporin
capaciousness
copper-captain
copper-pyrites
caprification
copple-crowned
capellmeister
copyrightable
copartnership
curtain-raiser
cerebrospinal
corn-chandlery
correlatively
correlativity
cornet-à-piston
carpet-bedding
carpet-bombing
carte-de-visite
cartelisation
cartelization
correspondent
corresponsive
corresponding
carpet-sweeper
carpet-slipper
coreferential
cerographical
cardinalatial
carnivalesque
cardinalitial
cartilaginous
cardiographer
carriage-drive
carnification
certification
cornification
certificatory
corrigibility
cardiological
carrion-flower
carcinomatous
carcinologist
carnivorously
cervicography
corridor-train

13 c□r□i

carrier-pigeon
coreligionist
coralliferous
coralligenous
Corolliflorae
corollifloral
ceruloplasmin
ceremonialism
ceremoniously
chromatically
chromatograph
chromatophore
chrematistics
chronobiology
chronographer
corinthianise
corinthianize
chronological
Caryocaraceae
corporateness
cordocentesis
carbonisation
carbonization
corrosiveness
△**carboniferous**
cercopithecid
Cercopithecus
corrosibility
corroborative
corroboration
corroboratory
carbonylation
cartridge-belt
Christianness
Christianlike
christianiser
christianizer
Christmas-tide
Christmas-time
chrysanthemum
chrestomathic
Christologist
chrysophantic
chrysophilite
circumambient
circumambages
circumduction
circumductory
circumflexion
circumference
circumfluence
carburisation
carburization
Curculionidae
circumjacency
circumstances
circumspectly
circumscriber
corruptionist
circumvallate
circumventive

circumvention
Casuarinaceae
casualisation
casualization
cosmeceutical
cost-efficient
cost-effective
cosmetologist
Cassegrainian
case-hardening
cysticercosis
casting-weight
casuistically
customariness
cosmochemical
cosmothetical
customisation
customization
custodianship
cosmopolitism
cosmopolitics
cytochemistry
catechistical
catecholamine
catechumenate
catechumenism
cytodiagnosis
categorically
categorematic
cattle-lifting
catalytically
cat-o'-nine-tails
cathodography
cotton-picking
cytopathology
catercornered
catastrophism
catastrophist
churchmanship
church-officer
church-service
causelessness
cauterisation
cauterization
chuck-farthing
chuckle-headed
counselorship
coursing-joint
cruiserweight
counting-house
court-bouillon
courteousness
counter-parole
counter-caster
counteractive
counteraction
counter-weight
counterfeiter
counterfeitly
counterchange
countercharge

counterbidder
counter-signal
counter-fleury
countermotion
counter-poison
counterspying
counter-attack
counterstroke
counter-jumper
coxcombically
cryobiologist
chylification
chymification
cryptographic
cryptographer
crystal-gazing
cryptological
crystallinity
cryptanalysis
cryptesthesia
diacatholicon
dramatisation
dramatization
dramaturgical
dead-colouring
diabetologist
diametrically
dialectically
diageotropism
draggle-tailed
draught-screen
draught-engine
draught-animal
diaphragmatic
deathlessness
diaphanometer
diachronistic
diathermanous
diaphototropy
drawing-master
drawing-pencil
dualistically
drainage-basin
draining-board
diagnostician
diamond-beetle
diamond-powder
dialogistical
drag-parachute
dead-reckoning
draftsmanship
dialypetalous
debauchedness
declaratively
declamatorily
declaratorily
dictatorially
deciduousness
decrepitation
deceivability
deceitfulness

decriminalise
decriminalize
dichlamydeous
decelerometer
documentarise
documentarize
documentation
documentalist
documentarist
documentarily
decomposition
decompressive
decompression
decontaminate
decontaminant
dichotomously
deceptiveness
deceptibility
deck-passenger
decerebration
decortication
doctrinairism
decarbonation
dichrooscopic
decarboxylase
Dicotyledones
dactyliomancy
dactylography
deducibleness
deductibility
dodecaphonism
dodecaphonist
daddy-long-legs
dreadlessness
dieselisation
dieselization
dyed-in-the-wool
dwelling-house
dwelling-place
dreamlessness
dress-improver
dressing-table
defeasibility
diffarreation
defibrination
defibrillator
deficientness
defectiveness
defectibility
differentiate
defencelessly
defensibility
deformability
defervescence
defervescency
deferentially
deforestation
diffusiveness
diffusibility
diffusion-tube
dog-periwinkle

13 d□u□l

daguerreotype
daguerreotypy
dignification
digestibility
dog's-tail-grass
deglutination
driving-mirror
drinkableness
drink-offering
drill-sergeant
drilling-lathe
deipnosophist
dollarisation
dollarization
delectability
Dolichosauria
Dolichosaurus
dolichocephal
deliciousness
delightedness
dolphinariums
dulcification
dilapidations
deliquescence
delirifacient
deliriousness
dilettanteism
deleteriously
domiciliation
demi-caractère
demyelination
damageability
damnification
demolishments
demolitionist
dimensionless
demonological
diminishingly
demonstrative
demonstration
demonstratory
domestication
demythologise
demythologize
dematerialise
dematerialize
dimethylamine
demiurgically
dunderheadism
dangerousness
dancing-master
densitometric
denticulation
dynamogenesis
Dendrocalamus
dendrological
do-nothingness
denationalise
denationalize
Dioscoreaceae
△diotheletical
△dyotheletical
△dyothelitical
deoch-an-doruis
deoxidisation
deoxidization
dioristically
deodorisation
deodorization
deontological
deprecatingly
deprecatorily
dipleidoscope
Dipterocarpus
dipping-needle
dephlegmation
deplorability
diplomatology
Diprotodontia
diprotodontid
depersonalise
depersonalize
diphthongally
dermatoplasty
dermatologist
dermatography
derecognition
directionless
darning-needle
dereligionise
dereligionize
derequisition
derestriction
derivationist
disparateness
disparagement
discapacitate
disparagingly
dastardliness
dishabilitate
disharmonious
dispassionate
dismantlement
distastefully
distant-signal
disnaturalise
disnaturalize
disobediently
disobligation
disobligatory
disobligement
désobligeante
disobligingly
disadvantaged
desperateness
dissemblingly
dismemberment
disseveration
disseminative
dissemination
dissepimental
disfellowship
dysmenorrheic
dysmenorrheal
dysmenorrhoea
disrespectful
disheartening
dispersedness
dyspeptically
disceptatious
disreputation
disaffectedly
disaffirmance
desegregation
disagreeables
despicability
distinctively
distinguished
distinguisher
dissimilation
dissimilarity
dispiritingly
dissimilitude
disciplinable
dissimulative
disfiguration
dissimulation
disfigurement
displeasingly
desulphuriser
desulphurizer
displantation
desultoriness
disilluminate
disillusioned
disembarkment
disemployment
disembodiment
disengagement
disinterested
disintegrable
disintegrator
disinvestment
disinhibition
disinhibitory
disinvigorate
disposability
disconcertion
disconformity
dispositively
dispositioned
dispositional
discommodious
discommission
disconnection
discoloration
dishonourable
dishonourably
disgospelling
dispossession
discontiguity
discontiguous
discontentful
discontenting
discontinuity
discontinuous
dissoluteness
dissolubility
discomycetous
disappearance
disappointing
disequilibria
desirableness
distributable
disgracefully
destructively
distractively
distractingly
destructivist
destructivity
destructional
discreditable
discreditably
disordinately
desertisation
desertization
dispraisingly
disarticulate
discriminator
descriptively
descriptivism
disproportion
distressfully
distrustfully
distressingly
discretionary
disestimation
disassimilate
disputatively
disputability
disjunctively
dysfunctional
disquietingly
disqualifying
disguisedness
disgustedness
dispurveyance
detrimentally
determinately
determinative
determination
deterministic
deteriorative
deterioration
detestability
deuteragonist
deuterogamist
deuteroscopic
Deuteronomist
daughter-in-law
double-banking
double-coconut
double-chinned
double-concave

13 d□u□l

double-crosser
double-dealing
double-density
double-fronted
double-founted
double-glazing
double-hearted
double-jointed
double-meaning
double-mouthed
double-natured
double-or-quits
double-shotted
double-shuffle
double-tongued
dauntlessness
developmental
devolutionary
devolutionist
divertisement
diversifiable
divertibility
diverticulate
devastatingly
divisibleness
division-lobby
devotionalist
devotionality
downcast-shaft
downrightness
dexterousness
dextrocardiac
epanadiploses
epanadiplosis
evangeliarium
evangeliarion
evangelically
evangelistary
exaggeratedly
examinability
examinational
elaborateness
evaporability
États-Généraux
exanthematous
enantiomorphy
enantiodromia
enantiodromic
enantiotropic
embranglement
embracingness
Eubacteriales
embrittlement
embellishment
embarrassment
embourgeoised
embryogenesis
embryological
exclamational
△eucharistical
eschatologist
△encyclopaedia
encyclopaedic
encyclopedism
encyclopedian
encyclopedist
excrescential
ecclesiolater
ecclesiolatry
encompassment
encomiastical
excommunicate
eccentrically
encroachingly
enchondromata
Encephalartos
encephalocele
encephalotomy
encephalogram
exceptionable
exceptionably
exceptionally
encapsulation
excortication
excursiveness
excusableness
eschscholtzia
excessiveness
excitableness
encouragement
encouragingly
exclusiveness
endearingness
endeavourment
endocrinology
endometriosis
endurableness
endosymbiotic
endosmometric
emerald-copper
even-Christian
energetically
elephantiasis
elephant's-ears
elephant's-foot
everlastingly
exemplariness
exemplifiable
execrableness
epeirogenesis
epeirogenetic
electrisation
electrization
electrifiable
electrovalent
electromagnet
electroscopic
electrocement
electromerism
electrometric
electioneerer
electrophilic
electrochemic
electrophorus
electrothermy
electroplater
electromotive
electro-optics
electrography
electrostatic
electrocution
electrotypist
efficaciously
effectiveness
effectualness
efflorescence
effervescible
effervescence
effervescency
eagle-flighted
ergonomically
engine-turning
eigenfunction
eighteen-pence
eighteen-penny
ergatomorphic
exhibitionism
exhibitionist
ethologically
Ephemeroptera
Echinodermata
ethanolamines
ethnocentrism
ethnolinguist
ethnobotanist
ethnographica
enhypostatise
enhypostatize
epinastically
Eriocaulaceae
epigeneticist
epidermolysis
epitheliomata
epiphenomenon
enigmatically
epicondylitis
epidotisation
epidotization
epitrachelion
epigrammatise
epigrammatize
epigrammatist
emigrationist
existentially
enjoyableness
△enlightenment
evocativeness
egocentricity
exothermicity
exobiological
egotistically
econometrical
economisation
economization
ecotoxicology
explanatorily
euphausiacean
expectorative
expectoration
expeditionary
expeditiously
△expressionism
expressionist
expandability
expendability
expansiveness
expensiveness
expansibility
exponentially
Euphorbiaceae
explosiveness
expropriation
exportability
expurgatorial
empire-builder
experimentist
empyreumatise
empyreumatize
expostulative
expostulation
expostulatory
emphysematous
exquisiteness
Eurocommunism
Eurocommunist
egregiousness
earth-chestnut
earth-movement
earth-motherly
earthly-minded
erroneousness
Europocentric
Etruscologist
essentialness
eosinophilous
east-north-east
exsanguineous
ensanguinated
eusporangiate
east-south-east
extravagation
extravasation
extragalactic
extravagantly
extravascular
extracellular
extrametrical
estrangedness
extra-physical
extralimitary
extrapolative
extrapolation
extrapolatory
extraposition

Words marked △ may be spelled also with a capital letter

extraordinary
extratropical
extrajudicial
extra-axillary
△establishment
entrepreneuse
extrinsically
entomological
extemporarily
entomophagous
entomophilous
entomostracan
extenuatingly
extendability
extensiveness
extendibility
extensibility
extensionally
extinguishant
entertainment
exteroceptive
exterminative
extermination
exterminatory
exterritorial
Enteropneusta
estate-bottled
educatability
educationally
equidifferent
equidistantly
ecumenicalism
equilibration
ebullioscopic
equinoctially
equiponderate
equiponderant
equipotential
equestrianism
equisetaceous
equitableness
equivocalness
environmental
eavesdropping
erythematosus
erythrophobia
erysipelatous
Egyptological
franchisement
Franco-Russian
flagellomania
flagellantism
flame-coloured
featherweight
feather-bonnet
feather-stitch
feather-duster
frank-tenement
Frankeniaceae
fragmentation
fragmentarily
Flammenwerfer
flannel-flower
fractionalise
fractionalize
fractionalism
fractionation
fractionalist
fractiousness
feature-length
fibrovascular
fictionalised
fictionalized
facultatively
factorability
factorisation
factorization
facetiousness
fiddle-faddler
fiddle-pattern
field-emission
flesh-pressing
feeding-bottle
fuel-injection
free-marketeer
free-selection
frequentative
frequentation
freezing-point
fugaciousness
figure-casting
figure-weaving
fair-and-square
fringe-dweller
fridge-freezer
fringilliform
frighteningly
faithlessness
flight-feather
frightfulness
frivolousness
flint-knapping
flirtatiously
filibustering
filibusterism
filibusterous
felicitations
filterability
folk-etymology
full-fashioned
falsification
feloniousness
fellow-citizen
fellow-feeling
fellow-servant
follow-through
filipendulous
fundamentally
fantastically
finger-breadth
finger-pointer
fencing-master
funambulation
funambulatory
functionalism
functionalist
fonctionnaire
floccillation
floodlighting
flower-de-leuce
flower-service
foolhardiness
floristically
floricultural
foot-land-raker
foot-passenger
flourishingly
frontogenesis
floating-point
floutingstock
formalisation
formalization
ferociousness
furaciousness
forgetfulness
fermentitious
forefeelingly
formidability
ferrimagnetic
fertilisation
fertilization
fortification
fortississimo
fortitudinous
ferricyanogen
forejudgement
foreknowingly
foreknowledge
foraminiferal
forementioned
forensicality
ferromagnetic
ferro-chromium
ferroelectric
ferroconcrete
ferrosoferric
forgottenness
ferrocyanogen
fire-resistant
fire-resisting
foreshadowing
foresightless
first-begotten
fortunateness
formularistic
fortune-teller
fortune-hunter
foster-brother
fissiparously
fishing-tackle
fishing-ground
fossilisation
fossilization
fossiliferous
fasciculation
fatigableness
futurological
feudalisation
feudalization
founder-member
foundation-net
flugelhornist
flügelhornist
frumentaceous
frumentarious
fluvio-glacial
feuilletonism
feuilletonist
frustratingly
faultlessness
fruitlessness
favorableness
fixed-interest
gradationally
granddaughter
grandfatherly
grandiloquent
grandiloquous
grandmotherly
gracelessness
graphological
gnathonically
gravitational
gravimetrical
granitisation
granitization
gratification
graminivorous
glaciological
gladiatorship
graticulation
grammatically
glamorisation
glamorization
grappling-hook
grappling-iron
glass-painting
glass-grinding
granuliferous
granulomatous
go-as-you-please
gubernatorial
ghetto-blaster
great-grandson
gigantomachia
guilelessness
grief-stricken
Gaidhealtachd
geitonogamous
guiltlessness
galvanisation
galvanization
galvanometric
galvanoplasty

galactosaemia
galactorrhoea
golden-crested
gillie-wetfoot
Galeopithecus
gymnastically
gumple-foisted
gambling-house
gymnospermous
gametogenesis
Gemütlichkeit
gynodioecious
gonadotrophic
gonadotrophin
gender-bending
gynaecomastia
gynaecologist
gynaecocratic
gentianaceous
gentle-hearted
gentlemanship
gentlemanlike
gentlemanhood
gentlewomanly
gynomonoecism
gynandromorph
goniometrical
generalisable
generalissimo
generalizable
generationism
genethlialogy
genotypically
genetotrophic
genito-urinary
globalisation
globalization
geotactically
geoscientific
goose-barnacle
geotechnology
grotesqueness
geometrically
globetrotting
geocentricism
geochemically
geochronology
glorification
good-King-Henry
ground-angling
groin-centring
ground-officer
good-naturedly
grown-junction
geopolitician
geomorphogeny
geomorphology
geotropically
grouse-disease
glossographer
glossological
geostationary
globuliferous
Germanisation
Germanization
Germanophilia
garnetiferous
garnisheement
garlic-mustard
gyromagnetism
gerund-grinder
gerontophobia
gerontophilia
gerontologist
gerontocratic
garrulousness
gerrymanderer
gasteropodous
gesticulative
gesticulation
gesticulatory
gastrocnemius
gastroenteric
gastrological
gastronomical
gathering-peat
gathering-coal
Grumbletonian
gluconeogenic
gauntlet-guard
governing-body
glyphographic
glyphographer
glycosylation
glyptographic
heave-offering
heave-shoulder
heaven-kissing
Heath-Robinson
hyalinisation
hyalinization
headquartered
heat-resistant
heartlessness
healthfulness
heart-sickness
heartbreaking
heart-stricken
heart-stirring
hybridisation
hybridization
hubristically
hibernisation
hibernization
habitableness
hobby-horsical
hacking-jacket
hide-and-go-seek
Hydrangeaceae
hydraulicking
hydraulically
hydrarthrosis
hedge-marriage
hedge-accentor
hydropathical
hydromagnetic
hydrogenation
hydrocephalic
hydrocephalus
hydrometrical
hydromedusoid
hydrochloride
hydrokinetics
hydro-airplane
hydroelectric
hydrosomatous
hydrocracking
hydrostatical
hydrosulphide
hydrosulphite
hydroxylamine
hydrodynamics
haematogenous
haematologist
heebie-jeebies
haemodialysis
hieroglyphics
hieroglyphist
hierogrammate
haemorrhoidal
High-Churchism
High-Churchman
high-explosive
high-muck-a-muck
hygroscopical
hygrometrical
hagiographist
high-stomached
high-watermark
heir-portioner
hair-splitting
hole-and-corner
half-evergreen
Hellenistical
Hildebrandism
helter-skelter
half-heartedly
hole-in-the-wall
helminthiasis
helminthology
holometabolic
heliometrical
hollow-hearted
heliotropical
helispherical
half-sovereign
Holothuroidea
hallucinative
hallucination
hallucinatory
hemicellulose
homochromatic
Hammerklavier
homoeomorphic
homoeroticism
homoeopathist
homoeothermic
homoeothermal
homogenetical
homoiothermic
homoiothermal
homologically
homologoumena
humble-mouthed
homiletically
homomorphosis
Hymenomycetes
hymenopterous
homeoteleuton
homeothermous
homeomorphism
homeomorphous
hemiparasitic
Hemerobaptist
hemispherical
homosexualism
homosexualist
homosexuality
hematogenesis
hematopoiesis
hematopoietic
homeward-bound
hunger-marcher
hunger-striker
Huntingdonian
hunting-spider
hunting-ground
handkerchiefs
hundredweight
honorifically
honeycomb-moth
heortological
haphazardness
heptasyllabic
hypocycloidal
hypochondriac
hypochondrium
hyphenisation
hyphenization
hypoglycaemia
hypoglycaemic
hypomenorrhea
hypsophyllary
hypnotisation
hypnotization
hypno-analysis
hippopotamian
hypophosphite
hyperparasite
hypercalcemia
hypersarcosis
hypernatremia
hyperactivity
hypervelocity

13 i□m□t

hypermetrical
hypermetropia
hypermetropic
hyperphysical
hyperphrygian
hyperhidrosis
hyperglycemia
hypertrophied
hypertrophous
hypercritical
hyperesthesia
hyperesthetic
hypersthenite
hypereutectic
hyposulphuric
hypothecation
hare-and-hounds
hermaphrodite
hermeneutical
horsefeathers
horse-sickness
horse-milliner
horse-and-buggy
herpetologist
horse-wrangler
hard-heartedly
hurricane-lamp
hurricane-deck
horripilation
herniorrhaphy
horticultural
harmonisation
harmonization
herborisation
herborization
harbour-master
haruspication
heresiologist
heresiography
horizontality
hysteranthous
histiophoroid
histrionicism
Hutchinsonian
heteroblastic
heteroclitous
heterochronic
heterocarpous
heterogeneity
heterogeneous
heterogenesis
heterogenetic
heteromorphic
heteroplastic
heteropterous
heterosporous
heterostrophy
heterostylism
heterostylous
heterothallic
heterothermal
heterotrophic
hound-trailing
housewifeship
housewifeskep
housemistress
house-breaking
heuristically
hexobarbitone
hexactinellid
hexadactylous
hazardousness
inaudibleness
inanimateness
imaginariness
imaginatively
italicisation
italicization
inappreciable
inappropriate
inattentively
inadvertently
incredibility
incredulously
inclinational
incriminatory
incompatibles
incompetently
incommiscible
incompossible
incommunicado
incombustible
incombustibly
incantational
inconsciently
incandescence
inconvenience
incondensable
inconversable
incontestable
inconvertible
incontestably
inconvertibly
inconsecutive
inconsequence
incense-burner
inconceivable
inconceivably
inconvincible
inconsiderate
incontinently
inconsistence
inconsistency
inconsonantly
inconspicuous
incongruously
inconstruable
incurableness
incarceration
incorrectness
incardination
incorporative
incorporating
incorporation
incorporeally
incuriousness
incorruptible
incorruptibly
incorruptness
incessantness
Indianisation
Indianization
indoctrinator
indifferently
indefatigable
indefatigably
indelibleness
indolebutyric
induplication
independently
indiscernible
indiscernibly
indispensable
indispensably
indistinctive
indistinction
indissociable
indisposition
indissolvable
industrialise
industrialize
industrialism
industrialist
indescribable
indescribably
industriously
indissuadable
indissuadably
indeterminate
indeterminacy
indeterminism
indeterminist
individualise
individualize
individualism
individuation
individualist
individuality
inegalitarian
inelaborately
ineffableness
inefficacious
inefficiently
ineffectively
ineffectually
ideographical
inexhaustible
inexhaustibly
inevitability
ineligibility
inexorability
inexplainable
inexpectation
inexpediently
inexpressible
inexpressibly
inexpensively
inexperienced
inerrableness
identicalness
ineducability
infeasibility
infraposition
infraspecific
infectiveness
inflexibility
inflexionless
infallibilism
infallibilist
infallibility
infundibulate
infinitesimal
inflorescence
infuriatingly
informatician
informational
inferentially
influentially
infructuously
ingeniousness
ingenuousness
ingurgitation
Ichthyosauria
ichthyologist
inhomogeneity
inhomogeneous
inharmonicity
inhospitality
imitativeness
inimitability
idiomatically
idiorrhythmic
idiosyncratic
injudiciously
injuriousness
ill-favouredly
Illecebraceae
illocutionary
illegibleness
illogicalness
illuminations
island-hopping
ill-considered
illustriously
illustrissimo
immediateness
immunifacient
immunological
immunotherapy
immarcescible
immiscibility
immutableness
ismaticalness
immaterialise

13 i□m□t

immaterialize
immaterialism
immaterialist
immateriality
immovableness
innocuousness
ignominiously
iontophoresis
iontophoretic
inner-directed
innovationist
innoxiousness
isobarometric
inoperability
isomerisation
isomerization
isometrically
isogeothermic
isogeothermal
inofficiously
inoffensively
isoagglutinin
inorganically
isochronously
isodimorphism
isodimorphous
isoelectronic
iconomaticism
inodorousness
inopportunely
inopportunity
inobservation
isostatically
inobtrusively
inoculability
implacability
impracticable
impracticably
impractically
impeccability
impecuniosity
impecuniously
△**impressionism**
△**impressionist**
impignoration
implicatively
impalpability
impulsiveness
impoliticness
impolitically
imponderables
impenetration
improbability
improvability
improvisation
improvisatory
improvisatrix
improvidently
impropriation
impermanently
imperialistic
imperseverant
imperceptible
imperfectible
imperceptibly
imperfectness
impertinently
impartibility
impartialness
impermissible
impermissibly
impersonalise
impersonalize
imperforation
impersonation
impersonality
imperiousness
imparipinnate
importunately
imperturbable
imperturbably
impassability
impassiveness
impossibilism
impossibilist
impassibility
impossibility
impostumation
imputableness
impetuousness
inquisitively
inquisitional
inquisitorial
irreclaimable
irreclaimably
irrecognition
irreciprocity
irrecoverable
irrecoverably
irredeemables
irrefrangible
irrefrangibly
irreligionist
irreligiously
irreplaceable
irreplaceably
irrepleviable
irrepressible
irrepressibly
irresponsible
irresponsibly
irritableness
irretrievable
irretrievably
irrationalise
irrationalize
irrationalism
irrationalist
irrationality
irreverential
instantiation
instantaneity
instantaneous
insubordinate
insubstantial
insociability
insectivorous
insectologist
insidiousness
inspectorship
insufficience
insufficiency
insignificant
instigatingly
inspirational
instinctively
instinctivity
instinctually
inspiritingly
institutively
institutional
insolvability
insolubleness
insensateness
insinuatingly
insensitively
insensibility
insensitivity
insupportable
insupportably
instructively
instructional
inscriptively
inscriptional
insusceptible
insusceptibly
insatiateness
insatiability
intravasation
intravascular
intracavitary
intranational
intraparietal
intracapsular
intrapetiolar
intracellular
intra-arterial
intransigeant
intransigence
intransigency
intramuscular
integumentary
intricateness
intrinsically
intellectuals
intelligencer
intelligently
intemperately
intensiveness
intangibility
intentionally
iatrogenicity
introversible
iatrochemical
introspective
introspection
introgression
intercalative
intercalation
intergalactic
interlacement
interlaminate
interradially
△**international**
interparietal
intermarriage
interjaculate
interoceptive
interscapular
interrelation
intermetallic
interferingly
interpetiolar
intermediator
intercellular
interferogram
interpersonal
interdentally
interjectural
interpilaster
intersidereal
interdigitate
intermittence
intermittency
interpolative
interrogative
interlocation
interpolation
interrogation
interrogatory
interposition
intercommunal
intercolonial
interlocution
intercolumnar
interlocutory
interlocutrix
interspecific
interspersion
interbreeding
intertropical
intercropping
interpretable
interpretress
interproximal
interestingly
interosculate
interosculant
interstratify
interstellary
interlunation
interpunction
intercurrence
interruptedly

Words marked △ may be spelled also with a capital letter

intrusiveness
invidiousness
involucellate
involuntarily
inventiveness
invendibility
invincibility
inventorially
inviolateness
inviolability
invariability
invisibleness
investigative
investigation
investigatory
Jacobinically
jack-crosstree
judiciousness
judge-advocate
judgement-hall
judgement-debt
judgement-seat
Judaistically
Judas-coloured
juglandaceous
jiggery-pokery
Johnsonianism
jollification
jumping-spider
Jamestown-weed
Jenny-long-legs
Japano-Chinese
jargonisation
jargonization
jurisprudence
jerry-building
justificative
justification
justificatory
jet-propulsion
journey-weight
jawbreakingly
jawdroppingly
juxtaposition
Kidderminster
Kletterschuhe
knight-marshal
knights-errant
knight-service
knick-knackery
△knickerbocker
kaleidoscopic
Kenyapithecus
kangaroo-apple
kangaroo-grass
kangaroo-thorn
kindergärtner
kind-heartedly
kindly-natured
kinematograph
kinesiologist
kinesipathist
kinesitherapy
knock-for-knock
knowledgeable
knowledgeably
kapellmeister
kiss-and-make-up
kissing-comfit
kiss-in-the-ring
kittenishness
kitchen-garden
kitchen-midden
kittly-benders
kettledrummer
kitty-cornered
knuckle-headed
knuckleduster
loathsomeness
leather-jacket
leather-winged
leather-lunged
leasing-making
labialisation
labialization
librarianship
labefactation
labyrinthical
labyrinthitis
laboriousness
liberationism
liberationist
lackadaisical
lickerishness
lichenologist
lecherousness
lectisternium
lycanthropist
lactobacillus
Lycopodiaceae
Lecythidaceae
ludicrousness
lady-in-waiting
Liebfraumilch
laevorotation
laevorotatory
left-handiness
lifting-bridge
life-preserver
life-rendering
logographical
lignification
logarithmical
legislatively
legislatorial
light-fingered
lightning-tube
light-emitting
lightsomeness
lighthouseman
light-spirited
leishmaniases
leishmaniasis
leishmanioses
leishmaniosis
Leibnizianism
laissez-passer
lampadephoria
lymphatically
lymphotrophic
Lamellicornia
lamellibranch
lemon-coloured
Lamarckianism
limitlessness
long-descended
lance-sergeant
line-engraving
lantern-pinion
lance-corporal
linsey-woolsey
line-fisherman
landing-ground
land-measuring
land-ownership
longsuffering
land-surveying
languishingly
linguistician
Lepidodendron
lepidopterist
lepidopterous
Lepidostrobus
lipogrammatic
leptocephalic
leptocephalus
leptophyllous
leptospirosis
laryngectomee
laryngoscopic
laryngologist
listening-post
Lasiocampidae
lissotrichous
lethargically
letter-carrier
letter-founder
letter-heading
lithesomeness
letter-perfect
letter-quality
letters-patent
litigiousness
lattice-girder
lattice-bridge
luteinisation
luteinization
Latin-American
lithotriptist
lithontriptic
lithontriptor
leucaemogenic
launching-ways
launching-site
laughableness
laughing-stock
leucitohedron
leuco-compound
leuko-compound
leukocythemia
Louis-Quatorze
level-crossing
lavender-water
liver-coloured
livery-servant
lawn-sprinkler
lexicographic
lexicographer
lexigraphical
luxuriousness
lozenge-shaped
measuring-tape
measuring-worm
mechanisation
mechanization
mycobacterium
machine-pistol
machine-gunner
mocking-thrush
machicolation
Machiavellism
Machiavellian
microwaveable
microcassette
macrodactylic
macroeconomic
microeconomic
microscopical
microdetector
macrocephalic
microcephalic
micrometrical
microfelsitic
microphyllous
macropinakoid
macrodiagonal
microlighting
macroglobulin
microanalysis
microtonality
macromolecule
microcosmical
microporosity
microcomputer
micro-organism
microcracking
microprinting
microgranitic
microsurgical
micronutrient
macaronically
mycotoxicosis
mediatisation
mediatization

13 m□d□a

mediatorially
medicamentary
middle-bracket
muddle-brained
middlebreaker
Middle-Eastern
modernisation
modernization
moderatorship
△mediterranean
mnemotechnics
mnemotechnist
magnanimously
megacephalous
magnetisation
magnetization
magnetomotive
magnetosphere
magneto-optics
megaherbivore
magnification
magnificently
magniloquence
megaloblastic
megalopolitan
megalosaurian
Maginot-minded
magnoliaceous
magisterially
megasporangia
megastructure
might-have-been
magazine-rifle
Mohammedanise
Mohammedanize
Mohammedanism
maiden-tongued
maiden-widowed
maid-of-all-work
mainstreeting
Meistersinger
malacological
maliciousness
malacophilous
malacostracan
melodramatise
melodramatize
melodramatist
maladminister
milk-dentition
melodiousness
maladroitness
maladaptation
maladjustment
mallemaroking
malleableness
millefeuilles
millennianism
millenniarism
millennialist
mulberry-faced
Malthusianism
multicamerate
multicapitate
multiramified
multinational
multipartyism
multicellular
Malpighiaceae
multifilament
mellification
mollification
multilinguist
multidigitate
multivibrator
multiskilling
multiplicable
multiplicator
mellifluently
mellifluously
millionairess
multicoloured
multilobulate
multiloculate
multiloquence
multipresence
multigravidae
multigravidas
multi-authored
multitudinary
multitudinous
multinucleate
multicultural
melanochroous
melancholious
malariologist
Melastomaceae
△millstone-grit
molluscicidal
mammaliferous
mummification
momentariness
momentousness
memorableness
membranaceous
man-management
manganiferous
Manichaeanism
monochromatic
monochromator
monocotyledon
monodactylous
mine-detection
mind-expanding
manufacturing
manifold-paper
manifestative
manifestation
mini-flyweight
monographical
manageability
monogrammatic
managerialism
managerialist
mundificative
mundification
monomolecular
monometallism
monometallist
mononucleosis
meningococcic
meningococcal
meningococcus
mangold-wurzel
manipulatable
monopsonistic
monophosphate
monophthongal
△monophysitism
Monarchianism
mineralogical
mini-submarine
many-sidedness
ministerially
monosyllabism
monosymmetric
monostrophics
monothalamous
monotrematous
△monotheletism
△monothelitism
monotelephone
monstrousness
mensurability
money-grubbing
mortal-staring
miracle-monger
meridionality
marketability
marketization
mercerisation
mercerization
myrmecologist
marsh-samphire
mirthlessness
morphographer
morphogenesis
morphogenetic
morphological
merchandising
merchandizing
morphinomania
morphophoneme
mercilessness
marriage-lines
morning-prayer
mortification
morbillivirus
marsipobranch
morale-booster
marble-hearted
mirror-writing
Myristicaceae
Morisonianism
meritoriously
martyrologist
mismanagement
misobservance
musicological
mesocephalism
mesocephalous
musicotherapy
misadvertence
misadventured
misadventurer
master-builder
misperception
miscegenation
masterfulness
messenger-wire
mesmerisation
mesmerization
miscellaneous
master-mariner
master-passion
mispersuasion
Messerschmitt
mystery-monger
mischief-maker
mischievously
misshapenness
mystification
mashie-niblick
mastigophoric
mastigophoran
muscle-reading
misemployment
mass-marketing
mesencephalic
mesencephalon
misunderstand
misunderstood
misanthropist
misconception
misgovernment
misconjecture
miscomprehend
miscorrection
misappreciate
miserableness
misproportion
mistrustfully
mistrustingly
mesaticephaly
masculineness
mutualisation
mutualization
mitochondrial
mitochondrion
mathematicise
mathematicize
mathematicism
mathematician
mother-of-pearl

Words marked △ may be spelled also with a capital letter

metafictional
metagrabolise
metagrabolize
metagrobolise
metagrobolize
matchlessness
matchboarding
metrification
matrilineally
matrifocality
matrimonially
matriculation
matriculatory
metallisation
metallization
metalliferous
metallography
metallurgical
metempiricism
metempiricist
metamorphoses
metamorphosis
metonymically
mutton-dummies
meteoriticist
Methodistical
meteorologist
methodologist
mutton-thumper
metaphosphate
metoposcopist
metapsychical
metaphysician
materfamilias
materialistic
motor-traction
metastability
moulding-board
mouse-coloured
mouthwatering
mouthbreather
maurikigusari
mourning-bride
mourning-coach
mourning-cloak
mourning-piece
mourning-stuff
mountebankery
mountebanking
mountebankism
mountains-high
mounting-block
mowing-machine
myxoedematous
maxillofacial
muzzle-loading
mezzo-sopranos
△**neanderthaler**
near-sightedly
Nyctaginaceae
nectariferous
nickel-and-dime
nickeliferous
nickel-plating
nucleoprotein
noctivagation
nick-nackatory
necromantical
necroscopical
necessariness
necessitarian
necessitation
necessitously
needle-pointed
nefariousness
niggardliness
neglectedness
negligibility
night-warbling
night-watchman
night-wanderer
nightmarishly
negotiability
nightclubbing
night-tripping
no-holds-barred
noiselessness
neighbourless
neighbourhood
nullification
noli-me-tangere
nomographical
nymphaeaceous
nomenclatural
nominatively
numerological
numismatology
nemathelminth
namby-pambical
namby-pambyish
namby-pambyism
non-pathogenic
non-observance
non-accessible
non-scientific
non-acceptance
non-accidental
non-regardance
nondescriptly
Nintendinitus
non-resistance
non-negotiable
nonsensically
non-persistent
non-returnable
non-aggression
non-biological
non-classified
non-concurrent
non-conclusive
non-conducting
non-forfeiting
nonconforming
△**nonconformist**
nonconformity
non-collegiate
nannoplankton
non-commercial
non-cognizable
non-compliance
non-compounder
non-contagious
non-specialist
non-appearance
non-productive
non-production
non-proficient
non-attendance
non-functional
non-fulfilment
non-judgmental
Neo-Lamarckism
Neo-Lamarckian
Neo-Kantianism
Neo-Melanesian
neoclassicism
neoplasticism
Neo-Plasticism
neoclassicist
neologistical
neogrammarian
nephelometric
nephrological
naphthylamine
normalisation
normalization
normativeness
noradrenaline
nervelessness
nerve-wracking
north-eastward
north-easterly
north-westward
north-westerly
northerliness
nursing-father
narrowcasting
narcotisation
narcotization
narco-analysis
narcohypnosis
nostalgically
Netherlandish
netting-needle
nitrification
nitwittedness
nitroparaffin
nationalistic
nitrobacteria
nitro-compound
notoriousness
nature-worship
neuraminidase
neurasthenlac
neurovascular
neuropathical
neurolinguist
neurofibromas
neuroblastoma
neurotoxicity
neurocomputer
neuroethology
neuromuscular
neurosurgical
novocentenary
navigableness
newfangleness
orange-blossom
oraculousness
occidentalise
occidentalize
Occidentalism
Occidentalist
orchesography
orchestration
orchestralist
orchidomaniac
orchidologist
occasionalism
occasionalist
occasionality
old-clothesman
odd-come-shorts
operativeness
overabounding
overabundance
over-anxiously
overbearingly
over-breathing
overcredulity
overcredulous
over-confident
overexcitable
over-exquisite
overflowingly
oreographical
overhastiness
overindulgent
overinsurance
overmultitude
oleomargarine
oceanographic
oceanographer
oceanological
overqualified
oneiroscopist
overstatement
oversubscribe
overvaluation
offhandedness
olfactologist
officiousness
off-reckonings
offensiveness

Words marked △ may be spelled also with a capital letter

13 o□g□n

organogenesis
organotherapy
ophthalmology
ophiomorphous
ochlocratical
other-directed
otherworldish
oligopolistic
onirocritical
oligocythemia
opisthobranch
opisthography
objectivation
objectiveness
objectivistic
objectionable
objectionably
obliviousness
omnicompetent
ornamentation
owner-occupied
owner-occupier
ornithischian
ornithichnite
ornithomantic
ornithophobia
ornithologist
obnoxiousness
Orobanchaceae
odonatologist
onomatopoesis
onomatopoetic
onomastically
ozone-friendly
odoriferously
ovoviviparous
omoplatoscopy
odontoglossum
odontological
odontophorous
odontornithes
oppignoration
opprobriously
opportuneness
opportunities
opportunistic
oppositionist
oyster-catcher
oyster-fishery
obstetrically
obstinateness
observational
obstructively
obstructional
obsessionally
octocentenary
ostreiculture
ostreophagous
outsettlement
outrecuidance
ontogenically
ontologically
ostensibility
orthopaedical
osteopetrosis
orthopinakoid
orthodiagonal
orthosilicate
orthognathism
orthognathous
ortho-compound
orthographist
orthostichous
osteomyelitis
outspokenness
otter-trawling
obtuse-angular
outstandingly
obtrusiveness
octave-coupler
onychophagist
phalansterism
phalansterian
phalansterist
peaceableness
peacelessness
peace-offering
prayerfulness
phanerogamous
planetologist
pease-porridge
phase-contrast
plate-printing
peach-coloured
pharisaically
plagiocephaly
planimetrical
platiniferous
Plagiostomata
plagiostomous
pianistically
plagiotropism
plagiotropous
platinum-blond
platitudinise
platitudinize
platitudinous
phallocentric
pearl-shelling
pharmacognosy
pharmacopoeia
pharmaceutics
pharmaceutist
plasmodesmata
psammophilous
pragmatically
plaintiveness
phaenological
peacock-throne
peacock-flower
peacock-copper
prairie-oyster
plausibleness
practicalness
plantie-cruive
plantain-eater
phantasmalian
phantasmality
platycephalic
pharyngoscope
pharyngoscopy
platyrrhinian
pebble-glasses
pococurantism
pococurantist
pocket-picking
packing-needle
pucciniaceous
pycnidiospore
pickle-herring
pycnoconidium
picture-palace
picture-window
picturesquely
pedicellariae
pedagogically
pudding-headed
pudding-sleeve
pidginisation
pidginization
paddle-steamer
pedantocratic
podophthalmus
Podostemaceae
pedestrianise
pedestrianize
pedestrianism
preparatively
preparatorily
premandibular
Pre-Raphaelite
Pre-Raphaelism
prevarication
predatoriness
prefatorially
prefabricated
prefabricator
precautionary
prematureness
presbyacousis
presbytership
phencyclidine
prescientific
prescriptible
preoccupation
pseudo-archaic
preadolescent
pseudomonades
pseudomorphic
pre-adamitical
preadmonition
preadaptation
preferability
pretendership
premeditative
premedication
premeditation
preteriteness
predefinition
pretermission
pretermitting
preternatural
preterperfect
Pherecrataean
presentiality
predestinator
pretentiously
precentorship
preserving-pan
psephological
plethorically
predicamental
predicatively
predicability
presidentship
precipitately
precipitative
plebification
precipitation
preliminaries
preliminarily
precipitantly
precipitously
premillennial
pteridologist
plesiosaurian
paediatrician
prehistorical
prefigurative
prefiguration
prefigurement
plenitudinous
phellogenetic
phelloplastic
pneumogastric
pneumonectomy
pneumatically
pneumatolysis
pneumatolytic
pneumatometer
pneumatophore
preambulatory
pre-engagement
prerogatively
piezomagnetic
preconception
preponderance
preponderancy
phenomenalise
phenomenalize
phenomenalism
phenomenalist
phenomenality
phenomenology

Words marked △ may be spelled also with a capital letter

phenothiazine
preconisation
preconization
predomination
predominantly
premonishment
prepositively
prepositional
premonitorily
piezoelectric
paedomorphism
prepossessing
prepossession
precopulatory
preordainment
preprogrammed
preordination
plentifulness
plectognathic
plenteousness
plectopterous
prejudicative
prejudication
prejudicially
presumptively
phenylalanine
pterylography
pigheadedness
pigeon-chested
pigeon-fancier
pigeon-hearted
pigeon-livered
Philadelphian
privateersman
privatisation
privatization
primatologist
peirastically
philanthropic
psilanthropic
principalness
principalship
pricelessness
prizefighting
philhellenism
philhellenist
priming-powder
primitiveness
poikilothermy
primigravidae
primigravidas
prick-me-dainty
prick-the-louse
prismatically
philomathical
prison-breaker
primordialism
primordiality
primogenitary
primogenitive
primogenitrix
primogeniture
Psilophytales
philosophical
philosophiser
philosophizer
poisonousness
pointlessness
printing-house
printing-press
pointing-stock
polyadelphous
palpable-gross
paleanthropic
Paleanthropus
palebiologist
pelican-flower
polychromatic
polycarbonate
polycythaemia
polecat-ferret
polydactylism
polydactylous
polydaemonism
palaeobiology
palaeobotanic
polyembryonic
palaeoclimate
palaeocrystic
palaeoecology
pulselessness
palaeographic
palaeographer
palletisation
palletization
pelletisation
pelletization
pulverisation
pulverization
palaeontology
Palaeotherium
palaeozoology
polygalaceous
polygonaceous
phlogisticate
Phlegethontic
polyhistorian
palmification
pollicitation
polliniferous
Polemoniaceae
palingenesist
palynological
polynomialism
palindromical
paleoecologic
paleopedology
paleobiologic
paleoclimatic
paleobotanist
poliomyelitis
Polypodiaceae
polyphloisbic
Peloponnesian
polyprotodont
polypropylene
pilgrim-bottle
polysyllabism
polysyllogism
polysynthesis
polysynthetic
polythalamous
palatableness
polytechnical
pompier-ladder
pentadactylic
pentadelphous
panharmonicon
Pantagruelism
Pantagruelian
Pantagruelion
Pantagruelist
pentastichous
pentasyllabic
penicillinase
penicilliform
panic-stricken
ponderability
panleucopenia
△**pandemoniacal**
ponderousness
panaesthetism
Pan-Africanism
panegyrically
pantheistical
penthemimeral
Punchinelloes
panchromatism
pantheologist
pencil-compass
pennilessness
pinking-shears
pontificality
pantisocratic
pandiculation
peninsularity
pentobarbital
panspermatism
panspermatist
panophthalmia
pendragonship
pangrammatist
penuriousness
punishability
panpsychistic
penetratively
penetratingly
penetrability
punctiliously
penitentially
pendulousness
penny-farthing
penny-pinching
prosaicalness
propaedeutics
probabilities
probabilistic
protanomalous
proparoxytone
phonautograph
proterandrous
proverbialise
proverbialize
proverbialism
proverbialist
proteoclastic
phonendoscope
phonetisation
phonetization
progenitorial
proteinaceous
prolegomenary
prolegomenous
proterogynous
process-server
processionary
processioning
pooper-scooper
professoriate
professorship
proleptically
Protestantise
Protestantize
Protestantism
protectionism
projectionist
protectionist
protectorless
prosectorship
protectorship
profectitious
prosecutorial
prosecutrices
prosecutrixes
procès-verbaux
pro-chancellor
prophetically
profitability
provincialise
provincialize
provincialism
provincialist
provinciality
promiscuously
proliferative
proliferation
proliferously
promise-breach
prolification
prohibitively
provisionally
profit-sharing
problematical
pro-and-conning

13 p□o□n

prognosticate
protolanguage
provocatively
promotability
prosopagnosia
phonocamptics
protoactinium
photoreceptor
photoperiodic
photochemical
photochromism
photochromics
Protochordata
protochordate
photophoresis
propositional
proto-historic
photoelectric
photoelectron
photo-emission
pronounceable
pronouncement
protonotarial
protonotariat
Protococcales
photocopiable
prosopopoeial
prosopography
photovoltaics
protospataire
phonographist
photographist
proconsulship
proportionate
proportioning
Photostatting
prospect-glass
prospectively
phosphoretted
phosphorylase
phosphorylate
phosphuretted
procreational
propraetorial
proprietorial
propraetorian
proprioceptor
procrastinate
progressively
progressivism
progressivist
progressional
prostaglandin
plotting-paper
prosthodontia
prostatectomy
procuratorial
pronunciation
protuberation
protuberantly
producibility
pepper-and-salt
popping-crease
papilliferous
Papilionaceae
papillomatous
peptonisation
peptonization
papaprelatist
paper-hangings
paper-fastener
paper-mulberry
papaveraceous
pervasiveness
phreatophytic
Parnassianism
parabolically
perichondrial
perichondrium
perscrutation
paradoxically
porcelaineous
△perpendicular
perseveration
perseveringly
pyrheliometer
porcellaneous
purse-snatcher
perfectionate
perfectionism
△perfectionist
perfervidness
paraffin-scale
paragraphical
peregrination
peregrinatory
perigastritis
parthenocarpy
perihepatitis
parking-ticket
porridge-stick
participative
participating
participation
participatory
participantly
participially
partition-wall
perditionable
partitionment
parliamentary
parliamenting
parliament-man
parti-coloured
particularise
particularize
particularism
particularist
particularity
parallactical
parallelistic
parallelogram
purple-in-grain
paraleipomena
paralipomenon
perplexedness
pyramidically
paramagnetism
paramenstruum
pyrimethamine
perambulation
perambulatory
paramyxovirus
parencephalon
parenthetical
perennibranch
phrenological
Pyrenomycetes
perinephritis
phrenetically
personalistic
parrot-disease
purposelessly
parrot-fashion
periodisation
periodization
periodicalist
purposiveness
periodontitis
perspicacious
perspectively
perspectivism
perspectivist
perspicuously
peripherality
paraphernalia
pyrophosphate
parapophysial
peripatetical
parapsychical
parapsychosis
partridge-wood
perishability
pyrosulphuric
parasynthesis
parasynthetic
parasyntheton
perissodactyl
phraseologist
parasitically
pyrotechnical
puritanically
perityphlitis
pyretotherapy
Portulacaceae
perdurability
permutability
perfunctorily
porcupine-wood
percussion-cap
percussionist
perlustration
perivitelline
party-coloured
party-spirited
postclassical
post-communion
passementerie
passenger-mile
posterization
Passeriformes
post-existence
possessionate
possessionary
possessorship
pasigraphical
puss-gentleman
paschal-candle
paschal-flower
pestiferously
possibilities
pessimistical
passion-flower
piscicultural
pusillanimity
pusillanimous
postliminiary
postliminious
post-modernism
post-modernist
postmenstrual
post-operative
post-traumatic
post-tensioned
postulational
posture-master
phthalocyanin
pitch-farthing
pitched-roofed
petrification
patrilineally
patrifocality
patrimonially
patriotically
potamological
potentiometer
pathogenicity
petrochemical
petrophysical
petroliferous
patronisingly
patronizingly
pathognomonic
Pythonomorpha
petrocurrency
paterfamilias
paternalistic
putty-coloured
potty-training
pluralisation
pluralization
plumbisolvent
plumbosolvent
pauperisation

Words marked △ may be spelled also with a capital letter

pauperization
prudentialism
prudentialist
prudentiality
pruning-shears
pluripresence
powdering-room
powdering-gown
powerlessness
power-assisted
phylacterical
psychoanalyse
psychoanalyze
psychoanalyst
psychiatrical
psychobiology
psychodynamic
psychographic
psychogenesis
psychogenetic
psychohistory
psychokinesis
psychokinetic
psychological
psychometrics
psychometrist
psychrometric
psychrophilic
psychopathist
psychophysics
physharmonica
psychasthenia
psychosomatic
psychosurgery
psychotherapy
physiographic
physiographer
physiognomist
physitheistic
physicianship
physiological
physiotherapy
phyllophagous
phylloquinone
phytochemical
phytoplankton
phytotoxicity
phycoerythrin
quatch-buttock
Quaker-buttons
quaternionist
qualitatively
qualificative
qualification
qualificatory
quasi-contract
quadricipital
quadrifoliate
quadrifarious
quatrefeuille
quadrigeminal

quadragesimal
quadrilocular
quadrillionth
quadrilingual
quarrelsomely
quadrilateral
quadriliteral
quadrumvirate
quadringenary
quadrennially
quadruplicate
quadruplicity
quadraphonics
quadrophonics
quadripartite
quadrisection
quadrivalence
quartz-crystal
quartodeciman
quartz-halogen
quartziferous
quartermaster
quarterdecker
quarter-hourly
quarter-gunner
quantivalence
questioningly
questionnaire
querulousness
quincentenary
quincuncially
quingentenary
quick-scenting
quick-tempered
quicksilvered
quick-answered
Quinquagesima
quinquevalent
quinquivalent
quintillionth
quilting-frame
quilting-party
quintuplicate
quizzing-glass
quotation-mark
quodlibetical
Rhadamanthine
reacclimatise
reacclimatize
rhabdomantist
reaffirmation
realisability
realizability
realistically
road-metalling
reapplication
reappointment
realpolitiker
rearrangement
rhapsodically
reattribution

reactionarism
reactionarist
Rhaeto-Romanic
Rhaeto-Romance
rebecca-eureka
robe-de-chambre
rabble-rousing
rectangularly
Rickettsiales
receivability
rectipetality
recriminative
recrimination
rectification
recriminatory
rectilinearly
receiving-ship
receiving-line
receiving-room
rectitudinous
recollectedly
recalcitrance
recommendable
recommendably
recombination
recomposition
recomfortless
recompression
reconcilement
reconsolidate
reconnoiterer
reconstituent
reconstructor
receptiveness
receptibility
reciprocative
reciprocating
reciprocation
reciprocality
recessiveness
recitationist
recrudescence
recrudescency
recrystallise
recrystallize
radialisation
radialization
reducibleness
reductiveness
redeemability
radiesthesist
redding-straik
redeliverance
rudimentarily
Redemptionist
riding-clothes
radiolabelled
radio-actinium
radioactivity
radiotelegram
radioteletype

radiolocation
reduplicative
reduplication
redissolution
redevelopment
re-examination
re-embarkation
re-endorsement
re-enforcement
reefing-jacket
re-edification
re-eligibility
roe-blackberry
rheumatically
re-exportation
refractometer
refocillation
reflexiveness
reflexibility
reflexologist
reflectograph
refrigerative
refrigeration
refrigeratory
Rafflesiaceae
reformability
refurbishment
reference-mark
referentially
reforestation
refashionment
regimentation
rag-and-bone-man
regardfulness
regurgitation
register-plate
registrarship
right-thinking
righteousness
rehabilitator
reimbursement
rainbow-chaser
rainbow-tinted
reincarnation
reinforcement
rhinoscleroma
rhizomorphous
reinstatement
reintegration
reinterrogate
railway-stitch
rejuvenescent
roller-bearing
rollerblading
roller-bandage
rollercoaster
roller-skating
religiousness
roll-on-roll-off
rallying-point
remeasurement

13 r□m□e

rumlegumption
rumbledethump
rumelgumption
Romano-British
romanticality
reminiscently
remonstrative
remonstration
remonstratory
remonstrantly
ramapithecine
remorselessly
remissibility
remittance-man
rent-collector
ranz-des-vaches
röntgenoscopy
renegotiation
Ranunculaceae
randomisation
randomization
rensselaerite
root-and-branch
rhopalocerous
rhombohedrons
rhombporphyry
reorientation
rhodochrosite
republicanise
republicanize
republicanism
republication
rapaciousness
reprehensible
reprehensibly
representable
representment
re-presentment
representamen
replenishment
reptiliferous
repulsiveness
reproachfully
rapprochement
repetitionary
repetitiously
requisiteness
restaurant-car
Russification
resolvability
resplendently
resynchronise
resynchronize
restoratively
Russocentrism
Russocentrist
restrictively
risorgimentos
rust-resistant
resuscitative
resuscitation
resistibility
rusty-coloured
ritualisation
ritualization
retranslation
rutherfordium
retributively
rattle-brained
retentiveness
retinoscopist
rationalistic
retroactively
retroactivity
ratiocinative
ratiocination
ratiocinatory
retromingency
retroflection
retrospective
retrospection
retrogressive
retrogression
round-the-clock
round-tripping
rough-and-ready
reunification
revocableness
revaccination
revictualling
revolutionary
revolutionise
revolutionize
revolutionism
revelationist
revolutionist
revendication
revindication
reverberative
reverberation
reverberatory
reversibility
reversionally
reverentially
rhyparography
stalagmometer
stalagmometry
stalagmitical
stalactitical
stalactitious
shabby-genteel
scambling-days
searchingness
starch-reduced
staccatissimo
swaddling-band
scandal-bearer
scandalmonger
shamefastness
shamelessness
shapelessness
statelessness
state-of-the-art
seal-engraving
statesmanship
statesmanlike
stagecoaching
stagecoachman
scalenohedron
slate-coloured
skateboarding
Shakespearean
Shakespearian
snaffle-bridle
slaughterable
scaphocephaly
scathefulness
staphylococci
staphyloplasy
spathiphyllum
swashbuckling
scaling-ladder
scarification
stabilisation
stabilization
staminiferous
spadicifloral
station-master
statistically
stalking-horse
small-and-early
scarlet-runner
swallow-tailed
spasmodically
stainlessness
shadowcasting
seaworthiness
sharpshooting
scalpelliform
scalping-knife
statute-barred
scapulimantic
scapulomantic
shalwar-kameez
star-ypointing
sublanceolate
submandibular
submachine-gun
subeditorship
sabrerattling
sabre-rattling
subdeaconship
subternatural
sable-coloured
subterraneous
subversionary
subject-object
subventionary
subreptitious
subsequential
subserviently
subtilisation
subtilization
subdivisional
subsistential
sublieutenant
suballocation
subclavicular
subindicative
subindication
subinvolution
subcommission
subcontractor
sub-postmaster
sub-post-office
subcontiguous
subcontinuous
subpopulation
subspeciality
subappearance
subequatorial
subtriangular
subprefecture
subordinately
subordinative
subordinating
subirrigation
subordination
suburbicarian
subtropically
subtriplicate
substantively
substantivise
substantivize
substantivity
substantially
substitutable
substructural
subjunctively
sacramentally
sacralisation
sacralization
socialisation
socialization
secretaryship
secretiveness
successlessly
successionist
successorship
sick-feathered
Saccharomyces
saccharimeter
saccharometer
saccharimetry
succinctorium
sacrificially
section-cutter
secondariness
sacrosanctity
sectorisation
sectorization
sociolinguist
sociologistic
sycophantical

sacerdotalise
sacerdotalize
sacerdotalism
sacerdotalist
sick-thoughted
seductiveness
sedimentation
sedimentology
sadomasochism
sadomasochist
sodomitically
sedentariness
side-splitting
seditiousness
scenarisation
scenarization
spelaeologist
steganopodous
steganography
sketchability
speechfulness
Sterculiaceae
Spencerianism
stercoraceous
stercorarious
steadfastness
Swedenborgian
stereographic
speleological
skeletogenous
stereoscopist
stereotropism
stereotypical
sleight-of-hand
stethoscopist
seeming-simple
specification
sterilisation
sterilization
sneak-thievery
speaking-voice
swelled-headed
smelling-salts
spermatoblast
spermatogenic
spermatophore
Spermatophyta
spermatophyte
spermatorrhea
spermatotheca
seek-no-further
stern-foremost
Stegocephalia
stenophyllous
skeuomorphism
stenographist
steeplechaser
sleeplessness
sheepshearing
stepping-stone
step-parenting
sheep-stealing
sherry-cobbler
sweet-savoured
spectacularly
sweet-tempered
smelting-house
smelting-works
spectroscopic
spectrometric
spectrography
spectatorship
speculatively
suffocatingly
suffraganship
suffragettism
soft-sectoring
safety-deposit
suffumigation
signal-to-noise
sagaciousness
suggestionism
suggestionist
significative
signification
significatory
significantly
sigmoidectomy
sigmoidoscope
sigmoidoscopy
sugar-refinery
sugar-refining
sightlessness
schwärmerisch
schadenfreude
Schwenkfelder
sphagnicolous
sphagnologist
sphygmography
scholarliness
scholasticism
schematically
sphingomyelin
schoolgirlish
school-leaving
school-marmish
schoolteacher
school-trained
sphericalness
spherocytosis
spheroidicity
spheristerion
schutzstaffel
schizocarpous
schizaeaceous
schizogenesis
schizogenetic
schizomycetic
Schizomycetes
schizophrenia
schizophrenic
Schizophyceae
spindle-legged
spindle-shanks
spindle-shaped
spinelessness
spine-chilling
seine-shooting
spine-tingling
spifflication
swinge-buckler
shingle-roofed
swinging-block
sailing-master
suicidologist
spiritousness
spirit-rapping
spiritualness
spiritualiser
spiritualizer
stick-in-the-mud
sticking-point
skirl-in-the-pan
stillroom-maid
seismographic
seismographer
seismological
swimming-baths
stigmatically
skinny-dipping
spinning-house
spinning-jenny
spinning-wheel
Scientologist
ship-of-the-line
stirpiculture
skittle-ground
shiftlessness
Saint-Simonism
Saint-Simonian
Saint-Simonist
scintillation
scintilliscan
skirting-board
snifting-valve
scintiscanner
spinuliferous
self-awareness
self-abasement
self-addressed
sulfacetamide
sulfathiazole
sulfanilamide
syllabication
self-adjusting
self-annealing
self-appointed
self-approving
self-assertive
self-asserting
self-assertion
self-assurance
self-balancing
self-criticism
self-collected
self-communion
self-contained
self-conscious
self-condemned
self-confessed
self-conceited
self-confident
self-confiding
self-convicted
self-conjugate
self-consuming
salaciousness
sale-catalogue
solicitorship
self-deceitful
self-deception
self-defeating
self-denyingly
solidungulate
solidungulous
self-dependent
self-direction
self-discharge
self-dispraise
selfe-despight
self-executing
self-existence
self-enjoyment
silver-mounted
sylleptically
silver-tongued
solifidianism
self-financing
self-forgetful
self-fertility
self-governing
sulphadiazine
sulphonylurea
self-hypnotism
sulphureously
sulphur-bottom
sulphuretting
self-inductive
self-induction
self-indulgent
self-infection
self-inflicted
salpingectomy
selling-plater
salviniaceous
self-injection
self-important
soldierliness
self-insurance
sylvicultural
self-judgement
self-knowledge
self-levelling
solemnisation

13 s□l□m

solemnization
self-murdering
self-motivated
splinter-proof
selenographic
selenographer
splanchnocele
splanchnology
splendiferous
selenological
splenetically
self-operating
salmonellosis
salmon-fishing
syllogisation
syllogization
self-opinioned
syllogistical
self-publicist
self-publicity
self-pollution
self-propelled
self-professed
self-possessed
self-recording
sclerocaulous
sclerodermite
sclerodermous
self-referring
self-regarding
self-righteous
scleromalacia
self-repeating
self-repugnant
scleroprotein
self-reproving
self-restraint
self-revealing
self-reverence
self-slaughter
self-sacrifice
self-sterility
self-sufficing
self-shielding
self-supported
self-surrender
self-surviving
self-sustained
self-satisfied
splutteringly
self-treatment
self-tormentor
silk-throwster
somnambulance
somnambulator
sympathectomy
sympatholytic
sympathetical
semi-automatic
semi-barbarism
semi-barbarian
semiconscious
semiconductor
semicarbazide
semi-evergreen
symmetrically
summer-seeming
symphyseotomy
symphysiotomy
sempiternally
somniloquence
sympiesometer
symbiotically
simplificator
simple-hearted
semimenstrual
semiochemical
symbolisation
symbolization
semioviparous
Semnopithecus
symbolistical
symbolography
semipalmation
semiporcelain
semi-permeable
semiperimeter
semiparasitic
simarubaceous
semi-sagittate
semasiologist
sempstressing
somatological
symptomatical
sumptuousness
somatotrophic
somatotrophin
sensationally
syntactically
synecphonesis
synecological
sansculottism
sansculottist
synecdochical
senselessness
sententiously
synchondroses
synchondrosis
synchronicity
synchronistic
synchronology
synchronously
synthetically
syndicalistic
sentimentally
sensitisation
sensitization
sensitiveness
sensibilities
synallagmatic
single-chamber
single-hearted
sindonologist
sunworshipper
synaposematic
synarthrodial
seneschalship
sinistrorsely
sanctifyingly
sanctimonious
sanitarianism
sanitationist
sandy-laverock
stop-and-search
stomatoplasty
scorched-earth
stoicheiology
scorchingness
stoechiometry
stoichiometry
stop-consonant
spondylolysis
swordsmanship
suovetaurilia
smokelessness
Scoleciformia
stone-coloured
smoke-consumer
spokespersons
sponging-house
soothfastness
scorification
Scotification
shock-absorber
stocking-soles
stockbreeding
swollen-headed
scolopendrine
scolopendrium
stoloniferous
stopping-place
smooth-chinned
smooth-dittied
short-tempered
sportsmanship
sportsmanlike
shooting-match
spontaneously
smooth-tongued
sportswriting
supranational
supratemporal
suprasensible
suprachiasmic
supramolecule
supra-axillary
septentrional
septentriones
syphilisation
syphilization
syphilophobia
syphilologist
sophistically
sophisticated
sophisticator
supplementary
supplantation
suppositional
supercalender
supersalesman
superlatively
supernational
supercautious
supersaturate
separableness
superabundant
superaddition
superfetation
supervenience
supersensible
supersensibly
superphysical
superfineness
superficially
supervirulent
superfluidity
superfluously
supereminence
superannuable
superannuated
superdominant
superposition
supercollider
supernormally
supercomputer
supercolumnar
superorganism
superordinate
superordinary
supercriminal
supercritical
separationism
separationist
superstitious
superhumanise
superhumanize
superhumanity
supernumerary
supersubtlety
supersymmetry
sequestration
sequentiality
surface-active
surface-vessel
serialisation
serialization
sarcastically
scrobiculated
strobilaceous
scribbling-pad
sericiculture
sericulturist
seroconverted
Saracen's-stone

Words marked △ may be spelled also with a capital letter

structuralism
structuration
structuralist
structureless
screech-martin
screech-thrush
serjeant-at-law
sergeant-major
sarmentaceous
serpent-lizard
surreptitious
streetwalking
sprightliness
surchargement
survivability
straightforth
straight-pight
sorbitisation
sorbitization
strikebreaker
serologically
shrill-tongued
scrumptiously
strombuliform
spring-cleaner
stringentness
serendipitist
serendipitous
strenuousness
syringomyelia
string-pulling
strengthening
strangulation
surrogateship
sorrowfulness
sarcophaguses
Serbo-Croatian
strophiolated
streptocarpus
streptokinase
Syrophoenicia
streptococcic
streptococcal
△streptococcus
scripophilist
scripturalism
scripturalist
strato-cumulus
stratigraphic
stratigrapher
strategically
stretcher-bond
stratospheric
scrivenership
straw-coloured
spray-painting
systematician
systematology
supercollate
suspender-belt
systemisation
systemization
sustentaculum
sustentacular
suspectedness
suspicionless
sesquiplicate
sesquiterpene
satanicalness
satiricalness
squeamishness
soundproofing
squeezability
snuff-coloured
spunging-house
south-eastward
south-easterly
south-westward
south-westerly
southerliness
skulking-place
squanderingly
squandermania
saurognathous
Sauropterygia
sculpturesque
square-bashing
square-dancing
square-pierced
squirarchical
soul-searching
△sovietologist
savanna-wattle
savanna-forest
seventeenthly
sewing-machine
Saxifragaceae
sexagesimally
sexploitation
Scyphomedusae
stylistically
Thalamiflorae
thalamifloral
thanatophobia
thanatography
thalassocracy
thalattocracy
tram-conductor
traceableness
trade-weighted
tradesmanlike
trapezohedral
trapezohedron
travel-stained
travel-tainted
traffic-lights
teachableness
traditionally
toad-in-the-hole
thanklessness
tracklessness
thank-offering
thankworthily
traumatically
thaumatolatry
traumatonasty
thaumaturgism
thaumaturgics
thaumaturgist
train-spotting
tranquilliser
tranquillizer
transparently
translational
transnational
translatorial
transactinide
transactional
transcendence
transcendency
transfer-paper
transferrable
transferrible
transversally
transpersonal
transientness
transshipment
transshipping
transmination
transpiration
transpiratory
transliterate
transmigrator
transmissible
transmittable
transmittible
transmittance
transplanting
translocation
transpositive
transposition
transformable
transportable
transportedly
transport-ship
transportance
transcribable
transcriptase
transcriptive
transcription
transgressive
transgression
transisthmian
transistorise
transistorize
transatlantic
transit-circle
transitionary
transmutative
transmutation
translucently
transfusively
translucidity
tractableness
toastmistress
Tractarianism
tobaccanalian
table-skittles
tablespoonful
tubuliflorous
tuberculation
ticket-of-leave
ticket-writing
tachistoscope
tickly-benders
technicalness
technological
technopolitan
tachometrical
tachymetrical
tachygraphist
tiddledywinks
treacherously
thenceforward
thereinbefore
theriomorphic
theologically
theologoumena
trellis-window
thermobalance
thermochemist
thermodynamic
thermographic
thermographer
thermogenesis
thermogenetic
thermonuclear
thermoplastic
thermophilous
thermosetting
thermotherapy
thermotropism
theanthropism
theanthropist
Theopaschitic
theorematical
theoretically
treasure-chest
treasure-house
treasurership
treasure-trove
trestle-bridge
theatricalise
theatricalize
theatricalism
theatricality
tremulousness
tricarboxylic
trisaccharide
trilateralism
trilateration
trilateralist
tricarpellary
thimblerigged

13 t□i□b

thimblerigger
thiocarbamide
twiddling-line
Third-Worldism
toilet-service
thing-in-itself
tritheistical
trichological
trichromatism
trichopterist
trichopterous
triliteralism
trilingualism
trickle-charge
thick-wittedly
thick-pleached
triple-crowned
thigmotropism
triangulately
triangulation
triangularity
triboelectric
trigonometric
tricorporated
trisoctahedra
thiosulphuric
triatomically
triethylamine
tributariness
tritubercular
tribuniticial
tribunitician
triquetrously
trisyllabical
talkativeness
telecommuting
teleconverter
telecottaging
telegrammatic
telemarketing
telencephalic
telencephalon
talent-spotter
teleportation
telerecording
tolerationism
tolerationist
telescopiform
telautography
televangelism
televangelist
televisionary
time-beguiling
time-bettering
time-consuming
temperateness
temperamental
temperability
tamper-evident
tempest-beaten
tempest-tossed
tempestuously
tumbler-switch
temporariness
temporalities
temporisation
temporization
tomboyishness
temporisingly
temporizingly
tumorgenicity
tumorigenesis
timbrophilist
temerariously
temptableness
time-trialling
tantalisation
tantalization
tentativeness
tantalisingly
tantalizingly
Tenebrionidae
tenaciousness
tender-hearted
tenpenny-piece
tangentiality
tendentiously
tonsillectomy
tintinnabulum
tintinnabular
tenant-in-chief
tent-preaching
tenosynovitis
tongue-doubtie
tongue-in-cheek
tongue-lashing
tongue-twister
tenovaginitis
thoracentesis
Tropaeolaceae
thoracoplasty
troublesomely
troublousness
twopenceworth
twopenny-piece
two-pennyworth
thought-reader
thoughtlessly
trophoblastic
toothache-tree
trophallactic
troth-plighted
toothsomeness
tooth-ornament
trophotropism
troglodytical
trolling-spoon
thoroughbrace
thoroughgoing
thorough-paced
thousand-pound
trouser-pocket
trouser-button
trout-coloured
topographical
typographical
topside-turvey
topologically
tippling-house
tape-recording
taphrogenesis
topsy-turvydom
terra-japonica
threateningly
tartarisation
tartarization
three-farthing
three-per-cents
threepenn'orth
threefoldness
three-cornered
torrentiality
terrestrially
tercentennial
tariffication
terminatively
terminability
terminational
tergiversator
territorially
thrillingness
thremmatology
thrombophilia
thrombokinase
tyrannosaurus
turbocharging
terrorisation
terrorization
turbo-electric
tortoise-plant
tortoiseshell
terpsichoreal
terpsichorean
thresher-shark
thresher-whale
thrashing-mill
threshing-mill
thrasonically
teratogenesis
teratological
throttle-lever
throttle-valve
turquoise-blue
throwing-stick
throwing-table
tarry-fingered
tastelessness
Testicardines
testification
testificatory
tetrabasicity
tetrahedrally
tetrachloride
Tetrabranchia
tetrastichous
tetradynamous
tetrasyllabic
tetrasyllable
tithe-gatherer
tattie-howking
tattie-lifting
titillatingly
tittle-tattler
Titanotherium
totipalmation
tetartohedral
thunder-darter
thunder-master
thunder-bearer
thunder-shower
thunderstrike
thunder-stroke
thunderstruck
true-disposing
touchableness
truthlessness
thurification
trunk-breeches
tautometrical
tautophonical
tautochronism
tautochronous
Teutonisation
Teutonization
tautologously
tauromorphous
trumpet-shaped
trumpet-flower
tsutsugamushi
trustlessness
trustworthily
toxicological
toxicophagous
tax-deductible
taxonomically
toxoplasmosis
Thymelaeaceae
thyroidectomy
trysting-place
trysting-stile
unabbreviated
unambiguously
unambitiously
unaccompanied
unaccentuated
unascertained
unaccountable
unaccountably
un-Americanise
un-Americanize
unamiableness
uralitisation
uralitization
uranographist

unapostolical
unapprehended
unappreciated
unapprovingly
unappropriate
unassuageable
unassimilable
unassimilated
unarticulated
unanticipated
unadulterated
unadventurous
unadvisedness
unbiassedness
umbraculiform
umbrella-plant
umbrella-stand
unblessedness
unbridledness
unbelievingly
umbelliferous
unbendingness
unbrotherlike
unbeseemingly
unboundedness
unchastisable
unchastizable
uncleanliness
uncreatedness
urchin-snouted
uncalculating
uncompanioned
uncommendable
uncommendably
uncompetitive
uncompensated
uncomplicated
uncomplaisant
uncomplaining
uncomfortable
uncomfortably
uncontainable
unconsciously
unconcealable
unconcernedly
unconcernment
unconsecrated
unconversable
uncontestable
unconvertible
uncontentious
unconjectured
unconceivable
unconceivably
unconsidering
unconditioned
unconditional
unconformable
unconformably
unconstrained
unconjunctive
unconsummated
unconquerable
unconquerably
uncloudedness
uncoordinated
unco-ordinated
uncooperative
unco-operative
uncertainness
unceremonious
unchristianly
uncircumcised
uncourtliness
undifferenced
undulationist
undeliverable
undomesticate
undepreciated
underhandedly
underpainting
undercarriage
underachiever
under-shepherd
underniceness
underfinished
underclassman
underclothing
undergraduate
underprepared
underestimate
understrapper
underutilised
underutilized
understanding
underexposure
undescendable
undescendible
undiscernible
undiscernibly
undiscernedly
undistempered
undistinctive
undisciplined
undiscomfited
undissociated
undishonoured
undiscouraged
undescribable
undistributed
undistracting
undeservingly
undisturbedly
undiscussable
undiscussible
undisguisable
undisguisedly
undutifulness
undeterminate
undauntedness
undeviatingly
undividedness
undiversified
unevangelical
unexaggerated
unembellished
unembarrassed
unexceptional
unexclusively
unexemplified
unelectrified
unenforceable
urethroscopic
urediniospore
unenlightened
unemotionally
unexplainable
unexpressible
unexpensively
unexperienced
unearthliness
uneatableness
unestablished
unentertained
unequivocally
unfeelingness
unflinchingly
unfeignedness
unfalteringly
unfamiliarity
unforgettable
unforgettably
unforthcoming
unforgiveness
unforeseeable
unforeskinned
unfortunately
unfashionable
unfashionably
unguardedness
ungrammatical
ungainsayable
ungenuineness
ungentlemanly
unhealthfully
unhealthiness
unhurtfulness
unicameralism
unilateralism
unicameralist
unilateralist
unilaterality
uninaugurated
unimaginative
universalness
uninflammable
uninformative
uninforceable
uninfluential
uninhabitable
unilluminated
unillustrated
unimpeachable
unit-packaging
unimpregnated
unimpressible
unimpassioned
uninquisitive
uninstructive
unintelligent
unintentional
unintermitted
uninteresting
uninterrupted
unjustifiable
unjustifiably
unknowingness
unlearnedness
unlimitedness
unmeaningness
unmacadamised
unmacadamized
unmedicinable
unmindfulness
unmentionable
unministerial
unmurmuringly
unmistakeable
unmistakeably
unmistrustful
unmitigatedly
unnecessarily
unneighboured
unneighbourly
unnaturalness
unnaturalised
unnaturalized
unoriginality
unobstructive
unobtrusively
unpracticable
unpractically
unpreoccupied
unprecedented
unpresentable
unpreventable
unpretentious
unpredictable
unpredictably
unpleasurable
unpleasurably
unphilosophic
unpolarisable
unpolarizable
unpunctuality
unprophetical
unprovided-for
unpromisingly
unprovisioned
unprovocative
unprogressive
unperpetrated
unperfectness
unperceivable

13 u□p□r

unperceivably
unperceivedly
unpurchasable
unpersuadable
unpasteurised
unpasteurized
unpitifulness
unputdownable
unqualifiable
unqualifiedly
unquestioning
unreasoningly
unreclaimable
unreclaimably
unrecognising
unrecognizing
unrecollected
unrecommended
unrecompensed
unrecoverable
unrecoverably
unregenerated
unrighteously
uprighteously
unreliability
unrelentingly
unremembering
unremorseless
unremittently
unremittingly
unreplaceable
unrepresented
unreplenished
unreprimanded
unreprievable
unrepentingly
unreproachful
unreproaching
unrestfulness
unrestingness
unresistingly
unreturningly
unscavengered
unsparingness
unstaunchable
unsubstantial
unsociability
unstercorated
unsteadfastly
unspecialised
unspecialized
unspectacular
unspeculative
unsightliness
unscholarlike
unsuitability
unskilfulness
unspiritually
unstigmatised
unstigmatized
unsaintliness
unsalvageable
unsaleability
unselfishness
unsoldierlike
unsympathetic
unsymmetrical
unsymmetrised
unsymmetrized
unsensational
unsentimental
unsmotherable
unspottedness
unsupportable
unsupportedly
unsuperfluous
unsurpassable
unsurpassably
unserviceable
unshrinkingly
unscrutinised
unscrutinized
unsustainable
unsusceptible
unsuspectedly
unsettledness
unsatisfiable
unsavouriness
untraversable
ultrafiltrate
ultra-distance
ultra-virtuous
ultra-tropical
untransparent
untransmitted
untransformed
untremblingly
untheological
untrespassing
untaintedness
Ustilaginales
ustilagineous
untamableness
untenableness
untunableness
untunefulness
utterableness
unterrestrial
unthriftiness
unthriftyhead
up-to-the-minute
up-to-the-moment
untrustworthy
unvitrifiable
unwhistleable
unwillingness
unwelcomeness
unwomanliness
unwholesomely
unwarrantable
unwarrantably
unwarrantedly
unworldliness
unworkmanlike
unwithdrawing
unwithholding
unwittingness
vraisemblance
vibrationless
vibracularium
vice-admiralty
vice-consulate
victimisation
victimization
Vaccinioideae
victimologist
vacillatingly
vacuolisation
vacuolization
vectorisation
vectorization
vice-president
vice-principal
vicariousness
vocationalism
videocassette
vegetarianism
voicelessness
villagisation
villagization
volcanisation
volcanization
vulcanisation
vulcanization
vulgarisation
vulgarization
volta-electric
volcanologist
vulcanologist
Voltaireanism
Voltairianism
valedictorian
vulnerability
velvet-fiddler
villeggiatura
volumenometer
velt-mareschal
voluntariness
voluntaristic
Valerianaceae
volatilisable
volatilizable
viniculturist
veneficiously
venographical
vindicability
vindicatorily
Vansittartism
venerableness
ventriloquise
ventriloquize
ventriloquial
ventriloquism
ventriloquist
ventriloquous
venereologist
venturesomely
venturousness
viol-de-gamboys
violoncellist
vapourishness
verbalisation
verbalization
vernalisation
vernalization
versatileness
variable-pitch
variable-sweep
vernacularise
vernacularize
vernacularism
vernacularist
vernacularity
voraciousness
verifiability
verbigeration
varnishing-day
verbification
versification
verticillated
vertiginously
versicoloured
vermiculation
verumontanums
verisimilarly
veritableness
visualisation
visualization
visceroptosis
visionariness
viscometrical
viscosimetric
viticulturist
vitrification
vitelligenous
vote-splitting
vouchsafement
vaulting-horse
vaulting-house
vivaciousness
vivisectional
vivisectorium
vivisepulture
vexillologist
vexatiousness
what-d'ye-call-'em
what-d'ye-call-it
weather-headed
weather-beaten
weather-bitten
weatherometer
weather-driven
whaling-master
wearisomeness

wrapping-paper
wide-awakeness
wide-stretched
whereinsoever
weeding-chisel
wheeler-dealer
white-favoured
white-breasted
weight-lifting
whithersoever
weight-watcher
waiting-vassal
writing-master
writing-school
whiskerandoed
whirling-table
whipping-cream
whipping-cheer
whimsicalness
whistled-drunk
whistle-blower
whistling-shop
well-appointed
well-beseeming
well-connected
well-conducted
well-developed
walking-papers
walking-ticket
walking-orders
will-o'-the-wisps
well-preserved
well-regulated
well-respected
wills-o'-the-wisp
well-thought-of
well-warranted
well-worked-out
wamble-cropped
women-children
woman-suffrage
wonderfulness
winterisation
winterization
wonder-working
wonder-wounded
winding-engine
winding-strips
winkle-pickers
woodcock's-head
whoremasterly
wood-engraving
whoremistress
wholesomeness
whole-coloured
wrong-headedly
wool-gathering
woollen-draper
wappenshawing
word-blindness
worldly-minded
worthlessness
work-hardening
word-processor
word-splitting
Wordsworthian
wasterfulness
washing-liquid
washing-powder
washing-bottle
waspish-headed
wet-and-dry-bulb
water-vascular
water-carriage
waterflooding
watering-house
watering-place
watercolorist
water-softener
water-sprinkle
water-breather
waterproofing
water-standing
wayfaring-tree
xylographical
X-inactivation
xanthochroism
xanthochromia
xanthochroous
xanthopterine
xiphiplastral
xiphiplastron
xiphophyllous
xerodermatous
xerophthalmia
yachtsmanship
yieldableness
yellow-bellied
yellowishness
yuppification
yesterevening
yestermorning
zygodactylism
zygodactylous
zygapophyseal
zygapophysial
zymotechnical
Zingiberaceae
zincification
zinkification
zoogeographic
zoogeographer
zoophysiology
zoosporangium
zoopsychology
Zarathustrism
Zarathustrian

14 a□a□a

anacardiaceous
amaranthaceous
amateurishness
anachronically
arachnological
avariciousness
anamnestically
anagrammatical
Acanthocephala
anarthrousness
Amaryllidaceae
ambidextrously
Albigensianism
ambulancewoman
arboricultural
ambassadorship
archaeometrist
Archaeornithes
archaeological
archaeozoology
Asclepiadaceae
archgenethliac
alcoholisation
alcoholization
acclimatisable
acclimatizable
architectonics
archiepiscopal
accomplishable
accomplishment
accumulatively
acceptableness
accustomedness
accountability
accountantship
addressability
androcephalous
andromedotoxin
audiometrician
androdioecious
andromonoecism
audio-frequency
alder-buckthorn
alexipharmakon
adenocarcinoma
anesthesiology
affectionately
affectlessness
aggrandisement
aggrandizement
aggressiveness
Anglo-Israelite
angiostomatous
Augustinianism
angustifoliate
apheliotropism
achondroplasia
achromatically
aphoristically
alimentiveness
arithmetically
anisodactylous
azidothymidine
aristocratical
adiathermanous
acknowledgment
allegorisation
allegorization
alloiostrophos
allelomorphism
allopathically
all-overishness
armamentariums
administratrix
administration
administrative
admissibleness
aromatherapist
apodeictically
above-mentioned
aforementioned
apothegmatical
apophthegmatic
abominableness
apoplectically
apologetically
alphabetically
alphamerically
alphanumerical
apprehensively
appreciatively
apprenticehood
apprenticement
apprenticeship
amphibological
appendicectomy
Appendicularia
approach-stroke
asparagus-stone
aerobiotically
aerobiological
agrobiological
agriculturally
Africanisation
Africanization
aerodynamicist
aeroelastician
aerohydroplane
agroindustrial
air-vice-marshal
aerenchymatous
arrondissement
aeronautically
air-conditioned
aircraftswoman
aerospace-plane
agrostological
across-the-table
across-the-board
associationism
abstemiousness
aesthesiogenic
Aussichtspunkt
adscititiously
auspiciousness
absent-mindedly
abstractedness
abstractionism
abstractionist
absorbefacient
absorptiometer
absorptiveness
asset-stripping
asseveratingly
antiarrhythmic
attractiveness
autobiographer
autobiographic
autocratically
articulateness
anticonvulsant
anticonvulsive
autocoprophagy
anticipatorily
anticipatively
antediluvially
antidepressant
authentication
artificialness
anti-federalism
anti-federalist
astigmatically
antagonisation
antagonization
attainableness
auto-intoxicant
anti-Jacobinism
artillery-plant
antilymphocyte
antimonarchist
attemptability
altimetrically
antimetathesis
actinobacillus
astrogeologist
astrophysicist
astrologically
astronomically
antiodontalgic
antiphlogistic
antiphonically
antaphrodisiac
antiperspirant
antiperistasis
antiphrastical
antipathetical
antiquarianism
autoradiograph
after-mentioned
anthropography
anthropologist
anthropometric
anthropophobia

Words marked △ may be spelled also with a capital letter

14 c□l□r

anthropophobic
anthropopathic
anthropophuism
auto-suggestion
antiseptically
antiscriptural
altitudinarian
attitudinarian
attitudinising
attitudinizing
antithetically
autotypography
altruistically
aquifoliaceous
advocate-depute
advantageously
adventitiously
asynchronously
asymmetrically
asymptotically
bear-animalcule
boarding-school
bladder-campion
brachycephalic
brachydiagonal
brachydactylic
brachypinakoid
black-marketeer
blank-cartridge
beautification
bibliomaniacal
bacteriologist
bacteriostasis
bacteriostatic
back-projection
backscratching
bed-sitting-room
bread-and-butter
breeding-ground
bletheranskate
blepharoplasty
breakfast-table
bremsstrahlung
breathing-while
breathing-space
breathlessness
bridge-building
blithesomeness
Bristol-diamond
blistered-steel
blister-plaster
boisterousness
Baluchitherium
bill-discounter
ballet-mistress
belletristical
bull-headedness
billiard-marker
belt-tightening
beneficialness
banana-fingered
benzodiazepine
banqueting-hall
biomathematics
bronchiectasis
broncho-dilator
blood-sacrifice
blood-bespotted
bloodthirstily
△brobdingnagian
blood-consuming
blood-poisoning
biogeochemical
biometeorology
biodegradation
blockade-runner
bioelectricity
bioclimatology
book-mindedness
bioengineering
biographically
bioluminescent
biosystematics
barrage-balloon
bargain-counter
Burschenschaft
berberidaceous
birth-strangled
burling-machine
barrister-at-law
barometrically
bird-of-paradise
borough-English
bastardisation
bastardization
Basidiomycetes
beseechingness
Bashi-Bazoukery
batrachophobia
batrachophobic
butter-fingered
butterfly-screw
bathing-machine
bathing-costume
bituminisation
bituminization
buttress-thread
bathygraphical
bougainvillaea
bouleversement
bowdlerisation
bowdlerization
characterology
characteristic
chalcographist
chancellorship
changeableness
chargeableness
clash-ma-clavers
charitableness
clavicytherium
cradle-snatcher
Charley-pitcher
cyanobacterium
cyanoacetylene
cyanocobalamin
chacographical
classification
classificatory
class-conscious
claustrophobia
claustrophobic
Chaetodontidae
chaptalisation
chaptalization
coastguardsman
cabbage-lettuce
cabinet-edition
cabinet-pudding
cock-a-doodle-doo
cyclanthaceous
cack-handedness
coconut-matting
cyclobarbitone
cyclopentolate
cucurbitaceous
cadaverousness
coelanaglyphic
chevaux-de-frise
creditableness
cleansing-cream
chemoreceptive
Chenopodiaceae
chemoautotroph
chemosynthesis
cheirographist
cheiromantical
clear-starching
coessentiality
climatological
chivalrousness
coincidentally
chincherinchee
child-resistant
crinkle-crankle
crinkum-crankum
chicken-hearted
chicken-livered
cairngorm-stone
chimney-sweeper
clitoridectomy
clitter-clatter
collapsability
collapsibility
calico-printing
calligraphical
colliquescence
calamitousness
colonel-in-chief
calorification
chlorpromazine
chlorite-schist
chloritisation

14 c□l□r

chloritization
colour-sergeant
comparableness
commandantship
compatibleness
campanological
compassionable
campanulaceous
commensurately
commensuration
compensational
commentatorial
commissionaire
commissaryship
Camelopardalis
complexionless
composing-stick
commodiousness
common-or-garden
compossibility
commonsensical
comprehensible
comprehensibly
compunctiously
compurgatorial
communications
communion-table
communion-cloth
campylotropous
consanguineous
contagiousness
cantankerously
concavo-concave
conscienceless
conscriptional
centenarianism
condescendence
concelebration
convexo-concave
contemporanean
contemperation
contemperature
contemptuously
condensability
concessionaire
contesseration
conversational
conversaziones
convertibility
concentrically
conventionally
conceivability
conservational
conservatorium
conservatively
cinchonisation
cinchonization
canthaxanthine
confidentially
continentalism
continentalist
conditionality
contiguousness
continuousness
conglobulation
conglomeration
conclusiveness
conglutination
conglutinative
cinematography
convocationist
cannonball-tree
consociational
censoriousness
conformability
conformational
Convolvulaceae
conspiratorial
contracyclical
contractedness
contractionary
contradictable
contradictious
centrifugalise
centrifugalize
centrifugation
contrafagottos
△**congregational**
contraindicant
contraindicate
controllership
centralisation
centralization
contraposition
contrapositive
centripetalism
contrarotating
Congressperson
congratulation
congratulatory
congratulative
concretisation
concretization
controvertible
controvertibly
constitutional
construability
constructional
constructively
constructivism
contumaciously
censurableness
conjunctivitis
contumeliously
centuplication
conquistadores
consubstantial
convulsiveness
conductibility
consuetudinary
Crouched-friars
chordamesoderm
co-ordinateness
chondromatosis
chondrogenesis
chondrophorine
chondrocranium
cholelithiasis
cholecystotomy
cholinesterase
cloak-and-dagger
chorographical
cross-marketing
cross-reference
cross-sectional
cross-infection
crossing-warden
Crossopterygii
croque-monsieur
capparidaceous
captain-general
copper-bottomed
capriciousness
Caprifoliaceae
cyproheptadine
capitalisation
capitalization
coquettishness
cornet-à-pistons
correligionist
correspondence
correspondency
cardinal-bishop
cardinal-deacon
cardinal-priest
curvilinearity
cardiomyopathy
carcinomatosis
carcinogenesis
carcinological
corticotrophin
corticosteroid
cardiothoracic
cardiovascular
corolliflorous
chromodynamics
caramelisation
caramelization
chromatography
chromatosphere
chronometrical
cercopithecoid
cartographical
cartridge-paper
Christ-cross-row
Christocentric
Christological
circumambience
circumambiency
circumambulate
circumbendibus
corpuscularian
corpuscularity

Words marked △ may be spelled also with a capital letter

circumforanean
circumferentor
circumgyration
circumgyratory
circumlocution
circumlocutory
circumlittoral
circumnutation
circumnutatory
circumnavigate
circumposition
circumstantial
circumspection
circumspective
circumscissile
corruptibility
circuitousness
circumvolution
cost-accountant
cost-accounting
Castanospermum
cosmeceuticals
castle-building
cosmochemistry
cystolithiasis
cosmopolitical
cosmographical
castrametation
catechetically
catachrestical
catechumenical
catechumenship
catadioptrical
Catherine-wheel
cytogeneticist
categorisation
categorization
cotemporaneous
cathodographer
courageousness
Crutched-friars
cruciverbalism
cruciverbalist
counsellorship
counterbalance
counter-salient
counter-passant
counter-battery
countermeasure
countershading
counterchanged
counterskipper
counter-opening
counter-trading
countersubject
counter-current
counter-culture
country-dancing
coxcombicality
cryobiological
cryptococcosis
cryptaesthesia
cryptaesthetic
crystallisable
crystallizable
crystallomancy
cryptorchidism
cryptosporidia
diamantiferous
diaheliotropic
dialectologist
diaphanousness
diachronically
diathermaneity
death-practised
diaphototropic
diagnosability
diamondiferous
dragon-standard
deceivableness
decolonisation
decolonization
decolorisation
decolorization
decommissioner
decimalisation
decimalization
decompoundable
decontaminator
deconsecration
deconstruction
dechristianise
dechristianize
decorativeness
dicotyledonous
dactyliography
dodecasyllabic
dodecasyllable
diesel-electric
dress-rehearsal
dressing-jacket
dyer's-greenweed
defeasibleness
daffadowndilly
deflagrability
defibrillation
differentially
differentiator
defenestration
definitiveness
diffractometer
daguerreotyper
degenerateness
dogtooth-violet
digitalisation
digitalization
dog's-tooth-grass
drill-husbandry
do-it-yourselfer
deliberateness
deliberatively
delectableness
dolichocephaly
delightfulness
dolomitisation
dolomitization
deliverability
demobilisation
demobilization
democratically
demonetisation
diminutiveness
demonetization
demoralisation
demoralization
demi-semiquaver
dinoflagellate
dynamo-electric
dynamometrical
denominational
denominatively
denitrificator
dinitrobenzene
denazification
dioscoreaceous
depreciatingly
dipterocarpous
depolarisation
depolarization
diplomatically
deplorableness
diplostemonous
departmentally
deposit-receipt
dermatoplastic
dermatological
dermatographia
dermatographic
deregistration
derogatoriness
durchkomponirt
Durchmusterung
disdainfulness
disacknowledge
disaccommodate
disadventurous
disregardfully
dysteleologist
Disneyfication
dysmenorrhoeal
dysmenorrhoeic
discerpibility
disrespectable
distemperature
dispensability
distensibility
dispensational
dispensatorily
dispensatively
dessert-service
dissertational
disceptatorial
disserviceable

disaffiliation
disaffirmation
disaggregation
despicableness
despitefulness
dispiteousness
distinguishing
dispiritedness
disciplinarian
disciplinarium
displeasedness
desulphuration
displenishment
desalinisation
desalinization
disillusionary
disillusionise
disillusionize
disembarkation
disimpassioned
disambiguation
disembowelment
disemboguement
disincarcerate
disengagedness
disinteresting
disinheritance
disintegration
disintegrative
disinfestation
disinvestiture
disingenuously
disenthralment
disenchantment
disenchantress
disinclination
disinformation
disincorporate
disentrainment
disenfranchise
disencumbrance
disposableness
discombobulate
discomboberate
disconcertment
discomfortable
disconformable
despoticalness
dissociability
discommendable
discount-broker
disconnectedly
discountenance
disjointedness
discolouration
discourteously
discouragement
discouragingly
disconsolately
disconsolation
discontinuance
discontentedly
discontentment
dissolutionism
dissolutionist
dissolubleness
dissolvability
disapplication
disappointment
disapprobation
disapprobatory
disapprobative
disappropriate
disapprovingly
disequilibrate
disequilibrium
disarrangement
distributional
distributively
distractedness
destructionist
disorderliness
disorientation
discriminately
discriminating
discrimination
discriminatory
discriminative
disgruntlement
discretionally
disassociation
disattribution
disputatiously
disputableness
disqualifiable
disfurnishment
disquisitional
discursiveness
disgustingness
disgustfulness
dissymmetrical
data-processing
detestableness
detoxification
daughterliness
daughters-in-law
double-breasted
double-barreled
double-declutch
double-flowered
double-stopping
double-tonguing
double-threaded
dividing-engine
devil-on-the-neck
devalorisation
devalorization
davenport-trick
divertissement
diverticulated
diverticulitis
diverticulosis
devitalisation
devitalization
devotionalness
dexamphetamine
dextrorotation
dextrorotatory
daylight-saving
dazzle-painting
exacerbescence
evangelicalism
evangelisation
evangelization
egalitarianism
examine-in-chief
Elasmobranchii
enantiomorphic
enantiostylous
emblematically
embellishingly
embourgeoising
eschatological
exclaustration
encyclopaedian
encyclopaedist
encyclopedical
excrementitial
ecclesiologist
ecclesiastical
Ecclesiasticus
excommunicable
excommunicator
encephalopathy
encephalograph
exceptionalism
excruciatingly
endoradiosonde
endosmotically
epexegetically
even-handedness
eternalisation
eternalization
eleutheromania
electrovalency
electrogenesis
electioneering
electrochemist
electrothermal
electrothermic
electrotherapy
electronically
electrogilding
electrobiology
electrowinning
electroplating
electromotance
electroforming
electro-optical
electro-osmosis
electrostatics
electroculture
effeminateness

Words marked △ may be spelled also with a capital letter

effervescingly
eigen-frequency
echocardiogram
exhilaratingly
ethnobotanical
ethnologically
ethnographical
etherification
enharmonically
exhaustibility
exhaustiveness
Elizabethanism
epidemiologist
Epidermophyton
evil-mindedness
enigmatography
epigrammatical
epistolography
epistemologist
existentialism
existentialist
eulogistically
exothermically
econometrician
evolutionistic
emphaticalness
expedientially
expressionless
expressiveness
expansionistic
explorationist
euphorbiaceous
empire-building
experienceless
experientially
experimentally
empyreumatical
euphuistically
Eurocentricity
edriophthalmic
Euro-Parliament
early-Victorian
exsanguination
ex-servicewoman
extra-parochial
extracanonical
extravehicular
extraneousness
extraforaneous
extra-condensed
extracorporeal
extractability
extrinsicality
extemporaneity
extemporaneous
entomostracous
extensionalism
extensionality
extinguishable
extinguishment
eutrophication
entertainingly
enterocentesis
esterification
extortionately
enthronisation
enthronization
enteropneustal
enterprisingly
enthusiastical
enthymematical
equiangularity
educationalist
eburnification
equiponderance
emulsification
erythropoiesis
erythropoietin
etymologically
flamboyant-tree
flagelliferous
flagellomaniac
fraternisation
fraternization
flat-footedness
flaughter-spade
featherbedding
flagitiousness
flag-lieutenant
fibrocartilage
factitiousness
facinorousness
fiddle-faddling
federalisation
federalization
French-Canadian
French-polisher
free-handedness
feeble-mindedly
free-spokenness
figurativeness
fringillaceous
flight-recorder
friendlessness
faint-heartedly
fairy-godmother
fallaciousness
folding-machine
falsifiability
fellow-creature
fellow-commoner
filiopietistic
follow-my-leader
fellow-townsman
fully-fashioned
Finlandisation
Finlandization
fundamentalism
fundamentalist
fundamentality
fantasticality
fantastication
finger-alphabet
finger-painting
finger-pointing
fingerprinting
fingers-breadth
food-controller
flowery-kirtled
frolicsomeness
floriculturist
footplatewoman
footplatewomen
frontierswoman
forward-looking
fermentability
fermentescible
forthrightness
farthingsworth
formidableness
ferrimagnetism
forbiddingness
far-sightedness
fortifications
foraminiferous
ferro-manganese
ferromagnesian
ferromagnetism
foreordination
ferroprussiate
forisfamiliate
foreseeability
foreshortening
forethoughtful
furfuraldehyde
fortune-telling
fortuitousness
fire-worshipper
foster-daughter
fastidiousness
fashionmonging
fatherlessness
fatiguableness
futtock-shrouds
foundation-stop
fructification
fivepenny-piece
fives-and-threes
favourableness
glanduliferous
Grace-and-Favour
grace-and-favour
gram-equivalent
grangerisation
grangerization
Gnathobdellida
graphitisation
graphitization
grammaticaster
gregariousness
greisenisation
greisenization
greywacke-slate

galvanoplastic
galactophorous
galactopoietic
galeopithecoid
galeopithecine
gold-of-pleasure
gelatinisation
gelatinization
genealogically
gynaecological
gender-specific
gentleman-cadet
gynomonoecious
gynandromorphy
gentrification
generalissimos
generalisation
general-purpose
generalization
genethliacally
genethlialogic
gooseberry-bush
gooseberry-fool
gooseberry-moth
gooseberry-wine
geometrisation
geometrization
glove-stretcher
geocentrically
goodfellowship
good-for-nothing
good-humouredly
geothermometer
geolinguistics
groundbreaking
groundlessness
geognostically
geopolitically
geomorphogenic
geomorphologic
geographically
geostrategical
geosynchronous
gerontological
gyrostabiliser
gyrostabilizer
Gasteromycetes
gutter-merchant
glucocorticoid
Gewürztraminer
heaven-directed
heavenly-minded
heathenishness
heather-mixture
heather-bleater
heather-bluiter
heather-blutter
heavier-than-air
headmastership
heart-searching
heart-heaviness
healthlessness
Hebraistically
hobbledehoydom
hobbledehoyish
hobbledehoyism
hebetudinosity
hickery-pickery
huckleberrying
hydromagnetics
hydrocephalous
hydromechanics
hydronephrosis
hydronephrotic
hydrogeologist
hydrocellulose
hydro-aeroplane
hydrophobicity
hydrobiologist
hydropneumatic
hydrocoralline
hydrologically
hydroponically
hydrocortisone
hydrographical
Hydropterideae
hydrosulphuric
hydroextractor
hydrodynamical
hierarchically
haematogenesis
haematopoiesis
haematopoietic
hieroglyphical
Hierosolymitan
hierogrammatic
hierographical
hyetographical
high-handedness
highly-seasoned
high-mindedness
hygroscopicity
hagiographical
hygrographical
high-principled
high-priesthood
holier-than-thou
helminthologic
holometabolism
holometabolous
heliosciophyte
heliographical
halfpennyworth
Haloragidaceae
hallucinogenic
half-wellington
humidification
homoeomorphism
homoeomorphous
homoeothermous
homoeoteleuton
homogenisation
homogenization
homoiothermous
Hamamelidaceae
hemispheroidal
humoursomeness
hunter-gatherer
hunting-leopard
hunting-grounds
handicraftsman
handkerchieves
hen-and-chickens
hundred-per-cent
hunt-the-slipper
honourableness
hypoallergenic
hypocritically
hypochondriasm
hypochondriast
hypocoristical
hypodermically
hippety-hoppety
hypomagnesemia
hypomenorrhoea
hypomixolydian
hippopotamuses
haplostemonous
hypophysectomy
hypercatalexis
hypercalcaemia
hyperbatically
hypernatraemia
hyperacuteness
hypersensitise
hypersensitive
hypersensitize
hyperaesthesia
hyperaesthesic
hyperaesthetic
hyperventilate
hyperglycaemia
hyperinflation
hyperbolically
hyperconscious
hypertrophical
hypercriticise
hypercriticism
hypercriticize
hypostatically
hyposulphurous
hepaticologist
hypothetically
hephthemimeral
hypothyroidism
hermaphroditic
hereditability
hereditariness
horrendousness
horse-godmother
herpetological
herring-fishery
horticulturist

Words marked △ may be spelled also with a capital letter

harmoniousness
horror-stricken
heresiographer
hysterectomise
hysterectomize
hospitableness
histopathology
histogenically
histochemistry
historiography
histoplasmosis
histologically
histolytically
histrionically
hesitation-form
heterochromous
heterochronism
heterochronous
heteromorphism
heteromorphous
heterophyllous
heterospecific
heterosomatous
heterostrophic
heterothallism
heterozygosity
Hexactinellida
inaccurateness
inadequateness
imaginableness
inalienability
Italianisation
Italianization
inapprehension
inapprehensive
inappreciation
inappreciative
inapproachable
inapproachably
inappositeness
inauspiciously
inarticulately
inarticulation
inartificially
inalterability
inartistically
inadvisability
incidentalness
incredibleness
incogitability
inclinableness
incommensurate
incompleteness
incommodiously
incompressible
incommunicable
incommunicably
inconscionable
inconveniently
inconsequently
inconsiderable
inconsiderably
inconsistently
incontiguously
inconclusively
incontrollable
incontrollably
inco-ordination
incapacitation
incorporeality
incestuousness
incautiousness
indubitability
indecomposable
indecipherable
indoctrination
indecorousness
indecisiveness
indifferentism
indifferentist
indefiniteness
indigenisation
indigenization
indemonstrable
indemonstrably
indomitability
indiscerptible
indistinctness
indiscoverable
indisposedness
indescribables
indestructible
indestructibly
indiscreetness
indiscriminate
indiscreteness
indeterminable
indeterminably
indivisibility
inexcusability
ineffectuality
inevitableness
idealistically
inexorableness
inexpiableness
inexpressibles
inerrabilility
identification
inestimability
inframaxillary
Infralapsarian
infrangibility
infeasibleness
inflation-proof
inflammability
infrastructure
infectiousness
inflexibleness
inflectionless
infopreneurial
ingratiatingly
ingloriousness
inhabitiveness
ichthyosaurian
ichthyolatrous
ichthyophagous
ichthyological
ichnographical
inharmoniously
inimitableness
initialisation
initialization
idiopathically
iniquitousness
ill-naturedness
illegitimately
illegitimation
illimitability
ill-intentioned
ill-conditioned
illustrational
illustratively
illiterateness
immobilisation
immobilization
immaculateness
immoderateness
immunochemical
immunogenicity
immunogenetics
immunoglobulin
immunophoresis
immunosuppress
immiserisation
immiserization
immitigability
immethodically
innumerability
inner-direction
inordinateness
inoperableness
inorganisation
inorganization
isodiametrical
ivory-porcelain
implacableness
implausibility
impracticality
implementation
impregnability
impressibility
impressionable
impressiveness
imponderabilia
improvableness
improvvisatore
imparidigitate
impermeability
imperfectively
imperviability
imperviousness
imparisyllabic
imperturbation

14 i□p□s

impassableness
imposthumation
impassibleness
impoverishment
inquisiturient
irrecognisable
irrecognizable
irreconcilable
irreconcilably
irreducibility
irrefutability
irrelativeness
irremovability
irreplevisable
irreproachable
irreproachably
irreproducible
irreparability
irrespectively
irresolubility
irresoluteness
irresponsively
irrestrainable
irresuscitable
irresuscitably
irrevocability
insufficiently
insignificance
insignificancy
inspirationism
inspirationist
institutionary
insalubriously
insensibleness
insanitariness
inseparability
insuperability
insuppressible
insuppressibly
insurrectional
instrumentally
insurmountable
insurmountably
inscrutability
insusceptively
insatiableness
intrafallopian
intra-abdominal
intramercurial
intramedullary
intramolecular
intra-articular
intransigeance
intransigently
intransitively
intransmutable
intractability
integrationist
intuitionalism
intuitionalist
intrinsicality
intellectually
intelligential
intelligentsia
intelligentzia
intolerability
intempestively
intempestivity
intangibleness
intentionality
iatrochemistry
introductorily
intermaxillary
Internationale
interactionism
interactionist
interdependent
interpenetrant
interpenetrate
interferential
intermediately
intermediation
intermediatory
interpellation
interferometer
interferometry
intercessional
intercessorial
interjectional
intersectional
intersexuality
interlineation
interlingually
intermigration
intermittently
interplanetary
interambulacra
intermolecular
intercommunion
intercommunity
interconnector
interconnexion
interior-sprung
interlocutrice
interlocutress
interspatially
intergradation
interpretation
interpretative
interpretively
interestedness
interpunctuate
interruptively
intertwinement
intertwiningly
intussuscepted
invincibleness
inviolableness
invariableness
inveterateness
△**jack-by-the-hedge**
Jack-in-the-green
Johannisberger
jingoistically
jurisdictional
justifiability
jusqu'auboutist
joukery-pawkery
knapping-hammer
kneading-trough
Kremlinologist
knight-bachelor
knight-banneret
knight-errantry
knickerbockers
knitting-needle
kindergartener
kinetheodolite
knotenschiefer
knowledge-based
know-nothingism
Kupferschiefer
karstification
keratinisation
keratinization
kissing-strings
leaden-stepping
leather-mouthed
leading-strings
libidinousness
libertarianism
liberalisation
liberalization
labyrinthodont
licentiousness
lecythidaceous
lieutenantship
life-expectancy
left-handedness
luggage-carrier
lugubriousness
legalistically
lignocellulose
legislatorship
light-heartedly
light-flyweight
legitimisation
legitimateness
legitimization
lighter-than-air
Leibnitzianism
lumbersomeness
lymphangiogram
lamellirostral
long-headedness
luncheon-basket
longitudinally
longs-and-shorts
languorousness
linguistically
long-windedness
lyophilisation
lyophilization

Words marked △ may be spelled also with a capital letter

lepidodendroid
lapidification
lipogrammatism
lipogrammatist
leptodactylous
loquaciousness
larger-than-life
laryngoscopist
laryngological
lasciviousness
letter-of-marque
lithochromatic
lithographical
lithontriptist
lithonthryptic
liturgiologist
lateralisation
lateralization
latitudinarian
louping-on-stane
leucocythaemia
leucocytopenia
leukocytopenia
leucocytolysis
leukocytolysis
love-in-idleness
levelling-staff
lavender-cotton
loving-kindness
low-temperature
lexicographist
measurableness
measuring-wheel
moccasin-flower
macadamisation
macadamization
mock-heroically
macro-marketing
micro-marketing
microbarograph
macrodactylous
macroeconomics
microeconomics
micro-meteorite
microdetection
macrocephalous
microcephalous
micropegmatite
microseismical
microchemistry
microminiature
microbiologist
microinjection
macromolecular
micrologically
microcomponent
microcomputing
macrosporangia
microsporangia
microprocessor
microstructure
microtunneling
macroevolution
microevolution
mucoviscidosis
medicalisation
medicalization
medicamentally
Middle-American
middle-distance
muddleheadedly
meddlesomeness
meditativeness
magneto-elastic
magneto-optical
magniloquently
megalomaniacal
megasporangium
megasporophyll
megatechnology
megavertebrate
Mohorovicician
maidenhair-tree
maintenance-man
Meistersingers
major-generalcy
majesticalness
multarticulate
Malacopterygii
malacostracous
malodorousness
millenarianism
multiracialism
multifariously
multifactorial
milking-parlour
multiple-choice
multiplication
multiplicative
multifoliolate
multinucleated
multicuspidate
multi-ownership
mylonitisation
mylonitization
malcontentedly
malappropriate
melastomaceous
militarisation
militarization
malfunctioning
memorandum-book
memory-resident
Monochlamydeae
monocarpellary
monochromatism
manifold-writer
manageableness
monolingualism
Monoplacophora
monoprionidian
monophthongise
monophthongize
mineralisation
mineralization
monosaccharide
ministerialist
Menispermaceae
△**monotheletical**
monotheistical
monotonousness
munition-worker
money-scrivener
myocardiopathy
Mephistopheles
Mephistophelic
Mephistophilis
Mephostophilus
morganatically
miraculousness
marketableness
market-gardener
murdering-piece
marvellousness
myrmecophagous
myrmecophilous
myrmecological
Marcgraviaceae
Marchantiaceae
morphinomaniac
morphophonemic
marriage-broker
marriage-favour
marble-breasted
marble-constant
meretriciously
martyrological
miscalculation
misacceptation
misadventurous
misadvisedness
misdescription
mysteriousness
miscellanarian
Mesdemoiselles
mismeasurement
misogynistical
mischief-making
mastigophorous
misimprovement
misinterpreter
misanthropical
misinformation
misinstruction
misgovernaunce
miscomputation
miscontentment
misapplication
massproduction
misappropriate
misarrangement
mistranslation
mushroom-anchor

Words marked △ may be spelled also with a capital letter

14 m□s□t

mesaticephalic
mispunctuation
mosquito-weight
meticulousness
mathematically
mathematicised
mathematicized
Mitteleuropean
Mittel-European
matresfamilias
matriarchalism
metalinguistic
metallogenetic
metallographer
metallographic
mettlesomeness
metempsychoses
metempsychosis
methodicalness
mythologically
metropolitical
meteorological
methodological
metaphorically
metaphosphoric
metoposcopical
metapsychology
metaphysically
motivelessness
motivationally
mourning-border
mountaineering
muzzle-velocity
△neanderthaloid
△nebuchadnezzar
noctambulation
nectareousness
nyctaginaceous
nuclear-powered
nuclearisation
nuclearization
necessarianism
neck-sweetbread
Nudibranchiata
nudibranchiate
nievie-nick-nack
Nietzscheanism
neglectfulness
night-wandering
night-blindness
night-flowering
night-foundered
night-fossicker
neighborliness
number-cruncher
numberlessness
nymphomaniacal
nimble-fingered
nominalisation
nomenclatorial
nominalization

numismatically
nematodiriasis
namby-pambiness
non-performance
non-belligerent
nonsensicality
non-restrictive
non-destructive
non-chromosomal
nondisjunction
non-electrolyte
non-involvement
non-concurrence
non-comedogenic
non-conformance
non-communicant
non-committally
non-compearance
non-co-operation
non-contentious
non-operational
nonotechnology
non-judgemental
neocolonialism
neocolonialist
Neopythagorean
north-eastwards
north-westwards
north-north-east
north-north-west
narcocatharsis
narrow-mindedly
narcosynthesis
norepinephrine
norm-referenced
norethisterone
nutritiousness
nitrocellulose
nitroglycerine
naturalisation
naturalization
nature-printing
noteworthiness
neuropathology
neuroradiology
neuroscientist
neurobiologist
neurofibrillar
neurofibromata
neuroblastomas
neuroendocrine
neuroanatomist
neurologically
neurocomputing
Neuropteroidea
neurohypnology
neutralisation
neutralization
newfangledness
newspaper-woman
newsworthiness

orange-coloured
orange-squeezer
oncogeneticist
oecumenicalism
onchocerciasis
old-gentlemanly
odd-come-shortly
old-established
overcompensate
over-confidence
overcapitalise
overcapitalize
overcorrection
over-determined
overestimation
oleaginousness
open-handedness
overindulgence
open-mindedness
ocean-greyhound
overprotective
overproduction
overpopulation
overpoweringly
oneirocritical
over-refinement
overspecialise
overspecialize
overscrupulous
over-the-counter
overwhelmingly
off-off-Broadway
organ-harmonium
organometallic
organisability
organiser-purse
organisational
organizability
organizer-purse
organizational
ophthalmoscope
ophthalmoscopy
ophthalmometer
ophthalmometry
opinionatively
onirocriticism
oligopsonistic
oligocythaemia
opisthoglossal
opisthocoelian
opisthocoelous
opisthographic
obligatoriness
osmoregulation
omnibenevolent
omnicompetence
Ornithodelphia
ornithodelphic
ornithophilous
ornithological
ornithomorphic

Words marked △ may be spelled also with a capital letter

omnium-gatherum
orobanchaceous
onomatopoiesis
otolaryngology
oppressiveness
oophorectomise
oophorectomize
obsequiousness
observableness
obstructionism
obstructionist
obstreperously
outward-sainted
outlandishness
outrageousness
optoelectronic
ottrelite-slate
ostrich-feather
optimalisation
optimalization
optimistically
ostentatiously
octingentenary
osteodermatous
orthochromatic
orthophosphate
Osteoglossidae
osteoarthritis
osteoarthrosis
orthographical
orthopterology
oxyhaemoglobin
prayerlessness
plane-polarised
plane-polarized
planet-stricken
planing-machine
pharmacologist
pharmacopoeial
pharmacopoeian
pharmacopolist
pharmaceutical
plasmapheresis
pragmaticality
pragmatisation
pragmatization
piano-accordion
Praeraphaelite
praiseworthily
practicability
Plantaginaceae
plant-formation
phantasmagoria
phantasmagoric
plague-stricken
platycephalous
public-spirited
pococuranteism
picture-gallery
picture-writing
pachydactylous
pachydermatous
precariousness
predaciousness
prefabrication
plea-bargaining
presbyterially
preaching-house
preaching-cross
prescriptively
prescriptivism
prescriptivist
pseudo-archaism
pseudaesthesia
preadolescence
pseudomembrane
pseudomorphism
pseudomorphous
pseudonymously
pseudepigrapha
pseudepigraphy
pseudosolution
pseudosymmetry
pseudoscorpion
predeterminism
predeterminate
predevelopment
preferentially
premeditatedly
predesignation
predesignatory
prenegotiation
pre-Reformation
presentability
preventability
presentimental
predestinarian
predestination
predestinative
presentational
presentiveness
preventiveness
preservability
psephoanalysis
plethysmograph
precipitinogen
premillenarian
plenipotential
pteridophilist
predisposition
predictability
phelloplastics
pneumoconiosis
pneumoconiotic
pneumodynamics
pneumokoniosis
pneumatologist
pleonastically
phenobarbitone
piezomagnetism
preconcertedly
preponderantly
pyelonephritic
pyelonephritis
piezochemistry
precociousness
paedomorphosis
preconsonantal
preposterously
preoperational
prearrangement
Pleuronectidae
pleurapophyses
pleurapophysis
pre-established
pleasure-giving
pleasure-seeker
pressurisation
pressurization
prettification
plectognathous
pretty-pretties
presupposition
presumptuously
phenylbutazone
pterylographic
pugnaciousness
pugilistically
pig-in-the-middle
pigeon-breasted
pigeon-fancying
philanthropist
psilanthropism
psilanthropist
pribble-prabble
prince-imperial
principalities
poikilothermal
poikilothermic
prick-the-garter
prison-breaking
philosopheress
philosophaster
philosophistic
philologically
prioritisation
prioritization
prittle-prattle
printing-office
point-to-pointer
painter-stainer
palmatipartite
polyacrylamide
palaeobiologic
palaeobotanist
polyembryonate
palaeoclimatic
palaeoecologic
palaeographist
palaebiologist
palaeanthropic
Palaeanthropus
palaeopedology

phlegmatically
palagonite-tuff
polemoniaceous
polymerisation
polymerization
polynucleotide
palingenetical
paleopathology
paleomagnetism
paleoecologist
paleogeography
pillow-fighting
paleophytology
paleobiologist
paleolimnology
paleoanthropic
Paleoanthropus
paleobotanical
paleozoologist
paleographical
paleontography
paleontologist
paleoethnology
Polyplacophora
polysaccharide
polishing-paste
polishing-slate
polysyllabical
polysynthetism
palato-alveolar
politicisation
politicization
polytheistical
palatalisation
palatalization
pamphleteering
pentadactylism
pentadactylous
pinnatipartite
pennatulaceous
Pontederiaceae
Panhellenistic
pincer-movement
Pentecostalist
Pan-Americanism
pentobarbitone
pantomimically
pantopragmatic
pantographical
pancreatectomy
punctuationist
penetrableness
penny-a-linerism
penny-in-the-slot
pennystone-cast
propagandistic
propaedeutical
probabiliorism
probabiliorist
proscriptively
proud-stomached

Protevangelium
phonematically
proletarianise
proletarianism
proletarianize
prosencephalic
prosencephalon
proceleusmatic
progenitorship
propeller-blade
professionally
professorially
proventriculus
projectisation
protectiveness
projectization
prothonotarial
prothonotariat
profitableness
promise-keeping
promise-breaker
promise-crammed
providentially
prohibitionary
prohibitionism
prohibitionist
propitiatorily
prodigiousness
propitiousness
protistologist
prognosticator
photocatalysis
photocatalytic
phototelegraph
photoperiodism
photorealistic
photosensitise
photosensitive
photosensitize
photochemistry
photobiologist
photoelectrode
protoplasmatic
photo-engraving
protozoologist
protospathaire
Prototracheata
photogrammetry
photographical
provost-marshal
proportionable
proportionably
proportionally
proportionless
proportionment
photoluminesce
prolocutorship
photosynthesis
photosynthetic
phosphor-bronze
phosphorescent

phosphoprotein
prosperousness
proprietorship
proprioceptive
procryptically
procrastinator
progressionary
progressionism
progressionist
protrusiveness
prosthodontics
prosthodontist
procuratorship
pronunciamento
productibility
productiveness
peppermint-drop
papilionaceous
popularisation
popularization
paradigmatical
paroemiography
pyrheliometric
purse-snatching
perfectibilian
perfectibilism
perfectibilist
perceptibility
perfectibility
portentousness
perceptiveness
paragrammatist
parthenocarpic
porphyrogenite
pertinaciously
perfidiousness
perniciousness
pernicketiness
parliament-cake
parliament-heel
parsimoniously
permissibility
permissiveness
particularness
purple-coloured
parallelepiped
parallelopiped
parallel-veined
paraleipomenon
paralinguistic
pyramidologist
peremptoriness
parenchymatous
pyrenomycetous
paronomastical
pardonableness
personableness
purposefulness
Periophthalmus
periodontology
parlour-boarder

person-to-person
perlocutionary
pyrophotograph
pyrophosphoric
paraphrastical
periphrastical
peripateticism
parapsychology
partridge-berry
pararosaniline
perishableness
Perissodactyla
phraseological
parasitologist
paratactically
pyrotechnician
peritoneoscopy
percutaneously
perturbational
porcupine-grass
persuasibility
percussion-fuse
percussion-lock
persuasiveness
Pasteurelloses
Pasteurellosis
pasteurisation
pasteurization
possessiveness
postindustrial
pestilentially
Passifloraceae
passionateness
pisciculturist
post-millennial
postmenopausal
postmastership
post-production
postpositional
postpositively
Petrarchianism
Petrarchianist
Pythagoreanism
phthalocyanine
patresfamilias
patrialisation
patrialization
petticoat-tails
patriarchalism
potentiometric
petrochemistry
petrophysicist
pathologically
petrologically
petrographical
potassium-argon
Plumbaginaceae
plumbisolvency
plumbosolvency
pluviometrical
pluto-democracy

Prussification
power-amplifier
psychoanalysis
psychoanalytic
psychochemical
psychodramatic
psychodynamics
psychographics
psychogenetics
psycholinguist
psychometrical
psychoneuroses
psychoneurosis
psychoneurotic
psychophysical
psychosomatics
psychotechnics
physiognomical
phyllotactical
Phytolaccaceae
phytopathology
phytogenetical
phytogeography
quadrigeminate
quadrigeminous
quadragenarian
quadrangularly
quadrisyllabic
quadrisyllable
quantification
quattrocentism
quattrocentist
quartz-porphyry
quarter-gallery
quantitatively
quaquaversally
querimoniously
question-master
quincentennial
quicksilvering
quicksilverish
quinquagesimal
quinquevalence
quinquefarious
quinquennially
quinquefoliate
quinquecostate
quilting-cotton
quintessential
quizzification
quodlibetarian
reading-machine
reaping-machine
reasonableness
reappraisement
reacquaintance
roadworthiness
rabbeting-plane
rabbit-squirrel
Rabelaisianism
rebelliousness

ribonucleotide
robes-de-chambre
robustiousness
rectangularity
recrementitial
Rochelle-powder
rocket-launcher
Rickettsiaceae
receivableness
rectilinearity
receiving-house
receiving-order
recollectively
recalcitration
recolonisation
recolonization
recommencement
recommendation
recommendatory
reconnaissance
reconsecration
recondensation
reconciliation
reconciliatory
reconstitution
△**reconstruction**
reconstructive
rice-polishings
recapitulation
recapitulatory
recapitulative
recurvirostral
recitation-room
recoverability
radicalisation
ridiculousness
radicalization
redeemableness
riding-breeches
redintegration
riding-interest
radiotelemeter
radiotelephone
radiotelephony
radiotelegraph
radioresistant
radiosensitise
radiosensitive
radiosensitize
radiochemistry
radio-frequency
radio-astronomy
radio-strontium
radioautograph
redistillation
redistribution
redistributive
rheumatologist
refrangibility
refractoriness
reflexological

14 r□f□e

reflectography
reflectionless
reflectiveness
reformationist
regressiveness
regularisation
regularization
regeneratively
regardlessness
rehabilitation
rehabilitative
rhinencephalic
rhinencephalon
reinforcements
rhinoceros-bird
Rhinocerotidae
Rhizophoraceae
reimplantation
reintroduction
reinvigoration
rejuvenescence
relentlessness
relinquishment
rampageousness
remedilessness
rummelgumption
rumbledethumps
rumblegumption
rummlegumption
reminiscential
remonetisation
remonetization
remarkableness
remorsefulness
remoralisation
remoralization
Rembrandtesque
rambunctiously
rangatiratanga
röntgenography
ranunculaceous
rhombenporphyr
reorganisation
reorganization
repudiationist
reprehensively
representation
re-presentation
representative
reprogrammable
reproductively
reproductivity
repetitiveness
requisitionary
requisitionist
Rosicrucianism
respectabilise
respectability
respectabilize
respectfulness
Russianisation
Russianization
restitutionism
restitutionist
resultlessness
resinification
restorationism
restorationist
restorableness
responsibility
responsiveness
Russo-Byzantine
restrictionist
rostrocarinate
resurrectional
restrainedness
resistlessness
retransmission
retaliationist
retinoblastoma
retroreflector
retrocognition
retro-operative
retrogradation
roundaboutedly
roundaboutness
rough-and-tumble
revalorisation
revalorization
revengefulness
revitalisation
revitalization
revivification
rewardableness
rhyparographer
rhyparographic
rhynchophorous
stalactitiform
scandalisation
scandalousness
scandalization
standard-bearer
slanderousness
shamefacedness
scaremongering
Shakespeariana
stagflationary
snaggletoothed
slaughterhouse
slaughterously
scaphocephalic
scaphocephalus
staphylococcal
staphylococcus
station-manager
stationariness
spatiotemporal
spawning-ground
seasonableness
seat-of-the-pants
star-of-the-earth
star-of-the-night
stamping-ground
snapping-turtle
slantendicular
slantindicular
slatternliness
scatterbrained
shatter-brained
statuesqueness
Sabbatarianism
Sabbath-breaker
subgenerically
submergibility
subterrestrial
submersibility
subjectiveness
subjectivistic
subaggregation
subminiaturise
subminiaturize
submicroscopic
submissiveness
subalternation
subinfeudation
subinfeudatory
subinsinuation
subconsciously
subcontrariety
subcontracting
subcontinental
subarborescent
subassociation
substantivally
substantialise
substantialism
substantialist
substantiality
substantialize
substantiation
subatmospheric
substitutional
substitutively
substitutivity
subcutaneously
sacramentalism
sacramentalist
sacramentarian
successionally
successionless
successfulness
successiveness
sacchariferous
saccharisation
saccharization
sacrilegiously
sectionisation
sectionization
secularisation
secularization
sacrosanctness
sociobiologist
sacrococcygeal

sycophantishly
securitisation
securitization
spelaeological
steganographer
steganographic
speechlessness
speech-training
stereoisomeric
stereometrical
siege-artillery
stereospecific
stereotactical
shelf-catalogue
shepherd's-purse
specialisation
specialization
shell-limestone
steel-engraving
spermiogenesis
spermatogenous
spermatogonium
spermatophytic
spermatorrhoea
stegocephalian
stegocephalous
sceuophylacium
scenographical
steeplechasing
steeple-crowned
sheep-whistling
sleepy-sickness
spectacularity
sweet-and-twenty
spectroscopist
spectrological
spectrographic
stertorousness
soft-conscienc'd
sufferableness
suffructescent
segregationist
suggestibility
suggestiveness
Schwenkfeldian
sphaerocrystal
sphygmographic
scholastically
schematisation
schematization
school-divinity
schooner-rigged
schoolmasterly
schoolmistress
schoolteaching
schismatically
schizognathous
schizomycetous
schizophyceous
skimble-skamble
spindle-shanked
swindge-buckler
stiletto-heeled
swingling-stock
stichometrical
spiritlessness
spirit-stirring
spiritualistic
spirituousness
sticky-fingered
shillingsworth
shilly-shallier
seismometrical
stigmatiferous
stigmatophilia
stigmatisation
stigmatization
scientifically
spirochaetosis
spironolactone
snipper-snapper
snip-snap-snorum
spinthariscope
scintillascope
scintilloscope
scintillometer
shifting-boards
self-accusation
self-accusatory
self-affrighted
self-admiration
self-abnegation
self-assumption
self-absorption
self-advertiser
salubriousness
solubilisation
solubilization
silicification
self-compatible
self-comparison
self-commitment
self-complacent
self-condemning
self-consequent
self-confidence
self-consistent
self-conviction
self-correcting
solecistically
solicitousness
solidification
self-dependence
self-discipline
self-displeased
self-destroying
self-determined
self-developing
self-effacement
self-explaining
self-expression
self-employment
self-enrichment
silversmithing
self-flattering
self-fulfilling
self-fulfilment
self-generating
self-government
sulphacetamide
sulphanilamide
sulphurisation
sulphurization
sulphathiazole
self-heterodyne
self-inductance
self-indulgence
self-immolation
self-importance
self-interested
self-justifying
salamander-like
self-management
self-motivating
salmon-coloured
self-preserving
self-punishment
self-propelling
self-protecting
self-protection
self-protective
self-proclaimed
self-propulsion
self-possession
saltpetre-paper
self-rectifying
self-regulating
self-regulation
self-regulatory
self-repression
self-repugnance
sclerophyllous
self-respecting
self-respectful
self-restrained
self-revelation
self-sufficient
self-suggestion
self-supporting
self-sustaining
self-sustenance
self-satisfying
solitudinarian
self-tormenting
somnambulistic
somnambulation
semi-centennial
semiconducting
semicarbazones
semicircularly
semicrystallic
semi-elliptical
symmetrophobia

14 s□m□e

symmetrisation
symmetrization
simultaneously
simplification
simplificative
simplistically
semi-occasional
semi-officially
symbolicalness
semaphorically
simaroubaceous
semasiological
sempstress-ship
symptomatology
sensationalism
sensationalist
sansculotterie
sansculottides
synchronically
sentimentalise
sentimentalism
sentimentalist
sentimentality
sentimentalize
singing-gallery
single-breasted
synonymousness
synaposematism
sinistrorsally
sanctification
sanguification
sensualisation
sensualization
sanguinariness
sanguinivorous
sporangiophore
sporangiospore
stomachfulness
stomatogastric
Scombresocidae
stoicheiometry
stoechiometric
stoichiometric
sword-swallower
shove-halfpenny
stocking-stitch
shoulder-height
sporotrichosis
swoopstake-like
stout-heartedly
Scottification
short-sightedly
Supralapsarian
suprasegmental
sapphire-quartz
sophistication
supplicatingly
supplementally
saponification
supposititious
suppositionary
supercargoship
supersaturated
supernaturally
superabundance
superabsorbent
superscription
supercelestial
superterranean
supersensitive
soporiferously
superphosphate
superficialise
superficiality
superficialize
superciliously
supervisorship
superelevation
super-flyweight
superambitious
supereminently
superimportant
superintendent
superintending
superinfection
superincumbent
superannuation
superinduction
superconductor
superconfident
supersonically
supernormality
supercontinent
superfoetation
supererogation
supererogatory
supererogative
superessential
superstruction
superstructure
superstructive
superovulation
superexcellent
septuagenarian
sequaciousness
spread-eagleism
Sarraceniaceae
serratirostral
surpassingness
scrubbing-board
scrubbing-brush
scribbling-book
strobilisation
strobilization
strabismometer
seroconversion
sericitisation
sericitization
straddle-legged
street-credible
sergeant-at-arms
serjeant-at-arms
serpentiningly
serpent-worship
surefootedness
sprightfulness
serviceability
strikebreaking
shrill-shriking
spring-cleaning
spring-carriage
servomechanism
strepsipterous
scrupulousness
Syrophoenician
surprisingness
stratification
stratigraphist
stratigaphical
stretching-bond
scratchbuilder
scrutinisingly
scrutinizingly
sustainability
systematically
suspensibility
susceptibility
susceptiveness
suspiciousness
sesquipedalian
sesquipedality
sesquisulphide
soteriological
satisfactorily
stumbling-block
soul-confirming
squadron-leader
soul-destroying
stupendousness
slug-foot-second
south-eastwards
south-westwards
south-south-east
south-south-west
skunk-blackbird
Sturmabteilung
sauropterygian
squirearchical
scurrilousness
stultification
△sovietological
savanna-sparrow
saxifragaceous
thalassography
travelling-wave
trapezohedrons
traffic-manager
traffic-calming
traffic-returns
traffic-signals
Trachypteridae
traditionalism
traditionalist

Words marked △ may be spelled also with a capital letter

traditionality
traditionarily
tragicomically
thaumatography
thaumaturgical
traumatisation
traumatization
transcaucasian
Transcaucasion
transvaluation
transcendental
transcendently
transferential
transversality
transfer-ticket
transvestitism
transsexualism
transliterator
transmigration
transmigratory
transmigrative
transmissional
transmissively
transmissivity
transpicuously
transplantable
transformistic
transformation
transformative
transmogrified
transport-rider
transportingly
transportation
transitionally
transitoriness
transitiveness
transcutaneous
transfusionist
traitorousness
Traducianistic
tobacco-stopper
tablespoonfuls
tabularisation
tabularization
tabernacle-work
tacheometrical
technicoloured
tachygraphical
tide-waitership
theocratically
trencher-friend
trencher-knight
tremendousness
theriomorphism
theriomorphous
therianthropic
theologoumenon
thermochemical
thermodynamics
thermoelectric
thermalisation
thermalization
thermometrical
thermophyllous
thermotolerant
Theopaschitism
theosophically
theatricalness
tree-worshipper
thimblerigging
thiobarbituric
third-programme
trimethylamine
tripersonalism
tripersonalist
tripersonality
trichobacteria
trichomoniasis
triphenylamine
trichinisation
trichinization
trichophytosis
trichotomously
Trinitarianism
tridimensional
trivialisation
trivialization
trinitrophenol
trinitrotoluol
trickle-charger
trinkum-trankum
triple-tonguing
triconsonantal
triconsonantic
trisoctahedron
trituberculism
trituberculate
teleconference
talking-machine
telejournalism
telejournalist
telangiectasia
telangiectasis
telangiectatic
tallow-chandler
teleologically
teleprocessing
telephonically
telephotograph
telepathically
telesmatically
telescopically
Teletypesetter®
teletypewriter
telautographic
televangelical
temperamentful
tumbling-barrel
tumultuousness
tomfoolishness
tumorigenicity
tinsel-slipper'd
tintinnabulant
tintinnabulary
tintinnabulate
tintinnabulous
tendovaginitis
troubleshooter
thought-reading
thoughtfulness
Trochelminthes
trophoneurosis
two-dimensional
thoroughbraced
two-for-his-heels
tropologically
topsy-turviness
threadbareness
three-halfpence
three-halfpenny
three-farthings
thriftlessness
tariff-reformer
terminableness
tergiversation
tergiversatory
turbine-steamer
torsion-balance
territorialise
territorialism
territorialist
territoriality
territorialize
terminological
thromboplastin
tyrannicalness
turbo-generator
terror-stricken
thrashing-floor
threshing-floor
terotechnology
through-ganging
turquoise-green
testamentarily
testimonialise
testimonialize
tetradactylous
tetrachotomous
tetrasporangia
△tetragrammaton
tatterdemalion
tittle-tattling
thunderousness
tautologically
trumpet-tongued
text-processing
thysanopterous
thymelaeaceous
thyrotoxicosis
unavailability
unaccomplished
unaccommodated
unaccounted-for

Words marked △ may be spelled also with a capital letter

14 u□a□f

unaffectedness
unacknowledged
unavoidability
uranographical
unapprehensive
unappreciative
unapproachable
unapproachably
unappropriated
unaspiringness
unacquaintance
unassumingness
unattractively
unauthenticity
unartificially
unalterability
unbearableness
umbrageousness
unbecomingness
unbusinesslike
unclassifiable
uncheerfulness
uncultivatable
uncomprehended
uncompromising
uncommunicated
uncommunicable
uncontaminated
unconscionable
unconscionably
unconfederated
uncongeniality
uncontemplated
unconventional
unconciliatory
unconsolidated
uncontradicted
uncontrollable
uncontrollably
uncontrolledly
uncontroverted
uncertificated
uncorroborated
unchristianise
unchristianize
uncircumcision
uncrystallised
uncrystallized
undecomposable
undecipherable
undiminishable
undemonstrable
undomesticated
undeniableness
undervaluation
underdeveloped
under-secretary
undermentioned
under-clerkship
undernourished
under-constable
underpopulated
undergraduette
understrapping
understandable
understandings
understatement
undespairingly
undesignedness
undiscoverable
undiscoverably
undesirability
undistractedly
undeservedness
undeterminable
uterogestation
unexpectedness
unextinguished
unentertaining
unenterprising
unenthusiastic
unflappability
unflatteringly
unfaithfulness
unfriendedness
unfriendliness
unforeknowable
unfruitfulness
ungracefulness
ungratefulness
ungraciousness
ungroundedness
unhandsomeness
unhesitatingly
unincorporated
universalistic
universitarian
unidentifiable
utilitarianise
utilitarianism
utilitarianize
unidirectional
unilluminating
uniformitarian
unintellectual
unintelligible
unintelligibly
unintermitting
unintoxicating
unknightliness
unknowableness
unmaintainable
unmalleability
unmannerliness
unmanufactured
unmentionables
unmerchantable
unmarriageable
unmercifulness
unmathematical
unmatriculated
unmetaphorical
unmetaphysical
unmaterialised
unmaterialized
unostentatious
unpraiseworthy
unpracticality
unpreparedness
unpretendingly
unpremeditated
unpremeditable
unpoeticalness
unprepossessed
unpleasantness
unpresumptuous
unprofessional
unpropitiously
unproportioned
unprosperously
unproductively
unproductivity
unpurchaseable
unpassableness
unquestionable
unquestionably
unreadableness
uproariousness
unrecognisable
unrecognisably
unrecognizable
unrecognizably
unreconcilable
unreconcilably
unreciprocated
unrecapturable
unreflectingly
unrightfulness
unreliableness
unromantically
unremunerative
unremorsefully
unreproducible
unresolvedness
unresponsively
unrestrictedly
unreservedness
unrestrainable
unrestrainedly
unrhythmically
unsectarianism
unsociableness
unsuccessfully
unsuitableness
unspiritualise
unspiritualize
unsplinterable
unsympathising
unsympathizing
unsophisticate
unstrengthened
unsurmountable
unscrupulously

Words marked △ may be spelled also with a capital letter

unscripturally
unsystematical
unsystematised
unsystematized
unsisterliness
unsuspectingly
unsuspiciously
unsatisfaction
unsatisfactory
ultra-Neptunian
ultramicrotome
ultramicrotomy
unthankfulness
ultrasonically
ultramontanism
ultramontanist
ultracrepidate
untranslatable
untranslatably
untransferable
untransmutable
ultrastructure
unthinkability
unthinkingness
Ustilaginaceae
untameableness
ultimogeniture
ultroneousness
unthoughtfully
untruthfulness
untowardliness
unvanquishable
unwatchfulness
unyieldingness
vibroflotation
vice-chancellor
vice-consulship
vociferousness
victoriousness
vice-presidency
vicar-apostolic
vicesimo-quarto
videotelephone
vigesimo-quarto
vegetativeness
vaingloriously
volcanological
vulcanological
vulnerableness
voluminousness
volumetrically
voluptuousness
valerianaceous
valetudinarian
volatilisation
volatilization
vindictiveness
venereological
verse-mongering
verticillaster
verisimilitude
vasodilatation
vasodilatatory
vespertilionid
Vaticanologist
vitrescibility
vitriolisation
vitriolization
vitalistically
vitilitigation
vituperatively
viviparousness
vivisectionist
what-d'you-call-'em
what-d'you-call-it
wearing-apparel
weak-mindedness
weaponschawing
weeding-forceps
wheeler-dealing
weightlessness
weighing-bottle
weight-training
weight-watching
whippersnapper
whittie-whattie
whistle-blowing
well-acquainted
Weltanschauung
Wilhelmstrasse
willing-hearted
well-thought-out
wonder-stricken
winning-gallery
window-dressing
window-shopping
whole-heartedly
woollen-drapery
wappenschawing
worcesterberry
worshipfulness
word-processing
westernisation
westernization
washing-machine
withering-floor
water-repellent
water-resistant
watertightness
watering-trough
watercolourist
water-breathing
xylopyrography
xylotypography
xanthomelanous
xiphihumeralis
yttro-tantalite
yttro-columbite
Zygobranchiata
zygobranchiate
Zygophyllaceae
zingiberaceous
zinziberaceous
zinckification
zincographical
zoophytologist
Zoroastrianism

15 a□a□r

anacreontically
anaesthesiology
anaesthetically
acanthocephalan
amaryllidaceous
ambulance-chaser
arboriculturist
asclepiadaceous
acclimatisation
acclimatization
architecturally
Archichlamydeae
archiepiscopate
archiepiscopacy
accommodatingly
ancestor-worship
accountableness
andromonoecious
Americanisation
Americanization
adenocarcinomas
adenohypophyses
adenohypophysis
acetyl-salicylic
affranchisement
argumentatively
angustirostrate
achondroplastic
achromatisation
achromatization
atherosclerosis
atherosclerotic
abiogenetically
Aristotelianism
adjutant-general
ankylostomiasis
acknowledgeable
acknowledgeably
acknowledgement
all-changing-word
allotriomorphic
atmospherically
armoured-cruiser
annihilationism
Annunciation-day
anomalistically
apocalyptically
apophthegmatise
apophthegmatize
apophthegmatist
Apollinarianism
acousto-electric
alphabetisation
alphabetization
alpha-chloralose
amphitheatrical
appendicularian
approachability
appropinquation
appropriateness
acquisitiveness
agriculturalist
African-American
aerodynamically
air-chief-marshal
acrimoniousness
agranulocytosis
air-conditioning
aircraft-carrier
Aussichtspunkte
assimilationist
anticlericalism
anticholinergic
antichristianly
autodidacticism
autographically
anti-Gallicanism
antimonarchical
automorphically
astronavigation
authoritatively
astrodynamicist
antepenultimate
antiperistalsis
antiperistaltic
arterialisation
arterialization
autoradiography
Attorney-General
attorney-general
anthropobiology
anthropocentric
anthropogenesis
anthropological
anthropomorphic
anthropophagite
anthropophagous
anthropopathism
anthropopsychic
anthroposophist
autoschediastic
antitrinitarian
antivivisection
adventurousness
blameworthiness
brachycephalous
brachydactylous
brachistochrone
blast-furnaceman
bibliographical
back-calculation
bacteriological
bacchanalianism
bed-and-breakfast
before-mentioned
bomb-calorimeter
boning-telescope
banqueting-house
bronchoscopical
broadmindedness
blood-and-thunder
bloodcurdlingly
blood-guiltiness
biogeochemistry
biogeographical
broken-heartedly
biotechnologist
biodestructible
bio-astronautics
biostratigraphy
bioluminescence
bioavailability
bargain-basement
Bartholomew-tide
basidiomycetous
butterfly-flower
butterfly-orchid
butterfly-orchis
beta-thalassemia
chamberlainship
clandestineness
chargé-d'affaires
cradle-snatching
coconsciousness
cockneyfication
Caesalpiniaceae
Czechoslovakian
chenopodiaceous
chemopsychiatry
chemoattractant
crease-resistant
crease-resisting
criminalisation
criminalization
crimping-machine
co-instantaneity
coinstantaneous
cold-bloodedness
collenchymatous
cold-heartedness
Callitrichaceae
calendarisation
calendarization
colposcopically
chloramphenicol
compassionately
compartmentally
commendableness
compendiousness
competitiveness
complementation
complementarily
complementarity
compotationship
comfortlessness
comprehensively
comprehensivise
comprehensivize
compressibility
communalisation
communalization
computerisation
computerization

communicatively
communicability
combustibleness
cineangiography
canvas-stretcher
conscientiously
conscriptionist
condescendingly
congealableness
contemplatively
contemptibility
contemporaneity
contemporaneous
confessionalism
confessionalist
concessionnaire
conversationism
conversationist
conceptualistic
convertible-term
consentaneously
conventionalise
conventionalize
conventionalism
conventionalist
conventionality
contentiousness
consecutiveness
consequentially
conceivableness
conservationist
conservatorship
cannibalisation
cannibalization
considerateness
consideratively
confidentiality
configurational
continuation-day
cinemicrography
cinematographic
cinematographer
consolation-race
connoisseurship
convolvulaceous
conspicuousness
contractability
contractibility
contradictively
contradictorily
controllability
confrontational
contrapropeller
congratulations
contravallation
controversially
canisterisation
canisterization
constitutionist
constructionism
constructionist
conjunctiveness
conjunctionally
consumptiveness
conquerableness
consubstantiate
cholangiography
chondrification
cloud-cuckoo-land
cholecalciferol
cholesterolemia
cholecystectomy
cholecystostomy
choriocarcinoma
cross-laterality
crossing-sweeper
crossopterygian
cephalochordate
caprifoliaceous
Capernaitically
cerebrovascular
correlativeness
correspondently
correspondingly
carriage-forward
carcinogenicity
carnivorousness
cardiopulmonary
ceremoniousness
chromatographic
chromoxylograph
Corynebacterium
chronologically
carpometacarpus
Caryophyllaceae
corporification
Christadelphian
chrestomathical
Christy-minstrel
circumambagious
circumferential
circumforaneous
circumincession
circuminsession
circumnavigable
circumnavigator
circumstantiate
circumstantials
circumspectness
circumscribable
circumscriptive
circumscription
corruptibleness
circumvallation
castanospermine
cosignificative
cosmopolitanism
cataclysmically
catheterisation
catheterization
cytogenetically
categoricalness
catch-as-catch-can
catallactically
cytomegalovirus
△catholicisation
△catholicization
churrigueresque
courtmartialled
courts-bouillons
countermandable
countervailable
counterfesaunce
counterfeisance
counter-security
counter-flowered
countermovement
counterirritant
counter-proposal
counter-pressure
counter-evidence
cryoprecipitate
crypto-communist
crypto-Christian
crystallisation
crystallization
crystallography
cryptosporidium
diamagnetically
diaheliotropism
draughtsmanship
draught-proofing
diaphragmatitis
diaphototropism
diastereoisomer
decalcification
decolourisation
decolourization
decommissioning
decomposability
decontaminative
decontamination
decipherability
doctrinarianism
decarbonisation
decarbonization
decarburisation
decarburization
diesel-hydraulic
dyer's-yellowweed
dressing-station
differentiation
defencelessness
diffrangibility
daguerreotypist
degenerationist
dehypnotisation
dehypnotization
deindustrialise
deindustrialize
drilling-machine
dolichocephalic
deleteriousness

Words marked △ may be spelled also with a capital letter

15 d□m□c

democratisation
democratization
democratifiable
demagnetisation
demagnetization
demulsification
demonstratively
demonstrability
demystification
dimethylaniline
denitrification
dephlogisticate
Diprotodontidae
departmentalise
departmentalize
departmentalism
dermatoglyphics
dermatomyositis
direction-finder
director-general
durchkomponiert
dorsiventrality
dorsibranchiate
dissatisfaction
dissatisfactory
de-Stalinisation
de-Stalinization
dishabilitation
disharmoniously
dispassionately
distastefulness
disobligingness
desacralisation
desacralization
disadvantageous
dysteleological
disrespectfully
dishearteningly
dispensableness
dessertspoonful
disreputability
disaffectedness
disaffectionate
disafforestment
disagreeability
distinctiveness
distinguishable
distinguishably
distinguishment
displeasingness
desilverisation
desilverization
disillusionment
disimprisonment
disentanglement
disinterestedly
disenthrallment
desensitisation
desensitization
disinflationary
disentrancement
dissociableness
dyslogistically
discommodiously
discommendation
dysmorphophobia
discontinuation
discontinuously
dissolvableness
disorganisation
disorganization
disgracefulness
destructiveness
destructibility
distractibility
desertification
disarticulation
descriptiveness
disproportional
distressfulness
distrustfulness
discretionarily
disassimilative
disassimilation
disputativeness
disquisitionary
desexualisation
desexualization
detribalisation
detribalization
determinability
dithyrambically
double-barrelled
double-facedness
dividend-warrant
devil-worshipper
developmentally
diversification
devitrification
dextrophosphate
emancipationist
evangelicalness
evangelistarion
enantiomorphism
enantiomorphous
exchangeability
encyclopaedical
excrementitious
ecclesiological
ecclesiasticism
encomiastically
excommunicative
excommunication
excommunicatory
encephalography
energy-efficient
everlastingness
exemplificative
exemplification
eleutherodactyl
eleutherophobia
eleutherophobic
eleutherococcus
electrification
electromagnetic
electroacoustic
electronegative
electrotechnics
electrometrical
electrochemical
electrothermics
electrophoresis
electrophoretic
electrokinetics
electroanalysis
electropositive
electrodynamics
electromyograph
enfranchisement
efficaciousness
ergatandromorph
exhibitionistic
echinodermatous
ethnolinguistic
ethnomusicology
etherealisation
etherealization
episcopalianism
Eriocaulonaceae
epidemiological
epitheliomatous
epistemological
éclaircissement
ecotoxicologist
expeditiousness
euphemistically
expressionistic
experientialism
experientialist
experimentalise
experimentalize
experimentative
experimentalism
experimentation
experimentalist
earthshattering
edriophthalmian
edriophthalmous
Europeanisation
Europeanization
extra-illustrate
extraordinaries
extraordinarily
extra-provincial
extrajudicially
extra-curricular
entrepreneurial
entomologically
extemporariness
extemporisation
extemporization
extensification
extensivization

Words marked △ may be spelled also with a capital letter

externalisation
externalization
exteriorisation
exteriorization
ebullioscopical
equalitarianism
equiprobability
erythroleukemia
Erziehungsroman
flamboyante-tree
feather-boarding
fragmentariness
fractionisation
fractionization
Frenchification
French-polishing
field-sequential
free-heartedness
freezing-mixture
fifth-generation
Fifth-monarchism
Fifth-monarchist
flibbertigibbet
faithworthiness
fellow-traveller
fantasticalness
ferro-molybdenum
first-generation
formularisation
formularization
fissiparousness
fashionableness
four-dimensional
foundation-stone
foul-mouthedness
flutter-tonguing
grandiloquently
gravitationally
granitification
gramophonically
granulitisation
granulitization
Gleichschaltung
greenery-yallery
great-grandchild
gris-amber-steam'd
gillie-white-foot
gentlemanliness
Gentleman-at-arms
gynandromorphic
goniometrically
good-conditioned
gooseberry-stone
geochronologist
good-naturedness
gnotobiological
gnotobiotically
geomorphogenist
geomorphologist
glossographical
gastroenteritis
Götterdämmerung
gathering-ground
gluconeogenesis
governor-general
hearing-impaired
health-conscious
hobbledehoyhood
hackney-coachman
hydropathically
hydrometallurgy
hydrobiological
Hydrocorallinae
hydrostatically
hydrodynamicist
hyetometrograph
hierogrammatist
high-gravel-blind
heir-presumptive
holocrystalline
Hellenistically
half-heartedness
helminthologist
heliotropically
half-wellingtons
homochlamydeous
hemochromatosis
hemicrystalline
homogeneousness
humanitarianism
homeopathically
hendecasyllabic
hendecasyllable
hypochondriacal
hypochondriasis
hypomagnesaemia
hypnotisability
hypnotizability
hypno-anesthesia
hypophosphorous
hypopituitarism
hypercatalectic
hyperadrenalism
hyperthyroidism
hypercorrection
hypercritically
hepaticological
hypoventilation
hard-and-fastness
hermaphroditism
herb-Christopher
hereditarianism
hereditarianist
hermeneutically
harvest-festival
hard-heartedness
hospitalisation
hospitalization
historiographic
historiographer
heterocercality
heterochromatic
heterodactylous
heterogeneously
heterosexuality
hexachlorophane
hexachlorophene
inaccessibility
imaginativeness
inadmissibility
inapprehensible
inapplicability
inappropriately
inattentiveness
inalterableness
inadvisableness
incredulousness
incalculability
incomparability
incompatibility
incommensurable
incommensurably
incomprehensive
incomprehension
incommutability
incommunicative
inconsequential
inconsiderately
inconsideration
incentivisation
incentivization
inconsolability
inconspicuously
incongruousness
incapaciousness
incorrigibility
indubitableness
indefeasibility
indefinableness
indefensibility
indigestibility
indemnification
indomitableness
indistinctively
indisciplinable
indissolubility
indistributable
indisputability
indeterminately
indetermination
individualistic
indivisibleness
inexcusableness
ineffaceability
inefficaciously
ineffectiveness
ineffectualness
ideographically
inexpugnability
inexplicability
inexpensiveness
inestimableness
inextensibility

15 i□e□u

inequitableness
infrangibleness
inflammableness
infrastructural
infundibuliform
infinitesimally
ichthyodorulite
ichthyodorylite
injudiciousness
ill-favouredness
illimitableness
illustriousness
immunochemistry
immunologically
immunopathology
immensurability
immortalisation
immortalization
innumerableness
inoperativeness
isoperimetrical
inofficiousness
inoffensiveness
icositetrahedra
isoimmunization
inopportuneness
inobtrusiveness
implausibleness
impracticalness
impecuniousness
imprescriptible
impressionistic
imponderability
impenetrability
improvisatorial
improvvisatrice
impermeableness
imperviableness
imperishability
importunateness
inquisitiveness
inquisitorially
irreconcilement
irreducibleness
irreductibility
irredeemability
irrefragability
irrefutableness
irreligiousness
irremissibility
irremovableness
irrepealability
irreprehensible
irreprehensibly
irreparableness
irresolvability
irresistibility
irretentiveness
irrationalistic
irrevocableness
irreversibility

instantaneously
insubordinately
insubordination
insubstantially
insignificative
insignificantly
inspirationally
institutionally
insensitiveness
inseparableness
insuperableness
instructiveness
insurrectionary
insurrectionism
insurrectionist
instrumentalism
instrumentation
instrumentalist
instrumentality
inscrutableness
intrapreneurial
intransigentism
intransigentist
intransmissible
intractableness
intramuscularly
intrinsicalness
intellectualise
intellectualize
intellectualism
intellectualist
intellectuality
intelligibility
intolerableness
intemperateness
intensification
introsusception
interfascicular
intertanglement
interlamination
internalisation
internalization
internationally
interjaculatory
interscholastic
interdependence
interpenetrable
interferometric
interpersonally
intertentacular
interjectionary
interventionism
interventionist
interchangeable
interchangeably
interchangement
interdigitation
interambulacral
interambulacrum
interrogatively
intercollegiate

interconnection
intercolonially
intermodulation
interconversion
interpretership
interprovincial
interestingness
interosculation
interstratified
intersubjective
intertwistingly
intussusceptive
intussusception
invulnerability
involuntariness
Jack-in-the-pulpit
Jack-of-all-trades
Johnny-head-in-air
Jungermanniales
junior-flyweight
jurisprudential
jerry-come-tumble
justifiableness
jusqu'auboutisme
jusqu'auboutiste
juxtapositional
knick-knackatory
knitting-machine
kilogram-calorie
kind-heartedness
knowledgability
kerbstone-broker
kitchen-gardener
katathermometer
Lob-lie-by-the-fire
labour-intensive
lackadaisically
lactovegetarian
logographically
logarithmically
light-headedness
light-mindedness
lymphadenopathy
lamellirostrate
landing-carriage
landscape-marble
long-sightedness
lepidopterology
lophobranchiate
lissencephalous
letters-of-marque
lithochromatics
low-spiritedness
lexicographical
meadow-saxifrage
mechanistically
Michaelmas-daisy
mechanoreceptor
mechanomorphism
machine-washable
machine-readable

macroscopically
microscopically
microtechnology
micropegmatitic
Microchiroptera
microphotograph
microbiological
micromillimetre
micromicrocurie
micromicrofarad
microdissection
microelectronic
microanalytical
macrocosmically
macrosporangium
microsporangium
microsporophyll
microprocessing
mucosanguineous
medicine-dropper
Middle-Easterner
middle-of-the-road
middle-stitching
Megacheiroptera
magneto-electric
magisterialness
maintainability
malacopterygian
mole-electronics
multilateralism
multilateralist
multilingualism
multiarticulate
maldistribution
multitudinously
multinucleolate
malconformation
malpractitioner
malpresentation
malassimilation
miniaturisation
miniaturization
manic-depressive
monochlamydeous
Monocotyledones
monocrystalline
manneristically
manoeuvrability
montmorillonite
Monarchianistic
mineralogically
menispermaceous
monosymmetrical
maneuverability
Mephistophelean
Mephistophelian
margaritiferous
meroblastically
market-gardening
marsh-cinquefoil
morphophonemics
mortiferousness
marriage-licence
marriage-portion
Marsipobranchii
myristicivorous
meritoriousness
messenger-at-arms
miscellaneously
misbecomingness
mischievousness
misintelligence
misconstruction
misappreciative
misappreciation
misapprehensive
misapprehension
misproportioned
mistrustfulness
mesaticephalous
musculo-skeletal
methamphetamine
mathematisation
mathematization
metalinguistics
metamathematics
Methodistically
metropolitanate
metropolitanise
metropolitanize
mythologisation
mythologization
materialisation
materialization
materfamiliases
materialistical
near-sightedness
noble-mindedness
nucleosynthesis
necromantically
necessitousness
nightmarishness
neighbourliness
number-crunching
nomographically
numismatologist
nemathelminthic
Nemathelminthes
nondescriptness
non-belligerency
nonsensicalness
non-intervention
non-intrusionist
non-commissioned
non-contributory
non-professional
non-profit-making
non-attributable
non-attributably
non-judgmentally
Neo-Christianity
nepheline-basalt
north-eastwardly
north-westwardly
north-countryman
norm-referencing
nothingarianism
notwithstanding
nationalisation
nationalization
nitro-derivative
nitrogenisation
nitrogenization
natureknowledge
neurophysiology
neurolinguistic
neurobiological
neurofibrillary
neuroblastomata
neuroanatomical
neuropsychiatry
neuropsychology
neurohypophyses
neurohypophysis
new-Commonwealth
overbearingness
overdevelopment
overforwardness
open-heartedness
oceanographical
overpreparation
oneirocriticism
organophosphate
ophthalmoscopic
ophthalmophobia
ophthalmoplegia
ophthalmologist
Ophioglossaceae
ochlocratically
oligonucleotide
opisthognathous
Opisthobranchia
objectification
omnibenevolence
omnidirectional
owner-occupation
ornithodelphian
ornithodelphous
ornithorhynchus
odoriferousness
odontostomatous
opprobriousness
observationally
obstructionally
ostreiculturist
optoelectronics
ontogenetically
orthophosphoric
orthopsychiatry
onychocryptosis
phase-difference
peasecod-bellied
peasecod-cuirass

pharisaicalness
plagiostomatous
platitudinarian
pharmacognosist
pharmacognostic
pharmacokinetic
pragmaticalness
peacock-pheasant
practicableness
plantaginaceous
phantasmagorial
Platyhelminthes
public-relations
packet-switching
pycnodysostosis
picture-restorer
picture-moulding
picture-postcard
picturesqueness
pedagoguishness
Pre-Raphaelitish
Pre-Raphaelitism
Pre-Raphaelistic
phenakistoscope
△presbyterianise
△presbyterianize
△presbyterianism
preacquaintance
pseudoephedrine
pseudohexagonal
pseudepigraphic
predeterminable
preferentialism
preferentialist
preternaturally
presentableness
pretentiousness
presentationism
presentationist
preservationist
precipitousness
plenipotentiary
predictableness
prehistorically
pneumatological
phenomenalistic
phenomenologist
prepositionally
preformationism
preformationist
phenolphthalein
preconstruction
prepossessingly
pleuropneumonia
pleasurableness
pleasure-seeking
prestidigitator
phenylketonuria
phenylketonuric
Philadelphaceae
philanthropical
philosophically
printing-machine
pyknodysostosis
police-constable
polychlorinated
polychloroprene
polycrystalline
palaeoanthropic
Palaeoanthropus
palaeobiologist
palaeobotanical
palaeoethnology
palaeoecologist
palaeographical
palaeogeography
palaeolimnology
palaeomagnetism
palaeontologist
palaeontography
palaeopathology
palaeophytology
palaeozoologist
pulchritudinous
paleichthyology
paleopathologic
paleoecological
paleogeographic
paleogeographer
paleopedologist
paleobiological
paleozoological
pulmobranchiate
pillow-structure
paleontological
paleoethnologic
polyphloesboean
Polyprotodontia
polishing-powder
polysyllabicism
polysynthetical
polyunsaturated
pantechnicon-van
pencil-sharpener
pantopragmatics
panophthalmitis
Pan-Presbyterian
penetrativeness
punctiliousness
probationership
phonautographic
prosenchymatous
phonemicisation
phonemicization
phoneticisation
phoneticization
properispomenon
professionalise
professionalize
professionalism
processionalist
proof-correcting
prohibitiveness
problematically
prognosticative
prognostication
provocativeness
photomacrograph
phototelegraphy
photo-mechanical
photorefractive
photodegradable
photosensitiser
photosensitizer
photozincograph
photolithograph
photomicrograph
photoelasticity
photoconductive
photoconducting
protozoological
photojournalism
photojournalist
protospatharius
photogrammetric
provost-sergeant
proportionately
proportionality
photomultiplier
photoxylography
prospectiveness
phosphorescence
phosphorylation
procreativeness
proprietorially
programmability
procrastinative
procrastinating
procrastination
procrastinatory
progressiveness
pronunciamentos
propylitisation
propylitization
pergamentaceous
paradoxicalness
perpendicularly
pyro-electricity
paroemiographer
perfectionistic
paragraphically
paraheliotropic
parthenogenesis
parthenogenetic
parliamentarism
parliamentarian
parliamentarily
parliament-hinge
parliament-house
particularistic
parallelepipeda
paralinguistics
perfluorocarbon

Words marked △ may be spelled also with a capital letter

parenthetically
phrenologically
personalisation
personalization
purposelessness
personification
perspicaciously
perspicuousness
pyrophotography
portrait-gallery
portrait-painter
peristaltically
parasympathetic
perissodactylic
perissosyllabic
parasiticalness
pyrotechnically
perfunctoriness
party-government
postconsonantal
passenger-pigeon
pessimistically
pusillanimously
post-millenarian
post-Reformation
post-synchronise
post-synchronize
postulationally
Pithecanthropus
Patripassianism
paterfamiliases
plumbaginaceous
paulo-post-future
poverty-stricken
powdering-closet
psychobiologist
psychobiography
psychochemistry
psychographical
psychogenetical
psychogeriatric
psychohistorian
psychologically
psychometrician
psychrometrical
psychopathology
psychophysicist
psychosomimetic
psychosynthesis
psychotherapist
psychotomimetic
physiographical
physiologically
physicochemical
physiotherapist
phytogeographic
phytogeographer
quatercentenary
quasi-historical
quarrelsomeness
quadruplication
quadripartition
quarter-sessions
quartermistress
questionability
question-begging
quick-wittedness
quick-conceiving
quinquagenarian
quintuplication
reafforestation
Rhamphorhynchus
reapportionment
readvertisement
recrementitious
receiving-office
recollectedness
reconvalescence
reconcilability
reconsideration
reconsolidation
reconstitutable
recoverableness
rudimentariness
riding-committee
radio-telegraphy
radiogoniometer
radio-gramophone
redetermination
rheumatological
re-establishment
refrangibleness
refreshment-room
refortification
regionalisation
regionalization
right-handedness
right-mindedness
rainbow-coloured
reindustrialise
reindustrialize
reinterrogation
railway-carriage
railway-crossing
romanticisation
romanticization
remonstratingly
remorselessness
röntgenotherapy
renormalisation
renormalization
rhombencephalon
rhombenporphyry
reprivatisation
reprivatization
reproachfulness
repetitiousness
respectableness
resurrectionary
resurrectionise
resurrectionize
resurrectionism
resurrectionist
resurrection-man
resurrection-pie
resourcefulness
ritualistically
rate-determining
retrievableness
rationalisation
rationalization
retroreflective
retrospectively
retrogressively
retrogressional
roundaboutation
roundaboutility
round-shouldered
riverworthiness
Rhynchobdellida
Rhynchocephalia
stalagmitically
stalactitically
shabby-gentility
standoffishness
standardisation
standardization
slave-trafficker
scaphocephalous
swathling-clouts
staphylorrhaphy
swathing-clothes
Sabbath-breaking
△sublapsarianism
subterraneously
subject-superior
subcivilisation
subcivilization
subintellection
subintelligence
subintelligitur
subcommissioner
sub-postmistress
subspecifically
suburbanisation
suburbanization
subordinateness
sober-mindedness
substratosphere
substantiveness
substantialness
substitutionary
socialistically
successlessness
second-adventist
second-in-command
secundogeniture
sociolinguistic
sociobiological
sycophantically
saddler-sergeant
saddler-corporal
sedimentologist

15 s□d□m

sadomasochistic
steganographist
speechification
stereochemistry
stereoisomerism
seeming-virtuous
spermatoblastic
spermatogenesis
spermatogenetic
smelting-furnace
spectroscopical
speculativeness
softly-sprighted
significatively
Schrecklichkeit
sphaerosiderite
schillerisation
schillerization
Sphenisciformes
school-inspector
schoolmastering
schoolmasterish
spheroidisation
spheroidization
schistosomiasis
schizo-affective
schizophrenetic
stiff-neckedness
sticking-plaster
shilly-shallying
seismographical
stigmatophilist
spirochaetaemia
stilpnosiderite
self-abandonment
self-affirmation
syllabification
self-approbation
self-advancement
self-complacence
self-consequence
self-considering
self-confidently
self-consistency
self-constituted
self-capacitance
self-documenting
self-degradation
self-deprecating
self-destructive
self-destruction
self-determining
self-development
self-examination
self-explanatory
self-explication
self-forgetfully
self-fertilising
self-fertilizing
Selaginellaceae
self-humiliation
sulphinpyrazone
sulphureousness
self-improvement
self-importantly
self-liquidating
selenographical
self-opinionated
syllogistically
self-observation
self-preparation
solipsistically
self-pollination
self-propagating
self-portraiture
self-questioning
self-realisation
self-realization
sclerodermatous
self-registering
self-resemblance
self-slaughtered
self-substantial
self-sacrificing
self-sufficiency
self-sustainment
self-sovereignty
self-vindication
sympathomimetic
sympathetically
semicrystalline
semidocumentary
symmetricalness
semi-independent
semi-logarithmic
semimanufacture
Semi-Pelagianism
semisubmersible
semitransparent
symptomological
symptomatically
sensation-monger
synecologically
synecdochically
sententiousness
synchronisation
synchronization
synchronistical
synchronousness
single-heartedly
synarthrodially
synergistically
sinistrodextral
sanctimoniously
singularisation
singularization
stoicheiometric
stoechiological
stoichiological
sword-and-buckler
swothling-clouts
shoulder-clapper
shoulder-slipped
shoulder-shotten
scolopendriform
slotting-machine
spontaneousness
shoot-from-the-hip
septentrionalis
septentrionally
supplementation
supplementarily
saprophytically
suppositionally
supportableness
supercalendered
superlativeness
superpatriotism
supernaturalise
supernaturalize
supernaturalism
supersaturation
supernaturalist
superabundantly
superadditional
superheterodyne
superficialness
superfluousness
superplasticity
superimposition
superintendence
superintendency
superincumbence
superincumbency
superinducement
superconductive
superconducting
superconfidence
superordination
superstitiously
superstructural
superexcellence
superexaltation
spread-eaglewise
sarraceniaceous
scribaciousness
scribbling-paper
sericiculturist
sarcenchymatous
sergeant-drummer
surreptitiously
serviceableness
straightforward
strombuliferous
serendipitously
shrink-resistant
servomechanical
strephosymbolia
scripture-reader
stratigraphical
stretcher-bearer
scratchbuilding
systematisation

Words marked △ may be spelled also with a capital letter

systematization
susceptibleness
sesquicentenary
sesquicarbonate
south-eastwardly
south-westwardly
slumpflationary
seventeen-hunder
thanatognomonic
thalassographic
thalassographer
thalassotherapy
teacher-governor
thankworthiness
traumatological
training-college
tranquilization
tranquilizingly
transparentness
translationally
transubstantial
transactionally
transferability
transliteration
△transfiguration
transfigurement
transplantation
transilluminate
transposability
transpositional
transmogrifying
transportedness
transcriptively
transcriptional
transgressively
transgressional
transmutability
transmutational
tuberculisation
tuberculization
ticket-collector
Tectibranchiata
tectibranchiate
technologically
technostructure
therapeutically
treacherousness
theriomorphosis
therianthropism
thermochemistry
thermodynamical
theorematically
treasonableness
theosophistical
thiobarbiturate
trinitrobenzene
trinitrotoluene
thick-headedness
thick-wittedness
trigonometrical
trisoctahedrons

thin-skinnedness
thirtysomething
trisyllabically
telegraphically
telephotography
telestereoscope
temperamentally
tamper-resistant
tempestuousness
tentaculiferous
tender-heartedly
tendentiousness
tungsten-halogen
tongue-and-groove
thoracocentesis
two-pair-of-stairs
troubleshooting
troublesomeness
thoughtlessness
thoroughgoingly
topographically
typographically
threepenceworth
threepennyworth
thromboembolism
tarsometatarsal
tarsometatarsus
through-composed
testament-dative
tetrasporangium
Tetrabranchiata
tetrabranchiate
Tetractinellida
tetrasyllabical
tatterdemallion
totalitarianism
thunder-stricken
true-heartedness
trustworthiness
toxicologically
trypanosomiasis
unavailableness
unaccommodating
unascertainable
unavoidableness
unapostolically
unapprehensible
unauthenticated
unauthoritative
unalterableness
unadvisableness
unchangeability
unchallengeable
unchallengeably
uncompanionable
uncompassionate
uncomplaisantly
uncomplainingly
uncomplimentary
uncomprehensive
uncomprehending

uncommunicative
unconscientious
unconsciousness
unconcernedness
unconsentaneous
unconditionally
uncanonicalness
uncontroversial
unconstrainable
unconstrainedly
uncooperatively
unco-operatively
unceremoniously
unchristianlike
uncircumscribed
undemonstrative
underhandedness
under-the-counter
underemployment
under-production
under-privileged
underestimation
understandingly
undistinguished
undisciplinable
undisappointing
undesirableness
undetermination
unexceptionable
unexceptionably
unexceptionally
unforgivingness
unfortunateness
unfossiliferous
ungrammatically
ungentlemanlike
unhealthfulness
unimaginatively
unidiomatically
unintentionally
unintermittedly
uninterpretable
uninterestingly
uninterruptedly
unnecessariness
unobjectionable
unobjectionably
unobtrusiveness
unpeaceableness
unpractisedness
unprecedentedly
unpremeditation
unprepossessing
unphilosophical
unprotectedness
unprotestantise
unprotestantize
unprofitability
unpronounceable
unproportionate
unprogressively

15 u□p□r

unparliamentary
unpatriotically
unqualifiedness
unrecommendable
unreconciliable
unreconstructed
unrighteousness
unrelentingness
unremittingness
unstatesmanlike
unseaworthiness
unsubstantiated
unsteadfastness
unspeakableness
unselfconscious
unsymmetrically
unsportsmanlike
unsophisticated
unsuspectedness
unsatisfiedness
ultracentrifuge
unteachableness
ultramicroscope
ultramicroscopy
ultrafiltration
ultrasonography
ultra-Protestant
untransferrable
untransmigrated
untransmissible
untractableness
untrustworthily
unverifiability
unwholesomeness
vice-chamberlain
vicissitudinous
victualling-yard
victualling-ship
victualling-bill
videoconference
vehicle-actuated
Völkerwanderung
vindicativeness
ventriloquially
ventriloquistic
venturesomeness
violinistically
vertiginousness
vasoconstrictor
viscosimetrical
viscoelasticity
vascularisation
vascularization
weatherboarding
wringing-machine
weighing-machine
whirling-machine
well-conditioned
well-intentioned
well-upholstered
wondermongering
windscreen-wiper
wrong-headedness
word-association
warrantableness
world-shattering
world-without-end
warm-heartedness
withdrawing-room
xylotypographic
xeroradiography
zygophyllaceous
zoogeographical
zoophysiologist
zoophytological

Words arranged according to
EVEN LETTERS

b**a**b**a**
caba
Cama
capa
casa
Dada
data
fa-la
Gaea
gaga
Gaia
gala
ha-ha
haka
Java
kaka
△kama
kana
kara
kata
kava
la-la
△lama
lana
lava
mama
mana
mara
masa
△maya
nada
naga
Naia
Naja
nala
nana
napa
paca
papa
Pará
para
paua
pawa
raca
raga
raja
Rama
△rana
ra-ra
rata
Saba
saga
sama
taha
taka
tala
tana
tapa
tara
ta-ta
tava
tawa
taxa
vara
vasa
waka
Yama
b**arb**
carb
daub
gamb
garb
iamb
jamb
△lamb
b**anc**
laic
marc
narc
saic
talc
Waac
b**ald**
△band
△bard
baud
bawd
card
Dard
daud
dawd
eard
fand
fard
gaed
gaid
gaud
gawd
hand
hard
haud
kaid
laid
△land
lard
laud
maid
mand
mard
maud
NAND
nard
paid
pand
pard
rag'd
raid
△rand
said
sand
△sard
wadd
Wafd
waid
wald
wand
wan'd
ward
yald
△yard
yaud
b**a**b**e**
bade
bake
bale
bane
bare
base
bate
baye
cade
cafe
café
cage
cake
came
cane
△cape
care
case
cate
cave
dace
dale
dame
Dane
dare
date
daze
eale
ease
face
fade
fake
fame
fane
fare
fate
fave
faze
gade
gage
gale
game
gane
gape
gare
gate
gave
gaze
hade
hake
hale
hame
hare
hate
have
haze
jade
jake
△jane
jape
kade
kaie
kale
kame
lace
lade
lake
lame
lamé
△lane
lare
lase
late
lave
laze
Mace®
mace
made
mage
make
male
mane
mare
mase
mate
maté
maze
△name
nape
nare
nave
naze
△pace
page
△pale
pane
pape
pare
pate
pâté
pave
pavé
PAYE
race
rade
rage
rake
rale
râle
rape
rare
rase
rate
rave
raze
sade
safe
sage
sake
saké
sale
same
sane
sate
save
Saxe
tace
take
tale
tame
tane
ta'ne
tape
tare
tate
vade
vale
vane
vare
vase
wade
wage
wake
wale
wame
wane
ware
wase
wate
wave
wawe
Yale®
yale
yare
yate
b**aff**
barf
caff
calf
cauf
daff
faff
gaff
haaf
haff
half
kaif
lauf
naff
naif
naïf
raff
Waaf
waff
waif
△wakf
△waqf
yaff
zarf
b**ang**
cang
dang
darg
fang
gang
hagg
hang
kang
lang
magg
mang
marg
pang
ragg
rang
sang
Taig
△tang
T'ang
vang
wang
△yang
△b**ach**
bash
△bath
cash
dash
each
eath
fash
gash
gath
hash
hath
lakh
lash
lath
Mach
mash
math
nach
oath
pash
path
rach
rash
rath
sash
tach
tanh
tash
tath
wash
B**a**b**i**
bani
cadi
capi
dali
dari
gadi
haji
Jawi
kadi
kaki
△kali
kami
kati
kazi
magi
mali
mani
maxi
Nazi
Paki
Pali
qadi
rabi
ragi
raki
rami
rani
saki
Sami
sari
sati
tabi
taki
tali
taxi
vagi
vali
wadi
wali
△yagi
zati
h**adj**
hajj
b**ack**
balk
bank
bark
bask
bauk
calk
cark
cask
cauk
cawk
dank
dark
dawk
faik
fank
gawk
hack

4 □a□l

haik
hank
hark
hask
hawk
△jack
jark
lack
laik
lank
lark
lawk
mack
maik
mark
mask
mawk
nabk
naik
nark
pack
paik
△park
pawk
rack
raik
rank
sack
Salk
sank
sark
tack
talk
tank
task
wack
walk
wank
wark
wauk
yack
△yank
zack
B**a**a**l**
báel
bail
ball
bawl
call
carl
caul
dahl
Dáil
△earl
fail
fall
farl
Gael
gall
gaol
Gaul

hail
hall
harl
haul
jail
jarl
kail
mail
mall
marl
maul
nail
pail
pall
paul
pawl
rail
sail
saul
Taal
tael
tail
tall
vail
wail
△wall
waul
wawl
y'all
yawl
b**a**l**m**
barm
calm
caum
farm
gaum
haem
halm
harm
hawm
kaim
ma'am
maim
malm
marm
naam
palm
Saam
saim
warm
wasm
b**a**r**n**
bawn
△cain
cann
damn
darn
dawn
earn
fain
faun

fawn
gain
gaun
hain
harn
Jain
jann
kain
kaon
lain
larn
lawn
△main
maun
naan
nain
△pain
pawn
rain
raun
rawn
sain
sawn
ta'en
tarn
vain
△wain
warn
yarn
yawn
c**a**p**o**
dado
dago
fado
faro
gajo
gapó
halo
haro
jato
kago
kayo
lazo
mako
mano
Nato
paco
Pavo
sago
taco
taro
b**a**r**p**
calp
camp
carp
caup
damp
gamp
gasp
gaup
gawp

harp
hasp
jasp
jaup
lamp
Lapp
palp
parp
ramp
rasp
salp
samp
tamp
tarp
vamp
warp
wasp
yapp
yaup
yawp
b**a**u**r**
bawr
carr
daur
fair
gair
gaur
haar
hair
laer
lair
maar
mair
mawr
Nair
pair
parr
sair
tahr
vair
waur
yarr
b**a**a**s**
bags
bars
bass
bats
bays
cans
caps
cats
Dabs
dais
dams
days
ears
eats
hass
jass
jaws
kans

lags
lass
mags
Mars
△mass
nabs
naos
oafs
Oaks
oats
pads
pais
pass
pays
rags
rams
rats
sans
sass
says
tabs
tags
taps
tass
taws
wats
ways
yaws
b**a**f**t**
baht
bait
Balt
bant
bast
batt
bayt
cant
can't
cart
cast
daft
dalt
dant
dart
daut
dawt
△east
fact
fart
fast
gait
gant
gart
gast
haet
haft
ha'it
halt
ha'n't
hart
hast

haut
kant
kart
lant
last
malt
mart
mast
matt
oast
pact
pant
part
past
raft
rait
rant
rapt
rast
salt
△sant
saut
tact
tait
tart
tatt
taut
tawt
vant
vast
vaut
wadt
waft
wait
want
wart
wast
watt
b**a**b**u**
baju
balu
bapu
masu
Rahu
raku
ratu
tabu
tapu
tatu
vatu
c**a**l**x**
faix
falx
faux
lanx
Manx
b**a**b**y**
cagy
caky
cany
cavy

Davy
easy
fady
gaby
gamy
gazy
hazy
jasy
jazy
lacy
△lady
laky
lazy
many
△mary
maty
mazy
nary
△navy
oaky
oary
pacy
paly
racy
sagy
taky
vary
wady
waly
wany
wary
wavy
waxy
yawy
zany
j**a**z**z**
razz
a**b**b**a**
obia
A**b**i**b**
a**b**a**c**
a**b**e**d**
abid
'zbud
a**b**b**é**
able
abye
oboe
o**b**o**l**
e**b**o**n**
T-**b**a**r**
A**b**o**s**
ibis
Ibos
obos
a**b**e**t**
abut
obit
ybet
i**b**e**x**
a**b**l**y**

Words marked △ may be spelled also with a capital letter

obey
a**cta**
octa
s**cab**
A**C**/D**C**
a**cid**
ecad
ecod
iced
scad
△scud
a**che**
acme
acne
acre
ecce
eche
oche
scye
s**cag**
scog
scug
a**cyl**
scul
s**cam**
scum
icon
scan
e**cco**
echo
s**cop**
scup
a**cer**
icer
scar
scur
e**cht**
scat
scot
scut
e**cru**
s**caw**
scow
a**chy**
icky
scry
E**dda**
idea
odea
o**dic**
a**dze**
edge
idée
idle
idol
idyl
odal
odyl
udal
A**dam**
Edam
idem
E**den**
Odin
e**ddo**
odso
A**dar**
odor
A**des**
ados
△ides
odds
udos
a**dit**
edit
a**daw**
a**dry**
D-day
eddy
edgy
idly
V-day
b**ema**
△beta
ceca
deva
feta
gena
geta
Jena
keta
leva
mega
mela
mesa
peba
pela
sena
sera
seta
tela
Veda
△vega
△vela
vena
Vera
weka
weta
Xema
zeta
B**eeb**
herb
kemb
kerb
Serb
verb
wemb
a**esc**
merc
b**ead**
bend
dead
deed
deid
feed
fee'd
fend
feod
feud
geld
head
heed
heid
held
hend
herd
lead
lend
lewd
mead
meed
meld
mend
need
nerd
pend
read
redd
reed
rend
seed
seld
send
tea'd
teed
tee'd
teld
tend
veld
vend
weed
weid
weld
△wend
yead
yeed
yeld
yerd
Zend
b**ede**
bene
bere
bete
bête
cede
cere
cete
dele
deme
dene
dere
feme
fere
fête
gene
gêne
gere
△hebe
he-he
hele
heme
here
hete
jeté
leke
leme
lere
lese
leve
leze
Mede
mene
mere
mese
mete
meve
meze
mézé
nene
nete
névé
peke
△pele
pene
père
rede
reke
rete
sele
semé
sere
sese
teme
tene
tête
vele
were
we're
we've
wexe
yede
yeve
zeze
b**eef**
deaf
delf
jeff
kerf
leaf
neif
pelf
reef
reif
seif
self
serf
teff
terf
b**erg**
leng
meng
peag
tegg
yegg
b**eth**
eech
hech
kesh
lech
mesh
nesh
pech
pegh
sech
tech
yeah
yech
b**eni**
cedi
deli
Devi
feni
kepi
meri
nevi
peni
peri
semi
yeti
b**enj**
b**eak**
beck
berk
deck
deek
desk
feck
geck
geek
heck
jerk
keck
keek
leak
leek
meek
merk
neck
nerk
neuk
peak
peck
peek
penk
perk
reak
reck
reek
reik
seek
seik
serk
teak
weak
week
welk
yelk
yerk
yesk
yeuk
b**ell**
ceil
cell
ceòl
deal
deil
dell
feal
feel
fell
geal
heal
heel
heil
△hell
he'll
herl
jeel
jell
keel
kell
△leal
meal
mell
merl
mewl
neal
peal
peel
pell
real
reel
seal
seel
seil
sell
teal
teel
teil
tell
veal
veil
vell
weal
weel
weil
well
we'll
yell
zeal
b**eam**
berm
deem
derm
△fehm
ferm
germ
△geum
helm
herm
leam
neem
neum
perm
ream
seam
seem
Sejm
team
teem
term
△vehm
weem
yelm
a**eon**
bean
been
bein
△dean
deen
dern
eevn
eev'n
fern
gean
hern
hewn
jean
keen
kern
lean
mean
mein
nemn
neon
pean
peen
pein
peon
pern
rean
reen
rein
sean
seen
sewn
Tean

Words marked △ may be spelled also with a capital letter

4 □e□o

teen
tern
vein
Venn
wean
ween
yean
zein
a**ero**
bego
△deco
demo
△hero
keno
Lego®
leno
memo
pepo
peso
redo
rego
repo
seco
sego
veto
zero
b**eep**
△deep
geep
heap
help
hemp
hesp
Jeep
keep
kelp
kemp
leap
leep
lerp
neap
neep
peep
reap
repp
seep
temp
veep
weep
yelp
b**ear**
beer
dear
deer
fear
feer
gear
hear
heir
Herr
jeer

keir
lear
leer
lehr
leir
meer
near
ne'er
pear
peer
rear
sear
seer
seir
serr
tear
teer
tehr
veer
wear
weir
year
b**ees**
ceas
cens
cess
deus
fegs
feis
fess
gens
geos
hers
jess
△keys
lees
△lens
less
'less
△mess
mews
ness
nets
news
peas
pecs
reds
reis
reps
seas
sens
seps
sess
tems
vers
yes's
Zeus
b**eat**
beet
belt
bent

best
△celt
cent
cert
debt
deft
delt
dent
feat
feet
felt
fent
fest
fett
geat
geit
gelt
gent
gest
heat
heft
hent
hept
hest
jeat
jest
△kelt
kent
kept
kest
leat
leet
△left
△lent
lest
Lett
meat
meet
melt
ment
neat
nest
nett
newt
next
peat
pelt
pent
pert
pest
reft
rent
rest
seat
sect
△sekt
sent
sept
sett
sext
teat

telt
tent
test
text
vent
vert
vest
vext
weet
weft
△welt
went
wept
wert
△west
yelt
yest
yett
zest
b**eau**
Bedu
genu
Jehu
Jesu
menu
Peru
tegu
zebu
d**eev**
derv
perv
d**eaw**
meow
jeux
a**ery**
bevy
defy
demy
deny
dewy
eely
eery
hery
levy
rely
reny
sexy
tedy
△very
Ge**ëz**
Jeez
lezz
E**fik**
△a**fro**
a**far**
u**fos**
E-**fit**®
a**ffy**
iffy
ofay
a**gha**

agma
egma
a**ged**
egad
igad
a**gee**
ague
ogee
ogle
ogre
ygoe
a**gog**
u**gli**®
e**gal**
o**gam**
a**gen**
agin
agon
Ogen
a**gio**
Igbo
a**gar**
eger
a**ges**
eggs
egis
O**gpu**
e**ggy**
ugly
△**rhea**
shea
Shia
shwa
Thea
whoa
c**hub**
c**hic**
choc
△c**had**
chid
khud
shad
shed
she'd
shod
thud
whid
who'd
g**hee**
shoe
thae
thee
whee
c**hef**
c**hug**
shag
shog
thig
thug
△whig
p**hoh**

shah
c**hai**
Shri
Thai
c**hik**
dhak
b**hel**
chal
dhal
shul
a**hem**
cham
chum
sham
shim
them
wham
whim
whom
c**hin**
chon
△khan
phon
△shan
shin
shun
'shun
than
then
thin
thon
when
whin
s**hmo**
shoo
thro
thro'
c**hap**
chip
chop
ship
△shop
whap
whip
whop
c**har**
cher
khor
shir
thar
thir
Thor
whe'r
whir
m**hos**
ohos
phos
rhos
rhus
shes
she's

this
thus
who's
c**hat**
chit
chut
ghat
khat
phot
phut
shat
shet
shit
shot
shut
that
what
whet
△whit
whot
c**hou**
thou
thru
c**hiv**
shiv
c**haw**
chew
△chow
dhow
phew
shaw
shew
show
thaw
thew
whew
whow
a**hoy**
chay
shay
they
whey
c**hez**
chiz
phiz
whiz
b**iga**
Bixa
dika
disa
dita
diva
giga
gila
hila
hiya
kina
kiva
lima
lira
mica

Words marked △ may be spelled also with a capital letter

mina
Mira
△nipa
△pica
pika
pila
piña
pipa
pita
rima
riva
riza
sida
sika
sima
Siva
tika
vina
visa
Vita®
vita
viva
zila
d**i**e**b**
limb
nimb
sibb
zimb
d**i**s**c**
fisc
zinc
b**i**n**d**
bird
died
eild
find
gied
gild
gird
hied
hild
hind
jird
kild
kind
lied
lind
mild
mind
pied
rind
sild
sind
tied
tind
vied
vild
△wild
wind
yird
a**i**d**e**

aîné
bice
bide
bike
bile
bine
bise
bite
cine
ciné
ciré
cite
cive
dice
dike
dime
dine
dire
dite
dive
eine
fife
fike
file
fine
fire
five
gibe
gite
gîte
give
hide
hike
hire
hive
jibe
jive
kibe
kike
kine
kipe
kite
lice
Lide
life
like
lime
△line
lire
lite
live
mice
mike
mile
mime
mine
mire
mise
mite
nice
nide

nife
Nike
△nine
nite
pice
pike
pile
pine
pipe
pisé
pize
rice
ride
rife
rile
rime
rine
ripe
rise
rite
rive
sice
side
sike
sile
sine
sipe
sire
site
size
tice
tide
tige
tike
tile
△time
tine
tire
tite
△vice
vide
vile
vine
vire
vise
visé
vite
vive
wice
wide
wife
wile
wine
wipe
wire
wise
wite
wive
yike
yite
zite

b**i**f**f**
fief
jiff
lief
miff
nief
niff
riff
tiff
ziff
b**i**g**g**
bing
biog
ding
ging
hing
△king
ling
△ming
ping
rigg
ring
sing
ting
wing
zing
b**i**s**h**
dich
dish
fish
high
hish
kish
kith
lich
lith
nigh
pish
pith
rich
sich
sigh
Sikh
sinh
sith
△tich
wich
wish
with
d**i**v**i**
dixi
fini
hi-fi
hili
kiwi
△midi
mini
miri
nidi
nisi
pili

pipi
simi
siri
tiki
tipi
titi
wili
ziti
b**i**l**k**
bink
birk
bisk
△dick
dink
dirk
disk
fink
firk
fisk
gink
hick
jink
kick
kink
△kirk
lick
link
lirk
lisk
mick
milk
mink
mirk
△nick
oink
pick
pink
rick
rink
risk
sick
silk
sink
tick
tink
wick
wink
yirk
△b**i**l**l**
birl
ciel
cill
cirl
dial
dill
dirl
fill
gill
girl
hill
jill

kill
lill
mill
nill
n'ill
nirl
pill
pirl
rial
riel
rill
sial
sill
till
tirl
vial
vill
viol
virl
wiel
will
yill
f**i**l**m**
firm
gism
jism
pium
riem
Sium
a**i**r**n**
bien
cion
Dian
Finn
firn
gien
ginn
girn
hisn
his'n
jinn
kiln
kirn
lien
limn
linn
△lion
mien
pion
pirn
sien
sign
winn
Xian
Zion
B**i**r**o**®
bito
ciao
cito
dido
fico

Fido
figo
filo
fino
△giro
jiao
kilo
kino
lido
Lilo®
lilo
limo
lino
mico
milo
mino
miso
rivo
sijo
silo
Tico
tiro
vino
vivo
wino
g**i**m**p**
jimp
kilp
△kipp
limp
△lisp
pimp
ripp
risp
simp
wimp
wisp
b**i**e**r**
birr
fiar
girr
kier
liar
lier
pier
tiar
tier
tirr
vier
A**I**D**S**
airs
bias
bios
bits
cits
dibs
dies
digs
diss
fils
fits

4 □i□t

gios
hiss
kiss
Lias
lips
mirs
△miss
nibs
oils
pics
Pils
pins
pips
piss
pits
Riss
siss
tits
vibs
wits
yips
a**in't**
airt
bint
bitt
cist
dict
△diet
dint
dirt
ditt
fiat
fist
fitt
gift
gilt
girt
gist
hilt
hint
hipt
hist
jilt
kilt
kist
lift
lilt
lint
list
'list
milt
mint
mist
mitt
mixt
oint
Pict
piet
pint
rift
riot

ript
ritt
sift
silt
sist
tift
tilt
tint
tipt
vint
wilt
win't
wist
A**inu**
aitu
Dieu
lieu
rimu
M**IRV**
mirv
△v**iew**
j**inx**
minx
a**iry**
△city
dixy
fiky
lily
limy
liny
miny
miry
mity
mixy
nixy
oily
piny
pioy
pipy
pity
pixy
ricy
rimy
sizy
tidy
tiny
viny
vizy
wily
winy
wiry
f**izz**
gizz
hizz
jizz
mizz
△ritz
tizz
zizz
a**jee**
a**jar**

A**jax**
e**kka**
okra
okta
skua
O**Ked**
skid
ski'd
a**kee**
Skye
s**kag**
skeg
skug
s**kol**
s**kim**
a**kin**
ikon
skin
s**keo**
skio
s**kep**
skip
s**ker**
skyr
s**kis**
i**kat**
skat
skit
s**kaw**
skew
o**kay**
skry
a**lfa**
alga
alma
flea
glia
ilea
ilia
ilka
Olea
olla
plea
ulna
ulva
b**lab**
bleb
blob
blub
club
flab
flub
glib
glob
pleb
slab
slob
slub
b**loc**
flic
a**lod**

blad
bled
clad
clod
fled
glad
gled
glid
olid
pled
plod
sled
slid
'slid
a**lae**
albe
alee
alme
△aloe
blae
blee
blue
clue
else
flee
floe
flue
glee
glue
olpe
plié
slae
slee
sloe
slue
ylke
c**lef**
b**lag**
clag
cleg
clog
flag
fleg
flog
gleg
glug
plug
slag
slog
slug
b**lah**
g**lei**
vlei
f**lak**
E**lul**
a**lum**
clam
clem
flam
glam
glim

glom
glum
plim
plum
slam
△slim
slum
ylem
b**lin**
clan
élan
flan
glen
plan
a**lso**
alto
Clio
oleo
olio
a**lap**
blip
clap
clip
clop
flap
flip
flop
glop
plap
plop
slap
slip
slop
△a**lar**
blur
flor
slur
a**las**
alls
alms
Alps
Glis
olds
plus
a**lit**
blat
blet
blot
Blut
clat
clot
flat
flit
glit
glut
plat
plot
slat
slit
slot
slut

c**lou**
S**lav**
a**lew**
alow
blew
blow
claw
clew
clow
flaw
flew
flow
glow
△plow
slaw
slew
slow
f**lax**
flex
flix
flox
flux
ilex
ulex
a**lay**
alky
ally
blay
bley
clay
cloy
elmy
flay
fley
gley
illy
oldy
play
ploy
slay
sley
a**mla**
emma
a**mid**
a**mie**
smee
ympe
s**mog**
smug
a**mah**
umph
i**mpi**
a**mok**
a**myl**
△i**mam**
△a**men**
G-man
omen
a**mbo**
ammo
umbo

a**mir**
emir
omer
smir
smur
a**mis**
emys
Xmas
e**mit**
omit
smit
smut
ympt
e**meu**
ombu
ombú
s**mew**
A**mex**
E**mmy**
a**nna**
anoa
anta
Inca
inia
k**nob**
knub
snab
sneb
snib
snob
snub
s**ned**
snod
a**nce**
ante
knee
once
snee
snye
unbe
unce
unde
undé
k**nag**
snag
snig
snog
snug
a**nkh**
inch
a**nti**
inti
unci
a**nal**
anil
a**nan**
anon
a**nfo**
anno
info
ingo

inro
into
onto
unco
undo
Unio
unto
k**n**a**p**
knop
snap
snip
g**n**a**r**
knar
knur
oner
snar
a**n**a**s**
ana's
anis
ants
anus
ends
gnus
onus
g**n**a**t**
inst
knit
knot
knut
onst
snot
unit
u**n**a**u**
a**n**e**w**
anow
enew
enow
gnaw
knew
know
snow
o**n**y**x**
Pnyx
e**n**v**y**
inby
inky
inly
only
b**o**b**a**
boma
bona
bora
coca
coda
△cola
coma
coxa
Doña
dona
dopa
Dora
fora
Hova
hoya
iota
jota
kola
kora
loma
lota
mola
mona
mora
mowa
moxa
moya
noma
nova
roma
Rosa
△rota
soca
soda
sofa
soja
sola
△soma
sora
soya
toea
toga
tola
tosa
vola
Xosa
yoga
zoea
zona
b**o**m**b**
boob
cobb
comb
doab
doob
forb
△sorb
tomb
womb
d**o**u**c**
torc
zoic
b**o**l**d**
bond
bord
coed
cold
cond
cord
dowd
foid
fold
fond
food
ford
foud
goad
gold
△good
gowd
hoed
hold
hond
hood
kond
load
loid
△lord
loud
mold
mood
MOT'd
△pond
pood
road
roed
△rood
sold
sord
toad
toed
told
void
woad
wold
wood
△word
yold
yond
you'd
b**o**d**e**
boke
bole
bone
bore
code
△coke
cole
come
cone
cope
core
cose
cote
cove
coze
doge
dole
dome
done
dope
dose
dote
dove
doze
fone
fore
gole
gone
gore
hoke
hole
home
hone
hope
hore
hose
hote
hove
howe
jobe
joke
jole
Jove
kore
lobe
lode
loge
loke
lome
lone
lope
lore
lose
lote
love
lowe
mode
moke
mole
mome
mope
more
mose
mote
moue
move
moze
node
nole
nome
none
nope
nose
note
n'ote
no'te
oose
ooze
poke
△pole
pome
pone
△pope
pore
pose
posé
pote
robe
'robe
rode
roke
role
rôle
Rome
rone
rope
rore
rose
rosé
rote
roué
rove
soke
sole
some
sone
sore
to-be
toge
toke
tole
tome
tone
tope
tore
tose
tote
toze
vole
vote
woke
wore
wove
yode
yoke
yore
yowe
zone
b**o**f**f**
coff
coif
coof
corf
doff
dowf
goaf
goff
golf
goof
gowf
hoof
houf
howf
koff
loaf
loof
poof
pouf
roof
sowf
toff
wolf
woof
wowf
yoof
b**o**n**g**
boyg
dong
gong
hogg
hong
long
mong
'mong
Moog®
nogg
nong
pong
rong
song
tong
b**o**o**h**
bosh
both
cosh
coth
dosh
doth
gosh
Goth
hogh
josh
koph
loch
losh
loth
moch
moth
nosh
pooh
posh
qoph
roch
soph
tosh
yogh
f**o**c**i**
hoki
Holi
lobi
loci
lo-fi
Loki
modi
moki
mooi
nodi
nori
not-I
roji
roti
Sofi
soli
sori
topi
tori
yogi
yoni
b**o**a**k**
bock
bonk
△book
bosk
bouk
cock
conk
cook
cork
dock
doek
dook
dork
folk
fork
Gonk®
gonk
gook
gouk
gowk
△hock
hoik
honk
hook
howk
△jock
jook
jouk
konk
kook
lock
look
mock
monk
mook
nock
nook
nork
pock
polk
ponk
pook
pork
pouk
△rock
rook
soak
sock

4 □o□l

sook
souk
tock
tonk
took
touk
volk
wock
work
yock
yolk
york
youk
zonk
zouk
b**oil**
boll
bool
bowl
coal
coil
coll
cool
cowl
doll
dool
dowl
eorl
foal
foil
fool
foul
fowl
goal
goel
gool
gowl
howl
joll
jowl
kohl
loll
moil
moll
mool
moyl
Noel
Noël
noil
noll
noul
nowl
△poll
pool
roil
roll
rotl
roul
soil
soul
sowl

toil
toll
tool
wool
yowl
b**oom**
coom
corm
doom
dorm
foam
form
gorm
holm
loam
loom
norm
poem
roam
room
roum
soom
soum
sowm
toom
worm
zoom
b**oon**
born
bo's'n
bos'n
boun
coin
conn
coon
corn
doen
down
eoan
foen
föhn
foin
Goan
goon
gown
hoon
horn
Joan
△john
join
koan
loan
loin
loon
lorn
loun
lown
moan
△moon
morn
mown

noon
Norn
noun
nown
poon
porn
pown
roan
roin
roon
soon
sorn
sown
toon
torn
toun
town
woon
worn
zoon
b**oko**
bolo
boyo
bozo
coco
coho
dodo
dojo
gobo
gogo
go-go
hobo
△homo
joco
jomo
kolo
koto
lobo
loco
logo
loto
Moho
mojo
moko
mono
Moro
no-go
no-no
poco
pogo
polo
ro-ro
soho
so-ho
solo
so-so
toco
to-do
toho
toko
yo-ho

yo-yo
zobo
c**omp**
coop
co-op
coup
cowp
dorp
doup
dowp
golp
goop
gorp
holp
hoop
loop
loup
moop
Mopp
moup
noop
noup
pomp
poop
romp
roop
roup
soap
soop
soup
sowp
yomp
yoop
zopp
b**oar**
Boer
boor
bowr
coir
cour
doer
door
dorr
dour
four
goer
goor
hoar
hoer
hour
jour
loir
loor
lour
mohr
△moor
poor
pour
roar
soar
sour

torr
tour
voar
your
b**obs**
boss
bots
bows
boys
coms
cons
coss
cows
Cox's
dods
does
dogs
dohs
doss
dows
foes
foss
gods
goes
Goss
goys
hoas
hohs
hols
hops
hors
hoss
hots
jobs
joes
joss
koss
loos
loss
löss
lots
△mods
Mohs
moss
noes
nous
oons
oops
pons
pops
poss
pots
sods
sols
soss
sous
toes
togs
tons
tops
toss

woes
wots
b**oat**
bolt
boot
bort
bott
bout
coat
coft
coit
Colt®
colt
coot
Copt
△cost
cott
doat
doit
dolt
don't
dort
dost
dout
dowt
font
foot
fort
△goat
gout
goût
holt
hoot
△host
hout
jolt
loft
loot
lost
lout
lowt
moat
moit
molt
moot
mort
most
mott
nott
nout
nowt
oont
poet
polt
pont
poot
port
post
pott
pout
ront

root
rort
rost
rout
rowt
soft
soot
sort
sout
toft
tolt
toot
tort
tost
tout
towt
volt
wont
won't
woot
woo't
wort
wost
yont
△m**otu**
non-U
tofu
△tolu
zobu
c**oax**
co-ax
hoax
roux
b**ody**
bogy
bony
boxy
coky
cony
copy
cory
cosy
coxy
cozy
dogy
domy
dopy
dory
doty
doxy
dozy
fogy
foxy
fozy
goby
go-by
goey
gory
holy
homy
△joey

Words marked △ may be spelled also with a capital letter

joky
logy
lory
moly
mony
mopy
nosy
nowy
oosy
oozy
poky
poly
pony
pory
posy
poxy
roky
ropy
rory
rosy
Soay
△toby
tody
toey
△tony
Tory
towy
mozz
pozz
epha
epic
spec
spic
apod
sped
spud
apse
épée
spae
spie
spue
spag
opah
spek
spik
opal
Spam®
J-pen
△open
span
spin
spun
upon
oppo
upgo
spar
spur
apes
EPNS
EPOS
epos

opus
upas
spat
△spet
spit
spot
spiv
spaw
spew
△apex
apay
spay
spry
upby
upsy
aqua
arba
area
aria
arna
orca
orra
proa
urea
Ursa
urva
Arab
△crab
crib
drab
drib
drub
frab
grab
△grub
krab
prob
croc
eric
uric
ared
arid
brad
bred
brod
cred
crud
drad
grad
grid
irid
prad
△prod
trad
trod
arle
arse
brae
bree
Brie
△cree

dree
erne
Erse
frae
free
gree
grue
orfe
orle
pree
tree
trie
true
trye
urdé
urge
Graf
△prof
tref
areg
brag
brig
brog
crag
drag
dreg
drug
frag
frig
△frog
grig
grog
prig
prog
trig
trog
trug
arch
pruh
arak
drek
trek
aril
aryl
oral
Ural
vril
arum
brim
Brum
cram
crim
DRAM
dram
drum
from
gram
grim
grum
pram
prim

PROM
prom
tram
trim
Urim
Aran
bran
△bren
cran
gran
gren
grin
△iron
trin
tron
△wren
arco
Argo
arvo
brio
broo
ergo
Kroo
proo
trio
urao
crap
crop
drap
drip
drop
frap
grip
prep
prop
trap
trip
tryp
wrap
arar
brer
brrr
Ares
aris
arms
△arts
bras
ergs
Eros
fris
gris
iris
kris
orts
pros
prys
très
urus
aret
brat
△brit

brut
crit
drat
erst
fret
frit
grat
grit
grot
prat
trat
tret
△trot
writ
△frau
prau
Urdu
arew
arow
a-row
braw
brew
brow
craw
crew
crow
draw
drew
drow
frow
grew
grow
prow
trew
trow
vrow
Brix
crux
oryx
prex
Prix
△army
'Arry
arty
△bray
dray
drey
fray
gray
grey
orby
orgy
pray
prey
tray
trey
troy
urdy
X-ray
Druz
friz

trez
ossa
used
esne
esse
isle
Esth
asci
Asti
Tshi
åsar
ksar
tsar
user
uses
isn't
psst
ashy
Esky®
esky
espy
I-spy
etna
stoa
stab
stob
stub
atoc
otic
sted
stud
ethe
stie
stye
stag
etch
itch
étui
atok
it'll
STOL
VTOL
atom
item
stem
stum
eten
Eton
△sten
stun
otto
atap
atop
stap
step
stop
star
stir
utas
Utes
utis

état
stet
stot
staw
stew
stow
stay
stey
aula
aura
buba
buna
duma
dura
guga
gula
huia
hula
huma
juba
juga
△jura
luna
Musa
puja
pula
puma
puna
pupa
rusa
Ruta
sura
tuba
tufa
tuna
yuca
yuga
zupa
bulb
curb
dumb
numb
fusc
auld
△bund
burd
cued
curd
duad
fund
guid
hued
Kurd
muid
nurd
ould
△quad
quid
quod
rudd
rued

4 □u□e

rund
sudd
sued
suid
surd
tund
turd
a**une**
buke
△bute
cube
cure
curé
cute
duce
dude
△duke
dule
dune
dupe
dure
euge
fume
fuse
fuze
gude
gule
huge
hule
iure
jube
juke
June
jure
△jute
juve
luce
luge
luke
lune
lure
lute
luxe
mule
mure
△muse
mute
nude
nuke
Nupe
puce
puke
pule
pure
rube
rude
rule
rume
rune
ruse
rusé

supe
sure
△tube
tule
tune
yuke
△yule
b**uff**
bumf
cuff
cuif
duff
fuff
guff
△gulf
huff
humf
luff
muff
nuff
puff
ruff
surf
tuff
turf
zurf
b**ung**
burg
dung
fung
hung
lung
mung
quag
rung
△sung
b**ush**
cush
dush
eugh
gush
hush
lush
much
mush
ouch
ouph
pugh
push
rukh
rush
ruth
such
sukh
tush
e**uoi**
fuci
kuri
muti
puri
Sufi

Tupi
Tupí
Zuni
Zuñi
b**uck**
buik
bulk
bunk
burk
busk
cusk
duck
dunk
dusk
fuck
funk
guck
gunk
huck
hulk
hunk
husk
junk
luck
lurk
lusk
△muck
murk
musk
oulk
△puck
pulk
punk
ruck
rusk
suck
sulk
sunk
tuck
△turk
tusk
yuck
b**uhl**
△bull
burl
cull
curl
dual
duel
dull
fuel
full
furl
gull
gurl
hull
hurl
lull
muil
mull
murl

null
nurl
pull
purl
wull
△c**ulm**
mumm
quim
turm
Würm
b**urn**
curn
duan
durn
guan
gurn
Huon
muon
ourn
quin
ruin
sunn
tuan
turn
vuln
yuan
a**uto**
△bubo
budo
bufo
duro
euro
huso
judo
Juno
ludo
muso
ouzo
sumo
yuko
b**ump**
burp
cusp
dump
gulp
gump
hump
jump
lump
mump
pulp
pump
quep
quip
quop
△rump
rurp
sump
tump
yump
b**urr**

curr
duar
furr
guar
huer
muir
nurr
puer
puir
purr
suer
b**uss**
buts
cups
cuss
dubs
duds
dues
duos
fuss
guns
guts
guys
huis
huss
lues
muss
nuts
ours
outs
puss
runs
Russ
suds
suss
tuts
wuss
△a**unt**
buat
bunt
bust
butt
cuit
cult
cunt
curt
duct
duet
dunt
dust
fust
gust
hunt
hurt
just
luit
lunt
lust
munt
must
mutt

oust
punt
putt
quat
quit
runt
rust
suet
suit
tuft
yuft
yurt
g**uru**
juju
ju-ju
kudu
kuku
kuru
luau
lulu
pudu
puku
pulu
ruru
△sulu
Susu
tutu
△zulu
y**unx**
b**uoy**
bury
busy
duly
duty
fumy
△fury
guly
hugy
△judy
July
jury
puly
pumy
puny
quay
quey
ruby
ruly
tuny
yuky
b**uzz**
fuzz
Günz
lutz
putz
quiz
tuzz
u**vea**
a**vid**
ivy'd
e**voe**

a**val**
evil
oval
o**vum**
e**ven**
oven
a**ver**
ever
over
A**ves**
e**vet**
a**vow**
s**wab**
swob
a**wed**
owed
swad
o**wre**
swee
twae
twee
s**wag**
swig
twig
a**wdl**
AWOL
hwyl
twal
d**wam**
swam
swim
swum
s**wan**
twin
s**wap**
swop
e**wer**
ower
i**wis**
'twas
ywis
s**wat**
swot
twat
twit
a**way**
awny
awry
M-way
owly
sway
swey
tway
s**wiz**
i**xia**
a**xle**
a**xel**
axil
exul
e**xam**
a**xon**

Words marked △ may be spelled also with a capital letter

4 □Z□S

exon
oxen
e**x**p**o**
o**x**e**r**
a**x**e**s**
axis
exes
△e**xit**
c**y**m**a**
eyra
Lyra
myna
s**y**n**c**
d**y**a**d**
dyed
eyed
fyrd

kynd
rynd
synd
tynd
tyn'd
wynd
a**yre**
byke
byre
byte
cyme
dyke
dyne
eyne
eyre
fyke
fyle

gybe
gyre
gyte
gyve
hyke
hyle
hype
kyle
kyne
kyte
lyme
lyne
lyre
lyse
lyte
pyne
pyre

ryfe
ryke
rype
syce
syke
syne
sype
tyde
tyke
tyne
type
tyre
tyte
wyte
zyme
a**y**a**h**
myth

wych
D**y**a**k**
g**y**a**l**
myal
ryal
l**y**a**m**
c**y**a**n**
hyen
hymn
Lyon
syen
wynn
g**y**r**o**
hypo
pyro
sybo
typo

tyro
g**y**m**p**
tymp
d**y**e**r**
oyer
a**y**e**s**
byes
eyas
eyes
nyas
oyes
c**y**s**t**
eyot
kyat
pyat
pyet
pyot

ryot
xyst
l**y**n**x**
△jynx
lynx
e**yry**
gyny
o**y**e**z**
m**z**e**e**
a**z**y**m**
a**z**a**n**
d**z**h**o**
c**z**a**r**
tzar
U**z**i**s**

Words marked △ may be spelled also with a capital letter

5 □a□a

B**a**h**a**i
Baha'i
△bajan
Bajau
balas
banal
Banat
basal
basan
bazar
cabal
cabas
cacao
caman
camas
canal
carap
carat
daman
damar
daraf
datal
Dayak
falaj
fanal
farad
fatal
galah
Galam
gamay
gayal
gazal
hadal
hakam
halal
hamal
hanap
haram
jalap
japan
Javan
jawan
kabab
kahal
kaiak
Kanak
karat
kayak
Kazak
lagan
lahar
lavas
lazar
macaw
△madam
makar
malar
malax
Malay
marae
marah
Masai
Mayan
△nahal
naiad
Naias
naras
nasal
natal
naval
nawab
Nayar
△paean
pagan
palas
palay
panax
△papal
papaw
pavan
pawaw
Qajar
qanat
rabat
radar
rajah
ramal
rasae
ratan
rayah
Sabal
Sakai
salad
salal
saman
sapan
Saran®
Satan
satay
sawah
△tacan
talak
talaq
talar
tamal
tapas
tasar
Tatar
tavah
vagal
varan
vasal
watap
zakat
zaman
b**a**r**b**e
bar-b-q
barbs
Caaba
cabby
carby
Darby
daube
dauby
gabby
gamba
gambo
garbe
garbo
iambi
jambe
jambo
jambu
Kaaba
lay-by
mamba
mambo
maybe
△rabbi
samba
sambo
sauba
tabby
taube
warby
yabby
zambo
b**a**c**c**a
bacco
baccy
banco
barca
batch
caeca
casco
catch
dance
darcy
fancy
farce
farci
farcy
fasci
ganch
gaucy
gawcy
haick
hance
hanch
hatch
lance
lanch
larch
latch
lauch
△march
match
△nance
△nancy
narco
narcs
natch
pance
Parca
parch
Pasch
patch
rance
ranch
ratch
saice
saick
sauce
sauch
saucy
talcy
watch
yacca
b**a**d**d**y
baldy
banda
Bände
bands
bandy
bardo
bards
bardy
bawdy
caddy
Candu
candy
cardi
cards
cardy
daddy
dandy
faddy
gandy
garda
gaudy
hands
handy
hards
hardy
lai-do
l-and-l
kandy
labda
laldy
lande
lardy
lauds
Mahdi
mardy
Nandi
nandu
△paddy
panda
pandy
pardi
pardy
ragde
rands
randy
sands
△sandy
tardy
vardy
waddy
waide
B**a**b**e**e
△babel
bagel
baked
baken
△baker
baler
based
bases
bated
caber
cadee
cadet
caged
cagey
cakes
cakey
camel
cameo
caneh
caper
carer
caret
carex
Carey
cater
cates
cavel
caver
daker
Dalek
dared
dares
dated
Datel®
dater
daven
dazed
dazer
eager
eared
easel
eaten
eater
eaves
faced
facer
facet
fader
faker
fakes
famed
fated
Fates
favel
fazed
galea
△games
gamey
gaper
gapes
gases
gated
gavel
gayer
gazer
haček
Hades
haler
harem
hater
haven
haver
haves
hazel
hazer
jaded
jäger
jakes
james
japer
jasey
△javel
jawed
kaneh
Karen
label
laced
lacet
lacey
laded
laden
lager
laker
lapel
lares
laser
lated
laten
later
latex
laver
layer
macer
△maker
mamee
maned
maneh
manes
manet
maser
mater
matey
maven
mazer
naked
naker
named
namer
names
nares
nates
navel
navew
oaken
oaker
oared
oases
oaten
oater
oaves
paced
pacer
paces
pacey
pager
pages
palea
palet
paned
panel
paper
pareo
parer
pareu
paseo
pated
paten
pater
paved
paven
paver
payed
payee
payer
racer
races
raged
ragee
rager
rakee
raker
ramee
ramen
ranee
raper
rased
rated
ratel
rater
rates
ravel
raven
raver
rayed
razed
razee

saber
saker
salep
sales
salet
samel
samen
samey
sared
saree
sated
saved
saver
savey
sawed
sawer
sayer
tabes
tacet
taken
taker
talea
taler
tales
tamer
tapen
taper
tapet
Taser®
taser
tater
taver
tawer
taxed
taxer
taxes
vales
valet
vaned
varec
wader
wafer
wager
wages
waked
waken
waker
wakes
waler
wales
wamed
waned
waney
wares
water
waved
waver
waves
wavey
waxed
waxen
waxer
yager
yamen
yawey
b**a**ff**y**
calfs
daffy
gaffe
halfa
halfs
Jaffa
Naafi
samfu
△taffy
waefu'
waifs
waift
wauff
yarfa
b**a**d**g**e
baggy
bangs
barge
cadge
cadgy
cargo
dagga
daggy
darga
fadge
fango
faugh
gadge
gauge
haugh
jaggy
kanga
kaugh
laigh
large
largo
laugh
madge
maggs
manga
mange
mango
mangy
marge
naggy
panga
parge
radge
raggy
range
rangy
saggy
saiga
sarge
sargo
saugh
taggy
taiga
tanga
tangi
tango
tangy
targa
targe
waugh
b**a**s**h**o
bathe
baths
cache
dacha
eathe
hashy
hatha
kacha
kasha
lathe
lathi
laths
lathy
macho
mashy
maths
nache
nacho
oaths
△pacha
△pasha
pashm
paths
rache
raphe
raphé
rathe
sadhe
sadhu
tache
tacho
takhi
washy
yacht
△b**a**n**i**a
baric
△basic
basil
basin
basis
batik
bavin
cabin
cadie
calid
calif
calix
camis
canid
Canis
capiz
Carib
cavie
cavil
danio
daric
Datin
David
davit
facia
Fagin
fakir
gamic
gamin
habit
hakim
harim
Hasid
jagir
Kafir
kalif
kamik
kamis
labia
labis
Ladin
lakin
lamia
lapis
Latin
lawin
madid
△mafia
mafic
magic
malic
malik
mania
manic
Manis
maria
marid
matin
mavin
mavis
△maxim
nadir
Nasik
nazir
△oasis
panic
panim
Paris
patin
patio
pavid
pavin
pavis
rabic
rabid
radii
radio
radix
ramie
ramin
rapid
ratio
ravin
sabin
△sahib
sakia
△salic
salix
Samit
sapid
sarin
sasin
satin
savin
sayid
tabid
tacit
tafia
Tajik
takin
Tamil
tamin
tamis
tap-in
tapir
tapis
tatie
△tatin
tawie
taxis
vakil
valid
vapid
varix
vatic
wazir
zamia
b**a**n**j**o
gadje
ganja
gauje
hadji
hajji
kanji
lapje
zanja
B**a**c**k**s
balk'd
balks
balky
barky
darky
gawky
Haikh
haiku
hanky
hawks
jacks
Jacky
laika
lanky
larky
latke
lawks
maiko
manky
marks
mawky
narky
paiks
pakka
palki
parka
parki
parky
pawky
ranke
ranks
sanko
sarky
tacky
talks
talky
△tanka
tanky
wacke
wacko
wacky
walks
wanky
yakka
b**a**d**l**y
balls
bally
baulk
bayle
cable
calla
caple
cauld
caulk
daily
dalle
dally
dault
eagle
early
easle
fable
farle
fatly
fault
gable
gaily
gally
△gault
hable
haily
hallo
halls
haply
hauld
haulm
hault
hayle
kails
kayle
ladle
laxly
macle
madly
maile
manly
△maple
marle
marls
marly
matlo
nabla
nalla
padle
pagle
palla
pally
paoli
paolo
parle
parly
patly
raile
rails
rally
rawly
rayle
sable
sadly
salle
sally
sault
tabla
table
tails
tally
tauld
vails
vault
walla
walls
△wally
wanle
wanly
waulk
yauld
b**a**l**m**y
barmy
calms
calmy
damme
gamma
gamme

Words marked △ may be spelled also with a capital letter

5 □a□n

gammy
gaumy
halma
hammy
△haoma
jammy
kaama
kamme
karma
lammy
magma
mamma
mammy
padma
palmy
Parma
rammy
Saame
Sabme
Sabmi
salmi
Salmo
Sammy
tagma
talma
tammy
b**a**'i**n**g
banns
canna
canny
carny
daine
daint
daunt
daynt
faine
fains
faint
fanny
fauna
fayne
gains
garni
gaunt
hadn't
harns
hasn't
haunt
Jaina
jaunt
kaons
laund
lawny
mains
manna
maund
nanna
nanny
naunt
pains
paint

panne
Patna
raine
rains
rainy
rayne
saine
△saint
sauna
saunt
Sawny
sayne
Taino
taint
'taint
tanna
taunt
tawny
varna
vaunt
wanna
yawny
b**a**b**o**o
bacon
baloo
baron
bason
baton
bayou
cabob
caboc
cagot
△calor
canoe
canon
cañon
capon
capos
capot
carob
carol
carom
caxon
dados
Dagon
dagos
fados
fagot
fanon
favor
gajos
galop
gapós
gazon
gazoo
halo'd
halon
halos
haros
havoc
jabot

Jacob
jatos
kabob
kagos
kapok
Karoo
kayos
kazoo
labor
Lagos
Mâcon
macon
Magog
magot
mahoe
△major
makos
manor
manos
maron
maror
mason
△mayor
nabob
nagor
napoo
pacos
paeon
pagod
parol
racon
radon
ratoo
rayon
razoo
razor
sabot
sajou
△salon
salop
sapor
sarod
saros
savor
△savoy
Saxon
sayon
taboo
tabor
tacos
talon
taroc
tarok
taros
tarot
tatou
△taxol
taxon
taxor
valor
vapor

△wagon
wahoo
ya-boo
△yahoo
yakow
yapok
yapon
c**a**l**p**a
campo
campy
carpi
dampy
gappy
gaspy
happy
harpy
jaspe
jaspé
kalpa
kappa
nappa
nappe
nappy
palpi
pampa
pappy
paspy
Ralph
raspy
salpa
sampi
sappy
△talpa
tappa
taupe
waspy
yappy
zappy
b**a**i**r**n
bajra
bajri
barre
barré
cabré
cadre
caird
cairn
Capri
carry
dairy
darre
eagre
fa'ard
faery
fairy
faurd
fayre
garre
hairy
harry
karri

kauri
labra
laird
lairy
laura
lavra
macro
maire
Maori
marry
nacre
naira
narre
padre
pagri
paire
pairs
parry
raird
sabra
sabre
sacra
saury
taira
tarre
tarry
tayra
vairé
vairy
warre
zabra
zaire
b**a**l**s**a
basse
bassi
basso
bassy
caese
canst
carse
causa
cause
'cause
daisy
earst
false
farse
Farsi
fatso
gadso
gassy
gauss
gawsy
hadst
halse
Hansa
Hanse
harsh
Hausa
hause
hawse

karst
karsy
lapse
Lassa
lassi
lasso
lassu
maise
manse
marsh
massa
massé
massy
mayst
paisa
paise
palsy
pansy
parse
Parsi
passé
patsy
pause
paysd
raise
rasse
saist
salsa
salse
sansa
sasse
sassy
say-so
sayst
taish
tansy
tarsi
tasse
tawse
valse
waist
warst
△b**a**n**t**u
Bart's
basta
baste
basto
batta
batts
batty
cacti
canto
canty
carta
carte
caste
catty
darts
△earth
faith
Fanti

fasti
fatty
gaitt
Gantt
garth
haith
hasta
haste
hasty
haute
janty
jarta
katti
laith
△laity
Malta
malty
△manta
manto
manty
masty
matte
Nantz
nasty
natty
panto
pants
panty
parti
parts
party
pasta
paste
pasty
patte
patté
patty
raita
△rasta
ratty
saith
Sakta
Sakti
salto
salts
salty
Santa
sauté
tanti
tanto
tarty
taste
tasty
Tatts
tatty
vasty
vaute
vawte
waite
waits
walty

Words marked △ may be spelled also with a capital letter

waltz
wants
wanty
warty
waste
yarta
yarto
△zante
babul
bahut
△cajun
camus
capul
caput
Datuk
datum
Fagus
favus
Gadus
△galut
gamut
garum
Janus
jarul
kaput
larum
Larus
lay-up
△magus
mahua
manul
manus
maqui
mazut
oakum
ramus
sagum
salue
Sarum
sarus
△tabun
tabus
taluk
talus
Taxus
vacua
vague
vagus
value
varus
wamus
Yakut
calve
carve
carvy
Fauve
halva
halve
larva
malva
mauve

naeve
naevi
naive
naïve
navvy
Parvo
Saiva
salve
salvo
savvy
valve
varve
waive
Yahve
fatwa
mahwa
Yahwe
barye
calyx
satyr
baize
darzi
gauze
gauzy
hamza
jazzy
kanzu
karzy
lazzi
lazzo
maize
matza
matzo
sadza
tazza
tazze
wanze
zanze
abeam
abear
abram
abray
E-boat
H-beam
I-beam
obeah
Q-boat
U-boat
abaca
abaci
aback
abide
abode
a'body
X-body
abbey
abcee
abies
abled
abler
ablet

absey
objet
abaft
aboil
abrim
abrin
absit
Eblis
Iblis
obiit
abele
obeli
oboli
U-bolt
A-bomb
H-bomb
aband
abuna
abune
ebony
obang
T-bone
U-bend
Z-bend
abbot
abhor
ablow
abord
abore
abort
mbira
ybore
abase
abash
abask
abuse
abysm
abyss
obese
abate
about
Abrus
above
abaya
abuzz
éclat
ictal
occam
ocean
octad
octal
sceat
Sclav
scrab
scrae
scrag
scram
scran
scrap
scrat
scraw

scray
yclad
scuba
acock
scads
scudi
scudo
scuds
ackee
acred
acres
F-clef
G-clef
icker
ocher
△ocker
ocrea
octet
scree
screw
ycled
scaff
sci-fi
scoff
scuff
scuft
acrid
actin
ictic
scail
sclim
scrim
scrip
acold
icily
oculi
P-Celt
Q-Celt
scala
scald
△scale
scall
scalp
scaly
scold
sculk
scull
sculp
T-cell
scamp
schmo
acini
Iceni
icing
scand
scant
scena
scend
'scend
scene
scent

scone
ycond
accoy
acton
actor
ichor
McCoy
scion
scoog
scoop
scoot
scrod
scrog
scrow
scapa
scape
'scape
scapi
scopa
scope
Scops
acari
acerb
acorn
ochre
ochry
scare
scarf
scarp
scart
scary
score
scorn
scurf
T-cart
scuse
'scuse
acute
scath
scatt
Scots
scuta
scute
ictus
occur
scaud
scaup
scaur
scoug
scoup
scour
△scout
scrub
scrum
schwa
scowl
scowp
scuzz
addax
adman
ad-man

adrad
ideal
ydrad
adobe
edict
educe
educt
adder
adeem
adieu
adred
advew
edged
edger
idler
udder
ydred
edify
adage
addio
ad-lib
admin
admit
admix
Eddic
sdein
aduki
addle
adult
edile
idyll
oddly
odyle
Adam's
edema
Adeni
adunc
OD'ing
add-on
adiós
CD-ROM
idiom
idiot
odeon
odsos
adapt
adept
adopt
L-dopa
adore
adorn
adust
Idist
odism
odist
add-to
adyta
adsum
odeum
odium
odour

adown
adays
sdayn
bedad
begad
began
begar
begat
bekah
belah
belay
bemad
bepat
beray
cecal
cedar
debag
debar
decad
decal
decay
dedal
defat
degas
delay
deman
denay
deray
dewan
dewar
fecal
femal
feral
fetal
feuar
genal
gerah
getas
geyan
Hecat
hejab
hemal
he-man
hepar
hexad
jehad
jelab
kebab
kenaf
kesar
leear
legal
leman
medal
Medau
mesal
metal
pecan
pedal
pekan
penal

Words marked △ may be spelled also with a capital letter

5 □e□b

perai
Pesah
petal
petar
re-bar
recal
recap
redan
regal
regar
rehab
relax
relay
reman
renal
renay
repay
resat
resay
Sebat
sedan
segar
selah
sepad
sepal
serac
sérac
serai
seral
setae
Teian
telae
tepal
terai
teras
Texan
△texas
Vedas
△vegan
velar
venae
venal
debby
△derby
gerbe
herby
kembo
lesbo
△melba
o'erby
△rebbe
webby
yerba
beach
beech
belch
bench
cerci
Decca®
de-ice
deuce

fence
fetch
hence
heuch
keech
ketch
leach
leech
letch
leuch
Mecca
mercy
peace
peach
peece
pence
Perca
perce
perch
reach
react
recce
recco
reccy
reech
Reich
retch
secco
teach
tench
terce
teuch
vetch
△welch
wench
beads
beady
bends
bendy
deedy
fendy
geode
heads
heady
heedy
kendo
leads
leady
Mehdi
mends
△neddy
needs
needy
nerdy
perdu
perdy
ready
reddy
reede
reedy
seedy

teade
△teddy
Vedda
veldt
weeds
weedy
Yezdi
zerda
aedes
bedel
bedew
begem
beget
belee
benet
beret
besee
beset
betel
bevel
bever
bewet
bezel
celeb
Ceres
debel
defer
Deneb
desex
deter
devel
Dewey
eeven
feces
fever
fezes
gemel
genet
heben
△hevea
hewed
hewer
jebel
jewel
kevel
keyed
leger
lemel
lenes
leper
levee
level
lever
mêlée
mered
merel
mesel
meted
meter
nebek
nebel

neper
nevel
never
newel
penes
peter
rebec
rebel
refel
refer
relet
remen
remex
renew
reney
repel
reset
revel
revet
Seder
sedes
Seger
semée
semen
sesey
seven
sever
sewed
sewel
sewen
sewer
sexed
sexer
seyen
teaed
Tebet
te-hee
telex
temed
tenet
tepee
△terek
teres
Tevet
tewel
Texel
veney
vexed
vexer
weber
xebec
Xeres
yeses
yeven
yewen
zebec
Zener
beefs
beefy
deify
delfs

delft
feoff
leafy
neafe
reffo
reify
selfs
serfs
terfe
beige
belga
cerge
deign
feign
hedge
hedgy
heigh
henge
heugh
hewgh
kedge
kedgy
ledge
ledgy
legge
leggy
leugh
menge
merge
neigh
peggy
reggo
reign
renga
sedge
sedgy
serge
terga
teugh
venge
verge
wedge
wedgy
weigh
fecht
hecht
Lethe
meshy
meths
Pecht
Peght
techy
wecht
aecia
aegis
aerie
aesir
bedim
befit
begin
belie

besit
betid
Bevin
bewig
cedis
ceria
ceric
debit
demic
demit
denim
derig
△devil
eerie
fecit
felid
Felis
fetid
gelid
genic
genie
genii
genip
geoid
△helix
hemic
hemin
jerid
kefir
kelim
legit
lenis
lepid
levin
Levis®
levis
△lewis
lexis
media
△medic
Melia
melic
melik
meril
merit
mesic
metic
△metif
Metis
△métis
nelis
nepit
Pekin
penie
penis
peril
petit
pewit
rebid
récit
redia

redid
redip
refit
régie
rejig
re-jig
relic
relie
remit
remix
renig
renin
resin
resit
retie
revie
semie
semis
sepia
△seric
serif
serin
sewin
telia
telic
tenia
tepid
tewit
Vedic
vegie
venin
vezir
xenia
xeric
Zenic
Meiji
beaky
becke
decko
decks
dekko
fenks
△gecko
geeky
jerks
jerky
kecks
leaky
nerka
Neski
peaky
pecke
perky
pesky
reaks
reeky
weeke
weeks
welke
welkt
be-all

belle
bells
belly
ceili
cella
cello
'cello
dealt
fella
felly
ferly
gelly
gerle
heald
hello
jeely
jello
jelly
kelly
meal'd
mealy
medle
merle
neeld
neele
nelly
newly
realm
realo
redly
reels
repla
reply
seeld
seely
sella
selle
sells
teals
tell'd
telly
tesla
veale
vealy
veily
△weald
welly
wetly
yealm
b**e**a**m**y
derma
△fehme
femme
fermi
gemma
gemmy
heame
herma
herms
jemmy
lemma

neemb
neume
pelma
reame
reams
reamy
regma
seame
seamy
terms
△vehme
weamb
b**e**a**n**o
△being
benne
benni
benny
cerne
feint
fenny
ferny
gerne
henna
henny
jeans
△jenny
jeune
ken-no
kerne
leant
leany
Lemna
leone
Lerna
Lerne
meane
means
meant
meany
meint
meiny
mesne
meynt
penna
penne
penny
peony
reins
renne
segno
seine
senna
teend
teene
teens
teeny
teind
tenné
tenno
tenny
terne

veena
veiny
weeny
wenny
b**e**b**o**p
befog
begot
below
berob
besom
besot
béton
celom
decor
décor
decoy
demob
demon
demos
depot
detox
Devon
dévot
felon
fetor
gemot
△genoa
genom
helot
heroe
heron
jeton
kebob
lemon
lenos
mebos
Médoc
melon
memos
meson
metol
me-too
peeoy
pekoe
pepos
pesos
redox
rejón
repos
repot
segol
segos
sekos
Señor
sepoy
seron
serow
seton
telos
tenon
tenor

venom
xenon
Xerox®
Zeno's
zeros
d**e**l**p**h
dempt
heaps
heapy
hempy
keeps
kelpy
kemps
kempt
leaps
leapt
nempt
peepe
peppy
seepy
Serps
Tempe
tempi
tempo
tempt
'tempt
vespa
weepy
b**e**a**r**d
beare
beery
berry
ceorl
deare
dearn
deary
decry
deere
derry
feare
ferry
geare
genre
Genro
Gerry
heard
heare
heart
hejra
△henry
herry
△jerry
Jewry
leare
learn
leary
leery
lepra
mear'd
meare
merry

metre
△metro
△métro
△negro
peare
pearl
peart
pedro
peery
perry
petre
△petri
rearm
rears
reird
repro
△retro
retry
seare
serra
serre
serry
tears
teary
terra
terry
tetra
veery
verry
weary
weird
yeard
yearn
years
zebra
△b**e**a**s**t
cease
cense
cesse
deism
deist
dense
desse
feast
feese
fesse
geese
geist
gesse
gesso
heast
heist
herse
Jesse
lease
leash
least
leese
leish
mease
Mensa

mense
mensh
merse
messy
meuse
neese
neist
newsy
pease
peise
perse
perst
peyse
reast
reest
reist
reuse
sease
seise
seism
sensa
sense
sessa
tease
temse
tense
terse
verse
verso
verst
weise
△welsh
wersh
yeast
b**e**a**t**h
benty
berth
betty
cento
certy
death
△deity
delta
depth
derth
felty
festa
fetta
gents
gents'
genty
geste
heath
hefte
hefty
hertz
jetty
kelty
kente
lefte
lefty

lenti
lento
lepta
meath
meaty
meith
mento
mesto
neath
'neath
netty
peaty
pelta
pesto
△petty
reata
reate
recta
recti
recto
rente
resty
rewth
seity
septa
set-to
teeth
tenth
tenty
terts
testa
teste
testy
texts
vertu
vesta
weete
wefte
yenta
yesty
zesty
b**e**a**u**t
beaux
begum
begun
bemud
bevue
Cebus
cecum
debug
debus
debut
début
degum
demur
femur
fetus
gebur
genus
get-up
Jesus

5 □e□v

jésus
ledum
lemur
let-up
△negus
nevus
nexus
rebus
rebut
recur
regur
rerun
revue
sebum
sedum
segue
serum
set-up
tenue
velum
venue
△venus
zebub
bevvy
deave
deeve
delve
heave
heavy
helve
keeve
kerve
leave
leavy
neive
nerve
nervy
peavy
peeve
perve
reave
reeve
reive
selva
senvy
serve
servo
verve
weave
deawy
fetwa
bedye
beryl
cetyl
Debye
herye
ceaze
feeze
heeze
Jeeze
leaze

leeze
lezzy
mezze
mezzo
neeze
peaze
peize
seaze
seize
senza
teaze
weize
afear
aflaj
offal
oflag
after
offer
often
affix
Afric
afrit
afald
afoot
'sfoot
afara
afire
afore
yfere
afoul
eggar
ogham
agger
aglee
aglet
agley
agree
agued
egger
egret
ngwee
ogee'd
ogler
ugged
agoge
again
agrin
ngaio
oggin
ogmic
Ugric
agila
agile
Agama
agami
agene
agent
aging
agone
agony
ngana

Ngoni
Nguni
agios
aglow
agood
igloo
agape
Egypt
igapó
aggri
aggro
aggry
agora
agast
agist
egest
agate
a'gate
aguti
agave
ogive
agaze
ahead
aheap
cheap
cheat
Chian
chiao
ihram
phial
sheaf
sheal
shear
Shiah
shoal
shoat
thrae
thraw
uhlan
wheal
whear
wheat
Chubb®
dhobi
Sheba
chace
chack
chaco
check
chica
chich
chick
chico
chock
choco
chuck
△phoca
shack
shock
shuck
thack

theca
thick
whack
which
chide
chode
khadi
kheda
rhody
shade
shady
cheek
cheep
cheer
chief
chiel
Khmer
pheer
sheel
sheen
sheep
sheer
sheet
shied
shiel
shier
shies
shlep
shmek
shoed
shoer
shoes
shred
shrew
shyer
theek
thief
three
threw
wheel
wheen
chafe
chaff
chaft
chufa
chuff
shaft
shift
theft
thoft
wheft
whiff
whift
ahigh
phage
shogi
thagi
thegn
thigh
shchi
chain

chair
choir
ohmic
sheik
thaim
theic
their
thrid
khoja
shoji
thuja
△cheka
choke
choko
choky
khaki
shake
shako
shakt
shaky
ahold
ahull
△chalk
chela
child
△chile
chili
chill
choli
chyle
dhole
dholl
f-hole
ghyll
jhala
phyla
phyle
shale
shall
shalm
shalt
shaly
shelf
shell
she'll
shill
shily
shola
shule
shuln
shuls
shyly
thelf
thilk
thill
thole
tholi
Thule
△whale
whelk
whelm

whelp
while
whilk
whole
who'll
champ
chimb
chime
chimo
chimp
chomp
chump
chyme
rhime
rhomb
rhumb
rhyme
shama
shame
Shema
thema
theme
thumb
thump
thyme
thymi
thymy
zhomo
ahent
ahind
ahint
bhang
chank
chant
△china
chine
chiné
△chink
chino
chunk
chynd
ohone
phang
phene
phone
'phone
phony
△rhine
rhino
rhone
rhyne
shand
Shang
shank
sha'n't
shan't
shend
shent
shine
shiny
Shona

shone
shunt
thana
thane
thank
thine
thing
think
thong
whang
whine
whiny
chaos
choof
chook
△choom
pheon
△phlox
△sheol
△she'ol
shmoe
shook
shool
shoon
shoot
shrow
theow
thiol
throb
throe
throw
whoop
whoot
chape
chaps
chips
chops
shape
shaps
shope
whipt
chara
chard
chare
chark
charm
charr
chars
chart
chary
chère
chert
chirk
chirl
chirm
chirp
chirr
chirt
chord
chore
churl

Words marked △ may be spelled also with a capital letter

churn
churr
mhorr
phare
shard
shar'd
share
shark
sharn
sharp
sherd
shere
shire
shirk
shirr
shirt
shore
shorn
short
shura
there
therm
third
thirl
thorn
thorp
uhuru
whare
wharf
where
whirl
whirr
whore
whorl
whort
c**h**a**s**e
chasm
chess
chest
chose
chuse
ghast
ghest
ghost
phase
phese
shash
shush
these
those
whish
whisk
whiss
whist
whose
whoso
Xhosa
c**h**o**t**a
chott
chute
dhoti
photo
rhyta
shite
shits
shote
shott
shute
theta
thete
Thoth
△white
△whity
c**h**o**u**t
choux
ghaut
ghoul
△rheum
shout
shrub
shrug
shtum
shtup
thou'd
thous
thrum
uh-huh
whaup
whaur
c**h**a**v**e
chevy
chive
chivy
shave
sheva
Shiva
shive
shove
who've
c**h**e**w**y
shawl
shawm
shewn
shown
showy
thawy
thews
thewy
thowl
c**h**a**y**a
khaya
shaya
shoyu
they'd
thuya
c**h**i**z**z
ghazi
whizz
b**i**g**a**e
cigar
cimar
cital
dinar
dital
divan
diwan
filar
final
hi-hat
hijab
hilar
jihad
kisan
ligan
lilac
limax
linac
liras
micas
Midas
minae
minar
minas
nicad
Nicam
nidal
nikau
Nisan
nival
△nizam
pi-jaw
pilau
pilaw
pipal
pirai
rimae
rival
riyal
Sican
simar
sisal
sitar
Sivan
sizar
tical
tidal
△titan
△vicar
vinal
viral
vital
vitas
vivat
wigan
witan
zigan
B**i**b**b**y
bilbo
bimbo
dibbs
kimbo
Limbi
△limbo
nimbi
Nimby
Niobe
ribby
timbó
zimbi
a**i**t**c**h
biccy
Binca®
birch
bitch
cinch
cinct
circa
circs
cisco
diact
disco
ditch
filch
finch
fitch
hilch
hitch
linch
milch
mince
misca'
mitch
niece
piccy
piece
pièce
pilch
pinch
pitch
since
ticca
tinct
△titch
vinca
△wicca
wilco
wince
winch
witch
yince
zilch
zinco
zincy
b**i**d**d**y
birds
diddy
dildo
diode
giddy
Hindi
Hindu
kiddo
kiddy
kinda
kindy
middy
minds
misdo
rindy
Sindi
tiddy
tilde
vifda
vilde
vivda
widdy
wilds
winds
windy
a**i**d**e**d
aider
aînée
airer
bided
bidet
biker
biped
biter
cider
cimex
citer
civet
diced
dicer
dicey
diker
dikey
dimer
diner
dived
diver
Dives
dizen
eider
eisel
fiber
fifer
filed
filer
filet
finer
fines
fired
firer
fiver
fives
fixed
fixer
gibel
giber
gilet
given
giver
hider
hiker
hired
hirer
hi-tec
hiver
hives
△hizen
jiber
jiver
kidel
kiley
libel
liber
lifer
liger
liken
liker
limen
limes
limey
lined
linen
liner
lines
liney
liter
lived
liven
liver
lives
miler
mimer
miner
miser
miter
mixed
mixen
mixer
mizen
niger
nisei
niter
nixes
oiled
oiler
Picea
piked
piker
pilea
pilei
piler
piles
piney
piped
△piper
pipes
pixel
Ribes
ricer
ricey
rider
Rigel
△riley
rimed
rimer
ripen
riper
risen
riser
rites
rived
rivel
riven
river
rivet
Sicel
sided
sider
sides
Sikel
silen
siler
silex
sinew
△siren
siver
sixer
sixes
sized
sizel
sizer
Tibet
tiger
tiled
tiler
tiles
timed
timer
△times
△tinea
tined
tired
titer
vibes
vibex
video
viner
vinew
viper
vireo
vires
vitex
viver
vives
vixen
widen
wiles
winey
wiper
wired
wirer
wires
wives

Words marked △ may be spelled also with a capital letter

5 □i□f

wizen
yikes
zibet
zineb
zizel
j**i**f**f**y
miffy
niffy
b**i**g**g**y
bilge
bilgy
binge
bingo
bingy
ciggy
dinge
dingo
dingy
dirge
fidge
hinge
△jingo
jirga
kidge
Kings
liege
ligge
linga
lingo
lingy
midge
minge
mingy
misgo
piggy
pingo
ridge
ridgy
siege
singe
tinge
virga
virge
Virgo
wilga
winge
wings
wingy
zingy
b**i**g**h**a
bight
dicht
dight
dishy
eight
fiche
fichu
fight
fishy
hight
hithe
kight
kithe
lichi
licht
light
lithe
litho
miche
might
niche
night
pight
pithy
richt
△right
rishi
sidha
sight
sithe
tichy
tight
tithe
△vichy
wight
withe
withy
b**i**f**i**d
bikie
ci-gît
cilia
civic
civil
digit
dinic
dixie
finis
kilim
kinin
licit
lie-in
likin
limit
linin
lipid
livid
mimic
Minié
minim
mirin
mix-in
nihil
nitid
nixie
oidia
pipit
pixie
ricin
rigid
Rigil
sigil
Sinic
sirih
sit-in
tibia
tie-in
Tilia
timid
vigia
vigil
virid
visie
visit
Vitis
vivid
vizir
wifie
zip-in
△n**i**n**j**a
Rioja
wilja
d**i**c**k**y
dinky
dirke
finks
jinks
kicks
kinky
licks
links
micky
milko
milky
minke
mirky
picky
pinko
pinky
pisky
risky
sicko
silky
sinky
Sitka
ticks
ticky
tikka
wicky
winks
zinke
zinky
a**i**o**l**i
aïoli
aisle
aizle
△bible
bield
billy
birle
dilli
dilly
dimly
field
fille
filly
fitly
gilly
girly
hillo
hilly
lisle
mille
mirly
nirly
piel'd
pills
qibla
rifle
rille
sidle
sield
sigla
silly
tilly
title
villa
villi
viola
viold
wield
wills
willy
yield
b**i**o**m**e
disme
films
filmy
gimme
gismo
gizmo
hiems
△jimmy
limma
pigmy
sigma
b**i**o**n**t
Diana
diene
eigne
fiend
fient
finny
giant
ginny
hiant
hinny
jinni
jinns
kiang
liana
liane
liang
ligne
linny
Lions
ninny
piano
piend
△pinna
pinny
pions
piony
riant
sient
signs
tinny
'tisn't
viand
visne
winna
a**i**d**o**s
bidon
bigot
bijou
bipod
Biros
bison
bitos
ciaos
cibol
dicot
didos
divot
eikon
ficos
figos
finos
gigot
giron
giros
jigot
kid-on
kikoi
kilos
kinos
Libor
lidos
limos
linos
livor
miaow
micos
mid-on
milor
milos
△minor
minos
misos
△nicol
nidor
Nilot
ninon
niton
picot
pi-dog
pilot
pilow
piñon
△pinot
piton
pivot
rigol
rigor
rivos
silo'd
silos
siroc
Ticos
tigon
△timon
△tiros
vigor
vinos
vison
visor
vizor
△widow
winos
zip-on
c**i**p**p**i
dippy
gilpy
gimpy
gippo
gippy
hippo
hippy
jimpy
kippa
lippy
△nippy
pippy
timps
tippy
Wimpy®
wimpy
wispy
yippy
zippo
zippy
a**i**e**r**y
cirri
diary
fiars
fibre
fibro
fiere
fiery
fiord
firry
hijra
kirri
liard
liart
△libra
litre
livre
micra
micro
mikra
mitre
nitre
nitry
picra
piert
tiara
Tisri
titre
b**i**r**s**e
birsy
bitsy
cissy
didst
dipso
ditsy
first
gipsy
giust
kiosk
miasm
midst
'midst
mimsy
△missa
missy
nisse
rinse
sissy
tipsy
b**i**o**t**a
birth
bitte
bitts
bitty
dicta
dicty
diota
dirty
ditto
ditty
△fifth
fifty
filth
firth
fisty
fitte
gilts
girth
hilts
kilty
kitty
linty
lists
mifty
miltz
minty
mirth

Words marked △ may be spelled also with a capital letter

misty
Mitty
nifty
ninth
nitty
pietà
piety
pinta
pinto
piste
△pitta
riata
rifte
rifty
sieth
silty
Sitta
sixte
sixth
sixty
tilth
tinty
titty
virtu
vista
visto
vitta
width
witty
ficus
fit-up
gibus
gigue
hilum
hilus
miaul
Mimus
minus
mix-up
nidus
nisus
picul
Picus
pikul
pilum
pilus
pin-up
pious
pipul
pique
piqué
risus
simul
sinus
Sioux
sirup
situs
tie-up
tip-up
titup
virus
bivvy
civvy
divvy
kieve
lieve
mieve
nieve
rieve
sieve
silva
viewy
pioye
△sibyl
vinyl
diazo
ditzy
dizzy
fizzy
Mirza
piezo
pizza
ritzy
tizzy
winze
ajwan
eject
ojime
djinn
fjord
akkas
skean
skear
skoal
skran
skids
skeer
skeet
skied
skier
skies
skiey
skyer
skyey
skiff
skoff
skegg
skail
skein
sklim
skrik
Akela
P-Kelt
Q-Kelt
skald
skelf
skell
skelm
skelp
skill
skulk
skull
skimp
akene
skank
skene
skink
skint
skunk
skeos
skios
okapi
skart
skirl
skirr
skirt
skyre
ukase
skate
skatt
skite
skyte
skive
skivy
okays
alaap
Alban
△algae
algal
alias
Allah
allay
almah
altar
alway
bleak
blear
bleat
bloat
clean
clear
cleat
cloak
cloam
eliad
Elian
Elsan®
elvan
fleam
float
gleam
glean
glial
gloat
ileac
△iliac
Iliad
Ilian
ollav
plead
pleat
ploat
sloan
ulnae
ulnar
alibi
all-be
clubs
fly-by
glebe
gleby
globe
globy
plebs
slubb
alack
Alice
△black
block
clack
cleck
click
clock
cluck
elect
flack
fleck
flick
flock
glacé
△place
plack
plica
pluck
slack
slice
slick
Vlach
blade
blude
bludy
clade
elide
elude
glade
glady
glede
glide
glode
slade
slide
albee
aldea
alder
alien
allée
allel
Allen
alley
almeh
aloed
aloes
alter
blaes
bleed
bleep
△blues
bluey
claes
cleek
cleep
elder
elmen
elpee
elver
elves
fleer
△fleet
flier
flies
fluey
flyer
gleed
gleek
gleet
glued
gluer
gluey
olden
older
plied
plier
plies
sleek
sleep
sleet
slier
slued
slyer
ulcer
aleft
aloft
bluff
cleft
cliff
clift
cloff
flaff
fluff
gliff
glift
pluff
'slife
align
elegy
éloge
elogy
glogg
ology
plage
aloha
alpha
elchi
algid
algin
alkie
all-in
allis
blain
bluid
claim
eldin
elfin
Elgin
eloin
elsin
flail
flair
fluid
glaik
glair
oldie
oleic
olein
plaid
plain
plait
slaid
slain
sloid
sluit
ulmin
ulyie
ulzie
alike
bloke
cloke
flake
flaky
fluke
fluky
glike
slake
ylike
alula
slily
slyly
blame
△blimp
blimy
clame
clamp
climb
clime
clomb
clomp
clump
e-la-mi
elemi
flame
flamm
flamy
fleme
flimp
flume
flump
Flymo®
glume
llama
plumb
plume
plump
plumy
slime
slimy
slo-mo
slump
ulema
aland
alang
aline
A-line
alone
along
bland
blank
blend
blent
blind
blini
blink
blond
blunk
blunt
clang
clank
cline
cling
clink
clint
clone
clonk
clung
clunk
eland
flank
fling
flint
flong
flung
flunk
gland
glans
glent
glint
klang
llano
olent
plane
'plane
plank
plant
pling
plink
plong
plonk
plunk

5 □l□o

slane
slang
slant
sling
slink
slung
slunk
Algol
allod
allot
allow
alloy
aloof
altos
blood
bloom
bloop
cloop
cloot
elbow
△flood
floor
Fluon®
fluor
gloom
gloop
gluon
kloof
oleos
olios
pleon
plook
sloom
sloop
sloot
alapa
aleph
clepe
clipe
clipt
clype
Elaps
elope
△elops
flype
glyph
slept
slipe
slips
slipt
slope
slops
slopy
slype
alarm
alary
alert
alure
blare
blore
blurb

blurt
Clare
claro
clart
clary
clerk
flare
flary
flirt
flora
flory
flurr
glare
glary
glory
slurb
slurp
ultra
blasé
blash
blast
bless
blest
bliss
blist
blush
clash
clasp
class
△close
flash
flask
flesh
flisk
flosh
floss
flush
glass
glisk
gloss
plash
plasm
plast
plesh
plush
slash
slish
slosh
sluse
slush
alate
all-to
blate
blatt
blite
blitz
clote
cloth
elate
elite
élite

elute
flats
flite
flitt
flota
flote
flute
fluty
flyte
glitz
illth
klutz
plate
platy
Pluto
slate
slaty
sloth
zloty
album
algum
all-up
almug
Alnus
aloud
blaud
claut
cloud
clour
clout
flour
flout
glaum
glaur
Glaux
glout
ileum
ileus
△ilium
oleum
plouk
Ulmus
alive
blive
clave
cleve
clove
glove
Oliva
olive
slave
slive
slove
alowe
blown
blows
blowy
clown
flawn
flawy
flews

flown
flaxy
aleye
aliya
alkyd
alkyl
allyl
playa
sloyd
blaze
cloze
glaze
glazy
gloze
plaza
amban
amman
embar
embay
imbar
omlah
omrah
smear
umiak
ameba
amice
amici
amuck
smack
smock
amide
imide
amber
ameer
Ampex®
embed
ember
emcee
emeer
emmer
emmet
emmew
imbed
immew
impel
smeek
umbel
umber
amigo
image
imago
omega
imshi
imshy
amain
ambit
amnia
amrit
△e-mail
immit
immix

impis
smaik
△smoke
smoko
smoky
amble
ample
amply
emule
imply
small
smalm
smalt
smell
smelt
smile
smolt
ymolt
amend
amene
ament
amine
amino
among
emend
emong
imine
ambos
△ammon
embog
embow
embox
impot
smoor
smoot
umbos
ambry
amort
D-mark
emery
emure
△imari
ombre
ombré
smarm
smart
smirk
smirr
smore
umbra
umbre
amass
Amish
amiss
amuse
omasa
smash
amate
Amati
amity
emote

empty
smite
smith
smote
umpty
Y-moth
amour
ampul
embus
imaum
imbue
ombus
ombús
smout
amove
emove
smowt
Emmys
amaze
anear
annal
annat
antae
antar
Anzac
eniac
Incan
in-car
ingan
in-law
inlay
Intal®
Invar®
knead
snead
sneak
sneap
unbag
unbar
uncap
undam
ungag
unhat
Uniat
unlaw
unlay
unman
unpay
unsay
untax
enact
knack
knock
snack
sneck
snick
snuck
V-neck
anode
cnida
snide

angel
anger
anker
annex
ended
endew
enmew
ensew
enter
Enzed
indew
index
infer
inker
inlet
inner
inset
inter
kneed
knee'd
kneel
oncer
one-er
onset
sneer
snoek
unbed
undee
undée
under
unfed
unget
unked
unket
unled
unlet
unmet
unmew
unpeg
unpen
unred
unset
unsew
unsex
unwed
unwet
in-off
knife
on-off
snafu
sniff
snift
snuff
unify
anigh
antic
anvil
enfix
entia
Indic
indie

Words marked △ may be spelled also with a capital letter

infix
intil
Inuit
inwit
on-dit
snail
unbid
undid
unfit
unfix
unhip
unkid
unlid
unlit
unpin
unrid
unrig
unrip
untie
until
untin
unwit
unzip
enoki
ensky
snake
snaky
snoke
ancle
anele
△angle
Anglo
anile
ankle
incle
ingle
inkle
inula
knell
knelt
knoll
onely
snell
△uncle
anima
anime
animé
anomy
enema
enemy
gnome
mneme
anana
an-end
anent
Anona
inane
jnana
ancon
anion
annoy

end-on
endow
enjoy
enrol
envoi
envoy
indol
ingot
inion
onion
on-job
snood
snook
snool
snoop
snoot
unbox
uncos
ungod
ungot
△union
unsod
unwon
inapt
inept
snaps
snipe
snips
snipy
unapt
angry
antra
antre
Anura
enarm
enorm
entry
enure
gnarl
gnarr
inarm
Indra
indri
inerm
inert
infra
inorb
intra
intro
inure
inurn
knarl
knurl
knurr
snare
snark
snarl
snary
snirt
snore
snort

unarm
△angst
anise
gnash
inust
knish
knosp
snash
snush
enate
snath
uneth
unite
unity
ankus
annul
endue
ennui
ensue
incur
incus
incut
indue
Injun
input
knout
oncus
onkus
snout
uncus
uncut
undue
undug
ungum
knave
knive
gnawn
knowe
known
snowk
snowy
inbye
bobac
bobak
bogan
bolas
borak
borax
bowat
boyar
boyau
cohab
comae
comal
copal
△coral
coram
cowal
cowan
coxae
coxal

domal
donah
Donat
dorad
Doras
dotal
douar
Douay
dowar
focal
foray
fouat
gobar
gonad
gopak
goral
gowan
hogan
horal
Hovas
Jonah
joram
joual
jowar
koban
Kodak®
Koran
lobar
local
logan
loral
loran
lotah
lovat
lowan
loyal
modal
molal
molar
molas
monad
monal
△monas
moral
morat
moray
nodal
nomad
no-man
nopal
notal
novae
novas
noway
noxal
noyau
podal
pokal
polar
Pomak
poral

powan
Qoran
rolag
romal
△roman
romas
roral
rotal
rowan
royal
sofar
sokah
solah
solan
solar
soman
somas
△sonar
soral
sowar
today
toga'd
Tokaj
△tokay
toman
tonal
topaz
Torah
toran
total
vocab
vocal
volae
volar
Wodan
△woman
Wotan
yojan
zoeae
zoeal
zoeas
Zohar
zonae
zonal
bobby
bombe
bombé
bombo
boobs
booby
cobby
combe
combo
combs
comby
corbe
dobby
Dolby®
doubt
forby
gobbi

gobbo
gombo
hobby
howbe
kombu
lobby
looby
mobby
nobby
pombe
sorbo
womby
yobbo
△zombi
bocca
bonce
botch
coach
coact
cocci
cocco
conch
couch
dolce
douce
△force
hoick
hooch
hotch
loach
mooch
mouch
nonce
notch
poach
ponce
poncy
pooch
porch
potch
pouch
roach
rotch
sonce
souce
souct
sowce
torch
touch
voice
vouch
yoick
zocco
bonds
boody
borde
condo
cords
coudé
doddy
dowdy

fonda
fonds
foody
fordo
goldy
good-o
goods
goody
Gouda
horde
howdy
loads
Lords
lordy
mondo
moody
noddy
poddy
roads
ronde
rondo
rowdy
soddy
solde
soldi
soldo
sonde
sorda
sordo
toady
todde
toddy
tondi
tondo
woods
woody
words
wordy
zonda
bogey
bohea
boned
boner
bones
boree
borel
borer
botel
bowed
bowel
bower
bowes
bowet
boxen
△boxer
codex
cokes
coley
△comer
comet
coney

5 □o□f

cooed
cooee
cooey
coper
cored
corer
corey
cosec
coset
coved
coven
cover
covet
covey
cowed
cower
coxed
Coxes
cozen
domed
donee
Donet
doper
dopey
doree
doseh
doted
doter
dover
dowed
dowel
dower
doyen
dozed
dozen
dozer
fogey
fomes
forel
forex
fouet
fovea
foxed
foyer
godet
gofer
golem
goner
gooey
hogen
hokey
holey
homer
homey
honer
honey
hooey
hoper
hosed
hosen
hoses
hotel
hoten
hovel
hoven
hover
jodel
joker
jokey
joyed
koker
lobed
loden
loner
loper
lorel
losel
losen
loser
lover
lovey
△lower
lozen
model
modem
moder
mohel
Monel®
moner
money
moped
moper
mopes
mopey
morel
mores
Mosel
Moses
mosey
moted
motel
moten
motet
motey
moved
mover
mowed
mower
Nobel
nomen
△nones
nonet
nosed
noser
nosey
noted
noter
novel
nowed
△nowel
noyes
podex
poked
poker
pokes
pokey
poler
poles
poley
poney
porer
poser
posey
power
robes
rodeo
△roger
roker
Romeo
Roneo®
roneo
roped
roper
ropes
ropey
rosed
△roses
roset
rover
rowel
rowen
rower
rozet
sober
soger
soken
soler
soles
soree
sorel
sorex
sowed
sower
toged
token
toned
toner
toney
topee
topek
toper
totem
towel
tower
toyer
voces
volet
vomer
voter
vowed
vowel
vower
Woden
woken
women
wooed
wooer
woven
wowee
woxen
yodel
yokel
zoned
zooea
c**o**m**f**y
go-off
goofy
hoofs
houff
howff
loofa
loofs
poofy
roofs
roofy
sol-fa
sowff
toffy
woofy
b**o**d**g**e
boggy
bongo
borgo
bouge
bough
coign
conga
congé
congo
corgi
cough
dodge
dodgy
doggo
doggy
donga
dough
foggy
forge
forgo
gorge
gouge
Hodge
hongi
hough
jougs
lodge
longa
longe
longs
lough
moggy
podge
podgy
pogge
ponga
pongo
pongy
porge
porgy
rouge
rough
soggy
sorgo
sough
tonga
tongs
tough
vouge
wodge
wonga
wongi
b**o**c**h**e
bodhi
bothy
docht
foehn
gosht
hoo-ha
△mocha
mochy
moths
mothy
Sophi
Sophy
Sotho
tophi
toshy
vozhd
b**o**g**i**e
bolix
bonie
boric
bovid
bowie
cobia
cogie
colic
colin
comic
conia
conic
conin
covin
dogie
dolia
Doric
Doris
dovie
dowie
Eolic
eosin
folia
folic
folie
folio
gonia
goyim
iodic
△ionic
logia
logic
logie
loric
loris
lotic
louis
modii
moria
motif
movie
moxie
nomic
noria
no-win
oobit
oorie
podia
polio
posit
potin
powin
robin
Romic
roric
rorid
rorie
rosin
rosit
rotis
rozit
sodic
solid
sonic
Tobit
toe-in
tonic
topic
toric
torii
toxic
toxin
tozie
vogie
vomit
yogic
yogin
yowie
zooid
zoril
△zowie
h**o**d**j**a
kopje
pooja
b**o**o**k**s
booky
bosky
cocky
conky
cooky
corky
docks
dorky
folks
forky
hokku
honky
hooka
hooky
jocko
kooky
locks
looks
mocks
nooky
poaka
poake
pocky
polka
pooka
porky
pouke
rocks
rocky
rooky
socko
socks
vodka
wonky
works
yolky
yonks
Yorks
zooks
b**o**d**l**e
bogle
boule
boult
bowls
coals
coaly
coble
colly
cooly
could
coyly
do-all
doilt
doily
dolly
doole
dowle
doyly
fogle
folly
fonly
foulé

Words marked △ may be spelled also with a capital letter

fowls
foyle
goals
godly
golly
goold
gooly
holla
hollo
holly
hooly
hotly
jolly
joule
jowly
koala
lolly
lowly
moble
molla
molly
moola
mooli
mools
mooly
mould
Mouli®
mouls
moult
moyle
noble
nobly
noils
nould
n'ould
noule
poilu
polls
△polly
pools
poule
poulp
poult
roble
roily
Rolls
rotls
roule
socle
soily
soole
sowle
soyle
toile
toils
tools
voilà
voile
voulu
wolly
woold

△world
would
yodle
you'll
c**o**m**m**a
commo
comms
commy
coomb
coomy
dogma
dolma
dooms
doomy
dormy
douma
foamy
forme
gormy
homme
horme
korma
loamy
momma
mommy
△norma
pommy
rooms
roomy
rowme
△tommy
worms
wormy
b**o**i**n**g
boink
bonne
bonny
boong
borne
borné
bound
bowne
conne
corni
corno
cornu
corny
count
doing
Donna
donne
donné
doona
downa
△downs
downy
found
fount
foyne
going
gonna

horns
horny
hound
joint
△koine
KOing
loins
loons
loony
lound
lownd
lowne
moong
moony
morne
morné
mound
△mount
noint
'noint
nonny
no-one
Norna
nouns
nouny
poind
point
porno
pound
pownd
powny
poynt
ronne
round
rownd
royne
sonne
sonny
sound
sownd
sowne
toing
tonne
towny
wound
xoana
young
zoons
b**o**k**o**s
bolos
boron
bosom
boson
Cobol
cocoa
cocos
codon
cohoe
cohog
cohos
colon

color
dodos
dojos
dolor
donor
gobos
hobos
homos
honor
hoo-oo
jokol
kolos
kotos
kotow
locos
△logos
lolog
lotos
mojos
mokos
monos
moron
Moros
motor
nohow
nomoi
nomos
no-nos
no-no's
polos
potoo
robot
ro-ros
rotor
Sodom
Solon
solos
sopor
tocos
to-dos
tohos
tokos
topoi
topos
Wolof
c**o**a**p**t
compo
compt
coopt
co-opt
coppy
corps
coupe
coupé
coypu
golpe
gompa
goopy
hoppy
koppa
loipe

loopy
loupe
moppy
morph
oomph
poppa
poppy
poupe
poupt
roopy
roupy
soapy
soppy
soupy
zoppo
b**o**a**r**d
boart
boord
bourd
bourg
bourn
coarb
cobra
copra
courb
courd
coure
court
cowry
Dobro®
doorn
doura
dowry
fours
goary
△goura
gourd
hoard
hoary
hoord
houri
hours
howre
kokra
koori
loord
lorry
loure
loury
Moera
Moira
moire
moiré
moory
morra
morro
mourn
mowra
poori
poort
powre

roary
soare
sopra
sorra
sorry
worry
you're
yourn
yours
yourt
zorro
b**o**a**s**t
boose
boost
bossy
bouse
bousy
bowse
△coast
coost
copse
copsy
corse
corso
doest
dorsa
dorse
douse
dowse
foist
△fossa
fosse
godso
goose
goosy
gorse
gorsy
gosse
hoast
hoise
hoist
hoosh
horse
horst
horsy
△house
howso
joist
joust
loast
loess
loose
lossy
louse
lousy
lowse
moist
moose
mopsy
△morse
mossy

mouse
moust
mousy
noise
noisy
noose
Norse
poesy
poise
popsy
posse
poyse
roast
roist
roosa
roose
roost
rouse
roust
royst
sonse
sonsy
souse
sowse
toast
toise
Topsy
torse
torsi
torsk
torso
tossy
touse
tousy
towse
towsy
woosh
worse
worst
zoism
zoist
a**o**r**t**a
bolts
booth
boots
booty
botte
botts
botty
coate
coati
contd
Conté
conte
conté
conto
costa
coste
costs
cotta
couth

5 □o□u

doeth
don'ts
dorts
dorty
dotty
foots
footy
forte
forth
△forty
fouth
fowth
goats
goaty
goety
gotta
gouty
hosta
how-to
jolty
jonty
kofta
loath
lofty
los'te
lotto
molto
monte
month
motte
motto
motty
mouth
△north
ponty
porta
Porte
porty
potto
potty
pouty
roate
ronte
roots
rooty
rorty
route
routh
rowth
softa
softs
softy
soote
sooth
sooty
sorts
△south
sowth
tooth
toots
torte

totty
volta
volte
wootz
worth
youth
bogus
bolus
bonus
bosun
bo'sun
cogue
△comus
donut
focus
forum
hocus
ho-hum
hokum
Horus
jorum
jotun
kokum
lobus
locum
locus
△lotus
modus
△mogul
mohur
Momus
mop-up
mopus
Morus
△motus
nodus
notum
Notus
novum
pop-up
rogue
roguy
roque
solum
solus
sorus
Soyuz
togue
ton-up
tonus
top-up
toque
torus
vogue
woful
yokul
convo
hoove
loave
moove
poove

poovy
Soave
solve
volva
volve
wolve
you've
dohyo
gonys
Kotys
polyp
polys
Tonys
bonza
bonze
booze
boozy
cobza
colza
gonzo
motza
pozzy
toaze
touze
touzy
towze
towzy
woozy
apeak
Apgar
apian
appal
appay
ephah
speak
speal
spean
spear
speat
spial
splat
splay
sprad
sprag
sprat
spray
spyal
uplay
uptak
apace
epact
epoch
space
spacy
speck
specs
spica
spice
spick
spicy
apode

epode
spade
spado
spide
△spode
apeek
apnea
appel
après
mpret
opter
spaer
speed
speel
speer
spied
spiel
spies
spred
spree
sprew
upjet
upled
upped
upper
upsee
upset
upsey
spiff
apage
spahi
apaid
aphid
aphis
April
apsis
épris
Optic®
optic
spain
speir
split
spoil
sprig
sprit
uptie
spake
spike
spiky
spoke
apple
apply
aptly
spald
spale
spall
spalt
speld
spelk
spell
spelt

spile
spill
spilt
spule
spume
spumy
opine
spane
spang
spank
spend
spent
spina
spine
spink
spiny
spunk
upend
up-end
apiol
apoop
apron
ephod
ephor
EPROM
eprom
Epsom
ippon
oppos
speos
spoof
spook
spool
spoom
spoon
spoor
spoot
sprod
sprog
up-bow
epopt
opepe
apart
apert
apery
aport
appro
opera
opéra
spard
spare
spark
spart
sperm
spire
spirt
spiry
spore
sport
spurn
spurs

spurt
spyre
apish
apism
spasm
sposh
spate
spite
spitz
spots
sputa
appui
appuy
opium
spaul
spout
sprue
sprug
uprun
spawl
spawn
spewy
epoxy
apayd
spayd
upbye
equal
squab
squad
squat
squaw
squeg
equid
equip
squib
squid
squit
squiz
Equus
Ardas
aread
areal
arear
argal
argan
Arian
A-road
arrah
arras
array
artal
△arval
Aryan
bread
break
bream
briar
broad
creak
cream
croak

Croat
dread
dream
drear
dryad
freak
friar
graal
great
groan
groat
kraal
oread
organ
orval
praam
prial
pro-am
tread
treat
△triad
△trial
Trias
troad
troat
urban
ureal
urial
urman
urnal
wreak
araba
Araby
aroba
bribe
drabs
dribs
grabs
grebe
oribi
probe
tribe
urubu
areca
brace
brach
brack
bract
brick
broch
brock
crack
crick
crock
cruck
Draco
dreck
erect
erica
erick
Eruca

Words marked △ may be spelled also with a capital letter

eruct
frack
fract
frock
△grace
grece
grice
gryce
orach
oracy
price
prick
pricy
Pruce
trace
track
tract
treck
trice
trick
trock
truce
truck
wrack
wreck
wrick
a**r**e**d**d
arede
brede
bride
△credo
crude
erode
grade
gride
grody
gryde
irade
predy
pride
prude
trade
tride
trode
uredo
a**r**c**e**d
Ardea
ardeb
△ariel
Aries
arles
armed
armet
arrêt
arses
artel
breed
breem
breer
brief
brier
△creed
△creek
creel
creep
cried
crier
cries
cruel
cruet
dried
drier
dries
dryer
erred
erven
freed
freer
freet
fried
frier
fries
fryer
greed
Greek
△green
grees
greet
grief
gruel
orbed
order
oriel
ormer
preen
pried
prief
prier
pries
proem
pryer
treen
tried
trier
tries
tryer
urdee
urdée
urger
urned
wrier
wryer
yrneh
a**r**e**f**y
craft
croft
draff
draft
drift
graff
graft
griff
grift
grufe
gruff
kraft
trefa
triff
b**r**o**g**h
dregs
drugs
grège
grego
tragi
o**r**t**h**o
prahu
A**r**g**i**e
argil
armil
aroid
arris
arsis
artic
braid
brail
brain
broil
Bruin
bruit
craig
drail
drain
droil
droit
△druid
erbia
Ernie
frail
fraim
freit
fruit
△grail
grain
graip
grein
groin
krait
orbit
orcin
orgia
orgic
ornis
orpin
orris
preif
proin
traik
trail
T-rail
train
trait
treif
Troic
ureic
vraic
b**r**a**k**e
braky
broke
crake
drake
grike
gryke
iroko
proke
trike
troke
wroke
b**r**i**l**l
brûlé
drill
drily
drôle
droll
dryly
frill
grill
krill
prill
prole
proll
tra-la
trild
trill
troll
trull
truly
urali
Urals
wryly
a**r**a**m**e
aroma
brame
breme
brume
crame
cramp
creme
crème
crême
crime
crimp
cromb
crome
crumb
crump
drama
drome
frame
fremd
frump
grama
grame
grime
grimy
groma
grume
grump
premy
prima
prime
primo
primp
primy
promo
Proms
tramp
trema
tromp
trump
a**r**e**n**a
aren't
brand
brank
brent
brine
bring
brink
briny
brond
Bronx
brunt
crane
crank
crena
crine
crone
cronk
crony
drank
drant
drent
D-ring
drink
drone
drony
drunk
franc
△frank
frena
frond
front
grand
grant
grind
grone
grunt
irons
irony
krang
krans
kranz
kreng
krona
króna
krone
orang
orant
O-ring
prana
prang
prank
prent
prink
print
prone
prong
pronk
prune
prunt
trant
trend
trine
trona
tronc
trone
trunk
urena
urent
urine
wring
wrong
wrung
yrent
△a**r**b**o**r
ardor
argol
argon
argot
ariot
armor
arrow
arson
arvos
brood
brook
brool
broom
crook
croon
cruor
droog
drook
drool
droop
ergon
ergot
error
Freon®
freon
griot
groof
groom
M-roof
Orion
Orlon®
orlop
prion
prior
proof
trior
trios
troop
try-on
urson
vroom
wroot
c**r**a**p**e
craps
crapy
crepe
crêpe
crept
crepy
crêpy
crypt
drape
drops
drupe
erupt
grape
graph
grapy
gripe
grips
grope
grype
grypt
props
trape
traps
tripe
tripy
trope
wraps
wrapt
yrapt
I**r**a**q**i
a**r**d**r**i
ard-ri
arere
brere
crare
crore
drere
frère
frore
frorn
frory
prore
urari
a**r**i**s**e
arish
arose
artsy
brash
brass
brast

Words marked △ may be spelled also with a capital letter

5 □r□v

brisé
brisk
brose
brush
brust
crash
crass
cress
crest
crise
crisp
△cross
cruse
crush
crust
crusy
dress
drest
dross
△druse
drusy
erase
erose
frass
fresh
frisk
frist
frost
frush
frust
grasp
grass
grese
grise
grist
grisy
gross
Irish
prase
presa
prese
△press
prest
prise
prism
prose
proso
prosy
pryse
trash
trass
tress
trest
trist
truss
trust
tryst
wrast
wrest
wrist
arête

arett
Arita
broth
brute
crate
crith
crwth
Erato
frate
frati
frith
fritz
froth
grate
grith
grits
irate
orate
prate
pratt
praty
Proto®
△proto
tratt
trite
troth
trots
truth
urate
urite
wrate
wrath
write
wrote
wroth
arcus
argue
△argus
arnut
croup
crout
drouk
fraud
fry-up
grouf
group
grout
△kraut
orgue
proud
proul
trout
Ursus
vrouw
brava
brave
bravi
bravo
breve
crave
cruve

drave
drive
drove
grave
gravy
greve
△grove
preve
△privy
prove
Provo
trave
yrivd
brawl
brawn
braws
brown
crawl
crewe
crowd
△crown
drawl
drawn
drown
frown
frowy
growl
grown
prawn
prowl
trawl
trews
wrawl
braxy
druxy
prexy
proxy
Greys
Oriya
proyn
X-rays
braze
brize
craze
crazy
croze
Druze
frize
frizz
froze
graze
grize
Oryza
prize
Asian
assai
assay
asway
eskar
essay
Islam

Oscan
Oscar
oshac
pshaw
psoas
usual
dsobo
tsuba
psych
aside
A-side
B-side
ashen
△ashes
ashet
asker
askew
aspen
asper
asses
asset
aster
as-yet
esker
esses
Essex
ester
islet
issei
osier
usher
usnea
Osage
Tsuga
usage
V-sign
ASCII
Asdic
aspic
astir
aswim
g-suit
osmic
ossia
Ossie
ostia
Q-ship
esile
istle
psalm
dsomo
ysame
asana
usen't
ascot
assot
escot
estoc
estop
f-stop
psion

psyop
estro
psora
Q-sort
usure
usurp
usury
ascus
astun
issue
pseud
△atlas
atman
attap
attar
ethal
ottar
stead
steak
steal
steam
stean
stear
stoae
stoai
stoas
stoat
strad
strae
strap
straw
stray
U-trap
stubs
U-tube
stack
stich
stick
stock
stuck
étude
stade
stedd
stede
study
ether
etwee
other
otter
steed
steek
steel
steem
steen
steep
steer
stied
sties
stoep
strep
strew

styed
styes
utter
staff
stiff
stuff
étage
stage
stagy
stogy
itchy
atria
atrip
△attic
ethic
ettin
staid
staig
stain
stair
steil
stein
△stoic
stoit
stria
strig
strip
atoke
stake
stoke
atilt
atoll
ettle
Itala
stal'd
stale
stalk
stall
stela
stele
stell
stilb
stile
still
stilt
stole
stoln
stull
stulm
style
styli
stylo
utile
atimy
atomy
etyma
stamp
steme
stime
stimy
stoma

stomp
stumm
stump
styme
atone
atony
ctene
Etons
stand
stane
stang
stank
stend
stent
sting
stink
stint
stond
stone
stong
stonk
stonn
stony
stung
stunk
stunt
ethos
stood
stook
stool
stoop
stoor
strop
strow
stroy
atopy
étape
n-type
p-type
staph
steps
stept
stipa
stipe
stope
stupa
stupe
otary
stare
stark
starn
starr
stars
start
stere
stern
stire
stirk
stirp
store
stork

Words marked △ may be spelled also with a capital letter

storm
story
sture
sturt
styre
uteri
U-turn
stash
stoss
ytost
state
styte
stoun
stoup
stour
stout
strum
strut
stave
stive
stivy
stove
stews
stewy
stown
ataxy
△ethyl
stays
aurae
aural
auras
bubal
buran
Cuban
curat
ducal
ducat
dural
eupad
fugal
fural
furan
gulag
gular
human
△judas
jugal
jumar
jural
jurat
kulak
kulan
Lucan
lunar
mural
Musak
Muzak®
nugae
pumas
pupae
pupal
pupas
quean
quoad
Quran
Qur'an
△rubai
rudas
rumal
Ruman
rural
subah
sugar
sumac
surah
sural
surat
tubae
tubal
tubar
tubas
tunas
yulan
zupan
bubby
bumbo
busby
cubby
dumbo
fubby
△gumbo
hubby
jumbo
jumby
nubby
outby
△rugby
rumba
rumbo
subby
tubby
turbo
bunce
bunch
bunco
butch
culch
curch
cutch
dunce
dunch
△dutch
guaco
gulch
hunch
hutch
juice
juicy
junco
kutch
lunch
lurch
mulch
mulct
munch
Musca
Musci
mutch
ounce
punce
△punch
quack
quich
quick
runch
succi
sulci
Turco
yucca
buddy
bundu
Bundy®
cuddy
cundy
curdy
duddy
fundi
funds
fundy
△guide
gundy
hurds
muddy
Munda
oundy
outdo
puddy
quids
ruddy
suede
suède
auger
aurei
buret
buses
Butea
buyer
cubeb
culet
culex
cumec
cupel
curer
cusec
cutey
cuvée
duper
duvet
fumes
fumet
fusee
fuzee
gules
julep
luces
Luger®
luger
lumen
Lurex®
luter
luxes
muley
murex
mused
muser
muset
muted
numen
Nupes
ousel
outed
outer
ouzel
pubes
puker
puler
Pulex
puree
purée
Purex
puzel
△queen
queer
quiet
ruler
△rules
rumen
Rumex
runed
rupee
suber
sujee
super
tubed
△tuber
tubes
tuned
tuner
tupek
tutee
buffa
buffe
buffi
buffo
buffs
cuffo
fuffy
gulfy
huffy
luffa
puffy
quaff
quiff
ruffe
sulfa
surfy
tuffe
turfs
turfy
budge
buggy
bulge
bulgy
bungy
burgh
dungy
durgy
fudge
fuggy
fungi
gunge
gungy
gurge
judge
lunge
lungi
△lurgi
lurgy
mudge
muggy
mulga
mungo
nudge
outgo
pudge
pudgy
puggy
punga
purge
ruggy
surge
surgy
vuggy
vulgo
aught
buchu
bushy
cushy
duchy
gushy
hushy
lushy
musha
mushy
nucha
oucht
ought
ouphe
pushy
qui-hi
ruche
rushy
sushi
tushy
△wushu
audio
audit
△aulic
aumil
auric
auxin
bunia
burin
buy-in
cubic
cubit
Cufic
cumin
△cupid
curia
curie
curio
cutie
cutin
cut-in
cutis
dulia
fugie
fusil
humic
humid
hutia
Kufic
lucid
ludic
lupin
lurid
mucic
mucid
mucin
mudir
mujik
music
musit
nubia
nudie
oubit
ourie
pubic
pubis
pudic
pugil
pumie
Punic
pupil
purim
purin
putid
put-in
quail
quair
quoif
quoin
quoit
Rubia
rubin
rudie
runic
run-in
rupia
rutin
Sufic
Sufis
tulip
tumid
tunic
tupik
Yupik
bunje
bunjy
Ouija®
ouija
bucko
bucku
bulky
bunko
burka
burke
busky
ducks
ducky
dumka
dumky
dusky
funky
gucky
hulks
hulky
hunks
hunky
husks
husky
junky
△lucky
mucky
murky
musky
pucka
pukka
pulka
punka
quake
quaky
sucks
sulks
sulky
Tunku
Turki
tusky
yucky
yukky
bugle
build
built
△bulla
bully
burly

Words marked △ may be spelled also with a capital letter

cully
curly
dully
duple
duply
fugle
fully
Guelf
guild
guile
guilt
gully
gurly
gusla
gusle
gusli
guyle
hullo
hully
hurly
murly
nulla
pusle
quale
qualm
quell
quill
quilt
quoll
ruble
rumly
sully
surly
tulle
d**u**m**m**y
duomi
duomo
guimp
gumma
gummy
lumme
lummy
mummy
pulmo
queme
rummy
rusma
summa
Suomi
tummy
turme
yummy
b**u**n**n**y
burnt
cuing
curny
dunno
dunny
funny
guana
guano

gunny
Luing
quant
quena
quina
quine
quint
quonk
ruana
ruing
ruins
runny
suing
suint
Sunna
Sunni
sunny
tunny
a**u**l**o**i
aulos
autos
budos
buroo
buxom
duros
duroy
euros
eusol
furol
furor
futon
guyot
humor
husos
jupon
juror
kudos
ludos
mucor
musos
muton
ouzos
pudor
put-on
rumor
run-on
sudor
sumos
sutor
Tudor
tumor
tutor
yupon
b**u**m**p**h
bumps
bumpy
buppy
cuppa
dumps
dumpy
duppy

gulph
guppy
humph
humpy
jumps
jumpy
lumpy
mumps
pulpy
puppy
purpy
quipo
quipu
rumpy
sumph
tumpy
turps
yuppy
b**u**r**q**a
b**u**r**r**o
burry
curry
durra
fuero
furry
guard
guiro
gurry
hurra
hurry
kukri
kurre
lubra
lucre
lurry
mucro
mudra
Munro
murra
murre
murry
outré
quare
quark
quart
quern
query
quire
quirk
quirt
Quorn®
sucre
Sudra
surra
sutra
tuart
tugra
b**u**i**s**t
bulse
bursa
burse

burst
bussu
cuish
curse
cursi
curst
dulse
dunsh
durst
fubsy
fussy
guess
guest
guise
gussy
gutsy
guyse
hurst
hussy
muist
mulse
mulsh
mumsy
musse
mussy
nurse
pudsy
pulse
△purse
pursy
pussy
quash
quasi
quest
quist
sudsy
tuism
Tutsi
wurst
a**u**n**t**y
bunty
busty
butte
butty
cutto
cutty
duets
duett
dusty
furth
fusty
gusto
gusty
gutta
gutty
junta
junto
jutty
kurta
lusty
△mufti

muntu
Muntz
musth
musty
nutty
punto
punty
purty
putti
putto
putty
quite
quits
quota
quote
quoth
quyte
runty
rusty
rutty
suety
suite
suits
tuath
tufty
tutti
tutty
a**u**g**u**r
cut-up
durum
Eurus
fucus
fugue
Fusus
Gueux
humus
jugum
△lupus
mucus
put-up
queue
Rubus
run-up
sunup
tuque
c**u**r**v**e
curvy
guava
murva
suave
vulva
b**u**n**y**a
butyl
Kuo-yü
quayd
queyn
Surya
b**u**a**z**e
buzzy
furze
furzy

fuzzy
huzza
huzzy
kudzu
muzzy
a**v**g**a**s
avian
uveal
e**v**i**c**t
e**v**a**d**e
i**v**i**e**d
e**v**o**h**e
a**v**a**i**l
avoid
ovoid
e**v**o**k**e
a**v**a**l**e
mvule
ovoli
ovolo
ovule
uvula
a**v**a**n**t
Avena
avens
avine
evens
event
ovine
a**v**i**o**n
evhoe
a**v**e**r**t
evert
every
ivory
ovary
overt
a**v**a**s**t
avise
aviso
kvass
ovist
e**v**i**t**e
ovate
a**v**i**z**e
avyze
s**w**e**a**l
swear
sweat
tweak
A**W**A**C**S
swack
twice
△s**w**e**d**e
a-**w**e**e**k
aweel
awned
awner
dweeb
owler
owlet

owner
owsen
sweel
sweep
sweer
sweet
tweed
tweel
'tween
tweer
tweet
twier
twoer
twyer
s**w**i**f**t
s**w**a**g**e
o**w**c**h**e
a**w**a**i**t
owrie
swain
sweir
twain
a**w**a**k**e
awoke
d**w**a**l**e
dwalm
dwell
dwelt
dwile
kwela
swale
swaly
swell
swelt
swill
swoln
twill
'twill
twilt
△s**w**a**m**i
swamp
a-**w**i**n**g
bwana
dwang
dwine
owing
swang
swank
swine
△swing
swink
swone
swung
twang
twank
twine
twink
Twins
twiny
e**w**h**o**w
swoon

swoop
swapt
swept
swipe
swopt
award
aware
awarn
awmry
awork
dwarf
F-word
sward
sware
swarf
swarm
swart
swerf
swire
swirl
sword
swore
sworn
'twere
twerp
twire
twirl
twirp
awash
ewest
swash
swish
Swiss
twist
aweto
swath

swats
swith
swits
twite
awful
dwaum
swoun
swy-up
two-up
awave
swive
'twixt
aways
swayl
bwazi
Swazi
axial
axman
exeat
expat
Oxfam
exact
exode
exude
oxide
excel
exeem
exies
expel
oxter
axoid
ex-div
oxlip
axile
exalt
△exile

exult
ixtle
exeme
oxime
exine
axiom
expos
extol
ox-bot
ox-bow
exert
extra
exurb
exist
exits
ox-eye
bylaw
byway
cycad
cymar
gynae
gyral
△hyrax
lyyar
mynah
pygal
pyral
rybat
symar
△syrah
typal
tyran
zygal
sybbe
lynch
synch

Hyads
hynde
kynde
tynde
cyder
dykey
hyleg
△hymen
hyper
lycée
Pyrex®
ryper
sycee
syker
syren
syver
tyler
tyned
tyred
xylem
nyaff
hypha
hythe
kythe
lythe
sythe
Tyche
Typha
tythe
ayrie
cylix
△cynic
eyrie
Eytie
gynie
hylic

hyoid
kylie
kylin
kylix
Kyrie
lyric
lysin
lysis
myoid
pyoid
pyxis
△sybil
typic
xylic
Xyris
zymic
ayelp
cycle
cyclo
gyeld
myall
nyala
myoma
pygmy
rymme
ayont
by-end
dying
eying
gynny
hyena
hying
kyang
lying
nying
tying

vying
cyton
gyron
hypos
hyson
kyloe
lysol
nylon
pylon
syboe
sybow
△synod
sysop
typos
tyros
xylol
zygon
gyppo
gyppy
lymph
myope
myops
nymph
sylph
aygre
Cymry
△hydra
hydro
lyart
Lycra®
myrrh
gypsy
kydst
lyssa
nyssa
Eyeti

fytte
lytta
synth
typto
xysti
gyrus
Pyrus
syrup
sylva
xylyl
izzat
Czech
azide
Aztec
Uzbeg
Uzbek
azygy
azoic
ozeki
△azyme
azine
ozone
Azeri
azure
azurn
azury
izard
azote
azoth
pzazz

6 □a□a□a

bahada
bajada
balata
banana
baraza
batata
cabala
cabana
cañada
Carapa
dagaba
Havana
jacana
jaçana
jataka
kabala
kabaya
kamala
△kanaka
karaka
katana
Malaga
mañana
maraca
nagana
palama
panada
△panama
papaya
Paraná
pataca
samara
satara
taiaha
tamara
zapata
△bayard
cafard
canard
farand
hazard
maraud
mazard
nasard
navaid
tabard
tarand
vaward
Banate
canapé
carafe
damage
eatage
facade
façade
galage
garage
gavage
hamate
karate

lanate
lavage
△madame
malate
manage
oarage
palace
palate
parade
parage
pavage
pavane
rafale
ramate
ravage
salade
sarape
savage
savate
takahe
tamale
vacate
wakane
zarape
lalang
padang
parang
satang
zamang
calash
camash
gamash
Kazakh
paraph
Tanach
calami
jawari
manati
nagari
Pahari
palagi
safari
salami
tamari
tatami
uakari
Wahabi
carack
damask
padauk
saxaul
Balaam
napalm
salaam
papain
samaan
wabain
babaco
catalo
galago

kakapo
lavabo
macaco
Navaho
Navajo
paramo
rabato
bazaar
ram-air
badass
camass
cavass
harass
kababs
kavass
madams
naiads
vakass
basalt
caract
galant
karait
naiant
natant
savant
talant
vacant
gagaku
tamanu
Caranx
canary
datary
△galaxy
malady
panary
papacy
salary
Tatary
vagary
bazazz
pazazz
balboa
cambia
lambda
baobab
earbob
iambic
tambac
barbed
dabbed
day-bed
gabbed
nabbed
tabbed
tan-bed
babble
△barbie
bauble
bawbee
bawble

cabbie
dabble
faible
gabble
gamble
garble
hamble
jabble
jambee
lambie
lay-bye
marble
rabble
ramble
wabble
wamble
warble
yabbie
gasbag
△lambeg
ragbag
ratbag
casbah
kasbah
jambok
△zambuk
barbel
gambol
jambul
sambal
carbon
rabbin
bamboo
gabbro
yah-boo
barber
camber
dabber
dauber
gabber
gambir
harbor
jabber
jamber
lamber
nabber
sambar
sambur
tamber
yabber
garbos
iambus
jambos
lay-bys
mambos
rabbis
sambos
zambos
barbet
gag-bit

gambet
gambit
hagbut
rabbet
rabbit
sabbat
talbot
wabbit
hatbox
haybox
jawbox
pay-box
tar-box
babbly
carboy
dawbry
day-boy
marbly
tarboy
wambly
fascia
kaccha
calcic
calced
rancid
raucid
talced
eatche
gauche
gaucie
manche
mascle
Parcae
raucle
sancai
caecal
cancel
faecal
faucal
laical
△marcel
parcel
pascal
rancel
rascal
tarcel
caecum
talcum
cancan
earcon
falcon
farcin
garçon
△gascon
Marcan
mascon
fascio
gaucho
rancho
sancho

ear-cap
madcap
calcar
△cancer
dancer
lancer
lascar
rancor
saucer
calces
cascos
caucus
darcys
faeces
falces
fasces
fauces
lances
mancus
narcos
saccos
catcht
fat-cat
faucet
lancet
mascot
ramcat
waucht
Manchu
catchy
patchy
talcky
bardic
Dardic
banded
barded
candid
caudad
fanded
gadded
handed
landed
padded
parded
sanded
wadded
warded
baddie
caddie
candie
candle
caudle
daddle
daidle
Dandie
dandle
dawdle
faddle
haddie
handle

lac-dye
laddie
laldie
paddle
paidle
pardie
raddle
randie
saddle
taddie
waddie
waddle
wandle
Yardie
bandog
lapdog
wardog
gardai
sandhi
haiduk
zaddik
caudal
daedal
fardel
jandal®
pardal
sandal
sardel
△vandal
fandom
mandom
randem
random
tandem
Dardan
farden
garden
hadden
hagden
hagdon
hand-in
harden
hard-on
lardon
madden
maidan
△maiden
pardon
randan
randon
sadden
warden
nandoo
nardoo
vaudoo
wandoo
hard-up
paid-up
bandar
candor
carder
dander
gadder
gander
hander
ladder
Länder
lander
larder
lauder
madder
mandir
padder
pandar
pander
raider
sadder
sander
sawder
wander
warder
zander
caddis
bandit
pandit
saidst
landau
saddhu
May-dew
caudex
baldly
bawdry
hardly
laidly
law-day
lay-day
man-day
mayday
pay-day
tawdry
bauera
camera
catena
favela
galena
Ganesa
kamela
lagena
pakeha
patera
tapeta
valeta
zabeta
zareba
maleic
fag-end
hareld
lag-end
salewd
taberd
tag-end
barege
barège
camese
△carême
facete
galère
gamete
kabele
manège
Na-Dene
paleae
raceme
sagene
sapele
taleae
valete
samekh
varech
tapeti
△**favell**
rameal
vakeel
hareem
baleen
careen
casein
casern
cave-in
cavern
fade-in
have-on
lateen
Ramean
Sabean
sateen
take-in
tavern
gazebo
make-do
sapego
fade-up
make-up
rave-up
take-up
wake-up
career
fadeur
laveer
pasear
cameos
capers
caress
havers
jabers
kamees
papers
tavers
waders
waters
cadent
caveat
gayest
haven't
jacent
lament
latent
latest
manent
mayest
parent
patent
sayest
talent
tavert
bateau
cadeau
gateau
gâteau
bakery
barely
basely
calefy
eatery
fakery
gaiety
gamely
gamesy
jadery
lamely
lately
madefy
namely
napery
palely
papery
rakery
rarefy
rarely
safely
safety
sagely
samely
sanely
tabefy
tamely
tawery
wafery
watery
wavery
yarely
kameez
△**maffia**
raffia
taffia
baffle
Caffre
gaufre
raffle
waffle
yaffle
zaffre
bagful
barful
canful
capful
earful
hatful
jarful
lapful
lawful
manful
panful
sapful
vatful
waeful
halfen
samfoo
gaffer
gaufer
△kaffer
△kaffir
zaffer
farfet
haffet
haffit
carfax
carfox
barfly
day-fly
gadfly
mayfly
naffly
saw-fly
waffly
kangha
Pangea
bagged
banged
fagged
fanged
gagged
hagged
hanged
jagged
lagged
nagged
ragged
sagged
tagged
tanged
wagged
zagged
bangle
bargee
cangle
cangue
daggle
dangle
dargle
fangle
gadgie
gaggle
Gamgee®
gamgee
gangue
gargle
haggle
jangle
langue
maigre
malgre
malgré
mangle
maugre
paigle
raggee
raggle
taggee
taigle
tangie
tangle
waggle
wangle
mangal
mangel
Targum
jargon
laggen
laggin
largen
margin
pangen
tangun
waggon
wangan
wangun
dayglo
Day-Glo
bang-up
hang-up
△**badger**
banger
cadger
dagger
danger
gagger
ganger
gauger
hangar
hanger
Jaeger®
jaeger
jagger
laager
lagger
langur
manger
nagger
△ranger

6 □a□g□s

saggar
sagger
sangar
sauger
tagger
yagger
fangos
haggis
largos
sargos
sargus
tangos
valgus
baggit
catgut
caught
faggot
gadget
garget
haught
maggot
naught
parget
raught
target
taught
waught
pang-fu'
dangly
gangly
jangly
laughy
mangey
margay
tangly
waggly
mashua
△raphia
pathic
washed
daphne
lathee
mashie
mazhbi
kathak
pachak
Gadhel
fathom
mayhem
pashim
sachem
fat-hen
lathen
machan
Pathan
Sathan
sazhen
washen
wash-in
Pakhto

Pashto
lash-up
mayhap
wash-up
basher
bather
Cathar
dasher
△father
gather
jaghir
Jashar
Jasher
lasher
lather
masher
rasher
rather
washer
bathos
hachis
laches
machos
nachos
pathos
rachis
raphis
tachos
cachet
sachet
cachou
Pakhtu
Pashtu
bashaw
cashaw
cashew
haw-haw
eathly
gashly
rashly
sashay
cafila
calima
capita
Carica
△carina
Dalila
farina
kafila
kamila
la-di-da
lamina
Latina
△manila
marina
maxima
patina
qasida
sahiba
salina

saliva
tahina
vagina
zariba
maniac
manioc
panisc
ravin'd
taxied
varied
barite
camise
canine
caribe
dacite
Danite
dative
facile
famine
gamine
habile
halide
halite
Hamite
karite
labile
larine
malice
marine
maxixe
narine
native
patine
pavise
ranine
rapine
ratine
ratiné
ratite
ravine
Sabine
saline
samite
sasine
satire
sative
savine
tajine
tamine
tamise
vagile
vahine
valine
valise
wahine
walise
tariff
baaing
baking
basing

bating
caging
caking
caning
caring
casing
caving
cawing
daring
dating
earing
eating
facing
fading
gaming
gaping
gating
having
haying
hazing
japing
jawing
lacing
lading
lasing
lawing
laying
making
maying
naming
paging
paling
paring
paving
paying
racing
raging
raking
raping
raring
rating
raving
rawing
saring
saving
sawing
saying
taking
taming
taring
tawing
taxing
wading
waking
waning
waving
waxing
banish
barish
caliph

Danish
dawish
eadish
famish
garish
Hadith
harish
jadish
lakish
lamish
Lapith
latish
lavish
marish
oafish
palish
papish
pariah
parish
radish
rakish
ravish
rawish
sakieh
Salish
vanish
Cabiri
ragini
samiti
tahini
wakiki
wapiti
Danisk
panick
panisk
Daniel
facial
garial
gavial
labial
narial
parial
racial
radial
samiel
Babism
barium
favism
kalium
labium
laxism
magism
malism
Maoism
nanism
Nazism
papism
racism
radium
Ramism

sadism
Sapium
Taoism
Valium®
banian
camion
cation
Fabian
fanion
gabion
kalian
kation
Latian
magian
Malian
malign
Marian
nasion
nation
Parian
radian
ration
Sabian
Salian
Samian
talion
Walian
wanion
Zabian
calico
caligo
casino
katipo
Ladino
Latino
manito
matico
magilp
cahier
caviar
pavior
rapier
varier
basics
capias
caries
danios
facies
ladies
ladies'
△matins
patios
rabies
radios
radius
rapids
ratios
sanies
taxies
Babist

Words marked △ may be spelled also with a capital letter

galiot
lariat
laxist
malist
Maoist
Marist
papist
racist
Ramist
rapist
sadist
Samiot
tanist
Taoist
tapist
jabiru
Malibu
cagily
cavity
easily
family
gasify
hazily
ladify
laxity
lazily
matily
mazily
Nazify
pacify
parity
racily
ramify
rarity
ratify
salify
sanify
sanity
satiny
vanity
warily
wavily
waxily
masjid
sanjak
Tadjik
gaijin
garjan
hanjar
jamjar
banjos
kanjis
matjes
fan-jet
ramjet
banjax
backra
markka
sabkha
tankia
backed
hawked
marked
masked
narked
racked
ranked
tacked
tanked
vacked
cackle
darkie
darkle
fankle
hackee
hackle
hankie
hawkie
mackle
palkee
parkee
parkie
rankle
tackle
talkie
wankle
Yankee
yankie
haikai
kaikai
Naskhi
saikei
jackal
barkan
barken
calkin
catkin
daikon
darken
gaskin
harken
malkin
mawkin
nankin
napkin
parkin
talk-in
walk-in
walk-on
back-up
jack-up
mark-up
walk-up
backer
balker
banker
barker
calker
canker
cauker
cawker
dacker
daiker
gawker
hacker
hanker
hawker
janker
lacker
laiker
larker
marker
masker
packer
parker
racker
ranker
sacker
tacker
talker
tanker
tasker
wacker
△walker
wanker
wauker
yacker
yakker
yanker
faikes
maikos
sakkos
sankos
tankas
backet
banket
basket
casket
gasket
hawkit
jacket
lasket
market
nacket
packet
racket
tacket
darkey
darkly
hackly
hawkey
jacksy
lackey
lankly
parkly
rankly
dahlia
halloa
paella
pallia
lablab
Gaelic
△gallic
garlic
ballad
balled
callid
fabled
failed
gabled
macled
maelid
mailed
marled
nailed
palled
pallid
pat-lid
sailed
sallad
tabled
tailed
walled
bailee
bailie
caille
faille
mallee
pallae
rallye
sallee
saulge
saulie
taille
tailye
wallie
bablah
nallah
pallah
wallah
bailli
maulvi
fallal
hallal
sallal
Baalim
mallam
vallum
ballan
ballon
callan
caplin
Caslon
fallen
fall-in
gallon
hallan
kaolin
lallan
marlin
maslin
raglan
ratlin
Gallio
halloo
ballup
call-up
cat-lap
dallop
earlap
gallop
oar-lap
wallop
bailer
bailor
batler
bawler
caller
fabler
faller
gaoler
hailer
hauler
jailer
jailor
mailer
nailer
pallor
parlor
railer
sailer
sailor
samlor
tailor
tatler
vallar
wailer
waller
callus
caules
caulis
dalles
gallus
hallos
△majlis
matlos
Pallas
Rallus
sables
tables
ballat
ballet
ballot
batlet
cablet
callet
camlet
caplet
carlot
eaglet
gablet
gallet
gaslit
haglet
hamlet
harlot
haslet
haulst
mallet
pallet
raylet
sallet
samlet
tablet
tallat
tallet
tallot
taslet
varlet
wallet
maglev
ballow
callow
fallow
gallow
hallow
mallow
matlow
sallow
tallow
wallow
hallux
△**bailey**
ballsy
barley
bawley
faulty
galley
parlay
parley
railly
valley
vaulty
waylay
Y-alloy
kalmia
caimac
haemic
karmic
Tarmac®
tarmac
calmed
dammed
jammed
maimed
palmed
rammed
△talmud
warmed
lammie

Words marked △ may be spelled also with a capital letter

6 □a□m□g

mammae
mammee
Palmae
palmie
malmag
warmth
haemal
hammal
mahmal
mammal
wadmal
wadmol
hammam
marmem
badman
bagman
barman
batman
cabman
caiman
carman
cayman
daemon
daimen
daimon
farm-in
gagman
gammon
gasman
haemin
harman
harmin
lawman
law-man
layman
madman
△mammon
ragman
salmon
taxman
△vatman
warman
daimio
warm-up
bammer
dammar
dammer
farmer
gammer
hammer
jammer
lammer
mammer
palmar
palmer
rammer
tammar
warmer
yammer
lacmus

Lammas
magmas
salmis
wammus
dammit
mammet
marmot
maumet
mawmet
haymow
calmly
warmly
Tammuz
maunna
pa'anga
taenia
tannic
zarnec
canned
damned
darned
fanned
hained
maenad
manned
pained
panned
tanned
vanned
wanned
cannae
faunae
jaunce
jaunse
launce
paunce
pawnce
△pawnee
raunge
sannie
sarnie
vaunce
pad-nag
gaunch
hainch
haunch
launch
paunch
raunch
tannah
cannel
carnal
darnel
fannel
faunal
tarnal
wannel
magnum
painim
paynim

bainin
cannon
magnon
Saanen
tannin
bagnio
catnap
catnep
catnip
sannup
banner
canner
darner
dauner
dawner
earner
fanner
fawner
gainer
garner
lanner
mainor
manner
pawner
tanner
vanner
warner
faints
faunas
magnes
pannus
Tainos
bag-net
Bannat
basnet
cannot
carnet
'gainst
gannet
garnet
magnet
oak-nut
walnut
satnav
larnax
Magnox®
magnox
barney
carney
dainty
fainly
fainty
gainly
jaunty
mainly
△maundy
maungy
painty
sarney
△sawney

Tannoy®
tannoy
tawney
vainly
vaunty
dagoba
Lakota
macoya
Masora
pagoda
pakora
payola
samosa
sapota
yaqona
haboob
day-old
gadoid
ganoid
haloed
haloid
kayoed
laroid
Samoed
cajole
camote
capote
favose
galore
hamose
lanose
matoke
parole
pavone
radome
ramose
vadose
vamose
far-off
lay-off
pay-off
barong
kalong
sarong
galosh
caroli
satori
barock
padouk
paiock
pajock
yapock
cagoul
jarool
waboom
baboon
batoon
cacoon
ganoin
gazoon

lagoon
Mahoun
maroon
racoon
ratoon
sagoin
saloon
manoao
palolo
saloop
favour
△labour
savour
tabour
valour
vapour
cabobs
dadoes
dagoes
famous
favous
haloes
hamous
kabobs
kaross
kayoes
majors
patois
ramous
taboos
tarots
cavort
dacoit
dakoit
far-out
galoot
lavolt
layout
mahout
mazout
pay-out
ragout
rag-out
way-out
barony
△calory
canopy
jalopy
paeony
parody
savory
△saxony
yarpha
calpac
Naypic
capped
happed
lampad
lapped
mapped

napped
rapped
sapped
tapped
wapped
warped
cample
dapple
lappie
magpie
rappee
salpae
sample
sapple
taupie
tawpie
wampee
waspie
yappie
hatpeg
kalpak
carpal
carpel
lappel
palpal
rappel
wampum
dampen
happen
hatpin
jampan
map-pin
parpen
sampan
sanpan
sappan
taipan
tampon
tarpan
tarpon
yaupon
Sappho
camper
capper
carper
damper
dapper
gasper
gauper
gawper
hamper
harper
jasper
lapper
mapper
napper
pamper
pauper
ramper
rapper

Words marked △ may be spelled also with a capital letter

rasper
sapper
tamper
tapper
vamper
wapper
warper
yapper
yawper
zapper
campos
campus
carpus
gaupus
gawpus
jaspis
kalpis
lampas
mawpus
palpus
pampas
pappus
salpas
wampus
bampot
carpet
jampot
lappet
Rajput
rat-pit
sawpit
tan-pit
tappet
tappit
pawpaw
camply
damply
barque
△basque
caique
caïque
calque
casque
haique
Jacque
lasque
manqué
marque
masque
sacque
saique
yanqui
garrya
latria
△varroa
capric
fabric
lauric
matric
tanrec

tauric
barred
caprid
darred
garred
haired
hatred
jarred
labrid
manred
marred
nacred
paired
ramrod
sacred
tarred
warred
waured
wax-red
bajree
cabrie
faerie
tagrag
jarrah
barrel
carrel
laurel
lauryl
parral
parrel
patrol
sacral
saurel
Bairam
labrum
marram
marrum
sacrum
vagrom
barren
carron
Dacron®
farren
garran
garron
hadron
latron
macron
matron
napron
natron
patron
rat-run
warran
warren
barrio
hairdo
Karroo
larrup
satrap

Capris
Labrus
labrys
Laurus
macros
madras
Maoris
narras
tarras
Taurus
walrus
barrat
barret
cabrit
carrat
carrot
garret
garrot
hairst
labret
parrot
tabret
waurst
barrow
farrow
harrow
marrow
narrow
tarrow
yarrow
matrix
fairly
warray
warrey
△**cassia**
fatsia
nausea
tarsia
Vaisya
parsec
capsid
gassed
halsed
Hassid
lapsed
passed
dassie
falsie
hassle
laesie
laisse
lassie
Parsee
passée
tassie
warsle
massif
taisch
sansei
causal

damsel
eassel
eassil
hansel
haysel
pausal
ransel
tahsil
tarsal
tarsel
tassel
varsal
vassal
balsam
hansom
passim
ransom
causen
damson
kamsin
parson
raisin
ramson
Samson
sarsen
camsho
catsup
△**caesar**
causer
falser
gasser
halser
hassar
hawser
kaiser
mahsir
Mauser
parser
passer
pauser
raiser
bassos
cassis
fatsos
gadsos
lapsus
lassos
masses
passus
tarsus
basset
tasset
wadset
samshu
padsaw
carsey
causey
gansey
jansky
karsey

marshy
nay-say
caltha
kantha
maltha
mantra
mantua
Raetia
△tantra
Baltic
haptic
lastic
lactic
mantic
mastic
nastic
nautic
tactic
batted
canted
casted
fantad
fantod
fatted
hatted
malted
mantid
masted
matted
parted
patted
raited
ratted
salted
tasted
vatted
wafted
wanted
warted
wasted
bastle
battle
battue
cantle
castle
cattle
daftie
dartle
dartre
dautie
dawtie
Fantee
hantle
jantee
mantle
mattie
pattée
pattle
rattle
saithe

tattie
tattle
tawtie
wattle
ragtag
tautog
nautch
canthi
baetyl
battel
Cantal
cartel
cautel
dactyl
hartal
mantel
martel
pastel
pastil
santal
wastel
bantam
factum
fantom
pactum
partim
tam-tam
barton
batten
caftan
canton
captan
carton
Caxton
dalton
danton
fan-tan
fasten
fatten
hapten
harten
hasten
kaftan
kanten
latten
marten
martin
panton
pantun
partan
parton
patten
rattan
ratten
ratton
santon
Tartan®
tartan
tauten
wait-on

Words marked △ may be spelled also with a capital letter

6 □a□t□o

wanton
tattoo
laptop
ragtop
baiter
banter
barter
baster
batter
baxter
cantar
canter
cantor
captor
carter
caster
△castor
cauter
daftar
darter
△easter
factor
faitor
falter
faster
fatter
fautor
gaiter
△garter
gas-tar
gaster
halter
hatter
kantar
karter
laster
latter
martyr
△master
matter
natter
palter
panter
parter
paster
pastor
patter
rafter
ranter
raptor
raster
ratter
saeter
salter
santir
santur
sartor
△tartar
taster
tatter

vatter
wafter
waiter
wanter
waster
yatter
bastos
cactus
cantos
cantus
factis
mantis
mantos
pantos
pastis
saltos
saltus
sautés
wastes
rat-tat
tautit
tattow
daftly
earthy
fastly
gantry
lastly
paltry
pantry
partly
pastry
raptly
rattly
saltly
tartly
tautly
vastly
wastry
canula
datura
facula
△garuda
lacuna
Laputa
macula
manuka
masula
mazuma
natura
papula
radula
ranula
tabula
taluka
valuta
Varuna
yakuza
caduac
salue'd
tabued

valued
cayuse
lagune
macule
manure
mature
nasute
△nature
papule
parure
rasure
razure
salute
Baluch
galuth
hamuli
kabuki
ramuli
saluki
Canuck
Kanuck
△casual
manual
vacuum
Paduan
Papuan
saguin
Saturn
taguan
baguio
Basuto
lanugo
gazump
faquir
jaguar
valuer
△maquis
values
kaputt
yaourt
Basutu
maguey
raguly
salvia
carved
salve'd
valved
varved
garvie
jarvie
larvae
halvah
Jahveh
Yahveh
carvel
larval
marvel
valval
varvel
carven

mauvin
calver
carver
halver
marver
salver
salvor
taiver
valvar
waiver
calves
canvas
cauves
halves
naeves
naevus
parvis
salvos
tan-vat
jarvey
savvey
fatwa'd
bagwig
earwig
talweg
fatwah
wah-wah
Yahweh
earwax
paxwax
calxes
baryta
satyra
sayyid
haüyne
Kabyle
papyri
banyan
baryon
canyon
karyon
lawyer
△magyar
sawyer
Pamyat
raiyat
gay-you
larynx
ladyfy
razzia
dazzle
razzle
hamzah
matzah
matzoh
banzai
ranzel
Tarzan
jazzer
mahzor

mamzer
panzer
patzer
matzas
matzos
tazzas
matzot
aboard
abraid
ablate
ablaze
abrade
oblate
obtain
abrazo
abdabs
ablaut
oblast
abbacy
obeche
abacus
ibices
abided
ibidem
obtend
abrégé
abseil
abbess
abbeys
obsess
abject
ablest
absent
object
obtect
obtest
obvert
yblent
ybrent
ubiety
oblige
abeigh
obeism
obiism
obsign
ablins
oboist
abelia
abolla
abulia
obelus
obolus
obi-man
Abroma
absorb
abroad
'sblood
oblong
abloom
abvolt

ubique
aborne
sbirri
aboral
Oberon
sbirro
iberis
aburst
uberty
abased
abuser
abated
obital
abator
obiter
abatis
abattu
abound
absurd
obtund
ybound
abduce
abjure
obdure
objure
obtuse
ablush
abouts
abduct
abrupt
ibexes
obeyer
scramb
achage
octane
octave
sclate
sclave
scrape
scraye
sclaff
ack-ack
acrawl
scrawl
scrawm
octavo
éclair
Octans
octant
sceatt
X-craft
occamy
C-cubed
icebox
scabby
acacia
icicle
icecap
acedia
acidic

Words marked △ may be spelled also with a capital letter

acidly
eczema
schema
sclera
accend
screed
accede
achene
ocreae
scheme
sclere
screak
schelm
scream
screen
Access®
access
ackers
uckers
accent
accept
octett
scient
yclept
ochery
screwy
Scogan
scried
accite
acmite
active
scribe
scrike
scrine
scrive
scliff
aching
acting
scaith
tchick
schism
action
schizo
scrimp
schist
script
acuity
acajou
achkan
scilla
scolia
Scylla
scaled
scalae
sculle
ocelli
schlep
ocular
scalar
scaler
Eccles
oculus
△scales
sculls
ocelot
sculpt
scolex
accloy
scampi
scamel
acumen
scummy
iconic
scenic
sconce
scunge
acanth
acinus
econut
acknew
acknow
scanty
scungy
echoic
accord
echoed
ecbole
eclose
ochone
scrobe
T-cloth
o'clock
accoil
school
schorl
scroll
scrowl
scroop
echoer
across
echoes
scrows
T-cross
accost
schout
ectopy
scopae
scyphi
scapus
scopas
ochrea
scarpa
scoria
scarab
sciroc
acarid
scared
scarr'd
accrue
écarté
écurie
J-curve
scarce
scarre
scerne
scorse
scarph
scarth
scorch
octroi
scarer
scorer
acarus
Acorus
scarfs
Scarus
accrew
ochrey
scarey
scarry
scurfy
scurry
scurvy
△scotia
acetic
Scotic
scathe
scythe
scatch
△scotch
scutch
schtik
acetal
acetyl
scutal
scutum
acater
scoter
acates
scatty
Scotty
accuse
acture
△scouse
scruze
scruff
scouth
actual
scruto
scrump
octuor
schuss
Scrubs
acquit
occult
schuit
schuyt
scrunt
occupy
scaury
scowth
ectype
scryde
scryne
scryer
scazon
scuzzy
Eddaic
adland
adward
adnate
ideate
'sdeath
admass
ad-mass
edible
adverb
addend
adread
adhere
advene
addeem
adieus
△advent
advert
adieux
adagio
eddied
admire
advice
advise
sdaine
edging
eddish
oddish
sdeign
addios
addict
adrift
Idoist
oddity
odd-job
addled
idolum
Adamic
odd-man
Adonia
Adonic
Edenic
Adonai
Adonis
adsorb
addoom
adjoin
adnoun
add-ons
adoors
eddoes
odious
adroit
idiocy
adipic
adorer
odds-on
adytum
editor
adduce
adjure
adsuki
adzuki
odeums
adduct
adjust
befana
gelada
Gemara
medaka
petara
retama
terata
zenana
bedaub
decarb
aefald
belaud
demand
herald
petard
regard
relaid
remand
repaid
repand
resaid
retard
reward
wesand
weyard
wezand
aerate
became
bedaze
behave
bejade
belace
belate
bename
berate
betake
beware
cerate
cetane
debase
debate
decade
decane
decare
deface
defame
dégagé
delate
derate
female
Hecate
hexane
legate
let-a-be
menace
menage
ménage
metage
metate
negate
New-Age
new-age
pedate
pelage
pesade
rebate
redate
reface
regale
relate
remade
remake
rename
resale
retake
sebate
sedate
senate
serape
sesame
sewage
tenace
velate
behalf
decaff
rehang
serang
bedash
detach
Pesach
rehash
seraph
teraph
decani
Dewali
dewani
gelati
Nepali
debark
demark
reback
remark
re-mark
repack
becall
befall
bemaul

6 □e□a□m

bewail
derail
detail
devall
jezail
mesail
mezail
recall
rerail
retail
serail
tenail
becalm
cedarn
demain
detain
regain
remain
retain
gelato
legato
melano
pedalo
rebato
decamp
revamp
repair
dedans
kebabs
lemans
megass
metals
repass
bejant
bezant
decant
defast
depart
desalt
hexact
△levant
nefast
pedant
pesant
pezant
recant
recast
redact
repast
secant
sejant
tenant
tewart
zelant
belamy
denary
fegary
legacy
petary
senary

telary
tetany
bezazz
cembra
jerboa
lesbic
terbic
nebbed
redbud
seabed
tebbad
verbid
webbed
feeble
kebbie
pebble
remble
Seabee
semble
bedbug
lebbek
nebbuk
reebok
gerbil
herbal
jerbil
verbal
Berber
herbar
member
lesbos
hen-bit
yes-but
dew-bow
△**bembex**
△bembix
peg-box
red-box
feebly
pebbly
deuced
fenced
peacod
recced
△**deccie**
fescue
rescue
seiche
cercal
mescal
pencel
pencil
tercel
beacon
deacon
leucin
percen
re-echo
tercio
Velcro®

redcap
teacup
de-icer
fencer
mercer
cercus
fences
recces
reccos
seccos
hep-cat
mercat
tercet
beachy
descry
leachy
peachy
reechy
tetchy
vetchy
serdab
geodic
herdic
Wendic
beaded
bedded
bended
gelded
headed
leaded
reeded
seeded
sended
tedded
tended
wedded
weeded
wended
beadle
bendee
cendré
heddle
meddle
need-be
needle
peddle
perdie
perdue
reddle
teddie
tendre
vendee
vendue
red-dog
keddah
zendik
feodal
feudal
sendal
beldam

seldom
deaden
dead-on
head-on
herden
leaden
lead-in
ledden
read-in
redden
reeden
tendon
verdin
head-up
send-up
bedder
bender
deader
deodar
feeder
fender
gelder
gender
header
leader
lender
melder
mender
needer
pedder
reader
redder
reeder
render
seeder
sender
tedder
tender
Veadar
vender
vendor
wedder
weeder
welder
weldor
vendis
geddit
re-edit
verdet
verdit
meadow
deadly
heyday
lewdly
needly
pet-day
verdoy
genera
geneva
Hedera

meseta
nepeta
oedema
pereia
peseta
pesewa
Reseda
réséda
semeia
Seneca
senega
telega
terefa
veleta
zereba
reverb
Aeneid
befeld
behead
beheld
defend
depend
jereed
legend
△nereid
remead
remeid
reread
seméed
tele-ad
bemete
delete
hexene
kebele
lexeme
recede
re-cede
red-eye
remede
renege
retene
revere
secede
sememe
△serene
severe
terete
vegete
venewe
hereof
Benesh
secesh
Tebeth
seseli
Yemeni
bedeck
nebeck
rebeck
zebeck
bedell

befell
cereal
merell
newell
redeal
reheel
△repeal
reseal
resell
retell
reveal
beseem
beteem
redeem
telesm
bemean
Berean
beseen
decern
demean
herein
hereon
Nemean
secern
serein
Verein
△wedeln
Herero
hereto
hetero
teredo
beweep
meneer
meteor
rehear
rêveur
veneer
cereus
△jewess
merels
recess
revels
revers
sevens
behest
bepelt
bereft
bewept
cement
deceit
decent
defeat
defect
deject
dement
desert
detect
detent
detest
devest

Words marked △ may be spelled also with a capital letter

gerent
hereat
△recent
recept
refect
regent
regest
reheat
reject
relent
repeat
repent
reseat
resect
resent
revert
revest
sedent
select
détenu
réseau
teledu
Telegu
celery
hereby
heresy
merely
remedy
revery
severy
tepefy
venery
deific
leafed
reffed
sexfid
neaffe
Newfie
keffel
netful
penful
pepful
deafen
heifer
reefer
telfer
reffos
perfet
Ceefax®
bee-fly
belfry
deafly
deffly
medfly
perfay
wet-fly
zeugma
Belgic
begged
legged

menged
pegged
sedged
wedged
beagle
dengue
feague
gee-gee
league
meagre
reggae
teagle
Teague
veggie
wedgie
beegah
length
beigel
Bengal
tergal
red-gum
tergum
pen-gun
beggar
hedger
kedger
ledger
legger
leiger
lenger
merger
seggar
venger
verger
height
keight
weight
Tengku
geegaw
gewgaw
peshwa
tephra
method
lechwe
lethee
rechie
tee-hee
seahog
bethel
lethal
methyl
seghol
derham
△pelham
pea-hen
sephen
techno
reship
aether
hether

kephir
lecher
menhir
nether
pether
Senhor
tether
wether
△zephyr
Tethys
red-hat
red-hot
tewhit
heehaw
nephew
hegira
hejira
hemina
jemima
medina
Nerita
Peziza
△regina
retina
vesica
zeriba
celiac
heliac
begild
begird
behind
belied
defied
denied
levied
period
rebind
relied
remind
renied
revied
rewind
aedile
bedide
belike
belive
bemire
beside
betide
betime
bêtise
cerise
cerite
debile
decide
décime
defile
define
delice
demise

deride
derive
desine
desire
device
devise
feline
ferine
△levite
mediae
Medise
Medize
nerine
nerite
pelite
penile
petite
rebite
recipe
recite
rediae
refine
regime
régime
regive
relide
reline
relive
remise
repine
reside
resile
re-site
retile
retime
retire
revile
revise
revive
rewire
sedile
Semite
senile
serine
teniae
Venice
venire
venite
belief
relief
besing
feeing
hewing
hexing
seeing
sewing
teaing
teeing
vexing
besigh

ceriph
fetich
fetish
Jewish
nebish
newish
perish
relish
seriph
zenith
△**gemini**
periti
Yezidi
medick
aerial
Belial
denial
fecial
ferial
fetial
genial
medial
menial
mesial
penial
redial
refill
retial
serial
telial
venial
xenial
aecium
cerium
cesium
helium
Medism
medium
merism
Nerium
sepium
sexism
tedium
telium
Vedism
verism
xenium
benign
Delian
design
Fenian
△legion
lesion
△median
mesian
region
resign
re-sign
medico
merino

pepino
megilp
belier
defier
denier
métier
relier
senior
verier
bekiss
cecils
defies
demies
demiss
denims
genius
medius
merils
merits
nelies
regius
relics
remiss
series
vegies
begift
begirt
delict
demist
depict
desist
dewitt
heriot
legist
Nesiot
oecist
relict
remint
resist
sexist
Vedist
verist
Zenist
review
re-view
meninx
bepity
cecity
dewily
eerily
ferity
geminy
lenify
lenity
levity
verify
verily
verity
feijoa
Seljuk

Words marked △ may be spelled also with a capital letter

6 □e□j□y

deejay
dee-jay
beaked
decked
necked
peaked
recked
deckle
heckle
keckle
reekie
reskue
seckle
selkie
Neskhi
seckel
teckel
beckon
jerkin
meeken
merkin
perkin
reckan
reckon
weaken
welkin
beaker
decker
jerker
keeker
leaker
pecker
△seeker
deckos
dekkos
geckos
becket
reskew
bed-key
feckly
kecksy
meekly
weakly
weekly
realia
Aeolic
belled
ceiled
celled
gelled
heeled
keeled
peeled
sealed
veiled
wealk'd
cellae
felloe
jeelie
keelie
mealie
nellie
wellie
jet-lag
peg-leg
redleg
reflag
verlig
Beulah
fellah
health
keblah
sealch
sealgh
wealth
△**bedlam**
beflum
peplum
replum
vellum
berlin
Ceylon
leglan
leglen
leglin
merlin
merlon
replan
Teflon®
tellen
tellin
vellon
dewlap
cellar
dealer
de-blur
feeler
feller
healer
heeler
heller
keeler
Kevlar®
mealer
medlar
pedlar
peeler
reeler
sealer
seller
tellar
teller
vealer
cellos
hellos
jellos
Mejlis
peplos
peplus
realos
△tellus
leglet
Merlot
pellet
reflet
reglet
vellet
△zealot
bellow
△fellow
mellow
reflow
yellow
deflex
reflex
reflux
berley
deploy
fealty
leally
lealty
medley
mellay
o'erlay
really
re-ally
realty
replay
sell-by
dermic
△fehmic
△vehmic
deemed
desmid
gemmed
helmed
hemmed
red-mad
teamed
teemed
gemmae
hermae
meemie
sepmag
dermal
vermal
vermil
desman
fenman
gemman
gemmen
△german
germen
germin
hetman
leg-man
merman
penman
red-man
seaman
sermon
tegmen
vermin
yeoman
yeomen
yes-man
beamer
reamer
seamer
seemer
teamer
teemer
termer
termor
dermis
Geomys
Hermes
Jeames
kermes
kermis
lemmas
Termes
△vermes
vermis
besmut
cermet
fewmet
helmet
hermit
pelmet
permit
semmit
Tex-Mex
seemly
termly
hernia
neb-neb
pen-nib
fennec
neanic
kenned
leaned
Leonid
penned
Pernod®
Seanad
veined
beanie
meanie
meinie
peenge
pennae
séance
beenah
fennel
gennel
kennel
kernel
pennal
regnal
ternal
vennel
vernal
weanel
hennin
Memnon
pennon
rennin
lean-to
deaner
henner
keener
kenner
penner
seiner
tenner
weaner
beanos
feints
segnos
tennis
bennet
ben-nut
dennet
gennet
jennet
kennet
Nernst
peanut
peinct
rennet
sennet
sennit
begnaw
dernly
keenly
leanly
meanly
meiney
teensy
teenty
fedora
femora
hebona
Pecora
pelota
redowa
remora
Señora
serosa
xeroma
desorb
resorb
heroic
behold
△beyond
devoid
keloid
new-old
peloid
record
reload
remoud
resold
retold
reword
second
zeroed
aerobe
become
before
begone
behote
behove
Belone
belove
cenote
decode
decoke
delope
démodé
demote
denote
depone
depose
devote
dévote
genome
hexose
ketone
ketose
merome
metope
perone
peyote
rebore
recode
redone
remote
remove
repone
repose
resole
revoke
rezone
setose
veloce
venose
behoof
let-off
re-roof
set-off
tee-off
belong
debosh
zeroth
neroli
bemock
betook
retook

Words marked △ may be spelled also with a capital letter

rework
befool
befoul
behowl
bemoil
ben-oil
betoil
defoul
reboil
recoil
retool
befoam
deform
megohm
reform
re-form
bemoan
besoin
ceroon
dehorn
heroin
heroon
reborn
recoin
rejoin
renown
seroon
zeloso
recoup
bezoar
detour
devoir
devour
memoir
retour
tenour
velour
betoss
cerous
deboss
demons
heroes
kebobs
Merops
serous
venous
vetoes
besort
decoct
dégoût
dehort
deport
detort
devout
get-out
let-out
refoot
report
repost
resort
retort
revolt
set-out
betony
felony
gelosy
gemony
lemony
melody
memory
pelory
leipoa
besped
helped
keypad
leaped
lepped
neaped
peapod
repped
deepie
kelpie
kemple
kewpie
people
semple
sempre
teepee
△temple
weepie
sea-pig
tempeh
peepul
pen-pal
bedpan
deepen
hempen
hen-pen
reopen
tenpin
weapon
beeper
helper
Hesper
keeper
△kelper
kemper
Keuper
leaper
peeper
pepper
reaper
semper
temper
△vesper
weeper
yelper
delphs
herpes
tempos
bespat
bespit
bespot
despot
keppit
sexpot
teapot
deeply
teapoy
jerque
△**kerria**
ferric
metric
tenrec
bedrid
betrod
feared
geared
Hebrid
meered
metred
retrod
seared
tetrad
beurre
beurré
dearie
decree
degree
féerie
George
hearie
hearse
Leerie
pearce
peerie
retree
reurge
searce
serrae
terrae
lea-rig
dearth
hearth
search
bedral
ferrel
neural
petrel
petrol
retral
tetryl
verrel
betrim
megrim
retrim
feerin
hen-run
Herren
neuron
perron
serran
Terran
weirdo
bedrop
beer-up
rewrap
bearer
hearer
jeerer
nearer
rearer
tearer
△terror
wearer
cerris
debris
débris
degras
derris
hearts
henrys
métros
nebris
repros
retros
serras
Sèvres
terras
Weirds
berret
ferret
learnt
pearst
regret
searat
secret
terret
territ
decrew
Hebrew
redraw
betray
bewray
dearly
defray
hearsy
hearty
near-by
nearly
pearly
rearly
verrey
yearly
geisha
felsic
Persic
hersed
jessed
new-sad
seised
sensed
versed
heaste
△jessie
keksye
lessee
measle
pensée
persue
mensch
jet-ski
meishi
pe-tsai
deasil
mensal
pensel
pensil
teasel
versal
vessel
weasel
jetsam
jetsom
pensum
semsem
sensum
geason
jetson
kelson
lessen
lesson
messan
nelson
peason
pepsin
person
reason
season
seisin
telson
tenson
ven'son
versin
cessio
mess-up
censer
censor
cesser
geyser
keasar
leaser
lesser
lessor
Mensur
sensor
teaser
tensor
verser
census
lenses
menses
mewses
senses
sepses
sepsis
versos
versus
yesses
bed-sit
eel-set
pet-sit
verset
leasow
seesaw
feisty
△jersey
kersey
measly
Mersey
reasty
reesty
yeasty
△**bertha**
centra
Dectra®
△kentia
tertia
Celtic
gestic
hectic
Keltic
lentic
Lettic
pectic
peptic
septic
belted
bestad
bested
bestud
betted
debted
heated
heptad
jetted
letted
melted
netted
pentad
petted
retted
seated
teated
tented
vented
vested
vetted
wetted
△**beetle**

berthe
centre
certie
debtee
fettle
feutre
gentle
jestee
keltie
kettle
leetle
leftie
lettre
meathe
mentee
mestee
mettle
nestle
nettle
pestle
pettle
seethe
settee
settle
tee-tee
teethe
tentie
testee
ventre
vertue
Westie
cestui
cental
dental
dentel
dentil
festal
lentil
meatal
mental
Pentel®
pentel
rectal
rental
septal
ventil
△vestal
centum
mentum
rectum
restem
septum
tectum
beaten
dentin
deuton
jetton
lectin
△lenten
lepton
melton
neaten
nekton
newton
pecten
pectin
seiten
seston
sextan
sexton
teston
Teuton
weeten
△**gentoo**
beat-up
peg-top
pent-up
redtop
beater
belter
bestar
bestir
better
bettor
center
debtor
dexter
felter
fester
fetter
fewter
getter
heater
hector
jester
kelter
lector
lentor
letter
mentor
nectar
nester
Nestor
neuter
pelter
pester
petter
pewter
rector
reiter
renter
rester
seater
sector
setter
teeter
tenter
tester
tetter
vector
venter
welter
wester
yester
zester
centos
certes
cestos
cestus
depths
gentes
lentos
meatus
mentos
rectos
rectus
rentes
set-tos
set-to's
testes
testis
vestas
dectet
septet
sestet
sextet
bestow
dentex
meat-ax
Semtex®
tettix
vertex
centry
deathy
deftly
featly
gently
gentry
heathy
meetly
neatly
nettly
nextly
peltry
pertly
sentry
vestry
beluga
Betula
cedula
cesura
fecula
△ferula
△medusa
mezuza
nebula
regula
remuda
tegula
veduta
benumb
defus'd
fecund
gerund
refund
re-fund
retund
secund
segued
aemule
Beaune
bemuse
cerule
ceruse
cesure
deduce
defuse
defuze
delude
deluge
demure
denude
depute
detune
ferule
heaume
jejune
legume
nebule
nebulé
peruke
peruse
rebuke
recule
recure
recuse
reduce
refuge
refuse
refute
relume
repure
repute
resume
résumé
retune
retuse
secure
seduce
setule
tenure
vedute
velure
venule
bepuff
rebuff
returf
bebung
bedung
besung
rehung
Senusi
beduck
begunk
debunk
becurl
refuel
sequel
sexual
△**beduin**
beguin
béguin
repugn
return
re-turn
sequin
Regulo®
regulo
tenuto
repulp
femurs
lemurs
serums
tenues
tenuis
bedust
deduct
degust
Jesuit
penult
reduit
reluct
requit
result
Telugu
beauty
decury
deputy
nebuly
penury
rebury
pelvic
cervid
fervid
heaved
leaved
nerved
peeved
reeved
revved
weaved
keavie
oeuvre
renvoi
devvel
nerval
serval
vervel
weevil
△**heaven**
Hesvan
△kelvin
leaven
verven
beaver
delver
heaver
leaver
nerver
peever
reaver
reiver
server
weaver
weever
beeves
delves
heaves
leaves
nerves
pelves
pelvis
selvas
selves
velvet
vervet
cervix
lenvoy
peavey
renvoy
red-wud
deawie
peewee
wee-wee
meawes
peewit
key-way
leeway
seaway
deixis
bedyed
bedyde
desyne
menyie
re-type
Wemyss
Aegypt
fezzed
bezzle
heezie
teazle
benzal
benzil
benzol
benzyl
meazel
teazel
seizin
tenzon
weazen

Words marked △ may be spelled also with a capital letter

geezer
seizer
fezzes
mezzos
afeard
afraid
aflame
efface
affair
off-air
offcut
off-day
afield
offend
effere
effete
afresh
affear
affeer
effeir
afters
affect
afreet
effect
eftest
△**afghan**
affied
affine
office
effing
offing
offish
affirm
effigy
off-job
off-key
afflux
efflux
afford
afloat
afront
effort
Eftpos
offput
affrap
affret
affray
effray
offset
effuse
Q-fever
afawld
affyde
Aglaia
iguana
agname
agnate
O-grade
agnail
ignaro

aghast
egg-box
eggcup
Agadic
Agadah
agreed
agrégé
agleam
egress
ogress
eggery
agogic
agnise
agnize
agrise
agrize
aguise
aguize
ignite
ageing
agoing
a-going
ogling
aguish
ogrish
ageism
egoism
Ugrian
ngaios
ageist
egoist
egoity
uglify
uglily
eggler
egally
agamic
ogamic
agamid
agenda
mganga
agonic
egence
eggnog
Ngunis
agency
egency
age-old
ogdoad
ignore
ugsome
T-group
ignomy
agapae
Egeria
agaric
agorot
egesta
kgotla
agouta

agouti
agouty
ogival
agryze
agazed
choana
ohmage
phrase
sheave
theave
thrave
wheare
thrang
sheath
thrash
chiack
chyack
shrank
thwack
thrall
chiasm
thrawn
cheapo
chiaus
shears
she-ass
thraws
'sheart
thwart
cheapy
phrasy
sheafy
shoaly
phobia
phobic
Ghebre
thible
shibah
chibol
Theban
Gheber
ghubar
Thebes
Shebat
△thibet
chubby
shabby
cha-cha
chacma
chicha
Thecla
chicle
phocae
thecae
chichi
chi-chi
shtchi
thecal
chicon
chocho

chocko
shacko
thicko
whacko
chucks
phocas
shucks
checky
chicly
choccy
thicky
whacky
khodja
Chadic
rhodic
chided
shaded
rhodie
shaduf
whidah
whydah
chadar
chador
chider
shoder
Rhodes
shades
shadow
chuddy
shoddy
chaeta
phaeic
chield
shield
shrewd
thread
three-D
cheese
pheere
pheese
pheeze
△phoebe
thieve
threne
wheeze
thresh
wheech
wheesh
phreak
shreek
shreik
shtetl
phlegm
Phleum
sheepo
threap
threep
cheers
sheers
sheets

wheels
shiest
shyest
threat
cheeky
cheery
cheesy
△sheeny
sheepy
sheety
wheely
wheezy
shufti
chafer
shofar
chafts
chuffy
shifty
shufty
whiffy
bhagee
chigoe
chigre
chagan
shogun
thuggo
shaggy
Shaiva
sheila
chaîné
chaise
choice
Shiite
shrike
shrine
shrive
theine
thrice
thrive
thyine
shying
shaikh
sheikh
shyish
shriek
shrink
shtick
shrill
thrill
chrism
Shiism
thairm
theism
shairn
shrimp
chains
theirs
thrips
Christ
shrift

theist
thrift
thrist
bhajee
bhajan
shojis
chakra
chokra
chukka
Shakta
shiksa
choked
shaked
shikse
bhakti
chokri
Shakti
shekel
shaken
chikor
choker
chukar
chukor
shaker
shikar
shakos
chokey
Khalka
Khalsa
Shelta
Thalia
thulia
cholic
whelk'd
chelae
childe
chylde
shelve
khalif
chilli
phalli
shalli
thalli
tholoi
khilim
Philem
phylum
shalom
sholom
whilom
chalan
phyllo
choler
thaler
whaler
△**pholas**
tholos
tholus
whiles
chalet

6 □h□l□y

khalat
khilat
shalot
whilst
chalky
chilly
shelfy
shelly
shelty
shelvy
whally
whelky
whilly
wholly
ahimsa
rhumba
shamba
chemic
thymic
rhymed
shamed
themed
rhombi
thymol
shaman
whammo
chimer
rhymer
shamer
chimes
shamus
Themis
thymus
chammy
chemmy
chummy
shammy
shamoy
shimmy
thumby
whammy
whimmy
whimsy
khanga
thanna
phenic
phonic
shined
chance
change
'change
△chinee
shinne
thence
whence
whinge
chinch
thanah
bhindi
phenol
phenyl
phonal
rhinal
khanum
phenom
phonon
thin'un
Shinto
chenar
chinar
phoner
shiner
thenar
whiner
chinks
chinos
rhinos
thanks
things
whenas
chenet
why-not
nhandu
chenix
chancy
chanty
△chinky
chunky
phoney
shandy
shanny
shanty
shindy
shinny
shinty
shonky
thingy
thinly
whinny
chintz
chroma
△shroud
shrowd
choose
chrome
shoole
△shrove
throne
throve
throwe
shroff
throng
whoosh
dhooti
she-oak
shlock
shmock
shtook
phloem
shtoom
shoo-in
thrown
chromo
shmoes
throes
whoops
throat
choosy
dhooly
phooey
theory
chapka
shaped
chypre
rhaphe
chapel
chopin
shapen
shippo
shaper
chappy
chippy
choppy
shoppy
whippy
cheque
chequy
charka
charta
chorda
chorea
choria
dharma
dharna
dhurra
khurta
△sharia
△sheria
△sherpa
shirra
Theria
thoria
cherub
choric
chared
shared
ahorse
charge
chargé
chirre
choree
thorpe
thyrse
wharve
kharif
sharif
sherif
△church
Thorah
gharri
thyrsi
bharal
chiral
choral
thiram
Charon
Chiron
△sharon
shoran
thoron
△chi-rho
gherao
cherup
sharer
shorer
charas
Charis
charms
charts
chorus
pharos
shares
sharps
Shires
shorts
therms
wharfs
Bharat
charet
thirst
thorax
charry
cherry
cherty
chirpy
gharry
sharny
sherry
shirty
shorty
thirty
thorny
wherry
whirly
whirry
Shiraz
Phasma
phasic
physic
Chasid
phased
chasse
chassé
chaste
ghesse
bhisti
chesil
chisel
chosen
Xhosan
physio
chaser
phases
phasis
△rhesus
theses
thesis
whisht
chasmy
chesty
ghosty
phossy
whisky
chatta
whatna
phatic
photic
rhotic
thetic
shited
whited
shotte
chetah
thatch
thetch
chatti
chital
rhythm
chaton
chitin
chiton
photon
phyton
rhyton
shut-in
whaten
whiten
ghetto
whatso
rhetor
photos
whites
chatty
chitty
shitty
△whitey
should
chaufe
chouse
chauff
chough
sheuch
sheugh
shough
though
thrush
wheugh
shmuck
shrunk
shtuck
shtumm
rheums
chaunt
thrust
rheumy
shaved
chèvre
shavie
shivah
shovel
thivel
cheven
chevin
shaven
shivoo
shaver
shiver
shover
shives
chevet
chivvy
shewed
showed
thewed
chewie
chowri
shewel
thowel
chewer
shower
thawer
thewes
chewet
chowry
rhexis
they're
they've
they'll
wheyey
rhizic
phizog
ghazal
ghazel
Bimana
cicada
cicala
gitana
piñata
piraña
piraya
Pitaka
pitara
sifaka
tinaja
vihara
vimana
bicarb
ligand
△lizard
ribald

Words marked △ may be spelled also with a capital letter

riband
ribaud
rizard
visaed
vizard
wisard
wizard
binate
dilate
finale
fixate
hidage
hirage
kinase
libate
ligase
ligate
linage
lipase
micate
mid-age
milage
mirage
pipage
pirate
rivage
silage
silane
tirade
tisane
vidame
visage
vivace
pilaff
△siwash
Bihari
Divali
Diwali
miladi
eirack
hijack
limail
air-arm
disarm
misaim
dizain
sixain
gitano
mikado
virago
midair
finals
vitals
aidant
dicast
dikast
libant
bigamy
binary
digamy
Hilary
litany
milady
piracy
vicary
vivary
bizazz
pizazz
limbec
limbic
niobic
air-bed
big-bud
dibbed
disbud
fibbed
gibbed
jibbed
limbed
nibbed
nimbed
pig-bed
ribbed
diable
dibble
dimble
fimble
jirble
kibble
liable
nibble
nimble
timbre
viable
wimble
bin-bag
kit-bag
Liebig
jibbah
kirbeh
gimbal
timbal
gibbon
Lisbon
ribbon
bibber
dibber
disbar
fibber
gibber
jibber
libber
limber
mimbar
minbar
timber
Air-bus®
air-bus
bilbos
bimbos
△limbos
Limbus
nimbus
timbós
gibbet
tidbit
titbit
nimbly
Riccia
kincob
diacid
minced
viscid
zinced
circle
fiacre
fitché
miscue
kimchi
litchi
discal
fiscal
tincal
nincom
nincum
sitcom
△viscum
niacin
oilcan
piecen
siccan
viscin
wiccan
zircon
gilcup
hiccup
oil-cup
air-car
circar
kit-car
mincer
piecer
pincer
siccar
sircar
wincer
circus
ciscos
discos
△discus
pieces
Pisces
viscus
zincos
gib-cat
Kit-Cat
kit-cat
Tib-cat
tipcat
bitchy
fitchy
hitchy
pitchy
titchy
wincey
witchy
zincky
siddha
windac
gilded
girded
kidded
lidded
minded
misdid
ridded
rinded
tinded
winded
birdie
diddle
dièdre
dildoe
dindle
fiddle
girdle
kiddle
kindle
△middle
piddle
riddle
tiddle
widdle
windle
pie-dog
siddhi
Sindhi
dik-dik
Mindel
tindal
diadem
dirdam
dirdum
△wisdom
bidden
Diodon
gilden
hidden
linden
midden
milden
ridden
sindon
Hindoo
giddap
giddup
wind-up
bidder
binder
birder
cinder
didder
finder
gilder
girder
hidder
hinder
kidder
kinder
lieder
minder
pinder
ridder
siddur
sirdar
tinder
wilder
winder
dildos
windas
mildew
△window
air-dry
fiddly
kindly
midday
mildly
six-day
tiddly
vildly
wildly
cinema
kinema
pineta
tineid
viséed
bireme
misère
Nicene
picene
silene
kilerg
△sileni
ripeck
cineol
eisell
lineal
pineal
tineal
pileum
Gideon
live-in
pigeon
side-on
wigeon
wivern
△cicero
libero
line-up
pile-up
diseur
fineer
linear
biceps
citess
divers
Fifers
oilers
pileus
videos
vireos
vivers
bident
bisect
digest
direct
divert
divest
eident
piment
rident
silent
Tibert
virent
wisent
cicely
cidery
fikery
finely
finery
likely
lively
livery
misery
nicely
nicety
ninety
nitery
oilery
pinery
rifely
ripely
rivery
sinewy
tigery
tilery
timely
titely
vilely
vinery
vively
widely
wifely
winery
wisely
miffed
misfed
piaffe
piffle
riffle

6 □i□f□l

siffle
aidful
bibful
dinful
fitful
sinful
tinful
wilful
biffin
tiffin
differ
liefer
niffer
pilfer
titfer
filfot
misfit
kid-fox
lingua
digged
dinged
figged
gigged
hinged
jigged
minged
pigged
ridged
rigged
ringed
singed
tigged
wigged
winged
zigged
biggie
bingle
ciggie
dingle
gidgee
giggle
gilgie
gingle
higgle
jiggle
jilgie
jingle
kidgie
kingle
lingle
mingle
niggle
piggie
pingle
single
tingle
widgie
wiggle
fisgig
fizgig

△**binghi**
gilgai
nilgai
gingal
jingal
lingel
ridgel
ridgil
zingel
lingam
air-gun
biggin
biogen
fingan
liggen
mingin
pidgin
piggin
six-gun
△virgin
gingko
airgap
bigger
binger
digger
dinger
finger
ginger
jigger
lidger
lieger
ligger
linger
nigger
Pinger®
pinger
ridger
rigger
ringer
sieger
singer
virger
winger
zinger
air-gas
bilges
bingos
biogas
dinges
dingus
oil-gas
pingos
fidget
giggit
lingot
midget
mid-gut
nidget
widget
witgat

nilgau
dingey
dinghy
giggly
jiggly
jingly
kingly
niggly
singly
tingly
wiggly
lithia
Mishna
Mithra
lithic
dished
niched
tithed
kishke
lichee
eighth
highth
mishmi
Tishri
withal
dirham
dirhem
lichen
nigh-on
richen
siphon
sithen
within
righto
bishop
high-up
hip-hop
mishap
cipher
cither
dither
either
fisher
△higher
hither
lither
micher
mither
nicher
sigher
tither
wisher
wither
zither
eights
fishes
lights
lithos
nights
pithos

riches
rights
sithes
tights
wishes
mishit
with-it
Vishnu
eighty
highly
linhay
mighty
nighly
nighty
richly
minima
silica
lilied
pitied
tidied
cilice
dirige
divide
divine
finite
fixive
liaise
lipide
Milice
picine
pinite
ribibe
simile
tibiae
virile
visile
visite
visive
aiding
ailing
airing
biding
biking
biting
dicing
diving
filing
fining
firing
fixing
giving
hiding
hieing
hiring
kiting
liking
liming
lining
living
mining

niding
pieing
piling
piping
△riding
rising
siding
sizing
tiling
timing
tiring
△viking
wiping
wiring
Fifish
fikish
finish
minish
nicish
widish
bikini
miriti
tisick
filial
finial
simial
tibial
bivium
cilium
civism
Lilium
minium
oidium
sizism
bilian
minion
pinion
simian
Sirian
△titian
virion
vision
aikido
libido
virino
cimier
pitier
tinier
visier
vizier
wizier
civics
limits
Sirius
tibias
tinies
oikist
qiviut
sizist
timist

vibist
milieu
airily
citify
dimity
fixity
jiminy
minify
nidify
oilily
tidily
tinily
vilify
vivify
wilily
wirily
kibitz
gidjee
jigjig
jig-jig
jig-jog
jimjam
finjan
ninjas
picked
pinked
ricked
ticked
wicked
zinked
birkie
dickie
fickle
kie-kie
kinkle
mickle
pickle
pinkie
rickle
sickie
sickle
silkie
tickle
tinkle
winkle
Nikkei
nickel
dinkum
nickum
birken
firkin
girkin
kirkin'
libken
milken
misken
pipkin
sicken
silken
simkin

Words marked △ may be spelled also with a capital letter

6 □i□p□r

siskin
ticken
wicken
ginkgo
dikkop
kick-up
link-up
pick-up
bicker
bilker
dicker
jinker
kicker
licker
linker
milker
nickar
nicker
picker
ricker
risker
sicker
sinker
sirkar
ticker
tinker
wicker
winker
yicker
yikker
pinkos
picket
ticket
wicket
wisket
dickey
dickty
hickey
△mickey
miskey
rickly
sickly
tickey
tickly
tinkly
Lib-Lab
sialic
aisled
billed
dialed
hilled
milled
misled
nilled
nirled
titled
willed
billie
diploe
gillie
girlie
nirlie
vielle
willie
dialog
mid-leg
pin-leg
kiblah
zillah
nielli
billon
diplon
fill-in
Hielan'
riglin
rivlin
sialon
tiglon
villan
violin
billy-o
niello
Rialto
fillip
birler
filler
Hitler
killer
miller
pillar
rifler
siller
tiller
titler
villar
violer
willer
killas
titles
villus
aiglet
billet
diglot
fillet
firlot
giblet
giglet
giglot
gillet
gimlet
jillet
kidlet
killut
millet
nirlit
oillet
piglet
piolet
riblet
rillet
violet
willet
Kisleu
pillau
Kislev
billow
pillow
willow
diplex
bieldy
mislay
wieldy
willey
mia-mia
filmic
Micmac
dimmed
nimmed
rimmed
diamyl
△dismal
gimmal
hiemal
airman
binman
disman
firman
gigman
hit-man
Kirman
oilman
pieman
pig-man
pin-man
pitman
'simmon
tinman
miombo
bitmap
bismar
dimmer
firmer
gimmer
gimmor
kimmer
limmer
nimmer
simmer
Zimmer®
zimmer
gimmes
gismos
gizmos
litmus
kismet
dismay
firmly
sienna
zinnia
bionic
finnac
Finnic
picnic
pionic
binned
dinned
finned
ginned
nid-nod
pinned
pioned
sinned
tinned
dinnle
fiancé
girnie
jinnee
minnie
nix-nie
pinnae
pinnie
pirnie
tinnie
wienie
winnle
nig-nog
Dipnoi
dirndl
ginnel
girnel
lienal
lionel
signal
simnel
lignum
finnan
lignin
mignon
kidnap
dinner
finner
ginner
girner
limner
pinner
pioner
signer
△signor
sinner
tinner
Wiener
winner
pianos
viands
dip-net
linnet
lionet
oilnut
pignut
pinnet
pirnit
signet
sinnet
minnow
winnow
jitney
kidney
linney
lionly
pioney
riancy
aikona
eidola
kia-ora
lipoma
mimosa
bifold
lipoid
milord
siloed
viroid
bizone
citole
dipole
ditone
filose
kinone
Nilote
Nivôse
picoté
pilose
pinole
ribose
rimose
virose
mid-off
rip-off
tip-off
zip-off
qigong
simorg
kibosh
tifosi
titoki
nim-oil
rigoll
til-oil
biform
simoom
Aizoon
bicorn
disown
Minoan
simoon
gigolo
kimono
tifoso
vigoro
giaour
rigour
vigour
didoes
limous
minors
Nilots
pilous
rimous
timous
tiroes
vinous
virous
dim-out
fit-out
rig-out
bijoux
dipody
simony
biopic
hippic
dipped
hipped
hispid
limpid
lipped
nipped
pipped
ripped
sipped
tipped
zipped
dimple
disple
fipple
hippie
hirple
lippie
Nippie
nipple
pimple
ripple
simple
sipple
tipple
wimple
yippee
simpai
dispel
kirpan
lippen
Nippon
oil-pan
pigpen
pippin
Rippon
tiepin
wippen
diaper
diapir
△dipper
kipper

Words marked △ may be spelled also with a capital letter

6 □i□p□s

lisper
nipper
ripper
simper
sipper
tipper
yipper
zipper
cippus
gippos
hippos
hippus
limpet
pit-pat
sippet
tinpot
tippet
piupiu
Tippex
Tipp-Ex®
biopsy
dimply
gilpey
jimply
limply
pimply
ripply
simply
bisque
cinque
cirque
risque
risqué
sierra
midrib
mihrab
citric
nitric
picric
ric-rac
vitric
fibred
kinred
Nimrod
pierid
sirred
tiara'd
tiered
tierod
cierge
fierce
kierie
lierne
pierce
sirree
tierce
tiercé
ti-tree
diarch
hijrah

sirrah
fibril
mitral
nitryl
Vibram®
citrin
citron
fibrin
fiorin
micron
mikron
vibrio
riprap
rip-rap
sitrep
mirror
cirrus
△citrus
fibros
micros
miurus
Pieris
vivres
pierst
pig-rat
tirrit
fin-ray
air-sea
fiesta
miasma
mid-sea
siesta
vizsla
air-sac
biased
pissed
birsle
fissle
hirsle
kiss-me
missee
tissue
kirsch
kitsch
diesel
hirsel
kissel
missal
missel
tinsel
jissom
lissom
bisson
gipsen
Nissen
fiasco
finsko
giusto
sissoo
piss-up

kisser
rinser
cissus
dieses
diesis
dipsas
dipsos
lisses
miasms
miosis
misses
missis
missus
nisses
misset
jigsaw
pit-saw
rip-saw
linsey
mid-sky
milsey
mimsey
missay
pigsny
pigsty
tinsey
winsey
sistra
wiltja
biotic
cistic
fistic
miotic
tic-tac
tietac
bitted
cisted
ditted
fitted
gifted
kilted
listed
pioted
pitted
tilted
tinted
vista'd
witted
bistre
bittie
filtre
histie
kiltie
kirtle
kittle
lintie
little
mistle
pintle
tiptoe

tittle
virtue
vittae
vittle
wintle
distal
distil
kittul
lintel
listel
pistil
pistol
rictal
vistal
wittol
diatom
dictum
victim
biotin
bitten
kitten
listen
litten
mitten
piston
pitten
Wilton
bistro
tiptop
tittup
ziptop
bister
bitter
bittor
bittur
dieter
fictor
filter
fitter
hitter
jitter
kilter
lictor
lifter
linter
lister
litter
milter
minter
△mister
nipter
pitter
qintar
rioter
ritter
sifter
sinter
sister
sittar
sitter

tilter
tinter
titter
viator
victor
winter
witter
cistus
dittos
hiatus
pintos
rictus
vistos
diktat
dittit
dittay
filthy
kittly
riotry
vintry
wintry
wistly
cicuta
fibula
ligula
pilula
situla
tipula
vicuña
liquid
dilute
disuse
figure
fixure
ligule
ligure
minute
misuse
pilule
titule
Vimule®
simurg
kiaugh
pituri
lifull
ritual
vidual
visual
Siouan
liquor
lituus
fiaunt
minuet
misust
piquet
△kikuyu
titupy
silvae
mizvah
silvan

liever
riever
silver
Milvus
silvas
bigwig
tie-wig
wigwag
wigwam
viewer
tiswas
tizwas
dimwit
nitwit
airway
midway
viewly
jinxed
biaxal
diaxon
dioxan
dioxin
pinxit
Libyan
minyan
Pinyin
cityfy
piazza
fizzed
fizzle
mizzle
pizzle
sizzle
vizzie
zigzag
fizzen
gizzen
mizzen
fizzer
rizzar
rizzer
rizzor
diazos
mizzly
Ojibwa
djebel
ejecta
ujamaa
djinni
ajowan
sklate
skeary
skibob
akedah
skidoo
Ski-doo®
ekuele
skreen
sklent
skeely

Words marked △ may be spelled also with a capital letter

skeery
skliff
skiing
skying
skaith
skeigh
skyish
skrimp
skolia
△**skylab**
skelum
skills
skelly
skilly
skolly
skyman
akimbo
skimpy
skinny
skoosh
okapis
skippy
skarth
skerry
skurry
sketch
skater
skates
skrump
skivie
skiver
skivvy
skewed
skewer
skyway
okayed
ukiyo-e
skryer
albata
alpaca
cloaca
Alcaic
Altaic
algate
alkane
alnage
cleave
eluate
fluate
gleave
old-age
oleate
please
sleave
sleaze
Sloane
ullage
ulnare
bleach
ollamh
pleach
Alhagi
alkali
△**almain**
Altair
always
eluant
olfact
pliant
Albany
Almany
bleaky
bleary
floaty
gleamy
sleazy
globed
global
globin
clubby
flabby
glibly
globby
Old-Boy
old-boy
plebby
slabby
slobby
slubby
placed
placid
cleché
cliché
cloche
flèche
plicae
eltchi
flocci
glycol
plical
flacon
glycin
ulicon
Alecto
placer
slicer
blacks
blocks
flicks
flocks
glacis
ilices
slacks
elicit
placet
placit
blocky
clucky
plucky
Elodea
alidad
bladed
sleded
slided
bludge
bludie
fledge
gledge
kludge
pledge
sledge
sludge
aludel
eluder
glider
slider
blades
all-day
cloddy
clodly
fledgy
gladly
sludgy
alteza
alkene
allege
allele
cleeve
fleece
sleeve
fleech
sleech
aldern
alpeen
altern
albedo
alleys
Elaeis
pliers
albeit
albert
client
eldest
eluent
fluent
oldest
sliest
slyest
almery
bluely
bluesy
fleecy
gleety
sleeky
sleepy
sleety
sleezy
olefin
cliffy
clifty
fluffy
pluffy
alogia
alegge
blague
plague
flugel
flügel
plagal
flagon
plug-in
slogan
alegar
alight
blight
elegit
flight
ill-got
plight
slight
'slight
bluggy
claggy
cloggy
flaggy
plaguy
slaggy
althea
all-hid
elchee
Elohim
elshin
old-hat
ultima
allied
illiad
Pleiad
albite
Aldine
allice
△alpine
alsike
alvine
blaise
blaize
glaive
gloire
illipe
illite
plaice
sluice
bluing
elding
flying
gluing
plying
slairg
ulling
bluish
elfish
elvish
gluish
oldish
sleigh
slyish
Alpini
allium
Albion
eloign
ultion
albino
Alpino
ultimo
allies
glaiks
△plains
plaint
bluidy
glairy
ploidy
sluicy
sloken
ulikon
flakes
flukey
alalia
slalom
alumna
blamed
flamed
plumed
flambé
alumni
flamen
fly-man
old-man
clamor
glamor
clumps
glumps
slimes
flemit
climax
blimey
clammy
clumpy
clumsy
flimsy
glumly
glumpy
plummy
plumpy
slimly
slimsy
slummy
slumpy
planta
clinic
clonic
plongd
blende
blonde
blonde®
blunge
elance
flange
flense
glance
plonge
plunge
blanch
blench
clench
clinch
clunch
elench
flanch
flench
flinch
planch
plinth
clonal
plenum
blanco
planar
planer
blinis
blinks
clints
clonus
Elanus
glands
llanos
Olenus
slangs
elanet
planet
blanky
blenny
clingy
flinty
flunky
plenty
plonky
slangy
slinky
blintz
glioma
algoid
almond
alcove
aldose
ill-off
klooch
sloosh
alsoon
allons
almous
Cloots
ellops

Words marked △ may be spelled also with a capital letter

6 □l□o□t

all-out
almost
bloody
bloomy
floosy
floozy
gloomy
gloopy
sloomy
Clupea
aliped
elapse
clip-on
slip-on
slap-up
slip-up
eloper
klepht
flappy
floppy
slippy
sloppy
claque
clique
cloqué
plaque
cliquy
gloria
cleric
all-red
florid
alerce
florae
floral
plural
alarum
aldrin
florin
alarms
claros
clarts
flares
floras
Glires
claret
floret
clarty
clergy
flirty
flurry
slurry
alisma
clusia
glossa
plasma
closed
plused
plaste
plissé
△flysch

closer
flaser
clasts
pluses
ulosis
closet
blashy
classy
flashy
fleshy
flisky
flossy
flushy
glassy
glossy
plashy
plushy
sloshy
slushy
elytra
clitic
alated
fluted
plated
slated
blithe
clothe
blotch
clatch
clutch
fletch
flitch
glitch
slatch
glutei
flotel
gluten
platan
platen
pluton
blotto
Clotho
elater
elutor
fluter
plater
slater
ulster
cloths
flatus
plates
ulitis
zlotys
blotty
clotty
flatly
glitzy
plotty
pleura
allude

allure
almuce
blouse
clause
flaune
flouse
illude
illume
ill-use
cleuch
cleugh
clough
floush
pleuch
pleugh
△plough
sleuth
slouch
slough
illupi
albugo
albums
flaunt
cloudy
fleury
floury
glaury
clivia
Slavic
gloved
slived
clavie
Slovak
O-level
Y-level
alevin
cloven
eleven
elevon
flavin
sliven
sloven
claver
clever
clover
flavor
glover
△oliver
plover
slaver
sliver
claves
clavis
clevis
cloves
gloves
olivet
slavey
blowed
clawed

flawed
flewed
flowed
slewed
blowie
blowse
blowze
flow-on
blow-up
slow-up
blower
flower
glower
blowsy
blowzy
flyway
slowly
alexia
alexic
alexin
flaxen
△klaxon
elixir
flexor
plexor
ilexes
plexus
clayed
cloyed
flayed
gleyed
played
slayed
alkyne
aliyah
E-layer
flayer
player
slayer
clayey
blazed
glazed
blazon
glazen
blazer
glazer
blazes
impala
ambage
embace
embale
embase
empale
empare
imbase
immane
impale
impave
smeath
embank

embark
imbark
immask
impark
embail
emball
emparl
imparl
embalm
impawn
impair
empart
impact
impart
umlaut
smeary
amebic
imidic
smudge
Amidol®
emydes
amidst
amadou
smiddy
smudgy
amoeba
impend
ampere
ampère
impede
emmesh
immesh
smeech
smeeth
embers
ambery
empery
umbery
smegma
émigré
amigos
imagos
smight
smoggy
smugly
amrita
△empire
imbibe
smoile
umpire
impish
omnium
amnion
Emmies
impies
omnify
smoked
smoker
smokos
amelia

emblic
emulge
smalti
amylum
emblem
smalto
ambler
smiler
smalls
umbles
amulet
omelet
smilet
implex
smilax
employ
smalmy
smelly
amomum
amtman
amenta
omenta
omened
amende
emunge
amends
amoove
emmove
impone
impose
smooch
smooth
imbosk
emboil
emboss
imboss
embost
import
impost
embody
emboly
imbody
omerta
omertà
amerce
amorce
embrue
emerge
imbrue
umbrae
smirch
Amtrak
amoral
umbral
umbrel
umbril
am-dram
embryo
umbras
amoret

Words marked △ may be spelled also with a capital letter

imaret
improv
imbrex
smarmy
smarty
smirky
smirry
smurry
amused
omasal
omasum
amuser
emesis
tmeses
tmesis
emetic
smatch
smutch
amatol
Amytal®
amytal
emetin
smiter
smithy
smutty
△empusa
ampule
émeute
empuse
immune
immure
impure
impute
smeuse
smouse
ambush
smouch
impugn
amours
amount
embusy
B-movie
smoyle
△amazon
antara
indaba
inyala
enjamb
enlard
inlaid
inland
inward
onward
unhand
unlaid
unmard
unpaid
unsaid
anlace
anlage
ansate
encage
encase
encave
enface
engage
engagé
enlace
ennage
enrace
enrage
enragé
ensate
entame
incage
incase
incave
infame
infare
ingate
inhale
inlace
inmate
innate
insane
intake
invade
unbare
uncage
uncape
uncase
uncate
undate
unease
Uniate
unlace
unlade
unmade
unmake
unrake
unsafe
untame
unware
in-calf
unhang
aneath
encash
sneath
uneath
unlash
incavi
enrank
unbark
unmask
unpack
untack
end-all
engaol
entail
enwall
infall
inhaul
inwall
onfall
unnail
unvail
encalm
ungain
enhalo
incavo
encamp
unhasp
unfair
unhair
annals
in-laws
endart
enfant
enrapt
indart
infant
intact
uncart
unfact
unlast
angary
infamy
sneaky
uneasy
unwary
enable
snebbe
snubbe
unable
ink-bag
anabas
Anubis
knobby
knubby
snobby
snubby
onycha
ink-cap
knicks
anicut
Sno-cat®
knacky
anodic
cnidae
snudge
unedge
anodal
enodal
anadem
one-day
entera
injera
ennead
indeed
intend
on-lend
unbend
undead
unfeed
unhead
unlead
unread
annexe
enlevé
entêté
incede
indene
infere
inhere
sneeze
unhele
undeaf
unself
enmesh
inmesh
sneesh
undeck
unmeek
anneal
enseal
unheal
unleal
unreal
unreel
unseal
unseel
unveil
unweal
unwell
enseam
inseam
inseem
unhelm
unseam
unteam
Andean
intern
undern
unhewn
unrein
unseen
unsewn
endear
ensear
unbear
undear
ungear
unless
inbent
incept
incest
indent
infect
infeft
infelt
infest
ingest
inject
insect
insert
intent
invent
invert
invest
unbelt
unbent
unfelt
unkent
unkept
unmeet
unnest
unpent
unrent
unrest
unseat
unsent
untent
unwept
ingénu
sneery
sneezy
unredy
unific
sniffy
snifty
snuffy
△enigma
Onagra
onager
anight
knight
knaggy
snaggy
snugly
inched
unshed
unshod
unshoe
anthem
inship
unship
anchor
anther
inches
unshot
unshut
anyhow
unthaw
angina
intima
engild
engird
envied
enwind
invis'd
inwind
unbind
ungild
ungird
unkind
untied
unwind
ancile
Andine
endite
endive
enfire
engine
ensile
entice
entire
incise
incite
indite
ingine
in-line
inside
intime
intine
intire
invite
Kneipe
ondine
on-line
onside
on-site
undine
unfine
unhive
unlike
unlime
unline
unlive
unripe
untile
unwire
unwise
unwive
anting
ending
enring
inning
onding
unking
enrich
inwith
unlich
unwish
uncini
antick
enlink
inwick
unlink
unpick
infill

6 □n□i□m

uncial
unwill
indium
infirm
unfirm
ensign
enzian
Indian
indign
angico
indigo
antiar
envier
inlier
antics
gneiss
Indies
on-dits
'snails
unbias
undies
unkiss
anoint
engirt
enlist
indict
insist
unbitt
ungilt
ungirt
unwist
in-situ
enmity
entity
snaily
unmiry
untidy
△antlia
angled
ankled
unclad
unglad
unglue
analog
unclog
unplug
inulin
inclip
angler
antler
Anglos
anklet
englut
inflow
onflow
unclew
influx
anally
snelly
anemia

gnamma
anemic
anomic
gnomic
mnemic
anomie
gnomae
animal
enamel
gnomon
mnemon
one-man
enamor
animus
enemas
gnomes
ynambu
ananke
anonym
unsnap
ananas
unknit
unknot
Ancona
ancora
△angola
△angora
Annona
entomb
enwomb
intomb
untomb
enfold
in-bond
infold
inroad
intoed
in-toed
in-word
uncord
unfold
ungord
unhood
unload
unlord
unsold
untold
ancome
Ankole
anyone
encode
encore
engobe
engore
enmove
enrobe
enzone
income
indole
in-joke

insole
intone
invoke
inwove
oncome
one-one
snooze
unbone
uncope
undone
unlove
unpope
unrobe
unrope
unyoke
one-off
unroof
enlock
inlock
inwork
uncock
uncork
undock
unhook
unlock
unwork
enroll
ensoul
entoil
in-foal
insoul
uncoil
uncool
uncowl
unfool
unroll
unsoul
enform
inform
unform
enjoin
inborn
intown
inworn
unborn
ungown
unmown
unsown
untorn
unworn
inhoop
unhoop
indoor
undoer
unmoor
endoss
ingoes
snooks
enroot
inmost

oncost
unbolt
unboot
uncolt
unlost
unroot
unsoft
unwont
incony
oniony
snoopy
snooty
snoozy
unholy
uniped
unipod
unsped
unspi'd
inspan
unspun
sniper
unspar
inkpot
snappy
snippy
unique
anuria
oniric
inbred
unbred
untrod
enerve
enfree
entrée
unfree
untrue
anarch
enarch
inarch
anorak
antrum
engram
ingram
ingrum
untrim
intron
entrap
enwrap
inwrap
unprop
unwrap
snarer
snorer
indris
intros
Andrew
undraw
anerly
energy
gnarly

in-tray
knurly
snarly
snorty
unpray
entrez
ink-sac
unused
enisle
inisle
snaste
unison
aneses
anesis
enoses
enosis
gnoses
gnosis
unisex
anatta
anetic
united
snathe
knitch
snatch
snitch
instal
instil
unital
Gnetum
anatto
one-two
instep
unstep
unstop
instar
uniter
unstow
knotty
snotty
Anoura
induna
infula
insula
pneuma
ungula
ensued
endure
ennuyé
ensure
incuse
induce
infuse
inhume
injure
insure
intuse
unrude
unrule
unsure

untune
engulf
ingulf
unturf
unhung
unsung
anough
enough
inrush
onrush
annuli
incubi
unhusk
untuck
annual
uncurl
unfurl
ungual
unturn
Anguis
ungues
unguis
incult
induct
indult
Innuit
insult
intuit
unhurt
unjust
unsuit
anbury
injury
snouty
unbury
unbusy
unduly
unruly
snivel
uneven
knives
gnawed
unawed
unowed
knawel
answer
gnawer
knower
anyway
one-way
anoxia
anoxic
undyed
uneyed
enzyme
oneyre
ungyve
oneyer
encyst
snazzy

Words marked △ may be spelled also with a capital letter

6 □o□d□r

posada
somata
sonata
torana
totara
yojana
comarb
△mosaic
Romaic
sodaic
coward
dotard
Poland
Roland
togaed
toward
woman'd
bocage
borage
borane
borate
bovate
comate
cowage
dog-ape
dogate
donate
dosage
dotage
douane
folate
forage
forane
homage
iodate
lobate
locale
locate
lorate
lovage
mopane
morale
nocake
nomade
nonage
nonane
notate
noyade
pomace
pomade
potage
romage
rosace
rotate
socage
solace
sorage
togate
to-name
towage
volage
voyage
zonate
Zouave
gobang
kobang
bodach
fogash
potash
pot-ash
jowari
mopani
Romani
souari
△mohawk
Polack
monaul
morall
no-ball
to-fall
you-all
domain
sodain
△dorado
pomato
potato
robalo
solano
tomato
vorago
hot-air
mohair
corals
morals
morass
noways
potass
△royals
sowans
vocals
Volans
cobalt
comart
dopant
dotant
go-cart
go-kart
monact
sonant
tonant
tooart
volant
vorant
nogaku
boyaux
△botany
covary
donary
goramy
gowany
horary
nomady
nonary
notary
oogamy
Romany
rosary
△rotary
volary
votary
zonary
tombac
tombic
tomboc
bobbed
box-bed
combed
dobbed
forbad
forbid
hotbed
jobbed
lobbed
mobbed
morbid
robbed
sobbed
wombed
bobble
cobble
comble
corbie
doable
dobbie
dog-bee
double
foible
forbye
gobble
hobble
hombre
jobbie
mobbie
mobble
nobble
rouble
sombre
wobble
zombie
dor-bug
bosbok
tombak
corbel
bobbin
bonbon
corban
dobbin
booboo
bomber
cobber
comber
dobber
goober
jobber
robber
somber
towbar
bombos
combos
morbus
sorbus
yobbos
combat
fox-bat
gobbet
hobbit
nobbut
sorbet
wombat
woobut
woubit
fog-bow
bombax
Bombyx
bobbly
bow-boy
cowboy
doubly
lowboy
potboy
tomboy
wobbly
concha
lorcha
coccid
forced
roscid
voiced
△bosche
bouche
bouché
bouclé
conche
couché
douche
louche
potche
rotche
touché
coccal
coucal
low-cal
non-com
non-con
toucan
honcho
poncho
mob-cap
toecap
boxcar
concur
forcer
soccer
voicer
coccos
coccus
conchs
Dorcas
△forces
hoicks
yoicks
zoccos
bobcat
doocot
doucet
forçat
low-cut
tomcat
cou-cou
roucou
moo-cow
coccyx
botchy
coachy
conchy
notchy
poachy
poncey
pouchy
touchy
bonduc
Nordic
aoudad
bonded
codded
corded
dodded
doodad
fonded
fordid
godded
hooded
loaded
nodded
podded
rodded
sordid
voided
woaded
wooded
worded
boddle
boodie
boodle
coddle
condie
doddle
doodle
fondle
fondue
foodie
hoddle
hoodie
howdie
noddle
noodle
poodle
poudre
roadie
toddle
voidee
woodie
fog-dog
hopdog
hot-dog
doodah
good-oh
houdah
howdah
pondok
bordel
Goidel
ooidal
rondel
condom
goddam
bolden
cordon
godden
god-den
golden
hodden
hoiden
holden
houdan
hoyden
△jordan
loaden
louden
sodden
soldan
wooden
hoodoo
koodoo
voodoo
hold-up
bonder
bordar
△border
codder
conder
condor
dodder
donder
fodder
folder
holder
loader
moider
nodder

6 □o□d□s

polder
ponder
pouder
powder
solder
sowder
voider
wonder
yonder
rondos
tondos
voudou
row-dow
boldly
box-day
coldly
fondly
goodly
hobday
lordly
loudly
Monday
woodsy
bodega
modena
monera
novena
solera
womera
dog-end
token'd
to-rend
cohere
Docete
Eocene
foveae
pop-eye
toneme
cosech
△joseph
Molech
moneth
no-tech
boleti
soneri
copeck
kopeck
△boreal
foveal
lozell
Nowell
roseal
sorell
zooeal
boreen
come-on
govern
Korean
love-in
△modern

moreen
nosean
poleyn
poteen
solein
solemn
voteen
bolero
comedo
forego
korero
non-ego
pomelo
Toledo
torero
bo-peep
coheir
dog-ear
howe'er
poseur
to-tear
voyeur
bogeys
Boreas
bowels
coleus
covers
dozens
fogeys
moneys
movers
novels
pokeys
powers
rodeos
Romeos
Roneos
soleus
sowens
volens
vowels
vowess
cogent
covent
covert
docent
dolent
domett
foment
forest
honest
loment
lowest
modest
molest
moment
motett
nocent
ponent
potent

rodent
sobeit
to-rent
coteau
pole-ax
△bowery
comedy
comely
foreby
homely
lonely
lovely
lowery
moiety
oogeny
popery
ropery
rosery
rosety
solely
sorely
towery
volery
gowf-ba'
confab
coffed
hoofed
poufed
roofed
sol-fa'd
woofed
bouffe
coffee
coffle
poffle
pouffe
toffee
loofah
boxful
joyful
potful
woeful
Corfam®
boffin
bowfin
coffin
coffer
confer
doffer
goffer
golfer
gowfer
hoofer
loafer
△rolfer
roofer
wolfer
woofer
comfit
confit

konfyt
low-fat
non-fat
soffit
confix
dogfox
forfex
bob-fly
botfly
dor-fly
hop-fly
gorgia
loggia
cogged
dogged
fogged
gorged
hogged
jogged
logged
nogged
pongid
sogged
togged
bodgie
boggle
boogie
bougie
coggie
coggle
coigne
congee
doggie
dongle
goggle
google
joggle
loggie
moggie
morgue
pongee
poogye
porgie
soigné
soogee
soogie
toggle
tongue
woggle
googol
△mongol
solgel
sol-gel
Dodgem®
△gorgon
hoggin
longan
moggan
Morgan
morgen

noggin
pop-gun
potgun
gorgio
sorgho
bodger
codger
cogger
conger
cougar
dodger
△dogger
fogger
forger
hogger
jogger
lodger
logger
longer
monger
sodger
bongos
borgos
pongos
sorgos
bouget
bought
bowget
dought
forgat
forget
forgot
fought
gorget
hogget
loggat
'mongst
mought
nougat
nought
rotgut
rought
sought
congou
coggly
doughy
goggly
googly
longly
morgay
roughy
boshta
lochia
△gothic
Sothic
mothed
bothie
mochie
towhee
hoo-hah

kowhai
nochel
bothan
Cochin
eothen
Goshen
lochan
boo-hoo
forhoo
yoo-hoo
dog-hep
dog-hip
nosh-up
bother
cosher
fother
gopher
josher
kosher
mother
nosher
pother
rother
tocher
tosher
tother
t'other
tophus
log-hut
rochet
top-hat
Tophet
moshav
forhow
no-show
pochay
po'chay
poshly
coaita
conima
copita
dolina
lorica
nomina
vomica
oomiac
zodiac
bodied
copied
gobiid
honied
monied
bodice
bolide
boride
bovine
comice
conine
cosine
cotise

Words marked △ may be spelled also with a capital letter

6 □o□l□s

docile
doline
dorise
dorize
iodide
iodine
iodise
iodize
iolite
△ionise
△ionize
mobile
moline
motile
motive
norite
no-side
notice
novice
nowise
△oolite
podite
police
polite
solive
somite
sopite
tonite
votive
boding
boning
boring
bowing
boxing
coding
coming
cooing
coping
coving
doning
doping
doting
dozing
foxing
goring
hoeing
holing
homing
joying
lobing
loping
loring
losing
loving
lowing
moving
mowing
nosing
poking
poling
posing
robing
roding
roping
roving
rowing
sowing
toeing
toling
toning
towing
toying
woning
wooing
yoking
zoning
boyish
cowish
dotish
dovish
eolith
goyish
modish
mopish
morish
△polish
popish
Romish
tonish
toyish
solidi
yogini
Kodiak
Morisk
oomiak
△**jovial**
monial
Novial
oorial
podial
social
tomial
bonism
corium
dolium
Dorism
eonism
folium
holism
iodism
Ionism
ionium
lolium
monism
nomism
podium
porism
sodium
Sofism
tomium
yogism
Aonian
Dorian
Eolian
gonion
Ionian
Jovian
logion
lotion
morion
motion
notion
Popian
potion
solion
bonito
domino
dosi-do
loligo
solito
vomito
zorino
copier
cosier
cozier
foliar
hosier
rosier
bodies
bogies
conics
fogies
folios
golias
holies
modius
monies
movies
pokies
polios
sonics
Tonies
aorist
bonist
codist
forint
holist
Ionist
loriot
modist
monist
△soviet
bodily
codify
comity
cosily
gorily
holily
homily
hominy
modify
moyity
nosily
notify
novity
oozily
policy
polity
ropily
rosily
rosiny
Torify
hobjob
conjee
poojah
moujik
log-jam
donjon
popjoy
soojey
cocked
corked
forked
hooked
pocked
soaked
worked
yolked
zonked
bookie
cockle
cookie
folkie
honkie
kookie
nookie
rookie
△yorkie
hookah
bodkin
docken
dodkin
joskin
look-in
morkin
soaken
work-in
cock-up
hook-up
lock-up
mock-up
bosker
△cocker
conker
cooker
corker
corkir
docker
forker
hocker
honker
hooker
howker
korkir
locker
looker
mocker
porker
△rocker
soaker
tonker
worker
yonker
yorker
jockos
bosket
cocket
docket
dooket
locket
nocket
pocket
pookit
poukit
rocket
socket
booksy
cocksy
donkey
folksy
hockey
hookey
horkey
jockey
low-key
monkey
holloa
boiled
bolled
bowled
cowled
doiled
foiled
howled
jowled
mobled
polled
pot-lid
rolled
soiled
souled
toiled
boulle
collie
coolie
coulée
doolie
dowlne
goalie
goolie
mollie
noulde
poulpe
voulge
bow-leg
dog-leg
loglog
coolth
koolah
mollah
moolah
tol-lol
coelom
Moslem
bollen
codlin
goblin
gollan
gowlan
koulan
moulin
norlan'
pollan
pollen
poplin
roll-on
woolen
collop
dollop
foul-up
gollop
lollop
roll-up
boiler
bowler
coaler
collar
cooler
dollar
fowler
gollar
goller
holler
howler
jowler
loller
moiler
poller
poplar
△roller
sollar
soller
toiler
toller
tooler
yodler
boules
coulis
dowlas
hollos

Words marked △ may be spelled also with a capital letter

moulds
oodles
collet
goblet
goglet
goslet
howlet
job-lot
toilet
tonlet
follow
go-slow
hollow
mob-law
bollix
pollex
Pollux
coolly
doyley
foully
gooley
hooley
jolley
motley
mouldy
podley
volley
woolly
yowley
cosmea
holmia
cosmic
formic
holmic
hormic
doomed
formed
roomed
wormed
commie
coombe
dormie
roomie
Bokmål
cormel
formal
formol
normal
pommel
bowman
common
cowman
dodman
dolman
dolmen
foeman
foemen
fogman
hodman
log-man

Mormon
△norman
potman
rodman
Rouman
socman
topman
towmon
toyman
boomer
Colmar
commer
dormer
former
roamer
roemer
roomer
wormer
commis
commos
cormus
cosmos
dolmas
houmus
kosmos
commit
commot
format
mommet
motmot
commix
cornea
cornua
goanna
goonda
joanna
hobnob
Cognac
poonac
zoonic
conned
corned
donned
downed
gowned
horned
mooned
morned
wonned
bonnie
bounce
donnée
Downie®
Hornie
jounce
loonie
lounge
Moonie
pointe
poonce

pounce
pownie
rounce
townee
townie
tonnag
cornel
nounal
zoonal
xoanon
coiner
conner
corner
downer
horner
joiner
moaner
mooner
nooner
sooner
sorner
bounds
doings
donnés
hounds
points
pounds
rounds
sounds
zounds
bonnet
cobnut
cornet
donnat
donnot
hornet
non-net
posnet
sonnet
tow-net
fornix
bouncy
bounty
coonty
county
gooney
△johnny
mornay
Mounty
pointy
powney
rouncy
townly
woundy
corona
jojoba
korora
Pomona
Eozoic
conoid

kobold
locoed
no-good
toroid
toxoid
zonoid
bog-ore
botoné
comose
coyote
ionone
jocose
lobose
mopoke
morose
nodose
no-hope
porose
sobole
tofore
torose
hop-off
bogong
oolong
so-long
golosh
△moloch
colobi
bogoak
mocock
Mohock
cocoon
cohorn
cojoin
Eozoon
godown
go-down
Motown®
comodo
corozo
rococo
rotolo
yo-ho-ho
bow-oar
colour
dolour
honour
notour
Bofors
bosoms
cohoes
colons
colors
comous
dodoes
goboes
hoboes
iodous
joyous
locoes

mojoes
nodous
no-noes
noyous
porous
torous
cohort
co-host
cop-out
not-out
volost
gomoku
bosomy
colony
corody
gobony
monody
monosy
motory
nobody
oology
polony
sodomy
cowpea
hoop-la
copped
couped
hopped
looped
lopped
mopped
pooped
sopped
topped
torpid
wopped
copple
corpse
coupee
couple
doppie
hoopoe
hopple
koppie
popple
soapie
souple
topple
toupee
oompah
compel
gospel
vorpal
pompom
coppin
coupon
gowpen
hog-pen
holpen
loipen

loupen
pompon
tompon
morpho
poo-poo
joy-pop
bopper
comper
cooper
copper
couper
△dopper
hooper
hopper
looper
lopper
mopper
popper
romper
soaper
souper
topper
torpor
yopper
compos
corpus
bowpot
compot
cowpat
forpet
forpit
hotpot
loupit
moppet
poppet
poppit
roopit
roupit
toupet
cowpox
comply
△pompey
popply
mosque
torque
boorka
moorva
cobric
con-rod
forrad
horrid
torrid
boorde
bourne
△bourse
coarse
coerce
corrie
course
cowrie

Words marked △ may be spelled also with a capital letter

gourde
hoarse
Lowrie
Moerae
pourie
roarie
soirée
source
sourse
toorie
tourie
bodrag
toerag
tow-rag
fourth
hoorah
Moirai
borrel
Bovril®
corral
sorrel
worral
worrel
fogram
pogrom
forren
poprin
sovran
gooroo
hooroo
journo
horror
pourer
roarer
soarer
tourer
boards
gourds
kouros
morris
morros
zorros
forrit
hog-rat
torret
worrit
borrow
morrow
sorrow
forray
gourdy
hooray
hourly
Norroy
pomroy
poorly
sourly
foussa
gossib
corsac
bossed
fossed
hoised
Mossad
poised
soused
tossed
cossie
donsie
fo'c'sle
fossae
mossie
mousie
mousle
mousmé
mousse
nousle
possie
pousse
sonsie
sowsse
tousle
borsch
bonsai
consul
dorsal
dorsel
dossal
dossel
dossil
fossil
housel
morsal
morsel
norsel
podsol
tolsel
tonsil
torsel
woosel
dorsum
Possum®
possum
'possum
cousin
foison
godson
gossan
horson
loosen
poison
poyson
tocsin
toison
tossen
worsen
gossip
toss-up
△**bowser**
cooser
dorser
dosser
douser
dowser
fossor
josser
moiser
motser
mouser
poiser
posser
rosser
rouser
tonsor
tosser
touser
△towser
worser
wowser
corsos
gooses
horses
houses
louses
noesis
noises
souses
torsos
comsat
corset
cosset
dowset
lowsit
posset
bow-saw
log-saw
bolshy
forsay
fousty
goosey
gousty
horsey
mousey
toasty
tolsey
contra
footra
foutra
△noctua
rostra
aortic
Coptic
goetic
noetic
nostoc
poetic
△pontic
Toltec
zoetic
booted
costed
cotted
cottid
doited
dotted
foetid
footed
hotted
jotted
lofted
lotted
moated
motto'd
potted
rooted
rotted
routed
sotted
totted
wonted
wotted
boatie
bootee
bottle
coatee
cootie
costae
dottle
footie
footle
foutre
goatee
goitre
goutte
hogtie
hottie
jostle
loathe
montre
mottle
pontie
postie
pottle
rootle
softie
soothe
sortie
toetoe
tootle
tottie
toutie
wortle
sontag
hootch
toitoi
aortal
boatel
coital
costal
coutil
foetal
fontal
hostel
mortal
pontal
pontil
portal
postal
postil
bottom
montem
tom-tom
bolt-on
boston
bouton
cotton
gotten
looten
molten
moutan
mouton
ponton
rottan
rotten
soften
torten
too-too
boater
bolter
coater
colter
copter
co-star
coster
cottar
cotter
couter
doater
doctor
dorter
douter
foetor
footer
foster
fouter
goiter
hooter
hotter
jolter
jotter
lofter
loiter
looter
low-tar
mooter
mortar
mouter
△pooter
porter
poster
potter
pouter
powter
rooter
rorter
roster
rotter
router
sorter
soutar
souter
sowter
tolter
tooter
totter
touter
zoster
Boötes
coitus
contos
Cortes
costus
cottus
foetus
fortes
fortis
lottos
months
mouths
nostos
pontes
portas
pottos
sortes
tortes
youths
doitit
tomtit
kowtow
cortex
vortex
costly
couthy
forthy
hostry
loathy
mostly
mouthy
poetry
portly
rootsy
softly
toothy
tootsy
worthy
youthy
copula
gopura
koruna
morula

motuca
Podura
rosula
rotula
torula
Yoruba
zonula
toluic
jocund
rotund
cohune
colure
conure
lobule
locule
module
nodule
solute
vocule
volume
volute
zonule
zonure
coburg
gomuti
lobuli
loculi
moduli
toruli
bohunk
mocuck
Podunk
toluol
column
jötunn
colugo
gomuto
modulo
voguer
forums
locums
moguls
coquet
locust
loquat
robust
roquet
yogurt
voguey
corvid
corvée
louvre
coeval
hooven
bovver
Hoover®
hoover
louver
soever
solver
wolver
corves
△corvus
hooves
loaves
looves
wolves
corvet
convex
volvox
convey
convoy
cobweb
bobwig
cotwal
kotwal
doo-**wop**
godwit
wou-wou
bowwow
powwaw
powwow
wow-wow
forwhy
Norway
bonxie
coaxer
hoaxer
coryza
corymb
cotyle
covyne
oocyte
polype
polypi
ronyon
bowyer
polyps
Toryfy
boozed
foozle
mozzie
mozzle
nozzle
sozzle
touzle
borzoi
donzel
podzol
gozzan
zoozoo
bonzer
boozer
momzer
nozzer
rozzer
howzat
boozey
sozzly
tolzey
appaid
appayd
spraid
uphand
uphaud
upland
upward
L-plate
opiate
T-plate
update
upgaze
upmake
uprate
uptake
sprang
upgang
uphang
splash
sprack
sprawl
sprain
appair
sphaer
optant
upcast
upwaft
yplast
apiary
speary
epocha
ipecac
spaced
spiced
△**apache**
specie
spicae
apical
epical
spacer
spicer
apices
specks
spicas
spacey
speccy
specky
epodic
apodal
apedom
spader
spider
spades
spados
spadix
spuddy
append
spread
spredd
upheld
uplead
upsend
apiece
ephebe
sphene
sphere
speech
ephebi
appeal
upwell
spleen
uplean
speedo
upheap
upkeep
upleap
appear
sphear
upbear
uprear
uptear
uppers
sprent
upbeat
up-beat
uprest
speedy
sphery
spiffy
spoffy
apogee
epigon
spight
spigot
ypight
spahee
upshot
epeira
optima
upbind
uphild
upwind
up-wind
aplite
éprise
épuisé
△ophite
optime
splice
spline
sprite
up-line
uprise
upside
spliff
spaing
△spring
spying
upping
uppish
uplink
upfill
uphill
up-till
Ophism
option
aphids
optics
speiss
splits
spoils
splint
spoilt
sprint
uplift
uprist
uptilt
△**sphinx**
uppity
spiked
spoken
spikes
opaled
spalle
spulye
epilog
spilth
△**apollo**
apples
epulis
opulus
upblow
upflow
apeman
epimer
spammy
spined
spence
sponge
spunge
spinal
spinel
eponym
opener
spinar
spinet
upknit
openly
spinny
spongy
spunky
apnoea
aplomb
opioid
uphold
appose
aptote
opcode
oppose
splore
upcome
uprose
sprong
splosh
uplock
uplook
upboil
upcoil
uproll
uptorn
uptown
uproar
apport
opt-out
sprout
upmost
uproot
aphony
spooky
spoony
epopee
apepsy
opaque
aporia
Sparta
spirea
spiric
sparid
spired
a-per-se
sparge
sparke
sparre
sparse
sperre
sperse
spurge
spurne
uphroe
updrag
eparch
sparth
spiral
operon
upwrap
sparer
sparks
sports
sperst
△spirit
aperçu
éperdu
updraw
upgrew
upgrow
sparky
sparry
sporty
spurry
upbray

Words marked △ may be spelled also with a capital letter

eposes
opuses
sposhy
aphtha
spathe
spetch
spital
sputum
spot-on
apathy
spotty
upstay
spauld
epaule
spouse
spruce
sprung
sprush
upgush
uprush
spruik
upcurl
upfurl
uphurl
oppugn
upturn
spruit
spouty
spavie
spavin
up-over
spivvy
spewer
spawny
upsway
apexes
spayad
spryer
uprest
spryly
epizoa
apozem
squama
equate
squame
△square
squash
squawk
squail
squall
equant
squeak
squeal
Aquila
equine
équipe
squire
squiff
squish
squill

squirm
squier
squirr
squids
squint
squirt
equity
squiny
arcana
argala
armada
errata
organa
argand
Briard
errand
friand
Ormazd
arcade
arcane
breare
crease
create
dreare
ergate
grease
greave
ornate
preace
prease
triage
troade
urbane
areach
breach
breath
broach
creach
creagh
eriach
preach
wreath
wroath
argali
arrack
orgasm
ordain
preamp
dryads
Greats
groats
oreads
trials
Arnaut
arrant
breast
creant
criant
dreamt
errant

triact
truant
Arcady
creaky
creamy
creasy
croaky
dreamy
dreary
freaky
friary
greasy
treaty
ersatz
△arabic
arable
criblé
treble
tribal
arabin
graben
briber
prober
arabis
Erebus
probit
crabby
drabby
drably
grubby
pre-buy
trebly
erucic
graced
priced
broché
Brücke
△crèche
croche
orache
△oracle
troche
uracil
drachm
bracer
gricer
grocer
pricer
tracer
tricar
trocar
arccos
braces
crocus
cruces
fracas
△graces
grices
précis
traces

tracks
tricks
fricht
precut
tricot
bricky
cricky
drecky
pricey
tricky
uredia
iridic
eroded
traded
bridge
bridie
bridle
cradle
dredge
drudge
fridge
grudge
trudge
bridal
credal
iridal
gradin
grader
trader
credos
grades
gradus
irides
trades
credit
aridly
cruddy
Friday
fraena
freez'd
friend
breese
breeze
creese
freeze
frieze
Graeae
greece
greese
greete
griece
grieve
kreese
preeve
priefe
prieve
breech
creesh
ordeal
orcein

arrear
breeks
briefs
cruels
greens
orders
uraeus
ardent
argent
arpent
arrect
arrest
driest
freest
orgeat
△orient
priest
urgent
urtext
wriest
wryest
artery
breezy
briery
creeky
creepy
freely
freety
greedy
greeny
griesy
gryesy
ornery
orrery
troely
prefab
trifid
griffe
trifle
armful
artful
ireful
urnful
Gräfin
gryfon
prefer
drafts
profit
orifex
prefix
crafty
draffy
drafty
drifty
dry-fly
bregma
tragic
frigid
brigue
brogue

dragée
drogue
Progne
grigri
frugal
brogan
△dragon
grog-on
origan
origin
orogen
trigon
trogon
Trygon
grog-up
droger
fragor
gregos
tragus
troggs
aright
bright
fright
frigot
wright
gru-gru
bragly
craggy
draggy
dreggy
druggy
△froggy
groggy
trigly
Brahma
Orphic
arched
orchid
Archie
Brahmi
archil
orchel
orchil
graham
archon
arghan
arshin
△brehon
orphan
urchin
archer
△arches
△orchis
orthos
orchat
archly
arnica
orbita
pruina
troika

Words marked △ may be spelled also with a capital letter

6 □r□i□d

urtica
braird
araise
Argive
arkite
arride
arrive
arsine
braide
braise
braize
bruise
cruise
cruive
ermine
fraise
froise
Graiae
graile
graine
greige
orcine
oreide
oroide
orpine
praise
preife
proine
pruine
ureide
ursine
arcing
crying
drying
erring
froing
frying
proing
prying
trying
urging
urning
arrish
dreich
droich
dryish
graith
wraith
erbium
truism
proign
brails
brains
fruits
grains
orgies
aroint
'Arriet
artist
fruict
brainy
freity
fruity
grainy
orbity
frijol
Trojan
tri-jet
arcked
grakle
broken
kraken
wroken
broker
proker
drakes
irokos
trek-ox
crikey
aralia
arolla
brolga
frolic
Uralic
grille
grilse
proleg
arilli
prelim
Dralon®
trillo
proler
frills
armlet
pre-let
prolix
brolly
drolly
frilly
orally
trilby
trolly
gramma
premia
uremia
bromic
dromic
eremic
uremic
premed
gramme
premie
tremie
trémie
trompe
grumph
dromoi
brumal
primal
crimen
crumen
dromon
crambo
cremor
framer
primer
tremor
trimer
cramps
crumbs
dromos
grumps
primos
Primus®
primus
promos
trumps
fremit
gromet
prompt
premix
brumby
crampy
crimpy
crumby
crummy
crumpy
drumly
frumpy
Grammy
grimly
grumly
grumpy
primly
trimly
Aranea
crania
Urania
irenic
ironic
uranic
branle
brenne
bronze
cringe
frenne
fringe
Fronde
grande
grange
grunge
△orange
prance
prince
trance
transe
branch
brunch
cranch
crunch
drench
△french
Granth
trench
wrench
pranck
crenel
crinal
trinal
uranyl
urinal
crinum
frenum
kronen
uranin
bronco
drongo
eringo
eryngo
franco
gringo
pronto
ironer
kroner
kronor
krónur
pruner
branks
crants
Erinys
Kronos
prunes
prunus
trunks
Uranus
brunet
cronet
erenow
brandy
branky
brahny
bronzy
cranky
cranny
franzy
frenzy
fringy
granny
grungy
pranky
tranny
trendy
krantz
areola
arroba
areole
arkose
broose
△creole
croove
droome
groove
orgone
oriole
triode
brooch
ariosi
arioso
arroyo
arbour
ardour
armour
arrows
proofs
troops
try-out
ormolu
argosy
armory
arrowy
briony
broody
broomy
bryony
droopy
grooly
groovy
priory
grappa
tropic
draped
trepid
tripod
uropod
craple
frappé
graple
griple
grippe
triple
trophi
drupel
propel
propyl
crepon
drop-in
fripon
trapan
trepan
crypto
troppo
draper
griper
groper
proper
cripes
drapes
grapes
gripes
trapes
tripos
armpit
drapet
crappy
crepey
croppy
drappy
drippy
dropsy
grapey
grippy
prepay
preppy
trappy
tripey
triply
trophy
Griqua
frorne
crural
froren
dry-rot
arista
crissa
crista
crusta
friska
frusta
erased
irised
crosse
crusie
frisée
graste
grysie
triste
wrasse
△**prusik**
cresol
trisul
arcsin
arisen
grison
orison
prison
aristo
fresco
presto
eraser
groser
priser
proser
crases
crasis
crises
crisis
crisps
irises
krises
preses

Words marked △ may be spelled also with a capital letter

prisms
uresis
urosis
uruses
cruset
groset
preset
prosit
brashy
brassy
brisky
brushy
crispy
crusty
dressy
drosky
drossy
frisky
frosty
grassy
grisly
prismy
prissy
trashy
tressy
trusty
wristy
protea
△arctic
△cretic
critic
erotic
iritic
uretic
grated
X-rated
pratie
wrethe
writhe
cratch
crotch
crutch
fratch
grutch
wretch
brutal
crotal
protyl
trotyl
arctan
△breton
Briton
craton
Cretan
cretin
croton
erg-ten
gratin
proton
△triton

grotto
bruter
crater
cratur
frater
grater
krater
orator
prater
pretor
ureter
writer
Brutus
gratis
iritis
frutex
pre-tax
bratty
fratry
fretty
frothy
gritty
grotty
pretty
truthy
wrathy
trauma
around
ground
Ormuzd
arbute
argute
armure
arouse
brouze
croupe
crouse
croûte
grouse
ordure
triune
troule
troupe
trouse
brough
crouch
drouth
grouch
grough
trough
arguli
arguer
trouts
draunt
irrupt
argufy
croupy
groupy
grouty
trouty

trivia
graved
gravid
proved
prevue
drivel
frivol
gravel
grovel
travel
craven
driven
graven
proven
craver
driver
drover
graver
prover
trover
bravos
△graves
Provos
travis
trevis
brevet
cravat
grivet
grovet
privet
trivet
crowed
browse
drawee
drowse
frowie
prawle
growth
crewel
trowel
prewyn
brew-up
brewer
drawer
grower
pre-war
brewis
browst
frowst
brawly
brawny
browny
browsy
crawly
drowsy
frowsy
frowzy
growly
wraxle
cruxes

orexis
praxis
prayed
arayse
argyle
grayle
groyne
proyne
trayne
Argyll
crayon
Troyan
brayer
crayer
prayer
aroynt
greyly
crazed
prized
△brazil
drazel
frazil
brazen
frozen
grazer
prizer
frizzy
espada
Tswana
Asgard
island
usward
ashake
ashame
aslake
astare
escape
estate
osmate
V-shape
askari
assail
aswarm
escarp
askant
aslant
assart
astart
usable
isabel
ash-bin
isobar
usably
psocid
△psyche
ash-can
psycho
used-up
usedn't
ascend

yshend
Essene
osteal
esteem
astern
ossein
asleep
asmear
assess
assets
ascent
aspect
assent
assert
astert
ostent
ashery
astely
esnecy
osiery
useful
isogon
usager
usages
asthma
ischia
isohel
eschar
eschew
espied
ashine
aspine
aspire
assize
essive
oscine
aswing
aspick
Ostiak
aswirl
espial
ostial
osmium
ostium
ascian
assign
Ossian
ustion
Eskimo
espies
assist
T-shirt
aseity
ossify
ash-key
psylla
asylum
ashlar
ashler
ostler

Psalms
tsamba
Ostmen
isomer
usance
ashore
aslope
astone
osmose
assoil
aswoon
esloin
essoin
astoop
osmous
asport
aspout
assort
assott
escort
astony
isopod
ash-pan
ash-pit
Ostrea
escroc
psoric
astral
escrol
estral
asarum
ashram
estrum
T-strap
usurer
estrus
Osiris
tsuris
astrut
esprit
escrow
Astrex
astray
estray
osprey
tsetse
tsotsi
isatin
Ishtar
Isatis
Ashura
oscula
osmund
assume
assure
astute
oscule
escudo
pseudo
issuer

Words marked △ may be spelled also with a capital letter

6 □s□u□t

asquat
psywar
Ostyak
ottava
strata
steard
strand
Utgard
ethane
steale
steane
steare
strafe
strake
straff
attach
strath
attack
attask
straik
Y-track
atlatl
attain
atwain
Q-train
strain
strawn
stramp
strass
strays
stealt
strait
steady
steamy
strawy
stable
stobie
atabeg
atabek
atabal
stably
stubby
atocia
stacte
stucco
sticks
stocks
sticky
stocky
stadda
stadia
stedde
stodge
studio
steddy
stodgy
Athena
Strega®
attend
steeld

Athene
ethene
steeve
stieve
strene
itself
streak
streek
atweel
streel
stream
atween
Etnean
strewn
others
steels
stress
attent
attest
△street
steedy
steely
steepy
steery
stifle
staffs
stuffy
stigma
staged
stigme
stogie
stager
stagey
stogey
stuggy
etcher
striga
attire
étoile
striae
stride
strife
strike
Strine
stripe
strive
a'thing
string
stying
k'thibh
staith
strich
at-risk
atrial
atrium
Ethiop
étrier
ethics
stairs
atwixt

strict
strift
stripy
atokal
stoker
stakes
stokes
△italic
stoled
stolid
stelae
stalag
etalon
stolen
stolon
stalko
stelar
stylar
stalls
stylos
stylus
stilet
stylet
otalgy
stalky
stilly
stilty
stemma
atomic
etymic
stemme
stimie
stymie
stomal
ataman
etymon
stamen
stumer
stumps
stumpy
stanza
atonic
ethnic
stoned
stance
stanze
stonne
stanch
stench
stanck
atonal
stuns'l
stonen
stanzo
stingo
stinko
atoner
stoner
stinks
stingy

stinty
Atropa
stroma
stromb
strond
stroud
at-home
attone
otiose
stooge
stoope
strobe
strode
stroke
strove
strong
strook
stroll
stroam
attorn
strown
stroup
stools
strout
utmost
△utopia
atopic
etypic
stupid
staple
steppe
stipel
step-in
stop-go
step-up
stupor
stapes
stipes
pteria
stirra
yttria
athrob
steric
yttric
eterne
starve
sterve
stirre
storge
starch
sterol
iterum
pterin
stereo
attrap
starer
storer
Pteris
starts
stirps

stores
uterus
attrit
storax
styrax
starry
storey
stormy
sturdy
ptisan
ptoses
ptosis
stasis
statua
static
stated
statue
stitch
statal
statim
stater
stator
otitis
△states
status
stithy
struma
stound
attune
strung
stoush
stouth
struck
strunt
stoury
staved
stived
Ativan®
steven
stiver
stover
staves
stawed
stewed
stownd
stowre
stewer
stower
ataxia
ataxic
ptyxis
stayed
ethyne
stayne
stayre
stay-on
stayer
curara
kumara
Purana

Tupaia
yukata
Judaic
aubade
aurate
butane
cubage
curare
curate
fumage
furane
humane
jubate
jugate
lunate
luxate
mucate
murage
mutate
nutate
outage
pupate
rugate
sudate
tubage
tubate
musang
queach
sumach
curari
gurami
jupati
kumari
ourali
ourari
rubati
out-ask
aumail
eucain
fusain
supawn
bumalo
fugato
fumado
rubato
turaco
durant
jumart
jurant
mutant
nutant
subact
curacy
eutaxy
lunacy
lunary
muzaky
queasy
queazy
sudary

Words marked △ may be spelled also with a capital letter

sugary
hubbub
bulbed
cubbed
dubbed
numbed
outbid
rubbed
rum-bud
subbed
sunbed
surbed
turbid
bubble
bum-bee
△bumble
burble
fumble
Guebre
humble
jumbie
jumble
mumble
nubble
outbye
rubble
rumble
suable
subbie
tumble
bumbag
humbug
gubbah
jubbah
bulbel
bulbil
bulbul
jumbal
dubbin
nubbin
tulban
turban
△pueblo
bulbar
bus-bar
cumber
durbar
Gueber
lubber
lumbar
lumber
number
outbar
rubber
tubber
bumbos
gumbos
jumbos
rumbos
turbos

burbot
numbat
rubbet
rubbit
surbet
turbit
turbot
sunbow
outbox
aumbry
bubbly
busboy
dumbly
humbly
jumbly
nubbly
numbly
rubbly
rumbly
suably
cutcha
fulcra
kutcha
puncta
juiced
muscid
muscae
muscle
nuncle
quiche
tusche
succah
buccal
furcal
sulcal
Tuscan
△vulcan
nuncio
puncto
hub-cap
juicer
succor
buncos
cuscus
guacos
juncos
juncus
ruscus
succès
succus
sulcus
Turcos
dulcet
mudcat
muscat
dun-cow
bunchy
muscly
outcry
punchy

△buddha
sundra
tundra
mundic
budded
funded
rudded
buddle
bundle
burdie
cuddie
cuddle
Culdee
curdle
duddie
fuddle
fundie
guddle
huddle
hurdle
muddle
nurdle
puddle
ruddle
rundle
subdue
Suidae
sundae
pug-dog
sundog
numdah
purdah
sundri
dumdum
durdum
quidam
burden
cudden
cuddin
guidon
gulden
hudden
hurden
lurdan
lurden
pudden
sudden
tundun
huddup
dudder
dunder
funder
furder
△guider
judder
mudder
murder
pudder
rudder
sudder

sunder
fundus
Turdus
pundit
subdew
sundew
cuddly
puddly
Purdey®
Sunday
sundry
eureka
murena
superb
but-end
butene
mug-ewe
quaere
Sûreté
tuyère
humeri
ourebi
puteli
cuneal
luteal
puteal
museum
Augean
dudeen
Humean
Judean
lucern
lutein
luzern
tureen
pukeko
pumelo
tupelo
tuxedo
auteur
fureur
auceps
aureus
duress
duvets
fumets
lumens
funest
humect
lucent
outeat
ouvert
pudent
queest
bureau
cutely
cutesy
dukery
dupery
hugely

humefy
mutely
nudely
purely
queeny
rubefy
rudely
rudery
surely
surety
tumefy
puffed
ruffed
turfed
cuffle
duffle
guffie
muffle
purfle
ruffle
surfie
cupful
dueful
duffel
fulfil
gutful
jugful
mugful
rueful
tubful
cuffin
muffin
nuffin
puffin
ruffin
turfen
buffer
duffer
furfur
puffer
suffer
sulfur
surfer
buffet
outfit
tuffet
subfeu
curfew
guffaw
outfox
suffix
outfly
purfly
quagga
bugged
fulgid
hugged
jugged
lugged
lunged

rugged
sun-god
tugged
turgid
budgie
bungee
bungie
bungle
burgee
burgle
guggle
gurgle
juggle
jungle
luggie
lungie
muggee
puggie
puggle
jungli
cudgel
fungal
subgum
buggan
buggin
durgan
kurgan
outgun
burgoo
gung-ho
budger
△bugger
Bulgar
bulger
bulgur
burger
fulgor
hunger
lugger
mudger
mugger
nudger
nuggar
purger
rugger
sungar
tugger
turgor
vulgar
fungus
Judges
mungos
outgas
Tungus
vulgus
△budget
nugget
quight
bungey
hungry

6 □u□h□a

jungly
quaggy
tughra
bushed
hushed
pushed
euchre
nuchae
qui-hye
rushee
tushie
nurhag
quahog
muzhik
burhel
bushel
muchel
Mughal
nuchal
Durham
fulham
humhum
eughen
euphon
Kuchen
rushen
tuchun
Pushto
tu-whoo
push-up
author
gusher
husher
lusher
musher
Nuphar
outher
pusher
rusher
wuther
rushes
cushat
lum-hat
outhit
sunhat
Pushtu
cushaw
lushly
muchly
oughly
Auriga
cubica
Judica
Lucina
lumina
numina
Punica
rumina
Tulipa
buried

busied
dutied
Lusiad
rubied
audile
augite
dunite
fusile
futile
gunite
humite
Lucite®
lumine
lupine
munite
murine
musive
mutine
nubile
pumice
purine
rubine
rusine
rutile
supine
sutile
busing
buying
cueing
during
luging
luting
musing
outing
puling
rueing
ruling
tubing
tuning
dudish
mulish
Munich
punish
quaich
quaigh
rudish
rupiah
buriti
burial
autism
cubism
curium
dudism
Humism
mutism
nudism
purism
Sufism
bunion
dupion

durian
durion
fusion
Humian
Julian
Tupian
turion
Zunian
Zuñian
subito
△**junior**
punier
audios
curios
kumiss
quoits
rubies
aurist
cubist
cueist
curiet
Humist
juliet
jurist
lutist
nudist
purist
quaint
queint
quoist
aurify
bulimy
busily
humify
munify
mutiny
nudity
punily
purify
purity
rubify
bunjee
bunjie
jug-jug
gurjun
outjet
outjut
buckra
funkia
Gurkha
pulkha
quokka
Turkic
busked
fucked
husked
musked
sucked
tusked
buckie

buckle
huckle
junkie
luckie
muckle
muskle
puckle
ruckle
runkle
suckle
sunkie
muskeg
punkah
sukkah
bunkum
bumkin
buskin
dusken
lucken
rumkin
sucken
suck-in
sunken
tuck-in
cuckoo
duikep
fuck-up
muck-up
bucker
bulker
bunker
busker
ducker
duiker
△dunker
duyker
fucker
hunker
husker
△junker
kunkar
kunkur
lunker
lurker
△mucker
pucker
△quaker
sucker
tucker
Tunker
tuskar
tusker
yucker
bunkos
ruckus
turkis
bucket
busket
junket
musket

sucket
Sukkot
sunket
tucket
duskly
turkey
qualia
quelea
mucluc
public
curled
guiled
mulled
bullae
humlie
ouglie
outlie
ruelle
tuille
putlog
Guelph
Gullah
mullah
nullah
quelch
nuclei
mukluk
suslik
fullam
Muslim
dualin
dunlin
fullan
muflon
murlan
murlin
muslin
pull-in
pull-on
purlin
sullen
duello
burlap
Dunlop
pull-up
bugler
buller
burler
butler
culler
curler
cutler
fuller
guiler
guller
guslar
guyler
hurler
muller
outler

puller
purler
sutler
cullis
hullos
auklet
buglet
bullet
cullet
cutlet
duplet
gullet
gurlet
juglet
mullet
nutlet
outlet
pullet
runlet
sublet
sunlit
curlew
outlaw
duplex
Ku-Klux
burley
dually
guilty
gulley
hurley
mulley
outlay
pulley
qualmy
wurley
mummia
Suomic
bummed
gummed
hummed
mummed
summed
bummle
hummle
summae
nutmeg
bummel
hummel
kümmel
mulmul
pummel
hummum
Burman
busman
culmen
cummin
cupman
gunman
musmon
outman

subman
summon
tutman
bummer
cummer
fulmar
hummer
mummer
murmur
rummer
summar
summer
duomos
hummus
submit
summat
summit
muu-muu
lummox
bunnia
duenna
guinea
quanta
quinoa
quinta
Hunnic
muonic
quinic
burned
dunned
punned
ruined
sunned
turned
vulned
duende
nuance
quince
quinie
quinte
quinze
numnah
quench
Sunnah
nudnik
funnel
gunnel
quinol
runnel
△tunnel
guenon
turn-in
turn-on
guango
quango
burn-up
turnip
turn-up
burner
cunner

gunner
punner
ruiner
runner
turner
wunner
guanos
burnet
gumnut
gurnet
punnet
runnet
Tuanku
curney
gurney
quinsy
△aurora
cupola
judoka
mucosa
rucola
cuboid
fucoid
mucoid
dumose
furole
furore
quooke
rugose
cut-off
put-off
run-off
bugong
dugong
oulong
judogi
zufoli
suborn
zufolo
Euro-MP
humour
huzoor
rumour
tumour
aurous
buboes
dumous
fumous
humous
mucous
putois
rufous
rugous
bug-out
buy-out
cut-out
dugout
rubout
eulogy
sulpha

cupped
cusped
cuspid
humped
pumped
pupped
supped
tupped
dumple
purpie
purple
rumple
supple
△yumpie
△yuppie
huppah
curpel
△humpen
lumpen
luppen
jump-up
bumper
cupper
dumper
gulper
humper
jumper
lumper
mumper
pulper
pumper
Rumper
supper
quipos
rumpus
Vulpes
output
pulpit
puppet
put-put
sumpit
Quapaw
furphy
humpty
murphy
numpty
purply
supply
tumphy
pulque
murrha
nutria
cupric
lubric
rubric
furred
outred
putrid
currie
durrie

quar'le
quarte
runrig
Tuareg
gurrah
hurrah
tugrik
burrel
musrol
murram
quorum
murren
murrin
outrun
quarto
Führer
burros
fueros
△guards
guiros
hubris
mucros
Munros
gutrot
turret
burrow
furrow
tutrix
hurray
murray
murrey
quarry
quirky
sunray
surrey
quartz
cuesta
△russia
subsea
cursed
cussed
gutsed
pulsed
sussed
Aussie
bursae
cuisse
gussie
nursle
puisne
pursue
tussle
hussif
Bursch
putsch
tussah
tusseh
bukshi
muesli
munshi

Russki
bursal
cursal
gunsel
mussel
pussel
russel
tussal
outsum
△bunsen
tutsan
bursar
curser
cursor
cusser
fusser
guiser
gutser
hussar
nurser
pulsar
purser
pusser
quasar
sudser
tusser
busses
cursus
tussis
gusset
outset
outsit
russet
subset
sunset
pursew
gun-shy
pudsey
puisny
Russky
lustra
quotha
cultic
fustic
fustoc
luetic
rustic
bunted
busted
gutted
hutted
jutted
nutted
putted
quited
runted
rusted
rutted
suited
tufted

tutted
△auntie
bustee
bustle
buttle
cup-tie
cuttle
cuttoe
gustie
guttae
guttle
hurtle
hustle
justle
lustre
mustee
puntee
puttee
puttie
quethe
rustle
rustre
subtle
suttee
suttle
turtle
cultch
quatch
quetch
quitch
duetti
buntal
curtal
subtil
custom
multum
quotum
tum-tum
△burton
button
luiten
lutten
muntin
mutton
pultan
pulton
pultun
putten
sultan
suntan
duetto
bust-up
dust-up
outtop
aunter
Auster
△bunter
buster
butter
cuiter

6 □u□t□s

culter
cutter
duster
guitar
gunter
gutter
hunter
hurter
Kultur
luster
muster
mutter
nutter
ouster
punter
putter
quoter
rutter
suitor
tufter
cultus
custos
duetts
juntos
Muftis
puntos
quotas
quotes
fustet
Muftat
tut-tut
surtax
auntly
curtly
curtsy
justly
subtly
sultry
suttly
aucuba
lucuma
lunula
Luzula
mutuca
suburb
queued
cupule
curule
euouae
future
jujube
lunule
mutule
nucule
puture
suture
tubule
eunuch
cumuli
tumuli

mutual
mutuum
auburn
autumn
lucumo
△**august**
tumult
augury
humusy
luxury
curved
fulvid
outvie
pulvil
vulval
culver
pulver
quaver
quiver
vulvar
curves
turves
curvet
survew
kurvey
purvey
survey
suivez
outwin
pulwar
tulwar
outwit
runway
subway
lunyie
gunyah
yum-yum
bunyip
huzza'd
fuzzle
guzzle
muzzle
nuzzle
puzzle
wuzzle
puzzel
buzzer
guizer
gutzer
nuzzer
putzes
aviate
aviary
ovibos
avocet
avidin
evader
avidly
availe
avails

evejar
evoker
avulse
évolué
evolve
evulse
svelte
uvulae
ovular
uvular
uvulas
evilly
ovally
avenge
△avenue
evince
avanti
avenir
evener
evenly
evzone
uveous
Evipan®
Svarga
averse
overdo
overgo
overby
overly
Avesta
ovisac
avisos
avoset
kvetch
avital
avatar
ovator
avoure
avouch
avaunt
evovae
avowed
avowal
avower
avowry
avoyer
sweard
awhape
awrack
aweary
sweaty
two-bit
swabby
kwacha
owl-car
twicer
swaddy
a'**where**
tweeze
twyere

awheel
sweets
tweeds
sweert
owlery
sweeny
sweepy
sweety
tweedy
tweely
tweeny
twight
twiggy
ewghen
awhile
twaite
awning
aweigh
owlish
sweirt
awaked
awaken
awoken
△**twelve**
twilit
owelty
twilly
swampy
swimmy
kwanza
twined
swinge
twinge
twiner
swink't
swanky
swanny
swingy
twangy
twenty
awsome
ywroke
awrong
swoosh
awmous
swiper
swipes
swipey
two-ply
Swarga
Swerga
awmrie
swarve
swerve
swarth
swaraj
dwarfs
swords
owerby
qwerty

swardy
swarty
swirly
twirly
swashy
swishy
twisty
swathe
awatch
swatch
switch
twitch
awetos
ewftes
swathy
swound
'twould
swoune
swivel
sweven
swivet
swownd
swowne
two-way
swayed
swayer
awayes
excamb
expand
oxland
exhale
oxgate
oxgang
oxtail
extant
extasy
Exocet®
exedra
exodic
△**exodus**
exceed
expend
extend
oxhead
extern
excess
except
expect
expert
exsect
exsert
extent
exogen
oxygen
ox-bird
excide
excise
excite
expire
extine

extirp
expiry
axilla
exilic
oxalic
oxslip
oxalis
oxymel
axeman
examen
exomis
exempt
exonic
exonym
extold
△oxford
expose
exposé
exhort
export
extort
exopod
exequy
exarch
axises
exotic
exited
excuse
exhume
expugn
exeunt
ox-eyed
Aymara
pyjama
aye-aye
by-lane
byname
by-name
cytase
gyrate
hypate
lynage
lyrate
mygale
zymase
pygarg
bypath
dynamo
bypass
by-past
byzant
dynast
gyrant
tyrant
bye-bye
dyable
nybble
dybbuk
cymbal
gymbal

Words marked △ may be spelled also with a capital letter

symbol
tymbal
fynbos
Syncom
eye-cup
dyadic
syndic
kynded
pye-dog
gylden
Hyades
syndet
hyaena
Cybele
pyrene
xylene
myself
rypeck
△lyceum
wyvern
eyeful
fylfot
kyogen
myogen
syngas
Pythia
mythic
Pythic
hyphae
lychee
hyphal
zythum
hyphen
△python
syphon
△typhon
cypher
sypher

mythos
mythus
sythes
typhus
Myrica
Syriac
eyliad
myriad
byline
bylive
by-time
lysine
pyrite
zymite
dyeing
eyeing
pyeing
typing
tykish
cytisi
hylism
lyrism
Syrism
Lydian
Syrian
Tyrian
Zyrian
lyrics
hylist
lyrist
typist
syrinx
typify
ryokan
cyclic
eyelid
syrlye
myelin

myelon
Syalon®
cycler
cyclos
cyclus
nyalas
by-plot
eyalet
eyelet
by-blow
bye-law
byrlaw
by-play
pyemia
pyemic
gymmal
Nyanja
nyanza
cyanic
gymnic
hymnic
hypnic
pycnic
pyknic
hymned
byrnie
hymnal
hypnum
cyanin
pycnon
pyoner
Hypnos
cygnet
gynney
Lycosa
myxoma
Pyrola
xyloma

zygoma
ayword
byroad
byword
cymoid
cytoid
hypoid
jymold
xyloid
zymoid
bygone
cymose
cytode
dynode
gyrose
pyrope
tylote
xylose
zygose
zygote
zymome
cyborg
kybosh
by-work
by-form
byroom
tycoon
dyvour
cymous
gyrous
pylons
syboes
sybows
tyroes
myopia
myopic
gypped
gyppie

tympan
nympho
gyppos
eye-pit
sylphy
hydria
pyuria
Cymric
hydric
synroc
cybrid
cyprid
hybrid
cypris
cyprus
hybris
hydros
byssal
gypsum
myosin
hyssop
byssus
cyeses
cyesis
Hyksos
myosis
cystic
myotic
mystic
cystid
Eyetie
myrtle
tystie
xystoi
hyetal
△system
syntan
oyster

xyster
Myrtus
syrtes
syrtis
xystos
xystus
syntax
lyfull
Tyburn
dysury
syrupy
sylvia
sylvae
sylvan
sylvas
lynxes
hydyne
syzygy
izzard
Azrael
ozaena
azygos
Szekel
azalea
azolla
Ozalid®
Azania
azonic
azonal
mzungu
azione
czapka
dzeren
azotic
tzetse

Words marked △ may be spelled also with a capital letter

7 □a□a□a

bananas
baracan
Canajan
carabao
caracal
caravan
caraway
Cataian
Catalan
catapan
Catayan
faraday
faraway
Galahad
Halakah
halavah
jacamar
jamadar
kahawai
kajawah
layaway
macadam
Malayam
Malayan
maracas
nacarat
pajamas
palamae
palatal
Pan-Arab
patamar
qabalah
Ramadan
rat-a-tat
Sabaean
Sabahan
sagaman
Saharan
sarafan
Satanas
tamarao
tamarau
tanadar
waratah
yatagan
caramba
catawba
△balance
balancé
Jamaica
navarch
Tabasco®
vacance
vacancy
valance
calando
kabaddi
tamandu
cabaret
cadaver
camaïeu
caramel
caravel
damages
falafel
galabea
galatea
hanaper
lazaret
manager
manatee
naiades
palaver
panacea
Papaver
parapet
para-red
ravager
Saracen
tabaret
tanager
Wahabee
Falange
galanga
sarangi
calathi
earache
Falasha
Halacha
Maratha
Marathi
navarho
panache
paratha
sagathy
samadhi
tamasha
baladin
canakin
cap-a-pie
cap-à-pie
carabid
carabin
dataria
fanatic
faradic
galabia
gazania
jalapic
jalapin
Latakia
malacia
malaria
manakin
Mazarin
nagapie
Nasalis
navarin
paladin
Panagia
patagia
Patarin
ramakin
ratafia
salamis
Sarapic
Sarapis
△satanic
savarin
tabanid
talaria
tamarin
Tamarix
Tataric
vanadic
karaoke
malarky
banally
batable
capable
cavalla
cavally
datable
eatable
fadable
fatally
hatable
makable
manacle
namable
nasally
pacable
papable
papally
parable
parafle
payable
ratable
ratably
salable
salably
savable
sayable
takable
tamable
taxable
taxably
vatable
mahatma
paracme
salaams
caranna
carauna
lasagna
lasagne
rabanna
savanna
talaunt
camaron
caracol
catalog
catalos
galagos
gasahol
kakapos
lavabos
laxator
macacos
magalog
marabou
matador
Navahos
Navajos
pakapoo
Panadol®
parador
parados
paradox
paragon
paramos
parasol
△parazoa
sabaton
sacaton
salamon
sapajou
Tagalog
Tagálog
talayot
catalpa
bagarre
catarrh
cavalry
macabre
palabra
△tanagra
waza-ari
zamarra
zamarro
babassu
bagasse
Bahaism
Bahaist
Dadaism
Dadaist
fadaise
karaism
Lamaism
Lamaist
malaise
Sabaism
Bahaite
canasta
catasta
Karaite
Maranta
namaste
rabatte
Sabaoth
Bahadur
Balanus
△calamus
Calanus
Carabus
caracul
databus
△karakul
labarum
ladanum
macaque
Tabanus
vacatur
Varanus
paranym
palazzi
palazzo
cambial
catboat
day-boat
jambeau
pap-boat
Zambian
rag-baby
hawbuck
iambics
layback
payback
sambuca
sawbuck
zambuck
carbide
gambado
lambada
man-body
naebody
babbler
bas-bleu
bawbees
cambrel
dabbler
darbies
gabbler
gambier
gambler
gambrel
garbled
garbler
has-been
jambier
mad-bred
marbled
marbler
marbles
rabbler
rambler
tabbied
wabbler
warbler
cabbage
cabbagy
camboge
gamboge
garbage
cambric
garboil

Words marked △ may be spelled also with a capital letter

7 □a□d□n

lambkin
parboil
bar-bell
barbola
barbule
cabbala
falbala
hagbolt
kabbala
lamb-ale
patball
pay-bill
ragbolt
sawbill
tap-bolt
waxbill
waybill
bambini
bambino
canbank
carbine
dabbing
daubing
ear-bone
gabbing
hatband
hayband
jambone
jawbone
lambent
nabbing
rabbins
rabboni
rawbone
Ray-Bans®
salband
tabbing
dambrod
day-book
gabbros
gas-buoy
jambool
law-book
rag-book
Banbury
Barbary
catbird
daubery
gabbard
gabbart
garbure
halberd
halbert
Hamburg
hauberk
lambert
may-bird
tambura
tanbark
cambism
cambist
earbash
gambist
iambist
lambast
rag-bush
tarbush
△babbitt
barbate
dabbity
hay-bote
rabbits
rabbity
Sabbath
Barbour®
cambium
harbour
jambeux
tambour
jambiya
lamboys
Bacchae
barchan
car-coat
day-coal
fascial
faucial
gas-coal
panchax
paschal
pascual
bawcock
dawcock
haycock
cascade
falcade
saccade
sarcode
catched
catchen
catcher
darcies
fancied
fancier
farcied
hatchel
hatcher
hatches
hatchet
larchen
latchet
manchet
Märchen
marcher
marches
mascled
matched
matcher
Nancies
narceen
parched
patched
patcher
ranched
rancher
raschel
ratchet
satchel
saucier
talcked
watcher
watches
watchet
calcify
farcify
△bacchic
bacchii
macchie
sarcoid
carcake
gas-coke
oatcake
pancake
bascule
bauchle
calculi
catcall
falcula
law-calf
mancala
masculy
saccule
sacculi
saucily
vascula
sarcoma
balcony
calcine
dancing
farcing
fascine
larceny
Marconi®
marconi
nascent
talcing
vaccine
fauchon
gauchos
halcyon
Manchoo
pak-choi
raccoon
ranchos
salchow
sanchos
baccara
baccare
cascara
d'accord
lancers
mascara
cap-case
carcase
carcass
△fascism
△fascist
laicise
sarcasm
talcose
baccate
calcite
falcate
laicity
marcato
paucity
saccate
Bacchus
calcium
catchup
farceur
jacchus
patch-up
rancour
raucous
sanctum
Sanctus
sarcous
talcous
laicize
bandeau
band-saw
cardiac
handbag
handcar
handjar
handsaw
hard-pan
land-law
landman
land-rat
Landtag
land-tax
Mazdean
Pandean
sandbag
sandman
Wardian
yardman
habdabs
caddice
candock
cardecu
daddock
haddock
Maddock
paddock
pandect
candida
baddies
bandied
candied
candies
dandler
dawdler
handier
handled
handler
handsel
handset
hard-set
ländler
mandrel
paddler
pardner
raddled
saddler
waddler
dandify
hand-off
bandage
faldage
fardage
yardage
baldric
Baldwin
Band-aid®
band-aid
baudric
bawdkin
gaudgie
hard-hit
mandril
maudlin
sandpit
Vaudois
hardoke
may-duke
△vandyke
zaddiks
bawdily
candela
dandily
gaudily
handily
hardily
mandala
mandola
pardale
rag-doll
sandfly
tardily
balding
bandana
banding
candent
farding
gadding
gardant
△gardens
jamdani
landing
madding
nandine
padding

7 □a□d□o

pardine
sanding
sardana
sardine
wadding
warding
yardang
band-box
bandook
bandrol
caldron
cardoon
caudron
eardrop
hands-on
hard-got
hardtop
hard-won
lardoon
mandioc
Pandion
pandoor
sandbox
sandboy
sand-hog
tandoor
wardrop
bandora
bandore
bandura
caldera
gaudery
laddery
mandira
mandora
△pandora
pandore
pandura
pay-dirt
sanders
yard-arm
baddish
baldish
bardash
caddish
caddyss
faddish
faddism
faddist
hardish
Kaddish
maddest
Mahdism
Mahdist
maidish
maidism
pay-desk
Qaddish
rag-dust
saddest
saddish
saidest
sawdust
bandits
caudate
△mandate
candour
carduus
eardrum
handful
handgun
handout
hand-out
hard-run
pandour
sardius
taedium
vaudoux
tardive
hagdown
lay-down
man-days
baseman
camerae
cameral
cameras
case-law
caseman
catenae
catenas
cateran
caveman
△danelaw
daresay
faceman
gamelan
gametal
gateman
gateway
kamerad
lace-man
laneway
lateral
Lateran
name-day
paterae
raceway
rate-cap
sazerac®
tapetal
wakeman
zareeba
cadence
cadency
faience
faïence
fayence
ha'pence
latence
latency
patency
valence
valency
calends
fazenda
kalends
capelet
caperer
caterer
cat-eyed
faceted
gateleg
havened
haverel
lakelet
lameter
latexes
layered
paperer
racemed
ravener
sad-eyed
sakeret
tagetes
tapered
taperer
Tasered
wagerer
wakened
wakener
watered
waterer
wavelet
waverer
face-off
rake-off
take-off
Fabergé
have-a-go
pace-egg
parerga
saw-edge
catechu
Ganesha
Babesia
camelid
capelin
Galenic
gametic
hare-lip
javelin
malefic
paresis
paretic
racemic
ramekin
rarebit
ravelin
tabetic
valeric
basenji
cadelle
canella
Capella
dazedly
eagerly
fadedly
gabelle
gazelle
hazelly
jadedly
Javelle
labella
lamella
mace-ale
nacelle
nakedly
padella
parella
parelle
△patella
sabella
sacella
save-all
zanella
maremma
caserne
cayenne
ha'penny
Karenni
pageant
taverna
camelot
catelog
gazebos
have-not
mamelon
matelot
name-son
page-boy
paletot
saveloy
waveson
lace-ups
Cabeiri
camelry
Madeira
pareira
vanessa
vareuse
cavetti
cavetto
G-agents
galeate
galette
gaseity
△gazette
jadeite
Janeite
Lacerta
layette
magenta
majesty
maleate
navette
palette
paneity
ramenta
V-agents
baleful
baneful
bateaux
cadeaux
cage-cup
cajeput
careful
caseous
dareful
easeful
fade-out
fateful
gaseous
gateaus
gâteaux
gazeful
hateful
haveour
mazeful
race-cup
rageful
rameous
takeout
taleful
tapetum
wakeful
wameful
cadenza
cat-flap
earflap
half-cap
half-day
half-pay
halfway
saffian
fat-face
maffick
baffler
gauffer
haaf-net
maffled
palfrey
raffler
rat-flea
tax-free
waffler
caffein
hafflin
halflin
halfwit
mafflin
Mayfair
parfait
rag-fair
bagfuls
caffila

Words marked △ may be spelled also with a capital letter

canfuls
fanfold
hatfuls
jarfuls
jawfall
panfuls
vatfuls
daffing
gaffing
half-one
naffing
pakfong
payfone
ratfink
damfool
jaw-foot
saffron
half-ape
carfare
fanfare
hayfork
Kaffers
Kaffirs
oak-fern
salfern
warfare
wayfare
batfish
catfish
gabfest
garfish
hagfish
raffish
sawfish
taffeta
taffety
half-cut
gangway
hangman
pangram
tangram
Haggada
raggedy
baggies
bangled
cargoes
dangler
fangled
gangrel
haggler
jangler
langrel
langued
languet
laugher
mangler
mangoes
Pangaea
tangled
tangler
tangoed
wangler
baggage
langaha
bargain
ganglia
languid
sangria
tanghin
baggily
largely
mangold
nargile
nargily
oak-gall
rangoli
tangelo
May-game
pangamy
sangoma
Targums
bagging
banging
fagging
gagging
ganging
gauging
hanging
jagging
lagging
margent
nagging
pangene
panging
pargana
ragging
sagging
tagging
tangent
wagging
waygone
zagging
hangdog
jargoon
languor
daggers
day-girl
faggery
haggard
jaggery
laggard
raggery
Rangers
saggard
taggers
waggery
bargest
haggish
largess
largish
margosa
waggish
gargety
haughty
maggoty
naughty
paughty
hangout
valgous
gang-bye
bathyal
cathead
each-way
fat-head
lashkar
mashlam
mashman
mash-vat
nashgab
Paphian
pathway
rachial
raghead
rawhead
saphead
warhead
washday
washrag
yakhdan
yashmak
cathode
kathode
raphide
rawhide
cashier
dasheen
machree
Maghreb
tar-heel
yachter
kachcha
naphtha
bashlik
bathmic
Daphnia
daphnid
△kashmir
machair
Maghrib
mashlim
mashlin
yachtie
dasheki
dashiki
cathole
ear-hole
jawhole
lapheld
manhole
rat-hole
fathoms
nathemo
sashimi
bashing
dashing
kachina
lashing
lathing
machine
manhunt
mashing
saphena
washing
cash-box
cathood
dash-pot
fashion
machzor
manhood
tachyon
washpot
wanhope
bathers
Cathari
Cathars
fashery
fathers
gathers
hachure
jaghire
kacheri
lathery
saxhorn
washers
washery
hashish
pachisi
rathest
tachism
tachist
machete
bashful
bathtub
Bauhaus
gashful
△kashrus
△kashrut
man-hour
mashlum
mash-tub
mash-tun
Pakhtun
Pashtun
washout
wash-out
washtub
cachexy
basilar
Caliban
Canidae
capital
capitan
Cariban
caritas
Dalilah
datival
fajitas
Gadidae
habitat
Harijan
janizar
laminae
laminar
Laridae
latitat
magical
Mahican
marital
matinal
maximal
paginal
△radical
Ranidae
Ratitae
sahibah
salival
talipat
taxicab
taximan
taxiway
vaginae
vaginal
vaginas
vanitas
Vatican
wanigan
marimba
paxiuba
△carioca
tapioca
Matilda
basinet
△cabinet
caliber
calices
calipee
caliper
caliver
carices
galilee
habited
lamiger
lamiter
latices
Latiner
Malines
mariner
marines
matinee
matinée
patined
radicel
radices
ravined
sakiyeh

salices
salicet
samisen
satinet
tabinet
taliped
talipes
varices
satisfy
havings
makings
ratings
savings
takings
babiche
caliche
kamichi
Lapiths
malicho
taniwha
basidia
Cabiric
canikin
davidia
Fatimid
Hamitic
Hasidic
Hasidim
lacinia
manikin
maximin
△pacific
Palilia
△papilio
Ramilie
salicin
satiric
Tamilic
panicky
bacilli
barilla
calicle
cariole
Daniell
dariole
lapilli
mamilla
△manilla
manille
maniple
maxilla
panicle
papilla
patible
rabidly
radiale
radicle
rapidly
ravioli
sanicle
tacitly
validly
vanilla
vapidly
variola
variole
cariama
nations
patient
radiant
rations
salient
sapient
taxiing
valiant
variant
bar-iron
calicos
cami-top
Capitol
caribou
casinos
galipot
halidom
halimot
haricot
janitor
Ladinos
malison
manihoc
Manihot
manitou
maticos
parison
paritor
sadiron
saligot
talipot
warison
calibre
cariere
caviare
laniard
laniary
Babilism
△mafiosi
△mafioso
Naziism
balista
batiste
jacinth
labiate
△radiata
radiate
△sagitta
Samiote
satiate
satiety
variate
variety
badious
cacique
carious
cazique
fatigue
garigue
habitué
habitus
halibut
halitus
haviour
Lalique
maximum
Panicum
paviour
Salique
sanious
△saviour
vagitus
various
Panjabi
manjack
man-jack
banjoes
Mas-John
mah-jong
zanjero
backpay
backsaw
barkhan
Gaekwar
Gaikwar
hack-saw
jackdaw
jackman
jarkman
markkaa
markkas
markman
packman
pack-rat
packway
parkway
sabkhah
sabkhat
tank-car
Walkman®
walkway
tap-kick
backset
backsey
bark-bed
cackler
hackler
hackles
hacklet
hackney
△jackeen
nankeen
tackled
tackler
talkies
Zadkiel
package
sackage
tankage
banksia
hawkbit
jacksie
lack-all
lankily
pawkily
tackily
back-end
backing
balking
banking
barking
carking
gaskins
hacking
hawking
lacking
mankind
marking
packing
parking
racking
Rankine
ranking
sacking
sarking
tacking
talking
tanking
tasking
vacking
walking
yanking
backhoe
backlog
backlot
back-row
hack-log
jackpot
markhor
backare
cankery
hackery
jankers
tankard
dankish
darkish
hawkish
jackass
larkish
mawkish
parkish
rackets
rackett
rackety
tackety
hackbut
sackbut
sackful
tankful
walk-out
lackeys
Sankhya
carload
fabliau
hallian
hallway
kail-pat
mailbag
mail-car
mailman
mailvan
oakleaf
pallial
Paulian
pay-load
rail-car
railman
railway
tableau
earlobe
wallaba
wallaby
carlock
daglock
earlock
fallacy
△gallice
laylock
oar-lock
padlock
raploch
warlock
ballade
May-lady
caulker
dailies
dallier
earlier
earlies
gaulter
haulier
nail-bed
railbed
rallied
rallier
sallied
tablier
tailles
tallied
tallier
tallies
vaulted
vaulter
wallies
waulker
bailiff
hayloft
haulage

Words marked △ may be spelled also with a capital letter

tallage
tally-ho
baillie
haploid
mail-gig
marl-pit
racloir
tabloid
taillie
tailzie
tall-oil
waylaid
catlike
lac-lake
man-like
saclike
warlike
day-lily
gallfly
hallali
may-lily
tail-fly
caulome
gas-lime
Kallima
oak-lump
ballant
balling
bawling
bay-line
cabling
callant
calling
calluna
carline
carling
catling
cauline
darling
daylong
eanling
fabling
failing
falling
fatling
gadling
gallant
galling
garland
gatling
halling
harling
kaoline
Karling
Lallans
lalling
lawland
madling
mailing
malling
marline
marling
nailing
oakling
palling
pallone
Pauline
railing
ralline
ratline
ratling
sailing
sapling
tabling
tail-end
tailing
tallent
tanling
wailing
walling
warling
wauling
wawling
ball-boy
balloon
call-box
call-boy
earldom
Gaeldom
galleon
Gallios
galliot
galloon
hallion
hallyon
kail-pot
mailbox
maillot
nail-rod
paillon
tallboy
Walloon
fahlerz
fahlore
failure
gallery
mallard
maulers
maulgre
May-lord
nailery
tailard
vallary
warlord
Baalism
ballast
carlish
Carlism
Carlist
earless
gallise
Gaulish
hapless
hatless
lawless
law-list
napless
oarless
pay-list
rayless
sacless
sapless
tallish
taplash
taxless
wayless
Baalite
fat-lute
gallate
tallith
bail-out
ballium
balls-up
callous
call-out
fall-guy
fallout
fall-out
gallium
gallnut
malleus
pailful
pallium
parlour
parlous
railbus
wailful
baclava
baklava
Pahlavi
△pavlova
gallows
matlows
Mawlawi
sallowy
tallowy
valleys
wall-eye
gallize
Cadmean
nagmaal
oatmeal
palm-cat
pap-meat
wadmaal
Calmuck
gammock
hammock
Kalmuck
mammock
man-made
larmier
malmsey
palmiet
barmaid
barmkin
palm-oil
balmily
hammily
harmala
sawmill
wadmoll
tagmeme
calmant
carmine
catmint
caymans
damming
farming
garment
haemony
harmans
harmine
harmony
jamming
jasmine
lamming
maiming
payment
ragment
raiment
ramming
salmons
sarment
Tammany
varment
varmint
warming
wayment
daimios
palmtop
daymark
earmark
farmery
mammary
May-morn
palmary
palmyra
saimiri
waymark
badmash
farmost
harmost
marmose
oak-mast
palmist
rammish
warmish
basmati
magmata
mammate
mammoth
Marmite®
marmite
palmate
tagmata
cadmium
harmful
palmful
balneal
dawn-man
gainsay
harn-pan
taeniae
taenias
Barnaby
wannabe
bannock
cannach
jannock
pannick
zarnich
Kannada
daunder
daunter
fainted
haunted
haunter
jauntee
Laender
launder
maunder
nainsel'
nannied
nannies
painted
painter
pannier
sainted
saunter
tainted
taunter
vaunted
vaunter
carnify
damnify
magnify
sawn-off
carnage
pannage
tannage
wainage
paunchy
raunchy
jauntie
cannily
cannula
faintly
fannell
gauntly
paenula
saintly
magnums
canning
cannons

7 □a□n□o

damning
darning
dawning
earning
fanning
fawning
haining
manning
panning
tanning
vanning
warning
yawning
bagnios
daunton
maintop
rainbow
wannion
cannery
garners
gauntry
laundry
manners
tannery
badness
carnose
earnest
farness
fatness
faunist
gabnash
garnish
gayness
harness
Jainism
Jainist
laxness
madness
mannish
mannose
pannose
patness
rawness
sadness
tarnish
varnish
waeness
wanness
wannish
bainite
Cainite
gahnite
kainite
magnate
magneto
mannite
Samnite
tannate
gainful
hafnium
hahnium
mainour
painful
carneys
caporal
majorat
man-o'-war
Masorah
mayoral
samosas
samovar
tatouay
j'adoube
barocco
capouch
patonce
baconer
baloney
baronet
bayonet
cacolet
cajoler
calomel
caloyer
caromel
damosel
damozel
favored
favorer
halogen
haroset
jaconet
parolee
Rasores
Samoyed
tabooed
taborer
taboret
taloned
valonea
wagoner
katorga
basoche
caroche
galoche
panocha
Aaronic
caloric
△calorie
camogie
canonic
Canopic
carotid
carotin
galopin
△jacobin
Japonic
△laconic
lanolin
mahonia
malonic
masonic
paeonic
parodic
parotic
parotid
parotis
sagouin
saponin
saronic
Saxonic
taborin
△valonia
bazooka
bazouki
gazooka
matooke
paiocke
pajocke
palooka
talooka
cagoule
kagoule
panoply
baronne
façonné
ganoine
kayoing
Madonna
Mahound
gasohol
manoaos
palolos
cacoepy
jaloppy
△camorra
△canonry
favours
masonry
savoury
vapours
vapoury
baboosh
Barotse
caboose
carouse
jalouse
papoose
vamoose
zamouse
cahoots
calotte
dacoity
dakoiti
fagotti
fagotto
garotte
gavotte
hap'orth
lavolta
baroque
Canopus
carolus
jacobus
madoqua
cacodyl
kakodyl
paronym
tan-ooze
pampean
salpian
calpack
earpick
manpack
rampick
ratpack
Tampico
tappice
ba'spiel
camp-bed
dappled
day-peep
lamprey
nappies
sampler
sapples
rampage
dauphin
nauplii
△sapphic
garpike
lampuka
lampuki
rampike
happily
lamp-fly
maypole
tadpole
campana
capping
carping
damping
gasping
happing
jampani
kampong
lamping
lapping
mapping
napping
parpane
parpend
parpent
rampant
ramping
rapping
rasping
salpinx
sapping
T'ai-p'ing
tamping
tapping
vamping
wappend
wapping
warping
zampone
zamponi
camphor
campion
harpoon
lampion
lampoon
marplot
Rajpoot
rampion
tampion
bagpipe
Campari
carpark
carport
jaspery
lampern
lampers
mappery
pampero
rampart
rampire
rapport
sampire
vampire
dampish
gampish
harpist
Lappish
mappist
pappose
Rappist
vampish
wampish
waspish
waypost
palpate
Rappite
warpath
earplug
pappous
banquet
basqued
lacquer
lacquey
marquee
masquer
parquet
racquet
marquis
Pasquil
Pasquin
fair-day
fairway
pairial
pair-oar
patrial
saurian
△taurean

Words marked △ may be spelled also with a capital letter

Zairean
saprobe
barrace
barrack
barrico
caprice
carrack
carract
carrect
carrick
farruca
hatrack
hayrick
matrice
parrock
patrick
patrico
tarrock
hag-ride
hayride
tan-ride
barrier
cairned
carried
carrier
farrier
hair-eel
hairnet
harried
harrier
married
marrier
parried
tarried
tarrier
vaurien
caprify
sacrify
barrage
farrago
lairage
caproic
darrain
gag-rein
hairpin
labroid
ram-raid
sauroid
naartje
paprika
bairnly
caerule
carrell
fairily
favrile
laurels
marrels
payroll
pay-roll
safrole
hadrome
macramé
macrami
Barrens
barring
cab-rank
cadrans
Cairene
caprine
earring
fairing
farrand
farrant
jarring
ladrone
latrant
latrine
madroña
madrone
madroño
manrent
Marrano
marring
padrone
padroni
pairing
sacring
tarring
taurine
vagrant
warrand
warrant
warring
wauring
barrios
bar-room
carrion
carry-on
gadroon
hairdos
maormor
patriot
patroon
taproom
taproot
warrior
satrapy
Macrura
padrero
patrero
tabrere
fairish
labrose
lairise
madrasa
matrass
matross
Maurist
sacrist
caprate
carroty
garrote
nacrite
narrate
parroty
haircut
nacrous
natrium
sabreur
marrowy
narrows
darrayn
lairize
bass-bar
batsman
Capsian
capstan
cat's-ear
cat's-paw
darshan
daysman
daystar
gadsman
magsman
marshal
oarsman
Pan-Slav
passman
rakshas
ramstam
tapsman
tar-seal
sassaby
car-sick
cassock
hassock
lassock
ransack
passade
passado
wayside
banshee
dabster
daisied
Dansker
falsies
fatsoes
gagster
hag-seed
hamster
harshen
harslet
hayseed
kamseen
lassoed
lassoes
mahseer
maister
mawseed
mayster
paisley
palsied
pansied
parsley
parsnep
passkey
sarsden
sarsnet
tapster
tarsier
wabster
waisted
waister
yapster
falsify
salsify
massage
passage
paysage
sapsago
sausage
catskin
catsuit
caustic
karstic
lawsuit
Mao-suit
parsnip
payslip
vassail
warship
wassail
Baisaki
capsule
falsely
harshly
Jap-silk
Marsala
Salsola
tassell
balsamy
gaysome
Lakshmi
△satsuma
waesome
bausond
cassino
cassone
dapsone
gassing
lapsang
paisano
parsing
passant
passing
pausing
raising
ramsons
tar-sand
bassoon
caisson
earshot
mansion
△passion
samshoo
tap-shoe
tar-spot
caesura
Hansard
maestri
maestro
maistry
mansard
Massora
matsuri
samsara
tapstry
bassist
falsish
falsism
Parsism
cassata
falsity
varsity
wadsett
caesium
caestus
danseur
masseur
passout
saksaul
Tarsius
cassava
massive
passive
cat's-eye
janskys
Vaishya
capsize
man-size
caltrap
cartway
castral
Dantean
dart-sac
factual
fast-day
Haitian
Kantian
lacteal
Laotian
maltman
manteau
mantram
mantrap
Mantuan
martial
Martian
partial
Raetian
raftman
rat-trap
saltcat
salt-fat
tactual

Words marked △ may be spelled also with a capital letter

7 □a□t□b

Watteau
xantham
xanthan
zaptiah
cattabu
mastaba
Caltech
cantico
castock
factice
haptics
hattock
Lactuca
lattice
mastich
mattock
nautics
tactics
bastide
fantads
fantods
battler
canteen
cantlet
cantred
cantref
castled
earthen
fanteeg
farthel
farther
fartlek
gantlet
maatjes
manteel
mantlet
mantoes
martlet
mast-fed
mauther
mawther
△narthex
oak-tree
pad-tree
panther
panties
pantler
△partlet
partner
pasties
ratteen
rattler
saltier
saltoed
sautéed
tartlet
tattler
waltzer
wastrel
wattled
wattles
zabtieh
zaptieh
caitiff
cast-off
laithfu'
mastiff
part-off
Tartufe
cartage
lastage
vantage
waftage
wantage
wastage
wattage
cantrip
△captain
eastlin
factoid
fantail
gastric
gastrin
mastoid
mattoid
nartjie
rat-tail
rattlin
sautoir
tag-tail
△tantric
wagtail
want-wit
xanthic
xanthin
partake
battels
battill
cantala
Castile
cattalo
cattily
daytale
earthly
hartely
hastily
kantela
kantele
Kartell
nastily
nattily
nautili
pantile
saltily
tactile
tastily
tattily
daytime
laytime
Maytime
pastime
ragtime
wartime
baiting
banteng
banting
basting
batting
bay-tine
cantina
canting
casting
darting
easting
Fastens
fasting
fatting
halting
hatting
karting
lactone
Lagting
lantana
lasting
malting
Martini
Martini®
martini
matting
mattins
paktong
pantine
panting
parting
pasting
patting
raiting
ranting
ratting
saltant
salting
tantony
tartana
tartane
tartine
tasting
tatting
vatting
wafting
waiting
wanting
wasting
bastion
caltrop
cantdog
cantion
caption
cartoon
caution
faction
Gasthof
hautboy
paction
partook
saltbox
taction
warthog
Zantiot
bastard
battero
battery
capture
castory
cattery
cautery
dastard
eastern
factory
facture
gaiters
garters
laetare
lantern
martyry
mastery
mattery
nattery
parture
pastern
pasture
pattern
rapture
rattery
saltern
saltire
tantara
△tartare
Tartary
tatters
tattery
wafture
wastery
baptise
baptism
△baptist
cattish
Dantist
fantasm
fantast
fantasy
fastish
fattest
fattish
Kantism
Kantist
lactase
lactose
maltase
△maltese
maltose
rattish
Saktism
saltish
tactism
tartish
battuta
cantata
cantate
hastate
lactate
partita
partite
saltate
saltato
vastity
cab-tout
canthus
faitour
hauteur
Mantoux
mastful
pantoum
paste-up
rastrum
santour
tactful
tantrum
caitive
captive
factive
tantivy
Fastext
martext
baptize
canulae
canulas
fabular
faculae
facular
hamular
hanuman
lacunae
lacunal
lacunar
Laputan
maculae
macular
natural
pabular
paludal
papulae
papular
radulae
radular
ramular
samurai
tabulae
tabular
calumba
caducei
calumet
manumea
manurer
natured
papules

Words marked △ may be spelled also with a capital letter

raguled
saluter
babuche
Baluchi
capuche
manumit
pagurid
paludic
parulis
patulin
raoulia
Tamulic
mazurka
yamulka
zakuska
zakuski
casuals
vacuole
vaguely
vacuums
calumny
tabuing
babudom
baguios
Basutos
lanugos
galumph
capuera
daquiri
January
saburra
saguaro
saouari
vaquero
babuism
casuist
vacuist
faculty
fatuity
Nahuatl
vacuate
vacuity
valuate
baculum
cajuput
famulus
fatuous
hamulus
pabulum
ramulus
vacuous
Jacuzzi®
jacuzzi
Latvian
garvock
vaivode
waivode
navvied
salvoes
salvage
mauvais
mauvein
naevoid
naively
naïvely
valvula
valvule
carving
mauvine
parvenu
salving
△calvary
carvery
halvers
taivers
taivert
canvass
Fauvism
Fauvist
harvest
Jahvism
Jahvist
naivist
parvise
Saivism
Yahvist
larvate
naïveté
naiveté
naivety
naïvety
Saivite
salvete
valvate
carve-up
narwhal
waiwode
waywode
hag-weed
man-week
matweed
mayweed
oarweed
ragweed
tarweed
cat-walk
gadwall
jaywalk
maxwell
warwolf
batwing
lapwing
lauwine
waxwing
barwood
camwood
dagwood
oak-wood
rag-wool
sapwood
catworm
day-work
hayward
haywire
lapwork
madwort
maw-worm
nayward
nayword
ragwork
ragworm
ragwort
saw-wort
vanward
war-worn
waxwork
wayward
wayworn
bagwash
car-wash
fan-wise
mapwise
Yahwist
Manxman
Marxian
Marxism
Marxist
bauxite
man-year
satyral
barytes
calyces
calyxes
lazy-bed
baby-sit
barytic
katydid
ladykin
satyric
satyrid
calycle
ladyfly
taxying
varying
Babylon
baryton
dasypod
ladycow
Babygro®
dasyure
halyard
lanyard
tanyard
babyish
calypso
easy-osy
ladyish
ladyism
zanyism
manyata
Dasypus
ladybug
marybud
papyrus
jazzman
dazzler
matzahs
Tadzhik
jazzily
calzone
calzoni
canzona
canzone
canzoni
fanzine
jazz-pop
madzoon
matzoon
mamzers
mazzard
matzoth
bazzazz
pazzazz
△abraxas
Abbasid
ablator
abrazos
abscind
abscond
obscene
abactor
obscure
abscess
abscise
absciss
abidden
abiding
Abaddon
abreact
absence
abreast
obverse
obsequy
observe
abigail
abthane
obligee
abridge
obligor
ebriose
absinth
ebriate
ebriety
obviate
oblique
obvious
abalone
obelion
obolary
abolish
ebbless
obelise
obelisk
ability
obelize
abomasa
abandon
ebonise
ebonist
ebonite
ebonize
abroach
abdomen
abiosis
abiotic
obconic
abrooke
abjoint
obloquy
absolve
Iberian
obtrude
uberous
abysmal
abyssal
abashed
abusage
abusion
obesity
abusive
abettal
abuttal
obitual
ebbtide
abetted
abetter
abutted
abutter
abattis
abstain
abettor
abature
abjurer
abought
ébauche
aboulia
obovoid
obovate
abaxial
abeyant
Achaean
Achaian
octaval
scraich
scranch
△scratch
scrauch
△achates
ectases
scraper
scraggy
scraigh
scraugh
ectasis
oceanic

7 □c□c□l

△oceanid
octadic
sciarid
sciatic
scrapie
accablé
actable
octapla
scrawly
acharné
scranny
scrawny
Actaeon
ichabod
octagon
octavos
échappé
schappe
scrappy
schanse
acharya
schanze
iceboat
scabbed
scabies
scabrid
iceball
ice-belt
scabble
scybala
iceberg
ice-blue
acacias
ecocide
acyclic
scuchin
ice-cold
Acadian
scudded
scudder
scudler
acidify
scedule
scuddle
academe
academy
acidity
scleral
△science
screech
screich
acceder
schemer
screwed
screwer
ycleped
acreage
screigh
icteric
icterid
screaky

écuelle
ack-emma
Acheron
echelon
ycleap'd
ycleepe
Acmeism
Acmeist
accents
ocreate
octette
icterus
screw-up
screeve
scherzi
scherzo
ice-free
scoffer
scaffie
scuffle
ice-foot
aciform
scaglia
Scoggin
ecthyma
Acrilan®
actinal
scribal
scriech
scritch
scriber
accinge
accidie
aclinic
acridin
actinia
actinic
schisma
echidna
scriene
actinon
schizos
scrimpy
eclipse
echinus
occiput
achieve
scrieve
ocellar
schlich
schlock
occlude
scalade
scalado
scalder
scalled
scalpel
scalper
scolder
sculler
ecology

acclaim
oceloid
P-Celtic
Q-Celtic
scaldic
sculpin
Iceland
scalene
scaleni
scaling
scallop
scolion
scollop
acaleph
schlepp
oculist
schloss
acolyte
acolyth
oculate
aculeus
ocellus
scumbag
schmeck
schmock
schmuck
scamper
schmoes
Scomber
scumber
scummed
scummer
scamble
schmelz
scumble
schmooz
scandal
scanned
scanner
scented
scunner
iconify
acantha
Scandic
scantle
scantly
schnell
economy
schnook
schnaps
scenary
scenery
schnorr
acinose
iciness
iconise
aconite
ichnite
acinous
acknown
iconize

acrobat
scholar
scrotal
accoied
accoyed
acrogen
acroter
October
scooped
scooper
scooter
scroggy
△scrooge
scrouge
acromia
ecbolic
ectopia
ectopic
octofid
scholia
accoyld
schoole
schools
scrowle
scroyle
account
echoing
ectozoa
octopod
accompt
accourt
accoast
echoise
echoism
echoist
sciolto
eclogue
octopus
scrotum
acronym
echoize
icepack
scepter
scupper
acapnia
scepsis
△sceptic
scapple
scapula
scopula
sceptre
sceptry
scopate
scyphus
acarian
accrual
ochreae
scoriac
scoriae
Acarida
acorned

scarfed
scarlet
scarped
scarper
scarred
scarves
scorner
scorper
scorser
scarify
scorify
écorché
acaroid
acerbic
ochroid
Scorpio
scurril
Acarina
acarine
eccrine
ocarina
scoring
acerose
actress
accrete
acerate
acerous
ochrous
Scirpus
scissel
scissil
acushla
scissor
Scotian
schtick
schtuck
Scotice
scatted
scatter
scutter
scythed
scyther
acetify
Scotify
scutage
Scotchy
ichthic
Scottie
acutely
scatole
scuttle
scytale
scotoma
scotomy
acetone
schtook
schtoom
ecotype
acetose
△ecstasy
Scotism

Words marked △ may be spelled also with a capital letter

Scotist
acetate
scutate
acatour
acetous
ichthys
acaudal
accusal
scrubby
scrunch
accused
accuser
ictuses
scauper
scourer
scouser
scouter
scruffy
scourge
acouchi
acouchy
scourie
scrutin
octuple
scruple
scrummy
scrutos
scrumpy
acquire
actuary
accurse
accurst
acquest
acquist
scourse
acquite
actuate
scrunty
Sciurus
scavage
scowder
scowrer
scowrie
ectypal
acrylic
ecdysis
scrying
scazons
advance
ideally
adharma
od's-bobs
oddball
edictal
eductor
edacity
educate
adrenal
addenda
adherer
odd-even

uddered
adverse
idlesse
edifice
edified
edifier
adagios
admiral
admirer
advices
advised
adviser
adhibit
sdeigne
advisor
odaller
udaller
od's-life
idyllic
odd-like
idolise
idolism
idolist
odalisk
odylism
adulate
idolize
adamant
oddment
Adamite
edental
adenoid
identic
odontic
adenoma
adenine
adonise
oddness
Odinism
Odinist
Odonata
adonize
idiotcy
od-force
idiotic
odzooks
adjoint
adjourn
adapted
adapter
adopted
adopter
edaphic
adeptly
adaptor
adipose
adermin
odorant
address
addrest
adpress

odorate
odorous
oddsman
△odyssey
edition
adjunct
adducer
odoured
adjudge
adaxial
eddying
ceramal
decadal
decanal
getaway
jemadar
megabar
megarad
tetanal
welaway
debauch
hexarch
medacca
mesarch
penance
recatch
rematch
tenancy
xerarch
regards
veranda
bedazed
behaved
belated
belayed
bemazed
benamed
betaken
cedared
cerated
Cetacea
debased
debaser
debater
decayed
defacer
delayed
delayer
dewater
fedayee
felafel
legatee
medaled
medalet
menacer
metaled
metamer
métayer
pedaled
penates
rebater

related
relater
relayed
remanet
renayed
repaper
retaken
retaker
velamen
velated
deraign
derange
melange
mélange
relâche
seraphs
Bedawin
ceramic
cerasin
dedalic
denarii
fedarie
gelatin
hematic
hematin
heparin
hepatic
hexadic
keramic
keratin
megabit
melanic
melanin
nematic
Nepalis
pelagic
regalia
relaxin
remanié
sebacic
sematic
senarii
serafin
Serapic
Serapis
tetanic
vedalia
veganic
velaria
velaric
venatic
xerafin
xerasia
aefauld
cenacle
debacle
débâcle
default
hexapla
legally
mesally

metally
penally
regally
retable
seeable
tenable
venally
bepaint
besaint
betaine
delaine
demaine
demayne
depaint
dewanny
pesaunt
remains
repaint
aerator
belabor
celadon
decagon
decapod
delator
hexagon
hexapod
legator
legatos
levator
megafog
megaron
megaton
melanos
△metazoa
pedalos
peraeon
relator
senator
telamon
venator
zelator
genappe
hetaera
hetaira
Megaera
remarry
bécasse
because
degauss
delapse
megasse
relapse
defaste
penalty
pesante
regatta
Vedanta
devalue
△pegasus
petasus
renague

7 □e□b□a

revalue
△senatus
tetanus
△lesbian
membral
remblai
sea-beat
Serbian
Berbice
kebbock
kebbuck
nebbich
redback
setback
wetback
herblet
pebbled
verbify
herbage
cembali
cembalo
netball
verbals
geebung
henbane
seabank
verbena
webbing
red-book
temblor
△gerbera
herbary
newborn
redbird
seabird
sea-born
herbist
herbose
nebbish
verbose
bed-bath
herbous
sea-blue
terbium
berceau
dew-claw
pea-coat
pea-crab
redcoat
Sercial
teuchat
meacock
peacock
percoct
petcock
seacock
deicide
beached
beechen
belcher
bencher

geechee
leechee
leuchen
merchet
peacher
perched
percher
reached
reacher
recceed
reccied
rescued
rescuer
teacher
welcher
wencher
mercify
deictic
helcoid
percoid
reechie
teachie
teach-in
descale
key-cold
percale
rescale
re-scale
leucoma
newcome
o'ercome
welcome
Aeschna
descant
descend
descent
fencing
leucine
Meccano®
peccant
percine
rescind
hen-coop
reactor
tercios
percept
mercery
△mercury
peccary
rescore
metcast
pen-case
percase
percuss
leucite
ketchup
mesclum
mesclun
peccavi
red-cowl
beadman

dead-cat
deadpan
dead-pay
headman
headway
herdman
seed-lac
Vendean
lewdsby
heyduck
vendace
verdict
bendlet
dead-men
dead-set
headset
leidger
meddler
needler
needles
peddler
readier
readies
reedbed
seedbed
re-edify
send-off
headage
vendage
wendigo
headrig
readmit
seedlip
seed-oil
tendril
Veddoid
deedily
headily
needily
readily
seedily
beldame
beading
bedding
bending
dead-end
deodand
feeding
feuding
gelding
heading
leading
lending
mending
pendant
pendent
pending
reading
redding
reeding
seeding

sending
tedding
tendenz
verdant
wedding
weeding
welding
dendron
dew-drop
feedlot
herdboy
seedbox
tendron
readapt
readopt
feodary
feudary
Jeddart
perdure
verdure
weedery
berdash
feudist
geodesy
herdess
key-desk
reddest
reddish
vendiss
Wendish
deodate
verdite
deedful
heedful
lead-out
needful
read-out
let-down
meadowy
set-down
dead-eye
bedeman
bederal
bemedal
federal
△general
Genevan
hederal
Peneian
peregal
pesewas
renewal
Senecan
several
telefax
terefah
vegetal
veteran
beseech
decency
defence

Rebecca
recency
regence
regency
remercy
tedesca
tedesco
delenda
nereids
bejewel
fevered
geneses
Jezebel
leveret
meseled
Nemeses
referee
reneger
renewer
reverer
seceder
teletex
venerer
demerge
deterge
remerge
revenge
reweigh
telergy
dépêche
bedevil
benefic
benefit
ceresin
demerit
generic
△genesis
genetic
heretic
nemesia
△nemesis
pedesis
pedetic
reverie
selenic
senecio
telesis
venefic
zetetic
beseeke
deleble
merells
vexedly
beteeme
dejeune
demeane
demesne
Gehenna
sejeant
develop
hebenon

Hereros
heteros
pereion
reredos
semeion
telecom
temenos
teredos
benempt
receipt
bebeeru
bepearl
cerebra
jewelry
pereira
revelry
△terebra
decease
defense
demerse
recense
release
reverse
reversi
reverso
rêveuse
teleost
beneath
celesta
celeste
dejecta
démenti
détente
genette
memento
seventh
seventy
vedette
aeneous
Benelux
cereous
détenue
gerenuk
renegue
réseaus
réseaux
revenue
sexed-up
bereave
deceive
deserve
receive
reserve
reseize
beef-ham
A-effect
geofact
perfect
perfidy
beef-tea
deified
deifier
feoffee
feoffer
leaflet
self-fed
leafage
serfage
deaf-aid
jeofail
jetfoil
sexfoil
beefalo
dew-fall
dewfull
menfolk
merfolk
penfold
seafolk
tenfold
perfume
perfumy
beffana
leafing
reefing
reffing
self-end
selfing
feoffor
seafood
self-sow
serfdom
ten-foot
webfoot
deiform
eelfare
fee-farm
fen-fire
leafery
perform
sea-fire
welfare
bedfast
gemfish
jewfish
net-fish
perfuse
redfish
selfish
selfism
selfist
serfish
leafbud
peafowl
seafowl
Belgian
verglas
yeggman
beagler
beignet
feigned
△leaguer
leughen
Neogaea
veggies
weighed
weigher
lee-gage
heigh-ho
lengths
lengthy
penguin
weigh-in
Bengali
bergylt
pergola
seagull
weigela
wergild
bergama
begging
geogeny
geogony
hedging
legging
Neogene
o'ergang
pegging
reagent
wedging
beggary
belgard
bergère
sea-girt
leggism
lengest
Newgate
tergite
weights
weighty
bee-glue
Heshvan
lethean
recheat
redhead
recheck
Methody
beshrew
fechter
lethied
tee-heed
meshuga
Cepheid
Mechlin
nephric
technic
keyhole
techily
beshame
bethumb
bethump
beshine
beshone
bethink
meshing
methane
methink
rethink
nephron
perhaps
reshape
becharm
Becher's
beghard
bewhore
Jethart
lechery
leghorn
rechart
Senhora
Peshito
rechate
Cepheus
beehive
yeshiva
seahawk
Cebidae
decimal
Delilah
devisal
Felidae
Felinae
feminal
fenitar
genipap
genital
genizah
geoidal
helical
heliman
helipad
jemidar
lexical
medical
metical
Mexican
Oedipal
pedicab
pelican
pemican
recital
reginal
retinae
retinal
retinas
retiral
revisal
revival
seminal
seminar
semitar
vesicae
vesical
bewitch
dehisce
mediacy
menisci
periods
bedizen
bemired
besides
betided
betimes
decibel
decided
decider
defiler
definer
deliver
demirep
denizen
derider
desirer
deviled
devilet
devisee
deviser
femiter
helices
helixes
pedicel
penises
perigee
recipes
reciter
refined
refiner
regimen
reliver
remiges
repiner
resider
resiner
retired
retiree
retirer
reviler
reviser
reviver
semiped
veliger
vetiver
Yezidee
Zezidee
besiege
seringa
bedight
behight
Belisha
benight
betight
ceviche
delight
fetiche
Jericho

Words marked △ may be spelled also with a capital letter

7 □e□i□i

relight
aecidia
cecitis
deficit
delimit
deliria
felicia
Geminid
Geminis
legitim
levitic
lewisia
neritic
pelitic
periwig
revisit
sebific
sedilia
Semitic
sericin
tenioid
betitle
cedilla
delible
gelidly
hemiola
legible
legibly
pedicle
petiole
reticle
retitle
tepidly
vehicle
vesicle
vexilla
mediums
melisma
seriema
verismo
beginne
defiant
deviant
hemione
lenient
mediant
reliant
resiant
benison
debitor
demigod
devisor
genitor
helicon
heritor
leg-iron
lexicon
medicos
melilot
merinos
pea-iron
pericon
peridot
perigon
retinol
revisor
revivor
semi-log
sericon
venison
periapt
deciare
devilry
Félibre
retiary
hérissé
△métisse
pelisse
periost
sepiost
veriest
deviate
genista
mediate
rebirth
seriate
teniate
bezique
decidua
dedimus
detinue
devious
helibus
Oedipus
perique
peritus
relique
repique
residua
residue
retinue
serious
tedious
believe
relieve
relievo
Mes-John
perjink
perjure
perjury
weekday
peekabo
deckled
geckoes
heckler
necklet
vetkoek
leakage
necktie
deskill
perkily
peskily
seakale
serkali
leukoma
decking
Jenkins
jerking
lekking
necking
peaking
pecking
reeking
weekend
desktop
peckish
bee-kite
△aeolian
bell-jar
bellman
heel-tap
hell-cat
keelman
meal-man
realgar
reelman
refloat
sealwax
jellaba
deflect
fetlock
genlock
hemlock
neglect
pellach
pellack
pellock
re-elect
reflect
replace
replica
wedlock
Wenlock
yelloch
ceilidh
seclude
bellied
Cellnet®
hellier
jellied
mealies
re-alter
replied
replier
Wealden
well-fed
wellies
well-set
jellify
sell-off
well-off
geology
keelage
negligé
négligé
neology
realign
fellahs
healthy
wealthy
declaim
new-laid
reallie
realtie
reclaim
sea-like
cellule
heal-all
deplume
réclame
reclimb
Tellima
beeline
Bellona
berline
ceiling
dealing
decline
deplane
devling
feeling
fenland
gelling
healing
heeling
Hellene
hem-line
herling
keeling
keyline
lee-lane
merling
peeling
recline
red-line
reeling
replant
sealant
sealine
sealing
seeling
setline
telling
veiling
welling
wetland
yelling
zealant
begloom
bell-boy
bellhop
hell-box
hellion
keelson
reallot
Realtor®
realtor
rebloom
well-won
wet-look
yealdon
dewlapt
declare
deplore
meal-ark
pedlary
sealery
cellist
'cellist
cellose
declass
hellish
keyless
legless
realise
△realism
realist
reclose
recluse
rellish
sexless
deflate
deplete
fellate
mellite
neolith
Peelite
perlite
reality
reflate
replete
zeolite
becloud
gealous
jealous
kellaut
perlous
sell-out
zealful
zealous
beslave
hellova
helluva
Mevlevi
Pehlevi
replevy
bellows
mellowy
yellows
yellowy
realize
besmear
Permian
vermian
Bermuda

Words marked △ may be spelled also with a capital letter

new-made
beamlet
Heimweh
jemmied
meemies
seamset
dermoid
desmoid
germain
mermaid
seamaid
vermeil
beamily
gemmule
vermell
vermily
beaming
desmine
ferment
gemming
geomant
germane
Germans
hemming
hetmans
lemming
reamend
reaming
seeming
segment
teaming
teeming
tegmina
termini
verminy
fermion
gemmery
seamark
beamish
bee-moth
fermata
fermate
fewmets
gemmate
lemmata
permute
regmata
termite
fermium
teemful
new-mown
aeonian
Aetnean
beanbag
hernial
Lemnian
lernean
Kennick
redneck
re-enact
beinked

dernier
hennaed
meander
pennied
pennies
reannex
re-enter
reinter
veinlet
vernier
reunify
peonage
teenage
deontic
kennels
pennill
Reynold
eevning
ferning
keening
kenning
kerning
leaning
△leonine
meaning
pennant
pennine
penning
regnant
remnant
renning
seining
veining
vernant
lean-tos
re-endow
reunion
ternion
beanery
deanery
fernery
hennery
re-entry
rein-arm
△reynard
ternary
fennish
fewness
kernish
newness
peonism
redness
setness
teentsy
wennish
wetness
Zennist
kernite
keynote
neonate
peanuts

pennate
reunite
ternate
dernful
heinous
veinous
beknave
beknown
fern-owl
neo-Nazi
deposal
femoral
Jehovah
△menorah
men-o'-war
nemoral
removal
repoman
reposal
Seconal®
serosae
serosas
Veronal®
veronal
xeromas
redoubt
debouch
deforce
devoice
heroics
rejoice
retouch
seconde
secondi
secondo
seconds
begored
beloved
besomed
betoken
decoder
demoded
deposer
devoted
devotee
Helodea
kerogen
leg-over
meioses
me-tooer
oenomel
recover
re-cover
recower
rejoneo
rejones
remodel
removed
remover
reposed
tenoner

venomed
xerotes
regorge
aerobic
△bedouin
begonia
celomic
cenobia
cerotic
demonic
demotic
deposit
genomic
hedonic
henotic
kenosis
kenotic
ketosis
meconic
meconin
meiosis
meiotic
melodic
mesonic
Metonic
metopic
nepotic
Neronic
Pelopid
peloria
peloric
reposit
xerosis
xerotic
recoyle
remould
demount
heroine
reboant
rebound
recount
re-count
redound
refound
remount
repoint
resound
rewound
zeroing
aerosol
decolor
Mesozoa
metopon
begorra
demonry
devoirs
felonry
helotry
heronry
memoirs
recoure

rejourn
velours
zedoary
delouse
Genoese
heroise
heroism
rehouse
remorse
bemouth
reroute
velouté
aerobus
decorum
pelorus
refocus
seropus
Xenopus
zero-sum
behoove
devolve
resolve
revolve
meronym
metonym
heroize
bespeak
net-play
respeak
respray
Tempean
△templar
bespice
henpeck
respect
bespeed
deep-fet
deep-sea
deep-set
jeepney
keepnet
perplex
telpher
templed
templet
△tempter
seepage
serpigo
△delphic
delphin
despair
despoil
vespoid
bespake
bespoke
seppuku
leg-pull
reapply
redpoll
respell
serpula

7 □e□p□n

despond
dew-pond
heaping
helping
keeping
kemping
leaping
perpend
perpent
repping
respond
△serpent
tenpins
terpene
vespine
weeping
yelping
peep-toe
besport
deep-fry
jeepers
jeopard
lempira
leopard
peppery
respire
seaport
sexpert
tempera
tempore
tempura
△vespers
bedpost
despise
hey-pass
tempest
bespate
despite
respite
bespout
eelpout
helpful
jerquer
mesquin
mesquit
re-equip
bear-cat
beer-mat
betread
cerrial
decrial
hearsay
meercat
meerkat
△ne'erday
retread
retreat
re-treat
retrial
tear-gas
bedrock
defrock
derrick
detract
metrics
rebrace
re-erect
refract
retrace
retract
secrecy
terrace
tetract
verruca
débride
degrade
detrude
regrade
regrede
tetrode
bearded
berried
debrief
decreed
decreet
decried
decrier
deerlet
ferried
hearken
hearted
hearten
henries
learned
learner
Negroes
pearled
pearler
Perrier®
perrier
regreet
reorder
retried
serried
terreen
terrier
wearied
yearner
petrify
redraft
terrify
beerage
ferrugo
peerage
sevruga
verruga
beardie
detrain
Geordie
georgic
Hebraic
△negroid
pearlin
pedrail
recruit
refrain
retrain
retrait
terrain
weirdie
zebroid
heureka
bed-roll
Cedrela
dearnly
febrile
ferrule
heartly
merrily
peartly
wearily
weirdly
zebrula
zebrule
begrime
megrims
neuroma
reframe
reprime
bearing
cedrine
feering
gearing
hearing
herring
jeering
key-ring
leering
neurine
neurone
pébrine
Petrine
pew-rent
regrant
regrind
reprint
searing
tearing
terrane
terrene
terrine
veering
wearing
year-end
zebrina
zebrine
bedroom
gearbox
heirdom
legroom
rear-dos
redroot
reproof
weirdos
bedropt
decrypt
Ferrara
pedrero
petrary
△terrors
bearish
bed-rest
beprose
defrost
depress
heiress
heurism
leg-rest
leprose
leprosy
metrist
nearest
necrose
△negress
neurism
peeress
rearise
recross
redress
re-dress
refresh
regress
repress
re-press
reprise
seeress
wearish
zebrass
bed-rite
betroth
cedrate
Debrett
ferrate
ferrety
ferrite
Negrito
neurite
regrate
retrate
rewrite
rewrote
secreta
secrete
secrets
serrate
defraud
fearful
ferrous
leprous
petrous
regroup
tearful
deprave
deprive
redrive
reprive
reprove
repryve
decrown
reprize
beeswax
censual
deiseal
felspar
geishas
△hessian
Jersian
Jew's-ear
key-seat
lensman
mensual
△messiah
△messias
newsman
Persian
redsear
seismal
sensual
Telstar
persico
seasick
bedside
depside
leg-side
seaside
bee-skep
feaster
gessoes
heister
hepster
keister
leisler
leister
measled
measles
Meissen
oersted
Perspex®
webster
welsher
densify
versify
message
beastie
cesspit
deasoil
deistic
hership
leg-spin
mess-tin
Perseid
redskin
seismic
vessail
netsuke

Words marked △ may be spelled also with a capital letter

beastly
densely
hersall
herself
messily
pensile
sensile
sessile
tensely
tensile
tersely
beesome
jessamy
pessima
ceasing
jessant
leasing
peasant
pepsine
persant
persona
persons
retsina
sensing
teasing
versant
versine
versing
weasand
cession
gemsbok
leg-show
mersion
neuston
newsboy
peascod
pension
session
tension
tersion
version
wet-shod
bedsore
berserk
censure
dessert
leasure
leisure
measure
pessary
seasure
sensory
seysure
tessera
Persism
△persist
sensism
sensist
density
felsite
sensate
tensity
versute
Celsius
deasiul
pea-soup
Perseus
reissue
pensiv'd
pensive
tensive
zemstva
zemstvo
leasowe
peishwa
beltman
beltway
bestead
bestial
central
dextral
dextran
gentian
meat-man
neutral
oestral
peat-hag
peatman
rent-day
rest-day
tertial
tertian
test-ban
text-man
textual
Vectian
ventral
vestral
bedtick
bestick
bestuck
lettuce
pentact
pentice
peptics
restock
testacy
cestode
pentode
peptide
△testudo
bestrew
centner
centred
feather
fettler
genteel
heathen
heather
hen-toed
jettied
kestrel
leather
meat-tea
mettled
neither
peat-bed
rentier
reutter
seethed
seether
seltzer
settled
settler
tent-bed
test-bed
vent-peg
weather
web-toed
beatify
certify
left-off
rectify
restaff
restiff
testify
centage
lentigo
restage
tentage
tentigo
ventage
ventige
vertigo
vestige
weftage
gertcha
beatnik
benthic
bestain
bestrid
centric
certain
cestoid
deltaic
deltoid
dentoid
Deutzia
dextrin
felt-tip
lentoid
penthia
pertain
rectrix
Septrin®
tectrix
testril
ventail
westlin
pertake
beet-fly
bestill
deathly
fertile
△gentile
△gestalt
heftily
meat-fly
meatily
pettily
reptile
restyle
sectile
sextile
tent-fly
tenthly
test-fly
testily
textile
bedtime
centime
centimo
leptome
rectums
septime
teatime
beating
Beltane
belting
betting
bez-tine
dentine
destine
destiny
felting
gestant
getting
heating
heptane
jesting
jetting
leptons
letting
meeting
melting
neoteny
Neptune
nesting
netting
pelting
pentane
pentene
peptone
petting
reptant
resting
retting
seating
sestina
sestine
setting
△sextans
△sextant
tenting
testing
ventana
venting
vesting
vetting
weeting
westing
wetting
benthos
destroy
festoon
keitloa
lection
menthol
mention
neutron
peat-bog
rection
section
septuor
settlor
sextuor
testoon
△**gestapo**
peg-tops
red-tape
bestorm
betters
centare
century
dentary
denture
feature
fetters
gesture
hectare
lectern
lecture
lecturn
leotard
lettern
letters
nectary
peatary
peatery
perturb
rectory
△restart
restore
rettery
sectary
testern
texture
venture
△venturi
vesture
vettura
△western
yestern
dentist
Kentish

7 □e□t□t

leftish
leftism
leftist
lentisk
Lettish
pectise
pectose
peltast
pentise
pentose
peptise
pertuse
pettish
Ventôse
ventose
wettish
dentate
gestate
meltith
peltate
restate
septate
sestett
sextett
tektite
testate
centaur
centrum
featous
jestful
lentous
meat-tub
nestful
oestrum
oestrus
pestful
restful
tentful
tent-guy
tertius
zestful
centavo
festive
restive
meat-axe
mestiza
mestizo
pectize
peptize
cesural
cesuras
decuman
Ketubah
medusae
medusan
medusas
mezuzah
nebulae
nebular
nebulas
perusal
refusal
refutal
regulae
regular
secular
tegulae
tegular
nelumbo
defunct
felucca
sebundy
beaufet
bemused
cerumen
cesures
deluded
deluder
genuses
lemures
peruked
peruser
rebuker
rebuses
reduced
reducer
refugee
refuser
refuter
reputed
requiem
securer
seducer
tenured
rejudge
remuage
resurge
penuche
penuchi
beaufin
decuria
legumin
Lemuria
△petunia
refugia
repunit
sequoia
beguile
decuple
medulla
rebuild
recuile
sequela
setuale
tequila
beguine
béguine
genuine
returns
sequent
tenutos
requere
require
beauish
bequest
repulse
request
Senussi
requite
requote
tenuity
jejunum
Réaumur
△regulus
remueur
seculum
Telugus
tenuous
Xenurus
decurve
recurve
seruewe
Servian
service
pervade
bevvied
heavier
heavies
oeuvres
selvage
heave-ho
vervain
heavily
nervily
nervule
servile
weevily
cervine
fervent
heavens
heaving
leaving
nervine
revving
servant
serving
weaving
beavery
nervure
peevers
pervert
servery
△dervish
peevish
nervate
Servite
velvety
fervour
nervous
servewe
legwear
between
seaweed
wee-weed
hen-wife
seawife
reawake
sea-wolf
setwall
werwolf
redwing
seewing
redwood
red-wood
bedward
bedwarf
bed-work
dew-worm
eelworm
felwort
keyword
leeward
legwork
network
o'erword
seaward
seaware
seaworm
sea-worn
webworm
wetware
weyward
New-Wave
new-wave
betwixt
Zeuxian
re-exist
zeuxite
recycle
kerygma
belying
defying
denying
levying
relying
renying
revying
benzoic
benzoin
Neozoic
benzole
benzene
benzine
seizing
weazand
seizure
benzoyl
bezzazz
affable
affably
effable
affaire
affairs
off-beam
offbeat
off-come
X-factor
off-duty
offence
effendi
offered
offeree
offerer
offeror
affeard
affear'd
affeare
offense
effects
off-fore
offhand
African
affined
officer
offices
affiche
offload
afflict
ufology
off-line
aftmost
sfumato
pfennig
afforce
efforce
affoord
Y-fronts
offpeak
off-peak
off-plan
off-road
sferics
affront
offside
off-spin
off-site
offscum
offtake
effulge
off-ward
affying
agnamed
agraffe
agrapha
agnatic
agravic
iguanid
oghamic
ignaros
agraste
egg-bird
egg-cell
agaçant
egg-case
egg-cosy

Words marked △ may be spelled also with a capital letter

ague-fit
ogreish
igneous
egg-flip
Ogygian
agogics
egghead
agrised
igniter
against
agilely
agelong
agelast
ageless
agility
egality
agamoid
eggmass
agamous
aginner
agonise
agonist
agonize
agnomen
ignorer
agnosia
ignoble
ignobly
aground
egg-plum
aggrace
aggrade
igarapé
aggress
aggrate
agister
agistor
ego-trip
egotise
egotism
egotist
agitate
agitato
egotize
eggwash
choanae
choanas
pheazar
phrasal
cheapen
cheater
phraser
sheared
shearer
sheaved
sheaves
theater
wheaten
sheathe
sheaths
sheathy
cheapie
thiamin
cheaply
chiasma
chiasmi
chiasms
phratry
theatre
shiatsu
Chianti
shmaltz
thwaite
thiasus
chlamys
shiatzu
chobdar
she-bear
shebeen
Chablis
Thebaic
Thebaid
shabble
shebang
rhabdom
rhubarb
phobism
phobist
chabouk
chibouk
rhabdus
choc-bar
△choctaw
choc-ice
shy-cock
Chechen
checker
chicken
chocker
shicker
shochet
shocked
shocker
shucker
thicken
thicket
whacked
whacker
whicker
Chicago
chéchia
check-in
chuckie
phacoid
rhachis
chuckle
shackle
thickly
chicana
chicane
△chicano
phocine
thickos
whackos
chicory
shicksa
thecate
check-up
thick'un
chaddar
Cheddar
chuddah
chuddar
khaddar
Rhodian
chidden
shedder
shidder
shudder
thudded
whidded
whidder
shadily
chiding
shading
chaddor
shadoof
rhodora
rhodium
rhodous
khediva
khedive
shadowy
chaetae
cheetah
shreddy
threads
thready
cheeper
cheerer
cheesed
chiefer
sheeted
shtetel
thieves
wheeled
wheeler
whoever
whyever
wheenge
wheesht
cheerio
choenix
phoenix
phrenic
Rhaetia
Rhaetic
wheelie
cheerly
chiefly
sheerly
shtetls
wheedle
wheeple
wheezle
phlegmy
shoeing
phaeton
sheepos
threnos
Wheeson
chiefry
phaeism
phrensy
bheesty
thretty
Phoebus
threave
chaffer
chuffed
shafted
shafter
shifted
shifter
whiffer
whiffet
shuffle
whiffle
chiffon
shofars
Chogyal
chigger
shagged
shogged
thigger
thuggee
whigged
chagrin
thiggit
shoggle
shoggly
chignon
thuggos
shehita
Ahriman
△shaitan
shrinal
shriech
shritch
chained
shrived
shrivel
shriven
shriver
thrived
thriven
thriver
aheight
sheikha
shright
x-height
Shiitic
shrilly
thrilly
whaisle
whaizle
chrisom
shrimpy
thrimsa
△christy
thrifty
thristy
shrieve
shakudo
chukker
shakoes
shakily
shekels
shaking
chikhor
chikara
△shakers
shikari
chekist
shake-up
challah
challan
Chilean
chiliad
Chilian
ghilgai
shalwar
shellac
thalian
chalice
Shylock
Chaldee
chalder
Chelsea
childed
childer
chilled
chiller
phellem
philter
shelled
sheller
shelter
shelves
thalweg
thiller
whelked
chylify
khalifa
chalcid
challie
challis
cheloid
chillis
ghillie
phallic
phallin
sheltie
shilpit
thallic

7 □h□l□

childly
thalami
chalone
chelone
cholent
choline
phalanx
whaling
shallon
shallop
shallot
shallow
cholera
choltry
philtre
whalery
whilere
thylose
wholism
wholist
chalutz
chelate
thulite
chillum
△phallus
thallus
thulium
chalaza
champac
champak
shimaal
chamade
chamber
chamfer
chamlet
chimley
chimney
chumley
shammed
shammer
shammes
shimmer
shimmey
thumbed
thumper
whammed
whimmed
whimper
whimsey
chymify
chamois
khamsin
rhombic
Thummim
shamble
shambly
thimble
whample
whemmle
whimple
whomble
whommle
whummle
rhyming
shamans
thymine
rhomboi
rhombos
shampoo
chambré
chimera
chimere
chamise
chamiso
chemise
chemism
chemist
Rhemish
Rhemist
rhymist
Thomism
Thomist
Shemite
themata
chymous
Rhamnus
rhombus
Thammuz
chinwag
khanjar
thannah
whangam
phonics
chancel
chancer
chances
chancey
changer
changes
△channel
channer
chanter
chantey
chunder
△chunnel
chunner
chunter
shanked
shantey
shoneen
shunned
shunner
shunter
thankee
thanker
thinker
thinned
thinner
thonder
thonged
thunder
whangee
whene'er
whinger
thanage
rhonchi
chantie
△chindit
△chinkie
phone-in
shindig
think-in
shingle
shingly
phoneme
shining
whining
chanson
chantor
△chinook
phantom
ahungry
bhangra
chancre
chantry
chondre
chondri
shandry
△chinese
Rhenish
shiness
shyness
khanate
phenate
phonate
rhenium
chanoyu
chintzy
chloral
theorbo
thrombi
shrouds
shroudy
chooser
choosey
chromel
phloxes
shooter
theorem
throned
thrower
whoopee
whooper
through
chaotic
chloric
chlorin
chookie
chromic
chronic
△phlomis
shoogie
theoric
throw-in
shoofly
shoogle
shoogly
chromos
chronon
shmoose
throaty
whoobub
shmooze
chapeau
chapman
chappal
chuppah
shiplap
shipman
shipway
shophar
shopman
whipcat
whipsaw
chaplet
chapped
chapter
chipped
chipper
chopped
chopper
shipmen
shipped
shippen
shipper
shopped
shopper
whapped
whipped
whipper
whippet
whopped
whopper
chappie
chippie
rhaphis
shapely
chopine
shaping
shippon
shop-boy
whip-top
chapess
chapati
chupati
shape-up
shipful
shopful
chequer
chordae
chordal
chorial
gharial
△shariat
△sheriat
Sherpas
thereat
theriac
therian
thermae
thermal
whereas
whereat
cherubs
thereby
whereby
charade
charged
charger
charges
△charley
charmed
charmer
charnel
charred
charter
chirper
chordee
sharded
sharker
Shar-Pei
sharpen
sharper
sherbet
shereef
shirker
shirred
shorten
thorned
thyrses
wharves
where'er
wherret
whirler
whirred
whirret
whorled
sheriff
thurify
charkha
churchy
△charlie
charpie
chervil
choreic
choroid
dhurrie
gherkin
sharpie
sherris
shortie
therein
thermic
Thermit®
theroid

Words marked △ may be spelled also with a capital letter

thyroid
wherein
charily
chorale
chortle
sharply
shortly
thirdly
whirtle
charing
chorine
pharynx
sharing
shoring
chariot
charpoy
cheroot
chorion
gheraos
Pharaoh
thereof
thereon
Thermos®
whereof
whereon
therapy
charism
cherish
chorism
chorist
whereso
whorish
Bharati
charity
thereto
thirsty
thorite
whereto
charqui
chirrup
choreus
churrus
thorium
thyrsus
chorizo
chasmal
Chesvan
physics
bhistee
chasmed
chasten
chessel
chesses
chested
Chislev
ghessed
shaster
shyster
whisker
whisket
whiskey

whisper
chasmic
Chassid
chassis
phasmid
ghastly
ghostly
thistle
thistly
thyself
whistle
chasing
physios
shastra
chesnut
château
khotbah
khutbah
shittah
whittaw
photics
chatted
chattel
chatter
chitter
chutney
khotbeh
shatter
shitted
shotted
shotten
shutter
thether
thither
thother
whate'er
whatten
whether
whetted
whetter
whither
whitret
whitter
shut-off
thatcht
chetnik
shittim
whatsis
whatsit
shottle
shuttle
whitely
whittle
rhatany
rhytina
shiting
whiting
ghettos
shit-hot
whatnot
whitlow

chutist
photism
whitish
shotgun
shotput
shut-out
Whitsun
shut-eye
thruway
shrubby
chaunce
thrutch
chaufer
chaumer
rheumed
shouter
chaunge
theurgy
thought
chauvin
thrummy
Shavian
shaving
Cheviot
chevron
Shavuot
shivery
showman
chowder
shawley
Shawnee
show-off
showghe
shawlie
showbiz
showily
chewink
showing
thawing
showbox
showery
thrymsa
wheyish
chayote
whizzed
whizzer
rhizoid
rhizome
rhizine
bimanal
didakai
die-away
Nicaean
picamar
pitapat
pitarah
Sinaean
timarau
aidance
finance
viranda

virando
citadel
didakei
dilated
dilater
filabeg
filacer
filazer
hicatee
lie-abed
limacel
limaces
minaret
vilayet
visaged
giraffe
hidalga
hidalgo
hibachi
piranha
△cidaris
dibasic
dika-oil
△filaria
jigajig
jig-a-jig
piratic
tilapia
Titania
△titanic
△titanis
Vinalia
vis-à-vis
vitamin
vivaria
zizania
bidarka
ziganka
citable
disable
disally
finable
finagle
finally
fixable
hirable
likable
livable
mirable
miracle
misally
mixable
ridable
sizable
vitally
digamma
gisarme
sixaine
dilator
disavow
girasol

gitanos
jigajog
limaçon
mikados
mirador
picador
tinamou
viragos
bizarre
rivalry
simarre
filasse
Sivaism
tirasse
vinasse
ailanto
Sivaite
piragua
bivalve
kit-boat
Niobean
pigboat
dieback
finback
limbeck
tieback
bilboes
dibbler
kimboed
nibbler
timbrel
wimbrel
yibbles
fimbria
air-bell
diabolo
gimbals
hip-belt
oil-belt
piebald
pinball
timbale
big-band
dibbing
disband
fibbing
gibbing
hip-bone
jibbing
mirbane
nibbing
ribband
ribbing
rib-bone
ribbons
ribbony
jib-boom
disbark
fibbery
fig-bird
filberd

7 □i□b□s

filbert
gilbert
libbard
limbers
misborn
oil-bird
tilbury
timbers
airbase
diabase
gibbose
air-bath
hip-bath
kibbutz
limbate
niobate
niobite
oil-bath
gibbous
limbous
niobium
niobous
Circean
pit-coal
bibcock
biocide
discide
zincode
air-crew
aitches
biccies
birchen
Circaea
circled
circler
circles
circlet
ciscoes
discoed
discoer
ditcher
filcher
finched
fitchée
fitchet
fitchew
hitcher
kitchen
linchet
piccies
pilcher
pinched
pincher
pitched
pitcher
tinchel
witchen
zincked
zincify
discage
ribcage

biscuit
circlip
circuit
discoid
kinchin
zincoid
oil-cake
air-cell
miscall
piccolo
vincula
Zincala
Zincali
Zincalo
discant
fir-cone
hircine
mincing
Miocene
piscina
piscine
wincing
zincing
air-cool
jim-crow
pilcrow
discept
hiccupy
miscopy
discard
discern
discerp
discord
discure
pilcorn
pincers
piscary
rip-cord
sincere
tip-cart
viscera
circusy
die-cast
diocese
discase
discuss
giocoso
miscast
pincase
viscose
siccity
zincite
linctus
minceur
viscous
zincous
birdman
diedral
findram
misdeal
misdial

misdraw
wildcat
windbag
piddock
viaduct
windock
diddler
dildoes
fiddler
fiddley
girdled
girdler
hindleg
kiddier
kiddies
kindler
kindred
lip-deep
mindset
misdeed
misdeem
misdiet
misdoer
piddler
pig-deer
riddler
tiddled
tiddler
tiddley
Windies
windage
windigo
disdain
Siddhis
giddily
windily
bidding
binding
birding
eilding
finding
gilding
girding
hilding
kidding
lindane
minding
misdone
ridding
wilding
winding
air-drop
bird-dog
diadrom
jib-door
windrow
Windsor
bindery
cindery
finders
pindari

tindery
windore
kiddush
middest
piedish
pin-dust
wildish
Yiddish
biodata
misdate
giddy-up
hind-gut
mindful
oil-drum
windgun
lie-down
mildewy
pindown
sit-down
windows
bikeway
bipedal
fire-bar
fireman
firepan
five-bar
five-day
△liberal
lineman
literal
live-oak
mineral
pikeman
pile-cap
sidebar
side-bar
sidecar
sideman
sideral
Tibetan
tideway
tile-hat
vinegar
virelay
wide-gab
wine-sap
wireman
wiretap
wireway
licence
silence
vivency
limeade
videnda
bigener
cinerea
dimeter
fibered
fire-new
hive-bee
libelee

libeler
livener
minever
pie-eyed
pig-eyed
pikelet
pin-eyed
pipe-key
ridered
rivered
riveret
riveted
riveter
sidemen
sinewed
tile-red
videoed
vinewed
widener
wizened
hive-off
disedge
diverge
hireage
kitenge
lineage
mileage
cimelia
cinerin
dimeric
Dioecia
eidetic
eirenic
fivepin
kinesis
kinetic
limelit
limepit
lived-in
mimesis
mimetic
ninepin
niterie
piperic
silesia
Sirenia
sirenic
tide-rip
viremia
viremic
cineole
firefly
fixedly
micella
micelle
mineola
miserly
mixedly
nigella
tigerly
tiredly

Words marked △ may be spelled also with a capital letter

vitelli
vixenly
Viyella®
dilemma
aileron
bibelot
dice-box
filemot
firebox
firedog
firepot
liberos
live-box
livelod
pi-meson
viceroy
vine-rod
viretot
dirempt
firearm
sidearm
△viverra
cineast
disease
diseuse
diverse
fideism
fideist
fineish
finesse
jive-ass
license
misease
niceish
sizeism
sizeist
ailette
biretta
dinette
liberty
lineate
minette
pileate
pimento
pipette
vidette
direful
firebug
hideous
hideout
lifeful
line-out
mixed-up
niveous
piceous
pileous
pinetum
pipeful
piteous
silenus
timeous

wileful
wipeout
Minerva
misfeed
piaffer
piffler
pigfeed
riffler
airfoil
milfoil
tinfoil
kinfolk
miffily
misfall
misfell
misfile
pinfold
pitfall
sixfold
tinfuls
disfame
△tiffany
tiffing
airflow
bigfoot
fiefdom
six-foot
difform
disform
misfare
misfire
misform
piffero
pilfery
pin-fire
diffuse
liefest
pig-fish
pinfish
sitfast
ziffius
diagram
dingbat
gingham
lingual
ringman
ring-taw
ringway
Virgoan
dingoes
giggler
higgler
jingler
jinglet
jingoes
kinglet
lingoes
mingler
niggler
piggies
pingler

pingoes
ringlet
singles
singlet
tingler
wiggler
wing-led
winglet
diagrid
king-hit
king-pin
nilgais
pilgrim
pinguid
pinguin
ringbit
ringgit
gingall
gingili
△lingula
riggald
singult
virgule
biogeny
digging
figging
gigging
hinging
jigging
ligging
misgone
pigging
ridging
rigging
ringent
ringing
singing
sirgang
tigging
tinging
wigging
zigging
Zingana
Zingane
Zingani
Zingano
kingdom
king-rod
pidgeon
widgeon
figgery
fingers
gingery
Midgard
niggard
niggery
piggery
wiggery
Zingara
Zingare
Zingari

Zingaro
biggest
biggish
disgest
disgust
jiggish
piggish
riggish
fidgets
fidgety
virgate
hip-gout
kingcup
nilgaus
vingt-un
misgave
misgive
disgown
airhead
big-head
dish-rag
fish-day
fish-fag
fish-way
high-hat
highman
highway
lichway
mishear
Mishnah
Mithras
pinhead
pithead
Xiphias
fighter
fish-net
high-fed
high-key
highmen
high-set
kishkes
lighted
lighten
lighter
mishmee
nighted
Richter
righten
righter
sighted
sighter
tighten
fishify
cichlid
fishgig
fish-oil
lithoid
Mishnic
nightie
xiphoid
airhole

dishelm
lichtly
lightly
lithely
nightly
pightle
pinhole
pithily
rightly
sightly
Sinhala
tightly
wightly
dishome
diphone
dishing
fishing
miching
nithing
sighing
sithens
tithing
wishing
fish-god
highboy
high-low
high-top
right-oh
right-on
rightos
mishapt
bichord
bighorn
cithara
cithern
dichord
die-hard
dishorn
dithery
fishery
kithara
pig-herd
tinhorn
withers
zithern
highest
highish
mightst
Sikhism
lithate
lithite
dishful
fishful
lithium
mid-hour
pithful
sighful
wishful
without
Ziphius
eightvo

Words marked △ may be spelled also with a capital letter

7 □i□h□w

lich-owl
fisheye
bifilar
digital
finical
liminal
militar
mimical
minicab
minicam
mini-car
minimal
minimax
similar
simitar
sinical
vicinal
bilimbi
viliaco
cimices
citizen
divider
diviner
filibeg
Filices
limited
limiter
limites
Minitel
miniver
minivet
similes
vibices
visitee
visiter
filings
finings
fixings
linings
tidings
viliago
rikishi
bidie-in
divisim
finikin
militia
minikin
mirific
silicic
vivific
finicky
hijinks
kibitka
civilly
licitly
lividly
ribible
rigidly
risible
silicle
timidly

visible
visibly
vividly
ripieni
ripieno
didicoi
didicoy
divisor
kirimon
liaison
libidos
midiron
Nitinol
pig-iron
silicon
similor
Vidicon®
visitor
biliary
ciliary
miliary
mimicry
riviera
rivière
tiniest
Ciliata
ciliate
filiate
miniate
nimiety
viciate
vitiate
bilious
bivious
fidibus
milieus
milieux
minibus
minimum
minimus
mini-sub
nimious
pili-nut
pitiful
Ricinus
siliqua
silique
simious
vicious
vidimus
rilievi
rilievo
disject
disjoin
misjoin
jinjili
jimjams
pig-jump
disjune
linkman
milk-bar

milkman
milk-pan
pickmaw
silk-man
dinky-di
dinkies
milk-leg
pickeer
pickled
pickler
pickles
pinkoes
sickbed
sickled
tickler
tinkler
winkler
kick-off
zinkify
linkage
sinkage
ricksha
milkily
riskily
silkily
dickens
kirking
licking
milking
picking
pinking
sinking
ticking
winking
zinking
hip-knob
kirkton
linkboy
milk-cow
milk-sop
misknow
hickory
pickery
winkers
pinkish
sickish
rickets
rickety
milk-run
riskful
sick-out
wickiup
pickaxe
pink-eye
billman
disleaf
disleal
disload
fig-leaf
milldam
Millian

mislead
pig-lead
uillean
airlock
air-lock
dialect
Diplock
hillock
hip-lock
killick
killock
misluck
niblick
pillock
rim-lock
sillock
ziplock
billies
dialled
dialler
fielded
fielder
fitlier
hillmen
killdee
vialled
wielder
willies
yielder
airlift
mid-life
biology
pillage
tillage
village
diploid
mislaid
sialoid
sirloin
villain
villein
dislike
liplike
mislike
riblike
siclike
wiglike
pig-lily
sillily
diploma
dislimb
dislimn
millime
aiblins
air-lane
airline
aisling
billing
biplane
birling
birlinn

cieling
dialing
dilling
diplont
dislink
filling
girlond
hidling
hidlins
Hieland
Hielant
hirling
kidling
killing
kitling
△midland
mid-Lent
milling
pigling
pilling
rifling
rigling
rivlins
sibling
tilling
titling
villany
violent
violone
willing
witling
billion
billy-oh
gillion
hilltop
jillion
killcow
killjoy
million
niellos
pill-box
pillion
witloof
zillion
diglyph
pillory
Sillery
titlark
aidless
aimless
airless
biblist
bitless
dialist
dialyse
finless
girlish
kinless
lidless
lipless
pipless

Words marked △ may be spelled also with a capital letter

ribless
rimless
sinless
tieless
villose
violist
wigless
willest
witless
giblets
tillite
violate
millrun
pill-bug
vialful
villous
willful
mislive
billowy
pillowy
willowy
mill-eye
dialyze
pigmean
pigmeat
gimmick
mimmick
titmice
mismade
filmset
airmail
pigmoid
riempie
sigmoid
mismake
△dismals
oil-mill
ailment
diamond
dimming
△dinmont
figment
fitment
pigment
rimming
siamang
siemens
filmdom
miombos
pismire
pit-mirk
air-miss
biomass
dimmish
dismask
dismast
dismiss
filmish
kirmess
midmost
△siamese
titmose
bismuth
mismate
sigmate
mim-mou'd
dismayd
dismayl
mizmaze
siameze
dipnoan
Linnean
bionics
finnack
finnock
minnick
minnock
pinnace
pinnock
tie-neck
winnock
zip-neck
Dionaea
fiancée
Limnaea
lioncel
pinnoed
pioneer
pionies
dignify
lignify
signify
lignage
signage
blontic
lianoid
finnsko
giantly
Pianola®
pinnula
pinnule
misname
sirname
visnomy
binning
dinning
ginning
limning
pianino
pinning
pioning
signing
sinning
tinning
winning
midnoon
Signior
diandry
giantry
ginnery
kiln-dry
signary
△signora
△signore
signori
signors
signory
bigness
dimness
disnest
Finnish
fitness
hipness
lignose
lioness
lionise
lionism
pianism
pianist
Sienese
witness
Zionism
Zionist
big-note
dignity
lignite
pinnate
lion-cub
signeur
lionize
bifocal
bilobar
bimodal
bipolar
bitonal
bivouac
bizonal
digonal
dipolar
Filofax®
kilobar
pivotal
divorce
divorcé
Minorca
sirocco
zimocca
bigoted
bilobed
disobey
litotes
mitogen
mitoses
Nilotes
picotee
pivoted
pivoter
Siporex®
visored
vizored
widower
nihonga
timothy
ciboria
cipolin
gironic
kilobit
limosis
mitosis
mitotic
Nilotic
nimonic
pilotis
sinopia
sinopis
virosis
binocle
pinocle
bicorne
eidolon
gigolos
girosol
kiloton
kimonos
dimorph
bigotry
Titoism
Titoist
ricotta
ridotto
riposte
risotto
vicomte
linocut
pirogue
display
disprad
misplay
dispace
nit-pick
six-pack
dimpled
diopter
dispred
pimpled
rippier
rippler
ripples
ripplet
simpler
simplex
tippler
kippage
limpkin
silphia
simpkin
nippily
oil-palm
air-pump
dipping
dispend
dispone
hipping
limping
lipping
lisping
lispund
nipping
pimping
pipping
pit-pony
ripping
sipping
timpani
timpano
tipping
zipping
biophor
pitprop
dip-pipe
airport
bit-part
dioptre
dispark
dispart
disport
nippers
diapase
dispose
dispost
hippish
wimpish
dispute
picquet
diarial
diarian
diurnal
lip-read
misread
Nitrian
Pierian
sierran
disrobe
microbe
oil-rich
pibroch
vitrics
nitride
pierced
piercer
tiaraed
tierced
tiercel
tiercet
midriff
nigrify
nitrify
vitrify
pierage
vitrage
diarchy
air-raid
air-rail
fibroid
fibroin

7 □i□r□o

Giardia
ligroin
milreis
tigroid
vitrail
vitrain
fierily
misrule
nitrile
diorama
fibroma
citrine
disrank
firring
microns
migrant
mikrons
sirring
tigrine
vibrant
Vitrina
vitrine
disroot
hip-roof
△pierrot
vibrios
vitriol
digraph
disrupt
library
cirrose
diarise
diarist
digress
diorism
fibrose
Midrash
nitroso
piarist
tigress
tigrish
bit-rate
cirrate
citrate
diorite
disrate
librate
migrate
misrate
nitrate
nitrite
picrate
picrite
titrate
vibrate
vibrato
cirrous
citrous
fibrous
Librium®
nitrous

vitraux
vitreum
diarize
disseat
kinsman
miasmal
miasmas
mitsvah
Rigsdag
Riksdag
Rissian
airsick
dissect
airside
biassed
diaster
fibster
hipster
linseed
minster
misseem
misstep
oil-seed
pigsney
Pilsner
til-seed
tipster
kiss-off
tipsify
kitschy
airship
cirsoid
cissoid
hirstie
jib-sail
kidskin
kinship
kip-skin
Liassic
miasmic
midship
missaid
missuit
niks-nie
oilskin
pigskin
pigsnie
pissoir
sibship
firstly
fissile
himself
missile
oil-silk
rissole
tipsily
lissome
winsome
biasing
Diasone®
dissent

ginseng
hissing
linsang
lip-sync
missend
missent
missing
rinsing
sinsyne
airstop
fiascos
fission
ginshop
hip-shot
mission
pie-shop
piss-pot
ribston
Riksmål
rim-shot
ripstop
dissert
fissure
piastre
missish
hirsute
fissive
missive
midsize
air-trap
dip-trap
fist-law
lift-man
mint-man
mistral
victual
Vietnam
virtual
bittock
diptych
distich
mistico
tietack
tintack
viatica
pintado
riptide
bistred
dirt-bed
dirtied
dittoed
fifteen
fifties
fig-tree
fin-toed
fir-tree
kirtled
mint-new
mista'en
mist-net
oil-tree

sixteen
sixties
tiptoed
vintner
vistaed
vittles
distaff
lift-off
mintage
vintage
dirt-pie
distain
histoid
histrio
littlin
pigtail
pintail
victrix
mistake
dirtily
distill
distyle
fictile
fifthly
fistula
mistell
mistily
mistold
niftily
ninthly
pistole
sixthly
wittily
airtime
big-time
mistime
biltong
bitting
dietine
distant
distend
distent
distune
dittany
fitting
histone
hitting
kittens
kitteny
listing
misting
mistune
mittens
pitting
rioting
sifting
Sistine
sittine
sitting
tilting
tinting

witting
bistros
cistron
diction
fiction
lift-boy
miction
mistook
mixtion
pint-pot
biotype
tintype
tittupy
bistort
bittern
bitters
cistern
cittern
dietary
△diptera
distort
disturb
fixture
gittern
history
jitters
jittery
linters
littery
midterm
misterm
mistery
mixture
picture
sintery
△victory
winters
wintery
dietist
fittest
Pictish
pietism
pietist
Pittism
riotise
tittish
biotite
dictate
Hittite
listeth
nictate
△pittite
vittate
wistiti
bittour
fistful
giltcup
listful
mistful
riotous
sistrum

Words marked △ may be spelled also with a capital letter

7 □l□c□e

wistful
fictive
Miltown®
diethyl
riotize
fibular
figural
ligular
pilular
simular
situlae
titular
vitular
bitumed
bitumen
dilutee
diluter
disused
figured
minutes
misuser
rivulet
sinuses
tituped
liquefy
divulge
liturgy
simurgh
viduage
hirudin
minutia
silurid
piously
vihuela
visuals
diluent
minuend
piquant
dilutor
kikumon
sit-upon
sinuose
liquate
pituita
pituite
sinuate
situate
viduity
△limulus
liqueur
mimulus
Silurus
sinuous
viduous
dibutyl
Rigveda
civvies
divvied
milvine
△nirvana
sievert
silvern
silvery
lievest
△mid-week
misween
pigweed
midwife
witwall
miswend
miswent
viewing
fir-wood
airward
die-work
figwort
misword
ribwork
ribwort
tinware
Midwest
pigwash
airwave
midwive
biaxial
dioxide
Pinxter
dioxane
mid-year
pixy-led
Digynia
sibylic
disyoke
misyoke
bicycle
biryani
minyans
pitying
tidying
jipyapa
mitzvah
diazoes
dizzied
sizzler
fizzgig
dizzily
Cinzano®
fizzing
dizzard
gizzard
rizzart
bizzazz
pizzazz
djibbah
Ojibwas
ejector
ijtihad
Mjölnir
sjambok
ajutage
akvavit
skiable
sky-bred
ikebana
skyborn
sky-blue
skyclad
skidpan
skidded
skidder
skudler
skeeter
skreigh
skiffle
skegger
sky-high
skyhook
skriech
skriegh
skyjack
ski-jump
skelder
skelter
skilled
skillet
skulker
P-Keltic
Q-Keltic
skaldic
skellie
skollie
skulpin
ukelele
ukulele
skyline
skolion
skylark
skellum
skilful
skimmed
skimmer
skummer
skimmia
okimono
skinker
skinned
skinner
skin-pop
skinful
skepped
skipped
skipper
skippet
skepsis
skeptic
skepful
skirret
skirted
skirter
ekistic
skysail
skitter
sketchy
skatole
skittle
skuttle
skating
skiving
ekpwele
skyward
skew-put
okaying
alcázar
almanac
cloacae
cloacal
flea-bag
flyaway
ilkaday
Alcaics
pliancy
alcaide
alcalde
alcayde
algates
aliases
alkanet
allayer
alnager
bleared
bleater
bloated
bloater
cleaner
clearer
cleaved
cleaver
floatel
floater
gleaner
gloater
pleaded
pleader
pleased
pleaser
pleated
pleater
sleaved
alfalfa
alkalis
Alsatia
Eleatic
ellagic
fleapit
gliadin
olearia
ulnaria
bleakly
cleanly
clearly
flyable
pliable
pliably
Almaine
cleanse
illapse
alfaquí
clean-up
iliacus
club-law
clubman
flyboat
plebean
blabbed
blabber
blubbed
blubber
clabber
clobber
clubbed
clubber
flubbed
ill-bred
slabbed
slabber
slobber
slubbed
slubber
plebify
globoid
elf-bolt
flybelt
globule
flybane
flyblow
flybook
ale-bush
globose
globate
glebous
globous
clachan
glacial
placcat
placebo
blacken
blocked
blocker
blucher
clacker
cliché'd
clicker
clicket
clocked
clocker
flacker
flacket
flecked
flecker
flicker
glacéed
glacier
placket
plucked
plucker

7 □l□e□i

slacken
slacker
slicken
slicker
slocken
flaccid
placoid
blackly
slackly
slickly
alicant
glucina
glycine
placing
slicing
△elector
olycook
ulichon
electro
placard
plectra
plectre
alecost
glucose
glycose
elocute
placate
placita
plicate
floccus
alodial
alidade
cladode
bladder
bludger
cladder
clodded
fledged
gladded
gladden
glidder
pledgee
pledger
pledget
plodded
plodder
sledded
sledger
slidden
slidder
cludgie
gladdie
gliding
sladang
sliding
gladdon
pledgor
cladism
cladist
alodium
gladful

gladius
bluecap
gleeman
illegal
fluence
fluency
already
alférez
aliened
alienee
alleged
alleger
alleyed
altered
bleeder
bleeper
cleeked
fleeced
fleecer
fleerer
Kleenex®
sleeken
sleeker
sleeper
sleeved
sleever
ulcered
albergo
alledge
allegge
allergy
sleechy
algesia
algesis
aloetic
cleekit
Elzevir
sleekit
blue-sky
alveole
alveoli
elderly
fleetly
sleekly
alterne
blueing
fleeing
albedos
alienor
blue-rot
glue-pot
algebra
allegro
alveary
sleepry
altesse
Alberti
bluette
clued-up
gleeful
blue-eye

altezza
fly-flap
bluffer
cliffed
clifted
flaffer
bluffly
olefine
plafond
aliform
fly-fish
elegiac
flag-day
plug-hat
blagger
clagged
clogged
clogger
flagged
flogged
glugged
plaguey
plugged
plugger
slagged
slogged
slogger
slugger
elegant
all-good
elegise
elegist
elogist
oligist
blighty
flighty
elogium
plagium
elegize
allheal
althaea
all-hail
fly-half
alchemy
alchymy
Althing
ale-hoof
elfhood
alchera
alphorn
althorn
elkhorn
Elohist
almirah
fluidal
Pléiade
Pleiads
Alcides
claimer
eloiner
glaiket

glaived
plaided
plaited
plaiter
sleided
alright
sleight
albinic
albitic
alginic
fluidic
glaikit
glairin
ileitis
illicit
plainly
albinos
cloison
ellipse
slàinte
fly-kick
olykoek
flokati
flyleaf
elfland
ululant
ululate
alumnae
alameda
alamode
clamber
clammed
clamper
climbed
climber
clumber
clumper
flamfew
glimmer
glommed
plumber
plummet
plumpen
plumper
slammed
slammer
slimmed
slimmer
slumber
slummer
plumage
alembic
Olympia
Olympic
plumbic
plumpie
plumply
plumula
plumule
slimily
aliment

alimony
alumina
clamant
clement
element
flaming
Fleming
flummox
plumcot
alamort
plumery
slumbry
alumish
blemish
△flemish
glimpse
plumist
plumose
climate
plumate
alumium
alumnus
clamour
glamour
Olympus
plumbum
plumous
alannah
Cluniac
plantar
blanket
blended
blender
blinded
blinder
blinked
blinker
blunder
blunger
blunker
clanger
clinger
clinker
flanged
flanker
flannel
flannen
flinder
flinger
flunkey
glandes
klinker
planned
planner
planter
plonker
plunder
plunger
plunker
slander
slanger

Words marked △ may be spelled also with a capital letter

slanted
slender
slenter
slinger
slinker
slinter
elenchi
glenoid
glonoin
Plantin
Tlingit
alonely
blandly
blankly
blindly
bluntly
planula
slantly
alanine
clangor
plenipo
llanero
planury
plenary
allness
alongst
illness
oldness
planish
plenish
plenist
slyness
alength
alunite
planxty
flâneur
blintze
Alcoran
Alkoran
also-ran
gliomas
klootch
all-over
allowed
almoner
blooded
bloomer
blooper
flooded
floored
floorer
flyover
allonge
△clootie
floosie
floozie
fluoric
gliosis
illogic
plookie
alforja
aloofly
bloosme
alsoone
alcohol
pleopod
almonry
allonym
alcorza
clypeal
glyptal
klipdas
slipway
clapnet
clapped
clapper
clip-fed
clipped
clipper
flapped
flapper
flipper
plopped
slapped
slapper
slipped
slipper
slopped
clippie
clupeid
glyphic
glyptic
ale-pole
alepine
clip-ons
sloping
flip-dog
flip-top
fly-past
clypeus
cliquey
aliquot
Floréal
floreat
glareal
cleruch
alarmed
blarney
blurred
claroes
gloried
slurper
slurred
clarify
glorify
clarain
clarkia
floruit
alertly
clerkly
alarums
pleroma
plerome
clarini
clarino
flaring
glaring
alerion
clarion
clerisy
florist
oloroso
clarity
flare-up
all-star
alms-man
Elysian
glossal
allseed
all-seer
alms-fee
blasted
blaster
△blessed
blister
blusher
blushet
bluster
clasher
clasper
classed
cluster
clyster
flasher
flasket
fleshed
flesher
flushed
flusher
fluster
glassen
glasses
glisten
glister
glosser
oldster
plashet
plaster
plushes
plussed
plusses
slashed
slasher
sloshed
plusage
classic
classis
clastic
close-in
elastic
elastin
Glossic
plasmic
plasmid
plasmin
plastic
plastid
pliskie
closely
fleshly
closing
plusing
blesbok
blossom
elf-shot
elision
elusion
fly-slow
plessor
plosion
closure
elusory
Flustra
alyssum
close-up
Elysium
elusive
plosive
elytral
flat-cap
flotsam
flytrap
glottal
gluteal
plateau
pluteal
slot-car
blather
blatted
blatter
blether
bletted
blither
blotted
blotter
clatter
clitter
clothed
clothes
clotted
clotter
clutter
flatbed
flatlet
flatted
flatten
flatter
flitted
flitter
flutter
glitter
glutaei
glutted
platted
platter
plotted
plotter
slather
slatted
slatter
slither
slitter
slotted
slotter
flotage
blotchy
glottic
glottis
plottie
all-time
old-time
blatant
flotant
flutina
fluting
flyting
platane
platina
plating
slating
elation
elution
elytron
fletton
glutton
platoon
cloture
olitory
elitism
élitism
elitist
élitist
flutist
clotbur
elytrum
gluteus
plotful
pluteus
elative
clausal
pleurae
pleural
flaunch
flounce
flouncy
aliunde
albumen
allurer
clouded
clouted
clouter
fleuret
ileuses
ill-used
plouter

7 □l□u□h

claucht
claught
flaught
slouchy
sloughy
albumin
alluvia
plaudit
ploukie
albugos
aleuron
blaubok
bloubok
blouson
fleuron
pleuron
flaunty
Glaucus
eluvial
Flavian
fluvial
pluvial
clavier
flivver
klavier
Slavify
elevens
flavine
flavone
gloving
olivine
Slovene
Slavdom
clivers
clovery
olivary
plovery
slavery
slavish
Slavism
clavate
elevate
eluvium
flavour
blowsed
blowzed
clowder
plowter
alewife
blow-off
flowage
blowfly
ill-will
all-wing
blowing
ellwand
flowing
glowing
slowing
blowjob
elmwood

plywood
all-work
blawort
blewart
blow-dry
flowers
flowery
slowish
blewits
blowgun
blow-out
flexile
flexion
fluxion
flexure
plexure
fluxive
ally-taw
claypan
play-day
play-way
play-act
playlet
playpen
play-off
clay-pit
allying
cloying
flaying
playing
ally-tor
play-box
playboy
clayish
playbus®
playful
glazier
glazing
glozing
alizari
impalas
ambatch
ambages
embased
empanel
impanel
ommatea
embargo
embathe
empathy
imbathe
Amharic
impavid
amiable
amiably
embayld
impaint
empaire
empayre
ambassy
amearst

ampassy
embassy
impasse
embaste
impaste
impasto
amabile
smacker
smicker
smicket
smectic
smickly
emicant
omicron
emicate
smidgen
smudger
smidgin
smeddum
amoebae
amoebas
empeach
emperce
impeach
ambered
ammeter
umbered
immerge
amnesia
amnesic
amoebic
imperia
imperil
emperor
impearl
immense
immerse
amnesty
omneity
impetus
amygdal
imagoes
smuggle
imagine
imaging
imagery
△imagism
imagist
umwhile
amphora
ammiral
imbiber
impinge
empight
empiric
omnific
ambient
omniana
ambitty
impiety
omniety

impious
omnibus
smoke-ho
smokily
smoking
amalgam
amildar
implead
emplace
implode
implied
smelled
smeller
smelter
smolder
ymolten
amplify
amyloid
emulsin
emblema
emplume
ambling
amylene
emplane
implant
smiling
embloom
emulsor
smaltos
implore
amylase
emulate
implate
implete
emulous
emblaze
imamate
amental
omental
amender
emonges
amenage
amentia
emanant
eminent
amongst
emongst
amanita
amenity
emanate
amentum
omentum
ominous
ammonal
immoral
umbonal
ambones
embowed
embowel
embower
empower

imbower
imposer
umbones
ammonia
embolic
emporia
ampoule
embound
impound
embosom
imbosom
imports
embogue
embolus
embread
Umbrian
amtrack
embrace
emerods
emersed
smarten
impregn
smaragd
umbrage
ambroid
embraid
embroil
smartie
emerald
smartly
amarant
Amerind
amorant
amorini
amorino
imprint
embryon
embryos
umbrere
amorism
amorist
amorosa
amoroso
empress
emprise
imbrast
impresa
imprese
impress
imprest
umbrose
embrute
emeriti
emirate
imbrute
amorous
umbrous
embrave
improve
embrewe
embrown

Words marked △ may be spelled also with a capital letter

7 □n□h□l

imbrown
Ameslan
ambs-ace
ames-ace
smashed
smasher
amusing
amosite
smash-up
amusive
emitted
emitter
emptied
emptier
empties
omitted
omitter
smatter
smitten
smother
smutted
umpteen
S-matrix
smytrie
emptily
smittle
emetine
imitant
amation
emotion
emption
amatory
imitate
amateur
amative
emotive
amputee
imputer
smouser
ampulla
imburse
impulse
empyema
amazing
endarch
enhance
infancy
infarct
unlatch
innards
inwards
onwards
unhandy
unhardy
annates
ansated
Antares
engaged
△engager
enraged
inhaler
inlayer
invader
kneader
sneaked
sneaker
unbaked
unbated
undated
uneared
uneaten
unfaded
unfamed
unfazed
ungazed
unjaded
unladen
unmated
unnamed
unpaced
unpaged
unpanel
unpaper
unpared
unpaved
unraced
unraked
unrated
unravel
unsated
unsaved
untaken
untamed
untaxed
unwaged
unwaked
unwares
unwater
unwayed
enlarge
enrange
Inkatha
antacid
entasis
inhabit
insanie
invalid
unwarie
entayle
envault
unhable
unmanly
unvaile
uncanny
unpaint
unsaint
unhappy
ondatra
unmarry
infaust
inhaust
andante
annatta
annatto
inearth
infanta
infante
unearth
unfaith
unhasty
unlaste
sneak-up
antbear
anybody
enabler
knobbed
knobber
snubbed
snubber
knobble
knobbly
knubble
knubbly
snabble
ink-blot
antbird
Anobium
knacker
knicker
knocker
snicker
snicket
unacted
unscrew
V-necked
gnocchi
onychia
insculp
knuckle
knuckly
unscale
enactor
knock-on
inscape
△unicorn
unscary
unicity
knock-up
unidea'd
unideal
snodded
snoddit
snidely
anodyne
anodise
anodize
enteral
indexal
kneecap
knee-cap
knee-pad
knee-pan
inherce
unperch
unteach
underdo
unheedy
unready
unweldy
anoeses
enterer
entêtée
indexer
indexes
ingener
integer
invexed
kneeled
kneeler
one-eyed
sneerer
sneezer
unbeget
unfeued
unmeted
unsewed
unsexed
unvexed
enfeoff
undeify
ant-eggs
inveigh
undergo
anaemia
anaemic
angelic
Angevin
annelid
anoesis
anoetic
antefix
endemic
enteric
inherit
△interim
invenit
angerly
injelly
undealt
antenna
inbeing
△inferno
interne
unbeing
unmeant
angekok
enderon
enfelon
enteron
envelop
envenom
unbegot
unkempt
unheard
unheart
unlearn
unweary
incense
intense
inverse
unherst
unleash
unsense
entente
in-depth
ingesta
Insecta
unneath
untenty
angelus
ingénue
knees-up
unbegun
innerve
inweave
unnerve
unreave
unreeve
unweave
ink-feed
sniffer
snifter
snuffer
unified
unifier
unoften
onefold
snaffle
sniffle
snuffle
snuffly
knifing
uniform
ink-fish
anagram
snagged
snigger
snugged
anagoge
anagogy
sniggle
snuggle
endgame
anthrax
enthral
inthral
uncheck
encheer
enwheel
enchafe
anthoid
enchain
inchpin
unchain
ant-hill

7 □n□h□n

enshell
inshell
unchild
unshale
unshell
Anthony
enchant
in-thing
unshent
unthink
unshoot
unshape
unwhipt
encharm
inkhorn
inshore
onshore
on-shore
uncharm
unchary
unshorn
enchase
enthuse
inchase
inphase
enrheum
unshout
anchovy
unshewn
unshown
anginal
antigay
antiwar
indican
infimae
inqilab
intimae
unvital
unhitch
unwitch
unfilde
antigen
enfiled
enginer
enliven
enriven
enticer
incised
inciter
indices
inditer
infidel
insider
insides
insinew
invitee
inviter
knaidel
unaided
unaimed
unaired
uncited
unfiled
unfired
unfixed
unhired
unlimed
unlined
unmixed
unoiled
unrimed
unrisen
unriven
unrivet
unsinew
unsized
untiled
untired
unwiped
unwived
innings
unhinge
enlight
insight
undight
unright
unsight
incipit
incivil
indicia
inhibit
insipid
oneiric
uncivil
anticke
unpinkt
Enfield
entitle
infield
unfitly
angioma
ancient
antient
anziani
insigne
andiron
angicos
antilog
endiron
environ
incisor
indigos
unvisor
onliest
anxiety
ungirth
unwitty
annicut
antique
anxious
envious
infimum
invious
uncinus
snakily
unaking
unskan'd
snakish
Anglian
antliae
unclean
unclear
uncloak
englobe
inglobe
anelace
△anglice
inflect
inflict
unblock
unplace
include
unglued
anglify
analogy
unplait
unslain
unalike
enflame
inflame
unplumb
unplume
angling
aniline
anklong
anklung
endlang
endlong
enplane
incline
inkling
unblent
unblind
unsling
unslung
antlion
engloom
unclipt
analyse
analyst
anglist
enclasp
enclose
endless
enflesh
English
inclasp
inclose
inulase
unalist
unbless
unblest
unclasp
unclose
unflesh
unflush
anility
inflate
encloud
uncloud
enclave
enslave
unalive
unglove
unblown
analyze
cnemial
f-number
anomaly
anemone
unsmart
animism
animist
endmost
gnomish
gnomist
animate
enemata
enomoty
unsmote
enamour
onymous
Ananias
unsneck
in-kneed
in-and-in
inanely
anonyma
ensnare
ensnarl
insnare
unsnarl
onanism
onanist
oneness
inanity
unknown
Angolan
insofar
unmoral
unroyal
unvocal
unwoman
enforce
inforce
invoice
unvoice
inroads
ancones
annoyed
annoyer
endogen
endowed
endower
enjoyer
incomer
intoner
inwoven
oncogen
snooded
snooker
snooper
snoozer
unbowed
uncover
ungored
unhoped
unloved
unmoved
unnoted
unposed
untoned
unwooed
unwoven
unyoked
unzoned
engorge
enrough
ungorg'd
unrough
anionic
encomia
entomic
entopic
entotic
inconie
Indocid®
unsolid
ennoble
snoozle
ungodly
unmould
unnoble
enround
inbound
inconnu
ingoing
injoint
ongoing
on-going
unbound
undoing
unfound
unjoint
unmount
unround
unsound
unwound
endozoa
entozoa
unbosom
inboard
indoors
onboard
on-board

Words marked △ may be spelled also with a capital letter

unhoard
endorse
indorse
in-house
unhorse
unhouse
unloose
unroost
unsonsy
insooth
oncosts
uncouth
unsoote
unworth
involve
antonym
indoxyl
unspeak
inspect
unspide
knapped
knapper
snapped
snapper
snipped
snipper
snippet
unspied
unspoke
inaptly
ineptly
knapple
unaptly
unspell
unspilt
sniping
unspent
inspire
anapest
unequal
anyroad
entreat
inbreak
intreat
untread
engrace
infract
unbrace
unfrock
untrace
intrada
intrude
untride
enarmed
gnarled
gnarred
inbreed
knarred
knurled
snarled
snarler
snorkel
snorter
unarmed
undried
unfreed
unorder
untried
unurged
engraff
engraft
indraft
ingraft
anarchy
android
aneroid
energic
energid
engrail
engrain
entrail
entrain
inertia
ingrain
introit
unbroke
angrily
entrall
entrold
inertly
introld
snirtle
untruly
enframe
enprint
entrant
inbring
intrant
snaring
snoring
undrunk
unwrung
encrypt
entropy
ancress
encrust
engrasp
engross
entrism
entrist
entrust
incross
incrust
ingress
ingross
intrust
uncross
undress
untruss
untrust
encraty
ingrate
uncrate
untruth
unwrite
anurous
ingroup
onerous
snarl-up
engrave
on-drive
indrawn
ingrown
uncrown
ungrown
anorexy
unusual
aniseed
gnasher
Knesset
one-step
unasked
anosmia
endship
△gnostic
oneself
inkspot
one-shot
one-stop
Oniscus
gnathal
initial
instead
onstead
unstrap
D-notice
unstack
unstick
unstock
unstuck
another
ensteep
knitted
knitter
knotted
knotter
snotter
unities
unsteel
unstuft
on-stage
snatchy
gnathic
snottie
unstaid
unstrip
enstyle
install
instill
knittle
anatomy
anytime
enstamp
one-time
instant
uniting
anattos
enation
unction
unition
in-store
unitard
unitary
anatase
unitise
instate
unstate
unitive
unitize
angular
annular
infulae
inhuman
insular
ungulae
unhuman
enounce
injunct
annulet
endurer
end-user
ennuied
ennuyed
ensurer
incudes
inducer
infuser
inhumer
injurer
inquiet
insured
insurer
snouted
uncured
unfumed
unguled
unqueen
unquiet
unruled
unsured
untuned
unruffe
indulge
aneurin
indulin
indusia
insulin
unlucky
in-built
unbuild
unbuilt
anguine
ensuing
unburnt
unfunny
unguent
unsunny
engulph
ingulph
enguard
enquire
enquiry
inquere
inquire
inquiry
unguard
anguish
inburst
inquest
insulse
uncurse
unpurse
annuity
unquote
annulus
incubus
incurve
andvile
knevell
knavery
knavish
snowcap
snowman
unswear
snow-ice
anywhen
ensweep
snow-fed
unowned
unsweet
unswai'd
indwell
indwelt
inkwell
know-all
snowily
entwine
inswing
intwine
knowing
untwine
knowhow
know-how
unswept
unaware
unsworn
anywise
endwise
entwist
intwist
snowish
untwist
anyways
endways
anaxial

7 □n□x□c

inexact
ungyved
enzymic
envying
inlying
undying
untying
innyard
snuzzle
gonadal
Mozarab
oolakan
tokamak
copaiba
joyance
monarch
nomarch
noyance
polacca
△romance
sonance
sonancy
tobacco
toparch
monarda
notanda
towards
dowager
forager
foramen
forayer
gowaned
homager
kokanee
nodated
nonaged
po-faced
potager
Romanes
rosacea
rosaker
royalet
socager
togated
voyager
zonated
botargo
gouache
Bobadil
bonamia
boracic
botanic
cohabit
conaria
domatia
folacin
gonadic
komatik
Koranic
logania
monacid

monadic
nomadic
novalia
podalic
Polaris
potamic
Romanic
rosalia
solatia
somatic
Sotadic
vocalic
volatic
romaika
coracle
coralla
dowable
focally
locally
losable
lovable
loyally
modally
morally
movable
movably
nodally
no-fault
notable
notably
potable
ropable
rowable
royally
tonally
totally
towable
vocable
vocally
volable
womanly
Cocagne
cocaine
hosanna
moraine
posaune
romaunt
sodaine
borazon
donator
dorados
dos-à-dos
hob-a-nob
Mogadon®
monaxon
nonagon
polaron
robalos
rotator
solanos
conacre

podagra
polacre
sowarry
Molasse
morassy
Mosaism
potassa
Romansh
Zolaism
coranto
dopatta
loyalty
royalty
volante
bonasus
conatus
notaeum
pomatum
popadum
solanum
totanus
Volapük
copaiva
bonanza
bogbean
corbeau
forbear
Hobbian
rowboat
Sorbian
towboat
hogback
roebuck
sowback
forbade
forbode
bobbles
bomblet
cobbler
doubler
doubles
doublet
double-u
doubted
doubter
gobbler
gombeen
hobbler
lobbyer
low-bred
nobbler
nombles
wobbler
yobboes
zombify
corbeil
howbeit
nombril
cowbell
dog-belt
dogbolt

fog-bell
loobily
low-bell
nobbily
tombola
tombolo
bobbing
bowbent
combine
cowbane
dobbing
dogbane
fog-bank
hopbind
hopbine
jobbing
mobbing
robbing
sobbing
sorbent
boobook
logbook
low-brow
top-boot
bobbery
bombard
bombora
cowbird
forbore
Homburg
jobbery
Lombard
low-born
mowburn
poe-bird
poy-bird
robbery
wosbird
yobbery
bobbish
bombast
combust
hobbish
Hobbism
Hobbist
mobbish
Sorbish
soubise
yobbish
yobbism
Corbett
Moabite
sorbate
sorbite
comb-out
box-coat
conceal
conchae
conchal
dog-crab
Joycean

morceau
ponceau
Roscian
topcoat
concoct
gorcock
concede
concedo
botcher
bouchée
coachee
coacher
conches
concrew
couchee
couchée
moocher
moucher
notched
notchel
notcher
poacher
potcher
pouched
torcher
touched
toucher
vouchee
voucher
wotcher
boscage
soccage
coccoid
conceit
conchie
log-chip
Noachic
rotchie
toeclip
hoe-cake
box-calf
cow-calf
doucely
zoccolo
coxcomb
non-come
concent
doucine
porcine
voicing
volcano
gorcrow
ponchos
torchon
concept
concupy
forceps
concern
concert
concord
dogcart

Words marked △ may be spelled also with a capital letter

no-score
popcorn
sorcery
concise
concuss
corcass
low-cost
boycott
doucets
dowcets
toccata
douceur
Jobclub
Roscius
concave
bondman
cordial
good-day
△goodman
Gordian
hoodman
mondial
roadman
road-map
roadway
rondeau
woodman
woodwax
córdoba
conduce
conduct
hordock
howdy-do
soldado
boodied
doodler
fondler
good-den
good-e'en
goodies
hog-deer
road-bed
roe-deer
soldier
toadied
toddler
wondred
bondage
condign
cordage
pondage
sondage
wordage
boudoir
conduit
foudrie
hordein
lordkin
mondain
non-drip
woodsia
condole
condyle
dowdily
gondola
hold-all
moodily
rowdily
sondeli
wordily
condemn
goddamn
bonding
codding
condone
cording
cow-dung
folding
fondant
fordone
holding
loading
Londony
lording
mordant
mordent
nodding
podding
road-end
roading
rodding
rondino
sodding
sordini
sordino
tondini
tondino
voiding
wording
good-now
good-son
road-hog
tordion
Borders
bordure
doddard
doddery
goldarn
moidore
powdery
rondure
Wonders
coldish
foodism
△goddess
goldish
goodish
loudish
wordish
cordate
cordite
fold-out
foodful
gold-bug
Gordius
hoodlum
Hordeum
woodcut
hoedown
low-down
top-down
dogdays
goldeye
good-bye
Docetae
forecar
fore-day
forelay
foreman
forepaw
foreran
foresaw
foresay
gomeral
hoseman
love-day
Mohegan
molerat
nosebag
nosegay
nose-rag
note-pad
polecat
rodeway
rokelay
ropeway
rosebay
sokeman
someday
someway
tonepad
cogence
cogency
Moresco
potence
potencé
potency
morendo
bone-bed
boneset
cogener
coherer
covelet
covered
coveted
cozener
doe-eyed
dovelet
foreleg
foremen
foresee
forever
Gore-Tex®
honeyed
hose-net
hoveled
however
Joneses
lobelet
Lorelei
lovered
modeled
modeler
moneyed
moneyer
nose-led
notelet
pop-eyed
powered
rose-red
toweled
towered
come-off
foreign
lozenge
lozengy
somewhy
bone-oil
coletit
comedic
cometic
coterie
Docetic
dovekie
forelie
fox-evil
Gobelin
△godetia
go-devil
gomeril
Homeric
Homerid
lobelia
polemic
poperin
roper-in
rosehip
soredia
tonemic
tonetic
totemic
toxemia
toxemic
zooecia
corella
foveola
foveole
loverly
modelli
modello
morello
Moselle
notedly
novella
novelle
rosella
roselle
roseola
rozelle
soberly
vowelly
codeine
doyenne
fore-end
someone
boleros
boredom
Comecon
comedos
copepod
dovecot
foretop
holesom
moneron
pomelos
pomeroy
popedom
somehow
sorehon
toheroa
Toledos
toreros
bone-dry
forearm
tone-arm
bone-ash
Couéism
Couéist
doveish
moreish
nor'-east
poseuse
codetta
dogeate
dozenth
fouetté
foveate
honesty
lomenta
lorette
modesty
mofette
momenta
mozetta
nonette
nonetti
nonetto
novelty
podestà
polenta
poverty
roseate
Rosetta
rosette
rosetty

7 □o□e□u

bodeful
△boletus
coteaux
cover-up
doleful
foregut
forerun
hopeful
pokeful
rosebud
rose-bug
rose-cut
pole-axe
homelyn
non-flam
pooftah
pouftah
Wolfian
wolfram
confect
confide
coffret
comfrey
hop-flea
△pomfret
poofter
pouffed
poufter
sol-faed
woofter
solfège
forfair
forfeit
wolfkin
boxfuls
cot-folk
goofily
Norfolk
potfuls
souffle
soufflé
topfull
confine
forfend
golfing
loafing
△rolfing
roofing
wolfing
Corfiot
hoofrot
hotfoot
mouflon
rooftop
tomfool
wolf-dog
bonfire
comfort
confirm
conform
zoeform

codfish
confess
confest
confuse
cowfish
dogfish
hog-fish
toffish
wolfish
confute
conflux
loofful
congeal
couguar
loggias
long-day
low-gear
Morglay
songman
Vosgean
Vosgian
torgoch
fougade
boggler
boogied
congree
cougher
doggrel
goggled
goggler
goggles
joggled
long-leg
mongrel
pongoes
poogyee
roughen
rougher
soignée
tongued
tongues
toughen
wongied
foggage
long-ago
long-oil
roughie
toughie
foggily
roughly
soggily
toughly
Dodgems®
dodgems
zoogamy
co-agent
cogging
dodging
dogging
doggone
forging

forgone
hogging
jogging
lodging
logging
longing
nogging
sogging
togging
zoogeny
zoogony
gorgios
longbow
lorgnon
sorghos
boggard
boggart
boy-girl
cowgirl
dodgery
doggery
forgery
gougère
hoggery
joggers
mongery
toggery
congest
doggess
doggish
hoggish
longest
longish
doughty
foughty
loggats
noughts
zorgite
congius
congrue
songful
sorghum
forgave
forgive
bodhrán
bowhead
dog-head
go-ahead
△godhead
hop-head
hothead
lochial
log-head
Loghtan
mophead
moth-eat
Pooh-Bah
pot-head
tow-head
Gothick
toshach

cowhide
boshter
cochlea
cowheel
moshvei
potheen
cowhage
co-chair
pochoir
bothole
doghole
foxhole
mochell
pothole
toehold
top-hole
bow-hand
cowhand
forhent
fox-hunt
moshing
nothing
boyhood
godhood
hoghood
pothook
coehorn
coshery
cothurn
cowherb
cowherd
foghorn
mothery
non-hero
noshery
nowhere
pochard
pothery
yoghurt
dobhash
sophism
sophist
göthite
oophyte
box-haul
jodhpur
dorhawk
goshawk
Loghtyn
bolivar
Bovidae
comical
comital
conical
corival
cotidal
domical
holiday
logical
loricae
Mohican

nodical
nominal
somital
topical
toxical
zooidal
cowitch
goyisch
△morisco
oomiack
to-pinch
codices
conifer
dominee
folioed
fomites
ioniser
ionizer
lobiped
lorimer
loriner
molimen
molinet
moniker
no-fines
nominee
porifer
posited
rooinek
rosined
rotifer
soliped
sorites
vomited
borings
cotinga
foliage
Moringa
moriche
potiche
tonight
bodikin
codicil
cohibit
colitis
comitia
conidia
domicil
dominie
gobioid
gonidia
gonidic
hominid
monilia
motivic
notitia
oolitic
politic
△robinia
solicit
somitic

Words marked △ may be spelled also with a capital letter

soritic
colicky
bouilli
codilla
codille
docible
foliole
gorilla
Modiola
mouillé
Moviola®
rouille
solidly
zorille
zorillo
coniine
motions
notions
totient
bog-iron
bonitos
box-iron
copilot
co-pilot
dominos
dosi-dos
Honiton
horizon
monitor
non-iron
norimon
positon
soliton
tow-iron
zorinos
colibri
goliard
hosiery
poniard
rosiere
topiary
foliose
Corinth
foliate
△goliath
modiste
sociate
society
comique
copious
corious
holibut
modicum
noxious
solidum
solidus
vomitus
conject
conjoin
toe-jump
goujons
conjure
conjury
bonjour
bookman
folkway
Hock-day
Lockian
lockjaw
lockman
lockram
mooktar
rocklay
rock-tar
workbag
workday
workman
yolk-sac
cockade
mockado
booklet
cockled
cockles
△cockney
look-see
porkies
rockier
Rockies
boskage
corkage
dockage
lockage
mockage
soakage
cockshy
workshy
booksie
cockpit
hook-pin
pockpit
pork-pie
rock-oil
rokkaku
cockily
rock-elm
rockily
book-end
booking
corking
docking
Dorking
god-king
honking
mocking
rocking
soaking
socking
working
bowknot
kolkhoz
rock-cod
topknot
workbox
worktop
bonkers
conkers
cookery
jookery
joukery
mockers
mockery
monkery
pockard
rockery
rookery
bookish
dockise
Lockist
lookism
monkish
rookish
Yorkish
Yorkist
box-kite
bookful
cookout
forkful
lockful
lock-nut
lockout
lookout
soukous
workful
work-out
cockeye
donkeys
monkeys
sockeye
dockize
Boolean
coalman
coaltar
coal-tar
cobloaf
coeliac
pollman
poll-tax
roll-bar
rouleau
souldan
tollman
toolbag
toolbar
toolman
woolfat
woolman
Zoilean
would-be
bollock
collect
cowlick
dorlach
hoolock
pollack
pollicy
pollock
Porlock
potlach
rollick
rollock
rowlock
collide
collude
roulade
boulder
boulter
bowlder
coal-bed
colleen
collier
coulter
dollied
dollier
dowlney
foulder
goolies
holloes
△jollies
jollyer
moulder
moulten
poulder
poulter
woolded
woolder
woolled
woollen
woolsey
worlded
jollify
low-life
mollify
collage
college
moulage
noology
soilage
tollage
zoology
holla-ho
colloid
couloir
douleia
toolkit
godlike
rodlike
toylike
godlily
jollily
lowlily
worldly
coulomb
fog-lamp
bogland
boiling
bowline
bowling
codling
colling
Collins
coolant
cotland
cowling
foiling
fooling
fopling
forlana
forlend
forlent
fowling
godling
golland
gosling
gowland
hog-line
holland
hotline
howling
logline
lowland
morling
norland
oodlins
pollent
polling
rolling
soiling
toiling
tolling
tooling
topline
towline
yowling
coal-box
dolldom
moellon
rollmop
roll-top
toe-loop
toolbox
toylsom
collops
boilery
bollard
collard
foolery
forlore
forlorn
foulard
Lollard
pollard
poulard
pouldre
poultry
soilure

7 □o□l□s

coalise
coolish
dollish
fogless
foolish
forlese
godless
goulash
jobless
joyless
mollusc
mollusk
rodless
sonless
toeless
topless
toyless
wouldst
Zoilism
Zoilist
Coalite®
collate
hoplite
jollity
pollute
zoolite
zoolith
bowlful
rollout
soulful
toilful
poll-axe
gooleys
volleys
coalize
holm-oak
Wormian
dormice
Formica®
hommock
commode
commodo
boomlet
foamily
formula
hot-melt
pommelé
roomily
booming
coaming
command
commend
comment
△commons
commune
dooming
dormant
foaming
formant
forming
gormand
hog-mane
hormone
Normans
noumena
roaming
Rommany
rouming
souming
torment
tormina
towmond
towmont
boom-box
hoummos
mormaor
Mormops
commère
foumart
fox-mark
Kommers
woomera
wormery
bog-moss
cosmism
cosmist
koumiss
topmast
topmost
commote
commute
formate
cormous
doomful
holmium
roomful
commove
cooncan
corneal
cornual
gownman
horn-mad
Johnian
moineau
noonday
poundal
somnial
tonneau
connect
cornice
dornick
downa-do
poinado
tornade
tornado
boonies
bouncer
bounded
bounden
bounder
corn-fed
counsel
counted
counter
données
down-bed
founder
hornlet
joannes
joinder
jointed
jointer
lounder
lounger
△moonies
moonlet
moonset
mounted
mounter
poinder
pointed
pointel
pointer
pounced
pouncet
pounder
rounded
roundel
rounder
sounder
wounder
younger
younker
coinage
cornage
tonnage
coontie
council
hobnail
△johnnie
moonlit
Mountie
poon-oil
toenail
bonnily
cornfly
jointly
roundle
roundly
soundly
tonnell
youngly
zoonomy
coining
conning
donning
fornent
horning
joining
loaning
looning
morning
nooning
poynant
ronning
sorning
town-end
wonning
coondog
cornrow
downbow
gownboy
moon-bow
moon-god
country
donnard
donnart
donnerd
donnert
foundry
joinery
cognise
Cornish
cornist
coyness
donnish
donnism
Goanese
hog-nose
hornish
hornist
hotness
lowness
moonish
nowness
roinish
roynish
so-and-so
soonest
tonnish
townish
bornite
cognate
connate
connote
cornett
cornute
cornuto
hornito
youngth
zoonite
hornbug
hornful
horn-nut
moanful
round-up
worn-out
connive
mooneye
romneya
cognize
cocopan
coronae
coronal
coronas
locoman
soroban
sororal
morocco
boloney
bosomed
cojones
△colonel
colones
coroner
coronet
coyotes
ionomer
monomer
no-hoper
popover
poroses
soboles
vocoder
borough
soroche
boronia
colobid
colonic
coronis
monodic
monofil
monosis
moronic
oogonia
Polonia
polonie
porosis
robotic
rosolio
sorosis
mono-ski
corolla
monocle
Bologna
cologne
pogoing
to-torne
to-worne
corozos
hobodom
homolog
monocot
Monodon
monopod
potoroo
rococos
rotolos
Solomon
colours
coloury
honours
sojourn
colossi
hoboism

Words marked △ may be spelled also with a capital letter

hop-oast
molossi
poloist
soloist
cocotte
coconut
colobus
homonym
toponym
compear
Gosplan
compact
coppice
hospice
torpedo
torpids
compeer
complex
compter
coupler
couplet
Doppler
hopples
kouprey
morphew
pompier
poppied
torpefy
compage
Solpuga
△complin
△dolphin
low-paid
morphia
morphic
cowpoke
compile
Gospels
hop-pole
pompelo
soapily
soppily
company
comping
componé
compony
dopping
forpine
gowpens
hopping
looping
lopping
mopping
pompano
popping
sooping
sopping
topping
volpino
wopping
complot

morphos
pompion
pompoon
soapbox
soupçon
tompion
cob-pipe
compare
compart
compère
comport
coopery
coppery
corpora
coupure
foppery
oospore
poppers
rompers
row-port
zoopery
compass
compast
compose
compost
foppish
hoop-ash
lompish
poppish
porpess
rompish
compete
compote
compute
towpath
hog-plum
nonplus
pompous
coequal
rorqual
bosquet
bouquet
conquer
docquet
rocquet
torqued
jonquil
bourlaw
courlan
doormat
doorway
four-oar
journal
Locrian
moorman
moor-pan
poor-law
to-break
correct
morrice
nourice

porrect
sourock
touraco
comrade
corrade
corrida
corrode
corrody
joy-ride
boarder
bourder
bourrée
coarsen
courier
courser
courses
Fourier
fourses
gourmet
hoarder
hoarsen
journey
log-reel
moorhen
mourner
poursew
sorrier
tourney
worried
worrier
horrify
torrefy
courage
moorage
porrigo
bourkha
Goorkha
do-or-die
to-brake
borrell
courtly
four-ale
hoarily
log-roll
lorrell
moorill
noursle
sorrily
woorali
wourali
gourami
no-trump
courant
dourine
horrent
louring
mooring
pouring
roaring
soaring
soprani

soprano
souring
torrent
touring
△bourbon
△bourdon
boxroom
fourgon
godroon
journos
moorlog
morrion
poor-box
poor-oot
soursop
corrupt
towrope
horrors
Moorery
woorara
boarish
boorish
low-rise
Mooress
△moorish
nourish
poorish
sourish
to-brusd
tourism
tourist
votress
co-write
morrhua
pour-out
poursue
zoarium
borstal
box-seat
coastal
cob-swan
dog's-ear
Dogstar
mobsman
moss-hag
rodsman
topsman
Cossack
dog-sick
fossick
hopsack
hop-sack
nonsuch
pot-sick
toisech
bow-side
△gorsedd
topside
torsade
boasted
boaster

bobsled
bolster
booster
△coaster
conster
corslet
corsned
cowshed
dogsled
dossier
foister
hoister
holster
jouster
lobster
lokshen
mobster
moisten
monster
mousmee
roaster
rodster
roister
rooster
rouster
royster
toasted
toaster
worsted
consign
corsage
borscht
bolshie
bonsoir
conseil
corsair
cowslip
doe-skin
dogship
dogskin
donship
foxship
godship
hog-skin
non-skid
non-slip
nonsuit
poussin
sonship
souslik
sow-skin
toastie
topsail
topsoil
topspin
toustie
△worship
forsake
mousaka
bossily
console

7 □o□s□m

consols
consult
fossula
loosely
lousily
moistly
noisily
nousell
tossily
woosell
c**o**n**s**u**m**e
noisome
noysome
toysome
woesome
b**o**u**s**i**n**g
consent
godsend
Hobson's
horsing
housing
mousing
rousant
rousing
sossing
sousing
tossing
tousing
b**o**w**s**h**o**t
copshop
forsloe
forslow
forsook
gorsoon
gossoon
hoosgow
hotshot
monsoon
non-stop
poisson
pop-shop
potshop
torsion
tosspot
toyshop
g**o**s**s**i**p**y
c**o**n**s**o**r**t
goosery
morsure
mousery
tonsure
c**o**n**s**i**s**t
possess
z**o**i**s**i**t**e
H**o**t**s**p**u**r
c**o**r**s**i**v**e
torsive
b**o**a**t**m**a**n
Comtian
contrat
costean
footbar
foot-jaw
footman
footpad
footway
Fortran
fox-trap
koftgar
mootman
Noetian
portman
portray
postbag
postman
postwar
root-cap
rostral
b**o**r**t**s**c**h
contact
conteck
dog-tick
low-tech
mortice
poetics
portico
b**o**u**t**a**d**e
tostada
b**o**o**t**l**e**g
bottled
bottle-o
bottler
bow-tied
box-tree
costrel
cottier
cowtree
dottled
dottrel
fontlet
footmen
△forties
fortlet
goateed
goitred
hop-tree
hostler
loathed
loather
moither
mottled
mottoed
mottoes
mouther
norther
poitrel
posteen
pouther
röntgen
rootlet
sonties
soother
souther
toothed
f**o**r**t**i**f**y
mortify
pontiff
pontify
b**o**t**t**e**g**a
cortège
cottage
footage
hostage
montage
pontage
portage
postage
pottage
rootage
voltage
b**o**b**t**a**i**l
contain
cottoid
couthie
doitkin
△footsie
fox-tail
goat-fig
hoatzin
noctuid
nostril
postfix
routhie
tootsie
tortrix
voltaic
b**o**a**t**-**f**ly
coctile
cortile
cortili
goutfly
hostile
loathly
loftily
monthly
noctule
pontile
soothly
sootily
tortile
youthly
b**o**t**t**o**m**s
contemn
costume
zootomy
b**o**a**t**i**n**g
bolting
bottine
bottony
coating
contend
content
contund
cottony
doating
dotting
footing
fortune
hosting
hotting
houting
jotting
løgting
looting
lotting
montane
montant
mooting
norteña
norteño
portend
portent
posting
potting
pouting
rooting
rotting
routine
routing
sorting
sotting
soutane
tontine
tortoni
totting
wotting
c**o**c**t**i**o**n
coition
control
dogtrot
footboy
footrot
foot-ton
foxtrot
fox-trot
goat-god
hot-trod
jogtrot
pontoon
porthos
portion
postbox
post-doc
soft-top
Tom-trot
z**o**o**t**y**p**e
c**o**n**t**o**r**t
costard
couture
doctors
lottery
loutery
montero
monture
nocturn
non-term
postern
posture
pottery
torture
tottery
voiture
Zostera
c**o**l**t**i**s**h
Comtism
Comtist
contest
contuse
cottise
doltish
goatish
hostess
hottest
hottish
loutish
mortise
mostest
ooftish
poetess
poetise
portess
softish
sottish
wottest
c**o**s**t**a**t**e
portate
wotteth
c**o**n**t**o**u**r
dortour
nostrum
portous
postbus
rostrum
routous
c**o**s**t**i**v**e
tortive
c**o**t**t**o**w**n
dogtown
c**o**n**t**e**x**t
zootaxy
b**o**s**t**r**y**x
p**o**e**t**i**z**e
c**o**p**u**l**a**r
gopuram
jocular
lobular
locular
modular
morular
nodular
popular
torulae
vocular
Yoruban
zonular

Words marked △ may be spelled also with a capital letter

7 □p□l□e

Columba
rotunda
boluses
columel
focused
focuses
hocused
ioduret
locules
moguled
noduled
non-user
volumed
volumes
voluted
zonulet
tohunga
torulin
volubil
volutin
nonuple
soluble
voluble
volubly
wofully
coquina
roguing
toluene
voguing
colugos
gomutos
△völuspa
goburra
roguery
roguish
voguish
coquito
△locusta
robusta
toluate
lobulus
loculus
modulus
nocuous
torulus
Zonurus
nouveau
convict
couvade
voivode
louvred
convoke
△lowveld
convene
convent
corvine
dogvane
hop-vine
solvent
wolving
convert

couvert
poovery
wolvish
solvate
volvate
convive
woiwode
cow-weed
hogweed
pop-weed
forwent
morwong
boxwood
dogwood
logwood
boo-word
forward
forwarn
forworn
godward
hogward
lobworm
norward
nor'ward
woe-worn
hogwash
nor'-west
bow-wave
coaxial
coexist
body-bag
bogy-man
copycat
cotylae
holydam
polygam
polyact
cotyles
loxygen
polymer
polypes
Corypha
coryphe
polynia
holy-ale
polyoma
bodying
bowyang
copying
Corydon
fogydom
polygon
polypod
Polyzoa
hop-yard
bogyism
copyism
copyist
fogyish
fogyism
Toryish

Toryism
Kotytto
corylus
polypus
△toby-jug
polynya
foozler
sozzled
boozily
woozily
boozing
momzers
forzati
forzato
booze-up
aplanat
apparat
apsaras
splatch
upcatch
upwards
apparel
opiated
speaker
speared
sprayed
sprayer
sprayey
upmaker
splashy
aphagia
aphasia
aphasic
aplasia
apraxia
sprawly
spraint
spray-on
sphaere
upraise
appalti
appalto
upvalue
△apician
epochal
spacial
special
epicede
épicier
species
specter
specify
epacrid
epacris
speckle
specula
spicily
spicula
spicule
upscale
epicene

spacing
apocope
epicarp
epicure
spectra
spectre
spicery
epicism
epicist
opacity
spicate
opacous
spadger
spadoes
apadana
spidery
epidote
apodous
spodium
apteral
spaeman
spheral
appeach
spredde
ephebes
speeded
speeder
speeler
sphered
spieler
spreagh
aphelia
aphesis
aphetic
apperil
apteria
ephebic
ephelis
sphenic
spheric
splenic
spleeny
apiezon
ephebos
speedos
up-tempo
ephedra
spheare
appease
aplenty
ephebus
speed-up
upheave
apteryx
spreaze
spreeze
apogeal
apogean
epigeal
epigean
epigram

spignel
apagoge
epagoge
apogamy
epigene
epigone
△epigoni
epigons
epigyny
upchuck
upcheer
spyhole
apehood
upshoot
upthrow
upwhirl
apsidal
oppidan
optical
optimal
uprisal
aphides
apsides
épuisée
splicer
spoiled
spoiler
uppiled
uprisen
upriver
upsides
spairge
spriggy
springe
springy
spright
upright
uptight
yplight
epeirid
Ophidia
△ophitic
options
apricot
epsilon
upsilon
ypsilon
ophiura
optimum
spikily
spikery
spelean
applied
applier
spalted
spelder
spelled
speller
spelter
spilled
spiller

7 □p□l□g

apology
speldin
spulyie
spulzie
upclimb
opaline
opulent
spiling
up-along
upflung
apollos
epulary
upclose
epilate
spilite
applaud
upblown
ipomoea
spumous
sponsal
spinach
spinode
spancel
△spandex
spaniel
spanker
spanned
spanner
spencer
spender
spinner
spinnet
spinney
spondee
sponger
spin-off
apanage
open-air
opuntia
spongin
spunkie
spangle
spangly
spindle
spindly
spinule
open-end
opening
open-top
opinion
sponson
sponsor
spin-dry
spun-dry
aptness
Spanish
spinose
spinate
spinous
spinout
spun-out
spondyl
splotch
apposer
opposer
speoses
spoofer
spooler
spooney
spoorer
splodge
splodgy
aphonia
aphonic
aphotic
aptotic
opsonic
opsonin
appoint
upbound
upgoing
upwound
apropos
uphoard
uphoord
upcoast
uphoist
uprouse
apports
upspeak
upspear
apoplex
apepsia
upspake
upspoke
△spartan
sporran
spuriae
spurway
upbreak
oporice
upgrade
sparger
sparred
sparrer
spersed
spiraea
sporter
spurner
spurred
spurrer
spurrey
eparchy
sparthe
sperthe
sparkie
sparoid
spermic
spiroid
upbraid
uptrain
up-train
sparely
sparkle
sparkly
spirtle
sporule
spurtle
spireme
epergne
operand
operant
sparing
spirant
upbring
upfront
up-front
uptrend
approof
sparrow
appress
apprise
operose
oppress
upbrast
epurate
operate
spirits
spirity
éperdue
approve
updrawn
upgrown
apprize
episode
ape-shit
apostil
spasmic
spastic
apishly
△apostle
△epistle
opuscle
episome
opossum
aphthae
spatial
apothem
epithem
epithet
spathed
spattee
spatter
spitted
spitten
spitter
spotted
spotter
sputter
upstage
spathic
sputnik
upstair
apetaly
spatula
spatule
spittle
epitome
épatant
upstand
upstood
epitaph
epitope
upstare
upstart
apatite
upstate
epitaxy
spousal
appuied
appuyed
epaulet
spouter
splurge
splurgy
upsurge
upbuild
appulse
upburst
spawner
upsweep
upswell
upswing
upswept
upswarm
epaxial
epoxide
aphylly
uplying
spryest
epizoan
epizoic
epizoon
squamae
squabby
squacco
squaddy
aquafer
squared
squarer
squashy
aquaria
aquatic
aquavit
squalid
squawky
equable
equably
equally
squails
squally
equator
squalor
squatty
squelch
squeaky
equerry
aqueous
squeeze
squeezy
Equidae
equinal
squinch
squitch
aquifer
aquiver
squiffy
squidge
squidgy
squishy
equinia
squilla
squills
squirmy
squinny
△aquilon
equinox
areaway
arrayal
creance
triarch
truancy
errands
friande
arcaded
arrased
arrayer
breaded
breaker
briared
broaden
creamer
creaser
croaker
dreaded
dreader
dreamed
dreamer
dryades
ergates
greaser
greaten
greater
greaves
groaner
oreades
treader
treater
wreaked
wreaker
arraign
arrange
breathe
breathy
preachy

wreathe
wreaths
wreathy
break-in
creatic
creatin
erratic
organic
△priapic
triacid
triadic
triatic
broadly
dreadly
errable
friable
friarly
greatly
treacle
treacly
treadle
triable
△creator
organon
treason
triaxon
preasse
breadth
arcanum
Arnaout
break-up
erratum
organum
Priapus
treague
organza
Arabian
drybeat
grab-bag
Grobian
crybaby
arabica
tribade
tribady
crabbed
crabber
cribbed
crubeen
drabber
drabbet
drabler
dribber
driblet
drubbed
grabbed
grabber
grubbed
grubber
problem
triblet
crab-oil
frabbit
brabble
cribble
drabble
dribble
dribbly
fribble
grabble
gribble
grubble
prabble
pribble
proball
tribble
wrybill
armband
prebend
proband
probang
tribune
bribery
preborn
arabise
Arabism
Arabist
probate
probity
tribute
arabize
Araceae
brecham
brochan
crucial
crucian
fractal
△grecian
proctal
trochal
trucial
brocade
precede
brachet
bracken
bracket
bricken
brocked
Brocken
brocket
cracked
cracker
cricket
crickey
crochet
crocked
crocket
drucken
erected
erecter
fracted
frocked
fructed
pricier
pricker
pricket
proceed
trachea
tracked
tracker
tricker
trochee
trocken
trucker
wracked
wrecker
crucify
brocage
trucage
arachis
braccia
braccio
breccia
brickie
brockit
bruchid
cricoid
crocein
ericoid
orectic
practic
truckie
brickle
bricole
bruckle
crackle
crackly
dry-cell
erectly
freckle
freckly
gracile
grackle
grockle
prickle
prickly
trickle
trickly
truckle
drachma
bracing
brucine
Dracone®
dracone
gricing
iracund
tracing
erector
precook
precool
proctor
Procyon
tractor
precept
triceps
brocard
dry-cure
grocery
procure
tracery
tricorn
△grecise
Grecism
precast
precess
precise
process
tricksy
uricase
brucite
grecque
tractus
△trochus
urachus
precava
△grecize
graddan
gradual
Irideae
irideal
iridial
iridian
predial
pridian
triduan
dry-dock
predict
produce
product
traduce
bridled
bridler
brodded
dredger
drudger
gridder
grodier
prodded
trodden
trudgen
trudger
prodigy
sraddha
brodkin
trade-in
cruddle
crudely
gradely
griddle
treddle
Urodela
urodele
credent
erodent
gradine
gradini
gradino
mridang
prudent
trading
trident
uredine
uridine
bridoon
predoom
prudery
tridarn
iridise
prudish
aridity
credits
crudity
erudite
gradate
predate
erodium
iridium
triduum
uredium
bradawl
predawn
iridize
arsenal
creedal
freeman
freeway
trueman
ardency
oriency
urgence
urgency
arreede
Friends
breeder
briered
creeper
dry-eyed
freebee
freemen
freezer
friezed
Froebel
greener
greeted
greeter
grieced
griever
orderer
praeses
creeshy
pre-echo
arsenic
creepie
ermelin
freebie
freesia

7 □r□e□l

Friesic
greenie
griesie
preemie
troelie
uraemia
uraemic
briefly
cruells
cruelly
greenly
griesly
gryesly
orderly
freeing
orleans
freedom
praetor
treetop
pre-empt
arrears
free-arm
arietta
ariette
cruelty
greenth
Croesus
fraenum
orifice
preface
prefect
proface
prefade
crofter
draftee
drafter
drifter
grafter
grifter
grufted
proffer
trifler
griffin
traffic
trefoil
triffic
triffid
armfuls
gruffly
profile
trifoly
truffle
urnfuls
profane
draft-ox
dry-foot
griffon
prefard
preform
triform
dry-fist
profess
profuse
profits
drag-bar
drag-man
frogman
grogram
program
trigram
brigade
tragedy
bragged
brogged
cragged
dragged
dragnet
drogher
droguet
drugged
drugger
drugget
fragged
frigged
frigger
frogged
froglet
prigged
prigger
trigger
trogged
druggie
frogbit
grigris
arugula
draggle
fragile
gregale
tragule
wriggle
wriggly
origami
trigamy
brigand
oregano
origane
orogeny
progeny
dragoon
E-region
triglot
Gregory
a-rights
frigate
archway
Brahman
Orphean
orthian
preheat
archlet
arsheen
orphrey
bruhaha
archaic
△brahmin
armhole
trehala
arshine
errhine
prehend
arch-foe
orthros
archery
orchard
Orphism
△archeus
Orpheus
archive
arrival
artisan
orbital
ordinal
ordinar
arbiter
armiger
braided
brained
broider
broiler
bruiser
cruiser
drainer
dry-iced
ermined
fruited
fruiter
grained
grainer
greisen
groined
orbiter
ordinee
praiser
praises
trailer
trained
trainee
trainer
arriage
droichy
freight
cruisie
druidic
prairie
traikit
armilla
article
Braille
frailly
greisly
treille
orcinol
traitor
arriéré
arriero
orgiast
traipse
artiste
frailty
Orvieto
project
traject
frijole
prejink
trekked
trekker
brokage
Prakrit
arcking
broking
erl-king
brokery
Fraktur
Grallae
Trullan
Uralian
trilobe
armlock
prelacy
prelect
prelude
preludi
cruller
driller
grilled
Grolier
kruller
proller
trilled
troller
trolley
pro-life
orology
trilogy
urology
brulyie
brulzie
trellis
arc-lamp
prelims
erelong
praline
proline
prolong
Trilene®
trollop
arblast
armless
artless
braless
oralism
orality
prelate
prelaty
prolate
trilith
uralite
urolith
arillus
Krilium®
trilbys
frampal
grammar
gremial
tramcar
tramway
trimtab
trumeau
cromack
grimace
primacy
bromide
brimmed
brimmer
brommer
brummer
crammed
crammer
cramped
crampet
crimmer
crimper
crumpet
drummed
drummer
grommet
grummet
krimmer
premier
primmed
primmer
prommer
trammed
trammel
tramper
trampet
trimmed
trimmer
trommel
trumpet
primage
Aramaic
Brummie
crampit
cremsin
crombie
drumlin
gremlin
△kremlin
primsie
bramble
brambly
crimple
crumble
crumbly

Words marked △ may be spelled also with a capital letter

crumple
drumble
frumple
grimily
grumble
grumbly
primely
primula
trample
tremble
trembly
tremolo
briming
bromine
△cremona
crimina
crimine
crimini
dromond
framing
primine
priming
tromino
crampon
crimson
gramary
△primary
primero
uromere
Arimasp
bromism
cramesy
gramash
grumose
premise
premiss
promise
bromate
cremate
eremite
primate
promote
brimful
brumous
frame-up
grampus
grumous
premium
primeur
premove
Araneae
brinjal
cranial
frontal
grandad
grandam
grannam
Iranian
iron-pan
trangam
trental

truncal
△uranian
irenics
tranect
wryneck
grenade
uranide
branded
brander
bran-new
brinded
bringer
bronzed
bronzen
bronzer
cringer
drinker
drunken
Erinyes
fringed
fronded
fronted
grandee
granfer
granger
granted
grantee
granter
grinded
grinder
grinned
grinner
grunter
orangey
prancer
printer
pronged
prunted
tranced
tranter
trinket
trunked
wringed
wringer
wronger
cranage
branchy
bronchi
broncho
crunchy
Frenchy
Granthi
tranche
araneid
bran-pie
crinoid
frantic
grannie
prenzie
trannie
transit

trenail
prancke
brangle
bransle
brantle
brindle
Brinell
crankle
cringle
crinkle
crinkly
crunkle
frankly
frenula
grandly
granola
granule
gruntle
prankle
pronely
trangle
trindle
tringle
trundle
wrangle
wrinkle
wrinkly
wrongly
grandma
erg-nine
ironing
pruning
urinant
broncos
crannog
drongos
eryngos
franion
fronton
grantor
gringos
grunion
princox
pronaoi
pronaos
transom
grandpa
Granary®
granary
trinary
urinary
brinish
crinose
dronish
dryness
ironise
ironist
trenise
uranism
urinose
wryness

crenate
crinate
crinite
erinite
granita
granite
pronate
pronota
△trinity
uranite
urinate
bran-tub
cranium
proneur
pronoun
trankum
trinkum
uranium
uranous
urinous
ironize
areolae
areolar
Kroo-man
ortolan
preoral
arboret
brooder
crooked
crooner
cruores
cryogen
groover
triolet
triones
trooper
brioche
Armoric
cryonic
drookit
ergodic
prootic
troolie
criollo
croodle
ariosos
arroyos
Bryozoa
creosol
Kroo-boy
armoire
armoury
arnotto
trionym
crop-ear
cryptal
prepack
prepuce
tropics
tripody
cropped

cropper
crupper
drapier
dripped
droplet
drop-net
dropped
dropper
frapped
frappée
fripper
grapnel
gripped
gripper
prepped
prophet
prop-jet
propped
trapped
trapper
triplet
Triplex®
triplex
tripped
tripper
trippet
wrapped
wrapper
propage
cryptic
drappie
drip-tip
erepsin
graphic
Graphis
krypsis
prepaid
tripsis
trophic
trypsin
tryptic
aripple
cripple
dropfly
dropple
grapple
gripple
propale
propyla
tripoli
tripple
griping
prepone
propane
propend
propene
propine
propone
trepang
crypton
gryphon

7 □r□p□r

krypton
drapery
drip-dry
grapery
gropers
prepare
tripery
oropesa
prepose
propose
tropism
tropist
cropful
drop-out
trap-cut
trapeze
briquet
croquet
prequel
croquis
orarian
araroba
ardrigh
ard-righ
prurigo
trireme
orarion
prerupt
arm-rest
prorate
orarium
artsman
cristae
crusian
crustae
crustal
crystal
Drusian
Frisian
trishaw
trisect
crusade
crusado
drostdy
preside
prisade
prisado
prosody
brasier
brasset
brisken
brisket
brushed
brusher
cresset
crested
crisper
crosier
crossed
crosses
crushed
crusher
Dresden
dressed
dresser
freshen
fresher
freshet
△fresnel
Frisbee®
frisker
frisket
frosted
grasper
grasser
grisled
pressed
presser
Prestel®
prosper
tressed
tressel
trussed
trusser
trusses
trustee
truster
tryster
wrester
prosify
presage
prisage
brassie
crispin
drastic
eristic
griskin
pressie
prosaic
prussic
trysail
droshky
briskly
bristle
bristly
crassly
crisply
crossly
dry-salt
freshly
grisely
gristle
gristly
grossly
grysely
pre-sell
prosily
trestle
trisula
wrestle
irksome
presume
triseme
trisome
trisomy
urosome
art-song
Krishna
present
prosing
aristos
Bristol
creston
dry-shod
erasion
erosion
frescos
frisson
grysbok
pressor
prestos
brasero
brisure
drosera
erasure
frisure
grosert
irisate
brush-up
brusque
crissum
friseur
frustum
grassum
press-up
pre-stun
trismus
erosive
fretsaw
Grotian
△protean
urethan
erotica
protect
tritide
brothel
brother
critter
dratted
erathem
fretted
fritted
fritter
gritter
grutten
pre-teen
pretzel
prithee
prythee
pr'ythee
trotted
trotter
writhen
written
wrythen
brutify
frutify
gratify
protégé
fratchy
arctiid
arctoid
oratrix
proteid
protein
write-in
britska
britzka
brattle
brittle
brittly
crotala
crottle
fritfly
irately
prattle
protyle
tritely
erotema
eroteme
Tritoma
bruting
gratiné
grating
orotund
prating
pretend
protend
tritone
Tritons
△writing
Brython
grottos
krytron
oration
fratery
friture
△oratory
preterm
protore
urethra
British
brutish
cretism
erotism
pretest
protest
protist
crittur
fretful
proteus
protium
tritium
write-up
pretext
prothyl
arousal
traumas
braunch
craunch
frounce
graunch
praunce
trounce
grounds
arguses
arouser
crouper
graupel
grouper
grouser
grouter
prouler
trouper
trouser
trouses
trouter
brought
draught
drought
drouthy
fraught
froughy
grouchy
wrought
droukit
groupie
proudly
trouble
croupon
croûton
triumph
arcuate
arbutus
arduous
argulus
gravlax
trivial
crevice
privacy
bravado
privado
provide
bravoes
brevier
preview
Bravais
drive-in
prevail
travail
travois
provoke
bravely
drevill
gravely

Words marked △ may be spelled also with a capital letter

7 □s□u□n

privily
travels
craving
crivens
driving
droving
graving
prevene
prevent
provand
provant
provend
provine
proving
bravery
bravura
gravure
preverb
proverb
previse
proviso
provost
treviss
breveté
brevity
gravity
pravity
private
privity
trivium
crowbar
drawbar
grow-bag
brawler
brawned
browser
crawler
crowded
crowder
crowned
crowner
crownet
drawler
draw-net
drowner
growler
oreweed
prowler
trawler
brewage
Brownie®
△brownie
crowdie
prawlin
crewels
brewing
drawing
growing
crow-toe
draw-boy
draw-top

Erewhon
artwork
brewers'
brewery
drawers
froward
prewarm
prewarn
dry-wash
pre-wash
prowess
frowsty
brewpub
grown-up
proximo
bruxism
drayman
grey-lag
greyhen
drayage
argyria
traybit
treybit
grayfly
fraying
greying
praying
Gruyère
prayers
'Arryish
greyish
grey-out
preyful
trayful
cruzado
brazier
crazies
crozier
frizzed
grazier
wrizled
prezzie
crazily
drizzle
drizzly
frazzle
frizzle
frizzly
grizzle
grizzly
grazing
trizone
assagai
Tswanas
askance
ashamed
assayer
escapee
escaper
essayed
essayer

T-shaped
U-shaped
V-shaped
yslaked
ascarid
ascaris
Asianic
Asiatic
askaris
Aspasia
astatic
Islamic
ismatic
astatki
assault
astable
Ismaili
Israeli
Osmanli
usually
ascaunt
escalop
Astarte
esparto
Tsabian
isobare
isobase
isobath
asocial
psychic
isochor
psychos
usucapt
psych-up
asudden
tsaddik
tsaddiq
isodoma
isodont
assegai
isleman
essence
assever
isoetes
osiered
osselet
osseter
asperge
ascesis
ascetic
askesis
astelic
asteria
asterid
osteoid
osteoma
asperse
asteism
osseous
isogram
isagoge

Isegrim
isogamy
isogeny
tsigane
ash-heap
escheat
ischial
oscheal
isohyet
ash-hole
asphalt
asshole
pschent
asthore
esthete
ischium
isthmus
asphyxy
estival
astilbe
ascites
ashiver
assizer
assizes
Oscines
assiege
ascidia
ascitic
aspidia
aspirin
ossific
ossicle
ostiole
assigns
Eskimos
ostiary
osmiate
ostiate
osmious
isokont
△psalter
psyllid
asylums
asklent
isoline
useless
isolate
Ishmael
isomere
Ostmark
asinico
asunder
isonomy
tsunami
asinine
Asmoday
escolar
asconce
estover
osmosis
osmotic

psionic
estoile
astound
esloyne
essoyne
espouse
Isopoda
asepses
asepsis
aseptic
aspread
csárdás
estreat
Osirian
ascribe
escribe
astrict
estrich
ostraca
ostrich
astride
estrade
usurped
usurper
astroid
ostraka
escroll
ashrama
astrand
c-spring
G-string
tsarina
usuring
tsardom
estrepe
tsarism
tsarist
usuress
asprout
estrous
usurous
asprawl
isospin
ash-tray
isatine
isotone
isotron
isotope
isotopy
isotype
esotery
oscular
osmunda
assumed
assured
assurer
assuage
escuage
tsouris
asquint
issuant

7 □s□u□o

escudos
esquire
estuary
ossuary
T-square
osculum
asswage
asexual
astylar
espying
atlases
steaded
stealed
stealer
steamed
steamer
strawed
strawen
strayed
strayer
strange
attaché
ptyalin
steamie
stearic
stearin
attaskt
attaint
straint
athanor
attaboy
ethanol
strappy
stealth
straits
stratum
stratus
stibial
stabbed
stabber
stabler
stables
stubbed
atabrin
atebrin
stabile
stibble
stubble
stubbly
stibine
stibium
stacked
stacker
stacket
sticked
sticker
stocker
atactic
stichic
stickit
stickle
stichoi
stichos
stucco'd
stuccos
etacism
itacism
otocyst
stick-up
stuck-up
stachys
stadial
stodger
studded
studden
studied
studier
studies
stiddie
staddle
studdle
student
studios
stadium
stretch
steeled
steepen
steeper
steerer
strewed
strewer
utterer
atresia
etaerio
etheric
steekit
sthenic
streaky
steeple
steeply
utterly
streamy
étrenne
attempt
atheise
atheism
atheist
steep-to
streets
streety
stretta
strette
stretti
stretto
strewth
atheous
atheize
staffer
stiffen
stifled
stifler
stuffed
stuffer
stiffly
ataghan
stigmas
Stygian
stagger
stagily
staging
étagère
stagery
etchant
etching
ethical
△stoical
strigae
stained
stainer
staired
stoiter
strides
Striges
striker
striped
stripes
stripey
strived
striven
striver
strings
stringy
staithe
strigil
staidly
utricle
atriums
stridor
ethiops
athirst
striate
atokous
Italian
stellar
italics
atelier
stalked
stalker
stalled
stelled
stiller
stilted
stilter
stollen
étalage
otology
otalgia
styloid
stalely
stelene
Italiot
Stilton
stylise
stylish
stylist
utilise
athleta
athlete
otolith
stylate
stylite
utility
atalaya
stylize
utilize
stomach
stammel
stammer
stamper
stemlet
stemmed
stemmer
stempel
stomper
stummed
stummel
stumper
stymied
ethmoid
stemple
stimuli
stumble
stumbly
atamans
etymons
stamens
stamina
stamnoi
stamnos
stembok
stemson
atomise
atomism
atomist
itemise
stomata
atomize
itemize
Etonian
stengah
stand-by
standee
standen
stander
staniel
stannel
stanyel
stinged
stinger
stinker
stinted
stinter
stonied
stonker
stunned
stunner
stunted
stenchy
ctenoid
stand-in
stannic
stencil
utensil
atingle
stonily
stoning
stanzos
stentor
stingos
stonern
stand-to
stand-up
△ottoman
attonce
attones
stooden
stooker
stooped
stooper
stroken
stroker
strowed
strower
atrophy
strophe
atropia
atropin
etiolin
stoolie
strobic
strooke
strodle
Atropos
stroppy
stopgap
△utopian
stapler
stepney
stepped
stepper
stopped
stopper
stopoff
stop-off
stupefy
stypsis
styptic
stapple
stipple
stipule
stopple
stipend
stoping
stupent
stepson

Words marked △ may be spelled also with a capital letter

utopism
utopist
step-cut
△eternal
sternal
stirrah
attract
otaries
starken
star-led
starlet
starred
starter
starved
sterlet
stirpes
stirred
stirrer
storied
stories
△sturmer
storage
starchy
ptarmic
pteroic
starlit
starnie
steroid
athrill
pteryla
starkly
startle
startly
sterile
sternly
iterant
otarine
staring
styrene
uterine
pterion
stardom
stereos
starers
stir-fry
attrist
attrite
iterate
starets
staretz
start-up
sternum
stirrup
sturnus
yttrium
ataraxy
storeys
etesian
stashie
stishie
stushie

stasima
atishoo
a-tishoo
statice
statics
statued
stetted
stotter
stutter
stately
statant
station
Stetson
stature
statism
statist
statute
stative
strumae
staunch
étourdi
stouten
strudel
Etruria
stoutly
attuent
attuite
strunts
stovies
stoving
atavism
stew-can
stewpan
stowage
stewing
stowing
stewpot
athwart
steward
staying
curaçao
cutaway
Judaean
nunatak
oulakan
runaway
subadar
durance
Judaica
surance
mutanda
aurated
duramen
lunated
Musales
mutagen
putamen
subarea
sudamen
sugared
nuraghe

nuraghi
queachy
bubalis
cumarin
Fumaria
fumaric
lunatic
puparia
Puranic
subacid
subarid
Sudanic
suramin
turacin
tutania
autarky
rusalka
aurally
buyable
curable
ducally
dupable
durable
durably
fugally
humanly
jurally
mutable
mutably
rulable
rurally
sueable
tunable
tunably
eucaine
lucarne
△muraena
bugaboo
butanol
curaçoa
curator
Euratom
fugatos
fumados
fusarol
rubatos
subatom
turacos
sumatra
dumaist
Judaise
Judaism
Judaist
dupatta
mulatta
mulatto
Bubalus
punalua
subaqua
sub-aqua
Judaize

bugbear
bum-boat
cudbear
gunboat
mud-boat
outbrag
sunbeam
sunbeat
tugboat
buy-back
cutback
jumbuck
outback
Purbeck
runback
bumbler
burbler
fumbler
humbles
jumbler
mumbler
numbles
outbred
rumbler
tumbler
tumbrel
lumbago
gumboil
ouabain
quiblin
tumbril
sunbake
quibble
△sunbelt
bugbane
cubbing
cumbent
dubbing
gubbins
husband
lumbang
numbing
rubbing
subbing
tubbing
turband
turbant
turbine
turbond
gumboot
nun-buoy
pueblos
Bunbury
dun-bird
fubbery
lubbard
△numbers
outburn
rubbers
rubbery
sunbird

sunburn
turbary
cubbish
furbish
kurbash
rubbish
subbase
surbase
tubbish
mudbath
sunbath
surbate
turbith
bulbous
bumbaze
humbuzz
dulcian
Dunciad
sun-clad
surcoat
tulchan
succuba
succubi
succade
suicide
bunched
bunches
butcher
futchel
guichet
gutcher
juncoes
luncher
lurcher
mulcted
muncher
muscled
puncher
putcher
quacker
quicken
succeed
dulcify
culchie
muscoid
quickie
cupcake
furcula
quackle
quickly
curcuma
outcome
succumb
buccina
mud-cone
muscone
nuncios
outcrop
puccoon
punctos
subcool

7 □u□c□r

duncery
succory
dulcose
muscose
nutcase
outcast
success
succise
succose
succuss
dulcite
furcate
juncate
Succoth
sulcate
fulcrum
fuscous
punch-up
punctum
putchuk
Quechua
Quichua
succour
succous
△muscovy
quadrat
subdean
subdual
suidian
sundial
burdock
puddock
ruddock
subduce
subduct
sundeck
fuddled
fuddler
huddled
hundred
hurdies
hurdler
hurdles
muddied
muddler
puddler
ruddied
ruddier
rundled
rundlet
subdued
subduer
mundify
guidage
mueddin
quadric
quiddit
quodlin
turdoid
muddily
quiddle
ruddily
rundale
ducdame
quidams
budding
burdens
duodena
funding
△guiding
lurdane
mundane
nundine
pudding
turdine
bundook
gumdrop
outdoor
puldron
turdion
duddery
outdare
outdure
sundari
burdash
Kurdish
Luddism
tun-dish
Luddite
outdate
surdity
humdrum
put-down
rubdown
rundown
run-down
sundown
funeral
gudeman
humeral
juvenal
lumenal
mudéjar
numeral
puberal
ruderal
subedar
tutelar
tutenag
rudesby
lucency
pudency
quiesce
tumesce
pudenda
bug-eyed
cupeled
murexes
quieten
quieter
auberge
outedge
queechy
aurelia
auxesis
auxetic
eugenia
eugenic
eutexia
numeric
queenie
subedit
suberic
suberin
aureola
aureole
cure-all
jumelle
nucelli
△pucelle
queenly
queerly
quietly
rubella
rubeola
museums
lucerne
lugeing
dukedom
eugenol
juke-box
mu-meson
pukekos
tupelos
tuxedos
Euterpe
funèbre
jug-ears
duresse
eupepsy
rulesse
aureate
aureity
burette
buvette
cuneate
cunette
curette
cuvette
fumette
fumetti
fumetto
lunette
musette
ouverte
puberty
bureaus
bureaux
dureful
duteous
hugeous
humerus
luteous
museful
quietus
tubeful
tuneful
duvetyn
huff-cap
mudflap
mudflat
ruffian
runflat
surfman
turfman
outface
suffect
suffice
surface
sulfide
muffled
muffler
purfled
quaffer
ruffled
ruffler
funfair
furfair
huffkin
surfeit
buffalo
cupfuls
fulfill
huffily
jugfuls
mugfuls
outfall
puffily
Suffolk
tubfuls
zuffoli
zuffolo
buffing
duffing
luffing
puffing
sulfone
surfing
turfing
buffoon
outflow
outfoot
puff-box
bus-fare
gunfire
puffery
dun-fish
huffish
lubfish
mudfish
muffish
pupfish
subfusc
subfusk
suffuse
sunfast
sunfish
tubfast
tubfish
suffete
sulfate
sulfite
turfite
burghal
burglar
Jungian
subgoal
aufgabe
bungler
△burgher
juggler
outgoer
outgoes
puggled
puggree
burgage
luggage
fungoid
tung-oil
cudgels
cupgall
dung-fly
nutgall
buggane
bugging
bulgine
bulging
fulgent
hugging
jugging
juggins
lugging
lunging
mugging
muggins
outgone
pugging
pungent
purging
rugging
sugging
surgent
surging
tugging
turgent
burgeon
dudgeon
dungeon
gudgeon
△guignol
murgeon
outgrow
sunglow
surgeon
budgero

Words marked △ may be spelled also with a capital letter

buggery
busgirl
Hungary
puggery
surgery
burgess
muggish
outgush
puggish
suggest
nuggety
outgate
△vulgate
bulghur
burghul
fulgour
fungous
lungful
outgive
rug-gown
bush-cat
△bushman
cuphead
jughead
lum-head
mukhtar
subhead
tushkar
hushaby
bushido
dudheen
euchred
Fuehrer
luthier
tushker
push-off
Buphaga
nurhags
kuchcha
bush-tit
fuchsia
push-pin
tughrik
bush-fly
lughole
muchell
mudhole
mushily
out-half
bushing
euphony
gushing
pushing
ruching
Ruthene
cubhood
cushion
euphroe
fushion
mudhook
nunhood
nut-hook
pushrod
Pushtoo
euphory
futhark
futhorc
futhork
Kuh-horn
luthern
outhire
outhyre
tushery
duchess
Cushite
Kushite
Kurhaus
outhaul
pushful
push-out
push-tug
Pushtun
quahaug
ruthful
cubical
cubital
kufiyah
luminal
Muridae
musical
pupilar
△puritan
rufiyaa
Surinam
Lusiads
culices
jubilee
juniper
Jupiter
△lucifer
lucigen
mucigen
murices
pubises
quoiter
tubifex
bubinga
rupiahs
augitic
bulimia
bulimic
culicid
cutikin
fusidic
juridic
mudiria
tunicin
audible
audibly
auricle
cubicle
cuticle
funicle
fusible
fusilli
humidly
lucidly
luridly
tumidly
tunicle
audient
auditor
humidor
musimon
△rubicon
curiosa
furioso
ju-jitsu
puniest
dubiety
muriate
bulimus
cubitus
curious
dubious
dutiful
euripus
furious
lulibub
rubious
Punjabi
subject
subjoin
outjump
outjest
buckram
bucksaw
junkman
musk-bag
musk-cat
muskrat
musk-sac
Turkman
buckeen
buckler
buckoes
suckler
turkies
Turkmen
Turkify
bulkily
cuckold
duskily
huskily
luckily
murkily
muskily
suck'ole
sulkily
bucking
busking
cucking
duck-ant
ducking
fucking
hulking
husking
lurking
muskone
quaking
sucking
tusking
bucksom
duck-coy
musk-cod
musk-pod
Dunkirk
hunkers
ouakari
puckery
buckish
duskish
luskish
murkish
puckish
Turkess
Turkish
Sukkoth
sunkets
tuck-out
buck-eye
bullbar
bullbat
hurlbat
nucleal
nuclear
outleap
Pullman
pull-tab
quillai
Tullian
lullaby
bullace
bullock
gunlock
mullock
putlock
rullock
nuclide
builded
builder
bullied
bull-pen
cullied
curlies
duelled
dueller
fuelled
fueller
full-fed
guelder
guilder
gullied
gullies
outlier
purlieu
queller
quilled
quillet
quilted
quilter
sullied
wurlies
nullify
qualify
fullage
sullage
built-in
Guelfic
mullein
murlain
nucleic
nuclein
purloin
ruellia
surloin
tuilyie
tuilzie
nutlike
sunlike
surlily
mud-lump
mug-lamb
sublime
sunlamp
bulling
culling
curling
cutline
dunlins
Euglena
furlana
furlong
hurling
Juglans
nulling
outland
outline
purline
purling
△bulldog
bullion
cullion
duellos
full-hot
mullion
nucleon
outlook
quillon
rullion
burlaps
bullary
butlery
cutlery
dullard

7 □u□l□s

guildry
gullery
mudlark
sutlery
Auslese
budless
bugloss
bullish
cubless
cutlass
dualism
dualist
dullish
euclase
fullest
fullish
gullish
gunless
gutless
hueless
outlash
outlast
publish
sumless
sunless
bullate
duality
nullity
quality
sublate
build-up
built-up
bull-pup
full-out
nucleus
pull-out
outlive
gulleys
hurleys
pulleys
wurleys
nutmeal
Würmian
bummock
hummock
mummock
outmode
mummied
mummify
rummage
duumvir
turmoil
bummalo
mulmull
pug-mill
rummily
augment
bumming
butment
fulmine
gumming
humming
hutment
mumming
summand
summing
summons
mummery
nummary
summary
summery
budmash
Burmese
durmast
outmost
quamash
rummish
submiss
summist
Suomish
surmise
furmety
furmity
gummata
gummite
pug-moth
summate
gummous
hummaum
outmove
quantal
quinnat
quintal
quintan
quondam
dunnock
furnace
guanaco
huanaco
duendes
funnies
nuanced
quannet
quintet
Quonset
turnkey
turnoff
turn-off
aulnage
dunnage
gunnage
tunnage
quinche
quantic
quinoid
quintic
funnily
sunnily
outname
surname
burning
cunning
dunning
funning
guanine
gunning
punning
quinine
quinone
ruining
running
sunning
tunning
turning
guangos
munnion
quangos
runnion
dunnart
gunnera
gunnery
gurnard
nunnery
quinary
turnery
burnish
dulness
dunnish
fulness
furnish
Hunnish
nunnish
outness
pug-nose
rumness
Sunnism
dunnite
quinate
ruinate
Sunnite
burnous
burn-out
muonium
quantum
ruinous
turndun
turnout
aurorae
auroral
auroras
autocar
automat
autovac
cupola'd
cupolar
humoral
mucosae
sudoral
cut-over
Euronet
humogen
Nurofen®
out-over
aurochs
bubonic
bucolic
dulosis
dulotic
eulogia
out-owre
autopsy
judoist
autobus
autocue
autonym
gunplay
outplay
outpray
auspice
mudpack
outpace
suspect
guppies
jump-jet
outpeep
outpeer
purples
rump-fed
sumpter
jump-off
pulpify
yuppify
bumpkin
culprit
dumpbin
lumpkin
pumpkin
bumpily
dum-palm
duopoly
jumpily
lumpily
pulpily
bumping
cupping
lumping
pupping
rump-end
supping
suspend
suspens
tupping
vulpine
pumpion
subplot
guipure
gunport
outpart
outport
purport
△purpura
purpure
support
suspire
dumpish
lumpish
mumpish
outpost
purpose
suppose
surpass
cuspate
turpeth
jump-cut
outpour
pulpous
sulphur
surplus
Quapaws
suppawn
cumquat
kumquat
outroar
quartan
surreal
currach
outrace
outride
bur-reed
burrhel
curried
currier
furrier
guarded
guardee
hurried
ouvrier
quarrel
quarter
quartet
queried
sucrier
putrefy
curragh
outrage
ouvrage
duarchy
murrain
quartic
bunraku
buirdly
burrell
puerile
supreme
suprême
supremo
currant
current
furring
guaraná
Guaraní
guarani
murrine
outrank
purring

Words marked △ may be spelled also with a capital letter

subring
guerdon
gunroom
murrion
outroop
outroot
quartos
sunroof
eutropy
guy-rope
outrope
bulrush
cuirass
currish
guarish
outrush
querist
sucrase
sucrose
sunrise
tutress
burrito
cuprite
cut-rate
eucrite
guérite
outrate
quorate
cuprous
Quercus
furrowy
guereza
quartzy
cumshaw
fur-seal
Hulsean
kursaal
outsoar
outspan
outstay
pursual
Russian
Tuesday
tussock
outside
subside
subsidy
bukshee
bursted
bursten
burster
cuisser
funster
guesser
guesten
jukskei
munster
outstep
punster
pursuer
△quashee
quester
Russify
gunship
ludship
lugsail
nunship
outsail
outswim
pursuit
△quashie
quassia
subsoil
sunsuit
tumshie
fussily
ourself
outsell
outsole
fulsome
subsume
bussing
cuisine
cursing
guising
gutsing
nursing
subsong
fuss-pot
gumshoe
gunshot
mudscow
mugshot
outshot
questor
rum-shop
suasion
sunspot
bursary
Bursera
cursory
guisard
nursery
suasory
subsere
tussore
subsist
Hussite
pulsate
russety
burst-up
gutsful
cursive
jussive
suasive
tussive
outsize
△austral
dustman
dust-pan
fustian
lustral
Muftiat
muntjac
muntjak
nuptial
out-tray
quetzal
quittal
suntrap
buttock
custock
eustacy
futtock
justice
lustick
puttock
quetsch
subtack
custody
burthen
bustier
bustler
cup-tied
curtsey
custrel
cuttoes
duetted
further
guttier
hustler
lustres
murther
nut-tree
puttied
puttier
quitted
quitter
rustler
rustred
subteen
turtler
justify
Austric
curtail
curtain
dustbin
huitain
sustain
outtake
out-take
cuittle
ductile
dustily
eustyle
fustily
lustily
Mustela
mustily
nuttily
outtalk
outtell
pustule
rustily
subtile
customs
run-time
rut-time
bunting
busting
butt-end
buttons
buttony
curtana
cutting
duotone
gutting
hunting
hutting
jutting
munting
mustang
muttons
muttony
nutting
putting
quiting
rusting
rutting
subtend
suiting
sultana
suntans
tufting
tutting
yu-stone
auction
duettos
pultoon
quittor
ruction
suction
tuition
subtype
austere
bustard
buttery
culture
custard
gutters
multure
mustard
nurture
nuttery
outturn
pulture
rupture
tuatara
vulture
vulturn
cultish
cultism
cultist
curtesy
eustasy
runtish
ruttish
curtate
guttate
oustiti
gustful
hunt's-up
hurtful
lustful
lustrum
punt-gun
surtout
furtive
subtext
augural
cupular
jugular
lunular
sutural
tubular
tumular
suburbs
augurer
fucused
fucuses
futures
sutured
pupunha
lupulin
subunit
tubulin
bubukle
autumny
queuing
gurudom
lucumos
fuguist
guruism
auguste
cumulus
tumulus
purview
surview
suavely
curving
pulvini
culvert
quavery
quivery
subvert
curvate
curvity
outvote
suavity
vulvate
fulvous
survive
survewe
outwear
outwick

Words marked △ may be spelled also with a capital letter

7 □u□w□e

burweed
cudweed
outweed
outweep
huswife
gunwale
outwalk
out-wall
outwell
mugwump
outwent
outwind
outwing
nutwood
budworm
bug-word
bugwort
bulwark
cutwork
cutworm
lugworm
mudwort
mugwort
outward
outwork
outworn
sunward
tutwork
outwash
Pugwash
sunwise
outwith
juryman
jurymen
ruby-red
buoyage
quayage
butyric
queynie
guayule
buoyant
burying
busying
rubying
jury-box
buzz-saw
Günzian
hutzpah
guzzler
huzzaed
muzzler
puzzler
quizzed
quizzer
quizzes
buzz-wig
muezzin
fuzzily
muzzily
buzzing
subzone

buzzard
subzero
kunzite
aviator
ivy-bush
avocado
ovicide
evacuee
Avicula
evictor
evocate
Ovidian
oviduct
evident
avidity
ivresse
aviette
aviform
oviform
ovoidal
uveitic
uveitis
evolver
evolute
ovulate
even-odd
avenger
evangel
eventer
oven-tit
evening
aventre
evanish
dvandva
avionic
Ivorian
ovarian
overeat
overfar
overlap
overlay
overman
overpay
overran
overtax
avarice
overact
averred
averted
ivoried
ivories
overfed
overget
overnet
overred
overren
over-rev
oversea
oversee
overset
oversew

average
overage
over-age
Avertin®
dvornik
overbid
overhit
overlie
overall
over-all
overfly
overply
overtly
evertor
overjoy
oversow
overtop
overarm
Everest
ivorist
overuse
evirate
Avernus
overbuy
overdue
overrun
overawe
overdye
overeye
Avestan
Avestic
evasion
evasive
ovation
evitate
avoutry
uva-ursi
swearer
sweated
sweater
swabbed
swabber
swobber
twibill
awlbird
twoccer
swidden
swaddle
twaddle
twaddly
twiddle
twiddly
Swedish
two-down
owre'lay
owl-eyed
sweeney
sweeper
sweered
sweeten
tweeter

two-eyed
△sweetie
awheels
sweetly
tweedle
swifter
swiftly
twafald
twifold
twofold
twyfold
two-foot
two-four
swagman
swagged
swagger
swigged
swigger
twiggen
twigger
swaggie
Swahili
two-hand
two-inch
awaking
dwelled
dweller
swallet
swelled
sweller
swelted
swelter
swiller
swollen
twelves
twilled
owl-like
ewe-lamb
swaling
two-line
swallow
sweltry
aweless
awnless
△twelfth
swamper
swimmer
ewe-milk
owl-moth
gwiniad
gwyniad
Owenian
twankay
swing-by
ewe-neck
swanker
swankey
swinger
swinked
twinned
twinset

twinter
swindge
swankie
dwindle
swindle
swingle
twangle
twinkle
twining
swinery
Owenism
Owenist
swinish
twoness
Owenite
twin-tub
swooned
swapped
swapper
swopped
swopper
two-pair
swipple
two-part
dwarfed
dwarves
swarded
swarmer
swerver
sworder
twirler
swarthy
twiscar
swasher
swisher
Swisses
twisted
twister
two-step
awesome
twasome
twosome
twistor
swatted
swatter
swither
Switzer
swotted
swotter
twitted
twitten
twitter
switchy
twitchy
twattle
two-time
two-tone
swounds
'swounds
awfully
awkward

Words marked △ may be spelled also with a capital letter

swaying
swazzle
swizzle
swozzle
twizzle
extatic
oxy-acid
axially
exhaust
expanse
exacter
exactly
exscind
exactor
exocarp
execute
exedrae
oxidant
exoderm
exodist
oxidase
oxidise
exudate
oxidate
oxidize
ox-fence
externe
axle-box
excerpt
exhedra
expense
extense
exogamy
exigent
exegete
axe-head
excheat
extinct
excited
exciter
expired
exhibit
exciton
excitor
expiate
axillae
axillar
exilian
exclude
explode
exalted
exclaim
explain
exploit
explant
oxblood
explore
axolotl
exility
oxalate
exclave
example
exempla
exemple
examine
exomion
Oxonian
axinite
oxonium
exposal
exposed
exposer
expound
exports
extreat
exurban
uxorial
extract
extrude
exarchy
exordia
extrait
exurbia
extreme
express
exarate
excreta
excrete
exergue
oxy-salt
exotica
oxytone
excusal
expunct
excuser
exhumer
expunge
expurge
excudit
excurse
expulse
exuviae
exuvial
oxazine
Aymaran
Aymaras
lyra-way
pyjama'd
pyjamas
bycatch
hyraces
hyraxes
lyrated
dynamic
hydatid
myiasis
pyralid
△pyralis
pyramid
pyramis
synaxis
dyeable
gyrally
rybauld
Lycaena
tyranne
tyranny
Zygaena
dynamos
synapse
dynasty
synapte
eye-beam
bye-byes
cymbalo
eyeball
eyebolt
pyebald
symbole
myrbane
eyebrow
eye-bath
lyncean
lynchet
hyacine
syncope
syncarp
synchro
hylding
eye-drop
lyddite
byreman
Hygeian
hymenal
type-bar
△mycetes
typeset
synergy
mycelia
pyaemia
pyaemic
pyretic
pyrexia
pyrexic
synesis
lyceums
hyperon
xylenol
bynempt
hyped-up
eye-flap
synfuel
myogram
nylghau
syngamy
Pythian
mynheer
Lychnic
lychnis
typhoid
eye-hole
wych-elm
by-thing
eyehook
typhoon
mythise
mythism
mythist
tychism
Lythrum
pythium
typhous
mythize
cynical
lyrical
symitar
typical
cylices
kylices
lymiter
pyrites
pyxides
myringa
△syringa
syringe
pyritic
pyxidia
hygiene
lyricon
xylitol
Syriasm
cytisus
Dyticus
Mytilus
wysiwyg
eyeliad
syllabi
byplace
byrlady
dyslogy
myology
cycloid
hyaloid
myalgia
myalgic
myeloid
myeloma
cycling
cyclone
dyeline
hyaline
△cyclops
cyclist
eyelash
eyeless
myalism
hyalite
pygmean
pygmoid
Lyomeri
Nyanjas
by-and-by
cyanide
hymnody
Lymnaea
hypnoid
lying-in
dyingly
lyingly
vyingly
cyanine
hymning
hypnone
hymnary
cyanise
gymnast
hymnist
kyanise
cyanate
cyanite
kyanite
pycnite
syenite
cyanize
kyanize
gyrocar
synodal
xylomas
zygomas
bycoket
bygones
bywoner
hypogea
pyrogen
tyloses
tyrones
xylogen
zymogen
Byronic
dysodil
gyronic
hypoxia
hypoxic
mycosis
mycotic
pyloric
pyrosis
sybotic
sycosis
synodic
synovia
tylosis
xylonic
Xylopia
zygosis
zygotic
zymosis
zymotic
by-going
gyronny
lycopod
mylodon
tylopod
dyvoury
hyloist

Words marked △ may be spelled also with a capital letter

7 □y□o□u

Nynorsk
pylorus
pyropus
hyponym
synonym
lymphad
nymphae
nymphal
ryepeck
dyspnea
nymphet
lyophil
nymphic
sylphid
syrphid
nymphly
gypping
tympana
tympani
tympano
tympany
nymphos
symptom
Syrphus
△cyprian
hydride
dyarchy
hydroid
myrrhic
△pyrrhic
pyrrole
rye-roll
cyprine
hydrant
Cypriot
myrrhol
cypress
gytrash
hydrate
hydrous
hydroxy
dyester
byssoid
cypsela
byssine
eye-shot
eye-spot
eyesore
myosote
myotube
mystify
syntagm
cystoid
systole
systyle
cystine
syntony
synthon
mystery
cyathus
hypural
zymurgy
dysuria
dysuric
pyruvic
Sylvian
sylvine
sylvite
Tynwald
eye-wink
dye-wood
dye-work
eye-wash
Czechic
tzaddik
tzaddiq
tzigany
azygous
Szekler
Szekely
Azilian
azulejo
tzimmes
azimuth
azymite
azymous
Azanian
ozonise
ozonize
azurean
czardas
azurine
czarina
czardom
czarism
czarist
azurite
azotise
azotous
azotize

8 □a□a□u

caracara
jararaca
jararaka
katakana
lava-lava
maharaja
Mahayana
matamata
Ramayana
sasarara
takamaka
saraband
carapace
catalase
database
malaxage
malaxate
palamate
paravane
vanadate
parasang
calabash
Malagash
calamari
maharani
databank
tamarack
paravail
Fanagalo
galapago
cataract
paravant
calamary
Malagasy
harambee
balanced
valanced
Jamaican
balancer
navarchy
tamandua
kalamdan
qalamdan
malander
marauder
hazardry
habanera
Kamadeva
karateka
lavatera
Mahadeva
parabema
Samaveda
Sama-Veda
tapadera
bayadère
Canarese
Fagaceae
Gadarene
Japanese
Javanese
Kanarese
Macanese
Nazarene
paramese
paranete
Taxaceae
galabeah
maravedi
Nazarean
panacean
tara-fern
jalapeño
tapadero
malapert
parakeet
parament
camaïeux
Japanesy
lamasery
savagely
savagery
paraffle
paraffin
carangid
canaigre
harangue
galangal
radar-gun
barathea
calathea
Halachic
Halachah
△marathon
matachin
Ramadhan
yataghan
rajaship
tabashir
calathus
cavatina
galabiya
salaried
tamarind
baladine
banalise
banalize
basanite
calamine
calamite
canalise
canalize
carabine
catamite
faradise
faradize
fayalite
Japanise
Japanize
kamacite
laxative
macarise
macarize
magazine
mazarine
nasalise
nasalize
Nazarite
paganise
paganize
△palatine
papalise
papalize
△paradise
parasite
Patarine
rabatine
sanative
saxatile
taxative
Wahabite
zaratite
garaging
managing
maraging
salading
dahabieh
galabiah
galabieh
paganish
Tanalith®
vagarish
hara-kiri
tarakihi
tamarisk
malarial
palatial
patagial
cabalism
caladium
faradism
fatalism
macarism
navalism
paganism
papalism
paradigm
patagium
ranarium
samarium
satanism
savagism
vanadium
Wahabism
Bahamian
Batavian
Canadian
halation
Hawaiian
lavation
malarian
natation
pacation
ranarian
Tatarian
taxation
vacation
palamino
△cavalier
gasalier
canaries
vagaries
cabalist
calamint
Fanariot
fatalist
garagist
Lazarist
papalist
safarist
salariat
Satanist
banality
calamity
capacity
fatality
nasality
natality
rapacity
sagacity
salacity
satanity
damaskin
namaskar
malarkey
caballed
halalled
canaille
parallel
macallum
rataplan
caballer
dataller
eatables
parallax
marasmic
marasmus
japanned
savannah
japanner
carap-nut
Casanova
matadora
parabola
paranoea
paranoia
Saratoga
catacomb
paranoic
Garamond
paranoid
vagabond
caracole
matadore
parabole
paragoge
sagamore
zabaione
macaroni
carap-oil
parafoil
lavaform
macaroon
parazoan
parazoon
talapoin
cacafogo
tapacolo
paramour
tamanoir
vavasour
lavaboes
rabatoes
vanadous
Datapost®
gadabout
layabout
marabout
racahout
tacahout
lavatory
natatory
paradoxy
paralogy
sanatory
vavasory
mad-apple
Oak-apple
paragram
paradrop
palabras
zamarras
zamarros
banausic
badassed
harassed
rat-arsed
tanaiste
damassin
harasser
macassar
hamartia
Marattia
basaltic
galactic
tac-au-tac
cadastre
calanthe
lamantin
canaster
varactor
tarantas
vacantly
macahuba
malamute

Words marked △ may be spelled also with a capital letter

8 □a□a□u

tapaculo
catapult
paraquat®
Paraguay
catalyse
catalyze
paralyse
paralyze
catalyst
kazatzka
kala-azar
damboard
garboard
lap-board
larboard
pax-board
wayboard
sawblade
vambrace
madbrain
jambeaux
barbecue
barbicel
barbican
Barbados
gambados
waybread
pax-brede
daybreak
parbreak
has-beens
gambogic
Darbyite
lamb-like
babbling
baubling
dabbling
gabbling
gambling
garbling
lambling
marbling
rabbling
rambling
saibling
tabbying
wabbling
wambling
warbling
Cambrian
lambskin
carbolic
kabbalah
jambolan
tan-balls
zambomba
carbamic
carbonic
△rabbinic
rawboned
carbonyl
galbanum
garbanzo
bambinos
sawbones
tabbinet
lambency
gabbroic
gabbroid
lambdoid
tarboosh
gambroon
barbeque
barbaric
jamboree
Hamburgh
carbaryl
tamburin
harborer
jabberer
carburet
barberry
bayberry
hagberry
tayberry
waxberry
lambaste
gambeson
barbasco
iambuses
gambetta
sabbatic
barbated
rabbeted
barbette
barbital
rambutan
rabbiter
Babbitry
rabbitry
tamboura
mawbound
faubourg
hatbrush
tarboush
tar-brush
cambiums
carboxyl
jambiyah
barchane
calceate
fasciate
catch-all
bacchant
bar-chart
farcy-bud
cascabel
matchbox
patch-box
saucebox
watchbox
△nancy-boy
fascicle
farcical
saccadic
sarcodic
bar-coded
watchdog
Sarcodes
marchesa
calcrete
marchese
pasch-egg
parchesi
pancheon
ranchero
pancreas
sauciest
hatchery
hatchety
patchery
calcific
fanciful
watchful
catchfly
lancegay
bacchiac
man-child
cancrine
narceine
batching
catching
fancying
Fasching
hatching
matching
patching
ranching
talcking
watching
dabchick
Bacchian
falchion
fauchion
panchion
sanction
bacchius
patchily
sanctify
sanctity
carcajou
latchkey
marcella
cancelli
saeculum
vasculum
calcular
saccular
vascular
calculus
saccules
sacculus
lancelet
rascally
marchman
ranchman
watchman
sarcomas
calcanea
garcinia
vaccinia
nascence
calcanei
vaccinal
mancando
falconer
larcener
parcener
Maecenas
balconet
carcanet
falconet
sarcenet
falconry
nascency
fasciola
cancroid
fasciole
parclose
pad-cloth
waxcloth
watch-out
manciple
saucepan
calcspar
catch-pit
calcaria
carceral
caschrom
mascaron
baccarat
△fascista
rascasse
saucisse
Fascisti
narcissi
△fascismo
Fascists
mancuses
narcoses
narcosis
narcotic
falcated
lanceted
dancette
dancetté
caecitis
dancetty
calc-tufa
farceuse
calc-tuff
law-court
hatchway
handmaid
landward
yardland
yardwand
baldpate
card-case
card-game
handmade
hardbake
hardface
hardware
landrace
maid-pale
mandrake
aardvark
hardback
hardhack
hardtack
laid-back
landmark
sandbank
sand-lark
band-call
hand-ball
handrail
hardball
landfall
land-haul
landrail
waldrapp
band-pass
land-laws
landmass
handcart
handfast
sand-cast
sand-dart
bandeaux
landlady
laudable
mandible
laudably
cardecue
caudicle
raddocke
Sadducee
handicap
caudices
Pandects
lah-di-dah
candidal
candidly
gaudy-day
bald-head
hand-held
hardhead
land-herd
handbell
daydream
hardbeam
hand-sewn
hard-fern

Words marked △ may be spelled also with a capital letter

Mandaean
sandheap
sand-peep
Landseer
Landwehr
baldness
handless
hardness
landless
maidless
paddlers
wardress
handiest
saddlery
cardigan
hay-de-guy
sandshoe
dandy-hen
bardship
hardship
land-ship
wardship
landwind
yardbird
hardline
land-line
land-mine
landside
dandriff
bandying
bardling
daidling
handling
paddling
sandling
waddling
band-fish
dandyish
land-fish
sandwich
baldrick
baudrick
hand-pick
handbill
hand-mill
landfill
land-girl
mandrill
sandhill
dandyism
Gandhism
Mahdiism
Mazdaism
Mazdeism
Paddyism
Gandhian
Gandhist
handlist
Mahdiist
Mazdaist
tawdrily

vandyked
zaddikim
baudekin
landskip
Baedeker
daedalic
Vandalic
hard-a-lee
sardelle
sand-flag
△magdalen
mandolin
caudillo
gardyloo
handclap
landslip
pardalis
bandelet
handplay
pandemia
pandemic
Landsmål
cardamom
cardamum
bandsman
bandyman
cardamon
handyman
landsman
mandamus
randomly
bandanna
△gardenia
sardonic
hardened
tap-dance
△cardinal
labdanum
laudanum
fandango
Mandingo
gardener
hardener
pardoner
Pandanus
hand-knit
sardonyx
maidenly
wardenry
mandioca
cardioid
handhold
hardwood
landlord
maidhood
card-vote
handsome
hard-core
wardmote
wardrobe
aardwolf

hands-off
tandoori
handbook
handwork
hard-rock
land-roll
hand-loom
landform
sandworm
wardroom
bawd-born
hand-horn
waldhorn
wardcorn
land-poor
△baudrons
eardrops
bald-coot
hand-post
sandwort
hard-copy
caldaria
mandorla
land-crab
sandarac
laddered
wandered
banderol
falderal
△mandarin
wanderoo
handgrip
larderer
△wanderer
landdros
land-army
panderly
sawdusty
faldetta
caudated
banditti
bandster
mandator
sand-star
carditis
banditry
sand-dune
dandruff
handcuff
hard-luck
sandpump
handfuls
handover
sandiver
pandowdy
caudexes
Kalevala
baseband
baselard
face-card
△lakeland

racecard
saleyard
savegard
waveband
bakeware
caretake
casemate
catenane
catenate
lacerate
latewake
macerate
makebate
namesake
nametape
paleface
racemate
tapenade
waterage
Danelagh
racepath
bareback
baresark
cakewalk
face-mask
lacebark
baseball
race-ball
date-palm
jazerant
lacerant
name-part
catenary
dateable
hateable
makeable
nameable
rateable
saleable
takeable
tameable
tapeable
paper-boy
rateably
saleably
cadenced
face-ache
babeldom
calendar
calender
kalendar
lavender
taberdar
calendry
paper-day
danegeld
gapeseed
pale-dead
rapeseed
lace-leaf
Bakewell

farewell
harebell
rakehell
cameleon
gate-vein
male-fern
Pareoean
paderero
paterero
bateleur
cameleer
cave-bear
hare's-ear
bareness
baseless
baseness
bateless
careless
materess
dateless
easeless
faceless
fadeless
fameless
gameness
gateless
haleness
hateless
lameness
lateness
makeless
maneless
mateless
nameless
paleness
rareness
safeness
sageness
sameness
saneness
sateless
tameless
tameness
tapeless
vaneless
wageless
wakeless
wareless
waveless
bakemeat
basement
batement
casement
danegelt
easement
fakement
gazement
haterent
lavement
mazement
pavement

Words marked △ may be spelled also with a capital letter

8 □a□e□g

saw-edged
parergon
oak-egger
water-gas
catechol
waterhen
mageship
mateship
canephor
case-shot
cagebird
rarefied
tape-tied
Bakelite®
bale-fire
baregine
base-line
cameline
capeline
date-line
facetiae
galenite
gate-fine
lakeside
laterite
maderise
maderize
malefice
palewise
racemise
racemize
rare-ripe
sagenite
tapelike
tapeline
Vaseline®
wakerife
wavelike
cageling
catering
lacewing
layering
papering
ravening
salering
tapering
valeting
wakening
watering
wavering
babelish
camelish
hamewith
waterish
△maverick
cane-mill
material
matériel
Babeeism
babelism
Galenism
racemism
Jamesian
Naperian
Sahelian
Salesian
valerian
gaselier
face-lift
Galenist
maledict
water-jet
kabeljou
capeskin
camellia
labelled
lapelled
panelled
ravelled
lamellae
patellae
waterlog
date-plum
labellum
sacellum
Waterloo
gabeller
lamellar
patellar
patellas
satelles
capellet
dalesman
dayes-man
gavelman
salesman
talesman
waterman
caverned
cayenned
maternal
paternal
taverner
cabernet
hazelnut
base-load
cameloid
cane-toad
case-load
galenoid
gatefold
harewood
pagehood
barebone
dane-hole
gamesome
matelote
racemose
take-home
sawed-off
bale-dock
cagework
capework
casebook
casework
gamecock
gavelock
havelock
laverock
garefowl
case-worm
gapeworm
saleroom
tapeworm
waveform
base-born
careworn
fade-down
take-down
kakemono
tape-loop
racegoer
gazeboes
have-nots
ravenous
waverous
bareboat
barefoot
gatepost
hanepoot
hare-foot
lace-boot
category
waterpox
carefree
date-tree
name-drop
water-ski
cavesson
caper-tea
palestra
maieutic
majestic
galeated
gazetted
lamented
talented
patentee
parental
ramentum
gamester
man-eater
patentor
mazeltov
latently
patently
tapestry
malemute
Mameluke
tape-lure
wage-push
palebuck
ramequin
mameluco
makeover
maneuver
takeover
fade-away
takeaway
waterway
pale-eyed
panegyry
saufgard
half-face
halfpace
saw-frame
half-calf
half-ball
taffrail
half-mast
fat-faced
sad-faced
daffodil
canfield
gasfield
half-dead
hayfield
half-beak
half-term
half-year
calfless
naffness
half-text
caffeine
calf-time
half-life
half-pike
half-size
half-tide
half-time
baffling
halfling
maffling
waffling
caffeism
halflins
half-pint
half-tint
calfskin
half-blue
matfelon
lawfully
manfully
hawfinch
calf-love
half-done
half-hose
half-note
half-sole
half-tone
half-loaf
half-cock
half-moon
half-door
half-hour
half-boot
saffrony
gas-fired
half-bred
far-forth
tafferel
fanfaron
warfarin
warfarer
wayfarer
half-step
taffetas
far-flung
half-butt
kaffiyeh
gangland
hatguard
rat-guard
vanguard
gang-rape
langrage
language
margrave
langlauf
gang-bang
bar-graph
bang-tail
hangnail
Sangraal
Sangrail
malgrado
Sangrado
matgrass
oat-grass
hangable
tangible
mangabey
tangibly
Haggadic
Haggadah
jaggedly
raggedly
bargeese
cargeese
gangrene
Sangreal
sap-green
vargueño
fangless
pangless
barghest
hangnest
laughful
Langshan
hangbird
hangfire
narghile
sanguine
dangling
gaggling

gangling
jangling
laughing
tangling
tangoing
wangling
way-going
languish
ganglion
gangliar
sanglier
tangoist
narghily
sanguify
nargileh
pangolin
bargello
tangelos
nargilly
pangamic
Targumic
bargeman
gangsman
war-gamer
manganic
margined
mangonel
marginal
Manganin®
△waggoner
daggings
hangings
garganey
tangency
bargoose
cargoose
gas-globe
mangrove
waygoose
langspel
margaric
sangaree
hanger-on
margarin
kangaroo
badgerly
largesse
sargasso
pargeted
targeted
bangster
daughter
gangster
laughter
pargeter
gadgetry
pang-full
hangover
law-giver
gargoyle
washland
hashmark
washball
oathable
warhable
washable
cachucha
cathedra
cathodic
cathodal
washed-up
rachides
raphides
cashmere
hasheesh
bashless
cashless
nathless
pathless
rashness
Panhagia
pathogen
kachahri
naphthol
pashmina
lathlike
rathripe
washwipe
yachting
Kashmiri
bathmism
taghairm
Cathaian
wash-dirt
parhelia
rachilla
Valhalla
Walhalla
△catholic
Gadhelic
pachalic
parhelic
pashalik
bachelor
cachalot
cacholot
sachemic
Baphomet
bauhinia
raphania
tachinid
pachinko
lashings
Raphanus
Sathanas
washings
bathrobe
mashloch
cash-book
washbowl
bathroom
washroom
Pakhtoon
fashions
fashious
cachepot
bathorse
pad-horse
sawhorse
warhorse
Mathurin
vacherin
gatherer
lathyrus
fatherly
cathisma
tachisme
tachiste
machismo
Lachesis
mathesis
rachises
bathetic
Japhetic
pathetic
rachitic
catheter
cathetus
rachitis
bathcube
cathouse
madhouse
tap-house
△kashruth
man-hours
Pakhtuns
Pashtuns
wash-away
cachexia
cathexes
cathexis
Cathayan
calisaya
Camisard
badinage
camisade
capitate
carinate
cavitate
fatigate
kamikaze
laminate
lapidate
Latinate
marinade
marinate
maritage
navigate
paginate
palisade
radicate
saginate
salivate
sanitate
vaginate
validate
Varidase®
calipash
capitani
hari-kari
mahi-mahi
capitayn
camisado
capitano
palisado
habitans
harigals
habitant
latitant
radicant
vaginant
janizary
laminary
lapidary
salivary
sanitary
satiable
variable
cabin-boy
panic-buy
variably
mariachi
maniacal
cariacou
havildar
zamindar
Sapindus
samizdat
variedly
marinera
saliceta
Balinese
casimere
Galilean
caginess
calipers
easiness
gaminess
haziness
laziness
matiness
maziness
raciness
wariness
waviness
waxiness
zaniness
manifest
navicert
wariment
facilely
natively
basinful
Faringee
Maxim-gun
daring-do
malinger
daringly
gapingly
ragingly
ravingly
savingly
takingly
Lapithae
Manichee
padishah
caliphal
parishen
Salishan
papisher
ravisher
vanisher
garishly
lavishly
rakishly
basilica
cavitied
ladified
ramified
ratified
salified
Catiline
kalinite
laciniae
Latinise
Latinize
maritime
maximise
maximize
Nazirite
salicine
sanidine
sanitise
sanitize
satirise
satirize
vaticide
basilisk
basidial
familial
basidium
fakirism
△familism
Hasidism
Latinism
Marinism
nativism
pacifism
Basilian
Cabirian
Galician
magician
Parisian
pavilion
Tahitian

8 □a□i□i

Tamilian
familiar
gasifier
pacifier
ratifier
canities
papilios
Ramilies
Familist
had-I-wist
Hasidist
Latinist
Marinist
maximist
nativist
pacifist
satirist
basicity
calidity
caninity
facility
lability
Ladinity
lapidify
Latinity
△nativity
rabidity
rapidity
salinity
sapidity
vagility
validity
vapidity
magicked
panicked
radialia
cavilled
panicled
mamillae
maxillae
papillae
Ramillie
panislam
carillon
papillon
vanillin
bacillar
caviller
mamillar
papillar
variolar
△bacillus
facially
labially
racially
radially
kakiemon
talisman
hacienda
Panionic
talionic

gabioned
patience
radiance
salience
sapience
valiance
variance
△national
rational
maligner
malignly
radiancy
saliency
valiancy
mariposa
yakimona
manifold
marigold
tapiroid
baritone
camisole
farinose
halicore
halimote
laminose
palinode
varicose
yakitori
gasiform
Janiform
maniform
napiform
natiform
paliform
ramiform
raniform
variform
vasiform
cavicorn
naricorn
makimono
calicoes
halitous
manitous
Califont®
palimony
palinody
Vanitory®
vanitory
Calippic
calibred
taxiarch
marigram
variorum
janitrix
radiuses
papistic
sadistic
Taoistic
radiated
Labiatae

parietal
sagittal
varietal
Calixtin
sapi-utan
banister
canister
ganister
magister
radiator
varistor
△haliotis
papistry
tanistry
babirusa
Canicula
capitula
Kaliyuga
navicula
vaginula
fatigued
habitude
latitude
manicure
radicule
vaginule
habitual
taciturn
fatigues
Wahiguru
carjacou
banjoist
lap-joint
mah-jongg
marjoram
zanjeros
backband
backhand
backland
backward
backyard
lackland
parkland
parkward
back-date
bank-rate
backlash
backwash
backpack
hark-back
talkback
backfall
rack-rail
back-hair
darkmans
Walkmans
bankable
talkable
walkable
backache
tacked-on

lackaday
markedly
backveld
hawkweed
tack-weld
back-heel
hawkbell
jack-bean
barkless
dankness
darkness
lankness
nankeens
rankness
sackless
saikless
backbeat
back-seat
rack-rent
talkfest
packaged
packager
backchat
talkshow
backbite
backfile
backfire
backside
balkline
hawklike
jack-pine
parklike
waukrife
darkling
tackling
bank-high
jack-high
backfill
back-lill
bank-bill
walkmill
walk-mill
waukmill
backlift
back-lilt
backlist
banksman
marksman
tacksman
markings
mackinaw
back-comb
backbond
back-load
backword
pack-load
backbone
back-rope
bank-note
darksome
lack-love

packfong
hawk-moth
backwork
bank-book
hack-work
rackwork
task-work
bankroll
Jack-fool
backroom
darkroom
backdown
mark-down
talk-down
back-door
back-foot
backmost
hackbolt
jackboot
backspin
larkspur
cankered
jack-tree
Valkyrie
Walkyrie
mackerel
walker-on
jackaroo
jackeroo
backdrop
tank-trap
bankerly
jacketed
marketed
racketed
hackette
backstop
marketer
racketer
basketry
racketry
pack-mule
sackfuls
tankfuls
bankrupt
walk-over
walk-away
hawk-eyed
Macleaya
fahlband
gaillard
galliard
halliard
△kailyard
palliard
railcard
sail-yard
ball-game
fail-safe
malleate
palliate

Words marked △ may be spelled also with a capital letter

tailgate
tailrace
talliate
vaultage
wayleave
kaoliang
caillach
ballpark
fall-back
hallmark
mailsack
tailback
bail-ball
pall-mall
tail-lamp
galleass
galliass
jail-bait
mail-cart
fabliaux
tableaux
gallabea
gallabia
bailable
fallible
mailable
sailable
fallibly
caulicle
Gallican
mallecho
cable-car
ballocks
halluces
table-cut
garlicky
palladic
Rallidae
balladin
balled-up
balladry
pallidly
nail-head
railhead
wallsend
banlieue
carl-hemp
tailleur
gall-less
nailless
railless
sailless
tailless
tallness
wall-less
bailment
earliest
raillery
faultful
ladleful
tableful
lallygag
l'allegro
daylight
fanlight
gaslight
tally-ho'd
faulchin
ballyhoo
tally-hos
hailshot
mailshot
call-bird
gaol-bird
jail-bird
fail-dike
nail-file
tail-like
tailpipe
caulking
dallying
rallying
sallying
tallying
vaulting
sailfish
wallfish
ball-girl
call-girl
Gaullism
Harleian
Gaullist
rallyist
faultily
haploidy
tabloidy
tailskid
mail-clad
hallaloo
ballclay
gallumph
bailsman
Paul's-man
sally-man
tallyman
table-mat
vallonia
parlance
parlando
badlands
garlands
railings
tail-ends
tailings
ballonet
nail-bomb
bailbond
railroad
△calliope
call-note
nail-hole
tail-rope
badly-off
taglioni
bail-dock
ballcock
eagle-owl
ballroom
mailroom
sailroom
tail-boom
ball-gown
hall-door
hall-moot
mail-boat
sail-boat
tail-coat
wallwort
tailspin
calliper
galloper
walloper
gallipot
galleria
tailored
ballyrag
mail-drag
mailgram
cauldron
pauldron
taileron
wallaroo
fall-trap
eagle-ray
sailorly
ballista
galluses
balletic
balloted
galleted
palleted
ballotee
raclette
tarlatan
varletto
tabletop
harlotry
varletry
halloumi
kail-runt
day-level
gallivat
hallowed
wallowed
wallower
Mawlawis
cableway
Galloway
wall-eyed
waylayer
farm-hand
farmyard
caimacam
naumachy
gammadia
Talmudic
warmed-up
calmness
gaumless
harmless
warmness
mammifer
earmuffs
lammiger
dalmahoy
palm-wine
wagmoire
kaimakam
haymaker
law-maker
way-maker
Mammalia
mammilla
yarmulka
yarmulke
harmalin
palm-play
tagmemic
sarmenta
daemonic
daimonic
harmonic
salmonid
gammoner
salmonet
rag-money
farm-toun
warm-boot
palmiped
qaimaqam
palm-tree
balmoral
Palmerin
hammerer
Parmesan
marmoset
harmosty
Sarmatia
dalmatic
haematic
magmatic
palmitic
Sarmatic
palmated
palmette
haematin
palmitin
palmetto
gas-motor
mammetry
maumetry
mawmetry
razmataz
badmouth
panmixia
panmixis
barnyard
gainsaid
mainland
mainyard
rainband
raindate
taeniate
vauntage
manna-ash
rain-wash
sannyasi
mainsail
rainfall
maintain
gainsays
fainéant
mainmast
balneary
cannabic
damnable
gainable
tannable
wannabee
cannibal
cannabin
cannabis
paint-box
damnably
barnacle
pannicle
wainscot
maenadic
saintdom
manna-dew
main-deck
nainsell
rainwear
fainness
gainless
painless
rainless
saintess
vainness
vauntery
magnific
vauntful
carnifex
nannygai
pawnshop
launcher
rain-bird
jaundice
mainline
fainting
haunting
jaunting
nannying
painting
taunting

Words marked △ may be spelled also with a capital letter

8 □a□n□i

vauncing
vaunting
faintish
nannyish
saintish
saintism
Laingian
daintily
jauntily
pannikel
cannikin
mannikin
pannikin
larnakes
magnolia
cannulae
cannular
cannulas
gauntlet
carnally
tarnally
paynimry
earnings
fannings
gainings
cannonry
taenioid
nainsook
mainboom
sainfoin
barn-door
maindoor
carneous
raincoat
rainbowy
lagnappe
bannered
mannered
gauntree
rain-tree
Ragnarök
bannerol
raindrop
banneret
lanneret
mannerly
magnesia
vainesse
farnesol
magnetic
mannitol
magneton
fainites
magnetos
samnitis
gannetry
mainstay
carnauba
painture
tainture
carnival

panorama
sayonara
△savoyard
baronage
cabotage
malonate
sabotage
wagonage
sago-palm
marocain
gado-gado
mako-mako
mahogany
babouche
barouche
farouche
pabouche
baroccos
razor-cut
caboodle
canoodle
Ganoidei
Saxondom
carotene
gasogene
gasolene
gazogene
Masorete
haroseth
Masoreth
Carolean
Jacobean
△napoleon
caboceer
saboteur
baroness
bayonets
canoness
mayoress
cajolery
barometz
banoffee
wagonful
toboggan
caboched
caboshed
pahoehoe
basophil
cabochon
parochin
Zalophus
capoeira
Carolina
japonica
maiolica
majolica
canopied
parodied
camomile
canonise
canonize

caponise
caponize
Caroline
datolite
favorite
gasoline
Jacobite
jarosite
lanoline
Maronite
pavonine
saponite
Saxonise
saxonite
Saxonize
Taborite
taconite
valorise
valorize
vaporise
vaporize
canoeing
fagoting
tabooing
baronial
cacomixl
manorial
rasorial
laconism
Saxonism
Taxodium
Baconian
Bajocian
Catonian
Favonian
Jacobian
Laconian
Maeonian
Maronian
pavonian
Racovian
△salopian
Saxonian
palomino
caponier
gasolier
sabotier
calorist
canoeist
canonist
parodist
Saxonist
majority
saponify
havocked
carolled
masoolah
caroller
Damocles
wagon-lit
paroemia

lagoonal
marooner
ratooner
naloxone
malodour
canorous
saporous
savorous
valorous
vaporous
batology
cacodoxy
cacology
Mayology
taxonomy
magot-pie
favoured
laboured
savoured
vapoured
barogram
nanogram
tabourin
favourer
labourer
vapourer
tabouret
savourly
parousia
jalousie
carousal
carousel
damoisel
carouser
galowses
famously
panoptic
garotted
garotter
barostat
maroquin
paroquet
man-of-war
calotype
kalotype
paroxysm
paronymy
camphane
vamplate
warplane
gas-plant
hat-plant
palpable
tappable
palpably
salpicon
gazpacho
pappadom
camphene
earpiece
say-piece

harp-seal
campness
dampness
lampreys
waspnest
samplery
campagna
zampogna
camp-shot
campfire
camphine
camphire
campsite
dauphine
samphire
sapphire
sampling
△sapphism
campaign
Tarpeian
nauplius
sapphics
parpoint
sapphist
paspalum
pamphlet
rampsman
jampanee
sarpanch
harpings
raspings
rampancy
earphone
lamphole
pappoose
pay-phone
ratproof
war-proof
lamp-room
lamp-hour
lamppost
bagpiper
cap-paper
rag-paper
tar-paper
bagpipes
Pan-pipes
vampiric
rampired
camporee
rapparee
pamperer
tamperer
Capparis
pamperos
dapperly
lampasse
campuses
carpeted
lappeted
hampster

8 □a□t□e

rampauge
manpower
tax-payer
△jacquard
lacqueys
marquess
basquine
marquise
vanquish
daiquiri
narquois
hair-band
caproate
carriage
hair-wave
laureate
marriage
patriate
carryall
carry-all
hair-ball
hair-tail
hauriant
capricci
barracan
barracks
barricos
matrices
carrycot
sabre-cut
Capridae
Labridae
fairydom
Maoridom
harridan
Labrador
manrider
sacredly
fair-lead
hairbell
barriers
fairness
hairless
haurient
farriery
caprifig
garrigue
warragle
madrigal
warragal
warragul
warrigal
kauri-gum
larrigan
tarragon
darraine
hairlike
hairline
pairwise
carrying
dairying

harrying
marrying
parrying
tarrying
fairyism
darraign
larrikin
caprylic
barrulet
sapremia
sapremic
harrumph
haeremai
lacrimal
lacrymal
dairyman
yarraman
barranca
hadronic
Caprinae
patronne
matronal
patronal
safronal
safranin
barranco
warrener
madroños
Marranos
matronly
vagrancy
warranty
pair-bond
cabriole
capriole
carriole
hair-work
gairfowl
hair-worm
carry-ons
nacreous
carry-out
macropod
sauropod
sapropel
satrapal
sacraria
Saururae
macrural
hairgrip
Laurasia
madrassa
lacrosse
madrasah
garrison
sarrasin
warrison
sacristy
cabretta
Mahratta
garreted

parroted
barrette
garrotte
carritch
parritch
barrator
narrator
parroter
barratry
parrotry
carraway
narrowly
matrixes
rat-rhyme
sarrazin
rakshasa
cab-stand
hatstand
camstane
nauseate
palstave
ratsbane
tasswage
palstaff
haystack
pass-back
sawshark
cat's-tail
laystall
rat's-tail
camshaft
lay-shaft
naissant
nauseant
lapsable
passable
passible
raisable
passably
passibly
massacre
capsicum
waesucks
massicot
hassocky
Hassidic
passados
mansuete
ear-shell
mass-bell
passless
cat's-meat
far-spent
passment
pay-sheet
pauseful
marsh-gas
sapsagos
day-sight
batswing
lassoing

canstick
cat-stick
malstick
mapstick
Parsiism
△faustian
△gaussian
day-shift
manshift
karstify
baasskap
Marsilea
Marsilia
tasseled
mamselle
sassolin
capsular
causally
tasselly
vassalry
balsamic
marsh-man
ransomer
parsonic
Sassanid
raisonné
cassinos
paisanos
bassinet
sarsenet
mansonry
massoola
basswood
password
tarsioid
camstone
capstone
lapstone
ragstone
camshoch
fatstock
mass-book
pass-book
lasslorn
mansworn
Mass-John
pap-spoon
ram's-horn
maestoso
caesious
mansions
nauseous
cat's-foot
marsport
passport
tarsiped
Tarsipes
pansophy
caesurae
causerie
sanserif

Massorah
caesural
kaiserin
caesuras
maestros
Passeres
Sanscrit
Sanskrit
hausfrau
passer-by
cassette
falsetto
masseter
danseuse
masseuse
Passover
causeway
man-sized
capsizal
gastraea
eastland
eastward
castrate
tartrate
xanthate
canthari
castrati
pastrami
fastback
fast-talk
cant-rail
fastball
castrato
last-gasp
Gasthaus
manteaus
manteaux
vartabed
pantable
partible
tastable
wastable
earth-bag
wait-a-bit
canticle
particle
pastiche
pasticci
nautical
tactical
canticum
canticos
masticot
canticoy
mastodon
tarted-up
day-to-day
cattleya
masthead
wartweed
xanthene

Words marked △ may be spelled also with a capital letter

8 □a□t□e

paste-eel
Pantheon
xanthein
daftness
fastness
fattrels
gastness
hartbees
mastless
mattress
partners
saltiers
saltless
saltness
tactless
tartness
tautness
vastness
waitress
wartless
wastness
farthest
maltreat
battle-ax
Bartlemy
lactific
earth-fed
pantofle
Tartuffe
△faithful
tasteful
wasteful
fantigue
martagon
gas-tight
earth-hog
Banthine®
gantline
ianthine
part-time
rattline
salt-mine
wartlike
wastrife
xanthine
bantling
eastling
farthing
Lagthing
mantling
naething
rattling
sautéing
tattling
waltzing
wattling
baitfish
saltfish
paitrick
malt-mill
wanthill

Baathism
Ba'athism
partyism
Tantrism
Xanthium
Bactrian
malt-kiln
Parthian
Sartrian
Xanthian
eastlins
Baathist
Ba'athist
Tantrist
wait-list
paltrily
partaken
lantskip
partaker
kantikoy
battalia
mantilla
dactylic
△tantalic
pantiled
△bastille
pastille
nastalik
Santalum
tantalum
pantalon
santalin
martello
nasta'liq
batteler
dactylar
daytaler
cattalos
Dactylis
nautilus
naythles
△tantalus
mantelet
wastelot
earthman
raftsman
Rastaman
ragtimer
tautomer
caatinga
Castanea
galtonia
cantoned
pattened
tartaned
laitance
pastance
cantonal
tautonym
santonin
saltando

fastener
fattener
hastener
hastings
saw-tones
castanet
earth-nut
martinet
tartanry
wantonly
xanthoma
cartload
cartroad
tattooed
gantlope
raft-rope
salt-cote
Zantiote
part-song
dart-moth
fantoosh
gag-tooth
jaw-tooth
sawtooth
canthook
partwork
maltworm
hawthorn
lanthorn
tattooer
watt-hour
caltrops
captious
cautious
dartrous
factious
fastuous
hautbois
lacteous
xanthous
eastmost
faltboat
raft-port
salt-foot
saltwort
wartwort
earth-pea
Xantippe
Zantippe
patty-pan
hag-taper
bacteria
Hatteria
martyria
bacteric
△tartaric
battered
nattered
raftered
raptured
tattered

batterie
parterre
Sauterne
Tartarie
pastoral
pastural
cast-iron
hapteron
calthrop
banterer
barterer
capturer
natterer
palterer
patterer
cantoris
halteres
Raptores
Tartarus
bastardy
dastardy
easterly
latterly
masterly
pastorly
△tartarly
fantasia
mantissa
bartisan
partisan
cactuses
saltuses
hastated
factotum
maltster
Partitur
mastitis
gastrula
sastruga
Xanthura
zastruga
cartouch
saltbush
sastrugi
zastrugi
salt-junk
fauteuil
gastfull
wastfull
malt-dust
tastevin
earthwax
castaway
bartizan
partizan
sapucaia
carucage
carucate
hamulate
jaculate
lacunate

maculate
maturate
radulate
saturate
tabulate
vapulate
lacunars
saturant
lacunary
salutary
valuable
valuably
caruncle
faburden
gazunder
talukdar
Saturday
caducean
caduceus
maturely
babushka
△capuchin
baculine
baculite
daturine
fabulise
fabulize
lazulite
lazurite
matutine
paludine
sabuline
manuring
naturing
manurial
masurium
naturism
paludism
Laputian
pagurian
fabulist
naturist
caducity
maturity
Hanukkah
vacuolar
casually
casualty
manually
Saturnia
saturnic
laburnum
lacunose
maculose
paludose
papulose
ramulose
sabulose
Januform
caducous
fabulous

pabulous
paludous
papulous
patulous
ramulous
sabulous
kalumpit
haruspex
manubria
saburral
calutron
saguaros
vaqueros
paduasoy
baguette
maquette
haqueton
baluster
valuator
salvable
Calvados
salvific
aasvogel
mauvaise
mauveine
navvying
valvulae
valvular
valvelet
Salvinia
galvanic
tadvance
halve-net
calvaria
calvered
malvasia
malvesie
larvated
fauvette
war-weary
cam-wheel
ragwheel
man-weeks
earwiggy
tarwhine
batwoman
day-woman
laywoman
madwoman
rag-woman
△tamworth
wanworth
catworks
gas-works
waxworks
wanwordy
radwaste
waywiser
gas-water
tar-water
faux-naïf

banxring
bauxitic
capybara
easy-care
baby-talk
lazy-jack
Davy-lamp
man-years
Caryocar
Ganymede
lady-fern
lady-help
cagyness
gamyness
satyress
laryngal
larynges
ladyship
ladybird
ladyfied
calycine
ladylike
satyrisk
calycled
babyfood
babyhood
calycoid
ladyhood
manyfold
barytone
lady-love
baby-doll
easy-goer
many-root
Babygros
Dasyurus
lawyerly
calypsos
calyptra
kalyptra
manyatta
caryatic
caryatid
karyotin
calycule
larynxes
many-eyed
zarzuela
dazzling
manzello
calzones
canzonas
canzonet
jazz-rock
gadzooks
marzipan
mahzorim
mamzerim
jazz-funk
abradant
Abbaside

ablative
abrasive
abbatial
obeahism
ablation
abrasion
oblation
Abram-man
obtainer
oblatory
obscurer
abscissa
abscisse
abscisin
abacuses
obedient
abidance
abnegate
Abderite
Ibsenite
Ibsenism
Abderian
Ibsenian
obtemper
obtected
absentee
objector
abjectly
absently
obsequie
observer
abdicate
obligate
obligati
obligato
abdicant
obeisant
obligant
aboideau
aboiteau
abridger
obliging
oblivion
obsidian
abricock
ebriated
absinthe
obliquid
abampere
abomasal
abomasum
abomasus
T-bandage
abundant
ébéniste
ebenezer
abrogate
absonant
absorbed
absorber
obsolete

ebionise
Ebionite
ebionize
ebionism
abnormal
△abhorrer
△absolute
obvolute
absolver
ubiquity
mbaqanga
aberrate
aberrant
obtruder
Aberdeen
eburnean
aborigen
aborigin
abortive
aborning
abortion
abessive
abuttals
abstract
obituary
abatable
obstacle
abetment
abutment
abetting
abutting
abstrict
abutilon
abat-jour
abattoir
abat-voix
absterge
abstruse
obstruct
obdurate
obturate
obduracy
ybounden
absurdly
abducent
obtusely
ablution
obtusity
abductee
abductor
abruptly
obi-woman
abeyance
abeyancy
oceanaut
scrabbed
Scrabble®
scrabble
scramble
scratchy
scrag-end

écraseur
scragged
scraggly
sciatica
scraping
Occamism
Accadian
occasion
Oceanian
oceanids
Occamist
scramjet
scrawler
scrammed
scrap-man
sciaenid
scrannel
octaroon
octapody
scrapped
scrapple
eclampsy
schapska
schantze
scrattle
octantal
sceattas
scabbard
iceblink
scybalum
Scabiosa
scabious
scabrous
icebound
ice-cream
scuchion
acicular
acid-head
acidness
scudding
academia
academic
acidosis
schemata
acierage
acierate
scienced
sciences
screechy
screeder
sclerema
sclereid
acoemeti
icterine
sclerite
scheming
screwing
achenial
achenium
△ockerism
schellum

screamer
Achernar
screener
scleroma
scleroid
sclerose
ocherous
sclerous
acre-foot
eclectic
accepted
screwtop
accentor
accepter
acceptor
scienter
schedule
screever
scherzos
icefield
ecofreak
scoffing
scuffler
scofflaw
scaffold
Schizaea
activate
echinate
scribble
scribbly
schiedam
accident
△occident
actively
scriggle
achingly
scriggly
acridine
actiniae
actinide
scribing
actinism
actinium
activism
scribism
actinian
actinias
activist
acridity
activity
achillea
schiller
schimmel
actinoid
echinoid
schizoid
ochidore
Echinops
schizont
acrimony
scrimped
scrimply
scoinson
ecliptic
scripted
scrimure
achiever
aculeate
ocellate
scalable
eco-label
△scolecid
scoleces
scolices
scilicet
schlocky
ice-ledge
occluder
scalados
scullery
ecologic
schläger
scalding
scalping
scolding
sculling
scaldini
scallion
scullion
scaldino
scalpins
scaly-leg
scalenus
scolioma
Acalepha
acalephe
Scolopax
schleppy
Scalaria
scalprum
scelerat
ocularly
ecclesia
occlusal
occlusor
sculpsit
oculated
scolytid
sculptor
Scolytus
scalawag
scamping
scumming
scampish
scomfish
scumfish
scambler
schmaltz
ecumenic
schmooze
scammony
scombrid
scimitar
schnecke
scenical
scandent
scentful
acanthin
acanthus
scanning
scenting
scandium
Scandian
scansion
scontion
scanties
scantily
scantity
economic
sceneman
scincoid
schnapps
scenario
aconitic
aconitum
acknowne
ectosarc
accolade
accorage
octonary
scrowdge
accorder
ectoderm
acrolein
echoless
ectogeny
scoopful
scroggie
scrouger
eclogite
scooping
acrolith
acromial
acrotism
scholium
sciolism
acromion
eclosion
scholion
sciolist
schooled
scrolled
scrounge
schooner
accounts
scoop-net
Ochotona
Octopoda
ectozoic
acrosome
ectozoan
ectozoon
octoroon
ichorous
sciolous
echogram
acrostic
accoutre
accouter
scrofula
octopush
scuppaug
scuppers
Scopolia
scopelid
scapulae
scapular
scapulas
Scopelus
scaphoid
sceptred
sceptral
acerbate
acervate
ochreate
scordato
scarabee
scirocco
acorn-cup
Scaridae
acaridan
accredit
scarless
scarcely
scornful
scorched
scorcher
scirrhus
scurrile
scarfing
scarping
scarring
scorning
scarfish
△scorpion
scurrier
Scorpios
Scorpius
acerbity
scarcity
scurvily
achromat
scarmoge
acarpous
ochreous
scarious
scorious
ectropic
scarf-pin
eccrisis
eccritic
ecostate
ice-skate
acescent
scissile
acosmism
scission
acosmist
icestone
scissors
scissure
Scotland
Scotican
scattery
scutiger
scutcher
Scottice
scathing
scatting
Scottish
Scythian
Scottify
scutella
ocotillo
scuttler
scotomia
Scotsman
scotomas
scotopia
scotopic
scot-free
ecstasis
ecstatic
ecotoxic
ichthyic
acaudate
accurate
ecaudate
occupate
occupant
accuracy
scrubbed
scrubber
scrunchy
McGuffin
scourger
acquight
scouther
occupied
acauline
sciurine
accusing
scouring
scouting
occupier
acquaint
scrutiny
scrupler
scruples
octuplet
actually
scrummed
sciuroid
acaulose
scrumpox

Words marked △ may be spelled also with a capital letter

acquired
occurred
acquiral
accursed
acoustic
occulted
accustom
actuator
occultly
scavager
scavenge
scowther
scawtite
scowling
advanced
adjacent
idealise
idealize
ideative
idealism
adnation
ideation
idealist
ideality
Adiantum
idocrase
educable
educible
eduction
adscript
edacious
educated
educator
edgeways
addendum
edgeless
idleness
adherent
udderful
adhesive
edgewise
adhesion
idlehood
edgebone
addebted
edifying
odograph
ad-libber
edginess
additive
advising
addition
advisory
addicted
admitted
adultery
bdellium
idyllian
idyllist
odalique
adularia

idoliser
adulator
idolater
idolatry
idolizer
Adamical
oddments
Adamitic
odometer
udometer
odometry
Edentata
aduncate
edentate
adenoids
odontist
aduncity
identify
identity
adynamia
adynamic
adenomas
odontoma
odontoid
aduncous
adenitis
od's-nouns
△advocate
advocaat
advocacy
idiolect
admonish
idiotish
idiotism
ideology
ideogram
addorsed
advowson
odiously
adroitly
advoutry
adaptive
adoptive
adaption
adoption
adequate
adequacy
adorable
adorably
Odyssean
adessive
adespota
editress
adjutage
adjutant
adjuvant
adducent
adjuring
adductor
adjuster
adjustor

mesaraic
métayage
separate
seladang
megawatt
relaxant
legatary
bedabble
démarche
menarche
revanche
heraldic
retarded
veranda'd
rehandle
verandah
demander
regarder
retarder
rewarder
heraldry
rewarewa
Lebanese
legalese
metamere
Nepalese
Serapeum
Cesarean
cetacean
fedayeen
Pegasean
bejabers
decadent
remanent
pedately
sedately
Pelasgic
deranged
bedaggle
redargue
resalgar
seraphic
detached
seraphim
teraphim
xeraphim
seraphin
metaphor
regather
Hepatica
velamina
déraciné
gelatine
hematite
hepatise
hepatite
hepatize
ketamine
legalise
legalize
legatine

melamine
melanite
metalize
negative
penalise
penalize
petaline
relative
sedative
sepaline
serafile
set-aside
tetanise
tetanize
velarise
velarize
debasing
defaming
delaying
derating
medaling
menacing
metaling
pedaling
relaxing
renaying
repaying
retaking
megalith
terakihi
geraniol
betacism
geranium
legalism
melanism
petalism
regalism
teratism
△veganism
velarium
aeration
△dedalian
delation
deration
gelation
legation
negation
△pelagian
regalian
relation
sedation
venation
vexation
Zelanian
behavior
pedalier
ceramics
denarius
senarius
ceramist
legalist

medalist
metalist
regalist
denazify
femality
feracity
legality
megacity
regality
tenacity
venality
veracity
remarked
bedarken
remarker
medallic
metallic
bewailed
detailed
Heraclid
medalled
metalled
pedalled
petalled
tenaille
befallen
seraglio
teraflop
derailer
hexaplar
pedaller
retailer
hexaglot
metaplot
becalmed
demanned
detainee
relaunch
detainer
regainer
retainer
cedar-nut
pecan-nut
Decapoda
hematoma
Hexapoda
lecanora
melanoma
Metabola
metanoia
Nematoda
teratoma
hecatomb
metazoic
ceratoid
hematoid
keratoid
nematoid
petaloid
sepaloid
sesamoid

8 □e□a□o

teratoid
tetanoid
keratose
let-alone
megadose
megapode
nematode
hexafoil
metazoan
metazoon
belabour
melanous
pedaloes
petalous
rebatoes
sepalous
megavolt
dekalogy
demagogy
hexapody
negatory
pedagogy
petalody
sepalody
vexatory
behappen
pétanque
remarque
gematria
hetairia
debarred
hetaerae
métairie
hetairai
decagram
hexagram
veratrum
betatron
bevatron
negatron
veratrin
repairer
hetairas
zelatrix
relapsed
relapser
xeransis
semantra
gelastic
pedantic
semantic
Vedantic
xerantic
behatted
defatted
departed
repartee
decanter
departer
△levanter
recanter
recaptor
redactor
remaster
cerastes
pedantry
secantly
tenantry
tenacula
velatura
denature
peracute
resalute
megabuck
megabyte
megadyne
bedazzle
keyboard
lee-board
pegboard
seaboard
teaboard
membrane
verbiage
jet-black
neoblast
semblant
bee-bread
herb-beer
herbless
verbless
herbaged
keybugle
kerbside
seablite
pebbling
feeblish
redbrick
gerbille
cembalos
herbelet
redbelly
verbally
reabsorb
pembroke
new-blown
temblors
herbaria
membered
seaborne
berberis
Cerberus
dew-berry
fen-berry
peaberry
teaberry
nebbishe
Nembutal®
verbatim
verboten
deuce-ace
leachate
bescrawl
pew-chair
merchant
penchant
pencraft
perceant
reactant
seacoast
seacraft
berceaux
petchary
fencible
peccable
peacocky
Percidae
deicidal
leechdom
deucedly
bescreen
nescient
perchery
merciful
peaceful
heich-how
descried
merchild
describe
descrive
perceive
reactive
zecchine
kerchief
fetching
leaching
letching
perching
reaching
recceing
reccying
rescuing
teaching
zecchini
pea-chick
reaction
△reichian
Teucrian
zecchino
rescript
tetchily
Leucojum
teocalli
aesculin
mescalin
percolin
Aesculus
tercelet
henchman
henchmen
newcomer
welcomer
peacenik
med'cinal
seicento
deaconry
peccancy
seacunny
deschool
leachour
cercaria
mercuric
geocarpy
leachtub
leucitic
seecatch
Mercator
teuchter
berceuse
selcouth
hen-court
reoccupy
bedcover
peccavis
dead-hand
headband
headland
reed-band
reed-rand
headcase
headrace
reedmace
seedcake
seedcase
feedback
headmark
dead-fall
dead-wall
headrail
deuddarn
headlamp
dead-cart
headfast
beddable
beddy-bye
readable
vendible
weldable
readably
vendibly
berdache
headache
pendicle
headachy
deadhead
dead-head
feed-head
seed-leaf
Weldmesh®
weldmesh
dead-deal
seldseen
headgear
deadness
deedless
headless
heedless
leadless
lewdness
needless
seedless
seedness
weedless
weldless
dead-beat
dead-heat
dead-meat
headrest
needment
readiest
weldment
hey-de-guy
headship
feldsher
dead-shot
headshot
rendzina
dead-wind
reed-bird
bendwise
dead-fire
deadline
dendrite
feed-line
feed-pipe
headline
head-tire
leadline
needfire
readvise
reed-pipe
seedlike
seed-time
der-doing
headring
meddling
peddling
reedling
seedling
yeldring
seed-fish
herdwick
dead-lift
Seidlitz
pendulum
verdelho
pendular
seed-plot
feudally
hebdomad
beadsman
headsman
herdsman
leadsman
seedsman

Words marked △ may be spelled also with a capital letter

Mesdames
ready-mix
reddenda
tendance
tendence
vendange
perdendo
reddendo
deadener
leadenly
pendency
read-only
tendency
verdancy
dead-wood
dendroid
headword
reed-rond
dead-rope
headnote
headrope
seadrome
seed-lobe
headlong
deadlock
dead-lock
dead-work
headlock
headwork
herd-book
yeldrock
bead-roll
head-boom
headroom
dead-born
seed-corn
dead-bolt
headmost
seed-coat
feldspar
verdured
gendarme
lead-free
reed-wren
renderer
tenderer
verderer
verderor
feldgrau
tenderly
geodesic
vendetta
geodetic
seedy-toe
reedstop
lewdster
verditer
vendeuse
dead-pull
feed-pump
head-butt

headhunt
readjust
demerara
serenata
metewand
meteyard
rereward
beverage
defecate
delegate
federate
generale
generate
hebetate
leverage
regelate
relegate
renegade
renegate
selenate
serenade
serenate
sewerage
telesale
vegetate
venerate
ceterach
telepath
telemark
femerall
renegado
benefact
generant
hebetant
pederast
relevant
revenant
se-tenant
telecast
vegetant
delegacy
federacy
federary
femetary
resemble
December
remember
defenced
Seleucid
tedesche
tedeschi
defended
beheadal
rebeldom
tenendum
defender
degender
nereides
legendry
seven-day
repetend

△reverend
Genevese
teleseme
terebene
venereal
mezereum
mezereon
venerean
pederero
hereness
redeless
cerement
decedent
deferent
deselect
referent
reselect
reverent
Serevent®
teletext
tenement
vehement
cemetery
serenely
severely
bedeafen
feverfew
telergic
merengue
demerger
revenger
revenges
sewer-gas
petechia
telethon
secesher
telechir
celeriac
Genesiac
jeremiad
remedied
weregild
benefice
ceresine
deletive
pelerine
redefine
reremice
rerevise
selenide
selenite
telecine
televise
Vegemite®
vegetive
legering
receding
renewing
sewering
feverish
herewith

Jeremiah
fedelini
Benedick
remedial
helenium
selenium
telefilm
deletion
Hegelian
Menevian
redesign
selenian
Venetian
peperino
genetics
senecios
△benedict
derelict
remediat
reverist
Fête-Dieu
teleview
celerity
heredity
legerity
readdify
serenity
severity
temerity
bevelled
debelled
jewelled
levelled
newelled
rebelled
refelled
repelled
revelled
reveille
sewellel
Peterloo
beveller
jeweller
△leveller
rebeller
△repealer
repeller
reteller
revealer
reveller
rebellow
redeploy
teleplay
bedesman
meresman
peterman
peter-man
△redeemer
tenesmus
beseemly
hereunto

déjeuner
demeanor
betel-nut
depeinct
Denebola
Hereford
dene-hole
develope
werewolf
behemoth
peperoni
feverous
generous
Hereroes
selenous
telecoms
temerous
teleport
ceremony
deletory
feretory
hegemony
telegony
repeople
hereupon
bepepper
cerebric
meteoric
deferred
deterred
referred
rehearse
△tenebrae
terebrae
rere-arch
research
re-search
cerebral
deferral
referral
cerebrum
herefrom
telegram
teletron
△tenebrio
deferrer
veneerer
terebras
sewer-rat
genetrix
deceased
demersed
recessed
reversed
releasee
demersal
reversal
releaser
releasor
reverser
recesses

8 □e□e□t

reversis
reversos
dementia
fenestra
Nemertea
telestic
bewetted
dejected
demented
repeated
reverted
revetted
selected
nepenthe
recentre
resettle
selectee
pedestal
cementum
sebesten
bee-eater
begetter
bepester
besetter
cementer
defector
deserter
detector
receptor
reheater
rejecter
rejector
repeater
repenter
resenter
resetter
selector
semester
mementos
decently
recently
revestry
revenued
verecund
hebetude
reperuse
henequen
henequin
bedeguar
reneguer
bejesuit
sederunt
bereaved
deserved
received
reserved
receival
bereaven
deceiver
decemvir
deserver

receiver
reserves
never-was
hereaway
Teletype®
beefcake
leaf-base
self-hate
self-made
self-same
leaf-fall
perfecta
red-faced
perfecti
deifical
perfecto
leaf-scar
reoffend
hen-flesh
selfheal
self-help
deafness
leafless
selfless
selfness
self-left
sea-fight
serfship
belfried
leaflike
self-life
self-like
serflike
deifying
self-will
reaffirm
self-pity
beefalos
menfolks
perfumed
perfumer
reef-knot
beef-wood
selfhood
serfhood
self-love
leaf-roll
leaf-soil
self-born
self-sown
seafront
self-lost
telferic
perforce
renforce
seafarer
renforst
re'nforst
new-found
deaf-mute
self-rule

leaf-curl
key-fruit
keffiyeh
leg-guard
sea-grape
weighage
bergfall
berghaan
eelgrass
sergeant
neighbor
bergmehl
Neogaean
pea-green
sea-green
sengreen
seigneur
meagrely
vengeful
hedgehog
lengthen
hedge-hop
re-ignite
fee-grief
beagling
feigning
sea-going
weighing
Yenglish
seignior
hey-go-mad
bergamot
bergenia
geogonic
mergence
vergence
leggings
reagency
vergency
Wedgwood®
peignoir
geognost
weigh-out
geognosy
seignory
hedgepig
kedgeree
hedgerow
beggarly
heighten
lee-gauge
rephrase
bethwack
bethrall
methodic
menhaden
methadon
beshadow
neshness
meshugga
meshugge

nephrite
tephrite
technics
cephalic
kephalic
methylic
cephalad
cephalin
kephalin
lethally
bechamel
béchamel
mechanic
bechance
methanal
methanol
Nethinim
methinks
nephroid
dethrone
mesh-work
recharge
seahorse
Sephardi
lethargy
△bethesda
Mephisto
methysis
hen-hussy
Peshitta
mephitic
Peshitto
mephitis
seahound
bee-house
hen-house
yeshivah
yeshivas
yeshivot
resinata
perisarc
△medicaid
celibate
cemitare
decimate
dedicate
defilade
delibate
delicate
depilate
derivate
geminate
heritage
hesitate
levigate
levirate
levitate
△medicare
medicate
meditate
merimake

remigate
resinate
seminate
vesicate
teriyaki
Medibank
mericarp
pedipalp
pericarp
semitaur
genitals
dedicant
hesitant
vesicant
celibacy
delicacy
retiracy
seminary
deniable
leviable
reliable
deniably
reliably
mediocre
heliacal
meniscus
periodic
begirded
rekindle
devildom
bewilder
heliodor
reminder
zemindar
beniseed
Pekinese
beriberi
helideck
perigeal
perineal
periderm
perineum
Medicean
Oedipean
perigean
deviless
dewiness
eeriness
sexiness
desinent
pediment
penitent
redirect
regiment
renitent
resident
reticent
sediment
sepiment
delivery
peripety

Words marked △ may be spelled also with a capital letter

8 □e□l□e

refinery
senilely
periagua
bewigged
meringue
Feringhi
besieger
rejigger
meninges
vexingly
perished
zenithal
lecithin
decipher
perisher
Jewishly
newishly
Neritina
verified
aegirine
aegirite
decisive
definite
derisive
feminine
feminise
feminize
feticide
genitive
Leninite
lenitive
lewisite
medicine
melilite
melinite
redivide
regicide
resinise
resinize
retinite
Semitise
Semitize
sericite
Tebilise
Tebilize®
deviling
refining
repining
retiring
reviling
reviving
semi-ring
devilish
peridial
remigial
aecidium
delirium
devilism
feminism
Leninism
peridium
Semitism
venidium
decision
derision
Geminian
lenition
Lewisian
meridian
petition
recision
religion
revision
sedition
bénitier
verifier
Semitics
verities
feminist
Leninist
Semitist
debility
felicity
felinity
feminity
gelidity
resinify
revivify
senility
tepidity
devilkin
hemiolia
hemiolic
devilled
pedicled
perilled
petioled
megillah
tefillah
periblem
vexillum
Sémillon
tefillin
petiolar
periplus
aerially
genially
medially
mesially
serially
venially
bedimmed
melismas
nepionic
befinned
legioned
resigned
defiance
deviance
lenience
reliance
resiance
perianth
regional
beginner
designer
resigner
hemionus
benignly
deviancy
leniency
semicoma
helicoid
pezizoid
resinoid
retinoid
semibold
lepidote
pericope
peridote
perigone
semi-dome
Seminole
semitone
tedisome
demi-wolf
periboli
aeriform
reniform
retiform
setiform
demijohn
demi-jour
desirous
geminous
perilous
resinous
demi-volt
heliport
semi-soft
decisory
derisory
petitory
revisory
hemiopia
hemiopic
semi-opal
semi-arid
demiurge
pedigree
decigram
lexigram
Ménière's
genitrix
heritrix
herisson
lewisson
geniuses
heliosis
teniasis
demissly
remissly
meristic
periotic
semiotic
veristic
befitted
remitted
belittle
remittee
redistil
remittal
meristem
seriatim
helistop
demister
depicter
depictor
deviator
mediator
register
remitter
remittor
resistor
selictar
deviltry
registry
retinula
vesicula
deciduae
demi-lune
geniture
pedicure
perilune
refigure
reticule
semilune
semi-mute
semi-nude
pediculi
decidual
residual
semibull
residuum
heniquin
deciduas
medieval
believer
desilver
reliever
relievos
reviewal
reviewer
semi-axis
perigyny
Heliozoa
serjeant
Medjidie
verjuice
vee-joint
△benjamin
perjured
perjurer
deck-hand
neckband
deck-game
necklace
verkramp
peekaboo
neckweed
neckbeef
neckgear
neckwear
feckless
meekness
reckless
weakness
neckline
penknife
heckling
keckling
reckling
weakling
weakfish
leukemia
leukemic
reckoner
weakener
Geckones
deck-load
peak-load
neck-bone
desk-work
beak-iron
beck-iron
neckatee
weak-eyed
hellward
weel-far'd
dealbate
hell-gate
oeillade
telltale
tell-tale
well-made
wet-lease
heel-ball
keelhaul
weel-far't
fellable
healable
sellable
tellable
pellucid
pellicle
replicon
replacer
hellicat
Helladic
secluded
welladay
wellhead
well-read
pell-mell
well-seen

fellness
realness
veilless
wellness
zealless
bell-tent
defluent
hell-bent
refluent
well-kept
bellyful
pellagra
geologic
neologic
belly-god
aeglogue
negligee
negligée
verligte
geologer
penlight
red-light
△**sealyham**
fellahin
bellbind
bell-bird
hellfire
hell-fire
hell-kite
meal-tide
mealtime
realtime
seal-pipe
bellying
replying
dealfish
well-nigh
well-wish
Wellsian
velleity
△**oerlikon**
sealskin
cellular
beplumed
wealsman
Hellenic
reclined
declinal
bed-linen
jetliner
recliner
dealings
feelings
wetlands
well-knit
feelgood
feel-good
bellcote
bell-rope
healsome
hell-hole
meal-poke
well-done
mealworm
hell-born
well-born
well-worn
well-to-do
well-doer
bellwort
keelboat
jelly-pan
telluric
declared
hell-bred
well-bred
cell-free
meal-tree
tellural
cellarer
declarer
cellaret
déclassé
feblesse
realiser
mellitic
perlitic
zeolitic
reclothe
declutch
Neo-Latin
fellatio
belleter
deflater
deflator
geolatry
zealotry
jealouse
reillume
well-hung
bellpush
bell-pull
bell-buoy
gealousy
jealousy
replevin
beslaver
Mevlevis
newly-wed
beflower
bellower
deflower
reflower
fellowly
mellowly
wellaway
deflexed
reflexed
reflexly
Wesleyan
Vellozia
realizer
permease
permeate
team-mate
re-embark
neomycin
pemmican
gemma-cup
new-model
Bermudan
Bermudas
beamless
helmless
seamless
seemless
teemless
termless
germaine
teamwise
term-time
jemmying
seemlier
bedmaker
helmsman
tegmenta
Germanic
sermonic
vermined
helminth
△**renminbi**
△**germinal**
terminal
sermoner
terminer
beam-ends
△terminus
sermonet
geomancy
seamanly
yeomanly
yeomanry
geomyoid
reimpose
teamwork
gemmeous
reimport
re-embody
△**vehmique**
mesmeric
re-emerge
besmirch
kermesse
dermatic
hermetic
pelmatic
helmeted
besmutch
deemster
geometer
seamster
teamster
fermatas
geometry
vermouth
seamount
rein-hand
re-engage
penny-bun
vernicle
penny-dog
fern-seed
meunière
penneech
penneeck
lernaean
reindeer
beinness
keenness
leanness
meanders
meanness
reinless
reinsert
re-invent
reinvest
penny-fee
teenaged
nennigai
teenager
sennight
se'nnight
deanship
fernshaw
hernshaw
fernbird
meantime
bean-king
weanling
yeanling
deontics
re-enlist
fern-ally
kernelly
vernally
reinsman
pennoned
pernancy
beanpole
mean-tone
reinform
mean-born
cernuous
penny-pig
△**gesneria**
wet-nurse
penn'orth
jeanette
reinette
neonatal
reinfund
ceinture
reinfuse
reinsure
lean-burn
reanswer
xeromata
Legoland
decorate
denotate
derogate
desolate
detonate
helotage
lemonade
meconate
pejorate
perorate
relocate
renovate
resonate
segolate
zero-base
zero-rate
cenotaph
reposall
mesocarp
debonair
aerodart
aeronaut
resonant
xenogamy
demobbed
redouble
débouché
heroical
penoncel
resorcin
rejoicer
heroicly
lemon-dab
secondee
keloidal
beholden
beholder
bepowder
△recorder
seconder
secondly
Genovese
kerosene
telomere
peroneal
mesoderm
melodeon
zero-zero
demoness
peroneus
deforest
deponent
redolent
reforest
behovely
recovery
remotely

Words marked △ may be spelled also with a capital letter

8 □e□r□e

belonger
besought
xenophya
oenophil
heroship
geropiga
melodica
semolina
Señorita
veronica
demoniac
aerolite
cenobite
demonise
demonize
genocide
kerosine
leporine
meionite
melodise
melodize
memorise
memorize
mesolite
pemoline
peroxide
serotine
tenorite
xenotime
becoming
beloving
besoming
aerolith
demolish
regolith
xenolith
△menomini
memorial
cenobium
demonism
hedonism
helotism
meconium
me-tooism
metopism
nepotism
pelorism
Peronism
peyotism
besonian
bezonian
demonian
demotion
Devonian
devotion
melodion
Neronian
remotion
Senonian
Geronimo
Aerobics®

aerobics
Bedouins
hedonics
melodics
demonist
demotist
hedonist
Jehovist
melodist
nepotist
Peronist
peyotist
tenorist
detoxify
ferocity
remodify
serosity
velocity
venosity
besouled
recoiler
récollet
deformed
△reformed
re-formed
bepommel
deformer
△reformer
recommit
reformat
renowned
denounce
renounce
besognio
bemoaner
dehorner
renowner
aerobomb
Cenozoic
Mesozoic
menopome
merosome
aerofoil
jeroboam
rehoboam
tenoroon
decolour
decorous
felonous
nemorous
venomous
secodont
aerology
aeronomy
cetology
demology
gemology
menology
merogony
oecology
oenology

pedology
pelology
penology
serology
sexology
tenotomy
decouple
recourse
resource
begorrah
metopryl
aerogram
mesotron
devourer
△democrat
reborrow
repoussé
Senoussi
heronsew
gerontic
besotted
retorted
revolted
deportee
begotten
dehorter
reporter
resorter
retorter
revolter
aerostat
hemostat
devoutly
reposure
resolute
revolute
resolved
resolver
revolver
reconvey
men-of-war
aerodyne
cenocyte
cerotype
genotype
hemocyte
serotype
meronymy
metonymy
deep-laid
bed-plate
helpmate
jetplane
jet-plane
keepsake
key-plate
seaplane
template
hemp-palm
neoplasm
pea-plant

geophagy
keepsaky
vespiary
helpable
respects
hen-padle
Vespidae
bespread
deep-read
hemp-seed
resplend
neoprene
set-piece
reappear
deepness
helpless
besprent
deepfelt
helpmeet
neopagan
despight
peep-show
helpline
Memphite
mesprise
mesprize
neophile
semplice
tempting
Delphian
Memphian
dewpoint
bespoken
serpulae
zeppelin
Responsa
geoponic
weaponed
response
tenpence
keypunch
reopener
tenpenny
weaponry
geophone
neophobe
peep-hole
weephole
leaprous
deepmost
hesperid
tempered
leap-frog
temporal
vesperal
pepperer
temperer
Hesperis
Hesperus
hen-party
jeopardy

despisal
despiser
despotic
herpetic
despatch
dempster
sempster
despotat
ten-pound
deep-dyed
geophyte
neophyte
seaquake
verquere
mesquine
mesquite
verquire
jerquing
bearward
near-hand
rearward
decrease
degrease
ferriage
gear-case
recreate
pearl-ash
reproach
deer-park
rear-rank
beerhall
near-gaun
pearmain
reordain
rear-lamp
deer-hair
recreant
retroact
segreant
February
bearable
tearable
terrible
wearable
bearably
terribly
terraced
tetracid
verrucae
metrical
jerrican
jerrycan
terraces
verrucas
tetradic
degraded
begrudge
perradii
bear-lead
befriend
defreeze

8 □e□r□e

derrière
pearl-eye
refreeze
repreeve
repriefe
reprieve
retrieve
deer-neck
bear's-ear
dearness
fearless
gearless
heirless
nearness
peerless
regreets
searness
tearless
rearrest
reorient
febrific
petrific
terrific
pea-rifle
dearnful
weariful
retrofit
tetragon
verrugas
bedright
heirship
searcher
bearbine
bepraise
Hebraise
Hebraize
nearside
pearlite
rearmice
retraite
berrying
dearling
decrying
ferrying
learning
pearling
retrying
wearying
yearling
yearning
deer-lick
near-silk
Hebraism
negroism
Georgian
Georgics
hearties
pearlies
pearlins
Hebraist
retraict
retraitt
rear-view
heartily
bearskin
deerskin
terrella
petrolic
Negrillo
heartlet
neurally
retrally
ferryman
merryman
neuromas
neuronic
serranid
befringe
refringe
bedrench
retrench
neuronal
petronel
tetronal
bearings
Serranus
zebrinny
fearsome
yearlong
yearbook
heirloom
deerhorn
deer-horn
ferreous
hen-roost
rearmost
cecropia
heartpea
tetrapla
tetrapod
neuropil
terrapin
decrepit
necropsy
détraqué
perruque
terraria
pear-tree
retrorse
rear-arch
tetrarch
pear-drop
heart-rot
petrosal
reprisal
new-risen
necrosis
neuroses
neurosis
Letraset®
ferritic
heuretic
Nearctic
necrotic
neuritic
neurotic
ferreted
serrated
△decretal
detrital
ferritin
secretin
ferreter
regrater
regrator
detritus
metritis
Negritos
neuritis
serratus
aegrotat
secretly
rearouse
pear-push
beer-pump
depraved
deprived
deprival
reproval
reprover
regrowth
tearaway
tetraxon
defrayed
betrayal
defrayal
betrayer
defrayer
terrazzo
messmate
messuage
persuade
perswade
redshare
seascape
Teasmade®
bed-staff
newshawk
redshank
Jews'-harp
Jew's-harp
newscast
redstart
feasible
leasable
reusable
sensible
tensible
feasibly
sensibly
peasecod
versicle
bedsocks
persicot
Messidor
feast-day
bedstead
reascend
kenspeck
△newspeak
△seaspeak
deisheal
newsreel
seashell
peesweep
eel-spear
menswear
newsless
reassess
bed-sheet
reascent
reassert
feastful
menseful
senseful
messages
mem-sahib
fess-wise
newswire
perspire
redshire
beesting
beeswing
feasting
newsgirl
seismism
reassign
jet-skier
beastily
perseity
sensilla
tessella
teaseled
mersalyl
teaseler
weaseler
verselet
weaselly
pessimal
pessimum
verse-man
Welshman
Bessemer
yersinia
reasoned
seasoned
personae
teosinte
personal
seasonal
reasoner
seasoner
personas
peasanly
keeshond
felstone
gemstone
keystone
pea-stone
seashore
ten-score
penstock
cesspool
sesspool
mess-room
newsroom
gemshorn
Mess-John
teaspoon
velskoen
sensuous
sessions
redshort
menstrua
sensoria
lease-rod
leisured
measured
tesserae
mensural
tesseral
Mensuren
measurer
measures
bedstraw
pea-straw
setscrew
felsitic
reassume
reassure
beestung
persaunt
pea-soupy
zemstvos
peishwah
feast-won
yea-sayer
left-hand
leftward
Lettland
peat-land
text-hand
westward
berthage
centiare
peat-hagg
reattach
left-bank
peat-bank
best-ball
meatball
reattain
restrain
bestiary
△tertiary

Words marked △ may be spelled also with a capital letter

textuary
vestiary
vertebra
death-bed
beatable
bed-table
gettable
lettable
rentable
testable
denticle
lenticle
pentacle
tentacle
testicle
hectical
lenticel
vertical
verticil
death-cap
death-cup
vertices
pentadic
bestadde
testudos
pettedly
septleva
meathead
neat-herd
aesthete
bestreak
peat-reek
bestrewn
leathern
yestreen
deftness
feetless
heathens
leathers
lectress
meatless
meetness
neatness
nextness
pertness
rectress
restless
seatless
tentless
textless
weetless
peetweet
sentient
vestment
feathery
heathery
leathery
beatific
pettifog
deathful
vestigia
heptagon
△pentagon
vertigos
heath-hen
peatship
bestride
dextrine
gentrice
nestlike
perthite
tentwise
ventaile
vent-pipe
beetling
centring
fettling
left-wing
nestling
restring
seething
settling
teething
ventring
testrill
centrism
Hertzian
neutrino
destrier
fewtrils
westlins
centoist
centrist
restrict
gentrify
lent-lily
dentalia
Reptilia
gentilic
Pentelic
dentelle
vent-plug
sextolet
festally
mentally
rectally
rent-a-mob
pentomic
septimal
testamur
leptonic
neotenic
Newtonic
tectonic
Teutonic
sentence
centinel
pectinal
sentinel
lentando
centones
pectines
bentwood
centroid
bestrode
centrode
dextrose
peat-hole
rest-home
vent-hole
pentroof
jestbook
tent-work
textbook
benthoal
sept-foil
bestrown
meltdown
next-door
peat-moor
dextrous
feateous
featuous
oestrous
peat-moss
ventrous
vent'rous
vertuous
beetroot
westmost
centuple
septuple
sextuple
Zentippe
gestapos
heatspot
dentaria
septaria
neoteric
bettered
lettered
nectared
textured
vestured
rent-free
sesterce
heptarch
pentarch
gestural
pectoral
rectoral
sectoral
textural
vestural
deuteron
setter-on
setter-up
hectorer
lecturer
letterer
pesterer
pewterer
restorer
venturer
vesturer
features
death-ray
hectorly
westerly
pertused
jettison
pentosan
centeses
centesis
meatuses
rectitic
dentated
septette
sestette
sextette
teetotal
teetotum
testatum
sestetto
sectator
testator
rectitis
rest-cure
test-tube
centrums
destruct
centaury
aestival
festival
leftover
centavos
bestowal
bestower
neotoxin
geotaxis
vertexes
ventayle
sentry-go
mestizas
mestizos
denudate
depurate
peculate
regulate
bequeath
mezuzahs
débutant
depurant
petulant
recusant
penumbra
benumbed
renumber
nelumbos
zerumbet
semuncia
peduncle
befuddle
bemuddle
secundum
refunder
beau-pere
cerulean
cerulein
teru-tero
feculent
relucent
tegument
temulent
demurely
jejunely
securely
bemuffle
gefuffle
kefuffle
beauffet
requight
penuchle
△nenuphar
reduviid
beauxite
cerusite
delusive
deputise
deputize
Jebusite
lemurine
nebulise
nebulize
reguline
regulise
regulize
relumine
resupine
xenurine
reducing
reputing
seducing
segueing
reburial
tenurial
nebulium
peculium
refugium
decurion
delusion
lemurian
Peruvian
refusion
Venusian
Venutian
△vesuvian
△peculiar
beauties
Merulius
beautify
jejunity
repurify
security
sedulity

8 □e□u□l

tequilla
republic
medullae
sequelae
beguiler
medullar
medullas
sexually
remurmur
resubmit
sequined
returnee
sequence
refusnik
returnik
returner
lemuroid
medusoid
levulose
setulose
jelutong
mezuzoth
nebulous
sedulous
setulous
tenuious
Beaufort
delusory
demurred
recurred
required
demurral
delubrum
demurrer
requirer
debussed
Senussis
Jesuitic
besuited
rebutted
requited
petuntse
petuntze
rebuttal
requital
rebutton
rebutter
requiter
seductor
Jesuitry
decurved
recurved
resurvey
teguexin
requoyle
perviate
cervical
services
△services
selvedge
revved-up

Fervidor
fervidly
heaviest
servient
selvagee
weeviled
venville
nervular
cervelat
nervelet
weevilly
pea-viner
leavings
servants
fervency
heavenly
pervious
beavered
perverse
renverse
renverst
velveret
pelvises
Helvetic
velveted
servitor
cervixes
eelwrack
webwheel
reawaken
dey-woman
leg-woman
penwoman
seawoman
pen-wiper
bedwards
seawards
redwater
seawater
re-expand
re-export
cetywall
hexylene
Terylene®
demyship
Lecythis
lecythus
lekythos
merycism
Pepysian
beryllia
desyatin
dewy-eyed
benzoate
seizable
weazened
terzetta
terzetti
terzetto
off-and-on
off-board

off-break
off-comer
off-drive
offended
offender
aftereye
afferent
efferent
effetely
offering
affeered
affected
affecter
effecter
effector
after-tax
efficacy
iffiness
official
effigies
affinity
affirmer
affiance
effierce
affluent
effluent
afflated
afflatus
effluvia
sfumatos
pfenning
Afro-jazz
afforest
Afro-rock
offprint
off-piste
sforzati
sforzato
affright
effraide
affronté
affrayed
off-shake
off-stage
off-shakt
offsider
off-sales
offshore
eftsoons
offshoot
off-sorts
ofttimes
effulged
effusive
affusion
effusion
aflutter
off-white
off-wards
aguacate
eglatere

agraphia
agraphic
agraphon
agnation
agrarian
Ignatian
yglaunst
ignaroes
egg-apple
egg-bound
agaçante
agacerie
agedness
egg-dance
ague-cake
agrémens
agrément
agreeing
agrestic
agrestal
egg-fruit
egg-glass
ugliness
aguishly
ignition
aglimmer
agrimony
ignitron
egoistic
aglitter
agalloch
ngultrum
Agamidae
egomania
agentive
agential
Aganippe
agonised
agonized
agiotage
ignorant
ignominy
agrology
agronomy
agnostic
egg-plant
Egyptian
egg-purse
aggraced
aggrieve
agar-agar
Ygdrasil
ageratum
eggshell
egestive
egg-slice
egestion
egg-spoon
egg-timer
egg-tooth
△**agitprop**

agit-prop
agitated
agitator
egg-whisk
thraward
pheasant
thrawart
thearchy
shraddha
thraldom
Theaceae
wheatear
cheaters
cheatery
sheathed
shear-hog
thrasher
Theatine
thiamine
thiazide
thiazine
cheating
phrasing
sheading
shealing
shearing
shoaling
thwacker
phialled
shearleg
shearman
chiasmas
chiasmus
shrapnel
whoa-ho-ho
thrapple
theatric
shea-tree
theatral
chiastic
thwarted
Rh-factor
thwarter
shmaltzy
thwartly
shea-nuts
shabrack
thebaine
shabbily
rhabdoid
Shabuoth
rhubarby
chechako
Phocidae
Phocaena
checkers
chickens
thickety
shechita
shocking
shucking

Words marked △ may be spelled also with a capital letter

whacking
thickish
chuckies
check-key
△phacelia
shackles
chaconne
chicaner
chicanas
chicanos
check-off
thickoes
whackoes
checkout
check-out
chiccory
chickpea
thickset
shuddery
cheddite
shedding
thudding
whidding
shoddily
shadblow
rhodanic
who-dun-it
shaddock
Rhodesia
Rhodites
shadbush
khedival
she-devil
shadower
shoelace
wheel-cut
shredded
shrewdie
sheepdog
chiefdom
threaden
Whieldon
sheep-dip
shielder
shredder
threader
shrewdly
Phoebean
chiefess
shoeless
chiefest
chiefery
thievery
cheerful
chee-chee
threshel
Phaethon
thresher
sheeling
sheeting
shieling

thieving
wheeling
wheezing
sheepish
shrewish
thievish
cheewink
shlemiel
shoebill
phrenism
Rhaetian
cheerios
cheekily
cheerily
wheezily
sheerleg
wheedler
phlegmon
three-man
wheelman
threnode
shoehorn
threnody
shred-pie
sheep-pen
shlepper
threapit
threepit
sheep-pox
three-ply
shoetree
sheep-run
sheep-rot
phreatic
bheestie
sheet-tin
threaten
three-way
chaffery
Shafiite
chaffing
shafting
shifting
whiffing
shiftily
whiffled
shuffler
whiffler
shofroth
chiffons
chaffron
shag-bark
rhagades
shagreen
thuggery
Whiggery
Whigship
shagpile
chugging
shagging
shogging

thigging
whigging
Whiggish
thuggism
Whiggism
shaggily
shigella
shogunal
shagroon
phthalic
phthalin
chthonic
phthisic
phthisis
shehitah
shiitake
thridace
chair-bed
choirboy
sheikdom
choicely
Khoikhoi
Shaivite
sheiling
shriving
thriving
Shaivism
shrieker
shrinker
thriller
chainlet
chrismal
chainman
chairman
choirman
shrimper
Chrissie
thrissel
thlipsis
thripses
chainsaw
theistic
Christie
thristle
christom
christen
Christly
shrieved
shrieval
shakable
shake-bag
chokidar
Shaktism
Shekinah
shake-out
shikaree
shake-rag
chillada
choliamb
Chaldaic
chiliasm

chiliast
phyllary
childbed
philabeg
philibeg
chaliced
pholades
while-ere
Chaldean
Chellean
sheltery
khalifah
shelf-ful
shellful
khalifat
khilafat
whole-hog
phyllite
shell-ice
thalline
childing
chilling
shelling
shelving
shilling
childish
phallism
thallium
chillies
chillily
cholemia
cholemic
thalamic
Philomel
whaleman
thalamus
philamot
philomot
Chelonia
chalonic
phalange
phalloid
phelloid
phylloid
thalloid
phyllode
phyllome
shalloon
shallows
thallous
phyllody
cheliped
chilopod
chalkpit
chyluria
choleric
phylarch
chaldron
children
thyloses
thylosis

phyletic
chelator
shelduck
chalazae
chalazas
shamiana
chummage
shammash
champart
shamable
chemical
△chimaera
themself
chambers
champers
shimmery
shameful
whim-wham
chumping
shamming
thumping
whamming
whimming
champion
whimsily
shambles
chamelot
shamanic
thumbnut
rhomboid
shampoo'd
shamrock
shampoos
thumbpot
chimeric
whimbrel
chamfron
chambray
chemurgy
chamisal
shamisen
thumbs-up
chamises
chamisos
phimosis
shamuses
rhematic
thematic
ohmmeter
whomever
chinkara
khansama
whiniard
whinyard
chantage
phantasm
phantasy
thingamy
thanedom
Rhinodon
thanadar

Words marked △ may be spelled also with a capital letter

8 □h□n□d

whinid'st
Shandean
channels
chinless
shunless
thinners
thinness
thinnest
△chancery
thundery
thankful
phenogam
shanghai
rhonchal
chin-chin
rhonchus
whinchat
whinnied
phengite
chunking
shunning
shunting
thanking
thinking
thinning
thinnish
Ghanaian
Chanukah
phenolic
phenylic
shingled
chenille
chandler
shingler
shingles
chinampa
phonemic
Chinaman
shinbone
phinnock
thin-sown
phantomy
chenopod
thin-spun
chondral
chondrin
phoner-in
△chondrus
phenetic
phonetic
rhinitis
shantung
whenever
thankyou
chlorate
chromate
thio-salt
throbbed
thrombin
theorbos
thrombus
thio-acid
shrouded
chlordan
chromene
thronged
thiophil
thiophen
choo-choo
chloride
chlorine
chlorite
chromite
rhyolite
theorise
theorize
shooting
throwing
whooping
chromium
shootist
theorist
theodicy
rheocord
rheotome
theosoph
chlorous
shoot-out
throw-out
chaology
rheology
theogony
theology
theonomy
thropple
thiourea
theocrat
chloasma
whoopsie
throated
throstle
throttle
rheostat
shipyard
shipmate
whiplash
whipjack
whiptail
chaplain
chapeaux
shapable
△shepherd
chapless
chappess
choppers
shipless
shipment
chip-shop
chop-chop
whipbird
rhaphide
ship-tire
whiplike
chipping
chopping
shipping
shopping
whapping
whipping
whopping
shop-girl
rhopalic
chapelry
shipload
whipcord
rhapsode
chapbook
shipworm
whipworm
shopworn
rhapsody
chaptrel
chaperon
chapatti
chupatti
chapiter
whipster
chipmuck
chipmunk
chequers
Chordata
theriaca
choriamb
chordate
shortage
thirlage
wharfage
sherwani
shortarm
charlady
pharmacy
cherubic
thurible
cherubim
cherubin
whirlbat
whorlbat
thoracic
characid
thoracal
characin
thoraces
sharp-cut
short-cut
whoredom
short-day
Thursday
thirteen
charneco
Cherkess
charmful
therefor
thurifer
wherefor
chiragra
choragic
choregic
choragus
choregus
churchly
thermite
charming
charring
chirping
chording
churning
sharking
sharping
shirring
shirting
thirding
wharfing
whirling
whirring
churlish
sharpish
shortish
△chartism
△phormium
thermion
thirties
wherries
△chartist
phorminx
chirpily
shirtily
Cherokee
shiralee
therblig
chorally
shareman
shireman
shoreman
churinga
charango
chorioid
thyreoid
thyrsoid
charlock
△sherlock
charcoal
churn-owl
short-oil
share-out
thereout
whereout
theropod
charisma
chorused
Pharisee
whoreson
chorisis
charoset
sharp-set
thornset
Sheraton
thirster
Charites
△thorough
chirrupy
wherever
thyroxin
thoraxes
C-horizon
chasuble
physical
physicky
Chasidic
phosgene
chasseur
thisness
thusness
whiskers
whispers
chastely
whiskery
whispery
chestful
ghastful
△phosphor
khuskhus
chastise
Cheshire
thuswise
ghosting
whisking
△thespian
chastity
physalia
whistled
shashlik
whistler
physalis
chessman
chestnut
Shoshone
Shoshoni
phisnomy
physique
physeter
thesauri
Cheshvan
whosever
△shetland
châteaux
Whiteboy
thetical
whitecap
shithead
white-eye
chattels
thatness
whatness
shattery
Photofit®

Words marked △ may be spelled also with a capital letter

photofit
whitefly
photogen
thatched
thatcher
chitchat
white-hot
chatline
chat-line
what-like
chatting
shitting
shotting
shutting
whetting
whitling
shot-clog
white-leg
whittler
chattles
rhythmic
rhythmed
rhythmal
rhythmus
△photinia
whitener
shithole
shothole
shutdown
ghettoes
white-out
photopia
photopic
chutzpah
whitepot
photopsy
rhetoric
shot-free
whittret
Rhytisma
phytosis
white-tie
whitster
whatever
thataway
thousand
thrum-cap
shoulder
shouldn't
shouldst
chauffer
theurgic
shauchle
shouther
thoughts
shauchly
shouting
ghoulish
shrunken
thrummed
thrummer

shtupped
chausses
chaunter
chounter
thruster
chauntry
choultry
Shivaite
Shivaism
cheville
shoveler
chevalet
chivalry
Shavuoth
Shevuoth
chevrony
cheverye
chivaree
shivaree
cheverel
cheveril
cheveron
shiverer
showyard
showcase
chewable
thawless
thewless
thowless
chow-chow
shawling
showgirl
showroom
showdown
showboat
chawdron
whey-face
Phrygian
Cheyenne
chayroot
choy-root
whizbang
rhizobia
whizzing
rhizopod
rhizopus
Himalaya
Hinayana
hiragana
Minamata
bigarade
divagate
titanate
vicarage
vicarate
dilatant
gigawatt
divan-bed
sidalcea
finances
dinarchy

vizarded
bilander
filander
risaldar
virandos
misandry
ribaldry
ribaudry
wizardly
wizardry
Bixaceae
Limaceae
Vitaceae
pita-hemp
rivaless
△titaness
vicaress
bivalent
divalent
filament
ligament
vizament
giraffid
hidalgas
hidalgos
hibachis
kinakina
dilative
finalise
finalize
fixative
limacine
liparite
Picariae
rivalise
rivalize
△simazine
titanite
vitalise
vitalize
vitamine
vitative
silaging
niramiai
bifacial
bilabial
filarial
riparial
vicarial
finalism
sinapism
△titanism
titanium
vitalism
vivarium
bibation
cibation
citation
dilation
fixation
himation

libation
ligation
limation
misalign
nidation
picarian
riparian
Sicanian
Titanian
bigamist
digamist
finalist
timariot
visagist
vitalist
tiramisu
dicacity
finality
hilarity
minacity
rivality
vitality
vivacity
hijacker
disabled
rivalled
miracles
misallot
disallow
pita-flax
viraemia
viraemic
disarmer
disannul
disannex
lima-wood
pinacoid
pinakoid
girasole
pinafore
rigatoni
linalool
disadorn
picaroon
rigadoon
bigamous
bimanous
biparous
biramous
digamous
titanous
viragoes
citatory
dilatory
filatory
libatory
minatory
didapper
disapply
misapply
disagree

filagree
binaural
cicatrix
disarray
misarray
bioassay
dicastic
didactic
gigantic
Silastic®
silastic
Sinaitic
didactyl
disaster
pilaster
pinaster
ailantos
simaruba
disabuse
filature
fixature
ligature
picayune
bimanual
pirarucu
air-brake
rim-brake
midbrain
bioblast
timbrel'd
tie-break
limbmeal
limbless
diablery
misbegot
gibbsite
nibbling
air-brick
nimbyism
witblits
air-built
diabolic
cimbalom
disbench
air-bends
jibbings
ribbonry
timbered
airborne
disburse
misbirth
airburst
bilberry
nisberry
diabasic
nimbused
bimbashi
disbosom
nimbuses
diabetic
bimbette

8 □i□b□t

diabetes
air-brush
disbowel
pilchard
jib-crane
gimcrack
jimcrack
disclaim
aircraft
miscible
vincible
biscacha
bizcacha
viscacha
vizcacha
milch-cow
ditch-dog
biocidal
miscreed
discrete
Circaean
pinchers
discreet
bitchery
witchery
miscegen
pinchgut
pinch-hit
diactine
mischief
cinching
circling
discoing
filching
pinching
pitching
witching
zincking
dipchick
biscuity
bitchily
circuity
hitchily
zinckify
vinculum
circular
discolor
miscolor
piacular
piccolos
fiscally
zircaloy
Zircoloy®
pitchman
winchman
zirconia
zirconic
piscinae
diaconal
piccanin
piecener
piscinas
discinct
discandy
pince-nez
cinchona
disclose
oilcloth
discrown
disclost
hiccuped
disciple
mince-pie
linchpin
sinciput
visceral
miscarry
diocesan
circussy
hiccatee
circiter
piscator
cincture
discoure
lincture
tincture
hiccough
discount
miscount
piecrust
△viscount
air-cover
discover
Biscayan
hindward
wildland
windward
birdcage
birdbath
birdcall
windfall
windgall
windsail
air-drain
airdrawn
windlass
misdealt
biddable
diadochi
diddicoy
bindweed
birdseed
hindhead
misdread
bindi-eye
birds-eye
bird'seye
hindlegs
kindless
kindness
mildness
mindless
piedness
rindless
vildness
wildness
windless
misdight
windship
birdshot
bird-lice
bird-life
birdlike
bird-lime
Hinduise
Hinduize
wildfire
wildlife
windpipe
birdwing
fiddling
hindwing
kindling
middling
misdoing
piddling
riddling
windring
windmill
Hinduism
kindlily
vindaloo
windblow
diademed
misdempt
misdonne
riddance
findings
sindings
hiddenly
jim-dandy
wildwood
airdrome
wind-rode
windrose
birdsong
windsock
wildfowl
lindworm
wild-born
fiddious
bird-bolt
hindfoot
hindmost
piedmont
mind-body
Pindaric
wildered
pindaree
siddurim
hinderer
mind-cure
windsurf
mindfuck
wild-duck
windburn
misdoubt
windowed
bird-eyed
wild-eyed
Cinerama®
cider-and
hiveward
sideband
sideward
tideland
timecard
vineyard
Airedale
filename
liberate
likewake
literate
liveware
pipe-case
siderate
tide-gate
tidewave
limewash
sidepath
literati
fire-back
firemark
fire-walk
Kitemark
kite-mark
likewalk
pipe-rack
sidewalk
tidemark
fireball
live-rail
sidewall
time-ball
vine-gall
riverain
literato
firedamp
wire-hair
fireman's
sideways
ci-devant
libelant
life-raft
live-bait
cinerary
literacy
literary
siserary
vicenary
vinegary
river-bed
citeable
hireable
likeable
liveable
rideable
sizeable
silenced
wiseacre
libeccio
cider-cup
ricercar
silencer
fire-edge
Tineidae
videndum
disendow
fireweed
pike-head
△miserere
tiger-eye
vine-leaf
cinereal
live-well
sidereal
wire-heel
nineteen
vice-dean
wire-sewn
ciseleur
rice-beer
fineless
fineness
fireless
hiveless
lifeless
likeness
niceness
pipeless
rifeness
ripeness
riteless
tideless
timeless
tireless
viceless
vileness
wideness
wifeless
wireless
wiseness
witeless
hive-nest
lifebelt
life-rent
virement
videofit
river-god
river-hog
dimethyl
fireship
sideshow
fire-bird
liveried

Words marked △ may be spelled also with a capital letter

rice-bird
dimerise
dimerize
fireside
five-line
hivelike
lifelike
lifeline
life-size
lifetime
likewise
mimetite
nine-mile
pipelike
pipeline
piperine
pipe-wine
riverine
sideline
siderite
sidewise
sirenise
sirenize
viperine
wifelike
wise-like
zibeline
hireling
libeling
nidering
riveting
sideling
tireling
vice-king
videoing
wiseling
file-fish
line-fish
liverish
pipefish
tigerish
tilefish
viperish
vixenish
fire-risk
limerick
sidekick
biserial
tidemill
time-bill
dimerism
dioecism
tigerism
limekiln
Milesian
Sikelian
sirenian
fivepins
kinesics
kinetics
niceties

ninepins
nineties
Siceliot
Sikeliot
fidelity
livelily
ciderkin
wineskin
bi-weekly
libelled
rivelled
vine-clad
libellee
rice-glue
fire-flag
fire-plug
vitellin
sideslip
libeller
micellar
vitellus
fire-plow
cineplex
dice-play
fire-clay
lineally
pipeclay
linesman
riverman
sidesman
tidesman
nine-inch
hibernal
Zigeuner
pigeonry
dive-bomb
fire-bomb
firewood
fivefold
lifehold
lime-wood
livelood
ninefold
pinewood
sideroad
wifehood
wivehood
cicerone
fire-bote
lifesome
literose
nine-hole
sidenote
time-zone
tiresome
wirewove
lifelong
livelong
sidelong
ciceroni
fire-hook

firelock
firework
life-work
pilework
pipework
sidelock
tide-lock
wirework
dice-coal
pine-wool
fireworm
pile-worm
wireworm
live-born
time-worn
rice-soup
dimerous
libelous
viperous
diner-out
lifeboat
mile-post
nine-foot
pilewort
pipewort
mirepoix
widebody
fire-opal
fine-spun
lifespan
wide-open
wide-area
dimetric
lime-tree
pipe-tree
dihedral
disenrol
mire-drum
dihedron
fire-trap
vine-prop
firearms
sidearms
firebrat
liver-rot
river-rat
fine-draw
wiredraw
bi-yearly
linearly
diseased
licensed
cineaste
cinéaste
licensee
finesser
licenser
licensor
diversly
dicentra
lineated

pileated
rivetted
bidental
pipe-stem
fire-step
sidestep
bisector
digester
director
mimester
sin-eater
pimentos
videotex
directly
misentry
silently
ciselure
fine-tune
fire-tube
sinecure
Nibelung
tile-hung
bisexual
ritenuto
pipefuls
lifebuoy
lime-twig
giveaway
give-away
hide-away
riverway
live-axle
fire-eyed
wide-eyed
nine-eyes
airframe
giff-gaff
niffnaff
riff-raff
hip-flask
diffract
pig-faced
airfield
midfield
misfield
oilfield
disflesh
siffleur
piffling
misfaith
misfeign
misfalne
fitfully
sinfully
wilfully
sinfonia
disfrock
zip-front
oil-fired
air-force
pilferer

pifferos
diffused
diffuser
disfavor
oil-gland
disgrace
disgrade
misgraff
jingbang
airgraph
biograph
diagraph
ring-bark
ring-mark
ring-walk
ringtail
ring-tail
ring-wall
dingbats
nit-grass
rib-grass
ringhals
misgraft
diggable
singable
zingiber
liegedom
wingedly
kingless
ringless
wingless
wingbeat
pinguefy
siege-gun
kingship
wing-shot
king-bird
disguise
king-like
king-size
linguine
misguide
ringside
ring-time
ringwise
giggling
higgling
kingling
mingling
niggling
pingling
ridgling
singeing
singling
sing-sing
tingeing
tingling
wingding
jingoish
kingfish
tinglish

8 □i□g□i

Yinglish
linguini
ring-dial
jingoism
jingoist
linguist
cingulum
kingklip
lingular
singular
gingelly
king's-man
liegeman
Virginia
biogenic
Diogenic
diagonal
virginal
diggings
virginly
kinghood
kingwood
diagnose
kid-glove
ringbone
ring-dove
ding-dong
Ping-Pong®
ping-pong
singsong
ringwork
ringworm
gingkoes
lip-gloss
king-bolt
kingpost
ring-bolt
wingspan
king-crab
fingered
jiggered
disgorge
lingerie
lingerer
ziggurat
king-crow
gingerly
diegesis
fidgeted
lingster
ringster
oil-gauge
ring-pull
disgavel
gingival
misgiven
ridgeway
ring-dyke
diaglyph
ginglymi
Mithraea

Mishnaic
Mithraic
△highland
nigh-hand
lichgate
lichwake
night-ape
mishmash
wish-wash
fish-hawk
highjack
fishball
fish-tail
highball
hightail
pithball
fish-farm
dishable
fishable
tithable
dishabit
light-box
dithecal
nightcap
night-dog
eight-day
withheld
high-tech
fish-meal
eighteen
fish-weir
high-gear
△highness
nighness
pithless
richness
high-test
mightest
rich-left
night-foe
lightful
mightful
rightful
night-fly
pishogue
night-hag
eighthly
withwind
fish-dive
fishwife
high-five
high-rise
pithlike
Vichyite
fighting
lighting
righting
sighting
lightish
rightish
tightish

high-risk
ditheism
eighties
ditheist
rightist
mightily
nightjar
fishskin
fish-glue
night-man
siphonic
lichened
sithence
biphenyl
diphenyl
siphonal
lichenin
dishonor
lichanos
siphonet
dichroic
cichloid
fish-pond
highroad
withhold
fish-bone
high-lone
Nichrome®
wishbone
fish-hook
night-owl
high-born
eight-oar
highmost
tithe-pig
high-bred
withered
dishorse
litharge
pilhorse
pith-tree
pichurim
hitherto
higher-up
ditherer
disherit
highbrow
withdraw
withdrew
litherly
dichasia
biphasic
richesse
sightsee
fish-stew
air-house
dishouse
ginhouse
fish-guts
dishevel
eightvos

tightwad
digitate
litigate
militate
mitigate
sibilate
silicate
tidivate
titivate
vicinage
vizirate
biriyani
dividant
litigant
△militant
mitigant
sibilant
vigilant
△visitant
limitary
military
vivipary
pitiable
vitiable
cicisbei
sigisbei
cicisbeo
sigisbeo
pitiably
△hibiscus
viliacos
dividend
vilipend
airiness
dividers
liminess
miriness
oiliness
pitiless
siziness
tidiness
tininess
wiliness
wiriness
diligent
dirigent
diriment
liniment
miniment
vivisect
divinely
finitely
viliagos
gibingly
finished
finisher
Filipina
oiticica
citified
vilified
ciminite

civilise
civilize
digitise
digitize
divinise
divinize
divisive
filicide
liripipe
minibike
minimise
minimize
miticide
rigidise
rigidize
silicide
similise
similize
sinicise
sinicize
viricide
viridite
viticide
dividing
limiting
visiting
diminish
dividivi
piri-piri
minidisk
lixivial
minipill
vizirial
dirigism
lixivium
minimism
△nihilism
silicium
Sinicism
virilism
civilian
division
Milicien
Sicilian
viridian
Filipino
Pilipino
vitiligo
vilifier
vivifier
civilist
minimist
nihilist
civility
divinify
divinity
lividity
nihility
rigidify
rigidity
silicify

timidity
vicinity
viridity
virility
vividity
mimicked
mimicker
mini-skis
visibles
filially
visioned
visional
pimiento
visioner
cicinnus
ripienos
silicone
Visigoth
filiform
piliform
pisiform
liripoop
sibilous
midi-coat
filioque
miliaria
filigree
siriasis
disinter
minister
sinister
vitiator
ministry
silicula
disinure
finitude
ridicule
silicule
dividual
kibitzer
misjudge
disjoint
hip-joint
disjunct
jiu-jitsu
ninjitsu
ninjutsu
kirkward
kirkyard
milkmaid
rickyard
nickname
kickback
milk-walk
nick-nack
pickback
rick-rack
tick-tack
hickwall
kickball
silktail
milk-warm
rinkhals
kickable
linkable
dinky-die
wickedly
dickhead
milk-weed
silkweed
pick-me-up
diskless
milkless
pinkness
sickness
tick-shop
kickshaw
rickshaw
sicklied
milklike
tickling
tinkling
milkfish
ticklish
tick-tick
sicklily
jickajog
kinkajou
nickelic
nickeled
pick-'n'-mix
sickener
pickings
jirkinet
milkwood
mirksome
sinkhole
milk-loaf
linkwork
picklock
tick-tock
sickroom
silkworm
kickdown
ginkgoes
kink-host
milkwort
pinkroot
wickered
milk-tree
pickerel
bick-iron
licker-in
picker-up
tinkerer
zikkurat
sickerly
picketed
ticketed
diskette
nicky-tam
linkster
picketer
Pinkster
ricketty
tick-over
miskeyed
pink-eyed
billiard
mill-hand
milliard
willyard
diallage
disleave
milliare
millrace
rillmark
milltail
uilleann
villiago
willyart
milliary
sillabub
tillable
violable
willable
dilly-bag
fillibeg
millibar
billyboy
violably
pirlicue
biblical
billy-can
hillocky
dislodge
villadom
killadar
silladar
field-dew
billhead
mill-head
pillhead
millième
misleeke
Niflheim
killdeer
will-less
fitliest
diplegia
dialogic
dialogue
killogie
diplogen
villagio
pillager
villager
mislight
silly-how
millrind
hillside
kill-time
dialling
fielding
yielding
bill-fish
mill-girl
disloign
niellist
diploidy
villainy
disliken
misliker
hielaman
rifleman
gig-lamps
diplomat
violence
airliner
bin-liner
cislunar
milliner
fillings
hidlings
△midlands
billfold
girlhood
millpond
nielloed
billbook
billhook
hillfolk
mill-work
pillworm
millions
hill-fort
pillwort
diplopia
filliped
milleped
milliped
Lilliput
rifle-pit
millirem
dieldrin
gillaroo
jillaroo
killcrop
dialyser
biolysis
dialyses
dialysis
△dielytra
dialytic
villatic
billeted
filleted
misletoe
ciclaton
mirliton
violater
violator
gillyvor
billowed
pillowed
willowed
williwaw
disloyal
diplozoa
dialyzer
filmland
firmware
filmable
gimmicky
dismoded
pigmaean
firmless
firmness
giambeux
pin-maker
wig-maker
dismally
diamanté
diamonds
pin-money
filmgoer
biomorph
mismarry
sigmatic
mismated
mismetre
mismatch
diameter
viameter
biometry
titmouse
bigmouth
dismount
Zionward
Biennale
kirn-baby
winnable
cinnabar
binnacle
pinnacle
picnicky
dianodal
limnaeid
Siennese
Viennese
Linnaean
signieur
giantess
signless
lientery
midnight
dianthus
bien-aimé
lionlike
fiendish
kirn-milk
biennial
giantism
signaled
signaler

8 □i□n□l

signally
bionomic
cinnamic
fisnomie
visnomie
cinnamon
misnomer
bignonia
mignonne
pianinos
winnings
minneola
kiln-hole
dipnoous
ligneous
signpost
pinniped
Diandria
signoria
vigneron
Dionysia
pianiste
finnesko
lignitic
limnetic
pinnated
signeted
bien-être
pianette
vignette
tinnitus
biannual
winnowed
winnower
Disneyfy
lipomata
bilobate
pilotage
dinosaur
Minotaur
bifocals
kilowatt
misogamy
disorbed
divorcee
divorcée
divorcer
siroccos
Girondin
disorder
misorder
linoleic
virogene
linoleum
mid-ocean
timoneer
Minoress
vinolent
pinochle
piroshki
pirozhki
Sinophil
finochio
ricochet
simoniac
cimolite
licorice
limonite
Minorite
nicotine
picotite
pisolite
sinopite
Timonise
Timonize
pivoting
vigorish
binomial
ciborium
rigorism
Timonism
nicotian
Tironian
rigorist
simonist
Timonist
minority
pilosity
vinosity
pilotman
pivot-man
widowman
ritornel
disowner
Dinornis
liposome
ribosome
ditokous
nidorous
rigorous
timorous
vigorous
kilovolt
kidology
misology
Sinology
sitology
vinology
virology
kilogram
lipogram
kilogray
Limousin
△sikorsky
timously
ridottos
risottos
risoluto
biconvex
kilobyte
Linotype®
ribozyme
misogyny
airplane
dioptase
dispeace
displace
misplace
tinplate
bioplasm
air-plant
bioplast
displant
pie-plant
tippable
hippydom
limpidly
dispread
misplead
jimpness
limpness
oil-press
diopside
disprize
misprise
misprize
rippling
simpling
pin-prick
△silphium
simplism
mid-point
mispoint
misprint
pinpoint
simplist
simplify
Hispanic
diapente
dispence
dispense
disponee
disponge
dispunge
fippence
sixpence
disponer
rispings
sixpenny
misproud
biophore
diaphone
displode
disprove
disproof
oil-paper
diapiric
dioptric
hippuric
zippered
disperse
dispurse
hipparch
kipperer
simperer
Hippuris
dispirit
disposed
disposal
diapason
disposer
dispatch
rispetti
rispetto
disputer
dispathy
lispound
diapause
displume
air-power
cinquain
disquiet
misquote
rib-roast
microbic
microbar
microbus
didrachm
microcar
wirricow
Pieridae
Pierides
microdot
pier-head
hirrient
fiercely
nitrogen
diarrhea
diarchic
diarchal
libraire
migraine
piercing
fibrilla
dioramic
fibromas
vibronic
citrange
vibrancy
citreous
vitreous
cirriped
mirrored
hierarch
hierurgy
micrurgy
vibrissa
nitrosyl
nigrosin
diereses
dieresis
diuresis
fibrosis
hidrosis
dicrotic
dioritic
diuretic
fibrotic
hidrotic
hieratic
aigrette
libretti
libretto
migrator
vibrator
vibratos
misroute
tirrivee
tirrivie
nitroxyl
miasmata
piassaba
piassava
first-aid
airspace
diastase
dissuade
misshape
misstate
tipstaff
pig's-wash
airshaft
piss-a-bed
kissable
missable
rinsable
rinsible
Dipsacus
△dipsades
first-day
diastema
airspeed
misspend
pisshead
misspeak
misspell
hipsters
jib-sheet
misspelt
misspent
dissight
pinscher
bit-slice
disseise
disseize
biassing
Riesling
tinsmith
dipstick
lipstick
pigswill
midships
tinsnips
tipsy-key
tinseled

Words marked △ may be spelled also with a capital letter

dissolve
lip-salve
missilry
tinselly
tinselry
lissomly
lip-synch
△pilsener
rinsings
△diaspora
misshood
bioscope
diascope
diaspore
diastole
dip-slope
oilstone
ribstone
sixscore
tinstone
die-stock
kinsfolk
linstock
fiascoes
miasmous
fissiped
fissured
disserve
minstrel
airstrip
diestrus
airscrew
Dioscuri
kiss-curl
minshuku
dissever
missives
jigsawed
diastyle
fistiana
tilt-yard
filtrate
misteach
liftback
mint-mark
distrail
gilt-tail
cistvaen
distrain
kistvaen
air-to-air
victuals
distract
distrait
bistable
liftable
pintable
tiltable
ditty-bag
ditty-box
bittacle

fistical
viaticum
tic-tac-to
distichs
misticos
birthdom
pintados
birthday
giftedly
gilt-head
lintseed
disthene
fistmele
fiftieth
sixtieth
distress
listless
△mistress
riftless
tintless
victress
mistreat
ointment
mirthful
histogen
vintager
airtight
giftshop
diatribe
girtline
pint-size
uintaite
birthing
dirtying
dittoing
littling
fiftyish
misthink
lift-girl
mistrial
histrion
histrios
district
filthily
mistaken
fistulae
biathlon
fistular
fistulas
pistolet
distally
wittolly
diatomic
mistimed
mittimus
miltonia
diatonic
Miltonic
mittened
distance
pittance

Nintendo®
listener
fittings
siftings
distinct
virtuosa
dirt-road
giltwood
histioid
virtuose
Vietcong
virtuosi
gift-book
tint-tool
Piltdown
virtuoso
dirt-poor
virtuous
tilt-boat
tittuped
pitty-pat
cisterna
listeria
△victoria
wistaria
wisteria
historic
littered
wintered
dipteral
littoral
pictural
dipteran
sitter-in
gift-wrap
titterer
dipteros
pictures
bitterly
sisterly
winterly
distaste
cistuses
hiatuses
dietetic
mistitle
dictator
lift-pump
distrust
mistrust
bistoury
mistryst
disusage
figurate
ligulate
misusage
simulate
titubate
figurant
simulant
titubant

titulary
liquable
liquidus
liquidly
virulent
minutely
liturgic
disunite
figuline
figurine
minutiae
virucide
vituline
tituping
diluvial
fiducial
diluvium
simulium
dilution
diluvian
diluvion
disunion
Siculian
Silurian
figurist
△silurist
piou-piou
disunity
aiguille
ritually
visually
viburnum
piquancy
liguloid
siluroid
sinusoid
bibulous
bicuspid
titupped
liquored
liquesce
sinuated
situated
sinuitis
nieveful
divvying
disvalue
sirvente
silverly
silvatic
disvouch
viewdata
fin-whale
viewable
pin-wheel
viewless
mid-wifed
miswrite
airwoman
pig-woman
bijwoner

airwards
mid-wived
midwives
mixy-maxy
tityre-tu
zizyphus
cityfied
Vinylite
pixy-ring
didymium
digynian
dicyclic
sibyllic
minyanim
pityroid
hidy-hole
didymous
digynous
dihydric
dihybrid
sitz-bath
mitzvahs
zigzaggy
dizzying
mizzling
sizzling
piazzian
mitzvoth
diazepam
pizzeria
ejective
ejection
djellaba
Mjöllnir
tjanting
skean-dhu
Akkadian
skiagram
skiatron
skidding
skydiver
skeechan
skokiaan
skullcap
skilless
skillful
skylight
skelping
skilling
skulking
skillion
skelloch
skeletal
skeleton
skimming
skimping
skimpily
skene-dhu
skinhead
skin-deep
skinless

8 □k□n□i

skanking
skinking
skinning
skinfood
akinesia
akinesis
eklogite
skipjack
skepping
skipping
skirling
skirting
skirmish
skerrick
akaryote
skyscape
ekistics
sketcher
skittish
skittles
skewbald
skewback
skewness
ekpweles
skywards
okey-doke
altarage
clearage
cleavage
flea-bane
floatage
floatant
pleasant
Alhambra
clean-cut
clear-cut
oleander
Oleaceae
Ulmaceae
pleaseth
cleaners
cleavers
alcahest
alkahest
Almagest
bleacher
alkaline
alkalise
alkalize
allative
elvanite
flea-bite
gliadine
illative
aliasing
allaying
bleating
bloating
cleaning
clearing
cleaving
floating
gleaming
gleaning
gloaming
pleading
pleasing
Albanian
Alsatian
illation
alkalies
alkalify
sleazily
algaroba
alkaloid
albacore
fleasome
clear-out
fleawort
aleatory
alcatras
elf-arrow
cleanser
oleaster
pliantly
pleasure
clearway
clubland
slobland
club-face
glabrate
club-haul
clubable
club-head
glibness
glibbery
slabbery
slobbery
club-line
blabbing
blubbing
clubbing
flubbing
ill-being
slubbing
clubbish
slobbish
clubbism
plebeian
clubbist
flabbily
glabella
globulin
globular
globulet
globally
alebench
olibanum
clubroom
fly-blown
glabrous
slyboots
club-foot
clubroot
ale-berry
globated
clubrush
clochard
blockade
blockage
glaciate
placcate
flock-bed
placable
placebos
clackbox
blackboy
placably
blackcap
black-cat
placidly
clichéed
all-clear
black-fox
glucagon
glycogen
elf-child
elective
blacking
blocking
clecking
clicking
clocking
glacéing
slicking
blackish
blockish
election
flection
alacrity
pluckily
glycolic
blackleg
placeman
placemen
placenta
glyconic
glucinum
floccose
blackout
glyceria
electric
glyceric
glycerol
glyceryl
electrum
plectrum
electron
glycerin
plectron
electros
plectres
electret
glucosic
glycosyl
glacises
plicated
placitum
block-tin
blacktop
elicitor
flichter
floccule
flocculi
glad-hand
clodpate
gladiate
eludible
bludgeon
pledgeor
gladness
bladdery
gliddery
sliddery
fly-drive
cladding
clodding
gladding
plodding
sledding
sledging
cloddish
clodpole
gladiole
gladsome
gladioli
clodpoll
alienage
alienate
ulcerate
blueback
alterant
alleycat
blueweed
bluebell
sleeveen
blueness
clueless
sleepery
alder-fly
allergic
alberghi
allergen
elder-gun
blue-chip
bluebird
△algerine
elsewise
ilmenite
bleeding
bluewing
fleering
fleeting
sleeking
sleeping
sleeving
bluefish
alienism
Algerian
allerion
ulterior
alienist
alterity
sleepily
fluellin
alveolar
alveolus
alderman
aldermen
alternat
Alderney
△bluenose
gleesome
fluework
bluegown
ulcerous
bluecoat
sleep-out
allegory
sloetree
allegros
blue-grey
alveated
cliental
alley-tor
alley-taw
fluently
alleluia
flue-cure
sloebush
bluebuck
alleyway
blue-eyed
sloe-eyed
aldehyde
olefiant
ill-faced
gliffing
cly-faker
all-fired
ill-faste
ill-fated
ill-faurd
all-fours
all-fives
sluggard
elegiast
flagrant
plagiary
slug-a-bed
eligible
eligibly
alogical
blagueur
slugfest

Words marked △ may be spelled also with a capital letter

plug-ugly
flagship
clagging
flagging
flogging
glugging
plugging
slagging
slogging
sluggish
plaguily
flagella
oligemia
elegance
elegancy
flagpole
flag-worm
slughorn
aligarta
oliguria
slogorne
oligarch
alighted
blighted
flighted
plighted
blighter
plighter
slightly
all-giver
alphabet
△glühwein
blah-blah
alchemic
elkhound
ale-house
although
ultimata
alginate
alligate
ultimate
plein-air
claimant
plainant
ultimacy
Pleiades
albiness
alaiment
plainful
sleigher
△almighty
albitise
albitize
algicide
fluidise
fluidize
plaiding
plaining
plaiting
plainish
albinism

alpinism
illinium
illision
fluidics
alpinist
algidity
fluidify
fluidity
plaidman
alliance
eloigner
cleidoic
albicore
ellipses
ellipsis
elliptic
cloister
plaister
slaister
illiquid
altitude
blokeish
elflocks
clambake
plumbate
plum-cake
slam-bang
△plumbago
blamable
blamably
flambéed
glumness
slimness
slimmest
flambeau
flummery
glimmery
plumbery
slumbery
blameful
plumaged
△olympiad
Alemaine
plumbite
slimline
blimbing
clamming
climbing
clumping
glomming
plumbing
slamming
slimming
slumming
blimpish
glumpish
plumpish
slimmish
plumbism
Olympian
△olympics

clammily
clumsily
flimsily
flymaker
glumella
plumulae
flim-flam
plumular
flamelet
plumelet
aluminum
flamenco
flamingo
elements
clamancy
clemency
slumlord
plimsole
glam-rock
slummock
△plimsoll
plumbous
alum-root
plumiped
plum-tree
climatic
climatal
clematis
flammule
plum-duff
Plymouth
blinkard
blindage
elongate
plantage
plantain
Plantago
plank-bed
clangbox
clinical
Blenheim
blinders
blinkers
flannels
flinders
glanders
planless
plangent
blankety
allnight
blind-gut
flanched
planched
clanship
clincher
flincher
elenchus
planchet
△klondike
blanking
blending

blinding
blinking
clanging
clanking
clinking
flinging
glancing
planking
planning
planting
plonking
plunging
slanging
slanting
blandish
bluntish
clannish
slangish
Blennius
flintify
flintily
slangily
bloncket
planulae
planular
plantlet
clonally
clansman
clinamen
Klansman
clangour
plenipos
plant-pot
clinique
planuria
flânerie
llaneros
plenarty
elenctic
planetic
plankton
glandule
plantule
blanquet
△klondyke
gliomata
allocate
allopath
pleonasm
Eldorado
allosaur
pliosaur
pleonast
allogamy
Pliocene
bloomers
bloomery
gloomful
blood-hot
bloodied
fluoride

fluorine
fluorite
blooming
flooding
flooring
glooming
allodial
algorism
allodium
Ultonian
bloodily
gloomily
Algonkin
floodlit
algology
blood-red
allotted
allottee
blood-tax
blood-wit
floodway
clypeate
slipcase
slippage
slipware
slap-bang
slap-dash
flapjack
slapjack
sliprail
slop-pail
elephant
flippant
oliphant
alopecia
clappers
slippery
slipshod
slip-shoe
slop-shop
slapshot
elaphine
flip-side
clapping
clipping
flapping
flipping
plopping
slapping
slipping
slopping
clapdish
clap-sill
glyptics
floppily
sloppily
clip-clop
clop-clop
flip-flap
flip-flop
slipslop

8 □l□p□n

slipknot
clupeoid
slip-dock
slopwork
slop-bowl
slipform
flypaper
claptrap
klephtic
flypitch
slip-over
aliquant
claqueur
eloquent
cliquish
cliquism
clarsach
clerical
altrices
cleruchy
clerkdom
floridly
clerkess
florigen
all-right
clerihew
flurried
alarming
blurring
blurting
flirting
glorying
slurring
clerkish
flirtish
alarmism
altruism
ultraism
alarmist
altruist
ultraist
florally
plurally
clarence
△florence
clarinos
clarinet
gloriosa
gloriole
glareous
glorious
flare-out
glory-pea
ultrared
plurisie
alfresco
all-risks
olorosos
eldritch
all-round
ale-stake
elastase
glissade
plussage
glossary
flush-box
blastema
alms-deed
glosseme
fly-speck
claspers
fly-sheet
ill-spent
blistery
blustery
clustery
flustery
plastery
blissful
blushful
glassful
flesh-fly
flashgun
glossina
allspice
glassine
Glassite
blasting
blessing
blushing
clashing
clasping
flashing
flossing
flushing
plashing
plussing
slashing
sloshing
alms-dish
classism
classics
plastics
classist
classify
flashily
glassify
glassily
glossily
classman
glassman
blastoid
blast-off
alms-folk
elf-shoot
glasnost
blossomy
plastral
alastrim
klystron
plastron
allsorts
fly-spray
closeted
blastula
floscule
oldsquaw
plus-twos
platband
flatmate
flatware
flatback
plateasm
flatways
plateaus
blattant
plateaux
clotebur
cloth-cap
elatedly
△flathead
glutaeal
flittern
slattern
blathers
blethers
clatters
flatness
flitters
glutaeus
plotless
ill-treat
blithely
clattery
flattery
glittery
slattery
slithery
sluttery
plateful
slothful
blotched
fletcher
clutches
flatwise
all-thing
blatting
bletting
blotting
clothing
clotting
flatling
flatting
flitting
fly-tying
glutting
platting
plotting
slitting
slotting
flatfish
flattish
sluttish
clothier
glitzier
glitzily
clitella
flotilla
glutelin
platelet
glutamic
ill-timed
plateman
old-timer
platanna
platinic
△platonic
△plutonic
platinum
Platanus
plethora
flatlong
flatworm
platform
flatuous
flatboat
flat-foot
gluttony
platypus
ulstered
clithral
clitoral
elaterin
flatiron
clitoris
Ulothrix
platysma
flatuses
fly-tower
cloudage
ill-usage
alguacil
flounder
fly-under
sloughed
plougher
sloucher
allusive
illumine
illusive
plaudite
plausive
alluring
clouding
flourish
alluvial
illuvial
alluvium
illuvium
allusion
alluvion
Claudian
illusion
plaudits
flautist
cloudily
pleurisy
cloudlet
alburnum
glaucoma
aleurone
glaucous
illusory
claustra
bleuâtre
flaunter
clausula
alguazil
clavicle
clavecin
claviger
cleveite
Slavonia
Slavonic
eleventh
slovenly
slovenry
Pluviôse
pluviose
olive-oil
pluvious
clovered
slaverer
cleverly
clavated
elevated
Olivetan
elevator
slivovic
blowhard
blow-back
clawback
slowback
blowball
blowlamp
glowlamp
flywheel
clawless
flawless
slowness
clownery
blowpipe
clowning
blowfish
clownish
blowhole
slowpoke
glow-worm
slowworm
blowdown
slow-down
claw-foot
flowered
Old-World
old-world

Words marked △ may be spelled also with a capital letter

flowerer
floweret
slow-burn
alewives
flexible
flexibly
flax-seed
flix-weed
Flextime®
flax-mill
flax-lily
△gloxinia
flax-comb
flexuose
flexuous
fluxions
flexural
plexuses
flax-bush
play-mare
playmate
clay-bank
playback
clay-marl
playable
cloyless
cloyment
play-debt
clay-pipe
playtime
playbill
playgirl
Illyrian
play-list
clay-cold
claymore
cloysome
playsome
playbook
playroom
play-goer
playsuit
blizzard
blazoner
blazonry
blazered
alizarin
impanate
emmarble
smear-dab
ommateum
immanent
immanely
empathic
immanity
imparity
smearily
embarked
embanker
empacket
embalmer

impannel
embarred
impaired
empatron
impairer
impasted
impasto'd
embattle
imparter
amiantus
impastos
immature
Emmanuel
Immanuel
emaciate
amicable
amicably
smectite
smacking
smocking
emiction
emictory
omadhaun
smidgeon
smudgily
amidmost
amadavat
amperage
amnesiac
amberite
emperise
emperize
imbecile
emperish
imperial
imperium
impetigo
impelled
impeller
umbellar
amberoid
amoeboid
amberous
empeople
immersed
Emmental
embezzle
amygdala
amygdale
emigrate
emigrant
smugness
smuggled
smuggler
imaginal
imaginer
imagines
amygdule
Amphibia
omphalic
omphalos

omohyoid
amphipod
amphoric
amphorae
emphases
emphasis
emphatic
umpirage
ambivert
imminent
immingle
impishly
ambition
ambiance
ambience
omnivore
omniform
omnivory
empierce
ameiosis
amniotic
immitted
embitter
imbitter
imminute
smokable
smoke-box
smoke-dry
smallage
empleach
impleach
small-arm
implicit
impledge
smilodon
emulgent
smeltery
smileful
emulsive
smaltite
implying
smelling
smelting
smallish
emulsion
emulsify
smalmily
emplonge
implunge
emulsoid
amelcorn
umble-pie
smallpox
implorer
smallsat
amuletic
omelette
emulator
impluvia
amplexus
employed

employee
employer
emblazon
emendate
emendals
amenable
amenably
emongest
amandine
eminence
eminency
immolate
umbonate
embolden
emborder
empolder
imborder
impolder
immodest
immoment
imponent
impotent
smoothie
smoothen
smoother
smoothly
ammoniac
embodied
ammonite
immobile
impolite
imposing
ammonium
embolism
emporium
impolicy
impocket
ammonoid
embossed
empoison
embosser
immortal
importer
imposter
impostor
omoplate
omophagy
smorzato
smartass
emery-bag
embraced
American
embracer
amaracus
embraces
imbrices
umbriere
emergent
amortise
amortize
emerging

smartish
emersion
smarmily
ombrella
umbrella
umbrello
imprimis
amorance
amaranth
embryoid
embryons
improper
smørbrød
ambrosia
empressé
impresse
imprison
embrasor
amorosos
umbratic
umbrated
umbrette
amoretti
amaretto
amoretto
emeritus
emeraude
improver
emissary
amusable
amusedly
emissile
emissive
omissive
amissing
smashing
emission
omission
amusette
imitable
emetical
umptieth
smithers
smithery
smothery
emitting
emptying
omitting
smuttily
imitancy
amitosis
emptysis
amitotic
imitator
amethyst
ambulate
amputate
ambulant
smoulder
smouldry
impudent

8 □m□u□e

impurely
immunise
immunize
umquhile
immunity
impunity
impurity
ampullae
impugner
empurple
impurple
embusqué
embussed
empyreal
empyrean
empyemic
empyesis
amazedly
endamage
indagate
inhalant
unbarbed
unhatch'd
sneak-cup
enhancer
unbanded
uncandid
unwarded
unsaddle
inlander
inwardly
onwardly
unnaneld
unmade-up
innately
insanely
unsafely
unsafety
unwarely
unwatery
unlawful
enlarged
ungauged
unhanged
unpanged
entangle
untangle
enlargen
endanger
enlarger
uncaught
untaught
unbathed
uncashed
undashed
unpathed
unsashed
unwashed
unwashen
ingather
uneathes
unvaried
annalise
annalize
indamine
infamise
infamize
innative
invasive
unnative
engaging
inlaying
sneaking
sneaping
uncaring
unfading
unlading
unmaking
unsating
enravish
sneakish
uniaxial
invasion
annalist
insanity
sneakily
uneasily
unwarily
unbacked
unbanked
unbarked
unhacked
unmarked
unmasked
unpacked
unracked
untackle
unmasker
unpacker
uncalled
unfabled
ungalled
unhailed
unmailed
unsailed
untailed
unwalled
unfallen
intaglio
entailer
inhauler
enwallow
unhallow
unfaulty
one-armed
undammed
unharmed
unmaimed
unwarmed
encaenia
undamned
unearned
unfanned
unmanned
unpained
unsained
untanned
unwarned
enraunge
unpannel
ungainly
Ansafone®
infamous
undamped
unsapped
untapped
unwarped
ensample
encarpus
unbarred
unhaired
unmarred
unpaired
untarred
unfairly
intarsia
uncaused
unhalsed
unraised
envassal
sneaksby
unbaited
unhatted
unsalted
untasted
unwanted
unwasted
unmantle
unfasten
one-acter
annattos
infantry
unvalued
Antabuse®
undazzle
anableps
snobbery
enabling
snobling
snubbing
snobbish
snubbish
snobbism
anabolic
inkberry
anabasis
anabatic
unabated
unobeyed
snack-bar
unicycle
knackers
knickers
knockers
inscient
knackery
enactive
inactive
inscribe
onychite
unactive
enacting
knocking
unaching
knackish
onychium
enaction
inaction
unscaled
inoculum
unicolor
insculpt
anaconda
aniconic
ensconce
insconce
anechoic
anecdote
inscroll
knockout
enacture
inedible
Cnidaria
unadored
inedited
unedited
unrepaid
antedate
enterate
under-age
antenati
underarm
unrepair
antepast
interact
underact
untenant
underbid
unwebbed
enfeeble
ensemble
under-boy
underbuy
unfenced
intercom
intercut
undercut
enneadic
intended
unbedded
unbended
undeeded
underdid
unheeded
unleaded
unneeded
unseeded
untended
unwedded
unweeded
underdog
unfeudal
unseldom
engender
entender
Enzedder
intender
untender
antecede
knee-jerk
unbeseem
Angeleno
knee-deep
interess
antevert
indecent
inherent
interest
unbereft
undecent
undesert
underfed
underfur
unbegged
unhedged
enveigle
inveagle
inveigle
enneagon
sneeshan
sneeshin
untether
unnethes
△**angelica**
Annelida
antefixa
undefied
andesine
andesite
ankerite
anserine
inferiae
undefide
unbelief
entering
indexing
sneering
sneezing
unseeing
knee-high
endemial
ungenial
endemism
ingenium
annexion

Words marked △ may be spelled also with a capital letter

inhesion
unbenign
anterior
inferior
interior
unsexist
under-jaw
invecked
undecked
unrecked
angekkok
unfelled
unhealed
unpeeled
unsealed
unveiled
underlie
unhealth
underlap
underlip
annealer
unveiler
entellus
underlet
interlay
underlay
unreally
endermic
unhelmed
unseamed
underman
intermit
intermix
unseemly
unkenned
unpenned
unreined
unweaned
unweened
unyeaned
antennae
enceinte
internee
antennal
enkernel
infernal
internal
unkennel
antennas
infernos
internet
unheroic
anaerobe
antelope
envelope
kneehole
anteroom
ante-post
undevout
unhelped
unreaped

unpeople
Interpol
underpin
unheppen
unweapon
untemper
underpay
endeared
inferred
interred
unfeared
ungeared
unpeered
enhearse
inhearse
unhearse
anhedral
integral
underrun
an-heires
unlearnt
unsecret
interrex
undersea
unleased
unsensed
unversed
Anderson
unperson
unreason
unseason
incenser
incensor
Intelsat
underset
intersex
undersay
undersky
enfested
indebted
indented
infefted
inserted
invected
inverted
unbelted
unheated
unmelted
unnetted
unseated
untented
untested
unvented
unvetted
unwetted
incentre
intertie
ungentle
unsettle
invertin
unbeaten

knee-stop
ancestor
anteater
enfetter
inceptor
indenter
infector
injector
inserter
inventor
inverter
invertor
investor
onsetter
unfetter
undertow
ancestry
intently
ungently
unmeetly
infecund
annexure
insecure
underuse
unsexual
unnerved
interval
endeavor
once-over
interwar
underwit
underway
endeixis
unseized
unafraid
knife-box
snuffbox
knife-boy
snifters
snuffers
sniffing
snuffing
unifying
sniffily
sniffler
snuffler
unifilar
sniffles
snuffles
knife-man
snugness
snuggery
anagogic
snagging
snugging
sniggler
knightly
anaglyph
inchoate
inch-tape
ensheath

enthrall
inthrall
unshaded
unshadow
enshield
unthread
inchmeal
enshrine
inshrine
unthrift
on-the-job
unshaked
unshaken
anthelia
anthelix
enthalpy
anthemia
unrhymed
unshamed
unchancy
enshroud
unshroud
enthrone
unthrone
inch-worm
unshaped
unshapen
enchoric
unshared
encharge
one-horse
uncharge
unchurch
anchoret
enchased
unchaste
unchosen
anthesis
enthetic
unthatch
unshrubd
unshaved
unshaven
unchewed
unthawed
Anthozoa
intifada
unvizard
anti-fade
enfilade
ensilage
envisage
indicate
intimate
uncinate
antimask
antitank
incitant
indicant
intimacy
unribbed

enviable
inviable
unviable
unlimber
enviably
encircle
ungilded
ungirded
unlidded
unminded
engirdle
enkindle
unriddle
unwisdom
unbidden
unhidden
unridden
unkindly
antisera
one-idea'd
indigene
inficete
unlineal
anti-hero
engineer
inkiness
incident
indigent
indigest
indirect
enginery
entirely
entirety
snailery
unlikely
unlively
untimely
unwifely
unwisely
unwilful
enridged
unhinged
unrigged
unringed
untinged
unwigged
unwinged
unkingly
unfished
unwished
antiphon
anti-chip
antiship
unbishop
encipher
uncipher
antithet
unpitied
anticize
incisive
infinite

8 □n□i□i

undivine
enticing
inviting
ungiving
unliving
untiring
indicial
unfilial
incivism
indicium
intimism
oncidium
undinism
envision
incision
antiriot
intimist
infinity
intimity
unfixity
untidily
anticked
antiskid
unlicked
unlinked
unmilked
unpicked
unpinked
unsicker
unfilled
unmilled
unrifled
untilled
untitled
unwilled
unwieldy
undimmed
unfilmed
Indiaman
angiomas
infirmly
insignia
unpinned
unsigned
untinned
ancients
ensigncy
antidote
Antilope
antinode
antipode
antipole
antipope
anti-lock
anti-roll
ensiform
unciform
anticous
environs
indigoes
antibody
antilogy
antimony
antinomy
incisory
undipped
unripped
enfierce
encierro
gneissic
unbiased
unkissed
unmissed
Anointed
unbitted
undinted
unfitted
ungifted
unlisted
unsifted
indictee
unvirtue
anointer
antistat
incisure
intitule
antirust
unviewed
antitype
snake-oil
snake-pit
angklung
antliate
enallage
unpliant
unilobed
unilobar
analecta
unplaced
unsliced
Anglican
analects
included
influent
analogic
analogue
analogon
in-flight
unallied
analcime
analcite
unsluice
unslaked
analemma
inflamed
unblamed
inflamer
inclined
unclench
one-liner
unbloody
antlered
unclosed
analyser
encloser
incloser
analyses
analysis
enclisis
unclassy
analytic
enclitic
inflated
unelated
enclothe
unclothe
unclutch
inflator
inflatus
uncloudy
enslaved
ungloved
uncloven
enslaver
unblowed
unflawed
enflower
inflexed
unplayed
unglazed
analyzer
inimical
animalic
animally
gnomonic
mnemonic
unsmooth
unamused
animatic
animated
animater
animator
unimbued
unamazed
inundate
inundant
one-night
unknight
unanchor
unenvied
unending
unaneled
on-and-off
uninured
endosarc
un-Mosaic
untoward
annotate
innovate
insolate
intonate
intonaco
endocarp
endogamy
uncombed
unforbid
untombed
undouble
unforced
unvoiced
enforcer
unfolded
unhooded
unloaded
unlorded
unwooded
unworded
unsodden
inholder
unfolder
unloader
unsolder
unlordly
oncogene
endoderm
entoderm
unsolemn
enforest
indolent
innocent
insolent
unhonest
endogeny
ontogeny
uncomely
unhomely
unlovely
unroofed
snootful
unjoyful
engorged
unforged
ungorged
unrouged
unbought
unforgot
unfought
unsought
unbodied
unmonied
indocile
unionise
unionize
unpolite
annoying
incoming
intoning
oncoming
unboding
unloving
unmoving
unmodish
unpolish
unsocial
encomium
△unionism
encomion
△**unionist**
snootily
unholily
unbooked
uncooked
undocked
unlocked
unlooked
unworked
onlooker
unsocket
engouled
enrolled
uncowled
unpolled
unsoiled
unsouled
enroller
informed
undoomed
unformed
unwormed
informal
unformal
uncommon
informer
insomnia
uncoined
uncoyned
ungowned
unmoaned
announce
inconnue
enjoiner
ongoings
unbonnet
endozoic
entozoic
one-on-one
entozoal
endozoon
entozoon
encolour
unjoyous
oncology
oncotomy
ontology
unlopped
unsoaped
incorpse
uncouple
unholpen
unsoured
endorsed
enmossed
unhoused
unpoised
unroused

Words marked △ may be spelled also with a capital letter

endorsee
unloosen
unpoison
endorser
entoptic
enzootic
unpoetic
intorted
unbolted
uncoated
unfooted
unposted
unrooted
unrotted
unsorted
unwonted
ungotten
unrotten
uncostly
unworthy
encolure
involute
insomuch
unsolved
endodyne
antonymy
anaphase
knapsack
knapscal
knapweed
ensphere
insphere
one-piece
unsphere
anapaest
snippety
snapshot
knapping
snapping
snipping
snappish
snap-link
unspoilt
snappily
unspoken
unipolar
unopened
snip-snap
anaphora
end-paper
inspired
unspared
snap-brim
inspirer
inspirit
Anoplura
unsprung
uniquely
inequity
△iniquity
encrease

enervate
increase
increate
inornate
inurbane
uncreate
encroach
unpreach
inerrant
undreamt
entreaty
inarable
unbraced
ungraced
unpriced
untraced
entr'acte
ungraded
untraded
encradle
unbridle
intruder
intrados
unfriend
enfreeze
engrieve
unfreeze
unbreech
unpriest
unartful
intrigue
androgen
anarchic
anorthic
enarched
anarchal
energise
energize
unpraise
knurling
snarling
snorting
unerring
inertial
entryism
untruism
entrails
entryist
enormity
unbroken
engramma
unframed
unprimed
entremes
intromit
encrinic
unironed
unpruned
entrance
infringe
intrince

entrench
indrench
intrench
encrinal
engroove
ingroove
enormous
inermous
intrepid
undraped
unproper
entrepot
entrepôt
infrared
antrorse
introrse
unbrused
unbraste
entresol
enfrosen
unarisen
unprison
enuresis
undrossy
untrusty
anoretic
enuretic
unpretty
unargued
unground
engraved
unproved
engraven
undriven
unproven
engraver
ingrowth
anorexia
anorexic
ungrazed
unprized
unfrozen
inkstand
unusable
unusably
one-sided
gnashers
unuseful
ants'-eggs
unespied
inessive
inustion
unisonal
oniscoid
inkstone
anasarca
anestrum
Ångström
angstrom
anestrus
anisette

inositol
inasmuch
initiate
one-track
unsteady
instable
unstable
unitedly
anathema
knotweed
on-stream
knitwear
instress
knotless
snottery
unstuffy
snatcher
snitcher
gnathite
anything
gnatling
knitting
knotting
unstring
snottily
Gnetales
knittles
anatomic
unatoned
instance
instinct
instancy
knot-hole
one-to-one
knotwork
unctuous
anatropy
unstarch
unstated
unstitch
unstrung
unstruck
instruct
unstayed
Annulata
Ungulata
angulate
annulate
inaurate
incubate
indurate
inhumane
inhumate
insulate
intubate
undulate
ungulate
insurant
undulant
uncurbed
undubbed

unrubbed
unturbid
encumber
unbudded
unfunded
unguided
unbundle
unburden
unsued-to
unmuffle
unruffle
unpurged
enhunger
indulger
unvulgar
an-hungry
unburied
enlumine
induciae
induline
induviae
infusive
enduring
ennuying
indusial
induvial
aneurism
indusium
infusion
unsucked
untucked
unbuckle
insucken
Anguilla
annulled
unculled
uncurled
undulled
unpulled
annually
unguilty
ungummed
unsummed
unburned
unsunned
unturned
inguinal
innuendo
annulose
undulose
anourous
incubous
undulous
infusory
anguiped
unsupple
incurred
unfurred
enquirer
inquirer
unburrow

8 □n□u□t

intuited
unhunted
unquoted
unsuited
inductee
unsubtle
unbutton
enaunter
inductor
inputter
insulter
industry
unjustly
incurved
uncurved
aneurysm
unmuzzle
univocal
univalve
snivelly
unevenly
universe
unavowed
snowball
snowfall
snow-capt
knowable
anywhere
snowless
snowshoe
snowbird
snowlike
snowline
snowslip
snow-hole
snowboot
snowdrop
answerer
unawares
enswathe
inswathe
unswathe
snowbush
unswayed
snow-eyes
inexpert
encyclic
ankylose
enhydros
encysted
rotavate
soda-lake
coranach
bonamani
tomahawk
bonamano
nowadays
donatary
Monarcho
romancer
tobaccos

monarchy
nomarchy
toparchy
mokaddam
notandum
colander
Polander
pomander
solander
cowardly
cowardry
monandry
towardly
Moraceae
Rosaceae
vocalese
Sotadean
voyageur
votaress
covalent
god-awful
pot-au-feu
coxalgia
Cocaigne
coraggio
botargos
podargus
do-naught
monachal
Jonathan
borachio
Monachus
pot-ashes
foramina
sonatina
boracite
botanise
botanize
conative
coramine
donative
dopamine
focalise
focalize
localise
localize
locative
monazite
moralise
moralize
nodalise
nodalize
nomadise
nomadize
notarise
notarize
polarise
polarize
Romanise
Romanize
rotative

royalise
royalize
sodalite
sodamide
solanine
solarise
solarize
tonalite
topazine
totalise
totalize
vocalise
vocalize
vocative
volatile
womanise
womanize
Romanish
tovarich
tovarish
womanish
conarial
domanial
gonadial
monaxial
notarial
conarium
domatium
donatism
localism
modalism
monadism
moralism
nomadism
Romanism
rosarium
royalism
solarism
solarium
solatium
somatism
vocalism
conation
donation
dotation
Horatian
jobation
Kolarian
lobation
location
Moravian
nodation
notation
Novatian
novation
Polabian
potation
△rogation
Romanian
rosarian
Rotarian

rotation
solation
vocalion
vocation
zonation
douanier
botanist
Donatist
localist
△loyalist
modalist
moralist
Romanist
△royalist
solarist
somatist
vocalist
votarist
locality
modality
molality
molarity
morality
nodality
polarity
sodality
tonality
totality
vocality
voracity
so-called
totalled
rocaille
corallum
moraller
movables
notables
tomalley
toxaemia
toxaemic
morainic
domainal
morainal
johannes
bona-roba
Coca-Cola®
iopanoic
nonanoic
coracoid
homaloid
Polaroid®
comatose
Vodafone®
oogamous
pomatoes
potatoes
tomatoes
voragoes
donatory
moratory
potatory

rogatory
rotatory
tomatoey
bob-apple
zoiatria
podagric
sowarree
monaural
podagral
Moharram
potassic
Romansch
mocassin
bonassus
molasses
cobaltic
monastic
△romantic
cofactor
go-faster
corantos
logboard
mopboard
hot-brain
zooblast
bombycid
morbidly
sowbread
sombrero
cobblers
combless
tombless
cobblery
sombrely
morbific
doubtful
bombsite
combwise
womblike
cobbling
doubling
doubting
hobbling
lobbying
not-being
wobbling
boobyish
boobyism
hobbyism
zombiism
hobbyist
lobbyist
gorblimy
corbeled
morbilli
tombolos
gor-belly
pot-belly
combined
Sorbonne
combings

bobbinet
tolbooth
doubloon
sombrous
bobby-pin
sorbaria
forborne
row-barge
zomboruk
dobber-in
mowburnt
cowberry
△dogberry
foxberry
sorbuses
sorbitic
combated
sorbitol
hobbitry
fogbound
pot-bound
boob-tube
fox-brush
mouchard
conchate
conclave
non-claim
couchant
morceaux
ponceaux
forcible
boschbok
touch-box
voice-box
forcibly
△coccidia
Coccidae
coachdog
conceder
roncador
forcedly
concrete
torchère
dog-cheap
botchery
louchely
force-fed
forceful
pouchful
voiceful
coccyges
colchica
godchild
coactive
conceive
botching
coaching
couching
notching
poaching
torching
touching
dobchick
coaction
Noachian
torchier
conceity
touchily
Roccella
concolor
torcular
Cocculus
zoccolos
coachman
Golconda
volcanic
joncanoe
log-canoe
toucanet
conchoid
zoochore
souchong
box-cloth
mouchoir
poaceous
zoochory
concepti
forcipes
hotchpot
concerti
concerto
sorcerer
moccasin
zoocytia
concetti
concetto
concause
conclude
concours
Foucault
hoactzin
Gondwana
bondmaid
food-card
woodland
woodward
woodyard
bold-face
good-dame
woodwale
wordgame
good-lack
holdback
woodlark
cordwain
gold-wasp
moldwarp
holdfast
Bordeaux
rondeaux
foldable
fordable
voidable
rondache
conducti
toddy-cat
soldados
rowdedow
rowdydow
sordidly
cold-weld
pondweed
word-deaf
woodmeal
rood-beam
how-d'ye-do
toodle-oo
goodyear
boldness
coldness
cordless
fondness
foodless
goldless
goodness
hoodless
lordless
loudness
roadless
top-dress
voidness
woodless
woodness
wordless
road-test
soldiery
bondager
woodshed
lordship
woodchip
woodchat
roadshow
woodbind
woodwind
goldsize
goodsire
goodtime
goodwife
mondaine
pond-life
roadside
△woodbine
woodlice
woodpile
boodying
fondling
fordoing
lordling
toadying
toddling
yoldring
dowdyish
food-fish
goldfish
rowdyish
toadfish
toadyish
hoodwink
goodwill
dowdyism
rowdyism
toadyism
goodlier
dog-daisy
non-dairy
woodskin
Goidelic
bordello
jordeloo
condylar
toadflax
gondelay
wordplay
moody-mad
bondsman
goadsman
roadsman
woodsman
condense
toe-dance
voidance
cordiner
Londoner
gold-ends
holdings
lordings
rondinos
tondinos
voidings
goldenly
mordancy
woodenly
cordwood
hoodooed
woodhole
woodnote
woodwose
wordlore
woodroof
cold-work
road-book
woodcock
woodwork
wordbook
wood-wool
woodworm
wood-born
wondrous
foldboat
rood-loft
toad-spit
bordered
doddered
powdered
wondered
bouderie
foedarie
rood-tree
folderol
ponderal
borderer
dodderer
fodderer
ponderer
solderer
wonderer
corduroy
yonderly
road-user
lordosis
lordotic
goadster
loadstar
roadster
woodruff
toadrush
woodrush
sow-drunk
doldrums
rondavel
wood-evil
cordovan
holdover
foldaway
hobdayed
boneyard
forehand
foreland
foresaid
foreward
homeland
homeward
noseband
Romeward
Roseland
bone-cave
bone-lace
code-name
copemate
coverage
cozenage
foredate
forename
home-made
love-hate
Lovelace
moderate
notecase
somegate
tolerate
toleware
yoke-mate
rose-rash
comeback
fore-rank

8 □o□e□a

mopehawk
rope-walk
coverall
dovetail
foresail
home-farm
forewarn
rope-yarn
moderato
power-amp
someways
cosecant
cotenant
covenant
forecast
foremast
forepart
forepast
honey-ant
molecast
tolerant
cometary
monetary
novenary
rosemary
hover-bed
honey-bee
loveable
moveable
poseable
ropeable
honey-bag
money-bag
honeybun
November
hover-bus
homeobox
money-box
moveably
bone-ache
novercal
hover-car
Rome-scot
bone-idle
comeddle
fore-edge
fogeydom
noveldom
Poseidon
toreador
honeydew
honey-dew
nose-herb
bonehead
coleseed
forehead
forelend
foreread
pokeweed
sorehead
novelese

somedele
nose-leaf
rose-leaf
tone-deaf
foredeck
forepeak
bone-meal
forefeel
foretell
hose-reel
somedeal
foremean
foreseen
forebear
boneless
coreless
doneness
goneness
homeless
hopeless
loneness
loveless
moveless
noseless
noteless
roseless
soleness
soreness
toneless
voteless
zoneless
bodement
coherent
coregent
forefeet
forefelt
forehent
forelent
forewent
homefelt
love-feat
love-nest
love-seat
movement
non-elect
non-event
powerful
hover-fly
lozenged
somewhen
dogeship
foreship
popeship
comether
together
somewhat
foreshew
foreshow
forelimb
forewind
lovebird

cohesive
coteline
covetise
dolerite
dovelike
foreside
foretime
home-fire
home-life
homelike
hosepipe
lobeline
lovebite
monetise
monetize
nosedive
noselite
novelise
novelize
polemise
polemize
rope-ripe
roselike
soberise
soberize
solecise
solecize
sometime
somewise
vomerine
vowelise
vowelize
covering
coveting
foreking
forewing
honeying
lowering
modeling
nose-ring
popeling
rogering
sobering
toweling
towering
fogeyish
novelish
pokerish
rosefish
yokelish
homesick
lovesick
rose-pink
bone-mill
molehill
mote-hill
soredial
soterial
bogeyism
Docetism
fogeyism

nobelium
novelism
solecism
soredium
tokenism
totemism
Wodenism
zooecium
Bohemian
cohesion
comedian
Rogerian
hotelier
motelier
Gobelins
polemics
Docetist
forebitt
forelift
novelist
noverint
polemist
solecist
totemist
homelily
lovelily
foreskin
moleskin
bowelled
coverlid
hovelled
modelled
rowelled
towelled
vowelled
novellae
foreplan
hoveller
modeller
yodeller
△borealis
modellos
morellos
novellas
coverlet
coleslaw
foreslow
foreplay
role-play
bogey-man
Doberman
lodesman
moneyman
governor
solemnis
cokernut
love-knot
rose-knot
foreknow
modernly
solemnly

Copepoda
rose-comb
foretold
foreword
popehood
rosewood
solenoid
yoke-toed
borecole
borehole
dolesome
dove-cote
forebode
foregone
holesome
jokesome
lonesome
lovesome
nose-cone
rotenone
wobegone
love-song
codebook
forelock
homework
lovelock
morepork
notebook
ropework
rosebowl
foredoom
comedown
forenoon
home-born
home-town
lovelorn
foregoer
covetous
colewort
forefoot
foremost
honewort
lobe-foot
rose-root
fore-body
somebody
dowel-pin
homespun
honeypot
Moresque
dog-eared
dowel-rod
home-bred
lop-eared
rose-tree
love-drug
fox-earth
rose-drop
home-brew
forensic
honey-sac

Words marked △ may be spelled also with a capital letter

8 □o□i□h

coleuses
homeosis
somerset
Rodentia
domestic
homeotic
toreutic
forested
rosetted
forestal
lomentum
momentum
tomentum
fomenter
△forester
go-getter
lodestar
molester
nonettos
cogently
Coventry
covertly
forestay
forestry
honestly
modestly
momently
nocently
non-entry
potently
rose-hued
molecule
nonesuch
rosebush
bone-dust
love-suit
molehunt
moreover
rove-over
dove-eyed
mole-eyed
golfiana
box-frame
conflate
hog-frame
loaf-cake
hoof-mark
roof-rack
goofball
korfball
bouffant
dog-faced
confocal
confider
confrère
coiffeur
dowfness
hoofless
roofless
hoofbeat
solfeggi
dogfight
rooflike
sol-faing
wolfling
wolf-fish
sol-faism
forfairn
Wolffian
forfeits
conflict
sol-faist
wolfskin
gonfalon
moufflon
joyfully
woefully
confined
gonfanon
confiner
confines
Corfiote
soffioni
confront
conferva
coffered
conferee
rooftree
comforts
confused
confetti
confound
coiffure
forfault
longhand
bongrace
fox-grape
longcase
long-wave
roughage
long-haul
long-tail
longwall
poignado
long-hair
congrats
cowgrass
dog-grass
log-glass
longways
lopgrass
rotgrass
poignant
zoograft
congiary
doggy-bag
dough-boy
doggedly
rough-dry
long-head
Congoese
Congreve
ronggeng
long-term
jongleur
longueur
△**congress**
long-legs
longness
songless
congreet
lodgment
songfest
tong-test
longship
rough-hew
yongthly
songbird
long-life
long-line
long-nine
long-time
longwise
songlike
coughing
forgoing
goggling
joggling
tonguing
roughish
toughish
long-firm
Hodgkin's
Mongolic
coagulum
forgeman
Gorgonia
congenic
zoogenic
doggoned
congener
lodgings
doughnut
co-agency
zoogloea
conglobe
foxglove
longsome
mongoose
songbook
longhorn
mongcorn
gorgeous
long-togs
longboat
rough-out
long-spun
boughpot
doggerel
hoggerel
gorgerin
longeron
fougasse
Golgotha
boughten
foughten
Loaghtan
gongster
songster
tongster
long-stay
longeurs
longeval
forgiven
God-given
cowheard
mothball
top-heavy
cochleae
poshteen
cochlear
poshness
dochmiac
forhaile
po'chaise
dochmius
Rochelle
potholer
bonhomie
bothyman
nowhence
nothings
forhooie
pooh-pooh
sopheric
cothurni
sopherim
oophoron
Lothario
cosherer
cothurns
motherly
pochette
hot-hatch
foxhound
cot-house
cowhouse
dog-house
hothouse
log-house
pothouse
lothfull
jodhpurs
yoghourt
moshavim
boniface
cogitate
dominate
loricate
motivate
nominate
rosinate
solidare
solidate
volitate
komitaji
solidago
holidays
dominant
toxicant
volitant
docimasy
poticary
solidary
solitary
sociable
sociably
zodiacal
Moriscos
Gobiidae
louis-d'or
lonicera
Porifera
Rotifera
bonibell
coliseum
domineer
bodiless
boniness
boxiness
cosiness
coxiness
dopiness
doziness
foxiness
foziness
goriness
△holiness
nosiness
ooziness
poriness
ropiness
rosiness
lorikeet
moniment
bovinely
politely
foliaged
jowing-in
boringly
cooingly
dotingly
hopingly
jokingly
losingly
lovingly
mopingly
movingly
posingly
rovingly
wooingly
eolithic
polished
polisher
△**dolichos**

8 □o□i□h

boyishly
modishly
mopishly
popishly
tonishly
toyishly
codified
modified
notified
domicile
eolipile
homicide
lonicise
lonicize
logicise
logicize
mobilise
mobilize
monitive
positive
soricine
totitive
volitive
vomitive
folioing
ionising
ionizing
positing
vomiting
solidish
politick
conidial
gonidial
conidium
Doricism
gonidium
logicism
Molinism
solidism
dominion
logician
monition
nolition
position
Socinian
volition
politico
codifier
modifier
notifier
policies
politics
homilist
logicist
Molinist
solidist
docility
mobility
motility
motivity
nobility
solicity
solidify
solidity
tonicity
toxicity
popinjay
monicker
bouillon
cotillon
modiolar
Coriolis
△modiolus
zorillos
son-in-law
jovially
socially
non-ionic
éolienne
motional
notional
doridoid
hominoid
soricoid
zopilote
rosin-oil
coliform
coniform
covinous
dominoes
modiwort
monitory
vomitory
Eohippus
positron
goliardy
forinsec
komissar
kolinsky
aoristic
holistic
logistic
monistic
nomistic
poristic
sovietic
foliated
societal
podiatry
lodicula
moribund
lodicule
solitude
modicums
howitzer
forjudge
goujeers
conjugal
logjuice
moo-juice
conjoint
Dow-Jones
conjunct
conjurer
conjuror
△nonjuror
book-hand
bookland
cookmaid
dockland
dockyard
folkland
bookcase
book-mate
cookware
folk-tale
workfare
workmate
book-oath
bookmark
pockmark
rock-lark
cocktail
forktail
rock-fall
Hock-days
hock-cart
lockfast
bookable
cookable
lockable
mockable
workable
booked-up
polka-dot
forkedly
workaday
worky-day
forkhead
rockweed
workweek
monk-seal
rock-hewn
book-lear
workwear
bookless
workless
book-debt
bookrest
bookshop
pork-chop
workshop
cockshot
cockshut
cockbird
rock-bird
booklice
dockside
Hock-tide
corkwing
porkling
rockling
monkfish
rockfish
lockpick
workgirl
fork-lift
cocknify
rock-alum
locksman
Mon-Khmer
workings
corkwood
monkhood
rock-wood
workload
booklore
cork-sole
folklore
worksome
folk-song
bookwork
cookbook
rock-cook
rock-cork
rockwork
workbook
workfolk
bookworm
cookroom
hook-worm
workroom
book-post
cockboat
cockloft
folkmoot
workboat
cockspur
corktree
folk-free
cockerel
looker-in
looker-on
cock-crow
docketed
pocketed
socketed
jockette
sockette
cockatoo
lockstep
rocketer
rocketry
cocksure
folk-tune
dock-dues
forkfuls
work-over
lockaway
rockaway
soakaway
cockeyed
Cockayne
woolward
coalface
toll-gate
kohlrabi
woolpack
△woolsack
coalball
goalball
roll-call
rouleaus
foulmart
toll-bait
rouleaux
rollable
tollable
coolabah
coolibah
coolibar
box-lobby
follicle
pollicie
pollical
hoolican
foolscap
bollocks
pollices
soul-scat
soul-scot
hollidam
collider
colluder
cow-leech
dog-leech
roll-neck
woolfell
coolness
foulness
goalless
soilless
soulless
toilless
fowl-pest
colliery
toplofty
collegia
collogue
lollygag
collagen
hooligan
colleger
lowlight
holla-hoa
tool-shed
woolshed
soul-shot
coalmine
poolside
poulaine
poultice
boulting
jollying
moulding

Words marked △ may be spelled also with a capital letter

moulting
woolding
coalfish
foul-fish
tolldish
soul-sick
souldier
no-claims
woollies
doolally
loblolly
coelomic
coolamon
nobleman
noblemen
dolly-mop
pollinia
pollinic
coplanar
topliner
Hollands
Lowlands
moslings
moulinet
toilinet
dollhood
world-old
toilsome
holly-oak
woolwork
boll-worm
tool-room
fool-born
toil-worn
Coalport
foalfoot
goalpost
lolloped
collapse
lollipop
colloque
colloquy
collyria
collared
dollared
toll-free
pouldron
solleret
Lollardy
Mollusca
coalesce
△coulisse
noblesse
dolly-tub
poplitic
zoolitic
polluted
toileted
roulette
toilette
potlatch
bog-Latin
dog-Latin
collator
pollster
polluter
zoolater
toiletry
zoolatry
dog-louse
low-lived
low-level
top-level
roll-over
golliwog
gollywog
polliwig
polliwog
pollywig
pollywog
follow-on
follow-up
follower
hollowly
volleyed
wool-dyed
jolleyer
volleyer
formiate
room-mate
doom-palm
doum-palm
wormcast
formable
cosmical
dolmades
doomsday
wormseed
foamless
formless
gormless
dormient
tommy-gun
topmaker
formulae
formalin
formular
formulas
formally
normalcy
normally
doomsman
hormonic
hog-maned
commence
communal
hormonal
noumenal
torminal
noumenon
commando
commoner
coamings
commoney
commonly
dormancy
Hogmanay
zoomancy
wormwood
roomsome
wormhole
formwork
coumaric
commerce
commerge
zoomorph
non-moral
boom-iron
coumarin
tommy-rot
formerly
cosmesis
cosmetic
dogmatic
poematic
roomette
non-metal
commuter
doomster
noometry
pommetty
zoometry
dormouse
roomfuls
cornland
downland
downward
join-hand
townland
corn-cake
moonface
moon-gate
poundage
somniate
mooncalf
poontang
loanback
moonwalk
town-talk
cornball
downfall
down-haul
horntail
moon-ball
moonsail
round-arm
fountain
△mountain
tonneaus
downcast
mountant
tonneaux
boundary
corn-baby
coenobia
loanable
hobnobby
corniced
cornacre
corniche
cornicle
fornical
tornadic
joined-up
tornados
Tom-noddy
horngeld
moonseed
coinhere
corn-beef
hornbeak
rowndell
hornbeam
moonbeam
mounseer
countess
hornfels
hornless
moonless
pointers
rounders
townless
cornrent
downbeat
youngest
cornific
somnific
fountful
joint-fir
△roentgen
moonshee
township
Zoanthus
moonshot
downwind
coincide
cornpipe
down-line
downpipe
downside
downsize
downtime
hornpipe
low-noise
moonrise
noontide
noontime
bouncing
bounding
founding
lounging
mounting
poinding
pointing
rounding
sounding
townling
wounding
moon-fish
roundish
youngish
cornmill
downhill
hornbill
horn-rims
corn-kist
bouncily
woundily
coonskin
townskip
cornflag
roundlet
downflow
downplay
zoonomia
zoonomic
pornomag
cognomen
gownsman
soundman
townsman
mornings
fornenst
download
poon-wood
down-come
downhole
down-home
moonroof
coon-song
cornmoth
hornbook
hornwork
moonrock
joint-oil
cornworm
hornworm
down-town
torn-down
downpour
corneous
cornloft
count-out
downmost
horn-pout
hornwort
moonwort
cornered
donnered
down-trod
bountree
control
coenurus
cognosce
goings-on

Words marked △ may be spelled also with a capital letter

8 □o□n□s

zoonoses
zoonosis
zoonitic
zoonotic
bonneted
cornuted
top-notch
cornetti
cornetto
round-top
cornutos
hornitos
cornetcy
corn-cure
jointure
roundure
downrush
cornhusk
downturn
conniver
cognovit
moon-eyed
coenzyme
Notogaea
toxocara
honorand
cohobate
coronate
rotovate
sororate
coronach
monomark
monorail
motorail
coco-palm
monocarp
podocarp
colorant
roborant
sonorant
coronary
homogamy
honorary
monogamy
porogamy
motor-bus
Monoecia
monoacid
motor-car
moroccos
conoidic
conoidal
poloidal
toroidal
do-gooder
locoweed
Holocene
Togolese
solonets
homogeny
jocosely

monogeny
morosely
nomogeny
solonetz
cocoa-fat
toboggan
toboggin
do-nought
colophon
colonise
colonize
dolomite
monoxide
motorise
motorize
polonise
polonize
robotise
robotize
sodomise
△sodomite
sodomize
sororise
sororize
monolith
nohowish
bobolink
colonial
monomial
motorial
oogonial
sororial
coronium
motorium
oogonium
polonism
polonium
Boeotian
Dodonian
Polonian
Solonian
Colonies
robotics
colonist
monodist
monotint
motorist
oologist
jocosity
morosity
nodosity
porosity
sonority
sorority
motor-jet
co-worker
monocled
cocoplum
rosoglio
monoglot
motorman

notornis
cocoanut
coloboma
Podogona
holozoic
coco-wood
coronoid
corocore
horologe
locomote
monomode
monopode
monopole
monotone
soporose
iodoform
corocoro
doloroso
△locofoco
dolorous
sonorous
soporous
conodont
homodont
monodont
colotomy
dosology
doxology
homology
homotony
horology
lobotomy
monogony
monology
△monopoly
monotony
nomology
nosology
podology
pomology
posology
tocology
tokology
topology
△coloured
honoured
coco-tree
hologram
logogram
monogram
nomogram
sonogram
tomogram
colourer
honourer
mobocrat
monocrat
tomorrow
colossal
colossus
molossus

joyously
holoptic
Holostei
yokozuna
monohull
sonobuoy
motorway
gonocyte
holotype
homodyne
homotype
logotype
monocyte
△monotype
topotype
homonymy
homotypy
monogyny
toponymy
Zoophaga
soapland
tow-plane
volplane
soapbark
soap-ball
complain
cow-plant
zoophagy
compadre
poppadum
hopped-up
souped-up
gospodar
hospodar
torpedos
torpidly
codpiece
complete
morpheme
oosphere
toe-piece
morphean
compress
hot-press
Morpheus
soapless
box-pleat
compleat
complect
solpugid
compages
complied
complice
compline
comprise
co-optive
loop-line
morphine
porpoise
zoophile
coupling

morphing
complish
co-option
Pompeian
sorption
complier
comprint
zoophily
compulse
compiler
nonpolar
pompelos
cow-pilot
jogpants
pompanos
toppings
volpinos
top-proud
loophole
poppy-oil
soaproot
soapwort
corporal
zooperal
copperas
corporas
non-party
composed
compesce
porpesse
composer
hospitia
not-pated
compital
hospital
computer
zoopathy
compound
soapsuds
Porphyra
Zoophyta
zoophyte
porphyry
torquate
cotquean
△conquest
mosquito
non-quota
door-yard
gourmand
moor-band
moorland
door-case
kourbash
four-pack
doornail
four-ball
four-part
pot-roast
horrible
pourable

Words marked △ may be spelled also with a capital letter

poor's-box
horribly
touracos
worricow
worrycow
porridge
corridor
forrader
joy-rider
court-day
horridly
torridly
hoarhead
hog-reeve
four-leaf
yourself
doorbell
bourgeon
fourteen
dourness
journeys
poorness
sourness
sorriest
coarsely
courtesy
hoarsely
sobriety
horrific
mournful
non-rigid
porrigos
lorry-hop
fourthly
coercive
sourdine
to-bruise
boarding
coursing
courting
hoarding
mourning
sourcing
worrying
boarfish
coarsish
poortith
sorryish
door-sill
poorwill
coercion
boursier
courtier
to-broken
no-frills
courtlet
doorsman
doors-man
no-trumps
doorknob
courante
Sobranje
Sobranye
moorings
sopranos
sovranly
sovranty
botryoid
fourfold
sour-cold
botryose
foursome
hourlong
moorcock
moorfowl
poor-John
doorpost
four-foot
moor-poot
moor-pout
boortree
bourtree
pourtray
coprosma
touristy
Socratic
doorstep
doorstop
Botrytis
go-around
tournure
sourpuss
poursuit
corrival
co-driver
borrowed
sorrowed
borrower
sorrower
soaraway
sour-eyed
four-eyes
moussaka
mossland
potshard
constate
jobshare
log-slate
Lonsdale
potshare
moss-hagg
toiseach
forslack
foxshark
hog's-back
mossback
borstall
coxswain
bobstays
constant
forswatt
possible
horse-boy
houseboy
possibly
Popsicle®
goose-cap
horsecar
loose-cut
lopsided
house-dog
mouse-dun
consider
topsides
monstera
forspend
△godspeed
hogshead
potsherd
top-shelf
goose-egg
forspeak
top-shell
zoosperm
Holstein
dogsleep
forswear
△monsieur
mouse-ear
dog's-meat
forspent
boastful
houseful
noiseful
horsefly
housefly
goosegob
goosegog
hoosegow
sous-chef
cowslip'd
conspire
solstice
boasting
coasting
hoisting
housling
roasting
roisting
roysting
toasting
god-smith
forswink
joy-stick
mopstick
non-stick
bonspiel
pot-still
Volscian
moistify
forsaken
mousekin
bonsella
consulta
podsolic
consoler
consular
tonsilar
corselet
moss-flow
dorsally
consommé
Comsomol
Komsomol
hoastman
hoistman
horseman
houseman
Norseman
consumer
gossamer
consumpt
nonsense
loosener
poisoner
housings
Volsungs
cousinly
cousinry
Cotswold
dog's-nose
fog-smoke
forswore
hog-score
moss-rose
potstone
roestone
rot-stone
top-stone
zoospore
forsooth
forsworn
voussoir
couscous
kouskous
hot-short
dogsbody
dog's-body
zooscopy
gossiped
gossypol
gossipry
tonsured
conserve
construe
coistrel
coistril
coystrel
coystril
moss-crop
bowsprit
house-sit
corseted
cosseted
fossette
noisette
housetop
house-tax
corsetry
moisture
low-slung
forswunk
hoistway
horseway
powsowdy
boss-eyed
postcava
coat-card
△portland
postcard
post-paid
△boatrace
bootlace
contrate
footpace
footpage
foot-race
mortgage
mort-safe
postdate
postface
rostrate
rout-cake
software
voutsafe
foot-bath
footpath
koftgari
postnati
boot-jack
coatrack
footmark
postmark
softback
boattail
contrail
football
footfall
moot-hall
root-ball
softball
mortmain
contrair
root-hair
bootlast
contract
contrast
portlast
portrait
root-fast
contrary
costmary
mortuary
noctuary
loo-table

8 □o□t□b

mootable
portable
sortable
bontebok
cottabus
kottabos
post-obit
monticle
postiche
soutache
cortical
poetical
vortical
Toltecan
post-echo
morticer
cortices
porticos
vortices
Cottidae
hotted-up
rootedly
bolthead
goatherd
goatweed
goutweed
jolthead
mort-head
nowt-herd
softhead
portière
bottle-oh
fortieth
boat-deck
footwell
mortbell
soft-sell
northern
△southern
footgear
footwear
bootless
coatless
doctress
footless
fortress
fostress
portress
rootless
softness
sootless
wontless
footrest
rout-seat
sortment
mortific
pontific
loathful
mouthful
soothful
toothful
worthful
youthful
pontifex
cottaged
portague
portigue
Portugee
cottager
cottagey
soft-shoe
poetship
mostwhat
contline
contrite
contrive
doctrine
goethite
port-fire
portoise
port-wine
rootlike
tortoise
footling
goatling
jostling
loathing
mortling
mottling
non-thing
northing
routeing
softling
soothing
southing
tott'ring
fortyish
goatfish
monteith
bootlick
dog-trick
forthink
boatbill
foothill
moot-hill
voltaism
poetries
worthies
contrist
fortuity
port-winy
toothily
worthily
bootikin
cootikin
goatskin
Montilla
tortilla
coutille
footslog
portolan
portulan
noctilio
Portaloo®
hosteler
cost-plus
soft-slow
hostelry
mortally
postally
zootomic
bottomed
costumed
Northman
routeman
bottom-up
costumer
contempt
bottomry
continua
fortuned
boutonné
continue
fontange
portance
sortance
bostangi
fontanel
contango
continuo
montanto
softener
tontiner
contents
norteñas
norteños
root-knot
don't-know
moltenly
rottenly
boat-load
foothold
roothold
softwood
bolthole
bolt-rope
boothose
contrôlé
footnote
foot-rope
footsore
porthole
postcode
postpone
postpose
soft-core
zoetrope
zoothome
zootrope
boat-song
dogtooth
goat-moth
boat-hook
boot-hook
footwork
koftwork
controul
soft-boil
footworn
poltroon
soft-soap
goitrous
porteous
porthors
tortious
tortuous
footpost
goutwort
hoot-toot
hout-tout
poltfoot
zootypic
southpaw
boutique
montaria
dog-tired
tortured
tottered
boot-tree
cost-free
goat's-rue
nocturne
post-free
doctoral
dotterel
postoral
postural
△southron
contorno
fosterer
loiterer
mouterer
posturer
potterer
torturer
totterer
monteros
doctorly
porterly
souterly
contessa
portesse
cortisol
mortiser
soothsay
southsay
costated
toe-to-toe
footstep
aortitis
footrule
postlude
footmuff
foot-pump
non-toxic
zootoxin
cortexes
vortexes
copulate
lobulate
loculate
modulate
populace
populate
rosulate
conurbia
columbic
Columban
conurban
Columbus
homuncle
corundum
mocuddum
jocundly
rotundly
document
monument
co-author
roburite
solutive
focusing
hocusing
vogueing
botulism
populism
locution
non-union
solution
volution
roturier
populist
volumist
coquilla
toquilla
coquille
nonuplet
columned
columnal
columnar
volutoid
nodulose
torulose
nodulous
populous
locutory
colubrid
d'oeuvres
focussed
hocussed
mofussil
coquette
locustae
moquette
roquette
loquitur

Words marked △ may be spelled also with a capital letter

coquitos
coquetry
robustly
souvlaki
solvable
Corvidae
convolve
convulse
nouvelle
volvulus
convince
Corvinae
convener
convenor
souvenir
solvency
louvered
converge
converse
poxvirus
pop-visit
corvette
non-voter
convexed
convexly
conveyal
conveyer
conveyor
dog-weary
forweary
cobwebby
dog-whelk
bobwheel
cogwheel
joy-wheel
cow-wheat
dog-wheat
box-wagon
bob-white
non-white
toywoman
forwards
godwards
forwaste
dog-watch
fob-watch
pomwater
Norweyan
coextend
polygala
holydame
polymath
ponytail
corybant
polygamy
polypary
polyacid
molybdic
copy-edit
copyread
hony-seed

polygene
polyseme
polytene
polygeny
polymery
polysemy
coryphee
polyphon
bodyline
body-line
iodyrite
polypide
polypine
polypite
ponyskin
polyglot
Polymnia
polyonym
bowyangs
polyzoic
copyhold
cotyloid
holy-rood
polypoid
polysome
bodywork
copybook
cony-wool
polyzoan
polyzoon
polypous
hoky-poky
polygony
polypody
polysomy
roly-poly
polyuria
polyarch
rosy-drop
bodysuit
polyaxon
polygyny
foozling
colza-oil
douzeper
momzerim
mozzetta
bozzetti
bozzetto
bouzouki
appanage
uplander
upwardly
apparent
spragged
sprangle
upcaught
splasher
upgather
aphasiac
aphanite

optative
speaking
upmaking
apiarian
apiarist
sprackle
up-market
appalled
sprawler
spearman
sphagnum
spraints
sprauncy
speakout
upraised
aplastic
sprattle
splatter
epiblast
space-age
speciate
spectate
spiccato
epicycle
epicedia
epicedes
specific
apocrine
speckled
speculum
spiculum
specular
spicular
epicalyx
apically
epically
spaceman
specimen
spicknel
Apocynum
spacious
specious
spectral
spectrum
spicated
epicotyl
spadices
spadeful
spudding
upadaisy
spadille
spadillo
epidemic
spademan
spadones
spadroon
epidural
apodosis
epidotic
speed-cop
uppercut

splendid
spredden
splendor
spreader
appendix
ephemera
appetent
speedful
aphetise
aphetize
appetise
appetite
appetize
spaewife
speeding
apperill
splenial
apterism
apterium
splenium
aphelian
aphelion
Ephesian
spherics
splenius
speedily
sphenoid
spheroid
apterous
upreared
appearer
apres-ski
après-ski
appeaser
spreathe
spreethe
upsetter
appestat
spherule
upheaval
speedway
epifocal
opificer
spiffing
spoffish
apograph
epigraph
spyglass
apogaeic
epigaeal
epigaean
apagogic
epagogic
Spigelia
apogamic
epigamic
epigones
epigeous
spageric
spagiric
spagyric

upcheard
upthrust
apricate
oppilate
optimate
speisade
spoilage
opsimath
spritely
spoilful
sphingid
sprigged
springed
springle
springal
springer
sphinges
uppishly
aphicide
optimise
optimize
uprising
Aprilish
Ophitism
optimism
aphidian
Aprilian
ophidian
optician
optimist
sprinkle
optional
split-new
ypsiloid
split-off
apricock
ophiurid
ophiuran
splitted
uplifted
uptilted
splinter
splitter
sprinter
uplifter
aptitude
sphinxes
spuilzie
spritzig
spritzer
spikelet
spekboom
spillage
spoliate
spalpeen
spelaean
spellful
apologia
epilogic
apologue
epilogue

8 □p□l□i

Apolline
applying
spalling
spelding
spelling
spilling
epyllion
spilikin
opulence
apple-pie
epilepsy
appliqué
speldrin
opalised
epulotic
spilitic
epilator
applause
spillway
Apollyon
opalized
spy-money
epimeric
apomixis
spondaic
Spaniard
spendall
spunyarn
open-cast
openable
opinable
opinicus
epanodos
openness
spanless
spinneys
spintext
spin-text
spinnery
spinifex
apanaged
up-anchor
spanghew
spanking
spanning
spending
spinning
sponsing
sponsion
spinnies
spongily
spangled
open-plan
spangler
spanglet
spanemia
eponymic
spanemic
spongoid
span-long
openwork

spontoon
open-door
spandrel
spandril
epinosic
Upanisad
epinasty
spinette
spinster
spansule
open-eyed
up-to-date
splotchy
upholder
opponent
spoofery
spookery
spoonfed
spoon-fed
apronful
spoonful
aphorise
aphorize
apposite
epsomite
opposite
opposing
spooming
upcoming
spookish
aphorism
opsonium
aphorist
spookily
spoonily
uplocked
sprocket
upfollow
apron-man
uptowner
Epyornis
aphonous
optology
sprouted
uprootal
uprooter
spyplane
upsprang
Epiphany
epopoeia
apoplexy
upspring
epipolic
opopanax
epiploic
epiploon
upsprung
apophyge
epiphyte
opaquely
approach

spar-hawk
spur-gall
spermary
operable
sparable
spiracle
sporidia
sporadic
Sparidae
upgrader
spurless
aperient
sparsely
sportful
opera-hat
appraise
sportive
sparling
sparring
sperling
spirling
sporting
spurling
spurning
spurring
sparkish
spur-rial
spurrier
sparsity
sportily
spirilla
sparkler
sporular
sparklet
spirally
spermous
spurious
appriser
operetta
apyretic
operatic
spirated
spirited
aperitif
apéritif
operator
spiritus
opercula
Spergula
aperture
approval
approver
upgrowth
apyrexia
sparaxis
spur-ryal
Sporozoa
apprizer
apostate
apostasy
episodic

episodal
episperm
epistler
episemon
episcope
epispore
apospory
episcopy
upas-tree
apositia
apositic
opuscula
opuscule
epistyle
spatfall
epithema
spot-weld
△**spätlese**
apothegm
upstream
epithems
spotless
sputtery
spiteful
spitcher
epitrite
△spitfire
spitting
spotting
upstairs
spottily
spatular
epitomic
epitonic
△**spetsnaz**
△spetznaz
spathose
upstroke
spittoon
aphthous
epitases
epitasis
apatetic
spousage
spousals
sprucely
appuying
spouting
opiumism
spruiker
upturned
oppugner
aplustre
splutter
upcurved
spivvery
spavined
spaw-well
spawning
spryness
sphygmic

sphygmus
Squamata
aquacade
squamate
squabash
aquanaut
squabble
squaccos
squaddie
squander
squalene
squarely
squasher
equalise
equalize
squaring
squarish
squarial
aquarium
aquarian
equation
Aquarius
aquatics
aquarist
aquatint
equality
squawker
equalled
squailer
squaller
squawman
squaloid
squamose
squamous
squadron
squarson
squatted
squattle
squatter
squamula
squamule
aqualung
squelchy
squeegee
squegger
squeaker
squealer
aqueduct
squeezer
equipage
squirage
equitant
squireen
squiress
squirely
squiffer
squiggle
squilgee
squiggly
aquiline
equities

Words marked △ may be spelled also with a capital letter

equinity
equivoke
equipped
squirrel
squinter
squirter
breakage
preamble
cream-bun
triarchy
organdie
trial-day
arrasene
Briarean
Priapean
arbalest
armament
ornament
arcanely
creamery
dreamery
ornately
urbanely
dreadful
dreamful
freakful
groanful
wreakful
triangle
arranger
arraught
breathed
wreathed
wreathen
breather
broacher
preacher
treacher
wreather
Arianise
Arianize
Armalite
Aryanise
Aryanize
creatine
creative
ergative
kreatine
organise
organize
treatise
urbanise
urbanite
urbanize
arcading
breaking
croaking
dreaming
drearing
groaning
treading
treating
broadish
freakish
triaxial
Arianism
ordalium
organism
priapism
trialism
Arcadian
△creation
Croatian
Graafian
Orcadian
ordalian
greasies
arbalist
arcanist
organist
triadist
trialist
creakily
croakily
dreamily
drearily
greasily
organity
triality
urbanity
break-jaw
breaskit
trialled
treadler
orgasmic
Armagnac
ordainer
breadnut
cream-nut
ergatoid
creasote
kreasote
break-out
freak-out
creatrix
Triassic
triapsal
orgastic
breasted
arrantly
errantly
errantry
truantry
armature
creature
treasure
△treasury
break-vow
broadway
cribbage
cribrate
trabeate
tribrach
crab-yaws
dry-bible
probable
probably
tribadic
drabness
crablike
crabwise
cribbing
drubbing
grabbing
grubbing
drabbish
crabbily
cribella
cribbled
drabbler
dribbler
fribbler
grabbler
dribblet
tribally
tribunal
crab-wood
cribrose
cribwork
cribrous
frabjous
tribasic
drabette
tributer
crab-nuts
orichalc
trochaic
braccate
brockage
croceate
cruciate
eructate
trackage
tractate
truckage
wreckage
proclaim
prochain
armchair
fructans
crucible
brickbat
tricycle
brocaded
fricadel
Dracaena
tracheid
preceese
tracheae
bracteal
tracheal
dry-clean
prochein
crackers
proceeds
priciest
crockery
trickery
graceful
wrackful
wreckful
crucifer
crucifix
trichina
crocoite
erectile
erective
fructive
practice
practise
practive
procaine
proclive
tractile
tractive
trichite
trochite
bricking
cracking
fracking
frocking
pricking
tracking
tricking
trucking
wrecking
brackish
trickish
practick
trochisk
brachial
brachium
erection
fraction
friction
traction
practics
fructify
trickily
crackjaw
trochlea
freckled
oracular
tricolor
truckler
bracelet
bractlet
tricklet
drachmae
drachmai
trackman
truchman
truchmen
truckman
drachmas
△draconic
arachnid
brick-nog
cracknel
trecento
areca-nut
precinct
procinct
trachoma
trichoid
trichord
trochoid
urochord
fructose
orecrowe
trichome
broccoli
gracioso
araceous
croceous
gracious
precious
tractors
crackpot
precepit
tric-trac
brick-red
precurse
tricorne
brockram
procurer
tractrix
précised
dricksie
crocuses
brick-tea
cricetid
brocatel
Cricetus
brochure
fracture
preclude
trackway
trachyte
graduand
bride-ale
eradiate
graduate
bride-bed
credible
erodible
gradable
tradable
credibly
△tridacna
producer
traducer
trudgeon
aridness
gradient

Words marked △ may be spelled also with a capital letter

8 □r□d□e

grodiest
drudgery
prideful
tradeful
prodigal
Bradshaw
fredaine
bridging
brodding
cradling
grudging
prodding
trudging
drudgism
brodekin
predella
tredille
gridelin
urodelan
brideman
credenda
credenza
mridanga
uredinia
credence
prudence
uredines
prodnose
prodrome
trade-off
prodromi
gridlock
gridiron
gradatim
creditor
predator
proditor
traditor
crudités
Bradbury
praecava
freehand
arsenate
freebase
tree-calf
free-fall
treenail
artefact
brief-bag
green-bag
friended
Greekdom
friendly
free-reed
Praesepe
freeze-up
freeness
treeless
trueness
praefect
pre-elect
greenery
grieful
greenfly
arpeggio
breeched
triethyl
treeship
breeches
free-shot
arsenide
arsenite
Graecise
Graecize
breeding
briefing
creeping
freezing
△greeking
greening
greesing
greeting
grueling
ordering
Friesish
Greekish
greenish
arterial
free-will
praedial
proemial
Graecism
Armenian
△artesian
Friesian
greenies
pre-exist
prie-dieu
breezily
free-city
greedily
orsellic
orielled
orseille
true-blue
urceolus
greenlet
freedman
freedmen
Armenoid
freehold
freeload
argemone
arsehole
Freefone®
gruesome
true-love
free-soil
freeborn
true-born
grievous
free-cost
free-port
Freepost®
true-bred
greegree
oriented
arrestee
△**oriental**
arrester
arrestor
Argestes
ardently
priestly
urgently
driftage
draft-bar
trifecta
trifocal
urnfield
drift-ice
crofting
grafting
trifling
draffish
gruffish
graffiti
graffito
greffier
craftily
triffidy
truffled
profiler
artfully
irefully
profaner
drift-net
driftpin
proforma
pro-forma
triforia
profuser
profiter
profound
drift-way
bregmata
prograde
trigraph
braggart
cragfast
fragrant
pregnant
tragical
frigidly
preggers
progress
trigness
fragment
froggery
groggery
priggery
grog-shop
drag-shot
dragline
bragging
briguing
brogging
dragging
drugging
fragging
frigging
frogging
frogling
prigging
trogging
broguish
frog-fish
priggish
priggism
proggins
druggist
Erdgeist
wriggler
brigalow
frugally
cragsman
dragoman
dragsman
Trigynia
erogenic
orogenic
trigonic
dragonné
original
trigonal
origanum
oreganos
dragonet
dry-goods
oragious
tragopan
frog-spit
Fragaria
progeria
erigeron
gregatim
brighten
frighten
dragster
brightly
armgaunt
drag-hunt
triglyph
Orpheans
prohibit
orthicon
△**orthodox**
Archaean
△**archaeus**
archness
orthoepy
archaise
archaize
archwise
prehnite
archaism
archaist
orchella
orchilla
prehuman
arch-mock
arch-poet
orthopod
trahison
orchesis
orthoses
orthosis
orchitic
orthotic
orchitis
archduke
archlute
art-house
try-house
archival
archives
ordinand
drainage
fruitage
grainage
irrigate
irritate
ordinate
urticate
arm-in-arm
artifact
irritant
ordinant
urticant
ordinary
fruit-bud
fruit-bat
brainbox
draisene
armigero
artiness
△druidess
trainers
orpiment
broidery
fruitery
fruitful
fruit-fly
erringly
pryingly
tryingly
ornithic
graithly
prairied
arginine
artifice
draisine
fruitive
troilite
braiding

bruising
fruiting
graining
groining
praising
trailing
training
brainish
frailish
Prairial
Braidism
druidism
troilism
Arminian
fruition
irrision
Orbilius
troilist
vraicker
articled
brailler
articles
fruitlet
trail-net
Arvicola
arvicole
pruinose
train-oil
irrisory
brainpan
arbitral
arrieros
artistic
truistic
frailtee
Orvietan
artistry
bruilzie
prejudge
frijoles
trekking
praktics
brakeman
broken-in
brokenly
brake-van
arillate
grillade
grillage
arillary
trilobed
preludio
trolleys
drollery
prolific
pro-lifer
urologic
prologue
arc-light
Araldite®
drilling
drolling
frilling
grilling
trilling
trolling
drollish
trillium
orillion
trillion
frillies
trilbies
trollies
trollius
trilemma
prolamin
prolonge
arilloid
arillode
gralloch
trilloes
trollopy
prolapse
breloque
prelatic
uralitic
prolixly
drammach
crummack
trumeaux
gramoche
dromical
bromidic
premedic
drumhead
premiere
première
cromlech
gromwell
Aramaean
brimless
grimness
grumness
primness
trammels
trimness
drumbeat
erumpent
trumpery
crimeful
grumphie
dram-shop
Brumaire
drumfire
Frimaire
grimoire
tramline
brimming
cramming
cramping
drumming
primming
tramming
tramping
trimming
trumping
drumfish
frumpish
trampish
Aramaism
cramoisy
grumpily
bromelia
Tremella
crumpled
promulge
bromelin
frampler
grumbler
premolar
trampler
trembler
trembles
tremolos
primally
criminal
crumenal
trominos
fromenty
frumenty
frampold
tramroad
primrose
trombone
crummock
drammock
drummock
crumhorn
krumhorn
cramboes
primrosy
cromorna
krameria
trimeric
cremorne
cromorne
gramarye
premorse
Trimurti
trimaran
gramercy
premised
promisee
cremosin
promiser
promisor
premises
frame-saw
kromesky
aromatic
dramatic
eremitic
primatic
trematic
eremital
primatal
prometal
gram-atom
tram-stop
cremator
promoter
promotor
prompter
trimeter
fremitus
Primates
promptly
Drambuie®
drymouth
brim-full
cram-full
premiums
primeval
Craniata
brancard
drunkard
iron-sand
brandade
frondage
frontage
ironware
truncate
bran-mash
ironbark
transact
irenical
ironical
irenicon
granddad
front-end
frondeur
grandeur
princess
frondent
transect
transept
grindery
orangery
princely
frank-fee
prankful
trunkful
wrongful
transfer
transfix
cranefly
branchia
bronchia
branched
prong-hoe
tranship
brancher
drencher
trencher
bronchos
bronchus
△trenches
tranchet
Araneida
brandied
crannied
frenzied
brandise
bronzite
iron-mine
Ironside
prentice
'prentice
transire
bringing
bronzing
cringing
drinking
grinding
grinning
grunting
prancing
pranking
printing
trunking
wringing
brandish
Frankish
prankish
brindisi
iron-sick
prandial
cronyism
eryngium
francium
Orangism
trunnion
frontier
bronzify
crankily
trendily
Brunella
△prunella
uranylic
brindled
gruntled
iron-clad
wrinkled
crenelle
prunelle
frenulum
franklin
prunello
granular
trundler
wrangler
frontlet
iron-clay
brinkman
frontman

8 □r□n□m

transmit
transmew
ordnance
brand-new
ironwood
frondose
ironwork
princock
frontoon
araneous
drongoes
eryngoes
wrongous
print-out
brine-pan
brine-pit
Arenaria
dry-nurse
front-row
iron-gray
iron-grey
prenasal
grandson
frenetic
granitic
uranitic
crenated
crinated
brunette
prenatal
pronotal
pronotum
pronator
urinator
transude
transume
tranquil
craniums
areolate
arrogate
priorate
△**argonaut**
arrogant
preorder
arboreta
arboreal
armozeen
prioress
cryogeny
armozine
arsonite
brookite
cryolite
ergotise
ergotize
erionite
trioxide
crooning
drooking
proofing
droogish

armorial
troopial
ergotism
creolian
Triodion
cryonics
arborist
armorist
arsonist
creolist
errorist
droopily
priority
criollos
brooklet
creosote
kreosote
arborous
creodont
bryology
oreology
arboured
armoured
ergogram
cryotron
groo-groo
armourer
brood-sac
cryostat
cropland
dry-plate
griptape
prophage
prophase
triplane
triptane
wrappage
kreplach
gripsack
trap-ball
trap-fall
frappant
proppant
trippant
tropical
tripedal
tripodal
drip-feed
drop-dead
drophead
grapheme
drop-leaf
trappean
frippery
prophecy
prophesy
trippery
trophesy
drop-shot
arapaima
dropsied

trophied
drop-ripe
dropwise
eruptive
graphite
traplike
trephine
tripwire
cropping
dripping
dropping
frapping
gripping
prepping
propping
trapping
tripling
tripping
wrapping
drop-kick
graphium
eruption
graphics
dry-point
pre-print
Trappist
preppily
propylic
crippled
propylon
trippler
propolis
drupelet
tripeman
araponga
arapunga
crepance
prepense
propense
propanol
trapunto
triploid
triphone
triptote
droplock
traprock
trip-hook
drop-goal
trapdoor
drop-wort
prop-root
troparia
prepared
creperie
preparer
properly
property
proposal
proposer
crepitus
propound

cropfull
cropfuls
wrapover
triptych
prophyll
trapezia
truquage
truqueur
frequent
prurient
prorogue
prurigos
pruritic
pruritus
brassard
aristate
crispate
cristate
crustate
dressage
dry-stane
frescade
ore-stare
pristane
prostate
trespass
brassart
grossart
erasable
crossbar
crossbow
trashcan
crosscut
presidia
prosodic
presidio
crusader
crusados
cross-eye
triskele
urostege
grosbeak
ark-shell
drisheen
△**brussels**
trossers
△**crescent**
△prospect
Prospekt
trashery
friskful
pressful
tristful
trustful
pressfat
presager
groschen
brassica
prescind
crescive
prestige

pristine
brisling
brushing
crashing
crossing
crushing
dressing
frisking
frosting
grasping
grassing
gressing
pressing
trussing
trusting
briskish
crossish
freshish
tristich
Irishism
prosaism
Erastian
pression
Prussian
trustier
crispies
prosaist
brassily
crustily
friskily
frostily
Prussify
trashily
trustily
prusiked
Griselda
cresylic
bristled
wrestler
crosslet
wristlet
trisemic
trisomic
Erysimum
freshman
Irishman
pressman
proseman
prose-man
trashman
presumer
crash-mat
presence
prisoner
presents
fresh-new
frescoed
prismoid
dry-stone
dry-stove
iriscope

Words marked △ may be spelled also with a capital letter

brush-off
grass-oil
frescoer
bristols
frescoes
griseous
gross-out
uroscopy
urostomy
crashpad
prosopon
cross-ply
cross-rib
preserve
fresh-run
braseros
grisgris
gris-gris
cross-row
crosstie
dress-tie
frisette
grisette
frustule
pressure
tressure
frustums
crossway
presbyte
prostyle
urostyle
frottage
protease
tritiate
urethane
bratpack
pratfall
protract
writable
critical
erotical
protocol
tritical
Triticum
frutices
erythema
frotteur
brothers
druthers
oratress
pre-teens
grittest
frothery
grateful
trothful
truthful
wrathful
froth-fly
protégée
crotched
crutched

wretched
britches
cratches
bratchet
crotchet
brattice
brettice
trotline
bratling
fretting
fritting
trotting
writhing
brattish
erethism
pretties
frothily
gratuity
prettify
prettily
wrathily
writhled
crotalum
prattler
Crotalus
brittley
brutally
prytanea
tritonia
protonic
cretonne
gratinée
pretence
pretense
protense
△**writings**
proteose
proto-ore
write-off
fretwork
grattoir
trottoir
grottoes
trot-cozy
critique
pratique
criteria
ureteric
urethrae
ureteral
urethral
△**brethren**
oratorio
Arcturus
urethras
preterit
writerly
britzska
Protista
bretesse
erotesis

protases
protasis
erotetic
protatic
protrude
△**protozoa**
brouhaha
traumata
croupade
frautage
groupage
arguable
arquebus
arguably
trouncer
grounded
grounden
grounder
trouvère
△**fräulein**
trouveur
groupers
trousers
argument
argutely
crousely
fraudful
proudful
troutful
trauchle
brougham
draughts
draughty
droughty
braunite
Ursuline
drouking
grouping
grouting
trouting
proudish
troupial
Freudian
argufier
croupier
groupist
triunity
troubled
troubler
grouplet
troutlet
croupous
ordurous
orgulous
trout-rod
frou-frou
arcuated
triumvir
creutzer
kreutzer
breviate

proviant
breviary
drivable
provable
provably
provided
provedor
provider
providor
bravados
privados
crivvens
provoker
groveled
traveled
trivalve
travelog
groveler
traveler
gravelly
trevally
gravamen
province
cravenly
previous
traverse
proviral
Proverbs
provirus
crevasse
provisor
provisos
travesty
breveted
crevette
graviton
gravitas
privates
grave-wax
driveway
browband
drawback
drawable
growable
brown-bag
drownded
draw-leaf
draw-well
draw-gear
browless
trowsers
browbeat
growlery
brow-tine
erewhile
brawling
browning
browsing
crawling
crowning
drowning

frowning
growling
prowling
trawling
brownish
crawfish
crow-bill
Brownism
Brownian
Brownist
drowsily
crownlet
trewsman
drawings
trawl-net
draw-down
brownout
crowfoot
frowards
brewster
frowster
draw-tube
wraxling
proximal
Fraxinus
greyness
argyrite
trey-tine
grayling
crayfish
grey-fish
grey-coat
tray-trip
trayfuls
grey-eyed
prizable
cruzados
cruzeiro
grizzled
brazilin
grizzler
prizeman
Trizonia
Brezonek
trizonal
brazenly
brazenry
grazioso
escalade
escalate
escapade
estacade
escalado
escapado
estancia
islander
escargot
astatine
Islamise
Islamite
Islamize

Words marked △ may be spelled also with a capital letter

8 □s□a□i

ashaming
assaying
essaying
essayish
escapism
Islamism
ossarium
escalier
espalier
escapist
essayist
escallop
assailer
escalope
escarole
assassin
aspartic
espartos
osnaburg
isabella
ash-blond
isobront
isobaric
isochasm
isocracy
isocheim
isochime
isocline
psychism
C-section
psychics
psychist
psychoid
isochore
isocryme
isodicon
isodomum
isodomon
asperate
assegaai
osier-bed
assemble
assemblé
assembly
Essencia
ascender
usheress
osteogen
asperger
asperges
ushering
asterisk
B-Special
especial
asterism
Essenism
Asterias
asperity
esterify
esteemed
islesman

asteroid
asperous
assessor
asbestic
assenter
assentor
asserter
assertor
asbestos
osteitis
usefully
usufruct
isagogic
isogamic
isogonic
isogonal
isogloss
asphodel
isthmian
eschalot
ischemia
ischemic
asthenia
asthenic
ischuria
aspheric
esthesia
esthetic
eschewal
eschewer
asphyxia
aspirate
estimate
estivate
oscitate
ostinato
Ustilago
aspirant
oscitant
espiègle
ossified
oscinine
aspiring
ascidium
aspidium
ascidian
astigmia
aseismic
Ossianic
assignee
assiento
assignor
assignat
assisted
ash-leach
isolable
psilocin
△psaltery
isologue
psellism
△psalmist

psalmody
psilosis
psilotic
Psilotum
isolator
psammite
isomeric
isomorph
isometry
isonomic
Isengrim
asynergy
assonate
assonant
ascorbic
Asmodeus
astonied
essonite
astonish
Estonian
psionics
essoiner
astomous
estopped
estoppel
espousal
espouser
assorted
assotted
assorter
aseptate
esophagi
ash-plant
isopodan
Isoptera
isoprene
isopleth
psephite
psephism
ostracod
ostracon
estridge
esurient
astragal
estrogen
ostreger
usurping
ostrakon
psoralen
astringe
estrange
usurious
espresso
tsaritsa
tsarevna
ash-stand
isostasy
tsessebe
asystole
isospory
isothere

isotherm
isotonic
isotropy
isotopic
esoteric
tsutsumu
osculate
osculant
issuable
issuably
esculent
astutely
pseudery
assuming
pseudish
astucity
Esquimau
issuance
espumoso
esquisse
Assyrian
ashy-grey
stearage
stearate
stravaig
stramash
athanasy
straicht
straucht
stranded
straddle
atrament
strategy
straggle
strangle
étranger
stranger
straight
straught
straggly
attached
straw-hat
steadied
atrazine
Ottamite
ptyalise
ptyalize
stearine
steatite
steading
stealing
steaming
steaning
straying
ptyalism
strabism
ottavino
steadier
stradiot
steadily
steamily

stratify
attacker
strammel
strained
straunge
strainer
steatoma
stratose
strap-oil
stratous
strapped
strapper
steapsin
Atlantic
straiten
Atlantes
Atlantis
stealthy
straitly
stub-nail
stibnite
stabbing
stabling
stubbing
stablish
stubbled
stibbler
stubborn
stoccata
stockade
staccato
sticcado
sticcato
stoccado
stickful
stacking
sticking
stocking
stiction
stockist
stickily
stockily
stickjaw
stickler
stockman
stuccoed
stuccoer
stocious
stockpot
studfarm
stedfast
studding
studying
stodgily
studbook
studwork
studious
stadiums
steerage
strewage
ytterbia

Words marked △ may be spelled also with a capital letter

8 □t□r□o

atremble
steenbok
steelbow
attercop
ethercap
ettercap
stretchy
attendee
attender
etcetera
ethereal
strepent
utterest
steevely
stievely
streigne
strength
streight
Strephon
Atherina
atherine
athetise
athetize
etherise
etherize
atheling
steeling
steening
steering
steeving
strewing
uttering
steepish
etherial
etherism
Athenian
etherion
etaerios
etherist
etherify
strelitz
streaked
streaker
steepled
steelman
steelmen
streamer
étrennes
atheroma
athetoid
attemper
stressed
stressor
attested
streeted
attester
attestor
attentat
Strepyan
staffage
stifling

stuffing
stiffish
stuffily
stigmata
staggard
stagnate
stagnant
stegodon
staggers
itchweed
atchieve
itch-mite
Stahlism
Stahlian
strigate
striddle
stridden
strident
stringed
stringer
Atticise
Atticize
ethicise
ethicize
strigine
attiring
staining
steining
striking
striping
striving
Atticism
ethicism
stoicism
ethicist
strickle
strinkle
stricken
Strimmer®
strigose
Strigops
Ethiopic
stripped
stripper
striated
striatum
atwitter
strictly
attitude
utriculi
stairway
stake-out
stallage
stellate
stillage
stalwart
stolidly
stilbene
stall-fed
stilbite
stalking

stalling
stilling
stilting
stiltish
stallion
stellion
stillion
stellify
stultify
stallman
Atalanta
Italiote
stalkoes
utiliser
ptilosis
styluses
athletic
stiletto
utilizer
stemmata
stumpage
atomical
stomachy
stampede
stampedo
stemless
ptomaine
stamping
stemming
stumming
stumpily
stumbler
stimulus
stamened
atomiser
stomatic
stomatal
stembuck
atomizer
stanzaic
standard
stinkard
stunkard
stannate
Stone-Age
stone-age
stunsail
△**stannary**
ethnical
stonefly
stanchel
stancher
stanchly
stannite
standing
stinging
stinking
stinting
stonking
stunning
standish

Stundism
Stundist
stingily
stone-mad
stuntman
stanhope
standoff
stand-off
stenlock
stentour
stannous
stanzoes
stonerag
ethnarch
stoneraw
sting-ray
stenosed
stenoses
stenosis
stenotic
stromata
etiolate
strombus
stroddle
strongyl
stronger
strongly
strophic
stooshie
strobila
atropine
Ottomite
strobile
stooping
stroking
strowing
strobili
atropism
atrocity
otiosity
strooken
stroller
attorney
atropous
atmology
ethology
etiology
stropped
stroupan
strontia
atmolyse
atmolyze
stepdame
stephane
stoppage
stuprate
stopbank
utopiast
atypical
etypical
stapedes

stupidly
stopless
stepwise
stepping
stopping
stapelia
stippled
stipuled
stippler
stipular
stopcock
step-down
stop-loss
stipites
stopover
star-pav'd
star-gaze
sternage
storable
star-read
sturgeon
starkers
starless
starters
stirless
startful
stormful
pterygia
sterigma
staragen
starched
starcher
sturdied
eternise
eternize
starlike
sternite
sturnine
starling
starring
starting
starving
△sterling
stirring
storming
Storting
storying
starfish
startish
eternity
starrily
stormily
sturdily
startled
pterylae
startler
storeman
iterance
sturnoid
stereome
yttrious

Words marked △ may be spelled also with a capital letter

8 □t□r□o

starwort
pteropod
starspot
starosta
sternson
starosty
uteritis
stardust
sternway
ataraxia
ataraxic
storeyed
stasimon
otoscope
statuary
statable
statical
statedly
stitched
stitcher
stitches
stetting
stotinka
stotinki
stotious
statured
étatisme
étatiste
statuses
Etruscan
étourdie
struggle
struthio
stoutish
Etrurian
strummed
strummel
strumose
strumous
strumpet
strutted
strutter
stived-up
stovaine
stowlins
stewpond
stowdown
stowaway
ethylate
staysail
ethylene
stayless
stayaway
rutabaga
pupa-case
runagate
Gujarati
nunataks
lunanaut
subabbot
Judaical
autarchy
muqaddam
mutandum
subaudio
subahdar
Musaceae
Rutaceae
Sudanese
subagent
humanely
nuraghic
eulachan
eulachon
oulachon
putamina
sudamina
bubaline
curarine
curarise
curarize
curative
eutaxite
humanise
humanize
mutative
putative
ruralise
ruralize
sugaring
tuna-fish
puparial
humanism
puparium
ruralism
sudarium
aularian
duration
Eurasian
lunarian
lunation
Lusation
luxation
mutation
nudation
nutarian
nutation
pupation
Rumanian
sudation
Turanian
humanist
lunarist
lutanist
muralist
ruralist
audacity
fugacity
furacity
humanity
queasily
rurality
autarkic
durables
autacoid
humanoid
fumarole
fusarole
bumaloti
ducatoon
hula-hoop
fumadoes
runabout
curatory
fumatory
juratory
mutatory
nugatory
sudatory
eupatrid
subacrid
subaural
Muharram
Muharrem
curatrix
Jurassic
Rumansch
Judaiser
curassow
mulattos
cunabula
hula-hula
cubature
Quaalude®
subacute
punaluan
subadult
eucaryon
eukaryon
eucalypt
eucaryot
eukaryot
△rubaiyat
Judaizer
cupboard
outboard
dumb-cane
hub-brake
outbrave
sunbeamy
curbable
hubbuboo
Quebecer
turbocar
turbidly
outbreed
subbreed
outbreak
dumb-bell
curbless
dumbness
numbness
turbofan
lumbagos
surbahar
dumb-show
purblind
sunblind
sun-blind
curbside
jumboise
jumboize
bumbling
burbling
humbling
mumbling
rumbling
tumbling
sun-blink
turbojet
sunbaked
quibbler
furbelow
rumbelow
tunbelly
turbaned
turbined
turbinal
turbines
sunblock
nut-brown
cumbrous
cumbered
cumberer
lumberer
numberer
outburst
sunburnt
sunburst
Burberry
lubberly
lumberly
△mulberry
sunberry
surbased
subbasal
rubbishy
surbated
sunbathe
Subbuteo®
outbound
dulciana
Furcraea
fulcrate
punctate
purchase
surcease
pub-crawl
subclaim
guacharo
lug-chair
outclass
subclass
nunchaku
runcible
succubae
punch-bag
Mulciber
succubas
succubus
Muscidae
muscadel
suicidal
duncedom
muscadin
Muscadet
mud-clerk
hurcheon
luncheon
huncheon
puncheon
putcheon
butcher's
butchery
cutchery
quackery
quick-fix
subchief
bunching
butching
muscling
zucchini
function
junction
munchies
munchkin
mutchkin
curculio
furcular
muscular
surculus
buncombe
curcumin
Dutchman
Dutchmen
Turcoman
dulcimer
Dulcinea
Puccinia
succinic
△vulcanic
succinyl
Buccinum
succinct
subchord
bum-clock
putchock
luscious
outcross
sun-cured
subcosta
outcaste
subcaste
quickset
furcated

Words marked △ may be spelled also with a capital letter

sulcated
dulcitol
muscatel
juncture
punctule
puncture
punctual
Quechuan
Quichuan
fulcrums
subcrust
Guicowar
gurdwara
quadrate
quadrans
quadrant
quiddany
fundable
guidable
buddleia
outdwell
fundless
hundreds
sundress
ruddiest
purdahed
quadriga
sun-dried
outdrive
bundling
fuddling
hurdling
muddying
puddling
ruddying
outdrink
Buddhism
sundries
Buddhist
quiddity
quiddler
guidance
outdance
duodenal
nundinal
duodenum
pundonor
puddings
puddingy
suddenly
suddenty
quadroon
outdoors
sundrops
subduple
sundered
murderee
subdural
murderer
sunderer
cul-de-sac
outdated
suedette
punditry
quidnunc
dun-diver
superadd
fuselage
gude-dame
numerate
pucelage
suberate
superate
tutelage
rugelach
Gujerati
lukewarm
suzerain
numerals
funerary
numeracy
numerary
tutelary
tuneable
auger-bit
superbly
tubercle
Lupercal
pudendal
pudendum
queendom
queerdom
funereal
tube-well
superego
mule-deer
muleteer
cureless
cuteness
hugeness
muteness
nudeness
pureness
rudeness
ruleless
sureness
tubeless
tuneless
suberect
supergun
dukeship
tumefied
duvetine
euxenite
gudesire
gudewife
juvenile
Puseyite
queenite
quietive
suberise
suberize
sure-fire
tubelike
△yuletide
cupeling
dukeling
queening
quieting
queerish
eugenism
eumerism
lutecium
lutetium
Puseyism
quietism
aurelian
Eusebian
Lutetian
Sumerian
superior
Dukeries
eugenics
eugenist
lutenist
quietist
queerity
superjet
aureoled
cupelled
luteolin
rubellan
superloo
nucellar
bucellas
duxelles
nucellus
queenlet
superman
supernal
fumerole
suberose
tubenose
tuberose
fusel-oil
numerous
suberous
tuberous
tuxedoes
eudemony
pure-bred
dule-tree
funebral
eupepsia
suversed
superspy
cuneatic
eupeptic
eutectic
pubertal
quaestor
supertax
nubecula
quietude
subequal
tubefuls
duvetyne
subframe
sufflate
suffrage
outflash
outflank
puffball
pug-faced
surfaced
sufficer
surfacer
gulfweed
outfield
subfield
bun-fight
gunfight
outfight
puffbird
surfbird
outfling
purfling
ruffling
surffish
gunflint
turf-clad
ruefully
sulfinyl
outfrown
subfloor
buff-coat
sulfuric
buffered
furfural
furfurol
furfuran
sufferer
dumfound
puff-puff
outflush
suffixal
mudguard
outguard
burgrave
outglare
subgrade
cutglass
nut-grass
sunglass
dung-cart
burglary
huggable
luggable
surgical
ruggedly
turgidly
dungmere
hung-beef
dung-heap
bung-vent
judgment
jugglery
surgeful
quagmire
bungling
juggling
lungeing
outgoing
lung-fish
dung-hill
hungrily
quagmiry
bungalow
pungence
subgenre
subgenus
burganet
burgonet
△burgundy
fulgency
pungency
bunghole
mungoose
dung-fork
lung-book
mungcorn
subgroup
lungwort
Bulgaric
budgeree
dungaree
puggaree
tung-tree
fulgural
budgeros
budgerow
hungerly
vulgarly
Tungusic
funguses
Tunguses
tungstic
budgeted
tungsten
gurgoyle
bushwalk
push-ball
push-cart
bush-baby
euphrasy
euphobia
Dukhobor
bushveld
lushness
muchness
ruthless
suchness
Cuthbert
bushfire
euphuise

8 □u□h□i

euphuize
fuchsine
fuchsite
push-bike
rushlike
suchlike
suchwise
rush-ring
△euphuism
euphuist
subhumid
subhuman
euphonia
euphonic
ruthenic
Duchenne
bush-rope
mushroom
cushions
hush-boat
cushiony
euphoria
Eutheria
euphoric
out-Herod
Lutheran
eucharis
duchesse
fughetta
zuchetta
Cushitic
Kushitic
nuthatch
zuchetto
bughouse
gunhouse
mug-house
nuthouse
outhouse
hush-hush
bush-buck
push-pull
Pushtuns
push-over
Tunicata
dubitate
fumigate
△jubilate
mucilage
muricate
musicale
mutilate
pumicate
pupilage
pupilate
ruminate
supinate
suricate
tunicate
sukiyaki
nudicaul

subimago
Buridan's
fumigant
jubilant
luminant
ruminant
rutilant
tulipant
culinary
luminary
pupilary
dutiable
△guaiacum
fusileer
mutineer
business
puniness
muniment
rudiment
futilely
supinely
musingly
pulingly
punisher
mulishly
mutinied
purified
auditive
culicine
cutinise
cutinize
fugitive
pulicide
punitive
subitise
subitize
quailing
mudirieh
judicial
pugilism
rubidium
audition
munition
musician
punition
auxiliar
fusilier
purifier
nudities
burinist
luminist
pugilist
cupidity
futility
humidify
humidity
humility
lucidity
nubility
pudicity
tumidity

tunicked
musicker
auricled
pupillar
audience
julienne
tubicole
auriform
cubiform
fusiform
muriform
nubiform
tubiform
luminous
muticous
mutinous
nubilous
numinous
auditory
fumitory
punitory
cutie-pie
Tubigrip®
furiosos
autistic
cubistic
juristic
muriatic
puristic
Sufistic
muriated
quaintly
△auricula
furibund
pudibund
rubicund
Punjabee
cunjevoi
junk-yard
buckrake
muck-rake
buck-wash
Gurkhali
duck-hawk
rucksack
duck-tail
musk-ball
musk-cavy
lucky-bag
lucky-dip
bulkhead
duckweed
lunkhead
buckbean
muckheap
buik-lear
Buckley's
duskness
luckless
sucklers
tuskless

ruckseat
buckshee
tuckahoe
junk-shop
buckshot
duck-shot
buckling
duckling
junk-ring
suckling
duckbill
tuck-mill
puckfist
buckskin
musk-plum
Turkoman
buskined
junkanoo
suckener
duck-pond
duckmole
funkhole
murksome
suck-hole
muck-worm
buckhorn
bunkered
suckered
buckaroo
buckeroo
Quakerly
junketed
huckster
musketry
muckluck
buckayro
Quillaia
Quillaja
full-face
full-page
nuclease
nucleate
sublease
bull-calf
fullback
pull-back
full-sail
outlearn
gullable
gullible
bully-boy
curlicue
purlicue
publican
bullocky
publicly
bullhead
bull's-eye
bull-beef
fuel-cell
dullness

fullness
nullness
purlieus
full-pelt
guileful
full-aged
duologue
mulligan
sunlight
bullwhip
bullshit
bullgine
full-time
nucleide
suilline
building
bull-ring
bullying
cullying
duelling
fuelling
gull-wing
outlying
qualming
quilling
quilting
sullying
qualmish
bullyism
cullyism
duellist
full-tilt
guiltily
sublimed
fugleman
quillman
quill-nib
muslined
sublunar
outlands
muslinet
sullenly
bulldoze
bullnose
duelsome
full-bore
nucleole
bull-hoof
bully-off
nucleoli
full-cock
bull-horn
hull-down
pull-down
quill-pen
bullfrog
bullyrag
mullarky
burletta
bulletin
furlough

Words marked △ may be spelled also with a capital letter

turlough
bulldust
buplever
pullover
mulloway
outlawry
duplexer
dull-eyed
full-eyed
gunlayer
guimbard
hummable
hummocky
outmoded
rummager
nutmeggy
mummying
duumviri
duumvirs
Gurmukhi
gunmaker
nummular
fulminic
pulmonic
summoner
pulmones
furmenty
turmeric
bummaree
submerge
submerse
outmarch
dummerer
murmurer
summerly
surmisal
surmiser
gummosis
outmatch
gunmetal
summital
luxmeter
Pulmotor®
summitry
surmount
quandang
turnback
turn-back
quintain
quandary
ruinable
runnable
guanacos
huanacos
burnt-ear
quintett
aulnager
outnight
bunny-hug
quencher
quinsied
burnside
Burnsite
quantise
quantize
quintile
turnpike
Burnsian
quantify
quantity
dunnakin
turnskin
quinella
tunneled
quenelle
tunneler
euonymin
euonymus
turnings
turnsole
quandong
quantong
turncock
turn-down
turncoat
turnspit
runner-up
pug-nosed
muenster
burnouse
buln-buln
quincunx
turnover
automata
cupolaed
autocade
auto-da-fé
automate
subovate
tutorage
△autobahn
autocarp
autoharp
Euromart
autogamy
dupondii
cuboidal
fucoidal
suborder
humoresk
aurorean
European
tutoress
Euroseat
autogeny
rugosely
Kuroshio
eulogise
eulogize
suboxide
tutorise
tutorize
tutoring
sutorial
tutorial
eulogium
europium
tutorism
Ausonian
Huronian
Junonian
sutorian
autogiro
eulogies
eulogist
humorist
dumosity
fumosity
gulosity
mucosity
rugosity
Jugoslav
Jugo-Slav
Yugoslav
Yugo-slav
suborner
Eurobond
autosome
sumotori
humorous
rumorous
sudorous
tumorous
bunodont
autology
autonomy
autotomy
ourology
humoured
rumourer
autocrat
Eurocrat
autopsia
Rumonsch
autoptic
culottes
tucotuco
tug-of-war
autodyne
autolyse
autolyze
autotype
autogyro
sulphate
humpback
hump-back
jump-ball
suppeago
supplant
culpable
jumpable
culpably
auspices
puppy-dog
cuspidal
puppodum
puppydom
jumped-up
cuspidor
subpoena
pump-head
pump-well
rumpless
suppress
jump-seat
supplely
puppy-fat
jump-shot
supplied
cut-price
outprice
outprize
sulphide
sulphite
surplice
surprise
tump-line
dumpling
lumpfish
puppyish
purplish
quippish
sumphish
pulpmill
supplial
puppyism
gumphion
gumption
subprior
supplier
murphies
supplies
gunpoint
outpoint
lumpy-jaw
subpolar
suspence
suspense
tuppence
rum-punch
lumpenly
tuppenny
pulpwood
pumphood
jump-rope
rump-bone
sulphone
sunproof
pump-room
rump-post
mudpuppy
purpuric
cutpurse
purpurin
purposed
supposed
supposal
supposer
purposes
supposes
pulpited
pulpitum
sumpitan
pulpiter
quipster
pulpitry
puppetry
sulphury
outpower
musquash
huaquero
surquedy
guardage
outreach
guardant
surrebut
curricle
lubrical
rubrical
guéridon
outrider
putridly
aubrieta
ouvrière
quartern
quarters
nutrient
quartett
furriery
outright
quarried
murrhine
quartile
currying
hurrying
querying
quirkish
guardian
outreign
quarrier
quartier
quirkily
guerilla
murrelet
outremer
supremos
outrance
Quirinal
guaranis
mucrones
Quirinus
curranty
currency
guaranty
cupreous

muir-poot
muir-pout
eutropic
outroper
quart-pot
eutrophy
bulrushy
△guernsey
aubretia
eucritic
turreted
burritos
Quirites
surround
muirburn
outrival
sur-reyn'd
surroyal
outstand
bud-scale
outstare
purslane
substage
substate
sunshade
fuss-ball
purslain
outsmart
puissant
pursuant
questant
suasible
pussy-cat
tussocky
pulsidge
outsider
outsides
cursedly
outspend
outspeak
nutshell
outswell
mug-sheep
outsleep
outswear
outspent
pulsific
purseful
outsight
Burschen
mudslide
outshine
sunshine
guessing
nursling
outswing
pursuing
questing
quisling
gunsmith
ouistiti
gunstick
Russniak
question
huissier
outskirt
sunshiny
pulsejet
pulsojet
vulsella
subsolar
subsonic
nuisance
purse-net
cussword
outscold
gunstone
mudstone
rubstone
sunstone
puss-moth
gunstock
outscorn
outshoot
outsport
rum-shrub
subshrub
subserve
humstrum
outstrip
cursitor
pulsator
bursitis
numskull
cum-savvy
substyle
outsized
subsizar
purtraid
purtrayd
cultrate
lustrate
suitcase
dust-bath
dust-ball
quatrain
nuptials
dustcart
subtract
gustable
quotable
suitable
quotably
suitably
mustache
rustical
justicer
subtidal
custodes
buttress
curtness
ductless
dustless
huntress
hurtless
justness
lustless
rustless
suitress
furthest
guttiest
quit-rent
quotient
rust-belt
subtlety
multifid
multifil
multigym
cultigen
dust-shot
buntline
lustrine
subtribe
wurtzite
duetting
hustling
lustring
puttying
quitting
rustling
turtling
outthink
Austrian
duettino
curtains
duettist
subtrist
multeity
sultrily
cuitikin
outtaken
pustular
subtilly
subtilty
Funtumia
customed
buttyman
huntsman
puntsman
customer
subtonic
sultanic
subtense
hustings
suitings
dust-hole
punt-pole
gust-lock
dust-bowl
lustrous
ructions
dust-coat
subtopia
multiped
multiple
multiply
multi-ply
lustique
Suctòria
cultured
quatorze
cultural
guttural
nurtural
putter-on
multurer
musterer
mutterer
nurturer
kurtosis
eustatic
guttated
subtitle
surtitle
subtotal
rum-ti-tum
subtrude
tub-thump
lustrums
cultivar
cumulate
cupulate
jugulate
lunulate
subulate
tubulate
tumulary
suburbia
suburban
cucumber
cucurbit
furuncle
luculent
muculent
purulent
guruship
autunite
Eugubine
lupuline
queueing
futurism
futurist
luxurist
futurity
Lucullic
Lucullan
mutually
Musulman
autumnal
Huguenot
cumulose
rugulose
tubulous
susurrus
Augustan
augustly
subucula
durukuli
tucutuco
sucurujú
surucucu
subvocal
outvoice
outvalue
pulville
pulvilli
pulvilio
suivante
outvenom
pulvinar
pulvinus
quivered
subverse
subviral
culverin
quaverer
subverst
curvated
curveted
curvital
outvoter
vulvitis
survival
survivor
surveyal
kurveyor
purveyor
surveyor
outweary
outwrest
outweigh
outworth
outwards
outworks
sunwards
outwatch
cut-water
quixotic
quixotry
duty-paid
butyrate
ruby-tail
jurymast
butylene
busyness
△eurythmy
quayside
eucyclic
buoyance
buoyancy
busybody
duty-free
zugzwang
fuzz-ball
quizzery

Words marked △ may be spelled also with a capital letter

huzzaing
puzzling
quizzing
quizzify
subzonal
buzzword
pulza-oil
aviation
aviarist
aviatrix
evacuate
evacuant
evocable
avocados
evection
eviction
evocator
evadable
oviducal
avidness
evidence
avadavat
avifauna
availful
availing
avoision
evaluate
evulgate
evilness
evolvent
avulsion
evulsion
evil-doer
uvularly
uvulitis
evil-eyed
ovenware
Svengali
aventail
evenfall
evenness
evangely
eventful
oven-bird
eventide
evincive
avenging
eventing
evenings
ovenwood
evensong
even-down
evanesce
aventure
eventual
avionics
oviposit
overhand
overlaid
overland
overlard
overhale
overlade
overname
overpage
overrake
overrate
overtake
overgang
overhang
overrash
overwash
overrack
overrank
overtalk
overtask
overcall
overfall
overgall
overhaul
oversail
overlain
overhair
overpass
overcast
overmast
overpart
overpast
everyday
overfeed
overhead
overlend
overread
overleaf
oversell
overveil
overteem
overseen
overween
overkeep
overleap
overbear
overhear
overpeer
overseer
overwear
overyear
overseas
averment
overbeat
overheat
overhent
overkest
overlent
overneat
overwent
aversely
averages
overshoe
over-shoe
overshot
overkind
overwind
aversive
overbite
overfine
overgive
overlive
overnice
override
overripe
overside
oversize
overtime
overtire
overwise
averring
overking
overwing
overfish
overfill
overkill
aversion
eversion
overlier
overview
overskip
over-club
overclad
overslip
overalls
overplus
overblow
overflow
overcloy
overplay
△everyman
oversman
overknee
ivory-nut
overbold
overfold
overfond
overhold
overload
△overlord
overloud
oversold
overword
evermore
everyone
ovariole
overcome
overdone
overdose
overrode
overtone
overwore
overlong
overbook
overcook
overlock
overlook
overwork
overboil
over-cool
oversoul
overtoil
overworn
overdoer
ovarious
overcoat
overpost
overspin
overfree
overarch
overbrim
overcrop
overtrip
overbrow
overcraw
overcrow
overdraw
overgrow
overstep
ovaritis
overstay
overfund
overrule
overture
overruff
overhung
overmuch
overbulk
overfull
overburn
overturn
overjump
overdust
overbusy
overswim
everyway
oversway
overhype
evasible
svastika
evitable
kvetcher
avoutrer
avowable
avowedly
a-weather
awearied
swealing
swearing
sweating
tweaking
own-brand
swabbers
swabbing
twichild
twoccing
two-digit
swaddler
twaddler
twiddler
Swadeshi
Zwieback
sweet-bay
tweeness
tweezers
two-edged
sweeping
sweeting
sweetish
tweedler
sweep-net
owreword
owrecome
sweet-oil
sweetpea
sweetsop
sweep-saw
two-faced
Swiftian
swiftlet
Owl-glass
Ewigkeit
swagshop
swagging
swigging
swagsman
twigsome
two-horse
swaining
swainish
Kwakiutl
own-label
swelldom
twelvemo
owl-light
twilight
swelchie
dwelling
swelling
swilling
swellish
swell-mob
swill-tub
swimwear
swimming
swimsuit
swan-mark
swanherd
swan-neck
swannery
twi-night
twinship
swan-shot
swanlike
awanting
swanking
swanning
swinging
twanging

Words marked △ may be spelled also with a capital letter

8 □w□n□i

twinling
twinning
swingism
twenties
swanskin
swan-skin
swindler
twinkler
swan-song
twin-born
swankpot
swine-pox
swine-sty
twin-axis
swooning
two-piece
swap-shop
swapping
swopping
swaption
twopence
twopenny
two-power
sword-arm
sword-cut
swarming
swerving
dwarfish
dwarfism
sword-law
swordman
owerloup
two-start
two-sided
two-speed
swastika
swashing
swishing
swissing
twisting
two-score
owl-train
twittery
switchel
twitcher
swatting
swotting
twitting
twattler
two-timer
swayback
sway-back
swayling
excavate
exhalant
ox-warble
expander
expandor
axiality
execrate
exocrine

exacting
exaction
executer
executor
executry
oxidiser
oxidizer
extended
expender
extender
exoergic
expedite
exterior
ox-pecker
excelled
expelled
expellee
external
externat
excerpta
axle-tree
exhedrae
extensor
expenses
expected
exserted
exceptor
expecter
expertly
exigeant
exigible
exiguity
exogamic
exigence
exigency
exiguous
exegesis
exegetic
exchange
excitant
expirant
expiable
exciting
expiring
excision
ex-libris
expiator
exultant
axillary
explicit
excluded
exploded
excludee
excluder
exploder
△explorer
exemplum
examplar
exemplar
examinee
examiner

eximious
oxymoron
oximeter
exanthem
exponent
ox-tongue
extolled
extoller
axiology
exhorter
exporter
exposure
axoplasm
exoplasm
exophagy
exequial
exequies
exorable
Oxbridge
extruder
extrados
exarchal
exercise
exertive
exorcise
exorcize
exordial
exorcism
exordium
exertion
exorcist
extremer
extremes
uxorious
extrorse
expresso
excretal
excreter
exergual
existent
axe-stone
exosmose
exospore
oxytocic
oxytocin
exitance
exoteric
exotoxic
exotoxin
exhumate
excubant
excuse-me
expunger
excusive
excursus
exuviate
pyjamaed
cynanche
synarchy
bylander
gynandry

hypalgia
synaphea
dynamise
dynamite
dynamize
lyra-wise
△sybarite
sycamine
tyramine
lyra-viol
cymatium
dynamism
gyration
dynamics
pyramids
dynamist
tyrannic
zygaenid
tyrannis
hydatoid
hyracoid
sycamore
gyratory
dynatron
synapses
synapsis
dynastic
synaptic
synanthy
synastry
eye-black
myoblast
cymbidia
ryebread
symbolic
cymbalos
eyebrows
symbiont
syncline
lynch-law
hyacinth
syncopic
syncopal
lynchpin
dyschroa
syncarpy
syncytia
syndical
syndings
syndrome
syndesis
syndetic
Cyrenaic
lykewake
type-face
lykewalk
typecast
myxedema
hymeneal
hymenean
Pyrenean

tyreless
lysergic
synergic
synergid
synechia
lyre-bird
type-high
hymenial
mycelial
pyrexial
gynecium
hymenium
mycelium
Hyperion
hypernym
mycetoma
pyrenoid
type-body
synedria
synectic
ryeflour
myograph
syngraph
eyeglass
nylghaus
syngamic
dysgenic
myogenic
pyogenic
lychgate
mythical
Typhoean
Typhoeus
syphilis
hyphenic
pythonic
Tychonic
△typhonic
hyphened
kyphosis
kyphotic
dye-house
symitare
dytiscid
Dytiscus
myriadth
cylinder
syringes
typified
cytisine
pyridine
pyritise
pyritize
pygidial
cynicism
hylicism
lyricism
pygidium
pyxidium
typifier
hylicist

Words marked △ may be spelled also with a capital letter

lyricist
Cyrillic
kyrielle
hygienic
mytiloid
lyriform
pyriform
pyritous
myriapod
myriopod
Syriarch
myristic
syrinxes
gymkhana
syllabub
syllabic
syllable
syllabus
cyclical
Hyblaean
byrlakin
cyclamen
cyclonic
eyeliner
cyclopic
△cyclopes
cycloses
cyclosis
kyllosis
pyelitic
myelitis
pyelitis
eye-level
wye-level
cycleway
dyslexia
dyslexic
△myrmidon
pygmaean
dysmelia
dysmelic
myomancy
symmetry
pyengadu
cyanogen
gynny-hen
ayenbite
pyonings
hymn-book
cyanuret
gymnasia
gymnasic
cyanosed
lyings-in
cyanosis
hypnosis
pycnosis
cyanotic
hypnotic
syenitic
hypnotee
hypogaea
myxomata
xylomata
zygomata
hylobate
xylocarp
gyroidal
xyloidin
hypogene
pyroxene
Tyrolese
hypogeal
hypoderm
hypogeum
hypogean
Tyrolean
hypothec
by-motive
cytokine
cytosine
dysodile
gyrolite
mylonite
tyrosine
Xylonite®
xylonite
zylonite
synovial
Byronism
sybotism
syconium
hypocist
by-corner
Pyrosoma
Tylopoda
cytosome
hypobole
lysosome
pyrosome
sycomore
mylodont
zygodont
cytology
mycology
typology
xylology
zymology
kymogram
synopses
synopsis
synoptic
gyrostat
pyrostat
cynosure
dysodyle
gyrodyne
lysozyme
pyrolyse
pyrolyze
pyroxyle
hypogyny
hyponymy
synonymy
Nymphaea
symplast
dysphagy
sympodia
dyspneic
eye-piece
by-speech
dyspneal
nymphean
lyophile
sylphide
symphile
nymphish
sylphish
symphily
tympanic
tympanal
tympanum
dyspnoea
lymphoma
lymphoid
lyophobe
symploce
symphony
dyspepsy
symposia
dyspathy
sympathy
Symphyla
cyprides
Ayurveda
Tyrrhene
hydrogen
myrrhine
hydremia
hydromel
Hydromys
cyprinid
hydranth
Cypriote
pyrrhous
hydropic
hydropsy
hydroski
hydroxyl
eye-rhyme
△hydrozoa
eyeshade
eyestalk
gypsydom
eyesight
Ayrshire
hyoscine
gypsyism
eye-salve
gypseous
rye-straw
syssitia
myositis
myosotis
dyestuff
ryotwari
dystocia
mystical
Tyrtaean
by-street
syntagma
syntagms
cysteine
oystrige
systolic
systemic
systemed
dystonia
myotonia
dystonic
myotonic
syntonic
syntonin
eye-tooth
dystopia
mystique
hysteria
hysteric
nystatin
cystitis
syntexis
pyruvate
sylviine
△sylvaner
sylvatic
dye-works
eye-water
lynx-eyed
syzygial
syzygies
Ozacling®
izvestia
azulejos
ozoniser
ozonizer
czaritsa
czarevna
tzatziki
azoturia

9 □a□a□a

catamaran
maharajah
Malayalam
Nabataean
tacamahac
calamanco
calavance
caravance
catafalco
jacaranda
sarabande
caravaned
caravaner
maharanee
camanachd
maranatha
catabasis
katabasis
katabatic
macadamia
Pan-Arabic
parabasis
paralalia
parataxis
balalaika
palatable
palatably
man-at-arms
paravaunt
galapagos
Kalamazoo®
malaxator
Navaratra
Navaratri
paramatta
taraxacum
paparazzi
paparazzo
canal-boat
carambola
carambole
cavalcade
canal-cell
△damascene
kalanchoe
parasceve
bavardage
calandria
farandole
farandine
gabardine
marauding
cat-and-dog
man-and-dog
malanders
hazardous
hazardize
dahabeeah
lamaserai
palace-car
paralegal
tapaderas
zapateado
Japaneses
palaverer
parameter
parapeted
taxameter
cadaveric
catalexis
catamenia
△hamamelis
paralexia
paramecia
paramedic
Saracenic
bagatelle
panatella
savagedom
tapaderos
catalepsy
karateist
cabaletta
cabalette
lazaretto
fabaceous
fagaceous
sagapenum
taxaceous
paraffine
paraffiny
Varangian
harangued
haranguer
carangoid
salangane
△falangism
△falangist
Walachian
panachaea
tabasheer
cataphyll
pararhyme
catarhine
matachina
matachini
Malathion®
malachite
parachute
barathrum
Carabidae
dahabiyah
fanatical
galabiyah
paradisal
Samaritan
satanical
Tabanidae
Varanidae
carabiner
dahabiyeh
galabiyeh
karabiner
tanalised
tanalized
barasinga
maharishi
balanitis
Nazaritic
paradisic
parasitic
camarilla
sabadilla
tamarillo
capacitor
caparison
lavaliere
Wahabiism
garagiste
palafitte
Wahabiite
capacious
malarious
rapacious
sagacious
salacious
vagarious
damaskeen
palankeen
kalamkari
lazar-like
caballine
caballing
halalling
caballero
cataclasm
cataclysm
cataplasm
△paraclete
△balaclava
cataplexy
rabatment
Balaam-box
Balaamite
Marasmius
japanning
Jagannath
parabolas
paradoxal
paranoiac
cataloger
paradores
paradoxer
baragouin
catabolic
catatonia
catatonic
katabolic
macaronic
macaronis
madarosis
natatoria
parabolic
paragogic
paralogia
paranoeic
parapodia
paratonic
sanatoria
datacomms
catamount
paramount
cacafogos
tapacolos
paramorph
calaboose
babacoote
catalogue
paragogue
macaw-palm
palampore
damasquin
palanquin
catarrhal
hamadryad
maladroit
parabrake
tanagrine
paragraph
calabrese
gala-dress
canal-rays
banausian
camass-rat
Malaysian
Dadaistic
lamaistic
rajahship
tayassuid
harassing
palaestra
cadastral
bay-antler
macaw-tree
△tarantula
galantine
rabatting
tarantara
galactose
tarantass
tarantism
cacafuego
paracusis
malagueña
tapaculos
Kamasutra
paraquito
carap-wood
sapanwood
salaryman
catalyser
catalyzer
paralyser
paralyzer
catalysis
catalytic
paralysis
paralytic
paranymph
vambraced
parbuckle
sarbacane
carbachol
Barbadian
Cambodian
Barbadoes
gambadoes
cambiform
gambogian
Lambegger
tarboggin
tabbyhood
Cambridge
gambolled
garbology
jambolana
cabbalism
cabbalist
jambalaya
carbamide
carbamate
carbonade
carbonado
carbineer
carbinier
harbinger
wambenger
carbuncle
lambently
jawboning
carbanion
garbanzos
Carbonari
carbonise
rabbinism
rabbinist
carbonate
rabbinate
rabbinite
sanbenito
carbonize
zamboorak
bamboozle
barbarian
gas-burner
hamburger
harborage
cambering
jabbering
Barberton
barbarise
barbarism
carburise
barbarity
carburate

barbarous
barbarize
carburize
barbastel
barbascos
cambistry
gas-bottle
barbitone
barbotine
rabbeting
sabbatine
jawbation
talbotype
Babbittry
sabbatise
sabbatism
lambitive
sabbatize
harbourer
tabbouleh
tambourin
lamb's-wool
carbazole
bacchanal
panchayat
wanchancy
calceated
fasciated
pancratic
saccharic
saccharin
catchable
danceable
fanciable
matchable
patchable
watchable
bacchante
bacchants
△saccharum
Maccabean
hatchback
Maccabees
dance-band
fascicled
calcicole
ear-cockle
fascicule
fasciculi
catch-crop
match-cord
sarcocarp
watchcase
march-dike
march-dyke
calcedony
Sarcodina
cascadura
rancidity
cauchemar
gauchesco
gaucherie
rancheria
rancherie
parchedly
rancheros
Parcheesi®
haecceity
fancy-free
calcifuge
bacciform
falciform
lanciform
sacciform
dance-hall
raccahout
rascaille
lance-jack
caecilian
matchlock
canceleer
cancelier
cancelled
marcelled
parcelled
sarcology
vasculums
hatchling
masculine
rascaldom
calculary
calculose
fanciless
matchless
rascalism
calculate
falculate
laccolite
laccolith
rascality
sacculate
calculous
calcimine
catchment
hatchment
parchment
parcimony
sarcomere
sarcomata
calcaneal
calcanean
Mancunian
vaccinial
gasconade
balconied
tap-cinder
carcinoma
falconine
parcenary
gasconism
larcenist
sauciness
fascinate
lancinate
vaccinate
calcaneum
calcaneus
larcenous
vaccinium
lanceolar
gas-cooled
patchocke
patchouli
patchouly
match-play
Sarcoptes
sarcoptic
catchpole
catchpoll
marchpane
mancipate
Cancerian
camcorder
barcarole
calcarine
gas-carbon
cancerate
cancerous
rancorous
saucerful
Caucasian
fancy-sick
Caucasoid
fascistic
pancosmic
sarcastic
saucisson
marcasite
narcissus
dancettee
dance-tune
narcotine
falcation
narcotise
narcotism
narcotist
narcotize
raucously
sanctuary
catchweed
lance-wood
matchwood
catchword
fancywork
patchwork
watchword
cardiacal
dandiacal
landwards
bald-faced
baldpated
hand-paper
sandpaper
cardialgy
land-yacht
sand-yacht
bald-eagle
card-table
landdamne
bandwagon
galdragon
paediatry
hardparts
hard-paste
gaudeamus
land-value
bandy-ball
paddy-bird
bandobast
Laodicean
Sadducean
dandy-cock
hand-screw
sand-screw
baldachin
landscrip
lardy-cake
baldicoot
bandicoot
mad-doctor
landscape
dandy-cart
labdacism
Sadducism
manducate
candidacy
candidate
Candlemas
handlebar
hard-metal
raddleman
saddlebag
saddle-lap
sand-devil
paddle-box
saddlebow
candlenut
land-reeve
dandified
hands-free
dandyfunk
land-agent
hardihead
band-wheel
handshake
hardshell
maid-child
cardphone
hardihood
card-sharp
land-shark
cab-driver
hardliner
hard-wired
sandpiper
baudricke
land-pilot
Gandhi-ism
bandwidth
△daedalian
fardel-bag
landslide
bandelier
bandoleer
bandolier
sandalled
paedology
bandoline
land-plane
△magdalene
mandoline
sand-blind
bandoleon
caudillos
dandelion
land-flood
mandilion
△mandylion
bandalore
bandolero
handclasp
hand-glass
sandblast
sandglass
vandalise
vandalism
lardalite
waldflute
vandalize
landamman
Landsmaal
pandemian
cardamine
hardiment
randomise
randomize
Dardanian
Sardinian
sardonian
card-index
tap-dancer
Valdenses
Waldenses
sand-snake
fandangle
maddingly
gardening
hardening
maddening
pardoning
bandoneon
bandonion
fandangos
Mandingos
bawdiness

9 □a□d□o

faddiness
gaudiness
handiness
hardiness
maidenish
sandiness
tardiness
landforce
mandiocca
baldmoney
handtowel
hardnosed
landloper
land-loper
Land-Rover®
wardrober
cardboard
hardboard
eard-house
dandiprat
dandyprat
handspike
sandspout
baldaquin
ealdorman
garderobe
sandarach
bard-craft
handcraft
bandbrake
handbrake
banderole
dandy-roll
mandarine
wandering
handgrips
ganderism
hand-press
hardgrass
landdrost
paederast
panderess
panderism
pandurate
caldarium
panderous
landgrave
waldgrave
hard-drawn
caddis-fly
yardstick
candytuft
handstaff
bandstand
band-stone
handstand
Landsting
△sandstone
faldstool
laudation
pandation
handsturn
Landsturm
laudatory
mandatary
mandatory
sandstorm
laudative
cardpunch
hard-cured
hard-ruled
landaulet
handcuffs
paedeutic
paideutic
landowner
handiwork
handywork
cameraman
barefaced
camerated
caretaker
casemaker
casemated
face-saver
lace-paper
lacerated
pacemaker
ratepayer
camera-shy
lake-basin
lacerable
laterally
talegalla
macerator
matelasse
matelassé
cave-earth
rare-earth
saleratus
laser-beam
camelback
paperback
raven-bone
wagenboom
Camembert
caper-bush
calembour
mareschal
paper-coal
paper-clip
layer-cake
canescent
latescent
Paleocene
tabescent
water-cool
water-core
paper-case
patercove
raven-duck
calendrer
calendric
eavesdrip
calendula
gaberdine
haberdine
eavesdrop
cavendish
make-peace
make-ready
base-level
wavemeter
cafeteria
dare-devil
papeterie
parenesis
rakehelly
madeleine
pademelon
patereros
tax-exempt
baneberry
naseberry
vade-mecum
take-leave
maleffect
paper-file
waterfall
hare's-foot
waterfowl
paleogaea
galengale
malengine
Paleogene
habergeon
paper-girl
Watergate
mane-sheet
page-three
makeshift
cane-chair
date-shell
name-child
rakeshame
waveshape
canephora
canephore
catechise
catechism
catechist
catechize
Camelidae
Galenical
baseliner
haverings
lateritic
sagenitic
materials
facetious
parecious
kabeljouw
gavelkind
Sabellian
labelloid
lamelloid
waterlily
canellini
capelline
labelling
panelling
ravelling
waterline
tabellion
lamellose
panellist
paperless
waterless
baseplate
face-cloth
face-plate
faveolate
lamellate
name-plate
paleolith
patellate
satellite
wavellite
paper-mill
ravelment
watermark
Falernian
case-knife
careenage
pageantry
cageyness
eagerness
fadedness
mare's-nest
mateyness
nakedness
satedness
taperness
maternity
paternity
cavernous
gate-money
gate-tower
late-comer
Malebolge
categoric
paregoric
wake-robin
case-bound
gaze-hound
macédoine
racegoing
kakemonos
bakeboard
baseboard
base-court
bakehouse
gatehouse
panegoism
racehorse
warehouse
wasegoose
bakeapple
paper-pulp
cameo-part
davenport
palempore
face-cream
racetrack
paper-reed
sage-green
canefruit
canebrake
cameo-rôle
lace-frame
wavefront
page-proof
salesroom
cane-trash
careerism
careerist
gatecrash
sagebrush
oakenshaw
wapenshaw
haversack
waterside
watershed
cadetship
water-ski'd
caressing
haversine
raree-show
water-shot
caressive
cadential
lacertian
palestral
maieutics
case-study
gazetteer
parentage
have-at-him
mare's-tail
palestric
wapentake
date-stamp
vasectomy
bakestone
gazetting
hare-stane
lacertine
lamenting
panettone
panettoni
parenting
△valentine
balection
caseation
paleotype

Words marked △ may be spelled also with a capital letter

calenture
cane-sugar
date-sugar
waveguide
balefully
banefully
carefully
fatefully
hatefully
wakefully
mamelucos
face-guard
safeguard
waterweed
laserwort
navelwort
paperware
paperwork
waterwork
water-worn
taperwise
caterwaul
water-wave
safetyman
yakety-yak
panegyric
rarefying
Paleozoic
half-hardy
half-baked
half-faced
half-caste
mafficker
half-adder
bafflegab
halfpence
palfreyed
parfleche
Rafflesia
ramfeezle
halfpenny
carfuffle
calf's-foot
lay-figure
half-cheek
half-shift
half-shell
half-hitch
half-miler
half-timer
halflings
half-light
half-title
gas-filled
jaw-fallen
half-blood
half-close
half-plate
raffinose
raffinate
ray-fungus
half-royal
calfdozer
half-dozen
mayflower
oar-footed
safflower
saffroned
calf-bound
half-bound
half-pound
half-round
half-price
half-track
fanfarade
half-breed
malformed
tax-farmer
half-frame
fanfarona
warfaring
wayfaring
Sanforise
half-truth
half-crown
Sanforize
ham-fisted
raffishly
gas-fitter
hamfatter
half-sword
languaged
pay-gravel
gaugeable
laughable
laughably
barghaist
Langobard
Largactil®
Haggadist
vargueños
languette
larghetto
MacGuffin
bargainer
langridge
tanghinin
languidly
narghilly
ganglions
gangliate
hang-glide
gangplank
rangeland
bargellos
Targumist
bargander
jargoneer
laggingly
bagginess
jargonise
jargonist
largeness
manganese
manginess
ranginess
manganate
manganite
marginate
manganous
jargonize
baignoire
gangboard
langspiel
bargepole
Pan-German
sangfroid
haggardly
bangsring
margarine
△tangerine
badger-dog
△kangaroos
gargarise
gargarism
margarita
margarite
dangerous
gargarize
mangostan
haggishly
waggishly
laughsome
sargassos
pargasite
sargassum
gadgeteer
targeteer
maggot-pie
haughtily
naughtily
faggoting
pargeting
targeting
largition
rangatira
mangetout
gang-punch
langouste
mangouste
law-giving
parge-work
bathwater
fat-headed
sapheaded
washbasin
bath-salts
bathybius
cachectic
cathectic
yacht-club
cathedral
rachidial
rachidian
Sanhedrim
Sanhedrin
pachyderm
washed-out
cashierer
machmeter
cachaemia
cachaemic
tachogram
pathogeny
bath-sheet
dash-wheel
dachshund
naphthene
eachwhere
bakhshish
kathakali
mashallah
gasholder
waghalter
pathology
cacholong
parhelion
natheless
batholite
batholith
bathylite
bathylith
tachylite
tachylyte
washcloth
nachtmaal
cat-hammed
sachemdom
nathemore
Bathonian
ham-handed
dashingly
manhandle
panhandle
taphonomy
machinery
machinist
washiness
machinate
saphenous
washing-up
bath-towel
fashioner
machzorim
Pakhtoons
dashboard
washboard
bathhouse
bath-house
washhouse
tachypnea
parhypate
jaghirdar
washerman
bacharach
bath-brick
catharses
catharsis
cathartic
katharsis
gathering
Mathurine
ratheripe
catharise
Catharism
Catharist
lathyrism
ratherest
ratherish
catharize
yachtsman
cache-sexe
Manhattan
pathetics
washstand
bashfully
bashawism
lachrymal
haphazard
latitancy
garibaldi
harigalds
camisades
laminated
patinated
radicated
vaginated
waribashi
Laminaria
palilalia
sanitaria
basically
capitally
fatigable
habilable
habitable
habitably
laminable
magically
manically
maritally
maximally
navigable
navigably
radically
vaginally
camisados
capitanos
laminator
navigator
Caribbean
panic-bolt
marischal
parischan
mariachis

Words marked △ may be spelled also with a capital letter

9 □a□i□c

radicchio
fatiscent
variscite
zamindari
zamindary
basipetal
taoiseach
calibered
salimeter
tasimeter
taximeter
gaminerie
capitella
varicella
taxidermy
manifesto
satinetta
satinette
lapideous
salicetum
satisfice
satisfied
satisfier
basinfuls
rapid-fire
radiogram
taking-off
galingale
lamington
malingery
variegate
Manichean
ravishing
vanishing
caliphate
basilical
basilican
fatidical
pacifical
satirical
vaticinal
basifixed
laminitis
lapidific
vaginitis
basilicon
marinière
laciniate
malicious
magicking
panicking
maniplies
Ramillies
caliology
hagiology
Mariology
palillogy
radiology
varioloid
maxillula
papillule
radial-ply
papilloma
cavilling
vacillant
bacillary
capillary
mamillary
maxillary
papillary
labialise
labialism
papillose
racialism
racialist
radialise
sapidless
hariolate
mamillate
marialite
papillate
papillote
radiality
vacillate
variolate
variolite
papillous
variolous
laticlave
labialize
radialize
talismans
radionics
gabionade
galiongee
gabionage
Salientia
patiently
radiantly
rationale
rationals
saliently
sapiently
valiantly
△malignant
Fabianism
Fabianist
magianism
rabidness
rapidness
Sabianism
sapidness
tacitness
validness
vapidness
malignity
latifondi
manifolds
halitosis
halitotic
saxitoxin
makimonos
Napierian
taligrade
Saxifraga
saxifrage
hagiarchy
marigraph
janitress
calibrate
wapinshaw
janissary
magistral
varieties
radiately
Calixtine
Pakistani
raciation
radiation
radiothon
satiation
variation
banisters
magistery
radiatory
sagittary
macintosh
sagittate
caliatour
radiative
variative
basifugal
canicular
capitular
manipular
navicular
radicular
sapi-outan
vaginulae
saliaunce
halieutic
variously
fatiguing
marihuana
marijuana
babirussa
caciquism
habituate
capitulum
basin-wide
satinwood
yakity-yak
Varityper®
salicylic
ramifying
ratifying
salifying
Mao-jacket
banjulele
Jack-sauce
backwards
parklands
parkwards
backwater
bank-paper
lack-Latin
tank-wagon
tanka-boat
hawksbill
walkabout
back-pedal
back-bench
barkeeper
hackneyed
Yankeedom
hackberry
lack-beard
Yankeeism
bank-agent
packaging
lark's-heel
packsheet
back-shift
jackshaft
back-chain
gawkihood
backshish
mark-white
backfisch
backpiece
pack-cinch
backbiter
lack-linen
rank-rider
darklings
back-light
backsight
backfield
darkfield
back-block
jack-block
backslide
jackalled
Raskolnik
back-slang
Jack-a-Lent
jack-plane
back-cloth
back-plate
bark-cloth
pack-cloth
sackcloth
Jack-slave
hackamore
jacksmith
jackknife
balkingly
jack-snipe
△balkanise
balkiness
gawkiness
lankiness
larkiness
pawkiness
tackiness
wackiness
talking-to
△balkanize
task-force
backwoods
backboned
hawk-nosed
bark-bound
back-board
backcourt
bark-louse
dark-house
pack-horse
backspace
backspeer
backspeir
back-spaul
backtrack
Valkyries
jack-fruit
lack-brain
pack-train
pack-drill
hankering
back-cross
cankerous
task-group
Valkyriur
back-crawl
hawkishly
mawkishly
△jack-straw
market-day
market-man
bank-stock
△marketeer
racketeer
jack-staff
packstaff
backstage
backstall
marketing
racketing
saskatoon
talkathon
walkathon
basketful
talkative
backstays
jack-stays
rack-punch
backswing
pack-twine
backsword
dalliance
gaillarde
sail-maker
tailgater
wallpaper
Gaeltacht

9 □a□n□e

malleable
talliable
kailyaird
paillasse
palliasse
gallabeah
gallabiah
gallabieh
table-beer
Wallabies
ballabile
ballabili
table-book
day-labour
gallabiya
Paulician
vallecula
gally-crow
warlockry
gaelicise
gaelicism
△gallicise
△gallicism
gaelicize
△gallicize
Palladian
wallydrag
balladeer
balladine
called-for
balladist
callidity
pallidity
△palladium
palladous
sallee-man
cailleach
rail-fence
eagle-eyed
gaol-fever
jail-fever
mallee-hen
mailmerge
paillette
ballsed-up
ladlefuls
cauliform
cablegram
calligram
panlogism
tailwheel
tally-hoed
tail-rhyme
faulchion
eagle-hawk
cailliach
tailpiece
gauleiter
nail-biter
bailliage
tail-light
Carlylean
table-leaf
hallalled
haplology
cable-laid
mail-plane
sailplane
tableland
tailplane
fallalery
Carlylese
Carlylism
faultless
sailcloth
mallemuck
table-maid
waulkmill
Paulinian
Laplander
mallander
mallender
tail-ender
gallonage
gallantly
gallingly
gallinule
railingly
wailingly
caulinary
gallantry
garlandry
earliness
kaolinise
manliness
Paulinism
Paulinist
day-length
kaolinite
gallinazo
kaolinize
malleolar
railwoman
mail-coach
call-money
gallooned
ballpoint
rail-borne
rail-motor
sailboard
tailboard
wallboard
jailhouse
malleolus
Fallopian
gallopade
Callippic
Gallophil
galloping
walloping
callipers
gallopers
sallyport
harlequin
gas-liquor
tan-liquor
gaol-break
jail-break
parlor-car
sailor-man
galleried
mail-order
cauldrife
mail-train
ballerina
ballerine
sailoring
tailoring
ball-proof
ball-dress
jaileress
nail-brush
tailoress
ballasted
ballistic
haplessly
lawlessly
tallyshop
gallisise
callosity
gallisize
mahlstick
maulstick
tailstock
table-talk
balloting
galleting
gallstone
hailstone
hallstand
marlstone
ballot-box
lallation
△maelstrom
kallitype
hail-storm
tablature
palletise
varletess
Hallstatt
palletize
callously
Pavlovian
gallivant
Hallowmas
bailiwick
gallowses
Hallowe'en
paulownia
tallow-dip
wallowing
eaglewood
tableware
table-work
galliwasp
sallowish
tablewise
tallowish
waylaying
parleyvoo
balmacaan
Barmecide
haemocoel
tarmacked
naumachia
panmictic
haemocyte
gammadion
Talmudist
mammiform
mammogram
bar-magnet
tacmahack
palm-civet
haymaking
haymakers
mammalian
mammillae
farm-place
marmalade
mammalogy
harmaline
△warmblood
marmelise
barm-cloth
△carmelite
marmelize
tagmemics
Tasmanian
harmonica
harmonics
garmented
lawmonger
man-minded
warmonger
salmonoid
gammoning
badminton
balminess
barminess
harmonise
△harmonist
mammonish
mammonism
mammonist
Harmonite
mammonite
harmonium
sarmentum
harmonize
palm-honey
harmdoing
palm-court
farmhouse
palmhouse
palmipede
hammerman
marmoreal
palmarian
barmbrack
hammering
yammering
hammerkop
hammer-toe
farmeress
marmarise
marmarize
haemostat
paymaster
say-master
palmistry
Dalmatian
farmstead
harmattan
Sarmatian
haematoid
palmately
haematoma
harmotome
calmstone
caumstone
malmstone
gammation
palmation
palmettos
haematite
palmitate
calmative
palm-sugar
harmfully
Gammexane®
△barmizvah
△basmizvah
△batmizvah
fainéance
faineancy
gainsayer
rainmaker
rainwater
rain-gauge
bain-marie
sannyasin
taeniasis
paintable
lagniappe
lawn-party
△paintball
dannebrog
Barnabite
barnacled
barnacles
launderer
maunderer
panniered
saunterer

9 □a□n□e

painterly
magnifico
magnified
magnifier
saintfoin
nannyghai
nanny-goat
carnahuba
raincheck
mainsheet
raunchily
sainthood
jaundiced
mainliner
raintight
pannikell
carnelian
pannelled
saintlike
saintling
cannelure
vainglory
carnalise
carnalism
carnalist
dauntless
taintless
cannulate
carnality
magnalium
rain-cloud
carnalize
cannonade
cannoneer
cannonier
fawningly
warningly
yawningly
canniness
faintness
gauntness
raininess
tawniness
lawnmower
rainbowed
rain-bound
haanepoot
mannequin
Wagnerian
mainbrace
bannerall
mainframe
rain-print
rainproof
laundress
mainprise
△mannerism
△mannerist
paintress
Wagnerism
Wagnerist

Wagnerite
magnesian
bannister
gannister
garnishee
garnisher
tarnished
tarnisher
varnisher
faunistic
saintship
earnestly
garnishry
carnosity
magnesite
magnesium
Parnassus
magnetics
magnitude
dae-nettle
day-nettle
caen-stone
rain-stone
carnation
damnation
magnetron
tarnation
barnstorm
damnatory
garniture
rainstorm
magnetise
magnetism
magnetist
carnotite
magnetite
magnetize
gainfully
painfully
Carnivora
carnivore
taint-worm
Caenozoic
Cainozoic
Kainozoic
jaborandi
Haloragis
panoramic
saponaria
favorable
favorably
razorable
vaporable
mako-makos
capotasto
mayoralty
pavonazzo
razor-back
razor-bill
razor-clam
capocchia

man-orchid
baroscope
paroicous
major-domo
Mahometan
baronetcy
barometer
bayoneted
can-opener
gasometer
manometer
razor-edge
Masoretic
Samoyedic
sapogenin
cacodemon
barometry
gasometry
manometry
nanometre
majorette
vaporetti
vaporetto
wagonette
pay-office
camouflet
razor-fish
parochial
halophobe
halophile
halophily
cacophony
halothane
parochine
saxophone
masochism
masochist
halophyte
Aaronical
canonical
laconical
parodical
Zapodidae
Maeonides
tamoxifen
vaporiser
vaporizer
calorific
Jacobinic
Jacobitic
parotitis
vaporific
sapodilla
zapotilla
halobiont
palominos
caponiere
laborious
havocking
Damoclean
wagonload

panoplied
carolling
favorless
wagon-lits
paroemiac
paroemial
marooning
baboonery
baboonish
taxonomer
cacotopia
Salomonic
taxonomic
vasomotor
lagomorph
masonried
savourily
vapouring
barograph
Camorrism
Camorrist
labourism
labourist
vapourish
favourite
Labourite
manor-seat
jalousied
majorship
mayorship
panoistic
wagons-lit
cacoëthes
dacoitage
catoptric
garotting
fagottist
raconteur
caroluses
manoeuvre
vaporware
cacodylic
canopying
parodying
campeachy
campeador
palpebral
jam-packed
pay-packet
rag-picker
rampicked
tan-pickle
gazpachos
jaspidean
campodeid
lampadary
lampadist
dapple-bay
camp-fever
raspberry
salpiform

Malpighia
rampaging
lampshade
camp-chair
harp-shell
lamp-shell
sapphired
lamplight
nauplioid
rat-poison
lamp-black
rappelled
carpology
lamp-glass
mappemond
tamponade
carpenter
tamponage
campanile
campanili
campanula
carpingly
gaspingly
rampantly
raspingly
happening
campanero
carpentry
campanist
gaspiness
happiness
nappiness
sappiness
harpooner
lampooner
camphoric
rasp-house
bagpiping
gaspereau
wapper-jaw
Walpurgis
tampering
barperson
damp-proof
layperson
jasperise
lampbrush
pauperess
pauperise
pauperism
vampirise
vampirism
jasperous
jasperize
pauperize
vampirize
waspishly
campesino
carpetbag
carpet-bag
carpet-bed

Words marked △ may be spelled also with a capital letter

tappit-hen
carpeting
palpitant
wasp-stung
camp-stool
carpet-rod
palpation
tappet-rod
raspatory
palpitate
tarpaulin
tax-paying
sasquatch
banqueted
banqueter
lacquerer
parqueted
Jacquerie
hacqueton
marquetry
parquetry
banquette
harquebus
pasquiler
matriarch
patriarch
tarriance
fair-faced
hair-waver
macro-axis
macrobian
carry-back
Lauraceae
△patrician
barracuda
barricade
barricado
macrocode
matricide
parricide
patricide
barracker
barricoes
patricoes
△batrachia
capriccio
matricula
fabricant
latrociny
barracoon
macrocopy
Capricorn
macrocosm
fabricate
macrocyte
Dalradian
hag-ridden
macrodome
manriding
parrhesia
sapraemia
sapraemic
sacrifice
sacrifide
caprifoil
barrefull
caprifole
capriform
dairy-farm
tauriform
carrageen
cat-rigged
farragoes
iatrogeny
Tarragona
cairngorm
fairyhood
hairpiece
ram-raider
darraigne
parrakeet
caerulean
patrolman
barrelled
bas-relief
lap-roller
laurelled
patrolled
patroller
barrelage
macrology
patrology
sacrilege
sacralgia
bairnlike
fairylike
fairyland
Maoriland
matriliny
patriliny
sacralise
caprylate
garrulity
haircloth
natrolite
saprolite
barrelful
garrulous
sacralize
dairymaid
lacrimals
matrimony
patrimony
sacrament
lacrimary
lacrymary
lacrimose
lacrimoso
lacrymose
lagrimoso
carronade
cab-runner
warranted
warrantee
warranter
matronage
patronage
jarringly
safranine
barrancos
warrantor
hairiness
matronise
patroness
patronise
tarriness
matronize
patronize
pair-royal
cabriolet
gadrooned
garryowen
patriotic
dayr'house
pair-horse
hairspray
Sauropoda
kauri-pine
madrepore
parroquet
hairdrier
hairdryer
fairy-ring
hair-brush
hair-grass
macrurous
sacrarium
Laurasian
madrassah
sacristan
barrister
lairdship
patristic
hadrosaur
bairn-team
barret-cap
parrot-jaw
barretter
garreteer
garrotted
garrotter
hairst-rig
carrytale
fairytale
hairstyle
bairn-time
latration
narration
day-return
gas-retort
narratory
parrot-cry
Mauritius
narrative
carrousel
Harrovian
galravage
marrowfat
marrow-men
marrowsky
harrowing
narrowing
sabre-wing
barrow-boy
marrowish
saprozoic
marshalcy
fan-shaped
man-slayer
Hanseatic
Pan-Slavic
raiseable
ranshakle
camstairy
waistboat
waistbelt
hause-bane
waistband
waistcoat
cassocked
ransacker
sapsucker
false-card
passadoes
waist-deep
pad-saddle
Hassidism
camsheugh
haustella
panspermy
far-seeing
camsteary
baksheesh
Parseeism
sassafras
falsified
falsifier
massagist
paysagist
pass-check
waist-high
hawsehole
day-school
falsehood
wassailer
capsaicin
day-sailor
wassailry
mausolean
tahsildar
hause-lock
cat-silver
hanselled
mamselles
tasselled
vassalage
tarsalgia
damselfly
marshland
tasseling
waistline
capsulary
capsulise
causeless
pauseless
vassaless
capsulate
causality
sassolite
mausoleum
capsulize
baisemain
facsimile
Balsamina
kalsomine®
parsimony
passament
passement
cassimere
massymore
Sassanian
Sassenach
cassonade
passenger
parsonage
cassingle
pausingly
Cassandra
falseness
gassiness
harshness
Jansenism
Jansenist
massiness
parsonish
Samsonite®
Vaishnava
batswoman
oarswoman
passional
passioned
haustoria
marsupial
passepied
sans-appel
pansophic
hawsepipe
marsupium
Caesarean
Caesarian
lapstreak
wasserman
passers-by
cassareep
lapstrake

9 □a□s□r

casserole
dayspring
hamstring
hamstrung
maistring
passerine
kaiserdom
cassaripe
mag-stripe
sassarara
Caesarism
Caesarist
kaiserism
Massorete
palsgrave
lassitude
wadsetter
cassation
causation
falsettos
causative
cassoulet
far-sought
massively
passively
passivism
passivist
passivate
passivity
balsawood
cassowary
falsework
marshwort
pansexual
△balthasar
△balthazar
Matthaean
eastwards
castrated
rag-trader
saltwater
cantharid
cantharis
martially
partially
tactually
cantharus
gastraeum
lanthanum
earth-bred
pantables
cantabile
cantabank
earthborn
earth-bath
Cactaceae
tactician
△canticles
pasticcio
party-call
latticini

latticino
faithcure
manticora
manticore
facticity
masticate
tacticity
vastidity
paste-down
cattleman
Martlemas
rattlebag
Bartlemew
saltpeter
wattmeter
sautéeing
panthenol
Parthenon
battle-cry
saltpetre
gastnesse
hartlesse
pantheism
pantheist
battle-axe
earthflax
Tartufian
earthfall
pantoffle
cactiform
△rastafari
earthfast
Tartufish
Tartufism
cartogram
pantagamy
castigate
fastigium
saltchuck
cartwheel
hartshorn
pantihose
mastoidal
captaincy
last-ditch
fantailed
fat-tailed
part-timer
rat-tailed
wart-biter
cartridge
eastlings
partridge
gastritis
Xanthippe
captainry
party-jury
partaking
Castalian
castellan
Castilian

Tantalean
Tantalian
cattaloes
martelled
battology
cartilage
cartology
tautology
cantilena
earthling
maltalent
pantiling
santolina
wasteland
battalion
malt-floor
martellos
pantaleon
△pantaloon
cartulary
cartelise
cartelism
cartelist
casteless
dactylist
faithless
tactilist
tantalise
tantalism
tasteless
pantalets
tactility
tantalate
tantalite
cantaloup
castellum
cautelous
tantalous
cartelize
salt-glaze
tantalize
pantomime
battement
Baltimore
caste-mark
mattamore
Daltonian
Martinmas
Waltonian
santonica
bastinade
bastinado
bartender
East-ender
Fasten-e'en
cartonage
dartingly
haltingly
lastingly
pantingly
rantingly

waitingly
battening
cantoning
fastening
fattening
rattening
cantiness
Cantonese
cantonise
cattiness
△daltonism
fattiness
hastiness
nastiness
nattiness
pastiness
saltiness
tartiness
tastiness
tattiness
wantonise
wasteness
castanets
cantonize
wantonize
factional
pactional
xanthomas
bastioned
cautioner
salt-money
saltworks
eastbound
gastropod
cant-board
cautionry
dartboard
Xanthoura
cart-horse
cart-house
malt-horse
malt-house
masthouse
salt-horse
tattooist
xanthoxyl
zanthoxyl
rantipole
bacterial
bacterian
cantorial
factorial
lactarian
latter-day
raptorial
sartorial
sartorian
Tartarean
Tartarian
cart-track
fast-track

vantbrace
easterner
master-key
Sauternes
wasterife
factorage
pasturage
waiterage
bacteroid
castor-oil
latter-wit
bastardly
dastardly
pastorale
bantering
cauterant
factoring
faltering
mastering
raftering
waitering
yattering
lanterloo
martyrdom
masterdom
tantarara
bacterise
cauterise
cauterism
factorise
martyrise
ranterism
rapturise
rapturist
tartarise
vant-brass
masterate
pastorate
bacterium
castoreum
martyrium
masterful
matterful
rapturous
sartorius
wasterful
bacterize
cauterize
factorize
martyrize
rapturize
tartarize
Baltoslav
Bantustan
baptismal
Cartesian
earth-star
fantasied
fantastic
cattishly
saltishly

Words marked △ may be spelled also with a capital letter

baptistry
fantastry
fantasise
fantasist
Dantesque
fantasque
fantasize
party-size
vastitude
cast-steel
cart's-tail
factotums
earth-tone
jactation
lactation
mactation
partition
saltation
partitura
saltatory
factitive
partitive
cartouche
pantoufle
tactfully
captivate
captivity
part-owner
earthwolf
zante-wood
earthward
earthwork
earthworm
pantryman
manurance
saturated
lacunaria
laquearia
maturable
naturally
saturable
tabularly
jaculator
saturator
tabulator
valuables
larum-bell
majuscule
ranunculi
facundity
nature-god
cacuminal
matutinal
paludinal
Baculites
datum-line
casualise
casualism
valueless
vacuolate
casualize

Saturnian
saturniid
saturnine
saturnism
saturnist
vagueness
haruspicy
galumpher
manubrial
bahuvrihi
casuarina
Paludrine®
salubrity
manubrium
casuistic
casuistry
maquisard
palustral
vacuation
valuation
fatuitous
vacuously
Yajurveda
Malvaceae
larvicide
carvacrol
Sarvodaya
larviform
△sauvignon
laevigate
malvoisie
larvikite
marvelled
varvelled
laevulose
valveless
Calvinism
Calvinist
galvanise
galvanism
galvanist
naiveness
naïveness
galvanize
salvarsan
canvasser
harvester
valvassor
calvities
△salvation
salvatory
Galwegian
law-writer
jaywalker
Rauwolfia
Darwinian
Darwinism
Darwinist
waxworker
waywardly
war-wasted

cat-witted
fat-witted
Manxwoman
marxisant
padymelon
laryngeal
karyogamy
easy-chair
calycinal
satyrical
Satyrinae
many-sided
labyrinth
manyplies
karyology
Maryology
lady-smock
lady's-maid
lazy-bones
lazy-tongs
easy-going
baby-tooth
caryopses
caryopsis
Magyarise
Magyarism
Magyarize
karyosome
caryatids
karyotype
calyptera
calyculus
Zanzibari
ranzelman
manzellos
gauziness
jazziness
manzanita
wayzgoose
balzarine
lazzarone
lazzaroni
gauze-tree
ablatival
abactinal
absconder
obscenely
obscenity
obscurely
obscurant
obscurity
abscissae
abscissas
abscessed
abscisses
abscissin
obedience
'sbodikins
abodement
abidingly
abnegator

abseiling
obsecrate
obversely
obsession
obversion
obsessive
objectify
abjection
objection
obreption
obtention
obvention
objective
obsequial
obsequies
obsequent
△observant
observing
obeisance
abdicable
abdicator
obligatos
oblivious
ébrillade
obsignate
ebriosity
obviation
obliquely
obviously
obliquity
obbligati
obbligato
ebullient
obeliscal
abolition
abominate
obumbrate
abondance
abundance
abundancy
Ebenaceae
abandoned
abandonee
abrogator
absorbent
absorbing
absorbate
obcordate
obsolesce
abdominal
obconical
ebionitic
obnoxious
abnormity
abnormous
abhorrent
abhorring
abbotship
obvoluted
obvolvent
ibuprofen

aberrance
aberrancy
obtruding
Abernethy
eburneous
△aborigine
obtrusion
obtrusive
abortuary
abysmally
abashedly
abashless
abasement
abashment
obeseness
abusively
abstainer
abatement
obstinacy
abstinent
obstinate
obstetric
obstruent
obturator
obfuscate
abounding
obtundent
absurdism
absurdist
absurdity
about-face
objurgate
ablutions
about-ship
abduction
abruption
about-turn
obovately
sciamachy
scrabbler
scrambler
scrabbing
scrapbook
scratcher
scratches
Octandria
octameter
octahedra
scrapegut
scraggily
scragging
scrapheap
McNaghten
octachord
Sciaridae
sciatical
oceanides
occasions
octaploid
scrawling
scramming

Words marked △ may be spelled also with a capital letter

sclaunder
sciaenoid
achaenium
octagonal
octapodic
eclampsia
eclamptic
scrappily
scrapping
octastich
octastyle
ice-action
scrapyard
scablands
scybalous
acock-bill
aciculate
acyclovir
scuddaler
acidified
acidifier
acidulent
acidulate
acidulous
academics
academism
academist
acidfreak
schematic
screwball
screecher
screeding
screw-down
accedence
sclereide
echeveria
schechita
icterical
Icteridae
scleritis
Acheulean
Acheulian
scheelite
screaming
octennial
screening
scleromas
sclerosal
sclerotal
sclerosed
scleroses
sclerosis
sclerotia
sclerotic
sclerotin
screw-pile
accension
accession
accessary
accessory
accentual

sciential
eclectics
eccentric
acceptant
scientise
scientism
scientist
acceptive
scientize
scheduled
scheduler
screeving
screw-worm
scaff-raff
scagliola
Ockhamism
Ockhamist
echinated
actinally
scribable
activator
scribbler
accidence
achimenes
scrivener
occipital
accipiter
Achillean
schilling
octillion
scrimmage
echidnine
actionist
Actinozoa
schizopod
écritoire
scrippage
scrimpily
scrimshaw
scriptory
△scripture
schistose
schistous
schiavone
scallawag
aculeated
ocellated
scaly-bark
ochlocrat
schlocker
scolecoid
scald-crow
scolecite
occludent
schlieren
scaldfish
ecologist
scaldhead
scaldings
scalelike
scaleless

scalpless
schlemiel
schlemihl
acclimate
Icelander
Icelandic
scaliness
scalloped
scoliosis
scoliotic
Acalephae
acalephan
schlepped
schlepper
ocularist
scelerate
ecclesial
scaldship
occlusion
occlusive
acoluthic
scolytoid
sculpture
acellular
acclivity
acclivous
scalework
scallywag
scummings
scambling
scumbling
schmaltzy
ecumenics
ecumenism
acuminate
acuminous
scombroid
schmutter
scamp-work
schnecken
aciniform
acanthoid
acanthine
sconcheon
scuncheon
acanthous
scintilla
ichnology
iconology
scantling
scentless
ichnolite
economics
economise
economism
economist
economize
scantness
schnapper
schnorkel
schnorrer

scenarios
scenarise
scenarist
scenarize
iconostas
schnitzel
aconitine
schnauzer
ichneumon
schnozzle
scholarch
acrobatic
echolalia
octonarii
scholarly
scrog-bush
scrog-buss
scroddled
accordant
according
accordion
acropetal
acrogenic
acroteria
ectogenic
scoopfuls
acrophony
ectotherm
ectophyte
acronical
scholiast
schoolbag
schoolday
schoolman
school-age
octoploid
schooling
scrolling
schoolboy
schoolery
ectoblast
ectoplasm
scrounger
octopodes
sciosophy
acropolis
ectomorph
accompany
acrospire
accourage
ectocrine
Octobrist
accoutred
octostyle
octopuses
acronycal
acronymic
Octogynia
sceptered
scapegoat
sceptical

acupoints
scopeloid
scapulary
scapeless
scapolite
scopulate
scapement
ecophobia
scaphopod
Scyphozoa
acariasis
Scorpaena
scarabaei
scaraboid
Aceraceae
acaricide
scarecrow
sciroccos
scorecard
acaridean
acaridian
scorodite
scorrendo
scarpetti
scarpetto
scarified
scarifier
scart-free
scorifier
scare-head
scirrhoid
scorching
scirrhous
Ecardines
scarpines
scorpioid
scurriour
acarology
scare-line
scoreline
ectropion
ectropium
scarf-ring
scarfskin
accretion
accretive
scorbutic
scarfwise
ice-skater
écossaise
acescence
acescency
ecosphere
scissorer
ecosystem
acetabula
Scoticism
scytheman
scattered
scatterer
scatheful

Words marked △ may be spelled also with a capital letter

△scotified
scutiform
Scotchman
scutching
scutcheon
scutellar
scatology
acetylene
ocotillos
scutellum
acetamide
scotomata
acuteness
ecstasied
Scotistic
ecstasise
ecstasize
ichthyoid
occupance
occupancy
accusable
scrutable
scrutator
accumbent
scrubbing
scoundrel
scrumdown
acquiesce
scouthery
Sciuridae
scourings
scrubland
actualise
actualist
actuality
actualize
scrummage
scrumming
scrutoire
actuarial
occurrent
occurring
acquittal
acoustics
acquitted
occulting
actuation
occultism
occultist
occupying
scavenger
ecdysiast
scuzzball
scazontes
scazontic
adiabatic
adnascent
Edwardian
adjacency
adiaphora
idealiser
idealizer
idealless
idealogue
advantage
edibility
edictally
educement
education
educatory
educative
Adrenalin®
adrenalin
adverbial
adherence
adhesions
udderless
adversely
admeasure
adversary
adversity
advertent
advection
adventure
Adventist
advertise
adjective
adventive
advertize
adderwort
edificial
Oddfellow
Adi-Granth
admirance
admirable
admirably
advisable
advisably
Admiralty
ad-libbing
advisedly
adviceful
adminicle
admission
admissive
admitting
addiction
admixture
addictive
odd-jobman
odd-jobber
adulterer
edelweiss
adulthood
addlement
odalisque
odd-lotter
Odelsting
adulation
adulatory
adamantly
adumbrate
udometric
ademption
Adamitism
edematose
edematous
aduncated
odontalgy
adenoidal
identical
identikit
Identi-Kit
adenomata
odontomas
Adansonia
adenosine
odonatist
idiomatic
advocator
adsorbent
adsorbate
ideophone
idiophone
adnominal
idiotical
admonitor
idioticon
idioblast
idioplasm
adjoining
ideologic
ideomotor
ideologue
ideograph
idiograph
advoutrer
adaptable
adipocere
adoptious
adeptness
adiposity
adornment
adoringly
addressed
addressee
addresser
addresses
adpressed
addressor
adoration
odorously
eduskunta
editorial
adjutancy
adjuvancy
adjunctly
adducible
odourless
adduction
adductive
iddy-umpty
megafarad
separates
metabasis
metabatic
debatable
get-at-able
reparable
reparably
repayable
separable
separably
megafauna
separator
megagauss
separatum
pedal-bone
cedar-bird
cevapcici
bepatched
debauched
debauchee
debaucher
decalcify
renascent
megascope
defaecate
defalcate
demarcate
Decandria
Hexandria
celandine
demandant
demanding
pen-and-ink
regardant
regarding
retardant
rewarding
wet-and-dry
decaudate
retardate
nefandous
regardful
rewardful
△temazepam
decadence
decadency
Hexateuch
recalesce
remanence
remanency
hexameter
metapelet
melanemia
menagerie
metameric
belatedly
cesarevna
Decameron
decametre
hexahedra
secateurs
megadeath
megahertz
revalenta
cepaceous
ceraceous
cetaceous
debateful
sebaceous
setaceous
Pelasgian
debagging
selachian
seraphims
megaphone
seraphine
seraphins
decathlon
refashion
decachord
hexachord
melaphyre
semaphore
metaphase
Hepaticae
hepatical
relatival
venatical
feralised
feralized
velarised
velarized
ceratitis
hematinic
hepatitis
keratitis
pedatifid
cebadilla
cevadilla
menadione
relations
decalitre
reradiate
retaliate
behaviour
feracious
nefarious
tenacious
veracious
vexatious
seraskier
repackage
Heraclean
defaulter
hexaploid
metalloid
befalling
bewailing
medalling
metalline
metalling
pedalling

Words marked △ may be spelled also with a capital letter

9 □e□a□l

medallion
seraglios
tenaillon
megaflora
medallist
metallise
metallist
metaplasm
metallize
debarment
recalment
repayment
besainted
remainder
demanning
retaining
degarnish
decagonal
decapodal
decapodan
hexagonal
melanomas
keratoses
telamones
teratogen
demagogic
hematosis
keratosis
melanosis
melanotic
melatonin
metabolic
pedagogic
megajoule
peraeopod
belamoure
ceratodus
decalogue
demagogue
pedagogue
melampode
megaspore
remarqued
repairman
relay-race
zelatrice
debarring
mepacrine
petaurine
veratrine
debarrass
Dekabrist
hetaerism
hetaerist
hetairism
hetairist
petaurist
repassage
relapsing
delapsion
decastich
hexastich
semantics
semantide
bez-antler
pecan-tree
oenanthic
decastyle
hexastyle
Melastoma
semanteme
defatting
departing
desalting
△levantine
recaption
redaction
semantron
decastere
departure
depasture
megastore
recapture
repasture
Xenarthra
pedantise
pedantism
rebaptise
rebaptism
se-baptist
decantate
devastate
cerastium
pedantize
rebaptize
hematuria
megacurie
melanuria
melanuric
megabucks
devaluate
tenaculum
cedarwood
medaewart
metalwork
Decagynia
Hexagynia
megacycle
bedazzled
semblance
sea-beaten
herb-Paris
semblable
semblably
herbicide
verbicide
herb-Peter
pebble-bed
redbreast
verballed
cembalist
herbalism
herbalist
verbalise
verbalism
verbalist
verbality
verbalize
Serbonian
temblores
cerberean
cerberian
herbarian
verbarian
herb-grace
berberine
herborise
herborist
verberate
herbarium
herborize
eel-basket
nebbisher
verbosely
verbosity
Verbascum
sea-bather
rebbetzin
bed-bottle
seabottle
kerbstone
herbivora
herbivore
herbivory
perchance
reactance
sex-change
merciable
peaceable
peaceably
perceable
reachable
rescuable
teachable
beach-ball
peach-blow
leuco-base
beccaccia
leucocyte
nescience
leucaemia
leucaemic
teacherly
percheron
new-create
beccafico
mercifide
beech-fern
perciform
hercogamy
beachhead
bench-hole
describer
perceiver
zecchinos
△herculean
d'escalier
pencilled
penciller
percaline
vetchling
pencil-ore
fenceless
merciless
mescalism
peaceless
reachless
retchless
teachless
percolate
Neocomian
welcoming
benchmark
beech-mast
Hercynian
percental
descended
descender
peccantly
mercenary
rencontre
deaconess
hercynite
bed-closet
mercaptan
peach-palm
peace-pipe
teacupful
cercariae
cercarian
△mercurial
red-carpet
geocarpic
mercerise
mercurise
mercurate
mercurous
mercerize
mercurize
mercy-seat
Reichsrat
Reichstag
Leicester
percussed
percussor
Leuciscus
bescatter
peach-tree
leucotome
leucotomy
peacetime
reacquire
reactuate
beech-wood
peach-wood
descrying
dead-march
readvance
dead-water
feed-water
head-water
tea-dealer
lead-paint
pendragon
hendiadys
beddy-byes
weedicide
pendicler
mendicant
headscarf
mendacity
mendicity
re-educate
reddleman
headpeace
headreach
dead-level
needle-tin
beadledom
seed-pearl
headlease
lend-lease
needleful
needle-gun
heddle-eye
re-edifier
verdigris
deid-thraw
headchair
headshake
head-rhyme
headphone
needy-hood
seldshown
headpiece
headliner
headlines
hen-driver
jet-driven
pen-driver
headlight
dendritic
seed-field
veldskoen
Mendelian
pendulums
penduline
seed-plant
feudalise
feudalism
feudalist
Mendelism
feudality
headcloth
pendulate

Words marked △ may be spelled also with a capital letter

pendulous
dead-alive
feudalize
ready-made
neodymium
reed-knife
bendingly
pendently
verdantly
deadening
reddendos
headiness
heediness
neediness
readiness
reediness
seediness
weediness
reddendum
redding-up
tendinous
head-woman
seed-coral
dead-doing
headboard
bead-house
deadhouse
feldspath
reed-organ
gendarmes
seed-drill
headframe
deodorant
rendering
tendering
bead-proof
herd-groom
deodorise
head-crash
headdress
readdress
reed-grass
tenderise
read-write
verdurous
weed-grown
deodorize
tenderize
geodesist
deadstock
feedstock
geodetics
headstick
headstock
feedstuff
headstall
seed-stalk
headstone
perdition
rendition
vendition
feudatory
heedfully
needfully
ready-wash
meadow-rue
relevance
relevancy
severance
hederated
leveraged
serenader
vegetated
telepathy
federarie
generalia
telematic
deferable
delegable
generable
generally
referable
relegable
renewable
reverable
severable
severally
vegetable
vegetably
venerable
venerably
defecator
generator
renegados
revelator
venerator
pederasty
severalty
peter-boat
resembler
hereabout
seneschal
beseeched
beseecher
decencies
remercied
level-coil
redescend
senescent
telescope
telescopy
jewel-case
repercuss
beheading
defendant
dependant
dependent
depending
Defenders
legendary
legendist
deference
reference
reverence
vehemence
vehemency
referenda
telemeter
tête-bêche
telegenic
cerebella
pedereros
redevelop
telemetry
venereous
hereafter
sevenfold
jewelfish
bevel-gear
beleaguer
detergent
revenging
Betelgeuz
revengive
fever-heat
petechiae
petechial
repechage
telepheme
telephone
telephony
telephoto
generical
genetical
heretical
venefical
beneficed
benefited
redeliver
televiser
teredines
benedight
Genesitic
selenitic
televisor
remediate
terebinth
selenious
reaedifye
genealogy
teleology
peneplain
rebel-like
bevelling
debelling
jewelling
leger-line
levelling
peneplane
rebelling
refelling
repellant
repellent
repelling
revealing
revelling
rebellion
jewellery
cerecloth
beseeming
besetment
bevelment
deferment
determent
determine
redeeming
revetment
nevermore
decennial
perennial
sexennial
hereunder
teleonomy
secernent
decennary
vexedness
belemnite
perennate
perennity
decennium
demeanour
developed
developer
△pele-tower
hegemonic
heterosis
heterotic
peperomia
semeiotic
telegonic
telepoint
heterodox
heteropod
pereiopod
△pele-house
reredorse
reredosse
reremouse
heteronym
reserpine
rehearsal
rerebrace
rehearser
redecraft
meteoroid
cerebrums
bebeerine
celebrant
deferring
deterrent
deterring
Dexedrine®
gemel-ring
penetrant
peregrine
referring
rehearing
terebrant
veneering
tenebrios
telegraph
meteorism
meteorist
tenebrism
tenebrist
tenebrose
celebrate
celebrity
cerebrate
desecrate
meteorite
penetrate
tenebrity
terebrate
meteorous
revel-rout
tenebrous
petersham
Teleostei
bedelship
reversely
reversing
decession
demersion
detersion
recension
recession
reversion
△secession
necessary
remeasure
necessity
teleosaur
defensive
detersive
recessive
celestial
fenestral
nemertean
nemertian
select-man
semestral
Terentian
metestick
telestich
fever-tree
mementoes
Nepenthes
seventeen
seventies
seventhly
begetting
besetting
△celestine
merestone

Words marked △ may be spelled also with a capital letter

9 □e□e□t

nemertine
relenting
repeating
repentant
revetting
deception
defection
dejection
desertion
detection
detention
reception
refection
rejection
resection
retention
selection
debenture
deceptory
defeature
dejectory
mesentery
refectory
repertory
retexture
sedentary
defeatism
defeatist
celestite
cementite
dementate
tête-à-tête
deceitful
resentful
deceptive
defective
detective
receptive
rejective
resentive
retentive
revertive
selective
reperusal
reservoir
deserving
receiving
decemviri
decemvirs
reservist
jewel-weed
remedying
beefeater
self-faced
self-abuse
perfecter
perfectly
perfector
perfectos
leaf-metal
leafleted

self-begot
renfierst
kerfuffle
red-figure
pen-friend
self-pious
beefaloes
new-fallen
self-slain
bedfellow
gerfalcon
jerfalcon
pew-fellow
self-image
feoffment
perfumery
deafening
leafiness
self-doubt
bee-flower
leaf-nosed
webfooted
leaf-mould
self-rowld
self-worth
leaf-trace
self-pride
leaf-green
performer
telferage
perfervid
perforans
perforant
seafaring
self-wrong
perfervor
self-trust
welfarism
welfarist
perforate
self-drive
sea-fisher
selfishly
perfusion
perfusate
perfusive
beefsteak
self-study
leaf-stalk
self-build
self-built
Delftware
self-aware
fee-faw-fum
sergeancy
vengeance
geography
zeugmatic
vengeable
vengeably
weighable

hedgebill
hedge-born
hedge-bote
neighbour
weigh-bauk
berg-adder
berg-cedar
Kerguelen
feignedly
lengthily
lengthful
penguinry
seigniory
Vergilian
bengaline
sedgeland
Bengalese
vengement
△bergamask
bergomask
pergunnah
bergander
merganser
beggingly
legginess
Reaganism
Reaganite
seignoral
geognosis
Zeuglodon
beggar-man
beggardom
vee-gutter
Neo-Gothic
weightily
weighting
wedgewise
déchéance
red-headed
nephralgy
Rechabite
methadone
pethidine
methodise
Methodism
△methodist
methodize
red-heeled
tee-heeing
rechlesse
reshuffle
meshugaas
nephogram
tephigram
metheglin
technical
red-haired
nephritic
nephritis
tephritic
technique

tephillah
penholder
pew-holder
nephology
tephillin
methylene
nepheline
nephalism
nephalist
netheless
cephalate
lethality
methylate
nephelite
segholate
cephalous
bethumbed
mechanics
redhanded
bethankit
mechanise
mechanism
mechanist
techiness
mechanize
dethroner
nephrosis
nephrotic
tephroite
recharter
recherché
lethargic
Sephardic
Sephardim
Senhorita
lecherous
methystic
Zechstein
mephitism
réchauffé
bethought
methought
yeshivahs
yeshivoth
perinaeal
perinatal
semi-bajan
demi-lance
hesitance
hesitancy
dedicated
dedicatee
medicated
meditated
cevitamic
genitalia
genitalic
decidable
decimally
definable
definably

demisable
derivable
derivably
desirable
desirably
devisable
helically
heritable
heritably
levigable
lexically
medicable
medically
revisable
revivable
revivably
seminally
veritable
veritably
decimator
dedicator
depilator
hesitator
Semi-Saxon
Pedipalpi
demitasse
perinaeum
△peripatus
perikarya
devil-crab
Meliaceae
periscian
meniscoid
dehiscent
desiccant
heliscoop
periscope
desiccate
zemindari
zemindary
periodate
remindful
mediaeval
semi-metal
venireman
desinence
penitence
penitency
renitency
residence
residency
reticence
reticency
bedizened
decimeter
deliverer
perimeter
demi-deify
demi-devil
peripetia
decidedly

deliverly
refinedly
reticella
retiredly
decimetre
hemihedry
perimetry
delineate
femineity
serinette
deviceful
sericeous
devil-fish
meningeal
Feringhee
teeing-off
besieging
Pekingese
redingote
benighted
benighten
benighter
delighted
perishing
periphery
fetichise
fetichism
fetichist
fetishise
fetishism
fetishist
fetichize
fetishize
feticidal
genitival
Helicidae
levitical
medicinal
Neritidae
regicidal
regiminal
semifinal
veridical
reminisce
deciliter
feliciter
mediciner
felicific
peridinia
retinitis
semi-rigid
sericitic
derisible
deliriums
deficient
definiens
deliriant
desipient
recipient
resilient
helipilot

decilitre
religiose
religioso
delicious
delirious
demipique
Leviticus
redivivus
religieux
religious
seditious
heli-skier
periaktos
Periclean
aetiology
heliology
semiology
megillahs
hemialgia
semifluid
petiolule
semiplume
devilling
pericline
perilling
pétillant
sea-island
decillion
penillion
vexillary
aerialist
genialise
periblast
periclase
periplast
serialise
serialism
serialist
aeriality
feuilleté
geniality
legislate
megilloth
petiolate
sepiolite
seriality
veniality
genialize
serialize
bedimming
devilment
refitment
remitment
melismata
defiantly
leniently
semiangle
beginning
benignant
designing
legionary

regionary
Fenianism
fetidness
gelidness
tepidness
benignity
designate
gelignite
designful
Meliboean
demi-monde
pericones
semivowel
demi-gorge
peridotic
resinosis
semisolid
semitonic
heliborne
periboloi
peribolos
semicolon
perimorph
demi-volte
peribolus
Menippean
hemispace
hemiopsia
perisperm
semi-Arian
periproct
peritrich
semi-truck
pedigreed
denitrify
devitrify
Félibrige
demiurgic
helidrome
peridrome
pericrany
semi-grand
hemitrope
serigraph
heritress
meliorism
meliorist
denigrate
denitrate
meliorate
meliority
remigrate
seniority
demiurgus
retiarius
semibreve
heliostat
devil's-bit
devilship
peninsula
demission

remission
remissory
tediosity
régisseur
demissive
remissive
△leviathan
registrar
revictual
hemistich
semiotics
geriatric
mediatrix
mediately
peristyle
seriately
peristome
befitting
besitting
penistone
refitting
remittent
remitting
resistant
resistent
depiction
deviation
mediation
seriation
heliotype
heliotypy
decistere
depicture
deviatory
Hemiptera
mediatory
periptery
mediatise
helictite
depictive
mediative
resistive
mediatize
pedicular
reliquiae
reticular
retinulae
retinular
semilunar
vehicular
vesiculae
vesicular
deviously
seriously
tediously
reliquary
residuary
deciduate
deciduous
deliquium
△pediculus

residuous
△reticulum
believing
relieving
hemicycle
pericycle
verifying
perilymph
heliozoan
heliozoic
serjeancy
serjeanty
bed-jacket
pea-jacket
verjuiced
Seljukian
perjurous
jerkwater
deck-cargo
leuko-base
leukocyte
beekeeper
leukaemia
neckverse
herkogamy
deckchair
neckpiece
weeknight
neckcloth
berkelium
weak-kneed
weekender
reckoning
jerkiness
leakiness
perkiness
deskbound
desk-bound
deckhouse
leukotome
leukotomy
hellwards
hell-hated
well-famed
belly-ache
weel-faird
weel-faur'd
weel-faurt
well-faurt
jellybean
beslobber
beslubber
bellibone
belly-band
welly-boot
hellebore
deflected
fetlocked
neglecter
reflected
reflecter

deflector
reflector
bellicose
replicate
vellicate
bell-metal
refluence
wellbeing
well-meant
veilleuse
Beelzebub
well-set-up
belly-flop
jelliform
jellyfish
geologian
neologian
jet-lagged
red-legged
reflagged
pellagrin
negligent
geologise
geologist
neologise
neologism
neologist
geologize
neologize
fellaheen
healthily
wealthily
cellphone
healthful
heel-piece
declaimer
reclaimer
well-aimed
well-given
well-lined
well-oiled
well-timed
hell-black
△celluloid®
bell-glass
cellulase
cellulose
realmless
cellulite
belle-mère
bedlamism
bedlamite
beglamour
wellanear
ceilinged
sex-linked
vellenage
tellinoid
feelingly
healingly
reelingly

tellingly
declinant
reclining
red-lining
Ceylonese
△hellenise
Hellenism
Hellenist
mealiness
replenish
ceylanite
ceylonite
declinate
reclinate
well-known
△hellenize
well-woman
bell-tower
△peel-tower
red-looked
well-borer
hellhound
sealpoint
well-doing
well-found
△peel-house
wellhouse
dewlapped
aeolipile
aeolipyle
well-spent
cellarman
Keplerian
tellurian
telluride
beglerbeg
de-blurred
well-tried
cellarage
declarant
tellurion
cellarist
tellurise
deflorate
hell-broth
tellurate
tellurite
cellarous
tellurium
tellurous
tellurize
beplaster
déclassée
realistic
hellishly
reclusely
realising
reblossom
reclusion
seclusion
reclusory

reclusive
seclusive
red-letter
pelletify
Bellatrix
Neolithic
deflation
depletion
fellation
fellatios
reflation
repletion
Sellotape®
sellotape
depletory
pellitory
pelletise
zealotism
depletive
pelletize
bell-punch
jealously
well-built
zealously
keelivine
keelyvine
declivity
re-elevate
declivous
fellow-man
reflowing
yellow-boy
yellowish
deflexion
defluxion
reflexion
deflexure
reflexive
realizing
permeance
permeable
permeably
germicide
vermicide
vermicule
Bermudian
desmodium
vermifuge
vermiform
termagant
Geomyidae
mermaiden
seemlihed
vermeille
seemliest
gemmology
reimplant
permalloy
vermilion
hermandad
segmental

tegmental
Germanice
fermented
geomancer
germander
segmented
sermoneer
geomantic
beamingly
germanely
seemingly
germinant
permanent
sermoning
beaminess
Germanise
Germanish
Germanism
Germanist
jemminess
△pelmanism
seaminess
sermonise
terminism
terminist
germinate
hetmanate
terminate
verminate
germanium
tegmentum
verminous
Germanize
sermonize
newmarket
tee-marker
mesmerise
mesmerism
mesmerist
mesmerize
bee-master
desmosome
kermesite
hermetics
besmutted
permitted
permitter
hermitage
dermatoid
geometric
geometrid
dermatome
gemmation
termitary
hermitess
lemmatise
pegmatite
permutate
gemmative
lemmatize
reimburse

seemlyhed
herniated
lean-faced
seannachy
reinhabit
Zernebock
penny-bank
Lemnaceae
sennachie
meandered
reindeers
beanfeast
penniform
meanwhile
fernticle
kennel-man
kennelled
pennyland
beingless
pennalism
penniless
vernalise
vernality
vernalize
neonomian
reanimate
Memnonian
pennoncel
meaningly
teknonymy
beingness
Mennonite
penninite
re-enforce
reinforce
re-endorse
reinvolve
reinspect
reinspire
penny-post
meandrian
Wernerian
Deinornis
penny-rent
re-entrant
wernerite
meandrous
Keynesian
Wednesday
benne-seed
benni-seed
deinosaur
rennet-bag
veinstuff
beanstalk
pennatula
reinstall
ternately
jenneting
veinstone
resnatron

Words marked △ may be spelled also with a capital letter

9 □e□r□a

vernation
means-test
reinstate
ceanothus
Pernettya
reinsurer
heinously
Jenny-wren
penny-wort
penny-wise
neo-Nazism
aeromancy
belomancy
ceromancy
oenomancy
resonance
memoranda
decorated
desolater
zero-rated
aerotaxis
celomatic
melomania
melomanic
oenomania
xenomania
denotable
deposable
memorable
memorably
removable
removably
revocable
revocably
revokable
meiofauna
decorator
desolator
detonator
renovator
resonator
menopause
redoubted
demobbing
recombine
resorbent
retoucher
bee-orchis
reconcile
rejoicing
fetoscopy
decoy-duck
beholding
recording
△secondary
recordist
recondite
redolence
redolency
aerometer
decoherer

mekometer
oenometer
pedometer
pew-opener
recoveree
recoverer
hecogenin
xenomenia
devotedly
reposedly
xeroderma
recoveror
aerometry
behoveful
reposeful
recomfort
reconfirm
lemonfish
decongest
besom-head
aerophobe
xenophobe
xenophoby
oesophagi
xerophagy
aeroshell
mesophyll
nemophila
oenophile
oenophily
xenophile
xerophily
aerophone
Oenothera
telophase
xerochasy
aerophyte
mesophyte
xerophyte
Belonidae
genocidal
Meropidae
meropidan
serotinal
memoriter
△menominee
pelorised
pelorized
aerolitic
cenobitic
memorials
Peronismo
aerobiont
defoliant
devotions
négociant
negotiant
depositor
repositor
defoliate
negotiate

Peronista
felonious
ferocious
melodious
véronique
recollect
re-collect
remoulade
rémoulade
mesogloea
aeroplane
mesoblast
decollate
décolleté
reformade
reformado
recommend
reformism
reformist
deformity
recountal
reconnect
denouncer
refounder
rejoinder
renouncer
recoinage
bemoaning
besognios
recognise
recognize
hemoconia
serotonin
aeromotor
melocoton
mesomorph
xeromorph
merozoite
melon-pear
aerospace
recompact
decomplex
decoupage
découpage
devonport
decompose
recompose
reconquer
△democracy
menorrhea
resources
xenograft
aerotrain
bezoardic
aerodrome
melodrama
melodrame
velodrome
devouring
aerograph
cerograph

memoirism
memoirist
xenocryst
democraty
heronshaw
bemonster
meroistic
perovskia
lemon-sole
rehousing
detorsion
retorsion
repossess
refortify
reportage
xerostoma
befortune
besotting
remontant
reporting
repotting
revolting
veloutine
decoction
decontrol
detortion
reboation
retortion
decocture
Mecoptera
decoctive
retortive
resoluble
désoeuvré
reconvene
resolvent
revolving
reconvert
lemon-weed
genotypic
hemolysis
hemolytic
metonymic
zelotypia
net-player
reapparel
temptable
red-plague
henpecked
respecter
bespeckle
hen-paddle
telpheric
hey-presto
serpigoes
despoiler
peep-sight
delphinia
geophilic
Memphitic
neophilia

hen-paidle
Delphinus
pemphigus
leg-puller
red-polled
neopilina
serpulite
Melpomene
despumate
geoponics
responder
responser
terpenoid
bespangle
weepingly
responsor
terpineol
serpentry
responsum
deep-toned
geophones
neophobia
neophobic
merpeople
reappoint
Hesperian
desperado
jeoparder
peppering
pepperoni
tempering
pepper-box
pepper-pot
temporary
temporise
temptress
desperate
temperate
deiparous
leaperous
leaporous
deep-drawn
temporize
Herpestes
pen-pusher
heapstead
perpetual
bespatter
bespotted
herpetoid
cespitose
despotism
despotate
geophytic
neophytic
becquerel
recreance
recreancy
retreaded
rearrange
heartache

9 □e□r□a

Wehrmacht
learnable
△lehrjahre
△béarnaise
ferry-boat
heartbeat
reprobacy
heart-bond
heartburn
reprobate
retribute
metrician
retrocede
refracted
retracted
sea-rocket
neurochip
febricula
febricule
terricole
terracing
detractor
refractor
retractor
negro-corn
serricorn
metricise
metricist
reprocess
verrucose
deprecate
febricity
metricate
verrucous
metricize
heart-dear
Hebridean
Hebridian
perradial
reproduce
bedridden
betrodden
retrodden
degrading
depredate
tetradite
perradius
degree-day
reprieval
retrieval
deer-fence
gear-lever
hearkener
pearl-eyed
retriever
pearl-edge
learnedly
decreeing
bear-berry
deerberry
georgette

heart-free
metrifier
petrified
retroflex
terrified
terrifier
febrifuge
heartfelt
serrefile
bear's-foot
terraform
deprogram
ferrogram
neurogram
pearl-gray
petrogram
reprogram
△tetragram
pearl-grey
neuroglia
bedraggle
segregate
hearth-tax
negrohead
gearwheel
tearsheet
gearshift
deprehend
reprehend
searching
near-white
hearth-rug
Hebraical
negroidal
recruital
debruised
Hebraiser
Hebraizer
pearlised
pearlized
recruiter
pearlings
rear-light
heartikin
pearlitic
retroject
petrolled
metrology
necrology
neurology
petrolage
petrology
tetralogy
neuralgia
neuralgic
heartland
heartling
Negrillos
beardless
heartless
weariless

febrility
neurility
serrulate
petroleum
pétroleur
merry-make
decrement
detriment
herriment
herryment
merriment
recrement
reprimand
terramara
terramare
neuromata
derring-do
derringer
herringer
serranoid
jeeringly
leeringly
terrenely
veeringly
wearingly
metronome
beeriness
merriness
Petrinism
weariness
weirdness
beer-money
deer-hound
year-round
beer-house
deer-mouse
rear-dorse
rearhorse
rearmouse
tetrapody
bedropped
metroplex
necrophil
negrophil
neuropath
détraquée
tetrarchy
terrorise
terrorism
terrorist
terrarium
terrorful
terrorize
pearl-spar
heart-sick
defroster
depressed
heartseed
medresseh
redresser
refreshen

refresher
repressed
pearl-sago
heuristic
peirastic
bearishly
heartsome
wearisome
represent
re-present
depressor
detrusion
jerry-shop
repressor
heart-sore
leprosery
leprosity
betrothal
heir-at-law
gear-stick
negritude
négritude
betrothed
regretted
rewritten
secretage
tear-strip
△decretals
red-rattle
necrotomy
neurotomy
ferreting
regrating
detrition
neuration
secretion
serration
ferrotype
decretory
secretary
secretory
serrature
△territory
decretist
necrotise
regretful
decretive
secretive
necrotize
rearousal
defrauder
fearfully
tearfully
rearguard
retroussé
reproving
sea-roving
retrovert
depravity
heartwood
zebra-wood

pearlwort
Hebrewess
Hebrewism
tetroxide
defraying
terrazzos
newspaper
persuader
reistafel
Teeswater
geostatic
△messianic
sensually
feiseanna
news-value
leaseback
lease-band
fen-sucked
Persicise
persecute
Persicize
Menshevik
persienne
penstemon
△messieurs
neesberry
densifier
versified
versifier
cease-fire
versiform
messaging
newsagent
news-sheet
leasehold
beasthood
geosphere
deistical
seismical
hem-stitch
Jew's-pitch
beastings
beestings
ressaldar
tessellae
tessellar
teaselled
teaseller
weaseller
beastlike
yeastlike
lease-lend
perseline
teaseling
ceaseless
menseless
newsflash
senseless
tenseless
pensility
tensility

Words marked △ may be spelled also with a capital letter

sensillum
pease-meal
Welsummer
gelsemine
gessamine
jessamine
persimmon
pessimism
pessimist
gelsemium
yersiniae
yersinias
messenger
personnel
personify
personage
teasingly
lessoning
reasoning
seasoning
peasantry
denseness
messiness
newsiness
personise
tenseness
terseness
hessonite
pepsinate
personate
personize
newswoman
sessional
tensional
versional
pensioner
versioner
newshound
bedspread
censorial
censorian
jetstream
jet-stream
menstrual
redstreak
sensorial
tesseract
newstrade
berserker
keystroke
berserkly
leisurely
sensorily
△jews'-trump
cee-spring
gee-string
jesserant
measuring
newsprint
feast-rite
geyserite

menstruum
sensorium
pease-soup
celsitude
bed-settee
bed-sitter
jet-setter
pet-sitter
versatile
Jew's-stone
news-stand
cessation
sensation
tessitura
sensitise
sensitive
sensitize
pea-souper
reassurer
tee-square
pensively
persevere
peaseweep
fesse-wise
leastwise
leastways
leftwards
westwards
besteaded
meat-eater
melt-water
tent-maker
centrally
dextrally
neutrally
textually
ventrally
perttaunt
restraint
vertebrae
vertebral
death-bell
vestibule
depth-bomb
death-blow
heathbird
west-about
petticoat
heathcock
menticide
pesticide
tentacled
geotactic
death-cell
tentacula
fettucine
fettucini
Celticism
Celticist
Kelticism
Pentecost

pepticity
septicity
verticity
ventiduct
death-damp
c'est-à-dire
peptidase
death-duty
gentleman
sentience
sentiency
bestrewed
feathered
gentlemen
settle-bed
weathered
kentledge
aesthesia
aesthesis
aesthetic
genteelly
weatherly
centreing
reattempt
heathenry
Weltgeist
△zeitgeist
neutretto
kettleful
ventifact
certified
certifier
rectified
rectifier
testified
testifier
neat's-foot
death-fire
dentiform
lentiform
restiform
septiform
tectiform
heath-fowl
centigram
hectogram
pentagram
vestigial
vertigoes
heptaglot
vestigium
textphone
centrical
rectrices
tectrices
restringe
neoteinia
perthitic
centriole
certainly
left-field

ventricle
neutrinos
certainty
reptilian
rentaller
festilogy
festology
pentalogy
pestology
pentalpha
reptiloid
deathlike
fertilely
pentylene
pestilent
deathless
depthless
fertilise
gentilise
gentilish
gentilism
mentalism
mentalist
fertility
gentility
mentality
pectolite
sectility
tent-cloth
ventilate
dentalium
fertilize
gentilize
destemper
September
centumvir
septemfid
septemvir
peat-smoke
septimole
sentiment
△testament
testimony
vestiment
pentamery
death-mask
Neptunian
Newtonian
pectineal
sextantal
tectonics
centenier
sentencer
septennia
centinell
jestingly
meltingly
peltingly
pentangle
rectangle
weetingly

pertinent
centenary
septenary
centonist
heftiness
jettiness
meatiness
Neptunist
peptonise
pettiness
sextoness
testiness
Teutonise
Teutonism
Teutonist
bentonite
centonate
destinate
festinate
pectinate
neotenous
neptunium
peptonize
Teutonize
sectional
destroyed
destroyer
oestrogen
benthonic
geotropic
leitmotif
leitmotiv
westbound
dextrorse
neat-house
penthouse
pesthouse
rest-house
west-north
centipede
heptapody
peat-spade
pentapody
septuplet
sextuplet
vertiport
red-tapism
red-tapist
centurial
hesternal
letter-gae
mentorial
nectareal
nectarean
nectarial
Nestorian
rectorial
sectarial
sectarian
sectorial
septarian

9 □e□t□r

tectorial
tentorial
textorial
vectorial
yesterday
deuteride
peat-creel
perturbed
perturber
restarter
△westerner
setter-off
heptarchy
pentarchy
sestertia
death-roll
featurely
bettering
centering
gettering
hectoring
lettering
mentoring
nectarine
reiterant
vectoring
venturing
vetturini
vetturino
weltering
westering
centurion
letterbox
bent-grass
hectorism
neoterise
neoterism
neoterist
rectoress
sectorise
texturise
vectorise
death-rate
deuterate
dexterity
lectorate
rectorate
reiterate
tenth-rate
deuterium
dexterous
nectarous
pesterous
septarium
setter-out
tentorium
tetterous
venturous
test-drive
yestereve
neoterize

sectorize
texturize
vectorize
deathsman
pertussal
tea-taster
pertussis
pettishly
centesimo
leptosome
death-song
pentosane
pertusion
dentistry
pertusate
ventosity
death-trap
Pentothal®
peat-stack
seat-stick
beatitude
certitude
rectitude
Weltstadt
pettitoes
testatrix
neat-stall
teetotums
leptotene
dentation
dentition
gestation
mentation
reptation
septation
sestettos
tentation
testation
gestatory
jettatura
vestiture
destitute
restitute
gestative
tentative
centaurea
kent-bugle
restfully
zestfully
Centaurus
festively
restively
leftovers
aestivate
festivity
festivous
delta-wing
deathward
pentoxide
vestryman
petulance

petulancy
recusance
recusancy
securance
Jerusalem
tegulated
deludable
rebukable
refusable
refutable
refutably
regularly
reputable
reputably
resumable
secularly
securable
tegularly
tenurable
depurator
peculator
regulator
débutante
penumbral
betumbled
decumbent
recumbent
refurbish
nelumbium
semuncial
requicken
sepulcher
demulcent
sepulchre
sequacity
beau-ideal
gerundial
delundung
redundant
secundine
fecundate
fecundity
gerundive
feculence
feculency
temulence
temulency
oecumenic
refusenik
reputedly
teru-teros
beauteous
ceruleous
rebukeful
refulgent
resurgent
securitan
nebuliser
nebulizer
Jebusitic
deducible

reducible
delusions
pecuniary
repudiate
vedutista
vedutisti
beautiful
decubitus
pecunious
penurious
gemütlich
genuflect
medullary
republish
sexualise
sexualism
sexualist
medullate
sexuality
sexualize
rebutment
sequencer
sequinned
béguinage
genuinely
repugnant
refurnish
desulphur
resurrect
fenugreek
demurrage
decurrent
demurring
recurrent
recurring
requiring
reguerdon
jequirity
menuisier
requester
sequester
demulsify
debussing
decursion
recursion
repulsion
revulsion
sequestra
cerussite
decussate
requisite
decursive
recursive
repulsive
revulsive
desuetude
requitted
penultima
rebutting
reductant
reluctant

resultant
resulting
deduction
reduction
seduction
desultory
sepulture
Jesuitism
reductase
degustate
reluctate
resultful
deductive
reductive
seductive
tenuously
pervicacy
belvedere
fervidity
heavy-duty
serviette
pelviform
net-veined
vervelled
weevilled
servilely
sexvalent
tervalent
nerveless
servilism
servility
fervently
leavening
servantry
heaviness
nerviness
leavenous
perverter
renversed
fervorous
peevishly
pervasion
Leavisite
pervasive
Helvetian
servitude
velveteen
velveting
nervation
nervature
helvetium
nervously
sea-walled
net-winged
networker
bed-worthy
seaworthy
seawardly
hen-witted
deoxidise
deoxidate

Words marked △ may be spelled also with a capital letter

deoxidize
re-examine
hedyphane
Hesychasm
Hesychast
recyclist
beryllium
denyingly
Aepyornis
dehydrate
rehydrate
demystify
benzidine
benzoline
mezzanine
mezzotint
terzettos
aflatoxin
off-chance
off-colour
off-centre
off-cutter
offerable
after-clap
after-crop
aftercare
afterdeck
after-damp
offending
efference
aftergame
afterglow
afterheat
afterings
offerings
after-life
aftermost
aftermath
afternoon
oftenness
offensive
effectual
aftertime
affecting
affection
offertory
affective
effective
afterward
afterword
offhanded
Africaner
Afrikaner
affidavit
Afrikaans
office-boy
officinal
efficient
officiant
affiliate
officiate

officious
affirmant
affianced
afflicted
affluence
effluence
ufologist
off-limits
afflation
effluvial
effluvium
affluxion
effluxion
Afro-Asian
effortful
off-putter
sforzandi
sforzando
sforzatos
affricate
aforehand
affrended
affronted
affrontee
affrontée
aforesaid
aforetime
offseason
offsaddle
off-stream
off-street
offspring
off-the-peg
effulgent
effulging
sgian-dubh
sgraffiti
sgraffito
agnatical
Iguanidae
iguanodon
eglantine
egg-beater
Yggdrasil
agreeable
agreeably
ignescent
agréments
egregious
agreement
ague-proof
egression
agrestial
ignitable
ignitible
agriology
agalactia
agelastic
Agamemnon
egomaniac
agonistes

agonistic
agonising
agonizing
ignorance
ignorable
ignoramus
agnominal
agronomic
Agapemone
egg-powder
aggrieved
aggregate
égarement
aggressor
aggravate
agistment
egotheism
egotistic
agitation
agitative
agateware
pheasants
thearchic
theandric
phraseman
cheapener
theaceous
chiarezza
sheatfish
shear-hulk
sheathing
thrashing
cheap-jack
chiacking
thwacking
phialling
shearling
thralldom
wheatmeal
chiasmata
cheapness
shoalness
thrasonic
whoa-ho-hoa
theatrics
thwarting
wheatworm
shoalwise
chlamydes
chlamyses
chlamydia
shebeener
shibuichi
chubb-lock
Ghibeline
shubunkin
chibouque
chabazite
chickadee
chickaree
cha-cha-cha

shockable
chechaqua
chechaquo
checkbook
phycocyan
thecodont
checkered
shickered
thickener
thicketed
thick-eyed
whichever
shochetim
chock-full
chuck-full
shock-head
thickhead
chuckhole
phacoidal
Shechinah
shechitah
rhachides
rhachises
rhachitis
thick-knee
phycology
chickling
chuckling
thick-lips
checklist
chocolate
chocolaty
phacolite
phacolith
checkmate
chicaning
chicanery
thickness
checkrail
checkrein
checkroom
thickskin
thick-sown
check-till
chickweed
shadberry
chidlings
shadeless
rhodolite
rhodamine
whodunnit
rhodanise
shadiness
rhodanate
rhodonite
rhodanize
rhodopsin
Rhodesian
khedivial
khedivate
shadowing

shoemaker
cheekbone
wheelbase
three-card
sheepcote
shield-may
shielduck
three-deck
threadfin
rhoeadine
shielding
shredding
shield-arm
cheesevat
phrenesis
phrenetic
threnetic
sheet-feed
sheepfold
threefold
three-foot
three-four
cheechako
sheer-hulk
threshold
shoeshine
threshing
sheep-hook
phlebitis
phrenitic
phrenitis
sheet-iron
sheet-lead
sheep-lice
shoeblack
shtetlach
sheerlegs
thief-like
chiefling
three-line
wheedling
cheerless
chiefless
shredless
shrewmice
threonine
threeness
phaenogam
threnodic
chaetodon
chaetopod
three-pair
three-pile
three-part
three-star
chiefship
sheep's-bit
sheepskin
threesome
Thyestean
Thyestian

9 □h□e□t

phrentick
chieftain
threatful
sheepwalk
wheelwork
sheep-wash
theftboot
theft-bote
chafferer
chaffinch
shuffling
whiffling
whifflery
shaftless
shiftless
theftuous
shag-eared
thighbone
phagocyte
phagedena
chagrined
shogunate
thegither
shaggy-dog
chihuahua
phthalein
phthalate
chthonian
shlimazel
shriveled
choiceful
chain-gear
choir-girl
sheikhdom
cheilitis
shrinkage
shrieking
shrinking
shriek-owl
chairlift
shrilling
thrillant
thrilling
chainless
shrimping
chainshot
Christian
Christmas
thriftier
thriftily
chainwork
shakeable
chokebore
chokecoil
chokedamp
shakedown
choke-full
shakiness
choke-pear
Shakerism
Chekovian

Chaldaean
shillalah
chiliarch
phillabeg
shillaber
chiliagon
chaldaism
chalybean
whaleboat
shellback
whaleback
whole-body
whalebone
shellbark
chalybite
tholobate
thylacine
chelicera
cholecyst
sheldduck
shellduck
sheltered
shelterer
challenge
cholaemia
cholaemic
chalkface
shelf-fuls
wholefood
cheliform
shellfire
shellfish
khalifate
philogyny
phylogeny
whale-head
shell-hole
childhood
cheloidal
phillibeg
shelf-life
whole-life
philology
chilblain
childlike
shelflike
shell-like
shell-lime
childless
shell-less
cholelith
chalumeau
wholemeal
Philomela
Philomene
shelf-mark
shell-marl
philomath
Thelemite
chelonian
phalangal

phalanger
phalanges
phalanxes
△philander
phalangid
phelonion
childness
chillness
wholeness
phellogen
shallowly
phyllopod
philhorse
Chilopoda
△philippic
philopena
shell-pink
phylarchy
choleraic
sheldrake
shelfroom
phalarope
Philister
chelaship
thalassic
wholistic
wholesale
wholesome
shell-sand
thelytoky
philately
chelation
phalluses
thalluses
child-wife
shellwork
Phillyrea
whillywha
chalazion
shamianah
champaign
shameable
champagne
chemicked
thymocyte
thymidine
chambered
chamberer
chamfered
whimperer
chimaerid
whimberry
champerty
shamefast
rhamphoid
thumb-hole
whimsical
thumbkins
thumblike
rhumb-line
shambling

thumbling
chameleon
rhymeless
shameless
themeless
thumbless
champlevé
chamomile
thumb-mark
thumbnail
△shamanism
shamanist
shampooed
shampooer
shambolic
shammosim
chamfrain
chemurgic
thumb-ring
chimerism
chemostat
rhymester
Thomistic
chemistry
chymistry
thumbtack
chemitype
chemitypy
shamateur
rhombuses
rhyme-word
shemozzle
shimozzle
khansamah
thin-faced
chincapin
chinkapin
phantasim
shunnable
thinkable
phantasma
phantasms
shankbone
thenabout
Phenician
shanachie
phonecard
phenacite
ahungered
channeler
phonmeter
thunderer
whencever
chandelle
thin-belly
whingeing
whinberry
chanteuse
chanceful
changeful
phonogram

rhonchial
shanghai'd
thanehood
thinghood
Rhynchota
phansigar
phengites
thankings
Chantilly
Chanukkah
phenakism
phenakite
phenology
phonology
rhinology
shingling
Chandler's
chandlery
shineless
thankless
phenolate
phonolite
rhinolith
phonemics
phenomena
shiningly
whiningly
phoniness
shininess
thingness
whininess
whensoe'er
chincough
phantosme
Rhineodon
Shintoism
Shintoist
phonopore
chondrify
chancroid
chondroid
chondrule
Shangri-la
chinaroot
Phanariot
chantress
chondrite
chancrous
thundrous
thaneship
chinstrap
phenetics
phonetics
thanatoid
think-tank
whinstone
whunstane
phonation
phenotype
phonotype
phonotypy

phonatory
phonetise
phonetism
phonetist
thanatism
thanatist
Chinatown
phonetize
thingummy
chinovnik
△chinaware
shantyman
whinnying
throwaway
theomancy
chromakey
theomachy
theopathy
chromatic
chromatid
chromatin
chronaxie
rheotaxis
theomania
shootable
chloracne
throwback
throbbing
theorbist
thrombose
chlordane
shrouding
throw-down
rheometer
theoretic
chlorella
shoot-'em-up
shroffage
cheongsam
throughly
thronging
throngful
theophagy
theophany
thiophene
rheochord
chronical
theoriser
theorizer
chloritic
chromidia
rhyolitic
chronicle
theorique
throbless
chromogen
theologer
theosophy
chlorosis
chlorotic
rheologic
theogonic
theologic
theotokos
theologue
theocracy
Theobroma
rheotrope
theocrasy
throwster
thio-ether
throttler
throatily
chip-based
shapeable
chaprassi
chaprassy
chuprassy
chipochia
rhipidion
rhipidate
rhipidium
chapleted
whipper-in
shipshape
rhaphides
shop-floor
chapeless
rhopalism
shapeless
chipolata
rhapontic
whipcordy
choplogic
rhapsodic
shippound
whip-round
chipboard
shipboard
shopboard
chophouse
chop-house
chaparral
shipwreck
whip-graft
chaperone
shopfront
shophroth
chapstick
chopstick
whipstock
whipstaff
whipstall
ship-owner
chequered
charlatan
thereaway
theriacal
shirralee
Third-Ager
sherwanis
thermally
thornback
Charybdis
thornbill
cherubims
charabanc
char-à-banc
shirtband
shorebird
thornbush
Characeae
short-coat
character
shortcake
sharecrop
short-cord
churidars
charge-cap
charge-man
chartered
charterer
sharpener
sharp-eyed
shortener
Thargelia
charmeuse
chargeful
sherifian
shortfall
therefrom
wherefrom
therefore
wherefore
chiragric
shortgown
churchman
churchway
short-head
cherchef't
church-ale
shorthold
churching
shorthand
third-hand
shorthorn
churchism
short-haul
thermical
Thersitic
whirligig
△thermidor
thereinto
thirtieth
whereinto
short-life
chirology
chorology
therology
Charolais
shoreline
charmless
chartless
choralist
shirtless
shoreless
short-list
thornless
cheralite
chirality
theralite
churnmilk
pheromone
shire-moot
cherimoya
chirimoya
pharyngal
pharynges
pharynxes
chironomy
chariness
sharpness
shortness
thereness
whereness
charwoman
chernozem
chorionic
pharaonic
thermotic
charlotte
chiropody
Theropoda
therapsid
whirlpool
therapist
chart-room
third-rate
sharesman
shoresman
thirdsman
shore-side
cherished
chorister
pharisaic
sharkskin
dharmsala
whorishly
chorusing
sharp-shod
shortstop
thyristor
charoseth
charities
thorntree
thirstily
short-time
thyratron
short-term
thirstful
thereupon
whereupon
thereunto
whereunto
Theravada
charivari
thorow-wax
shoreweed
whirlwind
churr-worm
shareware
shoreward
therewith
wherewith
short-wave
thyroxine
wherryman
cherry-pie
cherry-pit
cherry-bob
thirtyish
chorizont
physician
physicked
physicism
physicist
Chasidism
chastened
chastener
whiskered
whisperer
whosoever
chassepot
ghastfull
phosphide
phosphene
phosphine
phosphate
phosphite
Phasmidae
Chassidic
shashlick
chiselled
chiseller
ghostlike
whistling
phaseless
Thysanura
ghastness
chest-note
phaseolin
chaseport
thesaurus
shotmaker
whittawer
whitebeam
whitebait
whitebass
whitecoat
photocell
photocopy
rhotacise
rhotacism
rhotacize
chatterer

shattered
shuttered
white-face
photogram
photogene
photogeny
phytogeny
whitehead
Whitehall
thatching
shotfirer
chitlings
phytology
châtelain
whittling
photolyse
whet-slate
rhythmics
rhythmise
rhythmist
rhythmize
photonics
chitinoid
whitening
whiteness
chitinous
whatsoe'er
ghettoise
Whitworth
ghettoize
photophil
photopsia
shotproof
rhetorise
rhetorize
Photostat®
white-seam
white-shoe
phytotomy
whetstone
phytotron
phototype
phototypy
whitewall
whitewing
whitewood
whiteware
whitewash
chatoyant
thousands
rheumatic
rheumatiz
thaumatin
shrubbery
shouldest
thrum-eyed
chauffeur
shrugging
theurgist
thoughted
thoughten
shrublike
shoutline
shrubless
thrumming
shtupping
thrusting
thrust-hoe
chevrette
chevalier
shovelled
shoveller
chivalric
shaveling
chevelure
shovelful
chavender
chevroned
shivering
showmanly
chawbacon
chowkidar
showpiece
showbizzy
showplace
shawlless
showiness
shewbread
showbread
showering
showerful
whey-faced
chrysalid
chrysalis
chrysanth
chiyogami
phlyctena
whizz-bang
△rhizobium
rhizocarp
rhizocaul
rhizoidal
Rhizopoda
Himalayan
dilatancy
jigamaree
dilatable
dilatator
financial
financier
disanchor
vitascope
disaccord
Ricardian
ribaudred
vivandier
girandola
girandole
filanders
hit-and-run
tip-and-run
tie-and-dye
bicameral
bilateral
bivalence
bivalency
divalency
mirabelle
silageing
cigarette
gigahertz
vivamente
filaceous
limaceous
micaceous
vinaceous
disaffect
giraffoid
giraffine
disaffirm
lilangeni
sisal-hemp
piratical
misavised
vitaliser
vitalizer
mirabilia
△mirabilis
cigarillo
vivariums
bivariant
bilabiate
bivariate
vicariate
visagiste
bibacious
bifarious
dicacious
hilarious
minacious
vicarious
vivacious
misallied
misallege
rivalling
rivalless
mica-slate
piña-cloth
disarming
misaunter
disavowal
simarouba
disavouch
pinafored
disanoint
viragoish
disappear
cisalpine
dika-bread
cicatrice
cicatrise
cicatrize
misassign
rivalship
Sivaistic
sizarship
vicarship
Dinantian
gigantean
didactics
digastric
disattune
dicastery
disattire
gigantism
bipartite
ribattuta
ailanthus
sitatunga
hibakusha
misadvise
disbranch
air-bubble
misbecome
Timbuctoo
disbodied
diablerie
oil-beetle
nimblesse
Kirbigrip®
kirbigrip
kirby-grip
misbehave
air-bridge
fimbriate
Hizbollah
Hizbullah
disbelief
misbelief
diabology
diabolise
diabolism
diabolist
liability
viability
diabolize
Gibbonian
Ribbon-man
Ribbonism
disbursal
timber-man
disburden
Limburger
oil-burner
timbering
gibberish
misbeseem
misbestow
gibbosity
kibbutzim
gibbously
mischance
mischancy
discharge
mischarge
pinchbeck
aitchbone
pinchcock
circadian
piccadell
piccadill
diacodion
pitch-dark
viscidity
diacodium
kitchener
discredit
miscredit
miscreant
nipcheese
tip-cheese
miscreate
witchetty
pisciform
pitchfork
pinchfist
miscegene
miscegine
hitch-hike
diactinal
discoidal
diacritic
diactinic
circuitry
witchknot
discalced
witchlike
zinc-bloom
pieceless
circulate
niccolite
discolour
miscolour
oil-colour
mincemeat
piecemeal
witchmeal
discumber
discomfit
discommon
discandie
mincingly
circinate
diaconate
cincinnus
zirconium
air-cooled
cinchonic
pitch-pole
pitch-poll
hiccuping
pitchpine
pitchpipe
wincopipe
sincipita

Words marked △ may be spelled also with a capital letter

sinciputs
discerner
dip-circle
sincerely
piece-rate
sincerity
viscerate
discursus
hircosity
viscosity
pitch-tree
piscatrix
piscatory
siccative
dischurch
cinctured
linctuses
discourse
lincrusta
viscounty
piacevole
discovert
discovery
air-cavity
witch-wife
piece-work
diachylon
diachylum
hindrance
windwards
bird-table
find-fault
vindicate
middleman
misdeemed
middle-age
tie-dyeing
fiddle-bow
hindberry
bird's-foot
hind-wheel
wind-shak'd
windshake
wind-chill
windthrow
disdained
middlings
riddlings
hindsight
windtight
Mindelian
rix-dollar
bird-alane
bird-alone
windblown
misdemean
vindemial
windingly
bird's-nest
giddiness
windiness
hiddenite
bird-lover
windhover
windborne
windbound
bird-house
bird-louse
wild-goose
yird-house
windbreak
misdirect
hindbrain
kilderkin
hinder-end
niddering
wildering
tinderbox
windproof
Pindarise
Pindarism
Pindarist
wildgrave
Pindarize
Yiddisher
misdesert
windstorm
mind-curer
mindfully
wind-swift
kiddywink
windowing
windswept
hivewards
sidewards
fire-eater
fire-water
life-saver
limewater
mine-layer
pipe-layer
rice-water
tidewater
tide-gauge
cinematic
cineramic
cineraria
kinematic
literatim
disenable
liberally
life-table
literally
miserable
miserably
timetable
cinerator
fife-major
liberator
literator
time-lapse
literatus
river-boat
disembody
riverbank
disembark
libecchio
timescale
virescent
libeccios
kinescope
ninescore
ricercare
ricercata
Big-endian
eider-duck
videodisc
eiderdown
vice-regal
fivepence
line-fence
ninepence
pike-perch
diaereses
bigeneric
diaeresis
fivepenny
ninepenny
vicereine
life-weary
nine-metre
wineberry
cinereous
river-flat
linen-fold
videogram
disengage
air-engine
divergent
diverging
oil-engine
river-head
rivet-head
bioethics
side-wheel
vice-chair
hidey-hole
rivet-hole
sideshoot
firethorn
time-share
wirephoto
kinetical
mimetical
vicesimal
vigesimal
Viperidae
pine-finch
timepiece
life-sized
sidelined
sidelines
videlicet
firelight
limelight
pipe-light
sidelight
sideritic
minefield
rice-field
eirenicon
ninetieth
dioecious
river-jack
firefloat
wipe-clean
fireplace
kite-flyer
riverlike
divellent
libellant
libelling
niderling
vitelline
zibelline
life-blood
fire-alarm
vitellary
fiberless
fire-blast
riderless
riverless
sinewless
wineglass
lineality
lineolate
libellous
lineament
Hibernian
vicennial
pigeon-pea
wide-angle
mire-snipe
fixedness
givenness
hibernise
mixedness
tiredness
Gibeonite
hibernate
Simeonite
hibernize
firewoman
piperonal
tire-woman
life-force
cicerones
fire-power
fire-robed
hive-honey
nineholes
sidebones
Ciceronic
siderosis
fireworks
hide-bound
lime-hound
sideboard
firehouse
pine-house
fine-tooth
timenoguy
Didelphia
didelphic
didelphid
Didelphis
pineapple
disemploy
misemploy
Didelphys
fire-break
firebrick
pipe-track
sidetrack
wisecrack
lime-green
ricegrain
fire-drake
timeframe
firebrand
fire-irons
viverrine
fire-arrow
fireproof
firecrest
rice-grass
side-dress
winepress
biserrate
fire-grate
linearity
line-grove
fine-drawn
wiredrawn
five-a-side
riverside
diversify
fideistic
diversely
finessing
river-sand
dimension
diversion
licensure
diversity
hideosity
tiger's-eye
fire-stick
livestock
vine-stock
dipeptide
river-tide
disesteem
liberties
misesteem

9 □i□e□t

pikestaff
directrix
disentail
lifestyle
disentomb
lipectomy
diverting
eigentone
firestone
libertine
△limestone
milestone
minestone
pipestone
rivetting
sin-eating
tile-stone
wine-stone
bijection
bisection
digestion
direction
lineation
videotape
△directory
divesture
fire-storm
line-storm
bidentate
dioestrus
digestive
directive
divertive
videotext
vice-queen
direfully
hideously
piteously
timeously
sideburns
ritenutos
fireguard
lifeguard
bile-ducts
binervate
mine-owner
riverweed
wideawake
river-wall
fixed-wing
liver-wing
tiger-wood
sideswipe
liverwort
liveryman
life-cycle
niff-naffy
misfeasor
difficile
difficult
diffident
siffleuse
disfigure
misfallen
oil-filled
△zinfandel
miffiness
fin-footed
six-footer
tit-for-tat
pilferage
different
misfaring
pilfering
pifferari
pifferaro
disforest
diffusely
diffusion
diffusive
diffluent
disfluent
disfavour
ring-canal
ring-dance
disgracer
kingmaker
ring-gauge
biography
lingually
qinghaosu
tinguaite
piggyback
ridgeback
piggy-bank
ridge-bone
disgodded
ring-fence
ringleted
single-sex
king's-evil
single-end
singleton
vingt-et-un
misguggle
ring-shake
king's-hood
disguised
disguiser
king-sized
misguided
misguider
pilgrimer
ringsider
bilge-keel
Virgilian
singalong
ting-a-ling
liege-lord
Cingalese
liegeless
lingulate
virgulate
singultus
ring-small
jiggumbob
Virginian
ring-snake
ringingly
singingly
virginals
dinginess
minginess
virginity
biogenous
virginium
diagnoses
kingdomed
ring-money
diagnosis
king-cobra
misgrowth
singspiel
king-apple
ridge-pole
bilge-pump
gingerade
kingcraft
fingertip
hip-girdle
niggardly
finger-end
fingering
jingo-ring
lingering
niggerdom
ridge-rope
niggerish
niggerism
ring-cross
gingerous
disgusted
piggishly
misgotten
ridge-tile
fidgeting
ringstand
misgiving
misgovern
ginglymus
Highlands
bigheaded
dish-faced
dishwater
high-taper
mid-heaven
pigheaded
lithiasis
fightable
rightable
sightable
withhault
Mithraism
Mithraist
fish-garth
Mithraeum
fightback
fishyback
light-ball
night-bell
right-bank
nightbird
fish-scrap
pithecoid
night-crow
night-cart
lithocyst
dithecous
nightclub
light-dues
Nithsdale
right-down
high-level
tightener
righteous
tithe-free
eightfoil
eightfold
nightfall
eightfoot
eight-foot
light-foot
nightfire
light-fast
night-fowl
mishegaas
nightgear
dichogamy
nightgown
tight-head
highchair
sight-hole
diphthong
right-hand
eight-hour
nighthawk
Cichlidae
lithoidal
Xiphiidae
xiphoidal
Ziphiidae
high-viced
highlight
eightieth
tight-knit
fish-slice
high-place
tight-lace
△high-flier
△high-flyer
nightlife
lithology
night-line
nightlong
sightline
dishallow
△dithelism
high-blest
high-class
lightless
nightless
rightless
sightless
Sinhalese
dish-cloth
△dithelete
fish-plate
dish-clout
high-blown
high-flown
light-mill
nightmare
nightmary
dishumour
mishanter
fish-knife
siphonage
lichenoid
mishandle
sighingly
siphuncle
lightning
dishonest
fishiness
lichenism
lichenist
lichenose
lightness
litheness
pithiness
rightness
tightness
siphonate
dishonour
lichenous
dichromat
fish-woman
dish-cover
dishtowel
high-toned
pinhooker
dichromic
dithionic
fish-joint
dichroism
fish-louse
dichroite
fish-spear
high-speed
mishappen
bishopric
lithopone
bishopdom
bishopess
fisherman

Words marked △ may be spelled also with a capital letter

sight-read
night-robe
high-grade
fish-creel
high-dried
△bilharzia
night-rail
Richardia
night-rule
dithyramb
ciphering
withering
high-proof
tightrope
citharist
night-rest
witherite
high-grown
withdrawn
dichasial
eightsman
sightsman
night-side
sightseer
lightship
lithistid
night-soil
eightsome
lightsome
lithesome
sight-sing
nightspot
Xiphosura
△diphysite
dichasium
night-tide
dichotomy
lithotome
lithotomy
night-time
withstand
withstood
withouten
wishfully
fish-guano
Vishnuism
Vishnuite
nightwear
night-walk
right-wing
withywind
nightward
night-work
rightward
light-year
biohazard
militancy
sibilance
sibilancy
vigilance
digitated
Filicales
pixilated
digitalin
digitalis
militaria
civically
dividable
finically
limitable
litigable
mitigable
similarly
visitable
divinator
mitigator
sibilator
visitator
vigilante
bilimbing
Liliaceae
Tiliaceae
viliacoes
miniscule
biliteral
diligence
niaiserie
dividedly
limitedly
citizenry
midinette
siliceous
vimineous
viticetum
disinfect
misinform
disinfest
bilingual
dining-car
viliagoes
fining-pot
riding-rod
vikingism
disinhume
finishing
Tisiphone
bicipital
Cimicidae
libidinal
mirifical
miticidal
viricidal
civilised
civiliser
civilized
civilizer
digitiser
digitizer
virilised
virilized
dirigible
divisible
divisibly
dirigisme
Miliciens
siciliana
siciliane
siciliano
Filipinos
dimidiate
dirigiste
lixiviate
cilicious
litigious
lixivious
silicious
finicking
mimicking
midi-skirt
miniskirt
finickety
disillude
sitiology
Dixieland
sigillary
limitless
ciliolate
sigillate
titillate
disimmure
visioning
pimientos
visionary
lividness
rigidness
ripienist
timidness
visionist
vividness
bipinnate
vivianite
silicosis
silicotic
minibreak
vizierial
Minitrack®
citigrade
filigreed
filigrain
filigrane
mini-dress
visitress
vizierate
vizirship
dimissory
viciosity
vitiosity
sinistral
air-intake
misintend
filiation
miniation
vitiation
miniature
minirugby
Ricinulei
ridiculer
bilirubin
biliously
pitifully
viciously
siliquose
dividuous
disinvest
vilifying
vivifying
air-jacket
disjaskit
nick-nacky
kirkyaird
pickaback
dicky-bird
pickadell
pickadill
rinky-dink
sickleman
milk-vetch
milk-fever
Nickie-ben
pickeerer
sicklemia
lickpenny
milk-shake
pick-thank
milk-white
kickshaws
sick-tired
milk-float
nickelled
milk-gland
nickeline
nickeling
nickelise
nickelous
nickelize
milken-way
winkingly
sickening
milkiness
pinkiness
riskiness
silkiness
zinkenite
milk-molar
risk-money
kink-cough
Dicksonia
nickpoint
milk-house
milk-tooth
pick-tooth
pickapack
sink-a-pace
wink-a-peep
tinkering
△pinkerton
lickerish
silk-grass
sickishly
nickstick
rickstick
ricketily
kickstand
Minkstone
picketing
rickstand
ticketing
kick-start
milk-sugar
milk-punch
pick-purse
sicknurse
billiards
dill-water
misleader
misleared
niellated
diallagic
wieldable
yieldable
villiagos
billabong
rifle-bird
dialectal
millocrat
Violaceae
billycock
pillicock
dialectic
millscale
biblicism
biblicist
dislocate
birlieman
killdeers
fieldfare
villiform
killifish
billy-goat
sialogram
mirligoes
villagree
villagios
villagery
biologist
dialogise
dialogist
dialogite
dialogize
mill-wheel
hill-billy
misliking
gillflirt
jillflirt
titleless

9 

wieldless
dial-plate
sialolith
diplomacy
millimole
diplomate
willemite
Finlander
uitlander
villanage
villenage
millennia
violently
willingly
violin-bow
millenary
millinery
diclinism
hilliness
silliness
violinist
diclinous
villanous
willpower
nielloing
billboard
millboard
fill-horse
gill-house
mill-horse
billionth
millionth
mill-tooth
zillionth
millepede
millipede
fillipeen
mislippen
filliping
millepore
Millerian
pilloried
pillar-box
Hitlerism
Hitlerist
pillarist
pillorise
Hitlerite
millerite
pillorize
fieldsman
fillister
Willesden
aimlessly
girlishly
sinlessly
witlessly
rifle-shot
dislustre
villosity
rillettes
billeting
filleting
millstone
violation
ciclatoun
violative
fieldvole
mill-owner
billowing
fieldward
fieldwork
willowish
pillow-cup
diplozoon
gimmickry
diamagnet
sigmoidal
pin-making
bismillah
gimmalled
gismology
gizmology
dismality
dismember
firmament
pigmental
Simmental
air-minded
diamonded
pigmented
wit-monger
mismanage
dismantle
biomining
filminess
gigmanity
bit-mapped
Cimmerian
rigmarole
dismissal
diametral
biometric
diametric
film-strip
sigmation
sigmatron
sigmatism
dismaying
dismayful
lion-tamer
picnicked
picnicker
pinnacled
finnochio
dianoetic
lienteric
lioncelle
lion-heart
significs
dignified
lignified
signified
signifier
ligniform
gianthood
signalman
lignaloes
lign-aloes
signalled
signaller
limnology
fiend-like
signaling
pianolist
signalise
pinnulate
signalize
bionomics
sinningia
winningly
signboard
pinnipede
kidnapped
kidnapper
signorial
kiln-dried
△signorina
signorine
signorini
△signorino
pignerate
pignorate
diandrous
Dionysiac
Dionysian
witnesser
giantship
pianistic
Minnesang
dianetics®
vignetter
pinnately
dignitary
signatory
signature
signeurie
winnowing
piano-wire
kidney-ore
Fibonacci
pivotally
lidocaine
pilot-boat
Aizoaceae
finocchio
biconcave
divorcive
Girondism
Girondist
Dinoceras
milometer
Nilometer
tin-opener
linolenic
mitogenic
filoselle
kilometre
misoneism
misoneist
kilohertz
pirouette
pilot-flag
pilot-fish
Sinophile
Sinophily
widowhood
dinothere
binominal
Dipodidae
nicotined
limonitic
nicotinic
pisolitic
disorient
nicotiana
bifoliate
simonious
pilot-jack
disoblige
filoplume
cipollino
misoclere
pilotless
hit-or-miss
visor-mask
ginormous
ritornell
liposomal
ribosomal
filopodia
kilojoule
Sinologue
dimorphic
nicompoop
simon-pure
timocracy
eidograph
minorship
timorsome
limousine
bimonthly
bilobular
bilocular
binocular
picocurie
Dicotylae
kilocycle
displayed
displayer
cisplatin
hippiatry
dispraise
mispraise
hippocras
air-pocket
fig-pecker
hip-pocket
mispickel
nit-picker
hippodame
cispadane
hispidity
limpidity
diapyesis
diapyetic
hippiedom
simpleton
displease
misplease
simplesse
misprised
simplices
silphiums
disprison
simpliste
dispelled
hippology
dispensed
dispenser
dispondee
limpingly
lispingly
nippingly
rippingly
lippening
nippiness
Nipponese
timpanist
disproval
disproved
disproven
rib-plough
disprofit
dispeople
disproove
dispersal
air-piracy
dioptrics
hit-parade
disperser
dispurvey
pimpernel
diaphragm
disparage
nipperkin
bioparent
diapering
simpering
Hipparion
diapirism
dioptrate
disparate
disparity
hippurite

Words marked △ may be spelled also with a capital letter

wimpishly
disposing
disposure
simpatico
lippitude
disputant
dispauper
△piepowder
diaphysis
Lippizana
lip-reader
diurnally
gier-eagle
pier-table
microbial
microbian
micro-brew
hierocrat
microcode
ditrochee
microchip
vibracula
didrachma
nigricant
misreckon
microcopy
microcard
microcosm
fibrocyte
microcyte
hieracium
hierodule
nitriding
pieridine
aigre-doux
tiercelet
tierceron
pierrette
nitrified
vitrified
microfilm
cirriform
fibriform
microform
mitriform
vitriform
hierogram
microgram
disregard
misregard
diarrheal
diarrhoea
diarrheic
vibraharp
librairie
mitraille
livraison
fibrillae
fibrillar
hierology
micrology
fibrillin
fibroline
tirra-lyra
disrelish
fibreless
pier-glass
fibrolite
microlite
microlith
misrelate
Vitrolite®
micro-mini
micromesh
fibromata
vibrantly
fieriness
fibrinous
cirrhosis
cirrhotic
vibriosis
Vitreosil®
vitriolic
cirrhopod
cirripede
disrupter
disrepair
micropsia
micropyle
micropump
disruptor
micropore
misreport
disrepute
librarian
hierarchy
mirroring
vibrissae
dioristic
Midrashim
nitro-silk
tigrishly
microsome
nigrosine
Nigritian
hieratica
nigritude
vibratile
microtome
microtomy
microtone
nitratine
libration
librettos
migration
nitration
titration
vibration
fioritura
fioriture
libratory
migratory
vibratory
dicrotism
dicrotous
vibrative
Vitruvian
gilravage
microwire
mitre-wort
microwave
dissuader
kidstakes
misshaped
misshapen
piss-taker
rijstafel
tipstaves
tipstaffs
diastasic
diastasis
diastatic
miasmatic
biostable
rinseable
mid-season
first-born
dissocial
dissected
dip-sector
dissector
dissident
diosgenin
sissified
first-foot
kissagram
kissogram
kitschily
first-hand
biosphere
dip-switch
disshiver
biestings
disseisin
disseizin
disseisor
disseizor
tinselled
air-splint
firstling
tinseling
missilery
dieselise
dissolute
fissility
dieselize
midsummer
dissemble
dissembly
dissimile
lissomely
winsomely
die-sinker
△dissenter
dissunder
hissingly
missingly
dissonant
tipsiness
gilsonite
kinswoman
pigsconce
dib-stones
Dioscorea
missioner
diastolic
kinsfolks
fissipede
dissipate
airstream
midstream
big-screen
air-strike
pin-stripe
sisserary
first-rate
kieserite
first-time
hirsutism
pipsqueak
dissaving
pit-sawyer
missaying
mint-sauce
filtrable
virtually
distraint
distraite
Cistaceae
dietician
distichal
big-ticket
fisticuff
pistachio
viaticals
viaticums
witticism
gilt-edged
histidine
tittlebat
fifteener
sixteener
kintledge
diathesis
diathetic
diathermy
sixteenmo
littleane
tiptoeing
mistletoe
fifteenth
sixteenth
diatretum
histogram
pictogram
mistigris
histogeny
vintaging
dirt-cheap
lintwhite
uintahite
pintailed
pint-sized
mistaking
tint-block
distilled
distiller
lintelled
pistoleer
pistolled
tip-tilted
dittology
histology
girthline
fistulose
mirthless
vistaless
biathlete
fistulous
distemper
mistemper
histamine
birthmark
diatomist
victimise
diatomite
victimize
Miltonian
dittander
oil-tanker
distantly
fittingly
hintingly
siftingly
wittingly
dirtiness
kittenish
Miltonism
mistiness
niftiness
tintiness
wittiness
distingué
fictional
dictyogen
diatropic
virtuosic
Victrolla®
victrolla
virtuosos
tittupped
tittuping
cisternae
dietarian
diet-bread

diuturnal
historian
Listerian
pictorial
viatorial
Victorian
dirt-track
distorted
disturbed
disturber
filter-bed
pistareen
historify
bitter-pit
filter-tip
pictarnie
binturong
diet-drink
disthrone
sistering
tittering
victorine
bitterish
dipterist
historism
Listerise
Listerism
victoress
winterise
birth-rate
micturate
dipterous
jitterbug
litter-bug
Listerize
winterize
pietistic
dietitian
dietetics
lintstock
dictatrix
siltstone
dictation
nictation
siltation
dictatory
dictature
nictitate
pint-stoup
mint-julep
mistaught
riotously
wistfully
tittivate
kittiwake
birthwort
widthwise
widthways
titubancy
simulated
dilutable
figurable
titularly
simulator
simulacra
simulacre
figurante
minuscule
simulcast
bifurcate
bisulcate
hirundine
liquidise
liquidate
liquidity
liquidize
△minuteman
virulence
virulency
minute-gun
liquefied
liquefier
liturgics
liturgist
divulgate
Siluridae
Tipulidae
virucidal
Hirudinea
sinusitis
fiduciary
minutiose
ritualise
ritualism
ritualist
visualise
visualist
visuality
ritualize
visualize
biguanide
piquantly
titupping
Liguorian
Ripuarian
liquorice
liquorish
divulsion
sinuosity
divulsive
pituitrin
sinuately
liquation
sinuation
situation
pituitary
situtunga
sinuously
silvering
silverise
silverize
mid-wicket
rigwiddie
midwifing
midwifery
viewphone
tim-whisky
mid-winter
witwanton
viewiness
rigwoodie
viewpoint
airworthy
nitwitted
midwiving
bipyramid
Didynamia
airy-fairy
cityscape
Sisyphean
lily-white
△sibylline
bicyclist
Sibyllist
pityingly
dizygotic
dimyarian
Himyarite
pixy-stool
pizzicato
zigzagged
pizzaiola
dizziness
mizzonite
diazonium
sitzkrieg
diazeuxis
ejaculate
ejectment
djellabah
T-junction
skiamachy
skiascopy
Ukrainian
skiagraph
skedaddle
skidproof
sky-diving
skeesicks
ski-flying
ekphrasis
skrimmage
skyjacker
ski-jumper
skijoring
ski-kiting
skill-less
skylarker
skaldship
akoluthos
skilfully
skunkbird
skin-diver
skin-tight
skinflick
skinflint
skinny-dip
skinny-rib
skeptical
skip-tooth
skyrocket
skirtings
skirtless
sketchily
skatepark
skew-table
skew-whiff
okey-dokey
clearance
pleasance
cloacalin
cleavable
floatable
pleadable
clearcole
almandine
pleaseman
sleazebag
bleareyed
clear-eyed
albarelli
albarello
oleaceous
ulmaceous
alpargata
bleaching
bleachers
bleachery
cloacinal
pleadings
allayment
bleakness
cleanness
clearness
aleatoric
alkalosis
algarroba
algarrobo
cloakroom
albatross
alcarraza
cleanskin
clearskin
cleansing
allantoic
allantoid
allantois
altar-tomb
olfaction
olfactory
clianthus
olfactive
pleasurer
clearwing
altarwise
clubbable
ill-boding
blubbered
slabberer
slab-sided
glabellae
glabellar
globalise
globalism
globulite
flabellum
globulous
globalize
alabamine
clubwoman
clubhouse
elaborate
alabaster
globosity
fly-bitten
slabstone
globe-trot
fly-by-wire
clabby-doo
alack-a-day
olecranal
electable
olecranon
blackbuck
slack-bake
blackball
blackband
block-book
blackbird
block-coal
blackcock
alicyclic
glycocoll
placoderm
clackdish
elucidate
placidity
slickered
flechette
fléchette
blackface
Blackfeet
Blackfoot
blackfish
clock-golf
blackgame
blackhead
blockhead
blockhole
flaccidly
blackjack
blacklead
glycollic
blacklist
fleckless

Words marked △ may be spelled also with a capital letter

placeless
plackless
blackmail
placement
allcomers
placentae
placental
placentas
ale-conner
blackness
slackness
slickness
glucinium
electoral
electrode
glyceride
electrify
plectrums
glycerine
plectrons
alectryon
electress
electrise
electrize
glucoside
glycoside
block-ship
plicately
elocution
placation
plication
elocutory
placatory
placitory
plicature
floccular
fluctuant
electuary
fluctuate
flocculus
blackwood
blockwork
clockwork
blackwash
clockwise
ale-draper
clodpated
gladiator
blade-bone
bladdered
ill-deedly
cladogram
fledgling
glidingly
slidingly
gladioles
gladiolus
Clydeside
cladistic
Gladstone
bladework
Aldebaran
allemande
alienable
allenarly
alterable
illegally
alienator
albescent
altercate
all-ending
allegedly
blaeberry
△bluebeard
blueberry
fleet-foot
allergist
Elaeagnus
fleeching
alpenhorn
elsewhere
sloethorn
illegible
illegibly
allegiant
blue-rinse
alleviate
blue-black
sleepless
alveolate
elaeolite
alternant
fleetness
glueyness
sleekness
alternate
allegoric
albespine
albespyne
blue-green
algebraic
blueprint
bluegrass
eldership
sleepsuit
clientage
clientele
clientèle
bluestone
albertite
alleluiah
flue-cured
aloes-wood
cliff-face
cliffhang
cly-faking
bluffness
fly-fisher
All-father
elegiacal
clogdance
flagrance
flagrancy
flag-waver
sluggabed
Oligocene
oligaemia
plague-pit
flugelman
flagellum
alignment
sloganeer
elegantly
sloganise
uliginose
uliginous
sloganize
flageolet
sloggorne
sloghorne
slughorne
oligopoly
oligarchy
flagstick
ill-gotten
flagstaff
flightily
blighting
flagstone
slighting
slightish
flagitate
plightful
ill-headed
ill-hedded
ill-haired
alchemise
alchemist
ill-humour
alchemize
Elohistic
alphasort
claimable
alligator
alligarta
ultimatum
Pleiocene
plain-cook
plain-darn
illiberal
altimeter
altimetry
glaireous
cleithral
allicholy
sleighing
illimited
illicitly
plain-Jane
Altiplano
eloinment
pleiomery
fluidness
plainness
plaid-neuk
albinotic
cloisonné
albinoism
plainsman
plainsmen
ellipsoid
altissimo
plainsong
cloistral
plaintiff
slaistery
plaintful
plaintive
altitudes
plainwork
ill-judged
slakeless
flakiness
fluke-worm
alalagmos
ululation
plumdamas
slammakin
blameable
blameably
climbable
flammable
plumbagos
slimeball
plume-bird
climactic
clampdown
climb-down
slumberer
flambeaus
flambeaux
plumbeous
alum-shale
clamshell
flame-leaf
blameless
flameless
plumbless
plumeless
plumulose
alum-slate
plumulate
plume-moth
alimental
elemental
ill-manned
Alemannic
clamantly
clemently
flamingly
eliminant
flamencos
flamingos
aluminise
plumpness
sliminess
aluminate
eliminate
aluminium
aluminous
aluminize
glomerule
glomeruli
glamorise
alembroth
glomerato
clamorous
glamorous
slumbrous
glamorize
flame-tree
alum-stone
plum-stone
climature
climatise
climatize
clamourer
élongated
clinoaxis
plantable
glengarry
slingback
blind-coal
clinician
clonicity
plangency
blinkered
blunderer
glandered
plunderer
slanderer
slant-eyed
flannelly
slenderly
plenteous
blindfold
clingfilm
blindfish
flanching
flinching
glenoidal
Glenlivet®
klondiker
plentiful
blond-lace
flintlock
plant-lice
planuloid
plant-like
plantling
plenilune
plant-lore
blindless
plantless
Olenellus

9 □l□n□m

alinement
aloneness
blandness
blankness
blindness
bluntness
plenipoes
planarian
Planorbis
plenarily
klinostat
plantsman
alongside
blind-side
planisher
slinkskin
slingshot
slung-shot
plenitude
plane-tree
planetoid
planation
planetary
glandular
slangular
klendusic
clinquant
slinkweed
blindworm
slantwise
slantways
klondyker
allowance
allopathy
allocable
allowable
allowably
allocarpy
pleonaste
blood-bird
blood-bath
almond-oil
blood-dust
fluoresce
ill-omened
oleo-resin
pleonexia
allowedly
allometry
blood-fine
blood-feud
floodgate
bloodheat
floorhead
kloochman
kloochmen
allophone
Fluothane®
illogical
algorithm
Algonkian
blood-line
alloplasm
bloodless
bloodlust
bloomless
allotment
floodmark
aloofness
alcoholic
fluorosis
allomorph
Algonquin
allograft
blood-rain
bloodroot
elbow-room
allograph
allotrope
allotropy
oleograph
fluorspar
bloodshed
bloodshot
floodtide
ileostomy
allotting
allostery
allottery
floodwall
bloodwood
blood-worm
blood-wite
bloodying
flippancy
flap-eared
aliphatic
slop-basin
flappable
slap-happy
alopecoid
slippered
flip-chart
slop-chest
Clupeidae
elopement
slopingly
slip-coach
slop-pouch
Glyptodon
clapboard
clipboard
slip-board
flophouse
clapbread
flaptrack
slapstick
klephtism
slop-built
slopewise
clappy-doo
clepsydra
eloquence
plaquette
floreated
floriated
alarm-bell
albricias
altricial
cleruchia
clerecole
clericals
clericate
clericity
Florideae
floridean
floridity
alarmedly
clarified
clarifier
glorified
floriform
flirt-gill
ultra-high
all-ruling
pluralise
pluralism
pluralist
plurality
pluralize
flaringly
glaringly
clarendon
alertness
clarionet
pluripara
flare-path
clerkship
floristic
floristry
claret-cup
clergyman
flurrying
elastance
glissandi
glissando
plasmatic
classable
glossator
flashback
flashbulb
class-book
glass-crab
flashcube
closedown
blusterer
clustered
plastered
plasterer
blessedly
all-seeing
glassfuls
glass-gall
closehead
blast-hole
blaspheme
blasphemy
fleshhood
flesh-hook
classical
fleshings
classific
glossitis
classible
plastisol
plastique
close-knit
glasslike
fleshling
blissless
blushless
classless
fleshless
flesh-meat
blastment
fleshment
classmate
closeness
flushness
alms-woman
elastomer
flash-over
plasmodia
plus-fours
alms-house
blast-pipe
alms-drink
classroom
glass-rope
blush-rose
flustrate
blustrous
closeting
flesh-tint
blastular
floscular
elusively
fleshworm
glassware
glasswork
glasswort
flûte-à-bec
flute-bird
plutocrat
blatherer
bletherer
clatterer
flatterer
slate-gray
slate-grey
cloth-hall
blotching
glottides
glottises
flatlings
ulotrichy
glitziest
elutriate
clitellar
plutology
plate-like
flatulent
clitellum
glutamine
platemark
glutamate
Plutonian
△platonics
platinoid
blatantly
plutonomy
platinise
Platonise
Platonism
Platonist
Plutonism
Plutonist
slatiness
glutenous
glutinous
platinous
plutonium
platinize
Platonize
plethoric
Ulsterman
plate-room
plot-proof
clathrate
elaterite
elaterium
plate-ship
platitude
flotation
blutwurst
cloth-yard
flouncing
cloud-capt
fleurette
ploughman
flaughter
ploughmen
slaughter
ploughing
slouching
ploughboy
eleutheri
Aleurites
illuminer
flourishy
pleuritic
pleuritis
plausible
plausibly
album-leaf

Words marked △ may be spelled also with a capital letter

9 □m□r□c

cloudland
cloudless
clout-nail
alburnous
clout-shoe
claustral
plaustral
flaunting
claustrum
clausulae
clausular
fluviatic
olive-back
slavocrat
clavicula
clavicorn
claviform
slave-fork
slave-hunt
Slovakian
clavulate
Slavonian
Slovenian
elevenses
aliveness
Slavonise
olivenite
Slavonize
Slavophil
clovepink
Oliverian
ill-versed
flavoring
slavering
cleverish
flavorous
gloves-off
slavishly
clove-tree
clavation
elevation
elevatory
slivovica
slivovitz
slivowitz
olive-yard
slow-march
slow-paced
blow-valve
flowmeter
flowchart
clew-lines
flyweight
flowingly
glowingly
blowtorch
slowcoach
slow-hound
flower-bed
flowerage
flowering
flowerpot
flower-bud
alewashed
ill-wisher
flax-wench
plexiform
fluxional
flexitime
play-actor
played-out
plaything
flay-flint
clay-slate
Alcyonium
claytonia
play-world
play-going
playhouse
play-spell
playgroup
playfully
blizzardy
alizarine
imbalance
immanacle
impacable
immanence
immanency
embargoed
embargoes
empathise
empathize
ommatidia
impavidly
impatiens
impatient
ambagious
embarking
emballing
embalming
embayment
empanoply
embarring
impairing
embarrass
embassade
ambassage
embassage
empaestic
impassion
impassive
impartial
embattled
impastoed
impaction
impactite
amianthus
impactive
emaciated
smock-race
emication
amidships
imidazole
amoebaean
impedance
imperator
umber-bird
impeacher
impeccant
embedding
impendent
impending
Ember-days
imperfect
amber-fish
ambergris
immediacy
imbecilic
impeticos
impetigos
immediate
imperious
amberjack
umbellule
impellent
impelling
embellish
umbellate
embedment
Immelmann
empennage
impennate
emmetrope
impetrate
immensely
ampersand
immersion
immensity
Emmenthal
impetuses
impetuous
Ember-week
embezzler
amperzand
smug-faced
amygdalin
imageable
Amygdalus
smuggling
imageless
imagining
imaginary
imaginist
imagistic
amphibian
amphibole
amphiboly
omphacite
amphigory
omphaloid
ampholyte
amphioxus
Amphipoda
emphysema
emphasise
emphasize
emphlyses
emphlysis
imminence
imminency
impingent
impinging
empirical
umbilical
ambitious
umbilicus
immigrant
immigrate
immission
amniotomy
immitting
immixture
omnibuses
impiously
ambiguity
ambiguous
smoke-ball
smoke-bomb
smokebush
smokehood
smoke-jack
smokeless
smokiness
smoke-room
smoke-sail
smoketree
impleader
small-arms
small-bore
small-coal
emplecton
implicate
emplectum
implodent
emulgence
impliedly
amplified
amplifier
small-hand
amyloidal
emollient
emolliate
smell-less
smileless
emolument
implement
emblemise
emblemata
emblemize
smilingly
ampleness
smallness
gmelinite
amblyopia
amylopsin
emplaster
emplastic
amplosome
emblossom
implosion
implosive
smell-trap
amplitude
small-time
emulation
impletion
emulative
small-town
emulously
impluvium
implexion
amendable
emendable
emendator
amendment
eminently
amenities
emanation
emunction
emanatory
emunctory
emanatist
emanative
amenaunce
ominously
immorally
immovable
immovably
imposable
immolator
emboscata
impotence
impotency
immodesty
smoothing
smoothish
impolitic
emporiums
impounder
△immortals
impostume
important
importune
imposture
embodying
omophagia
omophagic
smorzando
smart-alec
embreathe
smartarse
improbity
Americana
embracing

Words marked △ may be spelled also with a capital letter

9 □m□r□c

embraceor
embracery
imprecise
embrocate
imbricate
imprecate
americium
embracive
imprudent
emergence
emergency
embroglio
imbroglio
amorphism
amorphous
embroider
amornings
umbrella'd
amaryllid
amaryllis
umbrellos
amoralism
amoralist
impromptu
amarantin
Amerindic
embrangle
imbrangle
smartness
Amarantus
embryonal
embryo-sac
embryonic
embryotic
ombrophil
ambrosial
△ambrosian
Amerasian
embrasure
impresari
amorosity
embrittle
umbratile
amarettos
ambrotype
amorously
improving
improvise
smartweed
embrazure
amassable
smasheroo
amissible
omissible
amassment
amusement
amusingly
impsonite
omittance
Ametabola
smatterer
smothered
smotherer
umpteenth
emptiness
emotional
emptional
amatorial
amatorian
imitation
imitative
emotivism
ambulance
immutable
immutably
imputable
imputably
ambulator
amputator
ambulacra
ambuscade
ambuscado
impundulu
impudence
amourette
immunogen
amaurosis
amaurotic
△ombudsman
Ombudsmen
embussing
impulsion
impulsive
empyreuma
Ambystoma
amazement
△amazonian
amazingly
amazon-ant
amazonite
unbalance
undamaged
unmanaged
incapable
incapably
uncapable
uneatable
unfadable
unmakable
unmanacle
unnamable
unpayable
unsalable
unsatable
unsayable
untamable
untamably
indagator
inhalator
ungarbled
unharbour
unhatched
unmatched
unwatched
Antarctic
enranckle
enhancive
unhandled
unsaddled
unhandily
uncandour
ungazed-at
unpapered
unwakened
unwatered
uncareful
unbaffled
untangled
unbashful
inhabiter
invalidly
in-patient
invariant
insatiate
insatiety
unsatiate
unmasking
unpacking
unmanlike
unwarlike
engarland
unfailing
ungallant
intaglios
inharmony
inpayment
unharming
unharmful
undaunted
unhaunted
unpainted
untainted
uncannily
unsaintly
undawning
unharness
incarnate
ungainful
unpainful
endamoeba
entamoeba
unrazored
uncanonic
unsavoury
unhappily
unmarried
sneak-raid
unpalsied
encaustic
unpartial
unearthed
encanthis
infantile
unearthly
andantino
infantine
unhasting
unhatting
unwasting
incaution
enrapture
unbaptise
unbaptize
unnatural
unmanured
unmatured
unsaluted
infatuate
unvarying
undazzled
anabranch
Anobiidae
inebriant
inebriate
inebriety
inebrious
unobvious
anabolism
anabolite
inability
snub-nosed
anabiosis
anabiotic
unabashed
knob-stick
ink-bottle
anacharis
unactable
knock-back
knock-down
inscience
knackered
knickered
anucleate
enucleate
knocker-up
inscriber
onychitis
knock-knee
Anschluss
inoculate
unicolour
enactment
unscanned
unscented
aniconism
aniconist
anecdotal
unscarred
unscathed
unscythed
anacruses
unaccused
unscoured
anacrusis
unadmired
unadvised
snideness
unadapted
unadopted
cnidarian
unadorned
inodorous
antenatal
ink-eraser
undebased
undecayed
undefaced
undelayed
unrebated
unrelated
unrelaxed
enterable
inferable
intenable
unseeable
untenable
endecagon
inter-arts
underbear
interbred
underbred
interbank
inselberg
underbush
underbite
underclad
underclay
undercoat
intercede
unreached
endeictic
angel-cake
unwelcome
intercrop
undercook
undercool
intercept
undercard
undercart
undercast
intercity
underclub
interdeal
underdraw
interdict
underdeck
underdoer
unheedily
unreadily
intendant
interdine
unbending
underdone
unheeding

Words marked △ may be spelled also with a capital letter

engendure
interdash
unheedful
unneedful
indecency
inference
inherence
inherency
unrenewed
unsevered
entelechy
Angelenos
interesse
interests
undeceive
undeserve
unreserve
interface
unperfect
underfeed
interfold
underfelt
underfong
underfund
angel-food
interflow
underflow
underfoot
interfere
underfire
angel-fish
interfuse
underfish
unselfish
under-five
undergrad
inveigler
unfeigned
unweighed
intergrow
undergird
undergown
antechoir
sneeshing
underhand
underhung
angelhood
angelical
antefixal
endemical
indexical
undecimal
antefixes
endenizen
undecided
undefiled
undefined
undesired
unmerited
unrefined
unrevised
undelight
andesitic
enteritis
indelible
indelibly
intenible
inheritor
ingenious
unserious
unbelieve
interject
interjoin
underkeep
interknit
underking
interleaf
intellect
interlace
interlock
interlude
unhealthy
underlaid
underlain
annealing
index-link
interline
interlink
underline
underling
unfeeling
unveiling
interlope
interlard
angerless
indexless
unrealise
unrealism
unreality
unjealous
unzealous
unrealize
envermeil
annexment
interment
undermine
ungermane
unseeming
intermure
innermost
undermost
internode
unpennied
indemnify
antennule
internals
unmeaning
antennary
internist
Inverness
indemnity
undernote
unbeknown
knee-cords
enveloped
envenomed
unbeloved
unremoved
unrevoked
anaerobic
anhedonia
anhedonic
knee-holly
knee-joint
indecorum
interplay
unbespeak
underplay
interpret
underpeep
unpeopled
unperplex
untempted
interpage
underpaid
unbespoke
interpone
underplot
underprop
underpart
interpose
underpass
unhelpful
enhearten
unbearded
unhearsed
unlearned
unwearied
knee-drill
endearing
inferring
integrand
integrant
interring
unbearing
under-ring
unfearing
under-roof
unheard-of
interrupt
under-ripe
unredrest
integrate
integrity
underrate
unfearful
underseal
intersect
underside
intensify
undersign
undersoil
intensely
inversely
underself
undersell
incessant
unceasing
uncessant
undersong
intension
inversion
undershot
incensory
intersert
insensate
intensate
intensity
intensive
inversive
undersaye
ancestral
intestacy
underta'en
ungenteel
unsettled
entertain
incertain
uncertain
entertake
undertake
infertile
insectile
undertime
annectent
intestine
onsetting
undertane
undertint
undertone
unresting
unweeting
inception
indention
infection
ingestion
injection
insection
insertion
intention
invention
undertook
indenture
insectary
inventory
invertase
intestate
anoestrum
anoestrus
unrestful
incentive
inceptive
infective
ingestive
intentive
invective
inventive
antelucan
unsecular
unberufen
undeluded
unrebuked
unreduced
unrefuted
unsecured
unseduced
unbeguile
ungenuine
ingenuity
ingenuous
in-service
interview
intervein
intervale
intervene
unnerving
unpervert
undervest
innervate
endeavour
innerwear
underwear
in-between
knee-swell
interwind
underwing
underwood
interwork
underwork
interzone
uneffaced
ineffable
ineffably
unifiable
snuff-dish
unoffered
knife-edge
snuffling
knifeless
snuff-mull
uninformed
uniformly
knife-rest
enigmatic
sniggerer
sniggling
knightage
Anaglypta®
ensheathe
insheathe
unsheathe
anthracic
encheason
anthocyan
unchecked

9 □n□h□c

unshocked
unshackle
anthocarp
uncheered
unchained
unshrived
unshriven
unchrisom
unthrifty
inshallah
enchilada
enshelter
inkholder
inshelter
anthology
anthelion
anchylose
enthymeme
anthemion
enchanted
enchanter
one-handed
unchanged
unshunned
unthanked
anthropic
unwhipped
unshapely
anchor-man
enchorial
anchor-ice
uncharged
uncharmed
uncharnel
uncharted
anchorage
anchoress
anchorite
uncharity
anthurium
unghostly
on-the-spot
unshutter
enrheumed
anchoveta
antipapal
uncinated
antipathy
inaidable
unaidable
unlikable
unlivable
unridable
unsizable
untirable
△indicator
antipasto
antiscian
engiscope
insincere
enkindled

unkindled
unriddler
unbinding
unwinding
unmindful
engine-man
inside-car
incidence
indigence
indigency
on-licence
enlivener
unripened
unsinewed
antigenic
antihelix
antivenin
unlived-in
unmixedly
antiserum
untimeous
snail-fish
angiogram
unmingled
enlighten
unlighted
unsighted
antitheft
unsightly
antiphony
unsighing
unwishing
antichlor
unwishful
ancipital
antiviral
inhibiter
undivided
unlimited
unvisited
anticivic
insipidly
invisible
invisibly
uncivilly
incipient
insipient
inhibitor
intimiste
antivirus
insidious
invidious
unpitiful
unsickled
anticking
unwinking
knaidloch
kneidlach
infielder
snail-like
anticline

infilling
unwilling
ancillary
anti-flash
inviolate
infirmary
angiomata
infirmity
antiknock
indignify
undignify
anciently
indignant
ancientry
Indianise
Indianist
unfitness
indignity
Indianize
antidotal
antinodal
antipodal
anti-novel
△antipodes
unpiloted
antimonic
antinomic
antitoxic
antitoxin
indigotin
antinoise
unripping
antispast
indispose
antitrade
unpierced
antitragi
encierros
antitrust
unbiassed
gneissoid
snail-slow
gneissose
ungirthed
unwittily
insistent
unfitting
unsisting
unwitting
indiction
undiluted
unfigured
indirubin
antiquely
anxiously
enviously
antiquark
antiquary
antiquate
antiquity
insinuate

antitypal
antitypic
unpitying
ink-jerker
snakebird
snakebite
innkeeper
Inuktitut
unskilled
snakelike
unskilful
unskimmed
unskinned
snakiness
snakeroot
snakeskin
snakeweed
snakewood
snakewise
unallayed
uncleaned
uncleared
unpleased
unpleated
uncleanly
unclearly
unpliable
unpliably
ankle-boot
inflicter
unelected
unplucked
analectic
inflictor
anglicise
anglicism
anglicist
anglicize
unfledged
unpledged
including
influence
unaltered
analgesia
analgesic
influenza
Englified
one-legged
unaligned
unclogged
unplagued
unplugged
inelegant
analogise
analogist
analogous
analogize
unclaimed
unplained
unplaited
ankle-jack

unplumbed
inclement
Englander
unblended
unblinded
unblunted
unplanked
unplanned
unplanted
inclining
inglenook
ingleneuk
unalloyed
unblooded
unfloored
unclipped
analeptic
△anglophil
unslept-in
ingle-side
Englisher
unblessed
unclassed
unfleshed
unglossed
inelastic
uncleship
endlessly
unfleshly
analysand
inclusion
enclosure
Englishry
inclosure
anglesite
inclusive
englutted
unblotted
unclothed
inflation
inflative
unclouded
unillumed
onslaught
ingluvial
ingluvies
inflowing
angleworm
anglewise
inflexion
influxion
inflexure
unamiable
anamneses
unimpeded
anamnesis
anemogram
enamelled
enameller
anemology
unsmiling

Words marked △ may be spelled also with a capital letter

animalise
animalism
animalist
animality
anomalous
animalize
gnomonics
mnemonics
unamended
mnemonist
unimposed
enamorado
unamerced
enumerate
inamorata
inamorato
inumbrate
animistic
onomastic
Mnemosyne
unamusing
animosity
unemptied
unsmitten
animating
animation
animatism
enamoured
unengaged
Anonaceae
unentered
unindexed
unsnuffed
ananthous
unincited
uninvited
enunciate
unanxious
unenvious
unknelled
un-English
anonymise
anonymity
inanimate
unanimity
anonymous
unanimous
anonymize
inaneness
unendowed
anandrous
onanistic
inanition
inunction
uninjured
uninsured
unknowing
unenvying
annoyance
unlocated
unsolaced
endogamic
enjoyable
enjoyably
unlosable
unlovable
unmovable
unmovably
unpotable
unroyally
unwomanly
annotator
innovator
intonator
undoubted
uncombine
untouched
ensorcell
unvoicing
endoscope
endoscopy
unconcern
uncordial
unfolding
unloading
incondite
indolence
indolency
innocence
innocency
insolence
oncometer
onion-eyed
uncovered
unmoneyed
endogenic
oncogenic
ontogenic
unmovedly
unhopeful
unconfine
unconform
uncongeal
endophagy
angophora
endophyte
entophyte
Unionidae
unlogical
unionised
unionized
unmotived
unnoticed
unpoliced
unrosined
endomixis
unpolitic
indocible
unsolidly
encomiums
encomiast
innoxious
inworking
onlooking
unworking
unbookish
unmoulded
ungodlike
ungodlily
unworldly
ennobling
enrolling
untoiling
endoblast
endoplasm
entoblast
incommode
endowment
engoûment
enjoyment
enrolment
informant
endosmose
insomniac
announcer
encounter
unbounded
uncounted
unfounded
unjointed
unmounted
unpointed
unrounded
unsounded
unwounded
unsoundly
incognito
unbosomer
ontologic
endomorph
oncomouse
uncoupled
endorphin
encolpion
endosperm
endospore
encompass
encolpium
incorrect
unmourned
unsourced
unworried
encourage
entourage
uncourtly
endocrine
inpouring
incorrupt
uncorrupt
envoyship
onion-skin
intorsion
endosteal
En-Tout-Cas®
oncostman
entoptics
uncouthly
infortune
unfortune
intortion
Angostura
endosteum
unpopular
involucel
involuted
unfocused
insoluble
insolubly
involucre
innocuity
innocuous
insolvent
antonymic
oncolysis
oncolytic
endolymph
uniplanar
snaphance
unapparel
anaplasty
knapscull
inspector
anopheles
insphear'd
snipefish
unspoiled
knapskull
unapplied
unspilled
inspanned
inaptness
ineptness
unaptness
inopinate
unopposed
anaphoric
kniphofia
one-parent
unsparing
uniparous
unspotted
anaptyxis
unsquared
inequable
unequable
unequally
inerrancy
end-reader
increaser
uncreated
undreaded
undreamed
untreated
unwreaked
enwreathe
inbreathe
inwreathe
unwreathe
inorganic
inerrable
inerrably
anorectal
entrechat
intricacy
Antrycide®
infracted
unfrocked
untracked
anorectic
infractor
unprecise
entrecôte
intricate
introduce
unpredict
unbridged
unbridled
uncrudded
ungrudged
untrodden
inerudite
snare-drum
unfreeman
snorkeler
unordered
energetic
unorderly
enfreedom
intriguer
androgyne
androgyny
intrigant
anarchial
anarchise
anarchism
anarchist
anorthite
anarchize
engrained
engrainer
ingrained
unbraided
unbruised
undrained
unpraised
untrained
introitus
introject
entralles
undrilled
andrology
onirology
△andromeda
entrammel
untrimmed

Words marked △ may be spelled also with a capital letter

9 □n□r□m

uncrumple
enurement
increment
inurement
encrimson
entremets
incremate
uniramous
unfranked
unprinted
engrenage
intrinsic
unwrinkle
angriness
inertness
encrinite
ungroomed
encrypted
entrapper
uncropped
unpropped
entropion
unprepare
entropium
engrossed
engrosser
unbrushed
uncrossed
undressed
ungrassed
unpressed
untressed
untrussed
untrusser
intrusion
intrusive
unfretted
unwritten
ingrately
unwriting
incretion
Encratism
un-British
Encratite
energumen
inbrought
indraught
inwrought
unfraught
unwrought
onerously
unprovide
unprovoke
ungravely
engraving
engravery
introvert
uncrowded
uncrowned
undrowned
ingrowing

unbrizzed
unashamed
unassayed
unessayed
anastasis
anastatic
unusually
unessence
unushered
gnostical
unisonant
unisonous
uniserial
anestrous
inusitate
unassumed
unassured
unisexual
initialed
initially
initiator
Gnetaceae
unstocked
unstudied
anathemas
unuttered
unstifled
unstuffed
instigate
snatchily
snitchers
unethical
unattired
unstained
unstriped
Anatolian
installed
instilled
unstilled
inutility
unstamped
anatomise
anatomist
anatomize
unstinted
instantly
gnathonic
inotropic
unstopped
unstopper
△unitarian
unstirred
unsterile
knotgrass
enstatite
institute
unitively
unstaying
endurance
insurance
undulancy

angulated
annulated
indurated
undulated
pneumatic
endurable
endurably
incunable
incurable
incurably
inhumanly
insularly
insurable
uncurable
untunable
untunably
incubator
insulator
unhumbled
untumbled
incumbent
unsuccess
inculcate
infuscate
uncurdled
unsubdued
unsued-for
intumesce
unqueened
inquietly
unqueenly
unquietly
indumenta
unduteous
untuneful
unruffled
anguiform
unguiform
anhungred
indulgent
insurgent
endungeon
inrushing
unmusical
inaudible
inaudibly
inducible
infusible
indusiate
induviate
infuriate
incurious
indubious
injurious
uncurious
undutiful
unsubject
unluckily
unfuelled
unquelled
unsullied

unqualify
aneuploid
annulling
inquiline
uncurling
unbuilt-on
annualise
annualize
annulment
inburning
unturning
innuendos
unfurnish
inquinate
untutored
△infusoria
pneumonia
pneumonic
unsuspect
anguipede
unrumpled
inculpate
unguarded
unhurried
incurrent
incurring
inquiring
uncurrent
inquorate
anguished
unguessed
unpursued
incursion
insulsity
incursive
injustice
unburthen
encurtain
uncurtain
inductile
annuitant
inputting
insultant
insulting
unsuiting
induction
intuition
unhurtful
inductive
intuitive
inaugural
incubuses
incurvate
incurvity
unmuzzled
unavoided
snivelled
sniveller
univalent
unavenged
universal

knaveship
knavishly
snow-water
snowscape
unswaddle
knowledge
snowberry
snow-white
snowfield
snowfleck
snowflick
indweller
snowflake
snow-blind
snowblink
inswinger
knowingly
snowiness
snowbound
snowboard
snowdrift
snow-broth
untwisted
snowstorm
inexactly
unextinct
unexcited
unexpired
unexalted
unexposed
unextreme
enzymatic
untypable
engyscope
untypical
undyingly
ankylosed
ankylosis
anhydride
anhydrase
anhydrite
enhydrite
anhydrous
enhydrous
cobalamin
Mozarabic
locatable
rotatable
copataine
Rotavator®
woman-body
rocambole
woman-born
monarchal
tobaccoes
Holarctic
monarchic
romancing
somascope
mosaicism
mosaicist

non-access
cowardice
cowardree
Monandria
hob-and-nob
hot-and-hot
forage-cap
lorazepam
covalency
God-a-mercy
Rotameter®
copacetic
kopasetic
logaoedic
pomace-fly
dogaressa
moraceous
pomaceous
rosaceous
volageous
coral-fish
botargoes
cotangent
coraggios
notaphily
toxaphene
Vodaphone
borachios
womanhood
monachism
monachist
Fomalhaut
botanical
foraminal
monadical
tovarisch
cohabitee
localiser
localizer
moraliser
moralizer
polarised
polariser
polarized
polarizer
Romaniser
Romanizer
totaliser
totalizer
vocaliser
vocalizer
womaniser
womanizer
logarithm
notabilia
tomatillo
covariant
cohabitor
rotavirus
solacious
souari-nut
voracious
womankind
Corallian
coralloid
womanlike
△coralline
rotaplane
totalling
womanless
corallite
forasmuch
Johannean
monadnock
Johannine
cocainise
cocainism
cocainist
vocalness
cocainize
nonagonal
monatomic
monaxonic
moratoria
rosa-solis
coral-rock
zoiatrics
coral-reef
copatriot
coralroot
podagrous
potassium
Monastral
Mozartean
Mozartian
copartner
corantoes
rowan-tree
monactine
monastery
cobaltite
vocabular
comatulid
totaquine
vol-au-vent
coralwort
doubtable
porbeagle
bomb-happy
bow-backed
corbicula
forbiddal
forbidden
forbidder
morbidity
double-bar
bomb-ketch
dor-beetle
doubleton
double-you
sombreros
soubrette
combretum
double-axe
wobbegong
woebegone
bombshell
gorblimey
pot-boiler
bomb-sight
corbeille
corbelled
corbeling
gobbeline
doubtless
hobbyless
bombilate
bobbin-net
Hobbinoll
sobbingly
combining
nobbiness
Sorbonist
bombinate
combinate
torbanite
top-booted
zoobiotic
sorb-apple
bomb-squad
Roxburghe
Lombardic
robber-fly
bombardon
bomb-proof
Hobbesian
bobbysock
sodbuster
bombastic
yobbishly
bombasine
combustor
booby-trap
bog-butter
combatant
combating
tombstone
sorbitise
combative
sorbitize
tomboyish
bombazine
concealer
moschatel
touchable
notchback
touchback
concubine
concocter
concyclic
concoctor
coccidium
touchdown
concierge
bob-cherry
concreate
couchette
force-feed
pouchfuls
coccygeal
coccygian
touch-hole
coach-hire
coach-horn
porcpisce
conceited
conchitis
torchière
colchicum
coachload
conciliar
dog-collar
porcelain
torch-lily
coachline
force-land
touchline
forceless
touchless
voiceless
coccolite
coccolith
forcemeat
coxcombic
voice-mail
box-camera
coxcombry
touchmark
volcanian
concenter
volcanoes
colcannon
concentre
△jobcentre
douceness
volcanise
△volcanism
△volcanist
concentus
volcanize
voice-over
no-account
Corchorus
forcepses
force-pump
porcupine
doucepere
forcipate
conceptus
concordat
torch-race
concerned
concerted
zoechrome
concertos
Socceroos
sorceress
sorcerous
worcester
vouchsafe
concisely
torch-song
colcothar
boycotter
toccatina
Touchtone®
touchtone
bog-cotton
touch-type
zoocytium
concluded
concourse
Foucault's
boschveld
concavely
concavity
coachwhip
coachwood
torchwood
touchwood
coachwork
bold-faced
gold-laced
goodfaced
road-maker
toad-eater
top-drawer
woodwaxen
cordially
woodscrew
conductor
mordacity
conductus
conducive
condiddle
boodie-rat
road-metal
gold-fever
toodle-pip
soldierly
noodledom
poodle-dog
goodyears
road-sense
cowdie-gum
doodlebug
woodreeve
cordiform
hot-dogger
condignly
road-agent
good-cheap
woodchuck
cold-short
goldfinch

9 □o□d□i

Cordaites
goldminer
good-sized
non-driver
goodnight
goldfield
good-willy
goldfinny
goldsinny
goodliest
pondokkie
roadblock
woodblock
Cordelier
gondolier
condyloid
condyloma
condolent
cordyline
word-blind
bordellos
coldblood
gold-cloth
gold-plate
bond-slave
condemned
goddamned
condiment
goldsmith
wordsmith
Jordanian
Londonian
condenser
Domdaniel
mordantly
noddingly
goldenrod
woodentop
Cobdenism
dowdiness
goodiness
hoydenish
hoydenism
Londonese
Londonise
Londonish
Londonism
moodiness
rowdiness
Soudanese
woodiness
wordiness
coadunate
Cobdenite
golden-eye
Londonize
bondwoman
rood-tower
wood-borer
roadworks
hood-mould

hoodooing
road-borne
wordbound
roadhouse
voodooism
voodooist
woodhorse
woodhouse
woodlouse
woodmouse
loudmouth
hordeolum
coadapted
good-speed
doddipoll
doddypoll
toddy-palm
goldspink
gowdspink
woodspite
bordereau
holderbat
wordbreak
gold-brick
roadcraft
woodcraft
road-train
doddering
foddering
soldering
wondering
goldcrest
toadgrass
foederati
ponderate
ponderous
wonderful
wonderous
cold-drawn
corduroys
soi-disant
roadstead
goldstick
foodstuff
cordotomy
bondstone
goldstone
loadstone
toadstone
woodstone
condition
toadstool
coadjutor
low-downer
row-dow-dow
moudiwart
moudiwort
mowdiwart
mowdiwort
Mondayish
co-tenancy

love-match
polemarch
rope-dance
sovenance
tolerance
fore-caddy
homewards
Romewards
code-named
forenamed
homemaker
lovemaker
notepaper
pome-water
robe-maker
rope-maker
rosewater
forecabin
coveralls
covetable
pole-vault
tolerable
tolerably
dodecagon
moderator
tolerator
sokemanry
bone-earth
foretaste
honey-bear
powerboat
moveables
moneybags
money-bill
honey-blob
bower-bird
honey-bird
Morescoes
honeycomb
honey-cart
lower-case
lower-deck
hôtel-Dieu
power-dive
coherence
coherency
forereach
foreteach
dose-meter
foreweigh
sovereign
oogenesis
oogenetic
yoke-devil
Rome-penny
bone-weary
pokeberry
love-feast
côtelette
foreteeth
novelette

solenette
womenfolk
dove's-foot
foreigner
monergism
rowel-head
foreshock
fore-wheel
nose-wheel
love-shaft
love-child
somewhile
forethink
something
foreshore
love-charm
somewhere
hope-chest
foreshewn
foreshown
Homeridae
polemical
nose-piece
rosefinch
fore-cited
noveliser
novelizer
sometimes
forenight
foresight
lovelight
doleritic
cohesible
dope-fiend
coheritor
Docetists
korediate
monecious
moleskins
womenkind
foreskirt
foregleam
bone-black
foreslack
someplace
nosebleed
rose-elder
bowelling
dowelling
modelling
rowelling
towelling
gore-blood
pole-clipt
dowerless
foreclose
honeyless
loverless
moneyless
powellise
Powellism

powerless
towerless
vowelless
covellite
forecloth
locellate
nose-flute
△powellite
soleplate
powellize
Dobermann
honeymoon
homeomery
lowermost
copes-mate
jokesmith
novennial
solemnify
come-and-go
governall
foreanent
governing
no-meaning
governess
modernise
△modernism
△modernist
notedness
soberness
solemness
solemnise
modernity
solemnity
foreknown
jobernowl
modernize
solemnize
forewoman
rose-topaz
foreboder
foretoken
forewomen
home-comer
love-token
rope-soled
ropeworks
foregoing
forepoint
homebound
horehound
solenodon
forecourt
dove-house
fore-horse
rope-house
foretooth
Coregonus
forespeak
powerplay
mole-spade
coreopsis

Words marked △ may be spelled also with a capital letter

love-apple
rose-apple
forespend
forespent
hoverport
hovel-post
homeopath
honeypots
fore-brace
rope-trick
towel-rack
homecraft
home-croft
forebrain
towel-rail
forefront
love-arrow
coheiress
rose-cross
voyeurism
home-truth
dove-drawn
home-grown
coseismal
forensics
honey-seed
nor'-easter
coseismic
coverslip
rowel-spur
foresteal
forest-oak
homestead
honey-trap
potential
domestics
toreutics
novelties
forestage
forestair
forestall
forest-fly
homestall
colectomy
lobectomy
topectomy
copestone
forestine
go-getting
hone-stone
lodestone
momentany
bolection
dog-eat-dog
coverture
love-story
momentary
motettist
potentise
tomentose
nonentity
potentate
molestful
momentous
tomentous
potentize
molecular
love-juice
boletuses
homebuyer
home-ruler
forejudge
dolefully
hopefully
bodeguero
home-guard
yo-heave-ho
go-between
homeowner
come-o'-will
moneywort
poker-work
wolfsbane
Confucian
Forficula
roofscape
forficate
confidant
confident
confiding
cowfeeder
confrérie
wolfberry
coiffeuse
solfeggio
configure
forfaiter
forfeiter
top-flight
boyfriend
moufflons
vow-fellow
roof-plate
confining
goofiness
coffinite
hoof-bound
wolfhound
roof-board
corfhouse
confronté
cofferdam
confervae
confervas
conformal
loaf-bread
△comforter
conferred
conferrer
confirmed
confirmee
confirmer
conformer
goffering
hoofprint
solferino
confirmor
loaferish
cod-fisher
confessed
rodfisher
confestly
wolfishly
confessor
confusion
confiseur
godfather
△confiteor
comfiture
confiture
solfatara
confluent
roof-guard
poignancy
long-dated
long-eared
long-faced
long-range
zoography
forgeable
tonga-bean
hobgoblin
dough-ball
Longobard
longicorn
roughcast
rough-draw
longaeval
tonguelet
toughener
tongue-tie
mongrelly
boogieing
goggle-box
borghetto
lorgnette
God-gifted
lodge-gate
long-chain
longshore
rough-hewn
long-lived
long-sixes
Mongolian
△mongoloid
coagulant
coagulase
Congolese
Mongolise
△mongolism
coagulate
longcloth
Mongolize
lodgement
songsmith
zoogamete
zoogamous
congenial
gorgonian
roughneck
gorgoneia
longingly
bogginess
dogginess
fogginess
gorgonise
podginess
roughness
sogginess
toughness
morganite
zoogenous
zoogonous
gorgonize
mongooses
zoogloeic
longhouse
long-coats
lodgepole
doggerman
long-track
box-girder
conger-eel
congeries
hop-garden
songcraft
rodgersia
mongering
Gongorism
Gongorist
congested
Moygashel®
moygashel
doggishly
hoggishly
roughshod
gong-stick
longitude
forgather
forgetter
forgotten
doughtily
forgetful
forgetive
songfully
congruent
congruity
congruous
forgiving
longevity
longevous
hotheaded
mop-headed
moth-eaten
not-headed
tow-headed
pothecary
gothicise
Gothicism
Gothicist
gothicize
lophodont
cochleate
lothefull
potholing
top-hamper
bonhommie
sophomore
Gothamist
Gothamite
bonhomous
cochineal
fox-hunter
mob-handed
pot-hanger
pot-hunter
mochiness
Tocharian
Tokharian
coshering
△mothering
Lotharios
mothproof
Tocharish
Tokharish
cothurnus
mother-lye
sophister
sophistic
sophistry
nowhither
dominance
dominancy
jouisance
comitadji
cogitable
comically
conically
logically
nominable
nominally
topically
toxically
dominator
motivator
nominator
corivalry
solitaire
bonilasse
Rosinante
Rozinante
comitatus
yohimbine
Politburo
dowitcher

9 □o□i□c

Moriscoes
koniscope
Coniferae
policeman
poriferal
poriferan
rotiferal
dosimeter
focimeter
konimeter
homiletic
dosimetry
nobilesse
politesse
Cominform
Kominform
coping-saw
sociogram
moviegoer
towing-net
boning-rod
loving-cup
holing-axe
dominical
Dominican
Dorididae
homicidal
Hominidae
political
Soricidae
soritical
domiciled
mobiliser
mobilizer
politicly
boliviano
dominions
volitient
politicos
solicitor
nobiliary
noviciate
novitiate
politique
gorillian
sociolect
moniplies
dosiology
koniology
sociology
gorilloid
gorilline
movieland
cotillion
modillion
nonillion
foliolose
socialise
△socialism
△socialist
foliolate

joviality
socialite
sociality
socialize
motion-man
coriander
motionist
notionist
solidness
polianite
soliloquy
sociopath
hodiernal
topiarian
posigrade
goliardic
monitress
topiarist
solipsism
solipsist
logistics
covin-tree
foliation
sociation
Comintern
foliature
Komintern
sovietise
sovietism
goniatite
sociative
sovietize
coticular
lodiculae
Solifugae
copiously
noxiously
rosin-weed
codifying
modifying
notifying
hobjobber
Poujadism
Poujadist
conjugant
conjugate
conjoined
conjuring
nonjuring
forjaskit
forjeskit
cockmatch
folk-dance
bookmaker
rockwater
rock-basin
pockmanky
cock-padle
workmanly
worktable
cocklaird

tonka-bean
corkscrew
cockscomb
cock's-comb
mockadoes
booked-out
cockleman
rock-perch
workbench
boxkeeper
jockteleg
zoo-keeper
cockneyfy
cocklebur
folk-weave
cocksfoot
fork-chuck
worksheet
rock-shaft
lock-chain
bookshelf
cook-chill
cock-a-hoop
monkshood
Yorkshire
workpiece
cockfight
folk-right
rock-pipit
Cockaigne
workplace
Volkslied
look-alike
bookplate
rock-flour
locksmith
dog-kennel
mockingly
soakingly
boskiness
cockiness
corkiness
forkiness
rockiness
moskonfyt
workwoman
cockroach
workforce
book-token
corkborer
hook-nosed
rock-borer
cock-robin
folkloric
rock-solid
rock-socks
workfolks
look-round
rock-bound
Doukhobor
corkboard

booklouse
cockhorse
cookhouse
lockhouse
workhorse
workhouse
△volksraad
rock-brake
rock-'n'-roll
lookers-on
dock-cress
rockcress
workerist
cock-broth
mockernut
monk's-seam
jockstrap
cockateel
cockatiel
rocketeer
forky-tail
bookstall
yolk-stalk
bookstand
docketing
Folketing
honky-tonk
pocketing
socketing
bookstore
pocketful
rock-guano
cockswain
donkey-man
monkey-bag
monkey-jar
monkey-pot
jockeyism
monkeyish
monkeyism
monkey-nut
monkey-run
foolhardy
low-loader
toolmaker
mouldable
△pollyanna
fool-happy
colleague
jollyboat
roll-about
hoolachan
collected
collector
collocate
collodion
poulterer
mollified
mollifier
poultfoot
holly-fern

collegial
collegian
bow-legged
dog-legged
• collagist
zoologist
colligate
lowlights
collegium
jollyhead
lowlihead
hollyhock
loll-shrob
colloidal
coal-fired
coalminer
coalfield
coal-black
mould-loft
hoplology
worldling
tol-lolish
mould-made
jolliment
Moslemism
Coelomata
coelomate
collimate
mollymawk
collinear
non-linear
pollen-sac
Hollander
△lowlander
lollingly
dolliness
godliness
jolliness
lowliness
nobleness
soiliness
pollinate
pollinium
soul-force
poll-money
foilborne
soil-bound
coalhouse
coolhouse
doll-house
tollhouse
toolhouse
goalmouth
tollbooth
collapsar
lolloping
lollipops
colloquia
bowler-hat
forlornly
foolproof

Words marked △ may be spelled also with a capital letter

foul-brood
Lollardry
coal-brass
goslarite
collyrium
coelostat
molluscan
molluskan
coulisses
foolishly
godlessly
joylessly
toylesome
collision
collusion
dolly-shop
pollusion
collusive
non-lethal
popliteal
dog-letter
mollities
toilet-set
cowl-staff
bolletrie
zoolatria
zoolithic
pollutant
coalition
collation
pollution
collotype
collative
pollutive
soul-curer
soulfully
colluvies
world-view
boulevard
worldwide
Tod-lowrie
following
Hollywood
holloware
mouldwarp
jolleying
doomwatch
doomsayer
worm-eaten
Dormobile®
cosmocrat
formicant
formicary
formicate
commodore
commodity
cormidium
cosmogeny
cosmogony
topmaking
pommelled

sommelier
cosmology
formulaic
boomslang
Commelina
formulary
formalise
formalism
formalist
formulise
formulism
formulist
normalise
formality
formulate
normality
formalize
formulize
normalize
non-member
commendam
commensal
common-law
Rosminian
Roumanian
Roumansch
commander
commenter
low-minded
tormented
tormenter
commonage
rooming-in
tormentil
zoomantic
commingle
foamingly
commoning
communing
commandos
commentor
△communion
hodmandod
topminnow
tormentor
△communard
communise
△communism
△communist
foaminess
loaminess
Mormonism
Normanise
Normanism
roominess
comminate
comminute
△community
Mormonite
cosmonaut
tormentum

torminous
communize
Normanize
wormholed
zoomorphy
bog-myrtle
cosmorama
boomerang
commorant
cormorant
rosmarine
woomerang
commissar
Holmesian
job-master
tommy-shop
committal
commutual
cosmetics
dogmatics
committed
committee
formatted
formatter
godmother
dot-matrix
zoometric
coemption
commotion
cosmotron
dormition
formation
dogmatory
dormitory
dogmatise
dogmatism
dogmatist
commutate
dormitive
formative
normative
dogmatize
corn-salad
going-away
roundarch
downwards
horn-maker
moon-faced
moonraker
countable
woundable
loon-pants
connubial
bonnibell
mound-bird
coenobite
soundbite
sound-bite
coenobium
Cornaceae
connected

connecter
low-necked
connector
moonscape
townscape
coenocyte
fornicate
poinadoes
tornadoes
point-duty
count-down
round-down
lounge-bar
rounceval
roundelay
round-eyed
young-eyed
pointedly
counselor
pounce-box
bounteous
townsfolk
corniform
hound-fish
round-fish
born-again
hornyhead
Roundhead
joint-heir
moonshine
moonshiny
pounching
roundhand
down-throw
moonphase
hobnailed
soundings
downright
moonlight
cornfield
pointillé
poinciana
councilor
△bountiful
cornelian
point-lace
moon-glade
poenology
cornflake
countline
foundling
moonblind
somnolent
youngling
boundless
countless
jointless
pointless
soundless
woundless
loincloth

cornflour
cognomens
cognomina
cornemuse
zoonomist
moon-knife
foiningly
bonniness
downiness
horniness
jointness
looniness
roundness
soundness
youngness
downforce
cornborer
going-over
moon-loved
boondocks
coonhound
down-going
townhouse
cornopean
John-apple
downspout
Cointreau®
cornbread
corner-man
hornwrack
downgrade
Boanerges
down-train
cornbrake
corncrake
downtrend
corner-boy
cornbrash
foundress
jointress
pointsman
roundsman
youngster
countship
tonnishly
cognisant
coenosarc
goings-out
sonneteer
downstage
downstair
round-trip
cornstalk
youngthly
cornstone
hornstone
moonstone
cognation
cognition
connation
sonnetary

9 □o□n□t

cornetist
sonnetise
connotate
cognitive
connotive
sonnetize
moonquake
down-quilt
moanfully
downburst
coenourus
connivent
downswing
jointworm
joint-worm
roundworm
woundwort
connexion
Johnny-raw
bountyhed
down-gyved
down-lying
cognizant
Dodonaean
Notogaean
pogo-dance
coronated
monolater
monolayer
logomachy
monomachy
Colocasia
homogamic
homotaxic
homotaxis
honoraria
monobasic
monogamic
monomania
Notogaeic
porogamic
motorable
Novocaine®
Rotovator®
rotovator
monolatry
△holocaust
ionopause
polonaise
novodamus
motor-boat
motor-bike
solonchak
motorcade
motoscafi
motoscafo
monorchid
hodoscope
horoscope
horoscopy
poroscope
poroscopy
monoecism
do-gooding
do-goodery
do-goodism
colonelcy
bolometer
coco-de-mer
coroneted
hodometer
monometer
potometer
tonometer
logopedic
monogenic
monomeric
poromeric
monoceros
bolometry
hodometry
horometry
tonometry
Notonecta
box-office
homophobe
goloshoes
Lotophagi
monophagy
homophile
homophyly
iodophile
logophile
toxophily
monorhyme
colophony
do-nothing
homophone
homophony
monophony
monorhine
gonophore
ionophore
monochord
notochord
molochise
monophase
holophote
holophyte
logothete
nomothete
molochize
monodical
monopitch
colonitis
colorific
dolomitic
dolorific
honorific
sodomitic
soporific
coyotillo
notoriety
doronicum
notorious
mono-skier
coralline
locoplant
monocline
monoplane
corollary
homoplasy
monoamine
colonnade
cocooning
cocoonery
△bolognese
homopolar
gonococci
horologer
tokoloshe
homoeosis
homoeotic
homotonic
horologic
monologic
monotonic
Solomonic
topologic
corocoros
homoeobox
locofocos
locomotor
homomorph
Notodonta
homologue
monocoque
monologue
colour-mag
colourman
colourway
mobocracy
monocracy
monotroch
nomocracy
coloureds
gonorrhea
logorrhea
sojourner
homograft
loxodrome
loxodromy
monodrama
monotreme
Nototrema
colourant
colouring
holocrine
hodograph
holograph
homograph
logograph
logogriph
monograph
Monotropa
nomograph
rotograph
sonograph
tomograph
colourise
colourist
motocross
colourful
colour-sup
pomoerium
colourize
homousian
Molossian
motor-ship
monopsony
colosseum
monostich
colostric
monostyle
colostomy
co-routine
co-portion
Homoptera
monoptote
colostrum
monocular
colobuses
monopulse
cocoa-wood
homotypal
toponymal
copolymer
co-polymer
holotypic
homonymic
homotypic
Monogynia
monotypic
toponymic
golomynka
monoxylon
colocynth
zoophagan
comptable
complaint
comprador
zooplasty
poppycock
compacted
hop-picker
hop-pocket
compactly
coppicing
compactor
torpedoer
torpedoes
dog-paddle
hooped-pot
torpidity
pompadour
completed
completer
cosphered
morphemic
morphetic
complexly
coupledom
soapberry
complexus
poppy-head
comprisal
dolphinet
loop-light
zoophilia
comptible
compliant
compelled
compeller
gospeller
corpulent
gospelise
gospelize
compander
companied
compendia
hoop-snake
rompingly
toppingly
companing
component
compandor
companion
cosponsor
soapiness
soppiness
gowpenful
topping-up
gomphoses
gomphosis
morphosis
morphotic
zoophobia
zoophoric
soap-works
zoophorus
pompholyx
soupspoon
corporeal
Popperian
corporify
cooperage
nonpareil
comptroll
co-operant
coopering
coppering
godparent
poppering
non-person
copperish

Words marked △ may be spelled also with a capital letter

zooperist
cooperate
co-operate
corporate
porporate
nonparous
compasses
composter
corpuscle
foppishly
rompishly
corposant
composure
△composite
pomposity
torpitude
compotier
hospitage
soopstake
hospitale
competent
computant
soapstone
computist
hospitium
nonplused
pompously
potpourri
porphyria
porphyrin
porphyrio
zoophytic
complying
torquated
coequally
△conqueror
mosquitos
non-reader
courbaril
doorn-boom
non-racial
correctly
corrector
court-card
fourscore
comradely
Notre-Dame
corrodent
joy-riding
corridors
torridity
courtesan
courtezan
fourpence
journeyed
journeyer
tourneyer
bourgeois
Courtelle®
worriedly
fourpenny

Lowrie-tod
tournedos
Monroeism
Monroeist
courbette
courgette
courteous
horrified
torrefied
board-foot
cobriform
toeragger
board-game
corrigent
corrugate
worryguts
door-cheek
four-wheel
coordinal
co-ordinal
mournival
mournings
coercible
coercibly
corralled
court-leet
log-roller
coprology
courtlike
courtling
four-flush
hour-glass
coprolite
coprolith
correlate
door-plate
hourplate
no-trumper
worriment
fogramite
fogramity
doorknock
hog-ringer
porrenger
porringer
hour-angle
louringly
roaringly
soaringly
sopranini
sopranino
hoariness
sopranist
sorriness
godrooned
sourdough
boar-hound
hoarhound
pourpoint
four-hours
pourboire

sour-gourd
four-horse
poorhouse
poor-mouth
boar-spear
corrupter
corruptly
sobriquet
court-roll
poor's-roll
boardroom
courtroom
hoar-frost
sour-crout
Fourcroya
pourtrayd
nourisher
courtship
touristic
boorishly
sourishly
worrisome
copresent
corrasion
corrosion
bourasque
corrosive
door-stead
doorstone
hoar-stone
nouriture
Socratise
coarctate
Socratize
poursuitt
boardwalk
borrowing
sorrowing
boerewors
gourd-worm
worrywart
sorrowful
courtyard
four-by-two
coprozoic
constancy
lossmaker
Mössbauer
moustache
constable
houseboat
horseback
possibles
roast-beef
house-bote
housecoat
consocies
fossicker
△coxsackie
house-carl
worst-case

goose-club
mouse-deer
house-duty
bolstered
corsleted
holstered
howsoever
roisterer
roysterer
bobsleigh
△bolshevik
poussette
roussette
dorsiflex
housefuls
goosefoot
horse-foot
goose-fish
fog-signal
consigned
consignee
consigner
consignor
Monsignor
goose-girl
kok-saghyz
loosehead
Rorschach
horsehide
horsehair
household
mouse-hole
house-hunt
mouse-hunt
gooseherd
noosphere
conspirer
conscient
conscious
forsaking
loose-leaf
tonsillar
joss-block
consultee
consulter
house-leek
houselled
norseller
consulage
coastline
house-line
mossplant
consultor
dog-salmon
boastless
fossilise
horseless
houseless
noiseless
consolute
consulate

fossulate
fossilize
horsemeat
roast-meat
housemaid
noisomely
consuming
horsemint
rousement
gossamery
house-mate
Jonsonian
poison-gas
poison-oak
sons-in-law
goose-neck
goosander
cousinage
voisinage
rousingly
consonant
bossiness
horsiness
looseness
lousiness
moistness
mossiness
noisiness
worseness
consensus
consonous
poison-nut
poisonous
poison-ivy
monsoonal
torsional
forswonck
hopscotch
dogshores
non-smoker
zooscopic
zoosporic
dosshouse
joss-house
lobscouse
dog's-tooth
jobsworth
horseplay
gossiping
gossypine
horsepond
Gossypium
fossorial
tonsorial
conscribe
constrict
construct
conserver
consorted
consorter
construer

consortia
constrain
bowstring
bowstrung
box-spring
houseroom
conscript
goustrous
monstrous
moss-grown
goose-step
possessed
goose-skin
horseshoe
possessor
mouse-trap
joss-stick
poss-stick
corsetier
forsythia
horsetail
mouse-tail
corseting
cosseting
top-sawyer
housewife
horsewhip
pousowdie
goose-wing
copsewood
coastward
housework
louse-wort
coastwise
non-sexist
mooseyard
pontianac
pontianak
portrayal
postnasal
postnatal
boot-faced
bootmaker
mortgagee
mortgager
portrayer
root-eater
rostrated
toothache
Nostratic
footfault
mouthable
hootnanny
mortgagor
contralti
contralto
contrasty
posthaste
softpaste
mortician
foeticide
porticoed
porticoes
corticoid
monticule
poeticule
forthcome
toothcomb
conticent
zootechny
contactor
poeticise
poeticism
vorticism
vorticist
vorticose
corticate
vorticity
posticous
poeticize
contadina
contadine
contadini
contadino
Southdown
bottle-gas
soft-pedal
voltmeter
pontlevis
zoothecia
northerly
southerly
bottle-imp
pottle-pot
hostlesse
north-east
poetresse
south-east
zootheism
bottleful
portreeve
pontifice
volte-face
fortified
fortifier
mortified
mortifier
mouthfeel
mouthfuls
coltsfoot
soothfast
△forty-five
Portuguee
cottaging
contagion
contagium
voltigeur
youthhead
goat's-hair
soft-shell
youthhood
mouth-harp
doctrinal
Noctuidae
post-viral
bobtailed
container
contrived
contriver
postrider
tortrices
no-strings
footlight
fortnight
tortricid
foothills
rostellar
bootblack
fortalice
noctiluca
portulaca
soothlich
hosteller
postiller
fortilage
nostology
sortilege
sortilegy
costalgia
nostalgia
nostalgic
sootflake
toothlike
hostilely
monthling
northland
portolani
portolano
postulant
southland
postilion
mortalise
mouthless
toothless
worthless
footcloth
footplate
hostility
mortality
mortcloth
postulate
tortility
rostellum
mortalize
contumacy
mouth-made
contemned
contemner
contemper
costumier
contumely
contemnor
northmost
southmost
zootomist
continual
pottingar
cottonade
boutonnée
contender
contented
continued
continuer
pontoneer
pontonier
pottinger
routineer
cotton-gin
joltingly
poutingly
routinely
△continent
softening
contangos
continuos
△hottentot
post-entry
dottiness
goutiness
loftiness
Montanism
Montanist
pottiness
routinise
routinism
routinist
sootiness
voltinism
fortunate
sostenuto
continuum
souteneur
totting-up
fortunize
routinize
postwoman
soft-goods
contrôlée
pontooner
portioned
portioner
postponer
softcover
soft-nosed
zootrophy
portfolio
zoetropic
foot-pound
root-bound
footboard
moot-court
boathouse
footloose
moot-house
porthouse
posthorse
posthouse
root-house
toothpick
dottipoll
coeternal
doctorial
nocturnal
contorted
co-starred
couturier
voiturier
fosterage
porterage
boat-train
cotter-pin
sooterkin
doctorand
footprint
fostering
loitering
pottering
root-prune
rostering
torturing
tottering
contornos
foster-son
posterior
coat-dress
doctoress
Pooterism
porteress
posturist
soft-grass
doctorate
posterity
Southroun
torturous
contessas
contested
contester
poetaster
route-step
sottisier
doltishly
loutishly
sottishly
loathsome
toothsome
youthsome
cortisone
contusion
poetastry
contusive
bootstrap
rootstock
fortitude
footstalk
foot-stall

portatile
coatstand
font-stone
mort-stone
footstool
hortation
sortation
sortition
footsteps
hortatory
hortative
portative
contoured
routously
costively
boatswain
howtowdie
northward
southward
toothwort
mouthwash
north-west
south-west
toothwash
forthwith
post-synch
lobulated
nodulated
non-usager
jocularly
popularly
joculator
modulator
Columbian
△columbine
columbary
columbate
columbite
columbium
homuncule
homunculi
coruscant
coruscate
loquacity
toluidine
jocundity
rotundate
rotundity
conundrum
volumeter
columella
toruffled
Roquefort
voluminal
Zonuridae
coquilles
Lotus-land
locuplete
columnist
wofulness
torulosis

Solutrean
Solutrian
docudrama
colubrine
volucrine
rogueship
roguishly
focussing
hocussing
coquetted
volunteer
coculture
voluntary
nocuously
cocuswood
Norueyses
souvlakia
convector
convocate
convolute
dog-violet
non-verbal
converter
polverine
wolverene
wolverine
convertor
wolvishly
non-voting
solvation
convivial
convexity
Norwegian
porwiggle
boxwallah
pot-waller
forwander
bow-window
forwarder
forwardly
nor'wester
nor'-wester
sou'-wester
coaxially
coaxingly
cony-catch
polywater
polymathy
corydalis
polybasic
Polygamia
polygamic
corybants
polymasty
corymbose
molybdate
molybdous
polygenic
polymeric
polylemma
cotyledon

polyhedra
body-check
coryphaei
polyphagy
bodyshell
coryphene
polyphone
polyphony
polythene
polyphase
copyright
polypidom
polyvinyl
monyplies
polyploid
polyglott
polyamide
polyomino
polyonymy
Houyhnhnm
polyandry
polygonal
polytonal
polyzonal
polyconic
polyposis
polyzooid
polymorph
polyzoary
polygonum
Polyporus
cohyponym
holy-cruel
polyarchy
polygraph
polyester
polyptych
polystyle
holystone
body-curer
bodyguard
polyaxial
Polygynia
polytypic
pozzolana
booziness
wooziness
monzonite
douzepers
appanaged
apsarases
aplanatic
speakable
ups-a-daisy
apparatus
spraickle
sprauchle
uplandish
apparency
speakeasy
sphacelus

splay-foot
spearfish
spragging
spearhead
splashily
splashing
apparitor
appalling
sprawling
spearmint
sphagnous
Appaloosa
sphaerite
upmanship
splatting
spearwort
opobalsam
specially
spectacle
spectator
spiccatos
specialty
spicebush
epicyclic
epicedial
epicedian
epicedium
epicleses
epiclesis
specified
epicritic
spicilege
spaceless
speckless
apiculate
speculate
spiculate
epicenter
epicentre
spiciness
apocopate
△epicurean
epicurise
epicurism
epicurize
spaceship
spacesuit
space-time
spec-built
space-walk
△apocrypha
apodictic
spadefuls
spadefish
spodogram
spadillio
spadelike
opodeldoc
spodumene
epedaphic
epidermal

spiderman
epidermic
epidermis
spadesman
spadassin
epidosite
spadework
speedboat
speedball
spleuchan
up-perched
upper-case
appendage
appendant
sphendone
splendent
spreading
splendour
ephemerae
ephemeral
ephemeras
appetence
appetency
apheresis
epaenetic
ephemerid
ephemeris
splenetic
ephemeron
après-goût
speechify
sprechery
speechful
spherical
appetiser
appetizer
ephelides
speerings
splenitis
appetible
spreckled
Up-Helly-Aa
appealing
appellant
upwelling
speedless
appellate
uppermost
spleenish
spleenful
△sphenodon
upheaping
ephedrine
speedster
appertain
upsetting
spherular
speedwell
apteryxes
apoenzyme
epigraphy

9 □p□g□e

spaghetti
epigaeous
Spigelian
apogamous
epigynous
spagerist
spagirist
spagyrist
upcheered
up-Channel
upthunder
optimates
opsimathy
optically
optimally
sphincter
Ophiuchus
iprindole
epainetic
spriteful
April-fish
spoilfive
springlet
springald
springily
sprigging
springing
△springbok
uplighted
uplighter
upaithric
sprightly
uprightly
Epeiridae
speirings
apsidiole
aphidious
sprinkler
uplinking
ephialtes
ophiology
upfilling
ophiolite
ophiuroid
apriorism
apriorist
apriority
spoilsman
spritsail
splitting
sprinting
uplifting
upsitting
splintery
spikefish
spike-nail
spikenard
spikiness
spike-rush
spokesman
spokesmen
spokewise
appliance
appliable
spellable
spoliator
spellbind
spulebane
spulebone
epilobium
applicant
apple-cart
applicate
spelldown
apologise
apologist
epilogise
epilogist
apologize
epilogize
spellican
spillikin
apple-jack
apple-John
opal-glass
spelunker
opulently
spillover
epileptic
speldring
spilosite
apple-tree
epilation
epulation
apple-tart
applauder
apple-wife
apomictic
spymaster
spinnaker
sponsalia
spendable
epinician
spinacene
epinicion
up-and-down
spongebag
spinneret
spanaemia
spanaemic
open-heart
spongeous
open-weave
spiniform
open-chain
open-field
sponsible
spongiose
spongious
epinikian
epinikion
spangling
spindling
spineless
spinulose
spinulate
spinulous
eponymous
open-ended
spininess
opinioned
up-and-over
open-armed
spin-dried
spin-drier
spin-dryer
spindrift
Upanishad
epinastic
spinosity
open-steek
epineural
spondulix
Spinozism
Spinozist
opsomania
opposable
epeolatry
ephoralty
spoonbait
spoonbill
upholding
opponency
optometer
optometry
spoon-feed
spoonfuls
splodgily
optophone
spoonhook
aphoriser
aphorizer
appointed
appointee
upbounden
appointor
up-country
upholster
opportune
sprouting
uprooting
apportion
spoonwise
spoonways
apophasis
apophatic
epiphanic
epipolism
epiphragm
epiphytal
apophyses
epiphyses
apophysis
epiphysis
epiphytic
sportance
spermaria
spermatia
spermatic
spermatid
sportable
approbate
up-pricked
spiracula
sporocarp
sporocyst
sporidial
sporidesm
sporidium
sparterie
sparsedly
sparteine
spirogram
sporogeny
spirogyra
apartheid
epirrhema
apprehend
spur-whang
eparchate
appraisal
appraiser
upbraider
X-particle
spirillar
sparklies
uptrilled
sparkling
spareless
sparkless
spiralism
spiralist
spireless
sportless
spirality
sporulate
spirillum
apartment
optronics
sporangia
sparingly
apartness
apertness
spareness
spur-royal
aperiodic
spare-part
sporophyl
sportsman
spiraster
operosely
apprising
oppressor
operosity
spiritual
spirituel
spare-time
operating
spiriting
epuration
épuration
operation
spiration
spiritism
spiritist
spiritoso
spiritful
spiritous
aperitive
operative
opercular
upbrought
up-draught
upwrought
operculum
upgrowing
spirewise
sporozoan
apprizing
epistases
apostatic
epistasis
epistatic
epistaxis
spasmatic
episodial
epistemic
apostille
apishness
episcopal
epistoler
epistolet
△apostolic
epistolic
△spasmodic
opusculum
spatially
apathaton
sputterer
apathetic
apothecia
epithesis
epithetic
epitheton
spot-check
spotlight
spatulate
apetalous
epitomise
epitomist
epitomize
epitapher
epitaphic
upstaring
epitaxial

Words marked △ may be spelled also with a capital letter

spauld-ill
epaulette
spout-hole
upgushing
spoutless
oppugnant
upburning
upturning
up-current
up-putting
spluttery
apivorous
spewiness
upsy-daisy
aphyllous
sphygmoid
epizootic
epizeuxis
aquabatic
squabbler
squabbish
aquarelle
squamella
square-cut
aquaphobe
squashily
equaliser
equalizer
squalidly
aquariums
aquariist
aquatinta
squawking
aquaplane
equalling
squailing
squalling
equalness
squatness
squamosal
aquarobic
aquaboard
aquadrome
squadrone
squarrose
squatting
squelcher
squegging
squeakily
squeaking
squeakery
squealing
squeamish
squeezing
squinancy
squirarch
equitable
equitably
squiralty
equivalve
squibbing
squireage
aquilegia
equisetic
squiredom
equisetum
equipment
equivocal
equipoise
equivoque
equipping
squirrely
squinting
squirting
squitters
squint-eye
breakaway
ergataner
arracacha
pre-adamic
breakable
treatable
great-aunt
dreamboat
breakback
broad-brim
broadbill
broadband
friarbird
organ-bird
greatcoat
cream-cake
bread-corn
broadcast
Triandria
errand-boy
Dryasdust
breakdown
break-even
organelle
ervalenta
ornaments
trial-fire
breakfast
arraigner
triangled
triangles
breadhead
preachify
breathily
dreamhole
preachily
breathing
preaching
triathlon
treachery
breathful
treachour
erratical
organical
organised
organiser
organized
organizer
armadillo
irradiant
irradiate
ortanique
broad-leaf
creamlaid
breadline
dream-land
treadling
trialling
broadloom
dreadless
dreamless
triallist
wreakless
treadmill
arrayment
treatment
area-sneak
breakneck
broadness
greatness
triatomic
trialogue
organ-pipe
breadroom
breadroot
creatress
broadside
breast-fed
breastpin
broadtail
breaktime
dreamtime
triactine
proactive
creatural
treasurer
break-wind
creamware
broadwise
creamwove
broadways
organzine
crab-faced
trabeated
probeable
trebuchet
trabecula
tribadism
crab's-eyes
crabbedly
cribellar
tribology
drabbling
fribbling
aryballos
fribblish
tribalism
tribalist
tribeless
cribellum
prebendal
Orobanche
arabinose
Trubenise
tribunate
Tribunite
Trubenize®
prebiotic
crab-louse
crab-apple
tribesman
proboscis
arabesque
crabstick
grubstake
probation
probatory
tributary
probative
traceable
traceably
trackable
tractable
tractably
tractator
bricabrac
bric-à-brac
track-boat
trackball
brickclay
Ericaceae
frock-coat
precocial
tricycler
tricyclic
precocity
procacity
crocodile
precedent
preceding
procident
procedure
brick-dust
crackdown
tracheide
cricketer
crocheted
proceeder
bracteole
procreant
tracheary
précieuse
bracteate
brochette
procreate
Tracheata
tracheate
crucified
crucifier
cruciform
eruciform
truck-farm
wreckfish
crackhead
Bruchidae
practical
precoital
trichinae
trichinas
Trochidae
practised
practiser
proclisis
proclitic
proctitis
trachitis
trichitic
triclinic
trochilic
Fructidor
brachiate
fractious
practicum
practique
trachinus
trochilus
brick-kiln
trochlear
truck-load
oricalche
crackling
freckling
prickling
trickling
truckling
truculent
bractless
frockless
graceless
priceless
traceless
trackless
trickless
truceless
gracility
oraculous
tricolour
truchmans
△draconian
Uriconian
Arachnida
pre-cancel
arachnoid
△dracontic
cracknels
precentor
△draconism
erectness
preconise

9 □r□c□n

priciness
precincts
proconsul
preconize
pro-choice
Urochorda
trichosis
tricrotic
graciosos
practolol
precipice
preceptor
trackroad
procuracy
groceries
precurrer
traceried
trichroic
trichrome
urochrome
precursor
procaryon
procaryot
tricerion
procuress
procerity
procureur
cracksman
precisian
fricassee
processed
trickster
crocosmia
tricuspid
precisely
tricksome
précising
prick-song
precision
processor
truck-shop
precisive
Brechtian
precatory
fricative
precative
fructuary
fructuate
fructuous
brickwall
prickwood
brickwork
trachytic
Brachyura
brickyard
graduated
bridgable
gradually
tradeable
graduator
Iridaceae

Traducian
predicter
bridecake
predicant
traducing
predictor
eradicate
predacity
predicate
tridactyl
dredge-box
grudgeful
predefine
predigest
tredrille
predikant
predilect
iridology
prideless
trade-last
tradeless
credulity
credulous
urodelous
mridamgam
bridemaid
trademark
tridymite
mridangam
tridental
Uredineae
uredinial
tridented
prudently
tradename
crudeness
credendum
uredinium
uredinous
prodromal
prodromic
prud'homme
prodromus
Gradgrind
bridesman
bride's-man
tradesman
predesign
prudishly
eruditely
iridotomy
erudition
gradation
predation
△tradition
gradatory
predatory
proditory
traditors
predative
traditive

Bradburys
Bradbury's
predevote
bridewell
freelance
grievance
trierarch
irrelated
free-range
freezable
△freemason
greenback
green-bone
order-book
breed-bate
pre-embryo
proembryo
arc-en-ciel
friedcake
brief-case
friending
breezeway
free-bench
creepered
green-eyed
trieteric
arle-penny
truepenny
freeze-dry
freeze-out
greengage
pre-engage
arpeggios
freesheet
freewheel
pre-echoes
creep-hole
breeching
freephone
greenhand
greenhorn
arsenical
free-diver
free-liver
free-rider
tree-lined
artemisia
arteritis
praesidia
pre-exilic
arteriole
arseniate
arsenious
triecious
Orwellian
Greekling
gruelling
briefless
Greekless
griefless
orderless

irreality
urceolate
greenmail
praeamble
triennial
tree-snake
briefness
cruelness
greenness
Orleanism
Orleanist
freewoman
△free-lover
freewomen
praecoces
praenomen
free-board
tree-house
freebooty
free-space
pre-employ
pre-emptor
greegrees
arrearage
tree-trunk
brier-root
greenroom
△greensand
grief-shot
orienteer
priest-rid
freestyle
tree-stump
△argentine
Argentino
freestone
priestess
argentite
orientate
pro-estrus
arrestive
irregular
praeludia
Greenwich
greenweed
brier-wood
greenwood
treenware
greenwash
proenzyme
oriflamme
drift-bolt
orificial
prefacial
trifacial
trifocals
proffered
profferer
prefigure
trefoiled
preflight

drift-land
truffling
craftless
driftless
profilist
trifolium
profanely
gruffness
profanity
preferred
preferrer
triformed
triforium
craftsman
draftsman
dry-fisted
professed
drift-sail
profusely
professor
profusion
profiteer
profiting
prefatory
profluent
drift-weed
driftwood
craftwork
prefixion
fragrance
fragrancy
frogmarch
pregnance
pregnancy
frog-eater
orography
urography
bregmatic
pragmatic
pregnable
programme
tragedian
brigadier
frigidity
brogueish
drag-chain
drug-fiend
fragilely
traguline
wriggling
tragelaph
frugalist
fragility
frugality
dragomans
trigamist
trigamous
trigynian
dragonfly
originals
brigandry

Words marked △ may be spelled also with a capital letter

dragoness
dragonise
dragonish
dragonism
Origenism
Origenist
aragonite
originate
erogenous
trigonous
trigynous
urogenous
dragonize
prognoses
prognosis
draghound
frogmouth
gregarian
Gregorian
Gregarina
gregarine
progestin
frigatoon
drug-store
frightful
tregetour
drag-queen
orthoaxes
Brahmanic
orthoaxis
trihybrid
Archibald
Orchideae
trihedral
trihydric
trihedron
orchidist
orthodoxy
orthoepic
arch-felon
archaiser
archaizer
Brahminee
arthritic
arthritis
Brahminic
arch-fiend
archology
prehallux
archilowe
archimage
archangel
orphanage
archontic
arch-enemy
prehensor
orphanism
arthrosis
arthropod
orthopedy
orthoptic
Arthurian
arch-druid
orpharion
archeress
orchestic
orchestra
architect
orthotics
arch-stone
orthotone
archetype
architype
orthotist
archducal
archduchy
archivolt
archivist
artisanal
arrivance
arrivancy
irritancy
ordinance
urticaria
drainable
irrigable
irritable
irritably
trailable
trainable
irrigator
irritator
ordinaire
trainband
fruit-cage
fruitcake
braincase
brain-dead
armigeral
cruiseway
praiseach
broiderer
fruiterer
praiseful
frying-pan
Orpington
Irvingism
Irvingite
freighter
ornithoid
artichoke
fraîcheur
druidical
△artificer
arrivisme
arriviste
vraicking
treillage
armillary
arpillera
artillery
Braillist
brainless
fruitless
trail-less
trainless
argillite
orgillous
frailness
traitorly
drainpipe
arbitrage
orris-root
arbitrary
arbitress
traitress
arbitrate
arbitrium
brainsick
orgiastic
croissant
traipsing
drain-trap
△armistice
fruit-tree
drain-tile
articular
orbicular
irriguous
fruitwood
brainwash
brain-wave
projector
prejudice
prejudize
frikkadel
brake-fade
Prakritic
brakeless
urokinase
brokerage
prokaryon
prokaryot
brakes-man
brake-shoe
arillated
trilobate
Trilobita
trilobite
prolicide
frolicked
prolactin
prelector
preludial
urolagnia
orologist
prologise
urologist
prologize
drill-hole
trellised
brilliant
trillions
prolamine
trilinear
prolonger
drollness
trollopee
prolepses
prolepsis
proleptic
prolapsus
arblaster
drillship
artlessly
prolusion
prelusory
prolusory
prelusive
prelatial
trilithic
urolithic
prolately
prelation
prolation
trilithon
prelature
proletary
prelatess
prelatise
prelatish
prelatism
prelatist
uralitise
prolative
prelatize
uralitize
grillwork
prolixity
△brummagem
grammatic
crammable
drum-major
cramp-bone
crampbark
promachos
cremocarp
trump-card
dromedare
dromedary
primaeval
trumpeted
trumpeter
drum-belly
trampette
trumped-up
bromoform
cramp-fish
Cro-Magnon
krummhorn
tramlined
tramlines
trimmings
cramp-iron
bromeliad
crumblies
bromelain
grimalkin
brambling
Crimplene®
crumpling
grumbling
primuline
trampling
tremblant
trembling
tremolant
tremulant
crimeless
gremolata
primality
tremolite
tremulate
tremulous
Dramamine®
Gramineae
promenade
trominoes
prominent
brominism
griminess
premonish
primeness
criminate
criminous
primrosed
trampolin
primipara
primarily
cramp-ring
trimerous
cremaster
trimester
premosaic
promuscis
promising
promissor
crumb-tray
primatial
primitiae
primitial
primitias
dramatics
drumstick
Trematoda
trematode
trematoid
trimetric
prime-time
brimstone
brimstony
prompting
cremation
premotion
promotion

Words marked △ may be spelled also with a capital letter

9 □r□m□t

prompt-box
crematory
dramaturg
premature
prompture
aromatise
dramatise
dramatist
eremitism
△primitive
promotive
trimethyl
aromatize
dramatize
framework
grandaddy
frontager
iron-cased
truncated
drinkable
grantable
printable
transaxle
grand-aunt
brinjarry
prongbuck
prenubile
pronuclei
wry-necked
trunk-call
transcend
crankcase
irenicism
grenadier
wrongdoer
grenadine
Orangeman
cranreuch
orangeade
brandered
princelet
trinketer
Frankenia
orange-tip
princekin
drunkenly
trancedly
transenna
transeunt
princedom
cranberry
trinketry
Orangeism
princesse
transfect
gronefull
trunkfuls
wrong-foot
transfard
transform
transfuse
trunkfish
branchiae
branchial
bronchial
Frenchman
printhead
branchlet
Frenchmen
Frenchify
drink-hail
transhume
branching
trenchand
trenchant
wrenching
truncheon
branchery
pronghorn
trenchard
franchise
trunk-hose
Araneidae
crinoidal
frenzical
principal
Crinoidea
iron-miner
iron-sided
Ironsides
principia
frangible
franticly
principle
transient
brand-iron
frontiers
grandiose
crenelled
wrinklies
irenology
uranology
urinology
Franglais
granuloma
brandling
brangling
crinoline
front-line
trunk-line
wrangling
prunellos
granulary
frontless
granulose
printless
crenelate
crenulate
granulate
granulite
translate
granulous
trinomial
trunk-mail
grandmama
ironsmith
transmute
transmove
Brunonian
pronuncio
droningly
brand-name
brininess
crankness
frankness
grandness
proneness
wrongness
uraninite
francolin
Prontosil®
transonic
ironworks
iron-bound
front-page
drone-pipe
grandpapa
transpire
transport
transpose
trunk-road
front-rank
brandreth
prankster
transship
trans-ship
dronishly
pranksome
grandsire
uraniscus
prenotify
granitoid
trinitrin
ironstone
arenation
crenation
prenotion
pronation
urination
crenature
granitise
granitite
urinative
granitize
orang-utan
pronounce
transumpt
granivore
transvest
frontward
trunk-work
frontwise
frontways
pranayama
brondyron
Grundyism
trendyism
arrogance
areolated
ergomania
Areopagus
crookback
broomball
cryoscope
cryoscopy
preoccupy
broom-corn
preordain
areometer
cryometer
ergometer
eriometer
kryometer
cryogenic
crookedly
arboreous
arboretum
erroneous
o're-office
arrow-head
Bryophyta
bryophyte
Armorican
Oriolidae
creolised
creolized
brooklime
proofless
prooemion
proof-mark
prooemium
ergonomic
proofread
cryoprobe
arrowroot
broomrape
ergograph
groomsman
priorship
troop-ship
arrow-shot
areostyle
preoption
preocular
brookweed
arrowwood
trionymal
orepearch
crop-eared
cryptadia
crop-marks
prepacked
drop-scene
drop-scone
trepidant
propodeon
propodeum
tripudium
fripperer
graphemic
prophetic
gruppetti
gruppetto
uropygial
propagule
propagate
uropygium
cryptical
dropsical
graphical
trephiner
droppings
trappings
wrappings
graphitic
graphicly
propriety
prepollex
propelled
propeller
propylaea
tropology
crapulent
crepoline
crippling
propylene
propulsor
grapeless
propylite
crapulous
trepanned
trepanner
gripingly
gropingly
treponema
treponeme
proponent
crepiness
drepanium
cryptogam
triploidy
drop-forge
proptosis
cropbound
wrapround
cryptonym
draperied
draperies
properdin
drop-drill
troparion
drop-press
grapeseed
tropistic
crepuscle

Words marked △ may be spelled also with a capital letter

9 □r□t□t

trapesing
grapeshot
prepostor
tripe-shop
preputial
trap-stick
grapetree
trap-stair
△tripitaka
crepitant
drip-stone
dropstone
prepotent
crepitate
grapevine
tripe-wife
triptyque
trapezial
trapezoid
trapezium
trapezius
croquante
frequence
frequency
triquetra
briquette
croquette
Iroquoian
prorector
prerecord
triradial
prurience
pruriency
prorogate
drerihead
ore-rested
prerosion
ororotund
proration
ore-raught
Aristarch
Crustacea
crustated
urn-shaped
prismatic
prostatic
crushable
graspable
crossbeam
truss-beam
crossbuck
crossbred
crossbill
crossband
wristband
crossbite
frostbite
dress-coat
arcsecond
prosector
trisector
prosecute
presidial
prosodial
prosodian
president
presidios
prosodist
presidium
crescendo
crosiered
cross-eyed
freshener
brasserie
triskelia
tristesse
crossette
cross-fade
crossfall
brush-fire
crossfire
crossfish
press-gang
trisagion
crosshead
grasshook
preschool
eristical
prosaical
Aristides
tristichs
grisaille
irascible
irascibly
prescient
brassiere
brassière
trustiest
prussiate
prescious
crossjack
cross-kick
prusiking
preselect
drysalter
frostlike
bristling
crashland
grassland
wrestling
crestless
crustless
frostless
graspless
trustless
proselyte
prosimian
gris-amber
dressmake
grist-mill
irksomely
erasement
presuming
pressmark
presentee
presenter
frost-nail
pre-senile
presently
briskness
crassness
crispness
crossness
freshness
grossness
Irishness
prosiness
prisonous
crossover
uroscopic
frescoing
frescoist
grass-plot
crossroad
prescribe
proscribe
preserver
preserves
cross-ruff
grosgrain
pre-shrink
pressroom
prescript
proscript
erostrate
frustrate
prostrate
dress-suit
cross-sill
crosstree
trashtrie
cross-talk
irisation
crash-test
prosateur
crosstown
grossular
orestunck
pressures
tressured
proseucha
proseuche
brusquely
try-square
prescutum
crosswalk
crosswind
brushwood
brushwork
crossword
frostwork
presswork
crosswise
presbyter
presbytic
presbyope
presbyopy
Bretwalda
protoavis
prothalli
write-back
frithborh
protected
britschka
graticule
triticale
△protector
Briticise
Briticism
criticise
criticism
eroticise
eroticism
eroticist
fruticose
triticism
Briticize
criticize
eroticize
write-down
erythemal
fritterer
prothesis
prothetic
brotherly
tritheism
tritheist
brutified
gratified
gratifier
froth-fomy
Arctogaea
frithgild
protogine
protogyny
dratchell
erstwhile
fratching
crotchety
fratchety
Arctiidae
erethitic
proteinic
brutelike
truthlike
brittlely
brattling
crotaline
gratulant
brutalise
brutalism
brutalist
crotalism
frothless
trothless
truthless
wrathless
brutality
gratulate
brutalize
protamine
Aretinian
pretended
△pretender
arytenoid
Britannia
Britannic
cretinoid
gratingly
pratingly
protonema
protanope
protandry
Britoness
bruteness
cretinise
cretinism
triteness
gratinate
cretinous
prytaneum
cretinize
prothorax
trot-cosey
Brittonic
Brythonic
trattoria
trattorie
arctophil
fraternal
oratorial
△oratorian
pretermit
erythrina
troth-ring
criterion
oratorios
erythrism
preterist
writeress
erythrite
preterite
triturate
craterous
protostar
Britisher
protester
bretasche
protistic
brutishly
protestor
grotesque
gratitude
gritstone
prototype

Words marked △ may be spelled also with a capital letter

9 □r□t□t

writative
proteuses
fretfully
bratwurst
protoxide
prettyish
prettyism
protozoal
protozoan
protozoic
protozoon
araucaria
traumatic
groupable
grauncher
trouncing
groundman
groundsel
groundage
grounding
groundhog
ground-ash
groundnut
ground-ivy
Argus-eyed
trousered
trout-farm
draughter
grouchily
draught-ox
wrought-up
troubling
troutling
troutless
troublous
proudness
triumphal
proud-pied
triumpher
fraudsman
trousseau
fraudster
Proustian
croustade
arcuation
irruption
proustite
irruptive
arduously
triumviri
triumvirs
triumviry
driveable
proveable
proveably
trivially
provocant
Dravidian
gravadlax
bravadoes
privadoes
provident
providing
provedore
gravidity
travailed
provoking
drivelled
driveller
gravelled
grovelled
groveller
travelled
traveller
trivalved
privilege
gravel-pit
groveling
prevalent
traveling
trivalent
graveless
frivolity
frivolous
gravamina
Provençal
preventer
provender
provinces
graveness
drove-road
preverbal
pre-vernal
traversal
traversed
traverser
travertin
provisoes
yravished
prevision
provision
provisory
provostry
gravy-soup
brevetted
privateer
privately
breveting
privation
privatise
gravitate
privative
privatize
graveyard
draw-table
crow's-bill
crown-bark
tri-weekly
crowberry
crow's-foot
trawl-fish
crown-head
draw-sheet
growthist
drowsihed
dry-waller
trowelled
troweller
trawl-line
crewelist
crownless
draw-plate
brownness
brown-nose
crow's-nest
brow-bound
grewhound
brew-house
crowfoots
crown-post
frowardly
prowessed
crow-steps
crow-quill
crownwork
proximate
proximity
argy-bargy
graywacke
greywacke
arty-farty
greybeard
arsy-versy
arhythmia
arhythmic
tray-cloth
prayingly
greyhound
dray-horse
prayerful
greystone
frizzante
cruzadoes
cruzeiros
Brazilian
brazilein
brazeless
prozymite
craziness
assayable
escapable
escalator
asparagus
ashamedly
essayette
estafette
Ascaridae
ismatical
ascarides
estaminet
Islamitic
Ismailian
assaulter
assailant
establish
Ismailism
Israelite
espagnole
usualness
Kshatriya
aspartame
ash-bucket
usability
ash-blonde
isobathic
isocratic
isocyclic
isochimal
isoclinal
psychical
isoclinic
psychogas
psychoses
isochoric
psychosis
psychotic
usucapion
isochrone
isocrymal
tsaddikim
tsaddiqim
isodomous
isodontal
Isidorian
esperance
Esperanto
assembler
ascendant
ascendent
ascending
osteoderm
osmeteria
usherette
ashen-grey
aspergill
osteogeny
ascetical
osteology
aspen-like
osteopath
aspersoir
ushership
△ascension
aspersion
aspersory
ostensory
ascensive
aspersive
ostensive
aspectual
essential
ascertain
osteotome
osteotomy
asbestine
assertion
assertory
asbestous
assentive
assertive
asafetida
isagogics
isogamete
isogamous
isogenous
asthmatic
ischiadic
ischiatic
escheator
isohyetal
ischaemia
ischaemic
asphalter
asphaltic
asphaltum
Esthonian
asphyxial
oscitancy
estimable
estimably
aspirator
estimator
ostinatos
astichous
ascitical
aspidioid
oscillate
ostiolate
espionage
assientos
ossifraga
ossifrage
assistant
ossicular
assiduity
assiduous
ossifying
Isokontae
isokontan
psalm-book
psalteria
isologous
Psyllidae
esplanade
esclandre
asplenium
isallobar
psalmodic
asclepiad
asclepias
Asclepios
Asclepius
ashlaring
ashlering
ostleress

Words marked △ may be spelled also with a capital letter

psaltress
uselessly
psalm-tune
isolation
isolative
asymmetry
psammitic
esemplasy
isomerase
isomerise
isomerism
isomerous
isomerize
isometric
asymptote
isoniazid
asyndetic
asyndeton
isinglass
isonomous
asininity
asynergia
isenergic
assonance
ascorbate
osmometer
osmometry
escopette
associate
asmoulder
assoilzie
astounded
estoppage
estopping
ascospore
espousals
escortage
iso-octane
esophagus
isopodous
psephitic
isopolity
asepalous
isopropyl
psoriasis
psoriatic
escribano
ostracean
Ostracoda
Ostracion
ostracise
ostracism
astrocyte
ostracize
astraddle
astrodome
estradiol
esurience
esuriency
usurpedly
astrofell
astragals
Ostrogoth
astrakhan
astrolabe
astrology
estrildid
ashramite
astringer
estranged
estranger
astrantia
astronomy
astronaut
estrapade
astrophel
espressos
Astroturf®
tsarevich
isostatic
isosceles
isosteric
Psittacus
isotactic
isotheral
isotropic
esoterica
esoterism
Ashtaroth
Ashtoreth
assurance
pseudaxis
assumable
assumably
assurable
assumedly
assuredly
assuaging
assurgent
astucious
issueless
Esquimaux
espumosos
pseudopod
pseudonym
assumpsit
estuarial
estuarian
estuarine
esquiress
assuasive
assuetude
asexually
stratagem
stramaçon
stramazon
steamboat
strategic
steadfast
straggler
strangler
strangles
strangely
strap-game
étrangère
strangury
strap-hang
steam-haul
steadicam®
steatitic
ottavinos
steadiest
strawlike
strapline
strayling
strapless
attainder
straining
steatosis
stratonic
strappado
strapping
stearsman
straw-stem
steamship
Atlantean
Utraquism
Utraquist
strapwort
strawworm
steadying
stableman
stableboy
stabilise
stabilate
stability
stabilize
stoccatas
staccatos
sticcados
sticcatos
stoccados
sticheron
stockfish
stockhorn
stockinet
stockings
stichidia
stockless
stocklist
atacamite
stockpile
stackroom
stockroom
stocktake
stickwork
stockwork
stackyard
stockyard
studiedly
studentry
utterance
athematic
steerable
utterable
Athenaeum
steenbras
steel-blue
ytterbium
steel-clad
stretched
stretcher
attendant
athetesis
ethereous
steel-gray
steel-grey
etherical
strelitzi
streakily
streaking
steenkirk
atheology
steerling
utterless
stream-ice
streamlet
stream-tin
streaming
strewment
uttermost
otherness
steepness
utterness
athetosic
athetosis
athetotic
attempter
steersman
atheistic
stressful
streetcar
streetage
attention
streetboy
streetful
attentive
attenuant
attenuate
strenuity
strenuous
steelwork
otherwise
steelyard
stiffener
stiffness
staffroom
staff-tree
stiffware
stag-dance
stagnancy
stigmatic
stegodont
staggered
staggerer
stage-name
staginess
stegnosis
stegnotic
staghound
Stagirite
Stagyrite
stegosaur
Stahlhelm
itchiness
ethically
stoically
steinbock
staircase
stridence
stridency
strifeful
strikeout
stairfoot
string-bag
stringily
strigging
stringent
stringing
Stringops
stairhead
steinkirk
strip-leaf
stairlift
stridling
stripling
stainless
staidness
Ethiopian
stripping
striation
striature
stricture
strictish
utricular
utriculus
stairwell
stairwork
stairwise
stokehold
stokehole
stellated
stylebook
stillborn
stiltbird
stylobate
stalactic
italicise
Italicism
italicize
stolidity
stalk-eyed
stellerid
stiltedly
stall-feed

9 □t□l□f

styliform
otologist
still-head
still-hunt
still-life
stalkless
styleless
stylolite
Ptolemaic
stalemate
staleness
Stalinism
Stalinist
stillness
stalworth
stillroom
stylistic
stylishly
athletics
utilities
stilettos
stellular
stomachal
stomached
stomacher
stomachic
stoma-care
atomicity
stammerer
ethmoidal
etymology
stimulant
stimulate
staminode
staminody
staminoid
staminate
atomistic
standards
stingaree
stannator
stoneboat
stingbull
stink-bird
stonechat
ethnocide
stone-cold
stonecrop
ethnicism
stonecast
atonicity
ethnicity
stone-dead
stone-deaf
stander-by
stintedly
cteniform
stingfish
stonefish
standgale
stanching
stonehand
stanchion
stinkhorn
stone-hard
stenciled
ethnology
stone-lily
atonalism
atonalist
stingless
stintless
stoneless
atonality
△atonement
atoningly
stoniness
stenopaic
stone-pine
standpipe
itineracy
ethnarchy
itinerant
itinerary
itinerate
stoneshot
Stenotype®
stenotypy
stonewall
stinkwood
stoneware
stonework
stonewort
etiolated
stromatic
stoolball
strouding
atmometer
strongman
strongyle
strongbox
strongarm
strongest
strongish
atrophied
strobilae
atrocious
strobilus
attollens
attollent
strolling
attorneys
ethologic
stroupach
stropping
strossers
strontian
strontium
atmolysis
stopwatch
stepbairn
stapedial
stupidity
stapedius
stupefied
stupefier
stepchild
styptical
stoplight
stippling
stipulary
stipulate
stop-frame
stop-press
stuporous
stipitate
etiquette
stargazer
stargazey
storiated
eternally
storybook
stormbird
attribute
stirabout
storm-cock
ataractic
attractor
athrocyte
steradian
Pteridium
stornelli
stornello
sternebra
storiette
storyette
Styrofoam®
styrofoam
sternfast
pterygial
pterygoid
pterygium
otorrhoea
starchily
attrahens
attrahent
starshine
Storthing
ptarmigan
Sturnidae
starlight
sternitic
startling
sterilant
storyline
startlish
sterilise
stormless
ottrelite
sterility
sterilize
sternmost
staringly
star-anise
starkness
sternness
stercoral
starboard
Pteropoda
star-apple
sternport
sternpost
stardrift
star-proof
storeroom
star-crost
stir-crazy
pterosaur
uterotomy
starstone
attrition
iteration
iterative
sterculia
sternward
stasidion
Ctesiphon
état-major
statocyst
stutterer
statuette
stitching
statehood
stitchery
statelily
stateless
statolith
statement
stational
stationer
stateroom
statesman
△stateside
statistic
statutory
statewide
strumatic
stauncher
staunchly
struggler
stouthrie
strumitis
strumming
stoutness
strutting
attuition
structure
attuitive
stevedore
stovepipe
atavistic
stownlins
stewardry
stewartry
staymaker
strychnia
strychnic
itsy-bitsy
nunataker
Gujarathi
sugarally
sugar-cube
autarchic
subarctic
sugarcane
subahdary
out-and-out
subagency
mujahedin
mutagenic
tularemia
tularemic
cutaneous
musaceous
rutaceous
tufaceous
sugar-free
Judas-hole
subapical
sudaminal
Tupaiidae
Lubavitch
eutaxitic
mujahidin
subacidly
butadiene
audacious
fugacious
furacious
humankind
autarkist
Judas-kiss
sugarloaf
humanlike
sugar-lump
sugarless
eudaemony
humanness
ruralness
Jugannath
lunarnaut
fumarolic
fumatoria
subatomic
runaround
subalpine
sugarplum
subaerial
Judaistic
subahship
subastral
Judas-tree
mulattoes
subaction
subaltern

Words marked △ may be spelled also with a capital letter

Burakumin
Duralumin®
duralumin
Euraquilo
eucalypti
eucaryote
eukaryote
cumbrance
subbranch
cupbearer
sunbeamed
sunbeaten
quebracho
gutbucket
outbacker
Quebecker
Québecois
rudbeckia
mum-budget
turbidite
turbidity
bubble-car
tumble-car
bumble-bee
humble-bee
humble-pie
numble-pie
Bumbledom
tumble-dry
humblesse
bubble-gum
tumble-bug
humbugged
humbugger
cubby-hole
lumbrical
sunbright
dumb-piano
lumbricus
numbskull
dumb-cluck
quibbling
turbulent
suability
gubbinses
husbandly
numbingly
husbandry
tubbiness
turbinate
dumbfound
zumbooruk
turboprop
lumberman
subbureau
sunburned
lumber-pie
lumbering
rubberise
rubberize
furbisher
rubbishly
bulbosity
nutbutter
rum-butter
sunbather
curbstone
outbounds
bulbously
bum-baylie
mumchance
punctated
purchaser
surcharge
cunctator
guacharos
punctator
subclause
outcrafty
quickbeam
hunchback
punch-ball
succubine
quick-born
succubous
punch-bowl
Juncaceae
punch-card
muscadine
muscleman
quickener
quick-eyed
succeeder
butcherly
cutcherry
zucchetto
quick-fire
lunch-hour
subclimax
punctilio
zucchinis
subcellar
muscology
quicklime
succulent
curculios
juiceless
sulcalise
surculose
musculous
sulcalize
guacamole
curcumine
dulcamara
△vulcanian
buccaneer
buccanier
surcingle
subcantor
succentor
juiciness
quickness
vulcanise
△vulcanism
△vulcanist
runcinate
succinate
succinite
vulcanite
vulcanize
Turcophil
turcopole
punch-prop
susceptor
nuncupate
succursal
subcortex
hut-circle
muscarine
subcostal
quickstep
quicksand
successor
dulcitude
lunch-time
Dulcitone®
furcation
guncotton
sulcation
succotash
suscitate
subcaudal
punctured
puncturer
succourer
punctuate
Muscovian
muscovado
△muscovite
subcavity
quadratic
auld-warld
subduable
subdeacon
quadratus
guidebook
bundobust
duodecimo
fuddle-cap
ruddleman
hundreder
cuddeehih
quadrella
subduedly
hundredor
Dundreary
hundredth
cul-de-four
gum-digger
quadrigae
bus-driver
quodlibet
quadrifid
cuadrilla
quadrille
burd-alane
guideline
guideless
subdolous
fundament
Dundonian
humdinger
mundanely
puddening
duodenary
curdiness
muddiness
ruddiness
mundanity
burdenous
mundungus
purdonium
outdoorsy
guidepost
subdermal
subdorsal
sundering
murderess
murderous
Bundesrat
Bundestag
guideship
quadruman
quadruped
quadruple
quadruply
subdivide
sundowner
Oudenarde
△mudéjares
Gujerathi
eumelanin
numerable
numerably
numerally
superable
superably
numerator
numeraire
numéraire
superbrat
superbold
superbity
ouzel-cock
tubercled
supercoil
queen-cake
supercold
tubercule
lutescent
pubescent
quiescent
rubescent
rufescent
tumescent
supercool
pudendous
Juneberry
superette
subereous
superfine
cuneiform
queen-fish
superfast
superfuse
superflux
aubergine
pug-engine
supergene
superglue
superheat
auger-hole
queenhood
superhero
superhive
numerical
Eumenides
juvenilia
subeditor
quaeritur
quaesitum
museology
queen-like
cupelling
pure-blood
queenless
rubellite
luteolous
supermini
supermart
outermost
tunesmith
luteinise
queerness
quietness
supernova
luteinize
eudemonia
eudemonic
juke-joint
Euterpean
queen-post
superpose
superplus
funebrial
superrich
runecraft
mugearite
superstar
supersede
supersafe
supersoft
queenship
rulership
supersalt

9 □u□e□s

supersell
quietsome
queen's-arm
queen-size
curettage
eutectoid
superthin
tubectomy
humectant
juneating
subentire
humectate
Bucentaur
humective
rune-stave
nubeculae
dune-buggy
duteously
hugeously
musefully
tunefully
supervene
supervise
outerwear
auger-worm
tumefying
suffragan
ruffianly
surficial
sufficing
surfacing
suffocate
puff-adder
ruff-a-duff
surfperch
cuffuffle
curfuffle
buff-wheel
surfeited
surfeiter
buffaloes
fulfilled
fulfiller
subfamily
muffin-cap
muffin-pan
muffineer
puffingly
huffiness
puffiness
turfiness
sulfonate
wulfenite
duffing-up
sulfonium
sunflower
surfboard
turf-spade
turf-drain
furfurole
suffering
dufferdom
dufferism
sulfurate
furfurous
huffishly
suffusion
suffusive
buff-stick
muffettee
outfitter
buffeting
sulfation
sulfatase
suffixion
fungibles
fungicide
ruggedise
turgidity
ruggedize
Ausgleich
fungiform
fungoidal
outgoings
ruggelach
cudgelled
cudgeller
bungaloid
surgeless
judge-made
judgement
bulgingly
fulgently
pungently
tuggingly
turgently
subgenera
bulginess
mugginess
pudginess
surgeoncy
dungeoner
outgrowth
Bulgarian
Hungarian
vulgarian
dungarees
bugger-all
fulgurant
Bulgarise
vulgarise
vulgarism
fulgurate
fulgurite
vulgarity
fulgorous
fulgurous
hungerful
lung-grown
Bulgarize
vulgarize
Tungusian
suggester
judgeship
fungosity
budgeting
purgation
budgetary
purgatory
tungstate
purgative
outgiving
rug-headed
Dukhobors
subhedral
bush-metal
bushwhack
push-chair
rushlight
bushelman
busheller
euchology
euphemise
euphemism
euphemize
Ruthenian
euphenics
euthenics
bug-hunter
mug-hunter
authentic
gushingly
pushingly
bushiness
euphonise
euphonism
euthanasy
euthenist
mushiness
oughtness
pushiness
rushiness
euphonium
ruthenium
euphonize
bushwoman
cushioned
cushionet
euchloric
bush-house
lush-house
mushmouth
authorial
eutherian
bushcraft
bush-fruit
euphorbia
authoring
wuthering
authoress
authorise
authorish
authorism
Eucharist
Lutherism
Lutherist
authority
rush-grown
authorize
zuchettas
△eurhythmy
zuchettos
push-start
outhauler
Euphausia
euphausid
pushfully
ruthfully
push-cycle
dubitancy
jubilance
jubilancy
luminance
muricated
mutilated
rutilated
tunicated
puritanic
Ruritania
cubically
dubitable
dubitably
judicable
ludically
musically
fumigator
judicator
mutilator
ruminator
subimagos
supinator
luminaire
Rubiaceae
quail-call
auriscope
subincise
music-demy
luminesce
luciferin
rubicelle
muniments
rudiments
Juniperus
pumiceous
rubineous
audiogram
tuning-key
tuning-peg
tuning-pin
audiphone
punishing
Munichism
Culicidae
juridical
lunitidal
municipal
Pulicidae
humiliant
munitions
auxiliary
judiciary
humiliate
judicious
musicking
fusillade
audiology
pupillage
pupillary
curialism
curialist
eudialyte
pupillate
audiencia
fusionism
fusionist
humidness
lucidness
luridness
tumidness
lunisolar
tubicolar
auditoria
audiophil
quail-pipe
music-rack
tulip-root
auditress
tutiorism
tutiorist
juniority
ludicrous
pupilship
curiosity
dubiosity
furiosity
tulip-tree
audiotape
auricular
cuticular
funicular
curiously
dubiously
dutifully
furiously
funiculus
tulipwood
mutinying
purifying
nutjobber
outjockey
subjected
subjacent
subjugate
Punjaubee
muck-raker

Words marked △ may be spelled also with a capital letter

buck-wagon
Puck-hairy
huckaback
buckyball
Turkicise
Turkicize
hunky-dory
luckie-dad
luck-penny
duck's-foot
buckwheat
musk-sheep
musk-shrew
tusk-shell
buck's-horn
buckthorn
buckshish
duckshove
buckskins
musk-plant
cuckoldom
cuckoldry
duck's-meat
Turkomans
muckender
quakingly
bulkiness
duskiness
funkiness
huskiness
junkiness
luckiness
muckiness
murkiness
muskiness
punkiness
quakiness
sulkiness
musk-pouch
suck-holer
buckhound
buckboard
duck-board
bunkhouse
bucktooth
Euskarian
tuckerbag
Junkerdom
Quakerdom
tuckerbox
Junkerism
Quakeress
Quakerish
Quakerism
buckishly
duskishly
junketeer
musketeer
bucketing
junketing
musketoon
hucksteryy
bucketful
mucksweat
turkey-hen
buckayros
bull-dance
curlpaper
cut-leaved
full-faced
nucleated
rue-leaved
nucleator
bully-beef
bugle-band
public-key
bugle-call
full-scale
duplicand
publicise
publicist
duplicate
duplicity
publicity
publicize
Euclidean
bull-beans
guillemot
oubliette
tuillette
nullified
nullifier
qualified
qualifier
mudlogger
bullwhack
guildhall
gully-hole
bugle-horn
bullfinch
full-timer
purloiner
bullfight
full-blood
full-blast
guileless
guiltless
qualmless
pullulate
full-blown
sublimely
subliming
Muslimism
sublimise
sublimate
sublimity
sublimize
outlinear
sublinear
Ausländer
cullender
outlander
sublunary
burliness
curliness
surliness
sublunate
nucleolar
bulldozer
bull-nosed
mullioned
guilloche
cullionly
full-bound
bull-board
nucleolus
full-speed
full-split
nullipara
nullipore
full-cream
full-orbed
butlerage
fullerene
full-front
bully-rook
full-dress
bull-trout
full-grown
guildsman
publisher
sublessee
dualistic
bullishly
sublessor
outlustre
burlesque
sublethal
bully-tree
qualitied
qualities
subletter
bulletrie
sublation
outlaunce
outlaunch
bugle-weed
quillwort
hummocked
submicron
mummy-case
submucosa
submucous
mummified
mummiform
nutmegged
duumviral
hummeller
pummelled
surmullet
nummuline
nummulary
bummaloti
nummulite
submental
augmented
augmenter
summonses
Augmentin®
outmantle
culminant
fulminant
augmentor
pulmonary
dumminess
gumminess
rumminess
culminate
fulminate
Pulmonata
pulmonate
fulminous
submentum
summing-up
submerged
submersed
summerset
summarily
murmuring
submarine
summering
summarise
summarist
murmurous
summarize
surmaster
submissly
surmising
gummosity
submitted
submitter
summiteer
submatrix
summation
gummatous
summative
guinea-pig
turntable
turnabout
turn-screw
burnt-cork
pugnacity
quinidine
turn-penny
quintette
quintetti
quintetto
tunny-fish
turnagain
△bunny-girl
quenching
quantical
quinoidal
funnelled
funnel-net
funnel-web
tunnelled
tunneller
tunnel-net
quinoline
quinolone
tunneling
outnumber
buonamani
buonamano
furniment
quinonoid
burningly
cunningly
punningly
runningly
funniness
sunniness
turnround
turnip-fly
turnip-top
subnormal
Turnerian
nunneries
quintroon
vulnerary
vulnerate
runners-up
burnisher
furnished
furnisher
turnstile
turnstone
nunnation
ruination
furniture
subneural
quintuple
ruinously
quinquina
subniveal
subnivean
guanazolo
cupolated
Mucorales
autogamic
automatic
aurorally
humorally
automaton
autolatry
out-of-body
autoscopy
mutoscope
ouroscopy
autos-da-fé
out-of-door
out-of-date
dupondius
auxometer

Words marked △ may be spelled also with a capital letter

9 □u□o□e

autogenic
autotelic
suboffice
humongous
autophoby
autophagy
Europhile
Lusophile
autophony
bucolical
autotimer
sudorific
eulogiums
autogiros
autopilot
autopista
autoflare
humorless
autoclave
tug-of-love
buxomness
autosomal
autonomic
autotoxin
sumotoris
autopoint
ouroboros
autoroute
autofocus
Eurospeak
autocracy
dulocracy
Eurocracy
autograft
autocrime
autograph
autotroph
autocross
tutorship
Junoesque
suboctave
subocular
autoguide
tucotucos
out-of-work
autolysed
autolyzed
autolysis
autolytic
autocycle
autogyros
Autolycus
pump-water
sulphatic
vulpicide
nutpecker
suspected
suspicion
auspicate
cuspidore
cuspidate
subpoena'd
yuppiedom
puppyhood
supplicat
surprisal
surpliced
surprised
surpriser
suppliant
bumptious
gumptious
mumpsimus
sumpsimus
sulphinyl
bumpology
suspended
suspender
suspenser
suspensor
bumpiness
dumpiness
jumpiness
lumpiness
pulpiness
vulpinism
vulpinite
sulphonic
pulpboard
purpureal
out-porter
supporter
out-parish
suppurate
dumpishly
lumpishly
mumpishly
purposely
supposing
purposive
turpitude
pulpiteer
puppeteer
put-putted
pulpstone
subpotent
bump-start
culpatory
jump-start
lump-sugar
outpourer
sulphuret
sulphuric
sumptuary
sumptuous
gunpowder
supplying
subphylum
surquedry
turquoise
guardable
turribant
guard-book
rubrician
curricula
currycomb
△hurricane
hurricano
lubricant
lubricate
lubricity
rubricate
lubricous
outredden
putridity
puerperal
quartered
aubrietia
quercetin
guardedly
hurriedly
quarterly
quartette
quartetti
quartetto
quercetum
putrefied
surrogacy
outrigger
subregion
subrogate
surrogate
murrained
surreined
guerrilla
outraigne
surrejoin
currajong
kurrajong
curry-leaf
outrelief
guardless
puerilism
puerility
querulous
supremacy
supremely
nutriment
querimony
supremity
guaranies
guarantee
gunrunner
outrunner
quarenden
quarender
rum-runner
surrender
currently
purringly
guarantor
surrendry
furriness
mucronate
outrooper
eutrophic
eutrapely
eutropous
guardrail
guardroom
guardsman
quirister
buprestid
Buprestis
guardship
guard-ship
hubristic
currishly
sunrising
run-resist
Cupressus
buhrstone
burrstone
nutrition
turret-gun
lucrative
nutritive
burrawang
currawong
quarryman
quarry-sap
quarrying
quartzose
quartzite
puissance
pursuance
substance
Dunstable
guessable
pursuable
puissaunt
subsacral
bumsucker
subsecive
outsiders
subsidise
subsidize
pussyfoot
bursiform
subschema
putschist
subsoiler
gumshield
outskirts
Mussulman
vulsellae
Kunstlied
musselled
Mussulmen
ourselves
subsellia
nurselike
nurseling
nun's-flesh
pulseless
subsultus
vulsellum
Quasimodo
nursemaid
fulsomely
subsample
cuisinier
nuisancer
cursenary
out-sentry
curstness
fussiness
gutsiness
mussiness
pursiness
outspoken
Russophil
bursarial
cursorial
outspread
subscribe
substract
substruct
sunstruck
subseries
sunscreen
outstrain
outstrike
sunstroke
cursorily
outspring
guest-room
subscript
cursorary
sussarara
questrist
pulse-rate
substrata
substrate
subsystem
pulsatile
nurse-tend
russeting
pulsation
cursitory
pulsatory
mussitate
pulsative
cursively
suasively
guesswork
guestwise
pulse-wave
substylar
quittance
australes
cultrated
outtravel
quetzales
Luftwaffe

Words marked △ may be spelled also with a capital letter

rusty-back
justiciar
rusticial
mustachio
rusticise
rusticism
rusticate
rusticity
rusticize
custodial
custodian
quotidian
custodier
furtherer
murtherer
dust-devil
suttletie
sutteeism
justified
justifier
multifoil
dusty-foot
multiform
butty-gang
fustigate
lustihead
dustsheet
butt-shaft
multihull
lustihood
sustained
sustainer
duettinos
curtilage
fustilugs
quitclaim
subtilely
musteline
pustulant
puftaloon
subtilise
ductility
pustulate
subtilety
subtility
pustulous
curtalaxe
subtilize
multimode
customary
custumary
customise
customize
Huttonian
mutton-ham
suntanned
juttingly
subtenant
sustinent
subtenure
dustiness

fustiness
gustiness
lustiness
mustiness
nuttiness
rustiness
sultaness
austenite
sultanate
outtongue
tuitional
subtropic
subtopian
multipede
multiplet
multiplex
multipara
juxtapose
auctorial
butter-fat
butter-pat
cut-throat
gutter-man
Hunterian
suctorial
suctorian
subtorrid
austerely
butterfly
butterine
dust-brand
guttering
muttering
nurturant
vulturine
butter-box
dustproof
rust-proof
culturist
dust-brush
guitarist
vulturish
vulturism
austerity
butterbur
buttercup
butternut
putter-out
vulturous
cutty-sark
multitude
subtitles
curtation
gustation
guttation
luctation
quotation
quotition
ructation
dust-storm
gustatory

gustative
quotative
multiuser
hurtfully
lustfully
furtively
cultivate
multi-wall
tuptowing
cumulated
lunulated
tubulated
Tubularia
suturally
purulence
purulency
humungous
eunuchoid
eunuchise
eunuchism
eunuchize
lupulinic
luxuriant
luxuriate
luxurious
queue-jump
Lucullean
Lucullian
mutualise
mutualism
cucullate
mutuality
mutualize
lucumones
susurrant
lucubrate
susurrate
augurship
subursine
Augustine
tucutucos
curviform
vulviform
surveille
pulvillar
pulvilled
pulvillio
pulvillus
pulvinule
pulvinate
subversal
culver-key
subverter
pulverine
quavering
quivering
pulverise
quiverish
pulverous
quiverful
pulverize

subvassal
curvesome
curvetted
curveting
curvation
curvature
curvative
surviving
surveying
nut-wrench
nut-weevil
jut-window
outworker
subwarden
tutworker
outwardly
outwitted
quixotism
Eumycetes
Eutychian
eurytherm
jurywoman
jurywomen
duty-bound
muzzle-bag
puzzle-peg
puzzledom
quizzical
puzzolana
buzzingly
fuzziness
muzziness
aviatress
ovibovine
evacuator
avocation
evocation
evocatory
evocative
oviductal
evidently
oviferous
Avogadro's
evaginate
ovigerous
evagation
avoidance
available
availably
avoidable
ivy-leaved
evolvable
avalanche
evolution
ovulation
evolutive
ovalbumin
aventaile
oven-ready
evangelic
avengeful

avant-goût
evincible
evincibly
événement
eventrate
evanition
avuncular
eventuate
evaporate
evaporite
oviparity
oviparous
overcatch
overmatch
overwatch
overdated
overladen
overtaken
avertable
overhaile
overpaint
overhappy
overcarry
overhaste
overhasty
overvalue
everybody
overscore
overpedal
overperch
overreach
overreact
overheads
oversexed
over-sexed
overweigh
avertedly
overmerry
overweary
overcheck
overshade
over-shoes
overwhelm
overshine
overshoot
overthrow
overshirt
overpitch
overrider
overripen
oversized
overtimer
overdight
overnight
oversight
avertible
eversible
overskirt
△everglade
overalled
oversleep

9 □v□r□l

overgloom
overflush
overplast
overcloud
overblown
overflown
overglaze
overinked
overcover
overjoyed
overpower
overtones
overtower
overgorge
overbound
overcount
overgoing
overmount
overwound
overboard
Averroism
Averroist
overpoise
overroast
ivory-palm
overspill
overspend
overspent
overgreat
overprice
overtrick
over-trade
evergreen
overgreen
overdraft
overgrain
overtrain
overtrump
overprint
overproof
overdress
overgrass
overpress
overtrust
overwrest
overwrite
overproud
overdrive
overcrowd
overgrown
overgraze
overprize
overissue
overstock
overstudy
ivory-tree
oversteer
overstrew
overstaff
overstuff
overstain
overstand
overstink
overstunk
overstare
overstate
overruler
overtures
overbuild
overlusty
uvarovite
overswear
everywhen
overswell
over-exact
over-exert
overlying
avisement
avisandum
avascular
evasively
eviternal
ovotestes
ovotestis
evitation
avouterer
avizefull
avizandum
sweatsuit
swear-word
two-by-four
two-bottle
twice-born
ewe-cheese
twice-laid
twice-told
two-decker
twaddling
twiddling
sweepback
sweetcorn
'tween-deck
sweetener
sweet-flag
sweetfish
sweet-gale
sweepings
Owle-glass
ownerless
sweetmeal
sweetmeat
sweetness
ownership
sweet-talk
sweetwood
sweet-wort
swift-foot
swiftness
two-footed
twiforked
twiformed
two-forked
twyforked
twyformed
two-fisted
swaggerer
swag-belly
two-headed
two-handed
two-hander
sweirness
awakening
two-leafed
two-leaved
sweltered
twalpenny
twelvemos
twa-lofted
two-legged
swallower
twalhours
two-lipped
twelfthly
swimmable
swimmeret
swampland
two-masted
two-master
swingboat
swing-back
ewe-necked
twin-screw
swing-door
swansdown
swans-down
swingeing
swine-fish
swinehood
swineherd
Zwanziger
twentieth
twin-birth
Zwinglian
swindling
swingling
twangling
twinkling
twin-plane
twiningly
swan-goose
twin-track
swinishly
swingtree
swingtail
swing-wing
twentyish
twenty-two
sweptback
two-parted
owl-parrot
sweptwing
sword-bean
swart-back
sword-belt
sword-bill
swarm-cell
sword-cane
swordfish
sword-hand
swarajism
swarajist
sword-knot
swordlike
swordless
awareness
swartness
two-roomed
swordplay
sword-rack
swordsman
sword-tail
twoseater
twistable
awesomely
two-storey
awestruck
awestrike
twostroke
swashwork
twitterer
switchman
switching
twitching
twattling
two-timing
awfulness
swivelled
swivel-gun
swivel-eye
awkwardly
tway-blade
exhalable
excavator
excambion
excambium
excaudate
expatiate
Excalibur
excarnate
exhausted
exhauster
expansile
expansion
expansive
exuberant
exuberate
exactable
execrable
execrably
exactment
exactness
exactress
executrix
executant
execution
executory
executive
ixodiasis
exodermal
exodermis
exudation
oxidation
exudative
exceeding
extendant
expediter
expedient
expeditor
exteriors
excellent
excelling
expellant
expellent
expelling
extermine
externals
excerptor
extempore
excerptum
extensile
△excelsior
extension
extensity
excessive
expensive
extensive
excentric
exsertile
exceptant
excepting
expectant
expecting
exception
exsection
exsertion
expertise
exceptive
expertize
axle-guard
extenuate
ex-service
exoenzyme
exigeante
exogamous
exigently
oxygenise
oxygenate
exogenous
oxygenous
oxygenize
exegetics
exegetist
oxy-halide
exchanger
△exchequer

Words marked △ may be spelled also with a capital letter

excitancy
excisable
excitable
expirable
extincted
exsiccant
expiscate
exsiccate
oxy-iodide
exciseman
excitedly
exhibiter
excipient
exhibitor
extirpate
ex-librism
ex-librist
Axminster
expiation
expiatory
exultance
exultancy
explicate
exaltedly
explainer
exploiter
exilement
exploring
exclusion
explosion
exclosure
exclusory
exclusive
explosive
expletory
expletive
exemplify
exemplary
examinant
examining
examinate
exemption
exanthema
exanthems
exanimate
exonerate
axiomatic
exposable
Oxfordian
exponible
expositor
excoriate
exfoliate
extolling
extolment
expounder
extorsive
extortion
exposture
extortive
exopodite
exequatur
uxorially
uxoricide
extractor
extricate
extradite
exarchist
exarchate
exerciser
exercises
exorciser
exorcizer
exordiums
extremely
excrement
extremest
extremism
extremist
extremity
extrinsic
exergonic
extrapose
extrorsal
expressly
extrusion
extrusory
extrusive
exaration
excretion
exoration
excretory
excretive
extraught
extravert
extrovert
existence
exosphere
exosporal
exostoses
exosmosis
exosmotic
exostosis
exoticism
excusable
excusably
exsuccous
expurgate
exculpate
excurrent
excursion
expulsion
exquisite
excursive
expulsive
pyracanth
gynaecoid
gynaeceum
gynaecium
rybaudrye
synangium
hydathode
synapheia
dynamical
Pyralidae
pyramidal
dynamiter
pyramides
pyramises
pyramidic
△sybaritic
pyramidon
hypallage
zygaenoid
zygaenine
tyranness
tyrannise
tyrannous
tyrannize
synagogal
dynamotor
synagogue
cymagraph
by-passage
synanthic
Byzantine
synaptase
zygantrum
cymbidium
cymbiform
eyebright
symbolics
cymbaloes
symbolled
symbology
cymbalist
symbolise
△symbolism
symbolist
symbolize
symbiosis
symbiotic
dyscrasia
syncretic
synclinal
syncoptic
syncopate
dyschroia
synchrony
syncytial
syncytium
synchysis
syndicate
syndactyl
syndromic
hymenaeal
hymenaean
Mycenaean
Pyrenaean
hyperbola
hyperbole
Aylesbury
hypercube
type-metal
cynegetic
hyperemia
hyperemic
myxedemic
syneresis
hymeneals
Pyreneans
pyreneite
type-genus
hyperfine
lysergide
hypergamy
synergise
synergism
synergist
synergize
pyrethrin
△pyrethrum
Hyaenidae
Hypericum
hyperlink
hypermart
hypernymy
cybernate
byrewoman
hyperopia
lyme-hound
Mycetozoa
cyberpunk
synedrial
synedrion
lyme-grass
typewrite
synedrium
synectics
tylectomy
dysentery
hypertext
Lymeswold®
myofibril
gyrfalcon
eye-glance
myography
syngamous
dysgenics
syngeneic
myoglobin
ayahuasco
wych-hazel
Typhaceae
mythicise
mythicism
mythicist
mythicize
typhoidal
typhlitic
typhlitis
wych-alder
mythology
syphiloid
syphiloma
syphilise
syphilize
mythomane
△typhonian
hyphenise
hyphenism
△pythoness
hyphenate
hyphenize
mythopoet
Cytherean
Xyridales
cynically
lyrically
typically
wyliecoat
Syriacism
cylindric
lysimeter
lysigenic
synizesis
syringeal
Mytilidae
pyritical
hygienics
hygienist
Syrianism
hypinosis
pyridoxin
Myriapoda
myriorama
Myristica
typifying
synkaryon
syllabics
syllabled
syllabify
syllabary
syllabise
syllabism
syllabize
dyslectic
cyclicism
cyclicity
Wyclifite
pyelogram
myologist
syllogise
syllogism
syllogize
cycloidal
cyclolith
cyclamate
hyalonema
hyalinise
cyclonite
hyalinize
cyclopean
cyclopian
△cyclopses

Words marked △ may be spelled also with a capital letter

9 □y□l□p

syllepses
syllepsis
sylleptic
cyclorama
eyeleteer
cyclotron
byrlaw-man
cyclizine
myrmecoid
myomantic
lyam-hound
lyomerous
symmetral
symmetric
△lyonnaise
cyaniding
hymnodist
pycnidium
hypnogeny
hypnoidal
hymnology
hypnology
cyanamide
dyingness
wyandotte
gymnasial
gymnasien
gymnastic
pyknosome
gymnosoph
gymnasium
hypnotoid
cyanotype
hypnotise
hypnotism
hypnotist
hypnotize
gynney-hen
hypogaeal
hypogaean
myrobalan
gyromancy
pyromancy
Hylobates
pyrolater
hypomania
hypomanic
hypotaxis
pyromania
typomania
zygomatic
pyrolatry
hypocaust
hyponasty
gyrovague
hypogaeum
gyroscope
pyroscope
synoecise
synoecism
synoecete
gynoecium
synoicous
synoecize
myxoedema
xyloidine
cytometer
eye-opener
pyrometer
xylometer
zymometer
cytopenia
hypoxemia
hypoxemic
pyrogenic
pyroxenic
zymogenic
hypoderma
cytometry
pyrometry
hypogeous
mycophagy
Xylophaga
xylophage
cymophane
pyrophone
sycophant
xylophone
gynophore
hylophyte
zygophyte
mycorhiza
Lycosidae
synodical
xylorimba
cytokinin
mylonitic
synovitic
synovitis
myxovirus
synoekete
gyroplane
cytoplasm
hypoblast
pyroclast
tycoonery
bytownite
tycoonate
cytotoxic
cytotoxin
hypotonia
hypotonic
mycologic
mycotoxin
zymologic
hylozoism
hylozoist
hypocotyl
zygosperm
zygospore
gynocracy
cymograph
kymograph
xylograph
hypocrisy
hypocrite
synodsman
hyson-skin
synopsise
synopsize
hypostyle
pygostyle
synoptist
cytolysis
mylohyoid
pyrolysis
pyrolytic
pyroxylic
pyroxylin
synonymic
zymolysis
zymolytic
dysphagia
dysphagic
dysphasia
dysplasia
dyspraxia
lymphatic
nymphalid
nymphaeum
sympodial
sympodium
nymphical
Syrphidae
lyophilic
nymphlike
sylph-like
tympanist
dyspnoeal
dysphonia
dysphonic
dysphoria
dysphoric
dyspnoeic
lyophobic
symphonic
symptosis
symptotic
dyspepsia
dyspeptic
symposiac
symposial
symposium
sympathin
sympatric
symphysis
symphytic
Symphytum
mydriasis
mydriatic
hydrocele
by-product
hygrodeik
hybridoma
hybridise
hybridism
hybridity
hybridous
hybridize
△ayurvedic
hydraemia
hydrofoil
pyorrhoea
by-ordinar
hydrology
hygrology
hydrolyse
hydrolyte
hydrolyze
hydrangea
cyprinoid
hydronaut
hydriodic
Pyrrhonic
hydroptic
hygrophil
hydropult
hydrostat
hygrostat
hydrosoma
hydrosome
hygristor
hydration
hydraulic
hydrovane
dyer's-weed
dyer's-weld
hydroxide
hydrozoan
hydrazoic
hydrazine
hydrozoon
eyeshadow
eye-splice
eyestrain
eye-string
gypsywort
Myrtaceae
dystectic
syntactic
syntectic
cystocele
cystocarp
mysticism
cystidean
myrtle-wax
syntheses
dysthesia
dysthetic
synthesis
synthetic
mystified
mystifier
cystiform
mystagogy
nystagmic
nystagmus
Cystoidea
△ayatollah
hyetology
systaltic
nyctalops
cystolith
systemise
systemize
bystander
syntonise
syntonous
syntonize
dystrophy
dystopian
hysterics
mysteries
oyster-bed
hysteroid
cystotomy
dysthymia
dysthymic
Sylviidae
Sylviinae
sylvanite
sylvinite
ozocerite
tzaddikim
tzaddiqim
izvestiya
dziggetai
ozokerite
azimuthal
ozonation
azeotrope
czarevich

Words marked △ may be spelled also with a capital letter

Bananaland
Malayalaam
calamancos
calamander
salamander
Naiadaceae
caravaneer
macadamise
macadamize
palatalise
palatalize
caravaning
carapacial
Pan-Arabism
datamation
malaxation
Panamanian
Mahayanist
parawalker
caravanned
caravanner
catafalque
Malabar-rat
paratactic
maladapted
damasceene
Lamarckism
Lamarckian
maraschino
parascenia
hazardable
maladdress
parabemata
damageable
manageable
manageably
zapateados
paraselene
manageress
savageness
management
Japanesery
caramelise
caramelize
papaverine
catamenial
managerial
△paramecium
Saracenism
paramedico
cadaverous
papaverous
Japanesque
parametric
japan-earth
parametral
catalectic
cataleptic
cabalettas
lazarettos
malapertly

paraffinic
Carangidae
haranguing
paraphrase
cataphract
paraphrast
Nabathaean
paraphilia
paraphonia
cataphonic
paraphonic
marathoner
paraphasia
paraphasic
paraphyses
paraphysis
parathesis
paradisaic
capacitate
mazarinade
palatinate
paradiddle
taradiddle
parapineal
paradisean
carabineer
barasingha
damagingly
jamahiriya
paradisiac
fanaticise
fanaticize
parasitise
parasitize
vanadinite
law-abiding
parakiting
natalitial
paradisial
fanaticism
Nazaritism
panaritium
parasitism
paradisian
carabinier
capability
Patavinity
ratability
salability
tamability
taxability
vacationer
parasitoid
samariform
calamitous
cavalierly
parabiosis
paralipses
paralipsis
cabalistic
fatalistic

parabiotic
canaliculi
paraglider
lavallière
paraplegia
paraplegic
paralleled
parallelly
zabaglione
parablepsy
caballeros
paraglossa
paramnesia
paraenesis
paragnosis
paraenetic
palaeogaea
paranoidal
Palaeocene
Palaeogene
catalogize
palagonite
parabolise
parabolize
paragonite
paralogise
paralogize
palaeolith
lavatorial
natatorial
parapodial
catabolism
katabolism
natatorium
paralogism
parapodium
sanatorium
Patagonian
macaronics
macaronies
parabolist
paradoxist
paranormal
paramouncy
Palaeozoic
paraboloid
laparotomy
malacology
satanology
paradoctor
paradoxure
cataloguer
palaeotype
hamadryads
Pan-African
catarrhine
cavalryman
catarrhous
paratroops
malapropos
harassedly

harassment
samarskite
Eatanswill
radarscope
palaestric
palaestral
bagassosis
parastichy
wag-at-the-wa'
vacantness
tarantella
pararthria
catastasis
parastatal
catacumbal
△ragamuffin
cacafuegos
malaguetta
catapultic
paraquitos
canary-seed
canary-bird
canary-wood
paralympic
day-boarder
babblative
lambdacism
gas-bracket
fatbrained
madbrained
iambically
barbed-wire
babblement
gabblement
rabblement
parbreaked
jaw-breaker
law-breaker
lambrequin
cabbage-fly
garbageman
wabbliness
wambliness
Balbriggan
dabblingly
ramblingly
wamblingly
warblingly
barbellate
gambolling
carbonnade
rabbinical
carbonados
carbuncled
carbon-copy
sanbenitos
lambdoidal
gabbroitic
namby-pamby
Camberwell
barbershop

barber-shop
hamburgher
halberdier
cat-burglar
jabberwock
law-burrows
carbureter
carburetor
farborough
Yarborough
ear-bussing
gay-bashing
gambit-pawn
sabbatical
Sabbath-day
balbutient
rabbitfish
Babbittism
lamb's-tails
salbutamol
rabbit-hole
barbituric
harbourage
harbour-bar
tambourine
carboxylic
saccharase
saccharate
bacchanals
wanchancie
saccharide
saccharine
saccharise
saccharize
pancratium
fasciation
pancratian
pancratist
saccharify
cat-cracker
cacciatora
saccharoid
cacciatore
saccharose
sauce-alone
marchantia
bacchantes
matchboard
patchboard
Maccabaean
catch-basin
patchcocke
sarcocolla
fascicular
fasciculus
farcically
catch-drain
rancidness
calcedonio
satchelled
pancreatic

10 □a□c□e

pancreatin
Manchester
fancifully
watchfully
calciferol
watchguard
watchglass
cancrizans
manchineel
sanctified
△sanctifier
sanctities
fan-cricket
calceiform
cancriform
sanctimony
calc-sinter
sanctitude
match-joint
parcel-bawd
cancellate
calculable
calculably
parcelwise
rascal-like
cancelling
parcelling
rascallion
parcel-gilt
sarcolemma
marchlands
cancellous
narcolepsy
vascularly
calculuses
laccolitic
calculated
sacculated
calculator
matchmaker
match-maker
watchmaker
parchmenty
dance-music
marcantant
calcinable
gasconader
malcontent
carcinogen
watch-night
carcinomas
carcinosis
balconette
fascinator
vaccinator
falcon-eyed
calceolate
lanceolate
raccoon-dog
cancionero
Marcionite

Marcionist
Sarcophaga
sarcophagi
sarcoplasm
catchpenny
cascarilla
barcarolle
mascarpone
calcareous
saucerfuls
Marcgravia
saucer-eyed
marcescent
Lancashire
matchstick
narcissism
pancosmism
narcissist
march-stone
watchstrap
rat-catcher
calcitonin
watchtower
jaw-crusher
Manchurian
lascivious
hard-handed
handmaiden
cardialgia
sandbagged
sandbagger
hardbacked
hand-basket
hand-gallop
hard-earned
mandragora
paediatric
hand-barrow
cardcastle
sandcastle
bandmaster
land-waiter
yard-master
land-values
mandibular
dandy-brush
handicraft
manducable
hand-screen
Sadducaean
handicuffs
pandectist
lardaceous
candidness
handedness
handy-dandy
randle-balk
saddleback
saddle-fast
bald-headed
hand-weeded

hard-headed
saddleless
hand-sewing
candlefish
candlewick
saddlebill
handselled
daydreamer
candlewood
paddle-wood
saddle-nose
saddle-sore
candle-coal
saddleroom
hand-me-down
candle-doup
paddle-boat
candle-tree
randle-tree
saddletree
paddy-field
dandy-fever
Tardigrada
tardigrade
gaudy-green
paedagogic
paedagogue
hay-de-guise
cardiganed
hay-de-guyes
dandy-horse
bawdy-house
land-pirate
sand-binder
tawdriness
dawdlingly
hard-riding
land-mining
maudlinism
hard-billed
hard-fisted
hard-bitten
candelabra
candelilla
sandalwood
bandoleros
band-clutch
bardolatry
landammann
randomwise
tandemwise
paddymelon
△pandemonic
randomiser
mandamuses
randomizer
hand-in-hand
maidenhair
pardonable
pardonably
sardonical

maidenhead
maidenweed
jardinière
maiden-meek
pardonless
gaudy-night
wardenship
maidenlike
tap-dancing
Waldensian
padding-ken
cardinally
landing-net
maidenhood
Mandingoes
Sandinista
Sandinismo
hand-to-hand
land-jobber
card-holder
landholder
handsomely
hard-fought
hand-lotion
handworked
land-locked
hard-boiled
cardiology
land-louper
sand-hopper
cardiogram
cardboardy
hard-gotten
paedophile
handspring
land-spring
madder-lake
balderdash
ladder-back
Wanderjahr
land-bridge
land-breeze
pandermite
sanderling
banderilla
badderlock
gander-moon
sandgroper
paederasty
pandurated
wanderlust
caddis-case
candescent
caddis-worm
faldistory
handstaffs
paedotribe
band-string
Landsthing
handstaves
land-lubber

eard-hunger
land-hunger
eard-hungry
hard-pushed
paedeutics
paideutics
sandsucker
vaudeville
paddy-whack
land-owning
tawdry-lace
barehanded
case-harden
face-harden
gametangia
lacerative
face-saving
cameration
catenarian
catenation
laceration
maceration
racemation
laterality
barebacked
race-walker
baseballer
wage-earner
camerawork
calefactor
malefactor
lake-lawyer
paperboard
water-brain
laverbread
waterborne
water-borne
paper-birch
paperbound
water-bound
paper-chase
watercraft
salesclerk
watercress
paper-cigar
tapescript
watercolor
calescence
canescence
latescence
tabescence
paper-cloth
dame-school
paleaceous
camel-corps
parenchyma
waterdrive
fazendeiro
calendries
calendarer
sacerdotal

Words marked △ may be spelled also with a capital letter

bareheaded
barelegged
gate-legged
wavelength
make-weight
make-belief
Madelenian
game-dealer
tale-teller
tape-record
patereroes
gamekeeper
gate-keeper
babelesque
mace-bearer
talebearer
carelessly
fadelessly
namelessly
casemented
pace-setter
paper-faced
waterflood
waterfront
waterglass
pace-egging
paper-gauge
catechumen
canephorus
catechiser
catechesis
catechetic
catechizer
rarefiable
base-minded
wateriness
maledicent
maleficent
taperingly
waveringly
ease-giving
maleficial
lace-pillow
materially
javelin-man
valerianic
lageniform
hare-lipped
babesiasis
babesiosis
sauerkraut
Hakenkreuz
paper-knife
△magellanic
camerlengo
camerlingo
matellasse
satellitic
lamellated
satellites
safe-blower
paper-mâché
paper-maker
watermelon
taseometer
tabernacle
Capernaite
capernoity
maternally
paternally
camelopard
face-to-face
face-powder
malevolent
hate-monger
categorise
categorize
Jamesonite
date-coding
categorial
Caledonian
Cameronian
categories
categorist
careworker
caseworker
faceworker
pace-bowler
racecourse
ravenously
barefooted
case-bottle
hateworthy
nameworthy
waterproof
waterquake
paper-ruler
Palearctic
care-crazed
cameo-shell
watersmeet
wapenschaw
water-skied
water-skier
raven's-bone
waterspout
caper-sauce
raven's-duck
lamentable
patentable
lamentably
majestical
parentless
talentless
watertight
tapestried
mare's-tails
Lacertilia
parentally
malentendu
parenthood
paleotypic
talent-spot
man-entered
parenteral
face-fungus
hamesucken
base-burner
baserunner
page-turner
saleswoman
waterworks
panegyrise
panegyrize
panegyrist
malfeasant
mafficking
half-a-crown
daffodilly
half-a-dozen
bafflement
half-length
gauffering
palfrenier
half-yearly
halfe-horsy
gaff-rigged
bafflingly
caffeinism
halfwitted
half-kirtle
half-sister
lawfulness
manfulness
yaffingale
half-cocked
half-dollar
half-volley
half-hourly
gas-furnace
kaffir-boom
calf-ground
far-fetched
half-duplex
half-hunter
batfowling
margravate
margravine
Sangradoes
barge-board
mangabeira
ragged-lady
jaggedness
raggedness
daggle-tail
tangleweed
tanglement
marguerite
tanglesome
gangrenous
tanglefoot
larghettos
baggage-car
sanguinary
sanguinely
laughingly
tanglingly
languished
languisher
sanguinity
ganglionic
gangliform
gangliated
hang-glider
rangelands
Targumical
laggen-gird
tangential
marginalia
jargonelle
marginally
gauging-rod
pangenesis
pangenetic
marginated
△gargantuan
languorous
Panglossic
Langerhans
rangership
margaritic
large-scale
mangosteen
targetable
pargetting
daughterly
gangbuster
gargoylism
gas-guzzler
Rachmanite
Rachmanism
sad-hearted
yacht-built
Nachschlag
Sanhedrist
cathode-ray
cashiering
cash-keeper
tachograph
tachygraph
pathogenic
pathognomy
naphthalic
naphthenic
pathfinder
gashliness
△bathmizvah
△catholicon
Catholicos
pathologic
nathelesse
batholitic
bathylitic
tachylitic
tachylytic
fathomable
fathomless
sachemship
fathom-line
baphometic
mathematic
bathometer
bathymeter
fathometer
pachymeter
tachometer
tachymeter
bathymetry
tachometry
tachymetry
cachinnate
bathing-box
washing-day
machinegun
bathing-hut
rat-hunting
panhandler
taphonomic
machineman
mashing-tub
machinator
fashionist
wash-bottle
tachypnoea
fatherland
cash-credit
fatherless
fathership
fatherlike
fatherhood
bathyscape
pathetical
washateria
washeteria
bashawship
cashew-nuts
lachrymals
lachrymary
lachrymose
palisander
Caricaceae
Salicaceae
capitalise
capitalize
laminarise
laminarize
radicalise
radicalize
capitalism
Radicalism
sanitarium
Vaticanism
capitation
cavitation
habitation

10 □a□i□a

janizarian
laminarian
lamination
lapidarian
lapidation
latitation
nanisation
nanization
navigation
pagination
patination
radication
sagination
salivation
sanitarian
sanitation
validation
galimatias
capitalist
lapidarist
maximalist
sanitarist
Vaticanist
radicality
sanitarily
magi-marker
habitaunce
palisadoes
saxicavous
habilatory
caricature
parischane
hagiocracy
maniacally
fatiscence
habit-cloth
palindrome
facileness
nativeness
capitellum
varicellar
taxidermic
taxidermal
native-born
laniferous
lanigerous
saliferous
gaminesque
tasimetric
manifestos
manifestly
salicetums
tariffless
satisfying
faying-face
radiograph
panic-grass
casinghead
savingness
takingness
cariogenic
radiogenic
baking-soda
malingerer
variegated
variegator
Manichaean
garishness
lavishness
rakishness
banishment
famishment
lavishment
ravishment
vanishment
Manicheism
facilitate
habilitate
pacificate
vaticinate
pacifiable
salifiable
habiliment
maxi-single
lapidified
pacificism
facilities
pacificist
vaginismus
Parisienne
salicional
radiciform
caliginous
familiarly
familistic
nativistic
laciniated
hagiologic
radiologic
capillaire
maxillulae
bacillemia
panislamic
maxilliped
Radiolaria
radiolysis
radiolytic
variolitic
mamillated
papillated
hagiolater
Mariolater
variolator
papillitis
hagiolatry
Mariolatry
habit-maker
talismanic
Papiamento
radiometer
variometer
ration-card
nationless
malignment
nationwide
sapiential
salientian
nationally
rationally
malignance
malignancy
nationhood
ration-book
marionette
manifolder
manifoldly
varicocele
capitoline
saxicoline
janitorial
capitolian
Mabinogion
varicosity
Cavicornia
salicornia
calico-wood
facinorous
ranivorous
saxicolous
varicotomy
calico-tree
babiroussa
calico-bush
palimpsest
radiopager
radiophone
radiophony
radiopaque
bacitracin
caligraphy
pasigraphy
calibrator
taxi-driver
ladieswear
wapinschaw
radiosonde
hagioscope
radioscope
radioscopy
patisserie
pâtisserie
magistrand
magistrate
magistracy
papistical
Haliotidae
sagittally
varietally
Sagittaria
radiotoxic
capitulate
manipulate
paniculate
capitulant
capitulary
patibulary
fatiguable
latifundia
Caligulism
halieutics
manicurist
habitually
taciturnly
radiculose
balibuntal
pari-mutuel
salicylate
salicylism
varitypist
lap-jointed
panjandrum
hackmatack
jack-rabbit
back-handed
cack-handed
kack-handed
pack-saddle
back-hander
backwardly
backmarker
backpacker
backgammon
jackhammer
tank-farmer
jack-rafter
taskmaster
hawksbeard
tanka-boats
rackabones
fat-kidney'd
lackadaisy
Jack-a-dandy
backvelder
Yankeefied
hawk-beaked
lark-heeled
hackneyman
park-keeper
Kafkaesque
bark-beetle
rack-renter
parkleaves
back-office
pack-thread
backsheesh
bank-cheque
backbiting
rank-riding
hawk-billed
Jacky-Jacky
back-blocks
backslider
maskalonge
packing-box
barkentine
napkin-ring
marking-ink
pack-animal
maskanonge
maskinonge
marking-nut
mackintosh
Parkinson's
jackanapes
back-to-back
backworker
sack-posset
jackbooted
backspacer
hanky-panky
back-spauld
banker-mark
cankeredly
back-friend
Jack-priest
marker-flag
marker-bomb
cankerworm
background
dark-ground
walk-around
maskirovka
ear-kissing
basket-case
basketball
market-hall
racket-tail
jack-straws
marketable
market-bell
back-street
packet-ship
backstairs
basket-hilt
talky-talky
walky-talky
back-stroke
packet-note
basketwork
market-town
packet-boat
backstitch
basketfuls
yackety-yak
back-number
hackbuteer
lacklustre
lackluster
tankbuster
bankruptcy
markswoman
galliambic
palliament
△parliament
oak-leather

Words marked △ may be spelled also with a capital letter

wall-washer
palliative
wall-facing
tagliarini
malleation
palliation
Paulianist
railwayman
palliatory
ball-barrow
calliature
ballabiles
gallabiyah
gallabiyeh
Wallachian
valleculae
vallecular
cauliculus
tablecloth
fallacious
rally-cross
Callicarpa
table-cover
pallidness
table-d'hôte
palladious
nail-headed
bailieship
mallee-bird
earlierise
earlierize
hail-fellow
mallee-fowl
pall-bearer
cauliflory
galloglass
tally-hoing
ballyhooed
gaultheria
ballsiness
faultiness
rallyingly
nail-biting
malleiform
hallalling
sail-flying
halleluiah
hallelujah
ball-flower
wallflower
ball-player
Gallomania
table-music
garlandage
mallanders
mallenders
sallenders
Laplandish
falling-off
kaolinosis
kaolinitic

tablanette
gallinazos
wall-to-wall
railroader
ballooning
balloonist
wall-rocket
Mallophaga
Gallophile
Gallophobe
tailor-made
tailormake
sailorless
tailor-bird
galleryite
sailorlike
ballerinas
caulescent
pallescent
ballistite
ballistics
eagle-stone
tablespoon
table-sport
tally-trade
ballet-girl
palletiser
palletizer
parlour-car
ball-buster
tallow-face
fallowness
sallowness
fallow-chat
gallows-lee
tallywoman
galley-west
halloysite
galley-worm
△barleycorn
barley-bree
barley-broo
Barmecidal
tarmacadam
man-machine
naumachiae
tarmacking
naumachias
naumachies
haemoconia
palmaceous
mammectomy
parmacitie
Talmudical
maimedness
calmodulin
warmed-over
palm-kernel
harmlessly
mammograph
mammogenic

salmagundi
salmagundy
carmagnole
haemolysis
haemolytic
harmonical
harmonicon
Salmonidae
harman-beck
Haemanthus
Tammanyite
salmon-pink
Tammanyism
salmonella
sarmentose
harmonious
sarmentous
warming-pan
harmoniser
△salmanaser
garmenture
harmonizer
△salmanazar
palm-grease
hammerhead
hammerless
May-morning
hammer-fish
palm-branch
hammer-pond
hammerlock
palmer-worm
marmarosis
Lammas-tide
ragmatical
palmatifid
Karmathian
haematinic
palmettoes
haematuria
haematosis
△barmitsvah
△barmitzvah
△basmitsvah
△basmitzvah
△batmitsvah
△batmitzvah
map-mounter
palm-butter
mammy-wagon
mainlander
taeniacide
gainsaying
rainmaking
balneation
maintained
maintainer
taeniafuge
cannibally
cannabinol
paint-brush

panniculus
manna-croup
wainscoted
launcegaye
rannle-balk
garnierite
maundering
sauntering
mainpernor
painlessly
magnifical
Magnificat
magnifying
manna-grass
faint-heart
rain-shadow
daintiness
jauntiness
paintiness
hauntingly
tauntingly
vauntingly
gaingiving
mainlining
pawnticket
pain-killer
rannel-balk
carnallite
Parnellite
cannellini
Parnellism
cannelloni
cannel-coal
manna-larch
gauntleted
rain-plover
capnomancy
cannon-game
cannonball
cannon-shot
rainforest
balneology
rain-doctor
mainspring
day-nursery
wainwright
pawnbroker
laundry-man
Laundromat®
laundrette
bannisters
garnishing
varnishing
carnassial
Parnassian
magnetical
mainstream
gainstrive
painstaker
walnutwood
garnet-rock

magnetiser
magnetizer
day-neutral
ca'ing-whale
paintworks
halocarbon
Sapotaceae
cacodaemon
laboratory
pagoda-tree
malo-lactic
capodastro
capotastos
razor-blade
paroecious
baronetage
halogenate
baronetess
cajolement
tapotement
Jacobethan
Hanoverian
cacogenics
Napoleonic
carotenoid
nanosecond
halogenous
barometric
gasometric
manometric
salopettes
vaporettos
camouflage
law-officer
camoufleur
canophobia
panophobia
canophilia
basophilic
cacophonic
halophytic
manor-house
canonicate
canonicals
saponified
gadolinite
Jacobinise
Jacobinize
favoritism
gadolinium
Jacobinism
Jacobitism
laconicism
Carolinian
calorifier
caloricity
canonicity
carotinoid
vaporiform
canonistic
halobiotic

Words marked △ may be spelled also with a capital letter

10 □a□o□i

parodistic
cacomistle
Mahommedan
mayonnaise
madonnaish
paronomasy
maconochie
cacotopian
Zaporogian
batologist
Mayologist
taxonomist
vaporosity
malodorous
canorously
valorously
vaporously
vapour-bath
favourable
favourably
mavourneen
favourless
savourless
laboursome
gamotropic
laeotropic
cacography
cacotrophy
Camorrista
razor-shell
famousness
razor-strop
panoptical
panopticon
catoptrics
raconteuse
manoeuvrer
manoeuvres
△paronychia
calotypist
paroxysmal
paroxytone
paronymous
Ramphastos
rajpramukh
cappuccino
rampacious
jaspideous
marprelate
harpy-eagle
dapple-grey
Malpighian
rampageous
dauphiness
sapphirine
campaigner
carpellate
carpellary
rappelling
rampallian
wampumpeag
parpen-wall
wappenshaw
salpingian
campanular
campaniles
sappanwood
damping-off
campaneros
camphorate
lampholder
harpooneer
lampoonery
wax-proofed
wasp-tongu'd
wasp-tongue
harpoon-gun
Camptonite
lampoonist
carphology
damp-course
carpophore
jasperware
rapportage
vampire-bat
rapporteur
dapperness
sapperment
dapperling
lapper-milk
bar-parlour
tatpurusha
campground
wapper-eyed
campesinos
campestral
lappet-head
day-patient
tappet-ring
carpet-moth
tappet-loom
tarpauling
lamp-burner
masquerade
banqueteer
banqueting
lacquering
man-queller
parquetted
harquebuse
harquebuss
marquisate
pasquinade
pasquilant
vanquisher
matriarchy
patriarchy
laurdalite
patrialise
patrialize
hair-waving
map-reading
patrialism
laureation
patriation
patriality
fair-haired
hair-raiser
fairy-beads
macrobiota
macrobiote
patriciate
fairy-cycle
macrocycle
matricidal
parricidal
patricidal
barricados
barracking
batrachian
capriccios
matricliny
matrocliny
patricliny
patrocliny
matricular
sarracenia
barracoota
capricious
lauraceous
macrocarpa
fabricator
barracouta
sacredness
hair-pencil
fair-headed
fair-leader
matrifocal
patrifocal
sacrificer
macroflora
macrofauna
carragheen
iatrogenic
saprogenic
Caerphilly
fair-minded
carrying-on
sacroiliac
laurvikite
ram-raiding
day-release
matrilocal
patrilocal
patrolling
rag-rolling
barrel-bulk
barrelfuls
tauromachy
barramunda
barramundi
fairy-money
parramatta
lacrimator
lacrymator
barrenness
patronless
Fahrenheit
matronship
farrandine
matron-like
warrandice
warrantise
warranting
lawrencium
Laurentian
Lawrentian
matronymic
patronymic
matronhood
barrenwort
barring-out
patroniser
patronizer
capreolate
hair-powder
warrioress
matryoshka
fair-boding
gadrooning
patriotism
macrophage
Sauropsida
hairspring
macroprism
fair-spoken
sapropelic
madreporic
saprophyte
fairground
bairn's-part
wanrestful
Saurischia
laurustine
patristics
sacrosanct
fairy-stone
macrospore
narratable
sabretache
hairstreak
parrot-beak
garrotting
parrot-fish
parrot-bill
Maoritanga
Mauretania
sabre-tooth
parrot-coal
barratrous
galravitch
narrowcast
marrowless
narrowness
marrow-bone
narrow-boat
barrow-tram
△macrozamia
cassia-bark
nauseative
nauseating
Pan-Slavism
pay-station
Pan-Slavist
hamshackle
ramshackle
ranshackle
mass-market
marshalled
marshaller
tarsia-work
Marshalsea
daisy-chain
waistcloth
falsidical
haustellum
man-stealer
panspermia
panspermic
camsteerie
mansuetude
false-faced
falsifying
pausefully
passiflora
marsh-fever
Cassegrain
far-sighted
passageway
day-scholar
marshiness
wassailing
causticity
caespitose
easselward
easselgate
marshlocks
tassel-gent
hanselling
tasselling
damselfish
cassolette
ransomable
ransomless
baisemains
facsimiled
facsimiles
cassumunar
passimeter
passamezzo
raising-bee
parsonical
raisonneur
parson-bird
maisonette

Words marked △ may be spelled also with a capital letter

10 □a□v□l

passionate
mansionary
passionary
Cassiopeia
haustorium
bassoonist
Passionist
nauseously
pansophism
pansophist
hawser-laid
man-servant
marsh-robin
cat's-cradle
masspriest
Caesarship
kaisership
hansardise
hansardize
cat's-brains
Massoretic
Sanskritic
saussurite
lansquenet
daisy-wheel
palsy-walsy
causewayed
capsizable
fast-handed
gastralgia
bastnäsite
carthamine
partialise
partialize
tartrazine
Watteauish
Kantianism
martialism
partialism
castration
martialist
partialist
factuality
partiality
tactuality
pastmaster
earth-board
pasteboard
hartebeest
earthbound
masticable
pasticheur
fantoccini
particular
nautically
tactically
latticinio
cactaceous
mastectomy
participle
masticator
mastodynia
fastidious
hartie-hale
rattle-pate
tattle-tale
rantle-balk
wattlebark
rattle-head
pantheress
battlement
battleship
tattie-shaw
wattlebird
pantherine
pantherish
saltcellar
tattie-claw
battledore
wattlework
battledoor
rattle-trap
waitperson
tactlessly
pasty-faced
Tartuffish
Tartuffism
Tartuffian
faithfully
tastefully
wastefully
fastigiate
saltigrade
pantagraph
pantograph
paste-grain
lactogenic
castigator
earth-house
battellant
earthiness
paltriness
partridges
tattlingly
battailous
day-tripper
jaw-twister
last-minute
cantillate
martellato
tautologic
earth-light
pastellist
pantaloons
manteltree
tantaliser
nautiluses
cantaloupe
cantilever
tantalizer
pantomimic
cartomancy
tautomeric
lactometer
tantamount
earthmover
cartonnage
martingale
parting-cup
bastinaded
Fastens-eve
Battenberg
Battonberg
wantonness
cantonment
panton-shoe
martensite
bantingism
tartanalia
casting-net
Battenburg
xanthomata
cautionary
factionary
santioneer
gag-toothed
gap-toothed
saw-toothed
cartoonish
cartoonist
factionist
Bartholmew
Gastropoda
gastronome
gastrosoph
gastrology
gastronomy
gastrotomy
xanthopsia
captiously
cautiously
factiously
earth-plate
pantophagy
cartophile
cartophily
tautophony
wastepaper
earthquake
master-card
master-hand
masturbate
lattermath
natterjack
Tattersall
factorable
pasturable
bastard-bar
raft-bridge
masterless
matterless
parturient
cartwright
factorship
mastership
pastorship
mastermind
rafter-bird
bastardise
bastardize
Eastertide
Eastertime
easterling
bastardism
△nasturtium
lanternist
latter-mint
saltarelli
saltarello
pastorally
bacteremia
bacterioid
masterhood
waiterhood
patter-song
masterwork
latter-born
tartareous
eastermost
lattermost
masterwort
gasteropod
△**canterbury**
wanthriven
lactescent
baptistery
earth-shine
fantastico
earth-smoke
lactoscope
pantoscope
earth-table
cantatrice
factitious
pasteurise
pasteurize
pasteurism
Carthusian
Malthusian
Pasteurian
ear-trumpet
salt-butter
captivance
wait-a-while
panty-waist
earthwoman
earthwards
pantrymaid
pastrycook
bartizaned
value-added
paludament
naturalise
naturalize
tabularise
tabularize
naturalism
jaculation
maculation
maturation
papulation
salutation
saturation
tabulation
vapulation
naturalist
salutarily
jaculatory
salutatory
tabulatory
maculature
manuscript
caruncular
majuscular
Ranunculus
caoutchouc
matureness
nature-cure
nature-myth
Janus-faced
lanuginose
baculiform
raduliform
lanuginous
paludinous
naturistic
manumitted
maquillage
casualness
vacuolated
datum-level
calumniate
△**saturnalia**
calumnious
naturopath
makunouchi
fabulosity
fabulously
datum-plane
haruspical
haruspices
daguerrean
jaguarondi
jaguarundi
saouari-nut
salubrious
balustrade
lacustrine
palustrine
palustrian
balustered
larvicidal
malvaceous
salvifical
marvelling

Words marked △ may be spelled also with a capital letter

10 □a□v□l

marvellous
valvulitis
galvaniser
galvanizer
salverform
canvasback
harvest-bug
harvest-fly
harvestman
canvas-work
calves'-foot
parvovirus
day-wearied
war-wearied
jaywalking
ear-witness
Marxianism
baby-walker
many-headed
satyresque
satyagraha
laryngitic
laryngitis
baby-ribbon
baby-minder
lady-killer
calyciform
satyriasis
baby-sitter
karyolymph
karyolysis
Maryolater
Maryolatry
many-folded
Babylonish
Babylonian
palynology
papyrology
karyoplasm
barysphere
Dasyuridae
lady's-smock
calyptrate
raiyatwari
caryatidic
caryatidal
caryatides
karyotypic
calyculate
baby-jumper
razzmatazz
dazzlement
dazzlingly
Ranzellaar
lanzknecht
manzanilla
canzonetta
canzonette
Abraham-man
abranchial
oblateness
oblational
obtainable
obtainment
ebracteate
abscission
obediently
'sbuddikins
abnegation
abreactive
abreaction
abbey-laird
able-bodied
abbey-piece
object-ball
abjectness
objectless
object-soul
obsequious
observable
observably
observance
observancy
observator
abdication
obligation
obligatory
obliterate
obligement
abridgable
abridgment
obligingly
obsidional
absinthism
obbligatos
ebullition
ebullience
ebulliency
obeliscoid
abominable
abominably
abominator
abundantly
abonnement
abrogative
abrogation
absorbable
absorbedly
absorbency
obsoletely
obsoletism
obsoletion
abiogenist
ebionitism
abdominous
abnormally
Oblomovism
absorptive
absorption
abhorrence
abhorrency
absolutely
absolutism
absolution
absolutist
absolutory
absolvitor
ubiquarian
ubiquitary
ubiquinone
ubiquitous
aberration
eburnation
aberdevine
Übermensch
△aboriginal
abortively
aborticide
abortional
Aberglaube
obtruncate
Aberdonian
abbreviate
Abyssinian
obituarist
abstracted
abstracter
abstractor
abstractly
abstemious
abstention
abstinence
abstinency
abiturient
abstergent
abstersive
abstersion
obstetrics
abstrusely
obstructer
obstructor
obdurately
abjuration
obduration
objuration
obturation
abjunction
obfuscated
absurdness
obtuseness
éboulement
obnubilate
ablutomane
abruptness
above-board
above-named
oceanarium
scrambling
ocean-basin
scratching
scratchily
scratch-wig
octandrian
octandrous
scrapegood
octamerous
octahedral
octahedron
ocean-going
scraggling
octangular
actability
occasional
occasioner
octaploidy
Sciaenidae
Sclavonian
oceanology
schalstein
scrag-whale
icebreaker
scabbiness
scabridity
scabrously
a-cockhorse
aciculated
acidifying
academical
acidimeter
acidimetry
schematise
schematize
schematism
acieration
schematist
eczematous
screech-owl
accelerate
accelerant
acre-length
schefflera
scleriasis
screenplay
screenings
scleromata
scleroderm
sclerotise
sclerotize
sclerotial
sclerotium
sclerotomy
Acherontic
schemozzle
accessible
accessibly
accentuate
acceptable
acceptably
acceptedly
scientific
acceptance
acceptancy
scherzandi
scherzando
scoffingly
scaffolage
scaffolder
ecphractic
ecthlipses
ecthlipsis
ecchymosed
ecchymosis
ecchymotic
ecphoneses
ecphonesis
activation
scribbling
scritch-owl
activeness
scrivening
accidented
accidental
△occidental
scaithless
activities
acriflavin
scrimmager
schismatic
actionable
actionably
schizocarp
Echinoidea
schizoidal
echinoderm
Achitophel
actinolite
Schizopoda
schizogony
scrimpness
schipperke
scrimshank
scriptoria
scriptural
achievable
ocellation
scaldberry
ochlocracy
ecological
scoldingly
oculomotor
schlimazel
Iceland-dog
Scillonian
schlepping
ecclesiast
Scolytidae
sculptress
sculptured
sculptural
sculduddry
acolouthic
acolouthos
scampishly
ecumenical
acuminated

Words marked △ may be spelled also with a capital letter

Scombridae
Scombresox
scandalise
scandalize
scandalled
scandalous
iconoclasm
iconoclast
iconically
scenically
acanaceous
acinaceous
scintiscan
scantiness
scintigram
iconolater
iconolatry
economical
iconomachy
economiser
iconomatic
iconometer
iconometry
economizer
scansorial
iconoscope
acrobatism
octonarian
acrobatics
octonarius
scrog-apple
scholastic
accoucheur
accordable
accordance
accordancy
acromegaly
octogenary
acroterial
acroterium
acroterion
octodecimo
ectodermic
ectodermal
acrogenous
ectogenous
scooped-out
octohedron
acrophobia
acrophonic
ectophytic
acrolithic
sciolistic
scrobicule
tchoukball
schoolmaid
schoolward
school-mate
school-ma'am
school-marm
schooldays
schooltide
schooltime
scrollwise
schoolgirl
octoploidy
schoolwork
schorl-rock
scrollwork
schoolroom
school-bred
acroamatic
accountant
accounting
scrounging
ectoenzyme
octopodous
ectomorphy
accomptant
accomplice
accomplish
eccoprotic
echopraxia
echopraxis
accostable
accoutring
accoutered
octopusher
scrofulous
acronychal
acronymous
octogynous
acephalous
scapegrace
scepticism
scyphiform
Scopelidae
scapulated
Scaphopoda
scyphozoan
scape-wheel
acervately
scarlatina
acervation
scorpaenid
scordatura
scoreboard
scarabaeid
scarabaean
scarabaeus
aceraceous
ochraceous
scaredy-cat
accredited
scarceness
scarcement
acarpelous
scarifying
scornfully
ecardinate
scurfiness
scurviness
scurrility
scorpionic
scurrilous
scarf-joint
achromatic
achromatin
Scaramouch
scorzonera
acarophily
acorn-shell
accrescent
scoresheet
ice-skating
ecospecies
icosahedra
acesulfame
Icosandria
scissor-leg
acetabulum
acetabular
scotodinia
scatheless
scatter-gun
scattering
Scotifying
Scotchness
scattiness
scathingly
Scottified
Scotticise
Scotticize
Scotticism
scutellate
acotyledon
scuttleful
acetylenic
acatalepsy
scotometer
scatophagy
Scotophile
Scotophobe
scaturient
eco-tourism
Scotswoman
ichthyosis
ichthyotic
accurately
accusative
occupative
accubation
accusation
occupation
accusatory
accumbency
scoutcraft
accusement
scrutineer
accusingly
scrutinise
scrutinize
scrutinous
acquainted
actualités
scrummager
acquirable
occurrence
accursedly
acoustical
occultness
acquitment
acquitting
accustomed
accultural
accumulate
scrupulous
scavengery
scavenging
scowdering
scowlingly
schwarzlot
acrylamide
Edwardiana
adjacently
Ndrangheta
'Ndrangheta
adiaphoron
ideational
idealistic
edibleness
edaciously
adactylous
adrenaline
adrenergic
adhesively
adderstone
adder's-wort
adversaria
advertence
advertency
adventurer
advertiser
adjectival
edifyingly
additament
admirative
admiration
admiraunce
advisatory
advisement
advice-boat
admiringly
adhibition
additional
administer
△adriamycin®
sdeignfull
advisorate
admissible
admittable
admittedly
admittance
Adullamite
idioclast
adulterate
adulterant
adulteress
adulterine
adulterise
adulterize
adulterous
adelantado
edulcorate
edulcorant
odd-looking
addle-pated
adolescent
idolatress
idolatrise
idolatrize
Odelsthing
idolatrous
adamantean
adamantine
idempotent
Adamitical
odontalgia
odontalgic
adenectomy
identified
identifier
odontomata
odontocete
odontogeny
odontolite
odontology
edentulous
adenovirus
idiopathic
advocation
advocatory
adsorbable
idiolectic
idiolectal
admonitive
admonition
admonitory
ideologist
adsorption
idiot-proof
ideography
odiousness
adroitness
adaptative
adaptation
adaptively
edaphology
adequately
adequative
odorimetry
editorship
adjuration
adjuratory
adjunctive

Words marked △ may be spelled also with a capital letter

adjunction
sdrucciola
adjudgment
adjudicate
adjustable
adjustably
adjustment
△devanagari
metagalaxy
separately
relaxative
reparative
separative
separatism
defamation
relaxation
reparation
separation
separatist
melanaemia
defamatory
reparatory
separatory
metacarpal
metacarpus
separatrix
megaparsec
metatarsal
metatarsus
pedal-board
debauchery
revanchism
revanchist
△renascence
melancholy
megascopic
defalcator
bel-accoyle
demandable
regardable
rewardable
regardless
rewardless
retardment
verandahed
heraldship
rehandling
decandrian
hexandrian
decandrous
hexandrous
herald-duck
sewage-farm
sexagenary
debateable
femaleness
sedateness
debasement
debatement
defacement
rebatement
regalement
legateship
Sexagesima
dewatering
cesarevich
metamerism
Melanesian
decamerous
hexamerous
hexametric
decahedral
hexahedral
decahedron
hexahedron
metalepsis
metaleptic
metacentre
meganewton
decadently
△dewar-flask
pelargonic
hemangioma
metaphrase
metaphrast
detachable
seraphical
detachedly
decathlete
detachment
megaphonic
Metatheria
metaphoric
metathorax
metaphysic
metatheses
metathesis
metathetic
decapitate
delaminate
deracinate
desalinate
gelatinate
repaginate
revalidate
negatively
relatively
debasingly
debatingly
defacingly
delayingly
menacingly
megalithic
desalinise
desalinize
gelatinise
gelatinize
keratinise
keratinize
relativise
relativize
negativism
relativism
ceramicist
negativist
relativist
negativity
△relativity
tenability
relational
venational
gelatinoid
gelatinous
keratinous
behavioral
legalistic
melanistic
retaliator
remarkable
remarkably
recallable
Heraclidan
dérailleur
derailment
recallment
retailment
Heracleian
hexaplaric
metallurgy
metaplasia
metaplasis
hexaëmeron
detainable
regainable
retainable
detainment
regainment
retainment
repainting
penannular
melanomata
teratomata
megalosaur
Nematoidea
hematocele
teratogeny
pedal-organ
devalorise
devalorize
melaconite
metabolise
metabolite
metabolize
revalorise
revalorize
senatorial
venatorial
demagogism
metabolism
pedagogism
pedagogics
decalogist
decapodous
hematology
hepatology
keratotomy
nematology
teratology
hematocrit
ceratopsid
melanocyte
nematocyst
decampment
pedal-point
remarriage
repatriate
repairable
repair-shop
decagramme
metastable
tenantable
pedantical
tenantless
department
tenantship
hexactinal
xenarthral
recapturer
metastases
metastasis
metastatic
devastator
devastavit
denaturant
denaturise
denaturize
decagynian
hexagynian
decagynous
hexagynous
herb-garden
keyboarder
semblative
lesbianism
kerb-market
membranous
herbicidal
herbaceous
Serbo-Croat
pebble-ware
pebbledash
kerb-vendor
feebleness
herb-bennet
Jew-baiting
Leibnizian
verballing
verbena-oil
red-blooded
herb-Robert
kerb-trader
membership
Herbartian
Selbornian
herbariums
sea-bathing
descramble
bedchamber
leuchaemia
neoclassic
merchantry
leucoblast
peach-bloom
leechcraft
peacockery
peacockish
peacock-ore
leucocytic
peccadillo
beech-drops
leucoderma
teschenite
peacherino
geochemist
reschedule
beccaficos
mercifully
peacefully
beachfront
henceforth
deactivate
reactivate
bescribble
tetchiness
reactively
kerchiefed
perceiving
reactivity
fen-cricket
reactional
descriptor
pencil-case
pencil-lead
pencilling
beach-la-mar
perchloric
percolator
peacemaker
percentage
descendant
descendent
deaconship
Fescennine
mercantile
percentile
descending
descension
deaconhood
geocentric
bedclothes
deschooler
teichopsia
leucoplast
percipient
mercaptide

Words marked △ may be spelled also with a capital letter

perceptive
perception
leucopenia
peace-party
perceptual
teacupfuls
redcurrant
percurrent
percursory
merceriser
mercerizer
Reichsland
Reichsrath
Reichsbank
reichsmark
percussant
percussive
percussion
rescission
peach-stone
rescissory
percutient
seecatchie
gem-cutting
reacquaint
reaccustom
rencounter
henchwoman
henchwomen
peach-water
head-banger
headmaster
hendecagon
mendicancy
veldschoen
mendacious
needle-case
needle-bath
lead-pencil
dead-weight
beadleship
needlefish
beadlehood
needlecord
meddlesome
needle-book
needlework
seed-vessel
heedlessly
needlessly
dead-centre
dead-nettle
head-centre
dead-letter
feed-heater
hey-de-guise
hey-de-guyes
headcheese
headsheets
headphones
reed-thrush
deadliness
dead-lights
dead-finish
tea-drinker
tendrilled
tendrillar
weedkiller
dendriform
fer-de-lance
hebdomadal
hebdomadar
hebdomader
seldomness
ready-money
Geodimeter®
ready-mixed
reading-boy
leadenness
pendentive
tendential
geodynamic
perdendosi
tendinitis
tendonitis
seed-potato
dendroidal
head-to-head
dendrophis
dendrobium
headworker
dendrology
dendrogram
o'er-drowsed
readoption
headsquare
perdurable
renderable
perdurably
genderless
tenderness
tenderfeet
leadership
readership
lead-arming
tenderling
perdurance
gelder-rose
tenderloin
tenderfoot
deodoriser
tenderiser
leaderette
dead-ground
deodorizer
tenderizer
geodesical
geodetical
head-stream
ready-to-eat
deadstroke
headstrong
ready-to-sew
head-lugged
head-hugger
yerd-hunger
yerd-hungry
head-bummer
headhunter
Zend-Avesta
beadswoman
seed-oyster
rendezvous
generalate
telecamera
△resedaceae
telepathic
federalise
federalize
federative
generalise
generalize
generative
revelative
seven-a-side
vegetative
vegetating
federalism
Genevanism
defecation
delegation
denegation
federation
generation
hebetation
regelation
relegation
renegation
△revelation
vegetarian
vegetation
veneration
telematics
federalist
generalist
generality
generalled
renewables
oedematose
oedematous
revelatory
generatrix
pederastic
telecasted
benefactor
telecaster
relevantly
resemblant
resembling
Decembrist
rememberer
Decemberly
hereabouts
Seleucidae
Seleucidan
telescreen
Rebeccaite
redescribe
beseeching
Rebeccaism
defenceman
senescence
telescopic
aerenchyma
cenenchyma
mesenchyme
defendable
dependable
dependably
dependacie
dependance
dependence
dependency
decelerate
degenerate
regenerate
degeneracy
regeneracy
reverencer
referendum
sereneness
severeness
televérité
cerebellic
bejewelled
cerebellum
cerebellar
telerecord
degenerous
pedereroes
tête-de-pont
telemetric
tenemental
reverently
vehemently
revengeful
detergence
detergency
Betelgeuse
genethliac
telephonic
telephoner
telechiric
lederhosen
jewel-house
hereticate
rededicate
hereditary
veterinary
remediable
remediably
Genesiacal
répétiteur
remediless
beneficent
redelivery
feverishly
△benedicite
meperidine
repetitive
selegiline
benefiting
beneficial
repetition
television
geneticist
hereditist
bedevilled
remedially
Venetianed
veneficous
heresiarch
benefitted
deregister
reregister
Benedictus
televisual
televiewer
repealable
resealable
revealable
revealment
genealogic
teleologic
bedellship
repellance
repellence
repellancy
repellency
rebellious
redeemable
redeemably
redeemless
determined
determiner
telesmatic
secernment
teleonomic
telegnosis
decennoval
Never-Never
never-never
redecorate
heterogamy
heterotaxy
Heterocera
benevolent
heterogeny
penelopise
penelopize
developing
ceremonial
hegemonial
hegemonism
ceremonies

semeiotics
hegemonist
generosity
teleworker
Heteropoda
heretofore
telegonous
heterocont
heterodont
heterokont
selenodont
heterodoxy
heterogony
heterology
heteronomy
selenology
semeiology
generously
temerously
reredorter
werewolves
heterodyne
redemptive
redemption
sevenpence
sevenpenny
peremptory
redemptory
metempiric
deferrable
penetrable
referrable
referrible
penetrably
telebridge
tenebrific
researcher
rehearsing
penetralia
deterrence
penetrance
penetrancy
veneer-moth
tenebrious
telegraphy
meteoritic
celebrated
genevrette
meteorital
celebrator
desecrater
desecrator
penetrator
telewriter
cerebritis
Lebensraum
defeasible
defensible
releasable
reversible
defensibly
reversedly
Peter-see-me
teleostean
nécessaire
defenseman
defeasance
seven-score
teleostome
Teleostomi
demeasnure
fenestrate
revestiary
deceptible
defectible
delectable
detectable
detectible
detestable
receptible
rejectable
rejectible
repeatable
revertible
delectably
detestably
receptacle
dejectedly
dementedly
repeatedly
△seventh-day
seventieth
nepenthean
desertless
recentness
relentless
selectness
relentment
resentment
regentship
regent-bird
repertoire
semestrial
pedestrian
derestrict
△fenestella
Nemertinea
repentance
resentence
deceptious
dejections
mesenteric
beweltered
debentured
mesenteron
tête-à-têtes
deregulate
reregulate
vegeburger
rere-supper
deceivable
receivable
reservable
deceivably
deservedly
reservedly
decemviral
denervated
lever-watch
Pelecypoda
heresy-hunt
self-danger
self-taught
pen-feather
self-parody
self-hatred
self-raised
self-abuser
perficient
perfective
self-acting
perfection
self-action
perfidious
self-regard
self-feeder
self-seeder
self-severe
leafleteer
self-deceit
new-fledged
leafleting
self-denial
self-seeker
self-repose
leafletted
self-mettle
red-figured
leaf-sheath
self-binder
self-giving
self-rising
self-killed
self-willed
self-filler
self-killer
beef-witted
perfoliate
self-slayer
self-glazed
self-unable
leaf-insect
self-inject
newfangled
leaf-mosaic
reafforest
self-loving
self-moving
self-motion
self-cocker
self-rolled
self-bounty
self-colour
leaf-hopper
self-poised
leaf-spring
self-breath
perforable
leaf-bridge
self-profit
self-praise
ley-farming
performing
perfervour
perforated
perforator
perforatus
self-driven
beef-brewis
self-esteem
net-fishery
net-fishing
sea-fishing
Neofascism
Neofascist
self-styled
self-murder
beefburger
self-ruling
deaf-mutism
leaf-cutter
self-exiled
geographic
geographer
Belgravian
verge-board
weighboard
neighborly
weigh-bauks
meagreness
seigneurie
vengefully
lengthways
lengthwise
lengthsman
weigh-house
penguinery
neogenesis
neogenetic
seignorage
Bergsonism
Bergsonian
zeuglodont
geognostic
ledger-bait
vergership
ledger-line
weightless
nephralgia
hen-hearted
déshabillé
methodical
Methedrine®
béche-de-mer
technetium
nephograph
technicise
technicize
nephridium
technicism
technician
technicist
rechristen
cephalagra
nephologic
methyldopa
cephalopod
methylated
cephalitis
methomania
mechanical
methinketh
technofear
nephropexy
methionine
dethroning
Aethiopian
technopole
nephrology
nephrotomy
technology
technocrat
reshipment
hetherward
netherward
lethargied
lethargise
lethargize
hen-harrier
nethermore
nethermost
Methuselah
nephoscope
mephitical
medicament
sexivalent
delicately
decimalise
decimalize
dedicative
derivative
devitalise
devitalize
hesitative
medicalise
medicalize
medicative
meditative
recitative
retinalite
revitalise
revitalize
recitativi
genitalial
seminarial

Words marked △ may be spelled also with a capital letter

decimalism
revivalism
tepidarium
decimation
dedication
delibation
deligation
deliration
denization
depilation
derivation
gemination
hesitation
levigation
leviration
levitation
medication
meditation
recitation
remigation
seminarian
semination
velitation
vesication
recitativo
decimalist
revivalist
seminarist
feminality
seminality
demi-cannon
dedicatory
depilatory
hesitatory
vesicatory
pedipalpus
medicaster
hesitantly
retinacula
perikaryon
beribboned
redisburse
bewitchery
bewitching
mediocrity
heliacally
seriocomic
dehiscence
meliaceous
periscopic
meniscuses
desiccator
rediscount
rediscover
behindhand
periodical
behind-door
bewildered
desiderata
deliberate
desiderate

delineable
demirepdom
peripeteia
semiterete
desireless
defilement
definement
refinement
repinement
retirement
revilement
revivement
aedileship
desiderium
perihelion
peripetian
semi-weekly
peridermal
ceriferous
sebiferous
setiferous
setigerous
perimetric
hemihedral
perimetral
perineural
hemihedron
peritectic
pedimented
pedimental
regimental
delineator
residenter
penitently
delineavit
beliefless
reliefless
heliograph
melic-grass
vexingness
mediagenic
meningioma
periegesis
meningitis
periphrase
perishable
relishable
perishably
perithecia
Jewishness
newishness
delightful
benighting
periphonic
Hemichorda
peripheric
peripheral
decipherer
semichorus
periphyton
debilitate

delimitate
felicitate
legitimate
revisitant
legitimacy
verifiable
semicircle
decisively
definitely
derisively
femininely
genitively
periwigged
deridingly
repiningly
retiringly
revilingly
revivingly
devilishly
revivified
decivilise
decivilize
definitive
legitimise
legitimize
semi-divine
femininism
legitimism
△peridinium
recidivism
definition
peridinian
redivision
legitimist
recidivist
feminility
femininity
legibility
periwinkle
penicillin
definienda
deficience
desipience
recipience
resilience
meridional
revisional
△petitioner
religioner
deficiency
recipiency
resiliency
demi-ditone
felicitous
veridicous
semicirque
feministic
semi-liquid
definitude
religieuse
heli-skiing

genialness
hemiplegia
hemiplegic
periclinal
petiolated
feuilleton
heliolater
legislator
heliolatry
medium-term
melismatic
heliometer
designable
designedly
resignedly
designless
designment
resignment
Helianthus
semi-uncial
regionally
benignancy
hemianopia
designator
semi-annual
semi-double
helicoidal
peritoneal
peritoneum
lepidolite
peridotite
perigonial
perigonium
Heliconian
decinormal
lexicology
meritocrat
desirously
perilously
resinously
semipostal
melicotton
helicopter
Cecidomyia
hemisphere
semi-opaque
heliophyte
delinquent
relinquish
peritricha
reciprocal
heritrices
semi-drying
decigramme
hemicrania
hemitropic
hemitropal
lexigraphy
serigraphy
denigrator
meliorator

heritrixes
remissible
periosteal
periosteum
remissness
mediastina
redissolve
△peninsular
aeciospore
helioscope
teliospore
periastron
registrant
registrary
heriotable
resistible
resistibly
mediatress
resistless
belittling
rebirthing
Cerinthian
geriatrics
pediatrics
geriatrist
peristylar
peristomal
desistance
desistence
remittance
△resistance
heliotrope
heliotropy
heliotypic
sericteria
registered
hemipteral
peripteral
hemipteran
heliotaxis
geniculate
pediculate
reticulate
semilunate
vesiculate
Pediculati
reticulary
semilucent
reliquaire
pedicurist
tediousome
vesiculose
meticulous
pediculous
periculous
deliquesce
semiquaver
believable
relievable
medievally
reviewable

Words marked △ may be spelled also with a capital letter

perimysium
hemicyclic
pericyclic
hemizygous
perigynous
serjeantry
perjinkety
perjinkity
perjurious
weak-handed
necklacing
verkrampte
leukoblast
leukocytic
jerked-meat
leukoderma
weak-headed
deckle-edge
beekeeping
sea-keeping
deck-tennis
fecklessly
recklessly
weak-minded
weakliness
weak-hinged
weak-willed
Berkeleian
leukemogen
jerkinhead
weekending
Neo-Kantian
leukoplast
leukopenia
deck-bridge
peckerwood
deck-quoits
well-padded
bellhanger
dealbation
well-marked
fell-walker
peelgarlic
well-earned
cellobiose
pellucidly
neglectful
deflective
neglective
reflective
reflecting
deflection
neglection
re-election
reflection
pellicular
sexlocular
replicator
secludedly
sealed-beam
belladonna
belly-dance
hellbender
well-beseen
bell-wether
well-heeled
wellie-boot
deflagrate
jellygraph
negligible
re-eligible
negligibly
geological
neological
reflagging
negligence
pellagrous
healthcare
healthless
healthsome
bell-shaped
well-chosen
well-thewed
declaimant
reclaimant
well-minded
bell-ringer
well-wished
seal-fisher
well-wisher
declaiming
well-liking
well-sinker
bell-siller
well-willer
well-placed
cellulosic
weeldlesse
cellulated
cellulitis
belly-laugh
bell-flower
sex-limited
ceilometer
bellamoure
declinable
reclinable
peel-and-eat
heulandite
declension
telling-off
Bedlington
wellington
declinator
sealing-wax
reallocate
reel-to-reel
fellmonger
meal-monger
well-to-live
well-boring
well-formed
well-gotten
cellophane®
wellspring
well-spoken
mellophone
mefloquine
declarable
deplorable
deplorably
well-graced
declaredly
dealership
tellership
bellarmine
de-blurring
cellar-flap
cellar-book
declarator
real-estate
realisable
declassify
reclassify
depletable
red-lattice
belletrist
aeolotropy
well-judged
reillumine
well-turned
fellrunner
bell-turret
yellowcake
yellowback
yellowhead
yellow-weed
fellow-heir
mellowness
yellowness
fellowship
yellowbird
yellow-yite
yellow-girl
yellow-wood
yellow-root
yellow-wort
deflowerer
reflexible
deployment
realizable
permeative
permeation
germicidal
vermicidal
vermicelli
vermicular
gemmaceous
geomedical
desmodiums
reim-kennar
vermifugal
permafrost
termagancy
seemlihead
seemliness
seemelesse
segmentate
segmentary
germinable
terminable
reaming-bit
terminably
sermonical
helminthic
hetmanship
penmanship
seamanship
beam-engine
fermentive
seamanlike
Terminalia
terminally
permanence
permanency
sermoniser
terminuses
sermonette
terminator
sermonizer
Dermaptera
Dermoptera
red-murrain
mesmerical
new-married
Weimaraner
mesmeriser
mesmerizer
permissive
permission
desmosomal
permutable
hermetical
hermitical
seamstress
dermatogen
geometrise
geometrize
permitting
geometrist
hermit-crab
permethrin
dermatoses
dermatosis
pegmatitic
dermatitis
Pelmatozoa
seannachie
penny-a-line
pernoctate
pennycress
pernickety
vernacular
pennaceous
pernicious
Deinoceras
meandering
re-entering
△neandertal
ferntickle
fernticled
leontiasis
lean-witted
re-enlister
kennel-maid
kennelling
kennel-coal
meaningful
tennantite
reunionism
reunionist
deontology
herniotomy
penny-plain
penny-piece
penny-pinch
reinspirit
reincrease
Bernardine
re-entrance
re-entrancy
pennyroyal
lemniscate
penny-stane
vernissage
tennis-ball
tennis-shoe
penny-stone
teinoscope
Pennisetum
ferniticle
fernyticle
deinothere
pennatulae
pennatulas
teeny-weeny
pennyworth
memorandum
zero-valent
derogately
desolately
melomaniac
decorative
demoralise
demoralize
denotative
depolarise
depolarize
derogative
devocalise
devocalize
memorative
pejorative
remoralise
remoralize

Words marked △ may be spelled also with a capital letter

10 □e□p□s

zero-rating
decoration
denotation
derogation
desolation
detonation
pejoration
peroration
relocation
renovation
revocation
aerobatics
meiofaunal
derogatory
desolatory
revocatory
debonairly
menopausal
aeronautic
aerotactic
resonantly
resorbence
deforciant
heroicness
rejoiceful
penoncelle
reconciler
heroically
heroi-comic
resorcinol
rejoicings
mesoscaphe
debouchure
second-hand
second-rate
recordable
second-best
secondment
recondense
beforehand
rejoneador
remoteness
denotement
denouement
dénouement
devotement
revokement
beforetime
demonetise
demonetize
remonetise
remonetize
mesomerism
xerodermia
xerodermic
xenogenous
aerometric
redolently
lemon-grass
belongings
aerophobia

genophobia
kenophobia
xenophobia
zelophobia
aerophobic
zelophobic
oesophagus
henotheism
henotheist
hemophilia
mesothorax
telophasic
mesophytic
xerophytic
demotivate
denominate
detoxicate
peroxidase
detoxicant
depositary
negotiable
demoniacal
velocipede
Menominees
becomingly
Mesolithic
demolisher
demobilise
demobilize
depositive
peroxidise
peroxidize
cenobitism
lenocinium
demolition
deposition
reposition
re-position
demoticist
kenoticist
désorienté
devotional
serotinous
depository
repository
mesohippus
aerobiosis
aerobiotic
hedonistic
Jehovistic
nepotistic
xenobiotic
defoliated
defoliator
negotiator
hemoglobin
recoilless
decollated
decollator
deformable
reformable

reformados
deformedly
recommence
aero-engine
debonnaire
redounding
resounding
nero-antico
recogniser
reioyndure
rejoindure
recognizer
decolorate
decolorant
Demogorgon
decolonise
decolonize
decolorise
decolorize
recolonise
recolonize
aerologist
aeronomist
gemologist
oenologist
pedologist
penologist
serologist
sexologist
tenotomist
melocotoon
demonology
zero-coupon
mesomorphy
meconopses
meconopsis
decorously
venomously
mesosphere
decompress
recompress
recoupment
resorptive
decoupling
desorption
resorption
recompence
recompense
decomposer
decompound
reconquest
hemorrhage
leiotrichy
besom-rider
devourment
aerogramme
aérogramme
menorrhoea
seborrhoea
hemorrhoid
aerotropic

aerography
cerography
demography
venography
xerography
democratic
repoussage
reconsider
remorseful
perovskite
demoiselle
repoussoir
remortgage
decoctible
reportable
besottedly
reportedly
devoutness
deportment
xerostomia
recontinue
hemoptysis
hemostasis
aerostatic
hemostatic
demodulate
depopulate
repopulate
resolutely
resolutive
devolution
resolution
re-solution
revolution
resolvable
resolvedly
revolvency
serotyping
hemocyanin
geophagism
temptation
geophagist
geophagous
neoplastic
tea-planter
respectant
despicable
despicably
henpeckery
respectful
respective
respecting
bespeckled
telpherage
perplexing
perplexity
telpherman
bedpresser
helplessly
deep-seated
hemp-nettle

telpherway
serpigines
deoppilate
despairful
temptingly
neophiliac
despairing
delphinium
besprinkle
deep-sinker
delphinoid
pemphigoid
geophilous
pemphigous
ten-pointer
reap-silver
leg-pulling
△**neapolitan**
geoponical
weaponless
despondent
respondent
weapon-shaw
responsive
serpentine
serpentise
serpentize
desponding
responsory
deep-rooted
pepper-cake
respirable
temperable
leopard-cat
desperados
Hesperides
deep-freeze
vesper-bell
keeperless
leopardess
keepership
jeopardise
jeopardize
reappraise
sexpartite
vespertine
peppermill
peppermint
temporally
temporalty
kempery-man
temperance
peppercorn
jeopardous
pepperwort
temporiser
respirator
deep-browed
temporizer
despisable
tempestive

Words marked △ may be spelled also with a capital letter

10 □e□p□t

perpetrate
perpetuate
despotical
sempstress
despiteful
despatches
perpetuity
despiteous
ten-pounder
geophysics
desquamate
seaquarium
perquisite
degreasant
retreatant
beer-garden
rearmament
reproacher
recreative
reorganise
reorganize
neorealism
recreation
neorealist
beer-parlor
ferro-alloy
beer-barrel
recreantly
neuroblast
heartbreak
jerry-built
reprobance
heart-blood
heart-block
tetrabasic
reprobater
reprobator
retributor
depreciate
meerschaum
leprechaun
leprechawn
refractary
deprecable
detractive
refractive
retractile
retractive
tetractine
detracting
refracting
detraction
re-erection
refraction
retraction
metrically
tetrachord
retrochoir
detractory
neurectomy
refractory

terracotta
terracette
deprecator
refracture
degradable
reproducer
searedness
serradella
serradilla
petrodrome
recrudesce
depredator
pearl-diver
near-begaun
decreeable
befriender
near-legged
tetraethyl
hearse-like
debriefing
retrieving
tear-jerker
fearlessly
peerlessly
febrifugal
petrifying
terrifying
wearifully
retrograde
beard-grass
ferrograms
segregable
retrogress
heart-grief
bedraggled
Tetragynia
neurogenic
tetragonal
petroglyph
searchable
tetrahedra
searchless
gearchange
gear-change
pear-shaped
Herrnhuter
ferry-house
heartiness
pearliness
wearyingly
yearningly
recruiting
Hebraicism
Hebraistic
metrologic
necrologic
petrolling
neurilemma
neurolemma
petroleous
neurolysis

serrulated
petrolatum
necrolater
necrolatry
pétroleuse
Terramycin®
merrymaker
metromania
neuraminic
necromancy
petromoney
Tetramorph
tetrameral
tetrameter
hearing-aid
detruncate
Serranidae
ferronière
year-on-year
refringent
retransfer
merry-night
beer-engine
ferrandine
petronella
metronomic
metronymic
retransmit
Herrenvolk
Tetrandria
ne'er-do-weel
ne'er-do-well
deer-forest
fearsomely
pearmonger
dearbought
fearnought
rear-boiled
heortology
beer-bottle
rear-dorter
neuroplasm
tetrapodic
△neuroptera
terreplein
necrophile
negrophile
decryption
ferro-print
necrophily
metropolis
necropolis
tetrapolis
tetraploid
necrophobe
negrophobe
tetraptote
neuropathy
heart-quake
perruquier
terrorless

retrorsely
tetrarchic
Petrarchal
Petrarchan
terra-rossa
terroriser
terrariums
terrorizer
heartsease
heart's-ease
petrissage
depressant
pearl-shell
decrescent
retrospect
refreshful
degressive
depressive
redressive
regressive
repressive
depressing
refreshing
tetrastich
degression
depression
regression
repression
heuristics
decrassify
serrasalmo
tetrasemic
pearl-stone
tetraspore
heart-spoon
necroscopy
leproserie
metrostyle
tetrastyle
secretness
redruthite
secretaire
dew-retting
regretting
tetrathlon
tetratomic
serrations
heart-throb
neurotoxic
neurotoxin
tetrotoxin
seersucker
deprivable
depravedly
retrovirus
pearl-white
heart-whole
pear-switch
heartwater
defrayable
defrayment

leastaways
felspathic
dessiatine
dessyatine
Persianise
Persianize
persuasive
sensualise
sensualize
Messianism
sensualism
persuasion
geostatics
Messianist
sensualist
sensuality
gensdarmes
persuasory
newscaster
sex-starved
△belshazzar
sensibilia
pease-brose
versicular
persicaria
persecutor
reassemble
reassembly
newsreader
news-vendor
kenspeckle
newsdealer
persiennes
pensieroso
newsletter
bed-swerver
persiflage
persifleur
versifying
message-boy
deaspirate
perspirate
set-stitch'd
jeistiecor
feistiness
measliness
reastiness
yeastiness
beeswinged
seismicity
geoscience
redshifted
tessellate
teaselling
dense-media
verse-maker
leishmania
densimeter
tensimeter
densimetry
personable

Words marked △ may be spelled also with a capital letter

reasonable
seasonable
reasonably
seasonably
reasonless
seasonless
pepsinogen
kersantite
personalia
personally
personalty
seasonally
personhood
personated
Kensington
personator
tersanctus
cessionary
pensionary
newsmonger
versionist
pensionnat
seismology
seismogram
sensuously
peashooter
newsworthy
fesse-point
menstruate
censurable
leisurable
measurable
mensurable
censurably
leisurably
measurably
measuredly
censorship
perstringe
censorious
menstruous
news-writer
menstruums
sensoriums
persistent
persistive
verse-smith
pease-straw
jet-setting
sensitised
sensitiser
sensitized
sensitizer
reissuable
reassuring
Welshwoman
kerseymere
Jew's-myrtle
left-handed
neat-handed
bestraddle
death-adder
left-hander
leftwardly
westwardly
bestraught
Benthamite
bestialise
bestialize
centralise
centralize
neutralise
neutralize
oestradiol
Benthamism
bestialism
centralism
neutralism
textualism
Cestracion
centralist
neutralist
Septuagint
textualist
bestiality
centrality
dextrality
neutrality
West-Banker
test-market
restrained
pea-trainer
restrainer
death-agony
rest-harrow
neat-cattle
beetmaster
peat-caster
Vertebrata
vertebrate
vestibulum
vestibular
pettichaps
petty-chaps
pesticidal
septicidal
meatscreen
fettuccine
tentaculum
heptachlor
lenticular
tentacular
testicular
nectocalyx
hectically
septically
vertically
septicemia
geotechnic
heptachord
pentachord
rent-a-crowd
testaceous
pettedness
testudinal
testudines
text-editor
centre-half
nettle-rash
centre-back
centre-rail
featherbed
settleable
heathendom
beetlehead
nettle-cell
gentleness
settlement
centre-fire
centreline
genteelise
genteelize
heathenise
heathenize
nettlelike
weatherise
weatherize
feathering
leathering
weathering
genteelish
heathenish
nettle-fish
genteelism
heathenism
Wertherism
Wertherian
aesthetics
kettle-pins
peat-reeker
bestseller
geothermic
geothermal
weatherman
centrefold
gentlehood
best-before
mettlesome
nettlesome
gentlefolk
nettle-tree
kettledrum
wentletrap
restlessly
vestmented
rest-centre
vestmental
neutrettos
beetle-eyed
beatifical
dentifrice
certifying
rectifying
testifying
centigrade
hectograph
pentagraph
vectograph
Heptagynia
Pentagynia
heptagonal
pentagonal
lentigines
vertigines
pentahedra
rent-charge
bestridden
cestoidean
left-winger
rectricial
tectricial
gentrifier
centricity
ventricose
ventricous
felt-tipped
restricted
beetmister
centrifuge
ventricule
ventriculi
death-knell
ventilable
Pentelican
gestaltism
centillion
septillion
sextillion
Gestaltist
pestilence
reptilious
Sertularia
gentilesse
fertiliser
centilitre
hectolitre
centiliter
ventilator
dentaliums
fertilizer
centumviri
septemviri
septemvirs
Celtomania
Keltomania
lentamente
pentimenti
pentimento
Heptameron
Pentameron
centimetre
hectometre
centimeter
heptameter
pentameter
peg-tankard
septennate
nesting-box
sextonship
centennial
sentential
septennial
septennium
rectangled
pertinence
pertinency
melting-pot
Heptandria
Pentandria
rent-an-army
pectinated
certiorari
lectionary
centroidal
centromere
seltzogene
festoonery
peltmonger
neutrophil
sectionise
sectionize
destroying
geotropism
vest-pocket
centrosome
deltiology
penthouses
dextrously
feateously
left-footed
left-footer
dextrogyre
deutoplasm
heptapodic
pentapodic
pentaprism
pentapolis
pentaploid
heath-poult
letter-card
perturbate
better-ball
yesterdays
perturbant
restorable
neoterical
letterhead
yesteryear
betterness
fetterless
letterless
betterment
pesterment
heptarchic
hectorship

10 □e□t□r

lectorship
mentorship
rectorship
dexterwise
letter-file
westernise
westernize
pewter-mill
sestertium
westernism
letter-clip
pectorally
texturally
reiterance
letter-bomb
letter-wood
fetterlock
letter-book
tenterhook
yestermorn
nectareous
bettermost
setterwort
reiterated
see-through
yestereven
death's-head
hectostere
Leptospira
tea-tasting
pentastich
lentissimo
leptosomic
centesimal
Kentish-man
Vertoscope®
Kentish-rag
pentastyle
beatitudes
death-token
pentathlum
heptathlon
pentathlon
teetotally
pentatomic
pentstemon
heptatonic
pentatonic
heatstroke
penteteric
death-throe
restitutor
Heptateuch
Pentateuch
restaurant
centaurian
destructor
lentivirus
bestowment
deathwards
deathwatch

death-wound
vestry-room
get-up-and-go
Betulaceae
bequeathal
dehumanise
dehumanize
depurative
regularise
regularize
regulative
reputative
secularise
secularize
secularism
denudation
depuration
deputation
peculation
recusation
refutation
regulation
reputation
Verulamian
secularist
regularity
secularity
depuratory
regulatory
petulantly
benumbment
decumbence
recumbence
decumbency
recumbency
penumbrous
nelumbiums
denunciate
repurchase
defunctive
defunction
peduncular
sequacious
sepulchral
refundable
Gesundheit
refundment
seguidilla
redundance
secundines
redundancy
gerundival
recuperate
rejuvenate
remunerate
requiescat
demureness
jejuneness
recureless
reputeless
secureness

deducement
securement
seducement
rejuvenise
rejuvenize
oecumenism
tegumental
temulently
refulgence
resurgence
refulgency
resupinate
Securitate
repudiable
delusively
rebukingly
seducingly
securitise
securitize
beautician
beautifier
securities
dehumidify
tenurially
delusional
cecutiency
medusiform
securiform
aeruginous
ceruminous
leguminous
velutinous
peculiarly
repudiator
refuelable
△republican
medullated
returnable
returnless
sequencing
sequential
repugnance
repugnancy
Beaujolais
Lemuroidea
nebulosity
nebulously
sedulously
resumptive
resumption
demurrable
requirable
recurrence
decurrency
recurrency
menu-driven
Venus-shell
sequestrum
decussated
requisitor
delustrant

deductible
rebuttable
requitable
Jesuitical
resultless
seductress
requiteful
reluctance
reluctancy
sepultural
heavy-armed
serviceman
cervicitis
fervidness
heavy-laden
pelvimeter
servomotor
pelvimetry
heavenward
heaven-sent
servant-man
serving-man
heaven-born
heaven-bred
perviously
perversely
perversive
perversion
perversity
beaver-wood
beaver-tree
fervescent
velvet-leaf
servitress
velvet-pile
velvet-crab
velvet-duck
betweenity
werwolfish
networking
bed-wetting
deoxidiser
deoxidizer
recyclable
kerygmatic
dehydrater
dehydrator
benzocaine
Benzedrine®
mezzo-forte
mezzo-piano
mezzotinto
benzpyrene
effaceable
effacement
affability
aficionado
afterbirth
offenceful
offendedly
offendress

effeteness
after-guard
aftergrass
after-image
effeminate
effeminacy
effeminise
effeminize
after-light
afterpiece
afterpains
affeerment
aftershave
afterswarm
aftershaft
aftersales
aftershock
effectuate
effectible
affectedly
affectless
effectless
oftentimes
affettuoso
aftertaste
effervesce
afterworld
afterwards
Africander
Afrikander
Africanise
Africanize
Africanism
Africanist
efficacity
Africanoid
office-girl
office-book
affiliable
affinitive
officially
officialty
efficience
efficiency
officiator
affirmable
affirmance
effigurate
afflictive
afflicting
affliction
off-licence
affluently
effloresce
effleurage
affordable
afrormosia
effortless
off-putting
sforzandos
affricated

Words marked △ may be spelled also with a capital letter

10 □h□l□s

affrighted
affrighten
effrontery
affrontive
affronting
off-spinner
offsetable
effulgence
effusively
egg-and-dart
eglandular
age-bracket
egg-binding
egocentric
egg-capsule
Yggdrasill
agrégation
ignimbrite
ignipotent
egoistical
agglutinin
agentivity
agonisedly
agonistics
agonizedly
ignoration
ignorantly
ugsomeness
ignobility
Ugro-Finnic
agronomial
agronomics
agrologist
agronomist
agapanthus
Egyptology
egurgitate
aggrandise
aggrandize
aggressive
aggression
aggravated
ego-tripper
agitatedly
pheasantry
phraseless
wheatfield
sheathless
sheathfish
sheathbill
phialiform
whoa-hoa-hoa
choanocyte
theatrical
cheapskate
wheatsheaf
shear-steel
Wheatstone
thwartways
thwartedly
thwartship
thwartwise
shea-butter
shearwater
chlamydate
chlamydial
shabracque
shebeening
chubbiness
shabbiness
Ghibelline
shibboleth
rhabdolith
rhubarbing
checkclerk
thickening
chucker-out
chickenpox
thick-grown
chocaholic
chocoholic
shockingly
checklaton
shecklaton
chocolatey
phocomelia
checkpoint
shock-proof
shockstall
chockstone
thick-skull
chock-tight
shuddering
shoddiness
thuddingly
Rhodymenia
whodunitry
rhodophane
khidmutgar
khediviate
shadowcast
shadowless
Rh-negative
shoemaking
chrematist
chief-baron
sheep-biter
wheel-clamp
wheelchair
three-cleft
shield-hand
shield-maid
shieldrake
threadbare
thread-lace
shieldwall
thread-cell
shieldless
shrewdness
shieldlike
shieldling
Rhoeadales
threadworm
cheesecake
cheese-head
phrenesiac
cheesemite
cheesewire
cheesewood
sheep-faced
cheerfully
sheet-glass
cheechakos
cheechalko
wheelhorse
wheelhouse
cheekiness
cheeriness
cheesiness
wheeziness
sheepishly
shrewishly
thievishly
phoenixism
Phoenician
sheep-louse
phlegmonic
phlegmasia
phlegmatic
sheet-metal
shrewmouse
phlebolite
threnodial
phaelonion
threnodist
Chaetopoda
phaenology
phlebotomy
phrenology
phaenotype
shlemozzle
three-phase
sheep-plant
cheekpiece
three-piece
three-point
three-piled
threepence
threepenny
three-parts
three-pound
cheekpouch
sheepshank
phrensical
three-sided
sheep's-head
three-speed
threescore
sheep's-foot
sheep's-eyes
shoestring
thief-taker
threatened
threatener
cheektooth
chiffchaff
chuff-chuff
shaft-horse
chuffiness
shiftiness
chaffingly
shuffle-cap
chiffonier
Whiggarchy
whiggamore
shag-haired
phagocytic
phagedaena
phagedenic
shagreened
shagginess
Whiggishly
phthisical
phthisicky
Thailander
chainbrake
chairborne
Rheinberry
chairbound
shriech-owl
shritch-owl
choiceness
thriveless
shrinelike
shriveling
shrivelled
shriche-owl
thrivingly
rhoicissus
shrinkpack
shrinkable
shrink-wrap
shrillness
chair-organ
cheirology
cheironomy
chain-smoke
Christmasy
theistical
Christless
thriftless
thriftiest
Christlike
Christhood
shrievalty
chainwheel
chairwoman
chokeberry
shakuhachi
Chekhovian
choliambic
chiliarchy
shellacked
chiliastic
chalkboard
chalybeate
childbirth
shellbound
thale-cress
phylactery
chylaceous
chelicerae
thalictrum
shelldrake
pholidosis
shillelagh
challenged
challenger
sheltering
Childermas
chalcedony
wholegrain
cholagogic
cholagogue
thill-horse
chalkiness
chilliness
shelliness
childishly
phallicism
Chalcidian
thalliform
philologic
philologue
philologer
chalumeaux
shale-miner
shell-money
philomathy
phalangeal
whaling-gun
phalangist
phyllotaxy
phalloidin
phylloxera
phelloderm
chalcocite
shallowing
Phyllopoda
phallocrat
whole-plate
chilopodan
philopoena
philippina
philippine
Philippise
Philippize
Philippian
childproof
shellproof
Philistean
△philistine
Philistian
thalassian
wholesaler

10 □h□l□s

chalkstone
shellshock
philosophe
philosophy
child-study
philatelic
phillumeny
wholewheat
philoxenia
whillywhaw
shellycoat
Rhamnaceae
shammashim
chemiatric
chimpanzee
chemicking
chemically
thymectomy
chamaeleon
chambering
shimmering
whimpering
chamber-lye
chamberpot
chimneypot
Chambertin
themselves
shamefaced
shamefully
thumb-index
whimsiness
thumpingly
thumbikins
champignon
thimbleful
thimblerig
chemonasty
rhomboidal
rhomboides
whomsoever
thumbpiece
thumbprint
shame-proof
chimerical
chambranle
thimerosal
rhyme-royal
thumbstall
thumbs-down
thumbscrew
chemisette
chemotaxis
shamiyanah
Rhyniaceae
phantasime
shin-barker
thin-walled
phantasmic
phantasmal
phantastic
phantastry

Rhineberry
thenabouts
chinachina
phonically
rhinoceros
rhinocerot
phenacetin
phenocryst
changeable
thunderbox
changeably
thunder-egg
chanceless
changeless
thunbergia
thunder-god
channelise
channelize
changeling
thundering
chandelier
channelled
chancellor
chunderous
thunderous
changeover
thankfully
Rhinegrave
Chinagraph®
phonograph
phenogamic
Phenogamae
shanghaied
shanghaier
△chinchilla
thinginess
thinkingly
rhinolalia
chandlerly
phonolitic
phenomenal
phenomenon
phonematic
phonometer
shenanigan
phantomish
whensoever
phonophore
rhinophyma
shandrydan
phanerogam
chondromas
chondritic
chondritis
chank-shell
△rhinestone
rhinoscope
rhinoscopy
phonetical
rhinotheca
phenotypic

phonotypic
thanatosis
thingumbob
chinquapin
rhinovirus
shunt-wound
shandygaff
phoneyness
shantytown
theomaniac
chloralism
chromatics
chloralose
theomantic
chromatype
thromboses
thrombosis
thrombotic
shroud-laid
shroudless
throneless
theotechny
Shrovetide
theoretics
throne-room
thiopental
throughout
throughput
throughway
theophobia
theophanic
theophoric
chloridate
chlorinate
theodicean
chloridise
chloridize
chlorinise
chlorinize
Rh-positive
chromidium
chlorinity
chronicity
chronicler
Chronicles
phlogistic
phlogiston
thrown-silk
theopneust
theologate
chromomere
theosophic
chlorophyl
chromophil
theosopher
phlogopite
theodolite
theologise
theologize
theologian
rheologist

theogonist
theologist
chionodoxa
chromosome
chloroform
theonomous
chronology
chromogram
chronogram
chronotron
chloroquin
chlorodyne
chromotype
thiouracil
rheotropic
theocratic
throw-stick
throat-band
throat-lash
throttling
throatwort
throat-full
thiocyanic
chaptalise
chaptalize
whiptailed
chapfallen
chopfallen
chaplaincy
chaplainry
shipmaster
whippeting
shopkeeper
shopaholic
whippiness
ship-rigged
shop-lifter
shop-in-shop
ship-holder
rhapsodise
rhapsodize
rhapsodist
shopsoiled
Rhipiptera
shipwright
chaparajos
chaparejos
shipbroker
chopsticks
whip-stitch
cheque-book
choriambic
choriambus
thereanent
thermalise
Thermalite®
thermalize
pharmacist
thereamong
thereabout
whereabout

whirl-about
thereafter
whereafter
whirlblast
cherubical
shortbread
Charybdian
cherubimic
charabancs
char-à-bancs
shard-borne
third-class
Characidae
charactery
churn-drill
Charadrius
short-dated
charge-card
charge-hand
ahorseback
chargeable
chargeably
chargeless
sharp-edged
shortening
shereefian
thirteenth
Cherkesses
charleston
sheriffdom
chirograph
choregraph
shore-going
chirognomy
churchward
churchyard
church-rate
thornhedge
churchless
churchgoer
charthouse
whorehouse
chirpiness
shirtiness
thorniness
wharfinger
phorminges
charmingly
churlishly
thermionic
thermistor
Charollais
short-lived
chiromancy
cherimoyer
Charentais
pharyngeal
chironomic
chironomid
chironomer
Chironomus

Words marked △ may be spelled also with a capital letter

sharp-nosed
thyrsoidal
short-order
chersonese
charioteer
thermophil
lherzolite
thermopile
thermotics
chardonnay
thermoform
chordotomy
thermology
thermogram
thermostat
Chiroptera
third-party
Charophyta
shire-reeve
chirurgeon
chirurgery
sherardise
sherardize
short-range
△chartreuse
dharmshala
churn-staff
wheresoe'er
pharisaism
shortsword
short-track
charitable
charitably
charity-boy
thirstless
chartulary
thereunder
whereunder
thoroughly
whereuntil
Theravadin
sharawadgi
sharawaggi
shirtwaist
shorewards
whirlybird
Thirty-nine
thirtyfold
cherry-coal
chessboard
physicking
physically
chasse-café
chasteness
whispering
ghastfully
phosphoric
phosphorus
phosphoret
phosphuret
phosphatic

whiskified
Chassidism
chiselling
thysanuran
chasmogamy
physiology
physiocrat
ghost-write
chessylite
Shetlandic
Shetlander
shotmaking
chittagong
chittaroni
whitebeard
whity-brown
whatabouts
thetically
photodiode
shutterbug
chatterbox
chattering
chittering
shuttering
whitterick
white-faced
photoflood
photograph
photogenic
phytogenic
photoglyph
white-heart
thatchless
chattiness
shittiness
Phytolacca
châtelaine
photolysis
photolytic
rhythmical
rhythmless
photometer
photometry
photonasty
Ahithophel
whatsoever
photophily
photophobe
photophone
photophore
photophony
rhetorical
chitarrone
white-slave
whitesmith
phototrope
whitethorn
phototropy
phototypic
phytotoxic
phytotoxin

phototaxis
Whitsunday
khitmutgar
white-water
chatoyance
chatoyancy
thousandth
rheumatise
rheumatize
thaumasite
rheumatism
rheumatics
rheumatoid
△chautauqua
shouldered
Chaucerism
Chaucerian
chaudfroid
chauffeuse
theurgical
thoughtful
shoutingly
ghoulishly
chauvinism
chauvinist
chaulmugra
chaud-mellé
thruppence
thruppenny
chaussures
chauntress
shave-grass
shove-groat
Shivaistic
shovelhead
shovelling
shovelnose
chivalrous
shovelfuls
chevrotain
chevesaile
chevisance
whewellite
chewing-gum
showboater
showerless
showground
showjumper
thixotrope
thixotropy
chrysalids
chrysophan
chrysolite
chrysotile
phlyctaena
phlyctenae
rhizogenic
whizzingly
rhizomorph
rhizoplane
Rhizophora

rhizophore
dilatation
divagation
disavaunce
disanalogy
pit-a-patted
△sinarchism
mica-schist
sinarchist
didascalic
vizard-mask
vivandière
hit-and-miss
misandrist
ritardando
misandrous
△dinanderie
minauderie
dilacerate
disamenity
cicadellid
picaresque
Titanesque
ligamental
nidamental
nidamentum
sisal-grass
hidalgoish
hidalgoism
cibachrome
dilapidate
disanimate
divaricate
vitaminise
vitaminize
vitalising
vitalizing
miracidium
viraginian
vitalities
disability
livability
ridability
cigarillos
limaciform
viraginous
filariasis
vitalistic
tirailleur
misallying
pinacoidal
pinakoidal
pinakothek
dilatorily
limacology
bigamously
disappoint
disapprove
disapparel
△sinarquism
sinarquist

cicatricle
cicatrices
binaurally
disarrange
misarrange
bizarrerie
cicatrixes
didactical
disastrous
pilastered
bipartisan
picayunish
bimanually
miraculous
dika-butter
bivalvular
disadvance
misadvised
litany-desk
air-bladder
Zimbabwean
riebeckite
nimbleness
tie-breaker
misbehaved
limb-girdle
nibblingly
fimbriated
diabolical
disbelieve
misbelieve
big-bellied
ribbon-weed
ribbon-seal
disbenefit
ribbonfish
ribbon-worm
timbrology
timberland
timberyard
timber-mare
timber-head
limber-neck
disbarment
disburthen
Gilbertine
kimberlite
limburgite
timberline
Gilbertian
Gibberella
timber-toes
timber-tree
diabetical
kibbutznik
pin-buttock
air-brushed
discharger
wit-cracker
disclaimer
mischanter

Words marked △ may be spelled also with a capital letter

10 □i□c□b

pitch-black
discobolus
witchcraft
viscachera
piccadillo
piccadilly
discrepant
kitchendom
discretely
kitchen-fee
pitcherful
discretive
discretion
biochemist
miscreance
miscreancy
miscreated
miscreator
Winchester
Winchester®
discreetly
piscifauna
zincograph
piece-goods
hitch-hiker
witch-hazel
circuiteer
bitchiness
pitchiness
filchingly
pinchingly
witchingly
kinchin-lay
circuitous
disculpate
miscellany
circulable
piccalilli
zinc-blende
disc-floret
circularly
zincolysis
circulator
disc-flower
lincomycin
discommend
circumvent
circumcise
circumflex
circumpose
discommode
discompose
nincompoop
discomfort
mischmetal
viscometer
viscometry
circumduce
circumfuse
circummure
miscompute
circumduct
cincinnate
diaconicon
disconcert
disconnect
disconsent
discontent
misconceit
miscontent
miscanthus
circensial
circensian
Vincentian
piccaninny
misconster
misconduct
pince-nezed
cinchonine
cinchonise
cinchonize
air-cooling
tinctorial
cinchonism
zinc-worker
disclosure
discipline
discophile
pinchpoint
pinchpenny
Discophora
sincipital
discarnate
discordant
miscorrect
discordful
discursive
discerning
discursion
discursist
diachronic
discursory
discussive
die-casting
air-cushion
△circassian
discission
discussion
pin-cushion
pitchstone
discutient
discourage
dischuffed
discounsel
discoursal
miscounsel
discourser
diacaustic
diacoustic
discounter
pie-counter
viscountcy
discoverer
pitch-wheel
pitchwoman
ditch-water
winceyette
misdrawing
windfallen
windjammer
wildcatter
wildebeest
vindicable
windscreen
vindictive
bird-scarer
vindicator
fiddleback
fiddle-back
mind-bender
mind-reader
fiddlehead
misdeemful
middle-aged
riddle-like
misdeeming
kiddiewink
mind-healer
fiddlewood
middlemost
bird-pepper
middlebrow
mindlessly
dildo-glass
hirdy-girdy
windshield
wind-shaken
bird-cherry
kindliness
disdainful
riddlingly
bird-hipped
bird-witted
bird-skiing
Diadelphia
windflower
vindemiate
hiddenness
biodynamic
midden-cock
hiddenmost
wildfowler
giddy-paced
bird-spider
kind-spoken
mild-spoken
hinderland
hinderlans
wilderness
rinderpest
wilderment
tinder-like
nidderling
hinderlins
wind-broken
Cinderella
hinderance
hindermost
Hindustani
Yiddishism
pied-à-terre
windsurfer
yird-hunger
yird-hungry
wind-sucker
windowpane
windowless
window-shop
windowsill
window-bole
tiddlywink
wire-dancer
sidesaddle
fire-warden
Piperaceae
vinegar-eel
vinegar-fly
liberalise
liberalize
literalise
literalize
mineralise
mineralize
piperazine
life-saving
pipe-laying
time-saving
vinegarish
bipedalism
cinerarium
liberalism
literalism
cineration
liberation
literation
sideration
kinematics
liberalist
literalist
mineralist
liberality
literality
literarily
kite-marked
fire-walker
linebacker
wire-walker
fire-basket
life-jacket
bimetallic
cinema-goer
bipetalous
dipetalous
disepalous
liberatory
mineralogy
dive-dapper
pine-carpet
time-barred
wire-haired
pine-barren
fire-raiser
five-parted
mile-castle
fire-master
tide-waiter
wine-taster
literature
fiberboard
disembogue
disembroil
disembosom
disembowel
disenchain
disenchant
rivercraft
firescreen
widescreen
libecchios
virescence
disenclose
five-o'clock
Oireachtas
river-drift
disendowed
aide-de-camp
life-tenant
file-leader
vicegerent
viceregent
nineteenth
pike-keeper
timekeeper
lifelessly
timelessly
tirelessly
pine-beetle
life-renter
pine-beauty
time-served
time-server
wizen-faced
fire-office
riverfront
mimeograph
fiberglass
disengaged
divergence
divergency
liver-grown
pine-chafer
river-horse
time-sharer
time-thrust
fire-shovel

Words marked △ may be spelled also with a capital letter

kinesipath
wine-bibber
like-minded
sidewinder
vine-mildew
livelihead
likeliness
liveliness
timeliness
wifeliness
fivefinger
five-finger
five-eighth
line-fisher
tigerishly
cimetidine
piperidine
life-giving
pipelining
time-killer
likelihood
livelihood
misericord
viperiform
vitellicle
fire-blight
kite-flying
fire-plough
dice-player
mixed-media
dilemmatic
mileometer
river-mouth
pigeon-pair
disennoble
hibernacle
Vireonidae
pigeon-wing
pigeon-toed
pigeonhole
pigeon-post
ride-and-tie
dive-bomber
tiresomely
wide-bodied
siderolite
Ciceronian
fire-policy
literosity
mine-worker
wireworker
life-rocket
wine-cooler
vice-county
bioecology
diseconomy
dike-louper
sideboards
vice-consul
viperously
life-mortar

siderostat
widespread
cider-press
didelphine
fixed-price
didelphian
diremption
fine-spoken
pipe-opener
videophone
didelphous
disespouse
five-square
line-squall
Viverridae
pileorhiza
△viverrinae
pipe-wrench
vine-branch
pile-driver
wine-grower
wiredrawer
disenslave
life-estate
riverscape
licensable
diseaseful
widershins
fiberscope
licentiate
disentrail
disentrain
silentiary
digestible
divertible
divestible
digestedly
sidestream
directness
directress
silentness
divestment
misentreat
sidestreet
Directoire
disentwine
bimestrial
liberty-man
dilettante
dilettanti
five-stones
minestrone
sidestroke
licentious
disenthral
bidentated
disentitle
Nibelungen
fine-tuning
sinecurism
sinecurist

wire-puller
bisexually
lime-burner
file-cutter
mine-hunter
eigenvalue
disenvelop
disenviron
fixed-wheel
sideswiper
liverwurst
river-water
pin-feather
disfeature
misfeature
difficulty
diffidence
midfielder
fitfulness
sinfulness
wilfulness
niffy-naffy
disfurnish
difformity
difference
differency
misfortune
diffusible
diffusedly
disfluency
Singhalese
biographic
diagraphic
biographee
biographer
air-grating
wing-walker
ring-tailed
ringmaster
hinge-bound
king's-chair
siegecraft
ringleader
singleness
minglement
ring-necked
singlehood
gigglesome
single-foot
singletree
single-step
single-eyed
king-of-arms
pilgrimage
kingliness
ring-finger
minglingly
nigglingly
kingfisher
pilgrimise
pilgrimize

disguising
pinguidity
ginglimoid
kinglihood
linguiform
jingoistic
linguistic
linguister
linguistry
Pinguicula
pinguitude
hinge-joint
Ringelmann
Lingulella
singularly
diagometer
diagonally
virginally
singing-man
virginhood
virgin-born
biogenesis
diagenesis
biogenetic
diagenetic
disglorify
ring-porous
diagnostic
wing-footed
wingspread
ridge-piece
fingermark
fingernail
digger-wasp
jigger-mast
didgeridoo
finger's-end
niggerhead
fingerless
king-archon
niggardise
niggardize
fingerling
niggerling
disgarnish
pilgarlick
gingersnap
fingerhold
fingerhole
fingerbowl
fingerpost
king's-spear
disgustful
disgusting
disgestion
jiggety-jog
witgatboom
king-at-arms
disgruntle
gingivitis
siegeworks

bilge-water
high-handed
fish-ladder
△highlander
dishwasher
Lithuanian
highjacker
high-ranker
light-armed
highwayman
fish-farmer
Mishnayoth
high-raised
big-hearted
high-tasted
dishearten
fish-manure
high-vacuum
fish-carver
night-blind
dishabille
high-octane
pichiciago
night-chair
nightclass
lithoclast
night-cloud
night-churr
right-drawn
nightdress
Lithodomus
lighterage
lightening
high-necked
high-heeled
lighterman
Michaelmas
eighteenth
eighteenmo
high-reared
fish-kettle
light-faced
rightfully
lithograph
night-glass
hip-huggers
lithoglyph
diphtheria
diphtheric
night-heron
lighthouse
night-house
mithridate
high-minded
highbinder
mightiness
lighting-up
fish-finger
highlights
tightishly
ditheistic

Words marked △ may be spelled also with a capital letter

10 □i□h□i

high-kilted
high-placed
tight-laced
tight-lacer
lithologic
night-light
Wilhelmine
high-flying
right-lined
sightlines
diphyletic
△ditheletic
night-latch
litholatry
lithomancy
lithomarge
wishing-cap
siphonogam
night-night
tithingman
fishing-rod
dishonorer
high-energy
dishonesty
bichromate
dichromate
dithionate
withholden
withholder
light-organ
fishmonger
dichromism
high-souled
high-roller
light-o'-love
diphyodont
dichroitic
dichlorvos
right-of-way
lithophane
bishopweed
nightpiece
xiphopagic
xiphopagus
bishop-bird
lithoprint
night-palsy
eightpence
eightpenny
light-proof
lithophysa
lithophyse
lithophyte
hitherward
high-priced
nightrider
hitherside
highermost
hithermost
disharmony
disherison
disheritor
night-raven
fish-trowel
withdrawal
withdrawer
nightstand
nightshade
night-steed
night-spell
air-hostess
night-sight
Lithistida
nightstick
nightshirt
eightscore
night-stool
vichyssois
xiphosuran
light-table
high-street
light-tight
lithotrite
lithotrity
dichotomic
lithotomic
night-taper
high-strung
light-tower
mishguggle
fishburger
silhouette
fish-gutter
rightwards
wishy-washy
night-watch
digitately
digitalise
digitalize
disimagine
limitative
militarise
militarize
mitigative
similative
visitative
militarism
minimalism
viviparism
digitation
divination
limitarian
limitation
litigation
mitigation
pixilation
sibilation
tidivation
titivation
△visitation
militarist
minimalist
finicality
militarily
similarity
viviparity
viviparous
divinatory
mitigatory
sibilatory
militantly
sibilantly
vigilantly
cicisbeism
disincline
disinclose
liliaceous
tiliaceous
biliverdin
citizeness
divineness
divineress
finiteness
citizenise
citizenize
miniseries
piliferous
vitiferous
pitilessly
vivisector
diligently
dining-hall
diving-bell
riding-whip
bilinguist
visiogenic
riding-hood
riding-robe
dining-room
living-room
tiring-room
riding-boot
riding-coat
riding-crop
firing-step
diving-suit
riding-suit
disinhibit
disinherit
nidificate
Filicineae
filicinean
divisively
diminished
rigidified
silicified
minimising
minimizing
virilising
virilizing
civilities
libidinist
risibility
visibility
militiaman
sicilienne
divisional
sicilianos
digitiform
libidinous
nihilistic
similitude
simillimum
bimillenia
mini-floppy
Sigillaria
sigillarid
pixillated
titillator
visionless
visionally
bipinnaria
ricinoleic
Visigothic
ripidolite
visitorial
digitorium
minivolley
fimicolous
limicolous
nidicolous
viticolous
Ciliophora
disimprove
misimprove
visiophone
viziership
limitrophe
ministrant
ministress
sinistrous
ministeria
tibiotarsi
disinthral
sinisterly
mini-buffet
minibudget
mini-budget
diminutive
diminution
diminuendo
siliculose
nidifugous
ridiculous
filibuster
disinvolve
midi-system
Lipizzaner
disjection
misjoinder
disjoining
disjointed
disjunctor
sinke-a-pace
sick-making
nick-nacket
sick-fallen
rick-barton
silkscreen
pickedness
wickedness
sickle-cell
fickleness
sicklebill
pick-cheese
sickliness
tinklingly
ticklishly
dickcissel
sick-listed
rick-lifter
nickelling
nickumpoop
Dickensian
pickaninny
ticking-off
link-motion
pick-pocket
Ginkgoales
kicksorter
ticker-tape
sickerness
wickerwork
silkgrower
tickety-boo
picket-line
rickettsia
picket-duty
rickburner
gillravage
Williamite
misleading
hillwalker
diallagoid
villiagoes
silly-billy
fieldboots
millocracy
dialectics
biblically
violaceous
dielectric
rifle-corps
digladiate
diplodocus
dilly-dally
will-lessly
tilly-fally
millefiori
biological
rifle-green
sialagogic
sialogogic
sialagogue
sialogogue

Words marked △ may be spelled also with a capital letter

villagioes
villainage
villeinage
villainess
wieldiness
hill-digger
yieldingly
villainous
dislikable
dislikeful
millilitre
diplomatic
millimetre
fieldmouse
millennial
millennium
villanelle
willy-nilly
tirling-pin
tillandsia
Villanovan
bibliomane
millionary
bibliopegy
bibliophil
pillionist
bibliopole
bibliology
bibliopoly
pill-popper
billposter
fieldpiece
girlfriend
tillerless
millwright
pillorying
bill-broker
tiller-rope
pillar-root
dialysable
millesimal
fieldstone
billet-head
millet-seed
mill-stream
billet-doux
gimlet-eyed
tilly-vally
pillow-lava
pillowcase
pillow-lace
willowherb
pillow-bere
pillow-beer
pillowslip
willy-willy
pilliwinks
fieldwards
fieldworks
disloyally
disloyalty
dialyzable
mismeasure
biomedical
dismalness
cismontane
pigmentary
Piemontese
mismanners
Simmenthal
airmanship
diamantine
Riemannian
dismantler
bit-mapping
biomorphic
air-marshal
mid-morning
Kilmarnock
dismissive
dismission
dismissory
biometrics
bigmouthed
sign-manual
cinnabaric
lignocaine
picnicking
Limnaeidae
bienséance
dignifying
lignifying
signifying
pianoforte
midnightly
fianchetti
fianchetto
fiendishly
biennially
simnel-cake
signalling
pinnulated
cinnamonic
mignonette
piano-organ
kirn-dollie
Pinnipedia
kidnapping
dinner-pail
dinnerless
dinner-time
dinner-gown
sign-writer
pianissimo
piano-stool
pinnatifid
vignettist
pinnatiped
disnatured
biannually
Finno-Ugric
lion-hunter
kidney-bean
Disneyfied
Hitopadesa
Mimosaceae
bilocation
misogamist
bimodality
bipolarity
bitonality
bivouacked
misocapnic
lipomatous
pilocarpin
Pilocarpus
Dinosauria
dinosauric
tibouchina
disordered
disorderly
picosecond
digoneutic
pirouetter
air-officer
disorganic
sitophobia
lipochrome
ricocheted
pilot-house
simoniacal
nicotinism
tirocinium
cipollinos
riboflavin
disownment
ritornelle
ritornelli
ritornello
filopodium
kidologist
misologist
Sinologist
vinologist
virologist
rigorously
timorously
vigorously
pilot-plant
dimorphism
dimorphous
kilogramme
lipography
mimography
timocratic
misobserve
birostrate
bijouterie
vicomtesse
binoculars
zidovudine
bidonville
pilot-whale
△mixolydian
misogynist
misogynous
bioplasmic
diaphanous
hippiatric
dispraiser
Hippocrene
nit-picking
hippocampi
limpidness
hippodrome
diapedesis
diapedetic
ripple-mark
dispredden
simpleness
dimplement
displenish
nipplewort
displeased
hippogriff
hippogryph
disprinced
ripplingly
simplified
misprision
simplifier
simplicity
biopoiesis
simplistic
jippi-jappa
dispelling
hippomanes
dispondaic
dispensary
cispontine
Pimpinella
ripping-saw
disprofess
disprovide
displosion
hippophagy
hippophile
hippophobe
dispersant
dioptrical
disparager
dispersive
dispersion
dispersoid
dispermous
hippuritic
dispirited
disparates
air-passage
disposable
disposedly
dispossess
dispassion
dispositor
disputable
disputably
hippety-hop
dispatcher
dispatches
dispiteous
Piepowders
△diophysite
biophysics
Lippizzana
Lippizaner
disqualify
cinquepace
cinquefoil
disquieten
disquietly
lip-reading
misreading
rip-roaring
diurnalist
rib-roaster
fibreboard
fibroblast
microbiota
microburst
microcrack
hierocracy
micrococci
ditrochean
microcline
vibraculum
jinricksha
aigre-douce
pierceable
fierceness
bierkeller
microfiche
nitrifying
microflora
microfarad
microfauna
cirrigrade
hierograph
micrograph
vibrograph
fibreglass
nitro-group
ditriglyph
hieroglyph
diarrhoeic
diarrhoeal
diorthosis
diorthotic
cirrhipede
migraineur
piercingly
vitrailled
migrainous
giardiasis
mitre-joint
jinrikisha

Words marked △ may be spelled also with a capital letter

10 □i□r□l

fibrillate
fibrillary
hierologic
micrologic
microlight
citrulline
fibrillose
fibrillous
tirra-lirra
miarolitic
microlitic
hierolatry
hieromancy
nigromancy
micrometre
micrometer
nitrometer
vibrometer
micrometry
fibrinogen
Dibranchia
citronella
Hieronymic
vitriolate
vitriolise
vitriolize
vitreosity
Cirrhopoda
hierophant
hiera-picra
Cirripedia
higry-pigry
disruptive
microprism
△disruption
microprint
micropylar
micropolis
microphone
microprobe
vibraphone
microphyte
hierarchic
hierarchal
mirrorwise
microscale
mitre-shell
disrespect
nigrescent
vitrescent
digressive
microseism
digression
microskirt
nicrosilal
microsomal
fibrescope
microscope
microspore
hieroscopy
microscopy
fibrositis
diprotodon
librettist
microtomic
microtonal
vibrations
picrotoxin
gilravager
gilravitch
mitre-wheel
biorhythms
nitrazepam
first-aider
dissuasive
piss-taking
dissuasion
miasmatous
dissuasory
wit-snapper
diastaltic
dissociate
first-class
dissective
dissecting
dissection
dissidence
diastemata
diaskeuast
misseeming
misspelled
linseed-oil
dissheathe
first-floor
first-fruit
biospheric
pig-sticker
midshipman
bioscience
dissoluble
dissilient
dissolvent
missel-bird
dissolving
tinselling
disselboom
Tinseltown
missel-tree
kieselguhr
lissomness
sinsemilla
dissembler
dissimilar
dipsomania
jimson-weed
die-sinking
dissenting
dissension
dissonance
dissonancy
missionary
missionise
missionize
ripsnorter
six-shooter
dissipable
dissipated
dissertate
disservice
lip-service
minstrelsy
pin-striped
rijsttafel
dissatisfy
dissevered
bissextile
Vietnamese
air-traffic
distraught
dirt-eating
virtualism
filtration
virtualist
virtuality
victualled
victualler
tilt-hammer
mistrayned
distrainee
distrainer
distrainor
distracted
mint-master
ritt-master
histoblast
fisticuffs
pistachios
rib-tickler
biotically
cistaceous
distichous
giftedness
△eisteddfod
pittie-ward
little-ease
△diothelete
littleness
virtueless
△diothelism
kittle-pins
diathermic
diathermal
sixteenmos
distressed
distresser
listlessly
mistressly
fifty-fifty
mirthfully
Dictograph®
pictograph
histogenic
filthiness
wintriness
distringas
diatribist
histrionic
distribute
mistakable
mistakenly
distilland
distillate
pistillate
pistillary
distilment
distillery
histologic
pistol-whip
distilling
pistolling
pistillode
histolysis
histolytic
mist-flower
victimless
victimiser
hitty-missy
Tintometer®
mixty-maxty
victimizer
listenable
birthnight
distensile
distensive
distension
distention
kitten-moth
fitting-out
mitten-crab
listener-in
distinctly
distinguée
dictionary
distrouble
misthought
diatropism
fictionist
virtuosity
histiology
virtuously
dirt-rotten
histiocyte
birthplace
tittupping
fifty-pence
fifty-penny
Dictaphone®
△victoriana
hinterland
littermate
disturbant
filterable
historical
pictorical
bitterness
sisterless
birthright
picture-hat
distortive
sisterlike
wintertide
wintertime
bitter-king
bitterling
disturbing
winterkill
Cistercian
distortion
diuturnity
winter-clad
bitterwood
sisterhood
victorious
bitter-root
litter-lout
bitter-spar
picture-rod
birthstone
dietetical
uintathere
dictatress
fictitious
distruster
mistrysted
figurative
simulative
figuration
nidulation
simulation
titubation
titularity
simulatory
simulacrum
sipunculid
minuscular
Didunculus
bifurcated
liquidness
liquidiser
liquidator
liquidizer
minute-hand
vituperate
minute-jack
lieutenant
figurehead
minute-bell
diluteness
minuteness
figurework
minute-book
minute-drop
virulently
liquefying
disulfiram

Words marked △ may be spelled also with a capital letter

liturgical
divulgence
bituminate
dijudicate
dilucidate
Simuliidae
hirudinean
bituminise
bituminize
disutility
fiducially
hirudinoid
bituminous
hirudinous
visualiser
visualizer
biquintile
sinusoidal
bibulously
bisulphate
disulphate
bisulphide
disulphide
liquescent
bicultural
pit-village
misventure
silver-bath
silverback
silvertail
silverweed
silverside
silverling
silverfish
silverbill
silver-gilt
silverskin
view-halloo
viewlessly
viewfinder
tim-whiskey
miswandred
disworship
misworship
viewership
miswording
Midwestern
nitwittery
didynamian
didynamous
vinylidene
pityriasis
disyllabic
disyllable
dicynodont
Himyaritic
pizzicatos
zigzaggery
zigzagging
dizzyingly
sizzlingly

piezometer
mizzen-sail
mizzen-mast
fizzenless
diazeuctic
skibobbing
skedaddler
skaithless
skrimshank
skyjacking
ski-jumping
sky-jumping
skikjöring
skillfully
skulkingly
skylarking
akolouthos
skelly-eyed
skimmingly
skimpingly
skinniness
skin-tights
skin-diving
skene-occle
skippering
skip-kennel
Skupshtina
skippingly
skepticism
skirmisher
ekistician
sky-surfing
skyscraper
skateboard
sketchable
sketchbook
skittishly
ski-touring
skeuomorph
sky-writing
skew-corbel
cloacaline
floatation
almacantar
pleasantly
pleasantry
float-board
altar-cloth
alcaicería
illaudable
illaudably
sleazeball
albarellos
flea-beetle
allargando
bleariness
sleaziness
illatively
floatingly
gloatingly
pleadingly

pleasingly
alkalinise
alkalinize
alkalinity
pliability
oleaginous
flea-bitten
altazimuth
altarpiece
algarrobos
altar-rails
cleansable
altar-stone
float-stone
clearstory
olfactible
pliantness
illaqueate
ill-advised
bleary-eyed
alablaster
clubmaster
club-headed
slubbering
glebe-house
ill-behaved
flabbiness
slabbiness
klebsiella
flabellate
globularly
fly-by-night
alabandine
alabandite
club-footed
elaborator
plebiscite
glaciation
glacialist
blackamoor
blackboard
blockboard
black-bully
blackberry
click-clack
block-chain
placidness
elucidator
slackening
blackfaced
blackguard
glycogenic
blackheart
blockhouse
pluckiness
electively
electivity
flaccidity
flick-knife
glycolysis
glycolytic

elecampane
clockmaker
electorate
electoress
electorial
Clactonian
glaciology
Plecoptera
flock-paper
electrical
clock-radio
electrogen
electromer
electronic
placer-gold
glycosidic
blacksmith
Blackshirt
slickstone
glucosuria
glycosuria
glucosuric
glycosuric
flycatcher
blackthorn
flocculate
flocculent
blackwater
glad-hander
gladiatory
pledgeable
all-dreaded
fledgeling
bladder-nut
ill-defined
ploddingly
fly-dumping
gladsomely
clodhopper
Clydesdale
Clydesider
cladistics
gleemaiden
Alcelaphus
alterative
illegalise
illegalize
ulcerative
alienation
allegation
alteration
ulceration
illegality
bluejacket
elderberry
albescence
sleevehand
blue-pencil
fleeceless
sleeveless
allegeance

fleece-wool
Illecebrum
bluey-green
allergenic
blue-cheese
fleechment
bluethroat
sleepiness
sleetiness
fleeringly
fleetingly
allegiance
ulteriorly
blue-rinsed
alleviator
alveolitis
aldermanic
aldermanly
aldermanry
alternance
alternatim
alternator
blue-tongue
allegorise
allegorize
allegorist
blue-rocket
olde-worlde
blue-collar
blue-bonnet
ulcerously
bluebottle
bluebreast
algebraist
allegretto
sleekstone
alpenstock
fluentness
clientship
sleepy-head
fly-flapper
clofibrate
old-fogyish
fluffiness
fly-fronted
all-firedly
fly-fishing
ill-founded
plagiarise
plagiarize
flag-waving
plagiarism
plagiarist
flag-basket
flagrantly
oligoclase
plaguesome
plague-sore
plague-spot
clogginess
flagginess

10 □l□g□i

sluggishly
Flagellata
flagellate
flagellant
flugelhorn
flügelhorn
Glagolitic
oligopsony
oligarchic
oligarchal
flight-deck
flightless
slightness
flagitious
alphabetic
Alzheimer's
allhallond
allhallown
allhollown
All-Hallows
alchemical
alphameric
alphametic
Alphonsine
alcheringa
ultimately
alligation
plainchant
claircolle
alliaceous
alliterate
illiterate
sluicegate
illiteracy
oleiferous
Albigenses
albinistic
eloignment
altisonant
altitonant
elliptical
cloistress
plaintless
cloistered
cloisterer
flake-white
ill-looking
clamjamfry
glumaceous
slumberful
glimmering
slumbering
slammerkin
slumberous
blamefully
plume-grass
flame-grill
clamminess
clumpiness
clumsiness
flimsiness

old-maidish
old-maidism
Plumularia
Flamingant
alimentary
elementary
eliminable
flaminical
△clementine
flamingoes
eliminator
flamboyant
plum-colour
clomiphene
glomerular
glomerulus
plumassier
climatical
ill-matched
alang-alang
alineation
elongation
plantation
blind-alley
planoblast
clinically
blind-drunk
blonde-lace
plunderage
flunkeydom
slenderise
slenderize
blanketing
blundering
flunkeyish
flunkeyism
flannelled
glance-coal
glanderous
plunderous
slanderous
flindersia
plangently
klangfarbe
planigraph
allnighter
flint-heart
planchette
plant-house
ilang-ilang
clinginess
flintiness
slanginess
glancingly
slangingly
slantingly
clannishly
glandiform
plentitude
plenilunar
plant-louse

blancmange
clinometer
planimeter
planometer
clinometry
planimetry
flanconade
glendoveer
clangorous
plenishing
alongshore
clingstone
clinkstone
slingstone
plane-table
planetical
planktonic
planetaria
ill-natured
klendusity
glandulous
blanquette
slang-whang
clanswoman
ylang-ylang
clonazepam
allowances
allopathic
glyoxaline
allocation
algolagnia
allogamous
gliomatous
allopatric
Allosaurus
pleonastic
floorboard
elbow-chair
klootchman
floorcloth
almond-tree
almond-eyed
altogether
all-obeying
all-overish
aldohexose
allometric
pleonectic
blood-guilt
blood-group
algophobia
allotheism
oleophilic
allophonic
pleochroic
allochiria
blood-horse
bloodhound
fluoridate
fluorinate
bloodiness

gloominess
fluoridise
fluoridize
Pliohippus
floodlight
blood-money
alcoholise
alcoholize
alcoholism
algologist
pleomorphy
sloop-of-war
fluorotype
blood-plate
flood-plain
Algonquian
allotropic
oleography
blood-royal
bloodstain
bloodstone
bloodstock
Bloomsbury
blood-sized
altostrati
allosteric
allocution
illocution
altocumuli
blood-wagon
floodwater
allonymous
bloody-eyed
all-play-all
blepharism
flippantly
clapperboy
clappering
flapperish
slipperily
slop-seller
clapped-out
floppiness
slippiness
sloppiness
clypeiform
slipsloppy
clapometer
flapdoodle
glyptodont
pluperfect
flap-dragon
all-purpose
flyposting
slipstream
flypitcher
slip-string
slop-bucket
eloquently
cliquiness
flirtation

clarabella
floribunda
ultrabasic
clarichord
alarm-clock
oleraceous
floridness
florideous
ultrafiche
clarifying
glorifying
clergiable
alarmingly
flirtingly
altruistic
florilegia
pleromatic
Clarenceux
△florentine
ultroneous
gloriously
plerophory
alarm-radio
ultra-rapid
florescent
floristics
ultrasonic
ultrashort
clerestory
ultrasound
all-rounder
clergyable
glissandos
Alismaceae
glossarial
glossarist
ill-starred
flash-board
flesh-broth
flesh-brush
clish-clash
glass-coach
glass-cloth
closed-door
cluster-cup
blister-fly
blistering
blustering
clustering
glistering
plastering
Glaswegian
blusterous
flesh-eater
glass-faced
blissfully
blasphemer
flash-house
glasshouse
elasticate
classiness

Words marked △ may be spelled also with a capital letter

flashiness
fleshiness
glassiness
glossiness
blushingly
plastilina
classified
classicise
classicize
elasticise
elasticize
Plasticine®
plasticise
plasticize
classicism
classifier
classicist
elasticity
plasticity
plastidule
flashlight
plesiosaur
clistogamy
plasmogamy
plastogamy
Blastoidea
blastomere
blastoderm
plasmodesm
blossoming
plasmodial
plasmodium
plasmosoma
blastopore
plasmosome
blastocoel
glossology
glasnostic
plasmolyse
plasmolyze
blastocyst
flash-point
clostridia
close-stool
flosculous
glassworks
plutocracy
elatedness
glitterand
platteland
glitterati
blitheness
blethering
blithering
flattering
glittering
slatternly
blithesome
flatterous
clothes-peg
clothes-pin
blottesque
cloth-eared
plate-fleet
slothfully
plate-glass
glottidean
clottiness
glitziness
plottingly
sluttishly
elytriform
elutriator
blitzkrieg
all-telling
flatulence
flatulency
plutolatry
plate-layer
glutaminic
flutemouth
Platonical
gluttonise
gluttonize
gluttonish
gluttonous
glottology
flat-footed
fly-tipping
plate-proof
platypuses
ulsterette
almucantar
cloud-built
cloudburst
cloudberry
flaunching
fleur-de-lis
fleur-de-lys
allurement
albumenise
albumenize
glauberite
ploughland
ploughgate
plough-tail
ploughman's
ploughable
plough-team
slaughtery
ploughwise
plough-tree
plough-iron
albuminate
illuminate
△illuminati
illuminant
cloudiness
allusively
illusively
alluringly
floutingly
flourished
albuminise
albuminize
illuminism
Eleusinian
illuminist
albuminoid
albuminous
plauditory
glauconite
pleurodont
pleurotomy
cloudscape
illustrate
fluviatile
fluvialist
slavocracy
clavicular
clavichord
olivaceous
glove-fight
clove-hitch
glove-money
eleventhly
slovenlike
eleven-plus
Slavophile
Slavophobe
cloverleaf
cleverness
flavorless
flavorsome
olive-shell
flavescent
flavouring
all-weather
clew-garnet
slow-gaited
clownishly
slow-moving
slow-motion
slow-footed
flower-head
flower-bell
flowerless
flower-show
flower-girl
blow-by-blow
flexi-cover
△plexiglass
flexihours
pleximeter
pleximetry
alexanders
fluxionary
fluxionist
claymation
play-acting
playschool
playleader
playfellow
allycholly
Alcyonaria
playwright
play-writer
playground
blizzardly
emparadise
imparadise
immanation
impanation
embasement
empalement
impalement
immaterial
empanelled
immanental
embargoing
empathetic
smeariness
ommatidium
amiability
impatience
ambagitory
embankment
embarkment
imparlance
embalmment
impalpable
impalpably
impairment
impassable
impassible
impassably
impassibly
ambassador
embassador
impartable
impartible
impartibly
impartment
△immaculate
immaculacy
immaturely
impaludism
immaturity
Ambarvalia
emaciation
smickering
smock-faced
smock-frock
amido-group
smudginess
imperative
impeccable
impeccably
impeccancy
impendence
impendency
ember-goose
impediment
impenitent
impeditive
imbecility
imperilled
imperially
amoebiform
immeritous
amoebiasis
umbellifer
umbellated
immemorial
emmenology
ampelopses
ampelopsis
emmetropia
emmetropic
impersonal
immeasured
Emmentaler
impervious
smifligate
Empfindung
emigration
amygdaloid
emigratory
imaginable
imaginably
imaginings
emphractic
amphibrach
amphibolic
amphibious
amphictyon
amphimacer
amphimixis
Amphineura
amphiscian
emphysemic
emphatical
amphoteric
Amphitryon
ambivalent
omniparity
omniparous
amritattva
immiscible
omniscient
umpireship
immiserise
immiserize
omniferous
omnigenous
ambidexter
imminently
ambisexual
impishness
umbilicate
empiricism
imbibition
empiricist
Ampicillin®
omnipotent

10 □m□i□o

Ambisonics®
ambisonics
omnivorous
embittered
impictured
embitterer
imminution
smokeboard
smoke-black
smoke-dried
smokehouse
smokeproof
smokestack
smoketight
amalgamate
ampliative
ampliation
implacable
implacably
amylaceous
implicitly
smell-feast
amplifying
smalminess
smelliness
emollition
emulsifier
emblements
emoluments
emblematic
emalangeni
ameliorate
Amblyopsis
small-pipes
implorator
Amblystoma
emplastrum
emplastron
emulatress
small-tooth
implexuous
employable
employment
emblazoner
emblazonry
emendation
amendatory
emendatory
amanuenses
amanuensis
amino-group
emancipate
emancipist
eminential
amenorrhea
immoralism
immolation
umbonation
immoralist
immorality
immovables

embouchure
emboldener
immoderate
immoderacy
immoveable
empoverish
impoverish
embowelled
amboceptor
immodestly
impotently
smoothpate
smoothness
smooth-shod
smooth-bore
ammoniacal
ammoniacum
embodiment
impolitely
imposingly
immobilise
immobilize
immobilism
imposition
immobility
embolismic
embolismal
ammoniated
impoundage
embonpoint
amyotrophy
impossible
embossment
empoisoned
importable
immortelle
immortally
impostumed
importance
importuner
importancy
imposthume
imipramine
omophagous
omophorion
emery-board
improbable
improbably
imbroccata
umbraculum
emery-cloth
imprudence
amerceable
amercement
embruement
imbruement
smørrebrød
emergently
impregnate
impregnant
smaragdine

smaragdite
embroglios
imbroglios
umbrageous
emarginate
amerciable
smarminess
embroidery
smirkingly
umbrellaed
emerald-cut
umbrelloes
imprimatur
ombrometer
Amaranthus
amarantine
imprinting
Amerindian
embryonate
embryogeny
embryology
embryotomy
ombrophile
ombrophobe
emery-paper
improperly
impressive
impression
impresario
impressure
umbratical
embryulcia
improvable
improvably
improviser
emery-wheel
embrowning
Emi-Scanner®
emissivity
emasculate
ametabolic
smithcraft
emetically
smithereen
smother-fly
smattering
smothering
smuttiness
amatorious
amateurish
amateurism
imputative
ambulation
amputation
impugation
imputation
ambulatory
ambulacral
ambulacrum
ambuscados
impureness

immurement
impudently
ambushment
ammunition
impudicity
impugnable
impugnment
immunoblot
immunology
ampussy-and
impuissant
amazedness
Amazon-like
Angaraland
unbalanced
unhazarded
Incaparina
unsalaried
indagative
indapamide
unparadise
indagation
inhalation
incapacity
unmanacled
unparallel
indagatory
enjambment
unbarbered
unwatchful
infarction
unsanctify
uncandidly
inwardness
unhardened
unpardoned
unmaidenly
unhandsome
incandesce
unnameable
unsaleable
untameable
untameably
innateness
insaneness
unsafeness
unwareness
encasement
enfacement
engagement
enlacement
enragement
incasement
uncared-for
unwavering
unmaterial
unlabelled
unpanelled
unravelled
unraveller
unmaternal

unlamented
unparented
unpatented
untalented
unparental
unlawfully
unmanfully
intangible
untangible
intangibly
enlargedly
ensanguine
endangerer
encashment
unfathomed
unfathered
ungathered
unfatherly
unpathetic
insalivate
invaginate
invalidate
inhabitant
insanitary
unsanitary
insatiable
invariable
unsatiable
unvariable
insatiably
invariably
sneakiness
uneasiness
unwariness
engagingly
sneakingly
unfadingly
unravished
sneakishly
unpacified
unratified
invaliding
invalidism
unfamiliar
invalidity
uniaxially
invariance
annalistic
unsatiated
untalked-of
infallible
unbailable
unfallible
unmailable
infallibly
entailment
unhallowed
anharmonic
enharmonic
inharmonic
ungainsaid

untainting
ungarnered
unmannered
unmannerly
endamoebae
entamoebae
antagonise
antagonize
infamonise
infamonize
uncanonise
uncanonize
antagonism
antagonist
unlaboured
infamously
encampment
unhampered
unpampered
uncarpeted
inmarriage
unfairness
engarrison
unpassable
unransomed
intactness
unfaithful
untasteful
sneak-thief
unfastened
andantinos
infanthood
incautious
enraptured
unbattered
ungartered
unmastered
unpastured
unpastoral
unbaptised
incantator
unbaptized
insalutary
invaluable
unvaluable
invaluably
andalusite
Andalusian
infatuated
unladylike
unobtained
snobocracy
unobscured
inobedient
unobedient
knobkerrie
unobserved
knobbiness
unabridged
snubbingly
snobbishly
anabolitic
unabsolved
anabaptise
anabaptize
anabaptism
△anabaptist
unscramble
snick-a-snee
knockabout
anaclastic
Anschauung
unscabbard
unacademic
unscreened
anucleated
unaccented
enschedule
inactivate
knackiness
inactively
inactivity
uneclipsed
unscripted
knick-knack
knock-kneed
inoculable
unscalable
knuckle-bow
anacolutha
inoculator
unicameral
onocentaur
uneconomic
unicentral
anecdotage
anecdotist
unschooled
knickpoint
unsceptred
unscorched
anacardium
anachronic
unicostate
inaccurate
inaccuracy
unoccupied
unacquaint
unscrupled
anacoustic
anacrustic
unactuated
knackwurst
knockwurst
unidealism
cnidoblast
ineducable
uneducable
uneducated
unedifying
unadmiring
unadmitted
anadyomene
anadromous
inadaptive
inadequate
inadequacy
unadjusted
inseparate
unheralded
unregarded
unretarded
unrewarded
underagent
unrelative
undelaying
anhelation
annexation
indexation
inveracity
unveracity
unremarked
unbewailed
unmetalled
unrecalled
undebarred
unrepaired
untenanted
underactor
under-board
interbrain
interbreed
underbuild
underbelly
inselberge
underborne
underburnt
underbough
underbrush
interchain
underclass
under-craft
interceder
under-clerk
undercrest
unmerciful
unpeaceful
undescried
unreactive
undercliff
intercalar
unwelcomed
intercross
undercroft
interclude
undercover
enterdeale
underdrain
incendiary
invendible
unbendable
unreadable
unvendible
intendedly
unheededly
underdress
intendment
underdrive
intendance
intendancy
unrendered
untendered
engenderer
untenderly
engendrure
ingenerate
intemerate
intenerate
inveterate
inveteracy
undefended
sneezeweed
unreverend
antecedent
enlevement
enlèvement
unreverent
unrevenged
knee-length
unremedied
unrepealed
unrepelled
unrevealed
ante-bellum
unredeemed
sneezewood
ungenerous
sneezewort
undeterred
underearth
uncerebral
unreversed
antecessor
interested
undefeated
undetected
unrepeated
unrepented
unresented
unreverted
unrelentor
indecently
inherently
antepenult
undeceived
undeserved
unreceived
unreserved
undeserver
interfaith
unperfumed
underfloor
interferon
interferer
intergrade
underglaze
unwedgable
undergoing
unfeigning
unweighing
enneagonal
undergrove
intergrown
undergrown
encephalic
encephalin
encephalon
enkephalin
unmechanic
antechapel
untethered
unseminar'd
indelicate
ingeminate
inseminate
indelicacy
undeniable
unreliable
knee-timber
undeniably
ante-Nicene
enregiment
incedingly
sneeringly
unperished
unrelished
unverified
indecisive
indefinite
undecisive
unfeminine
undesiring
unmeriting
unrepining
indecision
endemicity
infelicity
unbedimmed
unbedinned
undesigned
unbenignly
undecimole
undesirous
unperilous
inheritrix
anteriorly
inferiorly
interiorly
unremitted
unresisted
enregister
unbelieved
unrelieved
unbeliever
unperjured

Words marked △ may be spelled also with a capital letter

10 □n□e□j

underjawed
unreckoned
unweakened
interleave
underlease
unhealable
unsellable
untellable
interlaced
unwellness
underlying
underlinen
interlunar
interloper
undeclared
undeplored
unrealised
unfellowed
unmellowed
underlayer
unrealized
endermical
intermodal
underminde
underminer
intermarry
endermatic
unhelmeted
intermezzi
intermezzo
underneath
internodal
internment
internship
underntime
infernally
internally
undernamed
Enneandria
undernoted
once-for-all
unrejoiced
unheroical
unrecorded
unseconded
unbeholden
enterocele
unbesought
unbecoming
unreposing
enterolith
unreformed
unrenowned
indecorous
angelology
enterotomy
unreported
ante-mortem
unbegotten
unresolved
interphase
interplant
underplant
unhelpable
interplead
enterprise
underprise
underprize
unbespoken
interpolar
unweaponed
underpants
interphone
underproof
unpeppered
untempered
interposal
interposer
unrespited
under-power
underquote
ance-errand
once-errand
inferrable
inferrible
integrable
unbearable
unpeerable
untearable
unwearable
unbearably
unmetrical
endearment
interregna
interregal
interreges
unsearched
unwearying
integrally
interramal
integrator
undepraved
undeprived
unreproved
unbetrayed
understand
interspace
interstate
understate
infeasible
insensible
unfeasible
unsensible
insensibly
unsensibly
underspend
understeer
interstice
undershirt
underskirt
unlessoned
unreasoned
unseasoned
undersense
incessancy
understood
underscore
understock
insensuous
undershoot
understory
underscrub
undershrub
uncensored
uncensured
unleisured
unmeasured
underslung
understudy
undersexed
enneastyle
undersized
ingestible
injectable
insertable
inventable
inventible
unbeatable
unlettable
intertidal
invertedly
ancestress
intentness
inventress
unmeetness
infeftment
insentient
investment
intertwine
unsettling
under-trick
intertrigo
intertwist
undertaken
undertaker
undertimed
under-tunic
undertoned
intestinal
intestines
anoestrous
incestuous
infectious
intentions
enfestered
unbettered
unfeatured
unfettered
unlettered
unrestored
indentures
unbestowed
interurban
integument
insecurely
unrecuring
interunion
insecurity
unbeguiled
unreturned
unrequired
unrequited
undervoice
intervolve
undervalue
unleavened
intervener
intervenor
unbeavered
intervital
interweave
underwhelm
underwrite
underwired
underworld
angel-water
underwater
interwound
unseizable
interzonal
knife-board
snuff-brown
unoffended
unaffected
uneffected
inefficacy
sniffiness
snuffiness
sniffingly
unofficial
unifoliate
snaffle-bit
knife-money
uniflorous
knife-point
snuff-paper
uniformity
snuff-taker
Onagraceae
enigmatise
enigmatize
enigmatist
sniggering
anagogical
knagginess
Unigenitus
knightless
knighthood
anaglyphic
anaglyptic
enthraldom
anthracene
inchoately
unsheathed
anthracite
inchoative
inchoation
enthralled
anthracoid
unshackled
unshadowed
unshielded
unthreaded
uncheerful
unshifting
unchristen
unshakable
unshakably
unshakenly
anthelices
anchylosed
anchylosis
anthemwise
anthomania
unthankful
enchanting
unchanging
unthinking
unshingled
Anthonomus
unphonetic
enthronise
enthronize
anthropoid
anthophore
antheridia
anchorless
anchor-ring
uncharming
anthersmut
anchor-hold
anchoretic
anchoritic
unthorough
enthusiasm
enthusiast
unchastely
unchastity
unthatched
unshrubbed
unshowered
intimately
antipathic
entitative
incitative
indicative
anti-racism
incitation
indication
intimation
invitation
anti-racist
unrivalled
indicatory
invitatory

Words marked △ may be spelled also with a capital letter

antimasque
antimatter
untimbered
invincible
invincibly
Antiochene
indiscrete
indiscreet
encircling
Antiochian
intinction
encincture
unkindness
unhindered
antiaditis
incinerate
unliterary
enticeable
unlikeable
unliveable
unrideable
unsizeable
antivenene
entireness
unlikeness
unripeness
unwiseness
enticement
incitement
inditement
invitement
anti-Semite
indigenise
indigenize
unlifelike
unwifelike
infidelity
anti-heroic
engine-room
indigenous
unlicensed
antisepsis
antiseptic
indigested
undigested
undirected
undiverted
undivested
incidental
indigently
indirectly
antiserums
unkinglike
unwithheld
enrichment
insightful
unrightful
Antichthon
infighting
in-fighting
antitheism
Antichrist
antitheist
antiphonic
antiphonal
antiphoner
unwithered
antitheses
antithesis
antithetic
annihilate
anticipate
infinitate
intimidate
invigilate
anticipant
infinitant
infinitary
unmilitary
untidiness
incisively
infinitely
enticingly
incitingly
invitingly
untiringly
unfinished
infinitive
inhibitive
anticivism
inhibition
incivility
insipidity
invisibles
unfilially
incipience
insipience
incipiency
incisiform
ancipitous
inhibitory
antibiosis
antibiotic
unvitiated
infinitude
individual
individuum
unpickable
unsinkable
inviolable
unfillable
untillable
inviolably
unbiblical
unyielding
unwieldily
anticlimax
anticlinal
unpillared
anxiolytic
inviolated
unfilleted
unviolated
unpillowed
infirmness
infirmarer
undismayed
ensignship
indignance
unsinnowed
unwinnowed
antimonate
invigorate
invigorant
undivorced
Indigofera
△antipodean
antilopine
antimonide
antimonite
indicolite
indigolite
antimonial
antisocial
incisorial
antinomian
environics
antilogous
oneirology
snail-paced
indisposed
undisposed
undisputed
antifreeze
antitragus
antidromic
antiproton
unbiasedly
snail-shell
angiosperm
gneissitic
infiltrate
indictable
unbirthday
anointment
enlistment
indictment
unlistened
insistence
indistinct
insistency
unvirtuous
unhistoric
unfiltered
unsistered
unsisterly
antistatic
infibulate
undivulged
unliquored
antiquated
insinuator
antisyzygy
snake-house
snake's-head
snakestone
unpleasant
unbleached
unpleasing
uncleansed
unilabiate
unclubable
unilobular
angleberry
ankle-biter
ankle-chain
ingle-cheek
inflective
inflictive
inflection
infliction
unilocular
includable
includible
angledozer
unaltering
unsleeping
influenzal
ineligible
ineligibly
analogical
unflagging
inelegance
inelegancy
analphabet
Anglo-Irish
encloister
uncloister
unblamable
unblamably
△anglomania
inclemency
inclinable
unblenched
unblinking
unilingual
unbloodied
unallotted
△anglophile
unslipping
△anglophobe
△anglophone
ineloquent
unclerical
antler-moth
inglorious
analysable
unblissful
unblushing
Englishism
anglistics
Englishman
Anglo-Saxon
inflatable
analytical
englutting
unilateral
uniliteral
unploughed
unplausive
inflexible
inflexibly
unplayable
analyzable
unimpaired
unimparted
inimically
animadvert
anamnestic
anemograph
unimagined
unemphatic
unsmiled-on
enamelling
enamellist
unimplored
animalcula
animalcule
unemployed
anemometer
anemometry
unamenable
gnomonical
mnemonical
unsmoothed
unembodied
unimposing
unimmortal
anemophily
un-American
enamorados
anamorphic
unsmirched
enumerator
inamoratas
inamoratos
unimproved
unamusable
onomastics
inimitable
inimitably
animatedly
enamouring
inundation
unentailed
uninuclear
anonaceous
unintended
unannealed
unendeared
unindeared
uninfected
uninvested
unknighted
one-nighter

10 □n□n□g

unknightly
unanchored
enunciable
unenviable
unenviably
unendingly
unenriched
uninviting
unentitled
enantiomer
enantiosis
enunciator
uninflamed
unanalysed
unenclosed
uninclosed
unanalytic
uninflated
unenslaved
unanalyzed
unanimated
unenforced
uninforced
uninformed
uninvolved
uninspired
unknowable
unanswered
untowardly
innovative
annotation
innovation
insolation
intonation
invocation
unmorality
endogamous
innovatory
invocatory
unromantic
entombment
undoubtful
undoubting
insouciant
unforcible
enforcedly
unforcedly
endoscopic
unfordable
enfoldment
unpowdered
intolerant
unloveable
unmoveable
unmoveably
unforeseen
engouement
incoherent
unhoped-for
unhomelike
Indonesian

endodermic
endodermal
endodermis
ungoverned
unforetold
endogenous
undomestic
unforested
unmolested
indolently
innocently
insolently
uncoffined
unconfined
unconfused
unfoughten
encoignure
unforgiven
endothelia
untochered
unmotherly
endophytic
entophytic
entophytal
endorhizal
innominate
intoxicate
incogitant
intoxicant
insociable
unsociable
unsociably
snootiness
unholiness
unpolitely
annoyingly
intoningly
unlovingly
unpolished
unmodified
unpolicied
unnoticing
indocility
insolidity
unsolidity
unsocially
encomienda
unconjugal
unlockable
unworkable
enrollment
ensoulment
entoilment
insoulment
unpolluted
endopleura
informally
uncommonly
endosmosis
endosmotic
uncommuted

enjoinment
insomnious
unbonneted
incognitos
incoronate
endopodite
oncologist
ontologist
entomology
endomorphy
uncoloured
unhonoured
incomplete
incompared
incorporal
incomposed
insobriety
encourager
endocrinic
endocrinal
endocritic
unborrowed
inconstant
unconstant
endorsable
unpossible
unboastful
unforsaken
unconsoled
unhouseled
unconsumed
unpoisoned
uncorseted
unpoetical
unwontedly
unworthily
unbottomed
unfortuned
unsoftened
undoctored
unfostered
untortured
unmortised
involution
unpopulous
involucral
involucrum
unfocussed
insolvable
unsolvable
insolvably
insolvency
antonymous
unhouzzled
unapparent
unspeaking
gnaphalium
unappalled
snaphaunce
snaphaunch
anaplastic

unspecific
inspective
inspection
inappetent
anopheline
unappeased
anapaestic
snappingly
snappishly
unuplifted
inaptitude
ineptitude
inspanning
inapposite
knap-bottle
end-product
inoperable
inspirable
inoperably
snapdragon
unipartite
unsporting
unapprised
unspirited
inspirator
unapproved
inspissate
anaphylaxy
anaptyctic
inequation
inequality
unequalled
uniqueness
iniquitous
inurbanely
unarranged
unbreached
unbreathed
encroacher
enervative
entreative
enervating
entreating
increasing
uncreating
undreading
undreaming
enarration
enervation
inurbanity
unordained
entreasure
untreasure
unbribable
ungraceful
infraction
ungracious
incredible
uncredible
incredibly
unproduced

introducer
enuredness
inuredness
ingredient
ungrudging
onirodynia
intradoses
unfriended
unfriendly
untrueness
unbreeched
inbreeding
androecial
androecium
energetics
unpriestly
unartfully
unprofaned
unprofited
infragrant
intriguant
unpregnant
intriguing
androgenic
intrigante
unoriginal
unfrighted
anarchical
unorthodox
infrahuman
anarthrous
inordinate
inordinacy
unordinary
unfruitful
snarlingly
snortingly
unerringly
inartistic
unartistic
unbrokenly
unprolific
untrampled
oniromancy
intramural
unpromised
entremesse
undramatic
unprompted
unprincely
unbranched
untrenched
entrancing
inbringing
unwrinkled
encrinitic
encrinital
untranquil
undrooping
unarmoured
enormously

Words marked △ may be spelled also with a capital letter

10 □o□a□c

intrepidly
entrapment
enwrapment
enwrapping
encryption
androphore
Entryphone®
unprepared
unproperly
infraposed
unproposed
infrequent
unfrequent
introrsely
incrassate
inerasable
inerasible
unerasable
inerasably
inerasibly
increscent
introspect
untrustful
ingressive
engrossing
undressing
untrussing
ingression
infrasonic
unprisoned
oniroscopy
infrasound
ingratiate
uncritical
ingrateful
ungrateful
untruthful
unarguable
unarguably
ungrounded
untroubled
unprovable
unprovided
unprovoked
unprizable
unassailed
ink-stained
one-sidedly
unascended
unusefully
anesthesia
ink-slinger
gnashingly
unossified
Gnosticise
Gnosticize
unaspiring
Gnosticism
anastigmat
unassigned
unassisted
unisonally
unisonance
anastomose
gnoseology
gnosiology
end-stopped
unescorted
uniseriate
anastrophe
anisotropy
inosculate
inesculent
unassuaged
unassuming
unattached
initialise
initialize
initiative
initialing
initiation
unsteadily
initialled
unstrained
initiatory
unstrapped
gnotobiote
unitedness
unattended
unstreamed
unstressed
unattested
instigator
knottiness
snottiness
unstringed
unstripped
unstriated
installant
instalment
instilment
installing
instilling
unutilised
unutilized
anatomical
unatonable
unstanched
unstinting
instantial
unitholder
unstooping
unctuosity
anatropous
unctuously
unstarched
instituter
institutor
institutes
instrument
instructor
insurancer
inhumanely
undulately
incubative
indurative
unhumanise
unhumanize
undulating
insularism
angulation
annulation
incubation
induration
inhumation
insulation
intubation
undulation
pneumatics
angularity
annularity
inhumanity
insularity
incunables
incubatory
undulatory
incunabula
uncurbable
incumbency
uncumbered
unnumbered
annunciate
injunctive
injunction
inculcator
unpunctual
unbundling
unburdened
innumerate
innumeracy
untuneable
inducement
innumerous
indumentum
inquietude
insufflate
unruffable
unsurfaced
engulfment
anguifauna
indulgence
insurgence
indulgency
insurgency
anhungered
unbudgeted
insulinase
unruliness
unruliment
enduringly
unpunished
unpurified
injudicial
aneurismal
unpuckered
untuckered
unsublimed
inquilinic
unqualited
Anguillula
unsummoned
unsummered
unsurmised
unguentary
unturnable
unquenched
innuendoes
infusorial
infusorian
inculpable
inculpably
unsupplied
unpurposed
incurrable
innutrient
unquarried
unhurrying
incurrence
inquirendo
unfurrowed
inquisitor
annuntiate
insultable
unquotable
unsuitable
unsuitably
unjustness
insultment
industrial
uncustomed
unbuttoned
inductance
unbuttered
uncultured
unnurtured
inaugurate
unpurvaide
incurvated
unpurveyed
unsurveyed
aneurysmal
unmuzzling
knave-bairn
univocally
unavailing
univoltine
snivelling
univalence
univalency
unevenness
uneventful
univariate
univariant
university
unovercome
inevitable
inevitably
unavowedly
unswearing
snow-capped
anywhither
unawakened
indwelling
snowplough
snowblower
angwantibo
snowmobile
snow-wreath
answerable
answerably
one-worlder
answerless
unswerving
untwisting
unswayable
onyx-marble
unexpanded
unexacting
unexecuted
unoxidised
unoxidized
inextended
unextended
unexcelled
unexpected
inexpiable
inexpiably
unexciting
unexpiated
inexplicit
unexcluded
unexplored
unexampled
unexamined
inexorable
inexorably
inexistant
inexistent
untyreable
unhygienic
encyclical
unsymmetry
ankylosaur
enzymology
unsympathy
enhydritic
encystment
Solanaceae
Mosasauros
woman-built
loganberry
rowan-berry
romancical
comanchero
woman-child

monarchise
monarchize
monarchial
monarchism
Monarchian
monarchist
mosaically
coparcener
towardness
cowardship
monandrous
locateable
voyageable
solacement
Romanesque
womanfully
lovat-green
woman-grown
notaphilic
woman-hater
coradicate
co-radicate
cohabitant
soda-siphon
logarithms
womanishly
rosaniline
tonalitive
volatilise
volatilize
movability
non-ability
notability
volatility
tomatillos
notarially
non-aligned
covariance
notational
rotational
vocational
monadiform
foraminous
voraginous
bonamiasis
donatistic
modalistic
moralistic
Romanistic
colatitude
Mohammedan
homaloidal
Monaxonida
topazolite
moratorium
Tobagonian
monadology
potamology
somatology
somatotype
podagrical

conacreism
non-arrival
no-man's-land
logan-stone
monastical
romantical
copartnery
cobalt-blue
monactinal
woman-tired
vocabulary
novaculite
vocabulist
Volapükist
notaryship
forbearant
forbearing
Hobbianism
hot-brained
Bombycidae
corbiculae
morbidness
forbidding
morbidezza
double-page
double-take
double-bank
double-park
double-talk
double-bass
doubleness
sombreness
double-gild
sombrerite
double-flat
gombeen-man
double-knit
doubletree
bomb-vessel
double-hung
hobble-bush
double-dyed
double-eyed
doubtfully
hobby-horse
wobbliness
doubtingly
hobblingly
pot-boiling
soubriquet
gor-bellied
pot-bellied
corbelling
morbillous
Gorbymania
bobbin-lace
combinable
Sorbonical
Sorbonnist
hot-blooded
booby-prize

comburgess
Homburg-hat
Colbertine
Norbertine
torbernite
bombardier
robber-crab
combustive
combustion
dog-biscuit
bobbysoxer
combatable
hop-bitters
nonchalant
moucharaby
touch-and-go
conclavist
notch-board
coachbuilt
concoctive
concoction
hot-cockles
forcedness
torch-dance
concretely
concretise
concretive
concretize
concretism
concretion
concretist
cow-chervil
forcefully
coach-horse
poachiness
touchiness
conceitful
touchingly
colchicine
coactivity
conchiglie
conchiolin
conchiform
colchicums
touch-judge
conciliate
conciliary
torchlight
zooculture
coxcomical
dolcemente
touch-me-not
non-content
concinnity
coccineous
concinnous
forcing-pit
concentric
concentred
volcanised
volcanized

conchoidal
hog-cholera
zoochorous
conchology
touch-plate
touch-piece
concipient
conceptive
△conception
voiceprint
touch-paper
forcipated
hotchpotch
conceptual
coacervate
concordant
concurrent
non-current
concertina
concerning
concurring
concordial
concertino
torch-staff
vouchsafed
concessive
concussive
nowcasting
concession
concussion
touchstone
cowcatcher
concettism
concettist
toccatella
conclusive
concluding
conclusion
conclusory
low-country
woodlander
coadjacent
gold-washer
good-father
cordialise
cordialize
bordraging
road-making
toad-eating
cordiality
loudhailer
cordwainer
loadmaster
pond-master
good-nature
woodcarver
conducible
rood-screen
conductive
conduction
mordacious

cordectomy
hoddy-doddy
sordidness
rowdy-dowdy
moudiewart
mowdiewart
roadheader
road-mender
bowdlerise
bowdlerize
cordierite
cowdie-pine
soldiering
bowdlerism
woodpecker
goodfellow
moudiewort
mowdiewort
hoodie-crow
gold-beater
hot-dogging
goody-goody
woodshrike
woodthrush
bond-timber
word-finder
goodlihead
woodpigeon
goodliness
lordliness
gold-digger
good-liking
non-drinker
good-sister
goldilocks
toddy-ladle
cordillera
Cordeliers
socdolager
socdoliger
socdologer
sogdolager
sogdoliger
sogdologer
condylomas
condolence
rondoletto
lordolatry
sordamente
condensate
condonable
woodenhead
soddenness
woodenness
condensery
gold-end-man
hoydenhood
hodden-grey
foudroyant
loud-voiced
bond-holder

Words marked △ may be spelled also with a capital letter

good-mother
wood-boring
good-looker
woodworker
cold-rolled
road-roller
good-morrow
wondrously
roadworthy
borderland
wonderland
ponderable
road-bridge
borderless
ponderment
wonderment
borderline
ponderance
ponderancy
wonderwork
foederatus
woodgrouse
condescend
toddy-stick
conditions
coadjutant
loud-lunged
roadrunner
good-humour
coadjutrix
wood-cutter
bondswoman
goodlyhead
how-do-you-do
rope-dancer
forehanded
cote-hardie
rose-garden
rope-ladder
moderately
foretaught
forefather
foregather
colemanite
corelative
lovemaking
rope-making
moderatism
monetarism
corelation
moderation
Pomeranian
toleration
monetarist
rope-walker
fore-hammer
fore-damned
love-favour
Monegasque
rose-laurel
moderatrix
covenanted
forecasted
covenantee
forecastle
covenanter
covenantor
forecaster
tolerantly
honeybunch
money-bound
lower-class
hovercraft
honey-chile
honey-crock
fore-advise
roberdsman
molendinar
lovey-dovey
bone-headed
soreheaded
foreseeing
foreteller
yoke-fellow
hopelessly
movelessly
tonelessly
copesettic
rose-beetle
rove-beetle
bonesetter
honey-eater
love-letter
coherently
poker-faced
womenfolks
powerfully
honey-guide
foreignism
towel-gourd
foreshadow
rose-chafer
boneshaker
somewhiles
somewhence
towel-horse
forechosen
dower-house
powerhouse
home-thrust
note-shaver
foreshewed
foreshowed
rose-window
lovelihead
comeliness
homeliness
loneliness
loveliness
cohesively
forefinger
covetingly
coweringly
hoveringly
loweringly
soberingly
toweringly
come-hither
pokerishly
polemicist
zone-ticket
comedienne
comédienne
home-signal
rose-lipped
pome-citron
comedietta
Docetistic
novelistic
solecistic
tokenistic
totemistic
rose-tinted
forebitter
dowel-joint
hogen-mogen
money-maker
honeymonth
homeomeric
homeomorph
honey-mouse
hover-mower
fore-and-aft
governable
Copernican
modernness
solemnness
△government
rose-engine
governance
governante
moderniser
solemniser
governessy
modernizer
solemnizer
rose-combed
solenoidal
money-order
dolesomely
lonesomely
love-monger
coregonine
fore-notice
foreboding
home-coming
polemonium
love-potion
somebodies
homeworker
poke-bonnet
dove-colour
rose-colour
cometology
ponerology
forecourse
covetously
lobe-footed
loveworthy
noteworthy
Coleoptera
coleoptile
hokey-pokey
homeopathy
foreordain
coleorhiza
love-broker
foreground
home-brewed
vowel-rhyme
honey-stalk
sobersides
tower-shell
womenswear
honey-sweet
lover's-knot
honey-stone
somersault
potentiate
hovertrain
powertrain
potentiary
come-at-able
comestible
domestical
cosentient
rodent-like
money-taker
potentilla
robertsman
forest-born
forest-bred
forest-tree
code-number
forerunner
Rome-runner
bodegueros
fore-quoted
molehunter
honey-wagon
bowerwoman
wolframite
God-fearing
Wolfianism
conflation
confabular
confection
non-fiction
confidante
confidence
confidency
confederal
toffee-nose
solfeggios
forfaiting
forfeiture
joyfulness
woefulness
confinable
dog-fancier
tomfoolery
bow-fronted
confirmand
conferment
conferring
confirming
coffer-fish
conformist
conformity
△conference
conférence
solferinos
confervoid
non-ferrous
confiscate
confessant
confusable
confusible
confusedly
cod-fishery
cod-fishing
rodfishing
confession
confiserie
confutable
solfataric
solfataras
confounded
forfeuchen
forfoughen
confluence
zoographic
zoographer
poignadoes
long-haired
poignantly
dough-baked
rough-draft
doggedness
congregate
congregant
long-headed
tongueless
long-legged
tongue-tied
mongrelise
mongrelize
tonguelike
toughening
non-gremial
mongrelism
long-termer
tongue-work
longaevous
toggleiron

tonguester
borghettos
goggle-eyed
doughfaced
rough-grind
rough-hound
rough-house
rough-hewer
long-winded
doughiness
topgallant
coagulable
googolplex
coagulator
zoogonidia
gorgoneion
Gorgonzola
congeneric
noogenesis
congenetic
morganatic
congenital
conglobate
zoogloeoid
gorgeously
hodgepodge
rough-rider
loggerhead
longprimer
songwriter
congestive
congestion
rough-stuff
songstress
forgettery
forgetting
long-staple
congruence
congruency
forgivable
wonga-wonga
Sophoclean
tophaceous
cochleated
Nothofagus
dochmiacal
moth-flower
sophomoric
fox-hunting
pot-hunting
nothingism
dog-handler
job-hopping
lophophore
motherland
mother-cell
motherless
tocherless
mother-city
motherhood
tocher-good
bothersome
mother-to-be
motherwort
mother-spot
oophoritis
moth-hunter
solivagant
nominately
cogitative
comitative
dominative
nominalise
nominalize
nominative
nominalism
solidarism
cogitation
domination
ionisation
ionization
lorication
motivation
nomination
solitarian
toxication
volitation
nominalist
solidarist
comicality
logicality
solidarity
solitarily
topicality
topi-wallah
docimastic
dominantly
coriaceous
foliaceous
morigerate
vociferate
vociferant
noticeable
noticeably
motiveless
politeness
noviceship
homiletics
novicehood
coniferous
morigerous
pomiferous
poriferous
rotiferous
solipedous
vociferous
towing-path
Cotingidae
lovingness
holing-pick
moving-coil
robing-room
roping-down
rowing-boat
toxiphobia
polishable
boyishness
modishness
mopishness
tonishness
toyishness
polishment
polishings
dolichurus
Dolichotis
nobilitate
solicitant
modifiable
notifiable
soricident
positively
solidified
cohibitive
politicise
politicize
soliciting
positivism
cohibition
politician
solifidian
positivist
docibility
positivity
politicker
positioned
positional
volitional
bolivianos
moniliform
moliminous
politicoes
solicitous
moniliasis
solicitude
jovialness
socialness
sociologic
bouillotte
movie-maker
porismatic
goniometer
goniometry
sociometry
motionless
Polianthes
notionally
totipotent
eosinophil
monitorial
volitorial
vomitorium
Morisonian
codicology
docimology
toxicology
horizontal
rosin-plant
sociopathy
goliardery
solid-state
forinsecal
Louis-Seize
rotisserie
rôtisserie
logistical
monistical
poristical
goliathise
goliathize
Corinthian
podiatrist
societally
policy-shop
hobjobbing
conjecture
conjugally
conjugated
Conjugatae
non-joinder
conjointly
conjunctly
conjurator
rock-rabbit
cock-paddle
work-harden
rock-badger
bookmaking
pockmarked
bookmarker
workbasket
cocktailed
fork-tailed
rock-salmon
pockmantie
dock-master
workmaster
cockabully
rockabilly
cock-a-bondy
kookaburra
forkedness
hookedness
cockneydom
cockneyish
cockneyism
cork-heeled
bookseller
workfellow
mock-heroic
folk-memory
rock-temple
workpeople
bookkeeper
lock-keeper
cockteaser
cockchafer
workaholic
rock-lizard
rock-ribbed
bookbinder
cocksiness
folksiness
folk-singer
rock-violet
cork-tipped
pockpitted
cockyleeky
cockalorum
poikilitic
working-day
looking-for
locking-nut
book-holder
mock-modest
bookmobile
folklorist
Doukhobors
rock-hopper
topknotted
work-to-rule
you-know-who
folk-speech
mock-orange
cockernony
mock-privet
forkit-tail
rocksteady
rock-steady
pocketless
cockatrice
pocket-comb
pocket-hole
pocket-book
lockstitch
pocketfuls
rock-turbot
cocksucker
book-muslin
cork-cutter
rock-butter
monkey-gaff
monkey-rail
monkey-tail
jockeyship
monkey-rope
donkey-work
monkey-boat
donkey-pump
monkey-pump
monkey-suit
Coolgardie
wool-carder
toolmaking
wool-packer
poll-parrot

Words marked △ may be spelled also with a capital letter

coalmaster
colleagued
mouldboard
world-class
doulocracy
collective
bollocking
collecting
porlocking
rollicking
rollocking
collection
follicular
colliculus
coelacanth
collocutor
coolheaded
goal-tender
Zollverein
foolbegged
cowl-necked
goalkeeper
poll-degree
soullessly
boll-weevil
mollifying
toploftily
collegiate
Howleglass
zoological
collagenic
collegiums
loll-shraub
doll's-house
wool-winder
mouldiness
goalkicker
wool-picker
fowl-plague
Collembola
coelomatic
collimator
coulometer
coulometry
Hollandish
Bollandist
fowling-net
cooling-off
rolling-pin
pollenosis
Moulinette®
poplinette
toilinette
pollinator
pollen-tube
wool-comber
toilsomely
rollcollar
coal-porter
woolsorter
foul-spoken
colliquate
colliquant
colloquise
colloquize
colloquial
colloquium
colloquist
tollbridge
dollarless
dollarship
Lollardism
poultroone
collar-work
collarette
collyriums
wool-driver
wool-grower
Rolls-Royce®
worldscale
coalescent
molluscoid
molluscous
collatable
pollutedly
toiletries
mollitious
zoolatrous
collotypic
collateral
douloureux
toolpusher
coal-cutter
hot-livered
hollow-ware
world-weary
hollowness
noblewoman
noblewomen
hollow-eyed
woollyback
volleyball
woollybutt
doomsaying
worm-eating
commeasure
cosmically
formicaria
formidable
formidably
cosmodrome
commodious
coomceiled
room-fellow
formlessly
cosmogenic
cosmogonic
room-ridden
formaliter
cosmolatry
commentate
commandant
commentary
commonable
commonweal
commandeer
commonness
commandery
gormandise
gormandize
commanding
tormenting
gormandism
commingled
commonalty
communally
noumenally
commonhold
communique
communiqué
comminuted
Commiphora
cormophyte
zoomorphic
commercial
coumarilic
cosmoramic
commissary
commission
commissure
commutable
cosmetical
dogmatical
noematical
commitment
committing
formatting
dogmatiser
commutator
dogmatizer
hot-mouthed
commixtion
commixture
corn-maiden
downwardly
somniative
moonraking
foundation
down-market
downfallen
mountained
roundabout
somniatory
moon-raised
corn-factor
down-easter
point-blank
hobnobbing
town's-bairn
△donnybrook
youngberry
coenobitic
pornocracy
connective
connection
corniculum
cornaceous
cornucopia
fornicator
horned-pout
mountebank
counteract
counterbid
pouncet-box
loundering
counselled
corn-dealer
counsellor
founderous
round-eared
countersue
counterspy
poinsettia
round-faced
loan-office
Zoanthidae
moonshiner
zoanthropy
Zoantharia
roundhouse
bounciness
coincident
loungingly
soundingly
woundingly
corn-miller
councillor
horn-rimmed
councilman
cornflakes
hornblende
somnolence
somnolency
somniloquy
bonnilasse
cornflower
moon-flower
cognominal
somnambule
round-mouth
down-and-out
round-nosed
loan-holder
Johnsonese
boondoggle
Johnsonism
Johnsonian
downlooked
corncockle
corn-dollie
horn-footed
conniption
soundproof
corn-spirit
cornerback
cornerways
cornerwise
countryman
cornbrandy
cognisable
cognisably
coenosteum
cognisance
joint-stock
joint-stool
hounds-foot
soundtrack
round-table
down-at-heel
downstream
top-notcher
moonstrike
cornettino
downstairs
cornettist
downstroke
pornotopia
cornstarch
connatural
non-natural
moonstruck
jointuress
cornhusker
downturned
corn-cutter
connivance
connivence
connivency
townswoman
Johnny-cake
gooneybird
cognizable
cognizably
cognizance
logopaedic
△coromandel
monovalent
monomachia
monomaniac
roborating
homotaxial
honorarium
coloration
coronation
monogamist
homogamous
monogamous
monocarpic
coloratura
cocoa-beans
motor-coach
rotorcraft
motor-cycle
monorchism
monoecious

10 □o□o□c

horoscopic
poroscopic
conoidical
homogenate
Homorelaps
homocercal
jocoseness
moroseness
homogenise
homogenize
monogenism
logopedics
monogenist
homogenous
monocerous
monogenous
bolometric
iodometric
holohedral
holohedron
colorectal
notonectal
homosexual
solonetzic
honor-guard
tobogganed
tobogganer
holophrase
homophobia
monophobia
nosophobia
homophobic
monophobic
monothecal
monotheism
monotheist
topophilia
homothally
monorhymed
homophonic
monophonic
monorhinal
monochroic
monochrome
homochromy
monochromy
tocopherol
monochasia
monophasic
holophytic
nomothetic
holophotal
nomothetes
holodiscus
monolithic
dolomitise
dolomitize
sororicide
colonially
sororially
monoplegia

monoclinic
monoclinal
monoclonal
motor-lorry
homoblasty
homoplasmy
motormouth
colonnaded
holoenzyme
homologate
homoeopath
gonococcic
gonococcal
gonococcus
homoeomery
homologise
homologize
lobotomise
lobotomize
locomobile
locomotive
monologise
monologize
monopolise
monopolize
monopodial
nosocomial
△horologium
monopodium
locomotion
Solomonian
horologist
monologist
monopolist
nomologist
nosologist
podologist
pomologist
topologist
homologous
homotonous
monotocous
monotonous
locomotory
pogonotomy
dolorously
sonorously
notodontid
ionosphere
colourwash
colourfast
colourable
△honourable
colourably
honourably
gonorrheic
gonorrheal
colourless
honourless
sojourning
loxodromic

honours-man
gonorrhoea
logorrhoea
colour-code
doxography
holography
horography
logography
monography
nomography
nosography
sonography
tomography
topography
homoerotic
mobocratic
monocratic
colour-supp
joyousness
porousness
no-nonsense
colossuses
monostylar
Podostemon
colostrous
goloptious
holosteric
monopteral
monopteron
monopteros
homoousian
coconut-oil
monoculous
coconut-shy
monogynian
toponymics
homonymity
homocyclic
monocyclic
homozygote
homonymous
homozygous
monogynous
monoxylous
monohydric
monohybrid
Notoryctes
complanate
compearant
complacent
co-optative
non-playing
coaptation
co-optation
complainer
compradore
zoophagous
zooplastic
compaction
compactify
torpidness

torpedoist
torpedo-net
corpse-gate
comprehend
complement
couplement
completely
completive
dopplerite
completion
complexion
morphemics
complexify
complexity
completory
compressed
compressor
box-pleated
complected
complicate
complicant
complicacy
compliable
compliment
dolphin-fly
morphinism
zoophilism
zoophilist
complicity
soup-ticket
compliance
compliancy
zoophilous
compulsive
gospellise
gospellize
compelling
compulsion
corpulence
corpulency
pompelmous
compulsory
compilator
compensate
cowpuncher
porpentine
companying
louping-ill
compendium
hopping-mad
componency
topping-out
morphogeny
compromise
low-profile
zoophobous
morphology
complotted
colportage
comparable
comparably

copperhead
colporteur
torporific
compursion
corporeity
corporally
cow-parsley
dog-parsley
copperwork
copperworm
comparison
comparator
co-operator
corporator
romper-suit
composedly
torpescent
compassing
compassion
colposcope
coppy-stool
colposcopy
Compositae
compositor
composture
corpuscule
compatible
computable
hospitable
compatibly
hospitably
low-pitched
compatriot
hospitaler
competence
competency
competitor
compotator
computator
compounder
nonplusing
compluvium
nonplussed
non-payment
porphyrite
porphyrios
zoophytoid
porphyrous
coequality
conqueress
conquering
mosquitoes
journal-box
four-handed
journalese
tournament
journalise
journalize
tourmaline
journalism
journalist

Words marked △ may be spelled also with a capital letter

pourparler
four-parted
corroboree
court-baron
courtcraft
nourice-fee
corrective
correction
porrection
four-o'clock
porraceous
correctory
fourscorth
corrodible
horridness
torridness
hoar-headed
coarseness
hoarseness
four-leafed
four-legged
courtesied
bourgeoise
cowrie-pine
sourdeline
poor-relief
journeying
Fourierism
journeyman
fourteenth
fourteener
coursework
sourcebook
door-keeper
four-letter
four-seater
four-leaved
yourselves
horrifying
torrefying
mournfully
corrigible
corregidor
Bourignian
corrigenda
courageous
corrugated
corrugator
fourth-rate
fourchette
courthouse
poor's-house
co-ordinate
hour-circle
gourdiness
coercively
mourningly
worryingly
coercivity
tourbillon
courtierly
four-figure
nourriture
tourniquet
corralling
log-rolling
coprolalia
coprolitic
four-in-hand
torrent-bow
four-inched
torrential
sopraninos
horrendous
botryoidal
godrooning
Bourbonism
Bourbonist
door-to-door
four-colour
four-footed
four-poster
coprophagy
corruptive
correption
corruption
four-square
pourtrahed
pourtraict
corrosible
morris-pike
nourishing
copresence
co-presence
correspond
Morris-tube
four-stroke
corrivalry
sorrowless
board-wages
four-by-four
moustached
moustaches
constative
gobsmacked
codswallop
cod's-wallop
box-spanner
rouseabout
roustabout
Constantia
constantan
non-starter
constantly
horse-bread
consubsist
bossyboots
gooseberry
housebound
consecrate
consociate
housecraft
consectary
non-society
fossicking
hop-sacking
horse-cloth
horse-coper
tossicated
considered
pousse-café
loss-leader
bolshevise
bolshevize
mousseline
bolstering
roistering
bolshevism
Mousterian
bolshevist
dog's-fennel
boisterous
roisterous
roysterous
lobster-pot
conspectus
consuetude
horse-faced
gooseflesh
horseflesh
boastfully
goosefoots
dorsifixed
coastguard
dorsigrade
goose-grass
consignify
Monsignore
Monsignori
Monsignors
horse-gowan
constipate
conspirant
conspiracy
worshipful
topsoiling
solstitial
non-swimmer
conscience
worshipped
worshipper
moss-litter
constitute
forsakenly
consultant
tonsillary
consolable
non-soluble
horse-leech
consilient
consulship
consultive
consulting
houselling
dog-soldier
consultory
tonsilitic
corselette
tonsilitis
horselaugh
consummate
consumable
consumedly
noisemaker
consimilar
howsomever
poison-fang
poisonable
foisonless
cousinship
consension
bousingken
consonance
consonancy
cousinhood
consensual
dog's-tongue
non-smoking
comstocker
zoosporous
gobstopper
mousepiece
house-proud
sousaphone
house-party
horsepower
consequent
goose-quill
conservant
horse-rider
consortism
consortium
constraint
constringe
monstrance
monstruous
consistent
mouse-sight
possessive
possession
horseshoer
consistory
possessory
corsetière
horse-thief
horse-tamer
topsy-turvy
moisturise
moisturize
mossbunker
horse-woman
popsy-wopsy
coastwards
contraband
contrabass
foot-candle
contravene
contrahent
voetganger
boat-racing
bootmaking
costeaning
foot-racing
Noetianism
contradict
contrarily
root-fallen
footballer
contraflow
goat-sallow
contraplex
foot-warmer
hootnannie
costean-pit
foot-patrol
contraprop
zoothapses
zoothapsis
portmantua
contracted
portmantle
postpartum
post-partum
contractor
postmaster
contraltos
goat's-beard
northbound
southbound
toothbrush
potty-chair
foeticidal
PostScript®
postscript
vorticella
ponticello
postocular
vorticular
fonticulus
monticulus
poetically
vortically
post-echoes
corticated
tosticated
contactual
foetidness
rootedness
wontedness
contadinas
Cortaderia
Pontederia
zootherapy
soft-headed
bottle-feed

bottle-head
bottle-neck
pottle-deep
jostlement
bootlegger
röntgenise
röntgenize
southering
bottle-fish
zoothecial
cottierism
zoothecium
boat-necked
post-bellum
△rottweiler
northerner
△southerner
southernly
bottle-nose
hop-trefoil
contrecoup
contre-jour
bottle-tree
postperson
tortfeasor
bootlessly
bottlefuls
Pontefract
pontifical
pontifices
post-office
fortifying
mortifying
youthfully
Montagnard
Portuguese
Portugaise
forthgoing
contiguity
contagious
contiguous
post-chaise
post-Nicene
Voltairean
costliness
portliness
rootsiness
toothiness
worthiness
contritely
loathingly
soothingly
footlights
fortuitism
Voltairism
contrition
Voltairian
fortuitist
postliminy
bootlicker
foot-licker
soft-billed
goat-willow
soft-finned
fortuitous
contribute
Portakabin®
postillate
rostellate
noctilucae
nostologic
sortileger
hostelling
tortellini
postillion
montelimar
portolanos
postulancy
postulatum
postulator
postulates
bottom-land
zootomical
bottomless
bottomness
contemning
bottom-fish
nostomania
coati-mondi
coati-mundi
portamenti
portamento
bottommost
route-march
voltameter
continuate
cottontail
continuant
cottonseed
cottonweed
rottenness
contendent
contingent
contending
cotton-mill
contention
low-tension
pontonnier
continuity
fontanelle
fontinalis
continence
forty-niner
continency
hootananny
hootenanny
cottonwood
cotton-boll
cotton-worm
coetaneous
continuous
portentous
continuums
post-modern
controvert
mouth-organ
zootrophic
soft-bodied
nootropics
portfolios
portionist
tortuosity
controlled
soft-boiled
controller
tortiously
tortuously
foxtrotted
polt-footed
soft-footed
postcoital
post-mortem
bogtrotter
fortepiano
mouthpiece
soft-spoken
south-polar
mouthparts
toothpaste
nostopathy
souterrain
montero-cap
footbridge
torturedly
jolterhead
couturière
forthright
doctorship
contortive
co-starring
fosterling
doctor-fish
contortion
fox-terrier
coeternity
foster-home
coat-armour
posteriors
montbretia
port-crayon
contestant
toothshell
poetastery
contesting
fortissimo
costus-root
foetoscopy
soothsayer
bootstraps
hoity-toity
goat's-thorn
hoots-toots
voetstoots
houts-touts
root-rubber
goatsucker
portcullis
posthumous
footguards
zootsuiter
worthwhile
northwards
southwards
post-exilic
contexture
contextual
Montezuma's
loculament
copulative
popularise
popularize
copulation
lobulation
modulation
nodulation
population
volutation
jocularity
modularity
popularity
copulatory
holus-bolus
columbaria
homuncular
homunculus
loquacious
jocundness
columellae
volumetric
documental
monumental
lotus-eater
solubilise
solubilize
non-utility
solubility
volubility
solutional
poculiform
voluminous
coquelicot
roquelaure
coquimbite
columnated
populously
hocus-pocus
Colubridae
voluptuary
Locustidae
robustness
coquetting
coquettish
goluptious
robustious
voluptuous
pohutukawa
convective
convictive
convictism
convection
conviction
louvre-door
convulsant
pot-valiant
convulsive
convulsion
convalesce
convoluted
mouvementé
non-vintage
convenable
convenient
convincing
convention
convenance
△conventual
non-violent
conversant
convertend
convergent
conversely
convertite
converging
conversion
louver-door
convexedly
convexness
conveyable
conveyance
woe-wearied
cobwebbery
pot-wabbler
pot-wobbler
Boswellise
Boswellize
Boswellism
Boswellian
forwarding
hot-working
coexistent
polyvalent
polymathic
corydaline
polyhalite
polygamist
body-cavity
body-warmer
jouysaunce
jovysaunce
polygamous
polycarpic
polymastia
corybantic
polymastic
polydactyl

Words marked △ may be spelled also with a capital letter

corybantes
polyactine
molybdenum
molybdosis
polymerase
polysemant
polymeride
polymerise
polymerize
polygenism
polymerism
Polynesian
polygenist
polygenous
polymerous
polyhedric
polyhedral
polyhedron
Polychaeta
polychaete
coryphaeus
polychrest
polyphagia
polytheism
polytheist
Polyphemic
Polyphemus
polyphonic
polychroic
polychrome
polychromy
polyphasic
polyrhythm
cotyliform
polydipsia
polyhistor
polyploidy
polyclinic
polyominos
polyanthus
polyonymic
Polyandria
copyholder
polynomial
Polypodium
polytocous
body-popper
corylopsis
rosy-footed
polycotton
polygraphy
polycrotic
copywriter
polystylar
polyatomic
Polypterus
hony-suckle
polytunnel
cony-burrow
polyaxonic
copy-typing
polygynian
polycyclic
Polyhymnia
polygynous
polyhydric
polyhybrid
pozzolanic
monzonitic
pozzuolana
mozzarella
aplanatism
splanchnic
upwardness
spray-dried
sphacelate
speakerine
sphalerite
apparelled
aplacental
apparently
splash-back
splashdown
optatively
speakingly
apparition
spear-point
spray-paint
sphaeridia
aphaeresis
spear-shaft
epiblastic
specialise
specialize
specialism
speciation
specialist
speciality
spectacled
spectacles
spectatrix
spaceborne
spiceberry
spacecraft
epicycloid
speciesism
speciesist
specifical
specifying
△apocalypse
speculator
apiculture
epicanthic
epicanthus
epicentral
epicondyle
speciocide
speciosity
spaciously
speciously
spaceplane
spectrally
apochromat
apocarpous
epicuticle
spacewoman
apocryphal
apocryphon
spadiceous
epididymis
spudding-in
apodeictic
epideictic
epidemical
spodomancy
epidendrum
epidiorite
spiderlike
epidermoid
spiderwork
spiderwort
epidotised
epidotized
splenative
upper-class
apperceive
upper-crust
appendices
splendidly
splendrous
spread-over
appendixes
sphereless
spherelike
ephemerist
ephemerous
speedfully
spreaghery
speechless
speech-song
speediness
appetitive
appetising
appetizing
appetition
sphericity
appealable
spleenless
spleenwort
sphenoidal
spheroidal
sphenogram
spherocyte
appearance
appeasable
spherulite
upperworks
apterygial
Apterygota
spiflicate
epigraphic
epigrapher
apagogical
epagomenal
epigenesis
epigenetic
epiglottic
epiglottis
spagerical
spagirical
spagyrical
epigastric
oppilative
optimalise
optimalize
aprication
oppilation
split-brain
upside-down
upsideowne
springhase
springtail
springhaas
spring-cart
springhalt
Sphingidae
springhead
springless
springlike
springtide
springtime
springwood
springwort
springbuck
uppishness
sprightful
upright-man
split-image
aphidicide
ypsiliform
optimistic
sprinkling
uphillward
ophiologic
ophicleide
ophiolitic
ophiolater
ophiolatry
split-level
ophiomorph
opsiometer
optionally
epeirogeny
Ophiuridae
spoilsport
splintwood
sphinxlike
spokeshave
spoliative
spallation
spoliation
spoliatory
spuleblade
spellbound
applicable
applicably
spellcheck
applicator
epiloguise
epiloguize
apologetic
spellingly
spillikins
epilimnion
spelunking
speleothem
Apollonian
speleology
opalescent
upflashing
apolitical
applausive
applauding
apolaustic
apple-woman
epimeletic
apomorphia
spumescent
spondaical
open-handed
eponychium
spinaceous
spongeware
spongebags
spongeable
Spencerian
Spenserian
spancelled
spongewood
sponge-down
open-hearth
spinnerule
spinigrade
epentheses
epenthesis
epenthetic
open-minded
sponginess
spunkiness
spankingly
sponsional
spongiform
spaniolate
spaniolise
spaniolize
sponsorial
opinionist
spin-bowler
spongology
spin-doctor
epanaphora
spinescent
spinstress
spinsterly
open-stitch

up-and-under
spondylous
opsomaniac
splotchily
spoondrift
opposeless
spoonerism
spookiness
appositely
oppositely
appositive
oppositive
apposition
opposition
aphoristic
appointive
optologist
uproarious
apron-stage
upholstery
éprouvette
epiplastra
apoplectic
apopemptic
epiphonema
apophthegm
epiphytism
opaqueness
spermaceti
approaches
sparganium
spermarium
spermatium
Spartacist
spermaduct
opprobrium
appreciate
spiraculum
spiracular
opera-cloak
upgradable
sporadical
aphrodisia
sparseness
spur-heeled
sportfully
spirograph
opera-glass
sparagrass
Sparagmite
sporogonia
sportiness
sportively
spur-winged
sportingly
sparkishly
appraisive
spermicide
upbraiding
spermiduct
apartments
spirometer
spirometry
apprentice
upbringing
sporangial
sporangium
spuriosity
spermogone
spuriously
spirophore
sporophore
sporophyte
sporophyll
sportswear
oppressive
oppression
spiritedly
spiritless
operettist
spirit-blue
spirituous
operculate
approvable
approvance
sperm-whale
approximal
sperrylite
sporozoite
apostatise
apostatize
epispastic
episodical
epistemics
episternal
episternum
spasticity
spissitude
aposematic
episematic
opisometer
apostolate
episcopate
episcopant
episcopacy
epistolary
apostolise
apostolize
episcopise
episcopize
epistolise
epistolize
epistolist
spasmodist
aposporous
episiotomy
apostrophe
epistrophe
spatiality
ophthalmia
ophthalmic
spot-barred
epithemata
apothecary
opotherapy
spot-welder
sputtering
apothecial
epithelial
apothecium
epithelium
epithermal
apotheoses
apotheosis
spotlessly
spitefully
spatchcock
spitchcock
spottiness
spittlebug
epitomical
epitomiser
epitomizer
upstanding
spatangoid
apotropaic
apotropous
epitaphian
epitaphist
spathulate
spauld-bone
spouseless
spruceness
epaulement
opium-eater
upsurgence
upbuilding
oppugnancy
upbursting
splutterer
upbuoyance
epexegeses
epexegesis
epexegetic
spoylefull
epizootics
aquamanale
squabasher
aquamanile
aquamarine
squamation
aquabatics
squandered
squanderer
square-face
square-sail
squarehead
squareness
squarewise
square-toed
square-toes
aquaphobia
aquaphobic
squashable
equability
equanimity
squalidity
squamiform
equanimous
aquaplaner
equatorial
aquarobics
squamosity
aquafortis
squadroned
squadronal
squamulose
squelching
squeteague
equestrian
squeezable
squeeze-box
equiparate
squirarchy
equivalent
equitation
squirality
squireship
squirelike
squireling
squirehood
squirearch
equivocate
equipotent
squirrelly
squint-eyed
squint-eyes
pre-Adamite
breakables
broad-arrow
preadapted
breadboard
breadberry
broad-based
broadbrush
broadcloth
breadcrumb
errand-girl
triandrian
breakdance
triandrous
greaseband
greaseball
Armageddon
arcaneness
ornateness
urbaneness
greasewood
ornamental
arbalester
ornamenter
dreadfully
break-front
breadfruit
arraigning
triangular
broad-gauge
breathable
triathlete
breathless
wreathless
breath-test
preachment
treacherer
irradicate
drearihead
creaminess
dreaminess
dreariness
freakiness
greasiness
weariment
creatively
dreamingly
freakishly
creatinine
organicism
urbanities
organicist
creativity
ergativity
friability
armadillos
organismic
organismal
irradiance
creational
irrational
irradiancy
drearihood
drearisome
urbanistic
arbalister
dreadlocks
ordainable
great-niece
ordainment
organogeny
arragonite
treasonous
urbanology
organogram
triaconter
ergatogyne
broadpiece
breakpoint
organ-point
preappoint
prearrange
proairesis
triapsidal
broadsheet
cream-slice
bread-stick
broadsword

Words marked △ may be spelled also with a capital letter

breadstuff
breastrail
breast-feed
breast-deep
truantship
breast-high
triactinal
breast-knot
breastbone
breastwork
breast-pump
great-uncle
creaturely
braaivleis
tread-wheel
dreamwhile
dream-world
breakwater
tribrachic
Grobianism
cribration
trabeation
trabeculae
trabecular
trebleness
problemist
crabbiness
drabbiness
crib-biting
Brobdignag
cribriform
aryballoid
tribometer
prebendary
frabjously
erubescent
erubescite
arabesqued
Grubstreet
crab-stones
crackajack
proctalgia
eructation
△tractarian
fractality
proclaimer
trochanter
crackbrain
tricycling
tricyclist
ericaceous
precocious
procacious
Crocodilia
Crocodilus
precedence
procidence
precedency
procedural
trachelate
cricketing
crocheting
proceeding
procoelous
Trachearia
prick-eared
brick-earth
tracheated
procreator
tracheitis
brickfield
crucifying
gracefully
Cruciferae
precognize
trace-horse
practicals
practisant
trochiscus
trickiness
trickishly
crocoisite
trichinise
trichinize
practising
triclinium
practician
erectility
proclivity
tractility
fractional
frictional
tractional
trichinose
trichinous
brachiopod
Trichiurus
trichiasis
brecciated
practiques
truckle-bed
truculence
cracklings
truculency
oracularly
prick-louse
bricklayer
tracklayer
procumbent
brickmaker
precompose
tricameral
arachnidan
precondemn
preconceit
preconcert
fricandeau
Dracontium
trecentist
iracundity
precentrix
draconites
preconsume
proctorage
trochoidal
urochordal
proctorise
proctorize
troctolite
proctorial
tricrotism
graciosity
preciosity
tricrotous
oryctology
proctology
trichology
trichotomy
trochotron
graciously
preciously
trichogyne
precipiced
preceptive
dry-cupping
preceptial
preceptory
precipitin
procurable
tractrices
precursive
precordial
trichroism
trichromic
Greco-Roman
trichromat
procaryote
precarious
precursory
procurator
tricostate
fricasseed
precession
procession
track-scout
processual
trick-track
brocatelle
groceteria
tricoteuse
preclusive
precaution
preclusion
brickworks
trachytoid
brachydome
brachylogy
brachyural
procrypsis
procryptic
brachyaxis
gradualism
eradiation
graduation
gradualist
graduality
predecease
tradecraft
eradicable
predicable
producible
traducible
predictive
productile
productive
traductive
prediction
production
traduction
iridaceous
predaceous
predacious
iridectomy
eradicated
eradicator
Bridgerama
bridle-hand
bridle-path
bridgeable
bridgehead
bridle-rein
bridgeless
bridle-wise
bridle-road
cradlesong
bridge-work
gradienter
trade-falne
pridefully
prodigally
bridegroom
prodigious
drudgingly
grudgingly
prednisone
predentate
tridentate
Tridentine
credential
prudential
Uredinales
gridlocked
bride-price
bridesmaid
bride's-maid
bride's-cake
uredo-stage
iridescent
iridosmine
predestine
bradyseism
iridosmium
predestiny
predispose
uredospore
tradesfolk
uredosorus
creditable
creditably
traditores
predevelop
freelancer
trierarchy
free-handed
irrelative
irrelation
free-market
free-labour
freemartin
pre-embryos
proembryos
greencloth
free-school
green-drake
friendless
friendship
friendlies
friendlily
irrelevant
irremeable
irremeably
breezeless
free-select
irreverent
Froebelism
Froebelian
free-verser
greenfield
greenfinch
arpeggiate
arpeggione
greenheart
breechless
greenhouse
free-minded
breeziness
greediness
pre-eminent
creepingly
grievingly
free-fisher
free-diving
praesidium
irreligion
pre-exilian
arse-licker
araeometer
araeometry
creepmouse
free-for-all
free-fooder
freeholder
freeloader
praenomens
gruesomely

Words marked △ may be spelled also with a capital letter

10 □r□e□o

praenomina
praecocial
praetorial
praetorium
praetorian
free-soiler
irrenowned
grievously
free-footed
freebooter
praepostor
irresolute
Greenpeace
pre-emptive
pre-emption
free-spoken
arles-penny
free-trader
cruet-stand
greensward
greenshank
greenspeak
greenstick
kriegspiel
greenstone
greenstuff
araeostyle
arrestable
arrestment
priestship
priest-like
priest-king
priestling
freestyler
orientally
priesthood
orientated
orientator
praemunire
tree-burial
praeludium
freedwoman
freedwomen
proficient
arefaction
prefecture
proffering
draft-horse
profligate
profligacy
craftiness
draftiness
triflingly
griffinish
griffinism
triffidian
graffitist
trafficked
trafficker
trifoliate
truffle-dog

artfulness
irefulness
prefulgent
profulgent
truffle-pig
profundity
prefrontal
trifurcate
preferable
preferably
preferment
preferring
preference
trifarious
professing
profession
profitable
profitably
profitless
profoundly
profluence
prefixture
orographic
prognathic
urographic
pragmatise
pragmatize
drag-racing
pre-glacial
pragmatism
pragmatics
pragmatist
trigrammic
programmed
programmer
braggartly
fragrantly
pregnantly
tragically
tragicomic
tragacanth
frigidness
drug-addict
bragadisme
triggerman
fragmented
fragmental
cragginess
dregginess
grogginess
braggingly
priggishly
trigeminal
frog's-march
frog's-mouth
brigandage
dragonnade
Trogonidae
dragonhead
brigandine
brigantine

dragonlike
dragon-fish
originally
dragon-root
dragon-tree
orogenesis
orogenetic
urogenital
originator
progenitor
frog-hopper
prognostic
proglottis
troglodyte
△krugerrand
frigorific
gregarious
brightness
frightened
brightsome
frightsome
bright-work
bright-eyed
drug-pusher
drug-runner
triglyphic
arthralgia
arthralgic
Brahmanism
orthoboric
prohibiter
prohibitor
orthoclase
orthocaine
Orthoceras
orchideous
orthodromy
archdeacon
orthoepist
orthograph
archegonia
orthogenic
orthogonal
arch-chimic
arch-pirate
archbishop
archaicism
Brahminism
archaistic
arch-flamen
Archimedes
archontate
archonship
prehensile
prehensive
prehension
orphanhood
prehensory
arthromere
orpheoreon
Arthropoda

archeology
orthopraxy
orthopedia
orthopedic
△orthoptera
orthopaedy
orthoprism
orthoptics
orthoptist
orthopnoea
orthophyre
Arthuriana
arch-priest
orcharding
archerfish
orchardist
orchardman
orchestics
prehistory
orchestric
orchestral
architrave
arrhythmia
arrhythmic
orthotonic
orthotropy
orthotopic
archetypal
Urticaceae
ordinately
irrigative
irritative
urticarial
fruitarian
irrigation
irritation
ordination
urtication
ordinarily
dreikanter
brainchild
cruisewear
fruiteress
praiseless
greisenise
greisenize
broidering
armigerous
fruitfully
craigfluke
freightage
freight-car
ornithopod
ornithosis
braininess
praisingly
trailingly
artificial
fruit-knife
treillaged
armillaria

armipotent
arvicoline
traitorism
traitorous
drainpipes
brainpower
arbitrable
arrière-ban
arbitrager
arbitrator
brainstorm
artistical
Articulata
articulate
articulacy
projectile
projective
projecting
projection
trajection
trajectory
projecture
prejudiced
brake-block
crakeberry
trekschuit
brokenness
broken-down
prokaryote
drakestone
brake-wheel
Araliaceae
trilobitic
trilobated
prolicidal
frolicking
prelection
trilocular
frolicsome
prolocutor
preludious
trolleybus
trolley-car
trolley-man
grille-work
prolifical
orological
urological
prologuise
prologuize
brilliance
trillionth
brilliancy
Ural-Altaic
prolongate
trilineate
prelingual
trilingual
Trollopean
trolloping
trollopish

Words marked △ may be spelled also with a capital letter

Trollopian
drill-press
grillsteak
prelatical
trilateral
triliteral
prolixness
prolixious
grammarian
grammatist
gramicidin
premedical
trumpeting
trammelled
trammeller
trammel-net
brome-grass
primogenit
Bramah-lock
frame-house
grumpiness
trimmingly
promulgate
drumbledor
tremolandi
tremolando
tremolitic
frame-maker
tromometer
tramontana
tramontane
promenader
trimonthly
criminally
prominence
prominency
gramineous
tremendous
promontory
premonitor
trampoline
trombonist
grimlooked
framboesia
△gramophone
gramophony
primiparae
primiparas
tremorless
trimorphic
primordial
primordium
premarital
fremescent
promiseful
promissive
Arimaspian
promissory
promptuary
promotable
dramatical
eremitical
primatical
prometheum
Promethean
promptness
arsmetrick
promethium
prompt-note
prompt-book
prompt-copy
dramaturge
dramaturgy
wry-mouthed
primevally
premaxilla
iron-handed
truncately
truncation
ironmaster
transactor
front-bench
pronuclear
pronucleus
grandchild
transcribe
△trinacrian
transcript
irenically
ironically
arenaceous
grand-ducal
transducer
granddaddy
drink-drive
wrongdoing
granadilla
grenadilla
orange-peel
fringeless
grangerise
grangerize
orange-wife
princelike
bronze-wing
cringeling
princeling
trinketing
Grangerism
orange-lily
orange-wood
princehood
orange-root
orange-tree
princessly
transeptal
wrongfully
transferee
transferor
transfuser
transgress
transgenic
brant-goose
brent-goose
branchiate
branchless
trench-feet
branch-line
trenchancy
bronchiole
branch-work
trench-coat
trench-foot
franchisee
franchiser
bronchitic
bronchitis
grant-in-aid
brand-image
frangipane
principate
frangipani
Franciscan
crankiness
trendiness
drinking-up
cringingly
grindingly
gruntingly
prancingly
prankingly
princified
transitive
iron-mining
principial
principium
transition
fringillid
iron-willed
principled
principles
frantic-mad
trunnioned
transience
transiency
transitory
iron-fisted
iron-witted
transistor
iron-liquor
crenellate
trundle-bed
translucid
granulomas
crinolined
iron-glance
translunar
granularly
uranalysis
urinalysis
granulitic
crenulated
granulated
crinolette
granulater
granulator
translator
trunk-maker
grandmamma
pronominal
drink-money
transmuter
urinometer
uranometry
grand-niece
pronuncios
pruning-saw
brontosaur
iron-worded
ironmonger
Francophil
transonics
craniology
craniotomy
wrongously
transplant
prenuptial
pronephric
pronephros
transposal
transposon
transposer
transputer
granophyre
grandstand
trans-shape
crankshaft
crank-sided
cranesbill
crane's-bill
trans-sonic
grindstone
triniscope
urinoscopy
trinitrate
frenetical
wrong-timed
transudate
pronounced
grand-uncle
pronouncer
tranquilly
transvalue
transverse
front-wheel
frontwards
printworks
brandy-ball
brandy-snap
ergomaniac
Areopagite
areolation
arrogation
Eriocaulon
artocarpus
argonautic
arrogantly
trioecious
cryoscopic
cryogenics
cryometric
arrow-grass
ergophobia
cryophilic
troop-horse
eriophorum
cryophorus
proof-house
broodiness
droopiness
broodingly
droopingly
prioritise
prioritize
Ordovician
priorities
ergodicity
ordonnance
cryoconite
ergonomics
bryologist
ergonomist
oreologist
crio-sphinx
brood-pouch
armourless
armour-clad
areography
oreography
broomstaff
proof-sheet
broomstick
pro-oestrus
ergosterol
wrap-rascal
trap-ladder
drop-hammer
propraetor
oropharynx
prepuberty
tropically
drupaceous
tripudiate
tripudiary
prophetess
tripleness
graplement
prophesied
tripperish
trophesial
prophetism
prophesier
graphemics
tropaeolum
tropaeolin

Words marked △ may be spelled also with a capital letter

10 □r□p□e

tripterous
drop-letter
grapefruit
propagable
propagulum
△propaganda
propagator
tripehound
triplicate
graphicacy
preppiness
trappiness
trippingly
graphitise
graphitize
trephining
eruptivity
triplicity
eruptional
graphitoid
uropoiesis
proprietor
propellant
propylaeum
prepollent
propellent
propelment
tropologic
propulsive
propelling
propulsion
crapulence
propulsory
grape-louse
tripinnate
propendent
prepensely
propensely
prepensive
propensive
trepanning
propension
propensity
treponemas
treponemes
propionate
cryptogamy
tryptophan
graptolite
Trophonian
cryptology
graphology
trophology
cryptogram
proproctor
tropopause
tropophyte
preparedly
properness
propertied
tripartite

tripartism
proportion
preparator
wraparound
proposable
prepossess
crêpe-soled
grapestone
prepositor
crepuscule
propitiate
prepotence
prepotency
triphthong
propitious
propounder
cropduster
tripe-woman
gripe-water
prepayable
prepayment
Triphysite
trapeziums
pre-qualify
triquetral
triquetrum
frequenter
frequently
craquelure
triradiate
pruriently
prerelease
proratable
crossandra
crustacean
prostatism
crispation
crustation
prestation
cross-armed
trespasser
crispbread
crossbreed
crossbench
crossbones
fresh-blown
frostbound
crossbower
crossclaim
crosscheck
trisection
criss-cross
trisectrix
prosecutor
presidiary
prosodical
presidency
presidiums
fresherdom
crescendos
arms-length

urostegite
proscenium
triskelion
prosperity
presternum
prosperous
crescentic
crescented
prospector
prospectus
brass-faced
crossfield
trustfully
dressguard
grass-green
presageful
presignify
grass-grown
dress-goods
urosthenic
prostheses
prosthesis
prosthetic
trust-house
brassiness
crustiness
drossiness
friskiness
frostiness
grassiness
grisliness
trashiness
trustiness
crushingly
friskingly
graspingly
pressingly
trustingly
tristichic
prosaicism
prescience
cristiform
Aristippus
prosciutti
prosciutto
crassitude
prostitute
trisulcate
prosilient
drysaltery
crosslight
presumable
presumably
dressmaker
cross-match
drosometer
present-day
prisonment
presentive
presential
Krishnaism

presension
prismoidal
gressorial
prostomial
prostomium
uroscopist
aristology
aristocrat
crosspiece
drosophila
erysipelas
presuppose
crash-proof
cross-party
crosspatch
crossroads
prescriber
proscriber
cross-refer
presurmise
grass-roots
frustrated
cross-staff
dress-shirt
cross-stone
frost-smoke
presetting
proseuchae
pressurise
pressurize
bressummer
brusquerie
grasswrack
brushwheel
Irishwoman
presswoman
wristwatch
freshwater
presbytery
presbytism
presbyopia
presbyopic
Proteaceae
tritiation
prothallia
prothallic
prothallus
protracted
protractor
protective
protecting
protection
protocolic
critically
tritically
△cretaceous
triticeous
protectory
protectrix
brother-man
arytaenoid

protreptic
brutifying
gratifying
gratefully
truthfully
wrathfully
Arctogaeic
Arctogaean
erotogenic
wretchedly
protohuman
frothiness
grittiness
prettiness
wrathiness
writhingly
fratricide
bratticing
crithidial
erethismic
trithionic
proteiform
gratuitous
proteinous
erethistic
Trotskyite
Trotskyism
Trotskyist
fritillary
prattlebox
Crotalidae
gratillity
crotalaria
erotomania
arithmetic
pretendant
pretendent
protensive
writing-ink
pretension
pre-tension
protension
orotundity
protensity
protonemal
pratincole
protanopia
tritanopia
protanopic
tritanopic
writing-pad
trattorias
grotto-work
proteolyse
protoplasm
protoplast
arctophile
arctophily
protopathy
Protophyta
protophyte

Words marked △ may be spelled also with a capital letter

triternate
oratorical
writership
fraternise
fraternize
fraternity
protervity
erythritic
urethritic
triturator
ureteritis
urethritis
Fratercula
△protestant
protostele
Britishism
frithsoken
frithstool
grith-stool
prototypal
protrudent
protrusile
protrusive
protrusion
truth-value
protoxylem
protozoans
trou-madame
traumatise
traumatize
traumatism
arcubalist
trouvaille
troubadour
ground-bass
groundmass
groundbait
groundedly
groundsell
groundless
groundling
groundsill
groundplot
groundsman
ground-hold
ground-dove
groundwork
groundprox
arguteness
trousering
trouser-leg
trou-de-loup
argumentum
proud-flesh
fraudfully
crouch-ware
fraughtage
draught-bar
draughtman
draught-net
croupiness
troubledly
triumphant
triumphery
triumphing
trousseaus
trousseaux
troutstone
trout-spoon
fraudulent
triumviral
trivialise
trivialize
trivialism
triviality
provocable
crève-coeur
provection
provocator
providable
△providence
proveditor
prevailing
provokable
gravel-walk
privileged
travelogue
drivelling
gravelling
grovelling
travelling
travel-sick
prevalence
trivalence
prevalency
trivalency
travelator
travolator
grave-maker
gravimeter
gravimetry
Provençale
driving-box
cravenness
prevenient
preventive
provincial
prevention
provenance
prevenancy
graveolent
previously
driverless
travertine
traversing
proverbial
gravestone
provisions
gravity-fed
brevetting
Gravettian
provitamin
privatiser
privatizer
Drawcansir
brewmaster
crew-necked
trawlerman
browbeater
brownfield
drowsihead
brawniness
drowsiness
drawlingly
frowningly
growlingly
prowlingly
crewellery
arc-welding
trowelling
crewelwork
crow-flower
growing-bag
brow-antler
drawing-pen
drawing-pin
brown-noser
ore-wrought
Erewhonian
drawbridge
Brownshirt
brownstone
drawstring
draw-string
crown-wheel
proximally
fraxinella
grey-haired
grey-headed
grey-wether
dray-plough
trey-antler
argyrodite
traymobile
grey-coated
prayerless
arty-crafty
prizefight
brazil-wood
brazen-face
brazenness
prizewoman
asparagine
escalation
escaladoes
escapadoes
escalatory
astarboard
estanciero
escapeless
escapement
assafetida
estatesman
Islamicise
Islamicize
isoaminile
Asiaticism
Islamicist
ascariasis
essayistic
assailable
assailment
escallonia
escalloped
Ismailitic
Israelitic
escamotage
astacology
escapology
assay-piece
escarpment
escadrille
espadrille
isoantigen
usableness
isabelline
isocyanide
isochasmic
isocheimic
isocheimal
psychicism
psychicist
psychiater
psychiatry
psychopath
psychopomp
psychogony
psychology
psychogram
Psocoptera
usucapient
usucaption
isochronal
isodynamic
Isoetaceae
assemblage
osteoblast
osteoclast
osteocolla
ascendable
ascendible
ascendance
ascendence
ascendancy
ascendency
asseverate
osmeterium
aspergilla
osteogenic
asceticism
asteridian
asperities
asterisked
especially
asteriated
Osteolepis
Asteroidea
asteroidal
osteopathy
osteophyte
assessable
ostensible
ostensibly
assessment
aspectable
assertable
assentient
asbestosis
assentator
asafoetida
usefulness
isogametic
isogenetic
isoglossal
isoglottic
isoglottal
escheatage
escharotic
ischuretic
asphyxiate
asphyxiant
estimative
aspiration
estimation
estivation
oscitation
aspiratory
oscitantly
ossiferous
assibilate
assimilate
aspiringly
osmiridium
aspidistra
oscillator
astigmatic
assignable
assignment
ossivorous
osmidrosis
assistance
estipulate
isokinetic
Ashkenazim
psilocybin
psalterium
psalterian
psellismus
psalmodise
psalmodize
psalmodist
ashlar-work
isoleucine
Ishmaelite
asymmetric

Words marked △ may be spelled also with a capital letter

10 □s□m□e

Asymmetron
psammophil
isomorphic
isometrics
asymptotic
isoniazide
asyntactic
asynchrony
asynartete
isentropic
astomatous
assonantal
associable
astonished
assoilment
astounding
assortment
ascomycete
esophageal
isopterous
asepticise
asepticize
asepticism
Ostpolitik
psephology
usurpative
usurpation
usurpatory
usurpature
ascribable
asarabacca
escribanos
ostracodan
ostrich-egg
astrictive
ostrichism
astriction
ostraceous
esuriently
△astragalus
estrogenic
usurpingly
astrologic
astrologer
astrolatry
astrometry
estrangelo
astringent
astronomic
astronomer
usuriously
ascription
escritoire
tsarevitch
isoseismic
isoseismal
asystolism
isosporous
tsesarevna
psittacine
isothermal
isotropism
isotropous
Esculapian
osculation
ustulation
osculatory
usquebaugh
escutcheon
astuteness
assurgency
pseudimago
assumingly
pseudocarp
pseudoacid
pseudocode
pseudology
pseudobulb
assumptive
△assumption
asexuality
assythment
stravaiger
Athanasian
strawboard
strawberry
ethambutol
stiacciato
stracchini
stracchino
strandflat
strandwolf
strategics
strategist
atramental
straggling
straighten
straightly
attachable
attachment
strathspey
steakhouse
Stradivari
steadiness
steaminess
stealingly
stratified
strabismic
strabismal
strabismus
stratiform
attackable
attainable
strainedly
attainment
attainture
steatocele
stramonium
strabotomy
stratocrat
strapontin
strappados
stearsmate
Uto-Aztecan
straitness
steamtight
stealthing
stealthily
straitened
atracurium
stibialism
stablemate
stableness
stubbiness
stabbingly
stubble-fed
stabiliser
stabilizer
stubbornly
sticharion
sticcadoes
sticcatoes
stochastic
stockhorse
stickiness
stockiness
stockinged
stockinger
stichidium
stichology
stock-still
stickybeak
stodginess
stadholder
studiously
otter-board
attendment
attendance
attendancy
ethereally
streperous
otherguess
strengthen
othergates
otter-hound
strepitant
steeliness
steepiness
strepitoso
strepitous
strelitzia
strelitzes
streamless
streamline
streamling
athermancy
stream-gold
streamered
attempered
steersmate
stressless
Etheostoma
otter-shrew
streetward
otter-trawl
streetlamp
attestable
streetwise
streetroom
attentions
street-cred
streetfuls
attenuated
attenuator
otherwhere
otherwhile
otherworld
steelworks
stiffening
stuffiness
stiflingly
stigmatise
stigmatize
stigmatism
stagnation
stigmarian
stigmatist
stigmatose
stagnantly
stagecoach
stagecraft
stag-headed
staggering
steganopod
ethicality
strideways
stridelegs
strifeless
stripeless
attirement
strife-torn
stridently
stringhalt
stringless
stringendo
stringency
stripiness
strikingly
strivingly
strigiform
strinkling
strip-poker
strippings
striptease
strictness
strictured
stridulate
stridulant
stridulous
Italianate
stellately
Italianise
Italianize
Italianism
Italianist
stillatory
stalwartly
stillbirth
stalactite
stolidness
stallenger
stylograph
stalagmite
stillhouse
stiltiness
stallinger
stellified
stultified
stillicide
stultifier
stelliform
ateleiosis
stylolitic
Ptolemaean
Ptolemaist
stylometry
stolenwise
stylopised
stylopized
still-stand
utilisable
stylistics
stilettoed
stellulate
still-video
utilizable
stemmatous
stomachful
stomachous
stammering
stamp-hinge
stemwinder
stumpiness
stimulable
stumblebum
stimulancy
stimulator
stimpmeter
stomatopod
stomatitis
Stannaries
stand-alone
stonebrash
stonebreak
stone-blind
stone-broke
stony-broke
stoneborer
stone-crazy
ethnically
standers-by
stone-eater
stenograph
stanchable
stanchless

Words marked △ may be spelled also with a capital letter

stanchness
stonehorse
stinginess
stingingly
stinkingly
stintingly
stunningly
stenciling
stencilled
stenciller
stonemason
stentorian
stannotype
stenopaeic
standpoint
Ctenophora
ctenophore
itinerancy
stone's-cast
standstill
stone-still
stinkstone
stenotopic
etiolation
stroganoff
stromatous
otioseness
strong-knit
stronghold
strongroom
strophiole
strobilate
stoopingly
strobiline
strobiloid
attornment
atmologist
ethologist
atmosphere
stepdancer
stepladder
step-parent
stepfather
stephanite
utopianise
utopianize
utopianism
stupration
stupidness
stupefying
stypticity
step-sister
stipellate
stipulator
stupendous
stepmother
staphyline
staphyloma
sternalgia
sternalgic
eternalise
eternalize
stargazing
starvation
eternalist
sternboard
storyboard
stormbound
stern-chase
attractant
attractive
attracting
attraction
uterectomy
starveling
stormfully
storefront
sterigmata
Pterygotus
starchedly
star-shaped
storehouse
starriness
storminess
sturdiness
startingly
stirringly
steriliser
pterylosis
sterilizer
pteranodon
stark-naked
start-naked
stereocard
stercorate
stereobate
stercorary
starmonger
stertorous
stereotomy
storiology
stereogram
stereopsis
stereotype
stereotypy
stormproof
star-bright
sternsheet
stork'sbill
sternwards
sternworks
starry-eyed
state-aided
statecraft
statically
stuttering
statuesque
stitchwork
stitchwort
stationary
stationery
statistics
statoscope
statutable
statutably
staunching
ythundered
étourderie
Struldbrug
attunement
struggling
stouthrief
struthioid
struthious
stoutherie
staurolite
structured
structural
stavesacre
stewardess
ethylamine
strychnine
strychnism
stay-at-home
sugarallie
tularaemia
tularaemic
sugar-baker
subarcuate
autarchist
Judaically
sugar-candy
put-and-take
cup-and-ball
subaudible
cup-and-ring
subacetate
subaverage
mujaheddin
humaneness
curateship
mutagenise
mutagenize
subangular
sugarhouse
queasiness
sugariness
humanities
curability
dupability
durability
mutability
subacidity
sueability
durational
mutational
nutational
humanistic
autarkical
Muhammadan
Muhammedan
eudaemonia
eudaemonic
euharmonic
Muraenidae
curatorial
fumatorium
sudatorium
subatomics
Eurafrican
subarticle
mulattress
eubacteria
hupaithric
rub-a-dub-dub
subacutely
subaqueous
subaquatic
eucaryotic
eukaryotic
eucalyptol
eucalyptus
quebrachos
curbmarket
dumb-waiter
Purbeckian
turbidness
tumble-cart
curbvendor
tumbleweed
humbleness
mumble-news
mumblement
tumblerful
dumbledore
rubble-work
tumbledown
bumble-foot
outbreath'd
outbreathe
tumble-dung
humbuggery
humbugging
purblindly
fumblingly
humblingly
jumblingly
mumblingly
rumblingly
bumbailiff
lumbricoid
Mumbo-Jumbo
mumbo-jumbo
tunbellied
rumbullion
outbalance
turbulence
turbulency
turbulator
husbandage
husbandman
lumbang-oil
turbinated
rum-blossom
cumbrously
zumbooruck
lumber-yard
lumberjack
outbargain
rue-bargain
lumber-camp
curbtrader
rubberneck
rubberwear
cumberless
numberless
cumberment
lumber-mill
cumbersome
lumbersome
lumber-room
rubber-room
rubbishing
sunbathing
dumbstruck
outbluster
bubbly-jock
surcharged
surcharger
cunctative
subcranial
cunctation
punctation
subclavian
nutcracker
cunctatory
outclassed
Munchausen
subchanter
subchapter
subcharter
nunciature
subcabinet
succubuses
juncaceous
suicidally
succedanea
punch-drunk
subchelate
butchering
quickening
succeeding
zucchettos
quick-firer
bunch-grass
quick-hedge
bunchiness
subceiling
punctilios
functional
puschkinia
auscultate
subcalibre
subcaliber
punch-ladle

succulence
quick-lunch
succulency
dulciloquy
muscularly
subculture
subcompact
outcompete
quick-match
Vulcanalia
subcentral
buccinator
succinctly
lusciously
suscipient
susceptive
Turcophile
subception
Turcophobe
subcordate
muscardine
subcarrier
muscarinic
subcircuit
successful
successive
succussive
quick-stick
succession
succussion
quick-sandy
lunch-table
quicktrick
quickthorn
punctulate
punctually
subcrustal
punctuator
muscovados
Muscovitic
Dutchwoman
Dutchwomen
quick-water
subdialect
subdeanery
quadrangle
quadratics
quadratrix
quadrantal
quadrantes
quadratura
quadrature
buddy-buddy
subduction
duodecimal
duodecimos
subdecanal
outdacious
fuddy-duddy
humdudgeon
hurdle-race

muddlehead
subduement
out-dweller
quadrennia
cuddlesome
pundigrion
hurdy-gurdy
quadrireme
quadriceps
quadrisect
quadrivial
quadrivium
quadriller
quadricone
quadripole
quadriform
Buddhistic
cul-de-lampe
pudding-bag
suddenness
burdensome
pudding-pie
pundonores
duodenitis
fund-holder
dunderpate
dunderhead
rudderless
sunderment
wunderkind
rudder-fish
sunderance
dunderfunk
Bundesrath
Bundesbank
Bundeswehr
Quadrumana
quadrumane
quadruplet
quadruplex
quadrumvir
subdivider
Tuberaceae
Juvenalian
numeration
superation
superalloy
lukewarmth
lukewarmly
suzerainty
superaltar
superacute
superbrain
superbness
superclass
queencraft
superclean
Lupercalia
tuberculum
tuberculin
tubercular

pubescence
quiescence
tumescence
quiescency
supercargo
superdense
super-duper
Jugendstil
superexalt
euhemerise
euhemerize
quietening
Euhemerism
eugenecist
euhemerist
superfecta
superfluid
supergrass
supergiant
supergroup
aubergiste
superheavy
Bucephalus
superhuman
Judenhetze
juvenilely
rune-singer
eugenicist
juvenility
tuberiform
mucedinous
superiorly
Puseyistic
quietistic
superlunar
Aureomycin®
supernally
gubernator
sure-enough
supernovae
supernovas
superorder
superoxide
eudemonism
eudemonics
numerosity
tuberosity
autecology
numerology
numerously
surefooted
superposed
superpower
super-royal
Queensland
superstate
supersharp
superseder
superspeed
auger-shell
supersweet

supersonic
superstore
mutessarif
supersound
supersaver
quaestuary
lutestring
rupestrian
supertonic
supertitle
puberulent
puberulous
bureaucrat
supervisee
supervisal
supervisor
superwoman
suretyship
surf-bather
ruffianish
ruffianism
suffragism
sufflation
suffragist
surfcaster
surfactant
sufficient
surfaceman
tuffaceous
outfielder
bufflehead
buff-jerkin
bumfreezer
suffigance
gunfighter
surfeiting
surf-riding
ruefulness
fulfilment
fulfilling
buffalo-nut
muffin-bell
luffing-jib
buffoonery
outflowing
sufferable
sufferably
subfertile
sufferance
rumfustian
suffisance
subfuscous
outfitting
dumfounder
curfew-bell
sulfhydryl
burglarise
burglarize
subglacial
sunglasses
fungicidal

surgically
ruggedness
turgidness
dung-beetle
judgmental
luggage-van
quagginess
bunglingly
jugglingly
cudgelling
nudge-nudge
subgeneric
outgeneral
subgenuses
subglobose
△juggernaut
budgerigar
fungus-gall
turgescent
suggestive
outgassing
suggestion
humgruffin
dung-hunter
rush-candle
bushranger
Buchmanite
subheading
Buchmanism
bushwalker
bush-harrow
bushmaster
bush-lawyer
ruthlessly
bush-shrike
euphuistic
bushelling
oughtlings
euphonical
cub-hunting
euphonious
ruthenious
euthanasia
Euthyneura
rush-holder
euchlorine
mushroomer
Euphrosyne
euphoriant
authorless
authorship
euphorbium
rutherford
Authorized
eurhythmic
push-stroke
jumhouriya
euphausiid
push-button
ouvirandra
Punicaceae

Words marked △ may be spelled also with a capital letter

dubitative
judicative
puritanise
puritanize
ruminative
luminarism
puritanism
dubitation
fugitation
fumigation
jubilation
judication
lumination
Lusitanian
mutilation
rumination
Ruritanian
supination
luminarist
musicality
pupiparous
fumigatory
judicatory
duniwassal
Ruminantia
jubilantly
ruminantly
judicature
muliebrity
rubiaceous
luciferase
supineness
Luciferian
auriferous
luciferous
muciferous
nubiferous
nubigenous
nuciferous
pupigerous
tulip-eared
rudimental
audiograph
tuning-fork
punishable
mulishness
punishment
music-house
munificent
fugitively
humidifier
audibility
fusibility
judicially
munifience
musicianer
musicianly
rubiginose
culiciform
cupidinous
fuliginous
rubiginous
pugilistic
humiliator
humidistat
numismatic
audiometer
eudiometer
fusionless
rupicoline
auditorium
luminosity
nucivorous
rupicolous
tubicolous
musicology
luminously
mutinously
audiophile
nudibranch
music-shell
pumie-stone
subintrant
juristical
puristical
quaintness
auriculate
funiculate
lucifugous
subjective
subjection
surjection
subjectify
subjugator
subjoinder
outjetting
outjutting
buck-rabbit
muck-raking
buck-basket
musk-mallow
Aufklärung
duck-legged
Turkmenian
junk-dealer
huckle-bone
lucklessly
musk-beetle
duckshover
muck-midden
duck-billed
cuckoldise
cuckoldize
husking-bee
subkingdom
sucking-pig
cuckoo-spit
duck-footed
junk-bottle
muckspread
lucky-piece
Quaker-bird
dukkeripen
huckstress
musket-rest
musket-shot
junketings
Turko-Tatar
bucketfuls
buck-jumper
turkey-cock
turkey-trot
full-handed
nuclearise
nuclearize
nucleation
full-sailed
full-manned
hurlbarrow
hullabaloo
hurly-burly
publicness
duplicator
outlodging
bull-headed
full-length
bull-beggar
bull-necked
bull-beeves
nullifying
qualifying
guilefully
mudlogging
mulligrubs
full-circle
guiltiness
full-rigged
full-winged
qualmishly
dull-witted
sublimable
subliminal
sublimated
muslin-kale
sullenness
outlandish
nulla-nulla
Euglenales
sublingual
nucleolate
full-voiced
full-bodied
guillotine
nucleoside
nucleotide
nucleonics
bullionist
full-cocked
nucleosome
bull-roarer
full-bottom
butlership
gully-raker
dull-browed
bullet-head
subletting
bullet-tree
sunlounger
full-summed
guilty-like
outmeasure
mummy-cloth
submucosae
submucosal
submediant
curmudgeon
mummifying
nutmegging
duumvirate
pummelling
nummulitic
nummulated
submontane
Kuomintang
summonable
submanager
fulmineous
Pulmonaria
humming-top
summerlike
summertide
summertime
curmurring
submersion
submariner
summerwood
cummerbund
surmisable
submissive
submission
summitless
hug-me-tight
submitting
surmounted
surmounter
mummy-wheat
subnuclear
quinacrine
pugnacious
quink-goose
quenchable
quenchless
quantitive
quantifier
tunnelling
surnominal
turning-saw
quinaquina
turnbroach
vulnerable
runner-bean
turnaround
subnascent
burnishing
burnettise
burnettize
subnatural
turnbuckle
quintuplet
quinsy-wort
automatism
humoralism
automation
automatist
humoralist
Euromarket
autogamous
automatons
suborbital
autoscopic
subordinal
out-of-doors
bufotenine
autogenics
autoteller
suboceanic
autogenous
humoresque
Tudoresque
subofficer
tumorgenic
autophobia
autophagia
autochthon
autotheism
autotheist
Eurocheque
autodidact
Mucorineae
Eurovision
tutorially
eulogistic
humoristic
Euroclydon
autoplasty
tuboplasty
Yugoslavic
auto-immune
bubonocele
automobile
automotive
autonomics
autonomist
autologous
autonomous
humorously
humourless
humoursome
autography
autocratic
autoerotic
Eurocratic
autostrada
autoptical
suboctuple

10 □u□o□u

Eurotunnel
sulphatase
pump-handle
sulphation
pulp-cavity
hump-backed
supplanter
suspectful
pump-action
auspicious
suspicious
lumpectomy
suppedanea
cuspidated
subpoenaed
rumple-bane
supplejack
suppleness
subprefect
supplement
suppletive
suppletion
pumple-nose
purple-born
suppletory
suppressed
suppressor
purple-hued
supplicate
supplicant
surprising
bumpkinish
suppliance
dumpy-level
mumping-day
suspenders
pulp-engine
suspensive
turpentine
out-pension
suspension
turpentiny
suspensoid
jumping-off
suspensory
sulphonate
sulphonium
jump-jockey
subprogram
rumpy-pumpy
Tupperware®
supperless
suppertime
supportive
supporting
subphrenic
outperform
suspirious
supporture
supposable
supposably
supposedly
purposeful
surpassing
outpassion
out-patient
puppet-show
put-putting
puppet-play
sulphurate
surplusage
sulphurise
sulphurize
outpouring
lumpsucker
sulphurous
supplyment
supply-side
musquetoon
surrealism
quartation
surrealist
burr-walnut
curriculum
curricular
rubrically
lubricious
lubricator
rubricator
putridness
quarterage
quarter-boy
quarrender
quarter-day
quartering
quarter-ill
puerperium
quarrelled
quarreller
quarteroon
quarter-saw
putrefying
outrageous
surrogatum
puir's-hoose
guardhouse
puir's-house
quarriable
quirkiness
hurryingly
queryingly
quercitron
sucralfate
supralunar
burramundi
currant-bun
guaranteed
quarantine
gunrunning
rum-running
Quirinalia
mucronated
suprapubic
subreptive
subreption
eutrapelia
quersprung
suprarenal
putrescent
putrescine
cuirassier
quernstone
turret-ship
Turritella
nutritious
subroutine
furrow-weed
burrow-duck
quartz-mill
quartz-rock
quartzitic
Russianise
Russianize
Russianism
outstation
substation
Russianist
puissaunce
puissantly
pursuantly
nurse-child
bumsucking
subsection
subsidiary
outside-car
cursedness
cussedness
quesadilla
subsidence
subsidency
subspecies
outspeckle
Aussiedler
substellar
substernal
outsweeten
sub-Saharan
nursehound
guest-house
pursuivant
nun's-fiddle
gunslinger
mudslinger
outswinger
guessingly
pursuingly
questingly
subsoiling
questionee
questioner
subspinous
substitute
Mussulmans
Russellite
subsultive
subsellium
mussel-plum
russel-cord
subsultory
curselarie
subsumable
pulsimeter
pulsometer
nursing-bra
guest-night
Cuisenaire
purse-pride
Russophile
purse-proud
Russophobe
subsequent
subsurface
subscribed
subscriber
subshrubby
bursarship
pursership
tusser-silk
nurseryman
gut-scraper
outstretch
substratal
substratum
subsistent
purse-seine
subsessile
outsetting
sunsetting
Pulsatilla
pulsatance
fuss-budget
numskulled
subtrahend
australite
fustianise
fustianize
Australian
lustration
fustianist
nuptiality
Australorp
subtracter
subtractor
rustic-ware
justiciary
multicycle
Eustachian
mustachios
multocular
rustically
rustic-work
pultaceous
rusticated
rusticator
lustreware
turtleback
turtleneck
lustreless
subtleness
cuttlefish
cuttle-bone
turtledove
huntiegowk
quatrefoil
turtle-soup
hurtlessly
multifaced
putty-faced
tuftaffeta
tuftaffety
justifying
Guttiferae
multigrade
sultriness
austringer
rustlingly
sustaining
cultriform
lust-dieted
bur-thistle
putty-knife
multilobed
Mustelidae
subtilness
Mustelinae
multiloquy
custom-made
customable
multimedia
customised
customized
sustentate
button-back
button-ball
hunting-box
hunting-cog
hunting-cap
hunting-cat
buttoned-up
muttonhead
subtangent
mutton-chop
sultanship
just-in-time
sustentive
sustention
mutton-fist
fustanella
purtenance
sustenance
subtenancy
buttonhold
button-wood
buttonhole
button-hook

Words marked △ may be spelled also with a capital letter

austenitic
button-bush
mutton-suet
auctionary
tuitionary
auctioneer
subtropics
lustrously
multiphase
multiplane
multiplied
multiplier
multipolar
butter-bake
quaternate
subterrane
butter-ball
quatorzain
subterrain
△**quaternary**
culturable
nurturable
buttery-bar
butterhead
subterrene
butter-bean
butter-bird
butter-wife
muster-file
butter-dish
butter-fish
butter-milk
quaternion
quaternity
culturally
gutturally
butterdock
muster-book
mustard-oil
muster-roll
butter-boat
butterwort
butter-tree
subterfuge
put-through
run-through
butter-bump
multi-stage
cutty-stool
multistory
multi-track
tut-tutting
quotatious
pultrusion
rust-bucket
tub-thumper
tuft-hunter
cultivable
multivocal
multivious
cultivator

cumulative
cumulation
suturation
tubularian
tubulation
tubularity
tubulature
cucurbital
furuncular
futureless
luculently
purulently
futurition
luxuriance
luxuriancy
cucumiform
cumuliform
futuristic
cucullated
autumnally
futurology
lugubrious
lucubrator
tumultuate
tumultuary
augustness
tumultuous
curvaceous
curvacious
outvillain
pulvilling
pulvillios
pulvilised
pulvilized
subvention
pulvinated
suaveolent
culvertage
pulverable
culver-keys
subvariety
subversive
subversion
pulveriser
pulverizer
curvetting
survivable
survivance
purveyance
surveyance
mugwumpery
outwrought
tutworkman
outwitting
bunya-bunya
ruby-throat
jury-rigged
July-flower
eurypterid
Eurypterus
jury-rudder

quizmaster
puzzle-head
puzzlement
quizziness
puzzlingly
tuzzi-muzzy
tuzzy-muzzy
fuzzy-wuzzy
evacuative
evacuation
Aviculidae
Avicularia
aviculture
evidential
availingly
evaluative
evaluation
evolvement
evil-minded
evil-worker
evolutions
ivy-mantled
even-handed
avenaceous
avengeress
avengement
evincement
evangelise
evangelize
evangelism
evangeliar
△**evangelist**
avant-garde
even-minded
evanescent
avanturine
aventurine
eventually
avvogadore
avgolemono
evaporable
evaporator
ovipositor
overhanded
overlander
overcaught
overraught
overrashly
overdaring
overlaying
overlaunch
overlabour
overcanopy
overmantel
overmaster
overmatter
ivory-black
overabound
avaricious
averseness
overweight

over-refine
overreckon
overpeople
overleaven
overoffice
overthwart
overshadow
Averrhoism
Averrhoist
overcharge
over-the-top
overthrust
overshower
overridden
overbidder
avertiment
overnicely
overtimely
overwisely
ever-living
overriding
overwinter
overplaced
Everglades
oversleeve
overflight
overglance
overslaugh
overflowed
overinform
overinsure
overdosage
overboldly
overfondly
overbought
overworked
overlocker
overlooker
overcolour
ovariotomy
everyplace
overspread
overpriced
overbridge
overfreely
overgreedy
overpraise
overground
overgrowth
overstrain
overstress
overstride
overstrike
everything
overstrong
overstrung
overstruck
overstayer
overburden
overruling
overrunner

overturner
oversupply
oversubtle
everywhere
overexcite
overexpose
eviscerate
eviternity
avouchable
avouchment
sweath-band
sweatiness
sweatpants
sweatshirt
sweat-shirt
Swadeshism
sweetbread
sweet-briar
sweet-brier
'tweendecks
sweetening
sweetheart
tweediness
sweepingly
sweetie-pie
△**tweedledee**
Tweedledum
sweepstake
sweep-seine
sweet-stuff
tweet-tweet
sweetwater
sweet-water
swaggering
owlishness
sweltering
twelvefold
twelve-note
twelve-tone
twilighted
swellingly
Twelfth-day
swampiness
swimmingly
swan-maiden
swine-drunk
twi-nighter
swingingly
twangingly
twin-sister
swingle-bar
twinflower
swing-music
swan-upping
swing-swang
swing-shelf
swinestone
swing-stock
twi-natured
twy-natured
swan-mussel

Words marked △ may be spelled also with a capital letter

swing-wheel
twenty-five
twentyfold
twenty-four
swooningly
sword-blade
swordcraft
sword-dance
swerveless
sword-guard
sword-grass
dwarfishly
swordproof
sword-stick
swarm-spore
Owlspiegle
twittering
zwitterion
switchback
switchgear
swatchbook
switch-over
twittingly
swivelling
swivel-hook
two-wheeled
two-wheeler
awkwardish
two-year-old
excavation
exhalation
expandable
exsanguine
ex-cathedra
expatiator
expatriate
expansible
expansibly
exhaustive
exhaustion
axe-breaker
oxy-bromide
exobiology
exuberance
exuberancy
execrative
execration
execratory
exactingly
exactitude
exacerbate
executable
executress
executancy
exocytosis
oxidisable
oxidizable
expendable
extendable
extendible
extendedly
exheredate
expeditate
experiment
expeditely
expeditive
expedition
expedience
experience
expediency
exteriorly
excellence
△excellency
externally
excerpting
excerption
extemporal
extensible
expectable
expectably
expectedly
exceptless
expertness
expectance
expectancy
exceptious
extenuator
exaggerate
exogenetic
oxygenator
exiguously
exegetical
exhilarate
exhilarant
excitative
excitation
expiration
excitatory
expiratory
extinctive
extinction
exsiccator
extincture
excitement
extinguish
excitingly
exhibitive
exhibition
exhibitory
extirpable
extirpator
exaltation
exultation
exultantly
explicable
explicator
explicitly
excludable
exulcerate
exploitage
exultingly
exploitive
explosible
examinable
examinator
eximiously
oxymoronic
exenterate
ox-antelope
axinomancy
exonerator
axiomatics
excogitate
expositive
exposition
expository
exfoliator
axiologist
exportable
exophagous
exopoditic
exurbanite
exprobrate
excruciate
extractant
extricable
uxoricidal
extractive
extraction
extradotal
exorbitate
exorbitant
uxorilocal
excrementa
extramural
extraneity
extraneous
uxoriously
expressage
extrusible
excrescent
expressive
expression
extra-solar
expressman
expressure
expressway
exasperate
exospheric
exosporous
exoticness
exotically
exothermic
exothermal
exoterical
exhumation
excusatory
expunction
exsufflate
expurgator
expugnable
exculpable
excursions
excursuses
exuviation
synaxarion
pyracantha
gynandrism
synandrium
gynandrous
synandrous
hypalgesia
hypalgesic
dynamitard
△sybaritish
△sybaritism
pyramidion
dynamicist
pyramidist
gyrational
dynamistic
tyrannical
Lycaenidae
Tyrannidae
Zygaenidae
△hyracoidea
dynamogeny
synaloepha
synaeresis
dynastical
tyrant-bird
hypanthium
synanthous
dysarthria
hypaethral
hypaethron
hypabyssal
myoblastic
cymbidiums
symbolical
symboliser
symbolizer
hye-battel'd
dyscrasite
synclastic
syncretise
syncretize
syncretism
syncretist
syncopated
syncopator
myocardial
myocardium
synchronic
synchronal
syncarpous
eye-catcher
syndicator
syndactyly
synderesis
syndetical
Pyrenaeans
Cyperaceae
Wykehamist
hyperaemia
hyperaemic
hyperacute
hyperbolic
hyperbolas
hyperbaric
hyperbatic
hyperbaton
typescript
synecdoche
hyperdulia
syneidesis
typesetter
hyperfocal
hypergolic
synergetic
pyrethroid
Lysenkoism
hypermania
hypermanic
cybernetic
cybernated
pyrenocarp
type-holder
mycetozoan
mycetology
pyretology
synecology
typewriter
cyberspace
hyperspace
hypersonic
hypertonic
dysenteric
type-cutter
cynghanedd
dysgraphia
dysgraphic
myographic
Syngenesia
pyogenesis
syngenesis
syngenetic
ayahuascos
Lythraceae
Lychnapsia
mythically
typhaceous
mythiciser
mythicizer
pythogenic
Pythagoras
mythologic
mythologer
syphilitic
mythomania
hyphenated
typhlology
mythopoeia
mythopoeic
Myricaceae

Words marked △ may be spelled also with a capital letter

Xyridaceae
typicality
cylindrite
cylindroid
myriadfold
lysigenous
myringitis
syringitis
pyrimidine
mytiliform
gyniolatry
pyridoxine
myrioscope
dyskinesia
myeloblast
syllabical
syllabuses
by-election
cyclically
cyclo-cross
Wycliffite
cyclograph
eye-legible
myological
syllogiser
syllogizer
cycloidian
hyalomelan
hyalophane
hyaloplasm
cyclopedia
cyclopedic
cycloramic
cyclostome
cyclostyle
eyelet-hole
cyclothyme
symmetrise
symmetrize
symmetrian
hypnagogic
hypnogogic
hypnogenic
pycnogonid
hypnoidise
hypnoidize
cyanometer
pycnometer
pyknometer
cyanophyte
gymnasiast
gymnosperm
gymnastics
pycnospore
gymnosophy
gymnasiums
pycnostyle
Lyon-at-arms
hypnotiser
hypnotizer
Pyrolaceae
pyromaniac
pyrogallic
pyrogallol
hypoxaemia
hypoxaemic
hypogaeous
myxomatous
hypotactic
pyromantic
zygodactyl
zygocactus
synoecious
gyroscopic
pyro-acetic
myxoedemic
pyrotechny
pyromeride
pyroxenite
hypodermic
hypodermal
hypodermis
pyrogenous
xylogenous
cytometric
pyrometric
hypocentre
hypotenuse
cynophobia
gynophobia
mysophobia
pyrophobia
gynophobic
pyrophobic
xylophagan
hylotheism
hylotheist
cynophilia
xylophonic
sycophancy
cytochrome
xylochrome
pyrophoric
△pyrophorus
hypophyses
hypophysis
hypotheses
hypothesis
hypothetic
mycorhizal
tyrosinase
mylonitise
mylonitize
Tyrolienne
hypoplasia
mycoplasma
hylozoical
hypocorism
△lycopodium
hypodorian
cytologist
mycologist
typologist
zymologist
hylotomous
xylotomous
zygomorphy
gyrocopter
zygosphene
cymotrichy
mycorrhiza
zygobranch
kymography
pyrography
typography
xylography
gynocratic
hypocritic
synoptical
hypostress
hypostases
hypostasis
synostoses
synostosis
gyrostatic
hypostatic
pyrostatic
pyrolusite
myxomycete
zygomycete
pyroxyline
synonymise
synonymize
hypolydian
synonymist
synonymity
hypogynous
synonymous
hyoplastra
dysplastic
dysphemism
lyophilise
lyophilize
sylphidine
symphilism
symphilous
tympanitic
tympanites
tympanitis
nympholept
lymphokine
dysprosium
symphonion
symphonist
lymphogram
lymphocyte
symposiast
sympathise
sympathize
sympathies
Sympetalae
symphyseal
△dyophysite
symphysial
symphylous
dyer's-broom
hygrochasy
hydrically
hydrochore
hybridiser
hybridizer
Tyrrhenian
hydrograph
hygrograph
hydragogue
pyorrhoeic
pyorrhoeal
pyrrhicist
hydrologic
hydrolysis
hydrolytic
hydromania
hydromancy
hydrometer
hygrometer
hydrometry
hygrometry
Cyprinidae
by-drinking
pyrrhotine
pyrrhotite
Pyrrhonism
Pyrrhonian
Pyrrhonist
hydrophane
hydroplane
cypripedia
hydrophily
hydropolyp
hydroponic
hydrophone
hygrophobe
hydropathy
hydropower
hydrophyte
hygrophyte
hydrospace
hydrosomal
hydrosomes
hydroscope
hygroscope
hydrotheca
hydrotaxis
hydraulics
hydrazides
byssaceous
myasthenia
myasthenic
hypsometer
hypsometry
byssinosis
eye-spotted
gypsophila
hypsophobe
hypsophyll
eye-servant
eye-service
eyas-musket
Hyoscyamus
mystically
myrtaceous
cystectomy
cysticerci
△dyothelete
△dyothelite
synthesise
synthesize
synthetise
synthetize
△dyothelism
synthesist
synthetist
mystifying
syntagmata
hyetograph
mystagogic
mystagogue
mystagogus
nystagmoid
nyctalopia
nyctalopic
nyctalopes
systemless
systematic
hyetometer
cystinuria
cystinosis
syntenoses
syntenosis
nyctinasty
dystrophia
dystrophic
dystrophin
oyster-bank
oyster-park
oyster-farm
hysterical
hystericky
oyster-wife
mystery-man
synthronus
mysterious
hysteresis
synteresis
hysteretic
hysteritis
cystoscope
cystoscopy
cystostomy
dysthymiac
Tyburn-tree
eye-witness
azobenzene
azeotropic
czarevitch

11 □a□a□a

Calabar-bean
calamancoes
catafalcoes
Palaearctic
paramaecium
camaraderie
paraparesis
paraparetic
caravanette
parasailing
caravanning
farawayness
malakatoone
lalapalooza
catacaustic
caravansary
paramastoid
taratantara
parabaptism
maladaptive
Malacca-cane
parascience
maraschinos
parascender
damascening
parascenium
paraldehyde
Camaldolese
Camaldolite
cat-and-mouse
hazardously
parabematic
paracetamol
paraselenae
paragenesia
paragenesis
paragenetic
paranephric
paranephros
Pan-American
paramedical
Saracenical
paramedicos
paraleipses
paraleipsis
Paracelsian
managership
parapenting
paraffin-wax
paraffinoid
paraffin-oil
Pan-Anglican
paraphraser
paraphraxia
paraphraxis
catachresis
paraphrenia
kalashnikov
paraphiliac
Marathonian
cataphonics
Panathenaea
Panathenaic
parathyroid
Mahabharata
pataphysics
'pataphysics
parachutist
capacitance
fanatically
satanically
parasitemia
magazine-gun
parasitical
carabiniere
carabinieri
malariology
vacationist
caparisoned
parasitosis
cavalierish
cavalierism
canalicular
capaciously
rapaciously
sagaciously
salaciously
canaliculus
maladjusted
damask-steel
catallactic
cataplectic
parallactic
paragliding
paralleling
parallelise
parallelism
parallelist
parallelize
capableness
salableness
savableness
tamableness
parablepsis
parableptic
paraglossae
paraglossal
cataclasmic
cataclastic
cataclysmic
parabolanus
laparoscope
laparoscopy
paramoecium
vagabondage
vagabondise
vagabondish
vagabondism
vagabondize
Japanophile
malacophily
satanophany
katabothron
katavothron
parabolical
paradoxical
paragogical
Paradoxides
ratatouille
natatoriums
sanatoriums
paramountcy
paramountly
paramorphic
cataloguise
cataloguize
palaeotypic
hamadryades
maladroitly
catadromous
katadromous
paratrooper
paragrapher
paragraphia
paragraphic
malapropism
paracrostic
parapsychic
harassingly
Marantaceae
paranthelia
rabattement
catastrophe
parasuicide
catapultier
paratyphoid
catalytical
paralympics
canary-grass
carbocyclic
marble-paper
marble-edged
jawbreaking
rabble-rouse
cabbage-moth
cabbage-palm
cabbage-root
cabbage-rose
cabbage-tree
cabbagetown
cabbage-worm
garbologist
cabbalistic
carbonadoes
carbonalite
carbonylate
Carbonarism
carbonation
carbuncular
jabberingly
Carborundum®
jabberwocky
barbaresque
carburetted
carburetter
carburation
carburetion
carburettor
barbarously
barbastelle
gambit-piece
Sabbathless
rabbet-joint
△sabbatarian
Halbstarker
barbiturate
harbour-dues
harbourless
saccharated
bacchanalia
Barclaycard
wax-chandler
pancratiast
cat-cracking
paschal-lamb
fascia-board
sauce-crayon
farcicality
fasciculate
calcicolous
sarcocystis
parchedness
hatchettite
calcifugous
bacciferous
calciferous
marchioness
sarcoidosis
sanctifying
lance-knecht
lance-knight
cancellated
sacculiform
vasculiform
rascalliest
masculinely
masculinise
masculinist
masculinity
masculinize
narcoleptic
vascularise
vascularity
vascularize
matchlessly
laccolithic
calculating
calculation
sacculation
vasculature
calculative
tan-coloured
matchmaking
watchmaking

Words marked △ may be spelled also with a capital letter

11 □a□e□l

sarcomatous
marconigram
dancing-girl
sarcenchyme
carcinology
carcinomata
fascinating
lancinating
calcination
fascination
lancination
vaccination
vaccinatory
larcenously
lanceolated
calceolaria
cancioneros
sancho-pedro
sarcophagal
sarcophagus
patch-pocket
Nancy-pretty
catch-phrase
mancipation
mancipatory
calcariform
canceration
rancorously
marcescible
Lancastrian
latch-string
watchspring
laicisation
narcissuses
catch-the-ten
rat-catching
raucousness
sanctuarise
sanctuarize
baccivorous
laicization
hardwareman
handbagging
hand-painted
paediatrics
paediatrist
handfasting
sand-casting
laudability
mandibulate
Sadduceeism
May-December
handicapped
handicapper
landscaping
landscapist
manducation
manducatory
candidiasis
paedodontic
candidature
handkercher
hand-feeding
randle-perch
candleberry
paddle-wheel
paddle-shaft
candlelight
saddleg-irth
handselling
saddlecloth
candle-power
saddle-nosed
paddle-board
hard-hearted
hard-wearing
tap-dressing
land-measure
candlestick
paddle-staff
maidservant
tardy-gaited
handshaking
sand-thrower
card-sharper
hard-visaged
bandeirante
landfilling
hard-hitting
landsknecht
sand-skipper
candelabras
candelabrum
bandoleered
bandoliered
bandy-legged
paedologist
Magdalenian
fardel-bound
baddeleyite
△pandemoniac
△pandemonian
Sandemanian
△pandemonium
landing-beam
Pandanaceae
hard-and-fast
landing-gear
garden-glass
cardinalate
maddeningly
garden-house
landing-ship
land-jobbing
landholding
landlordism
hardworking
cardiomotor
hand-to-mouth
cardiograph
hardmouthed
cardophagus
paedophilia
paedophilic
Wanderjahre
hand-breadth
land-grabber
panduriform
dandy-rigged
hard-grained
hand-promise
wanderingly
mandarinate
balderlocks
gander-month
hard-pressed
paederastic
handwritten
handwriting
handwrought
landgravine
waldgravine
landgravate
sanderswood
candescence
caddishness
faddishness
paedotrophy
△waldsterben
land-steward
landaulette
hand-running
maceranduba
camera-ready
barefacedly
gametangium
calefacient
race-walking
kamelaukion
name-calling
wage-earning
rate-capping
Rabelaisian
calefaction
labefaction
madefaction
malefaction
rarefaction
tabefaction
calefactory
malefactory
calefactive
rarefactive
sauerbraten
Water-bearer
camel-backed
rateability
saleability
tameability
paleobotany
paper-credit
watercolour
water-cooled
water-cooler
catercorner
paper-cutter
cater-cousin
watercourse
calendrical
fazendeiros
calendering
calendarise
calendarist
calendarize
haberdasher
paper-enamel
watered-down
pad-elephant
dare-devilry
make-believe
safe-deposit
safe-keeping
cameleopard
pale-hearted
talebearing
paper-feeder
paper-folder
water-finder
paleography
navel-gazing
water-heater
game-chicken
paper-hanger
catechismal
catechistic
catechising
catechetics
catechizing
pale-visaged
malefically
maleficence
watering-can
watering-cap
watering-pot
lateritious
palebiology
materialise
materialism
materialist
materiality
materialize
laterigrade
malediction
valediction
maledictory
valedictory
maledictive
facetiously
Canellaceae
lamellicorn
lamelliform
patelliform
waterlogged
face-flannel

11 □a□e□l

gaberlunzie
camerlengos
camerlingos
Paleolithic
satellitise
satellitize
safe-blowing
paper-making
paper-muslin
tabernacled
bare-knuckle
capernoited
Capernaitic
capernoitie
paternalism
cavernulous
△paternoster
cavernously
navel-orange
café-concert
safe-conduct
malevolence
paper-office
gametophyte
categorical
pace-bowling
warehousing
Laserpicium
Caterpillar®
caterpillar
salesperson
Laserpitium
safe-breaker
safe-cracker
hare-brained
pan-European
name-dropper
make-or-break
gatecrasher
water-skiing
paper-sailor
caressingly
navel-string
caper-spurge
parentheses
panesthesia
parenthesis
parenthetic
paresthesia
panentheism
panentheist
palestrical
patent-right
lacertilian
Palestinian
Valentinian
lamentingly
patent-rolls
parent-craft
lamentation
balefulness
banefulness
carefulness
fatefulness
gaseousness
hatefulness
wakefulness
pâte-sur-pâte
rate-cutting
dame's-violet
paper-weight
cave-dweller
lake-dweller
safety-catch
panegyrical
panegyricon
malfeasance
half-landing
half-baptise
half-baptize
baffle-plate
halfpennies
baffle-board
half-hearted
half-measure
half-leather
half-century
half-checked
caffeinated
half-binding
haaf-fishing
half-blooded
half-integer
halfendeale
half-and-half
malfunction
half-holiday
half-pounder
calf-country
gaff-topsail
MacFarlane's
fanfaronade
half-brother
raffishness
gas-fittings
half-starved
vanguardism
margraviate
hangability
tangibility
ragged-Robin
Haggadistic
languescent
sang-de-boeuf
rangefinder
large-handed
sanguinaria
sanguineous
laughing-gas
languishing
languidness
Sanguisorba
pan-galactic
hang-gliding
mangalsutra
large-minded
bargemaster
Targumistic
tangentally
ramgunshoch
badging-hook
bagging-hook
jagging-iron
marginalise
marginalism
marginalist
marginality
marginalize
Gargantuism
Gargantuist
Panglossian
haggardness
kangaroo-rat
kangaroo-hop
daggerboard
dangerously
waggishness
barge-stones
tax-gatherer
haughtiness
naughtiness
targa-topped
gangsterdom
gangsterism
maggotorium
gangbusting
langoustine
laughworthy
gas-guzzling
cash-railway
Bashi-Bazouk
cachectical
machicolate
cash-account
tachycardia
cathedratic
pachydactyl
pachydermal
pachydermia
pachydermic
cashierment
Machaerodus
wash-leather
pathography
tachygraphy
pathogenous
naphthalene
naphthalise
naphthalize
wash-gilding
Machairodus
△bathmitsvah
△bathmitzvah
parheliacal
△catholicise
△catholicism
catholicity
△catholicize
△panhellenic
pathologist
bachelordom
bachelorism
batholithic
bathylithic
mathematics
bathymetric
tachometric
tachymetric
mathematise
mathematize
washing-blue
washing-line
machine-made
taphonomist
washing-soda
bathing-suit
machine-shop
machination
wash-and-wear
machine-work
fashionable
fashionably
tacheometer
tacheometry
tachyphasia
bathophobia
pathophobia
taphephobia
taphophobia
cathartical
father-in-law
washerwoman
Sachertorte
bathyscaphe
bathysphere
yachtswoman
catheterism
bashfulness
lachrymator
haphazardly
marivaudage
farinaceous
salicaceous
maximaphily
sanitariums
radicalness
radioactive
caricatural
satiability
variability
panic-buying
ratiocinate
radiocarbon
Taliacotian

Words marked △ may be spelled also with a capital letter

11 □a□l□t

labiodental
palindromic
lapidescent
facinerious
varicelloid
radicellose
varicellous
taxidermise
taxidermist
taxidermize
manifestoes
latiseptate
cabinetwork
satisfiable
satisficing
daring-hardy
Hagiographa
hagiography
radiography
gaming-table
caaing-whale
palingenesy
eating-house
gaming-house
eating-apple
gazing-stock
paving-stone
variegation
Manichaeism
ravishingly
vanishingly
parishioner
fatidically
pacifically
satirically
facilitator
habilitator
pacificator
vaticinator
habiliments
paripinnate
familiarise
familiarity
familiarize
laciniation
maliciously
lapidifying
Marie-Jeanne
Bacillaceae
bacillicide
bacillaemia
bacilliform
lapilliform
mamilliform
papilliform
hagiologist
Mariologist
radiologist
papillulate
panislamism
panislamist
carillonist
maxillipede
radiolarian
capillarity
racialistic
vacillating
cavillation
hariolation
mamillation
vacillation
variolation
vacillatory
capillitium
maxim-monger
panic-monger
radiometric
Janian-faced
marionberry
nationalise
nationalism
nationalist
rationalise
rationalism
rationalist
nationality
rationality
nationalize
rationalize
malignantly
ration-money
salinometer
Dasipodidae
californium
janitorship
latirostral
radiopaging
radiophonic
papier-mâché
pasigraphic
calibration
hagioscopic
panic-struck
magistratic
calisthenic
sagittiform
Hamiltonian
variational
magisterial
sagittarian
canisterise
magisterium
Sagittarius
canisterize
paniculated
capitularly
manipulable
manipulator
fatigue-duty
latifundium
habitudinal
latitudinal
fatiguingly
variousness
taciturnity
habituation
mariculture
panjandarum
bank-manager
back-ganging
backpacking
rack-railway
tank-farming
dark-lantern
bankability
talkability
backscratch
backscatter
backbencher
tack-welding
park-officer
backfitting
back-blocker
backsliding
maskallonge
rat-kangaroo
walking-beam
hacking-coat
walking-cane
packing-case
backing-down
park-and-ride
walking-song
wauking-song
back-loading
talk-you-down
bank-holiday
back-country
backbreaker
Baskerville
back-draught
hawkishness
mawkishness
△basket-maker
market-value
basketweave
basket-chair
market-place
market-woman
racket-court
market-house
market-price
racket-press
talkatively
yackety-yack
Jack-pudding
tankbusting
galliambics
mail-catcher
galliardise
tagliatelle
balls-aching
mail-carrier
call-barring
gally-beggar
gally-bagger
fallibilism
fallibilist
fallibility
day-labourer
cauliculate
valleculate
caulicolous
Gallicanism
hallucinate
sallee-rover
ball-bearing
hall-bedroom
tail-feather
hälleflinta
fault-finder
cauliflower
calligraphy
haplography
calligramme
cauligenous
ballyhooing
rallying-cry
baillieship
warlikeness
wallclimber
cable-length
fallalishly
faultlessly
Carlylesque
Maglemosian
gallimaufry
rallentando
ball-and-claw
calling-crab
garlandless
gallantness
marlinspike
Paulinistic
balloon-back
sailboarder
balloon-vine
callipygean
callipygous
ball-breaker
pallescence
Vallisneria
Callistemon
tables-d'hôte
cable-stitch
haplessness
hatlessness
lawlessness
saplessness
tally-system
ballot-paper
call-at-large
Callitriche
balletomane

11 □a□l□t

tabletopped
parlour-maid
callousness
ball-busting
Gallovidian
cablevision
tallow-catch
tallow-faced
gallows-bird
gallows-free
gallows-foot
Gallowegian
sallow-thorn
fallow-finch
gallowglass
eagle-winged
gallowsness
gallows-ripe
gallows-tree
galley-foist
barley-break
barley-brake
barley-broth
barley-sugar
palm-cabbage
map-measurer
haemocyanin
Talmudistic
May-meetings
warm-hearted
farm-offices
mammiferous
mammography
haemoglobin
mammillaria
mammalogist
man-milliner
warm-blooded
salmonberry
harmonogram
haemangioma
salmonellae
salmonellas
garmentless
harmoniphon
harmonistic
mammonistic
carminative
mammoplasty
haemophilia
haemoptysis
balm-cricket
lammergeier
lammergeyer
haemorrhage
haemorrhoid
law-merchant
△balmorality
hammercloth
palmyra-nuts
hammer-brace
gammerstang
palmyra-wood
haemostasis
haemostatic
haematocrit
haematocele
haematology
palmatisect
mammoth-tree
harmfulness
fainéantise
paint-bridge
cannibalise
cannibalism
damnability
cannibalize
cannabinoid
wainscotted
wainscoting
maintenance
launderette
magnifiable
carnificial
magnificoes
magnificent
manniferous
manna-groats
rain-chamber
raunchiness
jaunting-car
wag-'n-bietjie
rannell-balk
manna-lichen
saintliness
dauntlessly
taintlessly
cannon-metal
magnanimity
magnanimous
fawningness
cannon-proof
maintopmast
maintopsail
carnaptious
saintpaulia
pawnbroking
laundry-maid
manneristic
Wagneresque
tarnishable
harness-cask
garnishment
earnestness
mannishness
harness-room
varnish-tree
magnesstone
garnet-paper
magnetician
painstaking
carnationed
barnstormer
gainfulness
painfulness
carnivorous
taboparesis
saponaceous
sapotaceous
papovavirus
cacogastric
nasogastric
capodastros
baton-charge
gamogenesis
baronetical
favoredness
Napoleonism
Napoleonist
napoleonite
majoretting
parochially
canophilist
halophilous
saxophonist
cacophonous
nasopharynx
masochistic
canonically
laconically
vaporisable
vaporizable
vasodilator
majoritaire
Valoniaceae
calorimeter
vaporimeter
calorimetry
Carolingian
Jacobinical
Jacobitical
parotiditis
cavo-rilievo
halobiontic
Baconianism
laboriously
saponifying
Madonna-lily
madonnawise
paronomasia
batological
taxonomical
lagomorphic
panomphaean
savoir-faire
savoir-vivre
nasofrontal
vapouringly
savouriness
cacographer
cacographic
gamotropism
vasopressin
vasopressor
favouritism
carousingly
wagonwright
paronychial
wasp-waisted
malpractice
palpability
cappuccinos
Campodeidae
ear-piercing
Campbellite
camp-meeting
sampler-work
carpogonium
lamp-chimney
Cappah-brown
naupliiform
lamplighter
harpsichord
pampelmoose
pampelmouse
pamphleteer
carpentaria
wappenschaw
damping-down
campaniform
salpingitic
salpingitis
campanology
campanulate
parpen-stone
camphorated
lamprophyre
wapper-jawed
cappernoity
tamper-proof
dampishness
waspishness
carpospores
campestrian
malposition
carpet-snake
palpitation
panpsychism
panpsychist
masquerader
marqueterie
Jacqueminot
marquessate
lacquer-tree
barquentine
pasquinader
marquisette
matriarchal
patriarchal
carriageway
marriage-bed
far-reaching
hair-raising
tarry-breeks

Words marked △ may be spelled also with a capital letter

tauroboliu m
macrobiotic
saprobiotic
fairy-butter
patricianly
macrocyclic
barricadoes
matriclinic
matroclinic
patriclinic
patroclinic
capriccioso
matriculate
latrocinium
barrack-room
sacrocostal
macrocosmic
fabrication
fabricative
macrodactyl
tarradiddle
labradorite
fair-dealing
fair-seeming
fair-weather
sacrificial
macrofossil
carrageenan
carrageenin
barrage-fire
madrigalian
madrigalist
macrogamete
farraginous
saprogenous
carryings-on
fairniticle
larrikinism
laurel-water
patrol-wagon
caprolactam
saprolegnia
sacrilegist
matrilineal
matrilinear
patrilineal
patrilinear
patrolwoman
barrel-house
barrel-organ
garrulously
matrimonial
patrimonial
sacramental
lacrimosely
lacrymosely
lacrimatory
lacrymatory
warrantable
warrantably
patronising
pairing-time
patronizing
carrion-crow
pair-bonding
patroonship
sauropodous
sauropsidan
sapropelite
madreporite
saprophytic
hairbreadth
hair-trigger
hair-brained
hairdresser
sabre-rattle
saurischian
patristical
laurustinus
macroscopic
hairstylist
Mauretanian
narratively
narrow-gauge
harrowingly
marrow-bones
fairnyticle
Falstaffian
marshalling
rapscallion
Pan-Slavonic
batsmanship
marshalship
oarsmanship
false-bedded
passibility
passacaglia
car-sickness
waistcloths
daisy-cutter
maisterdome
maysterdome
haustellate
panspermism
panspermist
parsley-pert
falsifiable
passage-boat
salsuginous
cat's-whisker
caustically
causticness
tassell-gent
marshlander
causelessly
pauselessly
marshmallow
marsh-mallow
facsimilist
passamezzos
bauson-faced
passing-bell
maisonnette
passing-note
bar-sinister
sarsen-stone
cassiopeium
passionless
Passiontide
Marsupialia
pansophical
mass-produce
kaisar-i-Hind
hamstringed
mansard-roof
Sanskritist
palsgravine
basset-hound
cassiterite
causatively
saussuritic
sansculotte
sansevieria
varsovienne
massiveness
passiveness
mantua-maker
want-catcher
cantharidal
cantharides
lanthanides
cantharidic
fast-talking
part-payment
factualness
martialness
bastnaesite
partibility
parti-coated
party-coated
Pantocrator
lattice-leaf
particulate
earth-closet
participial
participant
participate
tautochrone
mastication
masticatory
lattice-work
mastodontic
rattle-pated
battle-piece
battlefield
pantheology
battleplane
farthermore
farthermost
rattlesnake
tattie-bogle
bastle-house
rattle-brain
battledress
pantheistic
partnership
waitressing
gastrectomy
castle-guard
earthenware
saltierwise
lactoflavin
△rastafarian
lactiferous
lactifluous
fastigiated
cartography
pantography
vantageless
castigation
castigatory
faith-healer
nautch-girls
earth-hunger
fact-finding
farthingale
part-singing
mastoiditis
captainship
castellated
Santalaceae
dactylogram
tautologise
tautologism
tautologist
tautologous
tautologize
mantelshelf
mantelpiece
dactylology
earthliness
pantalooned
bastel-house
faithlessly
tastelessly
tantalising
Tantalus-cup
pantaletted
pantalettes
salt-glazing
tantalizing
saltimbanco
bad-tempered
pantomimist
saltimbocca
tautomerism
tautometric
earthmoving
canting-coin
bastinadoed
bastinadoes
bastinading
martensitic
waiting-list

11 □a□t□n

waiting-maid
tautonymous
lastingness
waiting-room
martinetism
casting-vote
gastromancy
gastroscope
xanthophyll
Xanthochroi
Bartholomew
gastrologer
gastronomer
gastrosophy
gastronomic
gastrostomy
fast-forward
Xanthoxylum
Zanthoxylum
cartophilic
earth-pillar
party-pooper
pantophobia
tautophonic
earthquaked
sartorially
Tattersall's
master-mason
masturbator
bactericide
fast-breeder
bacteraemia
factory-gate
master-wheel
masterpiece
master-clock
martyrology
pasture-land
saltarellos
master-class
pastoralism
pastoralist
pastureless
raptureless
easternmost
garter-snake
banteringly
falteringly
yatteringly
dastardness
bacteriosis
master-joint
Gasteropoda
Fastern's-e'en
factory-ship
cauterising
pattern-shop
part-writing
parturition
masterfully
rapturously
wasterfully
canterburys
bastard-wing
saltirewise
cauterizing
Earthshaker
Baltoslavic
baptismally
pantisocrat
lactescence
hatti-sherif
fantastical
cattishness
saltishness
pantoscopic
pantothenic
earth-tremor
hart's-tongue
partitioner
haptotropic
raptatorial
saltatorial
jactitation
partitively
△pasteurella
pastourelle
pasteuriser
pasteurizer
tactfulness
captivating
captivaunce
faithworthy
hasty-witted
malt-extract
east-by-north
east-by-south
sapucaia-nut
natural-born
saourari-nut
naturalness
manufactory
manufacture
carunculate
carunculous
manumission
manumitting
maquiladora
vacuolation
vacuum-clean
calumniator
saturnalian
naturopathy
baculovirus
haruspicate
saburration
harum-scarum
casuistical
valuational
facultative
fatuousness
vacuousness
salvability
vaivodeship
waivodeship
salvageable
carvel-built
parvanimity
Calvinistic
larviparous
harvest-home
harvest-mite
harvest-tick
bay-windowed
waywardness
man-watching
fauxbourdon
papyraceous
baby-farming
calycanthus
barycentric
laryngology
laryngismus
laryngotomy
labyrinthal
labyrinthic
baby-sitting
Maryologist
lady's-mantle
many-tongued
baby-bouncer
caryopteris
caryopsides
lady-trifles
calypsonian
caryatidean
calyptrogen
razzamatazz
gauze-winged
abracadabra
abranchiate
ablatitious
ablactation
abecedarian
abactinally
abscondence
obsceneness
obscurement
obscureness
obscuration
obediential
abbey-lubber
obtemperate
obsecration
obsessional
absenteeism
object-glass
obtestation
objectively
objectivise
objectivism
objectivist
objectivate
objectivity
objectivize
observantly
observingly
observation
observatory
observative
obliterated
obliterator
abridgeable
abridgement
obsidionary
obliviously
obsignation
obsignatory
obliqueness
obviousness
obliquation
obliquitous
ebulliently
abolishable
abolishment
abolitional
abomination
obumbration
abandonedly
abandonment
ob-and-soller
absorbingly
obsolescent
abiogenesis
abiogenetic
abdominally
abhominable
obnoxiously
abnormalism
abnormality
abhorrently
abortionist
obtrusively
abbreviator
abusiveness
abstraction
abstractive
abstriction
obstriction
abstentious
abstinently
obstinately
obstipation
obstetrical
obstruction
obstructive
obfuscation
obfuscatory
obmutescent
objurgation
objurgatory
objurgative
ablutionary
about-sledge

Words marked △ may be spelled also with a capital letter

above-ground
scratchback
scratch-coat
scratchless
scratch-work
eccaleobion
scrapepenny
octave-flute
octahedrons
octahedrite
sclate-stane
scragginess
octachordal
scrawlingly
achaenocarp
octagonally
scrappiness
ocean-stream
octastichon
McCarthyism
McCarthyite
icebreaking
scabbedness
scaberulous
acidifiable
academician
academicals
academicism
acidanthera
schematical
screech-hawk
screwdriver
accelerando
accelerator
icteritious
schecklaton
screamingly
octennially
screen-wiper
screencraft
sclerocauly
sclerometer
scleroderma
sclerophyll
sclerotioid
sclerotitis
acre-breadth
accessorial
accessorily
accessorise
accessorize
accentually
eclecticism
eccentrical
Scientology®
scientistic
acceptation
acceptivity
screw-wrench
scherzandos
ecofriendly
scaffoldage
scaffolding
scribacious
schizanthus
scriveboard
accidentals
octingenary
actinically
occipitally
accipitrine
octillionth
schillerise
schillerize
acriflavine
schismatise
schismatize
actinometer
schizogenic
Echinoderma
scripophile
scripophily
Schizophyta
schizophyte
acrimonious
schizopodal
Actinomyces
scrimpiness
scrimshandy
scrimshoner
scriptorial
scripturism
scripturist
scriptorium
Schistosoma
schistosome
schistosity
achievement
scale-armour
ochlocratic
scoleciform
acclamation
acclimation
acclamatory
acclimatise
acclimatize
scolopendra
ochlophobia
ochlophobic
scalariform
scalpriform
ecclesiarch
ecblastesis
sculpturing
sculduddery
sculduggery
acolouthite
acclivitous
scamblingly
ecumenicism
acumination
scandaliser
scandalizer
acinaciform
ichnography
iconography
scenography
Acanthaceae
scintillant
scintillate
iconologist
econometric
scincoidian
scant-o'-grace
iconostasis
acknowledge
scholar-like
scholarship
accoucheuse
accordantly
accordingly
acromegalic
acropetally
ectogenesis
ectogenetic
octodecimos
acrocentric
ectothermic
scholiastic
scrobicular
schoolwards
schoolchild
schorlomite
schoolgoing
schoolhouse
schoolcraft
ectoblastic
ectoplasmic
ectoplastic
accommodate
accountancy
accountable
accountably
account-book
echo-sounder
ectomorphic
octonocular
accomptable
accompanier
accompanist
ectotrophic
accoutering
schottische
acronymania
scepterless
scuppernong
acupressure
scapigerous
sceptically
scyphistoma
scopolamine
acupuncture
scopophilia
scopophilic
scopophobia
sceptreless
scoriaceous
scorpaenoid
scarabaeoid
scarabaeist
schrecklich
scarlet-bean
schreech-owl
acarpellous
scorchingly
Scorpionida
acarologist
scaremonger
X-chromosome
Y-chromosome
achromatise
achromatism
achromatous
achromatize
△scaramouche
scoring-card
eccrinology
accrescence
icosahedral
icosahedron
icosandrian
icosandrous
scissor-bill
scissortail
scissorwise
Scotlandite
scatterable
scatteredly
scattergood
scatterling
scattershot
scythe-stone
Scotchwoman
Scotch-Irish
Scottifying
scuttlebutt
acatalectic
acataleptic
Scitamineae
scotomatous
Scotophilia
Scotophobia
Scotophobic
ichthyoidal
ichthyology
ichthyolite
ichthyornis
ichthyosaur
accusatival
scoundrelly
acaulescent
acquiescent
scruffiness
scouthering

11 □c□u□i

scrutiniser
scrutinizer
octuplicate
scoutmaster
scrumptious
sceuophylax
actuarially
acquirement
acquisition
acquisitive
acquittance
acoustician
accustomary
acculturate
occultation
accumulator
schwärmerei
advancement
adiathermic
adiaphorism
adiaphorist
adiaphorous
od's-bodikins
educability
adscription
educational
adverbially
adverseness
adversarial
adversative
advertently
advertorial
adventuress
adventurism
adventurist
adventurous
advertising
adjectively
edification
edificatory
admiralship
advisedness
advisership
addititious
adminicular
sdeignfully
adulterator
addle-headed
idyllically
adelantados
edulcorator
adolescence
idempotency
adumbration
adumbrative
identically
identifying
adenomatous
odontogenic
odontophore
odontoblast
odontologic
odontograph
odonatology
idiotically
idioblastic
idioglossia
ideological
idiomorphic
adjournment
ideographic
idiographic
ideopraxist
△adoptianism
adoptianist
△adoptionism
adoptionist
od's-pitikins
odoriferous
addressable
odorousness
editorially
adjudgement
adjudicator
idoxuridine
reparations
pedal-action
perambulate
decarbonise
decarbonate
decarbonize
decarburise
decarburize
rebarbative
debauchedly
recalculate
debauchment
revaccinate
melancholia
melancholic
debarcation
defalcation
demarcation
metaldehyde
retardation
retardatory
retardative
regardfully
hexateuchal
recalescent
hematemesis
metagenesis
metagenetic
hexadecimal
sexagesimal
cesarevitch
cesarewitch
belatedness
debasedness
relatedness
decameronic
sewage-works
senate-house
hexahedrons
hexametrise
hexametrist
hexametrize
metacentric
hepatectomy
metasequoia
derangement
pelargonium
cerargyrite
metaphrasis
metachrosis
metaphorist
Megatherium
metaphysics
metathesise
metathesize
megavitamin
tetanically
venatically
desalinator
Geraniaceae
Pedaliaceae
selaginella
gelatiniser
gelatinizer
metasilicic
semasiology
deracialise
deracialize
negationist
Pelagianism
relationism
relationist
behaviorism
behaviorist
legatissimo
metafiction
reradiation
retaliation
retaliatory
retaliative
behavioural
nefariously
tenaciously
veraciously
vexatiously
debarkation
demarkation
mésalliance
beta-blocker
metalliding
metallogeny
Heracleidan
metalloidal
tenableness
hexaplarian
metallurgic
metaplastic
Heraclitean
demagnetise
demagnetize
megalomania
metasomatic
petalomania
hexagonally
hepatoscopy
keratometer
teratogenic
melanochroi
keratophyre
melanophore
nematophore
demagogical
pedagogical
nematodirus
hematoblast
megaloblast
nematoblast
megatonnage
megalopolis
teratologic
metamorphic
ceratopsian
senatorship
demagoguery
pedagoguery
demagoguism
pedagoguish
pedagoguism
hematolysis
hematoxylin
Hematoxylon
depauperise
depauperate
depauperize
repatriator
desacralise
desacralize
désagrément
hetaerismic
hetairismic
△renaissance
metapsychic
délassement
hexastichal
pedantocrat
pedanticise
pedanticism
semanticist
pedanticize
xeranthemum
département
redactorial
melanterite
metastasise
metastasize
devastating
decantation
devastation
recantation

Words marked △ may be spelled also with a capital letter

repartition
devastative
devaluation
revaluation
metalworker
membraneous
pebble-stone
herb-of-grace
verbigerate
Leibnitzian
Verbenaceae
herb-trinity
verberation
kerb-crawler
leg-business
verboseness
deobstruent
herbivorous
merchandise
merchandize
merchantman
merchantmen
merchanting
peach-brandy
peccability
leucocratic
peacock-blue
peacock-fish
peacock-like
beachcomber
fetch-candle
peccadillos
leucodermal
leucodermia
leucodermic
geochemical
peacherinos
teacherless
leucaemogen
rescue-grass
benchership
teachership
hercogamous
deictically
describable
perceivable
perceivably
men-children
reactionary
reactionist
description
descriptive
peace-keeper
pencil-cedar
Aesculapian
perchlorate
mercilessly
pencil-stone
percolation
fence-lizard
reach-me-down
peacemaking
peace-monger
welcomingly
welcomeness
beech-marten
beach-master
descendable
descendible
mercenarily
mercenarism
deschooling
leucoplakia
percipience
percipiency
perceptible
perceptibly
peace-parted
henchperson
mercurially
leucorrhoea
mercuration
leach-trough
Neo-Catholic
head-banging
dendrachate
verde-antico
readability
vendibility
weldability
headscarves
re-education
perduellion
needlewoman
needlepoint
needlecraft
needcessity
needlestick
readvertise
needle-furze
dendritical
tendrillous
readmission
Kendal-green
feudalistic
pendulosity
dead-clothes
pendulously
mendelevium
Vendémiaire
hebdomadary
seldom-times
ready-monied
reading-book
redding-comb
reading-desk
Heldentenor
weeding-fork
weeding-hook
tendencious
tendentious
verd-antique
redding-kame
reading-lamp
geodynamics
pendant-post
reading-room
dendrolatry
dendrometer
dendroglyph
headborough
reed-sparrow
feldspathic
leader-cable
gendarmerie
dead-freight
verdureless
pedder-coffe
tenderfoots
fender-stool
perduration
reed-drawing
tender-dying
reddishness
head-station
venditation
ready-to-wear
heedfulness
needfulness
headhunting
merdivorous
meadow-grass
meadow-brown
ready-witted
meadowsweet
têtes-à-têtes
lese-majesté
lese-majesty
leze-majesty
severalfold
telepathise
telepathist
telepathize
generations
Revelations
temerarious
generalling
hemeralopia
generalship
telecasting
benefaction
tepefaction
benefactory
remembrance
resemblance
reverberant
Decemberish
reverberate
telescience
defenceless
telescopist
Telescopium
revendicate
defeudalise
defeudalize
legerdemain
dependingly
serendipity
Defenderism
regenerable
decelerator
regenerator
referendums
never-ending
referendary
deleterious
téléférique
venereology
cerebellums
teleselling
cerebellous
redetermine
renewedness
decerebrise
decerebrate
decerebrize
Telemessage®
deferential
referential
reverential
deselection
reselection
venesection
tenementary
pedetentous
never-fading
revengeless
revengement
revengingly
level-headed
hebephrenia
hebephrenic
telephonist
generically
genetically
hereditable
heretically
venefically
beneficence
redeliverer
telekinesis
telekinetic
leze-liberty
beneficiary
beneficiate
repetitious
veneficious
heresiology
bedevilling
bedevilment
Hegelianism
deteriorism
deteriorate
deteriority

Benedictine
benefitting
benediction
dereliction
remediation
benedictory
benedictive
seven-league
beneplacito
genealogise
genealogist
teleologism
teleologist
genealogize
repellantly
repellently
repellingly
Aeneolithic
determinacy
beseemingly
determinant
determinism
determinist
determinate
perennially
sexennially
hereinafter
telegnostic
perennation
heterotaxis
developable
heteroscian
heteroecism
benevolence
heterocercy
werewolfery
werewolfish
werewolfism
hegemonical
renegotiate
ceremonious
teleworking
heteroclite
development
telecommand
telecommute
derecognise
derecognize
heterotopia
heterotopic
heterospory
heterograft
heterotroph
selenograph
△heterousian
telecottage
heterostyly
telecontrol
Heteroptera
heterotypic
deserpidine
level-pegged
redemptible
betel-pepper
metempirics
cerebriform
meteorogram
desegregate
telearchics
researchful
penetralian
meteorology
cerebralism
cerebralist
meteorolite
telegrammic
teleprinter
peregrinate
peregrinity
telegrapher
telegraphic
cerebroside
tenebrosity
meteoritics
terebratula
penetrating
celebration
cerebration
desecration
penetration
terebration
celebratory
penetrative
gegenschein
reverseless
releasement
defeasanced
recessional
reversional
secessional
reversioner
necessarian
necessaries
necessarily
necessitied
desensitise
necessitate
necessitous
defensative
desensitize
Teleosaurus
defensively
recessively
cement-water
fenestrated
celestially
vedette-boat
receptacula
cenesthesia
cenesthesis
telesthesia
telesthetic
seventeenth
pedestalled
repentantly
repentingly
resentingly
refectioner
perestroika
mesenterial
refectorian
selectorial
sedentarily
cement-stone
cementation
delectation
detestation
cementatory
deceitfully
resentfully
deceptively
defectively
retentively
selectively
detectivist
receptivity
retentivity
selectivity
desexualise
desexualize
bereavement
deservingly
decemvirate
reservation
reservatory
bevel-wheels
self-harming
self-damning
self-tapping
self-raising
self-basting
self-mastery
perfectible
perfectness
deification
reification
self-feeding
self-defence
self-delight
self-reliant
self-seeking
self-neglect
self-feeling
self-healing
self-sealing
self-devoted
self-respect
self-tempted
self-despair
self-reproof
self-centred
self-fertile
leafletting
self-service
self-serving
self-denying
self-relying
self-affairs
self-offence
fee-fi-faw-fum
self-charity
self-winding
self-limited
self-figured
self-misused
self-elected
leaf-climber
self-blinded
self-planted
self-closing
perfumeless
self-imposed
deaf-and-dumb
web-fingered
self-invited
perfunctory
self-induced
self-knowing
self-conceit
self-concept
self-concern
self-loading
self-covered
self-powered
self-cocking
self-locking
self-mockery
self-command
self-torment
self-worship
self-content
self-control
self-torture
self-opening
self-opinion
performance
self-created
performable
beef-brained
self-trained
self-pruning
welfaristic
perforation
perforative
selfishness
self-assumed
self-assured
self-starter
self-sterile
self-subdued
leaf-cushion
reef-builder
self-support
leaf-cutting

Words marked △ may be spelled also with a capital letter

self-culture
self-evident
self-evolved
self-excited
self-example
self-express
weighbridge
neighboring
neighbourly
bergschrund
leaguer-lady
leaguer-lass
feignedness
seigneurial
wedge-heeled
lengthiness
hedge-hyssop
seigniorial
seigniorage
hedging-bill
begging-bowl
Reaganomics
hedge-priest
hedge-parson
wedge-shaped
hedge-school
wedge-tailed
weightiness
weight-train
hedge-writer
Rechabitism
methodology
Methodistic
dephlegmate
nephrectomy
lethiferous
meshuggenah
meshuggeneh
technically
nephritical
Technicolor®
cephalocele
nephologist
cephalalgia
cephalalgic
methylamine
nephelinite
Cephalopoda
Cephalaspis
cephalotomy
methylation
mechanician
mechanicals
mechanistic
tephromancy
nephropathy
technomania
nephrolepis
technophobe
technophile
technopolis
technocracy
technomusic
netherwards
lethargical
netherlings
netherworld
netherstock
lecherously
bewhiskered
mechatronic
Mekhitarist
refinancing
pericardiac
pericardial
pericardian
pericardium
peripatetic
pelican-fish
leviratical
derivatives
recitativos
semipalmate
pericarpial
Pedipalpida
perigastric
demi-bastion
retinacular
retinaculum
deniability
reliability
recirculate
bewitchment
heliochrome
heliochromy
desiccation
desiccative
rediscovery
periodicity
revindicate
devil-dodger
periodontal
periodontia
bewildering
deliverance
perihepatic
deliverable
mediaevally
deliberator
desideratum
delitescent
revivescent
peripeteian
perigenesis
perinephric
pedicellate
bedizenment
peridesmium
refinedness
retiredness
hemihedrism
perineurium
denizenship
demi-pension
desinential
penitential
pericentral
residential
pericentric
regimentals
delineation
redirection
venisection
sedimentary
delineative
delivery-man
delivery-van
Rediffusion®
heliography
meningocele
besiegement
besiegingly
periphrases
periphrasis
perishables
perithecial
perithecium
delightedly
meliphagous
delightless
perichylous
benightment
perishingly
fetichistic
fetishistic
delightsome
△helichrysum
sedigitated
genitivally
levitically
medicinable
medicinally
veridically
semicircled
reminiscent
resipiscent
reviviscent
periwigging
verisimilar
peridiniums
penicillate
Penicillium
definientia
deficiently
resiliently
petitioning
petitionary
religionary
revisionary
seditionary
petitionist
religionise
religionism
religionist
revisionism
revisionist
definiendum
religionize
retinispora
semi-diurnal
religiosity
defiliation
deliciously
deliriously
religiously
seditiously
revivifying
semi-skilled
periglacial
semiologist
semi-ellipse
vexillology
legibleness
decillionth
legislation
vexillation
legislature
periclitate
legislative
medium-dated
relic-monger
mediumistic
heliometric
legionnaire
regionalise
regionalism
regionalist
regionalize
benignantly
designingly
defiantness
hemianopsia
hemianoptic
designation
resignation
designatory
designative
semi-annular
peritonaeal
peritonaeum
retinoscope
retinoscopy
Perigordian
demigoddess
medico-legal
Lepidosiren
peritonitic
peritonitis
meritorious
hemimorphic
perimorphic
retinospora
meritocracy
helicograph

semi-monthly
Lepidoptera
Lepidosteus
helispheric
hemispheric
heliophobic
perispermal
perispermic
menispermum
semi-aquatic
delinquency
reciprocant
reciprocate
reciprocity
demiurgeous
demiurgical
semi-trailer
pericranial
defibrinise
defibrinate
pericranium
defibrinize
serigrapher
lexigraphic
serigraphic
hemitropous
melioristic
demigration
denigration
denitration
melioration
remigration
meliorative
sepiostaire
mediastinal
periostitic
periostitis
mediastinum
perissology
peninsulate
helioscopic
series-wound
registrable
hemistichal
semiotician
mediatrices
peristalsis
peristaltic
peristalith
peristomial
befittingly
remittently
resistingly
mediateness
dexiotropic
heliotropic
heliotropin
mediatorial
peristerite
hemipterous
sericterium
resistively
resistivity
geniculated
pediculated
reticulated
vesiculated
Pedicularis
reticularly
semi-jubilee
deviousness
seriousness
tediousness
pediculosis
sericulture
semi-tubular
medievalism
medievalist
believingly
desilverise
desilverize
deck-passage
leukocratic
leukodermal
leukodermia
leukodermic
deckle-edged
weak-hearted
neck-herring
weak-sighted
heckelphone
weak-kneedly
leukoplakia
leukorrhoea
neckerchief
peckishness
fell-walking
keelhauling
beblubbered
helleborine
belly-button
reflectance
neglectable
replaceable
pellucidity
replacement
bellicosely
bellicosity
perlocution
replication
vellication
well-advised
belly-dancer
belle-de-nuit
well-behaved
peelie-wally
well-defined
well-derived
well-desired
well-meaning
well-beloved
oeil-de-boeuf
bell-heather
gelliflowre
celliferous
melliferous
mellifluent
mellifluous
deflagrable
negligeable
deflagrator
realignment
negligently
belligerent
neologistic
well-thumbed
healthiness
wealthiness
healthfully
reclaimable
reclaimably
bell-ringing
seal-fishing
well-wishing
well-sinking
declamation
deplumation
reclamation
declamatory
well-entered
feelingless
well-endowed
replenished
replenisher
Hellenistic
wellingtons
declination
reclination
declinatory
declinature
well-covered
realpolitik
well-looking
reallotment
bell-founder
well-founded
well-rounded
bell-foundry
bell-housing
Della-Robbia
well-trodden
well-ordered
hellgramite
deploringly
well-groomed
well-dressed
telluretted
declaration
defloration
deploration
declaratory
declarative
hellishness
leglessness
recluseness
sexlessness
perlustrate
realisation
well-stacked
zeolitiform
belly-timber
repleteness
deglutinate
aeolotropic
bellettrist
deglutition
deglutitory
deglutitive
well-judging
jealoushood
fell-lurking
fell-running
jealousness
zealousness
repleviable
mellivorous
re-elevation
declivitous
yellow-belly
bellows-fish
yellow-ammer
reflowering
reflexology
deflexional
reflexively
reflexivity
Wesleyanism
realization
permeameter
vermiculate
vermiculite
vermiculous
geomedicine
desmodromic
Fehmgericht
Vehmgericht
gemmiferous
dermography
geomagnetic
termagantly
de-emphasise
re-emphasise
de-emphasize
re-emphasize
gemmologist
gemmulation
sea-milkwort
permanganic
fermentable
segmentally
helminthoid
helminthous
terminology
reamendment

Words marked △ may be spelled also with a capital letter

permanently
germaneness
seemingness
Germanophil
Germanistic
Germanesque
germination
termination
vermination
terminatory
germinative
terminative
hermeneutic
gemmiparous
re-emergence
permissible
permissibly
permittance
hermeticity
seamstressy
helmet-shell
geometrical
Geometridae
dermatology
termitarium
permutation
vermivorous
penny-a-liner
reincarnate
teeny-bopper
weeny-bopper
kernicterus
re-enactment
reinterment
reinterpret
reintegrate
△neanderthal
reinsertion
re-invention
ferntickled
geanticline
reinflation
reanimation
pennoncelle
meaningless
teknonymous
Mennonitism
re-endowment
re-encourage
reintroduce
tennis-match
tennis-court
fernitickle
fernytickle
neonatology
reinstation
reinsurance
heinousness
pennyweight
pennywinkle
penny-wisdom
memorandums
memorabilia
decorations
aeronautics
redoubtable
recombinant
debouchment
deforcement
rejoicement
rejoicingly
second-rater
second-floor
second-class
secondarily
recondition
recordation
second-guess
recoverable
rejoneadora
cenogenesis
merogenesis
merogenetic
xenogenesis
xenogenetic
mesocephaly
devotedness
removedness
reposedness
telocentric
reposefully
oesophageal
hemophiliac
mesothelial
oenophilist
mesothelium
xerophilous
pelotherapy
serotherapy
aerobically
denominable
denominator
Begoniaceae
demoniacism
velocimeter
velocipeder
velocimetry
Merovingian
cenobitical
aerobiology
genouillère
memorialise
memorialist
refocillate
memorialize
demonianism
devotionist
negotiatrix
defoliation
negotiation
feloniously
ferociously
melodiously
recollected
aeroelastic
ceroplastic
meroblastic
mesoblastic
xenoglossia
xenoplastic
décolletage
decollation
reformadoes
renormalise
reformulate
renormalize
recommender
Mesoamerica
recommittal
deformation
leg-of-mutton
△reformation
re-formation
reformatory
reformative
demountable
reconnoiter
reconnoitre
recountment
recognition
recognitory
recognitive
demonolater
demonomania
demonolatry
metoposcopy
xenodochium
aerological
gemological
oenological
pedological
penological
serological
sexological
demonologic
mesomorphic
xenomorphic
xeromorphic
demonocracy
decolourise
decolourize
hero-worship
seroconvert
cenospecies
decomposite
tenorrhaphy
hemorrhagic
menorrhagia
resourceful
aerobraking
devouringly
seborrhoeic
demographer
cerographic
demographic
venographic
xerographic
xerotripsis
aerotropism
democratise
democratist
democratize
Depo-Provera®
zero-grazing
belowstairs
remorseless
deconstruct
reconstruct
△remonstrant
demonstrate
remonstrate
repossessor
decorticate
Demosthenic
gerontology
reportingly
revoltingly
gerontophil
reportorial
aerostatics
aerostation
dehortation
deportation
dehortatory
dehortative
demodulator
depopulator
Belorussian
devolvement
aerodynamic
metonymical
lemon-yellow
temptatious
Neoplatonic
net-practice
respectable
respectably
respectless
bespreading
resplendent
perplexedly
Hepplewhite
telpherline
neopaganise
neopaganism
serpiginous
neopaganize
peep-through
delphically
Terpsichore
Delphinidae
delphiniums
despoilment
tempolabile

11 □e□p□l

geopolitics
despumation
weapon-schaw
despondence
despondency
respondence
respondency
reaping-hook
serpentinic
responsible
responsibly
responsions
serpentlike
keeping-room
weeping-ripe
serpent-star
leaping-time
reupholster
deep-mouthed
reapportion
desperadoes
hesperidium
leap-frogged
Hesperiidae
reappraisal
vespertinal
reappraiser
sempervivum
temporality
temperament
leopard-moth
pepperiness
peppercorny
temporaries
temporarily
pepper-grass
temporising
desperately
temperately
desperation
respiration
respiratory
temperature
temperative
deep-drawing
leopard-wood
temporizing
tempest-tost
tempestuous
perpetuance
perpetrable
perpetuable
perpetually
perpetrator
perpetuator
bespattered
herpetology
sempiternal
sempstering
sempiternum
helpfulness

geophysical
sesquipedal
mesquinerie
perquisitor
sesquialter
sesquioxide
rebroadcast
merry-andrew
reproachful
tear-falling
beer-parlour
bear-baiting
retroaction
retroactive
bear's-breech
retrobulbar
detribalise
terribility
wearability
detribalize
meprobamate
heartbroken
necrobiosis
necrobiotic
pearl-barley
pearl-button
reprobation
retribution
reprobatory
retributory
reprobative
retributive
refractable
retraceable
retractable
depreciator
tetracyclic
retrocedent
verruciform
tetractinal
terricolous
ferro-chrome
detractress
deprecating
deprecation
metrication
deprecatory
deprecative
tetradrachm
tetradactyl
regredience
débridement
tetradymite
Petrodromus
degradation
depredation
depredatory
retrievable
retrievably
tear-jerking
hearse-cloth

learnedness
heart-easing
reorientate
neurofibril
retroflexed
ferriferous
pearl-fisher
retrofitted
ferrography
petrography
reprography
deprogramme
reprogramme
tetragynian
ferruginous
terrigenous
tetragonous
tetragynous
refrigerant
refrigerate
segregation
segregative
petroglyphy
tetrahedral
tetrahedron
hearth-penny
searchlight
reprehender
yeard-hunger
searchingly
yeard-hungry
hearth-money
hearth-brush
hearth-stone
Hebraically
near-sighted
detrainment
recruitment
metrologist
necrologist
neurologist
petrologist
retrolental
neuroleptic
heartlessly
wearilessly
serrulation
merrymaking
pearl-millet
detrimental
recremental
gerrymander
jerrymander
necromancer
necromantic
recriminate
tetramerism
tetramerous
pearl-mussel
dedramatise
terremotive

dedramatize
herring-bone
herring-buss
ferro-nickel
refringency
herring-gull
refrangible
searing-iron
ferronnière
retranslate
dégringoler
herring-pond
tetrandrian
tetrandrous
pearl-oyster
rear-roasted
tetrapodous
neuropteran
tetrapteran
tetraplegia
tetraplegic
necrophilia
necrophilic
retrophilia
necropoleis
tetraploidy
necrophobia
necrophobic
negrophobia
decrepitude
neuropathic
decrepitate
petropounds
pearl-powder
terraqueous
retro-rocket
Petrarchian
Petrarchise
Petrarchism
Petrarchist
tetrarchate
Petrarchize
terroristic
heart-shaped
decrescendo
refreshener
depressible
repressible
repressibly
heart's-blood
serrasalmos
wearisomely
△refreshment
representee
representer
representor
bearishness
necroscopic
tetrasporic
terrestrial
heart-struck

heart-strike
heart-string
heart-strook
leprosarium
regrettable
regrettably
neuroticism
tetratheism
tear-stained
deerstalker
serratulate
betrothment
neurotomist
secretional
neurotrophy
neurotropic
secretarial
secretariat
territorial
territoried
regretfully
secretively
heart-urchin
defraudment
fearfulness
tearfulness
retroussage
tetravalent
depravement
deprivement
depravingly
reprovingly
sex-reversal
depravation
deprivation
reprivatise
deprivative
reprivatize
persuadable
felspathoid
persuasible
re-establish
sensualness
Weismannism
Messiahship
newscasting
feasibility
sensibility
tensibility
versability
seasickness
persecution
persecutory
persecutive
Wensleydale
reascension
reassertion
perspective
message-girl
bersaglieri
dessignment
news-theatre
leaseholder
deistically
perspirable
verslibrist
perspicuity
perspicuous
tessellated
weasel-faced
sessile-eyed
beastly-head
persulphate
beastliness
pensileness
ceaselessly
senselessly
verse-making
leesome-lane
leishmaniae
leishmanias
verse-monger
gelseminine
pessimistic
densimetric
personified
personifier
geosyncline
personalise
personalism
personalist
personality
seasonality
personalize
personpower
yersiniosis
weasand-pipe
personating
personation
personative
pensionable
sessionally
tensionally
seismonasty
seismoscope
seismometer
tensiometer
seismometry
tensiometry
tensionless
teaspoonful
seismologic
seismograph
men-servants
Bessarabian
tessaraglot
tea-strainer
keystroking
measureless
measurement
Sensurround®
geostrophic
geostrategy
mensuration
mensurative
persistence
persistency
versatilely
versatility
sensational
sensitively
sensitivity
reassurance
pensiveness
perseverant
persevering
perseverate
pentlandite
gentianella
neutraliser
neutralizer
restraining
peat-casting
tectibranch
vertebrated
vertebrally
destabilise
rentability
destabilize
petticoated
depth-charge
pentacyclic
septicaemia
geotactical
pentactinal
Pentacrinus
tentaculoid
denticulate
gesticulate
tentaculate
tentaculite
testiculate
verticality
Deutschmark
Weltschmerz
geotechnics
penteconter
geotectonic
leptocercal
festschrift
Pentecostal
sextodecimo
leptodactyl
pentadactyl
testudinary
death-duties
gentlemanly
weatherable
leather-back
leather-coat
weathercock
feather-edge
gentlenesse
heathenesse
leatherette®
weather-fend
tent-pegging
feather-head
leather-head
aesthetical
centrepiece
penthemimer
bestselling
nettle-cloth
weathermost
leather-neck
genteelness
settledness
gentlewoman
gentlewomen
centreboard
feather-pate
beetlebrain
feather-star
weather-worn
weather-wise
septifragal
certifiable
certifiably
rectifiable
certificate
testificate
pettifogger
pestiferous
septiferous
centigramme
hectogramme
pentagynian
lentiginose
heptagynous
lentiginous
pentagynous
tentiginous
vertiginous
dentigerous
get-together
pentahedral
pentahedron
Westphalian
bestridable
centrically
centripetal
restringent
ventriloquy
Westminster
restriction
restrictive
centrifugal
ventricular
ventriculus
reptilianly
pestologist
rectilineal
rectilinear

11 □e□t□l

pestilently
deathliness
de-Stalinise
de-Stalinize
gentilhomme
sertularian
gentilitial
gentilitian
ventilation
ventilative
pentamidine
sentimental
testamental
testamentar
testimonial
vestimental
centimorgan
death-marked
pentamerism
Septembrist
heptamerous
pentamerous
centimetric
Teutonicism
pertinacity
geitonogamy
Pelton-wheel
mentonnière
sententious
sentinelled
pertinently
meltingness
centenarian
pentandrian
septentrial
septentrion
heptandrous
pentandrous
septenarius
festinately
pectinately
destination
festination
pectination
pentangular
rectangular
mentholated
centrobaric
destroyable
mentionable
sectionally
Berthon-boat
benthoscope
oestrogenic
Neotropical
Weltpolitik
textbookish
pentaploidy
rectipetaly
perturbance
perturbable
vectorially
centuriator
perturbator
reattribute
vectorscope
perturbedly
deuterogamy
leptorrhine
heptarchist
yesternight
featureless
textureless
westernmost
pesteringly
venturingly
Deuteronomy
deuteranope
letterboxed
tenterhooks
letter-board
teeter-board
setter-forth
letterpress
lectureship
venturesome
death-rattle
letter-stamp
deuteration
reiteration
△restoration
reiterative
restorative
nectar-guide
dexterously
venturously
pentastichs
pettishness
rectiserial
death-stroke
pectisation
peptisation
teetotaller
teetotalism
pentathlete
restatement
gestational
gestatorial
destitution
restitution
restitutory
restitutive
tentatively
left-luggage
restfulness
zestfulness
destruction
restructure
destructive
pentavalent
restiveness
festivities
aestivation
vestry-clerk
west-by-north
west-by-south
pentazocine
pectization
peptization
ferulaceous
decumbently
recumbently
decumbiture
denunciator
pedunculate
sepulchrous
resuscitant
resuscitate
redundantly
fecundation
denumerable
denumerably
recuperable
remunerable
recuperator
rejuvenator
remunerator
rejuvenesce
oecumenical
tegumentary
beauteously
rebukefully
regurgitant
regurgitate
delusionist
decurionate
vesuvianite
Leguminosae
pecuniarily
peculiarise
peculiarity
peculiarize
repudiation
repudiative
beautifully
penuriously
refuellable
reduplicate
beguilement
beguilingly
republisher
genuflexion
genuineness
beaumontage
verumontana
resurrector
requirement
decurrently
recurrently
sequestered
demulsifier
sequestrant
sequestrate
decussately
decussation
requisition
requisitory
decursively
repulsively
requiteless
requitement
penultimate
reluctantly
desultorily
degustation
reluctation
degustatory
resultative
deductively
reductively
seductively
tenuousness
deçurvation
serviceable
serviceably
pervicacity
serviceless
heavy-headed
helve-hammer
heavy-handed
merveilleux
nervelessly
heavenwards
servant-girl
servant-lass
servantless
servant-maid
servantship
leaving-shop
pervertible
△beaverboard
nervuration
peevishness
pervasively
velvet-paper
leave-taking
neovitalism
neovitalist
velvetiness
servitorial
nervousness
heavyweight
between-maid
betweenness
betweentime
reawakening
Welwitschia
re-expansion
deoxidation
deoxygenise
deoxygenate
deoxygenize
deoxyribose
re-existence

Words marked △ may be spelled also with a capital letter

Hesychastic
demyelinate
beryliosis
dehypnotise
dehypnotize
dehydration
rehydration
Mezzogiorno
benzylidine
mezzotintos
off-Broadway
off-coloured
aficionados
afterburner
offenceless
after-dinner
after-effect
aftergrowth
aftersupper
offensively
effectually
affectingly
affectional
affectioned
affectation
affectively
effectively
affectivity
offhandedly
efficacious
office-block
officialdom
officialese
officialism
officiality
afficionado
efficiently
affiliation
officiously
affirmingly
affirmation
affirmatory
affirmative
afforcement
Afrocentric
Afro-centric
affrication
affricative
affrightful
affranchise
offscouring
offset-litho
off-the-shelf
effulgently
aguardiente
eglandulose
egg-and-spoon
agnatically
agrarianism
agranulosis
egregiously
agriproduct
agriculture
agglomerate
agglutinant
agglutinate
egalitarian
egomaniacal
agonistical
agonisingly
agonothetes
agonizingly
Ignorantine
ignoramuses
ignominious
agrobiology
ignobleness
agrological
agronomical
agnosticism
agrostology
aggradation
aggregately
aggregation
aggregative
agoraphobia
agoraphobic
aggravating
aggravation
egotistical
phrasemaker
phraseogram
phraseology
chiaroscuro
thrasonical
theatricals
theatricise
theatricism
theatricize
theatre-goer
thwartships
chiastolite
thwartingly
theanthropy
chlamydeous
rhabdomancy
Rhabdophora
rhabdomyoma
chick-a-biddy
chock-a-block
phycocyanin
thick-coming
chicken-feed
shock-headed
thick-headed
shock-horror
shackle-bolt
shackle-bone
phycologist
chuckle-head
thick-lipped
chocolatier
phycomycete
phycophaein
thick-ribbed
whichsoever
check-string
thick-witted
rhododaphne
shad-bellied
shuddersome
whodunnitry
rhodium-wood
shadowiness
shadowgraph
sheet-anchor
wheelbarrow
three-bottle
sheep-biting
three-colour
sheet-copper
wheel-cutter
threadmaker
thread-paper
three-decker
threadiness
cheeseparer
phrenetical
threnetical
cheesecloth
cheeseboard
cheesewring
cheesepress
sheet-feeder
sheep-farmer
cheechakoes
three-handed
Phaethontic
cheerleader
three-leafed
three-leaved
three-legged
wheedlesome
phlegmonoid
phlegmonous
sheep-master
three-masted
three-master
three-nooked
Phaenogamae
phaenogamic
chaenomeles
phaenomenon
chaetognath
phrenologic
three-parted
sheet-rubber
three-suited
sheep-silver
three-square
chieftaincy
chieftainry
threatening
three-volume
wheelwright
chaff-cutter
chaff-engine
shufflingly
shiftlessly
whiffletree
chafing-dish
chafing-gear
chiffonnier
theftuously
whigmaleery
phagocytism
phagocytose
phagedaenic
rhagadiform
shagge-eared
shaggedness
shigellosis
thigmotaxis
phagophobia
phthiriasis
chain-driven
shrivelling
choice-drawn
shriekingly
shrinkingly
shrink-proof
thrillingly
choirmaster
chrismatory
cheiromancy
cheirognomy
cheironomer
cheironomic
chrisom-robe
Cheiroptera
chainplates
chairperson
choirstalls
chainstitch
chain-smoker
choirscreen
△christiania
Christianly
Christmassy
Christogram
Christology
christingle
christening
Christendom
thriftiness
Christ-cross
chokecherry
shellacking
shell-crater
phylacteric
chelicerate
thalidomide
challenging
philhellene

11 □h□l□e

shelterless
chalcedonic
chalcedonyx
whole-footed
cheliferous
chyliferous
whale-fisher
Chilognatha
philogynist
philogynous
whole-hogger
whole-hoofed
Chillingham
phillipsite
shell-jacket
philologian
philologist
whole-length
chylomicron
childminder
philomathic
philanderer
whaling-port
cholinergic
phalanstery
phyllomania
phyllotaxis
Thallophyta
thallophyte
phylloclade
shallowness
cholestasis
cholesteric
cholesterin
thalassemia
thalassemic
cholesterol
wholestitch
wholesomely
philosopher
philosophic
whole-souled
thelytokous
shelftalker
philatelist
wholly-owned
chalazogamy
rhamnaceous
rhumb-course
chamaephyte
Chimaeridae
chamberlain
chambermaid
chimney-nuik
chimney-nook
champertous
chymiferous
Rhamphastos
whimsically
championess
thimble-case
thimblefuls
chameleonic
shamelessly
rhyme-letter
thimbleweed
thumb-marked
shamanistic
rhombohedra
chemurgical
rhyme-scheme
chemosphere
Thomistical
chemotactic
chemotropic
shameworthy
shimmy-shake
chantarelle
phantasiast
phantasmata
thingamyjig
thingamybob
rhinocerote
thunderbolt
thunderbird
thunderclap
thunder-dart
chanterelle
thunderhead
thunder-like
channelling
chancellery
chancellory
thunderless
chance-comer
change-house
thenceforth
whenceforth
thunder-peal
changefully
phonofiddle
phonography
phenogamous
rhynchocoel
rhynchodont
shanghaiing
chinoiserie
thinking-cap
chanticleer
thin-skinned
phenologist
phonologist
rhinologist
thingliness
chandlering
shinplaster
thanklessly
phonemicise
phonemicist
phonemicize
phenomenise
phenomenism
phenomenist
phenomenize
shunamitism
shenanigans
shiningness
phantomatic
chansonette
chansonnier
rhinoplasty
phonophobia
rhinorrhoea
chancroidal
Chondrostei
Phanerozoic
thanksgiver
rhinoscopic
phonetician
phoneticise
phoneticism
phoneticist
phoneticize
thanatology
thanatopsis
phonotypist
thingumajig
thingumabob
thankworthy
shinty-stick
theomachist
thrombocyte
throbbingly
theorematic
theotechnic
theoretical
theocentric
thiopentone
through-bolt
throughfare
throughgaun
theophobiac
theophobist
theophagous
chrominance
chaotically
chronically
chlorinator
chlorimeter
chlorimetry
thio-alcohol
chloanthite
theopneusty
chromoscope
chronoscope
chlorometer
chronometer
chlorometry
chronometry
chlorophyll
chromophore
theosophise
theosophism
theosophist
theosophize
rheological
theogonical
theological
theologiser
theologizer
theodolitic
chloroplast
chromoplast
chromosomal
chronologer
chronologic
theomorphic
chloroprene
chronograph
chloroquine
theobromine
rheotropism
Theocritean
throat-latch
throatiness
throat-strap
thiocyanate
chapeau-bras
Chippendale
shepherdess
shopkeeping
whipping-boy
whipping-top
shop-lifting
Rhopalocera
shapeliness
whippletree
rhapsodical
ship-breaker
shopbreaker
chaperonage
shipbuilder
chequerwork
chequerwise
chars-à-bancs
charlatanic
charlatanry
chartaceous
thereabouts
whereabouts
therebeside
chart-buster
short-change
Pherecratic
shortcoming
characinoid
thoracotomy
chargesheet
charge-house
chargenurse
sheriffalty
sharefarmer
thuriferous
sheriffship

chirography
choregraphy
chorography
chiragrical
sharp-ground
churchwards
shareholder
short-handed
churchwoman
churchgoing
thermically
Thersitical
choroiditis
thyroiditis
thermionics
sherris-sack
shirtlifter
chirologist
chorologist
charmlessly
sharemilker
whoremonger
chiromantic
Theromorpha
whoremaster
pharyngitic
pharyngitis
thermotaxic
thermotaxis
theriolatry
thermonasty
thermoscope
thermometer
thermogenic
thermometry
thermophile
chordophone
thermotical
thermocline
tharborough
theriomorph
choreograph
thermograph
thermoduric
thermolysis
thermolytic
chiropodial
chiropodist
chiropteran
short-priced
thornproofs
share-pusher
Therapeutae
therapeutic
chirurgical
charismatic
short-staple
sharksucker
wheresoever
phariseeism
shirt-sleeve
pharisaical
cherishment
whorishness
short-spoken
third-stream
Thyrostraca
chorisation
theretofore
charity-girl
thirstiness
thyrotropin
short-termer
charcuterie
thoroughwax
thorough-pin
short-winded
therewithal
wherewithal
sharp-witted
therewithin
cherry-stone
thirty-twomo
chorization
Phasmatidae
Phasmatodea
physiciancy
physicianer
physicalism
physicalist
physicality
whiskerando
whiskeyfied
chastenment
phosphonium
phosphorise
phosphorism
phosphorate
phosphorite
phosphorous
phosphorize
phosphatide
phosphatise
phosphatize
chastisable
whistleable
thistledown
whistlingly
ghastliness
ghostliness
whistle-stop
thysanurous
physiolater
chasmogamic
physiolatry
thesmothete
ahistorical
physiognomy
physiologic
physiologus
physiocracy
whist-player
whosesoever
physitheism
thesauruses
ghost-writer
whisky-liver
phytoalexin
photo-ageing
photoactive
white-billed
△whiteboyism
Whitechapel
white-collar
photocopier
photochromy
phytochrome
chitterling
shatter-pate
whitleather
thitherward
whitherward
photo-finish
photography
phytography
photoglyphy
white-headed
white-haired
white-handed
thatch-board
Thatcherism
Thatcherite
shuttlecock
phytologist
white-listed
shuttlewise
rhythmicity
photometric
photonastic
whiting-time
whatsomever
whitlow-wort
phytophagic
photophilic
photophobia
photophobic
photophonic
photoperiod
rhetorician
photo-relief
white-rumped
photoresist
phytosterol
photosphere
whitishness
phototactic
white-tailed
phytotomist
phototropic
whitethroat
shit-stirrer
Whitsuntide
white-winged
whitewasher
chitty-faced
rheumateese
rheumatical
rheumaticky
Chautauquan
thaumatrope
thaumaturge
thaumaturgy
shrubbiness
shrubberied
shouldering
thoughtcast
thoughtless
thought-sick
thought-wave
thrummingly
chaulmoogra
cheval-glass
shovelboard
shaving-soap
shiveringly
showmanship
shawnee-wood
showeriness
showerproof
show-stopper
showjumping
thixotropic
chrysalides
chrysalises
chrysarobin
chrysoberyl
chrysocolla
chrysocracy
chrysoprase
wheyishness
phlyctaenae
rhizocarpic
rhizogenous
rhizomatous
rhizanthous
rhizosphere
pit-a-patting
bicarbonate
Micawberish
Micawberism
financially
vicar-choral
disaccustom
ritardandos
bilaterally
disaventure
filamentary
ligamentary
filamentous
ligamentous
disaffected
vicar-forane
disafforest
vinaigrette

Words marked △ may be spelled also with a capital letter

11 □i□a□h

cigar-holder
Sivatherium
rival-hating
dilapidated
piratically
△titanically
dilapidator
rifacimenti
rifacimento
vivacissimo
bifariously
hilariously
vicariously
vivaciously
misalliance
disablement
mid-Atlantic
disarmament
disannuller
Titanomachy
pinacotheca
disapproval
cicatricula
cigar-shaped
disassemble
disassembly
giganticide
didacticism
gigantology
didactylous
misanthrope
misanthropy
gigantesque
bipartition
ailanthuses
litany-stool
vinblastine
misbecoming
kibble-chain
misbegotten
fimbriation
disbeliever
misbeliever
diabolology
liabilities
disbandment
ribbon-grass
timbromania
timbrophily
timber-hitch
gibberellic
gibberellin
misbestowal
nimbostrati
gibbousness
disbowelled
gimcrackery
misclassify
aircraftman
finch-backed
pitchblende
miscibility
vincibility
piscicolous
hircocervus
discrepance
discrepancy
kitchenette
biochemical
circle-rider
kitchen-maid
biocoenoses
biocoenosis
biocoenotic
yince-errand
kitchen-sink
miscreation
miscreative
miscreaunce
kitchenware
witch-finder
zinciferous
discography
zincography
miscegenist
miscegenate
pinch-hitter
kinchin-cove
diacritical
kinchin-mort
biscuit-root
vincristine
mischievous
miscellanea
discalceate
circularise
circularity
piacularity
circularize
circulating
circulation
circulatory
circulative
discoloured
discomycete
circumciser
discomfited
circumflect
circumpolar
circumsolar
circumvolve
circumspect
viscometric
circumlunar
circumfused
misconceive
discontinue
misconstrue
cinchoninic
disceptator
disciplinal
discipliner
discophoran
pitchperson
discordance
discordancy
witch-ridden
miscarriage
discernible
discernibly
discerpible
air-corridor
discardment
discernment
diachronism
sincereness
diachronous
pitch-roofed
discerption
discerptive
discussable
discussible
discotheque
discothèque
biocatalyst
piscatorial
viscousness
discoursive
diacoustics
discourtesy
viscountess
piscivorous
bird-catcher
bird-fancier
birdwatcher
pieds-à-terre
windbaggery
misdiagnose
vindication
vindicatory
vindicative
middle-earth
mind-bending
mind-reading
fiddle-de-dee
riddle-me-ree
middle-sized
mind-healing
pit-dwelling
middle-class
kindredness
middle-world
kind-hearted
kindredship
girdlestead
windlestrae
windlestraw
fiddlestick
bird-nesting
giddy-headed
windcheater
diadelphous
mind-blowing
misdemeanor
sindonology
biodynamics
middenstead
wildfowling
piedmontite
hinderlands
Windbreaker®
Biedermeier
widdershins
bird-brained
hinderlings
hinderingly
kinderspiel
misdescribe
mind-numbing
windsurfing
wind-sucking
mindfulness
misdoubtful
misdevotion
window-barne
tiddlywinks
fire-watcher
wire-dancing
CinemaScope®
wide-watered
witenagemot
piperaceous
time-bargain
wide-ranging
kinematical
literaliser
literalizer
mineraliser
mineralizer
tire-valiant
fire-walking
fire-balloon
kite-balloon
bimetallism
bimetallist
liberalness
literalness
cinema-organ
fire-marshal
vice-marshal
lifemanship
fire-raising
mine-captain
wine-tasting
literatured
literaryism
disembodied
liveability
disemburden
disembitter
river-bottom
liver-colour
disencumber
linen-draper

Words marked △ may be spelled also with a capital letter

river-dragon
aides-de-camp
vice-admiral
river-driver
vicegerency
time-release
aide-mémoire
wise-hearted
life-rentrix
time-service
time-serving
tiger-flower
tiger-footed
divergement
bioengineer
divergently
divergingly
rivet-hearth
side-wheeler
dicephalous
nikethamide
line-shooter
mine-thrower
widechapped
time-sharing
kinesipathy
eidetically
mimetically
wine-bibbing
Ribesiaceae
rice-biscuit
vine-disease
Kimeridgian
fivefingers
fire-fighter
firelighter
limelighted
pipe-lighter
line-fishing
cineritious
cine-biology
ciné-biology
kinesiology
time-killing
misericorde
kinesiatric
life-history
pipe-cleaner
time-pleaser
divellicate
miserliness
fire-flaught
libellously
river-mussel
hibernacula
△hibernicise
Hibernicism
△hibernicize
pigeon-berry
pigeon-chest
pigeon-flier
pigeon-flyer
pigeonholer
pigeonholes
pigeon-house
hide-and-seek
hibernation
viceroyalty
dive-bombing
fire-bombing
kinetoscope
sideropenia
siderophile
kinetochore
wireworking
kinetograph
fire-worship
viceroyship
fine-toothed
fire-control
Didelphidae
disemployed
pipe-dreamer
firecracker
line-printer
fire-crested
vine-dresser
vine-fretter
wine-growing
wiredrawing
diversified
dimensional
dimensioned
linen-scroll
disenshroud
disentrance
disentrayle
liberty-boat
liberticide
diverticula
kinesthesia
kinesthesis
kinesthetic
directrices
misestimate
libertinage
disentangle
divertingly
bicentenary
libertinism
directional
pipe-stapple
pipe-stopple
directorial
libertarian
disenthrall
direct-grant
disenthrone
△directorate
divestiture
digestively
directivity
wire-pulling
bisexuality
direfulness
hideousness
piteousness
life-support
minesweeper
Minenwerfer
riverworthy
time-expired
misfeasance
diffraction
diffractive
misfeatured
difficultly
diffidently
biofeedback
sinfonietta
rinforzando
differentia
differently
pilferingly
misfortuned
zip-fastener
diffuseness
diffusively
diffusivity
disfavourer
disgraceful
disgracious
wing-walking
ring-carrier
ring-fencing
single-phase
single-digit
single-entry
single-soled
single-cross
singlestick
misguidance
pilgrimager
disguisable
ring-winding
disguisedly
misguidedly
linguistics
singularise
singularism
singularist
singularity
singularize
singing-bird
rigging-loft
rigging-tree
wing-and-wing
diagnosable
kingdomless
diagnostics
finger-paint
pilgarlicky
disgarrison
fingerglass
fingerplate
lingeringly
fingerboard
△gingerbread
fingerprint
finger-grass
fingerstall
fingerguard
disgustedly
piggishness
ring-straked
fidgetiness
ring-stopper
disgruntled
king-vulture
misgovernor
tiggywinkle
king's-yellow
△mithradatic
Mithraicism
Highlandman
pigheadedly
right-angled
fish-packing
high-ranking
fish-farming
high-battled
night-attire
highfalutin
pichiciagos
night-cellar
diphycercal
lithochromy
lithodomous
high-feeding
fish-bellied
eighteenmos
high-hearted
high-tension
high-density
high-mettled
righteously
light-footed
night-flower
nightfaring
tight-fisted
night-flying
lithography
dichogamous
lithogenous
light-headed
light-heeled
diphthongal
light-handed
night-hunter
right-handed
right-hander
diphthongic
diphtheroid
△mithridatic

11 □i□h□i

high-pitched
nightingale
highlighted
highlighter
high-sighted
tight-lacing
light-legged
lithologist
tightly-knit
high-alumina
sightliness
highblooded
mishallowed
tight-lipped
litholapaxy
sightlessly
△ditheletism
△dithelitism
light-minded
right-minded
nightmarish
wishing-bone
fishing-frog
siphonogamy
lichenology
fishing-line
dishonorary
dishonestly
wishing-tree
dishonourer
wishing-well
dichromatic
dichroscope
high-powered
high-rolling
fish-torpedo
high-voltage
wishtonwish
right-of-ways
sight-player
xiphopagous
night-porter
lithophysae
lithophytic
tithe-paying
hitherwards
sight-reader
high-profile
tichorrhine
withershins
dithyrambic
witheringly
Michurinism
disharmonic
wither-wrung
citharistic
highwrought
highbrowism
night-season
sightseeing
rights-of-way
lithosphere
sight-singer
vichyssoise
night-shriek
△diphysitism
eight-square
lithotritic
lithotritor
lithotripsy
right-to-life
dichotomise
dichotomist
lithotomist
dichotomous
lithotomous
dichotomize
withstander
high-stepper
without-door
wishfulness
fish-gutting
dishevelled
lightweight
night-waking
night-walker
light-winged
right-winger
night-worker
sightworthy
highly-sexed
minicabbing
limitations
finicalness
vigilantism
disinclined
viridescent
virilescent
limitedness
limited-over
citizenship
misidentify
vivisection
vivisective
disinfector
misinformer
riding-habit
bilingually
dining-table
riding-rhyme
riding-light
riding-skirt
riding-cloak
hiding-place
tiring-glass
riding-glove
tiring-woman
diving-board
biting-louse
riding-horse
tiring-house
diving-dress
Livingstone
civilisable
civilizable
mirifically
vinificator
visiting-day
diminishing
divisionary
civilianise
△divisionism
divisionist
civilianize
digitigrade
dimidiation
lixiviation
litigiously
rigidifying
bimillenary
visibleness
sigillarian
limitlessly
disillusion
disillusive
titillating
pixillation
sigillation
titillation
titillative
pig-ignorant
Titianesque
disimprison
sitiophobia
misinstruct
vicissitude
sinistrally
pipistrelle
sinistrorse
ministerial
disinterred
ministering
disinterest
miniaturise
miniaturist
sinisterity
ministerium
tibiotarsus
miniaturize
diminuendos
biliousness
pitifulness
viciousness
viniculture
viticulture
misjudgment
disjunction
disjuncture
disjunctive
tick-tack-toe
tick-tack-too
nick-nackery
tickle-brain
zinkiferous
silk-thrower
milk-thistle
milk-livered
Pickwickian
milk-kinship
pickelhaube
nickel-ochre
nickelodeon
nickel-bloom
lick-platter
nickel-steel
pinking-iron
sickeningly
pick-and-pick
milking-time
silkworm-gut
pick-your-own
lickspittle
lickerishly
pinkishness
sickishness
picket-fence
ricketiness
rickettsiae
rickettsial
rickettsias
ticket-punch
picket-guard
tickettyboo
milk-pudding
sicknursing
billiard-cue
gillravitch
hillwalking
milliampere
hill-pasture
dialectally
diplococcus
dialectical
field-cornet
dislocation
villication
digladiator
dislodgment
millefleurs
gillyflower
sialography
dialogistic
title-holder
bill-chamber
dislikeable
killikinick
dislikeness
sillimanite
diplomatics
diplomatese
diplomatise
diplomatist
diplomatize
violoncello

Words marked △ may be spelled also with a capital letter

millenniums
willingness
millenarian
millenarism
violinistic
villanously
bibliomancy
bibliolater
bibliomania
bibliolatry
billionaire
millionaire
bibliopegic
millionfold
bibliotheca
bibliophile
bibliophily
bibliopolic
pillion-seat
will-worship
△lilliputian
pillar-saint
sialorrhoea
tiller-chain
millisecond
aimlessness
airlessness
girlishness
sinlessness
witlessness
billsticker
billets-doux
midlittoral
millet-grass
pillow-fight
pillow-block
fieldworker
air-mechanic
biomedicine
filmsetting
filmography
diamagnetic
sigmoidally
dismembered
firmamental
diamond-back
diamond-dust
diamorphine
mismarriage
dismissible
dismastment
diametrally
diametrical
biomaterial
dismutation
dismayfully
fiançailles
sign-painter
winnability
cinnabarine
pilniewinks

bienséances
lion-hearted
signifiable
significant
significate
pianofortes
ninny-hammer
giant-killer
kinnikinick
limnologist
simnel-bread
lignum-scrub
lignum-swamp
winningness
winning-post
piano-player
dinner-dance
dinner-wagon
sign-writing
pignoration
Wienerwurst
cinnarizine
piano-school
Minnesinger
pinnatisect
Finno-Ugrian
lignivorous
pinnywinkle
Disneyesque
kidney-stone
Disneyfying
mimosaceous
bivouacking
kilocalorie
lipomatosis
pilocarpine
divorceable
divorcement
disordinate
mitogenetic
widowerhood
disobedient
Tironensian
misoneistic
bimolecular
sin-offering
disorganise
disorganize
Sinophilism
dinotherium
ricochetted
ricocheting
mitotically
minoritaire
bifoliolate
bisociation
bisociative
pilot-jacket
disobliging
ritornellos
Sinological

virological
bicorporate
ritournelle
mimographer
mixotrophic
lipoprotein
binocularly
ribonucleic
liposuction
dicotyledon
pinocytosis
diaphaneity
hippiatrics
hippiatrist
Diophantine
hippeastrum
Hippocratic
hippocampal
hippocampus
hippodamist
hippodamous
hippodromic
mispleading
fipple-flute
displeasant
displeasing
displeasure
simpliciter
simplifying
hippologist
dispensable
dispensably
dispensator
△hispanicise
hispanicism
△hispanicize
disprovable
diaphoresis
diaphoretic
disproperty
jimpson-weed
hippopotami
diapophyses
diapophysis
dispersedly
misperceive
diaphragmal
disportment
simperingly
limp-wristed
disparately
dispiriting
mispersuade
disposingly
wimpishness
disposition
diapositive
dispositive
dispatchful
disputation
disputative

biophysical
Lippizzaner
cinquecento
△milquetoast
disquietude
disquieting
disquietful
disquietous
disquietive
microampere
rib-roasting
hierocratic
micrococcal
micrococcus
fibrocement
fibrocement®
microcephal
jinrickshaw
microcosmic
nitrocotton
vitrifiable
microfiches
microfiling
microfloppy
microfossil
hierography
micrography
microgamete
nitrogenase
nitrogenise
nitrogenous
nitrogenize
microgroove
diarthrosis
Cirrhipedia
microinject
vitraillist
mitrailleur
fibrillated
hierologist
micrologist
microlithic
misrelation
disremember
misremember
micrometric
nitrometric
microneedle
citronellal
nitraniline
Hieronymian
Hieronymite
Micronesian
hierophobia
hierophobic
microphonic
microporous
microphytic
hierarchism
hierurgical
mirror-glass

11 □i□r□r

mirror-image
nigrescence
vitrescence
dioristical
microswitch
vitrescible
nitrosamine
tigrishness
microscopic
nitrosation
microtubule
diprotodont
Niersteiner
vibratility
microtomist
librational
vibrational
lip-rounding
microwriter
lip-smacking
first-attack
dissociable
dissociably
Dipsacaceae
dissectible
air-sickness
AIDS-related
diastematic
linseed-cake
misspelling
linseed-meal
Einsteinian
einsteinium
missheathed
kiss-me-quick
first-footer
first-fruits
pig-sticking
midshipmate
dissolvable
dissyllable
dissilience
dissolutely
dissolution
dissolutive
dissymmetry
dissembling
dissimilate
dissimulate
dipsomaniac
disseminule
lissomeness
winsomeness
disseminate
dissentient
dissentious
dissonantly
kiss-and-tell
fissionable
diascordium
ripsnorting
dissepiment
first-person
fissiparism
fissiparity
fissiparous
dissipation
dissipative
tin-streamer
dissertator
diastrophic
bias-drawing
pissasphalt
missishness
first-strike
hirsuteness
victuallage
victualling
victualless
distracting
distraction
distractive
rib-tickling
eisteddfods
mistreading
△diotheletic
rinthereout
diathermacy
diathermous
littleworth
virtue-proof
distressing
distressful
fifteenthly
sixteenthly
dittography
pictography
nitty-gritty
histrionics
histrionism
distributee
distributer
distribuend
distributor
distillable
Distalgesic®
histologist
mirthlessly
distempered
mistempered
victimology
histaminase
distensible
listening-in
distantness
listeners-in
sitting-room
fitting-shop
distinction
distincture
distinctive
distinguish
histiocytic
disturbance
filter-paper
historiated
pictorially
bitter-earth
picture-book
dipterocarp
picture-card
picture-cord
historicise
historicism
historicist
historicity
historicize
winterberry
historiette
picture-goer
winter-bloom
victoryless
sister-in-law
disthronize
listeriosis
picture-play
bitter-apple
wintergreen
picture-rail
bitter-cress
picturesque
Pinteresque
micturition
littérateur
bittersweet
winter-sweet
picture-wire
diatessaron
distasteful
Nietzschean
pietistical
pittosporum
dictatorial
nictitating
nictitation
riotousness
wistfulness
distrustful
mistrustful
tittivation
birth-weight
sinupallial
simulacrums
air-umbrella
sipunculoid
bifurcation
biquadratic
Liquidambar
liquidation
figure-dance
lieutenancy
minute-watch
vituperable
vituperator
minute-while
minute-glass
liquefiable
divulgement
divulgation
diluvialism
diluvialist
dilutionary
disunionist
aiguillette
ritualistic
ailurophobe
ailurophile
bicuspidate
disulphuret
disulphuric
liquescence
liquescency
situational
sinuousness
silver-white
silversides
silversmith
silveriness
silver-point
silver-grain
silver-stick
silvestrian
rib-vaulting
lily-livered
disyllabify
disyllabism
ejectamenta
ejaculation
ejaculatory
ejaculative
ejector-seat
sky-aspiring
sky-coloured
skillcentre
skilligalee
skilligolee
skeletonise
skeletonize
skulduddery
skulduggery
skilfulness
skimmington
skin-popping
skeptically
skirmishing
sketchiness
skittle-ball
skating-rink
plea-bargain
alkalescent
all-American
bloatedness
ill-affected
clear-headed

Words marked △ may be spelled also with a capital letter

bleach-field
alkalimeter
alkalimetry
clean-limbed
cleanliness
pliableness
clean-living
olla-podrida
clean-shaven
ill-assorted
olfactology
illaqueable
pleasurable
pleasurably
pleasureful
clubmanship
clubability
flabbergast
globeflower
globigerina
all-building
plebeianise
plebeianism
plebeianize
globularity
Globerigina
elaborately
elaboration
elaboratory
elaborative
alabastrine
Black-and-Tan
black-and-tan
black-a-vised
black-boding
black-beetle
placability
black-browed
blackbirder
blockbuster
black-coated
elucidation
elucidatory
elucidative
placket-hole
all-cheering
slickenside
flickertail
black-figure
black-fellow
black-fisher
blackheaded
place-hunter
slack-handed
electioneer
flaccidness
place-kicker
alycompaine
blackmailer
place-monger
black-market
flock-master
Placentalia
electorship
Plectoptera
electrician
electricity
electrocute
electrified
electrolier
electrology
electrolyse
electrolyte
electrolyze
electronics
electrotint
electrotype
electrotypy
glycosylate
block-system
elicitation
flocculence
fluctuating
fluctuation
sledge-chair
fly-dressing
bladder-worm
bladderwort
sliding-rule
clodhopping
gladioluses
ill-disposed
Gladstonian
gladfulness
altercation
altercative
all-electric
elder-flower
sleek-headed
elsewhither
alleviation
alleviatory
alleviative
alder-leaved
elderliness
blue-blooded
sleeplessly
aldermanity
glue-sniffer
alternately
alternating
alternation
alternative
allelopathy
allegorical
allegoriser
allegorizer
allelomorph
algebraical
allegrettos
allez-vous-en
sleepwalker
old-fogeyish
cliffhanger
ill-favoured
elegiacally
sluggardise
sluggardize
flag-wagging
flag-captain
eligibility
Oligochaeta
oligochaete
oligochrome
aleggeaunce
flag-officer
clog-almanac
flagellated
flagellator
oligomerous
sloganising
sloganizing
plagioclase
plagiostome
Plagiostomi
blightingly
slightingly
flightiness
flagitation
alphabetise
alphabetize
allhallowen
ill-humoured
plein-airist
illiberally
plaice-mouth
Albigensian
allineation
ill-informed
illimitable
illimitably
glaikitness
illicitness
claim-jumper
pleiomerous
cloisonnage
plainstanes
clairschach
ellipsoidal
plain-spoken
plainstones
Pleistocene
ellipticity
cleistogamy
pleiotropic
plaintively
illiquidity
altitudinal
illiquation
clairvoyant
climacteric
climactical
slimmed-down
glimmer-gowk
slumberland
slumberless
slumbersome
plumber-work
Glumiflorae
glumiferous
plumigerous
T-lymphocyte
clam-chowder
alembicated
old-maidhood
plumularian
blamelessly
plum-blossom
elementally
ill-mannered
elimination
eliminatory
eliminative
flamboyance
flamboyancy
flamboyante
plume-pluckt
glomerulate
glomeration
clamorously
glamorously
slumbrously
blemishment
climatology
flammulated
plum-pudding
Plymouthism
Plymouthist
Plymouthite
glamourpuss
slum-dweller
blameworthy
clanjamfray
clindamycin
clinochlore
plano-convex
blunderbuss
flannelette
slenderness
clandestine
plenteously
blanketweed
blind-felled
planogamete
flinchingly
clench-built
plantigrade
plentifully
planuliform
clinometric
planimetric
plantocracy
plenipotent
planisphere

11 □l□n□s

plantswoman
blind-storey
planetoidal
planetology
planetarium
glandularly
clenbuterol
blunt-witted
allocatable
allopathist
gliomatosis
blood-bought
klootchmans
fluorescein
fluorescent
alto-relievo
cliometrics
aldopentose
blood-flower
blood-frozen
elbow-grease
blood-guilty
allocheiria
pleochroism
illogically
fluorimeter
algorithmic
alto-rilievo
alloplastic
bloodletter
gloom-monger
fluoroscope
fluoroscopy
fluorometer
algological
pleomorphic
allotropism
allotropous
blood-spavin
bloodsucker
bloodstream
bloodsprent
altostratus
blood-typing
altoruffled
allopurinol
altocumulus
floorwalker
bloody-faced
bloody-bones
bloody-sweat
blepharitis
elephantoid
elephantine
clapperclaw
flapperhood
slipperwort
kleptomania
glyptotheca
kleptocracy
glyphograph

flap-mouthed
all-powerful
flirtatious
clericalism
clericalist
blarney-land
ultrafilter
floriferous
florilegium
pluralistic
ultra-modern
ultramarine
Clarencieux
glaringness
plerophoria
florescence
ultrasonics
pluriserial
ultraviolet
clergywoman
alismaceous
plasmatical
close-bodied
close-banded
glass-blower
close-barred
flesh-colour
glass-cutter
cluster-bean
flusterment
blessedness
clyster-pipe
glossectomy
plasterwork
class-fellow
close-fisted
glass-gazing
blasphemous
close-handed
close-hauled
elasticated
classically
elastically
plessimeter
plessimetry
plasticiser
plasticizer
elasticness
plasminogen
classifying
class-leader
fleshliness
close-lipped
blushlessly
fleshmonger
flesh-market
glossolalia
blastogenic
elastomeric
Elastoplast®
blastocoele

glasnostian
glossodynia
plasmolysis
plasmolytic
clostridial
clostridium
close-reefed
elusoriness
flustration
glassworker
plate-armour
flat-earther
plate-basket
plutocratic
clothes-line
clothes-pole
clothes-prop
blotchiness
blotting-pad
ulotrichous
elutriation
plutologist
flatulently
ill-tempered
glutaminase
Platanaceae
Platonicism
plutonomist
△platinotype
glutinously
plethorical
platforming
glottogonic
plate-powder
platyrrhine
Ulsterwoman
plateresque
slate-writer
plate-warmer
glaucescent
slaughterer
ploughshare
sleuth-hound
eleutherian
plough-staff
plough-stilt
illuminance
illuminable
illuminator
albugineous
flourishing
pleuritical
illusionism
illusionist
illuviation
albuminuria
cloudlessly
glauconitic
pleurodynia
fleurs-de-lis
fleurs-de-lys

illustrated
illustrator
illustrious
flauntingly
cloud-topped
clavecinist
Clavicornia
slave-driver
clavigerous
slaveholder
Slavonicise
Slavonicize
olivine-rock
pluviometer
cleverality
slaveringly
clovergrass
glove-shield
slavishness
slave-trader
flavourless
flavoursome
slow-release
ill-wresting
slow-sighted
old-womanish
claw-and-ball
flowingness
flower-clock
floweriness
flower-stalk
flexibility
cloxacillin
flexography
pleximetric
Alexandrian
△alexandrine
alexandrite
flax-dresser
play-actress
playing-card
alcyonarian
clay-brained
player-piano
playfulness
Elizabethan
embarcation
empanelling
empanelment
immanentism
immanentist
immarginate
impatiently
embarkation
imparkation
amiableness
emparlaunce
ommatophore
embarrassed
empassioned
impassioned

Words marked △ may be spelled also with a capital letter

11 □n□a□e

impassively
impassivity
impartially
impartation
impastation
amicability
emmenagogic
emmenagogue
impeachable
imperceable
impeachment
impenetrate
imperfectly
imperforate
immedicable
impenitence
impenitency
impedimenta
impetigines
imperialise
imperialism
imperialist
imperiality
imperialize
imperilment
immediately
immediatism
imperiously
embellisher
umbellately
impermeable
impermeably
impermanent
emperorship
impetration
impetratory
impetrative
immenseness
impersonate
Emmenthaler
impertinent
impecunious
impetuosity
impetuously
imperviable
imagination
imaginative
amphibology
amphibolite
amphibolous
amphictyony
amphimictic
amphipodous
amphiprotic
amphipathic
△amphisbaena
amphetamine
emphyteusis
emphyteutic
ambilateral
ambivalence
ambivalency
omnipatient
omnifarious
omniscience
empiecement
ambiversion
impingement
empirically
immitigable
immitigably
empiricutic
ambitiously
impignorate
omnipotence
omnipotency
omniformity
omnipresent
immigration
embittering
ambiguously
smokelessly
smokescreen
emplacement
implacental
implication
implicative
smallholder
emulsionise
emulsionize
amyloidosis
emolumental
implemental
small-minded
emblematise
emblematist
emblematize
Amelanchier
smilingness
imploringly
imploration
imploratory
small-screen
implausible
implausibly
emulousness
amplexicaul
amino-acetic
amentaceous
amenability
aminobutene
emancipator
amontillado
amenorrhoea
emanational
ominousness
imponderous
immoveables
embowelling
embowelment
embowerment
empowerment
immomentous
smooth-faced
smooth-paced
ammophilous
smooth-bored
impolitical
impoliticly
impoundable
impoundment
Amboina-wood
Amboyna-wood
amyotrophic
immortalise
immortality
immortalize
emboîtement
impostumate
importunacy
importantly
importunely
importuning
importunate
importunity
importation
imposthumed
smörgåsbord
improbation
impractical
umbraculate
embracement
embracingly
Americanise
Americanism
Americanist
Americanize
imprecisely
imprecision
imbricately
embrocation
imbrication
imprecation
imprecatory
imprudently
umbriferous
impregnable
impregnably
amorphously
embroiderer
amerciament
embroilment
umbrella-fir
umbrella-ant
amaranthine
embryonated
embryologic
impropriate
impropriety
emery-powder
ambrosially
impressible
impressment
impresarios
smart-ticket
umbratilous
amorousness
improvident
improvement
improvingly
improvisate
smartypants
smarty-boots
emasculator
amusiveness
ametabolism
imitability
ametabolous
smithereens
empty-headed
empty-handed
empty-nester
emotionable
emotionally
emotionless
emetophobia
amatorially
Smithsonian
smithsonite
imitatively
amateurship
amativeness
amethystine
ambuscadoes
smouldering
ampullosity
immunogenic
immunotoxic
immunotoxin
immunoassay
amour-propre
impuissance
impulsively
empyreumata
amazon-stone
unpalatable
unpalatably
unhazardous
incapacious
unparagoned
enjambement
unharboured
unmatchable
unmasculine
enhancement
incarcerate
unhandseled
unsandalled
unpardoning
unhandiness
incardinate
unwandering
incalescent
annabergite

11 □n□a□e

unravelling
unravelment
untamedness
ungazed-upon
infangthief
ensanguined
enlargement
unpathwayed
unfashioned
ingathering
inhabitance
inhabitancy
unnavigated
inhabitable
innavigable
innavigably
unhabitable
unnavigable
unsatisfied
invalidhood
unsatirical
unmalicious
invalidness
inhabitress
insatiately
unsatiating
unhackneyed
intagliated
unmalleable
uncalled-for
entablement
unfailingly
ungallantly
unmanliness
unballasted
entablature
ungarmented
unharmfully
undauntable
unpaintable
incarnadine
undauntedly
untaintedly
unjaundiced
encarnalise
encarnalize
uncanniness
ungarnished
unharnessed
untarnished
unvarnished
△incarnation
uncanonical
uncanonised
uncanonized
unlaborious
unsavourily
unlabouring
unhappiness
unmarriable
unbarricade
unwarranted
unpatriotic
encapsulate
incapsulate
unpassioned
infanticide
infantilism
unpatterned
unfaltering
incantation
incantatory
infantryman
infantrymen
unsaturated
unnaturally
insalubrity
infatuation
incarvillea
unharvested
inobedience
inobservant
unobservant
unobserving
snobography
inebriation
unabolished
unabrogated
unobnoxious
snobbocracy
inobtrusive
unobtrusive
unscratched
knocked-down
Anacreontic
snickersnee
enucleation
unscheduled
inscribable
inscription
inscriptive
knick-knacky
knuckle-bone
knuckle-head
unicolorate
unicolorous
anacoluthia
anacoluthon
inoculation
inoculatory
insculpture
inoculative
unicellular
unicoloured
onychomancy
anecdotally
unscholarly
onychophagy
Onychophora
anecdotical
unicorn-moth
anachronism
anachronous
knock-rating
unscissored
inscrutable
inscrutably
unaccusable
unaccusably
inedibility
inadvertent
inadvisable
unadvisable
unadvisably
unadvisedly
unidiomatic
inadaptable
unadaptable
anadiplosis
unaddressed
inodorously
unseparated
inseparable
inseparably
ungetatable
unget-at-able
unseparable
undebauched
undemanding
unregarding
unrewarding
unveracious
interallied
unrecalling
unremaining
interatomic
kneecapping
knee-capping
interactant
interaction
underaction
interactive
underbearer
interbedded
underbidder
underbudget
underbreath
underbridge
under-bonnet
underbitten
interchange
undercharge
unpeaceable
unreachable
unteachable
intercedent
undescribed
unperceived
intercalary
intercalate
unwelcomely
intercensal
undescended
unrescinded
unmercenary
intercooled
intercooler
underclothe
intercepter
interceptor
intercostal
intercessor
intercrural
intercourse
undercovert
interdealer
under-driven
unfeudalise
unfeudalize
underdamper
interdental
unbendingly
unheedingly
unreadiness
interdepend
infeudation
unheedfully
unneedfully
incendivity
undelegated
inseverable
unvenerable
△independent
undepending
antependium
antecedence
antecedents
unbeneficed
unbenefited
unrevealing
unbeseeming
undeveloped
under-espial
unreceipted
underexpose
unrehearsed
anteversion
unnecessary
inferential
enterectomy
interesting
unrelenting
unrepentant
unrepenting
unresenting
unresentful
unreceptive
unretentive
undeserving
interfacial
unperfectly
interfacing
underfulfil
enfeoffment

Words marked △ may be spelled also with a capital letter

index-finger
unperformed
unselfishly
interfusion
interfluent
interfluous
unwedgeable
unfeignedly
underground
Interglossa
intergrowth
undergrowth
enneahedral
enneahedron
untechnical
encephaloid
encephaline
enkephaline
encephalous
antechamber
underhanded
underhonest
unmechanise
unmechanize
inheritance
unmeditated
angelically
endemically
indefinable
indefinably
inheritable
undecidable
undefinable
undesirable
undesirably
unmeritable
inseminator
indehiscent
undelivered
undecidedly
unmeritedly
unbenighted
undelighted
unperishing
unreligious
endemiology
unbeginning
unbenignant
undesigning
indesignate
unpedigreed
inheritress
anteriority
inferiority
interiority
unbefitting
undeviating
unremittent
unremitting
unresisting
ungenitured
ingeniously
indeciduate
indeciduous
unbelieving
interjacent
interjector
underkeeper
interleaves
intellected
unreflected
interludial
intelligent
unhealthily
unhealthful
unreclaimed
interlinear
index-linked
unfeelingly
interlining
undeclining
interlunary
△interlingua
underlooker
unrealistic
underletter
interleukin
intermedial
intermeddle
intermedium
undermanned
unfermented
unsegmented
intermingle
undermining
interminate
undermasted
intermezzos
internecine
internecive
internodial
indemnified
antenniform
internalise
infernality
internality
internalize
internuncio
unmeaningly
enneandrian
enneandrous
interneural
unbeknownst
unmemorable
unremovable
angelolatry
unretouched
unrejoicing
unrecovered
unreposeful
angelophany
anaerobiont
enterovirus
unmelodious
envelopment
unrecounted
enterotoxin
anterograde
interosseal
enterostomy
interocular
underpraise
unrespected
interpreter
unperplexed
enterpriser
underpriced
undespoiled
interpolate
intemperant
untempering
intemperate
unweariable
unweariably
knee-tribute
interracial
unrefracted
interradial
interradius
unreprieved
unlearnedly
unweariedly
unterrified
interrogant
interrogate
interregnum
anteorbital
integrality
endearingly
interrupted
interrupter
interruptor
undepressed
unredressed
unrefreshed
integration
integrative
unfearfully
unreproving
undershapen
understated
unpersuaded
incense-boat
intersperse
undersleeve
intensified
intensifier
undersigned
under-school
interspinal
underseller
incensement
incessantly
unceasingly
unreasoning
intenseness
intensional
understorey
unpensioned
undershorts
interseptal
undersupply
insessorial
intersertal
interscribe
unleisurely
understrata
insensately
incensation
insensitive
intensative
intensitive
unsensitive
intensively
under-sawyer
intersexual
ancestrally
unrestraint
insecticide
insentience
insentiency
unfeathered
unweathered
anaesthesia
anaesthesis
anaesthetic
ungenteelly
unsettledly
investments
uncertified
unrectified
insectifuge
insectiform
investigate
intertribal
entertainer
uncertainly
intertrigos
underthirst
incertainty
uncertainty
undertaking
insectology
infertility
ungentility
unsentenced
intertangle
unrestingly
unweetingly
undertenant
insertional
intentional
intentioned
undestroyed

ancestorial
intertarsal
inventorial
unsectarian
unperturbed
underthrust
indexterity
insectarium
incertitude
indentation
infestation
investiture
investitive
inventively
Insectivora
insectivore
incentivise
incentivize
unregulated
ensepulchre
antemundane
infecundity
unreducible
unbeautiful
unrepugnant
unreturning
unrequisite
antenuptial
unreluctant
ingenuously
interviewee
interviewer
underviewer
undervaluer
intervallic
intervallum
intervening
interventor
unperverted
innervation
underwriter
underweight
underworker
unseaworthy
underwiring
snuff-colour
unification
snuff-dipper
unoffending
inoffensive
unoffensive
ineffectual
unaffecting
ineffective
unofficered
inefficient
inofficious
unofficious
snaffle-rein
uniformness
knife-switch
snuff-taking
onagraceous
enigmatical
unagreeable
unigeniture
anagnorisis
anthracitic
enthralling
enthralment
anthracnose
anthracosis
anthocyanin
uncheckable
unshockable
unthickened
anthochlore
unshrinking
enchainment
unchristian
unthriftily
unshakeable
unshakeably
unsheltered
anthologise
anthologist
anthologize
Enghalskrug
unchildlike
unwholesome
anthomaniac
unshunnable
unthinkable
enchantment
enchondroma
enchantress
anthropical
enchiridion
antheridium
unchartered
unsharpened
ink-horn-mate
anchor-stock
antherozoid
unchastened
Anthesteria
unchastised
unchastized
unthought-of
anchovy-pear
anticathode
antipathist
antijamming
△antijacobin
△anti-Jacobin
inviability
undisclosed
undiscerned
insincerely
insincerity
undiscussed
untinctured
unmindfully
incinerator
anti-feedant
anti-federal
antihelices
anti-Semitic
enlivenment
unfixedness
anti-heroine
unhidebound
engineering
anniversary
undiverting
antineutron
indigestion
indirection
indigestive
untimeously
indifferent
angiography
inking-table
undisguised
unhingement
undiagnosed
antiphrasis
unsighed-for
unwished-for
unlightened
unrighteous
antithalian
antiphonary
unwithering
unlightsome
unwithstood
unmitigated
antivitamin
individable
undividable
unmitigable
unmitigably
unvisitable
annihilator
anticipator
invigilator
undividedly
unlimitedly
unfinishing
infinitival
uncivilised
uncivilized
indivisible
indivisibly
antibilious
incipiently
insipiently
insipidness
insidiously
invidiously
unpitifully
individuate
unwinkingly
entitlement
unwillingly
inviolately
infirmarian
undignified
indignantly
ancientness
unwitnessed
indignation
oneiromancy
invigorator
oneiroscopy
antinomical
antimoniate
antimonious
antifouling
environment
oneirodynia
angioplasty
undispensed
antispastic
india-rubber
unvitrified
antirrhinum
unbiassedly
undissolved
unfiltrable
infiltrator
undistilled
insistently
unfittingly
unwittingly
unlistening
antistrophe
undistorted
undisturbed
antimutagen
unliquefied
Antiburgher
antiqueness
anxiousness
enviousness
antiquarian
antitussive
antiquities
insinuating
antiquation
insinuation
insinuatory
insinuative
antioxidant
antipyretic
antitypical
anticyclone
unpityingly
snake-hipped
unskilfully
snakishness
uncleanness
unclearness
unclubbable

inelaborate
unelaborate
ineluctable
Anglicanism
inalienable
inalienably
inalterable
inalterably
unalienable
unalienably
unalterable
unalterably
influential
Anglo-French
inelegantly
analogously
analphabete
Anglo-Indian
inflammable
inflammably
unblameable
unblameably
△anglomaniac
inclemently
unslumbrous
unblemished
unblindfold
unblenching
unflinching
Anglo-Norman
inclination
inclinatory
unallowable
unflappable
unflappably
△anglophilia
△anglophilic
△anglophobia
△anglophobic
△anglophonic
ineloquence
Anglo-Romani
unflustered
unplastered
unclassical
endlessness
inclusively
analyticity
uncluttered
inflatingly
unillumined
unplausible
unplausibly
enslavement
unflavoured
inflexional
inimicality
unimpeached
unimpededly
anemography
unambitious

unambiguous
unsmilingly
anomalistic
animalcular
animalcules
anemometric
unamendable
gnomonology
unimportant
anemophobia
anamorphous
unimpressed
enumeration
enumerative
onomasticon
unamusingly
animatingly
unemotional
unemotioned
animatronic
uninhabited
uninucleate
uninscribed
anencephaly
uninventive
unenchanted
uninchanted
uninhibited
uninvidious
enunciation
enunciatory
enunciative
uninflected
un-Englished
inanimately
inanimation
anonymously
unanimously
unannotated
unenjoyable
uninforming
unannounced
uninspiring
inenarrable
uninitiated
unendurable
unendurably
unenquiring
uninquiring
unknowingly
unknownness
uncomatable
endocardiac
endocardial
endocardium
unmoralised
unmoralized
unpolarised
unpolarized
unromanised
unromanized

unvocalised
unvocalized
undoubtable
unforbidden
undoubtedly
insouciance
unconcealed
enforceable
untouchable
unconcocted
unconceived
enforcement
unconcerned
unconcerted
unsoldierly
intolerance
intolerable
intolerably
infomercial
encomendero
incoherence
incoherency
oncogenesis
ontogenesis
ontogenetic
unloverlike
unforeknown
endometrial
endometrium
unhopefully
unforfeited
uncomforted
unconfirmed
unconfessed
engorgement
uncongenial
unforgotten
incongruent
incongruity
incongruous
unforgiving
endophagous
endothelial
endochylous
endothelium
Indo-Chinese
endothermic
entophytous
incogitancy
unmotivated
incogitable
indomitable
indomitably
innominable
Intoximeter®
intoximeter
unpolitical
unsolicited
unsocialism
unsociality
endomitosis

encomiastic
innoxiously
unlooked-for
uncollected
enfouldered
ennoblement
ungodliness
endoplasmic
endoplastic
incommodity
informality
uncommended
untormented
informatics
uncommitted
unformatted
information
informatory
informative
uncountable
unsoundable
unwoundable
unconnected
unboundedly
unfoundedly
unsoundness
incognisant
unconniving
incognizant
incoronated
antonomasia
entomophagy
entomophily
ontological
endomorphic
uncompacted
uncompleted
incompliant
uncompliant
uncompelled
uncompanied
incorporeal
endospermic
incorporall
incorporate
incomposite
incompetent
uncomplying
unconquered
uncorrected
incorrectly
uncourteous
encouraging
incoercible
Indo-Iranian
uncorrupted
endotrophic
incorruptly
unnourished
inconstancy
unmoistened

Words marked △ may be spelled also with a capital letter

11 □n□o□s

inconscient
inconscious
unconscious
endorsement
inconsonant
unpossessed
unmortgaged
unfortified
unmortified
uncontrived
uncontemned
incontinent
unsoftening
uncouthness
unfortunate
unportioned
uncontested
unmodulated
unpopulated
unpopularly
involucrate
involuntary
innocuously
unconvicted
involvement
unconvinced
unconverted
unspeakable
unspeakably
unspecified
inappetence
inappetency
unappealing
anaplerosis
anaplerotic
snapshooter
unsprinkled
unipolarity
anaphorical
unappointed
inopportune
inspiringly
unsparingly
unipersonal
unspiritual
inspiriting
inspiration
inspiratory
inoperative
inspirative
unoperative
unapproving
inspissated
inspissator
unapostolic
anaphylaxis
inequitable
inequitably
unequitable
unequivocal
entreatable
increasable
unbreakable
untreatable
increaseful
intreatfull
unbreathing
unpreaching
inorganised
inorganized
unorganised
unorganized
entreatment
intractable
intractably
untraceable
untractable
unpractical
unpractised
onirocritic
infracostal
unprocessed
intricately
anfractuous
infructuous
unfructuous
incredulity
incredulous
intradermal
energetical
snorkelling
engraftment
unpreferred
unprofessed
unprofiting
intriguante
unoriginate
androgenous
androgynous
unorthodoxy
enarthrosis
anarchistic
anorthosite
undrainable
engrailment
entrainment
inertia-reel
unprojected
engrammatic
ungrammatic
untrembling
untremulous
incremental
incriminate
encrimsoned
unpromising
intromitted
intromitter
incremation
undrinkable
unprintable
intrenchant
enfranchise
intrinsical
infrangible
infrangibly
intrepidity
unprophetic
infrequence
infrequency
incrassated
uncrushable
incrossbred
encrustment
engrossment
entrustment
unpresuming
intrusively
intrasexual
unprotected
intrathecal
unbrotherly
ungratified
unprotested
ingratitude
onerousness
undriveable
unprovident
unprovoking
untravelled
unprevented
intravenous
untraversed
inescapable
unescapable
unashamedly
unusualness
anisocercal
inessential
unessential
unassertive
unaspirated
gnostically
inestimable
inestimably
unassisting
anisomerous
anastomoses
anastomosis
anastomotic
uniserially
△angst-ridden
anisotropic
inusitation
unisexually
gnatcatcher
unsteadfast
initialling
unattainted
instability
gnotobiosis
gnotobiotic
inutterable
unutterable
unutterably
unattending
instreaming
unattempted
inattention
inattentive
unattentive
instigation
instigative
snatch-thief
snatchingly
snatch-purse
unstainable
unstaidness
installment
instantiate
instinctual
instinctive
gnathonical
unstoppable
unstoppably
unit-pricing
unitisation
instatement
institorial
institution
institutist
institutive
instaurator
unstaunched
instruction
instructive
snotty-nosed
unitization
pneumathode
pneumatical
incunabular
incunabulum
encumbrance
inturbidate
unhusbanded
incumbently
unpurchased
annunciator
unquickened
unsucceeded
unguiculate
inculcation
inculcatory
inculcative
unsuccoured
unsubduable
infundibula
innumerable
innumerably
insuperable
insuperably
intumescent
unqueenlike
unquietness

Words marked △ may be spelled also with a capital letter

indumentums
untunefully
insufflator
unfulfilled
indulgently
unvulgarise
unvulgarize
ingurgitate
inauthentic
unauthentic
unmutilated
indubitable
indubitably
unmusically
injudicious
unguligrade
incuriosity
infuriating
infuriation
incuriously
injuriously
undutifully
unsubjected
uncuckolded
unluckiness
induplicate
unqualified
inquilinism
inquilinity
inquilinous
unpublished
unqualitied
unaugmented
unsubmerged
unmurmuring
unquantised
unquantized
unburnished
unfurnished
inquination
pneumonitis
input-output
unsuspected
unsuspicion
unsurprised
unsuspended
unsupported
unsurpassed
inculpation
inculpatory
unguardedly
unhurriedly
inquiringly
inquirendos
unguerdoned
enquiration
innutrition
inquiration
△inquisition
inquisitive
unburthened
unjustified
uncurtailed
uncurtained
unsustained
industrials
industrious
inductility
insultingly
inductional
intuitional
unhurtfully
inductively
intuitively
intuitivism
inductivity
inaugurator
unluxuriant
unluxurious
incurvation
incurvature
unevidenced
unavailable
unavailably
unavoidable
unavoidably
univalvular
unavertable
universally
unavertible
knavishness
unsweetened
unawakening
unswallowed
angwantibos
knowingness
snow-goggles
know-nothing
one-worldism
answerphone
unawareness
snow-dropper
snowsurfing
unexcavated
inexhausted
unexhausted
inexecrable
inexactness
inexecution
inexpedient
unexperient
inextension
inexpensive
unexpensive
inexpectant
unexpectant
inexcitable
unexcitable
unexplained
unexploited
unexclusive
unexercised
unexpressed
inexistence
inexcusable
inexcusably
unsyllabled
undyingness
encystation
non-academic
solanaceous
Bonapartean
Bonapartism
Bonapartist
comancheros
monarchical
coparcenary
coparcenery
tobacconist
tobacco-pipe
Tom-and-Jerry
nonagesimal
Monadelphia
notaphilism
notaphilist
foraminated
botanically
nomadically
somatically
totalisator
totalizator
Loganiaceae
polariscope
polarimeter
solarimeter
polarimetry
coraciiform
logarithmic
foraminifer
tomatilloes
Moravianism
Novatianism
Novatianist
Rotarianism
voraciously
coralliform
coralloidal
movableness
notableness
womanliness
non-allergic
Mohammedism
God-almighty
botanomancy
somatogenic
potamogeton
moratoriums
somatoplasm
somatologic
somatotonia
somatotonic
potato-bogle
bog-asphodel
dolabriform
non-abrasive
monasticism
romanticise
romanticism
romanticist
romanticize
monasterial
woman-vested
forbearance
Bombacaceae
corbiculate
forbiddance
forbiddenly
double-faced
double-eagle
double-fault
double-edged
hobbledehoy
double-agent
double-check
double-shade
doublethink
double-sharp
double-lived
double-digit
double-blind
double-ender
double-entry
double-speak
double-space
double-cross
womb-leasing
cobblestone
corbie-steps
double-stout
double-Dutch
double-quick
morbiferous
non-believer
doubtlessly
bombilation
lobby-member
Sorbonnical
bonbonnière
bombination
combination
combinatory
combinative
borborygmic
borborygmus
bombardment
Dogberrydom
Dogberryism
Hobbistical
combustible
combustious
tolbutamide
tomboyishly
nonchalance
concealable

Words marked △ may be spelled also with a capital letter

11 □o□c□a

concealment
torchbearer
forcibility
concubinage
concubinary
concubitant
coccidiosis
concrescent
zoochemical
conceivable
conceivably
conceitedly
touch-in-goal
non-clinical
conceitless
monchiquite
conciliable
conciliator
concolorate
concolorous
tow-coloured
coxcombical
concomitant
volcanicity
concentered
volcanology
forcing-pump
concentring
concentrate
zoocephalic
conceptacle
concipiency
conceptious
forcipation
conceptuses
concernancy
concordance
concertante
concurrence
concurrency
concernedly
concert-goer
concertinos
concernment
torch-staves
vouchsafing
concessible
torch-singer
conciseness
touch-screen
concatenate
touch-typist
conclusions
coadjacency
bond-washing
wood-sanicle
word-painter
cordwainery
cordialness
loadsamoney
bondmanship
cold-casting
good-natured
woodcarving
conductance
road-scraper
conductible
conducement
conducingly
conductress
coeducation
poodle-faker
cold-welding
road-mending
word-perfect
Goldbergian
toddlerhood
bowdleriser
bowdlerizer
soldierlike
cold-hearted
load-bearing
soldiership
top-dressing
bold-beating
gold-beating
bond-service
bondservant
word-of-mouth
condignness
gold-digging
condolement
condylomata
condolences
cold-blooded
rondolettos
condolatory
non-delivery
condemnable
condominium
goldsmithry
condensable
goldenberry
zoodendrium
coadunation
condonation
coadunative
roadholding
cold-forging
road-hoggish
good-looking
good-morning
voodooistic
loudmouthed
loudspeaker
toad-spotted
toad-spittle
ponderingly
wonderingly
ponderosity
good-brother
wood-fretter
ponderation
ponderously
wonderfully
condisciple
wordishness
nondescript
goddess-ship
rood-steeple
condottiere
condottieri
woody-tongue
conditional
conditioned
conditioner
soldatesque
goddaughter
coadjutress
woodcutting
word-puzzler
non-dividing
good-evening
molecatcher
bower-anchor
Dodecandria
dodecaphony
rope-machine
moderations
pole-vaulter
dovetailing
forepayment
forewarning
rose-campion
foremastman
dodecastyle
Dodecagynia
honey-badger
moveability
money-broker
hover-barrow
ion-exchange
nomenclator
honeycombed
power-driven
Poseidonian
molendinary
power-diving
foreseeable
co-dependant
co-dependent
forereading
home-defence
sovereignly
sovereignty
fore-recited
forevermore
home-keeping
non-electric
non-election
novelettish
novelettist
non-elective
comet-finder
foreignness
rose-cheeked
nonetheless
forethinker
josephinite
foreshorten
somewhither
forethought
polemically
tonetically
Lobeliaceae
foresighted
soteriology
rose-diamond
foresignify
△bohemianism
nose-nippers
non-existent
hotel-keeper
honey-locust
moneylender
powerlessly
foreclosure
role-playing
hogen-mogens
money-making
sober-minded
coterminous
honeymooner
money-market
homeomorphy
homeomerous
home-and-away
home-and-home
love-in-a-mist
modernistic
foreknowing
vomeronasal
forevouched
gobe-mouches
rosewood-oil
comedogenic
homeworking
foretopmast
comeuppance
coleopteral
coleopteran
coleopteron
fore-spurrer
none-sparing
homeopathic
code-breaker
mole-cricket
bone-breccia
home-crofter
pomegranate
voyeuristic
homeostasis
homeostatic
honey-sucker

Words marked △ may be spelled also with a capital letter

honeysuckle
honey-suckle
money-spider
sober-suited
doveishness
money's-worth
homesteader
potentiated
potentially
comestibles
rodenticide
domesticise
domesticate
domesticity
domesticize
home-stretch
forestaller
honest-to-God
momentarily
fomentation
forestation
molestation
momentously
molecularly
dolefulness
hopefulness
forequarter
honey-waggon
lonely-heart
non-feasance
conflagrant
conflagrate
confabulate
forficulate
confidently
confidingly
△confederacy
△confederate
coffee-maker
coffee-table
toffee-nosed
toffee-apple
configurate
forfeitable
coefficient
conflicting
confliction
conflictive
gonfalonier
confineless
confinement
△god-forsaken
comfortable
comfortably
conferrable
confirmable
conformable
conformably
confirmator
confarreate
comfortless
confiscable
confiscator
pop-fastener
confessedly
toffishness
confutement
confutation
confutative
forfoughten
confluently
congealable
zoographist
congealment
long-waisted
zoografting
hobgoblinry
rough-coated
congregated
rouge-et-noir
longwearing
Congressman
long-measure
rough-footed
rough-handle
long-visaged
long-sighted
lodge-keeper
rough-legged
long-clothes
coagulation
congelation
coagulatory
coagulative
long-playing
tough-minded
congenially
zoogonidium
longanimity
longanimous
congenerous
loggan-stone
morgenstern
longinquity
long-tongued
doggy-paddle
loggerheads
Gongoristic
congestible
doggishness
hoggishness
rough-spoken
rough-string
forgettable
forget-me-not
doughtiness
forgetfully
songfulness
long-purples
congruously
forgiveness
lophobranch
Lochaber-axe
nothing-gift
Cochin-China
nothingness
doch-an-doris
mother-naked
mother-water
rother-beast
mother-right
fothergilla
mother's-mark
mother-in-law
non-harmonic
motherboard
mothercraft
botheration
sophistical
Bodhisattva
nominatival
dominations
totipalmate
comicalness
logicalness
corivalship
sociability
Politbureau
vociferance
vociferator
homiletical
policewoman
notice-board
police-court
domineering
nociceptive
police-judge
Moringaceae
doting-piece
towing-bitts
boxing-glove
poking-stick
poting-stick
coping-stone
toxiphobiac
toxiphagous
solid-hoofed
politically
domiciliary
domiciliate
politicking
codicillary
volitionary
Socinianism
solidifying
sociologese
sociologism
sociologist
docibleness
nonillionth
socialistic
solifluxion
goniometric
sociometric
notionalist
cosignatory
toxicomania
totipotency
toxicogenic
gonimoblast
toxicologic
monitorship
conirostral
soliloquise
soliloquist
soliloquize
sociopathic
Louis-Quinze
Rosicrucian
poliorcetic
positronium
non-issuable
solipsistic
logistician
Louis-Treize
goniatitoid
moribundity
copiousness
noxiousness
moxibustion
pomiculture
non-invasive
conjectural
conjecturer
conjugality
conjugating
conjugation
conjugative
conjunction
conjuncture
conjunctiva
conjunctive
conjuration
workwatcher
workmanlike
dock-warrant
workmanship
workability
book-account
cook-general
cockleshell
cookie-shine
bookselling
mock-heroics
bookkeeping
book-learned
rock-leather
workaholism
work-sharing
nook-shotten
bookbinding
bookbindery
Volkskammer
poikilocyte

Words marked △ may be spelled also with a capital letter

11 □o□k□l

Volkslieder
cockaleekie
cock-a-leekie
hook-climber
rock-climber
working-beam
cock-and-bull
mockingbird
booking-hall
working-over
rock-and-roll
rocking-tool
sockdolager
mock-modesty
sockdoliger
rock-forming
sockdologer
you-know-what
lock-forward
cock-sparrow
rock-sparrow
rock-breaker
cookery-book
bookishness
dockisation
pocketphone
pocket-piece
pocket-sized
pocket-glass
pork-butcher
pock-pudding
monkey-wheel
monkey-shine
monkey-block
monkey-gland
monkey-board
monkey-bread
monkey-grass
dockization
wool-carding
foolhardise
foolhardize
cool-tankard
pollyannish
colleaguing
world-beater
collaborate
collectanea
collectable
mollycoddle
collectedly
collectible
collections
folliculose
folliculous
mould-candle
pop-lacrosse
collocation
collocutory
boulder-clay
goal-tending
soul-fearing
wool-bearing
mould-facing
toplofical
world-famous
collegianer
collagenase
hooliganism
collagenous
colligation
colligative
goalkicking
soul-killing
soul-sleeper
hoplologist
worldliness
worldly-wise
loblolly-bay
loblolly-boy
Coulommiers
noble-minded
collembolan
coulometric
collimation
hollandaise
collenchyma
rolling-mill
pollen-grain
coplanarity
pollination
wool-combing
foul-mouthed
collapsable
collapsible
colliquable
colloquiums
boiler-maker
poultry-farm
roller-skate
Rollerblade®
rollerblade
forlornness
roller-towel
coelurosaur
wool-growing
coalescence
dollishness
foolishness
godlessness
joblessness
joylessness
toplessness
collusively
toilet-table
toilet-glass
toilet-cloth
coalitional
coalitioner
toilet-cover
wool-stapler
soulfulness
follow-board
doomwatcher
cosmocratic
formicarium
formication
commodities
cosmography
zoomagnetic
cosmogonist
room-divider
cosmologist
formularise
formularize
formalistic
formulation
commemorate
commendable
commendably
commensally
commendator
commentator
communicant
communicate
tormentedly
commonsense
common-shore
gormandiser
gormandizer
commonplace
communalise
communalism
communalist
commonality
communalize
commandment
communistic
commination
comminution
comminatory
comminative
cosmopolite
cormophytic
Kommersbuch
zoomorphism
non-marrying
cosmosphere
commiserate
solmisation
commissural
cosmetician
cosmeticise
cosmeticism
cosmeticize
cosmothetic
cosmotheism
cosmetology
dogmatology
non-metallic
commotional
formational
commutation
commutative
normatively
solmization
roundarched
foundations
fountain-pen
mountaineer
mountain-top
horn-madness
moon-madness
mountainous
connubially
round-backed
coenobitism
bonne-bouche
connectable
connectedly
cornice-hook
connectible
connections
corniculate
cornucopian
cornice-pole
townscaping
cornice-rail
fornication
John-a-dreams
point-device
point-devise
countenance
mountenance
counterbuff
counterbond
counterblow
counterbore
counterbase
counterdraw
coinherence
counterfect
counterfeit
counterfoil
counterfort
counter-glow
coinheritor
counselling
countermand
countermine
countermark
countermure
countermove
pointedness
roundedness
counterpace
counterplea
counterpane
counter-plot
counterpart
down-hearted
counter-roll
counterseal
countersign

Words marked △ may be spelled also with a capital letter

countersink
countersunk
counter-time
down-setting
town-meeting
counter-turn
bounteously
counter-view
countervail
counter-vote
counterwork
counter-work
corniferous
somniferous
pornography
cornigerous
round-headed
down-the-line
horny-handed
zoanthropic
Eoanthropus
zoantharian
coincidence
coincidency
downlighter
moonlighter
pointillism
pointillist
connoisseur
down-sitting
bountifully
pound-keeper
round-leaved
poenologist
town-planner
hornblendic
somnolently
pointlessly
soundlessly
cognominate
connumerate
pound-master
Nornamesque
somnambular
somnambulic
morning-gift
morning-gown
coenenchyma
morning-land
morning-room
morning-tide
down-to-earth
moon-goddess
Johnsoniana
loan-society
point-of-sale
townspeople
corn-cracker
down-trodden
countrified
countryfied

country-folk
country-rock
country-seat
countryside
cornerstone
down-draught
countrywide
hounds-berry
cognoscente
cognoscenti
cognoscible
tonnishness
hound's-tooth
point-source
bonnet-piece
joint-tenant
cognateness
cognitional
bonnet-rouge
pornotopian
non-naturals
connotation
connotative
cognitively
cognitivity
coinsurance
cornhusking
hornswoggle
town-dweller
round-winged
monocardian
logopaedics
logodaedaly
monovalence
monovalency
logomachist
sonofabitch
cologarithm
honorariums
monocarpous
coronagraph
monolatrous
holocaustal
holocaustic
motor-bandit
cocoa-butter
horoscopist
motor-driven
homogenesis
homogenetic
monogenesis
monogenetic
homogeneity
homogeneous
homogeniser
homogenizer
jocoserious
colonelling
Monodelphia
monodelphic
holohedrism

cotoneaster
colonelship
holobenthic
homocentric
go-to-meeting
locorestive
tobogganing
tobogganist
monothecous
monophagous
monophthong
homothallic
podophyllin
△monothelism
△monothelete
△monothelite
toxophilite
Podophyllum
homophonous
monochromat
monochromic
holothurian
homothermal
notochordal
homothermic
Nototherium
monochasial
△monophysite
monochasium
holophytism
colorimeter
colorimetry
monolingual
honorifical
sodomitical
colonialism
colonialist
notoriously
corolliform
monoclinous
monoblepsis
holoblastic
homoblastic
homoplastic
toxoplasmic
motor-launch
homoeopathy
gonococcoid
colonoscope
colonoscopy
homoeomeric
homological
horological
monological
nomological
nosological
pomological
posological
topological
monopoliser
monopolizer

Mohorovicic
homoeomorph
homomorphic
monomorphic
coronograph
homoiousian
rodomontade
monologuise
monologuist
monologuize
Monocotylae
homopolymer
ionospheric
homosporous
Zonotrichia
colour-blind
loxodromics
sojournment
Monotremata
gonorrhoeal
gonorrhoeic
honour-bound
honour-point
doxographer
horographer
logographer
monographer
nomographer
nosographer
sonographer
topographer
holographic
logographic
monographic
nomographic
nosographic
tomographic
topographic
monocrystal
colouration
homoerotism
rotogravure
coconscious
monopsonist
Zoroastrian
Soroptimist
homopterous
cohortative
pococurante
mononuclear
coconut-milk
coconut-palm
monoculture
hop-o'-my-thumb
toponymical
homozygosis
homozygotic
monozygotic
monomyarian
compearance
complacence

11 □o□p□a

complacency
zooplankton
complainant
complaining
complaisant
compactedly
compactness
torpedinous
completable
complexness
copple-crown
compression
compressure
low-pressure
compressive
copple-stone
compaginate
loup-the-dyke
complicated
comprimario
dolphinaria
comprisable
compliments
dolphin-fish
coupling-box
Pompeian-red
compliantly
non-priority
top-priority
compellable
compulsitor
compilement
corpulently
pompelmoose
pompelmouse
compilation
compilatory
compensator
compendiums
compendious
componental
companioned
compunction
rouping-wife
Comptometer®
non-provided
morphologic
morphotropy
complotting
copper-faced
corporeally
compurgator
copper-beech
non-partisan
comptroller
copperplate
corporality
compartment
comportment
coppersmith
copperworks
corporately
co-operating
co-operation
corporation
corporatism
corporatist
comparative
co-operative
corporative
compassable
torpescence
compossible
foppishness
rompishness
composition
compositous
compositive
corpuscular
poppet-valve
hospitaller
hospitalise
hospitality
hospitalize
competently
computerese
computerise
computerate
computerize
competition
compotation
computation
compotatory
competitive
computative
pompousness
nonplussing
zoophytical
porphyritic
conquerable
torque-meter
bouquetière
tonquin-bean
gourmandise
gourmandism
pourparlers
corroborant
corroborate
correctable
correctible
correctness
Torridonian
Corrodentia
comradeship
bourgeoisie
courteously
journey-work
courtesying
corrigendum
porriginous
corrugation
four-wheeled
four-wheeler
co-ordinates
co-ordinator
coercimeter
tourbillion
coercionist
courtierism
coprolaliac
courtliness
four-flusher
correlation
correlative
doorknocker
mooring-mast
torrentuous
four-pounder
coprophagan
coprophagic
coprophilia
corruptible
corruptibly
horripilant
horripilate
corruptness
bourtree-gun
△voortrekker
nourishable
non-resident
coprosterol
board-school
boardsailor
nourishment
horrisonant
boorishness
horrisonous
corrosively
doorstepped
doorstepper
coarctation
bourguignon
douroucouli
moorbuzzard
sorrowfully
non-standard
moustachial
Podsnappery
loose-bodied
possibilism
possibilist
possibility
torsibility
house-broken
consociated
consecrator
horse-collar
mouse-colour
consecution
consecutive
horse-couper
horse-dealer
horse-doctor
horse-drench
considering
considerate
dog's-mercury
conspecific
non-specific
constellate
tous-les-mois
zoospermium
consternate
coessential
worsted-work
house-factor
goose-flower
dorsiferous
house-father
consignable
consignment
Moeso-gothic
moss-cheeper
householder
house-hunter
constipated
worshipable
conspirator
hot-spirited
low-spirited
worshipless
Monseigneur
worshipping
consciously
constituent
constitutor
conspicuity
conspicuous
housekeeper
consultancy
consolidate
consilience
fossil-fired
mossbluiter
tonsillitic
tonsillitis
dorsolumbar
loose-limbed
consolement
noiselessly
horse-litter
consolatrix
consolation
consolatory
consummator
howsomdever
consimility
noisomeness
consumerism
consumerist
housemaster
toastmaster
house-mother
consumption

Words marked △ may be spelled also with a capital letter

consumptive
boysenberry
morsing-horn
nonsensical
consentient
poison-gland
consonantal
consonantly
poison-sumac
poisonously
consanguine
comstockery
comstockism
torsiograph
hog-shouther
houseparent
consequence
non-sequence
conservancy
conservable
construable
conservator
constricted
constructer
horse-racing
constrictor
constructor
horse-riding
horseradish
constrained
consortiums
bowstringed
moss-trooper
monstrosity
monstrously
possessable
consistence
consistency
loosestrife
moisturiser
moisturizer
constuprate
housewifely
housewifery
goose-winged
contradance
nostradamic
contrabasso
Nostradamus
foot-lambert
boot-catcher
Portlandian
contra-tenor
contrayerva
contrariety
contrarious
footballing
footballist
foot-tapping
contractual
portmanteau
contractile
contraction
contraption
contracture
portraiture
portraitist
contractive
contrastive
portability
contubernal
contactable
porte-crayon
vorticellae
mortice-lock
torticollis
ponticellos
monticulate
corticolous
monticolous
monticulous
forthcoming
zootechnics
postscenium
cost-account
tostication
tooth-drawer
contredance
mottle-faced
bottle-party
cost-benefit
contretemps
Pont-l'Évêque
bootlegging
bottle-chart
mont-de-piété
bottle-blond
bottle-glass
northermost
southermost
loathedness
northernise
northernism
southernise
southernism
northernize
southernize
bottle-nosed
bottle-gourd
bottle-green
soft-hearted
bottle-brush
north-easter
south-easter
zootheistic
post-tension
soft-centred
fortifiable
pontificals
pontificate
mouth-friend
mortiferous
soothfastly
vortiginous
soft-shelled
mouth-honour
contrivance
containable
contrivable
doctrinally
doctrinaire
post-lingual
fortnightly
Tortricidae
bootlicking
containment
post-vintage
contributor
postillator
post-glacial
noctilucent
noctilucous
footslogger
root-climber
southlander
loathliness
worthlessly
hostilities
postulation
postulatory
contumacity
hot-tempered
volt-amperes
bottom-heavy
contemnible
bottom-glade
contemplant
contemplate
contaminant
contaminate
bottom-grass
continuance
continuable
continually
continuator
contingence
contingency
contentedly
continuedly
Montenegrin
boutonnière
contentious
contentless
fortuneless
contenement
contentment
continental
hootananie
hootenannie
continently
contango-day
cottonmouth
Montanistic
fortunately
fortune-tell
rottenstone
post-vocalic
foot-soldier
postponence
controverse
controversy
montgolfier
controlling
portionless
controlment
poltroonery
boot-topping
bogtrotting
foxtrotting
tooth-picker
coeternally
nocturnally
footbreadth
Fontarabian
poltergeist
foster-child
conterminal
contorniate
post-primary
loiteringly
potteringly
torturingly
totteringly
root-pruning
posteriorly
mortarboard
porterhouse
porter-house
torturesome
foster-nurse
contestable
mortise-lock
loathsomely
toothsomely
doltishness
goatishness
loutishness
sottishness
hostess-ship
soothsaying
footstooled
hortatorily
hortatively
boat-builder
post-nuptial
noctivagant
noctivagous
costiveness
northwardly
southwardly
north-wester
south-wester
post-exilian
modularised

11 □o□u□b

modularized
populariser
popularizer
columbarium
conurbation
coruscating
coruscation
lotus-eating
documentary
Lotus-eaters
notungulate
loculicidal
locutionary
non-unionist
solutionist
volubleness
columniated
columnarity
volumometer
colubriform
roguishness
locust-years
voluntarily
voluntarism
voluntarist
voluntative
nocuousness
solvability
convictions
convicinity
convocation
voivodeship
louvre-board
Convallaria
convulsible
convulsions
pot-valorous
non-volatile
coevolution
convolution
convolvulus
convenience
conveniency
conventicle
convincible
convenances
non-violence
conversance
conversancy
conversable
conversably
gouvernante
convergence
convergency
convertible
convertibly
louver-board
convivially
conveyancer
pot-walloner
pot-walloper
forwandered
bow-windowed
forwardness
coextension
coextensive
coexistence
cony-catcher
polycarpous
polydactyly
corybantism
polymastism
polyactinal
molybdenite
copy-editing
copyreading
polygenesis
polygenetic
polytechnic
polyhedrons
polypeptide
polycentric
rosy-cheeked
polyphagous
Polyphemian
polyphonist
polychromic
polychroism
polyhistory
polyglottal
polyglottic
polyonymous
polyandrous
polygonally
polygonatum
rosy-bosomed
polymorphic
body-popping
polyzoarial
polyzoarium
Polytrichum
polygraphic
polycrystal
polycrotism
Polystichum
polystyrene
body-builder
polyculture
polyhydroxy
apparatchik
apparatuses
sphacelated
apparelling
apparelment
speakership
splay-footed
splashboard
splashproof
Aphaniptera
appallingly
sphagnology
aplanospore
sphaeridium
ipratropium
upcast-shaft
appartement
upvaluation
specialiser
specializer
specialogue
spectatress
spectacular
ipecacuanha
epicheirema
specifiable
specificate
specificity
spacefaring
apocalyptic
speculatrix
speculation
speculatory
speculatist
speculative
epoch-making
Apocynaceae
apocopation
spectrogram
spectrology
spectrality
epidiascope
spud-bashing
apodictical
epidemicity
spodomantic
epidendrone
apodyterium
ipselateral
appeachment
spread-eagle
splendidous
spreadsheet
spreadingly
splendorous
Ephemeridae
splenetical
ephemerides
splenectomy
speechmaker
speechifier
speech-crier
speechcraft
spherically
appealingly
appellation
appellative
spleenstone
spheroidise
spheroidize
speedometer
spherometer
appearances
appeasement
appeasingly
appertinent
spherulitic
spifflicate
epigraphist
apogamously
epigenesist
epigenetics
epigastrium
ophicalcite
ipsilateral
sphincteral
sphincteric
springwater
spring-clean
upping-block
springiness
springboard
springhouse
sphingosine
upping-stock
upping-stone
sprightless
uprightness
ophidiarium
ophiologist
oppignerate
oppignorate
opeidoscope
epeirogenic
Ophiuroidea
split-second
split-screen
upliftingly
spokeswoman
spokeswomen
apple-blight
spellbinder
application
applicatory
applicative
spelaeology
spelaeothem
epilogistic
apologetics
Apollinaris
apollonicon
epileptical
appleringie
opalescence
spill-stream
apple-squire
apoliticism
apomictical
apomorphine
spumescence
spontaneity
spontaneous
spine-basher
spinach-beet
spang-cockle

Words marked △ may be spelled also with a capital letter

up-and-coming
spinnerette
spaniel-like
open-hearted
spiniferous
spinigerous
spindle-legs
epanalepses
epanalepsis
Spenglerian
spinelessly
open-and-shut
opinionated
opinionator
spin-bowling
span-counter
sponsorship
open-mouthed
epinephrine
spinescence
spinsterial
spinsterian
spendthrift
spinsterdom
spinsterish
spondulicks
aponeuroses
aponeurosis
aponeurotic
spondylitic
spondylitis
spondylosis
Spinozistic
optometrist
splodginess
appointment
upholsterer
apron-string
upholstress
opportunely
opportunism
opportunist
opportunity
epiplastral
epiplastron
epipetalous
epiphytical
apophyllite
epiphyllous
spermatheca
spermaphyte
spermatical
spermatozoa
opprobrious
approbation
approbatory
approbative
appreciable
appreciably
appreciator
Spirochaeta
spirochaete
spiraculate
sportcaster
sporocystic
upgradeable
opera-dancer
aphrodisiac
Aphrodisian
upgradation
spirography
sparagmatic
sporogenous
sporogonium
sphragistic
appraisable
spermicidal
spiraliform
sparklingly
spirillosis
sparklessly
sporulation
apartmental
spirometric
sporangiola
sporangiole
sparingness
sparrow-bill
spermophile
spermophyte
sparrow-hawk
spermogonia
appropriate
appropinque
sporophoric
sporophytic
operoseness
sportswoman
appressoria
spiritually
spiritualty
spirituelle
operational
spiritistic
operatively
operculated
Spergularia
approvingly
approximate
apostatical
spasmatical
spessartine
spessartite
spastically
epistilbite
apostleship
episcopally
aposiopesis
aposiopetic
apostolical
epistolical
spasmodical
episepalous
apostrophic
apostrophus
epithalamia
epithalamic
spathaceous
ophthalmist
spatterdock
spatterdash
apathetical
epithelioma
spottedness
apotheosise
apotheosize
spatterwork
Epstein-Barr
apotropaism
epitrochoid
Apatosaurus
epitaxially
epithymetic
opium-smoker
appurtenant
spluttering
spawning-bed
sphygmogram
sphygmology
aquanautics
squandering
square-dance
aquarellist
square-built
squashiness
squalidness
aquaplaning
equableness
aquafortist
squarsonage
squattiness
aquaculture
squeakingly
squeakiness
squeamishly
equibalance
squirarchal
equilateral
equivalence
equivalency
Equisetales
Equisetinae
squirearchy
equilibrist
equilibrate
equilibrity
equilibrium
equidistant
equiangular
equivocally
equivocator
equipollent
equinoctial
squintingly
aquiculture
pre-adamical
pre-adamitic
preadaptive
preambulary
preambulate
bread-basket
cream-cheese
broadcasted
broadcaster
breadcrumbs
broad-church
preaudience
breakdancer
grease-heels
greaseproof
ornamentist
triangulate
arraignment
arrangement
Argathelian
breathalyse
breathalyze
breathiness
preachiness
broach-spire
treacherous
treachetour
erratically
organically
organisable
organizable
Arcadianism
creatianism
creationism
creationist
irradiation
organistrum
irradiative
broad-leaved
friableness
treacliness
dreadlessly
dreamlessly
broadminded
preadmonish
great-nephew
preannounce
dreadnaught
dreadnought
treasonable
treasonably
ergatomorph
ergatocracy
creatorship
preacquaint
groatsworth
organ-screen
breastplate
breadthwise

11 □r□a□t

breadthways
breadwinner
probabilism
probabilist
probability
trabeculate
treble-dated
problematic
crabbedness
Brobdingnag
tribologist
brabblement
tribalistic
tribulation
tribunicial
tribunician
tribuneship
tribunitial
tribunitian
bribery-oath
erubescence
erubescency
Proboscidea
proboscides
proboscises
tribeswoman
arabisation
probational
probationer
tributarily
arabization
arm-chancing
brace-and-bit
proclaimant
crocodilian
crocidolite
precedented
precedently
trackerball
proceedings
crackerjack
bracteolate
druckenness
trachearian
tracheotomy
procreation
procreative
truck-farmer
cruciferous
price-fixing
crucifixion
precognosce
practicable
practicably
practically
trichinella
preclinical
precritical
Trachinidae
Trochilidae
fractionlet
fractionary
fractionise
fractionate
fractionize
trichinosis
trichinotic
Brachiopoda
brachiation
fractiously
Procellaria
prickle-back
trickle-down
tracklement
precolonial
truculently
prickliness
brucellosis
prickly-pear
oracularity
gracelessly
pricelessly
tracelessly
tracklessly
tricoloured
oraculously
crackleware
bricklaying
tracklaying
brickmaking
Pre-Cambrian
wreckmaster
fricandeaux
preconceive
arachnoidal
arachnology
precontract
precentress
proconsular
pre-conquest
△dracunculus
proctodaeal
proctodaeum
proctoscope
proctoscopy
Urochordata
urochordate
trochometer
trochophore
Procyonidae
trichomonad
Trichomonas
proctorship
Trichoptera
procephalic
preceptress
precipitant
precipitate
precipitous
procerebral
procerebrum
procurement
prochronism
trichronous
procaryotic
procuration
triceratops
procuratory
brickshaped
tracasserie
preciseness
tricksiness
precautions
precautious
Procrustean
fructuation
cruciverbal
track-walker
brachyprism
brachyurous
credibility
predeceased
predictable
predictably
predicament
producement
traducement
traducingly
bradycardia
predecessor
eradication
predication
predicatory
eradicative
predicative
bridgeboard
bridge-house
bridge-drive
trade-fallen
prodigalise
prodigality
prodigalize
dredging-box
predilected
griddle-cake
iridologist
credulously
bridemaiden
predominant
predominate
tridominium
credentials
prudentials
gradiometer
urediospore
bradypeptic
iridescence
prudishness
tradeswoman
iridisation
gradational
traditional
gradationed
traditioner
predatorily
bridewealth
iridization
irreparable
irreparably
trierarchal
free-falling
freemasonic
△freemasonry
artefactual
greenbottle
irrelevance
irrelevancy
Broederbond
irreverence
true-seeming
true-devoted
free-hearted
true-hearted
freeze-frame
irretention
pre-election
△irredentism
△irredentist
irreceptive
irretentive
greengrocer
freethinker
free-thought
pre-eminence
irreligious
arse-licking
arterialise
arterialize
irremission
irremissive
arteriotomy
pre-existent
green-keeper
orderliness
irreflexion
araeometric
triennially
free-and-easy
irremovable
irremovably
irrevocable
irrevocably
praecordial
freeloading
free-tongued
greenockite
Graeco-Roman
praetorship
tree-worship
freebooting
freebootery
irresoluble
irresolubly
pre-emphasis

Words marked △ may be spelled also with a capital letter

pre-emptible
treecreeper
kriegsspiel
orientalise
Orientalism
Orientalist
orientality
orientalize
Argentinian
priestcraft
arrestation
orientation
irrecusable
irrecusably
irrefutable
irrefutably
irregularly
irreducible
irreducibly
irreduction
green-wellie
oriel-window
drift-anchor
proficience
proficiency
prefectship
prefectural
draft-dodger
prefigurate
trafficator
trafficking
trafficless
drift-mining
profaneness
profanation
profanatory
trifurcated
preferrable
professedly
profuseness
craftswoman
profit-taker
prefatorial
prefatorily
profiterole
prognathism
prognathous
pragmatical
pragmatiser
pragmatizer
programming
△braggadocio
braggartism
tragicomedy
tragedienne
tragédienne
frigidarium
triggerfish
trigger-fish
craggedness
progression
progressism
progressist
△progressive
fragmentary
frugiferous
fragileness
Tragelaphus
grog-blossom
draggle-tail
dragonnades
dragon's-head
originality
Origenistic
crag-and-tail
progenitrix
origination
progeniture
originative
dragoon-bird
Troglodytes
troglodytic
frigorifico
Gregarinida
progestogen
bright-field
frightening
frighteners
frightfully
drug-running
frugivorous
Brahmanical
orthoborate
△prohibition
prohibitory
prohibitive
orthocentre
Orchidaceae
orchidology
orthodontia
orthodontic
orthodromic
orchid-house
arch-heretic
orthoepical
archaeology
orchiectomy
orthography
archegonial
orthogenics
archegonium
archaically
archdiocese
Brahminical
arch-villain
Archimedean
archangelic
archenteron
urchin-shows
prehensible
arrhenotoky
arthropathy
arthroscopy
arthrodesis
archeometry
arthropodal
arthrospore
orthopraxis
orthopedics
orthopedist
orthopteran
orthopaedic
orthopteron
△archipelago
orthophyric
arch-traitor
arch-prelate
orthostatic
orthostichy
orthoscopic
prehistoric
orchestrina
orchestrion
orchestrate
architraved
orthotropic
archdukedom
archduchess
urticaceous
urticarious
dreikanters
trail-blazer
train-bearer
argie-bargie
trailbaston
artiodactyl
arrivederci
traineeship
Ornithogaea
ornithology
Ornithopoda
ornithopter
ornithosaur
Arminianism
artillerist
brainlessly
fruitlessly
pre-ignition
traitorhood
traitorship
arbitrageur
arbitrament
arbitrement
arbitrarily
arbitratrix
arbitration
brainsickly
brain-teaser
articulated
orbiculares
orbicularis
articulable
orbicularly
articulator
projectment
prejudicial
pre-judicial
prejudicant
prejudicate
prejudgment
prokaryotic
araliaceous
Grallatores
argle-bargle
drill-barrow
prelibation
prolocutrix
prolocution
prolificacy
prolificity
proliferate
proliferous
prolegomena
drill-harrow
brilliantly
trellis-work
troll-my-dame
preliminary
drill-master
prolongable
proleptical
drill-plough
artlessness
prelusorily
prelusively
prolateness
proletarian
proletariat
prelateship
grammatical
grammalogue
promycelium
eremacausis
premedicate
bromidrosis
premeditate
primaevally
trumpet-call
trumpet-fish
grummet-hole
Cromwellian
trammelling
premiership
trumpet-tree
trumpet-tone
trumpet-wood
primigenial
primogenial
Bramah-press
crémaillère
trombiculid
promulgator
bramble-bush
Primulaceae

Words marked △ may be spelled also with a capital letter

11 □r□m□l

tremblement
grumblingly
tremblingly
tremolandos
tremulously
tromometric
priming-iron
criminology
criminalese
criminalise
criminalist
criminality
criminalize
prominently
bromination
crimination
premonition
criminatory
premonitory
criminative
premonitive
priming-wire
trampoliner
cramboclink
dromophobia
gramophonic
primiparity
primiparous
trimorphism
trimorphous
dram-drinker
primariness
fremescence
promiseless
promisingly
trimestrial
promiscuity
promiscuous
dramaticism
trimetrical
primatology
promotional
Trimetrogon
crematorial
dramaturgic
prematurely
prematurity
crematorium
primateship
promptitude
primitively
primitivism
primitivist
brimfulness
premovement
premaxillae
transandean
transandine
transalpine
transaction
transceiver
transcriber
transcalent
arenicolous
transductor
Trinidadian
drink-driver
orange-tawny
frondescent
drunkenness
iron-hearted
orange-grass
grandeeship
orange-stick
craniectomy
transection
transeptate
transfigure
transfinite
transferral
frankfurter
transferred
transferrer
transformed
transformer
transferrin
transferase
uriniferous
transfusion
transfusive
grandfather
transfixion
uranography
Grenzgänger
crinigerous
wrong-headed
branch-pilot
transhumant
trench-knife
crankhandle
trenchantly
crunchiness
Frenchiness
Frenchwoman
Frenchwomen
truncheoned
truncheoner
branchiopod
transhipper
trencherman
prong-horned
trencher-fed
frantically
principally
transitable
transit-duty
printing-ink
transilient
fringilline
transiently
franticness
grandiosely
grandiosity
crenellated
front-loaded
front-loader
translucent
granulocyte
translocate
granuliform
granulomata
translunary
franklinite
granularity
frontlessly
wranglesome
granolithic
trendle-tail
trindle-tail
trundle-tail
granulation
translation
translatory
granulative
translative
wrong-minded
transmanche
prenominate
transmarine
grandmaster
transmittal
grandmother
transmitted
transmitter
pruning-bill
crane-necked
pruning-hook
grand-nephew
Francomania
cranioscopy
craniometer
craniometry
ironmongery
Francophobe
Francophile
△francophone
iron-founder
craniognomy
iron-foundry
orang-outang
frontolysis
uranoplasty
transpadane
transpierce
frank-pledge
transponder
transportal
transported
transporter
grandparent
transparent
uriniparous
transposing
granophyric
front-ranker
front-runner
trunksleeve
print-seller
trans-sonics
dronishness
Uranoscopus
brine-shrimp
trendsetter
transsexual
trans-sexual
granitiform
Trinitarian
franc-tireur
graniteware
transuranic
pronouncing
tranquility
tranquilize
branfulness
brankursine
transvaluer
transversal
granivorous
transvestic
brandy-glass
arboraceous
Areopagitic
crookbacked
proof-charge
preoccupied
preoccupant
preoccupate
arborescent
Eriodendron
crookedness
erroneously
arrow-headed
creophagous
cryotherapy
eriophorous
cryophysics
cryobiology
bryological
oreological
arrow-poison
proof-puller
proofreader
armoured-car
armour-plate
areographic
oreographic
cryosurgery
areosystile
△propranolol
prepubertal
trepidation
trepidatory
drap-de-Berry
prophethood

Words marked △ may be spelled also with a capital letter

prophetical
prophetship
prophesying
propagation
propagative
crapehanger
crepehanger
trapshooter
cryptically
graphically
dripping-pan
crappit-head
crappit-heid
triphibious
graphicness
proprietrix
Trappistine
proprietary
prepollence
prepollency
propylamine
crapulosity
propylitise
propylitize
tropomyosin
trypanocide
friponnerie
treponemata
Trypanosoma
trypanosome
prepunctual
trepanation
propinquity
Cryptogamia
cryptogamic
graphomania
trophotaxis
cryptorchid
cryptogenic
cryptomeria
drop-forging
tryptophane
graptolitic
trophoblast
trophoplasm
graphologic
trophozoite
cryptograph
tropophytic
proper-false
proportions
tripersonal
preparation
preparatory
preparative
troposphere
preposition
pre-position
proposition
prepositive
crepuscular
propitiable
propitiator
tripetalous
crepitation
crepitative
drop-curtain
crop-dusting
tripe-visag'd
prophylaxis
triphyllous
trapeziform
trapezoidal
triquetrous
prerecorded
pruriginous
prorogation
prerogative
crustaceous
prismatical
prostatitis
crystalloid
crystalline
crystallise
crystallite
crystallize
crossbearer
crossbanded
crossbarred
trustbuster
frostbitten
press-button
crossbowman
dress-circle
grass-cutter
prosecutrix
prosecution
cross-dating
brissel-cock
trusteeship
crescentade
prospecting
prospection
prospective
crestfallen
presagement
cross-garnet
crash-helmet
preschooler
grasshopper
prosthetics
prosthetist
drastically
prosaically
prescindent
cross-infect
trysting-day
tristichous
prestigious
presciently
Erastianism
Priscianist
prosaicness
Prussianise
Prussianism
Prussianize
grossièreté
prestissimo
prescission
prosciuttos
prostitutor
cross-leaved
trisyllabic
trisyllable
bristlecone
preselector
prosiliency
bristle-fern
cross-legged
trisulphide
bristliness
gristliness
dress-length
bristle-tail
proselytise
proselytism
proselytize
bristle-worm
trestlework
dressmaking
presumingly
irksomeness
presumption
presumptive
presentable
presentably
prosenchyma
presentient
presentment
presentness
presanctify
gressorious
Bristol-milk
cross-or-pile
aristocracy
crescograph
prosopopeia
preservable
brass-rubber
Droseraceae
dress-reform
grass-rooter
pre-stressed
frustrating
frustration
prostration
cross-stitch
dress-shield
brise-soleil
cross-tining
brusqueness
prosauropod
prose-writer
trustworthy
presbyteral
presbycusis
prothalamia
proteaceous
prothallial
prothalloid
prothallium
dry-transfer
protractile
protraction
protractive
froth-blower
protuberant
protuberate
protococcal
Protococcus
protocolled
protocolise
protocolist
criticality
protocolize
protectoral
protectress
criticaster
erythematic
brotherhood
brotherlike
tritheistic
protogalaxy
protagonist
tritagonist
erotogenous
protogynous
froth-hopper
crotcheteer
brattishing
fratricidal
trithionate
prattlement
brittleness
brittle-star
protolithic
gratulation
gratulatory
erotomaniac
protomartyr
writing-book
writing-case
writing-desk
pretendedly
pretentious
protanomaly
protonemata
protandrous
protonotary
crithomancy
prothoraces
prothoraxes
prothoracic
proteolysis

11 □r□t□p

proteolytic
troth-plight
arctophilia
erotophobia
prêt-à-porter
protopathic
protophytic
fraternally
erythrocyte
crateriform
proterogyny
fraterniser
fraternizer
prothrombin
proterandry
frater-house
preterition
trituration
preteritive
preterhuman
Proterozoic
Britishness
brutishness
grotesquely
grotesquery
Brotstudien
Prototheria
truth-teller
protrudable
protrusible
fretfulness
arquebusade
arquebusier
trout-basket
groundsheet
ground-sloth
trous-de-loup
ground-robin
ground-to-air
groundspeed
groundburst
groundswell
trouser-clip
trouserings
trough-fault
trough-shell
wrought-iron
drouthiness
grouchiness
draughtsman
troublefree
troublesome
trouble-town
troublously
proud-minded
trout-stream
irruptively
groupuscule
fraudulence
fraudulency
arduousness
triumvirate
trivialness
drivability
provocation
provocatory
provocateur
provocative
grave-digger
providently
proveditore
prevailment
travail-pain
travail-pang
provokement
provokingly
gravel-blind
prevalently
trivalvular
frivolously
gravimetric
preventable
driving-band
prevenience
provenience
driving-gear
preventible
traversable
prevaricate
previsional
△provisional
provisorily
provostship
gravity-feed
privateness
gravitation
gravitative
privatively
browbeating
drawing-room
crowd-puller
frowardness
frowstiness
drawn-thread
proximately
proximation
Praxitelean
proxy-wedded
prayerfully
brazen-faced
prize-winner
estancieros
ashamedness
established
establisher
Israelitish
assay-master
escarmouche
assafoetida
assassinate
isoantibody
psychagogue
psychedelia
psychedelic
psychically
psychiatric
psychopathy
psychometer
psychodelia
psychodelic
psychogenic
psychometry
psychophily
psychologic
psychonomic
psychotoxic
psychomotor
psychodrama
psychograph
usucaptible
isochronise
isochronism
isochronous
isochronize
isodiaphere
Esperantist
assemblance
assemblyman
osteoclasis
osteodermal
osteodermic
isoelectric
osteography
△aspergillum
Aspergillus
osteogenous
aspergation
ascetically
osteologist
osteoplasty
osteopathic
osteophytic
ascensional
assessorial
aspersorium
ostensively
essentially
asbestiform
assentingly
assentation
ostentation
assertively
isogeotherm
escheatable
asthmatical
escheatment
Escherichia
tschernosem
esthesiogen
eschatology
aspheterise
aspheterism
aspheterize
asphyxiated
asphyxiator
aspirations
espièglerie
assimilable
ascititious
oscillogram
oscillating
oscillation
oscillatory
oscillative
astigmatism
Ossianesque
assignation
Istiophorus
assiduities
assiduously
isolability
isolecithal
psaligraphy
psilomelane
psalmodical
Asclepiadic
Psilophyton
uselessness
Psilotaceae
isomagnetic
esemplastic
psammophile
psammophyte
isomorphism
isomorphous
isometrical
asynartetic
osmotically
astonishing
association
associative
astoundment
asportation
assortative
Ascomycetes
isapostolic
ostreaceous
ostracoderm
ostracodous
ostrich-farm
ostrich-like
astrocytoma
Ostrogothic
Estrildidae
estramazone
astringency
estranghelo
astronomise
astronomize
ostreophage
ostreophagy
estrepement
astraphobia
escritorial

isorhythmic
tsesarevich
tsesarewich
psittacosis
isothenuria
isotonicity
esotericism
esotericist
Osmundaceae
assuredness
assuagement
astuciously
assubjugate
pseudoscope
pseudomonad
pseudomonas
pseudologia
pseudopodia
pseudomorph
pseudologue
pseudograph
pseudocubic
isoxsuprine
Assyriology
ptyalagogic
ptyalagogue
straw-colour
steam-driven
strategical
atramentous
strawflower
steadfastly
strangulate
strangeness
straightway
straight-arm
straightish
straight-cut
straight-out
attaché-case
strap-hanger
stramineous
atrabilious
stratifying
attainments
attaintment
stratopause
strabometer
stratocracy
steatorrhea
steatopygia
steam-roller
strap-shaped
strait-laced
Atlanticism
Atlanticist
Atharvaveda
steady-going
steady-state
stabilisers
stabilizers
stockbroker
stock-farmer
stockholder
stockinette
stockjobber
stickleader
stickleback
itacolumite
stactometer
stichometry
ptochocracy
stockpiling
stocktaking
studiedness
stadtholder
studentship
stretchless
attendement
etherealise
ethereality
etherealize
strengthful
steel-headed
Atherinidae
streakiness
steeplebush
steeplejack
streamlined
streamingly
streaminess
athermanous
etheromania
steel-plated
attemptable
stressed-out
atheistical
streetwards
streetscape
street-level
streetlight
streetsmart
attentional
attestation
attestative
attentively
strenuosity
attenuation
strenuously
otherwhiles
steelworker
stifle-joint
stiff-necked
staff-system
stigmatical
stagflation
stage-manage
steganogram
stage-player
stage-struck
△stegosaurus
Stahlhelmer
Stahlianism
itchy-palmed
ethicalness
stoicalness
Steinberger
staircasing
strikebound
stringy-bark
stringently
stringiness
stringboard
stainlessly
utricularia
stridulator
attitudinal
staktometer
stellarator
atelectasis
atelectatic
stalactical
stalactital
stalactited
stalactitic
stelleridan
stiltedness
stilbestrol
styliferous
stylography
stalagmitic
still-hunter
stalling-ken
stellionate
stellifying
stultifying
stallmaster
stylopodium
stilt-plover
stylishness
stylisation
utilisation
athleticism
stilettoing
utilitarian
stilt-walker
stylization
utilization
stomachache
stomachfuls
stomachical
stomachless
etymologise
etymologist
etymologize
stumblingly
stimulating
stimulation
stimulative
atom-smasher
staminodium
atomisation
stomatology
Stomatopoda
atomization
standardise
standardize
ethnobotany
stone-colour
stenocardia
stenochrome
stenochromy
stonecutter
stintedness
stuntedness
ethnography
stenography
stoneground
stanchioned
stencilling
ethnologist
stentmaster
standoffish
ctenophoran
standpatter
itinerantly
stone's-throw
stenotropic
stenotypist
stonewaller
stonewashed
strongyloid
strongpoint
atrociously
attorneydom
attorneyism
stroboscope
ethological
atmospheric
stepdancing
utopianiser
utopianizer
stephanotis
stopping-out
stipulation
stipulatory
stipendiary
stipendiate
stepbrother
staphylitis
storm-beaten
attribution
attributive
stern-chaser
attractable
Styracaceae
yttro-cerite
Pterichthys
pterodactyl
pteridology
yttriferous
starchiness
starch-grain
storekeeper

startlingly
stereobatic
stereotaxia
stereotaxic
stereotaxis
stereoscope
stereoscopy
stereometer
stereometry
stereophony
stereoblind
stereosonic
sternotribe
stereograph
stereoptics
stereotyped
stereotyper
stereotypic
star-crossed
storm-stayed
sternsheets
Pterosauria
star-studded
storyteller
attritional
stormtroops
storm-tossed
iteratively
sternutator
stasimorphy
stitchcraft
stateliness
statemented
stethoscope
stethoscopy
statesmanly
statistical
stateswoman
statutorily
staunchable
Etruscology
staunchless
staunchness
Struthiones
stauroscope
staurolitic
struttingly
attuitional
attuitively
stave-church
stevengraph
stewardship
ithyphallic
△ithyphallus
funambulist
funambulate
subarboreal
sugar-coated
autarchical
subaudition
suraddition
out-and-outer
mutagenesis
subaffluent
Fumariaceae
Lubavitcher
subaxillary
mutationist
subacidness
audaciously
suballiance
curableness
durableness
mutableness
tunableness
eudaemonics
eudaemonism
eudaemonist
auxanometer
Butazolidin®
fumatoriums
curatorship
subaerially
subarration
subassemble
subassembly
Judaisation
eubacterium
△judas-window
eucalyptole
Judaization
outbreeding
tumblerfuls
bubble-shell
tumble-drier
rubble-stone
bumble-puppy
bulbiferous
humbuggable
lumbaginous
lumbricalis
outbuilding
tumbling-box
Lumbricidae
mumbo-jumbos
Turbellaria
quibblingly
turbulently
nubbing-cove
husbandlike
husbandland
husbandless
turbine-pump
rubbing-post
dumbfounder
bumbershoot
turbo-ram-jet
rubber-cored
rubber-stamp
curb-crawler
mulberry-fig
rubbish-heap
rumbustical
rumbustious
subbasement
surbasement
bulbousness
purchasable
cunctatious
bunch-backed
hunchbacked
Mulciberian
quick-change
suicidology
succedaneum
butcher-bird
Muschelkalk
luncheon-bar
muscle-bound
quicken-tree
quick-freeze
quick-frozen
quick-firing
furciferous
dulcifluous
Munchhausen
Punchinello
punching-bag
subclinical
subcritical
punctilious
functionary
functionate
auscultator
succulently
subchloride
muscularity
musculation
musculature
subcellular
subcultural
Durchlaucht
vulcanicity
vulcanology
subcontract
subcontrary
buccinatory
succinctory
outcrossing
susceptance
susceptible
susceptibly
turcopolier
Turcophobia
nuncupation
nuncupatory
nuncupative
subcapsular
subcardinal
subcortical
pulchritude
quick-sticks
quacksalver
quicksilver
successless
subcategory
muscatorium
suscitation
punctulated
succourable
punctualist
succourless
punctuality
punctuation
punctuative
quick-witted
quadraphony
quadratical
subdiaconal
subdeaconry
auld-farrant
fund-raising
duodecimals
hurdle-racer
sundrenched
hundredfold
quadrennial
subduedness
quadrennium
muddy-headed
quodlibetic
quadrillion
quadriennia
subdelirium
fundamental
subdominant
pudding-pipe
pudding-time
quadrophony
murderously
outdistance
subdistrict
quadrupedal
subdivision
subdivisive
tuberaceous
rubefacient
tumefacient
lukewarmish
superabound
rubefaction
tumefaction
superactive
superbright
queer-basher
supercharge
supercherie
supercoiled
tuberculoma
tuberculise
tuberculose
tuberculate
tuberculous
tuberculize

Words marked △ may be spelled also with a capital letter

quiescently
superdainty
juvenescent
queene-apple
superficial
superficies
rule-of-thumb
superfamily
superfusion
superfatted
superfetate
superfluity
superfluous
superheater
Rudesheimer
Rüdesheimer
fume-chamber
eugenically
numerically
superinduce
superinfect
superimpose
superioress
superiority
superintend
superjacent
museologist
superlunary
queenliness
pure-blooded
cupellation
superlative
queez-maddam
supermarket
supernormal
supernatant
gubernation
supernature
autecologic
subeconomic
superoctave
superpraise
superphylum
funerreally
superrefine
queen-regent
supersubtle
supersedeas
supersedere
supersedure
Queensberry
supersleuth
supersafety
queen-stitch
supersonics
superscribe
superstruct
superscreen
superstring
superscript
eupepticity
curettement
supertanker
quaestorial
humectation
duteousness
hugeousness
tunefulness
bureaucracy
supervolute
supervision
supervisory
superweapon
suffragette
tufftaffeta
tufftaffety
surf-bathing
ruffian-like
surfcasting
sufficience
sufficiency
suffocating
suffocation
suffocative
sulfadoxine
buff-leather
subfreezing
buffalo-bird
buffalo-robe
suffumigate
muffin-fight
turfing-iron
sulfonamide
duffing-over
muffin-worry
sulfonation
luffer-board
huffishness
suffixation
burglarious
jungle-green
judgment-day
judgemental
burgomaster
rumgumption
surgeonfish
surgeonship
subglobular
fulguration
turgescence
turgescency
suggestible
purgatorial
purgatorian
gurgitation
purgatively
humgruffian
bushwalking
bushmanship
Dukhobortsy
rush-bearing
bushwhacker
push-bicycle
euchologion
bushelwoman
euphemistic
authentical
such-and-such
fushionless
mush-mouthed
cushion-tire
cushion-tyre
Lutheranism
subharmonic
authorcraft
Eucharistic
bushy-tailed
eurhythmics
eurhythmist
pushfulness
nudicaudate
punicaceous
subitaneous
puritanical
subimaginal
subimagines
nudicaulous
cubicalness
musicalness
subincision
subindicate
subindustry
ruridecanal
luminescent
businessman
rudimentary
fusing-point
music-holder
punishingly
juridically
municipally
purificator
munificence
munitioneer
auxiliaries
humiliating
humiliation
humiliatory
humiliative
judiciously
audiologist
burial-place
audibleness
pupillarity
tubiflorous
curialistic
fusillation
numismatics
audiometric
numismatist
Aurignacian
tulipomania
auditoriums
auditorship
tulip-poplar
subirrigate
Hudibrastic
ludicrously
music-seller
audiotyping
audiotypist
auriculated
auricularly
pudibundity
rubicundity
curiousness
dubiousness
dutifulness
furiousness
audiovisual
duniewassal
subjectless
subjectship
subjugation
subjunction
subjunctive
buck-washing
buck-passing
huckleberry
musk-thistle
muskellunge
sucking-fish
tucking-mill
luckengowan
luckenbooth
ducking-pond
sucker-punch
duskishness
luskishness
bucket-wheel
hucksterage
musket-proof
hucksteress
turkey-shoot
gull-catcher
nuclear-free
bull-mastiff
bull-baiting
gullibility
full-acorned
duplication
publication
duplicature
duplicitous
duplicative
quill-driver
bull-terrier
full-hearted
dual-density
qualifiable
nullifidian
qualifiedly
curly-greens
curly-headed

hurly-hacket
gully-hunter
pull-through
full-charged
bullshitter
quilting-bee
bullfighter
dull-sighted
full-fledged
full-blooded
guilelessly
guiltlessly
pullulation
sublimeness
sublimation
burling-iron
fulling-mill
curling-pond
sublanguage
nucleolated
nucleoplasm
full-mouthed
dual-control
nulliparity
nulliparous
fuller's-herb
dull-brained
full-frontal
bull-fronted
full-fraught
publishable
publishment
bullishness
sunlessness
guildswoman
sublittoral
pullet-sperm
bullet-proof
qualitative
dual-purpose
curlew-berry
subluxation
hurley-house
pulmobranch
tummy-button
culmiferous
gummiferous
submolecule
submultiple
nummulation
augmentable
humming-bird
fulminating
culmination
fulmination
fulminatory
summersault
submergence
bur-marigold
submarginal
outmarriage
submergible
submersible
murmuringly
summariness
summerhouse
murmuration
murmurously
submissible
submissness
surmistress
summit-level
summational
surmounting
guaniferous
burn-the-wind
turnpike-man
quintillion
cunnilingus
running-gear
running-hand
cunningness
Quantometer®
quantometer
quandong-nut
curnaptious
Turneresque
vulneration
burnt-sienna
furnishings
burnishment
furnishment
nunnishness
quincuncial
quinquennia
ruinousness
quinquereme
quinsy-berry
automatical
Tudorbethan
Euro-sceptic
subordinary
subordinate
autogenesis
auto-reverse
autocephaly
europeanise
Europeanism
Europeanist
europeanize
Eurocentric
autophagous
autochthons
autochthony
autochanger
autophanous
bucolically
autokinesis
autokinetic
tumorigenic
autoplastic
Yugoslavian
subornation
autonomical
automobilia
Euro-dollars
automorphic
out-of-pocket
autographic
autotrophic
autoerotism
autogravure
out-of-the-way
bumpsadaisy
culpability
suspectable
suspectedly
suspectless
suppedaneum
suppressant
suppression
suppressive
purpresture
puppy-headed
sulphhydryl
supplicavit
surprisedly
suppliantly
subprioress
bumptiously
jumping-bean
jumping-deer
suspenseful
jumping-hare
suspensible
jumping-jack
subpanation
supportance
supportable
supportably
purportedly
subparallel
purportless
supportless
pump-priming
supportment
out-paramour
supportress
suppuration
suspiration
suppurative
surpassable
purpose-like
purposeless
dumpishness
lumpishness
mumpishness
supposition
suppository
suppositive
puppet-valve
sulphurator
sulphureted
sulphureous
sumptuosity
sumptuously
puppy-walker
supply-sider
outquarters
Munro-bagger
surrebuttal
surrebutter
curriculums
turriculate
hurricanoes
supracostal
lubrication
rubrication
lubricative
puerperally
quarterback
quarter-bred
quarterdeck
quarter-evil
quarter-jack
quarrelling
quarrellous
guardedness
hurriedness
quarter-note
quarrel-pane
quarter-road
quarter-rail
quarter-seal
quarrelsome
quarter-sawn
quarter-tone
quarter-wind
putrefiable
cupriferous
subregional
subrogation
surrogation
quarrington
guerrillero
querulously
supremacism
supremacist
nutrimental
supremeness
△suprematism
△suprematist
cupro-nickel
currant-cake
current-cost
surrenderee
surrenderer
surrenderor
currant-loaf
currentness
currant-wine
cuir-bouilli
cuir-bouilly
putrescence

Buprestidae
putrescible
currishness
hurry-scurry
hurry-skurry
turret-clock
nutritional
lubritorium
lucratively
nutritively
surrounding
burrowstown
quarry-water
outstanding
substandard
Russianness
substantial
substantive
subscapular
purse-bearer
bursiculate
tussock-moth
tussac-grass
subspecific
nun's-veiling
pussyfooter
subschemata
Burschenism
mudslinging
questioning
questionary
questionist
substituted
substituent
mussel-scalp
mussel-scaup
mussel-shell
Mussulwoman
fulsomeness
subsumption
subsumptive
subsensible
Russophobia
Russophobic
subsequence
subscribing
Burseraceae
substractor
subservient
nurserymaid
cursoriness
substrative
subsistence
purse-seiner
purse-taking
guesstimate
nurse-tender
mussitation
suasiveness
pussy-willow
multi-access
multi-author
subtraction
subtractive
quotability
suitability
justiciable
mustachioed
multicolour
buttock-mail
furthcoming
subtacksman
justiceship
multicuspid
rustication
furtherance
hurtleberry
multiethnic
turtle-shell
furthermore
furthermost
furthersome
subtreasury
turtle-stone
justifiable
justifiably
multifidous
guttiferous
tutti-frutti
fustigation
hunt-the-gowk
sustainable
rumti-iddity
sustainedly
curtain-fire
punt-fishing
curtailment
sustainment
curtail-step
multijugate
multijugous
multilobate
multilineal
multilinear
ductileness
subtileness
fustilarian
fustilirian
pustulation
dusty-miller
customarily
custom-built
sustentator
hunting-crop
hunting-horn
multinomial
hunting-mass
multanimous
buttonholer
button-mould
hunting-seat
hunting-song
hunting-tide
Huntington's
multangular
hunting-whip
subtropical
hunt-counter
multiplexer
multiplexor
gutta-percha
multiparity
multiparous
multipotent
putty-powder
multiplying
butter-paper
Kulturkampf
multiracial
subterminal
quaternion'd
quaternions
butterflies
gutterblood
cultureless
gutturalise
butter-cloth
butter-plate
gutturalize
hunter's-moon
butter-knife
mutteringly
guttersnipe
austereness
butteriness
butter-woman
Kulturkreis
butter-print
surtarbrand
surturbrand
mustard-tree
mutteration
subterhuman
rupturewort
multispiral
multisonant
multistorey
multiserial
multiscreen
multistrike
hurtfulness
lustfulness
tub-thumping
tuft-hunting
multivalent
furtiveness
cultivation
quoteworthy
subumbrella
suburbanise
suburbanism
suburbanite
suburbanity
suburbanize
furunculous
Subungulata
subungulate
Cupuliferae
luxuriantly
luxulianite
luxuriation
luxuriously
lucubration
susurration
Augustinian
luxulyanite
surveillant
curvilineal
curvilinear
subvertical
pulverulent
culverineer
quaveringly
quiveringly
pulveration
subvitreous
survivalism
survivalist
outwardness
butyraceous
eurythermal
eurythermic
Eurypharynx
buoyantness
Runyonesque
jury-process
Eurypterida
eurypteroid
fuzzy-haired
quizzically
evocatively
evidentiary
evagination
avoirdupois
ovuliferous
evolutional
evil-starred
evangelical
evangeliary
evening-star
avant-propos
eventration
evanescence
evanishment
eventualise
eventuality
eventualize
evaporation
evaporative
oviparously
oviposition
overbalance
overhandled
overcareful

11 □v□r□a

overgarment
overpayment
overearnest
overhastily
△everlasting
overcasting
svarabhakti
overachieve
overreached
overdevelop
overtedious
over-zealous
overweening
overbearing
overmeasure
overleather
overweather
overheating
overthrower
overpitched
overbidding
overnighter
overviolent
overpicture
overblanket
overflowing
over-anxiety
over-anxious
overindulge
overlocking
overcorrect
overcoating
overforward
over-breathe
over-precise
overproduce
over-trading
overfreedom
overgrainer
overfreight
overbrimmed
overprepare
overwrestle
overdraught
overfraught
overwrought
overcrowded
over-drowsed
overgrazing
overstretch
overstuffed
overstrooke
averruncate
overrunning
overfulness
overburthen
everywhence
eviscerator
evasiveness
eviternally
sweater-girl
owner-driver
tweezer-case
sweetie-wife
sweepstakes
sweep-washer
swift-footed
twofoldness
swift-winged
swagger-cane
swag-bellied
twelve-penny
twalpennies
twelvemonth
swell-headed
swallow-dive
swallow-tail
swallow-wort
awelessness
Twelfth-cake
Twelfth-tide
swim-bladder
swing-bridge
swingeingly
swing-handle
swingle-hand
dwindlement
twanglingly
swingletree
swingometer
swan-hopping
swing-plough
twin-brother
swinishness
two-penn'orth
sword-bearer
sword-dollar
swarthiness
swordplayer
sword-shaped
zwischenzug
kwashiorkor
awesomeness
two-storeyed
awe-stricken
twitter-bone
switchblade
switch-plant
switchboard
swivel-chair
swivelblock
awkwardness
exsanguined
expatiation
expatiatory
expatiative
excarnation
exhaustible
exhaustless
expansional
expansively
expansivity
exuberantly
oxy-chloride
oxy-compound
executrices
executrixes
executioner
executorial
executively
exceedingly
expenditure
expeditious
experienced
expediently
exteriorise
exteriority
exteriorize
excellently
exterminate
externalise
externalism
externalist
externality
externalize
excerptible
extemporary
extemporise
extemporize
extensional
excessively
expensively
extensively
expectantly
expectingly
exceptional
expectorant
expectorate
expectation
expectative
extenuating
extenuation
extenuatory
extenuative
oxy-fluoride
exaggerated
exaggerator
oxygenation
oxy-hydrogen
exhilarator
expiscation
exsiccation
expiscatory
exsiccative
excitedness
ex-directory
extirpation
extirpatory
extirpative
explication
explicatory
explicative
Oxalidaceae
exaltedness
explainable
exploitable
exclamation
exclamatory
exclamative
explanation
explanatory
explanative
exploration
exploratory
explorative
exclusively
explosively
exclusivism
exclusivist
exclusivity
exemplified
exemplifier
exemplarily
exemplarity
examination
exanthemata
axonometric
exanimation
exoneration
exonerative
axiomatical
exposedness
exponential
excogitator
expositress
excoriation
exfoliation
exfoliative
excommunion
axiological
extorsively
excorticate
expostulate
extortioner
exhortation
exportation
exhortatory
exhortative
exorability
extractable
extractible
extrication
extradition
extrafloral
exorbitance
exorbitancy
exercisable
excremental
extremeness
excrementum
expromissor
extrinsical
expropriate
extrapolate

axerophthol
excrescence
excrescency
expressible
expressness
extravagant
extravagate
extra-virgin
extravasate
oxyrhynchus
exasperator
exoskeletal
exoskeleton
existential
exstipulate
exotericism
expurgation
expurgatory
expugnation
exculpation
exculpatory
exquisitely
excursively
cycadaceous
gynaecology
gynaecomast
pyrargyrite
dynamically
pyramidally
pyramidical
△sybaritical
hypallactic
tyrannicide
tyrannosaur
tyrannously
dynamometer
dynamometry
synagogical
dynamograph
synanthesis
synanthetic
Byzantinism
Byzantinist
lycanthrope
lycanthropy
symbolology
symbolistic
eyebrowless
synclinoria
hyacinthine
synchoresis
syncopation
myocarditis
synchromesh
synchronise
synchronism
synchronous
synchronize
synchrotron
eye-catching
syndyasmian
syndicalism
syndicalist
syndication
syndesmoses
syndesmosis
syndesmotic
cyperaceous
gyre-carline
hyperactive
hyperacusis
hyperboloid
hyperbolise
hyperbolism
hyperbolize
hyperborean
hypercharge
hypercritic
synecdochic
hyperdactyl
hyperdorian
hyperemesis
hyperemetic
myoelectric
typesetting
hypergamous
synergistic
hyperinosis
hyperinotic
hyperlydian
hypermarket
cybernetics
cybernation
type-founder
type-foundry
synecologic
Hymenoptera
hyperphagia
hyperplasia
type-species
cyberphobia
typewritten
typewriting
hypersthene
hypersomnia
hypersonics
hyperstress
hypertrophy
dysfunction
myographist
syngnathous
lythraceous
mythography
Pythagorean
Pythagorism
mythologian
mythologise
mythologist
mythologize
syphilology
mythomaniac
Pythonesque
hyphenation
lychnoscope
mythopoetic
mythopoeist
dysharmonic
xyridaceous
cynicalness
typicalness
cylindrical
lysigenetic
myringotomy
syringotomy
pyritohedra
syllabicate
syllabicity
syllabarium
cyclicality
pyelography
dyslogistic
syllogistic
cyclohexane
hyalomelane
cyclopaedia
cyclopaedic
cycloplegia
sylleptical
cyclosporin
cycloserine
cyclothymia
cyclothymic
myrmecology
myrmidonian
symmetrical
symmetallic
symmetalism
Hydnocarpus
hymnography
Pycnogonida
pycnogonoid
hypnogenous
hymnologist
hypnopaedia
hypnopompic
gymnorhinal
gymnasiarch
gymnastical
hypnotistic
Sydneysider
zygocardiac
hylopathism
hylopathist
pyroballogy
myxomatosis
xylocarpous
hypogastric
synoecology
synoeciosis
cytogenesis
cytogenetic
hylogenesis
pyrogenetic
pyrotechnic
zymotechnic
hypoaeolian
Tyronensian
hypotension
hypotensive
Myxophyceae
hypothecary
hypothecate
mycophagist
hylophagous
xylophagous
cynophilist
xylophilous
Zygophyllum
sycophantic
sycophantry
hypothenuse
xylophonist
cymophanous
hypothermal
hypothermia
hypothyroid
pyrophorous
hypophyseal
hypophysial
hypothesise
hypothesize
hypothetise
hypothetize
Byronically
synodically
zymotically
zymosimeter
pyrokinesis
hypolimnion
hyponitrite
hyponitrous
tyroglyphid
Tyroglyphus
hypoglossal
mycoplasmas
cytoplasmic
hypoblastic
hypoplastic
pyroclastic
zygopleural
pyrognostic
mycodomatia
cytological
Lycopodinae
mycological
typological
zymological
hypocorisma
hylomorphic
zygomorphic
gyrocompass
hylozoistic
by-your-leave
mycorrhizal

11 □y□o□r

typographer
xylographer
kymographic
mycotrophic
typographia
typographic
xylographic
pyrogravure
gynostemium
hypostrophe
synoptistic
hypostasise
hypostasize
gyrostatics
hypostatise
hypostatize
synonymatic
Myxomycetes
Zygomycetes
synonymical
synonymicon
hypocycloid
hypotyposis
lymphangial
Nymphalidae
hyoplastral
hyoplastron
sympodially
tympaniform
nymphomania
symptomatic
nympholepsy
symphonious
dyspeptical
dyspareunia
symposiarch
dyspathetic
sympathetic
sympathiser
sympathizer
sympathique
sympetalous
hydrobromic
Hydrocharis
hydrocyanic
hydrochoric
hydrocarbon
hydrography
hydrogenise
hydrogenate
hydrogenous
hydrogenize
hydra-headed
pyrrolidine
hydrologist
hydrolysate
hydromedusa
Cypro-Minoan
hydromantic
hydrometric
hygrometric
hydrometeor
Cyprinodont
cypripedium
Hydrophidae
hydrophilic
hydroponics
hydrophobia
hydrophobic
hydropathic
hydrophytic
hygrophytic
hydrophyton
dyer's-rocket
hydrargyral
hydrargyrum
hydrostatic
hydrosphere
hydrosomata
hygroscopic
hydrotactic
hydrothorax
hydrotropic
dysrhythmia
gypsiferous
hypsography
hypsometric
hypsophobia
syssarcoses
syssarcosis
hyoscyamine
syntactical
syntectical
cysticercus
△dyotheletic
synthetical
synthesiser
synthesizer
synthetiser
synthetizer
△dyothelitic
hyetography
syntagmatic
system-maker
systematics
systematise
systematism
systematist
systematize
system-built
nyctanthous
nyctinastic
nyctophobia
oyster-patty
oyster-wench
hysterogeny
oyster-shell
hysteroidal
oyster-field
oyster-plant
oyster-knife
oyster-woman
oyster-tongs
hysteresial
hysterotomy
nyctitropic
sylvestrian
azo-compound
ozoniferous
ozonosphere
ozonisation
ozonization
Azerbaijani
Azotobacter

Words marked △ may be spelled also with a capital letter

taramasalata
Bananalander
salamandrine
salamandrian
salamandroid
banana-bender
paralanguage
palatability
paramagnetic
caravansarai
caravanserai
paratactical
zalambdodont
palaebiology
parascending
balance-sheet
balance-wheel
Papaveraceae
macaberesque
parametrical
parade-ground
malapertness
paracentesis
cataphractic
paraphrastic
catachrestic
cataphyllary
paraphimosis
Panathenaean
parachronism
cataphoresis
cataphysical
Zarathustric
paradisaical
Tamaricaceae
Samaritanism
banalisation
banalization
canalisation
canalization
capacitation
faradisation
faradization
nasalisation
nasalization
parasitaemia
Paradiseidae
laxativeness
paradise-fish
Ramapithecus
paramilitary
paradisiacal
parasiticide
capabilities
paradigmatic
vacationless
Papanicolaou
paralipomena
parasitology
calamitously
catadioptric
cabalistical
canaliculate
catallactics
parallelwise
paraglossate
Balaam-basket
Balaamitical
paraenetical
paragnathism
paragnathous
labanotation
satanophobia
parapophyses
parapophysis
Palaeolithic
paradoxidian
catamountain
palaeobotany
paraboloidal
malacologist
paradoxology
paramorphism
para-compound
palaeography
catacoustics
Malacostraca
man-about-town
paradoxurine
parasphenoid
paragraphist
parapsychism
panaesthesia
paraesthesia
palaestrical
Marattiaceae
wag-at-the-wall
paranthelion
galactagogue
galactometer
catastrophic
hamartiology
paranthropus
hamarthritis
panarthritis
galactosemia
paraquadrate
paracyanogen
parasyntheta
pay-as-you-earn
rabble-rouser
marble-cutter
marbled-white
cabbage-white
carbohydrate
day-blindness
gambling-hell
lamb's-lettuce
rabbinically
carbonaceous
rambunctious
namby-pambies
barber-monger
rabbit-warren
wag-by-the-wall
rabbeting-saw
rabbit-sucker
tambourinist
harbour-light
bacchanalian
Panchatantra
calceamentum
saccharinity
saccharoidal
Marcobrunner
fasciculated
saccadically
hatchet-faced
pancreatitis
ratchet-wheel
fancifulness
watchfulness
sanctifiable
sanctifiedly
cancellarial
cancellarian
cancellation
tax-collector
pauciloquent
baccalaurean
parchmentise
parchmentize
sarcomatosis
Vacciniaceae
gas-condenser
malcontented
falcon-gentle
falcon-gentil
marconigraph
carcinogenic
lanceolately
raccoon-berry
Marcionitism
sarcoplasmic
sarcophagous
saucepan-fish
cancerphobia
panchromatic
Lancasterian
narcissistic
narcotically
narco-therapy
march-treason
marcatissimo
lasciviously
land-yachting
sand-yachting
hard-favoured
card-carrying
laudableness
mandibulated
paedobaptism
paedobaptist
Laodiceanism
paddock-stool
paedodontics
candle-paring
saddlebacked
candle-waster
handkerchief
saddle-shaped
candle-holder
△pandaemonium
hard-featured
hard-sectored
paedogenesis
paedogenetic
paedological
sandblasting
bardolatrous
paedomorphic
landing-craft
sardonically
pandanaceous
landing-field
maidenliness
Tardenoisian
cardinalship
cardinal-bird
landing-place
landing-stage
landing-speed
landing-strip
handsomeness
cardiologist
cardiography
paedophiliac
land-grabbing
banderillero
bandersnatch
gander-mooner
landgraviate
gas-discharge
hard-standing
land-lubberly
land-surveyor
vaudevillean
vaudevillian
vaudevillist
vase-painting
saleableness
tameableness
paleobiology
paleobotanic
Valenciennes
watercresses
paleoclimate
capercaillie
capercailzie
water-cooling
Water-carrier
paleocrystic
water-drinker
eavesdropped

Words marked △ may be spelled also with a capital letter

12 □a□e□d

eavesdropper
kaleidophone
calendar-line
haberdashery
kaleidoscope
sacerdotally
water-diviner
base-levelled
paleoecology
baselessness
carelessness
hatelessness
namelessness
tamelessness
water-flowing
paleographic
paleographer
water-gilding
sage-thrasher
café-chantant
catechetical
laterisation
laterization
maderisation
maderization
racemisation
racemization
watering-call
waveringness
watering-hole
waterishness
materialness
Sabellianism
patellectomy
gamesmanship
salesmanship
watermanship
paper-marbler
make-and-break
bare-knuckled
tabernacular
paleontology
gamesomeness
malevolently
categorially
ravenousness
△mademoiselle
warehouseman
cane-bottomed
water-parting
base-spirited
bare-breached
safe-breaking
safe-cracking
bate-breeding
name-dropping
water-spaniel
paper-stainer
water-soluble
water-strider
majesticness
majestically
parenthesise
parenthesize
gazetteerish
palette-knife
parenterally
Lamentations
valetudinary
lake-dwelling
paper-washing
caterwauling
paleozoology
half-marathon
raffle-ticket
half-measures
half-seas-over
half-timbered
half-integral
half-mourning
malformation
languageless
tangibleness
barge-couples
raggle-taggle
tangle-netter
tangle-picker
Languedocian
rangefinding
baggage-train
large-hearted
gang-there-out
sanguinarily
sanguineness
sanguiferous
languishment
sanguinolent
sanguivorous
mangel-wurzel
tangentially
marginal-unit
languorously
wagger-pagger
Pan-Germanism
badger-legged
gangsterland
daughterling
machicolated
pachycarpous
cathodograph
Pachydermata
pachydermous
cash-register
tachygraphic
tachygrapher
pathogenesis
pathogenetic
machairodont
Panhellenism
panhellenium
panhellenion
Panhellenist
pathological
bachelorship
bachelor-girl
bachelorhood
mathematical
mathematised
mathematized
cachinnation
cachinnatory
washing-board
cash-and-carry
bathing-dress
washing-house
taphonomical
machine-ruler
△washingtonia
machinations
tacheometric
fashiousness
lath-splitter
bathypelagic
Machtpolitik
tachyphrasia
father-lasher
oath-breaking
fatherliness
fathers-in-law
father-figure
katharometer
gathering-cry
katharevousa
rachischisis
pathetically
cathetometer
cashew-apples
lachrymation
lachrymatory
lachrymosely
lachrymosity
habitability
navigability
habitational
navigational
capitalistic
caricaturist
variableness
radiobiology
marimbaphone
sapindaceous
palindromist
lapidescence
radioelement
cabinetmaker
manifestable
manifestible
manifestness
satisfaction
satisfactory
satisfyingly
habit-forming
hagiographic
radiographic
hagiographer
radiographer
taxing-master
palingenesia
palingeneses
palingenesis
baking-powder
babingtonite
Manicheanism
facilitative
catilinarian
facilitation
gasification
habilitation
Nazification
pacification
palification
panification
ramification
ratification
salification
sanitisation
sanitization
vaticination
pacificatory
laticiferous
Papilionidae
pavilion-roof
vaginicoline
caliginosity
radio-isotope
lapidicolous
radicicolous
radicivorous
vaginicolous
basidiospore
capillaceous
hagiological
radiological
carillonneur
Mariolatrous
radiomimetic
talismanical
camiknickers
radionuclide
patience-dock
sapientially
manifoldness
calico-flower
varicoloured
latirostrate
radiophonics
radiophonist
radiesthesia
magistrature
kakistocracy
papistically
radio-therapy
calisthenics
radio-thorium

Words marked △ may be spelled also with a capital letter

variationist
paniculately
manipulative
capitulation
manipulation
capitulatory
manipulatory
fatigue-dress
latitudinous
habitualness
fatigue-party
salicylamide
parisyllabic
backwardness
talkee-talkee
walkie-talkie
Yankee-Doodle
back-lighting
taskmistress
Jack-a-lantern
Jack-o'-lantern
back-slapping
marksmanship
walking-frame
△jack-in-office
larking-glass
△jack-in-the-box
Parkinsonism
parking-place
packing-press
talking-point
packing-paper
walking-staff
packing-sheet
walking-stick
back-to-nature
sack-doudling
backwoodsman
backboneless
back-wounding
backbreaking
backtracking
cankeredness
marker-beacon
market-garden
basket-making
market-making
racket-tailed
racketeering
backstarting
racket-ground
basket-stitch
back-mutation
backswordman
malleability
Tagliacotian
mail-carriage
hallucinogen
hallucinosis
early-closing
fallaciously
nail-scissors
wallydraigle
Palladianism
balladmonger
nail-head-spar
gaol-delivery
jail-delivery
ball-bearings
fault-finding
calligraphic
calligrapher
galligaskins
waulking-song
caulking-iron
gallsickness
gall-sickness
rallentandos
gallinaceous
hallan-shaker
ballanwrasse
marline-spike
Darlingtonia
wallcovering
sailboarding
mallophagous
rail-splitter
lallapalooza
harlequinade
ball-breaking
cable-railway
table-rapping
cable's-length
Naples-yellow
eagle-sighted
callisthenic
ballet-dancer
ballet-master
cable-tramway
balletically
Wall-Streeter
balletomania
table-turning
Carlovingian
tallow-candle
gallows-maker
early-warning
farm-labourer
barmy-brained
mammee-sapota
harmlessness
Macmillanite
mammillarias
mammalogical
harmonically
harmonichord
warmongering
harmonograph
salmon-fisher
harmonometer
salmon-colour
harmoniously
harmoniphone
harmoniumist
haemophiliac
hammer-headed
haemorrhagic
haemorrhoids
haematoblast
haematolysis
haematemesis
haematoxylin
Haematoxylon
maintainable
damnableness
wainscotting
vaunt-courier
saunteringly
gainlessness
painlessness
magnifically
magnificence
caenogenesis
faint-hearted
launching-pad
faintishness
Magnoliaceae
carnal-minded
magniloquent
vainglorious
cannon-fodder
balneologist
Cain-coloured
Wagnerianism
mannerliness
laundry-woman
harness-maker
earnest-money
earnest-penny
magnetically
magnetograph
malnutrition
magnetometer
magnetometry
barnstorming
magnetisable
magnetizable
nasolacrymal
japonaiserie
paroccipital
gamopetalous
gamosepalous
baroreceptor
barometrical
gasometrical
manometrical
major-general
parochialise
parochialize
parochialism
parochiality
gamophyllous
cacophonical
cacophonious
majolicaware
canonisation
canonization
valorisation
valorization
vaporisation
vaporization
vasodilatory
saponifiable
nanoplankton
paroemiology
saloon-keeper
paronomastic
baron-officer
lagomorphous
canorousness
vaporousness
labour-saving
favouredness
raconteuring
manoeuvrable
man-of-war's-man
barodynamics
panpharmacon
palpableness
lampadedromy
campodeiform
lampadomancy
Cappagh-brown
happy-go-lucky
salpiglossis
camp-shedding
camp-sheeting
sapphire-wing
carpenter-ant
carpenter-bee
Campanularia
happenstance
lamprophyric
camp-follower
carpophagous
camp-preacher
pamperedness
lappered-milk
gas-permeable
camp-drafting
carpetbagger
lamp-standard
carpet-knight
carpetmonger
tappet-motion
Jacquard-loom
pasque-flower
vanquishable
vanquishment
matriarchate
patriarchate
patriarchism
carriage-paid
carriageable

Words marked △ may be spelled also with a capital letter

marriageable
laureateship
marriage-ring
marriage-bone
carriage-free
hair's-breadth
macrobiotics
iatrochemist
matriclinous
matroclinous
patriclinous
patroclinous
matriculator
capriciously
macrocephaly
Capricornian
macrodactyly
hairlessness
carragheenin
fairnitickle
sacroiliitis
sacrilegious
patrilineage
tauromachian
sacramentary
saprophagous
Macropodidae
macropterous
hair-splitter
madreporitic
Patripassian
saprophytism
hairdressing
barristerial
patristicism
sarrusophone
garret-master
sabre-toothed
barratrously
parrot-wrasse
narrow-minded
marrow-squash
carriwitchet
fairnytickle
manslaughter
nauseatingly
law-stationer
passableness
passibleness
waistcoateer
waistcoating
laisser-aller
laissez-aller
tapsieteerie
laisser-faire
laissez-faire
panspermatic
parsley-piert
tax-sheltered
passage-money
false-hearted
marsh-harrier
Marseillaise
Marsileaceae
salsolaceous
tapsalteerie
tassel-gentle
ear-splitting
passemeasure
passy-measure
facsimileing
haussmannise
haussmannize
parsimonious
passionately
mansion-house
rags-to-riches
Passion-music
nauseousness
May-September
sarsaparilla
passe-partout
mass-produced
basso-relievo
basso-rilievo
massaranduba
masseranduba
causationism
causationist
sansculottic
pansexualism
pansexualist
cantharidine
cantharidian
carte-blanche
earth-created
particularly
pantechnicon
participable
party-capital
participator
fastidiously
zantedeschia
rattle-headed
battlemented
cattle-lifter
cattle-plague
saltpetreman
battleground
tactlessness
maltreatment
faithfulness
tastefulness
wastefulness
cartographic
pantographic
cartographer
pantographer
Mastigophora
faith-healing
farthingland
farthingless
cantillation
cantillatory
dactylically
santalaceous
battological
cartological
tautological
pantaloonery
dactyliology
dactyloscopy
cantilevered
saltimbancos
bantamweight
pantomimical
bastinadoing
cantankerous
Martini-Henry
East-Indiaman
carton-pierre
fast-and-loose
canting-wheel
waiting-woman
factionalism
factionalist
xanthomatous
xanthochroia
xanthochroic
xanthochroid
Gastrocnemii
gastrosopher
gastronomist
gastropodous
captiousness
cautiousness
factiousness
xanthopterin
pantophagist
pantophagous
cartophilist
Dantophilist
lactoprotein
earthquaking
masturbation
masturbatory
bactericidal
halter-necked
Gastarbeiter
matter-of-fact
masterliness
mastersinger
lantern-jawed
pattern-maker
battering-ram
bacteriology
bacteriostat
masterstroke
master-at-arms
garter-stitch
canterburies
lantern-wheel
pattern-wheel
master-switch
earthshaking
Cartesianism
pantisocracy
fantasticate
fantasticism
fantasticoes
partisanship
haptotropism
saltationism
partitionist
saltationist
factitiously
saltatorious
gastrulation
Pasteurellae
Pasteurellas
party-verdict
part-exchange
paludamentum
salutariness
maturational
salutational
naturalistic
salutatorian
salutatorily
manufactural
manufacturer
valuableness
ranunculuses
papuliferous
salutiferous
paludicolous
maquiladoras
vacuum-packed
calumniation
calumniatory
calumniously
naturopathic
fabulousness
salubriously
salvifically
salvage-corps
marvellously
Salviniaceae
galvanically
carving-knife
galvanometer
galvanometry
galvanoscope
malversation
salver-shaped
harvest-feast
harvest-field
harvest-goose
harvest-louse
Salvationism
Salvationist
calycanthemy
baby-batterer
lady's-cushion

laryngectomy
laryngophony
laryngospasm
laryngoscope
laryngoscopy
dasyphyllous
Calyciflorae
labyrinthine
labyrinthian
karyokinesis
Maryolatrous
baby-snatcher
calycoideous
palynologist
papyrologist
many-coloured
lady's-slipper
lady's-thistle
razzle-dazzle
katzenjammer
oblanceolate
ebracteolate
obscurantism
obscurantist
obedientiary
abbey-counter
obsessionist
object-lesson
absent-minded
object-finder
obreptitious
obsequiously
Observantine
obligational
obligatorily
obliterative
obliteration
obliviscence
obligingness
absinthiated
ebullioscope
ebullioscopy
abolitionary
abolitionism
abolitionist
obsolescence
obsoleteness
obcompressed
absorptivity
absoluteness
absquatulate
ubiquitarian
ubiquitously
aberrational
aboriginally
abortiveness
abbreviation
abbreviatory
abbreviature
abstractedly
abstractness
obstreperate
obstreperous
abstemiously
obstropalous
obstropulous
obstetrician
abstruseness
obdurateness
obmutescence
obtuse-angled
obnubilation
above-the-line
scramblingly
scratchbuild
scratchbuilt
scratchiness
scratchingly
scraperboard
scraggedness
occasionally
oceanologist
oceanography
octastichous
octastrophic
scabbardless
scabrousness
academically
accelerative
acceleration
acceleratory
sclerenchyma
screenwriter
sclerodermia
sclerodermic
sclerometric
sclerophylly
accentuation
accentuality
eclectically
scientifical
eccentricity
Schizaeaceae
scribblement
scribblingly
acciaccatura
schindylesis
schindyletic
accidentally
occidentally
schismatical
action-taking
schizocarpic
Echinocactus
echinodermal
schizophrene
schizothymia
schizothymic
schizophytic
echinococcus
schizogonous
schizopodous
schizomycete
scrimshander
scripturally
scriptwriter
scrieveboard
eco-labelling
scullery-maid
ecologically
scalping-tuft
achlamydeous
acclimatiser
acclimatizer
Scolopacidae
scolopaceous
scolopendrid
ochlophobiac
ecclesiastic
Ecclesiastes
ecclesiology
sculpturally
scampishness
ecumenically
scandalously
iconoclastic
ichnographic
scenographic
acanthaceous
Scandinavian
Schneiderian
scanning-disc
scintillator
scintigraphy
iconomachist
economically
econometrics
econometrist
scene-of-crime
iconophilism
iconophilist
scene-painter
scene-shifter
ectoparasite
scholastical
accouchement
accordionist
octogenarian
octopetalous
octosepalous
acrogenously
scrophularia
acrophonetic
scrobiculate
school-taught
schoolmaster
schorlaceous
schoolfellow
school-leaver
school-divine
schoolboyish
school-friend
accommodable
accommodator
acroamatical
echo-sounding
accomplished
accomplisher
accompanyist
acrostically
octostichous
accoutrement
accouterment
acronychally
octosyllabic
octosyllable
scapegoating
scapegallows
scyphistomae
scyphistomas
scapulimancy
scapulomancy
scoptophobia
scoptophilia
scopophiliac
Scorpaenidae
Scarabaeidae
scarabaeuses
acaridomatia
acarodomatia
scarificator
scornfulness
scare-heading
scurrilously
ochroleucous
scoring-board
scissiparity
scissor-tooth
scatterbrain
scatteringly
scattermouch
Scottishness
scutellation
acetaldehyde
scatological
scitamineous
scatophagous
ecstatically
ichthyocolla
ichthyolitic
ichthyolatry
ichthyophagy
accurateness
accusatively
occupational
accusatorial
acquiescence
scrutinising
scrutinizing
scrutinously
acquaintance
accursedness
acoustically
accustrement

12 □c□u□u

accumulative
accumulation
scrupulosity
scrupulously
scavengering
ectypography
Edwardianism
idealisation
idealization
ideationally
advantageous
odd-come-short
edaciousness
educationist
adscititious
adverbialise
adverbialize
adhesiveness
adder's-tongue
adventitious
adjectivally
advisability
additionally
administrate
administrant
adminiculate
addictedness
addle-brained
adulteration
adulterously
edulcorative
edulcoration
idolatrously
identifiable
identifiably
odontomatous
odontophobia
odontophoral
odontophoran
Odontophorus
odontologist
odontography
idiothermous
idiorhythmic
admonishment
idiosyncrasy
adaptability
adaptiveness
adequateness
adorableness
editorialise
editorialize
adjunctively
adjudicative
adjudication
metagalactic
separateness
metalanguage
reparability
separability
beta-carotene
defamatorily
hexadactylic
perambulator
pedal-clavier
decalcomania
melancholiac
recalcitrate
recalcitrant
heraldically
regardlessly
sexagenarian
decalescence
recalescence
hexametrical
metaleptical
decaffeinate
Penang-lawyer
metaphrastic
seraphically
detachedness
hexachloride
metachronism
metathoracic
metaphorical
metaphysical
metathetical
decapitalise
decapitalize
recapitalise
recapitalize
decapitation
delamination
deracination
desalination
gelatination
hepatisation
hepatization
legalisation
legalization
penalisation
penalization
repagination
revalidation
tetanisation
tetanization
velarisation
velarization
negativeness
relativeness
petaliferous
metasilicate
rehabilitate
relativities
relativitist
negativistic
relativistic
relationless
relationship
relationally
hepaticology
behaviorally
recapitulate
behaviourism
behaviourist
seraskierate
metallically
metallogenic
Heracleitean
hexafluoride
metallophone
metallurgist
remainder-man
keraunograph
retainership
metagnathous
demagnetiser
demagnetizer
megalomaniac
metasomatism
teratomatous
Ceratosaurus
megalosaurus
hepatomegaly
hematogenous
keratogenous
melanochroic
senatorially
keratoplasty
hematologist
hepatologist
nematologist
teratologist
Nematomorpha
metamorphism
metamorphist
metamorphose
melanotropin
ceramography
nematocystic
pedal-pushers
repatriation
metapsychics
telaesthesia
telaesthetic
pedantocracy
pedantically
semantically
departmental
Telautograph®
tenant-at-will
denaturalise
denaturalize
desaturation
peradventure
metalworking
decasyllabic
decasyllable
legacy-hunter
bedazzlement
Rembrandtish
Rembrandtism
kerb-merchant
feeble-minded
pebble-powder
heeby-jeebies
verbenaceous
reabsorption
kerb-crawling
deuch-an-doris
merchandiser
merchandizer
teachability
neoclassical
merchantable
merchantlike
peace-breaker
peach-blossom
beachcombing
peacock-stone
leucocytosis
peccadilloes
geochemistry
rescheduling
mercifulness
peacefulness
henceforward
deactivation
reactivation
reactiveness
peace-keeping
tercel-jerkin
tercel-gentle
pencil-sketch
reach-me-downs
fence-mending
sexcentenary
tercentenary
mercantilism
mercantilist
descensional
geocentrical
peace-officer
leucoplastid
perceptivity
perceptional
leucopoiesis
mercurialise
mercurialize
mercurialism
mercurialist
Neo-Christian
Neoceratodus
percussively
percussional
percutaneous
reoccupation
bench-warrant
peace-warrant
peach-yellows
readableness
vendibleness
hendecagonal
mendaciously

Words marked △ may be spelled also with a capital letter

heedlessness
needlessness
reed-pheasant
headshrinker
bend-sinister
headmistress
readmittance
hebdomadally
ready-moneyed
dead-and-alive
Heldentenöre
Heldentenors
geodynamical
weeding-tongs
dendrologist
dendrologous
readaptation
feldspathoid
tender-hefted
Neo-Darwinism
Neo-Darwinian
Neo-Darwinist
geodetically
headquarters
readjustment
rendezvoused
rendezvouses
vegetatively
revelational
generatrices
benefactress
heterauxesis
remembrancer
remembrances
rememberable
rememberably
reverberator
beseechingly
telescopical
repercussive
repercussion
degenerately
degenerative
regenerative
degenerating
deceleration
degeneration
regeneration
regeneratory
teleservices
never-failing
gem-engraving
telergically
revengefully
hebephreniac
terephthalic
genethliacal
genethliacon
téléphérique
hereditament
hereditarian
veterinarian
hereditarily
remedilessly
beneficently
feverishness
repetitively
redefinition
beneficially
repetitional
televisional
veneficously
terebinthine
televisually
Gesellschaft
genealogical
teleological
levelling-rod
rebelliously
redeployment
determinable
determinably
determinedly
telesmatical
perenniality
Gemeinschaft
hereinbefore
redecoration
Hemerocallis
heterogamous
heterotactic
heterodactyl
heteroecious
heterocercal
heterosexism
heterosexist
heteromerous
benevolently
heterosexual
heterophylly
heterothally
heterochrony
renegotiable
semeiotician
ceremonially
heteroplasia
heteroblasty
heteroplasty
heteroclitic
telecommuter
Heterosomata
selenologist
heterogonous
heterologous
heteronomous
heteromorphy
Heterocontae
heterokontan
heterotrophy
selenography
generousness
telesoftware
heterostyled
△heteroousian
heterocyclic
heterozygote
heterozygous
level-pegging
redemptioner
Redemptorist
peremptorily
metempirical
meteorically
meretricious
meteorograph
meteorologic
teleprompter
peregrinator
telegraphese
telegraphist
meteoritical
terebratulae
terebratulas
cerebrotonia
cerebrotonic
reversionary
secessionism
secessionist
teleostomous
desensitiser
desensitizer
teleosaurian
Nepenthaceae
decentralise
decentralize
fenestration
receptaculum
receptacular
dejectedness
dementedness
nevertheless
resettlement
seventy-eight
neverthemore
relentlessly
rejectamenta
defectionist
receptionist
rejectionist
retentionist
cement-copper
detectophone
teleutospore
cementitious
deregulation
reregulation
lese-humanity
venepuncture
hebetudinous
deservedness
reservedness
receiving-set
receivership
heresy-hunter
self-sameness
self-catering
pen-feathered
self-absorbed
perfectation
perfectively
self-activity
self-schooled
self-occupied
self-educated
self-adhesive
self-identity
self-advocacy
perfidiously
self-reverent
self-deceived
self-deceiver
self-reliance
self-devotion
self-begotten
self-reproach
self-betrayal
selflessness
self-destruct
self-delusion
self-effacing
self-affected
self-thinking
self-directed
self-director
self-lighting
self-righting
self-disliked
self-violence
self-rigorous
self-distrust
self-cleaning
self-pleasing
perfoliation
self-elective
self-electing
self-election
self-glorious
self-flattery
self-employed
self-interest
self-endeared
self-anointed
newfangledly
self-analysis
self-involved
self-coloured
self-consumed
self-portrait
self-contempt
self-focusing
self-applause
self-approval
performative
self-creation

reefer-jacket
self-ordained
self-gracious
self-produced
perfervidity
Jeffersonian
self-prepared
self-critical
self-assembly
new-fashioned
perfusionist
self-standing
Newfoundland
self-murderer
self-judgment
self-luminous
self-evidence
self-exciting
self-exertion
self-existent
self-hypnosis
geographical
sergeantship
sergeant-fish
neighborless
neighborhood
neighbouring
hedge-creeper
veggie-burger
vengefulness
seigniorship
seignioralty
pergameneous
hedge-mustard
Zeuglodontia
geognostical
hedge-parsley
ledger-tackle
beggarliness
Geiger-Müller
hedge-sparrow
weight-lifter
tergiversate
hedge-warbler
methodically
dephlegmator
hephthemimer
technicality
technicolour
aethrioscope
Neohellenism
nephological
nephelometer
cephalometry
nephelometry
mechanically
methanometer
technobabble
technomaniac
dethronement
technophobia
technophobic
nephrologist
technologist
technography
technocratic
technostress
nephroptosis
methaqualone
Netherlandic
Netherlander
Mechitharist
methotrexate
mechatronics
hemiparasite
semiparasite
celibatarian
pericarditis
delicateness
semi-water-gas
delicatessen
medicamental
derivatively
meditatively
hesitatingly
definability
desirability
heritability
revivability
dedicational
derivational
revivalistic
semipalmated
dedicatorial
pelican's-foot
reliableness
meniscectomy
bewitchingly
seriocomical
heliocentric
heliochromic
rediscoverer
periodically
periodontics
periodontist
bewilderment
deliberately
semi-detached
deliberative
demineralise
demineralize
desiderative
remineralise
remineralize
mediaevalism
deliberation
desideration
Semi-Pelagian
mediaevalist
delitescence
revivescence
revivescency
periselenium
perinephrium
semipellucid
pedicellaria
semideponent
perimetrical
perineuritis
penitentials
penitentiary
residentiary
residentship
delivery-pipe
delivery-tube
semi-official
heliographic
heliographer
feeing-market
heliogravure
teeing-ground
periphrastic
benightening
perichaetial
perichaetium
delightfully
Hemichordata
decipherable
peripherical
decipherment
perichoresis
legitimately
debilitative
delimitative
demilitarise
demilitarize
debilitating
debilitation
delimitation
felicitation
feminisation
feminization
legitimation
revisitation
Semitisation
Semitization
verification
semifinalist
veridicality
verificatory
devil-in-a-bush
semicircular
reminiscence
resipiscence
reviviscence
resipiscency
reviviscency
semiliterate
decisiveness
definiteness
derisiveness
feminineness
decitizenise
decitizenize
resiniferous
seminiferous
retiringness
reciting-note
definitively
semi-finished
verisimility
definitional
verisimilous
semi-diameter
religionless
meridionally
felicitously
periwig-pated
aecidiospore
demi-distance
semiglobular
aetiological
semiological
legislatress
heliolatrous
semi-imbecile
devil-may-care
Legionnaire's
Legionnaires'
perionychium
resignedness
Helianthemum
semi-annually
semicomatose
demi-mondaine
lepidomelane
lexicologist
hemimorphite
hemimorphism
perimorphous
lexicography
meritocratic
desirousness
perilousness
hemispheroid
heliophilous
perispomenon
delinquently
semi-Arianism
reciprocally
peritrichous
semi-precious
reciprocator
semi-tropical
periostracum
semi-attached
registration
revictualled
heliotherapy
belittlement
peristrephic
resistlessly
redintegrate
geriatrician

Words marked △ may be spelled also with a capital letter

redistribute
meristematic
peristomatic
deviationism
heliotropism
deviationist
mediatorship
peristeronic
geniculately
reticulately
geniculation
pediculation
reticulation
vesiculation
venipuncture
meticulously
deliquescent
demi-culverin
devil-worship
semicylinder
pericynthion
serjeantship
benjamin-tree
leukocytosis
fecklessness
recklessness
weak-mindedly
leukemogenic
Pecksniffian
keeking-glass
neck-moulding
leukoplastid
leukopoiesis
weak-spirited
weal-balanced
well-balanced
well-mannered
well-favoured
pellucidness
neglectfully
reflectively
neglectingly
reflectingly
reflectivity
deflectional
reflectogram
Della-Cruscan
oeils-de-boeuf
well-educated
re-alteration
well-deserved
well-becoming
well-tempered
well-affected
mellifluence
deflagration
geologically
neologically
belligerence
belligerency
well-timbered
well-directed
well-disposed
well-pleasing
well-plighted
belly-landing
mealy-mouthed
replantation
declensional
declinometer
well-informed
selling-price
△wellingtonia
reallocation
de-alcoholise
de-alcoholize
bell-bottomed
well-breathed
hellgrammite
tellurometer
well-dressing
well-grounded
seclusionist
belletristic
deflationary
reflationary
deflationist
replevisable
yellowhammer
yellow-rattle
fellow-member
yellow-rocket
yellow-yowley
Velloziaceae
permeability
reimbattell'd
dermabrasion
vermiculated
permaculture
vermiculture
Fehmgerichte
Vehmgerichte
geomagnetism
geomagnetist
gemmological
permanganate
fermentative
fermentation
segmentation
Germanically
vermin-killer
Germanophile
Germanophobe
hermeneutics
hermeneutist
re-embodiment
reimposition
reimpression
permissively
hermetically
geometrician
permittivity
dermatophyte
deambulatory
reimbursable
re-engagement
pernoctation
vernacularly
perniciously
reannexation
reinvestment
△neandertaler
geanticlinal
reinvigorate
re-enlistment
fennel-flower
neonomianism
reunionistic
deontologist
reinspection
mean-spirited
Gesneriaceae
Keynesianism
tennis-racket
Jenny-spinner
tennis-player
deinotherium
reinstalment
penny-wedding
penny-whistle
teensy-weensy
resonance-box
desolateness
decoratively
denotatively
derogatively
pejoratively
demoralising
demoralizing
memorability
removability
revocability
derogatorily
serotaxonomy
debonairness
aeronautical
redoublement
deforciation
reconcilable
reconcilably
heroicalness
heroi-comical
record-sleeve
record-player
second-to-none
venom'd-mouth'd
recordership
second-strike
seronegative
rejoneadores
mesocephalic
xerodermatic
aeroneurosis
recomforture
decongestant
decongestive
decongestion
oesophagitis
henotheistic
mesothelioma
mesothoracic
denominative
denomination
depositation
detoxication
memorisation
memorization
peroxidation
demoniacally
velocipedean
aerosiderite
velocipedian
velocipedist
becomingness
zero-dividend
depoliticise
depoliticize
depositional
hemodialysis
devotionally
negotiatress
recollective
recollection
aeroplankton
ceroplastics
deformedness
aeroembolism
△mesoamerican
decommission
recommission
recommitment
refoundation
renounceable
denouncement
renouncement
resoundingly
reconnoitrer
recognisable
recognisably
recognisance
recognizable
recognizably
recognizance
decoloration
levorotatory
metoposcopic
seropositive
demonologist
mesomorphous
xeromorphous
decorousness
venomousness
decompressor
decomposable

Words marked △ may be spelled also with a capital letter

12 □e□o□r

leiotrichous
resourceless
melodramatic
hemorrhoidal
cerographist
democratical
deconsecrate
reconsecrate
remorsefully
reconstitute
demonstrable
demonstrably
remonstrance
demonstrator
remonstrator
repossession
gerontocracy
besottedness
below-the-line
gerontophile
gerontophobe
aerostatical
demodulation
depopulation
resoluteness
revolutional
△resolutioner
revolutioner
seropurulent
resolvedness
reconversion
reconveyance
aerodynamics
depolymerise
depolymerize
genotypicity
deepwaterman
deepwatermen
temptability
Neoplatonism
Neoplatonist
bespectacled
respectfully
respectively
resplendence
resplendency
perplexingly
reappearance
helplessness
hemp-agrimony
deoppilative
deoppilation
temptingness
despairingly
despoliation
geopolitical
weeping-cross
responseless
respondentia
serpent-eater
despondently

leaping-house
responsively
serpentinely
despondingly
serpentinise
serpentinite
serpentinize
serpentining
serpentiform
serpentinous
responsorial
serpent-stone
jet-propelled
pepper-caster
pepper-castor
leap-frogging
temporalness
temperalitie
respirometer
temporaneous
jeopardously
leopard's-bane
despisedness
perpetualism
perpetration
perpetuation
perpetualist
perpetuality
despotocracy
despotically
despitefully
herpetofauna
herpetologic
sempiternity
geophysicist
desquamative
desquamation
desquamatory
sesquitertia
perquisition
sesquialtera
neuroanatomy
reproachable
reproachless
decreasingly
learnability
recreational
neorealistic
bearableness
terribleness
heartbreaker
jerry-builder
neurobiology
heartburning
depreciative
ferricyanide
ferrocyanide
depreciation
retractation
depreciatory
tetracycline

detractively
retractively
detractingly
refractivity
retractility
tetrachordal
refractorily
tetrachotomy
get-rich-quick
retrocessive
reprocessing
retrocession
reproducible
reproductive
reproduction
tetradactyly
petrodollars
Tetradynamia
recrudescent
depredations
tetrodotoxin
retrievement
fearlessness
peerlessness
pearl-essence
neurofibroma
febrifacient
petrifactive
petrifaction
terrifically
retroflexion
retroflected
terrifyingly
heart-failure
terraforming
pearl-fishery
pearl-fishing
retrofitting
petrographic
reprographic
necrographer
petrographer
reprographer
tetragonally
ferrugineous
neurogenesis
petrogenesis
petrogenetic
refrigerator
merry-go-round
petroglyphic
tetrahedrite
tetrahedrons
reprehensive
reprehension
reprehensory
neurohormone
reordination
Hebraistical
dearticulate
retrojection

cedrelaceous
metrological
necrological
neurological
petrological
retromingent
recriminator
tetramorphic
Febronianism
detruncation
retrenchment
dégringolade
heortologist
heir-apparent
necrophagous
neuropterans
neuropterist
neuropterous
tetrapterous
necrophiliac
retrophiliac
necrophilism
negrophilism
negrophilist
necrophilous
retropulsive
retropulsion
metropolises
necropolises
metropolitan
tetrapolitan
necrophorous
neurypnology
neuropeptide
decrepitness
neuropathist
petrophysics
tetrarchical
metrorrhagia
heart-rending
terror-struck
decrustation
decrescendos
pearl-sheller
refreshfully
neurasthenia
neurasthenic
regressively
repressively
depressingly
refreshingly
tetrastichic
tetrastichal
regressivity
neuroscience
refreshments
representant
tetrasporous
neurosurgeon
neurosurgery
heart-service

heart-strings
depressurise
depressurize
neurotically
heart-to-heart
deerstalking
merrythought
neurotrophic
pearl-tapioca
secretariate
defraudation
depravedness
retroversion
heartwarming
heir-by-custom
newsmagazine
newspaperdom
newspaperism
newspaperman
persuasively
sensualistic
feasibleness
sensibleness
pease-bannock
pease-blossom
reassemblage
reassessment
perspectival
versificator
message-stick
deaspiration
perspiration
perspicacity
perspiratory
reassignment
Messeigneurs
verslibriste
tessellation
persulphuric
personifying
geosynclinal
leasing-maker
seasoning-tub
seismonastic
session-clerk
seismoscopic
seismometric
session-house
teaspoonfuls
seismologist
seismography
sensuousness
pease-pudding
menstruation
Besserwisser
sensorimotor
measuring-rod
censoriously
dessertspoon
geostrategic
persistently

persistingly
densitometer
sensitometer
densitometry
sensationism
sensationist
reassuringly
reassumption
perseverance
perseverator
Gentianaceae
left-handedly
septuagenary
Septuagesima
meat-salesman
reattachment
neutralistic
Septuagintal
restrainable
restrainedly
vertebration
destabiliser
vestibulitis
destabilizer
pentacrinoid
lenticellate
verticillate
nectocalyces
verticalness
verticillium
lenticularly
denticulated
testiculated
gesticulator
geotechnical
geotectonics
Pentecostals
death-dealing
sextodecimos
pentadactyle
pentadactyly
testudineous
weatherboard
feather-brain
heather-bleat
weather-bound
fent-merchant
leather-cloth
weathercloth
beetleheaded
feather-grass
leathergoods
featheriness
aesthesiogen
heathenishly
aestheticise
aestheticize
aestheticism
aesthetician
aestheticist
leather-knife

kettle-holder
weatherproof
beetle-browed
restlessness
Zeitvertreib
kettlestitch
beatifically
certificated
testificator
meat-offering
left-of-centre
pettifoggery
pettifogging
hectographic
pentagonally
pentahedrons
ventripotent
ventriloqual
restrictedly
pestological
centillionth
pestilential
dentilingual
bertillonage
gentilitious
septilateral
Pestalozzian
Septemberish
centumvirate
septemvirate
testamentary
vestimentary
Septembriser
Septembrizer
tectonically
Teutonically
pectinaceous
pertinacious
meeting-house
sententially
septennially
sentinelling
nesting-place
resting-place
melting-point
septentrions
resting-stage
resting-spore
jesting-stock
dextrocardia
sectionalise
sectionalize
sectionalism
sectionalist
centroclinal
Bertholletia
deltiologist
centrosphere
dextrousness
dextrogyrate
deutoplasmic

centuplicate
pentapolitan
heat-apoplexy
perturbative
sectarianise
sectarianize
Nestorianism
sectarianism
centuriation
perturbation
perturbatory
neoterically
letter-weight
welterweight
heater-shield
pectoriloquy
Deuteronomic
deuteranopia
deuteranopic
teeter-totter
deuteroplasm
letter-writer
deuteroscopy
dentirostral
rectirostral
reiteratedly
testosterone
centesimally
leptosomatic
pentateuchal
restaurateur
restauration
destructible
death-warrant
bequeathable
bequeathment
reputatively
secularistic
benumbedness
renunciative
denunciation
renunciation
denunciatory
renunciatory
pedunculated
resuscitable
resuscitator
recuperative
remunerative
recuperation
rejuvenation
remuneration
recuperatory
remuneratory
detumescence
oecumenicism
nebulisation
nebulization
resupination
delusiveness
dehumidifier

12 □e□u□i

deducibility
reducibility
denuclearize
genuflection
sequentially
nebulousness
sedulousness
beaumontague
verumontanum
resumptively
desulphurate
desulphurise
desulphurize
resurrective
△resurrection
tenuirostral
Berufsverbot
revulsionary
sequestrable
sequestrator
Jesuitically
reductionism
reductionist
serviceberry
pervicacious
servocontrol
servicewoman
heavy-hearted
merveilleuse
heaven-fallen
heavenliness
heaven-gifted
perviousness
nerve-racking
perverseness
renversement
velvet-scoter
servitorship
velvet-guards
between-decks
betweentimes
benzaldehyde
mezzo-relievo
mezzo-rilievo
mezzo-soprano
afterburning
effeminately
effectuation
effectuality
affectedness
affectionate
afterthought
effervescent
Afrikanerdom
office-seeker
office-bearer
office-holder
office-hunter
afficionados
effiguration
affluentness
efflorescent
afforestable
Afrocentrism
Afro-American
off-reckoning
affrightedly
affrightment
affrightened
affrontingly
aforethought
offscourings
off-the-record
effusiveness
effusiometer
egg-and-anchor
egg-and-tongue
egg-apparatus
agreeability
ignitability
uglification
ignitibility
egoistically
agribusiness
agricultural
agalmatolite
agglomerated
agglutinable
agglutinogen
agamogenesis
agent-general
agrochemical
agroindustry
agroforestry
agrobusiness
Egyptologist
aggressively
agathodaimon
pheasant's-eye
phraseograph
phraseologic
phrasemonger
sheath-winged
shealing-hill
chiaroscuros
theatrically
theatromania
theatrophone
theanthropic
rhabdosphere
thick-and-thin
chick-a-diddle
shockability
checkerboard
checkerberry
shockingness
checking-room
chuckie-stane
chuckie-stone
phycological
chocolate-box
Phycomycetes
thick-sighted
thick-skinned
thick-skulled
checkweigher
phycoxanthin
rhododendron
shudderingly
rhodomontade
Rhodophyceae
shadow-boxing
chrematistic
three-centred
thief-catcher
shield-maiden
Threadneedle
shield-bearer
shield-shaped
cheeseparing
cheesetaster
cheese-rennet
cheesemonger
cheesehopper
cheeseburger
cheesecutter
cheerfulness
threeha'porth
chaetiferous
sheeling-hill
shieling-hill
cheerishness
sheepishness
shrewishness
thievishness
phlegmagogic
phlegmagogue
phaeomelanin
three-monthly
phlegmatical
phaenogamous
phlebotomise
phlebotomize
phrenologise
phrenologize
phlebotomist
phrenologist
three-pricker
three-pounder
Phaeophyceae
three-quarter
sheep-stealer
sheepshearer
sheep-scoring
chieftainess
chrestomathy
phreatophyte
three-wheeler
shuffle-board
whigmaleerie
phagocytical
phagocytosis
Whiggishness
thigmotactic
thigmotropic
chain-breaker
chaise-longue
chain-gearing
thrivingness
shriving-time
sheiling-hill
shrill-voiced
shrill-gorged
chairmanship
cheiromantic
chrisom-cloth
cheirologist
cheirography
cheiropteran
christianise
christianize
Christianism
Christianity
thriftlessly
Christliness
Christolatry
christophany
Christ's-thorn
chiliahedron
philharmonic
chalcanthite
childbearing
child-bearing
childcrowing
chalicothere
△philadelphus
△philodendron
philhellenic
Phalaenopsis
whale-fishery
whale-fishing
phylogenesis
phylogenetic
whole-hearted
shillingless
shilling-hill
childishness
philological
philanthrope
philanthropy
phyllotactic
thallophytic
Chalcolithic
chalcography
phallocratic
chalcopyrite
cholerically
thalassaemia
thalassaemic
Philistinise
Philistinize
△philistinism
whole-skinned
shellshocked

Words marked △ may be spelled also with a capital letter

philosophess
philosophise
philosophize
philosophism
philosophist
phillumenist
cheluviation
shilly-shally
chalazogamic
whimperingly
chimney-sweep
shamefacedly
shamefulness
rhamphotheca
whimsicality
championship
Chimonanthus
rhombohedral
rhombohedron
chimerically
rhumb-sailing
thematically
chemotherapy
chemotropism
shamateurism
chymotrypsin
phantasmical
phantasmally
phonocamptic
rhinocerical
rhinoceroses
rhinocerotic
rhinocerotes
thundercloud
thunder-drive
chance-medley
thunderflash
thunderingly
thunderously
whencesoever
thunder-plump
thunder-sheet
thunder-stone
thunderstorm
thankfulness
phonographic
phonographer
Rhinegravine
Rhynchonella
Rhynchophora
phenological
phonological
rhinological
phenylalanin
phonemically
phenomenally
phengophobia
rhinoplastic
chondroblast
Phanerogamia
phanerogamic
Phanerogamae
rhinorrhoeal
rhinorrhagia
chondriosome
phanerophyte
chondrostian
phonasthenia
△thanksgiving
phonotactics
phonetically
phenotypical
phonotypical
thingummybob
thingummyjig
shunt-winding
thank-you-ma'am
chlorambucil
Theopaschite
theopathetic
chromaticism
chromaticity
thiobacillus
chromatogram
chromatopsia
thrombolytic
theorematist
theoretician
rheometrical
through-going
through-other
through-stane
through-stone
theophylline
chlorination
chlorimetric
thiodiglycol
theopneustic
theologaster
chlorometric
chronometric
theosophical
chromophilic
chromophonic
chronologise
chronologize
chronologist
chloroformer
chromosphere
theomorphism
chronography
theocratical
throttle-pipe
throstle-cock
phrontistery
thiosulphate
chaplainship
Rhipidoptera
shepherdless
shepherdling
chapterhouse
Chaplinesque
whipping-post
rhopaloceral
whip-and-derry
whippoorwill
shopbreaking
whip-grafting
shipbuilding
chiquichiqui
charlatanism
thereagainst
whereagainst
pharmaceutic
pharmacology
cherubically
thirdborough
chart-busting
short-changer
characterful
characterise
characterize
characterism
sharecropper
share-capital
short-circuit
thoracoscope
thoracostomy
Charadriidae
charter-chest
Thurberesque
Charterhouse
thirteenthly
charterparty
chorographic
chirographer
chorographer
church-parade
churchwarden
churchianity
churchpeople
shareholding
Churchillian
thereinafter
churlishness
Thermidorian
whortleberry
chorological
sharp-looking
Chironomidae
pharyngology
pharyngotomy
thermolabile
thermotactic
thermoscopic
thermometric
thermophilic
chordophonic
thermosiphon
Theriomorpha
thermocouple
Theriodontia
thermosphere
thermotropic
chartography
choreography
thermography
thermostable
thermostatic
chiropractic
chiropractor
chiropterous
sharp-pointed
Choripetalae
therapeutics
therapeutist
chirurgeonly
short-staffed
shirtsleeves
sharp-sighted
short-sighted
sharpshooter
sharp-tongued
sharp-toothed
thyrotrophin
short-termism
short-termist
therethrough
wherethrough
thoroughfare
thorough-bass
thoroughness
△thoroughbred
shirtwaister
Third-Worlder
cherry-laurel
thirty-second
cherry-pepper
thirty-twomos
chorizontist
whiskerandos
chesterfield
whisperingly
whisperously
chassé-croisé
phospholipid
phosphoresce
phosphaturia
chastisement
whistle-drunk
Thysanoptera
Thesmophoria
physiognomic
physiologist
physiography
physiocratic
whisky-frisky
white-bearded
white-bellied
phytobenthos
photobiology
photochemist
white-crested
white-crowned

12 □h□t□c

photocopying
photochromic
rhytidectomy
photoelastic
shatter-brain
photo-etching
chitterlings
shatterproof
thitherwards
whitherwards
white-fronted
photofission
photographic
phytographic
photographer
phytographer
photogravure
phytogenesis
phytogenetic
photogeology
photoglyphic
what's-her-name
phytohormone
what's-his-name
what's-its-name
photokinesis
white-knuckle
phytological
shot-blasting
white-livered
rhythmically
rhythmometer
photomontage
rhythmopoeia
phytonadione
phytophagous
photophilous
photo-process
photorealism
rhetorically
Photostatted
photospheric
photosetting
phototherapy
phototropism
photovoltaic
thousand-year
thousand-legs
thousandfold
rheumatismal
thaumatogeny
rheumatology
thaumatology
thaumaturgic
thaumaturgus
shoulder-high
thoughtfully
ghoulishness
chauvinistic
chivalrously
shaving-brush
shaving-stick
Rhizocephala
rhizocarpous
rhizogenetic
rhizophagous
rhizophilous
dilatability
bioavailable
disanalogous
disambiguate
air-ambulance
disaccharide
financialist
disaccordant
lizard-hipped
Pirandellian
bicameralism
bilateralism
dilaceration
bicameralist
disaventrous
disaffection
disaffiliate
disaggregate
vicar-general
dilapidation
divarication
vitalisation
vitalization
vitativeness
titaniferous
Sivapithecus
misallotment
disallowable
disallowance
disannulment
disannulling
Titanosaurus
dilatoriness
limacologist
misapprehend
disappointed
dicarpellary
cicatrichule
disagreeable
disagreeably
disagreement
disassociate
kinaesthesia
kinaesthesis
kinaesthetic
disassembler
didactically
gigantically
gigantomachy
disauthorise
disauthorize
disastrously
misanthropic
misanthropos
Sinanthropus
Simarubaceae
miraculously
disadvantage
disadventure
misadventure
misadvisedly
bibble-babble
gibble-gabble
ribble-rabble
nimble-witted
nimble-footed
air-breathing
misbehaviour
diabolically
misbelieving
timbromaniac
timbrologist
disbursement
nimbostratus
disbowelling
disclamation
mischanceful
pitch-and-toss
mischallenge
aircraftsman
pisciculture
pinchcommons
piccadilloes
viscoelastic
discreteness
discretively
circle-riding
discretional
biochemistry
kitchen-knave
biocoenology
pitcher-plant
kitchen-range
kitchen-stuff
discreetness
kitchen-wench
zincographic
discographer
zincographer
miscegenator
discriminate
discriminant
circuitously
miscellanist
miscalculate
circumjacent
circumscribe
Discomycetes
Discomedusae
discomedusan
circumcentre
discomfiting
circumcision
discomfiture
circumfluent
circumfluous
discommodity
air-commodore
circumlocute
discomposure
circumstance
circumnutate
circumfusile
circumfusion
discommunity
circumgyrate
discandering
disconnexion
disconnected
discontented
miscontented
air-condition
disconsolate
misconstruct
disceptation
discipleship
disciplinant
disciplinary
discophorous
discordantly
discursively
discorporate
discerptible
viscerotonia
viscerotonic
circassienne
viscosimeter
viscosimetry
discouraging
discountable
viscountship
discourteise
discourteous
discoverable
discoverture
bird-catching
bird-watching
misdiagnosis
Hildebrandic
vindictively
vindicatress
fiddle-faddle
middleweight
kiddiewinkie
middle-income
niddle-noddle
mindlessness
fiddlesticks
fiddle-string
tiddledywink
wind-changing
disdainfully
mind-altering
misdemeanant
misdemeanour
sindonophany
birding-piece

Words marked △ may be spelled also with a capital letter

12 □i□i□g

winding-sheet
bird's-nesting
hindforemost
mind-boggling
Hindoostanee
kindergarten
misdirection
hindquarters
biodiversity
fire-watching
cinematheque
cinemathèque
literariness
mixed-ability
liberalistic
literalistic
mineralogise
mineralogize
mineralogist
vinegar-plant
vinegarrette
disembrangle
disembellish
disembarrass
disenchanter
disendowment
time-bewasted
mine-detector
nineteenthly
lifelessness
timelessness
tirelessness
live-feathers
vice-chairman
kinesipathic
dimerisation
dimerization
tigerishness
fire-fighting
kinesiatrics
pinealectomy
wineglassful
Hibernianism
pigeon's-blood
hibernaculum
Hibernically
life-and-death
life-interest
pigeon-flying
line-engraver
tiresomeness
vice-governor
siderophilic
time-honoured
wine-coloured
site-specific
wide-spectrum
Liverpudlian
fixed-penalty
Didelphyidae
wisecracking
timed-release
birefringent
fireproofing
diseasedness
diversifying
diversionary
diversionist
disestablish
liberticidal
diverticulum
diverticular
wire-stringed
divertimenti
divertimento
dilettantish
bicentennial
dilettantism
licentiously
river-terrace
directorship
wire-stitched
miseducation
hire-purchase
pile-dwelling
wife-swapping
time-exposure
timely-parted
disfranchise
diffrangible
pin-feathered
bioflavonoid
misfeaturing
difficulties
kilfud-yoking
misformation
differentiae
differential
diffusedness
diffusionism
diffusionist
disgradation
biographical
diagrammatic
singableness
king's-cushion
ringed-plover
single-handed
single-parent
dingle-dangle
higgle-haggle
jingle-jangle
mingle-mangle
wiggle-waggle
disgregation
single-acting
single-action
single-decker
single-seater
single-minded
single-wicket
single-figure
wing-shooting
disguiseless
disguisement
linguistical
virgin's-bower
singing-hinny
ring-compound
diageotropic
biogeography
ring-dotterel
ring-armature
disgorgement
fingerlickin'
finger-and-toe
ring-dropping
disgustfully
disgustingly
ring-streaked
gingivectomy
fish-hatchery
right-and-left
fish-salesman
disheartened
highfaluting
night-brawler
night-crawler
nightclothes
nightclubber
high-reaching
eighteenthly
eighteen-hole
high-velocity
high-seasoned
rightfulness
night-fishery
lithographic
lithographer
light-hearted
diphthongise
diphthongize
diphtheritic
diphtheritis
mithridatise
mithridatize
mithridatism
high-five-sign
high-fidelity
ditheistical
lithological
△ditheletical
litholatrous
lightning-bug
lightning-rod
Siphonaptera
Siphonophora
siphonophore
dishonorable
dishonorably
siphonostele
wishing-stone
dichromatism
dichroscopic
withholdment
aichmophobia
high-sounding
high-coloured
dichrooscope
sight-playing
lithophagous
lithophilous
hip-hip-hooray
tithe-proctor
high-spirited
hip-hip-hurrah
sight-reading
cichoraceous
witheredness
high-priestly
bilharziasis
bilharziosis
dithyrambist
disharmonise
disharmonize
high-pressure
withdrawment
lithospermum
xiphisternum
lithospheric
sight-singing
fish-strainer
lithotritise
lithotritize
lithotritist
lithotriptic
lithotripter
lithotriptor
right-to-lifer
lithotomical
high-stepping
dishevelment
dishevelling
highty-tighty
highly-strung
visitational
militaristic
divinatorial
visitatorial
viviparously
mini-lacrosse
pitiableness
disincentive
Cicindelidae
liriodendron
viridescence
virilescence
pitilessness
disinflation
disinfectant
disinfection
misinformant
bilingualism
riding-master

12 □i□i□g

riding-school
disingenuity
disingenuous
disinherison
citification
civilisation
civilization
digitisation
digitization
minification
minimisation
minimization
nidification
vilification
vinification
virilisation
virilization
vivification
divisiveness
siliciferous
visiting-card
visiting-book
diminishable
diminishment
vitilitigate
visibilities
divisibility
libidinosity
silicicolous
libidinously
bimillennium
bimilleniums
mini-motorway
minicomputer
ministrative
ministration
sinistrality
disintegrate
disintricate
sinistrorsal
sinistrously
disinterment
sinisterwise
disinterring
misinterpret
diminutively
diminuendoes
ridiculously
vinicultural
filibusterer
miminy-piminy
niminy-piminy
misjudgement
disjointedly
sickle-celled
sickle-shaped
kickie-wickie
ticklishness
nickel-silver
milking-stool
kicking-strap
milk-and-water
misknowledge
milk-porridge
pickerel-weed
lick-trencher
wicket-keeper
ticket-office
ticket-holder
ticket-porter
ticket-writer
lickety-split
sick-building
mickey-taking
kicksy-wicksy
billiard-ball
misleadingly
Lillibullero
Lilliburlero
dialecticism
dialectician
dialectology
dislocatedly
digladiation
dislodgement
williewaught
tirlie-wirlie
will-lessness
millefeuille
biologically
rifle-grenade
diplogenesis
yieldingness
villainously
mill-sixpence
rifleman-bird
diplomatical
violoncellos
billingsgate
violin-string
bibliomaniac
bibliopegist
bibliophobia
mill-mountain
bibliologist
bibliopolist
pillion-rider
kill-courtesy
bibliography
Bible-pounder
miller's-thumb
field-spaniel
millisievert
millesimally
will-o'-the-wisp
Bible-thumper
tilley-valley
biomechanics
diamagnetism
pigmentation
diamond-drill
diamond-field
Simmenthaler
diamond-hitch
diamond-wheel
Jimmy-o'Goblin
jimmy-o'goblin
Kimmeridgian
mismatchment
biometrician
dismayedness
diencephalon
pinniewinkle
significance
significancy
significator
fiendishness
giant-killing
limnological
Bignoniaceae
limnophilous
ligniperdous
giant's-kettle
winnowing-fan
kidney-potato
mixobarbaric
pilot-balloon
disoperation
disobedience
△risorgimento
disorganised
disorganized
mitochondria
ricochetting
nicotinamide
simoniacally
disorientate
picornavirus
rigorousness
timorousness
vigorousness
ailourophile
ailourophobe
timocratical
ribonuclease
misogynistic
displaceable
displacement
misplacement
diaphanously
Hippocratise
Hippocratize
Hippocratism
hippocrepian
hippocentaur
ripple-marked
nipple-shield
simple-minded
displeasedly
displeasance
disprivacied
disprivilege
dispensative
dispensation
dispensatory
Hispanically
hispaniolise
hispaniolize
mispunctuate
mispronounce
dispropriate
hippophagist
hippophagous
hippopotamic
hippopotamus
diapophysial
dispiritedly
dispiritment
dispossessed
dispossessor
dispatch-boat
dispiteously
disputatious
dispauperise
dispauperize
biophysicist
disqualified
disqualifier
disquisitive
disquisition
disquisitory
disquietness
misquotation
microanatomy
nitro-aniline
fibroblastic
micro-brewery
microbalance
nitrobenzene
microbiology
microclimate
vibracularia
cirro-cumulus
misreckoning
microcephaly
microcopying
microcapsule
picrocarmine
microcircuit
vitro-di-trina
vitrifaction
vitrifacture
microfilaria
hierographic
micrographic
hierographer
micrographer
microgranite
microgravity
hierogrammat
disregardful
ditriglyphic
hieroglyphic
microhabitat

Words marked △ may be spelled also with a capital letter

piercingness
mitrailleuse
fibrillation
Gibraltarian
hierological
micrological
disrelishing
nitromethane
Dibranchiata
dibranchiate
fibrinolysin
vitriolation
diprionidian
vitreousness
hierophantic
misrepresent
micropterous
disruptively
nitrophilous
microprinted
bipropellant
vibraphonist
micropipette
disreputable
disreputably
microphysics
hierarchical
mirror-writer
nitroso-group
digressively
microseismic
digressional
microscopist
microsurgeon
microsurgery
cirro-stratus
microtubular
nitrotoluene
microtomical
migrationist
vibratiuncle
sir-reverence
microwavable
biorhythmics
misstatement
dissuasively
dissocialise
dissocialize
dissociative
dissociation
dissociality
fissicostate
tissue-typing
kirschwasser
bioscientist
missel-thrush
fissilingual
missummation
dissymmetric
dissemblance
dissimilarly

dissimulator
disseminated
disseminator
kissing-crust
dissenterish
dissenterism
first-nighter
biosynthesis
biosynthetic
dissentingly
missionarise
missionarize
dissipatedly
dissertative
tin-streaming
dissertation
diastrophism
fissirostral
biosatellite
dissatisfied
disseverment
disseverance
filtrability
distrainable
distrainment
mistranslate
distractible
distractedly
histochemist
eisteddfodic
eisteddfodau
birthday-book
birthday-suit
mixtie-maxtie
tittle-tattle
mistle-thrush
diathermancy
Little-endian
listlessness
mistressless
mistress-ship
mistreatment
mirthfulness
pictographic
histogenesis
histogenetic
Sittlichkeit
histrionical
distributary
distributive
distribution
mistakenness
distillation
distillatory
histological
Mitteleuropa
Mittel-Europa
diatomaceous
distemperate
tintinnabula
diatonically

distanceless
Nintendoitis
listenership
distinctness
fictionalise
fictionalize
Histiophorus
virtuosoship
virtuousness
disturbative
Victorianism
filter-passer
mixter-maxter
pitter-patter
historically
pictorically
winter-weight
winter-beaten
picture-frame
picture-house
sisterliness
sisters-in-law
historiology
winterbourne
victoriously
Picturephone®
winter-ground
dietetically
Uintatherium
fictitiously
dictatorship
distrustless
mistrustless
diethylamine
figuratively
figurability
sinupalliate
Sipunculacea
vituperative
vituperation
vituperatory
figure-caster
lieutenantry
liquefacient
liquefaction
liturgically
liturgiology
dijudication
dilucidation
Liguliflorae
liguliforal
sinusoidally
ailurophobia
ailurophobic
ailurophilia
ailurophilic
bibulousness
simultaneity
simultaneous
liqueur-glass
silviculture

mid-Victorian
misventurous
silver-beater
silver-glance
silver-plated
silver-voiced
Midwesterner
cityfication
pityrosporum
mizzen-course
skrimshanker
skullduggery
skillfulness
skinny-dipper
skipping-rope
skirt-dancing
skateboarder
skutterudite
skittishness
skittle-alley
sky-tinctured
skeuomorphic
pleasantness
pleasantries
Alhambresque
alkalescence
alkalescency
pleasingness
clear-obscure
clear-sighted
olfactometry
olfactronics
altaltissimo
illaqueation
pleasure-pain
pleasureless
clubbability
slubberingly
blabbermouth
globigerinae
slobbishness
flabellation
flabelliform
ill-beseeming
plebiscitary
globetrotter
black-and-blue
electability
elucubration
placableness
blackballing
blackbirding
blockbusting
blackcurrant
slockdolager
cliché-ridden
flickeringly
slickensided
glockenspiel
black-figured
black-fishing

12 □l□c□g

blackguardly
glycogenesis
glycogenetic
black-hearted
blacklisting
placentation
placentiform
placentology
Plectognathi
glaciologist
black-pudding
plecopterous
glucoprotein
glycoprotein
black-quarter
electrically
electrifying
electrograph
electrogenic
electrolysis
electrolytic
electromeric
electrometer
electromotor
electrometry
electron-volt
electro-optic
electroplate
electrophile
electropolar
electrosonde
electroscope
electroshock
electrotonic
electrotonus
electrotypic
electrotyper
elocutionary
elocutionist
flocculation
black-visaged
clock-watcher
gladiatorial
gladiatorian
sledgehammer
bladderwrack
cladogenesis
cloddishness
gladsomeness
cladosporium
alienability
alterability
Elaeagnaceae
sleeping-suit
illegitimate
illegitimacy
illegibility
alder-liefest
aldermanship
aldermanlike
glue-sniffing
ulcerousness
eleemosynary
bluestocking
sleepwalking
cliffhanging
old-fashioned
sluggishness
flagellation
flagellatory
flagelliform
sloganeering
plagiotropic
oligarchical
oligotrophic
flagitiously
alpha-blocker
alphabetical
alphamerical
alphanumeric
clairaudient
pleiochasium
plainclothes
all-inclusive
plain-dealing
illiterately
alliterative
illiberalise
illiberalize
alliteration
illiberality
altimetrical
plain-hearted
fluidisation
fluidization
illimitation
clair-obscure
all-important
ellipsograph
elliptically
cleistogamic
pleiotropism
altitudinous
clairvoyance
clairvoyancy
flammability
plumbaginous
clamjamphrie
blamableness
plumber-block
plummer-block
glimmeringly
slumberingly
slumberously
slumpflation
blamefulness
flame-grilled
alembication
flammiferous
plumbiferous
blimpishness
plumulaceous
alimentative
elementalism
alimentation
flamboyantly
plum-porridge
flame-thrower
flammulation
plano-concave
plano-conical
blanc-de-Chine
flannelboard
clinker-built
flannelgraph
blunderingly
slanderously
flint-hearted
clincher-work
glandiferous
slantingways
clannishness
blandishment
flint-knapper
clangorously
blennorrhoea
plenipotence
plenipotency
blind-stamped
planispheric
ill-naturedly
planetesimal
planet-struck
glandulously
slang-whanger
allowability
pleonastical
blood-brother
fluorescence
fluoridation
fluorination
illogicality
fluorimetric
floodlighted
glioblastoma
bloodletting
all-or-nothing
fluorocarbon
fluoroscopic
fluorometric
fluorochrome
pleomorphism
pleomorphous
blood-pudding
bloodstained
bloodsucking
fly-on-the-wall
bloodthirsty
bloody-minded
slip-carriage
elephant's-ear
flippantness
clapperboard
slipperiness
slop-clothing
kleptomaniac
glyphography
glyptography
kleptocratic
klipspringer
claptrappery
cliquishness
floriculture
plurilocular
pluriliteral
ultramontane
ultramundane
ultroneously
clarinettist
gloriousness
clare-obscure
ultrasensual
pluriseriate
all-roundness
slash-and-burn
glossarially
glass-blowing
close-cropped
glass-cutting
plasterboard
plasteriness
blusteringly
glisteringly
blister-steel
plasterstone
blissfulness
flashforward
blast-furnace
close-fitting
close-grained
classicalism
classicalist
classicality
plessimetric
classifiable
close-mouthed
Plesiosaurus
plasmosomata
glossologist
blastosphere
elasmobranch
glossography
flesh-pottery
close-tongued
blastulation
glassyheaded
Platt-Deutsch
bletheration
clothes-brush
clothes-horse
clatteringly
flatteringly
glitteringly
flitter-mouse

Words marked △ may be spelled also with a capital letter

blithesomely
flatterously
clothes-press
bletherskate
blatherskite
clothes-sense
ill-treatment
slothfulness
elytrigerous
sluttishness
Ulotrichales
plate-leather
platonically
platanaceous
alstroemeria
gluttonously
slate-writing
glaucescence
slouch-hatted
slaughterman
slaughterous
plough-jogger
ploughwright
eleutherarch
illuminative
illuminating
claudication
illumination
allusiveness
illusiveness
plausibility
pleurisy-root
cloud-kissing
glaucomatous
Pleuronectes
cloud-seeding
illustrative
claustration
illustration
illustratory
clavicembalo
slaveholding
eleventh-hour
slovenliness
cloven-hoofed
cloven-footed
pluviometric
clever-clever
clownishness
blow-moulding
flower-garden
flower-delice
flower-de-luce
flower-deluce
flexibleness
alexipharmic
playing-field
immaterially
embarquement
ambassadress
empassionate
impassionate
impartiality
embattlement
immaculately
immatureness
amicableness
imperatively
imperatorial
impercipient
imperceptive
impenetrable
impenetrably
imperfective
imperfection
imperforable
imperforated
immethodical
impedimental
impenitently
imperishable
imperishably
impetiginous
Umbelliferae
impermanence
impermanency
immemorially
ampelography
impersonally
impersonator
immersionism
immersionist
immeasurable
immensurable
immeasurably
impersistent
impertinence
impertinency
imperviously
embezzlement
emigrational
amygdaloidal
image-worship
amphibrachic
amphictyonic
amphigastria
omphalomancy
amphisbaenic
amphistomous
emphatically
amphitheatre
amphitropous
omnisciently
immiseration
ambidextrous
umbilication
imbibitional
ambitionless
omnipotently
impierceable
omnipresence
embitterment
amalgamative
amalgamation
small-clothes
implicitness
emollescence
smallholding
emolumentary
emblematical
implantation
ameliorative
amelioration
emblazonment
amenableness
emancipation
emancipatory
amentiferous
amontillados
immovability
imponderable
immoderately
immoderation
smooth-leaved
smooth-coated
smooth-spoken
smooth-browed
impoliteness
imposingness
embourgeoise
empoisonment
imposthumate
impregnation
umbrageously
amortisation
amortization
emargination
amortisement
amortizement
umbrella-bird
umbrella-tree
Amarantaceae
embranchment
embryologist
ombrophilous
impropriator
ombrophobous
empressement
impressively
imprisonable
imprisonment
improvidence
improvisator
smash-and-grab
omissiveness
amissibility
emasculation
emasculatory
imitableness
smotheriness
smatteringly
smotheringly
emotionalism
emotionality
amitotically
amateurishly
ambulanceman
imputatively
immutability
imputability
immunisation
immunization
immunologist
empyreumatic
unmanageable
unmanageably
endamagement
incapacitate
incapability
unsalability
unparalleled
uncatalogued
unwatchfully
unsanctified
unsanctioned
incalculable
incalculably
uncalculated
unvaccinated
uncandidness
one-and-thirty
unpardonable
unpardonably
unhandsomely
incandescent
incatenation
incalescence
unwaveringly
unlawfulness
enlargedness
entanglement
endangerment
unfathomable
unfathomably
inhabitation
insalivation
insanitation
invagination
invalidation
unsatisfying
engagingness
unfadingness
unvariegated
sneakishness
unpavilioned
unfamiliarly
unhabituated
unmarketable
unsailorlike
enharmonical
inharmonical
inharmonious
unharmonious
unmaintained

12 □n□a□n

ungainliness
antagonistic
unfavourable
unfavourably
unvanquished
unpatronised
unpatronized
unpassionate
uncapsizable
infanticidal
unfastidious
unfaithfully
antasthmatic
incautiously
antarthritic
unnaturalise
unnaturalize
unsaturation
insalubrious
unobtainable
inobediently
inobservable
unobservable
unobservedly
inobservance
unobservance
snobographer
snobbishness
anabaptistic
inabstinence
unobstructed
snack-counter
sneck-drawing
snicker-snack
inaccessible
inaccessibly
unacceptable
unscientific
unacceptance
inactivation
knocking-shop
unscriptural
unachievable
knick-knacket
knuckle-bones
knuckle-joint
unsculptured
uneconomical
anecdotalist
unaccredited
unicorn-shell
unicorn-whale
anacatharsis
anacathartic
unscottified
inaccurately
inoccupation
unacquainted
unaccustomed
unscrupulous
unidealistic
inadvertence
inadvertency
unadventrous
unadvertised
inadmissible
inadmissibly
unadulterate
unidentified
unadmonished
inadaptation
inadequately
inseparables
unrewardedly
under-and-over
underachieve
untenability
unremarkable
unrecallable
unrepairable
untenantable
underbearing
underblanket
interbedding
enfeeblement
underbuilder
interchanger
enterchaunge
interchapter
once-accented
unmercifully
unpeacefully
intercolline
intercalated
intercommune
interconnect
interconvert
underclothed
underclothes
intercropped
intercipient
interceptive
unperceptive
interception
intercurrent
undercurrent
intercession
intercessory
interclusion
underdrawing
incendiarism
interdictive
interdiction
interdictory
underdressed
interdigital
engenderment
underdevelop
intemerately
inveterately
inteneration
unremembered
undependable
△independence
△independency
unregenerate
unregeneracy
antecedently
unrevengeful
unbeneficial
antemeridian
unrepealable
unrevealable
unredeemable
indetermined
undetermined
ungenerously
uncelebrated
indefeasible
indefensible
indefeasibly
indefensibly
indefectible
indetectable
indetectible
undelectable
undetectable
unrepeatable
interestedly
unrepentance
undeceivable
undeservedly
unreservedly
unperfection
interfretted
interfoliate
interfemoral
underfunding
interfrontal
interfertile
unperforming
interference
unperforated
interfluence
interglacial
inveiglement
undergarment
unmethodical
unmethodised
unmethodized
encephalitic
encephalitis
unmechanical
under-hangman
unmechanised
sneeshin-mull
unmechanized
indelicately
unseminaried
unhesitating
ingemination
insemination
angelica-tree
indehiscence
undeliberate
unregimented
unperishable
undelightful
unverifiable
indecisively
indefinitely
unrepiningly
indelibility
infelicitous
undesignedly
unresistible
unremittedly
unregistered
antediluvial
antediluvian
unbelievable
unrelievable
unbelievably
unrelievedly
interjection
interjacency
unreckonable
underkingdom
interkinesis
interlobular
intellective
unreflective
unreflecting
intellection
interlocutor
intellectual
intelligible
intelligibly
intelligence
interlaminar
indeclinable
indeclinably
index-linking
interlingual
underletting
undermeaning
intermediate
intermediacy
intermediary
intermeddler
unseemliness
intermontane
intermundane
interminable
interminably
unterminated
intermissive
intermission
intermittent
intermaxilla
intermixture
indemnifying
internalised
internalized

Words marked △ may be spelled also with a capital letter

internuncial
internuncios
internetting
interorbital
unreconciled
unheroically
interoceanic
interoceptor
unbecomingly
anaerobiosis
anaerobiotic
unreformable
unrecognised
enteropneust
unrecognized
Enteromorpha
indecorously
undecomposed
undemocratic
unremorseful
interosseous
unreportable
enteroptosis
unresolvable
unrespective
interpretate
interpleader
interpretess
interpretive
interpleural
enterprising
undespairing
interpellate
interpellant
interpolable
interpolater
interpolator
unresponsive
underpinning
underpeopled
under-produce
intemperance
underperform
intempestive
underpassion
underpowered
underpayment
unreproached
unbefriended
knee-breeches
unterrifying
interrogable
unsegregated
interrogatee
interrogator
interregnums
unsearchable
unsearchably
unwearyingly
knee-trembler
underrunning
anteprandial
knee-crooking
interruptive
interruption
unrefreshing
unreprovable
understanded
understander
understaffed
unpersuasive
unsensualise
unsensualize
undersealing
interspatial
interstadial
intersection
unpersecuted
undersheriff
under-sheriff
interstellar
interspersal
intensifying
interstitial
underskinker
inter-science
interspinous
unreasonable
unseasonable
unreasonably
unseasonably
undersurface
unmeasurable
unmeasurably
interservice
uncensorious
understratum
unsensitised
unsensitized
intertraffic
unrestrained
Invertebrata
invertebrate
indebtedness
ungentleness
unsettlement
anaesthetise
anaesthetize
anaesthetics
anaesthetist
investigable
investigator
entertaining
intertwining
unrestricted
undertakable
unfertilised
unventilated
unfertilized
undertenancy
incestuously
infectiously
unbetterable
under-turnkey
entertissued
intertissued
intertexture
unsepulchred
underutilise
underutilize
unreturnable
unrepulsable
unrequitedly
intervocalic
intervenient
intervention
interwreathe
underwriting
interwrought
underwrought
under-workman
knife-and-fork
ineffaceable
ineffaceably
ineffability
snuff-dipping
unaffectedly
snifter-valve
knife-grinder
unofficially
inefficiency
unaffiliated
snaffling-lay
unifoliolate
anagrammatic
sniggeringly
anagogically
snaggleteeth
snaggletooth
knightliness
knight-errant
enthrallment
anthocarpous
unshadowable
uncheerfully
unthreatened
enshrinement
encheiridion
unshrinkable
unthriftyhed
unchristened
unchallenged
anthelmintic
unchangeable
unchangeably
unthankfully
enchantingly
unchangingly
unthinkingly
enchondromas
enthronement
unchronicled
anthropoidal
anthropogeny
anthropogony
anthropology
anthropotomy
anthophilous
unchaperoned
incharitable
uncharitable
uncharitably
anchoretical
anchoritical
antherozooid
enthusiastic
unchasteness
unrhythmical
unthoughtful
unchivalrous
anthoxanthin
antimalarial
antihalation
antiparallel
antimacassar
antibarbarus
antibacchius
envisagement
anticatholic
antipathetic
antirachitic
indicatively
anti-national
anti-Gallican
antiparticle
unmiraculous
enviableness
anti-abortion
undischarged
encirclement
indiscretely
indiscretion
indiscreetly
indiscipline
undiscipline
undiscordant
undiscerning
undiscording
angiocarpous
undiscovered
unriddleable
unkindliness
incineration
antimetabole
antipetalous
antisepalous
antiperiodic
unlikeliness
unliveliness
untimeliness
anti-Semitism
unlikelihood
engine-fitter
△antilegomena

Words marked △ may be spelled also with a capital letter

12 □n□i□e

indigenously
engine-driver
indigestible
indivertible
indigestibly
undivestedly
indirectness
antineutrino
incidentally
engine-turned
indifference
indifferency
angiogenesis
inking-roller
antiphrastic
unrightfully
antichthones
antitheistic
antiphonical
antiphonally
antithrombin
unwithholden
antithetical
annihilative
anticipative
annihilation
anticipation
intimidation
invigilation
anticipatory
intimidatory
anti-aircraft
incisiveness
infiniteness
invitingness
infinitively
undiminished
incivilities
invisibility
unlibidinous
antidiuretic
individually
unwieldiness
unyieldingly
undiplomatic
anticlerical
undismantled
antimnemonic
oneiromancer
invigoration
undisordered
antisocially
oneirocritic
indisputable
indisputably
undisputedly
undispatched
antifriction
anti-predator
antigropelos
antipruritic
unbiasedness
Angiospermae
angiospermal
indissoluble
indissolubly
undissolving
undissembled
angiostomous
angiosarcoma
infiltrative
infiltration
undistracted
unfittedness
unmistakable
unmistakably
unlistened-to
indistinctly
antistrophic
antistrophon
unvirtuously
unfilterable
unhistorical
undisturbing
infibulation
unliquidated
anticyclonic
snake-charmer
unpleasantly
unpleasantry
unpleasingly
unelaborated
inflectional
Anglocentric
analogically
unflaggingly
analphabetic
uncloistered
inflammation
inflammatory
unslumbering
unblinkingly
inclinometer
△anglophobiac
ineloquently
ingloriously
unblushingly
unclassified
inelasticity
Englishwoman
analytically
enclitically
unflattering
inflationary
inflationism
inflationist
unilaterally
unamiability
inimicalness
inimicitious
animadverter
anemographic
unimaginable
unimaginably
unembittered
unimolecular
animalculism
animalculist
unemployable
unemployment
gnomonically
unimportuned
unimportance
anemophilous
anamorphoses
anamorphosis
unimpressive
unimprisoned
mnemotechnic
animatronics
onomatopoeia
onomatopoeic
unimpugnable
unendangered
uninterested
anencephalia
anencephalic
unintegrated
unenthralled
unendingness
enantiomeric
enantiomorph
enantiopathy
enantiostyly
enantiotropy
uninfluenced
unanalysable
unanalytical
unanalyzable
unintroduced
uninstructed
unencumbered
unincumbered
unanswerable
unanswerably
endoparasite
untowardness
endocarditis
unvoyageable
unmoralising
unmoralizing
infotainment
unromantical
undoubtingly
unconcealing
insouciantly
inconcinnity
inconcinnous
unconcerning
inconclusive
unconclusive
inconclusion
intoleration
unforewarned
uncovenanted
intolerantly
indoleacetic
encomenderos
unforeseeing
incoherently
indomethacin
uncomeliness
unloveliness
Indo-Germanic
ungovernable
ungovernably
unmodernised
unmodernized
unforeboding
endometritis
snooperscope
uncomeatable
unconfinable
unconfinedly
unconforming
unconformity
unconfusedly
incoagulable
unforgivable
endophyllous
Oncorhynchus
incogitative
intoxicating
intoxication
unionisation
unionization
innominables
unnoticeable
unpoliteness
unlovingness
unpolishable
unmodifiable
antoninianus
unsolicitous
unsocialised
andouillette
unsocialized
endoskeletal
endoskeleton
entoplastral
entoplastron
informidable
unformidable
incommodious
unformalised
unformulated
unformalized
endosmometer
uncommonness
uncommercial
incommutable
incommutably
announcement
uncounselled

Words marked △ may be spelled also with a capital letter

insomnolence
incognisable
incognisance
oncornavirus
incognizable
incognizance
incoronation
entomologise
entomologize
entomologist
Entomostraca
incompletely
incompletion
incompliance
incomparable
incomparably
incorporeity
incorporated
incorporator
uncomposable
incompatible
incomputable
inhospitable
unhospitable
incompatibly
inhospitably
incompetence
incompetency
uncompounded
incorrodible
incorrigible
incorrigibly
inco-ordinate
incorruptive
incorruption
incorrosible
unnourishing
inconstantly
unconsecrate
unconsidered
unworshipful
unworshipped
inconsolable
inconsolably
unfossilised
unfossilized
inconsumable
inconsumably
unconsenting
inconsonance
inconsequent
unconstraint
inconsistent
unpossessing
unpoetically
unwontedness
incontiguous
indoctrinate
unworthiness
incontinence
incontinency
uncontrolled
unpopularity
undocumented
incomunicado
insolubilise
insolubilize
insolubility
involutional
endonuclease
Indo-European
uncoquettish
inconvenient
unconvincing
inconversant
unconversant
endosymbiont
unapparelled
snap-fastener
unspectacled
inspectingly
inspectional
inspectorate
inspectorial
snippetiness
unappetising
unappetizing
inappellable
unappealable
inappeasable
unappeasable
anapaestical
snapshooting
snappishness
inapplicable
unapplicable
inapplicably
unapologetic
unapplausive
inappositely
unapproached
unoppressive
inoperculate
inspissation
anaphylactic
inequipotent
iniquitously
unornamented
unornamental
unbreachable
unbreathable
unbreathed-on
encroachment
entreatingly
increasingly
intracranial
unproclaimed
unprocedural
ungracefully
androcentric
ungraciously
unprocurable
intracardiac
ineradicable
introducible
ineradicably
introductive
unproductive
introduction
introductory
ungrudgingly
uncreditable
unfriendship
unfriendlily
engraftation
unprofitable
unprofitably
intriguingly
unoriginated
unfrightened
unprohibited
anarchically
unorthodoxly
enarthrodial
anarthrously
inordinately
inordination
entraînement
unfruitfully
unerringness
snarling-tool
snarling-iron
inartificial
unartificial
unartistlike
inarticulate
unarticulate
inarticulacy
introjection
unprejudiced
unbrokenness
unprelatical
untrammelled
intramundane
untremendous
intromissive
intromission
intromittent
intromitting
entrancement
infringement
entrenchment
intrenchment
unfranchised
intrinsicate
intransigent
intransitive
unprincipled
untranslated
untransmuted
unpronounced
infraorbital
enormousness
entrepreneur
intrapreneur
unpreparedly
unpropertied
unpropitious
unfrequented
infrequently
unfrequently
incrassative
encrustation
incrassation
incrustation
incrossbreed
androsterone
unprosperous
untrustiness
intrusionist
oniroscopist
unprescribed
ingratiating
ingratiation
uncritically
ungratefully
untruthfully
unprettiness
unpretending
unprotesting
ungroundedly
intrauterine
untroubledly
unprovidedly
unprevailing
unprovokedly
unprivileged
introversive
introvertive
introversion
ingravescent
unassailable
one-sidedness
unascendable
unascendible
unusefulness
unaspiringly
anastigmatic
unassignable
unassistedly
unassociated
uniseriately
inosculation
inescutcheon
unassumingly
unisexuality
unsteadiness
unstratified
unattainable
unattainably
unstableness
gnotobiotics
gnotobiology
unstockinged

12 □n□t□e

anathematise
anathematize
unutterables
anotherguess
installation
instillation
anatomically
unstimulated
unstanchable
unctuousness
△unitarianism
unattractive
unsterilised
unsterilized
unstatutable
unstatutably
instauration
instrumented
instrumental
instructible
instructress
instructions
enstructured
unstructured
undulatingly
incurability
insurability
pneumaticity
pneumatology
incunabulist
encumbrancer
encumberment
annunciative
△annunciation
injunctively
unguiculated
insusceptive
unsuccessful
unsuccessive
unpunctuated
infundibulum
infundibular
intumescence
unsupervised
insufflation
insufficient
unsufficient
insufferable
unsufferable
insufferably
unauthorised
unauthorized
unpunishable
unpunishably
inaudibility
infusibility
injudicially
unmunitioned
insubjection
induplicated
anguilliform
unsublimated
one-upmanship
unsubmissive
unsubmitting
unguentarium
unquenchable
unquenchably
unquantified
invulnerable
unvulnerable
invulnerably
pneumothorax
pneumococcus
unsuspecting
inauspicious
unauspicious
unsuspicious
unsuppleness
unsuppressed
unsupposable
insurrection
innutritious
unsubsidised
unsubsidized
unquestioned
unsubscribed
intussuscept
inquisitress
invultuation
unsustaining
industrially
intuitionism
intuitionist
uncultivable
uncultivated
inauguration
inauguratory
untumultuous
uneventfully
universalise
universalize
Universalism
Universalist
universality
unoverthrown
snow-gatherer
knowableness
knowledgable
knowledgably
snow-in-summer
snowboarding
unswervingly
enswathement
inexpansible
inexhaustive
inexactitude
inexecutable
inexpedience
inexperience
inexpediency
inextensible
unexpectedly
inexpertness
inexpectancy
unextenuated
inextirpable
inexplicable
inexplicably
inextricable
inextricably
inexpressive
unexpressive
inexpungible
unexpurgated
inexpugnable
unexpugnable
inexpugnably
unhyphenated
encyclopedia
encyclopedic
Ankylosauria
Ankylosaurus
enzymologist
enhypostasia
enhypostatic
unsystematic
tobacco-heart
non-alcoholic
monarchistic
tobacco-pouch
non-addictive
cowardliness
towardliness
nonagenarian
monadelphous
Boraginaceae
cohabitation
focalisation
focalization
localisation
localization
moralisation
moralization
nomadisation
nomadization
polarisation
polarization
Romanisation
Romanization
solarisation
solarization
totalisation
totalitarian
totalization
vocalisation
vocalization
volatileness
polarimetric
womanishness
Foraminifera
non-alignment
vocationally
donatistical
morality-play
corallaceous
non-admission
somatotensic
somatopleure
potamologist
gonadotropic
somatotropic
gonadotropin
somatotropin
polarography
somatostatin
solar-powered
woman-queller
noradrenalin
non-absorbent
monastically
romantically
non-automatic
non-attention
vocabularied
vocabularian
forbearingly
roebuck-berry
bombacaceous
forbiddingly
bobby-dazzler
double-handed
Combretaceae
double-dagger
double-banked
double-manned
double-acting
double-headed
double-header
double-decked
double-decker
double-dealer
gobbledegook
double-charge
double-minded
double-biting
double-figure
non-breakable
double-glazed
double-tongue
double-locked
double-formed
double-dotted
double-bottom
double-storey
double-bubble
gobbledygook
sorbefacient
doubtfulness
bomb-disposal
mosbolletjie
morbilliform
combinations
Hobbesianism

Words marked △ may be spelled also with a capital letter

conclamation
nonchalantly
forcibleness
coachbuilder
concubitancy
coccidiostat
concremation
concrescence
concreteness
zoochemistry
force-feeding
forcefulness
voicefulness
conchiferous
moschiferous
touchingness
conciliative
porcellanise
porcellanite
porcellanize
conciliation
porcellanous
conciliatory
concelebrate
concelebrant
porcelainise
porcelainize
porcelainous
non-combatant
bow-compasses
non-committal
non-complying
concomitance
concomitancy
non-communion
volcanically
concentering
forcing-house
coscinomancy
concentrical
concentrator
hog-constable
non-conductor
conchologist
concupiscent
coacervation
concordantly
concurrently
concertinaed
concorporate
non-Christian
non-custodial
torch-thistle
Low-Churchism
Low-Churchman
conclusively
Gondwanaland
hoodman-blind
word-painting
conductivity
mordaciously
word-deafness
good-tempered
woodlessness
wood-offering
woodshedding
cold-shoulder
Cordaitaceae
condemnation
condemnatory
goldsmithery
wordsmithery
condensation
woodenheaded
sodden-witted
voiding-lobby
wood-engraver
cold-moulding
hood-moulding
wondrousness
coadaptation
conduplicate
good-breeding
powder-skiing
powdering-tub
wondermonger
wonder-worker
word-wrapping
wonder-struck
conditionate
conditioning
lord-superior
word-building
good-humoured
road-surveyor
woodburytype
dodecandrous
moderateness
dodecahedral
dodecahedron
dodecaphonic
tolerability
nose-painting
forecarriage
dodecagynian
dodecagynous
lower-bracket
moveableness
honey-buzzard
money-changer
nomenclative
nomenclature
non-Euclidean
honeycombing
power-dressed
fore-admonish
Domesday-book
co-dependency
tone-deafness
foreseeingly
homelessness
hopelessness
movelessness
tonelessness
non-executive
non-efficient
non-effective
powerfulness
foreign-built
money-grubber
togetherness
monetisation
monetization
novelisation
novelization
cohesiveness
covetiveness
foresightful
cohesibility
homesickness
coletitmouse
solecistical
non-existence
nomenklatura
nosebleeding
powerlifting
moneylending
foreclosable
homeomorphic
honey-mouthed
fore-and-after
governmental
governorship
foreknowable
solenoidally
foregoneness
lonesomeness
forebodement
foretokening
forebodingly
lovelornness
rose-coloured
cometography
none-so-pretty
covetousness
noteworthily
coleopterist
coleopterous
corespondent
homeopathist
code-breaking
home-produced
home-crofting
rope-drilling
power-sharing
forensically
money-spinner
non-essential
home-straight
homesteading
potentiation
potentiality
domesticable
domestically
lomentaceous
domesticated
domesticator
homeothermic
homeothermal
forestalment
forestalling
momentaneous
honey-tongued
molecularity
forejudgment
forequarters
come-by-chance
non-flammable
confabulator
Confucianism
Confucianist
non-fictional
confectioner
confidential
rooflessness
non-flowering
confrontment
confirmative
confirmation
conformation
confirmatory
conferencing
conferential
conférencier
god-forgotten
confiscation
confiscatory
confusedness
confessional
confessoress
confoundedly
zoographical
congratulate
congratulant
hobgoblinism
Volga-Baltaic
longicaudate
congregation
tongue-tacked
boogie-woogie
rough-grained
longshoreman
soughing-tile
long-distance
bougainvilia
dough-kneaded
congeniality
congenerical
logging-stone
doughnutting
congenitally
conglobation
conglomerate
zoogeography

12 □o□g□o

gorgeousness
conglobulate
hodge-pudding
longipennate
rough-perfect
long-breathed
loggerheaded
long-drawn-out
longitudinal
forgettingly
long-standing
conglutinate
conglutinant
rough-wrought
Rochelle-salt
sophomorical
nothingarian
doch-an-dorach
oophorectomy
motherliness
mothers-in-law
mother-liquor
motherfucker
sophisticate
solitariness
nominatively
motivational
volitational
nominalistic
holidaymaker
sociableness
sociobiology
morigeration
vociferation
police-manure
bodice-ripper
vociferosity
vociferously
Cominformist
potichomania
modificative
codification
mobilisation
mobilization
modification
nobilitation
notification
solicitation
modificatory
politicaster
positiveness
solidifiable
positivistic
volitionless
volitionally
solicitously
conidiophore
conidiospore
solifluction
sociological
porismatical
sociometrist
toxicophobia
eosinophilia
eosinophilic
monitorially
toxicologist
horizontally
soliloquiser
soliloquizer
poliorcetics
holistically
non-intrusion
vomiturition
solitudinous
vocicultural
policy-holder
conjunctival
dock-labourer
workableness
book-scorpion
rock-scorpion
cockieleekie
mock-heroical
book-learning
cookie-pusher
cockfighting
workmistress
rock-climbing
poikilotherm
cooking-apple
rocking-chair
working-class
booking-clerk
looking-glass
rocking-horse
cooking-range
rocking-stone
lock-hospital
pocket-pistol
monkey-jacket
monkey-hammer
monkey-flower
donkey-engine
monkey-engine
monkey-tricks
monkey-wrench
monkey-puzzle
toll-gatherer
pollyannaish
pollyannaism
world-beating
collaborator
colluctation
collectively
collectivise
collectivize
collectivism
collectivist
collectivity
folliculated
coelacanthic
bollock-naked
collectorate
soullessness
toploftiness
collegialism
collegiality
zoologically
loblolly-tree
coulombmeter
posliminious
dolly-mixture
collinearity
pollen-basket
bowling-alley
polling-booth
Coelenterata
coelenterate
bowling-green
fowling-piece
boiling-point
rolling-stock
toilsomeness
lollapalooza
colliquative
colliquation
colloquially
dollarocracy
roller-skater
rollerblader
roller-hockey
world-shaking
molluscicide
Molluscoidea
wollastonite
foolish-witty
pollutedness
coalitionism
coalitionist
soul-stirring
collaterally
boulevardier
world-wearied
collywobbles
Hollywoodise
Hollywoodize
hollow-ground
woolly-haired
woolly-headed
motley-minded
woolly-minded
doomwatching
commodiously
Doomsday-book
doom-merchant
formlessness
boy-meets-girl
cosmographic
cosmographer
zoomagnetism
cosmogonical
formaldehyde
cosmological
commemorable
commemorator
commensalism
Rosminianism
commendation
commentation
commensality
commendatory
communicable
communicably
communicator
commencement
△commonwealth
rooming-house
commandingly
tormentingly
common-riding
gormandising
gormandizing
Commandments
communion-cup
communitaire
commensurate
cosmonautics
cosmoplastic
cosmopolitic
cosmopolitan
commorientes
dormer-window
commercially
commissarial
commissariat
boomps-a-daisy
commissioned
commissioner
commiserable
commiserator
cosmetically
dogmatically
noematically
committeeman
dormitory-car
downwardness
foundational
foundationer
fountain-head
fountainless
mountainside
mountain-high
roundaboutly
connubiality
mound-builder
bound-bailiff
coenobitical
bonny-clabber
non-nucleated
connectively
connectivity
sound-carrier
fornicatress

Words marked △ may be spelled also with a capital letter

countenancer
counter-agent
mountenaunce
counterbrace
counterblast
counterbluff
countercharm
counter-claim
corn-merchant
countercheck
counter-drain
counter-flory
counter-force
counter-guard
counter-gauge
lounge-lizard
counsellable
counterlight
countermarch
counteroffer
jointer-plane
counterplead
counterpeise
counterpoise
counterpoint
counter-paled
counter-punch
counterproof
counterscarp
countershaft
counter-sense
counter-tenor
counter-wheel
counter-weigh
somnifacient
pound-foolish
pornographic
pornographer
corn-shucking
corn-chandler
loan-sharking
coincidental
coincidently
counting-room
jointing-rule
moonlighting
pointillisme
pointilliste
poenological
town-planning
somniloquise
somniloquize
somniloquism
somniloquist
somnolescent
somnambulate
somnambulant
somnambulary
round-mouthed
somnambulism
somnambulist
morning-after
morning-glory
down-and-outer
conning-tower
coin-operated
Donnerwetter
country-house
countrywoman
coenospecies
coenesthesia
hound's-tongue
moon-stricken
joint-tenancy
bonnet-monkey
point-to-point
connaturally
county-people
logodaedalic
logodaedalus
monomaniacal
toxocariasis
motor-bicycle
motorcycling
motorcyclist
monometallic
monopetalous
monosepalous
monogenistic
monodelphian
monodelphous
horometrical
Notonectidae
borough-reeve
holophrastic
monotheistic
homothallism
monothalamic
monophyletic
△monotheletic
toxophilitic
do-nothingism
monochromate
monochromasy
monochromist
homochromous
monophyodont
homothermous
ionophoresis
△monophysitic
nomothetical
monofilament
colonisation
colonization
motorisation
motorization
Polonisation
Polonization
solonisation
solonization
doloriferous
soboliferous
soporiferous
monolinguist
borosilicate
non-objective
corollaceous
holoplankton
notoungulate
homoeopathic
homologation
homopolarity
homoeomerous
homoiomerous
locomobility
locomotivity
monopodially
podoconiosis
monopolistic
homoeomorphy
monotonously
homomorphism
homomorphous
monomorphous
mono-compound
dolorousness
sonorousness
Notodontidae
rodomontader
homoeostasis
homoeostatic
homologumena
loxodromical
monodramatic
monographist
rotor-station
motor-scooter
colossus-wise
motor-tractor
monostichous
monostrophic
coloquintida
monocultural
co-polymerise
co-polymerize
monosyllabic
monosyllable
homonymously
complanation
complacently
morphallaxis
complaisance
Torpedinidae
completeness
complemental
complexioned
complexional
compressible
complicative
dolphinarium
complication
comprimarios
complimental
complimenter
non-poisonous
doppelganger
doppelgänger
compellative
compulsative
compellation
compulsatory
compulsively
compulsorily
compensative
compensation
compensatory
componential
companionate
companionway
compunctious
morphologist
morphotropic
morphography
pompholygous
corporealise
corporealize
corporealism
compurgation
corporealist
corporeality
compurgatory
copper-fasten
corporalship
copper-bottom
composedness
compatriotic
hospital-ship
zoopathology
zoophytology
conqueringly
conquistador
journalistic
horribleness
corroborable
corroborator
correctional
correctioner
correctitude
Torricellian
journey-bated
bourgeoisify
Fourieristic
corrie-fisted
fourteenthly
torrefaction
horrifically
horrifyingly
mournfulness
courageously
lorry-hopping
co-ordinately
co-ordinative
co-ordination
coerciveness

Words marked △ may be spelled also with a capital letter

12 □o□r□i

mourning-band
boarding-pike
mourning-ring
mourning-dove
courtierlike
correlatable
board-measure
court-martial
torrentially
horrendously
fourfoldness
coprophagist
coprophagous
coprophilous
poor-spirited
horror-struck
morris-dancer
non-residence
nourishingly
boardsailing
non-resistant
non-resisting
Socratically
doorstepping
corrivalship
constatation
moustache-cup
constabulary
horse-breaker
house-breaker
mouse-buttock
consecrative
consecration
consociation
consecratory
horse-courser
horse-dealing
considerable
considerably
considerance
topside-turvy
zoospermatic
boisterously
conspectuity
dorsiflexion
boastfulness
consignation
consignatory
non-scheduled
house-hunting
house-husband
constipation
worshipfully
roasting-jack
toasting-fork
toasting-iron
conspiringly
solstitially
conscionable
conscionably
constitutive
constitution
constituency
loose-jointed
horse-knacker
housekeeping
forsakenness
consultative
consultation
consultatory
tonsilectomy
consolidated
consolidator
tonsillotomy
consummately
consummative
consummation
consummatory
mouse-milking
horsemanship
cousin-german
consentingly
consentience
Hobson-Jobson
poison-sumach
consensually
forswornness
goose-pimples
gossip-monger
gossip-writer
consequences
consequently
△conservative
△conservatism
conservation
conservatory
conservatrix
constrictive
constructive
constriction
construction
constringent
moss-trooping
monstruosity
conscription
house-steward
consistently
possessively
possessioned
possessional
horseshoeing
consistorial
consistorian
house-sitting
horse-trading
house-trained
horse-trainer
coast-to-coast
forset-seller
fosset-seller
house-to-house
topsy-turvily
moistureless
mousquetaire
dorsiventral
house-warming
housey-housey
contranatant
contrabbasso
contrariness
contrariwise
contradictor
contrapposto
portmanteaus
portmanteaux
contractable
contractible
contractedly
contractural
portrait-bust
contrapuntal
mouth-breeder
porte-bonheur
contubernyal
contabescent
porte-cochère
monticellite
horticulture
non-technical
Southcottian
north-country
tooth-drawing
monts-de-piété
bottle-washer
postmeridian
bottle-slider
bottle-blonde
southernwood
northernmost
southernmost
bottle-holder
pottle-bodied
röntgenology
röntgenogram
bottle-opener
north-eastern
south-eastern
bootlessness
Post-Tertiary
soft-sectored
pontifically
loathfulness
youthfulness
mouth-filling
contignation
contagionist
contagiously
contiguously
doctrinarian
contriteness
contrivement
containerise
containerize
postliminary
postliminous
fortuitously
postmistress
contriturate
contributary
contributive
post-diluvial
contribution
post-diluvian
contributory
postillation
noctilucence
nostological
footslogging
footplateman
footplatemen
bottom-sawyer
zootomically
contumacious
contemplable
contumelious
contemplator
porte-monnaie
contaminable
contemporary
contemporise
contemporize
contemptible
contemptibly
contemptuous
noctambulism
noctambulist
continuative
contentation
continuation
cottonocracy
goat-antelope
contingently
lost-and-found
bolting-hutch
foot-and-mouth
continuously
portentously
doating-piece
postponement
low-thoughted
dogtooth-spar
postpositive
postposition
controllable
do-it-yourself
tortuousness
post-doctoral
fortepianist
forth-putting
foster-parent
foster-father
postgraduate
foot-dragging
forthrightly

Words marked △ may be spelled also with a capital letter

conterminate
conterminant
coat-trailing
contortional
conterminous
foster-sister
posture-maker
postprandial
costermonger
foster-mother
posteriority
contestation
north-seeking
poetastering
south-seeking
contestingly
Montessorian
mouth-to-mouth
Northumbrian
posthumously
north-western
south-western
contextually
post-synching
post-hypnotic
softly-softly
tootsy-wootsy
modulability
loquaciously
volumetrical
monumentally
voluminosity
voluminously
columniation
populousness
coquettishly
locum-tenency
voluptuosity
robustiously
voluptuously
voluntaryism
voluntaryist
convectional
louvre-window
convulsively
convulsional
convalescent
convincement
conveniently
convincingly
conventicler
conventional
conventioner
conversative
conversation
louver-window
convivialist
conviviality
conveyancing
conveyor-belt
pot-walloping

low-watermark
soixante-neuf
Polygalaceae
polygamously
Polyadelphia
molybdenosis
polypetalous
polysepalous
cotyledonary
polydemonism
cotyledonous
polyneuritis
body-checking
polytheistic
polyphyllous
polyphyletic
polyphyodont
polypharmacy
polyrhythmic
rosy-fingered
polysiloxane
polyhistoric
polyglottous
polyembryony
polyanthuses
body-snatcher
Polygonaceae
polytonality
rosy-coloured
polymorphism
polymorphous
pony-trekking
polyurethane
polyisoprene
polyethylene
body-building
polysyndeton
polycythemia
polysyllabic
polysyllable
polymyositis
apparatchiki
apparatchiks
sphacelation
speakerphone
apparentness
sprachgefühl
speaking-tube
apparitional
splay-mouthed
aplanogamete
spear-running
sphairistike
spear-thrower
sprat-weather
specialistic
spectatorial
epicycloidal
specifically
space-heating
Epacridaceae

speckledness
apiculturist
epoch-marking
apocynaceous
spaciousness
speciousness
Epicureanism
spectrograph
apochromatic
spectrometer
spectrometry
spectroscope
spectroscopy
specksioneer
epicuticular
specktioneer
epididymides
apodeictical
epideictical
epidemically
epidemiology
spider-legged
speedboating
upper-bracket
speedballing
appercipient
apperceptive
apperception
appendectomy
appendicitis
splendidness
splendidious
ephemerality
spiegeleisen
ephemeridian
speechmaking
sprechgesang
speechlessly
sprechstimme
splenisation
splenization
sphericality
appetisement
appetisingly
appetizingly
splenomegaly
ephebophilia
speedskating
apfelstrudel
appertaining
Speedwriting®
spiflication
epigrammatic
apagogically
apogeotropic
sphincterial
spring-heeled
springkeeper
spring-bladed
spring-loaded
Ophioglossum

sprightfully
optimisation
optimization
ophiological
ophiolatrous
ophiomorphic
ophiophagous
ophiophilist
spokespeople
spokesperson
apple-blossom
apologetical
Apollinarian
speleologist
apolitically
applausively
applaudingly
span-farthing
spine-bashing
spine-chiller
epencephalic
epencephalon
spinning-mill
spongicolous
spinulescent
opinionately
opinionative
spondoolicks
spongologist
epanorthoses
epanorthosis
spinstership
spinsterhood
opposability
splotchiness
optoacoustic
optometrical
appoggiatura
appositeness
oppositeness
appositional
oppositional
appointments
uproariously
apron-strings
epiphenomena
apoplectical
approachable
spermathecal
approach-shot
spermaphytic
sportability
spermatocele
spermatogeny
spermatozoic
spermatozoid
spermatozoal
spermatozoan
spermatozoon
spermatocyte
appreciative

12 □p□r□c

appreciation
appreciatory
sporadically
spurge-laurel
sportfulness
opera-glasses
sporogenesis
sphragistics
epirrhematic
apprehensive
apprehension
sportiveness
appraisement
sparking-plug
appraisively
spurtle-blade
sporangiolum
sparrow-grass
spermophytic
aperiodicity
spermogonium
spuriousness
appropriator
sporophorous
sportscaster
spire-steeple
sportsperson
oppressively
appressorium
sportswriter
spiritualise
spiritualize
spiritualism
△spiritualist
spirituality
operatically
spiritedness
spiritlessly
spirituosity
episodically
epistemology
opisthodomos
opisthograph
opisthotonic
opisthotonos
episcopalism
episcopalian
epistolarian
epistolatory
apostolicism
apostolicity
apostrophise
apostrophize
epithalamium
epithalamion
ophthalmitis
sputteringly
epitheliomas
apothegmatic
spotlessness
spitefulness
spittle-house
appurtenance
epexegetical
sphygmograph
sphygmometer
sphygmophone
sphygmoscope
square-rigged
square-rigger
equalisation
equalitarian
equalization
equanimously
equatorially
squattocracy
squeaky-clean
equestrienne
equiparation
equivalently
Equisetaceae
equisetiform
squirearchal
equilibrator
equidistance
equivocation
equivocality
equivocatory
equipollence
equipollency
equiprobable
squirrel-cage
squirrel-tail
equimultiple
organ-builder
great-bellied
bread-chipper
broadcasting
breakdancing
pro-and-conned
triadelphous
ornamentally
armamentaria
dreadfulness
breakfast-set
organ-grinder
organ-gallery
triangularly
breathtaking
great-hearted
breathlessly
breathalyser
breathalyzer
preachership
organisation
organization
urbanisation
urbanization
organiser-bag
organizer-bag
creativeness
freakishness
irrationally
organoleptic
urbanologist
organography
preamplifier
break-promise
preassurance
breastplough
breakthrough
breaststroke
breastsummer
creatureship
treasure-city
trabeculated
problematics
tribespeople
proboscidean
proboscidian
tribute-money
probationary
probouleutic
proclamation
proclamatory
orichalceous
traceability
preclassical
trochanteric
crackbrained
truce-breaker
precociously
price-cutting
precedential
bracket-creep
trocheameter
tracheophyte
tracheoscopy
tracheostomy
brickfielder
gracefulness
truck-farming
precognizant
precognitive
precognition
practicalism
practicalist
practicality
trichinellae
trichinellas
fructiferous
brackishness
trickishness
tractibility
practitioner
trichiniasis
frictionless
fractionally
fractionator
fructivorous
Trichiuridae
procellarian
pro-celebrity
pre-Columbian
oracularness
preconscious
tricentenary
pre-cancerous
brick-nogging
precondition
dracontiasis
arachnophobe
preconstruct
proconsulate
iracundulous
tractoration
trachomatous
trichophyton
proctorially
trichotomise
trichotomize
proctologist
trichologist
trichotomous
trochosphere
fractography
graciousness
preciousness
tricephalous
preceptorial
precipitance
precipitancy
precipitator
trichromatic
tricorporate
precariously
prechristian
pre-Christian
precisianism
precisianist
procès-verbal
fricasseeing
trickstering
tricuspidate
precessional
processional
processioner
precisionist
procathedral
preclusively
precautional
brachydactyl
brachycephal
brachygraphy
trachypterus
graduateship
Pre-Dravidian
gradualistic
credibleness
bride-chamber
Traducianism
Traducianist
predictively
productively

Words marked △ may be spelled also with a capital letter

productivity
productional
tridactylous
cradle-scythe
pridefulness
prodigiosity
prodigiously
predigestion
predilection
predominance
predominancy
prudentially
Gradgrindery
tradescantia
tradespeople
iridescently
predesignate
predestinate
predisposing
traditionary
traditionist
creditworthy
predetermine
proditorious
irrelatively
irrepairable
pre-embryonic
friendliness
irrelevantly
free-selector
irreverently
irremediable
irremediably
irrepealable
irrepealably
irredeemable
irredeemably
freeze-drying
irreversible
irreversibly
treelessness
arpeggiation
greengrocery
freewheeling
free-thinking
breech-loader
breeches-buoy
pre-eminently
freezing-down
greenishness
irreciprocal
irremissible
irresistible
irresistibly
irresistance
pre-existence
irreflective
irreflection
pre-eclampsia
irrealisable
irrealizable

irreconciled
gruesomeness
irreformable
irreformably
grievousness
irresolutely
irresolution
irresolvable
irresolvably
irrespective
irresponsive
irrespirable
irrefragable
irrefragably
irreprovable
irreprovably
araeosystyle
pre-establish
orienteering
priest-ridden
priestliness
free-standing
irregularity
irrebuttable
free-swimming
creepy-crawly
prefabricate
proficiently
prefectorial
draft-dodging
profligately
triflingness
prefoliation
craftmanship
prefloration
preformative
preformation
trifurcation
preferential
craftspeople
craftsperson
professional
professorate
professoress
professorial
profit-taking
profiteering
profitlessly
profoundness
progradation
orographical
programmable
programmatic
trigrammatic
△braggadocios
fragrantness
tragicalness
tragicomical
brigade-major
trigger-happy
priggishness

tragelaphine
progymnasium
dragon's-blood
trigonometer
trigonometry
progenitress
proglottides
troglodytism
gregarianism
frigorificos
gregariously
pregustation
progesterone
triglyceride
orthoboracic
orthocousins
orchidaceous
orchidectomy
orchidomania
orthodontics
orthodontist
orthodromics
archdeaconry
archaeometry
orthognathic
orthographic
orthographer
archegoniate
orthogonally
orthogenesis
orthogenetic
orchilla-weed
Archilochian
preheminence
prehensility
prehensorial
orphan-asylum
arthroplasty
orthopedical
orthopaedics
orthopaedist
orthopterist
orthopteroid
orthopterous
archipelagic
archipelagos
orchard-grass
orchard-house
orthorhombic
orthosilicic
prehistorian
orchestrator
architecture
orthotonesis
orthotropism
orthotropous
archetypical
drainage-tube
ordinariness
irritability
trainability

irrigational
trail-blazing
Artiodactyla
praiseworthy
fruitfulness
ornithogalum
Freightliner®
freightliner
ornithomancy
ornithomorph
ornithophily
Ornithischia
ornithoscopy
freight-train
training-ship
artificially
argillaceous
artilleryman
fruit-machine
traitorously
arrière-garde
train-spotter
artistically
articulately
articulation
articulatory
brainwashing
projectivity
projectional
prejudgement
broken-backed
broken-winded
broker-dealer
grallatorial
frolicsomely
Grolieresque
trolley-table
trolley-wheel
prolificness
prolifically
prolegomenon
trolling-bait
brilliant-cut
brilliantine
troll-my-dames
prolongation
prelapsarian
prelatically
tralaticious
Pralltriller
urolithiasis
proletariate
trilaterally
tralatitious
grammaticise
grammaticize
grammaticism
grammatology
frame-breaker
premeditated
Gram-negative

12 □r□m□e

trumpet-major
trumpet-shell
primigravida
primogenital
primogenitor
crimping-iron
Kremlinology
bromhidrosis
Bromeliaceae
promulgation
bramble-berry
primulaceous
bramble-finch
frumentation
graminaceous
criminogenic
tremendously
Premonstrant
premenstrual
gram-molecule
crambo-jingle
Gram-positive
trampolinist
gramophonist
pro-marketeer
primordially
promuscidate
promissorily
promethazine
dramatically
aromatherapy
crymotherapy
cremationist
dramaturgist
dramatisable
trimethylene
dramatizable
brimfullness
premaxillary
transaminase
frankalmoign
transactions
front-bencher
trinacriform
transcalency
transcendent
transduction
drink-driving
granodiorite
cringe-making
frondescence
princeliness
prince-bishop
orange-flower
Frankenstein
transfection
wrongfulness
transferable
transferring
transforming
transformism
transformist
transference
transfusable
transfusible
uranographic
uranographer
transgressor
transgenesis
urinogenital
prenegotiate
trench-plough
transhumance
French-polish
Branchiopoda
transhipment
transhipping
bronchoscope
bronchoscopy
△principality
frankincense
prenticeship
'prenticeship
frondiferous
printing-head
drinking-horn
drinking-bout
branding-iron
transitively
frangibility
transitivity
transitional
transiliency
Fringillidae
Grandisonian
transitorily
frontispiece
frontiersman
transit-trade
front-loading
crenellation
translucence
translucency
granulocytic
transleithan
wranglership
translatable
granulations
trinomialism
trinomialist
transmigrate
transmigrant
transmogrify
transmontane
transmundane
brinkmanship
pronominally
transmissive
transmission
transmutable
transmutably
transmitting
ironing-board
pruning-knife
brontosaurus
Franco-German
transoceanic
△francophobia
drongo-shrike
front-of-house
craniologist
drongo-cuckoo
bronco-buster
transplanter
transpacific
transpicuous
transpontine
transpirable
transportive
transporting
transparence
transparency
transposable
transshipper
trendsetting
frenetically
print-through
transuranium
transudation
transuranian
transudatory
pronouncedly
tranquilness
tranquillise
tranquillize
tranquillity
tranquilizer
transumptive
transumption
transversely
transversion
transvestite
transvestism
transvestist
brandy-pawnee
brandy-bottle
preoccupancy
proof-correct
troop-carrier
preordinance
preoperative
arborescence
arborisation
arborization
creolisation
creolization
Oreopithecus
cryoglobulin
proofreading
armour-bearer
armour-plated
cryptanalyst
trophallaxis
prepubescent
tripudiation
crêpe-de-chine
arsphenamine
triple-headed
propaedeutic
propheticism
triple-tongue
dropped-scone
triple-turned
trypaflavine
propugnation
propagandise
propagandize
propagandism
propagandist
crapehanging
crepehanging
trapshooting
triplication
eruptiveness
dropping-well
proprietress
tropological
grapple-plant
trypanocidal
preponderate
preponderant
propenseness
cryptogamian
cryptogamist
cryptogamous
trophotactic
graphophobia
trophobiosis
trophobiotic
cryptomnesia
cryptomnesic
cryptologist
graphologist
triphosphate
trophotropic
cryptography
cryptonymous
tropophilous
preparedness
tripartition
proportioned
proportional
troposcatter
grapeseed-oil
preposterous
prepossessed
tropospheric
crepusculous
propitiative
propitiation
propitiatory
triphthongal
propitiously
prophylactic

trapezohedra
frequentness
prerogatived
prerequisite
ororotundity
crystal-clear
cross-and-pile
crassamentum
crystal-gazer
crystallitis
prostanthera
prostacyclin
crossbencher
crossbanding
cross-buttock
brass-bounder
prosectorial
cross-current
prosecutable
crosscutting
cross-country
prosodically
presidentess
presidential
cross-examine
Trismegistus
prosperously
prospectuses
trustfulness
brassfounder
cross-grained
dressing-case
dressing-sack
graspingness
dressing-room
dressing-down
dressing-gown
trysting-tree
irascibility
prestigiator
Prussianiser
Prussianizer
prestissimos
prostitution
preselection
bristle-grass
cross-lighted
crash-landing
cross-linking
prosyllogism
trestle-table
cross-lateral
proselytiser
proselytizer
freshmanship
crash-matting
presumptuous
presentative
presentation
presentiment
presentially
cristobalite
Bristol-brick
Aristotelean
Aristotelism
Aristotelian
Aristophanic
aristolochia
aristocratic
griseofulvin
praseodymium
prosopopoeia
prosopopeial
cross-purpose
preservative
preservation
preservatory
brass-rubbing
prestriction
droseraceous
prescriptive
proscriptive
prescription
proscription
cross-section
cross-selling
Crassulaceae
crassulacean
grossularite
pressure-cook
grass-widower
presbyacusis
presbyterate
presbyterial
△presbyterian
presbycousis
prothalamium
prothalamion
protractible
protractedly
protuberance
trituberculy
protectively
protectingly
protactinium
criticalness
triticalness
protocolling
△protectorate
protectorial
criticisable
criticizable
erythematous
brother-in-law
protreptical
gratifyingly
gratefulness
truthfulness
wrathfulness
protagonists
wretchedness
proto-history
gratuitously
arithmomania
arithmometer
protomorphic
arithmetical
pretenceless
pretendingly
pre-tensioned
protonematal
writing-paper
writing-table
proteoglycan
prothonotary
protoplasmic
protoplasmal
protoplastic
arctophilist
write-protect
erythroblast
oratorically
pretermitted
erythromycin
erythropenia
urethroscope
urethroscopy
protestation
protestingly
protistology
grotesquerie
prototherian
truth-telling
prototrophic
prototypical
protrusively
pretty-spoken
pretty-pretty
protozoology
traumatology
group-captain
ground-feeder
groundlessly
ground-beetle
ground-pigeon
ground-cuckoo
proud-hearted
draughtboard
draught-hooks
draught-horse
draught-house
draughtiness
droughtiness
draught-proof
trouble-house
troublemaker
trouble-mirth
trouble-state
troubleshoot
trouble-world
Frauendienst
triumphalism
triumphalist
triumphantly
fraudulently
driveability
grave-clothes
providential
arfvedsonite
prevailingly
gravel-voiced
travel-soiled
preventative
Provence-rose
preventively
provincially
driving-shaft
driving-wheel
previousness
brevipennate
prevaricator
proverbially
provisionary
privateering
gravitometer
privat-docent
privat-dozent
drawlingness
drawing-frame
drawing-knife
growing-pains
growing-point
drawing-paper
drawing-table
praxinoscope
prayerlessly
prayer-monger
prizefighter
asparaginase
Islamisation
Islamization
espagnolette
astacologist
escapologist
assassinator
isobilateral
isocheimenal
psychiatrist
psychobabble
psychopathic
psychoactive
psychometric
psychosexual
psychoticism
psychologise
psychologize
psychosocial
psychologism
psychonomics
psychologist
psychotropic
psychography
isochromatic
psychrometer

Words marked △ may be spelled also with a capital letter

12 □s□c□r

psychrometry
isochronally
isodiametric
isodimorphic
assemblaunce
osteodermous
asseverating
asseveration
aspergillums
osteogenesis
osteogenetic
osteological
osteomalacia
osteoplastic
osteoporosis
osteopathist
Ascension-day
assessorship
osteosarcoma
essentialism
essentialist
essentiality
assentaneous
ostentatious
usufructuary
eschscholzia
eschatologic
asphyxiation
Ustilagineae
aspirational
ustilaginous
assimilative
assibilation
assimilation
ossification
aspiringness
oscillograph
oscilloscope
psilanthropy
Asclepiadean
isolationism
isolationist
Ishmaelitish
asymmetrical
psammophytic
asymptomatic
asymptotical
asynchronism
asynchronous
astonishment
associations
astoundingly
assortedness
isoprenaline
psephologist
isoperimeter
isoperimetry
astrocytomas
astrogeology
astrological
estrangement
astringently
astronomical
astronautics
usuriousness
astrophysics
user-friendly
isostemonous
tsesarevitch
tsesarewitch
isotretinoin
isothermally
esoterically
escutcheoned
assuefaction
pseudorandom
pseudomartyr
pseudomonads
pseudo-Gothic
pseudopodium
pseudography
pseudonymity
pseudonymous
pseudocyesis
straw-breadth
strangle-weed
stranglement
stranglehold
stragglingly
strangulated
straightways
straightedge
straightness
straightener
straightaway
Stradivarius
strabismical
stratigraphy
straticulate
stratotanker
steatomatous
stratosphere
steatorrhoea
stratocratic
steatopygous
straitjacket
stealthiness
stablishment
stabilisator
stabilizator
stubbornness
stickability
stockbreeder
stockbroking
stockingless
stocking-feet
stocking-sole
stocking-foot
stock-in-trade
stockjobbery
stockjobbing
stickler-like
stichometric
stichomythia
stichomythic
studdingsail
studding-sail
studiousness
strengthless
strengthener
otter-hunting
stoechiology
etherisation
etherization
strepitation
steeplechase
steeple-crown
atheological
etheromaniac
atheromatous
etheostomine
Strepsiptera
street-raking
streetwalker
streptococci
streetkeeper
streptomycin
streptosolen
otherworldly
steelworking
stiff-hearted
stegocarpous
staggeringly
stage-manager
steganograph
Steganopodes
stegophilist
stegosaurian
Stahlhelmist
stridelegged
stoichiology
strikingness
Strigiformes
stridulation
stridulatory
stridulantly
attitudinise
attitudinize
stakhanovite
stakhanovism
stalwartness
stalactiform
Stellenbosch
stylographic
stelliferous
stilboestrol
still-peering
athletically
stammeringly
etymological
etymologicum
etymologicon
stomatodaeum
△standardbred
standardiser
standardizer
stone-breaker
ethnocentric
stonecutting
ethnographic
stenographic
ethnographer
stenographer
stony-hearted
stanniferous
standing-room
ethnological
stonemasonry
standpattism
Stanislavski
ethnoscience
stonewalling
stromatolite
strong-minded
strongylosis
strophanthin
strophanthus
strophiolate
strobilation
strobiliform
attorneyship
stroboscopic
atmospherics
strontianite
stepdaughter
stapedectomy
stupefacient
stupefactive
stupefaction
stipulaceous
etepimeletic
stupendously
attributable
styracaceous
attractively
attractingly
athrocytoses
athrocytosis
pterodactyle
pteridomania
Pteridophyta
pteridophyte
pteridosperm
stormfulness
starchedness
eternisation
eternization
storekeeping
stercoranism
stercoranist
stereotactic
stereoacuity
stereoscopic
stereometric

stereophonic
stereochrome
stereochromy
storiologist
stertorously
stereotropic
stereography
stereoisomer
stereopticon
stereotyping
△star-spangled
pterosaurian
storytelling
sternutative
sternutation
sternutatory
stern-wheeler
otosclerosis
stutteringly
statuesquely
statementing
stethoscopic
statesperson
statistician
strugglingly
stout-hearted
stauroscopic
structurally
strychninism
subarachnoid
funambulator
subarcuation
cut-and-thrust
sun-and-planet
subabdominal
mutagenicity
subaggregate
ourang-outang
humanisation
humanitarian
humanization
ruralisation
ruralization
mutationally
turacoverdin
nugatoriness
subapostolic
subarrhation
subauricular
sugar-refiner
subalternate
subalternant
subalternity
subantarctic
duraluminium
eucalyptuses
cupboard-love
turbocharged
turbocharger
turbidimeter
curb-merchant
tumbler-drier
bubble-headed
hubble-bubble
rumble-tumble
purblindness
lumbriciform
turbellarian
nubbing-cheat
turbinacious
rubbing-stone
cumbrousness
lumber-jacket
numberlessly
curb-crawling
kurchatovium
succedaneous
luncheon-meat
luncheonette
Punchinellos
functionless
functionally
auscultation
auscultatory
subcelestial
subcommittee
subcommunity
subconscious
buccaneering
buccaneerish
subcontinent
vulcanisable
succinctness
bus-conductor
vulcanizable
lusciousness
Turcophilism
susceptivity
succussation
successantly
quick-scented
successfully
quick-sighted
successively
successional
quicksilvery
quacksalving
quick-selling
subcutaneous
punctulation
puncturation
subcivilised
subcivilized
Quadragesima
quadrangular
quadraphonic
quadraplegia
quadraplegic
subdiaconate
duodecennial
hurdle-racing
muddleheaded
hundred-gated
quadrivalent
quidditative
quadriplegia
quadriplegic
quadriennial
quadriennium
quadrinomial
subdelirious
muddy-mettled
duodenectomy
pudding-faced
pudding-plate
pudding-stone
quadrophonic
subduplicate
dunderheaded
wunderkinder
quadrumanous
subdivisible
numerability
lukewarmness
superannuate
queer-bashing
supercharger
superciliary
supercilious
tuberculosed
tuberculosis
tuberculated
queen-consort
superconduct
supercargoes
supercluster
queen-dowager
juvenescence
supereminent
superevident
euhemeristic
supererogate
supererogant
superficials
superfrontal
superglacial
supergravity
superhighway
superhumanly
superhumeral
superheroine
suberisation
suberization
juvenileness
tuberiferous
juvenilities
subeditorial
superimposed
superiorship
Puseyistical
superluminal
queen-meadows
supermundane
supermassive
gubernaculum
supernaculum
gubernacular
supernacular
supernatural
superordinal
superorganic
numerologist
numerousness
surefootedly
superovulate
superplastic
sun-expelling
superpolymer
superposable
superpatriot
superrealism
superrealist
superrefined
queen-regnant
superstardom
Queenslander
supersubtile
supersedence
superspecies
superstition
supersensory
supersensual
mutessarifat
superstratum
supersession
quaestionary
quaestorship
fume-cupboard
bureaucratic
supervenient
supervention
pufftaloonas
surface-craft
sufficiently
subfactorial
surface-to-air
sulfadiazine
buffalo-berry
buffalo-grass
outfangthief
buffing-wheel
surfboarding
furfuraceous
subfertility
subfeudation
subfeudatory
suffruticose
subglacially
Muggletonian
judgment-hall
judgment-debt
judgment-seat
judgement-day
hunger-bitten

Words marked △ may be spelled also with a capital letter

hunger-strike
hugger-mugger
suggestively
ruthlessness
rushy-fringed
bushwhacking
authenticate
authenticity
euphoniously
euthanasiast
cushion-plant
rush-bottomed
authorisable
authorizable
subhastation
eurhythmical
Euphausiacea
Euphausiidae
oughly-headed
dubitatively
ruminatively
ruminatingly
pupilability
mucilaginous
jurisconsult
jurisdictive
jurisdiction
luminescence
lucifer-match
businesslike
subinfeudate
tuning-hammer
municipalise
municipalize
purificative
municipalism
cutinisation
cutinization
futilitarian
humification
△purification
municipality
purificatory
fugitiveness
luminiferous
munificently
musicianship
munitionette
fuliginosily
fuliginously
pugilistical
audiological
burial-ground
musicologist
luminousness
mutinousness
numinousness
jurisprudent
Hudibrastics
subinspector
autistically
cubistically
juristically
puristically
curietherapy
subintroduce
fugie-warrant
subjectively
subjectivise
subjectivize
subjectivism
subjectivist
subjectivity
huckle-backed
buckle-beggar
lucklessness
quaking-grass
lurking-place
ducking-stool
muckspreader
Quaker-colour
bunko-steerer
sublibrarian
guild-brother
public-school
public-domain
quill-driving
curliewurlie
quill-feather
qualificator
fully-fledged
bull-of-the-bog
guilefulness
mulligatawny
full-throated
bullshitting
qualmishness
bullfighting
subliminally
Juglandaceae
sublineation
fuel-injected
outlandishly
Euglenoidina
curling-stone
nucleophilic
full-bottomed
△sublapsarian
bullet-headed
curmudgeonly
augmentative
augmentation
subminiature
outmanoeuvre
submergement
summer-weight
submissively
surmountable
submaxillary
pugnaciously
dunniewassal
quintessence
quenchlessly
quantivalent
quantitative
quantisation
quantization
turnpike-road
quantifiable
quantitively
cunnilinctus
running-board
burning-glass
burning-house
turning-lathe
burning-point
turning-point
subnormality
quinquenniad
quinquennial
quinquennium
autocatalyse
autocatalyze
automaticity
Euro-passport
suboccipital
subordinancy
suboperculum
subopercular
euroterminal
Eurocentrism
autodestruct
autochthones
sudoriparous
autodidactic
sudoriferous
autorickshaw
eulogistical
Euro-American
auto-immunity
autoantibody
automobilism
automobilist
automorphism
humorousness
autocritique
autoptically
dumortierite
run-of-the-mill
out-of-the-body
Eurosterling
Eurocurrency
mucopurulent
autoexposure
autohypnosis
outplacement
culpableness
auspiciously
suspiciously
supplemental
supplementer
suppressible
suppressedly
supplicating
supplication
supplicatory
subprincipal
rumpti-iddity
sumphishness
surprisingly
cupping-glass
suspensively
out-pensioner
jumping-mouse
suspensorial
suspensorium
sulphonamide
sulphonation
pumpernickel
purpose-built
purposefully
surpassingly
suppositious
sulphuration
sulphureting
sulphuretted
Humpty-dumpty
quaquaversal
surrealistic
Munro-bagging
supraciliary
turriculated
supracrustal
quarter-blood
quarter-bound
quarter-final
quarter-guard
quarter-horse
quarterlight
quarter-miler
quartern-loaf
quarter-plate
quarter-pound
quarter-round
quarterstaff
quarter-sawed
putrefacient
putrefactive
putrefaction
subreference
outrageously
guerrilleros
guardianship
surrejoinder
supramundane
querimonious
cuprammonium
currant-bread
guaranteeing
currant-jelly
supraorbital
nutritionist
nutritiously
surroundings

Words marked △ may be spelled also with a capital letter

burrowing-owl
quarrymaster
quartz-schist
quartz-iodine
substantiate
substantival
guest-chamber
tussock-grass
Russocentric
subsidiarily
subsidiarity
cuisse-madame
question-mark
questionable
questionably
questionless
substitutive
substitution
subsultorily
nursing-chair
Russophilism
Russophilist
Russophobist
subsequently
outspreading
subscribable
substraction
substruction
burseraceous
substructure
subservience
subserviency
subscriptive
subscription
outstretched
purse-sharing
quasi-stellar
purse-strings
nurse-tending
Australasian
quotableness
suitableness
△justicialism
multichannel
butty-collier
multicentric
multicentral
futtock-plate
multicipital
multicostate
multicauline
multidentate
turtle-necked
hurtlessness
buttress-root
subtreasurer
multifaceted
justificator
multifoliate
multiflorous
multiformity
multifarious
multigravida
multilobular
multilocular
fustillirian
multilingual
puftaloonies
multiloquent
multiloquous
multilateral
subtemperate
customs-house
huntsmanship
sustentative
sustentation
putting-cleek
multinuclear
mutton-headed
hunting-field
putting-green
hunting-knife
hunting-lodge
multinominal
hunting-sword
putting-stone
multungulate
mutton-cutlet
Austronesian
rust-coloured
multipresent
multiplicand
multiplicate
multipliable
multiplicity
multipartite
multipurpose
subterranean
subterjacent
lust-breathed
muster-master
quattrocento
butterscotch
buttery-hatch
hunter-killer
butterfly-bow
butterfly-nut
butter-cooler
subthreshold
butter-muslin
multiscience
multisulcate
multiseptate
multiseriate
multitasking
multivoltine
multivalence
multivalency
multivariate
multiversity
multivarious
cultivatable
multivitamin
cumulatively
subumbrellar
furunculosis
eunuchoidism
cupuliferous
Tubuliflorae
tubulifloral
queue-jumping
luxullianite
cumulonimbus
cumulocirrus
futurologist
lugubriously
tumultuation
tumultuously
curvicostate
curvicaudate
curvifoliate
surveillance
pulvilliform
culvertailed
subvertebral
pulverulence
pulverisable
curvirostral
pulverizable
vulvo-uterine
survivorship
surveyorship
outward-bound
quixotically
ruby-throated
eurythermous
burying-place
ruby-coloured
puzzle-headed
muzzle-loader
puzzle-monkey
quizzicality
buzzard-clock
evidentially
availability
evil-favoured
evil-tempered
evil-mindedly
evil-speaking
evolutionary
evolutionism
evolutionist
avant-courier
evangelicism
evangelistic
even-tempered
avant-gardism
avant-gardist
evening-dress
evanescently
evaporograph
evaporimeter
evaporometer
overcapacity
overrashness
over-cannoped
overcanopied
avariciously
overscutched
overschutcht
everydayness
overreaction
over-weighted
overpersuade
overwhelming
overkindness
overfineness
overniceness
overripeness
overfinished
oversimplify
overflourish
overinclined
over-and-under
overfondness
overlordship
overpowering
ovariotomist
overpopulate
overprepared
overpressure
overcrowding
overestimate
overstrained
ivory-towered
averruncator
overfullness
oversubtlety
overmultiply
everywhither
overexposure
overexertion
evisceration
avitaminosis
avowableness
sweet-and-sour
sweepingness
sweetishness
sweet-scented
sweet-toothed
swaggeringly
swagger-stick
swainishness
awe-inspiring
swell-mobsman
Twelfth-night
swimming-bath
swimming-bell
swimmingness
swimming-pond
swimming-pool
swinging-boom
swinging-post
swine-keeping

Words marked △ may be spelled also with a capital letter

Zwinglianism
Zwinglianist
swindle-sheet
twenty-fourmo
twenty-twenty
sword-breaker
sword-bayonet
dwarfishness
swashbuckler
two-sidedness
twitter-boned
twitteringly
swizzle-stick
oxy-acetylene
exsanguinate
exsanguinity
exsanguinous
expatriation
exhaustively
expansionary
expansionism
expansionist
exobiologist
execratively
exacerbation
executorship
exheredation
expeditation
experimented
experimental
experimenter
expediential
experiential
exterminable
exterminator
exteroceptor
extensimeter
extensometer
extensionist
expectorator
expectations
ex-serviceman
exaggerative
exaggeration
exaggeratory
exiguousness
exegetically
exchangeable
exchangeably
exhilarative
exhilarating
exhilaration
exhilaratory
excitability
extinguisher
exhibitively
exhibitioner
explicitness
exulceration
exploitative
exploitation
explantation
exclusionary
exclusionism
exclusionist
exalbuminous
exemplifying
examinership
exenteration
exanthematic
excogitative
excogitation
expositively
expositional
expostulator
extortionate
extortionary
extortionist
exophthalmia
exophthalmic
exophthalmos
exophthalmus
exprobrative
exprobration
exprobratory
excruciating
excruciation
extraditable
exercitation
exorbitantly
exercise-book
extralimital
extramundane
extramarital
expromission
extranuclear
extraneously
uxoriousness
expropriable
expropriator
extrapolator
extra-regular
extra-special
expressively
expressivity
expressional
extrasensory
extra-uterine
extravaganza
extravagance
extravagancy
extraversive
extroversive
extraversion
extroversion
exasperative
exasperating
exasperation
exospherical
exothermally
exoterically
exsufflation
exsufflicate
excursionise
excursionize
excursionist
gynaecocracy
gynaecologic
gynaecomasty
synadelphite
hydatidiform
pyramidology
tyrannicidal
tyrannically
dynamometric
zygapophyses
zygapophysis
dysaesthesia
synaesthesia
dysaesthetic
synaesthetic
dynastically
synantherous
Lymantriidae
lycanthropic
synarthroses
synarthrosis
symbolically
symbololatry
syncretistic
synclinorium
synchroflash
synchronical
synchroniser
synchronizer
synchroscope
syndactylism
syndactylous
syndetically
hyperalgesia
hyperalgesic
hyperacidity
hyperbolical
hypercorrect
synecdochism
hyperdactyly
myxedematous
Hypericaceae
hyperidrosis
type-founding
synecologist
hymenopteran
hyperplastic
hyperpyretic
hyperpyrexia
hypersthenia
hypersthenic
hypersensual
hypersarcoma
synectically
hyperthermia
hyperthermal
hypertensive
hypertension
hypertrophic
type-cylinder
myographical
Syngnathidae
syngenesious
mythographer
mythogenesis
nychthemeral
nychthemeron
mythological
mythologiser
mythologizer
pythonomorph
cylindricity
cylindriform
myringoscope
pyrithiamine
typification
pyritiferous
hygienically
pyritohedral
pyritohedron
syllabically
cyclographic
cyclandelate
cyclopropane
Byelorussian
Cyclostomata
cyclostomous
myrmecologic
Myrmecophaga
myrmecophile
myrmecophily
dysmenorrhea
symmetallism
ayuntamiento
hymnographer
cyanogenesis
hypnogenesis
hypnogenetic
gymnosophist
hypnotically
hypnotherapy
hypnotisable
hypnotizable
pyromaniacal
gyromagnetic
xylobalsamum
pyrotartrate
hypogastrium
zygodactylic
pyrotartaric
cytogenetics
pyrotechnics
zymotechnics
pyrotechnist
pyrometrical
hypothecator
pyrophyllite
hypothalamic

hypothalamus
pyrochemical
sycophantise
sycophantize
sycophantish
hypochondria
hypochlorite
hypochlorous
hypothetical
hypophrygian
gynodioecism
pyroligneous
cytoskeletal
cytoskeleton
hypoglycemia
hypoglycemic
pyro-electric
mycoplasmata
pyroclastics
hypoplastron
pyrognostics
hypognathism
hypognathous
mycodomatium
Lycopodineae
cytotoxicity
Lycopodiales
hypocoristic
pyromorphite
hylomorphism
zygomorphism
zygomorphous
hypotrochoid
cymotrichous
typographist
hypocritical
synoptically
hypostatical
hypoeutectic
hyposulphate
pyrosulphate
hyposulphite
zygomycetous
synonymously
Nymphaeaceae
lymphangitis
dysphemistic
nymphomaniac
symptomatise
symptomatize
nympholeptic
lymphography
hydrobiology
hygrochastic
hydrochloric
hydrodynamic
hybridisable
hybridizable
hydroelastic
hydrofluoric
hydrographic
hygrographic
hydrographer
hydrogenated
hydrogeology
hydrokinetic
hydrological
Hydromedusae
hydromedusan
aye-remaining
hydrophanous
hydrophilite
hydrophilous
hygrophilous
hydrophobous
hydropathist
hydrophytous
hydroquinone
hydrargyrism
hydrostatics
hydrotherapy
hydrothermal
hydrotropism
hydraulicked
hydrozincite
mysticalness
△dyotheletism
syntheticism
hyetographic
syntagmatite
mystagogical
dysteleology
system-monger
systematical
systematiser
systematizer
hysterically
hysterectomy
hysterogenic
hysteromania
mysteriously
nyctitropism
Tyburn-ticket
Tyburn-tippet
sylviculture
Czechoslovak
Azerbaijanis
azathioprine

Words marked △ may be spelled also with a capital letter

13 □a□a□a

palatableness
paramagnetism
maladaptation
Lamarckianism
rag-and-bone-man
hazardousness
papaveraceous
damageability
manageability
managerialism
managerialist
paraleipomena
paramenstruum
Saracen's-stone
paraffin-scale
paraphernalia
Zarathustrian
Zarathustrism
satanicalness
magazine-rifle
ramapithecine
parasitically
malariologist
paralipomenon
canaliculated
capaciousness
rapaciousness
sagaciousness
salaciousness
maladjustment
parallactical
parallelogram
parallelistic
maladminister
savanna-forest
savanna-wattle
palaeoecology
malacophilous
Japano-Chinese
Palaeotherium
parapophysial
macaronically
parabolically
paradoxically
palaeobiology
palaeoclimate
Balanoglossus
palaeobotanic
malacological
palaeozoology
palaeographer
palaeographic
palaeocrystic
malacostracan
palaeontology
Pan-Africanism
maladroitness
papaprelatist
paragraphical
parapsychical
parapsychosis
panaesthetism
catastrophism
catastrophist
galactorrhoea
galactosaemia
catalytically
paramyxovirus
canary-creeper
parasynthesis
parasynthetic
parasyntheton
marble-hearted
jawbreakingly
rabble-rousing
wamble-cropped
gambling-house
cabbalistical
△carboniferous
carbonylation
carbonisation
carbonization
bamboozlement
namby-pambical
namby-pambyish
namby-pambyism
barbarisation
carburisation
barber-surgeon
barbarousness
barbarization
carburization
harbour-master
narco-analysis
paschal-candle
paschal-flower
saccharimeter
saccharimetry
saccharometer
Saccharomyces
matchboarding
fasciculation
lance-corporal
calcification
narcohypnosis
sanctimonious
sanctifyingly
cancellariate
masculineness
matchlessness
calculational
△baccalaureate
carcinologist
dancing-master
carcinomatous
Vaccinioideae
sarcophaguses
calcariferous
panchromatism
cancerophobia
sarcastically
lance-sergeant
narcotisation
narcotization
paediatrician
pandiculation
tax-deductible
candidateship
handkerchiefs
candle-lighter
candle-dipping
Gaidhealtachd
candle-snuffer
hard-heartedly
land-measuring
paddle-steamer
maid-of-all-work
daddy-long-legs
sandy-laverock
△pandemoniacal
paedomorphism
randomisation
randomization
landing-ground
maiden-widowed
cardinalatial
cardinalitial
maiden-tongued
cardiological
jawdroppingly
cardiographer
banderilleros
land-surveying
land-ownership
sale-catalogue
case-hardening
barefacedness
calefactories
labefactation
water-breather
paleobiologic
paleobotanist
paleoclimatic
watercolorist
parencephalon
catercornered
water-carriage
eavesdropping
lavender-water
kaleidoscopic
sacerdotalise
sacerdotalism
sacerdotalist
sacerdotalize
tape-recording
paleoecologic
materfamilias
paterfamilias
waterflooding
paper-fastener
catecholamine
catechumenism
catechumenate
paper-hangings
catechistical
watering-place
watering-house
palebiologist
materialistic
Valerianaceae
valedictorian
facetiousness
lamellibranch
Lamellicornia
capellmeister
kapellmeister
paper-mulberry
paleanthropic
Paleanthropus
hare-and-hounds
paternalistic
categorematic
gametogenesis
categorically
paleopedology
waterproofing
Galeopithecus
water-standing
water-softener
water-sprinkle
parenthetical
talent-spotter
Jamestown-weed
water-vascular
safety-deposit
panegyrically
Rafflesiaceae
half-heartedly
half-sovereign
wayfaring-tree
half-evergreen
laughableness
pangrammatist
baggage-animal
laughing-stock
bargain-hunter
languishingly
mangold-wurzel
manganiferous
tangentiality
jargonisation
jargonization
badger-baiting
kangaroo-thorn
kangaroo-apple
kangaroo-grass
badger-drawing
dangerousness
daughter-in-law
Machiavellian
Machiavellism
machicolation
cathodography
mashie-niblick

Words marked △ may be spelled also with a capital letter

tachygraphist
pathogenicity
pathognomonic
naphthylamine
mathematician
mathematicise
mathematicism
mathematicize
bathymetrical
tachometrical
tachymetrical
washing-bottle
machine-gunner
washing-liquid
machine-pistol
washing-powder
taphrogenesis
gathering-coal
gathering-peat
panharmonicon
yachtsmanship
tachistoscope
haphazardness
Latin-American
sanitarianism
sanitationist
fatigableness
habitableness
navigableness
radio-actinium
radioactivity
variable-pitch
variable-sweep
Lasiocampidae
ratiocination
ratiocinatory
ratiocinative
palindromical
cabinetmaking
manifestation
manifestative
tariffication
hagiographist
palingenesist
Manichaeanism
satiricalness
Papilionaceae
maliciousness
radiolabelled
radiolocation
maxillofacial
papilliferous
papillomatous
labialisation
radialisation
vacillatingly
labialization
radialization
nationalistic
rationalistic
manifold-paper
Maginot-minded
Saxifragaceae
pasigraphical
radiesthesist
panic-stricken
radiotelegram
radioteletype
magisterially
caliature-wood
manipulatable
back-calculate
backwardation
backscratcher
lackadaisical
back-pedalling
hacking-jacket
packing-needle
walking-orders
walking-papers
△balkanisation
parking-ticket
walking-ticket
△balkanization
back-formation
jack-crosstree
marketability
talkativeness
marketization
parliament-man
parliamenting
parliamentary
malleableness
railway-stitch
ball-cartridge
sable-coloured
hallucination
hallucinatory
hallucinative
garlic-mustard
eagle-flighted
calligraphist
rallying-point
vaulting-horse
vaulting-house
faultlessness
mallemaroking
cable-moulding
sailing-master
ballast-heaver
callisthenics
table-skittles
tablespoonful
ballet-dancing
ballot-rigging
palletisation
palletization
panleucopenia
haemodialysis
palmification
mammaliferous
sarmentaceous
man-management
salmon-fishing
salmonellosis
harmonisation
harmonization
haemorrhoidal
Hammerklavier
haematogenous
haematologist
barnsbreaking
cannibalistic
barnacle-goose
magnificently
carnification
damnification
magnification
launching-site
launching-ways
magnoliaceous
magniloquence
dauntlessness
gauntlet-guard
magnanimously
darning-needle
rainbow-chaser
balneotherapy
rainbow-tinted
nannoplankton
lawn-sprinkler
garnisheement
varnishing-day
Parnassianism
Saint-Simonian
Saint-Simonism
Saint-Simonist
mainstreeting
garnetiferous
magnetomotive
magneto-optics
magnetosphere
magnetisation
magnetization
carnivalesque
carnivorously
favorableness
sadomasochism
sadomasochist
panophthalmia
cat-o'-nine-tails
Jacobinically
laboriousness
taxonomically
cacographical
vapourishness
baton-sinister
palpable-gross
lampadephoria
Malpighiaceae
camp-sheathing
campylobacter
salpingectomy
wappenshawing
Campanulaceae
campanologist
camphoraceous
rapprochement
Capparidaceae
pauperisation
tamper-evident
pauperization
waspish-headed
carpet-bedding
carpet-slipper
carpet-bombing
carpet-sweeper
panpsychistic
marriage-lines
carriage-drive
iatrochemical
matriculation
matriculatory
macrocephalic
macrodiagonal
macrodactylic
macroeconomic
carrier-pigeon
sacrificially
matrifocality
patrifocality
caprification
tarry-fingered
saurognathous
iatrogenicity
macroglobulin
maurikigusari
barrel-vaulted
barrel-chested
matrilineally
patrilineally
sacralisation
garrulousness
sacralization
macromolecule
matrimonially
patrimonially
sacramentally
tauromorphous
patronisingly
fair-and-square
patronizingly
carrion-flower
patriotically
Sauropterygia
hair-splitting
macropinakoid
sabrerattling
sabre-rattling
barristership
sacrosanctity
parrot-fashion
parrot-disease
narrowcasting

13 □a□s□a

mass-marketing
panspermatism
panspermatist
laissez-passer
falsification
Cassegrainian
causelessness
balsamiferous
Balsaminaceae
passementerie
passenger-mile
passion-flower
marsipobranch
Passeriformes
△caesaropapism
marsh-samphire
Vansittartism
basset-hornist
sansculottism
sansculottist
canthaxanthin
lactobacillus
lattice-bridge
earth-chestnut
lattice-girder
particularise
particularism
particularist
particularity
particularize
parti-coloured
party-coloured
participially
participantly
participating
participation
participatory
participative
tautochronism
tautochronous
carte-de-visite
battle-scarred
cattle-lifting
tattie-lifting
pantheologist
parthenocarpy
tattie-howking
battle-cruiser
rattle-brained
pantheistical
mastigophoran
mastigophoric
Pantagruelian
Pantagruelion
Pantagruelism
Pantagruelist
cartridge-belt
partridge-wood
dactylography
cartilaginous
tautologously
earthly-minded
dactyliomancy
tantalisingly
faithlessness
tastelessness
cartelisation
tantalisation
tantalizingly
cartelization
tantalization
earth-motherly
tautometrical
earth-movement
cantonisation
waiting-vassal
casting-weight
cantonization
xanthochromia
xanthochroism
xanthochroous
gastroenteric
gastrocnemius
gastrological
gastronomical
east-north-east
east-south-east
xanthopterine
tautophonical
master-mariner
master-passion
factorability
martyrologist
dastardliness
bacteriophage
bacteriolysin
bacteriolysis
bacteriolytic
gasteropodous
lantern-pinion
cauterisation
factorisation
tartarisation
master-builder
masterfulness
wasterfulness
cauterization
factorization
tartarization
Baltoslavonic
pantisocratic
fantastically
party-spirited
partitionment
partition-wall
Malthusianism
manufacturing
Ranunculaceae
nature-worship
casualisation
vacuolisation
casualization
vacuolization
haruspication
daguerreotype
daguerreotypy
Casuarinaceae
casuistically
facultatively
salviniaceous
galvanometric
galvanoplasty
Calvinistical
galvanisation
galvanization
laevorotation
laevorotatory
canvas-climber
baby-battering
Caryocaraceae
laryngectomee
laryngologist
laryngoscopic
many-sidedness
labyrinthical
labyrinthitis
lady-in-waiting
baby-snatching
palynological
ranz-des-vaches
obsessionally
objectionable
objectionably
objectiveness
objectivistic
objectivation
observational
obliviousness
ebullioscopic
absorbability
obnoxiousness
aboriginalism
△aboriginality
abortifacient
obtrusiveness
abyssopelagic
abstractional
abstractively
abstentionism
abstentionist
obstinateness
obstetrically
obstructional
obstructively
obtuse-angular
schadenfreude
octave-coupler
occasionalism
occasionalist
occasionality
oceanological
oceanographer
oceanographic
acidification
academicalism
schematically
screech-martin
screech-thrush
accelerometer
scleromalacia
sclerocaulous
sclerodermite
sclerodermous
scleroprotein
accessibility
acceptability
eccentrically
Scientologist
acceptilation
schizaeaceous
scribbling-pad
scrivenership
accidentalism
occidentalise
Occidentalism
Occidentalist
accidentality
occidentalize
accident-prone
actinobacilli
schizocarpous
schizogenesis
schizogenetic
Echinodermata
Schizophyceae
schizophrenia
schizophrenic
scripophilist
actinotherapy
acrimoniously
actinomorphic
Schizomycetes
schizomycetic
actinomycosis
scripturalism
scripturalist
ochlocratical
Scoleciformia
scalpelliform
scalping-knife
acclimatation
scalenohedron
scaling-ladder
scolopendrine
scolopendrium
ecclesiolater
ecclesiolatry
sculpturesque
scambling-days
ecumenicalism
scandal-bearer
scandalmonger
scintiscanner
scintilliscan

Words marked △ may be spelled also with a capital letter

scintillation
economisation
iconomaticism
econometrical
economization
scenarisation
scenarization
acrobatically
scholarliness
scholasticism
octocentenary
scrobiculated
school-marmish
schoolteacher
school-leaving
schoolgirlish
school-trained
accommodating
accommodation
accommodative
accompaniment
accoustrement
accoutrements
accouterments
scapulimantic
scapulomantic
acupuncturist
scaphocephaly
Scyphomedusae
acorn-barnacle
acaridomatium
acarodomatium
accreditation
scarlet-runner
scarification
scorification
scorched-earth
scorchingness
achromaticity
achromatopsia
scathefulness
acetification
Scotification
acotyledonous
acetylcholine
acatamathesia
ecotoxicology
ichthyologist
Ichthyosauria
acquiescently
acquiescingly
actualisation
actualization
scrumptiously
acquirability
acquisitively
acculturation
schutzstaffel
Schwenkfelder
schwärmerisch
acrylonitrile
adiabatically
advanced-level
adiathermancy
adiaphoristic
advantageable
odd-come-shorts
educatability
educationally
admeasurement
adventuristic
adventuresome
adventurously
advertisement
advertizement
admirableness
advisableness
administrable
administrator
admissibility
adumbratively
identicalness
adenoidectomy
odontophorous
odontoglossum
odontornithes
odontological
odonatologist
idiomatically
adsorbability
ideographical
idiorrhythmic
idiosyncratic
adaptableness
odoriferously
Addressograph®
separationism
separationist
separableness
hexadactylous
perambulation
perambulatory
decarbonation
decarboxylase
debauchedness
revaccination
melancholious
recalcitrance
wet-and-dry-bulb
regardfulness
megaherbivore
megacephalous
sexagesimally
dematerialise
dematerialize
nemathelminth
refashionment
metaphysician
metaphosphate
mesaticephaly
rehabilitator
semasiologist
denationalise
denationalize
metafictional
behaviourally
nefariousness
tenaciousness
vexatiousness
metalliferous
metallography
metallurgical
metallisation
metallization
megalosaurian
hematogenesis
teratogenesis
melanochroous
pedagogically
megaloblastic
hematopoiesis
hematopoietic
megalopolitan
teratological
metamorphoses
metamorphosis
megasporangia
metagrabolise
metagrobolise
metagrabolize
metagrobolize
metapsychical
metastability
pedantocratic
telautography
tetartohedral
Melastomaceae
tenant-in-chief
hexactinellid
devastatingly
megastructure
membranaceous
Serbo-Croatian
heebie-jeebies
pebble-glasses
verbification
verbigeration
Leibnizianism
verbalisation
verbalization
Berberidaceae
herborisation
herborization
deoch-an-doruis
merchandising
merchandizing
peaceableness
teachableness
neoclassicism
neoclassicist
peacock-copper
peacock-flower
peach-coloured
leuco-compound
peacock-throne
geochemically
leucaemogenic
reactionarism
reactionarist
descriptively
descriptivism
reacclimatise
reacclimatize
pencil-compass
mercilessness
peacelessness
tercentennial
fencing-master
geocentricism
peace-offering
cercopithecid
Cercopithecus
geochronology
mercerisation
mercerization
percussion-cap
percussionist
leucitohedron
pendragonship
dead-reckoning
needle-pointed
re-edification
feudalisation
pendulousness
feudalization
feeding-bottle
weeding-chisel
tendentiously
redding-straik
Dendrocalamus
dendrological
dead-colouring
perdurability
gender-bending
tender-hearted
deodorisation
deodorization
perditionable
headquartered
televangelism
televangelist
generalisable
generalizable
generationism
revelationist
vegetarianism
generalissimo
temerariously
telemarketing
venerableness
reverberation
reverberatory
reverberative
seneschalship

rebecca-eureka
defencelessly
level-crossing
mesencephalic
telencephalic
mesencephalon
telencephalon
telescopiform
revendication
serendipitist
serendipitous
reference-mark
deleteriously
venereologist
telerecording
decelerometer
redevelopment
decerebration
deferentially
referentially
reverentially
beleaguerment
genethlialogy
redeliverance
beneficential
heresiography
repetitionary
televisionary
dereligionise
dereligionize
beneficiation
repetitiously
veneficiously
heresiologist
deterioration
deteriorative
benedictional
redeemability
beseemingness
deterministic
determinately
determination
determinative
perennibranch
heterocarpous
Hemerobaptist
heterogenesis
heterogenetic
heterogeneity
heterogeneous
heterothallic
heterochronic
heterothermal
ceremonialism
renegotiation
ceremoniously
heteroblastic
heteroplastic
heteroclitous
developmental
telecommuting
derecognition
selenological
heteromorphic
heterosporous
selenographer
genetotrophic
heterotrophic
selenographic
telecottaging
heterostylism
heterostylous
heterostrophy
heteropterous
teleportation
teleconverter
Redemptionist
metempiricism
metempiricist
penetrability
desegregation
meteorologist
telegrammatic
peregrination
peregrinatory
Tenebrionidae
cerebrospinal
meteoriticist
penetratingly
penetratively
defeasibility
defensibility
reversibility
depersonalise
depersonalize
reversionally
remeasurement
necessariness
necessitarian
necessitation
necessitously
recessiveness
deceptibility
defectibility
delectability
detestability
receptibility
seventeenthly
pedestrianise
pedestrianism
pedestrianize
derestriction
sedentariness
desertisation
deceitfulness
deceptiveness
defectiveness
receptiveness
retentiveness
desertization
derequisition
deceivability
receivability
receiving-line
receiving-room
receiving-ship
defervescence
defervescency
self-balancing
self-satisfied
self-sacrifice
self-abasement
perfectionism
△perfectionist
perfectionate
self-addressed
selfe-despight
self-adjusting
self-regarding
self-dependent
self-reverence
self-levelling
self-revealing
self-referring
self-defeating
self-repeating
self-deception
self-deceitful
self-recording
self-reproving
self-restraint
self-fertility
self-repugnant
self-denyingly
self-shielding
self-financing
self-discharge
self-direction
self-righteous
reaffirmation
self-dispraise
self-slaughter
self-important
self-annealing
self-infection
self-injection
reefing-jacket
self-inflicted
newfangleness
self-enjoyment
perfunctorily
self-insurance
self-indulgent
self-induction
self-inductive
self-knowledge
self-conceited
self-condemned
self-governing
self-confident
self-confiding
self-confessed
self-forgetful
self-motivated
self-conjugate
self-collected
self-pollution
self-communion
self-tormentor
self-conscious
self-consuming
self-possessed
self-contained
self-convicted
self-opinioned
self-appointed
self-operating
self-approving
self-treatment
self-professed
perfervidness
self-propelled
self-criticism
self-asserting
self-assertion
self-assertive
self-assurance
self-sterility
self-murdering
self-sufficing
self-judgement
self-publicist
self-publicity
self-supported
self-surrender
self-sustained
self-surviving
self-awareness
self-executing
self-existence
self-hypnotism
hedge-accentor
neogrammarian
sergeant-major
neighbourhood
neighbourless
hedge-marriage
begging-letter
weight-watcher
weight-lifting
tergiversator
methodologist
Methodistical
dephlegmation
technicalness
nephelometric
cephalosporin
cephalisation
cephalothorax
cephalization
mechanisation
mechanization
nephrological
technological

Words marked △ may be spelled also with a capital letter

technopolitan
Netherlandish
lethargically
lecherousness
hemiparasitic
semiparasitic
demi-caractère
semi-barbarian
semi-barbarism
semicarbazide
peripatetical
medicamentary
pelican-flower
derivationist
recitationist
semi-sagittate
desirableness
veritableness
semipalmation
perigastritis
semiochemical
periodicalist
revindication
periodontitis
bewilderingly
periodisation
periodization
perihepatitis
perinephritis
semiperimeter
hemicellulose
pedicellariae
semi-permeable
△mediterranean
semimenstrual
penitentially
sedimentology
regimentation
sedimentation
sewing-machine
meningococcal
meningococcic
meningococcus
perishability
delightedness
perichondrial
perichondrium
peripherality
delirifacient
felicitations
verifiability
reminiscently
perivitelline
verisimilarly
penicilliform
penicillinase
meridionality
deficientness
deliciousness
deliriousness
religiousness
seditiousness
sericiculture
vexillologist
serialisation
feuilletonism
feuilletonist
legislatorial
legislatively
serialization
heliometrical
beginningless
semiporcelain
retinoscopist
semiconductor
Lepidodendron
meritoriously
genito-urinary
lexicographer
lexicographic
semiconscious
Lepidostrobus
lepidopterist
lepidopterous
helispherical
hemispherical
reciprocality
reciprocating
reciprocation
reciprocative
demiurgically
defibrillator
defibrination
lexigraphical
remissibility
perissodactyl
peninsularity
redissolution
revictualling
registrarship
resistibility
remittance-man
heliotropical
mediatorially
register-plate
mediatisation
mediatization
semi-automatic
deliquescence
sericulturist
deciduousness
semioviparous
semi-evergreen
perityphlitis
serjeant-at-law
deck-passenger
leuko-compound
leukocythemia
Berkeleianism
Neo-Kantianism
seek-no-further
well-warranted
neglectedness
reflectograph
well-beseeming
well-developed
well-respected
well-regulated
mellification
mellifluently
mellifluously
negligibility
re-eligibility
belligerently
neologistical
well-thought-of
healthfulness
celluliferous
Neo-Lamarckian
Neo-Lamarckism
declamatorily
selling-plater
seal-engraving
Hellenistical
replenishment
well-conducted
realpolitiker
well-worked-out
well-connected
well-appointed
deplorability
well-preserved
declaratorily
declaratively
realisability
belles-lettres
realistically
perlustration
deglutination
pelletisation
pelletization
yellow-bellied
fellow-feeling
fellow-servant
fellow-citizen
yellowishness
reflexibility
reflexologist
reflexiveness
realizability
re-embarkation
vermiculation
Neo-Melanesian
terminability
helminthiasis
helminthology
fermentitious
Germanophilia
seeming-simple
Germanisation
terminational
terminatively
hermeneutical
Germanization
hermaphrodite
geomorphogeny
geomorphology
mesmerisation
mesmerization
permutability
dermatography
geometrically
dermatologist
dermatoplasty
reimbursement
reincarnation
bernicle-goose
vernacularise
vernacularism
vernacularist
vernacularity
vernacularize
reinterrogate
reintegration
△neanderthaler
reunification
penny-farthing
Jenny-long-legs
pennilessness
vernalisation
vernalization
re-enforcement
reinforcement
deontological
herniorrhaphy
re-endorsement
penny-pinching
Semnopithecus
seine-shooting
reinstatement
hexobarbitone
tenovaginitis
memorableness
revocableness
recombination
reconcilement
lemon-coloured
secondariness
aerogenerator
mesocephalism
mesocephalous
xerodermatous
deforestation
reforestation
recomfortless
xerophthalmia
negotiability
demolishments
aerolithology
demolitionist
aerobiologist
refocillation
devotionalist
devotionality

Words marked △ may be spelled also with a capital letter

feloniousness
ferociousness
melodiousness
recollectedly
désobligeante
deformability
reformability
recommendable
recommendably
reconnoiterer
metoposcopist
serologically
Peloponnesian
demonological
seroconverted
decompression
recompression
decompressive
decomposition
recomposition
melodramatise
melodramatist
melodramatize
cerographical
venographical
reconstituent
reconsolidate
remorselessly
reconstructor
remonstrantly
demonstration
remonstration
demonstratory
remonstratory
demonstrative
remonstrative
gerontocratic
decortication
gerontologist
decontaminant
decontaminate
gerontophilia
gerontophobia
devolutionary
revolutionary
devolutionist
revolutionise
revolutionism
revolutionist
revolutionize
resolvability
aerodynamical
genotypically
metonymically
tenosynovitis
temptableness
neoplasticism
Neo-Plasticism
despicability
resplendently
perplexedness
terpsichoreal
terpsichorean
reapplication
geopolitician
△perpendicular
serpent-lizard
tenpenny-piece
reappointment
deipnosophist
sexploitation
jet-propulsion
temperability
temporalities
temperamental
pepper-and-salt
temporariness
temporisingly
temporisation
desperateness
temperateness
temporizingly
temporization
tempest-beaten
tempest-tossed
tempestuously
bespottedness
sempstressing
herpetologist
sempiternally
sesquiterpene
sesquiplicate
rearrangement
reproachfully
retroactively
retroactivity
Tetrabranchia
neuroblastoma
heartbreaking
jerry-building
tetrabasicity
retributively
ferricyanogen
ferrocyanogen
petrochemical
tetrachloride
neurocomputer
ferroconcrete
refractometer
petrocurrency
ferro-chromium
deprecatingly
deprecatorily
tetradynamous
recrudescence
recrudescency
ferroelectric
neuroethology
reorientation
neurofibromas
metrification
petrification
retroflection
retrogression
retrogressive
refrigeration
refrigeratory
refrigerative
tetrahedrally
reprehensible
reprehensibly
searchingness
near-sightedly
terra-japonica
petroliferous
neurolinguist
heartlessness
ferrimagnetic
ferromagnetic
detrimentally
neuraminidase
retromingency
gerrymanderer
necromantical
decriminalise
decriminalize
recrimination
recriminatory
recriminative
neuromuscular
retranslation
heortological
heir-portioner
neuropathical
decrepitation
petrophysical
terrorisation
terrorization
recrystallise
recrystallize
heart-sickness
pearl-shelling
retrospection
retrospective
ferrosoferric
neurastheniac
heuristically
peirastically
tetrastichous
heart-stirring
tetrasyllabic
tetrasyllable
wearisomeness
representamen
representable
representment
re-presentment
necroscopical
terrestrially
heart-stricken
neurosurgical
territorially
secretaryship
secretiveness
neurotoxicity
neurovascular
geostationary
sensibilities
versicoloured
rensselaerite
Meistersinger
perspectively
perspectivism
perspectivist
versification
perspicacious
geoscientific
perspicuously
senselessness
leishmaniases
leishmaniasis
leishmanioses
leishmaniosis
pessimistical
messenger-wire
personalistic
leasing-making
seismological
seismographer
seismographic
pease-porridge
mensurability
Messerschmitt
measuring-tape
measuring-worm
perscrutation
versatileness
densitometric
sensationally
sensitisation
sensitiveness
sensitization
perseveringly
perseveration
gentianaceous
left-handiness
velt-mareschal
pentobarbital
geotactically
verticillated
denticulation
gesticulation
gesticulatory
gesticulative
geotechnology
leptocephalic
leptocephalus
Testicardines
pentadactylic
pentadelphous
gentlemanhood
gentlemanlike
gentlemanship
weather-beaten

feather-bonnet
weather-bitten
weather-driven
feather-duster
gentle-hearted
weather-headed
aesthetically
penthemimeral
heat-resistant
leather-jacket
leather-lunged
bestsellerdom
gentlewomanly
weatherometer
centre-forward
beetlebrained
kettledrummer
beetle-crusher
feather-stitch
featherweight
leather-winged
beatification
certification
rectification
testification
certificatory
testificatory
pestiferously
vertiginously
centricalness
ventriloquial
ventriloquise
ventriloquism
ventriloquist
ventriloquous
ventriloquize
restrictively
centrifugally
centrifugence
reptiliferous
rectilinearly
deathlessness
fertilisation
fertilization
sentimentally
belt-and-braces
geitonogamous
sententiously
netting-needle
septentrional
septentriones
peptonisation
Teutonisation
rectangularly
peptonization
Teutonization
dextrocardiac
section-cutter
benthopelagic
geotropically
rent-collector
rectipetality
leptophyllous
tent-preaching
letter-carrier
Heath-Robinson
reattribution
letter-heading
letter-perfect
nectariferous
deuterogamist
deuteragonist
helter-skelter
feature-length
Deuteronomist
letter-founder
yestermorning
letters-patent
venturesomely
deuteroscopic
sectorisation
vectorisation
restoratively
letter-quality
dexterousness
venturousness
yesterevening
sectorization
vectorization
lectisternium
pentastichous
leptospirosis
heptasyllabic
pentasyllabic
rectitudinous
tentativeness
restaurant-car
destructional
destructively
destructivist
destructivity
refurbishment
resuscitation
resuscitative
gerund-grinder
rejuvenescent
beauteousness
regurgitation
deducibleness
reducibleness
penuriousness
Gemütlichkeit
republicanise
republicanism
republicanize
reduplication
republication
reduplicative
sequentiality
ceruloplasmin
verumontanums
desulphuriser
desulphurizer
sequestration
requisiteness
repulsiveness
deductibility
desultoriness
reductiveness
seductiveness
cervicography
nervelessness
heaven-kissing
heave-offering
heave-shoulder
pervasiveness
velvet-fiddler
nerve-wracking
betweenwhiles
seaworthiness
deoxidisation
deoxidization
re-examination
re-exportation
resynchronise
resynchronize
Lecythidaceae
demythologise
demythologize
demyelination
Kenyapithecus
mezzo-sopranos
affenpinscher
offensiveness
effectualness
effectiveness
effervescence
effervescency
effervescible
offhandedness
efficaciously
officiousness
affirmatively
efflorescence
Afro-Caribbean
affordability
afforestation
off-reckonings
affreightment
egocentricity
agreeableness
egregiousness
aggiornamento
agriculturist
agglomeration
agglomerative
agglutinating
agglutination
agglutinative
agents-general
agonistically
ignominiously
agrobiologist
agrostologist
Egyptological
aggravatingly
egotistically
phraseologist
thrashing-mill
thrasonically
theatricalise
theatricalism
theatricality
theatricalize
theanthropism
theanthropist
chlamydomonas
chlamydospore
rhabdomantist
shabby-genteel
shock-absorber
chicken-and-egg
chicken-hazard
phycoerythrin
chuck-farthing
chuckle-headed
thick-pleached
thick-wittedly
rhodochrosite
Rhadamanthine
shadowcasting
chrematistics
three-cornered
wheeler-dealer
Phlegethontic
phrenetically
threefoldness
three-farthing
threshing-mill
thresher-whale
thresher-shark
cheerlessness
thremmatology
Rhaeto-Romance
Rhaeto-Romanic
phaenological
phrenological
threepenn'orth
three-per-cents
sheep-stealing
sheepshearing
chieftainship
chrestomathic
threateningly
phreatophytic
shiftlessness
thigmotropism
phthalocyanin
thrillingness
shrill-tongued
Cheirotherium
cheirographer
cheiropterous
christianiser

christianizer
Christianlike
Christianness
Christmas-tide
Christmas-time
Christologist
Shakespearean
Shakespearian
shalwar-kameez
phylacterical
whole-coloured
cholecystitis
Philadelphian
challengeable
challengingly
philhellenism
philhellenist
chylification
Thalamiflorae
thalamifloral
philomathical
philanthropic
whaling-master
phalansterian
phalansterism
phalansterist
phellogenetic
phallocentric
phyllophagous
phelloplastic
chalcographer
chalcographic
phylloquinone
wholesomeness
thalassocracy
philosophical
philosophiser
philosophizer
thalattocracy
chimneybreast
chimney-corner
chymification
shamefastness
whimsicalness
Thymelaeaceae
chameleon-like
thimblerigged
thimblerigger
shamelessness
rhombohedrons
rhombporphyry
chemoreceptor
phantasmalian
phantasmality
phonocamptics
thunder-bearer
changeability
thunder-darter
chinkerinchee
change-ringing
thunder-master

thenceforward
thunder-shower
thunderstruck
thunderstrike
thunder-stroke
changefulness
phonographist
thing-in-itself
phenylalanine
shingle-roofed
thanklessness
phenomenology
phenomenalise
phenomenalism
phenomenalist
phenomenality
phenomenalize
phonendoscope
thank-offering
phanerogamous
rhinoscleroma
thanatography
phenothiazine
thanatophobia
phonetisation
phonetization
phonautograph
thankworthily
phencyclidine
thiocarbamide
Theopaschitic
chlorargyrite
chromatically
chromatophore
chromatograph
thrombokinase
thrombophilia
theorematical
theoretically
shooting-match
throwing-table
throwing-stick
phlogisticate
Chlorophyceae
theologically
chronobiology
chloroplastal
chronological
theologoumena
chloroformist
chlorobromide
chlorocruorin
chronographer
Chloromycetin
throttle-valve
throttle-lever
thiosulphuric
ship-of-the-line
whipping-cheer
chopping-block
chopping-knife

chopping-board
whipping-cream
rhopalocerous
shapelessness
rhapsodically
rhyparography
charlatanical
pharmaceutics
pharmaceutist
pharmacognosy
pharmacopoeia
Pherecrataean
characterless
thoracentesis
thoracoplasty
charge-capping
charge-coupled
thurification
chirographist
churchmanship
church-service
church-officer
thereinbefore
thyroidectomy
whirling-table
whereinsoever
chiromantical
whoremasterly
whoremistress
pharyngoscope
pharyngoscopy
thermobalance
thermogenesis
thermogenetic
thermosetting
thermophilous
thermochemist
thermotherapy
thermoplastic
theriomorphic
choreographer
thermographer
choreographic
thermographic
thermotropism
thermonuclear
thermodynamic
chorepiscopal
pharisaically
sharpshooting
short-tempered
charity-school
thorough-paced
thoroughgoing
thoroughbrace
Third-Worldism
sherry-cobbler
physharmonica
physicianship
phase-contrast
whiskerandoed

phosphorylase
phosphorylate
phosphoretted
phosphuretted
whistle-blower
whistled-drunk
whistling-shop
physiotherapy
physiognomist
physiological
physiographer
physiographic
physitheistic
△chateaubriand
white-breasted
photochemical
phytochemical
photocopiable
photochromics
photochromism
photoelectric
photoelectron
photo-emission
whithersoever
white-favoured
photographist
ghetto-blaster
phytoplankton
photophoresis
photoperiodic
photoreceptor
Photostatting
phytotoxicity
photovoltaics
what-d'ye-call-'em
what-d'ye-call-it
thousand-pound
rheumatically
thaumatolatry
thaumaturgics
thaumaturgism
thaumaturgist
thoughtlessly
thought-reader
cheval-de-frise
chrysanthemum
chrysophilite
chrysophantic
rhizomorphous
disaffectedly
disaffirmance
dilapidations
vicariousness
vivaciousness
miracle-monger
Titanotherium
disappearance
misappreciate
disappointing
disagreeables
cicatrisation

Words marked △ may be spelled also with a capital letter

cicatrization
disassimilate
disarticulate
gigantomachia
misanthropist
X-inactivation
simarubaceous
disadvantaged
misadventured
misadventurer
misadvertence
timbrophilist
Liebfraumilch
diabetologist
aircraftwoman
piscicultural
kitchen-garden
biochemically
discreditable
discreditably
discretionary
kitchen-midden
pitched-roofed
zincification
pitch-farthing
miscegenation
mischief-maker
discriminator
mischievously
miscellaneous
discoloration
circumjacency
circumvallate
circumscriber
discomycetous
circumference
circumvention
circumventive
discommission
circumfluence
circumflexion
circumambages
circumambient
discommodious
circumspectly
miscomprehend
air-compressor
viscometrical
circumstances
circumduction
circumductory
bioconversion
discontenting
disconcertion
disconnection
misconception
misconjecture
discontentful
discontiguity
discontinuity
discontiguous
discontinuous
disconformity
cinchonaceous
disceptatious
discapacitate
disciplinable
miscorrection
diachronistic
visceroptosis
viscosimetric
diacatholicon
Hildebrandism
vindicability
vindicatorily
fiddle-faddler
fiddle-pattern
Middle-Eastern
middlebreaker
middle-bracket
kind-heartedly
tiddledywinks
biodegradable
winding-engine
sindonologist
bidding-prayer
Bildungsroman
winding-strips
kindergärtner
Kidderminster
mind-expanding
kindly-natured
liberationism
liberationist
miserableness
mineralogical
cinematograph
kinematograph
disembodiment
disembarkment
liver-coloured
videocassette
vice-admiralty
life-rendering
mine-detection
bioenergetics
fire-resistant
fire-resisting
time-bettering
time-beguiling
eigenfunction
disengagement
dimethylamine
kinesipathist
line-fisherman
kinesitherapy
kinesiologist
fixed-interest
vitelligenous
pigeon-fancier
pigeon-hearted
hide-and-go-seek
pigeon-chested
pigeon-livered
line-engraving
hibernisation
hibernization
Ciceronianism
vice-consulate
time-consuming
side-splitting
disemployment
misemployment
time-trialling
birefringence
vice-principal
vice-president
life-preserver
diversifiable
dimensionless
digestibility
divertibility
diverticulate
wide-stretched
disestimation
dilettanteism
directionless
divertisement
disequilibria
wide-awakeness
livery-servant
disfigurement
disfiguration
disfellowship
diffarreation
differentiate
diffusibility
diffusion-tube
diffusiveness
disgracefully
Zingiberaceae
single-hearted
single-chamber
pilgrim-bottle
disguisedness
linguistician
pidginisation
pidginization
biogeographer
diageotropism
diagnostician
niggardliness
finger-pointer
jiggery-pokery
finger-breadth
disgospelling
disgustedness
misgovernment
high-watermark
pigheadedness
disheartening
dichlamydeous
dishabilitate
nightclubbing
light-emitting
eighteen-pence
eighteen-penny
righteousness
light-fingered
tithe-gatherer
diphthongally
High-Churchman
High-Churchism
lighthouseman
might-have-been
sightlessness
nightmarishly
fishing-ground
lichenologist
lightning-tube
lithontriptic
lithontriptor
fishing-tackle
dishonourable
dishonourably
dichrooscopic
xiphiplastral
xiphiplastron
xiphophyllous
disharmonious
light-spirited
lightsomeness
lithesomeness
right-thinking
night-tripping
lithotriptist
high-stomached
dichotomously
high-muck-a-muck
night-wanderer
night-warbling
night-watchman
high-explosive
filipendulous
bidirectional
vivisectional
vivisectorium
vivisepulture
riding-clothes
disinhibition
disinhibitory
diminishingly
divisibleness
division-lobby
litigiousness
disilluminate
limitlessness
disillusioned
titillatingly
mini-flyweight
visionariness
disintegrable
disintegrator
sinistrorsely

13 □i□i□t

ministerially
disinterested
mini-submarine
filibustering
filibusterism
viniculturist
viticulturist
filibusterous
disinvigorate
disinvestment
disjunctively
nick-nackatory
pickle-herring
winkle-pickers
sick-feathered
milk-dentition
zinkification
silk-throwster
sick-thoughted
nickeliferous
nickel-plating
nickel-and-dime
pinking-shears
lickerishness
ticket-of-leave
ticket-writing
Rickettsiales
tickly-benders
billiard-table
billiard-cloth
yieldableness
dialectically
viol-de-gamboys
gillie-wetfoot
field-emission
millefeuilles
villeggiatura
dialogistical
villagisation
villagization
dipleidoscope
diplomatology
violoncellist
millennialist
millennianism
millenniarism
bibliolatrist
millionairess
bibliolatrous
bibliothecary
bibliophagist
bibliophilism
bibliophilist
wills-o'-the-wisp
bibliological
bibliopolical
bibliographer
bibliographic
dialypetalous
Bible-pounding
will-o'-the-wisps
△millstone-grit
Bible-thumping
sigmoidectomy
sigmoidoscope
sigmoidoscopy
dismemberment
diamond-beetle
mismanagement
Birminghamise
Birminghamize
dismantlement
diamond-powder
diametrically
significantly
dignification
lignification
signification
significatory
significative
signal-to-noise
bignoniaceous
pianistically
disnaturalise
disnaturalize
disordinately
disobediently
risorgimentos
mitochondrial
mitochondrion
disobligement
disobligingly
disobligation
disobligatory
lipogrammatic
ailourophilia
ailourophilic
ailourophobia
ailourophobic
misobservance
Dicotyledones
diaphanometer
dispraisingly
displantation
simple-hearted
displeasingly
tippling-house
simplificator
dipping-needle
diaphototropy
disproportion
misproportion
hippopotamian
dispurveyance
dispersedness
misperception
diaphragmatic
disparagement
disparagingly
dispiritingly
disparateness
mispersuasion
disposability
dispossession
dispassionate
dispositional
dispositioned
dispositively
disputability
disputatively
biopsychology
disqualifying
cinque-spotted
disquietingly
microanalysis
nitrobacteria
microcracking
vibracularium
nitro-compound
microcomputer
microcephalic
microcassette
microcosmical
microdetector
microeconomic
nitrification
vitrification
microfelsitic
microgranitic
hierogrammate
hieroglyphics
hieroglyphist
microlighting
micrometrical
micronutrient
micro-organism
microprinting
nitroparaffin
microporosity
disreputation
microphyllous
librarianship
mirror-writing
disrespectful
dioristically
microscopical
microsurgical
Diprotodontia
diprotodontid
microtonality
vibrationless
fibrovascular
microwaveable
misshapenness
first-begotten
bioscientific
dissolubility
dieselisation
dissoluteness
dieselization
dissemblingly
dissimilarity
dissimilitude
dissimilation
dissimulation
dissimulative
dissemination
disseminative
kissing-comfit
kiss-in-the-ring
kiss-and-make-up
Dioscoreaceae
dissepimental
fissiparously
biosystematic
lissotrichous
disseveration
linsey-woolsey
distractingly
distractively
biotechnology
kitty-cornered
tittle-tattler
△diotheletical
diathermanous
distressingly
distressfully
histrionicism
distributable
mirthlessness
victimologist
victimisation
victimization
tintinnabular
tintinnabulum
lifting-bridge
Nintendinitus
listening-post
distant-signal
kittenishness
distinctively
distinguished
distinguisher
fictionalised
fictionalized
histiophoroid
filterability
Dipterocarpus
picture-palace
winterisation
picturesquely
picture-window
winterization
distastefully
dictatorially
mistrustingly
distrustfully
mistrustfully
kittly-benders
misunderstand
misunderstood
figure-casting
figure-weaving
ritualisation

visualisation
ritualization
visualization
biculturalism
silver-tongued
silver-mounted
airworthiness
nitwittedness
piezoelectric
piezomagnetic
skulking-place
skeletogenous
skinny-dipping
skirting-board
skirl-in-the-pan
skateboarding
sketchability
skittle-ground
skeuomorphism
cloak-and-sword
cleavableness
floating-point
olfactologist
clean-timbered
plebification
globuliferous
globalisation
globalization
elaborateness
globetrotting
black-and-white
blackberrying
clickety-clack
clickety-click
blackguardism
floccillation
electioneerer
ill-considered
gluconeogenic
old-clothesman
plectognathic
glaciological
plectopterous
electrochemic
electrocement
electrocution
electrifiable
electrography
electromagnet
electromerism
electrometric
electromotive
electro-optics
electroplater
electrophilic
electrophorus
electrostatic
electroscopic
electrisation
electrothermy
electrotypist

electrovalent
electrization
glycosylation
clock-watching
gladiatorship
bladder-cherry
Illecebraceae
illegibleness
sleeplessness
alternatively
allegorically
allelomorphic
algebraically
client-centred
ill-favouredly
oligocythemia
flagellantism
flagellomania
flugelhornist
flügelhornist
plagiocephaly
plagiotropism
plagiotropous
Plagiostomata
plagiostomous
oligopolistic
flight-feather
alphabetiform
alphabetarian
All-hallowmass
All-hallowtide
clairaudience
alligator-pear
sleight-of-hand
cleistogamous
cloister-garth
plaintiveness
blameableness
climacterical
climactically
flame-coloured
Flammenwerfer
climbing-frame
plumbisolvent
aluminiferous
plumbosolvent
glamorisation
clamorousness
glamorization
climatography
climatologist
plantain-eater
clinodiagonal
flannel-flower
clandestinely
clandestinity
plenteousness
blankety-blank
clincher-built
blanchisseuse
plantie-cruive

blandishments
plentifulness
flint-knapping
blindman's-buff
planimetrical
clinopinacoid
clinopinakoid
alongshoreman
plenitudinous
planetologist
oleomargarine
allowableness
blood-boltered
bloodcurdling
almond-blossom
allochthonous
illogicalness
floodlighting
bloodlessness
algologically
alcoholometer
alcoholometry
blood-relation
blood-relative
Bloomsburyite
illocutionary
blepharospasm
elephantiasis
elephant's-ears
elephant's-foot
clapperboards
clapperclawer
glyphographer
glyphographic
glyptographic
flirtatiously
floricultural
ultra-distance
clarification
glorification
ultrafiltrate
pluralisation
pluralization
pluripresence
floristically
ultra-tropical
ultra-virtuous
blister-beetle
glass-grinding
blasphemously
classicalness
clishmaclaver
plesiosaurian
blastogenesis
plasmodesmata
glossological
glossographer
flesh-pressing
glass-painting
slate-coloured
platycephalic

clothes-basket
Kletterschuhe
blotting-paper
plotting-paper
platiniferous
platinum-blond
plethorically
plate-printing
platyrrhinian
platitudinise
platitudinous
platitudinize
slaughterable
illuminations
floutingstock
flourishingly
plausibleness
illustrissimo
illustriously
claustrophobe
clavicembalos
fluvio-glacial
flower-de-leuce
flower-service
clay-ironstone
immarcescible
immaterialise
immaterialism
immaterialist
immateriality
immaterialize
imparipinnate
impalpability
embarrassment
impassability
impassibility
ambassadorial
impassiveness
impartialness
impartibility
impeccability
imperceptible
imperceptibly
impenetration
imperfectible
imperfectness
imperforation
imperialistic
immediateness
imperiousness
umbelliferous
embellishment
impermanently
impermissible
impermissibly
impersonalise
impersonality
impersonalize
impersonation
imperseverant
impertinently

13 □m□e□t

imperturbable
imperturbably
impecuniosity
impecuniously
impetuousness
amygdalaceous
emigrationist
imaginariness
imaginatively
amphigastrium
emphysematous
amphitheatral
amphitheatric
immiscibility
amniocentesis
ambidexterity
ambidexterous
empire-builder
ambitiousness
impignoration
omnicompetent
ambiguousness
smoke-consumer
smokelessness
small-and-early
implacability
implicatively
amplification
smelling-salts
smelting-works
smelting-house
immovableness
imponderables
smooth-chinned
smooth-dittied
smooth-tongued
impolitically
impoliticness
embourgeoised
impossibilism
impossibilist
impossibility
impostumation
importunately
omoplatoscopy
improbability
impracticable
impracticably
impractically
umbraculiform
embracingness
amorphousness
umbrella-plant
umbrella-stand
emerald-copper
amarantaceous
Amaranthaceae
embranglement
embryogenesis
embryological
impropriation
△impressionism
△impressionist
embrittlement
improvability
improvidently
improvisatrix
improvisation
improvisatory
imitativeness
amitryptyline
immutableness
imputableness
immunifacient
immunotherapy
immunological
impulsiveness
empyreumatise
empyreumatize
unmacadamised
unmacadamized
uneatableness
untamableness
uncalculating
incarceration
incardination
incandescence
unsaleability
intangibility
ensanguinated
unfashionable
unfashionably
insatiability
invariability
unsatisfiable
unfamiliarity
insatiateness
infallibilism
infallibilist
infallibility
inharmonicity
ungainsayable
undauntedness
untaintedness
unsaintliness
unsavouriness
unwarrantable
unwarrantably
unwarrantedly
encapsulation
sneak-thievery
unearthliness
unfalteringly
incantational
unpasteurised
unpasteurized
unnaturalised
unnaturalized
unnaturalness
unsalvageable
inobservation
inobtrusively
unobtrusively
unabbreviated
unobstructive
△knickerbocker
unaccentuated
knock-for-knock
inscriptional
inscriptively
knick-knackery
inoculability
knuckleduster
knuckle-headed
unicameralism
unicameralist
unscholarlike
onychophagist
unaccountable
unaccountably
unaccompanied
Anacardiaceae
anachronistic
anachronously
unscrutinised
unscrutinized
unscavengered
ineducability
inadvertently
unadventurous
unadvisedness
unadulterated
inodorousness
underachiever
indefatigable
indefatigably
annexationist
untenableness
interbreeding
underclassman
indescribable
indescribably
undescribable
unperceivable
unperceivably
unperceivedly
intercolumnar
intercolonial
intercalation
intercalative
intercellular
unwelcomeness
intercommunal
undescendable
undescendible
underclothing
intercropping
intercurrence
undercarriage
invendibility
interdigitate
interdentally
unbendingness
inner-directed
unremembering
independently
unregenerated
indeterminacy
unbeseemingly
indeterminism
indeterminist
indeterminate
undeterminate
unceremonious
underexposure
unnecessarily
inferentially
underestimate
interestingly
unrelentingly
unrepentingly
undeservingly
unperfectness
underfinished
interferogram
interferingly
unselfishness
undergraduate
unneighboured
unneighbourly
unfeignedness
intergalactic
encephalocele
encephalogram
Encephalartos
encephalotomy
underhandedly
unreliability
undeliverable
unmedicinable
indelibleness
undeviatingly
unremittently
unremittingly
unresistingly
ingeniousness
unbelievingly
interjaculate
interjectural
unreplaceable
interlacement
interlocutrix
interlocation
interlocution
interlocutory
intellectuals
intelligencer
intelligently
unhealthiness
unhealthfully
unreclaimable
unreclaimably
interlaminate
unfeelingness

Words marked △ may be spelled also with a capital letter

unreplenished
interlunation
intermediator
intermarriage
intermittence
intermittency
intermetallic
underniceness
antenniferous
unmeaningness
△international
interosculant
interosculate
unrecoverable
unrecoverably
interoceptive
anaerobically
unrecollected
unrecommended
unrecognising
Enteropneusta
unrecognizing
unrecompensed
unremorseless
underprepared
interpretable
interpretress
underpainting
interpilaster
interpolation
interpolative
interpunction
interproximal
interparietal
interpersonal
intemperately
interposition
unperpetrated
interpetiolar
unreproaching
unreproachful
undepreciated
interradially
unreprievable
unlearnedness
interrogation
interrogatory
interrogative
interrelation
unreprimanded
endearingness
interruptedly
unrepresented
unterrestrial
unpersuadable
understanding
interscapular
infeasibility
insensibility
incense-burner
intersidereal
under-shepherd
interspecific
interstellary
interspersion
unreasoningly
incessantness
understrapper
interstratify
insensateness
unsensational
insensitively
insensitivity
intensiveness
ungentlemanly
unsettledness
investigation
investigatory
investigative
entertainment
uncertainness
insectologist
unsentimental
unrestingness
intentionally
unmentionable
intertropical
inventorially
unrestfulness
infectiveness
inventiveness
insectivorous
integumentary
underutilised
underutilized
unreturningly
ungenuineness
ingenuousness
unserviceable
endeavourment
ineffableness
snuff-coloured
inoffensively
ineffectually
ineffectively
inefficacious
snifting-valve
inefficiently
inofficiously
snaffle-bridle
enigmatically
anagrammatise
anagrammatism
anagrammatist
anagrammatize
inegalitarian
knight-marshal
knights-errant
knight-service
unshrinkingly
unchristianly
unthriftyhead
unthriftiness
anthelminthic
unwholesomely
unphilosophic
enchondromata
anthropopathy
anthropolatry
anthropogenic
anthropometry
anthropophagi
anthropophagy
anthropophyte
untheological
anthroposophy
anthropomorph
anthophyllite
unchastisable
unchastizable
unwhistleable
anti-marketeer
antiballistic
antibacterial
invincibility
Antiochianism
uncircumcised
undiscomfited
undisciplined
undiscernedly
indiscernible
indiscernibly
undiscernible
undiscernibly
antiscorbutic
undiscussable
undiscussible
undiscouraged
unmindfulness
antinephritic
antigenically
antidesiccant
antiterrorist
undiversified
anti-personnel
antisepticise
antisepticism
antisepticize
engine-turning
undifferenced
indifferently
undisguisable
undisguisedly
△enlightenment
unrighteously
antichristian
unsightliness
undishonoured
unwithholding
unwithdrawing
unmitigatedly
infinitesimal
undividedness
unlimitedness
invisibleness
antimicrobial
antihistamine
unministerial
individualise
individualism
individualist
individuality
individualize
insidiousness
invidiousness
unpitifulness
individuation
inviolability
anticlockwise
anticlimactic
unwillingness
anticlinorium
inviolateness
insignificant
Indianisation
Indianization
antilogarithm
oneiroscopist
anti-modernist
anticoagulant
antisocialism
antisocialist
antisociality
antinomianism
environmental
anticorrosive
indispensable
indispensably
antispasmodic
indisposition
unvitrifiable
antiarthritic
antigropeloes
indissuadable
indissuadably
undissociated
indissociable
antipsychotic
angiospermous
unbiassedness
antiasthmatic
indissolvable
undistracting
undistributed
unmistakeable
unmistakeably
undistempered
unwittingness
indistinction
indistinctive
undistinctive
undisturbedly
unmistrustful
antisubmarine

13 □n□i□u

insinuatingly
antiquitarian
unskilfulness
Anglo-American
uncleanliness
unpleasurable
unpleasurably
inelaborately
unelectrified
anglicisation
Anglo-Catholic
anglicization
influentially
ineligibility
analogousness
unflinchingly
inclinational
inflorescence
unblessedness
Anglo-Saxondom
unilateralism
unilateralist
unilaterality
uncloudedness
unilluminated
unillustrated
inflexibility
inflexionless
unamiableness
unembarrassed
unimpassioned
animadversion
unimpeachable
unembellished
unimaginative
unambitiously
unambiguously
animal-worship
anomalistical
animalisation
animalization
anemometrical
un-Americanise
un-Americanize
unimpregnated
unimpressible
onomastically
inimitabiity
mnemotechnics
mnemotechnist
unsmotherable
unemotionally
onomatopoesis
onomatopoetic
uninhabitable
uninteresting
unintelligent
unintermitted
uninterrupted
unentertained
unintentional
enantiodromia
enantiodromic
unenlightened
unanticipated
enantiomorphy
enantiotropic
uninfluential
uninflammable
inanimateness
unenforceable
uninforceable
uninformative
uninstructive
uninquisitive
uninaugurated
unknowingness
unpolarisable
unpolarizable
innovationist
enjoyableness
unwomanliness
incombustible
incombustibly
unconcealable
inconceivable
inconceivably
unconceivable
unconceivably
unconcernedly
unconcernment
unsoldierlike
incondensable
unconditional
unconditioned
unforeseeable
ontogenically
unforeskinned
endometriosis
undomesticate
indolebutyric
uncomfortable
uncomfortably
unconformable
unconformably
unforgettable
unforgettably
incongruously
unforgiveness
insociability
unsociability
encomiastical
innoxiousness
unconjectured
unconjunctive
unworkmanlike
unworldliness
endosmometric
uncommendable
uncommendably
incommunicado
incommiscible
informatician
informational
unboundedness
inhomogeneity
inhomogeneous
entomophagous
entomophilous
ontologically
entomological
entomostracan
uncomplaining
uncomplaisant
uncomplicated
uncompensated
uncompanioned
incorporeally
incorporating
incorporation
incorporative
uncooperative
unco-operative
incompossible
encompassment
incompatibles
inhospitality
incompetently
uncompetitive
unconquerable
unconquerably
incorrectness
encouragement
encouragingly
uncoordinated
unco-ordinated
uncourtliness
endocrinology
incorruptible
incorruptibly
incorruptness
unconsecrated
inconsecutive
unconsidering
inconsiderate
insconsciently
unconsciously
inconspicuous
unconsummated
inconsonantly
inconsequence
inconstruable
unconstrained
inconsistence
inconsistency
unforthcoming
uncontainable
indoctrinator
uncontentious
incontinently
unfortunately
incontestable
incontestably
uncontestable
involucellate
insolubleness
involuntarily
innocuousness
insolvability
inconvenience
inconvincible
inconversable
unconversable
inconvertible
inconvertibly
unconvertible
endosymbiotic
unspecialised
unspecialized
unspectacular
unspeculative
inspectorship
anaphorically
inopportunely
inopportunity
inoperability
unappreciated
inappreciable
anaphrodisiac
unapprehended
unsparingness
inappropriate
unappropriate
unspiritually
inspiritingly
inspirational
unapprovingly
unapostolical
unspottedness
anaphylactoid
unequivocally
uncreatedness
encroachingly
inorganically
inerrableness
intra-arterial
unprecedented
unpracticable
unpractically
onirocritical
intracellular
intracapsular
intricateness
anfractuosity
infructuously
intracavitary
incredibility
unpredictable
unpredictably
unbridledness
incredulously
androdioecism
energetically
introgression

Words marked △ may be spelled also with a capital letter

unprogressive
unoriginality
unarticulated
ungrammatical
untremblingly
incriminatory
unpromisingly
intramuscular
untransformed
intrinsically
intransigence
intransigency
intransigeant
untransmitted
untransparent
intranational
unpreoccupied
entrepreneuse
unprophetical
intraparietal
infraposition
intrapetiolar
untrespassing
infraspecific
introspection
introspective
unpresentable
intrusiveness
untrustworthy
unbrotherlike
unpretentious
unprovocative
unprovided-for
unpreventable
untraversable
introversible
unprovisioned
intravasation
intravascular
unestablished
unascertained
unassimilated
unassimilable
anastigmatism
anisophyllous
unassuageable
unsteadfastly
unit-packaging
anathematical
inattentively
unstigmatised
unstigmatized
instigatingly
anythingarian
instantaneity
instantaneous
instantiation
instinctually
instinctively
instinctivity
gnathonically
unstercorated
institutional
institutively
unstaunchable
instructional
instructively
pneumatically
undulationist
endurableness
incurableness
untunableness
pneumatometer
pneumatophore
pneumatolysis
pneumatolytic
unpurchasable
insusceptible
insusceptibly
unsusceptible
unpunctuality
infundibulate
unputdownable
unsuperfluous
untunefulness
insufficience
insufficiency
ingurgitation
injudiciously
inaudibleness
infuriatingly
incuriousness
injuriousness
undutifulness
induplication
unqualifiable
unqualifiedly
unmurmuringly
pneumogastric
insubordinate
pneumonectomy
unsuspectedly
insupportable
insupportably
unsupportable
unsupportedly
unsurpassable
unsurpassably
unguardedness
insubstantial
unsubstantial
unquestioning
inquisitional
inquisitorial
inquisitively
unsuitability
unjustifiable
unjustifiably
unsustainable
industrialise
industrialism
industrialist
industrialize
industriously
unhurtfulness
unevangelical
universalness
inevitability
knowledgeable
knowledgeably
answerability
inexhaustible
inexhaustibly
inexperienced
unexperienced
inexpediently
inexpensively
unexpensively
unexceptional
inexpectation
unexaggerated
inexplainable
unexplainable
unexclusively
unexemplified
inexorability
inexpressible
inexpressibly
unexpressible
encyclopedian
encyclopedism
encyclopedist
△encyclopaedia
encyclopaedic
unsymmetrical
unsymmetrised
unsymmetrized
enhypostatise
enhypostatize
unsympathetic
non-accidental
Monarchianism
tobaccanalian
non-acceptance
non-accessible
morale-booster
non-aggression
boraginaceous
logarithmical
volatilisable
volatilizable
foraminiferal
vocationalism
voraciousness
coralliferous
coralligenous
Mohammedanise
Mohammedanism
Mohammedanize
cocainisation
cocainization
potamological
somatological
gonadotrophic
gonadotrophin
somatotrophic
somatotrophin
Romano-British
non-appearance
noradrenaline
woman-suffrage
romanticality
copartnership
cobaltiferous
non-attendance
roe-blackberry
double-banking
double-natured
double-dealing
double-meaning
double-hearted
double-density
double-shuffle
double-chinned
double-shotted
double-glazing
double-concave
double-tongued
double-founted
double-jointed
double-coconut
double-mouthed
double-fronted
double-crosser
double-or-quits
hobby-horsical
morbillivirus
combinability
combinatorial
combinatorics
non-biological
bombastically
sorbitisation
combativeness
sorbitization
tomboyishness
touchableness
non-classified
coachbuilding
concyclically
concretionary
non-cognizable
conceitedness
fonctionnaire
porcellaneous
non-collegiate
porcelaineous
voicelessness
non-commercial
coxcombically
non-compliance
non-compounder
concomitantly
non-contagious

volcanologist
non-conclusive
nonconforming
△nonconformist
nonconformity
concentricity
concentration
concentrative
volcanisation
non-concurrent
non-conducting
volcanization
conchological
Conceptionist
porcupine-wood
concupiscence
concupiscible
conceptualise
conceptualism
conceptualist
conceptualize
concernedness
concertinaing
concertmaster
vouchsafement
concessionary
concessionist
concatenation
concavo-convex
coachwhip-bird
good-naturedly
cordocentesis
conductorship
coeducational
road-metalling
soldierliness
cold-heartedly
good-King-Henry
condylomatous
word-blindness
cold-bloodedly
toad-in-the-hole
golden-crested
wood-engraving
woodcock's-head
word-splitting
ponderability
word-processor
powdering-gown
powdering-room
wonder-working
wonder-wounded
ponderousness
wonderfulness
condescending
condescension
nondescriptly
conditionally
coadjutorship
Wordsworthian
homeward-bound
polecat-ferret
dodecaphonism
dodecaphonist
tolerationism
tolerationist
moderatorship
power-assisted
nomenclatural
women-children
honeycomb-moth
coreferential
robe-de-chambre
forefeelingly
forementioned
lozenge-shaped
money-grubbing
foreshadowing
foresightless
coreligionist
cobelligerent
codeclination
powerlessness
homeomorphism
homeomorphous
hole-and-corner
hole-in-the-wall
governing-body
modernisation
solemnisation
foreknowledge
foreknowingly
modernization
solemnization
Polemoniaceae
vote-splitting
forensicality
domestication
homeothermous
homeoteleuton
potentiometer
momentariness
momentousness
forejudgement
bone-turquoise
confraternity
conflagration
confabulation
confabulatory
confectionary
confectionery
confidingness
confederation
confederative
coffee-housing
configuration
non-fulfilment
non-functional
confrontation
non-forfeiting
confarreation
confessionary
confessorship
confoundingly
rough-and-ready
congratulable
congratulator
tongue-lashing
long-descended
Congreve-match
tongue-in-cheek
tongue-doubtie
congressional
Congresswoman
tongue-twister
bougainvillea
coagulability
conglomeratic
zoogeographer
zoogeographic
forgottenness
forgetfulness
longsuffering
conglutinator
congruousness
cochleariform
mother-of-pearl
sophisticated
sophistically
sophisticator
bonheur-du-jour
nominatively
totipalmation
noli-me-tangere
homiletically
mowing-machine
dolichocephal
Dolichosauria
Dolichosaurus
solifidianism
domiciliation
solicitorship
bouillabaisse
sociologistic
sociolinguist
socialisation
socialization
poliomyelitis
goniometrical
toxicophagous
eosinophilous
Morisonianism
codicological
toxicological
horizontality
Louis-Quatorze
corinthianise
corinthianize
△sovietologist
solidungulate
solidungulous
conjecturable
conjecturally
non-judgmental
conjugational
conjunctional
conjunctively
work-hardening
book-canvasser
cock-of-the-rock
poikilothermy
booking-office
mocking-thrush
cook-housemaid
pocket-picking
folk-etymology
foolhardiness
wool-gathering
colleagueship
collaboration
collaborative
collectedness
collecting-box
collectorship
pollicitation
woollen-draper
collieshangie
soul-searching
jollification
mollification
moulding-board
boulting-hutch
worldly-minded
bowling-crease
polliniferous
roll-on-roll-off
colloquialism
colloquialist
roller-bandage
roller-bearing
roller-skating
rollerblading
rollercoaster
dollarisation
dollarization
molluscicidal
toilet-service
hollow-hearted
follow-through
commeasurable
cosmochemical
cosmeceutical
formidability
Commelinaceae
formularistic
formalisation
normalisation
formalization
normalization
commemoration
commemoratory
commemorative
communication
communicatory

communicative
commandership
communitarian
commensurable
commensurably
communautaire
cosmopolitics
cosmopolitism
commercialese
commercialise
commercialism
commercialist
commerciality
commercialize
commiseration
commiserative
commutability
cosmothetical
committeeship
cosmetologist
commutatively
normativeness
foundation-net
mountains-high
downcast-shaft
boundary-layer
boundary-rider
connecting-rod
connectionism
mountebanking
mountebankery
mountebankism
counter-attack
counteraction
counteractive
counterbidder
counterchange
countercharge
counter-caster
counter-fleury
counterfeiter
counterfeitly
coinheritance
counter-jumper
founder-member
countermotion
counselorship
counter-poison
counter-parole
counter-signal
counterstroke
counterspying
coenaesthesis
bounteousness
counter-weight
cornification
non-negotiable
corn-chandlery
mounting-block
counting-house
pointing-stock
downrightness
bountifulness
somniloquence
boundlessness
pointlessness
cognomination
connumeration
somnambulance
somnambulator
coin-in-the-slot
morning-prayer
Johnsonianism
soundproofing
hound-trailing
round-the-clock
round-tripping
cornet-à-piston
monodactylous
no-holds-barred
monometallism
monometallist
holometabolic
monotelephone
homogenetical
novocentenary
homosexualism
homosexualist
homosexuality
borough-monger
podophthalmus
monophthongal
monothalamous
△monotheletism
△monothelitism
do-nothingness
homochromatic
monochromatic
monochromator
Holothuroidea
monophosphate
△monophysitism
honorifically
sodomitically
notoriousness
Corolliflorae
corollifloral
toxoplasmosis
homoeopathist
monomolecular
homoeothermal
homoiothermal
homoeothermic
homoiothermic
homologically
topologically
homologoumena
homoeomorphic
homomorphosis
monocotyledon
monogrammatic
monotrematous
logographical
monographical
nomographical
topographical
colourisation
homoeroticism
colourization
monopsonistic
non-observance
motor-traction
Podostemaceae
monostrophics
pococurantism
pococurantist
coconut-butter
mononucleosis
monosyllabism
monosymmetric
complainingly
complaisantly
compactedness
complexedness
comprehension
comprehensive
complementary
pompier-ladder
copple-crowned
compressional
compagination
dolphinariums
complications
complimentary
morphinomania
compulsionist
popping-crease
compendiously
companionable
companionably
companionhood
companionless
companionship
morphogenesis
morphogenetic
morphophoneme
comprovincial
non-proficient
Compsognathus
morphological
morphographer
non-production
non-productive
copper-captain
comparability
pooper-scooper
non-persistent
corporateness
comparatively
dog-periwinkle
copper-pyrites
compassionate
colposcopical
compositeness
compositional
compatibility
compatriotism
non-pathogenic
computer-aided
computational
zoopsychology
zoophysiology
conquistadors
corroboration
corroboratory
corroborative
court-bouillon
porridge-stick
corridor-train
coarse-grained
courteousness
journey-weight
corrigibility
non-regardance
mourning-piece
mourning-cloak
mourning-coach
coursing-joint
boarding-house
mourning-bride
mourning-stuff
correlatively
correlativity
torrentiality
corruptionist
horripilation
corrosibility
correspondent
corresponding
corresponsive
non-resistance
corrosiveness
non-returnable
bourguignonne
sorrowfulness
horse-and-buggy
dog's-tail-grass
constableship
constablewick
Constantinian
house-breaking
possibilities
goose-barnacle
mouse-coloured
consecutively
consideringly
considerately
consideration
considerative
topside-turvey
non-specialist
constellation
constellatory
consternation

Words marked △ may be spelled also with a capital letter

13 □o□s□f

horsefeathers
non-scientific
conscientious
consciousness
conspicuously
consolidation
consolidative
tonsillectomy
fossiliferous
noiselessness
fossilisation
fossilization
horse-milliner
consimilarity
consimilitude
housemistress
toastmistress
consumptively
consumptivity
consentaneity
consentaneous
nonsensically
consenescence
consenescency
poisonousness
consanguinity
zoosporangium
go-as-you-please
consequential
conservatoire
constructable
constructible
constrainable
constrainedly
constringency
bowstring-hemp
boustrophedon
monstrousness
horse-sickness
possessionary
possessionate
possessorship
topsy-turvydom
conspurcation
constupration
horse-wrangler
housewifeskep
housewifeship
contrabandism
contrabandist
contralateral
contrafagotto
contrabassoon
foot-land-raker
contraterrene
contraception
contravention
contraceptive
toothache-tree
contradiction
contradictory
contradictive
contrariously
contrappostos
foot-passenger
contractility
contractional
contrapuntist
mouthbreather
contabescence
horticultural
volta-electric
northerliness
southerliness
röntgenoscopy
bottle-coaster
north-easterly
south-easterly
post-tensioned
postmenstrual
north-eastward
south-eastward
soft-sectoring
pontificality
fortification
mortification
cost-effective
cost-efficient
soothfastness
doctrinairism
tortoiseshell
tortoise-plant
Voltaireanism
postliminiary
postliminious
Voltairianism
contristation
contributable
Portulacaceae
nostalgically
postclassical
worthlessness
postulational
mortal-staring
contemplation
contemplatist
contemplative
contamination
contaminative
Contemptibles
root-and-branch
contentedness
continuedness
fortune-hunter
cotton-picking
contentiously
fortune-teller
fortunateness
post-modernism
post-modernist
controversial
controvertist
post-communion
tooth-ornament
iontophoresis
iontophoretic
post-operative
contortionism
contortionist
contortionate
posture-master
foster-brother
post-traumatic
posterization
fortississimo
loathsomeness
toothsomeness
potty-training
fortitudinous
noctivagation
boatswain-bird
north-westerly
south-westerly
north-westward
south-westward
mouthwatering
post-existence
contextualise
contextualize
volumenometer
documentalist
documentarily
documentarise
documentarist
documentarize
documentation
voluntariness
voluntaristic
convocational
convulsionary
convulsionist
convalescence
convalescency
conventioneer
conventionary
conventionist
conversazione
conversazioni
convertiplane
convexo-convex
polygalaceous
polycarbonate
polydaemonism
polydactylism
polydactylous
polyadelphous
polytechnical
polythalamous
polychromatic
polyphloisbic
copyrightable
polyhistorian
polyembryonic
polygonaceous
Polypodiaceae
polynomialism
polypropylene
polyprotodont
polycythaemia
polysyllabism
polysyllogism
polysynthesis
polysynthetic
splanchnocele
splanchnology
speaking-voice
aphanipterous
sphagnicolous
sphagnologist
spray-painting
spectatorship
spectacularly
specification
apocalyptical
speculatively
epicondylitis
spectrography
spectrometric
apochromatism
spectroscopic
apocatastasis
spadicifloral
apodictically
epidermolysis
epidotisation
epidotization
appendiculate
splendiferous
splenetically
Ephemeroptera
appeteezement
speechfulness
sphericalness
apheliotropic
spheristerion
appealingness
appellational
appellatively
spheroidicity
spherocytosis
appertainance
appertainment
spifflication
epigrammatise
epigrammatist
epigrammatize
epigeneticist
apogeotropism
spring-cleaner
sphingomyelin
uprighteously
sprightliness
ophiomorphous
oppignoration

epeirogenesis
epeirogenetic
splinter-proof
spokespersons
applicability
spelaeologist
speleological
apoliticality
apomictically
spontaneously
spine-chilling
epanadiploses
epanadiplosis
Spencerianism
spinning-jenny
spinning-wheel
spinning-house
sponging-house
spunging-house
spinuliferous
spindle-legged
spindle-shaped
spindle-shanks
spinelessness
epinastically
spine-tingling
spondylolysis
up-to-the-moment
up-to-the-minute
oppositionist
opportuneness
opportunistic
opportunities
apportionment
epiphenomenon
apophlegmatic
spermatogenic
spermatotheca
spermatophore
Spermatophyta
spermatophyte
spermatoblast
spermatorrhea
opprobriously
apprehensible
appropriately
appropriation
appropriative
appropinquate
appropinquity
sportsmanlike
sportsmanship
sportswriting
spiritualiser
spiritualizer
spiritualness
spirit-rapping
spiritousness
operativeness
approximately
approximation
approximative
opisthobranch
opisthography
apostolically
spasmodically
epitrachelion
ophthalmology
apathetically
epitheliomata
apothegmatise
apothegmatist
apothegmatize
spathiphyllum
splutteringly
sphygmography
squandermania
squanderingly
square-dancing
square-bashing
square-pierced
squeamishness
equestrianism
squeezability
squirarchical
equitableness
equisetaceous
equidifferent
equilibration
equidistantly
equivocalness
equiponderant
equiponderate
equipotential
Aquifoliaceae
equinoctially
pre-adamitical
breakableness
preadaptation
preambulatory
cream-coloured
pro-and-conning
armamentarium
ornamentation
breakfast-room
great-grandson
triangularity
triangulately
triangulation
breathing-hole
breathing-time
treacherously
breaking-point
irrationalise
irrationalism
irrationalist
irrationality
irrationalize
dreadlessness
dreamlessness
broadmindedly
preadmonition
preadolescent
organogenesis
organotherapy
triatomically
ergatomorphic
broad-spectrum
breast-feeding
treasure-chest
treasure-house
treasure-trove
treasurership
cribbage-board
probabilistic
probabilities
problematical
triboelectric
Brobdignagian
Orobanchaceae
tribunitical
tribunitician
tributariness
pro-chancellor
Tractarianism
traceableness
tractableness
procrastinate
cracker-barrel
procreational
practicalness
fractionalise
fractionalism
fractionalist
fractionalize
fractionation
△brachiosaurus
fractiousness
trickle-charge
gracelessness
pricelessness
tracklessness
oraculousness
prick-me-dainty
preconception
arachnoiditis
arachnologist
precentorship
arachnophobia
preconisation
proconsulship
preconization
trichological
trichopterist
trichopterous
precopulatory
precipitantly
precipitately
precipitation
precipitative
precipitously
tricarpellary
trichromatism
tricorporated
tricarboxylic
procuratorial
procès-verbaux
processioning
processionary
process-server
prick-the-louse
precautionary
brachydactyly
brachycephaly
brachypterous
predicability
producibility
predicamental
predicatively
fridge-freezer
bridge-builder
predefinition
credulousness
predominantly
predomination
prudentialism
prudentialist
prudentiality
urediniospore
tradesmanlike
predestinator
gradationally
traditionally
predatoriness
trade-weighted
free-marketeer
irreverential
free-selection
irredeemables
pre-engagement
triethylamine
breech-loading
arteriography
freezing-point
irreligionist
irreligiously
true-disposing
irreciprocity
irreplaceable
irreplaceably
irreclaimable
irreclaimably
irrepleviable
araeometrical
irrecoverable
irrecoverably
irrecognition
arsenopyrites
irresponsible
irresponsibly
irretrievable
irretrievably
irrefrangible
irrefrangibly

Words marked △ may be spelled also with a capital letter

13 □r□e□r

irrepressible
irrepressibly
grief-stricken
argentiferous
prefabricated
prefabricator
profectitious
prefigurement
prefiguration
prefigurative
traffic-lights
preferability
craftsmanship
draftsmanship
professoriate
professorship
profitability
profit-sharing
prefatorially
drag-parachute
pragmatically
progressional
progressively
progressivism
progressivist
fragmentarily
fragmentation
draggle-tailed
trigonometric
progenitorial
prognosticate
troglodytical
frighteningly
frightfulness
prohibitively
ortho-compound
archidiaconal
orthodiagonal
orchidologist
orchidomaniac
archaeologist
archaeometric
archaeopteryx
orthognathism
orthographist
orthognathous
Archegoniatae
archbishopric
archimandrite
urchin-snouted
orthopaedical
archipelagoes
orthopinakoid
orchesography
orthostichous
orthosilicate
prehistorical
orchestralist
orchestration
architectonic
architectural
drainage-basin
irritableness
brainchildren
groin-centring
vraisemblance
cruiserweight
ornithichnite
ornithologist
ornithomantic
ornithophobia
ornithischian
draining-board
artificialise
artificiality
artificialize
prairie-oyster
brainlessness
fruitlessness
arrière-pensée
arbitrariness
brainsickness
brainstorming
train-spotting
projectionist
prejudicially
prejudication
prejudicative
broken-hearted
prolification
proliferation
proliferative
proliferously
prolegomenary
prolegomenous
drilling-lathe
trolling-spoon
brilliantness
trellis-window
preliminaries
preliminarily
trilingualism
proleptically
drill-sergeant
trilateralism
trilateralist
triliteralism
trilateration
uralitisation
uralitization
grammatically
premedication
premeditation
premeditative
trumpet-flower
trumpet-shaped
primigravidae
primigravidas
primogenitrix
primogenitary
primogeniture
primogenitive
bromeliaceous
premillennial
Grumbletonian
tremulousness
frumentaceous
frumentarious
premandibular
criminologist
priming-powder
premonishment
premonitorily
criminousness
graminivorous
tram-conductor
primordialism
primordiality
promise-breach
promiscuously
promotability
primatologist
dramaturgical
prematureness
dramatisation
primitiveness
dramatization
transatlantic
drinkableness
transactinide
transactional
trunk-breeches
transcribable
transcription
transcriptase
transcriptive
crinicultural
transcendence
transcendency
granddaughter
Frankeniaceae
orange-blossom
fringe-dweller
transfer-paper
transferrable
transformable
transferrible
transfusively
grandfatherly
uranographist
transgression
transgressive
wrong-headedly
branch-officer
bronchography
franchisement
bronchoscopic
arundinaceous
principalness
principalship
transit-circle
printing-house
printing-press
transitionary
fringilliform
transientness
grandiloquent
grandiloquous
transisthmian
transistorise
transistorize
translucidity
translucently
translocation
granuliferous
granulomatous
translational
translatorial
transliterate
transmigrator
transmination
transmissible
transmittance
transmittable
grandmotherly
transmittible
transmutation
transmutative
pronunciation
pruning-shears
transnational
cranioscopist
frontogenesis
drink-offering
craniological
Franco-Russian
transplanting
transportance
transportable
transportedly
transparently
transpersonal
transport-ship
transpiration
transpiratory
transposition
transpositive
brinksmanship
transshipment
transshipping
frank-tenement
granitisation
granitization
pronounceable
pronouncement
tranquilliser
tranquillizer
transversally
Eriocaulaceae
preoccupation
preordainment
preordination
erroneousness
cryobiologist

Words marked △ may be spelled also with a capital letter

arboriculture
ergonomically
armoured-train
oreographical
cryptanalysis
trophallactic
propraetorial
propraetorian
propaedeutics
prophetically
Tropaeolaceae
triple-crowned
cryptesthesia
proprioceptor
wrapping-paper
proprietorial
grappling-hook
grappling-iron
preponderance
preponderancy
trophoblastic
cryptological
graphological
preprogrammed
cryptographer
cryptographic
trophotropism
proportioning
proportionate
preparatorily
preparatively
proparoxytone
prepossessing
prepossession
prepositional
propositional
prepositively
trapezohedral
trapezohedron
triquetrously
frequentation
frequentative
prerogatively
Pre-Raphaelism
Pre-Raphaelite
prostatectomy
crystal-gazing
prismatically
prostaglandin
crystallinity
crossbreeding
trisoctahedra
trisaccharide
cross-cultural
cross-crosslet
prosectorship
criss-cross-row
prosecutrices
prosecutrixes
prosecutorial
cross-dressing

presidentship
cross-division
prospect-glass
prospectively
brassfounding
cross-gartered
prosthodontia
cross-hatching
prosaicalness
dressing-table
trysting-place
trysting-stile
prescientific
dress-improver
trisyllabical
trestle-bridge
trustlessness
cross-magnetic
cross-matching
presumptively
presentiality
prison-breaker
aristocratism
prosopography
prosopagnosia
erysipelatous
prosopopoeial
cross-purposes
cross-quarters
cross-question
preserving-pan
prescriptible
frustratingly
cross-springer
crassulaceous
cross-vaulting
trustworthily
presbyacousis
presbytership
protoactinium
protuberantly
protuberation
tritubercular
Protococcales
protectionism
protectionist
graticulation
Protochordata
protochordate
protectorless
protectorship
erythematosus
brother-german
brotherliness
tritheistical
brothers-in-law
gratification
proto-historic
proteinaceous
brattice-cloth
protolanguage

truthlessness
brutalisation
brutalization
arithmophobia
arithmetician
pretendership
pretentiously
protanomalous
writing-master
writing-school
protonotarial
protonotariat
proteoclastic
troth-plighted
preternatural
preterperfect
proterogynous
pretermission
pretermitting
proterandrous
erythrophobia
urethroscopic
preteriteness
protospataire
Protestantise
Protestantism
Protestantize
grotesqueness
traumatically
traumatonasty
trout-coloured
ground-officer
ground-angling
trouser-button
grouse-disease
trouser-pocket
argumentation
argumentative
draught-animal
draught-engine
draught-screen
troublesomely
troublousness
provocatively
travel-tainted
travel-stained
frivolousness
gravimetrical
provincialise
provincialism
provincialist
provinciality
provincialize
driving-mirror
prevarication
proverbialise
proverbialism
proverbialist
proverbialize
provisionally
privateersman

privatisation
gravitational
privatization
grown-junction
drawing-master
drawing-pencil
crown-of-thorns
prayerfulness
prizefighting
island-hopping
estate-bottled
isoagglutinin
ismaticalness
△establishment
astacological
assassination
isobarometric
psychasthenia
psychiatrical
psychopathist
psychogenesis
psychogenetic
psychometrics
psychometrist
psychotherapy
psychophysics
psychokinesis
psychokinetic
psychobiology
psychohistory
psychoanalyse
psychoanalyst
psychoanalyze
psychosomatic
psychological
psychographic
psychosurgery
psychodynamic
psychrometric
isochronously
psychrophilic
isodimorphism
isodimorphous
assemblywoman
isoelectronic
aspergillosis
osteomyelitis
osteopetrosis
ostensibility
Ascensiontide
asset-stripper
essentialness
ascertainable
ascertainment
assentiveness
assertiveness
isogeothermal
isogeothermic
asthmatically
eschscholtzia
asthenosphere

Words marked △ may be spelled also with a capital letter

13 □s□h□t

eschatologist
Ustilaginales
ustilagineous
assistantship
assiduousness
psilanthropic
Psilophytales
psammophilous
isomerisation
isomerization
isometrically
associability
astonishingly
associateship
associativity
psephological
astrocytomata
astrodynamics
ostreiculture
estrangedness
ostreophagous
astrapophobia
astrophysical
isostatically
tsutsugamushi
pseudomonades
pseudomorphic
pseudo-archaic
Assumptionist
Assyriologist
straw-coloured
strategically
steadfastness
strangulation
straight-pight
straightforth
stratigrapher
stratigraphic
attainability
ethanolamines
stratospheric
strato-cumulus
Atlantosaurus
stabilisation
stabilization
staccatissimo
stockbreeding
stocking-soles
sticking-point
stick-in-the-mud
athematically
utterableness
stretcher-bond
other-directed
strengthening
stoechiometry
steeplechaser
atheistically
streetwalking
otter-trawling
streptococcal
streptococcic
△streptococcus
streptocarpus
streptokinase
attentiveness
strenuousness
otherworldish
stigmatically
stagecoachman
stagecoaching
Stegocephalia
steganography
steganopodous
strikebreaker
stringentness
string-pulling
stoicheiology
stoichiometry
stainlessness
attitudiniser
attitudinizer
stalactitical
stalactitious
italicisation
italicization
stalagmitical
stalagmometer
stalagmometry
stalking-horse
stoloniferous
stillroom-maid
stylistically
staminiferous
atomistically
stomatoplasty
ethnobotanist
stone-coloured
ethnocentrism
ethnographica
stenographist
ethnolinguist
stenophyllous
strombuliform
strophiolated
strobilaceous
atrociousness
ethologically
atmospherical
step-parenting
stopping-place
stepping-stone
stop-and-search
stop-consonant
staphyloplasy
staphylococci
attributively
pteridologist
stern-foremost
starch-reduced
stirpiculture
pterylography
sterilisation
sterilization
stercoraceous
stercorarious
stereoscopist
stereographic
stereotropism
stereotypical
star-ypointing
Sterculiaceae
États-Généraux
statelessness
stethoscopist
station-master
state-of-the-art
statesmanlike
statesmanship
statistically
statute-barred
Etruscologist
structuralism
structuralist
structureless
structuration
funambulation
funambulatory
Judas-coloured
audaciousness
fugaciousness
furaciousness
suballocation
subappearance
sugar-refining
sugar-refinery
Judaistically
Eubacteriales
turbocharging
rumbledethump
turbo-electric
bubble-chamber
humble-mouthed
tumbler-switch
mulberry-faced
bulbourethral
surchargement
subclavicular
quick-answered
suicidologist
muscle-reading
butcher's-broom
dulcification
Punchinelloes
punctiliously
functionalism
functionalist
Hutchinsonian
Curculionidae
subcommission
pucciniaceous
subcontiguous
subcontinuous
vulcanologist
subcontractor
vulcanisation
succinctorium
vulcanization
quick-scenting
successionist
quicksilvered
successlessly
successorship
quick-tempered
quadragesimal
quadraphonics
subdeaconship
quadrennially
muddle-brained
hundredweight
mundification
mundificative
quadrilateral
quadrivalence
quadrifarious
quadripartite
quadrigeminal
quodlibetical
quadrisection
quadringenary
quadriliteral
quadrilingual
quadricipital
quadrillionth
quadrifoliate
quadrilocular
fundamentally
pudding-headed
pudding-sleeve
quadrophonics
dunderheadism
quadruplicate
quadruplicity
quadrumvirate
subdivisional
superaddition
superannuated
superannuable
superabundant
supercriminal
supercritical
supercollider
supercolumnar
supercalender
tuberculation
supercomputer
supercautious
superdominant
supereminence
superficially
superfineness
superfetation
superfluidity
superfluously

Words marked △ may be spelled also with a capital letter

rumelgumption
superhumanise
superhumanity
superhumanize
subeditorship
superlatively
supernumerary
supernormally
luteinisation
supernational
gubernatorial
luteinization
superordinary
superordinate
superorganism
autecological
numerological
superposition
superphysical
supersubtlety
superstitious
supersalesman
supersymmetry
supersensible
supersensibly
supersaturate
bureaucratise
bureaucratist
bureaucratize
subequatorial
supervenience
supervirulent
suffraganship
suffragettism
surface-active
sulfacetamide
suffocatingly
surface-vessel
suffumigation
sulfanilamide
sulfathiazole
burglariously
judge-advocate
judgement-debt
judgement-hall
judgement-seat
hunger-marcher
vulgarisation
hunger-striker
vulgarization
suggestionism
suggestionist
authentically
authenticator
Euphorbiaceae
rutherfordium
△eucharistical
authorisation
authoritarian
authoritative
authorization

euphausiacean
puritanically
subindication
subindicative
audio-engineer
businesswoman
rudimentarily
punishability
judiciousness
audio-location
pusillanimity
pusillanimous
numismatology
musicotherapy
musicological
jurisprudence
subirrigation
ludicrousness
subinvolution
audiovisually
subject-object
subjunctively
cuckoo-spittle
Quaker-buttons
full-fashioned
bullock's-heart
sublieutenant
nullification
qualification
qualificatory
qualificative
rumlegumption
quilting-party
building-block
building-board
quilting-frame
guilelessness
guiltlessness
juglandaceous
sublanceolate
fuel-injection
nucleoprotein
dualistically
qualitatively
submachine-gun
mummification
submandibular
cummingtonite
summer-seeming
quincentenary
quingentenary
quantivalence
quintillionth
burning-mirror
burnt-offering
vulnerability
quincuncially
Quinquagesima
quintuplicate
quinquevalent
quinquivalent

autocatalysis
autocatalytic
automatically
autoschediasm
autoschediaze
subordinately
subordinating
subordination
subordinative
autocephalous
tumorgenicity
autochthonism
autochthonous
tumorigenesis
auto-digestion
autobiography
Europocentric
Eurocommunism
Eurocommunist
autoeroticism
sulphadiazine
supplantation
suspectedness
suspicionless
subprefecture
supplementary
purple-in-grain
gumple-foisted
yuppification
bumptiousness
suspender-belt
jumping-spider
sulphonylurea
subpopulation
eusporangiate
supercollate
purposelessly
sub-postmaster
sub-post-office
suppositional
purposiveness
sulphur-bottom
sulphuretting
sulphureously
sumptuousness
turquoise-blue
supra-axillary
outrecuidance
suprachiasmic
hurricane-deck
hurricane-lamp
quarterdecker
quarter-gunner
quarter-hourly
quartermaster
quarrelsomely
surrogateship
querulousness
supramolecule
supranational
quartodeciman

subreptitious
surreptitious
hubristically
suprasensible
supratemporal
quartz-halogen
quartziferous
quartz-crystal
outstandingly
substantially
substantively
substantivise
substantivity
substantivize
quasi-contract
Russocentrism
Russocentrist
subspeciality
puss-gentleman
Russification
questionnaire
questioningly
substitutable
pulselessness
nursing-father
outspokenness
subsequential
substructural
subserviently
purse-snatcher
subsistential
outsettlement
Australianism
multi-authored
multicellular
multicultural
multicoloured
putty-coloured
rusty-coloured
multicamerate
multicapitate
custodianship
multidigitate
quatrefeuille
rust-resistant
justification
justificatory
justificative
multifilament
multigravidae
multigravidas
quatch-buttock
subtriplicate
subtriangular
curtain-raiser
multilobulate
multiloculate
multilinguist
multiloquence
subtilisation
subtilization

13 □u□t□m

customariness
customisation
customization
sustentacular
sustentaculum
multinucleate
Huntingdonian
hunting-ground
mutton-thumper
button-through
hunting-spider
multinational
mutton-dummies
subtropically
Austroasiatic
multipresence
multiplicable
multiplicator
multipartyism
juxtaposition
subterraneous
subternatural
butter-biscuit
butter-fingers
quaternionist
butterfly-fish
butterfly-weed
multiramified
butter-and-eggs
multiskilling
multitudinary
multitudinous
quotation-mark
multivibrator
suburbicarian
Cucurbitaceae
tubuliflorous
luxuriousness
mutualisation
mutualization
futurological
cumulostratus
subventionary
subversionary
pulverisation
pulverization
suovetaurilia
survivability
sunworshipper
burying-beetle
burying-ground
muzzle-loading
quizzing-glass
Aviculariidae
evocativeness
availableness
avant-couriers
evangelically
evangeliarion
evangeliarium
evangelistary
avant-gardiste
even-Christian
evaporability
everlastingly
overhastiness
overvaluation
overabundance
overabounding
overbearingly
overflowingly
over-anxiously
overinsurance
overindulgent
over-confident
over-breathing
overcredulity
overcredulous
overstatement
averruncation
overqualified
oversubscribe
overmultitude
overexcitable
over-exquisite
ovoviviparous
swaddling-band
twiddling-line
Swedenborgian
owner-occupied
owner-occupier
sweet-savoured
sweet-tempered
swelled-headed
swollen-headed
dwelling-place
dwelling-house
swallow-tailed
swimming-baths
swinge-buckler
swinging-block
twopenceworth
twopenny-piece
two-pennyworth
swordsmanship
swashbuckling
expandability
exsanguineous
expansibility
expansiveness
exobiological
execrableness
expendability
extendability
extendibility
experimentist
expeditionary
expeditiously
extermination
exterminatory
exterminative
exteroceptive
extemporarily
exterritorial
extensibility
extensionally
excessiveness
expensiveness
extensiveness
exceptionable
exceptionably
exceptionally
expectoration
expectorative
extenuatingly
exaggeratedly
excitableness
extinguishant
exhibitionism
exhibitionist
exclamational
explanatorily
exclusiveness
explosiveness
exemplifiable
exemplariness
examinability
examinational
exanthematous
axiomatically
exponentially
excommunicate
exportability
excortication
expostulation
expostulatory
expostulative
extra-axillary
extracellular
extragalactic
extrajudicial
extralimitary
extrametrical
extrinsically
extraordinary
expropriation
extrapolation
extrapolatory
extrapolative
extraposition
extra-physical
excrescential
△expressionism
expressionist
extratropical
extravagantly
extravagation
extravasation
extravascular
existentially
exothermicity
excusableness
expurgatorial
exquisiteness
excursiveness
gynaecocratic
gynaecologist
gynaecomastia
gynandromorph
pyramidically
synallagmatic
tyrannosaurus
synaposematic
dynamogenesis
zygapophyseal
zygapophysial
synarthrodial
lycanthropist
symbolography
symbolistical
symbolisation
symbolization
symbiotically
synchondroses
synchondrosis
synchronicity
synchronology
synchronistic
synchronously
syndicalistic
dyed-in-the-wool
hyperactivity
hypercritical
hypercalcemia
synecdochical
hypereutectic
hyperesthesia
hyperesthetic
hyperglycemia
hyperhidrosis
hypermetrical
hypermetropia
hypermetropic
cyberneticist
hypernatremia
pyretotherapy
synecological
hymenopterous
Hymenomycetes
Pyrenomycetes
synecphonesis
hyperphrygian
hyperparasite
hyperphysical
hypersthenite
hypersarcosis
hypertrophied
hypertrophous
hypervelocity
dysfunctional
syphilologist
pyrheliometer
syphilophobia
syphilisation

Words marked △ may be spelled also with a capital letter

syphilization
Pythonomorpha
hyphenisation
hyphenization
cylindraceous
cylindrically
pyrimethamine
syringomyelia
Myristicaceae
syllabication
cyclodialysis
syllogistical
syllogisation
syllogization
Cyclanthaceae
hyalinisation
hyalinization
sylleptically
cyclospermous
myrmecologist
dysmenorrheal
dysmenorrhoea
dysmenorrheic
symmetrically
hypno-analysis
ayuntamientos
cyanoacrylate
pycnoconidium
pycnidiospore
gymnospermous
gymnastically
hypnotisation
hypnotization
cytopathology
gyromagnetism
zygodactylism
zygodactylous
mycobacterium
myxoedematous
pyrotechnical
zymotechnical
hypomenorrhea
hypothecation
Syrophoenicia
cytochemistry
sycophantical
hypochondriac
hypochondrium
hypophosphite
pyrophosphate
gynodioecious
cytodiagnosis
hypoglycaemia
hypoglycaemic
Lycopodiaceae
mycotoxicosis
gynomonoecism
typographical
xylographical
hyposulphuric
pyrosulphuric
hypocycloidal
nymphaeaceous
lymphatically
sympiesometer
symptomatical
lymphotrophic
dyspeptically
sympathetical
sympathectomy
sympatholytic
symphyseotomy
symphysiotomy
hydro-airplane
hydrocracking
hydrochloride
hydrocephalic
hydrocephalus
hydrodynamics
hybridisation
hybridization
hydroelectric
hydrogenation
hydrokinetics
hydromedusoid
hydromagnetic
hydrometrical
hygrometrical
Hydrangeaceae
hydropathical
hydrarthrosis
hydrostatical
hydrosulphide
hydrosulphite
hydrosomatous
hygroscopical
hydraulically
hydraulicking
hydroxylamine
hypsophyllary
syntactically
cysticercosis
△dyotheletical
synthetically
△dyothelitical
mystification
Nyctaginaceae
systemisation
systematician
systematology
systemization
oyster-catcher
oyster-fishery
mystery-monger
hysteranthous
sylvicultural
ozone-friendly

salamander-like
macadamisation
macadamization
palatalisation
palatalization
banana-fingered
paratactically
palaeanthropic
Palaeanthropus
palaebiologist
manageableness
Hamamelidaceae
Pan-Americanism
caramelisation
caramelization
cadaverousness
paraleipomenon
paraphrastical
catachrestical
paralinguistic
paradigmatical
parasitologist
calamitousness
catadioptrical
parallel-veined
parallelepiped
parallelopiped
savanna-sparrow
pararosaniline
palaeoecologic
palaeopedology
palagonite-tuff
palaeobiologic
palato-alveolar
palaeoclimatic
palaeobotanist
palaeographist
malacostracous
Malacopterygii
malappropriate
data-processing
paragrammatist
parapsychology
galactopoietic
galactophorous
marble-constant
marble-breasted
cabbage-lettuce
rambunctiously
namby-pambiness
Sabbath-breaker
rabbeting-plane
rabbit-squirrel
Sabbatarianism
saccharisation
saccharization
sacchariferous
Marchantiaceae
narcocatharsis
pancreatectomy
sanctification
malcontentedly
carcinogenesis
carcinological
carcinomatosis
Marcgraviaceae
narcosynthesis
lasciviousness
handicraftsman
handkerchieves
paedomorphosis
maidenhair-tree
pardonableness
cardinal-deacon
cardinal-bishop
cardinal-priest
cardiovascular
cardiothoracic
cardiomyopathy
lateralisation
lateralization
Rabelaisianism
paleoanthropic
Paleoanthropus
water-breathing
paleobiologist
paleobotanical
watercolourist
parenchymatous
lavender-cotton
paleoethnology
paleoecologist
paleographical
paleogeography
catechumenical
catechumenship
catechetically
watering-trough
valerianaceous
paleolimnology
lamellirostral
paleomagnetism
tabernacle-work
paleontologist
paleontography
Camelopardalis
categorisation
categorization
davenport-trick
galeopithecine
galeopithecoid
paleopathology
paleophytology
water-repellent
water-resistant
majesticalness
watertightness
valetudinarian
paleozoologist
daffadowndilly
half-wellington
halfpennyworth
malfunctioning
sanguinariness
bargain-counter
sanguification
sanguinivorous
languorousness
larger-than-life
daughterliness
daughters-in-law
rangatiratanga
Bashi-Bazoukery
pachydactylous
cathodographer
pachydermatous
bathygraphical
tachygraphical
Panhellenistic
pathologically
mathematically
mathematicised
mathematicized
bathing-costume
bathing-machine
washing-machine
tacheometrical
fashionmonging
fatherlessness
Catherine-wheel
capitalisation
capitalization
radicalisation
radicalization
Vaticanologist
radioautograph
radio-astronomy
radiochemistry
cabinet-edition
cabinet-pudding
satisfactorily
tariff-reformer
radio-frequency
hagiographical
palingenetical
lapidification
Basidiomycetes
papilionaceous
manifold-writer
facinorousness
calico-printing
saxifragaceous
radioresistant
radiosensitise
radiosensitive
radiosensitize
radio-strontium
radiotelegraph
radiotelemeter
radiotelephone
radiotelephony
fatiguableness
latitudinarian

 Words marked △ may be spelled also with a capital letter

cack-handedness
backscratching
Jack-in-the-green
talking-machine
back-projection
market-gardener
marketableness
△jack-by-the-hedge
parliament-cake
parliament-heel
hallucinogenic
fallaciousness
calligraphical
daylight-saving
haplostemonous
tablespoonfuls
ballet-mistress
parlour-boarder
early-Victorian
tallow-chandler
salmon-coloured
harmoniousness
haematogenesis
haematopoiesis
haematopoietic
palmatipartite
maintenance-man
painter-stainer
faint-heartedly
magniloquently
vaingloriously
cannonball-tree
magneto-elastic
magneto-optical
Haloragidaceae
barometrically
major-generalcy
vasodilatation
vasodilatatory
calorification
saponification
paroemiography
paronomastical
malodorousness
favourableness
rampageousness
sapphire-quartz
pamphleteering
campylotropous
wappenschawing
campanulaceous
campanological
capparidaceous
banqueting-hall
matriarchalism
patriarchalism
marriage-favour
marriage-broker
patrialisation
patrialization
sacrococcygeal

iatrochemistry
Sarraceniaceae
batrachophobia
batrachophobic
capriciousness
macrocephalous
macrodactylous
macroeconomics
macroevolution
Caprifoliaceae
barrage-balloon
fairy-godmother
cairngorm-stone
sacrilegiously
macromolecular
sacramentalism
sacramentarian
sacramentalist
macro-marketing
sauropterygian
matresfamilias
patresfamilias
barrister-at-law
sacrosanctness
macrosporangia
narrow-mindedly
falsifiability
Passifloraceae
far-sightedness
karstification
parsimoniously
passionateness
massproduction
sansculottides
sansculotterie
canthaxanthine
castrametation
particularness
fastidiousness
parthenocarpic
saltpetre-paper
castle-building
cartographical
pantographical
mastigophorous
partridge-berry
captain-general
cartridge-paper
farthingsworth
tautologically
dactyliography
pantomimically
cantankerously
Castanospermum
xanthomelanous
pantopragmatic
tatterdemalion
bastardisation
bastardization
martyrological
Gasteromycetes

bacteriologist
bacteriostasis
bacteriostatic
fantastication
fantasticality
factitiousness
Pasteurelloses
Pasteurellosis
pasteurisation
pasteurization
naturalisation
naturalization
tabularisation
tabularization
ranunculaceous
nature-printing
Baluchitherium
daguerreotyper
salubriousness
marvellousness
galvanoplastic
laryngological
laryngoscopist
labyrinthodont
dazzle-painting
absent-mindedly
obsequiousness
observableness
obligatoriness
abominableness
absorbefacient
absorptiveness
absorptiometer
eburnification
abstractedness
abstractionism
abstractionist
obstreperously
abstemiousness
obstructionism
obstructionist
above-mentioned
scratchbuilder
ocean-greyhound
schematisation
schematization
sclerophyllous
acceptableness
scientifically
scribbling-book
octingentenary
schismatically
actinobacillus
schizophyceous
schizognathous
schizomycetous
acclimatisable
acclimatizable
ecclesiastical
Ecclesiasticus
ecclesiologist

14 □c□m□r

Scombresocidae
scandalisation
scandalization
scandalousness
ichnographical
scenographical
Acanthocephala
scintillometer
scintillascope
scintilloscope
econometrician
acknowledgment
echocardiogram
scholastically
achondroplasia
schoolmasterly
schoolteaching
school-divinity
schoolmistress
accountability
accountantship
schooner-rigged
accomplishable
accomplishment
across-the-board
across-the-table
scaphocephalic
scaphocephalus
scurrilousness
scaremongering
achromatically
scatterbrained
Scottification
ichthyological
ichthyolatrous
ichthyophagous
ichthyosaurian
scrubbing-board
scrubbing-brush
scrutinisingly
scrutinizingly
sceuophylacium
accustomedness
accumulatively
scrupulousness
Schwenkfeldian
adiathermanous
idealistically
advantageously
odd-come-shortly
educationalist
adscititiously
adventitiously
administrative
administration
administratrix
edriophthalmic
admissibleness
adenocarcinoma
identification
advocate-depute
idiopathically
addressability
recalcitration
rewardableness
regardlessness
hen-and-chickens
megatechnology
megavertebrate
telangiectasia
telangiectasis
telangiectatic
metaphorically
semaphorically
metaphysically
metaphosphoric
mesaticephalic
metalinguistic
rehabilitative
denazification
desalinisation
desalinization
gelatinisation
gelatinization
keratinisation
keratinization
rehabilitation
semasiological
hepaticologist
legalistically
retaliationist
recapitulative
recapitulation
recapitulatory
remarkableness
metallographic
metallographer
metallogenetic
megalomaniacal
devalorisation
devalorization
revalorisation
revalorization
nematodiriasis
dexamphetamine
megasporangium
megasporophyll
metapsychology
departmentally
telautographic
melastomaceous
Hexactinellida
Rembrandtesque
feeble-mindedly
Leibnitzianism
berberidaceous
leucocythaemia
leucocytolysis
leucocytopenia
neocolonialism
neocolonialist
geocentrically
perceptiveness
perceptibility
cercopithecoid
percussion-lock
percussion-fuse
percutaneously
reacquaintance
headmastership
meddlesomeness
Mesdemoiselles
weeding-forceps
reading-machine
leading-strings
leaden-stepping
gender-specific
tendovaginitis
televangelical
telepathically
federalisation
federalization
generalisation
generalization
vegetativeness
generalissimos
general-purpose
beseechingness
telescopically
aerenchymatous
degenerateness
regeneratively
venereological
defenestration
revengefulness
genethliacally
genethlialogic
telephonically
telephotograph
hereditariness
hereditability
remedilessness
heresiographer
repetitiveness
beneficialness
deregistration
genealogically
teleologically
levelling-staff
rebelliousness
redeemableness
telesmatically
teleconference
heterothallism
heterophyllous
heterochronism
heterochromous
heterochronous
heterosomatous
heteromorphism
heteromorphous
heterospecific
telejournalism

Words marked △ may be spelled also with a capital letter

telejournalist
heterostrophic
heterozygosity
peremptoriness
metempsychoses
metempsychosis
penetrableness
meretriciously
teleprocessing
meteorological
defeasibleness
necessarianism
delectableness
detestableness
relentlessness
hebetudinosity
deceivableness
receivableness
receiving-house
receiving-order
Teletypesetter®
teletypewriter
self-management
self-satisfying
self-abnegation
self-absorption
perfectibilism
perfectibilian
perfectibilist
perfectibility
self-accusation
self-accusatory
self-advertiser
self-admiration
perfidiousness
self-generating
self-revelation
self-dependence
self-determined
self-developing
self-heterodyne
self-respectful
self-respecting
self-repression
self-restrained
self-rectifying
self-destroying
self-regulating
self-regulation
self-regulatory
self-repugnance
self-effacement
self-affrighted
self-discipline
self-displeased
self-flattering
self-employment
self-immolation
self-importance
self-interested
self-enrichment
newfangledness
self-indulgence
self-inductance
self-condemning
self-government
self-confidence
self-motivating
self-tormenting
self-commitment
self-complacent
self-comparison
self-compatible
self-correcting
self-consequent
self-consistent
self-possession
self-conviction
self-proclaimed
self-propelling
self-propulsion
self-preserving
self-protective
self-protecting
self-protection
self-assumption
self-sufficient
self-fulfilment
self-fulfilling
self-suggestion
self-punishment
self-supporting
self-justifying
self-sustaining
self-sustenance
self-explaining
self-expression
geographically
sergeant-at-arms
neighborliness
weighing-bottle
geognostically
weight-watching
weightlessness
weight-training
tergiversation
tergiversatory
methodicalness
methodological
hephthemimeral
technicoloured
dechristianise
dechristianize
Mephistophelic
Mephistopheles
Mephistophilis
Mephostophilus
semicarbazones
peripateticism
medicamentally
decimalisation
decimalization
devitalisation
devitalization
medicalisation
medicalization
revitalisation
revitalization
meditativeness
hesitation-form
recitation-room
semi-occasional
periodontology
deliberateness
deliberatively
deliverability
demi-semiquaver
semi-centennial
semi-officially
heliographical
periphrastical
perishableness
delightfulness
legitimateness
semicircularly
reminiscential
legitimisation
legitimization
resinification
revivification
sericitisation
sericitization
definitiveness
verisimilitude
semi-elliptical
legislatorship
semiconducting
lepidodendroid
peritoneoscopy
retinoblastoma
lexicographist
devil-on-the-neck
hemispheroidal
Menispermaceae
Periophthalmus
relinquishment
denitrificator
defibrillation
semicrystallic
Perissodactyla
heliosciophyte
resistlessness
redintegration
redistributive
redistribution
redistillation
meticulousness
serjeant-at-arms
leukocytolysis
leukocytopenia
weak-mindedness
neck-sweetbread
neglectfulness

14 □c□l□c

reflectiveness
reflectionless
reflectography
perlocutionary
well-acquainted
deflagrability
healthlessness
well-thought-out
geolinguistics
deplorableness
belletristical
fellow-commoner
fellow-townsman
fellow-creature
reflexological
reimplantation
fermentability
terminableness
fermentescible
helminthologic
terminological
hermaphroditic
geomorphogenic
geomorphologic
permissiveness
permissibility
dermatographia
dermatographic
geometrisation
geometrization
dermatological
dermatoplastic
penny-a-linerism
pernicketiness
perniciousness
△neanderthaloid
reinvigoration
penny-in-the-slot
reinforcements
reintroduction
pennystone-cast
pennatulaceous
memorandum-book
demoralisation
demoralization
depolarisation
depolarization
remoralisation
remoralization
decorativeness
derogatoriness
aeronautically
reconciliation
reconciliatory
recondensation
recoverability
terotechnology
demonetisation
demonetization
remonetisation
remonetization
denominatively
denominational
demobilisation
demobilization
detoxification
aerobiological
devotionalness
deposit-receipt
aerobiotically
recollectively
aeroelastician
recommendation
recommendatory
recommencement
decommissioner
reformationist
reconnaissance
metoposcopical
decolonisation
decolonization
decolorisation
decolorization
recolonisation
recolonization
seroconversion
aerospace-plane
decompoundable
democratically
deconsecration
reconsecration
remorsefulness
reconstitution
reconstructive
deconstruction
△reconstruction
gerontological
decontaminator
aerodynamicist
memory-resident
aerohydroplane
respectabilise
respectabilize
respectability
despicableness
respectfulness
geopolitically
weaponschawing
responsiveness
serpentiningly
responsibility
reaping-machine
serpent-worship
reappraisement
vespertilionid
peppermint-drop
temperamentful
Neopythagorean
despoticalness
sempstress-ship
despitefulness
herpetological
sesquipedalian
sesquipedality
sesquisulphide
neuroanatomist
reorganisation
reorganization
neuroblastomas
neurobiologist
depreciatingly
petrochemistry
retrocognition
neurocomputing
refractoriness
tetrachotomous
reproductively
reproductivity
tetradactylous
neuroendocrine
neurofibrillar
neurofibromata
retrogradation
petrographical
reprogrammable
△tetragrammaton
segregationist
heart-heaviness
reprehensively
neurohypnology
Hebraistically
neurologically
petrologically
ferrimagnetism
ferromagnetism
ferromagnesian
ferro-manganese
recrementitial
wearing-apparel
herring-fishery
refrangibility
bear-animalcule
retransmission
retro-operative
Neuropteroidea
metropolitical
neuropathology
ferroprussiate
petrophysicist
neuroradiology
retroreflector
Petrarchianism
Petrarchianist
terror-stricken
heart-searching
regressiveness
neuroscientist
representative
representation
re-presentation
tetrasporangia
territorialise
territorialize

Words marked △ may be spelled also with a capital letter

territorialism
territorialist
territoriality
serratirostral
newspaper-woman
sensualisation
sensualization
persuasiveness
persuasibility
Meistersingers
verse-mongering
personableness
reasonableness
seasonableness
geosynchronous
person-to-person
seismometrical
newsworthiness
censurableness
measurableness
measuring-wheel
censoriousness
dessert-service
geostrategical
bed-sitting-room
sensationalism
sensationalist
left-handedness
septuagenarian
centralisation
centralization
neutralisation
neutralization
restrainedness
pentobarbitone
petticoat-tails
verticillaster
Pentecostalist
pentadactylism
leptodactylous
pentadactylous
gentleman-cadet
featherbedding
heather-bleater
heather-bluiter
heather-blutter
aesthesiogenic
heathenishness
geothermometer
leather-mouthed
heather-mixture
mettlesomeness
seat-of-the-pants
centripetalism
belt-tightening
gentrification
restrictionist
centrifugalise
centrifugalize
centrifugation
rectilinearity
pestilentially
sentimentalise
sentimentalize
testimonialise
testimonialize
sentimentalism
sentimentalist
sentimentality
testamentarily
Weltanschauung
pertinaciously
centenarianism
rectangularity
sectionisation
sectionization
dextrorotation
dextrorotatory
death-practised
centuplication
perturbational
restorableness
text-processing
letter-of-marque
westernisation
westernization
nectareousness
restorationism
restorationist
restitutionism
restitutionist
destructionist
regularisation
regularization
secularisation
secularization
sequaciousness
rejuvenescence
oecumenicalism
△nebuchadnezzar
beautification
securitisation
securitization
repudiationist
desulphuration
resurrectional
requisitionary
requisitionist
resultlessness
recurvirostral
Gewürztraminer
serviceability
heavier-than-air
servomechanism
heaven-directed
heavenly-minded
lecythidaceous
benzodiazepine
effeminateness
after-mentioned
affectlessness
affectionately
effervescingly
Africanisation
Africanization
off-off-Broadway
aforementioned
agriculturally
egalitarianism
agrobiological
agroindustrial
agrostological
aggrandisement
aggrandizement
aggressiveness
phraseological
thrashing-floor
theatricalness
chicken-hearted
chicken-livered
chacographical
threadbareness
wheeler-dealing
three-farthings
three-halfpence
three-halfpenny
threshing-floor
phlegmatically
Chaetodontidae
sheep-whistling
shifting-boards
phthalocyanine
shrill-shriking
cheiromantical
cheirographist
Christocentric
thriftlessness
Christological
Christ-cross-row
Shakespeariana
cholecystotomy
shelf-catalogue
whole-heartedly
shillingsworth
philologically
shell-limestone
cholelithiasis
philanthropist
cholinesterase
phyllotactical
phelloplastics
chalcographist
child-resistant
thalassography
philosophaster
philosopheress
philosophistic
shilly-shallier
chemoautotroph
rhombenporphyr
chimney-sweeper
shamefacedness
thymelaeaceous

Words marked △ may be spelled also with a capital letter

thimblerigging
chemoreceptive
chemosynthesis
phantasmagoria
phantasmagoric
phenobarbitone
rhinoceros-bird
Rhinocerotidae
changeableness
chancellorship
thunderousness
rhynchophorous
chincherinchee
phenylbutazone
phonematically
rhinencephalic
rhinencephalon
Chenopodiaceae
chondrocranium
chondrogenesis
chondromatosis
chondrophorine
thiobarbituric
Theopaschitism
chromatosphere
chromatography
thromboplastin
through-ganging
chlorite-schist
chloritisation
chloritization
chronometrical
theosophically
theologoumenon
chromodynamics
chlorpromazine
theocratically
chaptalisation
chaptalization
shepherd's-purse
whippersnapper
rhyparographic
rhyparographer
chordamesoderm
pharmaceutical
thermalisation
thermalization
pharmacopoeial
pharmacopoeian
pharmacologist
pharmacopolist
therianthropic
characteristic
characterology
chargeableness
Charley-pitcher
chorographical
thermometrical
thermophyllous
thermochemical
thermoelectric
thermotolerant
theriomorphism
theriomorphous
thermodynamics
third-programme
short-sightedly
charitableness
thyrotoxicosis
thoroughbraced
phosphoprotein
phosphor-bronze
phosphorescent
whistle-blowing
thysanopterous
physiognomical
photobiologist
photochemistry
photocatalysis
photocatalytic
shatter-brained
photoelectrode
photo-engraving
photographical
photogrammetry
phytogenetical
phytogeography
whittie-whattie
Phytolaccaceae
photoluminesce
photoperiodism
phytopathology
photorealistic
photosynthesis
photosynthetic
photosensitise
photosensitive
photosensitize
phototelegraph
what-d'you-call-'em
what-d'you-call-it
rheumatologist
thaumatography
thaumaturgical
shoulder-height
thoughtfulness
thought-reading
shove-halfpenny
chivalrousness
chevaux-de-frise
Rhizophoraceae
vicar-apostolic
disambiguation
disaccommodate
misacceptation
disaffiliation
disaffirmation
disaggregation
vitalistically
disacknowledge
simaroubaceous
disapplication
misapplication
disappointment
disapprobative
disapprobation
disapprobatory
disapprovingly
disappropriate
misappropriate
disarrangement
misarrangement
disassociation
disattribution
misanthropical
miraculousness
disadventurous
misadventurous
misadvisedness
nimble-fingered
aircraftswoman
pisciculturist
discretionally
zincographical
bioclimatology
mischief-making
discriminately
discriminative
discriminating
discrimination
zinckification
discriminatory
circuitousness
miscellanarian
discolouration
miscalculation
circumnavigate
circumscissile
discommendable
circumbendibus
circumferentor
circumlittoral
circumambience
circumambiency
circumambulate
circumforanean
discomboberate
circumposition
discomfortable
discombobulate
circumlocution
circumvolution
circumlocutory
circumspective
circumspection
circumstantial
circumnutation
miscomputation
circumnutatory
circumgyration
circumgyratory
disconnectedly
discontentedly

Words marked △ may be spelled also with a capital letter

disconcertment
discontentment
miscontentment
air-conditioned
discontinuance
disconsolately
disconsolation
disconformable
cinchonisation
cinchonization
disceptatorial
disciplinarium
disciplinarian
discursiveness
discerpibility
diachronically
pincer-movement
discouragement
discouragingly
discountenance
discourteously
discount-broker
vindictiveness
fiddle-faddling
middle-distance
Middle-American
bird-of-paradise
biodegradation
disdainfulness
kindergartener
misdescription
window-shopping
window-dressing
fives-and-threes
liberalisation
liberalization
mineralisation
mineralization
cinematography
tide-waitership
disemboguement
disembarkation
disembowelment
disenchantress
disenchantment
disencumbrance
fivepenny-piece
bioelectricity
disenfranchise
eigen-frequency
disengagedness
bioengineering
vice-chancellor
kinetheodolite
vicesimo-quarto
vigesimo-quarto
pigeon-fancying
pigeon-breasted
rice-polishings
fire-worshipper
vice-consulship
vice-presidency
disentrainment
diverticulosis
diverticulated
diverticulitis
videotelephone
licentiousness
libertarianism
disenthralment
divertissement
disequilibrate
disequilibrium
life-expectancy
diffractometer
disfurnishment
differentially
differentiator
biographically
siege-artillery
zingiberaceous
single-breasted
jingoistically
linguistically
singing-gallery
diagnosability
biogeochemical
finger-painting
fingers-breadth
finger-alphabet
finger-pointing
fingerprinting
disgustfulness
disgustingness
disgruntlement
misgovernaunce
high-handedness
night-blindness
lithochromatic
lighter-than-air
night-flowering
night-fossicker
night-foundered
light-flyweight
lithographical
light-heartedly
xiphihumeralis
high-mindedness
diaheliotropic
Wilhelmstrasse
lithonthryptic
lithontriptist
high-priesthood
withering-floor
high-principled
night-wandering
highly-seasoned
digitalisation
digitalization
militarisation
militarization
viviparousness
disinclination
disincarcerate
disincorporate
vivisectionist
disinformation
misinformation
disinfestation
riding-interest
disingenuously
riding-breeches
disinheritance
dividing-engine
silicification
vitilitigation
libidinousness
disillusionary
disillusionise
disillusionize
filiopietistic
misimprovement
disimpassioned
dinitrobenzene
misinstruction
pig-in-the-middle
disintegrative
disintegration
sinistrorsally
ministerialist
misinterpreter
disinteresting
diminutiveness
ridiculousness
disinvestiture
disjointedness
milking-parlour
hickery-pickery
Rickettsiaceae
billiard-marker
dialectologist
bill-discounter
bioluminescent
diplomatically
willing-hearted
Finlandisation
Finlandization
millenarianism
bibliomaniacal
diplostemonous
pillow-fighting
mismeasurement
diamantiferous
diamondiferous
biomathematics
biometeorology
piano-accordion
lignocellulose
winning-gallery
pinnatipartite
Disneyfication
disorderliness
disorientation

14 □i□o□l

dinoflagellate
lipogrammatism
lipogrammatist
ribonucleotide
dicotyledonous
misogynistical
diaphanousness
displenishment
displeasedness
simplificative
simplification
simplistically
dispensatively
dispensability
dispensational
dispensatorily
mispunctuation
diaphototropic
hippopotamuses
dispiritedness
disposableness
disputableness
hippety-hoppety
dispiteousness
disputatiously
disqualifiable
disquisitional
microbiologist
microbarograph
microchemistry
nitrocellulose
microcomponent
microcomputing
microcephalous
fibrocartilage
microdetection
microeconomics
microevolution
vibroflotation
hierographical
hierogrammatic
disregardfully
nitroglycerine
hieroglyphical
microinjection
micrologically
microminiature
micro-marketing
micro-meteorite
vitriolisation
vitriolization
micropegmatite
microprocessor
hierarchically
disrespectable
vitrescibility
microseismical
Hierosolymitan
microsporangia
microstructure
microtunneling
dissociability
dissolvability
dissolubleness
diesel-electric
tinsel-slipper'd
dissolutionism
dissolutionist
dissymmetrical
kissing-strings
dioscoreaceous
dissertational
disserviceable
biosystematics
mistranslation
distractedness
histochemistry
tittle-tattling
diathermaneity
histogenically
histrionically
distributively
distributional
histologically
histolytically
Mitteleuropean
Mittel-European
distemperature
tintinnabulate
tintinnabulant
tintinnabulary
tintinnabulous
distensibility
distinguishing
histoplasmosis
histopathology
dipterocarpous
picture-gallery
historiography
victoriousness
picture-writing
Nietzscheanism
birth-strangled
figurativeness
vituperatively
lieutenantship
liturgiologist
bituminisation
bituminization
simultaneously
air-vice-marshal
nievie-nick-nack
silversmithing
zinziberaceous
piezochemistry
piezomagnetism
skimble-skamble
skunk-blackbird
cloak-and-dagger
plea-bargaining
oleaginousness
clear-starching
cleansing-cream
pleasure-seeker
pleasure-giving
blockade-runner
glucocorticoid
electioneering
black-marketeer
ill-conditioned
plectognathous
electrobiology
electrochemist
electroculture
electroforming
electrogilding
electrogenesis
electromotance
electronically
electro-osmosis
electro-optical
electroplating
electrostatics
electrotherapy
electrothermic
electrothermal
electrovalency
electrowinning
bladder-campion
alder-buckthorn
illegitimately
illegitimation
allegorisation
allegorization
allelomorphism
old-established
sleepy-sickness
oligocythaemia
plague-stricken
flag-lieutenant
flagelliferous
flagellomaniac
old-gentlemanly
slug-foot-second
oligopsonistic
flight-recorder
flagitiousness
alphabetically
alphamerically
alphanumerical
illiterateness
altimetrically
Albigensianism
illimitability
ultimogeniture
ill-intentioned
altitudinarian
Plumbaginaceae
plumbisolvency
alimentiveness
flamboyant-tree
plumbosolvency
climatological

Words marked △ may be spelled also with a capital letter

Plantaginaceae
blank-cartridge
slantendicular
slanderousness
plant-formation
slantindicular
planing-machine
plane-polarised
plane-polarized
plenipotential
ill-naturedness
planet-stricken
glanduliferous
allopathically
pleonastically
blood-bespotted
blood-consuming
all-overishness
alcoholisation
alcoholization
alloiostrophos
blood-poisoning
blood-sacrifice
bloodthirstily
blepharoplasty
ultracrepidate
floriculturist
altruistically
ultramicrotome
ultramicrotomy
ultramontanism
ultramontanist
ultroneousness
ultra-Neptunian
ultrasonically
ultrastructure
plasmapheresis
class-conscious
blistered-steel
blister-plaster
classification
classificatory
clash-ma-clavers
Elasmobranchii
platycephalous
pluto-democracy
bletheranskate
clitter-clatter
slatternliness
blithesomeness
flat-footedness
clitoridectomy
plethysmograph
pleurapophyses
pleurapophysis
slaughterhouse
slaughterously
flaughter-spade
eleutheromania
Pleuronectidae
illustratively
illustrational
claustrophobia
claustrophobic
clavicytherium
pluviometrical
glove-stretcher
flowery-kirtled
alexipharmakon
Elizabethanism
imparidigitate
imparisyllabic
impassableness
impassibleness
ambassadorship
immaculateness
imperfectively
immethodically
embellishingly
impermeability
imperturbation
imperviability
imperviousness
imaginableness
amphibological
emphaticalness
omnibenevolent
immiserisation
immiserization
ambidextrously
empire-building
immitigability
omnium-gatherum
omnicompetence
implacableness
emulsification
implementation
emblematically
implausibility
imponderabilia
immoderateness
impoverishment
immobilisation
immobilization
embourgeoising
imposthumation
impracticality
impregnability
umbrageousness
Amaryllidaceae
amaranthaceous
impressiveness
impressibility
impressionable
improvableness
improvvisatore
amateurishness
ambulancewoman
immunogenetics
immunogenicity
immunochemical
immunophoresis
immunoglobulin
immunosuppress
empyreumatical
incapacitation
unwatchfulness
unhandsomeness
untameableness
unmaterialised
unmaterialized
intangibleness
unmathematical
antaphrodisiac
insanitariness
insatiableness
invariableness
unsatisfaction
unsatisfactory
kneading-trough
inhabitiveness
unmalleability
enharmonically
inharmoniously
unmaintainable
unmannerliness
antagonisation
antagonization
unvanquishable
unmarriageable
unmatriculated
unpassableness
unfaithfulness
incautiousness
unmanufactured
insalubriously
knickerbockers
unscripturally
unacknowledged
unaccommodated
unaccounted-for
unaccomplished
anacardiaceous
anachronically
inaccurateness
inscrutability
unacquaintance
unscrupulously
inadvisability
unidentifiable
inadequateness
unidirectional
inseparability
interambulacra
unmetaphorical
unmetaphysical
interactionism
interactionist
unrecapturable
unmerchantable
under-clerkship
unmercifulness
indescribables

14 □n□e□c

intercommunion
intercommunity
interconnexion
interconnector
under-constable
intercessional
intercessorial
unreadableness
interdependent
inner-direction
underdeveloped
inveterateness
indeterminable
undeterminable
indeterminably
interestedness
undeservedness
unreservedness
interferometer
interferometry
interferential
intergradation
undergraduette
encephalograph
encephalopathy
unhesitatingly
undesirability
undeniableness
unreliableness
indecipherable
undecipherable
indecisiveness
indefiniteness
undesignedness
unreciprocated
interior-sprung
antediluvially
interjectional
unreflectingly
interlocutress
interlocutrice
intellectually
intelligential
intelligentsia
intelligentzia
interlineation
interlingually
intermediately
intermediation
intermediatory
intermigration
intermolecular
undermentioned
intermittently
intermaxillary
Internationale
undernourished
unreconcilable
unreconcilably
enterocentesis
unbecomingness
unrecognisable
unrecognisably
enteropneustal
unrecognizable
unrecognizably
indecorousness
indecomposable
undecomposable
unremorsefully
indemonstrable
undemonstrable
indemonstrably
unresolvedness
interplanetary
interpretative
interpretation
interpretively
enterprisingly
undespairingly
interpellation
unresponsively
interpenetrate
interpunctuate
interpenetrant
underpopulated
intempestively
intempestivity
unbearableness
unreproducible
interruptively
integrationist
understandable
understandings
understatement
interspatially
infeasibleness
insensibleness
under-secretary
intersectional
understrapping
intersexuality
unrestrainable
unrestrainedly
uncertificated
intertwinement
entertainingly
intertwiningly
unrestrictedly
intentionality
unmentionables
incestuousness
infectiousness
unsectarianism
indestructible
indestructibly
unremunerative
undervaluation
ineffectuality
unaffectedness
uniformitarian
anagrammatical
enigmatography
snaggletoothed
knight-bachelor
knight-banneret
knight-errantry
onchocerciasis
uncheerfulness
unchristianise
unchristianize
enthymematical
unthinkability
unthankfulness
unthinkingness
enthronisation
enthronization
anthropopathic
anthropometric
anthropophobia
anthropophobic
anthropophuism
anthropologist
anthropography
enthusiastical
unrhythmically
unthoughtfully
antipathetical
anti-Jacobinism
invincibleness
indiscreteness
indiscreetness
indiscriminate
antiscriptural
uncircumcision
indiscerptible
indiscoverable
undiscoverable
undiscoverably
antiodontalgic
antimetathesis
anti-federalism
anti-federalist
indigenisation
indigenization
antiperistasis
antidepressant
antiperspirant
antiseptically
incidentalness
indifferentism
indifferentist
antiphrastical
unrightfulness
antiphonically
antiphlogistic
antithetically
anticipatively
anticipatorily
undiminishable
indivisibility
inviolableness
unyieldingness

Words marked △ may be spelled also with a capital letter

insignificance
insignificancy
antimonarchist
oneirocritical
anticonvulsant
anticonvulsive
indisposedness
antiarrhythmic
angiostomatous
undistractedly
indistinctness
unsisterliness
antiquarianism
antilymphocyte
unpleasantness
inflectionless
inalienability
inalterability
unalterability
Anglo-Israelite
inflammability
inclinableness
unflappability
ingloriousness
unclassifiable
unflatteringly
inflation-proof
unilluminating
inflexibleness
anamnestically
inimitableness
onomatopoiesis
unintellectual
unintelligible
unintelligibly
unintermitting
unenterprising
unentertaining
unknightliness
unenthusiastic
enantiomorphic
enantiostylous
unintoxicating
unincorporated
unknowableness
untowardliness
endoradiosonde
unromantically
unconciliatory
inconclusively
intolerability
oncogeneticist
unforeknowable
undomesticated
unconfederated
uncongeniality
unsophisticate
incogitability
indomitability
unsociableness
incommodiously
incommunicable
uncommunicable
incommunicably
uncommunicated
incommensurate
endosmotically
entomostracous
uncomprehended
incompleteness
incompressible
uncompromising
incorporeality
uncorroborated
inco-ordination
infopreneurial
inconsiderable
inconsiderably
inconscionable
unconscionable
unconscionably
unconsolidated
inconsequently
inconsistently
uncontradicted
unpoeticalness
incontiguously
indoctrination
uncontemplated
uncontaminated
uncontroverted
incontrollable
uncontrollable
incontrollably
uncontrollably
uncontrolledly
inconveniently
unconventional
snipper-snapper
knapping-hammer
snapping-turtle
unsplinterable
snip-snap-snorum
inappositeness
inapproachable
unapproachable
inapproachably
unapproachably
inoperableness
inappreciative
unappreciative
inappreciation
inapprehensive
unapprehensive
inapprehension
unappropriated
unspiritualise
unspiritualize
inspirationism
inspirationist
iniquitousness
intra-abdominal
inorganisation
inorganization
inerrabilility
intra-articular
intractability
ungracefulness
unpracticality
onirocriticism
ungraciousness
androcephalous
incredibleness
unproductively
unproductivity
introductorily
androdioecious
unfriendedness
unfriendliness
intrafallopian
unprofessional
anarthrousness
inordinateness
unpraiseworthy
unfruitfulness
inartificially
unartificially
inartistically
inarticulately
inarticulation
Infralapsarian
intramedullary
unpremeditable
unpremeditated
andromedotoxin
intramolecular
andromonoecism
intramercurial
inframaxillary
untransferable
intrinsicality
intransigeance
intransigently
intransitively
infrangibility
untranslatable
untranslatably
intransmutable
untransmutable
unpreparedness
unproportioned
unprepossessed
unpropitiously
uncrystallised
uncrystallized
unprosperously
unpresumptuous
infrastructure
ingratiatingly
ungratefulness
untruthfulness
unpretendingly
ungroundedness

14 □n□s□d

anisodactylous
unostentatious
anesthesiology
inestimability
unaspiringness
unassumingness
initialisation
initialization
unstrengthened
knitting-needle
knotenschiefer
Gnathobdellida
unattractively
institutionary
instrumentally
pneumatologist
unpurchaseable
insusceptively
unsuccessfully
innumerability
insuperability
insufficiently
unauthenticity
indubitability
unbusinesslike
insurmountable
unsurmountable
insurmountably
pneumoconiosis
pneumokoniosis
pneumoconiotic
pneumodynamics
unsuspectingly
inauspiciously
unsuspiciously
insuppressible
insuppressibly
insurrectional
unquestionable
unquestionably
intussuscepted
inquisiturient
unsuitableness
angustifoliate
intuitionalism
intuitionalist
uncultivatable
unavailability
unavoidability
universalistic
universitarian
inevitableness
knowledge-based
know-nothingism
unexpectedness
inexpiableness
unextinguished
inexorableness
inexpressibles
inexcusability
encyclopedical
encyclopaedian
encyclopaedist
unsympathising
unsympathizing
unsystematical
unsystematised
unsystematized
tobacco-stopper
volatilisation
volatilization
foraminiferous
Johannisberger
potassium-argon
forbiddingness
double-barreled
double-declutch
hobbledehoydom
hobbledehoyish
hobbledehoyism
double-threaded
double-flowered
double-tonguing
double-breasted
double-stopping
non-belligerent
concretisation
concretization
conceivability
concelebration
non-comedogenic
non-compearance
coxcombicality
non-committally
non-communicant
non-contentious
volcanological
non-conformance
concentrically
non-concurrence
non-co-operation
porcupine-grass
non-chromosomal
worcesterberry
concessionaire
moccasin-flower
conclusiveness
concavo-concave
conductibility
bowdlerisation
bowdlerization
goodfellowship
gold-of-pleasure
condensability
folding-machine
good-for-nothing
roadworthiness
food-controller
word-processing
wonder-stricken
condescendence
non-destructive
nondisjunction
conditionality
good-humouredly
power-amplifier
dodecasyllabic
dodecasyllable
nomenclatorial
robes-de-chambre
foreseeability
non-electrolyte
foreshortening
norethisterone
forethoughtful
norepinephrine
soteriological
solecistically
love-in-idleness
polemoniaceous
noteworthiness
cotemporaneous
foreordination
money-scrivener
potentiometric
confidentially
tomfoolishness
conformability
conformational
longs-and-shorts
rough-and-tumble
congratulative
congratulation
congratulatory
△**congregational**
long-headedness
Congressperson
long-windedness
bougainvillaea
morganatically
conglomeration
conglobulation
longitudinally
conglutinative
conglutination
Rochelle-powder
oophorectomise
oophorectomize
sophistication
nominalisation
nominalization
motivationally
sociobiologist
motivelessness
vociferousness
forisfamiliate
loving-kindness
dolichocephaly
polishing-paste
polishing-slate
politicisation
politicization
solidification

Words marked △ may be spelled also with a capital letter

solicitousness
Rosicrucianism
holier-than-thou
△sovietological
solitudinarian
non-involvement
non-judgemental
conjunctivitis
cock-a-doodle-doo
mock-heroically
book-mindedness
poikilothermic
poikilothermal
joukery-pawkery
rocket-launcher
woollen-drapery
soul-destroying
coelanaglyphic
soul-confirming
collapsability
collapsibility
colliquescence
bouleversement
follow-my-leader
cosmochemistry
cosmeceuticals
formidableness
commodiousness
norm-referenced
cosmographical
commentatorial
commandantship
communications
commonsensical
communion-cloth
communion-table
common-or-garden
commensurately
commensuration
cosmopolitical
commissaryship
commissionaire
foundation-stop
mountaineering
roundaboutedly
roundaboutness
counterbalance
counter-battery
counterchanged
counter-culture
counter-current
counsellorship
countermeasure
counter-opening
counter-passant
countershading
countersubject
counterskipper
counter-salient
counter-trading
coincidentally
somnambulation
somnambulistic
country-dancing
point-to-pointer
cornet-à-pistons
monosaccharide
monocarpellary
non-operational
holometabolism
holometabolous
nonotechnology
homogenisation
homogenization
colonel-in-chief
borough-English
Monochlamydeae
monophthongise
monophthongize
monotheistical
△monotheletical
monochromatism
soporiferously
monolingualism
dolomitisation
dolomitization
Monoplacophora
corolliflorous
homoeoteleuton
homoeothermous
homoiothermous
Mohorovicician
homoeomorphism
homoeomorphous
monotonousness
honourableness
colour-sergeant
monoprionidian
Zoroastrianism
pococuranteism
coconut-matting
comprehensible
comprehensibly
complexionless
morphinomaniac
compensational
louping-on-stane
compunctiously
morphophonemic
compurgatorial
comparableness
non-performance
copper-bottomed
compossibility
compassionable
composing-stick
corpuscularian
corpuscularity
compatibleness
hospitableness
porphyrogenite
zoophytologist
mosquito-weight
conquistadores
courageousness
co-ordinateness
boarding-school
mourning-border
correligionist
horrendousness
corruptibility
horror-stricken
correspondence
correspondency
non-restrictive
gooseberry-wine
gooseberry-moth
gooseberry-fool
gooseberry-bush
consubstantial
consociational
boisterousness
coessentiality
consuetudinary
coastguardsman
horse-godmother
conspiratorial
worshipfulness
conscienceless
constitutional
nonsensicality
consanguineous
torsion-balance
dog's-tooth-grass
conservatively
construability
conservational
conservatorium
constructively
constructivism
constructional
conscriptional
possessiveness
topsy-turviness
contrafagottos
contradictable
contradictious
contraindicate
contraindicant
contrarotating
contrapositive
contraposition
contractedness
contractionary
postmastership
contracyclical
horticulturist
cost-accountant
cost-accounting
corticosteroid
corticotrophin
Pontederiaceae
postmenopausal

Words marked △ may be spelled also with a capital letter

röntgenography
north-eastwards
south-eastwards
fortifications
contagiousness
contiguousness
post-millennial
fortuitousness
footplatewoman
footplatewomen
contumaciously
contemperation
contemperature
low-temperature
contumeliously
contemporanean
contemptuously
noctambulation
continentalism
continentalist
continuousness
portentousness
north-north-east
north-north-west
fortune-telling
postindustrial
rostrocarinate
controvertible
controvertibly
dogtooth-violet
postpositively
postpositional
controllership
do-it-yourselfer
soft-conscienc'd
foster-daughter
post-production
forthrightness
contesseration
south-south-east
south-south-west
north-westwards
south-westwards
popularisation
popularization
loquaciousness
volumetrically
solubilisation
solubilization
voluminousness
coquettishness
robustiousness
voluptuousness
convocationist
convulsiveness
Convolvulaceae
conventionally
conversational
conversaziones
convertibility
convexo-concave
forward-looking
polysaccharide
polyacrylamide
polymerisation
polymerization
polytheistical
Polyplacophora
polyembryonate
polynucleotide
polysyllabical
polysynthetism
sphaerocrystal
specialisation
specialization
spectacularity
spectrographic
spectrological
spectroscopist
apodeictically
epidemiologist
Epidermophyton
spread-eagleism
appendicectomy
Appendicularia
speechlessness
speech-training
apheliotropism
epigrammatical
optimalisation
optimalization
spring-carriage
spring-cleaning
sprightfulness
optimistically
spelaeological
apologetically
open-handedness
spinthariscope
open-mindedness
spindle-shanked
opinionatively
aphoristically
optoelectronic
uproariousness
apoplectically
apophthegmatic
approach-stroke
spermatogenous
spermatophytic
spermatogonium
spermatorrhoea
appreciatively
spirochaetosis
apprehensively
spermiogenesis
apprenticement
apprenticeship
apprenticehood
sporangiophore
sporangiospore
spironolactone
oppressiveness
spiritualistic
spiritlessness
sporotrichosis
spirituousness
spirit-stirring
epistemologist
opisthocoelian
opisthocoelous
opisthographic
opisthoglossal
epistolography
ophthalmometer
ophthalmometry
ophthalmoscope
ophthalmoscopy
apothegmatical
spatiotemporal
spawning-ground
epexegetically
sphygmographic
squadron-leader
squirearchical
equiangularity
equiponderance
aquifoliaceous
bread-and-butter
armamentariums
breakfast-table
breathlessness
preaching-cross
preaching-house
breathing-space
breathing-while
organ-harmonium
organisability
organizability
organisational
organizational
organiser-purse
organizer-purse
organometallic
preadolescence
prearrangement
probabiliorism
probabiliorist
△brobdingnagian
pribble-prabble
orobanchaceous
Grace-and-Favour
grace-and-favour
procrastinator
precociousness
Trochelminthes
practicability
fructification
trichinisation
trichinization
trickle-charger
proceleusmatic
preconcertedly

arachnological
triconsonantic
preconsonantal
triconsonantal
trichobacteria
trichophytosis
trichomoniasis
trichotomously
precipitinogen
precariousness
procuratorship
prick-the-garter
cruciverbalism
cruciverbalist
brachydactylic
brachycephalic
brachypinakoid
brachydiagonal
procryptically
Trachypteridae
predictability
Traducianistic
productiveness
productibility
predaciousness
cradle-snatcher
bridge-building
prodigiousness
tridimensional
predesignation
predesignatory
predestinative
predestinarian
predestination
predisposition
creditableness
traditionalism
traditionalist
traditionality
traditionarily
predeterminate
predeterminism
predevelopment
irreparability
free-handedness
Praeraphaelite
irrelativeness
friendlessness
breeding-ground
irreplevisable
irremovability
irrevocability
irreconcilable
irreconcilably
irrecognisable
irrecognizable
tree-worshipper
irresoluteness
irresolubility
irrespectively
free-spokenness
irresponsively
irreproachable
irreproachably
irreproducible
irrestrainable
pre-established
irrefutability
irresuscitable
irresuscitably
irreducibility
prefabrication
traffic-calming
traffic-manager
traffic-returns
traffic-signals
preferentially
professionally
professorially
profitableness
pragmatisation
pragmatization
pragmaticality
tragicomically
progressionary
progressionism
progressionist
dragon-standard
progenitorship
prognosticator
gregariousness
prohibitionary
prohibitionism
prohibitionist
orthochromatic
archgenethliac
archiepiscopal
archaeological
archaeometrist
Archaeornithes
archaeozoology
orthographical
orthopterology
orthophosphate
architectonics
greisenisation
greisenization
praiseworthily
Ornithodelphia
ornithodelphic
ornithological
ornithomorphic
ornithophilous
artificialness
artillery-plant
traitorousness
articulateness
projectisation
projectization
frolicsomeness
prolocutorship
drill-husbandry
proletarianise
proletarianize
proletarianism
grammaticaster
premeditatedly
trumpet-tongued
Kremlinologist
premillenarian
tremendousness
gram-equivalent
promise-breaker
promise-crammed
promise-keeping
bremsstrahlung
aromatherapist
trimethylamine
transcendental
transcendently
transcutaneous
transcaucasian
Transcaucasion
grangerisation
grangerization
prince-imperial
orange-coloured
orange-squeezer
transformative
transformation
transfer-ticket
transformistic
transferential
transfusionist
uranographical
prenegotiation
French-Canadian
broncho-dilator
bronchiectasis
French-polisher
trencher-knight
trencher-friend
principalities
printing-office
transitiveness
transitionally
fringillaceous
transitoriness
frontierswoman
crinkle-crankle
transliterator
transmigrative
transmigration
transmigratory
transmogrified
transmissively
transmissivity
transmissional
pronunciamento
transplantable
transpicuously
transportation
transportingly

14 □r□n□p

transport-rider
transsexualism
trinitrophenol
trinitrotoluol
Trinitarianism
crinkum-crankum
trinkum-trankum
transvaluation
transversality
transvestitism
arrondissement
preoperational
prioritisation
prioritization
cryobiological
arboricultural
cryptaesthesia
cryptaesthetic
propaedeutical
triple-tonguing
triphenylamine
propagandistic
proprioceptive
graphitisation
graphitization
proprietorship
propeller-blade
tropologically
preponderantly
cryptorchidism
trophoneurosis
cryptococcosis
cryptosporidia
proportionable
proportionably
proportionless
proportionment
proportionally
tripersonalism
tripersonalist
tripersonality
preposterously
propitiatorily
propitiousness
trapezohedrons
croque-monsieur
pre-Reformation
crystallomancy
crystallisable
crystallizable
trisoctahedron
prosperousness
prosthodontics
prosthodontist
cross-infection
crossing-warden
dressing-jacket
Prussification
cross-marketing
presumptuously
presentability
presentational
prosencephalic
prosencephalon
presentiveness
presentimental
prison-breaking
Bristol-diamond
aristocratical
Crossopterygii
presupposition
preservability
cross-reference
dress-rehearsal
prescriptively
proscriptively
prescriptivism
prescriptivist
cross-sectional
pressurisation
pressurization
presbyterially
trituberculate
trituberculism
protectiveness
Crutched-friars
prettification
prittle-prattle
arithmetically
prothonotarial
prothonotariat
protoplasmatic
fraternisation
fraternization
erythropoiesis
erythropoietin
protospathaire
protistologist
Prototracheata
protrusiveness
Protevangelium
pretty-pretties
protozoologist
traumatisation
traumatization
groundlessness
groundbreaking
Crouched-friars
troubleshooter
proud-stomached
trivialisation
trivialization
providentially
travelling-wave
preventability
preventiveness
proventriculus
provost-marshal
greywacke-slate
prayerlessness
asparagus-stone
psychogenetics
psychotechnics
psychometrical
psychoneuroses
psychoneurosis
psychoneurotic
psychochemical
psychophysical
psycholinguist
psychoanalysis
psychoanalytic
psychosomatics
psychodramatic
psychographics
psychodynamics
isodiametrical
osteoarthrosis
osteoarthritis
osteodermatous
asseveratingly
Osteoglossidae
esterification
asset-stripping
ostentatiously
eschatological
Ustilaginaceae
astigmatically
psilanthropism
psilanthropist
Asclepiadaceae
asymmetrically
asymptotically
asynchronously
osmoregulation
associationism
psephoanalysis
ostrich-feather
astrogeologist
astrologically
astronomically
astrophysicist
pseudaesthesia
pseudepigrapha
pseudepigraphy
pseudoscorpion
pseudomembrane
pseudomorphism
pseudomorphous
pseudosolution
pseudo-archaism
pseudosymmetry
pseudonymously
straddle-legged
stratigaphical
stratification
strabismometer
stratigraphist
attainableness
stocking-stitch
stichometrical
sticky-fingered
stretching-bond

Words marked △ may be spelled also with a capital letter

steel-engraving
stoechiometric
etherification
steeplechasing
steeple-crowned
attemptability
strepsipterous
street-credible
stigmatisation
stigmatization
stigmatiferous
stigmatophilia
stegocephalian
stegocephalous
stagflationary
steganographic
steganographer
strikebreaking
stoicheiometry
stoichiometric
attitudinarian
attitudinising
attitudinizing
Italianisation
Italianization
stalactitiform
stultification
otolaryngology
stiletto-heeled
utilitarianise
utilitarianize
utilitarianism
stomachfulness
stamping-ground
etymologically
stumbling-block
stomatogastric
standard-bearer
ethnobotanical
ethnographical
ethnologically
strobilisation
strobilization
stupendousness
staphylococcal
staphylococcus
eternalisation
eternalization
Sturmabteilung
attractiveness
yttro-columbite
pteridophilist
star-of-the-earth
star-of-the-night
uterogestation
pterylographic
ottrelite-slate
stereotactical
stereometrical
stertorousness
stereospecific
stereoisomeric
yttro-tantalite
statuesqueness
stationariness
station-manager
stout-heartedly
subarborescent
subaggregation
subatmospheric
subassociation
subalternation
rumbledethumps
rumblegumption
turbo-generator
tumbling-barrel
turbine-steamer
numberlessness
lumbersomeness
number-cruncher
luncheon-basket
durchkomponirt
Durchmusterung
subconsciously
subcontinental
vulcanological
subcontracting
subcontrariety
susceptiveness
susceptibility
successfulness
successiveness
successionless
successionally
quicksilvering
quicksilverish
subcutaneously
punctuationist
quadragenarian
quadrangularly
muddleheadedly
hundred-per-cent
quodlibetarian
quadrigeminate
quadrigeminous
quadrisyllabic
quadrisyllable
fundamentalism
fundamentalist
fundamentality
murdering-piece
superambitious
superannuation
superabsorbent
superabundance
superciliously
supercelestial
superconfident
supercontinent
superconductor
supercargoship
superexcellent
superelevation
supereminently
supererogative
supererogation
supererogatory
superessential
superficialise
superficialize
superficiality
superfoetation
super-flyweight
superincumbent
superinduction
superinfection
superimportant
superintendent
superintending
supernormality
supernaturally
surefootedness
superovulation
superphosphate
supersonically
supersensitive
superstructive
superstruction
superstructure
superscription
supersaturated
superterranean
supervisorship
sufferableness
Kupferschiefer
furfuraldehyde
suffructescent
luggage-carrier
subgenerically
suggestiveness
suggestibility
euphuistically
authentication
mushroom-anchor
euphorbiaceous
jurisdictional
audio-frequency
subinfeudation
subinfeudatory
humidification
munition-worker
pugilistically
numismatically
audiometrician
Nudibranchiata
nudibranchiate
subinsinuation
subjectiveness
subjectivistic
huckleberrying
nuclearisation
nuclearization
nuclear-powered

14 □u□l□c

public-spirited
bull-headedness
fully-fashioned
quilting-cotton
outlandishness
burling-machine
submicroscopic
rummlegumption
rummelgumption
subminiaturise
subminiaturize
submergibility
submersibility
submissiveness
pugnaciousness
quintessential
quincentennial
quantitatively
quantification
vulnerableness
quinquecostate
quinquefoliate
quinquefarious
quinquagesimal
quinquennially
quinquevalence
autoradiograph
Euro-Parliament
Eurocentricity
mucoviscidosis
tumorigenicity
autobiographic
autobiographer
eulogistically
auto-intoxicant
autocoprophagy
humoursomeness
autocratically
auto-suggestion
autotypography
sulphacetamide
sulphathiazole
sulphanilamide
auspiciousness
suspiciousness
supplementally
purple-coloured
supplicatingly
surprisingness
suspensibility
purposefulness
surpassingness
suppositionary
supposititious
sulphurisation
sulphurization
jusqu'auboutist
quaquaversally
turquoise-green
quarter-gallery
outrageousness
Supralapsarian
querimoniously
eutrophication
suprasegmental
nutritiousness
quartz-porphyry
Russianisation
Russianization
substantialise
substantialize
substantialism
substantiation
substantialist
substantiality
substantivally
Russo-Byzantine
Aussichtspunkt
Burschenschaft
question-master
substitutively
substitutivity
substitutional
purse-snatching
multicuspidate
futtock-shrouds
buttress-thread
justifiability
multifactorial
multifoliolate
multifariously
hunt-the-slipper
sustainability
multinucleated
hunting-grounds
hunting-leopard
multi-ownership
multiple-choice
multiplicative
multiplication
hunter-gatherer
multiracialism
quattrocentism
quattrocentist
gutter-merchant
subterrestrial
butter-fingered
multarticulate
butterfly-screw
cucurbitaceous
lugubriousness
Augustinianism
tumultuousness
curvilinearity
outward-sainted
muzzle-velocity
quizzification
evil-mindedness
evolutionistic
even-handedness
evangelicalism
evangelisation
evangelization
overcapitalise
overcapitalize
avariciousness
overscrupulous
over-determined
over-refinement
over-the-counter
overwhelmingly
overindulgence
overpoweringly
over-confidence
overcompensate
overcorrection
overpopulation
overspecialise
overspecialize
ivory-porcelain
overproduction
overprotective
overestimation
two-dimensional
sweet-and-twenty
two-for-his-heels
swindge-buckler
swingling-stock
swoopstake-like
sword-swallower
exsanguination
exhaustiveness
exhaustibility
expansionistic
exacerbescence
experimentally
experienceless
expedientially
experientially
extemporaneity
extemporaneous
extensionalism
extensionality
exceptionalism
ex-servicewoman
oxyhaemoglobin
exhilaratingly
extinguishable
extinguishment
explorationist
exclaustration
examine-in-chief
excommunicable
excommunicator
extortionately
excruciatingly
extractability
extra-condensed
extracanonical
extracorporeal
extraforaneous
excrementitial
extrinsicality

extraneousness
extra-parochial
expressiveness
expressionless
extravehicular
existentialism
existentialist
exothermically
gynaecological
gynandromorphy
pyramidologist
tyrannicalness
synaposematism
dynamometrical
dynamo-electric
symbolicalness
myocardiopathy
synchronically
hyperaesthesia
hyperaesthesic
hyperaesthetic
hyperacuteness
hyperbolically
hyperbatically
hypercriticise
hypercriticize
hypercriticism
hypercalcaemia
hyperconscious
hypercatalexis
hyperglycaemia
hyperinflation
hypernatraemia
pyrenomycetous
hypersensitise
hypersensitive
hypersensitize
hypertrophical
hyperventilate
Pythagoreanism
mythologically
pyrheliometric
cyclobarbitone
cyclanthaceous
pyelonephritic
pyelonephritis
cyclopentolate
myrmecological
myrmecophagous
myrmecophilous
dysmenorrhoeic
dysmenorrhoeal
symmetrisation
symmetrization
symmetrophobia
cyanoacetylene
cyanobacterium
cyanocobalamin
hypomagnesemia
cytogeneticist
pyrotechnician
hypodermically
hypomenorrhoea
Syrophoenician
Zygophyllaceae
sycophantishly
hypochondriasm
hypochondriast
hypothyroidism
hypophysectomy
pyrophosphoric
hypothetically
pyrophotograph
mylonitisation
mylonitization
hypomixolydian
hypoallergenic
hypocoristical
gynomonoecious
Zygobranchiata
zygobranchiate
hypocritically
gyrostabiliser
gyrostabilizer
hypostatically
hyposulphurous
xylopyrography
xylotypography
synonymousness
lymphangiogram
lyophilisation
lyophilization
nymphomaniacal
symptomatology
hydro-aeroplane
hydrobiologist
hydrocellulose
hydrocephalous
hydrocortisone
hydrocoralline
hydrodynamical
hydroextractor
hydrographical
hygrographical
dyer's-greenweed
hydrogeologist
cyproheptadine
hydrologically
hydromechanics
hydromagnetics
hydronephrosis
hydronephrotic
Hydropterideae
hydropneumatic
hydroponically
hydrophobicity
hydrosulphuric
hygroscopicity
hyetographical
nyctaginaceous
dysteleologist
cystolithiasis
systematically
hysterectomise
hysterectomize
mysteriousness
azidothymidine

15 □a□a□e

paraheliotropic
katathermometer
paralinguistics
parasiticalness
catallactically
parallelepipeda
cataclysmically
palaeopathology
palaeomagnetism
palaeoecologist
palaeogeography
palaeophytology
paradoxicalness
palaeobiologist
palaeolimnology
palaeoanthropic
Palaeoanthropus
palaeobotanical
palaeozoologist
palaeographical
palaeontography
palaeontologist
palaeoethnology
malacopterygian
paragraphically
malassimilation
parasympathetic
Sabbath-breaking
bacchanalianism
catch-as-catch-can
sanctimoniously
vascularisation
vascularization
carcinogenicity
sarcenchymatous
malconformation
landscape-marble
saddler-corporal
hard-heartedness
saddler-sergeant
landing-carriage
hard-and-fastness
cardiopulmonary
maldistribution
paleobiological
paleichthyology
calendarisation
calendarization
rate-determining
paleoethnologic
paleoecological
materfamiliases
paterfamiliases
paleogeographer
paleogeographic
materialistical
materialisation
materialization
lamellirostrate
Capernaitically
paleontological
categoricalness
paleopedologist
paleopathologic
parenthetically
maneuverability
paleozoological
half-wellingtons
half-heartedness
bargain-basement
margaritiferous
△catholicisation
△catholicization
mathematisation
mathematization
machine-readable
machine-washable
fashionableness
gathering-ground
catheterisation
catheterization
manic-depressive
radio-gramophone
radiogoniometer
basidiomycetous
nationalisation
rationalisation
nationalization
rationalization
radio-telegraphy
magisterialness
canisterisation
canisterization
back-calculation
lackadaisically
hackney-coachman
Jack-of-all-trades
Jack-in-the-pulpit
market-gardening
packet-switching
railway-crossing
railway-carriage
parliament-hinge
parliament-house
parliamentarian
parliamentarily
parliamentarism
paulo-post-future
Callitrichaceae
warm-heartedness
maintainability
cannibalisation
cannibalization
rainbow-coloured
manneristically
magneto-electric
carnivorousness
sadomasochistic
panophthalmitis
paroemiographer
vasoconstrictor
labour-intensive
manoeuvrability
malpractitioner
Pan-Presbyterian
malpresentation
carpometacarpus
tamper-resistant
banqueting-house
marriage-licence
marriage-portion
carriage-forward
sarraceniaceous
macrocosmically
caprifoliaceous
warrantableness
Patripassianism
saprophytically
macrosporangium
macroscopically
marsh-cinquefoil
Caesalpiniaceae
tarsometatarsal
tarsometatarsus
passenger-pigeon
Marsipobranchii
particularistic
pantechnicon-van
parthenogenesis
parthenogenetic
party-government
castanospermine
gastroenteritis
Bartholomew-tide
pantopragmatics
tatterdemallion
bacteriological
earthshattering
fantasticalness
lactovegetarian
faithworthiness
natureknowledge
daguerreotypist
harvest-festival
canvas-stretcher
Caryophyllaceae
objectification
observationally
ebullioscopical
abiogenetically
obstructionally
scratchbuilding
oceanographical
éclaircissement
sclerodermatous
scribaciousness
scribbling-paper
schillerisation
schillerization
echinodermatous
schizo-affective
schizophrenetic
acrimoniousness

cripture-reader
chistosomiasis
chlocratically
cclimatisation
cclimatization
colopendriform
cclesiasticism
cclesiological
canthocephalan
cknowledgeable
cknowledgeably
cknowledgement
chondroplastic
choolmastering
choolmasterish
chool-inspector
ccommodatingly
ccountableness
caphocephalous
chrecklichkeit
chromatisation
chromatization
ositetrahedra
cetyl-salicylic
cotoxicologist
hthyodorulite
hthyodorylite
cquisitiveness
cousto-electric
dventurousness
driophthalmian
driophthalmous
denocarcinomas
denohypophyses
denohypophysis
dontostomatous
eographically
doriferousness
djutant-general
etamathematics
ecarbonisation
ecarbonization
ecarburisation
ecarburization
ecalcification
ed-and-breakfast
legacheiroptera
lemathelminthes
emathelminthic
eta-thalassemia
exachlorophane
exachlorophene
esaticephalous
elaginellaceae
etalinguistics
epaticological
emagnetisation
emagnetization
edagoguishness
esacralisation
esacralization
departmentalise
departmentalism
departmentalize
herb-Christopher
kerbstone-broker
peacock-pheasant
teacher-governor
descriptiveness
pencil-sharpener
new-Commonwealth
geochronologist
Neo-Christianity
hendecasyllabic
hendecasyllable
readvertisement
tendentiousness
tender-heartedly
meadow-saxifrage
defencelessness
serendipitously
degenerationist
deleteriousness
redetermination
telephotography
hereditarianism
hereditarianist
repetitiousness
determinability
heterodactylous
heterocercality
heterogeneously
heterosexuality
heterochromatic
ceremoniousness
developmentally
selenographical
telegraphically
penetrativeness
cerebrovascular
desensitisation
necessitousness
desensitization
seventeen-hunder
desertification
telestereoscope
desexualisation
desexualization
receiving-office
self-capacitance
self-sacrificing
self-observation
self-abandonment
perfectionistic
self-advancement
self-resemblance
self-determining
self-development
self-registering
self-realisation
self-realization
self-deprecating
self-degradation
self-fertilising
self-fertilizing
self-destruction
self-destructive
self-affirmation
self-vindication
self-liquidating
self-slaughtered
self-importantly
self-improvement
perfunctoriness
self-sovereignty
reafforestation
self-confidently
self-forgetfully
self-pollination
self-complacence
self-considering
self-constituted
self-consequence
self-consistency
self-portraiture
self-documenting
self-opinionated
self-approbation
self-propagating
self-preparation
self-sufficiency
self-humiliation
perfluorocarbon
self-substantial
self-questioning
self-sustainment
self-explication
self-explanatory
self-examination
sergeant-drummer
neighbourliness
weighing-machine
pergamentaceous
Methodistically
cephalochordate
nepheline-basalt
methamphetamine
mechanomorphism
mechanoreceptor
mechanistically
dephlogisticate
technologically
technostructure
Mephistophelean
Mephistophelian
semimanufacture
Semi-Pelagianism
sedimentologist
decipherability
medicine-dropper
sericiculturist
vehicle-actuated
semi-independent

15 □e□i□n

regionalisation
regionalization
semi-logarithmic
meritoriousness
lexicographical
lepidopterology
semidocumentary
menispermaceous
denitrification
devitrification
semitransparent
hemicrystalline
semicrystalline
perissodactylic
perissosyllabic
peristaltically
heliotropically
semisubmersible
desilverisation
desilverization
devil-worshipper
health-conscious
well-intentioned
Hellenistically
well-conditioned
well-upholstered
fellow-traveller
helminthologist
hermeneutically
seeming-virtuous
hermaphroditism
geomorphogenist
geomorphologist
dermatoglyphics
dermatomyositis
reinterrogation
deindustrialise
reindustrialise
deindustrialize
reindustrialize
xeroradiography
reconcilability
second-adventist
second-in-command
recoverableness
before-mentioned
hemochromatosis
recollectedness
meroblastically
renormalisation
renormalization
decommissioning
decolourisation
decolourization
decomposability
resourcefulness
democratifiable
democratisation
democratization
reconsideration
reconstitutable
reconsolidation
remorselessness
demonstrability
remonstratingly
demonstratively
refortification
decontamination
decontaminative
reconvalescence
aerodynamically
respectableness
perpendicularly
reapportionment
temperamentally
tempestuousness
sesquicarbonate
sesquicentenary
neuroanatomical
reproachfulness
Tetrabranchiata
tetrabranchiate
neuroblastomata
detribalisation
detribalization
neurobiological
Tetractinellida
jerry-come-tumble
retrievableness
neurofibrillary
retrogressional
retrogressively
neurohypophyses
neurohypophysis
near-sightedness
neurolinguistic
ferro-molybdenum
necromantically
recrementitious
refrangibleness
hearing-impaired
metropolitanise
metropolitanate
metropolitanize
neuropsychiatry
neuropsychology
neurophysiology
retroreflective
heir-presumptive
retrospectively
tetrasyllabical
refreshment-room
tetrasporangium
reprivatisation
reprivatization
re-establishment
peasecod-bellied
peasecod-cuirass
perspicaciously
perspicuousness
pessimistically
messenger-at-arms
personification
personalisation
personalization
seismographical
dessertspoonful
sensation-monger
Tectibranchiata
tectibranchiate
tentaculiferous
Gentleman-at-arms
gentlemanliness
feather-boarding
weatherboarding
vertiginousness
ventriloquially
ventriloquistic
de-Stalinisation
de-Stalinization
testament-dative
sententiousness
septentrionalis
septentrionally
dextrophosphate
letters-of-marque
venturesomeness
destructibility
destructiveness
secundogeniture
resurrection-man
resurrection-pie
resurrectionary
resurrectionise
resurrectionism
resurrectionist
resurrectionize
demulsification
serviceableness
servomechanical
dehypnotisation
dehypnotization
demystification
African-American
efficaciousness
affranchisement
agranulocytosis
agriculturalist
shabby-gentility
thick-headedness
thick-wittedness
phrenologically
threepenceworth
threepennyworth
chrestomathical
shrink-resistant
Christadelphian
Christy-minstrel
cholecalciferol
cholecystectomy
cholecystostomy
Philadelphaceae
philanthropical

Words marked △ may be spelled also with a capital letter

cholangiography
cholesterolemia
thalassotherapy
thalassographer
thalassographic
philosophically
shilly-shallying
chemoattractant
rhombencephalon
chamberlainship
rhombenporphyry
Rhamphorhynchus
chemopsychiatry
phantasmagorial
thunder-stricken
Rhynchobdellida
Rhynchocephalia
thin-skinnedness
phenakistoscope
phenylketonuria
phenylketonuric
phenolphthalein
phonemicisation
phonemicization
phenomenologist
phenomenalistic
chenopodiaceous
chondrification
phoneticisation
phoneticization
thanatognomonic
phonautographic
thankworthiness
thiobarbiturate
chromatographic
chloramphenicol
thromboembolism
theorematically
shoot-from-the-hip
through-composed
theosophistical
chronologically
chromoxylograph
pharmacokinetic
pharmacognostic
pharmacognosist
therianthropism
thoracocentesis
chargé-d'affaires
whirling-machine
churrigueresque
choriocarcinoma
thermochemistry
theriomorphosis
thermodynamical
therapeutically
pharisaicalness
thoroughgoingly
thirtysomething
physicochemical
phase-difference
phosphorylation
phosphorescence
physiotherapist
physiologically
physiographical
photoconducting
photoconductive
photodegradable
photoelasticity
photogrammetric
phytogeographer
phytogeographic
photojournalism
photojournalist
photolithograph
photo-mechanical
photomacrograph
photomicrograph
photomultiplier
photorefractive
photosensitiser
photosensitizer
phototelegraphy
photoxylography
photozincograph
rheumatological
shoulder-shotten
shoulder-clapper
shoulder-slipped
thoughtlessness
bioavailability
disaffectedness
disaffectionate
disafforestment
misapprehension
misapprehensive
misappreciation
misappreciative
disagreeability
disassimilation
disassimilative
disarticulation
bio-astronautics
disadvantageous
misbecomingness
aircraft-carrier
viscoelasticity
kitchen-gardener
discretionarily
air-chief-marshal
mischievousness
miscellaneously
circumnavigable
circumnavigator
circumvallation
circumscribable
circumscription
circumscriptive
discommendation
circumferential
circumambagious
circumincession
circuminsession
circumforaneous
discommodiously
circumspectness
circumstantials
circumstantiate
air-conditioning
discontinuation
discontinuously
misconstruction
viscosimetrical
windscreen-wiper
vindicativeness
Middle-Easterner
middle-of-the-road
kind-heartedness
middle-stitching
biodestructible
mineralogically
cinematographer
cinematographic
videoconference
dimethylaniline
vice-chamberlain
cinemicrography
cineangiography
diversification
disentrancement
disentanglement
direction-finder
director-general
disenthrallment
riverworthiness
diffrangibility
differentiation
disgracefulness
single-heartedly
singularisation
singularization
biogeochemistry
biogeographical
dishearteningly
dishabilitation
Pithecanthropus
lithochromatics
Michaelmas-daisy
light-headedness
right-handedness
diaheliotropism
light-mindedness
right-mindedness
nightmarishness
dithyrambically
disharmoniously
high-gravel-blind
withdrawing-room
dividend-warrant
disinflationary
riding-committee
disillusionment

15 □i□i□p

disimprisonment
vicissitudinous
misintelligence
sinistrodextral
disinterestedly
miniaturisation
miniaturization
ticket-collector
gillie-white-foot
bioluminescence
violinistically
bibliographical
field-sequential
pillow-structure
diamagnetically
significatively
disorganisation
disorganization
disobligingness
kilogram-calorie
displeasingness
dispensableness
diaphototropism
disproportional
misproportioned
diaphragmatitis
dispassionately
disputativeness
disquisitionary
microanalytical
microbiological
Microchiroptera
nitro-derivative
microdissection
microelectronic
hierogrammatist
nitrogenisation
nitrogenization
micromicrofarad
micromicrocurie
micromillimetre
micropegmatitic
microprocessing
microphotograph
disreputability
disrespectfully
microsporangium
microscopically
microsporophyll
microtechnology
Diprotodontidae
dissociableness
diastereoisomer
first-generation
dissolvableness
diesel-hydraulic
lissencephalous
fissiparousness
biostratigraphy
dissatisfaction
dissatisfactory
victualling-bill
victualling-ship
victualling-yard
distractibility
biotechnologist
distressfulness
fifth-generation
Fifth-monarchism
Fifth-monarchist
distinctiveness
distinguishable
distinguishably
distinguishment
picture-moulding
historiographer
historiographic
picture-postcard
picture-restorer
picturesqueness
distastefulness
distrustfulness
mistrustfulness
ritualistically
pleasurableness
pleasure-seeking
flibbertigibbet
all-changing-word
gluconeogenesis
electroanalysis
electroacoustic
electrochemical
electrodynamics
electrification
electrokinetics
electromagnetic
electromyograph
electrometrical
electronegative
electrophoresis
electrophoretic
electropositive
electrotechnics
electrothermics
ill-favouredness
oligonucleotide
plagiostomatous
alphabetisation
alphabetization
alpha-chloralose
Gleichschaltung
illimitableness
plumbaginaceous
slumpflationary
flamboyante-tree
blameworthiness
plantaginaceous
clandestineness
plenipotentiary
blood-and-thunder
bloodcurdlingly
blood-guiltiness
allotriomorphic
ultracentrifuge
ultrafiltration
ultramicroscope
ultramicroscopy
ultra-Protestant
ultrasonography
blast-furnaceman
glossographical
flutter-tonguing
Platyhelminthes
slotting-machine
platitudinarian
cloud-cuckoo-land
eleutherococcus
eleutherodactyl
eleutherophobia
eleutherophobic
pleuropneumonia
illustriousness
slave-trafficker
impenetrability
imperishability
impermeableness
immensurability
impecuniousness
imperviableness
imaginativeness
amphitheatrical
omnibenevolence
omnidirectional
smelting-furnace
implausibleness
emancipationist
imponderability
immortalisation
immortalization
importunateness
impracticalness
Americanisation
Americanization
amaryllidaceous
impressionistic
imprescriptible
improvvisatrice
improvisatorial
ambulance-chaser
immunopathology
immunochemistry
immunologically
incapaciousness
incalculability
unsatisfiedness
unparliamentary
uncanonicalness
unpatriotically
unobjectionable
unobjectionably
inobtrusiveness
unobtrusiveness
anacreontically

Words marked △ may be spelled also with a capital letter

inaccessibility
knick-knackatory
unaccommodating
onychocryptosis
inscrutableness
inadvisableness
unadvisableness
inadmissibility
unidiomatically
inseparableness
interambulacral
interambulacrum
interchangeable
interchangeably
interchangement
unpeaceableness
unteachableness
intercollegiate
intercolonially
interconversion
interconnection
interdigitation
interdependence
indeterminately
indetermination
undetermination
unceremoniously
underemployment
indefeasibility
indefensibility
unnecessariness
underestimation
interestingness
unrelentingness
antepenultimate
unselfconscious
interferometric
interfascicular
encephalography
underhandedness
indefinableness
undesirableness
unverifiability
unremittingness
interjectionary
interjaculatory
intellectualise
intellectualism
intellectualist
intellectuality
intellectualize
intelligibility
unhealthfulness
interlamination
intermodulation
indemnification
internalisation
internalization
internationally
unreconciliable
interosculation
unrecommendable
unreconstructed
undemonstrative
interpretership
under-privileged
interpenetrable
interprovincial
under-production
interpersonally
intemperateness
interrogatively
understandingly
intersubjective
intensification
interscholastic
interstratified
insensitiveness
ungentlemanlike
anaesthetically
anaesthesiology
under-the-counter
intertwistingly
intertentacular
intertanglement
ancestor-worship
incentivisation
incentivization
interventionism
interventionist
unseaworthiness
ineffaceability
inoffensiveness
ineffectualness
ineffectiveness
inefficaciously
inofficiousness
unchristianlike
unchallengeable
unchallengeably
unwholesomeness
unphilosophical
unchangeability
anthropopathism
anthropogenesis
anthropocentric
anthropophagite
anthropophagous
anthropobiology
anthroposophist
anthropological
anthropomorphic
anthropopsychic
anti-Gallicanism
undisappointing
uncircumscribed
indisciplinable
undisciplinable
antiperistalsis
antiperistaltic
indigestibility
unrighteousness
antichristianly
anticholinergic
annihilationism
infinitesimally
antivivisection
indivisibleness
individualistic
anticlericalism
insignificantly
insignificative
antimonarchical
oneirocriticism
indisputability
antitrinitarian
indissolubility
indistributable
indistinctively
undistinguished
inalterableness
unalterableness
inflammableness
unimaginatively
anomalistically
uninterestingly
unintermittedly
uninterpretable
uninterruptedly
unintentionally
enantiomorphism
enantiomorphous
unconcernedness
unconditionally
intolerableness
ontogenetically
incongruousness
unforgivingness
unsophisticated
indomitableness
encomiastically
incommunicative
uncommunicative
incommensurable
incommensurably
incommutability
entomologically
uncomplainingly
uncomplaisantly
uncomprehending
incomprehension
incomprehensive
uncomprehensive
uncomplimentary
uncompanionable
incomparability
uncooperatively
unco-operatively
uncompassionate
incompatibility
incorrigibility
inconsiderately
inconsideration

Words marked △ may be spelled also with a capital letter

15 □n□o□s

unconscientious
unconsciousness
inconspicuously
inconsolability
unfossiliferous
unconsentaneous
inconsequential
unconstrainable
unconstrainedly
unfortunateness
uncontroversial
involuntariness
unspeakableness
inapplicability
inopportuneness
inapprehensible
unapprehensible
inappropriately
unsportsmanlike
inspirationally
inoperativeness
unapostolically
inequitableness
intractableness
untractableness
unprecedentedly
unpractisedness
incredulousness
unprofitability
unprogressively
ungrammatically
unpremeditation
andromonoecious
intramuscularly
untransferrable
enfranchisement
intrinsicalness
intransigentism
intransigentist
infrangibleness
untransmigrated
intransmissible
untransmissible
unpronounceable
entrepreneurial
intrapreneurial
unproportionate
unprepossessing
infrastructural
introsusception
untrustworthily
unprotectedness
unprotestantise
unprotestantize
energy-efficient
unascertainable
inestimableness
unsteadfastness
gnotobiotically
gnotobiological
inattentiveness
knitting-machine
instantaneously
unstatesmanlike
institutionally
instrumentalism
instrumentalist
instrumentality
instrumentation
instructiveness
pneumatological
Annunciation-day
infundibuliform
innumerableness
insuperableness
unauthenticated
unauthoritative
indubitableness
injudiciousness
unqualifiedness
invulnerability
insubordinately
insubordination
unsuspectedness
insurrectionary
insurrectionism
insurrectionist
unsubstantiated
insubstantially
intussusception
intussusceptive
inquisitorially
inquisitiveness
angustirostrate
unavailableness
unavoidableness
knowledgability
inextensibility
inexpensiveness
unexceptionable
unexceptionably
unexceptionally
inexplicability
inexcusableness
inexpugnability
encyclopaedical
unsymmetrically
ankylostomiasis
Monarchianistic
totalitarianism
logarithmically
romanticisation
romanticization
non-attributable
non-attributably
bomb-calorimeter
double-facedness
double-barrelled
hobbledehoyhood
non-belligerency
combustibleness
conceivableness
non-commissioned
non-contributory
conceptualistic
concessionnaire
good-naturedness
cold-heartedness
cold-bloodedness
good-conditioned
powdering-closet
wondermongering
condescendingly
word-association
nondescriptness
mole-electronics
sober-mindedness
governor-general
homeopathically
poverty-stricken
confidentiality
configurational
confrontational
comfortlessness
confessionalism
confessionalist
congealableness
congratulations
tongue-and-groove
long-sightedness
zoogeographical
lophobranchiate
nothingarianism
sociobiological
police-constable
boning-telescope
dolichocephalic
polishing-powder
sociolinguistic
socialistically
goniometrically
cosignificative
toxicologically
solipsistically
non-intervention
non-intrusionist
non-judgmentally
conjunctionally
conjunctiveness
cockneyfication
Völkerwanderung
Lob-lie-by-the-fire
noble-mindedness
collenchymatous
foul-mouthedness
world-shattering
world-without-end
norm-referencing
formularisation
formularization
commendableness
communicability
communicatively

 Words marked △ may be spelled also with a capital letter

communalisation
communalization
cosmopolitanism
foundation-stone
roundaboutility
roundaboutation
counter-evidence
counterfeisance
counter-flowered
counterfesaunce
counterirritant
countermandable
countermovement
counter-pressure
counter-proposal
counter-security
countervailable
connoisseurship
round-shouldered
co-instantaneity
coinstantaneous
Johnny-head-in-air
homogeneousness
homochlamydeous
monochlamydeous
Monocotyledones
logographically
nomographically
topographically
holocrystalline
monocrystalline
coconsciousness
monosymmetrical
comprehensively
comprehensivise
comprehensivize
complementarily
complementarity
complementation
compressibility
compendiousness
non-professional
morphophonemics
non-profit-making
corporification
compartmentally
compassionately
colposcopically
hospitalisation
hospitalization
computerisation
computerization
compotationship
competitiveness
zoophysiologist
zoophytological
conquerableness
four-dimensional
correlativeness
courtmartialled
corruptibleness
correspondently
correspondingly
courts-bouillons
dorsibranchiate
gooseberry-stone
consubstantiate
consecutiveness
considerateness
consideratively
low-spiritedness
conscientiously
constitutionist
conspicuousness
consolation-race
consumptiveness
consentaneously
nonsensicalness
consequentially
conservationist
conservatorship
constructionism
constructionist
conscriptionist
dorsiventrality
contravallation
contradictorily
contradictively
contrapropeller
portrait-gallery
portrait-painter
contractability
contractibility
north-countryman
röntgenotherapy
post-Reformation
north-eastwardly
south-eastwardly
mortiferousness
doctrinarianism
post-millenarian
postulationally
contemplatively
contemporaneity
contemporaneous
contemptibility
continuation-day
contentiousness
controversially
montmorillonite
controllability
postconsonantal
Götterdämmerung
north-westwardly
south-westwardly
post-synchronise
post-synchronize
softly-sprighted
convolvulaceous
conventionalise
conventionalism
conventionalist
conventionality
conventionalize
conversationism
conversationist
convertible-term
notwithstanding
Corynebacterium
polychlorinated
polychloroprene
polyphloesboean
polyunsaturated
polycrystalline
Polyprotodontia
polysyllabicism
polysynthetical
sphaerosiderite
apocalyptically
speculativeness
spectroscopical
epidemiological
spread-eaglewise
appendicularian
speechification
Sphenisciformes
spheroidisation
spheroidization
Ophioglossaceae
Apollinarianism
spontaneousness
open-heartedness
optoelectronics
apophthegmatise
apophthegmatist
apophthegmatize
approachability
spermatogenesis
spermatogenetic
spermatoblastic
opprobriousness
spirochaetaemia
appropriateness
appropinquation
epistemological
Opisthobranchia
opisthognathous
episcopalianism
ophthalmologist
ophthalmoplegia
ophthalmophobia
ophthalmoscopic
epitheliomatous
equalitarianism
equiprobability
ergatandromorph
crease-resistant
crease-resisting
great-grandchild
treacherousness
irrationalistic
broadmindedness
treasonableness

15 □r□a□o

organophosphate
preacquaintance
problematically
probationership
procrastinating
procrastination
procrastinatory
procrastinative
procreativeness
practicableness
fractionisation
fractionization
brachistochrone
preconstruction
precipitousness
processionalist
brachydactylous
brachycephalous
predictableness
cradle-snatching
predeterminable
irreparableness
irrepealability
irredeemability
free-heartedness
true-heartedness
irreversibility
irretentiveness
greenery-yallery
freezing-mixture
irreligiousness
arterialisation
arterialization
irremissibility
irresistibility
irremovableness
irrevocableness
irreconcilement
irresolvability
irrefragability
irreprehensible
irreprehensibly
irrefutableness
irreducibleness
irreductibility
preformationism
preformationist
preferentialism
preferentialist
professionalise
professionalism
professionalize
pragmaticalness
programmability
progressiveness
fragmentariness
trigonometrical
prognostication
prognosticative
prohibitiveness
Archichlamydeae
archiepiscopacy
archiepiscopate
orthophosphoric
orthopsychiatry
prehistorically
architecturally
ornithodelphian
ornithodelphous
Erziehungsroman
ornithorhynchus
training-college
broken-heartedly
drilling-machine
crimping-machine
criminalisation
criminalization
gramophonically
transactionally
transcriptional
transcriptively
transfigurement
△transfiguration
transferability
transgressional
transgressively
wrong-headedness
Frenchification
French-polishing
bronchoscopical
printing-machine
wringing-machine
transilluminate
grandiloquently
translationally
transliteration
granulitisation
granulitization
transmogrifying
transmutability
transmutational
pronunciamentos
transplantation
transportedness
transparentness
transposability
transpositional
granitification
trinitrobenzene
trinitrotoluene
tranquilizingly
tranquilization
transubstantial
Eriocaulonaceae
proof-correcting
arboriculturist
cryoprecipitate
armoured-cruiser
proprietorially
propylitisation
propylitization
trypanosomiasis
crypto-Christian
crypto-communist
cryptosporidium
proportionality
proportionately
properispomenon
prepossessingly
prepositionally
Pre-Raphaelistic
Pre-Raphaelitish
Pre-Raphaelitism
crystallography
crystallisation
crystallization
trisoctahedrons
prospectiveness
dressing-station
crossing-sweeper
prestidigitator
trisyllabically
cross-laterality
gris-amber-steam'd
presentationism
presentationist
presentableness
prosenchymatous
Aristotelianism
crossopterygian
preservationist
trustworthiness
△presbyterianise
△presbyterianism
△presbyterianize
pretentiousness
preternaturally
erythroleukemia
protospatharius
protozoological
traumatological
argumentatively
draught-proofing
draughtsmanship
troublesomeness
troubleshooting
provocativeness
provost-sergeant
gravitationally
psychopathology
psychogenetical
psychogeriatric
psychometrician
psychochemistry
psychotherapist
psychophysicist
psychobiography
psychobiologist
psychohistorian
psychologically
psychosomimetic
psychotomimetic
psychographical

Words marked △ may be spelled also with a capital letter

15 □x□e□s

psychosynthesis
psychrometrical
assimilationist
isoimmunization
asclepiadaceous
isoperimetrical
astrodynamicist
ostreiculturist
astronavigation
pseudepigraphic
pseudohexagonal
pseudoephedrine
straightforward
stratigraphical
sticking-plaster
stretcher-bearer
etherealisation
etherealization
stoechiological
strephosymbolia
atherosclerosis
atherosclerotic
stiff-neckedness
stigmatophilist
steganographist
stoicheiometric
stoichiological
stalactitically
stalagmitically
stilpnosiderite
standardisation
standardization
ethnolinguistic
ethnomusicology
standoffishness
strombuliferous
Attorney-General
attorney-general
atmospherically
staphylorrhaphy
stereochemistry
stereoisomerism
humanitarianism
number-crunching
quick-conceiving
punctiliousness
durchkomponiert
musculo-skeletal
subcommissioner
susceptibleness
pulchritudinous
successlessness
subcivilisation
subcivilization
quick-wittedness
quadripartition
quadruplication
superadditional
superabundantly
supercalendered
tuberculisation
tuberculization
superconfidence
superconducting
superconductive
superexaltation
superexcellence
superficialness
superfluousness
superheterodyne
superincumbence
superincumbency
superinducement
superimposition
superintendence
superintendency
superlativeness
supernaturalise
supernaturalism
supernaturalist
supernaturalize
superordination
superplasticity
superpatriotism
superstitiously
superstructural
supersaturation
Jungermanniales
tungsten-halogen
euphemistically
authoritatively
rudimentariness
pusillanimously
numismatologist
jurisprudential
junior-flyweight
subintellection
subintelligence
subintelligitur
subject-superior
public-relations
nucleosynthesis
△sublapsarianism
pulmobranchiate
quinquagenarian
quintuplication
mucosanguineous
autoradiography
autoschediastic
subordinateness
Europeanisation
Europeanization
autodidacticism
automorphically
autographically
supplementarily
supplementation
sulphinpyrazone
supportableness
purposelessness
sub-postmistress
suppositionally
sulphureousness
jusqu'auboutisme
jusqu'auboutiste
quartermistress
quarrelsomeness
quarter-sessions
surreptitiously
substantialness
substantiveness
Aussichtspunkte
subspecifically
quasi-historical
questionability
question-begging
substitutionary
substratosphere
multiarticulate
justifiableness
multilingualism
multilateralism
multilateralist
multinucleolate
juxtapositional
subterraneously
quatercentenary
butterfly-flower
butterfly-orchid
butterfly-orchis
multitudinously
suburbanisation
suburbanization
evangelicalness
evangelistarion
everlastingness
overdevelopment
overbearingness
overforwardness
overpreparation
owner-occupation
two-pair-of-stairs
sword-and-buckler
swathing-clothes
swathling-clouts
swothling-clouts
experimentalise
experimentalism
experimentalist
experimentalize
experimentation
experimentative
expeditiousness
experientialism
experientialist
exteriorisation
exteriorization
externalisation
externalization
extemporariness
extemporisation
extemporization
extensification

Words marked △ may be spelled also with a capital letter

15 □x□e□s

extensivization
exchangeability
exhibitionistic
exemplification
exemplificative
excommunication
excommunicatory
excommunicative
extra-curricular
extra-illustrate
extrajudicially
excrementitious
extraordinaries
extraordinarily
extra-provincial
expressionistic
gynandromorphic
synarthrodially
synchronistical
synchronisation
synchronousness
synchronization
hyperadrenalism
hypercritically
hypercorrection
hypercatalectic
synecdochically
synergistically
synecologically
hyperthyroidism
mythologisation
mythologization
myristicivorous
syllabification
dyslogistically
syllogistically
dysmorphophobia
symmetricalness
hypno-anesthesia
pycnodysostosis
pyknodysostosis
hypnotisability
hypnotizability
hypomagnesaemia
cytomegalovirus
cytogenetically
pyrotechnically
hypoventilation
zygophyllaceous
sycophantically
hypochondriacal
hypochondriasis
hypophosphorous
pyrophotography
hypopituitarism
pyro-electricity
typographically
xylotypographic
lymphadenopathy
symptomatically
symptomological
sympathetically
sympathomimetic
hydrobiological
Hydrocorallinae
hydrodynamicist
hydrometallurgy
hydropathically
hydrostatically
dyer's-yellowweed
dysteleological
hyetometrograph
systematisation
systematization
Czechoslovakian

Words marked △ may be spelled also with a capital letter

ISBN
0550 19043 0

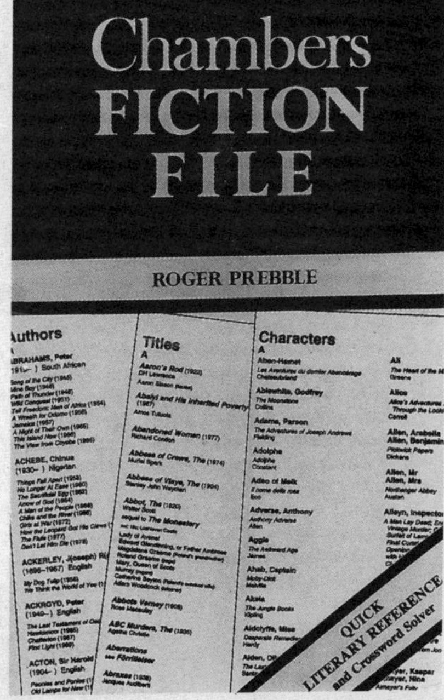

ISBN
0550 19033 3

ISBN
0550 19050 3

ISBN
0550 19025 2

ISBN
0550 19049 X

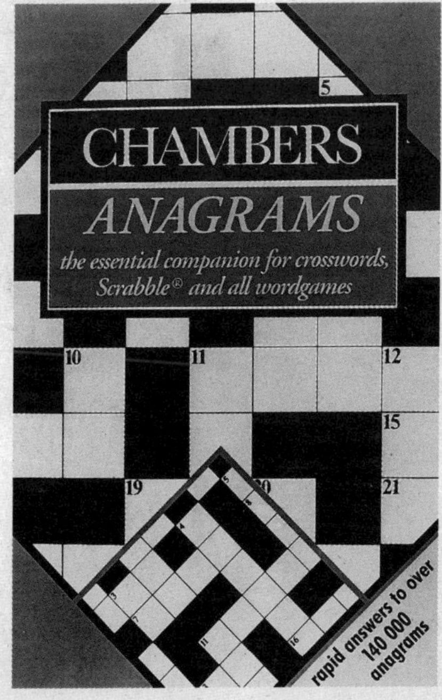

ISBN
0550 19048 1

Other

Chambers Games Titles

include the following

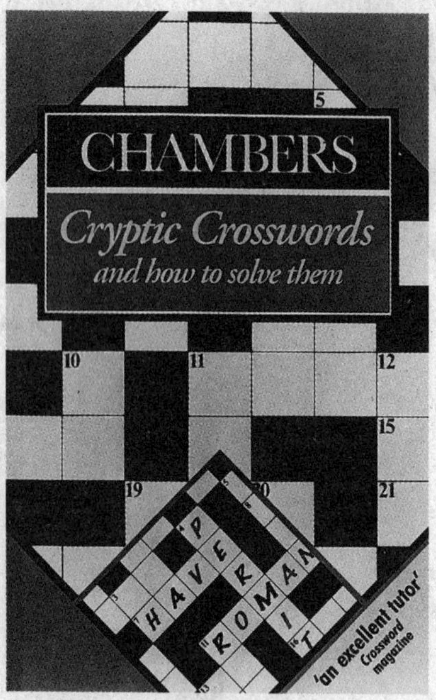

ISBN 0550 19047 3